The Wise
Encyclopedia
of Cookery

The Wise Encyclopedia of Cookery

One of the world's most definitive reference books on food and cooking

With 5100 recipes and over 500 illustrations, charts and diagrams

Grosset & Dunlap

A NATIONAL GENERAL COMPANY

New York

Copyright © 1971

BY

Wm. H. Wise & Co., Inc.

Previous Editions Copyright © 1948, 1951 by Wm. H. Wise & Co., Inc.

ISBN: 0-448-00639-1

Jacket courtesy of Karpy Custom Kitchens, Inc.
Photo by the Mort Engel Studio

Distributed by

Grosset & Dunlap, Inc., New York, N.Y.

Printed in the United States of America

Color Illustrations

Introduction

Cooking is coming in for a revival. In the midst of an era of mass produced, pre-cooked, packaged, processed foods, homemakers are turning away from the high priced prepared meals-in-one and back to their own kitchens, to the rich tradition of wholesome, old fashioned home cooking. Why? Because home cooking is more nutritious, less expensive and better tasting! And because, with proper preparation, efficient recipes, modern equipment and the lush variety of fresh foods available on local markets, distinctive and delicious home cooked meals take no longer to prepare than bland, packaged concoctions that fracture your weekly budget.

No style of cookery is outside the scope of today's cook. Tropical fruits blossom out in northern markets; all kinds and cuts of meat are obtainable locally; rich cheeses from abroad supplement extensive domestic production; grains, vegetables, dairy foods and seafood are available in abundance. More and more homemakers are deciding to get in on the fun of cooking exciting dishes, both new and old, and the pleasure of seeing their families thrive on nutritious, well prepared meals.

The WISE ENCYCLOPEDIA OF COOKERY, a long time culinary tradition in millions of homes, is designed for the bride and experienced homemaker alike. Newly revised for the modern cook, WISE COOKERY is a comprehensive handbook containing everything you need know about food, its purchase and preparation. This volume was put together with the idea that the good cook must have at her fingertips information on every culinary subject.

Valuable material on cooking procedures, suggestions for preparing foreign or unusual foods, fascinating and little known background material about the foods you eat are packed into the WISE ENCYCLOPEDIA. Tested, time saving recipes for old favorites as well as for interesting new dishes are organized in the convenient block form with ingredients listed first in bold letters. Tips on how to make the best use of foods and utensils on hand, how to organize the cooking of a meal and how to exercise imagination in meal preparation are here.

The homemaker will find all she need know about such food related subjects as camp cookery, high altitude cookery, barbecues, dinnerware, appliances, party foods and alcoholic beverages. Features on such timely items as health foods and fondue, and a glossary of foreign terms supplement the treatment of recipes.

You can make your own ice cream and candy, jar your own jellies and find out whether the savings gained is worth the effort of freezing your own foods.

Meal planning on a budget is discussed in the entry on menu planning. Weekly shopping lists and menus are illustrated. In addition hints and suggestions appear throughout the volume to aid homemakers in making the best of leftovers, in converting expensive ingredients into their more easily obtainable equivalents, and in using money saving food preparations to best advantage.

Numerous recipes have been especially prepared for the budget conscious homemaker. Luscious fruit desserts such as old fashioned peach shortcake, apple betty, and chocolate fudge cake require minimal preparation and seasonable or inexpensive ingredients. Economically prepared food garnishes include spicy apple rings for ham, orange sauce for baked chicken and quick tartar sauce for fish. Recipes for exotic curries, rice dishes, pickles and sauces call for low cost foods and depend on readily available spices for fullest flavor.

Subjects are organized alphabetically. Within each entry, recipes are listed alphabetically by name. In general recipes may be located by checking the listing for the recipe's main ingredient. For example, recipes for apple fritters and peach melba will be found under "apple" and "peach." Recipes with particular names in which no main ingredient or flavoring is noted will be found listed alphabetically under that name. Thus, a recipe for mulligatawny soup will be found under "mulligatawny."

Many recipes appear under the cooking techniques employed in their preparation. Directions for roast lamb will be found under "roast" and recipes for beef curry will be found under "curry." Variations of recipes, as in sauces, puddings, garnishes, frostings, are grouped with the parent recipes. An index in the back of the volume lists all recipes according to main ingredients. To locate a specific dish, check the entry under its name or primary ingredient. To find recipes for leftover rice—puddings, main courses—consult the index under "rice."

The successful cook approaches meal time with a certain joy, a relaxed mind. The Japanese instruct their cooks to leave problems at the door of the kitchen and to enter without worries. The most important ingredient you add to a meal is not listed in the recipe. You put in more than just food and spice. You put in love, care, imagination, a knowledge of your family's likes and dislikes and a skill that is the result of centuries of culinary experience. If you look upon cooking as a source of pleasure and satisfaction, both you and your family will be delighted with the results of your efforts.

THE PUBLISHERS

Acknowledgments

The information in this book is gathered from many sources, and many individuals and organizations must be thanked for their cooperation in making possible its compilation.

Much of the basic information on foods, their preparation, grading, marketing, and general standards was obtained from the United States Department of Agriculture, as represented by their many bulletins and publications. Among the many organizations — educational and commercial — to whom specific credit should be given for information, recipes, or material on which to base illustrations are:

The Agricultural Experiment Station of the University of Wyoming; the Agricultural Experiment Station, Colorado A and M College; Albro Packing Corporation; Allis Chalmers Manufacturing Company; Mr. Phil Alpert; Aluminum Cooking Utensil Company; American Badminton Association; American Central, Division AVCO Manufacturing Corporation; American Dry Milk Institute, Inc.; American Honey Institute; American Institute of Baking; American Limoges China Corporation; American Meat Institute; American Society of Refrigeration Engineers; American Soybean Association; American Spice Trade Association; American Stove Company; Association of Cocoa and Chocolate Manufacturers of the United States; Walter Baker, Chocolate and Cocoa Division, General Foods Corporation; Best Housekeeping Company; Birds Eye — Snider Division, General Foods Corporation; The Borden Company; British Information Service;

California Dried Fruit Research Institute; California Foods Research Institute; California Prune Marketing Program; Canned Salmon Industry; Carnation Milk Company; Club Aluminum Products Company; Cocoa Merchants' Association of America, Inc.; Corn Industries Research Foundation; Crosley Division, AVCO Manufacturing Company; Ecko Products Company; Englishtown Cutlery, Ltd.; Esquire, Inc.; Evaporated Milk Association; Family Circle Magazine; Florence Stove Company; Frigidaire Sales Corporation; Fruit and Syrup Manufacturers' Association; Fuller Brush Company; General Electric Company; General Mills, Inc.; Goetz Brewing Company; Gorham Company; Hershey Chocolate Corporation; International Association of Ice Cream Manufacturers; International Silver Company; Kelvinator, Division of Nash-Kelvinator Corporation; Kraft Foods Company;

Libbey Glass; Licensed Beverage Industry; Look Magazine; Millers' National Federation; Nash-Kelvinator Corporation; Nathan Straus-Duparquet, Inc.; National Association of Ice Industries; National Association of Margarine Manufacturers; National Canners Association; National Dairy Council; National Livestock and Meat Board; National Preservers Association; New York City, Department of Health, Bureau of Nutrition; Norge

Division, Borg-Warner Corporation; Oneida, Ltd.; Oyster Institute of North America; Pan-American Coffee Bureau; Poultry and Egg National Board; Publicity Associates, Inc.; Raytheon Manufacturing Company, Inc.; Refrigerating Engineering; Refrigeration Industry; Rice Millers' Association; A. I. Root Company;

Self-Rising Flour Institute, Inc.; Servel, Inc.; Tea Bureau, Inc.; "Tussocks", Bucks, England; Traubee Products, Inc.; United Fresh Fruit and Vegetable Association; United Fruit Company; United States Army, Quartermaster Corps; United States Department of Agriculture; United States Department of Commerce; United States Public Health Service; Victor Chemical Works; Virginia-Carolina Peanut Association; Josiah Wedgwood and Son; Westinghouse Electric Corporation; Wheat Flour Institute.

The illustrations are the work of the following associates of Sigman-Ward: Carl T. Sigman, William J. Ward, Jr., Fergus Retrum, William A. Patrick, Jane Vincil, Carl R. Kincherf, and Walter J. Karl.

In addition to the aforementioned organizations, credit for material used in the 1971 revision should be given to: American Dairy Association; E. I. du Pont de Nemours & Company, Inc.; General Electric Company; Miss Linda Stern. Color photographs were provided by the following organizations: Breakstone Sugar Creek Foods; Bureau of Commercial Fisheries; Campbell Soup Company; U.S. Department of Agriculture.

The Wise
Encyclopedia
of Cookery

A

A LA MODE. Literally, following the fashion. In cookery it applies to two quite different dishes: Beef (*which see*) braised with vegetables; and dessert, usually pie, served with a scoop of ice cream.

ABALONE. An extra large sea snail with flattened shell, the abalone is found chiefly along the shores of the Pacific Ocean. The shell is beautifully colored and polished on the interior and is important commercially in the manufacture of buttons, ornaments, and souvenirs. The central muscle of the creature is edible, and resembles a very large scallop. It is available fresh or canned, and in the Orient is dried. It is best minced and served in chowders, fish soups, canapes, and sandwiches. Its flavor is pleasantly strong and clamlike.

ABALONE

ABERTAM CHEESE. A hard cheese made from sheep's milk. It is native to Bohemia, in the region of Carlsbad.

ABRICOTINE. This is a delicious after-dinner cordial. It is made of old brandy distilled with an infusion of apricot extract.

ABSINTHE. This is a strong liqueur derived in part from certain oils of wormwood. It was usually served diluted with water and sweetened with sugar, gum sirup, or grenadine. The traditional method of serving involved the use of an absinthe spoon, a large pierced spoon, which fitted over the top of the glass. The absinthe was placed in the glass and a lump of sugar placed on the spoon. Cool water was then poured very slowly over the sugar and dripped through to the liqueur, turning it a milky color. When all the sugar was dissolved, the drink was ready.

The use of absinthe has been outlawed in France and in the United States because wormwood is a dangerous, habit-forming drug leading to mental derangement. In this country a liqueur called Pernod has a somewhat similar flavor and makes an acceptable substitute in mixed drinks calling for absinthe.

ACACIA. (a-ka′-sha). A genus of thorny, flowering trees or shrubs. The young flowers are used by the French chefs for making fritters.

ACETIC ACID. The sour acid noted in vinegar. It is the most common of the vegetable acids.

ACIDOPHILUS MILK. A fermented milk. *See* Milk.

ACID- AND ALKALI-PRODUCING FOODS. Too much importance need not be attached to selecting food with reference to its acid- and alkali-forming ingredients. Foods which seem to have an acid flavor and reaction during eating, such as oranges and lemons, are actually alkali in their reaction when absorbed into the blood stream.

If the list of acid-producing foods is studied, it will be found that a diet which consists largely of meat, eggs, bread, and cereals is acid-producing. If, however, a good amount of fresh fruits and vegetables are included, the diet will become more balanced. Plenty of milk, vegetables, and fruits, a sensible amount of eggs, meat, and fish, and one's quota of starch, sugar, and fat insure proper balance in the diet. *See* Diet *and* Menu.

Acid Producing Foods

Meat	Fish	Cereals	Dairy Products	Miscellaneous
beef	halibut, fresh	barley	cheese, Cheddar	corn, green or canned
bacon	oysters, fresh	bread, white	egg, yolk	crackers, soda
chicken	perch, fresh	bread, wheat	egg, white	cranberries
ham	salmon, canned	oatmeal	egg, whole	peanuts
mutton	salmon-trout	rice		prunes, raw or cooked
pork	sardines	dried cereals		walnuts
veal				

ALKALI PRODUCING FOODS

Vegetables		Fruits	
beans, lima, fresh	mushrooms	almonds	grape juice
beans, string, fresh	onions	apples	lemons
beets, fresh	parsnips	bananas	muskmelons
beets, greens	peas, fresh	coconuts	peaches, fresh
cabbage	potatoes, sweet	dates	pears
carrots	potatoes, white	figs, fresh	pineapple
celery	radishes	figs, dry	plums
cucumber	rutabagas	grapes	raisins, dried
lettuce	tomatoes		

ACIDULOUS WATERS. *See* ALKALINE AND MINERAL WATERS.

ACORN. Acorns are primarily used as local fodder for swine, but in earlier times several varieties of acorn served as one of the principle articles of human diet. The sweet acorn (*Q. esculus*) is still widely eaten in southern Europe and is prepared in the same way as chestnuts. In Turkey, acorns of several types, after being buried in the ground for some time, which removes the bitterness, are dried, washed, and ground with sugar, spices, and aromatics. The compound is called *palamonte*, and a food is made from it named *racahout*, which is much esteemed. The dwarf chestnut oak, a North American species, and several other species native to this country also produce edible acorns.

ACORN

The smooth brown acorn shell contains a fat kernel full of starch and oil, sometimes very bitter. In times of want the acorns from the white oak have not only provided bread and mush, but have been roasted, ground, and boiled to form a coffee substitute.

ACRID. This term is used to describe food which is sour, sharp, or tart, and has a tendency to pucker the mouth when eaten.

ADE. An ade is a drink of fruit juice and sweetened water. *See* LEMON.

ADSUKI BEAN. This bean is native to China and Japan, where it is grown for food.

ADULTERATION. Food adulteration consists of the addition of deleterious substances or fraudulent substitutions of cheaper foods without admission. In this country almost all food products are so abundant and cheap that adulteration offers small temptation to unscrupulous dealers. The Pure Food and Drug laws require that foods be labeled with their true contents, thus telling the consumer what he is getting and preventing illegal adulteration.

AERATED WATER. The name applies to the large class of beverages which are rendered sparkling by dissolving in them carbonic acid under pressure. The term does not include champagne or fermented ginger beer or any other carbonated beverage in which the carbonic acid gas is produced by the natural process of fermentation. Aerated water, or the more popularly known carbonated water or effervescent water, is always cooler as a beverage than plain water at the same temperature because the escaping gas carries off part of the heat stored in the water.

AFTERNOON TEA. A snack of light cakes and tea, served somewhere between three and five o'clock. At home, it may be served with or without formality, and is usually held at the later hour. In business establishments, many of which have adopted the custom for the sake of the "lift" derived by employees, it is usually served at three in the afternoon.

It is questionable as to when the custom of serving afternoon tea originated. Some see it as a contemporary of England's late seventeenth century coffee shops. Others attribute it to Anna, Duchess of Bedford (1788-1861). However, it is generally agreed that the function was started to alleviate hunger in days when light luncheons were served—and when the usual hour for dinner was eight o'clock in the evening. *See also* HIGH TEA, *and* KAFFEE KLATSCH.

AGAR AGAR. This vegetable isinglass or vegetable gelatin is prepared in Japan, and more recently in other countries. It is made from red, or gelidium, seaweed, which grows abundantly on the Atlantic and Pacific coasts of the United States. It is used in the making of gelatin desserts, jellies, soups, etc. and is marketed as slender sticks (slender kanten) and blocks (square kanten) as well as in powder form.

AGAVE. (1) This is another name for the American aloe.

AGAVE. (2) This is the name of a very intoxicating drink made by fermenting the sap of the aloe.

AGED EGGNOG. This is a form of eggnog (*which see*) prepared a month or so before it is to be used, and allowed to age.

AGUAJI. This is another name for the grouper (*which see*), a valuable food fish of the Caribbean.

AGUARDIENTE. A raw potent spirit distilled from either wine or molasses. It is similar in form to Brandy (*which see*) and is used mainly in Italy, Spain, Mexico, and parts of South America.

AKALA. (a-ka'-la). This shrub bears large, juicy, small-seeded, roundish, raspberry-like berries. It is native to the Hawaiian Islands. Some akala berries grow to two inches in diameter. The fruits are variously dark purplish and orange. Some are slightly bitter to taste, others, delicately sweet and flavored. Considered quite edible, the akala berry has often been compared to the raspberry or strawberry in taste.

AKEBIA (QUINATA). This is an edible fruit, about the same size and shape as a small banana, which is native to China and Japan. It is cultivated in the United States for ornamentation.

AKVAVIT. *See* AQUAVIT.

ALBACORE. The tuna fish (*which see*) and smaller related fish.

ALBUMIN. The transparent, viscous, nitrogenous substance found in blood and forming the chief and characteristic constituent of the white of an egg. It is soluble in water and coagulable by heat, alcohol, and strong acids.

Albumin burned in oxygen outside of the body is almost completely oxidized, but after oxidation within the body, about one third of its substance is excreted. Albumin, or the white of an egg, is altered physically, but not chemically, by processes of cooking. At about 134° F. delicate fibrillae of coagulated albuminous material begin to stretch through the substance and increase until the temperature reaches 160° F. At that point the fibrillae are so numerous that the entire mass is coagulated, but retains a soft or gelatinous consistency.

Eggs baked in puddings, or in any other manner, form one of the most insoluble varieties of albumin. A raw egg is ordinarily digested in the stomach in one and a half hours, but a baked egg requires from three and a half to four hours. The insoluble quality of albumin is further illustrated in the process of overcooking beefsteak. When strong heat is applied too long in the broiling, the albumin of the meat becomes dried, shriveled, and comparatively tasteless. Eggs cooked for persons with delicate digestions should be placed in water at a temperature between 170° F. and 180° F. and immersed for ten minutes. At the end of this time they will be of a uniform gelatinous consistency, very palatable, and not too tough to be readily acted upon by the gastric juices. If a cooking thermometer is not available, the water may be previously brought to the boiling point and then set aside for a moment or two to cool slightly. Eggs cooked in this manner are found to have the yolks more firmly coagulated than the white, which remains quite tender. A practical way of attaining the above result is to pour a quart of freshly boiled water over two eggs in a bowl and let them stand covered for ten to twelve minutes. This method is called coddling. *See* EGGS.

ALCOHOL. A liquid produced by a process which takes place in certain sugar-yielding substances (grains, molasses, sugar cane, fruits, etc.) by the action of an organized ferment, the yeast fungus, *Saccharomyces cerevisiae*. The chemical changes involved are complex, but the chief products are ethyl alcohol and carbon dioxide gas. Some glycerin, succinic acid, or other compounds may be formed. The fungus is always present in the air and when a suitable fluid is exposed to the air, fermentation proceeds. Two parts of sugar yield approximately one of alcohol.

Alcoholic drinks may be economically distilled from a great variety of cereals, vegetables, and fruits containing sugar or substances which can be artificially converted into sugar. There are no civilized races, and but few uncivilized or semi-civilized people, who do not practise some sort of distillation of alcohol from the materials most readily available.

Pure alcohol is transparent, colorless, agreeable in odor, strong and pungent in flavor, and highly volatile and inflammable. It burns with a pale blue smokeless flame.

ALCOHOL COOK STOVE (portable). *See* CAMP COOKERY.

ALCOHOLIC BEVERAGE. *See* BEER, BRANDY, GIN, LIQUEURS, RUM, WHISKEY, WINES, and individual beverages by name.

ALE. An alcoholic beverage made by fermenting malt and hops. Originally, it was a product of the northern countries of Europe, where there is no extensive wine production. Ale was once brewed only from malt, as distinct from beer which also contained hops, but since the 19th century much the same process has been used for both. *See* BEER.

ALE FLIP. An English drink sometimes called "One Yard of Flannel." The time of origin is not certain, but it may well date back to the 18th Century or earlier. *See* FLIP.

ALE POSSET. This is a mildly intoxicating drink made by curdling milk with ale and spices. *See* POSSET.

ALEATICO. The name given to wines made from the Aleatico grape, a species of the black Muscat. Originally made in Italy, this wine was used in England at the time of Chaucer. It may be either a medium-sweet, red table wine or a sweet, red dessert wine. It is served at room temperature or chilled, with entrees or with dessert depending on the type. *See also* WINE.

ALEBERRY. This is a warm English drink made from sweet small (weak) beer.

ALEBERRY

1 qt sweet small beer
2 tbsp fine oatmeal

Mix the beer and oatmeal. Let the mixture stand for two hours; then strain and boil it. After boiling, add sugar, wine, lemon juice, and nutmeg to taste. Serve hot and ungarnished, with a side dish of croutons, rusk, or similar bread.

ALELLA. A white table wine made in the vicinity of a Spanish village of the same name. It is sold in long fluted bottles. *See also* WINE.

ALEMTEJO CHEESE. A soft round cheese which is native to the province of Alemtejo, Portugal. It is made of the milk of sheep and the flowers of a kind of thistle. Goat's milk is often added in the smaller sizes.

ALEWIFE. A fish caught along the coast of America from the Gulf of Saint Lawrence to Chesapeake Bay. It exists in great abundance in Lake Ontario, where it is not uncommon to find immense schools of dead alewife floating on the surface of the water.

Closely allied to both the herring and the shad in shape and color, the various methods employed in the preparation of these fish may also be applied to the alewife. This inexpensive fish is called "gasperau" in Saint Lawrence Bay, "ellwife," and "sawbelly" in some localities, and is known as the "round pompano" in Bermuda. Several varieties of the alewife, considered inferior in quality, are used as fertilizer.

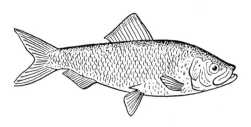

ALEWIFE

ALGARROBA. The fruit of the carob tree, also called St. John's Bread. *See* CAROB.

ALICANTE. A red wine of Spain, popular as a dessert wine in England during the 19th century.

ALKALI-PRODUCING FOODS. *See* ACID- AND ALKALI-PRODUCING FOODS.

ALKALINE AND MINERAL WATERS. (*See also* WATER) There are many spring waters which are used as beverages with or between meals. They possess, in addition to the properties of plain water, a mildly tonic effect due either to the carbon dioxide gas or salts, or both, which they may contain.

The effervescent or carbonic-acid waters are more highly charged with gas when sold in soft drinks or in siphons than when bottled. Fruit sirups are combined with soda, carbonic-acid, or other effervescent waters to make soda water and similar beverages. Ginger ale, sarsaparilla, etc. are made effervescent, and are often used as cooling and refreshing drinks.

Mineral waters may be classified as alkaline, saline, chalybeate, sulphurous, acidulous, arsenical, etc.

Thermal waters, like Poland water (a plain, carbonic-acid water), and Vichy, Johannis, Apollinaris, and Seltzer (effervescent carbonic-acid waters) are used mainly as agreeable table beverages, and to dilute spirits, wines, lemonade, etc. They are cooling, refreshing, and wholesome drinks.

A glass of Apollinaris or similar water taken an hour after a too heavy dinner promotes digestion and helps remove waste products from the system. Some waters are sold as natural lithia waters, but the quantity of lithium contained in any spring water is usually very small, and beverages of this class are generally reinforced artificially by lithium salts. Kronenquelle water is an alkaline lithia water from Obersalzbrunn, Silesia. Other lithia waters are found at Londonderry, New Hampshire, and at Amelie les Bains, and Royat, France.

Acidulous Waters. These waters, containing CO_2 in excess and but a slight amount of salts, may be obtained at Clysmic Spring, Wisconsin; Blue Lick, Kentucky, and Carlsbad (Dorotheenquelle) in Bohemia.

Alkaline Waters. These contain varying amounts of carbon dioxide, but their most important ingredients are the alkaline carbonates. They also contain sodium chloride and sometimes sodium sulphate. Generally speaking, the European waters are richer in alkalies than the American. A few of the places noted for their alkaline waters include: Vichy, France; Wiesbaden, Germany; Saratoga Springs, New York; Saint Louis Spring, Michigan; and Bethesda Springs, Virginia.

Alkaline and Saline Waters. On the advice of a physician these purges may be obtained at Bourbonne-les-Bains, France; Pullna, Bohemia (one of the oldest); Friedrichshall, Germany; Kissengen, Bavaria; Epsom, England; Crab Orchard, and Estill Springs, Kentucky; Bedford Springs, Pennsylvania; and Mount Clemens Spring, Michigan (this also contains iron). These waters should be taken either very cold or in a half-pint of very hot water, according to the directions of the physician. When taken in lukewarm water their taste is disagreeable.

Alkaline Sulfur Waters. Aix-les-Bains, Cauterets, Dax, and Luchon in France, Harrogate in England, and Neuendorf in Germany are but a few of the many European spas offering these waters. In the United States they flow from Richfield Springs, Sharon Springs, and Avon Springs in New York, as well as from White Sulphur Springs in West Virginia, and Hot Sulphur Springs in Arkansas.

These waters, containing sulfuretted hydrogen in addition to other ingredients, are much used in prescriptions for gout, rheumatism, obesity, and chronic eczema. They are often supplemented by a prescription of chalybeate waters.

Chalybeate Waters. Springs are found in Spa, Belgium; Saint Moritz, Switzerland; and Rock Enon, Virginia. Chalybeate waters, as prescribed by medical authorities, serve as tonics for the blood and nerves.

ALLEMANDE. A smooth yellow sauce used mainly for vegetables.

ALLEMANDE

2 cups veloute sauce
2 egg yolks
1 tbsp butter or 2 tbsp cream
Dash of nutmeg
1 tbsp lemon juice

Place the velouté sauce (*which see*) in the top of a double boiler over a low flame and simmer very slowly until it is reduced to half its original quantity. Place over boiling water. Beat the egg yolks and stir into the sauce. Add the rest of the ingredients. Cook over gently boiling water, stirring frequently, until thick and very creamy.

ALLERGY. Idiosyncrasies in respect to certain types of food are found to exist with some persons and according to medical authorities often continue throughout life. Thus, seafood, or strawberries, or chocolate, or almost any other food may cause hives or illness. Food allergies may be hereditary and may affect several members of one family. They are wholly independent of ordinary dyspeptic conditions.

ALLGAUER BERGKASE. A German hard cheese similar to Emmenthal, made from cow's milk. It comes in wheels weighing from 50 to 100 pounds.

ALLGAUER RAHMKASE. A German soft cheese made of cream, of the Limburger class, similar to Romadur (*which see*) but milder in flavor.

ALLIGATOR PEAR. This is the popular but incorrect name for the Avocado (*which see*).

ALLSPICE. The dried fruit of the West Indian pimento tree is called allspice because its flavor resembles a mixture of other spices, particularly cinnamon, nutmeg, and cloves. The tree grows to a height of about 20 feet. Soon after its blossoms fall the small berries are gathered by hand and dried in the sun. The berries are full grown at this time but not quite ripe. In drying they lose their green color and become a reddish brown. If allowed to ripen, the berries assume a dark purple color and become filled with a sweet pulp.

Allspice is usually sold ground, and is used for flavoring everything from soups, sauces, and preserves to meats, baked apples, and wine.

ALLSPICE

ALMOND. There are two chief types of almonds, the sweet (pink flowers) and the bitter (white flowers). When the unqualified term almond is employed in recipes,

it is generally understood that the sweet type is inferred. In California the nuts are harvested from August to October, dried

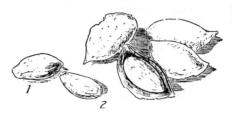

ALMONDS   1. Valencia   2. Jordan

for several days, and if discolored, as often is the case where the air is very humid, they are lightly sprayed with water and then treated with sulfur fumes to bleach the shell. There are two popular types of imported almonds, the Jordan and the Valencia. The Jordan contains a kernel that is plump and long, the Valencia, one that is plump and pointed at one end and broad at the other. Choice kernels are used for salting, and those of irregular size and shape are made into paste and butters.

HINTS ON USING ALMONDS

Almonds are easily shelled by a twist of the fingers. The so-called hard shell almonds may need a nut cracker, but the paper-shells break easily.

Almonds are easily blanched by pouring boiling water over them in a small pan and letting stand for several minutes. Drain off the water and slip off the skins with the fingers. Place the nuts on absorbent paper and allow to dry at room temperature for several hours or overnight. The blanched almonds may be cut into slivers with a sharp knife. To toast chopped or slivered almonds, spread them on a baking sheet and bake in a moderate oven (350° F.), stirring frequently.

For salted almonds, see the instructions under NUTS.

PURCHASING ALMONDS

Product	How Purchased	Weight	Yield by cups
Hard Shell	In shell	1 lb	1 cup meats
Paper Shell	In shell	1 lb	2 cup meats
Jordans	Meats	1 lb	3 cup meats
Valencias	Meats	1 lb	3 cup meats (generous)
Salted	Meats	1 lb	3½ cup meats
Butter	Glass jar	5 oz	⅓ cup

ALMOND CRESCENTS

4 oz butter
½ tsp almond extract
½ tsp vanilla
⅓ cup sugar, sifted
¾ cup chopped almonds
1 cup flour
¼ cup confectioners' sugar

Cream butter well; add the next three ingredients, and blend until smooth. Add the almonds. Sift the flour and add. Knead just enough to blend thoroughly. Divide dough in two and shape each half into a roll about an inch thick. Slice the rolls into ½ to ¾ inch lengths. Extend each piece into 1½ to 2 inch lengths by rolling between the palms. Bend these pieces into crescents, then place on ungreased baking sheets. Bake at 350° F. (moderate) for 20 minutes. Cool, then roll in confectioners' sugar. (Makes 3 dozen)

ALMOND CROISSANTS

½ cup shortening
½ cup sugar
Dash of salt
2 egg yolks
¼ cup finely crushed almonds
1 cup sifted flour (about)
1 egg white
1 tsp water
Chopped almonds

Cream together shortening, sugar and salt; beat in egg yolks, then finely crushed almonds. Gradually stir in flour until dough is stiff enough to handle; chill thoroughly. Roll ⅛-inch thick on lightly floured board; cut with small crescent-shaped cutter and place on greased baking sheet. Brush with egg white and water beaten together until frothy; sprinkle with chopped almonds and bake in moderately hot oven (375° F.) 12 minutes. (Makes 1½ dozen cookies)

ALMOND ICE CREAM

To a quart of vanilla ice cream (*see* VANILLA) add, when beginning to stiffen, ½ pound of blanched, coarsely ground or finely chopped almonds, two drops oil of almond, or ¼ teaspoon almond extract. Then complete freezing. (This recipe serves 6)

ALMOND PUDDING

3 tbsp butter or shortening
3 tbsp flour
⅓ tsp salt
¾ cup milk
3 eggs, separated
⅓ cup sugar
1 tbsp strong coffee
1 tsp vanilla
½ cup toasted shredded almonds

Melt the butter or shortening in the upper part of a double boiler and stir in the flour. Add the salt and gradually stir in the milk. Cook over hot water until mixture thickens, stirring constantly. Beat the egg yolks until thick with the sugar, then blend with the sauce. Stir in the coffee, vanilla, and almonds and finally fold in the stiffly beaten egg whites. Turn into a greased baking dish and bake in a moderate oven (350° F.) for 50 minutes or until firm. Serve at once with a chocolate or fruit sauce. (Any other kind of nut may be used, the pudding then assuming the name of the nut used.) (Serves 6)

ALMOND SWISS CREAM

1 tbsp (envelope) gelatin
¼ cup cold water
½ cup boiling water
1 cup sugar
1 pint heavy cream, whipped
½ tsp vanilla
¼ lb blanched almonds
12 marshmallows
12 candied or maraschino cherries
6 macaroons (coconut or almond)

Soften the gelatin in the cold water for about 10 minutes, then add the boiling water and sugar, stirring until the sugar and the gelatin are both dissolved. Cool, and when the mixture is beginning to congeal fold in the whipped cream and vanilla, then add the almonds, marshmallows and cherries cut into thin strips with scissors, also the macaroons crumbled with the fingers. Turn into 1 large mold or 8 individual ones. Chill until firm and unmold for serving. (Serves 8)

ALMOND BUTTER. *See* NUT BUTTER.
ALMOND EXTRACT. A solution of oil and bitter almonds, about one per cent alcohol of fair strength, used for flavoring cakes, pastries, ice creams, desserts, etc.

ALMOND PASTE. A preparation made of finely ground almonds that have been blanched, but not roasted. Used for making pastries, especially as a foundation for macaroons, and for marzipan (*which see*).

ALMOND PASTE

1½ cups finely ground almonds
¾ cup sugar
½ tsp salt
¼ cup water
Few drops almond extract (according to taste)

Mix dry ingredients, add to water, and cook for 20 minutes in a covered double boiler. Stir while cooling and add the almond extract. Pack the paste in a covered container and store in the refrigerator for 24 hours. Another variation of this recipe calls for the use of rosewater in place of the almond extract.

ALMOND SIRUP. An emulsion of mixed, ground kernels of sweet and bitter almonds (apricot or peach kernels may be substituted for bitter almonds) in barley sirup or in a sirup of orange-flower water and sugar. Ten parts of sweet almonds are generally used to three parts of bitter almonds. Almond sirup is used by bakers and pastry shops and by soda fountains for fancy iced beverages.

ALPINA LIQUEUR. This is a delicious, but fiery, pale golden-yellow liqueur made of spirit and distilled with an essence of fruit. It serves as a sweet cordial; it is usually served after dinner, but it is sometimes used to flavor certain cocktails. It is a product of Italy. *See also* LIQUEUR.

ALT KUHKASE. A German and domestic cheese also called Hand Cheese (*which see*).

ALTAR WINE. This is wine used for sacramental purposes. It is supposed to be "unadulterated fermented juice of the grape." *See also* WINE.

ALTENBURG CHEESE. A small flat cheese made of goat's milk which is a product of Germany.

ALTITUDE. For the effect of altitudes above 2500 feet above sea level on cooking processes see HIGH-ALTITUDE COOKERY.

ALUM. A chemical having a particularly astringent effect, alum is used in the preparation of pickles and maraschino cherries to give them crispness. The amount of alum left in such products usually amounts to less than two-tenths of one percent.

ALUMINUM. (*See also* KITCHEN EQUIPMENT.) Aluminum is a white, light metal of considerable strength that readily transmits heat. It is non-toxic and can be fabricated in many ways, which, in conjunction with its other properties, makes it well suited for many kitchen uses.

ALUMINUM FOIL

Aluminum may be rolled into exceedingly thin sheets that are used as bottle cap liners and as wrappings for perishable foods. The foil is now available in roll form for household use, and performs many cooking and storage functions. The foil can be wrapped around food to form an airtight and even watertight seal that does not insulate. It is especially adapted for storing foods in refrigerators and in some types of cooking where food components are boiled in the same pot but kept separate.

ALUMINUM WARE

The most common kitchen use of aluminum has been as a metal from which various utensils are made. In the majority of cases, these utensils are merely adaptations of similar utensils made of other materials, but some manufacturers offer aluminum utensils which, they claim, make possible new cooking techniques.

There are two basic types of aluminum ware found on the market today, the classification depending on the manufacturing process used.

Cast Aluminum. Though light in weight, cast aluminum usually has a heavy appearance. As the name would imply, it is made by pouring the molten metal into molds. The surface is usually grainy or "pebbled" because of the mold texture, but it may be given some sort of polish. The walls are comparatively thick. Vessels of this type heat quickly and evenly, holding their heat for long periods, which makes them well suited for slow cooking operations and for cooking foods that contain little water.

Stamped Aluminum. Aluminum vessels may also be fabricated from sheet metal. The surface is usually smooth and shiny, and the walls are thinner than those of cast vessels. Though they are quickly heated, they do not retain the heat, due to the thin walls. These vessels are thus better suited for quick cooking, boiling, and baking.

Purchasing Aluminum Ware

Cast aluminum vessels should be checked for imperfections of casting as well as to see how any separate sub-assemblies have been joined to the cast body. Stamped aluminum should not be too thin, lest it dent or warp easily, and the structure of any seams or joints should be examined.

Care and Cleaning of Aluminum

Aluminum is, by nature, a bright, shiny metal. Unless it has been specially treated, however, it will dull if not frequently used and washed. Aluminum vessels can be stained by food or water containing iron, sulfur, or alkalies. Eggs are particular offenders in this regard, and even soap, soda, or water softeners can stain aluminum if left in contact with it for any undue period of time. Such stains may disappear in the normal course of events if highly acid foods are cooked in the vessel.

Aluminum vessels should be washed in the regular manner. A fine grade of steel wool can be used to remove stains, the surface can be rubbed with lemon, or a weak solution of vinegar and water can be boiled in a stained vessel. Aluminum ware should be dried thoroughly before storing.

AMARANTE. This is one of the best white table wines of Portugal. It has body but little bouquet. It should be used when new and not allowed to age. *See also* Wine.

AMBERJACK

AMBER FISH. The great amber fish, or amberjack, is a food fish found in the Gulf of Mexico and around the West Indies. It sometimes attains a weight of 100 pounds. Small species are known as common amber, madregala, lemon fish, coronado; a species found off the Pacific coast is the highly prized yellow-tail. The various methods for preparation of cod,

halibut, or any large fish which may be cut into steaks can be used for this delicious fish.

AMBROSIA. In Greek mythology, this was a balsamic juice which served as the food of the gods and preserved their immortality. Mortals permitted to partake of ambrosia received additional beauty, strength, and swiftness, becoming in some measure akin to the gods. The name is sometimes erroneously applied to certain beverages.

AMER PICON. A stomachic and delicious aperitif made by distilling pure alcohol over oil of oats. It has an alcoholic content of 38 to 40 percent and is a product of France. Because it is quite bitter, it may be sweetened with a few drops of gum sirup, grenadine, or cassis, and then diluted with either plain or carbonated water. It is sometimes used as a flavoring for cocktails. *See also* Aperitif.

AMERICAN CHEESE. *See* Cheese and Cheddar.

AMIRAL. A butter sauce used mostly for boiled fish.

Amiral Sauce

1 cup melted butter
2 well-pounded anchovies
1 tsp chopped chives
A number of chopped capers
Thinly pared lemon peel
Juice of 1 lemon
Salt and pepper

To butter, add anchovies, chives, capers, and lemon peel. Let the mixture simmer over a gentle fire until the anchovies are well blended. Remove lemon peel, add lemon juice, salt and pepper to flavor, and serve hot.

AMONTILLADO. A popular type of moderately dry sherry (*which see*).

AMOROSO. A type of sherry which is darker and sweeter than Amontillado, but still considered dry. *See* Sherry.

AMOURETTE. A stomachic and refreshing long drink that has been popular in France since the prohibition of absinthe. It is not so fiery as absinthe and is violet-colored. It is usually drunk before meals, diluted with water, as an aperitif. *See* Aperitif.

ANCHOVY. Although of uncertain origin, these fish are members of the *Clupeidae* family. The anchovy is smaller than the herring, never exceeding four or five inches in length. The mouth is slit nearly as far as the eyes, and the gills are larger than those of the herring. Narrow, elongated, and covered with filmy scales, the backs of these fish are bluish-brown and the sides silver.

Anchovies are caught in the spring and summer during dark, moonless nights by means of artificial light which attracts and completely blinds them. They surround the numerous fishing boats, and the fishermen drop their nets, meanwhile beating the water and extinguishing the light. Anchovies are caught in this manner by the millions. After being cleaned, graded, and washed, they are placed in small kegs and arranged in layers with a little salt. This operation is repeated three or four times, the salt being renewed each time, before the anchovies are delivered to market. This method of preparing anchovies has been handed down through the centuries, having originated with the early Greeks and Romans.

Anchovies must be bought with care, since some, although well pickled and spiced with bay leaves, cloves, and pepper, are nothing but sprats, pilchards, alewives, or other inferior types of the herring family. The slender, soft-fibered anchovy of the Mediterranean, which rarely cruises farther north than Holland, is of the highest quality. The fillets come packed as straight strips or curled.

Pounding boned anchovy to a paste with mortar and pestle is the first step in the composition of many unusual sauces. Anchovies are seldom associated with cutlets or Wiener schnitzel, yet some American and European chefs specify in their recipes that boned filets of anchovy shall be used in garnishing the cutlets; and schnitzel a la Holstein is identified by a garnish of rolled anchovy filet on a slice of lemon.

The filet of anchovy used variously in hors d'oeuvre, antipasto, and smorgasbord, sharpens the appetite for both meat and drink; and when used in conjunction with certain fish and fowl it heightens the flavor.

Anchovy butter is a staple to be kept in jars on ice, ready to be spread lightly on a steak for broiling, or rubbed into a piquant sauce or a salad dressing. It is made by pounding boned and skinned anchovies in a mortar and mixing one part of the smooth paste with two parts of sweet but-

ter. If there is no mortar and pestle, however, prepared commercial anchovy paste can be used in the mixture, but it should be the rich heavy paste that comes in small earthen or glass jars. The same paste used in preparing smorgasbord, however, may be disguised by mixing tomato paste with it. The best anchovy paste mixed with heavy chili sauce or catsup also offers an excellent canapé. Anchovy paste can also serve as a foundation for more elaborate canapés of mussels, shrimp, lobster, whole anchovies or sardines, deviled eggs, and grilled walnuts.

A delicious dressing for a salad or for artichokes or broccoli is made by pounding two whole anchovies, boned and skinned, to a paste and blending with oil and vinegar, English mustard, an egg yolk, and minced parsley, chervil, chives, or capers, and seasoned with salt (very little is required) and mignonette pepper or freshly ground, black pepper.

Anchovy, regarded as a seasoning rather than a major ingredient, is effective in sauces for cold meats, poultry, and game; and some of the geniuses of the kitchen incorporate the essence in béarnaise ravigote, remoulade, and the standard basic Espagnole and demi-glace (*see* SAUCE). In Europe, bland, delicate fishes which are prepared by boiling and baking are stepped up to a keener piquancy with dashes of anchovy, but a practiced hand is required or the original delicacy is lost. The confirmed anchovy addict uses the larding needle (*which see*) and draws thin strips of the fish through roasts of meat, fowl, and game, to impart a tang of salt and a hidden flavor. If not overdone, the effect is pleasing. *See also* HORS D'OEUVRE.

ANCHOVY PEAR. This is the russet-colored fruit of a very ornamental West Indian tree that grows from 30 to 50 feet in height. The fruit, somewhat larger than a hen's egg, is pickled and eaten like the mango (*which see*), which it strongly resembles in taste.

ANCHOVY SAUCE. *See* BUTTER SAUCE.

ANCHOVY SPEAR. A small wood or plastic spear used to handle anchovies and similar small tidbits, rather than using a fork or the fingers.

ANCIEN IMPERIAL CHEESE. A small, flat cheese about two inches square and one-half inch thick. It is a native cheese of France and is also known by the names Petite Carré and Carré Affiné.

ANDALOUSE SAUCE. *See* Mayonnaise.

ANGEL CAKE. A light, frothy cake
made without shortening. *See* Cakes.

ANGEL FISH. A name applied to many
fishes, including the porgy (*which see*).

ANGELICA. (1) The name of several
quite different beverages, including:
(1) A pale yellow, very sweet, highly
aromatic liqueur made in Spain.
(2) A very sweet white wine formerly
made by the Mission Fathers in
California.
(3) A highly fortified white dessert wine
made in California.
(4) A mistelle used as a sweet alcoholic
base for making various aperitifs and
cordials. This is a product of southern California.

ANGELICA

ANGELICA. (2) There are over 50
varieties of the angelica plant, but *A. arch-
angelica* is the historic herb for culinary and
medicinal purposes, and it figures in the
Pharmacopoeia as *A. officinalis*. Angelica is
conspicuously exotic in appearance; yet it
is indigenous to Lapland, Iceland, the
Scandinavian countries, and the Alps. It
was domesticated in English gardens in
the 16th century, and Mary of Scotland
planted it at Holyrood and again in the
garden at Chatsworth House during her
imprisonment there.

Practically all parts of the plant are put
to some use—the leaves for herb tea, the
seeds for flavoring, the stout stems for
crystallized confection, the roots as food
and medicine, and the extracted oil in perfume. For the famous sweetmeat and the
candied angelica of the confectioners, the
stalks are boiled and peeled, then cooked
in sirup and crystallized. Angelica is used
in the compounding of gin, vermouth,
chartreuse, and benedictine. It was assert-
ed by one Dr. Fernie in 1897, that "Angelica taken somewhat freely as a sweetmeat will cause a distaste for alcoholic
liquors."

ANGLER. A European and American
marine fish that reaches a length of from
three to five feet. In the market, it always
comes dressed, the enormous head with its
large mouth removed, and the tapering
body skinned. It is used by the Italians and
is seldom seen in American markets not
patronized by them. Its flavor is somewhat
muddy.

It is given the name "angler" on account
of its habit of lying partly buried on the
sea floor, where it lures its prey with the
long appendages that rise from the top of
its large, flat head; these wave about like
lures at the end of a fisherman's line and
are drawn in as food of one kind or another approaches the large mouth, which
is always kept open to snap up any member of the unsuspecting finny tribe.

For cooking hints, *see* Fish.

ANGLISKAIA GORKAIA. A delicious after-dinner cordial made of old
brandy and distilled with an infusion of
apricots. *See* Liqueurs *and* Cordials.

ANGOSTURA. The bark of a shrub or
small tree of the Orinoco river valley of
South America. The outer surface is yel-
lowish-gray and is covered with small
warty, corky growths. The taste is very
bitter and aromatic. Its active constituent
is a volatile oil—hence its aromatic nature.
The bark is used by the natives as an anti-
malarial remedy and as a laxative. It is a
common ingredient in medicines and beverages, especially liqueurs, and it is widely
used to flavor foods.

It lends its name to a commercial brand
of Bitters (*which see*).

ANGOSTURA FIZZ. A non-intoxicating beverage made with egg white, bitters
and lime juice. *See* Fruit Drinks.

ANISE. Anise is an umbelliferous annual plant that is native to the Mediterranean region. It is extensively cultivated
for its seeds, the condiment oil of which is
used in making liqueurs, candy, bread,
and pastry. Its flavor is similar to that of
licorice. It has a stomachic, stimulating
effect and is used in medicine as a carminative. It is also served as a highly palatable

and soothing iced drink during the summer. When a teaspoonful is mixed with warm milk and a little honey, it serves to induce sleep. The oil can be procured either from the seed or from the stems and leaves.

ANISE

ANISEED. This is a name for the seeds of the Anise (*which see*).

ANISETTE. A colorless liqueur which has been made in France for over two centuries by the distillation of fennel, anise, and coriander seeds. It is fortified with pure brandy and sweetened with sirup. It is a particularly delicious afterdinner cordial. *See* LIQUEURS and CORDIALS.

ANNATTO, Anatto, or Arnotto. A small tree which grows in Central and South America and in certain parts of the West Indies. From its seeds comes a dark orange-red or yellowish-red dye which is used in coloring butter and cheese.

ANTIPASTO. The Italian name for hors d'oeuvres or appetizers (*which see*). The ingredients may be varied, but generally speaking, they must all be eaten with a fork.

APERITIF. An alcoholic beverage taken as an appetizer before a meal. It generally differs from the cocktail in being less potent, and it is frequently a "longer" drink. Also, the aperitif is not apt to be a mixed drink (as is a cocktail). *See* AMER PICON, AMOURETTE, DUBONNET, and VERMOUTH, *also* COCKTAIL, ALCOHOLIC.

APOLLINARIS. A strongly effervescent, alkaline mineral water from a spring near the Rhine. It is popular as a table water, as it has no taste. *See also* ALKALINE AND MINERAL WATERS.

APPENZELL CHEESE. A Swiss cheese which is similar to Emmentaler. It is made of cow's milk.

APPETITE. The desire for, or relish of, food or drink. When applied to food, it is announced by a slight sensation of fatigue and an empty feeling in the stomach. The appetite often appears with great suddenness, either independently or as a result of directing the attention to matters of food and eating. It may depart as suddenly, even without gratification, or it may vanish after the first few mouthfuls of food are eaten.

A voracious appetite sometimes occurs in children. This is called bulimia, which means excessive craving for food. It is by no means an indication of vigor and is often due to an irritated condition of the nerves of the stomach, which may be brought about by eating at irregular intervals. Such children are usually thin and are encouraged by ill advised parents to gorge themselves with food which they do not digest.

APPETITOST CHEESE. A Danish cheese which is made from sour buttermilk. It is popular among Danes in America and is made in this country.

APPETIZER. Appetizers include an unlimited assortment of food combinations that may be served as a preview to other refreshments. If they are to fulfill their purpose of piquing the appetite, they must be as attractive and as temptingly flavored as possible. There are three groups of appetizers: Cocktails, canapés, and hors d'oeuvres. (*See* COCKTAILS, CANAPES, AND HORS D'OEUVRES.)

COCKTAILS

These consist of fruit, vegetable, or sea food mixtures or of fruit or vegetable juices. They are served at the table to begin a meal, and the mixtures are usually accompanied by a nippy sauce. A peppy-flavored cocktail is always preferred to a sweet one; you can add lemon juice or ginger ale to fruit mixtures to achieve this flavor.

Most cocktails should be chilled thoroughly before serving. Add to them any elaborating touches you know. For example, freeze tiny pieces of the fruit in ice cubes to be served in fruit juices, or use colored or oddly-shaped ice. You can "frost" fruit-juice glasses just before serving by dipping their rims in lemon juice and then in sugar. Canapés, salted nut meats, cheese crackers or popcorn, pretzel sticks, and heated potato chips are good cocktail accompaniments.

CANAPES AND HORS D'OEUVRES

These appetizers can be made from any palatable morsel. They provide an excellent method of using left-overs, although their strong flavors and charming appearance connote luxury. They are usually eaten from the fingers or from cocktail picks, and they are usually served in the drawing or living room. Hors d'oeuvres, however, may be served in larger portions in the diningroom and eaten with a fork. Hors d'oeuvres and canapés may be served together, and they may be made of the same mixtures, but the distinction between the two resides in the fact that for canapés the mixture is always spread on a firm base.

Of course it is desirable to have appetizers looking as fresh as possible. For this reason, it is best to make as many advance preparations as possible before actually assembling them. If base, filling, or garnish is prepared ahead of time, store in a covered container in a refrigerator. Spend as little time as possible in actually making them; work very systematically using an assembly-line technique, that is, work with one kind at a time, and perform a particular operation on each of them before proceeding to the next operation. Make them uniform, and do not vary the garnishes on one kind of appetizer.

Canapés and hors d'oeuvres should be small and dainty and, if they are to be eaten with the fingers, easily handled. In this connection, toothpicks and cocktail picks are invaluable aids. Appetizers resemble motion picture previews in that they are calculated to create an anxiety for what is to come, but they differ in that they provide no actual sample of what is to come. In a word, it is not in good taste to repeat one food in different courses of the meal. Nor is it in good taste to combine too many foods. It is well to exercise restraint as well as initiative in preparing and garnishing these appetizers.

Garnishes are optional but, when used, they should be delicate, colorful, and generally in harmony with the rest of the appetizer. Butters, spreads, and other creamy mixtures may be forced through a pastry bag and tube and then used to border canapés. Borders and lines may also be made of chopped olives, chopped parsley, or chopped hard-cooked egg whites or yolks. Other popular garnishes are mint, pimiento, tiny pearl onions, nut meats, and watercress.

Attractive serving. Hors d'oeuvres and canapés may be served together in a special dish divided into compartments or on a large platter or tray. Place those of the same type together so that the arrangement will not seem haphazard. Arrange the tray so that the darker colors are on the outside and so that the finished picture is harmonious and artistic.

You may cut a cantaloupe, grapefruit, apple, or other fruit of similar shape in half, place the halves flat sides down on the tray, and stud them with hors d'oeuvres on toothpicks and surround them with canapés. If a pineapple is used, allow the leaves to protrude, and decorate each with a maraschino cherry.

You might hollow a large apple, fill it with mayonnaise, and surround it with cooked shrimp on cocktail picks for dipping. Or fill other fruit shells with anchovy paste and surround them with potato chips for dipping.

APPETIZER WINES. This is a general grouping of those wines that are served either as or with appetizers. *See* WINE.

APPLE. The apple has been used for centuries by almost every nation; it was probably one of the first fruits cultivated by man. It is mentioned in many legends of ancient times. Scandinavian folklore indicates the early existence of a belief that the apple was the only food of the gods and that it was through this fruit's peculiar properties that the gods acquired their wisdom. The Anglo-Saxon word *aple*, the German *apfel*, and the Celtic *avlan* are of common origin. The Latin *pomum*, meaning to drink, signifies the watery nature of the fruit.

Apples are generally classified as eating apples and cooking apples. Scientists agree that they are among the best health foods on the market. They contain Vitamins B and C and, contrary to current belief, proper cooking destroys but little of the Vitamin C. A juicy, ripe apple of any of the 200 species grown in the United States contains from eight to eleven per cent sugar, the essence of energy. However, only ripe apples should be eaten raw. Underripe apples contain a considerable percentage of starch, which is not easily digested; when stewed as applesauce, however, they form a palatable and digestible food that is particularly suitable for convalescents.

separate the apples by hand into different grades and place the apples on the proper belts, which deliver them to the sizing devices. As the fruit moves to the sizing machine, the inferior apples are removed. After being sized, the apples are deposited

APPLES   1. McIntosh   2. Red Delicious   3. Winesap   4. Whitney Crab

PREPARATION FOR MARKET

The quality of an apple from the consumer's point of view hinges upon the maturity of the apple when picked. Overmature apples may develop water core, an oily skin, or lose their color by the time they are picked. Premature apples are generally small, sour, poorly colored, and apt to develop apple scald in storage. The time elapsing from full bloom, when the first blossom petals fall, to maturity is the most reliable index as to when the apples should be picked. There is usually a period of five to twenty days in the season when the fruit is fully developed, yet still adhering well to the tree; picking should be done at this time.

The United States is far ahead of any other country in the production of commercial apples. Although they have been grown in the United States since early colonial times, production on a commercial scale dates from about the middle of the last century, when orchards were being developed in western New York.

The principal steps through which apples usually pass in well managed orchards from the time they are picked until they are packed and ready for shipment are as follows: In the orchard the apples are emptied from the picking bags into field crates, each of which holds about a bushel. These are hauled to the packing house. If it is necessary to remove spray, the fruit is then washed or brushed. Next it is delivered to the grading belt. Here the sorters

in packing bins, from which the containers are filled.

Grading. Apples are graded according to U.S. Government specifications. The highest grade classification is U.S. Fancy, which consists of apples of one variety, mature yet not overripe, carefully handpicked, clean, well formed, and free from decay or damage. Each apple of this grade must have the amount of color specified for the variety. U.S. No. 1 has the same requirements except that less color is required for red varieties. U.S. No. 1 Early Grade is made up of apples of one variety which meet the standards of U.S. Fancy Grade but require neither red color nor maturity. This grade applies to early varieties, which are more often used for cooking than eaten raw. The standards for U.S. Commercial are the same as for U.S. No. 1 except that less color is required. U.S. Utility is composed of apples of one variety, handpicked, mature but not overripe, and not seriously deformed or damaged. U.S. Utility Early is similar to the standards of U.S. Utility but need not be mature. In the combination of grades, at least 50% of the apples must meet the requirements of the higher grade apples. In U.S. Hail Grade, the apples must meet the requirements of U.S. No. 1 except that healed hail marks or marks where the skin was left unbroken are permitted. Apples which do not conform to any grade are Unclassified, while apples in bulk or open containers which do not meet the requirements of U.S. grades are Culls.

Food Value

	Water	Food Energy	Pro- tein	Fat	Carbo- hydrate	Cal- cium	Phos- phorus	Iron	Vita- min A	Thia- mine	Ribo- flavin	Ascorbic Acid	Nia. cin
Fresh Apples	84.1	64	.3	.4	14.9	6	10	.3	90	.04	.02	5	.2
Canned Apple- sauce	79.8	80	.2	.1	19.7	4	6	.2	60	.01	.01	1	trace
Dried Apple Nuggets	1.6	390	1.4	1.0	93.9	24	42	4.1	0	.05	.08	11	.5

Storage. In the important apple-producing districts and in markets, cold storage is in general use. Apples intended for sale later in the season should be placed in cold storage as soon as possible after packing in order to prevent their becoming mealy.

Hints on Buying

Each variety of apple is best suited for certain purposes. Dessert apples should be of medium size and good color. Tart fruit is best for general cooking purposes.

Since apples keep longer than most fruits, they can be bought in quantity and kept for future use. Some varieties have better keeping qualities than others, and each is in its prime at a certain season of the year. By referring to the tables, the housewife can determine her best buy in apples.

Hints on Preparation

All apples should be washed before use because of possible contamination from the spray usually placed on the trees during the period of growth. In peeling and removing the core about 20 per cent of the apple is wasted, but two pounds of cooking apples will easily make a 10-inch pie, six portions of applesauce, or about three dozen fritters.

One of the best explanations for the popularity of apples is that they lend themselves to a variety of cooking methods. Sautéed with diced beets and onions, they are ideal with roast beef, roast pork, and

Kinds or Varieties of American Apples, With Differences in Use

Table I

Name	Localities Grown	Market Months	Color	Diameter in Inches
Baldwin	East and West	Nov.	deep red	2¼ to 2½
Ben Davis	West	Nov.	red	2¼ to 2½
Crab apple	East and West	Nov.	red, yellow spots	1 to 1½
Delicious	West and S. West	Oct.	red	2¼ to 2½
Early Harvest	West and S. West	Sept.	yellow	2 to 2½
Golden Delicious	East and S. West	Nov.	yellow	2¼ to 3
Gravestein	West	Oct.	yellow and pink	2¼ to 3
Greening	East and West	Oct.	green	2¼ to 3
Jonathan	Universal	Oct.	bright red	2¼ to 3
McIntosh	Universal	Oct.	dark red	2 to 2½
Northern Spy	East	Oct.	red, yellow stripes	3 to 3½
Ribbston Pippin	West and S. West	Oct.	yellow	2¼ to 2½
Roman Beauty	West and S. West	Nov.	yellow, red stripes	2¼ to 2½
Spitzenberg	West and S. East	Nov.	red, dark red stripes	2¼ to 3
Stayman	West and S. West	Oct.	red, yellow stripes	2½ to 3
Wealthy	Universal	Oct.	yellow, red stripes	2½ to 3½
Winesap	West and N. East	Nov.	dark red	2 to 2½
Wolf River	West and S. West	Nov.	yellow, wide red stripes	3 to 3½
Worcester Pearman	West and S. West	Nov.	red	2¼ to 2½
Yellow Newton	West and S. West	Dec.	yellow spots and red stripes	2¼ to 2½

AMERICAN APPLES

TABLE II

Name	Acidity	Juiciness	Grades	Uses	
tart 1 Very acid	1 Juicy	1 Extra Fancy	1 Cocktail	7 Dessert
2 Sub acid	2 Mealy	2 Fancy	2 Candied	8 Garnish
3 Mild	3 Dry	3 C Grade	3 Cups	9 Eating
4 Very sweet	4 Coarse	4 Combination	4 Sauce	10 Cooking
		5 Orchard Run	5 Juice	11 Baking
			6 Salad	12 Combination
Baldwin	2	1	3	4,5,10,11
Ben Davis	3	3	3,4	6,7,8,10,12
Crab apple	2	1,2	1,2	2,5,7,8,10,12
Delicious	2	1,2	1,2	1,2,3,5,7,9
Early Harvest	3	1,2	3,4	4,5,6,7,8,9,10,11,12
Golden Delicious	3	1,2	1,2	1,2,3,5,7,9
Gravestein	3	1	2,3,4,5	5,7,8,9,10,11,12
Greening	2	1,2	3,4,5	4,5,6,7,8,10,11,12
Jonathan	2	1,2	2,3,4	4,9,12
McIntosh	3	1	2,3,4	5 7,8,9,10,11,12
Northern Spy	1	2	2,3,4	4,5,6,7,8,9,10,11,12
Ribston Pippin	3	1,2	1,2,3	1,2,3,5,6,7,9
Roman Beauty	1	1,2	1,2,3	5,7,8,11,12
Spitzenberg	3	1,2	1,2,3,4	5,8,10,12
Stayman	2	1,2	3,4,5	8,10,11,12
Wealthy	3	1,2	1,2,3,4,5	5,6,7,8,10,11,12
Winesap	1	3	3,4,5	7,8,10,11,12
Wolf River	2	4	2,3,4	7,8,10,12
Worcester Pearman	3	1	1,2,3	1,2,3,4,5,6,9
Yellow Newton	4	1	1,2,3	1,2,3,4,5,6,9

roast duck, as are apple quarters, richly candied like sweet potatoes. Baked apples, their cavities filled with raisins and brown sugar, served with or without cream as preferred, are a perfect dessert. Apples also enhance salads, fruit cups, fruit cocktails, brown bettys, and many other desserts. They also serve as a garnish to many vegetables and meats.

APPLE BETTY

2½ cups dry bread crumbs
9 medium-size tart apples
⅔ cup sugar
¼ tsp nutmeg
¼ tsp cinnamon
¼ tsp salt
Juice of 1 lemon
¼ cup water
2½ tbsp butter

Butter 8-cup casserole. Spread ⅓ of crumbs over bottom, then half of apples. Mix sugar, spices and salt, and scatter half this mixture over apples in casserole. Next deposit another ⅓ of crumbs, the remaining apples, and the remaining sugar mixture. Add last layer of crumbs and moisten evenly with juice and water. Top with bits of butter. Cover and bake at 350° F. (moderate) for 25 minutes. Uncover and bake 10 minutes more. Serve hot with cream, or cold with whipped cream. Dates, nuts, pineapple, or mincemeat may supplement apples.

APPLE BREAD CRUMB PUDDING

1 cup sugar
¼ tsp each ground cinnamon and nutmeg
¼ tsp salt
Grated rind 1 lemon
2 cups soft bread crumbs
3 cups pared cored sliced apples
2 tbsp butter, melted
¼ cup water
3 tbsp lemon juice

Combine the sugar, spices, salt, and lemon rind. Arrange in alternate layers in a greased baking dish, the crumbs, apples, and spice mixture, being sure to reserve a few crumbs for the topping. To these last, add the melted butter. Pour the combined water and lemon juice carefully into the dish, before putting on the topping. Now top with the buttered crumbs and bake in a moderate oven (350° F.) about 45 minutes. (Serves 4)

Apple Charlotte

1½ lb cooking apples
1 cup water
1 cup sugar
Strip of lemon rind
2 tbsp butter
Stale white bread

Peel and core 1½ pounds of cooking apples, and cut them in quarters. Stew them gently in the water, to which the sugar and the strip of lemon rind have been added. When apples are quite soft, add the butter, and mix thoroughly.

Cut the bread into thin slices. Dip these in hot melted butter, and line the bottom and sides of a deep pie-dish. Fill the dish with the stewed apples and cover with a layer of slices of stale bread dipped in melted butter. Sprinkle with sugar, and bake in a moderate oven (350° F.) until the top layer of bread is golden brown. Turn onto a warm dish, and pour some diluted apricot jam over it before serving.

Apple Chutney

3 green peppers
1 medium-sized onion
12 tart apples
1½ cups seeded raisins
1 tbsp salt
3 cups vinegar
1½ cups sugar
1½ tbsp ground ginger
1½ cups tart grape jelly
¾ cup lemon juice
1 tbsp grated lemon rind

Peel and core the apples. Put the peppers, onion, apples and raisins through the food chopper. Place in a large saucepan and add the remaining ingredients. Simmer about 1 hour, or until thick. Pour in sterilized jars and seal at once. (Makes 4 pints) *See also* CANNING.

Apple Cobbler

Place a layer of chopped apples in the bottom of a round pudding pan that has been well oiled. Sprinkle generously with sugar and a bit of grated nutmeg or cinnamon. Make a baking-powder biscuit dough (*which see*), adding enough extra liquid to make the mixture soft enough to drip from a spoon. Bake in moderate oven (350° F.) until the apples are soft and the crust brown—about 30 minutes. When done, turn the pudding upside down onto a plate so that the apples are on top. Serve with cream and sugar or with hard sauce.

Apple Compote

2 qt cooking apples
1 lb brown sugar
¼ lb butter

Pare and core apples; cut into ¼-inch slices. Arrange apples in a flat baking pan greased with part of the butter. Cover apples generously with sugar, and dot with remaining butter. Cover dish tightly and bake in moderate oven (375° F.) for about 30 minutes. Serve warm with heavy cream (either sweet or sour).

Apple Crisp

¼ cup all-purpose flour
⅔ cup firmly packed brown sugar
¼ cup butter
½ cup slightly crushed cornflakes
2 lb tart cooking apples (6 medium)
1 tbsp lemon juice

Mix flour, butter, and brown sugar with tips of fingers until thoroughly blended. Add cornflakes and mix well. Peel and slice apples into buttered baking dish, 10"x6"x2". Pack firmly, sprinkle with lemon juice, and top with cornflake mixture. Bake in a moderately hot oven (375° F.) for 30 minutes or until apples are tender. Serve warm or cold with cream. (Serves 4 or 5)

Apple Crumble

⅓ cup all-purpose flour
¾ cup firmly packed brown sugar
⅓ cup shortening (half butter)
4 cups pared sliced tart apples (5 to 6 medium)

Combine flour and brown sugar, and cut in shortening to make a crumbly mixture. Arrange sliced apples in bottom of greased, shallow baking dish (10"x6½"x2").

Sprinkle sugar mixture over top and bake in moderate oven (375° F.) for about 30 minutes or until top is golden brown and crunchy and apples are tender.

APPLE DELIGHT

1 tbsp gelatin
  (1 envelope)
¼ cup cold water
1 cup sugar
½ cup water
⅛ tsp salt
1 lb tart cooking apples
3 tbsp lemon juice
¼ tsp grated lemon rind

Soften gelatin in cold water. Boil sugar in the ½ cup water slowly for 3 minutes, counting time after boiling starts. Add salt and peeled, sliced apples (should be 3 cups); cover, simmer until tender. Remove from heat, stir in gelatin, then lemon juice and rind; cool. Pour into mold or bowl; chill until firm. Unmold and serve with custard sauce (cold) or cream. (Serves 4)

APPLE DUMPLINGS I
(Baking Method)

2 cups sifted pastry flour
2 tsp baking powder
⅓ tsp salt
4 tbsp shortening
⅔ cup milk (about)
6 peeled and cored baking apples
½ cup brown sugar
½ to ¾ tsp cinnamon
1 tsp lemon juice
½ cup sugar
½ cup boiling water

Sift the flour, baking powder, and salt together. Mix in the shortening. Add the milk, using just enough to form a light soft dough. Turn onto a floured board and roll out into an oblong sheet about ¼-inch thick. Cut into 6 equal-sized squares and place an apple in the center of each square. Fill the core cavities with the blended brown sugar and cinnamon, and sprinkle with the lemon juice. Wet the edges of the dough; then draw up over and around the apples, pinching the edges together so that they will not open while baking. Place side by side in a baking pan, and pour around the dumplings a sirup made by boiling the water and granulated sugar to-

gether for 3 minutes. The dough may be pricked in several places with a fork to lessen the likelihood of bursting while baking. Bake in a hot oven (400° F.) from 40 to 45 minutes or until apples are tender, basting occasionally with sirup in the pan. Serve hot with remaining pan sirup or with a lemon or vanilla sauce. (*See* SAUCES.)

APPLE DUMPLINGS II
(Steamed Method)

Steamed apple dumplings are prepared like baked dumplings. The dough-covered apples are placed in a buttered pan with room for expansion between them. The pan is tightly covered and placed in a steamer. The steaming time may vary from 1½ to 2 hours, depending on the size of the apples and the thickness of the dough. For a wintertime dessert, steamed apple dumplings are ideal. Serve them in a deep saucedish so that there will be room for plenty of sauce. Fluffy hard sauce with its refreshing lemon flavor is a perfect topping.

APPLE FRITTERS

2 fair-sized eating apples
Powdered sugar
2 tbsp flour
¼ tsp baking powder
1 egg, well beaten
¼ cup milk

Pare and core apples. Slice them and sprinkle with powdered, sifted sugar. Make a batter with flour, baking powder, egg, and milk. The consistency of the batter should be that of thick cream. Dip the slices of apples in this batter, and drop them in boiling fat. Take them out as soon as they are dark brown in color. Drain and serve with a sprinkling of powdered sugar.

APPLE HEDGEHOG

1 lb apples
Cream or custard
¾ lb sugar

Pare and core the apples. Add sufficient water to moisten the sugar. Put apples and sugar into a saucepan and boil until the mixture drops from a spoon. Put into a mold. When turned out, place strips of blanched almonds over it and cover with cream or custard (*which see*).

Apple Jelly

Apple jelly may be made from the parings and cores of tart apples used in canning. Discard all faulty parts. Cover with cold water and cook until quite tender. Strain twice. Measure and add ¾ cup of sugar for each cup of juice. Boil rapidly until the jelly stage is reached, then skim and pour at once into hot, sterilized glasses and seal.

Apple Mint Jelly

2 cups apple juice
1½ cups sugar
2 cups boiling water
1 cup mint leaves (tightly packed)

Pour the boiling water over the mint leaves, which have been washed and picked over, and allow to steep 1 hour. Press the juice from the leaves and add 4 tablespoons of this extract to the combined apple juice and sugar. Boil rapidly until the jelly stage is reached, color with a very few drops of green vegetable coloring and pour into hot, sterilized glasses. Seal.

Apple Muffins

2 cups sifted flour
2 tsp baking powder
½ tsp salt
½ cup sugar
½ tsp cinnamon
1 egg, beaten
1 cup milk
1 tbsp melted shortening
1 cup finely chopped raw apples

Sift the dry ingredients and moisten with the combined egg, milk, and shortening, stirring only enough to blend thoroughly. Add the chopped apples, turn into well greased muffin pans, and sprinkle the surface of each with cinnamon-sugar (2 tablespoons of sugar mixed with ½ teaspoon cinnamon). Bake in a moderately hot oven (350° F.) 25 minutes.

Apple Pan Dowdy

This very old New England apple dessert is served at many Fourth of July picnics. It usually marks the last appearance of apples until the next season's crop is gathered.

4 large tart apples
1 cup brown sugar
½ tsp cinnamon
¼ tsp nutmeg
⅓ tsp salt
3 tbsp butter
½ cup lukewarm water
Rich baking powder biscuit dough

Pare, core, and cut apples into eighths. Arrange them in a well buttered baking dish, and sprinkle with the brown sugar into which the spices and salt have been stirred. Dot with butter, and pour the water over all. Cover with a rich baking-powder biscuit dough (which see) rolled not more than ½ inch thick. Bake in a slow oven (300°-325° F.) for 25 to 30 minutes or until the crust is delicately browned and the apples are tender. Serve warm with plain, sweet, heavy cream or with your favorite hard sauce (which see).

Apple Pickles

7 lb green apples (unpeeled)
4 lb brown sugar
1 qt vinegar
1 cup water
1½ tsp cinnamon
1½ tsp cloves

Wash, quarter, and core the apples. Combine the sugar, vinegar, water, and spices, and boil (220° F.) until slightly thickened. Drop the apples into the sirup, and boil 10 minutes. Pack in sterilized jars, cover with hot sirup and seal. (Makes 6 pints)

Apple Pie I

4 tsp flour
A few grains salt
⅛ tsp each, ground cinnamon and nutmeg
Scant cup sugar
1 qt prepared apples
1 tbsp butter
Pastry for a two-crust pie

Sift the flour, salt, and spices and add to the sugar. Pare, core, and slice the apples and arrange in a pastry-lined pie plate (see Pastry) having the center apples higher than those around the edge. Sprinkle in the sifted dry ingredients and add the butter. Wet the edge of the crust with water, adjust the top crust, press the edges firmly together to seal, and make 2 or 3 gashes in the top to allow for escape of steam. Brush over with milk or cream, if desired, and let stand 5 minutes to dry. Bake in a hot oven (450° F.) for the first 10 minutes, then reduce to moderate (350° F.) and continue baking about 40 minutes longer or until the crust is done and the apples are tender.

APPLE PIE II

1 No. 2 can apples, drained
Scant ⅔ cup sugar
⅛ tsp each, ground cinnamon and nutmeg
¼ tsp salt
2 tsp quick-cooking tapioca
2 tsp butter, melted
Pastry for a two-crust pie

Combine all ingredients except the butter and pastry. Mix thoroughly and let stand for 1 hour to allow the tapioca to absorb part of the moisture, then complete the making of the pie as directed for Apple Pie I.

Any apple pie may be served either warm or cold, plain, with cheese, à la mode, or with light or whipped cream.

APPLE-PINEAPPLE-CRANBERRY PIE

2 cups sliced apples
½ cup crushed pineapple
½ cup halved cranberries
1 cup sugar
⅛ tsp salt
⅛ cup water or pineapple juice
Pastry for two-crust pie

Mix the apples, pineapple and cranberries with the sugar and salt and put over very low heat in a saucepan with enough water or juice to cover the bottom. Stir over heat for 15 minutes and cool for 3 hours. Line the bottom of a 9-inch pie pan with pastry, put in the filling and cover top with pastry, sealing edges. Bake at 450° F. for 10 minutes. Reduce heat to 350° F. and bake 35 minutes.

APPLE-PINEAPPLE BAKE

3 cups sliced apples
1 cup crushed pineapple
½ cup seeded raisins

½ cup sugar
⅛ tsp nutmeg
2 doz marshmallows

Grease a deep baking dish. Make alternate layers of apples, pineapple and raisins, and sprinkle with sugar and nutmeg. Bake 45 minutes at 350° F. Cover with marshmallows and brown.

APPLE-PRUNE STUFFING
(For Duck)

1 small onion, minced
2 tbsp butter
1½ cups bread crumbs
1 cup chopped celery
1 cup diced cooked prunes
1 cup tart apple, chopped
¼ tsp salt

Brown the onion in the butter, combine with all remaining ingredients, and blend thoroughly. *See* STUFFING.

APPLE-RAISIN STUFFING
(For Goose)

1 cup finely minced onion
3 cups diced, pared, cored apples
7 cups soft bread crumbs
1 cup seeded raisins
1½ tsp salt
⅛ tsp pepper
¼ cup sugar
¾ cup melted butter

Combine all ingredients and blend thoroughly. *See* STUFFING.

APPLE RINGS

1 cup sugar
¾ cup water
¼ cup vinegar
5 whole cloves
1 inch stick cinnamon
2 red apples
Red or green vegetable coloring
¼ cup cherry or currant jelly (optional)

Cook the sugar, water, vinegar, and spices together for 5 minutes. Meanwhile, wipe the apples with a damp cloth, but do not peel them. Core, cut crosswise into ½ inch slices, and cook slowly in the sugar sirup until transparent. Remove the apple slices carefully. Add the vegetable coloring to the sirup and cook until thick; then pour over the apple slices. Cool and arrange as a garnish. If desired, the centers from which the apple cores were removed may be filled with a bright colored jelly—cherry or currant. This makes a delicious meat garnish, especially when served with baked ham or pork.

APPLE SALADS

Apple Balls. (1) Combine with shredded white cabbage and shredded ham. Moisten with mayonnaise and serve in heart-lettuce cups. (2) Combine with finely chopped green pepper, seeded (or seedless) grape halves, and pitted, halved red cherries. Moisten with honey dressing and serve in lettuce cups. (3) Combine with cottage-cheese balls rolled in chopped chives, and cooked carrot balls. Moisten with French dressing to which a little prepared mustard has been added and serve on finely shredded raw spinach, finely shredded red cabbage, or crisp watercress. (2 balls of each to a portion.)

Apple Cup (Red-skinned, not peeled). (1) Fill with chopped celery, peas, and chopped nuts in equal parts, combined with mayonnaise. Serve on crisp lettuce. (2) Fill with mixed fruit salad moistened with French dressing and serve on crisp lettuce. (3) Fill with raspberry, orange, strawberry, lemon, or lime gelatin; combine while still liquid with chopped celery and chopped nuts. Serve on crisp green watercress with sour cream dressing.

Apple Cubes. Combine with orange and grapefruit sections, moisten with French dressing and serve in a nest of shredded raw spinach.

Apple Dice. Combine with diced celery, chopped nuts, and French dressing. Serve on a bed of shredded red cabbage.

Apple Sections. Combine with peach and tangerine sections (free from all skin and seeds) and moisten with currant jelly or cream cheese dressing. Serve on crisp lettuce.

Apple Slices. (1) Combine with banana slices and red raspberries and moisten with French dressing. Serve in a nest of crisp shredded white and red cabbage blended in equal parts. (2) Combine with quartered kumquats, moisten with French dressing, and serve on crisp lettuce, topping with a tomato slice. (3) Combine with sliced canned peaches and pineapple cubes. Mois-

ten with thin tomato mayonnaise (equal parts of mayonnaise and tomato juice) and serve garnished with watercress and finely chopped red cherries.

Apple Sticks. Combine with shredded red cabbage and shredded celery. Moisten with sour cream dressing, and serve on crisp romaine.

Apple Wedges. Combine with pear and orange sections, moisten with Russian dressing and serve in a nest of finely shredded red cabbage.

WALDORF SALAD

Combine equal quantities of diced apple, and diagonally sliced celery with chopped nuts to taste. Moisten with boiled dressing and garnish with crisp celery.

APPLE SNOW

3 large cooking apples
White of one egg
6 tbsp powdered sugar

Wash and dry three apples; prick them in a few places, and bake in moderate oven (350° F.) until soft. Remove the skin, and run the pulp through a sieve. Beat the egg white into a froth; add sugar gradually; then add apple pulp and beat it all together until thoroughly mixed, light, and soft.

APPLE ON A STICK

Skewer raw red apples in the blossom end, and then dip them in a hot sugar sirup which has been cooked to the brittle stage. The dipping must be done rapidly or the sirup will become too firm to coat the entire surface of the fruit. *See recipe for* STOCK SIRUP, *under* SIRUP.

APPLE SOUFFLE

3 cups sliced apples
⅓ cup water
2 eggs
½ cup sugar
Dash each, nutmeg, cinnamon, allspice
¼ tsp salt

Cook the apples and water gently until the apples are tender, then press through a coarse sieve. Beat the egg yolks with the sugar and spices; combine with the apples. Beat the egg whites and salt until stiff and dry, and fold into the first mixture. Turn into a well buttered casserole and bake in a moderate oven (350° F.) 15 to 20 minutes. Serve hot with hard sauce.

APPLE STRUDEL COFFEE CAKE

2 cups flour
2 tbsp sugar
1 tbsp baking powder
½ tsp salt
½ tsp cinnamon
¼ cup shortening
¼ cup grated cheese
¾ cup milk
1 cup sliced apples

Topping

1 tbsp butter
½ cup brown sugar
½ tsp cinnamon

Sift and resift the flour three times together with the sugar, baking powder, salt and cinnamon. Cream the shortening and cheese together and cut them into the dry ingredients. Add the milk and mix well to make a soft dough. Knead on a floured board for ½ minute and then level off the dough in a 9-inch pie pan. Insert the apples, edge down, over the top. Melt the butter and brush on the apples and dough. Then sprinkle top with the brown sugar and cinnamon. Bake in a moderately hot oven (400° F.) about 30 minutes, until apples and cake are done.

APPLE SURPRISE

Core and halve 3 apples of similar size. Cook until clear and red in a sirup made of equal parts of water, sugar, and red cinnamon candies. Lift out carefully and cool. Then fill each apple cavity with cranberry sauce blended with an equal bulk of drained prepared horseradish. Small apples prepared in this manner make a delicious garnish for fowl.

APPLE TAPIOCA

¼ cup quick tapioca
¼ tsp salt
2 cups boiling water
5 medium apples

½ cup sugar
1 tbsp butter
½ tsp cinnamon

Add tapioca and salt to water and cook in a double boiler for 15 minutes. Core and peel apples and arrange in a greased, deep baking dish. Fill centers with sugar, brush tops with melted butter and pour in tapioca. Sprinkle with cinnamon and bake at 350° F. until apples soften.

APPLE TART

1½ lb acid cooking apples
9 to 12 tbsp sugar
3 or 4 pats butter
½ lb rough puff pastry

Peel and core apples; slice and put in pan with sugar (amount varies according to taste), and butter. Cover the pan and stew on low heat for 15 minutes; then remove from the fire and let cool.

Prepare ½ lb rough puff pastry (*see* PASTRY) and line pastry tin with it; fill with the cold and partly stewed apple slices; brush over with sugar; and bake for 20 minutes. Serve cold with fresh cream.

APPLE TASTY

2 cups chopped apples
4 eggs
½ cup sugar
½ cup raisins
¼ cup chopped walnuts
2 tbsp brandy
¼ tsp cinnamon
½ tsp salt

Green-skinned, pie apples will provide good flavor for this dish. After paring and coring, chop the apples in ½-inch cubes. Separate eggs, beat yolks with sugar until light. Add other ingredients. Mix until well blended. Beat egg whites stiff and fold in. Pour batter into a deep-sided spring form and bake in a moderate oven (350° F.) for 25 to 35 minutes or until firm. Plain or whipped cream on top to serve. (Serves 6)

APPLE TURNOVER

2 good-sized apples
1 tbsp currants
1 tbsp sugar
½ tsp powdered cinnamon
1 tsp chopped mixed peel

Pare and finely chop apples. Mix all ingredients together. Make puff pastry dough (*see* PASTRY); roll in center to make thinner and to make oval in shape. Brush egg wash (1 egg yolk, and 2 tablespoons milk) on ½ of oval, and fill with chopped, tart apple mixture. Fold over and press gently to seal edge. Let rest 30 minutes. Bake at 450° F. for about 25 minutes. Brush with egg-white mixture and sprinkle with confectioner's sugar about 5 minutes before baking is finished.

APPLESAUCE

4 tart, juicy apples
½ cup water (approx.)
¼ cup sugar

Pare, quarter, and core apples; cut in eighths; add just enough water to steam fruit and keep from burning. Bring to a boil and cook (covered) slowly for 20 to 30 minutes or until soft. Add sugar, and simmer just long enough to dissolve sugar. Serve hot or cold. Applesauce may be spiced with cinnamon or cloves, and it should be sweetened to taste.

Applesauce may also be prepared by washing sound apples and cutting them into eighths, leaving the skin, core, and seeds. Cook in the same way as above, and rub through a sieve when the apples are soft. This will give a smooth sauce, which may be sweetened and spiced to taste.

APPLESAUCE CAKE

1 tsp cinnamon
½ tsp nutmeg
½ tsp ground cloves
½ tsp salt
1¼ cups cake flour, sifted
1 tsp baking soda
½ cup shortening
1 cup brown sugar
1 egg
1 cup tart applesauce
1 cup seedless raisins

Mix first 6 ingredients and sift 3 times. With large spoon, cream shortening and mix sugar evenly throughout. Add egg and beat until airy. Stir in applesauce lightly. Add flour mixture in three stages, beating thoroughly each time. Add raisins, being careful not to let them bunch at bottom. Empty into greased square pan (about 8″ square) and bake at 350° F. (moderate) for 45 minutes. Can also bake in layers or in muffin pans, baking at 350° F. for 30 minutes. Cake attains best flavor if not eaten for day or so. Wax paper or tight bread box will keep it moist.

APPLESAUCE FREEZE

2 cups applesauce
Grated rind small orange
1 tsp cinnamon
½ tsp nutmeg
2 tbsp sirup from preserved ginger
2 cups whipped, nonfat, dry milk solids

Mix applesauce with sirup, rind, and spices. Fold in whipped, nonfat, dry milk solids.

2½ cups crumbs
½ cup sugar
1 tsp cinnamon
6 tbsp melted butter
½ cup chopped nuts (if desired)

Mix crumbs, shortening, sugar, and spice. Sprinkle half on bottom of deep freezing tray. Top with applesauce mixture. Sprinkle with remaining crumbs. Freeze at fastest speed. Slice like brick ice cream.

BAKED APPLE

Eating apples, juicy and rather sweet, should be baked in their skins in a slow oven for a long time, 2 to 3 hours according to size. Cooking and acid apples are best baked after they have been peeled and put into a hot oven (400° F.) until soft. In either case, the apples should be cored and placed in a bakingdish, the bottom of which is covered with boiling water, before being baked. The center of the apple, after being cored, should be filled with sugar. Baked apples may be served either hot, straight from the oven, or quite cold with fresh cream.

CRAB APPLE JELLY

8 lb crab apples
Sugar
Water

Wash the apples, remove the stems and blossom tips, and cut out any blemishes.

Cut the apples in halves. Add water to barely cover and cook until soft. Crush lightly, then put into a jelly bag and let drip overnight. Next day, measure the juice and boil rapidly for 2 or 3 minutes. Add ¾ cup of sugar for each cup of juice. Stir until the sugar is completely dissolved, then boil rapidly for 15 minutes or until the jelly sheets from the spoon. Remove immediately from the heat, skim, and pour into hot, sterilized glasses. Seal.

DUTCH APPLE CAKE

2 cups flour
1 tbsp baking powder
½ cup sugar
½ tsp salt
⅓ cup cooking oil
1 egg
1 cup milk
4 large tart apples
1 tsp cinnamon
½ tsp nutmeg

Sift the flour, baking powder, half of the sugar and the salt together. Resift. Warm ¼ cup cooking oil and beat the egg with the milk. Add the warm cooking oil to the egg-milk mixture and blend. Add the liquid mixture to the dry ingredients and stir until barely blended. Then turn into a well greased rectangular cake pan and distribute an even thickness. Wash, peel, quarter and core the apples and then cut into eighths. Distribute the apples, sharp edge down, on top of the dough in rows. Mix the remaining sugar with the cinnamon and nutmeg and sprinkle over the top. Drip the remaining cooking oil over all. Bake for 30 to 35 minutes in a moderately hot oven (400° F.) until well browned. Serve while still warm, or reheat, with butter, Lemon Sauce (*which see*) or Hard Sauce (*which see*).

NUT CRUSTED APPLES

6 medium-sized apples
4 tbsp rich preserves
1 egg white, lightly beaten
½ cup soft bread crumbs
¼ cup brown sugar
¼ cup finely chopped nuts, any kind
1 cup water

Core the apples, removing a strip of skin about 1 inch wide from around the top of each, Fill the centers with apricot, peach, or other rich preserves. Coat each apple with the egg white. Combine the crumbs, sugar, and nuts, and use to top the apples, placed in a heavy baking pan. Pour the water around, and bake in a moderate oven (350° F.) until tender. (Serves 6)

POACHED APPLES

1 cup water
¼ cup lemon juice
2 cups sugar
1 tsp cinnamon
1 tsp nutmeg
1 tsp cloves
6 tart apples

Combine all ingredients except apples in a heavy, cast skillet or saucepan over a low heat until mixture reaches a slow boil. Wash and core the apples and then slice into rings. Drop rings into the sirup and cook until tender and browned. Remove from the sirup and serve while hot as a garnish for sausage or bacon.

SCALLOPED APPLES AND CHEESE

½ cup bread crumbs, toasted
4 to 6 apples
2 cups grated cheese
1 tsp salt
Milk
⅛ cup melted butter

Grease a baking dish liberally and put in half of the crumbs. Move the dish about so that the crumbs coat the sides and bottom; save remaining crumbs. Pare, core and slice the apples thin. Now, in the dish, form alternate layers of sliced apples and grated cheese sprinkled with salt until ingredients are exhausted. Add milk to top of apples. Blend the melted butter with remaining crumbs and sprinkle on top. Bake in a moderate oven (350° F.) until apples are tender, about 30 minutes.

STEWED APPLES

Pare apples, cut them into halves and then into quarters, and remove the cores. Cut the quarters into 2 or 3 lengthwise pieces, and place them in a saucepan with a very little water and sugar to taste—1½ tablespoons to 1 pound of apples is about the average. Bring to a boil, and then reduce the heat. Allow to simmer gently until done. Cool before serving, and serve with cinnamon and sugar.

SWEDISH APPLE CHARLOTTE

2½ lb fresh apples
1 cup sugar
½ cup water
½ stale brown loaf (about 2 cups breadcrumbs)
4½ oz butter (9 tbsp)

Pare, core, and cut the apples into thin sections. Cook into pulp with sugar and a very little water. Grate the loaf, and brown lightly in 6 tablespoons of the butter. Spread buttered and breadcrumbed tin with three layers of breadcrumbs and two of apples, the top layer being breadcrumbs. Bake for ½ hour in a moderate oven. Turn out and sprinkle with powdered sugar. Serve hot or cold, with whipped cream or vanilla sauce.

TAFFY APPLES

2 cups sugar
½ cup water
⅛ tsp cream of tartar
½ cup butter
1 tsp vinegar
½ cup cream
Apples

Be sure that the apples are washed and dried.

Combine the sugar and water in a large saucepan and bring slowly to boiling point, stirring just until the sugar is dissolved. Add the cream of tartar, butter, vinegar, and cream; cook, stirring constantly, to the soft crack state (290° F.). Remove from the fire and dip each apple, impaled on a skewer, into the sirup; then place on a buttered platter to harden.

If a caramel flavor is desired, use equal parts granulated and brown sugar.

UPSIDE DOWN APPLE GINGER BREAD

3 tart apples
2 tbsp butter
1¼ cups light brown sugar
1 egg, beaten
¼ cup shortening
½ cup molasses
1¼ cups all-purpose flour

¼ tsp salt
¾ tsp ground ginger
¼ tsp ground cinnamon
¾ tsp soda
½ cup sour milk or buttermilk

Core the apples, then peel and cut them into thin slices. Melt the butter in a heavy skillet with an ovenproof handle, and cover with one cup of the sugar. Arrange the apple rings in overlapping slices over the sugar.

Cream the shortening, gradually working in the remaining sugar, the egg, and the molasses. Sift the dry ingredients and add alternately with the milk. Pour over the apples in the pan and bake in a moderate oven (350° F.) ½ to ¾ of an hour. As soon as baked, invert onto a platter. Serve warm with whipped cream, cream cheese, or hard sauce.

Other fruits may be substituted for the apples. Modify the amount of sugar used according to the sweetness of the fruit.

APPLE BUTTER. Apple butter is prepared by cooking apple pulp (with or without spices) to the consistency of a thick paste suitable for spreading. Less sugar is used for fruit butter than for jams and marmalades. When cooked on top of the stove, fruit butters require slow cooking and frequent stirring to prevent burning. If cooked in the oven, they require only occasional stirring. Different kinds of apple butters are available in the markets.

APPLE CORER. See CUTLERY; see also KITCHEN EQUIPMENT.

APPLE JUICE. Unsweetened apple juice ranks high in popularity among fruit juices. The highest grade of apple juice is a more refined product than ordinary cider. Harmless yeasts and molds develop rapidly in juice, after it has been pressed from the apple. If this development is unchecked, the delicate apple flavor of the juice changes rapidly. By a special process, these organisms are destroyed at low temperature in high-grade canned apple juice without affecting the vitamin content, and the juice is then sealed in a vacuum. In addition, apple juice is put through very fine filters before canning. Cider, the less refined product, is put through rough, rather than fine, filters. An infinitesimal amount of benzoate of soda or another benzoate preparation is sometimes added to cider as a preservative. This is not done with apple juice. See also CIDER.

APPLE MINT. A member of the mint family, apple mint is used in mint juleps, lemonade and other ades, fruit salads, and certain desserts. It is also crystallized. Its flavor is rather more delicate than spearmint or peppermint.

APPLEJACK. A brandy made by distilling apple cider. The name is also given to a beverage produced by freezing hard cider. The distilled liquor is a strong apple-flavored cordial with a peculiarly pleasing taste. It forms the basis of many cocktails and punches. *See also* CIDER, COBBLER, SOUR.

APPLEJACK SHERBET

2½ cups apple juice
¼ cup sugar
1 tbsp lemon juice
¼ scant cup applejack
2 egg whites
⅛ tsp salt

Simmer the apple juice, sugar, and lemon juice for 10 minutes. Strain. Chill. Then pour into refrigerator tray and half freeze. Scrape out into an ice-cold mixing bowl and, gradually adding the apple-jack, beat with a chilled rotary egg beater until light. Return to the refrigerator tray and again freeze until mushy. Once more turn into the ice-cold mixing bowl and again beat until light with rotary egg beater. Now fold in the salt and stiffly beaten eggwhites, return to the tray and complete freezing without further stirring.

A fine digestive sherbet for service after the fish or roast at dinner (Serves 6)

APPLIANCES FOR THE KITCHEN. *See* KITCHEN EQUIPMENT.

APRICOT. The apricot is a yellow-colored fruit related to the peach. A native of North China, it was cultivated extensively in Armenia centuries ago, and it is now grown in all temperate countries. The best apricots come from France, while the greatest quantity of dried apricots come from California and Australia.

Apricots are usually picked when slightly immature, so that they may reach the market in good condition. The finest quality and best flavor, however, are found in fruit that has ripened on the tree. Because of its extreme perishability, such fruit is difficult to ship and is usually found in markets adjacent to the district in which it is grown. American shipping centers for this fruit are California, Oregon, and Washington.

Apricots do not contain as much sugar as apples and other fruits. They are wholesome when thoroughly ripe, if not eaten in excess. They agree well with some gouty persons and are even allowed to diabetics in moderate cases.

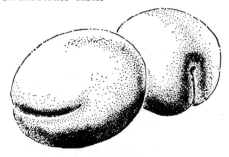

APRICOT

Well matured fruit is plump, fairly firm, and uniformly golden in color. It is in season during June, July, and August. Immature apricots are usually a greenish yellow in color. The flesh of apricots varies from firm to hard. By the time they reach the market, shriveling is often evident, and the typical apricot flavor is lacking. Fruits that have been bruised or injured should be avoided. The beginning of decay is usually indicated by softness verging upon mushiness and by a dull appearance.

Canned apricots may be either halved or whole. They are not peeled because the fruit bruises easily without its skin and because the skin is so tender that peeling is unnecessary. Whole canned apricots are excellent for salads and many desserts.

About two-thirds of the apricot crop is taken for drying. Dried apricots are rich in iron. A quick boiling of the dried fruit prepares it for use in cooking.

HINTS ON BUYING

Fresh apricots are sold by the pound (8 to 16) or the dozen. A pound will make approximately 2½ cups of cooked apricots. When fresh, they should be plump, fairly firm, and of a uniformly golden color. Ripe fruits should be covered and stored in the refrigerator. Slightly green fruit should first be ripened at room temperature.

Dried apricots are usually sold halved and unpeeled. They are graded according

Food Value

	Wa- ter	Food Energy	Pro- tein	Fat	Car- bohy- drate	Cal- cium	Phos- phorus	Iron	Vit. A Value	Thia- mine	Ribo- flavin	Nia- cin	Ascor- bic Acid
Fresh Apricots	85.4	56	1.0	.1	12.9	16	23	.5	2,790	.03	.04	.7	4
Canned Apricots	77.3	89	.6	.1	21.4	10	15	.3	1,350	.02	.02	.3	4
Dried Apricots	24	292	5.2	.4	66.9	86	119	4.9	7,430	.01	.16	3.3	12

to size. They should be stored in a dark, cool, dry place. Dried apricots have a deeper gold color than fresh, and their flavor has more character.

Canned apricots are graded according to the U.S. standards, and may be either whole or halved.

Hints on Preparation

To remove the skin from fresh apricots, immerse the fruit in boiling water for about 30 seconds to loosen the skin and then plunge into cold water to keep the fruit firm. To prevent discoloration, drop halves into a weak brine solution (1 tablespoon salt to 1 quart water) until ready for use.

Apricot Bavarian

1 tbsp gelatin
¼ cup cold water
¾ cup confectioners' sugar
1 cup apricot puree
¾ cup chilled whipping cream
2 tsp lemon juice

Soften gelatin in cold water for a few minutes; heat it in the top part of double boiler, stirring constantly, until it dissolves. Add gelatin and sugar to unsweetened apricot purée, *which see*. Mix thoroughly, and chill until somewhat thickened. Whip the cream, adding lemon juice when cream is moderately stiff; continue beating until thoroughly blended. Fold cream into the purée. Turn apricot-cream mixture into mold, and chill in refrigerator until set. (Serves 5)

Apricot Bread Pudding

1¼ cups bread crumbs
3 tbsp butter
⅔ cup milk
¾ cup sugar
1 cup cooked apricots
1 tbsp lemon juice
1 tsp lemon rind, grated
¼ tsp salt
2 eggs
6 to 8 apricot halves
¼ cup coconut, grated

Toast the crumbs, add the next 3 ingredients and bring to a slow boil in a saucepan while stirring. Put aside until cool and then add apricots (after chopping fine), lemon juice, rind and salt. Beat eggs and add. Blend well and turn into a greased baking dish. Arrange apricot halves to cover top, then sprinkle coconut. Bake, in a pan of hot water, at 350° F. until firm, about 45 minutes. (Serves 5)

Apricot Candy

¾ cup dried apricots
½ cup nut meats
¾ cup coconut
1 tsp grated orange rind
1 tsp grated lemon rind
1 tbsp lemon juice

Chop apricots, nut meats, and coconut. Mix well with orange and lemon rinds, and moisten with 1 tablespoon of lemon juice. Shape into small balls and roll in powdered sugar. (Approximately 50 small balls)

Apricot Compote

12 large apricots
2 cups cold water
1 cup sugar
½ cup brandy

Peel, halve, and stone the fruit. Boil sugar and water 10 minutes, removing any scum that rises. Put fruit in carefully. Let it simmer, being careful that it does not burn. When liquid is all absorbed, remove from fire, add brandy, and set in cool place until wanted.

APRICOT DUMPLINGS

2 cups milk
1 cup flour
3 tbsp butter
Fresh apricots

Melt the butter in the milk over a low flame and season with salt. When it simmers, stir in the flour and cook until it no longer sticks to the spoon. Spread this paste on a floured board and roll out very thin. Drop the ripe apricots into boiling water for a minute or so, and then remove the skin. Wrap the apricots in individual squares of paste, rolling them until they are smooth balls. Drop these dumplings into slightly salted boiling water and cook until they rise to the top. Drain them in a sieve carefully to avoid breaking. Serve with hot butter and sprinkle with powdered sugar and powdered cinnamon.

APRICOT FRAPPE

1 large can apricots
1½ cups sugar
1¾ cups water
1 tbsp lemon juice

Drain the fruit, cut it in small pieces, and place in a sieve while preparing the sirup. For sirup, combine the sugar and water in a saucepan, bring to boiling point, stirring until the sugar is dissolved, then cook 5 minutes. Cool, add the drained fruit and the lemon juice, and freeze either in hand freezer or in automatic refrigerator. If the former, freeze just until mushy; if the latter, freeze 2½ to 3 hours, stirring and scraping down once as soon as the mixture becomes a little mushy or about 30 minutes after the freezing process begins. (Serves 6)

APRICOT FRITTERS

1¾ cups flour
1¾ tsp baking powder
3 tbsp sugar
½ tsp salt
2 eggs
⅔ cup milk

1 cup canned apricots
2 tbsp lemon rind, grated
⅛ cup confectioners' sugar

Sift the first 4 ingredients together and then resift for complete blending. Beat the eggs and blend in the milk. Add the dry ingredients slowly, while stirring, and continue to beat until the mixture is smooth. Chop and drain the apricots. Blend the rind with the confectioners' sugar. Form small cakes of the apricots, cover with the rind-sugar, coat with batter and fry in deep fat at 375° F. until well browned to a fairly dark color. Remove, drain and serve hot. (Serves 4)

APRICOT ICE

½ cup sugar
2 cups boiling water
1 cup apricot juice
2 tbsp lemon juice

Combine the sugar and water, and cook 5 minutes, then add the fruit juice. Blend thoroughly, chill, turn into refrigerator tray, and freeze about 3 hours, stirring once when mushy. (Serves 4 to 6)

Almost any fruit juice may be similarly prepared.

APRICOT ICE CREAM

1 lb fresh apricots
1 cup boiling water
½ cup sugar
1 cup heavy cream, whipped
¼ cup evaporated milk, chilled
Grated rind ½ lemon
4 drops almond extract

Wash the apricots, and cook them with the boiling water over a very low flame for 10 minutes. Add the sugar, stir gently until this is dissolved, and cook 10 minutes longer or until the fruit is tender, then press fruit and juice through sieve. Measure 1 cup and set aside the remainder to use as a sauce for the ice cream. Now combine the 1 cup of apricot pulp with the whipped cream, with which the chilled evaporated milk and the flavorings have been blended. Freeze in refrigerator tray of automatic refrigerator about 4 hours, scraping and stirring the mixture from the bottom and sides of the tray at the end of the first hour. Serve with the chilled remainder of the apricot pulp as a sauce. (Serves 4 to 6) *See also* ICE CREAM.

APRICOT JAM

Wash the fruit carefully, then dip it into boiling water for about ½ minute or until the skins slip easily. Plunge the fruit at once into cold water for a few seconds, remove the skins, cut the fruit into halves, and discard the pits. To each pound of prepared apricots, allow ¾ pound of sugar, and 2 tablespoons of lemon juice. Crush the fruit, combine with the sugar in alternate layers, and let stand until some of the juice is extracted, that is, about 3 to 4 hours. Then heat slowly until the sugar is dissolved, stirring meanwhile. Bring to boiling and cook, stirring constantly, until the fruit is clear and the jam somewhat thick. Pour into hot sterilized jars and seal.

APRICOT MOUSSE

1 cup heavy cream, whipped stiff
2 egg whites, stiffly beaten
1 can apricots, drained and sieved
¼ cup granulated sugar
½ scant tsp salt
½ tsp almond extract
2 tbsp ground almonds

Combine gently, stiffly beaten egg whites and heavy cream, whipped stiff. Combine sieved apricot pulp (no juice), sugar, salt, flavoring extract, and blanched ground almonds; then add to combined egg whites and heavy cream. Blend well, but gently. Turn mixture into refrigerator tray and freeze 4 hours without stirring. You may use fresh apricot pulp or substitute apple sauce or apricot marmalade for canned apricots, if desired.

APRICOT NECTAR

Put 1 cup chilled apricot nectar (canned) into mixing bowl, add 2 teaspoons lemon juice, pinch of salt, 1 tablespoon sugar, and a large scoop of vanilla or New York ice cream. Beat until ice cream half melts. Serve at once. Makes 1¼ cups.

APRICOT NUT BREAD

1 cup apricots, dried
2 eggs
¾ cup sugar
1 tsp almond extract
Milk
2 tbsp shortening
2½ cups flour
4 tsp baking powder
1 tsp salt
⅓ cup nut meats, chopped

Rinse the dried apricots, letting them absorb as little moisture as possible. Cut up finely and put in about ¾ cup of warm water to soak for several hours. Beat eggs until light, then add sugar slowly while beating. Drain liquid off apricots; add milk to make one full cup. Add almond extract. Melt shortening and add to juice-milk mixture, then add apricots. Combine this with eggs. Sift flour, baking powder and salt together and add. Beat, add nuts and blend well. Grease a loaf pan thoroughly and line with waxed paper. Pour in mixture; let settle for a few minutes. Bake at 350° F. (moderate) for an hour and a quarter. Remove and cool.

APRICOT PIE

2 cups drained canned apricots
¼ cup sugar
1 package lemon-flavored gelatin
1½ cups apricot juice, hot
½ cup water
⅛ tsp salt
1 baked pastry shell
½ cup heavy cream, whipped

Combine apricots and sugar; chill. Dissolve flavored gelatin in hot or boiling apricot juice as directed on package. Add water and salt, and chill until mixture begins to thicken. Arrange apricots in baked pastry shell (*see* PASTRY); cover with slightly thickened gelatin mixture. Chill until firm, then pile whipped cream on pie. Canned peaches, pineapple, or cherries may be substituted if desired.

APRICOT CHIFFON PIE

1 tbsp gelatin
½ lb dried apricots
1½ cups water
3 eggs
¾ cup sugar
2 tbsp lemon juice
⅛ tsp salt
9-inch pre-baked pie shell

Soak the gelatin in ⅛ cup of water to soften. Soak the apricots in the remaining water over very low heat. After one hour, increase heat to simmer for 15 minutes. Press apricots and juice through a food mill or sieve to make a purée. Separate eggs and beat yolks in a double boiler, add half of sugar, the lemon juice, salt and apricot juice. Stir continuously, while cooking over hot water, until the mixture thickens. Add the gelatin and keep cooking and stirring until well dissolved. Cool until thick. Beat egg whites stiff, add remaining sugar and beat again until stiff. Then fold into the apricot mixture, blending thoroughly, and turn into the pie shell and chill in the refrigerator until well firmed. If preferred, garnish with whipped cream, sweetened.

APRICOT COCONUT CUSTARD PIE DE LUXE

3/4 cup sugar
4 tbsp flour
1/4 tsp salt
4 eggs
2 cups milk
1¼ cups shredded coconut
1 tsp vanilla
1½ cups cooked dried apricots
One 9-inch pre-baked pie shell

Prepare a custard (which see) with ¼ cup of the sugar, the flour, salt, egg yolks, and milk. As soon as thickened, remove from the fire and add one cup of the coconut, with the vanilla. Pour half of this mixture into the pre-baked pie shell (see PASTRY). Drain the apricots thoroughly, arrange half of them over the custard, then repeat the layers. Make a meringue (which see) with the egg whites and remaining sugar, pile on the filling, sprinkle with the remaining coconut, and place in a moderate oven (350° F.) until set and delicately colored. Serve cold.

APRICOT PRESERVES

6 cups firm, fresh apricot halves
6 cups sugar
1½ cups water

Wipe the fruit with a damp cloth. Halve and discard all pits but 8. Crack these and blanch the kernels. Combine the sugar and water in a saucepan and stir over a moderate heat until the sugar is dissolved. Add the blanched kernels and cook rapidly for 5 minutes to thicken the sirup. Put in the fruit and cook gently until tender but not broken. (All the fruit will probably not become tender with the same amount of cooking; therefore as the apricot halves soften, lift out onto a platter until all are tender.) Boil down the sirup until quite thick, take out the kernels, replace the fruit, and again bring to boiling point. Turn into small, hot, sterilized jars and seal. (Makes 3 pints)

APRICOT PUREE

Rinse, soak, and cook the apricots as described under stewed apricots (which see). Use a wooden spoon to force the cooked fruit through a sieve. Stir additional sugar into the pulp, if desired. The pulp or purée may be returned to the soup, or it may be used to make an apricot fool. To make this dessert, slowly stir in an equal amount of cream, add a pinch of salt, and chill.

APRICOT SALAD

3 apricots
3/4 cup olives, chopped
3/4 cup nut meats
Pepper
Salt
Mayonnaise

Peel apricots, cut in half, remove pit. Mix olives and nuts together and add a little mayonnaise. Fill apricot halves with this mixture. Add salt and pepper as desired. Serve on lettuce.

APRICOT SAUCE

1 cup sieved apricot pulp
1/4 cup sugar
1/3 cup apricot juice
1 tbsp lemon juice

Either stewed, fresh, or canned apricots may be used. Simmer the fruit, sugar, and juice for 10 minutes, stirring occasionally. Remove from the heat, and add the lemon juice. Serve hot or cold. (Makes 1 cup)

APRICOT SNOWBALLS

1 cup raw rice
Fresh apricots

Boil 1 cup of rice (*which see*) for 15 minutes or until tender. Wring out small pieces of cheesecloth (⅓ yard square) in hot water and lay over a small bowl. Spread the rice ⅛ inch thick over the cloth. Put an apricot in the center, filling the cavity in each half apricot with rice. Draw the cloth around until the apricot is covered smoothly with the rice. Tie tightly, and steam for 10 minutes. Remove the cloth carefully and turn the balls out on a platter. Serve with apricot sauce.

APRICOT SOUFFLE (Cold)

3 eggs
2 tbsp lemon juice
½ cup sugar
¼ tsp salt
1 tbsp gelatin
¼ cup cold water
⅔ cup apricot juice and pulp
½ cup cream, whipped, or evaporated milk, whipped

Beat the egg yolks slightly, add the lemon juice, sugar, and salt, and cook in a double boiler, stirring constantly, until the mixture thickens. Remove from the fire and add the gelatin, which has been softened in the cold water. Stir until dissolved. Beat in the apricot pulp and juice, using either freshly cooked, canned, or stewed dried apricots. If canned apricots are used, a little less sugar will be needed. Cool, and when almost at setting point, fold in the whipped cream or milk and the stiffly beaten egg whites. Turn into 1 large or several small wet molds. Chill, unmold, and garnish with apricot halves. (Serves 4 to 6)

APRICOT SPONGE

2 tbsp gelatin
⅓ cup cold water
1½ cups boiling water
21 apricots, stewed, sweetened
1½ tbsp lemon juice
8 egg whites

Let gelatin soak in cold water five minutes, then dissolve in boiling water. Chill until somewhat firm. Purée 14 apricots, add lemon juice, fold in. Beat egg white stiff and fold in. Place in mold. Chill until firm and festoon with rest of apricots.

APRICOT UPSIDE-DOWN CAKE

15 dried apricot halves
½ cup warm water
2½ tbsp butter
1 tbsp honey
½ cup brown sugar
⅔ cup granulated sugar
1 cup flour
1½ tsp baking powder
¼ tsp salt
¼ cup shortening
1 egg
¼ tsp vanilla extract
¼ tsp almond extract
¼ cup milk

Rinse apricots; let stand in water until pulpy. Using skillet (8″) with oven-proof handle, melt butter. Add honey, brown sugar and ⅓ cup granulated sugar. Add 2 tbsp water from apricots, boil 2 minutes, and turn off flame.

Now sift baking powder and salt with flour, 3 times. Cream shortening, blend in remaining granulated sugar. Add egg and flavorings and beat to a light froth. Beating thoroughly with each addition, add flour and milk in several stages, ending with flour. Distribute apricot halves over sirup in skillet and blanket them with batter. At 375° F. (moderate) bake about 25 minutes, until cake tests done. Leave cake in pan to cool slightly. Before removing from pan, loosen cake with knife blade at sides. Serve warm with lemon sauce or with whip cream. Almost any of the mild-flavored frostings (*which see*) goes well with this cake.

APRICOT WHIP

1 cup apricot puree
½ cup sugar
2 tbsp lemon juice
¾ cup whipping cream
2 egg whites

Sweeten apricot purée (*which see*) with ¼ cup sugar, add lemon juice. Whip cream firm; fold into apricot purée. Adding remaining sugar, beat egg whites until they reach a dry fluffiness. Fold into apricot-cream mixture. Whip is now ready for cold serving if preferred. To cook, empty into greased casserole. Set casserole in shallow pan of hot water. Bake in oven at 350°

F. (moderate) for 20 minutes. Next lower heat to 200° F. and bake 20 minutes more. Serve at once, as texture thickens in time. (Serves 6)

DRIED APRICOTS

Apricots should be left on the tree until they are perfectly ripe, but not overripe, to make the best dried fruit. They are generally harvested for drying by being shaken from the tree into a large sheet from which they are gently poured into cases holding about 35 pounds each. As soon as possible, these are carted to the cutting shed where the fruit is halved and pitted. They are placed, cut-side up, on trays and taken to the sulfur room, where they remain for eight to twelve hours. The trays are then removed and placed in the sun or in an evaporator. The dried fruit is taken from the tray and securely tied in clean calico bags. It is then stored in a cool, dry place; if exposed to heat it will become hard, lose weight, and deteriorate.

Grading. Apricots are graded in three classes. The first, U.S. No. 1, consists of apricots of one variety which are well formed, free from decay and damage, and mature, but not soft, overripe, or shriveled. U.S. No. 2 consists of apricots of one variety which are mature, but not overripe or shriveled and which are free from decay and serious damage.

Apricots which do not meet the requirements of either of these grades belong to the Unclassified grade.

APRICOT WHIP

1 cup stewed apricots, pitted
3 egg whites
¼ cup sirup from apricots
⅓ cup sugar
2 tsp lemon juice
⅛ tsp salt
Liqueur to flavor

Be certain apricots have been cooked enough for pulp to break apart easily. Beat egg whites lightly, then whip in other ingredients at moderate beating speed. Add liqueur to taste when nearly firm. Continue beating until firm and serve in individual sherbert glasses immediately. Or, serve in salad form, ringed by halved apricots over individual portion of lettuce or romaine. (Serves 6)

APRICOT WINE

Take 12 pounds of ripe apricots, wipe clean, and cut them into small pieces. Place them in 2 gallons of water and boil until the liquid has absorbed the flavor of the fruit. Then strain through a sieve and add 6 ounces of sugar for every quart of liquid. Boil again and skim repeatedly until scum ceases to rise. Pour into an earthen crock and let stand. Bottle the next day, putting a lump of sugar in each bottle.

DRIED APRICOT SHORTCAKE

1 recipe Shortcake
Stewed dried apricots
⅔ cup sugar, or to suit taste
Melted butter
Cream

Mix shortcake dough. Roll about ⅓ inch thick and cut with biscuit cutter of desired size. If crusty shortcakes are desired, lay biscuits all out on baking sheet; if less crusty ones are preferred, transfer half of them to baking sheet, brush with melted butter, and lay rest of rounds on top. Bake as directed for shortcake. To serve, place lower half of hot biscuit on serving dish, drizzle with melted butter, and spoon apricots and juice over them. Cover with top half of biscuit; spoon more apricots and juice over top. Serve immediately, with whipped cream, if desired. (5 generous servings)

OLD ENGLISH APRICOT PUDDING

1½ lb fresh apricots
¾ cup breadcrumbs
1 loaf stale white bread
½ cup sugar
1 tsp powdered cinnamon
Grenadine or fresh fruit juice

Blanch firm or even slightly underripe apricots, peel and halve them, crack the pits, and put the kernels in hot water for 20 minutes. Stew the apricots very slowly until tender in sirup sweetened according to the ripeness of the fruit. Place a layer of bread and butter in a buttered pie dish. Sprinkle it with sugar and the merest hint of powdered cinnamon. On this, place a layer of apricots and then some of the kernels. Moisten with grenadine or with fresh fruit juice. Repeat the layers until the dish is full, ending with bread buttered on both sides and sprinkled with bread-crumbs. Bake a half hour in a medium oven (350° F.).

STEWED DRIED APRICOTS

½ lb dried apricots
2 cups cold water
¼ cup sugar (optional)

Rinse the apricots in cold water, and then allow them to soak for about an hour. Put them into a saucepan with enough cold water to prevent burning (about 2 cups), and cover the saucepan. Heat to the simmering point. Simmer until the fruit becomes tender (about 30 minutes). Stir in the sugar (if desired) a few minutes before this point has been reached. Serve with cream.

APRICOT BRANDY. This is a highly flavored liqueur made in apricot-growing countries. There are two types, one in which brandy or other spirits are flavored with dried apricots, and the other in which the brandy is distilled directly from the fresh fruit and the crushed kernels of the pits. *See also* BRANDY *and* LIQUEURS.

APRICOT GLAZE. Used on fruit cakes to hold the decorations of fruit and nuts on the top of the cake.

APRICOT GLAZE

¼ lb dried apricots
1½ cups cold water
1 cup light corn sirup

Wash dried apricots. Cover them with water and let soak overnight or for several hours. Cook them in same water until very tender or for about 15 minutes. Drain off the cooking water through a fine sieve and rub through the sieve only half the apricots. Measure juice and purée. There should be ½ cup. Add 1 cup light corn sirup and boil rapidly for 2 or 3 minutes or until the mixture is clear. Remove from heat and use immediately, quickly applying to fruit cake with a pastry brush. If desired, decorations may be applied after the first coat of glaze, and a second coat applied over the decorations when the first coat has set. (Reheat glaze to boiling each time it is used.) Dry thoroughly before storing. (Enough to doublecoat 15 pounds of fruit cake)

APRICOT LIQUEUR. This is merely a sweetened apricot brandy of low alcoholic content.

AQUA VITAE. This Latin phrase once applied to distilled liquors, especially the brandies. Literally it means *water of life*, or, less literally, *the Elixir of life*. The French *Eau de vie*, the Swedish *Aquavit*, and the Celtic *Usquebaugh* are all based on the same idea.

AQUAVIT. A dry, clear white liquor containing 43 percent alcohol, distilled from grain, potatoes, or sawdust, and flavored with caraway seeds. It is a product of Sweden. Aquavit is served before or at the beginning of a meal.

ARCHBISHOP'S PUNCH. *See* PUNCH.

ARMADILLO

ARMADILLO. An armor-covered mammal indigenous to South America and the southwestern United States. The South American armadillos are much the larger. In recent years, these odd little creatures have become the target of gourmets. The armadillo has nocturnal habits and resembles the turtle in its love of fruits, roots, insects, and plants.

In preparing it for the table, the flesh is loosened from its carapace as in the case of terrapins. Because of its slightly musky taste, the flesh is flavored with spices and strong wines or some acidulation. Both clear and thick soups are also made from the meat.

ARMAGNAC. A liqueur of the brandy type, made from the marc residuum of grapes, which is boiled several times and then strained. It is a fiery and delicious after-dinner cordial, very dry and aromatized. It contains from 40 to over 50 per cent alcohol and is considered a good digestive. It is a product of France and is sometimes called "The Brandy of Lafayette." *See also* BRANDY, COGNAC, LIQUEURS, *and* WINE.

ARMAVIR CHEESE. A Russian cheese which is made of sour milk. It resembles HAND CHEESE (*which see*).

AROMATIC. Aromatic means spicy, pungent, or having a fragrant aroma.

AROMATIC HERBS. *See* HERBS.

ARRACK. This is a fiery liquor distilled from rice or molasses and commonly found in India and the Dutch Indies. Usually an amateur production somewhat on the order of American Moonshine, it has never enjoyed much more than local popularity.

ARTICHOKE. Two entirely different vegetables are known by this name, the French, or Globe artichoke, which is a green thistle-like head, and the Jerusalem artichoke which is a tuber. The Chinese artichoke is related to the Jerusalem.

French Artichoke. The dark green, sometimes purplish, heads vary in size from very small heads to those averaging four or five inches in diameter. The smaller heads are the better buy because they are usually more tender. One artichoke serves as one portion.

Artichokes, when served cold as a salad, are eaten with the fingers. Each leaf is pulled off and dipped in the accompanying sauce, and the tender end of the leaf is eaten. When the leaves have all been stripped off, the tender base is cut into pieces and eaten with a fork. Very small artichokes preserved in olive oil may be purchased for use as hors d'oeuvres. These are eaten in their entirety. Artichokes may also be served as a hot vegetable, and several unusual recipes are given below.

The artichoke has a delicate nutty flavor which is very delicious, but it is a curious fact that it does not go with certain beverages. Tea and most wines lose their flavor entirely when taken with artichokes.

BOILED ARTICHOKES

Remove the larger outside leaves of as many artichokes as desired, and cut off the stem close to the base. Clip off the hooked tips of the leaves. Separate the leaves carefully, and remove the prickly choke at the center of the head. Tie the head up with a piece of string so that it will keep its shape, and plunge into boiling, salted water to which a little vinegar or lemon juice has been added. Cook until the base is tender (15 or 20 minutes, depending upon the size). Remove from the water, drain, and remove the string. The artichoke is now ready to serve hot with melted butter or hollandaise sauce, or it may be cooled

and served with French dressing or a vinaigrette sauce.

ARTICHOKES PROVENCALE

Small artichokes
2 tbsp olive oil
2 carrots
1 clove garlic
1 onion
1 glass dry white wine
Hot water or stock
Salt and pepper

Mince the onions and dice the carrots. Heat 1 tablespoon of oil in a shallow pan, and add the onion and carrot. Place the artichokes base down in the pan, and sprinkle with the remaining oil and with salt and pepper. Cover the pan and cook slowly, being careful that the artichokes do not burn. When the onions and carrots begin to brown, add the wine and continue cooking slowly, uncovered, until the wine is reduced to half. Add the garlic and the hot water or stock, cover tightly, and continue cooking until the artichokes are tender. Serve the artichokes in a vegetable dish and strain the sauce over them, adding a few drops of lemon juice.

ARTICHOKE FRITTERS

The larger artichokes may be used for this dish, since only the bottoms will be used. Boil the artichokes as usual. When the bottoms are tender, drain. Remove and discard the leaves. Slice the bottoms into convenient sizes, and marinate them in a mixture of olive oil, lemon juice, salt, pepper, and chopped chives for several hours. Drain them on crumpled paper. Dip in a light fritter batter (*which see*) and fry in deep fat. Serve hot.

Jerusalem Artichoke. The Jerusalem artichoke is not often found in the market since it does not keep well, but it is easily grown in most sections of the country. The tuber has a pleasant flavor and makes an interesting change from potatoes. It resembles a potato but is more warty and misshapen. No adequate explanation is known for the name, since it apparently did not originate in the city of Jerusalem.

The Jerusalem artichoke should always be cooked in its jacket after being well washed and scrubbed. Then the skin may be peeled off easily.

Mashed Jerusalem Artichokes

1½ lbs firm Jerusalem artichokes
Salted water
Butter, salt, and pepper

Select tubers of uniform size and as smooth as possible. Wash them, scrubbing gently with a soft brush. Cook, covered, in boiling salted water for about 30 minutes or until tender. Overcooking will toughen the tubers. Drain, and strip off the skin. Mash the artichokes as you would potatoes, or put them through a ricer. Season with butter, salt, and pepper.

JERUSALEM ARTICHOKE

Cooked in this manner, the artichoke may be used in any way suitable for the potato. It may be used as a border for creamed dishes, or molded in a ring; mixed with cheese, it may be formed into small cakes and fried. The plain mashed artichoke may be formed into small balls and fried in deep fat. The boiled tubers may be diced and served cold, mixed in a salad.

Jerusalem Artichokes Au Gratin

Slice the boiled and peeled tubers into a baking dish and mix with a rich cream sauce. (*See* White Sauce) Cover with buttered crumbs and grated cheese and heat in the oven until the cheese melts.

Jerusalem Artichoke Souffle

2 cups mashed Jerusalem artichokes, thinned with a little cream
3 eggs, separated

Beat the egg whites to a stiff froth. Beat the yolks until light, and add them to the mashed artichokes. Season with salt and pepper. Fold in the beaten whites and turn into a buttered casserole. Bake in a hot oven until the soufflé begins to rise. Then lower the heat and bake for 20 or 25 minutes or until the soufflé is lightly browned. Serve immediately.

Stuffed Artichokes

Chill cooked artichokes, cut them in halves, and remove their inedible portions. Fill the artichoke bottoms with shrimp or crabmeat that has been marinated in French dressing. Serve with mayonnaise.

ARTILLERY PUNCH. *See* Punch.

ARVA. *See* Ava.

ASALI. An African liquor made by fermenting honey.

ASCIUTTO. An Italian term referring to a dry wine. *See also* Wine.

ASPARAGUS. This excellent vegetable was known in ancient Rome and is today grown in most parts of the world. Fresh asparagus in the vegetable market is one of the first signs of spring. Its season is short, but modern methods of canning and freezing make it available throughout the year.

Asparagus is rich in mineral salts and contains Vitamins A and B. It may be served hot or cold in many different dishes.

Hints on Buying

Two kinds of asparagus are found in the markets, white or blanched and green. The asparagus shoot grows from roots which are covered with earth. To form the white shoots, the earth is banked deeply over the roots in the same manner as celery is bleached. Because the light is prevented from reaching them, the stalks which grow up through the earth remain white. They are cut just as the tip shows through the ground. The white asparagus is believed to be somewhat milder in flavor than the green, and most of the crop is used for canning.

The green asparagus is the kind usually seen in the markets. The stalk should be green for almost its entire length, to insure tenderness. The white base is the part which grew in the ground and had time to toughen while the green shoot was reaching its proper length. Asparagus is usually sold by the bunch or by the pound. For the small family it is more advantageous to buy by the pound. A bunch of asparagus weighs about 3½ pounds.

Fresh asparagus is brittle with close compact tips. Its stem may be easily punctured with the finger nail. Spreading tips or limp stems indicate that the asparagus is wilted and probably has been picked too long.

ASPARAGUS

Canned Asparagus. Asparagus is canned as tips suitable for salad or garnishing, and as longer stalks to be used as a vegetable. Both the white and green types are available. The canning process changes the flavor of the asparagus slightly; it tends to destroy the delicate flavor of the fresh vegetable. Canned asparagus may be served cold or heated. It needs no additional cooking.

Asparagus soup may also be bought in cans. This is made from the stalks and tips which are not perfect enough for canning but are otherwise perfectly wholesome. Apart from its use as a soup it can be used in its condensed form as a delicious sauce for many dishes.

Frozen Asparagus. Modern quick-freezing methods are such that the frozen asparagus is very near the fresh in flavor and attractiveness. The spears are frozen whole or cut into small pieces; in either case, only the tender green portion is included. To prepare frozen asparagus for eating, drop the frozen mass into a little rapidly boiling, salted water, and cook it until the stalks are just tender. They then may be treated like the fresh vegetable.

Cooking Asparagus

Since asparagus grows in sandy soil, the tips and scales on the stalk are often filled with sand. For this reason, the stalks should be washed well in lukewarm water and the tips scrubbed gently with a soft brush. If the asparagus is not exceptionally young and tender, it is preferable to peel the stalks below the tips. This can be easily done with a peeling gadget such as is used for potatoes or carrots. The tough white bases of the stalks should be snapped off.

Since the tip of the asparagus is the tenderest part, it needs less cooking than the stalk. A special asparagus cooker—a deep, narrow kettle—can be purchased, or a double boiler may be used if the upper portion is inverted over the lower. In either case, the asparagus should be tied in a bunch. Bring the water in the kettle (or the lower portion of the double boiler) to a boil, add salt, and place the bunch of asparagus base down in the water. Then cover the kettle. In this way, the stalks cooking in the water and the tips cooking in the steam reach the same stage of tenderness. Asparagus cooks quickly (15 or 20 minutes). It is done when a fork pierces the stem easily. Do not overcook it.

Asparagus can be cooked in a covered skillet. Use a very little water, only enough to produce steam without boiling dry during the cooking process. Bring the water to a boil, add salt, and carefully lay the stalks in the skillet. Cover, and cook until the stalks are tender. The stalks on the bottom layer may cook more quickly than those on top, but there will be no significant difference.

Another method for cooking asparagus is to wrap the bunch in parchment cooking paper and place it in a kettle with enough boiling water to produce steam. Cook until the stalks are tender.

Before serving asparagus, drain it. Then serve it hot with melted butter or hollandaise sauce, or cool the stalks and serve them with a french dressing or vinaigrette sauce.

Asparagus combines well with many foods, and it may go into the making of a delicious and attractive luncheon dish. Place a thin slice of broiled ham on a slice of toast, and put a serving of cooked asparagus over this. Cover with grated cheese, and run it under the broiler until the cheese melts and bubbles. Chicken and asparagus may be combined in a rich cream sauce either in a casserole or on toast.

Asparagus and Ham Casserole

Diced cooked ham
Cooked asparagus cut in small pieces
Rich white sauce, not too thin
Chopped parsley and chives

Add the parsley and chives to the white sauce. In a casserole make alternate layers of ham, asparagus, and white sauce until the dish is filled, ending with a layer of sauce. Sprinkle the top with buttered crumbs, and bake in a moderate oven (350° F.) until the sauce bubbles and the crumbs are brown.

ASPARAGUS CUSTARD

1 can condensed asparagus soup
1¼ cups milk
1 tbsp grated onion
1 slice garlic
Dash of nutmeg
6 egg yolks
Salt and pepper
Croutons

Mix the soup, milk, onion, garlic, and nutmeg. Beat the egg yolks until light, adding the salt and pepper to taste. Beat the eggs into the asparagus mixture. Butter 6 custard cups. Drop a few croutons (*which see*) into each cup, and pour in the asparagus mixture. Bake in a moderate oven (325° F.) for about 45 minutes, or until set. Unmold and serve hot. (Serves 6)

JELLIED ASPARAGUS

Cold cooked asparagus
Hard-cooked eggs
Aspic

Prepare the aspic (*which see*). Slice the eggs into even slices. Use only the tender tips of the asparagus. Make a thin layer of aspic in the bottom of a loaf pan or mold. Let it set by chilling in the refrigerator. Lay a layer of sliced eggs on the aspic and cover with more aspic. Let set again. Make a layer of asparagus tips and cover them with aspic. Chill. Repeat these layers until the mold is full. Chill the mold until well set. Turn out on a bed of lettuce, slice and serve with a vinaigrette dressing.

ASPARAGUS MILANAISE

Place the stalks of cooked asparagus on an ovenproof serving dish. Cover the tips with grated Parmesan cheese. Pour melted butter over the cheese and brown quickly under the broiler.

CREAM OF ASPARAGUS SOUP

Cook the tips and stalks separately. Drain the tips and put them aside. When the stalks are soft, mash them and rub them through a sieve. Heat 2 cups of milk in the top of a double boiler. When a skin forms on the top of the milk, add 2 tablespoons of butter and 2 tablespoons of flour rubbed together into a smooth paste, stirring it in carefully so that it will not lump. Add the water in which the asparagus was cooked and the sieved pulp. Season to taste with salt and pepper. Add ½ cup of sweet cream and the tips. Heat the soup, but do not let it boil.

ASPIC. Aspic is a spiced, tart jelly made from brown or white meat stock alone or in combination with gelatin. It is used to enclose a variety of foods in a mold or to give a transparent coating of shining, sparkling finish. Various foods may be molded in aspic, such as stuffed olives, plain or stuffed tomatoes, eggs, poultry, fish, game, etc. *See also* SOUPS.

ASSAM. This is tea from the province of Assam in Northeastern India, which is one of the most important tea-producing areas in the world, from the standpoints of both quality and quantity. Assam teas are black or fermented. They are rich, thick, heavy teas which produce a strong, flavorful brew. Their leaves are frequently blended with those of less pungent varieties to obtain a milder flavor. The second flush (*which see*) Assams are especially prized. *See* TEA.

ASSMANNHAUSEN. This is one of the best known of the red Rhine wines (*which see*). It is a red table wine, thinner than most, but pleasing to the palate. *See also* WINE.

ASTI SPUMANTE. This is the best known sparkling wine of Italy. It is a sweet wine made from Moscato grapes. *See also* WINE.

AURORE SAUCE. A variation of white sauce. *See* SAUCE.

AURUM. A light golden Italian liqueur, aurum is highly aromatic but not overly sweet. *See also* LIQUEUR.

AUSLESE. The German word *auslese*, meaning *specially selected*, is used to designate those Rhine and Moselle wines made from the best grape bunches carefully sorted from the vintage. If this process has been carried to the point of picking the best grapes from the bunches, the terms *Goldbeerenauslese* or *Beerenauslese* are used, sometimes further qualified as *Feine* (Fine) or *Feinste* (Finest). *See also* MOSELLE *and* RHINE WINE.

AVA. An intoxicating beverage made by the Polynesian natives by fermenting a mash made from the roots of a pepper plant. It is also known as *Arva, Kava,* and *Yava.*

AVOCADO

AVOCADO. The avocado is sometimes called calavo and, mistakenly, alligator pear. It is the soft, green or purple, pear-shaped fruit of the tropical tree of the same name that is now grown in both California and Florida. When ripe, the fruit is soft and easily pared. The avocado has a delicate, buttery flavor that goes well with almost any kind of salad or fruit cup. It may be served alone when halved and with the large round pit removed, although many people find that a dash of lemon juice or of slightly sweetened vinegar adds zest to its mild flavor.

When mixed with cream cheese and a little lime juice, the avocado pulp makes an admirable spread for canapés. Cut in slices or diced, it forms a tasty base for salads of lettuce, endive, or tomatoes. It

purchased and laid aside until they become soft enough for use.

Avocados are easily bruised and injured. Bruising not only mars the appearance of the fruit but also affects the quality of the flesh. Bruised fruit should be avoided.

Sometimes the skin is marked by a light brown, irregular scabbing. This does not affect the quality of the flesh.

Decay can be detected by dark sunken spots which sometimes merge to form irregular patches, the surfaces of which are deeply cracked or broken. The flesh beneath these spots may be decayed. Avocados with broken or punctured skin should be carefully examined; such injuries allow ready entrance to decay organisms, and the flesh beneath the injury may be affected.

AVOCADO CANAPE

Mash the avocado and season with lemon and onion juice. Spread on toast strips. Top with a small piece of bacon and broil until bacon is crisp. Serve hot.

AVOCADO CHICKEN SOUP

2 tbsp flour
1 cup milk
2 cups chicken broth, concentrated
1 ripe avocado
1 stalk celery, chopped
1 tsp grated onion

Mix flour and ¼ cup milk to a thin paste, not adding all milk at once. Blend

FOOD VALUE

Water	Food Energy	Protein	Fat	Carbohydrate	Calcium	Phosphorus	Iron	Vit. A Value	Thiamine	Riboflavin	Niacin	Ascorbic Acid
65.4	265	1.7	26.4	5.1	10	38	.6	290	.12	.15	1.1	16

goes well with cocktail sauces, mayonnaise, and French dressing.

HINTS ON BUYING

Heavy, medium-sized avocados which have a bright, fresh appearance and which are fairly firm or are just beginning to soften, are usually the most desirable. After a little practice, the "feel" of the fruit will indicate this condition.

Avocados that have all the characteristics of quality except softness may well be

this into remaining milk. Boil chicken broth and add flour-milk mixture. Keep at a boil, stirring a few times until somewhat thick. Crush the avocado and press through sieve, leaving only fibers. Add avocado with juices, along with chopped celery and onion, to the soup. Needs salting, according to taste.

AVOCADO COCKTAILS

Tart Avocado Cocktail. Peel 2 avocados and dice them or shape them in balls. Dust lightly with salt, chill, and place them in cocktail glasses. Mix 1 cup of mayonnaise, ⅓ cup of orange juice, 2 tablespoons of lemon juice, 1 finely chopped hard-cooked egg, ¼ cup of ketchup, 2 teaspoons of horseradish, a few drops each of tabasco and Worcestershire sauces, and salt to taste. Chill this mixture, and pour it over the fruit. (Makes 6)

Filled Avocados. Chill small avocados and cut them in halves. Fill with marinated seedless grapes or with tomato juice cocktail.

Avocado-grapefruit Cocktail. Peel and dice or shape into balls 2 small ripe avocados. Combine with ½ cup of drained canned grapefruit. (Or use 3 avocados and omit the grapefruit.) Chill thoroughly. Prepare sauce by mixing ¾ teaspoon of tomato ketchup, 1 teaspoon of Worcestershire sauce, 1 teaspoon of lemon juice, and ¾ cup of whipped heavy cream. Mix half of the sauce with the fruit, and top with the remaining half. Chill thoroughly, and serve in cocktail glasses.

AVOCADO-FIG MOLD

1 pkg lime or lemon gelatin
2 cups boiling water
1 ripe avocado
1 grapefruit
1 cup canned figs
Olive, or other vegetable, oil

Stir gelatin into boiling water until dissolved and let cool. After peeling, slice avocado and grapefruit into small chunks. Coat a mold lightly with oil. Place third of fruit in pattern about bottom of mold. Securing the pattern with sufficient gelatin, chill until firm. Arrange remaining fruits in 2 or 3 more layers, covering each layer with gelatin mixture and allowing to set. Add remaining gelatin and chill until set. For salads, slice and serve over lettuce with mayonnaise, French dressing, sour cream or a cream dressing (*which see*).

AVOCADO ICE I

2 ripe avocados
⅓ tsp salt
3 limes (juice only)
1 tbsp lemon juice
½ lemon rind, grated
⅓ cup strained honey

Press the pulp of the peeled avocados through a coarse sieve or strainer. Add all remaining ingredients, blend thoroughly, turn into refrigerator tray, and freeze about 3 hours, stirring once when mushy. Serve in sherbet glasses as a dessert or as a meat accompaniment. (Serves 4)

AVOCADO ICE II

2 ripe avocados
¼ cup vinegar, sweetened slightly
¼ cup honey
¼ tsp salt
¼ tsp celery salt

Cut out avocado pulp, chop into small pieces and press through sieve. Combine avocado with all ingredients and blend thoroughly. Removing from refrigerator at least once to re-mix, freeze 3 to 4 hours.

AVOCADO ICE CREAM

3 ripe avocados, chilled
¾ cup dry sherry
¼ cup lemon juice
1 cup sugar
¼ tsp salt
1 cup milk
1 cup cream
1 tsp gelatin
⅛ cup boiling water

Peel and remove pits from avocados, crush to a fine consistency through sieve. Add sherry, lemon juice, sugar and salt, stirring briskly. When sugar is dissolved, add milk and cream. Dissolve gelatin in boiling water and stir thoroughly into avocado mixture. Now turn into ice tray of electric refrigerator and chill until thick. Remove, beat, return to tray and freeze firm. Add nuts if desired. (Makes 2½ pints)

AVOCADO MOUSSE

1 tbsp lemon gelatin
3 tender-ripe avocados
1½ tsp onion juice
1½ tbsp lemon juice
¾ tsp salt
¾ cup mayonnaise
¾ cup heavy cream
2 oranges
2 grapefruit

Soak gelatin in about ⅛ cup cold water to soften, then heat over hot water to dissolve. Halve, pit and peel the avocados, then pass through a food mill or sieve. Add onion and lemon juices, salt and mayonnaise. Stir in gelatin slowly. Whip cream stiff and fold in. Turn into precooled mold or molds and chill until thoroughly set. Peel the oranges and grapefruit, remove sections carefully and discard seeds. Chill plates or platter on which mousse is unmolded. Decorate with the orange and grapefruit sections. Also, if desired, minced watercress may provide additional decoration. A bed of lettuce is optional. (Serves 8)

For a slightly blander flavor, onion juice may be left out and lime used instead of lemon. Squeeze juice from 2 limes. Mince rinds fine and soak in juice for 2 minutes. Sieve out rind and stir juice into mashed avocado.

AVOCADO AND PERSIMMON SALAD

Peel avocados and slice lengthwise; marinate in French dressing (*see* SALAD DRESSINGS) for ½ hour. Place 4 slices alternately with 3 sections of grapefruit and chunks of persimmon on 5 crisp stalks of chicory on French endive on each salad plate. Serve with mayonnaise.

AVOCADO SALAD

3 avocados
½ cup tomato catsup
3 tbsp vinegar
2 tsp sugar
1 tsp Worcestershire sauce
½ tsp salt
Few drops tabasco

Arrange halves of avocado on crisp lettuce and top with Russian dressing.

AVOCADO SALAD SAN FRANCISCO

Cut the avocados in halves lengthwise and remove the pits. Blend all remaining ingredients. Pour 2 tablespoons of the sauce into each avocado half. Chill and serve as an appetizer salad. (Serves 6)

AYLER. This is one of the best white wines of the Saar Valley. *See also* WINE.

AZEITAO CHEESE. A soft Portuguese cheese made from goat's milk.

B

B AND B. This is a popular after-dinner cordial made of one part Benedictine (*which see*) and one part brandy.

BABA. A French cake, not too rich, generally soaked with rum and called Baba au Rhum. *See Cake.*

BACARDI. Bacardi is a kind of rum, originally distilled by a Cuban of the same name. It is used as a base for many drinks, especially cocktails. *See* RUM.

BACKSTEIN CHEESE. A brick-shaped German cheese similar to Limburger, *which see.*

BACON. The cured and smoked meat of the pig. Regular bacon, or breakfast-style bacon comes from the side of the hog; Canadian-style bacon comes from the loin. Hogs which yield the best bacon are leaner and longer in conformation than those yielding the best hams. The best bacon has a high percentage of lean to fat.

Because bacon is so easily and quickly prepared, it seldom receives sufficient attention. It should always be cooked at a low temperature to minimize shrinkage. The fat should never be allowed to get hot enough to smoke. Bacon may be prepared by broiling, baking, or panbroiling—depending largely on personal taste, convenience, and the amount to be cooked at one time. Thin bacon slices about six slices to the inch, or about eight or ten slices to the half pound.

To broil bacon, set the broiler at 400° F. and preheat for ten minutes. Place the strips of bacon on the broiler rack about three inches from the flame. Broil about 2½ minutes on each side for medium crispness, and turn only once. It will not be necessary to drain the bacon.

To panbroil bacon, place the strips of bacon in a cold frying pan over a moderate flame and cook until the fat becomes slightly opaque or yellow. Turn the slices and complete the frying. Pour off the fat as it accumulates. If bacon is liked especially crisp, drain the slices on soft paper.

To cook a large quantity of bacon, baking in the oven is suggested. Place the bacon strips on a rack in a shallow pan, not letting them overlap. Place the pan toward the top of the oven which has been set at 400° F. and bake until crisp. This method takes longer, but the bacon does not need to be turned or drained.

If it is necessary to keep bacon warm until it is served, it can be kept crisp by placing several thicknesses of soft paper on a rack and laying the cooked bacon on the paper. Place in a very cool oven (250° F.) until wanted.

To save time, when sliced bacon is chilled from storage in the refrigerator and does not separate readily, the entire package, or as much of it as is required, may be laid on the broiler rack. As soon as it starts to heat, the slices will separate. *See also* PORK.

BACON DISH. A covered platter designed to hold strips of bacon and keep them warm until served. *See* DISHES.

BADIAN. A Chinese fruit similar in flavor to Anise, *which see.*

BADIANE. This intoxicating beverage is derived in part from bitter almonds.

BADIANE

1 lb broken bitter almond meats
3 pt brandy
1 lb sugar
1 grated lemon peel
1 oz cinnamon
6 cloves
6 cups water

Mix all of the ingredients in a jar. Let the mixture stand for a month, and then strain it through a piece of flannel or similar cloth. Filter and then bottle it.

BADMINTON CUP. This wine cup is made of claret and herbs. It derives its distinctive flavor from the herbs; but these are always removed from the mixture as soon as the proper taste balance is achieved.

BADMINTON CUP I

1 bottle claret
1 bottle carbonated water
Sugar
Balm
Borage

Mix the ingredients in a bowl containing a large block of ice. Sugar the mixture to taste, and remove the herbs before their flavor becomes too strong.

BADMINTON CUP II

1 bottle claret
1 bottle carbonated water
2 large jiggers brandy
2 large jiggers port wine
2 oz powdered sugar
Lemon peel, thinly sliced
Balm sprigs
Borage sprigs

Peel the herbs, and place them in a large pitcher or jug. Add the other ingredients, and place the container in a refrigerator to chill until served. The herbs and lemon should be left in the mixture for but a short time, as explained above. This drink should not be mixed too far in advance, lest the carbonation be gone when served. It can be chilled in the usual punch or wine cup manner.

This wine mixture has a third version that can be used when the herbs are unavailable. If possible, however, at least the borage should be used as prescribed.

BADMINTON CUP III

½ fresh, peeled, medium-sized cucumber
Juice of 1 lemon (3 tbsp)
1 bottle carbonated water
1 large jigger curacao
1 bottle claret
2 large jiggers simple sirup
Nutmeg

Place the cucumber half in the bottom of a punch bowl or a similar container. Add the simple sirup, lemon juice, curacao, claret, and some nutmeg; mix well. Add ice to chill. Pour the carbonated water in, and stir gently.
See also WINE CUP and PUNCH.

BAIN-MARIE. (baN-ma re') French name for a multiple double saucepan which cooks foods in compartments without danger of burning. Hot water is used in the lower vessel, as in a double boiler, *which see.*

BAKED ALASKA. An elaborate-appearing dessert which is really very simple to make. A solid-frozen brick of ice cream is needed for this dessert. Furthermore, the ice cream should not contain water ice but should be made of milk or cream.

BAKED ALASKA

1 qt brick ice cream
1 layer sponge or pound cake
4 egg whites
1 cup confectioner's sugar

Cover a bread board or an oven plank with a piece of waxed or white paper. Make a meringue by beating the egg whites until stiff, gradually folding in three-fourths of the confectioner's sugar. The meringue should be light and dry. Now lay the cake on the papered board and place the ice cream upon the cake; the cake should extend about ½ inch beyond the ice cream on all sides. Cover completely with heavy coating of meringue. Dust surface well with rest of powdered sugar and place in very hot oven (475°–500° F.) until delicately browned. Serve at once.

BAKER. A name sometimes given to a vegetable dish that does not have a fitted cover. It is used to hold vegetables for serving at the table. *See* DISHES.

BAKING. The process of cooking by indirect heat in a confined space, as in a heated oven, through the medium of coal, gas, electricity, wood, charcoal, or oil, at temperatures from 250° F. to 450° F.

BAKING POWDER. Few homemakers stop to consider the value of baking powder. Until 1850 it was necessary to use homemade leavening agents—sour milk and soda, or soda and cream of tartar.

All baking powders contain three ingredients: (a) soda (the source of carbon dioxide); (b) acid (which sets the gas free from the soda); and (c) cornstarch or flour (which helps to keep the mixture dry). All baking powders are required by law to yield a definite amount of carbon dioxide gas. To that extent baking powders are similar. They differ though in the kind of acid used. Some contain two acid ingredients—calcium acid phosphate and sodium aluminum sulfate; these are called combination powders. Others, known as tartrate powders, contain cream of tartar or tartaric acid as the acid ingredient. Still others, the phosphate powders, contain calcium acid phosphate or sodium acid pyrophosphate.

TIME TABLE FOR BAKING
(See also High Altitude Cookery)

Food	Temperature (Deg. F.)	Time (Minutes)
Breads (quick)		
Baking powder biscuits	450	12–15
Corn bread	400	30
Fruit bread	350	1 hour
Muffins	425	25–30
Nut bread	325	1¼ hour
Breads (raised)		
Rolls	400–425	15–20
Whole wheat bread	425	10 min. and then
	350	1 hour
White bread	375–400	20 min. and then
	350	1 hour
Cakes		
Angel food	325	1¼ hours
Chiffon	325–350	45–55
Cup cakes	350–375	20–25
Fruit cake	250–300	1½–4 hours (depending on size)
Gingerbread	350	30
Jelly roll	350	20
Layer cake (¾–1 inch thick)	350	20–30
Loaf cake (1½–2½ inches thick)	325–350	1–1¼ hours
(over 2½ inches thick)	350	1 hour or more
Pound cake	275–325	1-2 hours
Sponge cake	325	1 hour or more
Cookies		
Most cookies	375–400	5–15
Fruit cookies	325–350	8–15
Molasses cookies	325–350	8–15
Chocolate cookies	325–350	8–15
Custard (cup)	325	35–40
Cream puffs and eclairs	450	20 and then
	350	for 25
Fish		
Whole or stuffed	500	15 and then
	400	for 40–50
Cut portion size	450	15–25
Fish casserole	350–400	20–25
Meats		
Ham, sliced	350	40–50
Meat pie (cooked meat)	350–500	15
Meat pie (uncooked meat)	350	1 hour or more
Meringue (for pies with cooked fillings)	350	15
Meringues	250–275	45–60
Pastry		
Pie shells	450	15
Tart shells	450	10–15
Pies		
Berry and fruit pies (canned and fresh)	425–450	15 and then
	350	20–30
Custard pies (uncooked mixture)	450	20 and then
	350	15
Dried fruit pies	425	10 and then
	350	30
Puddings		
Bread	350	35–45
Rice (raw)	300	2–3 hours
Souffles	325–350	30–35

Because different acid ingredients are used, baking powders differ in the speed of their reaction. This variation in speed means that there is a difference in the quantity of carbon dioxide gas liberated and lost during the mixing of batters. Consequently, each type of baking powder should be used in the amount best suited to it. Research has shown that one teaspoon of baking powder per cup of sifted flour is, in general, the proportion which gives the best results and the recipes in this book usually call for that quantity. It is perfectly safe to follow the proportions given in the directions that come with the particular brand of powder used. However, when baking in an altitude of more than 2,500 feet above sea level lesser quantities of leavening are used than normally. For information on this subject see HIGH ALTITUDE COOKERY.

Baking powder constitutes a very small part of any given recipe, yet it plays such an important role that it is often called "the biggest little thing in baking." One of the advantages of phosphate baking powder is that the baking can be delayed for a reasonable time (because of the powder's quick action) provided the dough or batter is covered and stored in a cool place in the meantime.

BAKING SODA. A by-product of common washing, or sal, soda, used in cooking. It is also known as sodium bicarbonate or bicarbonate of soda.

BALM. Although this fragrant herb of the mint family is a native of Europe, it is found growing wild in North America where it has escaped from gardens. It grows to a height of about two feet and is distinguished by small, two-lipped, white or rose-spotted flowers.

Balm leaves have a decided lemon odor and flavor and, in some places, the plant is known as "lemon balm." While the crushed leaves are used popularly in wine, punches, fruit drinks, and iced tea, a few chopped in with poultry dressing, or bruised and rubbed on steaks before broiling, add a pleasing tinge of flavor. The aromatic flavor of the leaves is generally recommended as an addition to soups, sauces, and desserts. Either fresh or dried leaves may be used.

BAMBOO SHOOTS. The young shoots of the bamboo plant which are cut when just appearing above ground are a favorite vegetable in the Orient. The shoots, which develop from an underground rootstock, are covered by tight thick overlapping sheaths which are stripped from the white shoots before cooking.

The larger specimens sometimes average several inches in diameter. In order that the plants may be allowed to develop lengthwise, they are sometimes cultivated like asparagus plant, that is, by banking.

The flavor of the bamboo shoot may be compared to the artichoke and it may also be prepared in the same manner. Boiling in salt water or deep-frying in hot peanut oil until crisp are two favorite methods of preparation. The shoots may also be served in soups or stews or salted and mixed with rice and butter. Fresh bamboo shoots may be difficult to find in this country but the canned product may be had in any large city. *See also* CHINESE COOKERY.

BANANA. The banana was discovered along the Indus River three centuries before Christ and brought to the New World in 1516.

In the 1670's William Dampier, an Englishman, went to Jamaica as a plantation manager. Having become very fond of bananas, he wrote the first book in English about them. In the book he suggests that "when banana fruit is only used for bread, it is roasted or boiled when it is full grown, but not yet ripe or turned yellow."

He continues, stating that "sometimes, for a change, natives eat a roasted banana and a ripe raw one which is instead of bread and butter. They sat very pleasant so, and I have made many a good meal in this quaint manner. Sometimes our Englishmen take six or seven ripe bananas and mashing them together, make them into a lump and boil them instead of a bag-pudding, which they call a buff-jacket, and this is a very good way for a change. This fruit makes also very good tarts; and the green plantain, sliced thin and dried in the sun and grated, will make a sort of flour (*see* BANANA FLOUR) which is very good to make puddings. A ripe plantain, sliced and dried in the sun, may be preserved a great while and then eaten like figs, very sweet and pleasant. The Darien Indians preserve them a long time by drying them over the fire, mashing them first and molding them into lumps. The Moskito Indians will take a ripe banana and roast it; then take a pint and one-half of water in a calabash; and squeeze the banana in pieces with their hands, mixing this with water; then they drink it off together; this they call 'mishlaw,' and it is pleasant and sweet and nourishing, somewhat like lamb's wool (as it is called) made with apples and ale."

before it is perfectly ripe. Bananas are shipped when still very green, and the fruit is often immature or irregularly ripened when eaten. Imperfectly ripened bananas are composed of starch; but as the natural ripening proceeds, the saccharine material is converted into a mucilaginous

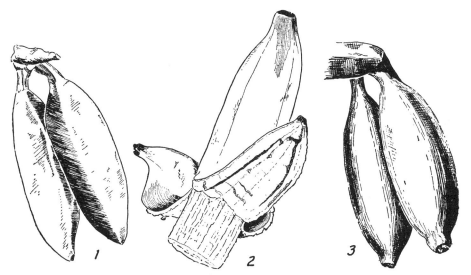

BANANAS   1. Plantain   2. Yellow   3. Red

The banana is a variety of the plantain, or *Plantago musa:* but the fruit is not so large or so hard as that commonly called plantain, and the flavor is far more delicate. There are many scores of varieties of the banana, ranging from the most delicate to the heaviest of the plantains. The bananas found in market are either the yellow or red types. The red are shorter and thicker and have a somewhat richer flavor. The banana varies in both digestibility and flavor.

In the West Indies and the Pacific islands, along the Congo, and throughout Central Africa, many natives look on bananas as their staple food. A diet consisting solely of this fruit will sustain life for a long period because of its relatively high nitrogen content as compared with that of sago, arrowroot, and similar carbohydrates. The percentage amounts to nearly five parts per hundred of the entire fruit, or one-fifth of the total solids. Grown on a given acreage, bananas will support a larger number of persons than wheat.

An apparent indigestibility of the banana is very often due to its being eaten

substance which, in turn, forms dextrine and glucose.

Dried or powdered bananas can be obtained in the market. This product is used in many dishes to give the flavor of fresh bananas when they are unavailable.

PREPARATION FOR MARKET

Since the fruit on a single banana plant is at various stages of development, it takes a practiced eye to select the bunches of proper grade for cutting and shipment. Cutting is done once or twice a week. Bananas are always harvested green, even when eaten in the tropics; if allowed to ripen on the plant, they lose their flavor. They are practically a continuous crop, fruit maturing nearly every month in the year.

Bananas are shipped "loose" (without box, crate, or wrapping of any kind) from the plantation to the ripening rooms. Until fully ripe they must be handled with infinite care, as they are subject to a too-rapid ripening on one hand and chill on the other.

Especially designed steamships are used for the successful transportation of bananas. Both refrigerator and naturally ventilated vessels are necessary. The problem is to carry the fruit well ventilated within a narrow range of temperature, because in the process of respiration, bananas absorb oxygen and yield carbon dioxide in large quantities. The fruit is inspected every few hours during the voyage and, on arrival, it undergoes weighing and a rigid inspection. Any fruit showing evidence of damage or a degree of maturity which forecasts early ripening is rejected for interior shipment and sold locally.

Grading refers to the fullness of the fruit when cut and is expressed as follows: ¾ full, full ¾, and full. Thin fruit is the opposite of full fruit. A banana "hand" is a bunch of bananas as it is cut from the stalk, and is composed of a number of "fingers" or individual bananas.

refrigerator, but should be kept in a dry, moderately warm room.

HINTS ON PREPARATION

Suit the preparation of the banana to its color. If it is tipped with green, it is partially ripe and its pulp is a little tart. Cook it in this stage by broiling, baking, or frying. If it is all yellow (with no green on the tips), the fruit is ready to eat or to cook; it will be delicious in waffles, puddings, cakes, or pies. If the skin is flecked with brown, the banana is in its prime and has a soft, mealy, fully ripe pulp. It should be eaten raw or used in a salad, fruit cup, or other dish calling for uncooked fruits. In the tropics green bananas and plantains are added to soups and stews just as vegetables are in the United States.

When preparing bananas for a pie filling, proceed as rapidly as possible and use

FOOD VALUE

Water	Food Energy	Pro- tein	Fat	Carbo- hydrate	Cal- cium	Phos- phorus	Iron	Vit. A Value	Thia- mine	Ribo- flavin	Nia- cin	Ascor- bic Acid
74.8	99	1.2	.2	23	8	28	.6	430	.09	.06	.6	10

HINTS ON BUYING

Properly ripened fruit should have an attractive color, a fresh appearance, firm pulp texture, and good strength of peel.

For immediate use, full-ripe fruit should be bought. Full-ripe bananas are frequently cheaper than those in the partly ripe or yellow-ripe stage. For use over a period of a few days or for cooking purposes, the partly ripe fruit should be purchased. If desired, this can be ripened at room temperature. Ripeness is indicated by the color of the skin. Good eating quality is indicated when the solid red or yellow color, depending on the variety, is flecked with brown. Most consumers know only these two varieties, the yellow being the more popular.

Inferiority is indicated by a badly discolored skin and a soft, mushy, sometimes discolored, flesh. In some instances the skin may be entirely brown or almost blackened and yet, if the flesh is fairly firm and not discolored, the fruit may be in prime eating condition.

Bruised fruit (blackened areas) should be avoided.

Bananas are sold by the pound, dozen, or hand. They should not be stored in the

a glass-bladed or a silver knife; this is to prevent darkening. The bananas may be sprinkled with a bit of lemon juice after being cut. A blend of lemon, orange, or lime juice sweetened with honey allows for a variety of flavors.

BAKED BANANAS

Peel slightly green-tipped or all-yellow bananas. Place them in a buttered baking dish and brush them with melted butter or margarine. Salt lightly. Bake in moderate oven (375° F.) for 15 to 18 minutes or until tender (when they can be easily pierced with a fork).

GLAZED BAKED BANANAS

Peel 4 bananas and place them, whole or cut in halves lengthwise, in a buttered baking dish. Sprinkle them with lemon juice. Bake them in a moderate oven (350° F.) for 20 minutes, glazing the tops by sprinkling sugar over them 5 minutes before removing them from the oven. Before serving sprinkle them with crumbs or nuts, if desired. For variety, bake bananas in cranberry sauce using 1⅓ cups of sauce. (Serves 4)

Banana Bread

2 tsp baking powder
¼ tsp soda
1 tsp salt
2 cups flour
⅔ cup sugar
⅓ cup shortening
2 eggs
1 tsp vanilla
3 bananas, well ripened

Mix first 4 ingredients and sift. Working sugar in, cream shortening until airy-light. Break eggs separately into shortening; beat thoroughly each time. Mash bananas with potato masher and stir into shortening. Add vanilla. Next add flour mixture in several parts, beating after each addition. Empty into pan of 8 x 4 inches. Bake at 350° F. (moderate) for 50 minutes. Do not slice until cool.

Banana Chutney

9 bananas, chopped
7 medium-sized onions, chopped
½ lb almonds
¾ lb dates, chopped
2 cups vinegar
3 cups fruit sirup, stewed or canned
¼ lb crystallized ginger, chopped
1½ tsp salt
1½ tsp curry powder
¾ lb seeded raisins

Mix first 4 ingredients with vinegar. Simmer for 25 minutes. Add sirup and remaining ingredients. Continue to simmer, stirring occasionally, until thick. Seal in heated jars. (Makes 6 pints)

Banana Cream Cocoa Cake

¼ cup cocoa
½ cup cake flour
¾ tsp baking powder
¼ tsp salt
2 eggs
½ tsp vanilla
1½ tbsp water
¾ cup sugar
2 ripe bananas

Combine first 4 ingredients and sift together until mixed. Separate eggs. Add vanilla, water and about half of sugar to

egg yolks; beat until somewhat thickened. Beat egg whites until firm, adding the rest of the sugar while beating. Mix yolk mixture lightly with sweetened egg white. Now add flour mixture gradually, stirring lightly until well mixed. Turn into shallow pan of about 9 x 12 inches, lined with plain paper. Bake at 375° F. (moderate) for 12 minutes. After cooling, cut cake in half. Cover one half with cream filling (recipe below). Slice bananas over filling, distributing evenly. Place other half on top and serve with whipped cream, or with a light dusting of confectioners' sugar. (Serves 6)

Filling

⅓ cup cornstarch
¾ cup sugar
½ tsp salt
2 cups milk
2 eggs
2 tbsp butter
½ tsp vanilla

Blend cornstarch, sugar and salt. Add milk a little at a time, stirring smooth. Heat in double boiler until fairly thick, stirring occasionally. Beat eggs lightly. Take about ½ cup of milk mixture and blend well with eggs. Mix this with rest of milk mixture, stirring briskly. Cover and cook 15 minutes longer, over boiling water. Removing from flame, blend in vanilla and butter. Allow to cool before spreading on cake. Shredded coconut may also be added after cooking.

Banana Cream Pie

10-inch pie shell, baked
1 cup sugar
½ cup flour
⅔ tsp salt
2½ cups milk
2 eggs
⅔ tsp vanilla
3 large, ripe bananas

Heat half of milk. Mix sugar, flour and salt in top half of double boiler. Pour in hot milk gradually, stirring until perfectly smooth. Add remaining milk and boil over flame, stirring often, until mixture thickens. Separate eggs and beat yolks thoroughly. Blend yolks with some of hot cream mixture taken from double boiler; then pour into rest of mixture. Cook 2 or 3 minutes over boiling water, continuing to stir. After removing from flame, stir in vanilla. Slice bananas over bottom of pie, distributing them evenly over the area but not too evenly in depth. Pour hot cream mixture over bananas and allow to cool. Now beat egg whites to a smooth and frosty meringue, beating in remaining sugar meanwhile. When meringue glistens, ladle it carefully over entire surface of filling. Place shell on baking sheet and bake at 350° F. (moderate) for 15 minutes or until meringue is tufted with brown patches. Cool.

BANANA CREOLE

Slice your bananas lengthwise into a buttered fireproof dish, and sprinkle them with brown sugar. Pour a glassful of rum over them, and cook the mixture in the oven until the sugar is dissolved.

BANANA CUTLETS

6 medium-ripe bananas
1/3 cup lemon juice (about)
1 cup crushed cornflakes
3 tbsp butter
Lettuce

Peel bananas and halve them crosswise. Dip them in lemon juice; then roll in cornflake crumbs. Saute them in butter until a golden brown. Serve on lettuce. (Serves 6)

BANANA DAINTY

4 very ripe bananas
2 cups whipped cream
1/2 tbsp orange or lemon juice

Peel and scrape the bananas; put them through a potato ricer or sieve and strain them. Add sugar and juice. Mix very lightly, and then fold in the whipped cream. Serve in glasses and garnish with sections of fruit. (Serves 6)

BANANA DOUGHNUTS

2½ cups flour
1 tsp salt
½ tsp soda
1½ tsp baking powder
½ tsp nutmeg
2 tbsp shortening
½ cup sugar
¾ tsp vanilla

2 eggs
1 large, ripe banana
¼ cup buttermilk
¼ cup flour

Mix and sift flour, salt, soda, baking powder and nutmeg. Working in sugar, cream shortening briskly. Beat in eggs and vanilla until thoroughly mixed and fluffy. After crushing bananas fine, mix with buttermilk and add to shortening mixture. Next stir in flour mixture in several parts, mixing well each time. Chill dough for half an hour. Very lightly dust rolling pin, rolling surface, and 2½" doughnut cutter with ¼ cup flour. Taking half the dough at a time, knead slightly and flatten to ⅜ inch with roller. Have at least 3 inches deep fat heated to 375° F. Cut out and fry several doughnuts at a time, turning frequently as they rise. Remove when well browned and drain on soft, absorbent paper. Apply sugar or cinnamon, if desired, before doughnuts are cool. Or, top with lime or lemon butter frosting. (Makes 2 dozen)

BANANA FRITTERS

1 cup all-purpose flour
1 tsp baking powder
1/3 cup sugar
1/6 tsp salt
1/8 tsp cinnamon
2 eggs
1/2 cup milk
6 large bananas, or equivalent

Mix first 5 ingredients and sift together. Beat eggs thoroughly, adding milk while beating. Pour into flour mixture and mix well. Slice each banana into 4 sections, cutting once across and once lengthwise. Coat each piece with batter and fry in deep fat over moderate flame. When golden brown, drain bananas and serve with a wine or liqueur sauce.

BANANA FROSTING

1 large ripe banana
3 cups confectioner's sugar
1½ tsp lemon juice
Salt

Crush the banana and gradually beat into it the sugar, lemon juice and salt. Spread between and on top of layer cake or use on small cup cakes.

Banana Fudge

⅔ cup milk
2 tbsp corn sirup
2 cups sugar
2 ripe bananas
½ tsp vanilla
2 tbsp butter

Heat milk and sirup, stirring in sugar until dissolved. Mash bananas fine and add to liquid. Cook over moderate flame, stirring occasionally. After 8 to 10 minutes, test with a small amount in cold water. When soft ball forms, take off flame and stir in butter and vanilla. Set pan in cold water to cool, then beat smooth. Empty into lightly buttered pan and cut when solid. (Makes 15 to 25 pieces)

Banana Grape Mold

1 tbsp gelatin
¼ cup water
2 cups grape juice
3 tbsp sugar
1 tsp lemon juice
3 bananas

Sprinkle water over gelatin and allow to soften. Heat about half of the grape juice to a boil and dissolve gelatin. Add remaining grape juice, sugar and lemon juice, dissolving sugar. Slice one banana and arrange as desired over bottom of mold. Pour over enough gelatin mixture to cover banana slices and chill. Then slice other bananas into remaining gelatin. Add to the partly filled mold and chill until firm. (Serves 5 to 6) Concentrated grape juice may be used. If so, dissolve gelatin into one cup of boiling water. Add only one cup of concentrated juice.

Banana Ice Cream

1 recipe vanilla ice cream
4 bananas
1 tbsp lemon juice
Dash of salt

Make 1 quart of vanilla ice cream according to the instructions under Ice Cream. Skin, scrape, and sieve the bananas and blend with the lemon juice and salt. When the ice cream is beginning to stiffen, stir in the banana pulp and finish freezing according to directions.

Banana Mousse

2 cups heavy cream
½ cup powdered sugar
2 egg whites
1¼ tsp vanilla
⅛ tsp salt
1 cup sliced bananas

Whip the cream until quite thick, fold in the sugar and continue beating until the mixture is stiff. Beat the egg whites until stiff, adding the vanilla and salt as they begin to stiffen. Combine the two mixtures and add the sliced bananas. Turn into refrigerator tray and freeze four hours. If preferred, turn the mixture into small paper cases or individual fancy molds and place in the refrigerator tray for freezing.

Be sure that the bananas are very thinly sliced and prepare them immediately before using lest they turn dark. (Serves 6)

Banana Newburg

Sprinkle brown sugar over fried bananas; add just enough sherry to make a sauce, and simmer for a few minutes. Serve hot as a meat accompaniment.

Banana-Nut-Mocha Cake

2 cups cake flour
1½ tsp baking powder
¼ tsp soda
⅔ tsp salt
½ tsp mace
½ cup shortening
1 cup sugar
2 eggs
3 bananas, mashed
1 tsp vanilla
1 tsp lemon juice
2½ tbsp milk
½ cup walnuts

Mix and sift flour, baking powder, soda, salt and mace. Cream shortening partially and churn in sugar until frothy. Beat in one whole egg at a time. Gradually add banana pulp, vanilla and lemon juice. Stir in flour and milk in several alternate parts until smoothly blended. Turn batter into 2 10-inch layer pans lined with wax paper. Bake at 350° F. (moderate oven) 20 to 25 minutes, or until cake tests as done. Carefully cool layers away from drafts before frosting. Spread tops with Mocha Frosting (*which see*) and decorate with nuts arranged in a pattern.

BANANA SCALLOPS

6 bananas, peeled
1 egg, slightly beaten
½ cup fine-sifted bread crumbs
1½ tsp salt

Cut bananas in 1-inch slices and dip them in mixture of egg and salt; drain, and then roll them in crumbs. Fry in hot deep fat (375° F.) for 1 to 2 minutes or until brown; drain on unglazed paper. Serve very hot. (Serves 6)

BANANA SNOW PUDDING

1 tbsp gelatin
¼ cup cold water
1 cup hot water
1 cup sugar
¼ cup lemon juice
3 egg whites
3 bananas

Soak gelatin for 5 minutes in cold water to soften, add hot water and heat to dissolve. Stir in the sugar and lemon juice, then cool or chill until thickened. Beat thoroughly. Whip egg whites stiff and fold in. Slice the bananas and distribute on bottom and sides of pre-chilled mold. Chill in refrigerator until firm. Unmold with quick dip in hot water. (Serves 6)

BANANA TOAST

3 ripe bananas
½ tsp salt
1 tbsp sugar
1 tsp lemon juice
1 tbsp butter
6 slices dry toast

Mash bananas; mix them with salt, sugar, lemon juice, and butter. Spread the mixture on toast, and place it in a hot oven (425°) for about 5 minutes. Serve hot with cream, if desired. (Serves 6)

BANANA TRIFLE

4 to 6 bananas
Apricot jam
¼ pt sherry
½ pt cream

Peel the bananas and cut them lengthwise, spread them with jam and lay them in a glass dish. Pour the Sherry over them, and allow them to soak. Just before serving, pour the cream, which should be half whipped, over them and garnish with some banana on the top.

FRIED BANANAS

Cut peeled bananas in halves crosswise, then lengthwise. Sprinkle with orange or lemon juice and dredge with seasoned flour. Sauté them in butter until they are delicate brown. Then sprinkle brown or powdered sugar over them. To serve with pork, sauté in sausage or pork drippings.

BANANA FLOUR. This flour is made by drying well-ripened and carefully selected bananas. It is highly nutritious and digestible. When thoroughly dried the banana is ground into a meal, having a white or pale grayish or yellowish color, and an agreeable, faintly aromatic odor and taste. The meal possesses decided advantages as a food for invalids and children. Tests have shown that an unboiled, saturated, aqueous solution of banana flour contains a very large percentage of sugar—from one-half to three-fourths as much as certain of the best-known prepared saccharine foods for infants, to which sugar has been artificially added. The finest banana flour, called *bananose*, was tested after an hour and a half of pancreatic digestion. It was found capable of developing twice as much sugar as the same quantity of oatmeal or farina, and approximately one and a half times as much sugar as cornstarch.

Banana flour made from the best quality of bananas can be made into a thin gruel by adding water or milk. Eaten with cream, it constitutes a delicious and highly nutritious dish suitable in cases of gastric irritability, acute gastritis, etc. For those desiring an acid flavor, lemon, orange, or grapefruit juice with powdered sugar may be used on the banana porridge.

BANBURY CHEESE. A small, round, soft English cheese, very rich in texture.

BANBURY TART. A mouth-watering combination of citrus peels and raisins baked in a pastry shell.

BANBURY TARTS

½ cup halved seeded raisins
½ cup sugar

1 slightly beaten egg
2 tbsp cracker crumbs
1 tsp grated orange or lemon rind
2 tbsp orange or lemon juice
Pastry

Combine the raisins, sugar, beaten egg, crumbs, and fruit rind and juice. Roll out any preferred pastry (see PASTRY) one-eighth inch thick and cut into five-inch squares. Moisten the edges with water, put a tablespoon of the filling in the center of each square, fold cornerwise into triangles and press the edges firmly together. Bake in a hot oven (450° F.) 15 to 20 minutes.

BANDED PICKEREL. A southern member of that fish family which is more extensively covered under Pickerel.

BANCHA. An inferior grade of coarse-leaved tea grown in Japan.

BANG. This old English beverage is made primarily of cider and ale.

BANG

1 pt warm ale
1 pt cider
2 large jiggers gin or whisky
Powdered sugar
Grated nutmeg
Grated ginger

Mix the ale and cider, add sugar and spices to taste, and pour the liquor in last. Serve warm.

BANNOCK. This flat, round unleavened bread is popular in Scotland and England where it is cooked in a primitive manner—on a hot hearth or griddle over the fire. It is usually made of oatmeal or barley meal. The turbot is sometimes called the "bannock-fluke."

BANYULS. A sweet, dark, ruby-colored dessert wine which is made in southern France. Its alcoholic content is about 16 percent. See WINE.

BAOBAB. This downy, ten-to-twelve-inch fruit grows on a low, thick-trunked tree (often 30 feet in diameter) found in Africa and, infrequently, in Florida. A strong woody shell encloses cells of a fibrous pulp with a subacid flavor. The leaves and bark of the tree are used to treat tropical fever, while its fruit is quite edible.

BAR SIRUP. Another name for simple sirup. See SIRUP.

BARBADOS GOOSEBERRY. This is a cactus plant native to the West Indies. The fruit of the plant is yellow, smooth, about as large as an olive, and considered edible by the natives. It is imported in small quantities to the United States.

BARBADOS WATERS. An early English name for rum, *which see.*

BARBARONE. This is a red table wine of the Barbera type (*which see*), but it is not necessarily made from Barbera grapes. It is a product of California. *See also* WINE.

BAOBAB FRUIT

BARBECUE. The term means a whole animal roasted or broiled in its entirety for a feast, or the feast at which such meat is served. Its origin is obscure, but probably is derived from the French *barbe-a-queue,* which means "from snout to tail." The word was in use in Virginia before 1700, and the institution of the barbecue is probably of southern origin.

In southern and western United States, a barbecue is an outdoor festival at which the "piece de resistance" is a beef or hog dressed whole and roasted on a spit over a pit fire. A large barbecue takes about twenty-four hours of preparation. First the meat is marinated for a number of hours and the fires prepared. Then the barbecue, or basting sauce is mixed according to carefully guarded formulas from minced peppers, garlic, herbs, tomatoes, lime juice, and sundry condiments. The animal is placed on a steel spit over the fire and the roasting begins. The spit is turned at regular intervals, and the basting is done by dipping new brooms in tubs of sauce and swabbing the meat evenly. It takes from dawn until high noon to roast a beef in this way, and at that time the outside crust is spicy and the meat is cooked through to the bones.

Home Barbecues

The outdoor preparation of meals has become increasingly popular in the United States, and the principle of the barbecue has been simplified to fit the smallest suburban yard. The home barbecue uses a fireplace or outdoor stove in place of a fire pit, and the equipment may vary from a simple portable charcoal grill to an elaborately constructed fireplace with ovens and flues.

The newer portable grills are far more convenient than the older brick type, having parts that do not rust. They are easily cared for and may be stored in the winter. Some barbecues have circular, movable wire racks upon which to cook; others supply a spit which may be turned by hand. This latter procedure, however, is rather tiresome to execute.

A small, homemade barbecue may be constructed of brick—cleaned old brick will do, with fire-brick for the inside of the oven. Bracing iron and a grill and even a ventilated door may often be found at a junkyard. Barbecues may also be constructed of flat stones, a method particularly suited to camp cookery.

The hibachi is a Japanese cooking stove similar to the barbecue grill. Usually made of heavy material, the hibachi has a lower section for the placement of hot coals and a grill above for cooking. This brazier-type stove is quite small and heavy, however, and is much more suited to an intimate indoor dinner than to a large lawn party. The Japanese maintain the tradition of cooking easily prepared foods directly at the dinner table with the use of a hibachi.

The secret of successful barbecue cooking is a good bed of coals. Leaping flames may be picturesque, but when it comes to cooking, a solid bed of glowing coals does the job. Whether charcoal, wood, or other fuel is used, light the fire sufficiently far in advance so that it will have burned down to coals when cooking starts. The grill is usually placed four or five inches above the coals. At this distance the heat is right for thorough cooking. Shish kabobs will be done in 20 to 30 minutes; hamburgers in

8 to 10 minutes; and larger pieces of meat will take 20 to 30 minutes to the pound.

Steaks, chops and frankfurters all lend themselves well to the barbecue style of cookery. Steaks should be well marbled but not fatty. Thin rather than very thick steaks cook best. Lower the rack very close to the coals initially in order to sear the juices into the meats. Then raise the rack and continue cooking.

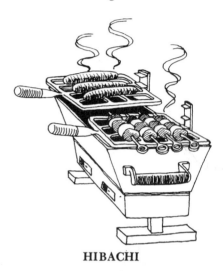

HIBACHI

Spareribs should be par-boiled before grilling. Fowls should be split in half down the back and grilled first on the bony side and then on the other side. All ingredients used in shish kebabs should cook at the same rate.

Necessary barbecue utensils include long-handled forks for turning meats, skewers for kebabs, asbestos potholders, pots for boiling water for vegetables and a device for controlling fire flare-ups.

Vegetables such as corn on the cob and potatoes may be wrapped in aluminum foil and embedded in coals for cooking. Tea and coffee cooked in open pots over a wood burning fire obtain a pleasant smoked flavor.

Barbecue sauces vary, and almost every successful outdoor chef has his private recipe for the sauce, as well as for the marinade which precedes the cooking. But whatever sauce is used, it should be applied lavishly while the meat is cooking, and additional sauce should be ready when the meat is ready to serve. Rolls may be toasted and spread with the sauce, ready for the meat. Sliced tomatoes and Bermuda onions marinated in vinegar, water, and salt, make a fine accompaniment.

MARINADE FOR BARBECUE I

4 cups wine vinegar
1 bottle red wine
1 tsp thyme leaves
12 sprigs parsley
2 bay leaves
4 shallots, cut in half
2 medium-sized carrots, sliced thinly
1 large onion, sliced thinly
2 cloves of garlic, bruised
1 tbsp salt
12 peppercorns, bruised

16 peppercorns
2 green peppers, chopped finely
3 juniper berries, bruised
4 sprigs thyme
6 sprigs parsley
4 bay leaves
6 sage leaves
½ cup salt

Place all the ingredients except the vinegar and stock in a saucepan and heat to the boiling point. Cook for 5 minutes, stirring constantly. Then add the vinegar and stock and bring to a boil again. Let boil up 3 or 4 times, and remove from the fire. Let the sauce cool. Place the meat in a deep earthenware dish and pour the cooled marinade over it. Let stand for several days in a cool place, or in the refrigerator,

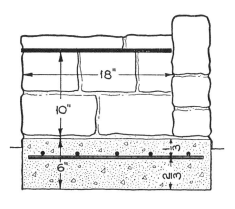

BARBECUE—FIREPLACE GRILL. A simple type for home garden construction.

Mix all the ingredients together. Place the piece of meat in a deep earthenware dish and pour over the marinade. Let stand in a cool place, or in the refrigerator, three or four days, turning the meat at least once a day. (Sufficient for a 5 or 6 pound piece of meat)

MARINADE FOR BARBECUE II

½ cup olive oil
4 cups vinegar
4 cups stock
6 small carrots, sliced thinly
12 small white onions, peeled and quartered
2 cloves of garlic, bruised
6 whole cloves

turning the meat at least once a day. (Sufficient for a 5 or 6 pound piece of meat)

BARBECUE SAUCE
(Dixie Style)

1½ cups cider vinegar
4 tsp lemon juice
3 tbsp Worcestershire sauce
½ lb butter or margarine
3 tbsp chile sauce
3 tbsp finely chopped onion
2 sour pickles, finely chopped
1 tsp finely chopped lemon peel
1 green pepper, finely chopped
1½ tsp light brown sugar
1 fresh sassafras leaf, lightly bruised

Place the vinegar, lemon juice, Worcestershire sauce, and butter in the top of a double boiler and allow the butter to melt. Meanwhile, place in a sauce pan and mix thoroughly all of the other ingredients, except the sassafras leaf. Stir the liquid so that the melted butter is blended well with the hot liquid and then add it to the mixed ingredients. Allow the sauce to simmer over a slow fire for 10 minutes, stirring constantly. Add the sassafras leaf for the last 3 to 5 minutes and then remove. Keep the finished sauce hot in the top of the double boiler until ready to serve on any kind of barbecued meat. (Makes about 2 cups)

BARBECUE SAUCE
(For Beef)

1 tbsp butter or margarine
1/3 cup minced onion
1/3 cup minced celery
2 tbsp brown sugar
2 tbsp vinegar
1 tbsp prepared mustard
2 tbsp Worcestershire sauce
1/4 tsp salt
Small piece of red pepper pod
1 cup tomato catsup
1 cup hot water
1 tbsp lemon juice

Melt the butter in a saucepan, add the onions and celery, and cook gently for 10 minutes. Add all the remaining ingredients except the lemon juice. Stir over a moderate flame until smooth and thickened. Just before taking from the stove, add the lemon juice. Serve with any dark meat, smoked meat, or frankfurters. (2 cups)

BARBECUE SAUCE
(For Lamb or Salmon)

1/2 cup water
1/2 cup tomato catsup
1 tbsp cider vinegar
1 tbsp Worcestershire sauce
1 medium-sized onion, chopped finely
1 tsp salt
1/2 tsp paprika
1/2 tsp chili powder
1/4 tsp black pepper
1/4 tsp red pepper

Mix the water, catsup, vinegar, and Worcestershire sauce in a saucepan. Add the chopped onion and allow to simmer

gently for 5 minutes. Mix the spices and salt and add enough of the hot liquid to form a paste. Continue adding liquid until the spices are of a creamy consistency. Then blend with the rest of the liquid and allow to simmer for 10 minutes. Keep hot in a double boiler until ready to baste the meat. (Makes about 1 cup)

BARBECUE SAUCE
(For Pork)

3/4 cup tomato catsup
2 1/2 tsp prepared mustard
2 tbsp granulated sugar
Dash of Worcestershire sauce
1/2 cup cider vinegar
2 tbsp melted butter or margarine
1 green pepper, finely chopped
1 large onion, finely chopped
1/2 cup sweet pickles, finely chopped
1/2 tsp lemon juice

Mix the catsup, mustard, and sugar; add the Worcestershire and vinegar and place in saucepan over low flame. Allow the mixture to simmer, but not to boil, for about 10 minutes. In another pan gently brown the pepper, onion, and pickles in the melted butter. Add liquid contents of the first pan and allow the whole to simmer for 5 minutes. Add the lemon juice about 1 minute before removing from the fire. This goes well with any kind of pork as well as with boiled beef tongue. (Makes about 2 1/2 cups)

BARBECUE SAUCE
(For Veal)

2 tbsp melted butter or margarine
4 tbsp dill pickle, diced
1/2 cup chili sauce
1/2 cup dill pickle juice
1 1/2 tsp Worcestershire sauce
2 drops tabasco sauce
3/4 tsp salt
1/2 tsp lemon juice

Melt the butter in a saucepan over a very low flame. Add the diced pickle and the chili sauce and mix thoroughly. Place the pickle juice in a bowl and add the Worcestershire, tabasco, and salt. Stir thoroughly. Add to the chili sauce mixture in the saucepan and cook, barely letting it simmer, for 10 minutes. Add the lemon juice and cook for another minute or so.

BARBEL. A European fresh water fish of the carp family. There are several species, all of which furnish a delicate flesh. The head is smooth and oblong and the upper jaw (with four barbels) is much longer than the lower. Its average length varies from twelve to eighteen inches, but barbels have been caught measuring three feet and weighing from fifteen to eighteen pounds.

BARBER FISH, also BARBER STURGEON or TENTHIDID. A kind of sturgeon, *which see.*

BARBERA. A type of red grape from which a wine of the same name is made, both in Italy and in California. A heavy-bodied red table wine, dry and tart, it is suited for use with meats and highly seasoned foods. It is served either at room temperature or slightly chilled. The quality of the wine varies considerably. *See also* WINE.

BARBEREY CHEESE. A small, soft, rennet cheese resembling camembert. It is also commonly known as Fromage de Troyes. Milk while still fresh and warm is coagulated with rennet. The uncut curd is put into a wooden mold having a perforated bottom. After being drained for three hours, the cheese is turned into an earthenware mold, the wooden one being removed after 24 hours. The cheeses are salted, dried in a well ventilated room, and ripened for about three weeks. In summer, the cheese is often sold without ripening. It is 5 or 6 inches in diameter and 1¼ inches in thickness.

BARBERRY. This is a shrub the red berries of which are made into preserves or jellies of a pleasant acid flavor. The common barberry, brought from Europe, grows abundantly in the New England states. Species native to Asia are used for ornamental purposes, and the fruits are not so good.

The fruit, which succeeds the yellow flowers of the shrub, ripens in the fall of the year. The young leaves are used as a salad or garnish in some localities.

BARBERRY JAM

Pick over the ripe barberries and put them into a heavy kettle, adding 2 cups of water for each 3 pounds of fruit. Cook very slowly over an asbestos mat until the fruit is soft. Press through a fine sieve, discarding the skins and seeds. Add an equal quantity of sugar to the pulp. Bring to a boil and boil about 15 minutes, or until it tests done. *See also* JAM.

BARBERRY

BARDE. Culinary term of the French cuisine, meaning a thin rasher or slice of pork fat used for covering or larding meat, fowl, or game, furred or feathered. It is used not only to protect the meat during cooking, but also to enrich its flavor.

BAR-LE-DUC. A delicious jam made of red or white currants, in which the whole berries are suspended in a clear jelly. It is a French creation, said to have been discovered by Perrin Lamothe, cellarer to Duke Robert, in 1364. While it is possible to make bar-le-duc at home, it is considerable work, since the berries must each be carefully pierced in order to retain their shape.

BARLEY. This grass is one of the oldest of the cultivated cereals. It was grown in ancient Egypt, and by the Greeks and Romans. Pliny regarded it as the most ancient food of mankind. It has been found in the lake dwellings of Switzerland in deposits belonging to the Stone Age. Ears of barley are represented plaited in the hair of the goddess Ceres, and are also shown on ancient coins. One of the sacred books of the Chinese claims that it was grown in China as early as 2000 B.C. It grows wild in western Asia—probably its original home. It is adapted to both warm and cold climates and has a wider range of distribution than any other cereal, being grown all over the temperate zones.

In the northern United States, the plant matures in about three months after being sown. It ranks very close to wheat in nutritive value; and cooked barley meal, like wheaten flour, contains gum, albuminoids, starch, and dextrin. As compared with wheat, barley contains more fat, salts, and indigestible cellulose, less protein, and less digestible carbohydrate.

Barley is prepared either as pot or starch barley (with the outer husk removed), pearled barley (the husked barley which has been subjected to a polishing process), and Scotch barley (the roughly ground grain). Barley meal is a wholemeal flour made by grinding barley.

Barley is not much used as a cereal in the United States, its chief use being for the preparation of malt for distilling. See MALT. However, it makes a good addition to meat broths and thick vegetable soups.

BARLEY WATER

½ oz pearl barley
¾ cup water
Salt to taste

Grind the barley in a coffee mill. Add the water and place in a saucepan. Boil for 20 minutes, add the salt, and strain the liquid. Keep in a cool place. Barley water should be made fresh daily.

WELSH BARLEY CAKES

Make a stiff dough with barley meal and skim milk. Roll out to a circle, about ¾ inch thick. Bake on a hot griddle. Split and serve with butter.

BARLEY-CORN. A grain of barley; also personified in verse as the famous John Barleycorn, the spirit of barley or malt liquor.

BARLEY MALT. Various proprietary breakfast cereals containing malted barley are called barley malt. See also MALT.

BARLEY SUGAR. Originally a confection of barley or barley water and sugar, flavored with acid, modern barley sugar is made of cane sugar and flavored with lemon. It generally comes as long transparent yellow strips.

BARLEY

BARLEY SUGAR STRIPS

3 cups sugar
2 cups water
1 lemon
⅛ tsp cream of tartar

Dissolve the sugar in the water; then add the thinly peeled lemon rind and the cream of tartar. Cook to the soft-ball stage (240° F.); then remove the lemon rind. Now add the strained juice of the lemon, and cook to the hard-crack stage (310° F.), taking care that the sirup does not burn and is of a delicate straw color. Turn at once into a generously buttered platter or slab, and when the candy begins to set, cut it in narrow strips. Then, when cool enough to handle, twist each strip. Keep in an airtight container in a cool place.

BAROLO. The best, or at least one of the best, of the red table wines of Italy. It comes from a small district of Piedmont. See also WINE.

BARRACUDA

BARRACUDA. The great barracuda of the Caribbean is said to have a more aggressively predatory nature than the man-eating shark with which it is often compared. This fish is man-sized, being almost 6 feet in length, 30 inches in girth, and weighing up to a little over 100 pounds.

Its long, pointed jaw is armed with razor-like teeth and its slender body cuts through the water with amazing speed.

Because of its ferocity, and the fact that it will strike at almost any moving object, the great barracuda has become a popular big game fish. However, its flesh is not considered edible. The smaller barracuda of the Pacific coast, and a species found in European waters, are used for food.

BARTENDING. Bartending—the art and science of preparing and serving intoxicating drinks—in the home can be a simple process or an involved ritual, depending on the whims of the home bartender.

Regardless of the degree of complexity, bartending is both an art and a science. It is a science because there are certain rules that must be followed, just as there are in all phases of cookery. But it is an art as well, for there is ample room within those rules for the little individual touches that make the difference between a commonplace product and a masterpiece. It is an art, too, because, in addition to mixing alcohol with flavoring, it involves mixing alcohol with people.

While the home bartender is never expected to be as skilled as the professional, he should learn when and how to serve those drinks he contemplates offering in his home. This is not too formidable a task, since it is possible to master a few simple drinks, all made from the same basic ingredients, one of which would be appropriate for almost any social occasion.

Though he is not expected to compete with the professional, the home bartender is faced with a greater responsibility than is the working apron-wearer. The guest in the home does not have the same freedom of choice and expression that he would have in a public house, and is, in a way, at the mercy of his host. The common laws of hospitality demand that the host serve drinks that are at least palatable.

Home Bar Equipment

While a certain amount of equipment is needed to mix drinks correctly, the bulk of it (or workable substitutes) can be found among the normal kitchen and home equipment. By virtue of borrowing and improvisation, the home bartender can mix satisfactory drinks with a minimum of outlay for special equipment.

Following is a list of the minimum items needed for a well-rounded bar service. Such individual items as require discussion are handled under their own headings elsewhere in this book.

Anchovy Spears or Toothpicks
Bar Spoon
Beer Can Opener
Beer Comb
Bottle Opener
Bottle Stoppers
Bowls
Cherry or Olive Fork
Coasters
Cocktail Shaker
Cocktail Strainer
Corkscrew
Cutting Board and Knife
Egg Beater
Glassware
Hammer
Ice Bucket and Tongs
Ice Chopper, Crusher and/or Pick
Jiggers
Juice Extractor
Juice Strainer
Lime Squeezer
Measuring Spoons
Mixing Glass (Graduated)
Muddler
Siphon Bottle
Straws (long and short)
Stirrers
Tray

Hints for the Home Bartender

Bottles and Cans. Though the cork is not now as common as it was in the past, it is often encountered in bar work. The cork must be removed whole, with as little disturbance to the contents of the bottle as possible. Particular care must be exercised in the case of the sediment-forming wines.

The preferred tool for cork removal is, of course, the corkscrew (*which see*); though, in emergencies, two thin but strong knife blades may be used. The blades are inserted between the cork and the glass on opposite sides and used with a combined lever-pulling action.

If corked bottles are to be stored for considerable periods of time, it is well to lay them horizontally, as is done with wines, so the liquid may touch the corks and keep them from drying out.

Carbonated beverages are commonly sealed with a crown or crimped metal cap, while liquor bottles use a screw cap. Some liquors are packed with a crimp cap that is held tight by means of a twisted wire. These caps are removed by raising the twist of wire, provided for this purpose. which relieves the tension.

A great variety of openers have been developed for use on the crown or crimped cap, all utilizing some phase of the lever principle. Any opener that functions and does not chip the bottle neck is suitable for bar work, though the wall mounted variety offer the advantage of being difficult to lose or mislay.

The crimped cap, once removed, should not be replaced by hand on a bottle of carbonated beverage. Not only are these caps bent out of shape on removal, but special crimping equipment is needed to reseat them properly. Unless the seal is air-tight, it is impossible to maintain pressure in a bottle, and a carbonated beverage will soon lose its effervescent properties. There are, however, many patented devices available which do provide a satisfactory seal.

Though rarely seen in America, there is also a special type of bottle designed for use with carbonated beverages, in which the bottle is sealed by means of a glass marble inside the neck. The gas pressure within the bottle holds the marble tightly against a ring in the neck. The bottle is opened by giving the marble a sharp blow with a special instrument. This breaks the seal by forcing the marble down; the gas escapes and the marble falls into a retaining chamber permitting the contents to be poured.

Some wide-mouthed bottles and jars are sealed by a special kind of metal cap known as the *anchor* lid. These may be opened by prying with the back of a table knife or using a special opener somewhat similar to the regular crimp cap opener, but having a wider pressure area. These caps may, if not too badly bent, be replaced by hand pressure.

Canned beverages, beer, fruit juices, etc., may be opened by using a regular can opener (*which see*), or by simply punching holes in the lid. In the latter case, two holes are always punched; one to let in air while the other functions as a pouring spout. There is also a special opener, commonly called a *beer can opener*, which punches a triangular hole in one motion.

Care must be taken when opening any carbonated or effervescent beverage, canned or bottled, lest it turn into a geyser.

The container should be well chilled, and it should never, never be shaken. A warm, well shaken bottle of beer can easily send half its contents to the ceiling with almost fire hose force. The cap should be removed from bottles with a single, rapid motion, to forestall foaming. In the case of canned beer, there are two schools of thought. One faction prefers to make a very small hole in the lid and wait for the gas pressure to be equalized before going further, while the other plunges right in, making the biggest openings possible as fast as possible. Since both techniques work, the option is one of temperament.

Cleanliness. Neatness and cleanliness are of paramount importance to good bartending. All utensils should be washed and put away as soon as possible after using, all spillage cleaned up at once, all cloths and towels used around the bar washed often, etc.

This business of washing and cleaning while you work may seem a bit extreme as opposed to the average male tendency of letting everything accumulate for one large cleanup at the close of operations, but it has many advantages. For one thing, the working area is less cluttered, and clean utensils are always available.

Cleanliness is important in bar work because the liquids handled are all of an organic nature. If constant vigilance is not maintained, things will become sticky and messy to handle, and the area will acquire odors. There may even be fermentation and decay, attraction of various insects, strong odors and possible health hazards.

Glasses should be washed in hot, soapy water, rinsed well in clear water, and polished with a dry cloth after drying by a towel or evaporation. This final polishing is important for more than just appearance, for normal washing procedures often leave a thin film of dried soap on the glass.

Special care must be taken when cleaning beer glasses. If there is any soap or grease film on the glass, it will be difficult, if not impossible, to draw a "head" on the beer. For the same reason beer glasses should not be washed or rinsed in water that has been used on glasses that have contained fruit juices.

Cocktail Shakers. There are enough shaker designs on the market to appeal to any taste and pocketbook. When purchasing, it should be remembered that the shaker will have to be shaken vigorously over prolonged periods of time. It will grow quite cold and often acquire a slippery coat of moisture from the humid air. Thus, the design selected should be one that will fit the user's hand firmly, and not be apt to go sailing across the room at the height of his exertions. The cover should be such that it will fit snugly and stay on during violent shaking.

When using the shaker, it should never be filled completely, else the whole intent of shaking will be thwarted. The shaker should only be filled to the one-half or two-thirds level so the contents will be free to churn.

Since shakers, especially metal ones, can get intensely cold and uncomfortable to handle during the mixing process, it is sometimes advisable to wrap a towel or some other insulating surface about them.

The motion of shaking is up to the individual, but it should be both vigorous and prolonged if it is to be effective.

Floating. Some drinks call for a liqueur or cream to be floated on the surface; others, as the pousse cafes, are made by floating a series of liqueurs on top of each other.

The trick in floating is to pour the topping liquid in such a manner that it does not mingle with the base liquid, but floats on top in its own layer. Always pour the liquids in the order given in the recipe, since the effect is based on the fact that a lighter liquid will naturally seek its own, higher level when added to a heavier one.

The floating may be accomplished by flooding the liquid carefully and gently down the side of the glass or along the shaft of a stirrer or spoon.

Perhaps the best way to float, is to place a spoon carefully on the base liquid so that the bottom of the spoon bowl is set into the liquid, but the inner part of the bowl is still dry. Then pour the next liquid slowly into the spoon bowl, taking care when removing the spoon that there is no stirring action. For the best effect, the spoon bowl should be horizontal with the surface and immersed to the very rim. A special spoon with a large shallow bowl set at right angles to the shaft is best for this purpose.

Frosting. Many recipes call for drinks to be served in "frosted" glasses, i.e., glasses that have a covering of ice crystals or frost on the outside. This effect is achieved by the condensation of atmospheric moisture on a sufficiently cold surface. It is to be desired, for, while it does not add to the actual taste of the drink, psychologically it suggests coolness and adds greatly to the drinker's total enjoyment.

The whole secret to frosting is to have the glass cold enough; otherwise, the moisture will condense in the form of water drops or "sweat," instead of the delicate white crystals of frost. Glasses may be chilled by placing them in a refrigerator or by packing them in cracked ice. In some cases, the glass may be frosted while mixing the drink, as in Daisies, if the drink itself contains enough finely cracked ice to sufficiently chill the glass.

Since the outer surface of the glass must be intensely cold to properly frost, thin walled glasses are far better for the purpose than their thicker brethren. Silver or metal cups and mugs, however, are far superior for frosting because they chill easier. Mint juleps, for example, are often served in silver cups for just this reason.

Garnishing. Garnishing is often called for in drink recipes; sometimes for appearance's sake only, sometimes as a definite requirement to achieve the desired taste. It is advisable first to determine the effect of a garnish before eliminating or varying it.

Twists of lemon peel, for example, are nearly always added for flavor and aroma. There is a definite technique to using lemon peel. The flavor and aroma come from strong oils that are contained in certain cells close to the outer surface of the rind. The white part of the skin is useless, indeed, often detrimental. In the olden days it was customary to obtain these oils by scraping the lemon skin surface with hard lump sugar, then using the oil-soaked sugar.

A more convenient way of using lemon peel, however, is to cut thin strips from the surface of the rind, as thin as possible, with little or none of the white part attached. When a drink is to be garnished, hold the strip closely over the drink's surface and twist it. This will rupture the cells and force the oil, in a fine spray, onto the surface of the liquid. Then drop the twisted peel into the glass. Since the oil is quite strong, not too large a piece is needed to achieve the proper effect; indeed, too large a piece would distort the proportions. This garnishing should always be done in the individual glass, never in the shaker or mixer.

When a drink is garnished with fruit (cherries, pineapple sticks, etc.) that is meant to be eaten, a toothpick or anchovy spear should be provided so the guest will not have to handle the fruit or go fishing for it among the ice with bare fingers. Sometimes these accessories are served in the drink, usually transfixing the cherry.

When canned or bottled fruits, particularly the preserved types, are used to garnish, they should first be removed from their container and the liquids in which they are packed completely drained off. These liquids, especially if chemical preservatives have been added, often have a strong, distinctive taste that can mar the flavor of the drink if too much is inadvertently added with the garnishing fruit.

Some recipes, particularly the wine punches, call for a garnishing of cucumber rind. Only thin slices of fresh cucumber rind should be used, and used sparingly, lest they predominate in the total flavor. These rinds are not twisted, as are the lemon, but are usually spiked over the side of the pitcher or bowl, though thin spirals may be dropped into the mixture.

Gin and Rum Drinks. There are two schools of thought regarding mixed drinks. One believes the taste of the liquor used should predominate, the other feels that each drink is an entity in itself, a distinct taste sensation. The epicure will hold to the latter school, feeling that if the taste of the liquor is desired it should be drunk straight, or in a highball, while a mixed drink should be a symphony, a blend of things that combine to form a harmonious whole, no one element jarring or predominating. Indeed, they will maintain that it is impossible to identify by taste alone the components of a properly blended drink.

Gin has a characteristic flavor that is hard to mask. One of the best ways of hiding it is to add a few drops of fresh lime juice to any gin drink that does not also contain a wine. Added in the proper proportions, the lime taste will not be discernible, but it will effectively "marry" the gin to the other components.

Certain rums also have the characteristic of standing out in a mixture. Here too, a few drops of fresh lime juice will act as a catalyst, though some use canned pineapple juice for the same purpose.

Measurements. (*See also* WEIGHTS AND MEASURES.) While the experienced professional may pour drinks, judging by the eye alone, the amateur had best use measuring devices if he is to get professional results.

If good tasting drinks are to be consistently produced, strict adherence to formulas is essential, and this involves the meticulous use of jiggers, graduated glasses, etc.

The exact capacity of all utensils used in bar work should be known. If it is not already marked on the instrument, it should be determined by comparison with a known standard.

For example, the handy bar spoon comes in a variety of designs, and hence, a variety of capacities. It should not be used as a teaspoon or tablespoon measure until its capacity has been checked.

If the mixing glass is not already graduated, this should be done. Using a known measuring device, fill it to various ounce or pint levels with water, marking the exact height of the liquid by scoring the outside of the glass lightly with the sharp edge of a jeweler's three cornered file or some similar instrument. Be sure that these marks are clear, accurate, and easily identified.

In using bitters, set up some standard so that a "dash" will always contain the same number of drops, approximately one sixth of a teaspoon. All bitters are highly concentrated and one or two drops more or less can have a noticeable effect in the drink.

Drink recipes are usually given in terms of "jiggers," or, in some cases, glasses. Find out exactly what the author means by these terms. In the bountiful days of the free lunch and nickel beer, a jigger, being the direct descendant of the whisky or "shot" glass, was thought of as being two liquid ounces. Inflation, however, has set in here, as in other fields, and the jigger has come to be commonly accepted as an ounce and a half. In some places the trend is fast carrying it down to even smaller sizes.

In the recipes given in this book, a jigger refers to an ounce and a half, while a large jigger means the two ounce size, and a small jigger calls for an amount of only one ounce.

The same general trend can be detected in other once common measures—a wine glass or a whisky glass, for example.

It would be well for the amateur to set up certain standard measurements that will produce known quantities of drinks, basing these standards on the equipment he has and the usual numbers of guests served, and to convert all recipes he wishes to use into those terms.

Recipes. When following a recipe for the first time, the amateur should first determine the measurement standards used. If the liquors are referred to by brand names (as they often are, for recipes are commonly distributed as a form of advertising) and he does not have those brands, he should make certain that he uses the same type of liquor that is called for. The recipe should be followed exactly.

Recipes, however, are not hard and fast rules. They are a known way of producing a certain tasting drink. If the drink is not to the taste of the maker, he should then vary the proportions until he is satisfied with the result. Once established, he should make a record of his personalized formula and follow it exactly in future mixing.

If the novitiate uses a number of bar manuals for reference, he is apt to be confused by seeing the same drink made differently by different authorities, or else appearing under different names in the various books. To save himself bewilderment, he should understand the reasons behind these discrepancies.

There is no Bureau of Standards for bar procedure. Drink recipes are largely a matter of local tradition. Conceived in some local establishment, a drink recipe was spread by word of mouth and memory by travelers who had sampled and found it to their liking. Since the memory is often poor, especially if the drink were good enough to warrant extensive sampling, or all the called-for ingredients not available in another locality, or another bartender felt it could be improved by slight variations, these transplanted offspring seldom bore much resemblance to the parent.

Then again, the reputation of an establishment was often made by some particular drink or drinks invented there. As an advertising move, these drinks were often christened in such a manner as to identify the house of origin. Often, if the drink were good enough, the formula or some essential detail in the making would be jealously guarded as a trade secret. As a business move, competing establishments would either vary the name and formula in the hopes of satisfying their trade with a better drink under a more diplomatic name, or else would attempt to imitate the secret recipe, producing a similar product but usually by different means.

Another factor is that, since the birth of drink recipes is a spontaneous affair, the same basic formulae would be independently conceived in different localities or countries and be given different names.

In the recipes given in this book, every possible attempt has been made to run down the original or the basic recipe and to list the accepted variations. However, it should be remembered that drink recipes are largely a matter of local tradition and a favorite subject for debate among epicures. The mint julep (*which see*) is a perfect case in point. Not even in the South, the acknowledged birthplace of the concoction, will you find universal agreement as to how it should properly be made.

Serving. Although a drink must be properly made if it is to be a good drink, the manner of service can greatly influence the enjoyment derived.

For one thing, cold drinks should be served cold and hot drinks hot. The lukewarm is never an enjoyable taste sensation.

Though cold drinks are made with ice, if a carbonated beverage, tea, lemonade, or other mixer is to be used, the mixer should be iced in advance, if possible. It is a simple matter to place these fluids in the refrigerator some hours before using, and this forethought will result in less melting of the ice, and hence less dilution, when the drinks are made.

Drinks should be served while fresh. They lose in flavor if they are prepared in advance and kept in the refrigerator or other storage place. Only the punches and some of the coolers take kindly to this type of treatment.

The cocktail shaker should be large enough to make one complete round for the assembled guests. If this is impractical, two shakers should be used. Shaken drinks, in particular, should be served fresh, and it is rather embarrassing for all concerned if one or two of the gathering have to sit thirstily by with waiting glasses while the host hurriedly reloads the shaker.

The glass can influence the enjoyment of a drink through psychological or other causes. *See* GLASSWARE.

If more than two persons are to be served, the drinks should be carried on a tray. The glasses are usually filled to the brim which means considerable weight will have to be held and carried carefully and steadily. The tray should be of such a design as to simplify this task. While decor is a factor in selecting a tray, the utilitarian purpose should not be forgotten. Far better a large, plain tray with big, sturdy handles, than a fragile, "cute" affair that will result in ruined rugs.

If cocktails or other drinks are to be served through a social evening or afternoon, it is customary to also serve some form of food, since most of these beverages have an appetizing effect. Pretzels, bread sticks, hard cooked eggs, sandwiches (*which see*) and canapés (*which see*) are appropriate.

Experience has built up a number of rules regarding the proper time and manner of wine service for which *see* WINE. While there are also rules for liquor, they have not been developed to the point of being a fine art. In either case, the best guiding principle is to balance common sense and personal experience with the materials at hand.

When liquor is planned as part of a meal, cocktails, and never a long drink, are served as an appetizer before the food. *See* COCKTAIL. Beer is sometimes used as a table beverage instead of wine, and goes best with meats and other heavy dishes. A brandy, liqueur or pousse café is served after the final coffee. Since the purpose of the after-dinner liqueur is mainly one of taste, it is served in small, almost minute, quantities.

During the winter, when warmth is desired, the heavy bodied liquors, especially the rums, are most appropriate. Hot drinks are excellent for serving after the guests have returned from some cold outdoor sport. Certain drinks have become associated with special seasons; thus, the Tom and Jerry is traditionally served at the time of the first snowfall, while the eggnog appears during the Christmas holidays. In areas where the practice of New Year's visiting is followed, a large bowl of eggnog is commonly kept on hand to serve calling groups.

In the summer, of course, a cooling action is desired in a drink. Sugar, because of its sweetness, tends to produce thirst, and because of its easily released energy, tends to raise body temperature. Thus, while sweet drinks may be desired for reasons of taste, they should be avoided as much as possible, or served only in the cool of the evening. Tropical drinks, which were, after all, designed for hot climates, are the best for summer service.

Since one of the main causes of summer thirst is the loss of body moisture through perspiration, the best summer drinks are "tall," well diluted ones that will offer the recipient ample cool liquid without excessive alcoholic content. Excessive alcohol in the summer defeats its own purpose by, in addition to other effects, raising body temperature through the release of energy.

A summer drink should always be served cold and with ample ice. There should be enough ice in the glass to last, and not melt away before the drink is finished. Not only will this keep the drink cold, but the sound of ice tinkling in a glass has a certain psychological suggestiveness of coolness. If possible, the glass should also be frosted, again suggesting coolness, this time through the medium of vision.

Stock. Though the commercial establishment stocks a wide variety of different brands and types of liquor, it is not at all necessary for the home bartender to go to such expense. Many of the bottles, particularly the liqueurs, are rarely used.

While a large assortment of potables is a decided asset, offering wide scope to the owner, careful study of the common drink recipes will show that a stock of three or four bottles will concoct a great variety of drinks, adequate to any normal social needs. A gin, a whisky (rye or bourbon—scotch is rarely used for mixed drinks), a vermouth and possibly a rum will give ample leeway. The other varieties may be added from time to time as needs arise or economics permit.

It may be necessary to vary some recipes to meet these limited conditions, but an adequate assortment of good recipes can be collected. It might be well, also, to collect some recipes that call for only one or two liquors to meet situations that might arise when the stock is low.

Though only a few liquors need be purchased, they should be the best liquors the buyer can justifiably afford. It has been said that there is no need to "waste" good liquor in a mixed drink, since no one can tell the difference, but this is a fallacy. The host who subscribes to it deludes no one but himself. Granted the flavor of a liquor may be hidden in a cocktail, no amount of ingredients or mixing will ever hide the roughness and after-effects of inferior liquor. A drink is never any better than its components.

The other ingredients commonly called for in drink recipes—fruits, eggs, spices, etc., are nearly always found among the normal household groceries.

Sugar. Since most drinks are made with iced fluids, making it difficult to dissolve granulated or lump sugar, the sugar normally used in bar work, unless otherwise specified, is of the powdered or confectioner's type.

If this is not available, simple sirup (*see* SIRUP) may be used in its place in the same proportions.

Tricks. If a siphon bottle (*which see*) of the type that can be carbonated by the user is included in the bar equipment, there are many things that can be done with it, other than making regular charged water. Various mixtures and blends may be placed in it and charged the same as water, producing novel effervescent drinks. For one thing, if certain of the still wines or some grades of applejack are so carbonated, they will taste very much like champagne.

If the charged water bottle is used in this manner, however, the liquids should not stay in it too long, and the bottle should be thoroughly cleaned lest a sticky sediment impede the operation of the mechanism.

A new type of mechanical mixer has been developed that opens vast vistas to the experimenter. Known as the Blendor, it is claimed that many hitherto impossible combinations may be blended in the device. In any event, any shaken drink can be mixed in it without the exertion demanded by the cocktail shaker. It is especially suited for heavily iced drinks such as the frozen daiquiri, which should come out looking more like a sherbet than a liquid if it is properly made.

There are some who object to the use of ice in drinks on the grounds that, as it melts, it dilutes the beverage, giving the last few sips a weak and watery taste. Several devices have been perfected to meet this difficulty. Varying in design, they are similar in principle; a fluid enclosed in a thin walled container. Placed in a refrigerator, the fluid freezes; placed in a drink, the device acts like an ice cube, but the fluid is confined to the container.

BASELLA. This is a climbing and trailing plant of the tropics, where it is cultivated as a pot herb. It has been introduced into the United States as a substitute for spinach, which it succeeds in season (from July until frost). It is decidedly mucilaginous when cooked. One variety bears edible tubers, and another furnishes a purple dye.

BASIL. This aromatic plant is native to India. A lady created by Keats in one of his poems buried her lover's head in a pot of basil. For ages basil has been held in high esteem. The ancient Greeks called it "the herb of kings." In old England it was considered a great honor to be presented with a pot of basil. The leaves of the plant are used in seasoning soups, steaks, duck, spaghetti sauce, and cheese and tomato dishes. Try adding basil to the water in which peas or potatoes are cooked.

BASIL

BASS. A number of spiny-finned fish of both fresh and salt water are known by this name. Most of them are excellent food fishes. The chief types are:

Black sea bass. The Romans called this fish *lupus*, meaning wolf, because of its voracity. Its oblong body is covered with scales which are unusually hard and rough. Its back is silvery blue in color. Its fine white flesh provides light flakes of delicious meat. The sea bass is a gamy fish, weighing from one-half pound to four pounds, and is found in Atlantic coastal waters from Cape Ann, Massachusetts to northern Florida. It is not an expensive fish, and is usually found in the markets either as the whole fish, or filleted.

Calico bass. Also called strawberry bass, this is a fresh-water fish of the Mississippi river and the Great Lakes. It is a small fish, weighing less than half a pound and it is mottled dark green on a silvery green background.

California white sea bass. A large fish, weighing from 50 to 100 pounds, which is related to the weakfish.

Channel bass. Also called red drum. It is silvery grey in color with wavy brown stripes, and sometimes a reddish tinge. In size, it ranges up to 40 pounds, but the best specimens for eating weigh about 10 pounds. It is found along the southern coasts and in the coastal rivers.

Large-mouthed black bass. Also known as straw bass. This is a freshwater fish which may weigh up to 20 pounds and reach a length of three feet. At its best for food, it weighs between 6 and 8 pounds.

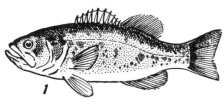

BASS   1. Large Mouth   2. Small Mouth

Small-mouthed black bass. One of the best of the game fishes, it is a fresh-water fish of wide distribution. It weighs between one-half and five pounds.

Striped bass, or rockfish. A game and food fish of the Atlantic coast, the striped bass has been introduced into Pacific waters. Its weight varies from half a pound to 75 or 100 pounds for an occasional giant. Its coloring is olive above and silvery yellow on the sides and below, marked with longitudinal black stripes.

White or silver bass. Found in the same waters of the Mississippi and Great Lakes as the rock bass, it has a much better flavor. It weighs from one to two pounds. The rock bass has soft flesh and is inclined to have a muddy flavor, so that it is not usually eaten.

Bass may be bought as the whole fish, fillets, or steaks, depending on the size. Bass may be baked, broiled, or fried.

BASTING. The process of moistening a roast during cooking with water, fat, pan liquid, or seasoning fluid. It is almost compulsory for a roast unless a covered roaster is used. The object is to return to the meat the juices and flavor which cook out during the roasting process and to prevent the meat becoming too dry. The basting process should be repeated several times during the cooking. Ordinarily a spoon or ladle is used; recently a gadget which resembles a bulb syringe has been put on the market. It is claimed to make the operation of withdrawing the liquid from the pan easier than scooping it out with a spoon.

BATFISH. *See* Red Gurnard.

BATTER. Two types of batter are generally thought of in connection with quick breads of various sorts. One is the pour batter and the other the drop batter. The pour, or thin, batter flows easily from a spoon or pitcher and varies in thickness from a popover mixture which is almost liquid to griddle-cake and waffle mixtures which are thicker. The drop, or thick, batter which is used for muffins and fritters does not pour readily, but drops in a soft mass from a spoon, or must be shaken or pushed from the spoon.

Batter for fritters should be liquid enough to coat the food mixture dipped into it. For meat, fish, vegetables, etc. the batter is not sweetened; but for fruit or other dessrt fritters the batter is often sweetened and flavored.

See also Griddle Cakes, Pancakes, Popovers, and Waffles.

Basic Fritter Batter

1 cup flour
1 tsp baking powder
½ tsp salt
1 egg, well beaten
¾ cup cold milk

Sift the dry ingredients together into a bowl. Combine the egg with the milk, mixing thoroughly with a rotary beater. Add all at once to the flour mixture and stir to make a smooth batter. Stir in the meat, fish, or vegetables, chopped or cut into small bits. Drop by spoonfuls into deep hot fat (375°–390° F.) and fry until golden brown. Drain on soft crumpled paper.

For fruit fritters, 2 tablespoons of sugar, more or less, depending on the sweetness of the fruit being used, should be sifted in with the dry ingredients.

BATTLEMAT CHEESE. A cheese, similar to, but softer than, Emmentaler cheese. It is a large round cheese about sixteen inches in diameter and four inches high. It weighs from forty to eighty pounds. This cheese is made in Switzerland and in the northern part of Italy.

BAUDEN CHEESE. A sour-milk cheese, essentially the same as Harzkase. This cheese comes in two shapes—conical and cylindrical. It is made in Bohemia and Silesia, and is locally known by the name Koppen.

BAUME. The hydrometric scale devised by a French chemist, Antoine Baumé. Baume hydrometers are still used by some manufacturers to determine the density of sirups for flavoring drinks and preserving fruits. They are gradually being replaced in most industries in the United States by standard hydrometers recommended by the U.S. Bureau of Standards.

BAVARIAN CREAM. A variation of soft custard (*which see*) into which gelatin and whipped cream are folded after the mixture is cooled. It is then chilled and unmolded for serving.

Bavarian cream may be flavored with a flavoring extract, with a dessert wine such as Madeira, sherry or port, with fruit or a combination of fruits, with fruit juice, or with a liqueur. The plain Bavarian creams may be served with almost any sweet sauce.

BAVARIAN CREAM

1 tbsp plain gelatin
¼ cup cold water
1½ cups milk, scalded
3 eggs, separated
⅓ cup sugar
1 tsp vanilla
½ cup whipping cream

Soften the gelatin in the water for 5 minutes. Add the milk and stir until the gelatin is dissolved. Beat the egg yolks until thick and the whites until stiff. Combine the egg yolks and sugar in the top of a double boiler. Add the gelatin mixture and cook over hot water for 5 minutes, stirring constantly, until the sugar is dissolved. Cool and chill until slightly thickened. Add the vanilla. Whip the cream until stiff and fold it into the mixture. Then fold in the beaten whites. Rinse a mold with cold water and pour in the mixture. Chill in the refrigerator until firm. (Serves 6)

BAY LEAF

BAY LEAF. The bay leaf grows on the sweet bay tree, a member of the laurel family that is native to the Mediterranean region. In ancient times the heads of honored persons were crowned with leaves of laurel or bay. One kind of bay rum, a medicinal and cosmetic, is composed principally of extract of bay leaf and alcohol. The bay leaf has a very powerful aromatic flavor.

Although the flavor of the dried leaf is strong enough to demand cautious use, the leaf is very popular as a seasoning for soups and stews and in sauces for meat and fish. It is excellent with chicken and with any tomato dish, and it is an integral part of the bouquet garni (*which see*). Stuffing for almost any roast bird requires the addition of bay leaf, and a bit of it goes well in boiled potatoes or boiled rice. It is a "must" in pickling solutions. One quarter of a medium-sized leaf is enough to permeate a pint of soup stock or a stew that will serve three.

BAYBERRY. This is the popular name of various small shrubs of the species *Myrica*. They are native to North America and to Britain and are known also by the names of candleberry and wax myrtle. The small leaf of California's Sierra Sweet Bay (*M. Hartwegii*) is used as a flavoring for fish, meats, sauces, etc. The flavor is similar to but more subtle than that of the bay leaf.

Bayberry candles are made from the waxy fruit of the shrub. The candles are prized for the delicate, pleasing aroma which they diffuse while burning and for their quality of being practically dripless. (Their wax being almost entirely consumed by the flame.) The latter feature is especially appreciated by homemakers who value their fine table linen.

The bayberry tree proper is of a different species (*Myrtaceae*) that grows in the West Indies. It is related to allspice and clove, *which see*. The leaves of this tree are used in making fine bay rum.

BEACH PLUM

BEACH PLUM (*Prunus maritima*). The wild beach plum is found on the sandy stretches of the eastern coast of the United States from New England to Virginia. The shrub stands from two to ten feet high, and bears dark green leaves that are formed like pointed ovals with saw-toothed edges.

Beach plums ripen in August and September. They are purple and round, and they vary from a half-inch to one inch in diameter. Birds vie with man in an effort to be the first to taste the juicy pulp of the fruit. The flavor varies from a not unpleasant bitterness to the tangy sweetness of the fully ripened fruit. The plums may be eaten raw, and they are delicious when made into jams and jellies. These are particularly tasty when served with roast pork or duck.

BEACH STRAWBERRY. This is a wild sweet variety of strawberry found along the Pacific coast. Its fruit is ripe during the spring and early summer.

BEAM TREE. This European and Asiatic tree (of the family *Malaceae*) reaches an average height of forty feet. It produces showy orange-red or scarlet fruits in the late spring. The fruit is acid and astringent and resembles that of the service-berry tree from which a kind of beer is made. The beam tree is closely related to the mountain ash.

BEAN. "Beans" may refer to the edible pods of the varieties which are eaten in their entirety, or to the shelled seeds of the more mature bean or of different varieties. In European cookery, *haricots* are the shelled seeds corresponding to our dried beans. Beans and peas together comprise the legumes.

FRESH BEANS

Snap Beans. The string bean or butter bean of the garden and fresh vegetable market is at its best when the seeds within the pod are very immature. Some varieties are green and some, commonly known as *wax beans*, are yellow. Different varieties differ in shape, being rounded or flat. In these days most of the varieties grown for market are practically stringless. The *haricots verts* of French menus are green string beans.

Lima Beans. Lima beans are sold fresh in the pods, or shelled and dried. There are two general classes, the large bean, and the small "butter bean" or "baby" lima bean. Since they are different varieties, the size has no bearing on the tenderness. Ordinarily the "baby" limas are more expensive, and many people consider them to have a more delicate flavor. Both varieties are dried.

Fava Beans. This is the "broad bean" of ancient history. While it has been a favorite in England for years, only recently has it been imported into the United States. It somewhat resembles the lima bean, except that the pod is rounder, and the beans within are globular in shape. When the broad bean is less than half grown, it may be eaten pod and all. When the beans are more mature, they should be shelled and used like lima beans.

Among other edible-podded beans are the asparagus bean and the runner bean.

FOOD VALUE

	Water	Food Energy	Protein	Fat	Carbohydrate	Calcium	Phosphorus	Iron	Vit. A Value	Thiamine	Riboflavin	Niacin	Ascorbic Acid
Fresh Snap	88.9	42	2.4	.2	7.7	65	44	1.1	630	.08	.10	.6	19
Green Lima	66.5	131	7.5	.8	23.5	63	158	2.3	280	.25	.14	.9	32
Canned Snap	94.0	19	1.0	0	3.8	27	19	1.4	410	.03	.05	.3	4
Canned Lima	80.9	72	3.8	.3	13.5	27	73	1.7	130	.03	.05	.5	8
Dried Common or Kidney	10.5	350	22.0	1.5	62.1	148	463	10.3	0	.60	.24	2.1	2
Dried Lima	12.6	341	20.7	1.3	61.6	68	381	7.5	0	.60	.24	2.1	2
Dried Cowpeas	10.6	351	22.9	1.4	61.6	80	450	7.8	0	.83	.23	2.2	2
Dried Soybeans	7.5	351	34.9	18.1	12.0	227	586	8.0	110	1.14	.31	2.1	Trace

Both bear exceptionally long pods which are tender and delicious when young. They are not often seen in the markets, but may be grown easily in the garden.

DRIED BEANS

Lima Beans. These are the shelled lima beans which have been dried. They make many delicious and inexpensive dishes.

Navy or "common" beans. These are the familiar, small white beans which are used for baked beans. A number of different kinds, varying somewhat in size, are included under this general name.

Kidney Beans. These are large, dark red, kidney-shaped beans which are often used for baked beans. It seems to be a matter of regional preference whether the navy or kidney beans are "real" baked beans.

Pinto Beans. These are the dotted pink beans of the western United States, the *frijoles* of the Mexicans.

Cowpeas. Black-eyed peas, or pea-beans, are small, whitish beans with a black spot at the eye. The cowpea has been used in the south to a greater extent than in the north. It is highly nutritious, and deserves more consideration than it has received. Black-eyed peas are the chief ingredient of Hopping John (*which see*) and of certain Creole dishes.

Soybeans. Only recently has the soybean been cultivated for human consumption. Formerly it was used for forage and to restore much-needed elements to the earth in crop-rotation plantings. The soybean is more valuable than any other dried bean so far as food value is concerned. However, it has a distinctive flavor which differs from the blandness of navy or kidney beans.

HINTS ON BUYING

Fresh Beans. Snap beans should be clean and fresh looking and so crisp that they snap in the fingers. All the beans should be at the same stage of maturity so that they will cook uniformly. One pound of fresh string beans will make four or five portions when cooked.

Unshelled lima beans should be plump and fresh looking and dark green in color. In many city markets it is now possible to buy the freshly shelled limas in small containers. These do not keep well and should be carefully examined before purchasing. The shelled limas should be plump with a tender skin and a delicate green color. If they are moist or slimy, they have started to spoil. A pound of unshelled lima beans will give about one-third of a pound, or one cup, of shelled beans, which will serve two persons.

The fava bean is similar to the lima, and the same criteria are applicable.

Dried Beans. At present these are usually sold packaged, and one need only buy a reliable brand to have uniformly sized, clean beans.

Canned Beans. Both green and yellow snap beans and fresh lima beans are canned. The snap beans are either cut in pieces or "frenched"—that is, cut lengthwise into thin slivers. The dried beans are most often canned as baked beans, although canned plain navy beans may be obtained for use in various dishes, many of foreign origin. The *garbanzos* of the Italian and Spanish markets are canned chickpeas, a variety of legumes.

Frozen Beans. Quick-frozen snap beans, either sliced or "frenched," form an excellent substitute for the fresh. Frozen lima beans of both the large and "baby" varieties are also available. Baked beans, too, are successfully frozen. Frozen beans should be dropped, unthawed, into a very little boiling salted water and cooked until tender. Then they may be treated as fresh beans.

HINTS ON PREPARATION

Young, tender beans need only to be washed and have the ends of the pods nipped off. Then they should be steamed in very little water until tender. Beans which have been "frenched" (cut in long narrow slivers) will cook more rapidly than those simply cut in pieces. An inexpensive gadget may be found in most variety stores which shreds the beans easily.

Butter Steamed Beans. A particularly delicious way to cook young beans is to melt a quantity of butter or margarine in a saucepan with a tightly fitting lid. Put the beans in and cover the pan. Steam in the butter over a low flame, shaking the pan often to prevent the beans from sticking.

Fresh beans need no more than salt and pepper and a lump of butter for seasoning, but a sprinkle of chopped tarragon leaves makes a pleasant flavor change. A sliver of garlic cooked with the beans also lends an intangible difference to the flavor. Sliced cooked beans with mayonnaise or French dressing makes an excellent salad.

Lima Beans. Limas should also be steamed to keep their flavor and nutrition. Season with salt, pepper, and butter. Older, tougher limas may be parboiled for a few minutes and then baked in various combinations to achieve tenderness.

Canned Beans. These need only to be heated and seasoned for serving. Be careful not to overcook them lest they become mushy.

Dried Beans. These must be soaked, usually overnight, before use. If you are in a hurry, the soaking time may be cut down by using boiling water and keeping the beans covered for several hours. Then long, slow cooking is in order.

Canned baked beans may be eaten straight from the can, but there are many ways of making them more interesting. For instance, prepare individual casseroles by placing thinly sliced frankfurters on the bottom. Add the beans which have been seasoned with a dash of sugar and grated onion. Cover the top with more thinly sliced frankfurters, brush with melted fat, and heat thoroughly in the oven. For an especially tangy flavor, pour a little catsup or chili sauce over the beans

BAKED BEAN CASSEROLE

A larger casserole is used for this dish. Cut skinless frankfurters in half crosswise and stand them upright around the edge of the casserole. Fill the center with beans.

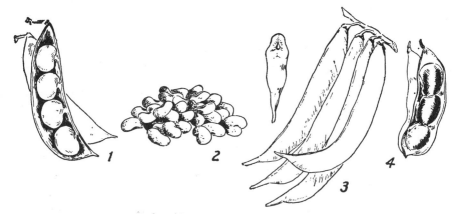

BEANS 1. Lima 2. Dried 3. Green 4. Soy

well seasoned with minced onion, thyme, and a little catsup, chili, or Worcestershire sauce. Top with wafer-thin slices of onion, brush the surface with butter or drippings, and bake in a moderate oven (375° F.) for about 40 minutes.

ARMENIAN STRING BEANS

5 tbsp olive oil
3 medium-sized onions, chopped finely
1 cup left-over chopped lamb
1 lb string beans, frenched
¼ cup bouillon
2 tomatoes, peeled and cut in thick slices

Heat the oil in a skillet, add the onion and lamb, and stir over a low flame until the onion is browned. Add the string beans and the bouillon, and cover the skillet. Cook until the beans are tender (about 15 minutes). Lay the tomato slices on top of the beans, cover tightly, and simmer for about 10 minutes longer. Season to taste with salt, pepper, and a dash of nutmeg and clove. (Serves 4)

BAKED STRING BEANS

Trim the ends from small beans, but leave them whole. Put them in a baking dish; add a good lump of butter or margarine, salt, pepper, and two or three small, peeled onions. Cover the dish tightly and set it in a moderate oven (350° F.) for an hour, or until the beans are tender.

SAVORY STRING BEANS

2 lb string beans
½ cup olive oil
1 cup finely sliced onions
1 tsp minced garlic
2 tsp salt
⅛ tsp pepper
¼ cup water
2 egg yolks, beaten

Remove the stems and tips from the beans and cut them into 2-inch lengths. Heat the oil in a pan having a closely fitting cover. Add the onions and the garlic, and cook until transparent. Add the beans, stir well, and add the seasonings. Add the water. Cover the pan and cook very slowly about 30 minutes, or until tender. Stir in the egg yolks just before serving. (Serves 6-8)

SCALLOPED STRING BEANS

¾ lb string beans, or 1 No. 2 can of beans
3 tbsp flour
3 tbsp butter
Salt and pepper
½ tsp Worcestershire sauce
1½ cups milk
¾ cup buttered crumbs
Paprika

If fresh beans are used, remove the stems and tips. Cut the beans into inch-long pieces, and wash them. Cook in a little boiling water until tender. Drain. Prepare a white sauce with the butter, flour, seasonings, and milk. Add this to the beans, turn into a greased baking dish, and sprinkle with the crumbs and paprika. Bake in a moderate oven (375° F). about 15 minutes, or until heated through. (Serves 4)

STRING BEAN, CABBAGE AND PEPPER SALAD

2 cups shredded cabbage
2 cups shredded cooked string beans
1 large green pepper, shredded
1 cup sour cream
Salt and pepper
⅓ cup washed capers
Fillets of anchovy
Quartered hard-cooked eggs

Have the cabbage shredded as fine as possible, then prepare as for cole slaw (which see). Drain very thoroughly and dry between two towels. Combine with the beans, pepper, sour cream, and seasonings. Chill and arrange in a salad bowl, sprinkling the capers over all and garnishing the base of the salad with the fillets of anchovy and quartered hard-cooked eggs. (Serves 6-8)

STRING BEANS COUNTRY STYLE

2 lb string beans
¼ lb salt pork or fat bacon
Water

Remove the stems and tips from the beans. Cut into inch-lengths and wash. Put into a saucepan with water to cover, and bury the pork or bacon in the center. Bring to the boiling point, cover tightly, and simmer from 2 to 2½ hours. Serve with the pork, pouring any remaining liquid over the beans. (Serves 6)

STRING BEANS CREOLE

1 onion, sliced
1 tbsp butter
1 cup cooked or canned tomatoes
½ bay leaf
½ tsp salt
½ green pepper, diced
1 whole clove
1 tsp sugar
1 No. 2 can string beans

Combine all the ingredients except the beans, and simmer for 15 minutes. Remove the bay leaf and clove, add the beans, and heat thoroughly. Fresh cooked beans may be used instead of canned beans. (Serves 4)

STRING BEAN SHORTCAKE

Prepare a baking powder biscuit dough (*see* BISCUIT). Prepare also creamed string beans and add to them 2 sliced hard-cooked eggs, a tablespoon of minced pimiento and a few drops of onion juice. Bake the shortcake dough as for any shortcake (*which see*), split, fill and top with the creamed beans. Other vegetables may be similarly prepared.

STRING BEANS WITH MUSTARD DRESSING

1 lb green string beans
1 egg yolk
1 tbsp prepared mustard
¾ cup milk, scalded
2 tsp vinegar
2 tsp butter or margarine
Salt and pepper

Remove the stems and tips, cut the beans into thin slices, and cook in a little boiling salted water until tender. Drain thoroughly. Beat the egg yolk with the mustard in the top of a double boiler, and add the scalded milk, stirring while adding. Place the boiler over hot water and cook, stirring constantly, until thickened. Add the vinegar, beans, butter, and seasonings, and serve piping hot. The sauce should be slightly curdled when served. (Serves 4)

CREAMED FRESH LIMA BEANS

Shell the lima beans, and cook them in boiling, slightly salted water until the beans are just tender. Drain. Season with salt and pepper. Scald ½ cup cream or rich milk

containing a bayleaf, 3 thin slices of onions, a clove, and a sprig of parsley. When hot, strain it over the beans and add a lump of butter. Serve immediately.

LIMA BEAN AND BACON CASSEROLE

1 lb small dried lima beans
2 small onions, quartered
1 bouquet garni
Small clove of garlic
Salt
8 peppercorns, gently bruised
½ cup onions, chopped
½ cup celery, chopped
¼ cup bacon or ham fat
2 tbsp butter or margarine
2 tbsp flour

Pick over the lima beans, and soak them overnight in enough water to cover them. Drain them, and recover with fresh water. Add the onions, bouquet garni (*which see*), garlic, salt, and peppercorns. Bring the mixture to a boil, lower the flame, and simmer gently until the beans are tender (about an hour). Meanwhile, mix ½ cup of onions with the chopped celery. Cook in bacon or ham fat in a skillet until the vegetables are tender. Drain the beans, reserving the liquid. Discard the garlic and the bouquet garni. Mix the beans with the onion and celery mixture, season to taste, and turn into a greased casserole.

Heat the butter or margarine, and blend in the flour without browning. When the mixture bubbles, stir in 1½ cups of the liquid in which the beans were cooked; ¼ or ½ cup of tomato catsup may also be added. Cook until thickened, stirring constantly. Pour this mixture over the beans, and arrange strips of bacon across the top. Bake in a moderate oven (350° F.) for about 40 minutes, or until the beans are tender and the bacon crisp and brown.

BAKED BEANS CREOLE

3 slices bacon, diced
½ cup minced onion
½ cup finely minced green pepper
1 medium-sized can oven-baked beans
Salt
1 cup canned or stewed fresh tomatoes
1 tsp sugar

Fry the bacon until crisp, and remove it from the pan. Brown the onion and green pepper in the bacon fat, and combine these with the bacon. Arrange the beans and bacon-vegetable mixture in alternate layers in a casserole. Add salt if needed. Blend the tomatoes and sugar and pour over all. Bake in a hot oven (425° F.) for about 30 minutes, or until the tomatoes thicken. (Serves 4)

BAKED FRIJOLES ARIZONA STYLE

2 lb pink or pinto beans
1 tsp salt
1 tsp soda
2 small white onions, minced
3 tbsp honey
Celery salt
Cayenne pepper
Small clove of garlic

Cover the beans with cold water overnight. In the morning, drain and cook with fresh water to which salt and soda have been added. Let the beans simmer until tender. Place onions and honey in the bottom of a casserole and cover them with drained beans. Add the seasonings. Rub the lid of the casserole thoroughly with the halved clove of garlic. Cover the casserole, and bake the beans in a hot oven (425° F.) until they are thoroughly tender. (Serves 6)

BEAN LOAF

3 cups cooked navy beans
1 small onion, minced
3 tbsp bacon fat
1 cup bread crumbs
1 egg
1½ tsp salt
1 cup evaporated milk

Mash the beans and combine them with all the other ingredients by stirring thoroughly. Turn the mixture into a well greased loaf pan and bake it in a moderate oven (375° F.) for about 45 minutes. Serve with catsup.

Bean loaf is excellent as a main dish on cold days. It is hearty and wholesome and appeals to everyone on cold, windy nights. It is a good meat substitute and a help to the food budget.

Slices of bean loaf make delicious sandwich fillings. Make the sandwiches with Boston brown bread, and serve with dill pickles.

BEAN ROAST

1 cup cooked white beans
1 cup peanuts
½ cup bread crumbs
1 tsp salt
Dash of pepper
½ cup milk

Pass the beans and peanuts together through the food chopper. Combine with the remaining ingredients and form the mixture into a loaf on a greased baking pan. Bake in a moderate oven (375° F.) about 30 minutes. Serve very hot with tomato sauce. If desired, strips of raw bacon may be arranged over the top of the loaf when it is half cooked. (Serves 4)

BEANS AND RICE, COUNTRY STYLE

2 cups red or black beans
2 qt water
3 onions
1 cup diced smoked ham or sausage
1 clove of garlic, sliced
⅛ tsp marjoram or thyme
4 cups hot cooked rice
1 tsp salt
2 tbsp butter

Wash the beans thoroughly, cover with 1 quart of lukewarm water, and let them stand covered overnight. In the morning, add the second quart of water to the beans with one onion, sliced. Bring all to a boil. Reduce the heat and simmer gently for about an hour and a half, or until the beans begin to soften.

If ham is used, dice it; if sausage, cook it until the fat flows freely and then dice it. Cook either until brown in a little fat. Drain the meat from the fat and add it to the beans. Mince the remaining onions and the garlic, and brown in the remaining fat. Add the marjoram or thyme and salt to the cooking beans. Stir thoroughly and continue to simmer until the beans are tender (about an hour). They should then be nearly dry. Add additional seasoning if desired.

Serve in the center of a large, deep platter. Surround with the rice into which the butter has been stirred. (Serves 6)

This recipe, in numerous variations, has long been a favorite. Its ingredients are readily available and the result is very tasty as well as filling, making a simple but satisfying dish.

Black Bean Soup I

1 cup black beans
1½ qt water
1 onion sliced
¼ lb salt pork
Salt and pepper
2 bay leaves
1 stalk celery
6 cloves
1 hard-cooked egg, sliced
1 lemon, sliced
Sherry

Soak the beans overnight. In the morning cook with the water, onion, pork, seasonings, and flavorings until the beans are tender, adding more water as necessary. Press through a coarse sieve, rubbing through all possible pulp. Extend with water or stock to give desired consistency. Reheat. Add the sherry and serve garnished with the egg and lemon slices. (Serves 6)

Black Bean Soup II

1½ cups black beans
1½ tbsp butter
¼ cup chopped onions
¼ cup finely chopped, green celery leaves
1 small carrot, scraped and chopped
1 small leek, washed and chopped
1 tsp celery salt
¼ tsp black pepper
4 or 5 grains of mustard seed
3 tbsp sherry wine
¾ cup sweet cream or rich milk
2 hard-cooked eggs
Thin slices of lemon

Soak the beans overnight in cold water. Drain, and place them in a soup kettle. Add a quart of cold water, and bring to the boiling point. Meanwhile, melt the butter in a skillet, and cook the onions, celery, and leek, stirring carefully, until they just begin to brown. Add the mixture to the beans and stir well. Add the salt, pepper, and mustard seed. Turn the flame low and cover the pot. Simmer 3 or 3½ hours (until the beans are very tender), adding more boiling water if necessary. Rub through a sieve and reheat the purée to the boiling point. Add the sherry and the milk or cream which has been scalded.

Do not boil again. Serve in bowls, sprinkling the chopped hard-cooked eggs over the surface and floating a thin slice of lemon in each portion. (Serves 8)

Bretonne Baked Beans

1½ cups pea beans
1 cup stewed tomatoes, fresh or canned
1 cup chicken stock or canned chicken bouillon
6 canned pimientoes, sieved
¼ cup minced green pepper
1 bouquet garni
2 whole cloves
1 thin slice garlic
1 onion, minced
¼ cup butter
2 tsp salt
¼ tsp freshly ground black pepper

Wash the beans in two or three separate waters. Cover them with water and let them soak overnight. In the morning drain, cover with fresh cold water, and allow to simmer until just tender. Drain, add all the remaining ingredients, turn into a casserole or bean pot, cover, and bake in a moderate oven (350° F.) until the beans have absorbed most of the liquid. (Serves 6)

Frijoles Mexicano

1¼ cups pinto beans
½ tsp soda
2 small cloves garlic
½ cup diced salt pork
1 tsp vinegar
Salt
1 small onion, sliced
3 tbsp bacon drippings
Grated cheese

Pick over the beans and wash them thoroughly. Cover them with cold water, add the soda, and soak them overnight. In the morning, add the garlic and salt pork, cover and cook them slowly in the same water in which they were soaked, adding more hot water from time to time to keep the beans well covered. They should be tender in about four hours, and when done there should be approximately 2 cups of liquid. Add the vinegar, and partly mash the beans with a potato masher. Add salt, if desired, together with the sliced onion. Heat the bacon drippings in a heavy pan, pour the beans in slowly, and stir them until they bubble. Cook about 10 minutes; then turn them into a greased baking dish, sprinkle them generously with grated cheese, and bake them in a hot oven (400° F.) for about fifteen minutes, or until the cheese is melted. (Serves 4)

KIDNEY BEAN SOUP

3 cups cooked or canned kidney beans
3 tbsp minced onion
3 tbsp minced celery leaves
¼ cup minced carrot
1 qt hot water
2 cups canned tomato
1 tsp salt
⅛ tsp pepper

Combine the beans, onion, celery, carrot, water and tomato. Bring slowly to boiling point and simmer very gently about 40 minutes or until the vegetables are tender, stirring frequently. Press through a sieve, season, and again bring to boiling point. Sprinkle with minced parsley and pass grated cheese and toasted whole wheat bread separately. (Serves 6)

MEXICAN BAKED BEANS

2 cups navy beans
6 cups cold water
½ cup olive oil
2 cups stewed tomatoes, fresh or canned
1 bunch of celery, diced small
1 medium-sized onion, minced
3 small sweet pickles, minced
½ cup stuffed olives, diced
1½ tsp salt
Pinch of cayenne pepper
Tiny pinch of chili pepper
½ cup grated cheese

Wash the beans in two or three separate waters; then soak them overnight in 6 cups of cold water. In the morning, turn the beans and the water in which they have been soaked into a heavy saucepan. Bring to the boiling point, reduce the flame, and let simmer for about an hour (until the beans are tender but not soft). Meanwhile, combine all the remaining ingredients except the cheese, and cook gently for a half hour. Stir thoroughly and pour the entire mixture over the beans which have been placed in a casserole or bean pot. Cover and bake in a slow oven (300°–325° F.) about 2 hours, after which sprinkle with

the cheese and return to the oven, uncovered, until browned. If desired, add 1½ cups of diced cooked ham to the beans when turning them into the bean pot.

NAVY BEAN SOUP

½ lb navy beans
1½ qt water
1 cup canned tomatoes
2 onions, finely chopped
1 small clove garlic, minced
½ cup celery tops, chopped
1 sprig parsley
1 carrot, diced
2 tbsp flour
1 cup milk
2 tbsp minced onions, additional
2 tbsp butter or margarine
2 tbsp vinegar
1 tsp salt
Dash of pepper

Wash and pick over the beans, cover with the water and let stand overnight. In the morning, simmer until tender in the same water, adding the tomatoes, onions, garlic, celery top and parsley tied together, and the carrot. When the vegetables are tender, take out the celery and parsley. Moisten the flour with the milk, add to the hot soup and again bring to boiling point, stirring constantly. Meanwhile, brown the 2 tablespoons of minced onion in the butter, add the vinegar and just before serving, stir these into the soup with salt and pepper. (Serves 6)

NEW ENGLAND BAKED BEANS I

4 cups pea beans
½ lb salt pork
2 tsp salt
2 tbsp brown sugar
⅓ cup dark molasses
½ tsp dry mustard
1 cup boiling water

Clean and wash the beans. Soak them overnight in enough water to cover them. In the morning, drain, cover with fresh cold water, and let them simmer in a closely covered saucepan until the skins burst. (To test, take a few beans on a spoon and blow on them gently. If the skins break readily, the beans are sufficiently cooked.) Turn both beans and water into a bean pot. Put the piece of salt pork which has been scraped and scored with a sharp knife into the beans so that the surface of the pork remains on top. Combine the salt, sugar, molasses, and mustard, add a cup of boiling water, and pour all over the beans, using additional water if necessary to cover them. Place the lid on the bean pot and bake in a slow oven (250°–300° F.) for about 6 hours, adding a little water occasionally as that in the pot evaporates. Uncover the bean pot during the last half hour of baking so that the pork and surface of the beans may brown. If desired, a small peeled onion may be placed in the bottom of the beanpot. Serve with Boston brown bread. (Serves 6 to 8)

The precaution of using a low temperature for baking beans had its origin in the Puritan fathers' decree that homemakers should do no work on Sunday. The beans were baked all day Saturday, eaten for Saturday supper, and also for Sunday breakfast, provided the stone oven was able to keep them hot over night.

NEW ENGLAND BAKED BEANS II

4 cups pea beans
2 slices fat salt pork
½ cup molasses
1 tsp dry mustard
½ tsp paprika
1 tsp finely minced onion
½ cup water in which beans were cooked

Prepare the beans for baking as directed in New England Baked Beans I. After they have simmered until tender, drain off and save any remaining liquid. Place a slice of the salt pork, in the bottom of a bean pot, pour in the prepared beans, and bury the second slice of pork in them. Combine the remaining ingredients, and pour them over the beans, lifting them with a spoon so that the seasonings may be evenly distributed. Cover the bean pot and bake as directed for New England Baked Beans I, uncovering for browning during the last half hour of baking. Beef stock or beef bouillon may be substituted for the bean water, if desired. (Serves 6 or 8)

SOUTH SEAS BAKED KIDNEY BEANS

2 no. 2 cans red kidney beans
½ lb bacon, sauteed
3 dill pickles, sliced thin
1 tsp salt
⅛ tsp pepper
1 tbsp grated coconut

Place one cup of the beans in the bottom of a casserole; add two slices of the bacon and one sliced pickle. Repeat the layers, seasoning each. Sprinkle the coconut over all, cover closely, and bake in a moderate oven (350° F.) for 30 minutes. (Serves 6)

SIMMERED RED BEANS AND SALT PORK

2 cups red beans
½ tsp soda
4 slices salt pork
1 onion, minced
1 carrot, minced
1 tsp sugar
Salt and pepper to taste

Pick over and wash the beans thoroughly. Cover them with cold water, add the soda, and soak them overnight. In the morning, drain, add fresh water to cover, and let simmer gently for about an hour. Meanwhile, cook the salt pork until crisp, remove from the fat, and cook the onion and carrot in the same fat until tender, stirring occasionally to prevent burning. Add the sugar and seasonings to the beans. Let simmer gently until the beans are quite tender and the water is absorbed. Garnish with the slices of salt pork. (Serves 6)

BEAR. Any of the largest carnivores of North America, formerly plentiful in the United States. Black, brown, and cinnamon bears are still to be found and may be hunted in season. The grizzly, once common in the West, is almost extinct. If they are killed instantly, before their anger is aroused, they provide flavorsome steaks for the lover of game foods. Otherwise, their adrenals are quickly activated and impart a very strong flavor to the meat. *See* GAME.

BEAR GRASS (*Xerophyllum*). Bear grass is a wild, edible member of the lily family, and is found throughout the mountains and dry hillsides of northwestern United States, and southwestern Canada. It is also called elk grass, squaw grass, and fire lily. Another member of the family, commonly called turkey beard, grows in dry areas from New Jersey to Florida.

The edible portions of the young plants are the bulbous rootstocks which may be roasted, and the tender stems which are prepared in the same manner as asparagus.

The most easily distinguishable features of the plant are the tall, tapering, un-branched stem, which may grow to a height of six feet, and the long, narrow, rough-edged leaves which emanate from the base of the stalk. The numerous, small flowers bloom only once every six or seven years, but, at that time, their creamy whiteness conspicuously covers the upper-most quarter of the stalk.

The name bear grass is also applied to two kinds of yucca (*which see*). These are found in the West, and the fruit and young stalks are edible.

BEARNAISE SAUCE. (bā ár nāz) A rich sauce, similar to mayonnaise in con-sistency, which is served with broiled fish and dark meats. True béarnaise sauce is never served hot or cold, but slightly warmed. It will separate and curdle if heated too much; if this happens the smooth texture may be restored by adding a few drops of cold water.

Bearnaise Sauce

1 cup white wine
1 tbsp tarragon vinegar
1 tbsp shallots, finely minced
Small sprig parsley, coarsely chopped
Small sprig tarragon, coarsely chopped
Small sprig chervil, coarsely chopped
2 peppercorns, bruised
3 egg yolks
Melted butter, about ¾ cup
Cayenne pepper
1 tsp mixed tarragon and chervil, minced

Place the wine, tarragon vinegar, shal-lots, parsley, coarsely chopped tarragon, chervil, and the peppercorns in the upper part of a double boiler. Cook over direct heat until reduced to ⅔ the original vol-ume. Strain through a fine sieve and return to the double boiler. Cool slightly. Set over hot water, not boiling, and beat in the egg yolks, using a wire whisk, adding melted butter alternately until the sauce is the consistency of mayonnaise. Season with the cayenne and minced herbs.

The secret of this sauce is the slow cook-ing of the egg yolks over hot water which should never reach the boiling point and the constant and rhythmic beating during the addition of the melted butter.

Sauce Bearnaise Tomate

When the béarnaise sauce has reached the consistency of mayonnaise, add ¼ its volume of thick tomato sauce or tomato purée, and omit the herbs. Serve with fish or meat.

BEATER. A device used to whip, beat, or blend liquids in cooking operations. While some of these operations may be per-formed with a spoon or fork, others, like whipping cream, are either tedious or im-possible without special apparatus.

The most familiar beater is the *egg* or *rotary beater*. In this device, two interlock-ing open-wire cages are made to revolve rapidly in opposing directions by means of a crank set on the shaft well above the liquid level.

There are, of course, many other var-iations. Some beaters twirl as the result of a plunger action when the handle is pressed down, while others have their blades set on a twisted flat shaft which is revolved by sliding a handle along its length.

Still other beaters do not have any mechanical action, but consist merely of a brush-like arrangement of wires set upon a handle or shaft, and all their motion must come from the user's hand and wrist. Beaters of this type are usually referred to as *flat beaters*, and while they are excellent for many kinds of work, they are not suited for producing stiff foams or froths.

Beaters are made in many sizes, and the housewife would do well to have more than one size and type of beater so that she can handle every type of food preparation without undue difficulty.

Purchasing Beaters

Regardless of design, beaters are com-monly made of metal. This metal should be corrosion resistant, and if plated, the plating should be complete and smooth. The beater should be sturdy enough to stand up under rugged use, and the blades, in particular, should be strong enough not to bend when they strike against the side of a pan. If the beater has a mechanical action, it should be simple and not apt to be jammed by food particles. All parts of the beater should be designed so that they may be easily cleaned.

See also KITCHEN EQUIPMENT *and* ELECTRIC MIXER.

BEATING. The purpose of beating is to incorporate a large amount of air into the mixture to be cooked. This is accomplished by the continual rapid turning over of a large part of the contents within the mixing bowl by means of a beater, whisk, or spoon.

BEATING

BEBIDA. This is the name of a very good rum made in Cuba and widely used in cocktails, punches, and other mixed drinks, hot and cold. It is also served as an after-dinner digestive. The name is derived from the Spanish *beber*, meaning "to drink."

BECHAMEL. A white broth-cream sauce combination, named after Louis de Bechamel, Marquis de Nointel, a palace functionary at the Court of Louis XIV of France, who used it frequently in planning the royal meals.

BECHAMEL SAUCE

2 tbsp fat
¼ cup ham and veal
1 onion
1 carrot
4 tbsp flour
1 pt milk
½ tsp salt
Pepper
Paprika
1 egg yolk

Melt the fat over low heat in a saucepan. Chop ham and veal very fine or run through a grinder. Slice onion and car-

rot very thin. Add ham, veal and onion to melted fat and brown slightly. Stir in flour slowly, so that it mixes well. Pour in milk slowly, while stirring to keep smooth, and then add carrot. Add salt and pepper and continue stirring until boiling starts. Heat may be increased to hasten boiling. Beat egg yolk and then beat a couple of tablespoons of the sauce into it. Return to pan with paprika and cook over a very low heat until yolk thickens. Strain.

BEECHNUT. The edible, triangular-shaped nut of the beech tree, of the genus *Fagus. See also* NUTS.

BEEF. The majority of the beef which is marketed comes from steers which have been specially raised for the meat trade. With the growing tendency in the United States toward smaller families, beef from heifers is preferred in many of the large cities. This beef is lighter in weight and gives correspondingly smaller cuts. Only steer and heifer beef can be graded United States prime. Meat from bulls, cows, and stags also find their way into market, but in lesser quantities, and the quality is generally inferior.

The United States government performs two services to the homemaker in the labeling of beef and other meats. It is a federal law that all beef which moves in interstate traffic must be inspected by government inspectors and bear the stamp of that inspection. This inspection weeds out diseased animals and those produced under unsanitary conditions. As a result such diseases as tuberculosis may not be transmitted through beef. As a general practice all the large meat packers have government inspectors in their plants and all meat is stamped no matter where it is to be sold. Meat that does not move in interstate commerce does not need this inspection, and unless there are state laws requiring it, locally grown beef will not be stamped. The seal is stamped in a harmless vegetable coloring over the carcass so that every cut will bear the mark. It reads "U.S. Inspected and Passed" with a number which is that of the packing house at which the animal was slaughtered, thus giving a control.

UNITED STATES GRADING

United States grading, on the other hand, is not compulsory and is only done

RETAIL CUTS

HIND SHANK

GROUND BEEF — HEEL OF ROUND

ROLLED FLANK — FLANK CUBES

FLANK STEAK — FLANK STEAK FILLETS

PLATE BOILING BEEF — ROLLED PLATE — SHORT RIBS

BEEF BRISKET — CORNED BEEF

KNUCKLE SOUP BONE — CROSS CUT FORE SHANK

ENGLISH CUT — ARM POT ROAST — ARM STEAK

WHOLESALE CUTS

ROUND

RUMP

LOIN END

FLANK — SHORT LOIN

PLATE — RIB

BRISKET — CHUCK

SHANK

RETAIL CUTS

ROUND STEAK — TOP ROUND — BOTTOM ROUND

ROLLED RUMP — RUMP ROAST

SIRLOIN STEAK — PIN BONE SIRLOIN STEAK

PORTERHOUSE STEAK — T-BONE STEAK — CLUB STEAK

STANDING RIB ROAST — ROLLED RIB ROAST — RIB STEAK

BLADE STEAK — BLADE POT ROAST

TRIANGLE POT-ROAST — SHOULDER FILET — BONELESS CHUCK POT-ROAST

ROLLED NECK — BONELESS NECK

BEEF CHART, showing principal cuts

when the packer requests the services of the government for this operation. Many packers have their own grades and so mark their meat, but these are rarely helpful to the housewife except to recognize the meat from a reputable packing house. There is no standardization among the various packers. United States grades, on the other hand, are identical for all packers.

Prime or Grade A-1. Prime or Grade A-1 beef consists of the very choicest of steer or heifer beef which has ideal conformation, finish, and quality. The carcass is relatively short and chunky and is heavily and uniformly fleshed. The rounds, loins, and ribs are well developed and rounded; the chucks and plates are unusually thick and compact. The cartilage is soft and pearly white; and the bones are relatively soft and red. The exterior surface of the carcass is entirely covered with a smooth creamy white layer of fat which does not

Food Value

Grade	Wa-ter	Food Energy	Pro-tein	Fat	Car-bohy-drates	Cal-cium	Phos-phorus	Iron	Vit. A Value	Thia-mine	Riba-flavin	Nia-cin	Ascor-bic Acid
Prime	47	406	13.7	39	0	8	148	2.1	0	.08	.11	3.7	0
Good	55	317	16.3	28	0	10	176	2.4	0	.10	.13	4.4	0
Commer-cial	60	268	17.5	22	0	10	189	2.6	0	.11	.14	4.7	0
Utility	66	201	18.8	14	0	11	203	2.8	0	.12	.15	5.1	0

usually exceed three-quarters of an inch in thickness. A slight excess or deficiency of fat will bar the animal from this grade. The flesh is firm and velvety, fine grained, and of a light cherry red color with an abundance of marbling (a fine network of fat through the red meat). As might be expected, relatively few animals fall within this category and these are usually purchased by large hotels, famous restaurants and others who will pay the top prices for prime beef. From the home maker's point of view, beef of this grade is an extravagance.

Choice or Grade 1. This is the best grade of beef ordinarily available to the housewife. The animal is probably slightly older than those graded Prime, and for this reason the cartilage may be slightly ossified and the bones somewhat grayer. There may be slightly more or less fat than indicated for Prime. The flesh is firm and velvety and of a good cherry red color, and there is plenty of marbling through the thicker cuts.

The best quality cow and bull carcasses are also graded Choice, but these do not compare in quality with steer or heifer beef. The meat is darker and there is almost no marbling.

Good or Grade 2. This is good quality beef, generally above average. The cuts are not as thick and heavy as they are on the higher grades, and the fat covering is not so evenly distributed. Usually the fat is firm and brittle and reasonably white, but it may have a yellowish tinge. The flesh is generally somewhat softer and somewhat darker in color than the higher grades. The thicker cuts show some marbling.

This grade of beef is an excellent buy for those who want good quality meat with economy. It is generally less wasteful, because it has less fat, than the higher grades. The flavor is good and it is generally tender. These three highest grades of beef come from cattle that have been finished on grain, since pasture-fed animals can seldom attain the weight and fat distribution required for top grading. For this reason the flavor is excellent. The fat is well distributed, and the meat is tender and juicy.

Medium, or Commercial, or Grade 3. This is usually the top grade assigned to beef that has not been finished on grain, and for this reason the flavor is not likely to be so fine as in grain-finished beef. This grade represents the middle point between the best and the poorest beef marketed. The fat covering is somewhat deficient and the cuts are inclined to be thin and angular. If the animal was over four years old the cartilage will be hard and white and the bones grayish or white and flinty. However, much younger beef falls within this grade and is correspondingly more tender. The fat is yellowish, and the meat soft and of a dark red color. There is little or no marbling. This grade of meat is economical in cuts which can be cooked in longer and slower ways than roasting and broiling.

Common, or Utility, or Grade 4. In this grade of beef the ratio of bones to meat is very high. The cuts are thin, and there is very little fat. The fat is generally yellowish white. The flesh is soft and watery and dark red in color. The chief recommendation for this grade is its economy, and the cuts are suitable for cooking only with moist heat.

Cutter, or Grade 5. Beef of this grade is due to poor feeding, lack of breeding, and old age. The meat is generally so high in bone ratio that few customers will buy it, and it is generally boned out and sold as boneless cuts in low-income districts. It is also used for making sausages. There is little or no fat, and the flesh is soft, watery, and dark in color.

Low Cutter, or Canner, or Grade 6. This grade includes nondescript carcasses of such poor quality that they cannot be sold as retail cuts. There is very little meat for the amount of bone, and the carcasses are generally boned out and the meat used for canning or for sausages. Ordinarily, very little Cutter or Low Cutter grade beef reaches the market, but after periods of extended droughts, when the cattle become emaciated, their carcasses can only be utilized in this way.

PREPARATION FOR MARKET

In the slaughterhouse the beef carcasses are split in nearly equal halves as part of the dressing operation, after being bled, skinned, and eviscerated. These halves are then either chilled or frozen, to await distribution to the retailer.

All commercial beef is either "fresh chilled" or "fresh frozen." This has nothing to do with quality or grade, and is concerned only with the processing. The meat packing plant contains a large chill or refrigerating room which is kept at a temperature between 34° and 38° F. The carcasses are placed in these rooms as the last step in the slaughtering operation to cool the meat and firm it up preparatory to shipping. After the meat has been in the room for 24 to 36 hours, it is thoroughly refrigerated, but not frozen. Fresh beef may be held for several weeks at this temperature, and prime beef is sometimes held for five or six weeks or longer to "age" it. Fresh chilled beef must be

RETAIL CUTS

Wholesale Cut	Retail Cut	Cooking Method
Round	Heel or Round	Braise or simmer
	Hind Shank	Soup or simmer
	Round Steak	Braise
	Top Round	Braise
	Bottom Round	Braise
Rump	Rolled Rump	Roast or Braise
	Rump Roast	Braise or roast
Flank	Rolled Flank	Braise
	Flank Stew	Stew
	Flank Steak	Braise
	Flank Fillets	Braise
Loin	Sirloin Steak	Broil or panbroil
	Pin Bone Sirloin	Broil or panbroil
	Porterhouse Steak	Broil or panbroil
	T-Bone Steak	Broil or panbroil
	Club Steak	Broil or panbroil
Plate	Plate Piece	Boil or braise
	Rolled Plate	Simmer or braise
	Short Ribs	Simmer or braise
Rib	Standing Rib Roast	Roast
	Rolled Rib Roast	Roast
	Rib Steak	Broil
Brisket	Brisket	Simmer
	Corned Beef	Simmer
Chuck	Blade Steak	Braise
	Blade Pot Roast	Braise
	Triangle Pot Roast	Braise
	Boneless Chuck Pot Roast	Braise
	Shoulder Fillet	Braise
	English Cut	Braise
	Arm Pot Roast	Braise
	Arm Steak	Braise
	Rolled Neck	Braise or stew
	Boneless Neck	Braise or stew
Foreshank	Knuckle	Soup
	Cross Cut Fore Shank	Soup or braise

shipped in specially refrigerated cars and ships in order to arrive in good condition.

Fresh frozen beef is prepared by placing in refrigerating rooms which are kept at a temperature between 5 and 10° F. The meat is frozen solid, and can be kept indefinitely provided the temperature is kept below freezing. The meat must be thawed before it can be used.

Although the freezing does not harm the meat in any way, most Americans have an aversion to frozen meat. For this reason, most of the beef sold at retail in this country is "fresh chilled," and the frozen meat is used for export.

Very few sides of beef are sold to the retailers; most of the beef is divided into forequarters and hindquarters before shipment. The line of severance lies along the ribs, and local trade customs decide how many ribs shall be left on the hindquarters. The number varies from none to five. The so-called Chicago, or western, method, which is the one most generally used, leaves one rib on the hindquarter. The cutting up of the quarters into wholesale cuts is again a process which differs in different cities. In the Chicago method, the hindquarters give the loin, round, rump, shank, and flank, whereas the forequarters give the rib, chuck, plate, brisket, and foreshank or shin. Many terms of local significance are used in various cities, which confuse comparisons of price and quality.

VARIETY MEATS

Brains. A great delicacy which may be prepared in various ways. *See* BRAINS.

Heart. Beef hearts are excellent stuffed and cooked long and slowly. *See* HEART.

Kidneys. Although beef kidneys are considered less desirable than those from smaller animals, they make wholesome food. To remove the alkaline odor from beef kidneys, parboil them first in salted water and drain. They may then be sautéed, stewed, or braised. In preparing the kidneys, if the butcher has not already done so, remove the fat and connective tissues. Do not overcook the kidneys; this will toughen them. *See* KIDNEYS.

Liver. Beef liver is less choice than calf's liver or lamb's liver, but good quality beef liver is certainly well worth the saving in price. *See* LIVER.

Lights. These are the lungs of the animal, which are not ordinarily used for food in this country. They are inexpensive, very nourishing, and can be mixed with other meats in appetizing dishes.

Sweetbreads. Beef sweetbreads (the thymus gland) are not ordinarily marketed, only those from young prime beef being saved. They may be used advantageously mixed with other kinds of sweetbreads. *See* SWEETBREADS.

Tongue. Beef tongues are available fresh, salted, or smoked. *See* TONGUE.

Tripe. The lining of the third stomach of

COOKING SCHEDULES

				Time (Minutes)		
Cut	Size	Method	Temperature	Rare	Medium	Well Done
Tenderloin Steak	1 inch	Broil or Panbroil	350° F.	7–8	8–9	10–11
	1½ inches	Broil or Panbroil	350° F.	8–9	10–11	12–15
	2 inches	Broil or Panbroil	350° F.	10–11	12–15	16–18
Sirloin and Porterhouse Steaks	1 inch	Broil or Panbroil	350° F.	10–12	14–16	18–20
	1½ inches	Broil or Panbroil	350° F.	14–16	18–20	22–25
	2 inches	Broil or Panbroil	350° F.	22–25	25–30	30–35
Chuck Steak (Prime only)	1 inch	Broil or Panbroil	350° F.	25	30	35
	1½ inches	Broil or Panbroil	350° F.	40	45	50
Hamburger	¾ inch	Broil or Panbroil	350° F.	8–10	12–15	15–18
Rib Roast	Per Pound	Roast	350° F.	18–20	22–25	30–35
Tenderloin or Filet	Per Pound	Roast	350° F.	10–12	14–16	18–20
Round	......	Braise	...... Simmer or Bake slowly	Brown for 15 minutes	1 hr.	1¼ hr.
Flank	......	Braise	Simmer or Bake slowly	Brown for 15 minutes	2 hr.	2¼ hr.
Less tender cuts	Per Pound	Stew or soup	Simmer	35–45min.		

the cow, tripe is delicious and digestible when tender and well cooked. It should be cooked at a low temperature, usually by stewing. *See* TRIPE.

HINTS ON PREPARING BEEF

Beef may be cooked by broiling, roasting, pot roasting or braising, and stewing or boiling. The choice of the cooking method is dictated by the cut to a great extent; see the table under Retail Cuts. Roast or broil a tender cut in an uncovered pan, adding no water. Water in a covered pan makes steam which cooks juice and flavor out of meat, and should only be used for less desirable cuts where the moist cooking is an advantage. Cook with moderate heat wherever possible, since this tends to make the meat more tender. The older method of searing a roast at high temperature and then turning the temperature down for the balance of the cooking is no longer considered the best method. Instead of sealing in the juices, which was its purpose, the searing actually dries out the meat and makes it less tender, and this method should therefore be avoided, though it is still often used.

Beef should be kept refrigerated until it is cooked, and not kept too long in any event. Chopped or ground beef, in particular, should be used as quickly as possible. The variety meats do not keep as well as do the regular cuts.

Beef is the better for being a little fat. If the particular piece is somewhat lean, add additional fat to it in cooking, either by tying it over a roast, or by using it to brown a pot roast or stew. By cooking at moderate temperatures, the drippings do not burn, and so can be rendered and used for subsequent cooking.

COOKING TIMES AND TEMPERATURE

In broiling meat, preheat the broiler at the indicated temperature for ten minutes before putting in the meat. If your broiler has no regulator, turn the flame on high, and place the rack so that the meat will be about three inches below the flame; at this point the temperature will be the indicated 350°. Turn the meat once during the broiling process. In roasting, if you use a meat thermometer, the reading should be 140° F. for rare, 160° for medium, and 170° for well done.

BEEF À LA MODE

4 lbs lean beef (rump or ribs)
1 slice fat salt pork
3 tbsp drippings
1 clove garlic
2 or 3 shallots
1 small bouquet garni
6 or 8 carrots
1 calf's foot
½ cup white wine
1 jigger brandy
12 small white onions
Salt and pepper

Marinate the salt pork in the brandy for 30 minutes. Then cut it in fine strips and use to lard the beef (*see* LARDING). Melt the drippings in a heavy pan with a tightly fitting cover. Brown the beef in the hot drippings. Have the butcher split the calf's foot in four. Add all the ingredients, except the carrots, and including the brandy which was used for the marinade. Leave the garlic, shallots, and onions whole. Cover the pan tightly and simmer very slowly for about 4½ hours. About two hours before the meat is done, add the carrots which have been cut in thick slices. Taste for seasoning, cover tightly, and continue cooking until the beef is tender. (Serves 6 or 8)

BEEF AND POTATO PUFF

2 tbsp drippings
2 tbsp chopped onion
2 tbsp chopped parsley
3 cups ground cooked beef (leftover)
3 cups mashed potato
1 cup gravy or milk
Salt and pepper
3 eggs, separated

Cook the onion and parsley for a few minutes in the drippings, until the onion is slightly yellowed. Mix together with the meat, potatoes, and gravy or milk. Season to taste with salt and pepper. Beat the egg whites until stiff and the yolks until thick and yellow. Stir the yolks into the meat mixture and then fold in the beaten whites. Pile lightly into a well greased baking dish and bake in a moderate oven (350° F.) for 1 hour, or until a knife inserted in the center comes out clean. Serve from the dish with a tomato sauce, if desired. (Serves 6)

Beef and Vegetable Soup

1 soup bone
2 qt water
2 cups celery and onion tops
Small piece red pepper
1 lb shin of beef
2 tbsp fat
1 cup each shredded carrot, celery, onion, string beans, and potatoes
Salt and pepper

Put the soup bone into a large saucepan with the water, the celery and onion tops and the red pepper loosely tied in cheesecloth. Simmer for 1 hour. Meanwhile, cut the meat into very small dice and brown these in the hot fat. Add to the soup and simmer until the meat is tender. Add the prepared vegetables all cut quite small and simmer until these are tender but not broken. Take out the bone and the cheesecloth bag, season, and slightly color with a little caramel. (Serves 6)

Beef Dumplings

⅔ lb ground lean beef
⅓ lb ground pork
1 cup soaked bread
⅓ tbsp barley
⅓ tsp sage
¼ tsp thyme
1 tbsp minced parsley or chives
Salt and pepper
1 egg, beaten

Blend all ingredients thoroughly, squeezing all possible water from the bread before adding to the meat. Form into balls the size of a small egg and cook in simmering soup' or stock about one hour. These dumplings may be served as a main dish with mashed potatoes, noodles, macaroni or spaghetti or boiled rice, and a green vegetable. (Serves 4 or 6)

Beef Strogonoff

1½ lbs tender lean beef
Salt and pepper
1½ tbsp butter
1½ tbsp flour
2 cups beef stock
1 tbsp tomato paste
4 tbsp sour cream, scalded
2 tbsp drippings
1 tbsp grated onion

Cut the meat into 1-inch cubes and sprinkle well with salt and pepper. Let stand in a covered dish for 2 hours in a cool place. In a saucepan melt the butter, stir in the flour, and cook, stirring constantly, over a low flame until the flour browns. Gradually stir in the beef stock and cook, stirring constantly, until the mixture boils and thickens. Strain through a sieve into a fresh saucepan and bring to a boil. Remove from the stove. Stir in the tomato paste and the sour cream. Replace on the stove, bring to a boil, and let simmer while the beef is prepared.

Melt the drippings in a skillet and add the meat and grated onion. Cook, turning frequently, until the meat is delicately browned. Add the meat to the sauce and let simmer for 15 or 20 minutes, or until the meat is tender. Serve immediately. (Serves 4)

Beefsteak Pie

1 lb lean raw chuck, round, flank or other beef
Flour
Salt and pepper
3 tbsp drippings
3 onions, sliced
2 cups cooked or canned tomatoes
1 cup cooked string beans
1 cup liquid in which beans were cooked
1 tbsp chopped parsley
Rich biscuit dough

Cut the beef in 1-inch cubes. Season the flour with salt and pepper and roll the meat in the seasoned flour. Heat the drippings in a deep skillet and brown the meat. Add the sliced onions and brown them. Add the tomatoes and the liquid from the beans. Cover the pan and simmer for 2½ or 3 hours, or until the meat is tender. If the stew needs to be thickened, make a paste of 1 or 2 tablespoons of flour with an equal quantity of water. Stir in a little of the hot stew and then return to the stew, stirring thoroughly. Cook a little longer, stirring constantly, until the sauce is smooth and thickened. Add the beans and the parsley and mix well. Put the stew into a shallow pan or baking dish.

Make a batch of biscuit dough (*which see*), using twice as much shortening as ordinarily. Roll out about ½ inch thick, to the size of the baking dish. Place on top of the meat filling, cut gashes in the top to allow steam to escape, and bake in a hot oven (425° F.) until the crust is well browned. Serve hot from the baking dish. (Serves 4)

BOILED BEEF

2½ lbs brisket, plate, chuck, or other beef
1½ tsp salt
Boiling water

Choose a piece of meat with some fat. Wipe with a damp cloth and place in a kettle. Add boiling water to half cover the meat. Cover the kettle and simmer until the meat is half done (about ¾ hour). Add the salt and more boiling water if necessary. Continue to simmer until the beef is tender. Boiled beef may be served hot or cold, with a horseradish sauce. (Serves 6)

HUNGARIAN GOULASH

2½ lbs lean round of beef
3 tbsp drippings
3 medium-sized onions, sliced thinly
Salt and pepper
1 tbsp paprika
1 blade marjoram
1 clove garlic, crushed
2½ lbs sauerkraut
1 tbsp butter
1 tbsp flour
1 cup sour cream
1 tsp caraway seeds

Cut the meat into 1-inch cubes. Melt the drippings in a skillet and brown the sliced onions. Skim out the onions and place in a stew pan. Brown the meat in the drippings and then turn the contents of the skillet into the stew pan. Season with salt and pepper, the paprika, marjoram, and garlic. Stir until the seasonings are blended and then add boiling water just to cover the meat. Simmer gently for 30 minutes. Add the sauerkraut and continue simmering for another hour, or until the meat is tender. Cream together the flour and butter and stir into the sauce, cooking until it is smooth and thickened. Add the sour cream and caraway seeds and cook for a few minutes longer. Serve very hot. (Serves 6 or 8)

Goulash should, of course, be served with noodles or rice. Noodles are the more traditional accompaniment, especially with Hungarian Goulash, but rice, or even potatoes, goes equally well.

PLANKED STEAK

Sirloin or tenderloin steak, 1½ or 2 inches thick
Mashed potatoes
Julienne carrots
Mushroom caps
Tomato slices
Cauliflower flowerets

Use a well seasoned plank (see PLANK) and brush it well with butter or melted drippings. Broil the steak in the usual manner for seven minutes, turning once to brown both sides. Make a border of mashed potatoes around the edge of the plank, using a pastry tube or spoon. Place the steak in position, snd season it with salt and pepper. Cut thick slices of tomato and place these around the steak. Place the mushroom caps, cup side up. Season tomatoes and mushrooms with salt and pepper and dot them with butter. Place the plank in a hot oven (400°–425° F.) and bake until the steak is done and the potatoes and vegetables done. Garnish with previously cooked julienne carrots and cauliflower and serve the whole dish sizzling hot.

POT ROAST WITH CRANBERRIES

3 lbs pot roast
Flour
2 tbsp fat
3 cups boiling water
2 cups raw cranberries
½ cup diced onions
½ cup diced celery
1 large bay leaf
6 sprigs parsley
2 whole cloves
6 whole peppercorns
1½ tsp salt

Wipe the meat and sprinkle with a very little flour, then brown on all sides in the heated fat. Add the water, cranberries (picked over and washed) and all remaining ingredients except the salt. Cover and bring to boiling point, then simmer very gently until the meat is tender, about 2½ hours, adding the salt when half done, and at that time, turning the meat over in the gravy. If necessary, thicken the gravy before serving with additional flour rubbed smoothly with cold water to moisten. (Serves 6)

Ragout of Beef

2 lbs lean raw chuck, round, flank, or
other beef
Flour
Salt and pepper
3 tbsp drippings
1 medium-sized onion, chopped
1 green pepper, chopped
1 cup chopped celery and leaves
2 tbsp chopped parsley
1 tbsp paprika

Cut the beef in 1-inch cubes. Season the flour with salt and pepper and roll the meat in the seasoned flour. Melt the drippings in a pan with a closely fitting lid. Brown the meat, adding the onion, pepper, celery, and parsley at the same time. Sprinkle in the paprika and add boiling water just to cover the meat. Cover the pan and simmer slowly for 2½ to 3 hours, or until the meat is tender. If desired, thicken the gravy with 1 or 2 tablespoons of flour mixed to a paste with an equal quantity of cold water. Stir in carefully and cook until smooth and thickened. Season to taste with additional salt and pepper. A little tomato catsup, chili sauce, or grated horseradish may be added to the sauce if desired. (Serves 4)

Rib Roast

A rib roast may be either a standing roast, i.e. with the bones in, or a boned and rolled roast. A standing roast is easier to carve if the butcher has sawed across the ribs where they meet the backbone and tied the chine bone in place. A standing rib roast should never be less than two ribs thick, otherwise it will tend to dry out too much in the roasting process.

Rub the surface of the roast with salt and pepper. Insert the meat thermometer so that the point is centered in the fleshiest portion without touching any bone. Place a standing roast in the pan, fat side up, resting on the rib bones. Place a rolled roast so that the fat side is on top. Roast uncovered according to the table until the meat is done or the thermometer registers the required temperature. Baste occasionally with the drippings; do not add water or other liquid. Remove the roast from the pan and keep it hot while you make the gravy from the drippings that remain in the pan.

The flavor of a roast is enhanced if several medium-sized onions are peeled and halved and laid on the meat when it is put in the oven. Potatoes may be roasted in the pan with the meat, or Yorkshire pudding (*which see*) may be prepared in it.

Russian Beef

3 lbs lean chuck, flank, round, or other
beef
3 tbsp cooking oil or drippings
1 medium-sized onion, minced
Salt and pepper
3 medium-sized fresh tomatoes
1 pint sour cream
Dash of paprika

Cut the meat into strips 1 inch by 3 inches. Heat the oil in a deep skillet having a well fitting cover. Brown the onion and the meat well, seasoning with salt and pepper as it cooks. Peel the tomatoes and cut into chunks. When the meat is well browned, add the tomatoes and sour cream and sprinkle in a good dash of paprika. Cover the pan and simmer very slowly about 2 hours, or until the meat is tender. If the sauce seems too thin, remove the cover during the last half hour and allow the sauce to cook down. Taste for salt and pepper. Be very careful that the sauce does not cook on to the bottom of the pan while the cover is off. Serve hot with potatoes or noodles. This is an excellent recipe for less tender cuts of meat since the action of the sour cream seems to tenderize even the toughest cuts. (Serves 6)

Sauerbraten
(Sour Pot Roast)

5 or 6 lb bottom round
For the marinade:
  8 whole cloves
  1 tsp whole peppercorns
  2 bay leaves
  2 branches celery leaves
  1 sprig thyme
  1 large onion, thinly sliced
  2 cloves garlic
  Salt
  Equal parts vinegar and water

Put the piece of meat into an earthenware dish, and pour the marinade over it, using sufficient vinegar and water to cover the meat. Cover the dish and let stand for three or four days, turning the meat twice a day.

For the sauce:

1 small can tomato paste
1½ cups beef stock
1 tbsp brown sugar
1 cup red wine
1 tbsp lemon juice
2 or 3 strips lemon peel
6 gingersnaps, crumbled
1 tbsp Worcestershire sauce

Remove the beef from the marinade and cook the marinade until it is reduced by one-half. In a heavy kettle melt a little beef drippings and sear the meat on all sides until it is brown. Add the marinade and all the rest of the ingredients. Cover the kettle and cook very slowly for 3½ or 4 hours, or until the meat is very tender. Remove the meat to a serving platter and keep warm. Strain the gravy and reheat if necessary. Serve very hot. (Serves 6 or 8)

Some people prefer to omit the garlic from the ingredients in the marinade, but it is so customary to include it that traditionalists will shudder if it is not present.

Sauerbraten may be made from other parts of beef than bottom round—the shoulder, for instance—and recipes will vary somewhat, especially in regard to the sauce.

Savory Stew

2 lb lean neck, plate, brisket, or flank
Flour
Salt and pepper
3 tbsp drippings
1 medium-sized onion, sliced
Boiling water

Cut the meat into inch cubes. Season the flour with salt and pepper and roll the meat in the seasoned flour. Melt the drippings in the stew pan and brown the meat well. Add the sliced onion and boiling water to cover. Put the lid on only part way and simmer slowly until the meat is tender, 2½ to 3 hours. Vegetables may be added about 30 minutes before the stew is done. Peel and quarter potatoes, peel and cut carrots into thick slices, peeled and sliced turnips, small whole onions, all make good additions to the stew. If the gravy is not thick enough when the meat is ready, stir 1 or 2 tablespoons of flour into a like amount of cold water. When the paste is smooth add it very carefully to the hot stew, stirring well to prevent lumping. Let the sauce cook up several minutes to thicken. (Serves 6)

Steak and Kidney Pie

2 lb rump steak
½ lb beef kidney
Salt and pepper
Shallots, minced
Parsley, minced
Beef stock
1 recipe of pastry

Cut the steak into small strips and sprinkle with salt and pepper. Remove the fat and membranes from the kidney and slice it. Sprinkle with salt and pepper. In a shallow casserole make alternate layers of beef and kidney, sprinkling each layer with shallots and parsley. Pack the meat in well, and nearly fill the dish. Pour in stock level with the top of the meat. Make a recipe of rich pastry (*which see*) and roll it as for a pie. Wet the edge of the casserole with cold water and place the pastry in position. Press it down well at the edges, sealing it to the dish. Cut a gash in the top to allow the steam to escape. Bake in a moderate oven (350° F.) for 1½ or 2 hours, or until the meat is tender. Serve from the casserole. (Serves 4 or 5)

Swiss Steak

3 lb round steak
½ cup flour
Salt and pepper
2 tbsp drippings
2 cups boiling water or stock
1 large onion, thinly sliced
1 bouquet garni
1 cup tomato paste
1 tsp prepared mustard

Season the flour with salt and pepper and rub into the steak. If the meat is not as tender as it might be, pound it with a mallet or the edge of a saucer while working in the flour. Melt the drippings in a heavy kettle and brown the meat well on all sides. Add the boiling water, onion, and bouquet garni. Let simmer for one hour. Then add the tomato paste and mustard, and continue simmering for another hour, or until the meat is tender. If desired, thicken the gravy with a little flour. (Serves 6)

YANKEE POT ROAST

2½ lb rump of beef
2 tbsp drippings
1 cup hot water or stock
2 medium-sized onions
Salt and pepper
2 medium-sized tomatoes
Pinch of ground ginger

Heat the drippings in a heavy pan or Dutch oven. Slice the onions and brown them in the drippings. Then add the meat and brown it well on all sides. Season with salt and pepper. Add the stock. Peel the tomatoes and cut them into chunks and add to the meat. Add the ginger. Cover the pot tightly and simmer very slowly for 3 hours, or until the meat is tender. (Serves 6)

BEEF ESSENCE. Several commercial products, in liquid or paste form, are available under this name. They are used to add flavor to meat preparations, and make a satisfactory substitute, with water, for beef stock when the latter is not available.

Beef essence made at home is quite different. It is a kind of broth which is sometimes fed to infants and invalids. To prepare the essence, cut one pound of lean round steak into very small cubes. Place the meat in a wide-mouthed jar and cover closely. Stand the jar in a pan of boiling water and keep just at the boiling point for several hours. The juice of the meat will be extracted without being diluted in any way. Strain out the bits of meat and serve the juice hot, with a little salt if desired or permitted.

BEEF JUICE. The juice may be extracted by scraping or squeezing slightly broiled tender steak. Broil for a minute or two on each side under a brisk flame. Then scrape the meat with a knife, discarding all the fibrous material. The tender pulp is readily digestible.

A simpler method is to place the seared meat in a meat press and squeeze out the blood and juice. This should be used immediately, preferably hot.

BEEF PEPTONE. This commercial product is a dark brown semi-solid paste with a strong meaty flavor and odor. One pound of this preparation represents eight pounds of fresh lean beef. In addition to the materials extracted from the beef, it contains additional proteins. Called by the culinary term "meat glaze" it is used to add flavor to sauces, soups, and gravies, and when diluted to the proper consistency, for glazing hot and cold meats or fowls. Several commercial variations of the product are on the market.

BEEF SOMATOSE. A commercial product used in invalid diets, somatose is a granular predigested meat powder which contains a large amount of albumin and is free of peptones. It has a yellowish color and a faint taste and odor. Dissolved in water it forms a light yellow solution having almost no taste or odor.

BEEF TEA. This preparation of beef is easily made at home for use in invalid diets. Cut tender lean beef into small cubes a quarter of an inch in diameter. In a large jar with a closely fitting lid steep the cubed beef in cold water for five or six hours. Use one pint of water to one pound of meat. At the end of this time, place the jar in a vessel of boiling water and keep just below the boiling point for twenty or thirty minutes. Do not allow the contents of the jar to boil. The tea is then strained and is ready for use.

BEER. The first historical records of brewing refer to it as a well-developed art. Certainly beer followed closely on the age of cultivation, and in Europe the Neolithic age of man began about 10,000 or 12,000 years ago. We know that Neolithic man cultivated and ate wheat, barley, and millet.

Evidence that a brewer lived and brewed his beer six thousand years ago was unearthed by archaeologists from the Museum of The University of Pennsylvania and the American School of Oriental Research during an expedition to Mesopotamia in 1935. One city after another was uncovered. When the level of the twelfth city was reached, a seal or drawing was found, baked in pottery, depicting two brewery workers stirring with long poles the contents of a brewery vat. Beer was made with bread, a special bread baked for the purpose, then mashed with barley malt and allowed to ferment. Some of this beer was flavored with cinnamon, some with dates and honey.

In 3000 B.C., in Egypt, barley and wheat were raised almost exclusively. There, too, breweries and bakeries were combined into the most important industry in the land. Egyptian legends attribute beer's introduction to a favorite goddess, Isis, mother of the gods, and the spirit of fertility. In the curious picture language which the Egyptians carved in the rocks of their temples and engraved upon pieces of baked clay, an early artist recorded a brewing recipe. Excavations of these tablets taken from ten graves have been pieced together by archaeologists into a total of twenty-three pictures showing the steps in making of *Hekit,* their barley-juice beverage.

The Greeks termed their beer *Zythos* while the Romans called theirs *Cerevesia,* this name being derived in part from that of the goddess of vegetation, *Ceres.* The first beer mash to be found was unearthed in Bezirk, a province of Rome. By a strange freak it had been preserved for almost 2000 years. During excavations in 1911, a large round jug was found hidden under the cellar stairs of a house built about the year 300 A.D. During the destruction and burning of the town, the jug remained intact, its contents sealed. An archaeologist proved through analysis that the dark brown mass was the oldest beer on record.

Charlemagne, King of the Franks (742–814 A.D.), became so interested in the process of brewing that he issued an order that all able beer masters should be sent to his court where he gave directions on best brewing methods. He elected his brew masters with the same care that he chose his councilors and leaders.

The Vikings believed that beer was the god-given liquor of heavenly Valhalla where heroes fallen gloriously on the battle-field were rewarded with an endless supply of *bior* which could be drunk forever from the skulls of their foes.

The Danes as far back as 860 A.D. under Gorm the Old, were acquainted with the art of brewing, and their ancient codes mention it as a most honorable profession. It is very probable that the Saxons introduced brewing into England, for ale or *alu* was used at coronations, wedding feasts, and religious ceremonies. About this same time well-equipped monastery brewers were turning out quantities of beer under the direction of monk master-brewers. These master-brewers developed the process of brewing into a fine art. They supervised the cultivation of various types of barley. They experimented with different waters. Most famous of the English brews was Burton, from Burton-on-Trent, where the monks found that the water of the river Trent made beer clear and sparkling.

Their "brown October ale" was brought to a perfection and celebrated throughout medieval times in poetry and song. The monks of England were as famed for their beer as the Trappists for their cheese and the Benedictines for their liqueurs.

Many of America's most eminent men of colonial and revolutionary times were brewers and tavern keepers. Samuel Adams, "Father of the Revolution," was the son of a brewer and a brewer himself. Thomas Chittenden, the first governor of Vermont, who was revered as the outstanding figure of that era, was a brewer and the keeper of a tavern.

MODERN BREWING

The first step in the process of brewing is the selection of barley with full, round, heavy, sweet grains of uniform quality—not a mixture of different crops. The grain is first steeped in cold water for a period of at least forty hours in order that it may soak up the utmost quantity of water. If the water during this time exhibits any signs of fermentation, it must be drawn off and replaced with cold water.

After the steeping, the grain is spread upon the floor of the malt house to a depth of about sixteen inches—an operation called "the couch." It is allowed to remain in this condition for from 24 to 26 hours; it is then turned by wooden shovels, and the depth of the couch is somewhat diminished. This process is repeated twice a day or oftener, and the depth of the barley is thus gradually diminished. In this state the barley absorbs oxygen from the air, and gives out carbonic acid, the temperature of the barley in the meantime being increased to a heat of 10° above that of the surrounding atmosphere.

During this stage the barley becomes covered with moisture and possesses an agreeable odor like that of apples. The appearance of the moisture has been termed "sweating." The interior of the grain by this time has undergone a transformation—from that of firmness to looseness, crumbling to powder between the fingers.

It is now taken to the kiln (large oven), and exposed to a heat of 90° F. which is gradually increased to 140° or even higher. The tiny rootlets which have begun to sprout are then cleared away, and the grain has become malt.

Brewers use three kinds of malt: pale or amber malt, brown or plain malt, and roasted or black malt. Only the first is fermentable; the second is employed to give flavor to beer; the third is used to give the dark color to porter and stouts. The last two malts are made by carrying the roasting process so far as to destroy the sugar—hence no fermentation is possible from them. In the roasted or black malt the sugar is charred by the heat to which it is exposed.

After the malt has been prepared, the brewing process is begun. This consists of several distinct operations. First, the malt is ground, either by millstones or iron rollers. The grist thus produced must be turned into mash. The ground malt is put into a mash-tub, and hot water is poured over it, which runs off by taps at the bottom of the tub. Successive quantities of hot water are run through the malt, and the worts (the resulting liquid) are blended and turned into a large copper boiler.

During the second operation, the hops are added and the liquor boiled. After boiling, the hops are strained out and the liquid passes into vessels to cool. When it has reached the proper temperature, the liquid passes into the fermentation tubes. There a quantity of yeast is added and fermentation takes place. When the sugar content has been lowered to the correct point, the yeast is cleared away and the liquid is put into casks to age. It is ready for consumption when it has aged sufficiently.

Beer varies greatly in its quality according to the way in which the brewing process has been carried on. The fermentation may be stopped at various points; if stopped early in the process, sweet ales result which become stronger as they age. If, on the other hand, the fermentation is carried on until the sugar is exhausted (and a large quantity of hops is added), pale bitter liquors are produced. The stronger the wort, the more sugar and alcohol result from the fermentation process.

ALE

Originally ale was the liquor brewed from malt without adding hops. However, since the 19th century, there is practically no difference in the process of brewing ale and beer, local tradition deciding whether the brew shall be called beer or ale. Strongly alcoholic ales are less popular than formerly, having been largely supplanted by the lighter varieties and by beer. The amount of hops used determines the bitterness of the ale. Bitter ale has been fermented to the point where it contains little sugar. Scotch ale, especially the Edinburgh brands, is pale in color and flavor. It is extremely vinous and similar in alcoholic content to some of the French clarets. It is mild in its effect and the taste of the hops does not predominate. American ales are very light, rarely containing more than 3 to $3\frac{1}{2}$ percent alcohol. They resemble English "table beer."

BOCK BEER

Bock beer is a sweet, heavy, dark brew with a higher alcoholic content than most beers. It is made from a mash of two-thirds barley malt and one-third wheat. The process originated at Einbreck, near Hamburg, Germany, between 1203 and 1256 A.D. The bock season lasts only a few weeks in March, and this beer is the last run of the winter types. See Bock Beer.

LAGER BEER

This term is properly applied only to those beers which are fermented in cool cellars by a slow process in which the yeast settles to the bottom of the vessels. In America it is applied indiscriminately to the light kinds of beer which are prepared by the slow process of fermentation. Much of this beverage, however, is not genuine lager beer for it has not lain a sufficient length of time in the cellar to deserve the title. It is more technically termed, and is known by the brewers as, *Schenkbier* or draught beer. Containing less alcohol than the genuine lager beer and less than the various kinds of ripened ales, it corresponds to what is known in America as "present use ales" (the new ales, commonly kept and sold in certain bars). Real lager beer is a light and pleasant summer beverage, but it has neither the nutritive nor the stimulating qualities that are generally claimed for it.

STOUT

Stout, which, like porter, has a dark color, is manufactured in the same manner as beer, except that black malt is used to give it the darker color.

BEER COMB. A small paddle, commonly made of wood or plastic, that is used to scrape the excess foam or "head" from the top of a freshly drawn glass of draft beer. Though made in many designs, it often resembles the familiar medical tongue depressor.

BEERENAUSLESE. A German word meaning specially selected. *See* Auslese.

BEESWING. This is a very fine, light sediment that often forms in old bottled port wines. Composed mainly of mucilage, it does not cling to the bottle as does the *crust*, or heavier sediment, but it does not mar the wine if it passes from the bottle in pouring. *See also* Port and Wine.

BEET. The garden beet is a small, edible relative of the sugar beet and the mangel (which is used for cattle feed). The green tops of young beets are excellent as a green vegetable, and the sweet roots make an attractive and colorful dish.

Early beets are usually marketed in bunches with the leaves left on, or cut back to a few inches. Fresh leaves of small, young beets should not be removed. They will make an extra vegetable, as greens. Late-crop beets are usually marketed with the tops removed. The medium-sized beets are the best at this time. Very small ones are runty, and the large ones are inclined to be tough. The beets should be smooth, free from blemishes, and firm. Flabby or shriveled beets are a poor buy.

Hints on Preparation

Beets lose their color if peeled before cooking. For this reason, beets should be cooked in their skins with a couple of inches of stem left on. When cooked, they are easily peeled. A little vinegar or lemon juice in the water also helps to retain their color. Cook covered in boiling water until the beets are tender, about 30 or 40 min-

utes for young beets, and possibly 2 hours for winter beets.

Wash and cook the tops as you would spinach, using only the water that clings

BEETS

to the leaves. Young leaves have a mild, agreeable flavor; when the beets are older, the greens are inclined to be strong.

Cold pickled beets are a delicious accompaniment to cold meats or fish. Grated raw beets may be added to a vegetable salad. Cooked beets, cut in narrow strips, also make a good addition to salad. Beets may be baked in the oven; they are even more delicious cooked in this manner than when they are boiled.

An easy way to prepare pickled beets is to save the liquor from sweet pickles. Heat it to the boiling point and pour it over cooked, peeled beets which have been placed in a screw-top jar. If the beets are very small, they may be left whole; otherwise, they should be sliced. Close the jar, chill, and keep in the refrigerator for several days to allow the flavor to permeate the beets. Rings of sliced raw onion may be added to the beets.

Food Value

Type	Water	Food Energy	Protein	Fat	Carbohydrates	Calcium	Phosphorus	Iron	Vit. A Value	Thiamine	Riboflavin	Niacin	Ascorbic Acid
Beets	87.6	46	1.6	.1	9.6	27	43	1.0	20	.03	.05	.4	10
Beet greens	90.4	33	2.0	.3	5.6	118	45	3.2	6,700	.05	.17	.3	34
Canned beets	89.4	39	1.0	0	8.7	15	29	.6	20	.01	.03	.1	5

BAKED BEETS

Wash the beets carefully, being careful not to break their skins. Arrange in a baking dish, cover, and bake in a moderate oven (350° F.) until tender. Peel.

BEETS IN ORANGE SAUCE

3 tbsp grated orange rind
2 tbsp lemon juice
⅓ tsp salt
1 tbsp flour
Pepper
Nutmeg
1 tbsp sherry wine
⅓ cup butter or margarine
3½ cups cooked sliced beets

Combine the rind and juice in the top of a double boiler. Stir in the flour and salt, a dash of pepper, and one of nutmeg. Blend until smooth and add the sherry. Cook in the top of the double boiler, over hot water, stirring constantly until it thickens. Add the butter or margarine, and stir until it melts. Add the beets, and heat through. Serve immediately. (Serves 6)

HARVARD BEETS

Small whole beets, cooked and peeled
2 tbsp butter
2 tbsp flour
1 cup water
¼ tsp onion juice
2 tbsp cider vinegar
¼ tsp salt
Pepper
1½ tsp sugar

Melt the butter, blend in the flour, and add the water. Stir over a moderate flame until the sauce boils and thickens. Add the remaining ingredients and the beets, and continue heating carefully until the beets are heated through. (Serves 6)

HONEYED BEET PRESERVES

2 lb strained honey
5 lb beets, cooked and peeled
2 tsp ground ginger
2 tsp lemon juice
1 lb chopped walnuts

Bring the honey to boiling point in a heavy saucepan placed on an asbestos mat.

Cut the cooked beets into shoestring strips and add to the honey with the ginger and lemon juice. Cook until thickened, stirring frequently; then add the chopped nuts and cook all about 10 minutes. Turn into hot sterilized jars and seal. (Makes 2 quarts) *See also* CANNING.

BEET JUICE

1 cup liquid from canned beets
1½ cups water
⅓ cup lemon juice
Salt and cayenne to taste

Mix the ingredients and chill thoroughly.

MASHED BEETS

Cook 3 bunches of beets in their skins until tender. Drain and cool slightly, and remove the skins. Trim off the roots and stems. Force the beets through a sieve or ricer into a saucepan. Add 3 tablespoons of butter or margarine, and season to taste with salt, pepper, and a teaspoon of sugar. Stir in 1½ tablespoons of lemon juice. Mix thoroughly and heat through. (Serves 6)

PICKLED BEETS

½ cup cider vinegar
¼ cup water
2 tsp dry mustard
½ tsp salt
⅓ cup sugar
½ tsp celery seed
2 cups sliced, cooked beets
1 medium onion, sliced

Heat the vinegar and water to boiling. Add the mustard, salt, and sugar. Blend until mixed, and let boil again; then pour over the combined celery seed, beets, and onion. Cover and place in the refrigerator to marinate overnight or longer. Serve cold.

STUFFED BEETS

6 tiny cooked beets
¼ cup French dressing
2 chopped sweet pickles
1 chopped hard-cooked egg
Dash of dry mustard
Salt and pepper

Marinate the beets in the French dressing for several hours. Mix the remaining ingredients, using a dash each of salt and pepper, and work them into a smooth paste. Hollow the beets and fill them with this paste. Serve cold. (Makes 6)

BEL PAESE CHEESE. A creamy rich Italian cheese, mild in flavor, and weighing about five pounds.

BELARNO CHEESE. A hard, rich Italian cheese.

BELL PEPPER. *See* Pepper.

BELLELAY CHEESE. This cheese was first made by monks in the Canton of Bern, Switzerland, in the 15th century and is now made exclusively in that locality. It is a soft rennet made from whole milk and is firmer than Limburger but not so firm as Emmentaler. The diameter of bellelay cheese is about seven inches and it weighs rom nine to fifteen pounds. It usually ripens in a year's time and can be kept for three or four years. Bellelay has a soft, buttery consistency and can be easily spread on bread. It is also known as *Tête de Moine* (Monk's Head).

BENEDICTINE. Possibly the oldest and best known of the liqueurs, benedictine was developed by the Benedictine monks of Fecamp, Normandy, in the year 1510 or earlier. It is still made in that region, and it is sold in distinctive bottles with the initials of the order, D.O.M. (Deo optimo maximo), on the label.

Very sweet and aromatic, benedictine is favored as an after-dinner cordial. It is also used in some of the mixed drinks. Following meals it is often served with an equal amount of brandy, the blend being known as *B and B*.

See also Liqueur and Cordial.

BERGAMOT. This is a type of orange. An oil used in the mixing of perfumes is distilled from its rind.

BERGQUARA CHEESE. A Swedish cheese, resembling Gouda. It was known in Sweden in the 18th Century.

BERLINER KUHKASE. Another name for Hand Cheese, *which see*.

BERRY. The name applies to small pulpy fruit, generally edible. The month of May marks the peak of the strawberry season with Louisiana, Florida, Virginia, and Maryland supplying most of the markets. Then, too, is the parade of blackberries, dewberries, blueberries, huckleberries, raspberries, gooseberries, and loganberries.

There are innumerable ways to prepare the many varieties which crowd the markets during the berry season. An uncooked dish like raspberry mallobet, or raspberries sugared and served in halves of cantaloupe, or berries that have been crushed fine with half their weight of sugar and frozen in their own syrup, will satisy the most delicate palate. Chilled berry whips, too, are an easy variation, made simply by beating up a cup of fruit pulp with an egg white and a fourth of a cup of powdered sugar. Marshmallow pudding with strawberries or other berries within and without is also refreshing. Strawberry chantilly, for which halved berries are chilled for 30 minutes in powdered sugar and two tablespoonfuls of rum and then folded into sweetened, whipped cream, or stiff egg whites, is a dessert certain to bring approval.

Berry pies and tarts, made from the fresh or the cooked fruit are perennial favorites as are berry muffins that turn breakfast or tea time into a festive occasion. Molded ices, sherbets, mousses, and ice creams concentrate delicate berry flavors in a way that lends glamour even to a simple meal of lamb or beef stew. Berries supreme, folded into stiffly whipped cream, are the busy homemaker's answer to the dessert problem at the end of a hastily prepared dinner.

The old controversy over the genuine type of shortcake still rages. There is a difference, purists insist, between shortcake proper and layer cake. One is made from biscuit dough; the other from sweet cake batter. The name of old-fashioned strawberry shortcake should never be given to sponge or layer cake dressed up with berries between and atop the layers, according to the purists.

The biscuit type, in single or multiple portions, is usually split open, as is the single-layer sponge, and then filled with fresh, juicy berries, and served warm with big, perfect berries set in whipped cream on top. The two or three layer or sponge cake has a filling of sliced berries and whipped cream, and is served cool. *See* Shortcake.

One of the berry desserts less known than shortcake is flummery (*which see*). Although huckleberry flummery is best made of berries newly picked and retaining their fresh aroma, preserved huckleberries will do.

For another berry dessert try sugared berries rolled up in hot, lightly buttered pancakes, which are dusted with sugar before being served with a pitcher of sweet cream.

All berries should have a fresh, clean, bright appearance and be free of dirt and moisture. A stained container often indicates leaky or damaged berries, and attention is called to the desirability of "turning out the berries" (if possible) before buying them.

Currants, bilberries, mulberries, blueberries, huckleberries, raspberries, blackberries, and gooseberries all contain considerable free acid and are moderately laxative, partly because of their seeds. Huckleberries and blueberries serve as laxatives when eaten with their seeds and skins. Blackberries have a similar effect. The expressed juice of red currants, raspberries, or blackberries makes a cooling and refreshing beverage when added to some effervescent water, such as Apollinaris or carbonic-acid water. The elderberry furnishes an astringent wine which is somewhat diuretic and sudorific.

For specific berries, see under name.

For berry dumplings, *see* DUMPLINGS.

BETTY. This dessert is made by placing alternate layers of sliced sweetened fruit and buttered bread crumbs in a baking dish. A small amount of fruit juice, or water is poured in, the top dotted with butter or margarine, and the dish baked in a moderate oven until the fruit is soft and the top brown and crisp. Betties may be made of apples, apricots, berries, peaches, plums, prunes, pineapple, and other fruits, all of which see.

BEVERAGE. An artificially prepared iquid, sometimes an intoxicant.

To relieve thirst all fluids which are not too sweet may be used, but tart beverages, such as acid lemonade or raspberry vinegar (also the effervescent carbonated waters) are generally the most acceptable.

As diuretics, mineral waters and carbonated waters are suggested. With many persons, coffee is also an active diuretic. So are beer, gin, champagne, and to a lesser degree, other forms of alcohol, and tea.

As diaphoretics, hot spirits, and water or hot tea may be used.

As diluents of the ingested food and of the waste material of the body the alkaline and carbonated effervescent or bland waters are the best.

As stimulants of the nerves and other organs, the milder forms of alcoholic beverages, diluted spirits, tea, and coffee are used.

As intoxicants, beers, ales, strong wines, champagne, and strong liquors are the most powerful agents. *Koumiss*, as originally made in the steppes of Russia, and many fermented substances, are also employed for the same purpose.

As demulcents, mucilaginous, farinaceous, and gelatinous beverages are used for fevers, etc. Such are decoctions of Iceland moss (cetraria) or Irish moss, barley or oatmeal water, arrowroot and other light gruels, solutions of gelatin, flaxseed tea, etc. When taken hot, they are soothing for coughs.

For use as tonics and to aid digestion, malt extracts, ales, light wines, clarets, Burgundies, diluted brandy or whisky, chalybeate, and arsenical waters, and alkaline waters can be taken before meals.

As astringents, red wines, and tea are of chief importance.

For nutrition, cocoa, chocolate, malt extracts, grape foods are excellent.

Many fruit essences and sirups are offered for sale for use in making cooling drinks and invalid beverages. When thoroughly reliable preparations are obtained they are perfectly harmless. Many are made with artificial flavoring. For example, mixtures of malic, citric, and tartaric acids are often substituted for lemonade. As a rule, it is better to extract the juice from the fresh fruit, and unless large quantities are required, this is almost as cheap. Unfermented grape juice is readily available and constitutes an excellent beverage for invalids, children, and adults, being wholly free from alcohol.

Root beer, sarsaparilla, and ginger ale are wholesome beverages. Ginger ale makes a useful drink for people who have overindulged in food or alcohol. They crave some beverage which has life and sparkle, and the ginger itself is helpful to the stomach. Grenadine makes a delicious beverage when diluted with plain or effervescent water or ginger ale.

CIDER, AND HERB BEERS

Mild stimulants have long been used to ward off coughs, colds, and the rigors of life. Cider for American breakfasts was going out of fashion at the close of the eighteenth century, but cider was still on American supper tables—one large mug at each end of the table. According to one authority, beer was the common drink of the first settlers, who "drank water only from necessity."

The settlers brought European traditions of herb beers, and herb teas, and later adapted them to local ingredients. Probably the earliest of indigenous beverages were the maple (*which see*) drinks made by the Indians. In late colonial times a sugar maple beer was described as a "very pleasant and salutary drink" touched up, as it were, with a dash of spruce essence. Whey, drained from milk curd, was another old-time hot weather drink and now it is sometimes taken livened up with sweetened fruit. It contains some of the protein, mineral, and vitamin values of whole milk.

The list of summer beverages is very long. Many of them invite experiment. Try a spoonful of jam to sweeten iced tea as the Russians do. Or peel a ripe peach and let it stand in the bottom of a glass of wine as the French do.

STANDARD MEASUREMENT FOR BEVERAGES

A mixing glass holds 12 ounces, or 8 jiggers, or 24 level tablespoons.

A jigger holds 1½ ounces, or 4 level tablespoons.

A pony glass holds 1 ounce, or 2 level tablespoons.

A sherry or port glass holds 2 ounces, or 4 level tablespoons.

A cocktail glass holds 2 ounces, or 4 level tablespoons.

A Bordeaux or Burgundy glass holds 4 ounces, or 8 level tablespoons.

A champagne glass holds 5 ounces, or 10 level tablespoons.

A tumbler holds from 8 to 12 ounces, or 16 to 24 tablespoons.

For recipes and other information concerning beverages *see* specific titles including BEER, CIDER, MILK, *etc.*

BIBLICAL WINES. Wine was, of course, made in biblical times. It is mentioned several times in the Scriptures, as indicated below.

Ahsis. This name for "perfumed" or aromatic wine appears five times. (Cant. viii, 2.)

Khemer, also *Khamar*. Used in eight different places, this is the poetic form of *Yayin*, or wine. (*See* Deut. xxxii, 14.)

Khometz. Means "poor" wine or vinegar.

Mesech. A mixture of wine with water or other ingredients.

Mimsach. Appearing only twice, this word has been translated as wine in Prov. xxiii, 30, and liqueur in Isaiah lxv, 11.

Schechar. This word, meaning wine, appears 23 times, especially in the sense of an intoxicating beverage. (*See* Prov. xxxi, 6 and 7.)

Soveh. Used only three times, it is not certain what type of wine is meant by this word. (*See* Isaiah i, 22.)

Tirosh. Used 38 times, this word means new wine or sweet wine. (*See* Joel ii, 24; Isaiah lxii, v. 8 and 9, etc.)

Yayin. The most-used name for wine in the Scriptures, this word appears no less than 140 times, from Gen. ix, 21 (the wine from Noah's vineyard), to Prov. xxi, 17. *See also* WINE.

BICARBONATE OF SODA. *See* BAKING SODA.

BIFFIN APPLE. This fruit is popular in England and is prepared for consumption by being baked in the oven, and then flattened or pressed into the form of a cake which is soft to the touch.

BIGARADE. A bitter-orange-flavored sauce.

BIGARADE SAUCE

Cut off thin, regular strips of rind from two bitter oranges and boil in plain water for five minutes; drain them and add them to about a pint or much reduced Espagnole Sauce (*which see*) and leave it on a gentle heat until the little pieces of rind are fairly soft. At time of serving, add the juice of an orange, a squeeze of lemon, and a little salt and pepper. This sauce is used mainly for poultry, game and especially venison. For Wild Duck Bigarade, *see* DUCK.

BILBERRY. *See* BLUEBERRY.

BILE. A secretion of the liver. *See* GALL.

BIN. In connection with wines, this is a wine cellar compartment in which filled bottles are stored. Since, as a general rule, all the wine in one bin is bottled and laid down together, bottles from the same bin are usually uniform in quality. *See also* WINE.

BIRD'S NEST SOUP. A Chinese soup. Only the gelatinous substance (allied to mucin) which lines the nest of a certain species of swallow is edible. It is used as the basis for a soup.

BISCUIT. A kind of hot bread, basically made of flour, shortening, and milk. Many variations of flavorings and handling are possible. Baking powder biscuits depend upon the comparatively large amount of shortening which goes into them for their tenderness. Baking powder biscuits may be rolled out, shaped into balls with the hands, or dropped from a spoon, depending on the amount of liquid which is added. If the biscuits are baked in muffin tins, they will be crusty on all sides. If they are laid close together on a pie plate or cookie sheet, they will rise high and be crusty top and bottom, with no crust between. If they are placed further apart, they will spread and not be so high.

Biscuits, like pie crust, should not be handled too much in mixing. The dry ingredients are sifted together and the shortening cut in with a pastry blender or mixed in quickly with the fingers. Only just enough liquid is added to make a dough which can be patted or rolled out. Or, if more liquid is added, drop biscuits are the result. Many people believe drop biscuits are more tender than rolled biscuits.

The basic biscuit dough may be used for quick cinnamon or fruit breads, for short cakes, and for topping for meat pies and fruit puddings. For sweet breads and puddings, the basic recipe is varied by adding a little sugar and shortening is used generously.

Baking powder biscuits may be prepared ahead of time and kept in the refrigerator for several hours until time to bake. They should be baked on an ungreased pan in a hot oven for from 12 to 15 minutes, or until the top is delicately browned. To reheat leftover biscuits, dip them quickly into hot water or milk, and bake them for three or four minutes in a hot oven (450° F.). Serve immediately.

Beaten biscuits are a southern biscuit which differ from baking powder biscuits in being hard and cracker-like.

BAKING POWDER BISCUITS

2 cups sifted all-purpose flour
2 tsp baking powder
½ tsp salt
4 tbsp shortening
¾ cup cold milk

Sift the flour, baking powder and salt together. Cut in the shortening with two knives or a pastry blender, until the mixture is the consistency of coarse meal. Stir in the milk to make a soft dough. Turn out on a slightly floured board, and knead for 30 seconds, or until the surface is smooth. Roll out ½ inch thick. Cut in 2-inch rounds with a floured biscuit cutter and bake on an ungreased baking sheet for 12 to 15 minutes in a very hot oven (450° F.). (Makes 15 biscuits)

VARIATIONS OF BAKING POWDER BISCUITS

Caraway Seed Biscuits. (For breakfast, afternoon tea, or coffee.) Cut the dough into rounds or other desired shape. Spread half the rounds with softened butter, sprinkle very lightly with caraway seeds, and cover with the remaining rounds. Bake at 450° F. for 15 minutes.

Cheese Biscuits. (For salad or appetizer tray.) Add ½ cup grated cheese to flour and shortening before adding milk or other liquid. Bake at 450° F. for 12 minutes.

Cinnamon Biscuits. (For tea.) Add ½ teaspoon ground cinnamon (or more if desired) to the flour before sifting. Bake at 450° F. for 12 to 15 minutes.

Honey Biscuits. (For afternoon tea or luncheon.) Make plain biscuits. Bake as directed and while still hot split in two. Spread the lower halves with butter beaten to a cream with equal parts of honey. Put the halves together and let stand for a few minutes in a cool oven. Serve hot.

Jam Biscuits. (For breakfast, luncheon, or tea.) Make plain biscuits. Roll and cut out as usual. Place on ungreased baking sheet. Make a deep depression in center top of each biscuit and fill with jam. Bake at 450° F. for 12 to 15 minutes.

Lemon Biscuits. (For tea and with seafood dishes.) Make plain biscuits and cut in 1½ inch rounds. Press a half lump of sugar dipped in lemon juice into the top of each biscuit. Sprinkle with grated lemon rind and bake at 450° F. for 10 minutes.

Orange Biscuits. (For afternoon tea or luncheon.) Make as for lemon biscuits, substituting orange juice and grated rind.

Raisin Biscuits. (For tea, coffee, or salads.) Add ½ cup chopped seedless raisins to the dry ingredients. Add the liquid and proceed as usual. Bake at 400° F. for 12 minutes.

Shrimp or Seafood Biscuits. (These biscuits are appetizers to accompany cocktails.)

Roll dough out ¼ inch thick. Cut into small rounds. Place a small spoonful of chopped seasoned shrimp or other seafood on half the rounds. Cover with a second round. Bake at 475° F. for 12 to 15 minutes.

Sour Cream Biscuits. (For breakfast, tea, or luncheon.) Use sour cream in place of milk, adding ½ teaspoon of soda to the cream before blending with the dry ingredients. Bake at 450° F. for 15 minutes. A somewhat richer biscuit.

Tomato Biscuits. (For salads.) Substitute tomato juice for milk. Bake at 450° F. for 15 minutes.

Beaten Biscuits

4 cups all-purpose flour
1 tsp salt
1 tbsp sugar
4 tbsp chilled lard
1 cup cold milk and water, half and half
Melted butter

Sift the dry ingredients three times. Cut in the lard with a pastry blender or two knives and add the milk and water. Mix to a stiff dough. Place a clean towel on a wooden block and place the dough on the towel. Beat with a wooden mallet until the dough is flattened out. Fold the dough together, sides into center, as it is flattened and continue beating for about 20 minutes, or until the dough snaps and crackles. Cut into small biscuits. Prick the top with a fork and brush over with melted butter. Bake in a moderate oven (350° F.) for 30 minutes.

Buttermilk Biscuits

2 cups sifted flour
½ tsp soda
2 tbsp shortening
¾ cup buttermilk

Sift together flour and soda. Add shortening, mixing well with a pastry blender or with two knives. Stir in buttermilk. Roll or pat the dough on a lightly floured board, cut with a round cutter, and place the biscuits in a hot greased pan. Bake in a hot oven (425° F.) for 15 minutes. Serve hot. (Makes about 15 biscuits)

BISCUIT CUTTER. A metal or plastic die used to cut individual biscuits from sheets of dough. They are usually round, but may have fanciful shapes. They are available as individual units, matched sets, or designed to cut several biscuits at one pressing. *See* Biscuit, *see also* Kitchen Equipment.

BISCUIT TORTONI. Mistakenly classified as ice cream, this type of frozen dessert is a mousse. It was created by the famous Italian restaurant man, B. Tortoni. It is served in individual paper cases, sprinkled with macaroon crumbs which have been soaked in sherry wine.

Biscuit Tortoni

¾ cup granulated sugar
¼ cup hot water
5 egg yolks
3 tbsp warm water
A few grains of salt
3 tbsp good sherry wine
2 cups heavy cream, whipped
½ cup finely cut or coarsely ground toasted almonds

Make a sugar sirup with the sugar and hot water, and allow it to boil 5 minutes, or until mixture reaches 234° F. (short thread). Beat the yolks with the water and salt. Remove the sirup from the fire, and pour the hot sirup over beaten yolk mixture, beating rapidly and constantly. Pour this mixture in top of double boiler, and set over gently bubbling water, stirring constantly until mixture is thick. Remove from hot water, cool, stir in sherry wine (more or less, according to taste), then strain mixture into whipped cream. Fill chilled paper cases; sprinkle top of each filled case with finely cut or coarsely ground toasted almonds. Place the cases in refrigerator tray, and freeze for 3 hours. *See also* Mousse.

BISMARCK HERRING. The fillets of herring with their roe are pickled in white wine and vinegar, seasoned with onion, carrot, salt and peppercorns. The resulting delicacy is usually served as hors d'oeuvre or as an appetizer.

BISMARK. This is an intoxicating English beverage made by combining a bottle of stout and a pint of champagne.

BISQUE. A thick rich smooth soup, usually made with a shellfish base. Modern quick cookery gives this name to a soup made with a white sauce base to which is added a puree of fish or vegetables.

A true bisque is made by marinating the shellfish overnight in a white wine court bouillon (*which see*). The fish is then cooked in the bouillon with fresh tomatoes until it is very tender. The fish is strained out and pounded in a mortar until it is smooth. It is then passed through a sieve and the purée returned to the bouillon. The soup is reheated, seasoned, and simmered until ready to serve. A soup tureen is heated and two or three well beaten egg yolks are put into it. The hot soup is then poured in, a little sweet cream and a small glass of sherry or brandy added, and the whole stirred well before serving.

See also various fish, shellfish, and vegetables, by name.

BITTERS. These aromatic or medicinal liquids are often spiritous, and sometimes have as high as 40 per cent alcoholic strength. Bitter herbs, leaves, roots, and substances such as orange rind, quassia, quinine, myrrh, cinchona bark, gentian, cascarilla, rhubarb, zedoary, angostura bark, calamus, and bryonia are used in making bitters. Juniper, peppermint, caraway, cloves, camomile, etc., are also used as flavoring agents. These concoctions are classed as (1) aromatic, (2) astringent, and (3) simple bitters. They are prepared by maceration or by distillation for medicinal uses, as beverages, or for use in cooking. The bitters possessing tonic qualities are regarded as beverages, some of which may be taken undiluted or mixed with water, plain or effervescent, and in tea, coffee, broth, or alcoholic drinks. Many fruit bitters, such as orange, peach, etc. (the name indicating the preponderant flavor), are made by reputable companies. There are many standard brands that have been on the market for so many years and are so well known that their trade names are considered generic, such as Fernet-Branca, Abbott's, Peychaud's, and Angostura. The last named contains no angostura bark, it is said, but was so called after the town of Angostura, Venezuela, where it was first made by an English army surgeon early in the nineteenth century. At any rate, each of these is made in accordance with a special recipe which is guarded with secrecy.

BITTO CHEESE. An Italian cheese of the Emmentaler group. It is a very hard cheese with small eyes. It is sometimes eaten fresh though more frequently allowed to ripen for two years before eating.

BLACK BUTTER. *See* BUTTER SAUCE.

BLACK CURRANT LIQUEUR. A liqueur made of black currants, brandy, and sugar, the French name for which is Cassis, *which see. See also* LIQUEURS.

BLACK-EYED PEA. An extremely nourishing legume used as a food staple for both humans and domestic animals. *See* BEAN.

BLACK HAW. (*Viburnum prunifolium*) Also called stag-bush, and sheepberry. A wild shrub of the honeysuckle family that bears edible fruits of bluish black color and about three-eighths of an inch in length.

BLACK HAW

The fruits are sweet and contain single, flat pits.

The black haw is found in an area bounded by southern New York and Connecticut, northern Georgia, eastern Kansas, and Michigan. The trunk is crooked and short and up to eight inches in diameter, but the branches spread over a disproportionately wide area and sometimes reach a height of thirty feet. The clustered white flowers are from two to four inches in diameter, the leaves are smooth, finely toothed, and ovate.

A southern variety (*V. rufidulum*) grows taller and bears larger fruit, which has a spherical pit. Its range is from Virginia, and Missouri, southward.

BLACK STRIPE. A beverage good either in summer or winter. Add a tablespoon of molasses to a wine glass of Santa Cruz rum. If made in summer, mix in a tablespoon of water and cool with chopped ice. If made in winter, place rum and molasses in a tumbler, and fill it up with boiling water. Put a little grated nutmeg on top in either season, and serve.

BLACK TEA. Tea that has been withered, fermented, and dried before it is packed for shipment. *See* Tea.

BLACKBERRY. The fruit of a small bush (*rubus*) which grows in any fertile soil where the moisture conditions are satisfactory. The wild blackberry has been cultivated on a commercial scale in America from the second half of the 19th Century. Dewberries are similar to blackberries, but trail along the ground, while blackberries are grown upright. Dewberries ripen about a week or two ahead of blackberries. Both are in season from June to August. Ripe berries have a lustrous black color; the unripe berries are green or red. In selecting blackberries, those of glossy black color with small seeds are the best quality. Overripe berries become dull black or gray.

There is also a novel form of blackberry which bears white fruit. It is not often grown commercially.

Preparation for Market

There are three federal grades of fresh blackberries. The first, U.S. No. 1, consists of blackberries or dewberries of one variety, which are firm, well colored, well developed, and not overripe, which are free from caps, mold and decay, and from damage caused by dirt or other foreign matter, shriveling, moisture, disease, insects, mechanical or other means. U.S. No. 2 consists of blackberries or dewberries of one variety which do not meet the standards U.S. No. 1 but do not contain more than 10% by volume of berries that have been seriously damaged from any cause. Not more than 1/5 of this amount may be affected by mold or decay. Unclassified consists of blackberries or dewberries which are not graded in conformity with the foregoing grades.

Hints on Buying

Quality in blackberries, and dewberries, is indicated by solid color, plumpness, and a bright, fresh appearance. Good berries should be free from dirt, trash, moisture, and adhering caps.

Wet or leaky berries should be avoided.

BLACKBERRY

A leaky condition is indicated by stained containers. Sometimes the stains are not evident until the containers are tilted. Leaky, soft or damaged berries are sometimes at the bottom or center of the container.

Decay can be easily seen by the presence of molds.

Berries with caps may be immature. A berry that has a number of green, unripe cells will not have as good flavor as one in which the cells are all one ripe color.

Blackberries are sold by the ½ pint, pint, or quart. 1 quart without caps measures 3¾ cups and will serve 4 to 6.

Canned blackberries are graded according to quality; top quality being U.S. Fancy, next, U.S. Choice, then U.S. Standard, U.S. Grade D, and U.S. Grade E, which is Water Grade or Pie Pack.

Hints on Preparation

Berries of all kinds are quite perishable and should be used on the day they are bought, if possible. One or two soft or moldy ones will spoil the others, so it is best to pick them over before storing. They can then be put in a clean bowl, covered and

Food Value

Water	Food Energy	Pro- tein	Fat	Carbo- hydrate	Cal- cium	Phos- phorus	Iron	Vit. A Value	Thia- mine	Ribo- flavin	Nia- cin	Ascor- bic Acid
84.4	65	1.2	.8	13.2	36	34	.9	320	.03	.07	.3	23

stored in the refrigerator. If hulled, wash and drain directly before serving.

BLACKBERRY BATTER PUDDING

⅓ cup butter or margarine
2 heaping tbsp sugar
2 well-beaten eggs
1 cup milk
2 cups flour
2 level tsp baking powder
½ tsp of salt
2 cups sugared blackberries

Cream butter with sugar, add eggs, then alternately add milk and flour, which has been sifted together with salt and baking powder. Beat well. Place a layer of the batter in a round cake pan which has been well buttered, and lightly floured. Cover with blackberries, and pour remaining batter over them. Bake in a moderate oven (350° F.) for 25 to 30 minutes. When done, spread the top with softened butter and a sprinkling of brown sugar. Run under flame a moment to melt the sugar. Serve with a hard sauce. (Serves 5 or 6)

BLACKBERRY BOUNCE

A refreshing drink that depends for its distinctive flavor upon both fruit and brandy. The preparation of the drink calls for a pound of sugar for each quart of stewed and strained blackberry juice. The brew is boiled for 5 minutes, skimmed, and cooled. A quart of brandy is added for each gallon of juice, and it is then spiced to taste.

BLACKBERRY COBBLER

1¼ qts blackberries
2 tbsp butter, melted
1 tsp lemon juice
Dough for 2 9-inch pie crusts, (see FLAKY
    PASTRY, see also PASTRY)
1½ tbsp flour
¾ cup sugar

Carefully wash and drain berries. Mix lightly with melted butter and lemon juice. Pat part of dough into even layer inside shallow pan or casserole. Blend flour with sugar and sift ½ mixture over lining of dough. Cover with berries. Sprinkle with balance of flour mixture. Cover with rolled-out pastry for top and trim. Pierce top with design for steam vents, or use a

pie bird to prevent steam from raising crust or making juices run over. Bake at 450° F. for 15 minutes. Reduce heat to 325° F. and bake 20 to 25 minutes longer. Serve either warm or cold. (Serves 4 to 6)

BLACKBERRY CORDIAL

Wash berries carefully in a colander, drain thoroughly, then place in top of a large double boiler. As the water heats, crush and stir the fruit thoroughly so that the juice flows freely. Turn into a cheesecloth bag previously wrung out of hot water and allow the juice to drip (as for jelly). Measure, and for each quart of blackberry juice add: 1 pound sugar, 1 tablespoon each ground cinnamon and nutmeg and 1½ teaspoons (each) ground cloves and allspice, tying all of these, in fine, doubled cheesecloth. Boil all together for 15 minutes. Remove the spices and skim the liquid thoroughly. When cold add ½ pint good French brandy to each quart of spiced juice. Bottle and seal tightly. This cordial improves with age and is often used as a pleasant remedy for diarrhea. Approximately 2 quarts of blackberries will be needed in order to prepare 1 quart of the juice.

BLACKBERRY DUMPLINGS

¾ cup sugar
½ cup water
1½ tsp lemon juice
⅛ tsp salt
1½ qts blackberries
2¼ cups flour
3 tsp baking powder
1½ tsp sugar
⅓ tsp salt
2½ tbsp butter
1 cup milk
1 tsp vanilla

Use saucepan of at least 4½ quarts capacity with tight lid. Stir in sugar, ½ cup water, lemon juice and ⅛ tsp salt. Heat over a low flame for 3 minutes. Wash and pick over berries, culling if needed, and add to liquid. Cover and simmer for 10 minutes. Mix and sift flour, baking powder, 1½ tbsp sugar and ¼ tsp salt. Soften butter and work into flour mixture. Add milk and vanilla; beat until smooth. Spoon batter onto berries. Simmer 25 minutes longer, keeping a tight cover in place. Serve berries ladled over the browned dumplings while still warm. (Serves 5 or 6)

BLACKBERRY FLUMMERY

7 to 9 tart shells made with Graham Cracker Pie Crust (*see* PASTRY)
1½ qts blackberries
¾ cup sugar
½ tsp cinnamon
1½ cups water
1 tbsp lemon juice
1½ tbsp cornstarch

Clean, rinse, and drain berries. Mix sugar with cinnamon; add with water and lemon juice to berries and boil. Gradually stir cornstarch into liquid and cook 20 minutes longer. When clear and thick remove from heat and chill. Turn into Graham Cracker tarts and top with whipped cream if desired.

BLACKBERRY JAM

Crush the berries, then heat thoroughly in their own juice. Press through a sieve to remove seeds, measure the pulp and liquid, and for every measured pint add one cup of sugar. Cook rapidly until thick, stirring constantly to prevent burning. Pour into hot, sterilized jars and seal. *See also* Jam.

BLACKBERRY, OR BRAMBLE, JELLY

Pick over some sound, ripe, but not over-ripe, blackberries and bake them in a moderate oven until they are quite soft. Pour them then into a jelly bag, a little at a time, fruit and juice as it comes, but remove all solid parts of one lot before putting in another. When you will have run all the juice in that way, add to it a pound of sugar per pint of juice and boil gently until the jelly sets. *See also* JELLY.

Blackberry jelly, as well as blackberry jam, are old favorites. They are rarely mixed with other fruits.

BLACKBERRY MOUSSE

1 pt blackberries
2 egg whites
Sugar
Whipped cream

Stew the blackberries and pass them through a sieve until you have at least a pint of purée. Sweeten it to taste and fold in the whites of eggs, beaten to a stiff froth. Then fold in the whipped cream and chill. Serve very cold. (Serves 4)

BLACKBERRY PANCAKES

1 cup flour
2 tbsp sugar
1 egg
1 cup blackberries
1 tbsp butter
1 cup milk

Mix together the flour, blackberries, sugar, egg yolk and milk to a smooth batter. Melt the butter and stir in, then add the stiffly beaten egg white. Heat a little butter in a frying pan and make small pancakes by covering the pan very thinly with the mixture. Brown on both sides. Serve hot, accompanied by vanilla ice cream. (Serves 4 or 6)

BLACKBERRY PAN DOWDY

2 cups canned blackberries, with sirup
⅔ cup sugar
¼ tsp salt
¼ tsp cinnamon
2 tbsp butter
Water
1 tsp lemon juice
Baking Powder Biscuit Dough (*see* BISCUIT), **prepared as below**

Drain berries, saving sirup, and turn into liberally buttered casserole. Cover with mixed sugar, salt and cinnamon. Dot with butter. Add water and lemon juice to berry sirup to make ½ cup; sprinkle over berries.

Prepare Baking Powder Biscuit dough in half quantity. Brush lightly with half-and-half mixture of egg white and water before and once during baking. Cover berries with dough about ½ inch thick. Bake at 300° F. to 325° F. (very moderate oven) 20 to 25 minutes, or until crust turns golden brown. Serve warm with cream or with Lemon Hard Sauce (*which see*).

BLACKBERRY PIE

1 recipe Flaky Pastry (*see* PASTRY)
1½ tsp lemon juice
¾ cup sugar

¼ tsp salt
2 tbsp flour
1 qt blackberries

Line 9-inch pie pan with dough. Mix all other ingredients with washed berries and turn into dough lining. Pinch down top crust and pierce in design to provide outlet for steam. Bake at 450° F. (very hot oven) for 10 minutes, then at 350° F. for 30 minutes.

BLACKBERRY PUDDING

2 cups blackberries
2 eggs
2 tbsp butter or margarine
¾ cup sugar
1 tsp baking powder
1 cup flour

Cream the butter, then add flour, sugar and beaten eggs. Then put in the black-berries. When all is well mixed, add the baking powder and a touch of carbonate of soda. Put in a mold and steam for 45 minutes. You can serve ice cream with this hot pudding, if desired; it makes a delicious combination.

Blueberries may be substituted for the blackberries in this recipe. (Serves 6)

BLACKBERRY ROLL

Baking powder biscuit dough
1 pint blackberries
½ cup sugar
Cinnamon

Prepare biscuit dough (which see); roll ½ inch thick. Place blackberries on dough and sprinkle with sugar and dust with cinnamon. Roll as for jelly roll; place, seam down, on greased baking sheet. Brush with butter and bake in hot oven (400° F.) for 25 to 30 minutes. Serve with foamy egg sauce (see SAUCE), or whipped cream. (Serves 6)

BLACKBERRY SHERBET

½ cup water
1 cup granulated sugar
¼ scant tsp salt
1 No. 2 can, or fresh, blackberries, sieved
2⅓ cups undiluted evaporated milk, chilled

Make a sugar sirup with water, sugar and salt, and cook until sirup spins a thin thread when poured from the tip of a spoon. Cool a little and stir in the sieved, strained blackberry juice. Cool, then chill. Stir in chilled evaporated milk, and freeze in hand freezer, using 6 parts ice and 1 part rock salt, until mixture is solid. Pack, using 4 parts ice and 1 part rock salt for 1 hour. Serve in chilled sherbet glasses, or orange cup, or placed over a well-chilled canned pineapple slice. (Makes 1 quart)

BLACKBERRY SHORTCAKE

Bring berries to a boil in hot sirup, using ½ to 1 cup sugar and ¼ to ½ cup water. Cool. Make shortcake (which see). Place lower half of hot biscuit on serving dish and spoon berries and juice over it. Cover with top half of biscuit, spoon more berries and juice over top. Serve immediately, with whipped cream, if desired.

BLACKBERRY WINE

Take fully ripe blackberries, mash them, and add a quart of berries to a quart of water. Let them stand over night. Then strain through a sieve and add ¾ pound of sugar to each quart of liquid and pour it into a cask when the sugar is dissolved. Add a gill of finings to each 20 gallons of liquid. The next day bung it and two months later bottle it.

STEWED BLACKBERRIES

1 qt blackberries
½ cup water
2 tsp lemon juice
⅛ tsp salt
⅔ cup sugar

Pick out any soft, bruised, or moldy berries. Rinse berries thoroughly but gently in cold water. Skim off any loose hulls. Drain, add ½ cup water and simmer under a cover for at least 15 minutes. Agitate berries several times while cooking to prevent clotting or sticking to the bottom. Add lemon juice, salt and sugar, stirring until sugar dissolves. Heat 3 minutes longer. Serve warm or cold, with heavy cream if desired. Do not re-heat.

BLACKBOARD. A kitchen blackboard can be a great convenience to the housewife. Hung in a prominent place on the wall, it can be used to jot down reminders for the next shopping expedition, notations as to the time when foods should be removed from the oven, etc. It is also a convenient place to leave notes for the children when they come in from school and the housewife is out of the house. Paper can be used for all of these tasks, it is true, but paper has a habit of getting lost. A simple slate or a sheet of coated cardboard of the type made for use in the nursery or children's playroom will suffice. If desired, a bulletin board (*which see*) may be used instead. *See also* KITCHEN EQUIPMENT.

BLACKFISH. An American fish which belongs to the *Labridae* species. It is found along the Atlantic coast from Maine to South Carolina.

Its original name was *tautog*, an Indian word meaning "sheep's head." Because of its dark coloring, it was given the name "blackfish." In parts of New England it is known as the "oyster fish." The blackfish is a very delicate and savory fish which may attain twenty pounds in weight and reach a length of three feet, although the average weight is from two and a half to three pounds.

The various methods of preparation for mackerel and pompano (*which see*) may be adapted to this fish.

BLACKHORSE FISH. Another name for sucker (*which see*).

BLACKSTRAP. Title given to the third-strike molasses (*which see*) utilized in the manufacture of cattle feed, in growing yeast and in the production of alcohol. In this the delicate constituents of the molasses are burned to bitter caramel; the sugar content is very limited.

BLADE. Certain spices such as mace come in two forms—*ground*, and in natural "blade" form. The word is also used of herbs and grains.

BLAEBERRY. Distorted name for blueberry.

BLANC MANGE. (bla mawnz) A dessert of French origin, the name of which means white food, which is made either with cornstarch, arrowroot, or Irish moss. This popular dessert is served molded and cold and has many variations.

CORNSTARCH BLANC MANGE

2 cups milk
3 tbsp cornstarch
⅛ tsp salt
⅓ cup sugar
⅔ tsp vanilla or other preferred flavoring

Scald one and a half cups of the milk; blend cornstarch, salt, and sugar and moisten with remaining milk. When perfectly smooth, pour the scalded milk over these, stirring constantly, then return to the saucepan and cook over hot water (double boiler) for 10 minutes, stirring constantly until thick and smooth. Cover and cook 10 minutes longer, stirring occasionally. Cool slightly, add the flavoring and turn into a mold which has been dipped into cold water. Chill and unmold for serving.

Arrowroot Blanc Mange. Substitute arrowroot for cornstarch in cornstarch blanc mange recipe.

Coconut Blanc Mange. As blanc mange begins to set, stir in 1 cup of coconut, fresh grated or canned moist.

Fruited Blanc Mange. As blanc mange begins to set, stir in 1 cup of fruit, fresh or canned, as cherries, crushed pineapple, berries.

Irish Moss Blanc Mange. Soften ⅓ cup of Irish moss in cold water to cover 15 minutes. Drain and add to 2 cups of milk. Cook in double boiler ½ hour without stirring. It thickens only on cooling.

All types of blanc mange are usually served with jam, jelly, light cream, boiled custard, or fruit, fresh or stewed.

BLANCH. To whiten by scalding or parboiling. A preliminary step sometimes used in food preparation. Also a banking up of earth surrounding the growing vegetables (such as celery) in order to keep off the sun and produce white stalks.

BLANQUETTE (blawn ket). A French stew, usually made with veal, with a creamy sauce, made slightly tart with lemon juice. *See* VEAL.

BLEACHING. Another term for blanch (*which see*).

BLEAK FISH. A small fresh-water fish belonging to the great carp family, common in European waters, and prepared in a manner similar to sprats (*which see*). The scales are lined with silvery pigment used in making artificial pearls.

BLEND. To mix food thoroughly; to mingle; to combine into one product.

BLENDER. *See also* KITCHEN EQUIPMENT. First developed as a bar accessory, the electric blender or liquidizer has proven itself to be invaluable in the kitchen. In both principle and operation, the blender differs radically from the electric mixer (*which see*), and is a supplement rather than a substitute for that useful instrument.

The blender usually consists of two parts: A small but powerful electric motor mounted in a metal base, and a separate, tall, thick-walled, covered mixing glass that has four sharp blades set on the bottom. The blades are revolved at high rates of speed by the motor through a small drive-shaft that protrudes from the base and engages the blade assembly through the bottom of the glass.

Because of the high rate of speed with which the blades revolve and their construction, they virtually emulsify any material that is placed in the glass, be it solid or liquid. The exact capacity of the blender depends on the design; some will grind coffee, others reduce any fruit or vegetable to a liquid, while others can handle little other than liquids.

The blender offers limitless possibilities. It can prepare soups, sauces, fruit and vegetable drinks, omelets, frozen desserts, and even batters, spreads, and dressings. With a blender, mixtures can be made that are otherwise either impossible or very difficult. It is a valuable asset for home bartending (*which see*).

Purchase and Use

There are several different model blenders available, most being rather similar in design and within the same general price range. They are quite expensive, but, if properly made, should be long-lived. Each model has different capacities and uses, and the purchaser should study them to see which more closely fits the family needs before making his selection. Whether bought originally for the bar or the kitchen, the full potentialities of the unit should be investigated, for they offer much in varying the menu and preparing healthful, tasty dishes. *See also* KITCHEN EQUIPMENT.

BLEU (blu). A French word meaning blue. *Pâté bleu* and *fromage bleu* are cheeses made from cow's milk in a manner imitative of Roquefort (*which see*). They are mottled, marbled, or veined with greenish blue. The term "bleu" is also applied to several kinds of cheese made in sections of the Auvergne and Aubrac mountains

and which are named Bleu d'Auvergne, Cantal, Guiole or Laguiole, and St. Flour. Other cheeses of this type are Queyras, Champoleon, Sarraz, and Journiac.

BLINIS. A small Russian pancake, often served with caviar or cheese.

Blinis

¾ lb buckwheat flour
1½ pints of milk
½ cup butter
Just under 1 oz. yeast
3 eggs
Pinch of salt

Dissolve the yeast in ½ pint of warm milk and make a dough with a little flour. Let this stand in a warm place for 2 hours. Then add the rest of the flour, the yolks of eggs, the salt, and the remaining warm milk. Mix thoroughly, but do not let the mixture get too thick. Lastly, add the whites of eggs beaten to a stiff froth and let stand for another ½ hour. Proceed in the same manner as in the making of pancakes, using a very small pan. *See* PANCAKES.

BLOATER. Selected smoked herring to which all the methods of preparation of smoked herring may be adapted. It is a national breakfast dish in England.

BLUE BLAZER. A hot alcoholic drink that is mixed by the rather spectacular method of pouring flaming whisky through the air between two mugs. The name comes from the characteristic blue flame of burning alcohol. Done properly, it looks as though a solid streak of blue fire were passing between the mugs.

Blue Blazer

1 large jigger whisky
1 large jigger boiling water
Powdered sugar, honey or rock candy
  to taste
Lemon peel

Place the whisky and boiling water in separate silver-plated mugs with large handles, the sweetening agent having been dissolved in the water. Ignite the whisky and mix by pouring from mug to mug three or four times. Smother flame if still burning, serve in six ounce glass with twist of lemon peel. *See also* BARTENDING. (Serves 1)

BLUE CRAB. A species of crab found along the Atlantic and Gulf coasts of the

United States, the dominant color of which is blue. *See* CRAB.

BLUE DORSET CHEESE. *See* BLUE VINNY CHEESE.

BLUE CHEESE. A domestic cheese, developed as a substitute for Roquefort (*which see*). Although made according to the same formulas, it may not by law be called Roquefort.

BLUE GILL. A North American perch, also called sunfish, *which see.*

BLUE PLATE. A grill plate with partitions to keep food separated. Originally the plates were made in a blue-patterned ware, which explains the name, but they may now be bought in a variety of makes and patterns in china and glass. Any type of meal can be served on these plates—company luncheons, oven dinners, vegetable plates, top-of-the-stove and broiled meals. The compartments prevent sauces from running into each other, and such vegetables as stewed tomatoes may be served on the same plate as the rest of the dinner, thus saving dish washing.

BLUE POINT OYSTER. Properly, an oyster grown in a certain section of Long Island waters. The name is used commercially and indiscriminately to designate a good-sized oyster which may come from any of the Atlantic waters or the Gulf of Mexico. *See* OYSTER.

BLUE VINNY CHEESE. A hard, flat, rich English cheese made from skimmed cow's milk. It is white with a blue vein through it.

BLUEBERRY. The berry of a number of *Vaccinium* bushes. Blueberry time starts in late May and lasts to mid-October. The cultivated crop in North Carolina is the first to be sent to market and then follow the crops from Maryland, Delaware, and Pennsylvania. In like order come the berries from New Jersey, Massachusetts, and Maine. By the end of the season New England and Nova Scotia are supplying the markets. The peak of the season is in June when blueberries pour into the markets from five producing centers. Most blueberries are brought into market by truck to insure their reaching the retail store in the shortest possible time. Picking is carried on in the early morning and the berries are in the wholesale market by nightfall.

There are few seeds in cultivated blueberries. They are sweet fleshed, tender skinned, with just enough tart flavor to give distinction to the fruit.

Generally the lighter blueberries with their dewy coats are known as blueberries, while the darker berries, some of which are nearly black, are known as "huckleberries." Blueberries have smaller seeds and are generally sweeter. West and south of New England, the general tendency is to group all varieties under the common name of huckleberry.

Blueberries, huckleberries, whortleberries and bilberries are marketed in canned and frozen forms which may be used for desserts.

VARIETIES OF BLUEBERRIES

Lowbush: most important commercial species. The fruit ripens during July and August. It is native in northeastern United States and parts of Canada. It usually grows from 6 to 18 inches high.

Highbush: Found growing wild from northern Florida to Maine and west to southern Michigan. Native of swamps, and moist woods, and moist high open fields. Grows in height from 10 to 15 feet.

Dryland: Native from Georgia and Alabama to Maine and westward to Michigan and Oklahoma. Grows in dry, relatively poor soil, to a height of 1 to 3 feet. The berries are light blue and have good flavor.

Evergreen: Native along Pacific coast from central California to British Columbia. Branches are important commercially for decoration. The berries are usually small and shiny black, and are used extensively in pies and otherwise in cooking. A large part of the crop is stored frozen for use by pie makers.

Mountain: Native of Cascade Mountains. Plants grow 3 to 5 feet high. Uniformly large well-flavored berries which are somewhat pear-shaped, black or maroon in color; juicy and tart.

Rabbiteye: Native to river valleys and the edge of woods in southern Georgia, Ala-

FOOD VALUE

Water	Food Energy	Pro- tein	Fat	Carbo- hydrate	Cal- cium	Phos- phorus	Iron	Vit. A Value	Thia- mine	Ribo- flavin	Nia- cin	Ascor- bic Acid
83.4	68	.6	.6	15.1	16	13	.8	280	.03	.07	.3	16

bama, and northern Florida. Berries are mostly black and not as attractive as blue. However, some varieties bear large, juicy aromatic blue fruit, which compares favorably with other species.

Canada Blueberry: commercial variety, harvested in Maine, and in the Adirondack Mountains.

BLUEBERRY

PREPARATION FOR MARKET

Cultivated blueberries are the aristocrats of the blueberry kingdom. The largest equal the size of blue grapes. The berries are picked and packed very carefully—two hundred to a quart box. Workers wear gloves so that the color or texture of the fruit will not be harmed and the boxes are made with side and corner openings with vents in the bottom to give the berries fresh air.

HINTS ON BUYING

Blueberries that are plump, fresh looking, clean, dry and free from leaves and trash, fairly uniform in size, and of a deep, full color throughout the lot, are usually of good quality.

Ripeness is indicated by the color, which may be blue, black, bluish-black or purplish. The seeds are small and inconspicuous, while huckleberry seeds are prominent, which make them less desirable.

Decay is usually indicated by the presence of molds. Freedom from moisture is essential to good quality berries. Moisture may be caused by natural breakdown, decay, or some form of mechanical injury. It should be looked for carefully.

Overripe fruit has a dull, lifeless appearance, and is often soft and watery. Berries held long after picking have a similar appearance and may be more or less shriveled.

Blueberries are sold by ½ pint, pint, or quart, and are graded according to quality with the usual U.S. Federal Grades, U.S. No. 1, U.S. No. 2, and Unclassified.

Blueberries are very perishable and should be used as soon as possible after being bought. They should be kept in a covered bowl in the refrigerator, and washed just before serving.

BLUEBERRY BETTY

3 cups blueberries
¼ cup sugar
Dash of salt
2 tbsp lemon juice
4 slices French toast
2 tbsp powdered sugar
¼ tsp nutmeg
Hard sauce

Rinse the berries and discard the culls. Add sugar, salt and lemon juice and cook over medium heat; then pour into shallow baking dish. Dice the toast (*which see*) and cover the berries. Mix powdered sugar and nutmeg and shake over top. Bake 30 minutes at 375° F. (moderate). Serve with hard sauce (*which see*). (Serves 5)

BLUEBERRY BUCKLE

1½ cups flour
2¼ tsp baking powder
⅔ tsp salt
⅓ cup sugar
⅓ cup shortening
1 egg
⅓ cup milk
2½ tsp lemon juice
1½ cups blueberries
⅓ cup flour
⅓ cup sugar (2nd)
½ tsp cinnamon
¼ tsp nutmeg
¼ cup butter

Blend and sift flour, baking powder and salt. Work shortening and sugar to a smooth creaminess. Beat in egg until puffy. In several turns, add flour mixture and milk, beating smooth after each addition. Empty into square or rectangular cake pan of about 70 square inches, lined with wax paper. Sprinkle lemon juice over all the blueberries and distribute them evenly over dough. Mix ⅓ cup flour, ⅓ cup sugar, cinnamon and nutmeg. Cut butter into small chunks and knead with fingers into flour mixture. Break this mass into loose pile of small crumbs and spread over blueberries. Do not pack crumbs. Bake at 350° F. (moderate) 50 minutes, or until tests done. (Serves 6)

BLUEBERRY CAKE

1½ cups cake flour
½ tsp salt
½ tsp soda
½ tsp baking powder
½ cup shortening
1 cup sugar
½ tsp cinnamon
2 eggs, beaten
½ cup milk
2 cups fresh or frozen blueberries

Sift flour, measure and resift 3 times with next three ingredients. Cream shortening with the sugar and cinnamon until smooth and soft. Add the eggs and beat until fluffy and light in color. Add the milk alternately with the dry ingredients, beating well after each addition. Gently fold in the blueberries. Pour into a greased 9 inch square cake pan 1¾ inches deep. Bake at 350° F. (moderate oven) for 45 minutes or until cake tests done. Serve warm or cold with lemon sauce (*which see*). (Serves 8)

BLUEBERRY COOKIES

3 cups flour
¾ tsp salt
3 tsp baking powder
1½ cups sugar
¾ cup shortening
2 eggs
1¼ cups blueberries
2 tsp lemon rind, grated
2½ tbsp walnuts, chopped
⅓ cup milk

Blend first 3 ingredients and sift. Working in sugar, cream shortening. Beat in eggs gradually. Add flour and milk in 3 parts each, beating smooth each time. Evenly stir in blueberries, lemon rind and nuts. Immediately drop batter onto greased baking sheets and bake at 385° F. (moderate) for 10 minutes or until firm. (Makes 36 good-sized cookies)

BLUEBERRY DESSERT

1 qt blueberries
¼ cup water
1 tsp lemon juice
½ cup sugar
Pinch of nutmeg
3 slices bread, buttered

Rinse blueberries; add water, lemon juice, sugar and nutmeg. Heat to a boil and remove from flame. Empty into shallow baking pan. Place bread halves in rows over berries. Bake at 425° F. for 10 minutes or until brown. (Serves 6)

BLUEBERRY FRITTERS

1 cup flour
2½ tbsp sugar
1 tsp baking powder
½ tsp salt
2 eggs
1 tbsp water
½ tsp lemon juice
1 cup blueberries

Mix and sift flour, sugar, baking powder and salt. Separate eggs; beat yolks with water and stir into flour mixture until smooth. Beat egg whites until stiff and fold into batter. Add blueberries. Have deep fat heated to 365° F. Drop in heavy spoonfuls of batter and fry 4 minutes, or until brown. Drain on absorbent paper. Serve with sauce. (Serves 6)

BLUEBERRY ICE CREAM

1 pt picked, washed, fresh or canned blueberries
½ cup granulated sugar
⅛ tsp salt
½ cup undiluted, evaporated milk
1 cup heavy cream, whipped

Blueberry Ice Cream and Blueberry Pie have been called two of the greatest achievements of the human race. Though not everyone will go so far, all will agree that life would be poorer without them.

Crush berries and combine with granulated sugar. Cook 5 minutes, then strain through a fine sieve. Add salt, and allow to cool, then strain again when cold, and add evaporated milk and fold in whipped cream. Freeze in refrigerator tray, stirring when mixture is frozen to a mush; then add whipped cream and freeze for 3 hours. *See also* ICE CREAM.

BLUEBERRY ICE-BOX PUDDING

1½ cups blueberries, stewed (*see* STEWED BLACKBERRIES, *substitute blueberries*)
⅓ cup sugar
2 tbsp lemon juice
¾ tbsp cornstarch
3 slices white bread, buttered
1 cup heavy cream
Cinnamon

Mix juice from blueberries with sugar, lemon juice and cornstarch. Heat until mixture boils thickly, stirring continuously. Stir in blueberries and cook another 5 minutes. Cut each bread slice into about 6 pieces. Beginning with bread, fill loaf pan with 4 alternate layers of bread and of blueberry mixture. Chill in refrigerator 1½ hours or until firm enough to be cut into squares. Beat cream until fluffy and spread on top. Sprinkle lightly with cinnamon. Chopped nuts or toasted coconut may be used instead of cinnamon. Canned blueberries may be substituted for fresh blueberries, using contents of No. 1 can. (Makes 5 or 6 portions)

BLUEBERRY PANCAKES

2 cups sifted flour
3 tsp baking powder
½ tsp salt
1 tbsp sugar
1 or 2 eggs well beaten
1½ cups milk (scant)
2 tbsp shortening, melted
1 cup fresh or drained canned blueberries

Mix and sift dry ingredients. Combine egg and milk; add flour mixture and beat until smooth; add shortening, and berries. Bake slowly on ungreased, hot griddle. Spread with butter, sprinkle with brown sugar, and roll, or serve plain with hard sauce (*which see*).

BLUEBERRY PIE

1 qt blueberries
1½ tbsp lemon juice
1 tbsp grated lemon rind
¾ cup sugar
¼ tsp salt

2 tbsp flour or 1½ tbsp quick-cooking tapioca
Pastry for a 2-crust pie

Wash, pick over, and drain the blueberries. Add the lemon juice and rind, the sugar, salt and flour or tapioca. Turn into a pastry-lined pie plate (*see* PASTRY). Moisten the rim of the bottom crust, put on the top crust and pinch the edges firmly together to seal. Make several slits in the top crust to allow for escape of steam, and bake about 40 minutes, having the oven very hot (450° F.) for the first 10 minutes, then reduce to moderate (350° F.) for the remainder of the baking.

BLUEBERRY ROLL

Prepare baking powder biscuit dough (*which see*); roll ½ inch thick. Sprinkle 1 pint washed, and drained blueberries on dough, and sprinkle with ½ cup sugar and 1½ tablespoons lemon juice. Roll as for jelly roll; place seam down, on greased baking sheet. Brush with butter and bake in hot oven (400° F.) for 25 to 30 minutes. Serve with lemon sauce (*which see*).

BLUEBERRY SHORTCAKE

See blackberry shortcake, substituting blueberries for blackberries.

BLUEBERRY SOUP

1 qt blueberries
2 qt water
Sugar
⅔ tbsp cornstarch
2 tbsp cold water
Whipped cream

Pick over the berries, then cook with the water for 1 hour. Strain through doubled cheesecloth, return to the saucepan (which has been rinsed with cold water to eliminate any seeds), sweeten to taste and thicken with the cornstarch moistened with the cold water. Cook 5 or 6 minutes, stirring constantly. Chill and serve garnished with whipped cream. (Serves 6)

BLUEBERRY TEA CAKE

1-egg cake batter (*see* CAKE)
1 to 1½ cups blueberries, drained
Confectioners' sugar

berries or huckleberries and turn remaining batter over top; bake as directed. Sprinkle with powdered sugar, cut in 3 inch squares and serve warm with butter for tea or supper. (Makes nine 3-inch-square portions)

Spiced Blueberry Molds

3 cups canned unsweetened blueberries
2 tbsp sugar
1 stick cinnamon
1 tsp whole allspice
1 tsp whole cloves
1½ tbsp gelatin
½ cup cold water
Dash of salt
2 tbsp vinegar
¼ cup lemon juice

Bring blueberries, sugar and spices to a boil and simmer 10 minutes, stirring constantly; force through a fine strainer to remove pulp and spices; measure and, if necessary, add water to make 2 cups. Soften gelatin in cold water 5 minutes; add to boiling fruit mixture and stir until gelatin is dissolved. Stir in salt, vinegar, and lemon juice, and pour into small individual molds; chill until firm. One quart fresh blueberries may be used; sort, wash and steam in double boiler about 20 minutes, adding spices after steaming 10 minutes. Then proceed as directed. (Makes approximately 10 small molds)

BLUEFISH. The bluefish is found in nearly all warm seas and is sometimes called "skipjack" or "skip-mackerel."

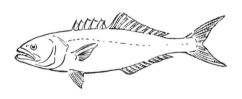

BLUEFISH

Bluefish are found practically all the year 'round off the eastern coast of the United States but appear in greater quantities during May, when they pursue the shoals of smaller fish while seeking spawning grounds close to the shore. These fish sometimes ascend the larger rivers, such as the Chesapeake or the Hudson as far as the tide sets, and blue fishing is consid-

ered great sport from Maine to the Carolinas.

An exceedingly voracious fish, it is one of the most destructive and remorseless bandits of the northern seashores. Swimming in large schools in pursuit of fish not much inferior to themselves in size, bluefish move along rapidly and swiftly like a pack of hungry wolves, destroying everything before them. Their trail is marked by bloodstains in the sea and fragments of fish too large to be swallowed whole.

The back of this fish is a beautiful bluish-green in color with small silvery blotches at the base. It grows rapidly, its average weight being three pounds and its length about eighteen inches.

The bad traits of this fish have not affected its popularity on American tables, and it is shipped by means of refrigerator cars to all points of the country. More than 8,000,000 pounds are handled annually in New York City. Either broiled, baked whole, or split, the bluefish furnishes an excellent dish. If the fish is to be stuffed, it is important not to forget to use lemon juice.

Young bluefish may either be broiled or baked—in a hot oven (400° F.)—filetted or prepared by any of the methods applied to filet of sole or flounder. Frozen fillets of bluefish should be thoroughly thawed before being cooked. *See also* Fish.

BLUNT-NOSED SHINER. This food fish is found along the southern coasts of North America. It is also called Moonfish, *which see.*

BOAL WINE. A delicious Madeira wine, luscious, rich in bouquet and fragrance, and flame red in color. *See* Madeira and Wine.

BOAR. The male swine or the wild European or American hog. The European boar provided the traditional Christmas feast of boar's head and lent itself to emblems of heraldry. *See* Wild Boar.

BOB WHITE. A name used indiscriminately to indicate any of the various quail found in the United States. The bird is called a partridge throughout most of the south. *See* Quail.

BOCK BEER. A special brew, made in the winter for spring use. The day it is put on sale is supposed to mark the arrival of spring. *See* Beer.

BODY. (I) A term used in the tea trade in describing strength of infused tea. Thus, a tea with a "full body" would be one that produced a rich, full flavored liquor that lacked bitterness. *See* TEA.

BODY. (II) A quality of wine caused by alcoholic strength in combination with sweetness and flavor, that leaves a lasting impression on the palate. The French refer to this quality as *corps. See* WINE.

BOERENKOOL SAUSAGE. A smoked country sausage, obtainable at most delicatessens. *See* SAUSAGE.

BOHEA. (Chinese; pronounced bo hee) An inferior tea produced in Java. Originally the word was used only for Chinese tea of the best quality which was grown in the Wu-i Hills of China. The tea beverage of the 18th century was known by this name.

BOHEMIAN SAUCE. *See* MAYONNAISE.

BOILED DRESSING. Delicious seasoned-to-taste, homecooked salad dressing still commands approval. Boiled dressing, for which there are a hundred variations, is especially good for fruit salads, or if preferred, it may be blended with sour cream —⅓ cream to ⅔ dressing—and used for cabbage slaw and potato salad.

STANDARD BOILED DRESSING

2 tbsp sugar
2 tsp flour
½ tsp salt
Few grains cayenne pepper
1 tbsp butter
2 egg yolks
½ cup vinegar
½ cup heavy cream, whipped

Mix the dry ingredients in the top of the double boiler, add the butter, the beaten egg yolks, and the vinegar (gradually). Cook over hot water, stirring constantly, until the mixture thickens. Remove from the fire and when cool, fold in the whipped cream.

This dressing is suitable for cole slaw, fruit salad, green salad, and mixed vegetable salad.

BOILED DRESSING

1 tsp salt
1 tsp dry mustard
1½ tbsp sugar
Few grains cayenne
2 tbsp flour
1 egg
1½ tbsp melted butter

¾ cup milk
¼ cup tarragon vinegar

Combine the salt, mustard, sugar, cayenne, and flour, and moisten with the beaten egg, melted butter and milk. When perfectly smooth, gradually add the vinegar and cook over hot water (double boiler) until thickened, stirring constantly. Strain and cool.

BOILED CARLTON DRESSING

½ cup rich chicken stock
½ cup tarragon vinegar
5 egg yolks
2 tbsp prepared mustard
Salt, pepper, cayenne
½ cup heavy cream
2 tbsp clarified butter

Reduce the chicken stock to half by boiling. Add the vinegar, place over hot water (double boiler), add the egg yolks, slightly beaten, also the seasonings. Cook, stirring constantly, until the mixture thickens. Strain, then add the heavy cream and clarified butter. Cool.

BOILED FRENCH CREAM DRESSING

1½ tsp sugar
1 tsp salt
½ tsp prepared mustard
Boiling water
½ cup oil
3 eggs
1 cup heavy cream
⅓ cup tarragon vinegar
1 tbsp grenadine sirup or Maraschino liqueur

Combine in the upper part of the double boiler the sugar, salt, mustard, and just enough boiling water to form a paste of mayonnaise consistency. Add the oil, then beat in the eggs, one at a time, to form a creamy dressing. Add the cream and vinegar and cook over hot water, stirring constantly, until the mixture thickens. Cool, add the grenadine or maraschino. This dressing will keep about two weeks under refrigeration.

BOILED FRENCH FRUIT DRESSING I

⅓ cup orange juice
1½ cups lemon juice

2 eggs
⅞ cup sugar
1 cup heavy cream
Dash of salt
Dash of nutmeg

Combine the fruit juices in the upper part of the double boiler. Add the eggs, slightly beaten with the sugar. Cook over hot water, stirring constantly, until the mixture thickens. Cool, and fold in the cream beaten to a stiff broth with the salt and nutmeg. Use for fruit salad or cocktail. This dressing will keep several weeks under refrigeration.

BOILED FRENCH FRUIT DRESSING II

2 eggs
3 tbsp clarified sweet butter
3 tbsp lemon juice
Dash each of salt and nutmeg
1 cup heavy cream
½ tsp celery salt
½ tsp orange extract
Slight grating orange rind
1 tsp grenadine sirup

Beat the eggs until very light, add gradually, stirring while adding, the butter, lemon juice, salt and nutmeg. Cook in the double boiler, stirring constantly and rapidly, until the mixture thickens. Cool, fold in the cream, beaten until stiff with the celery salt. Add also the orange extract, orange rind and sirup. This dressing keeps well under refrigeration.

BOILED LEMON DRESSING

1 tbsp flour
1 tbsp powdered sugar
⅔ tsp salt
Dash of nutmeg
2 egg yolks
2 tbsp cold water
1½ cups boiling water
1 tbsp clarified sweet butter
Juice 2 lemons
1 cup whipped cream

Combine in a double boiler the flour, sugar, salt and nutmeg. Add the egg yolks beaten with the cold water, and blend all thoroughly. Now gradually add the boiling water, stirring while adding, and cook over hot water until the mixture thickens, still stirring constantly. Stir in the butter, cool,

and just before using add the strained lemon juice and carefully fold in the whipped cream.

BOILED LOS ANGELES DRESSING

4 egg yolks
¼ cup oil
1 tbsp lemon juice
1½ tbsp wine vinegar
Salt
1 tsp prepared mustard
Dash of cayenne
1 cup heavy cream
1 tsp powdered sugar
2 tbsp grated horseradish
1 tbsp minced parsley

Beat the egg yolks slightly, add the oil, lemon juice, vinegar and seasonings and cook in a double boiler, stirring constantly, until the mixture thickens. Cool, and fold in the cream beaten stiff with the sugar, horseradish and parsley.

BOILED SOUR CREAM DRESSING

1½ tsp dry mustard
2 tsp powdered sugar
1 tbsp flour
3 egg yolks
4 tbsp clarified butter
¾ cup milk
½ cup lime juice
½ cup heavy sour cream

Combine in a double boiler the mustard, sugar and flour. Add the egg yolks slightly beaten, the butter, milk and lime juice. Cook over hot water, stirring constantly, until the mixture thickens. Strain, then add the heavy sour cream and beat all thoroughly.

For variation, add to 1 cup of the above, 1 tablespoon each of finely chopped pickled beets, sweet and sour gherkins and caviar.

BOILED SUZANNE PULLIG DRESSING

4 tbsp sweet butter
2 tbsp flour
Dash each of salt, pepper, cayenne and nutmeg
2 eggs
1 tbsp sugar
1 tsp prepared mustard
3 tbsp capers
1 tsp finely minced chives

Melt the butter in the upper part of the double boiler. Add the flour and seasonings and when smoothly blended, the well-beaten eggs, sugar and mustard. Cook, stirring constantly, until thickened. Cool, then fold in the capers and chives.

BOILER. (I) A chicken that is one year of age—or older. When boiled, fricasseed, or stewed, the more or less tough flesh has a fine flavor; but such a bird is not recommended for broiling, frying, or roasting. *See* CHICKEN.

BOILER. (II) A kitchen utensil. *See* KITCHEN EQUIPMENT.

BOILING. The process of cooking food in a chosen liquid at a temperature of 212° F. over direct heat. Usually, foods should be immersed in the boiling liquid, and the cooking time counted from the time the liquid begins to boil again. Note that adding fuel to the fire when water has once reached the boiling point will have no further effect than that of accelerating the rate of ebullition and evaporation without raising the temperature of the liquid or the immersed food.

If meat is being boiled, the operation, if continued for more than an hour, gradually converts the connective tissue of meat fiber into gelatin which is partially dissolved in water. The heat of the boiling water usually melts a little of the fat, which, since it cannot mix with the water, forms a coating on the surface. A small proportion of the juices of meat is drawn into the surrounding water, and the aqueous solution thus formed is termed "broth" or "bouillon."

The addition of salt to water in boiling fish, meat, or certain vegetables has a threefold action: (1) it acts directly on superficial albumin with coagulation taking place, (2) it slightly raises the boiling point of the water, (3) by increasing the density of the water, the juices are retained and a better flavor results.

If the salt is to be removed from meat, as in smoked or cured meats, the cooking may be begun in cold water which is slowly raised to the boiling point (212°). If excessively salty, pour off this first water and continue the process in fresh boiling water.

BOLOGNA SAUSAGE. (boe loe nyah) Composed of finely chopped beef, veal, and pork that has been well seasoned, smoked, and packed into a large sausage casing. *See* SAUSAGE.

BOMBAY DUCK. A familiar name for the bummalo, a small fish about the size of a smelt. It is caught in great quantities off the Indian Coast and is dried and canned as a relish. It is served as an accompaniment to curried dishes.

BOMBE. A frozen dessert made by lining a mold with a frozen, rich, sirupy custard (made from egg yolks and light sugar siryp) or water ice, the center cavity then being filled by another and different ice cream, mousse or parfait, to which stiffly beaten heavy cream has been added. The mold is then tightly sealed and the dessert refrozen.

TO LINE, FILL AND FREEZE A BOMBE MOLD

The mold should first be thoroughly chilled. This is very important for the lining or filling used is a frozen one, and if the mold is warm it will soften the mixture, thus requiring more time to freeze. Moreover it will be much more difficult to set it in place.

Use a spoon to place the ice into the mold and spread it evenly with the back of a chilled spoon or a spatula, making the lining layer from one-half to three-fourths inch thick. Next pack the filling into the center, also with a spoon, and fill the mold to overflowing. Place buttered paper over the surface, then put the cover on the mold and seal either with a strip of muslin dipped into melted fat or a strip of adhesive tape. Bury in ice and salt (one part salt to four parts ice) for at least three hours. The mold may be decorated with small pieces of fresh or candied fruit or nut meats. Unmold for service and decorate with whipped cream or fancy glacé fruits.

BOMBE MOLD

Bombes can be made in so many varieties, that only imagination limits the number of recipes that can be concocted. According to her budget, the homemaker can combine the ingredients, and make any type bombe she wishes. *See also* ICE, ICE CREAM, and PARFAIT.

BONBON SPOON. A serving spoon. See FLATWARE.

BONE MARROW. *See* MARROW.

BONING KNIFE. A special knife designed for use in separating meat from bones. *See* CUTLERY *and* CARVING.

BONITO. A salt water fish related to MACKEREL, *which see.*

BONNEKAMP. A very delicious, bitter cordial. It is used also as a flavor for certain drinks. A product of both Holland and Belgium. *See* CORDIAL.

BORAGE. Borage is an aromatic herb, the young, tender leaves of which are similar to cucumbers in smell and to oysters in taste. Their delicate flavor adds interest to salads, stews, cauliflower, and dried legumes. A borage leaf or two may garnish such cool drinks as summer punch and tomato juice cocktails, and a garnish of the blue flower spikes will add beauty as well as flavor. You can candy the flowers by brushing them lightly with egg white and sifting powdered sugar over them.

BORDEAUX. A popular type of French wine. About three-quarters of its production is Red Bordeaux, often called Claret, characterized by lightness, softness, and elegance of taste. The other quarter is White Bordeaux, which may be subdivided into Sauternes which are rather sweet, and Graves which are dry. *See* WINE.

BORDELAISE SAUCE. A rich sauce for red meat.

BORDELAISE SAUCE

Streaky salt pork or mild bacon
2 or 3 carrots
2 onions
1 stalk thyme
1 small bay leaf
1 cup white wine
2 or 3 whole shallots
6 whole peppercorns
Dash cayenne pepper
1 clove garlic
1 tbsp Espagnole sauce (which see)
Stock

Have a heavy iron pan or an earthenware casserole, not too large. Cover the bottom with thin slices of salt pork or bacon, cover these with diced carrots and onions, add thyme and bay leaf and place pan over a low heat to allow ingredients to sweat gently—that is, to bring out their juices slowly. When this is accomplished, add the wine, the whole shallots, peppercorns, a dash of cayenne, salt, if needed, and the garlic finely minced. Cook this very gently until the gravy produced is brown and sticky. Add the Espagnole Sauce and enough stock for your requirements. Boil up gently, skim to remove surface fat, and strain the sauce through a fine strainer. Return to pan and again reduce sauce by slow cooking. If preferred, red Bordeaux may be used instead of white wine. In this case, add a little lemon juice and some chopped parsley when serving. This sauce must be rather highly seasoned. It can be improved by adding at time of serving some poached beef marrow, cut into cubes, and a squeeze of lemon. (Makes approximately 1 cup)

BORECOLE. Another name for KALE, *which see.*

BORIC ACID. A white, crystalline compound, obtained from volcanic lagoons of Italy; also found in chemical combinations such as borax. According to the U.S. Pharmacopoeia, its use as food is forbidden.

BORSCHT. A Russian dish—a kind of stew made of duck, beef, and sausages, all cut into small sections, cooked in meat stock, and blended with *kwas* (beet juice) and sour cream, and garnished with shredded, cooked leeks, beets, and celery root. It may be served with *wastrousky*, a kind of rissoles, made of pastry stuffed with a paste made of cottage cheese, enriched with butter and egg yolks.

Borscht may also be applied to a soup, originally of Russia, Poland and Balkan countries, made of beets, water, onions, spareribs, lemon juice, and cream (Polish method). It is served either hot or cold. The Russian recipe contains breast of beef, water, and liquid from cooked beets, leeks cabbage, parsnip, celery, butter, salt, pepper, marjoram, and fennel. A heavy sour cream (three tablespoons for each serving) is offered as a garnish, and a whole boiled potato is placed in each serving plate of the soup.

BORSCHT

6 cups beef broth
1 cup each shredded carrots and beets
1 cup thinly sliced onions
1½ cups shredded cabbage
1 green pepper, shredded
Salt and pepper
½ cup canned tomatoes
½ cup thick sour cream

Combine the strained broth, carrots, beets and onions in a large saucepan and cook gently until tender. Add the cabbage, green pepper, salt and pepper to season rather highly, and cook 5 minutes or until the cabbage begins to soften, after which stir in the tomatoes and cook 5 minutes more. Serve in soup plates with a spoonful of thick sour cream on each portion. Dark rye bread thinly sliced should be passed with the soup. The soup will have a richer flavor if made some hours ahead of serving time and reheated. (Serves 6)

BOSTON BROWN BREAD. A moist, brown bread which is cooked by steaming rather than by baking. *See* BREAD.

BOSTON BUTT. The unsmoked, square cut from above the shoulder of pork. *See* HAM.

BOTTLED GAS. A natural or manufactured gas that comes compressed in portable steel tanks. It is used extensively in rural districts for cooking. *See* RANGES.

BOTTLED GAS RANGE. A gas range adapted to the use of bottled gas, *which see. See also* RANGE.

BOTTOMS. The lees or dregs that are formed in a bottle of wine by sediment. *See* WINE.

BOUCHE. A French word meaning *corked*, as in the case of a bottle.

BOUCHEE. (boo sha) A French term for small patty shells filled with meat or fish and usually served as appetizers.

BOUDANNE CHEESE. A French cheese made from cow's milk, either whole or skimmed. It is usually about eight inches in diameter and three inches high.

BOUILLABAISSE. (bool ya bas) No wine or liquor enters into the preparation of this interesting chowder, or stew, which originated in Marseilles, France. The original recipe called for twelve different kinds of fish listed below with corresponding English names or the name of the fish which may be substituted for those not available in any part of America.

1. Baudroie (Frog-Fish, also called Sea-Devil)
2. Congre (Conger, Conger Eel).
3. Dorade (Dory, also sometimes called John Dory).
4. Fielan (unknown in America). Small eel may be substituted.
5. Galiente (unknown in America). Substitute Grouper.
6. Grondin (Red Gurnard).
7. Langouste (Spiny lobster).
8. Merlan (Whiting).
9. Rascasse (unknown in America). Sea Bass may be substituted.
10. Rouquier (unknown in America). Eel may be used.
11. Sard (unknown in America). Substitute Haddock or Codfish.
12. Turbot (often erroneously called Halibut). Turbotin, a young Turbot.

BOUILLABAISSE A LA MARSEILLES I

½ cup olive oil
4 oz minced onion
2 oz leeks, chopped fine (white part only)
2 medium-sized fresh tomatoes (peeled and diced)
4 whole cloves of garlic (crushed)
1 tsp finely minced parsley
1 generous pinch saffron
1 large bay leaf
1 small sprig sarriette (common marum savory)
Salt and pepper
1 pinch of the top of fresh fennel

Heat the olive oil. Add all ingredients save the fish and cook until vegetables are transparent.

Add about 6 pounds of the above mentioned fish or substitutes, equal amounts of each variety. Cut the large fish into pieces, leave the smaller ones whole. (The whiting and red gurnard, being very tender, should be added only when the bouillabaisse has been boiling from 8 to 10 minutes.) Pour in sufficient cold water to cover the fish; season it with salt and pepper to taste, and let cook over a hot fire for 12 to 15 minutes. Place several slices of plain bread on a hot deep platter, preferably round. Pour the liquid over these and, on another platter arrange the fish, garnishing with the pieces of lobster. (Serves 6 generously)

Needless to say, this is a very filling dish —truly a meal in itself.

BOUILLABAISSE A LA MARSEILLES II

4½ pounds very fresh fish (see list) including a lobster if desired
2 large onions
3 whites of leeks
6 sliced tomatoes
2 or 3 cloves of garlic
1 laurel leaf
Generous pinch of saffron
Handful fennel leaves, chopped fine
⅔ cup best olive oil
4 tsp salt
½ tsp pepper

Clean the fish and cut them into large pieces. If lobster is used have it quartered and dressed by the dealer, or it may be prepared at home as directed under lobster, *which see*.

Pour 4 tablespoons of olive oil into a shallow saucepan and brown lightly the onions and whites of leeks. Add the tomatoes, cloves, saffron, laurel and fennel leaves. Over all place the lobster and all of the fish excepting the tender-fleshed whiting and red gurnard. Cover well with boiling water and add the salt and pepper. Pour in the rest of the olive oil and bring to a violent boil over a very hot fire for 10 minutes. The fast boiling insures a thick, well blended sauce. Add the whiting and red gurnard and again bring to a boil for another 10 or 15 minutes. Dry in the oven some thick slices of bread, place them in a hot tureen and pour the sauce over them as soon as it is done. The fish and lobster are served on another hot dish, covered with more bread and sauce.

Serve a dry, heady white wine with this bouillabaisse.

BOUILLON (boo yonh'). A clear soup which may be made of various kinds of meat. See POT AU FEU and SOUP.

BOUILLON SPOON. *See* FLATWARE.

BOULANGERE. (boo lan jer) French name given to a leg of lamb placed in a large earthenware baking dish, surrounded with potatoes, and baked or roasted.

BOUQUET. In wines, the odor or aroma, caused by the oxidation of various acids in the presence of alcohol. Wines lacking in natural acidity, then, have little or no bouquet, as is the case of many Italian wines. The bouquet is one of the greatest attributes of a wine, enhancing its value as a source of enjoyment. The bouquet of any wine should be *clean*, i.e., having no trace of mold, vinegar or decay. If a wine has a bad bouquet, it should be thrown away. *See also* WINE.

BOUQUET GARNI. The bouquet garni is a bunch of herbs used to season soups, stews, braised dishes, and sauces. Parsley, thyme, and bay leaves always form the foundation, and various other herbs may be added to these. The bouquet is tied together with string or tied in a cheesecloth bag and cooked with the dish it is to season. Always remove before serving.

BOURBON WHISKY. Liquor distilled from a fermented mash which is more than half corn. The name comes from the fact that the first whisky distilled in Kentucky was made from corn ground at a mill in Bourbon County. *See* WHISKY.

BOURGUEIL. A red table wine from France. *See* WINE.

BOURGUIGNONNE SAUCE. *See* BROWN SAUCE.

BOWFISH, or BOWFIN. A small, voracious, dark-colored fish found in the Great Lakes region, the Mississippi River, and in the eastern states. It is known locally as grindle, dogfish, mudfish, lake lawyer, marsh fish, choupique, and willow pike. It prefers the weedy marshes, and seeks the boggy places at night, returning to deeper waters by day. It may be caught with a spear (if fishing by lantern at night) or by hand, since it chooses shallow places for spawning. The soft pasty flesh of the fresh bowfish is not generally liked, but when it is salted and smoked, it is a delicacy. It may then be prepared in the same way as Finnan Haddie, *which see*.

BOWL COVERS. Bowl covers are circular pieces of treated cloth or flexible plastic material that have elastic strips sewn around the edges. They are designed to fit snugly over the top of bowls, saucers, and similar dishes, providing a seal that is virtually airtight and watertight.

Bowl covers are commonly used to protect foods in refrigerated storage against the possibilities of dehydration (*see* REFRIGERATOR) and odor transfer (*see* ICE REFRIGERATOR). They may also be used to protect cut melons, and for insect and dust protection when foods are stored in the pantry or on a shelf.

PURCHASING BOWL COVERS

Bowl covers are usually sold in matched sets, and the housewife would do well to see that she has enough of each size to meet her normal requirements. Many different materials are used in their construction, but the material should be thick enough to offer reasonable wear. The buyer should inspect the manner in which the elastic is affixed to the material, for that is often the point that wears out first. *See also* KITCHEN EQUIPMENT.

BOYSENBERRY. A berry similar to the raspberry in appearance, but larger and with larger seeds. It may be used like the raspberry or blackberry.

BRA CHEESE. A small, mild, soft, creamy Italian cheese.

BRACHETTO. An Italian red wine made sometimes as a still wine and other times as a sparkling wine.

BRAIN. The brains of beef, calf, sheep, and pork are considered delicacies, with calf's brains being the choicest.

Because of their extremely perishable nature, brains should be rushed from the market to the refrigerator, if not the saucepan. Their texture is very delicate and some preliminary treatment, such as parboiling, is imperative. Parboiling in slightly acidulated water, followed by plunging into cold water, firms the soft tissue and makes handling easier. After parboiling, brains are ready for baking, either plain or wrapped in bacon; frying in deep or shallow fat; scrambling with eggs; baking in tiny pastry cases, or serving with a tart sauce. In France boiled brains are served chilled on lettuce with either French dressing, or oil and lemon juice.

To prepare brains for almost any dish, wash, remove the membranes, soak the brains for twenty minutes in cold salted water, and drain. Parboil for about 15 minutes in a quart of water with either 1 tablespoon of vinegar or 2 tablespoons of dry, white wine; a sprig of parsley, tied up with a small bay leaf and a small stalk of celery; and 1 teaspoon of salt. If desired, a slice of onion and some slightly bruised peppercorns may also be added. Drain the cooked brains and pat dry. The brains may now be fried oyster style, or baked in the oven, after being dipped into seasoned flour, then into egg, and last into fine crumbs (bread, cracker, or even corn meal). If preferred, pour melted butter, or black butter (*which see*) over the breaded brains, and bake in a moderate oven (350° F.) until the crumbs are brown. Serve with a tart sauce—tartare, tomato, vinaigrette,

etc. Served in popover cases, in scrambled eggs, or with risotto, brains are a delicious addition to any meal.

BRAISE. Usually composed of a cup of coarsely chopped carrots, onion, and celery in equal parts; 1 bouquet garni (*which see*); a small bit of garlic, $\frac{1}{2}$ to $\frac{3}{4}$ cup of cold, cooked, chopped ham or ham trimmings, and 1 cup of liquid which may be either consommé, meat, or vegetable stock or fish or fruit stock for each 3 pounds of meat, fish, or vegetables. *See also* BRAISING.

BRAISIER. A cooking pot with a tight-fitting cover used especially for braising.

BRAISING. A method of cooking meat, fish, or vegetables in moist heat in a covered vessel at a temperature just below boiling. It is of value especially for cooking tough meat or meat which is too fresh or too young. The cover of the kettle—braisier —is so arranged as to reduce evaporation to a minimum. The meat becomes tender and flavorful as a result of the long cooking with the liquids which may be of many kinds. Spices may be added when the cooking is almost completed. The amount of fluid should be only enough to cover the meat, fish, or vegetables, and in this way the surrounding broth remains concentrated. Sometimes meat or fowl which is to be braised is first partially roasted, or seared. *See* BRAISE.

BRAMBLEBERRY. The English blackberry. *See* BLACKBERRY.

BRAN. The ground husk, or outer coat of wheat or other grains obtained in the process of flour-making. Its principal use is as a food for live stock. It may also be mixed with white flour to make brown or imitation graham bread, and is widely employed as a laxative—eaten with cereals, plain, or in muffins.

Bran contains carbohydrate material and the nutritive salts of wheat. If too much bran is consumed, however, it hastens peristalsis, and nutrition suffers because the food is hurried out of the alimentary canal before absorption is complete. When bread is eaten with food containing nitrogen and salts, white bread is preferable. Bran cakes or muffins may be purchased which are prepared expressly for the use of diabetics. *See* FLOUR.

BRAN BATTER BREAD

1½ **cups wheat bran**
1½ **cups hot water**

1 tbsp shortening
1½ tsp salt
⅓ cup molasses
1 cake compressed yeast
½ cup lukewarm water
5 cups flour

Mix wheat bran, hot water, shortening, salt and molasses. Let stand until cool. Add yeast softened in lukewarm water. Sift in about ½ the flour; beat well; add remaining flour to make soft dough. Cover and let rise in a warm place until double in bulk (about 1¼ hours). Beat and pour into greased bread pan. Let rise again until it fills the pan (about 45 minutes). Bake in a hot oven (400° F.) for 15 minut s, then reduce heat to moderate (350° F.) and finish baking, about 25 or 30 minutes.

BRAN RAISIN MUFFINS

1 cup sifted flour
1 tsp baking powder
½ tsp baking soda
½ tsp salt
1½ cups bran
½ cup seeded halved raisins
1 egg, well beaten
½ cup molasses
¾ cup milk
2 tbsp melted shortening

Sift the flour, baking powder, soda and salt; stir in the bran and raisins, and moisten with the combined egg, molasses, milk and shortening. Stir only enough to thoroughly blend and bake in well greased muffin pans in a hot oven (400° F.) 20 to 25 minutes.

BRANDADE. A French method of preparing salt or fresh cod, *which see.*

BRAND CHEESE. A German hand cheese made from sour-milk curd. During the manufacturing process it is moistened with beer. It weighs about a pound.

BRANDIED. A food or a dessert to which brandy (*which see*) has been added; or a fruit preserve the sirup of which is brandied.

BRANDY. Derived from the older *brandywine* or *brandwine* meaning "burnt wine," i.e., a spirit distilled from wine, the name has been shortened to its present form and given a broader meaning. Even as "wines" are made from fruits other than grapes, so are brandies distilled from almost any carbohydrate food. As in the case of wine, if something other than grape is used in the making, the name of the used ingredient is usually included on the label on the bottle; thus, Blackberry Brandy, Cherry Brandy, Plum Brandy, etc. As a general rule, when just the word brandy is used, it refers to a spirit distilled from the grape; either from wine or from the *marc*, the residue left in the wine press (*See* WINE). Cognac (*which see*) is a pure wine brandy.

Brandies are made in a variety of ways. They may be a direct distillate or they may be a blend of various distillates, flavored neutral spirits, etc. They contain from 45 to 60 percent alcohol by weight and may be colored, sweetened or flavored by added ingredients. They are aged in wooden casks before bottling, usually a minimum of from three to four years. Brandies improve with aging, up to a point which varies with the brandy, when they begin to deteriorate and must be bottled to prevent further evaporation. They are usually of a pale, amber color, but may be darkened with caramel. *See also* CORDIAL and LIQUEUR.

BRANDY MOUSSE

1 cup heavy cream
5 tbsp powdered sugar
⅛ tsp salt
2 egg whites
1 tbsp brandy

Whip the cream until quite thick, fold in the sugar and salt and continue beating until the mixture is stiff. Fold in the stiffly beaten egg whites to which the brandy has been added. Turn into refrigerator tray and freeze about 4 hours, stirring and scraping down in the pan when the mixture begins to stiffen. If desired, rum, white wine or a liqueur may be substituted for the brandy. (Serves 4) *See* MOUSSE.

BRANDY SAUCE

¼ cup butter
1 cup powdered sugar
2 tbsp brandy
2 eggs, separated
½ cup light cream

Cream the butter and sugar, combine carefully with the brandy, the egg yolks and the cream beaten together. Cook over hot water until the mixture thickens, then pour onto the well beaten egg whites, folding these in until blended.

BRANDY SNAPS

½ cup butter
1⅓ cups brown sugar, firmly packed
¾ cup white corn syrup
⅛ tsp salt
1½ tsp ground ginger
2¾ cups sifted all-purpose flour

Place first five ingredients in top of double boiler. Heat over boiling water, stirring until butter is melted and ingredients are well blended. Remove from heat, cool slightly, then add flour. Blend thoroughly. Chill dough thoroughly, then divide in four portions. Roll out one portion at a time on a lightly floured board to a very thin sheet about 1/16-inch thick. Cut in 2 inch rounds, place on greased baking sheets about ½ inch apart. Bake in a moderately hot oven (400° F.) cake rack to cool. Stored in tightly covered containers, these cookies will keep for several months. (Makes about 11 dozen)

BRANDY INHALER. See GLASSWARE.

BRANZA DE BRAILA. A Rumanian cheese. Another name for Teleme cheese.

BRASENOSE ALE. A heated, sweetened, ale mixture that was traditionally served at Brasenose College, Oxford University, on Shrove Tuesday. It was served in a bowl which was passed around the refectory following dinner. Much the same tradition was followed at other colleges, using a similar beverage called lamb's wool (which see).

BRASENOSE ALE

3 qt heated ale
Powdered sugar to taste
6 roasted apples

Served in a large bowl with the apples floating in the ale. See also PUNCH, LOVING CUP, and WINE CUP.

BRATWURST SAUSAGE. A small pork sausage. See SAUSAGE.

BRAUNSCHWEIGER SAUSAGE. A liver sausage. See SAUSAGE.

BRAWN. The flesh of the boar (when boiled, pickled, and pressed) or veal and pork trimmings, seasoned, spiced, and pressed. It can be purchased in bulk, can,

or sausage form and is used like sausage.

BRAZIL NUT. A South American nut which grows along the Amazon river. The tree, an evergreen, reaches 120 to 150 feet in height, with a diameter of six feet. It has yellowish-white flowers. The fruits, which weigh from one and a half to three pounds and measure three to six inches in diameter, contain from 12 to 22 nuts.

The harvesting of the nuts begins early in January, and a single worker can sometimes collect fifty pounds or more of Brazil nuts in a day. The annual yield of a mature tree varies from two to four hundred fruits, but in exceptional cases a single tree has produced five hundred or a thousand pounds of nuts in a single year. After the fruits are opened, the nuts are spread in the sun to dry. They are then washed by placing the nuts in a basket and dipping them in the river; the bad nuts rise to the surface and float away. The bulk of the crop is exported in the shell.

The Brazil nut has been introduced into the East Indies, Africa, and the West Indies, but it has not reached commercial importance in these regions. In Brazil the oil of the nut is used by the natives for lighting and cooking, but the major portion of the yield is used for the export trade,

BRAZIL NUTS

A pound of Brazil nuts in the shell will give 1½ cups of meats. Brazil nuts are

with the cheese and put the stalks together in three's, making a roll. Press firmly together, wrap in wax paper, and chill in the refrigerator for several hours. When ready to serve, slice the celery into quarter-inch slices with a very sharp knife. Each slice will resemble a pinwheel, with the cheese holding the whorls together.

Cooked celery makes a fine vegetable. Sliced and cooked in boiling salted water, it will be tender in ten minutes. It may be served with butter, or with a cream or cheese sauce. Celery braised in a little bouillon is also delicious.

BAKED CELERY AU GRATIN

> 2 stalks of celery
> 1½ cups cream sauce
> ½ cup grated cheese
> Buttered crumbs
> Salt and pepper

Wash the celery thoroughly, trim off the leaves, and cut the stems into convenient lengths. Cook in boiling salted water until just tender, and drain well. Grease a baking dish. Make layers of celery, cream sauce, and grated cheese, adding salt and pepper to taste. Finish up with a layer of cheese. Cover the top with a thick layer of buttered crumbs, and bake in a hot oven (425° F.) until the top is brown and the sauce bubbles. (Serves 6)

BRAISED CELERY

Wash the celery thoroughly, remove the leaves, and cut into convenient pieces. Place in a baking dish with enough meat stock just to cover. Season with salt and pepper. Cover the dish and bake in a hot oven (400° F.) for 25 minutes, or until the celery is tender. Serve very hot from the dish in which it was baked.

CELERY-CHEESE BALLS

> 1 cup finely chopped celery
> 1 package (3 oz) cream cheese
> Salt and pepper
> 2 tbsp finely chopped parsley
> Paprika

Mix the celery and cheese, and add salt and pepper. Shape the mass into 12 small balls. Roll these in parsley and dust them with paprika.

CELERY REMOULADE

Cut tender bleached stalks of celery into julienne strips. Marinate for an hour in French dressing. Drain, pressing slightly to remove any excess liquid. Mix with remoulade dressing (*which see*). Serve as individual portions in crisp lettuce leaves. Sprinkle chopped parsley and chopped chives over the top. An excellent accompaniment for fish.

CELERY STUFFING
(For Chicken, Pork, Veal)

> 3½ cups soft bread crumbs
> ½ tsp salt
> ¼ tsp sage
> ⅛ tsp thyme
> Dash of marjoram
> ¼ tsp pepper
> 4 tbsp melted butter
> ⅔ cup hot milk
> ¾ cup celery, finely cut

Combine the crumbs and seasonings, add the butter, and toss with a fork, then add the milk and celery, mixing all lightly. *See* STUFFING.

CREAM OF CELERY SOUP

> 1 medium-size onion, minced
> 1½ cups diced celery and leaves
> 1 bouquet garni
> 1 tbsp butter
> 1 tbsp flour
> 2 cups milk
> Salt, pepper, nutmeg
> 1 egg yolk
> 2 cups cream or undiluted evaporated milk

Boil the onion, celery and bouquet garni in salted water to cover for 30 minutes, or until the celery is tender. Scald the 2 cups of milk. Melt the butter and stir in the flour, cooking until it bubbles. Carefully pour in the scalded milk, stirring so it does not lump. Add to the celery mixture and cook for 10 minutes. Strain through a sieve into the top of a double boiler, mashing the celery to a puree. Place over boiling water, season with salt, pepper, and nutmeg. Scald the cream or evaporated milk, stir into it the egg yolk, well beaten, and add to the celery mixture. Heat to the boiling point, but do not let boil. Serve garnished with croutons. If desired, a part of the cooked celery may be reserved as pieces and added to the soup just before serving. (Serves 4 or 5)

CURRIED CELERY FRITTERS

1 cup flour
1 tsp baking powder
½ tsp salt
2 tsp curry powder
1 egg
¾ cup milk
1½ cups chopped raw celery

Sift the flour, baking powder, salt, and curry powder into a mixing bowl. Beat the egg thoroughly and beat in the milk. Add to the flour mixture all at once, and stir to make a smooth batter. Add the chopped celery and stir well. Drop by spoonfuls into deep hot fat and fry until golden brown. Serve hot. Other vegetables may be substituted for the celery.

STUFFED CELERY

Use only crisp, tender, white stalks of celery, and wash these in running water. Leaves may be disposed of or left on the stalks. Cut each stalk into 2 to 4 pieces, depending upon its size. If you choose, you may curl the ends by making short, narrow, parallel cuts in them, and then chill ng the celery in ice water. Dry, fill the grooves with one of the following mixtures, and chill thoroughly before serving.

Cream-cheese filling. Mix ½ package of cream cheese, 2 tablespoons of mayonnaise, 4 chopped stuffed olives, 2 tablespoons of minced nuts, and salt to taste.

Blended-cheese filling. Mix 1 package (3 ounces) of cream cheese, 1 tablespoon of Roquefort cheese, 1 tablespoon of butter, and salt to taste. Sprinkle with paprika.

Egg filling. Mix 1 finely-chopped hard-cooked egg, 2 tablespoons of mayonnaise, and salt and pepper to taste. Dust with paprika or minced parsley.

CELERY CABBAGE. Another name for Chinese cabbage, *which see.*

CELERY DISH. A dish or small platter designed to hold and serve celery at the table. *See* DISHES.

CELERY KNOB or **CELERIAC.** A good inexpensive winter vegetable that is not very common is celery knob, a member of the celery family that is cultivated for its turnip-like stem base. Its flavor is like celery.

The smaller size knobs are best; larger ones are likely to be hollow or woody. It may be served raw or cooked. Celeriac is one of the few vegetables that must be peeled before cooking. The skin is very tough and stringy.

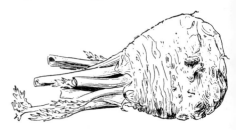

CELERY KNOB

Raw celery knob may be peeled and cut into julienne strips. Marinate the strips in French dressing for an hour, then drain, squeezing slightly to remove any excess liquid. Mix with mayonnaise and serve well chilled on crisp lettuce leaves. Drained crushed pineapple may be mixed with the celeriac.

Peeled and diced, celery knob may be cooked in boiling salted water and will be tender in ten minutes or so. A little vinegar or lemon juice added to the water will keep the celeriac white. The cooked celery knob can be served with butter or cream or hollandaise sauce, or it may be mashed. Like celery, it may be braised in meat stock.

CELERY KNOB BOURGEOISE

2 celery knobs
2 cups meat stock
4 tbsp butter or margarine
3 tbsp minced onion
2 tbsp minced green pepper
Salt and pepper
2 tbsp minced parsley
1 tbsp minced chives

Wash and peel the celery knob. Cut in small slices and simmer until tender in the meat stock. Drain and keep warm. In a saucepan, melt the butter and stir in the onion and green pepper. Cook, stirring constantly, until the onion and pepper soften. Add the celery knob and mix carefully so as not to break the pieces. Reheat and when ready to serve, season with salt

1 small onion and 2 anchovies very small. Cook in a little butter or margarine, and add ½ cup chicken stock, and a few drops of vinegar. Finish with 1 teaspoon chopped sweet herbs, and let simmer for a few minutes. Place the cauliflower in a serving dish and pour the sauce over it.

CAULIFLOWER POLONAISE

Cook the cauliflower, leaving the head whole. Melt 4 tablespoons butter or margarine and let brown. Stir in 2 hard-cooked eggs which have been finely chopped and 1 cup of fine bread crumbs. Mix well and pour over the cauliflower. Serve at once.

CAULIFLOWER SOUP

1 medium-sized cauliflower
2 tbsp butter or margarine
1 small onion, minced
2 tbsp flour
4 cups chicken stock
2 cups milk, scalded
Salt, pepper, and nutmeg

Steam the cauliflower until it is tender. Cut it in half. Press one half through a sieve and keep the other half warm. In a saucepan melt the butter and cook the onion until it is transparent, but not brown. Carefully stir in the flour and cook until it bubbles, stirring constantly. Add the chicken stock, stirring constantly. Mix the scalded milk with the sieved cauliflower, and stir it into the stock. Season with salt and pepper and a dash of nutmeg. Let boil up until it thickens slightly, stirring to prevent lumps. Break the half cauliflower into small flowerets and add to the soup. Heat thoroughly and serve immediately with croutons. (Serves 6 or 8)

CAVIAR. Caviar, in the strictest sense of the word, is the prepared roe of various species of sturgeon. But in recent years, the roe of various other fish has also been used to make caviar, because the supply of sturgeon roe has diminished to the point where it is entirely inadequate to meet the demand. These fish include: Spoon-bill, cat or paddlefish, salmon, whitefish, lake herring, carp, and codfish.

Only a comparatively few years ago the sturgeon was a very common fish in American waters. When caviar and smoked sturgeon became popular, the price of both these products rose rapidly, and fishermen found that sturgeon fishing was a very profitable occupation. As a result, the waters were overfished, and now the sturgeon has been nearly exterminated. Because of the scarcity of this fish, little caviar is prepared in the United States. In practically all cases, the fisherman who catches the female sturgeon prepares the caviar and either sells it to a local buyer or to one of the nearby wholesale markets.

The American process of preparing caviar is as follows: The sturgeon roe, immediately after its removal from the fish, is placed on a four-mesh sieve over a large mixing tube. The roe is rubbed back and forth on the sieve until the eggs pass through, leaving the membranes and connective tissue in the sieve. About a pound of Lunenburg salt or a half-pound of American dairy salt is sifted on to each 12 pounds of eggs. (Lunenburg salt is a German salt having a flavor particularly desirable in caviar.) Immediately after the addition of the salt, the mass is thoroughly mixed. At first it is sticky, but enough water is soon abstracted from the sturgeon eggs to dissolve the salt and form a brine. The mixing is continued for eight to ten minutes after which the mixture is allowed to stand 10 minutes or longer.

The eggs are then poured into sieves which hold eight to ten pounds of caviar and are allowed to drain for about an hour. The caviar is then poured into kegs and shipped to the canning factory where it is placed in cans or jars which are then sealed and pasteurized.

The methods used in Russia are much the same as those employed in America except that comparatively little is canned and much is prepared for export by pressing. Pressed caviar contains less water.

Genuine fresh caviar, made from sturgeon's roe, has large transparent grains of clear and brilliant color. It is considered a great delicacy and usually served as an appetizer on small crackers or bits of toast, with a simple garnish of sieved hard-cooked egg or onion juice. Perfectionists among gourmets insist that onion spoils the true flavor of the caviar.

Red caviar is made from the roe of the salmon.

CAVIAR BUTTER. *See* BUTTER SAUCES.
CAVY. *See* GUINEA PIG.
CAYENNE PEPPER. Cayenne pepper is a very hot, biting condiment that is

CELERIAC 238

ground from the fruits or seeds of several varieties of Capsicum (*which see*). Like paprika, it is a red powdery spice, but its color is not so bright as that of paprika. It should be used often but, because of its pungency, it should be used sparingly. It can accentuate delightfully the flavors of meat dishes, sea foods, soufflés, salads, sauces, and eggs.

CELERIAC. *See* CELERY KNOB.

CELERY

CELERY. The ancient Chinese credited celery with medicinal qualities and used it as a blood purifier. It was known in 16th-century Italy as an article of food, and spread from there to England and France, and eventually to America. In Chinese cookery celery is used as an ingredient to give crispness to their dishes.

Celery is ordinarily marketed as the whole stalk which contains the outer branches and leaves. Sometimes the outer branches are removed and the hearts are sold in bunches. Formerly celery was not

tender until it had been bleached, which gave the familiar white stalks and pale hearts with yellow leaves. Recently a new type of celery, known as pascal celery, is being grown for market. It needs no bleaching to be tender. It has an attractive light green color and is almost stringless, with a sweet flavor. Because it has not been bleached, it probably contains vitamins which are absent in the bleached plants.

Celery should be of medium length and thickness, with the branches brittle enough to snap easily. The leaves should be fresh looking. Limp branches and wilted or yellowed leaves indicate the celery has been kept too long.

The outer branches and leaves should not be discarded. They can be used in soup, for flavor in pot roasts, etc. The leaves, chopped finely, can be added to many dishes, and make a good substitute for celery seed in recipes calling for this seasoning.

HINTS ON PREPARATION

Celery should be thoroughly washed to remove any dirt which may lodge in the branches. If it is inclined to be stringy, the strings should be removed by pulling them down the length of the stalk.

The tender hearts of celery may be served as is, crisped by placing them in ice water in the refrigerator.

Celery curls make an attractive garnish. They are easily made by cutting tender celery into three- or four-inch length. Slit the pieces into narrow lengthwise slices, leaving a half inch base. Drop the pieces into ice water and place in the refrigerator for several hours. The narrow slices will curl back around the base. Celery stuffed with cheese, either roquefort-type, or any other easily spread tangy cheese, makes a favorite hors d'oeuvre.

For a special occasion, make celery pinwheels. Select tender stalks of even size. Mix roquefort-type cheese with cream cheese until it is soft and spreads easily. Or use the roquefort cheese spread which comes in jars. Fill the hollows of the stalk

FOOD VALUE

Water	Food Energy	Protein	Fat	Carbohydrate	Calcium	Phosphorus	Iron	Vit. A Value	Thiamine	Riboflavin	Niacin	Ascorbic Acid
93.7	22	1.3	.2	3.7	50	40	.5	0	.03	.04	.3	7

Lay on lightly floured board. Cover and allow to rest for about 10 minutes. Grease fingers lightly and roll each ball lightly back and forth until it becomes a cylinder of uniform thickness, 10 to 12 inches long, and not more than ⅜ inch thick. Lay on greased baking sheet. Cover and let rise until doubled in bulk (about 45 minutes). Using very light pressure, brush with mixture of one slightly beaten egg white blended with 1 tablespoon water. Leave plain, or with a very sharp knife make very shallow diagonal cuts across the top. Sprinkle with poppy or sesame seed if desired. Bake in a moderate oven (375° F.) until golden brown—from 8 to 10 minutes. Place a shallow pan of hot water on bottom of oven during baking to produce a crisp crust and beautiful brown color. For fancy bread sticks, make dough strips narrower and braid three together. Cut off ends neatly. Let rise until double in bulk, and bake in the same way.

CHAPATI
(Indian Bread)

Whole-wheat flour
Water
Salt

Put flour into a bowl and make a little indentation in the center. Add just enough water to make a very dry dough, adding a little salt. Knead well with the fingers and divide the dough into lumps the size of an egg. Roll out each on a floured board to the size and shape of a very thin pancake. Brown on both sides on an ungreased griddle. Press with a cloth before removing it from the griddle so that the air is expelled and the pancake automatically punctures. Eat the chapati while hot.

EASTER BREAD (RUSSIAN)

1 cup milk
1 lb all-purpose flour
6 oz butter
6 oz sugar
6 yolks of egg
4½ oz candied fruit
1 oz yeast

Dissolve the yeast in the warm milk, mix with half the flour and let it rise. Beat up the yolks of eggs with the sugar, and when the dough has risen mix the eggs with it

and the butter, melted. Then add the rest of the flour and the chopped fruit. Beat the mixture well and leave to rise again. Form into a long loaf or twist and bake in fairly quick oven (400° F.).

FIVE HOUR BREAD

2 cups scalded milk or boiled water
2 tbsp of butter, margarine or lard
2 tbsp sugar
1 tsp salt
1 cake compressed yeast
½ cup lukewarm milk
6 to 8 cups all-purpose flour

Add the sugar, shortening, and salt to the hot milk, and when lukewarm, add the yeast which has been dissolved in the ½ cup lukewarm milk. Then add enough flour to make a dough and knead and leave to rise in a warm place. The dough will be ready in about 3 hours. Form into loaves and place in greased pans. Leave to rise for 1 hour more. Bake in a moderately hot oven (375° F.) for 60 minutes. (Makes 2 loaves)

FRENCH BREAD

1 package dry granular yeast or 1 cake compressed yeast
1 cup lukewarm water
2 tsp sugar
1½ tsp salt
1 tbsp shortening
4 cups sifted all-purpose flour
1 egg white, beaten

Soften yeast in ¼ cup of the water. Let stand 10 minutes. To the remaining water add sugar, salt, shortening and 1 cup of the flour. Beat until very smooth. Add the yeast mixture and stir well. Thoroughly fold in egg white, then add flour to make a stiff dough. Turn out on lightly floured board, and knead until smooth and satiny, about 10 minutes. Place in a greased bowl, turn once to bring greased side up. Cover and let stand in a warm place (86° F.) out of drafts to rise until double in bulk (about 1 hour). Knead down.

If a Vienna or French loaf is to be made, cover and let rest 10 minutes; then form into a narrow rounded loaf about 14 inches long. Place on greased baking sheet on which white cornmeal or farina has been sprinkled. Make diagonal cuts with a very sharp knife every 2 inches about ⅛ inch deep.

If hard crusted rolls are to be made, divide kneaded dough into 18 portions. Cover and let rest 15 minutes. Form into rolls (Vienna Style) and place them 2½ inches apart on baking sheet treated as above. Brush rolls or loaf with a mixture of one slightly beaten egg white and 1 tablespoon water. Cover pans with damp cloth and let rise until double in size. Bake rolls in a moderately hot oven (375° F.) for 1 hour. Place shallow pan of boiling water on floor of oven to produce crustiness on loaf or rolls. After 10 minutes in oven, brush again with egg white mixture. After 20 minutes baking, brush again with egg white mixture. (Makes 1 large Vienna or French loaf or 18 small rolls)

HONEY FRENCH BREAD

1 to 1½ envelopes granulated yeast
½ cup lukewarm water
2 cups milk
2 tbsp butter
1 tbsp honey
1 tsp salt
5 cups all-purpose flour

Mix yeast with lukewarm water. Heat milk until lukewarm and add butter, honey and salt. When the butter is melted, add the yeast and water mixture and then mix in 5 cups of flour. Knead until the dough is smooth and does not stick to hands. Place the dough in a bowl, cover, and let rise in a warm place for about 2 hours, or until double in bulk. If the dough falls when touched lightly with the fingers, it has risen enough. Punch it down and let rise again for 45 minutes. Knead again, divide the dough in 3 parts, and shape into long cylinders about 1½ inches in diameter. Cover and let the loaves rise until double in bulk. Cut small diagonal slits about ¼ inch deep in the top of the loaves when half risen. Before baking, brush them with a little milk. Bake in a hot oven (400° F.) until they are crisp and golden. (Makes 2 loaves)

LIMPA (SWEDISH)

1 tsp granulated sugar
¼ cup lukewarm water
2 tsp caraway seed
1 tbsp salt

1 package dry granular yeast or 1 cake compressed yeast
1/3 cup brown sugar, or dark molasses
2 tsp grated orange rind
1¼ cups milk, scalded
½ cup water
3¼ cups sifted all-purpose flour
3 tbsp melted shortening
3 cups sifted rye flour

Stir the sugar into the lukewarm water. Add yeast and let stand 10 minutes. Add caraway seed, salt, sugar (or molasses) and orange rind to hot milk and cool to lukewarm. Combine milk mixture, water and yeast mixture and beat well. Add all but ¼ cup of the white flour and beat vigorously. Add cooled shortening and beat well. Stir in rye flour gradually to make a stiff dough. Sprinkle board with remaining flour, and turn out dough. Cover dough with bowl, let rest on board for 10 minutes. Knead quickly and lightly for 10 minutes. Round up into a ball and place in a greased bowl. Turn once to grease top. Cover and set in a warm place (86° F.) free from drafts until dough has doubled in bulk (1½ hours). Divide dough in half, round up each portion, cover and let rest for 10 minutes. Shape into loaves. Place in greased bread pans (8¼ by 4½ by 2¾ inches). Cover and let rise until double in bulk (1½ hours). Bake in a moderately hot oven (400° F.) 10 minutes. Reduce heat to moderate (375° F.) and continue baking for 40 minutes. Remove to cooling rack. Cool uncovered out of a draft. (Makes 2 loaves)

RYE BREAD

2 cups milk
1 tsp salt
3 tbsp brown sugar or ¼ cup molasses
2 yeast cakes
3 cups white flour
3 cups rye flour
1 tbsp caraway seeds

Scald 2 cups milk, add salt and brown sugar or molasses. Cool and add 2 cakes crumbled yeast. Stir in 3 cups white flour. Beat well and then stir in 3 cups rye flour. When smooth, turn dough onto lightly floured board and knead until elastic. Place in greased bowl, cover, and let rise until double in bulk. Add caraway seeds to dough, knead and shape into two loaves.

Place in greased pans, brush with butter and let rise until double in bulk. Bake in a moderately hot oven (375° F.) 45 to 60 minutes. The white flour may be reduced to 1 cup and 5 cups rye flour, used. This dough must be beaten. Unlike wheat breads, it will not be stiff enough to knead. (Makes 2 loaves)

SALT RISIN' BREAD

1 cup whole milk
2 tbsp granulated sugar
1½ tsp salt
⅓ cup white corn meal
1 cup lukewarm water
4¼ cups sifted all-purpose flour
2 tbsp lard

Scald milk. Remove from fire and stir in 1 tablespoon granulated sugar, the salt, and corn meal. Mix thoroughly and turn into a 2-quart jar or pitcher; cover, and set in a pan of water which is hot to the hand, or 120° F. Let the mixture stand, in the hot water, in a warm place for 6 to 7 hours, or until it has fermented.

When the gas escapes freely, stir in the water mixed with 1 tablespoon granulated sugar. Then stir in 2 cups sifted flour and beat thoroughly. Return the jar to the hot water bath (120° F.) and let the sponge rise until it is very light and full of bubbles. Turn the sponge at once into a large, warm mixing bowl and gradually stir in 2¼ cups sifted white bread flour, or just enough to make a stiff dough. Divide the dough in half, shape into loaves, and place in bread pans that have been generously greased with lard.

Note that so far no fat has been used. Now brush the loaves with 2 tablespoons lard melted to spreading consistency. Cover the two loaves with a light, clean, dry towel (or a double thickness of cheese-cloth), and let them rise in a warm place until the dough is 2½ times its original bulk. Bake in the oven at 375° F. for 10 minutes only, then lower the heat to moderate (350° F.) and continue baking for 25 minutes longer. You should further note that the sponge and dough of salt risin' bread require a higher temperature (120° F.) for rising than yeast mixtures. After the rising, the temperature of 120° F. should be kept as steady as possible. Home-made salt-risin' bread is not so light as yeast bread is, but it is moist and crumbly.

SODA BREAD
(Irish)

2 lb all-purpose flour
1 tsp bicarbonate of soda
1 cup sour milk or buttermilk
1 tsp salt
1 tsp cream of tartar

Mix together the dry ingredients and sift into a mixing bowl. Make a well in the center and stir in the milk, adding a little more if the mixture is too dry.

Mix well into a rather stiff dough. Divide into two and shape into rounds, prick the top with a fork and put in a greased, floured pan. Bake in a moderate oven (350° F.) for ¾ hour. (Makes 2 loaves)

WHITE BREAD

1 yeast cake
1 tbsp sugar
2 tbsp melted butter or shortening
2 tsp salt
6½ cups flour
2 cups lukewarm water

Add the sugar to the water, and stir in the broken yeast. When dissolved thoroughly, set it aside for about 10 minutes. Add the melted butter and salt; then gradually stir in 3 cups of flour and beat until smooth. Add balance of the flour, reserving some to place on the board. Knead dough on floured board until smooth and elastic and until all the flour is worked in. Place it in greased bowl, cover, and set it aside in warm place for about 2 hours, or until well risen. Mold it in two loaves, place them in well-greased bread pans, filling half full. Make a slight incision down center of each loaf. Cover, and let rise 1 hour or more. Bake in moderately hot oven from 45 to 60 minutes. (For milk bread substitute 2 cups of milk for the water plus ¼ cup water.) (Makes 2 loaves)

100% WHOLE WHEAT BREAD

½ cup brown sugar
⅔ cup lukewarm water
2 packages dry granular yeast or 2 cakes compressed yeast
1 tbsp salt
2 cups milk, scalded
6½ cups unsifted whole wheat flour
2 tbsp melted shortening

Stir 1 teaspoon of the sugar into the water; add yeast and let stand 10 minutes. Stir to blend well. Add remaining sugar and the salt to hot milk and cool to luke-warm. Stir softened yeast and add milk mixture and blend. Stir in 3 cups of the flour; add shortening and mix well. Add remaining flour gradually and mix thoroughly. Turn onto lightly floured board (use 2 tablespoons of all-purpose flour for kneading and shaping loaves) and knead 10 minutes. Place in a clean greased bowl; turn once to bring greased side up. Cover and allow to rise in a warm place (86° F.) away from drafts until doubled in bulk (about 1 hour). Turn out onto board again, divide in half. Round up each portion, cover, let rest 10 minutes. Shape into loaves and grease tops. Place in well greased pans (4½ by 8¼ by 2¾ inches.) Cover and set in warm place (86° F.) until light, and rounded tops come above sides of pans (about 1 hour). Bake in a moderately hot oven (400° F.) for 10 minutes. Reduce heat to moderate (375° F.) and bake 40 minutes longer. Remove from pan to wire rack; cool uncovered away from drafts. (Makes 2 loaves)

BREAD BOARD. A small, smooth, wooden board on which bread and other foods may be cut and sliced. It offers protection both to the knife edge and to table tops and other surfaces that would otherwise be endangered as the bread was sliced, as well as collecting the crumbs on an easily cleaned surface.

PURCHASING

The cost of the board is determined by the value of the wood that is used. Any reasonably hard wood will suffice, unless the housewife desires an ornate model for display purposes. The boards are usually made of several assembled pieces rather than a single slab of wood, so the manner of construction should be inspected. The board should be smooth, especially at the edges where there is danger of splinters, and the pieces should be joined evenly and without cracks, lest they offer crevices in which dirt and grease might collect.

CARE

If practical, it is wise to have separate cutting boards for bread, meat, and heavy duty chopping. The board should be wiped clean with a damp cloth; never washed, for excess moisture will cause warping and swelling. *See also* KITCHEN EQUIPMENT.

BREAD BOX. A ventilated box, usually built of sheet metal, that is used to store bread, rolls, etc. These boxes should be given a cool, shaded, dry location, and they are so designed as to give bread the proper amount of ventilation, postponing staleness and preventing mustiness. They are sometimes provided as part of a permanent kitchen cabinet, and are also available as separate units. *See also* BREAD and KITCHEN EQUIPMENT.

BREAD AND BUTTER PLATE. A flat plate, usually five inches in diameter, that is used to hold individual slices of bread and butter during the meal. It is placed to the left and rear of the dinner plate, with the butter knife resting on it. *See* DISHES, *see also* TABLE SETTING AND SERVICE.

BREAD CRUMBS. Bread crumbs have a place in a number of steamed and baked puddings. Some recipes call for soft crumbs and others for dry crumbs. Bread crumbs and fruit combine well in certain desserts such as Bettys. Dry bread crumbs are used as a topping for scalloped dishes, for coating croquettes, fish, and cutlets, and in place of part of the flour in many steamed desserts, muffins, unbaked pie shells, etc. If bread becomes stale, it can be thoroughly dried in a slow oven, rolled, and put through a sieve. For white crumbs, remove the crusts before drying. Soft bread crumbs are crumbs taken from the inside of a loaf of soft or fresh bread without including the crust. Bread crumbs may, or may not, be soaked in water, milk, or indicated liquid, but usually only the dry crumbs are soaked. Either dry or soft crumbs may be used as a topping. For au gratin seafood dishes, such as crabmeat au gratin or oyster scallop, bread crumbs make a perfect topping.

PREPARING BREAD CRUMBS

Save the bread for crumbs in a paper bag. Keep it tied and hanging so that the air can circulate through it, rather than in the bread box or a closed jar where it soon becomes moldy. Do not include buttered pieces of bread, as the butter soon becomes rancid. For fine, dry crumbs, put dried bread in a cloth bag, tie the open end, and roll it on a board with a rolling pin. Sift and re-roll the coarse crumbs.

white, sweet, and juicy flesh, without aroma. Only in a ripe melon can such quality be found.

Ripeness is usually indicated by a rind of yellow color and a softening at the blossom end. Immaturity is indicated by firmness and the whitish-green color of rind. The flesh of such melons is hard and often practically tasteless. Decay usually is in the form of dark, sunken, water-soaked patches that may be covered with a mold. The flesh of a melon affected by decay is not harmed if decay has not penetrated the rind. *See also* MELON.

CASEIN. The principal protein of milk, *which see.*

CASHEW NUT. A recent comer among nuts in the United States, the cashew nut, is now second in popularity to the peanut. As recently as 1923, only 100,000 pounds of these nuts were imported into the United States. Fifteen years later the story was very different; shipments for the year 1938 were more than 25,000,000 pounds. The natives of India and Haiti use the juice of the cashew nut for healing cuts and abrasions of the skin, besides eating it as a nut.

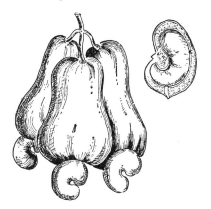

CASHEW NUT

To bring the cashews from India and still retain their tree-fresh taste was once thought to be impossible. Attempts at shipping cashew nuts usually ended in half or more of the shipment being flavorless and unfit for eating after the long voyage. But then came the cashews which are shipped in airtight tins. Now the cashew nuts on the market are packed by this special patented process and are always clean, tree-fresh, and full flavored.

The nut, either pickled or roasted, acquires a delicate flavor only after it is heated to a high temperature to drive off a considerable quantity of prussic acid which it naturally contains. This, however, is completely gone before the nut is released for commerce or offered as food.

The cashew does not grow in a shell at all, but instead is found hanging from an apple-like fruit on a kind of evergreen tree. The "apple" contains a milky juice which when fermented makes a delicious wine, and the wine distills to a spirit very much like rum.

Cashew nuts are used salted or in candy. They are not too satisfactory in baking because of their tendency to soften. A pound of cashews will yield four cups. *See also* NUTS.

CASING. The covering skin of sausage.

CASSAVA. *See* TAPIOCA.

CASSEROLE

CASSEROLE. A kitchen utensil, usually a shallow double-handled dish with a tightly fitting cover, which may be made of earthenware, glass, or metal. Also, the dish cooked in such a utensil.

Methods of cookery have much to do with results of the final dish. This is especially true when cooking meats, which fall broadly into two classes of prime and tougher cuts. How to make tougher cuts as tender and flavorful as choicer, more expensive prime cuts, is a problem for every homemaker. Good seasoning is one answer, and casserole cooking is another.

The casserole as a cooking utensil has an age-old history, and takes its historic place alongside other primitive pottery cooking vessels. Originally fashioned of clay or brick pottery, the earthenware casserole is still decidedly worthwhile as a cooking unit. It may be small or large, squat or high, but it isn't a casserole if it hasn't a cover. Only when there is a closely fitting cover, to prevent escape of food flavors, may the utensil be called a "casserole."

Those who advocate casserole cookery, point to the French, respected the world over for the excellence of their food, who through the ages have used casseroles, or pots and pans slow to heat and long to retain heat. It is to French pottery, finished within with a salt glaze; to the more costly copper, lined with block tin; to the cast-iron cocotte, the forerunner of the useful Dutch oven, that we owe such pleasures as the *made* French casserole dishes, or a potted duck. Snugly covered in one of these utensils, which may be put into the oven or used on top of the stove, food cooks with the minimum of labor to a home-maker, plus the maximum of flavor. She doesn't have to watch things while they are cooking either.

The casserole is brought to the table and the food served directly from it.

In contrast to the classic French casserole cookery, in which raw foods are cooked slowly inside a tightly lidded pot, the common or American-style casserole employs pre-cooked foods which are reheated together in an open baker or casserole dish. The American-style casserole, a noted budget and meal saver, provides the cook with an opportunity to utilize leftovers in an imaginative fashion.

Since most of the foods used in a casserole are pre-cooked or quick cooking, the actual cooking time of the dish should be kept short in order to insure the fullest flavor and nutritive value. Pre-cooked meats retain much of their natural juices which can be extracted if the meat is reheated at too high a temperature or for too long a time. The meat becomes shrivelled and the gravy, consequently, becomes thin.

Cooking temperatures should, therefore, not be allowed to rise above the simmering point. The casserole must be cooked uncovered to prevent sogginess. A gratinée crust is usually employed to protect the food, absorb excess grease and give the dish body. Casseroles may be cooked in a heat resistant utensil on top of the stove and then returned to the broiler to crisp the gratinée topping or they may be cooked from beginning to end in an uncovered casserole dish in the oven.

INGREDIENTS

While casserole ingredients vary with whatever is at hand, the dish itself usually combines two or three types of foods: pasta or rice, a mixture of vegetables and meats and a sauce. Often the pasta is omitted in favor of increased portions of meats and vegetables. The sauce may be cream, medium white, tomato, vinegar or brown gravy.

Cooked, frozen or diced fresh vegetables are used. If canned vegetables are used, they should be drained and added as near to the end of the cooking time as possible. Reserve the drained juices for making sauces or soups. In general, pre-cooked or canned meats, sausages, poultry and fish are used in a casserole, but fresh meats may be used if they are quick cooking.

Select seasoning appropriate to the various meats and vegetables: basil for lamb; thyme, savory and marjoram for chicken and veal; dill, caraway and basil for pork and fish; oregano for tomato sauce; coriander and cumin for gravies and white sauce. Use herbs and spices liberally.

BASIC RECIPE

A basic casserole recipe calls for about 2 cups of sauce, 1½ cups of meats and vegetables and 1 cup of pasta or rice. Proportions vary with different ingredients but in general the casserole should contain enough sauce to cover the other ingredients but not so much sauce that the dish becomes soggy.

Prepare the sauce in a large saucepan or heat resistant casserole and season. Add the frozen and fresh vegetables and cook until almost tender (about 5 minutes). Correct the seasoning. Stir in meats, canned or pre-cooked vegetables, rice or pasta. Turn the mixture into a casserole. Wipe the outside of the casserole before placing it in the oven so that no spilt-over burned food will be apparent when the dish is baked. Top with a mixture of buttered bread crumbs, crumbled Cheddar and paprika. Bake 15 to 20 minutes. Serve.

Substitute ingredients on hand for those listed in the basic recipe. Also see the index for listings of casserole recipes.

CHICKEN IN TOMATO SAUCE

Prepare a tomato sauce or use canned sauce or condensed tomato soup. Cut up onions, green pepper and carrots and add

straight down between the ribs (which may be garnished with paper frills, according to taste). If a stuffing is used, a portion of the stuffing should be given with each serving.

CARVING LEG OF LAMB

Rib Roast of lamb may be carved like a loin of veal.

PORK

Roast *Loin* of pork may be served with or without the tenderl in. The butcher should remove the back bone, and the rib bones should be carefully cut apart before cooking. As to its position on the platter, opinions differ. Some say meat uppermost; others, the reverse. It is really immaterial, but the carver must cut down between each two ribs, allowing one to each serving. Sometimes, when thinner slices are desired one slice may be cut with a bone, the next without.

With *Ham* a bone runs through near the center; the broader side gives the best cuts. A small, thick slice is often taken almost at right angles to the bone, served with a little portion of fat. Or the carver may begin at the thick end of the ham and proceed to cut thin slices right on to the narrow end.

Smithfield Ham is so rich and tender that very few thin slices give an ample serving. It is best to start at the back, letting the first cut be straight to the bone. A very sharp knife is needed.

FISH

On the whole, fish requires little carving. It is best to cut it with a silver server since other metal may affect the flavor. Care should be taken to preserve the large flakes if possible. The choicest portions are generally in the middle of a large fish. A planked fish should be cut through the center lengthwise. Small fish should be served individually without carving. A stuffed fish should have skewers and strings removed before serving. The cut being made from head to tail, the backbone is left on the platter.

Mackerel and *Bluefish*, split before cooking, are divided lengthwise, then subdivided into smaller portions.

Halibut is bought and served sliced, and is easy to cut lengthwise and crosswise to the small bone in the center.

Salmon, whether hot or cold, may be served whole. The head at the left is best, and slices should be cut starting at the central bones. Do not remove the skin; cut through it. Both the solid back flesh and the flakier portions belong in each portion.

Cod may be cut like salmon, but it breaks apart more easily.

POULTRY

Capon. A capon is carved somewhat like a turkey; that is, the legs should be separated from the body in a similar fashion,

CARVING HAM

and the dark meat of the second joint put aside to be served with the filets, which will be cut out of each side of the breast. One should be able to carve four or five filets from the breast on each side.

A simple trick in slicing the breast makes it easy to carve a fowl, be it a capon, chicken, turkey, or duck. Make deep cuts on the breast (about two inches apart) through the skin and flesh and down to the bone. Start the cuts at the ridge in the middle of the breast and go down the side at right angles to the ridge. Each of the sections of breast meat can then be lifted off and will have a layer of browned skin and rich fat on top.

CARVING TURKEY

Duck. Many a promising meal has gone to wreck because, when the duck is set before the head of the family, confusion is brought upon him by a shrill voice uttering these lines, ". . . We all of us prepare to rise when father carves the duck. . ." However, although the carving of a duck, goose, or pheasant is a little more complicated than that of a chicken, it is very easy after a little practice.

Place the duck on the platter with the tail to your left. Insert the fork between the right drumstick and thigh. Now run the point of a sharp knife around the leg, cutting the skin, using the fork to raise the leg toward yourself. Then place the knife underneath the leg and cut straight toward the tail, raising the leg with the point of the knife until you find the joint. Cut across the joint and remove the leg. Now insert the point of the fork in the bottom of the right wing, and carve from the top of the breast down to the wing joint, which you then easily sever with the point of the knife. Remove the left leg and wing in the same fashion. If the duck is large enough, slice the breasts. If it is small, split it from tail to neck and then cut across it, providing four portions. Proceed without haste, but with speed.

Goose. Because the goose is more fatty, the carving is easier. After removing the legs as indicated for duck, the breast slices are made directly from the top of the breastbone downward to the end of the wing.

Turkey. Carve a turkey exactly as you would carve a capon. However, since the wings and legs of a turkey (drumsticks) are more fleshy, slices may be carved from them.

Chicken. Carve a chicken exactly as you would carve a capon.

Small wild birds. Small wild birds are carefully split in two lengthwise from the breastbone downward. Then the legs and second joints are removed.

CARVING AID. A carving aid consists of a pair of stainless steel or plated metal prongs set in a handle. It is used to impale fowl and irregularly shaped meats to hold them steady for ease in carving. *See also* CARVING and CUTLERY.

CARVING KNIFE. *See* CUTLERY and CARVING.

CASABA MELON

CASABA MELON. A late variety of melon, which is usually ripened off the vine. It is large, almost globular, but may be somewhat pointed at the stem end. The rind is lightly ribbed and is somewhat wrinkled or furrowed lengthwise. Casaba melons of good quality have a soft, cream-

BROCCOLI SOUFFLE

⅓ cup butter
¼ cup flour
½ cup sweet heavy cream
½ cup chicken bouillon
3 egg yolks, well beaten
4 egg whites, stiffly beaten
1 tsp finely minced parsley
1 tsp finely minced chives
Salt and pepper
1½ cups cooked sieved broccoli
⅓ cup grated American cheese

Scald the cream with the chicken bouillon. Melt the butter and blend in the flour. Gradually stir in the liquid, and cook, stirring constantly, until the mixture thickens. Remove from the fire and add the egg yolks, parsley, and chives, and season with salt and pepper. Stir in the broccoli puree and the grated cheese. Lastly fold in the beaten whites of the eggs and turn into a buttered soufflé dish. Bake in a hot oven (400°–425° F.) for 25 minutes. Serve immediately. (Serves 4)

BROCCIO. A sour-milk cheese, made from sheep's milk. Made in Corsica.

BROCHETTE. A French term, meaning "skewered." *See also* KEBAB.

BROILER. (I) A young chicken, fit for broiling. *See* CHICKEN.

BROILER. (II) A broiler is a covered metal pan fitted with a wire rack, in which meats may be broiled. In most cases, the rack may be removed and the pan will double as a roaster. Broilers may also have a sizzling platter (*which see*) instead of a wire rack. The common broiler is designed to be used in the oven of a kitchen range, but there are special electrical units that incorporate a heating unit and are complete cooking devices in themselves. Broilers of this sort are equipped with controls and may be used to cook the food right at the table. *See also* RANGE, KITCHEN EQUIPMENT and ELECTRIC EQUIPMENT.

BROILING. The process of broiling or grilling is performed under a very hot flame or over hot coals or charcoal. A coating of coagulated albumin forms upon the outer surface of the meat while the albuminous material, or myosin, of the interior

TIME TABLE FOR BROILING

Cut		Size	Well Done	Time Medium	Rare
Beef:	Sirloin and Club Steaks	1 inch	18–30	14–16	10–12
		1½ inches	20–30	18–20	15–16
		2 inches	30–40	26–30	22–25
	Porterhouse	1 inch	20–32	16–18	12–15
	Top Round	1½ inches	25–35	22–25	18–20
	Chuck Steak	2 inches	30–36	28–30	25–28
	Tenderloin and Filet	1 inch	20–25	12–20	8–10
	Hamburger	¾ inch	12–25	10–12	8–10
Lamb:	Loin and Rib Chops	1 inch	20–28	15–18	——
		1½ inches	25–35	18–20	——
		2 inches	30–40	25–28	——
	Shoulder Chops	1 inch	20–28	15–18	——
		1½ inches	30–36	25–28	——
		2 inches	34–40	30–32	——
Pork:	Ham slice	¼ inch	13–16	12	——
		½ inch	24–30	15–20	——
	Bacon, sliced	(thin)	6	4	——
Liver:	(calf, lamb and beef)	½ inch	8–10	4–6	——
Fish:	(Filets, steaks or slices)	¼–½ lb.	6–12	5–10(do not
		¾–1 lb.	18–22	15–20	turn)
	Whole, small	not split	6–14	5–7	——
	Whole, medium	split	18–25	15–20 (do not
Chicken	——	1½ lb.	20–30	20*	turn)

*Broil for 10 minutes skin side down, turn, and broil ten minutes or more depending on size.

is gradually warmed and more slowly co-agulated. The outer coating prevents the evaporation of the juices of the meat (the nutrient parts) which, together with the extractive materials, are retained. Broiled meats, therefore, have a decided advantage in flavor over meat which has been stewed for a long time, although the latter may be equally tender and digestible.

In broiling, the heat should be strong when first applied and subsequently reduced to prevent charring of the surface. This reduction is accomplished either by moving the meat farther away from the fire, or by reducing the flame of the broiling oven. The process of broiling is conducted mainly by radiant heat, although there is slight convection through the air. It is, of course, necessary to prevent burning.

If the steak is properly broiled, it is slightly puffed in the center, but if badly broiled it is thin and dried out. Evaporation depends upon the extent of the surface of the meat, and for this reason thinly cut steaks or chops become comparatively dry and shriveled. Remember that the smaller the cut of meat to be broiled, the higher initial temperature to which its surface should be exposed and the briefer the cooking period. When very large steaks are broiled, it becomes necessary to sear them rapidly at a high temperature (500° F.), then reduce the heat to 350° F. for the remainder of the cooking. Be sure that the broiling oven is thoroughly preheated.

If the broiler does not have a regulating mechanism, the heat of 350° is attained by turning the flame high and placing the rack so that the surface of the food is about three inches from the flame. At this distance the temperature is just about 350° F.

Note: Preheat the oven broiler, pan, or grill for 10 or 15 minutes. Turn the meat once at half the broiling time, which is given in minutes in the table on the preceding page.

BROKEN TEA. Black tea leaves that have been broken or cut during the process of manufacture. Broken tea is generally not as popular in the United States as in the British Empire because of the stronger flavor when brewed. The term has no bearing on the quality of the tea.

BRONX COCKTAIL. A one-time favorite cocktail that has largely been supplanted by the Martini, which it closely resembles. Legend has it that the Bronx was first concocted by a New York bartender who had been challenged to produce something new and good in the way of mixtures, and was named after the Bronx Zoo by the maker because of the animals which some alcoholics thought they saw while in their cups. It was very popular during prohibition days because the ingredients were comparatively easy to get.

BRONX COCKTAIL

1 part dry gin
1 part dry vermouth
1 part orange juice

Shake thoroughly with cracked ice, strain into cocktail glasses.

As in the case of all popular cocktails, there are many variations on the basic recipe.

DRY BRONX COCKTAIL

1 part dry gin
1 part dry vermouth
1 slice orange
½ slice pineapple

First muddle the fruit slices well in a mixing glass, then pour them into a cocktail shaker, add the gin, vermouth, and cracked ice. Shake well and strain into cocktail glasses. Depending on the quantity made and the flavor desired, more fruit slices may be used.

SILVER BRONX COCKTAIL

4 parts dry gin
2 parts dry vermouth
2 parts sweet vermouth
1 part orange juice
1 egg white

Shake well with cracked ice, making sure egg white is thoroughly mixed, strain into cocktail glass.

See BARTENDING, *see also* COCKTAIL, ALCOHOLIC.

BROODKAASE CHEESE. A hard, flat cheese, native to Holland.

BROOK TROUT. A fresh-water food and game fish common to eastern North America. *See* TROUT.

BROTH. A thin soup made of the water in which meat has been simmered. Sometimes vegetables are added; barley or rice may be used as a thickener. The following broths may be made richer by allowing them to simmer for an hour longer than the time stated.

BEEF BROTH

1 lb lean beef
¾ tsp salt
Small piece bay leaf
1 qt cold water
1 lb bone (split by butcher)
Dash of pepper
Minced parsley

Cut meat in small chunks, remove fat. Place meat and bone in soup pot with salt, pepper and bay leaf fragment. Add water and bring slowly to a boil. Skim fat from surface. Then cover pot and allow to slowly simmer for 4 hours. Strain through cheese cloth, and add more seasoning if necessary. Allow to cool and again skim off fat. Serve hot after reheating in double boiler (do not allow to boil) and sprinkling with minced parsley. The broth may also be chilled and served as a jelly. Gelatin need not be added; the natural gelatin is sufficient.

CHICKEN BROTH

3 or 4 lb fowl
1 tsp salt
Minced parsley
Bouquet garni
1 small onion
2 qt cold water

Clean the bird and cut in small pieces. Place in pot with all ingredients excepting minced parsley. Add water and very slowly bring to a boil. Skim fat from surface, cover, and allow to simmer slowly for 3 hours. Strain through cheese cloth. Reheat in double boiler, sprinkle with minced parsley, and serve. *See also* SOUP.

BROUX DE NOIX. A liqueur made in France of crushed walnuts. Pure spirit of wine is re-distilled over the walnuts and aged. This liqueur is seldom exported from France.

BROWN. To seal the juices within a piece of meat by scorching the surfaces. *See* SEAR.

BROWN BETTY. (I) A student's drink that was very popular at Oxford and other English universities. Made of ale and other ingredients, it could be iced for summer consumption or heated for winter drinking, and was chiefly served at dinner.

BROWN BETTY

¼ lb brown sugar
1 pt water
1 lemon, sliced
Powdered cloves
Powdered cinnamon
½ pt brandy
1 qt ale
3 slices toast
Grated nutmeg
Grated ginger

The sugar is dissolved in the water, the sliced lemon added, and the mixture let stand for 15 minutes, usually in a large punch bowl. Then a small quantity (to taste) of cloves and cinnamon is added, the brandy and ale poured in, the toast floated on top sprinkled with the nutmeg and ginger. The drink is either iced or heated, depending on the season. *See also* BRASENOSE ALE, LAMB'S WOOL, PUNCH, and WINE CUP.

BROWN BETTY. (II) A pudding, better known as Betty, *which see.*

BROWN BREAD. A sweetish bread, traditionally served with Boston baked beans. *See* BREAD.

BROWN GRAVY. Made of meat juice, drippings, flour, etc. *See* GRAVY.

BROWN RICE. The milled rice grain from which only the husk has been removed as opposed to "paddy" or rough rice, and to "white" rice which is polished. Brown rice is more nutritious than white rice. *See* RICE.

BROWN SAUCE (ESPAGNOLE). Brown sauce is the base for most highly spiced sauces. Green pepper and tomato sauce combinations are richer and smoother if made with a brown sauce foundation. It is always made with a rich stock which may be combined with tomato puree, fruit juices, or vegetable stock, and even fish stock for fish sauces.

BASIC BROWN SAUCE

2 tbsp butter
3 tbsp flour
1 cup beef stock
½ tsp salt
Dash of pepper

Melt the butter, add the flour and cook the two together until thoroughly browned, stirring frequently, but not necessarily constantly, to prevent scorching, over a very low flame. Add the seasonings and the stock gradually, bring to boiling point and cook five minutes.

If desired, or if more convenient, bouillon cubes and water may be substituted for the meat stock. Also a slice of onion may be cooked with butter and flour if desired, and will make the sauce somewhat more savory.

The reason for the larger quantity of flour here is that in the browning of the flour, it loses some of its thickening properties.

This brown sauce is now ready to serve as the base for raisin, piquante, Madeira sauce, etc.

BROWN SAUCE VARIATIONS

Black Olive Sauce. To 1 cup of brown sauce add 1 dozen sliced black (ripe) olives. Suitable for almost any meat boiled or broiled.

Bourguignonne Sauce. Proceed as for Bordelaise Sauce (*which see*), adding 1 sprig of fresh parsley and 1 tablespoon of ground fresh mushrooms to the wine (which should be Burgundy) when reducing. Immediately before serving, add 1 tablespoon of butter, bit by bit. Suitable for broiled dark meat, eggs, and leftovers.

Cider Sauce. To 1 cup of brown sauce add 1 cup of the liquor in which the ham was cooked, reduced to $\frac{1}{3}$ its volume, a dash of cayenne, 1 teaspoon of grated white onion, 1 cup of cider reduced to $\frac{1}{3}$ its volume and $\frac{1}{4}$ cup of parboiled seedless raisins, optional. Suitable for roast ham or other smoked meat.

Currant Brown Sauce. To 1 cup of brown sauce add $\frac{1}{2}$ teaspoon of onion juice and $\frac{1}{4}$ cup of currant jelly. Suitable for cooked smoked meats.

Curry Sauce. To 1 cup of brown sauce, add 1 tablespoon of minced onion, slightly browned in butter, then blended with 1 teaspoon of curry powder moistened with cold brown sauce, and 1 teaspoon of tomato paste. Suitable for meat, fowl, vegetable, fish or eggs.

Hunter Sauce or Sauce Chasseur. Cook 1 tablespoon of thinly sliced onion, 1 tablespoon of thinly sliced fresh mushrooms, and 1 finely chopped shallot in 1 table-spoon of butter. When tender, moisten with $\frac{1}{2}$ cup of white wine then reduce to $\frac{1}{2}$ the original volume over a quick fire. Add 1 tablespoon of tomato puree and 1 cup of brown sauce, and immediately before serving, 1 tablespoon of butter, bit by bit, with 1 scant teaspoon blended, finely chopped parsley and tarragon. Suitable for grilled meats and game.

Jardiniere Sauce. To 1 cup of brown sauce add 1 tablespoon each of finely minced, cooked carrot, celery, and onion, 1 teaspoon each of finely minced parsley or chives, cooked diced string beans and small peas, and 1 teaspoon of minced pimento. Serve hot on grilled meats and leftovers, especially pork.

Madeira Sauce. To 2 cups of brown sauce, reduced to $\frac{1}{2}$ its original volume, add $1\frac{1}{2}$ tablespoons of Madeira wine. If too thick, thin with brown sauce. Suitable for roast dark meats or smoked meats.

Mushroom Brown Sauce. To 1 cup of brown sauce, add 1 cup of mushroom stock (mushroom trimmings cooked with water) reduced to $\frac{1}{4}$ its original volume, and, just before serving, stir in $\frac{1}{4}$ cup of sliced, fresh mushrooms cooked in a little butter, with 1 teaspoon of minced parsley. Suitable for meats, poultry and smoked meats.

Perigueux Sauce. Fry in butter 1 teaspoon of truffles, 2 large mushroom caps, a slice of garlic and a sprig of parsley, all finely minced. Brown, stirring constantly, then add to 1 cup of brown sauce with 2 or 3 tablespoons of white wine. Very appropriate for grilled meats, especially steaks and chops.

Piquante Sauce. Combine 2 tablespoons of white wine, 1 tablespoon vinegar and 1 teaspoon of minced shallots; reduce to $\frac{1}{2}$ its volume, add to 1 cup of brown sauce and just before serving, stir in 1 tablespoon of finely chopped sour pickles, 1 teaspoon each of minced parsley and chives, and a pinch of chopped tarragon. Suitable for pork, leftover meats and smoked meats.

Raisin Sauce. Carmelize 1 teaspoon of sugar with 1 teaspoon of vinegar. Combine with 1 cup of brown sauce and just before serving, stir in $\frac{1}{4}$ cup of seedless raisins plumped in hot water or stock, then thoroughly drain. Suitable for roast ham, pork, tongue or game.

Spaghetti Brown Sauce. To 1 cup of brown sauce add 1 clove of garlic, $\frac{1}{2}$ cup of raw ground beef, $1\frac{1}{2}$ tablespoons of chopped browned onion, a small leaf of fresh basil,

(starch-splitting) changes starch first to dextrin and finally to maltose, and maltase (maltose-splitting) may change a little of the maltose so formed, into glucose. In the stomach there are no enzymes acting on carbohydrates, but the digestion may continue under the influence of swallowed saliva for a time. In the pancreatic juice there is another amylase, which completes the splitting of starch to maltose, and then the intestinal maltase can reduce this to glucose, which will be absorbed. Cellulose cannot be digested and simply serves to add bulk to the diet.

Carbohydrates check albuminous waste and, like fats, yield both heat and mechanical work; hence good bread, sugar, and potatoes are all economical foods for the laborer. Unlike other classes of foods, however, they do not produce brawn, and do not to any great extent, enter into the actual structure of the tissues although the carbohydrates may be found existing as glycogen in some of the tissues, like the muscles and liver. In general, they seem to be more easily metabolized than fats or proteins. See also DIET and FOOD COMPOSITION.

CARBONATED WATER. See AERATED WATER and ALKALINE AND MINERAL WATERS.

CARBONATED WINES. Wines, red or white, dry or sweet, that are made effervescent by the introduction of carbon dioxide gas under pressure. This process is cheaper than the natural method of making effervescent wines by inducing fermentation in the bottle or, as in the bulk process, in a closed vat, and it is reflected in the price. These wines are stored and served in the same manner as all other sparkling wines. See WINE.

CARBORUNDUM. A trade name for silicon carbide, i.e., sand and carbon united under conditions of heat and pressure to form stone-like blocks of a remarkably tough, effective abraisve. As contrasted to stone (which see), it may be used "dry" to sharpen knives, etc. See also CUTLERY and KITCHEN EQUIPMENT.

CARDAMON. This is a perennial herb which grows to about twelve feet in India and somewhat higher in Ceylon. Its yellowish capsular fruit encloses angular aromatic seeds having a strong spicy odor and resembling anise in taste. True cardamon seeds are the fruit of the *Elettaria cardamomum* plant, but the seeds of the *Amomum*

cardamomum are sometimes sold as cardamons. The preferred variety of the seeds is known as "shorts."

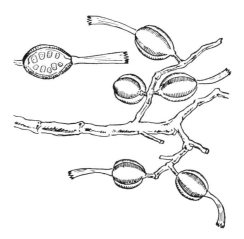

CARDAMOM SEED

The seeds are eaten whole or are used, whole or ground, as condiments, sometimes to replace cinnamon. They are chewed with betel nuts in the East; in this country they are sometimes chewed after drinking. They compliment coffee very nicely; a single seed will give new interest to a demitasse. They are used on Danish pastry and, ground, in grape jelly. A tincture of the oil derived from the seeds is used medicinally as a stimulant and as a carminative. The oil is sometimes used in colognes.

CARDINAL SAUCE. See WHITE SAUCE.

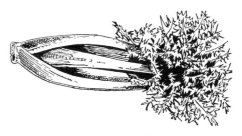

CARDOON

CARDOON. A close relative of the globe artichoke, the cardoon is cultivated for its roots and stalks. The main root is fleshy and tender, with a pleasant delicate flavor. It is best when boiled and served cold in a salad. The ribs of its large outside leaves are bleached and may be cooked and used as one would celery. The leaves are stripped from the midrib and any strings removed. Then the ribs are cut into short lengths and blanched in boiling salted water for 10 or 15 minutes. A few spoonfuls of vinegar added to the water will preserve the white color. Drain, and finish in any way suitable for celery.

Italian cooks prepare the parboiled cardoon by rolling the pieces in fine crumbs and sautéing them in olive oil. The dish is served with a thick well-seasoned tomato sauce.

CARIBOU. French name for reindeer, *which see.*

CARIGNANE. The name of a grape from which is made two types of wine; a dessert wine, notably in the Pyrénées Orientales in France, and a red table wine of the Claret type in California, both named after the grape. *See* GRAPE and WINE.

CARIOCA. A Cuban rum, next in favor to Bacardi. It is served as an after-dinner cordial, or as a long drink diluted with water, ginger ale, or carbonated water. It is also used in certain cocktails.

CAROB

CAROB. Also spelled caroub, and called Algarroba, locust bean, or St. John's bread. The sweet succulent pod of the carob tree which grows in Palestine and elsewhere along the Mediterranean. The entire fruit, excepting only its few small hard seeds, is edible, both fresh and dried. It is rich in sugar and fairly rich in protein. Its chief commercial value is as cattle food, but both the ground meal and a molasses-like sirup made from the pods are pleasing additions to the menu of humans.

Because of the sweet pulp, the dried pods are occasionally sold by peddlers and on the fruit stands as a cheap confection.

CAROID. Caroid is a vegetable digestive ferment made, like papoid, from the papaya or pawpaw, in the form of a dry yellowish powder. According to analysis, it retains a strong proteolytic action in acid, neutral, or alkaline medium. It softens and disintegrates proteides, coagulates milk like rennet, and is also amylolytic.

CAROTENE. A red, crystalline hydrocarbon found in yellow and green fruits and vegetables. It is the source of Vitamin A which is necessary to the normal growth and sight of animals. *See* VITAMIN.

CARP. The edible carp is a fresh water fish of the *Cyprinidae* family which is found in all parts of the world. It has a robust body, compressed, and covered with large scales. Its toothless mouth is rather small, with fleshy lips and four well developed barbels. In color the carp is dark olive, blending into brown on the upper part and shading off to a muddy light yellow on the ventral side.

Although the stories are not based on authenticated proof, several authors have told of carp which have lived for more than a hundred years. Certainly carps live long and may be domesticated, being easily tamed to feed out of the hand. In some countries, particularly in France, carp are raised in special ponds and may even be "caponized." These carp are fed almost exclusively on bread and have a particularly delicious flavor.

Individual carp may attain a weight of forty to fifty pounds, but the usual weight is much less, generally two to eight pounds. It lives in lakes and rivers, in sluggish water, where it feeds on vegetable matter. At the beginning of winter, the carp disappears into the mud, becomes torpid, and stops eating entirely until spring. So hardy is this fish that, when caught, it may be kept alive for days in wet moss, if properly fed, and consequently may be transported a good distance to market, arriving still alive.

Foamy Caramel Frosting

1¼ cups brown sugar
⅓ cup water
1 tsp vinegar
1 egg white
⅛ tsp salt
1 tsp vanilla extract
½ cup finely chopped blanched pistachio
  nuts

Place the sugar, water, and vinegar in a saucepan. Stir them until the sugar is dissolved. Cover, bring to boiling point, and continue boiling for three minutes. Remove, and stir in the unbeaten egg white with the salt. Beat the mixture with a rotary egg beater until it is thick enough to stand up in peaks. Add the vanilla and nuts.

CARAMELS. A rich soft candy, traditionally cut in small cubes. They may be varied in innumerable ways. Caramels, and indeed all candies containing cream or milk, must be cooked in a large saucepan as the mixture boils up high in the pan. In cutting caramels apart, use a long bladed, heavy knife with a "sawing" motion. *See also* Candy.

California Caramels

1 cup top milk
4 cups sugar, granulated or brown
⅔ cup molasses
½ cup butter
4 squares (oz) unsweetened chocolate
½ cup chopped nut meats
½ cup seedless raisins

Combine in a large saucepan the milk, sugar, molasses, butter, and chocolate. Cook over a very low flame, until the chocolate melts, stirring frequently; then continue cooking, stirring constantly until the mixture reaches the hard-ball stage (246° F.). Pour into a shallow, well greased pan over the nut meats and raisins. Cool, mark into squares, and cut apart with a heavy knife when cold. Wrap in waxed paper, and keep in an airtight container in a cool place.

Chocolate Caramels

3 squares (oz) unsweetened chocolate
1 cup sugar
¾ cup light corn sirup
¼ tsp salt
1½ cups heavy cream

Combine in a large saucepan the chocolate, sugar, corn sirup, salt, and half the cream. Place over a low flame, and stir constantly until the sugar is dissolved. Continue cooking, still stirring constantly, until the mixture reaches the soft-ball stage (238° F.). Now add another half cup of cream, and again cook to the soft-ball stage (238° F.), stirring constantly from the bottom of the pan. Finally add the third half cup of cream, and cook to the hard-ball stage (246° F.) always stirring constantly. Turn into a greased shallow pan. Do not scrape the pan. Let stand until cool, mark into squares, and cut apart when cold. Wrap in waxed paper and store in an airtight container in a cool, dry place.

Creamy Nut Caramels

2 cups sugar
2 cups light corn sirup
½ cup butter
¼ tsp salt
2 cups undiluted evaporated milk
1 tsp vanilla
1 cup halved blanched toasted almonds

Put the sugar, butter, and salt into a large saucepan, and bring slowly to the boiling point, stirring frequently. Slowly add the milk, so as not to stop the boiling, stirring meanwhile. Cook to the firm-ball stage (240° F.) stirring constantly. Add the vanilla, and quickly pour into greased or shallow pan over the almonds. When cool, mark into squares, and when cold cut and wrap each caramel in waxed paper. Store in an airtight container, and keep in a cool, dry place.

Maple Caramels

¼ cup granulated sugar
¼ cup brown sugar
¾ cup maple sirup
¼ cup corn sirup
½ cup heavy cream
1 tbsp butter
¼ tsp salt
⅓ cup toasted pecans

Cook together in a large saucepan the sugars, sirups, and cream to the firm-ball stage (246° to 250° F.). Remove from the

fire, add the butter, salt, and pecans. Turn
into a shallow, greased pan, cool, mark
into squares, and when cold cut apart, and
wrap in waxed paper. Store in an airtight
container in a cool, dry place.

RUM CARAMELS

2 cups sugar
2 cups light corn sirup
½ cup butter
1⅔ cups undiluted evaporated milk
2 tsp rum extract

Combine in a large saucepan the sugar
and sirup and cook to the soft-ball stage
(238° F.). Add the butter and when this is
melted, pour in the milk very slowly so as
not to check the boiling. Cook to the firm-
ball stage (246°–248° F.) stirring gently
but constantly. Add the flavoring and turn
into a greased pan. Cool, mark into squares
and when cold cut apart and wrap in
waxed paper. Store in an airtight container in a cool, dry place.

VANILLA CARAMELS

2 cups sugar
½ cup top milk
⅓ cup molasses
¼ cup butter
2 squares (oz) unsweetened chocolate
¼ cup broken pecans
2 tbsp blanched pistachio nuts, optional
1 tsp vanilla

Combine in a large saucepan, the sugar,
milk, molasses, butter, and chocolate. Cook
over a low flame until the chocolate melts;
then continue cooking, stirring constantly
to the firm-ball stage (246°–250° F.). Turn
into a shallow, greased pan over the nuts,
mark into squares, and when cold cut
apart and wrap in waxed paper. Store in
an airtight container.

CARAVELA. A dry Madeira wine,
usually served as an aperitif. It is light
amber in color.

CARAWAY. Caraway "seeds" are the
fruit of the *Carum carvi* a biennial plant
which grows in northern and central Europe and Asia and has been cultivated in
England and America for its seeds. The
plant has clusters of white or pinkish flowers. The aromatic seeds, tiny and ovate,
have a pleasant spicy flavor and, when
bruised, an agreeable odor.

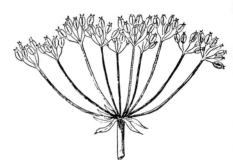

CARAWAY SEED

Caraway seeds are most widely used in
cheeses and pastries. They may be mixed
with cheese spreads and fillings for canapés
and hors d'oeuvres, or a few of them may
be sprinkled over these appetizers as a garnish. Caraways also improve the flavor of
mutton, liver, pork, and kidneys—they
should be added before the meat is cooked
—and of sauerkraut, cabbage, and French
fried potatoes. The aromatic oil that the
seeds yield is used by distillers to flavor
certain liqueurs (such as kümmel), and it
is used medicinally as a stimulant, mild
local anaesthetic, carminative, and antiseptic.

CARBOHYDRATES. The simplest carbohydrate is a sugar which cannot be
broken up into other sugars. Such a simple
sugar is called a monosaccharid. There are
two such common sugars in foods, glucose
and fructose; a third, galactose, is derived
from more complex sugars. Two simple
sugars, united chemically, make a double
sugar, or disaccharid; thus cane sugar, or
sucrose, will yield glucose and fructose,
while milk sugar, or lactose, will yield glucose and galactose, and maltose will yield
two portions of glucose. These three disaccharids are the only common ones.

Starches, dextrins, and cellulose, or vegetable fiber, are carbohydrates which are
made of many simple glucose groups, and
are hence called polysaccharids. All carbohydrates, to be used by the body, must be
reduced to simple sugars. Glucose therefore, needs no digestion, but the double
sugars must be split by enzymes into two
simple sugars. Each sugar has its special
enzyme, namely, sucrase (sucrose-splitting), maltase (maltose-splitting) and lactase (lactose-splitting).

The digestion of starches and dextrins
begins in the mouth, where amylase

bubbles appear on the surface of the cakes. Serve with butter and maple sirup.

Today buckwheat flour is usually mixed with wheat "middlings" in order to modify the flavor and make it more delicate. This combination makes a lighter batter and a sweeter one.

QUICK BUCKWHEAT CAKES

1½ cups buckwheat flour
½ cup white flour
4 tsp baking powder
½ tsp salt
1 egg, beaten
1½ cups milk
2 tbsp melted shortening
2 tbsp molasses

Sift together the flours, baking powder, and salt, and mix to a batter with the egg, milk, shortening, and molasses. Bake on a hot greased griddle. Serve with butter and sirup.

BUFFALO BERRY. An American fruit of the family *Elaeagnaclae* resembling the barberry (*which see*). It is cultivated in the western plains region. Generally round, tart, about the size of currants, it can be made into delicious jellies and preserves.

The name originated with the old custom of serving cooked berries as a sauce or accompaniment to buffalo meat.

BUFFALO BERRY

BUFFET. A long, low table, sideboard, counter, or cabinet, that is used to hold food for serving. The term is now applied to a meal where the food is arranged on such a buffet for the guests to help themselves.

This method of serving originated with the Russian *zakuski* or Swedish *smorgasbord*. In both cases, large tables are covered with

BUFFET SUPPER TABLE SETTING

a wide assortment of foods, attractive and appetizing, arranged in many dishes, so that each guest may pass from one to the other, choosing the portions he wishes.

The informal buffet is one of the easiest types of meals for the hostess to manage. It may vary in its degree of formality, with servants to pass the dishes, or it may be most informal, with the guests helping themselves and finding a seat, or standing up as they eat. A much larger group can be entertained in this way than at a sit-down meal.

The criterion of a suitable menu is that it may be eaten easily with a fork or spoon, and does not require the use of a knife to cut. Men, in particular, have an aversion to buffet meals at which they must juggle a plate, cutlery, cup and saucer, and whatever else is called for. If it is possible to set out small tables, such as bridge tables, at which people may sit to eat, this objection is removed. If space does not permit, small end tables may be used, or trays which fit on the lap or over the arms of the chair are a great help.

In any event, a buffet meal may consist of a one-dish centerpiece—a hot casserole in winter or a cold molded salad in summer, a tossed salad, rolls and butter (the rolls may be buttered in the kitchen for greater ease in serving), dessert, and beverage. With a menu such as this the main dish, salad, and bread go on one plate, and only a fork is needed with which to eat. Sandwiches may be added, as well as an assortment of relishes, or other garnishes appropriate to the dish. But good food, well cooked, and plenty of it, is more important than an elaborate menu.

BULLACE. A small tree of the *prunus* family, related to the sloe. The fruit of this tree is used in jams and jellies.

BULLETIN BOARD. A kitchen bulletin board may be constructed from a number of materials. Soft wood, the underside of linoleum, certain types of insulating or sound-proofing sheets, and like materials, at least one of which can usually be found in the cellar, can be attractively framed and hung conveniently on the kitchen wall. All manner of information, ranging from recipes clipped from the paper to notes for the children, can be pinned on it, where it will not get lost and will be prominently in view either as a reminder or as a reference. *See also* BLACKBOARD and KITCHEN EQUIPMENT.

BULLHEAD. Several varieties of catfish found in fresh waters of the United States. *See* CATFISH.

BULL'S EYE. A cooling, intoxicating drink made of brandy and hard cider.

BULL'S EYE

1 small jigger brandy
1 large jigger hard cider

Place in an 8-ounce highball glass, add 1 ice cube or equivalent, fill with ginger ale, stir gently and serve. (Serves one)

Ginger beer is sometimes used instead of ginger ale, and applejack may be substituted for the hard cider, if the latter is unavailable. If applejack is used, however, a small, rather than large, jigger should be used, since applejack is stronger. *See also* BARTENDING.

BUMMALO. A fish caught in great quantities off the Indian coast. They are dried and canned, to be used as a relish known as Bombay Duck, *which see*.

BUN. Generally a small sweetish cake, ordinarily eaten with coffee for breakfast. Many national variations are known, and in the United States the name is also given to a round soft roll used especially with hamburgers.

See also CAKE and ROLL.

BATH BUNS

1 lb flour
6 oz butter
1 oz yeast
½ cup milk
1 to 2 oz loaf sugar
2 eggs
5 oz powdered sugar
3 oz. sultana raisins
3 oz lemon peel

Rub the butter into the flour; warm the milk and cream the yeast with a little of it. Pour the milk and yeast into the middle of the flour. Add the beaten eggs. Beat very thoroughly, cover with a cloth, and put the dough to rise in a warm place until it doubles in size. This will take about 1½ hours. Add the powdered sugar, sultanas, and peel; beat well, and form into small, even-sized balls. Put into greased muffin tins and let them rise until they are double in size. Brush over with egg and milk, sprinkle with coarsely-crushed loaf sugar. Bake in a hot oven (400° F.) for 20 to 30 minutes.

CINNAMON BUNS

1 yeast cake
¼ cup lukewarm water
1/3 cup sugar
1 tsp salt
¾ cup scalded milk
2 eggs, well beaten
1 tsp grated lemon rind
4 cups all-purpose flour
½ tsp mace
¼ cup melted shortening

Soften the yeast in the warm water to which ½ teaspoon of the sugar has been added. Let stand for 10 minutes. Add the remaining sugar and salt to the scalded milk, stir well, and let cool to lukewarm. Combine the yeast mixture with the milk mixture and stir well. Sift the flour with the spice. Add the eggs, lemon rind, and half the flour to the milk-yeast mixture and beat until smooth. Beat in the cooled shortening, and then add the remaining flour and stir thoroughly. Turn out on a lightly floured board. Cover with a cloth and let rest for 10 minutes. Then knead for 10 minutes, until the dough is smooth and elastic. Do not use more than ¼ cup of flour for the kneading. Round up into a smooth ball, place in a greased bowl, and turn once to bring greased side on top. Cover with waxed paper and a clean towel and let rise in a warm place (about 86° F.) until the dough has doubled in bulk, about 1½ to 2 hours.

Divide the dough in two and roll each half into a rectangle about 8x14 inches and ¼ inch thick. Brush with melted butter and sprinkle with a mixture of ½ cup sugar and 4 teaspoons of cinnamon. Sprinkle with raisins and chopped nuts. Roll up as for a jelly roll. Cut into one-inch slices and place, cut side down, close together on a greased pan. Cover and let stand in a warm place until doubled in size. Bake in a moderate oven (375° F.) for 30 minutes. (Makes 24 buns)

HOT CROSS BUNS

1 yeast cake
¼ cup lukewarm water

1 cup milk
½ cup sugar
½ cup shortening
1 egg
¼ cup shredded citron
½ cup seedless raisins or currants
3-3½ cups sifted flour
¾ tsp salt

Soften the yeast in the lukewarm water. Scald the milk with the sugar and shortening, then cool to lukewarm. Add the softened yeast, then the beaten egg, citron, and raisins or currants, and finally the sifted flour and salt. Knead lightly, cover, and let rise in a warm place until doubled in bulk. Shape into buns, place side by side in a greased baking pan and again let rise until very light. Brush over with beaten egg or milk, and just before putting into the oven make a cross in the top of each with a sharp knife. Bake in a moderately hot oven (375-400° F.) about 20 minutes. After baking, sift powdered sugar over the tops of the buns. (Makes about 18 buns)

WILLIAMSBURG BUNS

1 cup milk
½ cup melted butter
2 tsp salt
½ cup sugar
2 yeast cakes
¼ cup warm water
3 beaten eggs
4½ cups flour
1 tsp nutmeg
1 tsp mace
1 wineglass sherry

Scald the milk, add the melted butter, salt and sugar. Cool to lukewarm. Add yeast cakes which have been dissolved in the warm water. Add eggs to liquids, then beat in well the flour, nutmeg, mace and sherry. Let the dough rise until double in bulk, turn it out and knead lightly. Fill greased muffin pans two-thirds full and let rise until light (about 20 minutes). Brush with melted butter and bake in a moderately hot oven (375° F.) about 20 minutes. (Makes about 36 small buns)

BURGER. *See* HAMBURGER.

BURGOO. A porridge; a thick gruel; a kind of thick oatmeal pudding. Also; a thick vegetable soup or stew, with beef and chicken forming a substantial part. This soup is cooked outdoors in huge iron kettles over a wood fire, and is usually served in pint-sized tin cups. *See also* BARBECUE and CAMP COOKERY.

"BURGUNDIES OF CHINA" TEA. These are fine, black teas of North China. *See* ICHANG.

BURGUNDY. Throughout the world Burgundy often means a dark red wine of more than average alcoholic content. In France Burgundy may be either red or white, and is produced in the former province of Burgundy. Much more red Burgundy is produced than white, and the best comes from the Cote d'Or region. The best known white Burgundy is Chablis, which has an unusual crisp flavor. *See also* WINE.

BURGUNDY CHEESE. A soft, white, loaf-shaped cheese weighing about four pounds. It is also known as *Fromage de Bourgogne.*

BURNED CREAM. A dessert made of carmelized sugar and custard, better known by its French name of creme brule, *which see.*

BURNET. A member of the rose family, this herb is native to Europe. It is also found in gardens as well as growing wild in North America. The plant bears spikes of small purple flowers. Its leaves are used for flavoring greens, salads, and beverages.

Young burnet leaves smell somewhat like cucumbers which, incidentally, they accompany very nicely; in fact, some gourmets maintain that in salads they are necessary complements to one another. Burnet leaves should be used in the preparation of both fine herbs and ravigote (*which see*). Both leaves and seeds are used to flavor vinegar.

BUTT. The thick end of a ham or shoulder. *See* HAM.

BUTTER. Butter is made from the fat of milk or cream and may be salted or not, and colored or not. It must contain less than 16 percent water and not less than 80 percent fat. Formerly butter was made on individual farms or dairies, and marketed through local grocers who shipped to jobbers, who in turn supplied the large cities. Now the butter trade is centralized in creameries to which the farmers deliver their cream daily, or the whole milk may be separated at the creameries and the skim milk returned to the farmers for use in feeding cattle and farm animals.

The cream is graded according to its suitability for making butter. The first grade contains cream which is sweet or slightly sour, but free from objectionable odors and tastes. The second grade includes all other cream. Some creameries, particularly those making sweet-cream butter have three grades, the first containing only sweet cream and the second sour cream which has no objectionable odor or flavor. All other cream goes in the third grade.

When the cream is received, it is weighed to determine the basis of payment to the farmer. It is then dumped into a receiving vat, passing through a wire screen which breaks up any lumps of cream. The cream is stirred and heated to about 90° F. as a preliminary to pasteurization. If the cream has been delivered by the farmers, it has probably developed a higher acidity to cream which has been separated at the creamery and not allowed to stand. Butter made from sour cream has an acid flavor and does not keep as well as butter made from sweet cream. It is therefore necessary to neutralize the acidity of the cream by the addition of milk of lime to the cream, which is being held at 90°.

The cream is then pasteurized to destroy the organisms which would impare its keeping qualities, and to give a more uniform product. Since the American public does not like a flat-tasting butter, and since the desirable as well as the undesirable organisms are destroyed by pasteurization, it is necessary to return a strictly controlled amount and kind of bacteria to the cream. The cream is then allowed to ripen until the desired flavor and condition are reached.

The cream is then churned, and if the color is not the conventional bright yellow which the trade finds desirable, vegetable coloring is added during the churning process. When the butter has all formed, the buttermilk is drawn off and the butter washed to remove any buttermilk remaining. The butter is then salted. Contrary to popular belief, salt does not improve the keeping qualities of butter; the American public has become used to salted butter and finds unsalted butter tasteless. In continental Europe and for the Jewish trade in the United States, unsalted butter is customary. The salt is worked into the butter until the butter has a tough, waxy and compact body.

4. Cover meat with hot broth or hot water, using about ½ to ¾ cup for each quart container. Leave 1 inch head space in jars; fill cans to top.
5. Work out air bubbles with knife. Add more liquid if needed to cover meat. Be sure to leave 1 inch head space in jars, and to fill cans to top.
6. Adjust jar lids or seal cans.
7. Process at once in the pressure canner at 10 pounds pressure (240° F.) for: Pint jars, 75 minutes; quart jars, 90 minutes; no. 2 cans, 65 minutes; no. 2½ and 3 cans, 90 minutes. Or in a boiling-water bath for 3½ hours.

HEART AND TONGUE

The heart and tongue are generally used as fresh meat. If you do wish to can them, follow directions for beef, veal, pork, lamb as hot packed, with these exceptions:

Heart. Remove thick connective tissue before cutting into pieces.

Tongue. Drop tongue into boiling water and simmer about 45 minutes, or until skin can be removed, before cutting into pieces.

SOUP STOCK

1. Make a fairly concentrated stock by covering bony pieces of chicken or other meat with lightly salted water and simmering until meat is tender. Cooking too long may cause·soup to lose flavor.
2. Skim off fat, and remove all pieces of bone; don't strain out meat and sediment.
3. Pour hot stock into containers to 1 inch of top in jars, to top in cans.
4. Adjust jar lids or seal cans.
5. Process at once in pressure canner at 10 pounds pressure (240° F.) for: Pint jars, 20 minutes; quart jars, 25 minutes; no. 2 cans, 20 minutes; no. 2½ cans, 25 minutes. Or in a boiling-water bath canner for 2½ hours.

CANTAL CHEESE. A very old variety of hard, rennet cheese, made from skimmed cow's milk. It is about 14 inches in diameter and weighs from 40 to 120 pounds. Also known as Auvergne, Auvergne Bleu, and Fourme.

CANTALOUPE. A variety of muskmelon, named after the castle of Cantaloupe, in the province of Ancona, Italy. It is found in many sizes and shapes. Through trade usage "cantaloupe" has become the name commonly applied to muskmelons grown in this country. Actually "cantaloupe" is the name which should be given to melons of a certain definite group grown in Europe. The flesh varies in color from a pinkish yellow to pale green.

VARIETIES

Commercially, cantaloupes are divided into three groups according to the color of flesh.

Pink Meat. The color of flesh is orange or pink throughout. The netting is not so heavy as that of either the green or salmon tints, but is usually well developed over the blossom end. With the exception of certain types which are slightly oval, pink-meated melons are elongated and somewhat pointed at both ends.

Salmon Tint. The flesh is normally greenish near the rind and salmon-colored toward the center. Immature melons of this group have flesh that is almost entirely green, while those of advanced maturity have almost entirely yellow or salmon flesh. The netting completely covers the melon; the shape is usually roundish.

Green Meat. The flesh is normally green from the center to rind. The netting completely covers the melon; the shape is roundish.

PREPARATION FOR MARKET

Cantaloupes require a fairly long growing season, with plenty of heat and sunshine, a dry atmosphere and sufficient soil moisture. They do not attain their highest flavor and best edible qualities unless allowed to become reasonably ripe on vigorous diease-free vines. Careful transporta-

FOOD VALUE OF CANTELOUPE

Water	Food Energy	Pro-tein	Fat	Carbo-hydrate	Cal-cium	Phos-phorus	Iron	Vit. A Value	Thia-mine	Ribo-flavin	Nia-cin	Ascor-bic Acid
94.0	23	.6	.2	4.6	17	16	.4	3,420	.06	.04	.8	33

tion experiments have shown that melons grown in the Imperial Valley of California to be shipped under refrigeration to the most distant eastern markets of the United States may remain on the vines until ripe enough for the stems to separate from the melons under a decided pressure of the thumb, and yet reach the consumer in excellent condition. Two stages of maturity

In judging the quality of cantaloupes, one should keep in mind the following points:

Sweetness, fine texture, and flavor are factors that determine quality in cantaloupes; one can expect to find them only in well matured fruit.

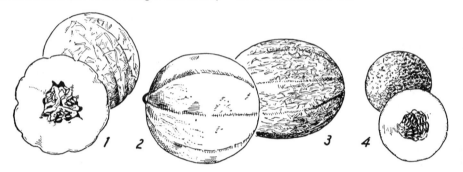

CANTALOUPES 1. **Pride of Wisconsin** 2. **Sunrise** 3. **Bender's Surprise** 4. **Minnesota Midget**

were included in these experiments, the one known as "full slip" by which the entire stem separates from the melon leaving a clean stem quality, the other known as the "half slip", by which about one-third of the width of the stem remains attached to the melon.

The melons are removed from the vine by placing the hand upon the melon, pressing upon the stem with the thumb or slightly lifting the melon from the ground. If the melon is sufficiently ripe the stem will separate under the pressure, showing that the melon is ready for gathering. Hampers, bushel baskets, crates, lug boxes, and numerous other types of containers are used for carrying the melon to the roadways. In most cases no picking containers are used, the melons being laid in piles. Canvas bags with shoulder straps are used extensively, but their tendency to bruise the melons is greater than that of baskets or crates. As a rule the melons are left in the picking baskets at the roadways until they are loaded into the wagons and they are usually hauled to the packing sheds in these containers. Whether the packing is done in a central or field packing shed the stock is usually sorted or graded as to maturity and defects as the melons are transferred from the field container to the packing bin.

The stage of maturity of a cantaloupe is indicated by the netting or veining on the surface and the condition of the scar at the stem end. The netting should be coarse, corky or grayish color, well developed, standing out in bold relief, and covering the surface to an extent depending on the class to which the variety may belong.

The green color of the immature rind should be a lighter shade and may have either a grayish or yellowish tinge.

The scar at the stem end should be slightly sunken and calloused, a condition which indicates that when the fruit is picked it separated readily and was not cut or gouged from the stem. Cantaloupes that show these characteristics are usually mature and usually have developed their full flavor and distinctive cantaloupe aroma.

A softening of the fruit at the blossom end is a supposed indication of ripeness, but as this softening can be induced by repeated pressure, too much reliance should not be placed on this test.

Over-mature cantaloupes are usually soft, watery and insipid. This condition is generally indicated by a very pronounced yellowing of rind showing through the netting.

Immature cantaloupes have a flesh that is generally hard, tough and flavorless.

3. Pack second joints and drumsticks. Have skin next to glass or tin. Fit breasts into center, smaller pieces where needed. Pack glass jars to about 1 inch of top; pack tin cans to top.

4. Set open jars or cans in large vessel with warm water about 2 inches below rim of containers. Cover vessel and heat at slow boil until meat in all containers is steaming hot and medium done (about 50 minutes in the cans, 75 in jars). If you have a thermometer, meat is heated enough when contents of center of jar registers 170° F.

5. Adjust jar lids, or seal tin cans.

6 Process at once in the pressure canner at 10 pounds pressure (240° F.) for:
Pint jars, 65 minutes; quart jars, 75 minutes; no. 2 cans, 55 minutes; no. 2½ and 3 cans, 75 minutes.
Or in a boiling-water bath for 3½ hours.

Raw pack, without bone.

Follow directions for raw-packed poultry with bone, with these exceptions:

Remove bone, but not skin, from meaty pieces before packing.

Boned chicken must be processed longer in the pressure canner than chicken with bone. Process at 10 pounds pressure for:
Pint jars, 75 minutes; quart jars, 90 minutes; no. 2 cans, 65 minutes; no. 2½ and 3 cans, 90 minutes.

GIBLETS

Because of flavor, it is best to can livers alone. Gizzards and hearts may be canned together. Since these are ordinarily canned and used in small quantities, directions are given only for pint glass jars and number 2 tin cans.

1. Put giblets in cooking pan. Cover them with broth made from bony pieces or with hot water. Cover the pan, and precook giblets until medium done. Stir occasionally.

2. If salt is desired, put level measure into clean, empty containers—½ teaspoon in each container.

3. Pack giblets hot to 1 inch of top in jars, to ½ inch of top in cans.

4. Cover giblets with hot broth or hot water. Leave 1-inch space at top of jars; fill cans to top.

5. Work out air bubbles with knife. Add more liquid, if needed, to cover meat. Be certain to leave 1-inch space in jars and to have cans filled to top.

6. Adjust jar lids, or seal cans.

7. Process at once in the pressure canner at 10 pounds pressure (240° F.) for:
Pint jars, 75 minutes; no. 2 cans, 65 minutes.
Or in a boiling-water bath for 3½ hours.

RABBIT

Prepare the meaty pieces, with or without bone, and pack and process as for chicken.

BEEF, VEAL, PORK, LAMB

For canning as large pieces, use loin and other cuts suitable for roasts, steaks, or chops. For canning as stew meat, use the less tender cuts and smaller pieces.

Cut away meat from bone. Set bones aside for use in broths or soups. Trim most of the fat away without unduly slashing the lean.

Cut into pieces that will slip easily into the containers; have the grain running lengthwise.

Hot pack.

1. Put meat in large shallow pan; add just enough water to prevent sticking. Cover pan and precook meat slowly until medium done, stirring occasionally for even heating.

2. If salt is desired, put level measure into clean, empty containers—½ teaspoon in pint jars or number 2 cans; ¾ teaspoon in 2½ cans, 1 teaspoon in quart jars or 3 cans.

3. Pack meat hot to 1 inch of top in jars, to ½ inch of top in cans.

4. Cover with meat juice, adding hot broth or water if needed. Again leave 1 inch head space in jars; fill cans to top.

5. Work out air bubbles with knife. Add more liquid if needed to cover meat. Be certain to leave 1 inch head space in jars and to fill cans to top.

6. Adjust jar lids or seal cans.

7. Process at once in the pressure canner at 10 pounds pressure (240° F.) for:
Pint jars, 75 minutes; quart jars, 90 minutes; no. 2 cans, 65 minutes; no. 2½ and 3 cans, 90 minutes.
Or in a boiling-water bath for 3½ hours.

Raw (cold) pack.

1. If salt is desired, put level measure into clean, empty containers—½ teaspoon in pint jars or number 2 cans; ¾ teaspoon in 2½ cans; 1 teaspoon in quart jars or 3 cans.
2. Pack containers with raw, lean meat. Leave about 1 inch head space in jars; fill cans to top.
3. Set open jars or cans in large vessel with warm water about 2 inches below rim of jar or can. Cover vessel and heat at slow boil until meat in all jars or cans is steaming hot and medium done (about 50 minutes in cans, 75 in glass jars). If you have a thermometer, meat is heated enough when center of container registers 170° F. Press meat down into tin cans ½ inch below rims, and add boiling water if needed to fill to top.
4. Adjust jar lids or seal cans.
5. Process at once in the pressure canner at 10 pounds pressure (240° F.) for: Pint jars, 75 minutes; quart jars, 90 minutes; no. 2 cans, 65 minutes; no. 2½ and 3 cans, 90 minutes. Or in a boiling-water bath for 3½ hours.

GROUND MEAT

For grinding, use small pieces or meat from the less tender cuts, but be sure that the meat is fresh, clean, and cold. Never mix in scraps of doubtful freshness as they may spoil a whole batch; don't use fat.

If desired, add 1 level teaspoon of salt to the pound of ground meat, mixing it well.

Hot pack.

1. Form ground meat into fairly thin cakes that can be packed in glass jars or tin cans without breaking.
2. Put meat cakes into cooking pan. Precook in oven until medium done or until, when cut into, red color at center of cakes is almost gone.
3. Pack cakes hot to 1 inch of top in jars, to ½ inch of top in cans.
4. Skim fat off drippings, and do not use the fat in canning.
5. Cover with meat juice, adding hot water if needed. Leave 1 inch head space in jars; fill cans to top.

6. Work out air bubbles with knife. Add more liquid if needed to cover meat. Be certain to leave 1 inch head space in jars and to fill cans to top.
7. Adjust jar lids or seal cans.
8. Process at once in pressure canner at 10 pounds pressure (240° F.) for: Pint jars, 75 minutes; quart jars, 90 minutes; no. 2 cans, 65 minutes; no. 2½ and 3 cans, 90 minutes. Or in a boiling-water bath for 3½ hours.

Raw pack.

This method is suitable only for tin cans. It is difficult to get canned ground meat packed this way out of jars.

1. Without forming cakes, pack raw ground meat solidly into tin cans level with the top.
2. Place open cans in large vessel with water about 2 inches below can rim. Cover vessel and heat at slow boil until meat in all cans is steaming hot and medium done (about 75 minutes). If you have a thermometer, meat is heated enough when center of can registers 170° F. Press meat down into cans about ½ inch below rim.
3. Seal cans.
4. Process at once in the pressure canner at 10 pounds pressure (240° F.) for: No. 2 cans, 100 minutes; no. 2½ and 3 cans, 135 minutes.

SAUSAGE

Use any tested sausage recipe, but omit sage as it is likely to give the canned sausage a bitter flavor. Use onion, garlic, and other spices very sparingly, because flavors change with processing and storing and the result may be undesirable.

Shape sausage meat into cakes. Precook, pack, and process like ground meat, hot packed.

CORNED BEEF

1. Wash the corned beef, and cut it into pieces suited to packing.
2. Cover meat with cold water; bring to a boil. If broth tastes very salty, drain and cover meat with fresh water, and parboil again.
3. Pack hot meat to 1 inch of top in jars, to ½ inch of top in cans.

¾ cup shortening (half butter)
2 cups dark brown sugar, firmly packed
1 egg, beaten
1 tsp vanilla
3 tbsp cream
1 cup chopped nuts
1 cup soft dates, chopped

Sift flour, measure, and resift 3 times with cream of tartar, soda, and salt. Cream shortening, blend in sugar, and add egg, vanilla, and cream; beat until smooth and fluffy. Add flour mixture and stir until well blended. Stir in nuts and dates. Shape in a roll, or divide in 2 or 3 portions and roll separately; wrap in waxed paper and chill in refrigerator overnight or for at least 4 hours. Slice thin with a thin-bladed very sharp knife, using a saw-like motion. Transfer to baking sheet, and bake in a moderately hot oven (400° F.) about 7 minutes, or until nicely browned. Remove the cookies to cake racks and allow to cool. (Makes about 5 dozen cookies, depending on size)

BUTTERSCOTCH ICE CREAM
(hand freezer)

2 cups scalded rich milk
1 tbsp flour
1 cup brown sugar
2 tbsp butter
1 whole egg, slightly beaten
¼ tsp salt
2 tsp vanilla extract
1 qt undiluted evaporated milk, or half milk, and half heavy cream

Cook sugar with butter in a heavy skillet or saucepan until melted and allow to boil 1 long minute. Add to scalded milk, stirring well. Beat slightly the whole egg with salt and flour, the flour added a small amount at a time, and pour milk over egg mixture slowly, stirring constantly. Cook over boiling water, for 10 minutes, stirring constantly for 5 minutes, then occasionally for the remaining 5 minutes. Should custard have a curdled appearance, it will disappear in freezing. Cool, and when cold add undiluted evaporated milk or half milk and heavy cream and vanilla extract. Strain through a fine sieve, and freeze in hand freezer, using 3 parts ice and 1 part rock salt. Pack or mold in 4 parts ice and

1 part rock salt. *See also* ICE CREAM. (Makes 2 quarts)

BUTTERSCOTCH PARFAIT

½ cup brown sugar
3 tbsp butter
½ cup hot water
2 egg yolks
2 cups heavy cream
1½ tsp vanilla
¼ tsp salt

Put the brown sugar and butter together in a heavy frying pan and stir constantly over a moderate heat until melted and thoroughly blended. Cook one minute, add the water and continue the cooking until the mixture is smooth and sirupy, about five minutes. Pour in a fine stream onto the beaten egg yolks, still beating constantly. Place over hot water (double boiler) and cook until light and fluffy. Chill, then fold in the cream whipped until stiff with the vanilla and salt. Freeze in automatic refrigerator or bury in ice and salt. *See also* PARFAIT. (Serves 6 to 8)

BUTTERSCOTCH PINWHEELS

2 cups all-purpose flour
3 tsp baking powder
½ tsp salt
⅓ cup shortening
⅔ to ¾ cup milk
⅓ cup melted butter
⅓ cup brown sugar, firmly packed
½ tsp cinnamon
2 tbsp corn syrup
¼ cup chopped nuts

Sift flour, measure and resift 3 times with baking powder and salt. Cut in shortening until particles are the size of rice grains. Add milk all at once, and stir quickly until dough stiffens. Turn out onto floured board and knead 8 to 10 times. Roll or pat dough carefully to a 9x12 rectangle, about ⅜ inch thick. Brush with 2 tablespoons of the butter, sprinkle with 2 tablespoons of the brown sugar mixed with cinnamon, and roll up from long side like jelly roll. Cut in 16 slices. Combine remaining butter, brown sugar, sirup and the nuts and put an equal amount in each of the 16 small buttered muffin pans. Place one slice, cut side down, in each. Bake in moderately hot oven (425° F.) for 15 to 20 minutes or until done and nicely browned. Serve hot with butter. (Makes 16 small pinwheels)

BUTTERSCOTCH RICE MOLD

⅓ cup rice
3 cups milk
1 cup brown sugar
¼ tsp salt
2 tbsp butter
1 tbsp gelatin
¼ cup cold water

Add salt and two cups of the milk, scalded, to the washed rice. Place in double boiler. Cook until nearly tender. Place sugar and butter in shallow pan. Cook slowly until very dark brown. Add this to the rice and cook until the sugar has melted and the rice is tender. After softening gelatin in water, dissolve it in the remaining cup of milk, also scalded. Add this to the rice mixture. Pour all into mold. Chill until firm. Serve with plain or whipped cream. (Serves 6)

BUTTERSCOTCH SAUCE

½ cup butter
½ cup brown sugar, firmly packed
1 tsp vanilla
1 egg yolk, well beaten
4 tbsp milk

Cream the butter thoroughly, gradually adding the sugar. When light and fluffy, add the vanilla, egg yolk, and milk, and beat well.

BUYING FOOD. *See* PURCHASING FOOD.

BYRRH. A French aperitif wine based on red wine, flavored with herbs and fortified with brandy. It has a slightly bitter flavor.

C

CABBAGE. Of ancient lineage, cabbage was well known to the ancient Romans who gave it considerable therapeutic value. It is one of the largest families of vegetables, being related to the cauliflower, Brussels sprouts, kale, and kohlrabi, all of which see. A recently imported member of the family is Chinese, or celery, cabbage, *which see.*

Cabbage proper is marketed in several varieties. The early or "new" cabbage forms conical or pointed heads. The Danish type forms hard compact heads and is the staple winter cabbage. The heads are tighter or looser depending on the variety. Savoy cabbage forms round heads of curly leaves. Red cabbage, on the other hand, is deep reddish purple in color and forms tight heads.

Hints on Preparation

Cabbage may be served raw, in slaw or salad, or it may be cooked. Red and white cabbage mixed in slaw makes an attractive color accent for the meal. Raw cabbage may be shredded with a special slicing board, or merely cut fine with a knife. Cold slaw is often fixed with an old fashioned boiled dressing, *which see.*

Cabbage should not be overcooked. The old fashioned method of boiling it in plenty of water has been found to destroy most of its valuable nutrients. For the best flavor, and the most health-giving results, cabbage should be steamed in the water which clings to it from washing. Cooked in this way, cabbage needs only salt and pepper and butter or margarine to be delicious.

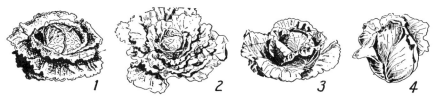

CABBAGE   1. Savoy   2. Early Flat Dutch   3. Round Head   4. Jersey Wakefield

Cabbage should be solid and hard, and the head should be heavy for its size. New cabbage is not usually so solid as the winter varieties. The outside leaves have usually been trimmed off and the stem cut close to the base of the head. Worm injury, decay, or yellowed leaves indicate inferior heads, but if the damage is not extensive, the affected parts may be cut away and the balance used to advantage. Cabbages in which the base of the leaves have separated from the stem are liable to be strong flavored and coarse, and should, of course, be avoided if possible.

One pound of cabbage will make about 3½ cups of shredded raw cabbage, or 2½ cups of cooked cabbage.

CABBAGE SLICER

Food Value

Water	Food Energy	Pro-tein	Fat	Carbo-hydrate	Cal-cium	Phos-phorus	Iron	Vit. A Value	Thia-mine	Ribo-flavin	Nia-cin	Ascor-bic Acid
92.4	29	1.4	.2	5.3	46	31	.5	80	.07	.06	.3	52

To prevent the odor of cabbage from permeating the house while cooking, place several slices of stale bread on top of the vegetable in a covered pan. The bread will absorb the odor, and should be discarded when the cabbage is cooked.

When cooking red cabbage, a small quantity of vinegar or lemon juice in the water will prevent its losing its color. *See also* COLE SLAW.

BIGOS (POLISH)

1 large head of cabbage
½ pound lean raw pork
½ cup chopped celery
½ cup chopped green pepper
3 medium sized green apples
1 small can tomato paste
1 No. 2 can Italian style tomatoes
1 bay leaf
3 whole cloves
1 small clove of garlic
Salt and pepper

Shred the cabbage and wash in cold water. Dry carefully, and sprinkle with a little salt. Let the cabbage stand to wilt slightly while you cut the pork in small cubes and brown it in a skillet in its own fat. Add the celery and green pepper and brown slightly. Scrape the mixture into a saucepan with a closely fitting lid, add the cabbage and the apples which have been pared, cored, and sliced thinly. Turn in the rest of the ingredients, mix thoroughly, and cover. Cook over a very low flame (275°–300° F.) for 1½ hours. This dish is even more delicious warmed up. (Serves 6)

CABBAGE AU GRATIN

Wash a good-sized head of cabbage and cut it in quarters. Steam it in salted water until tender. Drain well, and chop the cabbage. Place in a greased baking dish and pour over the cabbage 2 cups of rich cream sauce to which plenty of grated American cheese has been added. Top with buttered crumbs and bake in a hot oven (400° F.) until the crumbs are browned. (Serves 6)

CABBAGE PIE

Steam a large cabbage and drain thoroughly. Peel and slice six good-sized tomatoes. Grate a large onion. In a greased baking dish make alternate layers of cabbage leaves and tomato slices, sprinkling a little onion on each layer of tomatoes. Finish with a layer of tomatoes. Cover the top with buttered crumbs and place in a hot oven (400°–425° F.) until the crumbs are browned and the dish is heated through.

CABBAGE SOUP

½ medium-sized head new cabbage
1 large onion
1 large potato
3 cups milk
Salt and pepper
3 tablespoons butter
Grated cheese

Shred the cabbage and thinly slice both onion and potato. Cook in a heavy pan with about 4 tablespoons of water until the vegetables are tender. Mash very thoroughly to a pulp, add the milk, salt, pepper and butter, and reheat without actually boiling. Serve with a generous sprinkling of grated cheese. (Serves 3 or 4)

CREAM OF CABBAGE SOUP

1 medium-sized head of cabbage
3 large onions
1 green pepper
2 slices canned pimiento
1 bouquet garni
3 cups sweet milk
1 pint sour cream
Roux of 2 tbsp of butter and 2 tbsp flour

Shred the cabbage and the onions into a soup pot. Mince the green pepper and add it. Cover with boiling water and add the pimiento, chopped, and the bouquet garni. Cover the pot and simmer gently until the cabbage is tender, and the water reduced to half. Remove the bouquet garni, and season with salt and pepper to taste. Scald the milk and sour cream and add to the soup. Thicken with the roux and keep hot until ready to serve. Serve in bowls with grated Swiss cheese to be sprinkled on top. (Serves 6)

HOT SLAW

½ head of cabbage
2 tsp sugar

APPLESAUCE

Make applesauce, sweetened or unsweetened. Heat through, stirring to keep it from sticking to the pan. Pack hot to ¼ inch of top in jars, to top in cans.
Process for
Strained applesauce—
   Boiling-water bath:
      Pt. and qt. jars, 10 min.
      No. 2 cans, 10 min.
      No. 2½ cans, 15 min.
Unstrained applesauce—
   Boiling-water bath:
      Pt. and qt. jars, 5 min.
   Pressure canner:
      8 min. at 5 lb. pressure

APRICOTS

Select fully ripe, firm fruit of uniform size. Dip in boiling water for ½ minute, then quickly in cold water. Remove skins and pits, and cut fruit in halves. To prevent darkening, drop the halves into a salt-vinegar solution (2 tablespoons each of salt and vinegar per gallon of water). Drain just before heating or packing cold, and rinse thoroughly.
Hot pack. Cook in boiling sirup for about 5 minutes.* Pack hot fruit in hot, clean containers, placing halves in overlapping layers, rounded side up. Cover with boiling sirup.*
Process for—
   Boiling-water bath:
      Pt. jars, 20 min.
      Qt. jars, 25 min.
      No. 2 cans, 25 min.
      No. 2½ cans, 35 min.
Cold pack. Prepare fully ripe, firm fruit of uniform size as directed above. Pack raw fruit in clean, hot containers, placing halves in overlapping layers, rounded side up. Fill containers with boiling medium sirup.* If tin cans are used, exhaust them for 5 minutes.
Process for—
   Boiling-water bath:
      Pt. jars, 25 min.
      Qt. jars, 35 min.
      No. 2 cans, 25 min.
      No. 2½ cans, 35 min.
   Pressure canner (either pack):
      10 min. at 5 lb. pressure
*If desired for flavor, one cracked pit may be added to each quart of sirup; strain before filling jars.

BEETS, PICKLED

Cut off beet tops, leaving the root and 1 inch of stem. Wash beets, cover them with boiling water, and cook until tender. Skin and slice them. For sirup, use 2 cups of vinegar (or 1½ cups of vinegar and ½ cup of water) to 2 cups of sugar. Heat to boiling.
Pack hot beets in glass jars only. Cover with boiling pickling sirup. Add ½ teaspoon of salt per pint. Adjust jar lids. Process in boiling-water bath for 30 minutes.

BERRIES
(except strawberries)

Avoid crushing berries. Pick over, wash, hull or stem, and drain them.
Hot Pack (for firm berries). Add ½ cup of sugar to each quart of fruit. Cover pan, and bring to boil, shaking pan to keep berries from sticking. Pack jars to ½ inch of top and cans to top.
Process for—
   Boiling-water bath:
      Pt. and qt. jars, 15 min.
      No. 2 cans, 15 min.
      No. 2½ cans, 20 min.
Cold Pack (for red raspberries and other soft berries). Pack raw berries in hot, sterilized containers, shaking while filling for a full pack. Fill jars to ½ inch of top, cans to ¼ inch. Cover with boiling medium sirup (made with berry juice instead of water, if desired). If cans are used, exhaust from 3 to 5 minutes.
Process for—
   Boiling-water bath:
      Pt. and qt. jars, 20 min.
      No. 2 cans, 15 min.
      No. 2½ cans, 20 min.
   Pressure canner (both packs):
      10 min. at 5 lb. pressure
   Pressure canner (both packs):
      10 min. at 5 lb. pressure.

CHERRIES

Follow the method given for firm berries, adding a little water when heating unpitted cherries to keep them from sticking to the pan. Sweet cherries are usually canned whole without pitting while the sour ones are usually pitted. When cherries are not pitted, prick the skins with the tines of a fork to prevent shrinkage. The juice may be saved to prepare sirup.

Fruit Juices

Wash, pit (if desired), and crush ripe fruit. Heat slowly to simmering. Strain through a cloth bag. Add ½ to 1 cup of sugar (if desired) to a gallon of juice. Water may also be added. Heat juice, and fill the containers with it. Seal the containers, and process in water bath at simmering temperature (below boiling, 180° F.) for 20 minutes.

Fruit Purées

Use sound, ripe fruit. Wash and pit it. Cut large fruit in pieces. Simmer until soft, adding a little water if needed to keep from sticking. Put it through a strainer or food mill. Add sugar to taste. Heat again to simmering. Pack hot to ¼ inch of top in jars, to top in cans. Process in boiling-water bath for 20 minutes.

Peaches

Use the same method as for apricots.

Pears

Wash pears. Peel, halve, and core them. Continue as with apricots, using either hot or cold pack.

Plums

Select fully ripe plums. If they are to be canned whole, prick their skins to prevent shrinkage. Freestone varieties may be halved and pitted. Simmer to boiling in sirup or juice. If fruit is very juicy, you may heat it with sugar, adding no liquid. Pack hot into clean, hot containers, filling jars to ½ inch of top and cans to ¼ inch of top. Cover with boiling liquid. Process in boiling-water bath for 15 minutes for pt. jars, qt. jars, and no. 2 cans; for 20 minutes for no. 2½ cans. Processing may be completed in a pressure canner in 10 minutes at 5 pounds pressure.

Rhubarb

Wash rhubarb, and cut it into ½-inch pieces. Add ½ cup of sugar to each quart of rhubarb, and let stand to draw out juice. Bring to a boil, stirring to prevent sticking. Pack hot to ½ inch of top in jars, to top in cans; cover with hot sirup. Process in boiling-water bath, for 10 minutes, or in pressure canner for 5 minutes at 5 pounds pressure.

Sauerkraut

Heat well-fermented sauerkraut to simmering; do not boil. Pack hot sauerkraut in clean, hot containers, pressing down firmly. Fill jars to ½ inch of top, cans to ¼ inch of top. Fill containers with boiling hot sauerkraut juice.
Process for—
  Boiling-water bath:
    Pt. jars, 25 min.
    Qt. jars, 30 min.
    No. 2 cans, 15 min.
    No. 2½ cans, 20 min.

Strawberries

Wash and stem berries. Add ½ cup of sugar to each quart of fruit, and let stand to draw juice. Bring slowly to a boil, shaking the pan to prevent sticking. Pack hot to ½ inch of top in jars, to top in cans.
Process for—
  Boiling-water bath:
    Pt. and qt. jars, 15 min.
    No. 2 cans, 15 min.
    No. 2½ cans, 20 min.
  Pressure canner:
    5 min. at 5 lb. pressure

Tomatoes

Use only perfect, ripe tomatoes. Wash them thoroughly. To loosen skins, dip into boiling water for ½ minute, then dip quickly into cold water. Remove skins and cores.
Hot Pack. Quarter tomatoes. Bring to boil, stirring often. Pack hot in glass jars. Add ½ teaspoon of salt per pint. Process in boiling-water bath for 10 minutes.
Cold Pack. Quarter peeled tomatoes. Leave tomatoes whole or cut in halves or quarters. Pack, pressing gently to fill spaces. Add no water. Add ½ teaspoon of salt to each pint.
Process for—
  Boiling-water bath:
    Pt. jars, 35 min.
    Qt. jars, 45 min.
    No. 2 cans, 45 min.
    No. 2½ cans, 55 min.
  Pressure canner (either pack):
    5 min. at 5 lb. pressure

Cool the jars top side up. Give each jar enough room so that air can reach its entire surface. Never set a hot jar on a cold surface or in a draft. Don't slow the cooling by covering the jars.

Cans. Cool tin cans in cold, clean water, changing it as needed to cool them quickly; or cool them in running water. If the former method is used, take them out of the water while they are slightly warm so that they will dry in the air. Stagger cans if you stack them, so that air can get around them.

Selection and Preparation of Fruits and Vegetables

Select fresh, young, firm fruits or vegetables, and can them quickly. They should be canned within two hours of gathering but, if you must hold them, keep them in a cool, airy place, preferably in a refrigerator. Try to get local produce when buying fruits or vegetables to can. Try to use only perfect food; this will give the best flavor and appearance in the canned product. If the raw products are bruised or discolored in spots, these spots should always be removed.

Sort the fruits or vegetables according to size and ripeness to effect even cooking. Prepare only enough fruits or vegetables at one time for one canner load, about 6 or 8 jars. Wash them thoroughly in running water, if possible, or through several changes of water. If the latter method is used, lift fruits or vegetables out of the water before changing it, so dirt that has been washed off will not be drained back over them; rinse the pan thoroughly between washings. Avoid letting the food soak as this may cause a loss of food value. Handle fruits or vegetables gently to avoid bruising. In short, try to get food as perfect as possible and keep it as perfect and as clean as possible.

Yield of Canned Foods From Fresh

Fruits	
Apples	2½ to 3 lb.
Berries, except strawberries	5 to 8 cups
Cherries, as picked	6 to 8 cups
Peaches	2 to 2½ lb.
Pears	2 to 2½ lb.
Plums	2 to 2½ lb.
Strawberries	6 to 8 cups
Tomatoes	2½ to 3 lb.

Vegetables	
Asparagus	4 lb.
Beans, lima in pods	4 to 5 lb.
Beans, snap	1½ to 2 lb.
Beets, without tops	2½ to 3 lb.
Carrots, without tops	2½ to 3 lb.
Corn, sweet, in husks	6 to 16 ears
Okra	1½ lb.
Peas, green, in pods	4 to 5 lb.
Pumpkin	3 lb.
Squash, summer	2 to 2½ lb.
Sweetpotatoes	2½ to 3 lb.

This fruit and vegetable chart indicates the amount of certain fruits and vegetables that must be used to yield one quart of canned food. The yield from a bushel of fresh food is not given because the legal weight of a bushel varies in different states.

Sweetening Fruit

Sugar sirup. Sugar sirup may be used to sweeten fruit. Make sirup by boiling a mixture of sugar and water or sugar and fruit juice for five minutes. Then remove scum.

To extract juice, crush thoroughly ripe, sound, juicy fruit. Heat to boiling over a low heat. Strain through a jelly bag or another cloth.

Sirup	Sugar	Water or fruit juice	Yield
Thin	1 cup	3 cups	3½ cups
Medium	1 cup	2 cups	2½ cups
Heavy	1 cup	1 cup	1½ cups

Sirups may be thick or thin, depending on the acidity of the food and on the preference of the canner.

For juicy fruit. If you use the hot-pack method, you can add dry sugar to raw juicy fruit and then heat without added liquid. Use about ½ cup of sugar to a quart of fruit. Bring to a boil over a low heat. Pack fruit in the juice that cooks out.

Canning with corn sirup. If sugar is scarce, use light corn sirup or mild-flavored honey to replace as much as half the sugar called for in canning fruit.

Do not extend sugar with brown sugar, molasses, sorghum, or other strong-flavored sirups. Their flavor overpowers the fruit flavor, and some of them tend to darken the fruit. Saccharin is not recommended.

Canning without sweetening. Fruit may be canned without sweetening—in its own juice, in extracted juice, or in water. Sugar helps fruit to retain its shape, color, and flavor, but it is not needed to prevent spoilage. Process unsweetened fruit the same as sweetened. To sweeten fruits before serving, drain the liquid, dissolve sugar in it by heating for a few minutes, pour back over the fruit, and let stand for several hours.

DAY-AFTER-CANNING JOBS

When glass jars have cooled overnight, remove screw bands that have glass or metal lids underneath if you want to reuse them. If a band sticks, covering it for a moment with a hot, damp cloth may help to loosen it. Do not use force as this may break the seal.

Testing for leaks. If jars have been used, test seals by turning each jar partly over. Jars with self-sealing lids should be tested by tapping the centers of the lids with a spoon. A clear, ringing sound indicates a good seal. If you can in tin, examine seals when you wipe the cooled cans. Also set out any can that buckles and breaks its seams; too little food in the can or cooling too fast may cause this type of leak.

If a leaky spot is found, use the unspoiled food immediately or reprocess it as if it were fresh. Before re-using a jar or lid, check it for defects as directed. If there has been no leakage, store the containers and watch for signs of spoilage. Before storing canned food, wipe the containers clean and label them to show contents, date of canning, and lot number if more than one lot was canned in a single day.

Storing. Protect jars and cans of food against bad storage conditions—heat, freezing, and dampness. Warmth may cause canned food to lose quality. Hot pipes behind a wall sometimes make a shelf or closet too warm for storing food. Freezing may crack a jar or break a seal, thus admitting bacteria; it may also cause undesirable changes in flavor and texture. In an unheated place food may be protected by covering it with a blanket or wrapping it in paper. Dampness may corrode tin cans and metal lids of glass jars and eventually cause leakage.

GUARDING AGAINST SPOILAGE

Don't use canned food that shows any sign of spoilage. Inspect each container before opening it. Bulging can ends, jar lids, or rings, or a leak may mean that food has spoiled. After opening the container, look for other signs such as spurting liquid, an "off" odor, mold, or gas bubbles. Jellied broth and darkening of metal lids are not indicative of spoilage.

It is possible for canned vegetables to contain the poison causing botulism—a serious food poisoning—without showing signs of spoilage. There is no danger of botulism if the canner is in perfect order and if every canning recommendation has been followed accurately. But as a safety precaution, boil the food for ten to twenty minutes before tasting it. If the food looks spoiled or has an "off" odor during heating, destroy it. Burn it, or dispose of it in another way so that it will not be eaten by humans or animals.

CANNING FRUITS AND VEGETABLES

Directions for packing hot are given for all the foods in the list. For some fruits (among them tomatoes), directions for the cold-pack method are also given.

Canning experts strongly recommend the hot-water-bath canner for acid foods and the pressure canner for nonacid. However, some home canners have successfully canned acid foods in a pressure canner and Jars with self-sealing lids should be tested vice versa. Wherever possible, the processing times are given for both of these methods.

Note: These directions should be supplemented by all other relevant instructions that are given in the entire section on canning.

APPLES

Select a tart variety for best results. Wash, pare, core, and slice or quarter apples. To prevent darkening, drop the fruit into a salt-vinegar solution (2 tablespoons each of salt and vinegar per gallon of water) until it is ready for packing; rinse thoroughly, and drain. Precook for five minutes in thin boiling sirup. Pack hot fruit to $\frac{1}{4}$ inch of top in clean, hot containers. Cover with hot sirup, leaving $\frac{1}{4}$-inch head space in jars but filling cans to top.

Process immediately for:
    Boiling-water bath:
        Pt. jar, 15 min.
        Qt. jar, 20 min.
        Tin cans, 10 min.
    Pressure canner:
        10 min. at 5 lb. pressure

In butter cakes (*cont.*)
Heavy cake (cont.)
    Not mixed fast enough after milk
        was added
Crumbley consistency of cake
    Too much flour
    Too much shortening
    Too much baking powder or
        too much soda

In Sponge or Angel Cake:
If the cake is tough
    Too hot an oven
If heavy and small
    Oven too hot
    Ingredients were beaten too much
    Ingredients were not all at room
        temperature
    Cake removed from pan while still
        hot
Sticky or hard crust
    Baked too long
    Too much sugar
    Too hot an oven
Coarse grained cake
    Eggs not beaten well
    Ingredients were not thoroughly
        mixed

ANGEL FOOD CAKES

One might well ask, "What makes for perfection in angel food cake?" Correct procedure of measuring and mixing is extremely important for this type of cake. Cake flour gives a more tender, fluffy, finer grained cake and therefore should be used. Sugar should be both measured and sifted. The separating and beating of the egg whites requires special attention. It has been found that eggs separate more easily when cold, but the whites beat up to greater volume when they are at room temperature.

Fresh cream of tartar, which see, or another acid, such as lemon juice, is an essential ingredient of an angel cake. Without it the cake is cream colored rather than white, and, during the last few minutes of baking, the cake has a tendency to shrink. The action of the acid is not that of a leavening agent but rather that of a strengthener of the cell walls of the egg whites so that they retain their maximum size. Salt is necessary for the taste. Almond, lemon, vanilla, or combinations of flavors may be used depending on individual preference.

The basic recipe for angel food cake is as follows:

BASIC RECIPE

1½ cups superfine granulated sugar
1 cup cake flour
10 whites of eggs
**2 tbsp water—or 1 tbsp each water and
    lemon juice**
1 tsp cream of tartar
½ tsp vanilla
½ tsp almond extract
½ tsp salt

Separate the egg whites and allow them to stand at room temperature while mixing other ingredients. Sift the sugar. Sift the flour once before measuring. Add to the flour ½ cup sifted sugar and the salt. Re-sift three times to incorporate air which lightens the cake. Next, beat the egg whites with the water, or water and lemon juice, until the mixture is foamy. Add the cream of tartar and resume beating. It is important to stop beating the mixture when it is stiff enough to stand alone yet still has a moist, shiny appearance. Any preferred type of beater may be used, the rotary, flat, or electric mixer. The cake will be lighter if the beater is kept below the surface while beating. Gradually and gently whip into the egg whites, about 1 teaspoon at a time, the remaining cupful of sifted sugar. Fold in the vanilla and almond extract. Fold in gradually, about 1 tablespoonful at a time, the sifted flour and sugar mixture. Use a gentle folding motion and fold only until the sugar and flour are well blended with the egg whites. If overmixed the cake will be heavy and if undermixed the grain will be coarse. Pour batter into an ungreased, 9-inch tube pan and bake in a slow to moderate oven (300°-325° F.) about 1 hour. A low baking temperature is desirable for a tender cake. When finished, the crust should be a delicate brown and should not retain any imprint when it is lightly pressed. Invert pan on a rack and let stand until cake is cool (about 1 hour). The cake should then fall out easily.

The angel cake may be iced or left plain. Chocolate angel cake is made by substituting ¼ cup of cocoa for ¼ cup of flour in the above recipe. Sift the flour and cocoa together and proceed as for plain angel cake.

Butter Cakes

A butter cake consists of shortening, sugar, flavoring, eggs, liquid, flour, baking powder, and salt. The shortening helps the cake to be tender, while creaming (stirring and beating) creates a smoothness of texture. Butter "creams" well and gives a flavor that is well liked.

The sugar sweetens cake batter, helps it to brown and when well creamed with shortening, is largely responsible for what is known as a soft, velvety texture. A very fine granulated sugar gives the best results.

Eggs enrich, lighten, bind together and emulsify the fat with the liquid. According to the best modern methods for making butter cakes, whole unbeaten eggs are added one at a time to the creamed butter-and-sugar-flavoring mixture. Each egg should be thoroughly beaten into the mixture before the next is added. If pullet eggs (small eggs) are used, three should be in place of two average-sized ones.

Although water is the most commonly used liquid, milk, fruit juices, or wine may be substituted. Add about one-third of the liquid at a time, alternating with one-third of the dry, sifted ingredients.

The flour is the thickening agent or body of the cake. Cake flour makes the best cake, pastry flour is next, and all-purpose or bread flour, third. Cake flour is very fine, soft, and smooth. It contains more starch and less protein than the others. Its protein makes a more tender gluten and, consequently, a softer and more tender cake. Flour should be sifted once before measuring, and at least twice with the baking powder and salt.

The baking powder is the chief leavening agent. In general cakes need less baking powder than other flour mixtures because of the air creamed into the fat and sugar and beaten into the eggs (more of which are used than in most breads). Generally speaking, one level teaspoon is used for each cup of flour.

If an unsalted shortening is used, allow ½ teaspoon of salt for each cup of flour. With a salted shortening, ¼ teaspoon is enough. Add ⅓ of the sifted, dry ingredients to the first mixture of shortening, sugar, flavoring, and eggs and ⅓ of the liquid, and beat using a vigorous stirring motion until the mixture is smooth. Add the second third of liquid and dry ingredients; beat until smooth, and finally beat in the last third. Turn at once into greased pans and shake down to an even level surface.

The Baking. Failing thermostatic control a portable oven thermometer will prove invaluable to insure perfect baking. For layer cakes and cup cakes (butter) a moderate temperature (350°-375° F.) is best.

The following is an excellent recipe for a plain foundation butter cake which may be varied by the use of different fillings and icings.

Butter Cake

1 cup butter
1 cup sugar
1 tsp flavoring
2 eggs
2 cups sifted cake flour
2 tsp baking powder
½ tsp salt
¾ cup milk

Cream the butter until very light, gradually adding the sugar and continuing the beating until the mixture is light and fluffy. Add any preferred flavoring, then the eggs, one at a time, beating each in thoroughly. Add the sifted dry ingredients alternately with the milk and again beat until smooth. Turn the batter into greased cake pans and bake in a moderate oven (350°-375° F.) for about 25 minutes. After baking, place the cake (still in the pan) on a cooling rack for 3 or 4 minutes, then loosen the edges of the cake from the pan with a spatula and turn out onto the cooling rack. Be sure that the cake is always thoroughly cold before filling or icing.

Chiffon Cake

The chiffon cake, which offers something new in texture, has been developed very recently by home economists. Because it uses liquid shortening, there is no need to cream the shortening and sugar, and mixing is thus quicker and easier. The texture combines the lightness of sponge cake with the richness of a butter cake.

The basic recipe for chiffon cake is as follows:

Basic Recipe

2 cups flour
1½ cups sugar

3 tsp double action baking powder
1 tsp salt
½ cup cooking oil
7 eggs, separated
¾ cup cold water
2 tsp vanilla
Grated rind of one lemon (2 tsp)
½ tsp cream of tartar

Measure and sift together in a mixing bowl the flour, sugar, baking powder, and salt. Make a "well" and put in, in order, oil, 7 unbeaten egg yolks, water, vanilla and lemon rind. Mix well, gradually stirring in the flour. Measure 1 cup of egg whites and cream of tartar into large mixing bowl, and whip until whites form *very* stiff peaks. Pour egg yolk mixture gradually over whipped whites, gently folding with rubber scraper until just blended. Pour into ungreased pan at once. (Use 10-inch tube pan, 4 inches deep). Bake 55 minutes in slow, moderate oven (325° F.) then increase heat to moderate (350° F.) for 10 minutes. Remove from the oven and immediately turn pan upside down, placing tube part over neck of funnel or bottle. Let hang free of table, until cold. Loosen from sides and tube with spatula. Turn pan over and hit edge sharply on table to loosen.

The chiffon cake may be used plain or iced. A smaller cake may be made by halving all the ingredients, and using 4 eggs instead of the 7 called for above. If the cake is baked in a square cake pan, bake at 350° F. for 30 minutes. If a 9-inch tube pan is used, bake for 40 minutes at 325° F. and then bake for 10 minutes at 350° F.

FRUIT CAKES

Whether known as wedding cakes, or holiday cakes, the fruit cakes are rich dark, spicy mixtures, containing a proportionately great amount of fruits and nuts to the cake batter which holds them together. The traditional old English fruitcake is almost a fruit pudding, so rich and dark is it. However, modern homemakers prefer a somewhat simpler formula, and modern fruit cakes may be largely cake with a good addition of fruits. Many varieties of fruits are used, of course. White fruit cake uses light colored fruits and spices to keep a creamy color. Fruit cakes are never iced, except when they are to be used as wedding

cakes. For instructions for icing a wedding cake, *see* FROSTING, FILLING AND ICING.

The traditional dark holiday fruit cake is decorated on top with designs of cherries, citron, angelica, or other fruits, and blanched almonds or other nuts. An apricot glaze (*which see*) is used to hold the decorations in place.

Several variations of fruit cakes are given below.

CHRISTMAS CAKE

2¼ cups cake flour
1 tsp baking powder
½ tsp salt
½ cup shortening
½ cup butter
1 cup sugar
5 eggs
1 tsp lemon flavoring
1 tbsp brandy
¾ cup blanched, chopped, almonds
1 cup shredded, moist coconut
¼ cup candied lemon peel, chopped

Sift flour, measure; add baking powder, salt and sift again. Cream shortening and butter together; add sugar, cream until well blended. Add eggs one at a time, beating after each addition. If you use a mixer beat with slow speed throughout. Mix in lemon and brandy flavoring, almonds, coconut, and lemon peel. Stir in dry ingredients. Turn batter into greased and floured 9-inch tube pan. Bake in slow oven (300° F.) for 1¼ hours. When cooled store in airtight container.

KITCHENETTE WEDDING CAKE

⅔ cup butter or other shortening
2 cups sifted flour
¼ tsp soda
½ tsp salt
2 tsp lemon juice
1 tsp almond extract
6 egg whites
1¼ cups sifted powdered sugar
⅔ cup halved candied cherries
½ cup shredded citron
½ cup shredded blanched almonds

Cream the shortening. Add the soda and salt to the flour; resift, and gradually add to the shortening along with the lemon juice and almond extract. Beat egg whites until frothy, add powdered sugar, and continue beating until stiff. Combine with the first mixture and fold in the fruit and almonds. Turn into a greased pan lined with greased paper and bake in a slow oven (275° F.) about 1¼ hours.

New England Wedding Cake

1 lb sweet butter
1 lb sugar
12 eggs, separated
1 lb flour
1 tsp cloves
1 tsp nutmeg
1 cup brandy
1 cup sherry
2 lb seeded raisins, chopped
2 lb currants
1 lb citron, shaved thin
1 tsp cinnamon

Cream butter and add sugar gradually. Beat the egg yolks thick and add; whip in whites, beaten stiff. Dredge with ½ cup flour, sift remaining flour with spices, and stir into batter Add. wine and brandy. Stir in the dredged fruit, except the citron.

Line baking-pan with greased paper. Put part of the citron into the pan, then a layer of the mixed batter, alternating until all citron and batter is used.

Bake in steady slow oven (275° F.) for 4 hours. Allow cake to cool gradually in oven.

Rich Wedding Cake

1 lb shredded citron
1 lb halved crystallized cherries
1 lb diced crystallized pineapple
¾ lb shredded blanched almonds
¼ lb shredded candied orange rind
4½ cups sifted flour
3 tsp baking powder
1 tsp salt
2 cups butter
2 cups sugar
¾ cup wine or fruit juice
1 tsp vanilla
12 egg whites

Combine fruits and almonds. Sift three cups of flour with the baking powder and salt and sprinkle the remaining cup of flour over the fruits and almonds, stirring it in thoroughly. Cream the butter and sugar together, then add the sifted dry ingredients with the wine or fruit juice. Mix very

thoroughly and then work in the fruit-nut mixture and the vanilla. Finally fold in the stiffly beaten egg whites. Turn into a well-greased tube pan lined with greased paper and bake in a slow oven (275° F.) 2½ to 3 hours.

White Fruit Cake

⅔ cup butter
¼ tsp soda
6 egg whites
⅔ cup candied cherries
½ cup thinly-sliced citron
1⅞ cups flour
½ tsp lemon juice
1½ cups powdered sugar
⅓ cup blanched and shredded almonds
1 tsp almond extract

Cream butter, gradually add flour mixed and sifted with soda and lemon juice. Beat whites of eggs stiff. Add sugar. Combine mixtures, add cherries, almonds, citron and extract. Bake in greased deep cake-tin in moderate oven (350° F.) for 1 hour.

Sponge Cake

Plain sponge cake, sunshine cake, etc., all belong to the sponge cake family. They vary chiefly in the proportion of egg whites and yolks they contain. These cakes, with their delicate, airy texture, are ideal desserts. The sponge cake group, which includes all cakes made without shortening, is divided into two parts—the yellow loaf known as sponge, and the loaf of snowy whiteness known as angel food cake (*see above*).

Sponge Cake

1 cup sugar
1 tbsp lemon juice
½ tbsp grated lemon rind
1 tsp vanilla
5 eggs, separated
1 cup sifted cake flour
¼ tsp salt

Sift the flour at least three times. Beat the egg whites until frothy, gradually adding the salt. Continue beating until stiff enough to form peaks. Beat in the sugar, a little at a time, and continue beating until the mixture is no longer "grainy." Beat the egg yolks thoroughly, add lemon juice,

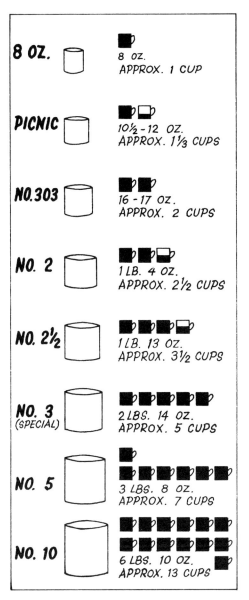

CANS. Chart showing sizes and capacities

CANNING. Home canning is indeed a delight to the homemaker. It enables her to serve out-of-season foods which have been preserved to retain the color, flavor, and nutritive value of the fresh foods; at the same time, it is highly economical. It is not so difficult as is generally supposed; in fact, the only requisites are cleanliness, fairly ordinary kitchen equipment, and the ability to follow directions with precision. Before beginning to can, it is advisable to study the methods, techniques, and equipment used in, and to have an understanding of the principle of, the process.

Tiny organisms that cause food spoilage are in the air, water, and soil at all times. Fresh fruits and vegetables also contain certain enzymes that may cause undesirable changes within the food. When these foods are canned, they are heated over a length of time, and to a degree, sufficient to stop the action of the enzymes and to destroy the elements of spoilage. At the same time, they should not be heated so long that their color, flavor, and nutritive value are impaired. The containers are sealed that no more organisms will enter them.

WARNING: Do not use canning powders or other chemical preservatives; some of them may be harmful. Sterilization by heat is more certain and much safer.

EQUIPMENT

The utensils used in canning are:
Shallow pans
Colander (for straining)
Wire basket or cheesecloth (for dipping)
Jar funnel
Quart measure
Measuring cup
Ladle or dipper
Measuring spoons
Jar tongs (to prevent burns)
Long-handled spoons
Stainless steel paring knives
Cutting knife and board
Scissors
Vegetable brush
Jars, covers, and rubbers (or tin cans and a sealer)
Pressure cooker or water bath (for processing)

Jars and lids. There are various types of jars, rubbers, and closures on the market. Home-canners should know how to use all types of jars and lids if every jar is to have a perfect seal.

There are four main types of closures made to fit the standard mason jar.

The original mason jar has a rubber shoulder ring and a one-piece screw top with a porcelain or lacquered metal lining. The porcelain is difficult to clean. This cover can be used repeatedly unless the porcelain loosens or breaks. If the jar is opened by prying up the cover, the cover may be dented so that it will make an imperfect seal if used again.

The two-piece glass and metal cover has a small rubber that is placed on the lid of the jar. The cover is held in place by a metal screw band. When the jars have cooled for twelve hours, the band should be removed to prevent rusting.

The wire-bail type jar has a glass lid that fits down on a rubber ring. The cover is held in place by two wire clamps or bails.

The two-piece metal cover containing a sealing compound is another type. The cover is lacquered metal with a composition rubber band. It is held in place by a metal screw band or clamp. Although the metal cap can be used but once, the screw band or clamp can be used often. It can be removed when the jars are cold.

The proper usage for each of the four closure types is given in the following chart:

use it to hold a new metal cap in place during processing. Since these jars are a little broader than a quart jar, they require a longer processing period. Process one and a half times as long as the time for a quart jars.

Tomatoes and fruits are sometimes canned in half gallon jars, but this size jar should never be used for meats and non-acid vegetables because of the slow penetration of heat. Even with the longer processing time required, foods may spoil.

Rubbers. New rubbers should be used each .time because the prolonged high temperature required for processing causes the rubber to deteriorate.

Tin cans. Tin cans may be used at home in place of glass jars, but canning in tin requires the use of a can sealer. This is practical only when more than 300 cans are needed for a family. Plain tin, C-enamel, and R-enamel are the types used in

Closure	When Canning	After Canning
Porcelain-lined cap; one-piece screw top	Fit wet rubber ring down on jar shoulder without stretching it unnecessarily. Fill jar; wipe the rubber ring and the jar rim clean. Then screw cap down firmly and turn it back ¼ inch.	As soon as the jar is removed from the canner, screw the cap down tightly to complete the seal.
Two-piece glass and metal cover	Fill jar, and wipe rim clean. Fit wet rubber ring on glass lid. Put the lid on the jar, rubber side down. Screw the band on until it is almost tight. Then turn back almost a quarter turn, but be sure that the jar and the band mesh. Caution: If band is screwed too tight, it may break.	As soon as the jar is removed from the canner, screw the band down tightly to complete the seal.
Wire-bail type of jar	Fit wet rubber ring on ledge at top of empty jar. Fill jar; wipe rubber ring and jar rim clean. Put on glass lid. Leave the short wire up; push the long wire over the top of the lid, fitting it into the groove.	As soon as the jar is removed from the canner, push the short wire down to complete the seal.
Two-piece metal cover with sealing compound	Fill jar; wipe rim clean. Put lid on with sealing compound next to glass. By hand, screw the metal band down tightly; do not use a wrench. When the band is screwed firmly, this lid has enough "give" to let air escape during the processing.	This jar seals automatically as it cools. Don't tighten the lid any further after removing the jar from the canner. Further tightening might break the seal.

The small-mouthed jars used as containers for food (such as coffee) can be used at home for canning fruits and tomatoes only. These jars require a small cover called a 63 millimeter. A metal cap with a composition rubber ring can be purchased for use on this type of jar. Boil the composition out of the original cover, and

home canning. Enameled cans are recommended for certain fruits and vegetables to prevent discoloring, but they are not necessary for a wholesome product.

C-enamel cans are recommended for:
Green lima beans
Corn
Carrots

production areas, so the harvested vegetables can be quickly brought to the plant for processing while fresh.

The fresh vegetables are washed in large vats of continuously circulating water or under sprays of water. Vegetables that must be peeled are specially treated to remove the peel or are put through mechanical peelers. The stems of such vegetables as green beans are automatically snipped off by specially designed cutting machines.

The vegetables are then spread on moving belts that carry them to workers who do any extra peeling or cutting necessary and remove undesirable pieces. Some vegetables such as peas may also be sorted into sizes by special equipment.

In the final processing of canned vegetables, the sealed cans are cooked under carefully controlled conditions of time and temperature and then quickly cooled. This is what insures the keeping quality of canned vegetables without refrigeration.

Today's processes provide wholesome products preserved at the peak of flavor.

ADVANTAGES OF CANNED FOODS

Canned foods are extremely practical. They can be transported any distance in any climate to be opened safe, wholesome, and ready for use. When opened, it needs only to be heated and served; this greatly reduces preparation and cooking time. The consumer has the assurance that the food has been properly cooked and seasoned.

The use of canned foods is economical. Canned meat, for instance, is already trimmed, and the purchaser pays only for what she will use. It is solid meat with no loss due to gristle, bone, or other waste products. It is packed in a form which does not yield food loss through shrinkage.

Canning concerns have established a commendable record for the safety and dependability of their products. A popular belief has existed to the effect that "ptomaine poisoning" is acquired through the use of canned foods, but this belief is foundationless. Food that has been sterilized and packed in air-tight containers cannot possibly be dangerous (unless, of course, the containers have since been damaged). Canned foods can be safely stored under a wide temperature range.

Whether to buy canned foods or to prepare them yourself. That canned foods possess all of the aforementioned advantages is undeniable, and it would be foolish to deny the utility of these products. They are probably most valuable as time-savers. On the other hand, it would be foolish to eliminate homemade foods from one's menus and to use only this modern, easier method.

Some canned foods cannot be recommended and others condemned. Each homemaker must determine which canned products fit her budget and her needs. Generally speaking, canned foods are less expensive than delicatessen products, but in some cases they are more so. In these cases it must be determined whether the amount of time saved is commensurate with the added cost.

If you have a baby, it may be worthwhile to compare the cost and convenience of various methods of preparing vegetables for him. You may prefer to strain some of the vegetables that you have prepared for the family, or you may prefer to buy vegetables canned especially for babies.

In connection with canned foods, a question arises as to whether home canning or dependence on commercially canned foods is preferable. Here again the decision must be left to the individual. If you wish to know whether it would pay to can certain fruits and vegetables, you might ask your State college of agriculture. You can find out, for example, the number of cans or jars that you may expect to fill by canning a half-bushel basket of pears and what you should figure as the yearly cost of the cans or jars.

If you have storage space, it is advisable to inquire about the price of a case (24 cans) of a food that your family uses often and compare it with the price of the same number of cans purchased individually.

LABEL INFORMATION

Most people want full value for their money when they buy canned foods; consequently, they are interested in both price and quality. The numberless brands, styles, varieties, and prices of canned foods available are indeed baffling unless the consumer has determined a reliable method of identifying quality. With U.S. Grade A, B, or C labels on canned fruits and vegetables, you can select the quality that best fits your purpose and purse. Without grade labels it is difficult to tell the quality of the product in a can. Prices and quality are not always proportionate. Nor do superlative terms such as Superb, Superfine, and Bestever, define quality.

U.S. Grades. "U.S." on a can label, or a shield embossed in one end of a can or jar, certifies that the product was processed under the continuous inspection plan of the Agricultural Marketing Service of the U.S. Department of Agriculture. Regardless of the grade designation, these foods are nutritious and wholly acceptable for human consumption. Otherwise, they could not be marketed in interstate commerce; the products would be illegal and subject to seizure under the consumer-protecting Federal Food, Drug, and Cosmetic Act.

U.S. Grade A ("Fancy") stands for top quality. It calls for near-perfection in color, size, and tenderness. There are few, if any, blemishes. This grade is desirable for special uses—for salads and dishes in which appearance is important.

U.S. Grade B ("Extra Standard") products are satisfactory for most meals, but they fall just a little short of U.S. Grade A in some respects. For example, they may be a little less tender.

U.S. Grade C ("Standard") is a good quality, but fruits and vegetables of this grade are not quite so uniform in color, size, and maturity as those of the A and B grades. Grade C is a wise choice for puddings, croquettes, and many other dishes.

Additional descriptive information on labels, such as the number of pieces in a can of apricots, the sieve size of peas, the strength of the sirup on fruits, and the net weight, also helps homemakers to make a wise selection.

Since the full measure of the edible contents of a package or can is required, the label on a jar of olives, for example, states the weight of the olives themselves or a numerical count. Since the government ruled that no piece of asparagus over four inches may be called a "tip," many packers now label their five-inch stalks "spears." It is a protection to both the consumer and the merchant.

Can sizes. Use the chart below as a guide in the selection of can sizes for fruits and vegetables. An adult size portion of canned vegetables usually measures about one-half cup.

STORAGE

Foodstuffs need not be removed from the can after it is opened; there is no danger of tin poisoning. But on the other hand, it is apparent that canned products are perishable; once the can has been opened, they are subject to contamination from the bacteria of the air just as is any fresh product. For that reason, it is not advisable to allow perishable foods to stand in open containers for any appreciable length of time unless they are kept very cold. Furthermore, although cold delays the growth of these bacteria, it does not entirely prevent it. Hence, foods cannot be kept in open containers in refrigerators indefinitely. Storage near steam pipes, radiators, furnaces, or kitchen ranges should be avoided.

Damaged containers. Containers should be sound and clean, free from rust and serious dents, and the ends should be flat or concave. Properly processed canned foods keep for long periods without spoilage unless damage to the can causes a leak. Bulging, swelling, leaking, or "flat sours" render cans potentially dangerous to the consumer. They should be refused or returned to the dealer to be destroyed immediately. Foods containing sulphur may discolor the inner surface of the can, but the stain is harmless.

CAN SIZES

Can	Average Net Weight	Average Cupfuls	Servings
8 oz.	8 ozs.	1	2
Picnic (No. 1 Eastern)	10½ to 12 oz.	1⅓	2
No. 303	16 to 17 oz.	2	4
No. 2	20 oz.	2½	4 to 5
No. 2½	29 oz.	3½	6 to 7
No. 3 (special)	46 oz.	5	7 to 10
No. 5 (for restaurants, etc.)	3 lb. 8 oz.	7	14
No. 10 (for restaurants, etc.)	6 lb. 10 oz.	13	26

with greased brown paper, and bake in a moderate oven (350° F.) about 1 hour.

JESSICA'S CAKE

2 cups sugar
1 cup butter
4 cups flour
6 eggs, separated
1 cup currants
Few raspings nutmeg
4 tbsp sherry or brandy

Cream the butter and sugar until very light, add the egg yolks and beat all together until light and creamy. Grate the nutmeg into the brandy and stir into the sugar mixture. Dredge currants with a little of the flour and stir the remainder into batter. Then add currants and fold in the stiffly beaten egg whites last. Pour into a well greased loaf pan and bake in a moderate oven (350° F.) about 1 hour, or until the cake tests done.

LADY CAKE

1 lb sugar
¾ lb sweet butter
1 lb flour
4 tbsp cornstarch
16 egg whites
Rose flavoring, lemon, or almond extract
½ tsp bak.ng powder

Cream the butter and sugar together with 8 egg whites. Sift the flour, cornstarch, and baking powder together and add to the creamed mixture. Beat the remaining 8 egg whites until very stiff and fold in gently. Stir in the flavoring, mixing lightly. Pour into small loaf pans which have been greased and paper-lined. Bake in slow oven (300° to 325° F.) for 1¼ to 1½ hours depending upon size of pans. Cover top and sides with vanilla frosting. *See* FROSTING. (Takes 2 cakes)

LADY BALTIMORE CAKE

2¼ cups cake flour
1½ tsp baking powder
½ tsp salt
½ cup butter or other shortening
1⅓ cups sugar
1 tsp vanilla
⅔ cup milk
4 egg whites

Sift the flour, measure and resift 3 times with baking powder and salt. Cream the butter thoroughly; add the sugar slowly and continue creaming until smooth and fluffy. Stir in the vanilla. Add sifted dry ingredients alternately with milk in 4 or 5 portions, beginning and ending with flour, and beating thoroughly after each addition. Fold in stiffly beaten egg whites. Turn batter into two 8-inch layer cake pans lined with thin, plain paper in bottom. Bake in a moderate oven (375° F.) about 25 minutes, or until cake is springy when lightly pressed with finger tips. Allow to cool in pans 5 minutes, then turn out onto cake racks, and cool thoroughly.

Make a double recipe of the Seven-minute Frosting (*see* FROSTING). Transfer about ⅓ of the icing to another bowl and quickly stir in the following ingredients:

12 maraschino cherries, well drained and chopped
½ cup finely chopped moist dried figs
½ cup chopped pecans

Spread between layers of Lady Baltimore Cake. Spread top and sides with rest of plain Seven-minute Frosting.

LIGHTNING CAKE

1 egg
½ cup sugar
1 cup flour
1 tsp baking powder
¼ tsp salt
¼ cup milk
3 tbsp melted butter
¼ tsp lemon extract

Beat the egg and add sugar while beating. Add the flour sifted with the baking powder and salt. Then add the milk, melted butter, and flavoring. Bake 25 minutes in greased cake-pans in a moderate oven (350° F.). Put together with any desired filling and frost. *See* FROSTING.

MOSS ROSE CAKE

2 cups cake flour
2 tsp baking powder
½ tsp salt
2 cups sugar
4 eggs
1 cup milk, scalded
½ tsp almond extract

Sift the flour, measure and resift 3 times with baking powder and salt. Place sugar in deep 1 quart bowl (small mixer bowl is convenient if electric mixer is used to make cake) and turn unbeaten eggs on top of sugar. A narrow bowl is needed to allow the beater to set well into the egg-sugar mixture. Beat with a rotary beater (or electric mixer on medium speed) for ten minutes, until mixture is very light and fluffy. Transfer to a larger bowl and fold in sifted dry ingredients in three portions. Add extract and the barely hot milk all at once and beat vigorously with a spoon about ½ minute until thoroughly blended. This is a very thin batter. Pour *immediately* into two 8-inch square pans 1¾ inches deep which have been lined on the bottom with greased paper. Bake in a moderate oven (350° F.) 25 to 30 minutes, or until cake springs back when touched gently on top. Let cool in pans for 10 minutes, then loosen sides if necessary and turn out on cake rack. Allow the cakes to cool thoroughly.

Put together with coconut frosting. *See* COCONUT.

MARBLE SPICE CAKE

2 cups sifted cake flour
1⅓ cups granulated sugar
½ tsp baking powder
1 tsp salt
2½ cups shortening
¾ cup milk
1½ tsp vanilla
2 eggs, unbeaten
1 tsp cinnamon
¼ tsp cloves
½ tsp allspice
½ tsp nutmeg

Have the eggs, milk and shortening at room temperature. Sift the first 4 ingredients into mixing bowl. Drop in the shortening. Add about ⅔ of the milk, then the vanilla and beat a minute. Add the eggs, beat 2 more minutes. Add remaining milk and beat 50 strokes. Divide batter in half. Add spices to one half. Drop batters alternately by tablespoonful in 10x10x2 inch pan lined on bottom with waxed paper, then greased. Bake at 375° F. for 35 to 45 minutes.

Cover cake with boiled frosting. *See* FROSTING.

MILK AND HONEY CAKE

½ cup shortening
½ tsp salt
½ tsp of vanilla
½ cup sugar
2 eggs
2 cups sifted flour
2½ tsp baking powder
½ cup undiluted evaporated milk
½ cup honey

Combine the shortening, salt and vanilla. Add the sugar gradually and cream until light and fluffy. Add the eggs, one at a time and beat thoroughly after each. Sift the flour and baking powder together 3 times. Combine honey and milk. Add a small amount of the flour mixture alternately with milk mixture to batter. Beat only until smooth after each addition. Pour into the pan, 8x8x2 inches, and bake in moderate oven (350° F.) for 50 to 60 minutes. Or pour into two greased 8-inch layer cake pans and bake at 350° for 25 minutes. Cover with white icing. *See* FROSTING.

OLD-FASHIONED NUT LOAF

2 cups sifted cake flour
2½ tsp baking powder
½ tsp salt
⅔ cup shortening
1 cup sugar
1 tsp vanilla
3 eggs
1 cup finely chopped walnuts
6 tbsp milk

Mix and sift the flour, baking powder and salt. Cream the shortening until soft and smooth; gradually add the sugar, creaming until fluffy. Add the vanilla and then beat in thoroughly one egg at a time; add the nuts and beat well. Add flour alternately with milk, beating until smooth after each addition. Turn into greased loaf pan and bake in moderate oven (350° F.) about 1¼ hours.

OLD-FASHIONED POUND CAKE

1 lb cake flour (4½ cups)
1 tsp baking powder
2 tsp nutmeg
1 lb butter (2 cups), scant
1 lb sugar (2¼ cups)

¼ cup lemon juice or 2 tbsp brandy
1 lb eggs (10), separated

Mix the flour, baking powder and nutmeg, and sift three times. Cream the butter until soft and smooth; add the sugar gradually, creaming until very fluffy; add the lemon juice and well-beaten egg yolks, beating very thoroughly. Fold in thoroughly the stiffly beaten egg whites, then the flour. Turn into two greased, paper-lined loaf pans and bake in slow oven (300°-325° F.) for 1¼ to 1½ hours. (Makes 2 loaves)

RUSSIAN LAYER CAKE

5 eggs, separated
1 cup granulated sugar
½ lemon, juice and grated rind
4 tbsp sifted potato flour
3 tbsp sifted white flour
Fine dry bread crumbs

Beat the egg yolks with sugar till very light. Add the strained lemon juice and rind. Add potato flour and white flour. Whip the egg whites till stiff and shiny and feed them in very slowly. Butter a cake pan or 2 layer pans and sprinkle lightly with fine dry sifted bread crumbs. Fill with cake mixture and bake 40 minutes in slow oven (325° F.). Let cool 20 minutes, before transferring to cake rack. Put together with lemon frosting. *See* LEMON.

SAND CAKE

8 tbsp butter
8 tbsp powdered sugar
4 tbsp ground rice
4 tbsp flour
2 tbsp potato flour
2 eggs, separated
½ tsp baking powder
Pinch of salt

Sift the flour, baking powder, salt, rice and potato flour together. Cream the butter and sugar, and add the yolks of the eggs, beating each one in separately. Beat the whites of eggs stiffly and fold these into the creamed butter and sugar, alternately with the dry ingredients, adding a little milk if necessary. Put the mixture into a greased loaf pan, and bake in moderately hot oven of 375° F. for about 40 minutes.
    When cooled, cover with boiled frosting. *See* FROSTING.

SCOTCH SNOW CAKE

1 lb arrowroot
½ lb pounded white sugar
½ lb butter
6 egg whites
Almond, vanilla, or lemon extract

Beat the butter to a cream; stir in the sugar and arrowroot gradually, at the same time beating the mixture. Whisk the whites of the eggs to a stiff froth, add them to the other ingredients and beat well for 20 minutes. Put in whichever of the above flavorings may be preferred; pour the cake into a greased tube pan and bake in a moderate oven (350° F.) for 1 to 1½ hours. Cover with vanilla frosting. *See* FROSTING.

SILVER WHITE CAKE

2 cups cake flour
2½ tsp baking powder
¼ tsp salt
1¼ cups sugar
½ cup butter, or shortening
¾ cup milk
1 tsp vanilla
3 egg whites, unbeaten

Be sure that all ingredients are at room temperature. Sift the flour, measure and resift 3 times with baking powder, salt, and sugar, the last time unto the large mixing bowl. Add the butter and ½ cup of the milk. Stir with a spoon to blend. Then beat 2 minutes with electric beater using low speed, or by hand with a wooden spoon. Scrape sides and bottom of bowl twice during beating. Add remaining ¼ cup of milk, vanilla, and egg whites and beat for 2 more minutes. Turn into two 8-inch layer cake pans, bottoms lined with thin, plain paper. Bake at 375° F. for 25 to 30 minutes or until cake tests done. Let cool in pan 5 minutes, then remove from pans onto cake racks to cool thoroughly. Put together with lemon filling and frosting. *See* LEMON.

SWEDISH CROWN CAKE

7 tbsp butter
1¾ cups powdered sugar
3 eggs, separated
2 tbsp grated potatoes
1½ cups ground almonds

Cream the butter and sugar with the yolks of egg, add the grated potatoes, working the mixture for 30 minutes. Add the ground almonds, mixing thoroughly, and finally add the whites of eggs, beaten to a stiff froth. Pour the mixture into a buttered cake pan which has been sprinkled with breadcrumbs and bake in a fairly cool (325° F.) oven for about 45 minutes. Let it stand for 15 minutes before turning out.

SODA CAKE

16 tbsp flour
Pinch of salt
½ tsp cream of tartar
Grated nutmeg
½ tsp bicarbonate of soda
9 tbsp butter
9 tbsp sugar
6 oz currants
½ cup sour milk (about)
1 egg

Grease well and flour a 6½ to 7 inch cake pan. Sift the flour, salt, bicarbonate of soda, cream of tartar and nutmeg into a bowl. Rub in the butter with the tips of the fingers until it resembles fine breadcrumbs, then add the currants and sugar and mix well. Stir in the beaten egg and sufficient sour milk to form a fairly soft mixture. Put into prepared tin and bake in a hot oven of 380° F. for the first 20 minutes or until the cake is golden brown, then lower the heat to 340° F. and bake for another 30 to 40 minutes. Put together with boiled frosting. *See* FROSTING.

SPICE CAKE

1¾ cups cake flour
2¼ tsp baking powder
¼ tsp salt
1 tsp cinnamon
½ tsp nutmeg
½ tsp cloves
Few grains of cayenne, if desired
2 tbsp boiling water
½ cup butter or shortening
1 cup sugar
2 eggs, separated
⅔ cup milk

Sift the flour, measure and resift 3 times with the baking powder and salt. Combine the spices and mix thoroughly with boiling

water. Cream the butter until soft and smooth, blend in ¾ cup of the sugar, and add the beaten egg yolks. Beat until light and fluffy. Stir in spice mixture; then add flour mixture and milk alternately, beginning and ending with flour and beating until smooth after each addition. Beat egg whites, add remaining ¼ cup sugar, and continue beating until very stiff; fold into batter. Turn into two 8-inch cake pans which have been lined with thin plain paper in bottom. Bake in a moderate oven (350° F.) for about 25 minutes, until springy when pressed lightly with the finger tips. Cool 5 minutes before removing from pans and then turn out and cool thoroughly on cake racks. Put together with orange frosting. *See* ORANGE.

TIPSY CAKE

1 loaf sponge cake
½ cup sherry or Madeira wine
2 cups milk
3 eggs
¼ cup sugar
1 tsp vanilla extract
½ cup blanched shredded almonds

Place the loaf of cake in a deep dish or glass serving bowl. Pour the wine over it. Make a custard (which see) from the milk, eggs, sugar, and flavoring. Cool the custard and pour over the wine-soaked cake. Strew the surface with the shredded almonds. Chill thoroughly before serving. (Serves 6)

VIENNESE RAISED CAKE

3 cups flour
2¼ tbsp powdered sugar
½ cup butter
1 oz yeast
3 eggs
Just under 1 cup milk
⅔ cup raisins and currants
2 dozen blanched almonds

Dissolve the yeast in a little warm milk. Put the flour in a bowl and make a well in the center. Put in the eggs, the melted butter, the sugar, and the dissolved yeast, stir all well together and finally add the raisins and currants. Pour the mixture into a fancy fluted tubular pan, which has been well greased and in which the almonds, blanched and sliced, have been strewn, filling the mold only ¾ full. Put it in a warm place,

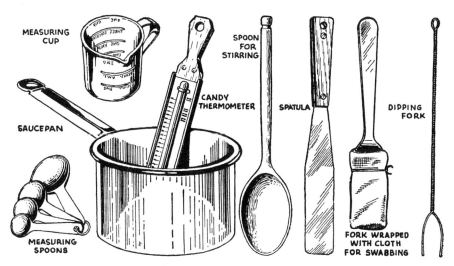

MEASURING CUP · SPOON FOR STIRRING · CANDY THERMOMETER · SPATULA · DIPPING FORK · SAUCEPAN · MEASURING SPOONS · FORK WRAPPED WITH CLOTH FOR SWABBING

CANDY MAKING EQUIPMENT

make your cream mixtures taste richer and smoother, intensify the flavors, and prevent graining.

Candy-Making Equipment

Candy Bars. These are used to form various sized spaces on the marble slab, into which are poured caramel and taffy mixtures. They can be arranged to hold various quantities of candy.

Candy Hook. Certain candy is improved by being pulled on a special hook, as the pulling makes it fluffier and lighter in color.

Caramel Cutter. This is a metal framework with transverse and longitudinal bars, which when pressed on the surface of caramel or taffy, mark it into a number of uniform small squares. The squares are then cut through with a knife.

Dipping Forks. Made of wire with two or three prongs or a loop at the end, these are used for lifting the dipped candies out of the coating mixtures.

Marble Slab. Although not absolutely necessary, a slab is convenient and useful. A large platter may be used instead.

Nougat Frames. These forms are not absolutely necessary, but their use does give nougat a professional touch. They are also useful in making candies of like consistency.

Saucepans. Several heavy-lipped pans, including two small ones, holding about one pint each for melting fondant and other minor operations are useful. They may be made of copper or aluminum.

Spatulas. These handy little utensils often take the place of spoons for stirring and beating mixtures or for scraping out pans.

Starch Tray. Any large, flat box or biscuit pan will do. A convenient size is 3x20 inches. The box is filled with clean, dry, sifted cornstarch, smoothed with a spatula or the blade of a knife. Impressions are made in the starch to form molds into which the candy mixture is poured, thus forming candies of various shapes and sizes according to the candymaker's whim. The candy mixture should fill each mold level with the top of the starch. Lift out the candies when set and dust off the starch. Always dry and sift the starch before storing for subsequent re-use.

The impressions may be made with the finger tips, a cork, a thimble, or any like object. For very fancy shapes small molds may be made of plaster, sealing wax, or paraffin. These are glued to a strip of wood (which should be longer than the starch tray) and pressed into the starch. Rubber mats that serve the same purpose as the starch tray can be purchased from any confectioner's supply house. They have innumerable designs and are easy to use but do not offer the opportunity for originality of execution that comes with the use of the starch tray.

Sugar Scraper. This is used to scrape up the sugar on the slab or platter. However, any broad-bladed spatula may be used.

Thermometer. The confectioner's thermometer is a most useful instrument to the candy maker. It enables one to tell at a glance when the different candies are ready to remove from the fire and is necessary from the standpoint of economy. Such thermometers are made of brass, copper, or other metals. The degrees indicated should be at least 350° F.

Tin Sheet or Tray. This should be of polished tin and is used for dropped chocolates.

Besides the above you will need: bowls, coloring (liquid or paste), containers (airtight), double boilers, egg beater, food chopper, funnel, knives, measuring cups and spoons, nutcracker, pastry brush, pastry tubes and bags, platters, rolling pin, scales, scissors, sieve (fine mesh), tin pans, waxed paper and wafer paper.

DEGREES OF BOILING SUGAR

Thread. At a point between 230° and 234° F. sirup reaches what is known as the "thread" stage, meaning that it spins a 2-inch thread when lifted from the mass on fork or spoon. If a longer thread is formed, it is known as the "great thread."

Soft-Ball. At a point between 234° and 240° F. (usually 238° F.) the soft ball stage is reached, meaning that when a little sirup is dropped into cold water it forms a soft ball which flattens on removal from water.

Firm-Ball. At a point between 244° and 248° F. the firm ball stage is reached, meaning that when a little sirup is dropped into cold water it forms a firm ball which does not flatten on removal from the water.

Note. When a boiling solution of sugar and water has passed the soft-ball degree, it may readily grain unless glucose (corn sirup) or some kind of acid is added. The danger may be guarded against also by melting the sugar very thoroughly before allowing it to boil, or still better, by brushing or sponging the sides of the pan during boiling so as to dissolve any hard particles or crystals which may form. Cream of tartar is the acid usually used to prevent granulation of the sirup. If too large a quantity is used, it will cause the sugar sirup to change color very rapidly, and the candies made or covered with it will be soft and sticky. Boiling sugar sirup intended for pulling, or such purposes, is all the better for the addition of a teaspoon (level) of glucose with the cream of tartar.

It is important to bear in mind that pure sugar and water shows no tendency to boil over. But all impurities or scum rising to the surface should be removed as soon as the sirup boils and then the boiling should be allowed to go on vigorously till the rrquired degree is reached.

Hard-Ball. At a point between 250° and 265° F. the hard ball stage is reached. This means that when a little sirup is dropped into cold water it forms a ball which is hard enough to keep its shape—yet plastic.

Soft-Crack. At a point between 270° and 290° F. the soft crack stage is reached. This occurs when the sirup separates into threads which are hard yet not brittle on bring dropped into cold water.

Hard-Crack. When the temperature of the sirup has reached between 300° and 310° F., a little sirup separates into hard brittle threads when dropped into cold water. This is known as the hard crack stage.

Note. The difference between soft-crack and hard-crack is easily found. If some of the sugar breaks with a slight noise and will not stick to the teeth, it is at the soft-crack stage. If you boil it again, and when tested it will quickly set hard and will easily snap when pressed, then it is at the hard-crack stage. Sugar at this stage passes rapidly to caramel and will burn if not attended to immediately.

CANDY TEMPERATURES

Type of Candy	Temperature (Farenheit)	Cold water test
Fudge, penuche, operas, maple, creams, etc.	234° to 236°	Soft ball
Fondant	238° to 240°	Soft ball
Caramels	246° to 248°	Firm ball
Taffies	265° to 270°	Hard ball
Butterscotch, toffee, etc.	290° to 300°	Crack
Brittles	300° to 310°	Hard-crack
Clear hard candies	310°	Hard-crack

ALMOND-PARMESAN FINGERS

3 tbsp chopped sweet almonds
3 tbsp butter
6 tbsp grated Parmesan cheese
3 tbsp minced parsley
3 tbsp heavy cream
Salt and pepper to taste
12 toast strips

Blanch the chopped almonds, and sauté them in butter until they are golden brown. Mix the remaining ingredients and spread the mixture on buttered toast strips. Garnish with finely chopped almonds, and heat thoroughly before serving. (Makes 12)

ANCHOVY-EGG CANAPES

Mix 3 tablespoons each of lemon and onion juice, and add a dash of cayenne. Drain 1 can of anchovy fillets, and marinate these in the mixture for ½ hour. Drain again, and place the fillets on 12 toast rounds. Border with 1 finely minced hard-cooked egg, dust with paprika, and garnish with watercress. (Makes 12)

ASPARAGUS CANAPES

12 thin slices of bread
6 thin slices boiled ham
Mustard
12 asparagus tips (cooked or canned)
Mayonnaise

Remove bread crusts. Cut ham slices in halves and trim them to fit the bread slices. Spread with mustard. Dip asparagus in mayonnaise, and place one tip at end of each prepared bread slice. Roll lengthwise, secure with a toothpick at each end, place on broiler rack in a preheated broiler, and turn to toast rolls. (Makes 12)

CANAPE TURNOVERS

Pastry
1 minced cooked chicken liver
2 slices bacon, broiled and minced
1 hard-cooked egg, chopped
2 tbsp minced parsley
¼ tsp curry powder
Salt
Paprika

Roll pastry (which see) very thin, and cut it in 2-inch squares. Mix the remaining ingredients, using only enough salt and paprika to season, and place 1 teaspoon of the mixture on each square. Fold the pastry into a triangle and press the edges together. Fry in hot deep fat (370° F.) until golden brown (3 to 5 minutes). Garnish with parsley. (Makes 24)

CAVIAR RISSOLETTES

Roll puff paste (which see) ¼ inch thick, and cut it in small rounds. Place 1 teaspoon of caviar, seasoned with lemon juice, in the center of each round. Wet edges and cover with a second round. Press edges together. Fry in hot deep fat (370° F.) until delicately browned (3 to 4 minutes). Drain on absorbent paper.

LOBSTER CANAPES

12 buttered toast rounds
Tartar sauce
⅜ cup chopped, sauteed mushrooms
1½ cup chopped, cooked lobster
Salt and paprika
3 tbsp grated Parmesan cheese
1½ tsp horseradish
Mayonnaise
Sliced, stuffed olives
Watercress

Spread untoasted sides of bread with tartar sauce, and cover with mixture of lobster meat and mushrooms. Dust with salt and paprika, and set in a cold place. Combine horseradish, cheese, and enough mayonnaise to make a creamy mixture. Press the mixture through a pastry bag, and then use it to border the canapés. In the center of each canapé place a slice of olive garnished with a sprig of watercress. (Makes 12)

PRETZEL AND CHEESE CANAPES

Work 1 package of cream cheese (3 oz.) to smoothness with a fork. Season it with paprika or with chopped olives, and place it in the hollows of small crisp pretzels. Crush other pretzels and sprinkle the crumbs over the cheese. Chill until ready to serve.

TOASTED NUT CANAPES

Cream ½ cup of butter. When it is soft enough to stir, stir in 1 cup of ground pecans and 2 tablespoons of Worcester-shire sauce. Spread the mixture on bread rounds. Toast until hot and serve at once.

Tomato Canapes

Place a thick slice of tomato on each round of toast. Dust with salt, paprika, and minced green pepper. Dot with butter. Top each with 1 tablespoon of grated cheese. Broil until tomatoes are soft and cheese is melted, and then serve at once. Thin slices of bacon may be substituted for the grated cheese.

Tomato and Shrimp Canapes

Place a thick slice of tomato on each round of toast. Place 2 or 3 marinated shrimp on top of each, and top with a dab of mayonnaise.

CANARD A LA PRESSE. French name for "Pressed Duck." *See* DUCK.

CANDLE. The efficient electric light has still to replace the candle for establishing a mood or a scenic effect at the dinner table. Candles are still widely used for lighting purposes at evening meals and especially at formal dinners. *See* TABLE SETTING AND SERVICE.

CANDLEBERRY. This is a waxy berry from which aromatic candles are made. It is better known as bayberry, *which see*.

CANDY. Human instinct often arrives at a truth while science toils after it at long distance. The mid-morning pick-me-up is an example. The little throng in the office building that gathers around the soft drink fountain, or the group in the factory cafeteria that takes a sweet drink, an order of ice cream, or some candy and goes back to work refreshed, is instinctively right. Dietitians pooh-poohed them for a long time, but now they are beginning to preach the doctrine that a sweet relieves fatigue.

The explanation is quite simple. Sugar is the energy producer for the body, just as gasoline is the fuel for the automobile. The simpler the sugar, the more readily it is converted into energy. Sugar is stored in the liver, and if the supply drops to a low level the muscles work at a disadvantage, and fatigue and fatigue-headaches result. The best sugars for the production of energy are the fruit sugars, but any sugar in any form is more rapidly converted into energy than starch. This does not mean that sugar will relieve everyone's fatigue.

The body cannot run without sugar. Even meat is partially converted into sugar in order to furnish energy. Those faddists and freak dietitians who abstain from sweets are simply defeating themselves because no matter what food the body assimilates it has to convert 75 percent of it into sugar in order to continue operating. So, the little group that takes its usual mid-morning and mid-afternoon pick up is following the wisest dictates of the most modern research of dietetic science.

Primitive man probably satisfied the craving of his "sweet tooth" with fruits, sweet herbs, and honey. To find the first written and pictured evidence of the importance of candy, one must turn to ancient Egypt. The Egyptians were the fathers of most things modern, including engineering, architecture, and chemistry. They were also the first people known to have made confectionery. True, their sweetmeats would seem crude in comparison with modern candy, but they were candies, nevertheless. The refining of sugar was an unknown art in those days, so the confectioner used honey as a sweetener. To this he added sweet herbs and spices. These confections were highly colored to attract the eye of the candy lover who, no doubt, found them quite delicious albeit very expensive.

Today, high grade commercial candies owe their distinction of flavor and appearance to the excellence of the raw materials used, and to the care with which they are mixed. In the deluxe candies, cream is used instead of thickened milk; butter instead of vegetable fat, and thick, rich coating chocolate is used for dipping. The better grades of hard candies contain good fruit flavors and safe colorings.

Home-made candies will always remain one of the most delightful and informal of holiday gifts. Happy the homemaker who has the knack of making them! It need not be a difficult task provided a few secrets of success have been mastered and the proper equipment is used.

Many homemakers are reluctant to try their hand because homemade candy, no matter how delicious when first made, gets dry and hard so quickly. The answer to this problem is to use glycerine. This pure, wholesome product has unique powers of absorbing and retaining moisture; a few drops added to your candies help keep them fresh for days. Glycerine will also

Poultry	*Calories per ounce*
Capon	62
Chicken' broiler	31
Chicken fowl	65
Goose	104
Squab	66
Turkey	85

Bread

Bread, brown	66
corn	64
gluten	72
rye	74
white	76
whole wheat	74
Rye Krisp	101
Zwieback	123
Crackers, graham	120

Sweets

Chocolate	178
Cocoa, dry	145
Honey	95
Maple Sugar	96
Maple Sirup	83
Molasses	81
Sugar, brown	112
white	116

Cereals

Barley meal	102
Buckwheat flour	101
Corn meal	108
Macaroni, cooked	26
Oatmeal, cooked	18
Pop Corn	117
Rice, cooked	32
Rye flour	102
Wheat cereal	60
Wheat flour, white	100
Wheat flour, whole	104

Dairy Products

Butter	225
Buttermilk	10
Cream	57
Cheese, American	135
Camembert	124
Cheddar	134
Cottage	32
Full cream	122
Limburger	105
Swiss	125

Dairy Products	*Calories per ounce*
Egg, whole, raw	45
white, cooked	16
yolk, cooked	106
Ice Cream	53
Kumiss	15
Milk, condensed	83
skimmed	17
whole	20
Oleomargarine	220
Olive Oil	252

Fresh Fruits

Apple	18
Apricot	17
Avocado	66
Banana	29
Blackberries	17
Cherries	22
Cranberries	16
Currants	23
Figs	24
Gooseberries	16
Grapes	29
Grape Juice	24
Guava	20
Huckleberries	21
Lemons	13
Mulberries	18
Muskmelons	12
Nectarines	19
Olives	26
Oranges	15
Peaches	12
Pears	19
Persimmons	40
Pineapple	13
Plums	13
Pomegranate	29
Raspberries	16
Strawberries	11
Tangerine	35
Watermelon	9

Dried Fruits

Apples	81
Apricots	81
Bananas	78
Currants	95
Dates	101
Figs	91
Peaches	78
Pears	102
Prunes	88
Raisins	100

Nuts	Calories per ounce
Almonds	180
Beechnuts	171
Brazil nuts	198
Butter nuts	210
Chestnuts	71
Coconut, fresh	175
dried	198
Filberts	197
Hickory nuts	208
Peanuts	163
Peanut butter	189
Pecans	206
Pine nuts	200
Pistachios	203
Walnuts	192

Vegetables

Artichokes	23
Asparagus	7
Beans, baked	38
green	41
Beets	12
Cabbage	9
Carrots	13
Cauliflower	9
Celery	5
Chard	11
Dandelion greens	18
Eggplant	8
Endive	40
Kohlrabi	9
Lentils, dried	101
Lettuce	6
Lima beans, green	36
dried	102
Mushrooms	13
Onions	14
Parsnips	19
Pepper, green	28
Peas, green	34
dried	104
Potato, sweet	54
white	32
Pumpkin	8
Radishes	9
Rhubarb	7
Rice	32
Spinach	7
Squash	14
Soy Beans	112
Tomatoes	7

CALVADOS. The apple brandy of France (not an applejack), with the full flavor of apple blossoms. A distinctive and strong spirit, made of pure distilled spirits of wine on apples after they have been pressed. Served between, during, and after meals in Normandy where it is known as *le trou Normand*—meaning to fill up the hole which may be left in the stomach after certain dishes. A very fine and powerful digestive.

CAMBRIC TEA. A weak tea to which is added about an equal quantity of hot milk, plus sugar to taste. It is usually accepted by children as a most satisfactory substitute for the stronger brew.

CAMBRIDGE CHEESE. A soft, rennet English cheese, made from cow's milk.

CAMEMBERT. A soft cheese made of cow's milk, to which a colorless fungus is added. The interior of the cheese is yellowish, waxy, creamy, and almost fluid in consistency, depending upon the ripeness. The rind is about ⅛ inch thick. The cheese is traditionally packed in wheels about four inches in diameter and one inch thick in a wooden box. It is a French product, believed to have originated in the Department of Orne in northwestern France about 1791. A domestic Camembert is also made.

CAMEMBERT GARNI

This is delicious served with fruits at the end of the meal. Select a not too soft camembert cheese. Scrape it with a sharp knife top, bottom, and sides to remove the crust entirely. Dip the whole cheese in sifted, dry, light bread crumbs, seasoned to taste with cayenne pepper and salt. (A few grains of nutmeg or cinnamon may be added to the crumbs, if desired.) Serve on a cheese platter on crisp, green leaves, such as vine leaves, geranium, etc., passing the cheese so that each guest may help himself. Serve crackers separately.

CAMOMILE. This daisy-like plant of the aster family is a native of Europe. In the wild state the head of the flower is yellow and the petals are white, but when cultivated the entire flower becomes white. It is distinguished by its strong aromatic odor and its bitter flavor. The plant has been long known to physicians as a diaphoretic and antispasmodic, and its use has always been more akin to the practice of medicine than to cookery. A blue, essential oil is extracted from the plant and has the same medicinal properties.

Camomile tea (formerly called tisane) is made of the fresh or dried flowers and drunk as a mild tonic. It was in great demand by members of the gentle sex in the eighteenth and nineteenth centuries. The tea is prepared as follows:

CAMOMILE TEA

1 level tsp dried camomile*
1 cup boiling water

*If the fresh herb is preferred use two rounded teaspoonfuls to each cup of boiling water.

Scald the cup and wilt the herb as instructed under TEA, and add the boiling water. Steep the brew for from 2 to 5 minutes and serve with sugar and lemon. *See also* TISANE.

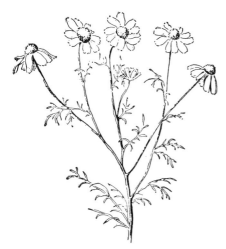

CAMOMILE

CAMPARI. A bitter vermouth wine, made in the Piedmont province of Italy and used for long refreshing drinks, to which is added a sweetening, such as cassis, gum sirup, grenadine, etc. Sometimes it is mixed with Amer Picon (half-and-half); then the sweetening is added, and carbonated water poured over. It contains from 16 to 18 percent alcohol.

CAMP COOKERY. True camp cookery consists of preparing food in the open by using utensils and heat sources that were either brought to the spot by the camper or improvised from materials found in the area. Though in many respects it closely resembles other forms of cooking, it is an art unto itself because of the unique circumstances under which it is practiced.

While camp cooking can be elaborate, in its simple form it is the most basic type of cooking ever done. It is the art of preparing food in the most direct manner, using a minimum of time, trouble, and equipment. It does not follow, however, that the products are inferior; indeed, to many the basic fare of the camp has a savor that cannot be matched in the finest of restaurants.

If one ever hopes to leave civilization behind for a week or two, then camp cooking is a thing he must learn. But the novice need not fear the task, for outdoor cooking is a very large part of the fun of camping. Nor is it too difficult an art to learn, if one is willing to profit by his mistakes and follow the advice of others more experienced in the way of the woods.

CONSIDERATIONS ON EQUIPMENT

A camper is limited to only such equipment as he may comfortably carry, and the cooking equipment is but a part of his total gear. The experienced camper will carry only what is basic, and as far as cooking is concerned, this is a surprisingly small percentage of the normal household kitchen equipment. The equipment that he does bring is usually purchased for different reasons than are similar items intended for kitchen use only.

Camping gear can be quite expensive, or it may be assembled from the shelves of the local dime stores and the discards from the kitchen. The camper should have special gear instead of borrowing from the kitchen, for he will often want items that, while similar, are of different construction than the ones in the kitchen. He should, however, beware of the gadgets which many stores will offer as the solution to all his camping problems. Rarely will complicated devices earn their way, justifying either their cost or their weight in the pack.

It is ridiculous for the camper to carry three separate items when one basic utensil will perform all three of the functions, nor is there any need for him to carry a heavy iron skillet when one made of a lighter metal will serve just as well. Since it is difficult to repair or replace a broken utensil in the woods, he must select only simple and sturdy vessels that will stand up under the rugged life of the trail. Not only should his gear be sturdy and light, but it should be compact as well; handles should fold, pots and pans should nest inside one another, and bulky objects either collapse or come apart for easy stowage.

The experienced camper will travel as "light" as possible. While the housewife often has difficulty finding sufficient space to store her many utensils, an experienced camper can carry his utensils, his food, and even his bedding on his back. A man can survive in the woods with but a knife and a pack of matches, if he must, and even the matches are not absolutely essential.

The amount of equipment that can be comfortably brought is governed largely by the method of transportation used by the camper. A man traveling by car or boat or with a string of pack animals can, of course, carry much more than a man on foot. A large party can carry more than a smaller group, and since the same basic items will often serve for several people as well as one, the larger group will have more room for "luxury" items than the smaller one that is burdened with essentials.

A permanent camp will often have many items already there, waiting to be used, thus relieving the campers of part of their normal burden. A party that is going into a permanent camp will carry different equipment than a group that is planning a long trip with only overnight stops. The purpose of the trip is another pertinent factor, for it may involve so much other gear as to leave little room for cooking equipment.

It can be seen that the optimum list of camp cooking equipment is a rather individual and highly flexible affair. There are too many factors involved to permit the setting of any hard and fast rules, and it is only through experience that the camper will learn what, to him, is the basic list of cooking equipment. In this respect, the novice is wise to follow the example set by experienced woodsmen.

The novice would do well to talk with experienced campers before planning his first trip; in fact, if he is going out of ready touch with civilization, there should be at least one experienced man in the party, for any wilderness can be dangerous to those not wise in its ways. He should also consult the Boy Scout Handbook and other works of a similar nature.

The following is by no means a complete list, but rather a discussion of some items of equipment peculiar to camp cookery to guide the novice in his thinking.

BASIC EQUIPMENT

There are many items of general camping equipment, such as axes, shovels, knives, and canteens, that are very useful in camp cooking, though their major applications lie in other fields. These, however, are things that the wise camper always brings, whether or not he contemplates cooking.

Can Opener. There are many variations of this instrument (*see* CAN OPENER), but the one selected for camping use should be sturdy, dependable, rust-proof, and large enough to handle all types of cans. The simple, non-mechanical type with a sharp blade of tool steel is the one usually adopted by the camper.

Cup. The camper's cup is usually larger than the household model. Not only does he want larger quantities of coffee when in the open, but he also uses his cup as a bowl for cereals, soups, desserts, etc., and even, at times, as a cooking utensil. The preferred material is a disputed point among campers, for each has advantages and drawbacks. Enamelware chips, crockery breaks, and it is difficult to drink a hot beverage from a cup made of any uncovered metal without burning the lips. Plastics are light and will protect the lip from the heat of the contents, but no plastic cup can be heated over a fire (*see* PLASTICS). Collapsible handles are convenient for storing, but the mechanisms should be dependable and not apt to give way when the cup is full.

Food Containers. The safe transportation of food in a crowded pack often presents problems. Canned foods are safe, but other types of food packages must be carefully stowed to prevent damage. Glass containers are not generally recommended because they are heavy and fragile. Cardboard containers and paper bags are also fragile, and, unless treated, easily damaged by water. Dry foods, such as coffee, flour, sugar, etc., are best carried in food bags made of heavy, water-resistant canvas. Not only is the food kept dry, but the bags may be rolled tighter as the food is used, thus decreasing the total bulk in the pack. Such bags may be made at home. Heavy, untreated canvas is often used rather than lighter, coated stock, for most water-proofing compounds have odors. The bags should be large enough to be securely folded over at the top when full, and have

9. *Boiling Foods*. The American Indians used to boil food in bark, wood, and fiber containers without burning the vessel. Though the process is possible, it is too tedious to be practical when there are so many other easier ways of cooking the same foods. The container must be watertight and can be constructed of any convenient material in any expedient way. The container is filled with water, the food dropped in, and the water heated by means of hot rocks which are taken from the fire and dropped directly into the water. The heat from the rocks is transferred to the water rather than the container, thus not burning the vessel, but the cool rocks have to be replaced by hot ones if it is to work.

10. *Other methods*. The examples given are merely basic; there are many ingenious methods of cooking certain foods under specific circumstances using only the resources of nature. Some are quite practical, while others are of interest only to the man desperately concerned with the problem of survival. If the subject is of interest to the reader, more specialized books should be consulted.

Cooking in the Mountain Camp. At high altitudes, the air pressure is lessened, with surprising effects on normal cooking practices. The mountain camper will find that he must modify many of his cooking techniques if he is to be successful. *See* HIGH-ALTITUDE COOKERY.

MENU

The same considerations of health and variety apply to the camp menu as to the kitchen menu. There is, however, one major difference. In the kitchen, meals are planned in accordance with family tastes and current food prices. While these considerations apply to the camper as well, he has problems unknown to the kitchen cook.

As previously discussed, not every kind of food can be safely brought on a camping trip. There are some that can be brought, but are very inconvenient to carry. And the camper must consider the utensils that he will have to do his cooking with, as well.

The menu for each trip is a highly individual affair that can only be determined by the circumstances peculiar to that trip. The ability of the cook should also be considered, for it would be rather pointless to plan meals that he is not fitted to prepare.

The important thing to do is to inject some variety and to make certain that the diet is well balanced, even if this means some inconvenience on the camper's part. It is also important to include some foods with laxative values (prunes, figs, etc.) on the menu, for campers often become constipated because of the change in diet or surroundings, and this condition can have serious results if it is neglected.

OUTDOOR SANITATION

To the housewife, the returning camper looks the epitome of filth. His clothes are black with soot and smell of wood smoke. He usually has several day's growth of beard and his face looks as though it were never washed.

All of this may well be true, but as far as his cooking equipment and camp site is concerned, the experienced camper is the soul of cleanliness. Cleanliness is harder to achieve in the woods than in the house, but for that very reason it is most important. Dirt and refuse breed germs, draw insects, and give off unpleasant odors. Not only can this make the camper's life unpleasant, but it can actually endanger it through disease. It takes but a small bit of grease on a mess kit to give the camper a serious case of dysentery.

Washing Dishes and Utensils. Rarely does the camper have the unlimited hot water of the housewife, nor does he have the large sinks and wide drainboards at his hand. But he does have an ample supply of dirt, and dirt, plain, ordinary dirt is one of the best cleansing substances man has ever discovered.

Camp gear gets filthier than kitchen gear. Pans are coated with grease and soot, and often, because of the uneven heat of some fires, food is burned in pans. But dirt will cut through anything. It can be used dry or in solution with water; swirled about in the bottom of utensils, or rubbed with the hand. Leaves or cloth may be used to protect the hand. Knives, tableware, etc., are stabbed directly into the ground until clean.

Dirt is an abrasive, which is why it is effective. Enamelware and plastics may receive the dirt treatment, but it should be gentle, lest they be overly scratched.

Everything, of course, should be washed with hot, soapy water following the scrubbing with dirt, but this pre-treatment will remove practically all of grease, food particles, soot, and other dirt, greatly simplifying the normal washing routine. Steel wool, dish rags, soap, and all of the other accessories to the washing operation may and should be used in camp. Bar soap is better than powder, however, for it is less affected by accidental moisture, easier packed, and can be used as a hand soap, as well. All of the normal precautions applied to dishwashing in the home hold for the camp as well, and the importance of absolute cleanliness cannot be too greatly stressed.

Refuse Disposal. There are no garbage men in the wilderness, but it is expected of the camper that he leave his site as clean and neat as it was when he found it. There are many important reasons for this, and they may all be summed up under two headings: consideration of others and personal comfort. Refuse should either be burned or buried, but never left lying about. A garbage pit should be dug when the site is opened, and all refuse that cannot be burned thrown in. Tin cans and glass containers should be smashed flat with an axe or stone before being thrown in the pit. Food refuse may be covered over with dirt as it is thrown in, to keep it from drawing insects, and when the camp is broken, the pit is refilled, possibly covered with stones to keep animals from digging it up to get at the garbage, and a sign posted indicating that this is a garbage pit and giving the date of closing. This step keeps later campers from inadvertently uncovering the pit when they dig their own.

Things that can be burned are either thrown into the fire as soon as discarded or saved for one grand burning. Nothing solid should be thrown into a stream or other water source, and soiled water should be poured on the ground instead of being thrown into a water source. The latrine should be located well away from any water source and is handled in exactly the same manner as the garbage pit.

FIRE PRECAUTIONS

Fire is an ever present danger in the woods, and the camper should be most careful in this respect. As previously stated, all underbrush should be cleared away from the vicinity of any fire, cooking or otherwise, and it is a wise precaution to build the fire on a stone base, where this is possible.

No fire should ever be left until the camper is positive that it is out. Being out does not mean that it is covered over and smouldering with no live coals or flames showing. Such a fire can be fanned back to destructive life days after the camper has left. The fire should be definitely out.

Water—in quantity—is the best fire extinguisher. It should be thrown on until there is no more smoke or hissing. If water is not available, then dirt or sand can be used. The camper should dig up the ground under the fire to make certain that roots in the ground are not burning. Forest fires are often started in this manner; roots beneath the cooking fire will catch and carry the fire quite some distance underground before it surfaces, and, this usually being long after the campers have left the site, becomes a dangerous thing.

When gasoline stoves are used, a chemical extinguisher should be kept on hand. If none is available, then a pile of sand or dirt should be kept in readiness. Never use water on any petroleum fire; it will never put it out and will only spread it, since gasoline and oil will float on water.

See also BARBECUE and PICNIC.

CAN OPENER. A device used to open tin cans. When canned foods came into popularity, much thought was given to the problem of opening the cans, with the result that there are now available a great many different types of openers.

The earliest and simplest model consists of a sharp blade that is forced into the metal and worked around the edge by means of a lever action against the rim of the can. As long as the blade is sharp, these devices are efficient, but they tend to leave dangerous, jagged edges as well as to mar the top surface of the food within the can.

There are many mechanical devices that are worked either by turning a key or a crank. This type functions by forcing a sharp cutting edge into the metal close to the rim and then forcing this knife edge around the rim of the can. This is accomplished by turning a serrated wheel which is pressed against the can.

A variety of electric can openers which work by means of round, revolving blades are available in wall mounted models. These may have knife sharpening or other attachments as desired.

in getting his fire started, or be so low on matches that he cannot risk using more than one to light the fire. There are many expedients he can use; gasoline, for example, though that is a dangerous practice and should be resorted to only under extreme emergency conditions. Gasoline should never be poured on live embers.

Fires may be started by using the powder from any sort of rifle or pistol shell. The paper stripped from a shotgun shell will also make good additional tinder. Certain plastic articles, especially the nitrates (celluloid, etc.) are inflammable, and a fountain pen casing, celluloid comb, or camera film, may sometimes be used as fire-making insurance. Waxed or oiled papers will burn with more than the usual amount of heat.

There are some chemical tinders on the market, little briquettes of compressed material, suitable for emergency use.

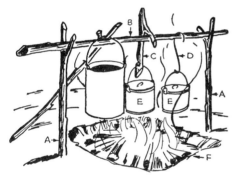

CAMP COOKING OVER A PIT FIRE
A. Uprights   B. Crossbar   C. Pothook (forked stick)   D. Pothook (heavy wire)
E. Nesting kettles   F. Fire pit

Cooking with a Fire

The ideal cooking fire should be as small, as hot, and as smokeless as possible. This is as good a definition of a bed of embers as there is, and that is the preferred cooking fire. A large roaring flame is valueless; the heat is uneven, the flames force the cook to stand well back, the vessels are blacked with soot, ash gets into the food, and smoke gets into the cook's eyes. The cook cannot perform his best work under those conditions.

The fire should be built high and roaring, at first, but the experienced cook waits until it has settled down to be a bed of glowing coals before he goes to work. If

there is no time for this cycle, then only a small fire is built.

METHODS OF SUSPENDING GAME OR POT OVER FIRE

Cooking With Utensils. Normal cooking procedure is followed when utensils are used. The chief difference between this and kitchen cooking is the heat source. The type and effectiveness of the heat control achieved by the outdoor cook depends upon his skill and upon the fireplace which he is using. Under good conditions, the camp cook will experience only slightly more difficulty than the kitchen cook.

Cooking Without Utensils. While pots and pans are very convenient, they are not, strictly speaking, essential, for it is possible to prepare many a tasty dish without their use. This sort of cooking may be used as an emergency measure when the utensils have been lost, as an expedient to extend the capacity of existing utensils or to lessen the numbers that need be carried, or as a way of getting more fun out of camping. Though foods are better prepared in utensils, the camp cook should know at least a few ways of getting along without them.

1. *Broiling.* Meats and even some vegetables and fruits may be broiled with ease over an ember bed. They may be broiled by *spitting*, i.e., by impaling them on long slender sticks of peeled green wood, searing the meat to keep the juices from escaping, and turning slowly over the fire until done. A *grill* may be constructed of green sticks and used to hold the food over the fire. In either case, the sticks must be watched to see that they do not burn through, and

growing saplings or slender limbs should be cut for the job (one of the few exceptions to the rule of never cutting growing wood). The wood selected should have a sweet tasting bark, lest it impart a bitter flavor to the food, and it should be peeled. Steel rods may also be carried for this purpose.

Meat may be broiled by *planking;* i.e., by cutting it thin and pegging it to a clean, smooth plank or wood slab that is placed close to the fire. It is well to lard such meat by also pegging down strips of bacon to keep it from being too dry.

KABOB COOKING

A *kabob* may also be made; a meal on a stick. Meat and various vegetables are cut to discs and squares of appropriate size and then impaled in sequence on a spit. The entire assembly is broiled over the fire and eaten directly from the spit. Meat, onion, carrot, potato, and onion is a typical kabob structure.

2. *Baking Fish.* Fish are easily baked without utensils. The carcass is thickly covered with mud or clay and buried in the embers. The cooking time varies from 15 to 30 minutes per pound, depending on the type of fish, thickness of clay, and heat of the fire. The clay or mud will bake hard in the fire and, when raked out, can easily be broken open. The skin of the fish, scales and all, will adhere to the clay, and it is not essential that the fish be gutted before baking, for the internal organs merely shrivel up when fish are baked by this method. When the cooked fish is split open, these organs may be easily removed, and leave no taste behind.

3. *Baking Fowl.* Small game birds and chickens may be baked in mud as described above, but these must first be cleansed and gutted.

4. *Baking Eggs.* Eggs may be baked in a fire, but it must be a gradual process, else they will explode. A small hole may be punched in the large end of the shell to let the air escape as the sac inside expands. The eggs may be covered with clay or mud or wrapped in wet leaves or paper, and buried under at least two inches of soil beneath the fire. They will be done in from 20 to 45 minutes.

5. *Baking Potatoes.* Potatoes may be thrown directly into the fire if you do not mind cutting away a thick, charred layer from the outside when done. It is better to wrap them in mud, or to bury them beneath the fire as previously described. Sweet potatoes will cook in less time than their Irish relations, which should be the first items on the fire so they will be done when the other foods are ready.

6. *Baking Corn.* Corn on the cob may be baked in much the same manner as are potatoes, first removing the cornsilk and wrapping the ear in its own husks before proceeding with the other preparations.

7. *Baking Bread.* A "twist" may be made without the aid of pan or oven, and makes a good companion to the kabob previously described. A biscuit dough is prepared, slightly thicker than usual, and worked into long thin rolls. These rolls are wrapped snake-fashion (spirals) about a spit and slowly turned over the fire until done.

TWIST COOKING

8. *Steaming Foods.* Meat, fish, fowl, and vegetables may all be steamed without the aid of utensils. Though there are variations, the processes are all basically alike. The food is first cleansed and prepared, and then wrapped in layers of some wet material: paper, cloth, leaves, etc. The package may be buried in the coals, but the usual practice is to bury it in the ground beneath the fire. Individual items are cooked in this manner, and in some cases, as in a clambake, layers of different foods are all put down in the same pit and cooked at once.

worse. Since campers are usually quite some distance from medical aid as well as the comforts of home, even a mild case of food poisoning can take on a very serious aspect in the wilderness.

The obvious solution is to rely on only non-perishable food forms, but though this can be done, it usually results in a rather monotonous diet. At least some perishables are welcome, if not essential.

In the winter, of course, there is no problem, but fortunate is the camper who has an ice chest and a supply of that cooling substance in the summer months. For obvious reasons, the camper rarely has this advantage and must turn to natural means for refrigeration.

The best and simplest refrigerator is a cool-running, ice-fed mountain spring or stream. The food is placed in water-tight containers and suspended in the water until needed.

If this is not practical, the camper may build an earth refrigerator by digging a hole in the ground, lining it with boards to restrain the dirt and insects, and by packing it with an insulating layer of grass, leaves, or similar materials. The hole is covered by a removable board which is also well padded with insulation of some sort. An arrangement such as this will keep foods cool, though it cannot be compared to an ice refrigerator. Deep caves or wells may also be found in the locale that will serve the same purpose.

The food may also be wrapped with a water-proof material, or otherwise protected against moisture, and covered with burlap or some other heavy, coarse cloth. If this cloth is kept wet, the resulting evaporation will have a cooling effect on the food underneath. However, this arrangement is an open invitation to insects and animals and must be constantly checked against their invasion.

Insects are another problem of the camp cook. Their role in food destruction is well known, but, the wilderness being their natural home, it is difficult to keep them out. Food should always be covered, and never placed directly on the ground where crawling insects may reach it. It is well to bring along some mosquito netting and construct some sort of insect-proof box to hold breads and similar foods.

Animals are a problem peculiar to the wilderness, for rarely, these days, do they invade the home. Animals of all sizes, ranging from vermin to the rather large bears, seem to like food just as much as do humans, and they show an amazing persistence and intelligence in seeking it out and, if not devouring it completely, ruining it for human consumption. The camper should inquire as to the type of wildlife he is apt to encounter in the region which he is planning to visit and learn the proper precautions. In some extreme cases, the food must be tied in tree forks, or even hung from tree limbs, but generally it is enough that it be placed in closed containers and kept off the ground.

The camper must also protect his food against the elements, for these can destroy as surely as insects or germs. A cloudless sky at sunset can still produce rain before dawn, and the food should always be kept under some sort of cover. The camper should also beware of harmless creeks that may suddenly flood the area, and, when packing the food for travel, see that it is properly done so that none will be crushed or otherwise ruined en route. If the food is carried separately, that is the last pack that should ever be permitted to fall in the river or get lost. *See also* FOOD PRESERVATION AND STORAGE.

WATER

Without water, cooking becomes quite difficult, and, in some cases, impossible. For this and other obvious reasons, water is one of the chief concerns of the camper. It is difficult for the camper to carry sufficient water to meet his daily requirements, especially if the trip is an extended one; yet, in certain types of terrain, as in the desert, that is what must be done. Even with the use of large containers, the camper must, under those circumstances, ration himself on water use and must therefore subsist mainly on fried, baked, and roasted foods.

In regions where water is available, the camper is still beset with problems, for water can be quite treacherous. Water can be polluted in a great many different ways, and it is difficult, without the aid of special equipment that the camper is not apt to carry, to tell whether or not the water is pure. In some cases, muddy, stale water can be quite safe (though hard on the palate), while the clearest of spring water may be laden with dysentery and even death.

It is most essential that the camper be very cautious about his water supply. That is, without doubt, the most important, basic rule of camping. He should always use only water that he knows to be pure, even if he must inconvenience himself to get it. If it is impossible to get water from a source of known purity, then the camper should purify his water before using it. There are no exceptions to this rule; a running stream will clear itself as it flows, but the sediment settling to the bottom does not carry the germs with it. Clear water is not necesssarily pure.

All sediment should first be removed from the water by either allowing it to settle and decanting the clear water, or by means of straining. The water should then be purified, and the simplest method is by means of boiling for an extended period. In high altitudes, this boiling should be done in a covered vessel, in some cases with a stone weighing the lid, to make certain that the water is boiling at high enough a temperature to kill off the germs (*see* PRESSURE COOKER and HIGH-ALTITUDE COOKERY). The flat taste natural to boiled water may be removed by pouring the water back and forth between two vessels.

If it is not convenient to boil the water, it may also be purified by adding four drops of iodine to every quart and letting it stand for at least 30 minutes before using. Potassium permanganate crystals may also be used. In addition, there are some commercial preparations available that can be used to chemically purify water at the camp.

The good camper will never deliberately pollute a water source, nor will he let this happen accidently, if it can at all be avoided. Heavily camped regions will often be posted to indicate good or bad water. The camper never tampers with these signs and trail etiquette demands that he post any further information that he knows to be true, especially concerning polluted water.

CAMP COOKING FUELS

Perhaps the most obvious difference between camp cooking and kitchen cooking lies in the cooking fuels and their manner of use.

Gasoline. The techniques of camp cooking most closely resemble those of the kitchen when the portable gasoline stove already discussed in this article is used.

In emergencies, gasoline may be used as a fuel without a special stove or burner, though extreme caution must be exercised. A stove is made by filling a large tin can with sand to within two inches of the top. The exposed metal is cut with equally spaced vertical strips and every other one is bent down so that a vessel may be rested on the rim and there will still be ventilation between it and the sand. The sand is saturated with gasoline and lit from a safe distance before the vessel is placed in the cooking position.

Chemical Fuels. As previously mentioned, there are many chemical fuels that are convenient to carry and that serve well for food-warming as well as emergency tinders. Few of these fuels are adapted to general cooking, however.

Charcoal. Charcoal is a manufactured fuel, being carbonized or charred wood. It burns with an intense, quiet, even, smokeless, flameless glow that makes an excellent cooking fire suitable for all types of operations. While not heavy, it is quite bulky, and a bit of a bother to transport. It is, however, frequently sold in camping or picnicing areas. Charcoal can be burned in a regular wood fireplace, or even on the ground, but the best results are to be achieved through the use of a special portable charcoal stove as previously discussed.

Coal. While coal is an excellent fuel, it is not well adaptable to camping. It is rarely naturally available in camping areas, is heavy and messy to carry, and requires special grates and devices to give a proper fire.

Wood. Wood is the natural camper's fuel, and by far the one most commonly used. Wood is found in almost every type of terrain, except for deserts and mountain peaks, and all the camper need carry is an axe or hatchet and a box of matches. Properly used, it makes an excellent cooking fire, and with the right type of fireplace, any sort of cooking may be done over a wood fire.

Deadwood is the only kind that should ever be used in a cooking fire. Green wood is difficult to burn, gives off more smoke than heat, and the boiling sap causes spark-scattering explosions. Ample deadwood will be found in any forest, if the camper will only look, and the beaches will offer driftwood, which, if dry, is an even better fuel than the deadwood of the forest. If a choice is possible, hardwood is to be preferred in a cooking fire, for it burns hotter and longer and gives better embers than does softwood. Woods that contain natural resins should be avoided, for while they will burn readily, they are also quite apt to produce smoke.

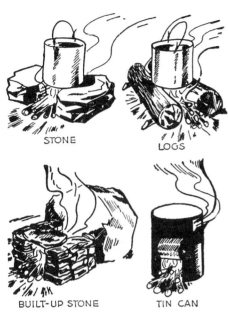

STONE   LOGS

BUILT-UP STONE   TIN CAN

CAMPFIRE COOKING

The Cooking Fire

Site Selection. The site should be selected with some care, with an eye to working space, wind, and fire prevention. A natural clearing of at least 20 feet in diameter, with the ground dry and sloping gently in one direction is the best location. Natural rock formations to serve as base, back wall, or building materials for the fire place are desirable. The underbrush should always be cleared away from the fire for at least 10 feet in all directions, and humus or root-filled soil should be avoided, if at all possible.

Fireplace. While one may cook over a simple open fire, a fireplace of some sort will enlarge both the ease and the scope of his operations. The elaborate outdoor fireplace as described in the article on barbecue (*which see*) is the best, but it is only practical for permanent camp sites. Such fireplaces are often provided in National Parks and similar reservations, or they may

be built by the camper at some location which he intends to frequent.

In the case of temporary or overnight camps, it is necessary to use one of a more quickly constructed design. As the illustrations suggest, the possibilities presented are endless. They range from simple trenches scuffed out by a heel to rather elaborate structures quickly assembled from flat rocks that happened to be lying in the neighborhood. The experienced camper approaches his fireplace problem with an open mind, building his fireplace to suit the conditions that are present. Nature will often have done more than half of the work by presenting him with natural rock formations or fallen trees that will require little modification to turn into a useful fireplace, and it is easier to use the materials on hand than go to searching for stones in a region in which there are few or to attempt to dig a trench if a region is mostly bare rock.

The basic fireplace design is a V-shaped trench or slot with the widest end facing the prevailing winds. As much of the fireplace as possible should be built of stone, for that material best reflects and holds the heat. If the fireplace has sidewalls of log or stone, cooking vessels may be rested on those and temperature control achieved by varying the depth of live coals in different sections of the slot. If the fireplace has no sidewalls, skillets are held by hand and pots and kettles may be suspended over the fire in a variety of different ways, as suggested by the illustrations.

REFLECTOR FIRE

Fuel. The camper should always try to gather his fuel while there is still light, for stumbling through the woods by means of a lantern or flashlight is not the easiest task in the world.

As discussed earlier, the camper should use only deadwood, except under emergency conditions. Live wood makes a very

TINDER
(PAPER, FUZZ-
STICK, SHAVINGS,
GRASS, LEAVES)

KINDLING
(SMALL SPLIT
WOOD, TWIGS,
BARK)

WOOD
(PROGRESSIVELY
LARGER TWIGS
AND STICKS)

STEPS IN BUILDING A FIRE

poor fuel, and the felling of trees is only wanton destruction. Any forest will provide more than an ample supply of fallen wood, simplifying the camper's task.

The firewood should be cut or split into lengths of suitable size for the fireplace, usually about a foot long and three inches in diameter. There should also be an equal supply of thinner stock of about half that diameter.

A supply of kindling is also necessary. This should consist of very dry wood, either splinters or narrow branches, ranging from a half inch to one inch in diameter. He will also need some tinder to start the fire. There are many practical types of tinder twigs or splinters that are a natural by-product of the wood-gathering, dry pine cones, paper, etc. Leaves and bark may also be used, but these must be very dry if they are to do more than smoulder.

If it is raining or if the region has recently been drenched, the camper need not despair. If he is unable to find any dry wood, he must remember that only the outside is wet, and if the larger pieces are split open, he will be able to garner enough dry pieces to start the fire. The wet wood may then be dried before use.

Fire Building. It requires no special luck or talent to start a fire with only one match; merely care and patience. The novice must remember that a fire has to be built up gradually, and he cannot hope to ignite a six-inch log with a single sheet of burning newspaper.

Paper makes excellent tinder, but it must be crumpled into loose balls if it is to work.

A layer of crumpled paper balls is covered lightly with small twigs, splinters, chips, etc., with slightly larger and more substantial material piled over this. The whole is roofed with a self-supported structure of kindling wood, and the larger material may be placed on this. The whole structure is loose and open to permit adequate ventilation. When the paper is ignited, if there is enough of each type of material, the fire will be passed from the smaller to the larger, at first slowly, and then rapidly. It is good practice to hold off the larger material until the fire has been well started, then stack it on gradually, taking care not to block the circulation.

If no or little paper is available, the fire may be started by building a small cone or tepee of very light tinder material. Larger material, and finally kindling wood, is loosely stacked about this inner cone. The lit match is held inside the cone, the flame licking the apex. A small ball of paper or cellophane placed inside the cone is also excellent. This fire will catch more slowly than if much paper is used, but the end is just as effective.

When the fire is fed, the larger logs must always rest on some sort of "andiron" so that the flames and air may reach the underside. A good fire may be ruined by improper feeding that blocks circulation. It must be remembered that judicious blowing or fanning will rouse smouldering embers into new life.

Emergency Tinders. There are times, especially when it is raining or snowing, when the camper may experience difficulty in getting his fire started, or be so low on matches that he cannot risk using more than one to light the fire. There are many expedients he can use; gasoline, for example, though that is a dangerous practice and should be resorted to only under extreme emergency conditions. Gasoline should never be poured on live embers.

Fires may be started by using the powder from any sort of rifle or pistol shell. The paper stripped from a shotgun shell will also make good additional tinder. Certain plastic articles, especially the nitrates (celluloid, etc.) are inflammable, and a fountain pen casing, celluloid comb, or camera film, may sometimes be used as fire-making insurance. Waxed or oiled papers will burn with more than the usual amount of heat.

There are some chemical tinders on the market, little briquettes of compressed material, suitable for emergency use.

CAMP COOKING OVER A PIT FIRE
A. Uprights   B. Crossbar   C. Pothook
(forked stick)   D. Pothook (heavy wire)
E. Nesting kettles   F. Fire pit

COOKING WITH A FIRE

The ideal cooking fire should be as small, as hot, and as smokeless as possible. This is as good a definition of a bed of embers as there is, and that is the preferred cooking fire. A large roaring flame is valueless; the heat is uneven, the flames force the cook to stand well back, the vessels are blacked with soot, ash gets into the food, and smoke gets into the cook's eyes. The cook cannot perform his best work under those conditions.

The fire should be built high and roaring, at first, but the experienced cook waits until it has settled down to be a bed of glowing coals before he goes to work. If

there is no time for this cycle, then only a small fire is built.

METHODS OF SUSPENDING GAME OR POT OVER FIRE

Cooking With Utensils. Normal cooking procedure is followed when utensils are used. The chief difference between this and kitchen cooking is the heat source. The type and effectiveness of the heat control achieved by the outdoor cook depends upon his skill and upon the fireplace which he is using. Under good conditions, the camp cook will experience only slightly more difficulty than the kitchen cook.

Cooking Without Utensils. While pots and pans are very convenient, they are not, strictly speaking, essential, for it is possible to prepare many a tasty dish without their use. This sort of cooking may be used as an emergency measure when the utensils have been lost, as an expedient to extend the capacity of existing utensils or to lessen the numbers that need be carried, or as a way of getting more fun out of camping. Though foods are better prepared in utensils, the camp cook should know at least a few ways of getting along without them.

1. *Broiling.* Meats and even some vegetables and fruits may be broiled with ease over an ember bed. They may be broiled by *spitting*, i.e., by impaling them on long slender sticks of peeled green wood, searing the meat to keep the juices from escaping, and turning slowly over the fire until done. A *grill* may be constructed of green sticks and used to hold the food over the fire. In either case, the sticks must be watched to see that they do not burn through, and

growing saplings or slender limbs should be cut for the job (one of the few exceptions to the rule of never cutting growing wood). The wood selected should have a sweet tasting bark, lest it impart a bitter flavor to the food, and it should be peeled. Steel rods may also be carried for this purpose.

Meat may be broiled by *planking;* i.e., by cutting it thin and pegging it to a clean, smooth plank or wood slab that is placed close to the fire. It is well to lard such meat by also pegging down strips of bacon to keep it from being too dry.

KABOB COOKING

A *kabob* may also be made; a meal on a stick. Meat and various vegetables are cut to discs and squares of appropriate size and then impaled in sequence on a spit. The entire assembly is broiled over the fire and eaten directly from the spit. Meat, onion, carrot, potato, and onion is a typical kabob structure.

2. *Baking Fish.* Fish are easily baked without utensils. The carcass is thickly covered with mud or clay and buried in the embers. The cooking time varies from 15 to 30 minutes per pound, depending on the type of fish, thickness of clay, and heat of the fire. The clay or mud will bake hard in the fire and, when raked out, can easily be broken open. The skin of the fish, scales and all, will adhere to the clay, and it is not essential that the fish be gutted before baking, for the internal organs merely shrivel up when fish are baked by this method. When the cooked fish is split open, these organs may be easily removed, and leave no taste behind.

3. *Baking Fowl.* Small game birds and chickens may be baked in mud as described above, but these must first be cleansed and gutted.

4. *Baking Eggs.* Eggs may be baked in a fire, but it must be a gradual process, else they will explode. A small hole may be punched in the large end of the shell to let the air escape as the sac inside expands. The eggs may be covered with clay or mud or wrapped in wet leaves or paper, and buried under at least two inches of soil beneath the fire. They will be done in from 20 to 45 minutes.

5. *Baking Potatoes.* Potatoes may be thrown directly into the fire if you do not mind cutting away a thick, charred layer from the outside when done. It is better to wrap them in mud, or to bury them beneath the fire as previously described. Sweet potatoes will cook in less time than their Irish relations, which should be the first items on the fire so they will be done when the other foods are ready.

6. *Baking Corn.* Corn on the cob may be baked in much the same manner as are potatoes, first removing the cornsilk and wrapping the ear in its own husks before proceeding with the other preparations.

7. *Baking Bread.* A "twist" may be made without the aid of pan or oven, and makes a good companion to the kabob previously described. A biscuit dough is prepared, slightly thicker than usual, and worked into long thin rolls. These rolls are wrapped snake-fashion (spirals) about a spit and slowly turned over the fire until done.

TWIST COOKING

8. *Steaming Foods.* Meat, fish, fowl, and vegetables may all be steamed without the aid of utensils. Though there are variations, the processes are all basically alike. The food is first cleansed and prepared, and then wrapped in layers of some wet material: paper, cloth, leaves, etc. The package may be buried in the coals, but the usual practice is to bury it in the ground beneath the fire. Individual items are cooked in this manner, and in some cases, as in a clambake, layers of different foods are all put down in the same pit and cooked at once.

9. *Boiling Foods.* The American Indians used to boil food in bark, wood, and fiber containers without burning the vessel. Though the process is possible, it is too tedious to be practical when there are so many other easier ways of cooking the same foods. The container must be water-tight and can be constructed of any convenient material in any expedient way. The container is filled with water, the food dropped in, and the water heated by means of hot rocks which are taken from the fire and dropped directly into the water. The heat from the rocks is transferred to the water rather than the container, thus not burning the vessel, but the cool rocks have to be replaced by hot ones if it is to work.

10. *Other methods.* The examples given are merely basic; there are many ingenious methods of cooking certain foods under specific circumstances using only the resources of nature. Some are quite practical, while others are of interest only to the man desperately concerned with the problem of survival. If the subject is of interest to the reader, more specialized books should be consulted.

Cooking in the Mountain Camp. At high altitudes, the air pressure is lessened, with surprising effects on normal cooking practices. The mountain camper will find that he must modify many of his cooking techniques if he is to be successful. *See* HIGH-ALTITUDE COOKERY.

MENU

The same considerations of health and variety apply to the camp menu as to the kitchen menu. There is, however, one major difference. In the kitchen, meals are planned in accordance with family tastes and current food prices. While these considerations apply to the camper as well, he has problems unknown to the kitchen cook.

As previously discussed, not every kind of food can be safely brought on a camping trip. There are some that can be brought, but are very inconvenient to carry. And the camper must consider the utensils that he will have to do his cooking with, as well.

The menu for each trip is a highly individual affair that can only be determined by the circumstances peculiar to that trip. The ability of the cook should also be considered, for it would be rather pointless to plan meals that he is not fitted to prepare.

The important thing to do is to inject some variety and to make certain that the diet is well balanced, even if this means some inconvenience on the camper's part. It is also important to include some foods with laxative values (prunes, figs, etc.) on the menu, for campers often become constipated because of the change in diet or surroundings, and this condition can have serious results if it is neglected.

OUTDOOR SANITATION

To the housewife, the returning camper looks the epitome of filth. His clothes are black with soot and smell of wood smoke. He usually has several day's growth of beard and his face looks as though it were never washed.

All of this may well be true, but as far as his cooking equipment and camp site is concerned, the experienced camper is the soul of cleanliness. Cleanliness is harder to achieve in the woods than in the house, but for that very reason it is most important. Dirt and refuse breed germs, draw insects, and give off unpleasant odors. Not only can this make the camper's life unpleasant, but it can actually endanger it through disease. It takes but a small bit of grease on a mess kit to give the camper a serious case of dysentery.

Washing Dishes and Utensils. Rarely does the camper have the unlimited hot water of the housewife, nor does he have the large sinks and wide drainboards at his hand. But he does have an ample supply of dirt, and dirt, plain, ordinary dirt is one of the best cleansing substances man has ever discovered.

Camp gear gets filthier than kitchen gear. Pans are coated with grease and soot, and often, because of the uneven heat of some fires, food is burned in pans. But dirt will cut through anything. It can be used dry or in solution with water; swirled about in the bottom of utensils, or rubbed with the hand. Leaves or cloth may be used to protect the hand. Knives, tableware, etc., are stabbed directly into the ground until clean.

Dirt is an abrasive, which is why it is effective. Enamelware and plastics may receive the dirt treatment, but it should be gentle, lest they be overly scratched.

Everything, of course, should be washed with hot, soapy water following the scrubbing with dirt, but this pre-treatment will remove practically all of grease, food particles, soot, and other dirt, greatly simplifying the normal washing routine. Steel wool, dish rags, soap, and all of the other accessories to the washing operation may and should be used in camp. Bar soap is better than powder, however, for it is less affected by accidental moisture, easier packed, and can be used as a hand soap, as well. All of the normal precautions applied to dishwashing in the home hold for the camp as well, and the importance of absolute cleanliness cannot be too greatly stressed.

Refuse Disposal. There are no garbage men in the wilderness, but it is expected of the camper that he leave his site as clean and neat as it was when he found it. There are many important reasons for this, and they may all be summed up under two headings: consideration of others and personal comfort. Refuse should either be burned or buried, but never left lying about. A garbage pit should be dug when the site is opened, and all refuse that cannot be burned thrown in. Tin cans and glass containers should be smashed flat with an axe or stone before being thrown in the pit. Food refuse may be covered over with dirt as it is thrown in, to keep it from drawing insects, and when the camp is broken, the pit is refilled, possibly covered with stones to keep animals from digging it up to get at the garbage, and a sign posted indicating that this is a garbage pit and giving the date of closing. This step keeps later campers from inadvertently uncovering the pit when they dig their own.

Things that can be burned are either thrown into the fire as soon as discarded or saved for one grand burning. Nothing solid should be thrown into a stream or other water source, and soiled water should be poured on the ground instead of being thrown into a water source. The latrine should be located well away from any water source and is handled in exactly the same manner as the garbage pit.

Fire Precautions

Fire is an ever present danger in the woods, and the camper should be most careful in this respect. As previously stated, all underbrush should be cleared away from the vicinity of any fire, cooking or otherwise, and it is a wise precaution to build the fire on a stone base, where this is possible.

No fire should ever be left until the camper is positive that it is out. Being out does not mean that it is covered over and smouldering with no live coals or flames showing. Such a fire can be fanned back to destructive life days after the camper has left. The fire should be definitely out.

Water—in quantity—is the best fire extinguisher. It should be thrown on until there is no more smoke or hissing. If water is not available, then dirt or sand can be used. The camper should dig up the ground under the fire to make certain that roots in the ground are not burning. Forest fires are often started in this manner; roots beneath the cooking fire will catch and carry the fire quite some distance underground before it surfaces, and, this usually being long after the campers have left the site, becomes a dangerous thing.

When gasoline stoves are used, a chemical extinguisher should be kept on hand. If none is available, then a pile of sand or dirt should be kept in readiness. Never use water on any petroleum fire; it will never put it out and will only spread it, since gasoline and oil will float on water.

See also Barbecue and Picnic.

CAN OPENER. A device used to open tin cans. When canned foods came into popularity, much thought was given to the problem of opening the cans, with the result that there are now available a great many different types of openers.

The earliest and simplest model consists of a sharp blade that is forced into the metal and worked around the edge by means of a lever action against the rim of the can. As long as the blade is sharp, these devices are efficient, but they tend to leave dangerous, jagged edges as well as to mar the top surface of the food within the can.

There are many mechanical devices that are worked either by turning a key or a crank. This type functions by forcing a sharp cutting edge into the metal close to the rim and then forcing this knife edge around the rim of the can. This is accomplished by turning a serrated wheel which is pressed against the can.

A variety of electric can openers which work by means of round, revolving blades are available in wall mounted models. These may have knife sharpening or other attachments as desired.

When canned beer was brought into the market, another type of opener came into popularity, the so-called *beer can opener*. This type engages the edge of the rim for leverage and, when the handle is raised, forces a sharp triangular point into the lid, making a large hole suitable for pouring liquids. A small airhole must be punched opposite the pouring hole for even liquid flow. Today an increasing number of beers, soft drinks and non–carbonated drinks come in tab top cans which may be opened without a beer can opener. Care should be taken that the tops of these cans are pointed away from the face while opening.

Purchasing

For kitchen use, the wall-mounted type of opener is best except for the highly specialized tasks of the beer can opener. Hand-held openers are as efficient, but they have a tendency to become mislaid or lost at the time of need. Whatever type is selected, it should function with a minimum of effort and do a smooth cutting job. Jagged edges on lids or cans can be dangerous to the fingers, and there is the possibility of small bits of metal breaking off and falling into the food.

If possible, the opener selected should be so designed as to either grip the lid or to raise it above the can level as it makes the final cut. In this way, it is possible to retrieve the cut metal circle before it falls back into the can.

The opener should be sturdy and well built, with as few moving parts as possible. It should be made of rust-proof material and should be reasonably easy to clean.

CANAPES. Canapés consist of bite-sized bits of savory food spread on edible bases and garnished or decorated. They lend themselves to an exciting variety of shapes, colors, and tastes, and they may be as simple or as elaborate as you like. Caviar and pâté de fois gras stand at the top of the luxury spreads; melted cheese at the top of the simpler ones. Women seem to prefer the former type and men the latter.

Canapés are served as snacks at cocktail and buffet parties, and their festive appearance lends a party atmosphere to the most casual of gatherings. They are passed at cocktail parties, but at buffet parties they may be served with hors d'oeuvres and eaten with a fork.

Of course both men and women prefer morsels of fresh and attractive appearance, and canapés require a good pit of coddling if they are to look as they should. Use very sharp cutting utensils to assure even shapes, and cover the bases so that the finished product will have a symmetrical appearance. Chill the canapés thoroughly before serving unless it is recommended that a particular sort be served warm. Any desired color can be achieved through the addition of vegetable coloring to the canapé butters.

DECORATIVE ARRANGEMENT FOR SERVING CANAPES

Garnishes should be carefully placed and then allowed to remain—pushing them about will spoil the canapé's neat, fresh appearance. Borders and lines should be as perfect as possible. Tiny watercress and parsley leaves should be left in their natural form and should be dropped on the centers of canapés. However, if they land closer to the outside, they should not be disturbed.

You can prepare limitless varieties of canapés. Following are suggestions for bases and spreads or fillings as well as for their combination. The recipes, intended for the inexperienced, are by no means strict formulas, but they may be adapted to suit individual tastes. As you grow in experience you will probably depend less and less on canapé recipes and more and more on concoctions of your own invention. *See also* Appetizers, Hors D'Oeuvres, and Cocktails.

Bread Canape Bases

Most kinds of bread can be used for canapé bases. The slices, however, should be ¼ inch thick, and the crusts must always be removed. The bread should then be cut into small shapes such as rounds, squares, diamonds, stars, hearts, oblongs, crescents, triangles, and strips. Toast or sauté in butter on only one side. Spread a mixture over the untoasted side and garnish as desired. Both toasting and buttering are optional.

If bread is to be used for rolled canapés, cut the crusts from very thin slices, cut the slices in halves or smaller pieces, spread with filling, roll lengthwise, secure with a toothpick at each end, and toast in broiler (or sauté in butter) while turning to brown evenly.

For rolled canapés use fresh bread, and for others use bread that is one day old.

PASTRY BASES

Roll pastry (*which see*) to a thickness of ⅛ inch, and cut it in whatever small shapes are desired. For variety these may be spread with peanut butter before baking; or they may be sprinkled with any of the following: celery seeds, caraway seeds, coriander seeds, paprika, cayenne, mustard, allspice, mace, grated cheese, or chopped nuts.

Roll puff paste (*which see*) to a thickness of ⅛ inch, cut it in small rounds, put two together to make small patty cases, and bake as directed. Fill them with any canapé filling or spread.

Fill miniature cream puff shells (*see* CREAM PUFFS) with such fillings as canapé butters and spreads, creamed mushrooms, and a mixture of deviled ham and cream cheese seasoned with catsup.

CANAPE CREPES

½ cup sifted flour
½ tsp salt
2 beaten egg yolks
1 cup water

Mix flour and salt. Mix egg yolks and water, combine the two mixtures, and beat until smooth. Bake on a greased griddle or frying pan. Cool, spread with a canapé filling, and roll. (Makes about 20)

BLINIS

These very small pancakes are widely used in Russia and Poland as canapé bases. *See* BLINIS. They can be served hot with caviar mixed with fresh sour cream and 1 tablespoon of melted butter, with pressed caviar, or with sliced smoked salmon.

RAMEKINS

Gather left over pastry scraps, roll them out evenly, and sprinkle with nicely-flavored grated cheese. Fold the paste in three, roll it again, and sprinkle it with cheese again. Roll it out and, with a paste cutter, shape small pieces as desired. Bake for 10 to 15 minutes in a brisk oven. Serve hot. Brushing the ramekins over with egg yolk before baking them adds to their appearance. Parmesan cheese is recommended above other kinds.

CHEESE PASTRY BASE

¾ cup sifted flour
⅛ tsp salt
½ cup butter
2 packages (6 oz.) cream cheese
1 tbsp cold water

Mix flour and salt. Blend in butter and cheese, using two knives or a pastry blender. Stir the water in, and chill the mixture. Roll the dough very thin, cut it in rounds, and bake in a very hot oven (450° F.) until lightly browned (about 10 minutes). This dough may be prepared several days before it is to be used, and then kept in a refrigerator. It may be served plain or used as a canapé base. (Makes about 100.)

If desired, sprinkle chopped nuts, caraway seeds, poppy seeds, or cinnamon and sugar over the baked pastries while hot.

CHEESE CRACKERS

1½ oz margarine
3 oz flour
4 oz grated cheese
Dash of salt
Dash of cayenne pepper
Yolk of 1 egg

Rub the margarine into the flour, and add the next three ingredients. Mix the egg yolk with a bit of cold water and add this. Work the mixture into a soft dough. Roll it very thin and cut it into small rounds. Bake in a moderate oven (350° F.) until golden brown. These cocktail crackers may be served plain or used as a canapé base.

PREPARED CANAPE BASES

There are many varieties of ready-to-use canapé bases on the market; these may be bread, cracker, or pastry mixtures. Thin crackers and wafers, flaked or shredded cereals, and potato chips make simple and attractive bases. To crisp or freshen, spread them over the bottom of a pan, and put this in a moderate oven (350° F.) for about 10 minutes.

DEVILED COCKTAIL CRACKERS

Mix butter, cayenne pepper, French mustard, anchovy paste, and salt. Spread the mixture liberally on flaky salted crackers, and grill them until sizzling. Grated cheese or tomato purée may be substituted for anchovy paste. These may be served plain or used as canapé bases.

PUFFED CRACKERS

Soak crackers in ice water for 8 to 10 minutes. Drain them on absorbent paper, place them in a greased pan, brush them with seasoned melted butter, and bake them in a very hot oven (450° F.) for 10 minutes. Reduce the heat to moderate (350° F.) and bake for 20 more minutes.

India puffs. Before baking the crackers, brush 18 of them with a mixture of 3 tablespoons of melted butter, ½ teaspoon of salt, ¼ teaspoon of paprika, and ¾ teaspoon of curry powder. (Makes 18)

Modifications of puffs. You may prepare cheese, nut, or caraway puffs by sprinkling the prepared crackers with grated cheese, finely chopped nuts, and caraway seeds, respectively. Then bake as directed above. Spread with a canapé butter, if desired, or serve plain.

CANAPE BUTTERS

Prepare any of the following butters by beating the listed ingredients into ¼ cup (4 tablespoons) of creamed butter.

Anchovy butter. 1 tablespoon of anchovy paste, ½ teaspoon of lemon juice, and a dash of paprika.

Cheese butter. ¼ cup of soft or grated cheese.

Chili butter. 2 tablespoons of chili sauce.

Chives butter. 1 tablespoon of finely minced chives and 1 teaspoon of lemon juice.

Chutney butter. 1 tablespoon of chutney.

Egg butter. 2 finely mashed hard-cooked eggs, ½ teaspoon of lemon juice, a dash of tabasco sauce, and salt and cayenne to taste.

Green savory butter. 3 tablespoons of spinach purée, 1 tablespoon of anchovy paste, 1 teaspoon of capers, a dash of paprika, and salt to taste.

Honey butter. ¼ cup of honey.

Horseradish butter. 2 tablespoons of horseradish.

Ketchup butter. 2 tablespoons of ketchup.

Lemon butter. A few gratings of lemon rind and 2 teaspoons of lemon juice.

Lime butter. A few gratings of lime rind and 2 teaspoons of lime juice.

Lobster butter. 1 tablespoon of lobster paste, ½ teaspoon of lemon juice, a dash of paprika, and a dash of dry mustard.

Mint butter. 2 tablespoons of finely chopped mint leaves and 1 teaspoon of lemon juice.

Mustard butter. 1 tablespoon of mustard.

Nut butter. 2 tablespoons of finely chopped, salted nuts.

Olive butter. 1 tablespoon of olive paste and ¼ teaspoon of lemon juice.

Onion butter. 1 teaspoon of onion juice.

Orange butter. A few gratings of orange rind and 2 teaspoons of orange juice.

Parmesan butter. 2 tablespoons of Parmesan cheese.

Parsley butter. 2 tablespoons of finely cut parsley and 1 teaspoon of lemon juice.

Peanut butter. ¼ cup of peanut butter, 1 teaspoon of honey, and salt to taste.

Pimiento butter. 2 tablespoons of mashed pimiento and 1 teaspoon of finely chopped pickles.

Roquefort butter. 1 tablespoon of Roquefort cheese.

Salmon butter. 1 tablespoon of salmon paste, 1 teaspoon of lemon juice, and a dash of cayenne.

Sardine butter. 1 teaspoon of sardine paste, ½ teaspoon of lemon juice, ½ teaspoon of onion juice, and a dash of paprika.

Shredded crabmeat butter. 1 cup of finely shredded crabmeat.

Shredded lobster butter. 1 cup of finely shredded lobster.

Watercress butter. 2 tablespoons of finely chopped watercress, 1 teaspoon of lemon juice, and a few drops of Worcestershire sauce.

Worcestershire butter. ¼ teaspoon of Worcestershire sauce.

MEAT SPREADS

Chicken liver spread. Mix ½ cup of chopped cooked chicken livers, 2 chopped hard-cooked eggs, 1 teaspoon of minced onion, salt to taste, and enough cream to moisten the mixture. Serve on crisp crackers, and garnish with parsley.

Chicken salad spread. Mix 1 cup of finely chopped chicken (cooked), 2 tablespoons of finely chopped celery, ½ cup of nut meats, and enough highly-seasoned mayonnaise to make a paste that will spread easily. Garnish with minced eggs.

Deviled ham spread. Mix 1 cup of deviled ham, 2 hard-cooked eggs, and 1 tablespoon of horseradish. Serve on toast rounds, and garnish with watercress.

Ham-cheese spread. Mix 1 cup of finely chopped boiled ham (cold), ¼ cup of grated American or Swiss cheese, ½ teaspoon of grated onion, and 1 teaspoon of ketchup. Serve on crackers, garnish with a bit of horseradish sauce, and dust with paprika.

Liverwurst spread. Remove the skin from ¼ pound of liverwurst and mash the meat with a fork. Add 1 tablespoon of mayonnaise, 1½ tablespoons of lemon juice, salt to taste, and enough cream to moisten. Serve on toast rounds, and garnish with onion butter.

Pâté de foie gras spread. Mix 3 tablespoons of pâté de foie gras, ¼ cup of cream, and seasoning to taste. Force the mixture through a sieve, and serve it on toast fingers. Garnish with parsley.

FISH SPREADS

Anchovy-cheese spread. Mix 1 part of chopped anchovy with 2 parts of cream cheese. Serve on crackers.

Caviar spread. Mix 3 tablespoons of caviar, 2 tablespoons of finely chopped white onions, and 1½ teaspoons of lemon juice. Spread on toast rounds, and garnish with minced hard-cooked egg.

Caviar-egg spread. Mix 2 tablespoons of caviar, 2 minced hard-cooked eggs, and enough mayonnaise to moisten. Spread on toast rounds.

Tuna fish spread. Mix ½ cup of shredded tuna, 1 tablespoon of lemon juice, 1 teaspoon of grated onion, and enough mayonnaise to hold the mixture together. Serve on toast, and garnish with small slices of lemon or with grated cheese.

Lobster spread. Substitute lobster for caviar in caviar-egg spread (above).

Shrimp spread. Add lemon juice, tabasco sauce, salt, and pepper to finely chopped shrimp. Spread on toast rounds. Garnish with pickled walnut.

Smoked fish canapés. Place strips of smoked salmon and smoked herring on toast fingers. Decorate edges with anchovy butter, and dust with chopped parsley.

CHEESE SPREADS

Cheese-onion spread. Mix ½ package (1½ ounces) of cream cheese, 1 tablespoon of minced onion, and enough cream to moisten. Season with salt. Serve on crackers or toast rounds. Sprinkle lightly with paprika, or garnish with a sprig of parsley. Or spread the mixture on slices of dried beef, roll these tightly, and cut them in 1-inch lengths.

Chili-cheese spread. Mix 1 package (3 ounces) of cream cheese with enough chili sauce to moisten. Serve on crisp potato chips and garnish with crumbled bits of crisp bacon.

Roquefort-chives spread. Mix Roquefort cheese with enough French dressing to moisten. Season with chopped chives, and serve on crackers.

Cheese-caviar spread. Combine cream cheese with enough cream to moisten. Shape it into tiny balls and roll these in caviar. Serve on small, lightly-buttered crackers.

Orange cheese spread. Mix 1 package of soft cream cheese, the rind of 1 orange, ¼ teaspoon of salt, and ⅛ teaspoon of paprika. Spread small bread shapes with mayonnaise or butter, cover them with the cheese spread, and top with chopped toasted pecan meats.

FRUIT SPREADS

Avocado spread. Pare avocados and mash the pulp with a fork. Season with lemon juice, lime juice, grapefruit juice, or minced onions, and with salt. Spread on crackers or toast rounds, and garnish with parsley. Or place a slice of tomato on toast and cover this with the spread. Or serve it as a dish in which to dip potato chips.

Guava-cheese spread. Spread cream cheese over bread or crackers, spread guava jelly over this, and sprinkle chopped nuts over the tops.

Almond-Parmesan Fingers

3 tbsp chopped sweet almonds
3 tbsp butter
6 tbsp grated Parmesan cheese
3 tbsp minced parsley
3 tbsp heavy cream
Salt and pepper to taste
12 toast strips

Blanch the chopped almonds, and sauté them in butter until they are golden brown. Mix the remaining ingredients and spread the mixture on buttered toast strips. Garnish with finely chopped almonds, and heat thoroughly before serving. (Makes 12)

Anchovy-Egg Canapes

Mix 3 tablespoons each of lemon and onion juice, and add a dash of cayenne. Drain 1 can of anchovy fillets, and marinate these in the mixture for ½ hour. Drain again, and place the fillets on 12 toast rounds. Border with 1 finely minced hard-cooked egg, dust with paprika, and garnish with watercress. (Makes 12)

Asparagus Canapes

12 thin slices of bread
6 thin slices boiled ham
Mustard
12 asparagus tips (cooked or canned)
Mayonnaise

Remove bread crusts. Cut ham slices in halves and trim them to fit the bread slices. Spread with mustard. Dip asparagus in mayonnaise, and place one tip at end of each prepared bread slice. Roll lengthwise, secure with a toothpick at each end, place on broiler rack in a preheated broiler, and turn to toast rolls. (Makes 12)

Canape Turnovers

Pastry
1 minced cooked chicken liver
2 slices bacon, broiled and minced
1 hard-cooked egg, chopped
2 tbsp minced parsley
¼ tsp curry powder
Salt
Paprika

Roll pastry (*which see*) very thin, and cut it in 2-inch squares. Mix the remaining ingredients, using only enough salt and paprika to season, and place 1 teaspoon of the mixture on each square. Fold the pastry into a triangle and press the edges together. Fry in hot deep fat (370° F.) until golden brown (3 to 5 minutes). Garnish with parsley. (Makes 24)

Caviar Rissolettes

Roll puff paste (*which see*) ¼ inch thick, and cut it in small rounds. Place 1 teaspoon of caviar, seasoned with lemon juice, in the center of each round. Wet edges and cover with a second round. Press edges together. Fry in hot deep fat (370° F.) until delicately browned (3 to 4 minutes). Drain on absorbent paper.

Lobster Canapes

12 buttered toast rounds
Tartar sauce
⅜ cup chopped, sauteed mushrooms
1½ cup chopped, cooked lobster
Salt and paprika
3 tbsp grated Parmesan cheese
1½ tsp horseradish
Mayonnaise
Sliced, stuffed olives
Watercress

Spread untoasted sides of bread with tartar sauce, and cover with mixture of lobster meat and mushrooms. Dust with salt and paprika, and set in a cold place. Combine horseradish, cheese, and enough mayonnaise to make a creamy mixture. Press the mixture through a pastry bag, and then use it to border the canapés. In the center of each canapé place a slice of olive garnished with a sprig of watercress. (Makes 12)

Pretzel and Cheese Canapes

Work 1 package of cream cheese (3 oz.) to smoothness with a fork. Season it with paprika or with chopped olives, and place it in the hollows of small crisp pretzels. Crush other pretzels and sprinkle the crumbs over the cheese. Chill until ready to serve.

Toasted Nut Canapes

Cream ½ cup of butter. When it is soft enough to stir, stir in 1 cup of ground

pecans and 2 tablespoons of Worcestershire sauce. Spread the mixture on bread
rounds. Toast until hot and serve at once.

TOMATO CANAPES

Place a thick slice of tomato on each
round of toast. Dust with salt, paprika, and
minced green pepper. Dot with butter.
Top each with 1 tablespoon of grated
cheese. Broil until tomatoes are soft and
cheese is melted, and then serve at once.
Thin slices of bacon may be substituted for
the grated cheese.

TOMATO AND SHRIMP CANAPES

Place a thick slice of tomato on each
round of toast. Place 2 or 3 marinated
shrimp on top of each, and top with a
dab of mayonnaise.

CANARD A LA PRESSE. French name
for "Pressed Duck." *See* DUCK.

CANDLE. The efficient electric light
has still to replace the candle for establishing a mood or a scenic effect at the dinner
table. Candles are still widely used for
lighting purposes at evening meals and
especially at formal dinners. *See* TABLE
SETTING AND SERVICE.

CANDLEBERRY. This is a waxy berry
from which aromatic candles are made. It
is better known as bayberry, *which see*.

CANDY. Human instinct often arrives
at a truth while science toils after it at long
distance. The mid-morning pick-me-up is
an example. The little throng in the office
building that gathers around the soft drink
fountain, or the group in the factory cafeteria that takes a sweet drink, an order of
ice cream, or some candy and goes back to
work refreshed, is instinctively right. Dietitians pooh-poohed them for a long time,
but now they are beginning to preach the
doctrine that a sweet relieves fatigue.

The explanation is quite simple. Sugar
is the energy producer for the body, just as
gasoline is the fuel for the automobile. The
simpler the sugar, the more readily it is
converted into energy. Sugar is stored in
the liver, and if the supply drops to a low
level the muscles work at a disadvantage,
and fatigue and fatigue-headaches result.
The best sugars for the production of
energy are the fruit sugars, but any sugar
in any form is more rapidly converted into
energy than starch. This does not mean
that sugar will relieve everyone's fatigue.

The body cannot run without sugar.
Even meat is partially converted into sugar
in order to furnish energy. Those faddists
and freak dietitians who abstain from
sweets are simply defeating themselves because no matter what food the body assimilates it has to convert 75 percent of it into
sugar in order to continue operating. So,
the little group that takes its usual mid-
morning and mid-afternoon pick up is
following the wisest dictates of the most
modern research of dietetic science.

Primitive man probably satisfied the
craving of his "sweet tooth" with fruits,
sweet herbs, and honey. To find the first
written and pictured evidence of the importance of candy, one must turn to ancient Egypt. The Egyptians were the fathers of most things modern, including
engineering, architecture, and chemistry.
They were also the first people known to
have made confectionery. True, their sweetmeats would seem crude in comparison
with modern candy, but they were candies,
nevertheless. The refining of sugar was an
unknown art in those days, so the confectioner used honey as a sweetener. To this
he added sweet herbs and spices. These
confections were highly colored to attract
the eye of the candy lover who, no doubt,
found them quite delicious albeit very
expensive.

Today, high grade commercial candies
owe their distinction of flavor and appearance to the excellence of the raw materials
used, and to the care with which they are
mixed. In the deluxe candies, cream is
used instead of thickened milk; butter instead of vegetable fat, and thick, rich coating chocolate is used for dipping. The
better grades of hard candies contain good
fruit flavors and safe colorings.

Home-made candies will always remain
one of the most delightful and informal of
holiday gifts. Happy the homemaker who
has the knack of making them! It need not
be a difficult task provided a few secrets of
success have been mastered and the proper
equipment is used.

Many homemakers are reluctant to try
their hand because homemade candy, no
matter how delicious when first made, gets
dry and hard so quickly. The answer to
this problem is to use glycerine. This pure,
wholesome product has unique powers of
absorbing and retaining moisture; a few
drops added to your candies help keep
them fresh for days. Glycerine will also

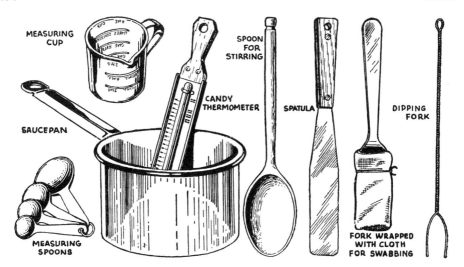

MEASURING CUP

SPOON FOR STIRRING

CANDY THERMOMETER

SPATULA

DIPPING FORK

SAUCEPAN

FORK WRAPPED WITH CLOTH FOR SWABBING

MEASURING SPOONS

CANDY MAKING EQUIPMENT

make your cream mixtures taste richer and smoother, intensify the flavors, and prevent graining.

Candy-Making Equipment

Candy Bars. These are used to form various sized spaces on the marble slab, into which are poured caramel and taffy mixtures. They can be arranged to hold various quantities of candy.

Candy Hook. Certain candy is improved by being pulled on a special hook, as the pulling makes it fluffier and lighter in color.

Caramel Cutter. This is a metal framework with transverse and longitudinal bars, which when pressed on the surface of caramel or taffy, mark it into a number of uniform small squares. The squares are then cut through with a knife.

Dipping Forks. Made of wire with two or three prongs or a loop at the end, these are used for lifting the dipped candies out of the coating mixtures.

Marble Slab. Although not absolutely necessary, a slab is convenient and useful. A large platter may be used instead.

Nougat Frames. These forms are not absolutely necessary, but their use does give nougat a professional touch. They are also useful in making candies of like consistency.

Saucepans. Several heavy-lipped pans, including two small ones, holding about one pint each for melting fondant and other minor operations are useful. They may be made of copper or aluminum.

Spatulas. These handy little utensils often take the place of spoons for stirring and beating mixtures or for scraping out pans.

Starch Tray. Any large, flat box or biscuit pan will do. A convenient size is 3x20 inches. The box is filled with clean, dry, sifted cornstarch, smoothed with a spatula or the blade of a knife. Impressions are made in the starch to form molds into which the candy mixture is poured, thus forming candies of various shapes and sizes according to the candymaker's whim. The candy mixture should fill each mold level with the top of the starch. Lift out the candies when set and dust off the starch. Always dry and sift the starch before storing for subsequent re-use.

The impressions may be made with the finger tips, a cork, a thimble, or any like object. For very fancy shapes small molds may be made of plaster, sealing wax, or paraffin. These are glued to a strip of wood (which should be longer than the starch tray) and pressed into the starch. Rubber mats that serve the same purpose as the starch tray can be purchased from any confectioner's supply house. They have innumerable designs and are easy to use but do not offer the opportunity for originality of execution that comes with the use of the starch tray.

Sugar Scraper. This is used to scrape up the sugar on the slab or platter. However, any broad-bladed spatula may be used.

Thermometer. The confectioner's thermometer is a most useful instrument to the candy maker. It enables one to tell at a glance when the different candies are ready to remove from the fire and is necessary from the standpoint of economy. Such thermometers are made of brass, copper, or other metals. The degrees indicated should be at least 350° F.

Tin Sheet or Tray. This should be of polished tin and is used for dropped chocolates.

Besides the above you will need: bowls, coloring (liquid or paste), containers (airtight), double boilers, egg beater, food chopper, funnel, knives, measuring cups and spoons, nutcracker, pastry brush, pastry tubes and bags, platters, rolling pin, scales, scissors, sieve (fine mesh), tin pans, waxed paper and wafer paper.

DEGREES OF BOILING SUGAR

Thread. At a point between 230° and 234° F. sirup reaches what is known as the "thread" stage, meaning that it spins a 2-inch thread when lifted from the mass on fork or spoon. If a longer thread is formed, it is known as the "great thread."

Soft-Ball. At a point between 234° and 240° F. (usually 238° F.) the soft ball stage is reached, meaning that when a little sirup is dropped into cold water it forms a soft ball which flattens on removal from water.

Firm-Ball. At a point between 244° and 248° F. the firm ball stage is reached, meaning that when a little sirup is dropped into cold water it forms a firm ball which does not flatten on removal from the water.

Note. When a boiling solution of sugar and water has passed the soft-ball degree, it may readily grain unless glucose (corn sirup) or some kind of acid is added. The danger may be guarded against also by melting the sugar very thoroughly before allowing it to boil, or still better, by brushing or sponging the sides of the pan during boiling so as to dissolve any hard particles or crystals which may form. Cream of tartar is the acid usually used to prevent granulation of the sirup. If too large a quantity is used, it will cause the sugar sirup to change color very rapidly, and the candies made or covered with it will be soft and sticky. Boiling sugar sirup intended for pulling, or such purposes, is all the better for the addition of a teaspoon (level) of glucose with the cream of tartar.

It is important to bear in mind that pure sugar and water shows no tendency to boil over. But all impurities or scum rising to the surface should be removed as soon as the sirup boils and then the boiling should be allowed to go on vigorously till the rrquired degree is reached.

Hard-Ball. At a point between 250° and 265° F. the hard ball stage is reached. This means that when a little sirup is dropped into cold water it forms a ball which is hard enough to keep its shape—yet plastic.

Soft-Crack. At a point between 270° and 290° F. the soft crack stage is reached. This occurs when the sirup separates into threads which are hard yet not brittle on bring dropped into cold water.

Hard-Crack. When the temperature of the sirup has reached between 300° and 310° F., a little sirup separates into hard brittle threads when dropped into cold water. This is known as the hard crack stage.

Note. The difference between soft-crack and hard-crack is easily found. If some of the sugar breaks with a slight noise and will not stick to the teeth, it is at the soft-crack stage. If you boil it again, and when tested it will quickly set hard and will easily snap when pressed, then it is at the hard-crack stage. Sugar at this stage passes rapidly to caramel and will burn if not attended to immediately.

CANDY TEMPERATURES

Type of Candy	Temperature (Farenheit)	Cold water test
Fudge, penuche, operas, maple, creams, etc.	234° to 236°	Soft ball
Fondant	238° to 240°	Soft ball
Caramels	246° to 248°	Firm ball
Taffies	265° to 270°	Hard ball
Butterscotch, toffee, etc.	290° to 300°	Crack
Brittles	300° to 310°	Hard-crack
Clear hard candies	310°	Hard-crack

General Hints on Candy Making

Use a little imagination in the shaping and decorating of the candies.

Add a pinch of cream of tartar for each 2 cups of sugar to help keep sirups from crystallizing.

When making chocolate fudge, try adding 4 or 5 teaspoons of grated orange peel as you beat it.

When a crystalline candy, such as fudge, reaches the degree called for in the recipe, remove it from the fire and cool to lukewarm, then and then only, beat it until the whole mixture has crystallized. The crystals will be large if you beat it while it is still hot.

Candy always tastes better to those who were "in at the making." So have the children around when making it.

Chocolate dipping needs an expert amateur. If you decide to experiment with it, make sure that you use dipping chocolate designed for this purpose, and melt it over warm, not hot water. Choose a clear, cool day rather than a damp, muggy one, for chocolate is temperamental.

When making fudge, add a cup of marshmallows, cut in small pieces, after beating the fudge and before turning it into a pan to cool.

Flavor fondant with a little candied orange peel, and roll it in shredded coconut. Or stuff pitted dates with halved walnuts, encased in fondant.

To make jumbo dates—those big, luscious ones confectioners show—press two pasteurized pitted dates together and stuff them as one.

After stuffing, some of the dates may be sugared by shaking them, a few at a time, in a paper bag containing sugar; or dates may be rolled in very finely chopped nut meats or shredded coconut.

A Valentine's Day sweet may be made as follows: Combine, and blend thoroughly 1 cup of sifted, cooked, dried apricots, ½ cup of finely chopped nuts, and ⅔ cup of fresh or shredded coconut. Stuff pitted dates, or figs, with this, and roll the dates in plain or colored sugar.

In beating candy use a large wooden spoon and never a rotary beater unless it is specified. Tilt the pan, and beat vigorously.

If you have no candy thermometer and must rely on the cold water test for "doneness," remember to take your candy off the fire while testing. Every second counts. To make the soft-ball test for fudge, take the pan off the fire, pour a teaspoon of the mixture into a shallow cup of very cold water, and see if you can gather this up in your fingers into a soft ball that will just hold its shape. If not, continue cooking and testing as the stage of consistency changes very quickly. If your fudge turns out to be too hard, add just enough liquid to it to melt it without burning, and then recook it.

Always remove with a dampened brush or swab any drops of sirup which may form on the sides of the saucepan while the candy is cooking, lest they cause crystallization.

For greasing pans, a bland oil instead of butter is favored by expert candy makers. This is because it does not contain the salt and moisture which butter ordinarily contains.

A number of recipes for miscellaneous candies are given below. See the well known types under their appropriate names, as Fudge, Brittle, etc.

Pulled Sugar

4 cups sugar
1 cup cold water
¼ tsp salt
1 tsp corn sirup
¼ tsp cream of tartar

Put the sugar, water, and salt into a saucepan; and stir till the sugar is dissolved. Then place it over a hot fire, and add the corn sirup and cream of tartar. Cook as quickly as possible to the hard-crack stage (310° F.) Immediately remove it from the fire. Dip the pan instantly into very cold water to check the boiling. Then pour the sirup on a slightly oiled slab or large platter, and as the edges cool, lift them toward the center, using a spatula. When cool enough to handle, roll into a ball, and pull with the fingers from the two sides, turning the edges over from side to side and into the center, pulling all parts evenly. The mass will soon take on a white sheen and become whiter and whiter. However, it should not become too cold. When shaping the pulled sugar into fancy forms, it should be pulled near the open door of a warm oven, but not overheated. With the sugar at this stage, you can make rose leaves, or whatever fancy dictates.

To Color Granulated Sugar

Place the desired amount of sugar upon a piece of stiff white paper; sprinkle over it a few drops of the desired edible food coloring and rub with a wooden spoon or between the hands until the coloring is distributed. Dry in a slow oven (300° F.), stirring occasionally, or rubbing the grains between the fingers to separate them. This sugar should be stored in an airtight container and in a dark, cool place.

Spun Sugar

4 cups sugar
2 cups cold water
1 tsp corn sirup
Pinch cream of tartar

Spinning sugar is very simple. It consists of drawing the hot sugar, which has been boiled to the hard-crack stage (310° F.) into strands as fine as hair, which will harden immediately and retain their form. The procedure begins prosaically enough as with any hard candy.

Dissolve the sugar in the water, then cook to the soft-crack stage (280° F.). Add the cream of tartar and corn sirup and continue cooking to the hard-crack stage (310° F.). Quickly remove from the heat and to prevent the sugar from changing its color, set the pan in cold water. Then remove it and place it in warm water.

Oil a rolling pin or the blade of a large knife, and hold it out straight with the left hand; then with the right hand dip a warm spoon into the sirup and shake it backward and forward over the rolling pin. The sugar will fall across the pin in long threads. Continue the operation until enough spun sugar is obtained. Then cut off the ends and press them as desired into large or small molds, or shape them in fancy designs on a slab.

Another method, often used by professionals, is as follows: While the sirup cooks to the hard-crack stage, lay out three steel bars on a stainless steel topped table or slab, two bars overlaying the third like three sides of an uncompleted square. These are to catch the sugar strands. Have a whip for sugar spinning, shaped like a miniature hearth broom, its brush part of steel wires instead of straw. Dip the whip gently into the sirup pot; raise it a second to let the sirup drip; then slowly and rhythmically raise your arm like a sower flinging seeds in a scattering arc. Fling the sirup high over your head in the general direction of the steel bars on the table before you; it will shoot in little silver arrows which follow the shape of a figure eight, then quickly fall to lie across the bars. The glass-like threads will pile high; and some will scatter to the floor beyond the table where a large sheet of white paper has been placed to catch any such. When the spinning is sufficient for a nest, or for whatever the intended use, cut the threads into lengths with a quick thrust of a carving knife.

A third method of spinning sugar is to oil the handles of two wooden spoons and fasten them with the ends over the edge of a table. Cover the floor below with a clean white paper. Then take a large fork, or two smaller forks, or an egg whisk, or a bunch of wires, dip that into the sirup and move it quickly back and forth over the oiled spoon handles. Continue until there is a mass of sugar threads resembling silk. The threads may be made either fine or coarse by moving the forks or spinners quickly or slowly.

If, in the course of spinning, the sirup becomes too firm to use, warm the pan over a very low flame and then resume the spinning process. The sirup may be colored, if desired. Spun sugar is used to decorate candies and cakes and also as a garnish for desserts. It must be kept in a very dry atmosphere and used as soon as possible after it is spun.

Practice will develop deftness and skill in handling all candy-making materials so as to get the best possible results. A most important factor in the production of good candy, as well as good food, is to not trust to guesswork, but to follow recipes carefully and to watch the thermometer.

Candying Flowers

Choice petals or entire flowers
1 oz gum arabic
1 cup water
1 tbsp corn sirup
1 cup sugar

You can use rose petals, pansies, violets, or mint leaves. Carefully dry the petals of the flowers without bruising them. Dissolve the gum arabic in half a cup of water over hot water. Let it stand until cold.

Then, using a soft brush, coat the flowers with the mixture. Run a needle and thread through the stem of each flower and hang them up to dry so that the flowers do not touch each other. Mix the corn sirup and sugar in ½ cup of water, bring to the boiling point, and cook to the soft ball stage (234° F.). Let stand until cold; then dip the gum-arabic-coated flowers gently into the sirup, remove, sprinkle them with fine granulated sugar, and place on waxed paper to dry.

CHOCOLATE DIPPING

Chocolate was first introduced as a candy, in tablet form, in 1662 by Antonio Carletti, pastry chef at the Royal Palace in Spain. Spain's ruler was the infant King Charles II (1661–1700). His mother, Queen Regent Maria Anna of Austria, soon after the discovery of this delicious sweet, sent great quantities of the candy to her friends in different parts of Europe.

Candy offers many interesting opportunities for the use of chocolate, from making simple fudge to the more delicate process of dipping various centers. Most types of candies lend themselves to chocolate coating, the more popular being French nougat creams, French hard nougats, fruit pàstes, flavored fondants, marzipans, and assorted liquid centers.

Several points should be kept in mind when dipping chocolates:

1. The temperature of the room should be from 60° to 65° F., absolutely dry and free from steam.

2. A dipping fork, which is very inexpensive, is necessary, and one candy only should be dipped at a time.

3. As a guide to determine the correctness of the dipping mixture, the first piece should be practically dry by the time the fifth center has been dipped.

4. If chocolate thickens while dipping, put more water in the lower part of the double boiler, but never add water to the chocolate itself.

5. Keep the dipped candies away from drafts—cold or hot.

6. Pack chocolate candies promptly in boxes lined with waxed paper; never expose them to the air for any length of time.

7. Any remaining dipping chocolate may be remelted or used for centers.

8. Chocolate, no matter the use, should be melted over hot, never boiling water,

as too high a temperature changes the flavor and color.

CANDIED ORANGE AND GRAPEFRUIT PEEL

Rinds of 4 oranges
Rinds of 2 grapefruit
3½ cups sugar
Water

Save fruit rinds until the desired amount is available, wrapping them in waxed paper and storing in the refrigerator. Now cover with cold water, bring to boiling point, drain, add fresh water, bring to boiling point again, drain a second time, cover with more cold water and simmer until the rinds are tender. Drain and cut rinds into strips with a knife or scissors. Combine the sugar with 1¾ cups water, bring to boiling point and cook the prepared fruit rinds in this sirup until they are clear and have absorbed most of the sirup itself. Cool, drain off any excess sirup and roll or toss the rind in granulated sugar. Store in airtight tins or jars.

Note: Dates, prunes and dried apricots may be stuffed with candied fruit rind and nuts.

CALIFORNIA CREAMS

1½ cups sugar
½ cup orange marmalade
1 cup undiluted evaporated milk
½ cup broken pecans

Combine in a saucepan the sugar, marmalade and milk, blend thoroughly and cook gently, stirring frequently, until the sugar is entirely dissolved; then continue cooking, without stirring, to the soft ball stage (236°–238° F.). Cool to lukewarm, add the pecans and beat until the candy holds its shape, then drop quickly from the tip of a teaspoon in small mounds onto waxed paper.

CHOCOLATE CREAMS

2 tbsp chocolate sirup
2 tbsp softened butter
1 tsp vanilla
About 1 cup confectioners' sugar
Melted chocolate

Combine the first four ingredients using a little more or less sugar according to consistency. Shape with the hands into small balls, then dip into melted chocolate (*see* CHOCOLATE DIPPING), invert onto heavy waxed paper and let stand, without moving, until chocolate is firm.

CREAM CANDY SQUARES

3 cups sugar
1 cup light corn sirup
1 cup undiluted evaporated milk
1 cup broken walnut meats
1 tsp vanilla

Combine sugar, corn sirup and milk, bring slowly to boiling point, stirring constantly, then continue cooking, stirring frequently, to the soft ball stage (236°–238° F.). Cool to lukewarm, add nuts and vanilla and beat until the candy begins to hold its shape; then turn into a 9x9 inch buttered pan and cut into squares when cold.

OPERA CREAMS

3 cups sugar
½ cup heavy cream
½ cup top milk or undiluted evaporated milk
1 tbsp corn sirup
2 tsp vanilla

Combine the sugar, cream, milk and corn sirup in a large saucepan and bring slowly to the boiling point, stirring constantly; then cook, still stirring constantly, to the soft ball stage (240° F.). Let stand for 1 minute, then pour gently onto a moistened slab or platter, cool to lukewarm, then beat vigorously until thick and smooth. Cover with a cloth and let the mass stand for about 1 hour, after which stir in the vanilla and knead until creamy, adding a little confectioners' sugar as needed to prevent sticking. Again let the mixture stand, covered, for about 3 hours, after which press into a square pan or pat out about ¾ inch thick. Cut into squares and place on waxed paper for at least 24 hours to harden, after which wrap in individual waxed papers.

CANETON. French name for duckling. *See* DUCK.

CANISTER. A metal case, a container, as for tea, coffee, or spices.

CANNED FOODS. In the eighteenth century a Parisian chef named Appert initiated a crude method of canning. Information about the process was introduced into the United States from England in the vicinity of 1818. However, canning had no scientific basis until the principles of fermentation formulated by Pasteur were applied to it in 1895. Today, from picking to packing for shipment, canning is a scientifically controlled industry. Consequently, the homemaker of today can provide a more varied and nutritive diet, and can devote far less time to the preparation of a meal.

The chief dietetic advantage of canned products is their retention of vitamins and mineral salts. Neither canned nor freshly cooked foods have the same vitamin content as the raw foods, but losses occur before canning or after food has been removed from cans, never while the food is in the cans. Canned fish and meats are excellent sources of vitamin A which helps to preserve good eyesight and to prevent germ infection. Canned milk, most canned meats, and some canned vegetables contain vitamin B which serves to prevent various nervous diseases. Vegetables are the chief sources of vitamin C, the antiscurvy vitamin. Nor does canning impair the food value of carbohydrates and proteins.

Prior to the development of the canning industry, foods were usually produced and consumed in the same locality: they were not imported or exported. In the interior of a continent the local drinking water, vegetables, and meats are likely to be marked by iodine deficiency. Since the local cows get little iodine in their hay and grass, their milk is likely to be similarly deficient. That is why many cases of goiter (which is often caused by lack of iodine) used to occur in inland countries, such as Switzerland, and in the central section of the United States. Today health officers attack this problem by adding iodine to table salt or another food material. The deficiency can also be overcome by including in the diet some iodine-rich foods produced elsewhere—fresh fish, oysters, or other sea foods shipped by refrigeration, and canned (as well as fresh) vegetables.

COMMERCIAL CANNING

Vegetables for canning are grown particularly for that purpose. The canning plants are usually located in the vegetable production areas, so the harvested vegetables can be quickly brought to the plant for processing while fresh.

The fresh vegetables are washed in large vats of continuously circulating water or under sprays of water. Vegetables that must be peeled are specially treated to remove the peel or are put through mechanical peelers. The stems of such vegetables as green beans are automatically snipped off by specially designed cutting machines.

The vegetables are then spread on moving belts that carry them to workers who do any extra peeling or cutting necessary and remove undesirable pieces. Some vegetables such as peas may also be sorted into sizes by special equipment.

In the final processing of canned vegetables, the sealed cans are cooked under carefully controlled conditions of time and temperature and then quickly cooled. This is what insures the keeping quality of canned vegetables without refrigeration.

Today's processes provide wholesome products preserved at the peak of flavor.

Advantages of Canned Foods

Canned foods are extremely practical. They can be transported any distance in any climate to be opened safe, wholesome, and ready for use. When opened, it needs only to be heated and served; this greatly reduces preparation and cooking time. The consumer has the assurance that the food has been properly cooked and seasoned.

The use of canned foods is economical. Canned meat, for instance, is already trimmed, and the purchaser pays only for what she will use. It is solid meat with no loss due to gristle, bone, or other waste products. It is packed in a form which does not yield food loss through shrinkage.

Canning concerns have established a commendable record for the safety and dependability of their products. A popular belief has existed to the effect that "ptomaine poisoning" is acquired through the use of canned foods, but this belief is foundationless. Food that has been sterilized and packed in air-tight containers cannot possibly be dangerous (unless, of course, the containers have since been damaged). Canned foods can be safely stored under a wide temperature range.

Whether to buy canned foods or to prepare them yourself. That canned foods possess all of the aforementioned advantages is undeniable, and it would be foolish to deny the utility of these products. They are probably most valuable as time-savers. On the other hand, it would be foolish to eliminate homemade foods from one's menus and to use only this modern, easier method.

Some canned foods cannot be recommended and others condemned. Each homemaker must determine which canned products fit her budget and her needs. Generally speaking, canned foods are less expensive than delicatessen products, but in some cases they are more so. In these cases it must be determined whether the amount of time saved is commensurate with the added cost.

If you have a baby, it may be worthwhile to compare the cost and convenience of various methods of preparing vegetables for him. You may prefer to strain some of the vegetables that you have prepared for the family, or you may prefer to buy vegetables canned especially for babies.

In connection with canned foods, a question arises as to whether home canning or dependence on commercially canned foods is preferable. Here again the decision must be left to the individual. If you wish to know whether it would pay to can certain fruits and vegetables, you might ask your State college of agriculture. You can find out, for example, the number of cans or jars that you may expect to fill by canning a half-bushel basket of pears and what you should figure as the yearly cost of the cans or jars.

If you have storage space, it is advisable to inquire about the price of a case (24 cans) of a food that your family uses often and compare it with the price of the same number of cans purchased individually.

Label Information

Most people want full value for their money when they buy canned foods; consequently, they are interested in both price and quality. The numberless brands, styles, varieties, and prices of canned foods available are indeed baffling unless the consumer has determined a reliable method of identifying quality. With U.S. Grade A, B, or C labels on canned fruits and vegetables, you can select the quality that best fits your purpose and purse. Without grade labels it is difficult to tell the quality of the product in a can. Prices and quality are not always proportionate. Nor do superlative terms such as Superb, Superfine, and Bestever, define quality.

U.S. Grades. "U.S." on a can label, or a shield embossed in one end of a can or jar, certifies that the product was processed under the continuous inspection plan of the Agricultural Marketing Service of the U.S. Department of Agriculture. Regardless of the grade designation, these foods are nutritious and wholly acceptable for human consumption. Otherwise, they could not be marketed in interstate commerce; the products would be illegal and subject to seizure under the consumer-protecting Federal Food, Drug, and Cosmetic Act.

U.S. Grade A ("Fancy") stands for top quality. It calls for near-perfection in color, size, and tenderness. There are few, if any, blemishes. This grade is desirable for special uses—for salads and dishes in which appearance is important.

U.S. Grade B ("Extra Standard") products are satisfactory for most meals, but they fall just a little short of U.S. Grade A in some respects. For example, they may be a little less tender.

U.S. Grade C ("Standard") is a good quality, but fruits and vegetables of this grade are not quite so uniform in color, size, and maturity as those of the A and B grades. Grade C is a wise choice for puddings, croquettes, and many other dishes.

Additional descriptive information on labels, such as the number of pieces in a can of apricots, the sieve size of peas, the strength of the sirup on fruits, and the net weight, also helps homemakers to make a wise selection.

Since the full measure of the edible contents of a package or can is required, the label on a jar of olives, for example, states the weight of the olives themselves or a numerical count. Since the government ruled that no piece of asparagus over four inches may be called a "tip," many packers now label their five-inch stalks "spears." It is a protection to both the consumer and the merchant.

Can sizes. Use the chart below as a guide in the selection of can sizes for fruits and vegetables. An adult size portion of canned vegetables usually measures about one-half cup.

STORAGE

Foodstuffs need not be removed from the can after it is opened; there is no danger of tin poisoning. But on the other hand, it is apparent that canned products are perishable; once the can has been opened, they are subject to contamination from the bacteria of the air just as is any fresh product. For that reason, it is not advisable to allow perishable foods to stand in open containers for any appreciable length of time unless they are kept very cold. Furthermore, although cold delays the growth of these bacteria, it does not entirely prevent it. Hence, foods cannot be kept in open containers in refrigerators indefinitely. Storage near steam pipes, radiators, furnaces, or kitchen ranges should be avoided.

Damaged containers. Containers should be sound and clean, free from rust and serious dents, and the ends should be flat or concave. Properly processed canned foods keep for long periods without spoilage unless damage to the can causes a leak. Bulging, swelling, leaking, or "flat sours" render cans potentially dangerous to the consumer. They should be refused or returned to the dealer to be destroyed immediately. Foods containing sulphur may discolor the inner surface of the can, but the stain is harmless.

CAN SIZES

Can	Average Net Weight	Average Cupfuls	Servings
8 oz.	8 ozs.	1	2
Picnic (No. 1 Eastern)	10½ to 12 oz.	1⅓	2
No. 303	16 to 17 oz.	2	4
No. 2	20 oz.	2½	4 to 5
No. 2½	29 oz.	3½	6 to 7
No. 3 (special)	46 oz.	5	7 to 10
No. 5 (for restaurants, etc.)	3 lb. 8 oz.	7	14
No. 10 (for restaurants, etc.)	6 lb. 10 oz.	13	26

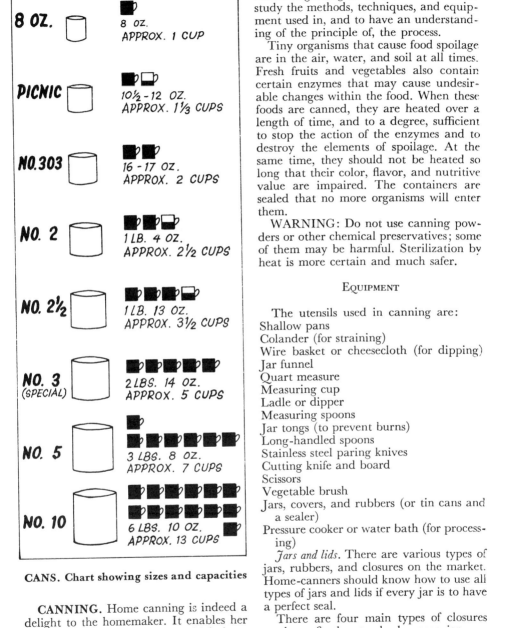

CANS. Chart showing sizes and capacities

ability to follow directions with precision. Before beginning to can, it is advisable to study the methods, techniques, and equipment used in, and to have an understanding of the principle of, the process.

Tiny organisms that cause food spoilage are in the air, water, and soil at all times. Fresh fruits and vegetables also contain certain enzymes that may cause undesirable changes within the food. When these foods are canned, they are heated over a length of time, and to a degree, sufficient to stop the action of the enzymes and to destroy the elements of spoilage. At the same time, they should not be heated so long that their color, flavor, and nutritive value are impaired. The containers are sealed that no more organisms will enter them.

WARNING: Do not use canning powders or other chemical preservatives; some of them may be harmful. Sterilization by heat is more certain and much safer.

EQUIPMENT

The utensils used in canning are:
Shallow pans
Colander (for straining)
Wire basket or cheesecloth (for dipping)
Jar funnel
Quart measure
Measuring cup
Ladle or dipper
Measuring spoons
Jar tongs (to prevent burns)
Long-handled spoons
Stainless steel paring knives
Cutting knife and board
Scissors
Vegetable brush
Jars, covers, and rubbers (or tin cans and a sealer)
Pressure cooker or water bath (for processing)

Jars and lids. There are various types of jars, rubbers, and closures on the market. Home-canners should know how to use all types of jars and lids if every jar is to have a perfect seal.

There are four main types of closures made to fit the standard mason jar.

The original mason jar has a rubber shoulder ring and a one-piece screw top with a porcelain or lacquered metal lining. The porcelain is difficult to clean. This cover can be used repeatedly unless the porcelain loosens or breaks. If the jar is

CANNING. Home canning is indeed a delight to the homemaker. It enables her to serve out-of-season foods which have been preserved to retain the color, flavor, and nutritive value of the fresh foods; at the same time, it is highly economical. It is not so difficult as is generally supposed; in fact, the only requisites are cleanliness, fairly ordinary kitchen equipment, and the

opened by prying up the cover, the cover may be dented so that it will make an imperfect seal if used again.

The two-piece glass and metal cover has a small rubber that is placed on the lid of the jar. The cover is held in place by a metal screw band. When the jars have cooled for twelve hours, the band should be removed to prevent rusting.

The wire-bail type jar has a glass lid that fits down on a rubber ring. The cover is held in place by two wire clamps or bails.

The two-piece metal cover containing a sealing compound is another type. The cover is lacquered metal with a composition rubber band. It is held in place by a metal screw band or clamp. Although the metal cap can be used but once, the screw band or clamp can be used often. It can be removed when the jars are cold.

The proper usage for each of the four closure types is given in the following chart:

use it to hold a new metal cap in place during processing. Since these jars are a little broader than a quart jar, they require a longer processing period. Process one and a half times as long as the time for quart jars.

Tomatoes and fruits are sometimes canned in half gallon jars, but this size jar should never be used for meats and non-acid vegetables because of the slow penetration of heat. Even with the longer processing time required, foods may spoil.

Rubbers. New rubbers should be used each time because the prolonged high temperature required for processing causes the rubber to deteriorate.

Tin cans. Tin cans may be used at home in place of glass jars, but canning in tin requires the use of a can sealer. This is practical only when more than 300 cans are needed for a family. Plain tin, C-enamel, and R-enamel are the types used in

Closure	When Canning	After Canning
Porcelain-lined cap; one-piece screw top	Fit wet rubber ring down on jar shoulder without stretching it unnecessarily. Fill jar; wipe the rubber ring and the jar rim clean. Then screw cap down firmly and turn it back ¼ inch.	As soon as the jar is removed from the canner, screw the cap down tightly to complete the seal.
Two-piece glass and metal cover	Fill jar, and wipe rim clean. Fit wet rubber ring on glass lid. Put the lid on the jar, rubber side down. Screw the band on until it is almost tight. Then turn back almost a quarter turn, but be sure that the jar and the band mesh. Caution: If band is screwed too tight, it may break.	As soon as the jar is removed from the canner, screw the band down tightly to complete the seal.
Wire-bail type of jar	Fit wet rubber ring on ledge at top of empty jar. Fill jar; wipe rubber ring and jar rim clean. Put on glass lid. Leave the short wire up; push the long wire over the top of the lid, fitting it into the groove.	As soon as the jar is removed from the canner, push the short wire down to complete the seal.
Two-piece metal cover with sealing compound	Fill jar; wipe rim clean. Put lid on with sealing compound next to glass. By hand, screw the metal band down tightly; do not use a wrench. When the band is screwed firmly, this lid has enough "give" to let air escape during the processing.	This jar seals automatically as it cools. Don't tighten the lid any further after removing the jar from the canner. Further tightening might break the seal.

The small-mouthed jars used as containers for food (such as coffee) can be used at home for canning fruits and tomatoes only. These jars require a small cover called a 63 millimeter. A metal cap with a composition rubber ring can be purchased for use on this type of jar. Boil the composition out of the original cover, and

home canning. Enameled cans are recommended for certain fruits and vegetables to prevent discoloring, but they are not necessary for a wholesome product.

C-enamel cans are recommended for:
Green lima beans
Corn
Carrots

R-enamel cans are recommended for:
Beets*
Berries
Cherries, red
Fruit juices
Plums
Pumpkin
Rhubarb
Sauerkraut
Squash
Strawberries
Sweetpotatoes
*Pickled beets must be packed in glass.

Use plain tin for:

Apples	Okra
Apricots	Peaches
Asparagus	Pears
Beans, snap	Spinach
Cherries, light	Peas
Meats	Tomatoes

The sizes used most in home canning are number 2 (which holds about 2½ cups or 20 ounces), number 2½ (which holds about 3½ cups or 28 ounces), and number 3 (which holds about 4 cups or 33 ounces).

Canners. Foods for canning are considered in two groups, depending on the amount of acid they contain. Fruits (including tomatoes), rhubarb, pimientos, and pickled products are acid foods; meats, poultry, fish, and vegetables are non-acid foods.

The recommended method for processing fruits and other acid foods is in a boiling-water bath at the temperature of boiling water (212° F.). For a boiling-water bath canner use any big, clean vessel that is deep enough so that the water can boil well over the tops of the containers, has a lid, and has a rack that will keep the jars from touching the bottom. (The rack may be of wire or wood; if possible, it should have partitions to prevent the jars from touching one another or falling against the sides of the canner.) A rack is not always necessary, however, if tin cans are used; these can be stacked in the canner.

If a steam-pressure canner is deep enough, it can be used as a water bath. Set the cover in place without fastening it, and have the pet cock wide open so that the steam will escape and no pressure will be built up.

The recommended method for processing nonacid foods is in a steam-pressure cooker. With a pressure cooker it is possible to obtain a temperature of 240° F. by applying ten pounds of steam pressure.

This high temperature kills the bacteria much more readily and thus reduces the danger of spoilage. Any reliable make of pressure cooker will prove satisfactory.

Adding small quantities of acid, such as lemon juice or vinegar, to a nonacid food does not change the acidity so that it can be treated as an acid food. This can be done only if enough acid is added to pickle the food, as in pickled beets. Nonacid vegetables can also be preserved by quick freezing, pit storing, drying, and salting

PREPARING EQUIPMENT

Steam-pressure canner. Clean the pet cock and safety valve openings by drawing a string or narrow strip of cloth through them. Do this at the beginning of the canning season and often during the season.

Check the pressure gage; an accurate gage is necessary to get the processing temperatures needed to preserve food. A weighted gage needs only to be thoroughly clean; but a dial gage, old or new, should be checked before canning. If it is off five or more pounds, it should be replaced. If it is off less than five pounds, merely make allowances for this. (For instance, if the gage reads two pounds too high, process the food at twelve pounds instead of the prescribed ten pounds.)

Wash the canner kettle well if it has not been used for some time. Wipe the cover with a soapy cloth, then with a damp, clean cloth; don't put it in water. Dry it well.

Jars and lids. Jars should be tested for a perfect seal and thoroughly washed. Unless the open kettle method is used, it is not necessary to sterilize the jars; thorough washing is sufficient. Discard any jars that have cracks, chips, or dents, because these defects can prevent airtight seals. Using jars and closures made by the same manufacturer may help to insure a perfect seal. Screw bands for glass and metal lids cannot be interchanged.

Wash glass jars and lids (except those with sealing compound) in hot soapy water, and rinse them well. Some metal lids with sealing compound should be boiled; most should be dipped in hot water. Follow the manufacturer's directions.

To test, place the lids on the jars (without rubbers) and screw them down. They are safe if it is impossible to insert a thin knife blade or your fingernail between the lid and the jar.

If necessary, adjust the vail on the lightning type jar. When the cover is placed on the jar without a rubber, there should be a slight but distinct "click", and the side clamp should go down with a "click." If you do not hear this sound, adjust the bail. To do this, remove the top wire and bend it down in the center (using the thumbs) to cause a slight dip. Holding the wire across the palm of the left hand, place the thumb in front of wire, and bend the end of the wire toward the center (using the right hand). Reverse and bend other end of wire. Replace on jar, and check again for click.

During the processing period place the jars, glass lids, and rings in a pan of warm water, and heat to just below boiling so they will be ready when the food is ready to pack. Lids with sealing compound should be dipped into hot water just before being placed on the packed jars.

Rubber rings. Scrub rings with a brush in hot soapy water. For each dozen rings use one tablespoon of baking soda to one quart of cold water, and put the rings in this solution. Boil uncovered for ten minutes, and rinse well. This will help to prevent the rubber rings from flavoring the food.

To test, bend the rubbers into folds; if they crack, discard them. Very good rubbers will return to their original shape after being stretched; but, since most will not, it is best not to test them by stretching. Fill the jars with water, place rubbers on them, screw the lids on, and invert the jars. If there is no seepage, they are safe.

During the processing period place wet rubber rings on the jars or lids as directed. Before sealing a jar, wipe the rim and rubber ring with a clean, damp cloth to remove food that might interfere with the seal.

Tin cans. See that cans, lids, and gaskets are in perfect condition. Discard cans that are dented, rusted, or badly bent, and lids with scratched or torn gaskets. Keep the lids in paper packing until they are ready for use. (The paper protects the lids from dirt and moisture.)

Just before use, wash the cans in clean water, and invert them to drain. Do not wash the lids; if these are dusty or dirty, wipe them with a damp cloth just before putting them on the cans.

Can-sealing machine. Sealers should be wiped off frequently on the days when they are in use to prevent corrosion and rusting. After each day of use, the machine should be washed in hot soapy water, rinsed carefully, and dried thoroughly.

If a sealer is used, be certain that it is properly adjusted. To test, put a little water into a can, seal it, and then submerge it in boiling water for a few seconds. If air bubbles rise from the can, the seam is not tight. Adjust the sealer according to the manufacturer's directions.

Utensils. Sterilize all other utensils to be used by washing them and then placing them in boiling water.

PACKING

Two methods. The term packing means filling the containers (jars or tin cans) with food. The cold pack and the hot pack are the two recommended methods of packing. In the cold pack method, the containers are filled with raw food or food that has been blanched (scalded and then dipped into cold water). The food is then covered with hot liquid, and the containers are sealed and processed immediately.

In the hot pack method, the food is precooked in boiling liquid and then drained before it is put into the clean, hot containers; it should be near boiling when it is being packed. Vegetables are precooked in boiling water; fruits are usually precooked in boiling sirup, but water and extracted juice are sometimes used. Tomatoes and other juicy fruits can be heated without added liquid. The precooking period varies in length with different foods; but fruits and vegetables are usually heated through, and meats are cooked until most of the pink color has disappeared.

The hot pack method is the most satisfactory for packing all nonacid and most acid foods. Any fruit can be packed cold, but this method is preferred only for tomatoes and certain berries.

Filling the containers. Food should be packed into the containers only moderately tight and then covered with enough liquid to fill the spaces around the food. (Follow special directions for filling containers when canning meats.) Raw foods are packed tighter than hot foods because they shrink during processing. Asparagus, string beans, beets, and carrots can be packed as closely as possible without crushing. Most foods can be pressed down in the containers with the fingers or with the

CANNING, filling the jars

bowl of a spoon. Greens should be pressed only lightly, and then cross-cut with a knife or scissors to the bottom of the jar to allow water to reach the center of the jar and air to escape. Corn, shell beans, and peas are shaken down; these are packed more loosely because they expand during processing.

Unless otherwise directed, fill jars to ½ inch of the top and cans to ¼ inch of the top. To allow for expansion, pack corn, shell beans, and peas only to 1 inch of top in jars and only to within ½ inch of top in cans.

Adding liquid and salt. Cover food in jars with liquid, leaving the prescribed head space, but fill cans to top with liquid, unless otherwise directed. For hot or cold pack it takes from ¾ to 1 cup of liquid to a quart glass jar or a number 2½ tin can to fill in around solid food.

Cooking liquid is recommended for packing most vegetables because it may contain minerals and vitamins dissolved out of the food. Boiling water is recommended when cooking liquid is dark, gritty, or strong-flavored, and it may be used if you haven't enough cooking liquid.

Salt is usually added to vegetables after they are covered with liquid. Unless otherwise directed, add ½ teaspoon of salt to each pint jar or number 2 can, and 1 teaspoon of salt to each quart jar or number 2½ can, of vegetables.

Fruits may be packed in hot sirup, water, or juice. Juicy fruits and tomatoes may be packed hot in the juice that cooks out when they are heated without added liquid. Tomatoes that are packed cold are pressed down in the containers so that they are covered with their own juice, and no liquid is added.

SEALING

Glass jars. After filling glass jars, work the blade of a table knife down the sides to remove air bubbles. Add more liquid if needed to cover food. Be sure to leave the prescribed head space at the top of each jar. Then adjust the jar lids as directed in the "When Canning" column of the closure chart on page 200, and process immediately.

Tin cans. The temperature of the food must be 170° F. or higher when tin cans are sealed. Food is heated to drive out the air and to help prevent discoloring and loss of flavor. Also, sealing hot prevents bulging of can ends and breaking of seams. You can get the right sealing temperature by packing food hot, or by heating it in open cans (exhausting), or both. Even when food is packed hot, you will need to reheat it before sealing the cans if the temperature has fallen below 170°. It is best to have a thermometer for checking temperatures of cans.

If it is found unnecessary to exhaust tin cans, work out the air bubbles after filling the cans. Add more liquid if needed to fill the cans to the top. Seal them at once, following the sealer manufacturer's directions, and process immediately.

To exhaust, place open, filled cans in a large kettle with boiling water about two inches below can tops. Cover the kettle, bring the water back to boiling, and boil for ten minutes. Remove cans from water one by one. Replace any liquid spilled from can by filling to the top with boiling liquid, possibly boiling water. Place a clean lid on the filled can, and seal it at once. Process immediately.

PROCESSING

Water-bath canner. For cold pack in glass jars, have water in the canner hot, but not boiling to prevent breakage. For all other packs have water boiling.

Put filled jars or cans on a rack in the canner. Add boiling water if needed to bring water an inch or two over the tops of the containers. Don't pour boiling water directly on glass jars. Put cover on canner.

Begin to count time as soon as the water comes to a rolling boil. Then boil gently and steadily for the time prescribed in the directions for the food you are canning. Add boiling water during processing if it is needed to keep the containers of food covered. As soon as the processing time is up, remove one container at a time with a jar lifter.

Pressure canner. Follow the manufacturer's directions for your own canner. Read the directions carefully before using it.

Put two or three inches of water in the bottom of the canner. Set filled containers on a rack in the cooker so steam can flow all around each jar. Tin cans may be staggered without a rack between layers. Fasten the cover securely so that no steam escapes, except through the open pet cock

or weighted gage opening. When steam escapes with a distinctly audible sound (after about ten minutes), close the pet cock or put on the weighted gage. Let pressure rise to ten pounds. Start counting time at the moment when right pressure is reached, and process for the time prescribed in the directions for the food you are canning. Keep the pressure constant by regulating the heat under the canner. Do not lower pressure by opening the pet cock. Keep drafts from blowing on the canner. When the time is up, slide the canner away from the heat.

Let the canner stand until the pressure is zero. Never try to rush the cooling by pouring cold water over the canner. When the pressure registers zero, wait a minute or two—no longer—and then slowly open the pet cock or remove the weighted gage. Unfasten the cover and tilt the far side up so that the steam escapes away from you. Spread a heavy cloth over the top of the canner. Lift the rack out of the canner by holding it through the cloth.

If you are using tin cans, release the steam in the canner as soon as the processing time has elapsed. To do this, open the pet cock or remove the weighted gage. Then remove the canner cover.

EFFECT OF ALTITUDE UPON PROCESSING

Water-bath canner. If you live at an altitude of 1,000 feet or more, you have to process food in a water bath for a longer time. For each 1,000 feet above sea level, add 1 minute to the processing time if the time called for is less than 20 minutes. If the time called for is more than 20 minutes, add two minutes for each 1,000 feet to the processing time.

Pressure canner. At altitudes above sea level it takes more than ten pounds of pressure to reach 240° F. Increase the pressure by one pound for each 2,000 feet altitude. A weighted gage may need to be corrected for altitude by the manufacturer.

IMMEDIATELY AFTER PROCESSING

Jars. As jars are taken from the canner, complete the seals at once, following as directed in the "After Canning" column of the closure chart on page 200. If any liquid has boiled out during the processing, seal the jar just as it is. Do not open it to add more liquid.

Cool the jars top side up. Give each jar enough room so that air can reach its entire surface. Never set a hot jar on a cold surface or in a draft. Don't slow the cooling by covering the jars.

Cans. Cool tin cans in cold, clean water, changing it as needed to cool them quickly; or cool them in running water. If the former method is used, take them out of the water while they are slightly warm so that they will dry in the air. Stagger cans if you stack them, so that air can get around them.

SELECTION AND PREPARATION OF FRUITS AND VEGETABLES

Select fresh, young, firm fruits or vegetables, and can them quickly. They should be canned within two hours of gathering but, if you must hold them, keep them in a cool, airy place, preferably in a refrigerator. Try to get local produce when buying fruits or vegetables to can. Try to use only perfect food; this will give the best flavor and appearance in the canned product. If the raw products are bruised or discolored in spots, these spots should always be removed.

Sort the fruits or vegetables according to size and ripeness to effect even cooking. Prepare only enough fruits or vegetables at one time for one canner load, about 6 or 8 jars. Wash them thoroughly in running water, if possible, or through several changes of water. If the latter method is used, lift fruits or vegetables out of the water before changing it, so dirt that has been washed off will not be drained back over them; rinse the pan thoroughly between washings. Avoid letting the food soak as this may cause a loss of food value. Handle fruits or vegetables gently to avoid bruising. In short, try to get food as perfect as possible and keep it as perfect and as clean as possible.

YIELD OF CANNED FOODS FROM FRESH

Fruits	
Apples	2½ to 3 lb.
Berries, except strawberries	5 to 8 cups
Cherries, as picked	6 to 8 cups
Peaches	2 to 2½ lb.
Pears	2 to 2½ lb.
Plums	2 to 2½ lb.
Strawberries	6 to 8 cups
Tomatoes	2½ to 3 lb.

Vegetables	
Asparagus	4 lb.
Beans, lima in pods	4 to 5 lb.
Beans, snap	1½ to 2 lb.
Beets, without tops	2½ to 3 lb.
Carrots, without tops	2½ to 3 lb.
Corn, sweet, in husks	6 to 16 ears
Okra	1½ lb.
Peas, green, in pods	4 to 5 lb.
Pumpkin	3 lb.
Squash, summer	2 to 2½ lb.
Sweetpotatoes	2½ to 3 lb.

This fruit and vegetable chart indicates the amount of certain fruits and vegetables that must be used to yield one quart of canned food. The yield from a bushel of fresh food is not given because the legal weight of a bushel varies in different states.

SWEETENING FRUIT

Sugar sirup. Sugar sirup may be used to sweeten fruit. Make sirup by boiling a mixture of sugar and water or sugar and fruit juice for five minutes. Then remove scum.

To extract juice, crush thoroughly ripe, sound, juicy fruit. Heat to boiling over a low heat. Strain through a jelly bag or another cloth.

Sirup	Sugar	Water or fruit juice	Yield
Thin	1 cup	3 cups	3½ cups
Medium	1 cup	2 cups	2½ cups
Heavy	1 cup	1 cup	1½ cups

Sirups may be thick or thin, depending on the acidity of the food and on the preference of the canner.

For juicy fruit. If you use the hot-pack method, you can add dry sugar to raw juicy fruit and then heat without added liquid. Use about ½ cup of sugar to a quart of fruit. Bring to a boil over a low heat. Pack fruit in the juice that cooks out.

Canning with corn sirup. If sugar is scarce, use light corn sirup or mild-flavored honey to replace as much as half the sugar called for in canning fruit.

Do not extend sugar with brown sugar, molasses, sorghum, or other strong-flavored sirups. Their flavor overpowers the fruit flavor, and some of them tend to darken the fruit. Saccharin is not recommended.

Canning without sweetening. Fruit may be canned without sweetening—in its own juice, in extracted juice, or in water. Sugar helps fruit to retain its shape, color, and flavor, but it is not needed to prevent spoilage. Process unsweetened fruit the same as sweetened. To sweeten fruits before serving, drain the liquid, dissolve sugar in it by heating for a few minutes, pour back over the fruit, and let stand for several hours.

DAY-AFTER-CANNING JOBS

When glass jars have cooled overnight, remove screw bands that have glass or metal lids underneath if you want to reuse them. If a band sticks, covering it for a moment with a hot, damp cloth may help to loosen it. Do not use force as this may break the seal.

Testing for leaks. If jars have been used, test seals by turning each jar partly over. Jars with self-sealing lids should be tested by tapping the centers of the lids with a spoon. A clear, ringing sound indicates a good seal. If you can in tin, examine seals when you wipe the cooled cans. Also set out any can that buckles and breaks its seams; too little food in the can or cooling too fast may cause this type of leak.

If a leaky spot is found, use the unspoiled food immediately or reprocess it as if it were fresh. Before re-using a jar or lid, check it for defects as directed. If there has been no leakage, store the containers and watch for signs of spoilage. Before storing canned food, wipe the containers clean and label them to show contents, date of canning, and lot number if more than one lot was canned in a single day.

Storing. Protect jars and cans of food against bad storage conditions—heat, freezing, and dampness. Warmth may cause canned food to lose quality. Hot pipes behind a wall sometimes make a shelf or closet too warm for storing food. Freezing may crack a jar or break a seal, thus admitting bacteria; it may also cause undesirable changes in flavor and texture. In an unheated place food may be protected by covering it with a blanket or wrapping it in paper. Dampness may corrode tin cans and metal lids of glass jars and eventually cause leakage.

GUARDING AGAINST SPOILAGE

Don't use canned food that shows any sign of spoilage. Inspect each container before opening it. Bulging can ends, jar lids, or rings, or a leak may mean that food has spoiled. After opening the container, look for other signs such as spurting liquid, an "off" odor, mold, or gas bubbles. Jellied broth and darkening of metal lids are not indicative of spoilage.

It is possible for canned vegetables to contain the poison causing botulism—a serious food poisoning—without showing signs of spoilage. There is no danger of botulism if the canner is in perfect order and if every canning recommendation has been followed accurately. But as a safety precaution, boil the food for ten to twenty minutes before tasting it. If the food looks spoiled or has an "off" odor during heating, destroy it. Burn it, or dispose of it in another way so that it will not be eaten by humans or animals.

CANNING FRUITS AND VEGETABLES

Directions for packing hot are given for all the foods in the list. For some fruits (among them tomatoes), directions for the cold-pack method are also given.

Canning experts strongly recommend the hot-water-bath canner for acid foods and the pressure canner for nonacid. However, some home canners have successfully canned acid foods in a pressure canner and Jars with self-sealing lids should be tested vice versa. Wherever possible, the processing times are given for both of these methods.

Note: These directions should be supplemented by all other relevant instructions that are given in the entire section on canning.

APPLES

Select a tart variety for best results. Wash, pare, core, and slice or quarter apples. To prevent darkening, drop the fruit into a salt-vinegar solution (2 tablespoons each of salt and vinegar per gallon of water) until it is ready for packing; rinse thoroughly, and drain. Precook for five minutes in thin boiling sirup. Pack hot fruit to ¼ inch of top in clean, hot containers. Cover with hot sirup, leaving ¼-inch head space in jars but filling cans to top.

Process immediately for:
Boiling-water bath:
Pt. jar, 15 min.
Qt. jar, 20 min.
Tin cans, 10 min.
Pressure canner:
10 min. at 5 lb. pressure

APPLESAUCE

Make applesauce, sweetened or unsweetened. Heat through, stirring to keep it from sticking to the pan. Pack hot to ¼ inch of top in jars, to top in cans.
Process for
Strained applesauce—
  Boiling-water bath:
    Pt. and qt. jars, 10 min.
    No. 2 cans, 10 min.
    No. 2½ cans, 15 min.
Unstrained applesauce—
  Boiling-water bath:
    Pt. and qt. jars, 5 min.
  Pressure canner:
    8 min. at 5 lb. pressure

APRICOTS

Select fully ripe, firm fruit of uniform size. Dip in boiling water for ½ minute, then quickly in cold water. Remove skins and pits, and cut fruit in halves. To prevent darkening, drop the halves into a salt-vinegar solution (2 tablespoons each of salt and vinegar per gallon of water). Drain just before heating or packing cold, and rinse thoroughly.

Hot pack. Cook in boiling sirup for about 5 minutes.* Pack hot fruit in hot, clean containers, placing halves in overlapping layers, rounded side up. Cover with boiling sirup.*
Process for—
  Boiling-water bath:
    Pt. jars, 20 min.
    Qt. jars, 25 min.
    No. 2 cans, 25 min.
    No. 2½ cans, 35 min.
Cold pack. Prepare fully ripe, firm fruit of uniform size as directed above. Pack raw fruit in clean, hot containers, placing halves in overlapping layers, rounded side up. Fill containers with boiling medium sirup.* If tin cans are used, exhaust them for 5 minutes.
Process for—
  Boiling-water bath:
    Pt. jars, 25 min.
    Qt. jars, 35 min.
    No. 2 cans, 25 min.
    No. 2½ cans, 35 min.
  Pressure canner (either pack):
    10 min. at 5 lb. pressure
  *If desired for flavor, one cracked pit may be added to each quart of sirup; strain before filling jars.

BEETS, PICKLED

Cut off beet tops, leaving the root and 1 inch of stem. Wash beets, cover them with boiling water, and cook until tender. Skin and slice them. For sirup, use 2 cups of vinegar (or 1½ cups of vinegar and ½ cup of water) to 2 cups of sugar. Heat to boiling.

Pack hot beets in glass jars only. Cover with boiling pickling sirup. Add ½ teaspoon of salt per pint. Adjust jar lids. Process in boiling-water bath for 30 minutes.

BERRIES
(except strawberries)

Avoid crushing berries. Pick over, wash, hull or stem, and drain them.

Hot Pack (for firm berries). Add ½ cup of sugar to each quart of fruit. Cover pan, and bring to boil, shaking pan to keep berries from sticking. Pack jars to ½ inch of top and cans to top.
Process for—
  Boiling-water bath:
    Pt. and qt. jars, 15 min.
    No. 2 cans, 15 min.
    No. 2½ cans, 20 min.
Cold Pack (for red raspberries and other soft berries). Pack raw berries in hot, sterilized containers, shaking while filling for a full pack. Fill jars to ½ inch of top, cans to ¼ inch. Cover with boiling medium sirup (made with berry juice instead of water, if desired). If cans are used, exhaust from 3 to 5 minutes.
Process for—
  Boiling-water bath:
    Pt. and qt. jars, 20 min.
    No. 2 cans, 15 min.
    No. 2½ cans, 20 min.
  Pressure canner (both packs):
    10 min. at 5 lb. pressure
  Pressure canner (both packs):
    10 min. at 5 lb. pressure.

CHERRIES

Follow the method given for firm berries, adding a little water when heating unpitted cherries to keep them from sticking to the pan. Sweet cherries are usually canned whole without pitting while the sour ones are usually pitted. When cherries are not pitted, prick the skins with the tines of a fork to prevent shrinkage. The juice may be saved to prepare sirup.

FRUIT JUICES

Wash, pit (if desired), and crush ripe fruit. Heat slowly to simmering. Strain through a cloth bag. Add ½ to 1 cup of sugar (if desired) to a gallon of juice. Water may also be added. Heat juice, and fill the containers with it. Seal the containers, and process in water bath at simmering temperature (below boiling, 180° F.) for 20 minutes.

FRUIT PURÉES

Use sound, ripe fruit. Wash and pit it. Cut large fruit in pieces. Simmer until soft, adding a little water if needed to keep from sticking. Put it through a strainer or food mill. Add sugar to taste. Heat again to simmering. Pack hot to ¼ inch of top in jars, to top in cans. Process in boiling-water bath for 20 minutes.

PEACHES

Use the same method as for apricots.

PEARS

Wash pears. Peel, halve, and core them. Continue as with apricots, using either hot or cold pack.

PLUMS

Select fully ripe plums. If they are to be canned whole, prick their skins to prevent shrinkage. Freestone varieties may be halved and pitted. Simmer to boiling in sirup or juice. If fruit is very juicy, you may heat it with sugar, adding no liquid. Pack hot into clean, hot containers, filling jars to ½ inch of top and cans to ¼ inch of top. Cover with boiling liquid. Process in boiling-water bath for 15 minutes for pt. jars, qt. jars, and no. 2 cans; for 20 minutes for no. 2½ cans. Processing may be completed in a pressure canner in 10 minutes at 5 pounds pressure.

RHUBARB

Wash rhubarb, and cut it into ½-inch pieces. Add ½ cup of sugar to each quart of rhubarb, and let stand to draw out juice. Bring to a boil, stirring to prevent sticking. Pack hot to ½ inch of top in jars, to top in cans; cover with hot sirup. Process in boiling-water bath, for 10 minutes, or in pressure canner for 5 minutes at 5 pounds pressure.

SAUERKRAUT

Heat well-fermented sauerkraut to simmering; do not boil. Pack hot sauerkraut in clean, hot containers, pressing down firmly. Fill jars to ½ inch of top, cans to ¼ inch of top. Fill containers with boiling hot sauerkraut juice.

Process for—
Boiling-water bath:
Pt. jars, 25 min.
Qt. jars, 30 min.
No. 2 cans, 15 min.
No. 2½ cans, 20 min.

STRAWBERRIES

Wash and stem berries. Add ½ cup of sugar to each quart of fruit, and let stand to draw juice. Bring slowly to a boil, shaking the pan to prevent sticking. Pack hot to ½ inch of top in jars, to top in cans.

Process for—
Boiling-water bath:
Pt. and qt. jars, 15 min.
No. 2 cans, 15 min.
No. 2½ cans, 20 min.
Pressure canner:
5 min. at 5 lb. pressure

TOMATOES

Use only perfect, ripe tomatoes. Wash them thoroughly. To loosen skins, dip into boiling water for ½ minute, then dip quickly into cold water. Remove skins and cores.

Hot Pack. Quarter tomatoes. Bring to boil, stirring often. Pack hot in glass jars. Add ½ teaspoon of salt per pint. Process in boiling-water bath for 10 minutes.

Cold Pack. Quarter peeled tomatoes. Leave tomatoes whole or cut in halves or quarters. Pack, pressing gently to fill spaces. Add no water. Add ½ teaspoon of salt to each pint.

Process for—
Boiling-water bath:
Pt. jars, 35 min.
Qt. jars, 45 min.
No. 2 cans, 45 min.
No. 2½ cans, 55 min.
Pressure canner (either pack):
5 min. at 5 lb. pressure

Tomato Juice

Use ripe, juicy tomatoes. Wash them, remove stem ends, and cut tomatoes into pieces. Simmer until softened, stirring often. Put through a strainer. Add 1 teaspoon of salt to each quart of juice. Reheat at once just to boiling. Pack boiling hot juice to ¼ inch of top in jars, to top in cans. Process in boiling-water bath for 15 minutes; in pressure canner for 5 minutes at 5 lbs. pressure.

Asparagus

Whole. Grade fresh asparagus for size. Wash, remove scales and tough ends; rewash. Place upright in wire basket or cheesecloth, and hold in boiling water which reaches just below the tips. Boil 3 minutes. Pack upright.

Diced. Wash asparagus; cut off scales and tough ends; rewash. Cut into 1-inch pieces. Cover with boiling water, and boil for 2 or 3 minutes. Pack hot.

Process for—
Boiling-water bath:
Pt. jars, 100 min.
Qt. jars, 120 min.
Pressure canner:
Pt. jars and all cans, 30 min.
at 10 lbs. pressure
Qt jars, 35 min.
at 10 lbs. pressure

Beans, Snap or String

Wash, string, and rewash beans. Cut or break into 1 or 2 inch pieces or leave whole, as desired. Precook until flexible. Pack.

Process for—
Boiling-water bath:
Pt. jars, 100 min.
Qt. jars, 120 min.
Pressure canner:
Pt. jars and all cans, 30 min.
at 10 lbs. pressure
Qt. jars, 35 min.
at 10 lbs. pressure

Beans, Lima or Shell

Wash, shell, and rewash beans. Precook for 3 minutes. Pack.

Process for—
Boiling-water bath:
Pt. jars, 160 min.
Qt. jars, 180 min.

Pressure canner:
Pt. jars and No. 2 cans, 50 min.
at 10 lbs. pressure
Qt. jars, 55 min.
at 10 lbs. pressure

Beets

Sort beets according to size. Cut off the tops, leaving the root and an inch of stem. Wash beets. Boil until skins slip off easily (15 to 20 minutes, depending upon size). Then skin and trim them. Leave baby beets whole. Cut medium or very large beets in ½-inch slices; halve or quarter very large slices. Work quickly to prevent bleeding. Pack, add cooking liquid, and process. Use the same processing time given for asparagus.

Beets, Pickled

See Canning Fruits and Other Acid Foods.

Carrots

Scrub carrots. Scrape them, or blanch them and slip off their skins. They may be sliced, diced, or left whole. Precook for 5 minutes, and pack. Use the processing time table given for asparagus.

Cauliflower

Wash cauliflower, and separate it into small flowerets. Soak it for 30 minutes in a salt solution (a tablespoon of salt to a quart of water). Precook for 3 minutes, and pack. Use the processing time table given for asparagus.

Corn, Cream Style

Husk corn and remove silk. Wash. Cut corn from cob at about center of kernel, and scrape cobs with the back of the knife. Add ½ as much water as corn. Heat to boiling, and pack* fairly loosely.

Process for—
Boiling-water bath:
Pt. jars, 180 min.
Pressure canner:
Pt. jars, 85 min.
at 10 lbs. pressure
No. 2 cans, 105 min.
at 10 lbs. pressure
*Use only pint jars and No. 2 cans.

CORN, WHOLE KERNEL

Husk corn and remove silk. Wash. Cut from cob at about two-thirds the depth of the kernel. Add half as much water as corn, enough to cover. Heat to boiling.
Pack, and process for—
Boiling-water bath:
Pt. jars, 160 min.
Qt. jars, 180 min.
Pressure canner:
Pt. jars and No. 2 cans, 60 min.
at 10 lb. pressure
Qt. jars, 70 min.
at 10 lbs. pressure

OKRA

Use small, tender pods. Wash. Remove stem ends without cutting pods. Cook for 1 minute in boiling water. Cut into 1-inch lengths or leave pods whole, as desired. Okra that is to be used in soups should be sliced.
Pack, and process for—
Water-bath canner:
150 min.
Pressure canner:
Pt. jars, 25 min.
at 10 lbs. pressure
Qt. jars, 40 min.
at 10 lbs. pressure

PEAS, GREEN

Shell and wash peas. Precook for 3 minutes. Pack fairly loosely.
Process for—
Boiling-water bath:
Pt. jars, 160 min.
Qt. jars, 180 min.
Pressure Canner:
Pt. jars and all tin cans, 45 min.
at 10 lbs. pressure
Qt. jars, 50 min.
at 10 lbs. pressure

PUMPKIN, CUBED

Wash, remove seeds, and peel pumpkin. Cut it into 1-inch cubes. Cover with water, and bring to a boil. Pack.
Process for—
Boiling-water bath:
210 min.
Pressure canner:
Pt. jars, 55 min.
at 10 lbs. pressure

Qt. jars, 90 min.
at 10 lbs. pressure
No. 2 cans, 50 min.
at 10 lbs. pressure
No. 2½ cans, 75 min.
at 10 lbs. pressure

PUMPKIN, STRAINED

Wash, remove seeds, and peel pumpkin. Cut into 1-inch cubes. Steam until tender (about 25 minutes). Put through food mill or strainer. Simmer until heated through, stirring to keep it from sticking to the pan. Pack; add no liquid or salt.
Process for—
Boiling-water bath:
210 min.
Pressure canner:
Pt. jars, 60 min.
at 10 lbs. pressure
Qt. jars, 80 min.
at 10 lbs. pressure
No. 2 cans, 75 min.
at 10 lbs. pressure

SAUERKRAUT

See under CANNING FRUIT AND OTHER ACID FOODS.

SQUASH, SUMMER

Wash squash. Trim ends, but do not peel it. Cut squash into ½-inch slices; halve or quarter to make pieces of uniform size. Cover with water, and bring to a boil.
Pack, and process for—
Boiling-water bath:
180 min.
Pressure canner:
Pt. jars, 30 min.
at 10 lbs. pressure
Qt. jars, 40 min.
at 10 lbs. pressure
No. 2 and 2½ cans, 20 min.
at 10 lbs. pressure

SQUASH, WINTER

Prepare, pack, and process like pumpkin.

SUCCOTASH

Prepare corn and beans according to the directions given for each. Combine them. Pack.

Process for—
Boiling-water bath:
Pt. jars, 160 min.
Qt. jars, 180 min.
Pressure canner:
Pt. jars, and No. 2 cans, 60 min.
at 10 lbs. pressure
Qt. jars, and No. 3 cans, 70 min.
at 10 lbs. pressure

SWEET POTATOES, DRY PACK

Wash sweet potatoes, and sort them according to size. Boil or steam until partially soft (20 to 30 minutes). Skin. Cut in pieces if large. Pack tight. Fill cans to tops, and fill jars to 1 inch of top, pressing gently to fill spaces. Add no salt or liquid.
Process for—
Boiling-water bath:
210 min.
Pressure canner:
Pt. jars, 65 min.
at 10 lbs. pressure
No. 2 cans, 80 min.
at 10 lbs. pressure
Qt. jars and No. 2½ cans, 95 min.
at 10 lbs. pressure

SWEET POTATOES, WET PACK

Wash sweet potatoes, and sort them according to size. Boil or steam until skins slip off easily. Skin, and cut in pieces. Pack jars to 1 inch of tops.
Process for—
Boiling-water bath:
200 min.
Pressure canner:
Pt. jars, 55 min.
at 10 lbs. pressure
Qt. jars and No. 2½ cans, 90 min.
at 10 lbs. pressure
No. 2 cans, 70 min.
at 10 lbs. pressure

CANNING MEATS

What to can. Beef, veal, mutton, lamb, pork, and rabbit are all successfully canned at home. So are various kinds of poultry—chicken, duck, goose, guinea, squab, and turkey. Meat of large-game animals may be canned like beef; that of game birds and small-game animals, like poultry.

Mixtures such as the following are not recommended for canning: chile con carne, hash and stews made with vegetables, head cheese, liver paste, pork and beans, scrapple, soups made with cereals and vegetables. Commercial canners succeed with these specialties because they have the needed equipment as well as laboratories to check their results. For the home canner, it is safer to can each food by itself and combine them when ready to serve.

Preparation of meat for canning. Can only meat from healthy animals that have been slaughtered and handled in a sanitary way. After killing, chill meat at once and keep it chilled until canning time, or else can the meat as soon as body heat left it. Chilled meat is easier to handle. Chilling calls for refrigeration or for weather that can be counted on to keep meat at 40° F. or lower. Meat held at temperatures near freezing may be canned at any convenient time within a few days after killing.

Avoid freezing of meat, if possible. If the meat does freeze, keep it frozen until canning time. Thawed meat is very perishable. Cut or saw the frozen meat into strips 1 or 2 inches thick just before canning.

It is best not to fry meat before canning. The brown crust that tastes so good in fresh-cooked chicken or steak becomes dry and hard, and the canned meat may even have a disagreeable flavor.

Salt does not help to preserve meat in canning, but you may add it for flavor if you wish. Ot it may be added when the food is used.

For the best flavored canned chicken, select stewing hens. Young birds need the same processing, often lack flavor, and may cook to pieces. To cut, it is best to cut away the edible pieces instead of drawing the bird.

For canning meat in large pieces, select cuts commonly used for roasts, steaks, or chops. Cuts that contain more connective tissue or bone and small pieces may be canned as stew meat, or ground meat or soup. Keep them clean and cold until ready to can.

Cleaning the utensils. For successful canning, every utensil and piece of equipment must be thoroughly clean.

Scrub metal, enamelware, and porcelain with hot, soapy water, and rinse with boiling water.

Cutting boards, table tops upon which meat has rested, and wooden utensils require "elbow grease" and special treatment if bacteria are to be kept under control. Scrape these, scrub them with hot soapy water, and rinse them with boiling water. Then disinfect them; use either a hypochlorite solution or a chloride of lime bleaching fluid diluted according to the directions on the can. Allow the solution to remain for about a half hour, and then wash it off with scalding water.

Don't allow meat to rest upon linoleum, for scalding and disinfecting are too harsh for this material.

Use cool water to rinse meat juices from cloths. Then wash the cloths in soapy hot water and boil them. Rinse them in the same kind of disinfectant you use for wood.

Yield of Canned Meat from Fresh

For a quart jar or a number 3 can, allow about:

5 to 5½ pounds of pork loin (untrimmed)
5 to 5½ pounds of beef rump (untrimmed)
3 to 3½ pounds of beef round (untrimmed)
4½ to 5½ pounds of chicken (dressed, undrawn) to be canned with bone
7 to 8 pounds of chicken (dressed, undrawn) to be canned without bone.

Directions

Canning experts strongly recommend the use of a pressure canner in processing meats. However, some home canners have successfully canned meat with the hot-water-bath method. Wherever possible, processing times are given for both methods.

Note: These directions for canning meats should be supplemented by all other relevant instructions given in the entire section on canning.

Canning Poultry

Hot pack, with bone.

1. Bone the breast, saw drumsticks off short, if desired, but leave bone in other meaty pieces such as second joints. Trim off all large lumps of fat. Sort pieces according to whether they are meaty or bony, and set giblets aside for separate canning.

2. Broth or hot water will be needed as liquid. Use bony pieces to make broth. Cover them with cold water, and simmer until meat is tender. Drain broth into a bowl; skim off fat. The remaining meat stripped from the bone may be canned as little pieces.

3. Pour hot broth or hot water over raw meaty pieces in cooking pan to cover meat. Put on lid, and precook until meat is medium done, or until, when cut, it shows almost no pink color at piece centers. Stir occasionally for even heating.

4. If salt is desired, put a level measure into clean, empty containers—½ teaspoon in pint jar or number 2 can; ¾ teaspoon in 2½ can; 1 teaspoon in quart jar or 3 can.

5. Pack second joints and drumsticks. Have skin next to glass or tin. Fit breasts into center, smaller pieces where needed. Leave about 1 inch head space above meat in glass jars; ½ inch in cans.

6. Cover meat with hot broth, using ½ to ¾ of a cup for each quart container. Leave 1 inch head space in jars; fill cans to top.

7. Work out air bubbles with knife. Add more liquid if needed to cover meat. Be certain to leave 1 inch head space in jars, and to fill cans to top.

8. Adjust jar lids, or seal cans.

9. Process at once in the steam pressure canner at 10 pounds pressure (240° F.) for: Pint jars, 65 minutes; quart jars, 75 minutes; no. 2 cans, 55 minutes; no. 2½ and 3 cans, 75 minutes. Or in a boiling-water bath for 3½ hours.

Hot pack, without bone.

Follow directions for hot-packed poultry with bone, with these exceptions:

Remove bone, but not skin, from meaty pieces. Poultry can be boned either raw or after precooking.

Boned poultry must be processed in the pressure canner longer than poultry with bone. Process at ten pounds pressure for: Pint jars, 65 minutes; quart jars, 90 minutes; no. 2 cans, 55 minutes; no. 2½ and 3 cans, 75 minutes. Or in a boiling-water bath for 3½ hours.

Raw (cold) pack, with bone.

1. Bone the breast, saw drumsticks off short, if desired, but leave bone in the other meaty pieces such as second joints. Trim off large lumps of fat. Sort pieces of meat according to whether they are meaty or bony. Set giblets aside for separate canning.

2. If salt is desired, put a level measure into clean, empty containers—½ teaspoon in pint jar or number 2 can; ¾ teaspoon in 2½ can; 1 teaspoon in quart jar or 3 can.

3. Pack second joints and drumsticks. Have skin next to glass or tin. Fit breasts into center, smaller pieces where needed. Pack glass jars to about 1 inch of top; pack tin cans to top.

4. Set open jars or cans in large vessel with warm water about 2 inches below rim of containers. Cover vessel and heat at slow boil until meat in all containers is steaming hot and medium done (about 50 minutes in the cans, 75 in jars). If you have a thermometer, meat is heated enough when contents of center of jar registers 170° F.

5. Adjust jar lids, or seal tin cans.

6 Process at once in the pressure canner at 10 pounds pressure (240° F.) for: Pint jars, 65 minutes; quart jars, 75 minutes; no. 2 cans, 55 minutes; no. 2½ and 3 cans, 75 minutes. Or in a boiling-water bath for 3½ hours.

Raw pack, without bone.

Follow directions for raw-packed poultry with bone, with these exceptions:

Remove bone, but not skin, from meaty pieces before packing.

Boned chicken must be processed longer in the pressure canner than chicken with bone. Process at 10 pounds pressure for: Pint jars, 75 minutes; quart jars, 90 minutes; no. 2 cans, 65 minutes; no. 2½ and 3 cans, 90 minutes.

GIBLETS

Because of flavor, it is best to can livers alone. Gizzards and hearts may be canned together. Since these are ordinarily canned and used in small quantities, directions are given only for pint glass jars and number 2 tin cans.

1. Put giblets in cooking pan. Cover them with broth made from bony pieces or with hot water. Cover the pan, and precook giblets until medium done. Stir occasionally.

2. If salt is desired, put level measure into clean, empty containers—½ teaspoon in each container.

3. Pack giblets hot to 1 inch of top in jars, to ½ inch of top in cans.

4. Cover giblets with hot broth or hot water. Leave 1-inch space at top of jars; fill cans to top.

5. Work out air bubbles with knife. Add more liquid, if needed, to cover meat. Be certain to leave 1-inch space in jars and to have cans filled to top.

6. Adjust jar lids, or seal cans.

7. Process at once in the pressure canner at 10 pounds pressure (240° F.) for: Pint jars, 75 minutes; no. 2 cans, 65 minutes. Or in a boiling-water bath for 3½ hours.

RABBIT

Prepare the meaty pieces, with or without bone, and pack and process as for chicken.

BEEF, VEAL, PORK, LAMB

For canning as large pieces, use loin and other cuts suitable for roasts, steaks, or chops. For canning as stew meat, use the less tender cuts and smaller pieces.

Cut away meat from bone. Set bones aside for use in broths or soups. Trim most of the fat away without unduly slashing the lean.

Cut into pieces that will slip easily into the containers; have the grain running lengthwise.

Hot pack.

1. Put meat in large shallow pan; add just enough water to prevent sticking. Cover pan and precook meat slowly until medium done, stirring occasionally for even heating.

2. If salt is desired, put level measure into clean, empty containers—½ teaspoon in pint jars or number 2 cans; ¾ teaspoon in 2½ cans, 1 teaspoon in quart jars or 3 cans.

3. Pack meat hot to 1 inch of top in jars, to ½ inch of top in cans.

4. Cover with meat juice, adding hot broth or water if needed. Again leave 1 inch head space in jars; fill cans to top.

5. Work out air bubbles with knife. Add more liquid if needed to cover meat. Be certain to leave 1 inch head space in jars and to fill cans to top.

6. Adjust jar lids or seal cans.

7. Process at once in the pressure canner at 10 pounds pressure (240° F.) for: Pint jars, 75 minutes; quart jars, 90 minutes; no. 2 cans, 65 minutes; no. 2½ and 3 cans, 90 minutes. Or in a boiling-water bath for 3½ hours.

Raw (cold) pack.

1. If salt is desired, put level measure into clean, empty containers—½ teaspoon in pint jars or number 2 cans; ¾ teaspoon in 2½ cans; 1 teaspoon in quart jars or 3 cans.
2. Pack containers with raw, lean meat. Leave about 1 inch head space in jars; fill cans to top.
3. Set open jars or cans in large vessel with warm water about 2 inches below rim of jar or can. Cover vessel and heat at slow boil until meat in all jars or cans is steaming hot and medium done (about 50 minutes in cans, 75 in glass jars). If you have a thermometer, meat is heated enough when center of container registers 170° F. Press meat down into tin cans ½ inch below rims, and add boiling water if needed to fill to top.
4. Adjust jar lids or seal cans.
5. Process at once in the pressure canner at 10 pounds pressure (240° F.) for:
   Pint jars, 75 minutes; quart jars, 90 minutes; no. 2 cans, 65 minutes; no. 2½ and 3 cans, 90 minutes.
   Or in a boiling-water bath for 3½ hours.

GROUND MEAT

For grinding, use small pieces or meat from the less tender cuts, but be sure that the meat is fresh, clean, and cold. Never mix in scraps of doubtful freshness as they may spoil a whole batch; don't use fat.

If desired, add 1 level teaspoon of salt to the pound of ground meat, mixing it well.

Hot pack.

1. Form ground meat into fairly thin cakes that can be packed in glass jars or tin cans without breaking.
2. Put meat cakes into cooking pan. Precook in oven until medium done or until, when cut into, red color at center of cakes is almost gone.
3. Pack cakes hot to 1 inch of top in jars, to ½ inch of top in cans.
4. Skim fat off drippings, and do not use the fat in canning.
5. Cover with meat juice, adding hot water if needed. Leave 1 inch head space in jars; fill cans to top.

6. Work out air bubbles with knife. Add more liquid if needed to cover meat. Be certain to leave 1 inch head space in jars and to fill cans to top.
7. Adjust jar lids or seal cans.
8. Process at once in pressure canner at 10 pounds pressure (240° F.) for:
   Pint jars, 75 minutes; quart jars, 90 minutes; no. 2 cans, 65 minutes; no. 2½ and 3 cans, 90 minutes.
   Or in a boiling-water bath for 3½ hours.

Raw pack.

This method is suitable only for tin cans. It is difficult to get canned ground meat packed this way out of jars.

1. Without forming cakes, pack raw ground meat solidly into tin cans level with the top.
2. Place open cans in large vessel with water about 2 inches below can rim. Cover vessel and heat at slow boil until meat in all cans is steaming hot and medium done (about 75 minutes). If you have a thermometer, meat is heated enough when center of can registers 170° F. Press meat down into cans about ½ inch below rim.
3. Seal cans.
4. Process at once in the pressure canner at 10 pounds pressure (240° F.) for:
   No. 2 cans, 100 minutes; no. 2½ and 3 cans, 135 minutes.

SAUSAGE

Use any tested sausage recipe, but omit sage as it is likely to give the canned sausage a bitter flavor. Use onion, garlic, and other spices very sparingly, because flavors change with processing and storing and the result may be undesirable.

Shape sausage meat into cakes. Precook, pack, and process like ground meat, hot packed.

CORNED BEEF

1. Wash the corned beef, and cut it into pieces suited to packing.
2. Cover meat with cold water; bring to a boil. If broth tastes very salty, drain and cover meat with fresh water, and parboil again.
3. Pack hot meat to 1 inch of top in jars, to ½ inch of top in cans.

4. Cover meat with hot broth or hot water, using about ½ to ¾ cup for each quart container. Leave 1 inch head space in jars; fill cans to top.
5. Work out air bubbles with knife. Add more liquid if needed to cover meat. Be sure to leave 1 inch head space in jars, and to fill cans to top.
6. Adjust jar lids or seal cans.
7. Process at once in the pressure canner at 10 pounds pressure (240° F.) for: Pint jars, 75 minutes; quart jars, 90 minutes; no. 2 cans, 65 minutes; no. 2½ and 3 cans, 90 minutes. Or in a boiling-water bath for 3½ hours.

Heart and Tongue

The heart and tongue are generally used as fresh meat. If you do wish to can them, follow directions for beef, veal, pork, lamb as hot packed, with these exceptions:

Heart. Remove thick connective tissue before cutting into pieces.

Tongue. Drop tongue into boiling water and simmer about 45 minutes, or until skin can be removed, before cutting into pieces.

Soup Stock

1. Make a fairly concentrated stock by covering bony pieces of chicken or other meat with lightly salted water and simmering until meat is tender. Cooking too long may cause·soup to lose flavor.
2. Skim off fat, and remove all pieces of bone; don't strain out meat and sediment.
3. Pour hot stock into containers to 1 inch of top in jars, to top in cans.
4. Adjust jar lids or seal cans.
5. Process at once in pressure canner at 10 pounds pressure (240° F.) for: Pint jars, 20 minutes; quart jars, 25 minutes; no. 2 cans, 20 minutes; no. 2½ cans, 25 minutes. Or in a boiling-water bath canner for 2½ hours.

CANTAL CHEESE. A very old variety of hard, rennet cheese, made from skimmed cow's milk. It is about 14 inches in diameter and weighs from 40 to 120 pounds. Also known as Auvergne, Auvergne Bleu, and Fourme.

CANTALOUPE. A variety of muskmelon, named after the castle of Cantaloupe, in the province of Ancona, Italy. It is found in many sizes and shapes. Through trade usage "cantaloupe" has become the name commonly applied to muskmelons grown in this country. Actually "cantaloupe" is the name which should be given to melons of a certain definite group grown in Europe. The flesh varies in color from a pinkish yellow to pale green.

Varieties

Commercially, cantaloupes are divided into three groups according to the color of flesh.

Pink Meat. The color of flesh is orange or pink throughout. The netting is not so heavy as that of either the green or salmon tints, but is usually well developed over the blossom end. With the exception of certain types which are slightly oval, pink-meated melons are elongated and somewhat pointed at both ends.

Salmon Tint. The flesh is normally greenish near the rind and salmon-colored toward the center. Immature melons of this group have flesh that is almost entirely green, while those of advanced maturity have almost entirely yellow or salmon flesh. The netting completely covers the melon; the shape is usually roundish.

Green Meat. The flesh is normally green from the center to rind. The netting completely covers the melon; the shape is roundish.

Preparation for Market

Cantaloupes require a fairly long growing season, with planty of heat and sunshine, a dry atmosphere and sufficient soil moisture. They do not attain their highest flavor and best edible qualities unless allowed to become reasonably ripe on vigorous diease-free vines. Careful transporta-

Food Value of Canteloupe

Water	Food Energy	Pro-tein	Fat	Carbo-hydrate	Cal-cium	Phos-phorus	Iron	Vit. A Value	Thia-mine	Ribo-flavin	Nia-cin	Ascor-bic Acid
94.0	23	.6	.2	4.6	17	16	.4	3,420	.06	.04	.8	33

tion experiments have shown that melons grown in the Imperial Valley of California to be shipped under refrigeration to the most distant eastern markets of the United States may remain on the vines until ripe enough for the stems to separate from the melons under a decided pressure of the thumb, and yet reach the consumer in excellent condition. Two stages of maturity

HINTS ON BUYING

In judging the quality of cantaloupes, one should keep in mind the following points:

Sweetness, fine texture, and flavor are factors that determine quality in cantaloupes; one can expect to find them only in well matured fruit.

CANTALOUPES 1. Pride of Wisconsin 2. Sunrise 3. Bender's Surprise 4. Minnesota Midget

were included in these experiments, the one known as "full slip" by which the entire stem separates from the melon leaving a clean stem quality, the other known as the "half slip", by which about one-third of the width of the stem remains attached to the melon.

The melons are removed from the vine by placing the hand upon the melon, pressing upon the stem with the thumb or slightly lifting the melon from the ground. If the melon is sufficiently ripe the stem will separate under the pressure, showing that the melon is ready for gathering. Hampers, bushel baskets, crates, lug boxes, and numerous other types of containers are used for carrying the melon to the roadways. In most cases no picking containers are used, the melons being laid in piles. Canvas bags with shoulder straps are used extensively, but their tendency to bruise the melons is greater than that of baskets or crates. As a rule the melons are left in the picking baskets at the roadways until they are loaded into the wagons and they are usually hauled to the packing sheds in these containers. Whether the packing is done in a central or field packing shed the stock is usually sorted or graded as to maturity and defects as the melons are transferred from the field container to the packing bin.

The stage of maturity of a cantaloupe is indicated by the netting or veining on the surface and the condition of the scar at the stem end. The netting should be coarse, corky or grayish color, well developed, standing out in bold relief, and covering the surface to an extent depending on the class to which the variety may belong.

The green color of the immature rind should be a lighter shade and may have either a grayish or yellowish tinge.

The scar at the stem end should be slightly sunken and calloused, a condition which indicates that when the fruit is picked it separated readily and was not cut or gouged from the stem. Cantaloupes that show these characteristics are usually mature and usually have developed their full flavor and distinctive cantaloupe aroma.

A softening of the fruit at the blossom end is a supposed indication of ripeness, but as this softening can be induced by repeated pressure, too much reliance should not be placed on this test.

Over-mature cantaloupes are usually soft, watery and insipid. This condition is generally indicated by a very pronounced yellowing of rind showing through the netting.

Immature cantaloupes have a flesh that is generally hard, tough and flavorless.

They are usually poorly netted and are sometimes called slick. The surface color showing through the netting is green, and frequently a small part of the stem adheres to the melon.

Bruised cantaloupes are undesirable for flesh as the bruised areas are usually soft, watery, and insipid.

Cantaloupes having growth cracks, unless freshly picked for immediate consumption, are undesirable since cracks provide for easy entrance of organisms which cause decay and souring of flesh.

Flabby or shriveled cantaloupes should be avoided, for they lack flavor and are likely to be fermenting.

Decay is indicated by soft, sunken spots on the surface and by mold or moisture on stem end.

Surface mold or mildew does not usually affect the edibility of fruit except when it has penetrated the rind, which it can do through broken or injured surfaces.

Cantaloupes are sold by the unit or pound, 2 pounds equaling 2 to 3 melons. One small melon serves two people, one large one, will serve 4 to 6 people.

Grading. Cantaloupe is graded according to quality by the United States Federal Grades. U.S. No. 1 consists of cantaloupe of one variety which are firm, mature, well formed, well netted and free from aphis honey dew, cracks, sunburn decay and from damage caused by dirt, moisture, hail, disease, insects or mechanical or other means. U.S. Commercial shall consist of cantaloupe which meet the requirements of U.S. No. 1, except for tolerance for number of defects. Not more than 20 percent may fall below the requirements of this grade. Unclassified consists of cantaloupe which have not been classified in accordance with the foregoing grades.

HINTS ON PREPARATION

Cantaloupe should be kept in a cool, dry place; or wrapped in several layers of waxed paper or an oil silk bag and put in the refrigerator. For best flavor, remove from refrigerator an hour or so before serving. It should be cool, but not cold. *See also* MELON.

CANTALOUPE AND BLACKBERRY SALAD

1 medium cantaloupe, chilled
1 pt fresh blackberries, chilled

Cut cantaloupe in wedges or rings, scoop out seeds and fiber from center and peel. Wash and drain blackberries. Arrange wedges or rings of melon on lettuce and fill center with berries. Serve with lime-honey dressing. *See* LIME. (Serves 5)

CANTALOUPE COCONUT MOLD

⅓ cup quick-cooking tapioca
2 cups water
¼ tsp salt
¾ cup strained honey
1 cup shredded coconut
¼ cup lemon juice
1 cup small cantaloupe balls (generous)
1 cup watermelon balls
Sweetened whipped cream

Shake the tapioca gently into the salted, rapidly boiling water and cook five minutes stirring constantly. Add the honey and coconut and continue cooking until the mixture thickens, stirring frequently. This will take about five minutes. Remove from the fire, add lemon juice, cool; then stir in the cantaloupe and watermelon balls. When the mixture cools and thickens, turn into a mold previously wet with cold water, and chill. Unmold and serve with whipped cream sweetened and flavored to taste. (Serves 4)

CANTALOUPE CUP COCKTAILS

As a cocktail, cantaloupe is excellent, either alone or with other fruits. Shape fleshy part into balls, using a vegetable ball cutter or cut in cubes. The following combinations will serve about 6 people.

MELON MINT COCKTAIL

Mix 3 cups cantaloupe cubes with 24 after-dinner mints, broken; chill.

CANTALOUPE FRUIT CUP

Mix 1½ cups each cantaloupe cubes and diced pineapple with ⅓ cup pineapple juice and 1½ tablespoons lemon juice. Serve in cocktail glasses, garnish with preserved green grapes.

CANTALOUPE CUP EPICURE

For each serving, allow half of a ripe cantaloupe. Remove seeds. Fill the fruit with wedges of fresh pineapple, grapefruit, and oranges. Garnish it with a few black-berries and small melon balls. Pour on as much port wine as possible without spill-ing. Set it in the refrigerator and chi l thoroughly.

Cubes of watermelon, honeydew, etc. mixed with Madeira wine, or sweet dessert wine may be substituted for the other fruit. You may also serve in sherbet glasses if desired.

CANTALOUPE CUP NEW YORKER

Cut a ripe, sweet cantaloupe in half and remove the seeds; brush the inside with a little brandy and fill the half cantaloupe with watermelon balls, fresh raspberries, and a few blackberries (fresh). The fruits should be well chilled. Serve on individual cold plates covered with a shiny green leaf. Serve powdered sugar.

CANTALOUPE DESSERT SALAD

Combine cantaloupe balls or cubes, diced bananas, quartered marshmallows, pecan halves, and Cooked Salad Dressing (See SALAD DRESSING). Serve on crisp let-tuce.

CANTALOUPE GOURMET

Cut a large ripe cantaloupe into halves; remove the seeds and divide each half into thirds. Pit one cup of sweet cherries and refill with chopped nut meats (any kind). Arrange the cherries neatly on pieces of melon, and pour over a few drops of Kirsch liqueur. Garnish with crisp sprigs of fresh mint before serving. (Serves 6)

CANTALOUPE PICKLES

Small cantaloupes
Vinegar
3 lb sugar
3 oz stick cinnamon
2 oz whole cloves
1 oz whole allspice

Select cantaloupes which are not too ripe, peel and cut into large cubes. Cover with mild vinegar and let stand 24 hours. Pour off the vinegar; then prepare a sirup allowing the amounts of sugar and spices specified to each quart of fresh vinegar. Boil down until thick, skim and simmer

the melons in this sirup for 20 minutes. Lift out with a perforated skimmer and pack in sterilized jars. Boil down the sirup until again thickened (the moisture from the melons will have thinned it somewhat), pour over the fruit in the jars and seal. *See also* CANNING.

CANTALOUPE PRESERVES WITH PEACHES

Use 12 peaches, peeled, stoned and sliced, 1 cantaloupe, peeled, seeded and sliced, and pulp of 3 oranges. Measure fruit; add ⅔ cup sugar to each cup fruit, let stand several hours before cooking. Cook, stirring frequently and gently, until fruit is clear and tender and sirup is thick. Turn into hot clean jars and seal at once. *See also* CANNING.

CANTALOUPE WALDORF SALAD

2 cups diced cantaloupe
1 cup diced apples
1 cup diced, fresh peaches
1 cup minced celery
¼ cup French Dressing
½ cup chopped nuts
Lettuce
1 cup Cream Mayonnaise

Combine fruits and celery; marinate in French dressing (*which see*) 10 minutes. Drain off excess dressing. Add nuts and serve on crisp lettuce on individual plates. Top with Cream Mayonnaise (*see* MAYON-NAISE). (Serves 6)

FILLED CANTALOUPE

Cut small melons in halves, remove seeds, imbed in ice and fill with clusters of cherries and fragments of ice.

CAPERS. The straggling caper bush, *capparis spinosa*, grows in the Mediterranean region and, to a limited extent, in the United States. It produces tulip-shaped flowers which, if fully formed, are large and white. Its tiny greenish flower buds have a pungent and slightly bitter taste. The midget buds are bottled and sold as "non-pareils" while the larger ones are sold in bulk as "capuchins" or "capotes." The seeds (sometimes called mountain pepper) and the berry-like fruit of capers are used in pickles, relishes, and similar condiment preparations. Pickled seeds of the nastur-tium are sometimes sold as capers, but these are considerably inferior to the genuine caper.

Capers enhance the flavor of salad dressings, meat sauces, and appetizers. They are usually sold in bottles, which should be kept tightly corked in a cool, dry place.

CAPLIN FISH or Icefish. A small smelt found in large numbers on the Arctic coast as far south as Cape Cod. They are very tasty and may be prepared in the same manner as SMELTS, *which see*.

CAPON. A capon is an unsexed rooster, seven to ten months old, weighing over four pounds. Its flesh is tender and the breast particularly fleshy and desirable. In a moderate oven a capon requires 25 minutes per pound for roasting. Quick rinsing in cold water is all the washing the capon will need.

It was under a Roman prohibition that the capon was created. The famous Fannian law, fixing the maximum of expenditures for a dinner or festival as well as on ordinary days, forbade having more than five guests on market days and more than three on other days, and prohibited the serving of any fowl at any repast except a hen, and this bird was not to be fattened. The useful hen and her unlaid eggs were to be sacrificed and the unproductive rooster was to be fed, to no purpose, for the rest of his days, immune from the butcher's block. The Fannian law set a shrewd surgeon thinking. He transformed a rooster into a capon by the now old and well-known surgical trick. Capons naturally grow fat without any infraction of the imperial Roman law against fattening chickens. Neither hen nor rooster, the capon was a huge success. Moreover, it was perfectly safe to eat him—he was "within the law." *See also* CHICKEN.

CAPSICUM. This is the name of a genus of plants which bear many-seeded berries. The fruits, known as chilies or peppers, are extremely hot and pungent. The fruits of one species are ground into paprika. The fruits of other species are used to make cayenne pepper. The capsicum fruits also go into the making of tabasco sauce. These capsicum derivatives are agreeable condiments, but some can be extremely virulent if they are used excessively. *See* CAYENNE PEPPER, CHILI, PAPRIKA, and PEPPER.

CAPSULE. The pod of the pea, the covering of the plantain, etc., are known as capsules. The plants that bear such coverings are often themselves known as capsules.

CARAMEL. A flavoring made by melting white sugar in a heavy skillet until it colors. It must be stirred constantly over a very low flame to prevent burning.

CARAMEL COLORING

A preparation easily made at home, of which a few drops added to sauces, soups, or gravies, give them a rich caramel color and will not change the taste. It is made of one part sugar and one-half part cold water. Put the sugar in an iron skillet and stir gently over a medium fire, until melted and browned almost black. Add the water gently—the mixture will steam and bubble violently at first. Cook slowly, still stirring, until the sugar dissolves and the liquid is a little thicker than water. If the liquid becomes too thick, add a little more water. When cool, strain and bottle. Shake the bottle before using. This preparation keeps indefinitely.

CARAMEL CAKE

2 cups sugar
1 cup boiling water
3 cups sifted cake flour
4 tsp baking powder
½ tsp salt
¾ cup shortening
1 tsp vanilla
2 eggs, separated

Melt ½ cup sugar in heavy pan over low flame, stirring until liquid becomes golden brown. Remove from heat and gradually stir in boiling water; then simmer until caramel is dissolved. Mix and sift flour, baking powder and salt. Cream shortening until soft and smooth; gradually add remaining 1½ cups sugar, creaming until very fluffy; beat in flavoring and well-beaten egg yolks. Add flour alternately with caramel sirup, beating until smooth after each addition; fold in thoroughly the stiffly beaten egg whites. Bake in 2 greased layer pans or in muffin pans in moderate oven (375° F.) about 25 minutes. (Makes 2 9-inch layers, or 30 cup cakes)

Ice with caramel frosting made by substituting 2 tablespoons caramel sirup for the vanilla in Seven-minute Frosting. *See* FROSTING.

Caramel Charlotte Russe

1 cup evaporated milk
1½ tsp gelatin
2 tbsp cold water
½ cup sugar
¼ cup boiling water
Few grains of salt
½ tsp vanilla

Chill milk thoroughly. Soften gelatin in cold water and set over hot water to dissolve. Caramelize the sugar, add the boiling water slowly and cook until caramel is dissolved. Add salt. Cool slightly and add dissolved gelatin. When the gelatin mixture begins to thicken, fold in the stiffly whipped milk and vanilla. Pour into a mold. (To make a more elaborate dessert; Add ¼ pound blanched almonds to the mixture and line the mold with lady fingers.) (Serves 6)

Caramel Custard

See Custard.

Caramel Fudge Sauce

1½ cups sugar
1 cup boiling water
1 tbsp butter
½ tsp vanilla

Melt sugar in heavy frying pan over slow heat; when light brown in color, remove from heat, stir in water, add butter and boil to a sirup or until a small amount forms a very soft ball when dropped into cold water (230° F.). Remove from heat, add vanilla and beat slightly; serve hot or cold. (Makes 1 cup)

Caramel Ice Cream

2 cups scalded milk
4 egg yolks, slightly beaten
¼ cup granulated sugar, caramelized
⅛ tsp salt
¼ cup granulated sugar
1 cup heavy cream
1½ tsp vanilla extract
¼ cup granulated sugar

Mix salt and egg yolks and ¼ cup granulated sugar (uncaramelized). To the scalded milk, add the caramelized granulated sugar and stir until thoroughly blended. Pour milk mixture over beaten egg yolk mixture, slowly and gradually beating well, and rapidly all the while. Now cook mixture over boiling water until it coats the spoon, stirring constantly. Cool, strain, add fresh heavy cream and vanilla, and freeze in hand freezer, using 3 parts ice, and 1 part of rock salt. When firm, pack or mold, using 4 parts ice and 1 part rock salt to complete freezing.

Caramel Sauce

1 cup sugar
1 cup water

Caramelize the sugar in a heavy pan. Add the water slowly, boil five or six minutes, and cool. If desired, strong coffee may replace part or all of the water, giving a particularly delicious sauce.

Caramel Sponge

¾ cup sugar
½ cup boiling water
1 tbsp gelatin (1 envelope)
¼ cup cold water
2 eggs separated
¼ tsp salt
1 cup milk
1 tsp vanilla
Whipped Cream

Put ½ cup of the sugar into a heavy metal saucepan or skillet, and stir constantly over direct heat until melted to an amber-colored liquid. Slowly add the boiling water and simmer until caramel is entirely dissolved, stirring occasionally. Cool for about 10 minutes. Soften gelatin in cold water for 5 minutes. Beat egg yolks, add salt and milk, and slowly stir in the caramel sirup. Return to saucepan and cook over low heat, stirring constantly until mixture just coats the spoon. Remove from heat and stir in the gelatin; add vanilla and chill. When mixture has become thick and sirupy beat the egg whites until stiff; add the remaining ¼ cup of sugar, and beat until thick and smooth; then whip the gelatin mixture until fluffy and add to the egg whites, folding lightly but thoroughly until well mixed. Pour into mold, bowl or sherbet glasses, and chill until firm. Unmold the dessert when stiff and garnish appropriately. Serve with whipped or plain cream. (Serves 5)

FOAMY CARAMEL FROSTING

1¼ cups brown sugar
⅓ cup water
1 tsp vinegar
1 egg white
⅛ tsp salt
1 tsp vanilla extract
½ cup finely chopped blanched pistachio
nuts

Place the sugar, water, and vinegar in a saucepan. Stir them until the sugar is dissolved. Cover, bring to boiling point, and continue boiling for three minutes. Remove, and stir in the unbeaten egg white with the salt. Beat the mixture with a rotary egg beater until it is thick enough to stand up in peaks. Add the vanilla and nuts.

CARAMELS. A rich soft candy, traditionally cut in small cubes. They may be varied in innumerable ways. Caramels, and indeed all candies containing cream or milk, must be cooked in a large saucepan as the mixture boils up high in the pan. In cutting caramels apart, use a long bladed, heavy knife with a "sawing" motion. *See also* CANDY.

CALIFORNIA CARAMELS

1 cup top milk
4 cups sugar, granulated or brown
⅔ cup molasses
½ cup butter
4 squares (oz) unsweetened chocolate
½ cup chopped nut meats
½ cup seedless raisins

Combine in a large saucepan the milk, sugar, molasses, butter, and chocolate. Cook over a very low flame, until the chocolate melts, stirring frequently; then continue cooking, stirring constantly until the mixture reaches the hard-ball stage (246° F.). Pour into a shallow, well greased pan over the nut meats and raisins. Cool, mark into squares, and cut apart with a heavy knife when cold. Wrap in waxed paper, and keep in an airtight container in a cool place.

CHOCOLATE CARAMELS

3 squares (oz) unsweetened chocolate
1 cup sugar
¾ cup light corn sirup

¼ tsp salt
1½ cups heavy cream

Combine in a large saucepan the chocolate, sugar, corn sirup, salt, and half the cream. Place over a low flame, and stir constantly until the sugar is dissolved. Continue cooking, still stirring constantly, until the mixture reaches the soft-ball stage (238° F.). Now add another half cup of cream, and again cook to the soft-ball stage (238° F.), stirring constantly from the bottom of the pan. Finally add the third half cup of cream, and cook to the hard-ball stage (246° F.) always stirring constantly. Turn into a greased shallow pan. Do not scrape the pan. Let stand until cool, mark into squares, and cut apart when cold. Wrap in waxed paper and store in an airtight container in a cool, dry place.

CREAMY NUT CARAMELS

2 cups sugar
2 cups light corn sirup
½ cup butter
¼ tsp salt
2 cups undiluted evaporated milk
1 tsp vanilla
1 cup halved blanched toasted almonds

Put the sugar, butter, and salt into a large saucepan, and bring slowly to the boiling point, stirring frequently. Slowly add the milk, so as not to stop the boiling, stirring meanwhile. Cook to the firm-ball stage (240° F.) stirring constantly. Add the vanilla, and quickly pour into greased or shallow pan over the almonds. When cool, mark into squares, and when cold cut and wrap each caramel in waxed paper. Store in an airtight container, and keep in a cool, dry place.

MAPLE CARAMELS

¼ cup granulated sugar
¼ cup brown sugar
¾ cup maple sirup
¼ cup corn sirup
½ cup heavy cream
1 tbsp butter
¼ tsp salt
⅓ cup toasted pecans

Cook together in a large saucepan the sugars, sirups, and cream to the firm-ball stage (246° to 250° F.). Remove from the fire, add the butter, salt, and pecans. Turn into a shallow, greased pan, cool, mark into squares, and when cold cut apart, and wrap in waxed paper. Store in an airtight container in a cool, dry place.

RUM CARAMELS

2 cups sugar
2 cups light corn sirup
½ cup butter
1⅔ cups undiluted evaporated milk
2 tsp rum extract

Combine in a large saucepan the sugar and sirup and cook to the soft-ball stage (238° F.). Add the butter and when this is melted, pour in the milk very slowly so as not to check the boiling. Cook to the firmball stage (246°–248° F.) stirring gently but constantly. Add the flavoring and turn into a greased pan. Cool, mark into squares and when cold cut apart and wrap in waxed paper. Store in an airtight container in a cool, dry place.

VANILLA CARAMELS

2 cups sugar
½ cup top milk
⅓ cup molasses
¼ cup butter
2 squares (oz) unsweetened chocolate
¼ cup broken pecans
2 tbsp blanched pistachio nuts, optional
1 tsp vanilla

Combine in a large saucepan, the sugar, milk, molasses, butter, and chocolate. Cook over a low flame until the chocolate melts; then continue cooking, stirring constantly to the firm-ball stage (246°–250° F.). Turn into a shallow, greased pan over the nuts, mark into squares, and when cold cut apart and wrap in waxed paper. Store in an airtight container.

CARAVELA. A dry Madeira wine, usually served as an aperitif. It is light amber in color.

CARAWAY. Caraway "seeds" are the fruit of the *Carum carvi* a biennial plant which grows in northern and central Europe and Asia and has been cultivated in England and America for its seeds. The plant has clusters of white or pinkish flowers. The aromatic seeds, tiny and ovate, have a pleasant spicy flavor and, when bruised, an agreeable odor.

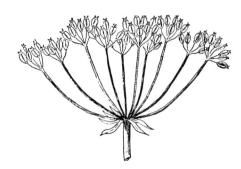

CARAWAY SEED

Caraway seeds are most widely used in cheeses and pastries. They may be mixed with cheese spreads and fillings for canapés and hors d'oeuvres, or a few of them may be sprinkled over these appetizers as a garnish. Caraways also improve the flavor of mutton, liver, pork, and kidneys—they should be added before the meat is cooked —and of sauerkraut, cabbage, and French fried potatoes. The aromatic oil that the seeds yield is used by distillers to flavor certain liqueurs (such as kümmel), and it is used medicinally as a stimulant, mild local anaesthetic, carminative, and antiseptic.

CARBOHYDRATES. The simplest carbohydrate is a sugar which cannot be broken up into other sugars. Such a simple sugar is called a monosaccharid. There are two such common sugars in foods, glucose and fructose; a third, galactose, is derived from more complex sugars. Two simple sugars, united chemically, make a double sugar, or disaccharid; thus cane sugar, or sucrose, will yield glucose and fructose, while milk sugar, or lactose, will yield glucose and galactose, and maltose will yield two portions of glucose. These three disaccharids are the only common ones.

Starches, dextrins, and cellulose, or vegetable fiber, are carbohydrates which are made of many simple glucose groups, and are hence called polysaccharids. All carbohydrates, to be used by the body, must be reduced to simple sugars. Glucose therefore, needs no digestion, but the double sugars must be split by enzymes into two simple sugars. Each sugar has its special enzyme, namely, sucrase (sucrose-splitting), maltase (maltose-splitting) and lactase (lactose-splitting).

The digestion of starches and dextrins begins in the mouth, where amylase (starch-splitting) changes starch first to dextrin and finally to maltose, and maltase (maltose-splitting) may change a little of the maltose so formed, into glucose. In the stomach there are no enzymes acting on carbohydrates, but the digestion may continue under the influence of swallowed saliva for a time. In the pancreatic juice there is another amylase, which completes the splitting of starch to maltose, and then the intestinal maltase can reduce this to glucose, which will be absorbed. Cellulose cannot be digested and simply serves to add bulk to the diet.

Carbohydrates check albuminous waste and, like fats, yield both heat and mechanical work; hence good bread, sugar, and potatoes are all economical foods for the laborer. Unlike other classes of foods, however, they do not produce brawn, and do not to any great extent, enter into the actual structure of the tissues although the carbohydrates may be found existing as glycogen in some of the tissues, like the muscles and liver. In general, they seem to be more easily metabolized than fats or proteins. *See also* DIET and FOOD COMPOSITION.

CARBONATED WATER. *See* AERATED WATER and ALKALINE AND MINERAL WATERS.

CARBONATED WINES. Wines, red or white, dry or sweet, that are made effervescent by the introduction of carbon dioxide gas under pressure. This process is cheaper than the natural method of making effervescent wines by inducing fermentation in the bottle or, as in the bulk process, in a closed vat, and it is reflected in the price. These wines are stored and served in the same manner as all other sparkling wines. *See* WINE.

CARBORUNDUM. A trade name for silicon carbide, i.e., sand and carbon united under conditions of heat and pressure to form stone-like blocks of a remarkably tough, effective abraisve. As contrasted to stone (*which see*), it may be used "dry" to sharpen knives, etc. *See also* CUTLERY and KITCHEN EQUIPMENT.

CARDAMON. This is a perennial herb which grows to about twelve feet in India and somewhat higher in Ceylon. Its yellowish capsular fruit encloses angular aromatic seeds having a strong spicy odor and resembling anise in taste. True cardamon seeds are the fruit of the *Elettaria cardamomum* plant, but the seeds of the *Amomum*

cardamomum are sometimes sold as cardamons. The preferred variety of the seeds is known as "shorts."

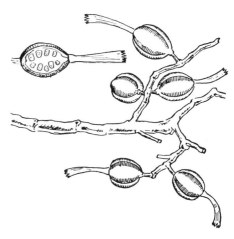

CARDAMOM SEED

The seeds are eaten whole or are used, whole or ground, as condiments, sometimes to replace cinnamon. They are chewed with betel nuts in the East; in this country they are sometimes chewed after drinking. They compliment coffee very nicely; a single seed will give new interest to a demitasse. They are used on Danish pastry and, ground, in grape jelly. A tincture of the oil derived from the seeds is used medicinally as a stimulant and as a carminative. The oil is sometimes used in colognes.

CARDINAL SAUCE. *See* WHITE SAUCE.

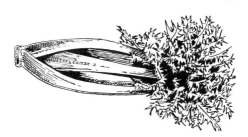

CARDOON

CARDOON. A close relative of the globe artichoke, the cardoon is cultivated for its roots and stalks. The main root is fleshy and tender, with a pleasant delicate flavor. It is best when boiled and served cold in a salad. The ribs of its large outside leaves are bleached and may be cooked and used as one would celery. The leaves are stripped from the midrib and any strings removed. Then the ribs are cut into short lengths and blanched in boiling salted water for 10 or 15 minutes. A few spoonfuls of vinegar added to the water will preserve the white color. Drain, and finish in any way suitable for celery.

Italian cooks prepare the parboiled cardoon by rolling the pieces in fine crumbs and sautéing them in olive oil. The dish is served with a thick well-seasoned tomato sauce.

CARIBOU. French name for reindeer, *which see.*

CARIGNANE. The name of a grape from which is made two types of wine; a dessert wine, notably in the Pyrénées Orientales in France, and a red table wine of the Claret type in California, both named after the grape. *See* GRAPE and WINE.

CARIOCA. A Cuban rum, next in favor to Bacardi. It is served as an after-dinner cordial, or as a long drink diluted with water, ginger ale, or carbonated water. It is also used in certain cocktails.

CAROB

CAROB. Also spelled caroub, and called Algarroba, locust bean, or St. John's bread. The sweet succulent pod of the carob tree which grows in Palestine and elsewhere along the Mediterranean. The entire fruit, excepting only its few small hard seeds, is edible, both fresh and dried. It is rich in sugar and fairly rich in protein. Its chief commercial value is as cattle food, but both the ground meal and a molasses-like sirup made from the pods are pleasing additions to the menu of humans.

Because of the sweet pulp, the dried pods are occasionally sold by peddlers and on the fruit stands as a cheap confection.

CAROID. Caroid is a vegetable digestive ferment made, like papoid, from the papaya or pawpaw, in the form of a dry yellowish powder. According to analysis, it retains a strong proteolytic action in acid, neutral, or alkaline medium. It softens and disintegrates proteides, coagulates milk like rennet, and is also amylolytic.

CAROTENE. A red, crystalline hydrocarbon found in yellow and green fruits and vegetables. It is the source of Vitamin A which is necessary to the normal growth and sight of animals. *See* VITAMIN.

CARP. The edible carp is a fresh water fish of the *Cyprinidae* family which is found in all parts of the world. It has a robust body, compressed, and covered with large scales. Its toothless mouth is rather small, with fleshy lips and four well developed barbels. In color the carp is dark olive, blending into brown on the upper part and shading off to a muddy light yellow on the ventral side.

Although the stories are not based on authenticated proof, several authors have told of carp which have lived for more than a hundred years. Certainly carps live long and may be domesticated, being easily tamed to feed out of the hand. In some countries, particularly in France, carp are raised in special ponds and may even be "caponized." These carp are fed almost exclusively on bread and have a particularly delicious flavor.

Individual carp may attain a weight of forty to fifty pounds, but the usual weight is much less, generally two to eight pounds. It lives in lakes and rivers, in sluggish water, where it feeds on vegetable matter. At the beginning of winter, the carp disappears into the mud, becomes torpid, and stops eating entirely until spring. So hardy is this fish that, when caught, it may be kept alive for days in wet moss, if properly fed, and consequently may be transported a good distance to market, arriving still alive.

Carp may be cooked by baking, boiling, frying, stewing, and is particularly good cooked in beer or wine. *See also* FISH.

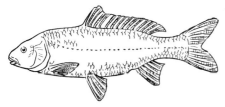

CARP

CARP COOKED IN BEER

1 medium-sized carp
1 medium-sized onion, sliced
2 or 3 carrots, sliced
2 bay leaves
Peel of 1 lemon, shredded
Juice of the lemon
1 tsp paprika
1 tsp cinnamon
2 tbsp gingersnap crumbs
2 tbsp vinegar
1 tbsp molasses
½ cup butter or margarine
Beer

Place the fish in a heavy saucepan or earthenware casserole. Brown the butter in a skillet. Add all the ingredients to the fish, using sufficient beer to cover the fish. Bring to a boil, and boil for 10 minutes. Then cover the pan and simmer for 15 minutes, until the fish is done. Transfer the fish to a hot platter and strain the sauce over it. Serve hot. (Serves 6)

CARP HUNGARIAN STYLE

1 large carp
Larding pork
3 medium-sized tomatoes
1 medium-sized onion
2 or 3 parsnips
1 cup sour cream
1 cup melted butter or margarine
1 tbsp paprika
Salt

Cut the salt pork into thin strips and with a larding needle (*see* LARDING) lard the back of the fish. Slice the tomatoes, onion, and parsnips thinly. Place the fish in a baking pan or ovenproof dish. Sprinkle

with salt and paprika, add the sliced vegetables, the melted butter, and the sour cream. Bake in a moderate oven (350° F.) until the carp is tender, basting frequently with the sour cream. (Serves 6 or 8)

CARP IN RED WINE

2 slices bacon
2 tbsp flour
1 tbsp butter
8 peppercorns
1 tbsp chopped parsley
1 tbsp chopped celery leaves
2 whole cloves
1 bay leaf
3 slices lemon
4 lb carp
Salt and pepper
2 cups hot water
1 cup fish stock
2 cups red wine
1 cup sliced fresh mushrooms

Cut the bacon in small pieces and brown in a large heavy kettle. Stir in the flour and butter and add the seasonings. Place the carp in the kettle and sprinkle with salt and pepper. Pour in the water and fish stock. Bring to a boil and then turn down the heat and simmer for 15 minutes. Stir in the wine and continue simmering until the flesh leaves the bones, about 1 hour. Carefully lift out the fish and place on a platter. Strain the sauce through fine cheesecloth into a saucepan and reheat to boiling. Sauté the mushrooms in a little butter and add to the sauce. Pour the sauce over the fish and garnish with lemon and parsley. Serve very hot. (Serves 6 or 8)

CARRÉ AFFINÉ CHEESE. Another name for Ancien Imperial cheese, *which see.*

CARROTS. A very ancient vegetable, our cultivated modern carrot was developed from the wild carrots of Europe and Asia. Carrots may be eaten raw or cooked, and are an excellent source of Vitamin A. Their yellow color is due to a substance called carotene.

HINTS ON PURCHASING

Carrots are marketed either as early or "new" carrots, or as late or winter carrots. The early carrots are usually sold in bunches with the greens on; the winter carrots have the tops removed. New carrots are gener-

	Wa-ter	Food Energy	Pro-tein	Fat	Car-bohy-drates	Cal-cium	Phos-phorus	Iron	Vit. A Value	Thia-mine	Riba-flavin	Nia-cin	Ascor-bic Acid
Carrots	88.2	45	1.2	.3	9.3	39	37	.8	12,000	.07	.06	.5	6
Canned Carrots	92.2	30	.5	.4	6.1	22	24	.6	12,000	.03	.02	.3	2

ally smaller and brighter in color than the later crop. With modern shipping facilities, the early carrots are found in city markets almost all year around, coming from the south during the winter.

Carrots should be firm and clean, well shaped and smooth. The greens should be fresh, but the carrot is not necessarily wilted if the tops have started to wither. Carrots which have split or grown in two tails are inclined to be woody and wasteful as well as poorly flavored.

Hints on Preparation

Carrots should be scraped as thinly as possible, never peeled. Very young new carrots need only to be scrubbed and may be cooked in their skins. Like most vegetables, carrots should be steamed in very little water, never boiled.

Carrot strips are a delicious addition to the raw vegetable plate. Cut in thin strips and chill in ice water to crisp them. Shredded raw carrots may be added to vegetable salads.

Tiny carrots may be cooked whole and rolled in chopped mint leaves for an attractive garnish with roast lamb. Carrots can be used in puddings and in pie in place of pumpkin or squash.

A particularly quick and delicious way to cook carrots is to shred them with a vegetable peeler and steam them for several minutes.

Baked Carrots

Use equal quantities of whole carrots, medium sized onions, and small potatoes. Peel the vegetables, but leave them whole. Place in a baking dish with enough melted margarine to half cover the vegetables. Sprinkle with salt and pepper. Bake for an hour in a moderate oven (350° F.), basting the vegetables frequently with the sauce. The potatoes will become crisp and the other vegetables will be delicious. This is an excellent vegetable to accompany roast beef or pot roast.

Carrot and Fig Conserve
(Creole Method)

1½ lb large firm carrots
1 large red beet
1½ cups seedless raisins
1 lb dried figs
1 large grapefruit
1 large lemon
2 large oranges
⅝ cups wine vinegar
2 cups water
3 lb sugar

Scrape and chop the carrots fine; peel and chop the beet fine; chop the raisins and figs fine. Shred or chop fine the rinds of the citrus fruits and combine all with the fruit juices, vinegar, water and sugar, in a large preserving kettle. Stir to blend thoroughly and let all stand together for three hours. Now stir again and cook gently, stirring constantly, until the mixture boils. Cook 40 minutes then turn into small sterilized jars and seal. (Makes about 10 pints)

Carrot Cookies

2 cups sifted flour
2 tsp baking powder
¼ tsp baking soda
¼ tsp salt
½ tsp cinnamon
½ tsp nutmeg
2 cups quick-cooking oatmeal
1 cup raisins
1 cup chopped nuts
½ cup shortening
1 cup grated raw carrots
1 cup honey
2 eggs well beaten

Mix and sift flour, baking powder, soda salt and spices; stir in oatmeal, raisins and nuts. Cream shortening; stir in carrots then honey and eggs; gradually stir in flour-nut mixture. Drop from teaspoon on greased baking sheet, flatten slightly and bake in moderate oven (350° F.) for 25 to 30 minutes. (Makes 3 dozen small cookies)

CARROT PUDDING

1 cup grated raw carrots
½ lb. fine dry bread crumbs
1 tsp nutmeg
2 tsp cinnamon
¼ tsp salt
¼ cup sherry
4 eggs
½ cup sugar
4 tbsp melted butter

Butter a large baking dish. Mix the grated carrots and crumbs with the seasonings and pour over the sherry. Beat the eggs until they are very light, and stir in the sugar, and melted butter. Pour over the carrot mixture, stirring thoroughly. Bake in a moderate oven (350° F.) about 45 minutes. Serve hot with any desired pudding sauce. (Serves 6)

CARROT TIMBALE

2 cups sliced carrots
1 egg plus 1 egg white
1 tbsp butter
Salt and pepper
Chicken broth
1 hard-cooked egg

Wash and scrape the carrots and slice thinly. Melt the butter in a saucepan, add the carrots, and steam for ten minutes, stirring to prevent burning. Add the chicken stock, enough to barely cover the carrots. Cook until the carrots are quite soft, then drain, and press through a sieve. Beat the whole egg and extra white together and stir into the mashed carrots. Season with salt and pepper to taste. Butter small timbale molds and lay a slice of hard cooked egg in the bottom of each. Fill each mold ⅔ full of the carrot mixture. Set in a pan of hot water, cover with greased paper, and bake in a moderate oven (350° F.) for 45 minutes. Turn out and serve with any desired sauce. (Serves 4)

CARROTS FLAMANDE

Wash and scrape 1 pound of carrots. Cut into half inch slices and braise in butter or margarine until tender. Place in a casserole and add 1 teaspoon sugar and a pinch of salt. Beat 3 egg yolks into ¼ cup sweet cream or rich milk, and stir in 1 tablespoon minced parsley. Pour over the carrots and heat thoroughly. Serve immediately. (Serves 6)

GLAZED CARROTS

Wash and scrape 12 new carrots. Place in a baking dish with 2 tablespoons of butter and ½ teaspoon salt. Pour over them 1 cup of canned apricot or other fruit juice. Cover. Bake in a moderate oven (375° F.) until tender, adding more liquid if necessary. Uncover the last 10 minutes to brown slightly. This makes a fine garnish for roasts.

CARVING. Carving at table is a social custom that grew up historically with the use of individual plates, knives, and forks. In the Middle Ages there were no forks—they came into being much later. Queen Elizabeth ate with her fingers—a touch of well bred conservatism which was preserved long after forks and spoons had come in for the common people. So the only carving that was really needed in medieval times was for such large fowls and joints as were too much for one portion. The roast was held by the carver by one corner and portions sliced off and presented to the guests on the flat of the knife. What his hand touched was thrown to the dogs.

Carving, like many other personal services, could not be done by a menial but only by a person of rank comparable to that of the guests. So, little wonder that for the English kings of the Middle Ages, carving was done by noblemen of high degree. Edward IV had four Carvers-in-Ordinary, with My Lord Willoughby as Carver-in-Chief. The royal retinue included also My Lord Buckingham, Cupbearer; Sir Richard Strangwicke, Chief Server; Sir Walter and eight other knights, together with eight other squires as Knights of the Hall, and extra servers.

An old book of the period called the "Boke of Nature," written by a man with the very modern name of John Doe, tells all about the "Kervyng of flesh" (carving of meat). You must lift a bird by the leg, detach a portion and poise it on the flat of the knife and pass it on; beef or roast meat was cut into a sort of endless strip.

What we think of as carving in the modern sense began when the Middle Ages gave way to the age of polite living. A great gulf separates us from the people who lived either in huge castles or in wattled huts—in "halls" without glass windows, or on floors that were bare earth covered with beaten rushes—and ate from a table that was called, and actually was, a "board."

Change that to the Jacobean and Georgian house with glass windows and snug dining rooms; add to that the delicacy of tea and coffee and the soft mist of tobacco smoke, and you will realize that the greatest revolutions are those least talked about in the history books. Such was the great kitchen revolution that took place over 200 years ago, a revolution which substituted individual plates and knives, forks, and napkins, for fingers grabbing in a dish.

Yet, oddly enough, until modern times, carving was a man's prerogative; women were not considered fit to be carvers.

The Art of Carving

Carving is considered an art, but its principles are easily learned. The novice will find a few general principles and an elementary knowledge of anatomy sufficient guidance. Practice in the kitchen before performance at the table will give the necessary confidence.

The fashion of carving at table is based on no mere tradition. Its purpose is to serve a dish piping hot in its most palatable form. The chief equipment needed is:
1. A platter (suitably hot or cold) large enough to hold not only the roast but the severed pieces as well.
2. Two sets of carving knife and fork. One set should have a sharp flexible knife eight or nine inches long and a two-pronged fork. This is for larger roasts. The second set should have a shorter, stiffer blade perhaps six inches long. This is used for smaller birds, steak, etc.

Poultry shears, a dressing spoon, a slicer, a knife rest, and a silver fish carver are useful accessories which may be added to the basic equipment.

The carver may sit or stand at his convenience. The usual procedure with roasts is to cut across the grain of the meat with swift sure strokes, not hacking or sawing in an untidy fashion.

Specific instructions are given below for most types of meat and poultry.

Beef

The heavy *Standing Rib Roast* is usually brought in standing upright on the platter. The carving fork should be pressed deep into the fleshy part of the joint, remaining there while thin slices are carved from the heavy end to the thinner.

The *Rolled Roast*, also placed on end on the platter is best left tied and skewered until, one by one, each string is cut and each skewer removed as the carver slices away the upper portions, cutting the meat crosswise from right to left.

A *Boneless Pot Roast* is sliced down vertically across the grain of the meat.

Steak, unlike most meats, is carved *with* rather than *against* the grain of the meat, since this cut is very tender. The strips so cut vary according to the thickness of the steak, but they are frequently an inch or more wide. Each guest is given a portion of the meat from both above and below the bone of the Porterhouse and the Club steak. Usually the meat is first cut free from the bone. The bone of a Sirloin steak is completely removed before the slicing begins. Individual steaks, such as Filet Mignon and the thin, small minute steaks, require no carving.

Tongue is carved in thin, crosswise slices. The tip and root may be reserved for use in sandwiches and also in omelets, scrambled eggs, and similar dishes.

Corned Beef, such as Brisket, should have the bones removed before serving and should then be sliced as usual across the grain.

Veal

Loin is often carved in vertical slices— with one rib to each portion, the rib bones having been severed from the back bone by the butcher.

Lamb

Leg of Lamb is placed before the carver with the heavier side farthest from him. With a left leg the bone which runs through it should be at the carver's right; with the right leg this bone should be at his left. Beginning either at the center or at the heavy end, the carver should slice the meat at right angles to the bone across the grain.

Crown Roast is the easiest possible roast to serve since the carver merely slices straight down between the ribs (which may be garnished with paper frills, according to taste). If a stuffing is used, a portion of the stuffing should be given with each serving.

CARVING LEG OF LAMB

Rib Roast of lamb may be carved like a loin of veal.

PORK

Roast *Loin* of pork may be served with or without the tenderl in. The butcher should remove the back bone, and the rib bones should be carefully cut apart before cooking. As to its position on the platter, opinions differ. Some say meat uppermost; others, the reverse. It is really immaterial, but the carver must cut down between each two ribs, allowing one to each serving. Sometimes, when thinner slices are desired one slice may be cut with a bone, the next without.

With *Ham* a bone runs through near the center; the broader side gives the best cuts. A small, thick slice is often taken almost at right angles to the bone, served with a little portion of fat. Or the carver may begin at the thick end of the ham and proceed to cut thin slices right on to the narrow end.

Smithfield Ham is so rich and tender that a very few thin slices give an ample serving. It is best to start at the back, letting the first cut be straight to the bone. A very sharp knife is needed.

FISH

On the whole, fish requires little carving. It is best to cut it with a silver server since other metal may affect the flavor. Care should be taken to preserve the large flakes if possible. The choicest portions are generally in the middle of a large fish. A planked fish should be cut through the center lengthwise. Small fish should be served individually without carving. A stuffed fish should have skewers and strings removed before serving. The cut being made from head to tail, the backbone is left on the platter.

Mackerel and *Bluefish*, split before cooking, are divided lengthwise, then subdivided into smaller portions.

Halibut is bought and served sliced, and is easy to cut lengthwise and crosswise to the small bone in the center.

Salmon, whether hot or cold, may be served whole. The head at the left is best, and slices should be cut starting at the central bones. Do not remove the skin; cut through it. Both the solid back flesh and the flakier portions belong in each portion.

Cod may be cut like salmon, but it breaks apart more easily.

POULTRY

Capon. A capon is carved somewhat like a turkey; that is, the legs should be separated from the body in a similar fashion,

CARVING HAM

and the dark meat of the second joint put aside to be served with the filets, which will be cut out of each side of the breast. One should be able to carve four or five filets from the breast on each side.

A simple trick in slicing the breast makes it easy to carve a fowl, be it a capon, chicken, turkey, or duck. Make deep cuts on the breast (about two inches apart) through the skin and flesh and down to the bone. Start the cuts at the ridge in the middle of the breast and go down the side at right angles to the ridge. Each of the sections of breast meat can then be lifted off and will have a layer of browned skin and rich fat on top.

CARVING TURKEY

Duck. Many a promising meal has gone to wreck because, when the duck is set before the head of the family, confusion is brought upon him by a shrill voice uttering these lines, ". . . We all of us prepare to rise when father carves the duck. . ." However, although the carving of a duck, goose, or pheasant is a little more complicated than that of a chicken, it is very easy after a little practice.

Place the duck on the platter with the tail to your left. Insert the fork between the right drumstick and thigh. Now run the point of a sharp knife around the leg, cutting the skin, using the fork to raise the leg toward yourself. Then place the knife underneath the leg and cut straight toward the tail, raising the leg with the point of the knife until you find the joint. Cut across the joint and remove the leg. Now insert the point of the fork in the bottom of the right wing, and carve from the top of the breast down to the wing joint, which you then easily sever with the point of the knife. Remove the left leg and wing in the

same fashion. If the duck is large enough, slice the breasts. If it is small, split it from tail to neck and then cut across it, providing four portions. Proceed without haste, but with speed.

Goose. Because the goose is more fatty, the carving is easier. After removing the legs as indicated for duck, the breast slices are made directly from the top of the breastbone downward to the end of the wing.

Turkey. Carve a turkey exactly as you would carve a capon. However, since the wings and legs of a turkey (drumsticks) are more fleshy, slices may be carved from them.

Chicken. Carve a chicken exactly as you would carve a capon.

Small wild birds. Small wild birds are carefully split in two lengthwise from the breastbone downward. Then the legs and second joints are removed.

CARVING AID. A carving aid consists of a pair of stainless steel or plated metal prongs set in a handle. It is used to impale fowl and irregularly shaped meats to hold them steady for ease in carving. *See also* CARVING and CUTLERY.

CARVING KNIFE. *See* CUTLERY and CARVING.

CASABA MELON

CASABA MELON. A late variety of melon, which is usually ripened off the vine. It is large, almost globular, but may be somewhat pointed at the stem end. The rind is lightly ribbed and is somewhat wrinkled or furrowed lengthwise. Casaba melons of good quality have a soft, creamy white, sweet, and juicy flesh, without aroma. Only in a ripe melon can such quality be found.

Ripeness is usually indicated by a rind of yellow color and a softening at the blossom end. Immaturity is indicated by firmness and the whitish-green color of rind. The flesh of such melons is hard and often practically tasteless. Decay usually is in the form of dark, sunken, water-soaked patches that may be covered with a mold. The flesh of a melon affected by decay is not harmed if decay has not penetrated the rind. *See also* MELON.

CASEIN. The principal protein of milk, *which see.*

CASHEW NUT. A recent comer among nuts in the United States, the cashew nut, is now second in popularity to the peanut. As recently as 1923, only 100,000 pounds of these nuts were imported into the United States. Fifteen years later the story was very different; shipments for the year 1938 were more than 25,000,000 pounds. The natives of India and Haiti use the juice of the cashew nut for healing cuts and abrasions of the skin, besides eating it as a nut.

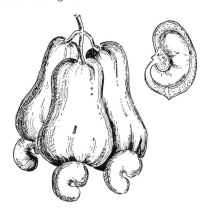

CASHEW NUT

To bring the cashews from India and still retain their tree-fresh taste was once thought to be impossible. Attempts at shipping cashew nuts usually ended in half or more of the shipment being flavorless and unfit for eating after the long voyage. But then came the cashews which were shipped in airtight tins. Now the cashew nuts on the market are packed by this special patented process and are always clean, tree-fresh, and full flavored.

The nut, either pickled or roasted, acquires a delicate flavor only after it is heated to a high temperature to drive off a considerable quantity of prussic acid which it naturally contains. This, however, is completely gone before the nut is released for commerce or offered as food.

The cashew does not grow in a shell at all, but instead is found hanging from an apple-like fruit on a kind of evergreen tree. The "apple" contains a milky juice which when fermented makes a delicious wine, and the wine distills to a spirit very much like rum.

Cashew nuts are used salted or in candy. They are not too satisfactory in baking because of their tendency to soften. A pound of cashews will yield four cups. *See also* NUTS.

CASING. The covering skin of sausage.

CASSAVA. *See* TAPIOCA.

CASSEROLE

CASSEROLE. A kitchen utensil, usually a shallow double-handled dish with a tightly fitting cover, which may be made of earthenware, glass, or metal. Also, the dish cooked in such a utensil.

Methods of cookery have much to do with results of the final dish. This is especially true when cooking meats, which fall broadly into two classes of prime and tougher cuts. How to make tougher cuts as tender and flavorful as choicer, more expensive prime cuts, is a problem for every homemaker. Good seasoning is one answer, and casserole cooking is another.

The casserole as a cooking utensil has an age-old history, and takes its historic place alongside other primitive pottery cooking vessels. Originally fashioned of clay or brick pottery, the earthenware casserole is still decidedly worthwhile as a cooking unit. It may be small or large, squat or high, but it isn't a casserole if it hasn't a cover. Only when there is a closely fitting cover, to prevent escape of food flavors, may the utensil be called a "casserole."

Those who advocate casserole cookery, point to the French, respected the world over for the excellence of their food, who through the ages have used casseroles, or pots and pans slow to heat and long to retain heat. It is to French pottery, finished within with a salt glaze; to the more costly copper, lined with block tin; to the cast-iron cocotte, the forerunner of the useful Dutch oven, that we owe such pleasures as the *made* French casserole dishes, or a potted duck. Snugly covered in one of these utensils, which may be put into the oven or used on top of the stove, food cooks with the minimum of labor to a home-maker, plus the maximum of flavor. She doesn't have to watch things while they are cooking either.

The casserole is brought to the table and the food served directly from it.

In contrast to the classic French casserole cookery, in which raw foods are cooked slowly inside a tightly lidded pot, the common or American-style casserole employs pre-cooked foods which are reheated together in an open baker or casserole dish. The American-style casserole, a noted budget and meal saver, provides the cook with an opportunity to utilize leftovers in an imaginative fashion.

Since most of the foods used in a casserole are pre-cooked or quick cooking, the actual cooking time of the dish should be kept short in order to insure the fullest flavor and nutritive value. Pre-cooked meats retain much of their natural juices which can be extracted if the meat is reheated at too high a temperature or for too long a time. The meat becomes shrivelled and the gravy, consequently, becomes thin.

Cooking temperatures should, therefore, not be allowed to rise above the simmering point. The casserole must be cooked uncovered to prevent sogginess. A gratinée crust is usually employed to protect the food, absorb excess grease and give the dish body. Casseroles may be cooked in a heat resistant utensil on top of the stove and then returned to the broiler to crisp the gratinée topping or they may be cooked from beginning to end in an uncovered casserole dish in the oven.

INGREDIENTS

While casserole ingredients vary with whatever is at hand, the dish itself usually combines two or three types of foods: pasta or rice, a mixture of vegetables and meats and a sauce. Often the pasta is omitted in favor of increased portions of meats and vegetables. The sauce may be cream, medium white, tomato, vinegar or brown gravy.

Cooked, frozen or diced fresh vegetables are used. If canned vegetables are used, they should be drained and added as near to the end of the cooking time as possible. Reserve the drained juices for making sauces or soups. In general, pre-cooked or canned meats, sausages, poultry and fish are used in a casserole, but fresh meats may be used if they are quick cooking.

Select seasoning appropriate to the various meats and vegetables: basil for lamb; thyme, savory and marjoram for chicken and veal; dill, caraway and basil for pork and fish; oregano for tomato sauce; coriander and cumin for gravies and white sauce. Use herbs and spices liberally.

BASIC RECIPE

A basic casserole recipe calls for about 2 cups of sauce, 1½ cups of meats and vegetables and 1 cup of pasta or rice. Proportions vary with different ingredients but in general the casserole should contain enough sauce to cover the other ingredients but not so much sauce that the dish becomes soggy.

Prepare the sauce in a large saucepan or heat resistant casserole and season. Add the frozen and fresh vegetables and cook until almost tender (about 5 minutes). Correct the seasoning. Stir in meats, canned or pre-cooked vegetables, rice or pasta. Turn the mixture into a casserole. Wipe the outside of the casserole before placing it in the oven so that no spilt-over burned food will be apparent when the dish is baked. Top with a mixture of buttered bread crumbs, crumbled Cheddar and paprika. Bake 15 to 20 minutes. Serve.

Substitute ingredients on hand for those listed in the basic recipe. Also see the index for listings of casserole recipes.

CHICKEN IN TOMATO SAUCE

Prepare a tomato sauce or use canned sauce or condensed tomato soup. Cut up onions, green pepper and carrots and add to sauce. Season with garlic, bay leaf, oregano, and pepper and cook until the vegetables are nearly tender. Stir in pre-cooked white or brown rice and shredded pre-cooked chicken. Turn the mixture into a casserole; top with buttered bread crumbs and grated Parmesan cheese. Bake for 15 to 20 minutes and serve.

Eggs in White Sauce

Sautée chopped onions in 4 tablespoons of butter or margarine. When the onions are golden, prepare a medium white sauce (which see) with the drippings and season with cumin, pepper, salt, coriander, tumeric and ginger. In a casserole arrange layers of pre-cooked brown rice, canned or cooked asparagus and okra and 4 to 6 hard boiled eggs cut in halves. Put a bunch of chopped fresh parsley into the sauce and pour over the ingredients in the casserole. Top with buttered whole wheat bread crumbs and crumbled cheese. Bake 15 to 20 minutes.

Ham and String Beans

Alternate layers of pre-cooked or parboiled medium noodles with layers of cooked ham strips and cut, fresh string beans. Cover with a cheese sauce (which see) flavored with celery tops and a pinch of sage. Top with buttered bread crumbs and bake uncovered for about 20 minutes.

Mushrooms and Corn

Prepare an onion sauce (which see) or use condensed cream of onion soup. Season with pepper, paprika and garlic and dry mustard. Add fresh or drained canned mushrooms, canned or frozen corn, chopped canned pimentos, cut fresh parsley and frozen peas. Cook slowly and add pre-cooked rice. Turn the mixture into a casserole and top with cracker crumbs and crumbled cheese. Bake.

CASSEROLE, ELECTRIC. An electrical appliance for one-dish meals, for baking potatoes, or warming food. It generally has a high and low heat control.

CASSIA. See Cinnamon.

CASSIS. The French name for black currants and a cordial made from black currants, brandy, and sugar. The cordial is served in a number of ways: alone, as a digestive liqueur; as a main ingredient in a number of different drinks; or as a sweet-

ening or flavoring agent in a number of others. See also Cordial, Currants, and Liqueur.

The name is also given to certain French wines, red, white and rose, that come from vineyards located a few miles southeast of Marseilles. Of these, the White Cassis is generally acknowledged as superior. See also Wine.

CASTELLO BRANCO CHEESE. A cheese similar to Serra da Estrella, which see.

CATAWBA WINE. Wine made from the Catawba grape, a native American species, widely cultivated in the middle and eastern states. The wine is generally amber in color, full-bodied, and rich in flavor. See also Grape and Wine.

CATFISH. The catfish, a small, fine fish of handsome appearance, is found in market from February to May and again in October and November. Catfish weigh from a quarter to three-quarters of a pound each, and have large, flat heads, a smooth, slimy, brown skin, with no scales at all on the back, and a whitish belly. The smaller the fish the better it is. It should be skinned before cooking.

A certain catfish of the genus arius is called "Easter" or "Holy Cross" fish because the shape of its skull and back show a distinct resemblance to Christ on the Cross. Each side of the body bears a faint figure of a kneeling person. These fish are edible and delicious, and run in exceptionally large schools during the Lenten season along the shores of South and Central America. Devoutly religious people abstain from eating them before Easter. The natives ingeniously prepare them and sell them as curiosities to visitors.

In the early 18th century, catfish and waffle suppers were as popular along the Schuylkill River near Philadelphia as hot dog roasts are today.

The various methods of preparation for small perch, and smelts may be adapted to this fine fish. See also Fish.

CATSUP or **KETCHUP.** A sauce used the world over, of which there are several varieties, such as cranberry catsup, cucumber catsup, grape catsup, tomato catsup, etc., usually served with either hot or cold cuts.

"Catsup," "catchup," and "ketchup" are derivations of the name of an East Indian pickle, formerly applied specifically to the boiled juice from salted mushrooms but now freely applied to various sauces consisting of the pulp—boiled, strained, and seasoned—of such fruits as indicated above, or vegetables, and even walnuts. It is not a relish, nor a pickle, but a sauce, which, besides being served with cold cuts, may be used also to add piquancy to made sauces, stews, etc. Most recipes for tomato catsup call for tomatoes (with or without onions), spices, vinegar, and sugar cooked together; a few recipes include green peppers. Since spices tend to darken the tomato color, home cooks put the whole or ground spices in a bag and suspend it in the kettle during the cooking period. When done, discard the spice bag, pour the sauce into small, sterilized jars or bottles, and seal. When cold, store in a cool dry place.

Mushroom Catsup

1 lb black mushrooms, *or* 3 oz dried Italian mushrooms
Rind of ½ lemon, washed in cold water
2 whole cloves
10 kernels peppercorns
1½ tsp salt
¼ tsp mace
1 lb beef (lean top roundsteak)
1 can French truffles (medium size)
2 cups water

Grind the beef, and boil it in two cups of water. Of this take one cup of bouillon to be used in the recipe.

The mushroom should be the wild variety, which can often be procured from the sidewalk stands maintained by Italians. (They are entirely different in flavor from the white cellar variety.) If these cannot be had, soak the dried Italian mushrooms in a little warm water for an hour. The wild mushrooms should be washed and rinsed in cold water. Break off the stems. Peel and discard the skins from the caps. Chop the stems and caps very fine. Put them in a saucepan in three cups of cold water, and let them simmer until the juice has been reduced one half. Add the salt, mace, and juice of the truffles. If you do not have a French pepper mill, place the mushrooms and cloves in a clean piece of cloth and crush them well with a hammer or a mallet. Mix these into the pan. Cut the lemon peel (no juice or pulp included) in strips the width of a match and add them. Add another cup of water to the

pan, and let it simmer until the liquid equals that of the fibrous contents. Then put in the beef stock, bring to the boiling point, and let stand for three hours.

Now with a large spoon, or still better a wooden potato masher, crush the mass until it assumes the consistency of a purée. Return it to the fire, and add the whole truffles. Let it simmer one hour. Remove the truffles. Strain the catsup by squeezing the juice well through a double cheesecloth first dipped into cold water then wrung almost dry. Chop the truffles as fine as possible. Add the chopped truffles to the catsup, and pour into hot, sterilized, small bottles or jars and seal. When cold store in a cool dry place. *See also* CANNING. (Makes 1 pint)

Grape Catsup

10 lb grapes
5 lb granulated sugar
1 tbsp salt
1 tbsp freshly ground pepper
2 tbsp ground cinnamon
1 tbsp ground cloves
1 tbsp ground allspice
1 qt vinegar

Pick over and wash the grapes, then crush in a large saucepan and cook without water until the juice flows freely. Press through cheesecloth or sieve to keep back skins and seeds. Combine pulp with all remaining ingredients, and simmer very slowly until of the desired consistency. Turn into sterilized jars and seal. Especially fine with fish, either cold or hot. *See also* CANNING.

Tomato Catsup

2½ qt sliced tomatoes (15 to 17 medium-sized)
¾ cup chopped onion
3-inch piece of stick cinnamon
1 tsp whole cloves
1 large garlic clove, chopped
1 cup vinegar
½ cup sugar
1¼ tsp salt
1 tsp paprika
Dash of cayenne pepper

Simmer the tomatoes and onions together for 20 or 30 minutes and press through a sieve. Tie the cinnamon, cloves and garlic into a thin clean white cloth. Add the spices to the vinegar and simmer for 30 minutes. Remove the spice bag. Bring the tomato puree to a boil and boil rapidly until it is reduced by half. Stir frequently to prevent sticking. Add the spiced vinegar, sugar, salt, paprika, and cayenne pepper to the tomato mixture. Boil rapidly, stirring constantly, about 10 minutes, or until slightly thickened. Pour into hot sterile jars, filling to the top, and seal. *See also* CANNING. (Makes 2 pints)

CATTY. The Chinese weight which, in the United States, is associated especially with tea. It is equal to 1⅓ pounds avoirdupois. *See also* KATI and CADDY.

CAUDLE. Hot, spiced mixtures that were popular in England during the 10th century for medicinal use. Chiefly used as a cold cure or preventative, they were also frequently given to women in childbed. While the majority used a red wine as a base, others used ale, some tea and spirits, and many were made devoid of any intoxicant or stimulant.

While there are a great many Caudle recipes, the following will serve as typical examples. *See also* MULLED WINE.

TEA CAUDLE

1 cup green tea (strong)
1 egg yolk
2 large jiggers white wine
Grated nutmeg
Powdered sugar

The tea is freshly made and placed in a saucepan over a slow fire. The egg yolk is thoroughly beaten and then mixed with the wine and with the nutmeg and sugar to taste, then the mixture is added to the saucepan, stirred well, and served while hot.

WHITE CAUDLE

1 tbsp powdered oatmeal
1 pint water
Sugar
Lemon juice
Nutmeg

The oatmeal is mixed with the water and let stand at least two hours before use. The mixture is then strained through a sieve, boiled, the other ingredients added to taste, and served while hot.

CAUL. A membrane covering the lower part of the intestines. It is used as a casing in sausage making. Pork caul is the one most preferred, lamb caul ranks second, while that of veal is the least desirable.

CAULIFLOWER. When properly cooked, cauliflower is one of the most delicious members of the cabbage family. Like broccoli, it is cultivated for its flowers, which form the compact white head which we call the cauliflower.

CAULIFLOWER

The long leaves which surround the "curd" or edible white portion while it is growing are usually cut down to an inch or so of the curd, and only enough leaves left on to be a protection in shipping. Large or small cauliflowers are equally good; size has no relation to age.

Prime cauliflower is solid and creamy white in color, with the outer leaves fresh and green. Spotting on the curd indicates the cauliflower is not so fresh as it might be. If the area affected is small, it may be cut away without too much waste. "Riciness" is the term used to describe the granular appearance when the flowerets have begun to grow. It is not objectionable unless it has progressed too far.

Cauliflower is also marketed quick-frozen. In this form, it can be cooked and used like the fresh vegetable.

HINTS ON PREPARATION

Cauliflower may be cooked whole, or broken into flowerets. Unless the head is very young, the stems should be thinly peeled up to the flower and any leaves removed. If the head is to be left whole, it is wise to soak it in lukewarm salted water for fifteen or twenty minutes to drive out any

FOOD VALUE

Water	Food Energy	Pro- tein	Fat	Carbo- hydrate	Cal- cium	Phos- phorus	Iron	Vit. A Value	Thia- mine	Ribo- flavin	Nia- cin	Ascor- bic Acid
91.7	31	2.4	.2	4.9	22	72	1.1	90	.10	.11	.6	69

insects which may be hidden within the head.

Cauliflower may be served raw in salads or with a raw vegetable tray for canapés.

Cauliflower is best when cooked closely covered in a small amount of water. A little lemon juice or sugar added to the water will keep the cauliflower white. It should be cooked until it is just tender; avoid overcooking which will make it mushy. Cooked in this way, cauliflower needs only salt and pepper and a little melted butter to be delicious. A whole cauliflower served with a golden cheese sauce poured over it is as attractive as it is good. There are innumerable ways to prepare this excellent vegetable.

BAKED CAULIFLOWER WITH CHEESE AND TOMATOES

Steam a head of cauliflower, leaving it whole. Drain it well. Place in a baking dish, head up. Pour over it 2 cups stewed tomatoes to which has been added 1 grated onion. Sprinkle over all a small cup of bread crumbs which have been mixed with ½ cup grated American cheese. Bake in a moderate oven (375° F.) until the crumbs are golden brown and the sauce bubbles. Serve immediately.

CAULIFLOWER FRITTERS

Steam and drain the cauliflower. Break up into small sprigs and season with salt, pepper, a little vinegar, and a sprinkling of chopped parsley and chives. Let stand for fifteen or twenty minutes. Drain away any liquid. Dip the pieces in batter and drop into deep hot fat. Fry until golden brown. Serve very hot.

CAULIFLOWER MOLD

1 medium-sized cauliflower
5 cups boiling water
3 tsp lemon juice
4 eggs, separated
Salt and nutmeg
2 tbsp melted butter

Break the cauliflower into flowerets and cook in the boiling salted water to which the lemon juice has been added. Cook uncovered for 15 minutes. Drain well and put the cauliflower through a ricer into a mixing bowl. Beat the yolks of the eggs until light and add to the cauliflower, beating well. Beat the egg whites stiffly with a few grains of salt and nutmeg and fold into the cauliflower mixture. Carefully stir in the butter. Butter a ring mold and carefully turn the mixture into the mold. Bake in a hot oven (400° F.) for 20 or 25 minutes, until the soufflé is well puffed and delicately browned. A knife inserted in the middle should come out dry. Unmold on a hot dish. (Serves 6)

CAULIFLOWER PICKLES

1 firm, white cauliflower
5 to 6 cups boiling water
2½ cups white vinegar
½ cup sugar
1 inch stick cinnamon
6 whole cloves
½ tsp salt
6 peppercorns

Discard all leaves and leaf stalk of the cauliflower, separate it into small flowerets, wash thoroughly and drain, then plunge into the boiling water to which a tablespoon of the vinegar has been added. Cook only 5 minutes (not long enough to soften the cauliflower). Drain thoroughly and pack in sterilized jars.

Meanwhile boil together for 10 minutes the vinegar, sugar, spices and seasonings, strain these over the cauliflower in the jars, having the pickle liquid come at least 1 inch over the cauliflower itself. Seal and let stand at least 2 days before using. A few pimiento rings may be scalded with the cauliflower and added when placing it in the jars. *See also* CANNING. (Makes 2 pints)

CAULIFLOWER PIEMONTESE

Cook a whole cauliflower and when done, serve with the following sauce. Chop

1 small onion and 2 anchovies very small. Cook in a little butter or margarine, and add ½ cup chicken stock, and a few drops of vinegar. Finish with 1 teaspoon chopped sweet herbs, and let simmer for a few minutes. Place the cauliflower in a serving dish and pour the sauce over it.

CAULIFLOWER POLONAISE

Cook the cauliflower, leaving the head whole. Melt 4 tablespoons butter or margarine and let brown. Stir in 2 hard-cooked eggs which have been finely chopped and 1 cup of fine bread crumbs. Mix well and pour over the cauliflower. Serve at once.

CAULIFLOWER SOUP

1 medium-sized cauliflower
2 tbsp butter or margarine
1 small onion, minced
2 tbsp flour
4 cups chicken stock
2 cups milk, scalded
Salt, pepper, and nutmeg

Steam the cauliflower until it is tender. Cut it in half. Press one half through a sieve and keep the other half warm. In a saucepan melt the butter and cook the onion until it is transparent, but not brown. Carefully stir in the flour and cook until it bubbles, stirring constantly. Add the chicken stock, stirring constantly. Mix the scalded milk with the sieved cauliflower, and stir it into the stock. Season with salt and pepper and a dash of nutmeg. Let boil up until it thickens slightly, stirring to prevent lumps. Break the half cauliflower into small flowerets and add to the soup. Heat thoroughly and serve immediately with croutons. (Serves 6 or 8)

CAVIAR. Caviar, in the strictest sense of the word, is the prepared roe of various species of sturgeon. But in recent years, the roe of various other fish has also been used to make caviar, because the supply of sturgeon roe has diminished to the point where it is entirely inadequate to meet the demand. These fish include: Spoon-bill, cat or paddlefish, salmon, whitefish, lake herring, carp, and codfish.

Only a comparatively few years ago the sturgeon was a very common fish in American waters. When caviar and smoked sturgeon became popular, the price of both

these products rose rapidly, and fishermen found that sturgeon fishing was a very profitable occupation. As a result, the waters were overfished, and now the sturgeon has been nearly exterminated. Because of the scarcity of this fish, little caviar is prepared in the United States. In practically all cases, the fisherman who catches the female sturgeon prepares the caviar and either sells it to a local buyer or to one of the nearby wholesale markets.

The American process of preparing caviar is as follows: The sturgeon roe, immediately after its removal from the fish, is placed on a four-mesh sieve over a large mixing tube. The roe is rubbed back and forth on the sieve until the eggs pass through, leaving the membranes and connective tissue in the sieve. About a pound of Lunenburg salt or a half-pound of American dairy salt is sifted on to each 12 pounds of eggs. (Lunenburg salt is a German salt having a flavor particularly desirable in caviar.) Immediately after the addition of the salt, the mass is thoroughly mixed. At first it is sticky, but enough water is soon abstracted from the sturgeon eggs to dissolve the salt and form a brine. The mixing is continued for eight to ten minutes after which the mixture is allowed to stand 10 minutes or longer.

The eggs are then poured into sieves which hold eight to ten pounds of caviar and are allowed to drain for about an hour. The caviar is then poured into kegs and shipped to the canning factory where it is placed in cans or jars which are then sealed and pasteurized.

The methods used in Russia are much the same as those employed in America except that comparatively little is canned and much is prepared for export by pressing. Pressed caviar contains less water.

Genuine fresh caviar, made from sturgeon's roe, has large transparent grains of clear and brilliant color. It is considered a great delicacy and usually served as an appetizer on small crackers or bits of toast, with a simple garnish of sieved hard-cooked egg or onion juice. Perfectionists among gourmets insist that onion spoils the true flavor of the caviar.

Red caviar is made from the roe of the salmon.

CAVIAR BUTTER. *See* BUTTER SAUCES.
CAVY. *See* GUINEA PIG.
CAYENNE PEPPER. Cayenne pepper is a very hot, biting condiment that is

ground from the fruits or seeds of several varieties of Capsicum (*which see*). Like paprika, it is a red powdery spice, but its color is not so bright as that of paprika. It should be used often but, because of its pungency, it should be used sparingly. It can accentuate delightfully the flavors of meat dishes, sea foods, soufflés, salads, sauces, and eggs.

CELERIAC. *See* CELERY KNOB.

CELERY

CELERY. The ancient Chinese credited celery with medicinal qualities and used it as a blood purifier. It was known in 16th-century Italy as an article of food, and spread from there to England and France, and eventually to America. In Chinese cookery celery is used as an ingredient to give crispness to their dishes.

Celery is ordinarily marketed as the whole stalk which contains the outer branches and leaves. Sometimes the outer branches are removed and the hearts are sold in bunches. Formerly celery was not tender until it had been bleached, which gave the familiar white stalks and pale hearts with yellow leaves. Recently a new type of celery, known as pascal celery, is being grown for market. It needs no bleaching to be tender. It has an attractive light green color and is almost stringless, with a sweet flavor. Because it has not been bleached, it probably contains vitamins which are absent in the bleached plants.

Celery should be of medium length and thickness, with the branches brittle enough to snap easily. The leaves should be fresh looking. Limp branches and wilted or yellowed leaves indicate the celery has been kept too long.

The outer branches and leaves should not be discarded. They can be used in soup, for flavor in pot roasts, etc. The leaves, chopped finely, can be added to many dishes, and make a good substitute for celery seed in recipes calling for this seasoning.

HINTS ON PREPARATION

Celery should be thoroughly washed to remove any dirt which may lodge in the branches. If it is inclined to be stringy, the strings should be removed by pulling them down the length of the stalk.

The tender hearts of celery may be served as is, crisped by placing them in ice water in the refrigerator.

Celery curls make an attractive garnish. They are easily made by cutting tender celery into three- or four-inch length. Slit the pieces into narrow lengthwise slices, leaving a half inch base. Drop the pieces into ice water and place in the refrigerator for several hours. The narrow slices will curl back around the base. Celery stuffed with cheese, either roquefort-type, or any other easily spread tangy cheese, makes a favorite hors d'oeuvre.

For a special occasion, make celery pinwheels. Select tender stalks of even size. Mix roquefort-type cheese with cream cheese until it is soft and spreads easily. Or use the roquefort cheese spread which comes in jars. Fill the hollows of the stalks

FOOD VALUE

	Food Energy	Pro-tein	Fat	Carbo-hydrate	Cal-cium	Phos-phorus	Iron	Vit. A Value	Thia-mine	Ribo-flavin	Nia-cin	Ascor-bic Acid
Water												
93.7	22	1.3	.2	3.7	50	40	.5	0	.03	.04	.3	7

with the cheese and put the stalks together in three's, making a roll. Press firmly together, wrap in wax paper, and chill in the refrigerator for several hours. When ready to serve, slice the celery into quarter-inch slices with a very sharp knife. Each slice will resemble a pinwheel, with the cheese holding the whorls together.

Cooked celery makes a fine vegetable. Sliced and cooked in boiling salted water, it will be tender in ten minutes. It may be served with butter, or with a cream or cheese sauce. Celery braised in a little bouillon is also delicious.

BAKED CELERY AU GRATIN

2 stalks of celery
1½ cups cream sauce
½ cup grated cheese
Buttered crumbs
Salt and pepper

Wash the celery thoroughly, trim off the leaves, and cut the stems into convenient lengths. Cook in boiling salted water until just tender, and drain well. Grease a baking dish. Make layers of celery, cream sauce, and grated cheese, adding salt and pepper to taste. Finish up with a layer of cheese. Cover the top with a thick layer of buttered crumbs, and bake in a hot oven (425° F.) until the top is brown and the sauce bubbles. (Serves 6)

BRAISED CELERY

Wash the celery thoroughly, remove the leaves, and cut into convenient pieces. Place in a baking dish with enough meat stock just to cover. Season with salt and pepper. Cover the dish and bake in a hot oven (400° F.) for 25 minutes, or until the celery is tender. Serve very hot from the dish in which it was baked.

CELERY-CHEESE BALLS

1 cup finely chopped celery
1 package (3 oz) cream cheese
Salt and pepper
2 tbsp finely chopped parsley
Paprika

Mix the celery and cheese, and add salt and pepper. Shape the mass into 12 small balls. Roll these in parsley and dust them with paprika.

CELERY REMOULADE

Cut tender bleached stalks of celery into julienne strips. Marinate for an hour in French dressing. Drain, pressing slightly to remove any excess liquid. Mix with remoulade dressing (*which see*). Serve as individual portions in crisp lettuce leaves. Sprinkle chopped parsley and chopped chives over the top. An excellent accompaniment for fish.

CELERY STUFFING
(For Chicken, Pork, Veal)

3½ cups soft bread crumbs
½ tsp salt
¼ tsp sage
⅛ tsp thyme
Dash of marjoram
¼ tsp pepper
4 tbsp melted butter
⅔ cup hot milk
¾ cup celery, finely cut

Combine the crumbs and seasonings, add the butter, and toss with a fork, then add the milk and celery, mixing all lightly. *See* STUFFING.

CREAM OF CELERY SOUP

1 medium-size onion, minced
1½ cups diced celery and leaves
1 bouquet garni
1 tbsp butter
1 tbsp flour
2 cups milk
Salt, pepper, nutmeg
1 egg yolk
2 cups cream or undiluted evaporated milk

Boil the onion, celery and bouquet garni in salted water to cover for 30 minutes, or until the celery is tender. Scald the 2 cups of milk. Melt the butter and stir in the flour, cooking until it bubbles. Carefully pour in the scalded milk, stirring so it does not lump. Add to the celery mixture and cook for 10 minutes. Strain through a sieve into the top of a double boiler, mashing the celery to a puree. Place over boiling water, season with salt, pepper, and nutmeg. Scald the cream or evaporated milk, stir into it the egg yolk, well beaten, and add to the celery mixture. Heat to the boiling point, but do not let boil. Serve garnished with croutons. If desired, a part of the cooked celery may be reserved as pieces and added to the soup just before serving. (Serves 4 or 5)

CURRIED CELERY FRITTERS

1 cup flour
1 tsp baking powder
½ tsp salt
2 tsp curry powder
1 egg
¾ cup milk
1½ cups chopped raw celery

Sift the flour, baking powder, salt, and curry powder into a mixing bowl. Beat the egg thoroughly and beat in the milk. Add to the flour mixture all at once, and stir to make a smooth batter. Add the chopped celery and stir well. Drop by spoonfuls into deep hot fat and fry until golden brown. Serve hot. Other vegetables may be substituted for the celery.

STUFFED CELERY

Use only crisp, tender, white stalks of celery, and wash these in running water. Leaves may be disposed of or left on the stalks. Cut each stalk into 2 to 4 pieces, depending upon its size. If you choose, you may curl the ends by making short, narrow, parallel cuts in them, and then chill ng the celery in ice water. Dry, fill the grooves with one of the following mixtures, and chill thoroughly before serving.

Cream-cheese filling. Mix ½ package of cream cheese, 2 tablespoons of mayonnaise, 4 chopped stuffed olives, 2 tablespoons of minced nuts, and salt to taste.

Blended-cheese filling. Mix 1 package (3 ounces) of cream cheese, 1 tablespoon of Roquefort cheese, 1 tablespoon of butter, and salt to taste. Sprinkle with paprika.

Egg filling. Mix 1 finely-chopped hard-cooked egg, 2 tablespoons of mayonnaise, and salt and pepper to taste. Dust with paprika or minced parsley.

CELERY CABBAGE. Another name for Chinese cabbage, *which see.*

CELERY DISH. A dish or small platter designed to hold and serve celery at the table. *See* DISHES.

CELERY KNOB or **CELERIAC.** A good inexpensive winter vegetable that is not very common is celery knob, a member of the celery family that is cultivated for its turnip-like stem base. Its flavor is like celery.

The smaller size knobs are best; larger ones are likely to be hollow or woody. It may be served raw or cooked. Celeriac is one of the few vegetables that must be peeled before cooking. The skin is very tough and stringy.

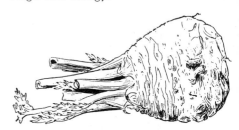

CELERY KNOB

Raw celery knob may be peeled and cut into julienne strips. Marinate the strips in French dressing for an hour, then drain, squeezing slightly to remove any excess liquid. Mix with mayonnaise and serve well chilled on crisp lettuce leaves. Drained crushed pineapple may be mixed with the celeriac.

Peeled and diced, celery knob may be cooked in boiling salted water and will be tender in ten minutes or so. A little vinegar or lemon juice added to the water will keep the celeriac white. The cooked celery knob can be served with butter or cream or hollandaise sauce, or it may be mashed. Like celery, it may be braised in meat stock.

CELERY KNOB BOURGEOISE

2 celery knobs
2 cups meat stock
4 tbsp butter or margarine
3 tbsp minced onion
2 tbsp minced green pepper
Salt and pepper
2 tbsp minced parsley
1 tbsp minced chives

Wash and peel the celery knob. Cut in small slices and simmer until tender in the meat stock. Drain and keep warm. In a saucepan, melt the butter and stir in the onion and green pepper. Cook, stirring constantly, until the onion and pepper soften. Add the celery knob and mix carefully so as not to break the pieces. Reheat, and when ready to serve, season with salt and pepper and add the parsley and chives. (Serves 4)

CELERY KNOB SAUTE

Wash and peel the celery knob and cut into quarter-inch slices. In a heavy pan having a tight-fitting cover melt some butter, margarine, or chicken fat. Add the slices of celery knob and cook covered over a very low flame, shaking every now and then to prevent sticking. When the slices are tender and delicately brown, season with salt and pepper and serve immediately. A particularly delicious way of cooking this vegetable.

MASHED CELERY KNOB

Wash and peel 2 celery knobs. Cut in small pieces and cook in boiling salted water to which is added 1 teaspoon of vinegar or lemon juice. When the pieces are very tender (about 15 minutes), drain thoroughly. Pass through a ricer, and season to taste with salt and pepper and a good lump of butter or margarine. Beat until light.

The mashed celeriac may be served in place of mashed potatoes. Or it may be used to garnish dishes in any of the ways mashed potatoes are used.

CELERY LEAVES. Sprinkle these over boiled potatoes, soups, chowders, and fish. Store them dry in tightly corked bottles. When sprinkled over the aforementioned foods they will regain their natural color and add a decorative touch.

CELERY SALT. Celery salt is a mixture of fine white salt and ground celery seed. Oyster stew, tomato juice and sauerkraut juice cocktails, clam bouillon, and potato and other salads have better taste appeal if seasoned with celery salt. Experiment with it as a substitute for ordinary salt on simple foods such as eggs.

CELERY SEED. Celery seed is derived from a herbaceous plant that is related to the vegetable celery. Try this aromatic seed with stews, pickling spices, hamburgers, canapé butters, vegetable salads, fish, meats.

CELLULOSE. Cellulose, which belongs to the class of carbohydrates, is the chief constituent of wood and of the walls of plant cells, and generally exists in various amounts in the different products of the soil. The outer layers of cereals and legumes are especially rich in cellulose. It is sometimes a hard substance, but in the earlier stages of plant growth, as in tender-leaf vegetables and fruits, and especially in berries, it is chemically combined with water in a more soluble and digestible form. Until quite recently cellulose was considered to be indigestible, but experiments have proved that a large percentage, before it becomes too mature and hardened, may be absorbed in the digestive canal, and if the foods are thoroughly masticated, from 25 to 50 percent are digested.

While, on an average, cellulose may give the body but little nourishment, it is of great importance in acting as roughage to promote the peristaltic movement of the intestines. The diet of man should contain some bulk in the form of more or less woody fibres, as the muscular wall of the intestine, if it has no work to do, becomes atrophied like every other muscle. The lack of cellulose in most cereal products and animal foods is one of the principal causes of constipation. *See also* FOOD COMPOSITION.

CEPES. *See* MUSHROOMS.

CERAMICS. One of the first crafts learned by man was the forming of useful and decorative objects from clay mixtures that are given durability through various processes of fire-hardening. Such objects have been found in the most ancient of ruins, and the craft persists today as a world-wide industry that manufactures much of the kitchenware and tableware used in the typical home.

The impact of ceramics upon cookery has been considerable, for the pots in which it is cooked and the dishes on which it is served have much to do with the type of food that is prepared and the final form which it assumes. The typical diet of a pioneer or a nomad (neither of whom is apt to carry much in the way of pots and dishes) as contrasted to the diet of the normal household is indicative of the culinary habits of the past when utensils were both scarce and expensive. The national dishes of any country run pretty much to type, and an investigation of the typical kitchen of that country will show ample cause for the characteristics assumed by the national dishes.

The potter's wheel has long been a source of inexpensive kitchen and table ware; and, as such, a blessing to the average home. The waterproof, easily cleaned ceramic glaze has been a boon to health and sanitation. Before the mass production of glazed dishes was developed, man had to turn to the metals and the woods for his dishes and serving plates. Until quite recently, metal objects were expensive. Wood is porous, and for that reason, no matter how much care is given to the utensils, presents a health hazard. The old Jewish law requiring a new set of kitchen and table ware each year was based, not on religious causes, but on the very real dangers to health presented by porous wood or unglazed pottery utensils.

Another feature of the ceramic industry is its versatility. It can produce an equally usable product to suit all tastes and pocketbooks, offering objects of great beauty to the wealthy, and yet giving those of lesser means practical utensils that are not necessarily unpleasing to the eye.

The mass production of metals has replaced much of the ceramic ware once used strictly for cooking purposes, and glass (*see* GLASSWARE) and plastics (*which see*) are offering competition in the field of tableware, but public taste still leans heavily to ceramics wherever their use is possible.

TYPES

In general, there are three types of ceramics that are used in the kitchen and on the table: *chinaware*, *earthenware*, and *pottery*.

Chinaware. Together with *porcelain*, this is among the finest types of ceramics made. Porcelain is rarely encountered in cooking utensils, but is sometimes used for the more expensive table service. There are several varieties of chinaware, all used more for tableware than cooking utensils. The differences, which any reputable dealer will gladly explain, lie in the number and types of clays, flints, and other materials used in the making and the precise methods of manufacture; all being too involved to warrant discussion here.

There are several tests for good chinaware. The material is translucent, and, if held to a strong light, the fingers on the back of the plate will cast a noticeable shadow. It has a musical ring when struck with a finger. Usually, the thinner objects are made from the better and more expensive grades of chinaware or porcelain.

The test used by the British Government to detect these materials for customs purposes depends on the fact that chinaware and porcelain are not absorbent or porous beneath the surface glaze. The glaze is removed by abrasion from a portion of the surface, and red ink placed on this exposed area. If the ink does not penetrate the material, then the object is either chinaware or porcelain.

Earthenware. By far the most common ceramic material, at least in culinary usage, there are many grades of earthenware, which, in the extremes, are comparable to both chinaware and pottery. Good earthenware is extremely durable and resistant to chipping and crazing. Earthenware objects made in a thickness proper to the grade of material used can stand up under an incredible amount of abuse, as anyone familiar with restaurant crockery knows. The material can be distinguished from chinaware by applying the tests mentioned previously. Earthenware is opaque and will not pass any shadows if held up to a light. It does not give off a musical ring if tapped. And, if the British test is applied, the material will absorb the ink.

Pottery. This is the crudest and weakest form of ceramics. It is subject to cracking, chipping, and crazing, and must be used in thicker cross-section than the other two materials. It has the roughest surface and the interior is extremely porous. There are even some forms of unglazed pottery that will pass water, and jars made of this material are used in tropical countries to keep water cool. This is possible because evaporation of the water on the surface keeps the temperature of the jar below that of the surrounding air.

Pottery objects are, however, very bright and colorful and can be quite decorative. They are greatly used in the so-called "peasant" art, and give a table a gay, fiesta mood. Any pottery used to hold food, however, should be glazed.

MANUFACTURE

Ceramic manufacture has evolved independently and almost spasmodically in different cultures throughout the years. It is world-wide in scope and has been known to practically every culture in all time, though some, of course, have developed the art to a higher extent than others. China, in particular, was making the finest

Brighten up an angel food tube cake with luscious, fresh strawberries for a spring-time treat. Use the basic recipe on page 153. Wash and chill the fruit while the cake is baking. Pile strawberries high in the indented center of the tube cake and dust lightly with confectioners' sugar. Fresh fruit adds a tangy taste to sweet baked goods. Try blueberries or pineapple slices on any unfrosted cake. The result is a dessert that's satisfying and light.

Top noodles with pot cheese dressing (see recipe on page 1046) for a light but filling dish. Or make a cottage cheese dressing by mixing equal parts of cottage cheese and sour cream and seasoning with salt and pepper. Use whole wheat or spinach noodles for variety.

Recipes for delicious Old Fashioned Sugar Cookies appear on page 336.

Broiled flounder tastes better with onions and tomatoes.
Spread the fillets, which have been seasoned with salt, pepper
and dill, with chopped vegetables and broil for 10 to 12 minutes or
until the fish is almost flaky. Then sprinkle the fish with shredded
Swiss cheese and return it to the broiler for 2 or 3 minutes longer. Serve with
asparagus and broad noodles or potatoes.
When choosing fresh fish, look for bright color, clear, unspotted skin,
clear, bulging eyes, red gills and firm, elastic flesh. All fish has a
characteristically strong odor; but fresh fish is free from any stale or sour
smell. Avoid fish that are limp, flabby or excessively dry.
Fish is always best when it is freshly caught. But, when fresh fish is
unavailable don't hesitate to choose from among quality frozen varieties.

High protein cheeses lend variety and appeal to nearly any dish. Crumble blue, Cheddar or tilsiter into salads. Broil Swiss or Munster on top of chops. For breakfast serve

Breakstone Sugar Creek Foods

A springtime delicacy,
cream of pea pods soup makes
use of leftover greens.

wedges of cheese with hot rolls, fresh fruit, butter and coffee. Stir cottage cheese, Edam or Gouda into frying scrambled eggs.

Today's eggs are fresher than ever — so fresh, in fact, that they're reluctant to leave their shells. To make perfectly peeled hard cooked eggs, use the oldest eggs in your refrigerator. Plunge them into cold water after cooking and then gently shell them. Raw broken out eggs have yolks centered in the firm, sometimes milky, white when they are freshest. Blood and meat spots are not harmful but may be extracted before using. Yolk and shell color are a matter of breeding and diet not related to the nutritive value of the eggs.

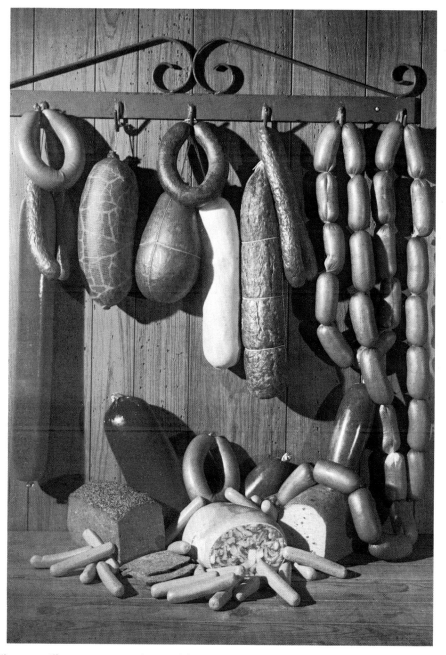

The versatile sausage can be used in soups, casseroles, sauces or as a main dish. Cold cuts make excellent sandwiches for picnics and parties. Try salami and fried eggs on rye bread or bologna with Swiss cheese and watercress on thick slices of white bread.

One of the most delicious warm weather soups, French Vichyssoise (the last "s" is pronounced) is traditionally served cold. A cream soup made of leeks and potatoes, Vichyssoise is inexpensively prepared. Serve the soup thoroughly chilled and garnished with chopped chives. Add bread sticks or rolls. See recipe on page 1218.

Delicate and flaky, crescent rolls can be served hot with cocoa or coffee in the morning for a Continental breakfast treat. Or serve these buttery rolls at a Sunday brunch party with wedges of cheese and consommé. Recipes for French, Austrian and Danish croissants appear on page 371.

of porcelains at a time when the rest of the world was making only the crudest of pottery. Archaeological excavations have found evidence that even older cultures in other parts of the world had developed the art to a high degree.

Ceramic manufacture, as we now know it, is pretty much basic and has been little changed through the years. Modern equipment has simplified much of the work involved and modern chemistry has given birth to more and better glazes, but in many respects they are only rediscovering the secrets of the ancients.

Clays, flints, and other mineral compounds are ground up and mixed with water (*blunging*), then blended to form the *slip* or watery clay compound that is the basic material. The slip is put through a *filter press* which removes most of the water, converting the material to a semi-solid plastic substance. It then goes to a *pug mill*, which, through rotary blades, further mixes the clay and extrudes it in the form of long, round sausages. The sausage is then formed into balls of suitable size and worked into shape, either on a potter's wheel, or by being pressed between plaster of paris molds. When the shaped object has dried to a *leather* or *cheese* hardness it is *turned* on a lathe to give it a smooth surface of the exact dimensions desired. Objects are also formed directly from the slip by casting in plaster molds which absorb the water, letting the clay harden.

The objects are now sent to the ovens for the initial or *biscuit* firing. When removed, they are hard, but unglazed. Designs are then placed on the surface either by hand painting or a transfer process. Next the objects are dipped in the *glaze*, a glass-like liquid, and, after drying, sent back to the ovens for the second or *glost* firing. Further ornamentation may then be done, and the object is given a final polishing and is ready for the market. *See also* DISHES.

CEREALS. Cereals take their generic name from Ceres, the Roman goddess of vegetation. Those in commonest everyday use are wheat, corn, rice, oats, rye, barley, and buckwheat, all of *which see*. From these a wide variety of flours, meals and breakfast foods are prepared, some being ready-to-eat, some requiring brief cooking, while others demand longer cooking.

The ready-to-eat cereals embrace flaked, puffed, and shredded grains, the products entering into their manufacture being wheat, bran, corn, rice, etc.

Cereals which need cooking include oatmeal, corn meal, the various granulated wheat and malt cereals, etc. Years ago all breakfast cereals demanded long home cooking, but today much of this preliminary preparation is done in the plants in which they are manufactured and packed. In all instances follow the manufacturers' directions as to the proportions to be used and the cooking time required.

With this wide variety of cereals from which to choose there is no longer any reason for sameness in a breakfast food. Nor should the service of these useful grains be confined to the first meal of the day, for cereals now enter into breads, muffins, griddle cakes and cookies; they may also be used in croquettes and meat loaves; they may serve as a topping for casserole dishes; they may be added to scrambled and creamed foods; they may appear on the appetizer tray—yes, you'll even meet them in the candy box!

CERVELAT. Originated in France, this short, rather thick and soft sausage is made of four-fifths beef and one-fifth pork. It may be eaten plain as an appetizer or cooked with sauerkraut or cabbage. *See* SAUSAGE.

CEYLON TEA. Any of the black teas grown on the island of Ceylon. They are more like those of South India than those of North India, but most of them have a unique flavor and richness all of their own. Except for some of the fine North India teas (such as Assams and Darjeelings), the Ceylons usually fetch the highest prices at the tea markets. They are grown from low to very high altitudes and vary widely in quality. *See also* TEA.

CH'A. (Chinese; tcha; tea, *which see*) The word *Ch'a* came into use about 725 A.D. Other Chinese words, used before that time to mean tea, included: *chaun, k'u t'u, ming, t'e,* and *t'u*. As some of these were names of other plants, borrowed to express tea, it is often difficult to ascertain from early Chinese writings that tea was the subject of discussion. The English of the early seventeenth century spelled it variously Chaa, and Chaw; in present day English slang it is often referred to as Char.

CHABLIS. A white table wine of the Burgundy family named after a small town in the Yonne Department of France, from whose neighboring vineyards have come the most famous of Chablis wines. It is a delicate, straw-colored wine, somewhat similar to Rhine Wine, but not as tart and having a fruitier flavor and more body. It can be made from one or more varieties of grapes; the Pinot blanc, Chardonnay, Burger, Golden Chasselas, and Green Hungarian being the most common.

Chablis is especially good with seafood and white meats. It is customarily served chilled.

See also BURGUNDY and WINE.

CHAFING DISH

CHAFING DISH. The chafing dish is a metal pan, with a water basin, which is heated by an alcohol lamp and used for cooking at the table. It is the ancestor of modern electric cooking vessels, and in its modernized version is the nucleus of informal entertaining.

Its chief advantage is that the cook need not be absent in the kitchen while the dish is being prepared. The guests enjoy the small ceremonial of chafing dish cooking, and the food can be kept piping hot until it is eaten.

The chafing dish with the water basin works on the principle of a double boiler and is used for preparing dishes that require slow cooking or for keeping prepared food hot. Without the water basin, the upper pan can be used like a skillet. The alcohol lamp is controlled by raising and lowering the wick, a larger flame being obtained by turning up the wick.

In preparing for chafing dish cooking, all of the ingredients should be gathered together on a tray, having been measured out in the kitchen. In this way the cook has only to combine the ingredients in the proper order, and there is no confusion of

supplies and utensils to spoil the effect of the party.

Dishes such as scrambled eggs, chicken à la king, lobster newburg, and spaghetti sauce are most often cooked in a chafing dish. Fondue (*which see*) is especially suited to this method of cooking.

CHAINTRE. A white table wine, of which there are two types, both made in France. One is a white Burgundy from Saône-et-Loire, and the other is a white Anjou wine from the district of Saumur. *See* WINE.

CHALYBEATE WATERS. Mineral waters containing iron. *See* ALKALINE AND MINERAL WATERS.

CHALYBON. A Greek wine from the vineyards of Lebanon.

CHAMBERTIN. A red table wine, one of the most famous of Burgundies. It comes from the vineyards of Chambertin, Commune of Gevrey-Chambertin, which have a number of owners; hence many Chambertin wines under different labels with varying qualities. *See also* BURGUNDY and WINE.

CHAMBRER. A French term, coming from *chambre* or room, meaning to bring a wine from cellar temperature to the warmer room temperature before it is served. *See* WINE.

CHAMOMILE. *See* CAMOMILE.

CHAMPAGNE. By far the most glamorous of all wines, the very name has become synonymous with expensive living, good taste and unrestrained celebration. Such a reputation must have been deserved, and Champagne has been earning her laurels as the Queen of Vintages since as early as the 6th century, when it was first mentioned in the will of Saint Remy, Bishop of Rheims. In the year 1387 when Vencesilaus, King of Bohemia and the Romans came to France for treaty talks with Charles VI, that worthy encountered the wines of the province of Champagne at Rheims, and decided on a several week's stay so that he might properly enjoy them. Francis I of France, Charles V of Spain and Henry VIII of England are but a few of the famous figures who have had personal vineyards at Ay, just to make certain of getting a supply of these wines.

Though the wines of Champagne had obviously made a sensation in those days, they were not the effervescent, nose-tickling, palate-exciting blends that are sold today. Champagne was then a still wine.

It was not until the middle of the 17th century, and then largely by accident, that the present form was developed. According to tradition, the vintage was rather poor one year and a Benedictine monk did some experimenting in an effort to save the wine. He blended various wines of the region and used a wooden "cork" rather than the then traditional oil-dipped flax plug to seal the bottles. This happy combination led to the discovery of Champagne in its present sparkling state, and further experimentation brought the wine to perfection.

Champagne is a fortified, blended, standardized sparkling wine. It is effervescent because of imprisoned gas caused by secondary fermentation. In color it is traditionally pale gold or straw to the eye, though it is also made in a pinkish shade. It is made in several degrees of sweetness.

French Champagne comes from vineyards in three distinct districts or regions:

1. The mountainous region of Rheims and nearby localities as Ambonay, Buzy, Mailly, Siller, Verzy, Verzenay, etc.

2. The slopes of Avize, with its famous hills of Avize, Cramont, Cuis, Grauves, Le Mesnil, Oget, etc.

3. The Valley of the Marne with Ay, Champillon, Cumieres, Dizzy, Epernay, Hautvilliers, Mareuil, Pierry, etc.

Champagne is also now made in other countries, as, in America, in upper New York State and in California.

MAKING CHAMPAGNE

Champagne is made by a very involved, very precise and very lengthy process, which accounts for its high price.

Champagne is made from both white and black grapes, but the first step is always to make a white table wine from these grapes (see WINE). These wines are then carefully blended, so that each will contribute its best characteristics to the finished product, and are mixed with a special yeast and some sugar, either cane sugar or a "liqueur" (in this sense, an older wine) or both, and then bottled. Special bottles capable of withstanding pressures up to 100 pounds per square inch are used, and the thick special corks are held in place by steel clamps. Even though special bottles are used, there is often considerable breakage as the secondary fermentation goes on in the bottle, the yeast converting the sugar into alcohol and gas. This gas which, un-

able to escape, builds up terrific pressures within the bottle, is the cause of the wine's effervescence. Under pressure it dissolves into the liquid, but as soon as the bottle is opened, it forms bubbles and causes the wine to froth and foam.

This second fermentation takes place while the bottles are laid on their sides in six foot piles in cellars. In addition to the desired gas, considerable unwanted sediment is also formed in the bottle. This is removed by a process known as *disgorging*. The bottles are placed neck down on special tables that have holes to hold the bottles at a 60 degree angle. Every day for about a two-month period each bottle is given a sharp rotary shaking by hand, causing the sediment to fall towards the cork. When the sediment has all settled on the cork, a skilled operator carefully removes the clamp which has been holding the cork in place. The internal pressure blows both the cork and the sediment out of the bottle, which is then immediately raised so that not too much of the wine will be lost.

Since, during this second fermentation, all of the sugar in the wine has been converted to other products, the wine is now too dry for many palates. As soon as it has been disgorged, the wine is sweetened (*dosed*) to various known standards, and recorked, this time using the commercial cork, wire basket and foil wrapping seen when one buys a bottle of champagne.

The bottles are now laid away in cellars, stored on their sides, for a further period of aging before they are sent to the market.

One variation in the disgorging process is to dip the neck in a freezing solution immediately before removing the cork. This sets up the sediment in a block of ice attached to the cork.

As can readily be seen, the process of champagne manufacture is by no means cheap. It involves extensive hand labor through a period of years.

A *bulk process* has been developed in an attempt to simplify the manufacture of sparkling wines. In this method, the secondary fermentation takes place in huge, glass-lined vats, the wines being bottled under pressure and the sediment being kept completely out of the bottle by means of filters or careful drawing from the top of the vat. Under American law, wines made by this method must announce that fact on their labels.

CHAMPAGNE CIDER

Types of Champagne

A Champagne that has not been *dosed* or sweetened at the time of disgorging is usually referred to as *brut* or *vin brut*. In this sense, *brut* means dry (*which see*), i.e., lacking in sugar. Champagnes are dosed to varying states of semi-sweetness, referred to variously as *extra-dry*, *dry* and *sec*. A sweet Champagne is called *doux*.

Champagne is basically a white table wine, but its manufacture gives it a universality in application that is equalled by few other wines. For most tastes it goes well with almost any food or dessert, is admirable when served alone, and can form the basis of many delightful mixed drinks and punches.

Because of its great cost, it has been restricted in use for most people to only those occasions of great state or celebration, a role which it plays with adequate ability. However, many excellent domestic champagnes are available at far lower prices than the imported brands.

It is properly served chilled, usually with the aid of an ice-bucket. The formal *Champagne Glass* (*see* GLASSWARE) is a *flute*, a six-inch, v-shaped, hollow-stemmed goblet with a round base. The purpose of the hollow stem is to display the effervescent quality of the wine. There is some objection to this type of glass because it is difficult to clean, but Champagne, and all chilled wines for that matter, should be served in some sort of stemmed goblet, usually a saucer-shaped glass, so the fingers will not have to touch the bowl when handling and thus heat the wine. The glass, regardless of size or shape, is never filled to the brim. *See* WINE, WINE CUP, PUNCH and GLASSWARE.

Champagne Cocktail

Place a lump of sugar, or 1 teaspoon of granulated sugar in a saucer-shaped glass. Add a drop or two of bitters to the sugar. Fill the glass with well chilled champagne and stir. Twist a small piece of lemon peel over the glass and drop the peel into the glass. A lump of ice may be added before pouring in the champagne.

This is the basic recipe. There are many variations, some calling for a jigger of cognac to be included, and some calling for a garnishing of fruit, usually pineapple sticks, cherries, and sliced orange.

Champagne Sherbet

½ cup granulated sugar
1 cup water
Grated rind of ½ lemon
Grated rind of 1 orange
¼ tsp salt
1 pint dry champagne, chilled
Juice of 1 lemon
Juice of 4 oranges
1 (extra) pt dry champagne, chilled

Make a sugar sirup with sugar and water, and boil until sirup spins a thin thread when dropped from the tip of a spoon; then stir in the lemon and orange rinds and salt. Let stand 10 minutes. Then stir in the previously chilled pint of champagne, juices of lemon and orange. Stir, chill, then freeze in hand freezer, using 5 parts ice and 1 part salt, until mushy. Stir and add the second pint of chilled champagne, stirring constantly. Pack and allow to stand in 6 parts ice and 1 part rock salt for 1 hour. Serve in well chilled sherbet glasses.

CHAMPAGNE CIDER. A light sparkling cider which may be made in the home.

Champagne Cider

5 gallons sweet cider
3 pt strained honey, or 1⅛ lb white sugar
½ cup skimmed milk, or 1 tsp dissolved isinglass
3 cups pure spirits

Add the honey or sugar to the cider in a crock. Stir the mixture well, cover the top with a clean cloth, and set the crock aside for a week. Then clarify the cider with the skimmed milk or isinglass. Add the spirits, and let stand for two or three days more. Then bottle the cider, fastening the corks on well with wire, or put into a small cask which can be bunged up tight. The wine will become effervescent after it stands.

"CHAMPAGNE OF TEAS." A name applied to Formosa Oolong teas, *which see*.

CHAMPOLEON CHEESE. A hard rennet cheese made from skimmed milk in the Department of Hautes Alpes in France.

CHAOURCE CHEESE. A soft, whole-milk cheese, resembling Camembert. It is four inches in diameter and three inches thick and is a product of the Department of Aube, France.

CHARQUI. (chahr kee) Known in this country as jerked beef or "jerky." The meat is cut into long strips and dried in the sun. It requires considerable soaking in water before it is fit for stewing or for the soup pot, and even then, it is inclined to be tough and fibrous. Its good points are that it keeps indefinitely and that it retains considerable nourishment. It is not to be confused with CHIPPED BEEF, *which see.*

CHAPON. A crust of bread, usually French bread, which is rubbed well with garlic and tossed with a mixed salad. In this way the garlic flavor is given to the salad without the danger of anyone finding a piece of garlic in his portion.

CHARD or **SWISS CHARD.** A form of beet grown only for the tops, chard is in the markets in the late summer and early fall. In effect, it is two vegetables in one, since the leaves may be cooked as greens and the white stems may be cooked like celery. In the home garden it is easily grown and is unique in its "cut and come again" characteristic.

SWISS CHARD

Drain well. They may be served hot with butter, cream sauce, or hollandaise sauce, or in any manner suggested for celery.

FOOD VALUE

	Food Energy	Protein	Fat	Carbohydrate	Calcium	Phosphorus	Iron	Vit. A Value	Thiamine	Riboflavin	Niacin	Ascorbic Acid
Water												
91.8	25	1.4	.2	4.4	105	36	4.0	2,800	.06	.13	.2	38

Chard does not ship well, and so is available only from local growers. The leaves should be crisp and tender, and the stalks fleshy and crisp. Coarse stems are likely to be stringy and tough. Wilted leaves and limp stems indicate that the chard has been picked too long.

HINTS ON PREPARATION

The flavor of chard is very delicate, rather like asparagus. It should always be steamed, never boiled, since boiling will remove all flavor. The leaves should be cooked like spinach, using only the water that clings to them from washing. A sliver of garlic or a dash of nutmeg adds a subtle flavor change to the greens. Cream of chard soup—made like cream of spinach soup— is a delicate and delicious luncheon or supper dish.

The white stems are prepared like asparagus or celery. Strip them carefully and cut into convenient pieces. Cook in very little boiling salted water until tender.

Chilled, they are delicious with French dressing or vinaigrette.

CHARD SWISS STYLE

¼ cup milk
2 slices of bread
⅓ cup dried mushrooms
2 leeks
3 tbsp chopped parsley and chives
½ cup chopped celery leaves
½ clove of garlic
4 cups cooked chopped chard greens
⅓ cup grated Swiss cheese
Salt, pepper, and nutmeg
4 eggs
½ cup fine bread crumbs

Break the bread into small bits and pour the cold milk over it. Let stand until the milk is absorbed. Soak the mushrooms in a little warm water, squeeze dry, and chop very fine. Clean the leeks and chop very fine. Add the mushrooms, leeks, parsley, celery leaves, and mashed garlic to the bread and mix the whole with the chard greens. Add the cheese. Season to taste with salt, pepper, and nutmeg. Add the unbeaten eggs, one at a time, beating well after each addition. Grease a baking dish thoroughly and turn in the chard mixture. Spread the crumbs over the top and dot with butter or margarine. Bake in a moderate oven (350° F.) for 30 minutes or until firm and well browned. (Serves 6 or 8)

CHARLOTTE RUSSE. A dessert composed of gelatin, whipped cream, and lady fingers originally named in honor of Princess Charlotte of France.

PLAIN CHARLOTTE RUSSE

1½ tsp plain gelatin
⅛ cup cold water
1 cup milk
¼ cup sugar
Pinch of salt
2 eggs, separated
½ tsp vanilla extract
½ cup whipping cream
Ladyfingers

Split the pairs of ladyfingers and line a spring mold with the fingers, rounded side out. Soften the gelatin in the cold water. In the top of a double boiler, scald the milk and stir in the sugar, salt, and gelatin. Stir, but do not allow to boil, until the sugar and gelatin are dissolved. Beat the egg whites until they are stiff and the yolks until they are thick and lemon colored. Stir a few spoonfuls of the hot milk mixture into the yolks and then return to the rest of the milk mixture. Cook, stirring constantly, until the mixture thickens and coats the spoon. Remove from the stove and cool. Add the vanilla, and then fold in the stiffly beaten egg whites, and the cream which has been whipped. Turn into the mold, cover, and set in the refrigerator to congeal. This will take 5 or 6 hours, or overnight.

When ready to serve, turn out and garnish with additional whipped cream and maraschino cherries. The vanilla extract may be replaced by rum or wine flavoring for a particularly delicious pudding. (Serves 5 or 6)

CHARLOTTE GLACE

1 tbsp gelatin
¼ cup cold water
⅓ cup powdered sugar
2 cups heavy cream
1 tsp vanilla
Ladyfingers
Whipped cream

Soften gelatine in cold water 5 minutes; dissolve over hot water. Beat sugar into cream, add vanilla and stir in gelatin; turn into cylindrical mold, pack in ice and salt, and freeze 3 hours. Unmold and garnish with whipped cream and ladyfingers. *See also* MOUSSE. (Serves 6)

FROZEN CHARLOTTE

1½ tsp gelatin
¼ cup cold water
2 cups heavy cream, whipped
½ cup confectioners' sugar
1 cup finely chopped pecans
2 tbsp wine
Macaroons

Soften gelatin in cold water 5 minutes; heat over hot water until dissolved. Add to whipped cream, mixing well; fold in sugar, pecans and flavoring. Line small molds with macaroons, fill with gelatine mixture and place in freezing compartment of automatic refrigerator; freeze two to four hours, or until firm. (Serves 6)

CHARTREUSE. (I) A highly renowned liqueur originally made by the Carthusian monks at the monastery, La Grande Chartreuse, near Grenoble, France, the motherhouse of the order. It was made according to a secret formula, supposedly a concoction of herbs from the slopes of the Dauphiné Valley and the finest of brandies. The formula was first given to the monks in 1607, when manufacture began, and was perfected by them in 1757, since remaining a secret that has defied analysis.

There were three types of Chartreuse made; a potent Green Chartreuse, an even stronger White Chartreuse, and a less potent, but much sweeter Yellow Chartreuse. All three are highly aromatic.

The White Chartreuse, labeled *Elixir des Pères Chartreux*, is no longer available, and only the green and yellow colored liqueurs are sold today.

When, in 1901, the monks were driven out of France by the persecution against religious orders, they transferred their distillery to Tarragona, Spain, and labelled their product Liqueur des Peres Chartreux.

The French Government sold the Chartreuse trademark and distilleries at auction, and they were used to produce an imitation Chartreuse sold with bottles and labels identical to the old Chartreuse made according to the secret recipe.

The only means of distinguishing between the bottles of the pre-1901 Chartreuse and the later product is by means of the printer's name on the label. On the left corner of the authentic Chartreuse label can be found *Lith. Alier* in very small letters, while the post-1901 labels merely have *Lith.* and lack the original printer's name. *See also* LIQUEUR.

CHARTREUSE. (II) A preparation of fish, meat, game, or vegetables in a casserole—the name signifies little more than its preparation in the casserole.

CHASCHOL DE CHASCHOSIS CHEESE. A hard, rennet cheese, made from the skim milk of cows. It is usually 18 to 22 inches in diameter, and 22 to 40 pounds in weight.

CHATEAU BOTTLED. A term used to refer to French wines that have been *Mis en bouteille au Château* (Put in the bottle at the Chateau), i.e., bottled by the same

CHECKERBERRY

people who made the wine and possibly even grew the grapes. Theoretically, this term is supposed to be confined to only the finest of wines worthy of the Chateau's reputation, and thus act as a sort of guarantee of quality, but this has been abused in some cases. It is, however, a guarantee of authenticity.

CHATEAU SAUTERNE. *See* SAUTERNE.

CHATEAUBRIAND. A steak which consists of a slice cut laterally from the thickest part of the tenderloin. It is the French form of the porterhouse steak and

must be at least three inches thick. It is broiled and served with béarnaise sauce (*which see*). The name was given to honor the great French writer and statesman of the Napoleonic era—Vicomte Chateaubriand.

CHAYOTE

CHAYOTE. This handsome member of the squash family originated in Mexico and is now cultivated in Florida. It is not too often found in market. It is about the size of an acorn squash with a green skin and the meat faintly tinged with green, like a honeydew melon. Its flavor is similar to the other squashes, but it is less flat than some.

Because it retains its firmness after cooking the chayote lends itself to many ways of preparation. It may be sliced, like eggplant, and coated with batter or dipped into cornmeal, and fried in deep fat. It may be halved and baked like the acorn squash, either with salt and pepper and butter, or with a stuffing. It can be boiled and mashed and seasoned with salt and pepper and butter. It makes an excellent addition to a curry.

If the chayote is very young and tender it may be cooked without peeling. Otherwise it should be peeled very thinly. The seeds should not be removed; they cook tender as do those of summer squash. *See also* SQUASH.

CHECKERBERRY. There are about 100 species of checkerberry, named *Gaultheria* for Doctor Gaultier of Quebec, Canada, which are known as boxberry, spiceberry, ground-berry, mountain tea, partridge-berry, etc. This evergreen shrub is found in cool, damp woods, chiefly under the shade of evergreens in Canada and the United States. The flowers are white, pink, or red. The berries are red and spicy, with a flavor resembling sweet birch. From the checkerberry an oil of wintergreen is extracted, used for flavoring candy, chewing gum, and certain medicinal products.

CHEDDAR. One of the oldest of English cheeses and one that has been successfully made in Canada and the United States, cheddar is made from cow's milk which has undergone a "cheddaring" process. Rennet is added to the whole milk and heated until a thick soft curd is formed. The whey is drained off, and the curd put through a mill which extracts the last of the whey. The curd is then salted, and pressed in a press for three days, being turned over each day. The shaped curd is then plunged into hot water to give it a tough thin rind, and the cheese greased on the outside with lard. The cheese is then wrapped in thin cloth to keep its shape and cured.

Good cheddar must set in the curing room, which is a dry, well ventilated room in which the temperature is maintained between 54° and 60° F., for at least three months before it can be used. At the end of six months it is considered mature, and after nine months it is "mellowed." A fine cheddar may be aged up to three years.

Cheddar cheese is traditionally shaped in flat wheels, and is orange in color. The flavor may vary from mild to sharp, depending on its age, and the consistency from soft to brittle, also depending on its age. A piece of really old Cheddar will crumble so that it can hardly be cut in slices and the flavor will be a sharply delicate nip.

American cheese, or "store" cheese, is a cheddar-type cheese. *See also* CHEESE.

CHEESE. The making of cheese probably predates the known history of man. There are references to it as far back as 2000 B.C. It is found mentioned in the Old Testament, in the palaces of forgotten kings, and at the feasts of Roman emperors.

Wandering Asiatic tribes brought the art of cheese-making to Europe, where it rooted deep and became one of the most important industries. In the years following the fall of the Roman empire, cheese-making was carried on under the wing of the church, and the peasants were taught the various methods of making it. Secret formulas for certain types were held as part of the wealth of the monasteries.

NATIONAL TYPES

Every country has its own distinctive type of cheese. In the valley of Emme in Switzerland, the Alpine peasant showed special skill in making the cheese known as Emmental, or Swiss, cheese. Equally famous is Gruyere, the French version of Swiss cheese. Limburg, Belgium, is the birthplace of Limburger, a fine, though odoriferous, soft cheese. Holland produces two picturesque cheeses, the Edam and Gouda. Both are covered with a brilliant red coating. Italy prides herself on Caccio Cavallo, a dry hard cheese very sharp on the tongue. Other Italian cheeses take their names from their place of origin, as Parmesan from Parma and Romano from Rome.

The little village of Chester on the river Dee in England originated a cheese which has been famous around the world since the days of Queen Elizabeth, the Cheshire cheese. Cheddar, Herkimer, and Stilton have a history and a romance, ancient and honorable. Dickens, Thackeray, and Boswell mention these sharp and flavorful cheeses. Famed in story and romance is the Stilton, with its semi-hard, white, crumbly body, streaked with blue mold. No less celebrated and better known is Cheddar, named for the quaint old village near the city of Bristol where it was first made. It was this cheese which was used as the model for American cheddar, or American cheese, commonly called "store cheese."

All cheese which is allowed to carry the name of Roquefort comes from a barren rocky region in France which one would think could scarcely provide herbage for the sheep whose milk is used to make the cheese.

DOMESTIC CHEESES

The production of cheese in the United States began with the early settlements, where it was made at home by crude methods. When the European emigrants started coming to the United States in appreciable numbers, they naturally brought their own methods of cheese-making. In New York and Pennsylvania the English and Dutch copied the Cheddar and Edam of their native countries. A Swiss colony in what is now Ohio started the production of Swiss cheese.

The first factory to make Cheddar, or American, cheese was established in Herkimer County, New York, in the middle of the 19th century. Cheese-making soon became an important industry and hundreds of small factories sprang up near the milk supplies. Wisconsin, with its ideal land and climate for dairy-farming, attracted the cheese-makers, and today some of the finest domestic cheeses come from Wisconsin. The Wisconsin Swiss cheese is equal in quality, texture, and flavor to the imported cheese.

Domestic cheeses are basically copies or adaptations of the old-world types. At their best they compare very favorably with the originals and are far less expensive. As in many other things, there is a tendency for the American processors to rush the product to the market, and much domestic cheese is insufficiently aged to be considered really fine.

duced during the manufacturing process. This gives them the characteristic bluish veining. Some cheeses are made of goat's milk; some of whole milk; others of skim cow's milk. All these variations give the individuality to the cheeses.

Process cheese is an American development in which the aging of the cheese is stopped at precisely the desired moment; the cheese is then packaged and can be stored and sold with the guaranty that it will always be uniform in taste and texture.

Cheese forms a highly nutritious article of food and, weight for weight, contains about twice as much protein as meat. The types of cheese differ somewhat in composition, but the table below gives the average.

FOOD VALUE

	Water	Food Energy	Protein	Fat	Carbohydrates	Calcium	Phosphorus	Iron	Vit. A Value	Thiamine	Riboflavin	Niacin	Ascorbic Acid
Cheddar type	39	393	23.9	32.2	1.7	873	610	.57	1740	.04	.50	.2	0
Cottage	74	101	19.2	.8	4.3	82	263	.46	30	.02	.29	.1	0
Cream	53.3	367	7.1	36.9	1.7	298	208	.17	2210	.01	.14	.1	0

CHEESE-MAKING

Cheese is the casein of milk, separated by rennet, which includes some of the fat and salts. There are many varieties, prepared in different ways, but the two chief classes are hard cheeses and soft cheeses. Hard cheeses are pressed and salted; soft cheeses are not.

Cheese is usually prepared from sweet milk. The coagulation is accomplished in a few minutes by the addition of the ferment, rennin, and the application of gentle heat. The casein may also be coagulated by the use of certain acids. Salt, in varying amounts, is added and the cheese pressed into a mold. The fluid which is squeezed out is called whey. The curd is then salted and dried on the surface by frequent turning in carefully controlled temperatures. The harder cheeses are given additional pressing and kept at higher temperatures. Cheese then must be aged and ripened, a process which involves carefully controlled fermentation. The riper a cheese, the greater its value, up to the point where it begins actual decomposition. During the ripening process the characteristic flavor and odor are developed.

Some cheeses such as Stilton and Roquefort have particular types of mold introduced

USING CHEESE IN THE MENU

The uses to which cheese may be put are practically limitless. As an appetizer it is served spread on crackers, or sliced, formed into small balls, or the whole Edam or similar cheese is set out with a cheese scoop. Cheese and green salad is a perfect combination. A gourmet's dessert consists of cheese and fresh fruit. Vegetables served with a cheese sauce, or with a topping of buttered crumbs and grated cheese take on additional interest. And there are a number of main dishes using cheese which form an economical and interesting variation for meat dishes.

In general, the American or Cheddar cheeses are used for cooked dishes, with Parmesan and such strongly flavored cheeses used for special flavor. The softer cheeses such as Camembert, Roquefort, Limburger and the like are used as appetizers or with salad or dessert. A piece of fine aged Cheddar, of course, is not to be used for grating on spinach au gratin, but rather saved to form the perfect end to a perfect dinner. Cottage cheese is used in salads and served with fresh fruits for a different luncheon or supper dish.

See also the individual cheeses by name in alphabetic sequence.

CHEESE BALLS

1 cup grated cheese
¼ cup bread crumbs
¼ tsp salt
¼ tsp paprika
Cayenne pepper
¼ tsp Worcestershire sauce
1 egg, separated
Deep, hot fat

Combine the grated cheese with the bread crumbs, salt, paprika, cayenne pepper, and the Worcestershire sauce. Blend thoroughly; then add the egg yolk, slightly beaten, and mix well. Finally fold in the stiffly beaten egg white. Shape the mixture into small balls, and roll them in fine, dry bread crumbs. When ready to serve, place them in a frying basket, and fry them in deep, hot fat (360°–375° F.) until golden brown. Drain on soft crumpled paper. Garnish with watercress.

CHEESE BEEF ROLLS

½ cup cottage cheese
1 tbsp chili sauce
Worcestershire sauce
Salt and pepper
6 small slices dried beef

Mix cottage cheese, chili sauce, a few drops of Worcestershire sauce, and salt and pepper to taste. Spread the mixture on slices of dried beef, roll tightly, and secure with toothpicks. A tasty hors d'oeuvre. (Makes 6)

CHEESE CAKE

1 package zwieback
½ cup melted butter
3 tbsp powdered sugar
3 eggs
1 cup fine granulated sugar
1 medium-sized lemon
½ tsp salt
½ tsp grated nutmeg
1 cup heavy cream, whipped stiff
1 tsp vanilla, optional
1 lb cottage cheese, sieved
½ cup bread flour, sifted twice

Crush the zwieback with a rolling pin and combine the crumbs with the butter and powdered sugar. Press half the mixture onto the bottom and sides of a well greased deep, round baking pan or spring mold. Beat the egg yolks until light and add the granulated sugar, gradually, beating while adding. Stir in the grated rind and juice of the lemon, the salt, nutmeg, the cream flavored with the vanilla, if used, and the flour. Mix all thoroughly, then rub through a sieve to insure absolute smoothness. Pour carefully into the prepared pan on top of the zwieback mixture and spread the remainder of this crumb mixture over the surface. Bake in a slow oven (250°–300° F.) for one hour, or until firm, then turn off the heat and leave the cheesecake in the oven for another 30 minutes.

Apricot Cheese Cake. Follow the above recipe, but put a layer of cooked, sieved, dried apricots on the zwieback crust before pouring in the cheese mixture, then proceed as indicated.

Pineapple Cheese Cake. Follow the above recipe, but put a layer of well-drained, crushed pineapple on the zwieback crust before pouring in the cheese mixture, then proceed as indicated.

Prune Cheese Cake. Follow the above recipe, but put a layer of cooked, sieved, rather firm prunes on the zwieback crust before pouring in the cheese mixture, then proceed as indicated.

In fact, almost any kind of cooked, sieved fruit pulp may be used as a foundation for cheese cake.

CHEESE CAKE WITH SOUR CREAM

12 graham crackers rolled to fine crumbs
¼ cup melted butter
3 eggs
⅓ cup sugar
⅛ tsp maple extract
⅛ tsp vanilla
Dash of salt
⅛ tsp cinnamon
12-oz package creamed cottage cheese
1 pt sour cream
6 drops almond extract
3 tbsp sugar

Combine graham cracker crumbs and butter. Mix thoroughly with fingers and pat into a 9-inch spring mold to make a thin bottom and side crust. Beat eggs and add next 6 ingredients, beating with a rotary beater. Pour into crust, and bake in moderate oven, (350° F.) 30 minutes. Remove from oven. Increase oven heat to

475° F. (hot). Immediately beat sour cream, almond extract and sugar together. Pour over cheese cake and return to 475° F. oven for 5 minutes. Remove to a cake rack to cool and then to refrigerator to chill. When chilled, run a knife around edge of cheese cake to loosen and release spring form. Garnish each slice with a teaspoon of tart jelly if desired. (Serves 6 to 8)

CHEESE CROQUETTES

3 cups hot riced potatoes
2 egg yolks, well beaten
¾ cup grated cheese, American, Parmesan or Swiss
A few grains cayenne pepper
1 tsp salt
1 tsp Worcestershire sauce
1 whole egg, beaten
Bread crumbs or cracker crumbs
Deep hot fat

Combine the potatoes, egg yolks, cheese and seasonings, blend thoroughly, divide into twelve portions and shape into small croquettes. Dip each in the egg, beaten with one tablespoon milk or water, then roll in the crumbs. Shake off any loose crumbs and immediately before serving fry golden brown in deep hot fat (360°–375° F.). Drain on soft, crumpled paper and use as a main luncheon dish or as an accompaniment to spinach, rice, or noodles, or other dishes.

CHEESE DROPS

2 tbsp butter
3½ tbsp flour
½ tsp salt
A few grains cayenne pepper, *or* Tabasco sauce to taste
2 tbsp grated cheese, American, Parmesan, Swiss, etc.
3 egg whites stiffly beaten
Paprika

Melt the butter, add the flour, stir until well blended, then remove from the fire. Add the salt, the cayenne or tabasco, the grated cheese. When well blended, fold in the stiffly beaten egg whites. Drop from the tip of a spoon to a greased cookie sheet. Sprinkle with paprika, and bake in a moderate oven (360° F.) about 10 minutes, or until brown. Serve hot as appetizers. (Makes about two dozen.)

CHEESE DUMPLINGS

3 tbsp butter or shortening
4 eggs
1 tsp salt
1 tsp Worcestershire sauce
A few grains cayenne
1 cup cottage cheese
½ cup flour
¼ cup dry bread crumbs

Cream the butter or shortening, add the beaten egg yolks, and beat to make a creamy mixture. Add the seasonings and cheese and blend well. (The cottage cheese should be pressed through a sieve or strainer.) Now add the flour and bread crumbs, and mix well. Lastly, fold in the stiffly beaten egg whites. Form into dumplings, the size of a walnut, and drop into rapidly boiling salted water, meat stock, or vegetable stock. Cover closely and allow to boil 10 minutes. Remove with strainer or slotted spoon, and place dumplings on hot cooked, chopped spinach, cooked greens, cooked macaroni, noodles or spaghetti. (Serves 6)

CHEESE FONDUE

1 tbsp butter
½ tsp flour (scant)
1 wine glass white wine
Salt and cayenne (a few grains)
¼ lb Swiss cheese
1 liqueur glass Kirsch
French bread

Melt the butter in an earthen casserole. Add the flour, scattering it over the butter, then the wine and salt and cayenne. Place over a very slow flame and bring to boiling point, stirring almost constantly. Add the cheese, grated or cut into small pieces, continuing to stir until the cheese is entirely melted and the mixture begins to bubble. Then stir in the Kirsch. Serve with French bread, untoasted, cut into three quarter-inch lengths. (The bread is to be dipped into the bubbling fondue and eaten from the fingers.) (Serves 8)

CHEESE FONDUE
(American Method)

2½ cups milk
2 whole eggs, plus 1 egg yolk
1 cup grated American cheese

Salt
Cayenne
4 egg whites
4 cups cubed bread
Cheese and butter to dot top

Scald the milk in a double boiler. Separate the eggs and beat the 3 yolks well. Add together with the cheese and seasonings; then stir until the cheese is melted. Finally fold in the stiffly beaten egg whites and pour the whole over the bread which has been placed in a generously buttered casserole. Dot with cheese and a little butter, set the casserole in a pan containing hot water and bake in a moderate oven (350° F.) 30 to 35 minutes, or until the fondue rises, sets to a delicate yet firm consistency, and is golden brown. Serve immediately. (Serves 6)

CHEESE FRITTERS

1 cup cooked rice
1 egg
1 tbsp milk
½ cup grated American cheese
2 tsp prepared mustard
¼ tsp salt
Dash of paprika
Flour
1 egg white
1 tbsp milk, additional
Fine bread or cracker crumbs

Combine the rice, the egg, slightly beaten, the milk, cheese and seasonings and blend all thoroughly. Shape into marble-sized balls and dredge lightly with flour. Then dip into the egg white beaten with the second tablespoon of milk and roll in the bread or cracker crumbs. Fry in deep hot fat (375° F.) until golden brown, drain on soft crumpled paper and garnish with watercress. (Serves 6)

CHEESE LOAF

½ lb American cheese
2 cup beans or lentils, cooked
½ tsp salt
¼ tsp white pepper
1 generous tsp grated onion
⅛ tsp thyme
⅛ tsp clove
⅛ tsp nutmeg
1 cup bread crumbs
1 tbsp melted butter

Pass the cheese and the beans or lentils through a food chopper. Add seasonings, flavorings, and bread crumbs, with the melted butter, adding, if too dry, a little milk, stock, or water. Turn the mixture onto a greased baking sheet, shape into a roll or loaf (or if preferred turn into a well greased loaf pan) and bake in a moderate oven (350° F.) about 45 minutes, basting occasionally with a little melted butter and water or stock. Serve with tomato or brown sauce. (Serves 6)

CHEESE MERINGUE PIE

1 cup cottage cheese, sieved
⅔ cup sugar
⅔ cup milk
2 egg yolks, well beaten
1 tbsp butter
¼ tsp salt
A dash of nutmeg
½ tsp vanilla
Pastry
Meringue

Combine all ingredients, except pastry and meringue, in the order given. Line a pie plate with pastry (*which see*), turn in the filling and bake about 35 minutes, having the oven hot (450° F.) for the first ten minutes, then reducing to moderate (350°–360° F.) for the remainder of the baking period. When done, cool slightly, then cover with meringue (*which see*) and return to a cool oven for a further 12 to 15 minutes to set and delicately color the meringue. (Makes one 9-inch pie)

CHEESE PLATTER

On a large platter arrange a Camembert cheese from which the crust has been scraped. Surround it with wedges or sections of other types such as Roquefort, Swiss, Bel Paese, Liederkranz, and cream cheese. Provide a cheese knife for service. Pass melba toast, cheese straws or other small hot biscuits or rolls and a variety of crackers, as well as thick slices of French bread and a pot of mustard.

CHEESE PUDDING

6 slices bread, ¼ inch thick, buttered
  and cubed
2½ cups grated American cheese
3 eggs

2½ cups milk
1 tsp salt
Few grains cayenne pepper
⅛ tsp each nutmeg, cloves and thyme
¼ tsp Worcestershire sauce
¼ tsp prepared mustard

Arrange the bread and cheese in alternate layers in a generously buttered casserole, having cheese for the top layer. Beat the eggs until light, add the milk and all remaining ingredients, blending thoroughly. Pour over the bread and cheese in the casserole, let stand half an hour, then bake in a slow oven (300°–325° F.) about one hour, or until a knife inserted in the center comes out clean. Serve immediately. (Serves 6)

CHEESE PUFFS

¼ cup butter
½ cup boiling water
½ cup flour
½ tsp salt
Dash of cayenne
4 drops tabasco
½ cup grated American cheese
2 whole eggs
1 egg white

Combine the butter and water in a saucepan and when boiling vigorously, add the flour, all at once, and stir and beat until perfectly smooth. The mixture will leave the sides of the saucepan and cling to the spoon in a ball. Remove from the fire, add seasonings and cheese and when these are blended into the first mixture, add one egg, unbeaten, and beat vigorously until the mixture is again smooth. Add the second egg and repeat the process. Finally, beat in the last egg white, and continue beating vigorously for four or five minutes. Drop small portions from the tip of a teaspoon (or press through a pastry bag using a plain tube) onto a greased baking sheet. Bake in a hot oven (400°–450° F.) 12 to 15 minutes. Serve very hot. These are a little on the order of a cream puff and are appropriate for tea, supper, at the cocktail hour or as appetizers.

CHEESE REFRIGERATOR CAKE

1 box (5 oz) Awieback
¼ cup sugar
1 tsp cinnamon

¼ cup melted butter
1 lb dry cottage cheese
3 eggs, separated
¾ cup sugar
1 tbsp cornstarch
3 tbsp lemon juice
1 tsp lemon rind

Roll zwieback fine with a heavy rolling pin. Combine crumbs with sugar and cinnamon and stir to blend. Add melted butter and mix well. Pat firmly in a thin layer on bottom and sides of an 8-inch spring mold pan. Bake at 400° F. (hot oven) 15 minutes. Cool on rack while mixing the filling. Force cottage cheese through a medium strainer into top of double boiler. Add egg yolks that have been beaten thoroughly. Combine sugar and cornstarch, blend to a paste with 1 tablespoon of the lemon juice and add to the cottage cheese. Cook until thickened, stirring occasionally. Let cool slightly, stir in remaining 2 tablespoons lemon juice, rind and fold in stiffly beaten egg whites. Turn into spring mold lined with zwieback crust and let chill in refrigerator for at least 2 hours before serving. (Serves 6 or 8)

CHEESE SOUFFLE

2 tbsp butter or margarine
2 tbsp flour
½ cup milk
Salt
Cayenne pepper
Dash of mustard
3 eggs, separated
1 cup grated sharp cheese

In a saucepan melt the butter and blend in the flour. Then gradually stir in the milk, and cook, stirring constantly, until the mixture boils and thickens. Add the seasonings to taste. Remove from the fire and cool slightly. Beat the egg whites until stiff and the yolks until thick and lemon colored. Add the beaten yolks to the milk mixture. Stir in the cheese, stirring until the cheese is melted. Finally fold in the beaten whites. Grease a baking dish and turn in the mixture. Bake in a moderate oven (350°–375° F.) approximately 30 minutes. To make an even top to the soufflé, run a knife around the surface of the mixture about 1 inch in from the edge of dish before putting it in the oven. Serve immediately. (Serves 4)

Cheese Spinach Soufflé. Follow recipe for Cheese Soufflé adding 1½ cups hot, finely chopped, well drained spinach sautéed in 1½ tablespoons butter and seasoned with 1 teaspoon grated onion.

Cheese Tomato Soufflé. Follow recipe for Cheese Soufflé substituting tomato juice or tomato juice cocktail for the milk in the basic recipe.

Cheese Shrimp Soufflé. Follow recipe for Cheese Soufflé adding 1½ cups cooked shrimps, finely chopped or ground, to the basic recipe.

Cheese Lobster Soufflé. Substitute lobster for shrimp in the preceding recipe. Either of these two may be seasoned with a dash of grated nutmeg.

CHEESE AND RICE SOUFFLE

½ cup cooked rice
1 cup milk, heated
1 cup grated American cheese
1 tsp butter
2 eggs
¼ tsp salt
A few grains cayenne pepper
A few grains nutmeg

Bring the milk slowly to scalding point in the upper part of a double boiler. Remove from the heat, add the cheese, butter and seasonings, and stir until thoroughly blended and the cheese partially melted. Combine with the beaten egg yolks and stir in the rice, being sure that the grains are thoroughly separated. Finally, fold in gently the stiffly beaten egg whites and turn into one large or 6 individual dishes lightly greased, filling them only about three-fourths full. Bake in a moderate oven (350° F.) 35–40 minutes if in one dish; 20 to 25 minutes if baked individually. If a crusty surface is liked place the baking dishes on the open oven shelf; if a more tender custard-like soufflé is desired, set them in a pan containing about two inches depth of hot water. (Serves 6)

CHEESE STRAWS

1 lb grated American cheese
4 tbsp butter or shortening
2 cups sifted flour
¼ tsp cayenne pepper
½ tsp salt
⅛ tsp each ground cloves and nutmeg
Salt

Grate the cheese into a bowl and mix it with the butter or shortening into a smooth paste, using the hands. Sift the flour with the cayenne pepper, salt, and spices. Sprinkle the flour mixture gradually over the cheese paste and knead the mixture to a pliable dough. Force the dough through a cooky press, using a small star plate, onto a cooky sheet. Cut into 2-inch lengths and sprinkle lightly with salt. Bake in a moderately hot oven (375°–400° F.) for 10 minutes, or until a delicate brown. Cool on a rack. These straws may be made in quantity as they keep well when packed between layers of wax paper in a covered tin and kept in a cool dry place. They may be served as appetizers, or with salads or at tea. (Makes about 7 dozen)

CHESTER CAKES

6 oz butter
6 oz sieved flour
6 oz grated Cheshire cheese
Salt and cayenne to taste
2 tbsp cream

Cream the butter, and work in the remaining ingredients. Blend the mixture with your hands, handling it as lightly as possible. When it is thoroughly blended, flour your hands and shape the dough into a ball. Allow this to rest for about an hour in a cool place. Roll it out ¼ inch thick and stamp this out in rounds of about the size of a fifty-cent piece. Bake in a moderate oven until golden brown. Allow to cool. Put together in pairs with a mixture of creamed butter and cheese. Reheat before serving.

CORN, CHEESE, AND TOMATO FONDUE

1½ cups milk
1½ cups corn, canned or cut from cob
1½ cups diced fresh or canned tomatoes
1½ cups soft bread crumbs
1¾ tbsp butter
1½ cups grated American cheese
3 eggs
Salt and pepper

Heat the milk in a double boiler, add the corn, tomatoes, crumbs, butter, and cheese. (Any other cheese which may be grated, such as Swiss, Stilton, Bel Paese, and Parmesan cheese may be used.) Stir until the cheese is melted, and the mixture begins to bubble. Now add the well-beaten eggs, and continue cooking gently for three or four minutes, stirring constantly. Season with salt and pepper and, if desired, add the spices. Stir and serve on freshly toasted and buttered bread or crackers, topping each serving with a poached egg, if desired. (Serves 6)

COTTAGE CHEESE BOWL

2 cups cottage cheese
2 cups thick sour cream
1 tbsp tarragon vinegar
4 tbsp minced chives
1 tsp sugar
1 tsp salt
¼ tsp white pepper
⅛ tsp paprika

Mix the sour cream with the sieved cottage cheese in a bowl. Add all remaining ingredients, mixing lightly. Line a salad bowl with salad greens, pour the cheese mixture carefully into the bowl, and dust with extra paprika. Serve as a luncheon or supper dish, or with potatoes which have been baked or steamed in their jackets. (Serves 6)

COTTAGE CHEESE MOUSSE

1 can condensed tomato soup
3 whole cloves
Rind of ½ lemon
¼ tsp onion juice
Salt and pepper to taste
1 tsp dry mustard
2 tsp Worcestershire sauce
1 envelope gelatin
1 cup cottage cheese, sieved
½ cup mayonnaise
1 cup sour cream, whipped

Combine the soup, cloves, and lemon rind in a saucepan, and bring to the boiling point. Remove from the fire, and add the seasonings and gelatin, which has been soaked in a little cold water for 2 or 3 minutes, stirring until the gelatin is entirely and completely dissolved. Cool; and when the mixture begins to set, remove the lemon peel and cloves. Beat in the cheese, alternately with the mayonnaise and blend thoroughly. Lastly, fold in the whipped sour cream, and turn into a large, wet ring mold or individual molds. Chill and unmold for service. (Serves 6)

COTTAGE CHEESE NUT LOAF

2 cups cottage cheese, sieved
1 cup nut meats, coarsely cut (any kind)
1 cup crushed corn flakes
1 tbsp grated onion
2 tbsp finely minced parsley
1 tbsp bacon fat
½ tsp salt
¼ tsp pepper
⅛ tsp each sage, thyme, cloves

Combine all ingredients, and blend thoroughly. Form into a loaf, and bake in a generously greased bread pan in a hot oven (375°–400° F.) about 45 minutes or until the top and sides are well browned. Turn onto a hot platter; garnish with pimientos, ripe olive, and watercress, and serve with tomato sauce. (Serves 6)

COTTAGE CHEESE SPREAD

Work into a pound of fresh cottage cheese enough sweet cream to moisten. Season with salt, pepper, a few caraway seeds, and finely minced chives. If liked, add also a teaspoon of onion juice and the same amount of Worcestershire sauce. Pack down solidly in a jar and let stand at least overnight before using. Serve with pumpernickel, thinly sliced rye bread, or crackers, and beer or ale. Small new potatoes cooked in their jackets are sometimes served with such a cheese spread.

CREAM CHEESE TARTS

½ cup butter
3 oz cream cheese
1 cup sifted all-purpose flour
About ¼ cup stiff tart jelly (grape)
1 egg yolk
2 tbsp milk
¼ cup chopped walnuts

Cream butter and cheese till well blended and fluffy. Add flour and knead to a smooth dough. Wrap and chill several hours. Roll dough ⅛ inch thick into a rectangle. Cut into 2-inch squares. Place ¼ teaspoon jelly on each square, in one corner. Beginning at this corner, fold edge over, completely covering jelly. Press down to seal and roll the squares diagonally. Turn into crescent shape. Brush with egg yolk mixed with milk. Sprinkle with nuts —or dip brushed surface into nuts. Place on greased baking sheets. Bake at 400° F. for 12 to 15 minutes. Cool on cake racks. Sprinkle with sifted confectioner's sugar. (Makes about 2½ dozen)

Frozen Cheese and Fruit Salad

One 3½ oz package cream cheese
¼ cup mayonnaise
½ tbsp lemon juice
½ tsp salt
2 tbsp fresh, chopped pineapple
¼ cup nut meats, chopped
1½ bananas, sliced
½ cup heavy cream

Combine all ingredients in the order given, turn into a refrigerator tray and freeze about 4 hours in automatic refrigerator, without stirring. Cut into slices or cubes and serve on lettuce, passing French dressing (*which see*) separately. (Serves 6)

Hot Cheese Nut Balls

1 cup grated American cheese
2 tsp flour
½ tsp salt
⅛ tsp cayenne
1 stiffly beaten egg white
¼ cup finely chopped nuts

Mix grated cheese, flour, salt, and cayenne. Fold in egg white and blend well. Shape mixture into small balls, and roll these in chopped nuts. Fry in hot deep fat (375° F.) until golden brown. Serve at once on cocktail picks. (Makes 15)

Pimiento Cheese Rolls

6 thin slices of bread
1½ tbsp mayonnaise
¼ cup pimiento cheese
Dried beef

Spread mayonnaise on the bread, cover with cheese, and top with dried beef. Roll lengthwise, cut each roll in half, and secure with toothpicks. Toast under broiler. Serve hot as hors d'oeuvres. (Makes 12)

Swiss Schnitzelbank Cheese Pot

2 Camembert cheeses
1 Liederkranz cheese
¼ lb. Roquefort cheese
½ lb butter
2 tbsp flour
2 cups cream
1 cup finely chopped olives
½ cup canned pimento, drained and chopped
Cayenne pepper

Scrape off the outer skins of the Camembert and Liederkranz cheeses. Put them into a copper or enamelled saucepan (not aluminum or iron, which will cause the mixture to turn black). Add the Roquefort cheese, butter, flour and cream, and simmer until melted into a smooth mass. Strain the mixture through cheese cloth or a sieve and work in the olives and pimiento. Season with cayenne pepper and pack into an earthenware pot or crock. Let stand several days to mellow.

Serve as a spread on pumpernickel or rye bread, or in small sandwiches for tea or cocktails. The spread will keep about two weeks in the refrigerator.

Welsh Rarebit

1 lb American cheese, well aged and sharp
⅓ cup beer or ale
1 tsp salt
1 tsp dry mustard
1 tsp paprika
¼ tsp white pepper
1 tsp Worcestershire sauce
2 whole eggs, well beaten

Shred the cheese and melt it with the beer or ale in a saucepan over direct heat, stirring constantly until the cheese is thoroughly melted and "follows the spoon around the pan." Add the seasonings alternately with the well beaten eggs. Stir rapidly and vigorously over direct flame for one minute. Serve on freshly made toast on sizzling hot plates. Beer or ale is the perfect accompaniment to this hearty dish. (Serves 6)

To make a Golden Buck, top the rarebit with a freshly poached egg.

CHEESE SAUCE. *See* White Sauce.

CHERIMOYA. The fruit of a small, sub-tropical tree found in the West Indies, Central America, Hawaii and elsewhere, which has been introduced into southern California. It varies from the size of an average apple up to a weight of 15 pounds. The pulp is white, juicy, with a custard-like center, of exceedingly fine flavor. It is also known under the name of "vegetable ice cream."

CHERIMOYA 1. Smooth 2. Tuberculate

CHERNA FISH. *See* GROUPER.

CHERRY. The cultivated cherries have been derived almost wholly from two European species: *prunus avium* and *prunus cerasus*. The varieties of *prunus avium* belong to three groups: 1. Geans or Guignes, which are divided into two kinds, Black, which has dark skin, and sweet, tender, dark flesh, and Red, which has pale skin, soft, sweet translucent flesh; 2. Bigarreaux or Hearts, are heart-shaped, firm light or dark, sweet fruit; and 3. Duke, which are light in color, and a somewhat acid fruit.

Sweet cherries are grown mostly in the western states and sour cherries are produced mostly in the eastern and Great Lakes states. Sweet cherries are used primarily for eating fresh, while sour cherries are used primarily for culinary purposes.

VARIETIES OF CHERRIES

The bulk of the commercial cherry crop is made up of a small number of varieties:
Sour varieties:
Richmond (Early Richmond). The importance of the Richmond cherry is due primarily to its relative season of ripening, which is about 7 to 10 days earlier than the Montmorency; also because of its hardiness. It is the most extensively planted sour cherry of its season.

Montmorency. This is by far the most extensively planted sour cherry, being preferred by the canners to other varieties.

English Morella. This is the principal sour variety planted to follow the Montmorency in sequence of ripening.
Sweet Varieties:
Of the some 20 varieties of sweet cherries produced commercially the following are the major varieties:

Tartarian. This variety is one of the most widely grown of the sweet sorts. The fruit is small, relatively, and not as firm as some of the other sweet sorts, but for home use it is an important variety. The color of the fruit is dark purplish black.

Napoleon (Royal Ann). This is doubtless the most important light-colored sweet cherry. The color is varying shades of bright red over a yellowish background.

Spanish (Yellow Spanish). This cherry has long been one of the most widely grown of all the sweet varieties, though it is now produced much less extensively than the Napoleon. The color is bright amber yellow, with a reddish blush, slightly mottled.

Windsor. On the basis of the quantity fruit produced, this variety is probably the most important midseason sweet cherry. The fruit is firm and ships well. While not as good in dessert quality as the Tartarian, it is a popular market sort in the section where it is grown. The color is very dark.

Schmidt. In some sections this variety is now attracting considerable attention. The fruit has the qualities of a good market cherry. It is also one of the sweet varieties most resistant to brown-rot. The color is purplish black.

Bing. The familiar large dark sweet cherry.

CHERRIES

Duke Varieties:
May Duke. This variety is one of the most widely grown of any in its group and

has many points of merit. It ripens its fruit over a long period.

Late Duke. The chief value of the Late Duke is, perhaps its late season of ripening, which is two to four weeks after the May Duke. It is suitable for home use and local markets rather than for long-distance shipping.

Philippe (Louis Philippe). This fruit has many points of merit, but unfortunately most growers report it to be entirely too unproductive for commercial purposes.

Preparation for Market

The manner in which cherries are picked is governed in a measure by the use that is to be made of them. When they are to be shipped to a distant market the stems must be left on the fruit. Nearby canners pay more for fruit without stems, which is pulled from the tree. When harvested with the stems, the picker grasps at one time the stems of several of the fruit in a cluster and strips them. If due care is exercised, the stems will remain firmly attached to the fruit and the spurs will not be broken or otherwise injured. It is not always an easy matter to decide just when cherries should be picked. Better flavor and quality are secured by allowing the fruit to remain on the tree as long as possible.

Various methods of handling the fruit after it is picked are followed by different growers. In some sections, it is packed in the orchard; in others, a movable packing house is provided. This house is built on runners, so that it may be moved readily from place to place by a team. In this case, the fruit is placed by the pickers in veneer boxes holding one quart, and the boxes are packed in 16-quart cases or crates. In some cases where a grower puts up a fancy pack, it is necessary to sort and hand pack carefully every box and basket.

Cherries are not well suited for long holding in storage, though sometimes they are held to advantage for a few days while the market is being cleared of an oversupply. Preferably they should be stored after grading and packing, as packed fruit cools more quickly, and is less subject to decay. Cherries intended for the frozen cherries trade are washed and then packed in barrels (with or without pitting) as soon as possible after picking. The barrels are then placed in cold storage where they remain until wanted by the trade.

A comparatively large percentage of both the sweet and sour cherry crop reaches the consumer either directly or indirectly through the tin can, the frozen barrel, or the glass jar.

Hints on Buying

Good quality in cherries is indicated by bright, fresh appearance, plumpness and good color. Well matured cherries are plump, firm, juicy, well colored in accordance with their variety and usually have a well developed flavor. Immature cherries are usually smaller than the average ripe cherries found in the container. They are generally hard, and of poor color; lack juice, and are likely to be very acid. Overmature or stale fruits are generally soft and of a dull appearance. They may be more or less shriveled, and they may be leaky. There is much waste in such fruit. A close examination should be made for worm injury. Cherries that have been bruised or otherwise mechanically injured are not desirable.

Cherries are graded according to the U.S. Federal grades. U.S. 1 consists of fresh cherries of one variety which are well formed, mature but not soft, overripe, or shriveled, and which are free from decay and damage caused by dirt or other foreign matter, skin breaks, cracks, scars or limb-rubs, bruises, scald hail, birds, russeting, disease, insects or mechanical or other means.

Cherries are sold by the pound, quart or lug (15 pounds). One pound of sweet cherries stemmed and pitted measures 2¾ cups and serves 4 or 5. One quart sour cherries, pitted, makes 2 cups.

Hints on Preparation

Always wash and pick over cherries. Wormy cherries will float. Drain well and spread on shallow tray in refrigerator.

Baked Cherry Tapioca

1½ cups canned sour cherries, drained
2½ cups cherry juice and water
2 tsp lemon juice
1½ tbsp melted butter
¾ cup firmly packed brown sugar
¾ tsp salt
Dash of nutmeg
⅓ cup quick-cooking tapioca

Combine ingredients in greased casserole, mixing well. Bake in moderately hot oven (375° F.) for 30 minutes, stirring every 10 minutes and again when removing from oven. Serve hot or cold with cream. (Serves 6)

CHERRY BOUNCE

Put perfectly ripe sweet cherries into a tub and mash them with a rolling pin, stones and all. To every five pints of cherries add a quart of rum. Let it stand a week and then strain through a flannel bag. To every gallon of bounce add ¾ pound of brown sugar. Bottle and let stand to ripen.

CHERRY BRANDY

10 lb sweet cherries
3 lb lump sugar
1 gallon brandy
1 oz bitter almonds, chopped

Take cherries, pound them and their stones in a mortar, add sugar and almonds. Put the mixture into a large stone jar, adding the brandy. Cover lightly and shake everyday for the first month and then occasionally for the next two months. Strain through a jelly bag and bottle for use. It should be kept for a year before use, since the flavor improves with age.

CHERRY COBBLER

3 tbsp quick-cooking tapioca
¾ cup granulated sugar
2 tbsp melted butter
Rich biscuit dough
1 cup canned, sour red cherry juice, mixed with
3 cups pitted sour red cherries

Combine tapioca, sugar, butter, and cherry juice with cherries. Stir well and turn into 6 individual buttered baking dishes. Roll biscuit dough (*which see*) ¼ inch thick, cut 6 equal rounds to fit top of individual cups; make a few slits to permit escape of steam and fit over each round, pressing dough against edge of each baking dish to seal. Bake 10 minutes in a very hot oven (450 deg. F.). Reduce heat to moderate (350° F.) and continue baking 10 to 15 minutes longer. Serve warm or cold. If desired, powdered sugar may be sprinkled over the tops. (Serves 6)

CHERRY COMPOTE

Put red cherries into a large shallow saucepan with just enough claret to cover them. Flavor with sugar and a pinch of cinnamon. Bring this slowly to the boil, and as soon as it boils, cover the pan and let the cherries simmer very gently (they should do no more than poach) for 10 minutes. Take the cherries out, reduce the sirup a little, and when it is cooling stir into it a tablespoon of red currant jelly for each pound of cherries. The compote should be served very cold and cream may be added.

CHERRY CREAM PUDDING

2 tbsp cornstarch
½ cup sugar
⅛ tsp salt
2 cups milk
3 eggs, beaten

Mix cornstarch, sugar, and salt in top of a double boiler. Add cold milk and stir until smooth. Cook over direct heat, stirring constantly until mixture boils and thickens. Slowly stir part of the hot mixture into the beaten eggs. Return to hot mixture in top of double boiler and continue to cook over boiling water for 2 minutes, stirring constantly to keep smooth. Remove from heat and cool. Prepare cherry cream sauce.

Thaw 1 pint slightly sweetened frozen cherries in refrigerator. (2 cups of canned cherries may be substituted.) Keep covered during thawing to prevent fruit from darkening. Drain off juice and stir 1 teaspoon of cornstarch into each ⅓ cup of juice. Cook over medium heat until thick and clear, stirring constantly. Add cherries and chill. When ready to serve, spoon cherry mixture into bottom of 5 individual serving dishes, then add the cream pudding (chilled) to cover. Top with whipped cream if desired. (Serves 5)

CHERRY CREAMS

½ cup butter
¾ cup unsifted XXXX sugar, firmly packed
⅛ tsp salt
½ tsp almond extract
¼ tsp vanilla
1 cup whole glazed cherries
1¼ cups sifted cake flour

CHERRY

Cream butter thoroughly, add sugar, salt and flavorings. Blend thoroughly. Add cherries and flour. Mix well. Pack into small loaf pan lined with waxed paper. Chill overnight. Slice with a thin-bladed, very sharp knife from ⅛ to ¼ inch thick, using saw-like motion. Place on ungreased baking sheets. Bake in a moderately hot oven (400° F.) for 7 to 10 minutes. Cool before removing from pans. (Makes about 3 dozen cookies)

CHERRY DUMPLINGS

See recipe for Blackberry Dumplings Mohawk. Fresh sour red cherries, pitted, may be used in place of the blackberries, but omit the lemon juice.

CHERRY FLAN

Make a flaky pastry (*see* PASTRY) and cover a round pie plate or flan pan. Make a pastry cream (*see* CREAM), using half milk and half cream. Fill the pastry with alternate layers of the cream and of cherries poached previously in a sirup of water and sugar. (A mixture of sweet and sour cherries that have been soaked in brandy is recommended.) Finally, a top layer of cream; bake in a slow oven (300° F.) and serve either hot or cold. *See also* FLAN.

CHERRY ICE

2 No. 2 cans sour pitted cherries
¼ cup granulated sugar
½ cup unstrained lemon juice
1 tbsp granulated gelatin
1 egg white, stiffly beaten

Drain cherries and measure 2 cups of the cherry juice, then boil for 5 minutes. Soak granulated gelatin in lemon juice for 5 minutes. Chop 2 cups of the cherries and stir in the softened gelatin mixture, then add to the hot cherry sirup. Stir well. Cool. When cold, rub mixture through a sieve, and pour into freezing trays of refrigerator. When frozen to a mush, turn mixture into a large bowl and beat well, using an egg beater, folding in at the same time the stiffly beaten egg white and the remaining whole cherries. Mold or place in refrigerator tray and freeze until firm (about 3 hours) stirring every 30 minutes until set. Then continue freezing without stirring until stiff. *See also* ICE.

CHERRY ICE CREAM

2 cups thin cream
1 cup sugar
2 cups cherries canned in sirup

Chop the drained cherries and add the sugar. Let stand for 15 or 20 minutes. Add the cream and freeze according to directions under ICE CREAM. This is best frozen in an ice cream freezer.

CHERRY JELLY

4 lb sour cherries
½ cup water
About 7 cups sugar (3 lb)
1 bottle liquid pectin (1 cup)

Wash, stem, and crush cherries. Add ½ cup water. Bring to a boil, cover, and simmer 10 minutes. Place fruit in bag; drain out juice. There should be about 3½ cups juice. Squeezing the bag will extract more juice, but the jelly will not be entirely clear. Measure 2 cups of sugar for each cup of juice into large saucepan. Mix thoroughly. Bring to a boil quickly over high heat. Add liquid pectin, stirring constantly. Bring to full rolling boil and boil hard ½ minute. Remove from fire, skim, pour quickly into hot sterilized glasses and cover with a thin film of melted paraffin. Cool and add a second layer of paraffin. Store in a cool dry place. (Makes 7 to 8 cups jelly) *See also* JELLY.

CHERRY-CURRANT JELLY

1½ lb ripe cherries
2 lb ripe currants
¾ cup water
7 cups sugar
½ bottle fruit pectin

To prepare the juice, stem (do not pit) and crush the cherries. Crush the currants and combine the fruits. Add the water, bring to boiling point, cover and simmer about 10 minutes. Turn into a jelly bag and press out the juice. Measure the juice (there should be 4½ cups) and sugar into a large saucepan. Mix well, bring to boiling point quickly, and at once add the pectin, stirring constantly. Bring to a full rolling boil and boil hard for half a minute. Remove from the fire, skim and pour quickly into hot, sterilized glasses. Seal. *See also* JELLY.

CHERRY KUCHEN

1 qt pitted red sour cherries
2 cups sifted flour
1 scant tsp soda
½ tsp salt
½ cup sugar
⅓ cup shortening
1 egg beaten, with
1 cup buttermilk (about)
2 tbsp butter

Wash the cherries. Sift together flour, soda, salt, and half the sugar. Cut in the shortening. Beat the egg slightly. Add two-thirds of the buttermilk to egg, and use to moisten the dry ingredients, using as much of the remaining buttermilk as necessary to make a soft dough.

Spread the dough about half an inch thick in a greased shallow baking pan (7x11 inches) building up a rim to hold in the fruit juice. Arrange the pitted cherries over the soft dough. Sprinkle them with the rest of the sugar, and dot with bits of butter.

Bake in a hot oven (400°–425° F.) for 40 minutes, or until the crust browns and the cherries are tender and look glazed. Remove from oven and place upon cake rack. Serve hot, or cool, with plain cream or ice cream. (Serves 6)

CHERRY LAURETTE

2 lb large black cherries
1 lb jar red currant jelly
2 tbsp brandy
1 lb sugar
2 lb raspberries
½ lemon
1 egg white

This is a particularly delicious dessert for hot weather. First make some raspberry water-ice as follows; crush the raspberries in a pint of cold water and strain. Make a sirup with 1 pint water and 1 pound sugar, cool and add the raspberry juice and lemon juice. Freeze the mixture and when half frozen fold in the stiffly beaten white of egg. While this is freezing, melt the currant jelly with the brandy, stone the cherries and add them to the melted jelly, then let cool. When ready to serve put a portion of raspberry ice on each plate and pour over some of the cherry sauce. *See also* ICE.

CHERRY MARLOW

½ lb marshmallows (about 32)
No. 2 tin sour, red cherries, or 2½ cups fresh pitted cherries
⅛ tsp salt
¼ tsp almond extract
1 cup whipping cream
1 tbsp lemon juice

Heat the marshmallows and juice drained from cherries over boiling water until marshmallows are melted but still fluffy. Remove from heat and stir in the finely chopped cherries. Add salt and almond extract, mix well, and chill thoroughly. Then whip cream until thick; add lemon juice and continue whipping until stiff. Fold cherry mixture into whipped cream, pour into freezing tray of mechanical refrigerator and freeze at the lowest temperature until firm, stirring once or twice if cherries tend to sink to the bottom. (Serves 5 or 6)

Note. If fresh cherries are used, add ¼ cup water to them and simmer in a covered pan until tender. Cool and drain before chopping.

CHERRY MARMALADE

2 lb pitted cherries
3 cups sugar
2 cups water
Lemon rind
Juice of 1 lemon
Orange rind
Juice of 1 orange

Combine cherries, sugar and water; simmer fifteen minutes and add juice and grated rind of lemon and orange. Continue cooking until sirup sheets from spoon. Remove from fire. Cool about 5 minutes, stirring frequently to prevent floating fruit. Pour into clean dry glasses, filling them to within ¼ inch of top. When cold and set, cover with paraffin, as directed for jelly; store in a cool, dry, dark place. *See also* JELLY and MARMALADE.

CHERRY AND PINEAPPLE MARMALADE

Wash, drain and pit the cherries, then pass through the food chopper. Peel and chop, shred, or grind the pineapple. Combine the two fruits, using ¾ cherries and ¼ pineapple. Measure and add two-thirds as much sugar as fruit and juice. Cook gently until thick and clear, stirring to prevent burning. Turn into sterilized jars and seal. *See also* MARMALADE.

CHERRY MOUSSE

1 No. 2 can red pitted cherries
2 tsp granulated gelatin
2 tbsp cold water
½ cup granulated sugar
1 tbsp lemon juice
⅛ tsp salt
1 cup heavy cream

Reserve a few whole cherries to garnish the mousse when unmolded. Rub the remaining cherries through a coarse sieve. Heat cherry pulp and juice to the boiling point; add gelatin which has been softened in cold water. Stir, then add sugar and lemon juice and salt and chill. Whip the cream to a custard-like consistency. When well-chilled, stir in the whipped cream and freeze in refrigerator tray until mushy; then scrape bottom and sides and beat for 2 minutes. Return to refrigerator and continue freezing for 3 hours, or until firm. *See also* MOUSSE for directions for molding and freezing in ice pail.

CHERRY PIE I
(Using canned cherries)

Pastry for 8-inch double crust
½ cup sugar, or to suit taste
⅛ tsp salt
3 tbsp flour or 1½ tbsp cornstarch
No. 2 can sour red cherries (2½ cups)
4 drops almond extract

Line pie pan with pastry (*which see*). Mix sugar, salt and flour together in saucepan; blend in juice drained from cherries (¾ to ⅞ cup). Cook over direct heat, stirring constantly until mixture boils and thickens. Remove from heat, add almond extract. Then turn drained cherries (1¾ cups) into pastry-lined pan and pour thickened juice over them. Roll out pastry for upper crust, cut a design for steam vents; moisten edge of lower crust with water, lay upper crust over it and press together; trim, let rest 10 minutes. Flute edge. Bake in a hot oven (450° F.) for 15 minutes until crust is lightly browned; then reduce heat to moderately slow (325° F.) and continue baking 15 minutes longer. Cool on cake rack before cutting.

CHERRY PIE II
(Using Fresh Cherries)

Pastry for 8-inch double crust
¼ cup flour or 2 tbsp cornstarch
¾ to 1 cup sugar
Pinch salt
1 qt sour red cherries (3 cups pitted)
4 drops almond extract
1 tbsp butter

Line pie pan with plain pastry (*see* PASTRY). Mix flour, sugar, and salt thoroughly and sprinkle about ⅓ of it over bottom of pastry-lined pan. Put the cherries in and sprinkle with rest of flour-sugar mixture; then sprinkle with extract. Dot with butter. Brush edges of lower crust with water before laying on top crust. Roll pastry for upper crust; cut a design for steam vents and lay over cherries; seal upper and lower edges together. Trim off excess dough, let rest 10 minutes and flute. Bake in a hot oven (450° F.) for 15 minutes; then reduce heat to moderately slow (325° F.) and bake 20 to 25 minutes longer, until cherries are done. Remove to cake rack to cool, 3 to 4 hours before cutting. Serve plain, with a wedge of sharp cheese, whipping cream, or a scoop of vanilla ice cream.

CHERRY CHIFFON PIE

No. 2 can red cherries, packed in sirup
1 tbsp gelatin (1 envelope)
3 eggs, separated
1 tbsp lemon juice
½ cup sugar
⅛ tsp salt
Baked 8-inch pie shell

Drain the cherries, saving the juice. Soften the gelatin in ¼ cup of the juice. Chop the cherries fine. Beat egg yolks in top of double boiler and add rest of cherry juice, lemon juice, and half the sugar. Cook over boiling water, stirring constantly until just thickened, about 5 minutes. Remove from heat, add softened gelatin, and stir until dissolved. Add cherries. Chill until mixture is thick and sirupy and begins to set. Beat egg whites with the salt until stiff, add the remaining sugar, and continue beating until very thick and smooth. Fold thoroughly but lightly into cherry mixture, and turn into cooled pastry shell (*see* PASTRY). Chill in refrigerator until firm. Serve with whipped cream, if desired.

CHERRY RELISH

4 cups sour cherries
1 cup seeded raisins
1/4 cup firmly packed brown sugar
1/2 cup honey
1/2 cup vinegar
1 tsp cinnamon
1/4 tsp cloves
3/4 cup pecans

Wash and pit the cherries; mix with raisins, sugar, honey, vinegar, and spices, bring to boil, and simmer 1 hour or until thick. Add nuts, turn into sterilized glass jars, and seal. (Yields 4 half-pint jars) *See also* CANNING.

CHERRY SAUCE

1 cup sieved cherry pulp
1/4 cup sugar
1/3 cup cherry juice
1 tbsp orange juice

Either stewed fresh or canned cherries may be used. Simmer the fruit, sugar and juice for ten minutes, stirring constantly. Remove from the heat, and add the orange juice.

CHERRY SHORTCAKE

To pitted cherries, add 1/2 to 3/4 cup sugar and 3 tablespoons water, and simmer 2 minutes, stirring until sugar is dissolved. Cool. Make shortcake (*which see*). Place lower half of hot biscuit on serving dish and spoon cherries and juice over it. Cover with top half of biscuit, spoon more cherries and juice over top. Serve immediately, topping with whipped cream, if desired.

CHERRY TARTS

Line tart tins with pastry (*which see*); trim and crimp the edges. Bake the crust in a brisk oven until brown. Spread on the crust a rich cream filling and set in it enough cherries to cover the whole surface. The cherries must be pitted first, and boiled in water and sugar. The sirup in which they are cooked is simmered, after the cherries are taken out, long enough to become quite thick, when it is used to glaze the cherries. Decorate the cold tarts by piping whipped cream around the edge. *See* CREAM.

CHERRY MERINGUE TART

1 qt tart cherries
1 cup granulated sugar
1/4 tsp salt
3 tbsp flour
1/8 tsp almond extract
2 egg whites
1/4 cup powdered sugar
1/2 tsp vanilla

Wash and pit cherries. Mix granulated sugar, salt, flour and flavoring: add to cherries and mix well. Turn into deep 9-inch pie plate, cover and bake in moderate oven (350° F.) for 30 minutes, or until fruit is tender. Beat egg whites until stiff, add powdered sugar gradually, beating until blended and add flavoring. Drop in 6 mounds on cherries and bake 15 minutes longer, or until meringue is lightly browned. (Serves 6)

CHERRY UPSIDE-DOWN CAKE

2 cups all-purpose flour
2 1/4 tsp baking powder
1/4 tsp salt
1 cup sugar
2 eggs, separated
1/2 cup milk
1/3 cup melted butter or margarine
No. 2 can unsweetened red cherries or
    2 1/2 cups pitted fresh cherries
1 tbsp brown sugar
1 tsp cinnamon

Sift flour, measure, and resift 3 times with baking powder, salt, and 3/4 cup of the sugar. Beat egg yolks, add milk and melted butter. Add milk mixture all at once to the flour mixture and stir quickly until batter is just smooth. Beat egg whites until fluffy, then beat in remaining sugar until stiff and glossy; fold thoroughly into batter; then fold in 1 cup well drained cherries. (Save juice for sauce.) Turn into baking pan lined with thin, plain paper (7 1/2 x 11 x 1 1/2 inches), and sprinkle top with brown sugar and cinnamon mixed together. Bake in a moderately hot oven (400° F.) for 35 minutes, or until cake tests done. Serve hot or cold with sauce made as follows:

Heat cherry juice to boiling. Blend 1 tablespoon cornstarch with 3 tablespoons sugar, add 3 tablespoons cold water, and mix to a smooth paste. Add to hot juice and stir over direct heat until sauce boils and thickens. Stir in a pinch of salt, 1 tablespoon butter, ⅛ teaspoon almond extract, and remaining cherries. Serve warm or cold over cake, top with whipped cream if desired. (Serves 6 to 8)

CHERRY UPSIDE-DOWN PUDDING

1½ cups all-purpose flour
1½ tsp baking powder
¼ tsp salt
½ cup butter or other shortening
1 cup sugar
1 egg, unbeaten
1 tsp vanilla
1 cup milk
¾ cup sugar
No. 2 tin sour red pitted cherries(2½ cups)
½ cup boiling water
Cream

Sift the flour, measure and resift 3 times with baking powder, and salt. Cream the butter, add the cup of sugar gradually and continue creaming until light and fluffy. Beat in the whole egg. Stir in vanilla. Add sifted ingredients alternately with milk, beginning and ending with flour and beating well after each addition. Turn into a greased 9-inch square pan 3 inches deep.

Prepare sauce by heating the ¾ cup of sugar, cherries, juice and boiling water, and pour it over the batter. Place in a moderate oven (350° F.) and bake for 35 to 45 minutes, or until pudding just begins to shrink from sides of pan, and top is golden brown. When baked, cherries and sauce will be on the bottom. Serve warm by spooning into individual dishes with some of cherry sauce over each serving. Top with whipped cream if desired. (Serves 8)

EGG PANCAKES WITH CHERRY SAUCE

1 cup milk
3 eggs, beaten
1 cup sifted flour
¾ tsp salt
1 tbsp sugar
3 tbsp shortening

Stir ½ cup of the milk into the eggs. Add the flour, salt and sugar all at once, and beat with a rotary beater until smooth. Add the remaining milk and mix thor-

oughly. Heat 1 teaspoon shortening in a 9-inch skillet and add ¼ cup of the batter. Rotate skillet slightly so that the batter runs to the edges all around. Bake until delicately browned on each side, turning once. Remove to a large plate, quickly spread with 3 tablespoons of cottage cheese filling, and roll. Continue baking and filling pancakes until all the batter is used. Arrange on a hot platter and serve with cherry sauce.

Cottage Cheese Filling

1 lb creamed cottage cheese
¾ tsp grated lemon rind
2 tbsp sugar
Dash of salt

Combine all of the ingredients together in the order given.

Cherry Sauce

½ lb sour pitted cherries
1 cup water
⅓ cup sugar
3 tbsp lemon huice
2 tbsp cornstarch
1 tbsp cold water

Simmer the cherries with the water, sugar and lemon juice for 10 minutes. Make a paste of the cornstarch and cold water and stir it into the cherry mixture. Cook until slightly thickened and clear. (Makes 10 pancakes)

MOLDED CHERRY NUT SALAD

1 tbsp gelatin
2 tbsp cold water
½ cup boiling water
2 tsp sugar
Dash of salt
¼ cup lemon juice
1 cup ginger ale
½ cup canned white cherries
¼ cup pecans
Lettuce
Mayonnaise

Soften gelatin in cold water 5 minutes and dissolve in boiling water. Add sugar, salt, lemon juice and ginger ale; chill. When slightly thickened, fold in cherries that have been seeded and stuffed with pecans. Turn into individual molds; chill until firm. Unmold on crisp lettuce and garnish with mayonnaise. (Serves 6)

WILD CHERRY WINE

Heat 16 quarts of wild cherries and 6 gallons of water to the boiling point. Simmer for 10 minutes and strain off the juice, pressing the cherries to extract it. Put the liquid into a large crock. Measure and add 3 pounds of granulated sugar to each gallon of juice. Mix thoroughly till sugar is dissolved and cool to lukewarm. Then add ½ cake of compressed yeast for each gallon of juice and ½ pound of chopped seedless raisins. Mix well. Cover the crock and allow the mixture to ferment for 5 days or until the bubbling has ceased. Stir well and add 1 pint of good brandy. Keep covered. At the end of three months, filter the wine and bottle it. This is best made in a stone crock or wine keg.

CHERVIL

CHERVIL. Chervil is a garden herb belonging to the parsley family, and it can be used to replace parsley in any recipe. Its flavor resembles that of parsley, but not very strongly—it is more delicate and also more aromatic. Because of their delicate flavor chervil leaves are usually accompanied by stronger herbs, such as chives, particularly in *bouquet garnis*. Chervil leaves are used to garnish or to season soups, salads, sauces, and appetizers, and they have a particular affinity for cheese, eggs, and beef.

CHESHIRE CHEESE. The oldest English cheese which was well thought of in the 17th century. It is made of cow's milk

and is supposed to owe its particular flavor to the saline content of the Cheshire soil on which the cows graze.

Cheshire cheese, which is a hard cheese like Cheddar, may come in white, red, or blue types. The white cheese is made from the uncolored milk; the red type has coloring added during the making. The blue cheese happens occasionally as the result of natural fungus action in the red cheese. A small proportion of red cheeses lose their color and develop a system of blue veins throughout the cheese, like Stilton or Roquefort. However, unlike these types, the fungus is not added deliberately to the Cheshire cheese. The blue cheese has a very fine rich flavor.

CHESTNUT. The native American chestnut, small and sweet, has been virtually eliminated by the chestnut blight which destroyed the trees about three decades ago. Experimentation is being carried on to develop a disease-resistant tree, but at the present time, the chestnuts which are found in market are imported.

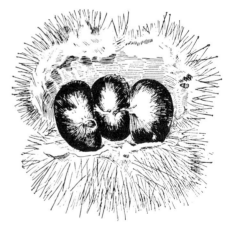

CHESTNUT

Chestnuts are best eaten cooked, and they may be roasted, boiled, or puréed. They are particularly delicious with brussels sprouts. Marrons glacés is a typically French preparation of preserved chestnuts. One pound of chestnuts in the shell will yield 2 cups of shelled meats.

To shell a chestnut, make a gash in the side of each shell with a sharp knife and place the chestnuts in boiling water for 15 minutes or so. Drain the nuts and remove the shell and the inner brown skin immediately. The nuts may also be heated in a hot oven (450° F.) for 20 minutes and the shell and skin removed with a knife.

BOILED CHESTNUTS

Blanch and shell the nuts and simmer, covered, in boiling salted water until just tender, 10 to 20 minutes. Drain well. Mash the chestnuts or put them through a ricer and season to taste with salt, pepper, and butter. Or the nuts may be left whole and combined with brussels sprouts.

CHESTNUT SOUP

1 small knuckle of veal
1 tsp salt
12 peppercorns
1 small slice garlic
2 bay leaves
Pinch of thyme
2 cloves
1 stalk celery, diced
2½ qt water
½ cup flour
1 qt boiled chestnuts
1 cup cream
2 eggs

Combine the veal with the seasonings and flavorings, add the water and simmer 1½ hours. Remove the veal knuckle and thicken with the flour blended smoothly with 1 cup of water, stirring while adding, and simmering for 5 minutes. Strain, then combine with the chopped, cooked, peeled chestnuts and the cream beaten with the eggs. Stir with a wire whisk until very hot but not actually boiling. Serve immediately. (Serves 6)

CHESTNUT STUFFING
(For Turkey)

2 lb Italian chestnuts
1 tbsp cooking oil
6 cups soft bread crumbs
½ cup melted butter
1 tbsp minced onion
2 tsp salt
1 tbsp chopped parsley
Dash of pepper

Make two ½ inch slits with a sharp knife in the shell of each chestnut. Place them in a deep saucepan with the oil and cook slowly for 5 minutes, shaking the pan fre-

quently. Then bake in a very hot oven (400° F.) for 5 minutes. Remove and cool until they can be handled. Remove shells and skins with the aid of a sharp knife, then mash the nuts and add them to the bread crumbs which have been blended with all remaining ingredients. *See* STUFF-ING.

CHIANTI. A medium-bodied, strongly flavored red table wine made from Sangioveto grapes; it is dry, fruity, and slightly tart. Originally an Italian wine, it is shipped and sold in unique straw covered *fiascos* or bottles. It is also made in California and other places.

Chianti goes well with red meats and all paste dishes, especially Italian dishes. It is served either at room temperature or slightly chilled. *See* WINE.

CHIAVARI CHEESE. A hard, rennet, sour-milk cheese made from the whole milk of cows. It is also known as Caccio Romano.

CHICK PEA. A plant, the roasted seed of which is known in the East as "pulse." *See* BEAN.

CHICKEN. Chicken ranks high as a digestible meat, the white meat being slightly more digestible than the dark, although there is little difference in the chemical composition. The meat of chicken is shorter fibered than most butcher's meats, and it is not interspersed with fat. Chicken fat is found in layers directly under the skin and surrounding the intestines.

In purchasing chickens, select birds which are fresh and plump, with well rounded breasts. In young immature birds the tip of the breast bone is flexible, and this is a good test of the tenderness of a chicken. The skin may be white or yellow, depending on the breed, but it should be thin, moist, and tender. The legs should be smooth, the feet limber, and the claws short.

MARKET CLASSIFICATIONS

The Department of Agriculture classifies chickens into seven classes according to age, sex, and weight.

Broilers. These are young chickens of either sex, eight to twelve weeks old, which do not weigh over 2½ pounds. They are sufficiently soft meated to be cooked by broiling.

Fryers. These are young chickens of either sex, fourteen to twenty weeks old, weighing between 2½ and 3½ pounds. They are sufficiently soft meated to be cooked by frying.

Roasters. These are young chickens of either sex, five to nine months old, weighing over 3½ pounds, and sufficiently tender to be cooked by roasting.

Stags. These are male birds with comb and spur development which shows them to be older than roasters, but not so mature as cocks. The flesh is slightly darkened and tougher than a roasting chicken.

Capons. These are unsexed male birds, seven to ten months old, and weighing over four pounds. Their flesh is very soft and tender.

Fowl. These are mature female birds, which may be any size and weight, and are suitable only for stewing or making soup.

Cocks. These are mature male birds, which may be any size and weight, and are comparable to fowl in quality.

UNITED STATES GRADES

There are four grades of dressed poultry which have been set up by federal standards.

U.S. Special. This grade includes young, fine-grained, soft-meated birds with broad full-fleshed breasts. The entire carcass is covered with fat and the skin is soft and glossy. The birds must be well bled, cleanly dressed, free of pin feathers, and have an empty crop. There must be no flesh or skin bruises or discolorations. The conformation of the bird must be perfect, with no crooked breasts or broken wing tips. The bird must be dry-picked or semi-scalded and dry packed.

U.S. Prime. This grade is only slightly below the special grade in quality. The breast may be not so broad, and the pin feathers may not have been entirely removed. No deformities or broken limbs are permitted. The birds may have had the crop removed and properly sewn up. They must be dry-picked or semi-scalded and dry packed.

U.S. Choice. Birds in this grade have fairly well fleshed breasts and a fair coverage of fat. They must be fairly well bled and dressed, but may show a few pin feathers. The crop must be practically empty. Slight bruises and abrasions, a crooked breast, or a broken wing or leg, if the bone does not protrude, are permitted.

U.S. Commercial. All birds which do not fit into the higher grades, but are considered fit for food are included in this grade. Badly bruised or emaciated birds, or those showing disease are not permitted.

PREPARATION FOR MARKET

Poultry which is raised for market is finished in one of two ways. It may be milk fed, which means that for six to ten days before the birds are killed they are fed milk with their ration. This bleaches the skin and flesh and gives a bird with fatty deposits throughout the muscle fiber. Grain fed poultry does not show these desirable qualities.

In slaughtering chickens, the two objectives are the complete removal of the blood and the feathers. The birds must be thoroughly bled, otherwise the flesh becomes discolored and the meat deteriorates rapidly. Poultry is picked by two methods—dry picking and scalding. Milk fed poultry is always dry-plucked. In the bleeding process, the muscles controlling the feathers become paralyzed and relaxed, and the feathers are easily removed. The large feathers are removed first, and then the pin feathers.

Poultry is scalded by plunging it into hot water. This relaxes the external tissues and makes removal of the feathers easy. The water must be hot enough to scald the feathers, but not hot enough to cook the skin. When this happens the skin is torn in removing the feathers. Scalding is almost never used in preparing broilers, fryers, and roasters and capons because the skin is much less attractive and the keeping qualities are considerably injured.

Poultry is usually sent to market without being drawn, but within recent years and with the improvement of refrigeration facilities, full drawn poultry has appeared on the market. After the poultry is dressed, the head, feet, and entrails are removed. The giblets are cleaned, wrapped in parchment or wax paper, and replaced in the body cavity. The entire carcass is then quick frozen and marketed in the frozen state. Advocates of this method claim that the flesh is much sweeter than when the bird is stored with the entrails in.

HINTS ON PREPARATION

Chicken is usually obtained from the butcher drawn and cut up, if it is to be stewed or fried. However, it is very simple to perform these operations in the home.

To draw a bird. Place the bird on a large sheet of paper. Before cutting off the feet, remove the tendons which connect with the drum sticks. Do this by making a cut about two inches long on the shank and lifting out the tendons with a skewer or hook. They will remain attached to the feet and can be cut off with the feet. Remove the oil sack at the back of the tail by cutting off down to the backbone and back to the tail.

Cut the neck skin down the back to the shoulder. Pull out the neck and cut it off close to the shoulder. Loosen the crop, gullet, and windpipe and very gently pull them away from the skin and out of the body. Cut them off where they enter the body. Be sure that you find the crop and remove it.

Turn the bird endwise and make as small an incision as possible from one-half inch below the end of the breastbone to

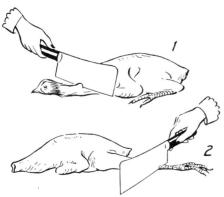

the vent. With practice, an amazingly small incision will serve. The cut must go through the fat, but should not cut the intestine. Insert the forefinger into the cut and lift up the intestine leading to the vent. Cut around the vent in a small circle.

Work two fingers into the cavity and locate the gizzard, which is at the center right of the bird. Grasp the gizzard firmly and pull gently but firmly until the entrails come out intact. It is important that they are not broken in the process since they will give a bad taste to the meat.

Lay the entrails on another piece of paper. Cut the gizzard away from its attachments. Clean the gizzard by cutting into one of its thick sides until the inner sac is reached, but do not cut this inner sac. Spread the two sides of the gizzard with the thumbs and peel it away from the inner sac. Discard the inner sac and lay the cleaned gizzard aside. Cut the heart away and place it with the gizzard. Lift the liver away from the intestines and find the gall sac on the under side. Slip the knife under the sac and cut it away, removing any part of the liver stained by the gall. This is extremely bitter and will spoil the liver for eating if it is not entirely removed. Save the liver with the other giblets. Carefully remove the fat surrounding the intestines and render it out for shortening. Chicken fat is very rich and can be used in place of butter in making pastry and cakes.

Rinse the giblets and the inside of the chicken with cool water to remove any bits of blood or other matter. Check that

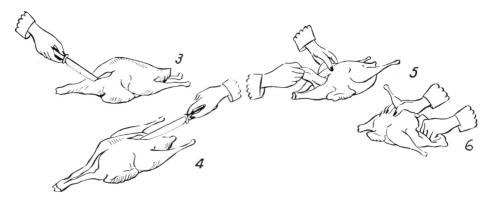

DRESSING A CHICKEN 1. Cutting off head and top of neck 2. Cutting off feet at end of drumstick 3. Making incision at base of neck 4. Making incision at base of abdomen 5. Removing crop, gullet and windpipe 6. Removing entrails

the lungs and kidneys, which cling to the carcass, have been removed. Drain the chicken well, wrap it, and store in the refrigerator until ready to use. Wrap the giblets separately and store them with the chicken.

STUFFING A CHICKEN

To cut up a chicken. A very sharp knife is the only tool required. The neck should be cut off and the crop, gullet, and windpipe removed as described above. Then cut up the bird as follows. Grasp one wing, pulling it up until the skin at the joint is taut. Slash through the skin, flesh, and joint, and do the same for the second wing. Fold the wing tips under the shoulder joints to keep a tidy piece.

Hold the leg out from the body until the skin is taut. Make a three-inch cut and notice how the leg separates from the breast meat. Cut the skin around the leg

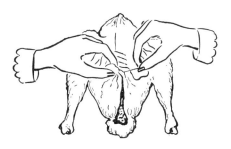

SEWING A CHICKEN

from the back nearly to the tail. Cut through the joint and press the leg back. Complete the cut through the tendons. Divide the legs into drum stick and thigh by cutting through the joint.

Lay the bird on its side. Slip two fingers into the opening where the wing was and loosen the lungs and the heart. Insert the knife into the wing opening with the sharp

edge away from you. Cut through the skin, following a straight line through the ribs to about one inch below the vent. Turn the bird and cut the other side the same way.

Now lay the bird so that the breast is up. Hold the tail end down firmly. Grasp the tip of the breast with the other hand and pull it back until the joints break. Cut around the vent to loosen the vent from the back section. Free the lungs from the ribs. Grasp the heart and liver firmly and pull the entrails together with the vent from the back. Cut the oil sac from the tail. The back and breast may be left whole or cut into two or three pieces depending on the size of the bird. Prepare the giblets as directed above. Wash and dry the pieces, and wrap and store in the refrigerator until ready to use.

TRUSSED CHICKEN

To bone a chicken. Have the bird plucked and singed, and head and feet removed, but do not have it drawn.

With a very sharp pointed knife (there are small boning knives made for the purpose) cut through the skin the entire length of the body, beginning at the neck. Scrape and cut the flesh from the backbone right down to the shoulder blade, being careful not to pierce the skin. Scrape the flesh from the shoulder blade and continue cutting around the wing joint, pointing the knife so that it scrapes the bone but never cuts through the skin. Do the same on the other side of the bird. Scrape the flesh from the second joints and the drum sticks. Sever the leg bones at their joints and draw them out of the flesh.

After the flesh has all been separated from the bones, the entire carcass with the entrails in place may be lifted out, leaving the fleshy part of the bird intact. It is then reshaped with stuffing and sewed up for roasting.

A boned chicken is a particularly special dish which is not really very difficult to prepare.

COOKING METHODS

Cooking times for poultry are generally given in terms of dressed weight. This means that the chicken should be weighed after the entrails have been removed in order to figure the time accurately.

Chicken should always be cooked to a well done state. This means that the meat has lost its pinkness and is white. To broil a chicken weighing two pounds to well done will take 35 to 45 minutes at 350° F. A roasting chicken weighing four or five pounds will require 1½ to 2 hours at 350°.

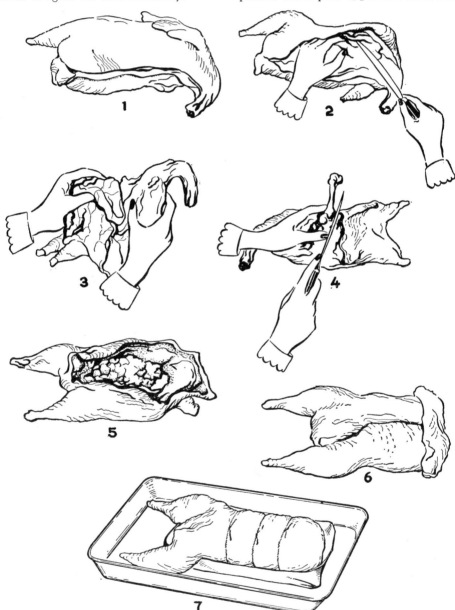

BONING A CHICKEN 1. External cuts 2. Loosening flesh 3. Removing flesh
4. Removing bones 5. Stuffing added 6. Envelope fold 7. Tied for roasting

A chicken to be stuffed and roasted should be trussed. Allow one cup of stuffing per pound of chicken. Rub the cavity of the bird with salt and insert the stuffing lightly. Fasten the opening by inserting small skewers across the opening and lacing with light cord. Put enough stuffing into the neck opening to plump out the neck and fasten the neck skin to the back with a skewer. Bring the tips of the wings up onto the back. Tie the drum sticks together and tie them securely to the tail.

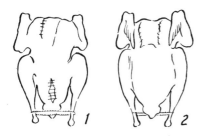

TRUSSED CHICKEN FOR ROASTING
1. **Breast up**   2. **Back up**

BOILED CHICKEN

Clean and wash a fowl and leave it whole or cut it in pieces, depending on the use for which it is intended. Add boiling water to half cover and cover the pot tightly. Simmer for 2 or 3 hours, or until tender. Add ½ teaspoon of salt per pound of chicken after the first hour of cooking.

BROILED CHICKEN

Have the bird dressed for broiling, with the backbone, neck, and wing tips removed. Have the broiler set at 350° F., or in a broiler without a regulator, turn the flame high and set the rack so that the chicken will be 3 inches from the flame. Place the chicken, skin side down, on a well greased preheated rack, and brush with melted butter, cooking oil, or other fat. Cook until slightly browned, seasoning with salt and pepper when partly cooked. Baste frequently with a little melted butter or fat mixed with water or chicken fat. Turn the bird skin side up, brush with more fat, season with salt and pepper, and continue broiling until done, basting frequently with the pan drippings. Allow 15 to 25 minutes for each side, depending on the size of the bird.

FRIED CHICKEN

Small chickens may be quartered and larger chickens cut into convenient pieces for frying. For each pound of chicken blend:

¼ cup flour
1 tsp paprika
½ tsp salt
⅛ tsp pepper

Rub the seasoned flour into the pieces of chicken. Heat enough fat in a heavy skillet to have ½ inch of melted fat. Any desired fat or cooking oil may be used. Start the meaty pieces first, slipping the less meaty pieces in as the chicken begins to brown. Avoid crowding; use two skillets, or remove the pieces as they are browned and keep warm until all are browned. As soon as the chicken is brown, reduce the heat and cook the chicken slowly until tender, 30 to 60 minutes, depending on the size of the chicken. Replace the pieces which have been kept warm, and as soon as all are a light tan in color, cover the skillet tightly. Turn the pieces two or three times during the cooking process so they brown evenly. If the cover does not fit tightly, or the bird weighs more than 3 pounds, it is a good idea to add about 2 tablespoons of water when the pan is covered. Uncover the pan during the last 15 minutes to recrisp the skin. When the chicken is done remove the pieces to a hot platter and prepare gravy from the pan drippings.

ROAST CHICKEN

Place the trussed bird on a rack in a shallow open roasting pan. Rub the skin with salt and pepper and brush with melted fat. Cover the top and sides of the bird with clean white cheesecloth which has been moistened with fat. Place the pan in an oven which has been preheated to 350° F. Do not add any water and do not cover the pan. Baste the chicken from time to time with the pan drippings. Roast for 30 to 45 minutes per pound, depending on the size of the chicken, allowing longer per pound for a smaller chicken than for a larger one. About three-quarters through the cooking time, turn the bird breast side up and finish cooking. The chicken is done when the thigh meat is soft when pinched. Do not pierce the skin with a fork as this allows juices to escape.

Remove the chicken to a heated platter, remove the skewers and string, and prepare gravy from the pan drippings.

STEAMED CHICKEN

Leave the chicken whole and place, breast up, on a rack in a large kettle. Add lightly salted water to the level of the rack and cover the kettle. Simmer until the bird is tender, 3 or 4 hours, adding more water as it boils away, but not letting the water level come above the rack. A steamed chicken has a particularly fine flavor for use in salads and other similar dishes.

ARROZ CON POLLO
(Rice with Chicken)

1 fryer, 3 to 3½ lb
½ cup olive oil
1 medium-sized onion, chopped
1¼ tsp salt
⅛ tsp pepper
1 clove garlic
1 tip bay leaf
3 cups canned tomatoes
1 cup raw rice
¾ tsp salt
6 pimiento-stuffed olives
1 green pepper

Disjoint the chicken and wipe the pieces. Cook gently in the hot olive oil until browned, turning occasionally to brown evenly. Remove the chicken. Cook the onion in the oil until transparent. Replace the chicken and add the salt and pepper, the tomatoes which have been heated to boiling, and the garlic and bay leaf. Wash the rice and add to the mixture. Sprinkle the ¾ teaspoon of salt over the surface. Cook gently over low heat or in a moderate oven (350° F.) until the rice is tender and fluffy and the liquid is absorbed, about 1 hour. Lift and stir the rice once after the first 15 or 20 minutes. Remove the garlic and bay leaf. Turn onto a warm platter and garnish with thin slices of olives and green pepper rings. (Serves 5 or 6)

CASSEROLE OF FOWL WITH VEGETABLES

4 to 5 lb fowl
Salt and pepper
Flour
2 tbsp butter or margarine
3 carrots
1 bunch celery
1 medium-sized onion
1 green pepper
1 cup hot water
1 cup milk

Cut up the fowl, season with salt and pepper, and sprinkle with the flour. Brown the pieces in the fat in a frying pan. Remove the browned pieces to a casserole. Chop the vegetables and pour them into the frying pan. Stir them around to absorb the fat. Then transfer them to the casserole with the chicken. Add a cup of hot water, and cover. Bake in a slow oven (275° F.) for 3 or 4 hours, or until the chicken is tender. Add more water from time to time if necessary. Just before serving, remove the pieces of fowl and skim off the excess fat. With 2 tablespoons of the fat mix 2 tablespoons of flour and stir into the milk. Add to the contents of the casserole. Cook for 10 minutes longer, season to taste, and pour the vegetable sauce over the chicken on a platter, or replace the pieces of chicken in the sauce and serve from the casserole. (Serves 6 or 8)

CHICKEN A LA KING

3 tbsp butter or margarine
1 cup diced mushrooms
2 tbsp minced green pepper
4 tbsp flour
⅔ tsp salt
⅓ tsp celery salt
⅛ tsp cayenne pepper
1½ cups milk
1 cup chicken stock
3 cups cooked chicken, cut in large dice
1 tbsp minced parsley
1 tbsp diced pimiento
2 egg yolks
3 tbsp sherry

Melt the butter and cook the mushrooms and green pepper in it for 5 minutes. Add the flour and seasonings and cook, stirring constantly, until smooth. Add the milk and chicken stock very slowly, stirring constantly. Bring to the boiling point, still stirring constantly, and simmer 5 minutes. Add the chicken, parsley, and pimiento, reheat thoroughly, and then stir in the egg yolks and sherry. Blend thoroughly and serve immediately, or keep warm over hot water. Serve on toast or in patty shells. (Serves 6 or 8)

Chicken a la Maryland

Have a frying chicken weighing about 2½ pounds split and the neck and backbone removed. Then quarter it, or cut into smaller pieces. Wipe the pieces thoroughly. Dip first into cold milk and then into seasoned flour. Cook golden brown in a heavy pan, using enough fat to half cover the chicken. Lift the pieces out as they brown and transfer them to another pan. Cover them closely and place the pan in a moderate oven (350°–375° F.). Continue cooking until the chicken is tender.

Meanwhile cook the neck, backbone, and wing tips with a little carrot, onion, parsley, and half a bay leaf in water to cover, until tender. Strain the liquid and use equal parts of this chicken stock and rich milk or cream to make a cream sauce (*which see*).

When the chicken is done, remove it to a hot platter, pour the cream sauce around it, and serve with corn fritters, strips of crisp bacon, and small potato croquettes.

Chicken and Mushrooms with Biscuit Rings

1 can condensed cream of tomato soup
1 can water, or bouillon, or meat stock
Leftover gravy and onions
Salt and pepper
2 cups diced cooked chicken
Baking powder biscuit dough

Heat the soup with the water, bouillon or meat stock, the gravy, and seasonings. Pour over the onions and chicken in a buttered shallow casserole. Roll out the biscuit dough (*which see*) on a slightly floured board, cut with a doughnut cutter and place the rings on top of the chicken mixture. Bake in a very hot oven (450° F.) 12–15 minutes. (Serves 6)

Chicken Cacciatore

1 fryer, 2½ to 3 lb
½ cup olive oil
1 onion, thinly sliced
3½ cups canned tomatoes, or 8 medium-sized tomatoes
1 clove garlic
1 tsp salt
¼ tsp pepper
½ cup white wine

Disjoint the chicken and wipe well. Cook slowly in the olive oil until golden brown, turning occasionally to brown evenly. Add the onions and cook until the onions are yellow and transparent. Add the tomatoes, garlic, salt, and pepper. Cover tightly and simmer until the chicken is tender and the tomatoes are reduced to a thick sauce, about 45 minutes. Add the wine the last 15 minutes of cooking. Remove the clove of garlic before serving. (Serves 4 or 5)

Chicken Croquettes

4 tbsp butter or margarine
5 tbsp flour
1 cup milk
½ cup chicken broth
3 cups ground cooked chicken
1 tsp finely chopped onion
1 tbsp chopped parsley
Salt and pepper
1 egg
1 tbsp water
Dry bread crumbs
Fat for deep frying

Make a thick cream sauce with the fat, flour, milk, and broth, and let it stand until cold. When the sauce is cold, add the chicken, onion, and parsley, and salt and pepper to taste. Mold the mixture into croquette shape. Beat the egg with the water. Dip the croquettes in this mixture, roll in the bread crumbs and let stand until ready to fry.

Heat the fat in a deep kettle to 350° F. Carefully place several croquettes at a time in a frying basket, lower slowly into the fat, and fry until brown. Remove the fried croquettes and drain on soft crumpled paper. Serve hot with a cream or mushroom sauce. (Serves 5 or 6)

Chicken Fricasse with Dumplings

Disjoint a fowl and place the pieces in a kettle. Add lightly salted water to cover, partly cover the kettle, and cook the fowl until tender. Simmer gently, do not allow to boil. The chicken will take 3 or 4 hours. When tender, remove the pieces from the broth and keep warm.

There should be 3 to 4 cups of broth in the kettle. Skim off the fat and measure the broth. For each cup of skimmed broth mix 1½ tablespoons of the fat with the same amount of flour. Stir several spoonfuls of the hot broth into the fat-flour mixture, and then pour the mixture back into the broth in the kettle. Cook the gravy until it is slightly thickened. Season to taste. Now make the dumplings.

3/4 cup sifted flour
2 1/2 tsp baking powder
1/2 tsp salt
1 egg
1/3 cup milk

Sift the flour, baking powder, and salt together. Beat the egg, add the milk, and mix with the dry ingredients. Drop by spoonfuls into the boiling chicken gravy. Cover tightly and cook for 15 minutes. The cover must not be removed while the dumplings are cooking.

Arrange the chicken on a platter, pour the gravy over, and add the dumplings.

CHICKEN GUMBO

1 small broiler
Seasoned flour
2 tbsp bacon fat
1 onion, diced
1/2 cup chopped tomatoes
1 cup finely chopped okra
1/2 green pepper, chopped
3 green onion tops, chopped
2 qt boiling water
2 tbsp chopped celery
1 tsp minced parsley
1/2 tsp thyme
1 bay leaf
1 carrot, diced
1 thin slice garlic
Salt and pepper

Disjoint the broiler as for frying and roll the pieces in seasoned flour. Heat the bacon fat in a heavy pan and brown the pieces of chicken in it. Cook the onion in the same fat until beginning to brown, then add the tomatoes, okra, green pepper and onion tops, and continue cooking, covered, for 10 minutes. Add all remaining ingredients and cook slowly, still covered, for 1 hour. Serve in soup plates putting a piece of chicken in each plate and passing well-broiled rice separately. (Serves 6)

CHICKEN LIVER HORS D'OEUVRES

Cut chicken livers in halves, wash them, and spread them with a mixture contain-ing equal portions of mustard and finely chopped olives. Cut slices of bacon in halves. Wrap a piece of bacon around each chicken liver, secure with toothpicks, and roll in bread crumbs. Bake in a hot oven (425° F.) for 10 to 15 minutes.

CHICKEN LOAF

4 1/2 tbsp butter or margarine
1/2 cup flour
1 cup chicken broth
1/2 cup milk
1 tbsp chopped onion
2 tbsp chopped green pepper
3 cups soft bread crumbs
4 cups chopped cooked chicken
Salt

Make a thick cream sauce with 4 table-spoons of the fat and the flour, broth and milk. In the rest of the fat cook the onion and pepper. Mix the sauce, cooked vegetables, bread crumbs, and chicken. Season to taste with salt. Put the mixture into a greased loaf pan and bake in a moderate oven (350° F.) until the loaf is well browned all over, from 1 to 1 1/2 hours. Serve hot or cold.

CHICKEN MARENGO

2 frying chickens, disjointed
2 tbsp olive oil
12 small white onions
2 1/2 cups boiling water
4 sprigs parsley
Pinch of thyme
1 sprig tarragon
2 dozen fresh mushrooms
Salt and pepper
Small clove of garlic
1 cup white wine
16 large pitted olives
4 egg yolks
2 tbsp flour
2 tbsp cold water

Wipe the pieces of chicken and sprinkle lightly with salt. Heat the olive oil in a large skillet and brown the chicken in it until golden brown. Peel the onions and parboil them. Drain and put them in a saucepan with the boiling water, parsley, thyme, tarragon, sliced mushrooms, salt and pepper, and garlic. Add the chicken, scraping out the oil from the skillet, and cook very gently, covered, for 30 minutes.

Remove the garlic and parsley and add the olives. Let them simmer a few minutes. Combine the egg yolks with the flour and cold water, making a smooth paste. Stir this into the hot liquid, and let cook, stirring constantly, until the sauce thickens. Serve very hot. (Serves 6)

CHICKEN MOUSSE

1 cup clear chicken broth
3 egg yolks
1 tbsp plain gelatin
1 tbsp cold water
1 cup ground cooked chicken (white meat)
½ cup ground toasted almonds
2 tbsp chopped parsley
½ tsp grated onion
Salt
Paprika
1 cup whipping cream

Beat the egg yolks and add to the broth. Cook over hot water until the mixture begins to thicken, then remove from the water. Soak the gelatin in the cold water and add to the hot mixture, stirring until the gelatin is dissolved. Add the chicken, almonds, parsley, onion, and season to taste with salt and paprika. Cool the mixture in ice water. Whip the cream and when the mixture begins to stiffen, fold in the cream. Have ready a mold rinsed out with cold water. Pour in the mixture, and set in the refrigerator to chill and become firm. When ready to serve, turn the mousse out and serve with crisp lettuce or watercress. (Serves 5 or 6)

CHICKEN PAPRIKA

1 fryer, 2½ to 3½ lb
⅓ cup flour
⅛ tsp pepper
1 tsp salt
¼ cup fat
½ cup finely chopped onion
1 tbsp paprika
2 or 3 tbsp hot water
2 tbsp flour
1 pint sour cream
Grated rind of 1 lemon
1 tbsp lemon juice

Disjoint the chicken. Mix the flour, salt, and pepper and rub it into the chicken. Brown the chicken in the hot fat and set

the pieces aside. Cook the onion in the fat until transparent. Replace the chicken and sprinkle the paprika and any remaining flour over the top. Add the hot water, cover tightly, and cook gently over low heat until the chicken is tender, 45 to 60 minutes. If necessary, add more water in tablespoon quantities, to prevent sticking. Remove the chicken and keep hot. Add the 2 tablespoons of flour to the juices in the pan and blend thoroughly. Cook over low heat until the mixture bubbles. Add the sour cream and cook, stirring constantly, until thickened. Simmer, covered, about 5 minutes. Add the lemon juice and rind and season well to taste. Replace the chicken and reheat to serving temperature. (Serves 4 or 5)

CHICKEN PUDDING

1 4-lb fowl, cut as for fricassee
1 large onion
4 whole cloves
6 whole peppercorns, slightly bruised
6 sprigs parsley
1 large bay leaf
6 sprigs celery top
¼ cup butter
2 tbsp flour
2 tsp salt
1 qt scalded nilk
8 eggs
⅛ tsp ground nutmeg

Wipe and pat dry the pieces of chicken. Place them in a stew pan and barely cover with cold water. Quarter the onion and stick a clove into each section, and add this with the peppercorns, parsley, bay leaf and celery to the chicken in the pan. Cover closely, bring slowly to the boiling point, then take off any scum which may appear on the surface. Reduce heat and simmer until the chicken is tender.

Meanwhile melt the butter, add the flour and salt, and, when smoothly blended, the milk, gradually. Stir until boiling and perfectly smooth. Beat the eggs until very light, then combine with the thickened milk, stirring vigorously lest the mixture curdle. Remove from the fire, arrange the well-drained portions of chicken in a buttered deep casserole and pour the custard over them. Sprinkle with the nutmeg, place the casserole in a pan of water, and bake in a moderate oven (350° F.) until the custard is firm and delicately brown, about 35 minutes. Serve hot or cold.

Chicken Salad

3 cups cooked chicken, cut into small dice
2 cups diced celery
¼ cup capers
½ cup chicken fat
½ cup vinegar
1 tsp onion juice
Dash of tabasco
Salt
Mayonnaise

Make a marinade of the chicken fat, vinegar, onion juice, tabasco, and salt. Pour this over the chicken and let stand for several hours, turning once or twice. Drain off the marinade, combine the chicken with the celery and capers, and mix with mayonnaise. Pile the salad in lettuce cups or fill scooped out tomatoes. Chill before serving. Garnish with hard cooked eggs and additional mayonnaise.

Chicken Souffle

½ cup butter or other fat
½ cup flour
2 cups milk
1 cup chicken broth
½ cup soft bread crumbs
3 cups ground cooked chicken
2 tbsp chopped parsley
Salt
4 eggs, separated

Make a thick white sauce with the fat, flour, milk, and broth. Beat the egg whites until stiff and the yolks until thick and lemon colored. Add the crumbs, chicken, parsley, salt to taste, and the beaten yolks to the sauce. Fold in the stiffly beaten egg whites. Turn the mixture into a greased baking dish, or in individual custard cups. Set in a pan of warm water and bake in a very moderate oven (325° F.) until the mixture is firm. The time required will be from 1½ to 1¾ hours. (Serves 5 or 6)

Chicken Vegetable Soup

1 qt strained chicken stock
⅔ cup asparagus tips, cut small
½ cup fresh green peas
½ cup finely minced green celery stalks
1 cup finely shredded spinach
2 tbsp butter
2 tbsp flour

Salt and pepper
½ cup scalded cream or undiluted evaporated milk
Paprika

Heat the stock to boiling point, add the asparagus, peas, and celery and simmer 10 minutes or until the vegetables are almost tender. Add the spinach and thicken with the blended butter and flour, stirring these into the soup with the salt and pepper. Cook, stirring constantly, until slightly thickened, then add the scalded cream or milk. Dust with paprika and serve with Melba toast or croutons. (Serves 4–6)

Jellied Chicken Bouillon

1 can concentrated chicken bouillon or consomme
Water
1 tbsp gelatin
Salt, pepper, celery salt
Worcestershire sauce

Dilute the bouillon or consommé with an equal bulk of water, reserving 2 tablespoons of this in which to soften the gelatin. Bring 1 cup of the mixture to boiling point, add the softened gelatin to it and stir until dissolved, then combine with the soup and add the seasonings. Chill very thoroughly. Break up lightly with a fork or cut into cubes and serve in bouillon cups. Top each with a teaspoon of salted whipped cream, or sprinkle lightly with minced parsley or chives, passing sections of lemon separately. (Serves 4)

Old-Fashioned Chicken Pie

4 lb fowl cut in pieces
½ lb lean pork
½ lb veal
4 cups water
1 large onion, quartered
2 sprigs celery, tied with
4 sprigs parsley, and
1 large bayleaf
6 peppercorns
Pinch of thyme
1 cup baby lima beans
½ cup diced carrot
2 tsp salt
1 cup fresh or canned corn
¼ cup flour
⅔ cup milk
Biscuit dough

Wipe the chicken pieces and giblets and place in a stew pan with the pork and veal. Add the water and all the seasonings. Boil for 5 minutes, reduce the heat, and simmer for an hour. Add the lima beans, carrots, and corn, and simmer for 30 minutes longer. Lift out the pieces of chicken and remove the skin and bones if desired. Place the pieces in a greased baking dish. Skim out the pork and veal, dice them, and add to the chicken. Remove the celery, parsley, and bayleaf and strain the broth. Add the lima beans, carrots, and corn to the chicken. Return the broth to the saucepan. Make a paste of the flour and milk and stir it into the hot broth. Cook, stirring constantly, until it thickens. Taste and correct the seasoning. Cover the chicken and vegetables with the sauce, and top with a biscuit dough, *which see*. Slash the top in several places to permit the steam to escape. Bake in a hot oven (425° F.) until the crust is brown, 25 to 30 minutes. (Serves 6 to 8)

SMOTHERED CHICKEN

1 fryer, 3½ to 4½ lbs.
1½ tsp salt
¼ tsp pepper
¼ tsp ginger
¼ cup flour
½ cup fat
2 cups cream or rich milk
¼ lb mushrooms, sliced

Disjoint the chicken. Mix the salt, pepper, ginger, and flour, and rub into the chicken pieces. Cook in the hot fat until golden brown. Sprinkle any of the remaining flour over the top. Heat the milk to boiling and pour over the chicken. Add more, if necessary, to half cover the chicken. Add the peeled and sliced mushrooms. Cover tightly and bake in a moderate oven (350° F.) until the chicken is tender, 1½ to 2 hours. (Serves 5 or 6)

CHICKEN FRYER. A chicken fryer is a large, covered pan, or high-sided skillet used primarily to cook chickens (*see* CHICKEN). It is, in effect, a Dutch oven, *which see*. *See also* KITCHEN EQUIPMENT.

CHICORY. There is considerable confusion in ordinary usage about the plants which are variously known as chicory, escarole, and endive.

Basically, there are two species of chicory: *C. intybus*, the large-rooted type properly called chicory, and *C. endivia* which

botanically is called endive. However, market terminology pays little attention to the botanical distinction.

The large-rooted chicory furnishes the roots which are roasted and ground for use in certain coffee blends. In the preparation, the roots are sliced, then roasted and ground as is coffee. The chicory has a

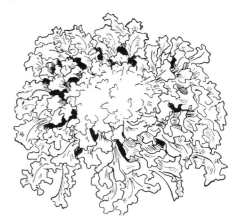

CURLY CHICORY

bitter flavor, and while it may be used as a substitute for coffee, it is generally used in this country as an added ingredient in certain blends of coffee to make the rather bitter brew which is liked by French and Spanish people.

This large-rooted type also produces the salad called French endive or Witloof chicory which is not too well known in the United States. By forcing the roots, the bleached salads called "Barbe de Capucin" or monk's beard, and Belgian endive are obtained. "Barbe de Capucin" is grown by digging the chicory roots before frost and cutting off at the tops. The roots are replanted in a warm dark cellar, horizontally, in moist soil. In a few weeks the roots have sprouted, and the pale slender leaves, curly and delicate, are six to ten inches long and ready for picking. Several crops will grow from the one planting of roots.

Belgian endive is grown from specially selected chicory roots. The tops are cut off and the roots cut into pieces about eight inches long. The roots are placed in the bottom of a deep trench which is filled with fine soil and covered with fertilizer to give heat. The shoots grow up through the soil, and in several weeks' time the plants are dug up and the heads cut off for market. The white heads are formed of a number of thick fleshy leaves four to six inches long and one or two inches wide which are pressed into a compact pointed head.

The botanical endive gives us two salads; the summer, or curly, chicory which has narrow, finely cut curly leaves, and escarole, which has broader and less curly leaves. Both of these salads are ordinarily green on the outer leaves with a bleached pale yellow heart. Both have a slightly bitter flavor and crisp quality which makes them an excellent addition to a mixed salad. They make an interesting change from lettuce, and are best served with a tart French dressing.

In buying chicory or escarole, or Belgian endive, look for crisp tender heads without excessive wilting. Slightly wilted heads can be revived by washing in water and chilling in the refrigerator. If the leaves have become brown, the head is not worth buying.

While many people know chicory as a salad, fewer know that it is a delicious vegetable when cooked. While it may be prepared like spinach, it is even better when braised. Both curly chicory and Belgian endive may be prepared according to the following recipe.

Braised Chicory

1 lb endive
Salt and pepper to taste
1 tbsp melted butter or margarine
Gravy or meat stock

Wash the endive in slightly warm water until it is free of sand and dirt. Shake the excess water off the leaves. Place the endive in a shallow heavy pan with a close-fitting cover. Add the salt and pepper, melted butter and just enough gravy or stock to prevent the leaves from sticking. Bake in a moderate oven or over a very low flame, for 15 or 20 minutes, until the endive is tender and pale brown.

CHIFFON CAKE. *See* Cake.
CHIFFON PIE. *See* Pies.
CHIFFONADE. A mixed green salad dressed with chiffonade dressing. *See* French Dressing.
CHILI. Chilies or chili peppers are the fruits of an herbaceous plant belonging to the Capsicum family. A single chili, broken, is sometimes added to soups and stews. Chili peppers are sometimes ground

into chili powder, and this is used to give tang to Mexican dishes such as *chili con carne*. Chili powder also lends an interesting flavor to tomatoes, shellfish, gravies, eggs, and corn. Chili sauce, another derivative, is excellent with frankfurters. Chilies are also used to make cayenne pepper, pickles, and chili vinegar. Chilies represent the strongest variety of Capsicum (*which see*); their flavor is fiery and pungent.

Chili con Carne

¼ lb beef suet
6 medium-sized onions
3 lb lean beef
6 fresh tomatoes
1 cup boiling water
2 cloves of garlic
2 slices dry bread
Chili powder
1 tbsp cider or red wine vinegar
1 tbsp brown sugar
Salt

Chop, then melt and heat the suet in a heavy frying pan. Slice the onions thinly and sauté them until golden brown. Take out the onions, and in the same hot fat sauté the beef which has been cut into ½-inch cubes. Cook the meat quickly to seal in the juices, then lift out.

In a large stewpan combine any remaining fat, the onions, the tomatoes, peeled and quartered and the boiling water. Now add the bread which has been thoroughly rubbed with the split garlic cloves, and allow to cook in the mixture for 5 minutes. Add the prepared meat and season with the chili powder using 1, 2, or 3 heaping tablespoonfuls according to your tolerance of pungent condiments. Cook gently for 30 minutes, then add the vinegar and sugar, with salt to taste. Do not allow the beef to disintegrate, but test frequently.

If you have eaten chili con carne in restaurants, or have used the canned product, and found it to be half beef and half beans, that is chili con carne con frijoles (with beans). Get from a Spanish or Latin-American grocer two pounds of Mexican bayo beans, frijoles, colorados, or garbanzos. Soak the beans over night, and next morning cook them in water to cover until they are tender. Drain well and add the beans to the chili about 15 minutes before it is ready to serve. Do not let the beans get too soft or broken.

There are many variations of chili con carne, and one of the most interesting uses green tomatoes instead of ripe. Use a dozen of the early green tomatoes and chop them rather fine. Later in the season, when they are larger and nearer ripe, scald them and remove the skins, and slice thin. Chili con carne made with green tomatoes has a piquancy that the ripe tomatoes do not give.

CHILI SAUCE

4 qt tomatoes (24 to 28 medium-sized)
2 cups chopped sweet red peppers
2 cups chopped onion
1 chili pepper, chopped
2 tbsp celery seed
1 tbsp mustard seed
1 bay leaf
1 tsp whole cloves
1 tsp ground ginger
1 tsp ground nutmeg
2 3-inch pieces stick cinnamon
1 cup firmly packed brown sugar
1½ cups vinegar
2 tbsp salt

Chop the tomatoes and combine with the sweet pepper, onion, and chili pepper. Put the celery seeds, mustard seed, bay leaf, cloves, ginger, nutmeg, and cinnamon loosely in a thin white cloth and tie the top securely. Add to the tomato mixture. Bring to a boil and simmer, stirring frequently, until the mixture is reduced by half. Add the sugar, vinegar, and salt. Boil rapidly, stirring constantly, for about 5 minutes. Remove the spice bag. Pour the chili sauce into hot sterile jars, filling the jars to the top. Seal. *See also* CANNING. (Makes 5 pints)

CHIMAJA. The root of a wild cherry tree native to Mexico. It is chopped, dried, and ground, and used as a condiment in Mexican cookery.

CHINAWARE. The name given to both a type of ceramic material (*see* CERAMICS), and to the dishes, cups, saucers, etc., made from that material. The name is derived from China, from which country came the first fine ceramics known to the present western world. *See also* DISHES.

CHINESE CABBAGE. Also known as celery cabbage, or by the Chinese names of *Pe Tsai* (peet say) and *Wong Bok*. This is an oriental member of the family which includes the cabbages and mustard, which has recently been introduced into American markets. The type most often seen, *Pe Tsai*, has long tapered heads, 14 to 16 inches long, of almost white leaves. The leaves and stalks are crisp and tender, and may be used in any way in which cabbage is used.

CHINESE CABBAGE

Sliced in convenient pieces, Chinese cabbage makes an interesting addition to a mixed green salad. It may be shredded and made into cole slaw. It may also be cooked and served in any of the methods given under cabbage. It has the added advantage of not having a strong odor while cooking.

CHINESE COOKERY. The Chinese believe that a wise man always eats well. For several thousand years, many more years than make up the entire history of

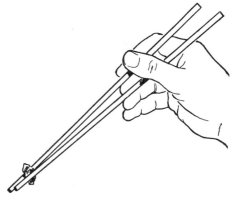

USING CHOPSTICKS

most countries, the Chinese have followed the traditions of fine cookery. Epicurus, famous Greek of fastidious taste, was a mere upstart in comparison with the old Chinese masters of the mysteries of soups, sauces, and savory foods.

Not only did the Chinese turn their kitchens into laboratories of succulent inven-

PLATE, PLAIN   SALAD   BREAD AND BUTTER   SOUP, PLAIN

CREAM SOUP AND STAND   CUP AND SAUCER, BREAKFAST   CUP AND SAUCER, TEA   CUP AND SAUCER, COFFEE   FRUIT SAUCER

OATMEAL SAUCER   BAKER, OVAL   VEGETABLE DISH, ROUND   SAUCE BOAT AND STAND, OVAL

SAUCE TUREEN AND STAND, ROUND   SOUP TUREEN AND STAND, ROUND   PLATE, SALAD, CRESCENT   EGG CUP, SINGLE

EGG CUP, DOUBLE   COFFEE POT, GLOBE   TEAPOT   CREAM   SUGAR BOX

CHINAWARE

tion, but they were among the first people to appreciate the value of glamour. So they gave names of poetic elegance to their foods. Exotic dishes were called "chicken giblets with cloud's ear," "dragon's well tea," or "snow fungi."

A good Chinese chef can, by some miracle, turn a humble pound of rice into an exquisite delicacy and transform a mixture of plebian vegetables into savory aristo-

crats. Like the French, the Chinese lay great stress on seasonings and sauces, but their seasonings are neither involved, difficult to obtain, nor expensive. Soy sauce, which is used to give piquancy to many of their dishes can be obtained in almost any grocery store. Some of the other ingredients may take a trip to a Chinese market, or the local Chinese restaurant to find, but many large grocers carry such things as bamboo shoots and water chestnuts.

Like the French, the whole culinary art of China depends on the art of blending. No one, for instance, knows how cabbage can taste until he has tasted it cooked with chicken as the Chinese do. The Chinese also believe in the contrast of textures in food, and for this reason use crisp noodles and pieces of water chestnut in an otherwise bland and soft dish. Most of their sauces are thickened with cornstarch and have a transparent thickness unlike sauces thickened with flour.

Chop suey and chow mein are not the start and finish of Chinese cookery. Several recipes are given below, more will be found throughout the text under such headings as Pork or the names of individual dishes.

CHAN FAR YOOK YUN
(Pork and crab balls)

1 lb pork
¼ lb water chestnuts
½ cup crab meat
2 oz dried mushrooms
2 eggs
1 tsp sugar
Pepper and salt
Soy sauce
Corn meal

Chop the pork, mushrooms, and water chestnuts very fine and mix with the crab. Season to taste with salt, pepper, and sugar. Form into balls about 1½ inches in diameter. Roll the balls in the cornmeal until they are well coated. Beat the eggs with a little cold water and roll the balls in it until they are coated. Heat a saucepan of oil to boiling, drop in the balls, and cook for 15 minutes. Drain thoroughly and serve with soy sauce. (Serves 6)

CHO LOW YU
(Sweet-sour fish)

1½ lb fillets of sole or flounder
1 tbsp finely chopped cucumber
1 tbsp Chinese pickled onions, chopped
1 tbsp chopped onion
1 tbsp fresh ginger
Peel of a good-sized lemon
2 cloves of garlic
2 cups vinegar
½ cup sugar

Sesame oil
Cornstarch
Salt and pepper
Soy sauce

Heat a little cooking oil in a skillet. Crush the garlic and cook in the oil for 2 or 3 minutes. Remove the garlic and put into the pan the vinegar, sugar, a few drops of soy sauce, and pepper. Thicken the sauce with a little cornstarch.

Skin the fish and fry the pieces in a large saucepan of boiling oil for 15 minutes. Drain well and put on a warm dish. Slice the ginger and onions into 1½-inch lengths. Bring the sauce to a boil. Add the cucumber, onions, ginger, and lemon peel, and cook for 5 minutes. Add a few drops of sesame oil and pour the sauce over the fish. Serve very hot. (Serves 5 or 6)

FOO YONG HY
(Crab omelet)

1 can crab meat
2 eggs

Beat the eggs thoroughly. Heat a little oil in a skillet. Add the crab, season with salt and pepper, and fry for a few seconds. Then add the beaten eggs, stir to mix the ingredients, and then cook until the egg is set. Serve immediately. (Serves 3 or 4)

LOONG HAR JAR MIN
(Fried lobster)

½ lb lobster meat
3 bundles fresh noodles
½ lb bean sprouts
¼ lb bamboo shoots
¼ cup dried mushrooms
½ cup sliced onions
Salt and pepper
Soy sauce
Cornstarch

Put the mushrooms in hot water and soak for 15 minutes. Remove the stems and slice the caps finely. Cut the bamboo shoots and lobster into thin slices. Heat a large saucepan of cooking oil to boiling and drop in the noodles. Cook for only a few seconds, until they are brown, and remove immediately. Drain and keep hot. Pour a little oil into a skillet and cook the lobster in the oil for 1 minute, turning it once. Add the bamboo shoots, bean sprouts, mushrooms, and onions, and cook them for another minute. Season with salt and pepper. Mix a scant teaspoon of cornstarch with a little cold water and stir into the lobster mixture. Add a few drops of soy sauce, and cook for a few minutes longer, until the sauce is thick and clear. Serve over the fried noodles, and pass additional soy sauce. (Serves 6)

CHINESE MUSTARD. An oriental mustard which is grown in many parts of the western world. The leaves are large and may be eaten uncooked as a salad, or cooked like spinach. Another variety, used by the Chinese in their cooking, is grown for the tuberous roots which resemble conical white turnips. They are prepared like our turnip.

CHINESE WATERMELON. Used to make preserves, the Chinese watermelon is a large, oblong fruit, nine to sixteen inches in length, with waxy, hairy skin, firm, white flesh, and cucumber-like seeds.

CHIPPED BEEF, or DRIED BEEF. Chipped beef is prepared, like corned beef, by pickling for a month. Then it is smoked for two days and dried for two weeks. After this it is sliced wafer-thin by machinery and is then ready for packing, either in cellophane rolls, in glass jars, or vacuum-packed in small cans. The meat used in its preparation is cut from lean top round, then cured until every fiber of the meat has been reached by the process. After this comes the oven drying, which removes most of the water from the meat, reducing it to a concentrated food and developing its individual toasty, smoky taste. The 2½-ounce size serves two persons nicely, the 3½-ounce pack is ample for four, while five ounces are sufficient for a family of five.

Dried beef, or chipped beef as it is sometimes called, combines best with starchy foods such as potatoes, rice, macaroni, or noodles. Creamed in its usual fashion it is delicious on popovers, baked potatoes, toast, or in patty shells. When crumbled and frizzled gently in a little butter it makes a savory addition to scrambled eggs, potato, or macaroni salad, or any bland food. High grade chipped beef in bulk is less expensive and just as satisfactory as the packaged meat. It keeps best when stored in a covered glass jar in the refrigerator.

For those who prefer it less salty, try this method: Pour boiling water over cut or chopped beef about 15 minutes before it is to be used. Drain the water off the beef, and finish cooking in the sauce or eggs or other dish. By being allowed to stand in the hot water, the beef will be partly cooked and tendered.

CHIPPED BEEF PANCAKES

5 medium-sized potatoes
2 eggs
⅔ cup shredded dried beef
½ cup flour
1 tsp baking powder
Salt if needed

Grate the raw potatoes and squeeze dry. Add the well-beaten eggs and beef, then the flour, baking powder and salt, if used—these last sifted together. Drop by spoonfuls onto a hot bacon-greased griddle or frying pan and when brown on one side, turn to brown the other. Serve very hot.

CHIPPED BEEF SHORTCAKE

Sprinkle poppy seeds on a sheet of biscuit dough (*see* BISCUIT). Spread with softened butter. Roll up like a jelly roll, cut into slices, and bake. When done, serve with creamed dried beef.

PATENT PARING KNIFE. This gadget may also be used for making chips.

CHIPS. Chips are cut wafer-thin crosswise from a raw, pared potato. The slices are dropped in cold water, patted dry in a cloth or absorbent paper, and then fried in hot deep fat (370–390° F.) for a few seconds (the potatoes meanwhile being stirred to prevent their sticking) or until crisp and golden brown. Drain on soft, crumpled paper. Serve hot or cold.

Parsnips, carrots, or turnips may be prepared in the same way.

CHIVES. The chive is a herb belonging to the onion and leek family. The plant, bearing lovely purplish flower pompoms, is sometimes grown for ornamental purposes. In some temperate climates it has been used as a vegetable. But chives are usually cultivated for their tender leaves. These are finely chopped and then used to flavor soups, stews, omelets, and salads. Their flavor is mild and similar to that of onions.

CHIVES

CHIVRY BUTTER. *See* BUTTER SAUCE.

CHOCOLATE. When Cortez returned to Spain from his explorations of Mexico, he brought with him the secret of a new beverage which the natives of the new world called "chocolatl." It was the product of the fruit of a tree which grew in Central America and the West Indies. The ancient Aztec word was "cacahoatl" which the Spaniards contracted to "cacao," and from which we get "cocoa." The new flavor found great favor among the Europeans, and its use spread rapidly. The trees are now grown in parts of South America, the East Indies, and in Africa.

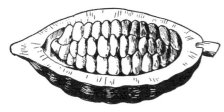

CHOCOLATE

It is well to understand the use of the various terms. Cacao is used in the trade to refer to the raw beans. Chocolate is the manufactured product when it appears in solidified form, such as bars. Cocoa is the pulverized bean from which part of the cocoa butter has been removed, and is a soft brown powder.

HARVESTING CACAO

The cacao tree grows 20 or 25 feet high and is covered with long pointed green leaves which are attached by short stalks alternately to opposite sides of the branches. The cacao flowers, which grow in clusters directly attached to the brown trunk or main branches of the tree, produce the cacao pod. The native workman severs the pod from the trunk with a curved knife, being careful not to touch the tuft from which it has sprung. The tuft will continue to bring forth new flower clusters which will form pods so long as it is not damaged. The ripe pod is eight inches long, three inches across, and weighs about a pound. It is rather oval in shape and has five ridges running from end to end.

The pod is opened with a cut of the knife, and it is seen that the shell is about a half inch thick and is filled with a pale pink, soft, sweet pulp in which are embedded 25 to 40 seeds. These seeds may vary in color from white, tinged with pink or yellow, to amethyst. The pulp is sweet, but the beans are very bitter and astringent. This is due to the presence of tannin compounds which have to be altered in the manufacturing process to give the rich sweetness of chocolate or cocoa.

The pods are collected, cut open, and the beans and pulp scraped out into baskets which are conveyed to the fermenting troughs. These are wooden troughs about four feet square and four feet high with perforated bottoms raised off the ground. The beans are shoveled into the box and covered with banana leaves to retain the heat which develops during fermentation.

The sweet pulp starts to ferment from the action of natural yeast organisms in the air. The pulp becomes liquid and runs out through the bottom of the box. The beans are turned over once a day, and this process is continued for two to six days, depending on the quality of the beans. The color of the bean changes from white or violet to brown or brownish red and the bitter astringent taste practically disappears.

The beans are then dried by exposing them to the sun and packed into sacks for shipment.

PREPARATION OF CHOCOLATE

The cacao beans are taken into the manufacturing plant, where the first step is a thorough cleaning to remove all foreign matter. Then the beans are roasted under carefully controlled temperatures. This makes the thin outer shells very brittle, and by passing them through special chambers, the shells are splintered off and blown out. The irregular fragments of beans are known as "nibs." The nibs pass through several cleaning operations to remove all the shell.

The nibs then pass to a milling machine, which consists of granite burrs. The nibs are ground and the heat developed by the friction liquefies the cocoa butter which constitutes about 54 percent of the bean. The result of this milling process is a rich dark liquor. The liquor now passes through steel rollers which grind the already small particles even finer. The liquor then passes into large tubs called "conches" which contain rollers. The liquid is continuously moved about in the conches to aerate it and further grind the particles for four days, when the chocolate will have reached its peak of flavor. The liquor is then fed into molds, tempered, and cooled. At this stage it forms the unsweetened cooking chocolate that is used for cakes, candy, and puddings.

If milk chocolate or sweet chocolate is to be made, milk and sugar in varying amounts is heated in huge kettles until the liquid portion is evaporated. The resulting taffy-like mass is added to the chocolate liquor and thoroughly mixed. Additional liquid is evaporated out and a coarse powder is the result. Cocoa butter is added to produce a heavy paste and the mixture is passed through a grinding machine. The pulverized paste goes to the conches where it is agitated for five days and then molded and packaged.

PREPARATION OF COCOA

The process of making cocoa is the same up to the formation of the liquor. The liquor is then compressed in hydraulic presses which squeeze out about half of the

cocoa butter, leaving behind a compressed cake of cocoa. These cakes are crushed and pulverized to a fine dry powder which is cooled, sifted, and packaged for market.

The Dutch in the East Indies discovered that treating the cacao nibs with certain alkalis gave a product of darker color, richer flavor, and finer aroma. So-called "Dutch-process" cocoa is made from cacao treated in this manner. Cocoa is described as "breakfast," or "high fat," cocoa, meaning that it contains not less than 22 percent of cocoa butter; or "medium fat" cocoa, meaning that it contains less than 22 percent of cocoa butter.

HINTS ON USING CHOCOLATE AND COCOA

In preparing recipes using chocolate, it is well to remember that chocolate burns easily. Chocolate should always be melted over hot water, and a chocolate cake should be baked at a slightly lower temperature (about 25° F. lower) than a plain cake. Too high a temperature will also change the flavor of chocolate. A square of cooking chocolate is equivalent to one ounce.

FOOD VALUE

	Wa-ter	Food Energy	Pro-tein	Fat	Car-bohy-drates	Cal-cium	Phos-phorus	Iron	Vit. A Value	Thia-mine	Riba-flavin	Nia-cin	Ascor-bic Acid
Chocolate, unsw'd	2.3	570	5.5	52.9	18	95	343	2.5	0	Trace	.24	1.1	0
Cocoa, dry	4.3	329	9.0	18.8	31.0	160	709	2.7	0	Trace	.39	2.3	0

If cocoa is to be substituted for chocolate in pudding, cake, or candy, it should be blended with the sugar or flour used in the recipe. Three level tablespoons of cocoa plus two teaspoons of shortening are the equivalent of one ounce of baking chocolate.

When cocoa is to be used as a beverage, it should be dissolved in a little cold water and the mixture stirred over a low flame until it is smooth and thick. Then additional cold milk or water is added, stirring constantly. When the mixture starts to foam it should be beaten with a rotary beater to prevent the formation of a scum. In this way, cocoa can be prepared in only one utensil. Hot chocolate can be prepared in the same way, using baking chocolate. Hot chocolate or cocoa is usually served with a topping of whipped cream.

Try a dash of nutmeg in the whipped cream. Children especially like a marshmallow added to the hot beverage.

Frosted chocolate is a simple summer drink. Blend one or two tablespoons of chocolate sirup with a glass of cold milk and top with a scoop of vanilla ice cream.

CHOCOLATE BAVARIAN

1 tbsp gelatin
1 tbsp cold water
¼ cup cocoa
⅛ tsp salt
½ cup sugar
1¼ cup water
½ tsp vanilla
2 tbsp melted butter
1½ cup whipping cream or evaporated
  milk

Soften gelatin in cold water. Dissolve over hot water. (Soften in a cup and set cup in a pan filled with boiling water. Turn off heat.) Mix cocoa, sugar, salt with cold water. Add dissolved gelatin, mixing thoroughly. Add melted butter and vanilla. Cool until mixture is thick and sirupy. Whip the cream or milk and fold in the chocolate mixture. Turn into mold and chill in refrigerator until set.

CHOCOLATE CAKE
(made with yeast)

1 cup butter
2 cups granulated sugar
3 eggs, separated
3 squares melted, unsweetened chocolate
1 cup cold milk
½ cake dry yeast
2¼ cups cake flour
½ tsp salt
½ tsp baking soda
1½ tsp vanilla or
1 tsp vanilla and
½ tsp almond extract

Cream the butter until light, gradually adding the sugar. Work in the well-beaten egg yolks, a little at a time, creaming and beating after each addition. Add 3 squares melted unsweetened chocolate alternately with 1 cup of milk, which has been mixed with ½ cake of dry yeast dissolved in ¼ cup of lukewarm water. Blend thoroughly. Sift 2¼ cups of cake flour with salt four times, and gradually add to first mixture.

Mix well, then fold in stiffly beaten egg whites; cover the bowl and place in the refrigerator overnight. In the morning stir in baking soda, dissolved in 3 tablespoons of hot water, and 1½ teaspoons of vanilla, or vanilla and almond. Blend thoroughly. Turn batter into two buttered cake pans (9x9x3 inches) and bake in a moderate oven (350° F.) for 40 to 45 minutes, or until firm. Cool, then cover with chocolate frosting (see CHOCOLATE).

CHOCOLATE LAYER CAKE

2 cups cake flour
¼ tsp soda
1½ tsp baking powder
½ tsp salt
⅓ cup cocoa
⅔ cup butter or shortening
1½ cups sugar
2 eggs, beaten
1 tsp vanilla
½ cup buttermilk
½ cup boiling water

Sift flour, measure and resift 3 times with next four ingredients. Cream shortening until soft, add sugar and blend thoroughly; add beaten eggs and beat vigorously until light and fluffy. Stir in vanilla. Add flour mixture alternately with buttermilk in several portions, beginning and ending with flour and beating well after each addition. Add boiling water all at once and stir quickly until smooth. Turn into 2 ungreased 8-inch cake pans which have been lined with thin plain paper in bottom. Bake in a moderate oven (350° F.) for 30 minutes. Cool in pans 5 minutes, then turn out onto cake rack to cool. Put together with chocolate or any desired filling. (See FROSTING AND FILLING)

DEVIL'S FOOD CAKE

2 cups cake flour
1½ cups sugar
¾ tsp salt
½ cup shortening
2 eggs
1 cup milk
1 tsp vanilla
2 squares (2 oz) unsweetened chocolate,
  melted and cooled
1 tsp baking soda
1 tbsp hot water

Sift the flour, measure and resift 3 times with sugar and salt. The last time sift directly into large mixing bowl. Add shortening (at room temperature), eggs, and ½ cup of the milk. Stir with a spoon to blend. Beat with an electric mixer using low speed or by hand with wooden spoon for 2 minutes by the clock. Scrape sides of bowl twice during beating. Add the combined vanilla, melted cooled chocolate, soda and water and the remaining milk. Beat for 2 more minutes. Pour into two 8-inch layer cake pans with bottoms lined with thin, plain paper. Bake at 350° F. for 20 to 25 minutes or until cake tests done. Cool 5 minutes before removing from pan. Put together with mocha frosting. (*See* MOCHA)

FUDGE CAKE

2 cups sifted cake flour
1½ tsp baking powder
½ tsp baking soda
½ tsp salt
½ cup shortening
1¼ cups firmly packed brown sugar
1 tsp vanilla
2 eggs
3 squares chocolate, melted
1 cup milk

Mix the flour, baking powder and soda and salt. Cream the shortening until soft and smooth; gradually add the sugar, creaming until fluffy; add the vanilla and beat in thoroughly one egg at a time, then the chocolate. Add flour alternately with milk, beating until smooth after each addition. Turn into greased pans or pan and bake; in 2 layer pans in moderate oven (350° F.) about 25 minutes; in square pan in moderately slow oven (325° F.) about 1 hour. Makes two 9-inch layers, or one 9-inch square cake. Put together with fudge frosting. (*See* FUDGE)

MANITOU BLACK CAKE

3 oz chocolate, melted
1 egg yolk, well beaten
1 cup milk
2 tbsp butter
1 cup sugar
½ cup milk
1½ cups flour
1 tsp vanilla
2 tsp baking powder
1 tsp soda

Mix the yolk of the egg with the milk and melted chocolate. Cook over the water until the mixture is thick and smooth. Remove from heat. Add the seven remaining ingredients in their order. Thoroughly beat in the flour before adding the baking powder and soda. Pour into a well greased pan, 12x9x1½ inches. Bake in moderate oven (375° F.). Cover with boiled frosting (*see* FROSTING). Cut in squares. This is a very rich cake, more like confection.

CHOCOLATE CHIP COOKIES

1 cup all-purpose flour
½ tsp salt
½ tsp soda
½ cup butter or shortening
⅓ cup granulated sugar
⅓ cup brown sugar, firmly packed
1 egg, beaten
½ tsp vanilla
½ tsp hot water
½ cup chopped nuts
10½ oz package semi-sweet chocolate chips

Sift flour, measure and resift 3 times with salt and soda. Cream the butter until smooth and soft, then add both sugars gradually and beat until fluffy. Add egg and vanilla and beat until light. Add sifted dry ingredients gradually, and mix well. Add hot water, then fold in the nuts and the chocolate chips. Drop by teaspoonfuls onto greased baking sheet. Bake in a moderate oven (375° F.) for 10 to 12 minutes. Remove to cake racks to cool. (Makes 30 to 50 small cookies.

CHOCOLATE CHIP CUP CAKES

2½ cups cake flour
2¼ tsp baking powder
½ tsp salt
½ cup butter
1 cup strained honey
½ cup sugar
3 eggs, separated
1 tsp vanilla
½ cup milk
1 cup semi-sweet chocolate chips

Sift the flour, measure and resift 3 times with baking powder and salt. Cream the butter until soft and smooth; add the honey and beat until fluffy, then add ¼ cup of the sugar and the egg yolks, and beat until light. Stir in the vanilla. Add flour mixture and milk alternately in 4 or 5 portions, beginning and ending with a portion of flour and beating until smooth after each addition. Beat egg whites until stiff and gradually beat in the remaining sugar. Fold in egg whites quickly and thoroughly in batter. Add the chocolate chips, stirring until just distributed. Dip into muffin tins lined with paper baking cups, or thoroughly greased, filling them to about two-thirds full. Bake in a moderate oven (350° F.) about 20 minutes, or until golden brown and springy when touched. Lift out onto cake racks to cool. Frost with chocolate frosting (see CHOCOLATE). (Makes 2 dozen cakes)

CHOCOLATE COCONUT PUDDING

2 squares unsweetened chocolate
3 cups milk
⅓ cup sugar
4 tbsp cornstarch
¼ tsp salt
2 eggs
1 tsp vanilla
¼ cup shredded coconut

Soften the chocolate in the upper part of the double boiler. Add the milk, heat, then beat with a rotary beater until well blended. Combine the sugar, cornstarch and salt, add a little of the hot chocolate mixture, stir until smooth, return to the double boiler and cool, stirring constantly, until the mixture thickens. Remove from the hot water, let cool slightly, and add the vanilla. Stir in the coconut and pour into individual serving dishes. Chill. Serve with cream. (Serves 6)

CHOCOLATE CREAM CUSTARD FILLING

1 tbsp gelatin
¼ cup cold water
1 square unsweetened chocolate
1 tbsp water
⅓ cup sugar
Dash of salt
½ cup milk
½ tsp vanilla
½ cup whipping cream

Soften gelatin in cold water. Melt chocolate over hot water. Add the 1 tablespoon water, blend well and stir in sugar and salt. Add milk gradually and cook until smooth and thickened, stirring constantly. Stir in

softened gelatin until dissolved. Remove from heat, add vanilla and chill until of consistency of a thin custard. Whip the cream until stiff and fold into chocolate mixture. Spread between layers of cake. *See* FROSTING AND FILLING.

CHOCOLATE CREAM ROLL

6 tbsp cake flour
6 tbsp cocoa
½ tsp baking powder
1 tsp salt
4 eggs
¾ cup sugar
1 tsp vanilla

Sift the cake flour once, measure, add the cocoa, baking powder, and scant teaspoon of salt, and sift together 3 times. Beat the egg whites until stiff, fold in gradually the sugar and then 4 egg yolks beaten until thick and lemon-colored, and flavored with 1 teaspoon of vanilla. Lastly fold in the flour mixture, a little at a time, blending well after each addition. Turn batter into a 15x10-inch pan which has been buttered and lined with greased paper to within ½ inch of edge. Bake in a hot oven (400° F.) 12 to 13 minutes. Quickly cut and trim off crisp edges of cake; invert on a damp cloth to cool; remove paper, and when cold spread with whipped cream. Roll as for jelly roll and serve well chilled. *See also* JELLY ROLL.

CHOCOLATE CUSTARD SAUCE

1 cup milk
2 squares chocolate
2 egg yolks
½ cup sugar
⅛ tsp salt
½ tsp vanilla

Heat milk and chocolate in top part of double boiler; when chocolate is melted, beat with rotary beater until smooth. Combine egg yolks, sugar and salt, gradually stir in milk chocolate, return to double boiler and cook stirring constantly, until mixture coats the spoon. Add vanilla; serve hot. (Makes approximately 1⅓ cups)

CHOCOLATE DROP COOKIES

2 cups all-purpose flour
1½ tsp baking powder

½ tsp salt
½ tsp soda
½ cup butter or shortening
½ cup brown sugar, firmly packed
½ cup granulated sugar
2 eggs, beaten
1 tsp vanilla
2 squares unsweetened chocolate, melted
¼ cup buttermilk

Sift flour, measure and resift 3 times with baking powder, salt and soda. Cream butter, add both sugars, and beat until smooth. Add eggs and beat until fluffy. Add vanilla. Stir in cooled melted chocolate. Add flour mixture and buttermilk alternately in 2 or 3 portions beginning and ending with flour. Drop by heaping teaspoonfuls onto greased baking sheets about 2 inches apart. Bake in a moderate oven (375° F.) for 12 minutes. Using a spatula or pancake turner, transfer to cake coolers, and cool before storing or serving. (Makes about 4 dozen.)

For chocolate-nut cookies, stir in ½ cup chopped pecans or walnuts after the last addition of flour.

CHOCOLATE FRAPPE

1 qt hot scalded milk
2 squares unsweetened chocolate melted
    over hot water
¼ cup granulated sugar
¼ tsp salt
1 tsp vanilla extract

Pour hot scalded milk over melted chocolate; stir in the sugar and salt, and cook, stirring frequently until mixture reaches the boiling point. Allow mixture to simmer for 5 minutes. Cool, add vanilla extract. Chill, and freeze in hand freezer, using equal parts of ice and rock salt. Serve in frappé glasses with a topping of plain whipped cream, forced through a pastry bag with a small fancy tube, and top (optional) with a roasted peanut, or an almond, or a toasted cashew nut.

CHOCOLATE FROSTING

½ cup butter
2¾ cups confectioner's sugar
2 egg yolks
2 squares (2 oz) unsweetened chocolate,
    melted
Cinnamon or vanilla

Cream the butter until very light, gradually adding the confectioner's sugar. Next work in the egg yolks, one at a time, then the chocolate, melted over hot water. Beat all very thoroughly and if desired flavor with ground cinnamon or a few drops of vanilla.

CHOCOLATE NUT FROSTING

4 tsp sweet butter
2 squares unsweetened chocolate, grated
¾ lb granulated or light brown sugar
½ cup thin cream or evaporated milk
    (undiluted)
⅛ tsp salt
1 tsp vanilla
1 cup chopped walnut meats

Melt a generous teaspoon of the butter in a saucepan, and swish it around the sides of the pan. Add the chocolate, sugar and cream or milk. Cook all over a gentle flame until a little dropped into cold water forms a soft ball (238° F.). Remove from the fire, add the remaining butter and the salt and cool to lukewarm, then add the vanilla and beat until of spreading consistency. Add the walnut meats to one third of the frosting and spread between the layers, then use the plain mixture on top and sides of the cake. (Sufficient for two 8-inch or 9-inch layers)

CHOCOLATE ORANGE FROSTING

2 tsp grated orange rind
¼ cup butter
2 cups sifted XXXX sugar, firmly packed
1½ squares unsweetened chocolate,
    melted
Pinch of salt
3 tbsp orange juice (about)

Combine orange rind and butter and cream until smooth and soft. Add about half the sugar, gradually blending well. Then add cooled melted chocolate and salt, and mix thoroughly. Add remaining sugar alternately with orange juice to produce a smooth spreading consistency. Spread on cake. (Makes enough for two 8-inch layers) *See also* FROSTING.

COCOA FROSTING

¼ cup cocoa
⅔ cup sugar

½ tsp salt
3 tbsp flour
1½ cups milk, scalded
1 egg
1 tbsp butter
½ tsp vanilla

Blend cocoa, sugar, salt and flour in top of double boiler; add milk and place over boiling water, stirring constantly until sauce thickens; then continue to cook for 10 minutes with occasional stirring. Beat egg thoroughly and stir in a little of the hot mixture; then return to the rest of the hot filling and cook 2 minutes longer; stirring constantly. Remove from heat, add butter and vanilla, and cool thoroughly, stirring occasionally to prevent the formation of a "skin" on the surface. Spread between and on top of the layers of cake. (Enough for two 8 or 9-inch layers) *See also* FROSTING.

CHOCOLATE ICE BOX PUDDING

6 slices white bread, ¼ inch thick
Melted butter
⅓ cup sugar
⅛ tsp ground cinnamon
1½ packages chocolate pudding
1½ cups evaporated milk
1½ cups water
¼ cup heavy cream

Cut the crusts from the bread and then cut it into fingers half an inch wide. Toast in a slow oven until dry and golden brown, after which dip into melted butter. Sprinkle with the blended sugar and cinnamon and return to the oven for a few minutes. Prepare the chocolate pudding mixture, using evaporated milk and water for the liquid, according to directions on the package. Arrange the bread fingers in six dessert glasses, pour in the pudding, cool and chill. Serve with whipped cream. (Serves 6)

CHOCOLATE ICE CREAM

1¼ cups sugar
1 tbsp flour
¼ tsp salt
2 eggs
2 squares unsweetened chocolate
2 cups milk
2 cups heavy cream
1 tbsp vanilla

Combine the sugar, flour and salt, then beat and add the eggs and blend until perfectly smooth. Melt the chocolate in the upper part of a double boiler, add the milk and bring to scalding point, stirring to blend thoroughly. Pour slowly over the egg mixture, stirring while pouring, then return to the double boiler and cook, over hot water, until thickened. Cool, strain and combine with the heavy cream, (unwhipped). Add the vanilla and freeze in hand freezer, using three parts ice to one part salt. Pack or mold using four parts of ice and one of salt. *See also* ICE CREAM. (Serves 6 or 8)

CHOCOLATE INDIANS

1 cup all-purpose flour
½ tsp salt
¼ tsp baking powder
⅓ cup cocoa
⅓ to ½ cup shortening (half butter)
1 cup sugar
2 eggs, beaten
1 tsp vanilla
¼ cup milk
⅔ cup moist raisins

Sift flour, measure, and resift 3 times with baking powder, salt, and cocoa. Cream shortening; add sugar gradually and continue creaming until thoroughly mixed. Add eggs and vanilla and mix well. Add the sifted dry ingredients in 2 or 3 portions alternately with the milk, stirring well after each addition. Stir in raisins and turn into a 11x7x1½-inch greased baking pan. Bake in a moderate oven (350° F.) for about 25 minutes. Allow to cool in the pan 10 or 15 minutes, then cut into cookies of desired size. (Makes 15 to 18 depending on size)

CHOCOLATE LEAVES

¾ cup pastry flour
⅞ cup confectioner's sugar
¼ tsp salt
4 oz almond paste
2 egg whites
1 tsp cold water
Bitter chocolate, melted

Combine the flour, sugar, and salt, and work them into the almond paste with a spatula. This is easiest done on a platter or marble slab. Beat the egg whites slightly with the cold water. Add half of the whites to the first mixture, continuing to work until it is completely smooth. Gradually add more of the egg white as needed. Add melted chocolate to taste, and the balance of the egg whites. The batter should be quite thin.

The traditional shape is an oak leaf which is obtained by the use of a metal stencil. This can be purchased in a large housewares store, or you can draw the shape and have the stencil cut from sheet metal. Leave not more than one inch margin around the leaf.

Grease and flour a cookie sheet. Lay the stencil in place, starting in one corner. With the spatula, apply the batter, pressing it smoothly over the stencil. Pick up the stencil carefully and move it to the next place, repeating the operations until the sheet is filled. Bake quickly in a hot oven (400°–425° F.). Remove from the oven and remove the leaves from the cookie sheet immediately.

When the cookies are cooled, coat each one with melted chocolate, sweet or bitter, depending on taste, and mark off the veins with a knife. Let the chocolate harden thoroughly and store in an airtight container in a cool dry place. The cookies are very thin, and this recipe makes a good quantity, depending on the size of the stencil.

CHOCOLATE MARLOW

1½ squares bitter chocolate
1 cup evaporated milk
16 marshmallows (¼ lb)
1 tsp vanilla extract
1 cup evaporated milk, chilled

Shave chocolate into top of double boiler. Add the milk and marshmallows and cook over boiling water until well blended. The mousse is very attractive if the marshmallows are not completely melted. Chocolate may be completely blended by beating mixture. When mixture is cold, add vanilla. Whip milk very stiff. Fold in chocolate mixture. Pour at once into cold freezing trays. (Makes 1 quart)

CHOCOLATE MOUSSE

2 squares unsweetened chocolate
½ cup powdered sugar

1 cup scalded milk
2 tsp gelatin
3 tbsp cold water
¾ cup granulated sugar
1 tsp vanilla
2 cups heavy cream
¼ tsp salt

Melt the chocolate over hot water, add the powdered sugar and stir until well blended, then carefully pour in the scalded milk. Place over moderate heat and bring slowly just to the boiling point, stirring constantly. Do not allow the mixture to really boil. Remove from the fire and add the gelatin, softened in the cold water, also the granulated sugar and vanilla. Strain through cheesecloth or a fine strainer. Chill and when beginning to thicken, beat with rotary beater until light and fluffy. Finally fold in the stiffly beaten cream to which the salt has been added. Freeze in automatic refrigerator about three hours. (Serves 6)

CHOCOLATE PARFAIT

½ cup water
½ cup sugar
¼ tsp salt
2 squares unsweetened chocolate
1 tsp gelatin
2 tbsp cold water
2 egg yolks
1 cup heavy cream
1½ tsp vanilla

Boil the sugar, water and salt until the sirup spins a thread when dropped from the tip of a spoon (230° F.), stirring only until the sugar is dissolved. Now add the chocolate, melted over hot water, also the gelatin softened in the cold water. Blend smoothly, then pour in a fine stream onto the well beaten egg yolks, beating constantly while pouring. Chill, stirring occasionally, and finally fold in the whipped cream and vanilla. Freeze in automatic refrigerator or bury in ice and salt. *See* PARFAIT. (Serves 6)

CHOCOLATE PIE

1¾ cups milk
⅞ cup sugar
4 squares unsweetened chocolate
½ tsp salt
2½ tbsp cornstarch

2 tbsp flour
1 whole egg plus 2 egg yolks
1 tbsp butter
1 scant tsp vanilla
9-inch pre-baked pie shell

Scald 1⅓ cups of the milk with the sugar, chocolate and salt in the upper part of the double boiler. When the chocolate melts beat with rotary beater until smooth. Moisten the cornstarch and flour with the remaining cold milk and when perfectly smooth, add to the mixture in the double boiler. Reheat and cook 5 minutes, stirring constantly, then remove from the fire. Beat the egg and yolks together and then beat into the chocolate mixture. Continue the cooking two minutes longer, stirring constantly. Cool slightly, add the butter and vanilla and when cold turn into the pre-baked pie shell. Top with a meringue made from the 2 egg whites beaten with 4 tablespoons of sugar. Place in a moderate oven (350° F.) to set and delicately color the meringue. If preferred, substitute whipped cream.

CHOCOLATE COCONUT PIE

1¾ cups milk
3 squares unsweetened chocolate
1 cup sugar
5 tbsp flour
½ tsp salt
2 eggs, separated
1 cup shredded coconut
1 teaspoon vanilla
9-inch pre-baked pie shell

Scald the milk with the chocolate in the upper part of the double boiler. When the chocolate is melted, beat with rotary beater until thoroughly blended. Combine ¾ cup of the sugar with the flour and salt, and add gradually to the chocolate mixture. Cook until thickened, stirring constantly, then continue the cooking for ten minutes longer, stirring occasionally. Pour a little of this cooked mixture over the beaten egg yolks, stirring while pouring; return all to the double boiler and cook 2 minutes longer. Now add the coconut and vanilla and when cold turn into the pre-baked pie shell, spreading evenly. Top with a meringue made with the egg whites and remaining sugar and place in a moderate oven (350° F.) until set and delicately colored. Serve cold.

CHOCOLATE REFRIGERATOR CAKE

2 squares unsweetened chocolate
1⅓ cups sweetened condensed milk
1 egg, separated
⅓ cup chopped preserved ginger
2 tbsp ginger sirup
½ tsp vanilla
Ladyfingers, split
Heavy cream, whipped

Melt chocolate in top part of double boiler, stir in condensed milk and cook until thickened. Stir 2 tablespoons chocolate mixture into beaten egg yolk; then add to remaining chocolate in double boiler and cook 3 minutes longer; cool. Stir in ginger, ginger sirup, and vanilla and fold into stiffly beaten egg white. Line bottom and sides of mold or loaf pan with waxed paper, then with ladyfingers, round sides out. Fill center with chocolate mixture, and if a loaf pan is used, arrange additional ladyfingers and chocolate mixture over top. Chill in the refrigerator at least 4 hours. Unmold, slice and serve with slightly sweetened whipped cream. (Serves 4 or 6)

CHOCOLATE SAUCE

2 squares unsweetened chocolate
1 cup water
2 cups sugar
Pinch of salt
2 tbsp butter
2 tsp vanilla

Cut the chocolate small, then cook over direct heat with the water until thick and smooth. Add the sugar and salt, bring to boiling point and cook three minutes. Stir in the butter and vanilla. This sauce keeps well if stored in an air-tight container and may be reheated as needed. One-half cup of cocoa may be substituted for the chocolate if desired.

CHOCOLATE SIRUP
(Made with Cocoa)

5 squares baking chocolate
2 cups boiling water
1¾ cups sugar
¼ cup light corn sirup
½ tsp salt

Melt the chocolate over hot water. Add the boiling water and place the pan over direct heat. Cook, stirring constantly, until smooth and thick. Add the remaining ingredients, and let bubble for several minutes, stirring occasionally. Cool and pour into a glass jar. (Makes 2½ cups)

CHOCOLATE SIRUP

1 cup cocoa
1½ cups sugar
½ cup light corn sirup
1½ cups water
¼ tsp salt
1 tsp vinegar
1 tsp vanilla

Combine all the ingredients except the vanilla and blend thoroughly. Heat over direct flame until the mixture boils, and then simmer for 5 minutes, stirring occasionally. Remove from the stove and add the vanilla. Cool and pour into glass jar. (Makes 2½ cups)

Both these sirups must be kept in the refrigerator.

CHOCOLATE SOUFFLE

3 tbsp butter
4 tbsp flour
¼ tsp salt
1 cup light cream
½ cup sugar
3 eggs
1 tsp vanilla
2 squares unsweetened chocolate

Prepare a heavy white sauce with the butter, flour, salt, and cream. Add the sugar and stir until dissolved. Combine with the well beaten egg yolks, the

vanilla, and the chocolate, previously melted over hot water. Finally fold in gently the stiffly beaten egg whites. Turn into a buttered baking dish, and bake in a moderate oven (350° F.) about 45 minutes. Serve hot with light cream or a marshmallow sauce. *See* MARSHMALLOW. (Serves 4 or 6)

CHOCOLATE NUT SOUFFLE

5 egg whites
¼ tsp salt
½ cup sugar
2 squares unsweetened chocolate
½ cup ground nuts

Beat the egg whites and salt until stiff and dry, gradually folding in the sugar. Meanwhile melt the chocolate over hot water and fold this into the egg whites together with the nuts. Pour into the well-greased top of a double boiler, cover, and cook over hot water about 45 minutes. Unmold and serve with whipped cream or a vanilla sauce. (Serves 6)

CHOP. (I) To cut in fine pieces with a sharp knife or other tool.

CHOP. (II) As applied to meat, chops, either mutton, lamb, veal, or pork, are cut from the rack or the loin. See each meat by name.

CHOP. (III) As commercially applied to Chinese tea, etc., it signifies either the grade—"first chop" then signifying first quality—or a special brand or lot. It is a Chinese custom-house seal or mark.

CHOP DISH. A type of small platter, so named because it is designed for use in serving chops at the table. *See* DISHES; *see also* PLATTER.

	LOIN	KIDNEY	RIB	FRENCHED RIB	BONELESS SHOULDER	BLADE	ARM	BUTTERFLY	SARATOGA
VEAL									
LAMB									
PORK									

CHOPS. Chart showing sources, shapes and names

CHOPPED MEAT. *See* HAMBURGER.

CHOPPING BOARD. A hardwood cutting board used in conjunction with a food chopper (*which see*). *See also* KITCHEN EQUIPMENT.

USING A KNIFE ON A WOOD CHOPPING BLOCK

USING A MINCING KNIFE IN A WOODEN BOWL

CHOPPING

CHOPPING BOWL AND KNIFE. A hardwood bowl and matching chopping knife (*see* FOOD CHOPPER) used to dice or chop foods. The bowl confines the food and makes the operation simpler than if a chopping board (*which see*) is used. *See also* KITCHEN EQUIPMENT.

CHOPSTICKS. Although eating with chopsticks seems foreign and exotic, it is not a difficult art to master, and takes only practice. In all but the most elaborate homes and restaurants, where silver-tipped ebony sticks are provided, chopsticks are made of bamboo. They are usually ten to twelve inches in length and three-sixteenths of an inch thick, tapering slightly, and they are rounded at the business end.

The Chinese do not pick up single grains of rice with chopsticks, nor do they eat soup with them. Spoons come with the soup, and rice is eaten by putting the edge of the bowl against the lower lip and flipping the contents into the mouth with the chopsticks. This requires a little practice. Real trouble starts when the novice tries to pick up a slippery fragment of fish, meat, or vegetable, or a slice of egg. Whether it is possible to learn the trick from written instructions is doubtful, but for the benefit of those who wish to try, we suggest they provide themselves with a pair of sticks, a dish of baked beans with sauce, and proceed as follows:

Put the right fist on the table, thumb up. Open the hand until the fingers are at right angles to the wrist. Lay one of the sticks in the crotch between the thumb and the palm of the hand and between the second and third fingers, so that the middle of the stock rests on the first joint of the third finger and is held down against it by the pressure of the thumb against the hand. Once in place, this stick is not moved again, the other being manipulated against it. Now the second stick is laid in place so that it lies across the tip of the second finger and the base of the forefinger. In this position it is held by the tip of the forefinger and the ball of the thumb. Having arranged the sticks with the tips meeting, the first trick is to learn to separate them with the first and second fingers and then to bring them together again.

When perfect at this, proceed to the picking up of a bean and getting it as far as the mouth without actually bending over the dish. A nonchalant ease is not likely to be acquired in a day, but diligent practice will at least enable one to appreciate the deftness of Oriental fingers.

CHOP SUEY. A thick so-called Chinese Stew.

BEEF CHOP SUEY

4 tbsp oil
½ cup diced onion
1½ lb diced raw round steak
1½ cups diced celery
½ cup water or stock
3 tbsp corn starch
¾ tsp salt
⅛ tsp pepper
1 tsp Chinese brown sauce
1 tbsp Chinese soy sauce
2 tbsp cold water
½ tsp brown sugar
1 can bean sprouts

Cook the onion and beef in the oil over a bright flame for five minutes, but do not brown. Stir constantly so as to sear all sides of the meat. Add the celery and water or stock, cover and simmer five minutes. Meanwhile combine the corn-starch, salt and pepper, Chinese sauces, cold water and sugar, blend until smooth, then stir into the first mixture, and again bring to boiling point with the well drained sprouts, stirring constantly to avoid burning or scorching. Serve with an abundance of plain boiled rice. Other meats may be substituted for the beef if preferred.

Chow Mein is similarly prepared, substituting Chinese fried noodles for the rice. In this case the noodles are first put onto the dish or platter, the meat-vegetable mixture being poured over them.

CHOW-CHOW. Any mixed vegetable pickle flavored with mustard or mustard seeds may be called chow-chow. Originally chow-chow was a Chinese sweetmeat consisting of pieces of orange peel, ginger, and other condiments in a thick sirup.

CHOW CHOW

1 qt finely chopped green tomatoes
3 cups finely chopped cabbage
½ cup finely chopped onion
½ cup finely chopped green pepper
¼ cup salt
2 tsp dry mustard
½ cup sugar
1 tsp celery seed
1 tsp mustard seed
1 tbsp horseradish
1 cup vinegar

Sprinkle layers of tomatoes, cabbage, onion, and green pepper with salt. Let stand overnight. In the morning squeeze the vegetables dry. Add the other ingredients and mix well. Pour into clean jars and cover. Keep in the refrigerator. This relish will keep for 2 or 3 weeks. (Makes 4 cups)

CHOW MEIN. *See* CHOP SUEY.

CHOWDER. The name comes from the coast of France, where the *chaudière* is a large cauldron in which the peasants and fishermen cook their soups and stews. Today each country, almost each region or state, has its own chowder. It may be made of clams, oysters, codfish, crab, eel, shrimp, and go under such native names as Zuppa di Baccala, Waterzoi, Gumbo, Bouillabaisse, or it may be made of vegetables and be peculiarly American.

Alas, what crimes have been committed in the name of chowder. Clam chowder is not bisque, not a Parisian potage, not a delicate broth for invalids. It is one of the heartiest of our national dishes. Let the devotees argue over the relative merits of Maine and Manhattan clam chowder; either is a satisfying dish. Manhattan chowder contains tomatoes; the Maine dish does not.

See also CLAM, CORN, MUSSEL and POTATO.

ORIGINAL NEW ENGLAND CHOWDER

"Take a dozen clams and one small onion," says a certain cook book, taking the name of clam chowder in vain. A dozen clams, forsooth. Take four or five dozen good soft clams, if you would serve six or eight hungry people. Then take six large onions and half a pound of the finest fat salt pork. Cut the pork in half-inch dice and brown slowly in an iron skillet. Slice the onions, thinly, into the pork fat, and brown evenly. Meanwhile wash the live clams, using a brush to get rid of all the sand and heat them slowly in a pan until the shells open. Save the juice, cut off the long necks, and remove the coarse membrane. Then chop half the clams, not too finely, and keep the rest whole. Put the pork, onions, clam juice, and a quart of boiling water into a kettle and add

3 large peeled tomatoes
1 bunch of leeks, cut fine
2 stalks celery, thinly sliced
2 carrots, diced
1 tbsp chopped parsley
Pinch of thyme
2 bay leaves
1 tsp salt
½ tsp black pepper
Pinch of nutmeg

Let the mixture boil up smartly. Then reduce the heat so the mixture simmers and add 3 large potatoes, diced. Prepare a roux by browning 2 rounded tablespoons of flour in 2 tablespoons of butter, and make it creamy and smooth by stirring in a little broth from the pot. Put the clams into the kettle, both chopped and whole, just before the potatoes are tender. Simmer slowly until the potatoes are just tender. Stir in the roux and add 2 large pilot biscuits which have been crumbled, a tablespoon of Worcestershire sauce, and a dash of tabasco sauce.

FISH CHOWDER

2 tbsp fat or drippings
1 large onion, thinly sliced
2 lb fresh cod or haddock
1 qt sliced raw potatoes
Water

1 tbsp butter
1 tbsp flour
2 cups milk
1 tsp salt
⅛ tsp pepper
2 tbsp minced parsley

Melt the fat in a large saucepan and cook the onion in it until light yellow. Discard all skin and bones of the fish and cut the flesh into inch cubes. Arrange these, with the potatoes, in the saucepan in layers, add water to barely cover and cook gently until the potatoes are just tender. Meanwhile blend the butter and flour smoothly, thin with a little of the hot fish liquor, return to the pan and stir until slightly thickened. Finally add the milk and seasonings and simmer five minutes. Just before serving sprinkle in the parsley. Crisp pilot crackers should be served with the chowder, while cole slaw and carrot strips are good accompaniments. (Serves 6)

SALT FISH CHOWDER

1½ lb salt codfish
¼ lb salt pork, diced
4 cups sliced raw potatoes
2 onions, sliced
Hot milk

Freshen the fish in lukewarm water, changing the water once. Drain very thoroughly. Cook the pork in a saucepan until the fat flows freely. Arrange in the pan the fish, potatoes, and onions, in layers, repeating the layers until all ingredients are used. Add hot milk to cover and simmer gently until potatoes and fish are tender. (Serves 4 or 6)

VEGETABLE CHOWDER

6 slices bacon, diced
2 onions, thinly sliced
1 qt hot milk
4 large potatoes, diced
2 cups canned lima beans
2 cups canned tomatoes
2 tbsp flour
1½ tsp salt
¼ tsp pepper

Cook the bacon in a frying pan until crisp. Lift out the bacon and cook the onions slowly until tender in the fat. Add to the hot milk with the potatoes and beans, simmer until both potatoes and beans are tender, add the tomatoes and the flour mixed smoothly with a little of the tomato juice. Season, bring to boiling point, and add the reserved bacon just before serving. (Serves 6)

CHRISTALINNA CHEESE. A hard rennet cheese made from cow's milk, which is a product of the canton of Graubunden in Switzerland.

CHRISTMAS MELON. Also called Santa Claus melon, *which see. See also* MELON.

CHROMIUM. Chromium is a hard metal that is exceptionally resistant to corrosion. It is commonly used as a plating, forming a protective coating over steel, copper, or some other metal. The plating possesses all of the properties of the parent metal, resisting stains and scratching. It greatly adds to the life of the utensil, as well as simplifying the cleaning problem. The surface, however, is bright, and tends to reflect rather than absorb heat, making such utensils poorly adapted for use on an electric range.

PURCHASING CHROMIUM-PLATED UTENSILS

The utensil should be judged as a utensil, realizing that the plating merely adds desirable features but cannot correct bad design. The plating itself should be smooth and free from blemish. Since the plating does wear out in time, the thickness of the coat determines the value.

CARE AND CLEANING OF CHROMIUM

Chromium plated utensils should be washed with soap and water, rinsed, and dried in the regular manner. Stains should always be removed with a polish, never with an abrasive for the latter would remove the plating as well as the stain. *See also* KITCHEN EQUIPMENT.

CHUB. A fish related to the carp which is found in southern waters. It may be cooked in any manner suitable for carp, *which see.*

CHUCK. A cut of beef, *which see.*

CHUFA. The small hard tuberous root of a grasslike plant native to the southern states is also called "earth almond" or "rush nut." They have a nutty flavor and are used like peanuts.

CHUPATTY. An unleavened pancake of coarse wheat flour which is the staple

CHUFA

native bread of northern India. It is shaped by hand and baked on a griddle.

CHURN. A vessel in which milk or cream is agitated to separate the oily globules and gather them as butter.

CHUTNEY. A pickle originally made in India. There are many varieties, but it is generally based on mangoes, with raisins, tamarinds, ginger, spices, etc. The manufactured and home-made chutneys in America are the tomato chutney, apple chutney, gooseberry chutney, peach chutney and banana chutney.

CHYLE. Milky fluid derived from chyme. It is an important medium whereby ingested fats are transferred to the blood.

CHYME. Pulp formed from food digested in the stomach by the action of the gastric juices.

CIDER. Cider made from ripe apples usually contains from four to eight percent alcohol, besides malic acid, extractives, sugar, and mineral salts. It is slightly laxative. The excess of carbonic acid generated by cider protects it from the atmospheric action, but when the gas disappears acetic fermentation converts the cider into vinegar. Cider is sometimes made from concentrated apple juice, which is added in the proportion of one part to twenty of water when ready for use. In other words, cider is a fermented beverage prepared from the juice of apples; it is not usually reckoned among the wines, nevertheless it belongs in the wine class with beverages made from currants, gooseberries, or other fruits. It is not as nutritious as beer or ale, but it is a very agreeable and mildly stimulating drink in hot weather—its acids assisting materially in quenching thirst.

Apples from which cider is made should not be permitted to fall on the ground; they ought to be hand-picked, or if shaken from the tree, coarse cloths or straw should be spread to catch the fruit and prevent bruising. All prematurely ripe and unsound apples should be rejected. If the weather is fine, the fruit may be exposed in the open air; if not, it should be placed in sheds or lofts until thoroughly ripened.

The usual way of making cider is to pound or grind the apples to a pulp by means of special machines. This pulp is then placed in a press and the juice pressed out. This juice should then be put into barrels and stored in a cellar where the temperature will not fall below 60° F. nor rise above 75° F. Active fermentation commences in a few hours and continues with the bung open until the hissing sound ceases.

The cider is then drawn off into clean barrels, separating it from its sediments; it is again bunged up for a few days, then opened, and the fermentation allowed to begin again. This second fermentation is much shorter. The cider is racked; the bungs must be tightly closed and the barrels kept in a cool place.

COMMERCIAL CIDER MAKING

The old-fashioned method of making cider—that used by individuals for home consumption—has been perfected by science for commercial purposes on a large scale.

Apples employed in the manufacture of cider may be divided into three categories: (a) The sweet, for their perfume; (b) the spicy, for their flavor; and (c) the tart, to give the required acidity.

As soon as apples are brought to the cider factory, they are sorted and placed in a pit where they will mature, the object being to develop certain principles and complete the malic acid reaction on the fruit, transforming its properties into sugar.

Thus prepared the apples are then conveyed through a hydraulic stone channel in which they are thoroughly washed by running water. Through another stone channel they are brought to the centrifugal grating machine which is composed of a large drum equipped with saw tooth blades, by means of which the slashing will be uniformly accomplished. The pulp thus obtained is left several hours in vats to permit its oxidation through contact with the air. It is at this stage that the juice acquires its individual and tempting amber color.

The next operation consists of the pressing of the pulp by means of a high pressure hydraulic press. For this the pulp is spread on heavy cloths in superimposed layers separated by wooden or rattan screens to permit the escape of the liquid. The first pressing over, the pulp must undergo a second one as the cells still contain a certain quantity of sugar. Before this second pressing, the cakes of pulp are submitted to the action of a disaggregator, which crumbles them to the desired consistency. Through a tube the crumbs are directed into vats. Water in the proper proportion is added. After a few hours the pulp is submitted to the second pressure.

The juices of the first and second pressing operations are frequently mixed in varying proportions, according to the quality of cider desired, and are then submitted to the fermentation. The juices obtained by pressure are generally placed in huge wooden vats, the insides of which are covered with a coat of a special varnish principally composed of a bituminous solution which will prevent corrosive action on the wood by the malic acids which cider contains. Experience has demonstrated that the glass vats successfully used in wine fermentation do not give good results in the fermentation of cider.

Before the fermentation process is started, the must, obtained by pressure, passses through the operation of cleansing, to clear away the insoluble matter which the liquid holds and also to remove any pectic substances which are found in a state near coagulation and which might easily render the must insoluble. However, the mixed juices which are more limpid and the juice from acid apples may be fermented without being cleansed.

The refining and cleansing of the must results from a biologic phenomenon which produces a kind of auto-fining called "defecation," toning down the sugar. Abandoned to itself, the must, after a few days, presents a peculiar appearance. A part of the pectin which it contains has been coagulated under the action of pectase and diastase and rises to the surface, forming a cap called "wild lees," while the larger lees have fallen down to the bottom (lees are the settlings of liquor, the sediments, the dregs). At the same time a kind of natural pasting occurs—the liquid is clear and freed almost completely of foreign matter and ferments. This is called in practice "between the lees."

This physico-chemical cleansing of the must is done by coagulating a part of the pectin (which see) contained in the juice of the coagulum. This is determined by a very slow fermentation of the yellow-brown cap mixed with the lees found at the bottom of the vessel. The defecation being made, the must is then drawn off and submitted to the fermentation proper which will last until all the sugar has disappeared from the liquid—that is, from four to five weeks.

Cider which is to be kept long is pasted by means of albumen of casein, gelatin, or isinglass; or it may be pasteurized. It may also be supplemented with tannin or treated with sulphuric anhydride.

Sparkling cider is obtained by a prolongation of fermentation after bottling by means of the addition of pure sugar, clarifying substances, and yeast. Certain sparkling ciders are made by the champagne method, (See CHAMPAGNE), but the process is very expensive, necessitating a large number of bottles and otherwise costly material. Cider is also rendered sparkling by the method of closed vats. This is only economical when a quantity of cider of approximately 220 gallons to 350 gallons, is to be handled. It is less expensive and is generally employed for sparkling cider to be exported. Gasified, or artificially made, sparkling cider is created by incorporating by means of special machines and at low temperature a certain quantity of catbonic acid gas. This cider does not possess the prolonged keeping properties of the champagne cider, but is an excellent product and costs much less.

As has been stated, the drawing off and bottling of cider must be made under pressure to eliminate the "flatness" of the liquid. The operation of bottling cider is facilitated by means of special machines which can wash, fill, cork, and label more than 6,000 bottles per hour without any production of foam, effervescence, or, on the other hand, any loss of gas. *See also* APPLE and BEVERAGE.

CIDER CAKE

4 cups sifted flour
3 tsp baking soda
¼ tsp salt
1 tsp cinnamon
1 tsp allspice
1 pound currants
½ cup shortening
1 cup sugar
4 eggs, separated
2 cups sweet cider

Mix and sift the flour, soda, salt and spices; mix about ½ cup with the washed and dried currants. Cream the shortening until soft and smooth; gradually add the sugar, creaming until fluffy, then add well-beaten egg yolks and beat thoroughly. Add flour mixture alternately with cider, beating until smooth after each addition; fold in thoroughly the stiffly beaten egg whites. Turn into greased loaf pan and bake in moderate oven (350° F.) about 1 hour. Cool the cake and turn out on a rack. Cover top and sides with a plain white icing. (*See* FROSTING)

CIDER GELATIN SALAD

1 tbsp gelatin
2 tbsp cold water
2 tbsp lemon juice
¼ cup sugar
1¾ cups hot cider
1½ cups diced apples
½ cup diced celery

Soften the gelatin in the combined cold water and lemon juice. Dissolve the sugar in the hot cider, add the softened gelatin and stir until this too is dissolved. Chill, and when beginning to thicken, stir in the apples and celery. Turn into previously wet individual molds and chill. Unmold and serve on lettuce, topping with mayonnaise and a sprinkling of chopped nuts. (Serves 6)

CIDER SAUCE

A variation of Brown Sauce, *which see.*
CIDER VINEGAR. *See* VINEGAR.
CINCHONA BARK. The bark of a tree growing in Peru which is used in the manufacture of some fortifying liquors, such as quinquina, and the like. It is also used in the manufacture of quinine. It contains a great amount of tannin.

CINNAMON

CINNAMON. Cinnamon is one of the most aromatic and one of the oldest known of spices. It is mentioned in the Old Testament as an ingredient in incense. It was formerly made into candles to be used only by kings. Oriental women used it to perfume their beds. The ancient Romans established it as the incense for their sacrificial and ceremonial fires. When a god was to be appeased or a departed spirit to be honored, they burned great quantities of cinnamon that its perfume might be wafted heavenward. They believed that the greater the amount of incense, the greater would be the pleasure of the deity or the spirit being honored.

Cinnamon proper is the prepared inner bark of the *Cinnamomum Aeylanicum* tree, a member of the laurel family, which is found chiefly in Ceylon. It does grow elsewhere, but Ceylon cinnamon has the best quality. The tree has ovate leaves, pale yellow blossoms, and acorn-shaped fruit, and it grows as high as thirty feet.

Saigon cinnamon is derived from the bark of the *C. Loureirii* which grows in Indo-China. Culiwan bark comes from the *C Culiwan*. Cassia is made from the bark of the *C. Cassia*, most of which comes from China. It is popularly known as and substituted for cinnamon, and it is also called "Chinese cinnamon" or cassia bark. Its flavor is very similar to that of cinnamon, but both its flavor and its fragrance are less agreeable than those of the genuine spice. Sassafras is also related to this group.

Cinnamon oil is extracted from many parts of the tree and used medicinally. The bark is ground and used as a spice. One of the steps in the preparation of cinnamon for the market involves its examination and assortment according to quality. The people who do this are obliged to taste and chew it. Very few are able to do this disagreeable job for more than three consecutive days.

As a spice cinnamon is primarily used with sweets; it accentuates a chocolate flavor delightfully. It also has a variety of uses in cookery, and it is becoming increasingly popular in beverages. Cinnamon (or cassia) sticks are served in hot drinks or used as muddlers in mulled wine. Cinnamon enhances the flavor of baked foods, apple and other fruit dishes, puddings, pickles, stews, sauces, and sweet potatoes. In the East it is sometimes used with meats and in coffee without the addition of cream and sugar.

CINNAMON CAKE

2 cups cake flour
1 tsp soda
½ tsp salt
2 tsp cinnamon
½ cup shortening (half butter)
1¼ cups light brown sugar, firmly packed
2 eggs
1 cup buttermilk

Sift the flour, measure and resift 3 times with soda, salt and cinnamon. Combine butter and other shortening and cream thoroughly. Gradually blend in the sugar; then add eggs and beat vigorously until mixture is light and fluffy. Add flour mixture and buttermilk alternately in 3 or 4 portions, beginning and ending with flour, beating well after each addition. Turn batter into two 8-inch layer cake tins, lined with thin, plain paper in bottom. Bake in a moderate oven (350° F.) for about 25 minutes or until springy when lightly pressed with fingertips. Cool in pan 5 minutes, then turn out on cake racks, sprinkle with powdered sugar or ice with coffee frosting. (*See* COFFEE)

CINNAMON COFFEE CAKE

Use ½ recipe of rich roll dough (*see* ROLL) for each coffee cake desired. After first rising, shape into a round, cover and let rest for 10 minutes. Roll out into a rectangle 8x14x⅜ inches. Spread with 2 tablespoons soft butter and sprinkle with a mixture of 1 tablespoon cinnamon and ⅓ cup sugar. Roll up snugly like a jelly roll starting at the longer side. Seal outside edge by pressing to the roll. Place in a straight line on a greased baking sheet with sealed edge underneath. With scissors, cut about ¾ way through the roll at 1 inch intervals. Twist the cut sections so they lie flat, turning one to the right, the next to the left, then to the right, and so on. There will be two rows of overlapping sections attached in the center. Brush with melted shortening, cover and let rise until doubled in bulk (about 1 hour). Bake in a moderate oven (375° F.) about 30 minutes. Cool on cake rack and ice with Confectioner's Icing (*see* FROSTING). (Makes 1 large coffee cake)

Chopped nuts may be added to the roll.

CINNAMON BUNS

Use ½ recipe of rich roll dough (*see* ROLL). Shape into a ball, cover and let rest for 10 minutes. Roll out into a rectangle 8x14x¼ inches. Brush with 2 tablespoons melted butter, sprinkle with a mixture of ¼ cup sugar and 2 teaspoons cinnamon and sprinkle with ½ cup raisins. Roll up as for jelly roll, starting at longer edge. Cut into 1-inch lengths, and place close together in a greased pan, cut side down. Cover and let rise until doubled in size in a warm place (86° F.), about 45 minutes. Brush tops with melted butter and sprinkle with more cinnamon and sugar. Bake in a moderate oven (375° F.) for 30 minutes, until nicely browned. (Makes about 12 rolls)

CINNAMON STARS

8 egg whites
2 cups granulated sugar
6 tsp cinnamon
2 tsp grated lemon rind
2 cups powdered sugar
2 cups finely-crushed almonds

Use electric mixer if possible. Beat egg whites to a froth and gradually beat in mixture of granulated sugar and cinnamon, sifting about ¼ cup at a time over top. Beat mixture until it becomes stiff, about 15 minutes.

Remove ½ cup of mixture and to the remaining mixture add the almonds and the lemon rind. Knead in thoroughly the powdered sugar. Roll out about ½ inch thick and cut with star-shaped cutter. Brush tops with the ½ cup of reserved mixture. Bake in moderate oven 350 deg. F. for 20 minutes or until very lightly browned. (Makes about 24 stars depending upon size of cutter used)

CINNAMON TOAST
See TOAST.

OLD-FASHIONED CINNAMON SUGAR COFFEE CAKE

1 recipe rich roll dough
⅔ cup light brown sugar, firmly packed
¼ cup flour
2 tsp cinnamon (or to su:t taste)
Dash of salt
¼ cup softened butter
⅔ cup chopped pecans, if desired

Make roll dough according to directions (see ROLL). After dough has risen until double in bulk, turn out on lightly floured board. Divide into two portions, round up and cover with bowls and let rest on board 10 minutes. Roll out each portion to fit a rectangular baking pan (7x11x1½ inches). Fit dough into greased pans, cover, and let rise in warm place (86° F.) until doubled in bulk, about 1 hour. Meanwhile prepare topping as follows: mix sugar, flour, cinnamon, and salt together thoroughly. Work in the soft butter to produce a coarse crumbly mixture. Stir in the nuts. Sprinkle over unbaked coffee cake. Bake in moderately hot oven (400° F.) for 15 minutes; then reduce heat to moderate

(350° F.) and bake 15 to 20 minutes longer. Serve warm with butter. (Makes 2 coffee cakes)

CINNAMON FERN. Another name for fiddlehead fern, *which see.*

CINZANO VERMOUTH. The king of Italian vermouths. It is well-known in the United States where it is widely used in numerous cocktails and as an apéritif. *See* VERMOUTH.

CISCO. A genus of fresh-water fishes of the Great Lakes region. The most important, because of its great abundance, is the lake herring. The choicest is the somewhat smaller cisco of Lake Tippecanoe. The recipes for bass, herring, mackerel, and perch may be adapted to this succulent and delicious fish.

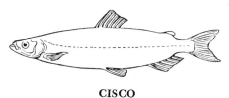

CISCO

CITRANGE. A hybrid fruit obtained by crossing the common sweet orange and the hardy but inedible trifoliate orange. The citrange varies in size and sweetness and is most often used in preserves and beverages.

CITRON

CITRIC ACID. A crystalline compound, white and sour, which is obtained from oranges, lemons, and limes. It is used as an artificial lemon flavor, and to make cooling drinks, particularly for use in fever. *See* Fruit.

CITRON. A fruit like a lemon, but larger and less acid in flavor, of which there are many varieties. The largest reach a length of nine inches and may weigh up to 20 pounds. The thick spongy rind is glacéed or candied and used in cakes and pastry much as orange and lemon peel are. It is greenish in color and has an agreeable tangy flavor.

Citron is usually bought by the piece, each piece representing half a fruit, and usually weighing about half a pound. The citron should be moist and slightly sticky; if it is hard and crystallized it has been kept too long and has dried out. For mixing into a cake citron should be cut in tiny dice or thin shavings.

CITRON MELON

CITRON-MELON. A species of watermelon, much smaller and rounder, which is inedible raw. It is used for making preserves.

Citron-Melon Preserves

6 cups sugar
6 cups water
1 6 lb citron-melon
6 oz ginger root
6 lemons, thinly sliced

Boil the sugar and water in a large kettle for 20 minutes; skim. Peel the melon, remove seeds and cut the fruit into pieces. Tie the ginger root loosely in cheesecloth and add with the prepared melon and lemon to the sirup. Simmer until the fruit is clear, about two hours, then turn into hot sterilized jars and seal. (Makes 3 quarts)

CITRUS. A genus of plants which contains a number of popular and useful fruits, all having a generally tart flavor. These include the orange, grapefruit, tangerine, citron, lemon, lime, and various hybrids, all of *which see.*

CIVET. (see vay) A culinary preparation which originated in France, made of rabbit, hare, or muskrat (*which see*).

(*Note:* This should not be confused with "Civet," a substance of musky odor which is secreted by the civet cat.)

Civet of Hare

1 hare
4 tbsp brandy
1¾ cups olive oil
Salt and black pepper
3 medium-sized onions
½ lb lean bacon or salt pork
2 tbsp flour
Red wine
7 or 8 sprigs parsley
1 large bay leaf
Small sprig thyme
Small whole clove garlic
2 dozen small white onions
2 dozen small mushroom caps
Fried bread

First collect and set aside the blood of the hare, with the liver, from which the gall should be very carefully removed. If the gall breaks, discard any part of the liver which it may touch.

Cut the head into four parts and cut the body and legs into convenient portions for serving. Place all of these in a large bowl, add the oil, salt, pepper and one of the onions cut into thin rings, and set aside to marinate for two hours, stirring frequently. Lift out the pieces of hare and pat dry. Meanwhile, cut the bacon or salt pork into small cubes, brown delicately then lift them out and set aside to keep hot. In the bacon or pork fat left in the pan, brown the remaining two onions, quartered, then put in the flour and brown this also. Next put in the pieces of hare and sear them on all sides. Add enough red wine to about half fill the pan, together with the parsley, bay leaf, thyme and garlic tied together. Cover and simmer gently about 45 minutes. Five minutes before serving thicken with the reserved blood slightly heated with a little **of** the sauce in which the hare was cooked; add also at this time the liver, cut into small cubes, and heat.

Transfer the portions of hare to another saucepan and strain the sauce over it. Add the cubed bacon or pork, together with the small white onions which have been parboiled and glazed, and the mushroom caps previously sautéed in a little butter. Reheat thoroughly. Serve in a deep platter, garnishing with heart-shaped pieces of bread fried in butter (croutons).

Civet of Hare Lyonnaise. Proceed as directed above, substituting small chestnuts cooked in meat stock and glazed for the mushrooms.

Rabbit may be prepared in the same manner.

CLABBER. Milk which has become thickened and sour by the natural action of lactic acid bacteria is called clabber. *See also* COTTAGE CHEESE and MILK.

CLAM. There are two species of clams which are of commercial importance, the soft, or long-necked clam, and the hard, or little-necked clam. The soft clams are found from Cape Cod north to the Arctic waters and the hard clams are found more abundantly south of the Cape. However, the ranges overlap considerably.

CLAMS   1. Quahog or Hard
2. Gasper or Soft

The soft clam lives in the tide flats, buried in the sand or mud that is alternately covered and exposed by the tide. When the tide is in, the clams push their long tube-like siphons up to the surface of the sand. Through the siphons, or necks, the clams draw in water laden with food and oxygen, and expel carbon dioxide and waste. When the tide goes out, the siphons are withdrawn, and a slight pit in the sand may show the location of the clam beneath.

The hard clam, which is known as the "quahaug" in New England, lives in deeper water. It may burrow into the bottom, but only deep enough to cover the shell,

since it does not have as long a siphon as the soft clam.

Soft clams are taken by digging, preferably when the tide is out, although they can be taken when covered by water. Soft clams must be taken by long-handled rakes or by dredging.

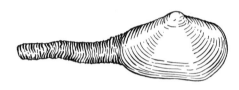

SOFT CLAM

The hard clam has a stronger flavor than the soft clam and is preferred for chowders. Small hard clams, of a size to be eaten raw on the half shell, are known as cherrystone clams.

STEAMED CLAMS

Soft clams are steamed open before being brought to the table. The first step is the "bearding" of the clam—that is, removing the black hood from the neck together with its trailing "veil." The hard clam is opened with an oyster knife, like an oyster. It is beardless.

RAZOR CLAM

The opened soft clams are served on a deep dish or large platter. An oyster or dinner fork may be used to remove the clam from its shell and the clam cap from the head. Most clam addicts, though, prefer using the fingers. At the side of each plate should be a small warm dish containing melted butter seasoned with lemon juice, and each clam should be dipped into this sauce before eating. The broth should be strained and served in cups, the clams often being dipped first into it, then into the butter.

Clams may be boiled, steamed, broiled, sautéed, baked, etc. Clams, both fresh and canned, deserve to be often used in more ways than in chowder (*which also see*).

good as it is. Tiny hard clams are prized raw or in a cocktail. Favorite clam combinations include clam fritters, scalloped clams, clams with spaghetti or noodles, clam pie, clam croquettes, creamed clams, clam cakes, clams in patty shells, deviled clams, and of course the clambake.

Many people think of clambakes as something to be enjoyed only in the summertime when friends get together—when a fire can be built on a beach for the cooking process. But as few as two people can have a "bake" merely with the aid of a large heavy saucepan or kettle and the kitchen range, the aroma of the steaming clams furnishing the salty atmosphere.

CLAM JUICE

3 tbsp lemon juice
3 cups clam juice
2 tbsp catsup
½ tsp grated onion or celery
Drop of tabasco or Worcestershire sauce
Salt to taste

Mix the ingredients and chill thoroughly. Strain before serving.

KITCHEN CLAMBAKE

4 qt hard clams
2 lb fish filets (cod, haddock or any other preferred fish)
2 lb pork sausages, optional
8 medium-sized carrots
8 medium-sized onions
4 small white potatoes
4 small sweet potatoes

Scrub the clams thoroughly to eliminate all sand, and place in the bottom of a large kettle. Cut the fish into four portions, wrap in parchment cooking paper, and place on top of the clams. Next lay in the sausages, also paper wrapped; then the carrots and onions which have been parboiled and drained and paper wrapped. Finally lay in the potatoes, scrubbed but not peeled. Add two cups of water, cover closely, and cook until the potatoes are tender, from half to three quarters of an hour. Remove paper bags before serving. The sausages flavor the vegetables nicely and the resultant broth is delicious. Butter or onion juice may be added to the broth-sauce in the pan, this being served separately in cups.

In corn season, two ears of corn per person may be added or substituted for the carrots.

NEW ENGLAND CLAM CHOWDER

½ lb salt pork, diced
2 medium-sized onions, sliced
3 cups diced raw potatoes
½ tsp salt
¼ tsp pepper
2 cups boiling water
1 qt clams, chopped
1 qt milk
2 tbsp butter
Crackers

Cook the pork until crisp, add the onions and cook about five minutes. Next put in the potatoes, seasonings, and water, cover, and simmer 10 minutes. Finally, add the clams with their liquor, the milk, and butter, and continue cooking until the potatoes are tender and the clams well plumped, about 10 minutes. Arrange crackers in hot soup dishes and pour the chowder over them, or serve crisp crackers separately. (Serves 4 or 6)

Either all soft clams or equal parts of hard and soft may be used. If soft shell clams are used the firmer portions should be finely chopped and cooked with the potatoes.

A *Manhattan Clam Chowder* differs from the New England type in that tomato juice or canned tomatoes are substituted for the milk. Also a sprinkling of thyme is used as the flavoring. Occasionally a little diced celery or carrot may be substituted for an equal amount of potato.

CLAM SPREAD

2 packages cream cheese
1 small can minced clams
1 smal onion
Salt and pepper
Worcestershire sauce

Drain the clams. Mash the cream cheese and soften with enough of the clam liquid so it spreads easily. Mix in the drained clams. Season with a little grated onion, salt and pepper to taste, and a drop of Worcestershire sauce. Pile into a bowl and serve with crackers or potato chips.

CLARET. Since the 12th century, this name has been applied to the red wines of Bordeaux by the British. The term has come to be applied to all red wines of the

CLARY

Bordeaux type (*see* BORDEAUX), though it is usually prefixed on the label by the country or state of origin, if other than France. This name has virtually supplanted the original name, Bordeaux, among English-speaking peoples.

Clarets are red table wines (*see* WINE); dry, medium-bodied, and rather sharp to the taste. They are made from a variety of grapes and usually have brilliant colors. They are especially suited for use with red meats and are served either at room temperature or slightly chilled. They are also widely used in a number of mixed wine drinks, especially punches and cooling summer concoctions.

See also PUNCH and WINE CUP.

CLARET GLASS. *See* GLASSWARE.

"CLARETS OF CHINA TEAS". Flavorsome black teas of South China. *See* PANYON TEA.

CLARIFY. As applied to liquid food or fat, the term means to render clear or limpid, to suppress the solid parts, or to separate the solids from the liquid.

An egg can be used to clarify soup or coffee. A slightly beaten egg added to boiled coffee or hot soup will coagulate and gather the fine particles which can

then be strained out, leaving a sparkling clear liquid.

See also RENDER.

CLARY. A garden herb, the leaves and flower of which are used as a food and in beverages. It is strong-scented mint originating in southern France and greatly cultivated in small gardens in America, tasting somewhat like a mixture of mint, wild sage, and muscatel sage. It is also used as a seasoning in egg dishes, and in drinks, such as clary tea, an infusion of the fresh or dried flowers. The leaves take the place of sweet woodruff in wine cups; and in beer and ale they replace hops.

CLEAR SOUP. A name given to clear consommé, which may be made of meat, or poultry, such as beef consommé or chicken consommé, or even occasionally to a fish bouillon, such as clam bouillon.

CLEAVER. A heavy, hatchet-like knife used primarily to chop through bones. *See also* CUTLERY.

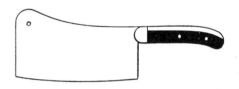

CLEAVER

CLOTTED CREAM. *See* DEVONSHIRE CREAM.

CLOUD BERRIES. The round, soft, red or yellowish fruit, somewhat like a raspberry, abundantly found in New England, sold fresh or canned and used for desserts, pies, and the like. All the recipes for raspberries, strawberries, and similar berries may also be used for this fruit.

CLOVES. Cloves are the dried flower buds of an East Indian tree belonging to the myrtle family. The freshly-gathered buds are crimson-colored, but they later acquire a deep brown cast. Because of their richly fragrant odor, cloves were first valued for their perfume. Long ago Chinese courtiers were required to hold cloves in their mouths while addressing their emperor. (This custom probably stemmed from the predilection of the Chinese for garlic.)

This spice has a warm, pungent, aromatic taste. It is used, either whole or ground, in the making of condiments, preserves, relishes, and candy. Whole cloves add a pleasant flavor to stewed fruits, pork and ham roasts, and canned soups. Remove them before these foods are served. Ground cloves enhance the flavor of baked goods, chocolate puddings, spiced wines, hot drinks, stuffings, and stews.

CLOVE

CLOVER CLUB. A cocktail supposedly named for a legal and literary club which met in a Philadelphia hotel where the blend is believed to have originated.

CLOVER CLUB

1 jigger dry gin
½ small jigger grenadine
½ small jigger lime juice
1 egg white

Place the ingredients in a cocktail shaker with cracked ice, shake well making sure egg white is thoroughly mixed, strain into cocktail glass. (Serves 1) *See* BARTENDING, *see also* COCKTAIL, ALCOHOLIC.

CLUB CHEESE. A typically American cheese prepared from well-ripened Cheddar with which pimientos are sometimes blended. It is packaged in small jars and also in waxed paper and tin foil. It is known as Snappy cheese.

CLUB SANDWICH. The club sandwich need not always be made of chicken. There are many other fillings suited to this type of sandwich, which is made with three slices of toast, arranged in tiers, with two

complete layers of fillings in between. Club, or three-decker sandwiches may also

CLUB SANDWICH

be made with plain bread, buttered, or spread with a creamed (flavored) butter. Club sandwiches may be served cold or hot; they may be cut in halves, from corner to corner—that is, diagonally, or in thirds, or quarters. First the lower layer is filled with a spread or a filling; topped with another slice of bread or toast, also filled with a spread or a filling, and finally topped

CLOUDBERRY

with a plain or toasted slice of bread. These are gently pressed together with the tips of the fingers and the sandwich knife, then cut according to fancy. When cut in thirds or quarters, they may be held together with decorative toothpicks.

CLUB SODA. A name commonly given to carbonated, or aerated, water (*which see*), especially when sold in bottles.

CLUB STEAK. A name for porterhouse steak from which the tenderloin has been removed and the ends trimmed.

COAGULATE. To change a cream or liquid food mixture into a curd-like mass.

COALFISH. Another name for pollock, a salt-water fish.

COAL RANGE. *See* RANGE.

COASTER. A receptacle or mat designed to be placed under a beverage glass to catch moisture that would otherwise mar furniture surfaces. This moisture is caused by spillage and overflow from the glass and by "sweating;" i.e., water droplets condensing on the surface of the glass, a common occurrence in the case of iced drinks.

Though the type and design of coasters are legion, the most favored ones have a rim of some sort to confine the liquid and a broken design on the surface. The rim should be large enough to comfortably hold the glass and still allow room for liquid collecting, and the design keeps the coaster from sticking to the glass due to an atmospheric seal being formed by the liquid if the glass fits smoothly.

COB. The woody spike of an ear of corn upon which the kernels grow. Corn on the cob is usually served hot with butter.

COBBLER. (I) A cooling, sweet, summer drink, made with a wine or liquor, fruit, sugar and shaved ice, usually sipped through straws. An American invention, the cobbler has enjoyed world-wide popularity.

As is often the case, there are many ways of mixing cobblers, and it is difficult to say which is the "basic" recipe.

APPLEJACK COBBLER

1 jigger applejack
½ tsp lemon juice
1 tbsp orange juice
1 tbsp maraschino

The ingredients are mixed in an old-fashioned cocktail glass (*see* GLASSWARE) with a goodly quantity of powdered or shaved ice. (Serves 1)

CATAWBA COBBLER

1 tsp powdered sugar
1 slice orange, quartered
2 large jiggers Catawba wine
Fruits in season

The sugar, orange slice and wine are placed in a large highball glass (*see* GLASSWARE) and mixed. The glass is then filled with powdered or shaved ice, garnished with fruit and the drink served with straws. (Serves 1)

CHAMPAGNE COBBLER

1 tbsp powdered sugar
2 thin slices orange peel
2 thin slices lemon peel
2 slices lemon
Berries in season
Champagne

Either a highball or a zombie glass (*see* GLASSWARE) is used. The sugar is dropped in the bottom with the citrus peels and the glass filled one third with powdered or shaved ice. The glass is then filled with champagne, stirred gently, and garnished with the lemon slices and berries. Serve with straws. (Serves 1)

CLARET COBBLER I

1 small jigger claret
1 small jigger simple sirup
Fruit slices in season

A goblet (*see* GLASSWARE) is filled with powdered or shaved ice, the wine and sirup added, stirred, and garnished with fruit, preferably orange and lemon. Serve with straws. (Serves 1)

CLARET COBBLER II

Made as the Catawba Cobbler, using claret.

PORT WINE COBBLER

1 jigger port wine
1 small jigger simple sirup
Fruits in season

Mixed and served as the Claret Cobbler I.

SHERRY COBBLER

Made as the Catawba Cobbler.

WHISKY COBBLER I

1 jigger whiskey
½ small jigger Curacao
1 slice lemon
Fruits in season

A goblet (*see* GLASSWARE) is filled with powdered or shaved ice, the ingredients added, stirred, garnished with fruit and served with straws. (Serves 1)

WHISKY COBBLER II

1 tbsp powdered sugar
1 large jigger whisky
1 tbsp pineapple sirup
Fruits and berries in season

The sugar, whisky and sirup are placed in the bottom of a large highball glass (*see* GLASSWARE), mixed, the glass filled with powdered or shaved ice, well garnished with fruits and berries and served with straws. (Serves 1)

COBBLER. (II) A deep dish dessert of the pie type, but without a bottom crust. The top crust is usually made of a biscuit-type dough rather than pastry. See the various fruits for recipes.

COBNUT. A species of the filbert and hazelnut family. The cobnuts are those with knobs of about the same length as the hazelnuts. When the nuts are ripe and have shed their husks, only an expert can be certain of their classification, for there are several kinds and sizes of each, but the hazelnuts, like the filberts, are generally oblong, and the cobs large, roundish, and angular. The filberts are those with fringed husks extending beyond the nuts, and the hazels have the husks shorter than the nuts.

COCK. A full-grown male of the domestic fowl.

COCKEREL. A young cock.

COCKTAIL, ALCOHOLIC. A short, iced, mixed drink made of one or more spirituous liquors combined with various flavoring ingredients, usually including bitters. Generally quite potent, cocktails are chiefly used as appetizers.

The origins of the cocktail are shrouded in doubt and dispute. Countries other than America have claimed its invention, but these claims are generally discounted; while in the United States there has been much debate as to the time, place and date that this type of mixed drink came into being and was given such an unusual name.

The bulk of the stories give the credit to one Betsy Flanagan, the widow of a Revolutionary soldier, who, it is said, operated a tavern at Four Corners, located in what is now Westchester County, New York State. According to the stories, the cocktail had been known prior to that time, but under different names. Mrs. Flanagan had acquired considerable local fame as a mixer of such drinks and her tavern was a popular resort for officers of that period. The stories all agree that she had a glass filled with cock or rooster tail feathers on the bar, but give different reasons as to how the feathers or "cock's tail" became identified with the drink.

Other localities have claimed the honor, giving many different stories that would explain the name. The town of Bladensburg, Maryland, for one, has gone on record, naming the year 1846 as the birthdate of the cocktail, while the state of Kentucky, famous for its bourbon and juleps, has also been named in at least one story.

Though its parentage may be in doubt, the birth, or at least the christening of the cocktail is overwhelmingly conceded to have happened in America. The cocktail developed and grew up as an American citizen, and it was as such that its fame became worldwide.

Though the cocktail was originally intended as an appetizer, it has come to be accepted as a mid-afternoon "pick-me-up" and as a commuter's drink, to be snatched between the office and the train. However, it was designed to be potent and was never intended for extended social drinking.

Just as the proper wine should be served with food, the proper cocktail should be served before the meal. Cocktail selection, however, is based more on the drink's capabilities than its taste, since any alcoholic mixture containing bitters will make a good appetizer.

For example, though all are extremely potent, some cocktails are faster in their action than others. Generally speaking, the *tart* or *dry* cocktails are "fast," while the *sweet* kind are "slow." If dinner is to be served immediately, a "fast" cocktail is in order, but if there is to be a delay, the "slow" sort should be served.

Cocktails are mixed in two ways; *shaking* and *stirring*. In the first case, the ingredients are placed in a cocktail shaker with cracked ice and vigorously agitated until thoroughly mixed. A stirred cocktail, and most cocktails made with wine fall into this category, is mixed in a mixing glass by being gently stirred with a long handled spoon. Since there is more dilution by melted ice in a shaken cocktail, the stirred drink is apt to be stronger. Too much depends, however, on the type and amount of ingredients used in each drink for this to be a general rule. For a detailed discussion of mixing methods, *see* BARTENDING.

The cocktail should be sipped, never gulped; and in serving, time should be allowed for this. If too many cocktails are served, or if they are served with the wrong timing, they can easily defeat their purpose by actually marring the drinker's enjoyment of the meal that follows.

The cocktail should be pleasing to the eye, as well as to the other senses, and for that reason, many are colored or are garnished with fruits, etc.

Most cocktails are served in stemmed goblets with a three or three and a half ounce capacity, though some require special glasses. *See* GLASSWARE.

Though the better known cocktails are fairly well standardized, both as to name and recipe, variations are common. Some basic cocktail recipes are listed alphabetically in this book. *See also* APERITIF, CORDIAL and LIQUEUR.

COCKTAIL, NON-ALCOHOLIC. This may take a variety of forms. As with all appetizers (*which see*), the recipes are extremely flexible, and the object is to make them as tasty and decorative as possible. The fruit and sea food mixtures are served at the table as the first course of dinner. The liquid cocktails may also be served at this time, but serving them in another room before going in to dinner seems to be more conducive to congeniality among the guests.

To give fruit an appetizing appearance remove all seeds, skin, and membrane from it, and chill or ice it thoroughly before serving. Arrange fruit cups in attractive patterns.

Fruit cup cocktails may be served in cocktail glasses, sherbet glasses, orange cups, or glass bowls. Some bowl-shaped glasses fit into long-stemmed ones and allow space for crushed ice between the two. Use very small pieces of a single fruit or combinations of fruits. Add sugar, and an additional sweetening agent if desired. Serve plain, with fruit juice, with gingerale, or with a nippy fruit dressing. Maraschino cherries and mint sprigs are among the more popular garnishes. Each serving should consist of about ½ cup of fruit mixture.

Iced fruit juices, plain or combined with other fruit juices or with gingerale, are served in cocktail glasses. You may sweeten them by adding honey, sugar, or a mixture of equal parts of sugar and water. Garnishing is optional. *See also* INDIVIDUAL FRUITS and SEAFOOD.

CITRUS FRUIT COCKTAIL

Mix 1⅛ cup of grapefruit juice, ⅜ cup of lemon juice, ¾ cup of orange juice, ½ cup of sugar, and 1½ cups of chilled carbonated water. Place the mixture in a cocktail shaker and shake vigorously. Serve at once in iced glasses. Garnish each cocktail with a sprig of fresh mint. (Serves 6)

FRUIT CUP COCKTAILS

Orange fruit cocktail. Combine orange sections, halved strawberries, and seedless grapes. Chill thoroughly.

Peach cocktail. Place 1 peach, peeled and diced, in each of 6 cocktail glasses. Sprinkle with powdered sugar. Mix ¾ cup of grape juice, ¾ cup of crushed ice, and ¼ cup of lemon juice. Pour this mixture over the peaches. Garnish each portion with mint leaves.

Cape Cod cocktail. Combine 2 diced apricot halves, 1 sliced banana, and ⅔ cup of cranberry sauce. Chill thoroughly, and serve in sherbet glasses.

Pineapple mint cocktail. Combine pineapple cubes, orange sections, cubes of mint jelly or pieces of after-dinner mints, and fruit juices. Chill thoroughly.

Grapefruit and strawberry cocktail. Cut 4 grapefruit in halves, remove the skins, and place the skins in cold water. Skin the grapefruit sections and combine them with 2 cups of strawberries. Sprinkle the fruit with powdered sugar and chill thoroughly. Line the skins with mint leaves and fill them with the fruit.

COCKTAIL SAUCES

Pink sauce. Mix 1 cup of mayonnaise, ½ cup of catsup, 1½ tablespoons of lemon juice, a few drops of tabasco sauce, and salt to taste. Serve with shrimp.

Sea food sauce. Mix 1 cup of mayonnaise, 2 tablespoons of catsup, 2 tablespoons of chili sauce, 1 tablespoon of tarragon vinegar, and 1 teaspoon of lemon juice.

Piquant sauce. Mix ⅓ cup of catsup, 1 teaspoon of onion juice, ½ teaspoon of tabasco sauce, and salt and pepper to taste. Chill thoroughly, and serve with fish.

Cocktail dressing. Mix ¼ cup of catsup, 1 tablespoon of lemon juice, 2 teaspoons of horseradish, a few drops of Worcestershire sauce, and salt and chopped celery to taste.

Shellfish cocktail sauce. Mix 2 tablespoons each of sugar, butter, chopped onion, and catsup with 6 tablespoons of mayonnaise. Chill thoroughly.

Raw oyster sauce. Mix 2 tablespoons each of chopped parsley and minced green onions, 3 tablespoons of oil and vinegar, 1 tablespoon each of chervil and chives, ½ teaspoon each of salt and Worcestershire sauce, and a few drops of tabasco sauce.

Tomato cream sauce. Fold ¼ cup of whipped heavy cream into ½ cup of condensed tomato soup or of tomato sauce. Add ½ teaspoon of lemon juice, and beat well. Serve with fruit mixtures.

COCKTAIL FORK. See FLATWARE.

COCKTAIL SHAKER. A metal or glass container in which liquids are mixed by means of vigorous agitation. Cracked ice is usually added to the liquids and serves the double purpose of chilling the beverage while aiding the mixing action. Its most common use is in the preparation of that class of drinks known as Cocktails (*which see*) from which the shaker derives its name.

There are a great many different designs and sizes of cocktail shakers. The simplest model is a plain, open, vase-like metal container that is sealed during shaking by a common glass, or a fitted metal cover. Other models have built in strainers and even spigots and pedestals.

See also BARTENDING.

COCKTAIL STRAINER. A device used to keep cracked ice, fruit skins, etc., back in the shaker or mixing glass when a drink is poured. It is commonly a coil of wire set around the rim of a circular sheet of metal. Various perforated devices are also used for this purpose, and those especially designed to be used with cocktail shakers, but not an integral part of the shaker, are also so called.

See also BARTENDING.

COCO DE MER. This nut is a member of the coconut family and grows on the Island of Seychelles in the Indian Ocean, which the natives firmly believe was the home of Adam and Eve, the nut being the "forbidden fruit." It is about eighteen inches long and five inches thick, resembling polished mahogany on one side and is covered with a coarse husk on the other.

COCO DE MER

COCONUT. Even if Robinson Crusoe had been cast up on a deserted island without chests, casks, ropes, food, gunpowder, and such necessities, he could have managed a happy existence provided coconut trees grew there. Recent scientific studies of the neglected coconut palm have been unexpectedly fruitful.

This remarkable tree matures at about seven or eight years of age and produces nuts for 70 or 80 years. The "meat" of the nut is nutritious and can be served in numerous ways, many of which were appreciatively described by Herman Melville, the 19th century novelist who lived among island natives for years.

The unripe fruit also provides a "milk" that is refreshing and wholesome. This remarkable beverage is always cool because the wall of the nut serves as an insulator against the heat. That is, every coconut is like a bottle of milk that "grows on ice." The juices have, in addition, a mild peptic reaction on the stomach which prevents indigestion.

But perhaps one does not like milk. In that case, there's still nothing to complain about. The roots are ground up and used like tea or coffee. This is an especially common practice in South India.

Not only does the coconut sustain life, it helps to prevent death and is the native's medicine chest. Because of an astringent substance in the tissue, coconuts are used as remedies for intestinal complaints and coughs, as poultices for rheumatic fever and indeed as a cure for all kinds of diseases. Even when a native is wounded, he has an antiseptic lotion ready which is made from the coconut. Toilet accessories are also extracted from it—the juice is used as a mouth wash and gargle; and tooth-powder is made out of coconut roots that have been roasted and ground.

When the tree, after a long productive life finally dies, its uses are not over. The wood can be used to build houses of great durability. Furniture made of it may be trimmed with ornamental carving and is also practical. Mattresses are made from the fibers of the coconut's husk. Housetops

are made of coconut leaves. The coconut uses as food is cooked over a fire of coconut wood. In Malabar and Ceylon, the roots of the dead palms are widely used as fuel. Stalks of the leaves are likewise burned. But the dried leaves are a source of illumination. They are lighted to become torches for "night traffic."

The coconut shell makes an excellent cup for drinking bouts, and even the beggar uses it as a "hat" to hold out for alms. But in the household the shell has its greatest use. It serves as a mixing bowl, a bathtub accessory, and a plate for eating. It is used for lamps, cups, saucers, spoons, ladles, ashtrays, and buttons. Few things invented by nature have proven as indispensable and of such all-around value as the coconut palm. "He who plants a coconut tree plants vessels and clothing, foods and drink, a habitation for himself and a heritage for his children."

Among the numerous edibles grown in Puerto Rico, the coconut runs an average of 25,000,000 nuts per year, with an average of 15 percent less during hurricane

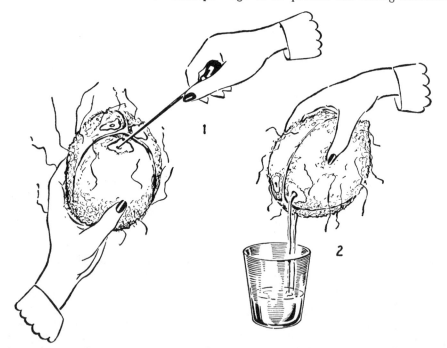

OPENING A COCONUT 1. Tap three soft areas at top of shell with ice pick or some other sharp instrument. 2. Pour out milk. 3. Revolve in hand, tap with hammer—not too hard—all over nut until hard shell cracks up and falls off. 4. After taps of hammer shell cracks up and falls off, leaving nut of meat. (not too hard with taps or shell falls apart and meat clings to shell.) 5. Take meat nut and slice up. 6. Slice of coconut meat.

years. The average output of a single tree, "tumbled" about 5 times a year, is 75 nuts—that is to say, 15 nuts to the gathering.

Copra is the general term applied to the meat of the nut. It is pressed and shipped in bulk from all tropical countries. It is used principally in the manufacture of oil and soap, as well as in the preparation of animal food.

VARIETIES OF PREPARED COCONUT

There are several kinds of prepared coconut—domestic manufacture, including (a) long shred (b) medium shred; and (c) short shred; and *partially* domestic manufacture (reprocessed), including also long, medium and short shred. The domestic manufacture is made of the best quality, sound, sweet coconuts shredded, desiccated in continental United States without removal of any oil, and processed with sugar, glucose, and glycerin, then properly flavored with salt; while the partially domestic manufacture, although being man-

ufactured in the same way as the domestic manufacture, requires reprocessing. Southern style, moist, shredded coconut, packed in hermetically sealed cans, is an excellent substitute for fresh grated coconut.

PREPARATION FOR MARKET

In Puerto Rico the coconut tumblers are trained from childhood and organized in a sort of trade association, the rates for tumbling, husking, grading and sacking being established.

Each tumbler is armed with a two-foot, razor-sharp machete and a two-foot length of one-inch rope cradled into a figure eight. Such is the equipment for taking to the air. These automatons (the tumblers) take a position at the base of a tree, clutch the figure-eight ropes between the big and second toes of each foot, lay the soles of their feet against the tree, half encircling the bole with the soles curved inward, insert a machete between their white, glistening teeth, and begin to climb. The rope, together with the pressure

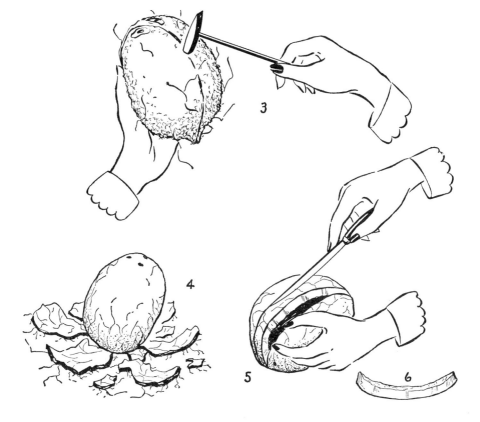

FOOD VALUE

	Wa-ter	Food Energy	Pro-tein	Fat	Car-bohy-drates	Cal-cium	Phos-phorus	Iron	Vit. A Value	Thia-mine	Ribo-flavin	Nia-cin	Ascor-bic Acid
Coconut, dry, shred'd	3.3	579	3.6	39.1	53.2	43	191	3.6	0	Trace	Trace	Trace	0

of the feet, insures a tight foothold as the climber reaches up, clutches the bole, and with a quick, froglike movement hitches his roped feet upward, repeating the gesture until he is 50 or 60 feet from the ground and within reach of the clustered coconuts.

Bracing himself against the outspreading fronds, he begins the sword play of the flashing machete, cleaving singles, doubles, trios, and whole branches of prime coconuts, which fall like bombshells on the damp ground.

COCONUT CHOCOLATE DREAMS

1/4 cup light corn sirup
2 cups sugar
1/2 cup water
2 cups grated fresh coconut
1/2 tsp vanilla
3 squares melted sweet chocolate

Combine the sirup, sugar, and water and cook over a low flame to the soft ball stage (238° F.). Cool to lukewarm, add the coconut and vanilla and beat and stir until creamy. Turn onto a slab or platter and pat with the palm of the hand into a thin sheet (about 3/8 inch thick) or roll out with a rolling pin dusted with powdered sugar. Pour the chocolate over evenly, and when cold, cut into squares.

COCONUT CONES

4 cups sugar
1 cup water
1/8 tsp cream of tartar
Grated coconut
1/2 tsp a mond extract
1/2 tsp vanilla

Combine sugar, water and cream of tartar, stir just until the sugar is dissolved, then cook, without stirring, to the soft-crack state (290° F.). Stir in coconut to thicken the mixture, so that it can be

molded. Flavor with the almond and vanilla, and when cool, shape into cones and place on waxed paper to dry.

COCONUT CREAM PIE

1/4 cup flour
1/2 cup sugar
1/4 tsp salt
1 1/2 cups scalded milk
3 eggs, separated
2 tbsp butter
1/2 tsp vanilla
1/2 cup moist shredded coconut
1/3 cup sugar
Baked 8-inch pie shell

Mix flour, 1/2 cup sugar, and salt in top of double boiler; add 3/4 cup of the scalded milk and stir vigorously until well blended. Add remaining hot milk and cook over direct heat until thick and smooth, stirring constantly. Beat egg yolks well, stir in a little of the hot mixture and pour back into the double boiler; cook over boiling water for 2 minutes, stirring constantly. Remove from heat and stir in butter and vanilla. Beat egg whites until stiff, and gradually beat in the 1/3 cup of sugar until very thick and smooth. Fold about 1/2 cup moist shredded coconut into the hot filling, then fold about 1/3 of the meringue into the mixture. Pour filling into pie shell and quickly pile over it the remaining meringue, being sure to touch the edges of the crust all around. Bake in a moderate oven (350° F.) and bake 12 to 15 minutes, or until golden brown. Cool on cake rack before cutting.

COCONUT DAINTIES

1 large fresh coconut
4 cups sugar
1 egg white
1/2 tsp almond extract
1/2 tsp vanilla

Grate the coconut (first removing all brown skin), and set aside ½ cup. Combine remaining coconut and sugar in a large saucepan with the water from the coconut and the beaten egg white. Cook over a low flame, stirring constantly from the bottom of the pan until the mixture begins to sugar. Remove from the fire, add the flavorings and beat until creamy. Drop by teaspoonfuls onto heavy waxed paper, sprinkle with the reserve grated coconut and cool. Store in a cool dry place.

If desired, 3 squares of grated unsweetened chocolate may be added to and cooked with the above ingredients.

COCONUT FINGERS

8 slices day-old white bread
1 cup sweetened condensed milk
1½ cups moist shredded coconut

Cut crusts from slices of bread and cut each slice into four strips. Dip slices of bread into condensed milk and then into coconut, covering all sides. Place on a greased baking sheet and bake in a moderately slow oven (325° F.) for 10 to 15 minutes or until delicately browned. Remove from pan at once. They become crisp on cooling. (Makes 32 fingers)

COCONUT ICING

Frost cake with 7-minute icing (*see* FROSTING) and immediately sprinkle the fresh icing with moist-pack grated coconut, being sure to cover sides as well as top of the frosted cake.

Variation: To make Moss Rose Icing, soak the coconut in 2 or 3 tablespoons of orange juice to which ¼ teaspoon of orange rind and 1 teaspoon sugar have been added. Squeeze moisture out of coconut, fluff up and sprinkle over icing.

COCONUT LEMON COOKIES

2¼ cups all-purpose flour
½ tsp soda
½ tsp salt
½ cup butter or shortening
¾ cup sugar
1 egg
1 tsp lemon rind
½ tsp lemon extract
1 cup grated coconut, firmly packed

Sift flour, measure and resift 3 times with soda and salt. Cream butter until soft and smooth; add sugar and beat until well blended. Add egg and beat until smooth and fluffy. Stir in lemon rind, lemon extract and coconut. Gradually blend in the flour mixture and turn dough into a small loaf pan which has been lined with waxed paper. Chill in refrigerator for several hours until firm; then turn out onto cutting board, strip off paper and cut into thin, uniform slices ⅛ inch thick or less, using a sharp, thin-bladed knife. Transfer cookies to greased baking sheet, and bake in a moderately hot oven (400° F.) for about 8 to 10 minutes or until nicely browned. Cool on cake racks. (Makes about 4 dozen)

COCONUT MILK

By "milk of coconut" Latin Americans mean the milky colored liquid that can be pressed from the coconut meat, and not the coconut water. It is prepared as follows. The coconut is first grated, then spread on a shallow pan, moistened with a little of the water from inside the coconut, and set in a warm oven for a few moments to loosen up the oils of the nut. The mass must by no means become hot—only slightly warmed, after which it is put into a strong though loose-woven cloth and wrung hard over a bowl until all the milk is expressed. What remains in the cloth resembles sawdust in appearance, and is discarded.

COCONUT-ORANGE CREAMS

1 tbsp butter
2 cups granulated sugar
¼ cup water
½ cup evaporated milk
2 tsp orange flower water
2 tsp orange juice
¼ tsp grated orange rind
2 cups moist shredded coconut

Melt the butter in the pan in which candy is to be cooked. Add sugar, water and milk and boil to soft ball stage (236° F.), stirring constantly. Cool and beat like chocolate fudge (*which see*). Add flavoring, rind and coconut, and knead into candy until creamy. Using about a tablespoon of candy, mold with the hands into even sized balls. Roll in additional coconut. (Makes 1½ pounds)

Note: Your druggist will supply the orange flower water.

FRESH COCONUT CAKE

1⅔ cups cake flour
1 cup sugar
¾ tsp salt
3½ tsp baking powder
⅓ cup shortening
½ cup coconut milk
¼ cup sweet milk
3 egg whites, unbeaten
1 tsp vanilla
Freshly grated coconut

Have all ingredients at room temperature. Sift the flour, measure and resift 3 times with the sugar, salt and baking powder, the last time into large mixing bowl. Add shortening and ½ cup of the two milks combined. Beat on low speed 2 minutes with electric beater (time exactly). Scrape batter from sides of bowl twice during the beating. Add remaining ¼ cup liquid, the egg whites and vanilla. Beat 2 minutes longer; scrape sides of bowl to keep batter smooth. Turn into two 8-inch layer pans, bottoms lined with thin, plain paper. Bake in a moderate oven (350° F.) for 25 minutes. Cool 5 minutes then turn out on cake racks to finish cooling. Put together with lemon filling (*see* LEMON) and frost with 7-minute icing. (*See* FROSTING). Sprinkle generously with freshly grated coconut.

ORANGE COCONUT SALAD

3 seedless oranges, peeled and sliced
Lettuce or romaine
½ cup moist coconut

Arrange a circle of thick overlapping orange slices on crisp lettuce with a light heap of coconut in the center. Serve with French dressing (*which see*) or lime honey dressing (*see* LIME). (Serves 5)

CODFISH. The codfish capital of the world is Gloucester, where "Cape Cod turkey" is handled by the ton and all other fish by the pound. Some day the whole history of codfish as a New England asset and institution may be written, and then perhaps the true story of Portuguese in-

fluence in the industry may come to light. It is significant that codfish is as substantial and important an asset to the Portuguese nation as the celebrated wines of Portugal. The people of that narrow but populous strip of the peninsula of southern Europe feast on prodigious quantities of sea food, and wash it all down with equally prodigious libations of good wine. While the grape never got a firm foothold on Puritan soil, it seems logical enough that the immigrant "Portagee" fisherman who came to the old colony in the early days must have had more than a little to do with the founding of a colossal industry, as well as the attendant customs and traditions that surround this New England industry.

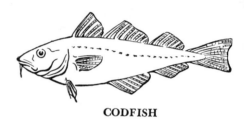

CODFISH

Codfish belongs to the *Gadidoe* family, of which there are more than 120 different species in the northern and temperate seas of each hemispheres. Its back is of a deep gray color, mottled with yellow, merging gradually into the silver-white of the lower parts. Like all white-fleshed fish, cod has its fat secreted in the liver as have the haddock, trout, flounder, smelt, perch, and others; while the oily fish such as the salmon, eel, mackerel, bluefish, shad, herring, etc., have the fat distributed throughout the flesh.

The cod feeds close to the bottom of the shores at about 25 to 50 fathoms and is a voracious and gluttonous fish. It reaches an average of three to three and one-half feet in length, and the average weight is from six to ten pounds, but some which have been caught measure five feet and weigh over 100 pounds.

It is an exceedingly prolific fish, and it has been estimated that from 9,000,000 to 10,000,000 eggs are contained in a single ovary of a female of three to three and one-half feet, weighing from 15 to 18 pounds; these eggs being equal in weight to one-half the total weight of the fish. During the spawning season from January to March, eggs may be seen floating in the water.

Cod Fishing

Shallow water cod, those caught off the rocky shores, are known as "Rock Cod"; while those taken from deep water are called "Off-shore Cod." The deep water cod are the better fish. A young cod, weighing one and a half to two pounds is known as scrod. The northern seas are the habitat of the cod, and cod-fishing in America, which is a great industry, is established principally along the banks of Newfoundland where the most important cod fisheries in the world have been located for many centuries. Saint Pierre and Miquelon Islands and the shores of the Atlantic Seaboard from Nova Scotia as far as the Gulf of Saint Lawrence are also busily occupied with cod fisheries.

More than 16,000 vessels including all nationalities and covering a stretch of approximately 500 miles long by 150 wide may be seen off the Newfoundland Banks during the fishing season beginning in May. During this time more than fifty million cods are caught.

Cod fishing is very interesting. As soon as the fish is taken on board the vessel, a specialist removes its head and bladder and puts them aside to be sold for the manufacture of by-products; then the liver is also removed to be utilized in the manufacture of cod liver oil, which has a well-known therapeutic value; the eggs also are set aside, to be used for sardine fishing. Then a second specialist takes hold of the fish; this is the "dresser" who bones the fish and crimps it, then cleans the abdominal cavity. The final specialist, the "packer," arranges the cod in the hold where it will receive its first salt, or be put into the frigid chamber or on ice, according to the destination and use of the fish. The further processes of drying and salting which are carried out on shore when the fish are unloaded, usually require about two months' time.

Although cod is in season throughout the year, it is at its best from September to the middle of December. Owing to its abundance, moderate price, and easy procurability, from an economic standpoint the cod ranks in the most important class of fish foods.

It assumes different names according to the mode of its preparation. For example, fresh cod is sometimes called "cabillaud" from the Dutch name of the fish, and when it is sold as taken from the water; green cod is the fish which is salted but not dried; dry cod is cod salted and dried; stockfish, the cod when dried but not salted, and so on.

Cod may be prepared by boiling, steaming, frying, sautéeing, baking and broiling or grilling. It is served with any of the sauces which are used with halibut, flounder, or turbot.

For information on salt cod, *see* Fish.

Baked Stuffed Cod

1 cod, about 3 lb
4 tbsp butter
1 small onion, finely chopped
1 cup soft bread crumbs
1/3 tsp thyme
1/4 tsp sage
1 tbsp minced parsley
1 hard-cooked egg, coarsely chopped
Salt and pepper
1/3 cup stock, milk, or water
4 slices salt pork

Wipe the fish with a damp cloth, rub over with one tablespoon melted butter seasoned with a little pepper and salt. Heat the remaining butter in a saucepan, and cook the onion in it until yellow, stirring frequently. Add bread crumbs, seasonings and flavorings with the egg and moisten with the stock, milk or water, using just enough to soften the crumbs but not make them too wet. Stuff the fish with this dressing and sew or skewer up the cavity. Lay the salt pork in a baking dish, put the fish on top, dredge with seasoned flour and pour 3/4 cup of water into the pan around the fish. Bake in a moderate oven (350° F.) allowing 15 minutes to the pound and baste with the liquid in the pan, adding a little more if necessary. Serve on a hot platter garnished with sections of lemon and parsley. (Serves 6)

Baked Cod with Crabmeat Dressing

1 cod, about 3 1/2 to 4 lb
1 tbsp melted butter
1 tsp lemon juice
1 1/2 cups flaked crabmeat, fresh or canned
1 tbsp grated onion
1/4 cup finely chopped celery

2 tbsp minced green pepper
⅛ tsp each thyme, sage, nutmeg and allspice
1 tsp salt
½ tsp pepper
¾ cup soft bread crumbs
1 beaten egg
4 slices bacon or salt pork

Wipe the fish with a damp cloth, then rub over with the melted butter to which the lemon juice and a little salt and pepper have been added. Blend the crabmeat, seasonings, flavorings and bread crumbs, and moisten with the beaten egg. Stuff the fish; then sew up or skewer the cavity. Place in a baking pan on the bacon or salt pork, and bake in a moderate oven (350° F.) allowing 15 minutes to the pound, basting frequently with the fat in the pan. Serve very hot accompanied by egg sauce or caper sauce, if desired. Garnish with parsley and lemon. (Serves 6)

BOILED COD

Sprinkle a solid piece of cod, 3 to 3½ pounds in weight, with salt and pepper. Place in a steamer and cook, over boiling water, 40 to 45 minutes or until the flesh can readily be separated into flakes. Remove skin and serve on a hot platter, garnishing with strips of dill pickle, parsley and sliced raw tomatoes topped with olives; or pour parsley sauce or egg sauce over the entire surface of the fish. If preferred, serve the sauce in a separate dish. (Serves 6 or 8)

BRANDADE DE MORUE
(Brandade of Salt Cod)

2 lb salt cod
Juice ½ lemon
5 tbsp olive oil
5 tbsp heavy cream
1 tbsp minced parsley
⅛ tsp white pepper
Dash of cayenne
Toast triangles

Soak the fish, skin side up, in several changes of cold water for 24 hours. Drain, then add enough cold water to cover and simmer gently for 30 minutes. Drain, and discard all bones and skin and shred the fish very finely. (The French cook uses a mortar and pestle to reduce the fish to a smooth paste but a heavy bowl and a fork and spoon will serve reasonably well.)

When beaten practically to a pulp, place the fish in a double boiler and, stirring with a wooden spoon, beat the lemon juice into it, then add the oil, slightly warmed, dropping it in gently from a spoon and never ceasing stirring until all is smoothly blended in. Add the cream in the same way, then stir in the parsley, pepper and cayenne. This is a typical brandade de morue, ready to serve on triangles of toast.

This is an excellent recipe for using salt cod. But the exalted masters of the French cuisine would never let it pass without some extra touches of elegance and refinement. Master Chef Escoffier suggests truffles, and probably would have added them in julienne strips, glistening black on the golden ream mound, with a border of crisp parsley and fluted crescents of puff paste. His recipe for *brandade de morue menagere* (home method) is much like the foregoing with the addition of finely mashed potatoes, which make the dish a little more bland, with the piquant tang of the codfish a little less pronounced. But he adds a dash of nutmeg and the merest touch of garlic.

BRANDADE OF FRESH CODFISH

For a brandade of fresh codfish, a boneless fillet should be poached in a court bouillon (*which see*) of white wine and water. Then it is drained and pounded or beaten to a paste, the rest of the process being the same as that for the salt codfish.

BROILED COD STEAKS

Wipe the fish, brush over with softened butter and sprinkle with salt and pepper. Cook on a well greased broiler at 350° F., turning to brown both sides. Steaks an inch thick will take 12 to 18 minutes to cook. Serve with plain melted butter, parsley butter or lemon butter, garnishing with parsley and sections of lemon.

FRIED COD STEAKS

Wipe the desired number of moderately thick cod steaks and toss in seasoned flour. Sauté in a little oil, fat from tried-out salt pork, or any preferred cooking fat, turning to brown both sides. Steaks an inch thick will take 10 to 12 minutes to cook. If salt pork is used, serve the pork scraps as a garnish to the fish.

KEDGEREE

2 tbsp butter
1 tbsp finely chopped onion
2 cups cooked flaked codfish
2 cups cooked rice
2 hard-cooked eggs, sliced
Salt
¼ tsp curry powder
½ cup heavy cream

Heat the butter in a sauce pan and cook the onion in it for three minutes, without browning. Add the fish, rice and eggs and salt if needed. Blend the curry powder with the cream, add this and cook all for two or three minutes, stirring constantly. Serve immediately on a very hot platter. While cod is delicious in kedgeree, other cooked fish such as halibut, fresh salmon or finnan haddie may be used. (Serves 6)

COFFEE. The history of coffee and coffee-drinking is full of picturesque interest from the legendary story of its discovery by an Arab observing the effect upon a flock of sheep browsing upon a certain shrub until they became elated and sleepless at night, to the unsleeping Balzac writing for fourteen hours on end on forty cups of coffee—as Dr. Johnson is said to have worked on forty cups of tea.

The coffee-temperament and the tea-temperament—so roughly, one might distinguish the French and the English. The French, of course, drink tea far more than they used to, as the English drink more coffee; but tea still remains the national drink of England and coffee that of America and (formerly, at least) of France.

Coffee, like all novelties, had to fight its way, and the objections urged against it are among the most curious examples of human absurdity, in England particularly. There, in *The Women's Petition Against Coffee*, published in 1674, it was complained "that it made men unfruitful as the deserts whence that unhappy berry is said to have been brought; that the offspring of our mighty ancestors would dwindle into a succession of apes and pigmies" if they continued drinking it.

But sensible Englishmen welcomed the use of this beverage among the laboring classes of society to wean them from strong liquors. An English writer observed in 1659 that "this coffee-drink hath caused a great sobriety among all nations: formerly

COFFEE

apprentices, clerks, etc., used to take their morning draughts of ale, beer, or wine, which often made them unfit for business. Now they play the good-fellows in this wakeful and civil drink."

The writer of a satirical poem entitled "A Cup of Coffee" wonders how any one can drink it instead of "Canary" and describes it as:

"A loathsome potion, not yet understood,
Syrup of soot, or essence of old shoes."

Among the coffee drinkers of France, those of the Ardennes—on the Belgian frontier—seem to be pre-eminent and have a special ritual. There they have been wont to take ten cups after dinner, and each cup has its special name: (1) *Café* (coffee); (2) *Gloria;* (3) *Pousse Café;* (4) *Goutte;* (5) *Regoutte;* (6) *Surgoutte;* ("Goutte" meaning, of course, "drop" in English, but for the French it means many drops of alcohol); (7) *Rincette;* (8) *Re-rincette;* (9) *Sur-rincette* (meaning a mouth-rinser, or "chaser") and (10) *Coup de l'étrier* (stirrup-cup).

In this progression of drinks *Gloria* (No. 2) is a coffee with a small glass of brandy in it, and all those that follow have *eau-de-vie* (brandy) added in ever increasing proportions.

Preparation for Market

Coffee consists of the berries or seeds of *Coffea arabica*, which are dried, roasted, ground, and subjected to infusion. The coffee beans are washed clean and picked over on the plantations, but they are cleaned once more after they are received by the importer who roasts and packs them. In the roasting plant they are put into a machine which rubs, tumbles, and rolls them about, while an exhaust fan sucks off the dust and bits of dirt loosened by this rubbing and rolling process. Then, if they are to be blended before roasting, the right percentage of each kind of green coffee is poured into another machine which stirs and tosses them about until they are thoroughly blended. Now the green coffee beans are ready for roasting.

The machine in which the coffee is roasted is a great metal cylinder full of small holes which revolves in a heated chamber or "oven." Inside the cylinder are metal flanges which, as the cylinder revolves, toss the beans about so that they roast evenly without burning. The coffee roaster takes care not to pack this cylinder too full, but allows plenty of room for the coffee beans to be tossed about as they roast.

The ovens are generally heated by coal, coke, or gas. Electric ovens have been tried, but they are not yet as popular as those heated by other means. At present most American coffee roasters prefer gas for heating their ovens. The heat is turned on slowly at first, until some of the moisture in the bean is driven off; then it is increased until a temperature of 450° Fahrenheit is reached. In ovens heated with coal or coke, roasting usually takes 25 to 30 minutes; gas ovens will roast the coffee in about 20 minutes.

During the roasting, the coffee beans undergo a great change. After they have been in the oven a short time they turn a yellowish brown, the color slowly deepening as they cook. Also, as the beans become heated they first shrivel up—then, when about half done, they begin to swell. At this point the roaster intensifies the heat and finishes the roasting as quickly as possible.

Every few minutes a few beans are taken out of the cylinder with a "trier," shaped something like a long spoon, to compare with the sample to be matched. When the color indicates that they are done, the heat is turned off, and both the cylinder and the coffee is cooled as fast as possible. There are two ways of cooling coffee in the cylinder. By the "wet method," the coffee is sprayed with a little water while the cylinder is still turning over and over. By the "dry method," big electric fans cool the cylinder of coffee rapidly. After this the coffee is emptied from the cylinder into a cooler, where the beans are stirred and tossed about while currents of cold air play over them.

Often there are small stones and bits of rubbish among the beans despite the processes they have been through, so as soon as the coffee is cold, it is transferred to the "stoner"—an interesting a r r a n g e m e n t through which a strong current of air is passed, this carrying the coffee beans through a pipe or "riser" into a big hopper. The stones, being too heavy for the air to carry away, are left behind in the stoner. The coffee is then ready for grinding.

Each kind of coffee—and there are over a hundred—has its own particular flavor, and coffees of various kinds are blended. The combination of several flavors is pleasanter than if one alone were used. Sometimes this blending is done before roasting. Sometimes the coffees are roasted, each kind by itself, and then combined. The methods chosen depend upon what the roaster thinks gives the best results. The man who decides the amounts of each kind that shall be blended is an important person in a coffee-roasting establishment. He must know how to recognize the different kinds of coffee and what flavor to expect from each. He must know how each crop of the various kinds is running, for often two crops from the same plantation will be different in flavor, yet coffee drinkers expect their coffee to taste the same every time they use it. And he must know one more thing—that is, what the people who buy his brand like. That is his guide in selecting the kinds of coffee he combines.

Coffee as a Beverage

The exhilarating effect of coffee is said to be caused by the ingredients caffeine, caffetannic, and caffeic acids, and a volatile oil developed during roasting. The coffee berry contains no starch; its principal carbohydrate is cane sugar or sucrose. The stimulant effect of coffee upon the nervous system is mainly due to the alkaloid caffeine, which is chemically identical with theine and possesses the same physiological properties, its action being chiefly upon the nerves and kidneys. Coffee also contains a little aromatic oil which is moderately stimulating to the nervous system. It has less oil than tea.

Coffee, when taken as a beverage, has well-marked physiological effects, chiefly upon the muscular, vascular, and nervous systems. It removes the sensation of fatigue in the muscles and increases their functional activity; it allays hunger to a limited extent; it strengthens the heart action, and constitutes a valuable cardiac stimulant in some forms of collapse by its moderate quickening effect upon the pulse and influence upon the vascular tone; it acts as a diuretic, and increases the excretion of urea; it has a mildly sudorific influence; it counteracts nervous exhaustion and stimulates nerve centers. It is used sometimes as a nervine in cases of migraine, and there are many persons who can sustain prolonged mental fatigue and strain by the use of strong black coffee.

Drunk in moderation, coffee is a mild stimulant to gastric digestion. In the bowels, coffee has an opposite effect to that of tea, for it stimulates peristalsis, and for many people, when drunk early in the morning, it possesses a distinctly laxative effect. It thus indirectly benefits the liver. Strong coffee with a little lemon juice or brandy is often useful in overcoming a malarial chill or a paroxysm of asthma. It is the universal testimony of army officers that coffee is indispensable for troops in service to relieve fatigue and improve their spirits. The stimulating and diuretic effect of coffee is more decided when it is taken into an empty stomach.

The nutrient value of coffee alone is too small to be considered, but the addition of sugar and milk, or cream, as in the case of tea, makes it a valuable food. It does, however, possess some effect in diminishing tissue waste. The very general fondness which exists for the taste of coffee makes it a useful means of flavoring many kinds of food for young and old, such as jellies, custards, cakes, pies, ice cream, etc.

Much argument has been expended on the relative digestibility and usefulness of tea and coffee, but about all that can be said definitely in regard to the matter is that many persons who can drink tea with impunity are made nervous and are kept awake by a similar quantity of coffee; whereas there are others who find that coffee aids their digestion, while tea interferes with it, and that it affects them in every way more agreeably than tea; and still a third class cannot take either tea or coffee without producing indigestion, insomnia, and nervousness. Speaking generally, coffee is believed in the United States to be more digestible and useful than tea, but in other parts of the world, especially in England, China, India, and Japan, tea is regarded as more beneficial than coffee. In equal weight, tea contains more than twice as much caffeine or, as it is also called "theine."

PREPARING COFFEE

At one time no one knew exactly why boiled coffee is spoiled coffee. Now scientists have discovered that the instant water begins to boil, oxides are precipitated which change the flavor. They have also discovered the reason why reheated coffee tastes so unpleasant. Waxy, resinous, insoluble, fats comprise about a fifth of the ground coffee. Cooling and reheating melts these fats and blends them into the brew. Coffee, which is used in practically every household in America at least once a day, deserves care in preparation. It is just as easy to make good coffee as it is to make poor coffee. Good coffee is clear and sparkling and of fine flavor.

General Directions. Be sure the coffee is correctly ground for your special method of brewing: *Fine* for drip pot; *Medium* for percolator; *Coarse* for "boiled" coffee; *Extra fine*—not pulverized—for vacuum type coffee maker.

Be sure the coffee pot, of whatever type, is clean; scald it with boiling water before each using.

Be sure to measure both coffee and water. Use two level tablespoons or one rounded tablespoon of ground coffee, for each coffee cup of water. If you desire stronger coffee, use more of it—longer brewing will not make it stronger without destroying the flavor.

Drip Pot Method. Measure two level tablespoonfuls of finely ground coffee for each cup into the dripper. If a filter paper is required, measure the coffee on top of the filter paper. Insert the water spreader. Measure the briskly boiling water and pour it into the dripper. Cover, keep hot, and allow the infusion to drip into the pot. Remove the dripper as soon as the water has filtered through the coffee. Cover the pot and serve at once.

Percolator Method. Measure the water into the scalded percolator. Use cold water for a percolator without a valve; use boiling water for a percolator with a valve. Measure into the basket two level tablespoonfuls of medium-ground coffee for each cup, place the basket in the percolator, insert the water spreader, and cover it. Percolate over moderate heat from five to eight minutes. Serve at once. Long percolating will spoil the flavor.

"Boiled Coffee Method." Measure two level tablespoonfuls of coarsely ground coffee for each cup into the scalded pot. Add an extra measure of coffee. Measure the briskly boiling water, and pour it over the coffee. Stir, cover, and let it simmer, not boil, from five to eight minutes. Settle it with a dash of cold water. Serve at once.

Vacuum Method. Measure the water into the bottom section. Put the top section in place with the rod or filter. Measure two level tablespoonfuls of extra finely ground coffee for each cup into the upper section, place on the stove. When all but a thin layer of water has been forced into the upper section, turn off the heat or remove from the stove. Stir just once. As soon as coffee has filtered back into the bottom section, remove the top. Serve at once while still piping hot.

After-Dinner Coffee (Demitasse). Make the coffee extra strong, using half again as much to twice the regular amount.

Café au Lait. Use equal parts of hot milk and freshly made strong coffee. Viennese *Café au Lait* is made by substituting all milk for water.

Syrian Method. This consists of strong black coffee, sweetened to taste and served with two or three cracked cardamon seeds in the bottom of each demitasse.

Turkish After-Dinner Coffee. A special coffee pot made of copper or brass, quite high and of tapering shape, is required for this. For each small cup of boiling water, allow a heaping tablespoon of pulverized coffee and one teaspoon of powdered sugar. Put the coffee, sugar, and briskly boiling water into the pot (never have this more than half full). Place over direct heat, and bring to the boiling point. Remove from the fire as the contents foams

up. Let settle. Repeat the boiling and settling process three times. Serve in very small cups.

Note: Turkish coffee pots are nickel lined, and are called *Racquie.* They have no cover, but a deep, curved-in rim. One may, if desired, add to each cup a drop or two of orange-flower water.

French Flaming Coffee (Café Brûle). In a bowl place 2 lumps of sugar, 2 pieces of lemon peel, 2 whole cloves—heads removed—a small stick of cinnamon, and a half glass of brandy. Blend well, set a match to the mixture, and let it burn for a half minute or so, stirring constantly with a metal spoon. Add ⅔ cup of strong coffee, strain into two heated demi-tasses and serve at once. (Serves 2)

Iced Russian Coffee. Melt ½ square of chocolate (*see* CHOCOLATE), stir in 3 or 4 tablespoons of sugar and a few grains of salt. Add ½ cup of undiluted evaporated milk, thin cream, or heavy cream, and bring to the boiling point, stirring constantly. When cold, pour into a pitcher with cracked ice, add 1½ cups of chilled strong coffee, and stir until well blended and ice cold. Serve in tall glasses. (Serves 2)

Frosted Coffee. Pour ½ cup of extra strong coffee into a shaker with about 2 tablespoons of cracked ice, and stir until it is thoroughly chilled. Add one scoop of vanilla ice cream, and shake vigorously. Turn into a tall glass, and top with a further small scoop of vanilla ice cream. Serve at once with straws. (Serves 1)

Coffee Chocolate Punch, Mexican Method. Combine 2 cups of chilled, extra strong coffee, ¼ cup of chocolate sirup, one cup of fresh cold milk, and a scoop of chocolate ice cream in a shaker containing cracked ice. Shake well and serve at once in small glasses. Vanilla ice cream may be substituted for the chocolate, if desired. (Serves 6)

Coffee Flip. Combine equal amounts of strong, chilled coffee and chilled, scalded milk. Top with whipped cream, forced through a pastry bag, and sprinkle with grated sweet chocolate, or chocolate shot.

Iced Coffee. In order to allow for dilution by ice, iced coffee must be made twice as strong as ordinary coffee. Pour the hot coffee directly over the ice cubes or crushed ice in the tall glasses used for serving. Be careful that the hot coffee lands on the ice before it touches the glass to avoid cracking the glass. Iced coffee can be sweetened before pouring or it can be sweetened to taste by the individual guest. In the latter case, use powdered rather than granulated sugar. Serve with heavy or whipped cream.

Another method of making iced coffee is to prepare double strength coffee, let it cool, and then pour into the ice cube trays of a refrigerator and let freeze exactly as though making regular ice cubes. These "coffee cubes" may be kept in the refrigerator until needed, at which time two or more cubes are placed in a tall glass and warm milk poured over them. The proportions of "coffee cubes," milk and sugar will be governed by individual taste.

To Make Coffee in Quantity

There are two well-known ways of making coffee in large quantities: the filtration or leaching method; and the boiling method.

After years of experiment, the filtration or leaching method has been recognized as the best because it accomplishes the desired result more scientifically, extracting the flavor but not the bitterness from the coffee. All chemical analyses have shown that filtration gives the best cup of coffee.

By filtration, or leaching, is meant the method in which a simple fine mesh cotton bag is fitted into the top of a coffee urn or pot, the ground, dry coffee placed therein, and the boiling water poured on and through the coffee. The water must be boiling. Draw off, then repour through the bag until the coffee is of the desired strength. After the last repouring, remove the bag and discard the grounds.

Hints on Coffee Making

(1) Be accurate in measurements of water and coffee.

(2) Remember that water must boil actively.

(3) Freshly boiled water is important. If water boils too long before using, it becomes stale and flat.

(4) Have the cups in which you serve the coffee hot.

(5) Don't over-percolate, overleach, or over-boil coffee.

(6) Coffee loses its flavor when exposed to the air.

(7) See that your coffee pot is in order, and that the lining is in good condition.

(8) If you use a leach bag, keep it immaculately clean.

(9) Be sure that your coffee is ground to the right degree of fineness.

(10) If you get muddy coffee in the leaching process, it is an indication that grounds or fine sediment are going through or over the bag.

(11) Coffee loses freshness from the moment it is ground. Fresh grinding is the secret of a good cup.

Coffee Bavarian

2 cups evaporated milk
1½ tbsp gelatin
3 tbsp cold water
1 cup sugar
⅓ cup water
3 egg yolks
⅛ tsp salt
½ cup strong coffee
1 tbsp sweet sherry flavoring

Chill milk thoroughly. Soak gelatin in the cold water. Boil sugar with the ⅓ cup water until the sirup spins a thread. Pour in a fine stream over the well beaten egg yolks, whipping briskly. Add salt. Dissolve soaked gelatin in hot coffee and add to egg mixture. When this is beginning to set, fold in the sherry flavoring and the milk that has been whipped stiff. Turn into a mold to set. Unmold and serve with sliced sugared peaches. (Serves 8)

Coffee Frappe

1 qt hot extra strong freshly made coffee
3 cups granulated sugar
¼ tsp salt
½ generous tsp vanilla
1 egg white, stiffly beaten

Combine sugar, salt and coffee (hot) and stir until sugar is thoroughly dissolved. Chill; then add vanilla extract and stir in stiffly beaten egg white. Freeze in hand freezer, using equal parts of ice and rock salt. Serve in frappé glasses, which have been well-chilled, and top with a rosette of whipped cream. *See also* FRAPPE.

Coffee Fruit Frosting

To mocha frosting (*see* MOCHA) add 2 tablespoons chopped candied cherries and

2 tablespoons sliced blanched pistachios before spreading on cake.

COFFEE ICE CREAM

Scald ⅓ cup of the milk to be used in the making of vanilla ice cream, with one-third cup of freshly ground coffee, then strain through a fine sieve or cloth and proceed as directed for vanilla ice cream. *See* ICE CREAM.

COFFEE JELLY

1 tbsp gelatin
¼ cup cold water
1½ cups clear, strong, hot boiled coffee
½ cup sugar
¼ tsp salt
1 tsp vanilla
Whipped cream

Soften the gelatin in the cold water, then dissolve with the sugar and salt in the hot coffee. Add the vanilla, turn into a previously wet mold and chill. Unmold and garnish with whipped cream. (Serves 4)
If preferred, use only 1¼ cups of hot coffee and 4 tablespoons of rum or brandy, stirring this last in just before molding.
Or, use 1 cup of very strong coffee, folding in ⅓ cup of heavy cream, whipped stiff just as the mixture is beginning to set.

COFFEE MOUSSE

½ tbsp granulated gelatin
2 tbsp cold water
1 cup very strong black coffee
1 tsp vanilla extract
¼ tsp salt
4 egg yolks, and
1 egg white, beaten together
3 tbsp good brandy
2 cups heavy cream, whipped stiff
1 cup granulated sugar

Soak the gelatin in cold water. Stir in very hot coffee to which has been added the sugar, and which has been boiled for 5 minutes or to a sirupy consistency. Pour over slightly beaten egg yolks and egg white, and beat together while hot, stirring briskly and constantly from bottom of saucepan to prevent curdling. Strain through double cheesecloth. Cool. Add

vanilla and brandy, then fold in the stiffly beaten heavy cream with the salt. Pour into mold or individual paper cups. If desired, and when using a large mold, you may pack in hand freezer pail, using equal parts ice and rock salt and allow to stand 2½ to 3 hours. If using refrigerator tray, freeze, if in paper cases, for 2½ hours; if large mold, freeze for 4 hours.

COFFEE PARFAIT

1 cup extra strong coffee
1 cup sugar
¼ tsp salt
3 egg yolks, slightly beaten
1 tbsp gelatin
¼ cup cold water
2 cups heavy cream whipped stiff
½ tsp vanilla

Make a custard with the coffee, sugar, salt and egg yolks. Strain while still hot, then add the gelatin which has been softened in the cold water and stir until this is dissolved. Chill, then fold in the whipped cream and vanilla and freeze in automatic refrigerator. *See* PARFAIT. (Serves 6 or 8)

COFFEE SHERBET

1¼ cups granulated sugar
1½ cups heavy cream
¼ tsp salt
2 cups very strong coffee
¾ cup heavy cream, whipped stiff
5 drops vanilla extract

Place sugar and 1½ cups unwhipped heavy cream in a saucepan and heat to the boiling point, stirring almost constantly. Remove from the fire and cool, then add salt and strong coffee. Freeze in hand freezer, using 3 parts ice and 1 part rock salt, until mushy; then stir in very gently the stiffly whipped heavy cream with the vanilla extract and freeze until solid. Pack into 4 parts ice and 1 part rock salt, after removing the dasher, for 1 hour. Serve in sherbet glasses which have been thoroughly chilled. *See also* SHERBET. (Serves 6 or 8)

COFFEE SNOWBALL PARFAIT

Have ready, molded, melon-shaped, a coffee parfait (*which see*). When ready to serve, unmold onto a well-chilled platter, covered with a large paper lace doily. Then, using a pastry bag with a small fancy rose tube, cover the entire surface of the parfait with small rosettes of unsweetened and unflavored whipped cream, each rosette the size of a nickle and close to one another so there is no uncovered spot. Onto each rosette, or dot, press very gently a small piece of candied angelica. Serve at once with a side dish of soft custard sauce flavored with maraschino liqueur.

COFFEE CLOTCH. *See* KAFFEE KLATSCH.

COFFEE CUP. Also called a breakfast cup, the cup used for individual coffee servings is generally larger than the tea cup. *See* DISHES.

dome set in the lid, on the inside the difference between the two is marked. The coffee grounds are held in a cylindrical metal basket with perforated top and bottom that fits snugly in the top of the pot slightly below the lid. The basket is supported by a hollow metal tube that, at one end, projects above the basket top and into the glass dome, and at the other, is fitted into a metal stand that rests on the bottom of the pot.

The percolator is filled with water to a point below the bottom of the perforated basket. When the water boils, steam pressure is built up inside the pot, which, pushing down on the surface of the water, forces the fluid up the hollow metal tube. When the water spurts out of the top of the tube, it is deflected downward by the glass dome

COFFEE MAKERS 1. Pot 2. Percolator 3. Drip 4. Vacuum

COFFEE MAKER. Though there are many possible ways of making coffee, there are only four techniques commonly used in the home. For that reason, the kitchen coffee maker will either be a *coffee pot*, a *percolator*, a *dripolator*, or a *vacuum coffee maker*.

Coffee Pot. The coffee pot is the simplest of all coffee makers. It consists merely of a pot in which the coffee and water are boiled, and has no internal mechanisms. The standard coffee pot is a straight-sided affair, with a simple spout set high on the body, a handle, and a r movable or hinged lid. It is usually made of metal.

Percolator. While in outward appearance, the percolator often greatly resembles the coffee pot with the addition of a clear glass

and sprays over the perforated top of the coffee basket. The water then seeps through the grounds, falling back into the bottom of the pot where it is again pushed up the tube.

This action is characterized by a bubbling or spurting, from which the percolator gets its name. It is very efficient, for the water cannot reach the coffee grounds until it has been heated to the correct temperature, and, by watching the color of the water as it splashes against the glass dome, the housewife can judge when the coffee has reached the desired strength.

Dripolator. Physically, the dripolator somewhat resembles a double boiler. It is built in two separate sections, an upper one and a lower one. The bottom of the upper section is perforated, and to it is attached a smaller removable container, also perforated on the bottom, which fits into the mouth of the lower section. The coffee, finely ground, is held in this small attached container between the two perforated bottoms. In operation, the two sections are assembled and the upper one is filled with boiling water. This water seeps or drips slowly through the coffee compartment and into the lower section. When the water has completely passed through, the upper section is removed for cleaning, and the lid, which usually rests on the upper section during the coffee making period, placed on the top of the lower section. The lower section is now used as a serving pot, being equipped with handle and spout.

Vacuum Coffee Maker. The vacuum coffee maker is the newest and most amazing addition to the list of coffee makers. It has an hourglass shape, consisting of two globes, usually glass, resting one on top of the other. The lower globe is almost a perfect ball, having only a small, circular opening at the top. The upper globe has a wide, open top, and a long tube projecting from the bottom that fits snugly through the opening of the lower globe. This tube reaches to approximately one-half inch from the bottom of the lower globe, and has a cloth glass or ceramic filter fitted at the top where it opens into the upper globe.

In operation, coffee grounds are placed in the upper globe and water in the lower. The unit is assembled, making certain that the seal between the two globes is airtight and that the tube is down as low as it can go into the lower globe. The unit is then placed on the range or other heating device, and the water in the lower globe heated. When the water boils, steam pressure is generated, forcing the water up the tube and into the upper globe, where it mingles with the coffee grounds. When all of the water that lies above the lower mouth of the tube has been forced into the upper globe, the heat is turned off. As the lower globe cools, the steam within is condensed, causing a vacuum to be formed. This vacuum sucks back all of the water from the upper globe, but the filter at the top of the tube holds back the coffee grounds. The upper section, tube and all, is then removed for cleaning, and the coffee served from the lower globe which has a pouring lip and cover.

PURCHASING

To some palates, these four different coffee makers produce four distinctly different types of coffee; while, to others, it is all coffee and their only requirements are that it be of a certain strength and temperature. Naturally, a family will want that type of apparatus that makes for them the superior coffee.

In the course of normal living, one will usually have ample opportunity to sample the product of at least the last three, if not all four, of these coffee makers, enabling the family to determine the desired type without going to the expense of purchasing all four.

Since basic design and price have been pretty much standardized among manufacturers, once the type of coffee maker desired has been established, the family can select their unit on the basis of personal needs and tastes.

Capacity is the most important single feature to be considered when selecting a coffee maker of a given type. It is far better to have a unit that is too large for the needs of the family than one that is too small. If the unit does not produce enough coffee for the family needs, it means that the entire process must be duplicated at least twice during each meal, for the grounds cannot be re-used. That this has decided disadvantages is, of course, obvious. Then too, one must always allow for the unexpected guest. It must be remembered that, while any unit can make less coffee than its full capacity, it cannot make more. In some cases, it might be well to purchase two units; one, very small, can be used to make one or two cups with a minimum of difficulty, while the other, large, will serve for family assemblies and even parties.

If one is not particular about the type of coffee maker, then the sole guides will be capacity, convenience, and price. The simple coffee pot is the cheapest of the four, but it is rapidly becoming defunct, for it is the most difficult and messy of the units to use. Unless the user is skilled, the product is quite apt to be inferior, while, with the other three, the process is practically automatic and fairly foolproof. Further, the other three types tend to keep the grounds out of the cup.

The price of a unit is usually determined by the material used in construction. Coffee makers are built of practically every metal, as well as glass, and are coming to make much use of plastic parts. Aluminum and glass are the most common materials, though "Sunday best" units are often made of silverplate, and enamelware is used for the cheaper and simpler units. The lower globe of a vacuum unit should be made of glass so that the user can determine the proper time to turn off the heat, but other than that the materials are virtually interchangeable in the various units.

In the dripolator, the water must be heated separately, and the unit itself is not placed on the range except to reheat the coffee. The other three devices, however, are heated directly over a flame or electric unit. It is possible to purchase special electric units that can be placed on the dining room table and used to make the coffee during the meal, if the coffee maker is of suitable design. While more expensive, such an arrangement can be a decided convenience under some circumstances. *See* ELECTRICAL EQUIPMENT.

There is a wide price range in coffee makers; the coffee pot being the cheapest, and the vacuum unit the most expensive. However, unless one is anxious for ornate outward design, suitable units may be found to fit any budget, and it should be remembered that it is the internal design of the unit and the skill of the user that determines the flavor of the coffee; not the external appearance. A well designed unit, regardless of cost, should make good coffee, and it is a far better practice to learn the mastery of one unit than to keep buying new ones in the hope of finding one that will "work."

CARE AND USE

If instructions are supplied with a new coffee maker, they should be followed, even though they may run contrary to the user's past practices. It is to be assumed that the manufacturer knows how the unit should be operated. One should be certain that only the proper grind of coffee is used with a unit, though the blend and the relative percentages of coffee and water are matters of personal taste.

The unit should be kept scrupulously clean at all times, if the coffee is not to take on strange, brackish flavors. It is advisable to use a brush (*see* BRUSHES) to clean the unit since they may usually be purchased in

special shapes to easily reach all corners of the device. Many units, especially of the vacuum type, are difficult to keep properly clean by other methods.

The unit should, of course, be given the care proper to the materials used in its construction. This care is discussed under the individual materials themselves elsewhere in this book. *See also* COFFEE and KITCHEN EQUIPMENT.

COFFEE MILL. *See* GRINDER.

COFFEE POT. *See* COFFEE MAKER; *see also* COFFEE.

COGNAC. This king among brandies is well known the world over, and its devotees extend well beyond the boundaries of France.

"Of all the gifts of the gods to man, wine is the most dear". . . . wrote a genial bard. Wine is, so to speak, the spontaneous offspring of the vine, but there is another product quite as precious which calls for man's industry. This is brandy, the liquid obtained by distilling wine. The best brandy, that most highly esteemed, without shadow of doubt is the cognac which comes from the Charente region. Properly speaking, only brandy from this region may be called cognac.

In the Charente the distillation of wine is a process which, from a chemical standpoint, consists in the separation by heat of liquids of different volatility. Figuratively speaking, this process has for its object the freeing of the spirit, as it were, of the wine, and in this way coaxing out its essential principle—an extremely delicate operation calling for ceaseless attention to apparently trifling details.

The process itself consists of several slow heating operations, and one must know how and when to stop. It exacts the sustained and undivided attention of the person carrying out the operation, who must possess sound practical experience as well as the happy knack which has been handed down as a family heritage from father to son. The peasant-distiller of the Charente, clad in his blue overalls and wearing mittens, is as proud of his ability as any belted earl is of his title of nobility.

The vines of the Charente, completely renewed with vines from America after the scourge of the last century, plunge their roots into a dry stony soil, poor, clayey by nature, and containing lime. Immediately after the grapes are picked, they are pressed. Then, without any drawing-off, "skins and all" as the popular expression goes, the juice is poured into the alembic or still.

The distilling apparatus in use in the Charente has remained unchanged for centuries. The distillation is carried out either under the supervision of the owners in person, by professional "burners," or by approved representatives of the commercial firms. The liquid as it flows from the still is colorless, with an alcohol percentage varying from 68 to 70. The cognac is then lodged in oak casks. The essence of the wood, as time goes on, blends with the liquor and gives it not only its characteristic odor but also its golden hue.

The casks are stored in cellars where light and air are excluded so far as possible, so that the cognac may mature gradually and not evaporate too quickly. As the cognac matures, it becomes more valuable. It is during this period of quiescence in the cellars, which may last for years (there are some cognacs more than 50 years old) that the mysterious transformation takes place which changes a liquid transparent like water, and harsh to the palate, into a beautiful amber-colored, delicate, mellow liquor with a natural "bouquet" reminiscent of the subtle, delicate scent of grape blossoms.

THE COGNAC REGION

The land of cognac is, in great part, formed by the basin of the sleepy river Charente whose limpid, blue, crystal-clear waters flow at one moment between swelling hills and, at another, amid green meadows. The river is navigable along the greater part of its course from Angoulême to its mouth, and it serves several small ports where come to mooring the barges which eventually will carry away the cognac.

The term cognac is applied exclusively to brandies distilled from grapes of a certain variety, gathered in areas enjoying an identically mild and moist climate, and possessing above all a calcareous soil. Cognac is manufactured in the following localities, listed in order of quality:

The Grande Champagne, comprising 21 communes of the arrondissement of Cognac.

The Petite Champagne, whose territory forms almost a belt around that of the Grande Champagne.

Les Borderies, situated to the north of the Grande Champagne.

Les Fins Bois, which territory forms a circle around the three preceding areas.

As one advances toward the Atlantic Ocean from the *Fins Bois* region, one passes through the zones of the *Bon Bois,* the *Bois Ordinaires,* and the *Bois à Terroir.*

Were we to classify the Charente brandies as Bordeaux wines are classified, we should say that the "Champagnes" and the "Borderies" constitute the great vintages, and the rest, the ordinary.

The precise date when the distillation of wine began in France is uncertain, but as far back as the year 1309, one of the French authors of that time, Arnautel de Villeneuve, a professor at the University of Montpellier, had already written in his book, *De Conservanda Juventute,* ". . . an ardent spirit called 'Eau de Vie' is drawn off by distillation. It is the quintessence of wine, the immutable or Golden Water. It prolongs life, hence its well-merited name 'Water of Life!'"

The various qualities of cognacs are usually indicated by stars—one, two, three, in ascending quality—but these have no age significance and the standards vary with different houses. Houses handling better brandies use letters to indicate quality: E, Especial; F, Fine; V, Very; O, Old; S, Superior; P, Pale; X, Extra; C, cognac. *See also* BRANDY.

COIN SILVER. *See* SILVERWARE.

COINTREAU. An after-dinner cordial of a crystal-like limpidity. It is also used to flavor many delicious cocktails, punches, cups, and other beverages. It is made of the peels of freshly picked and selected oranges and pure *Eau de Vie de Vin* (wine spirits). Its alcoholic content is 40 per cent. It is a peer among the cordials of France.

COLA. Various beverages made with sirup and extract of the cola nut, *which see.*

COLA NUT. The peoples of Africa probably used cola, or kola, at all times. This seed has in their different languages such names as "Kola," "Gouru," "Ombene," "Nagane," "Ouru," "Mendi," "Tureh," etc. The cola holds in Africa the position which tea, coffee, and cocoa occupies with other peoples; but it enjoys, to a certain extent, properties very superior to those of these other plants.

Before its introduction into Europe, the cola nut was an important article of commerce between the tribes of Africa; it was exported from coastal regions towards the interior, into the Lakes region, and, according to certain travelers, up to Mecca.

There exist in Occidental or West Africa many species or varieties but the cola nut which possesses the greatest world commercial or market value, comes from the Gold Coast, where it is named *"Goro de Gonsha."* In Senegal, as well as in the Soudan region, the cola is used as a stimulant; it quenches thirst, diminishes fatigue, permits long marches through the jungles, chases sleepiness, and is even considered aphrodisiac.

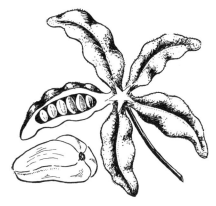

COLA NUT

The cola nuts are sometimes red, sometimes white inside. The red cola is furnished by the *cola acuminata*, the white cola by the *sterculia macrocarpa*. The red nuts are always more esteemed than the white; they both possess, however, the same properties, but the red nuts seem to be more active than the white. According to certain authorities, the cola trees which furnish exclusively red or white seeds are very rare. In general, the follicles contain white and red seeds mixed. To the natives the white cola is a sign of friendship, the red cola a declaration of war. It is by the cola that marriages are made in some regions; the white cola, received and returned to the sender, indicates that the suitor has been accepted, but if it be a red cola that is returned instead, everything is broken up.

In the upper Ivory Coast, the cola is the principal resource of the natives, not because they themselves consume it in great quantities, but because the nuts are bartered in northern markets. In these markets the cola nut is worth about five cents. A gun is worth from 1,500 to 2,000 nuts; a

spear, 500 nuts; a knife from 200 to 400 nuts; a saber from 600 to 700 nuts; cotton drawers, 1,000 nuts; an ox from 7,000 to 8,000 nuts; a captive is worth 10,000 colas; a rug is worth from 40 to 50 nuts; and a pound of rice is worth 10 nuts.

When the cola tree plantations belong to the community, as they often do, no one has the right to tear a branch from a tree or to pick seeds. At the harvest time, the fruits are distributed; the number of colas obtained varies according to age and social standing of the individual, but everybody, even the captives, receives some fruits. In most of the cola regions north of the equator the fine imposed by the native tribunals is usually one to be paid by a large sum of cola nuts. In French Guinea, the cola plays an important role in religious ceremonies, and it is planted in commemoration of a happy event. In the Niger region, the natives consume the fresh cola; they do not use the dry fruit. To keep the freshness of the nuts, they store them away in earthen pots. These nuts can be preserved and stay fresh for more than six months. The seed is especially employed by the Mohammedan tribes who offer it as a token of peace and friendship to all visitors.

The explorer Stanley mentioned cola trees near Lake Edward-Nyanza. "We were munching the cola nut," he says, "more for, one must admit, the health of our mouths, than to calm the pains in our stomachs."

It was in the Republic of Colombia that the cola tree (*cola acuminata*) was first introduced in America. The natives call it "Ecla." The cola acuminata is also found in Brazil, where it was probably introduced by the slave trade.

Outside of Africa, the cultivation of the cola tree has particularly developed in the West Indies. In Jamaica, a cola tree will produce at each harvest—and there are two a year—from 500 to 600 fruits, that is to say, from 100 to 110 pounds per tree per year.

The stimulating properties of the cola seed are due to the caffeine and the theobromine present in the seed in strong proportions; the aphrodisiacal properties may reside in an essential oil. The nut has no odor; its taste reminds one of that of acorns, but it is more astringent. When a piece of fresh cola is chewed for a long time, one perceives a sugary taste probably due to the transformation of starch into sugar by the saliva.

Besides the fruits, the cola tree gives a beautiful reddish wood used for turning and carving and for carpentry. It is hard and not very difficult to work. The cola acuminata can also be employed as dyeing material. For medicine, the only part employed is the seed.

COLANDER. A colander is a metal basket with a perforated bottom that is used for straining purposes. *See also* KITCHEN EQUIPMENT.

COLBERT BUTTER. *See* BUTTER SAUCE.

COLCANNON. An Irish preparation of cabbage. It is made of plenty of cabbage and potatoes, cooked and mashed together, and seasoned with butter, pepper, salt, and minced onion. Serve as a hot vegetable with a large lump of butter in the center.

COLD MEAT FORK. *See* FLATWARE.

COLD SLAW. Literally "Cold cabbage." More properly called "Cole slaw," *which see.*

COLE. Another name for the vegetable kale, *which see.*

COLE SLAW. One of the quickest and easiest salads to prepare—also one of the most popular—is cole slaw. It is made of shredded cabbage with the possible addition of shredded green and red pepper (pimiento) and finely sliced tart apples (with the bright red skin left on) all tossed together with mayonnaise or salad dressing. *See also* CABBAGE.

CREAMY COLE SLAW

1 large head of cabbage
⅓ cup tarragon vinegar
2 tbsp sugar
½ tsp salt
Pepper and paprika
½ cup minced green pepper
2 tbsp minced pimiento
¼ cup mayonnaise
¼ cup heavy cream

Shred the cabbage and soak in ice water for 30 minutes. Drain and dry thoroughly. Add the vinegar, sugar, salt, pepper, and paprika. Toss, and let marinate for an hour. Drain again, squeezing the cabbage slightly to remove any extra liquid. Add the pepper and pimiento. Whip the cream and mix with the mayonnaise. Pour over the cabbage mixture and toss thoroughly. Arrange on lettuce. (Serves 6)

PLAIN COLE SLAW I

Shred crisp cabbage very finely. Place in ice water with a little lemon juice, then drain. Add a grated carrot with a little minced green pepper or pimiento for their color value and moisten with any good boiled dressing or mayonnaise thinned with light cream or top milk. Serve very cold.

COLE SLAW II

Prepare cabbage as directed for Cole slaw I. After draining, marinate with a little French dressing and chill for one hour. Now combine with one cup finely chopped celery, one cup thinly sliced cucumber and one medium-sized onion, chopped fine, all previously chipped. At serving time add enough more French or other preferred dressing to moisten thoroughly.

COLLARD. A big, broad green of good flavor, belonging to the cabbage family, which may be prepared by the methods adapted to cabbage or other kinds of greens.

COLLARD

COLLINS. The family name for a group of summer drinks made by mixing a liquor with lemon or lime juice in a tall glass with ice and carbonated water. A true Collins should not be as tart as a Rickey (*which see*), but should not be so sweet as to impair its thirst-quenching properties. It is not as heavily iced as the Daisy (*which see*), its probable parent.

The Tom Collins is by far the most commonly seen member of this large family. It is the basic Collins recipe.

TOM COLLINS

1 jigger dry gin
½ lemon (juice)
1 tsp powdered sugar

The ingredients are placed in a collins glass (*see* GLASSWARE) with one or two ice cubes; the glass is filled with carbonated water and stirred gently. The drink is commonly served with a straw and garnished with a cherry and possibly thin slices of orange and lemon. (Serves 1)

Experienced mixers will sometimes add a few drops of lime juice to smooth out the gin flavor.

One school of thought calls for the sugar to be added last, and vigorously stirred, causing the drink to effervesce. If the drink is so mixed, it should be drunk rapidly, while still foaming; whereas, if mixed in the usual manner, it is intended to be sipped slowly, usually through a straw. If the drink is made so that it effervesces violently, it should not be garnished.

John Collins. A Tom Collins made with Holland gin.

Rum Collins. A collins made using Gold Label rum.

Whisky Collins. Whisky, rather than gin or rum, is used to make this collins.

COMFIT. An old-fashioned name given to certain sweetmeats, candy, or jam.

COMMISSION CHEESE. A skimmed-milk cheese which is much like Edam (*which see*) in manufacturing process and shape, although it is darker in color.

COMPORT. A compotier that is mounted on a pedestal or small stand. *See* COMPOTIER.

COMPOSITION OF FOOD MATERIALS. *See* FOOD MATERIALS, COMPOSITION OF.

COMPOTE. A combination of cooked, chilled fruits served as dessert. Perhaps because it is so simple to prepare, many homemakers have failed to recognize its real goodness. No recipe is actually needed for the average compote, since the homemaker can prepare one whenever she has a variety or two or three fruits on hand. Preferably one of the fruits should be colorful—like plums, either the green gage or the blue or Italian plums. Apricot halves lend color, too; then other fruits such as pear halves or pineapple chunks are included for their good flavor. A few sour cherries add a pleasant tang. Wine or liqueur may be added for flavoring, but this is not really necessary.

COMPOTIER. A large dish, bowl, or platter, often of ornate and unusual shape, that is filled with fruits (real or artificial), flowers, etc., and used as a centerpiece, being both decorative and functional. *See* DISHES, *see also* TABLE SETTING AND SERVICE.

COMPOUNDED BUTTERS. *See* BUTTER SAUCES.

CONDENSED MILK. Milk that has been evaporated and sweetened. *See* MILK.

CONDIMENT. Condiments are substances which are used as adjuncts to food, but which in themselves supply but little nourishment, their effect being mainly of a stimulating character either to the nerves of taste or secretion. They add flavor to otherwise insipid food, and relieve monotony in diet. Some condiments, such as mustard, contain a slight amount of nutritious material, but the total quantity of any of them which can be taken is so small in comparison with the bulk of the food that they can hardly be said to serve as nutrition.

Some foods are themselves so stimulating to the mucous membrane that they answer the double purpose of food and condiment combined. Such, for example, are onions and garlic. In the mouth, condiments produce an agreeable taste, with an increased flow of saliva, and the desire for food in the stomach is stimulated. They also increase the secretion of gastric juice.

With the exception of salt (*which see*) none of the condiments are absolutely indispensable in the sense of being essential for prolonging health, but so accustomed are all classes of men to their use from heredity or personal experience that, despite the aphorism of Plutarch that "hunger and salt should be man's sauce," without other relishes the appetite soon fails. There are many cases of feeble digestion and diminished activity of the gastric juice which are decidedly benefited by their use in moderation.

All the usual spices and condiments employed in cookery will be found elsewhere fully described together with hints for use in their alphabetical order. *See also* SEASONING.

CONFECTION. A title applied to sweetmeat or candies.

CONFECTIONERS' SUGAR. *See* SUGAR.

CONGER EEL. *See* EEL.

CONGIUS. A wine measure used by the Romans. It was a little larger than the modern gallon. *See* WEIGHTS AND MEASURES.

CONGOU. China black tea. *See* TEA.

CONSERVE. A conserve is a blend of several fruits and is made like jam. It may or may not contain nuts or raisins, or both. *See* individual fruits; *see also* JAM.

CHOP SUEY CONSERVE

1 lb seedless white grapes
1 doz red plums
1 large orange
4 lb fresh peaches
1 No. 2 can pineapple
Sugar

Wash the raw fruit; halve the grapes; pit and cut the plums into small pieces; slice the orange very thinly, discard seeds and quarter the slices; scald the peaches, remove skins and slice. Put the raw fruits into a large preserving kettle, add the pineapple juice and simmer gently for 30 minutes, stirring frequently. Now add the pineapple, diced. Measure the fruit and add ¾ cup of sugar for each cup of fruit. Continue to simmer slowly, stirring frequently, for one hour. Skim, if necessary, then turn into small sterilized jars and seal. (Makes 8 pints)

CONSOMME. *See* BOUILLON and SOUP.

JELLIED CONSOMME MADRILENE

Madrilene is the name of a clear canned soup that is manufactured by several leading soup companies. It is delicious when served in congealed form with salted crackers. Place the cans in the refrigerator 2 or 3 days before the soup is to be served. The soup will be congealed when the cans are opened. Open just before serving time, and turn into cups. Serve immediately, garnishing with a slice of lemon.

COOKIE. Cookies have national characteristics. French cookies, for instance, are the fanciest in appearance; German the spiciest. Italy's frequently have a base of anise oil and are made with almonds; Russia's are, for the most part, fried; and England's are somewhat massive and not unduly sweet. Oddly enough, there is no such thing as a truly American cookie.

One may use a basic dough and by cutting it into varied shapes or using different flavorings or frostings, or by adding a few nutmeats here, fruit or candied peel there, variety is easily acquired even with only one or two different mixes. Dainty cookies are good with dessert and with tea, and a filled cookie jar is an important asset in any family. It is just as easy to mix a large as a small batch, and soft molasses or spice cookies will actually improve if kept for a week or more. To keep cookies soft, just put a piece of bread in the jar or can in which they are stored. Ice-box cookies are time and energy savers. They can be made up at any convenient time well ahead of other holiday feast preparations, and the dough kept in the refrigerator ready to slice and bake as needed. *See also* BAKING.

BASIC COOKIE RECIPE

1 cup shortening
1 cup sugar
2 eggs
1½ tsp vanilla
2½ cups sifted flour
1½ tsp baking powder
½ tsp salt

Cream the shortening and sugar thoroughly together. Beat and add the eggs and vanilla. Work in the sifted dry ingredients, blending very thoroughly. Chill for at least an hour in the refrigerator, thus making it easy to roll out the dough without the addition of unnecessary flour. Roll out thinly and cut as desired. Place on cookie sheet, a little distance apart, and bake in a moderate oven (350°–375° F.) about 10 minutes, or until golden brown. Remove from the cookie sheet as soon as baked and cool on a perforated cake rack. (Makes about 5 dozen small cookies)

This basic recipe may be varied as follows:

Caramel Crisps. Substitute ⅔ cup brown sugar for the one cup white sugar.

Coconut Jumbles. Cut with a fluted cutter and sprinkle generously before baking with plain or colored coconut.

Fall Cookies. To the creamed shortening and sugar add two squares (ounces) melted chocolate and cut the cookies with a leaf-shaped cutter.

Filled Cookies. Cut dough into rounds and place on half of them a teaspoon of the following mixture: one-quarter cup chopped dates, five tablespoons peanut butter, one tablespoon corn sirup and one tablespoon water blended thoroughly. Top with remaining rounds of dough, from which, if desired, the centers may be cut with a thimble or tiny cutter.

Marmalade or Jam Triangles. Roll thinly, cut in 2-inch squares, spread lightly with marmalade or jam, moisten edges with milk, fold into triangles and press together, before baking.

Mother's Favorites. Substitute ⅔ teaspoon almond extract for the vanilla.

Nut Nibbles. Cut as desired and sprinkle before baking with finely chopped, toasted, cooled nut-meats.

Orange Crescents. Cut with a crescent-shaped cutter and sprinkle surface of cookies generously before baking with a mixture of 2 tablespoons granulated sugar and 1 teaspoon grated orange rind.

Spicy Cookies. Use 1 teaspoon ground cinnamon, ½ teaspoon ground nutmeg and ¼ teaspoon ground cloves in place of the vanilla, sifting them with the other dry ingredients.

DROP COOKIES

Drop cookies are one of the simplest and quickest types of cookies. Care must be taken not to put the batter on the cooky sheet too close to the next cookie, as it spreads in baking. Making each cooky the same size is advisable, so that all will take the same length of time in the oven.

MERINGUE COOKIES

Meringue cookies are apt to dry out if not eaten soon after baked. The egg whites used in meringue beat better if at room temperature. They should be beaten until they hold their shape, but not to the point of being dried out.

MOLDED COOKIES

Molded cookies are made from dough which is shaped and baked in the desired form. Most cookies prepared like this keep well.

REFRIGERATOR COOKIES

Refrigerator cookies are thin, crisp cookies, made from chilled dough. The chilling

takes several hours. The dough is sliced into equal sized cookies with a thin bladed sharp knife. Refrigerator cooky dough can be made in advance and stored for a few days in the refrigerator before use.

ROLLED COOKIES

Rolled cookies, which take the greatest skill in baking, provide the greatest variety and most originality in all cookie making. Every effort should be used to prevent the use of too much flour, as this makes the cookies lose in delicacy. If the dough is sticky, it should be chilled, before being rolled. In rolling, the barest minimum of flour should be used on the rolling pin and board.

BOWKNOTS

2 eggs
⅓ cup sugar
1 tbsp sweet cream
½ tsp cream of tartar
1 tbsp melted butter
¼ tsp salt
¼ tsp mace
Sufficient flour to make stiff dough
⅛ tsp soda

Beat the eggs without separating, add the sugar, cream and butter, then the flour, sifted with the other ingredients, roll small pieces of the dough into shapes the size and shape of a pencil, tie in single knots, fry in deep fat and roll in powdered sugar.

BUTTER COOKIES

1¾ cups all-purpose flour
¾ tsp baking powder
¼ tsp salt
⅔ cup butter
1 cup sugar
1 egg, well beaten
½ tsp vanilla
2 tbsp milk
¾ square (¾ oz) unsweetened chocolate, if desired

Sift flour, measure and resift 3 times with baking powder and salt. Cream butter thoroughly; add sugar, and continue creaming until well mixed. Stir in the well beaten egg. Add vanilla. Add sifted dry ingredients in 2 or 3 portions alternately with milk, beginning and ending with the flour mixture. If some chocolate cookies are desired, add chocolate which has been melted and cooled, to half the dough. Chill dough. Roll out ⅛ inch thick on a lightly floured board, and cut in desired shapes. A finish may be made by brushing with slightly beaten egg white, then placing blanched almonds split lengthwise, pieces of candied cherry, or chocolate shot, etc. on top. Bake on a greased baking sheet in a moderately hot oven (400° F.) for 8 to 12 minutes or until delicately browned. Cool on cake racks. (Makes about 3 to 4 dozen cookies)

BUTTER NUT BALLS

1 cup butter
½ cup sugar
2 eggs, separated
1 tsp lemon rind
2½ cups all-purpose flour
2 tbsp milk
1 cup chopped walnuts
12 to 15 glazed cherries

Cream butter till soft and smooth. Add sugar gradually, creaming after each addition. Blend in egg yolks, rind and beat until fluffy. Add half the flour, then milk and remaining flour. Knead slightly to blend thoroughly. Shape into balls the size of a walnut. Dip into slightly beaten egg white, then into nuts. Place on greased baking sheets. Press half a cherry in center of each cookie. Bake in a moderate oven (350° F.) for 20 to 23 minutes. Cool on cake racks. (Makes 2 to 2½ dozen cookies)

CHECKERBOARD AND RIBBON COOKIES

2½ cups all-purpose flour
¾ tsp baking powder
½ tsp salt
⅔ cup butter (or half butter, half shortening)
1 cup sugar
2 eggs, well beaten
1 tsp vanilla
1 square (1 oz) unsweetened chocolate, melted

Sift flour, measure, and resift 3 times with baking powder and salt. Cream butter, blend in sugar thoroughly, and add

eggs; beat until smooth and fluffy. Add vanilla, and stir in the flour mixture in several portions until smooth. Divide the dough in two portions and mix the warm melted chocolate into one portion, kneading with the hands or back of a spoon until well blended. Line a small bread loaf pan or a refrigerator freezing tray with waxed paper, and pack half the chocolate dough into the bottom in a uniform layer. Cover this with half the plain dough; then another layer of chocolate, and finally another layer of plain. Try to keep the layers uniform in thickness and smooth. Cover with waxed paper and chill overnight in the refrigerator.

Turn the layered loaf out onto waxed paper, on a molding board, and slice with a thin-bladed, very sharp knife, using a saw-like motion. To make checkerboard cookies, cut these slices ¼ inch thick, and lay four of them together, one on top of the other. The bottom one reading from the left will be striped; chocolate, white, chocolate, white; on top of that reading also from left goes white, chocolate, white, chocolate; the third is again, chocolate, white, chocolate, white, and the top slice is white, chocolate, white, chocolate. If dough has softened from handling, wrap these smaller loaves in waxed paper and again chill. Then slice thinly, place on a greased baking sheet, and bake in a moderate oven (375° F.) for 8 to 10 minutes, or until lightly browned. Transfer to cake racks to cool. (Makes about 5 to 6½ dozen)

FRUIT BARS

½ lb citron
½ lb pitted dates
½ lb raisins
½ lb figs
½ lb pecans
3 cups sifted all-purpose flour
2 tsp baking powder
¾ tsp salt
2 tsp ground cinnamon
2 tsp ground allspice
2 tsp ground nutmeg
2 tbsp butter
1 cup sugar
1 tsp vanilla
4 eggs
1 egg yolk
1 cup light molasses

Line a 10½x15x¾ inch baking pan with wax paper. Grease well. Cut citron into thick slices and grind with the rest of the fruit and nuts. Mix well with 1 cup of flour. Sift remaining flour 3 times with baking powder, salt and spices. Cream butter, sugar and vanilla thoroughly. Add eggs and yolk, one at a time, and beat thoroughly after each addition. Add molasses, then gradually stir in sifted flour mixture. Add ground fruit and nuts and mix well. Spread batter in the prepared pan and bake in a moderate oven (350° F.) for 20 to 25 minutes. Cool slightly in pan and drizzle with orange frosting, (see ORANGE). Cut into bars while still warm. Store in a tightly covered container. (Makes about 35 bars)

GUM DROP COOKIES

1 cup all-purpose flour
½ tsp baking powder
½ tsp salt
⅓ cup shortening, half butter
⅔ cup sugar
1 egg
½ tsp vanilla
2 tbsp milk
¾ cup spiced gum drops, cut in small pieces

Sift flour and measure; resift 3 times with baking powder and salt. Cream shortening; add sugar gradually and continue creaming until soft and smooth. Add well-beaten egg and beat until fluffy. Stir in vanilla. Add flour mixture alternately with milk, beating well after each addition. Add gum drops and stir to mix well. Drop by rounded teaspoonfuls onto a greased baking sheet about 2 inches apart. Bake in a moderately hot oven (400° F.) for about 10 minutes or until cookies are lightly browned. Remove immediately to cake racks; they become crisp as they cool. (Makes about 2½ dozen cookies)

NAPOLEON COOKIES

4 oz flour
3 oz butter
1 oz powdered sugar
1 oz ground almonds
1 yolk of egg
Jam

Cream butter and sugar together, add the sifted flour and the ground almonds and the yolk of egg and a teaspoon of water with it. Leave the dough for one hour. Roll out very thin and cut into small rounds with a cutter. Bake 10 minutes in a moderate oven. When cool, put raspberry jam between two cookies and place them together. (Makes 15 double cookies)

OLD-FASHIONED LACE COOKIES

1 cup all-purpose flour
1 tsp cinnamon
Dash nutmeg
¼ tsp salt
½ tsp soda
¾ tsp baking powder
½ cup butter
½ cup sugar
½ cup sorghum or other light-colored molasses
1 tsp lemon extract

Sift flour, measure and resift 3 times with spices, salt, soda and baking powder. Melt butter with sugar and molasses over boiling water and remove from heat. Add dry ingredients and lemon extract and beat until smooth; let stand over hot water for 5 minutes. Drop by half teaspoonfuls onto a greased baking sheet, 3 inches apart. Bake in a moderately slow oven (325° F.) for 10 minutes. Allow to cool for 2 or 3 minutes before removing from pan to cake rack with a spatula. (Makes about 5 dozen cookies)

The cookies are quite pliable when warm and can be shaped with the hands into cups or ruffles, or rolled into cones around the handle of a wooden mixing spoon.

OLD-FASHIONED SUGAR COOKIES
(Basic Sugar Cookie Dough)

2¼ cups all-purpose flour
2 tsp baking powder
½ tsp salt
½ cup butter
1 cup sugar
1 egg, beaten
¼ tsp lemon extract
¼ tsp vanilla
¼ cup milk
½ cup raisins, finely chopped

Sift flour, measure, then resift with baking powder and salt 3 times. Cream butter and sugar; add egg, and beat until smooth and fluffy. Stir in flavorings. Add dry ingredients in 2 or 3 portions alternately with the milk beginning and ending with flour and beating well after each addition. Stir in raisins. Chill dough and roll out ¼ inch thick on a lightly floured board. Sprinkle with granulated sugar, and cut with a 2 inch cookie cutter. Place on greased baking sheet and bake in a moderate oven (375° F.) for 8 to 10 minutes. (Makes about 3 dozen cookies)

Varieties of Sugar Cookies

Almond. Substitute ½ cup blanched almonds for the raisins. Otherwise make and bake as directed.

Butterscotch. Omit granulated sugar and raisins from basic recipe. Add 1 cup brown sugar firmly packed and ½ cup chopped pecans. Otherwise make and bake as directed.

Cherry. Substitute ½ cup finely chopped glazed cherries for the raisins. Otherwise make and bake as directed.

Lemon-coconut. Omit vanilla from basic recipe and add 1 teaspoon grated lemon rind. Substitute ½ cup moist shredded coconut, firmly packed for the raisins. Otherwise make and bake as directed.

Maple-pecan. Omit vanilla and raisins from basic recipe and add ¼ teaspoon maple extract and ½ cup chopped pecans. Otherwise make and bake as directed.

Sand Tarts. Make dough as directed in recipe. Roll out ⅜ inch thick. Cut with 2-inch cookie cutter, brush with slightly beaten egg white and sprinkle with a mixture of 2 tablespoons sugar and ¼ teaspoon of cinnamon. Bake as directed in recipe.

Spice. Omit vanilla and substitute brown sugar for granulated in basic recipe. Sift flour, measure and resift with baking powder, salt and add ½ teaspoon cinnamon, ¼ teaspoon cloves, and ¼ teaspoon nutmeg. Otherwise proceed as directed.

Pinwheel Cookies

2¼ cups all-purpose flour
¾ tsp baking powder
½ tsp salt
⅔ cup butter (or half butter, half shortening)

1 cup sugar minus 2 tbsp (⅞ cup)
1 egg, beaten
¾ tsp vanilla
2 tbsp milk
1 square (1 oz) unsweetened chocolate, melted

Sift flour, measure and resift 3 times with baking powder and salt. Cream butter or shortening, blend in sugar thoroughly, and add egg; beat until smooth and fluffy. Stir in vanilla. Add flour mixture and milk alternately in 2 or 3 portions, beginning and ending with flour. Divide dough into 2 equal portions; stir warm, melted chocolate into one portion, kneading with back of spoon until well blended, and chill in refrigerator for half an hour or longer. Sprinkle a towel lightly with flour and rub in gently with palm of hand. Place the 2 portions of dough on the towel about 12 inches apart. Roll out in rectangular shape (about 10 inches by 14 inches). Brush excess flour from top of dough and from all around the two sheets of dough Then brush *one* sheet of dough with slightly beaten egg white or milk. Lay other sheet on top by folding towel and dough over. Any torn or ragged places can be patted into shape. Again brush off excess flour and then again brush with egg white. Roll up the double sheet of dough beginning at the longer side of rectangle. Wrap snugly in sheet of waxed paper, retaining cylinder shape. Chill in refrigerator with the edge of roll on bottom. When ready to bake, remove paper wrapping, cut into thin uniform slices, using a thin-bladed sharp knife. Place cookies on a lightly greased baking sheet, and bake in a moderate oven (375° F.) for about 10 minutes, or until very delicately browned. (Makes about 3½ to 4 dozen cookies, the number depending on size) Keep in an airtight container.

Plain Refrigerator Cookies
(Basic Recipe)

2¼ cups all-purpose flour
½ tsp soda
½ tsp salt
½ cup butter or shortening
¾ cup sugar
1 egg
1 tsp vanilla

Sift flour, measure and resift 3 times with soda and salt. Cream butter until soft and smooth; add sugar and beat until well blended. Add egg and beat until smooth and fluffy. Stir in vanilla. Gradually blend in the flour mixture, and turn dough into a small loaf pan which has been lined with waxed paper. Chill in refrigerator for several hours until firm; then turn out onto cutting board, strip off paper and cut into thin, uniform slices ⅛ inch thick or less, using a sharp, thin-bladed knife. Transfer cookies to greased baking sheet, and bake in a moderately hot oven (400° F.) for about 8 to 10 minutes or until nicely browned. Cool on cake racks. (Makes about 4 dozen)

Varieties of Refrigerator Cookies

Cherry-citron. To basic recipe, add ⅛ teaspoon anise extract with the vanilla and lastly stir in ¼ cup sliced moist citron and ¼ cup sliced, moist, glazed (not maraschino) cherries. Shape, slice, and bake as directed.

Chocolate Almond. To basic recipe, add 1½ squares (1½ oz.) unsweetened chocolate, melted and cooled. Add chocolate to the creamed mixture before adding flour. Add ¼ teaspoon almond extract with the vanilla and lastly stir in ¼ cup chopped blanched almonds. Shape, slice, and bake as directed.

Lemon-coconut. Omit vanilla from basic recipe and add 1 teaspoon lemon rind and ½ teaspoon lemon extract. Lastly stir in 1 cup grated coconut, firmly packed. Shape, slice, and bake as directed.

Maple Walnut. To basic recipe add ½ cup chopped walnuts and ½ teaspoon maple extract. Shape, slice, and bake as directed.

Orange. Omit vanilla from basic recipe and add 1 teaspoon orange rind and ½ teaspoon orange extract. Shape, slice, and bake as directed.

Rocks

2½ cups all-purpose flour
1 tsp allspice
1 tsp cinnamon
½ tsp nutmeg
¼ tsp salt
⅔ cup shortening (half butter)
1½ cups sugar

3 eggs, beaten
½ tsp soda dissolved in 3 tbsp hot water
1 cup pecans or walnuts, chopped
1 cup moist seedless raisins, chopped, or
    1 cup currants

Sift flour, measure, and resift 3 times with the spices and salt. Cream shortening till soft and smooth, gradually blend in sugar, and add beaten eggs; beat until fluffy and light-colored. Stir in soda and water mixture; then add flour mixture in 2 or 3 portions, and stir until well blended after each addition. Fold in chopped nuts and raisins or currants. Drop by teaspoonfuls, at least 2 inches apart, on lightly greased baking sheet, and bake in a moderate oven (375° F.) for 15 minutes or until delicately browned. (Makes about 6 dozen cookies)

Rolled Honey Wafers

2 cups sifted flour
¼ tsp nutmeg
½ tsp cinnamon
1 cup shredded almonds
1 cup shortening
1 cup sugar
2 cups honey
2 eggs, well beaten

Mix and sift flour and spices; stir in almonds. Cream shortening until soft; beat in sugar, then honey and eggs; stir in flour-nut mixture. Drop small portions from teaspoon on greased bottom of inverted dripping pan, about 2 inches apart, and bake in slow oven (300° F.) about 12 minutes or until delicately browned. Cool 1 minute, then remove with spatula and roll, top side out, around handle of wooden spoon, or roll, cone-shaped, or fit into a cup. Keep in covered container to retain the crispness of the cookies. (Makes approximately 80 wafers)

Sponge Drop Cookies

3 eggs
¾ cup sugar
1 tsp flavoring
1 cup sifted flour
⅓ tsp salt
1 tsp baking powder

Beat the eggs until very light, gradually adding the sugar and beating thoroughly after each addition. Stir in the flavoring and finally, fold in gently the sifted dry ingredients. Line a baking sheet with well greased paper and drop the sponge mixture onto it from the tip of a spoon, a little distance apart to allow for spreading. Bake in a moderately hot oven (about 400° F.) until golden brown, about 10 minutes. (Makes about 3 dozen)

SPRITZ COOKIES

1 cup butter
¾ cup sifted granulated sugar
2 egg yolks
¼ tsp almond extract
2½ cups sifted all-purpose flour

Cream butter thoroughly. Add sugar gradually. Blend in unbeaten egg yolks. Stir in flavoring, then flour and mix thoroughly. Pack into cookie press by taking dough up in hands and shaping into cylinder. Drop into tube. Force through cookie press onto cold, ungreased cookie sheets, about 1 inch apart. Bake in moderate oven (375° F.) for 8 minutes or until a delicate brown. Remove cookies from pans onto cake racks while warm. If difficult to remove from pans, return to oven for a few minutes. Cool thoroughly. Store in air-tight container. (Makes 4½ dozen medium-sized cookies)

STUFFED COOKIES

2¼ cups all-purpose flour
1 tsp baking powder
¼ tsp salt
½ cup shortening (half butter, half lard)
1 cup sugar
1 egg
½ tsp vanilla
2 tbsp milk

Sift flour, measure and resift 3 times with baking powder and salt. Cream shortening, blend in sugar gradually, add egg and beat until smooth and fluffy. Stir in vanilla. Add sifted dry ingredients and milk alternately in 2 or 3 portions, beginning and ending with flour and beating well after each addition. Chill for at least an hour. Roll out on a lightly floured board

to about ⅛ inch thickness. Cut out with any desired shaped cookie cutter about 2 inches in diameter. Place half the cut-outs on lightly greased baking sheet. In center of each one place a teaspoon of the fruit filling (below) cover with another cookie, sandwich fashion, and press edges together firmly. Bake in a moderately hot oven (400° F.) for 6 to 8 minutes or until delicately browned. (Makes 2 to 2½ dozen, depending on size)

Filling

1 cup sugar
1 tbsp flour
1 cup seedless raisins
1 cup soft chopped dates
2 tbsp lemon juice
½ tsp grated lemon rind
Pinch of salt
¾ cup water

Blend sugar and flour and combine with remaining ingredients in saucepan. Cook over low heat, stirring constantly until well blended and thick. Mixture should actually boil about 3 minutes. Cool before using in cookies.

Other Fillings

Scant 2 cups flour
Yolks 4 eggs
3 tbsp powdered sugar
5 tbsp white wine, or water
Pinch of salt
Frying oil or good fat

Fig and Nut. Use ½ cup each of chopped figs and nuts in place of dates.

Mincemeat, jellied cranberry sauce or preserves. All are good fillers—and all ready to use, too!

WIRRE GEDANKEN
(Troubled Thoughts)

Work the flour and eggs with a knife, then add the other ingredients and knead for about 20 minutes. The paste should be light but quite firm. Mold into an oblong shape, cover with a bowl and let it stand for ½ hour. Now cut very small pieces from the paste and roll them out on a floured pastry board as thin as possible into rounds of about 3 inches. With a sharp knife make

4 small incisions in each round. Thread the handle of a wooden spoon in and out of these incisions. Have ready a small deep saucepan of boiling oil or fat. Dip the "Troubled Thought" in the hot fat, holding it with the wooden spoon. After about 1 minute, slip the spoon out as the "Troubled Thought" will be sufficiently cooked on one side, turn it carefully and cook the other side to a light golden color. Have ready a plate with confectioner's sugar and dip them in this while still hot, coating them equally all over. They should be very light and crumbly.

COOKIE CUTTER. A cookie cutter is a metal or plastic outline die used to cut cookie shapes from thin sheets of dough. It is quite similar to the biscuit cutter (*which see*), though usually of more fanciful outline. Cookie cutters and biscuit cutters may be used interchangeably for different effects of shape. *See also* KITCHEN EQUIPMENT.

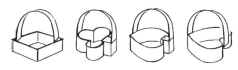

COOKIE CUTTERS

COOKIE JAR. A traditional household accessory and the major objective of many a childhood raid, the cookie jar is a large earthenware jar, with a tight-fitting lid, that is used to store cookies. Most decorative jars are not sufficiently airtight to keep cookies for longer than a day or two.

COOKIE PRESS. A cookie press is a convenient device that eliminates the necessity of rolling out the dough and cutting the individual cookies by hand. It consists of a wide, hollow tube with a plunger at one end and a die at the other. The cookie dough is placed in the tube, and, by means of the plunger, is forced out through the die to drop on the cookie sheet (*which see*) as a shaped piece. The plunger is usually controlled by a screw so that a uniform amount of dough may be forced out each time, and the die may be changed so that differently shaped cookies may be made. *See* COOKIE; *see also* KITCHEN EQUIPMENT.

COOKIE SHEET. A cookie sheet is a flat, thin, metal sheet on which cookies are baked. Any corrosion-resisting metal or coated metal may be used, provided that it is thin enough to transmit the heat quickly and evenly. The sheets may be plain, or they may have rolled or raised edges to give them rigidity and to prevent warping. The edges should not be too high, however, lest they interfere with the work. *See* COOKIE; *see also* KITCHEN EQUIPMENT.

COOKING AND COOKERY. The newcomer to cookery—whether a young person setting up a household for the first time or an older individual who is dabbling in the kitchen arts from curiosity—may be mystified or even discouraged, initially, by the seeming endless array of recipes, instructions and tricks of the trade shared by his more experienced fellows.

Actually, cooking has a logic that is firmly grounded in the principles of science—the techniques of cookery being based on the chemical changes that occur when foods are heated. For the new cook who attempts to learn the reasoning behind cooking rules, the art of cookery soon ceases to be a mystery. Confusion gives way to common sense and imagination combines with skill to produce wholesome and delicious meals.

SUGGESTIONS FOR THE NEW COOK

Before preparing a new recipe, review it carefully noting the ingredients, the timing and whether or not there are new techniques to be learned. A thorough reading of the entire entry concerned with the foods to be prepared enables the cook to discover hints on purchase and preparation.

For the first few meals, it is often wise to serve meal-in-one dishes or simple main courses based on recipes for familiar dishes such as pork chops, ham steak, fried chicken or veal cutlets. Easy to prepare side dishes—salad, frozen vegetables, fruit for dessert—minimize the problem of timing coordination and allow the cook to concentrate fully on the preparation of the new dish.

Experiment with new techniques in a relaxed situation before employing them in the preparation of a large dinner. If you have never made gravy, try cooking cheese sauce to be served on noodles one day for lunch to practice the gravy technique.

Avoid planning on more than one new recipe for any one meal. New recipes require more attention in their preparation and their timing is not completely predictable. Once the timing and cooking of several dishes have been mastered, the dishes may be combined to form a meal.

Meals can be exciting even when they are simple. Dress up new dishes and old alike with a variety of garnishes and side dishes. *See* DECORATING. The careful execution of recipes should not deter the new cook from experimenting with spices (*which see*) and seasoning foods to her own liking. Unfamiliar spices, however, should be used sparingly until the cook is sure of the results.

TIPS ON TIMING

Inexperienced cooks often find their biggest problem is coordinating all the dishes in a particular meal so that they are ready to be served at the same time. The most important factor in proper timing is to allow for the complete cooking of the entire meal. Decide upon the time dinner will be served; estimate the cooking time of the slowest cooking dish. (Extra time should be allowed for the pre-cooking preparation of foods.) Then, estimate the cooking time for each dish to be prepared and make up a time table of when the cooking of each separate food should begin. Such a chart could be tacked to the kitchen cabinet for reference.

When deciding on recipes to be used, check to see that not more than one recipe requires extensive last minute preparation. For example, it will be difficult for the new cook to make brown gravy for the potatoes at the same time that she must make cream sauce for the asparagus. The timing of recipes should be staggered so that it is not necessary to begin the preparation of two different dishes at the same time.

Ingredients can be treated so that their cooking time is lengthened or shortened according to the needs of the cook. For example, potatoes may be cut into small pieces for faster cooking or large pieces for slower cooking.

Many foods can be prepared and chilled before the cooking of the hot foods is begun. This procedure is particularly expedient when the main course is a quick cooking dish such as eggs, fish or liver. However, when the main course is a long cooking dish such as roast turkey, time might be saved by preparing salads, relishes, garnishes, desserts and dressings during the actual cooking time of the main dish.

Cut down on labor by combining tasks.

Thus, onions needed for three recipes can be cut at the same time. All cans may be opened at one time. For recipes that call for close watching and precise addition of ingredients, all necessary ingredients should be pre-measured and set aside until needed. Available manpower in the form of co-operative friends and curious children can be utilized in the execution of time consuming jobs such as the grating of potatoes or mixing of batter.

Par-boiling and blanching of various ingredients may usually be done hours before the cooking begins. Pots and pans should be coordinated so that the proper utensil is free when needed.

In the event that the cooking time for certain dishes has been wrongly estimated, keep the foods warm by placing them in covered dishes in a low temperature oven until serving time. Roasts have a built in safety cooking valve. If they appear to be almost finished when the rest of the meal is not, they can be removed from the oven and will continue cooking from internal heat. When the rest of the meal is nearly completed, the roast can be returned to oven to continue cooking more quickly. Ovens can also be used to keep foods such as pancakes, waffles, bacon and eggs warm while additional portions are being cooked.

PITFALLS TO AVOID

Inexperienced cooks often make the mistake of thinking that foods will cook faster if subjected to high heats. Actually, in the majority of cases, too high heats can severely damage the foods being cooked. *See* HEAT. The temperature suggested in the recipe should always be followed. In the case of oils and fats used for frying or sautéeing it is important that the heat be low enough so that the oil does not smoke. Deep frying (*which see*) has a technique all its own.

Sauces and gravies, likewise, must be cooked over low heat. Fish, eggs and liver —all quick cooking foods—are burnt by the application of high heats. Vegetables should be brought to a boil as rapidly as possible to prevent loss of vitamin C; but they should never be cooked at a boil. The temperature should be lowered to the simmering point once the boiling point has been reached. Follow the appropriate charts for the proper heats and cooking times of meats and baked goods. Remember that too high heats result in burning, unpleasant odor, breakdown of nutrients and impairment of flavors.

The problem of cooking foods before they have been thawed can be avoided by careful planning. Whenever at all possible, have meats thoroughly thawed before cooking. However, if it is necessary to cook meat that is frozen, try to prepare the meat in a sauce or gravy so that the loss in flavor is not readily noticed.

Cook frozen chicken in a pot with tomato sauce or juice and vegetables. Cover a roast in mushroom and onion soup, place in a covered pot and stew. Meat should not be soaked but simply run under cold water to remove the ice crystals. Broil frozen steaks and chops at very low temperatures so that the meats are virtually thawed by the time they begin to cook.

To avoid having to cook frozen meats, package meats so that they thaw more readily. Hamburger meat may be seasoned as soon as it is purchased, divided into patties or balls and frozen individually. These small clumps of chop meat will thaw quickly. The patties or balls may also be cooked frozen if time does not permit defrosting. Season and wrap chops and chicken parts individually for freezing. Meats that have been frozen and thawed usually cook more quickly than fresh meats.

RECIPE SUBSTITUTIONS

Since foods often have so much in common, they may often be treated in similar ways. There is, however, a certain skill involved in choosing the appropriate substitutions for recipe ingredients. In general, if the food you wish to substitute is similar in texture, color, species and density to the food in the recipe, substitution will be successful. Vegetables are particularly interchangeable. An unknown tuber may be cooked in the way potatoes are cooked. However, watch the timing with these foods. If the recipe calls for raw asparagus, tomatoes will cook too quickly and turn to sauce. Spinach may be used for greens in a salad but iceberg lettuce will not survive a recipe for creamed spinach.

Baking substitutions are much more tricky. In general, baking is a more precise art than cooking. Directions and ingredients must be followed to the letter for good results. If you wish to change the type of flour, sweetener or leavening agent that is called for, consult the appropriate cookbook entries. Small amounts of spices, however, may often be added to cake recipes with good results.

In the case of meats, consult the appropriate heading to determine whether the meat you have on hand can be used to best advantage in a particular recipe. Veal may be tender as a cutlet but it is not as fatty or flavorsome as beef. If you plan to make a stew, beef from the oft-used muscles of the steer will provide a tasty gravy whereas veal will loose both tenderness and its own very subtle flavor during prolonged cooking.

COOKING WITH WINE

The addition of wine is always best appreciated in cookery when it is used with discretion for flavoring purposes, a trifling amount conferring a subtly pervasive quality to the dish. The fundamental principle in wine cookery as in ordinary cookery, recognized by all good cooks, is that any flavoring agent introduced must never dominate the flavor of the principal food; each additional flavor or seasoning is merely for the purpose of accentuating the innate flavor of the food to which it must be subordinated and with which it must thoroughly blend (as the flavorings must with each other).

With soup, use a rather semi-sweet wine; with fish, a dry wine; with meat, a rather dry red wine, or Madeira or sherry; with game, a rather dry, red or white wine may be used, according to directions; with dessert, a semi-sweet or sweet wine. Certain desserts will be much enhanced by the use of rum, brandy, apple brandy, and the like.

Wine should never be combined with acid foods.

If eggs, milk, or cream are to be added, or butter to smooth a sauce, it should always be done after the wine.

To get the full benefit of a little spirits (brandy, for example) in certain dishes, it is advisable to pour it over the cooking food, touch a match to it and shake until the flame dies out. The flavor of the spirits will permeate the food subtly, raise the flavor, and instill aroma.

To retain every bit of the aroma of the wine or spirits, the cooking utensil must be kept closely covered as in braising.

In chilling wine-or-liqueur-flavored foods, the dish must be kept covered, even in the refrigerator.

When braising foods into which wine enters, the wine must be added with the meat, or fish, or game, or vegetables.

More wine must not be added to the food after it has been served. This would entirely spoil the dish, unless it is flamed, as for certain desserts.

It sometimes happens that homemakers have difficulties in freezing ice cream or other desserts with which rum has been mixed. If rum is whipped with the cream, the mixture will freeze without any trou le.

COON. An American game mammal; more correctly called RACCOON, *which see*.

COPPER WARE. Coppper was once greatly favored for the making of cooking vessels and other kitchen equipment. It is a bright, cheerful metal, quickly heated, reasonably durable, and light to handle. On the other hand, it is quite expensive, and difficult to clean. For this reason, it has been supplanted by other metals, notably aluminum, and solid copper vessels are now chiefly regarded as antiques. Because of its heat transmitting abilities, copper is often used in conjunction with other metals, especially stainless steel (*see* STAINLESS STEEL WARE). *See also* KITCHEN EQUIPMENT.

CORAL. The roe of the lobster, greatly used in French cuisine, to color butter, sauces, etc.

CORDIAL. A sweetened and aromatized spirit intended primarily to stimulate and invigorate the action of the heart and the circulation of the blood. As a general rule, the spirit used is flavored and scented after, not during, distillation, by means of *infusion* (*see* LIQUEUR).

Many cordials were developed, as were many brandies and liqueurs, by French monks in medieval days in their ceaseless quest for better medicines for the sick and feeble. With this rich heritage, France has taken the lead in the manufacture of fine brandies, cordials and liqueurs.

Cordials today are drunk more for their exceptional taste than their action on the heart, and are commonly served as after-dinner liqueurs as well as being used in various mixed drinks.

CORDIAL GLASS. *See* GLASSWARE.

CORIANDER SEEDS. The spicy seed of a small plant belonging to the parsley family is dried for use as a seasoning. The flavor of the aromatic coriander seed somewhat resembles the flavors of cumin and curry, but its usage differs from theirs. Coriander seeds are widely used in confectionery and sweetmeats, gingerbread, cookies, biscuits, mixed green salads, sausage, pork pie, and poultry seasonings. In the Orient a single seed is often added to a demitasse. Powdered coriander seed comprises the greater part of curry powder.

CORIANDER

CORING KNIFE. *See* CUTLERY; *see also* KITCHEN EQUIPMENT.

CORK EXTRACTOR. A device used to remove corks that have been forced down into the contents of a bottle, a common mishap in the case of wine. It consists of three long wires, each bent at one end, and all twisted together and attached to a handle at the other. The wires are thrust into the bottle and, by means of a sliding ring, closed over the cork, which is then removed by withdrawing the entire device.

CORKSCREW. A device consisting of some sort of pointed metal worm or auger, usually fitted to a handle, and often equipped with some means of applying leverage, that is used to remove corks from bottles.

Though the cork has seen its heyday of use, it is still frequently encountered, especially in the case of wine (*which see*). Of all the inanimate objects that seem strangely endowed with the power to resist the will of man, the cork is, perhaps, the most stubborn. For this reason, many people resign themselves to the inevitable and include a cork extractor (*which see*) in their equipment to retrieve the broken bits that are, in desperation, driven into the contents of the bottle.

The cork, however, should be removed in one piece, in suitable condition, if possible, for re-use. Much of the difficulty encountered is frequently due to the use of an improper corkscrew.

A scientific investigation into the subject has exploded many long-held beliefs about corkscrews. They found, for example, that a plain wire helix performed more satisfactory than a sharp auger-type worm. They also found, that while wine lovers prefer not to penetrate the entire cork for fear of disturbing sediment encrusted on the bottom of the cork, removal was easier if the worm did penetrate through the bottom, giving support to the pull.

In general, according to the findings of this investigation, the best corkscrews are those that are so constructed that the worm follows exactly the path cut by the point through the cork, that are long enough (over two inches) so that the worm projects out of the bottom of the cork but the shank does not enter the top, and that have some sort of leverage device to assist the user in extraction.

There are a great many corkscrews of varying designs on the market that meet those specifications. The homemaker would do well to get one of those, a husky corkscrew fitted with a large, comfortable handle, in short, one that works, and shun the novelty type with a miniature worm and a handle that is impossible to grip.

CORKY. A term applied to a wine that has been tainted by a foul-smelling or diseased cork. Such wine should be thrown out. The French refer to a corky wine as *bouchonne*.

CORN. Although historically and botanically, corn means any kind of grain, in the United States corn means maize, and in cookery this is generally true internationally. Two varieties of corn are commonly grown: field corn, which is used for fodder; and sweet corn, which produces the ears commonly thought of as "corn."

Sweet corn is a native of America, and was an important crop to the Indians of the Americas centuries before Columbus discovered the new world. The Icelandic sagas mention it as a product of the land to the west which the Norse sailors discovered in the 11th century. Because its origin is buried in antiquity, many legends were told concerning it.

An American Indian myth tells of a youth who went to the woods to fast to prepare for his approaching manhood. He built himself a hut, and wandered about it, praying that the Great Spirit might acknowledge him by sending him a gift for his people who were in great need. Finally, after several days of fasing, he was too

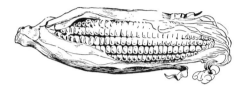

CORN

weak to move about, and lay on the ground. On the third day of this idleness, a youthful spirit appeared before him, dressed in flowing green plumes. The spirit commanded the Indian to rise and wrestle with him if he wished to get his heart's desire. After the exercise he was exhausted, and before he revived the spirit left. This was repeated for four days. On the fourth day the spirit said that he would return once more, on which occasion the youth would overcome him. He should then strip off his green clothes and bury them in the ground. If the mound over the clothes was tended and kept free from weeds, the young Indian would get his desire. The Indian defeated the spirit, and followed his directions. In a few days a plant grew out of the mound which bore ears of grain which were good to eat. This was the origin of the Indian corn.

The original Indian corn had vari-colored ears, sometimes blue, or black or red, or parti-colored. Modern horticulturists have developed the sweet corn as a white or yellow ear, since the colored ears do not meet acceptance in the market.

CORN AND CORN PRODUCTS

Corn is one of the richest sources of starch, and is thus an important energy food. One of its products is corn starch, which is used as a thickening agent in desserts and sauces. From the sugar content of corn is derived corn sirup which is used with pancakes and waffles and in many recipes. Corn oil is used as a salad and cooking oil. Laundry starch is also made from corn.

The corn kernels are dried, and then may be ground into corn meal which is usually thought of as a cereal, but may be used in making delicious breads and muffins. Hominy (*which see*) is corn prepared in a particular way.

Popcorn is a different variety of corn which has small kernels. When these are dried and exposed to heat, the starchy mass inside explodes through the outer skin of the kernel, and gives the familiar fluffy white morsels.

is prepared by slicing through the kernels and scraping the inner portions from the cob. The whole grain style is prepared by cutting the entire kernel from the cob without cutting through the kernel. The kernels are then processed in brine.

Frozen Corn. Corn is quick-frozen for market either on the cob or in the form of whole grains cut from the cob. In either case it is cooked and used like fresh corn.

Corn Meal. Corn meal, which may be either yellow or white, is prepared in two

FOOD VALUE

	Wa-ter	Food Energy	Pro-tein	Fat	Car-bohy-drates	Cal-cium	Phos-phorus	Iron	Vit. A Value	Thia-mine	Ribo-flavin	Nia-cin	Ascor-bic Acid
Canned Corn	80.5	77	2.0	.5	16.1	4	51	.5	200	.02	.05	.8	5
Fresh Corn	73.9	108	3.7	1.2	20.5	9	120	.5	390	.15	.14	1.4	12
Cornmeal (deger-minated)	12	355	7.5	1.1	78.8	10	140	1.0	0	.16	.09	.9	0
Cornmeal (whole grain)	12	365	9.1	3.7	73.9	18	248	2.7	0	.41	.12	1.7	0

HINTS ON BUYING

Fresh corn is at its best when it is picked from the stalk, husked, and cooked immediately. It is a particularly delicate vegetable. Once it is picked, the sugars in the kernel start turning to starch, and the ear loses its sweet flavor. The color of the kernels may be white or yellow, depending on the variety; current taste runs to the yellow types.

Fresh corn of good quality has a fresh-looking green husk with brown silk; the cob should be filled with plump milky kernels that are firm enough to offer slight resistance to pressure. Yellowed, or dried out husks are an indication of age or heat damage during shipping, and indicate that the corn has lost its flavor. Immature corn, in which the kernels are very small and not filled out, is unsatisfactory since it lacks flavor. Worm injury is not serious if it is confined to the tip since the damaged portion can be trimmed off easily. If it occurs further down the cob, the ear is less desirable. Corn should be examined for quality by pulling back the husk and examining the kernels.

Canned Corn. Corn is canned in two styles, cream and whole grain. The cream style

ways, known as old process and new process. The old process is also known as "water ground" or "stone ground." The original mills were turned by water power; modern mills are electric; but the chief characteristic of this type of grinding is that the corn is crushed between stones. The skin and germ are not removed before grinding and although some of them are bolted out, some part of the skin and most of the germ remain in the finished product, even when it is very finely ground. Many people consider stone ground meal to have a richer flavor because of the presence of the germ. Stone ground meal feels soft to the touch. Because of the presence of the germ, the meal will not keep as well as new process meal, and should be bought in small quantities. Stone ground meal is used to a greater extent in the south than in the north.

New process meal is ground between steel roller by very complicated machinery which break and remove the husk and germ almost entirely. This type of meal feels dry and granular to the touch, and will keep very well.

Because of the difference in the moisture content of the two types, it is difficult to interchange them in many recipes. For breads made with baking powder or eggs, or where the corn meal is mixed with white flour, the two types are practically interchangeable. For waffles and other types of bread the granular meal must be scalded before using. Many people believe that the new process meal requires longer cooking then stone ground meal.

Hints on Preparation

Corn on the cob is one of the most typical of American dishes. At its best the ears are freshly picked, husked and the silk removed, and plunged into rapidly boiling water. Not more than five minutes' boiling is necessary. Corn which is purchased in the market will need to be cooked ten to fifteen minutes, and if it is not so fresh as it should be, a little sugar in the water may improve the flavor. In either case, overcooking only toughens the kernels and removes the flavor. Nothing but salt and melted butter is needed with corn on the cob.

Corn which is slightly older, or which is to be eaten by people who cannot eat it from the cob may be prepared by cutting it from the cob and cooking it in milk or cream in the top of a double boiler for ten or fifteen minutes, depending on the age of the corn. For people with delicate digestions, the kernels may be slit and only the milky contents scraped from the cob with the back of a knife. This, heated with a little milk or cream, and salt and pepper, is a delicious dish.

Many western cooks prefer to cook corn in the husks, claiming that this improves the flavor. And, of course, in corn roasts and other forms of outdoor cooking, the husks are usually left on.

Fresh corn which is to be used in fritters or other prepared dishes should usually be parboiled before cutting from the cob. Then the kernels may be cut off whole, or the milk scraped out.

Corn Chowder I

1 cup fresh corn
1½-inch cube salt pork, diced
1 onion, sliced
1 qt potatoes, peeled and sliced
1 cup milk or cream
Salt and pepper
8 crackers

Fry the salt pork, add the onion, and cook until the onion is tender. Boil the peeled and sliced potatoes in 1 quart boiling water for 5 minutes. Add the fat and onion until the potatoes are soft. Add the corn and milk and bring to the scalding point. Add the butter and seasoning. Pour over the crackers and serve hot. (Serves 8)

Corn Chowder II

2 slices fat salt pork, diced
1 onion, diced
2 cups potatoes, cut in ½-inch cubes
3¼ cups boiling water
2 cups canned or fresh corn
1 tsp salt
⅛ tsp pepper
1¾ cups evaporated milk
1 tbsp butter
1 tbsp flour
Crackers

Cook the pork slowly in a large saucepan until the fat flows freely. Add the onion, cook 15 minutes, next put in the potatoes and water and simmer gently until the potatoes are tender. Add the corn, seasonings, and milk, and thicken with the blended butter and flour, stirring to mix smoothly. Pour over crackers in the serving dishes, or serve these separately. (Serves 4 or 6)

Corn Custard

2 cups scalded milk
½ green pepper minced finely
½ pimiento minced
1 tbsp minced onion
½ tsp salt
¼ cup chopped celery leaves
2 eggs slightly beaten
1½ cups corn cut from the cob
⅛ tsp pepper
Few grains of nutmeg

Combine all the ingredients and turn into a shallow buttered casserole. Place the casserole in a pan of hot water, and bake in a moderate oven (375° F.) about 30 minutes, or until the blade of a silver knife, inserted in the center, comes out clean.

If canned whole kernel corn is used, it should be well drained.

CORN FRITTERS

1 cup corn, fresh or canned
2 eggs
½ cup flour
½ tsp baking powder
⅓ tsp salt
Pinch of pepper

Place the corn in a bowl with the beaten eggs. Sift and add the dry ingredients and beat just until smooth. Drop by tablespoonfuls into deep hot fat, or sauté in shallow fat, turning to brown both sides. Drain on soft crumpled paper. Serve hot in place of potatoes with fried chicken, or with sirup as a light but delicious luncheon or supper dish.

If cream style corn is used, a little more flour may be required to make a batter of the proper consistency. Otherwise the method is the same.

CORN OYSTERS

8 ears of fresh corn
3 eggs, separated
½ tsp salt
¼ tsp white pepper
¼ cup sifted flour

Slit the kernels of the corn and scrape with the back of a knife. Beat the egg whites until they are stiff, adding a pinch of salt, and the yolks until they are thick and lemon colored. Combine the corn, egg yolk, salt, pepper, and flour and stir until smooth. Fold in the stiffly beaten egg whites. Drop the mixture by tablespoonfuls onto a well greased griddle or skillet. Cook on both sides until well browned. Serve at once. (Serves 6)

CORN PIE

Pastry or baking powder biscuit dough
1 tbsp softened butter
1 No. 2 can yellow corn
1 cup evaporated milk
⅔ tsp salt
1 tbsp minced green pepper
1 tbsp minced onion
1 tbsp minced parsley
1 egg
½ cup buttered crumbs
5 tbsp grated cheese

Line a 9-inch pie plate with the pastry or biscuit dough, building the rim up high. Spread with the softened butter to prevent the crust from soaking. Combine the corn, milk, salt, green pepper, onion, and parsley in a saucepan and heat thoroughly, stirring frequently. Remove from the fire and add the beaten egg. Pour into the prepared crust. Top with the crumbs blended with the cheese and bake about 30 minutes, having the oven very hot (450° F.) for the first five minutes, and then reducing the heat to 350° F. for the balance of the time. The pie is done when a silver knife inserted in the center comes out clean. Serve hot.

CORN PUFFS

2 eggs, slightly beaten
2 cups whole kernel corn
1 cup milk
¼ tsp paprika
½ tsp salt
1 tbsp minced chives
Few grains cayenne pepper
½ cup grated American cheese

Combine all the ingredients in the order given. Turn into six well buttered custard cups. Place in a pan of hot water and bake in a moderate oven (375° F.) 25 to 30 minutes, or until set. Unmold and serve with a white sauce or tomato sauce.

CORN SCRAMBLE

1 can condensed tomato soup
4 tbsp olive oil
1 tbsp finely minced onion
1 tbsp finely minced green pepper
1 can whole kernel corn
4 eggs
½ tsp salt
Pinch of pepper
1 tbsp paprika

Mix together the soup, oil, onion, pepper, and corn in a saucepan, and heat to the scalding point. Reduce the heat. Add carefully the well beaten eggs, and the seasonings. Stir rapidly and constantly while the mixture cooks, until it is set but not firm. Serve at once over toast, or in tomato or green pepper cups. A sprinkling of grated American cheese may be added just before serving. (Serves 4)

CORN SOUFFLE

2 tbsp butter
2 tbsp flour
1 cup milk
1 No. 2 can corn (whole kernel)
2 eggs
1 tsp salt
1/6 tsp pepper

Make a white sauce with the butter, flour, and milk. Separate the eggs and beat the whites until stiff and the yolks until thick and yellow. Drain the corn thoroughly. Add the corn to the white sauce with the seasoning and the beaten yolks. Fold in the stiffly beaten whites. Turn into a buttered baking dish or individual buttered custard cups. Bake in a moderate oven (350°-375° F.) about 30 minutes for the large dish or 18 to 20 minutes for the individual cups. Serve immediately.

If cream style corn is used, the amoun of milk should be slightly cut down.

CORN SOUP

2 cups whole kernel corn
1 pint boiling water
1 pint milk
1 slice onion
2 tbsp butter or margarine
2 tbsp flour
1 tsp salt
Dash of pepper
Dash of paprika

Fry the onion in the butter and stir in the flour. If raw corn is used, place it in the boiling water and boil 5 to 7 minutes. Add the milk to the corn and bring it to the scalding point. Thicken with the onion, flour, and butter mixture and add the seasonings. Heat, but do not let it boil. (Serves 4)

SCALLOPED CORN

1 cup milk
2 cups corn
1 cup bread or cracker crumbs
2 slices green pepper, diced
1 tsp salt
⅛ tsp pepper
2 tbsp butter

Place alternate layers of corn and bread crumbs in a greased baking dish, adding butter and seasonings to each layer. Pour over the milk and bake in a moderate oven (350°-375° F.) for 30 minutes.

SUCCOTASH

Cut enough corn from the cob to make 2 cups. Heat with a little milk, salt and pepper and a lump of butter. Cook until tender 2 cups of fresh lima beans and season with salt and pepper. Combine the corn and lima beans and reheat. (Serves 6 or 8)

Succotash may be made with fresh or canned corn and lima beans, or with dried lima beans which have been soaked and cooked until tender.

In parts of New England bits of salt pork are cooked with the corn; and in Massachusetts and Connecticut shell beans, not limas, are used.

CORN MEAL MUSH

Corn meal mush, which the Italians know as polenta, is made by cooking the meal in salted water. The simplest method, and one which prevents lumping, is to place the corn meal, cold water, and salt in the top of a double boiler. The proportions are 1 cup of meal, 1 to 1½ level teaspoons of salt, and 3½ to 4½ cups of water, depending on the length of time the mixture will be cooked. It is not necessary to stir the mixture. Place the top of the double boiler into the bottom containing boiling water and allow the mush to heat slowly, cooking half an hour or longer. Many people claim the mush should cook slowly as long as four hours. Just before serving remove the top of the boiler from the bottom and place over direct heat to let the mush boil for two or three minutes. It is necessary that the meal boil at some point in the cooking in order to give it a satisfactory flavor, but by doing it at this point there is no danger of its lumping.

Milk may be used in place of all or part of the water, if desired.

The mush is now ready to be used as a hot cereal, served with milk or cream and sugar, or as a vegetable with melted butter. A particularly delicious variation is to stir in grated cheese in the proportion of ½ cup to 1 cup of meal just before the mush is taken from the fire.

The cooked mush may be packed into a bread pan or other convenient pan and allowed to cool. When firm, it can be sliced and rolled in beaten egg and cracker crumbs and fried. This makes a delicious dish served with sirup. In Italy the polenta is usually spread out on boards in rather thin sheets. When cold it is cut in small squares which are rolled in beaten egg and crumbs and fried in deep fat. Polenta is usually served with cheese and a savory tomato sauce.

White corn meal may be cooked with buttermilk to make a dish which resembles cottage cheese in its flavor. Use 1 cup of corn meal to 6 cups of buttermilk, and 1 teaspoon of salt. The dish may be eaten hot, but is especially good cold, served with cream. For this it may be molded in custard cups.

CORN MEAL FRUIT GEMS

½ cup corn meal
1 cup white flour
3 tsp baking powder
6 tbsp sugar
2 tbsp melted butter
1 tsp salt
1 cup milk
1 cup raisins or currants
2 eggs
1 tbsp flour

Mix and sift the dry ingredients. Add the milk gradually, the well beaten eggs, and the melted butter. Dredge the raisins in the tablespoon of flour and add to the rest of the ingredients. Stir well. Bake in greased gem pans in a hot oven (400°-425° F.) for 25 minutes. (Makes 12 gems)

CORN MEAL PANCAKES

2 cups white flour
½ cup corn meal
1½ tbsp baking powder
1½ tsp salt
⅓ cup sugar
1½ cups boiling water
1¼ cups milk
1 tbsp melted butter
1 egg

Stir the meal into the boiling water and boil 5 minutes. Turn into a bowl. Mix and sift the dry ingredients and add to the meal. Beat the egg well and add it. Lastly add the melted butter. Stir well. Bake on a greased griddle. (Serves 6)

CORN MEAL WAFFLES

1½ cups boiling water
1 cup white corn meal
1½ cups milk
3 cups white flour
3 tbsp sugar
1¼ tbsp baking powder
1½ tsp salt
2 eggs, separated
2 tbsp melted butter

Cook the meal in the boiling water for 20 minutes. Mix and sift the dry ingredients. Beat the egg whites until stiff and the yolks until thick and lemon colored. When the meal is done, add the milk and dry ingredients, the beaten yolks and the melted butter, mixing thoroughly. Lastly fold in the stiffly beaten whites. Bake on a waffle iron. (Serves 6)

These waffles are somewhat heartier than regular waffles, and make an excellent base for creamed chicken or similar dishes.

CORN DODGER

1 cup yellow corn meal
½ cup all-purpose flour
1¼ tsp salt
1½ tsp baking powder
2 tsp sugar
1 cup milk
1 egg
2½ tbsp hot bacon drippings, or shortening

Lift corn meal lightly into measuring cup. Sift flour, measure and put into sifter with the cornmeal. Add salt, baking powder and sugar, and sift into mixing bowl. Add the milk and stir until smooth, then add unbeaten egg and beat well. Heat the drippings in a 10-inch heavy skillet in the oven until sizzling hot. Drain out drippings into the cornbread batter. Quickly beat drippings into the batter, then turn immediately into the hot skillet. Bake in a hot oven (450° F.) for 30 minutes, or until golden brown. Serve piping hot cut into pie-shaped pieces. (Serves 4 or 5)

Corn Muffins

1 cup yellow corn meal
1 cup white flour
3 tsp baking powder
½ tsp salt
3 tbsp sugar
1 egg
1 cup milk
3 tbsp melted shortening

Mix and sift the dry ingredients. Combine the well beaten egg, milk, and shortening. Add to the flour mixture, stirring only enough to blend. Fill greased muffin tins ⅔ full and bake in a hot oven (400°-425° F.) for 20 or 30 minutes, depending on the size of the muffin. (Makes 14 medium-sized muffins)
Corn muffins may be varied by adding crisp crumbled bacon to the batter.

Corn Pone

3 cups white corn meal
2 tsp salt
1½ tsp baking powder
¼ cup milk
About 1½ cups water
⅓ cup butter or shortening

Combine the corn meal, salt and baking powder and moisten with the milk to which enough water has been added to make a drop batter. Let stand 10 minutes, add the melted butter or shortening and shape with the hands into thin small pats about five inches long. Place in a greased pan and bake in a hot oven (425° F.) about 20 minutes. Serve very hot. (Makes 1½ dozen)

Corn Sticks

1 cup corn meal
1¼ cups milk
¾ cup white flour
2 eggs
¼ cup molasses
4 tsp baking powder
1 tsp salt
2 tbsp vegetable oil
2 tbsp butter

Scald the milk and pour over the corn meal. Mix thoroughly and let cool until lukewarm. Sift together the flour, salt, and baking powder and add to the cooled corn meal mixture. Add the molasses and the well beaten eggs. Then stir in the oil and melted butter. Pour mixture into well greased bread-stick pan and bake in a hot oven (400°-425° F.) for 20 minutes.

Crackling Bread

1 cup corn meal
¾ tsp salt
½ cup cracklings
Boiling water

Cracklings are the crisp brown particles that are left after pork fat has been rendered. If the cracklings contain a great deal of fat, place them while still warm in a piece of clean cheesecloth and squeeze out part of the fat. Add the salt to the corn meal and pour boiling water over it until it is of such consistency that it can be mashed with the hand. Add the cracklings, shape into cakes, and bake in a hot oven (400°-425° F.) until the cakes are brown.

Sour Milk Corn Bread

2 eggs
½ tsp salt
1 tsp sugar
2 cups sour milk
1 tsp soda
¼ cup flour
½ lb corn meal
¼ cup melted shortening

Beat the eggs, add the salt and sugar, then the milk into which the soda has been stirred. Combine quickly with the sifted flour and corn meal. Stir in the melted shortening, lightly but thoroughly. Turn into a hot greased shallow pan and bake in a moderate oven (350°-375° F.) for 30 to 35 minutes.
Fresh milk may be used in place of sour, in which case omit the soda and sift 2 teaspoons of baking powder with the flour.

Spoon Bread
(Virginia Method)

1 cup yellow or white corn meal
2 cups sweet milk, scalded
3 tbsp butter

3 eggs
1 tsp salt
1 tsp sugar
2 tsp baking powder

Add the corn meal to the scalded milk, stirring constantly to prevent lumping. Put in the butter and beat and blend until smooth. Cool slightly; add the well beaten egg yolks, beating while adding. Stir in the combined salt, sugar and baking powder, mix thoroughly, and finally fold in the stiffly beaten egg whites. Turn into a well buttered baking dish or casserole, previously made hot, and bake in a hot oven (400° F.) about 30 minutes. Serve hot. The bread will be quite soft and may be served with a spoon.

CORN FLOUR. Corn flour is corn meal which has been ground and bolted until it is as fine as wheat flour. It is used by bakers and in sausage making, but is not ordinarily found on the retail market. In England corn flour denotes corn starch, the substance used for thickening sauces and puddings.

CORN POPPER. A pan in which to pop corn. It may be intended for use over a stove or fire, or may be heated electrically. The poppers for use over a fire have a long handle; the electric poppers are more compact. Ideally a corn popper should have a window so that the corn may be watched. However, almost any metal container with a closely fitting top may be used as a corn popper.

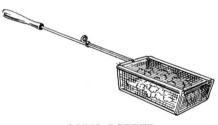

CORN POPPER

CORN SALAD. Another name for field salad, *which see.*

CORN SIRUP. Also known as sirup glucose. Corn sirup is manufactured from corn starch by treating it with an acid, the result being a wholesome article of food. Corn sirup varies in color from clear white to amber. It may be used as a table sirup or as sweetening, but it is not as sweet as cane sugar. It is particularly valuable in

candy-making because it does not crystallize and thus keeps the candy soft and of a desirable consistency.

It is possible to use corn sirup in preserving and canning, but special instructions are needed. It is also possible to use it as a sweetening in cake by making allowance for the extra liquid.

CORN STICK PAN. A corn stick pan is a baking pan somewhat similar to a muffin pan, but with the cavities shaped as individual ears of corn. The dough is, of course, baked in the shape of cavities, and the finished products are generally known as corn sticks. *See also* KITCHEN EQUIPMENT.

CORNED BEEF. Meat cured in a brine, much as with pickles. Originally it was preserved by dry salting—embedded or sprinkled with "corns of salt" (coarse). But as brining took the place of salting, the term still held, and we say "corned" beef instead of "brined" or pickled beef.

To cook corned beef, soak the meat in cold water for an hour (longer if very salty). Place in a kettle, and cover well with cold water, adding for each quart of water one teaspoon of vinegar. For 6 pounds of meat, add also a carrot and an onion. Simmer gently until tender, allowing 20 to 30 minutes per pound.

Cold cooked corned beef, sliced and prettily arranged with relishes on a cold platter, is a favorite for Sunday night suppers. You may serve a hot or cold horseradish sauce with it. This also makes a delightful sandwich combination.

CORNED BEEF AND CABBAGE

Cook corned beef as directed above, and about 20 minutes before the meat is done, wash the cabbage (a large head for the average family), quarter it, and add, cooking it right in the broth. Or cook the cabbage separately, shredding it if you like. To serve, lift the meat from the liquor, and drain well. Place on a large platter, surround with drained cooked cabbage, and top generously with melted butter. Peeled, halved potatoes may also be cooked with the meat and cabbage.

CORNED BEEF DE LUXE

4 lb brisket corned beef
8 potatoes
8 small white turnips

8 small carrots
8 small onions
1 large cabbage
Freshly grated horseradish
Mustard pickles

Soak the meat in cold water about one hour. Drain, cover with fresh cold water and bring very slowly to simmering point, never allow it to boil actively. Skim, if necessary, and continue the cooking until the meat is quite tender, three to four hours. Meanwhile prepare the vegetables according to their needs, and about half an hour before the beef is done put in the onions, carrots and turnips. The potatoes and cabbage will be cooked in separate pans, being sure not to overcook the latter. Slice the meat thinly for serving, garnish the platter with the colorful vegetables and serve with freshly grated horseradish and mustard pickles. This is sometimes known as New England Boiled Dinner.

CORNED BEEF HASH

A blend of cooked corned beef and and boiled potatoes which may be used in any desired proportions. Season with pepper, the meat is likely to make the hash sufficiently salty. Cook in a shallow pan, lightly greased, pushing the hash to one side of the pan when hot, that the surface may brown. Serve with tomato catsup or chili sauce, plain or topped with a poached egg. Corned beef hash is sometimes also turned into a deep pan and baked.

CORNED BEEF HASH (CANNED)

Canned corned beef hash is a time saver and the answer to many easy meals. Just turn into a pan, break up, heat and brown. Or, slice, roll in seasoned flour and brown. Again, slice, arrange in buttered shallow baking pan with a slice of onion or tomato on each round, season, brush with butter and broil.

CORNSTARCH. One of the most easily digested of starch foods, cornstarch is used for thickening sauces and puddings. Unlike flour, it cooks transparent, and will give a thickened translucent product. Cornstarch should always be dissolved in a little cold water before being added to a hot liquid, and it must be stirred constantly while boiling to prevent lumps.

For cornstarch pudding, see BLANC MANGE.

CORONADO. See AMBER FISH.

COS LETTUCE. Another name for romaine. See LETTUCE.

COSTMARY. This is a tansy-scented herb, the use of which coincides with that of TANSY proper (*which see*).

COSTMARY

COTELETTE. French name for cutlet.

COTHERSTONE CHEESE. A rennet cheese made from cow's milk. It resembles Stilton and is also known as Yorkshire-Stilton.

COTTAGE CHEESE. True to its name, cottage cheese probably originated with, or was most generously used by, the cottager or small farm-holder who thriftily utilized soured milk as a dish for his table. In old English manuscripts we find mention of *sawer ches*, and curious drawings showing the homemaker going through the various steps of making curds in her kitchen. Known in the cuisine of many lands under different names, as *smierkase*, pot cheese, etc., this solid form of pure milk, or semi-cheese as we might call it, enters into many famous as well as nourishing dishes. The special Easter dish of the Russians, *pascha*, is a well-blended mixture of cottage cheese (or cream cheese), pounded nuts and honey, packed into a decorative wooden mold of tower shape. When unmolded and wreathed with paper roses, it occupies the center of the heavily-laden Easter dinner table.

The Swedes, the Germans and the Austrians, all make distinctive dishes from cottage cheese. Some take the shape of filling for small pancakes, or fritters filled with cream cheese, or delicious morsels in breakfast breads. The familiar cheese cake is typical of the many cake mixtures to which this popular cheese is added, or it may be used as the lower layer of a fruit filling, as in pineapple-cheese pastry.

It blends so perfectly with various fruits and garnishes and adapts itself to so many different methods of serving in either hot or cold dishes, that the first essential is to become acquainted with some of these many delicious dishes. Almost every home-maker knows what a delightful combination cottage cheese and jam makes, yet few realize what an attractive, artistic dish can be made of it when placed in either ring or diamond shaped molds and served as a dessert with coffee and wafers, or almost any kind of berries, fresh or preserved.

In a salad or as a cold dish, served by itself, cottage cheese has few equals as a light lunch snack. For unusual flavors beat the cheese with a little sweet cream, and add such contrasted flavors as green chives, water cress, thinly sliced radishes, minced green pepper, or pimiento. These mixtures may be served on lettuce as salads, or spread on crackers as canapés.

Most nutrition specialists consider that a child needs an average of not less than a gram (0.03527 ounce) of calcium a day for the best rate of growth and for insuring good health. A quart of milk has little more than a gram of calcium—1.2 to be exact. Slightly more than half the calcium of milk is left in the whey when milk is converted into cottage cheese, but the remainder makes it still a good calcium food.

Home Made Cottage Cheese

To make cottage cheese at home, all that is necessary is to add part of a junket tablet to milk to make it coagulate, as one junket tablet is enough for three gallons of milk. A bit of arithmetic will easily decide what proportion to use for a smaller quantity. Dissolve the junket in cold water, add to the milk, and stir carefully until it is

evenly distributed. Let stand 12 hours, or overnight, at room temperature. Strain off the liquid through a white cotton cloth, such as a double cheesecloth, pressing all moisture out of the curd. Transfer to a dish. Season with salt and pepper, minced chives, or sugar. Or leave it entirely plain, or moisten with a little sweet cream.

Cottage cheese is a highly perishable product; it should be stored in the coolest place in your refrigerator, and be eaten as soon as possible. For other cheese recipes, see CHEESE.

COTTONSEED OIL. Composed principally of palmitin and olein, it is a valuable food. This oil and other vegetable oils are now frequently substituted for olive oil in the preparation and packing of various foods. Sardines which were formerly preserved in pure olive oil are now frequently packed in cottonseed and other oils. As a substitute for olive oil its use was greatly augmented by World War II.

COULIS. Strained juice from meat, fish, or poultry, thickened either with bread, flour, cornstarch, or other thickening agent.

COUMARIN. See TONKA BEAN.

COUPE. A frozen dessert. It is usually served in a special glass called a champagne coupe which is filled with a scoop of ice cream, garnished with whipped cream forced through a pastry bag and tube and decorated with candied fruits, chopped nuts, candied flowers, etc.

Coupe Baby's Dream

Garnish as many champagne coupes as required with a small scoop each of pineapple and raspberry ice cream. Between the two ice creams, arrange a line of small fresh strawberries, which have been washed and hulled, then soaked for 15 minutes in orange juice. Garnish each coupe with a small border of whipped cream, sweetened to taste and flavored with a few drops of vanilla extract. You may sprinkle a few crystallized violets, if available, over the whipped cream, which has been forced through a pastry bag with a small fancy tube. Serve at once.

Coupe Ganelin

2 squares grated chocolate
2 egg yolks, fresh and unbeaten
¼ cup heavy cream

2 tbsp powdered sugar
2 egg whites, stiffly beaten
6 scoops chocolate ice cream
Blanched chopped almonds (optional)

Combine the chocolate, egg yolks, and heavy cream, and whip, using rotary beater, until stiff and mixture holds up in peaks; then fold in the powdered sugar alternately with the stiffly beaten egg whites. Divide the mixture into six well-chilled champagne coupes. Place a scoop of chocolate ice cream in the center of each coupe, and dust, if desired, with blanched chopped almonds. Serve at once. (Serves 6)

COUPE HAVANA

2 cups honeydew melon, chilled then cubed small
1 rounded tbsp powdered sugar
⅛ tsp salt
1 tsp lime juice
1 cup mashed, sweetened strawberries
6 scoops vanilla ice cream
1 cup whipped cream

Chill the melon for at least 48 hours; peel and cube small; sprinkle with sugar, salt and lime juice. Divide mixture among 6 well-chilled champagne coupes. Place in center of each coupe a scoop of vanilla ice cream; cover the entire surface of each coupe with mashed sweetened strawberries and surround with a border of whipped cream, sweetened to taste and flavored with a few drops of vanilla extract, forced through a pastry bag with a small fancy tube. Serve at once.

COUPE JACQUELINE

Half-fill well-chilled champagne coupes with small cubes of fresh pineapple, soaked in a little brandy for 30 minutes, and thoroughly drained. Over this place a thin layer of apricots, sweetened to taste. Top with a small scoop each of pineapple and apricot ice cream, side by side, and between the two ice creams, arrange a line of well-chilled raspberries, which have been washed, hulled, then soaked for 15 minutes in orange juice. Garnish with a border of whipped cream, sweetened to taste and flavored with a few drops of maraschino liqueur, forced through a pas-

try bag with a small tube. The whipped cream may be tinted a delicate pink, if desired, or the whipped cream may be divided in two equal parts, each part tinted to taste. Serve at once.

COUPE JACQUES

Fill well-chilled champagne coupes with 2 scoops of ice cream, one lemon and the other strawberry, placed side by side. Between the two arrange a tablespoon of mixed fresh fruits, cubed very small and marinated in a little kirsch. Garnish with whipped cream, sweetened to taste and flavored with a few drops of vanilla extract, forced through a pastry bag with a small fancy tube. Serve at once.

COUPE PELL-MELL

1 pt vanilla ice cream
1 pt mixed fresh or canned fruit (prepared fruit for fruit cocktail)
Shredded, blanched almonds
Chocolate mint sauce
½ cup heavy cream, whipped

Prepare the fruit and chill. Prepare chocolate sauce as follows:

    ½ cup cocoa
    1 cup cold water
    2 cups granulated sugar
    ⅛ tsp salt
    1½ tsp vanilla extract
    ½ tsp essence of mint
    2 tbsp butter

Stir cocoa over direct heat with the water until smooth and thick. Add sugar and salt and stir until dissolved. Boil 3 long minutes, remove from the fire, and add vanilla and essence of mint (you may substitute ½ teaspoon more vanilla extract for essence of mint if desired); stir in butter, and when cold, store in an air-tight jar and keep in refrigerator until wanted. May be served hot, when reheated, with hot or warm dessert, and will keep very long in refrigerator.

Here is how to serve this delicious coupe. Divide the pint of vanilla ice cream equally among 6 well-chilled champagne coupes; likewise the fruit; then pour over two tablespoons of chocolate sauce; sprinkle each coupe with blanched, shredded almonds, and surround each coupe with a border of plain whipped cream, forced through a pastry bag with a small fancy tube. Serve at once. (Serves 6)

COUPE SABAYONNE

Beat 6 fresh egg yolks until thick, with 6 tablespoons of maraschino liqueur. Place over direct heat (low flame), and cook, stirring constantly from the bottom of the pan until mixture is of the consistency of mayonnaise. Allow to cool, fold in the stiffly beaten whites of 6 eggs. Chill well (about 2 hours) and when ready to serve, place a small scoop of vanilla ice cream in 6 well-chilled champagne coupes, and cover entirely with the sabayon cream. Stick in the cream a dozen (in each coupe) small sticks of blanched almonds. Serve at once. (Serves 6)

COUPE SUZETTE

In the bottom of a well-chilled champagne coupe, place 2 tablespoons of whipped cream, sweetened to taste and flavored with a few drops of vanilla extract. Place a scoop of pistachio ice cream in center, and sprinkle all around the ice cream 2 tablespoons of cleaned, rapidly washed and well-drained raspberries. Over the berries sprinkle a scant tablespoon of kirsch; top the entire surface with plain whipped cream (unsweetened and unflavored), forced through a pastry bag with a small fancy tube, and dust the entire surface with a tablespoon of maraschino cherries (green ones) chopped fine and squeezed through a clean cloth. Serve at once. (Serves 1)

COUPE VERNEUIL

Mash ½ dozen of large, ripe, well-washed, hulled fresh strawberries and combine with equal amount of sweetened, unflavored whipped cream. Chill well. When ready to serve, place the strawberry-whipped cream mixture in bottom of a well-chilled champagne coupe; place in center a scoop of macaroon ice cream; sprinkle with chopped pistachio nut meats; and cover the entire surface with whipped cream sweetened to taste and flavored with a few drops of vanilla extract, forced through a pastry bag, in pyramid shape that is pointed in center. Top with a large, nice, fresh strawberry. Serve at once. (Serves 1)

COURT BOUILLON. A French term indicating "short broth." Used in place of water when boiling various kinds of fish. There are several kinds in use, depending on the fish being cooked.

VINEGAR COURT BOUILLON

(For Large Pieces as Salmon or Large Trout)

2 qt cold water
⅔ cup vinegar
2 tbsp salt
2 small carrots, sliced
2 small onions, sliced
Few leaves of thyme
Small bouquet garni
12 peppercorns, slightly bruised

Place all ingredients, except the peppercorns, together in a fish kettle. Add the fish and cook gently just until tender, putting in the peppercorn 15 minutes before the fish is done.

White Wine Court Bouillon. (For Trout, Eel, Pike, etc.) Follow directions for Vinegar Court Bouillon, but use only one quart of water and substitute white wine for the vinegar.

Red Wine Court Bouillon. (For Trout, Carp and Fish Stew in general.) Follow directions for White Wine Court Bouillon, substituting red wine for white and adding one-third more of carrot and onions.

When fish are cooked with white or red wine court bouillon, they are usually served with a little of the broth containing some of the vegetable used, as a sauce. These vegetables should be always well done, the quantity of broth necessary reduced to a third of its original volume, and a little fresh butter added just before serving.

Milk or Cream Court Bouillon. (For large pieces of Turbot, Salmon, etc.) Cover the fish with salted cold water and add two-thirds cup of milk or cream for each quart of water with a peeled, seeded, slice of lemon. (No vegetables at all.)

COUS-COUS. A kind of polenta, made of coarsely ground semolina or cornmeal, steamed in beef, chicken, mutton stock, usually served separately with the meat or poultry used for the stock.

COW FISH. A sea fish common to North Carolina shores where it is considered excellent eating, baked or boiled in its bony shell. Occasionally a cow fish is caught as far north as Massachusetts, but this fish is a poor swimmer, its tail being like a rudder, its front part like a box. It has two horns or sharp spines projecting from its armored forehead. It is sometimes dressed and sold as skate wings or saddles, and belongs to the skate family (*which see*).

COWFISH

COW PEAS. *See* BEANS.

CRAB. Nature has attended to the matter of sanitation of the shores of the oceans and seas. To the lobsters, languostes, crabs, and other crustaceans, generally, have been assigned the task of keeping clean the immense areas of water. The stomach of these scavengers is perfectly equipped to receive all the refuse, to absorb and destroy it.

The crabs, of which there are more than a thousand species, are found all over the world and belong to the Arthropoda family. They supply food for edible fish, and are also esteemed as human food. The crab is in "berry" when the bristles of the under parts of the crab are crowded with red eggs. Even on the smaller crabs, there may be half a million, but on the mature and full-sized over two million eggs may be glued or impaled about the protected part of the crab's body. Prawns, those larger shrimp-like crustaceans, are netted, having eggs cluttering their curious legs. These eggs are guarded until hatching gives them means of escape.

With the crab eggs, this incubation takes many months. Not until summer warms up the sea-edges will the mother crab begin to brush off her young. The tiny crustaceans will not walk, but swim, looking first like young shrimp, then like lobsters, moulting three or four times before sinking to the sea floor, there to walk for the rest of their lives. These myriads of swimming crabs, so small that the sea-water is milky with them, are the relished food of countless fish from sea anemones to whales—hence, their millions.

The crab's growth is not gradual but by bounds, if not leaps. He carries his skeleton

outside his skin for protection, making it so hard that he cannot stretch it, nor can he add to it, as the oyster and clam do. When his armor becomes too tight, it must be cast off. This will not happen regularly but according to the plenitude of food he has found. His moulting is a very serious operation which must be done under the shelter of a stone or crevice in the rocks. Before growing he must reduce, withdrawing all the water possible from his system, and softening his muscles. The big shield on his back is loosened at the edges, to be finally pushed off.

Such castoffs are often seen on the shore. He draws up his legs and claws from their coverings and is a limp, defenseless creature when creeping from the old casing.

While soft, his skin expands, so the new armor must be larger. He has been carrying lime in solution in greater quantities than usual, and this begins to harden over his tender skin. He may eat up the smaller parts of his old skeleton to help in forming the new. He will be a finer fellow when he walks out again, but he is careful not to walk out too hurriedly. His gait seems curious to walkers on two legs. His footless, three-kneed legs move sideways; and, when he stops, he sits with legs forward and vicious claws before his legs, a defensive and an offensive attitude. Should he lose a leg in an encounter he may have an imperceptible limp until the next moult, when a new joint will appear, repairing the former damage.

The ebbing tide may leave him stranded, but that concerns him little. It is a youthful escapade to run from rock to rock or pool to pool in waterless air, as boys play in and out of water. Older crabs are more staid. They keep under water in the ebb-tide shallows. Several lie in an eelgrass pool, sheltered and well fed. One female, large as a man's head, resents disturbance, for underneath she bears her eggs.

MANY VARIETIES OF THE CRAB

These shellfish are found all along the Atlantic Seaboard down as far as Mexico.

From the waters of Chesapeake Bay alone, where the delicious *Blue* or *Common Crab* is found, hundreds of thousands are sent to market yearly, while huge quantities are also canned every year. The *King Crab*, sometimes called *Horseshoe Crab*, is found most plentifully at the mouth of the

Kennebec and Penobscot Rivers of Maine and along the Atlantic Seaboard as far as Mexico. In the southern states, it is called by the natives *Casserole Crab* from its resemblance to a saucepan or casserole. The *King Crab* is eaten only in the regions where found, and not being widely popular is seldom found in market.

The various methods employed in the preparation of the common crab may be adapted to these giant crabs.

Soft Shell Crabs, also known as *Shedders*, are crabs which have just shed their hard shell and are covered only by a soft skin; at this stage they are highly regarded by epicures. The little *Pea Crabs* or *Oyster Crabs* frequently found in oysters are most delicate and delicious morsels. They were known long before the days of Roman and Greek history.

The American Pacific Coast from Alaska to Mexico also provides the markets with huge quantities of common and large crabs, these latter known under the name of *Morro Crabs*.

PREPARING CRABS

Crabs should always be alive when purchased. To prepare soft crabs, stick a sharp knifepoint into the body between the eyes. Lift up the pointed ends of the shell and remove the spongy white fibers. Turn the crab on its back and remove the "apron" (ventral plaque) or small loose shell running to a point at about the middle of the under-shell. Wash the crabs and fry them at once. To prepare hard crabs, drop them headfirst into boiling salted water to cover, and cook for 20 minutes. Drain, rinse, and cool. Crack the shell and claws to obtain the meat.

Crabs are still a delicacy after the hard, new shell is grown. Behind that forbidding fortress is tender, flavorsome, white meat. Near the Chesapeake, where crabs are very plentiful, this meat may appear in one guise or another at nearly every meal. Boiled, it may be served simply with quartered lemon. Often it is served in neat little croquettes at the edge of the salad plate, or as a first course, or appetizer, or again as toothsome crab cakes delicately sautéed.

Perhaps the most highly esteemed of this host of luxuries from the sea are the soft-shelled crabs. Broiled or fried, soft-shelled crabs are delicious. When broiled, well seasoned melted butter is poured over them

as they come from the broiler. Although the usual way of frying soft-shelled crabs is the deep-fat method, many homemakers believe that sautéing is the best means of preserving the elusive flavor. Dusted with flour, the crabs are browned first on one side, then on the other. Serve garnished with parsley and cut lemon.

FRIED SOFT SHELLED CRABS

Clean the crabs, sprinkle with salt and pepper, roll in crumbs, then in beaten egg and again in crumbs. Fry in deep hot fat (360°–375° F.) 3 to 5 minutes. Drain on soft crumpled paper and serve with tartare sauce.

Being very light, the crabs will rise to the top of the fat while cooking and should be turned two or three times while frying.

SAVANNAH DEVILED CRABS

8 boiled crabs
4 large slices of bread, crumbled
¼ cup butter
1 tbsp Worcestershire sauce
Salt and pepper
Milk, to moisten
Tabasco sauce
Buttered crumbs

Remove the meat from the crabs and wash the shells carefully. Combine crabmeat, bread, butter, Worcestershire sauce, salt and pepper, and moisten with a little milk into which a dash of tabasco sauce has been stirred. The mixture should be rather soft. Pack loosely into the shells, top with buttered crumbs, and bake in a moderate oven (350° F.) until delicately browned and very hot.

CRABMEAT A LA KING

1 lb fresh or canned crabmeat, flaked
2 green peppers, finely chopped
¾ cup canned or fresh mushrooms, chopped
1 cup heavy cream
1 tsp salt
½ tsp paprika
⅛ tsp nutmeg
3 egg yolks
¼ cup sherry
1 tbsp minced chives

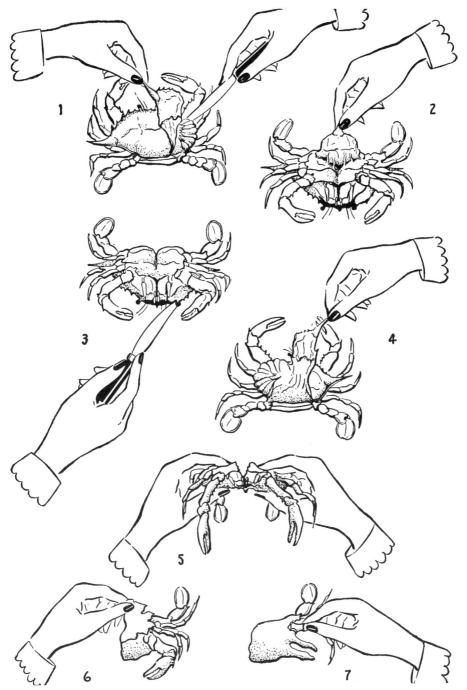

CLEANING A CRAB   1. Lift top shell and cut meat under both ends.   2. Lift up
pocket on under side and tear off.   3. Cut out eyes and area around them.   4. Tear off
all of top shell and then cut meat under both ends, lift up pocket on under side and tear
off.   5. Take crab, bottom up, and crack in half.   6. Skin off bottom shell.   7. Pull off
leg shells, leaving meat.

Combine crabmeat (carefully picked over), green peppers, mushrooms, cream, and seasonings. Simmer gently for 15 minutes, over boiling water, stirring frequently, but gently, so as not to mash the crab flakes. Add the egg yolks to the sherry and beat; then pour slowly into the crabmeat mixture, and continue to cook over a very low direct flame, stirring constantly, until slightly thickened, about two or three minutes. Serve at once on toast, in patty shells, or croustades.

CRABMEAT CAKES

1½ cups finely chopped raw potatoes
½ cup top milk
Dash each of cayenne, nutmeg and thyme
½ tsp salt
2 cups flaked crabmeat, fresh cooked or canned
2 eggs

Cook the potatoes in the milk over boiling water (double boiler) just until tender. Add seasonings, then the crabmeat and the eggs, slightly beaten. When blended, drop from a tablespoon onto a hot well greased griddle or heavy frying pan, brown slowly on both sides and serve hot with tartare sauce.

CRABMEAT COCKTAIL

Mix 1½ cups of flaked crabmeat with ½ cup of catsup and ⅓ cup of finely minced sour pickles. Chill, and serve in cocktail glasses. Or mix the flaked crabmeat with piquant sauce, *which see*. (Makes 6)

CRABMEAT SOUFFLE

1 cup crabmeat, fresh cooked or canned
3 tbsp butter
4 tbsp flour
1 cup milk, scalded
¼ tsp salt
⅛ tsp nutmeg
Dash of cayenne
1 tsp lemon juice
3 eggs

Pick over and flake the crabmeat. Melt the butter, stir in the flour, and when smoothly blended add the milk, stirring constantly over a low flame until smooth and thick. Add seasonings, cool, then work in the unbeaten egg yolks, crabmeat, and lemon juice, and fold in gently the stiffly beaten egg whites. Turn into a buttered soufflé dish or individual ramekins, set these in a pan of hot water and bake in a moderate oven (350° F.) until a knife inserted in the center comes out clean, 30 to 35 minutes if in large dish, 18 to 20 in small ones.

SAVORY CRABMEAT

1 pint crabmeat
3 eggs, beaten
½ cup butter
Pepper
½ tsp prepared mustard
½ tsp Worcestershire sauce
1 tsp salt
1½ cups rich or evaporated milk
1 tbsp minced green peppers
1 tbsp chives
1 tbsp parsley
½ cup buttered crumbs

Combine all ingredients except the crumbs. Turn into a deep buttered baking dish or casserole, sprinkle with the crumbs and bake in a moderate oven (350° F.) until piping hot and delicately browned. Serve immediately.

CRABAPPLE. The crabapple probably came from Siberia, northern China, and Manchuria, but has been cultivated for its fruit and flowers in China and Japan from time immemorial. The Chinese and Japanese have developed many forms differing in plant, fruit, and flower, more particularly in the flowers, these being of many colors, various sizes and in all degrees of doubling. The Siberian crabapple is the hardiest of the fruit trees. It grows quickly, thrives in many soils and bears year after year with increasing abundance.

Practically all the crabapples cultivated in the British Isles and the United States are hybrids of *Pyrrus malus* (the apple) and *Pyrus baccata* (the Siberian crabapple) and they are chiefly grown for their blooms, although their fruit is also used for the making of jams, jellies and preserves. *See* JELLY; *see also* APPLE.

The colorful crabapples are too sour to be eaten raw.

CRABAPPLE PICKLES

10 lb crisp, juicy Siberian crabapples
15 cups sugar
5 cups cider vinegar
5 cups water
1 tbsp whole cloves
2 tsp cassia buds
1 stick cinnamon

Wash crabapples thoroughly but do not remove stems. Pickle crabapples as soon as possible after picking before they become mellow. Well colored apples give the best looking product. Make a sirup by boiling the remaining ingredients for 3 minutes. Add 1¼ lb. apples (about 16 large) to approximately 2 cups of the boiling sirup for each quart jar. Simmer gently 1 to 2 minutes or until the apples crack slightly. Turn apples gently in the sirup once during the cooking. Pack carefully in quart jar, and cover with the boiling sirup. Seal according to the type of lid and process in boiling water bath for 15 minutes. Complete seal if necessary. Makes 8 quarts.

Note: Strain out spices when pouring sirup over apples in jars, if desired. The spices may darken the apples if they are left in the jar.

CRACKER MEAL. Crushed, sifted, unsweetened crackers (commercially packed) and used for coating croquettes, scallops, chops, cutlets and fish before frying. (*See* EGGING AND CRUMBLING.) Also as a topping for escalloped dishes and as a thickener for chowders. (*See also* CRACKERS)

CRACKERS. Crackers vary greatly in texture and flavor. The simplest type, such as water or milk crackers, are made with flour and water or milk, to which a little salt is added, after which they are baked until dry and crisp. If it is desirable to have them less crumbly, butter may be added in small quantity. The hard, unleavened type known as *ship biscuits, hard tack,* or *pilot biscuits* are so dry and firm that they are much less bulky than bread, and it is estimated that three-fourths of a pound of such biscuits is equivalent to one pound of bread in actual nutritive value.

Soda crackers, plain or salted, are most familiar and popular, as they are one of the most utilitarian of the wide variety offered the homemaker, in sanitary, convenient, packed form.

Any unsweetened cracker may be rolled or crumbled and used as a thickener for chowders, as an extender of the more expensive meat in a meat loaf, as a topping for escalloped dishes and in a score of other uses. (*See also* CRACKER MEAL)

Next in importance come sweet crackers to be eaten by themselves in place of the richer cake, to be crumbled as the base for many cake-type desserts, tortes, and ice box cakes, or for the making of crusts for certain pies, especially the popular chiffon type. Graham crackers are especially valuable for this particular purpose.

Rusks of all kinds may also be classed as crackers, their crumbs too being used in pastries and other desserts.

Crackers and cheese are too well known to need any eulogy and toasted crackers are quite literally at the bottom of many good looking and good tasting canapés and appetizers.

CRACKLING BREAD. *See* BREAD.

CRANBERRY. When the pilgrims landed in New England, the little crimson berry—now so popular on festal days—was a puny thing about the size of a pea,

CRANBERRY

growing wild in small patches. One gusty day down Cape Cod way, the sea broke through a strip of beach and spread a level three-inch carpet of sand over the best wild cranberry bog existing in those parts. When the people beheld the havoc of the storm the feeling was bitter. But when the smothered plants finally broke through the mantle of disaster, lo and behold, the harvest of berries was multiplied four times in quantity, size and flavor. Rough words against the elements died on the lips of the pilgrims and those who had spoken harshly of the rampant sea bestirred themselves to bring precious sand to aid in the

PREPARATION FOR MARKET

The loss between field and consumer has probably been greater with the cranberry than with any other fruit. Losses start in the field where sometimes as much as 30 percent of the crop is left by the pickers. A second loss occurs from natural shrink-

FOOD VALUE

	Wa- ter	Food Energy	Pro- tein	Fat	Car- bohy- drates	Cal- cium	Phos- phorus	Iron	Vit. A Value	Thia- mine	Riba- flavin	Nia- cin	Ascor- bic Acid
Cranber- ries	84.4	65	1.2	.8	13.2	36	34	.9	320	.03	.07	.3	23
Cranberry sauce	48.1	209	.1	.3	51.4	8	7	.3	30	—	.04	—	2
Dried cran- berries	4.9	409	2.9	6.6	84.4	82	22	3.4	660	.19	.18	.9	33

cultivation of all cranberries throughout the peninsula. So an ill wind brought riches upon its wings. Today the traveler through this section of New England gets a pleasant view of small, flat, vari-colored patches of earth given over to the propagation of the cranberry. It was originally called crane berry because the fruit hung from the multiple little stems or cranes, each berry by itself, and also from the appearance of the delicate little flower with its long central stamen which bears a real or fancied resemblance to the long bill of the crane.

KINDS OR VARIETIES

1. *Bennett.* Large size, oval in form, light red in color; late season; good keeper; will stand late picking.
2. *Centennial.* Largest variety grown in New Jersey; globose in form, light red in color; medium season; poor keeper.
3. *Early Black* (Late Red). Medium size, pearl-shaped to oval in form, dark crimson; early; fair keeper. It is the principal early sort in the East. The berries increase in size during early September and keep well if picked before they become too ripe.
4. *Howes* (Late Howe). Medium size, oval in form, good color; midseason; good keeper in western regions, but an uncertain keeper in Massachusetts. The leading variety in central Wisconsin, and among those liked best in the Oregon-Washington section.
6. *Searl* (Searl's Jumbo). Large size, oval in form, dark colored, midseason; fair keeper.

age of the berries due to respiration. Other losses occur from injury in handling the boxes of berries, in screening, and in packing, and often as a result of freezing and smothering.

Cranberries should be picked only when they are dry. They should not be gathered while the vines are wet. Experiments show that cranberries picked wet remain so a long time and generally do not keep well. They are picked three ways; first by hand picking, which has the advantage of getting most of the berries, when carefully done; second, by scooping with scoops or hand rakes, and third, by machinery, which is a very recent development and not yet widely used.

A foreman, 15 scoopers and 2 helpers make up a normal harvesting crew for a 15 acre field in Massachusetts. The helpers distribute the empty lug boxes, and pile them by a road and take the filled ones from the field. Hand barrows or wheeled barrows are commonly used in carrying the full boxes from the field to the roadsides. Little injury is done to the vines by carts or wheel barrows having pneumatic tires.

The berries are taken from the field to a storage house as quickly as possible after they are picked, particularly if the weather is hot. The direct effect of temperature on the life of cranberries and its indirect effect through the action of the fungi that cause decay make it doubly important that the berries be shaded in the field and cooled as soon as possible in storage if they are to remain first quality.

Cranberries vary in size and color according to the variety. They are rarely sold to the consumer under variety name. The most common on the markets are the rather large bright-red fruit and the small darker kind which are somewhat sweeter. All are sold by the pound or quart. One pound measures one quart and makes three to three and one-half cups of cooked sauce.

The consumer should look for lustrous berries, firm to the point of hardness.

HINTS ON PREPARATION

Sort berries without washing. Place in bowl or glass jar. Cover loosely and refrigerate. Wash just before using.

COOKED CRANBERRY APPLE SALAD

3 cups cranberries
1¾ cups water
1½ cups sugar
1 tbsp plain gelatin (1 envelope)
¼ cup cold water
2 apples, peeled
1 cup diced celery
Lettuce
Mayonnaise

Wash and pick over cranberries, cook covered until soft in the 1¾ cups water, then add sugar. Strain and rub pulp through sieve. Soften gelatin in the ¼ cup cold water. Reheat cranberry purée to boiling and add the softened gelatin, stirring until gelatin is dissolved. Pour a thin layer of cranberry gelatin into individual molds which have been rinsed in cold water. Chill in refrigerator until set; then arrange apple cut in thin wedges in design and pour in a little more gelatin to hold them in place; chill until set. Add rest of apples and celery to rest of gelatin mixture, pour into molds, and chill until firm. Unmold on lettuce leaves and serve with mayonnaise. (Serves 5)

CRANBERRY APPLESAUCE

2 cups cranberries
2 cups sliced apples
1 cup sugar
¾ cup water

Combine cranberries, apples, water and sugar. Cover and cook slowly until fruit is tender, about 20 minutes. Cool slightly and then beat with wire whip until fluffy and light.

Makes approximately 3 cups sauce.

CRANBERRY BORSCH

⅔ cup cranberries
1½ qt water
1 large onion, sliced
1 cup chopped cabbage
½ cup beet liquor
1 cup canned small beets
Salt
1 tbsp sugar
¾ cup sour cream
3 hard-cooked eggs

Boil cranberries in water about 10 minutes, or until skins have popped; force through sieve. Add onion and cabbage, and boil about 20 minutes or until soft. Add beet liquor and beets, cut in strips julienne style; season with salt and sugar, and pour into hot soup plates; add 2 tablespoons sour cream and half an egg sliced, to each plate. If served cold, chill thoroughly before serving. Garnish the cold soup with whipped sour cream or unsweetened fresh cream. (Serves 6)

CRANBERRY CAKE

2 cups cranberries
1 seedless orange
¼ cup seeded raisins
5 tbsp butter, melted
¾ cup sugar
1 package (14 oz) gingerbread mix
Heavy cream, whipped

Put the cranberries and orange through food chopper, using finest knife; mix with raisins. Pour melted butter into 9-inch square pan and sprinkle evenly with sugar. Spread the fruit mixture over top and cover with gingerbread mix, prepared according to directions on package. Bake in moderate oven (350° F.) for 40 to 50 minutes. Loosen cake from sides and bottom with spatula and turn out on cake plate. Serve with whipped cream. (Makes nine 3-inch squares)

Cranberry Catsup

4 lb cranberries
1 lb onions, chopped
2 cups water
4½ cups sugar
2 cups vinegar
1 tbsp each of:
cloves
cinnamon
pepper
allspice
salt

Combine cranberries, onions, water; cook until tender and rub through sieve. Add sugar, vinegar and cloves, cinnamon, pepper, allspice, and salt; boil until thick, pour into clean hot jars and seal at once. This should be somewhat thinner than tomato catsup. It has a tendency to thicken as it stands. (Makes approximately 3 pint jars catsup)

Cranberry Conserve

1 qt cranberries
1½ cups water
¼ lb seedless raisins, chopped
½ lb broken walnut meats
1 large orange, cut small
1½ lb sugar

Wash and pick over the cranberries, then cook in the water until all the berries have burst. Add all remaining ingredients and cook 25 minutes, stirring frequently and skimming if necessary. Turn into small sterilized jars and seal. (About 6 8-ounce glasses)

Cranberry Foamy Sauce

⅓ cup butter or margarine
1 cup confectioner's sugar
1 egg separated
¼ cup sweetened cranberry juice

Cream butter until soft; gradually beat in sugar, then egg yolk and cranberry juice. Just before serving fold in the stiffly beaten egg white. For variety flavor with 1 tablespoon brandy. Serve with steamed fruit pudding. (Makes approximately ¾ cup sauce)

Cranberry Frappe

1 qt hot strained unsweetened cranberry pulp
2 cups sugar
1 tbsp lemon juice
Grated rind 1 small orange

Combine the cranberry pulp and sugar and stir until the sugar is thoroughly dissolved. Cool, add the lemon juice and orange rind, chill and freeze using either hand freezer or automatic refrigerator. (*See* APRICOT FRAPPÉ.) (Serves 6 to 8)

Other berries, such as strawberries or raspberries, may also be used for frappés proceeding as indicated above, substituting the desired fruit for cranberries and possibly modifying the amount of sugar slightly for sweeter fruits.

Cranberry Ice

4 cups cranberries
2½ cups granulated sugar
3½ cups boiling water
⅛ tsp salt
½ cup orange juice
¼ cup lemon juice

Pick and wash cranberries. Combine sugar, water and salt and boil for 5 long minutes; add washed cranberries and cook 10 minutes longer, over a low flame, until berries are softened. Rub through a sieve, cool, then add combined orange and lemon juice. Chill, then freeze in refrigerator tray to a solid mush (about 2 hours). Serve in sherbet glasses.

Cranberry Jelly

1 lb (4 cups) cranberries
2 cups sugar
2 cups water

Pick over and wash cranberries in colander; drain. Boil cranberries and water about 20 minutes, or until skins are broken; force through sieve. Bring pulp to a boil, add sugar and boil 3 to 5 minutes, stirring until sugar is dissolved. Skim and pour into one large, or several small molds, or pour into jelly glasses; to keep jelly for some time, seal jars with paraffin. (Makes 1 large mold, or approximately 4 8-ounce glasses)

CRANBERRY JELLY WITH GRAPE

1 cup cranberry juice
1 cup tart apple juice
1 pt Concord grape juice
2¼ cups (1 lb) sugar

Mix juices and boil 5 minutes; skim, if necessary. Add sugar; stir until dissolved and boil rapidly until jelly sheets from edge of spoon. Pour into clean glasses. Paraffin when cool. (Makes 8 6-ounce glasses)

CRANBERRY JUICE COCKTAIL

2 cups cranberries
3 cups water
½ cup sugar
2 tbsp lemon juice

Cook cranberries and water about 5 minutes, or until skins pop open; strain through cheesecloth. Boil juice and sugar 2 minutes, stirring until sugar is dissolved; add lemon juice and chill thoroughly. Serve in small cocktail glasses. *See* GLASS-WARE. (Serves 6)

CRANBERRY MUFFINS

1 cup chopped raw cranberries
½ cup sugar
2 cups all-purpose flour
3 tsp baking powder
½ tsp salt
2 tbsp sugar
1 egg
1 cup milk
¼ cup melted shortening

Combine chopped cranberries and ½ cup sugar. Sift flour, measure and resift 3 times with baking powder, salt, and the 2 tablespoons of sugar. Beat egg, add milk and beat well; add melted shortening and immediately add all at once to dry ingredients, mixing until dry ingredients are just dampened; batter is not smooth. Stir in cranberries with the last few stirs until just distributed, and quickly dip batter into well-greased muffin pans, filling ⅔ full. Bake in hot oven (400° F.) for 20 to 25 minutes. (Makes 12 large or 16 medium muffins)

CRANBERRY PIE

Prepare 10-minute cranberry sauce (*which see*) slightly thickening it if desired, with cornstarch, tapioca, or flour. When cold turn into a 9-inch pastry-lined pie plate, place strips of pastry lattice fashion over the top and bake in a hot oven (450° F.) for 20 minutes, after which reduce to moderate (350° F.) and cook until the pastry is tender, about 15 minutes longer.

CRANBERRY PIE WITH RAISINS

1 recipe plain pastry
1 cup cranberries, cut in halves
1 cup raisins
¾ cup sugar
½ tbsp flour
Dash of salt
1 tbsp butter

Line a 9-inch pie plate with pastry. Mix together fruits and dry ingredients, and turn into pastry-lined plate; dot with butter and adjust top crust, or arrange lattice of pastry strips over top. Bake in hot oven (450° F.) 10 minutes, then reduce heat to moderate (350° F.) and bake 30 to 40 minutes longer.

CRANBERRY PUDDING

½ lb cranberries washed and cut in halves
½ cup butter
1 cup sugar
2 eggs beaten
3 cups freshly grated breadcrumbs
½ tsp cinnamon
½ tsp soda
2 tbsp finely cut orange rind
½ cup sultana raisins, scalded and chopped
¼ cup milk

1½ quart melon mold with cover, well buttered. Stir the butter hard with a wooden spoon until soft and creamy. Add the sugar and beat until light and fluffy. Add the eggs and beat thoroughly. Mix the breadcrumbs, cinnamon, and the soda and stir into the mixture. Add the orange rind, raisins and milk and mix well. Mix in the cranberries. Turn into a mold, cover, and steam for three hours. Serve with hard sauce flavored with brandy. (Serves 6)

CRANBERRY REFRIGERATOR CAKE

3 cups cranberries
1¼ cups water
⅓ cup seedless raisins
10 dates, finely cut
3 figs finely cut
⅓ cup chopped walnut meats
1 cup sugar
1 small sponge cake, sliced

Cook cranberries slowly in water until skins have popped; force through sieve. Add raisins, dates, figs, and nuts and mix; simmer, covered, for 5 minutes. Remove from heat and add sugar. Line a greased mold with sponge cake, add a layer of cranberry mixture, a layer of cake, and repeat, finishing with cake. Chill in refrigerator. Unmold and serve with whipped cream. (Serves 6 to 8)

CRANBERRY RELISH WITH CITRUS FRUITS

4 cups cranberries
1 orange
1 lemon
1 lime
1 cup sugar

Pick over and wash cranberries and put through food chopper, using fine knife. Wash orange, lemon and lime, slice and remove seeds and put through food chopper; mix with sugar and cranberries. Chill in refrigerator several hours before serving. This may be packed in scalded glasses and sealed with paraffin. Excellent with meats. (Makes approximately 1 quart relish)

CRANBERRY RING SALAD

4 cups cranberries
1½ cups sugar
1 cup water
1½ tbsp gelatin
¼ cup cold water
1 tbsp lime juice or lemon juice
⅔ cup coarsely chopped walnuts
1 cup diced celery
Watercress or endive
French dressing (*which see*)

Pick over and wash the cranberries. Boil the sugar and water together for five minutes. Add the berries and cook slowly, without stirring, until they burst (about 5 minutes). Soften the gelatin in the cold water, then dissolve in the hot sauce. Add the lime or lemon juice, cool and when beginning to thicken, stir in the walnuts and celery. Turn into a wet ring mold, chill and unmold for service. Garnish with watercress or endive and pass French dressing separately. If desired, the center may be filled with cottage cheese moistened with a little sour cream.

CRANBERRY SALAD I

1 orange
2 cups cranberries
¼ cup sugar
1 package lemon gelatin
1¾ cups water
Lettuce
Mayonnaise or boiled dressing

Peel the orange thinly, discarding all white membrane. Pass orange and rind through the food chopper with the cranberries, carefully picked over, washed and drained. Add the sugar. Prepare the gelatin according to the directions on the package, cool and when almost at setting point, combine the two mixtures. Turn into a previously wet mold, chill, unmold, and serve on lettuce with mayonnaise or a boiled dressing. (Serves 6)

CRANBERRY SALAD II

2 cups cranberries
½ cup water
1 cup sugar
1 (3½ oz) package cream cheese
¼ tsp salt
Dash cayenne
Dash nutmeg
Lettuce, watercress or other salad green
Mayonnaise

Pick over and wash the cranberries, add the water, and cook, gently mashing and stirring until boiling point is reached. Now cook vigorously for ten minutes, stirring frequently. Press through a sieve, add sugar and again bring to boiling point to make sure that the sugar is dissolved. Turn into a shallow wet pan, cool then chill and cut into cubes or into balls with a vegetable cutter. Season the cheese with salt, cayenne, and nutmeg, and mold it into small balls the size of the jellied cranberry. Arrange on shredded lettuce, watercress, or other salad green. Serve with mayonnaise.

OLD-FASHIONED CRANBERRY SAUCE

2 cups water
2 cups sugar
Grated rind 1 orange
4 cups cranberries

Cook together the water, sugar and orange rind for 5 minutes. Pick over, wash and add the cranberries, then cook just until the berries cease popping, about 5 minutes. Do not stir. Serve cold.

MOLDED CRANBERRY SAUCE

4 cups cranberries
2 cups water
2 cups sugar

Pick over and wash, then cook the cranberries and water together until all the berries burst. Strain, rubbing as much as possible of the pulp through the sieve. Add the sugar, stir until dissolved, then boil rapidly until a few drops tested on a cold plate jell, (220° F.) 12 to 15 minutes. Turn into a wet mold or molds and chill. Unmold for service.

CRANBERRY SHERBET

1 lb fresh cranberries
2 cups water
1¼ cups sugar
Grated rind 1 orange
1 cup orange juice
¼ teaspoon salt
Juice 1 medium-sized lemon
2 egg whites

Cook the washed, picked over cranberries and the water for 10 minutes, or until the berries burst. Rub through a fine sieve while still hot—there should be 2 cups of juice; if not, add enough hot water to compensate. Add the sugar, stir until dissolved, bring to boiling point, then remove from the fire and strain through doubled cheesecloth. Add the orange juice and rind,

the salt and lemon juice. Chill, fold in the stiffly beaten egg whites and freeze in hand freezer as directed. (Serves 6 to 8)

CRANBERRY STUFFING I

2 cups ground cranberries
½ cup butter
½ cup sugar
8 cups coarse fresh bread crumbs
2 tsp salt
¼ tsp pepper
1 tbsp sage
2 tsp thyme
½ cup chopped celery
3 tbsp minced parsley
1 cup water

Cook cranberries in butter slowly about 5 minutes, then stir in sugar. Mix together crumbs, seasonings, celery, and parsley; add with water to cranberry mixture, and cook about 8 minutes, or until blended, stirring constantly. Approximate yield, 6 cups stuffing or enough for large pork crown roast. (*See also* STUFFING)

CRANBERRY STUFFING II

1 cup chopped cranberries
¼ cup sugar
¼ cup chopped celery
2 tbsp minced parsley
¼ cup melted butter
4 cups dry bread crumbs
½ tsp sweet marjoram
1 tsp salt

Combine the berries and sugar, and let stand ½ hour. Sauté the celery and parsley in the butter, add the crumbs and seasonings, also the sugared fruit, and blend thoroughly. (*See also* STUFFING)

CRANBERRY TAPIOCA

3 tbsp quick-cooking tapioca
1½ cups boiling water
1½ cups cranberries
¾ cup cold water
¾ cup sugar
Grated rind of 1½ oranges

Add tapioca slowly to boiling water and cook 5 minutes or until clear, stirring constantly. Add cranberries to cold water and cook until berries pop; add sugar and orange rind and cook 5 minutes; stir in cooked tapioca and chill. (Serves 6)

SPICED CRANBERRY CONSERVE

3 qt cranberries
Grated rind 1 large orange
Grated rind and juice 1 large lemon
Juice 6 large oranges
2 cups seedless raisins, chopped
6 lb sugar
3 cups water
½ tsp ground mace
⅛ tsp ground allspice
2 tbsp cider vinegar
1 cup broken pecans

Place all ingredients, except the pecans, in a large kettle, first carefully washing and stemming the cranberries. Stir to blend thoroughly and let the mixture stand for three hours. Now bring slowly to boiling point and cook 30 minutes, stirring frequently. Skim if necessary, add the pecans, cook three minutes longer. Turn into small sterilized jars and seal. *See also* JAM. (About 6 pints)

STEAMED CRANBERRY PUDDING

2½ cups sifted flour
4 tsp baking powder
½ tsp salt
½ cup shortening
1 cup sugar
2 eggs, well beaten
½ cup milk
1½ cups cranberries
Cranberry sauce (*which see*), unjellied

Mix and sift flour, baking powder and salt. Cream shortening and add sugar gradually, beating thoroughly after each addition; beat in eggs. Add flour alternately with milk, beating until smooth after each addition; stir in cranberries. Turn into greased tube pan or other deep baking pan, filling pan ⅔ full; cover with greased paper. Place on rack in kettle of boiling water; have water come up half-way around pan. Cover kettle and steam 2 to 3 hours. Keep water boiling gently, adding more hot water as needed. Serve with cranberry sauce. (Serves 6)

CRAPE-FISH. Cod fish salted and pressed.

CRAPPIE. An edible fresh-water fish of the Mississippi valley.

CRAW. The first stomach or crop of a bird. It is edible.

CRAWFISH. See CRAYFISH.

CRAYFISH. The crayfish is one of Nature's wonders. Very tiny when born, it is enveloped in a shell which seemingly would deprive it entirely of elasticity, and prevent it from moving.

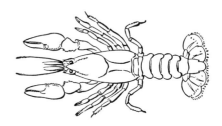

CRAYFISH

Growing up, it will change its dress. It lies on its back at the bottom of the river, shakes its tiny tail protruding from under the stiff shield, rubs its claws, moves its head, swings its feelers, flutters about, and inflates itself. All this is done patiently and methodically. Under these repeated exercises and efforts, the under part of its carapace splits open, and the crayfish emerges gradually, first the head, then the eyes, next the abdomen, claws, feelers, and finally the tail.

The crayfish is thus practically nude, having on just a filmy cellophane-like coat. Now once more it depends upon its own efforts, and immediately from its pores a viscous secretion is exuded, weaving a new dress to its shape. Very soon this shell-fish reappears on the sand of the river with a brand new and well fitting garment, coquettishly choosing the spot where the sun shines. This shellfish is its own architect, its own builder, its own dressmaker, and its own physician all at the same time. Nature has indeed marvellously attended to all the details.

The crayfish feeds on plants and animals. One of the simple water plants, Chara, furnishes it with lime for its skeleton. The mouth of the crayfish is just back of the mandibles and connects with the stomach by a short esophagus. The stomach is divided into two sections, the front possessing a grinding structure known as the gastric mill, which serves to shred and crush the food and prepare it for digestion in the rear section. The liver, or digestive gland, pours a fluid into the stomach, which prepares the food for absorption by the walls of the stomach and intestine. The intestine begins at the rear of the stomach and extends to the last segment.

The crayfish obtains oxygen from the water by means of gills which are well covered by the overhanging skeleton of the head-thorax region.

Hints on Preparation

Crayfish has been used for centuries for food in Europe, while in France crayfish breeding has been successfully practised for many years in order to increase the supply. In the United States frozen crayfish is openly sold under fancy names, such as South African Lobster Tails, Langoosta, Rock Lobster, Frozen Lobster Tails, Spiny Lobsters, etc. In cookery, crayfish, sometimes spelled crawfish is of three kinds: the small, used for pottages; the medium, used for garnishing; and the large, used in various cookery processes.

Crayfish should always be thoroughly washed and the green thread running the length of the tail should be removed, as with lobster. Practically all the recipes applied to shrimps and lobsters may be adapted to this delicious crustacean.

Crayfish a la Viennoise

Allow two or three crayfish for each serving, depending on their size. Cook in a white wine Court Bouillon (which see) about 15 minutes or until red. Lift them out and reduce the liquid in the pan by boiling until only a cupful remains. Thicken this to mayonnaise consistency with butter, season with paprika, pour over the fish and sprinkle with chopped parsley.

Crayfish Mariniere

3 dozen small crayfish
⅓ cup butter
2 tbsp finely chopped onion
2 tbsp finely chopped celery
White wine to cover
Salt and pepper
Butter (additional)
Lemon and parsley

Sauté the well washed crayfish in the ⅓ cup of butter with the onion and celery for about 10 minutes, or until the fish are red through and through. Pour the wine over them, season, and simmer about 15 minutes. Arrange in a mound on a hot platter and keep hot. Reduce the liquid remaining in the pan to one cupful by rapid boiling, strain, then beat in butter to thicken to mayonnaise consistency. Pour this sauce over the fish and sprinkle with minced parsley. Garnish with cut lemon and parsley. (Serves 6)

For crayfish à la Newburg, proceed exactly as for shrimp or lobster à la Newburg, which see.

CREAM. (I) The rich, fatty, aggregation of oil globules found in MILK, which see.

CREAMING

CREAM. (II) To work one or more foods until smooth and creamy with a spoon or spatula, rubbing the food against the sides of the mixing bowl until of the consistency of cream, as in creaming shortening, or shortening and sugar, in making cakes and cookies. Creaming may also be done with the hands or by using the slow speed on an electric mixer.

CREAM. (III) A rich filling for cakes, eclairs, cream puffs, flans, or fancy tarts. In warm weather pastries filled with cream must be kept under refrigeration to guard against food poisoning.

It is somewhat similar to a custard filling, but generally easier to handle in cooking than a true custard.

CREAM
(for Filling)

¾ cup sugar
⅓ cup flour
¼ tsp salt
2 tbsp butter
4 egg yolks
2 cups milk
1 tsp vanilla

Scald the milk and beat the egg yolks slightly. Combine the dry ingredients and mix with the eggs. Stir in enough milk to make a thin paste, and add to the remaining milk in the top of a double boiler. Cook for 5 minutes, stirring constantly and then cook 10 minutes longer, or until the mixture is thickened, stirring occasionally. Stir in the butter and remove from the hot water. Cool and add the vanilla. (Makes about 2½ cups)

CREAM PIE

1⅝ cups milk
½ cup sugar
½ tsp salt
¼ cup pastry flour
2⅔ tbsp cornstarch
1 whole egg plus 1 egg yolk
1 tbsp butter
½ tsp vanilla or other flavoring
9-inch pre-baked pie shell

Combine half the milk with the sugar and salt in the upper part of the double boiler. Stir until the sugar is dissolved, then place over a moderate heat and bring slowly to boiling point. Moisten the flour and cornstarch with the remaining milk and stir this into the scalded mixture. Add the beaten egg and egg yolk and cook over hot water (double boiler) five minutes, stirring constantly. Transfer to a cold bowl and add the butter and flavoring. When partly cooled, turn into the pre-baked pie shell. If desired, top with a meringue and place in a moderate oven (350° F.) to set and delicately color the meringue.

Coffee Cream Pie. Follow directions for cream pie substituting one cup of very strong coffee for one cup of the milk.

Peach Cream Pie. Arrange a layer of sliced peaches in the pre-baked pie shell before pouring in the cream mixture. Serve with a whipped cream topping.

CREAM CHEESE. A mild cheese made from rich cream, thickened by souring; or from sweet cream thickened with rennet. It may be wrapped in small tin foil or parchment paper packages weighing about three and a half ounces; or it may be in loaf form, packed in foil or parchment paper-lined boxes, and weigh from three to five pounds. This cheese is mildly acid, does not readily sour and keeps well. *See also* CHEESE.

CREAM NUT. *See* BRAZIL NUT.

CREAM PITCHER. Also called a *creamer;* a small jug used to dispense cream or milk at the table. *See also* DISHES.

CREAM PUFFS

CREAM PUFF. A very light, delicate, hollow puff of French origin, usually served as a dessert with a whipped cream or custard filling. Also used with savory fillings, sometimes even with chicken or lobster salad. Occasionally made very small and filled with some savory tidbit as cocktail accompaniments. *See also* PASTRY.

CREAM PUFF
(or Eclair Pastry)

1 cup boiling water
½ cup butter
1 cup pastry flour
3 eggs

Put boiling water and butter together in a saucepan and bring to boiling point. Sift, then add the flour all at once and cook, stirring constantly, until the mixture forms a smooth compact mass, leaving the sides of the pan clean. Now add the unbeaten eggs, one at a time, beating each in very thoroughly before adding the next

Then place in portions on a greased baking sheet, either by shaping with two spoons or forcing through a pastry bag using a plain tube. Allow enough space between the puffs for them to expand while baking. Bake in a hot oven (400° F.) about 30 minutes. When cool, with a sharp knife make a small cut in one side of each puff to admit the filling which can be forced in with a pastry bag and small tube.

The only difference between cream puffs and éclairs lies in the shape. Cream puffs are round, éclairs long and slender—this shape being best attained by forcing the mixture through a pastry bag.

Almost any kind of filling may be forced into cream puffs—such as custard cream filling, ice cream, chocolate cream filling, coffee custard cream filling, etc. If ice cream is used, fill the cream puffs at the moment of serving. Cream puffs or éclairs may be made from the size of a walnut to the size of a large egg. Cream puffs filled with sweetened, flavored whipped cream, either plain or colored, are an ideal tidbit for tea time, for dessert, or special parties. The cream puffs or éclairs may be iced with a thin butter icing in white, chocolate, or mocha—this last being very delicious and "French." The above recipe makes 12 large puffs or éclairs.

CREAM SAUCE. *See* WHITE SAUCE.

CREAM SOUP CUP. A large, double-handled cup that is somewhat broader and shallower than the regular soup cup, intended for individual servings of cream soups, etc. *See* DISHES, *see also* TABLE SETTING AND SERVICE.

CREAM SOUP SPOON. *See* FLATWARE

CREAM OF TARTAR. A product made for the argol deposit of grape juice after this is fermented. It has been known for generations as an ingredient in certain baking powders.

CREAMED BUTTER. *See* BUTTER SAUCES. *See also* CANAPE.

CREAMER. A common name for a *cream pitcher;* a small pitcher or jug used to dispense cream or milk at the table. *See also* DISHES.

CREME. A term used to distinguish those liqueurs, usually French, that have an unusual amount of sweetness. The term generally given in conjunction with the name of the plant or fruit whose flavor predominates in the liqueur.

Because of their extreme sweetness, these liqueurs are only served in small quantities, usually immediately following dinner, when served alone, and are more commonly used as flavoring ingredients in cocktails and other mixed drinks. One of their more colorful uses is in the spectacular POUSSE CAFE (*which see*).

Some of these liqueurs are:

Crème de Bananes. A sweet, banana-flavored liqueur.

Crème de Cacao. Made by distilling fine spirits over genuine cacao leaves, this sweet liqueur tastes of both cocoa and vanilla. One of the more popular liqueurs, it is served either alone or in cocktails.

Crème de Cassis. Sirupy, a dark ruby color that is almost black, this liqueur made of spirits and black currants is used both as a flavoring ingredient or is served alone, diluted with water, as a long drink.

Crème de Mandarine. A sweet liqueur made from pure, aged brandy and the peels of blood oranges.

Crème de Menthe. Possibly the most popular of liqueurs, it tastes of fresh mint and is made in two colors; green and white. It has an extremely refreshing taste and acts as a digestive. It is commonly served after dinner, either straight or poured over shaved ice, or between meals, diluted with water, in addition to use in various cocktails and other mixed drinks.

Crème de Moka. This sweet liqueur is made from old, fine spirits and the essential oil of Mocha coffee.

Crème de Noix. A sweet liqueur that is flavored with walnuts.

Crème de Noyau. A sweet liqueur, flavored with the crushed stones of fruits, commonly sloe cherries. Truly delicious, it is well suited to be served with desserts or used as a flavoring for some beverages.

Crème de Rose. A delicious pink liqueur that has the odor of roses.

Crème d'Orange. A dark, flame-colored after-dinner liqueur made of sun-ripened Spanish cherries and oranges that are infused with fine, aged brandy in France.

Crème de Violette. A sweet liqueur with the taste and odor of violets.

Crème d'Yvette. A sweet, violet-colored liqueur that was made in Connecticut, rather than France. *See also* LIQUEUR.

CREME BRULE. Translated as "burned cream," this delicious dessert is nothing more than custard with caramelized sugar. The sugar is caramelized in a skillet and when it is nice and brown, it is poured into the bottom of a fireproof baking dish. The dish is tilted and held for a few minutes so that the sugar will harden up the sides. Then a conventional baked custard mixture (*see* CUSTARD) is poured in, and the pudding baked in a pan of water as is an ordinary custard. When the pudding is chilled and just before serving, the top is sprinkled with more sugar, and the dish run under the broiler flame for a few seconds to melt and brown the topping. Then serve immediately.

CREOLE SAUCE. A sauce suitable for service with many things, omelets, poached eggs, fish and leftover dishes of meat, poultry and game.

CREOLE SAUCE

4 tbsp butter
1 large onion, sliced
1 large green pepper, sliced
½ cup sliced fresh mushrooms
1½ dozen small green olives
1 cup stock
1 No. 2 can tomatoes
Salt
Pepper
Cayenne
Small bay leaf
Small pinch of thyme
1 clove, crushed
1 tbsp sherry or white wine, optional

Melt and heat the butter and cook the onion and pepper in it over a moderate heat for about 5 minutes, stirring occasionally. Add the mushrooms, and the olives, stoned and quartered, and cook about 5 minutes longer. Now add the stock (which may be fish stock if the sauce is to be used with fish), the tomatoes, seasonings and flavorings, and simmer all gently for 20 minutes. Add the wine if used. The sauce is intended to be spicy although with a slightly sweet flavor.

CREPES. The French name applied to pancakes. (*See also* GRIDDLE CAKES AND BUCKWHEAT CAKES.)

CREPES SUZETTE. A delicate French pancake, served with a luscious rich sauce. There are several versions of these, the most popular of which is made as follows. There are three separate operations, the preparation of the orange butter, the making and baking of the crepes themselves, and finally the liqueur sauce.

ORANGE BUTTER

½ lb sweet butter
2 tbsp powdered sugar
Grated rinds 1 medium size orange and 1 medium size lemon
Dash of salt
Juice ½ orange

Cream the butter and sugar together and gradually add the combined remaining ingredients, continuing the creaming until throughly blended. Store, covered, in refrigerator until needed.

BATTER FOR CREPES

1 cup sifted pastry flour
2 tbsp sugar
⅓ tsp salt
3 eggs
1 cup milk

Sift together the flour, sugar and salt. Gradually add the eggs, unbeaten, and the milk, beating and stirring to make a perfectly smooth batter. Strain.

Butter very slightly a small frying pan about 5 inches in diameter (with two or three such pans one can turn out the crêpes much faster). Now pour a very small amount of the batter, about a tablespoon or just enough to cover the bottom of the pan, tilting this as the batter is poured in, so as to cover the entire bottom of the pan, very thinly. It is highly important that the cakes be thin. Turn with a spatula to cook and brown both sides, and keep hot. Grease the frying pan before each addition of batter, preferably using a pastry brush dipped in butter.

LIQUEUR SAUCE

This most important part of the recipe is prepared at the dining table. Have before you a chafing dish (blazer only), have also the stack of crêpes, the orange butter and three different liqueurs; Benedictine, Grand Marnier, and Cognac. Ignite the alcohol burner of the chafing dish or turn on electric current, and when the pan is warm, drop into it two tablespoons of the orange butter. When this is melted, put in four pancakes; with a spoon and fork toss and turn these about until thoroughly heated and coated with the orange butter. Now pour quickly over them two tablespoons of each of the liqueurs, strike a match, ignite the liqueurs, and allow them to burn for a few seconds, then fold the pancakes in half and fold again so that they are now folded in quarters. Serve three or four to a portion with the sauce remaining in the pan; then proceed to the next batch and repeat the operation. Serve on very hot plates.

CRESCENTS. (*Croissants* in French) A French crescent-shaped roll usually served for breakfast.

CRESCENTS

¼ cup butter
¼ cup sugar
2 cups scalded milk
½ yeast cake
¼ cup lukewarm water
3 beaten eggs
1 tsp salt
Flour
Butter

Cream the butter and sugar together and add to the milk when cooled to lukewarm, add also the yeast softened in the lukewarm water, together with the beaten eggs, salt and flour to make a light, soft dough. Knead thoroughly, brush over with

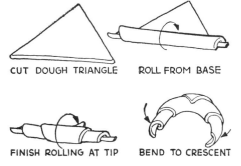

CUT DOUGH TRIANGLE   ROLL FROM BASE

FINISH ROLLING AT TIP   BEND TO CRESCENT

SHAPING CRESCENT ROLLS

butter and set aside to rise until very light, being sure that the dough is covered and kept in a place free from drafts, either cold or hot. Roll about ¼ inch thick cut into 5-inch squares, cutting these again diagonally into triangles. Brush with softened butter, and roll up beginning with the

wide end and rolling fairly tight. Shape by bringing both tips around into a half circle. Place on a lightly floured baking sheet, cover and let rise until doubled in bulk. Brush with beaten egg yolk to which a little milk has been added and bake about 20 minutes, having the oven hot (450° F.) for the first five minutes, then decreasing to 350° F. for the remainder.

For Danish or breakfast crescents proceed as directed above, sprinkling just before baking with finely chopped almonds.

AUSTRIAN CROISSANT

1 lb best flour
¼ lb butter
1 yolk of egg
½ oz salt
Scant 1 oz yeast
½ pt milk

Cream the yeast in 5 oz. of warm milk. Put the flour into a bowl, add the creamed yeast and work into a dough, neither too stiff nor too soft. Let it rise for about ½ hour, then add the rest of the milk and the salt and knead until the dough no longer sticks to the hands. Now roll out on a board and spread with the butter. Fold the dough, shape into a ball and let it stand in a cool place for several hours, or over night. Roll out the dough, cut into 5-inch lengths, roll each piece into a cylindrical shape and let stand for 10 minutes. Flatten them slightly and form into crescents and let them rise for another hour—then brush them over with a yolk of egg and bake in a moderate oven (350° F.).

CRESS. Cress is a general name for a group of peppery herbs including watercress, garden cress, and upland cress. All of these cultivated varieties are used as salads, garnishes, and condiments. They are also favored in the making of sandwiches and soups. *See also* WATER CRESS.

CREUSE CHEESE. A rennet, skimmilk, farm cheese. It is soft, yellow, and very flavorful.

CRIMP. (I) To gash a freshly caught fish on both sides of the body at intervals of about one and one-half inches, after which the fish is plunged into ice-cold water for about an hour, so that the muscle fibers contract firmly. Crimpling is done to keep the flesh firm and to retain the original flavor.

CRIMP. (II) Applied to pastry, particularly pies, the term denotes the operation of pressing the tines of a fork, or some similar instrument, down on the outer

CRIMPING PIE CRUST

edges of the uncooked pastry. In addition to providing a pleated decoration, crimping also tends to form a seal of any two-crust pastry edge, to the end that the filling is more firmly retained, and juices controlled. Slight moistening of the adjoining pastry edges with cool water before the crimping usually makes for a better seal.

CRISP. As applied to food, the adjective means somewhat firm and brittle, crumbling easily.

CRISSCROSSING TOP CRUST OF PIE

CRISS-CROSS. Applied to food, especially to pastry or pie, the term means crossing the top of a filled pastry shell or pie shell with several strips of pastry, *crossing* one another in different directions.

CROISSANT CHEESE. Small, soft, rich French cheese.

CROISSANTS. *See* CRESCENTS.

CROQUETTES. Savory rolls, balls or cones usually of fish, poultry or meat, crisp

on the outside and soft inside. To make them combine equal parts of thick white sauce and some cooked food such as minced chicken, fish, meat, or vegetables with appropriate seasonings. Spread about 1-inch thick on a platter and chill until firm enough to shape. Shape as desired, being sure to make them small. Dip into beaten egg, then roll in crumbs and fry golden brown in deep hot fat (390° F.). Drain on soft crumpled paper.

Croquettes may also be sautéed or baked in a hot oven but they will not then have such a crisp brown crust.

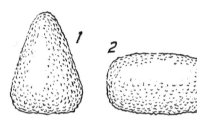

CROQUETTES 1. CONE 2. ROLLS

CROSNES. A small tuber resembling short strings of fat beads, which is little known in the United States. They are sometimes found in first class fruit and vegetable shops. Their taste is similar to the Jerusalem artichoke, but more delicate.

They are usually prepared by scrubbing with a stiff brush to remove the sand and boiling them in salted water 12 to 15 minutes, or until they are tender. They may be served hot with butter or a cream sauce. They make a delicious salad when marinated in French dressing and served with quartered tomatoes and water cress.

CRISSCROSSED PASTRY TOP

CROUSTADES. Bread shells made by cutting bread in 2-inch thick slices, then hollowing out the centers to form a box or a case. They are next brushed all over with melted butter, which may be highly seasoned or flavored and baked in a moderately hot oven (375°–400° F.) about 7 or 8 minutes, or until crisp and brown. Use as pâté cases on shells for any creamed mixture such as creamed fish, meat, poultry, or vegetables.

CROUTON. A small piece of bread, usually cube shaped, which has been browned by toasting, baking or frying and usually used as a garnish, especially for soups.

Preparation of croutons is easy. Form bread into ½ to ¾ inch cubes by successive cuts (slices, strips and cubes). Brown in single layers spread on a cookie sheet or shallow baking pan in a moderate (350° F.) oven. Turn as necessary to brown evenly. Additional flavor can be imparted by touching the cubes with melted butter or lightly buttering the slices of bread before cutting them into slices and cubes. Add other seasoning to taste.

CROWN ROAST. Either of lamb or pork, this is made from the rib chops using enough ribs (two racks or parts of two) to make a handsome crown. This is definitely

STUFFED CROWN ROAST OF PORK

a luxury or company dish. The chine bone or back bone is removed, but the chops are not separated. After trimming they are turned meat side inward and firmly tied together. When serving, the knife goes down between each two ribs from tip to base and the cut portion or serving lifted out (*see* CARVING). A crown roast is usually prepared by the butcher and may weigh from five to seven pounds.

Sometimes the roast is cooked plain, or again the center may be filled with minced

seasoned meat, partly the trimmings of the chops themselves, plus additional meat. The ends of the bones, which will have been trimmed, should be wrapped before cooking in thin strips of bacon or a cube of salt pork or a small potato may be impaled on each to prevent its burning during the roasting process. Before serving these protectors are removed and replaced by chop frills.

Cook like any roast.

CRUMB. The term means to envelop an article of food in bread crumbs or cracker crumbs after having previously dipped it in an adhesive liquid, such as egg or milk. *See also* BREAD CRUMBS.

CRUMPETS. A typical English breakfast or tea cake made of a very light batter and baked on a griddle. They are rarely made at home. Crumpets must be toasted before serving and are sometimes referred to as the "grub which makes the butter fly" as they use such a surprising quantity of butter.

CRUMPETS

1 pt warm milk
1 lb flour
¼ pt brewers' yeast
1 egg
1 oz butter
Pinch of salt

Mix all ingredients together; beat well and leave to rise until bubbles are formed on top, then bake them in small polished iron rings on top of an iron baking sheet. Crumpets may be cooked in an iron frying pan with moderate heat underneath. Turn when half done.

CRUST. (I) The hardened or browned external surface of any cooked dish or cut of meat, most often formed on oven-cooked items. Breads, casseroles, meats, etc. may form their own self-crusts during the cooking process. Pies, various other pastries and some casseroles usually have one or two pastry-crusts. A bottom crust merely supports the filling, while a top crust provides both a decorative cover and also a seal to hold in juices and aromas as desired.

CRUST. (II) The shell of any crustacean or other animal.

CRUST. (III) In wine, a form of sediment or *lees*, comprised chiefly of tartaric acid salts, that is formed by some of the red wines, Port especially, and adheres to the inside of the bottle. As is the case of all wine sediments, a crust in the bottle is a sign of age, and is not harmful, but should not be poured out in the glass. If reasonable care is exercised in pouring any crusted wine, the crust will not slip loose. *See* WINE.

CRUSTACEAN. A member of the *crustacea*, a division of the arthropods having crust-like shells, including lobsters, shrimps, crabs, barnacles, etc.

CRUSTAS. The name given to a class of American drinks that are somewhat similar to the COCKTAIL, ALCOHOLIC (*which see*), but are distinguished by having the glass lined with lemon peel and the rim frosted with sugar. A Crustas may be made from brandy, gin, rum or whisky and usually takes its name from the liquor used.

CRUSTAS
(Basic Recipe)

1 lemon
1 tsp simple sirup
2 dashes Angostura bitters
1 large jigger desired liquor (brandy, gin, rum, whisky)
Powdered sugar

A regular cocktail glass, small tumbler or wine glass may be used (*see* GLASSWARE). The lemon selected should be of the same size as the glass and have a bright, unmarred surface. The lemon is peeled in a thin, unbroken spiral and the peel used to line the inside of the glass. The rim of the glass is frosted by first rubbing it with a piece of the lemon to wet it and then dipping it in the powdered sugar. Enough finely shaven ice to fill the glass to the three quarter level is placed in a cocktail shaker together with the liquor, the simple sirup (or equivalent), the bitters, and about one teaspoon of strained lemon juice. A few dashes of maraschino may be added if desired. The ingredients are shaken well and poured, unstrained (ice and all), into the glass, prepared as above, which may also have fruit garnishing placed in the bottom. (Serves 1)

CRUSTED PORT. A Port wine that has formed a CRUST (*which see*) on the inside of the bottle. *See also* PORT.

CUBA LIBRE. A rum drink which has gained great popularity as a cooling summer beverage. Translated, the name means "Free Cuba."

CUBA LIBRE

1 jigger White Label rum
½ lime (juice)

Two ice cubes are placed in a ten ounce glass, the lime squeezed into it, the husk also dropped in, the rum added, and the glass filled with cola. It is stirred gently before serving. (Serves 1) *See also* RUM AND COKE, and BARTENDING.

CUBE STEAK. To cube steak requires a special machine, which presses the meat and imprints small cubes, breaking the fibers and rendering the meat more juicy and tender. The steaks, which are cut from sirloin tips or top round, are very popular. Cube steaks, seasoned with salt and pepper, are usually broiled.

CUCKOO GURNARD. *See* RED GURNARD.

CUCUMBER. Cucumbers are one of the vegetables which can trace their ancestry back through the ages. They are mentioned in the Bible, and several recipes for their use are found in the works of Apicius, who wrote during the first century.

CUCUMBER

Occasionally in a collection of old glass, a plain glass tube or cylinder resembling a lamp chimney with parallel sides will turn up. This may be an English cucumber glass, a device used at one time to make cucumbers grow straight. George Stephenson, of locomotive fame, is credited with their invention. Apparently he took great pride in the fine cucumbers he raised, but was distressed because they persisted in growing crooked. Finally he had a number of glass cylinders made in which he inserted the growing cucumbers. They then grew perfectly straight, and the tubes were adopted by other gardeners.

Modern horticulturists have given us a cucumber which grows practically straight of its own accord, and the somewhat bitter flavor for which they used to be known has been bred out. Some people find raw cucumbers hard to digest, and many do not know that cucumbers are delicious cooked.

A delicious tea sandwich is made by spreading white or whole wheat bread with cream cheese or pimiento cheese, covering with thin slices of cucumber which have been crisped in the refrigerator, and topping with another slice of bread spread with cheese.

FOOD VALUE

	Wa-ter	Food Energy	Pro-tein	Fat	Car-bohy-drates	Cal-cium	Phos-phorus	Iron	Vit. A Value	Thia-mine	Ribo-flavin	Nia-cin	Ascor-bic Acid
Cucum-ber	96.1	14	.7	.1	2.7	10	21	.3	260 (un-peeled)	.04	.09	.2	8

HINTS ON BUYING

Cucumbers for salad use should be firm, fresh looking, well shaped, and of good color. Some varieties are solid green when mature enough for slicing, but usually the tip is whitish with some white lines extending along the seams. These lines change from pale green to white, and finally to yellow, with age. Withered or shriveled cucumbers are tough and rubbery and bitter in flavor. Over-maturity is indicated by a puffy appearance and dull or yellowed skin. The flesh will be rubbery, the seeds hard, and the flesh in the seed cavity almost jellylike. While the cucumbers are no longer desirable for slicing, they may be used for certain types of pickles.

For pickling purposes, cucumbers from two to three inches long are generally used, but the most desirable are those of only one to two days' growth. The small prickly pickled cucumbers are commonly known as *gherkins*, but the true gherkin grows in the West Indies and Europe.

HINTS ON PREPARATION

Cucumbers blend well with tomatoes, lettuce, green peppers, and radishes in salads, especially in a tossed salad. They also combine well with pineapple and cabbage in a molded salad. Sliced very thin and marinated in French dressing they make a fine accompaniment to cold meat or fish. The professional flourish of scalloped edges to slices of cucumber is very easily attained by drawing the tines of a fork firmly down the length of the cucumber. The skin is removed in long strings, and the resulting scallops have green edges.

Creamed dishes may be served in cucumber cups which are simply made by cutting the cucumber into two-inch slices, hollowing out the slices, and cooking them in boiling salted water until they are just tender.

Cucumbers may be peeled and cut into convenient pieces and cooked in boiling salted water until just tender. Drain them well. Serve with hollandaise sauce. A particularly delicious way to serve hot cucumbers is to drench them with heavy cream which has been seasoned to taste with salt, pepper, and a few grains of nutmeg and cayenne pepper. Try this same dish made with sour cream.

Cucumbers may be fried by paring them and cutting them lengthwise into ⅓-inch slices. Pat them dry between towels, sprinkle with salt and pepper. Dip them first in crumbs, then in beaten egg, and then again in crumbs. Fry in deep hot fat (390° F.) until delicately brown, and drain on soft crumpled paper. Serve immediately and very hot.

BAKED STUFFED CUCUMBERS

4 medium sized cucumbers
½ cup chopped leftover cooked meat
1 tbsp butter
1 tbsp flour
1 cup milk
2 hard cooked eggs, chopped
1 tsp chopped parsley
1 tsp chopped chives
1 tsp grated onion
½ tsp chopped burnet leaves
½ cup celery diced very small
Salt, pepper, and nutmeg

Cut the cucumbers in half lengthwise and remove the seeds. Place in cold water for 15 minutes. Drain and parboil about 5 minutes in a small amount of boiling water.

Make a cream sauce of the butter, flour, and milk, and mix into it all the other ingredients. Fill the cucumbers with this mixture and top with buttered crumbs. Bake in a moderate oven (375° F.) about 20 minutes, or until the crumbs are browned. Serve very hot. (Serves 4)

CREAM OF CUCUMBER SOUP

Peel 3 medium-sized cucumbers and cut in half lengthwise. Remove the seeds and slice very thin. Melt 3 tablespoons of butter in a saucepan, and cook the cucumber slices, stirring constantly, until the cucumber is transparent. Do not let it brown. Sprinkle 1 tablespoon of flour over the mixture and blend well. Gradually stir in 6 cups of scalded milk. Bring again to the boil and let simmer 15 minutes, stirring constantly. Pour the mixture into a fine sieve and rub through into a saucepan. Replace on the stove and bring again to the boil. Season to taste with salt, pepper, and a dash of nutmeg. Remove from the fire and beat in 2 well beaten egg yolks, beating briskly. Lastly add 1 tablespoon of sweet butter. Serve very hot in bowls garnished with shredded toasted almonds. (Serves 6)

CUCUMBER-CHEESE SLICES

Cut a medium-sized cucumber in halves crosswise and pare it; scoop the seeds out, leaving the center hollow. Sprinkle salt about the inside of the cucumber, and drain it. Mix together 2 packages (6 ounces) of cream cheese, 2 tablespoons of chopped onion, ¼ cup of chopped green pepper, and enough paprika to give a reddish color to the mixture. Season with salt and pepper to taste and a few drops of Worcestershire sauce. Pack the mixture solidly into the cucumber cases. Marinate them in French dressing, and place them in a refrigerator to chill. Then cut the cucumber in slices of ¼-inch thickness, and place 3 slices on a small bed of crisp shredded lettuce. Garnish with strips of pimiento and with mayonnaise. Serve with French dressing or with mayonnaise. (Serves 6)

CUCUMBER COTTAGE CHEESE MOLD

3 large cucumbers
1 tbsp plain gelatin
1 tsp salt
2 tbsp grated onion
½ tsp paprika
1½ cups drained sieved cottage cheese

Peel and quarter the cucumbers and remove the seeds. Grate the cucumbers and strain, reserving juice and shreds. Soften the gelatin in the cucumber juice and then dissolve it over hot water. Season with salt, onion, paprika, and a little white pepper to taste. Let cool to lukewarm. Stir in the grated cucumber and let it get cold, but not set. Fold in the cottage cheese and mix well. Turn into a melon mold which has been wet in cold water, and chill for 2 or 3 hours in the refrigerator. When ready to serve, unmold onto a cold platter on a bed of crisp green watercress. Serve very cold with mayonnaise.

CUCUMBER TURMERIC PICKLES

6 large cucumbers
6 large onions
½ cup salt
1 lb brown sugar
1 qt vinegar
½ tsp turmeric
½ tsp white mustard seed
1 tsp celery seed

Wash, then slice the cucumbers very thin; peel and slice the onions, and let stand overnight (covered) with the salt. In the morning, drain, rinse with cold water, drain again, then cook with the sugar, vinegar and spices for 15 minutes, after which pack in sterilized jars and seal. (Makes 6 pints)

SCALLOPED CUCUMBER CASSEROLE

Wash and score 4 large cucumbers with the tines of a fork. Without peeling them, cut them into half-inch cubes, removing the seeds. Arrange a layer of the cubes in a generously greased casserole and season to taste with celery salt, pepper, and nutmeg. Sprinkle with 1½ teaspoons of grated onion mixed with 1 teaspoon of lemon juice and 1 tablespoon of water.

Spread ½ cup soft bread crumbs and dot with 1 tablespoon of butter or margarine. Repeat the layers until the casserole is full, finishing with a layer of crumbs. Cover and bake in a moderate oven (350°–375° F.) for 40 minutes. Uncover and bake 15 minutes longer, or until the top is nicely browned. Serve piping hot from the casserole. (Serves 6)

CUCUMBER MAYONNAISE SAUCE. *See* MAYONNAISE.

CUCUMBER SAUCE. *See* WHITE SAUCE.

CUMBERLAND SAUCE. This is especially suitable for cold cuts and smoked meats.

CUMBERLAND SAUCE

3 tbsp red currant jelly
2 tbsp port wine
2 tbsp orange juice
1 tbsp lemon juice
1 tsp dry mustard
1 tsp paprika
½ tsp ground ginger
3 tbsp thinly peeled orange rind, finely shredded and blanched

Melt the jelly over a low flame. Cool, then add the wine, fruit juices, seasonings and flavorings, and the orange rind which has been covered with cold water, brought to a boil and drained. Serve at room temperature.

CUMIN. Cumin is an annual herb, a member of the parsley family, that is native to Egypt and Syria. It is cultivated for its aromatic seeds. These have a somewhat bitter taste, and they are used as a condiment. They contain an oil that was formerly used for medicinal purposes.

Cumin is an ingredient in curry powder. Its flavor adds to those of cheese and sauerkraut, and it can be used generously with rice dishes. In Europe cumin seeds are used to season soups and pastry; in the Orient they are used in cooking meats. Their ability to stimulate the appetite recommends their use with canapé and hors d'oeuvre appetizers; they improve stuffed eggs particularly.

CUMQUAT. Another spelling for kumquat (*which see*).

CUP. (I) In its most common meaning, a cup is any small, open, bowl-shaped vessel intended primarily to hold liquids. It may be plain, or it may be fitted with one or more handles, and, in certain cases, it may also be equipped with a lid or cover. Cups are made from all suitable materials and have a variety of uses, both general and specialized. *See* DISHES, LOVING CUP, and GLASSWARE; *see also* TABLE SETTING AND SERVICE.

The term is also applied to certain beverage (*see* WINE CUP) and food (*see* FRUIT CUP) preparations that are served in cups or cup-like vessels, which, in some cases, are made from food itself.

A cup is also a common unit of measure in cooking practice. *See* WEIGHTS AND MEASURES.

CUP. (II) As applied to beverages, a cup may be made of one or of several fruits, or liqueurs, and may be served hot or cold, usually in crystal cups; hence their name. *See* WINE CUP.

CUP CAKES. Most cake batters can be used satisfactorily in making cup cakes. These are baked in muffin tins, at the same temperature as called for in the cake recipe, but for five minutes less than for the layers. *See* CAKES.

CURAÇAO. Cordials originally and still made in Curaçao in two colors, white and red, Curaçao is now also made in France, Belgium, and even Italy. Both kinds (white or red) are delicious after-dinner cordials with an orange tang.

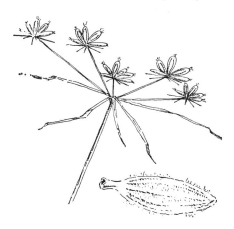

CUMIN

CURRANTS. The berry of the different sorts of *Ribes sativium*, or currant bushes. These fresh acid berries may be red, white or black. Their season is from June to the end of August. The less acid currants (white) may be eaten raw by themselves, in fruit cups or salads. Red currants are used in jam, jelly, beverages and pastries as well as alone raw, or with red raspberries. Black currants are used mainly in jelly, jam or cordial. All require washing and stemming before using. Bar le Duc was originally made from red currants.

Red and white currants have not been cultivated for more than four, or at most, five hundred years, and they are hybrids of at least three different wild species. The white currants are an albino strain of the red, and not a distinct variety, while the black are entirely different, being more closely related to the gooseberry than to the red currant.

CURRANTS

Dried Currants: The dried fruit of a practically seedless grape, smaller, darker, and much more tart than the seedless raisin. The word *currant* is a corruption of Corinth (Greece) which is the principal source of supply, though California furnishes a few. They are sometimes called Zante currants or Corinth currants to distinguish them from the Sultana raisins which are also called currants in certain localities.

VARIETIES OF CURRANTS

Red Varieties

Albert (Prince Albert, Rivers Late Red).—Berries medium to large, hang on the bushes well, season very late; clusters of good size.

Cherry—Berries large, becoming smaller, as the bush grows older, deep red, very acid, midseason.

Diploma—Berries very large, bright glossy red, mild subacid, clusters easily picked. Unexcelled for home use on account of its beauty and quality.

Fay—Berries large, dark red, acid, early to midseason; clusters with small berries at the ends, easy to pick.

Filler—Berries large, similar to Fay.

London Market (London Red)—Berries medium to large, deep red, rather acid, midseason to late.

Long Bunch Holland (Franco-German)—Berries medium size, light red, acid, season very late.

Perfection—Berries large, bright crimson, slightly subacid, midseason.

Pomona.—Berries medium to large, light red, subacid, midseason to late.

Red Cross.—Berries large, firm, light red, subacid. Hang on bushes well.

Red Lake.—Berries large, firm, light red, subacid. Promising new late variety with very large fruit and cluster.

Victoria (Raby Castle). Berries medium size, bright red, mild subacid.

Wilder.—Berries large, dark red, mild subacid.

White Varieties

White Grape.—Berries large, pale yellow, very mild flavor; clusters long, well filled.

White Imperial.—Berries large, pale yellow, almost sweet; clusters medium length, loose. A desirable variety; considered to have the best dessert quality of all currants.

Native American Varieties

Crandall.—Berries large, bluish black with a characteristic flavor somewhat unlike other black sorts; clusters rather small.

Golden Prolific.—Similar to the Crandall but with golden fruit.

PREPARATION FOR MARKET

Currants may be left on the bushes for a long time after they are ready for use, from four to six weeks, and with some varieties, even longer. Fruit that is intended for the general market should be picked and handled with great care. Injury to the skin furnishes an opportunity for the development of molds and bacteria which cause the fruit to spoil very quickly. Currants are picked by separating the stem of the cluster from the branches with the fingers, and not by grasping the clusters of berries and pulling them off. The berries are easily crushed.

HINTS ON BUYING

The currants should have a bright, clean, fresh appearance, with plump individual berries.

They are sold by the half-pint, pint or quart. One quart measures 3¾ cups and will serve 4 to 6. One pound of dried currants will yield 3 to 3⅜ cups.

When currants are to be used for jelly they should be slightly underripe as in that state of maturity the berries contain more pectin (the substance in the juice of the fruit which enables it to form jelly) than when thoroughly ripe. If the fruit is to be spiced, stewed or used for jams it should be fully ripe when picked.

HINTS ON PREPARATION

To store currants, spread on a shallow tray without washing. Remove soft or moldy currants. Cover with waxed paper and put in the refrigerator. Wash just before using.

BLACK CURRANT ICE

1 pt black currants
½ lb sugar
Squeeze of lemon
Fresh cream

Boil currants with sugar as if making jam. When the fruit is quite soft, pass through a fine sieve, add a squeeze of lemon and beat in as much fresh cream as you can spare. Freeze and serve.

BLACK CURRANT JAM

1 pt water
3 lb sugar
2 lb black currants

Boil sugar in a pint of water until it throws up large bubbles and is quite clear. Then add 2 lb black currants and boil 20 minutes or a little longer if necessary. Remove scum, pour into hot sterilized jars and seal.

BLACK CURRANT JAM ROLL

¼ lb suet
½ lb flour
Pinch of salt
Water
Black Currant jam

Chop suet finely and mix with flour and sufficient water to make stiff dough, not forgetting pinch of salt. Roll out and spread evenly with black currant jam; roll up, pinching the ends together, tie in a cloth and boil for about an hour.

BLACK CURRANT PUDDING

4 cups black currants
1 cup sugar
2 tbsp flour
½ tsp salt
Baking powder biscuit dough
(which see)

Wash currants well and remove all stems. Invert an all-metal measuring cup in center of a large pie pan and spread currants over bottom. Mix sugar, flour and salt and sprinkle over currants. Roll out dough to ½ inch thickness and cover pan and cup. Seal dough at edges and gash top of dough. Bake at 375° F. for 45 minutes. Serve hot, using juice in cup. (Serves 6)

BLACK CURRANT TEA

One of the old English household remedies for children with a cold, a hot drink made of black currant jam diluted in boiling water. Adults prefer to cure or to ward off colds with a stronger edition of the same nature, made by adding liquor.

CURRANT JELLY GRAVY

To each cup of brown gravy add a glass, or less, of currant jelly. Slices of a cold roast are delicious warmed in this gravy. Especially good with cold roast lamb.

CURRANT PRESERVES

2 qt red currants, washed and stemmed
2 large oranges, pulp and finely shredded peel
2 qt sugar
2 cups seeded or seedless raisins

Arrange currants, oranges and sugar in alternate layers in a large kettle. Let stand overnight. In the morning, bring slowly to a boiling point, stirring gently, and simmer for 25 minutes. Add the raisins and continue cooking until thickened. Turn into hot sterilized jars and seal. (Makes 2 quarts)

CURRANT AND RASPBERRY JELLY

1¼ qt red currants
1¼ qt ripe red raspberries
8 cups sugar
1 bottle pectin

Crush currants and raspberries thoroughly, then squeeze through jelly bag. Measure 3½ cups of juice and mix it thoroughly with the sugar in large kettle. Quickly bring to a full rolling boil and boil hard 2 minutes, stirring constantly. Add fruit pectin, bring again to a full rolling boil and boil hard ½ minute. Remove from heat, skim and pour. When cool, cover with paraffin. Makes approximately 12 6-ounce glasses.

HONEY AND CURRANT TARTLETS

1 recipe plain pastry (*which see*)
1 cup dried currants
⅓ cup sugar
1 tbsp lemon juice
1 tbsp honey
1 tbsp butter

Cook currants in water to cover until plump and water is practically evaporated; mix with ⅛ cup sugar and lemon juice, honey and butter. Roll pastry ¼ inch thick, cut in 4 inch circles and place scant tablespoon on half of each pastry circle. Wet edges with cold water and fold over to form half circle. Press edges together with floured fork, prick top and chill. Bake in hot oven (450° F.) about 15 minutes, until nicely browned. (Makes approximately 1½ dozen tartlets)

RED CURRANT JELLY

4 lb fully ripe currants
1 cup water
7 cups sugar
½ bottle liquid fruit pectin

To prepare the juice crush the fruit, add the water, bring to a rapid boil, cover and simmer eight to ten minutes. Turn into a jelly bag and press, or let the juice drip. Measure the juice (there should ·be five cups) and sugar into a large saucepan. Mix well, bring to boiling point over the hottest fire, and at once add the pectin, stirring constantly. Bring to a full rolling boil, and boil hard for half a minute. Remove from the heat, skim off any scum which rises to the surface, operating rapidly, and pour quickly into hot, sterilized glasses. Seal.

CURRANT BROWN SAUCE. *See* BROWN SAUCE.

CURRY. Curry is a condiment compounded from about sixteen spicy ingredients. It may occur as a powder or as a paste. The pulp of the tamarind pod is the usual base for curry paste, and turmeric is the most common base for curry powder. To these bases such spices as ginger, coriander, caraway, and cayenne pepper are added in varying proportions. Curry is so generally employed in Eastern cookery that it is often referred to as "the salt of the Orient."

In India curry condiments are prepared daily from fresh ingredients. It is necessary to substitute dry powder for the fresh ingredients in domestic curry, and this impedes the preservation of piquant tangs. Consequently, no American curry preparations seem to satisfy the critical judge. Most of the compounds used here are imported from England, but the critical gourmet will swear that curry can't be made outside of India.

A dash of curry will add the Oriental touch to chicken, shrimp, rice, and veal dishes. Curry dishes, complete with condiments and rice, are both nourishing and filling, so little need accompany them on the menu. Indians drink Darjeeling tea with them. A fruit or ice cream dessert will complete the meal. Curry dishes are international favorites.

A curry sauce adds to the flavor of meats, vegetables, fish, and eggs. Garlic, onions, lime juice, and coconut milk are essential ingredients of this sauce.

You can make a delicious cream soup by adding a curry mixture to a base of chicken stock. A teaspoon of curry will add zest to a can of tomato soup. Try it as well with other soups or with other tomato dishes, or sprinkle it lightly over scrambled eggs.

CURRY OF MEAT
(Recipe from India)

2 tbsp butter
2 tbsp finely minced onions
Rind of 1 lime, chopped
2 tbsp grated fresh coconut
1 pinch cardamon seed
2 small cubes green ginger root
1 tbsp curry powder
1 qt stock
2 lb meat, fowl, or fish
Boiled rice

Heat the butter, add the onion and lime rind and cook over a gentle heat until slightly browned, stirring frequently. Add the coconut, cardamom seed, ginger and curry powder. Allow these to cook very gently for 10 to 15 minutes, then add the stock and meat, using if possible lamb stock for lamb curry, chicken stock for chicken curry, etc. Simmer, covered, about an hour, or until the meat is tender. A little flour or rice flour moistened with stock or water may be added for thickening, if desired, though this is not usual. The main thing is to simmer very very slowly. Serve with hot boiled rice. (Serves 6 to 8)

Preparing the Rice. Dry, fluffy rice, each particle as separate from the next as a grain of sand on a sun-baked dune, is important to the excellence of any curry. For all curries are served with rice. Use unpolished Indian rice, if available. Wash well, boil 20 minutes, drain thoroughly, cover with a clean, dry cloth, and keep hot until served.

Curry sauce as described above can be used for scallops, crabmeat, lobster, shrimp, chicken, and vegetables. Chicken or vegetable broth, fresh or canned, may serve as the stock for the fish curry.

CURRY SAUCE. *See* BROWN SAUCE.

CURRY STUFFING. *See* ROAST DUCK under DUCK.

CUSH. A soup of English origin, very popular in New England. This very old dish is usually served in winter, and is made as follows:

Two cups of freshly made buttermilk cornbread should be fried in pork sausage (or bacon) fat, to which is added a medium-sized chopped onion. Brown the mixture well; then pour in a pint of whole, fresh milk. Season with salt and pepper,

bring to the boiling point, stirring constantly to prevent scorching, and serve sizzling hot with a pat of butter. (Serves 2)

CUSK. A fish similar to, but less delicate than cod.

CUSTARD. A combination of eggs and milk which may be sweetened or unsweetened, cooked in a double boiler as soft custard or baked, which gives it a jellylike consistency. *See also* BAVARIAN CREAM.

BAKED CUSTARD

3 eggs
2 tbsp sugar
Dash of salt
2 cups milk, scalded
1 tsp vanilla

Beat the eggs with the sugar and salt, then add the milk slowly, stirring constantly and mixing until the sugar is completely dissolved. Add the vanilla and turn the custard into slightly buttered custard cups (or one larger baking dish). Place in a pan of warm water and bake in a moderate oven (350° F.) 25 to 30 minutes. If baked in one dish allow a little longer baking period. Test by running a knife blade into the custard, if it comes out perfectly clean, not milky, the custard is done. Never allow the water in the surrounding pan to boil as this would make a honeycombed custard.

If the baked custard is to be served in the cup, and it is necessary that the top be browned, beat the eggs very well, instead of just slightly. This forms a foam that rises to the surface of the mold after the custard is poured in, and this foam browns beautifully during baking. This applies also to custard pie, as a pale-faced pie is not tempting nor appetizing. But when the eggs are well beaten, the custard, while just as creamy and smooth to the taste, is likely to contain air cells and not be quite as fine grained as a custard made from eggs beaten just enough to mix the whites and the yolks.

Apricot Custard. Place a stewed dried apricot half and a little juice in the bottom of each cup. Add custard, pouring against a spoon. Bake as directed.

Caramel Custard. Caramelize one-fourth cup of sugar and pour two teaspoons of it into each custard cup before pouring in the custard. Bake as directed. (Serves 6)

Chocolate Custard. Add one square (ounce) chocolate to the milk while scalding, being sure that the chocolate is thoroughly dissolved before adding to the eggs. Bake as directed. (Serves 6)

Coconut Custard. Add one-half cup shredded coconut to the custard before placing in the oven. Bake as directed. (Serves 6)

Coffee Custard. Substitute one cup strong freshly made coffee for one cup of milk. Bake as directed. (Serves 6)

Macaroon Custard. Add six crumbled macaroons with a little grated lemon or orange rind to the milk before adding to the eggs. Bake as directed. (Serves 6)

Maple Custard. Substitute maple for granulated sugar or use one-fourth cup of maple sirup. Bake as directed. (Serves 6)

Prune Custard. Place a layer of cooked, pitted prunes in the bottom of a buttered baking dish. Sprinkle with blanched chopped almonds and cover with custard. Bake as directed and serve cold, topped with sweetened, almond-flavored, whipped cream. (Serves 6)

SOFT OR BOILED CUSTARD

Either one or two whole eggs may be used to the cup of milk, one making a very thin custard, two a custard which is both heavier and richer. Sometimes the egg yolks only are used and for a richly flavored, well colored thick soft custard four egg yolks to the cup of milk should be taken.

Soft custards are used as dessert sauces, as delicate nourishing dishes for invalids or children, for blending with fruits and also as a base for many ice creams.

Sometimes as a matter of economy a little cornstarch is used as a substitute for part of the eggs but naturally this makes a less delicate, less nutritive custard.

BOILED SOFT CUSTARD

2 eggs, slightly beaten
1 tbsp sugar
Dash of salt
1 cup milk, scalded
½ tsp vanilla

Combine the eggs, sugar and salt in a bowl, add the scalded milk slowly, beating and stirring constantly. Return to the upper part of the double boiler and cook

over water which should never more than simmer, stirring constantly, until the custard thickens, shows faint traces in the wake of the spoon and coats the spoon itself. Cool slightly, add the vanilla and cool.

Where egg yolks alone are used in making a custard remember that the thickening will be more rapid than with whole eggs, so it is necessary to watch the custard constantly as it cooks.

Any desired flavoring may be used in a custard whether extract, freshly grated fruit rind or a sprinkling of spice such as cinnamon or nutmeg.

Apple Sauce Custard. Divide two cups of apple sauce among six custard cups or glasses, and chill. Add three-fourths teaspoon of gelatin softened in one tablespoon of cold water to one cup of boiled custard as soon as it comes from the fire. Stir thoroughly until the gelatin is dissolved, cool and when beginning to set pour over the apple sauce. Chill and serve topped with whipped cream flavored with vanilla. (Serves 6)

Praline Custard. Moisten six macaroons with one-third cup sherry and arrange in the bottom of a baking dish. Cover with boiled custard made with egg yolks only, top with a meringue made with the egg whites and sprinkle the surface generously with toasted sugared almonds. Bake in a moderate oven (350° F.) just until the meringue is a delicate brown and the sugar on the almonds begins to melt. Chill before serving. (Serves 6)

CUSTARD FILLING

1 tbsp flour
4½ tsp cornstarch
½ tsp salt
⅓ cup sugar
1¾ cups milk
1 egg, slightly beaten
1 tbsp butter
1 tsp vanilla

Combine dry ingredients thoroughly in top of double boiler. Add milk gradually and stir to blend. Heat to boiling over direct heat, stirring constantly. Reduce heat and continue to cook for 2 minutes. Stir a small amount hot mixture into the egg and return egg-mixture to double boiler and beat thoroughly. Cover and cook over hot water for 15 minutes, stirring occasionally. Add butter and vanilla. Cool before spreading between layers of cake. This filling is used in Blitz Torte and can be used in Boston Cream Pie. Enough for 8-inch cake.

CUSTARD PIE

4 eggs
6 tbsp sugar
Dash of salt
3 cups milk
1 tsp vanilla
Pastry
Grated nutmeg

Beat the eggs slightly, add the sugar, salt, milk and vanilla and stir to dissolve the sugar. Turn into a deep pie plate lined with pastry and brushed over with a little egg white reserved for the purpose. Dust lightly with nutmeg and bake in a hot oven (450° F.) for 10 minutes, then reduce to moderate (350° F.) and bake until the custard is set and the pastry tender, about 30 minutes longer.

Coconut Custard Pie. Follow directions for custard pie, adding ⅔ cup of shredded coconut to the custard mixture when placing in the pie plate.

Coffee Custard Pie. Follow directions for custard pie, substituting 1 cup of strong coffee for an equal amount of milk.

Cherry Custard Pie. Follow directions for custard pie, adding 1 cup of pitted canned cherries to the custard mixture when placing in the pie plate.

CUSTARD CUP. A custard cup is a small glass or earthenware cup or pot in which individual custards are cooked and served. See CUSTARD; see also KITCHEN EQUIPMENT.

CUT. Applied to cookery, the term refers to blending, such as cutting shortening into flour while making Pastry (*which see*).

CUSTARD APPLE. A tropical fruit having a soft, edible pulp. The common custard apple, a native of tropical America, is a large greenish or dark-brown fruit. The alligator-pear, sour-sop and sweet-sop are members of the genus. The chief North-American representative is the PAPAYA (*which see*).

The papaya tree grows to a height of 45 feet in favorable locations, the stem being sometimes ten inches in diameter. The fruit is a fleshy berry, three to seven inches

long, rather sweet, and edible when ripe in October. It thrives in southern Florida.

CUSTARD APPLE

CUTLERY. See also CARVING and KITCHEN EQUIPMENT. The knife, one of man's first tools, is still very important in the kitchen and on the table. Some specialized instruments have been developed to take over a few of its functions, but, by and large, the knife is still one of the most useful of kitchen tools.

Cutlery embraces all knives that are used primarily for cutting and slicing, i.e., ones with sharpened blades. Table knives may be classified as cutlery, but more commonly they are considered as a class apart and referred to as FLATWARE (*which see*).

TYPES

There are, of course, many different designs and styles of knives. Some are traditional, some are mere fads or novelties, others are experiments that may one day become traditional. Knives are typed by their intended use, which is usually determined by the blade shape. Though size is also a factor, it is the shape of the blade that determines the function.

Boner. Knives of this type have a short, narrow blade and a heavy, easily gripped handle. They are often equipped with finger guards. They are used to cut the meat away from bones, which is why they must be so shaped.

Bread. The traditional bread knife is simply a utility shape, ten inches or longer. It may be equipped with a special type of serrated edge.

Carver. Carving knives may always be recognized by their graceful, curving, swordlike lines. The blade always ends in a point that is slightly higher than the back of the blade at the haft. Carving knives are made in many sizes, usually ten inches or larger.

Clam. Used for opening clams, these knives have a blade about 3 inches long and ½-inch wide. The end is rounded and the back is thick in order to provide a better grip for the fingers as the knife is squeezed against the edge of the clam opposite the hinge. The edge of the knife is more wedge shaped than sharp.

Cleaver. A cleaver has a very broad, heavy blade and a relatively short handle. It is, literally, a meat-axe, being used with a hatchet-like motion to chop through both meat and bone. Because of the force of the blow, the cleaver must be used on some sort of chopping block, and the cutting edge, while sharp, is blunter in shape than that normally found on cutlery, for a thinner edge would chip.

Corer. A coring knife is one with either a circular or semicircular blade used to remove cores or to cut round holes in fruits and vegetables. It may have a further cutting edge inset on the side so that it may also be used as a paring knife.

French Cook. This, the traditional knife of the kitchen, is usually at least eight inches long and has a wide blade. The blade may be straight or pointed, but there is usually a slight rocking action along the "straight" length of the blade, suiting it for dicing and chopping operations as well as for straight cutting. The traditional knife of this type has an exceptionally wide blade.

Fruit. Because of the cellular structure of most fruits, knives of paring or utility shape are sometimes equipped with serrated edges specifically for use with fruit or vegetables.

Grapefruit. This knife has a thin, narrow blade with the end third or quarter bent or curved at a slight angle to the rest of the blade. The purpose of this is to duplicate the shape of a grapefruit segment, and the knife is used to cut individual citrus segments free from their membrane linings.

Oyster. This knife has a short, narrow, thick blade set in a large handle. It is used to pry open and separate the halves of oysters.

Parer. Used to pare fruits and vegetables, these knives usually have short blades, two or three inches in length, and are made with two different blade shapes. One blade is absolutely straight, while in the other, the cutting edge curves up to form a point. Each one is suited for different types of paring operations, and the housewife would do well to have at least one of each type.

Serrated Edges. Serrated edges are used for fruit and vegetable knives and also for some bread knives. They are practical in operation, but difficult to keep clean and rust-free.

Slicer. The slicer has a long, thin, narrow blade, usually of uniform width along the entire length. It may or may not terminate in a point. These knives, too, are made in many sizes, usually matching the carving knife.

Utility. This is the most general classification of all, and may be best defined by saying that it comprises all knives that do not fall into other categories. The blades are usually four inches in length or larger, and may be wide or narrow, depending on the manufacturer's ideas. They are, as the name implies, general utility knives, and every housewife, in time, acquires one or more favorite utility knives which she uses for every possible task, usually including many for which other tools have been developed.

CARVING SETS

Carving sets are used at the high point of the meal, to carve the main course. There is really no standard carving set; they can be very simple or quite elaborate, and the design will vary with the manufacturer. The basic set must contain a carving knife and a large, matching fork. The size of the knife is optional but is usually 10 inches or larger. In many sets there are two knives provided, a large one and a smaller one (8 or 9 inches) referred to as a *steak* knife or a *game* knife, depending on the manufacturer. A sharpening *steel* is often included. A carving set may also include a slicer for ham and similar meats. Others will have a pair of *game shears*, large scissors used to halve small fowl, bones and all. A final touch may be added in the form of a boner, and, in the case of fancy sets, a *carving aid* may also be included. This latter is a set of heavy prongs that is used to hold roasts and birds so they will not slip while under the knife. (*See also* TABLE SETTING AND SERVICE)

The combination of the above elements, as well as their exact size and shape, will vary with the manufacturer. There is just reason for this, since people often have decided opinions as to what constitutes the perfect carving utensil. Though proper tools are a definite aid, the secret to successful carving lies in the ability of the carver. See also CARVING.

PURCHASING CUTLERY

Knives are tools and should be thought of as such. A beautiful knife that will not hold an edge is worthless for anything other than display. A knife that is poorly balanced or difficult to hold can actually be dangerous to the user.

The most important element of any knife is, of course, the blade. It should be properly shaped and of a convenient length to do the job for which it is intended. It should take a good cutting edge and hold its sharpness through a reasonable period.

Blades are forged in one piece and are now commonly made of three kinds of steel: *carbon steel*, *vanadium steel*, and *stainless steel*. Stainless steel naturally resists corrosion and stains, while the other two types are usually chromium plated for the same purpose. The earlier steel knives do not have this plating, and there were forged iron blades made at one time.

As a general rule, stainless steel does not hold its edge as long as the other types, though some more expensive grades are quite good.

Knives are now made with two types of edges: the traditional, and the hollow ground. The traditional edge is made by pointing the full thickness of the blade into a V shape. The hollow ground edge is made by first making fairly wide concave grooves down both sides of the edge, and then sharpening the thin edge that is left. Since the hollow ground edge is thinner, it is easier to sharpen especially in inexperienced hands. Because it is thinner, however, it will lose its edge quicker and is more subject to nicking and chipping than is the traditional edge.

The handle is also important because the knife is a tool that must be held. The handle should be shaped to fit the hand, and there should be no danger of the fingers slipping onto the blade. If this possibility is present, there should be some sort of guard.

Knife handles are made of practically every known material. They should be sturdy and corrosion proof. They should not chip, dent, or warp. Good heavy duty handles are being made of compressed wood; these are clean and modern in appearance, and virtually indestructible. Whatever the material, the handle should be properly affixed to the blade. The type of kitchen knife where the handle is bonded to the blade by sturdy rivets which pass through both is to be preferred to those in which a short metal piece projecting from the blade is driven into a hollow handle. If the blade becomes loose it is worse than useless.

It is important that the knife as a unit has the proper balance. The desired balance will depend entirely on the function of the knife. For paring and boning use, the weight should all be in the handle so the blade may be guided with ease, for heavy duty carving and slicing the weight should lie in the blade, while it should be evenly distributed for light and general work. If the knife does not feel right, or if the weight is incorrectly distributed, the task of cutting will be made difficult.

Some forms of cutlery, fruit knives, bread knives, cake knives, etc., are now being molded out of plastic materials, the most commonly used being polystyrene (*see* PLASTICS). Plastic blades of this sort will perform their intended functions well, but cannot be used for general cutting purposes.

The number and type of knives needed will vary with the individual. Some people will make one or two knives do for every possible use, while others will want a specific tool for each task. Generally speaking, there should be at least two paring knives, two utility knives, and one French cook knife in the kitchen, while the carving set should have a carving knife, a fork, a slicing knife, and either a steel or stone for sharpening.

CARE OF CUTLERY

Cutlery must be sharp to be of use. Actually, the best way to sharpen cutlery of any sort is to hone it on a stone, much as straight razors are sharpened. Some skill is required for this operation, and the housewife is better advised to install some sort of sharpener in the kitchen for use on her inexpensive parer and utility knives.

The simplest sharpener is a plain carborundum slab. Carborundum is a remarkably tough abrasive that will readily grind away steel. Knives are sharpened by drawing them across the block in a cutting or slicing motion, using alternate sides for each stroke, and holding the blade at an angle of about 28 degrees. The motion is always made as though to cut the block, never in the opposite direction.

Another popular type of sharpener consists of either carborundum blocks or sharp steel disks that are held to form a V of the proper shape for a cutting edge. The cutting edge is drawn through this V until it is ground in the proper shape. This type of sharpener is the easiest to use, and may be installed permanently on a shelf or counter where it cannot be lost. It has, however, a tendency to wear away the knife more quickly than the other varieties by taking off more metal with each sharpening, and should never be used on carving knives and more expensive cutlery.

Carving knives should be sharpened by using either a steel or stone rod. Both of these implements have a gently abrasive edge and do not remove too much of the steel. The rod is held in one hand and the knife in the other and the action is similar to that used with the carborundum block. These instruments merely *dress* the edge; they do not hone or grind the knife. In time the edge will become too worn for the steel or stone to properly re-sharpen and it will be necessary to have the knife ground. This should be done by an experienced man, for it is, of necessity, a hand operation.

The knives should be stored in racks or cases for protection when not in use. It is poor practice to throw kitchen knives indiscriminately into a drawer, for not only may the edges be marred, but the hand may be sliced if one reaches in without looking. A rack hung on the wall out of the children's reach is the best solution to the knife storage problem. The carving sets may be stored with the silverware.

Knives should be washed separately to protect both the knives and the fingers. Reaching for a sharp blade beneath a masking blanket of soapsuds can be fraught with dangers. Cleansing powder or fine steel wool may be used on stainless steel or unplated metal blades, but if the blade has a chromium plating, as many do, only a non-abrasive polish should be used, to protect the plating. Care should also be exercised when sharpening plated knives to see that the abrasive touches only the edge and never the flat of the blade.

Knives should be thoroughly dry before they are put away, to prevent rusting. The sharpening steel, in particular, should be watched, for not only is it unplated and usually quite receptive to rust, but its rough surface is difficult to dry.

Finally, knives should be used as knives; never as screw drivers or levers.

CUTTING BOARD. A cutting board is a portable, smooth, hardwood board on which different materials may be cut. In general usage, the word has come to be applied to the paper cutter, a cutting board that has a metal edge and a hinged blade that can be brought down on this edge with a scissors-like motion. While boards of this type may be used in the kitchen, as far as the culinary vocabulary is concerned, a cutting board is a plain bread board, *which see.* More expensive kitchen cutting boards may be equipped with a hinged knife blade for chopping vegetables, but the blade is usually set in the wood and not placed at the edge, and the guiding rule of the paper cutter is lacking.

CUTTLE FISH. *See* Squid.

D

DAB. A flat fish of the flounder family.

DACE. A delicious, small, fresh-water fish, which may be prepared by all the methods applied to smelts.

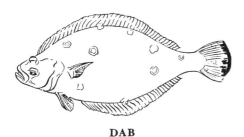

DAB

"DAGWOOD". A term which originated in the comic strips, used to denote a sandwich put together so as to finally attain such a tremendous size and infinite variety of contents as to stun the imagination, sight and stomach of all but the original maker. (*See also* SANDWICH)

DAIQUIRI. A rum drink that may be served either as a cool summer drink or as a cocktail.

DAIQUIRI

1 jigger White Label rum
½ lime (juice)
1 teaspoon sugar

Place in cocktail shaker with plenty of finely cracked ice, shake until thoroughly chilled, strain into cocktail glass. (Serves 1)

The Daiquiri, intended to be a cold drink, may also be served as a Frozen Daiquiri. The above recipe may be used, or, because of the dilution by melted ice in the glass, the following may be preferred.

FROZEN DAIQUIRI

1 large jigger White Label rum
1 lime (juice)
½ tsp sugar

Mix ingredients as above, strain into saucer type goblet (*See* GLASSWARE) that is filled with finely shaven ice, garnish with cherry or other fruit to taste, serve with short straw. This drink should be sipped slowly. (Serves 1)

See BARTENDING, *see also* COCKTAIL, AL-COHOLIC.

DAISY. A heavily iced alcoholic drink that closely resembles the COLLINS (*which see*) in recipe. An older drink, the Daisy in all probability was the inspiration for the Collins, which, simpler to make, has almost completely supplanted it in the public demand.

Daisies are made using brandy, gin, whisky and even some of the wines, and are often named for the liquor used. There are also several variations of the Daisy, elaborations of the basic recipe.

DAISY

1 jigger desired liquor (brandy, gin, whisky, etc.)
½ lemon (juice)
1 tsp sugar
1 dash grenadine

The ingredients are placed in a silver mug (a tall glass may also be used) that is half filled with cracked ice. The container is then filled with carbonated water, stirred, the drink garnished with fruit to taste, and served with a straw. (Serves 1)

One variation calls for the mug to be filled entirely with finely shaven ice, with only a little carbonated water added. The drink is stirred until the outside of the mug is frosted, and mint sprigs are added to the fruit garnishing.

The drink is sometimes mixed in a cocktail shaker with cracked ice and strained into a highball glass or mug where only one lump of ice is added and it is heavily garnished with fruit. In other cases, it is mixed

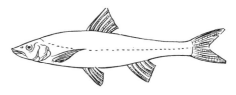

DACE

in a cocktail shaker, but ice and all is poured· into the mug without straining. Wine daisies should not be mixed in a shaker.

Lime juice is sometimes added, especially in the case of a gin daisy, and a teaspoon of brandy is often added to Daisies, other than the Brandy Daisy, either being mixed with the ingredients or floated on the top of the drink. See BARTENDING.

D'AMBERT CHEESE. Another name for Forez Cheese (*which see*).

DAME-JEANNE. *See* DEMIJOHN.

DAMEN CHEESE. A Hungarian cheese, also known as *Gloire des Montagnes*. It is a soft, uncured, rennet cheese made from cow's milk.

DANDELION. The humble dandelion, which is a good source of vitamins and minerals, is found in the markets in the early spring. Both wild and cultivated dandelions are marketed, the cultivated being somewhat more bleached in appearance than the wild, and may be more tender. In any event, young crisp plants are the most desirable, having the most delicate flavor.

Dandelions have a slightly bitter flavor which is different from that of most greens. The leaves may be served raw, in a mixed salad, or cooked like spinach.

The plants should be thoroughly washed and cleaned; a good deal of sand is likely to be found among the leaves, particularly when the dandelions have been home-gathered. The root should be cut off, and the plant quartered through the base. If the leaves are to be used in salad, they should be well drained and crisped in the refrigerator. A tart French dressing is all that is required.

To cook dandelion, put the washed plants into a saucepan and add just enough water to prevent burning. Cook until the leaves are thoroughly wilted. Drain the water, which is rather strong and should be discarded. The dandelion greens are then ready to serve as hot slaw, creamed, or simply seasoned with salt and pepper. Chopped crisp bacon and lemon juice makes an interesting variation. In Kentucky the dandelion greens are cooked with a piece of salt pork and seasoned with vinegar and pepper.

DANDELION WINE

15 qt dandelion blossoms
3 gal cold water
15 lb sugar
1 yeast cake
Juice of 1 dozen oranges
Juice of ½ dozen lemons
2½ lb raisins

FOOD VALUE

Water	Food Energy	Protein	Fat	Carbohydrate	Calcium	Phosphorus	Iron	Vit. A Value	Thiamine	Riboflavin	Niacin	Ascorbic Acid
85.8	52	2.7	.7	8.8	187	70	3.1	13,650	.19	.14	.8	36

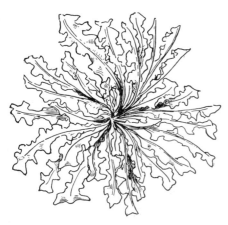

DANDELION

Place the blossoms in cold water and simmer for 3 hours. Then strain the liquid. Mix it with the sugar. Boil up, then strain through a cheesecloth. When lukewarm, add the yeast cake, and let the mixture stand for 2 or 3 days, skimming it each day. Add the juice of the oranges and lemons with the thinly peeled rinds of both oranges and lemons simmered for half an hour in a little water. There should be 5 gallons in all by measure. Put into a cask, and add the raisins. Leave the cask open for a day; then seal it tightly, and let it stand for 6 months before bottling. The wine improves with aging.

DANISH BLUE CHEESE. A hard, rich, 4-pound cheese. This is a Danish imitation of Roquefort.

DANISH EXPORT CHEESE. A small, flat, round Danish cheese.

DANISH PASTRY. A fairly rich pastry, usually made with raised dough and formed into individual portions about four to five inches in diameter before baking. Danish Pastries may be garnished with sugar, spices, nuts, icings, etc., as desired.

DANISH PASTRY

⅓ cup sugar
¾ cup lukewarm water
3 packages dry granular yeast or 3 cakes compressed yeast
1 tsp salt
¾ cup milk, scalded
5¼ cups sifted all-purpose flour
¼ cup shortening, melted
2 eggs
1 tsp vanilla
1¼ cups butter, thoroughly chilled

Stir 1 tablespoon of the sugar into water; add yeast and let stand for 10 minutes. Stir to blend well. Stir salt and remaining sugar into hot milk, cool to lukewarm. Combine yeast and milk mixtures thoroughly. Add 2 cups flour and beat to a smooth batter. Add shortening and mix well. Add eggs and vanilla and beat well. Gradually add all but ¼ cup of the remaining flour and mix thoroughly. Turn out on a lightly floured board (use remaining ¼ cup flour for kneading and shaping), cover, let rest 10 minutes. Knead lightly but thoroughly for 5 minutes. Place in greased bowl, turn dough over in bowl once to bring greased side up. Cover and let rise in a warm place (86° F.) until increased ¼ in bulk (20 to 30 minutes). Roll out on lightly floured board into a rectangle about ½ inch thick and about 14 inches by 18 inches. Use ½ of the butter and cut it into small bits, over the center third of dough. Fold over one side of dough to cover butter. Press edges together to seal in butter. Cut remaining butter in bits on top. Fold the remaining third of dough over the butter and press edges together to seal in butter. Shift dough ¼ turn on board and lightly roll out again in rectangle ½ inch thick. Fold each end of dough to center, then fold in half to bring open edges together. Place folded dough between 2 lightly floured sheets of wax paper and chill in refrigerator for 45 minutes. Roll out once more into a rectangle ½

inch in thickness. Again fold into fourths, cover and place in refrigerator for 4 or 5 hours or overnight. The rolling and folding spreads the chilled butter between thin sheets of dough and produces the puffy layers characteristic of Danish Pastry. Dough must be thoroughly chilled throughout so that butter is very firm. Cut dough into quarters and work with only ¼ at a time, returning balance to refrigerator. Work quickly so that the layers of butter do not soften. Roll out again to about ½ inch in thickness and cut out or shape as desired. Star or round cut outs, snails, braids or butterhorns (*see* PLAIN ROLL) are suitable shapes for this pastry. Place on greased baking sheets, cover and let rise in a warm place for about 1 hour.

Brush lightly with 1 slightly beaten egg white combined with 1 tablespoon cold water. Dust with sugar. Bake in a moderate oven (375° F.) for 15 to 18 minutes depending on size of rolls. Remove from pan to rack to cool. Brush with confectioner's icing (*see* FROSTING, FILLING AND ICING) and sprinkle with chopped nuts, if desired. (Makes 2 to 4 dozen)

DANSK SCHWEIZEROST CHEESE. A popular Danish cheese.

DANZIGER GOLDWASSER. An orange flavored *Goldwasser* (*which see*).

DARALAG CHEESE. Another name for *Bgug-Panir* cheese (*which see*).

DARJEELING. A variety of Black tea which is regarded by experts as the finest in the world. Grown high on the slopes of the Himalayas in Darjeeling, a district of the province of Bengal in Northern India. The pungent, distinctive flavor, at once rich and delicate, permeates the flavor of other teas. For that reason, this tea is blended into many American brands. Darjeeling is the one variety of Black tea which is also prized as a *straight* brew. It produces a handsome brew of a reddish color.

DASH. As applied to food measurement, a dash means a scant one-eighth of a teaspoon.

DASHEEN. A type of taro little known in this country, although it has been grown in the Southern States since 1913. Pliny, the Roman historian, mentioned taro as being an important food crop of Egypt. Captain Cook in 1778 called it an important food in the islands of the South Seas. Taro was introduced from China into the West Indies some two centuries ago.

There are two kinds of dasheens, known respectively as the corms, the larger roots, and the tubers, or smaller ones. The corms are rounded and flattened at the stem end like an old-fashioned wooden top. They have heavy, definitely marked circum-

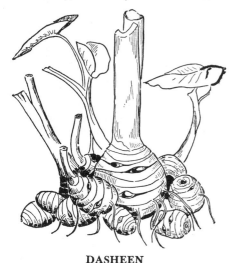

DASHEEN

ference rings and a light tan, somewhat shaggy covering. The tubers are similar but smaller in size and often irregular in shape. The flesh may be cream colored, but it is usually gray and may run in shades from gray to lavender, depending on the variety.

A starchy tuber, the dasheen has less moisture than the potato, the content of starch and protein being about one-half greater. The starch grain of the dasheen is among the smallest known in food plants. The mineral content is good, being over 1 percent. Preliminary reports prove conclusively that it contains Vitamins A, B, and C.

VARIED USES OF THE DASHEEN

From the *kalo* or taro, the Hawaiians make their famous *poi* by steaming, peeling, mashing, mixing with water, and straining the resulting mixture. This is allowed to stand a day or two (depending on the strength desired) to develop an acid taste, or longer if desired to ferment, when it makes a sort of tropical beer. This drink is also made in the West Indies under other names.

The dasheen is cooked very much like the potato. It is peeled and boiled, then mashed or riced. It is made into chips and hash. It is baked after a preliminary boiling, and a coating of oil is added to prevent the formation of a hard outer rind. Often the baked dasheen is stuffed with meat, or fish, or other green vegetables. It is also scalloped with cheese. In fact many of the recipes of potatoes can be used for dasheens if the homemaker remembers that the dasheen is much drier, and so needs more moisture and fat than the potato, for which it makes an excellent substitute.

DASHEEN FRITTERS

1 cup grated raw dasheen
1 cup white flour
1 tbsp sugar
½ tsp salt
2 tsp baking powder
½ cup milk

Mix the dasheen and the dry ingredients and add the milk. Drop heaping teaspoonfuls into deep hot fat and fry to a golden brown. Drain, sprinkle with powdered sugar and serve immediately. They are equally delicious with maple or sugar sirup.

DASHEEN PIE

2 cups boiled riced dasheen
¼ cup melted butter or margarine
¾ cup white sugar
½ tsp cinnamon
½ tsp nutmeg
1 egg, white and yolk beaten separately
2 cups milk
¼ lemon, juice and rind

Line a pie pan with pastry, building up a high edge. In a mixing bowl, mix the dasheen, shortening, sugar, cinnamon, nutmeg, yolk of the egg, milk and lemon juice and rind. Stir thoroughly, and fold in the beaten egg white. Pour into the unbaked pastry shell and bake in a hot oven (450° F.) for 10 minutes to set the crust. Turn down the oven to 350° and continue baking for 20 or 30 minutes, until a silver knife inserted in the middle comes out clean.

This filling may be baked as a pudding, without the crust, in a deep greased baking dish, or in individual custard cups.

SCALLOPED DASHEENS

Pare and slice raw dasheens, either tubers or corms. Grease a baking dish, and put the slices in in layers, seasoning each layer with salt, pepper, and butter or margarine. The addition of a few slices of onion brings out the dasheen flavor. Fill the dish, and pour in enough milk nearly to cover the dasheens. Bake in a moderate oven (350° F.) until the dasheens are tender and nicely browned on top. The dasheens will take only about two-thirds the time that scalloped potatoes take.

Grated cheese may be sprinkled on the layers of dasheen before baking, and cheese mixed with buttered crumbs sprinkled over the top.

STUFFED DASHEENS

Corms 3 or more inches in diameter are best for this dish. Clean the corm thoroughly either by scrubbing or scraping. Cut the base off squarely so that the corm will stand upright. With an apple corer and paring knife, cut a cylindrical hole 1½ inches in diameter from the top to within ¾ inch of the bottom. Cut the top of this core off for a plug. Hollow out the interior of the corm, leaving walls a good ½ inch thick. Parboil the corm for 10 minutes in well salted water. Prepare a filling of chopped leftover meat, well seasoned, and quite moist. Fill the corms with the stuffing, insert the plug, and place in a pan. Bake in a moderately slow oven (325° F.) until the corm is tender. Do not overbake. Serve immediately, cutting through the corm lengthwise into halves or quarters, depending on the size.

DATE. Fruit of the date palm. Dates have a history extending back thousands of years. They grow on date palms which sometimes reach a height of a hundred feet. The fruit grows in bunches weighing from 20 to 30 pounds. Three different species yield date fruit, date honey (a rich sirup made from the juice of the fresh fruit), date sugar, date sap (an intoxicating drink) and date palm flour (made from the pith of the tree). Date palms grow best in North Africa and Asia Minor, but in 1930 there were nearly 3,000 acres of date palms in the irrigated desert valleys of Arizona, California, and Nevada, and the U.S. Government has devoted time and money to developing our date culture.

The composition of dates varies and appears to depend somewhat upon variety, ripeness and age of the fruit. The weight of moisture in the flesh of uncured fruit is about 30% and of dry fruit is about 15%. Cured dates, having a moisture content of 20% contain about 2% each of protein, fat and mineral matter. Carbohydrate totals about 74%. The sugars alone amount to 60 to 65%. Dates furnish about 1,460 calories per pound at this composition. The mineral matter is made up of various elements such as calcium, phosphorous, iron and copper. Dates are a fair source of Vitamin A and Thiamin (Vitamin B). Apart from the pleasing variety dates offer to the diet, they are very valuable nutritionally.

KINDS OF DATES

Dates are classified as soft, semidry, and dry, depending on the softness of the ripe fruit. Another classification is according to the kind of sugar contained in the ripe fruit, invert-sugar dates containing mostly dextrose and glucose, and cane-sugar dates containing mostly cane sugar.

Most soft varieties are invert-sugar dates and most dry varieties are cane-sugar dates; some semi-dry varieties contain mostly invert sugars and others cane-sugar.

The common soft varieties include Khadrawy, Maktoom, Hayany, Dayri, Barhee, Braim, Kustawy, and Rhars, all of which are invert-sugar dates.

The common dry or bread varieties are the Thoory and Kenta, both of which are cane-sugar dates.

DATES

The common semidry varieties include Deglet Noor, Halawy, Saidy, Zahidi, and Sayer. The Deglet Noor is a cane-sugar date, whereas the other semidry varieties are invert-sugar dates.

The dry varieties usually contain only a little moisture when ripe and are non-perishable, whereas the soft and semidry varieties contain a considerable amount of moisture and are usually highly perishable if they are not dried by either natural or artificial means.

PREPARATION FOR MARKET

Dates are separated into lots of uniform ripeness in order to simplify handling during the ripening and curing processes. Dates are in the *khalal* stage, when the green color of the full-grown fruit turns to yellow or shades of red characteristic of the variety. Dates are in the *rutab* stage from the time the ripe color starts to appear and the flesh starts to soften until softening is complete and partial drying has occurred. *Tamar* dates are those that have dried out or cured enough to keep without spoiling. These terms are Arabic.

Dates ripen during the late summer and early fall. While in a green state they are firm, smooth, crisp and astringent. They attain full size and nearly full sugar content before the green color changes to the yellow or reddish color that is characteristic of the different varieties when ripening begins. As ripening continues, moisture is slowly lost by evaporation. This natural process of drying out of the flesh is called curing.

During a normal ripening season the dates of a single bunch, which may number as many as several hundred fruits, ripen a few at a time. Fruits of the highest quality are obtained by picking each day the dates which have reached a prime condition of ripeness and proper degree of curing. While ripening on the tree, the bunches may be covered with a paper or cloth to protect the fruit from rain, birds and insects.

HINTS ON BUYING

Fresh dates should be plump, lustrous, golden brown color, with smooth skin. They are sold by the package or pound. There are two general types of dates: the black, sweet, and meaty date with a thin skin such as the Fard, and the golden brown date with a coarse texture and a larger seed such as the Persian, Hallowi and Khadrawi. The Deglet Noor is a black date from Africa, but the California Mission date is somewhat similar. Dates are sold pitted and unpitted. They are graded according to size, firmness, and uniformity in the classifications: Extra Fancy, Fancy and Choice.

HINTS ON PREPARATION

One pound of dates equals 6 to 8 servings. When a recipe calls for one cup of dates, pitted dates are meant. When dates are to be used in smaller bits or cubes, as for cookies, lay the pitted dates on a wooden board and cut them with a sharp knife dipped frequently in cold water. A kitchen shears, dipped in cold water, may also be used. Do not try to mince dates for they will cohere in a sticky mass. Pitted dates make an excellent addition to a salad plate or fruit salad.

To store dates, put in refrigerator or in a cool, dry place. Fully cured dates are dry enough to keep without spoiling and can be packed in tight containers such as glass jars and coffee cans. These containers are insectproof and prevent further drying.

DATE CAKE DESSERT

1⅓ cups all-purpose flour
1 tsp soda
½ tsp salt
1 tbsp butter
1 cup sugar
1 egg, beaten
½ lb pitted dates
1 cup boiling water

Sift the flour, measure and resift 3 times with soda and salt. Blend butter and sugar well, and add beaten egg. Beat until mixture is light and fluffy. Cover chopped, pitted dates with the boiling water. Add to the creamed mixture alternately with the flour mixture, beginning and ending with flour and beating well after each addition. Pour into a greased pan (about 7x7x1½ inches) and bake in a moderate oven (375° F.) for 25 minutes or until it springs back to the touch. Serve warm or cold with Lemon Sauce (*which see*). (Serves 6 to 8)

DATE CREAM PUDDING

1 pt milk
4 tbsp sugar
1½ tbsp seed tapioca
½ lb pitted dates
1 egg

Cook milk and tapioca together for 15 minutes, then add the beaten yolk of egg and sugar and dates. Cook another 15 minutes. Remove from fire and fold in stiffly-beaten white of egg. Serve hot or cold. (Serves 4 to 6)

DATE GEMS

⅓ cup butter
1 cup powdered sugar
2 well-beaten eggs
½ cup milk
1¾ cup flour
2 tsp baking powder
½ tsp ground ginger
¼ tsp grated nutmeg
¼ tsp powdered cloves
1 cup chopped dates

Beat butter and sugar to a cream. Add eggs, milk, flour, baking powder, ginger, nutmeg, cloves and dates. Mix well and divide into buttered and floured pans and bake in a moderate oven for 25 minutes. Cool on a cake-rack and when cold decorate each with icing sugar moistened with orange juice and lemon. Top with pitted date.

DATE MOONS

½ lb dates
½ cup walnuts
4 tbsp candied ginger

Put dates, pitted, through the meat chopper, and add ½ cup walnuts and candied ginger coarsely cut. Knead and roll into sausages, using powdered sugar to prevent sticking. Serve cut in thin slices.

DATE PINWHEELS

1 lb pitted dates, cut up
½ cup water
½ cup sugar
2 cups all-purpose flour
½ tsp soda
½ tsp salt
½ cup butter
½ cup brown sugar, firmly packed
½ cup granulated sugar
1 egg, well beaten
½ tsp vanilla
1 cup finely chopped nuts

Put first 3 ingredients into saucepan and stirring constantly, cook until thick, from 2 to 3 minutes of actual boiling. Cool. Sift flour, measure, and resift 3 times with soda and salt. Cream butter until soft and smooth, blend in both sugars, add egg, beat until light and fluffy. Stir in vanilla. Stir in flour mixture and quickly work dough until smooth. Chill at least half an hour. Divide dough into 2 equal parts. Place one portion on lightly floured cloth and roll into a rectangle about ¼" thick. Combine date mixture with nuts and spread half the mixture evenly over the sheet of dough. Roll up like jelly roll the long way of the sheet, using cloth to facilitate rolling. Then wrap the roll snugly in waxed paper with the open edge of roll on bottom. Repeat with remaining dough and filling. Chill rolls until very firm, then slice thin using a sharp, thin-bladed knife. Place on lightly greased baking sheets and bake in moderately hot oven (400° F.) for 7 minutes or until lightly browned. Transfer to cake racks to cool. Makes 5 to 10 dozen cookies depending on diameter of rolls and thickness of cookies.

DATE TORTE SQUARES
Filling

½ cup pitted dates (2½ oz)
⅓ cup granulated sugar
¼ cup water
½ tsp lemon rind
½ cup chopped nuts

Cook dates, sugar and water about 3 minutes, stirring constantly until thickened. Cool. Add lemon rind and nuts.

Torte

⅔ cup all-purpose flour
½ tsp cinnamon
¼ tsp soda
¼ tsp salt
½ cup brown sugar, firmly packed
¾ cup quick-cooking rolled oats
½ cup melted butter

Sift flour, measure and resift 3 times with soda, cinnamon and salt. Add brown sugar, and rolled oats, mix thoroughly. Add butter and work with finger tips to a stiff crumbly dough. Divide in half. Pat one-half of dough into a uniform layer in a shallow 7 inch square pan. Spread with date filling, then crumble the remaining dough over the top in an even layer. Pat down gently. Bake at 325° F. (moderately slow oven) for 35 minutes. Leave in pan and cool thoroughly. Cut in squares. (Makes about 25 squares)

Fresh Fruit and Date Salad

1 small, well-ripened pineapple, chilled
2 well-ripened bananas
2 oranges, chilled
¼ lb dates, pitted and chopped
⅓ cup fruit salad dressing, chilled
Lettuce or romaine

Slice pineapple, peel slices, and cut in small wedges, discarding core of each slice. Peel and slice bananas and oranges; cut orange slices in quarters. Combine fruits quickly to prevent bananas from darkening, add dates and dressing (*See* SALAD DRESSING). Mix gently with as little manipulation as possible. Drop lightly into lettuce cups on individual salad plates. (Serves 5)

Pineapple Date Whip

⅔ cup whipping cream
1 tbsp lemon juice
1 cup crushed pineapple, drained
½ cup moist pitted dates, chopped
Pinch of salt
Sugar to suit taste

Have cream thoroughly chilled in refrigerator. Turn into chilled bowl and beat with a chilled rotary beater until thick; then add lemon juice and continue beating until quite stiff. Fold in the pineapple, chopped dates, and salt; then fold in sugar to suit taste, if any is required. Serve immediately. (Serves 5)

Steamed Date Pudding

1¼ cups sifted flour
2 tsp baking powder
¼ tsp salt
¼ package dates, cut small
2 tbsp butter
½ cup brown sugar
1 egg
¼ tsp vanilla
½ cup milk

Sift the dry ingredients and add the dates. Cream the butter, gradually add the sugar, then the well beaten egg and vanilla and work into these the fruit-flour mixture alternately with the milk. Turn into a well-greased mold, filling about ¾ full, cover with the lid or greased paper, and steam about three hours. Serve with lemon sauce. (Serves 4)

Stuffed Date Salad

Use pitted large dates; stuff with cream cheese or a spicy soft cheese moistened with mayonnaise and seasoned with salt and paprika. Serve 3 to a salad on a bed of crisp lettuce, romaine, escarole or watercress.

DAUPHIN CHEESE. A French cheese made in Flanders.

DAURADE. *See* GILT HEAD.

DEAF DUCK. *See* RUDDY DUCK *under* DUCK.

DECANTER. A narrow-necked glass container, equipped with a stopper, which is used to hold and serve wine, especially those wines that form sediments. *See* GLASSWARE *and* WINE.

DECANTING. In wines, the process of pouring a wine from the bottle into the decanter from which it will be served. The wine is usually poured through a cloth to screen out any sediment, cork particles, dust or other impurities that may have been in the bottle. While any wine may be served from a decanter for appearance's sake, decanting is almost essential in the case of a sediment-forming wine. *See* WINE, *see also* DECANTER.

DECIZE CHEESE. A French cheese made in the Nivernais region.

DECK, DECKER. These terms are applied to sandwiches to indicate that more than the normal two, i.e., top and bottom, slices of bread are used in the construction. These additional slices are used to separate different layers of filling, and the sandwich is usually held together by means of toothpicks. A *three-decker* is the normal size; beyond that they get unwieldy. *See* SANDWICH.

DECORATING. It would be hard to find a dish that could not profit from some form of decorating or garnishing. Appeal is enhanced by the addition of color, texture or flavor in the form of food accessories. Nutrition also profits from the inclusion of diverse elements in one meal.

Many dishes almost seem to demand

their traditional accompaniments. Lamb is usually served with mint sprigs or jelly. Pork calls for applesauce or garnishes made from apples, apricots, peaches or pineapple. Fish is incomplete without a wedge of lemon or lime. Besides what appear to be "natural" garnishes, a whole army of foods can be pressed into service as food decorations.

Olives and pickled cucumbers, cauliflower, carrots, tomatoes and peppers serve as tasty food accents. Fresh vegetables such as carrots, tomatoes, onions, celery, zucchini, sweet pepper, radishes can be cut into attractive shapes and used to adorn platters of meats. Fresh and canned fruits and melons may be served in the same way.

Greens in particular have decorative value for foods. Choose watercress, celery, or spinach leaves and other attractive greens to brighten up vegetables, fruits, salads and meats. Serve a baked tomato on a bed of lettuce; spoon mashed potatoes into cups made of kale or spinach.

Spices also may be used as effective garnishes. Paprika adds a delightful color to potatoes, macaroni, noodles and casserole crust. A little turmeric in the cooking water of rice adds interesting color and subtle flavor. Bruised fresh herbs used as plate garnishes exude a pleasing odor. Chopped chives and sprigs of parsley may be used liberally to good effect.

Among the more unusual garnishes that may be employed are nuts, especially almonds and walnuts, raisins, whole cardamons (floating in tea) and fresh flowers. Boiled eggs may be used sliced or grated; cheese may be grated on top of sauces; pimentos add spice and color.

DEEP DISH PIE. See PIE.

DEEP FAT FRYER. A deep fat fryer is essentially a wire mesh basket that can be lowered into a bath of boiling fat during the cooking operation (see FRYING). The basket has a handle, and is fitted with hooks that catch on the rim of the fat pan, thus keeping the basket off the bottom of the pan. The mesh is wide enough to permit ready access of the liquid, but fine enough to retain food placed inside. The fryer may be sold separately or in combination with a saucepan used to hold the fat. See also KITCHEN EQUIPMENT.

DEEP FAT FRYING. See FRYING.

DEEP WATER TROUT. See WEAKFISH.

DEER. See GAME.

DEERFOOT SAUSAGE. See SAUSAGE.

DEHYDRATION. Dehydration is the process of removing water from vegetables and fruits so that they will not decay. The process is simply a method of passing heated air over the fruits or vegetables at a temperature low enough to prevent changes in the cell structure, so that the fruit or vegetable retains its full food value, and the vital food salts are unaltered by heat, as happens when they are cooked. See also DRIED FRUITS.

DELICIOUS APPLE. See APPLE.

DEMERARA RUM. See RUM.

DEMIJOHN. A large glass bottle-like container with a bulging body and a long, narrow neck. Made in various sizes that range from one to ten gallons in capacity, it is usually encased in wicker with attached handles for carrying. It is used for the storage and shipment of wines and spirits, notably Madeira wine.

The name is the anglicised version of Dame-Jeanne, the original French name for a container of this sort.

DEMI-SEL CHEESE. A French cream cheese necessarily consumed where it is made because of its fragility and perishable nature. It is made on the same principle as domestic cream cheese (which see), but is softer, creamier, and lighter.

DEMITASSE. A small cup of black coffee, usually served after luncheon or dinner.

DEMITASSE CUP. About half the size of the regular coffee cup, it is a cup used for an individual serving of a demitasse or after-dinner coffee. See DEMITASSE, see also DISHES.

DERBYSHIRE CHEESE. A hard, round, rennet cheese made from the whole milk of cows in Derbyshire, England. The quality varies to such an extent that very few really good cheeses can be found. It is usually made in farm dairies, and because of this fact the size may vary with the size of the herd.

DESSERT. The dessert course writes finis to the meal. To make the ending a happy one the dessert must be well chosen. It must be in harmony with the dishes which have preceded it. If the first courses have been light, then a hearty dessert may be served for balance. If they have been rich and flavorful, a light dessert is to be preferred. Nor should the dessert repeat a food or flavor served elsewhere in the meal. Thus, if a fruit cup or fruit salad, or fruit cocktail, or a grapefruit has been served, a fruit dessert would make for monotony, and therefore should be avoided.

Generally speaking, with the substantial meal centered around meat or fish and the usual accompaniments, serve a light dessert, perhaps one of fruit. With a vegetable luncheon or dinner, a protein dessert with a custard foundation, such as baked custard, or custard pie, in winter sometimes mince pie or tarts, or a cake dessert, or cheese. Serve a starchy dessert, on the other hand, with a meal which has not included potatoes, spaghetti, or a similar starchy food, and a whipped cream dessert with the meal that has been fairly light and in which no other creamed dish has been served. *See also* BERRIES, CAKES, CUSTARDS, ICES, ICE CREAM, MOUSSES, PARFAITS, PIES, PUDDINGS, SHERBETS.

DESSERT DUMPLINGS. *See* DUMPLINGS.

DESSERT FORK. *See* FORKS *under* FLATWARE; *see also* TABLE SETTING AND SERVICE.

DESSERT KNIFE. *See* KNIVES *under* FLATWARE.

DESSERT PLATE. A small plate used for the serving of individual solid desserts, as pie, cake, etc. Usually flat and about seven inches in diameter, and can also serve as a luncheon or salad plate. *See also* DISHES.

DESSERT SPOON. *See under* SPOONS *in* FLATWARE.

DESSERT WINES. Those wines, usually very sweet, that go best with desserts or served alone. *See also* WINE.

DEWBERRY

DETERGENT. A detergent is any cleaning agent or solvent. In that sense, soap is a detergent, but the term has come generally to be applied to certain chemical formulations that are "soapless soaps." These detergents operate in much the same manner as does soap, by breaking the dirt and grease films into emulsions which are easily rinsed away, but do not leave the characteristic soap film so noticeable on glassware. By using a detergent, it is possible to minimize the dangers of films and spots if glasses and dishes are permitted to dry by evaporation following washing. *See* DISHWASHER; *see also* GLASSWARE.

DEVILED. As applied to food means a highly seasoned, chopped, ground, or whole mixture, served hot or cold.

DEVITALIZED FOODS. Foods badly prepared are devitalized foods. Foods should be so prepared that they retain, as nearly as possible, their natural elements. These elements will be partially, if not wholly destroyed by wrong methods of manufacture or wrong preparation in cooking.

The more natural the food comprising the diet, the more normal the health. What are natural foods? Natural foods are those which come to us in their unaltered state for our consumption. If foods require some method of preparation, such as milling or cooking, they should be so prepared that the natural elements will not be thrown out of harmony. We must imitate Nature, who in preparing foods in her laboratory, compounds them so that the elements contained in those foods harmonize.

DEVONSHIRE CREAM or CLOTTED CREAM. The cream is skimmed from scalded milk, so that albumin is coagulated with it. It is warmed over a slow fire, not above 150° F. Devonshire cream is delicious with preserved ginger, while clotted cream and maraschino form a nutritive drink.

DEVONSHIRE CREAM CHEESE. English cream cheese, made from pure cow's milk. It is shaped into small molds placed upon straw mats.

DEWBERRY. A trailing plant of the *rosaceae* family. Its prickly stems, leaves, and fruit resemble the blackberry, and all the methods of preparations of blackberries may be applied to dewberries. *See also* BERRIES.

DEXTROSE. *See* GLUCOSE.

DEXTRIN. A soluble carbohydrate formed from starch in its decomposition by acids, heat, or enzymes. It is in the intermediate state between starch and sugar. *See also* BREAD.

DIAMOND-BACK TERRAPIN. *See* TURTLES.

DIASTASE. A vegetable ferment which has the property of converting starchy foods into a soluble material called *Maltose.* It is soluble in water and weak alcohol, insoluble in stronger alcohol. Its advantage, as compared with similar ferments in the saliva and pancreatic juice, is considerable, and its strength enables it to dissolve starches when present in the proportion of only 1 to 2,000. Like the aforenamed ferments, it acts in alkaline solution, but, unlike them, it continues to operate in acid media.

Diastase is the peculiar substance which causes the ripening during germination of fruits and vegetables by converting their starches into dextrin and sugars. Hence fruit becomes more and more digestible as it ripens.

DICE. To cut food material into small cubes.

DIET. In the broad sense of the word, the individual's diet designates the food and beverages that he consumes regularly. In the narrow sense, it means a more or less strict allowance of food prescribed for the modification of particular physiological conditions. The purpose of regulating diets is to maintain optimum bodily health and efficiency. In this article we are concerned primarily with the nutritive value of food and secondarily with its digestibility, but every possible effort should be exerted to render it palatable as well. *See also* MENU PLANNING.

NORMAL FOOD REQUIREMENTS

The body is a working machine whose first requirement is fuel. Hence, the first consideration in the diet is an adequate daily intake of fuel to provide energy for the constant internal work that maintains life in the body and for the variable external work. In civilized communities, where cooking is a fine art, the number and variety of food preparations is so great that the appetite is often stimulated beyond the requirements of the system. In these cases more food is eaten than is necessary or desirable to maintain the best standard of bodily health and vigor.

The nature of the most favorable diet must naturally vary somewhat with individual constitutions and with external conditions. Cold, bracing weather inclines one to vigorous exercise and so increases the appetite as well as the need for food. A hot climate or season disposes man to languor and inactivity and so diminishes food requirements. The individual's state of health greatly modifies the amount and nature of food required. Feeble and inactive persons may live on a third or less of the ordinary ration. Other cogent factors are sex, size, expenditure of energy, and age. The active growing boy often eats more animal food than the adult, and the middle-aged man eats more than the aged. A man of seventy can preserve good health on a quantity of food that would soon starve his grandson.

The amount of food required daily by a healthy individual can be approximated with the aid of the charts given under CALORIES (*which see*). When computing the quantity it is necessary to consider as well the composition of the food. *See* PROTEINS. The estimates of different nutrition experts vary on the most favorable proportions of particular kinds of food in a mixed diet, but they more or less agree on the total amount. The chief difference of opinion occurs over the amount of fat to be eaten; but, as a general rule, when the amount of fat is decreased the carbohydrate estimate is correspondingly increased.

TABLE OF STANDARD DAILY DIET FOR
INFANTS AND CHILDREN
(Department of Agriculture, Bull. No. 54)

One meal for boy 14 to 16 years of age, inclusive, equivalent to 0.8 meal of man.
One meal for girl 14 to 16 years of age, inclusive, equivalent to 0.7 meal of man.
One meal for child 10 to 13 years of age, inclusive, equivalent to 0.6 meal of man.
One meal for child 6 to 9 years of age, inclusive, equivalent to 0.5 meal of man.
One meal for child 2 to 5 years of age, inclusive, equivalent to 0.4 meal of man.
One meal for child under 2 years of age equivalent to 0.3 meal of man.

A survey chart of dietary essentials, their uses, and their sources follows. For further information see MINERALS, VITAMINS, CARBOHYDRATES, and FATS.

Since few of our foods consist of a single foodstuff, and we are not likely to make even a single meal on pure fat, or pure protein, or pure carbohydrate, we are

TABLE OF DIETARY CONSTITUENTS AND NORMAL DAILY ADULT QUOTA

Required Element	Approx. Daily Amt. for Adult	Uses	Sources
Proteins	60 grams	Build and repair tissues, furnish energy, help indirectly to regulate body processes.	Meat, milk, eggs, dried legumes, cheese, fish
Calcium	.8 grams	Builds bones and teeth, a constituent of muscle and nerve tissues and of body fluids	Milk, cheese, vegetables, eggs, nuts
Phosphorus	1.32 grams	Works in conjunction with calcium to build bones and teeth, helps to prevent blood from becoming acid	Same as calcium and also fruits and whole grain cereals
Iron	15 milligrams	Gives the blood its ability to carry oxygen	Dried fruits and vegetables, green vegetables, meat (especially liver), eggs, whole grain bread and cereals
Iodine	.08 milligram	Constitutes part of the thyroid gland which regulates the body's use of energy	Iodized table salt, sea food

Common salt and other mineral substances are also essential to the daily diet. All of these, however, are probably present in a diet that includes adequate amounts of calcium, iron, and iodine.

Vitamin A	5000 International Units	Helps body to resist infection, prevents night blindness	Liver, fish liver oils, yellow and green fruits and vegetables, butter, milk, eggs
Vitamin B1 (Thiamine)	1.2 milligrams	Important to normal growth and digestion	Whole grain bread and cereals, liver and pork, dried peas and beans
Vitamin B2 (Riboflavin)	1.6 milligrams	Important to normal growth and to the reduction of oxygen	Meat, green leafy vegetables, milk, cheese, eggs
Niacin	16 milligrams	Aids the body in burning foods	Green leafy vegetables, fish, liver, lean meats
Vitamin C (Ascorbic acid)	57 milligrams	Is important to teeth, bones, and blood vessels and to the processes of oxidation and reduction	Green leafy vegetables, citrus fruits, tomatoes
Vitamin D	600 International Units	Important to the development and maintenance of healthy teeth and bones	Milk, eggs, fish liver oil, butter, liver, cream
Carbohydrates	—	Furnish energy	Vegetables, cane sugar, cereals
Fats	—	Furnish energy and give staying power to meals	Butter, cream, cheese, meat fat, lard, vegetable oils
Water	6 glasses	Essential constituent of all body tissues	
Cellulose	—	Aids normal functioning of intestines	Fruits, whole grain cereals, vegetables

Some Possible Substitutions in the Diet

These Foods	Sources of	May Be Substituted for
Fish, eggs, milk, cheese,* and dried legumes	Proteins	Meat and poultry
Whole-grain cereals and bread	Vitamin B, Calcium, Iron	White bread and refined cereals
Irradiated evaporated milk	Most of the food constituents	Fresh milk
Canned tomatoes, raw cabbage, cabbage salad, other fresh fruits in season	Vitamin C	Citrus fruits
Green and yellow vegetables, molasses, nut butters, and fortified margarines (containing vitamin A)	Vitamin A	Butter

In cooking, molasses may be substituted for white sugar
*An ounce and a quarter of American cheese is approximately equivalent to a fullsize glass of milk

certain of getting some building material in any diet. If a satisfactory diet pattern is followed one is assured of getting the proper quantities and kinds of vitamins, minerals, etc. It is not necessary then to calculate a certain amount of fats, etc. for the diet. The following daily diet plan provides all the nutrients normally necessary for the maintenance of health and efficiency. The foods may be taken in any form, single or compounded.

Milk Group—3 cups for children, 4 for teenagers, 2 for adults. Cheese may be substituted for some milk. Also, yogurt, sour cream and cottage cheese.

Vegetable-Fruit Group—4 servings, including 1 of citrus fruit or tomato (vitamin C) and 1 of dark green or yellow leafy vegetables (vitamin A). Serve both raw and cooked vegetables.

Meat Group—2 servings of 2 to 3 ounces lean, cooked meat, fish, poultry, 2 eggs, 1 cup cooked dried beans or lentils, or 4 tablespoons peanut butter.

Bread–Cereal Group—4 servings; whole grain, unbleached flour is preferred.

Water—about six glasses

Since sufficient amounts of fats and sugars are generally ingested as a result of cooking procedures, special allowances for these foods need not be made.

EATING WISELY

Many people have queer ideas about their health and physical condition. They prefer to adopt the dietary advice of quacks or faddists rather than follow the advice of scientists who have spent lifetimes in research. The vegetarian sect proclaims that there is evil in all edibles except vegetables: in actuality, the digestive apparatus is not designed to accommodate enough vegetable matter to fully nourish the human body. Vegetarians contend that meat is bad for the kidneys and liver, that it is hard to digest and causes high blood pressure. Yet Eskimos live on meat and blubber exclusively and exhibit no ill effects.

Undernourishment in this country seems to be most common among low income groups. One of the reasons resides in the fact that protein is probably the most important nutritional element and it is also the most expensive one. The diets of people in low income groups also tend to be lacking in mineral and vitamin content. This deficiency can, however, be overcome by careful planning, buying, and cooking. Expensive foods are not necessarily more nutritious than the inexpensive.

Improper cooking diminishes the value of many foods. Minerals and vitamins in vegetables, for example, are lost when the cooking liquor is discarded, or when they are cooked too long or in too much water. Cook vegetables in only a little water unless they are very strong-flavored. Cook them until they become tender but no longer. Don't add soda to preserve their color as the addition of soda will destroy some vitamins. If the cooking liquid is not to be served with the vegetable, it should be saved for gravy or soup.

Cereals provide an inexpensive source of energy. Whole or cracked grains have a higher mineral and vitamin content than milled grains. To achieve the most favorable flavor and food value cereals should be thoroughly cooked.

It is extremely sensible to follow a diet plan, but do not become a slave to it. In general, observe which foods agree with you and give you a sense of well-being and which foods seem to induce depression. And the best single bit of dietary advice we have heard was: "Never skimp on food." If it is necessary to economize, it is necessary to give particular attention to the provision of an adequate supply of protein, mineral, and vitamin matter.

from it. Fried foods are low in digestibility and are not recommended for invalids and children. Avoid also pastry, condiments, and excessive sweets.

Foods that will stimulate the appetite should be served to invalids especially. They should be attractive in appearance, and they should be served at the proper temperature. Small portions seem to be more appealing than large.

Cooked foods are generally more digestible than raw. To attain the maximum digestibility, cook protein foods at a low temperature and starchy foods at a high temperature. This is recommended for improved flavor and appearance as well as digestibility. The only starchy foods that

Food	Most Digestible Form
Meat	—chicken, bacon, lamb, veal, ground beef, fish
Cheese	—cottage cheese or cream cheese
Vegetables	—puréed or chopped
Soups	—strained vegetable soup or creamed soups
Fruit	—seedless fruits, cooked or puréed fruits, strained fruit juices. (Ripe bananas, contrary to an old popular opinion, are easily digested and, mashed, constitute a favorable food for infants.)
Cereal	—thoroughly cooked, served without sugar, cooked preferably in a double boiler, strained (for babies)
Salad	—shredded lettuce, raw tomatoes
Dessert	—ice cream, custard, simple puddings

FOOD FOR INVALIDS AND CHILDREN

One could not attempt to set down a standard diet for all invalids or children. They require more of the body-building substances, and it is recommended that the infant's diet be enriched by orange juice and fish liver oils; but the chief difference between these diets and those of average adults is that the child's foods should have an increased digestibility. This demand should help to determine both the nature of the food and the method of preparation.

Milk is probably the most important food for invalids and children, both because it contains most of the nutritional elements and because of its digestibility. Cocoa may be taken by both but, used excessively, it may cause indigestion. Eggs rank next in importance to milk but, if they must be omitted because of expense or allergy, vegetables and fruits can usually supply the same substances. Soft-cooked eggs are more digestible than raw ones. Poultry is an important food for invalids because it stimulates the appetite and because excellent broths are derived

should be given to babies are those that have been artificially predigested.

The most digestible forms should be given to infants between the ages of one and three and to invalids when desired.

SPECIAL DIETS

Patients having diseases need special diets formulated according to the particular disease. In diets for anemics the need for iron-rich foods such as liver and other meats, green vegetables, whole-grain cereals, and dried fruits is most stressed. Fish, lamb, beef, ham, chicken, tomatoes, asparagus, spinach, string beans, and milk are among the foods generally recommended for diabetic patients; sweets and starches are avoided.

Any special diet must be prescribed by a competent physician having a complete knowledge of the individual's physical condition. Before following even a general diet for convalescents, for reducing, or for gaining weight, you should consult your physician so that he may approve or modify it. Special diets are usually made to follow the normal diet plan as closely as possible.

THE CONVALESCENT'S DIET

What is said here of the convalescent's diet does not apply to a patient recovering from a special disease, as in a case of this sort the period of convalescence must be supervised by a physician. The standard convalescent diet is recommended only for the patient who has undergone a surgical operation or who is recovering from an infection. When the patient is able to take solid foods, the daily diet should consist of the following:

1 quart milk
1 egg (or at least 4 eggs a week)
1 serving of meat, fish, or poultry
1 green vegetable
1 yellow vegetable
1 serving of potatoes
2 servings of citrus fruit
Another fruit
Bread or cereal, preferably with every meal

This diet is high in mineral, protein, and vitamin (especially vitamin C) content, and it may or may not be low in roughage. In the past the tendency has been for convalescents to exist on a toast-and-tea sort of diet, but modern med cine recommends their being placed on a more substantial diet sooner in order to hasten recovery. If a softer or lighter diet than the above is desired, substitute cooked fruits for raw and decrease the portions of the other foods accordingly.

It may be seen that the above diet differs very slightly from that normally recommended. The difference between the two should reside in the method of preparation more than in the nature of the food. The convalescent's appetite must be tempted; consequently, a special effort should be made to render the food attractive and easily digestible. In connection with the latter, you might substitute fruit juices for fruit or you might purée the vegetables. Foods for the convalescent should not be irritating in any way; they should never be highly spiced.

LOSING WEIGHT

Include the following foods in your daily diet:

Milk, skimmed or buttermilk, 1 pint
Egg, 1 medium-sized
Bread, 3 slices of whole wheat or enriched white—or—2 slices of bread and 1 serving (¾ cup) of cooked cereal
Fruit or fruit juice, canned or fresh, 1 of the following:
  Grapefruit juice, unsweetened, ¾ cup
  Grapefruit, unsweetened, ½ medium
  ½ cup of unsweetened orange juice
  Sections of 1 medium orange
  1 cup of tomato juice
    —and—
  One or more additional servings of fruit without sugar or cream
Potato, white, 1 medium, boiled or baked in skin
Vegetable, 1 serving (½ cup) of one of the following steamed vegetables:
  Green leafy
  Peas
  Snap beans
  Broccoli
    —and—
  1 serving of one of the following: carrots, steamed or baked winter squash, steamed cauliflower, tomato
    —and—
  a raw vegetable or a salad. Use lemon juice or vinegar in place of a salad dressing.
Butter or fortified margarine—3 teaspoons on bread or used as a seasoning
Meat, poultry, or fish—1 generous serving of lean kinds. Liver or other organ meats should be eaten at least once a week.
Cottage cheese made with skimmed milk may be eaten every day, ½ cup to a serving.
Liquids—at least 6 glasses a day, but this should be taken between meals. Taken before a meal, water tends to stimulate the appetite; taken after, to stretch the stomach. Never take more than one cup of liquid at a meal.

Most cases of obesity result from an excessive calory intake with insufficient exercise. A good reducing diet, as that given above, is low in caloric content and in fats and carbohydrates, but it contains sufficient minerals, vitamins, and proteins to insure proper nourishment. Foods that must be especially avoided are sugar, candy, sodas, sundaes, soft drinks, rich desserts, cream, gravy, salad dressings, olives, bacon and other fat meat, and all fried foods. Liquor should also be omitted.

The above diet excludes all of the afore-mentioned foods and all between-meal snacks. It allows dessert only once a day. Serving of all foods should be of average size, and no second helpings should be taken. For best effects, supplement the diet with additional daily exercise. Check your weight regularly and see that the rate of weight loss is not too rapid. A loss of two pounds a week is a safe reducing speed. You may feel hungry when you begin this diet, but your stomach will soon adjust itself to a smaller amount of food.

Gaining Weight

The following high calory foods are recommended for the underweight person:

Apricots, dried, stewed, or sweetened
Avocado
Bacon, broiled
Brownies
Butter or margarine
Butterscotch sauce
Cheese, cream
Dates, pitted
Eggnog
Figs, dried
Honey, strained
Jam or jelly, commercial
Malted milk, chocolate
Peanut butter
Peanuts
Prunes, dried, stewed, or sweetened
Raisins, seedless
Soups, cream
Sugar, granulated
Wheat germ

General rules for gaining weight:

Eat three nourishing meals a day in pleasant, quiet surroundings

Take nourishing snacks and drinks between meals. If, however, this practice tends to impair the appetite for regular meals, limit extra snacks to bedtime.

Get plenty of sleep and rest.

Avoid exertion and fatigue. Very mild exercise before meals, however, may serve to stimulate the appetite.

Try to develop a peaceful frame of mind. Avoid worry and nervous tension.

Eat foods rich in thiamine (see Vitamins), as these seem to stimulate the appetite. Eat more sugar, sweets, and fats, and take larger servings.

Adjustment to a larger food intake should be gradual in order to avoid digestive difficulties.

Here is a sample day's menu:

Breakfast
Fruit juice or fruit with sugar and cream, if desired
Cereal, ¾ cup with milk or cream and with sugar
Toast, 2 or more slices with butter or margarine and jam or jelly
Milk or chocolate milk
Coffee with cream and sugar, if desired

Mid-morning snack
Milk or eggnog
Graham crackers

Luncheon
Creamed potatoes
Green beans
Salad of prunes stuffed with cream cheese served with mayonnaise
Raisin bread with butter or margarine and jam or jelly.
Fruit and cookies
Milk

Mid-afternoon snack
Malted milk or milk shake with ice cream

Dinner
Meat loaf and gravy
Sweet potatoes with butter or margarine
Beets in Harvard sauce
Beet greens with bacon garnish
Carrot, raisin, and banana salad with mayonnaise
Bread with butter or margarine and jam or jelly
Baked apple with cream, or custard pie, or cake
Milk
Tea, if desired

DIGESTION. Both the external temperature and the internal body heat influence digestive processes. The effect upon the system of the temperature of food and drink is also a matter for consideration.

Hot food and drinks in cold weather, cold food and beverages in hot weather, are instinctive with almost everyone, partly on account of mental association, and partly because of a temporary agreeable sensation exerted over body temperature. Sudden changes of heat or cold react upon the circulation, respiration, and nervous system in a variety of ways, and indirectly affect the digestive apparatus.

Emotions affect digestion. Most everyone has had the experience of being so upset that appetite fails and when you eat under such a condition the food is literally choked down. There is such a thing as functional dyspepsia, or, as it is often called, nervous indigestion. Tranquility is a splendid dish to be served at every meal. Strong mental emotion, such as fright, terror, or excessive excitement of any kind, inhibits the digestive functions both in the stomach and in the intestines. On the other hand laughter is one of the greatest helps to digestion, and the old custom among our forefathers of exciting laughter at table by jesters and buffoons was a wise procedure.

When fat is cooked in food, a good deal of it is converted into free fatty acids. Not being soluble in the watery digestive juices of the body, the digestive enzymes have to attack fats on the surfaces. So if fat which is swallowed is finely divided, digestive action is quicker. It also follows that the more liquid a fat is, the easier it is to emulsify it, that is, break it up into small particles. Hence fats that melt at or below body temperatures are more easily emulsified and more speedily digested.

DIKOYA. A variety of tea grown in one of the most productive districts of Ceylon. Dikoya teas are among the choicest of Black teas.

DILL. The dill is an aromatic European plant that belongs to the parsley family, and it bears yellow blossoms that turn into tiny fruits or seeds. The pungent leaves and seeds of the plant are used as condiments and as pickling agents. Dill is derived from the Norse *dilla*, meaning to lull, and it was formerly given to infants as a soporific.

Dill seeds have a rather acrid taste, and they serve to stimulate the appetite. The odor of dill is stronger and less agreeable than that of fennel. The two are closely related, but they are not identical. However, dill that is found growing wild in the United States is popularly called fennel.

Dill is used primarily to pickle cucumbers, but it should be used more extensively as a seasoning. Its finely-chopped fresh leaves add their fragrance to potatoes, stews, fish, cucumbers, vegetable salads, and broiled meats. Dill seeds will render cabbage, cauliflower, meat gravies, spaghetti sauces, fish sauces, turnips, sauerkraut, and soups (especially bean and borsch) more appetizing. Add a dash of dill to tomato sauce, or try using dill and celery in stewed tomatoes. Dill seeds resemble caraway seeds in flavor, and the two may be used interchangeably.

DINNER. The principal meal of the day. Dinner may be eaten at noon, but

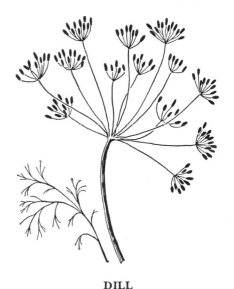

DILL

most commonly is eaten in the evening. *See* TABLE SETTING AND SERVICE.

DINNER FORK. *See* FLATWARE.

DINNER KNIFE. A large table knife used with meat courses. *See* FLATWARE.

DINNER PLATE. A flat plate, usually nine or ten inches in diameter. It is the largest individual plate used in table service. *See* DISHES, *see also* TABLE SETTING AND SERVICE.

DINNERWARE. *See* HOLLOW WARE.

DIPLES. A Greek, doughnut-like pastry, fried, then dipped in honey, and chopped raisins.

DIPLOMATE SAUCE. A sauce for boiled fish.

DIPLOMATE SAUCE

2 cups fish stock
1 cup white wine
1 generous tbsp lobster butter (*which see*)
½ cup scalded cream
Salt and pepper
2 tbsp coarsely chopped shrimp
2 tbsp coarsely chopped lobster

Reduce fish stock over a hot fire to 1 cup, and add 1 cup wine. Remove the pan from the fire and thicken sauce with lobster butter. Stir in cream and add salt and pepper to taste. Stir in shrimp and lobster. A little finely chopped truffle may also be added.

DIPPING CHOCOLATE. *See* CAN-
DIES.

DISGORGE. As applied to cookery, to
extract from a food what is useless, harmful, or detrimental. *Examples*: to remove the
drivel from snails; to remove the inedible
part of cucumbers or other vegetables; to
remove the excess of water or salt.

DISH DRAINING RACK. A dish
draining rack is a wire device designed to
hold plates and other dishes in a non-
touching, upright position so that they will
drain automatically after being washed.
While some are made of plain wire, the
better models have a rubber or plastic
coating to protect the dishes from possible
chipping or scratching. *See also* KITCHEN
EQUIPMENT.

DISHES. This term is applied to both
the vessels used to hold food at the table,
and the specific food preparations that are
served at the table. From this double
meaning it can be implied that plates and
platters do much more than merely hold
the food for the diner's convenience. They
enlarge the scope of food preparation, making possible appetizing arrangements of
food that, through their appeal to the eye,
greatly enhance their appeal to the stomach (*see* TABLE SETTING AND SERVICE).

Plates and platters have been made out
of a great many materials: wood chips,
palm leaves, precious metals, horn, and
pewter, to name but a few. Today, however, the common materials are ceramics,
glass, and plastics. Ceramic dishes are by
far in the majority, with glass coming
second in order of use. Plastic dishes are a
fairly new development and have not yet
been commonly accepted.

The available designs, styles, shapes and
sizes of dishes are legion and will satisfy
almost any taste and pocketbook. Since,
regardless of the cost, the purchase of a set
of dishes represents a major cash outlay for
the buyer, there are several factors that
should be carefully considered. The projected use and family needs, the numbers of
expected guests, the décor of the home and
the moods that will be established by the
table settings are all pertinent factors.
Whether the dishes, the silverware, or the
table linen will be purchased first is a matter of expediency and circumstances, but
it should be remembered that these three
elements, though not required to match,
should harmonize for the most effective
table settings.

When purchasing, it is well to select a
standard, so-called open stock pattern;
i.e., a dish design that will be manufactured for years to come. It will then be
possible to purchase matching replace-
ments at reasonable prices in later years.
An open pattern also makes it possible for
the family to add to their set from time to
time, as necessary. In the same vein, it is
possible for newly-weds to purchase only
the bare minimums when they first set up
housekeeping and money is needed for
many other expenses. They can then build
their set to any desired proportions later,
as circumstances permit. Also, should a
family desire an expensive set but lack the
immediate means, it is possible for them to
purchase the essentials in lower priced
ware and gradually build their better set,
one piece at a time.

The functionalism and durability of a
set of dishes should be considered as well
as the design. When purchasing, it is always well to approach exceptional *bargains*
with suspicious eyes. The manufacturing
may be inferior and the set may contain
many useless items. If the set is sound, but
priced below its obvious value, it may well
be a closed pattern or one whose manufacture has either been discontinued or will
be ended shortly. In that case, while the
purchaser will be getting value for his
dollar, he will be losing the advantages offered by an open pattern, as previously
explained.

There are many different items in a full
set of china. Many of them are alternative
items serving the same basic function, and
others (salt and pepper shakers, etc.) are
also available in silver and other materials.
Individual discretion will determine which
items are needed by the family.

Following is a list of the items usually
found in a chinaware set. To a lesser degree, the same or similar items will be
found in glass and plastics.

Dinner Plate. Used for individual settings,
this is the largest of the plates and is mainly restricted to main meal use. It is usually
ten inches in diameter.

Luncheon Plate. Similar in design to the
dinner plate, but usually only seven inches
in diameter.

Salad Plate. Used for serving individual
salads, this is generally the same size and
design as the luncheon plate. It may, however, be highly ornate or of unusual shape
and need not match the set.

Dessert Plate. Similar to the luncheon plate in size and design, this plate is used for individual servings of solid desserts as pies, cakes, etc.

Note: Though the size of luncheon, salad and dessert plates may differ in many sets, they can be identical, and one plate may serve all three functions.

Bread and Butter Plate. Usually a plain round plate approximately five inches in diameter. It is used to hold individual pieces of bread and butter.

Butter Dish. A large dish, usually covered, that holds a supply of butter for serving at the table; also a very small dish, sometimes called a Butter Chip used to hold an individual pat of butter, when butter is served in that manner.

Soup Dish. A large, shallow bowl or deep dish used for individual servings of soup.

Soup Cup and Saucer. A large, deep cup, usually double-handled, and frequently fitted with a lid to keep the contents warm, that is sometimes used for individual servings of soup.

Cream Soup Cup and Saucer. Similar to the soup cup, but broader and shallower; usually double-handled, but rarely fitted with a cover, it is intended for individual servings of cream soups, etc.

Soup Tureen. A large, frequently ornate, covered bowl designed to hold soup at the table. Individual servings are ladled out.

Tea Cup and Saucer. These cups are usually delicate in design and highly ornamented.

Coffee Cup and Saucer. Also called a *Breakfast Cup*, it is larger, and usually sturdier than the tea cup, for the morning coffee is usually served in a larger portion than the afternoon tea.

Demitasse Cup and Saucer. Also called a *Coffee Cup*, it is about half the size of the breakfast cup and often has straight sides. It is used for serving after-dinner coffee, when small quantities of a strong brew are desired.

Breakfast Bowl. A deep, straight, plain bowl used for dry cereals, etc.

Oatmeal Saucer. A wide, shallow bowl or deep saucer used for heated cereals.

Fruit Saucer. Similar to the oatmeal saucer, but smaller.

Vegetable Dish. A large, deep dish, round, square, or oval in shape, used to hold vegetables for serving at the table. It is frequently fitted with a cover to keep the contents warm. Uncovered vegetable dishes are sometimes called *bakers*, especially those of oval shape.

Sauce or Gravy Boat. A long, low, open pitcher, frequently resembling the hull of a boat in shape, that is used to dispense sauces, gravies, etc., at the table, either with a ladle or by pouring.

Sauce Tureen. A covered bowl, similar to the soup tureen, but smaller, from which sauces, gravies, etc., are dispensed at the table by ladling.

Platter. The general name for a large dish used to hold and serve meats, fish, etc., at the table. There are many sizes, shapes, and designs of platters, depending on their specific use. Some, for example, have engraved designs on the bottom to drain off the juice as the meat is carved. Platters are also known by several different names.

Oval Dish. A general name for an oval shaped platter, regardless of size.

Fish Dish. A large, oval platter used to serve fish.

Chop Dish. A small platter.

Muffin Dish. A large, round, covered platter used to serve heated muffins, toast, breads, etc.

Bacon Dish. A small, oval, covered platter designed to hold strips of bacon.

Egg Cup, Single. A small, egg-shaped cup designed to hold one or more soft cooked eggs. It has no handles.

Egg Cup, Double. A reversible, two-bowl cup, somewhat resembling an hourglass with unequal halves. One bowl is large enough to hold the contents of about two soft cooked eggs, while the other bowl is designed to hold the egg itself, if it is desired to eat it directly from the shell.

Toast Rack. A device somewhat similar to a letter rack, used to hold slices of toast upright.

Mustard Pot. A small, covered pot, usually with matching ladle, used to hold and dispense mustard.

Preserve Jars. These are similar to the mustard pot, but larger in size, and are used to hold and dispense honey, jam, marmalade, etc., at the table.

Jam and Butter Dish. A round, divided dish that is used to dispense the two items mentioned, usually at breakfast.

Cream Pitcher. Also called a *creamer*, it is a small container with a spout or lip and handle that is used to dispense cream or milk at the table.

Sugar Bowl. A small, covered bowl used to hold sugar.

Celery Dish. A long, narrow dish, either oval or rectangular, designed to hold stalks of celery. It is sometimes fitted with racks so that ice may be placed under the celery to keep it crisp but dry.

Salt Dish. A small, open, deep dish that is used to dispense salt at the table. It is preferred over the salt shaker in humid regions where salt is apt to become caked because of moisture in the air.

Compotier. A large dish that may be either highly ornate and made in the form of a leaf, fish, etc., or very simple; either shallow or deep; that is used to hold fresh fruits, nuts, wax fruits, flowers, etc., on the table. Often used as a center-piece, it can be left filled on the table as a decoration when the table is not in use.

Comport. A compotier mounted on a foot or pedestal. It is used in the same manner as a compotier.

Also included in a full set of china are various pickle dishes, sweets or candy dishes, nut dishes, salt and pepper shakers, cigarette boxes, match boxes, ash trays, jugs, pitchers, tea pots, coffee pots, and similar items. It must also be remembered that while the designs here described are basic, they are subject to much variation in each differently styled set.

The basic individual service unit is a five piece set, consisting of a dinner plate, a luncheon plate, a soup plate or bowl, a cup and a saucer. One such set is required for each member of the family and for each contemplated guest. If resources are limited, those are the components that should be purchased first. Fruit saucers, cereal bowls, salad plates and other accessories can come later. The number and type of platters and other service dishes needed depends entirely on the normal menu of the household, but it should be remembered that a lack of serving units will severely restrict the number and types of food preparations that can properly be set before the family. One large platter and two vegetable dishes will act as a bare minimum in this department, but the number should be increased as soon as possible.

See also CERAMICS, PLASTICS, GLASSWARE.

DISHWASHER. Several models of automatic dishwashers are available on today's market. You may choose from among convertible (portable to built-in) wood-topped and push button models in various sizes and colors.

The principle of operation is the same in all dishwashers, however. Utensils are subjected to high pressure jets of hot water (about 150 F.) combined with a special dishwashing detergent. Most dishwashers also have automatic drying units.

Dishes and utensils should be prepared for the automatic dishwasher in the same way that they are readied for hand washing. Bones and other large food wastes should be removed but rinsing is not necessary for the majority of modern appliances.

Load the upper and lower racks of the dishwasher in random fashion making sure that the items face the source of water without obstructing the water flow. Glassware should be placed on the shallow top rack only with care taken that the rims of the glasses rest securely on the bottom of the rack. Use a detergent specifically recommended for automatic dishwashers.

Special consideration should be given to the washing of the following items.

China. Most fine china and fine bone china, with a few exceptions, is machine washable. Antique, metal-trimmed, hand-painted or overglaze china should be hand washed, however. Consult the manufacturer's instructions for recommended detergents and cycles.

Plastics. Plastic dinnerware made from melamine plastic is machine washable. For other kinds of plastic, test one piece or write for the manufacturer's instructions. Teflon coated items may be washed in an automatic dishwasher. Light plastic items should be lodged securely on the top rack.

Silver. Sterling and silverplate are normally safe in a dishwasher. Do not wash silverplate in which the base metal is exposed as discoloration will appear. Do not wash silver and copper in the same load. Dirilyte items should be hand washed only.

Stainless Steel. Utensils and tableware wash perfectly in a dishwasher.

Aluminum. No pitting or warping will occur but some spotting may be caused by prolonged contact with detergent or by the minerals in the water. Color anodized aluminum such as that used for some water tumblers may fade. Do not wash with harsh detergent. *See* ALUMINUM.

Copper. Do not wash with silver. Utensils may spot or discolor from prolonged and direct contact with detergents.

Iron. Skillets should not be machine washed since the action will remove the rust resistant oil-seasoning of the metal put on by the manufacturer.

Wood. Use of an automatic dishwasher on wood will hasten warping, cracking and loss of finish.

DISHWASHING. Preparing a meal can be a pleasure—to many it is a hobby—and eating a meal has never been considered work. It is unfortunate that there must be an aftermath to every meal, an anti-climax in the form of many dirty dishes and cooking vessels. Cleaning these can hardly be considered fun, except under the most unusual of circumstances, but it is an essential step.

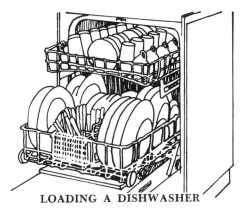

LOADING A DISHWASHER

Equipment

A minimum of equipment will cover most dishwashing needs. While a combination rag or sponge and plate scraper will effectively scour dishes, less energy is required to use a scouring device such as a sponge encased in plastic netting. Steel wool pads may be employed for very difficult scrubbing jobs.

Choose a mild soap or detergent in bar, flake or liquid form for most washing. If need be, silver polish, disinfectant (for appliances) or oven cleaner may also be employed. A rubber or plastic coated rack will hold drying dishes. Several soap and sponge holders are also useful.

There should be an adequate supply of dish towels. These may be made of any absorbent textile, but they should be lint-free.

DISHWASHER

Procedure

Before the dishes are stacked, they should be scraped as clean as possible. If they contain any material, such as egg yolk, that will harden, they should be rinsed off while it is still soft. Cups and glasses should be emptied and rinsed with clean water. The dishes should be stacked carefully, so that there is no possibility of any two becoming stuck together, or of the pile toppling over. China or glassware that has held ice or other cold substances should be given an opportunity to gradually warm before being placed in the water.

The water should be as hot as the hands will bear. Detergents should be used according to the directions on the box, and if soap is used, there should be adequate suds, but no free soap floating in the water.

Glassware (*which see*) should be washed first, before anything else is placed in the water. It is best to handle glassware individually, to prevent breakage through jostling. Chinaware comes next, and common sense will indicate how much should be placed in the dishpan at any one time. Mere soaking is not enough; each item should be well scrubbed with a cloth or brush. Silverware (*which see*) is washed next, before the cooking utensils.

If at any time during the operation the water becomes too cool, dirty, or greasy, it should be changed. Greasy water in particular is hazardous, for it is apt to coat everything with a thin grease film. It may be found necessary to add further soap or detergent as the washing progresses, but this should not be used as a substitute for fresh water.

Sharp knives should be washed individually, for otherwise the hands may be cut as they grope about in the water. A heavy object should never be placed on top of a fragile one in the water.

After being washed, the dishes should be rinsed in hot, clear water, and then dried. They may be rinsed by immersion or by pouring the water over them. If soap is used, the dishes should be dried by hand, lest water spots or soap film be left on the surface, but air-drying is permissible with some of the detergents. For appearance sake, a final polishing may be given with a clean, dry cloth.

Cooking Utensils. Because they are most subject to grease and charred foods, the utensils require special care. It is well to prepare each vessel as soon as it is released from use by scraping it out and filling it with water to soak. Frying pans, which are usually greasy, should have as much of the grease as possible poured out, be filled with water, and left to simmer while the other dishes are being washed. This water is poured down the drain, and will be found to carry most of the grease with it.

When food has burned in a vessel, much of the char can be removed by soaking and simmering, though care should be taken not to let substances like macaroni, noodles, etc., get down the drain where they might clog the pipes.

Steel wool can be used to remove stubborn particles, provided that the utensil is made of a suitable material. Silver polish can be used to remove stains on chromium plating, etc. Knives and similar sharp, pointed instruments should not be used to scrape, for they cause scratches and gouges in the surface.

Cooking vessels present particular problems because they often have rivets, rims, folds, and other hard-to-clean areas. In addition, they may be made up of components that require different individual care. Care must be taken at all times to make certain that the water does not become too dirty or greasy to properly clean.

Grease is the big problem in dishwashing. The only answers to grease are plenty of *hot* water, soap or detergent, and vigorous scrubbing. Wherever possible, the grease should be removed in solid form.

DISTILLED WATER. Water obtained by condensing steam. Distilled water is absolutely pure, but it has a flat or metallic taste from the absence of air and salts. It is now extensively used for drinking water, frequently on steamships at sea.

DITTANY. The famous herb "Dittany of Crete" (*Origanum dictamnus*) is a member of the mint family. It is, of course, native to Crete. It bears spikes of pink blossoms, but only its leaves are used for flavoring. These are wonderful in salads, especially fruit salads. They may be substituted for oregano, marjoram, or thyme (*all of which see*) in any recipe. In a word, they may be used to season almost any food. The dittany of the United States belongs to the same family and bears the botanical name of *Cunila origanoides*.

DIVINITIES. Divinities, nougats, and sea foams belong to the fudge family. These are a little more difficult to make, but once you have learned the fundamentals your candy-making repertoire will grow by leaps and bounds.

CHERRY COCONUT DIVINITY

2 cups sugar
⅔ cup water
½ cup light corn sirup
2 egg whites
1 tsp vanilla
⅛ tsp salt
½ can moist sweetened coconut, toasted and crumbled
¾ cup candied cherries, thinly sliced

Bring ½ cup of the sugar and ⅓ cup of the water to boiling point, stirring until sugar is dissolved, then cook to the soft ball stage (238° F.). In another saucepan, cook the remaining sugar, water and corn sirup to the firm ball stage (250°–252° F.) Remove from fire and cool slightly, then pour slowly over the stiffly beaten egg whites, beating constantly for about 1½ minutes or until the mixture loses its gloss. Now add the first sirup slowly, beating as before. Stir in the vanilla and salt and fold in the coconut and cherries. Turn immediately into a shallow buttered pan, spreading smoothly and when cold cut into small squares.

Broken nut-meats, chopped pitted dates or seedless raisins may be substituted for the candied cherries if desired.

HOLIDAY DIVINITY

2 cups sugar
⅓ cup light corn sirup
½ cup water or fruit juice

3 egg whites
⅛ tsp salt
⅓ tsp vanilla
½ cup diced candied cherries
¼ cup diced candied pineapple
½ cup toasted cooled halvéd almonds

Place the sugar, sirup and water or fruit juice in a saucepan, bring slowly to boiling point, stirring until the sugar is entirely dissolved, then cook to the hard ball stage (258°–260° F.). Remove from the fire and pour slowly over the stiffly beaten egg whites, beating and stirring briskly and consistently. Do not scrape the pan. Add salt and vanilla and beat until the candy holds its shape. Stir in fruit and almonds, turn into a waxed paper lined bread pan, smooth the surface and cool. Slice with a sharp knife, and keep covered in the container until ready to serve.

PEPPERMINT DIVINITY

3 cups sugar
½ cup light corn sirup
¼ tsp salt
2 egg whites
¾ tsp peppermint extract

Combine sugar, sirup and salt and bring gently to boiling point, stirring until the sugar is thoroughly dissolved, then continue boiling to the firm ball stage (246°–248° F.). Pour very slowly over the stiffly beaten egg whites, beating while pouring, and continuing the beating until the mixture holds its shape when dropped from the spoon. Add the peppermint extract, mix thoroughly and drop by teaspoonfuls onto waxed paper, or pour into a shallow buttered pan, spreading smoothly, and when cold cut into small squares.
Note. In the cooking of all divinities be sure to keep the sides of the saucepan wiped with damp brush or swab to avoid the formation of crystals.

DOCK. *See* SORREL.
DOGFISH. *See* GRAYFISH.
DOLCE-VERDI CHEESE. A hard, rich cheese made in Italy.
DOLLARFISH. *See* BUTTERFISH.
DOMACI BELI SIR CHEESE. A Yugoslavian cheese.
DOOAR. Black teas grown in the district of the same name in Bengal, India.

They are somewhat like the Assams, but less rich and pungent. Autumnal varieties are especially good, and are used in fine blends.
DORSET CHEESE. Another name for Blue Vinny Cheese (*which see*).
DOTTER CHEESE. A German cheese made of egg yolks and skimmed milk.
DOUBLE BOILER. A double boiler is really two saucepans, one set on top of the other. The lower one is filled with water, which, when boiled, heats the upper and thus cooks food without direct heat. (*See also* KITCHEN EQUIPMENT).

DOUBLE BOILER

DOUBLE-CREME CHEESE. A soft cream cheese made in many parts of France.
DOUBLE STANDARD SOUR. A mixed alcoholic drink. *See under* SOUR.
DOUGH. A soft mass of moistened and usually leavened flour or meal, prior to being baked, as bread, cake, etc. Also a soft pasty mass.
DOUGHNUTS. A tribe of prehistoric Indians is believed to have been the originators of the doughnut. Excavations recently made in the Southwestern part of the United States revealed among other relics petrified fried cakes with holes in them. Of course, nobody can know what mixture was used by the one who baked these cakes, but we are told that in appearance they closely resemble the doughnut as we know it today.

Although these aborigines may have been the first to make a fried cake with a hole in it, a doughnut of this shape is only a recent development in the baking industry. The doughnut, as we know it, is said by the experts to be a modern and up-to-date variety of a fried cake—the *olykolck*—which was brought to the New World by the early Dutch settlers. The popularity of this delicious cake spread so that it became a great favorite in every home, and because of this, there soon were many shops which specialized in the sale of doughnuts and coffee.

DOUGHNUT SHAPES

According to a student of the subject, it was in the middle of the 19th century that the modern doughnut was given the appearance so familiar to us. The idea of the hole came from a sea captain who was fond of doughnuts, although they gave him indigestion. He experimented with the doughnut dough, finally cutting holes in it with the top of a can. This arrangement served better to promote thorough baking, and the cakes were made more digestible.

Other varieties of the doughnut are the fried cake and the cruller, invented by a man named Krol. In his honor the cake was called "cruller." The dough used is similar to that of the doughnut, but it is made into twisted or other fanciful shapes.

 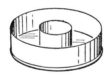

DOUGHNUT CUTTER

A Few Hints About Doughnuts

(1) Use as little flour as possible in rolling out the dough.

(2) Doughnuts will toughen if handled or kneaded too much. Roll and cut a few at a time.

(3) Absorption of the fat while frying makes doughnuts indigestible. The temperature of the fat while frying influences the amount absorbed. It should be from 360° to 375° F.

(4) Cook only a few doughnuts at a time, turning them frequently after they rise to the surface. Remove as soon as they are sufficiently brown, and drain on soft, crumpled paper.

(5) If the fat is too hot, the mixture breaks down into harmful compounds; if not hot enough, it soaks into the doughnut and makes it greasy.

(6) Greased-soaked doughnuts are usually the result of too much sugar.

(7) At least three inches of fat, or more according to the quantity of doughnuts to be fried, is required for good results. If you do not have a thermometer for deep fat frying, use the bread test. A cube of bread dropped into the hot fat should brown in one minute.

(8) To soften or freshen leftover doughnuts, place them in a paper bag or covered container, and reheat in a moderate oven (350° F.)

(9) The dough should be as soft as can be handled. Too soft a dough requires a heavily floured board for cutting, and the rings do not fry into plump puffs, but have unexpected lumps and bumps here and there.

(10) Try splitting old-fashioned doughnut just as you would English muffins, and toast them. Serve with honey, marmalade, or orange butter.

(11) Use orange frosting on chocolate doughnuts for a buffet or a Sunday supper. The flavor blending is excellent.

(12) You may, if desired, spice the doughnut dough before shaping it.

(13) The simplest way to sugar doughnuts after frying is to place a few in a paper bag with a spoonful of sugar, close the bag, and shake vigorously.

BISMARKS
(Jellied Doughnuts)

1 recipe rich roll dough (*which see*)
¼ cup tart stiff jam
Fat for frying
½ cup granulated sugar

Make dough according to directions but increase yeast to 2 packages dry granular yeast or 2 cakes compressed yeast. After dough has risen until double in bulk, turn out on lightly floured board and divide in 2 equal portions. Quickly round up portions and cover with bowls. Let rest on board 10 minutes. Roll out on lightly floured board to ¼ inch thickness. Allow to stand undisturbed 5 minutes. Cut with a

2 ½ inch cookie cutter that has been lightly dipped in flour. Again allow to stand 5 minutes. Place about ½ teaspoon jam in center of half the rounds and place a second round over the top of each, sandwich fashion. Seal the entire edge firmly by pressing with a fork or between the fingers. Cover and let stand in a warm place (86° F.) until double in bulk, about 45 minutes. Fry in deep fat heated to 350° F. until brown and crisp on both sides, about 5 minutes. Turn once during cooking. Drain on unglazed paper and transfer to a paper sack containing sugar while still warm. Shake to coat well. Makes about 20 Bismarks.

CRULLERS

¼ cup shortening
1 cup sugar
2 eggs, well beaten
3½ cups flour
4 tsp baking powder
1 tsp salt
¼ tsp ground nutmeg
¼ tsp ground cinnamon
1 cup milk

Cream the shortening and sugar together until very light. Add the eggs and when thoroughly blended, work in the sifted, dry ingredients alternately with the milk, mixing thoroughly after each addition. Roll out about half an inch thick on a lightly floured board, cut into strips about eight inches long and one inch wide, double together and twist, pinching the ends firmly together so that they will not break apart. Fry, drain, and sugar.

QUICK DOUGHNUTS

3 tbsp shortening
⅔ cup sugar
2 eggs, well beaten
3½ cups sifted flour
4 tsp baking powder
1 tsp salt
¼ tsp ground cinnamon (optional)
⅛ tsp ground cloves (optional)
⅛ tsp ground nutmeg (optional)
⅔ cup milk

Cream the shortening and sugar until light, add the eggs and blend thoroughly.

Sift together the dry ingredients and add, alternately with the milk, to make a dough of about the consistency of biscuit dough. (The amount of flour used may vary slightly so sift only three cups with the spices; it will be easy to add the remaining half cup if needed.) Roll out about half an inch thick on a floured board, using only enough flour on the board to prevent sticking, and cut with doughnut cutter. Fry, a few at a time, in deep hot fat (360°–375° F.), turning just as soon as the doughnuts rise to the top of the fat and turning again, once or more, during the frying. Drain on soft crumpled paper and when cool dust with powdered sugar.

For *chocolate doughnuts* add one and one-half squares (ounces) of melted chocolate to the milk, stirring to blend thoroughly.

RAISED DOUGHNUTS

1 yeast cake
1 cup milk, scalded and cooled
2 beaten eggs
1 tsp salt
¾ cup sugar
½ cup shortening
About 5 cups sifted flour

Crumble the yeast into a large mixing bowl, add the milk and stir and blend until the yeast is dissolved. Beat and add the eggs, salt and sugar, then the softened shortening and the flour, working all until smooth and using enough flour to make a light soft dough. Knead until smooth, then place in a greased bowl, brush with melted shortening, cover and allow the mixture to rise in a warm place, free from drafts, until doubled in bulk. Turn onto a lightly floured board, roll out about one-half inch thick and cut into rounds. Again let the doughnuts rise until light. Fry, a few at a time, in deep hot fat (360°–375° F.), turning just as soon as the doughnuts rise to the top of the fat and turning again, once or more, during the frying. Drain on soft crumpled paper and when cool dust with powdered sugar.

DOUX. A French term meaning sweet. *See* CHAMPAGNE.

DRAMBUIE. A clear, pale-brown, half-dry, and sparkling liqueur usually served as an after-dinner cordial. It has a delightful aroma. Made from Scotch whisky, it is a product of Scotland.

DREDGE. As applied to cookery, the term means to coat lightly, usually with flour or sugar, or mixed condiments.

DRESDENER BIERKASE CHEESE. Another name for Hand cheese (*which see*).

DRESS. As applied to food means to prepare for cooking or the table, as to dress a chicken, turkey, etc.

DRESSING. *See* STUFFING. As applied to salads, *see* SALAD DRESSINGS.

DRIED BEEF. *See* CHIPPED BEEF.

DRIED FRUIT. Before the Twentieth Century, dried f uits were largely imported. Now the United States leads the world in the production of raisins and prunes, and a large part of the figs we eat are grown here. Now dried fruits are often used in cakes, cookies, and other desserts, and meats are garnished with them. A slice of baked ham, with brown sugar, apricots, and a dash of powdered clove, is a new dish to many homemakers. Duck, chicken, beef, pork, and lamb have taken on new flavors from the addition of dried fruits or their juices while cooking. Cornmeal pudding is often enhanced by the addition of dried peaches, apricots, or prunes.

Today, dried fruits are not shriveled or withered fruits, as was the case before scientific methods of preparation were adopted. Strictly speaking, they should be considered fresh fruits from which the water has been evaporated.

DRYING AND PACKING

The fruits are dried on the ranches where they are grown. First, they are exposed for some hours to sulphur fumes to prevent decay, to preserve color, to discourage insects, to hasten drying, thus making it possible to retain vitamins. The residue of sulphur in the cooked fruit amounts to next to nothing. (Prunes are seldom sulphurized. They get a quick bath in a caustic solution, then a cold-water rinse.) Next, the fruit is laid under the rays of the sun for two to three weeks, then packed.

Packaging and distribution are modernized, the latter so much so that we have raisins, peaches, pears, apricots, figs, dates, and other dried fruits in all parts of the country the year round. Better packaging in air-tight cartons keeps the fruit moist, with the result that these evaporated fruits are not *dried*, and that fact radically affects their cooking or preparing processes.

VALUE OF DRIED FRUITS

Nutritionists have done much to extend the use of dried fruits by advocating the use of dried fruits in spring and summer as well as through the winter. According to tests made by dieticians, an anemic person can raise the hemoglobin count of his blood to normal by consuming a pound and a half of dried fruit a day. This is the approximate mineral equivalent of six to eight pounds of fresh fruit. Vitamins A, B, C, and the "protective" minerals are found in these dehydrated foods.

Many of the scientific health facts, cookery suggestions, and recipes having to do with dried fruits have come from the institute and testing kitchens of a man who believed in the health value of the fruits and their gustatory appeal. L. B. Williams of San Francisco and his staff have shown bakers how to popularize fruit breads, fruit breakfast pastries, and coffee rings, and have developed other uses for the formerly neglected fruits, all of which are preserved in their own sugar (glucose).

COOKING HINTS

In the old days when dried fruits were indeed dried and withered, it was necessary to soak them overnight or for at least eight hours. Today this is not only unnecessary but decidedly wrong. Quick cooking is the secret of success with these delicate fruit pulps, and quick cooking must be practised. It is entirely up to the cook whether these fruits shall be whole, shapely, and delicious, or whether they shall come out an unsightly, broken, or mashed mass.

Also, too many pieces of fruit should not be cooked at the same time. When we cook fresh fruits, like peaches, plums, or cherries, we put a few pieces at a time into water or sirup, and each piece has room in which to simmer but still retain its shape. The same method should be followed with evaporated fruits.

Apples. Absorb enough water to make their cooked bulk five times the original. Remove the particles of core. Rinse, cover with water, and boil 40 minutes. For fresh apple flavor, omit sugar. Or if desired, allow one quarter cup of sugar for each cup of fruit. Added flavor may be obtained with a few grains of salt.

Apricots. This fruit doubles in weight when cooked.

Rinse, cover with water, and boil 40 minutes. Allow, if desired, one quarter to one half cup of sugar for each cup of fruit, to taste.

Figs. Double in weight when cooked. Rinse, cover with water, and boil 20 to 30 minutes, depending on the condition of the fruit. Allow one tablespoon of sugar to each cup of fruit, and add for last 15 minutes of cooking.

Peaches. Triple in weight when cooked. Rinse, cover with water, boil five minutes, and remove skins. Cover with fresh water, and boil 45 minutes. Allow one quarter cup of sugar to each cup of fruit.

Pears. Triple in weight when cooked. Rinse, remove cores, cover with water, and boil 35 minutes. Allow one quarter cup of sugar for each cup of fruit.

Prunes. Double in weight when cooked. Rinse, cover with water, and boil from 45 to 60 minutes, depending on the condition of the fruit. Sugar is not needed, but from one to two tablespoons for each cup of prunes may be added if desired.

Raisins. Double in weight when cooked. Rinse. Allow one cup of water for each cup of raisins, boil ten minutes, and add one quarter to one half tablespoon of sugar for each cup of fruit.

Practically all foods shrink during the cooking process, but dried fruits are a notable exception. Raisins, dates, currants, and figs blend better with other ingredients if they are soaked for five minutes in a little boiling water. Use two tablespoons of boiling water for each half cup of fruit.

DRIED VEGETABLE. Each one has been placed under its initial letter. In modern manufacturing, there is little or no difference in the food constituents of the fresh and dried vegetables, but because water has been evaporated, we have a higher concentration of these constituents in the latter.

Dried vegetables rank next to cereals in importance as vegetable food. Like bread, they require thorough mastication, that is, they are very starchy, and improperly masticated starch is certain to cause digestive disturbances. They resemble meat, for they are rich in building material, in fact, containing twice as much per pound as meat.

All dried vegetables should be thoroughly cooked, preferably in meat or chicken stock. Being highly concentrated, they may well be blended with other foods.

DRINK STIRRER. *See* STIRRER.

DRINKS. *See* BEVERAGES, CORDIALS, LIQUEURS.

DRIPOLATOR. *See* COFFEE MAKER; *see also* COFFEE.

DRIPPINGS. As applied to meat drippings, there is nothing like bacon or sausage fat to use in sautéing or browning hashed brown and other fried potatoes. These fat drippings add flavor to many dishes, such as fried rice. Chicken fat makes a delicious shortening for biscuits or muffins or gingerbread.

DROP DUMPLINGS. *See* DUMPLINGS.

DRUMFISH. *See* SHEEPSHEAD.

DRY. A term applied to wines and wine mixtures to cover a taste sensation that lacks sweetness but is not necessarily tart or bitter.

See also WINE.

DRY CHEESE. A very hard German cheese, which is made expressly for home consumption in the winter. Also known as *Sperrkäse* and *Trockenkäse.*

DRY ICE. Carbon dioxide gas is frozen by first liquifying it under conditions of pressure and cold, and then suddenly releasing the pressure. The substance attempts to revert back to its normal state by expanding, thus causing the temperature to drop (*see* REFRIGERATION) low enough to precipitate the substance in the form of snow. These crystals are then compressed into cakes for commercial use.

Despite its snow-like appearance and cold temperature, dry ice is not really ice, for it does not contain solidified water. It is, however, truly dry, for it melts by evaporating back to its gaseous state, leaving no moisture behind.

It is colder than ice, having temperatures of 109 degrees *below* 0° F. and lower, and, pound for pound, dry ice will absorb nearly twice as much heat as will water ice. A ten-inch cube of dry ice will weigh about 45 pounds.

The gas given off by dry ice is generally harmless, being non-toxic, and (if there is no water present) non-corrosive. The material does require some care in handling, however, because of its extremely low temperatures. If dry ice is applied directly to the skin, severe burns can result.

Because of its temperatures and convenience, dry ice has many commercial applications, chief among them being the long-distance shipment of certain commodities. Perhaps its most familiar use is the refrigeration of ice cream in street vendor's carts.

See also ICE.

DUBONNET. An exceedingly rich, tonic wine or liqueur popular in France. Highly aromatic, of a beautiful garnet color, this appetizing wine is drunk in Europe at the beginning of a meal to promote appetite. It is highly praised by medical authorities. It is made of pure, best quality wine, special herbs, and cinchona oil imported from Peru. During the summer, diluted with water, it is a delightful, refreshing drink, and it is used in some cocktails. See APERITIF.

DUBONNET COCKTAIL

1 jigger Dubonnet
1 jigger dry gin

Stir in mixing glass with cracked ice, strain into cocktail glass; or, stir in chilled cocktail glass. In either case, garnish with twist of lemon peel. (Serves 1)

See BARTENDING, see also COCKTAIL, ALCOHOL.

DUCHESSE SAUCE. Tomato and Hollandaise sauces mixed together, with chopped ham and white wine added.

DUCK. (Domestic). The season for domestic duck begins in April and lasts until the end of November. Fresh winter duck and duckling found in the markets between November and April are from a few scattered growers who sell particularly to the Jewish trade. The reason most growers call a winter production halt is because ducks are difficult to raise when the weather turns bitter. Besides, the rest months give a chance to sell surplus summer ducks which have been quick frozen.

Within four to twelve hours after killing, the ducklings have been through the freezing operation and are packed, usually twelve to a box, ready for shipment to markets all over the world: to England, the Continent, Hawaii, South America, etc.

In September and October the fresh supply becomes smaller weekly, and during those months frozen ducks begin to appear in local markets as the fresh supply cannot keep up with the demand.

RAISING DUCKS FOR MARKET

On Long Island from Patchogue eastward through the Moriches, Eastport, and Speonk, a white blanket of ducks covers the land. The air vibrates with duck chatter. But these are not native Long Island birds. They are descendants of ducks which as recently as 1872 waddled about the imperial aviaries in China. They were royal ducks, and their descendants still are. The first nine of these ducks reached New York City on March 13, 1873, a date honored among Long Island duck growers.

Hatched with a voracious appetite which proves his undoing, the baby duck is fed and nursed by master husbandmen to attain the weight of five to six pounds in 10 to 12 weeks. Seldom does one find a duckling over that age in the market. It takes an average of 30 pounds of feed to bring a duckling to market size. Its diet is planned to give sweet tender breast flesh. Cornmeal, bran, flour, meal, meat scraps, milk, buttermilk, are all part of the youngster's diet—mixed with fresh greens and served as a semi-liquid or dry feed. Until a duck is two weeks old, and is allowed out into the sunlight, he must have his cod liver oil and minerals.

The first 48 hours after the duck cracks out of his shell, he is left in the bottom tray of the incubator, to keep dry and snug. Then his keeper moves him to a hot shed for five days; next into a cold shed (but even this is steam heated for his comfort). There the ducks are conditioned for ten days for the outdoor pens where they take up swimming in the sandy bottom creeks in water cleaned and replaced twice daily by the tides. When hatched the ducks look like balls of fat, butter gold. Slowly the color fades, and at eight weeks the duck is pure white, and his baby peep has changed to a deep bass quack.

SELECTION AND PREPARATION

Young ducks are plump, with very light, semi-transparent fat, soft breast bone, tender flesh, leg-joints which will break from the weight of the bird, fresh colored, and brittle billed. Their windpipes will break when pressed between the thumb and forefinger. One of the surest methods to determine the age of a duck is to open the wing fully. Near the beam-feather are two small, pointed, hard feathers. At the extreme end of the longest one a triangular groove will be found, if the bird is no more than a year old; if more than a year old, the bird has as many grooves as it is years old. Ducks for table purposes are best when one year old, but ducklings seldom reach more than three months. Almost all markets stock only ducklings, because the commercial raisers do not find that it is economical to keep the birds longer.

The world's finest ducks deserve the best efforts of the cook. Duck is prepared for roasting like chicken, except that trussing is not necessary as the legs are very short, and the wings are usually cut off at the joint. If stuffed (see STUFFING), operate as indicated for Turkey (which see). The fat from the roasting pan should be removed occasionally and the basting made with hot water rather than with the fat in the pan. For further information, see POULTRY.

BONED DUCKLING

Have the bird boned at the market, leaving the meat in one piece. Place it on a board, skin side down, and spread it with a dressing of ground veal, pork and ham combined with soft bread crumbs and highly seasoned with sage, thyme and allspice. Roll the bird up, and sew it securely into a piece of cheesecloth. Place the plump bundle in a stewpan with carrots, celery, turnips, and parsnip—the whole cut up, as indicated for Braise. An herb bouquet is added with wine, boiling water, or stock, barely to cover the bird and its vegetable garden. Simmer 2 to 2½ hours, according to weight. Then remove from the heat, but leave the duck in the stock an hour or longer until cool. Then lift it out until thoroughly cold. Next, remove the cheesecloth, trim the bird neatly, and place in a moderate oven (350° F.) for a few minutes to remove the excess fat. Brush over with beaten egg, sprinkle with crumbs, seasoned to taste with salt, pepper, and ground spices, and brown in the oven. A savory hot or cold dish, this may be served for a buffet or Sunday night supper.

BRAISED DUCKLING AND GLAZED ORANGES

5-lb duckling
Salt and pepper
1 cup orange juice
1 cup chicken bouillon
½ cup seedless raisins
Flour
1 small glass currant jelly
Glazed oranges and water cress

Have the duckling cut into portions. Wash and pat dry. Brown in a hot Dutch oven. Season with salt and pepper; add orange juice, consommé, and raisins. Cover and cook in a slow oven (300° F.) for two hours without disturbing. Remove the duckling to a hot platter, skim off as much fat as possible from the gravy. Add the currant jelly, and when melted, thicken the sauce with flour mixed smoothly with a little cold water, using about 1 tablespoon of flour for each cup of sauce. Pour the sauce over the duckling, garnish with glazed oranges and crisp watercress. (Serves 4)

CANARD A LA PRESSE
(Duckling Under Press)

Note: For this inimitable dish a special press is required, and the pressing operation is done right at the table. The duck should be rare.

Roast a duckling in the usual way, omitting the stuffing. Remove the legs, and set them aside for later use. Carve the breast into thin filets, and lay one against the other on a lukewarm dish. (Be sure the dish is not very hot.) Cut up the carcass, and press it with the special machine, sprinkling it the while with a half cup of good red wine. Collect the gravy as it runs, and to the gravy add a scant half teaspoon of brandy. With this gravy, thus flavored with the brandy, sprinkle the slices of breast, sandwiched as described. Place the dish itself on a chafing dish, or place the slices directly in the top of a chafing dish,

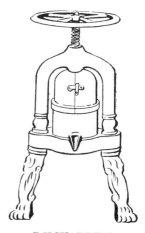

DUCK PRESS

and thoroughly heat, but do not allow them to boil. Serve immediately on warm plates, garnished with the grilled legs. (Serves 2 to 3)

DUCKLING CREOLE

5½- to 6-lb duck or 2 ducklings, disjointed
1 large onion, chopped
3 green peppers, chopped
¾ cup celery, finely chopped
1 small clove garlic
⅛ tsp each of thyme and cloves
2 generous tbsp butter
1 large tomato, peeled and quartered
1½ tsp salt
¼ tsp pepper
⅛ tsp paprika
½ cup water or stock
½ cup canned mushroom buttons, sliced
¾ cup condensed tomato soup
1 large green apple, peeled and quartered

Wash the ducklings and pat dry. Simmer the chopped vegetables in the butter in a large casserole or Dutch oven. Add the tomato and seasonings. Cover, and simmer for about 5 minutes; then add the pieces of duck and water or stock (or canned bouillon); cover and let simmer gently for 15 to 20 minutes. Add the mushrooms, tomato soup, and apple. Cover again, and simmer for 1½ hours, or until tender. Serve with either rice or potatoes. (Serves 6)

DUCKLING STEWED IN RED WINE

5-lb duckling
1 tsp salt
⅛ tsp pepper
2 large onions
3 sprigs fresh parsley, tied with
3 sprigs celery tops, and
1 large bay leaf
⅛ tsp thyme leaves
¼ cup good brandy
1 pint red wine
1 small carrot, thinly sliced
2 slices fat salt pork, chopped
1 tbsp olive oil
1 clove garlic, minced
½ lb fresh mushrooms, thinly sliced

Cut the duck into portions. Place in a large mixing bowl, and add all but the last 4 ingredients. Blend, and allow them to marinate at least 4 hours, stirring occasionally. Drain thoroughly, reserving the marinade. Heat the pork and olive oil in a casserole, and brown the drained duck pieces on all sides. Add the entire marinade, garlic, and mushrooms, and let simmer very gently for 1 hour. Serve from the casserole with rice. Wild rice is very appropriate. (Serves 4 to 6)

ROAST DUCKLING

Roast duckling is especially good if orange in some form is served with it. In its native China it was roasted, then served with a sauce made of orange juice and grated orange rind. In France, while the duck is roasting, a little of the fat is taken from the pan and sliced onions and carrots fried in it. Meanwhile, orange rind, cut into julienne strips, is simmered until tender either in chicken consommé or water to cover. This orange-flavored consommé is then added to the duck gravy in the roasting pan with a half cup of currant jelly and the whole heated together until the jelly is melted but never allowed to boil. The duck breast is served on toast surrounded by the onions, carrots and orange julienne strips and further garnished with orange sections. The gravy, with a tiny glass of kummel (*which see*) added, is then poured over all. If giblet gravy is preferred, use the recipe provided under the heading Gravy (*which see*).

Try a roast duckling with apples and cider sauce or champagne sauce if you prefer. For this, stuff the bird with diced celery; peel and core apples, arrange them around the duck in the roasting pan, then pour cider over all and use this for the basting.

Duck is prepared for roasting in the same manner as chicken except that little or no trussing is necessary since the legs are very short and the wings usually cut off at the joint. Both may, however, be lightly tied in place, if desired, always tieing under the back, never over the breast. If stuffed, proceed as indicated for turkey or chicken. The fat from the roasting pan should be poured off occasionally and the basting done with hot water or fruit juice rather than with the fat in the pan. For gravy, *see* GRAVY.

Young ducklings can be fried or broiled in the same manner as young chicken. Well boiled, fluffy rice or, better still, wild rice is especially good with duckling.

ROAST DUCKLING (*Curry Stuffing*)

1 5-lb duck
Salt and pepper
Curry stuffing
1 cup hot water
1 bay leaf
2 whole cloves
½ cup chopped celery tops

Wash the bird and cut off the neck. Sprinkle the inside with salt, and fill the cavity with curry stuffing (*see below*). Sew up the opening and truss or tie. Place in roasting pan with the hot water, bay leaf, cloves, and celery tops. Roast, having the oven very hot (500° F.), for the first 15 minutes, continue roasting at 350° F., allowing 25 minutes per pound (undrawn weight), basting frequently with the liquid in the pan and frequently skimming off the excess fat which accumulates in the pan. This dish is especially appropriate for hot weather. (Serves 4)

Curry Stuffing

2 tbsp minced onions
1 tsp salt
2 tsp curry powder
¼ tsp pepper
⅛ tsp thyme leaves
3 tbsp butter or shortening
1 tbsp vinegar
½ cup diced tart apple
½ cup cooked prune pulp
1 qt soft bread crumbs

Cook the onions, salt, curry powder, pepper, and thyme leaves in the butter or shortening for 5 minutes, stirring frequently. Then add all remaining ingredients and blend well. Cool before using.

ROAST DUCKLING
(Home Style)

1 5-lb duck
Fruit stuffing
Hot water and butter, for basting
4 tbsp flour

Wash the duck and cut off the neck. Fill the body cavity with your favorite fruit stuffing (*see* STUFFING). Fasten the opening with skewers or sew it up. Roast, having the oven very hot (500° F.) for the first 15 minutes to sear and brown it. Then reduce the temperature to moderate (350° F.), and continue roasting, basting frequently with hot water and butter, removing the excess fat as it accumulates in the pan and seasoning when half done. Allow 25 minutes per pound (undrawn weight). Meanwhile simmer the neck and giblets for 45 to 50 minutes in water to cover with a little onion and celery.

To make gravy: Drain and reserve the stock from the giblets. Chop the giblets, and brown them in 4 tablespoons of the drippings removed from the pan. Add the flour, and stir until smooth and brown, then add 2 cups of giblet stock, and stir until the gravy is smooth and thick. Cook 4 or 5 minutes, season, strain and serve hot. (Serves 4)

ROAST DUCKLING WITH ORANGE AND WINE SAUCE

5-lb duck
2 oranges, peeled and sliced
Salt and pepper
Hot water and butter for basting
2 cups bouillon or water
½ glass red wine
Orange sections and watercress

Prepare the duck for roasting. Stuff with the orange slices, sprinkle with salt and pepper, and roast, having the oven very hot (500° F.) for the first 15 minutes, then decreasing the temperature to moderate (350°–375° F.) for the remainder of the roasting time, 25 minutes to the pound (undrawn weight). Baste frequently with hot water and butter, pouring off any excess fat as it accumulates in the bottom of the pan.

Orange and Wine Sauce

For the sauce, cut the orange rind into julienne strips and simmer in the bouillon or water for ten minutes. Strain, and cook the giblets in this same stock for 25 to 30 minutes, or until tender. Add the orange strips, (originally cooked in stock), and press as much as possible of the giblets and orange through a fine sieve with the liquor in which they were cooked. Finally, add the wine and serve sizzling hot with the duck, garnishing with orange sections and watercress. (Serves 4)

WILD DUCKS

Black Duck. The black duck is essentially confined to the Eastern states, rarely migrating farther west than Kansas. Originally a diurnal-feeding species, like most ducks, persecution has taught the black duck to seek safety on the broad ocean during daylight hours, and to resort to inland ponds only after sunset for the purpose of feeding.

The black duck is excellent eating; and, as experiments prove that it can be reared in captivity, it may be raised for the market or used for restocking suitable localities. The Florida black duck is a closely allied cousin with similar habits, and is a resident of Florida and the Gulf Coast.

Blue-Winged Teal Duck. Formerly abundant and nesting over much of the eastern United States, this duck is now numerous only in the Middle West. It loves fresh water ponds and streams with mossy banks.

It migrates South early, and teal shooting in early September in some localities is one of the sporting events of the year. It is fond of wild rice, and is at its best when it has fattened on this nutritious seed.

Canvas-Back Duck. The canvas-back, perhaps the most famous of American waterfowl, has purchased its fame at a price. Now only the most wealthy epicure can afford to dine on canvas-back. Its exceptional gamy and indescribable flavor is due to the fact that its favorite food is wild celery, a long ribbon-like grass which grows in shallow ponds and estuaries. As this plant roots several feet under the surface, only the diving ducks can secure it. In Oregon and Washington, the canvas-back lives mainly upon *wapato*, a bulblike root formerly a staple article of food among Indians of those regions, and its flavor is fully as fine as the celery-fed canvas-back of the East. But in some parts of the country the canvas-back is in nowise superior to other ducks.

Few people know how the Canvas-Back Duck achieved its fame or how it fell heir to the name canvas-back. Fifty years ago Ward McAllister reigned as the aristo-cratic tycoon of New York and every year during the horse show, he gave an annual dinner to which four hundred guests flocked in full evening attire.

The game course was the canvas-back from Currituck Sound, North Carolina, where McAllister bought all his game. The method of shipping involved the use of specially designed canvas bags, which, by agreement, were returned to the shipper. All bills were made out "Fifty cents a pair. Canvas back." Thus the birds shipped north to satisfy the discriminating plutocrats became known as "canvas-backs" to the dealers, and by them were greatly extolled to customers, who concluded that the canvas-back duck was a king's morsel.

Green-Winged Teal Duck. Although still numerous in parts of the Far West, the green-winged teal has ceased to be common in the Atlantic states and may soon become extinct in this region. It does not frequent large lakes and open water, but shows a preference for fresh-water marshes and grass-fringed ditches. It is remarkable in how small a waterway a flock will hide and, if undisturbed, feed contentedly for hours. This teal is not so much of a diver, for the shallows in which it usually feeds do not require diving exercise.

Guichichi Duck. One of the most interesting birds is a native Panama duck that builds its nest in hollow trees. Its hatch is 13 or 14 eggs. As soon as the ducklings are old enough, the parents carry them in their bills, one at a time, to swamp. They are beautiful birds, with brown and white plumage. Properly prepared, it is one of the most delicious of the wild ducks.

Hooded Merganser Duck. The hooded merganser duck, the smallest and most beautiful of the ducks, ranges from Alaska to Mexico, and formerly was abundant in the East. It prefers still water ponds and rivers, and is often found in company with the wood duck. Its flesh is greatly preferred to that of the other two merganser ducks, which are a little too fishy for a real epicure.

Mallard Duck. The mallard is a very greedy and omnivorous duck, which eats all kinds of grain and small animal life. In the Far West it has the unique habit of resorting to stubble for waste grain, and the epicure, the connoisseur, and the gourmet need ask for nothing more delicious than a fat, corn-fed or wheat-fed mallard duck. This really fine duck is found in all parts of the world. Its size, abundance, and excellent flavor make it perhaps the most important of the duck family. Many of our domestic varieties are derived from it.

Mandarin Duck. See WOOD DUCK.

Merganser Duck. The narrow, serrate bill of this duck (sometimes called Goosander and in Canada Harle) as contrasted with the broad, smooth bills of most ducks would suggest that its habits differ from those of other ducks. The merganser's bill, with its saw-like teeth, is especially adapted to seizing and holding slippery prey of all kinds, including small fish, which constitute the most important part of its diet. It also eats water insects, frogs, and crayfish. It has a long, narrow body, eminently fitted for swift dives into water, where it spends much of its time. Cold weather and ice have no terrors for this fine bird, which may winter wherever open water is assured, provided food is abundant. It generally nests on the ground, but sometimes in hollows of trees.

Pato Real Duck. This muscovy is a large black bird with white markings on the wings. It weighs from three to eleven pounds. It flies only at dawn and dusk, and is easy to shoot on moonlight nights during the dry season. It likes to sit in the mud and feed on eel grass, water cabbage, wild rice, ginger root, and ragweed seed. It has a delicious gamy flavor, resembling that of the canvas-back.

Pintail Duck. This is one of the most beautiful ducks. It is easily recognized by its long, slender neck and elongated, pointed tail. The latter has caused it to be known in England as the Sea Pheasant. It is no longer common in eastern United States, but continues to exist in considerable number in the West. It is swift of wing, and an old pintail coming down wind will tax the nerve and skill of the most experienced hunter. Most wild ducks are fond of berries and in Alaska the pintail fattens on berries and becomes the most delicious duck of that region. It is one of the few ducks that braves the 2,000 mile trip from the Aleutians to Hawaii to winter in those sunny islands.

Red-Breasted Merganser Duck. This duck frequents salt water more than its relative, the plain merganser. It swims and dives with wonderful skill, and in clear, rapid mountains streams even the swift and wary trout is not safe from capture. It often hunts in company, a large flock advancing on a wide front, driving the fish before them and diving simultaneously, so that whichever way the fish darts a duck is there to get him. Roasted red-breasted merganser is a delight to the epicure.

Red Head Duck. This duck frequents the same feeding grounds as the canvas-back, dives just as well, and obtains its share of the coveted wild celery, so the epicure must possess a very delicate taste to distinguish red head ducks and canvas-backs. In fact, red heads are often sold as canvasbacks. It is more numerous east of the Rocky Mountains than west of them and while some of these ducks visit the bays and estuaries of the East Coast, its main preference seems to be for inland lakes and ponds where it subsists on various aquatic plants, insects, snails, acorns, beechnuts, etc. Such inland fed birds are not as tasty.

Ring Necked Duck. This is another tender morsel similar to the canvas-back. It is a fresh water species, an excellent diver, and gets its share of coveted wild celery.

Ruddy Duck. This ranges from one seacoast to the other and has a wide variety of names. In New England it is called the Dumb Bird and in the Potomac region the Rook. Names such as Deaf Duck and Fool Duck indicate its disposition, while Bull Neck and Spine Tail mark certain physical peculiarities. When swimming, its plump, round body and uplifted tail serve to easily distinguish it. The ruddy duck is extremely sociable and gathers in large flocks, sometimes in company with other species.

Formerly it was not esteemed by epicures and therefore little hunted, but as more highly priced species diminished in numbers, it has attracted more attention. In waters like the Potomac River, where it used to gather by the thousands in the fall, now only a few ruddy ducks remain. They are easily killed because they do not take wing when pursued but seek to escape by diving.

Wood Duck. Nature lavished the riches of color and design on many members of the duck family and critics can find subtleties of composition in duck plumage that outshine the gaudiest regalia of tropical parrots, sun birds, and humming birds. So, the diminutive, shy and retiring wood duck (also known as the Carolina Duck or the Summer Duck) stands as the peer of the world's feathered paragons of grace, symmetry, and beauty.

DUCK

420

Oddly enough, the genus *Aix* is represented by two species which dwell as far apart as America and China, and the superb wood duck's (*Aix sponsa*) picturesque and lovely cousin of the Orient is the mandarin duck (*Aix gelericulata*), whose charms are exquisite. For such close relatives, they differ sharply in make-up. The wood duck is all grace, in soft curves and flowing lines. But the mandarin duck was surely made to delight Chinese and Japanese painters and potters, and has its bizarre carnival costume elaborated with wing fans and a helmet that seems to be made of lacquered bronze.

The human mandarins of the Chinese aristocracy are classified in grades which are vaguely comparable to the European orders of nobility and knighthood. The official insignia of the seventh grade of civilian mandarins have a gold button on the ceremonial cap and a mandarin drake embroidered on the front of the robe. Hence, we gather that the duck owes its popularity and name to its intimate association with the nobility.

The wood duck, like the mandarin, is bred extensively on our Pacific Coast, but mostly from domestic stock, as it is a native game bird and the breeder must comply with the migratory bird regulations. When it was abundant, before plume and pot hunters threatened its extinction, it was indigenous to Canada and almost every state of the Union, so it thrives in the East as well as in California. At this time the hunter is restricted to one bird a season.

WILD DUCK COOKERY

A wild duck should always be served rare—18 to 20 minutes being the limit of roasting time. It should be placed in a very hot oven (500° F.) for five or six minutes; then the temperature decreased to moderate (350°–375° F.). Wild ducks, with the exception of canvas-backs, are fish eaters; and the homemaker, therefore, must take precautions to remove some of that fishy or muddy taste. Most gourmets agree that wild duck should be dry plucked. This may seem nearly impossible, but if you pour melted paraffin over the duck, and let it harden, most of the feathers, including the down, will come out when you rip it off.

Whatever amateurs may say to the contrary, a roasted wild duck must be profusely basted. Moreover, a wild duck is always singed and drawn, but never washed. Wipe it with a soft, damp cloth within and without. Cut off the pinions, and tie what is left of the wings to the body. A wild duck may or may not be stuffed, but a scant tablespoon of currant jelly or half a dozen cranberries, placed inside, will enhance the bird's flavor. Even a small duckling used for broiling should never be washed, but wiped with a damp cloth, or still better rubbed with good olive oil inside and out, seasoned with salt and pepper, and broiled as you would a chicken. It is advisable to lard it, that is, to cover with slices of bacon or pork fat. Lard the breast of any game bird to protect it against the intensity of the heat when roasting it, as well as to enhance its flavor. This will also add to the tenderness. Game, be it large or small, should be served instantly when done, as it then has the quintessence of flavor enhanced by the heat. *See also* ORANGE SAUCE.

ROAST WILD DUCK BIGARADE

Clean and singe a wild duck; rub it with lemon juice, then with salt and pepper, inside and out. Roast in the usual manner, basting frequently either with hot water to which may be added a little butter, or with game or meat stock, preferably veal stock. Cook very rare (about 18 to 25 minutes depending on the size and age of bird). Serve on a hot platter, garnishing with sections of peeled oranges, slices of lemon and crisp young watercress. Serve with bigarade sauce.

BIGARADE SAUCE

Remove all excess fat from the pan in which the duck was roasted; sprinkle in half a teaspoon of flour or, better still, the same amount of arrowroot or cornstarch, for two to three minutes. Now add two teaspoons of sugar, caramelized over a low flame and moistened with one tablespoon of wine vinegar, next the juice of half an orange (lemon juice may be substituted or the two blended). Immediately before serving, add one tablespoon of grated orange rind and one teaspoon of grated lemon rind.

If a gamy taste is desired, hang the duck in a cold place for a day or two, but never more than three days; this will also help to make the bird more tender, especially if old.

Appropriate for either canvas-back, red head, black duck or mallards.

WILD DUCK AU SANG
(Wild Duck in His Own Blood)

Like the domestic duck, wild duck may be prepared *au sang*. Kill the duck by a method which will insure no blood loss, then subsequently bleed it and save all the blood. Roast without stuffing to the desired point, about 20 minutes, having the oven very hot (500° F.) for the first five or six minutes, then decreasing the temperature to moderate (350°–375° F.). It should be so rare that when pricked with a fork drops of blood will ooze from the skin.

Slice the breast in thin filets and keep hot on a hot platter. With great care collect all the blood and with a fork crush the raw liver in it so as to obtain a soft paste, being careful first to remove the gall bladder and all connective tissue from the liver. To this paste add rapidly a few drops of lemon juice to prevent the blood curdling. Dust with freshly crushed peppercorns, a little salt, and a few grains of nutmeg. Moisten with a small glass of Zinfandel wine. Pour this sauce into a small saucepan or into the upper part of a double boiler or chafing dish, and heat gently, stirring constantly until the sauce changes color and texture, becoming a brown, soft, unctuous mass. Roll each piece of hot duck filet in the sauce and serve immediately. With a chafing dish the sauce can be prepared right at table. Burgundy is the correct wine to serve with this dish and with wild rice as the only accompaniment. However, brown rice may be substituted.

CURRANT GRAVY FOR WILD DUCK

Giblets of 1 duck
2 tbsp duck fat or butter
3 tbsp finely chopped celery
1 tbsp finely chopped onion
¼ tsp salt
2 tsp flour
Dash cayenne
½ tsp Worcestershire sauce
Dash tabasco
1 tbsp currant jelly

Before beginning to roast the duck, start giblets (and neck) simmering in a covered saucepan in enough water to cover. Add more water only if needed. Simmer until tender. Heat duck fat in skillet, add celery and onion and sauté until yellow and transparent. Mix salt, flour and cayenne and blend into butter. Add Worcestershire sauce, tabasco and the strained broth from giblets (concentrated to ½ cup). Stir until smooth and slightly thickened. Add jelly and stir until melted. Add finely cut giblets and meat from neck if desired. When duck is done, remove to hot platter, cover to keep hot. Skim off all but about 1 tablespoon fat. Add currant gravy to drippings and fat left in roasting pan, scrape well to loosen any browned residue, season to taste, heat to boiling and serve at once with duck. Makes 1 to 1½ cups gravy.

DUEL CHEESE. A small, rennet cheese made from cow's milk, originating in Germany.

DUKE OF CLARENCE MALMSEY. A very dry Madeira wine, light amber and reddish in color, produced by the use of several kinds of grapes. It has a tang and a wonderful bouquet. It is often served as an apéritif, and goes well with any cheese except cream cheese. *See* MADEIRA, *see also* WINE.

DULL. Any tea, the liquor of which is cloudy. *See also* TEA.

DULSE. Edible seaweed, is found in limitless quantities near the coasts of all continents and most islands. When dulse is fresh, it is brownish in color and often transparent in the sun. It has a delicious flavor. It is crisp and rather tough. To those who like its queer taste it is far superior to ice cream or candies.

Dulse is technically *Rhodymenia palmata* of the red seaweeds, found on the Atlantic coasts of Europe and America, and also on our Pacific Coast. One of the milder and pleasanter thrills of life is the poignant tang of the open sea and that is the flavor of dulse, if one savors it on the tongue after chewing some leaves slowly and reflectively. Fish and monsters of the deep graze and fatten on it, and it reaches our markets as the dulse and carrageen of the Atlantic, and as the *laver* and *agar-agar* of the Eastern seas.

On the island of Grand Manan, in the Bay of Fundy, dulsing is a great summer industry. After a high tide it is gathered

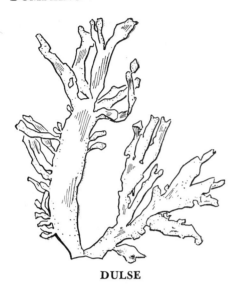

DULSE

by the dulsers after it has been torn loose from the sea bottom, packed in sacks, and brought to a beach of large, flat rocks, where the dulse is spread to dry, being turned once. When thoroughly dry, it is packed into sacks and barrels for shipment. Iodine is extracted from it.

Before iodine became widely known as a vital human need, the dulse, or delisk of Ireland and Scotland, enjoyed a period of high favor among American school children and some of their elders, and was sold more often as a treat than as a staple commodity. That was back in the days of gas lights and oil lamps, when the flavor of petroleum got into the corner grocer's sugar barrel; and some of us can still remember the great glass jars of puckery pickled limes that children bought with their pennies

The late Alfred W. McCann, investigating the ripe old age enjoyed by Cape Cod fishermen, observed that they received daily rations of iodine from eating fish that had lived on seaweed and other food. Further research convinced him that among people who subsisted on such a diet, arterio-sclerosis was virtually unknown. Other writers have attributed the large and healthy and long-lived families of the fishing villages along the coasts of Europe to nature's own preparation of iodine in their daily diet. In the Tyrol the dreaded goiter is prevalent, especially among women, but in the lowlands and along the shores, where fish is often the

only meat, and where stewed seaweed is a common vegetable, goiter is unknown and ancient mariners never have hardened arteries, high blood pressure, or apoplexy.

Carrageen, or Irish moss, is too mucilaginous to be used commonly as a vegetable but as a vegetable-gelatin for use in cooking it is an important article of commerce, like agar-agar of the Orient. The Chinese laver is another staple commodity of the East, as a vegetable and as an ingredient of soups, and it is also the chief food of the swallows that mysteriously build the nests that are exported to all quarters of the globe for making bird's nest soups for epicures. French and Italian peasants soak the dried leaves and boil them as a paste for broths and ragouts, and Irish, Scotch, and American fisher folk make them into soups and chowders with vegetables and herbs.

DUMPLING. The world's best culinary art has its roots in the cookery of peasants who evolved marvels in tireless efforts to make plain food savory, to avoid waste, to secure nourishment. One universal habit of cooks the world over has been to wrap choice morsels in leaves, dough, pastry, or puff paste, to be popped into hungry mouths without loss of juices, flavor, or aroma.

Hence we have the *dolmas* of Greece and the Levant, the *tamales* and *empanadas* of Hispanic peoples, the *koldunys* of Poland, the *kaldomars* of Sweden, the stuffed *blintzes* of the Slavs and Hebrews, the *ravioli* of Italy—and, on a grander scale, the majestic meat, fish, and game pies of Britain, never forgetting the *Vol au Vent* (*pâté*) of France.

Scarcely one of them is better than another, and not one falls short of lusciousness if you have a cosmopolitan palate, but we should pay homage to the ancestor of them all, the Chinese dumpling which was cooked to the taste of the great khans of Cathay when the tribesmen of Europe were still tearing raw meat from the bones of beasts with their teeth and hands. The hearty, exuberant, irrepressible Marco Polo harried all the Italian cooks from kitchen to kitchen with his tales of Chinese dumplings when he returned from his wanderings and *ravioli* was·created.

Chu-pao-pa and *su-gau*, the Chinese call them (there are other names in various provinces), and they are eaten in soup or with a sauce, just as we eat ravioli or bread dumplings in our soups. The only difference between the two forms is in the stuffing of the Chinese and the stuffing of the Italian. You can buy ravioli cutters and pastry jaggers in Italian and French shops, but even without them you can make the tiny morsels in disks, crescents, balls, squares, or other odd shapes according to your fancy. So it is with *chu-pao-pa.*

Apricot, peach, plum, prune, and other fruit dumplings may be made by the method described for apple dumplings. (*See* APPLE)

CHU-PAO-PA DUMPLINGS

For the dough, sift 3 cups of flour onto a mixing board or bowl, make a hollow in the center and pour into this 1 egg beaten with a dash of salt. Add just enough water or milk to moisten, then mix and knead into a smooth, firm dough. Place in the refrigerator for 1 hour, then roll out in thin sheets and cut into rounds or squares. Mince about ½ cup each of cooked chicken, pork, mushrooms, Chinese bamboo shoots (*which see*) and water chestnuts (*which see*), onion and celery. Moisten and bind the mixture with a beaten egg, a teaspoon of soy sauce and a little chicken stock. When thoroughly blended, divide among the pieces of dough. Moisten the edges of the dough with cold water, then fold or wrap and pinch all edges together firmly. Shortly before serving time, plunge into boiling chicken or veal stock and cook from 8 to 10 minutes depending on size. Serve the dumplings in Chinese chicken soup, or with a rich Chinese sauce.

DUMPLING OR RAVIOLI CUTTER

The dumplings may also be served on a bed of spinach or other cooked greens.

DESSERT DUMPLINGS

2 cups flour
2 tsp baking powder
⅛ tsp salt
2 tbsp sugar
1 egg, beaten
¾ cup milk
1 qt berries
1 cup water

Sift together the flour, baking powder, salt, and two tablespoons of sugar, and moisten with the beaten egg and milk. Drop from the tip of the spoon on top of the berries which have been brought to the boiling point with the water and the cup of sugar. Cover closely, and cook over a moderate heat for 15 to 20 minutes. Serve immediately, preferably with a wine hard sauce to bring out the delicate berry flavor.

DROP DUMPLINGS FOR STEW

1 cup sugar
1 cup flour
1 tsp baking powder
¼ tsp salt
2 tsp minced parsley
1 tsp grated onion
½ cup milk (about)

Sift the dry ingredients, stir in the parsley and onion, and moisten with the milk, using enough to make a drop or soft dough. The amount may vary slightly, depending on the flour. Drop small portions from the tip of a tablespoon or teaspoon into the boiling stew. As soon as all are in, cover the pan closely, and keep the stew boiling gently but steadily. Cook about 15 minutes, then arrange around the edge of the platter, turning the stew itself into the

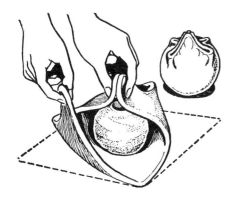

APPLE DUMPLING Shaping the dumpling

center. Gravy may be poured over the meat or served separately. Sprinkle a little parsley over all. After cooking the dumplings will probably be found to be sticking together, separate them as gently as possible, using two forks to tear them apart. Never lift the cover from the time the dumplings are put into the stew until the cooking is completed.

DUMPLINGS FOR MEAT PIE COVERING

2 cups flour
2 tsp baking powder
½ tsp salt
1 tsp poultry seasoning
1 tbsp shortening
2 eggs
About ⅓ cup milk

Sift the dry ingredients, cut in the shortening and moisten with the beaten eggs and milk, using enough of the latter to make a soft, drop dough. Arrange over meat, gravy and vegetables in one large or individual casseroles and bake in a moderately hot oven (375°–400° F.) 15 to 25 minutes depending on whether one large or several small pies are being made.

If desired, use a little less milk, roll or pat the dough out to fit the top of the casserole and cut into triangular sections like pie for serving. These dumplings may also be used for stew if desired.

FRENCH DUMPLINGS

1 egg
1 tbsp sweet cream
½ tsp salt
¼ cup butter, creamed
Flour
1 qt boiling consommé, bouillon, etc.

Beat the egg slightly with the cream and salt and add to the creamed butter with enough flour to make a mixture of about the consistency of a cake batter. Beat with a wooden spoon until the dough no longer clings to the spoon, then drop in tiny balls from the tip of a teaspoon into the boiling consommé, bouillon, or broth. Boil 5 minutes and use as a garnish for soups or stews or, if desired, serve as a main dish on creamed spinach or other greens.

DURIFF. A red table wine (*see* WINE) of the Burgundy type made from *Duriff*, or,

DUTCH OVEN

as they are also called, *Petite Sirah* grapes. A California wine. *See also* BURGUNDY.

DURRA. *See* SORGHUM.

DURUM WHEAT. Any of the varieties of hard wheat grown in Southern Russia, North Africa and North America. The flour is used chiefly for making alimentary pastes. *See also* PASTES.

DUST TEA. Green tea that has been reduced almost to powder. The quality varies according to the kind of tea from which it is made.

DUTCH OVEN. A covered skillet greatly used in home cookery, for almost any slow cooking. This handy cooking utensil should be seasoned before it is first used. It is generally made of cast iron, which is always covered with a thin coat of lacquer before it leaves the factory in order to prevent it from rusting during the period it is kept on the shelves of the warehouse or store. Before using, scour well inside and out, cover and all, with a good abrasive. Next, melt a generous amount of unsalted fat or vegetable oil, and brush it liberally on all parts of the kettle, even its sloping sides. Then place the utensil in a slow oven (275° F.) and bake it several hours occasionally opening the oven door to brush the sides and the cover with more of the fat. Remove from the oven when you no longer smell the odor of the lacquer, and use absorbent paper to remove all the fat. Wash in soap suds and rinse in clear hot water. The pot is now ready to use on the top of the range.

This type of Dutch oven is used for braising meats, and slowly simmering soups and stews.

Portable Dutch ovens, made of sheet iron, are described under the title CAMP COOKERY, *which see.*

E

EARTH NUT. Another name for peanut, *which see.*

EARTHENWARE. The name given to bowls, plates, cups, saucers, etc. made from a ceramic material of the same name. *See* CERAMICS; *see also* DISHES.

EASTER. Like many other church festivals, Easter is a mixture of both pagan and Christian customs. In old Norse mythology, the day was associated with the spring festival to welcome the return of new birth and awakening in crops and cattle. In fact, the very word "Easter" is derived from an old Saxon word meaning "rising."

Also, in India and China rabbits and eggs were symbols of reproduction and fertility, and were important features of another festival closely corresponding in date to our Easter. Therefore, it required little transition to include these symbols in a Christian festival occurring at the same period of the year.

Every land has quaint customs peculiar to the celebration of Easter. In the northern parts of England, the men once paraded the streets on Easter Sunday and claimed the privilege of lifting any woman they met three times from the ground, then demanding payment in a kiss!. Not unlike this, in Old Russia, when the Greek Orthodox Church was very strong, it was a rule that anyone could accost another on the streets on Easter Sunday and give him a triple kiss on the cheeks while saying "Christ Is Risen." Even the poorest peasant might so greet his Tsar. Extinguishing the hearth fire on Holy Saturday at sunset and re-lighting it with a candle blessed by the church is common in several lands. And the appearance of national dishes noted for their richness and epicurean quality, which have been absent during Lent, are the occasion for much feasting.

Homemakers today vie with one another in decorating Easter eggs and embellishing the family dinner table. Where spring is advanced, as in Italy and the Balkans, the populace takes to the open for their dancing and post-Lenten fetes. Hungary, Austria, Germany are countries where people celebrate the season with songs, merriment, and the exchange of gifts. In Poland, a pig's head, boiled and elaborately decked with flowers, is the principal food on the Easter table. Surrounding it are roast veal and hams, flanked by the popular Polish sausage highly spiced with garlic. Cakes of all kinds, adorned with sprigs of boxwood, are part of a feast that has for its centerpiece a large mold of butter in the shape of the Paschal Lamb; fresh, sweet butter making its appearance in the homes of all but the very wealthy only on important anniversaries.

There used to be an old English superstition that on Easter Sunday the sun danced or leaped as it came up above the horizon; and our forefathers used to get up very early on Easter morning to view the spectacle. Unfortunately the Devil always put a hill in the way, and so nobody ever got a chance to see the miracle.

Corn salad, which is also known as field salad, served with a herring cut in the shape of a man and known as "herring on horseback," was a customary dish in some parts of the world for Easter Day. Sometimes tansy was used to flavor cakes and sometimes it was put into the Easter pudding, which was a "custard greate."

Eggs, hard-cooked and colored, have been exchanged as Easter gifts for many centuries. Sometimes they are designed for eating, but more often for rolling on the green. Sometimes the Easter feast began as soon as the church clock recorded the midnight hour on Saturday. The food for the feast was brought to the church to be blessed.

"They roast their flesh and custards great, and eggs and radish store,
And trifles, clouted creame, and cheese and whatsoever more,
At first they list to eate, they bring into the Temple straight
That so the priest may hallow them with wordes of wond'rous waight."

Great roasts of young lamb, of ham and fowl, turned on the spit, graced the Easter feast, which, following the Lenten abstinence from meat, was as elaborate as means permitted.

EAU D'ARQUEBUSE. A very early French liqueur that was thought to have the power of curing all ills. No longer avail-

able, it was made in the vicinity of Lyons.
See also LIQUEUR.

EAU DE VIE. The French name for a
distilled spirit (water of life). The name of
the substance from which the spirit is distilled is usually affixed to the name, viz.,
Eau de Vie de Vin for Brandy (distilled from
wine), *Eau de Vie de Grain* for whisky, etc.
See also AQUA VITAE.

EAU DE VIE DE DANTZIG. A delicious liqueur with the taste and aroma of
cinnamon, having had for centuries a reputation for quality and goodness. Produced
in Germany, and generally served as an
after-dinner cordial.

**EAU DE VIE DE PRUNELLES DES
VOSGES.** A liqueur made in France. The
Vosges Mountains produce a very fine
species of sloe. These are picked while the
dew is still on them, crushed, seeds and
all, and then distilled over pure spirits of
wine. It is served as an after-dinner cordial.

ECHALOTE. French for shallot (*which
see*).

ECLAIR. A rich finger-shaped pastry
usually filled with cream and topped with
icing. An ice-cream eclair is filled with ice
cream. See CREAM PUFF.

EDAM CHEESE. A very famous product of Holland. It is hard, rennet cheese
made from skimmed milk. Cheese for export bears a Government mark guarantee-
ing the fat content to be at least 40 percent.
It is round in shape, but flattened at the
top and bottom. Edam cheese is molded,
but not milled like Cheddar. The outside
of this cheese is generally colored a brilliant
red, but for some markets it is colored yellow. The United States imports a large
quantity. Edam cheese is imitated in Denmark and Yugoslavia, as well as being
made in the United States.

EEL. The eel, although not a true ám-
phibian, creeps on the soil and swims in
the water, and has been known to survive
long droughts by burrowing into the muddy bottoms of dried-up rivers. It will eat
almost any kind of animal life from worms
and small fishes to the meat of warm-
blooded animals.

EEL

The life story of the eel reads like a
travelogue. The ribbonlike youngsters,
guided by some strange instinct, swim
thousands of miles of sea to return to the
streams which were the homes of their
parents. They travel in armies along our
shores in spring, entering tidal marshes and
estuaries. Rivers and ponds turn black
with baby eels. The males, however, soon
decide they have enough of it and, dropping out of the ranks, settle down near the
mouths of the rivers, while the females go
on. Neither cataracts, mill dams, nor dry
land can stop them.

At journey's end, the young eels settle
down to eat and grow. They grow rapidly,
adding a row of tiny scales with each year.
"Silver eels" they are called by their third
birthday. At eight years of age, they reach
maturity. Then there is a day of the year
when the eels are overcome with a strange
restlessness. They must go down to the
Sargosso Sea, and, come what may, no one
can prevent them. They are off to that
limited area between Bermuda and the
West Indian islands where they hatched
from the egg. The homesick hordes start
for the sea. They are skinned by damp
stones as they clamber over waterfalls.
They follow down the great rivers. Their
hour has come. (This is also the eel-fisher-
man's hour.) Should they fail to reach salt
water and the ocean's depth, their bones
soften, they can no longer eat, they die of
slow starvation.

The eel has minute scales imbedded in
the skin. The upper part of the body is
blackish in color, and the lower is yellowish when the eel is found in muddy water;
while the back is beautiful olive green and
the belly silver-white when the habitat is
clear water.

The reproduction of the eel has excited
the attention of naturalists since the days
of Aristotle. Where the eggs are laid is not
yet known, whether at the bottom or near
the surface. From five to twenty million
eggs are laid by each female, and the
eel dies after spawning once. The eels
caught in streams along the coast, dark
green in color, are those which do not
develop to the breeding stage. Some live
45 or 50 years.

Eel meat is sweet and there is very little
weight loss because the bones are small.
It has approximately the food value attributed to other fatty fish types. The medical council in its 1928 report stated that

"the body oil in eels (almost 30 percent of their whole substance) contains not only Vitamin D but almost as much Vitamin A," a striking confirmation of the medical contention that eels have a high dietetic value. When you purchase eels, pick them lively. Never choose a sluggish one.

Gulper Eel. A grotesque fish, seldom eaten, found in deep-sea waters off New York. This eel is almost all mouth, with an extremely tiny skull and a long, slender, tapering tail.

Capitone Eel. One of the largest eels, imported from Canada, and also one of the most tasty. The females are larger than the males, some weighing up to five pounds.

Conger Eel. A type of eel, found in the ocean. It attains a length of seven or eight feet, and is scaleless, grayish or dusty brown in upper coloring, silvery below. Prepare it the same as ordinary eels.

Hints on Preparation

Eel may be prepared in many ways: boiled or grilled, with tartar sauce or caper sauce; roasted rapidly, enrobed with a buttered paper, then served with a masterly sauce made with sweet oranges, or tangerines, and a small amount of Madeira wine; in aspic, as a fine summer luncheon; marinated, then rolled in soft, fresh bread crumbs and well-beaten eggs, fried and garnished with stuffed olives; boiled and served with ravigote sauce; larded with filets of anchovy, then roasted or baked; English style, hidden under a fine fritter batter and fried in deep fat; in matelotte, enhanced with small white onions which have been cooked in sugared butter; *au vert*, meaning cooked with aromatic herbs, such as sorrel, parsley, sage, thyme, etc. In all of these ways, besides many others, eel will prove a tasty treat.

If the eel is bought in the fish market it will be skinned and cleaned for you. However, if the eel is freshly caught, it may be necessary to perform the operation yourself. The easiest way to skin an eel is to impale it by a nail through the head to a wooden post or similar structure. With a sharp knife, cut through the skin just back of the head, completely encircling the head. Turn back the skin and peel off as you would a glove. When the eel is skinned, remove the head, tail, and entrails, wash in salt water, and cut into convenient pieces.

It is also possible to remove the skin by dipping the eel into simmering water until the skin is loosened. It can then be scraped off with a knife.

Baked Eel

2-lb eel, skinned, cut into 2-inch pieces
¼ cup olive oil
1 clove garlic
A pinch of thyme leaves
Juice of ½ lemon
Lemon slices
Parsley

Sprinkle blended salt and pepper over the pieces of eel. Heat the olive oil in a baking dish. Add the garlic, coarsely chopped, and the thyme. Place the eel in this hot mixture, squeeze a little lemon juice over it, and bake in a moderate oven (375° F.) for 25 to 30 minutes. Serve, garnished with lemon slices and parsley. (Serves 6)

Casserole of Eels

3-lb eel
Salt
½ cup flour
1 tsp salt
⅛ tsp pepper
¼ cup butter
12 small white peeled onions
Pinch of thyme
1 large bay leaf
Pinch of marjoram
Pinch of sweet basil
1 cup white wine
1 cup water
1 can button mushrooms

Skin the eel, clean thoroughly, and cut into 3-inch sections. Soak in cold salted water for one hour; drain, and pat dry. Roll in the blended salt and pepper; then brown in the melted butter. Transfer to a casserole, add the onions, thyme, bay leaf, marjoram, sweet basil, water and white wine. (Red wine may be substituted for white, if desired.) Cover and bake 35 minutes in a moderate oven (350° F.). Add the mushrooms, recover, and continue baking for 25 minutes longer. Serve sizzling hot. (Serves 6)

EFFERVESCENT WATER. See AER-
ATED WATER.

EGG. Eggs constitute a complete food.
The white of the egg, or albumen, contains
growth elements in the form of protein,
very similar to the protein in milk, but the
yolk has qualities which milk lacks. It has
more iron than milk. Its proteins are of
high quality and are easily digested. It is
as rich a source of Vitamins A and B as
milk, and it also contains Vitamin D. The
composition of the yolk is more complex.
Besides the protein vitellin, it contains
three fats, coloring matter, nuclein, leci-
thin, and salts of iron, calcium, magnesium, and potassium.

Although the structure of the egg (its
division into yolk and white) is familiar,
further study of details is interesting. Break
a fresh egg carefully into a saucer. The
shell is porous, allowing water to evaporate from the egg and air to enter. To this
porosity is due the fact that other substances may enter the egg, giving it an
unnatural flavor, and even hasten its deterioration. As moisture increases the porosity of the shell it should never be washed.
Within the shell is a fine membrane which
protects the white. The yolk is also divided
from the white by a delicate membrane,
which enables one to separate the yolk
from the white.

Careful examination reveals at each end
of the yolk a continuation of this membrane in the form of small cords which are
attached to each end of the shell, holding
the yolk evenly suspended in the center
of the shell. Rough handling or jolting
breaks this membrane and the yolk drops
to one side. Lift the white carefully with
a fork, and notice its elasticity. This co-
hesive property makes it possible to beat
air into the white until the whole mass becomes porous, full of air bubbles.

The egg white is in three or four layers:
an inner watery part, next to the yolk; one
or two jelly-like layers; and an outer watery white section. The yolk is creamy
rather than light when beaten, and a bit
of the yolk mixed in prevents the whites
from becoming light and dry when beaten.

The popular idea that hard-cooked eggs
are difficult to digest is without foundation.
Of course if they are gulped rapidly without proper mastication, discomfort may
result. But if the whites of hard-cooked
eggs are chopped fine, the yolk mashed,
and the two served upon bread or toast,
thus insuring thorough mastication, a dish
is produced that is of average digestibility
and that may be used for breakfast or
lunch without danger of causing indigestion.

Albumen, or the white of the egg, is
altered physically, but not chemically, by
process of cooking. At about 134° F. delicate fibrillae of coagulated albuminous
material begin to stretch through the substance, increasing with the temperature up
to 160° F. The fibrillae are so numerous
that the entire mass is coagulated, but is
still of a soft, or gelatinous, consistency.
Eggs baked in pudding, or in any other
manner, form one of the most insoluble
varieties of albumen possible. A raw egg
is ordinarily digested in the stomach in one
and a half hours, but a baked egg requires
from three to four hours.

The principle involved in this account of
the cooking of an egg is further illustrated
by the process of over-cooking beefsteak.
When strong heat is too long applied in
the process of broiling, the albumen of the
meat becomes dried, shriveled, and comparatively tasteless. So eggs, cooked for
persons with delicate digestions, instead of
being boiled in water at 212° F., should be
coddled, that is, placed in water at a temperature between 170° and 180° F., and
immersed for fully ten minutes. At the end
of this time they will be found of a uniform
gelatinous consistency, very palatable, and
tender enough to be readily acted upon by
the gastric juices.

The yolk actually coagulates at a lower
temperature than the white, although, as
eggs are commonly cooked, it does not
have an opportunity to coagulate first. In
the ordinary rapid cooking of eggs in boiling water, the white is firmly set before
there is time for the temperature of the
yolk to be thoroughly raised; consequently

FOOD VALUE

Water	Food Energy	Pro-tein	Fat	Carbo-hydrate	Cal-cium	Phos-phorus	Iron	Vit. A Value	Thia-mine	Ribo-flavin	Nia-cin	Ascor-bic Acid
74	158	12.8	11.5	.7	54	210	2.7	1140	.12	.34	.1	0

the yolk is softer than the white. The shell of the egg facilitates the slow cooking of the albumen by protecting the interior and preventing the escape of the contents through solution, just as in the cooking of fish or meat in water, the latter should be hot enough to immediately form an external coagulum of albumen sufficiently dense to prevent the diffusion of albuminous material and mineral salts into the water or liquid.

HINTS ON PURCHASING

The retail grades represent three classes of edible hen's eggs:

Fancy Grade. The top grade is known as the "fancy grade" and includes the selection of the finest quality of eggs of the day's lay. This grade is seldom available in retail stores, unless ordered in advance.

Grade A. The next highest grade is "Grade A." Any egg which falls below the standard for Grade A cannot legally be sold as fresh. This grade is limited and for that reason commands a high price.

Grade B. The next grade is known as "Grade B." Sometimes the question arises if, in buying Grade B eggs, the homemaker has bought the poorest quality eggs on the market. This is not so, for a Grade B egg is a United States standard and is of good table quality. The great bulk of eggs in commercial channels are of this grade. Grade B eggs are suitable for baking, frying, scrambling, omelets of all kinds, poaching, and all similar uses. They differ from Grade A in that a little more of their water content has evaporated, the air cell in the egg has become slightly tremulous, and the white of the egg has become less firm than that of the Grade A. As for food value, strictly Grade B eggs have qualities nearly equal to eggs sold under the Grade A specification. There should be no discrimination against the Grade B for it is considered satisfactory for almost any use.

Class C. Eggs of this grade are suitable for ordinary cooking.

Eggs with thin, glassy-looking shells that have a rather metallic sound when handled also are all right. Some hens habitually lay such eggs. The shells are not so porous as normal shells, and so keep the egg fresh a little longer. Unfortunately the outward appearance of an egg does not tell the whole story of quality. Only after the egg has been removed from the shell can the homemaker learn the quality of the egg, sometimes too late.

EGG COLOR

Shell Color. The shell color of eggs bears no fixed relation to the species of bird that lays them; nor does it affect the nutritive value of the egg. In other words, the color of the shell is not a criterion of its quality. The preferred shell color is a matter of individual taste, varying, strangely enough, with locality. Around Boston brown eggs are considered choice and fetch the highest prices, while in New York and elsewhere, white eggs are favored.

Yolk Color. Most homemakers first eye the yolk sharply, as they break open an egg. They know that the yolk should be well-centered in the white and should stand up in a nicely rounded form, that the membrane around it should not be easily ruptured, and that the germ should be undeveloped. But they are a bit hazy about yolk color and sometimes are suspicious of those of a deep orange hue. Actually the hen's diet to a large extent determines the yolk color.

During the spring the hens are hungry for growing things, and if given a chance eat an unusual amount of greens, with the result that the egg yolks are quite a bit darker yellow than when the chickens get less greens. Sometimes the range diet will even result in a yolk with a brown or green tinge—which does not affect its food value adversely, nor usually its flavor—but may hurt sales.

A rich orange-colored yolk in a fresh egg pretty clearly indicates the presence of a generous supply of Vitamin A. But a pale yolk may or may not mean a lack of it. If the hen has been kept away from greens but has been fed considerable cod liver oil, her egg yolk will be rich in both Vitamins A and D.

The White. Although it is the yolk which first commands the attention of the homemaker, she is equally critical of the white, especially if she wants to use it for leavening purposes. In the fresh egg it is nearly colorless, except for the two white cords extending from the yolk toward the ends of the egg.

As already stated, the egg white is in three, or sometimes four, layers: an inner watery white part next to the yolk, one or two jelly-like layers, and an outer watery white section. Most homemakers insist that the jelly-like part should at least equal the total of watery white. This part gradually loses firmness as it ages. Summer eggs are uniformly more watery than spring ones. But some hens always lay eggs that are watery. Research has not yet disclosed whether firm or watery layers are superior.

EGGS IN COOKING

Eggs are one of the most useful of the staple food products. They can be a part of any meal and of every course from appetizer to dessert. As a main luncheon dish they are difficult to surpass, for they are quickly and easily prepared.

Besides their principal use as a dish for breakfast, eggs are used as a thickening for sauces, soups, pie fillings, stuffings, salad dressings, custards, etc. They become a coating agent for dipping croquettes, cutlets, and other foods for frying. In muffins, cookies, croquettes, and some kinds of cakes, they are used as a binder to hold the other ingredients together. They improve the texture of frozen mixtures, because they act as a sort of wrapper around the crystals, preventing them from collecting in colonies. In soups they act as a clarifier. Mayonnaise, hollandaise, and similar emulsions demand eggs as a stabilizer. As a garnish for salads, cold meats, hot or cold fish, as well as for numerous vegetables, eggs have no rival. They enhance the flavor, color, and texture of products in which they are used, giving them more nutritive powers.

Eggs For Thickening. The reason that eggs can thicken sauces, soups, and custards is scientific but very easy to understand. Let us suppose you are making a custard. After beating the eggs, you combine them thoroughly with the milk until each tiny milk particle is incorporated with the egg; then you cook the blended mixture after flavoring to taste or according to given directions. You have seen how a poached egg "sets" when you drop it into hot liquid; the same thing happens in custard. The protein (albumen) of the egg quickly begins to coagulate or "set"; naturally the mi k must "set" or thicken, too, because your beating has made the two ingredients into one.

Eggs As A Leavening Agent. Eggs are a means of leavening. Chemists call the quality "viscosity" or "adhesiveness." If you

have ever tried to pick up a dropped egg, you know how adhesive it is. Annoying as this characteristic can be under certain circumstances, it is one of the main reasons that eggs are so valuable as a cooking ingredient. Just as soap suds, when beaten, turn into bubbles, so eggs develop multitudes of tiny air sacs as we beat them.

As a matter of fact, only the whites of eggs possess the power of leavening. Take their use in the making of sponge cake, for example. First, they gently and firmly entangle air in their tiny sacs; then, as the heat of the oven is applied, this air expands, stretching the walls of the sacs until they puff out like small balloons. It is the balloons that raise your cake. Since the walls of these sacs are made of albumen, which is toughened by too much heat, egg mixtures *must be cooked at a low or moderate heat* if they are to be tender. But the oven must not be too cool, because the little balloons collapse unless their albumen walls are hardened, ever so little, by cooking.

When you beat the egg whites for leavening, the rule is: Beat the whites until they are stiff enough to stand up and hold their shape, but do not beat them until they lose their glossy appearance. Egg whites beaten too much allow small bits to fly from the beater and the fluffy mass loses its shininess. This is the "dry" stage, and it is not satisfactory as a leavener.

In a frozen mixture these balloon-like sacs wrap themselves around the single crystals and prevent them from forming colonies. This film-forming property of eggs is especially valuable for freezing desserts without stirring them in a mechanical refrigerator, for instance, or packing them in ice and salt.

Eggs As A Stabilizer. When we add eggs to our mayonnaise, we are again calling these little air sacs to our aid. Just as their filmy walls close around the crystals in a frozen mixture, so they wrap drops of oil in their embrace to keep them from running together. When eggs are used in this way, they are called "stabilizers."

Eggs As A Binder. Eggs are a binder externally and internally. Externally they are used for croquettes, cutlets, and fritters (batter), for unless the food material is dipped in the eggs, the crumbs used will not stick and will drop to the bottom of the frying kettle.

We often use them to hold the ingredients together in fish balls, meat balls, hamburgers, croquettes, loaves, and all similar preparations requiring a binder. This is an internal binder. Although they bind the ingredients together, they also push them apart. By slipping their little films between the other particles of food, eggs prevent packing together in a hard lump.

Eggs As A Clarifier. We depend on an egg or egg shells to clear soup, coffee, or other food. As the heat is applied, the albumen of the egg coagulates, catching all the little undesirable particles that are floating around loose in the pot, kettle, or saucepan. This is called "clarifying."

Eggs As Antidotes For Poisoning. Whites of eggs may be used as antidotes for poison because of the ability of the albumen to coagulate and wrap the poison in an insoluble covering, thus protecting the delicate lining of the stomach.

COOKING EGGS

There are many methods of cooking eggs: soft-cooked, hard-cooked, coddled, poached (in butter, milk, bouillon, vegetable juices, water, wine, etc.), scrambled (plain or with the addition of fish, meat, or vegetables), shirred, fried, in omelets and soufflés.

In simple egg cookery, there are a few basic laws that must be observed if the egg is not to be too hard-cooked or underdone, watery when scrambled, or a flat, fallen omelet.

To Soft-Cook Eggs. To soft-cook eggs, so that they will have a tender white, start with the eggs in the shell in cold water to cover. Heat the water gradually to simmering, but do not let it boil. When it begins to simmer, cover the pan, remove it from the fire, and let it stand for a few minutes. The length of time depends on

the degree of softness to which you wish the eggs cooked, and on the number of eggs and size of the pan. Standing two minutes, will give you a three and a half minute egg; standing three minutes, a four minute egg, and so on.

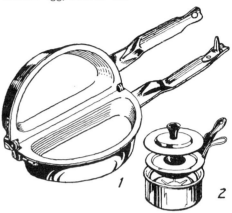

EGG COOKERS   1. Omelet pan
2. Individual poacher

To Fry Eggs (Pan-Fry). Heat butter or other fat half the size of a walnut in a small frying pan, and when fat begins to spread around the pan, slip two eggs, first broken into a saucer, into the fat. Cook over a very gentle flame until done, that is, until the white is coagulated, no longer. Should you want fried eggs turned over, toss the eggs—that is, flip them as you would a pancake, or turn them with a perforated pancake turner, to cook on the other side.

To Shirr Eggs. Melt a little butter in an individual shirred-egg dish, usually earthenware with a capacity of two eggs. Break the eggs into the dish, season with salt and pepper, and cook in the oven as slowly as possible. Serve in the same dish in which cooked.

To Make An Omelet. Most of us think we know how to make an omelet. Yet to make a good omelet requires practice, for to be successful, an omelet must be mellow inside, of an oval shape, pointed at both ends, plump in the middle, and of a golden brown color all over. The method, practiced by most good chefs, is as follows:

Break the eggs into a bowl and beat them thoroughly—the more beating, the lighter the omelet—then season to taste with salt and white pepper. Place a light frying pan, not a skillet, containing one scant teaspoon of butter (for two eggs), or

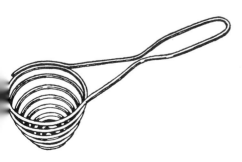

EGG COOLER

EGG

432

one tablespoon for six eggs, on a hot fire; let it become well heated, but not browned. Pour the eggs all at once into it, and with a fork or spatula quickly press the edges back toward the center as soon as they thicken. The soft part will run immediately to fill the space thus left vacant. Repeat until the eggs do not run. Bring the contents of the pan to the side nearest you. Then fold the omelet in half and let it slide toward the other side. Have a hot oval platter ready to receive the finished omelet.

If it is a composite omelet, that is, with an inside filling, have the filling ingredients all prepared before starting the omelet and, when the eggs are beginning to set, place the garnishing or filling in the center. Fold half of the omelet carefully over it like a turnover so as to form a covering. Brown a little, and invert onto a hot oval platter.

You may add a tablespoon or two of cream, evaporated milk, plain milk, or water to the beaten eggs for sake of economy, but the real omelet is made without the addition of these ingredients.

To Poach Eggs. Break each egg gently and separately into boiling water, salted or flavored with a little vinegar or lemon juice, in a shallow pan. Cover, and immediately remove from the fire. The egg itself will cool the water below the boiling point, while the sudden heat into which the egg falls will coagulate the outside enough to keep the egg whole while it cooks. The salt in the water helps to keep the egg whole; the vinegar or acid juice has the same effect. Both may be used. Do not let the water boil again. Let the egg stand in the covered pan until firm, about four or five minutes. Eggs may also be poached in consommé, tomato juice, or vegetable stock.

To Scramble Eggs. Beat the eggs until yolks and whites are mixed. Season to taste with salt and pepper, and turn the mixture into a frying pan (or into the top of a double boiler) containing, for six eggs, two tablespoons of melted butter. Cook slowly, stirring almost constantly to keep the mixture from sticking to the sides and bottom of the pan. When it is fluffy and creamy, remove it from the heat, and serve immediately. One-half cup of cold milk or tomato juice for each six eggs may be added, if desired, to the beaten eggs before cooking. Serve on toast or in scooped-out baked potatoes.

HINTS ON PREPARATION

For those of delicate digestion, eggs should be coddled rather than boiled—that is, placed in boiling water (one and a half cups for each egg) and kept in a warm place off the fire for twice as long as they are usually boiled.

Try preparing scrambled eggs in a double boiler, adding one tablespoon of cream or a thin white sauce for each egg. Season well, and add a chopped anchovy or two; then scramble.

At the sugar camps and in the home, it is a French Canadian custom to poach eggs in maple sirup.

In selecting eggs for cooking, remember that Grade A are best for poaching or soft cooking, as the white stands up well. Grade B are satisfactory for other table uses, and Grade C for cooking purposes.

Grading is based on appearance and interior quality, and has nothing to do with size. Large eggs are good for table service; medium eggs are best for baking purposes, as most recipes are built with the medium-sized egg in mind. An average medium egg weighs one and three-quarters ounces. Small eggs are good for soft cooking, but should be weighed for use in baking to make sure enough are used. Duck eggs contain more fat than hen's eggs.

When an egg rattles, if shaken, it is not fresh, because the air space inside the shell has become large through slow evaporation. Fresh eggs will sink when they are placed in a pan of water. Held in front of a candle or electric bulb in a dark room, they will appear clear.

Hard-cooked eggs look best when the yolk is firm and golden in color with no greenish ring between the white and the yolk. This green color develops when the eggs are subjected to too long or too violent cooking. Lower the eggs into simmering water and let them simmer for 20 minutes. Drain them at once, and cover them with cold water, changing the water twice during cooling. Shell just before serving or they dry into toughness on the surface.

Eggs separate more easily when cold than when warm. The whites beat up better at room temperature.

A generous pinch of baking soda added to the egg whites before they are beaten will make meringue stand up better.

To prevent a cracked egg from breaking when cooking, add a few drops of vinegar or lemon juice to the water in which it is cooked.

Very cold eggs sometimes crack when placed in boiling water to cook. This is easily prevented by puncturing the rounded end of each egg with a pin or needle before placing it in the water. Also, you will find it easier to remove the shells from hard-cooked eggs if you plunge them into cold water as soon as they are cooked.

If a bit of flour is sprinkled in the frying pan after bacon or ham has been cooked, eggs fried in their drippings will not stick to the pan.

When making a ham omelet, try adding a little mustard and a scant teaspoon of minced parsley or chives to the egg mixture.

USING LEFTOVER WHITES

Mayonnaise, and cooked salad dressings, mousses, many kinds of ice cream and certain cakes, as well as other desserts, call for the yolks of eggs only. Here are a few suggestions on how to use the leftover whites:

If the filling is removed from baked potatoes, mashed smoothly, beaten until fluffy with two or three stiffly beaten egg whites, some butter and seasoning, you have a deluxe baked potato. Pile the filling high in the potato shells, dot with butter or grated cheese, brown in the oven or under the flame of the broiler, or simply garnish with finely chopped parsley or chives.

Then there are puddings topped with meringue (*which see*) made by beating egg whites until stiff. Add granulated sugar very slowly according to the amount of egg whites, usually two tablespoons for each egg white, and beat until the sugar is dissolved. Then flavor as desired. It may then be placed in a moderate oven (350° F.) until set and delicately colored.

Cook leftover egg whites over hot water until firm; then dice and add to fish, potato, or vegetable salad, along with some whole hard-cooked eggs which have been sliced or quartered.

When preparing scrambled eggs, a few extra egg whites can be beaten in with the whole eggs.

One egg white
(1) For boiled frosting on loaf cake, using one cup of sugar.
(2) For confectioner's sugar frosting for a cake, using one cup of confectioner's sugar.

(3) For fruit whips—prune, apricot, apple snow, etc.
(4) For gelatin sponge, using 1 pint (2 cups) clear gelatin.
(5) For sherbert sauces.
(6) For meringue on small puddings, etc.
(7) For clearing one quart of soup or coffee, using shell also.
(8) For glazing small batch of cookies, rolls, etc.

Two egg whites
(1) For boiled frosting for layer cake.
(2) For almond macaroons.
(3) For larger quantities of all suggestions, for one egg white.

Three to six egg whites
(1) For marshmallow frosting.
(2) For white or silver cake.
(3) For meringues (pies and tortes, etc.).

One cup of egg whites
(1) For angel cake and similar cakes.
(2) For one dozen meringues or two dozen kisses.

USING LEFTOVER YOLKS

One egg yolk
(1) For one cup of mayonnaise.
(2) For glazing a dozen or so rolls, or one 8- or 9-inch pie.
(3) For egging and crumbing.
(4) For one eggnog.
(5) For pudding sauce.
(6) For confectioner's sugar frosting. *See* FROSTING.
(7) For plain blanc mange, etc.

Two egg yolks
(1) Equivalent of one whole egg for all baking purposes.
(2) For one pint of mayonnaise.
(3) For thickening one cup of milk for custards, timbales, etc.
(4) For French toast.
(5) For Hollandaise sauce (six servings).

Three egg yolks
(1) For muffins, cakes, cookies.

Four to eight egg yolks
(1) Gold cake (*see* CAKE) or cookies.
(2) Hot milk sponge cake.
(3) Rich soft custard.
(4) Yellow Jacket boiled frosting (*see* FROSTING).

BAKED EGGS WITH ALMONDS

2 cups tomato puree or condensed tomato
  soup
6 eggs
Salt and pepper
Finely minced blanched almonds
Buttered crumbs

Divide the purée or soup among six individual baking dishes or shirring dishes which can be sent to table. Break an egg into each, dust with salt and pepper, border with the almonds and top with buttered crumbs. Bake in a hot oven (400° F.) 10 to 12 minutes or until the eggs are set. (Serves 6)

CHEESE OMELET

8 eggs
6 tbsp water or milk
Salt and pepper
⅔ cup grated American or Swiss cheese
2 tbsp butter

Beat the eggs thoroughly, add the water or milk and seasonings, and blend well. Stir in the cheese. Heat the butter in a heavy frying pan without browning, turn in the egg mixture and cook as plain omelet (which see). Serve very hot.

The omelet may be made into a fluffy omelet by beating the yolks and whites of the eggs separately, adding the liquid, seasoning and cheese to the yolks, then folding in gently the stiffly beaten whites. Begin the cooking on top of the stove and finish browning the omelet in a moderately hot oven (375° F.). (Serves 6)

CREAMED EGGS AND DRIED BEEF ON TOAST

2 tbsp butter
2 tbsp flour
2 cups hot milk
½ tsp onion juice
¼ tsp pepper
¼ lb dried beef
5 hard-cooked eggs, sliced
Buttered toast
Water cress or parsley

Make a white sauce (which see) with the butter, flour, milk and seasonings. Pick the beef over, discarding any tough fiber, break or cut into small pieces, and add to the sauce with the eggs. Heat thoroughly, without boiling, and serve on toast, garnishing with water cress or parsley. (Serves 6)

CURRIED EGGS IN BROWN RICE RING

2 cups brown rice
2 tbsp butter
2 medium sized onions, coarsely chopped
4 tbsp flour
1 tbsp curry powder
2 cups chicken stock (or canned chicken
  bouillon)
1 cup heavy cream
Salt
6 hard-cooked eggs, quartered lengthwise
Chutney

Cook the rice (which see) until tender in plenty of boiling salted water, drain thoroughly and pack, not too firmly, in a well-buttered ring mold. A little before serving time, set the ring in a pan of hot water so as to heat the rice thoroughly.

Melt the butter in a saucepan and cook the onions in the butter until they are yellow and transparent but not brown. Add the flour and curry powder, and when smoothly blended, the stock or bouillon. Bring to boiling point and cook five minutes, stirring constantly. Now add the cream and season with salt. When again hot put in the eggs and let them heat through without actually boiling. Unmold the rice ring on a round platter, fill the center with the curry mixture and serve with any preferred chutney. (Serves 6)

EGGS FLORENTINE

Butter individual ramekins or casseroles and arrange ½ cup freshly-cooked, finely-chopped, well-seasoned spinach in each. Sprinkle the spinach with a teaspoon of grated cheese, make a slight hollow in the center and drop one or two eggs into each hollow. Dust with salt and pepper, cover with a rich cream sauce and sprinkle more cheese over all. Bake in a moderately hot oven (375° F.) 10 to 12 minutes, or until the eggs are set and the cheese delicately browned.

EGGS GOLDENROD

3 tbsp butter
3 tbsp flour
1 cup scalded milk
Salt and paprika
6 hard-cooked eggs
6 slices freshly made toast, buttered

Make a white sauce of the butter, flour and scalded milk in the usual way (*see* WHITE SAUCE). Separate the hard-cooked eggs, dice the whites, and add them to the sauce. Pour the sauce over the slices of toast, generously buttered, and sieve the hard-cooked yolks over the mixture. Serve at once. (Serves 6)

EGGS AU GRATIN

Place a tablespoon of heavy cream in each individual custard cup, ramekin, or baking dish. Break a whole fresh egg into each, season to taste, then top each with a tablespoon of buttered bread crumbs or a blend of buttered crumbs and cheese. Bake in a slow oven (300° F.) about 15 minutes, or until the eggs are set and the crumbs golden brown.

This dish may be varied by adding a spoonful of Worcestershire sauce.

EGGS WITH MUSHROOMS AND PEAS

2 tbsp butter
2 cups mushrooms, coarsely chopped
1 tbsp flour
½ cup milk
Salt and pepper
2 tbsp minced chives
1 tsp onion juice
½ cup canned or cooked peas
6 hard-cooked eggs, halved
Toast or bread cases
Paprika
Finely minced parsley

Heat the butter, add the mushrooms, and sauté for five minutes. Sprinkle in the flour, gradually add the milk and cook, stirring constantly, until the mixture boils, then add the seasonings and peas and when again boiling, the eggs. Heat thoroughly but do not allow the mixture to boil after the eggs are added. Serve on toast or in bread cases, dusting with the paprika and parsley. (Serves 6)

EGGS IN NEST

6 hard-cooked eggs, halved lengthwise
½ tsp salt
¼ tsp pepper or paprika
⅓ tsp prepared mustard
1 tsp lemon juice
1 tbsp mayonnaise
6 curled anchovies
Lettuce and mayonnaise
Tomato mold
2 cups tomato juice, heated
1 scant tsp salt
⅛ tsp pepper
1 tbsp gelatin
2 tbsp cold water
1 generous tsp Worcestershire sauce

Press the egg yolks through a sieve, then season with the salt, pepper or paprika, mustard, lemon juice, and mayonnaise, blending all thoroughly. Refill the whites with this mixture; then press the two halves together with a curled anchovy in the center of each egg.

Soften the gelatin in the cold water, then dissolve in the heated (not boiled) tomato juice. Season with the salt, pepper, and Worcestershire sauce. When it is almost at the setting point, pour a little of this tomato jelly in the bottoms of six individual molds, place an egg upright in each, and cover with the remaining tomato jelly. Chill until firm. Unmold onto lettuce, and serve with mayonnaise. (Serves 6)

EGGS PARMENTIER

3 cups hot well-seasoned mashed potato
1 tsp grated onion
3 tbsp butter
6 eggs
⅓ cup grated cheese
Water cress or parsley

Be sure that the mashed potatoes are perfectly smooth, and well seasoned with butter, salt and pepper and the grated onion. Divide into six portions and form hollowed-out nests of these on a well greased baking pan. The mixture may be placed on the pan with a spoon or passed through a pastry bag and tube. Put ½ tablespoon of butter in each nest, break in the raw eggs. Season with salt and paprika and top with the grated cheese. Bake in a slow oven (325° F.) 12 minutes, or until the eggs are set and the potato delicately browned. Transfer carefully to a platter and garnish with water cress or parsley.

If large-sized paper baking cups are available the nests may be made in these, and then served right in the cups. (Serves 6)

EGG TIMBALES

1 tbsp butter
1 tbsp flour
⅔ cup hot milk
4 eggs, separated
1 tbsp each minced parsley and chives
½ tsp salt
⅛ tsp white pepper
A dash each of garlic salt, celery salt, and cayenne pepper

Make a white sauce (*which see*) with the butter, flour and milk. Cool slightly, then add the egg yolks, beaten until thick and lemon colored, with the seasonings. Fold in the stiffly beaten egg whites, turn into six timbale molds or custard cups, set these in a pan of hot water and bake in a slow oven (300° F.) 25 to 30 minutes, or until the blade of a knife inserted in the center comes out clean. Let the timbales stand for 2 or 3 minutes out of the oven, then unmold and serve with cream of tomato sauce, curry sauce or plain cream sauce. (Serves 6)

FRIED STUFFED EGGS

6 hard-cooked eggs, halved lengthwise
5 finely chopped and pounded anchovies
½ cup soft bread crumbs
White pepper
2½ tbsp melted butter
Heavy cream
Egg and bread crumbs

Remove yolks from whites and press them through a sieve. Add the anchovies, crumbs, pepper, and butter, with enough cream to make the mixture soft enough to handle. Use to fill the cavities from which the yolks were taken. Place the egg halves together, pressing firmly. Dip first into beaten egg, then into bread crumbs and cook until golden brown in deep hot fat

(360°–375° F.). Drain on soft crumpled paper and serve immediately either on creamed spinach or other cooked green vegetable, or serve as a side dish with tartare sauce, figaro sauce or tomato sauce, all of *which see*.

Any of the filling mixture which is left over may be rolled into small balls, egged and crumbed the same as the eggs themselves and fried and used as a garnish.

If the two egg halves are fastened together with small wooden toothpicks before frying, danger of separation will be minimized. Remove these toothpicks before serving. (Serves 6)

POACHED EGGS WITH DEVILED HAM

6 slices freshly made toast
Butter
½ cup deviled ham
6 hot poached eggs
2 cups white or cheese sauce
Crisp water cress

Butter the toast generously, then spread with the deviled ham and arrange on a platter or for individual service. Place a freshly poached egg on each piece of toast, top with the sauce, garnish with water cress and serve immediately. (Serves 6)

SCRAMBLED EGGS WITH SHAD ROE

8 eggs
¼ cup cream
Salt and pepper
1½ to 2 tbsp butter
1 can or ½ lb shad roe
Paprika
Water cress

Beat the eggs, add the cream, and season to taste with salt and pepper (using white pepper). Melt the butter in a heavy frying pan or skillet. Pour in the egg mixture, and stir over a very low flame until just set. Turn onto a hot platter, sprinkle with paprika, and arrange on each side the roe, which has been lightly browned in butter on both sides. Garnish with crisp, green water cress. (Serves 6)

SHIRRED EGGS

Butter individual shirring dishes generously. Sprinkle with buttered crumbs and break one or two eggs over the crumbs. Season with salt and pepper, top with a further sprinkling of crumbs or a tablespoon of cream, or any good sauce as tomato or mushroom, for example. Bake in a slow oven (400° F.) 10 to 12 minutes and serve immediately in the dishes in which they were cooked.

SPANISH OMELET

2 tbsp butter
6 large onions
1 green pepper
1 red pepper
3 fresh tomatoes or 1 can tomato paste
1 lb mushrooms
Butter, additional
1 tbsp Worcestershire sauce
Salt and pepper
1 tbsp minced parsley
6 eggs
6 tbsp cream, milk or water
Parsley, chervil or water cress

Slice the onions thin, add to the first butter and stir and toss them about, over a moderate heat, until the rings are separated. Cover the pan and allow the onions to simmer gently until thoroughly tender and translucent. Then add the peppers, cut in slivers, first discarding stems, seeds and connecting tissue. Add also the tomatoes, peeled and sliced, (or the tomato paste) and continue the cooking until the peppers and tomatoes are tender. Add the Worcestershire sauce, salt and pepper, and minced parsley. Meanwhile, peel the mushrooms and sauté the caps in another pan with butter until they are brown and tender. (The stems should be minced and added to the first pan with the onions, peppers and tomatoes.) In a large heavy iron pan melt 2 tablespoons of butter, and using the eggs, cream, milk or water and seasonings, make a plain omelet (*which see*). As soon as this begins to set, puncture any bubbles, loosen the egg from the edges of the pan with a spatula and while still soft and custardy, but beginning to set, pour half of the sauce over one side of the omelet, fold the other side over, enclosing the sauce, and let stand over a low heat for a moment. Then invert onto a hot platter, pour the remaining sauce around the omelet, arrange the mushroom caps on top and pour the browned butter from the mushroom pan over all. Garnish with the parsley, chervil, or water cress (Serves 6 to 8)

STUFFED EGG APPETIZERS

Shell hard-cooked eggs, cut them in halves crosswise, and remove their yolks. The whites may then be filled with a variety of concoctions; you may use one of the following fillings or one of your own invention. The yolks are mashed or riced and then either combined with the filling or used as a garnish.

Deviled Eggs. Use 6 eggs. Combine the crushed yolks with 2 tablespoons of melted butter, 1 teaspoon of vinegar, ½ teaspoon of salt, ¼ teaspoon of dry mustard, ⅛ teaspoon of pepper, and an optional amount of liverwurst. Whip the ingredients into a smooth paste. Refill the whites. Garnish with paprika or chopped parsley. (Makes 12)

Crabmeat-stuffed eggs. Use 6 eggs. Mince the yolks and combine them with 1 cup of flaked crabmeat, 1 cup of finely-chopped celery, 2 tablespoons of chopped green pepper, 1 teaspoon of dry mustard, and ¾ cup of mayonnaise. Refill the whites. Garnish with tomatoes. (Makes 12)

Shrimp-stuffed eggs. Marinate shrimp in French dressing for 30 minutes. Moisten it with mayonnaise and a dash of Worcestershire sauce. Use the yolks as a garnish.

Caviar Monte Carlo. Combine the yolks with caviar, anchovy paste, and enough mayonnaise to hold the mixture together. Fill the whites and serve ungarnished. Alternate procedure: Combine caviar with lemon juice and grated onion, fill the whites with this mixture, serve them on thick tomato slices, and garnish with the minced yolks.

EGG BEATER. *See* BEATER.

EGG CHEESE. A Finnish cheese, made with fresh eggs.

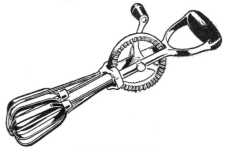

EGG BEATER

EGG COOKER. An electrical appliance for boiling eggs soft, medium, or hard. To shirr or poach eggs, use the inset dish.

EGG CUP. A small, specially designed cup without handles that is used to hold eggs as they are eaten. *See* DISHES.

EGG POACHER. An egg poacher is a metal device used to confine an egg to a given shape while it is being poached. *See* EGG; *see also* KITCHEN EQUIPMENT.

EGG SAUCE. *See* WHITE SAUCE and BUTTER SAUCE.

EGG SLICER. An egg slicer is a device used to cut a hard-cooked egg into slices or disks suitable for use in salads, sandwiches, and garnishings. While there are many different designs of this device in the stores, they agree in principle. The shelled, cooked egg is held in a depression while a grid of fine, parallel, equally spaced wires is pressed through it, making the cuts. The device may also be used on butter, cheese, and other hard-to-slice substances. *See also* EGG and KITCHEN EQUIPMENT.

EGGING AND BREADING, or **CRUMBING.** Enveloping an article of food in bread crumbs or cracker crumbs after having previously dipped it in an adhesive liquid such as eggs preparatory to frying. *See* CRUMB.

EGGNOG. This is a nutritious egg and milk drink, easily made at home. It contains sugar and is flavored with vanilla, fruit juice, chocolate, or wine. Brandy, whisky, or rum may be used according to taste. A basic recipe follows:

EGGNOG

1 egg, beaten
2 tsp sugar or honey
1 cup rich milk
½ tsp vanilla
Dash of nutmeg

Beat the egg and sugar together; then beat in the milk and vanilla. Serve cold in tall glasses with a light sprinkling of nutmeg. Omit the vanilla if other flavoring is used. To make a lighter fluffier eggnog, beat the yolk and white separately. Add the sugar, milk, and flavoring to the yolk, and fold in the white. (Serves 1)

AGED EGGNOG

Eggnog is very popular, especially during the holiday season. Some people maintain that eggnog is eggnog only when it has been mixed a month or two before the holidays and allowed to age. Once mixed, it is poured into a large open crock, covered with a cloth, and left untouched in a cool place until the proper date arrives. The standard ingredients of "nogs" comprise: ice, powdered sugar, the yolk (and sometimes the white) of a fresh egg, the liquor which will give its name to the "nog," and grated nutmeg. Milk is frequently an ingredient. Nogs are always served cold and should be shaken vigorously to thoroughly blend the egg (and milk, or cream, if included) with the other ingredients, so as to obtain a smooth drink of the consistency of rich creamy milk.

There are many recipes for eggnog, and a good one, whether made in advance or on the day it is to be drunk, is: 20 eggs, well beaten and stirred together with 2 pounds of sugar. Into this mixture pour 1½ pints of Jamaica rum and 2 quarts of brandy. When the whole has been well mixed, 5 or 6 quarts of cream (or of cream and milk, half and half) are slowly added, and carefully stirred to bring the mixture to velvet smoothness. (Serves 25)

CHRISTMAS EGGNOG

6 eggs
½ cup sugar
¾ cup rye whisky
⅓ cup Jamaica rum
1 cup whipped cream
Nutmeg

Beat the egg yolks until thick and lemon colored, then add the whisky and rum, a tablespoon at a time, beating constantly. Beat the egg whites until stiff, but not dry, and add gradually all but one tablespoon of sugar. Combine the two mixtures. Add the remaining sugar to the whipped cream, and fold it into the eggnog, reserving two tablespoons of cream. Serve in punch glasses, topping it with the remaining whipped cream and dusting each serving with grated nutmeg. (Serves 10)

CIDER EGGNOG

1 egg
½ tbsp powdered sugar
3 ice cubes
1 tumbler cider

Combine the egg, sugar, and ice cubes. Place these ingredients in a large tumbler and fill up with cider. Shake vigorously. (Serves 1)

EGGNOG ICE CREAM

6 eggs
½ cup sugar
¼ tsp salt
4 tbsp sherry
1 cup heavy cream
Nutmeg

Beat the egg yolks until thick, then add the sugar gradually and continue beating until this is thoroughly blended. Keep the mixture very cold while beating the egg whites, and salt until stiff. Combine the two mixtures. Add the wine gradually (rum or brandy may be substituted if desired) and lastly fold in the stiffly beaten cream. Freeze in automatic refrigerator for four hours without either scraping or stirring. When ready to serve sprinkle over each portion a dash of ground nutmeg or a slight grating from a whole nutmeg. (Serves 4 or 6)

EGGNOG SAUCE

2 cups light cream
3 egg yolks
½ cup sugar
1 tsp vanilla
Rum

Scald the cream. Beat the egg yolks and sugar together; combine with the cream and reheat, stirring continually, but do not allow the sauce to boil. Cool slightly, then add the vanilla and rum to taste.

EGGPLANT. The fruit of a plant which is a native of southern Asia, the eggplant is egg- or pear-shaped, and varies in length from several inches to a foot. The color ranges from white or yellow, to violet or purple; the eggplants found in our markets are generally the purple type.

Good eggplants are heavy and firm and of a uniform dark color. Those which are soft and flabby or shriveled are over-age or have been kept too long.

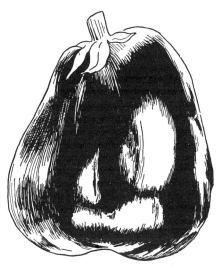

EGGPLANT

HINTS ON PREPARATION

In the Near East, from Greece to Asia Minor, the eggplant is baked in its skin, or stewed in oil or broth to conserve its flavor, rather than boiled in water to extract the flavor. While the eggplant is one of the minor vegetables commercially, it has been known for centuries. Some of the ancients believed it to be poisonous; in fact, it was known as *mala insana*, mad, or raging, apple, in the belief that it caused insanity. The custom of soaking eggplant in salt water before cooking it was a survival of the fear of its unwholesomeness.

In Turkey, Greece, the Balkans, Persia, and India, eggplant is combined with lamb or mutton in *kabobs*, the skewers reaching a length of two or three feet, and the broiling being done over an open fire or a charcoal brazier. For home cooking, ordinary metal skewers may be used, the squares of meat being alternated with squares of eggplant which has been parboiled in salted water, and then peeled and marinated for 15 minutes in a mixture of 3 tablespoons of

FOOD VALUE

Water	Food Energy	Pro- tein	Fat	Carbo- hydrate	Cal- cium	Phos- phorus	Iron	Vit. A Value	Thia- mine	Ribo- flavin	Nia- cin	Ascor- bic Acid
92.7	28	1.1	.2	5.5	15	37	.4	30	.07	.06	.8	5

olive oil and the juice of half a lemon. *See* KABOB.

For an unusual luncheon dish, take small eggplants and green tomatoes. Peel the eggplant and cut it and the tomatoes in half-inch slices. Dredge· with flour and season with salt, black pepper, and a little minced parsley. Then impale the slices of tomato and eggplant alternately on metal skewers, *à la brochette*. Grill them under the broiler, basting liberally with melted butter or cooking oil; or pan broil in plenty of butter or oil, turning the skewers constantly. Serve by pushing off the skewers onto slices of toast, and garnish the dish with crisp bacon.

EGGPLANT CAVIAR
(Poor Man's Caviar)

1 medium-sized eggplant
2 medium-sized onions
2 medium-sized cloves of garlic
3 medium-sized tomatoes, peeled
¾ cup olive oil
Salt and pepper

Wash the eggplant, but do not peel it Wrap it tightly in vegetable parchment paper, aluminum foil, or oiled paper. Place in a baking pan and bake in a moderate oven (350° F.) about 30 minutes, or until soft. Chop the onions and tomatoes into small bits. Crush the garlic with ½ teaspoon of salt. Unwrap the eggplant and peel it. Chop the eggplant into small bits. Continue chopping while adding slowly the onion, tomato, oil and garlic. Continue chopping until the mixture is blended thoroughly and the pieces are the size of caviar. Season to taste with salt and pepper, and chill thoroughly. Serve as an appetizer with melba toast and crackers. (Makes about 5 cups)

EGGPLANT FARCI

3 medium-sized eggplants
1 lb fresh mushrooms
1 large onion sliced thinly
6 slices fresh toast, crumbled
2 tbsp minced parsley
2 tbsp soy sauce
Black pepper
Dash of cayenne pepper
1 tsp brown sugar

Cut the eggplants in half lengthwise. With a sharp knife score the cut sides deeply; then saute the halves, cut side down, in olive oil until they are delicately browned. With a large spoon, carefully scoop out the pulp, leaving a shell about ¼ inch thick. Cut the pulp of the eggplant into small cubes. Peel and slice the mushrooms, caps and stems, and sauté in olive oil. Brown the onion slices in the same pan. Add the crumbled toast. Combine all of the ingredients, and fill the shells with this mixture, heaping them evenly. Sprinkle buttered crumbs over the top. Grease a large pan to hold the 6 shells and bake in a hot oven (400° F.) for 15 or 20 minutes, until thoroughly browned. Serve very hot. (Serves 6)

EGGPLANT PIE

1 small eggplant
4 tbsp butter or margarine
1½ lb shoulder of lamb, ground
1 egg, well beaten
1 medium-sized onion, minced
2 tbsp minced green pepper
Salt and pepper
Pinch of thyme
Pinch of sweet basil
1 cup tomato sauce
1 tbsp minced parsley
⅓ cup buttered crumbs

Slice the eggplant an inch thick, peel and quarter the slices, and sauté in the butter until tender. Combine all the remaining ingredients, except the bread crumbs. Place half of the lamb mixture in a greased baking dish, and cover with half the eggplant. Repeat the layers and top with the crumbs. Bake in a moderate oven (350° F.) for 45 minutes. Serve very hot. (Serves 6)

A tablespoon of curry powder added to the lamb mixture gives a delicious flavor. Olive oil may be used in place of the butter.

EGGPLANT SOUFFLE

2 large eggplants
2 tsp salt
1 large bay leaf
2 whole cloves
1 tbsp butter
2 eggs, slightly beaten

½ cup milk
½ tsp salt
⅛ tsp pepper
1 cup grated cheese
1 cup soft bread crumbs
2 tbsp buttered bread crumbs

Peel and slice the eggplant. Cook in 2 quarts of boiling water, to which the salt, bay leaf and cloves have been added, for about 20 minutes, or until tender. Drain, and discard the bay leaf and cloves. Mash the eggplant in a bowl, and work in the butter, eggs, milk, seasoning, grated cheese, and unbuttered crumbs, stirring well, Turn into a greased baking dish and sprinkle the top with the buttered crumbs. Bake in a moderate oven (350°–375° F.) until firm and brown on top, about 15 or 20 minutes. Serve at once in the dish in which it was cooked. (Serves 6)

FRENCH FRIED EGGPLANT

Peel the eggplant and cut into slender sticks, about ¼ inch thick. Dip in beaten egg which has been seasoned with salt and pepper, and then roll in crumbs. Fry in deep hot fat (375°–390° F.) 2 to 4 minutes, or until delicately browned and crisp. Serve very hot.

FRIED EGGPLANT

Peel the eggplant and cut in half-inch slices. Dredge in seasoned flour, or crumb with egg and crumbs, and fry in olive oil or other shortening until well browned on both sides.

STUFFED EGGPLANT

1 good-sized eggplant
3 slices bacon, diced
3 tbsp finely chopped green pepper
½ cup finely chopped celery
1 egg
2 cups soft bread crumbs
1¼ cups partly drained crushed pineapple
1 tbsp butter
Dash of paprika
Salt
Water or stock

Boil or steam the eggplant, unpeeled, until tender, about half an hour. Cut in halves lengthwise and carefully remove the pulp, leaving a shell about ¾ of an inch thick. Cut the pulp in small pieces. In a skillet cook the diced bacon until the fat runs freely. Add the pieces of eggplant and brown well. Add the green pepper and celery and cook until the celery is transparent. Add the crumbs, the well beaten egg, one cup of the pineapple, and the seasonings, and fill the eggplant shells with this mixture. Spread the remaining pineapple over the surface, and dot with butter or margarine. Place the eggplant in a pan, adding a little water or stock to prevent sticking. Bake in a moderate oven (350° F.) 30 to 35 minutes. Serve sizzling hot, slicing with a very sharp knife. (Serves 6)

ELLBOT. See HALIBUT.

EL REI SARCIAL WINE. A very fine, dry Madeira wine, appropriate for an aperitif.

ELBING CHEESE. A hard, rennet cheese made from cow's milk. It is known also as *Werderkäse* and *Nierderungskäse*. This is a German cheese.

ELDERBERRY. The eldertree was known to the ancients for its medicinal properties, and in England the inner bark was formerly administered as a cathartic.

According to old German folklore, the hat must be doffed in the presence of the eldertree; and in some of the English Midland counties a belief was once prevalent that the Cross of Christ was made from its wood and therefore it should never be treated with disrespect or used as fuel. However, Shakespeare and other writers mentioned that Judas hanged himself on an eldertree, and on this account, probably, to be crowned with elder was in olden times accounted a disgrace. In early time superstitious people in Denmark believed the tree was protected by the "Elder-mother" and that its flowers should not be

ELDERBERRY

plucked without the leaves and its wood should not be used for household furniture.

Elderflowers contain a volatile oil, and from them is distilled elderflower water, used in perfumes and lotions. The clusters of blossoms may be dipped in batter and fried like a fritter. The berries are used for wine and jelly.

Elderberry Jelly with Apple

2 qt elderberries, cleaned and stemmed
1 qt apples, stems and blossom ends removed
2 qt water
Sugar
Lemon juice

Put the elderberries and apples through a food grinder, then pour this mash into a preserving kettle. Add water and simmer, covered, for 15 minutes, stirring occasionally. Pour into a jelly bag and let drip overnight. Squeeze the bag until the pulp is dry. Measure the juice, add 1 cup of sugar and 1 tablespoon of lemon juice for each cup of juice. Bring to a rolling boil and boil vigorously until it sheets from the spoon. Remove from the fire immediately, skim, and pour into hot, sterilized glasses. Seal. See also Jelly.

Elderberry Wine

Pick elder blossoms from stems. Pack a 1-quart measure full, pressing down firmly.

COFFEE MAKER

Boil together 3 gallons water with 9 pounds granulated sugar for 5 minutes to a thin sirup. Add blossoms and mix well. Cool to lukewarm. Add 3 pounds seedless raisins, chopped, ½ cup lemon juice, strained, and 1 cake of compressed yeast. Put into large crock and let stand for 6 days, stirring 3 times daily. Strain and let stand for several months. Bottle or put into fruit jars. This light wine has the suggestion of a delicate champagne and keeps well for several years.

MIXER

ELECTRIC MIXER. Available in standard, portable or convertible models, the electric mixer is a time and energy saver for the baker and cook. When purchasing a mixer consider features such as multiple speed control, selective bowl sizes of heat resistant materials, chrome plated rotary beaters with no center shaft for easier cleaning, permanently lubricated motor. In the case of hand mixers, check for a light-weight, balanced handle and easy storability. Some hand mixers come with drink mixer attachments, too.

To clean the mixer, eject the beaters and immerse the beaters and bowls only in dishwater. Never immerse the head of the mixer. Wipe with a damp cloth.

ELECTRIC RANGE. See Range.

ELECTRICAL EQUIPMENT. Since the number and variety of time and labor saving electrical appliances offers so great a temptation to buy, the prospective consumer should take stock of her home and kitchen situation in determining which items are really most suitable to her needs.

Check for versatility. While many waffle irons will also grill sandwiches, fry bacon,

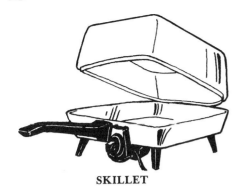

SKILLET

sausage and eggs, the cook might ulti-mately prefer a non-stick surface griddle which offers greater surface area, more heat control, and can double as an indoor barbecue for parties. Similarly an electric coffee maker is perfect for large crowds, but useless if yours is a tea drinking family.

While an electric knife may not be useful enough to merit the energy required to clean it, an electric can opener with a knife sharpening or ice crushing attachment may be a help in a family of young children who prepare their own lunches. It should be remembered that electric can openers are generally not equipped to open rimless cans and that the aluminum ends of cans will not be held by magnet attachments.

The blender (*which see*) has become one of the more versatile of electric appliances. Follow the manufacturer's instructions for use, remembering that a blender works in seconds not minutes. When preparing dry foods, blend small quantities at a time. To blend liquids and solids, always pour the liquid into the container first. Remove food

WAFFLE IRON

with a rubber spatula and never use a blender with the lid off the container.

The toaster (*which see*) is one implement that most families feel they can't do with-out. A homemaker who is fond of preparing toasted sandwiches might investigate the purchase of a small electric toasting oven which will not only toast bread on both sides by means of a reflector but will also toast breads, muffins, etc. with toppings such as cheese, tomato, sauce, ham.

Two items which may be indispensable or absolutely superfluous are the table broiler and electric skillet. These items be-come most useful when full scale oven and broiler appliances are not available, as for example, in some semi-furnished or kitch-enless rooms. In addition, individuals who

BLENDER

because of illness, paralysis or old age prefer to use table height appliances will find the broiler and skillet invaluable.

Skillets are useful for at-the-table cook-ing, frying, sautéeing, deep frying, stew-ing, simmering, keeping foods hot, steam-ing, pan broiling, boiling and even baking. Precise temperature control makes this a prized appliance of many cooks.

PURCHASE

Although the prime consideration in the purchase of an appliance is whether it fills a need without duplication, one should also consider whether it is well constructed, is easily cleaned and stored, whether a war-ranty and service are available and whether the design and construction are both ap-pealing and efficient. To be assured of

CAN OPENER

quality, purchase appliances which have been tested by the Underwriters Laboratory. The tag of approval should be visible on the item. Take care to ascertain that the tag applies to the entire finished product, however, and not just to one item used in the construction of the product.

CARE AND USE

Always check the wattage or amp rating stamped on every appliance purchased and never overload any electrical circuit with more than one high wattage appliance. A 15 amp circuit can usually handle appliances and lamps totaling 1700 watts without creating an overload.

Should a fuse blow, locate the cause and correct it. Replace the fuse promptly, never resorting to the expedient of a penny or other filler material. The use of extension cords with high wattage appliances should be avoided. If these must be used, care should be taken that an extension cord of the proper wattage is used. A 15 amp cord is adequate for any high wattage portable appliance.

Should a fire break out in an electrical appliance, disconnect the cord, if possible

and extinguish the fire with sand, dirt or electrical fire extinguisher. Never use water or even a regular fire extinguisher as these will only spread an electrical fire.

When using appliances with detachable cords or temperature control, always plug the cord or control into the appliance before connecting it to the wall outlet. To disconnect, remove the cord from the wall outlet first by pulling on the plug itself; then remove the cord from the appliance.

Unplug heating appliances directly after use and allow them to cool before washing. Never immerse an electrical appliance in water unless the item is specifically labeled immersible by the manufacturer. Clean appliances should be stored with the lids ajar to avoid musty odors. To wash a blender container, fill it about half full with warm water and drop of liquid detergent. Cover the container, replace it on the motor and blend for a few seconds at low speed. Rinse the container and lid and dry the parts thoroughly.

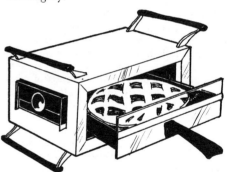

TABLE BROILER

ELISAVETPOLEN CHEESE. Another name for the Russian cheese, Eriwani, which is made from sheep's milk.

ELK. The elk, or moose deer, is one of the largest of the deer family. This game animal sometimes reaches enormous size. In the United States elk meat may be sold for food if the animal has been killed in accordance with the state regulations. Information may be obtained from the department of conservation, the Fish and Game Warden, or superintendents of Wild Life, or of Forestry, etc.

The price is very high, the meat being classified as game. It is cooked accordingly. The flavor is not too strong, if it is not hung too long. 48 hours are quite sufficient for a good elk steak to hang to be

GRIDDLE

juicy, tender, and fine-grained. Elk meat, especially from the leg, is flavorful and almost free of tendons and tissues. It possesses little natural fat, and needs to be larded with salt pork before cooking. Elk flesh is very light, digestible, and nourishing. Canadians hold it in high esteem and appreciate a roast buttock, or a round of elk, simmered gently in red wine with onions—plentifully stuck with whole cloves—parsnips, turnips, and leeks, until the wine is reduced to almost nothing. The roast is served with a sweet-sour shallot sauce or a Smitane sauce (*which see*); or an elk steak, from the round, pounded, marinated in white or red wine overnight, and very slowly broiled, may be served with one of the favorite game sauces.

The elk may be prepared by almost any of the methods applied to beef, as well as those for deer. However, elk meat requires a very slow cooking process, and the marinating should be of short duration, not exceeding 24 hours, unless one likes a gamey flavor. *See also* MOOSE.

ELLBOT. *See* HALIBUT.

EMMENTHAL CHEESE. So-called Swiss cheese is properly named Emmenthal cheese. It is a hard rennet cheese made from cow's milk with a mild, somewhat sweetish flavor, and is characterized by holes or eyes, about the size of a cent, one to three inches apart. Its shape is a huge wheel, weighing from 100 to 200 pounds.

In making Emmenthal cheese the milk is warmed slightly and the rennet added. When the curd is formed, it is broken up into small bits the size of a pea and put into a large kettle over a wood fire. The curd is heated to the proper temperature, while being stirred constantly, until the proper consistency is reached. The curd is lifted out of the kettle in a cloth and put into a mould, the top of which is designed so that it can be pressed down on the curd with increasing pressure. When the cheese has been pressed sufficiently, it is salted and sent to the ripening room. Here the cheeses mature under carefully controlled temperatures. The eyes of the cheese are formed by the rapid fermentation of the curd.

Similar cheeses are made in France, Italy, and Germany, and Gruyère is essentially the same kind of cheese. Genuine Swiss cheese is made in Switzerland, but a very good domestic Swiss cheese is made in the United States.

Swiss cheese is particularly good for cheese dishes and cheese toppings when the sharper cheeses such as Cheddar or Parmesan are not wanted. Ham and Swiss cheese is a classic sandwich combination. *See also* CHEESE.

EMRELETTES. Peeled seedless grapes which have been tinted green and flavored with crème de menthe. They are a commercial product and are used for garnishing fruit cups, salads, and the like.

EMULSION. A liquid mixture in which a fatty substance is suspended in minute globules, as in French dressing. Also a milky-appearing liquid.

ENAMELWARE. Enamelware vessels are made of iron or steel sheet that has had a glass-like material baked on the surface. Enamelware is made in many colors and patterns, all of varying durability. The enamel is by no means as durable as the metal underneath, being subject to chipping and flaking, but it serves to give the metal a sanitary, rust-proof surface. Enamelware is easy to clean and is widely used for pots, pans, and dishes; but never for skillets, griddles, or ovenware, where the intense dry heat would cause the porcelain coating to crack.

PURCHASING ENAMELWARE

Though the lighter shades of enamel are more pleasant to the eye, as a general rule the darker shades are more durable. The best and most durable enamelware has a triple coating, but it is also the most expensive.

Enamelware should have a smooth, flawless surface. Bubbles, chips, cracks, etc., are signs of weakness in the coating.

CARE AND CLEANING

Enamelware should never be used for any form of dry or waterless cooking because it may chip or crack under the heat. Care should be taken not to drop or bang this material, nor to subject it to sudden changes of extreme temperatures. A wooden spoon, rather than a metal one, should be used to stir the contents of an enamelware pan, and food particles should be removed from the sides and bottom by soaking, rather than scraping. If enamelware is ever chipped or cracked, it should be discarded, for there is danger of glasslike splinters of the vitrified material flaking off into the food while the vessel is being used.

Enamelware should never be scoured, nor should abrasives be used to clean it. Hard water scale may be removed by filling the vessel with water, adding a small amount of baking soda or lemon juice, and boiling the mixture for five or ten minutes. Discolorations may be removed from the surface by rubbing gently with a soft cloth and a paste of baking soda and water.

ENCHILADAS. A Mexican dish used in Texas, New Orleans, California, and other Pacific Coast states. *Enchiladas* are tortillas (*which see*) in layers with a sauce containing meat which may be made in a number of ways. The following recipe is an example:

ENCHILADAS

1 No. 2½ can tomatoes
1½ cups fresh pork, diced
Salt and pepper
2 tbsp finely chopped onion
1 crushed clove garlic
1 tbsp chili powder
Pancakes
Finely minced onion, additional
Grated Parmesan cheese

Bring the tomatoes to boiling point and add to them the pork (or use leftover cooked meat, either pork, veal, beef or chicken), salt and pepper to taste, with the 2 tablespoons of onion, the garlic and the chili, using more or less of this last, according to taste. Cover and simmer gently for 2 hours over a very low fire. At serving time have ready plenty of pancakes (*which see*), put one on a plate, pour one or two tablespoons of the hot sauce over it, top with a second pancake, then more sauce. Now sprinkle with 1 or 2

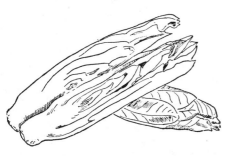

BELGIAN ENDIVE

teaspoons finely minced onion and a teaspoon of grated cheese, then a bit more sauce, to help the cheese melt. Each sandwich so made is a serving. Provide an extra bowl of minced onion and one of additional grated cheese for those who like a bountiful supply.

ENDIVE. *See* CHICORY.

ENGADINE CHEESE. A rennet cheese made in Switzerland from the whole milk of cows.

ENGLISH BISHOP. Another name for Archbishop's Punch. *See* PUNCH.

ENGLISH BREAKFAST TEA. A popular name applied to all China flavored blends of black teas, although, at first, it was intended to describe only the teas known as North China Congous. During colonial times these teas were popular with the English people as breakfast teas. The name was originated by Americans of the period—and it is little known in England.

English Breakfast teas are aromatic, strong, and without bitterness. They are popular in the United States.

ENGLISH DAIRY CHEESE. A very hard American cheese, much like Cheddar (*which see*). It is used for culinary purposes.

ENGLISH MUFFIN. The favorite breakfast hot bread of many people, usually served with plenty of butter and jam. They are also excellent for tea. Bake tender English muffins on your own griddle and serve them temptingly fresh and fragrant at a winter breakfast or afternoon tea party, or supper party. They take the place of rolls in the menu or may have a creamed mixture or a nippy rarebit poured over them.

ENGLISH MUFFINS

1 cup milk
3 tbsp butter
1½ tsp salt
2 tbsp sugar
1 yeast cake
¼ cup lukewarm water
1 beaten egg
4 cups sifted flour
Corn meal, to sprinkle, if desired

Scald the milk, pour it over the butter, salt and sugar, and stir until these are dissolved. Soften the yeast in the lukewarm water and when the milk mixture has cooled to lukewarm combine the two. Stir in the beaten egg and half the flour. Blend thoroughly, making sure that there are no lumps, and work in flour to make an elastic dough, using approximately two cups. Knead thoroughly. Cover and let stand in a warm place, free from drafts, until doubled in bulk, about one hour. Divide into small portions (about ⅔ of a cup). Knead and work so as to achieve a smooth surface, then roll out about one-half inch thick. Again let rise until doubled in bulk and bake on a heated griddle or heavy frying pan which may be very lightly sprinkled with corn meal. Let the heat be low and as the muffins rise, turn to brown both sides. They will take about 7 minutes on each side.

If rings, approximately 3½ inches in diameter, are available, the pieces of dough may be set in these for baking, thus insuring perfect roundness.

To serve, toast on both sides, then if desired break open with the fingers and toast the inside. Spread with plenty of butter.

ENTREE. An intermediate course. It usually refers, in America, to the main course.

ENTREMENT. The sweet course, usually dessert in the United States.

EPICURE. In the modern sense, the epicure is a gourmet—one who is fastidious in his food—a connoisseur. More restrained and more fastidious than the gourmand, he discovers the gradual degrees of excitation of which he is susceptible and never transgresses the limits he has imposed upon himself. He takes pride in considering the effect of food on his emotions, his judgment, his mind, and his character.

He gives special attention to food combinations and distinguishes what foods ought to form the basis of his meals from those that are mere accessories. In his opinion the gourmand indulges to excess, while the glutton requires the advice and treatment of the moralist or physician. The true epicure or gourmet takes discreet, often ecstatic delight in an excellent dish.

EPIGRAMMES. As applied to cookery, they may be lamb chops, or pieces of lamb breast, braised, broiled, or sautéed in butter, then boned, and placed under a heavy weight so that it is thoroughly flattened. When cold, the epigramme is then egged, breaded, and again broiled or sautéed in butter. Epigrammes may be served garnished with mixed cooked vegetables, asparagus, or any kind of mashed

ESCAROLE

cooked vegetable, such as potatoes, peas, carrots, spinach, etc., or with buttered peas or string beans.

EPOISSE. A soft rennet cheese made from whole or partly skimmed milk. It is a product of the Department of Cote d'Or in France.

EQUIPMENT FOR THE KITCHEN. See KITCHEN EQUIPMENT.

EQUIPMENT FOR OUTDOOR COOKERY. See BARBECUE and CAMP COOKERY.

ERCE CHEESE. A French winter and spring cheese made in Languedoc.

ERIWANI CHEESE. A Russian cheese made from sheep's milk. Different local names are *Karab, Tali, Kurini, Elisavetpolen,* and *Kasach.*

ERVY CHEESE. A soft, whole-milk, rennet cheese which resembles Camembert. It is made in wheels seven inches in diameter and weighing about four pounds.

ESCAROLE. A broad-leaved salad. See CHICORY.

ESPAGNOLE SAUCE. See BROWN SAUCE.

ESSENCE. A commercial preparation of meat, fish, or poultry, ready for use as flavoring.

EST EST EST. A golden Moscatello wine made in Montefiascone, in the Latium region, south of Rome. There are two types made, differing in sweetness, and of them, the sweeter is considered by many to be superior.

There is an interesting legend which would explain this rather unusual name. According to the story, a wealthy gentleman was travelling through Italy a great many years ago. Being a great epicure of wines, he sent his servant, also a man of sound taste, ahead to sample the wine of every inn along his route. Whenever the servant found a wine worthy of his master's palate, he would chalk the Latin word *est*, meaning "it is (good)," on the inn's sign, thus guiding his master to only the best stopping places.

When the servant encountered this particular wine, then known by a different name, he liked it so well that he chalked "EST EST EST" in great letters on the sign. The story further says that when the master arrived at the inn, he so concurred with his servant's judgment that he dis-

continued his journey and stayed there until, it is said, he died of over-indulgence.

ETOG. *See* CITRON.

ETUVE CHEESE. A Dutch cheese. It also comes half the full size, called *Demi-Étuve*.

EVAPORATED FRUIT. *See* DRIED FRUITS, which is the commoner term.

EVAPORATED MILK. Milk in which the water content has been reduced by evaporation. *See* MILK.

EVARGLICE CHEESE. A Yugoslavian cheese.

EXTRACT. *See* FLAVORING EXTRACT and SEASONING.

F

FALERNIAN WINE. One of the most highly praised wines of antiquity, classical prose and verse ring with hearty Roman applause for this famous wine grown near Falerno in the shadow of Mount Vesuvius. Both red and white wines are still being made from the grapes of those identical vineyards, but today they are held in low opinion. It is not known whether the wine has deteriorated through the years or if the tastes of the ancients differed from those of modern connoisseur.

FANNING. A term indicative of a small sized green tea. It bears no relation to the quality of the tea.

FARCE. A French term, meaning stuffing, *which see*.

FARINA. Generally speaking, finely ground wheat "middlings," or cornmeal, used in milk desserts or as a breakfast food. *See* WHEAT.

FARINACEOUS FOODS. Farinaceous foods are composed of flour of different kinds, and constitute a subdivision of starchy foods. The different starchy foods are derived from a variety of plant structures, including roots, tubers, bulbs, stems, pith, seeds, flowers, fleshy fruits, etc. Some, like the banana, are eaten raw, but the greater number require cooking. The starches derived from grain-bearing plants must be prepared by grinding and milling before cooking. About one-sixth of the protein of the various grain flours passes through the alimentary canal undigested.

In round numbers it may be stated that starch composes one-fifth of potatoes, one-half of peas, beans, wheat, rye, and oats (their flour contains more), and three-fourths of rice and Indian corn.

FARM CHEESE. Made in France and known also as *fromage à la pie, mou, maigre,* and *Fresne*, it is essentially the same as the cottage cheese of this country.

FASTING. The voluntary abstention from food for some moral or religious purpose, or as a means of combating illness. Although fasting may be contrary to man's instincts, its use as a form of ritual is of the greatest antiquity. In modern times men have fasted in order to protest against imprisonment and what they conceived to be injustice, as well as for political reasons, and sometimes only for notoriety.

Man dies of thirst much sooner than of starvation so that most fasting "championships" have been won lying inert in bed, keeping warm, and drinking plenty of water. Mahatma Gandhi fasted for as long as three weeks, during which time he partook of fruit juice mixed with water but abstained from food.

FASTING TO REDUCE

Reducing diets that are composed largely of milk or other liquids may lead to a type of starvation which can have serious results. The body needs a variety of foods to keep in good health.

Another fad which is harmful is the no-breakfast or no-lunch habit. Undue fatigue and physical distress may result if the body goes too long without food. A schedule of four light meals a day is closer to nature's plan than two meals. *See also* DIET.

FAT. All fats, regardless of their physical state—solid, plastic or liquid—or their origin—meat, milk, vegetable, or grain—are chemical compounds of carbon, hydrogen and oxygen. In carbohydrates (sugars and starches) the proportion of oxygen is such as to form water when the molecules are split up. (H_2O signifies that two atoms of hydrogen are combined with one atom of oxygen to produce one molecule of water.) In fats oxygen is not present in sufficient quantity to form water upon combustion of the molecules. The breakdown of fatty acids during digestion produces considerable heat. Thus, the energy value of fat in the body is nine calories per gram as opposed to that of carbohydrates and protein which is only 4 calories per gram. *See* CALORIES.

KINDS OF FATS AND THEIR USES

In baking shortenings produce tenderness by surrounding particles of starch and strands of gluten. In this way, the strands of gluten are kept short; hence the name "shortening." While lard (pig fat in a plastic state) is a popular shortening because it produces the most tender and flaky pastry, other fats have different baking advantages. Hydrogenated shortenings with emulsifiers allow for a higher ratio of sugar to flour and less liquid than plastic fat is required to reach optimum tenderness in pastry. *See* PASTRY.

Vegetable oils and hydrogenated shortenings that do not contain emulsifiers are ideal for frying and deep frying since they have high smoking points. The smoke point of lard varies while the temperature at which a hydrogenated shortening with added emulsifiers will burn is low. Since both butter and margarine have low smoke points they are not suitable for deep frying. However, they are excellent for sautéeing and slow frying which must be done over very low heat.

Fats should never be heated to smoking. At the smoke point, fats begin to break down and emit distasteful odors which adversely flavor food. Smoking fats lose nutritive value. Repeated use of a fat lowers the smoke point and foods absorb more fat, which is undesirable, when cooked in a fat with a low smoke point.

Remove crumbs and bits of food, which also lower the smoke point, by straining the fat through cheesecloth.

Liquid fats are used in the production of salad dressing and mayonnaise. Both French dressing and mayonnaise are emulsions of oil, vinegar or lemon juice and spices which are stabilized with egg yolk in mayonnaise and a cooked starch base in French dressing. In the home any variety of liquid vegetable, nut or grain oils may be used as salad oil. Clouding over of oils under refrigeration is natural and unharmful in oils that have not been "winterized" to eliminate this effect.

Butter, margarine, nut butters and certain rendered animal fats such as chicken fat are used as spreads, garnishes on hot foods and bases for gravies and sauces. Salt pork and pork fat are, in addition, diced and cooked with beans, lentils and greens as a flavoring. See individual headings of fats for further discussion.

STRUCTURE OF FATTY ACIDS

A pure fat is composed of molecules of glycerol to each of which one, two or three fatty acids are linked. Fatty acids may be likened to railway trains in which all of the cars, boxcars (carbons) are linked in a chain. A carboxyl group is at the engine of the train and a methyl group is at the caboose. These fatty acids are connected to the glycerol molecule at the carboxyl end.

We may imagine that a carbon, like a railway box car, has a maximum seating capacity. In the case of carbons no more than two hydrogens may be attached to each carbon. A fatty acid that is "booked up," that is one in which every carbon has the maximum two hydrogens attached to it, is called a saturated fatty acid.

When a total of two hydrogens (one each from two different carbons) are missing, the acid is known as a monounsaturated fatty acid. (Missing hydrogens occur in multiples of two.) A polyunsaturated fatty acid is missing four or more hydrogens to complete the chain.

The importance of polyunsaturates is a complicated question. The body needs sufficient amounts of many kinds of fatty acids—including saturated fats—in order to function properly. However, since recent studies show a relationship between the kinds of fats ingested and the build up of cholesterol in the blood, many physicians advise their patients with high blood cholesterol levels to cut down on excessive saturated fats intake.

Since the relationship between blood cholesterol and saturated fatty acids is not precisely defined and since the complete elimination of saturated fatty acids from the diet in favor of polyunsaturated fatty acids requires a large supplemental intake of vitamin E, individuals should consult their physicians before making any radical change in normal fatty acid intake.

Polyunsaturated fatty acids are found in largest quantity in liquid oils. Those oils which are highest in polyunsaturated fatty acids are safflower oil, sunflower oil, corn oil, soybean oil and cottonseed oil, in descending order. Sesame oil and peanut oil also rank high.

FELL. On the outside surface of a leg of lamb is a thin papery tissue known as the "fell." In older meat, mutton, for example, it is better to remove this fell, but in spring lamb it should be left on, as it will keep the meat in better shape and also serve as an automatic aid in basting. The fell will not affect the flavor while cooking. "Fell" is also the obsolete term for GALL, *which see*.

FENNEL. Fennel is an aromatic herb that belongs to the parsley family. It has the appearance of celery and the taste and aroma of anise (*which see*). Sugar-coated fennel seeds were eaten as a confectionery during the colonial period. Sweet, or garden, fennel is an Italian vegetable; it is served raw like celery, and it is sometimes cooked and blanched. Common fennel is cultivated for its leaves and seeds, both of which are used as condiments.

Fennel seeds add their aromatic flavor to such diverse foods as sweet pickles, cookies and other pastries, apple pie, and boiled fish. They are particularly popular in Scandinavian and Italian baking.

One type of fennel is found growing wild in some parts of the United States. It often grows to a height of about twelve feet and becomes a tremendous pest. *See* DILL. A different type is Florentine fennel, or finocchio (*which see*), which has only recently been introduced to American markets.

FENUGREEK. Fenugreek is an Asiatic herb that is cultivated for its seeds. The early Egyptians used it as today's physicians use quinine, and its seeds have been used extensively as a seasoning. Today fenugreek is used to impart a maple flavor to candy, but its chief contemporary use is as an ingredient of curry powder. Its flavor is rather bitter and its smell rather peculiar.

FENUGREEK

FERMENTED TEA. Better known as black tea. *See* TEA.

FERN. *See* FIDDLEHEAD FERN.

FERNET BRANCA. A very popular bitters produced in Italy. It is of a very dark brown color with a bitter quinine taste, and 40 percent alcoholic strength. It is used in certain cocktails and is mixed

with plain or mineral water as a long drink. It is a tonic, stomachic, and aperient.

FETTICUS. *See* FIELD SALAD.

FEUILLE DE DREUX CHEESE. A French cheese made in the Beauce region.

FEUILLETTE. A French name for Puff Paste, *which see*.

FIASCO. A traditional Italian bottle or flask, used for wines and oils, often used to export wines from Italy. It has a rounded bottom, a straw covering or jacket, and commonly holds two liters. A quart flask is called a *mezzo fiasco*, or half-flask.

FIDDLEHEAD FERN

FIDDLEHEAD FERN. Also called cinnamon fern. A kind of fern or brake that grows on the shores of streams. It gets its name from the fiddleheaded curve of the head of the frond.

The soft, budding stem of the fiddlehead fern has been long a well-known food in northern Maine, and is gathered in great quantities by the Indians on the Tobique River. After being thoroughly washed it is cooked like broccoli, although its flavor is a cross between that of asparagus and mushrooms. It is best cut when young and tender. Canned fiddlehead fern is available in fine grocery stores.

FIELD SALAD. This is one of several names given to a type of salad plant which has leaves shaped like a spoon. Among the many varieties, some form rosettes and some form heads. It has a slightly bitter taste which enhances a mixed salad containing lettuce, celery, and other salad vegetables. Field salad grows easily and matures both earlier and later than other salad plants.

Field salad varieties are also called corn salad, fetticus, fat hen, lamb's lettuce,

FIG   452

lamb's quarter, marsh salad, hog salad, and doucette. Italian corn salad is an entirely different plant.

FIELD SALAD

FIG. This fruit has a rich history merged in a mythical background. Pliny stated that in his time the fig tree under which Romulus and Remus were reared was pointed out as a sacred object. Xerxes, of ancient Per-

Immigrants from Europe and Asia brought cuttings of other varieties to America. The first cutting of Smyrna figs arrived in 1880. The result of its culture is the Calimyrna fig (meaning the Smyrna grown in California). French settlers brought cuttings from France to Louisiana, the most famous of which is the light green Celeste. As a consequence, we find a large number of varieties grown throughout the southern states.

Texas figs are dark and rich in flavor; because of their tough skin they are always skinned before canning. Some figs are canned from the fresh, and some from the dried fruit. Both are good and may be served right from the can. Many delicious desserts may be made from fresh, dried or canned figs.

Figs are unusually rich in iron. They also contain silicon, sulphur, and Vitamins A, B, C, and G.

Fig trees have no blossoms on their branches; the flowers are inside the fruit. This is why figs are so full of seeds.

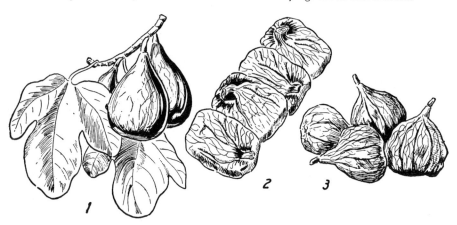

FIGS   1. Fresh   2. Dried   3. Pulled

sia, had the famous figs of Attica brought to him daily as a reminder that some day he must conquer the country that grew such fine fruit.

Franciscan Fathers brought the black fig, which is now known as the Mission or Black Mission Fig, to California in the 18th century. It is thought that they secured it from Mexico where it had been introduced by the Spanish missionaries who followed the Conquistadores. For almost a hundred years no other fig grew in the monastery gardens or on the ranches of California.

VARIETIES OF FIGS

California is the chief producing area of figs, giving us the Calimyrna, Adriatic, and Mission. The Calimyrna is almost white with a rich brown flesh. The Adriatic, originally imported from Italy about 1850, is smaller than the Calimyrna. Kadota figs are green, and are generally thought to have been brought to America from the shores of the Mediterranean. The Mission, or Black Mission, is dark purple, almost black, and looks black when dried.

The southeastern states furnish the Brown Turkey fig, the Brunswick, the Celeste, and the Magnolia.

HINTS ON BUYING

Fresh figs must be fully ripe to be of good quality. A ripe fig is fairly soft, or soft to touch and will vary in color from a greenish yellow to purplish or almost black depending on the variety. Varieties differ also in size.

Ripe figs sour and begin to ferment quickly, and fermentation proceeds rapidly. A characteristic odor is noticeable when figs begin to sour.

Bruised or mechanically injured fruit should be avoided for such fruit breaks down very quickly.

PREPARATION OF DRIED FIGS

The homemaker, who is about to make use of the new pack of dried figs in her holiday sweets, should remember that short soaking and quick cooking is the modern approved method of preparation. (*See also* DRIED FRUITS.) Rinse and drain the figs, cover them with water, and let them simmer for 20 minutes, depending on their softness.

Processed figs require no cooking and may be eaten "out of hand" as a natural confection. However, as a first step toward their use in cake, candy, etc., it is often preferable to pour boiling water over them, let them stand for 30 minutes; then drain, and use. Another good method is to rinse the figs and steam them over hot water for 20 minutes, or until tender. The "plumped" figs are then perfect for making into salads, confection stuffing or filling, and so on. To the cooking water may be added grated lemon or orange rind, whole cloves, cinnamon, or candied ginger to sharpen the somewhat bland flavor of the figs.

FIG-APRICOT DELIGHT

1 cup heavy cream, whipped
1 egg white, stiffly beaten
2 tbsp powdered sugar
½ cup finely diced figs
1 tbsp orange marmalade
½ cup cooked, diced, dried apricots
6 maraschino cherries
12 blanched almonds, shredded

Combine the whipped cream and egg white, fold in the sugar, marmalade, figs and apricots, blending thoroughly but gently. Turn into parfait or sherbet glasses, top each with a maraschino cherry, cut into daisy-like petals, and sprinkle with the almonds. Serve very cold. (Serves 6)

FIG CHARLOTTE

1 tbsp gelatin
¼ cup cold water
1 cup canned fig juice
⅓ cup sugar
⅛ tsp salt
1 tbsp lemon juice
⅛ tsp almond extract
1 cup canned figs
½ cup heavy cream, whipped

Soften the gelatin in the cold water. Combine the fig juice, sugar and salt in a saucepan. Bring to the boiling point and cook three minutes to dissolve the sugar thoroughly, then pour the softened gelatin and stir until this too is dissolved. Cool slightly, add the lemon juice and almond extract. Chill.

Cut half the figs (about 4) into slices and arrange in any desired design in the bottom of a previously wet mold. Fold the whipped cream carefully into the thickened (but not set) gelatin mixture and cover the figs in the mold with a layer of this. Dice the remaining figs, fold them into the remaining cream-gelatin mixture and use to fill up the mold. The work should be done quickly so that the first cream does not actually set before the second is poured over it. Chill. Unmold and garnish, if desired, with whipped cream. (Serves 6)

FIG DUMPLINGS

Use fresh figs, one for each dumpling. Enclose each in a square of biscuit dough and steam about 25 minutes. Serve with any desired sauce. See BISCUIT.

FIG FILLING

½ pound figs
6 pears, cored and pared
1 cup sugar
½ cup water

FIG   454

Chop figs and pears; add sugar and water, and cook until thick, stirring occasionally. (Makes approximately 1½ cups filling, or sufficient for two 9-inch layers)

FIG FRITTERS

1½ cups sifted flour
2 tsp baking powder
¼ tsp salt
1 whole egg plus 1 egg yolk
⅔ cup milk
¾ cup steamed cold dried figs

Sift the dry ingredients and mix to a batter with the egg, egg yolk, and milk, using enough milk to make a light drop batter. Dice or coarsely chop the figs and stir them into the batter. (If desired, a few drops of vanilla or almond extract may be added with the milk.) Drop the mixture from the tip of a tablespoon into deep hot fat (375° F.) and fry golden brown, turning to brown on all sides. Drain on soft crumpled paper and serve as hot as possible with hard sauce. (Serves 6)

FIG GINGER PUDDING

1 cup dried figs
1 egg
1 cup light molasses
½ cup melted shortening
2 cups sifted flour
1 tbsp ginger
¼ tsp salt
1 tsp baking soda
1 cup water

Rinse, stem, and coarsely chop the figs, then combine with the beaten egg, molasses, and shortening. Sift together the dry ingredients and add to the first mixture, alternately with the water, stirring and beating to blend thoroughly. Turn into one large or six small greased molds, cover with greased paper (or the cover of the molds) and steam; if in one large mold, 1½ hours, if in small molds about 45 minutes. Serve with vanilla custard sauce (*see* CUSTARD). (Serves 6)

FIG MOLD

1 lb dried figs
12 tbsp sugar

1 cup water
1 cup white wine
Strips of lemon rind
1 tbsp gelatin

Chop figs and put in saucepan with sugar, water, white wine, lemon rind, and simmer gently until figs are puffed out and tender. Dissolve gelatin in a little warm water and add. Pour mixture into mold and chill until set.

FIG PARFAIT

1 cup fig sirup
1 cup granulated sugar
2 egg whites, stiffly beaten
1 tsp grated orange rind
1 tbsp granulated gelatin
2 tbsp cold water
3 tbsp orange juice
¼ tsp salt
1 cup chopped canned figs (very fine)
1 cup heavy cream, whipped stiff
¼ cup chopped meats (optional)

Combine the fig sirup and sugar and boil until sirup spins a thread from the tip of a spoon. Immediately pour in a fine stream onto the stiffly beaten egg whites, beating briskly and constantly. Soak the gelatin in cold water and dissolve over hot water with the orange juice, salt, and grated orange rind, continuing beating until mixture is cold. Add to the egg mixture. Chill. Then fold in the chopped figs, alternately with whipped cream and chopped nuts (optional).

To freeze in a mechanical refrigerator pack in tray or mold and place in tray and freeze until firm, or about 2½ hours. To freeze in hand freezer pail, fill mold or molds to overflowing. Cover with buttered paper, then with buttered muslin, or cheesecloth around the rim, to prevent salt from entering into the creamy mixture; or rub butter around rim of the mold or molds. Use equal parts of ice and rock salt and freeze for 2 hours if in small molds or 3 hours if large molds. *See also* PARFAIT.

FIG PUDDING

½ lb dried figs
6 oz finely-chopped suet
2 well-beaten eggs

¼ lb flour
¼ lb sugar
Pinch of salt
1 cup milk

Chop figs finely and mix thoroughly with suet, flour, sugar, salt and eggs. Moisten with milk and pack the mixture into a greased mold. Steam for 3½ hours. (Serves 4)

Fig Tapioca

3 cups water
½ cup quick-cooking tapioca
½ cup sugar
¼ tsp salt
2 cups diced cooked figs
2 tbsp lemon juice
½ tsp grated lemon rind
½ tsp vanilla

Put the water in the upper part of a double boiler and bring to a boil over direct heat. Combine the tapioca, sugar and salt, shake gently into the water and again bring to boiling point, stirring constantly. Now set over the lower pan containing boiling water and cook five minutes longer. Add the figs, lemon juice, grated lemon rind, and vanilla and when partly cooled (when the mixture will be found to have thickened considerably) turn into serving dish and chill. Serve with plain or whipped cream. (Serves 6)

Fresh Figs Curacao

1 cup thick sour cream, partially whipped
5 tbsp Curacao liqueur
1 doz fresh figs, peeled and halved
1 tbsp brandy

Combine the cream and Curacao and separately combine the figs and the brandy. Let stand 15 minutes, then very gently fold the drained fig halves into the cream. Serve at once. (Serves 6)

Fresh Figs Flambee

Allow two fresh figs for each serving. Place in a fireproof dish and pour over them a little sugar sirup well flavored with brandy. Heat thoroughly, then, immediately before serving, sprinkle with sugar

and pour a little fresh brandy over each fig, allowing about one teaspoon for each serving. Light the brandy, and allow it to burn a minute or so, then top with whipped cream and serve immediately. It is nice to take the heated figs to the table and to pour and ignite the brandy there. Warm the brandy slightly before using.

Fresh Fig Marmalade

Wash the figs, place in a little water, and bring to boiling point. Measure and add an equal amount of sugar. Cook one hour, stirring constantly to prevent burning. Turn into sterilized jars and seal. *See* Marmalade.

Fresh Figs Melba

Arrange for individual service portions of vanilla ice cream. Press gently into these a fresh peeled Mission fig and top with a sauce made by crushing and straining 1 cup of fresh raspberries, adding ¼ cup of sugar and cooking to heavy sirup. This will be enough for six servings.

Rhubarb Fig Bar Dessert

1 lb rhubarb
¼ cup sugar
½ tsp lemon rind
½ lb fig bars
2 tbsp butter

Cut stem ends and leaves of rhubarb and discard. Wash well, drain and cut stalks into ½ inch lengths. Mix sugar and rind, sprinkle over rhubarb and mix well. Cut fig bars in small dice. Put a layer of fig bar cubes, then a layer of rhubarb into a glass baking dish (6 cup). Repeat until all are used, ending with a layer of fig bars on top. Dot with butter and bake in a moderate oven (375° F.) for 20 minutes or until rhubarb is tender. Serve warm. (Serves 6)

Spiced Fig Whip

½ cup sieved canned fig pulp
2 tbsp sugar
2 egg whites
⅛ tsp salt
⅛ tsp ground nutmeg
¼ tsp ground ginger
1 tsp lemon juice

Heat the fig pulp (drained, canned figs pressed through a sieve) with half the sugar, stirring constantly. As soon as the sugar is dissolved remove from the fire, cover and keep warm. Beat the egg whites until stiff, with the salt. Fold in the remaining sugar, sifted with the nutmeg and ginger. Add the lemon juice and combine with the fig mixture. Pile in a generously buttered soufflé dish, set in a pan containing hot water and bake in a moderate oven (350°–375° F.) until well risen and set, about 25 or 30 minutes. Serve immediately with the heated fig sirup or plain or with whipped cream as a sauce. (Serves 4)

STEAMED FIG PUDDING I

2½ cups all-purpose flour
½ tsp baking soda
2 tsp baking powder
1 tsp salt
1 tsp cinnamon
½ tsp ginger
½ tsp nutmeg
½ cup sugar
2 cups suet, chopped (½ lb)
1½ cups figs, chopped (1 lb)
1 cup raisins, washed
½ cup molasses
1 cup milk
2 eggs beaten
1 tsp vanilla

Sift flour, measure and resift 3 times with next 7 ingredients. Add finely chopped or ground suet, figs and raisins, and stir thoroughly to distribute. Combine the molasses, milk, eggs and vanilla and mix well. Add to the flour mixture and beat until well blended. Turn into well-greased mold or molds, filling ⅔ full. Cover securely and steam covered for 2 hours. Makes 5¾ cups of batter and will fill 3 No. 2 cans. Serve hot with brandy sauce (see BRANDY). (Serves 8 to 12)

STEAMED FIG PUDDING II

⅓ cup shortening
½ cup sugar
2 cups fine dry bread crumbs
1¼ cups scalded milk
3 eggs
¼ cup sifted flour

1 tsp baking powder
½ tsp salt
¼ tsp each ground cinnamon, cloves and nutmeg
½ cup chopped figs
½ cup seedless raisins

Cream the shortening and sugar, add the bread crumbs and milk, mix well and cool. Add the beaten eggs, then the sifted dry ingredients, the figs and raisins. Turn into a greased mold, filling it about three-fourths full. Cover closely with lid and greased paper and steam about 3 hours. Serve with hard sauce. (Serves 4–6)

FIGARO SAUCE. A Hollandaise sauce (*which see*) blended with tomato purée. To each one and a half cups of hollandaise, add three rounded tablespoons of tomato purée (canned or cooked), one tablespoon of finely chopped parsley, and a few grains of cayenne pepper. Salt to taste. Suitable for large pieces of boiled fish.

FILBERT. This is the nut of the bushy shrub or small tree of the Oriental hazel. Like butternuts, filberts are rich in fat and are frequently used in confections, cookies, etc. There are very few filberts grown in America, those found in our markets being imported from Italy and Turkey. *See also* NUTS.

FILBERT NUT

FILE. (*fee-lay*) Filé powder is derived from the tender young leaves of the sassafras tree. It is an essential ingredient of gumbo filé and of other Creole culinary preparations. Today this unique condiment is prepared and distributed by the remnants of the once-powerful Choctaws.

FILET. The French word *filet*, which is often Anglicized into "fillet," as applied to fish, poultry, game, or butcher's meat, refers to the flesh or any part of it which has been skilfully raised clear from the bones, and divided or not, as the manner in which it is to be served may determine.

It is the elegant French mode of dressing various kinds of fish, and even those which are not valued very highly afford an excellent dish when thus prepared. The fish to be fileted to advantage should be large. The flesh may then be divided down the middle of the back, separated from the fins, and raised clean from the bones with a very sharp knife. When thus prepared, the filets may be cut into attractive portions, dipped into yolk of egg, rolled in fine bread crumbs and fried in the usual way. By another method, the entire filet, if quite small, may be rolled (if large, divided and rolled) and fastened with thread, fine cord, or a short, thin skewer; then dipped in egg yolk, crumbed and fried, or steamed, sautéed, or grilled. Again, the filet may be well seasoned, floured, and sautéed in butter or any other fat a few minutes until done.

When the fish are not very large, they may be boned, without being divided down the middle, spread with butter or oil, discreetly seasoned, and each filet then rolled from tail to head in a small quantity of bread crumbs, seasoned with salt, pepper, and sometimes with spices, according to directions, or the fish are rolled in pounded lobster, mixed with a large portion of the coral, plus seasoning and butter. They are then laid in a dish, well covered with bread crumbs and butter, and baked from 10 to 15 minutes in a moderately hot oven until golden brown.

The filets may also be cut into small strips or squares, according to requirements, of uniform size, lightly dredged with seasoned flour and sautéed in butter over a brisk fire. They should be drained on soft crumpled paper and served with any prepared sauce, which may be a cream, a compounded butter, or a fancy sauce, or may be merely plain butter flavored with a teaspoon or more of minced parsley, chervil, chives, or any other aromatic herbs.

FILET MIGNON. A culinary term for a small thick tenderloin steak. *See* Beef.

FILET OF FLOUNDER. *See* Flounder.

FILET OF SOLE. On the subject of filet of sole, it is necessary to state that genuine sole is rarely found in American markets. It is imported from Europe and is thus prohibitively expensive. The filets sold under the name of sole are usually those of flounder or one of the related fishes. Gourmets insist that there is a distinct difference in the flavors.

FILLED CHEESE. A cheese like Cheddar, from which the butter fat is removed and other fats added during the processing.

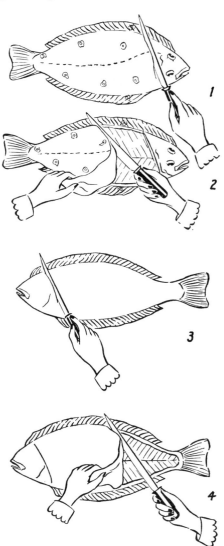

FILLETING FISH.   1. Cutting behind head on top.   2. Removing top filet.   3. Cutting behind head on bottom.   4. Removing bottom filet.

FILLING. *See* Frosting, Filling and Icing.

FILTER. A filter is a superior type of strainer (*which see*), being used to separate minute particles of solid matter from liquids. Filters can be made so fine as to separate certain kinds of liquids from other kinds, or even to remove germs from a solution, but devices of this nature are found only in laboratories.

Filters are based on the same principle as are strainers: that of having openings large enough to give passage to liquids, but too small for the solids to follow; but, because of the fineness of their operation, they are usually built differently than are strainers.

The most common kitchen filter is a simple pad made of several thicknesses of fine cloth. Such filters are used in certain types of coffee makers (*which see*), to strain fruit juices for jellies, etc. They may be purchased as manufactured units, or be made by the simple expedient of placing several thicknesses of cloth in a funnel. Paper may also be used for filtering purposes, but the action is slower and, unless the paper is of a special type, it is apt to burst under the pressure of the liquid.

Some coffee makers have solid glass filters: a roughened glass surface resting against a smooth glass surface, there being just enough clearance for the coffee to pass, but not enough for the grounds to follow.

In some cases, a filter may be installed in the water system. These commonly consists of a tank filled with sand, gravel, or some similar granular substance that filters the water as it passes through. In many cases, these filters also contain chemicals that soften the water, as well as filter it. *See also* Water Softener.

FIN DE SIECLE CHEESE. A French cheese made in Normandy.

FINANCIERE. A meat or vegetable sauce.

Financiere Sauce

1 cup brown sauce
½ cup chicken broth
Truffle trimmings
4 or 5 mushrooms
½ glass Sauternes or Madeira
Seasonings as desired

Heat the brown sauce (*which see*), add the chicken broth, the truffles, and the chopped mushrooms. Cook over a good heat until liquid is greatly reduced, then add the wine, a little at a time, after reducing the heat. Strain and serve hot.

FINE CHAMPAGNE. A first quality French brandy. *See* Brandy.

FINE SILVER. *See* Silverware.

FINES HERBES. This name refers to a combination of edible herbs that is used to give relish to many insipid dishes. It is well to have some prepared *fines herbes* on hand at all times. The recipe for a particular blend follows:

1 tsp burnet
1 tsp chives
2 tbsp thyme
2 tbsp savory
2 tbsp marjoram
2 tbsp dried parsley
1 tbsp sage
1 tbsp grated lemon rind
2 tbsp celery seeds
6 bay leaves

Finely powder all of the ingredients before measuring them. Then mix them thoroughly and sift. Keep in a tightly-covered jar or a tightly-corked bottle.

FINGER BOWL. A small glass bowl half filled with water that is brought to the table near the close of the meal for the diner to use in cleansing his fingers. It is used at formal functions and any meal that involves food of a type that is held in the hands while eating. The water is sometimes delicately scented and may have a few flower petals floating on the surface, but this is by no means necessary. If the food to be handled is very greasy, lemon juice may be added to the water to help cut the grease, but this is done only under those circumstances.

Individual finger bowls are always provided for the guests, and they are traditionally made of clear glass and are set on a lace or paper doily. When used they are brought to the table on the dessert service plates, along with the dessert silver, and are removed and set in their proper positions by the guests themselves, before the dessert is served. *See* Table Setting and Service.

The use of the finger bowl dates back to the pre-fork-and-spoon days when it was considered proper to eat nearly everything by using the fingers. Today, however, they are more a formality except on occasions when fried chicken or similar dishes are served, which accounts for their limited use.

FINGER ROLL. *See* ROLL.

FINING. In wine making, a process whereby a new or young wine is cleared by having a substance (finings) spread on the surface and settle to the bottom of the container, carrying with it all sediment, mucilage, or other impurities that might have been held in suspension in the wine. The most common finings are, for red wines, the whites of eggs; for white wines, isinglass or gelatin. Other substances, such as commercial powders, milk, or even fresh blood, are also used. *See* WINE.

FINNAN HADDIE. A smoked haddock. Legend has it that the name was derived from either of two towns in Scotland, Findon or Findhorn. *See also* HADDOCK and FISH.

FINNAN HADDIE BAKED IN MILK

2 lb finnan haddie
1½ cups rich milk, evaporated milk, or thin cream
1 bay leaf tied with
4 sprigs fresh parsley and
2 thin slices onion
Pepper
3 tbsp butter

If the finnan haddie is mildly salted, cover with boiling water and drain at once. Remove the bones carefully and, if desired, skin the fish. Place in a generously buttered shallow baking dish or casserole and pour the milk over. Add the herb bouquet, dust with pepper and dot with the butter. Bake in a moderate oven (350° F.) 20 to 25 minutes, or until the fish flakes separate easily when tested with a fork. Remove the herb bouquet before serving. Should a thicker sauce be desired, thicken the milk with a little flour after removing the fish. Pour the sauce over the fish to serve. (Serves 4)

FINNAN HADDIE A LA KING

3 lb finnan haddie
1 qt milk
½ cup butter or margarine
½ medium-sized onion, sliced
1 tbsp minced green pepper
1 tbsp minced pimiento
½ tsp paprika
1 scant tsp salt
4 tbsp flour
1 cup thin cream, scalded
1 cup milk (additional) scalded
1 or 2 tbsp sherry (or lemon juice)

Wash the fish quickly, pat dry, and place in a baking dish. Cover with the quart of milk. Let stand for one hour; then bake in a moderate oven (350° F.) for 30 minutes or until tender. Flake the fish, removing all bones and skin. There should be about 2 cups of fish. Cook the onion, green pepper, and pimiento in half the butter in the top of a double boiler for five minutes, stirring occasionally to blend well. Set over a very low flame; add the remaining butter, blend in the flour, paprika, and salt, and gradually stir in the combined scalded milk and cream (evaporated milk may be substituted for the cream), stirring constantly until the mixture is thick and smooth. Place over hot water, add the flaked fish and heat well. When ready to serve, add the sherry or lemon juice, and serve on toast, in heated patty shells, or in baked scooped out tomatoes, potatoes, or green peppers. (Serves 6)

FINO. A type of Sherry wine. *See* SHERRY.

FINOCHIO. Finochio is a bulbous Italian vegetable belonging to the fennel family. It was introduced to American markets by Italian truck gardeners within

FINOCHIO

the last few years. The demand for it has increased steadily as its excellent qualities as a vegetable to be eaten cooked or raw in salads have become more widely known.

Fennel is cultivated primarily for its fleshy, enlarged, leaf base. The ornamental foliage, though highly attractive, is of

rocks at the bottom of the sea. Some fish live in a depth of water which man cannot reach, while the orestias of Lake Titicaca swim in waters more than 12,000 feet above sea level.

The habits of many species of fish are sedentary. The fisherman knows that a certain trout or other fish will be found at a

FOOD VALUE

	Wa-ter	Food Energy	Pro-tein	Fat	Car-bohy-drates	Cal-cium	Phos-phorus	Iron	Vit. A Value	Thia-mine	Ribo-flavin	Nia-cin	Ascor-bic Acid
Cod	82.6	70	16.5	.4	0	18	189	.9	0	.04	.05	2.3	2
Mack-erel	77.2	98	19.0	2.5	0	21	218	1.0	0	.07	.07	4.2	2

little use after the leaf base is fully developed. When the fleshy knobs are about the size of a hen's egg, it is bleached as is celery for about two weeks or until pure white.

Finocchio stalks are very tender, and they have a unique flavor somewhat reminiscent of anise. Quartered and eaten raw with salt, they leave a pleasant, clean taste in the mouth. They make an interesting addition to a salad. They may be braised or steamed in any of the ways appropriate for celery, or they may be boiled and served with a cream sauce.

FIREPLACE. *See* BARBEQUE and CAMP COOKERY.

FISH. The empire of waters contains a vast number of fishes, some of which are inedible, but most of which serve as food for man. The Greeks and Romans, although not as advanced as modern man in the art of cooking, recognized the value of fish as a food. Their gastronomic discernment was supposed to be developed to such a point that they were able to tell from the taste just where the fish had been caught.

Although fish are red-blooded animals, their blood is cold, thus enabling them to live in the water. The liver of fish is very large in comparison with the size of the fish, and the oil derived therefrom is of medicinal value. Fish are generally reproduced by eggs, the size of which varies greatly. Their number runs into fantastic figures; certain species, such as the eel, lay ten million or more eggs at a time.

Fish exist in any degree of latitude or longitude where there may be water, whether fresh or salt. Certain species live on the high seas, others near the shore, while some choose as their habitat the

certain place in a certain month, be it lake, river, or sea. Other species appear to have the instinct of periodical migration, the sardines, cod, mackerel, and others visiting our shores periodically.

The herring has furnished material for some very fantastic tales in reference to its migration from the deep waters of the ocean to the shores, during the summer. In reality the necessity for spawning urges it to move shoreward in order to derive benefit from the heat of shallower waters which will cause a more rapid hatching of the eggs.

Fresh-water and salt-water fish differ in flavor, and there is even a difference to be detected between fish from running water and from lakes. Brook trout, for example, has a superior flavor to lake trout. The food supply also influences the flavor, and both fresh- and salt-water fish are better when taken from sandy and rocky rather than muddy bottoms.

The habits of the fish also have an effect on the quality and taste. The chequit, for instance, is so sluggish and easy to catch that it is sometimes called "lazy" and is known as "weakfish." It is watery and poorly flavored compared with the shad, a fish of more vigorous habits. The amount of fat also causes a difference in flavor. Such high-flavored fish as salmon and shad contain much fat. However, the distinctive flavors of mackerel and herring are apparently not due to fat, since their fat content is not so different from other highly fat fish. Fish varies in the dryness of the flesh, but there is no such thing as a tough fish; moreover the texture of the muscles is about the same in all parts of the fish, although there is a difference in flavor between the dark and white flesh when these both occur.

CURED FISH

Homemakers would probably use fish more often if it were not that many who live in inland communities find it difficult, if not impossible, to secure fresh fish. This objection may be overcome by using salted, quick roasted, or smoked fish. In addition, such fish is concentrated in food value and particularly tasty and appealing to the appetite. When we add another advantage, that of economy, it is easy to see why such fish should be used in the winter diet.

The salted varieties should, of course, be given a prolonged or overnight soaking to remove the excess salt. However, many types of salt fish come packed in convenient, easy-to-use form, such as canned codfish flakes, canned fish cakes, or balls, etc. Other fish, like filet of salt mackerel, haddock, etc., come packaged in convenient sections or portions for frying, baking, and other uses.

Salt herring is generally sold whole from the keg. This is a winter fish, admirably suited to simple hearty dishes of very low cost. Herring also makes a good salad or a fish jelly. Soaking overnight removes the too-strong flavor and prepares it for frying, broiling, or simmering in milk.

In the varieties of smaller cured fish we have brisling, sardines, and anchovy, all of which are wholesome and add flavor to starchy meals. For example, a sardine rarebit is an excellent pick-up lunch for the homemaker, while sardines used with spinach and noodles form an interesting dish. For the homemaker who prides herself on novelty in appetizers, sardines are a stand-by in endless combinations.

The delicatessen store, which stems from a foreign influence in foods, may display other and less-known salted and smoked varieties. Thus smoked whitefish is a delicacy and a treat, and a whole meal if only a hot boiled potato be added. Smoked salmon, when sliced paper-thin, is a most appetizing filler for tidbit sandwiches, or as a chief ingredient in a salad of potatoes, cucumbers, tomatoes, and even cooked or raw green vegetable salads.

Another delicacy is smoked sturgeon— rich, oily, and luscious. A very few slices of this fish go a long way when used with dark breads, pickles, cole slaw, etc.

While fish roe cannot strictly be classed as smoked or salted, nevertheless, it is a novelty which serves the same purpose. And while shad roe, fresh or canned, is usually high in price, there are other packs of roe, such as cod roe, which are excellent and less expensive. Extended by fried bacon and good hashed-browned potatoes, it makes a fine Sunday breakfast.

SMOKED FISH

Since smoked fish has its own special distinctive "smoked" flavor, little additional seasoning is necessary. Usually smoked fish is best cooked or prepared as plainly and simply as possible. When broiled just as they come and served with melted butter, these fish dishes are at their best.

But for the homemaker who does not like to use the broiler, it is good to note that a skillet or frying pan can be made to serve the purpose. Have the pan quite hot, put in a little butter, and when it is melted, lay in the fish. Cover, and cook for about ten minutes, turning once. By cooking with a cover, the escaping steam is percolated back onto the fish and develops a little gravy or sauce. Serve the fish on a very hot platter, pouring over it the butter-gravy from the pan, and serve it immediately with a section of lemon and a garnish of parsley or watercress.

A good fish on which to try this simple method is smoked finnan haddie, whether in the whole or canned form. Served with hot mashed potatoes, hot boiled rice, macaroni, noodles, or spaghetti, and a cream sauce, the homemaker can be sure that she is offering a nourishing, tasty dish which the whole family will enjoy. The addition of a little curry powder to the cream sauce gives an exotic and very pleasing new flavor.

In this connection, a smoked fish chowder must not be overlooked, for aside from the familiar fish and clam chowders, there are several most interesting smoked fish varieties made with pieces of white-meated smoked fish, such as finnan haddie, whitefish, etc. In all such chowders, flavor is enhanced, as in clam chowder, through the use of finely diced bacon or salt pork. Bulk is supplied by potatoes, crackers, or cubes of toasted bread. Additional nourishment is provided by the milk, which gives the right consistency to the chowder. *See* CHOWDER.

Another popular use for smoked or salted fish is the cake or patty, fried in a skillet or cooked in deep fat. Codfish cakes, or codfish balls are the most familiar example, but one may also have salmon cakes, smoked whitefish cakes, etc. Fish cakes are also obtainable canned or quick-frozen.

A great deal of the smoked fish to be found in our markets, especially of freshwater varieties, such as whitefish and carp, is smoked over a hickory fire. From Nova Scotia come the smoked cod filets which need no soaking, while some of the kippered herring on sale is from Canada. The flavor of the Canadian herring, somewhat less authoritative than that of English kippers, is due to the herring itself, rather than to any difference in processing.

It is a mistake to soak smoked fish. There is no excess salt to make soaking necessary, and the keen, smoky flavor is lessened by long immersion in water. Probably finnan haddie enjoys the greatest prestige among smoked fish. This and other smoked fish may be prepared as follows:

Steam the filets for 10 minutes, in one inch of milk brought to the boiling point. Let stand five minutes without further cooking, then lift out of the milk carefully, and broil. Serve with drawn butter. Or after the preliminary steaming, flake the fish and blanket it with a white or cream sauce, to which may be added a little sherry. Use the cooking milk for the sauce. *See* FINNAN HADDIE.

CHOOSING FRESH FISH

The inexperienced homemaker will be wise to find a reliable fish dealer and let him help in her fish selection. Knowing fish is a difficult matter for the novice. The table which follows may be used as a general guide in making the choice.

HINTS ON PREPARATION

Most people are in complete ignorance of the many varieties of fish of surpassing excellence. They do not realize that fish, whatever the kind, is a splendid investment not only for a varied diet, but also for the sake of health, and that fish can be economically prepared in countless delicious ways.

Fish deteriorates and decomposes much more rapidly than meat, and is at its best when cleaned and cooked just after being caught. Ice will preserve it a short time only. Bluefish caught in the surf, or trout in the brook, should be cooked immediately. Otherwise, they should be killed, and put on ice at once. If there is no ice, clean the fish, sprinkle the flesh with pepper and salt, wrap in a wet cloth, and set in a breeze or draught.

In selecting fish, see that the flesh feels firm and that the eyes are still bright. If you have a keen sense of smell, this will also guide you, although to the novice the odor of fish may be disagreeable even if untainted.

Cleaning and Scaling. The scaling and cleaning of fish are important first steps. In the city this may be done at the store or market. If it is to be done at home, clean the fish on a large piece of paper. Use a sharp, strong knife, and rub off the scales, working from the tail up to the head. (To skin a fish well, you should first watch an expert.) Cut through the skin of the abdomen, loosen it at the tail, and pull it off. Remove the head, open the abdomen, and take out the entrails. Roll these up in the paper on which the fish has been cleaned and dispose of it so there will be no odor.

Fish is boned by slitting the flesh down the back, and carefully separating the flesh from the side bones, finally pulling out the spine and attached bones, con-

TESTS FOR FRESHNESS OF FISH

Good Fish	Undesirable Fish
(1) Skin and color bright	(1) Skin dull, spotted, slimy; color pale or bleached
(2) Scales adhere strongly	(2) Scales loose
(3) Eyes clear, not sunken or wrinkled	(3) Eyes cloudy, wrinkled, sunken
(4) Gills red	(4) Gills yellowish, gray, brown
(5) Flesh firm and elastic	(5) Flesh flabby and soft; finger impressions remain
(6) Fresh odor, both exterior and gills	(6) Stale or sour odor, especially at gills
(7) Little slime on skin (usually clear slime on halibut)	(7) Skin slimy (usually); with some species, coagulated or lumpy
(8) Body rigid or stiff	(8) Body flabby or limp
(9) Body sinks in water (usually)	(9) Body floats in water if very stale, (though some good fish, if gassy, will float)

stantly keeping the knife blade close and parallel to the bone.

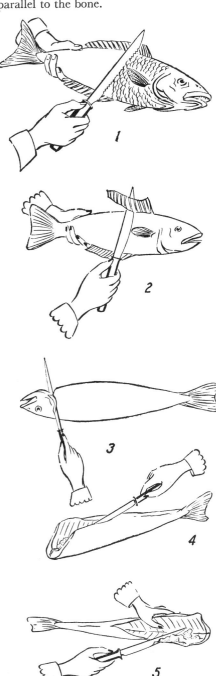

FISH   1. Scaling   2. Removing fins
3. Removing head   4. Slitting abdomen
5. Removing entrails

The strong odor clings to everything the fish touches. Wash the fish, the knife, and your hands in cold water and salt. Always pour the water in which the fish is washed or cooked into the sink at once, unless reserving it for fish soups, sauces, or chowders. Pour some salt in the trap and flush it with cold water. The utensils and dishes in which fish is served require very careful washing in several waters.

To Boil Fish

The connective tissues of fish soften and dissolve more readily than those of meat. Because of this characteristic, the fish readily "falls apart," or disintegrates, and the aim must be to prevent this. The protein is affected by cooking as in all other foods. The fat is melted. The connective tissue quickly softens. To avoid breaking the fish, it may be wrapped in cloth for boiling, and the water should only simmer. The coating (breading) of small fish or of slices of large fish with beaten eggs and crumbs, or batter, usually used for frying fish, tends to hold it together. In all cases, avoid overcooking. Fish is done when a fork easily pierces it and separates the flakes of flesh from the bone.

Boiling fish is considered to be the most delicate of all methods of cooking it, but because of the slippery skin and gelatinous consistency, it is difficult to boil fish so that its appearance will please the eye. To attain the best results, it is imperative to observe several rules:

1. Know the weight of the fish.

2. Bind the fish carefully in some fabric or cooking parchment. Coarse cheesecloth is excellent for this purpose.

3. The fish kettle must be large enough to accomodate the fish easily and the *cold water* (always used for large fish) must be well salted before the fish is placed in it, or the flakes of the fish will tend to separate.

4. For sliced fish, the water must be at the boiling point (212° F.) when the fish is put in, and should be in sufficient quantity to fully cover it, but not in excess, or the flavor will be washed away.

5. Keep the water boiling very slowly, after first coming to a boil, in order to "poach" the fish.

6. The slices must never be too thin.

7. Whether boiled whole or in slices, the fish should be removed at once as soon as it is done.

8. Like all white meat, the fish should always be fully done but never underdone, lest it be indigestible.

9. The cooking time varies according to size of the fish.

10. As a general rule, fish to be eaten hot should be cooked just before serving.

11. To keep boiling fish from creating a great deal of odor, wrap it in parchment paper rinsed with cold water rather than a cloth.

12. Cook fish bones and trimmings together with onion, celery leaves, sliced carrot, the seasoning and spices for the basis of a fish sauce.

13. For meals when fish is the main course, choose a tart dessert.

14. As a rule, fish boils in about 15 minutes, and is steamed in about 20. This varies according to size of the fish.

There are several recognized ways of boiling fish, each suited to the texture, size, and kind of fish to be boiled. If the fish is to be cooked whole, it is laid on the rack of the fish-kettle, usually of an elongated shape, first being scaled, cleaned, trimmed, and thoroughly washed in several waters. Then it is covered with cold, salted water, or the indicated liquid, and brought rapidly to the boiling point. It is skimmed thoroughly, and the cooking process continued by allowing it to simmer very slowly, without any sign of boiling until it is cooked to the desired degree.

The same process is applied to sliced or small fish, except that they are put into boiling water, instead of cold water, in order to sear the exterior as rapidly as possible, to prevent the fish from falling apart. It is necessary to concentrate all the juice and essence, as well as nourishing parts which the fish may contain and which escape in considerable degree when the fish is placed in cold water.

The addition of a tablespoon of vinegar or lemon juice or white wine to each quart and a half of water used for boiling the fish, and also the addition of a slice or two of carrot, onion, celery (as well as bay leaf and parsley tied together) enhances the flavor of the fish or the fish broth. The broth may then be used for sauce, fish soup, chowders, etc.

Fish may also be boiled in milk, to add more nutritive value. The various methods of cooking employed in the preparation of meats, may be applied to any kind of fish, except that the time of cooking varies.

Fish may also be stuffed in the same ways as chicken and meat. Leftover fish may be picked apart, mixed with cream sauce, and served as creamed fish, as an escalloped dish, baked, or moulded into balls or croquettes.

Filets: The handling of cooked filets (or slices) demands care, lest they break to pieces; a large broad spatula is the best tool. The cooking of fish filets should always be done just when ready to serve, to preserve the full flavor of the fish.

BROILING FISH

Broiling is assuredly the oldest method of cooking fish; and no new method surpasses it. The skin of small or thin fish serves to keep them in shape. Slices of halibut or salmon, or any kind of large fish, may be broiled with or without the skin removed. Rub the broiler with fat (oil, drippings, or any other kind of fat), lay the fish flesh side down, if whole and small, and set under the flame of the broiling oven. When done, place carefully on a heated platter, remove the skin if need be, sprinkle with salt and pepper, and spread with butter.

It is advisable to make a few incisions on the sides of small fish and on the sides and top—as far as the backbone—on a large fish to be broiled. This will facilitate cooking and prevent shriveling of the fish during the cooking process. The fish is then seasoned with salt and pepper to taste, oiled, greased or buttered, and placed on a broiler which has been preheated to prevent scorching.

DEEP FAT FRYING

The best deep-fat-frying medium for fish is oil, be it olive, vegetable, or animal oil. Whatever the fat used in frying fish, it should be used for fish alone, lest the other food take the flavor of fish. The fat used for frying fish should be very hot (390° F.), unless otherwise indicated, before the fish is plunged into it. Deep fried fish are usually either floured, breaded, or crumbed after being dipped in beaten egg, or may be dipped in batter. When the fish comes to the surface of the fat, it is done. It should be drained on soft crumpled kitchen paper (unglazed) or a towel, placed on a hot platter, garnished with parsley or cress and quartered lemon, and served at once. As a rule, sauces are never served with deep fried fish unless it be a tart, cold sauce, such as tartare, mayonnaise, or the like.

SAUCES FOR FISH

Boiled Fish. Boiled fish usually requires a tart, or sweet-sour sauce, such as sour cream sauce, tartare sauce, and similar sauces. Yet butter sauces, such as Hollandaise, plain melted butter or drawn butter, lemon butter, and the like, may be served. Horseradish, tomato, egg, and caper sauce also have an affinity for boiled fish.

Baked Fish. Baked fish is usually stuffed, when large, with a savory stuffing and hence requires a savory sauce, such as Spanish sauce, onion sauce, tomato and onion sauce, or a savory composite sauce.

Steamed Fish. Steamed fish is bland in flavor and requires a tart sauce such as those suggested for boiled fish.

Fried Fish. Fried fish is usually served with a cold sauce, such as Bohemian sauce, bourgeoise sauce, Dutch sauce, gribiche sauce, horseradish sauce with walnut, horseradish and cucumber sauce, ravigote sauce, remoulade (sharp) sauce, tartare sauce, with its many variations.

Cold Cooked Fish. Whatever the method in which the fish has been cooked, the same sauces as applied to fried fish may be used when fish is served cold.

RELISHES FOR FISH

The appropriate relishes for fish include: celery, celery and green pepper, pickled onions, cabbage in any style or form, cabbage and carrot, cucumber, cucumber relish, and sweet-sour beets, etc.

See the individual fishes for further information and recipes.

FISH BATTER I

1 cup sifted flour
⅔ cup cold milk
A few grains cayenne pepper
½ tsp salt

Moisten the flour with the milk, and season with the cayenne pepper and salt. Beat the mixture well until very smooth. Dip the fish into the batter, and sauté in a little fat in a shallow pan or fry in deep hot fat. (This method is usually used for small fish.)

FISH BATTER II

1 cup sifted flour
1 tbsp sugar
¼ tsp salt
⅔ cup cold water
½ tbsp oil
1 egg white beaten to a froth

Combine the flour, sugar, and salt, and moisten with the cold water. Beat well, then add the oil, and finally fold in the egg white. This is also used for small fish.

FISH CHOWDER

See CHOWDER.

FISH MOLD

1 tbsp gelatin
¼ cup cold water
2 egg yolks, slightly beaten
1 scant tsp salt
Few grains of white pepper
1½ tbsp melted butter
¾ cup cold milk
2½ tbsp lemon juice or mild vinegar
2 cups canned salmon, drained, skins and bones removed, or
2 cups canned tuna fish, well drained, or
2 cups crabmeat, drained and boned
1 tsp prepared mustard
Few drops of Worcestershire or tabasco sauce
Cole slaw

Soften the gelatin in the cold water. Combine the egg yolks, salt, pepper and mustard in the upper part of a double boiler. Add the butter, milk and lemon juice or vinegar and cook over boiling water, stirring constantly, until the mixture thickens. Now add the softened gelatin and stir until dissolved. Cool until almost at the setting point, then fold in the fish with remaining seasonings. Turn into a previously wet mold. Chill. When firm, unmold and garnish with cole slaw.

If desired, two different fish may be combined as salmon and crabmeat; or tuna and leftover boiled fresh fish. (Serves 4 to 6)

Variations. (1) Use a ring mold for the fish mixture. When serving fill the center

with thick cucumber sauce made as follows: Beat ½ cup of heavy cream until
stiff, season rather highly with salt, pepper
and mild vinegar or lemon juice, then fold
in one medium-sized cucumber, pared,
chopped and thoroughly drained.

(2) Add ½ cup of stiffly beaten cream or
evaporated milk to the fish mixture. Mold
as directed and at serving time unmold
and garnish with sliced cucumbers and
ripe olives.

(3) Instead of molding the fish mixture
use to fill large ripe tomatoes. Chill and
serve on a bed of lettuce or in a nest of
crisp green watercress, passing French
dressing separately.

NEW ENGLAND CODFISH CAKES

2 7-oz packages salt codfish
4 cups raw potatoes, diced small
⅓ cup butter
¼ tsp white pepper
1 egg, well-beaten

Put the codfish into a fine strainer and
pour warm water over it to rinse out some
of the salt. Drain thoroughly. Cook the
raw potatoes, diced, in boiling water for
15 minutes. Add little or no salt. Drain and
mash the potatoes. Combine the fish, potatoes, butter, pepper, and well-beaten egg.
Beat the mixture until it is fluffy. Shape into
cakes and fry in a little hot fat, turning to
brown on both sides. Drain them on soft,
crumpled paper and serve at once. (Serves
6)

The favorite New England method is to
try out fat salt pork, cook the fish cakes in
the fat, and serve the crisp fat itself as a
garnish.

NEW ENGLAND FISH BALLS

1 cup cooked fish (preferably white-
fleshed)
1 cup leftover mashed potatoes and
vegetables
1 beaten egg
1 tsp butter
⅛ tsp white pepper
Salt
Deep hot fat

Combine the cooked fish with the vegetables in equal parts. Add the beaten egg,

butter, and pepper. Taste for salt and add
it if needed. Drop the mixture from a tablespoon into the deep hot fat (375°–390° F.)
and cook until golden brown. Drain on
soft crumpled paper. Garnish with parsley
and cut lemon. (Serves 6)

FISH DISH. A specific type of platter
used to serve fish at the table. See DISHES.

FISH HOUSE PUNCH. An American
rum punch, famous since early colonial
days. General Washington and other Revolutionary leaders were among its admir-
ers. See PUNCH.

FIZZ. A sweetish alcoholic drink, commonly made of gin, that is so named
because of its highly effervescent nature.
Though the basic fizz recipe is very similar
to that of the Collins (which see), and to
many other drink types, it is mixed in a
shaker, which tends to increase its effervescent quality. This above resemblance,
however, is found only in the basic gin
fizz recipe; the other fizzes are more elaborate structures raised on this simple foundation. The fizzes are commonly served
in the summertime, for they are a refreshing, cooling drink. Cooling to everyone but
the maker, that is, for to be properly made,
a fizz must have prolonged, vigorous (almost violent) shaking.

GIN FIZZ

1 jigger dry gin
½ lemon (juice)
1 tsp powdered sugar

The ingredients are well shaken with
cracked ice, strained into a seven ounce
highball glass, and carbonated water is
added. (Serves 1)

Silver Fizz. Made the same as a gin fizz,
with one egg white added before shaking.

Golden Fizz. Made the same as a gin fizz,
with one egg yolk added before shaking.
The silver and golden fizzes are often made
in sequence to utilize the egg parts left over
after the first is mixed.

Royal Fizz. Made the same as a gin fizz,
with one whole egg added before shaking.
This is easier than separating the egg parts
as in the case of the golden or silver fizzes,
but yields less drinks per egg.

Any fizz may be served as a cocktail by
shaking extra hard and straining into a
cocktail glass without adding carbonated
water. The fizz can be shaken into a state

of almost solid foam, if the shaker is sufficiently persistent. *See* BARTENDING.

FLAN. A pastry filled with custard, fruit, or cream, similar to a tart. It is usually baked in a flan ring, which is a one-inch high band of metal joined in a square or ring which is used on a cooky sheet. In

FLAN PAN

using the flan ring, it is placed on the cooky sheet, lined with a sweet pastry, covered with wax paper, and weighted down with uncooked rice or dried beans. When the pastry is baked, the ring is removed, and the straight-sided pastry shell filled with any desired filling.

FLAN PASTRY

1½ cups all-purpose flour
¼ cup sugar
Pinch of salt
6 tbsp butter
4 egg yolks
1 tbsp cold water

Sift the flour onto a pastry board. Make a well in the center and pour in the balance of the ingredients. Mix with the fingers to a smooth paste, and mix in the flour with the heel of the hand until it is thoroughly combined. Roll out on a slightly floured board to fit an 8-inch flan ring. Place the ring on an ungreased cooky sheet, and carefully line with the pastry. Trim off the edges flush with the top of the ring. Line with wax paper and fill with dried rice or beans to prevent the crust from puffing up during baking. Bake in a moderate oven (350° F.) for 30 minutes, or until delicately browned. Remove the rice and paper and allow the pastry to cool. Then remove the

ring and place the pastry on a serving dish and prepare the filling.

FILLINGS FOR FLANS

1. Whipped cream, flavored with rum or any favorite liqueur, topped with black cherries, apricot halves, or other fruit.
2. Thick custard, flavored as desired and combined with almost any fruit.
3. Any of the cream pie fillings, topped with toasted nuts, or whipped cream.
4. Berries, sweetened to taste, and topped with whipped cream.
5. Ice cream, topped with fruit.
6. Lemon filling, topped with delicately browned meringue.

If a cream filling is used, it may be topped with sliced peaches, pears, apricots, or berries, and glazed with the following glaze, and then decorated with whipped cream.

GLAZE

3 tbsp tart jelly
2 tbsp water

In a saucepan, cook the jelly and water until it become sirupy. Cook, and brush over the fruit with a pastry brush.

FLANK. Part of the hindquarter of beef near the loin, from which are cut flank steaks. The larger part of the flank is frequently corned as the rump. *See* BEEF.

FLATFISH. *See* FLOUNDER.

FLATWARE. The general classification for all knives, forks, spoons, etc., as distinguished from the bowls, candlesticks and other items of hollowware (*which see*); in short, tools rather than utensils.

The term silverware is also applied to flatware; correctly so if the objects be made of silver or silver plate, for actually, flatware is a subdivision of silverware (*which see*).

MANUFACTURING

The method used to make silver flatware is basic for all materials, being changed only to meet special requirements of specific metals. There was a time when all knives, forks, and spoons were laboriously hammered out by hand from metal bars, but modern machinery has made mass production possible. If properly designed, the machine-made piece can rival the hand-made for beauty, and has the obvious advantage of exactly matching all the other pieces in the set.

The metal is received in the factory in the form of sheets from which are stampped the blanks, which for forks and spoons rather resemble miniature snow shovels. These blanks are rolled to distribute the metal in the proper thickness throughout the piece, cut to the proper shape, and have the design and proper curvature struck on both front and back. The pieces are then ground smooth, buffed, polished and otherwise finished.

Areas may be oxidized or chemically darkened to bring out the design, or the entire surface may be made to simulate the results of years of usage and careful polishing. Plated objects must, of course, go through the electro-plating tanks before the surface is given the final finishing.

The same basic procedure is used for knives, with the blades usually being formed from a bar of stainless steel. The handles are often hollow, being made in halves that are first soldered together, with the blade later being soldered in position.

Ivory and inlaid handles are attached by special methods, while plastic handles are usually molded directly on the piece.

TYPES

A complete set of flatware can run into a great many pieces, there being individual tools designed for use with practically every type of food known to man. While some elements are basic in all sets, the products of individual companies will differ in design and name. What to one company is a "grille" knife will be a "viande" knife to another, and while one company will manufacture a combination oyster-cocktail-pickle fork, another will have separate instruments for each of those functions.

In general, flatware may be divided into knives, forks, spoons, and serving implements.

Knives. The first eating implement (other than the fingers) used generally by man was the knife. The eating knife was usually a bit more refined than his dagger or hunting knife, and was used to carve, to serve, and to help get the food to his mouth. With time the other eating tools were devised, as well as specialized knives. Today we speak of the sharp carving

knives as cutlery (*which see*) and their blunter brethren as table knives. There are two main designs of table knives now popular; one with a relatively short handle and a long blade, the other being the reverse.

1. *Dinner Knife.* Used with meat courses, especially at dinner.

2. *Luncheon Knife.* Used with meat courses at all meals, with fish courses, and with desserts.

3. *Dessert Knife.* Used with dessert courses.

4. *Butter Spreader.* Used individually to spread butter and jam, also with cheese and crackers. It is either placed on the bread and butter plate, or (if no such plate is provided) above the service plate, but never with the other knives (*see* TABLE SETTING AND SERVICE).

5. *Fruit knives, fish knives,* and *steak knives* are other specialized table knives.

Forks. Basically a set of tines mounted on a handle, the manufacturers have expressed more latitude and variance in the design and conception of the fork than possibly any other eating instrument.

1. *Dinner Fork.* Matches the dinner knife in size and function; can also be used with a tablespoon for serving vegetables.

2. *Luncheon Fork.* A companion to the luncheon knife.

3. *Dessert Fork.* Used in conjunction with the dessert knife.

4. *Salad Fork.* As a general rule, this has wider tines than most forks and sometimes the outer edge of one tine is sharpened for cutting purposes. Used with salads that are served on separate plates; can also be used with fish, any sliced dessert, sandwiches, and all pastries.

5. *Oyster Fork.* Used with oysters and clams, seafood cocktails, and sometimes as a butter pick when individual pats of butter are served. It is the only fork that goes to the right of the spoons when the table is set (*see* TABLE SETTING AND SERVICE).

6. *Ice Cream Fork.* Used with firm ice cream and similar frozen desserts that are too solid to be easily handled with a spoon.

Spoons. Historically, the spoon is older than the fork and almost contemporary with the knife; for while the fingers can do all that a fork does, they can never handle liquids.

1. *Teaspoon.* The most common and widely used of the spoons. It is designed to

stir tea and coffee, but can also be used with any dessert of the type that is served in sherbert glasses, with fruit cocktails, and with grapefruit served in halves.

2. *Dessert* or *Oval Soup Spoon*. Used with desserts (when served on plates), soups (when served in a soup plate), and cereals; can also be used as a small serving spoon.

3. *Bouillon* or *Round Soup Spoon*. Used for soups both in cup and plate, bouillon, hot or jellied consomme, and chowders.

4. *Cream Soup Spoon*. Used with all soups both in cup and plate, cereals, and appropriate desserts.

5. *After-Dinner Coffee Spoon*. Used with demitasse and black coffee; also used as a serving spoon for relishes, etc.

6. *Iced Tea Spoon*. Used with all tall iced drinks.

7. *Grapefruit Spoon*. Used with fruits when served in halves; can be used as an emergency teaspoon.

SILVERWARE

Serving Implements. From the three basic eating tools there have been developed a number of implements for certain serving functions. Though, for the most part the family resemblance is unmistakable, they have sometimes taken strange forms.

1. *Tablespoon.* Used to serve vegetables, berries, casseroles, and salads; it is also handy as a kitchen spoon and as a measuring device.

2. *Cold Meat or Serving Fork.* Used to serve slices of cold meat, chops, bacon, fish, and (in conjunction with a table spoon) salad.

3. *Butter Knife.* Used to serve brick or bulk type butter; also for cheese and firm jellies.

4. *Jelly Server.* Used to serve firm jellies; also for certain cheeses, as cream or cottage.

5. *Gravy Ladle.* Used to dispense gravies and sauces for meats and desserts. If deep enough may be used as a soup label.

6. *Mayonnaise Ladle.* Smaller than the gravy ladle, it is better suited for the dispensing of whipped cream and thin sauces, but can be used for many of the gravy ladle's functions

7. *Soup Ladle.* Used to dispense soup; can be used as the above two ladles.

8. *Pierced Blade Pastry Server.* Used to serve cakes or pastries, fish or cutlets, and ice cream.

9. *Round Server.* Used to serve fish cakes, fried eggs, waffles, pancakes, meat patties, and similar flat, fragile foods.

10. *Bonbon Spoon.* Used to serve candies and salted nuts.

11. *Berry or Serving Spoon.* Used to serve berries, salads, puddings, vegetables, and casserole dishes.

12. *Sugar Spoon.* Used to serve powdered or granulated sugar.

13. *Sugar Tongs.* Used to serve lump sugar, may sometimes be used to serve ice cubes if large enough.

14. *Ice Cube Tongs.* Used to serve individual cubes or lumps of ice, may possibly be used for dispensing lump sugar if design is appropriate.

15. *Salad Sets.* Fork and spoon combinations that are used to serve salads. In some cases, the two units are combined in a sort of scissors.

16. *Lemon Fork.* Used to serve lemon slices; can also be used to serve pickles, etc.

17. *Pickle Fork.* Used to serve pickles, olives, lemon slices, etc.

18. *Olive Fork.* Used to serve olives, pickles, etc.; can also function as an oyster fork or butter pick if design permits.

19. *Cocktail Fork.* A general fork that frequently combines all the functions of the last three mentioned forks as well as those of the oyster fork.

PURCHASING FLATWARE

When purchasing flatware, the general principles given in the article on silverware (*which see*) should be followed. As has been seen, a complete set of flatware could contain a great number of individual pieces. However, not all of those pieces are essential for many serve dual functions. Flatware is normally sold in sets, each set offering a reasonably complete service for a specified number, usually multiples of two. The more expensive the set, of course, the more pieces included.

The essential individual setting is usually given as consisting of six pieces: a teaspoon, a soup spoon (cream or round), a luncheon knife, a luncheon fork, a salad fork and a butter spreader. These pieces are adequate to handle the normal mealtime needs. Additional pieces are, of course, desirable, for they at the very least eliminate the necessity of washing flatware pieces between courses, as sometimes happens if the number of available pieces is limited.

The number of possible guests expected for dinners should be considered when purchasing silver, of course. Once the essential individual services have been acquired, the service can be further built up, item by item. It is always well, for example, to have double the number of teaspoons as you have individual settings, for the spoon is often used in the course of the meal and needed later for coffee. Sets of dinner knives and forks can then be added, and the other pieces acquired according to the desires of the family. The exact nature of the full flatware set will depend largely on the needs of the family and the type of entertaining that is done.

Tablespoons are by far the most important items of serving implements. At least four should be provided for initially, and the other items added as needed.

FLAVORING. In the strict sense of the word, a flavoring agent is an extract or an essence that is used to impart a particular flavor to a foodstuff. It differs from a seasoning agent in that the latter does not impart its own flavor but merely heightens or tempers that of the food to which it is added. However, in cookery the two are closely related. *See* FLAVORING EXTRACT and SEASONING.

FLAVORING EXTRACT. Flavoring extracts are produced by dissolving the aromatic essential oils, or essences, in alcohol. Genuine vanilla extract and artificial extract, called "vanillin" and "coumarin" are chemically identical. For that reason it is quite difficult to distinguish between the two. In the case of the genuine article, however, there appears in the extract a certain percentage of the natural resin and gums that were in the vanilla beans. These do not show in the vanillin and coumarin. The homemaker may learn whether a flavoring extract is pure or an imitation by reading the label carefully. A flavoring extract is defined by the U.S. Department of Agriculture as "a solution in ethyl alcohol of proper strength of the sapid and odorous principles derived from an aromatic plant."

Here are the United States government specifications for the more popular flavoring extracts:

Lemon Concentrated Extract. Prepared from oil of lemon, lemon peel, or both, and ethyl alcohol proper strength, and contains not less than 20 percent by volume of oil of lemon and not less than 0.8 percent by weight of citral; stronger extracts not to exceed 60 percent of oil of lemon, providing labels clearly indicate strength of preparation offered.

Lemon Extract. Made from oil of lemon or lemon peel, or both, and ethyl alcohol of proper strength; not less than 80 percent by volume absolute ethyl alcohol, not less than 0.2 per cent by weight of citral, derived solely from oil of lemon, or peel.

Lemon Terpeneless Extract. Prepared by shaking oil of lemon with dilute ethyl alcohol, or by dissolving terpeneless oil of lemon of proper strength in dilute ethyl alcohol, and contains not less than 2 per cent by weigh of citral, derived solely from oil of lemon.

Non-Alcoholic Lemon Extract. A mixture of 20 percent by volume of oil of lemon (U.S.P. standard) and 80 percent by volume of cottonseed oil, which should be thoroughly refined, winter pressed, neutral, free from rancidity, giving a finished product clear and free from sediment and rancidity.

Orange Flavor Extract. Prepared from oil of orange or orange peel, or both, and absolute ethyl alcohol proper strength; contains not less than 80 percent by volume of ethyl alcohol, and not less than 5 percent by volume of oil of orange.

Orange Terpeneless Flavor Extract. Prepared by shaking oil of orange with dilute ethyl alcohol or by dissolving terpeneless oil of orange of proper strength in dilute ethyl alcohol, and shall correspond in flavoring strength to orange extract.

Non-Alcoholic Orange Flavor Extract. A mixture of 20 percent by volume of oil of orange (U.S.P. Standard) and 80 percent by volume of oil of cottonseed, the cottonseed oil to be thoroughly refined, winter pressed, sweet, neutral, clear and free from sediment and rancidity.

In general, flavoring extracts shall be a product conforming in name to the plant used as its flavoring principle, and produce a flavor and aroma of desirable quality.

Vanilla Concentrated Extract. Prepared, without added flavoring or coloring, from prime vanilla beans with or without glycerin; 100 cc. should contain soluble matters from not less than 100 grams of vanilla beans and not less than 30 percent by volume of absolute ethyl alcohol. When one part by volume is diluted with nine parts of dilute alcohol (40 percent by volume) the resulting mixture should comply with requirements for vanilla extract (*see below*) except for alcohol content. Label should indicate strength of product, and if not made directly from vanilla beans, should so state.

Vanilla 4 X Strength Extract. Prepared without added flavoring or coloring, from prime vanilla beans with or without sugar and/or glycerin. It should contain, in 100 cc., soluble matters from not less than 40 grams of vanilla beans and not less than 35 percent by volume of absolute ethyl alcohol. When, by volume, one part of product is diluted with three parts of dilute alcohol (40 percent by volume) resulting mixture shall comply with requirements for vanilla extract except for alcohol content. Label shall clearly indicate both strength of product, and if the product is not made directly from vanilla beans.

Imitation Vanilla Extract. (Artificially flavored and colored). A solution of vanillin and coumarin in dilute glycerol, containing 5 percent by volume of true vanilla extract, and colored with caramel.

It is well to buy reliable brands of flavoring extracts. While the initial cost may seem higher, the amount of extract used in any given recipe is so small that the net difference is almost negligible. Most average recipes call for one teaspoon of vanilla flavoring; the stronger extracts, such as almond, are measured in drops.

Because of the high alcohol content, flavoring extracts are extremely volatile. They should be purchased in small sizes and kept tightly closed to prevent evaporation. Also because of this characteristic, some of the flavor is dissipated in cooking or freezing. Thus an uncooked or unfrozen mixture may seem to be too highly flavored, but the cooking or freezing process will correct this.

FLIP. An intoxicating drink that has undergone an amazing transformation through the years, changing in every respect but the name.

The original Flips were forthright beer, wine or rum mixtures, served piping hot, being heated by the simple expedient of plunging a red hot poker directly into the bowl, pitcher or glass. A colonial American recipe for Flip, for example, called for beer or ale, rum and molasses in proportions determined more by availability than formula, and heated as already described. Raw eggs were sometimes added.

Another old Flip recipe, which does not demand the red hot poker treatment, is:

Ale Flip

1 pt ale
2 eggs
1 pinch ground nutmeg
1½ pinches ground cloves
2 tbsp sugar

The eggs and spices are beaten together thoroughly, the ale heated to the boiling point, but not allowed to boil, then poured over the egg mixture, stirring rapidly while pouring. The whole mixture is then poured from one container to the other until it thickens. Should it fail to thicken, the mixture is placed over a fire and stirred until proper consistency is reached. Served hot. Other spices may be added to the eggs and a small amount of brandy to the ale, if so desired. (Serves 1)

A visitor from the past would have difficulty recognizing the iced mixtures of today as Flip, but an evolution of sorts has taken place. The hot poker was a difficult impliment at best, and central heating systems and improved home insulation keep most of winter's chill from the bones of modern man. Today's Flips are iced, being mixed in a cocktail shaker. They must be shaken extra well, for they contain eggs which are difficult to mix properly with other ingredients. Many prefer to beat the eggs thoroughly before adding them to the mixture.

There are many versions of the modern Flip, all springing from the same basic recipe, and, in most cases, taking their names from the wine or liquor used.

Flip (Modern)

1 egg
1 tsp powdered sugar
1 jigger desired liquor (brandy, port wine, sherry, sloe gin, whisky, etc.)

The ingredients are shaken extra hard with cracked ice in a cocktail shaker and strained into a flip or cocktail glass (see Glassware).

Chocolate Flip. This is made, not with the addition of chocolate, as would be supposed from the name, but by using:

½ jigger sloe gin
½ jigger brandy

The gin and brandy are used as the liquor ingredients in the basic recipe.

Coffee Flip. As in the case of the Chocolate Flip, this drink is so named because of its similarity to the substance, rather than its actual use. Instead of the 1 jigger of liquor called for in the basic recipe, the following is used:

½ jigger brandy
½ jigger port wine

See also Bartending, and Cocktail, Alcoholic.

FLIP GLASS. See Glassware.

FLOATING BLADE VEGETABLE KNIFE. Also known as a patent peeler, as well as by a variety of trade names, the floating blade knife is a device designed to cut thin, even slices from irregularly shaped vegetables. It is used to pare vegetables, to cut potato chips, make garnishings, etc.

The distinguishing characteristic of this device is the so-called floating blade, which is a straight length of U-shaped steel with a narrow slot cut in the center. Both edges of this slot are sharpened so the instrument will operate when drawn in either direction. In operation, the rear edge of the slot does the cutting, while the front edge acts as a guard, regulating the depth of the cut. The blade is set loosely in a special handle or frame so that it has rotary "play," permitting it to follow the uneven contour of a vegetable. Because of this feature, it is able to peel potatoes and other vegetables in a most economical fashion, for, regardless of shape, the thickness of the paring will be uniform.

While they may be set in a traditional knife handle, these devices are frequently equipped with a specially shaped frame that may also have accessories for removing potato eyes and performing similar tasks. *See also* CUTLERY and KITCHEN EQUIPMENT.

FLOATING ISLAND. A dessert made of soft custard topped with meringue. The French make a similar dish with an uncooked meringue, which is called *Oeufs à la Neige* (Snow Eggs).

FLOATING ISLAND

4 eggs separated
⅛ tsp salt
3 tbsp sugar
2 cups scalded milk
½ tsp vanilla

Combine the egg yolks, sugar, and salt in the top of a double boiler. Gradually stir in the scalded milk. Place over boiling water and cook 5 minutes, stirring constantly, or until the mixture coats a metal spoon. Remove from the heat, add the vanilla, and pour into a serving dish. Cool quickly.

Make the meringue by beating the egg whites until stiff. Gradually beat in ¼ cup powdered sugar and a pinch of salt. Flavor with a drop of vanilla. If the custard has been placed in a heat-proof dish, drop the meringue in heaping spoonfuls on the cold custard and place under the broiler for a few minutes, until the meringue is delicately brown. Or the meringue may be dropped by spoonfuls onto a pan of just-boiling water and placed under the broiler. When browned, the individual puffs may be carefully removed from the water with a skimmer and placed on top of the custard. In either case, chill thoroughly before serving.

OEUFS A LA NEIGE

2½ cups milk
½ tsp grated orange rind
2 eggs
1 additional egg yolk
⅓ tsp salt
⅓ cup sugar
⅔ tsp vanilla

Scald the milk with the orange rind. Beat the eggs and extra yolk slightly with the salt, sugar, and vanilla in the top of a double boiler. Gradually add the scalded milk, stirring constantly. Place over boiling water and cook, stirring constantly, about 5 minutes, or until the mixture coats a metal spoon. Cool and pour into a serving dish.

Top with meringue made as follows. Beat two egg whites until foamy with a pinch of salt. Gradually beat in 4 tablespoons of powdered sugar, and continue beating until the meringue is very stiff. With a teaspoon, shape the meringue into egg-shaped forms and drop on the chilled custard. Serve the dessert very cold.

Chocolate Floating Island may be made by either of the above recipes. Melt 2 squares (ounces) of bitter chocolate with the milk, omitting the orange rind, and proceed as directed above.

FLOR ALPINA. A deliciously sweet, pale-golden colored, after-dinner Italian cordial. Rather strong, nearly 50 percent alcoholic content, it has a peculiar pleasing flavor, the suaveness of which gives it its well-deserved name, "Flowers of the Alps."

FLORENTINE. As applied to cookery, any composite dish which has spinach as a foundation.

FLOUNDER. A very small species of the *Pleuronectae* family of flat fish, the flounder closely resembles the imported sole and is often served under that name. This fish seldom measures more than 12 inches in length, while the average weight is from one to one and a half pounds. It is a well-liked, fine and delicate fish.

Better known, however, in America are the plaice, sometimes called fluke, or deep sea flounder, which sometimes weighs as much as 15 pounds and reaches a length of three feet. This variety of flounder is found on the market all the year around.

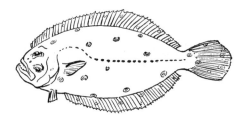

FLOUNDER

The plaice or fluke, commonly called the flounder, may be prepared like any flaky white-fleshed fish, such as the cod. Here are a few good "Flounder" recipes. *See also* FISH.

FILLETS OF FLOUNDER AMANDINE

4 tbsp butter or margarine
1 slice bacon, diced
½ small onion, thinly sliced
6 fillets of flounder
Flour
Salt and pepper
¾ cup sliced blanched almonds
1 tsp lemon juice

Heat half the butter in a large frying pan, and cook the diced bacon in it until it begins to brown. Add the onion and cook one minute, then put in the flounder which has been patted dry and dusted with the blended flour, salt, and pepper. Brown, on both sides. In another frying pan heat the remaining butter and brown the almonds in it. Arrange the fish on a hot platter with the bacon, but without the onion. Sprinkle with the almonds and pour over all a little melted butter (additional) to which the lemon juice and, if desired, a few drops of tabasco have been added. Garnish with parsley and sections of lemon. (Serves 6)

FILLETS OF FLOUNDER BAKED IN MILK

2 large fillets of flounder
Salt and pepper

1 very small onion, thinly sliced
1 tsp minced parsley
1 tsp minced celery top
A small piece of bay leaf
1 whole clove, optional
1½ cups milk
2 beaten egg yolks
2 tsp softened butter or margarine
¼ cup grated Parmesan cheese

Wash the fish and pat dry; season with salt and pepper and place in a buttered baking dish, sprinkling over it the onion, parsley and celery, with bay leaf and clove, if used. Pour the milk over, and bake in a moderate oven (350°–375° F.) until tender, about 15 minutes. Strain the liquor from the dish onto the beaten egg yolks and butter, add more seasoning if necessary, then pour back into the dish over the fish. Sprinkle with the grated cheese and put back into the oven for a few minutes to brown. Serve as soon as possible after the cheese is browned and the sauce slightly thickened. (Serves 2)

FILLETS OF FLOUNDER IN SOUR CREAM

6 fillets of flounder
Salt and pepper
Sour cream
1 tsp chives
Paprika
¼ cup mushrooms, thinly sliced
1 tsp parsley, finely minced

Arrange the flounder, washed and patted dry, in a buttered baking dish, season with salt and pepper, and pour in sour cream to a depth of half an inch. Dust with paprika and top with the mushrooms (canned or fresh), the parsley, and chives. Bake in a very hot oven (450° F.) 12 to 15 minutes or until tender. Serve immediately. (Serves 6)

FILLETS OF FLOUNDER SUZETTE AND LIZETTE

6 fillets of flounder
Salt and white pepper
2 tbsp melted butter or margarine
Slight grating of lemon rind
⅓ cup water, fish stock or clam bouillon
1 small bay leaf
1 whole clove

12 steaming clams
Hollandaise sauce
⅓ cup dry white wine
1 tbsp finely minced parsley
1 tbsp finely minced chives

Wash the fish and pat dry. Place in a shallow buttered baking dish, season with salt and pepper and pour the melted butter over, then sprinkle with the lemon rind. Now pour around the fish the water, stock or bouillon, add the bay leaf and clove and bake in a hot oven (400° F.) 15 minutes. Wash the clams in several waters, using a small brush to scrub them. Place in a saucepan without any water, and allow them to simmer over a very low flame until the shells open wide. Take out the clams, cut off and discard the necks, and add the clams to the Hollandaise sauce (*which see*) with the wine, parsley and chives. Remove the bay leaf and clove from the fish together with any liquid in the dish, and pour the reinforced Hollandaise sauce over the fish. Place under the flame of the broiling oven for a few minutes to brown. Serve at once in the same dish. (Serves 6)

FILLETS OF FLOUNDER WITH WINE

6 fillets of flounder
6 shallots chopped
½ cup fish stock
1 cup dry white wine
6 sprigs fresh parsley
3 sprigs green celery top
1 large bay leaf
6 whole peppercorns
2 whole cloves
⅓ cup heavy cream
1 tsp flour
Salt and pepper
¼ cup grated American cheese

Place the fillets, washed and patted dry, in a generously buttered baking dish with the shallots, the fish stock (made from fish trimmings), the wine, the parsley tied with the celery and bay leaf; add also the peppercorns, gently bruised, and the cloves. Place over a low flame and simmer 15 minutes. Lift out the fish and arrange on a hot fireproof platter. Strain the stock left in the baking dish, return it to the fire and bring to boiling point; add the cream and, when again boiling, thicken with the

flour and butter creamed together. Season with salt and pepper. Simmer gently for five minutes, then strain over the fish. Sprinkle with the grated cheese and place under the flame of the broiling oven to brown. Serve at once. (Serves 6)

STUFFED FILLETS OF FLOUNDER

6 fillets of flounder
2 tbsp butter or margarine
½ tsp grated onion
1½ cups soft bread crumbs
1 tbsp finely minced parsley
1 tsp minced green celery top
1 tsp minced chives
Butter and hot water for basting

Wash the fish and allow it to stand for 3 or 4 minutes in cold water to which a pinch of salt and a teaspoon of lemon juice have been added. Drain and pat dry. Melt the butter; add the onion and cook for a moment, without browning, then blend with the crumbs, parsley, celery and chives. Roll the fish fillets in this mixture dividing up any which is left over and laying it on the fish. Roll up and fasten each fillet with a toothpick or thread. Arrange in a generously buttered baking dish and bake in a hot oven (400°–425° F.) about 15 minutes, basting occasionally with a little blended butter and hot water. Serve with Hollandaise sauce (*which see*) or with cream sauce to which diced raw cucumber has been added. (Serves 6)

FLOUR. The basic ingredient of bread, pastry, and most cakes is flour, which is finely ground grain, or meal, which is grain more coarsely ground. The flour most widely used is made from wheat— either from the inner part of the grain, which makes white flour, or from the whole grain, which makes whole-wheat flour.

Wheat makes the best flour for most purposes because it contains proteins that combine in the presence of moisture to form gluten, which gives wheat doughs and batters a texture and character unlike any other bread mixtures. The gluten itself is the grayish-yellow, gummy substance that is left when the starch is washed out of wheat flour. The elasticity of dough is due to gluten, which expands and holds the gas bubbles given off as yeast ferments in the dough, or as a baking powder or soda and acid react when liquid is stirred into the dry ingredients of a quick bread.

The bread-making value of different types of wheat flour depends on the quantity and the quality of the gluten that can be developed in them. Flours are called "weak" if their gluten content is low in quantity or poor in baking quality. The nature and the amount of gluten in flour depend both on the kind of wheat from which the flour is made and on the milling. The wheats which make the "strongest" flours are grown mostly in the region between the Rocky Mountains and the Mississippi Valley, chiefly north and west of Missouri. The wheats grown in the more humid areas between the Great Plains and the Atlantic coast and most of the wheats of the Pacific coast are softer and less glutinous.

The homemaker and the baker want flour to suit specific purposes—that is, for bread, for pastry, or for cake. For bread, a strong flour is preferred, one that contains more gluten and less starch than other flours. (*See* BREAD) Cake and pastry flours are weak flours, milled from soft wheat. (*See* CAKE) All-purpose flours, as the term indicates, contain a moderate amount of gluten, giving them a strength between that of the typical bread and the typical cake flours. All-purpose flours are usually made by blending wheats or flours selected to produce the characteristics desirable for most kinds of baking.

Wheat Flour. Of the minerals and vitamins of wheat—especially iron, Vitamin B, and Vitamin G—the greater part are contained in the bran and germ, which are removed in the milling of white flour. Whole wheat, or graham flour, contains all the constituents of wheat in their natural proportions. Its baking strength, however, is less than white flour, and it does not keep so well.

In a diet that is limited in variety, and hence likely to be lacking in certain minerals and vitamins, some of the bread should be made from whole wheat flour. In a diet containing plenty of milk, eggs, fruit, and vegetables, the bran and germ of the wheat kernel are not so essential, but breads made from whole wheat flour add flavor and variety.

Bran (*which see*), the dark, fibrous portion of the wheat, is less completely digested than the rest of the kernel. As sold commercially, bran derives some food value from the starch as well as from the minerals and vitamins associated with the fibrous parts, but it is used chiefly for its laxative properties. In moderate quantities, and especially when finely milled in whole-wheat flour, bran is usually considered a desirable addition to the modern diet.

Rye Flour. In bread-making qualities, rye approaches wheat more nearly than does any other grain, and is, in fact, the only other grain that can be used alone successfully in yeast breads. The proteins of rye are similar to, though not identical with, those of wheat, and in food value the two grains are about the same, but rye flour makes a more sticky and less elastic dough than wheat flour.

Rye flour is marketed in four general grades—*dark, light, medium,* and *straight.* The dark flour includes some of the outer part of the grain; the light flour, the inner part or endosperm; and the medium grade is usually a blend of the light and the dark. The straight grade is all the flour produced in the milling of the rye, and normally consists of about 30 per cent dark flour and 70 percent light flour. Ordinarily the medium and straight-grade flours can be used interchangeably.

Bean Flours. Bean flours are made by grinding dry beans, whole or with the seed coat removed. They contain more protein than do the grain flours. But the proteins are different from those of wheat and rye, and bean breads are made by combining bean flour with wheat flour in proportions of about four or five of wheat to one of bean flour. This is done to avoid too much bean flavor and to get the benefit of the gluten in the wheat.

Soy-bean flour contains more protein, but less starch, than do wheat, rye, or other bean flours. The soy-bean proteins are more "efficient," that is, of higher nutritive quality than the proteins of other beans. Much of the soy-bean flour on the market is made of the whole or hull-free beans. Some of it, however, is made from the bean press cake, after the oil has been pressed out for other purposes. A very small quantity has the fat extracted by means of a chemical solvent. In the last case the flour contains much less fat than other bean flours and is used in smaller quantities in combination with wheat flour. All the bean flours are good sources of Vitamin B and rich in calcium and iron.

Flours, except whole wheat, should always be sifted once before measuring, and then dipped lightly into the measure and leveled. If they are packed into the measure, too much will be used. Whole wheat flour and meals should be stirred to lighten them; then they may be measured like other flours.

FLOWER CHEESE. A soft-cured, rennet cheese, made in England from the whole milk of cows. It is so named because petals of various kinds of flowers, such as roses or marigolds are added in the making.

FLUKE. *See* FLOUNDER.

FLUMMERY. A kind of custard pudding or blanc mange. A Colonial dessert which used to be made in Old Virginia to "please the eye as well as the palate" and sometimes the eye had the preference. Flummeries, elaborately decorated, were important dishes upon every well-set Virginia table. But there are also simple flummeries, such as:

GRAPE JUICE FLUMMERY

3 tbsp cornstarch
¼ tsp salt
½ cup sugar
Grated rind and juice of one lemon
2 cups grape juice

Sift together the cornstarch, salt and sugar and moisten with the lemon juice and a little of the grape juice, stirring until perfectly smooth. Scald the remaining grape juice over hot water (in a double boiler). Add the first mixture, then the lemon rind, and cook until thick, stirring almost constantly. When the mixture coats the spoon, turn into a wet mold and chill for several hours. Unmold and serve with plain cream, whipped cream, custard or other preferred sauce. (Serves 4)

FLUSH. A tea shoot. The second flush of a tea bush is generally believed to yield the best leaves.

FLUTING. As applied to cookery, the term means to press a pastry dough around the rim of the tin with the fingers, as in preparing pie for baking. *See* PIE.

FOAMY SAUCE. *See* BUTTER SAUCE.

FOLDING. As applied to cookery, the term means to combine the mixture very gently with another by cutting down through one, as in cake making. The best known method is as follows: Turn stiffly beaten egg whites, let us say, on top of the mixture with which the egg whites are to be combined. Cut down through the whole with the edge of a large spoon or spatula; bring the spoon along the bottom of the mixture, and then up and over the egg whites. Repeat this cutting and folding, as it is called, over and over again, until the egg whites disappear into the mixture, always working lightly and gently. Never stir after the egg whites are added.

FOLDING IN, using a rubber spatula

FOLLE BLANCHE. A white table wine of the chablis (*which see*) type, made in California from grapes of the same name.

FOND. A French word meaning "pan gravy."

FONDANT. Fondant is a creamy, smooth confection made of sugar, water, sometimes corn sirup, and some acid substance—cream of tartar or lemon juice. Its uses far surpass those of other candies because fondant not only forms the base of many delightful sweets, but is used for coating nuts, fruits, and other confections as well.

HELPFUL HINTS FOR FONDANTS

Every particle of sugar should be melted before the sirup is allowed to boil. If this precaution is not taken and the sugar, being partly dissolved, is allowed to boil, these crystals will not dissolve readily and may cause the sirup to grain.

Stirring or moving the pan after the sugar boils may cause the sirup to return to sugar.

Sirup should be allowed to cool before creaming the mass.

The cream of tartar is used to prevent too rapid crystallization of the sugar.

Add coloring and flavoring at the beginning of the beating process (if desiring one flavor and color for the entire batch). Otherwise, add the coloring and flavoring to the fondant as it is used in various candies.

Fondant should be allowed to ripen for at least two hours, longer if possible before using it to make candies.

DIPPING WITH FONDANT

Place two cups of fondant in the top of a double boiler. Heat it slowly. Do not let the water in the lower part boil, but keep it just below the boiling point. Stir only enough to blend, adding a few drops of stock sirup or boiling water if the mixture becomes too stiff. When melted add the coloring and flavoring desired or indicated, and stir as little as possible to avoid crystallization. Now remove from the heat, and lower the center, nuts or fruit, one at a time, into the mixture on a dipping fork. Draw the dipping fork lightly across the edge of the pan to remove any excess fondant, then invert the dipped candy or nut onto a slab, platter, or waxed paper, and, if desired, decorate with a bit of candied violet, rose leaf, or nut. Work as quickly as possible so that the fondant will not become too thick. In such case, however, add a few drops of boiling water to bring the mass back to the right consistency. See also CANDY.

MASTER RECIPE FOR FONDANT

3 cups sugar
1 cup water
⅛ tsp salt
1½ tsp corn sirup, cream of tartar or glycerin

Put the sugar, water and salt together into a saucepan and bring slowly to boiling point, stirring only until the sugar is entirely dissolved. Add the corn sirup, cream of tartar or glycerin and continue boiling, without stirring, to the soft ball

stage (238°–240° F.). Turn onto a slab or platter and cool to lukewarm (about 110° F.). Then beat and cream with a broad spatula, turning the sugar backwards and forwards, leaving no part unworked, until the whole mass becomes white and opaque. Now knead until very smooth and absolutely free from lumps, cover with a damp cloth and set aside in a cool place.

When using for centers, add any preferred flavoring, divide the fondant into portions and color and flavor each differently. Add also, if desired, finely chopped nuts, cocoanut, diced candied cherries or pineapple, grated orange rind, etc. Form the mixture into small balls, rolls, cubes or any preferred shape. Allow these to dry thoroughly (preferably overnight) before dipping in melted fondant.

BUTTER FONDANT

3 cups sugar
1 cup top milk
2 tbsp butter
⅛ tsp salt
1 tsp light corn sirup
1 tsp vanilla

Combine in a saucepan the sugar, milk, butter, and salt. Bring slowly to boiling point, stirring only until the sugar is thoroughly dissolved. Add the corn sirup, then cook to the soft ball stage (240° F.). Turn onto a platter or slab, moistened with cold water, cool to lukewarm, beat until creamy, then knead until perfectly smooth. Use only for centers, not for dipping.

CHOCOLATE FONDANT

To 1 pound of fondant add, while beating, 2 squares (or ounces) of melted chocolate, and 1 teaspoon of vanilla extract, or equal parts of vanilla and almond extract.

FRUIT FONDANT

Into 1 pound of unflavored fondant, knead chopped raisins, chopped dates, chopped figs, chopped candied fruits, or equal parts of the above and chopped nuts. Press into a flat cake about an inch thick and cut into bars. When dry, dip in melted chocolate or remelted fondant. Then sprinkle or decorate with chopped nut meats, such as almonds, pistachios, pecans, etc.

FONDANT FROSTING

2 cups sugar
1 cup water
2 tbsp light corn sirup

Put sugar, water and corn sirup in saucepan and stir over low heat until sugar is dissolved. Boil, covered, about 3 minutes to dissolve crystals that collect on sides of pan; then boil, uncovered and without stirring until small amount of sirup forms a soft ball when dropped into cold water (238° F.). Add just enough simple sirup (*see* SIRUP) to make it of right consistency to spread, or about 2 tablespoons, beating until smooth. If too thin, add more fondant; if too stiff, add more sirup. Keep hot in double boiler and prepare a small amount at a time. Tint delicately with a vegetable color paste rather than a liquid color which may thin frosting; flavor as desired. Use for small cakes; place cakes on wire rack to dry.

OTHER FONDANTS

Nut Patties. Shape the fondant into small balls, and flatten them into oblongs. Press a half pecan or other nut on top.

Chocolate Drops. Mold fondant into small balls and dip them in melted, sweet dipping chocolate. Invert on waxed paper to harden.

Fruit Bonbons. Shape fondant into small oblongs. Dip in remelted fondant, and press a bit of candied pineapple, ginger, or cherry on top.

Jam Sandwiches. While beating the lukewarm fondant, add a coloring corresponding to the jam to be used. When the fondant is cold, cut it into small squares, putting two squares together with a little jam. Dip in melted coating chocolate.

French Ribbon Creams. Work a pound of fondant until soft. Divide it into four equal parts. Leave one part white, and flavor with almond extract. To another part, add pistachio extract, green coloring, and chopped pistachio nuts. To the third part, add rose extract and color with red vegetable coloring. To the fourth part, add grated chocolate to taste, and flavor with vanilla. Knead the chocolate portion until smooth. Roll it out into a square ½ inch

thick. Work the white portion well. Roll it out the same size as the chocolate portion, and lay it on the chocolate portion. Now, mix the green portion, roll it out and lay it upon the white portion. Lastly, take the red portion, roll it out, and lay it upon the green portion. Press the whole together, as gently as possible, with a clean rolling pin, lightly dusted with confectioner's sugar. Trim the edges neatly, and let stand in a cool, dry place for an hour or longer to mellow and ripen. Cut into squares or thin slices and place on waxed paper to harden.

FONDUE. A Swiss favorite that derives its name from the French word "*fondre*," meaning "to melt," this dish is traditionally a melted cheese concoction eaten directly from the fondue pot or chafing dish (*which see*) with the aid of pieces of crusty bread. A wider application of the term includes a whole bevy of dishes created by varying one or more of the three elements required: cheese, wine and bread. Fondue cookery is ideal for informal entertaining or for special family treats and recipes may be adapted to serve as appetizer, snack or dessert recipes.

Fondue is not a difficult dish to make but its preparation takes constant vigilance. The mixture must be stirred constantly from the time the cheese is added to the wine until it has melted, about 10 minutes. It is important, also, that the heat of the mixture be low at the point that the cheese is added.

The dish is prepared directly at the stove in a saucepan and then transferred to a chafing dish which keeps the fondue warm while it is consumed. Guests are supplied with long forks or skewers with heat resistant handles. A piece of crusted French bread is spread onto the fork and dipped into the melted cheese sauce. The fondue thickens as it cooks at the table and the thick cheese crust which finally forms at the bottom of the pot is considered a delicacy by the Swiss. If the fondue becomes too thick at any point, it may be thinned slightly by the addition of a small amount of heated liquid—wine or whatever liquid has been used in the preparation of the fondue.

The traditional recipe (*see* CHEESE) is made with Swiss or Gruyere cheese and kirsch (*which see*) but any natural, unprocessed cheese may be used with any dry white wine and appropriate seasonings. For variety use pieces of fruit—apple, banana, pear, pineapple, orange—or meat—cooked cocktail sausages, ham, chicken, shrimp— as dippers. Also try raw vegetables such as celery, carrot, green pepper, cauliflower or mushrooms cut or broken into pieces. Brussels sprouts, potato puffs and French fried potatoes also work as dippers.

BEEF FONDUE

Cover and refrigerate 2 to 2½ pounds of beef tenderloin or sirloin, well–trimmed and cut into 1 inch cubes. Remove from refrigerator about 15 minutes before serving. Into a fondue pot, pour equal amounts of melted butter and salad oil to the depth of 1½ to 2 inches. Heat over medium heat to just below smoking point. With long–handled forks, guests spear pieces of meat and cook to taste. Remove to plates on which are an assortment of sauces (*which see*) and butters (*which see*). Anchovy (*which see*) butter, garlic butter, horseradish sauce, remoulade (*which see*) sauce and barbecue (*which see*) sauce make excellent accompaniments. Use a second fork to dip meat into sauces and to eat. Makes 4 to 6 servings.

CHEDDAR AND CRAB FONDUE

1 package (6 oz.) frozen crab meat, thawed
2½ cups (10 oz.) shredded Cheddar cheese
2 tbsp flour
1 cup sauterne
1½ tsp caraway seed

Drain crabmeat well and flake. Toss together cheese and flour. In saucepan heat sauterne until bubbles rise. Over low heat add cheese, ½ cup at a time, stirring until cheese is melted after each addition. Add crabmeat and caraway seed. Transfer to fondue pot. Serve with French bread cubes, toasted bread cubes or vegetable dippers. Makes 2½ cups.

FRUIT AND CHEESE FONDUE

In a 2–quart saucepan melt 2 tablespoons butter; stir in 2 tablespoons flour, ½ teaspoon nutmeg. Remove from heat; gradually stir in 1½ cups milk. Cook over medium heat, stirring constantly, until thickened. Cook 2 additional minutes. Remove from heat; stir in 2 cups (8 oz.) shredded Cheddar cheese and ⅓ cup crumbled blue cheese. If neces-

sary, return to heat to finish melting cheese. (Do not boil.) Serve as a dip for apple or pear slices, honeydew chunks or orange sections. Makes 2½ cups.

MUSHROOM–CHEESE FONDUE

2 cans (10½ oz. each) condensed cream of mushroom soup
4 cups (1 lb.) shredded Cheddar cheese
1 cup dairy sour cream
¼ cup prepared mustard
2 tsp Worcestershire sauce
¼ cup finely chopped chives

In a saucepan heat the soup. Over a low heat add the cheese, sour cream, mustard and Worcestershire sauce. Stir until the cheese is melted. Just before serving, stir in chives. Transfer to fondue pot. Serve with vegetable or fruit dippers or cocktail sausages. Makes 4½ cups.

TOMATO–SWISS FONDUE

4 cups (1 lb.) shredded aged Swiss cheese
¼ cup all-purpose flour
1 clove garlic, halved
2 cups tomato juice
½ tsp salt
½ tsp Worcestershire sauce
1 tsp crushed basil leaves

Toss together cheese and flour. Rub inside of saucepan with garlic; discard garlic. Add tomato juice and heat until bubbles rises. Over low heat add cheese, ½ cup at a time, stirring until cheese is melted after each addition. Add salt, Worcestershire sauce and basil. Transfer to fondue pot. Serve with cubes of French bread, vegetable dippers, cooked ham cubes or cooked shrimp. Makes 3½ cups.

FONTAINEBLEAU CHEESE. A French cream cheese made near Fontainebleau.

FONTINE CHEESE. A French cheese made in Franche-Comte.

FONTINA CHEESE. An Italian soft creamy cheese.

FOOCHOW OOLONG. An Oolong tea of China; named after the port from which it is shipped. Foochow Oolong is the most important of the China Oolongs; the others are known as Amoy Oolong, and Canton Oolong. *See* TEA.

FOOD CHOPPER. A double-bladed

semi-circular knife used to chop or dice fruits, vegetables, etc. The handle is located above the blades so that pressure may be exerted downward and the knife used with a rocking motion for greater efficiency. It can be used on a wooden cutting or chopping board, but is more commonly used in a wooden bowl. *See also* CHOPPING BOWL AND KNIFE.

FOOD CLASSIFICATION. The food we eat should serve a definite purpose. It should be utilized to build, repair, heat, energize or maintain the body. The foods which perform these functions may be divided into these three classes:

Class One: Those foods which act as antiseptics, eliminators, laxatives, and purifiers of the body.

Class Two: Those foods which build or rebuild the body, and which are known as building foods.

Class Three: Those foods which supply warmth and energy.

Class one is composed chiefly of raw fruits, and raw and cooked non-starchy vegetables. Class two consists chiefly of meats, fish, and legumes (cereals). Class three comprises starch, sugar, and fat.

FOOD COMBINATIONS

Every meal should be based upon the following nine essential principles, which must be observed when formulating all menus. To ascertain whether these principles are being observed, make a list of all the foods, and the proportionate amounts, eaten at each meal for six consecutive meals, and compare with these principles.

1. Eat natural foods, correctly prepared.
2. Every day's ration should include foods from each of the three food classifications listed above, with special emphasis on green vegetables and fresh fruits.
3. Eat no more than four kinds of food at any one meal; fewer are better.
4. Fruits and vegetables (properly prepared) should comprise the greater part of the total amount of food eaten daily. (This is necessary to supply the body with sufficient food salts.)
5. Every meal should include at least one variety of fruit or non-starchy vegetable. (These are anti-fermentative, anti-acid, anti-scorbutic, laxative, and purifying.)
6. Eat only one concentrated food at a meal. (Choose either meat, fish, eggs,

cheese, bread, cereal, rice, etc.) Use meat, fish, eggs, etc., at the night meal, and a starchy food at the noon meal, or if meat, fish, eggs, etc., is eaten at noon, omit at the night meal. Meat (a building food) should be eaten with little bread or other cereal foods (heat and energy foods), not because the combination is chemically incompatible, but because it gives two concentrated foods at the same meal. Two concentrated foods usually means overeating, even in the case of the hardest worker.
7. Never use commercial sugars and sirups in excess.
8. Dried sweet fruits, honey, maple sugar, and dark brown sugar do not combine well with starchy foods.
9. Acid fruits and acid vegetables (tomatoes) should not be eaten with very starchy foods. Starch digestion begins at the mouth, where normally the saliva is alkaline. If acid fruit is eaten with starch, the first essential step in the digestion of starch is interfered with, resulting in fermentation of the carbonic gas and alcohol.

The foregoing rules are intended to be used as a guide; to follow them slavishly leads to fadism in food. Certainly no one is going to suffer from enjoying pancakes with maple sirup for an occasional breakfast or spaghetti with tomato sauce for a tasty meal. It is the continual failure to observe the rules of balanced diet that lead to trouble.

See also MENU PLANNING.

FOOD MILL. A food mill is a device that forces vegetables and fruits through perforations, causing them to be puréed or riced. One typical design has a set of blades, operated by a crank, that press the food against a perforated metal shield. *See also* KITCHEN EQUIPMENT.

FOOD PRESERVATION AND STORAGE. Not the least of the problems that beset man in his struggle for existence is that presented by the perishable nature of the food which he needs for survival. Though now partially solved and rarely thought of as a major problem, the impact of that one difficulty upon history has been tremendous.

HISTORY

In the beginning, man was the prisoner of his food supply. Life was a grim struggle to meet the needs of the moment, for there was no known way to prepare for the future. The major portion of man's waking hours was devoted to foraging for food, a grim pursuit that overshadowed all other interests and may well account for the long blank prehistoric period that elapsed before civilization of any sort emerged.

Since man did not understand the true nature of food spoilage, he was restricted to those preservation methods that could be discovered accidentally. In time he learned to churn his milk to butter and cheese, to ferment his grape juice into wine and to salt, smoke, or dry his game and fish. He learned to grow crops, and the grains (which of themselves can be safely stored for reasonable periods) became his staple foods. He learned to domesticate animals, for they could be kept alive and slaughtered at need.

With these beginnings, cultures began to emerge. The pursuit of food was not so relentless now; man could store away foods for the long gaps between harvests and he had time for other things as well. But he was still a prisoner in many respects. A poor crop meant famine, and famine meant death or migration. Migration involved war with the owners of more fruitful crop lands, so cultures crumbled and changed as man prowled hungrily in search of food.

When man depended solely on local produce, menus were often flat and monotonous things. Only the wealthy could afford items that are today considered necessities. Fruit, unless you lived in a fruit-growing region, was unknown, and the vegetables you ate were the vegetables you grew. The different foods gradually spread through the world, but only by means of plantings and seeds, never by the shipment of the food itself. Thus, though the foods spread, they were restricted geographically to those areas suitable for their growth.

Not only were menus monotonous, they were rarely balanced. The knights of old were mighty men, but today's office worker is too large to comfortably wear a typical suit of armor. This increase in stature can hardly be due to an increase in exercise or outdoor living in this modern age. Not only has man added inches to his height, but he has also added years to his life expectancy. Modern medicine takes much of the credit, but a balanced diet is an important contributing factor, and such a diet would be difficult without present food preservation, storage and shipping methods.

In his search for food preservatives, man early learned that certain of the spices could help him. Nature is thoughtful and these spices were common in the sweltering orient where ice is rather a rarity. But food was spoiling in Europe as well, hence the rise of a thriving spice trade that gave impetutus to the wave of exploration that discovered and settled the New World.

Until fairly recently, food preservation as such was largely a matter of guesswork, for it was not until Pasteur and his followers unmasked the micro-world that the true nature of food spoilage was known. Once the basic principles were learned, there was a brief pause while industry learned to apply them, then the flood-gates were opened. These past few decades have seen tremendous strides made in the field of food preservation and handling. Canning, freezing, refrigeration, dehydration, etc., quickly came into being or were modified; shipping techniques were developed; pure food and drug laws passed; and in a comparatively short span of time the foods of the world came to be found in any season in any store and cases of food poisoning became so rare as to warrant headlines when they did occur.

WHY FOOD SPOILS

The development of modern food preservation methods is closely linked to the development of modern medicine, for they are both based to a great extent on an understanding of the micro-world. Food spoilage is quite similar to human disease for both are the result of microscopic infection.

By its very nature food is subject to microscopic invasion, even as are humans. All food is the product of either vegetable or animal life; while living, the plants and animals have a natural resistance against infection, but once dead, this resistance is gone. When food is gathered, then, it becomes merely a race to see whether man or the bacteria will win out.

The minute life that attacks food is quite similar to disease germs in many respects though their natural function is somewhat different. If nature merely sat back and permitted foods to grow and lie about unharmed, it would take but a few bumper harvests to crowd man right off the planet

But nature is very methodical and she has made arrangements to see that food, once grown, will be converted in form and structure back to the basic elements from which it was made so that these elements can be re-used in future food. This is an excellent plan for nature, and, indeed, makes life possible on this planet, but food undergoing this process of change is quite unusable for man.

The chief agents that attack foods are the yeasts that convert sugar into other substances, the various bacteria that produce acids and that break down nitrogenous matter (usually producing strong odors), and the many molds that thrive on the carbohydrates. There are others as well, and unless steps are taken, any one or any combination of them will proceed to multiply and prosper in the food, making it excellent fertilizer material, but unfit for human consumption.

These organisms reach the food in a number of ways, even as the human body is infected. The air is filled with them, flies and other insects carry them about, the ground in which foods are grown is a source of all manner of microscopic life, and some foods, notably the fruits, carry within them the seeds of their own destruction.

Most of these organisms have the ability to assume some inactive form, usually a spore, in which state they are carried about by one means or another until they lodge in a suitable home. Given the proper conditions of temperature and humidity, they become active, growing at the fantastic rate typical of the micro-organisms. When the material at hand has been converted, the organisms either die of themselves, are killed by their own products, or revert back to the inactive state until they again contact suitable breeding grounds.

METHODS OF FOOD PRESERVATION

At first glance the obvious solution to the problem of food spoilage would seem to be a change to substances that are not susceptible to spoilage. This, however, is impossible, for any such substance would be indigestible and useless as a food.

Since food spoilage is caused by micro-organisms of one sort or another, it follows then that there are four possible methods of preventing spoilage: keep them away from the food completely; if already in the food, remove them; leave them but take steps to impede their growth; and, finally, change the food to some form that will be less susceptible to attack, but still fit for consumption.

In general, no one of these means is enough; the successful procedures are all combinations.

Since the very air we breathe is laden with these organisms, it is manifestly impossible to prevent all possible bacteria contact throughout the entire handling of the food. But infection should never be encouraged, and the food kept as clean as possible at all stages.

Cooking. Cooking is more than a way of making food appetizing; it actually serves as a means of preservation. For one thing, the heat of cooking kills off most of the dangerous bacteria, for most bacteria are killed by temperatures greater than 176° F., especially if water is present, and the average cooking temperatures are 212° (boiling point of water) or greater. Cooking also somewhat alters the physical structure of the food, making spoilage more difficult than in the raw form.

Cooking thus renders the food relatively sterile, and it is theoretically possible to keep food indefinitely by means of repeated cooking. But cooking alone is not enough if the food is to be stored for a long period because of the dangers of re-infection.

Sterilization. Some microbes are capable of surviving, in spore form, temperatures up to 284° F. If the food is to be rendered completely sterile, then, it must be subjected to temperatures greater than that. Because of the effect on the food structure, this process is not applicable to all forms of food, for it gives some an unappetizing appearance. As in cooking, the food is subject to re-infection unless precautions are taken.

Pasteurization. Under this process, usually applied to milk, wines, and other liquids, the food is heated to a lower temperature than in sterilization and held at that for a stated period of time. Though not as complete as sterilization, it renders the food sufficiently sterile for all practical purposes. See PASTEURIZATION.

Canning and Bottling. Fortunately, the bulk of the organisms that cause food spoilage are of the *aerobe* class, i.e., can grow only in the presence of air. By placing cooked, pasteurized, or sterilized foods in sealed containers, two ends are accomplished. There is no possible danger of infection from the air, and any aerobe bacteria still present in the food, though not killed by the lack of air, are unable to grow and thus spoil the food. *See* CANNING.

Refrigeration. Though bacteria may be readily killed by heat, they have strong resistance against cold, being able to adapt themselves to spore forms that can withstand intensely cold temperatures. However, though cold does not kill them, it greatly impedes their activities. This feature has made home refrigeration one of the most practical methods of storing raw or fresh, or cooked foods for reasonable lengths of time, since the home ice refrigerator and mechanical refrigerator (*both of which see*) can economically produce temperatures that slow bacteria growth to practically a halt. The same principle has made practical the long-distance shipment of many foods.

Freezing. Though it is not practical to kill bacteria with cold temperatures, all biological activity ceases at freezing temperatures. This feature has made the long-duration storage of fresh foods possible, and, with recent developments both in knowledge and equipment, this type of food storage is fast coming into a position of prominence. *See* FREEZING FOODS.

Pickling and Salting. Salt, vinegar, and their derivatives have the power of impeding bacteria growth, and vinegar will even kill certain types of organisms. These methods were used by man long before the principles of food spoilage were understood, and are still used for certain types of food. The main disadvantage to these methods is that they impart a characteristic flavor to the food which, in some cases, is objectionable. *See* BRINE.

Spicing. Another long established method of food preservation. The fact that tropical cookery is redolent with spice-laden dishes is no mere quirk of palate, but rather a practical approach to the problem of food spoilage. *See* SPICE.

Chemical Preservatives. There are a great many chemicals that are efficient in killing micro-organisms, and, at one time or another, most of them have been used to preserve food. The main difficulty lies in the fact that many of these chemicals would kill humans as well, if used in sufficient quantities. Even though non-toxic, any chemical strong enough to impede or kill bacteria growth will, if in large enough

quantities, affect the stomach and digestion. They are also inclined to impart characteristic flavors and odors to the food. Practically every country including the United States now has stringent rules regarding the use of chemical preservatives. Only the safe chemicals and then only in safe amounts are permitted to be used. Such use, in America and many other countries, must be indicated on the label.

Dehydration. Most micro-organisms require water if they are to grow, and about the only ones that will readily develop on or in foods that have less than ten percent water content are a few of the molds. Foods that are naturally dry (grain, nuts, etc.) will keep for long periods by themselves, and man early learned to dry out fruits and meats by the heat of the sun or fires.

Commercial freeze drying is fast becoming an efficient means of dehydrating and preserving foods with a minimum loss of quality.

Other Methods. There are many other miscellaneous methods of preserving and storing foods that either apply to one specific food or have passed out of favor for other methods, though practical in themselves. Milk is evaporated, condensed and even dried. Meats are smoked. Eggs can be preserved by coating the shells with any one of a number of substances that result in an airtight seal. The same principle is now being tried experimentally with fruits and vegetables. The housewife of old, before the days of modern methods, had innumerable tricks that, though limited in application, were reasonably effective.

FOOD PRESERVATION AND STORAGE IN THE HOME

Food preservation and storage was, at one time, a rather involved process. Prepared foods not being generally available commercially, the housewife had to put up the bulk of her "preserves" herself. Since most fruits and vegetables do not keep well of themselves, the garden or farm surplus had to be put up in some cooked or pickled form if it were to last through the winter. Those that could keep by themselves were stored in bulk in the "root cellar" or its equivalent. The average housewife could not rely on the store for unseasonable fresh foods, for the stores were faced with exactly the same problems of storage and preservation as was she. The total effect was one of much work and large areas in the home being devoted only to storage. Further, there was a limit to her potential variety. Today, matters are somewhat different. There is a near endless variety of packaged foodstuffs available, aimed to suit every taste and pocketbook. Fresh foods are available both in and out of season, and, looking at it in one light, there is little absolute necessity for the housewife to have more than one or two day's supply of food in the house. There was a time when purchased packaged foods were looked upon with suspicion, but the food sold in the stores of today is as pure and safe as it can possibly be.

There are, however, decided advantages to storing food in the house, as many a harried housewife learned during the war years of shortages and rationing. A well-stocked grocery shelf gives the housewife an emergency supply to use in time of need. More important, ample storage space gives the housewife an opportunity to capitalize on food sales, by buying large quantities when prices are momentarily low.

As far as the canned and packaged goods are concerned, there are few precautions needed in their storage. The space selected should be ample in size, relatively cool and even-temperatured, and free from excessive dampness or moisture.

The preparation and storage of frozen foods is a science unto itself and is discussed under its proper heading. Fresh fruits and vegetables may be put up for long-term storage by means of canning or glassing, or may be kept for reasonable periods under circumstances proper to their individual natures, as discussed in the articles on the various items.

The extremely perishable foods—dairy products, meats, some fruits and vegetables—as well as the cooked foods must be kept under refrigeration. There are a wide variety of refrigerators and iceboxes available, designed for every purse and need, and no home need be without one. The method of food preparation and storage in refrigerators and iceboxes is discussed in the article on refrigerators, (*which see*). If the home has no such device, the perishable foods should be purchased from meal to meal, for any savings gained in quantity purchases would be more than offset by the resulting food spoilage through lack of proper storage facilities.

Though modern equipment and methods have greatly reduced the amount of food spoilage, constant vigilance must be exercised in the home. As has been seen, the possibilities of food becoming infected are ever-present, so constant care must be taken to minimize these possibilities and also to hamper the growth of any bacteria that may be present in the food.

Food, then, should be kept clean, covered, and cool, whether refrigerated or not. Insects should be discouraged and any kitchen and eating area, even at a summer cottage, must be screened. Perishables should be kept in the refrigerator as much as possible, especially during the summer, being removed only at need and replaced promptly.

Fortunately, most spoiled food can be quickly recognized as such, for food is spoiled as a result of physical change. Nature wisely provides us with many warning signals and has made these signals instinctively repulsive to us. Spoilage is usually indicated by discoloration, the presence of moldy growths, strong odors, acid or "wrong" flavors, surface sliminess, and softening or texture changes.

When those signs are detected, instinct should be followed and the food immediately discarded as unfit for consumption. Attempts to "save" the food by removal of spoiled parts, recooking, etc., are usually unwise, even though they might be effective. Mold, for example, is a surface growth and can be cut away, but it is reasonable to assume that if conditions were favorable for the growth of mold, other organisms might well have prospered within the food. Thus, the utmost discretion should be used when salvaging spoiled foods, and it is always wiser not to make the attempt.

It should be remembered that these physical signs are produced only by some of the bacteria that spoil food by "eating" it themselves, and that disease germs which sometimes infect food and are dangerous to man, do not, as a general rule, give any such warnings. Perishable foods, in particular, should only be purchased from reputable sources. Fortunately, present legislation together with modern handling procedure has practically removed the possibility of tainted foods reaching the market place.

FOOD PURCHASING. This is at all times an important matter, but the notable increase in food prices, during the past few years, has made it a matter of interest to every homemaker. The cost of food is only one item in the whole cost of living, and this is affected by many conditions in crop productions, manufacturing, by business generally throughout the nation, and by such abnormal conditions as those induced by war.

The cost of food may be considered from several points of view. The question of the cost for each individual a day and relation of cost and nutritive value will be studied in the following paragraphs as well as the proportion of the income to be spent for food.

Factors in Cost

Several factors must be taken into consideration when attempting to account for steadily rising prices. The amount of labor involved in producing a food materially affects its price. Meats, for instance, cost more than staple vegetable foods, like corn, wheat, or beans, because we must raise the corn first to feed the animals. Meat is as cheap as vegetable foods only when the animal can find its own food, as in the pioneer days of any country, when but a small part of the land is under cultivation. To the Pilgrim Fathers, meat was cheaper than corn in terms of labor, with deer and game at hand in the forest, while corn was raised with difficulty in small clearings. Meat production is now a tremendous industry in America, and the cost of production is very high. In former days cattle on the ranges of the West and Southwest found natural food, whereas now what they once fed upon is used for other purposes.

The transportation of food increases its cost. In one sense this is another form of labor. Each person who handles the food material on its way from producer to consumer adds an additional expense for the labor involved, and the consumer ultimately pays. We have heard much discussion of the "middleman," and the effort to bring the producer and consumer closer together. This means an attempt to do away with those who handle the product after it leaves the producer and before it reaches the consumer, whose employment usually adds considerably to the ultimate price of the product. And yet these "go-betweens" are necessary in a complex modern economy.

In transportation there is another element involved—the original cost of the means of transportation, of conveyance, plus natural wear and tear. The long distance railroad furnishes cold storage cars, and the cost of these and their maintenance affect freight rates. The farmer who carries his produce to market in an auto truck must have a return for the original cost of the truck and for keeping it in repair as well as the cost of gasoline and so forth necessary to run it.

The relation of demand to supply affects the price of food in a way easy to understand. Where the supply is permanently small and the demand widespread, the price of the particular food material will be high, and vice versa. Olive oil is a good example of the permanently high-priced food. California olive oil brings a high price not only because it is pure and well-flavored, but because many homemakers want it, and the industry is a small one compared to the great amount consumed in the United States. Many years are needed to establish an olive grove, and olive raising is not a popular way of making money, because it is slow.

We find a change in the use of cottonseed oil, a large supply and a relatively smaller demand making, in times of peace, a low price. At one time the belief was widespread that cottonseed oil was detrimental to health. This fallacy has been exploded and cottonseed oil has been shown to be nutritious and absolutely safe as a food commodity. The same is true of such other domestic oils as corn, peanut, and soy bean oils.

There are two things that the farmer can never feel absolutely sure of: (1) the kind of weather to expect from day to day, and (2) the general character of the season. Of course, the season affects the quality and the amount of any crop, and this in turn influences the price. Another aspect of the effect of season on food is this: A food is cheaper in its own locality when it is in season than it is at other times of the year when it has to be brought there from a distance.

Insects, pests, animal parasites, and plant diseases not infrequently spoil or even ruin a crop, and naturally the market price goes up with the smaller supply. Moreover, if the farmer succeeds in keeping his crop free from a particular pest, it means a more or less permanent increase in his expenses, for in fighting insects and fungi there is an outlay for machinery and chemicals and much labor is expended.

Other factors too must be reckoned with in the comparative prices of different foods. Some vegetables are more difficult to raise than others, even when the season is favorable, and the insects at least partly conquered. Some plants have more vitality than others, and grow under almost any condition of soil and moisture. The various diseases to which animals are subject also affect the prices of food. If a large number of cattle are found to have tuberculosis and are condemned as food, healthy cattle bring a higher price, because, again, the supply is small in relation to the demand.

WISE PURCHASING

We must also consider certain other factors in making food purchases. For instance, one may pay a smaller price in money for a poor food, but it may also prove poor economy. There may be more value in one good apple for five cents than in three wormy ones at the same price. Food in package form costs more than in bulk, and each fancy label adds a fraction to the cost. Plate-glass windows, beautiful ribbon decorations in a shop, the larger expense for rent on a fashionable street are all ultimately paid for by the consumer.

When prepared food of any kind is purchased one pays for raw material plus the cost of fuel and the labor involved in cooking and cleaning of utensils, etc. For example, the canned soup sold by any one of the best manufacturers must command a good price because so much time and labor are used in a careful inspection of all material employed and in keeping up a high standard of cleanliness, Remember, too, that whenever canned or cooked food appears on the table, these two items, fuel and labor, have necessarily been added to the cost of the raw materials. We may not pay cash for the labor involved in home cooked food, but it must be accounted for in time and energy. The homemaker who says "My time doesn't count," has a poor opinion of herself.

More and more cooked food, canned or otherwise, is taking its place in the market. When canned goods were first manufactured on a large scale, they comprised vegetables, fruits, meats, and fish; but we are now accustomed to a miscellaneous variety, including soups, baked beans, cooked vegetables, alimentary pastes, puddings, pudding sauces, hashed meat, shellfish, and even chicken. Bakery products have a larger sale than ever, and are now found in the smallest towns. In our large cities we find a "delicatessen shop" on almost every shopping street, where small portions of cooked meats, fowl, vegetables and salads may be purchased, and these stores are open even on Sunday. We should be duly appreciative of this innovation. The custom has grown up with the changes in our mode of living, especially in cities where the small apartment is common. Under these conditions it is difficult, if not impossible, in a small kitchen to prepare food that requires cooking slowly for a long time.

The canning and preserving of fruits in city dwellings is rare. First, the cost of the fruit is usually high in the city, and this plus the sugar and fuel, the labor, and the lack of storage space make home canning and preserving impracticable. Most homemakers have decided in favor of buying goods already canned, thus simplifying their housekeeping and insuring the purchase of nourishing foods. In the end it will probably be found that not only money but time and labor also have been saved.

SUGGESTIONS FOR BUYING

Fresh meat should be purchased on the day it is to be cooked, unless the refrigerator is sufficiently large to allow storage of the meat. Even then it should not be kept more than 24 hours. Meat should not be placed directly on ice. Fresh berries and delicate vegetables should be purchased on the day required for use. Butter and eggs may be purchased once a week; other semi-perishables in quantities depending on storage space.

It is economical to buy at least half a dozen lemons and the root vegetables in rather large quantities. Flour and sugar may be purchased by the small bag of at least five pounds; lump sugar, in boxes.

Breakfast cereals are best bought in packages, and it is wise not to buy too large a number at one time. It is better to purchase oftener and have fresher material. Coffee may ordinarily be bought in pound cans. Tea comes in closely sealed packages, one-fourth, one-half, and one pound. Cocoa is usually bought in ½-pound cans, but it is an economy to buy larger cans if it is frequently used. Macaroni, rice, and tapioca are commonly bought in packages, and the number purchased at one time must depend on how frequently they appear on the menu. Salt comes by the bag or box. Spices, ground, in small, tight boxes; whole spices in bulk, to be kept in tightly closed cans. Vinegar comes by the gallon, or in pint or quart bottles. Canned and preserved goods, singly or by the half dozen, dozen, or case. Bakery products should be purchased daily or every other day.

When food materials are delivered to the kitchen, have receptacles for each kind of food. (*See* KITCHEN EQUIPMENT.) Attend first to perishable foods. Put eggs away immediately. Wash and dry milk and cream bottles before putting them in the refrigerator. This is a good plan with lemons and other skin fruits, unless the quantity is too large—as during preserve making—in which case they should not be put into the refrigerator. Remove wrappings from meat, poultry, and fish, and place in the refrigerator. Fish should be covered so that its odor will not affect other foods. Vegetables like lettuce, celery, and spinach should be washed and picked over immediately. All semi-perishable foods should be put in a cool, dry place, and the non-perishables in their separate receptacles. Do not keep anything in paper bags, but save these bags for other uses.

Have a regular time for inspecting and for cleaning all the places and receptacles where food is kept. Do not allow any spilled food material to remain anywhere, and do not tolerate the presence of any material, cooked or uncooked, that shows the least taint. A keen sense of smell is a good servant here.

FOOD VALUE. The tables of food value given under the various headings in this book are based on data compiled by the Bureau of Human Nutrition and Home Economics of the U.S. Department of Agriculture. The percentages are given in terms of 100 grams of the edible portion of the food in question, and are average values for food energy, protein, fat, carbohydrate, three minerals, and the better known vitamins.

Water is given as a percent; food energy in terms of calories. Protein, fat, and carbohydrate are in terms of grams; calcium, phosphorus, and iron in milligrams. The Vitamin A value is given in terms of International Units, and the remaining vitamins in milligrams.

FOOL. A dessert made of cooked fruit and cream.

BERRY FOOL

1 qt berries (gooseberries, strawberries, etc.)
Sugar to taste
Pinch of salt
Cream or rich milk

Stew the berries with a very little water until they are soft. Rub through a sieve. Sweeten to taste and add a pinch of salt. For each 2 cups of pulp, 2 cups of cream are stirred in very slowly. Chill and serve very cold.

FOOTED TUMBLER. A conical shaped drinking glass set upon a foot or base. It often resembles stemware designs, but lacks the stem. *See* GLASSWARE.

FORBIDDEN FRUIT. An American liqueur made from brandy and grapefruit. It was originally made from shaddock, an early form of grapefruit. *See* LIQUEUR, *see also* GRAPEFRUIT.

FORCEMEAT. *See* STUFFING.

FORESHANK. *See* BEEF.

FOREZ CHEESE. A round cheese, ten inches in diameter and six inches high, with a flavor resembling Roquefort. It is sometimes called "d'Ambert," and is a product of France.

FORK. A fork consists of two or more prongs set on a handle and is primarily used to impale foods. It is the youngest member of the knife, fork, and spoon trio, mainly because it is not as essential as the other two instruments. Most of the fork's functions can be performed by the knife and spoon assisted by the fingers, and it was not until the present conception of table manners was born that the fork emerged from the kitchen, where it had been used to some extent.

Like the other implements, many specialized forms of the fork have been developed to meet certain needs. The table forks have flat, closely set tines that can be used as a scoop for many forms of food. *See* FLATWARE. Kitchen forks are usually built on a larger scale, having husky, wide-spaced tines, and long, sturdy handles, so they may be used to handle heavy pieces of meat, etc.

Because of the pressure normally exerted on a fork, they are commonly made of metal. Silver is the preferred material for table forks (see SILVERWARE), while the kitchen units are made of some rust-resisting metal form. Salad forks and other light-duty forks are sometimes made of wood or plastic. *See also* KITCHEN EQUIPMENT.

FORMAGELLE CHEESE. A small, soft-ripened, rennet cheese, made in Italy from cow's milk.

FORMAGGINI CHEESE. A name applied to several kinds of small Italian cheeses. *Formaggini di Leco* is a small, round, dessert cheese which weighs two ounces, and is made in Lombardy.

FORMAGGIO D'CAPRI. An Italian cheese made of goat's milk.

FORMOSA TEAS. Both Oolong and black teas are produced on Formosa, and it is to the former tea that this island in the western Pacific owes much of its fame. Formosa Oolongs are among the fine teas of the world. They have been called the "champagnes of teas" because of their pungent, delicately fruity flavor. Some of the Formosa Oolongs are now given three-quarter fermentation to make them more like the black teas that most Americans prefer. *See Tea.*

FORTIFICATION. In wine, this term refers to the addition of alcohol other than that naturally produced by fermentation within the must. The alcohol commonly used is grape brandy (*which see*), and fortification is usually done to check the fermentation while there is still sugar in the wine, thereby leaving it sweet. *See* WINE; *see also* PORT.

FOUETTER. (Fou et tay) French term for whipping eggs, etc.

FOWL. In present-day usage, an edible bird. It is more particularly applied to a chicken which is suitable only for boiling or steaming. *See* CHICKEN.

FRANKFURTER. *See* SAUSAGE.

FRAPPE. (I) The French word *frappé* means "chilled" or "iced." Frappés may be classified with water or fruit ices, and are not as rich as ice cream, parfait, or even sherbet. A frappé mixture has the coarsest texture of all the frozen dessert family, resembling coarse rock salt. It is used as a frozen mass in many punch bowls, frozen cup beverages, etc. It is usually

served either in parfait or sherbet glasses and sometimes topped with whipped cream.

Frappés are frozen to a mush in a hand freezer or in refrigerator trays. If a hand freezer is used, equal parts of ice and rock salt should be used. Any kind of fruit, canned or fresh, cut into small pieces may be added to a frappé, if desired. *See also* FROZEN DESSERTS.

ITALIAN FRAPPE

2 cups granulated sugar
3½ cups cold water
1½ cups grapefruit juice
½ cup lemon juice
Grated rind of 1 orange
1 cup orange juice
½ tsp grated lemon rind
1 tsp brandy

Make a sirup of sugar and cold water and boil 5 minutes. Add grapefruit juice, combined with orange and lemon juice and rind of orange and lemon; stir well and cool, then chill. When well-chilled, add brandy and freeze to a mush in hand freezer, using equal parts of ice and salt.

FRAPPE. (II) As used in drinks, frappé means an iced drink. Various liqueurs such as anisette may be served poured over shaved ice in a cocktail glass. The resulting concoction, anisette frappé, is sipped with a straw as the ice melts.

FREEZE. *See* ICE CREAM.

FREEZING FOODS. Coincident with the growth of the frozen food industry (*see* FROSTED AND FROZEN FOODS) has been the development of home preservation of food by refrigeration. For centuries homemakers have been aware of the significance of chilling food to preserve it, but only for the past ten years have they been aware of the tremendous potentialities in *freezing* food. Manufacturers have progressed steadily in the improvement of home freezing units, and the number of locker plants throughout the country has increased markedly. Many families have availed themselves of efficient, inexpensive storage space for their frozen foods. These families can preserve food for months, or even years, so that it retains nearly all of its original flavor, freshness, and nutrition.

The nutritive value of properly-frozen food is nearly equal to that of fresh food;

it should have substantially the same mineral, protein, and vitamin content. It is in the poor preparation, and not in the freezing, of foods that loss of nutritive value does occur. Proper treatment of the food before and after freezing is the homemaker's responsibility; the freezer does the rest.

The procedure for freezing foods is neither revolutionary nor difficult; it is far simpler than canning, for example. Supervising the freezing of food is not difficult, but more is involved therein than simply placing the food in a box or bag and dumping it into the freezer. If you keep the following seven steps in mind and follow all other relevant instructions with precision, you can be assured of success with frozen foods:

1. Have the necessary equipment ready in advance.

2. Select food of the best quality and of a variety recommended for freezing.

3. Prepare the food, following directions, as soon as possible after gathering.

4. Wrap or package it securely in a suitable moisture-vaporproof container.

5. Label and freeze it immediately.

6. Maintain correct storage temperature (0° F. or lower).

7. Cook or thaw and cook, according to what is recommended for the food.

HOME FREEZER OR COMMUNITY LOCKER

Locker plants. All locker plants have quick freezing and storage services for large quantities of food, and they are equipped to perform many other important services for the housewife. The housewife does not necessarily have to rent locker space in order to avail herself of these additional services. Of course not all plants offer the same services, so it would be well to investigate those given by your local locker plant.

It has been estimated that it is cheaper to rent locker space than to operate a home freezer, but certain of its disadvantages must be considered. The average locker holds a maximum of 250 pounds of frozen food, a relatively small amount if the family draws continuously from the frozen food supply. Often two lockers may be needed, or a locker can be used as an auxiliary to a home freezer. Transportation of food between locker and home must also be considered in the cost. Likewise, the temperature maintained in some locker

plants may not be low enough to prevent deterioration. (Storage temperatures should not rise above 0° F.)

Home freezers. The purchase of a home freezer is often an economically practical step; but just as often it can be a disaster. Families that profit most from such an investment are those that raise their own meat and vegetables. Families that have access to wholesale meat markets and can purchase a side of beef for much less money than the total cost of individual cuts may also find a home freezer an advantageous investment.

In general, however, it is wise to remember that the cost of foods that are purchased to be frozen is not less than the cost of foods bought for immediate consumption. A good deal of planning must be devoted to the purchase and uses of foods to be frozen in order to justify the price of the freezer itself. The homemaker must take advantage of the low prices of seasonal vegetables and fruits that may be frozen for consumption later in the year.

Each family must decide whether the cost of equipment will be sufficiently taken up in savings on the quantity purchase of foods bought at wholesale or bargain prices or harvested from gardens and preserved.

Often just the convenience of having a quantity of frozen food near at hand may be worth the expense of the freezer purchase and upkeep.

In view of your locale, means, family size, and special food habits, there is a type and size of home freezer to fit your needs. Generally speaking, they fall into three classes: (1) The chest-type, top-opening freezer has frosty holes or compartments for storing food. These freezers range in size from three to 50 cubic feet storage capacity. Most models having two or more compartments are so designed that the temperature of the compartments can be controlled individually. The smaller models often have a temperature-adjusting device so that the box may be used for either freezing or storing. (2) The upright, front-opening freezer resembles a household refrigerator in outward appearance. These range from four to 40 cubic feet in size. Some models have an inner door construction or drawers; others are merely fitted with shelves which serve as freezing surfaces. (3) Cooler-freezers combine a regular household refrigerator with a frozen food compartment. The small models are not equipped to freeze food—they merely provide storage space for food already frozen. Larger cooler-freezers may be had in sizes up to 760 cubic feet, enough to accomodate the storage needs of large farms or estates. These are the walk-in-type, combining cooler, freezer, and storage space, and they have separate compartments for quick-freezing food.

EQUIPMENT

No special equipment (other than packaging material) is needed for the preparation procedure. The items found in any well-ordered kitchen will be sufficient for this purpose. These include:
A few sharp knives
Mixing spoons
Measuring cups and spoons
Mixing bowls
Deep kettle (6 to 12 quart capacity) with lid
Wire-mesh basket or long-handled colander (for blanching)
Low rack (to hold basket or colander above water level)
Large pitcher (for making and chilling sirup)
Wide-mouthed canning funnel
Containers or packaging suitable for the food to be frozen
Labels
Also helpful are:
Kitchen shears
Berry huller
Vegetable scraper
Apple corer
Puréeing equipment (such as a food mill)

WHAT TO FREEZE

Most foods can be quick-frozen, but some are frozen and preserved better than others. The problem of what to freeze is, then, a comparative rather than a restrictive one. If your freezing and storage space is limited, it is best to freeze only those foods that freeze best.

As for meats, muscle cuts usually freeze better and have longer storage life than the organs—heart, liver, kidneys, etc. Ground meats, particularly sausage meat to which salt has been added, do not keep well over a long period of time.

Vegetables which are normally cooked and then eaten freeze well and retain their fresh-cooked characteristics. Radishes, lettuce, green peppers, celery, cabbage, and Chinese cabbage have their desirable crispness destroyed by freezing. If they are to be cooked or used for flavoring in other dishes, however, these vegetables freeze very well.

The banana is the only common fruit that cannot be successfully frozen. Other fruits can be frozen, though some better than others. It is more difficult to retain the characteristics of fresh fruits than that of fresh vegetables. Orange, grapefruit, and pineapple sections freeze very well in a prepared sugar sirup; avocados, persimmons, and watermelon are best frozen in a puréed form. Grapes, though they can be frozen, do not yield a very desirable frozen product.

Tomatoes preserved by freezing are no better than canned tomatoes, but they do produce a satisfactory product.

Baked goods and cooked dishes can usually be frozen with great success. Among the recommended baked goods are fruit-, corn starch-, or tapioca-filled pies; butter, angel, and sponge cakes; cupcakes; muffins; breakfast and dinner rolls; baking powder biscuits; and all kinds of bread. All kinds of bread, rolls, muffins, cupcakes, cakes, and fruit pies freeze well. Baking powder biscuits also freeze very well. The cooked foods that have been found satisfactory for freezing are listed on page 509.

Seafood, poultry, and game are successfully frozen. However, freezing large birds for roasting is wasteful of storage space in that packages should be as compact as possible if a freezer or locker is to hold enough food to be worthwhile.

Dairy products that freeze most successfully are eggs, butter, cheese, and cream. The butterfat in cream has a tendency to separate, but this failing can be overcome by homogenizing the thawed cream. The freezer preserves ice cream almost perfectly.

As a general rule, remember that you will take out of the freezer no better product than you put into it. Use only the best quality foods for freezing—those varieties which freeze best and the best obtainable grade of each variety.

Maturity is essential in fruits and vegetables, and the stage of maturity should be that which is most desirable for immediate table use. Unless otherwise stated, they should be young and tender. Overmature vegetables will produce a frozen product which is starchy and flavorless. Over-ripe fruit will be mushy after freezing, while green or partially ripe fruit will have a bitter taste and uneven texture. Fruits should have good, deep color with no, or at least a minimum of, green showing. Fruit should be tree- or vine-ripened wherever possible. The one exception is pears; these should be allowed to ripen off the tree. Look for crispness as well.

Select meat animals that are young and tender. Select only the best poultry—young, healthy, well-finished birds—as with all foods. Here again the fine quality of the frozen product is dependent upon careful selection.

PREPARATION

Food should be frozen as soon as possible after it is gathered or purchased. If, however, freezing cannot be undertaken at once, it is essential that you keep the food refrigerated until freezing time. Most foods are prepared for freezing much the same as they are for immediate use. Fruits require a special sweetening process; vegetables, a blanching process. Follow directions carefully for these processes.

PACKAGING

There are a variety of packages and wrappers available, some best used with one kind of food, some with another. Meat and poultry are usually more easily wrapped than boxed, but fruits and vegetables are always stored in bags, boxes, cartons, jars, or cans. These containers are made of many materials, among them metal, cellophane, laminated sheets of paper, cellophane or aluminum foil, viscose sheets, and vegetable parchment. Also important in packaging is stockinette, a tubular elastic woven material particularly suited to meat and poultry because of its ability to conform to irregular shapes and hold the inner wrap close against the food. Locker tape is especially designed to hold securely at low temperatures.

Two general rules about packaging are: (1) Do not lose time in the process. Pack the food while it is as fresh as possible, and then proceed immediately to the next step. (2) Try to avoid putting more food than will be consumed at one meal in one container; foods that have been thawed are very perishable.

Good packaging must prevent air from coming into contact with the food. At low temperatures air is very dry and will absorb moisture from improperly packaged food, leaving it dry, tough, and flavorless; this condition is known as "freezer burn." It must retain the flavor of the enclosed food and keep out other flavors. A suitable package is one that can be made airtight and impervious to moisture and vapor. It should absorb no water or fat and give no noticeable flavor to food; it should be rustproof, noncorrosive, sturdy enough to resist the rigors of freezing and storage, easy to fill, and designed so that the contents can be easily removed when frozen or partially thawed. It should have an effective, easy-to-handle seal, and it should be shaped to occupy a minimum of storage space. For this reason most containers are flat, rectangular, or cubical in shape.

Fruits and vegetables. Enameled metal cans or ordinary mason jars may be used for fruits and vegetables. Cans must be removed from the freezer with gloves, as the cold metal would otherwise stick to the fingers. Jars are undesirable in that they take up a good deal of space and become brittle at zero temperatures, and their narrow mouths do not permit easy removal of food.

Those packages that have been designed especially for freezing will probably prove most satisfactory. These may be flat, rectangular, top-opening boxes with an inner lining of moisture-vaporproof cellophane. (They are always overwrapped with moistureproof cellophane and heat-sealed.) Or they may be the flat, rectangular, end-opening type with a bag liner (needing no outer wrapping if the liner is heat sealed). There are also the cubical types with metal slip-in lids, and the cup-shaped and tub-shaped containers with slip-in lids, needing no heating-sealing. Special directions are given for the packaging of corn.

If head space is specified for fruits, fill the container only to about ¾ inch of the top. When the fruit is covered with sirup the head space should remain.

Meats, Poultry, and Fish. The most important thing to remember in packaging meats is to make the packages small enough so they will not require too much freezing time—one roast or large steak to a package, two medium steaks, 4 to 8 chops of hamburger patties, etc.

Some meats may be packed in the shallow rectangular, waxed paperboard cartons lined with moistureproof cellophane (such as are used for some vegetables), but larger sizes will be needed to accommodate the pieces. Cartons measuring 4 by 6 by 1½ inches deep are good size for hamburger or sausage. Larger ones (8 by 10 by 2½ inches) may be used for steaks and chops. Pack the cartons full, placing two sheets of cellophane between layers of meat and tucking the cellophane lining over and around the meat. Close the carton and label it. Then overwrap it with moisture-proof cellophane, and heat-seal the wrapping for best results. Fish steaks and fillets, small whole fish, cut-up chickens, and quartered broilers may also be packaged in this manner.

Roasts and bulky pieces are best wrapped in moisture-vaporproof paper or sheeting, then inserted in a stockinette. It is tied at the open end, pulled tightly around the meat, cut off, and tied at the other end. Never use plain butcher paper to wrap meat for freezing; it offers no protection during storage.

Baked goods, cooked dishes, etc. If these foods are frozen in the dish or pan in which they were cooked, they need only be wrapped in moistureproof cellophane or other sheeting and heat-sealed. There are paper pie plates and casseroles on the market which have been especially treated for use in both cooking and freezing. Fragile foods, such as angel cake, should be heat-sealed in moisture-proof wrapping and placed in a paper carton. Such foods as chicken à la king and spaghetti can be packed in the type of container used for fruits and vegetables. Cooked meats are packaged as are fresh meats. Soups may be poured into liquid-tight containers. Casserole dishes may be wrapped in moisture-proof cellophane, slipped into a stockinette, and tied.

Sealing the Package. Proper sealing of packages is essential, if foods are to be kept fresh, crisp, and tasty. The seal, no less than the packaging and wrapping material, makes the package airtight, moisture-proof, and vaporproof.

Sealing can be accomplished by heat, locker tape, the double or druggist's fold, or push-on and slip-in lids. Cellophane is sealed by heating the ends so that they fuse without scorching. Hold the open end firmly in a closed position and seal. This may be done with an ordinary curling iron, an old knife blade, or a hand iron. These should be hot enough to fuse the cellophane but not hot enough to scorch a newspaper. You can seal overlapping edges of outer wraps or the folded tops of bag liners in this manner, and bags are easily sealed by placing the heated metal across the open end a short distance above the level of the food within.

Materials which do not heat-fuse can be sealed by bringing the ends of the wrapping together at the top of the box and making a double fold—as the druggist does—then folding in the side edges and sealing all seams with locker tape.

Slip-in lids should be sealed with locker tape, after they are in place, for added protection. Seal the edges with one continuous strip of tape and fold it in snugly.

LABELING

Each package put into the freezer should first be labeled so that in the future the label will be able to give any desired information about the food. The contents and the date of packing should always be given. Date of packing is especially important with foods having a restricted storage life. The variety of fruit or vegetable used should also be given. This will be of value in determining which varieties freeze the best. Record as well the pack used for vegetables (dry or brine). You might also include the cut of meat used and its weight. If your frozen food is stored in a locker plant, it is well to write your name or locker number on the label.

In some states, permit number and transfer certificate are required by law to be posted with game stored in a locker plant.

FREEZING AND STORAGE TEMPERATURES

As a general rule, the quicker a product is frozen, the better its quality. For this reason, temperatures for quick freezing of food should be 0° F. or lower. Meat, poultry, and fish especially need quick freezing since the small ice crystals thus formed do not tend to rupture the cells as would the larger crystals formed by slower freezing. The more the cells are ruptured, the greater will be the leakage of vital juices from the food.

The speed with which a product freezes is not dependent on temperature alone, however. The size and shape of the package, the arrangement of the packages in the unit, and the means by which the food is frozen, such as air blast or metal freezing plates, affect the rate of freezing. For instance, it takes approximately fourteen hours to freeze a 3¾ pound roast in still air at 10° and about seven hours at the same temperature in an air blast.

Arrange the packages in the freezer so that air circulates between them, and so they are in close contact with the freezing surfaces of the compartment. Don't run the risk of attempting to freeze too much in a home freezer; follow the manufacturer's directions closely in this matter. If a large quantity of food is to be frozen, it is better and safer to take it to a locker plant for freezing, after which it can be stored in the home freezer.

Never place warm or hot foods in the freezer, as there is danger of spoilage from too slow freezing. When freezing such things as baked foods, let them cool before wrapping, and chill blanched fruits and vegetables before packaging.

To be sure that the temperature in the freezer remains at 0° F. or below, make it a practice to check it every day with a thermometer. Zero temperatures are recommended for all types of frozen foods.

A final reminder is to freeze food *immediately* after packaging. Any long delay may result in spoilage, or at best an inferior product. If freezing is done at a locker plant, place the packages in the refrigerator until the day's lot can be transferred. When transferring foods to and from a locker plant, it is advisable to use a corrugated paperboard box lined with newspapers to act as insulation.

BEFORE USING

Thawing. Do not allow vegetables to become thawed until you are ready to serve them at the next meal. Some foods should be completely thawed before cooking, others partially thawed, and some cooked in the solidly frozen state. When thawing is recommended, it should be done as slowly as possible; i.e., with the food on the lowest shelf of the refrigerator. If you have to hurry the thawing, the food can be placed on a work surface at room temperature. To reduce thawing time still further, place the frozen product in front of an electric fan. Food should always remain in the un-

opened package during thawing. Do not thaw more food than will be used at one meal; once thawed food is very perishable and must not be refrozen.

Cooking. Don't allow the food to become warm, but cook it while it is still chilled. Independent of the adjustment of cooking time, cook frozen foods as you would the fresh products. If you are cooking solidly frozen food, additional cooking time must be allowed.

PREPARATION OF VEGETABLES

The first step is thorough cleaning. Wash the vegetables carefully, taking care to remove all soil particles, and remove all imperfect portions. Greens especially should be carefully examined for soil particles and insects. Next, trim, cut, or slice the vegetable, as for cooking or table use.

Blanching. After the vegetables have been washed and cut or sliced in the proper size, they are ready for the most important step —blanching. Directions must be closely followed here to insure adequate blanching —neither too much nor too little. If done improperly, vegetables will lose flavor, color, and nutritive value. Unblanched vegetables can be preserved by freezing for only a short time before they begin to deteriorate, but proper blanching inactivates the enzymes in vegetables and checks the natural loss of flavor and color which takes place when vegetables stand for any length of time uncooked. Blanching helps to retain vitamins and is an effective destroyer of bacteria.

There are two methods of blanching, by water and by steam: water blanching is generally a more popular method, but steam blanching is recommended for some cut-up vegetables such as Frenched green beans, cut kernel corn, and diced turnips. Steam blanching conserves vitamins and minerals even better than water blanching, as there is not the nutritive loss when cut surfaces are exposed to steam that there is when immersed in boiling water.

Water blanching is accomplished by immersing about a pound of vegetables in boiling water for the period of time specified for that vegetable. The water in the kettle should be brought to a full rolling boil and the vegetables then placed in the wire basket or colander and immersed. The vegetables will cool the water slightly and a short time is required for the water to boil again. Do not count blanching time until the water comes to a rolling boil the second time and count the time accurately with a watch or clock. When water blanching, it is best to agitate the basket so that all surfaces of the vegetable are uniformly blanched. After removing the vegetables, chill them in iced water for one or two minutes; prolonged soaking will cause loss of flavor, as well as vitamins and minerals.

Steam blanching is much the same process except that the vegetables are blanched by steam rather than by water. Place about an inch of water in the kettle which should have a tight fitting lid and a low rack to keep the bottom of the wire basket or colander above water level. Bring the water to a boil, put in the vegetable-filled basket or colander, and cover tightly. Count blanching time when the vegetables are in place and covered.

Vegetable Packs. There are three possible ways of packing the vegetables after blanching. One is the dry pack, in which the vegetables are drained for a few moments after cooling then packed immediately in suitable containers. Another method is to cover the vegetables with a brine solution after placing them in containers. (The solution is made by adding one teaspoon of salt to each cup of water.) Brine pack is suitable for containers which are not wholly moisture-vaporproof, but tends to toughen vegetables and reduce their color. Also, brine packed vegetables must be defrosted and the brine removed before using. A third method, called "loose pack," is not recommended for the homemaker. The procedure here is to spread the vegetables on a tray, freeze them, remove them from the tray, and package them.

If brine pack is used, allow three quarters of an inch headroom for expansion of the contents during freezing. This allowance should always be made when freezing a liquid or semiliquid product.

Dry pack vegetables should fill the container *full*, so that as little air space as possible is left in the package. Use a funnel to fill containers with small whole, cut, or puréed vegetables, and shake the container while filling to pack it tightly. Large pieces, such as asparagus or broccoli, are packed by hand or with tongs to keep their shape. Leave about one-quarter inch headroom in a pint package of puréed vegetables, one half inch in a quart package.

Artichokes. Pull outer leaves from the globe until only the inner yellow or white leaves, free of all green, remain; cut off tops of buds and trim butt end to a cone. Wash hearts in cold water; blanch for 7 minutes in a solution containing 1 teaspoon of citric acid, or ½ cup of lemon juice, in 3 quarts of water. Chill for about 2 minutes in iced water, or for 5 minutes in running cold water; drain; and package.

Asparagus. Recommended varieties are: Mary Washington, Martha Washington (excellent and very good); Palmetto and Keystonian (good). Select stalks that are well colored and brittle and have tips that are tight and compact.

Asparagus toughens and loses flavor rapidly after harvest, so it should be packaged and ready for freezing within 3 hours after cutting. Use the upper 6 inches of the spears; separate stalks into small (⅜ to ¾ inch butt-end) and large (¾ to 1 inch butt-end). Wash in cold water and trim. The spear may be frozen whole or cut in 2-inch pieces before blanching. Steam-blanching is preferred. Steam-blanch small stalks 3½ minutes, large stalks 4½ minutes; or water-blanch small stalks 3 minutes, large stalks 4 minutes. Chill in ice water for 1 to 2 minutes, drain, and package. Handle tips carefully to preserve shape.

Beans, green shell. Recommended varieties are: French Horticultural, Lowe's Champion (excellent and very good); Bountiful, Giant Stringless, and Green Pod (good). Harvest while pods are still flexible, before they become dry. Shell a quantity of beans before starting to blanch, and do not wash them after shelling. Steam-blanching is preferred. Steam-blanch for 105 seconds, or water-blanch for 1 minute. Chill in iced water for about 1 minute, drain, and package.

Beans, green snap. The Kentucky Wonder is an excellent variety of pole beans, and the Blue Lake is very good. Lowe's Champion, Wisconsin Refugee, and Giant Stringless Green Pod are good varieties of bush beans. Harvest before the seeds in the pods become very prominent. The beans should break cleanly with no strings at the sides. Wash thoroughly within a few hours after harvesting. Snip off the tips. Small, tender beans (of 3 or 4 inches) may be frozen whole, cut in 1-inch lengths, or French sliced. Water blanching is preferable for whole or cut beans, steam-blanching for Frenched beans. Water-blanch cut beans for two minutes, whole beans for 2½ minutes. Steam-blanch Frenched beans for 2 minutes, cut beans 3 minutes, and whole beans 3½ minutes. Chill for 1 to 2 minutes, drain, and package.

Beans, Lima. Recommended pole beans: Challenger, King of the Garden, Giant Podded (good). Bush beans: Fordhook (excellent); Burpee's Bush, Clark's, Dreer Bush, Henderson, Baby Potato (good).

The green beans are the tender and tasty ones. Harvest while pods are well filled and still green. Use kitchen shears to cut off the tough edges of pods and gain easy access to the beans. Do not wash after shelling, and shell a quantity before blanching. Water blanching is preferred. Water-blanch small beans 1 minute, medium 1½ minutes, large 2 minutes. Steam-blanch small beans 2 minutes, medium 2½ minutes, large 3 minutes. Chill about 2 minutes in iced water, drain, and package.

Beans, Soy. Green Giant, Willomi, Bansei (excellent to very good); Hokkaido (good). Harvest while pods are well filled but still green. Soy beans are difficult to shell, but this can be done in conjunction with blanching. Water-blanch pods about 4 minutes, chill thoroughly for at least 2 minutes in iced water, and shell them directly into packages after they have *completely* cooled.

Beans, Wax. Round Pot Kidney is the only variety recommended. Prepare in the same manner as green shell beans (*which see*).

Beets. An excellent variety for freezing is Detroit Dark Red: Other varieties are satisfactory but may be inferior in color. Of these the Crosby is very good.

Fast growing young beets make the best frozen product. Cut off the tops and scrub the beets thoroughly in cold water. Cook, rather than blanch, in boiling water until tender (except the very small tender ones which may be frozen whole), then chill for about 2 minutes in iced water, rub off peels, and slice directly into packages. If small whole beets (1½ to 1¾ inch diameter) are desired, pare before blanching and steam-blanch (preferred) for 3½ minutes, or water-blanch for 2½ minutes. Chill about 2 minutes in iced water, drain, and package.

Beet Greens. Any variety may be used. Freeze beet greens as soon as possible after gathering, for they lose flavor and texture

rapidly. Wash thoroughly in cold water to rid them of soil particles. Discard any thick stems and yellowed leaves. Water-blanching is preferred for these; blanch 2 minutes while agitating the basket or colander. Steam-blanching time is 3 minutes. Chill about 2 minutes in iced water, drain, and package.

Broccoli. The Italian Green Sprouting variety is excellent. Other varieties will give a satisfactory frozen product. Stalks bearing tight, compact heads are of best maturity for freezing; harvest before the bud clusters flower. Wash thoroughly in cold running water; inspect carefully for insects, and discard coarse leaves. Cut head into pieces up to 1 inch in thickness and up to 7 inches in length; separate the stalks according to size before blanching. Water-blanching is preferred. Water-blanch small stalks 3 minutes, medium 4, and large 5; steam-blanch small stalks 4 minutes, medium 5, and large 6. Chill in running cold water for 4 to 5 minutes, drain, and package.

Brussels Sprouts. The Half Dwarf Improved and Long Island Improved varieties are good. Dark green, compact heads indicate a desirable stage of maturity. Cut sprouts from main stem and wash thoroughly in cold running water, trimming off coarse outer leaves and discarding insect-infested sprouts. Water-blanching is preferred. Water-blanch for 4 minutes; steam-blanch for 5 minutes. Then chill in cold running water for 6 to 8 minutes, drain, and package.

Cabbage. Savoy, Copenhagen, and Danish Ballhead are good varieties; others are satisfactory. Select tight, compact heads still tinged with green. Trim outer coarse leaves; then either shred with medium or coarse shredder, or separate into "leaves" with a sharp knife. Steam-blanching is preferred. Steam-blanch for 2 or water-blanch for 1½ minutes. Chill shreds in cold running water for 2 minutes, "leaves" for 3 minutes. Drain and package.

Carrots. Recommended varieties are Nantes Coreless and Amsterdam Coreless (excellent and very good) and Red Cored Chantenay (good). All other varieties freeze well but may be inferior in color. Small carrots are best for freezing. Select the fast-growing, first-of-the-season ones if possible. Cut off tops, wash in cold running water, and scrape. Carrots may then be frozen whole (the very small, tender ones), cut into ¼-inch slices, or put through a French slicer. Water-blanching is preferred. Water-blanch Frenched carrots 2 minutes, sliced 3 minutes, or whole 4½ minutes; steam-blanch for same periods. Chill in cold running water for about 5 minutes, drain and package.

Cauliflower. Recommended varieties are Forbes, White Mountain, Perfection, and Snowball (excellent and very good): and Erfurt (good). Select the solid, well-formed, snow white heads for freezing. Trim off outer leaves and base of stem; wash in cold running water. Cut head into pieces not thicker than 1 inch, and separate these into small and medium pieces before blanching. Water-blanching is preferred. Water-blanch small pieces 3 minutes, medium pieces 4 minutes; steam-blanch small pieces 4 minutes, medium pieces 5 minutes. Chill in cold running water 4 to 5 minutes, drain, and package.

Celery. The Pascal and Salt Lake varieties are good; others are satisfactory. Since frozen celery can only be used as a cooked product, the green varieties have the best flavor. Trim stalks as for table use, washing thoroughly in running cold water. Cut them into 1-inch pieces. Cook until tender by steaming or by cooking in a small amount of water. To chill, place in a shallow pan and float pan in cold water, stirring until product is cold. Package.

Chinese Cabbage. Mature heads will be well formed and solid. The Chihli variety is good for freezing. Cut individual leaves from base; wash thoroughly in cold running water, eliminating soil and foreign particles. Discard outer leaves which may be bruised. Water-blanching is preferred. Water-blanch for 70 seconds or steam-blanch for 2 minutes. Chill for about 5 minutes in cold running water, drain, and package.

Collards. Any variety freezes well. Wash thoroughly in cold running water, discarding stem and coarse leaves. Water-blanching is preferred; since the leaves of greens have a tendency to mat together during the blanching period, be sure to agitate the basket containing them up and down during the blanching period. Water-blanch for 2 minutes or steam-blanch for minutes. Chill in cold running water for minutes, drain, and package.

Corn, Sweet. White sweet corn does not give the fine flavor and attractive color that yellow sweet corn does. However, it is satisfactory for cut corn. The best varieties are Crosby Hybrid and Country Gentleman. Yellow sweet corn varieties recommended are Golden Cross Bantam, 8-Row Golden Bantam, Kingscrost Golden Bantam (excellent and very good); 14-Row Golden Bantam; Purgold, Seneca Golden, Maine Bantam, Lincoln, Indigold, and Aristogold Bantam (good). Other varieties of yellow sweet corn are recommended for cut corn only. Ears should be well developed, but kernels still milky when tested with the thumbnail. Silk of ears will be just dry at this stage of maturity.

Sweet corn loses flavor and texture rapidly after harvest, so freeze it as soon as possible. Husk, and eliminate those ears which are under- or overmature. To obtain the best possible product, blanch all corn on the cob whether or not it is intended for cut corn; if kernels are cut from cob before blanching, milk and flavor loss is likely to be great. Blanch no more than 6 ears at once. Steam-blanching is preferred. Steam-blanch small ears 6½ minutes, medium 8½, and large 10½; water-blanch small ears 6 minutes, medium 8½, and large 10½. Chill cobs in running cold water for at least 10 to 15 minutes. For freezing corn on the cob, drain a few seconds, wrap each ear individually in moistureproof cellophane, pack ears in large rectangular folding carton, overwrap carton with moistureproof cellophane, heat-seal, and freeze immediately.

For freezing cut corn, cut whole kernels from cob after chilling. To separate bits of cob from kernels, wash in large pan of cold water, letting kernels settle to the bottom and using a sieve or colander to skim out pieces of cob that come to the surface. Remove kernels from pan, drain and package.

If you prefer to cut kernels from cob before blanching, it is recommended that you steam-blanch only very small portions (about one cup) at a time for 2½ minutes. Cool immediately in running cold water for about 5 minutes, and eliminate bits of cob as described above.

Egg Plant. The Black Beauty and New Hampshire Hybrid varieties are good for freezing. Select medium-sized fruit so that seeds are tender and not too prominent.

Peel, and slice in ⅓-inch slices or dice in ⅓-inch cubes. Water-blanch for 4 minutes (preferred) or steam-blanch for 5 minutes. Chill the hot vegetable in running cold water for 2 minutes; then immerse it in a 2 percent citric acid solution (made by dissolving 1 tablespoon of citric acid, or ½ cup of lemon juice, in 2½ pints of cold water) for 2 minutes. Immerse again in running cold water for about 2 minutes and package. The citric acid treatment prevents this vegetable from darkening.

Kale. The Tall Curled Scotch and Dwarf Curled Scotch varieties give a fair frozen product. Wash thoroughly in cold running water. Discard main stem and any coarse leaves. Water-blanch for 70 seconds (preferred) or steam-blanch for 2 minutes. Agitate basket containing greens during the blanching period. Chill in running cold water for about 5 minutes, drain, and package.

Kohlrabi. The Early White Vienna variety is very good for freezing. This vegetable becomes bitter and stringy when overmature. Cut off tops. Wash thoroughly in running water. Peel, and dice in 1-inch cubes. Steam-blanch for 100 seconds (preferred) or water-blanch for 60 seconds. Chill for about 5 minutes in cold running water, drain, and package.

Mixed Vegetables. Select vegetables at the peak of maturity as for freezing separately. The following combinations can be used: succotash made with kernel corn and lima beans, green shell beans, or soy beans; peas and carrots; new potatoes and peas; kernel corn, peas, carrots, lima beans, and green beans.

Prepare for table use and blanch each vegetable separately, following the directions given for it. Chill, drain, and mix vegetables in proportions desired. Not all vegetables mature at the same time; if an out-of-season vegetable is to be used, use the frozen vegetable, thawed just enough to break the pack up, and mix it with the fresh. Package.

Mushrooms. Cultivated (*Agaricus campestris*) mushrooms are excellent for freezing. Select them with white, tight caps before they get too large. The medium and smaller sizes are best. Care should be taken not to bruise the mushrooms during handling. Plan to freeze them promptly to prevent deterioration. Wash them in cold running water, and cut off base of stem. They may be frozen whole, as buttons, or sliced. Sort whole mushrooms and buttons into small and large sizes for blanching. Steam-blanching is preferred. Avoid over-

blanching as this will cause excessive shrinking. Steam-blanch slices 3 minutes, small whole or button 3½, large 4½ to 6; water-blanch slices 2, button or small whole 3, or large 4 to 5½ minutes. Chill for two minutes in cold running water, then for 2 minutes in a 2 percent citric acid solution, and then for 2 more minutes in cold running water. (Prepare the citric acid solution by dissolving 1 tablespoon of citric acid, or ½ cup of lemon juice, in 2½ pints of cold water.) Drain well and package.

Mustard greens. The Florida, Broadleaf, Southern Giant, Curled, and Fordhook varieties are good for freezing. Wash thoroughly in cold running water, eliminating soil particles. Discard main stem and any coarse leaves. Water-blanch (preferred) for 50 seconds or steam-blanch for 90 seconds. Agitate basket containing greens during the blanching period. Chill in cold running water for 5 minutes, drain, and package.

New Zealand Spinach. Any variety will give only a fair frozen product. Small leaves are preferred. Wash thoroughly in cold running water, eliminating soil particles. Discard main stem. Water-blanch (preferred) for 70 seconds or steam-blanch for 2 minutes. Agitate basket containing greens during blanching period. Chill in cold running water for about 5 minutes, drain, and package.

Okra. The Green Velvet, Perkins, Long Pod, and Clemson Spineless varieties are good for freezing. Select pods that are young and tender. At this stage of maturity, stems will snap when pods are broken from plant.

Wash pods thoroughly to clean them of soil; discard stems. Separate into small and large pods. Steam-blanch (preferred small pods for 3 minutes and large ones for 4, or water-blanch small pods for 2 minutes and large ones for 3. Chill for 2 minutes in cold running water, drain, and package.

Parsnips. The Hollow Crown and Marrowfat varieties are excellent for freezing Mature parsnips which have been held in the ground during the winter are best.

Trim off tops. Wash in cold running water. Peel, and dice in ½-inch cubes or split lengthwise in ¾-inch sticks. Steam blanching is preferred. Steam-blanch cube for 100 seconds, sticks for 3 minutes; or water-blanch cubes for 60 seconds, stick

Low in fats, high in protein, inexpensive and easy to prepare, seafood has gained in popularity by leaps and bounds in recent years. A tasty and unusual seafood meal can be prepared in a matter of minutes by simply creating a new variation of the basic broiling, baking or frying recipe. Add wine or lime juice to baked fish. Pour sour cream sauce over broiled fish. Serve fried fish with horseradish and cucumber sauce. Tempting side dishes include raw spinach and mushroom salad with bacon and lemon, broiled tomatoes topped with cheese, delicately sauteed vegetables with soy sauce.

During the summer, that American favorite,
the sandwich, is transformed from a
midnight specialty into a full fledged main
course. Sandwich meals can actually be quite nutritious
and tempting. And they have the added advantage
of being light and easy to prepare.
Start with varieties of bread — rye, whole wheat, sourdough, white,
corn, pumpernickel, black. Then combine imagination and leftovers to make interesting new fillings. Pieces of chicken, turkey
and pork can be chopped up and mixed with mayonnaise, relish,
chopped onions, celery, peppers, mustard and horseradish in any
reasonable combination. Finely flaked leftover fish may be blended
with sour cream or mayonnaise and lemon juice, salt and pepper.
To add interest garnish plates with wedges of fresh fruit,
cheese, olives, pickles, eggs stuffed with crab meat,
shrimp, caviar or deviled egg filling.
Complete the dinner with fresh corn on the cob
or a salad plate, milk for children and
iced tea with lemon and mint for adults.

Look for plump
kernels, brown
silk and green
husk to insure
fresh, sweet
flavor in corn
on the cob.

Curry, the basic spice ingredient used in Indian cookery, is really a combination of several different spices. In Hindi the mixture is called garam masala which means "hot spice." A slab of stone and a stone rolling pin are used to grind the fresh spices — peppercorn, roasted cumin and coriander, ginger, cayenne pepper, shelled cardamom seeds, garlic, turmeric and others. The resulting paste is used to prepare stew-like dishes with meat, eggs, fish and vegetables. Liven up commercial curry with extra chili, cumin, coriander and ginger to obtain a more authentic Indian flavor.

Serve fish curry with boiled rice, tomato chutney, pan fried potatoes and okra. White rice can be cooked with turmeric for added color and aroma. Make a cooling raita by grating a cucumber, covering with salt and refrigerating for 30 minutes. When ready to serve, squeeze the water out of the cucumber and mix the meat with a pint of whipped yogurt. Dust lightly with curry powder

Charcoal grilled chicken is delicious basted with barbecue sauce or sprinkled with lemon juice. See Barbecue for tips on cooking and sauce suggestions.

Ratatouille, originating in Provence, France, is a delight to prepare and a pleasure to eat. Slice or cube approximately equivalent amounts of zucchini, eggplant, green pepper and tomato. Saute sliced onions and garlic in olive oil in a heavy saucepan. Arrange the rest of the vegetables in the skillet, seasoning with salt, pepper and additional olive oil. Simmer the ingredients slowly until done. Ratatouille is excellent as a vegetable side dish, a filling for crêpes or a sauce on rice.

How to keep a hungry,
young family happy
during those summer
picnic months?
Plenty of fresh fruit
and vegetables — apples,
peaches, tomatoes, corn,
melon — deep fried
chicken and buckets of
homemade cole slaw and
potato salad.
Hard cooked eggs, dough-
nuts, sandwiches and
cookies and lots of
lemonade and iced tea to
quench the inevitable
hot afternoon thirst.

for 2 minutes. Chill for 5 minutes in cold running water, drain, and package.

Peas. The following varieties are recommended for freezing: Thomas Laxton, Dark Podded Thomas Laxton (excellent); Improved Gradus, Gradus, Laxton's Progress, World's Record, Glacier, Morse's Market, Stratagem, Dwarf Alderman, Hendredfold, Stridealong, Little Marvel, Alderman (Telephone), President Wilson, Onward, Banqueteer Asgrow 40, Laxton's Cropper, Teton, Laxtonian, and Admiral Beatty (good). Slightly immature peas are better for freezing then those that are old and starchy. Pods should be well filled, but not hard and wrinkled. Shell a quantity before beginning to blanch, and do not wash peas after they have been shelled; discard those that are hard and starchy. Water-blanching is preferred. Water-blanch small peas for 45 seconds and large ones for 60, or steam-blanch small peas for 90 seconds and large ones for 2 minutes. Chill in cold running water for 3 minutes, drain, and package.

Peas, Blackeyed (Field Peas). The Grand Ramshorn, Bluegoose, and Crowder varieties are good for freezing. Harvest when pods are flexible but not dry. Proceed as for peas, above. Water-blanch (preferred) for 2 minutes, or steam-blanch for 3 minutes. Chill in cold running water for 3 minutes, drain, and package.

Peppers, Sweet. The California Wonder and Windsor varieties are good for freezing. Peppers should be well formed and crisp. Soft spots indicate overmaturity. Wash; discard stems and seeds. They may be frozen in halves or in slices, and either blanching method is satisfactory. Water-blanch slices 2 minutes, halves 3; steam-blanch slices 3 minutes, halves 4. Chill for several minutes in cold running water, drain, and package.

Potatoes, Irish. These varieties are good for freezing: Chippewa, Katahdin, Hoama, Bliss Triumph, Smooth Rural, and Green Mountain. Mature potatoes (with dry vines) should be dug before a frost and allowed to stand 30 days before freezing. New potatoes are dug when they are about 1 inch in diameter and then frozen immediately.

Mature potatoes freeze well only for French frying. Wash, peel, and cut into ¼-inch sticks. Either blanching method is satisfactory. Water-blanch for 2 minutes or steam-blanch for 3. Chill in cold running water from 3 to 5 minutes, drain, and package.

Wash new potatoes well to rid them of soil, and scrub vigorously to remove the tender skins. Steam-blanch those under 1 inch in diameter for 3 minutes, those 1 inch or over for 5 minutes. Chill in cold running water for 5 minutes, drain, and package.

Potatoes, Sweet. The Porto Rico and Nancy Hall varieties are good for freezing. Allow mature potatoes to cure for 30 days before freezing. Wash thoroughly to remove soil. Cook until soft, and let stand at room temperature to cool. Peel, and mash or slice. If potatoes are to be mashed, dip them (peeled) in a citric acid solution for 5 seconds. If they are sliced, dip slices in the solution. (Prepare the solution by dissolving 1 tablespoon of citric acid, or ½ cup of lemon juice, in one quart of cold water.) Package.

Pumpkin. All pie varieties freeze very well. Peel, and cut in 1-inch cubes. Steam the pumpkin until soft, then mash. Allow it to cool to room temperature before packing.

Rhubarb. The Macdonald, Ruby, Linnaeus, and Victoria varieties are excellent. Others yield a good product of good flavor, but have a less desirable color. The early spring cuttings give the best product. Select red-covered stalks. Cut off top leaves. Wash stalks in cold running water. Cut into 1-inch lengths. Water-blanch (preferred) for 90 seconds or steam-blanch for 2 minutes. Chill in cold running water for a few minutes and package.

Rutabagas. The Long Island Improved, American Purple Top, and Sweet German (Macomber) are the best varieties. Cut off tops, wash in cold water, peel, and dice in ½-inch cubes. Steam-blanching is preferred. Steam-blanch for 70 seconds or water-blanch for 60. Chill in cold running water for 3 minutes, drain, and package.

Spinach. Recommended varieties are: Nobel, Hollandia, King of Denmark, Viking, Virginia Savoy (excellent); Old Dominion, Princess Juliana, Prickly Winter, Viroflay, Broad Flanders, Long Standing Bloomsdale, and Victoria (good). In the East the savoy type spinach is superior to the broad leaf type; in the West the broad leaf type is slightly superior. Wash thoroughly in cold running water, eliminating soil particles. Discard the thick main stem. Water-blanch for 2½ minutes (preferred), or steam-blanch for 3½ minutes. Chill thoroughly in cold running water for at least 3 minutes, drain, and package.

Squash, Summer. Summer Crookneck and Zucchini are the only varieties recommended. Wash in cold running water. Slice in ½-inch slices. Water-blanch (preferred) for 3½ minutes or steam-blanch for 4½ minutes. Chill in cold running water for about 5 minutes, drain, and package.

Squash, winter. Golden Delicious and Golden Hubbard varieties are excellent; Green Hubbard and Blue Hubbard, good. Allow squash to ripen on the vine until the rind is hard. Peel, and cut in 1-inch pieces. Cook until tender in either steam or boiling water; steam is preferred. Mash, allow product to cool to room temperature, and package.

Swiss chard. Lucullus, Fordhook, and Ruby are excellent varieties. Others produce a good product. Wash thoroughly in cold running water. Discard main stems. Water-blanch (preferred) for 2 minutes, or steam-blanch for 3 minutes. Agitate basket containing greens during blanching. Chill in cold running water for 5 minutes, drain, and package.

Tomatoes. Select fully mature, firm, vine-ripened fruit. Wash and blanch tomatoes; steam- or water-blanch them for 2 minutes. Chill in cold running water for 5 minutes. Peel, and discard blossom ends and cores. Package.

Turnips. Purple Top Strapleaf, White Globe, and Purple Top White Globe are good varieties for freezing. Cut off tops, and wash turnips in cold running water. Peel, and dice in ½-inch cubes. Steam-blanch (preferred) for 70 seconds, or water-blanch for 60 seconds. Chill in cold running water for 5 minutes, drain, and package.

Turnip greens. The varieties grown especially for greens are best. Wash thoroughly in cold running water, eliminating coarse leaves as well as soil particles. Water-blanch (preferred) for 60 seconds, or steam-blanch for 100 seconds. Agitate basket containing greens during water-blanching period. Chill for 5 minutes in cold running water, drain, and package.

Using Frozen Vegetables

If your frozen storage facilities are in a locker plant, you may wish to bring several packages of vegetables home at one time. If you do this, the frozen vegetables may be kept safely in the freezing compartment of your refrigerator for 5 to 7 days.

Frozen vegetables may be cooked when they are solidly frozen, partly thawed, or completely thawed. Most vegetables are best cooked while they are still frozen. However, corn on the cob should always be completely thawed before cooking. Spinach and other greens should also be thawed, at least partly. Frozen vegetables that are to be used in casserole dishes will usually have to be thawed before they can be mixed with the other ingredients.

Brine-pack vegetables cannot usually be removed from the package until it is almost thawed, and you may have to allow them to thaw completely. Always cook them in the brine in which they were packed, adding no more water unless they boil dry. Serve them with the liquid remaining in the cooking vessel.

If you wish to serve a frozen vegetable for dinner, the package can be placed in the lowest part of the refrigerator in the morning. For quicker thawing, place it before an electric fan.

Every second saved during the cooking of the vegetables and every second saved in speeding them from range to table aids them in their retention of valuable nutrients. Hence, our vegetable cookery rules: (1) Cook in a small amount of water. (For most vegetables, ¼ to ½ cup of water is sufficient; for greens, a smaller amount of water is sufficient, and sometimes none is needed.) (2) Cook for the shortest possible time.

Have water boiling when you add the vegetables. Bring the water back to a boil and break up the pack of vegetables with a fork. This will cool the cooking water again, so bring it back to a boil; then turn to a lower heat and finish cooking. Count cooking time from the start of the last boiling period. Serve the vegetables immediately on cooking, dishing up the small amount of remaining liquid.

Since frozen vegetables have been blanched during their preparation for freezing, they require much shorter cooking periods than fresh vegetables. Following is a cooking time chart to guide you in cooking the more common vegetables. The time chart is only a guide because cooking time varies with variety, maturity, and size of pieces.

Asparagus...................5 to 8 min.
Beans, Green Snap or Wax..12 to 15 min.
Beans, Lima..............16 to 20 min.
Beets, Whole.............18 to 20 min.
Beets, Cubed or Sliced..Heat to Serving
                                          Temperature
Beet Greens..............10 to 12 min.
Broccoli...................5 to 7 min.
Brussels Sprouts.............3 to 4 min.
Carrots...................5 to 10 min.
Cauliflower.................5 to 8 min.
Corn, Whole Kernel and
                 on Cob...3 to 4 min.
Kohlrabi.................8 to 10 min.
Mushrooms..............10 to 15 min.
      (Sauté—do not cook in water)
Mustard greens...........12 to 15 min.
Peas.......................6 to 8 min.
Rhubarb.................10 to 12 min.
Spinach....................4 to 6 min.
Squash, Summer............4 to 6 min.
Squash, Winter........Heat to Serving
                                          Temperature
Swiss Chard..............8 to 10 min.
Turnips..................12 to 15 min.
Turnip Greens............15 to 20 min.

PREPARATION OF FRUITS

Whether fruits are sliced or packed whole, sweetening is an important step in their preparation. There are two ways of sweetening fruit. One is to add dry sugar to slightly crushed or cut-up fruit and stir gently until enough natural juice has been extracted to form a sirup. Obviously, only those fruits which have a high juice content, such as strawberries, raspberries, and cherries, can be prepared in this manner. Dry fruits such as peaches require a sugar sirup, prepared in advance and chilled, which is poured over them after they have been placed in the container.

Some fruits can be prepared either way—notably raspberries and strawberries. In the case of the latter a better result is obtained if they are sliced and mixed with dry sugar rather than frozen whole.

A few fruits may be frozen without sugar, namely cranberries and blueberries, but here again blueberries are better when slightly crushed and mixed with dry sugar.

Some fruits like apples, oranges, and grapefruit, prepared for table use or for use in cooking, are handled in the manner of vegetables—blanched, chilled and packed.

Peaches, apples, plums, apricots, pears and white cherries darken and discolor

rapidly when cut and exposed to air for any length of time. To reduce this darkening (oxidation), which changes the flavor as well as the color, add 1 teaspoon of ascorbic acid powder to each 4 cups of prepared sirup. Ascorbic acid is obtainable at drugstores and may be had in 100-mg. tablet form as well. Four tablets to each 4 cups of sirup will give a comparable solution. Ascorbic acid is concentrated Vitamin C in a readily assimilable form. The sirup when poured over the fruit will preserve much of its color and flavor during freezing and storage and subsequent thawing.

Sirups. Sirups are made by adding sugar to water, fruit juices, or corn sirup and allowing the mixture to stand, stirring occasionally, until the sugar is dissolved. Sirups should be chilled before packing with fruit in containers.

SIRUP CHART

Desired concentration	*Cups sugar per pint of water*
30%	1
40%	1 ⅔
50%	2 ½
60%	3 ½
65%	4 ½
70%	5 ½

When using corn sirup, remember that it is not as sweet as granulated sugar sirup, and therefore a greater proportion of corn sirup is necessary to provide sweetness equal to that of sugar sirup at any concentration. There are certain corn sirups obtainable today which are sweeter than ordinary corn sirup and very satisfactory for use in freezing fruit. A typical product is Sweetose White Sirup which is obtainable in five-pound jars.

CORN SIRUP

Desired concentration	*Water per 5-lb. jar of Sweetose*
50%	2 pts., 1 cup
60%	1 pt.
65%	1 cup
70%	½ cup

Use this sirup in the same manner as sugar sirup when higher concentrations are required.

Apples. Recommended varieties are: Greening, Baldwin, Northern Spy, Rome Beauty, Stayman Winesap, York Imperial,

Grimes Golden, (these varieties best for pie); Wealthy, Oldenburg (or Duchess), Jonathan, Yellow Newton Pippin, Spitzenburg, Stark, Cortland (very good); Gravenstein, McIntosh (satisfactory). Choose apples of good maturity, with a tight skin and bright color free from dark spots. They should be firm and not mealy.

To prepare, peel, core, and slice in twelfths. Slice only a few apples at a time to prevent their becoming discolored by exposure to air. Slice them into a weak brine solution (2 tablespoons salt per gallon of water) until you are ready to blanch. Steam-blanch for 90 seconds, chill in iced water, drain quickly, and package dry.

Another method is to use a chemical to preserve color. After slicing about 20 apples into the brine solution, make a fresh solution of sodium bisulfite or sodium sulfite dissolving 2 teaspoons of either chemical in 1 gallon of water. Sodium bisulfite and sodium sulfite can be purchased at a drugstore; buy either the U.S.P. or the C.P. grade. Only earthenware, stainless steel, glass, enameled, or aluminum ware should be used for this solution, and the same solution may be used for 4 or 5 lots of apples. Keep the slices immersed in the solution by covering the container with a plate or dish. After 5 minutes in the solution, remove the slices to an earthenware, china, or glass bowl and hold in the refrigerator for 4 or 5 hours before freezing. Package dry with no sugar or sirup.

Apricots. Of the varieties grown in California and the Pacific Northwest, the Tilton is the best; Royal, Blenheim, and Moorpark are very good. Apricots may be frozen whole or in halves, with or without skins. To peel, immerse fruit in boiling water for 15 to 30 minutes, then in running cold water for a minute or two, and rub off peels. If they are frozen with skins, wash in cold running water; then halve and pit, or leave whole. Pack into freezing container, allowing head space, and cover with 60 percent sirup. Close container.

Blackberries. Berries should be sweet, soft, plump, and glossy-skinned. Wash them thoroughly in cold running water or, preferably, in water containing ice. Clean them, and eliminate red and green berries. Fill freezing container, allowing head space; cover with 50 or 60 percent sirup; and close container.

Blueberries. In Maine and Massachusetts the wild low-bush and high-bush blue-

berry give an excellent frozen product. In New York and New Jersey the following varieties are excellent: Concord, Rubel, Pioneer, Rancocas, Cabot, and Jersey. In the Pacific Northwest states such varieties as the Rancocas, June, Concord, Katherine, Jersey, and Rubel varieties are very good; the Adams, Harding, Cabot, Grover Sam, and Alaska Wild are good varieties. Berries should be picked when sweet and soft.

Wash berries in cold running water or, preferably, in water containing ice. Pick out stems and leaves. Mix berries with dry sugar, using 5 or 6 pounds of fruit to 1 pound of sugar. Stir gently until juice is drawn from berries and sugar is partly dissolved. Fill container, allowing head space, and close it.

Alternate procedure: Same procedure as above, except no sugar or sirup is used; the berries are simply packed in the container. Pack container full.

Boysenberries. Follow the same directions as for blackberries.

Cantaloupe. Use only soft full-slip melons. Halve, scrape out seeds, and slice. Then peel off rind and hard flesh, and cut soft flesh into ½- to ¾-inch cubes. Mix cubes with sugar, using 1 pound of sugar to each 5 pounds of fruit. Stir until sugar is partly dissolved. Pack into containers, allowing head space, and close containers.

Cherries, sour and sub-acid. The Montmorency and English Morello varieties are the best sour cherry varieties. Some believe the Montmorency to be slightly superior to the English Morello. Cherries should be picked when soft-ripe. Wash them in water containing ice. Remove stems and pits. Add 1 pound of sugar to each 4 or 5 pounds of cherries; stir gently until sugar is partly dissolved in juice drawn from the cherries. Fill containers, allowing head space, and close them.

Cherries, sweet. The sweet cherry can give a very good product, but not as good as that of the sour cherry. Recommended varieties are: Lambert, Bing, Black Tartarian, Napoleon, Republican, Bacon, and Windsor. Soft, sweet, fully tree-ripened fruit should be used. Wash cherries in water containing ice. Remove stems. Pack, allowing head space; cover with 40 or 50 percent sirup; and close container.

Cranberries. Almost all of the New England and Massachusetts varieties freeze very well. Howes and Early Black varieties are somewhat superior. They should have a deep red, uniform color and a firm, glossy skin. Wash in cold running water. Remove stems, pieces of leaves, and poor berries. Pack container full and freeze dry, using no sugar or sirup.

Alternate procedure: Prepare berries as above. Cook them as you ordinarily would for cranberry sauce, adding sugar to taste. Let sauce cool to room temperature. Pour into container, leaving head space, and close it.

Currants. Almost any variety produces a very good frozen product, but the Perfection variety seems to be superior. Use fully ripe, bright red fruit. Wash it in cold running water or, preferably, in water containing ice. Remove stems. Add 1 pound of sugar for each 3 pounds of fruit, and stir gently until sugar is partly dissolved in the juice drawn from the fruit. Fill container, allowing head space, and close it.

Dewberries. Same as blackberries.

Figs. The Mission, Kadota, and Adriatic varieties are good for freezing. Use soft, fully tree-ripened fruit, not fruit that has begun to split or become sour. Wash in water containing ice, and eliminate fruit which is not properly ripe. Peel, if desired; pack container, allowing head space; cover with 50 or 60 percent sirup; and close container.

Gooseberries. All varieties produce an excellent frozen product. Use fully matured, soft-ripe berries. Remove stems and blossom ends. Wash in cold running water. Crush slightly, and add 1 pound of sugar to each 3 pounds of berries; stir gently until sugar is partly dissolved in juice drawn from berries. Fill container, allowing head space, and close it.

Grapefruit. The Duncan variety is excellent for freezing; the Marsh Seedling and Seedling are also very good. Fully matured, tree-ripened, soft fruit should be used. Immerse it for 3 minutes in boiling water, and cool in cold running water. Peel, remove all white membrane, break into sections, and remove section membranes and seeds. Pack in container, allowing head space; cover with 60 to 70 percent sirup; and close container.

Loganberries. Same as blackberries.

Mixed fruit. Many fruits can be combined to be frozen as a mixture for salads, fruit cocktails, and desserts. Select fruit for good maturity—soft-ripe but not mushy. Wash in cold water, or water containing ice; peel, core, pit, etc. according to individual directions given for each fruit. Then mix together in desired proportions. Package, allowing head space; cover with 60 or 70 percent sirup; and close packages.

If an out-of-season fruit is needed, use the frozen product. Allow it to thaw enough so that it can be mixed with the fresh fruits, but do not allow it to become warm before mixing it.

Suggested fruit combinations are: (1) pineapples, apples, cantaloupe, boysenberries or youngberries, red raspberries, and maraschino cherries; (2) apricots, boysenberries or youngberries, red raspberries, and pineapple; (3) sliced peaches and red raspberries; (4) sliced peaches and sliced strawberries; (5) apricots, pineapple, and cherries; and (6) pineapple, rhubarb, and strawberries.

Muskmelon. See cantaloupe.

Nectarines. The Stanwick and Gower varieties are excellent; the New Boy, very good. The procedure is the same as that given for peaches.

Oranges. The Valencia variety is superior to all others. The Florida Pineapple and Seedling varieties are also very good. Fully mature, tree-ripened fruit is best for freezing. To loosen peels, immerse in boiling water for 2 minutes, and cool in running cold water. Peel, break into sections, and remove all membranes and seeds. Pack sections, allowing head space; cover with 60 or 70 percent sirup; and close container.

Peaches. The yellow varieties are superior to the white varieties. The J. H. Hale variety is one of the best. The Hale Haven and South Haven varieties are also excellent; Eclipse, Elberta, Ideal, Massasoit, Marigold, Vedette, Viceroy, and Veteran are very good. The Sunbeam is also a good variety, but it gives a rather poor yield. Tree-ripened fruit is best. It should be soft-ripe but not mushy. To loosen skins, immerse in boiling water for about 1 minute, and then chill in cold water for 3 minutes. Rub skins off. Cut out bruised and imperfect portions. Peaches may be frozen in halves or in slices. For halves, remove pits and pack. For slices, slice sections around pit directly into container. Allow head space for either slices or halves. Cover peaches with 60 percent sirup and close container.

Pears. Pears do not give a particularly good frozen product, and the Bartlett is about the only variety that can be recommended. Care must be taken to select pears neither too green nor too soft and mushy. They should be picked green and left to ripen. Wash them in running cold water. Peel; cut out bruised and imperfect portions; core and quarter, or slice and dice if you prefer. Pack, allowing head space. Cover with 60 percent sirup, and close container.

Pineapples. Any of the standard market varieties are suitable for freezing. Select soft-ripe fruit. Top leaves will pull out easily at the desired stage of maturity. Peel; core; and slice, dice, or cut in wedges or sticks. Pack, allowing head space; cover with 60 percent sirup; and close container.

Plums and Fresh Prunes. The Italian prune is superior; the Stanley and Hungarian are excellent; the Redwing, Damson, Yellow Egg, and German prune varieties are also very good. Tree-ripened fruit is essential. It should be soft but not mushy, fully ripe, and sweet. Wash fruit in cold running water. Pit and quarter or halve it. Pack it, allowing head space; cover with 60 percent sirup; and close the package.

Raspberries. Black varieties: In New York and the Pacific Northwest the Bristol is superior to all other varieties; in Tennessee the Cumberland is best. The Cumberland, Plum Farmer, Munger, and Gregg varieties grown in the Pacific Northwest may also be used for freezing.

Purple varieties: The Sodus, Marion, and Columbian are best for freezing.

Red varieties: Wherever the Cuthbert variety is grown, it is superior to other varieties. In New England the Herbert is excellent; the Ranere, good. In New York the Viking and Milton are excellent; the Taylor and Lloyd George, very good. In the Middle Atlantic States the Latham, Chief, and Ranere (St. Regis) are excellent. In the Pacific Northwest the Washington is excellent; the Ranere, Lloyd George, Viking, Cayuga, Latham, Newburgh, and Ersking Park (very good); the Chief, King, Herbert, Antwerp, Utah, and Marlboro (good).

Select fully matured, soft-ripe, sweet fruit for the best frozen product. Pick berries while they are still plump. Clean berries by washing them in water containing ice. Eliminate those that are im-

mature, moldy, etc. Add 1 pound of sugar to each 4 or 5 pounds of berries. Stir gently until sugar is partly dissolved in juice drawn from berries. Fill container, allowing head space, and close it.

Rhubarb. Directions are given under vegetables.

Strawberries. Many varieties freeze well, but the following are superior: Marshall, Corvallis, Klondike, Vanrouge, Burgundy, and Blakemore. The Howard Supreme, Chesapeake, Big Joe, Big Late, Fruitland, Jersey Giant, Dunlap, Gandy, and Redheart are very good. Howard 17 (Premier), First Quality, Dorsett, Bliss, Fairfax, Lucky Strike, McClintock #98, Nancy Lee, Progressive, Missionary, Kellogg's Delicious, Parson's Beauty, Gibson, Kellogg's Marvel, Henderson, Aroma, Ettersburg #121, Catskill, and Culver are good. Select berries (vine-ripened) that are soft-ripe but not mushy. Full red color is essential to good flavor.

Wash berries in water containing ice. Hull, and eliminate berries which are immature or soft and mushy. Cut in $\frac{3}{8}$-inch slices, and add 1 pound of sugar for each 4 or 5 pounds of berries. Stir gently until sugar is partly dissolved in juice drawn from berries. Fill container, allowing head space, and close it.

Alternate procedure: Wash berries in ice water, eliminating berries that are immature, moldy, or mushy. Pack whole berries into container allowing head space, cover with 50 or 60 percent sirup, and close package.

Tomatoes. Directions are given under vegetables.

Youngberries. See Blackberries.

<h3 style="text-align:center">USING FROZEN FRUITS</h3>

Thawing time for fruits on the lower shelf of a refrigerator will range from 5 to 10 hours. It will take 3 or 4 hours at ordinary room temperature. Before an electric fan, the thawing time is reduced to about 1 hour. Fruits frozen in watertight packages may be placed in a pan of cold running water for thawing; this will take 40 to 45 minutes. If you are in a hurry to serve the frozen fruit, you may place the watertight package in lukewarm water (be sure that it is no hotter than this!) for 5 minutes and then transfer it to cold running water; a pint package will be thawed in about 30 minutes.

Do not let fruits thaw to too warm a temperature before serving, but try to time the thawing of fruits so they come to the table with a few ice crystals still glistening in the fruit. If you find this too cold, try dishing them out just before you sit down to begin the meal.

Frozen fruits may be used in preparing pies and other dishes as are fresh fruits. They make wonderful out-of-season up-side-down cakes, shortcakes, cobblers, muffins, fruit whips, ice creams, sherbets and ices, and salads. Thaw the fruit just enough so that you can work with it as you do with fresh fruit, but never allow it to become warmed up in the process of preparing pies or dessert dishes.

Frozen fruits make especially fine jams and jellies—even better than those made from the fresh fruit because freezing and thawing cause the juices to be released from the cells of the fruit and the natural fruit flavor and color to be dissolved into the juice.

When cooking with frozen fruit bear in mind that sugar has been added during the preparation for freezing, so allowances for this must be made. Additional sweetening is seldom needed when frozen fruits are used in pies, although berry juice may require thickening. Jams and jellies will, of course, need additional sugar, but add only enough to make the total amount (that added at the time of freezing plus that added at the time of cooking) equal the amount called for in the recipe.

Freezing Meats

The slaughtering and butchering will probably have to be done at a local locker plant or meat market. Unless you have experience and a suitable place for chilling and aging meat, the chances for waste and spoilage are too great a risk to run. It is wise, however, to be familiar with the various cuts of meat and how each can be frozen to best advantage, so that you can direct the meat cutter to get the maximum from the carcass.

For proper chilling, meat should be held in a room maintained at 32° to 34° F., and it should be chilled down to a temperature as close to 32° F. as possible. Thorough chilling is all that is necessary for pork, lamb, and veal; 24 hours is usually adequate, and it is advisable not to chill these meats much longer than 48 hours. This is especially important in the case of pork, the fat of which may turn rancid during storage if it is held for too long a period. Pork fat held in a cooler for not more than 48 hours at 32° F. before it is frozen, will remain in good condition for approximately one year when stored at 0° F. As for mutton, a better product will result if it is aged for a short period, from five to seven days, at 32° to 34° F. Aging tenderizes beef, so beef should be held for at least five days, preferably from eight to ten days.

When the family meat needs are smaller, the arrangement of a whole carcass for butchering may not be desired. Commercial cuts, or halves or quarters, may be purchased and then cut into whatever table cuts are desired. For example, a saddle of lamb may be purchased from the butcher who will cut it into chops and roasts, grind some for lamb patties, etc.

The cutting of a meat carcass for freezing is very different from the ordinary method of cutting. As much bone and fat as possible is removed in order to make the proportion of edible meat stored in the freezer as great as possible and, consequently, to conserve freezer space. A rolled roast, for example, occupies much less space than a standing rib roast; yet the two pieces yield the same proportion of edible meat. The size of roasts and steaks should be determined by the size of the family so that no more meat than is needed for cooking will be thawed at one time.

Beef cuts. Round. Can be cut into round steak, the top and bottom rounds of which may be cut of a thickness suitable for Swiss steaks. The heel and shank may be frozen for use as stew or soup meat or may be boned and ground for hamburg.

Rump. Fine for pot roasts. These may be boned and rolled, or they may be frozen with the bone, which does not add considerable bulk in this section.

Loin. From its large end come the sirloin and pin bone sirloin steaks; from the small end come the porterhouse, T-bone, and club steaks. These may be cut to any thickness desired; if you plan to use them for broiling, you will want them at least ¾ inch thick.

Flank. Can be made into flank steak for braising, cut up for stew meat, or ground for hamburg.

Plate. Can be cut into suitably-sized pieces to be used for boiling beef for soups and stews; it can be boned or rolled. The short ribs section can be cut from the plate and frozen separately.

Rib. The 2½-inch end piece may be cut off separately and used as short ribs; the remainder, cut up for roasts. It is better to have these roasts boned and rolled to conserve freezer space.

Brisket. The foreshank may be used as cuts for soups or stews, or it may be boned and ground for hamburg. The remainder can be made into corned beef or used for ground meat or stews.

Lamb cuts. Leg. The loin end may be cut off for roasting and three center cuts may be cut for broiling, leaving the shank end for stewing or braising. The leg may also be French style (whole leg with shank trimmed) or American style (loin end cut off and leg made into two roasts).

Loin. May be made into chops, or may be boned and rolled into roasts.

Rack. This, the fore part of the loin, may be made into rib chops or roasts.

Shoulder. Shoulder chops, boned and rolled roasts, and neck slices for stews come from this section.

Shank and Breast. This section may be used for stew meat, or it may be boned and ground for lamb loaf or patties.

Pork cuts. Ham. Fresh ham may be cut from the butt end and from the shank end. Use the center slices for steaks.

Rib section. Bacon and spareribs come from this section. The fatty portion may be used for salt pork or to make lard.

Loin. The outside fatty section can be used to make lard. Lean portion can be cut into loin or rib chops and roasts (preferably boned and rolled).

Butt. This section may be used for sausage meat; or it may be cut into a few blade steaks, the remainder to be used as boned and rolled roasts.

Jowls. May be used for bacon squares or in making pork sausage.

Veal cuts. Round. Round veal steaks, round roasts, boned and rolled rump roasts, and cut-up stew meat may be had from this section.

Loin. Loin chops, kidney veal chops, and sirloin steaks are desirable cuts from this section.

Rib. The small end may be cut into rib chops; the larger end, made into rolled rib roasts.

Breast. Can be cut up for stew meat, or boned and ground for veal loaf or patties.

Shoulder. The loin and shank side can be used for arm and blade steaks; the remainder, rolled into roasts and ground for patties and veal loaf.

Shank. Can be left intact or ground.

COOKING FROZEN MEATS

Meat may be thawed before or during the cooking process. In the case of large roasts, cooking is more uniform if the meat is at least two-thirds thawed before it is put into the oven. Small cuts of one or two pounds will thaw on the lower shelf of the refrigerator in five to ten hours; a four-pound roast will require 24 to 36 hours. This is the best way to thaw meats, but you may use either of the two methods given for speeding up the process. If a still quicker method is thought necessary, place the meat in a warm oven and let an electric fan blow into the oven.

When meat is completely or partially thawed, it is cooked in much the same manner as fresh meat. Stewing or braising meats may not have to be cooked as long as usual on account of the tendering effect of freezing, but solidly frozen roasts require from 15 to 20 more minutes of cooking time per pound than they otherwise would.

FREEZING POULTRY

Selection. The following information will be aid to you in selecting poultry for broiling, frying, etc.:

Broilers. 1 to 2½ pounds; 8 to 12 weeks old; smooth, thin skin; tender muscles with very thin connective tissue; small amount of fat under skin over the back; flexible tipped breastbone.

Fryers. 2½ to 3½ pounds; 14 to 20 weeks old; meaty enough to be disjointed and cut into serving pieces; noticeable layering of fat underneath the skin; same as for broilers except in size and age.

Roasters. Over 3½ pounds; 5 to 9 months old male; tender, soft-meated muscles; smooth skin; large enough and meaty enough to be roasted whole; excellent layering of fat underneath skin; flexible-tipped breastbone; connective tissue only slightly more developed than in fryer.

Capons. 4 pounds and over; 7 to 10 months old unsexed male; popular size, 6 to 7 pounds; full-breasted; yielding a high proportion of white meat.

Pullets. 2 ½ to 5 ½ pounds; 4 to 9 months old; similar to roaster except that body is shorter and plumper; flexible-tipped breastbone; smaller weights often used as fryers.

Fowls. Female of any weight; over 1 year old; thick, coarse skin; muscles well-developed with thick connective tissue; high proportion of fat underneath skin; breastbone no longer flexible.

Turkeys and Ducks. The same general characteristics given for roasters will help in the selection of turkeys and ducks. Both should be plump and full-breasted, preferably with short bodies. Hen turkeys are better if you desire them from 8 to 15 pounds; toms are better birds weighing from 16 to 25 pounds.

Killing the bird. Unless poultry is killed, bled, and plucked properly, an inferior product will result. Starve poultry for 24 hours before killing. Hang the bird by the feet and, with a knife in one hand (holding the bird's mouth open with the other hand), insert the point of the knife down the throat to sever the jugular vein. This will start the bleeding immediately. Insert the knife in the bird's mouth again, this time in the cleft of the roof of the mouth, running it back in a line between the eye and ear to pierce the third lobe of the brain. Give the knife a quarter turn to destroy brain tissues. After this procedure, main tail and wing feathers can be removed immediately.

The bird can also be plucked by the semi-scald method which will render over-scalding (cooking) impossible. For the latter method use water at 125° to 130° F. Dip the bird for 20 to 30 seconds, and then pluck. Pinfeathers may be removed by singeing or by the wax method. For the wax method birds are dipped or rolled in melted paraffin until their skins are coated, and then laid aside for a few minutes. When the coating is stripped off, the pinfeathers will come with it.

Poultry should be refrigerated overnight before being prepared for freezing.

Preparing fowl for freezing. Roasters. Remove head, shanks, and oil sac. Make as small a cut as possible in abdomen and draw carefully, making sure that lungs are completely removed. Wash in cold running water, and drain. Clean the giblets separately, and wrap them separately in moisture-proof paper; insert them in cavity of roaster. Package as roasts. *See also* CHICKEN.

Broilers. Remove head, shanks, and oil sac. Slit young, soft-boned birds down the back along the backbone, remove their entrails, and then cut them in two pieces along the breastbone. Wash the halves in cold running water and drain. Clean and wrap giblets separately; wrap them in moistureproof paper. Place two sheets of moistureproof paper between halves of bird, also place wrapped giblets between halves, and wrap for freezing as you would roasts.

Disjointing poultry. Remove head, shanks, and oil sac. Draw bird, and disjoint or cut up into serving pieces. Wash in cold running water and drain. Clean giblets separately and pack them separately in moistureproof paper. Pack the cut-up chicken in cartons such as are used for steaks.

COOKING FROZEN POULTRY

Poultry, especially roasters, should be completely thawed before being cooked. Broilers and cut-up poultry should at least be partly thawed, enough that the pieces can be separated. Allow 6 to 8 hours for a three-pound bird to thaw in the refrigerator. Except for the addition of extra cooking time for solidly frozen poultry, frozen poultry is cooked in the same manner as fresh.

FREEZING FISH

If fish are small, they may be frozen whole; medium-sized fish can be filleted if desired; large fish may be cut into steaks, into family-sized "chunks," or left whole for baking purposes.

To freeze small whole fish, scale, eviscerate, and wash thoroughly in cold running water. Cut off head, fins, and tail. Wrap each fish individually in moistureproof cellophane; then pack in a suitable-sized waxed carton. Package as steak.

To freeze fillets, scale, eviscerate, and wash in cold running water. Make a cut across body just below head and gill. With a very sharp knife and starting at the tail, run the knife lengthwise down the fish, first on one side and then on the other, to cut the flesh from the backbone. Pack fillets in the same manner as described for small whole fish.

To freeze fish steaks, scale, eviscerate, and wash in cold running water. Cut off head, fins, and tail. Use a very sharp knife to cut the fish crosswise in preparing steaks; retain one backbone vertebra in each steak. Cut chunks the same as steaks, but the pieces should be family size, about 5 to 6 inches long. Fish steaks are packaged the same as other steaks; chunks, the same as a roast. But fish may also be wrapped only in strong, heavy, moisture-vapor-proof paper and then tied or taped securely.

There is sometimes considerable leakage when lean fish is thawed, especially when it has been cut into steaks or fillets. Dipping these pieces in a ten percent brine solution for 20 seconds before they are wrapped and packaged will help to overcome this leakage. Use one pound of salt to four and a half quarts of water for the brine solution. It is not necessary to dip fatty fish.

Large whole fish may be given an ice glaze for protection during storage. Never skin a fish that you intend to ice-glaze. To ice-glaze, clean (scale, eviscerate, and wash) fish and then place it in the freezer without any wrapping. As soon as it is frozen, remove it and dip it in near-freezing ice water. Return it to the freezer for a few minutes to harden the glaze, and then repeat the process until a rather thick ice glaze has formed on the fish. Wrap the fish in moistureproof paper, and store it in the freezer. If not protected by paper, the ice glaze must be renewed every few weeks.

Thaw fish completely, and thaw it slowly whenever this is possible. Thawing time is 6 to 10 hours on the lower shelf of a refrigerator, 3 hours at room temperature, and about 2 hours in front of an electric fan.

FREEZING SHELLFISH

After oysters, clams, and scallops are shelled, wash them in a brine containing about one percent salt. Pack them, allowing head space, in a liquid-tight container such as is used for fruit. Steam or boil crabs and lobsters for 15 to 20 minutes, cool them, remove the meat from the shells, and package the meat dry in cartons or containers such as are used for fruits or vegetables. Freeze shrimp raw. Cut off and discard heads, wash and drain shrimps, and package them (with their shells) in the same type of containers recommended for fruits and vegetables.

Frozen shellfish should be completely thawed, but not warmed to room temperature, for use in cocktails. Shrimp, frozen raw, must first be cooked and then chilled before being served in cocktails. Those shellfish that are cooked before freezing should be completely thawed, also, for use in making salads. Partial thawing is sufficient if they are to be used in cooked dishes.

FREEZING GAME

All of the meat, fish, and poultry freezing rules apply to the freezing of wild game meats and fish. Game meat and fish are packaged, thawed, and cooked the same way as domestic meats and poultry and other fish. However, special field care is required.

There are three important things to remember about taking proper care of an animal bagged in the field: (1) proper bleeding and dressing, (2) quick cooling of the carcass; and (3) protection of cut or exposed surfaces from flies and other insects. Game fish should be protected from exposure to air and warm sun until they can be brought home or to camp.

Venison cuts are packaged in the same manner as the corresponding cuts of beef. All the carcass makes good eating in one way or another. Small four-footed game is eviscerated, skinned, washed in cold running water, and then packaged like roasting or like cut-up chickens. Game birds are preferably plucked by the wax method. They are then dressed and packaged the same as poultry.

FREEZING DAIRY PRODUCTS

Eggs. Eggs for poaching and frying can be frozen very successfully. Line muffin tins with paper muffin cups; carefully break an egg into each, being careful not to break the yolk. Freeze and, when frozen, remove the paper cups from the tins, pack them in a folding waxed carton, label, overwrap carton, and heat-seal.

Eggs for cooking purposes can be frozen either with the yolks and whites together or separated. Egg whites are simply packaged and frozen, but whole eggs and egg yolks must be mixed with sugar or corn sirup or with salt. Mix separate yolks with one tablespoon of sugar or corn sirup per cup of yolks or with one teaspoon of salt per cup of yolks. Mix whole eggs with one tablespoon of sugar or corn sirup, or with 1 teaspoon of salt, per two cups of eggs. Of course egg yolks that have been sweetened cannot be used for making mayonnaise, and vice versa. So keep most likely uses in mind while you are freezing eggs.

Eggs or yolks that have been mixed with sugar, corn sirup, or salt, may be packaged in one of three ways. Small paper muffin cups, as suggested above, are excellent for small amounts. Larger quantities may be poured into liquid-tight containers such as are used for fruits; allow $3/4$ to one inch of head space. Small portions may also be frozen in the refrigerator ice cube tray, using the divider. When frozen, remove the eggs as you would ice cubes—only much more carefully—and wrap each cube in moistureproof paper. Pack them in a folding carton for freezing storage.

Cheese. If wrapped in moisture-vapor-proof paper and heat-sealed, cheese can be frozen and held in storage for about six months at 0° F.

Butter, Lard. No special preparation or packaging is necessary to freeze butter or lard. It may be packed in tins lined with vegetable parchment paper, in waxed cartons lined with vegetable parchment paper or in parchment paper alone. It is a very satisfactory product.

Cream. Cream containing 40 per cent or more of butterfat can be frozen and stored for a few months without marked deterioration. First pasteurize the cream, if it has not been commercially pasteurized. Then package it in liquid-tight, heavily waxed containers like those used for fruits. Label and freeze immediately. Frozen cream should also be stored at the lowest possible storage temperature.

Using frozen dairy products. Eggs frozen for poaching or frying do not have to be thawed prior to cooking, but all other eggs must be completely thawed before they are used. Since the packages are small, they will thaw in a relatively short time. Frozen eggs should be used while they are still chilled, particularly when yolks have been frozen separately.

Cream, butter, lard, and cheese should always be completely thawed and then used in the same manner as the fresh. Frozen cream will be much smoother if, after it is thawed, it is put through a hand homogenizer.

FREEZING COOKED FOODS

The following cooked foods have been found satisfactory for freezing: cooked roasts and chops (with the exception of pork and pork products); roast chicken and turkey; cooked fowl to be used in making salads, creamed dishes, or meat pies; chop suey and chow mein; oven-baked beans; candied sweet potatoes; corned beef and corned beef hash; Creole spaghetti; spaghetti and meat balls; Spanish rice; beef, veal, and lamb stews; chicken à la king; Welsh rarebit; hamburg steaks; fish cakes; French fried potatoes; cottage fried potatoes; potato chips; mashed potatoes; pork and beans with tomato sauce; soups (asparagus, split pea, navy bean, mixed vegetable, beef broth); and many dessert dishes such as rice pudding, whipped gelatin desserts, and baked apples. Almost any hors d'oeuvres or sandwich fillings will freeze well.

Use your favorite recipe in preparing any of the above foods. It is better to undercook and underseason the food than to overcook or overseason it. If necessary, cooking can be completed when the food is heated at serving time. Seasonings sometimes undergo changes during freezing and storage, so it is best to add the right amount of salt or other seasoning at the time of reheating.

After foods have been cooked, cool them as quickly as possible. Use any packages or packaging materials suitable to the food or its container (if it is to be frozen in the dish in which it was cooked). Label and freeze foods. Most cooked foods do not keep well longer than three months, so plan to use them within a comparatively short time after freezing. Most cooked foods are of better quality if they are completely thawed before reheating.

FREEZING BAKED FOODS

It is difficult to distinguish between the freshly baked and the frozen products. Baked goods may be frozen either before or after they are baked. One thing in favor of baking breads and cakes before freezing them is the fact that this procedure considerably lengthens the storage life. Unbaked goods must be taken out of the freezer and used within comparatively short periods. Baked bread and rolls will keep well in the freezer for as long as one year. Unbaked yeast doughs have a storage life of two to three months. Baked cakes keep for six to eight months; baking powder cake batters should not be kept for longer than one month. Pies, whether baked before freezing or not, may be stored for as long as four months.

Pie that has been frozen before being baked is the only one of the baked products that does not need to be thawed before being used. All other unbaked products which have been frozen, should be thawed completely before being baked. If baked goods are to be thawed for serving, they can either be thawed to room temperature or they can be warmed in the oven for 20 to 30 minutes.

Ice Cream in the Freezer

You may purchase ice cream in quantity at your local drug store for storage in your home freezer, or you may make your own ice cream. The varieties of creams, ices, and sherbets you can make are limited only by your imagination. The freezer makes it easy to serve this nutritive and delicious food at any time. It might be used to dress up ordinary desserts into à la mode fare, or it might be used in sundaes.

Accidentally Thawed Foods

Foods are occasionally accidentally defrosted before you are ready to use them. Provided that no harmful change has taken place in the product, there is no reason why it should not be refrozen and saved. Fruit may have become fermented, but the most harmful possible result is that its juice might have an intoxicating effect. The flavor of the fruit may be impaired, but it will not be poisonous. If you do not wish to serve accidentally thawed fruits, you can make them into jams, jellies, or preserves.

Meats, poultry, and fish are subject to putrefactive spoilage. For this reason it is essential that you examine each package carefully before deciding whether or not it must be discarded. Spoilage can usually be detected by noting the odor. If it has a fresh odor and does not smell sour, it can be cooked and eaten without risk. It may also be refrozen, provided that the temperature of the product has not gone above 50° F.

When refreezing foods, it is bad policy to place a large quantity in the freezing cabinet at once because this will slow the refreezing. The best procedure is to remove all products from the cabinet and take them to a locker plant or commercial cold storage plant for refreezing. After they are frozen and the freezer is again operating at a temperature of 0° F., the foods may be returned to the home freezer.

The situation is somewhat different in the case of accidentally thawed shellfish and vegetables. Bacteria multiply rapidly in these products even at 50° F. and the bacterial count cannot be revealed by an odor. For this reason it is unwise to refreeze any of these foods after they have become completely defrosted, i.e., when they no longer contain any ice crystals. Packages still containing ice may be refrozen, provided that the freezing operation does not take more than 24 hours. If there is no locker plant or cold storage available where accidentally thawed foods can be refrozen quickly, it is better to avoid taking chances and to discard them.

FREEZING POINT. On the Fahrenheit scale, usually used in cookery, 32°. On the Centigrade scale, 0° is freezing.

FRENCH. To "French" means to prepare in the French fashion. To "French" rib lamb chops is to trim closely and then scrape the meat from the ends of the rib bones. To "French" green beans is to cut them in narrow slices lengthwise.

FRENCH BREAD. *See* Bread.

FRENCH COOK KNIFE. A knife with a wide tapered blade, much wider at the handle end than the handle. It is particularly useful for slicing and chopping, since the tip may be held on the board with the left hand, and the blade moved up and down with the right, without changing its position. *See* Cutlery.

FRENCH DRESSING. An emulsion of oil and vinegar, with seasonings, used as a salad dressing. French dressing can be varied in many ways and the wise homemaker will always have this basic dressing on hand. At least a quart may be prepared in advance, as it keeps well, and does not require refrigeration. In fact, French dressing thickens when chilled and must be brought back to room temperature to pour well.

The proportions of vinegar and oil may be varied to give a tarter dressing, but the following recipe is standard.

FRENCH DRESSING

3 cups oil
1 cup vinegar
1½ tbsp salt
½ tsp pepper

Blend all ingredients in a bottle or jar and shake violently. (Makes 1 quart)

FRENCH DRESSING VARIATIONS

Bar Le Duc Dressing. To 1 cup of French dressing, substituting lemon juice for vinegar, add 2 tablespoons of Bar le Duc jam.

Breslin Dressing. To 1 cup of French dressing add 1 tablespoon of finely chopped pistachio nuts and ½ tablespoon of finely chopped black truffles.

California Dressing. Substitute grapefruit juice for vinegar when preparing French dressing.

Chiffonade Dressing. To 1 cup of French dressing add 2 finely chopped hard-boiled eggs, 1 teaspoon of grated onion, 1 tablespoon of finely chopped parsley or chervil, 2 tablespoons of finely chopped pickled beets, and 1 teaspoon of finely chopped green olives. Blend thoroughly.

Chutney Dressing. To 1 cup of French dressing add, immediately before using, ½ cup of any preferred chutney. Blend thoroughly.

Columbia Dressing. Combine 1 teaspoon salt, 1 teaspoon prepared mustard, 1 tablespoon Worcestershire sauce and 1 cup of French dressing made with lemon juice. Using a piece of ice, stir and blend thoroughly for about 10 minutes until the mixture thickens. Take out the ice and keep the dressing in the refrigerator until needed. This may well be made up ahead as the longer it stands the better it is.

Cream French Dressing. To 1 cup of French dressing, made with lemon juice, add, just before using, 4 tablespoons of heavy cream. Stir thoroughly.

Whipped Cream French Dressing. Prepare as cream French dressing, substituting whipped cream for plain heavy cream.

Foamy Cream Dressing. Fold into cream French dressing 1 egg white, beaten until stiff but not dry.

Cream Cheese Dressing. Beat ½ package (1½ ounces) of cream cheese into ½ cup of French dressing. When smoothly blended, add a further ½ cup of French dressing and beat thoroughly.

Club Dressing. To 1 cup of French dressing add a little additional salt and pepper, 2 tablespoons of brandy, 2 tablespoons of tarragon vinegar and 6 tablespoons of olive oil. Blend thoroughly.

Currant Jelly Dressing. To 1 cup of French dressing, made with lemon juice, add 2 tablespoons of currant jelly.

Cucumber Dressing. To 1 cup of French dressing add 1 cup well drained, grated cucumber. Serve very cold. Especially good with fish salads.

Curry Dressing. Add very carefully 1 cup of French dressing to ⅓ teaspoon of curry powder which has been blended with ⅓ teaspoon of salt, beating constantly while blending.

Egg-Cheese Dressing. To 1 cup of French dressing add 1 teaspoon of sugar and a few drops of onion juice. Stir well, then add 1 hard-boiled egg, finely chopped, 4 tablespoons of grated American cheese, 1 tablespoon each of chopped parsley and chives, and 1 tablespoon each of chopped green pepper and red pimiento. Blend thoroughly.

Family Bowl Dressing. To 1 cup of French dressing add 2 tablespoons of Chili sauce, 1 tablespoon of drained, prepared horseradish and 1 tablespoon of minced chives. Rub the salad bowl with a cut clove of garlic before placing the selected salad greens in it. Pour the well-stirred dressing over and toss rapidly.

Farmer's Dressing. Put the selected salad greens in a bowl with a crust of bread which has been rubbed over with a cut clove of garlic, then cut into dice. Pour over all a cup of French dressing blended with a cup of drained canned tomatoes. Toss well before serving.

Fruit French Dressing. To ¾ cup of French dressing add 2 tablespoons each of strained lemon and orange juice, ¼ teaspoon of Worcestershire or similar sauce, 4 tablespoons of powdered sugar, and ¼ teaspoon each of prepared mustard and paprika. Beat well, and serve very cold.

Honey Dressing. To 1 cup of French dressing add 1 tablespoon each of strained honey, chopped parsley, and chives, and 1 teaspoon of drained, prepared horseradish. Blend thoroughly.

Mint Dressing (I). To ¾ cup of French dressing add 1 tablespoon of fresh mint, finely shredded with scissors, and a scant teaspoon of finely chopped shallot. Blend thoroughly. Good with meat salads, especially lamb.

Mint Dressing (II). To 1 cup of French dressing add 1 tablespoon of mint jelly, coarsely chopped.

Parisian Dressing. To 1 cup of French dressing add 1 scant teaspoon each of onion, parsley, chervil, chives, green pepper, and pimiento, all finely chopped and well blended. Stir thoroughly with a piece of ice until the mixture thickens, about 5 minutes. Remove the ice and keep in the refrigerator until needed.

Relish Dressing. To 1 cup of French dressing add 1 teaspoon each of finely chopped sweet gherkins, green pepper and beets, 1 scant teaspoon of finely shredded horseradish, and 1 teaspoon of catsup. Blend thoroughly.

Roquefort Cheese Dressing. To 1 cup of French dressing add 1½ ounces of Roquefort cheese, crumbled with a fork. Blend thoroughly.

Vinaigrette Dressing. To 1 cup of French dressing add 1 teaspoon each of chopped green olives, capers, chives, parsley and gherkins, and one finely chopped hard-boiled egg. Blend very thoroughly and chill.

Waldenstein Dressing. To 1 cup of French dressing add 1 hard-cooked egg yolk forced through a fine sieve, 1 teaspoon each of finely chopped chives, onion and parsley, and 2 fillets of anchovy, washed, dried and finely diced. Blend thoroughly. An excellent dressing for vegetable salads.

FRENCH FRYING. *See* FRYING.

FRENCH SAUCE. *See* WHITE SAUCE.

FRENCH TOAST. You may know it by another name, for it has been called German, Spanish, or Nun's toast, but French toast is really pan-fried bread. However there is no need to serve it the same way each time. It takes little time to turn out golden-brown, crunchy, yet tender slices of French toast. By serving with jelly or jam instead of sirup, or by sprinkling a mixture of cinnamon and sugar over it, you can secure considerable variety. Just the right savory flavor contrast can be obtained by serving it with crisp bacon or little link sausages.

From the ordinary, everyday ingredients likely always to be on hand, you are able to produce almost magically a truly delightful tidbit. All you need are butter, eggs, milk, and bread, preferably French bread. However, you may use plain bread, raisin bread, orange bread, etc., as French toast is only bread, sliced, dipped in beaten egg and milk, then fried. But spread it with hot applesauce and you have made a family favorite. Here is the standard formula for French toast:

Mix one slightly beaten whole egg and a half cup of cold milk. Cut the bread in slices, and dip them in the egg-milk mixture. Fry them in plenty of butter until well-browned on both sides. Serve with sirup, jelly, marmalade, or almost any sweet, as indicated above.

For variation, and as a healthful supper dish, try dipping the bread in condensed tomato juice mixed with beaten egg, and seasoned to taste with salt and pepper. Then fry either in butter or in hot, deep fat (380° F.). Drain on soft, crumpled paper and serve very hot.

FRICADELLE. The German name for meat ball or rissole.

FRICASSEE. The French name for a cooking process whereby meat is stewed and served with a white sauce made with the meat stock. Chicken and veal are most often prepared this way. *See* CHICKEN.

FRIED BREAD. *See* FRENCH TOAST.

FRIED CAKE. *See* DOUGHNUT.

FRIESCHE KAAS CHEESE. A soft cheese made in Holland.

FRIJOLES. (free ho lase) Spanish for beans, *which see.*

FRITTER. Food which has been dipped in batter and cooked either in deep hot fat or sautéed in butter or other fat. The food may be fruit, meat, poultry, or vegetables and may be uncooked, precooked, or leftover food. Fritters take their name from the foods from which they are concocted, as apple fritters, clam fritters, etc.

See also FRYING, BATTER, FRITTO MISTO, and individual fruits and vegetables.

FRITTO MISTO. An entrée which is an Italian favorite. *Fritto misto,* the "mixed fry" of Italy and of Italians wherever they may be, comes to the table in infinite variety, limited only by the cook's imagination. It may be a one-plate banquet for the vegetarian, a spectacular platter of richness and delicacy for the gourmet, or a glorified fish fry for the sea food lover, but it must come smoking and sizzling from the deep frying kettle, always shrouded in mystery. According to the theory or taste of the cook, the delectable morsels may be fried in crumbs, but quite often they appear in a puffy golden jacket of fritter batter. It is hard to say whether one is better than the other. The homemaker may go marketing for the ingredients of fritto misto, and buy anything or everything that fancy suggests; or she can prepare it on the impulse of the moment, if she has an emergency shelf in the pantry or a reserve stock of snacks.

Take a heaping cup of cold boiled rice and mix it lightly with a tablespoon of grated Parmesan cheese, salt, and white pepper, a slight grating of nutmeg, and a beaten egg. Form it into balls the size of a walnut, dip them in beaten egg, and roll them in finely grated bread crumbs.

You have, perhaps, some cold mashed potato. Mix it with a little minced parsley, or chives, seasoning, and one beaten egg. Form into balls the size of a walnut, dredge lightly with flour, then roll in beaten egg and crumbs. Fry in deep hot fat for "Rice Parmesan Cheese *Fritto Misto*."

Pick up the leftovers of cold meats—chicken, veal, beef, pork, lamb, tongue—and mince them together or separately, making a composite hash or as many varieties of balls as you have meats. Season with salt and black pepper, minced parsley, a little minced green pepper, a little grated onion, and a few grains of nutmeg. Mix with beaten egg, mold into balls or ovals, and roll in egg and crumbs. Fry in deep hot fat, drain, and serve.

Some of the meat may be left whole and trimmed into symmetrical shapes for frying in egg and crumbs; and whatever you may find of calf's liver, lamb's kidneys, sweetbreads, calf's brains, or chicken livers will add novelty to the ensemble.

Cauliflower is found on most of the plates of *fritto misto*, broken into sections and shaped nicely for frying; and there is a wide range of selection in artichoke hearts, bulbs of fennel, eggplant, vegetable marrow, summer squash, and ripe cucumbers.

Heat a frying kettle of olive oil to the boiling point, submerge the frying basket in it; then drop in the balls one by one, to keep them from sticking together. Let them fry to a rich golden brown, lift out the basket, and drain the balls on absorbent paper. Many homemakers will use lard, in spite of all that is sometimes said against it, and the results will be highly gratifying; yet a book might be written on the superiority of olive oil in all frying, and the incidental advantages to digestion, flavor, and even practical economy when olive oil is available.

Some Italian homemakers will tell you that *fritto misto* should always be in batter, and there is much to be said for it. There are few things more luscious than light, digestible fritters, and the method opens the way for an even greater variety of ingredients. The orthodox Italian batter is all eggs and without baking powder, yet some of the most distinguished French and Italian chefs use baking powder because one can be a little more certain of results. Proceed as follows:

BATTER

½ cup flour
1 tsp baking powder
3 eggs
Salt
White pepper
2 tbsp olive oil or melted butter

Sift together the flour and baking powder. Beat the eggs and add to the flour mixture, with salt and pepper to taste. Stir in the olive oil. Beat thoroughly. Dip the various bits of food in this batter and drop them quickly into smoking-hot oil (375° F.). As soon as they puff up and brown, lift them out and drain on soft crumpled paper.

A platter of fritters made by this method may reveal to the astonished and delighted diners such prizes as lobster, prawns, scallops, crab meat, oysters, clams, mussels, and bits of salmon and shad roe, accompanied by brown-crusted rice, potato, or macaroni or spaghetti balls, large mushrooms, cauliflower, broccoli, Brussels sprouts, marrons, okra, oysterplant, and balls of green corn and minced peppers, all coated in a crisp crust.

In preparing the batter for lobster, crab, and prawns, and for chicken, veal, liver, kidneys, and even game, a tablespoon of sherry or brandy adds piquancy and distinction. Berries and cubed fresh fruit may also be mingled in a *fritto misto*.

FROGS' LEGS. Frogs' legs, the gourmet's delight, a dish for the gods, are in season when oysters disappear from the market—that is, at the beginning of May. In fact, the official season for this delectable delicacy, this tender, flavorsome white meat that is famed far and wide as "better than chicken," begins on May first and continues through September.

Frogs are amphibians. They all begin life in the water, hatching from their eggs in the form of little fish-like tadpoles that vary in color from black to gray or dark brown. During their transformation into adult frogs they gradually develop legs, absorb their tails, and grow lungs that replace the gills with which they breathed while living under water. As adults, they are able to stay out of water for varying lengths of time, but the frog "drinks" his water by absorbing it through his skin, and if deprived of all moisture will quickly die. Despite this fact, some species live in trees; but the majority rarely stray far from the ponds and streams where the bull frog booms and the smaller members of the family trill or warble their cheerful songs throughout spring and summer.

Authoritative opinions differ as to the number of species of frogs that can be distinguished one from the other, but the lowest estimates are well up in the hundreds. However, only the legs of the larger frogs are suitable for use on the table, and the best known of these are the bull frog, leopard frog, and the pickerel frog. These big fellows weigh up to several pounds and sometimes measure 18 or 20 inches from the tips of their pointed noses to the toes of their outstretched legs. Some species are very colorful, being dressed in various combinations of brown and brilliant green. The under parts are usually quite light and may be intensely white or creamy in tone.

RAISING FROGS

Frogs are plentiful in this country, particularly in the South, and a large portion of those destined to provide legs to tickle the gourmets' palates are caught in the wild state. However, they also are raised commercially on an increasing scale.

The farmer of frogs chooses marshy land, fences it in, and either lets nature take its course or stocks the place with a species that is suitable for marketing as well as easily grown in his locale.

In the spring of her third year the female frog begins to lay eggs at the rate of from 20,000 to 30,000 a year. In 72 to 100 hours the eggs, or spawn, which are gathered in galvanized tubs, hatch into tiny tadpoles and are then transferred to troughs supplied with running water. A diet of ground beef and rolled oats is supplied, and, in due course, the tadpoles develop into frogs, salable the next year.

After attaining adulthood their diet is of insects, minnows, crawfish, and animalcules found upon the submerged foliage. Electric lights, hung around the pools close to the water, attract millions of insects, many of which fall into the water and help to fatten the frogs.

Frogs have many enemies. The giant water beetle preys on the tadpoles and young frogs, and raccoons, cranes, herons, turtles, snakes, and large fish enjoy their delicate flesh. Moreover, frogs are cannibals and have a great fondness for kinfolk. Segregation is necessary to keep down the mortality rate which is very high, at best.

It is quite simple to capture frogs that have been raised for market. The frog raiser walks around the special pool reserved for adult frogs and herds them from the banks into the water. Then the water is drained off until it concentrates in a shallow, central pool from which are lifted enough frogs to fill the orders on hand. The pool is then reflooded pending the next haul.

The hind legs of frogs are the only parts used for the table. If bought in the market they will already have been skinned; if the small boy of the family catches the frogs the legs must be separated from the bodies and then skinned before cooking. The skin is thin and loose and can be pulled off as the finger of a glove would be pulled. The weight of the Jumbo frogs' legs is up to six pounds to the dozen pair. As may be expected of such a delicacy, the retail price is high and varies according to the size of the legs—the largest commanding the highest prices.

Although frogs' legs are stocked by only a few retail fish dealers (the bulk going to restaurants), most dealers will order them for customers. Florida produces most of the frogs' legs used for the table. Other sections shipping them are Louisiana, Vermont, Quebec, New York, Alabama, Wisconsin, Maryland, and Delaware.

FRICASSEE OF FROGS' LEGS

2 tbsp butter
4 slices onion
1 bay leaf
A few sprigs parsley
A few sprigs celery top

1 whole clove
6 pair large frogs' legs
Flour
Salt and pepper
1 cup evaporated milk or thin cream
1 tbsp lemon juice
⅛ tsp grated nutmeg
Toast
Watercress

Melt the butter in a large frying pan. Add the onion and the bay leaf, parsley, celery top and clove tied together (bouquet garni). Lay in the frogs' legs previously washed, patted dry and dredged with the blended flour, salt and pepper, and cook, very gently, until tender and delicately browned, turning frequently. Remove from the pan. Add the milk or cream and cook over a gentle heat, stirring constantly, until the sauce is smooth and slightly thickened. Replace the frogs' legs, reheat, adding the lemon juice and nutmeg, and serve on hot buttered toast, garnishing with water cress. (Serves 6)

FRIED FROGS' LEGS

6 pair frogs' legs
Boiling milk
½ tsp salt
⅛ tsp pepper
1 tbsp lemon juice
Egg and bread crumbs
Deep hot fat

Cook the frogs' legs (washed and patted dry) gently in boiling milk, barely to cover, about three minutes. Drain. (The milk may be reserved and used for a fish sauce or soup.) Pat the legs dry, then marinate for one hour in the blended salt, pepper and lemon juice. Dip in egg and bread crumbs and either fry golden brown in deep hot fat (385° F.) or, if preferred, sauté in part butter, part shortening, turning to brown both sides. Garnish with watercress, cut lemon, and if desired, small bacon rolls. (Serves 6)

FROGS' LEGS GOURMET

Use as many frogs' legs as desired. Quickly wash the frogs' legs, and pat dry. Dip in undiluted evaporated milk or thin cream; then roll in seasoned flour, using

salt, pepper (white), and nutmeg to taste. Sauté in butter until golden brown on both sides. Arrange in a circle upon a sizzling hot platter, having four or five fried scallops in the center. Garnish with crisp water cress and a quartered lemon; and just before serving, squeeze a few drops of lemon juice over the whole, then pour over a freshly made brown butter sauce (see BUTTER SAUCE) to which finely chopped chives have been added. Serve with a side dish of creamed cucumber.

Fried frogs' legs may be served in a curry sauce, a highly spiced tomato sauce, or a Meuniere butter. They may also be prepared *a la King* or stewed.

FROMAGE A LA PIE. See FARM CHEESE.

FROMAGE DE BOURGOGNE. See BURGUNDY CHEESE.

FROMAGE DE CHEVRE. A hard goats' milk cheese made in France.

FROMAGE DE FOIN. Another name for Hay Cheese, a product of France.

FROMAGE PERSILLE. Another name for Gex Cheese. It is a hard rennet cheese made in France. It is marbled and bluish, resembling Roquefort.

FRONTIGNAN. A dessert wine made in Languedoc, it is rated as one of the best French sweet wines. It has a tawny color and improves with age. See WINE.

FROSTED. A term applied to an ice or frost covered glass used to serve drinks, usually intoxicating ones. Frosting is accomplished by chilling a glass or metal container to the point where atmospheric moisture will condense on the surface in the form of ice crystals. It adds to the enjoyment of any cold drink by visually suggesting coldness. See BARTENDING.

FROSTED AND FROZEN FOODS. Industry has come to realize almost overnight the advantages of the process known as "quick-freezing" food. Today some fifty producers are quick-freezing from one to a dozen products, and the recognized leader has over 50 items listed, including meats, poultry, fish, fruits, and vegetables.

"But freezing," the uninitiated say, "turns potatoes black, peas brown. It makes food flat; it kills flavor." Their minds flash back to what happened to the canned fruit caught by a cold spell. "The very look of a frozen food takes away the appetite." But *quick*-freezing is different.

Look through the microscope at a sliver of meat. The cell structure is like a honeycomb, and in both plant and animal tissue the cell contains a viscous fluid, holding a certain percentage of water in which are dissolved such salts as sodium, calcium, potassium, and magnesium—all making for fine flavor in food.

Slowly chill the meat sliver, watching the cell solution in which these salts are dissolved. It does not freeze evenly. Fresh water begins to crystallize out of the cellular and intercellular tissues, and the crystals become irregular and jagged. Slowly these grow, achieving a size many times that of the individual cell, their needle-point projections piercing the delicate walls. The meat holds its shape until it thaws; then that precious liquid which is no longer walled safely within the cell, leaks away, the meat becomes flabby and loses its flavor.

A scientist named Z. Plank, working more than thirty years ago, first reported on crystal formation within cells. He had no such practical thought as the freezing of vegetables or meat for the nation's dinner table. What he cared about was proving his theory that in freezing any fluid there is a certain temperature zone between 25° and 31° F. at which the biggest crystals are formed, when greatest cell damage occurs. He proved it.

Recent investigators went on from where Plank left off. Commercially-minded chemists made tests to see if rushing a food through this danger zone would not give a different type of crystal in the cells—smaller ones, they hoped. And their hopes came true. Quick-freezing, as the process is called, is done so rapidly at such extremely low temperatures, that only tiny crystals, infinitesimal in size are produced; these crystals are so minute that the cell walls are not damaged at all.

Every single food offers a set of problems all its own. Some freeze better than others, for all cell structure does not freeze and defrost in the same manner or at the same rate. Meat and fish have elastic cell walls. Fruits and vegetables have inelastic walls, yet by proper handling they can be quick-frozen and stored indefinitely in the same way as fish and meat.

Strawberries, now one of the most popular items in the quick-frozen list, required months of test freezing before the experts found the variety most suitable for color, texture, and flavor. It took one year of selecting proper varieties to meet all the rules for freezing, storing, defrosting, and serving. Laboratory experts were sent to the fields in Louisiana and followed the strawberry crop north as the season progressed. At the same time other experiments were going on in the Northwest. From these sample "freezes" of the nation's berry fields, only those that came through with perfect behavior were chosen.

Peas, the most popular vegetable, showed whimsies in the freezing process. Those high in sugar, of a dark color, the market-garden variety, are the best type. The laboratory and production experts devoted their attention to these, experimenting with 105 varieties, finally selecting but two types.

Once a variety was decided upon, soil experts made studies of planting areas as to chemical composition, degree of fertility, compiling detail upon detail as to amount of sunshine, rainfall, frost, and wind to expect. After the requisite acreage has been decided, the company's production man steps into the picture. His job is to spot a cannery or large farm in the neighborhood, and arrange for a lease. If this is not possible, the company may build its own plant, then contract for crops from neighboring farms.

From the choice of the seed, through the planting, cultivation, and harvesting, freezing, packing, and transporting, quick-freezing writes the rules. Processing machinery is moved from field to field. When a crop is at the exact ripeness, tenderness, and chemical composition nature intended it should be, the freezers are shuttled into the area by rail, four to a car. These look like huge refrigerators and each is a complete unit in itself, carrying its own compressors, motors, and brine-circulating apparatus.

COMMERCIAL FREEZING

Freezing may start in Texas with broccoli, spinach, or peas. From Texas the freezers may be pushed along into Louisiana and Florida when shrimp is at its best. Other freezers are rushed to Virginia's reddening strawberry fields. June brings the peas, beans, and spinach of New Jersey and New York to full maturity. Around the calendar, around the map, from coast to coast, the freezers travel, the vanguard of the nation's harvest, obtaining fruits and vegetables at their perfection.

In New Jersey you may see this company's largest truck farm in the East. Watch the pea harvesters at work. Tractors cut the fields much as a meadow is mowed. Trucks hasten the newly laid windrows to the viners for shelling. Viners are threshing machines of a sort, consisting of a reel with perforations and a series of paddles which operate in the same direction at different rates of speed, the reels separating the vines from the pods, the paddles stripping the pods, thus knocking out the peas. Dry cleaners eliminate all foreign materials, washing removes any juices acquired from vines or pods, blanching arrests enzymic action and accentuates the dark green color of the peas, a color which they hold throughout freezing, storing, and cooking. From the blancher the peas are cooled in water and conveyed to a quality separator.

After inspection automatic filling machines pour the peas into their cellophane-lined cartons. These are closed, wrapped in wax paper, self-sealed, placed in aluminum trays and thrust into the quick-freeze machines. All this harvesting, shelling, cleaning, packaging, and quick-freezing is done in a few short hours. Specially built, refrigerated rail cars are on hand to transport the pack to central warehouses. When a car reaches its destination, it is wheeled immediately into a warehouse where temperatures are kept at about zero. Transport from warehouse to dealer is by insulated truck, and for long distance delivery, special refrigerated trucks are used. Dealers pop the quick-frozen foods into refrigerated cases, where the packages are held at zero temperature until they are sold.

In New York City and the surrounding boroughs more than 1,500 markets carry quick-frozen products of the leading companies. The institutional distribution now covers the country. Hospitals were among the first users, dietitians and doctors being quickly convinced of the high quality of these selected products. Streamlined trains, airliners, ocean liners, where every inch of space counts, are turning with enthusiasm to quick-frozen foods. No shelling of peas and beans, no washing of spinach, no cutting or slicing of fruits, no dressing of poultry or trimming of meats. Knowing the exact number of servings to a package is a money-saving point. But not even an expert market man can accurately judge the number of portions to a bushel of spinach or a hamper of peas.

Could we foresee times of great calamity, flood, drought, wars, we might find in this infant industry a means to stock up enough in the "seven fat" years for the "seven lean." Quick-frozen foods, as far as scientists know, if kept at sufficiently low temperatures are practically immortal, be they sliced strawberries or steak. *See also* FREEZING FOODS.

FROSTFISH. A member of the cod family, the Tom Cod.

FROSTING, FILLING, AND ICING. There is not very much difference between a *filling* and a *frosting*, as very often frosting is used between layers of a cake as well as upon its top and sides. Sometimes what is called a "butter frosting" is used only as the filling. In this volume the terms "filling" and "frosting" are used interchangeably. As filling adds flavor to the cake, so frosting almost literally makes the cake by putting a good outward appearance on what otherwise might be a rather plain product.

However, frostings, and their similar fillings intended for beautification, also aim to give the final perfect flavor and sweet contrast to the cake's firm and distinctive texture. Many pound cakes, and rich mixtures like fruited loaves, do not actually require any topping or frosting, but most of the plain layer and loaf cakes, the cup cakes and small French cakes designed for afternoon tea use, should be finished with a frosting which fulfills all three requisites of color, flavor, and texture. In other words, cake and frosting are almost as closely associated as bread and butter. You may call it "icing" or "frosting"—it is the same thing—that sweet topping, but in culinary language the word "icing" is associated only with white.

There are two main types of frosting, one being the cooked variety, generally called "boiled frosting," and the other the uncooked. Each has its special technique.

COOKED FILLINGS AND FROSTINGS

The basis of all frostings is sugar; therefore one must understand sugar cookery and its various changes into sirup to make a successful cooked frosting which is neither too stiff nor yet so "runny" that it refuses to stay firmly on the cake. Granulated sugar is used in the standard, foundation boiled frosting. To prevent this hot sugar sirup from becoming so stiff as to crack or to be brittle (the same problem as in candy making) one must check temperatures carefully. Moreover, one must include as an important ingredient some sugar "stabilizer"—that is a product which will prevent the sugar from over-rapid return to a crystal or granular form. These stabilizers include corn sirup, marshmallows, or cream of tartar.

The process of making a perfect cooked frosting corresponds exactly with making creamy-textured, firm but not too hard or soft, candies (*see* CANDY). It corresponds also to making sirups for ice cream and other frozen desserts in which sirups are of great importance. Making meringue is similar, and so is the making of a parfait where hot sirup is carefully poured over beaten egg whites.

FROSTING A CAKE

The cake must be perfectly cold before spreading the filling or icing. If layer cakes are to be iced, it will be found more desirable to turn the layers upside down and spread the frosting on the bottom of the layer. This gives a smoother and more even surface. Brush any loose crumbs from the surface of the cake with a pastry brush. Spread the filling, being careful to keep the surface level. Lay the next layer on top and spread more filling, if it is a three-layer cake.

If the layers have a tendency to slide, they may be held in place with toothpicks until the filling has set.

When icing the top and sides of a cake, spread a thin layer of frosting over the cake, starting with the sides. Then repeat with a second, thicker layer. Work quickly so that the icing does not dry before you finish. The icing may be made with a smooth surface, but it is usually more attractive if swirls or other patterns are worked into it. This is easily done with a knife in the soft icing. For a round cake, a spiral starting at the outside and working into the center is an attractive finish. For a square or oblong cake try making parallel lines the length of the cake with a knife, and then cross these at right angles with similar lines. In a soft creamy frosting this will give an effect something like tucking. *See also* the various fruits and flavorings for frostings and fillings using these ingredients.

STANDARD FOUNDATION FOR BOILED FROSTING

1 cup sugar
1 tbsp white corn sirup
½ cup water, or
½ cup fruit juice
2 egg whites, stiffly beaten
A few grains salt
1 tsp flavoring
Coloring, if desired

Boil together the sugar, corn sirup, and water or fruit juice until the sirup "spins a long thread," or reaches 240° F. on a candy thermometer. Beat the egg whites and salt until stiff but not too dry. Pour the hot sirup very slowly over them, beating steadily and constantly until the sirup is all used and the frosting is of spreading consistency. Add flavoring and coloring, if desired, and spread on the cake or between the layers with a wide swirling motion. (Yields 2 cups)

DECORATIVE BOILED FROSTING

To make a decorative boiled frosting, all that is required is a slightly firmer consistency attained by cooking the sirup to a slightly higher degree (244° F.) so that the frosting may be forced or pressed out of a cake decorating tube in a thin but firm stream with which scrolls or flowers may be made or names, birthday or anniversary greeting written.

It is also possible to attain a firmer consistency by adding ⅛ to ¼ cup of sifted confectioner's sugar to the Standard Foundation Boiled Frosting.

SEVEN-MINUTE FROSTING

5 tbsp cold water
A few grains salt
1½ tsp white corn sirup
2 unbeaten egg whites
1 tsp flavoring
Coloring, if desired
1½ cups sugar

Combine all ingredients except flavoring and coloring in the upper part of a double boiler, and beat with a rotary egg beater until well mixed and blended. Place over vigorously boiling water, and continue to beat constantly and steadily for exactly seven minutes, no more and no less. The frosting should "stand in peaks." Remove from the water, and add flavoring and coloring, if desired. (Yields 2 cups)

Should a frosting become too thick perfect consistency may be restored by the addition of boiling water, but this must be added literally drop by drop, beating while adding.

In spreading cooked frostings whether used as fillings between the layers or to cover the top and sides of the cake, use a small, light spatula as this does the work easily and quickly.

VARIATIONS

Chocolate Frosting. To Standard Foundation Boiled Frosting or Seven-Minute Frosting, add 3 squares (ounces) of unsweetened chocolate which has been melted over hot water. Spread immediately on the cake.

Marshmallow Frosting. To Standard Foundation Boiled Frosting or Seven-Minute Frosting, add 12 quartered marshmallows to the hot mixture. Beat until smooth and of the proper spreading consistency.

Southern Seven-Minute Frosting. Substitute brown sugar for granulated sugar in Seven-Minute Frosting.

STANDARD BUTTER CREAM FROSTING

¼ cup butter
2 cups sifted confectioner's sugar
3 tbsp sweet or sour cream
1 tsp vanilla
Vegetable coloring, liquid or paste

Cream the butter and gradually work in ½ cup of the sugar, beating well, then add the remaining sugar alternately with the cream, still beating constantly. Finally add the vanilla and a very little coloring, if desired.

Fruit juices may be used in place of the cream, in which instance omit the vanilla. If orange juice is used add a slight grating of orange rind, or lemon rind with lemon juice.

STANDARD FOUNDATION CREAM FILLING

⅔ cup sugar
⅓ cup flour
⅓ tsp salt

2 whole eggs or 4 egg yolks
2 cups milk
1 tsp vanilla

Combine the dry ingredients and blend with the beaten eggs or egg yolks and enough milk to mix smoothly. Scald the remaining milk in a double boiler. Pour slowly over the first mixture, stirring constantly. Then return all to the double boiler and cook over boiling water for 5 minutes, stirring constantly, then 20 minutes longer with only occasional stirring. Cool and add the vanilla.

Coffee Cream Filling. Tie 2 tablespoons of ground coffee tightly in a double thickness of cheesecloth and scald with the milk in the above recipe. Strain and proceed as directed.

Chocolate Cream Filling. Melt 2 squares of unsweetened chocolate with the milk in the above recipe. Beat with a rotary beater until smooth, and proceed as directed. A little additional sugar may be desired.

Coconut Cream Filling. Follow directions for Standard Foundation Cream Filling, beating in ½ cup of shredded coconut, plain or toasted, to the cooked filling. If the coconut is toasted, let it cool thoroughly before adding it to the filling.

Butterscotch Cream Filling. Follow directions for Standard Foundation Cream Filling, substituting brown sugar for granulated sugar, and adding 2 tablespoons of butter to the hot cooked filling.

ALLEGRETTI FROSTING

2 (1-oz) squares of unsweetened
chocolate
¼ tsp butter

Frost the entire cake with Boiled Frosting or Butter Cream Frosting. Melt chocolate in top of double boiler, and stir in butter. When original frosting is dry, pour chocolate mixture around top edge of cake, allowing part of it to run down sides of cake. Cut cake when chocolate has cooled.

BUTTER FROSTING TO POUR

2 tbsp butter
1 cup sifted XXXX sugar firmly packed
1½ tbsp milk
½ tsp vanilla

Cream butter well, and add sugar and milk alternately, a little at a time, stirring until smooth after each addition. Stir in vanilla. When smooth, pour over the cake; let stand a few hours, if possible before cutting. (Sufficient for one 8-inch layer.) This frosting is frequently used on coffee cakes, tea rings, and plain cakes or cup cakes. Fruit juice, may be used in place of milk and vanilla.

BROILED FROSTING

3 tbsp butter or margarine
½ cup brown sugar, firmly packed
2 tbsp cream
½ cup shredded coconut

Melt the butter, and combine it with the remaining ingredients. Before the cake has cooled, spread the mixture over it. Place under broiler, as far from the source of heat as is possible. Broil until the frosting bubbles (a few seconds). Cut the cake while it is still warm, and serve either warm or cold. (Makes enough for an 8-inch-square loaf cake)

CINNAMON CRUNCH FROSTING

¾ cup brown sugar, firmly packed
1 tbsp cinnamon
⅓ cup flour
¼ cup melted butter or margarine
1 cup chopped nut meats
¼ cup milk or cream

Combine the brown sugar, cinnamon, and flour. Stir in the melted butter, nut meats, and milk or cream. When the cake has been removed from the oven, spread it lightly with frosting. Then place it under the broiler, about 3 inches away from the source of heat. While watching it carefully in order to prevent scorching, allow it to cook until the frosting bubbles (about 3 minutes). This is a popular frosting for spice cake or day-old cake. (Makes enough for a 12-by-8-inch loaf cake)

CONFECTIONERS' FROSTING I

½ cup shortening
2 to 2¼ cups confectioners' sugar
4 tbsp milk
¾ tsp salt
1 tsp vanilla

Cream the shortening until it becomes soft and fluffy. Add confectioners' sugar, milk, salt, and vanilla. Beat until the frosting is soft and creamy. (Makes enough for two 9-inch or three 8-inch layers.) This frosting may be served on one-layer cakes or on doughnuts, buns, or coffee cakes.

CONFECTIONERS' FROSTING II

1 egg white
3 cups confectioners' sugar, firmly packed
⅓ cup butter
Dash of salt
1 tsp vanilla
2 tsp cocoa butter, melted
2 tsp cream
Artificial coloring (optional)

Beat the egg white slightly, and blend it with 1 cup of sugar. Add the butter, salt, vanilla, and cocoa butter. Add the cream and the remaining sugar alternately, blending thoroughly after each addition. This frosting has a somewhat firmer consistency and is recommended for decorating cakes. Follow directions that accompany pastry tube. See also CAKE DECORATOR.

FROZEN DAIQUIRI. A heavily iced Daiquiri, (which see).

FROZEN DESSERTS. These have a base either of cream, plain or whipped, custard, fruit juice, or water. The general definitions are as follows:

Philadelphia Ice Cream. Light cream, sweetened and flavored.

French Ice Cream. A rich custard, sweetened, flavored, and enriched with added cream.

Ice Cream. Similar to French ice cream, but somewhat less rich.

Mousse. Whipped cream, flavored, sweetened and sometimes given body with a little added gelatin.

Parfait. Whipped cream enriched with egg yolks made into a type of smooth custard with sugar sirup.

Sherbet. An ice of water (or milk) given a slight body with gelatin or egg white.

Water Ice. Fruit juice, sweetened and extended with water.

Frappé. A rather coarse-textured water ice, frozen only to a mushy consistency.

In all frozen desserts, whether made with cream, custard, or water base, greater smoothness is insured by boiling the sugar to a sirup with a little liquid rather than adding it plain.

Any frozen dessert with a base containing a generous percentage of whipped cream can be successfully frozen in an automatic refrigerator, as for example mousses and parfaits. Sherbets and water ices, on the other hand, are best made with a hand freezer. However, they can be frozen in an automatic refrigerator provided they are taken out when partly frozen, turned into a bowl, vigorously beaten (to break up the ice crystals) then returned to the refrigerator and again beaten after a further half hour's freezing. A teaspoon of dissolved gelatin added for each cup of liquid provides for smoothness of texture. Sometimes, too, marshmallows are added as in the very popular marlows.

Every manufacturer of an automatic refrigerator issues a book of recipes and directions for its use. Follow the directions which are given therein in preparing frozen desserts. See also ICE, ICE CREAM, MOUSSE, PARFAIT, SHERBET, and individual fruits.

FRÜHSTÜCK CHEESE. An American cheese of the Limburger type. It is round in shape, and is two and one-half or three inches in diameter. Also known as Breakfast or Lunch cheese.

FRUIT. The varieties of fruits which are consumed in all countries are innumerable, and their uses are various. Sweet fruits no doubt largely composed the diet of primordial man, as they do of every primitive tribe today living outside of the Arctic Zone.

Speaking generally, fruits are composed largely of water, with starches, sugars, a vegetable jelly called "pectin," cellulose, and organic acids.

Pectin is a carbohydrate substance found in ripe pulpy fruits. It causes fruit to gelatinize when boiled.

The *organic acids* exist mainly in union with alkalis, forming compounds which are readily split up in the system, leaving the alkalis free to combine as carbonates or phosphates. Citric, the most important acid, predominates in lemons, limes, and oranges; tartaric acid in grapes; malic acid in apples, pears, peaches, apricots, gooseberries, and currants. Among the least acid of the common fruits are peaches, sweet pears, sweet apples, bananas, and prunes; moderately acid are strawberries. The most acid of all are currants, limes, and lemons.

Certain fruits also hold a little nitrogenous material, chiefly as albumins, but, as a rule, the starches and sugars predominate, and the nutritive value of any fruit depends chiefly upon them. Some also contain a small quantity of fat and waxy matter, and most of them have more or less pigment. Most fruits contain too much water to constitute an economical diet if eaten alone.

Fruits are commonly classified into stone-bearing fruits, pomes, citrus, berries, capsules, and pepos. Some, as the date, the plantain, and the banana, afford sufficient nutriment amply to support life for a long time; others, like the apple, are wholesome, but only slightly nutritious; while others again have little nutritive value and are mainly serviceable for their agreeable flavor, to furnish variety in the diet.

USES AND PROPERTIES OF FRUITS

The uses of the different fruits may be summed up as follows: (1) To furnish nutriment; (2) to convey water to the system and relieve thirst; (3) to introduce various salts (mineral salts) and organic acids which improve the quality of the blood and react favorably upon the secretions; (4) to act as antiscorbutics; (5) to act as diuretics, and to lessen the acidity of the urine; (6) to act as laxatives and cathartics; (7) to stimulate the appetite, improve digestion, and give variety in the diet; and (8) to serve as special "cures" for certain diseases, like the grape cure, although their specific action is very doubtful.

Fruits which afford the most nutriment are the banana, date, fig, prune, and grape. This is because of the large proportion of sugar which they contain. Fruits which contain the most water are muskmelons, watermelons, oranges, lemons, limes, grapefruits, and grapes. The antiscorbutic value of fruits is illustrated particularly by certain varieties which furnish abundant potash salts, as well as lime and magnesia. Among these are apples, lemons, limes, grapefruits, and oranges. The diuretic influence of fruits is in part due to their water, but chiefly to their organic acids and salts (mineral), which stimulate the circulation and probably also the activity of the renal epithelium.

As fruit ripens it absorbs more and more oxygen, and the tannin and vegetable acids which it originally contained are altered, so that it becomes less astringent and acid.

The starch is more or less completely turned into levulose or glucose, and soluble pectin is formed. The aroma and taste of ripe fruits depend upon the relative quantity of these different substances, together with various volatile ethers and oils. The sour fruits have either more acid or less sugar, and in the sweet fruits there is a preponderance of sugar which masks the acid taste. The more luscious the fruit, the more soluble sugars and special flavoring substances it contains.

The use of fruits as a common article of daily diet is highly beneficial, and the improvements which have been made of late years in methods of culture and means of rapid transportation, refrigeration, etc., make some varieties of fresh ripe fruits available in almost every climate in all seasons, while their increasing cheapness places them within reach of all classes.

Fruits, which nature develops more slowly than other products of the soil, receive for a longer time the beneficial influences of light, heat, and air. Under the continuous influence of the sun's rays, the elements of the soil, together with water and air, build up the millions of tiny fruit cells in which all the nourishing constituents are brought into the most perfect and soluble form. In the ripening of the fruit, the sun has taken the place of the cook and produced a morsel of exquisite flavor and wholesomeness, most agreeable, and meeting many demands of the body. Moreover, the water contained in fruits is in an absolutely pure state, distilled in nature's laboratory, and is, therefore, of great value in dissolving and removing impurities from the body.

While fruits eaten daily and in proper moderation are very wholesome, if they are eaten too freely, or if they are either insufficiently ripe or overripe, soft, and decomposing, they undergo malfermentation in the alimentary canal, and are likely to cause diarrhea, with colicky pains, cramps, and sometimes nausea and vomiting. Severe attacks of gastritis may, especially in children, be produced by indulgence in unripe apples, pears, cherries, berries, etc., and even fatal choleraic diarrhea has been occasioned by the indiscriminate consumption of fruits which have strongly laxative action.

The poorest time to eat fruit is at the conclusion of a very hearty dinner at which a considerable variety of food has already been consumed. Fruit generally is less wholesome when eaten out of its natural season. All fruits, such as berries, the seeds of which are eaten, are much less liable to produce intestinal irritation if taken with bread or other bulky starchy food. Raw fruit should always be well washed. The skin and seeds of the larger fruits and of grapes are quite indigestible.

Unfortunately, the value and necessity of fresh and dried fruit in the diet is much misunderstood and much underestimated by the American people. Fruits have been looked on as "dainties," "side dishes," or "tidbits," and are used or served usually to grace the table as a bouquet of flowers might do. Fruits have also been considered low in nutritive value as well as being expensive. Fruit is more than a "tidbit"; is a vital necessity in the diet; it is one of the most economical foods on today's market. To obtain the maximum value from fruit, it is necessary to know what fruits are best to eat, the proper way of preparing them, the most favorable time to eat them, and the foods with which they may be eaten. Inasmuch as many of the staple foods are deficient in valuable food salts (minerals) and are further robbed of them by the ordinary method of cooking, other foods, such as raw vegetables and raw fruits, must be supplied in the diet to partly if not wholly prevent the fermentation of foods deficient in food salts.

Economy in Buying Fruit

Since we should eat fruit daily, and not merely as a "treat," it is important to practise economy in buying it. Fresh fruits in season, and dried fruits are the cheapest. Canned fruit is economical when it is a product of one's own garden, or put up when some fruit has a low market price. Prices are so variable, even with one variety, that no definite sum can be given as a fixed price. Apples vary from 50 cents a bushel near the orchard and in season, to ten cents apiece for a fancy table variety in the winter. When buying fresh fruit, it is well to inquire the prices of the many kinds offered, note which is cheapest, and then observe whether the cheaper kind is such because it is abundant, or because it is of inferior quality. For cooking when the only cheap apples are spotted and bruised, it is best to buy dried or even canned apples. It is well to decide upon the fruit after you have studied the market conditions rather than before.

FRUIT FOR "EYE-APPEAL"

Fruits add color, flavor, and variety to meals. They are easily served, readily available, and economical. A fruit cocktail or canapé, served as a first course, stimulates the appetite; a fruit beverage such as orangeade, lemonade, limeade, pineade, etc., suggests a nice, long, cooling drink; a fruit salad adds a distinctive touch to any meal; while a dessert of fruit alone or combined with cream, cake, or pastry suggests a long list of concoctions which give just the right finish to a balanced meal.

Fruit cup with a ball of fruit ice on top, fruit drinks, such as cranberry or pineapple juice, fruit canapés, or fruit combinations, such as fresh pineapple with strawberries and melon balls, make excellent appetizers. Fruit salads are always appreciated either as a main course or as a small dinner salad. A newer type of fruit salad is made of the light flavored fruits with a sharp dressing served as a first course. Then there is the dessert salad made of heavier fruits and often a whipped cream dressing, which is salad and dessert.

Recently fruits have become a part of the main course, often taking the place of a vegetable. Some combinations are: (1) baked ham, glazed pineapple, and mashed sweet potato; (2) sirloin steak, baked banana, and broiled tomatoes; (3) ham cutlet, grilled grapefruit; (4) apple rings with lamb; (5) cubes of avocado added to cream of pea soup; (6) pot roast with a garnish of baked apples, filled with crushed pineapple; (7) lamb stew with cheese-filled pears garnished with mint jelly, etc.

Fresh fruits are always popular desserts and should be featured as much as possible when they are in "season." The variety of fruit desserts is limited only by the homemaker's imagination.

Fruit luncheon and dinner plates are becoming very popular. Here is one which will be enjoyed:

On a large salad plate first place crisp lettuce, then in the center a mound of red apple salad. Arrange around this cantaloupe balls, prunes stuffed with cottage cheese, sliced bananas marinated in orange juice, and fresh strawberries. The addition of fancy sandwiches or hot bread makes this a balanced meal and one sure to please.

FRUIT BUTTERS. A fruit butter is the product resulting from cooking fruit pulp with sugar (with or without spices) to the consistency of a thick paste suitable for spreading. Less sugar is used for butters than for jams and marmalades. Butters require very slow cooking and constant stirring to prevent burning when cooked on top of the stove, and it is a good idea to cook them over an asbestos pad. If cooked in the open, they require only occasional stirring.

The fruits most commonly used for butters are: tart apples, apricots, grapes, peaches, pears, plums, and quinces. Apple butter made with cider has an especially good flavor. Other combinations are apples and grape juice, apples and plums, and apples with quinces.

Use only sound, ripe fruit or firm portions of windfalls or culls. Wash the fruit thoroughly, and prepare it as follows:

Apples. Pare and slice. Use equal measures or weight of fruit and cider, or a half and half mixture of cider and water.

Apricots and Peaches. Scald, remove the skins and pits. Crush the fruit and cook it in its own juice.

Grapes. Remove the stems after washing and draining; crush, cook in own juice.

Pears. Quarter, remove the stems but not the cores and skins. Add half as much water as fruit.

Plums. Wash, crush, and cook in own juice.

Quinces. Wash, cut into small pieces, and remove the blossom ends, but leave the cores, seeds, and skins. Add water, using from one-half to equal quantities of water to fruit.

DIRECTIONS

Cook the fruit until it is quite soft, stirring constantly or very frequently. Press through a colander, then through a fine sieve, to remove all fibrous material and to give a smooth consistency. The quantity of sugar varies according to taste, but the usual proportion is half as much sugar as fruit pulp. Add one-fourth to one-half teaspoon of salt to each gallon of butter. Boil rapidly for one-half minute, then reduce the flame and cook very slowly, stirring almost constantly to prevent burning, unless you place an asbestos pad under the kettle.

As the fruit butter cooks down and becomes thicker, be sure the flame is low, to prevent any spattering. When the butter is thick enough, test it by pouring a small quantity on a cold plate. Cook until no rim of liquid separates around the edge of the butter.

Stir in the spices as desired; for example, one to two teaspoons of mixed ground spices to a gallon of butter. Use only fresh spices, and just enough to give a delicate flavor without obscuring the natural fruit flavor. Or if a light-colored fruit butter is desired, add whole spices tied loosely in cheesecloth while the butter is cooking. Pour the fruit butter while still scalding hot into sterilized containers, usually eight-oz. glasses, and seal. When cold, store in cool dry place.

See also CANNING.

FRUIT CAKE. *See* CAKE.

FRUIT CUPS. There is a subtle distinction between a fruit cocktail, a fruit cup, and a frozen cup. A fruit cocktail is essentially an appetizer; whereas a fruit cup is often served as a dessert, and a frozen cup, usually composed of fruit and ice cream, attractively dressed, is also a dessert. A fruit cup, like a cocktail, should be served very cold, and attractively decorated either with halved nuts, or small pompons of flavored, sweetened whipped cream, forced through a pastry tube, if desired.

The following fruit cups are only suggestions, and may be interchanged, according to circumstances or fancy. The fruits should be varied to take advantage of fruits which are in season. Furthermore, a fruit cocktail is usually less sweet, smaller in quantity, and more simple than a fruit cup.

Canned mixed fruits, alone or combined with fresh fruits, are usually used. Certain canned fruit combinations, for fruit-salad-making, consist of apricots, peaches, pears, pineapples, and maraschino-type cherries, as well as white seedless grapes. These fruits blend well in flavor and appearance, and together add a nourishing item to the fruit cup, especially when a few fresh fruits, in season, are added. Properly chilled, these mixed fruits make an excellent, economical, and light dessert.

SUGGESTIONS FOR FRUIT CUPS

Apricot, strawberry, and avocado.
Banana, blackberry, and raspberry.
Banana, orange, and raspberry.
Black currant, blueberry, and raspberry.

Cantaloupe, watermelon, and red currant.
Fresh fig, and pear balls.
Minted cantaloupe balls and blueberry.
Gooseberry and raspberry.
Seedless grape, avocado, and strawberry.
Grapefruit, apple, and cranberry.
Loganberry, orange, and nut.
Peach, pomegranate, and prune.
Pineapple, raspberry, and plum.
Cherry, date, and seedless grape.

Have all fruits thoroughly chilled before starting fruit cups. Pare, cube, dice, or cut into fancy shapes, using a fancy fruit cutter. Combine the fruit in a mixing bowl, and set in the refrigerator. When ready to serve, fill chilled glasses and garnish appropriately.

FRUIT DRINKS. Though fruit is one of the oldest forms of food, never have fruit juices been so widely used as beverages as in the past few decades. Modern science is largely responsible for this.

With fruits available and their value known, modern equipment has been developed that takes much of the labor from juice extraction. Now there are not only a great variety of juicers or extractors on the market, but there are also various mixers and blenders that further enlarge the fruit beverage possibilities. *See* KITCHEN EQUIPMENT.

Were this not enough, modern canning, bottling, freezing and even dehydration techniques offer year-round assortments of prepared juices that rival the fresh juices for taste and nutritive properties.

In America, at least, during normal peacetime conditions the fruits of the world are available in one form or another at the corner grocery store, and usually at reasonable prices. These fruits can and should play a vital role in the daily menu, supplying needed nutritive elements as they, through taste and attractive appearance, add zest to what might possibly otherwise be routine meals.

Almost any fruit juice is delicious when served purely as a juice. Diluted with water (plain or carbonated) and sweetened to taste, any fruit juice forms a delicious beverage.

But this by no means exhausts the possibilities. Fruit juices may be combined to form an endless variety of pleasing and healthful beverages. Fruit drinks can be served in many pleasing ways: as punches, cocktails, cooling afternoon drinks, refreshing mealtime beverages, at children's parties and when entertaining in general.

PREPARATION OF FRUIT DRINKS

A few recipes will be found at the end of this article and many others are included under their respective fruit headings.

Wherever possible, fresh juice is to be preferred in making fruit drinks, though prepared juices may be substituted. If prepared juices are used, it is well to first experiment with various brands to find one whose taste appeals to the family. Though modern methods are bringing forth juices that taste exactly like the fresh variety, some canned juices do have a different taste.

When fresh fruit juice is used, it should always be strained. Most fruits, when crushed, give off minute cells and pulpy matter, which, while often pleasant to the taste, have a tendency to give a fruit drink a rather muddy aspect if too much of the matter is allowed to mingle with the juice and then settle to the bottom.

While there are no rules as to the type of glass in which a fruit drink should be served (as there are with some alcoholic beverages), the glass selected should be appropriate as well as convenient. It should always be remembered that the eye has a great deal to do with the taste, and the optic nerves should be pampered as well as the palate.

For that reason, the clarity of the liquid and the appearance of the garnishings should be carefully considered. Straining will make it clear, but, if possible, the color should not be weak since that implies a watery drink and makes the tongue form a prejudgment. If necessary, some coloring matter should be added to give the drink a bright, attractive appearance.

The garnishings themselves are very important. They are usually slices, rings, or segments of either the fruit used to make the drink or some complementary variety. Peelings, cherries and berries are also widely used. Whatever the garnishing, it should be carefully prepared, cut evenly and arranged with some eye to the artistic effect. It is always much better to have too few garnishes than too many. One orange slice hooked over the side of the glass presents a much more attractive picture than five different varieties of fruit pieces floating in a solid mass.

Nor should the ice cubes used in cold fruit drinks be overlooked, for there is a potential source of attractive garnishing . The cubes may be prepared by first freezing a tray half filled with water, then carefully placing a cherry, mint sprig, or other garnish in the center of each cube compartment, completely filling with water and completing the freezing operation. Such cubes present a highly unusual and attractive appearance that more than repays the effort involved.

Tastes will differ, but as a general rule the best drinks are those that are not overly sweet or sour. Fruit acids have a tart, clean, refreshing taste that is marred by an overdose of sugar.

For cooling summer drinks, the tart varieties are the best. Sweet drinks may be served at the dinner table, but it must be remembered that too much sugar has a tendency to spoil the appetite, a rule that holds equally for adults as well as children.

ANGOSTURA FIZZ

White of 1 egg
1 large jigger Angostura bitters
1 tsp grenadine
1 tbsp thick cream
Juice of 1 lime

Shake thoroughly in a cocktail shaker with cracked ice and pour unstrained into a 6 or 8-ounce glass. Fill with carbonated water and garnish with a pineapple stick or other fruit. A good appetizer or thirst quencher. (Serves 1)

CITRUS MILK SHAKE

1 cup chilled strained orange juice
½ cup chilled grapefruit juice
½ cup evaporated milk
½ cup ice water
Pinch of salt
Dash of almond extract
2 tbsp powdered sugar
½ cup cracked ice

Mix well in a cocktail shaker, pour unstrained into tall glasses, serve immediately with straws. (Serves 3)

CRANBERRY FRUIT PUNCH

8 cups fresh cranberries
4 cups water

2 cups sugar
1 doz whole cloves
1 tbsp grated lemon peel
1 tbsp grated orange peel
¼ cup lemon juice
8 cups apple juice

The cranberries and the water are cooked in a covered kettle until the berry skins burst. The mixture is then forced through a sieve, and the sugar, cloves, and grated peel are added. This mixture is then allowed to cool, poured into a punch bowl with a large block of clear ice, stirred until chilled as the lemon and apple juice are added. Cider, either still or sparkling, may be substituted for the apple juice, if desired. Garnish with thin orange slices. (Serves 20)

FRUIT PUNCH

4 cups grape juice
1½ cups lemon juice
2 cups orange juice
5 cups water
Grated lemon peel to taste
Simple sirup or sugar to taste

The ingredients are mixed in a punch bowl with a large block of clear ice to chill. Juices, if fresh, are not strained, but seeds are removed. Garnished with fruit slices, mint sprigs, and small amount of cherries. (Serves 15)

FRUIT FIZZ

White of 1 egg
¾ cup sugar
½ cup lemon juice
1 cup orange juice
1 pinch powdered ginger
1 pinch allspice
1 pt chilled carbonated water

The egg white is well beaten, the sugar and spices added and the mixture beaten until stiff before the fruit juices are stirred in. The carbonated water is added last, being gently stirred. If desired, the spices may be omitted and ginger ale substituted for the carbonated water. Serve immediately in large glasses with ice. (Serves 8)

MOCK CRUSTA

2 limes (juice)
1 large jigger raspberry sirup
1 tsp grenadine

Rub the rim of a 6-ounce glass with lime peel and dip in powdered sugar, frosting a band about a half inch wide. Fill the glass with finely cracked ice and add the lime juice. Stir in the raspberry sirup, fill nearly to the brim with carbonated water, stir gently, then float the grenadine on top. Garnish with fruit in season and fresh mint sprigs. This is a non-alcoholic version of a long-famed drink (*See* CRUSTA). (Serves 1)

FRUIT JUICE. Better than tonics or "cures" are tangy fruit juices and similar foods attractively served just for the purpose of tempting lagging appetites and stimulating the flow of the digestive juices. Fruit juice cocktails have decided value in this line. They should be carefully blended and served tart and cold. Grapefruit juice and ginger ale in equal parts, white grape juice and egg cocktail, shaken with crushed ice, will prove excellent combinations.

For variation, serve fruit juice cocktails in small glasses, the rims of which have been rubbed with a slice of lemon, then dipped in powdered sugar. This makes a very attractive frosted rim around the edge of the glass. Do not use any sugar in the fruit juice mixture unless indicated and asked for.

FRUIT JUICE EXTRACTOR. *See* JUICER.

FRUIT KNIFE. Small kitchen knives of paring or utility shape are often called fruit knives because of their most common use. The term is specifically applied to such knives when they are equipped with serrated edges. *See* CUTLERY.

FRUIT PECTIN. A carbohydrate found in certain fruits, especially in apples and citrus fruits, which causes fruit to set when boiled with sugar as in jelly or jam. *See* PECTIN.

FRUIT SAUCER. A small but deep saucer used for individual servings of fruit, berries, etc. *See* DISHES.

FRY. *See* WHITEBAIT.

FRYER. A young, tender chicken, (*which see*).

FRYING. Frying as a cooking method has been in constant use since the days of the Romans, whose household records show that a large proportion of their foods were cooked in hot, and generally deep, oil. The Italians, descendants of the Romans, still prefer many foods cooked in hot olive oil; while the French feature foods cooked in a deep bath of hot fat, as witness the familiar French fried potatoes, potato chips, fritters of all kinds and shapes, and other delicacies. The Chinese, among the best cooks in the world, also emphasize cooking in oil, and any Chinese kitchen is recognized by the odor of heated peanut oil or sesame oil, which browns the noodles, shrimp or pork of Oriental specialties so perfectly.

Frying is a process of cooking in which the heat is transmitted by the contact of the food with melted fat, butter, or oil, and not by radiation, as in the case of broiling or roasting. The fat does not boil, for the food, as well as the fatty material itself, usually contains a considerable proportion of moisture, which, by being suddenly vaporized, produces the familiar spluttering which accompanies the process of frying.

Frying is less perfectly understood by cooks and homemakers than almost any other method of preparing food, and the process as usually carried out results in very unwholesome products. The pans used are too shallow, and both food and fat are likely to become scorched.

TECHNIQUE

The popular idea in regard to frying is that the fat used, whether butter, lard, drippings, or vegetable fats, is simply for the purpose of preventing food from adhering to the frying pan, but, from the explanation of the process given above, it is seen that this is not the case, and the best frying is done by immersing food completely in a bath of fat or oil. The prepared food is lowered in an open wire basket or netting into a deep pan which contains the fat, in which it is completely submerged. There is no danger of the fat soaking into the food if it is sufficiently hot and if the process is not too long continued because the water amid the fibers is boiling and driving out steam so rapidly that no fat can enter. But be sure the heat is well maintained until food is removed. Fritters cooked in this way are light and puffy from the sudden expansion of the water which they contain into large bubbles of steam, and are consequently decidedly more digestible.

Rightly done, deep fat frying is one of the most suitable cooking methods for cold weather, since the addition of fat in frying increases the food value of the dish and thus aids the body in resisting low temperatures. That is, the fat, oil, or shortening used is a source of energy and makes foods more nutritious. Some shortening and oils

supply important vitamins. Deep-fat-fried foods taste good because of the crisp, crunchy, nut-like brown crust formed over the food during the frying process. At the same time, the flesh or mixture of the food within is kept juicy, tender, and moist, protected as it is by this outer "crust."

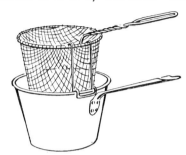

DEEP FAT FRYING OUTFIT

Again, many soft foods, almost shapeless in themselves (batters, doughs, soft fruits, seafoods, etc.) are given form and firmness when encased in a crisp "crust" achieved only by such frying. In summary, deep-fat-fried foods are tasty, attractive, and, if done correctly, tempting and eye-appealing.

The process of frying bears somewhat the same relation to boiling that the broiling of meat does, in that the heat employed is considerably greater. It is suddenly applied, and as a result the external surface of the food mass is coagulated and hardened before the juices in the interior have time to escape. For this reason, delicate fish, like trout, is much more highly flavored and palatable when fried than when boiled.

The boiling point of fats is very much above that of water, the vaporization of the latter being complete at 212° F. Between 300° and 500° F. may be required to vaporize the so-called volatile oils, but fats and oils used in cooking do not apply to this class, and when heated above 400° F. they turn dark brown or black and emit a disagreeable odor and smoke, leaving a nonvolatile carbon residue.

TYPES OF FATS

To properly fry foods in deep fat requires an oil or shortening which meets the conditions of neutral flavor, "high smoking point," and good keeping qualities. The flavor must be neutral, so that the food's own flavor will not be changed or lost in that of the fat. Whenever we eat a bit of fried food and taste "fat" and not "food," there has been a mistake made in the choice of fat.

Fats like butter, which are very delicious, sweet, and wholesome eaten uncooked, have a low smoking point—that is, they burn easily. When any fat breaks down, the poor results are indicated in the blue smoke which appears from the frying kettle. But if the fat has a high smoking point, it may be raised to a temperature of even 400° F. without smoke or bad effects on the cooking food.

Vegetable oils are most suited for deep-fat frying because they have this important high smoking point. Olive oil, peanut oil, cottonseed oil, in the form of pure liquid oils or when manufactured into solid form, are sweet, and wholesome frying media. In their latter form of white, glossy, smooth, creamy, solid fat, they are convenient because they do not tip or spill, and because they keep well, it being possible to use such fats over and over again.

The food to be deep-fat-fried must have some special preparation, or be such that it will form a crust in the hot fat, otherwise there would be no browning. It is easily

EQUIPMENT

A special thermometer for fat, and a modern French frying kettle are of great help to the homemaker. The French frying kettle consists of a heavy, flat-bottomed, narrow and straight-sided kettle equipped with a wire basket, both of which have handles easy to grasp. The prepared food, placed in the basket, is immersed in the deep fat heated to the proper degree (*see below*) in the kettle and lifted out when browning has been completed. Draining on soft crumpled paper follows. The special thermometer will register the high degrees of heat required for potato chips, French fried potatoes, croquettes, doughnuts, etc. Attached to one side of the kettle with the bulb submerged in the fat, it advises the homemaker of the exact temperature of the fat during the frying process and also between batches. If a deep fat frying thermometer is not used, the temperature of the fat may be tested with an inch-cube of bread. Fat is at the correct temperature for frying a cooked mixture if the bread cube becomes a golden brown in 40 seconds. For an uncooked mixture, the bread cube should brown in 60 seconds.

TIME-TABLE FOR DEEP FAT FRYING

Food	Temperature	Time
Croquettes, cutlets, fish balls, oysters, and usual cooked mixtures	375° to 390° F.	1 minute, or until browned
Doughnuts, fritters, and usual uncooked mixtures	360° to 385° F.	2 to 5 minutes
Fish	375° to 390° F.	3 to 6 minutes
French fried potatoes	390° F.	5 minutes

seen that flour mixtures, starchy doughs, and batters, are prime favorites among foods to be fried, resulting in the doughnut, cruller, or fritter. But if the food itself be moist or porous, then it must be made floury or starchy by means of an envelope. It is for this reason that every recipe for deep-fat frying of a moist food dictates that the food shall be dipped first in crumbs and then in egg. There must be a floury or starchy exterior if the food is to take on the rich golden hue so tasty and so crusty. This exterior protection, or envelope, may be supplied by rolling in flour, or in fine bread or cracker crumbs, or in crushed cereal flakes. Any starch will do, although each food seems to demand one type in preference to others for the most satisfactory finished coating.

FRYING PAN. A frying pan is a flat-bottomed, usually shallow, metal or glass vessel, fitted with a handle, that is used in surface cooking. The frying pan may be fitted with a cover, in which case it is also referred to as a chicken fryer or dutch oven (both of *which see*), or it may have none, in which case it is also known as a skillet or spider (both of *which see*).

At one time, most frying pans were made of cast iron, though this material has largely been supplanted today because of the weight factor. Sheet iron and sheet steel are used to make lightweight instruments, as well as aluminum. One of the newest is the pan made of heat-resisting glass.

Frying pans are used principally for frying, broiling, and, in some cases, baking purposes. Since the different materials have different rates of heat loss, not all frying pans are suited for all uses. They are made in different sizes, and usually have lips for pouring out the grease that results from frying operations. *See also* KITCHEN EQUIPMENT.

FRYING PAN

FTINOPORINO CHEESE. A Macedonian cheese, similar to Brinsen, made from sheep's milk.

FUDGE. Everybody loves fudge, and while it is one of the easiest candies to make, each step must be carried out accurately to insure a fine, smooth-textured product. Sugary fudge will not enhance your reputation as a candy-maker, nor will your friends appreciate being "spoon fed" should the fudge refuse to harden. *See also* CANDY.

CHOCOLATE FUDGE

2 cups sugar
2 squares chocolate
2/3 cup cream, milk or water
2 tbsp light corn sirup
1/4 tsp salt
1 tsp vanilla
2 tbsp butter

Combine the sugar, chocolate, cream, milk or water, sirup and salt in a large saucepan and bring slowly to boiling point, stirring constantly until the sugar is entirely dissolved and the ingredients blended. Continue cooking, without stirring, to the soft ball stage (238°-240° F.). Add the vanilla and cool, without stirring, to lukewarm (110° F.) then add the butter and beat briskly until the mixture is creamy and loses its gloss. Turn into a buttered square pan and when partly cooled, mark into squares, cutting apart when cold.

Should the mixture become too stiff and be difficult to spread in the pan the candy may be kneaded or a very little warm cream added to bring it back to spreading consistency.

FUDGE FILLING AND FROSTING

2 cups brown sugar
1/2 cup rich milk
2 squares chocolate, grated
1 tbsp butter
1/2 tsp vanilla

Place the sugar and milk in a saucepan, stir over a very low flame until the sugar is dissolved, then stir in the chocolate and continue stirring until this is melted. Beat a few seconds with a rotary egg beater to insure smoothness. Increase the flame and cook until the mixture forms a soft ball (238° F.) when dropped into cold water. Remove from the fire, add the butter, cool to lukewarm then add the vanilla and beat until of spreading consistency. Use one-third of the mixture as filling, and the remainder as frosting for top and sides of the cake.

Should the frosting become too firm to handle easily, it may be stirred over hot water for a few minutes until it again becomes creamy.

FUDGE SAUCE

2 squares bitter chocolate
1 tbsp butter
1/3 cup milk
1 cup granulated sugar
1/8 tsp salt
2 tbsp corn sirup
1/2 tsp vanilla extract

Melt chocolate and butter; stir in milk gradually. Add sugar, salt and corn sirup. Boil 5 long minutes, or until mixture reaches the very soft ball stage (236° F.). Serve hot over ice cream or puddings.

PENUCHE

2 tbsp butter
2 cups brown sugar
3/4 cup top milk
2/3 cup chopped nuts, raisins, or marsh-mallows

Although the main composition of this candy is fudge, it may be made in various ways, with raisins, marshmallow, etc. Combine the butter, sugar, and milk, and cook to the soft-ball stage (238° F.), stirring only until the mixture begins to hold its shape. Stir in the nuts, raisins, or marshmallows, and turn into a buttered shallow pan. Cut into squares when firm.

Sour Cream or Creole Fudge

4½ cups brown sugar
¼ tsp salt
2 cups sour cream
½ tsp vanilla
½ cup nut meats

Combine the sugar, salt and cream in a large saucepan, blend thoroughly and heat slowly, stirring constantly, until the sugar is dissolved; then cook to the soft ball stage (238° F.). Cool to lukewarm, then add the vanilla and nuts and beat until creamy. Turn into buttered square pan and when partly cooled, mark into squares, cutting apart when cold.

Uncooked Chocolate Fudge

½ lb sweet chocolate
2 tbsp butter
1 lb confectioner's sugar
⅛ tsp salt
1 tsp vanilla
2 beaten eggs
1 cup broken nut meats

Place the chocolate and butter in upper part of the double boiler, over hot water, and heat until the chocolate melts, stirring occasionally. Meanwhile, add the sugar, salt and vanilla to the eggs and blend thoroughly. Now combine the two mixtures, stir in the nut meats, spread in a buttered pan and chill. Cut into squares and wrap in waxed paper.

FULL. When refering to tea, means strength, without bitterness.
See Tea.

FUMET. One of the most important operations in cooking game is preparing game stock. This is very simple and easy to make.

Fumet

3 tbsp chopped, uncooked rather fat ham
1 medium-sized onion, minced
2 small shallots, minced
A pinch of thyme
1 bay leaf tied with 4 sprigs parsley
Trimming of any game
2 tbsp butter
2 tbsp Madeira wine
1 cup brown sauce (or chicken or veal stock)

Place the ham in the bottom of an earthenware casserole. Add the minced onion and shallots, thyme, bay leaf and parsley. To this add all the trimmings of game that you may have with two tablespoons of butter. Heat the mixture gradually and slowly, and cook, stirring often, until delicately colored. Then pour in the Madeira, and allow the whole to reduce to nearly nothing, stirring often to prevent scorching. Pour the brown sauce (*which see*) or stock over the mixture, and allow it to simmer very gently for 20 to 25 minutes. Strain through a fine sieve. Return the strained liquid to the saucepan and again reduce to nearly nothing—that is, to a kind of glaze. A teaspoon of this extract is quite enough to add game flavor to any kind of sauce used for game and will keep some considerable time under refrigeration in an airtight jar.

FYLDE CHEESE. A hard cheese, somewhat resembling Cheshire, made in Lancashire, England.

G

GAISKALI CHEESE. Another name for Ziegenkase cheese (*which see*).

GALANTINE. An elaborate, cold preparation of boned and seasoned chicken or veal, etc., served in its own jelly; a kind of aspic.

GALL OR BILE. The bitter, yellow, or green sh fluid secreted by the liver and stored in the gall bladders of animals. Formerly called fell. Gall aids the processes of digestion by helping to neutralize the gastric acids.

In removing the entrails of poultry and other animals the cook must be especially careful to prevent this fluid from touching the edible parts of the meat. If the gall bladder should be broken or cut, and the liquid allowed to drop on the meat, the portion splashed must be cut away; for, even though it is well washed, the contaminated section will retain the bitter flavor and will impart the taste to the rest of the food with which it is cooked.

GALLON. See WEIGHTS AND MEASURES.

GAME. The term applied to any wild or partially wild animal or bird, commonly used as food. Most game is protected by game laws and may be taken only during certain *open* seasons, and in definitely stated numbers and limitations

Game is one of the luxuries of the dinner table. It is healthful, savory and easy to digest, yet no branch of the art of cookery demands more knowledge and care on the part of the cook who may be entrusted with its preparation.

First, let us consider small feathered game. Take quail for example, that most delicate of birds which perhaps first came into prominence in the ancient days of the wandering of the Israelites in the wilderness. A plump quail pleases equally by its taste, its shape and its color. Its flavor is very evanescent and it may be prepared in many ways.

Woodcock is another example of a bird held in high esteem, delicious when roasted and served with an accompaniment of fried crumbs.

The merit of a pheasant consists largely in its flavorful gamy aroma. It is a dry-fleshed bird which needs great care in its preparation. It should always be hung for at least a week before cooking, if it is to be prepared for a connoisseur.

Many of the wild birds served on our tables are imported. From the fens and moors of Scotland we receive tender grouse; from Siberia the hazel hen and snow hen; from Norway the wild hen, from England partridge, and both black and white plover; while our quail comes largely from South America especially from Uruguay.

Most wild birds, whether from woodland or shore, need no extraneous aids in the way of spices or condiments to give them savor, flavor and piquancy, being sufficiently individual in their own right. Some of the larger ones lacking natural fat should be larded to enrich and nourish the meat. The main point in game cookery is that it should be cooked just to the indicated degree of doneness and be served sizzling hot.

Remember, too, that game birds in their fresh state have a flavor entirely different from what that flavor will be after hanging. With some, this hanging is done before plucking and drawing; with others, afterwards. Generally speaking, only pheasant, woodcock, and snipe require this preliminary operation, although sometimes quail and other birds are hung before cooking.

BONING A WILD BIRD

Clean and singe the bird as usual, then with a sharp pointed knife, beginning at the extremity of the wing, pass the knife down close to the bone cutting the flesh from the bone and being careful to keep the skin whole. Run the knife down each side of the breastbone then up the legs, always keeping close to the bone. Now, having completely separated bone from flesh, lay the bird flat on paper or towel, skin side down, fill with whatever stuffing or dressing is indicated, then fold the flesh over the stuffing, restoring the bird as nearly as possible to its original form and sew up all incisions made in the skin.

LARGER FURRED GAME

This class of game is well represented by venison. Herds of Alaskan reindeer provide us with tender steaks, appetizing roasts, delicious stews, succulent casseroles and tempting braised morsels. The widespread taste for game is not new, indeed it is actually a survival from our ancestors. Nevertheless, it is a generally accepted fact that game is definitely a man's dish, the inference being that women do not especially care for it. One reason for this may be that man likes to hunt as a sport not as a necessity, and when a hunt has been successful, the next step obviously is that he likes to see the result of his prowess on his dinner table.

Most of the game, both large and small, shot during the open seasons is privately consumed, so a hint or two regarding its preparation is necessary. While young deer may be cooked in its fresh state, hanging for a few days, and often marinating, is almost compulsory for really mature game. Remember that when marinating game, be it deer, bear, reindeer, etc., or any one of the smaller species, the longer the marinating, the stronger the gamey flavor, so this process is left entirely to individual taste. Twenty-four hours of marinating will leave the game, more or less, in its natural flavor; forty-eight hours will bring out the high strength of the game, and above that limit the game will be still stronger.

Deer, moose, elk, bear, and all kinds of large game are prepared as follows:

Bone the neck, then trim the meat to make a nice square portion, this to be used for stews and ragouts. Grind the trimmings with fresh pork, in equal proportion. Season with salt, pepper, sage and nutmeg. Use for sausage meat and meat loaf. Save the bones for stock for soup and consommé.

Bone, roll and tie the front legs (shoulders), then prepare a marinade of one part of sour red wine to two parts of water, with onions, garlic, celery, carrots, bay leaves, cloves, peppercorns, caraway seeds, salt and a little sugar. Marinate the meat in this for three days or four if desired really gamey. Roast in a hot oven, do not overcook, using the marinade to baste the roast and to make a not-too-thick gravy.

Use the ribs for chops: season with salt and pepper, dip into melted butter, and broil until medium done. Just before removing from the fire, season again with salt and fresh-ground, whole black pepper. No other seasoning is required.

Roast the hind legs the same as you would a leg of lamb or mutton. Rub the meat over, first with a mixture of salt and black pepper; then with a cut clove of garlic or, still better, rub the roasting pan with the garlic. Place the meat in the roasting pan and pour over it a No. 2 can of tomatoes. Add a stalk of celery, a small onion, sliced, two whole cloves, six sprigs of fresh parsley tied with large bay leaves, salt and pepper to taste. Roast until medium done, basting frequently with the drippings in the pan. When the meat is cooked, pour off any excess fat, leaving about two tablespoons. Add two tablespoons of flour, and brown the mixture in the roasting pan. Now pour in two cups of stock or canned beef bouillon blended with an equal part of the marinade, and simmer about five minutes. Then strain through cheesecloth. Now add a cup of red currant jelly, the juice of one orange and half a lemon with a little of the shredded rind of both, and reheat before serving.

Cut the short ribs into pieces of one or two ribs to the piece, and place them in a roasting pan. Cover with a No. 2 can of tomatoes, season with peppercorns and smoked salt. Add one large lay leaf tied with six sprigs of green celery tops, one-half small onion, sliced thin, two whole cloves, and a clove of garlic, and bake until the meat is well done and begins to separate from the bones. If during the roasting the meat looks dry, add some of the venison stock, or strained marinade, but do not add water. When the meat is tender, transfer it from the pan to a frying pan or skillet, and place in the oven to crisp. Serve with brown gravy, adding for each cup of this, one teaspoon of grated orange rind and a dash of nutmeg.

Make a stew of the flank, cutting the meat into one and a half inch cubes, dredging these with seasoned flour and searing them in a little hot fat. For each two pounds of meat put a tablespoon of butter into a stewpan and allow it to cook to a nut brown color without burning. Then add the meat, six or eight small peeled white onions and a clove of garlic sliced thin, and again brown for a few minutes. Cover this with venison stock, made from neck, bones, and trimmings, and cook all about 30 minutes. Finally add one cup of mushrooms, fresh or canned, one-fourth cup of sliced green pepper, one pint of red wine, with salt and black pepper (freshly ground) to season rather highly. Cover and simmer very slowly for 35 to 40 minutes.

Use the loin, filet, flank and rump for steaks and filet mignon.

Roast saddle, cimier or haunch, (all of which mean the same cut under different names), may include the rack and shoulders, or the rack and loin. The saddle is usually larded with long narrow strips of fat larding pork. The round may also be similarly prepared and cooked when the rack is attached to it. Either may be marinated or not, as preferred.

The liver of a young deer is as delicious a dish, when carefully cooked, as any liver with bacon.

The cooking of a cut of buffalo need hold no terrors for the homemaker fortunate enough to receive it. Like beef, it may be roasted in the oven or in an iron pot on the top of the stove, or cut in steaks and broiled over charcoal or under an electric broiler, exactly as a steak that is rare, medium, or well-done. Usually to remove the gamey edge from the flavor, the cut is marinated from twelve to twenty-four hours in the following marinade: 1 part vinegar to 3 parts of water. Wine or sherry may take the place of the vinegar. The time depends on the size of the meat cut, but ordinarily for a steak it is 12 hours, and for a large roast 24 hours, or more if one likes the marinade flavor. The longer the better, but the time should not be more than 48 hours. The same directions and the same rules apply to bison, bear, and in fact all large game.

CIVET OF DEER

8 lb deer meat (as above)
½ lb deer liver
½ lb salt pork
½ cup hare or rabbit blood
4 tbsp brandy
4 tbsp olive oil
2½ glasses red wine
4 sprigs of parsley
4 tops of green celery, tied with
2 bay leaves
2 small cloves of garlic, gently bruised
½ scant tsp thyme
1 tbsp flour
2 doz small white onions, peeled and sliced

2 doz small mushrooms, peeled, stems removed and sliced, caps quartered
Salt, pepper and a few grains of cayenne

Use shoulder, neck, breast and flank together with a generous ½ cup of hare or rabbit blood, to bind in at the last minute lest the stew be ordinary. The blood of the deer, whether young or old, cannot be used, as it does not keep long enough. Allow 8 pounds of meat for 6 persons, together with ½ pound of deer liver.

Prepare a marinade by using all of the above ingredients except the first four on the list. Cut the meat into serving portions and place in a bowl, cover with the marinade and let stand for 6 hours. While waiting, parboil ½ pound of salt pork and then dice into small cubes. When ready to prepare, fry the diced salt pork in shallow butter and drain as soon as brown.

In the same pan and fat, add the pieces of deer, well-drained and patted dry, and sear, turning to brown on all sides. Lift out the meat, place on a hot platter, and keep hot. To the fat remaining in the pan, add a generous tablespoon of flour and cook until golden brown. Return the pieces of fried pork and deer to the pan and moisten with the marinade, without straining this. Cover and bake in a moderate oven (350°–375° F.) for 40 minutes. Remove from the oven and set over a very low flame. Gradually heat the hare or rabbit blood almost to scalding point over hot water, and stir in ½ teaspoon of flour or ¼ teaspoon of arrowroot, moistened first with a little water.

When ready to serve, and only then, add the piece of deer liver, raw and cubed small, then the blood-flour mixture; stir, bring slowly to the scalding point (not to the boiling point) and serve on a very hot platter; garnish with small triangles of heart-shaped, fried-bread croutons.

GAME GARNISHES AND ACCOMPANIMENTS

All kinds of fruit garnishes are appropriate including prunes, oranges, pears, bananas, apples, grapefruit, kumquats, pineapple and peaches. These may be prepared in various ways such as fried, stewed, candied, broiled or baked.

Tart jellies, green peppers, pimientoes and practically all types of relish are also appropriate.

Boiled wild rice may be served with practically any type of game except quail. Truffles, fried hominy, small dumplings, tiny pancakes, triangles of baked puff pastry, fruit fritters and potato chips are all suitable accompaniments.

The wine or liquor served with game is a matter of choice—Burgundy and Champagne, or whisky and rum. The former school does not preclude the latter, both are right and two are usually combined in the dinners held indoors where wines are easily available.

GAME KNIFE. A game knife is a small carving knife suitable for use on wild fowl and small game. It may also be used as a steak knife. *See* CUTLERY; *see also* CARVING.

GAME SHEARS. Game shears are heavy duty scissors or shears that are used to cut fowl, especially game birds in halves or smaller portions, being strong enough to cut right through the bone. *See* CUTLERY; *see also* CARVING.

GAMMELOST CHEESE. A Norwegian cheese made from sour skim milk. It varies in weight from 24 to 65 pounds. For shipment it is packed in a chest with wet straw.

GAMMON. A ham or flitch of bacon, cured or dried by salting and smoking.

GANDER. A male goose. *See also* GOOSE.

GAR. Any of certain fishes having an elongate pikelike body, and long and narrow jaws. *See* PIKE.

GARFISH

GARBAGE DISPOSAL UNIT. A convenient solution to the rather unpleasant problem of handling garbage is offered in the garbage disposal unit that is incorporated into the sink drain. The strainer cover which normally protects the drain opening is removed and the garbage dumped down. It falls into the unit where strong metal teeth powered by an electric motor grind it up, bones and all. The garbage is thus converted into a soft mass that can be safely washed down the drainpipe with water, passing out through the house sewage system.

The unit can handle all forms of food garbage; but tin cans, glass, etc., must go into the trash bucket. It is claimed that some new models can handle glass. *See* KITCHEN EQUIPMENT and SINK.

GARBAGE PAIL. Because of the nature of many of the items that make up the family garbage, the kitchen garbage pail, as well as the outside garbage can should be covered, to keep odors in and insects out. The most practical units are those that consist of two sections. The outer shell has a lid that is au omatically raised by stepping on a foot treadle, while the inner bucket is removable, having a sturdy wire handle for carrying purposes. They are usually made of metal, the inner bucket galvanized and the outer shell given some protective but decorative coating.

The garbage can should be kept thoroughly clean. It is convenient to line the can with paper or to use treated paper bags to hold the garbage. These can be disposed of without the need of washing out the can each time. However, if any food has lain in the can, it should be scalded and disinfected, using any good household disinfectant. In this way odor and insects can be avoided.

The outside pail may very well be buried in the earth. Units come for this purpose with a heavy cover. These prevent dogs or other animals from upsetting the can or knocking the lid off. *See also* GARBAGE DISPOSAL UNIT and KITCHEN EQUIPMENT.

GARBANZO PEA. *See* CHICK PEA.

GARDEN BALM. *See* BALM.

GARDEN CRESS. Garden cress is usually found in gardens as a spring annual. It is the only species of peppergrass that is cultivated. *See* WATERCRESS.

GARLIC. Garlic is a bulbous European herb belonging to the lily family. The early Egyptians used it in both cooking and embalming. The ancient Romans believed it to possess magical powers. The ancient Greeks detested it. Even today it seems to be liked or disliked with intensity. It is a generally acceptable and pleasant flavoring agent when it is used with discretion in both method and amount.

The bulb of the plant contains smaller bulbs commonly called cloves (not to be confused with cloves proper). It has a penetrating smell and a strong, acrid taste. It might well be described as "just like onion only more so." It is similar to onion even in structure, but its effects are considerably more powerful.

Each clove can be removed without cutting the bulb so that very little odor escapes from the garlic until the clove is prepared for use. When the odor does escape it is accompanied by a small amount of oil that will stain anything it contacts—knife, board, or hands. This stain, rather than the garlic itself, will wrinkle a sensitive nose. Mastery of a few handling tricks will make you want to use, rather than omit, this flavoring agent in the recipes that call for *a clove of garlic, minced.*

A special board labeled "garlic and onions" should hang over the sink in the kitchen, and it should be used for nothing else. When desired, break a clove of garlic, from the bulb, hold it with a fork or a piece of paper toweling, and peel it. Still protecting the hands with the paper or the fork, cut the clove in tissue-thin slices. These will readily brown and practically dissolve in the cooking mixture; they need not be chopped any finer. To avoid a clinging odor, rinse the wooden cutting board and the paring knife (stainless steel) in cold water before washing them in hot soapy water.

If you are browning minced garlic for use in a cooked dish, avoid scorching it which gives it an extremely disagreeable taste. To add a subtle flavor to salads, rub a hard crust of bread back and forth over a cut clove of garlic, toss the crust with the salad, and then remove it.

Garlic is used to season many culinary preparations—salads, meats, vegetables, tomato dishes, spaghetti, cheese, and soups.

GARLIC

It is less acrid in warm climates, and there it is sometimes used as a food as well as a seasoning. In southern Europe and among Italians in the United States, it forms a part of almost every dish.

GARLIC BUTTER. *See* Butter Sauce.

GARLIC SALT. Rub a cut clove of garlic over coarse white table salt to prepare garlic salt. This mixture can be substituted for ordinary salt to enliven almost any food.

GARNISH. *See* Decorating.

GARUM. A sauce made of brine and small fish; also a pickle prepared from the gills or the blood of the tunny. In old times this sauce was made of that fish which the Greeks called *Garon.*

GAS RANGE. *See* Range.

GAS STOVE. *See* Range.

GASOLINE RANGE. *See* Range.

GASOLINE COOK STOVE (PORTABLE). *See* Camp Cookery.

GASPERGOU CROAKER. *See* Sheepshead.

GASTRIC JUICE. A thin, acid fluid secreted by the glands of the stomach—the chief digestive fluid, acting mainly on proteids.

GASTRONOMY. Gastronomy, according to Brillat-Savarin, is the rational knowledge of all that relates to man as an eater. Its object is to watch over the preservation of men, by means of the best nourishment possible. It arrives thereat by laying down certain principles to direct those who look for, furnish, or prepare the thing which may be converted into food. Thus it is

GARDEN BALM

gastronomy that sets in motion farmers, winegrowers, fishers, hunters, and the numerous family of cooks, whatever may be their title, or under whatever qualification they may disguise their occupation of preparing food.

Gastronomy is connected with natural history, by its classification of alimentary substances; with physics, by the investigation of their composition and their qualities; with chemistry, by the different analyses and decompositions which it makes them undergo; with cookery, by the art of preparing food and rendering it more agreeable to taste; with commerce, with the search for means to buy at the cheapest rate possible what is consumed by it, and selling to the greatest advantage that which is presented for sale; with political economy, by the resources which it furnishes to the authorities for taxation, and by means of exchange which it establishes among nations.

GAUTRIAS CHEESE. A round cheese which is a product of the Department of Mayenne, France.

GEECHEE LIMES. A condiment from Savannah, Georgia, made by a secret formula from a very tart, olive-like fruit that grows only on the banks of the Ogeechee River.

GEFULLTE FISH. A Jewish fish-dish, almost a "must" for the Friday night meal, made with half whitefish and half yellow pike. Some Jewish cooks include the flesh of carp, which gives rather a dark ball.

The fish is first boned, then put through a grinder, along with raw green pepper, onions, celery, and carrots. Salt and pepper are the only seasonings. This delicious mixture of fish is put in a wooden bowl, with one egg added for every pound of fish. Then the hard work starts in earnest, for this mixture must be chopped by hand for fully 20 minutes before it is formed into balls. Meanwhile the bones of the fish have been put into a kettle along with a little chopped carrot, onion and celery. These are covered with water and simmered for 15 minutes and the broth strained. Then the balls are cooked in this fish broth one and one-half hours over a very low flame. The juice in which the fish is cooked will jell when chilled and it makes a delicious accompaniment, either as jelly or as broth.

For an entrée, or main dish, serve a slice or two of fish ball on a lettuce leaf with a tablespoon of its jelly. Pickles, olives, and cooked carrots, cut in decorative designs, make appropriate garnishes. For a luncheon menu *gefüllte* fish may be served as a main dish, always cold, however, with vegetables. It is an unusual hors d'oeuvre, cut in very small slices and garnished with green pepper, parsley, and olives. Jewish women serve it, too, as a sandwich filler, cut into very thin slices and sandwiched with lettuce. Many Jewish homemakers insist that *gefüllte* fish is not *gefüllte* fish without horseradish.

Sometimes, instead of forming the mixture into balls, the fish having been taken from its natural skin, pounded, seasoned and prepared generally, is then replaced in the skin and cooked in the fish broth made from the bones and trimmings.

GELATIN. Gelatin is obtained by extraction from the white connective tissue in the skin, and from the bones of food animals, principally beef and veal.

In the early days homemakers made their own gelatin by boiling calves' feet for half a day, straining the broth through flannel (not once but several times), and finally clearing it with egg whites. Later hartshorn shavings and isinglass made from sturgeon's bladders were used in combination to make gelatin. Still, straining and clearing was a pre-requisite. Gelatin then was anything but cheap. At one time the isinglass cost $18.00 a pound wholesale.

The first attempt to prepare a commercial gelatin from bones was made by a Frenchman in 1681. Nothing came of the idea until after the French Revolution when many people in France were starving; then the French Government hoped to make gelatin improve the food of the poor. The French Academy of Medicine was asked to pass judgment on the product; they declared it nourishing food. Thereupon all public institutions and hospitals served gelatin in soups and broths; but the taste was unpleasant. People ate it because they had to. It was anything but a delectable dish, and a very distant cousin to the appetizing jellies we serve today.

There are two types of gelatin, the plain uncolored, and the kind called "dessert powder," which carries fruit flavors and contains but 10 to 12 percent gelatin, just enough to congeal a pint of liquid. The remainder of the powder consists of sugar, flavoring and coloring. Plain, unflavored gelatin is used for making jellied soups, consommé and bouillon, vegetable, meat

GELATIN

and fish jellies, also in making·coffee jelly. Fruited jellies may have either a plain un-flavored gelatin base or the dessert powder base which is already sweetened, flavored and colored. This last comment also ap-plies to lime, lemon, and orange jellies.

In manufacturers' testing kitchens, die-titians and chefs are constantly at work developing new uses for gelatin and devis-ing new standardized recipes for the home table. Indeed, gelatin is the busiest food in the kitchen. It gets into everything from soup to the afterdinner candies. It is at the same time called upon to beautify other foods and make palatable leftovers. Again, in frozen salads and desserts, gelatin is used to prevent excessive crystallization and coarse texture. Recipes that call for gelatin run into the thousands—so versatile is this old favorite.

Not only can we prepare simple, clear jellies from gelatin, but different methods give different results. Beating the jelly with a whisk or rotary beater as it begins to set produces a whip. Added beaten egg whites or whipped cream, by folding them in to the thickened jelly, gives a sponge or a Spanish or a Bavarian cream. Sometimes milk (instead of water) and both the yolks and whites of eggs are used for these des-serts. There is no clear distinction among them when it comes to their actual titles.

There are many ways of serving these fancy gelatins—piled in sherbet or parfait glasses, chilled, then topped with whipped cream which may be forced through a pas-try bag; or, you may combine alternate layers of plain and whipped gelatin in a mold, chill, and then unmold. Again, cube plain gelatin and when set, fold into the whipped mixture a combination of two colors, one light and one brilliant, for attractiveness.

DIRECTIONS FOR USING PLAIN GELATIN

Place cold water or other liquid called for in the recipe in a mixing bowl and sprinkle the gelatin on top of the liquid; let stand a few minutes to soften.

Add sugar and hot liquids, and stir until dissolved.

Add any remaining liquids and blend thoroughly.

If sliced or diced fruits, vegetables, meat, or fish are to be added and no special de-sign is desired or indicated, allow the mix-ture to thicken slightly, then stir the pre-pared food through the congealing jelly, thus keeping the fruit distributed.

Pour into a mold or plain bowl which has been rinsed in cold water and chill in the refrigerator.

To congeal or set gelatin salads, desserts or any kind of gelatin dishes quickly, pro-ceed as follows:

To the already softened gelatin add only enough hot water or other indicated liquid to completely dissolve it, then, when this is accomplished, add the remaining liquid, cold, and proceed thereafter according to recipe directions. Chilling in the bowl or other container surrounded by broken or crushed ice will also speed up the setting. With covered molds ice may be put on the cover, but be careful not to allow any ice or water to get into the molds themselves.

To unmold, immerse just to the top of the mold for a second in warm water, or wrap a hot cloth around the mold; slightly loosen the jelly at the edge, turning mold from side to side. Then place the serving dish on top of the mold, invert, and care-fully lift the mold off the jelly.

If the dish on which jelly is to be un-molded is first moistened with cold water it is an easy matter, should it not be exactly centered, to slide it into position. Or, put a lace paper doily on the mold before it is inverted onto the serving dish, then both doily and molded gelatin can be centered together.

In summer, without ice, it is sometimes desirable slightly to increase the amount of gelatin, or decrease the amount of liquid specified.

In order to utilize any fruit juices (fresh or canned) you may have on hand, the gelatin may be softened in cold fruit juices, or these fruit juices may be heated and substituted for all or part of the hot water in which the softened gelatin is dissolved. Delicious easy desserts are the result.

Always use fresh citrus fruit (orange or lemon) in making desserts and salads, and take advantage of the pure health-giving vitamins that these contain.

In combining fresh pineapple, juice or fruit, with gelatin, always first scald the pineapple, both fruit and juice. When using canned pineapple, this is not neces-sary as the pineapple has already been cooked.

Use leftover coffee for a coffee jelly, coffee Spanish cream, coffee cream pie, or mocha sponge.

An attractive molded salad containing fruit, vegetables, fish, meat or poultry may be served as the first course at a luncheon. (A good way to use leftovers.)

Canned soups are easily jellied, and are especially appetizing on a hot summer day. They should be more highly seasoned than when served hot.

Tiny jellied salads, fish loaves or aspic jellies, make most attractive appetizers or hors d'oeuvres.

Jelly may be molded in shallow pans and cut into fancy shapes with cutters— rabbits, pigs, etc. Use these to decorate cakes or ice cream for children's parties.

Ices and sherbets, as well as ice creams made with gelatin, may be chilled or frozen most satisfactorily in the trays of automatic refrigerators. *See* FROZEN DESSERTS.

FOUNDATION GELATIN BASE
FOR SALADS AND DESSERTS

1 tbsp gelatin
½ cup cold water
1 cup hot water
½ cup sugar
½ tsp salt
Dash of pepper
¼ cup mild vinegar or lemon juice

Soften the gelatin in the cold water. Add the sugar and seasonings to the hot water and stir until the sugar is dissolved. Combine with the softened gelatin, stir until this also is dissolved, reheating if necessary, then add the vinegar or lemon juice. Blend thoroughly and set aside to chill. When beginning to thicken, stir in the desired food ingredient from which the salad or dessert will take its name, probably either vegetable or fruit, using from one and a half to two cups. Turn into a mold which has been rinsed in cold water and chill. When firm, unmold and garnish as desired.

If canned fruit is to be molded use the fruit sirup as a part of the liquid and sugar, of course omitting salt and pepper. With fish, meat or vegetables, little or no sugar will be added, but some such seasoning as prepared mustard, Worcestershire or Chili sauce may be stirred in. (Serves 4 to 6)

GENEVA. A name sometimes given to Hollands, or Dutch Gin (*see* GIN). In this connection, it is actually a corruption of the French *Genièvre*, or gin, and does not,

as is often thought, have any connection with the city of Geneva.

GENIEVRE. The French name for Gin (*which see*), *genièvre* means juniper. It is a plain spirit flavored with juniper berries, either pure white or faintly straw-colored. The color is not due to the wood of the casks in which it is kept, but to caramel, which is added to the liquor.

GENIPAP or GENIPOP. The fruit of *Genipa Americana* of the West Indies and northern South America, is about the size of a small orange, and has a pleasant, vinous flavor. It is greenish white in color, is subacid, has a purple juice, and is prepared as a preserve, marmalade, or jam. In Surinam it is sometimes called *Marmalade Box*.

GENOISE. A cold sauce for cold or hot fish.

GENOISE SAUCE

3 large, blanched, bitter almonds
3 large, sweet almonds
½ tsp cream sauce II or a little unbeaten egg white
2 egg yolks
Salt and pepper to taste
1 cup olive oil
Juice of 1 small lemon
1 tbsp mixed fine herbs

Pound in a mortar the bitter and sweet almonds with the cream sauce (*which see*) or egg white. Force this paste through a fine strainer, add the egg yolks and salt and pepper, and beat thoroughly with a wire whisk. Add olive oil alternately with the lemon juice, drop by drop, beating continuously. When ready to serve, add the fine herbs, blanched for a minute or two in plain water, drained, and squeezed through a cloth. The herbs may include chervil, parsley, tarragon, chives and pimpernel.

GENTIAN. A flowering plant of various species, such as the yellow gentian of Europe, used medicinally and also for a hot beverage concoction. The fringed gentian of America with blue, delicately fringed flowers, is also used medicinally and for hot beverages.

GENTIANE. Flavored with the roots of the *Gentiana lutea*, an alpine plant, this is a digestive liqueur made in parts of France and Switzerland. *See also* LIQUEUR.

GERANIUM JELLY. If you have a rose geranium plant, you can make a deliciously flavored geranium jelly. Put one or two rose geranium leaves into boiling apple juice, allowing them to remain in the cooking sirup from four to six minutes, depending on the strength of flavor desired. If preferred, a very small rose geranium leaf may be put into each glass of finished jelly as soon as poured, and sealed in. *See* APPLE and JELLY.

GERMAN SILVER. Also called nickel silver. *See* SILVERWARE.

GERMAN TOAST. A pan-fried bread that is better known as French toast, *which see.*

GEROME CHEESE. A soft rennet cheese, similar to Munster, with a greenish appearance. Anise is sometimes incorporated before it is put into forms. It weighs from one-half to five pounds. It is considered excellent in winter, but less so in the summertime.

GERVAIS CHEESE. A rennet cheese made from a mixture of whole milk and cream. It is of the Neufchâtel group and can be eaten all the year round, but preferably during the summer.

GEWACHS. Found on the labels of Rhine and Moselle Wines, this German word means "the growth of," and is followed by the vineyard owner's name.

GEX CHEESE. A hard rennet cheese made from cow's milk. It is marbled and has a bluish appearance resembling Roquefort, Sassenage, and Septmoncel. It weighs 14 to 15 pounds. It is also known as Fromage Persillé. It is excellent in winter but not served in the summer.

GHEE. A clarified butter, used in Indian cookery.

GHERKINS. Small pickles, particularly the small prickly cucumber. Those of very small size are sometimes called "midgets." They are used for garnishing hot and cold platters.

GIBLETS. The "odds and ends" of poultry from which giblet gravy is made. Specifically, they are the liver, heart, and gizzard; more broadly, they include the neck, wing tips, and legs. *See* GRAVY.

GILL. (I) The breathing organ of a fish.

GILL. (II) A measure equaling half a cup. *See* WEIGHTS AND MEASURES.

GILT HEAD. A fish with a gray-silvered back and light green reflections. The belly is of a brilliant silver hue crossed with 18 to 20 golden stripes. It should be pre-pared the same way as sole or fillets of flounder (*which see*). The French call it *daurade.*

GIMLET. A cooling intoxicating drink made with gin, lime juice, and ice. There are many variations served under the name of Gimlet, involving bitters, fruit and carbonated water, but they are impostors belonging to the Collins, Rickey, and Sling families (*which see*).

The true Gimlet is mixed in a saucer type goblet (*see* GLASSWARE) filled with finely shaven ice. A dry gin and a sweetened preserved type of lime juice, such as is commonly used in the British tropical regions, are used.

GIMLET

1 part dry gin
1 part bottled lime juice

The ingredients are poured into an ice-filled goblet as described above, and stirred, usually with a small swizzle stick (*which see*). Serve with a short straw. (Serves 6)

The proportions should not be thought of as final, but are intended to be varied by the individual drinker until he has found that blend which most pleases him. For further discussion on drinks and drink recipes, *see* BARTENDING.

GIN. This name is a corruption of the French *genièvre*, meaning juniper, gin being a plain spirit flavored with juniper berries. Gin is the purest of all spirits, being distilled at a higher strength than other spirits. In Europe it is made of flour of rye, coarsely ground, barley malt and cold water, brought to a fermentation point, and then distilled and rectified over juniper berries. It is white or faintly straw-colored, the color being due to caramel, and generally not to the cask in which it is stored. Gin does not have to age to be potable.

In the U.S., the basis of gin is practically neutral alcohol so that it matters little from what it is distilled. Alcohol being flavorless and colorless, it is flavored at will and reduced in strength by the addition of distilled water. Coriander seeds, angelica root, or various essential oils and juniper are used, but the juniper berry gives the distinctive flavor to gin. The common juniper is a low, evergreen bush which grows in all parts of the world. It must be properly cultivated to produce berries of the finest flavor, the production of which is extensive. The great connoisseur of good liquor, Comte de Moret, son of Henry IV of France, is said to be responsible for the use of juniper berries in flavoring gin.

Gin is one of the oldest of spirits and for a long while it was used principally for its medicinal properties, and was frequently prescribed by physicians. It is made in almost all countries that do distilling—including Cuba, South America, Australia, China, Russia, South Africa, and the United States.

Three varieties are well known (1) *London*, "dry," (2) *Plymouth* or *Old Tom*, "sweet, ' and (3) Sloe gin, which is really a liqueur, and not a gin at all. *Hollands* is distilled from barley malt exclusively and the flavoring is ground up with the malt to make the mash. The Dutch distill their gin at a low proof, 94° to 98°, which produces a heavy spirit in body. It has so pronounced a flavor that it cannot be mixed with other ingredients to make cocktails.

Tom gin, also called ' Old Tom Gin" is said to have originated from the name of an old English distiller, Thomas Chamberlain, who sweetened his product and signed his name "Old Tom." It is very often used to make the drink known as *Tom Collins*.

Good gin should be smooth to drink straight, should have a delicate flavor and aroma, and should be crystal clear.

In France it is called *genièvre*; in Denmark and Norway, *schnaaps*; in Belgium, *genièvre* and sometimes, *hasselt*; Dutch gins, being different from English gins, are sold under the names of *Jenever*, *Geneva*, *Hollands* or *Schiedam*. *Geneva* is sold as soon as distilled: it has nothing to gain by being kept. Some European gins are aged as much as whisky is aged; some in old sherry wine casks, thus giving the gin a beautiful pale-yellow tint.

GINGER. A perennial, reedlike plant (*Zingiber officinale*) whose rootstalks provide the ginger used in cookery, beverages, and medicine. It is a native of several tropical countries, including India and China in southern Asia and it also flourishes in nearby Jamaica in the West Indies. Ginger was featured in Roman, Greek and Arabian cooking in the ages when its source of supply was kept secret by the crafty traders. Marco Polo (1250–1324), the adventurous Venetian traveler, speaks of it in his book of travels, and Sir John Mandeville (1300–1371) discourses on the "gode Gyngevere."

The roots grow into a shape that roughly resembles the palm and fingers and are therefore commonly referred to as "hands." After the roots are dug they are placed in baskets, and when enough baskets are ready the handles are looped through ropes held by two men, one at each end. Something like a tug of war then ensues for two hours; this is repeated the following day, so as to shake the roots free of scales and dirt, after which the roots are sun-dried for eight days; another good shaking and two more days of drying prepares them for export.

For culinary use ginger is cracked into small pieces and put through a refining process that reduces it to powder. Small cracked pieces are also used in making the assortment of spices used in pickl ng.

Preserved ginger, in sirup, and crystallized ginger are classified as confections and have achieved a high degree of popularity in this country. They are greatly prized in the Orient, especially in China, whence so much of the ginger root comes. Chinese and Indian curry powders nearly always contain ginger root. Native doctors still use ginger in several forms for many ailments. They recommend chewing a piece of the root to relieve toothache; a ginger plaster is prescribed to dull a headache; and ginger tea is given to stimulate the intestinal tract.

Ginger receives its odor from the oils it contains; its pungency comes from its resin; the lighter its color, the more "bite" it has.

GINGER

"To ginger" means *to put spirit into*, and that is exactly what ginger root does to anything with which it comes in contact, be it gingerbread, ginger ale, candy, or preserves. Old kings of the Orient used to nibble ginger that had been boiled in honey. Great-grandmama kept a little stone jar of candied ginger on the pantry shelf. Today we seem to be losing track of the fine practice of "gingering" our food. The largest use for this spice in the kitchen is in the flavoring of cookies and cakes. It also has a place in meat cookery. Pot roasts, for instance, may be rubbed with ginger before they are seared, or a little may be added to the brown gravy with which they are served. Sometimes ginger-snaps are used in the latter for the double purpose of flavoring and thickening. Beef tongue is also delicious served with a gingersnap sauce.

Preserved ginger is made as follows: It is washed and then boiled for 24 hours, after which it is soaked for a day in salt water. It is then washed once more, sun-dried, and boiled for half a day w th an equal weight of sugar and placed in jars for several days. It is once more boiled and finally sealed in jars.

GINGER CRISPS

½ cup butter
½ cup light molasses
½ cup sugar
1 tbsp vinegar
2 cups all-purpose flour
1 tsp cinnamon
½ tsp ginger
1½ tsp soda

Put butter, molasses, sugar, and vinegar into a saucepan and boil 3 minutes, stirring constantly. Remove from heat and cool. Sift flour, measure and resift 3 times with cinnamon, ginger, and soda. Add to the cooled butter mixture and blend well. Wrap in waxed paper and chill overnight or for several hours. Roll out on lightly floured board very thin ($^1/_{16}$th inch thick). Cut with a 2-inch cookie cutter. Place on greased baking sheet and bake in a moderate oven (375° F.) for 7 minutes. Remove from sheet while warm and place on rack to cool. Stored in air tight container, these cookies will keep for several months. (Makes 10 dozen very thin cookies)

GINGER ICE-BOX COOKIES

4 cups all-purpose flour
1 tsp soda
3½ tsp ginger
¼ tsp salt
1 cup shortening
½ cup light brown sugar firmly packed
¾ cup sorghum molasses
2 eggs, unbeaten

Sift flour, measure and resift 3 times with soda, ginger and salt. Cream the shortening, blend in the sugar, add the sorghum and eggs, and beat vigorously until smooth and fluffy. Then add the flour mixture and stir until thoroughly combined. Pack into a refrigerator freezing tray or small loaf pan lined with waxed paper and place in refrigerator to chill until very firm; or shape into roll and wrap in waxed paper before chilling. Do not freeze. When ready to bake, slice ⅛ inch thick with a thin-bladed, very sharp knife. Place on greased baking sheet and bake in a moderate oven (350° F.) for 15 to 18 minutes, or until nicely browned. The dough may be kept in the refrigerator several days if well wrapped, and sliced and baked as cookies are needed. (Makes about 6½ dozen cookies)

GINGER ICE CREAM

To a quart of vanilla ice cream, made as indicated, add, when beginning to stiffen, ½ cup preserved chopped ginger and 2 tablespoons ginger sirup. Complete freezing. *See* ICE CREAM.

GINGER SNAPS

2½ cups sifted flour
1 tsp salt
2 tsp baking soda
1 tsp ground cinnamon
1½ tsp ground ginger
1 cup molasses
½ cup shortening

Sift the flour, salt, soda, and spices twice. Heat the molasses to the bubbling point; then add the shortening (butter or vegetable shortening). Remove from the fire immediately and cool. Gradually stir in the sifted, dry ingredients. Blend thoroughly. Roll out to ⅛ of an inch thick upon a lightly-floured board, and cut into desired, fancy shapes with cutters dipped in flour. Bake on an ungreased baking sheet in a moderate oven (350° F.) 8 to 10 minutes. Cool. When cold, store in cookie jar, and keep in a cool dry place. (Makes about 6 dozen cookies)

GINGER ALE. A nonalcoholic, effervescent beverage impregnated with ginger, making a cooling and refreshing drink.

GINGER BEER. A fermented beverage flavored with ginger; very low in alcoholic content.

GINGERBREAD. Perhaps the oldest of all sweet cakes, gingerbread can trace its lineage back to days in Egyptian history. But it was really a Greek of the Island of Rhodes who invented it about 2800 B.C. Rhodes became so famous for its *melitates*, as it was called, perhaps because of its golden color, that all the countries around the Mediterranean, and even those beyond the Pillars of Hercules were crowding the port for their supplies of the delicious cakes. Besides their gingerbread made of flour, honey and of course, ginger, the Rhodians invented nougat, which was made of dried currants and almonds, a confection which like the *melitate*, has enjoyed undying popularity.

Ginger was in general use among all nations of the day, and in China and India had been an important article of commerce. In England, even before the Norman Conquest, it was, next to pepper, the most common of all spices. By the 13th century, gingerbread was a well-established food and Chaucer tells us that "they sette hym Roiall spicerye and Gingerbread."

In an old English manuscript there is set down a simple recipe for "gyngerbrede": "Take a quart of hony (honey) and seethe yt and skeme yt clene; take Saffroun (saffron), poundir Pepir (pepper), and throw ther-on: take grated Brede (bread) and make yt so styff that yt wol be cut into strippes; then take poudir (powdered) Cinammon and strew there-on y-now; then make yt square, lyke as thou wolt slyce yt; then when thou slycest hyt, caste Box leaves above, y-styked ther-on Cloves, and if thou wyll have yt Red, coloure yt with Saunderys y-now (Saunderys was red sandalwood). . ."

It was about this time that they began molding the gingerbread into fanciful shapes—men, birds, animals, and the letters of the alphabet. Sometimes these were given a coating of gilt, hence the expression "take the gilt off the gingerbread." Throughout the 16th century it was a common article of food and much favored as a gift of honor by workmen to their patrons, and by youngsters to their elders a symbol of respect. If it was to be a symbol of honor it often measured as much as three feet across and weighed more than 150 pounds, according to the nature of the occasion being celebrated.

It is said that at the time of the birth of Peter the Great, the Czar was presented with more than 125 loaves, the largest being in the shape of the arms of the city of Moscow. Two, of 100 pounds each, represented the double Imperial Eagle, while another reproduced the Kremlin with its turrets, surrounded by many horsemen.

Gingerbread, of course, has many variations. There is orange gingerbread, pineapple gingerbread, and all the fruit tribe gingerbread, Scotch gingerbread, mixed fruit gingerbread, molasses gingerbread, nut gingerbread, all made on the same basic principle—that is, with shortening, sugar, egg, molasses, flour, soda, spices, hot water, or fruit juice. If desired, it may be frosted or iced.

Served piping hot from the oven with whipped cream and a baked apple, it is a dessert fit for a king. Served with fresh or canned fruit, it is satisfying. All recipes for cake of this sort are simple and easy to prepare and for this reason they are popular with the busy homemaker.

GINGERBREAD MEN

2¾ cups all-purpose flour
½ tsp soda
1 tsp ginger
½ tsp cinnamon
½ tsp salt
½ cup shortening
¼ cup brown sugar, firmly packed
¾ cup light molasses
1 egg beaten
½ tsp grated lemon rind
1 tsp hot water
1 tsp vinegar

Sift the flour, measure and resift 3 times with soda, spices and salt. Cream the shortening and add the sugar in two or three portions, creaming each time until mixture is fluffy. Add molasses and egg and beat until smooth. Fold in the sifted dry ingredients gradually, then add lemon rind, water and vinegar and blend thoroughly. Cover dough and chill. Roll out small portions of the chilled dough at a time on lightly floured board to ¼ inch thickness. Cut in shape of snow men, Santa Clauses, etc., using cookie cutter, or a cardboard pattern. Transfer carefully to greased, floured baking sheets, using a pancake turner to do the lifting of the cookies and a spatula to carefully slide them off onto the sheet. Bake in a moderate oven (350° F.) for about 20 minutes or until cooked through and nicely browned. Transfer to a cake rack. Decorate with powdered sugar frosting, currants, candies, etc., to make faces, beards, buttons, etc. If the cutouts are intended for the Christmas tree, make a small hole before baking. (Makes 12 gingerbread men)

GINGERBREAD MUFFINS

½ cup butter and lard mixed
½ cup sugar
3 cups sifted flour
1½ tsp baking soda
½ tsp salt
1 tsp cinnamon
1 tsp ginger
½ tsp cloves
1 egg, beaten
1 cup New Orleans molasses
1 cup hot water

Cream the shortening and sugar, then add the sifted dry ingredients alternately with the egg, molasses and hot water. Beat until smooth. Bake in small, well greased muffin pans in a moderately hot oven (375° F.) about 20 minutes.

GINGERBREAD WAFFLES

2 cups sifted flour
1 tsp baking powder
1 tsp baking soda
⅔ tsp salt
1 tsp ground ginger
2 eggs
1 cup molasses
½ cup milk
6 tbsp melted shortening

Sift together all the dry ingredients and mix to a batter with the beaten egg yolks, the molasses and milk stirred together, and the melted shortening. Finally fold in the stiffly beaten egg whites. Bake at a slightly lower temperature than plain waffles because molasses burns readily. (Makes 6 to 8 waffles)

HOT GINGERBREAD SQUARES

½ cup butter or shortening
½ cup brown sugar
1 cup dark molasses
2 eggs
2½ cups sifted flour
¼ cup cocoa
2 tsp baking powder
1 tsp ground ginger
1 tsp ground cinnamon
½ tsp ground nutmeg
½ tsp ground cloves
½ tsp soda
½ tsp salt
¾ cup hot strong coffee or water

Cream the butter or shortening. Gradually add the sugar. When blended, beat in the molasses, then the eggs, one at a time, and beat well. Sift the dry ingredients together. Add the sifted dry ingredients alternately with the coffee or water, beating after each addition. The batter should be rather thin. Pour in a well greased shallow pan and bake in a moderate oven (350° F.) for 30 minutes. Divide into squares with two fork and serve hot with whipped cream, plain or flavored with a little molasses or grated cheese. Or serve with cream cheese softened with a little cream.

PLAIN GINGERBREAD

½ cup water
1 cup molasses
2¼ cup flour
1 tsp soda
½ tsp salt
1½ tsp ground ginger
¼ cup melted shortening

Combine the water and molasses. Sift the dry ingredients and stir into the first mixture, then add the melted shortening. Blend thoroughly and pour into a well greased or greased-paper-lined baking pan.

Bake in a moderate oven (350° F) for ½ to ¾ of an hour.

GINKGO. A Japanese tree cultivated in the United States for its handsome foliage and delicious nuts, which are much used in Japanese cookery.

GINSENG. A Chinese herb with an aromatic stimulant root. In China the root is used as medicine. *See also* HERBS.

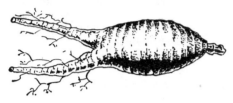

GINSENG

GISLEV CHEESE. A Danish, hard, rennet cheese made from the skim milk of cows.

GIZZARD. The second stomach of birds, in which the food is ground. It is used to make giblet gravy, first cleaning and removing the thick inner skin. *See* GRAVY.

GJETOST CHEESE. A Scandinavian goat's milk cheese.

GLACE. (I) Glacé is the transparent candy coating used to cover nuts and various dried frui s. Most fruits cannot be glacéd, as their own moisture would immediately destroy the clear coating Glacé is also used to make lollipops, wafers and many clear, hard candies.

BASIC RECIPE

2 cups sugar
⅔ cup water
⅛ tsp cream of tartar

Combine the sugar, water, and cream o f tartar in a small saucepan. Stir only until the sugar is dissolved; then cook to 310° F. Remove immediately from the fire, and dip the base of the saucepan into cold water to check the temperature rise, and the consequent slight discoloration. Then gently immerse in it perfect whole or half nut meats, sections of candied pineapple, whole candied cherries, small prunes which have been pitted carefully or other dried fruits by means of a candy-dipping fork. Allow any excess sirup to drain off. Then turn the coated candies upside down on an oil slab or platter to cool. They will harden almost immediately. The glacé sirup will thicken as it cools and may be gently reheated over a moderate flame.

Observe the following cautions very carefully: Be particular in measuring the cream of tartar; a very little helps to insure clarity, but too much makes the glacé sticky. If during the cooking process, drops of sirup are thrown up on the sides of the ; aucepan, they must be carefully removed with a small brush dipped in cold water, or a strip of cheesecloth tied around the tines of a fork The dipping of the fruits and nuts into glacé must be done with the utmost care and gentleness to avoid clouding.

Glacé which is left over after dipping fruits or nuts may be flavored with a drop or two of peach, apricot, lemon, vanilla, or other flavoring, including liquor. It may be delicately tinted with various colorings. Dropped from the lip of the saucepan unto oiled slab or platter, it will make dainty candy wafers about the size of a quarter.

Glacé is to a large extent a "weather candy"—that is, its crispness is affected by both heat and moisture. If glacé must be made in hot or damp weather, it is well to cook it to one or two degrees higher than the temperature indicated, to offset any tendency toward stickiness. *See also* CANDY.

GLACE. (II) In French terminology, glacé means iced, as with ice cream. Thus, meringue glacé is a meringue served with ice cream.

GLASS. (I) The common term for a drinking vessel made of glass. *See* GLASSWARE.

GLASS. (II) To "glass" a food means to preserve or store it in a glass container. *See* CANNING

GLASSED GOODS. This is a general term given to foods that are packed in glass containers. *See also* CANNING.

GLASSWARE. This term embraces all items of kitchen and table ware that are made of glass, as opposed to similar items made of ceramics (*which see*), plastics (*which see*), metal (*see* HOLLOW WARE), and other materials.

HISTORY

Glass is one of the oldest "made" materials known to man, there being definite evidence that glass was produced in Egypt about 1500 B.C., and very strong evidence that it was known and used as far back as 3000 B.C. It is interesting to note that a block of blue glass that very probably had been used for construction purposes has been unearthed in the Mesopotamian region in Iraq, especially in light of the current use of glass brick in modern architecture.

Though the Egyptians made large numbers of glass bottles and vessels, it remained for the Greeks to invent the blowpipe that facilitated the production of hollow glass objects and still is a basic instrument in glass manufacture. Among the other races that have made notable contributions to glassmaking are the Roman, Venetian, French, German, and English.

In America, the first glass factory was established at Jamestown in 1608, and later manufactured glass beads for trade with the Indians. America, too, has made important contributions to the science of glassmaking, especially in industrial fields, and the development of processing machines.

Though old in use and little changed in basic formula, glass has not been pushed aside by the newer materials. Indeed, its applications have increased rather than diminished through the years, and even now, for example, spun glass fibers are beginning to appear in the textile field.

MANUFACTURE

The principal materials used to make glass are silica sand, soda ash, and lime. These, or similar ingredients (the composition varies with the type of glass being made) are mixed together with bits of broken glass called *cullet*, and subjected to high temperatures in a furnace. The heat, usually in the neighborhood of 2,700 degrees Fahrenheit, changes this melange of solids into a molten mass of glass, the impurities and unmelted particles sinking to the bottom, leaving only pure glass at the surface. This molten glass is then formed and cooled into shape.

Blown Glass. The most interesting of all processes to watch, hand-blowing techniques have changed little through the years. The blower dips one end of his long iron blowpipe into the furnace and "gathers" a molten glob of glass at the end. By careful manipulation of the pipe and judicious blowing, he causes the mass to take the desired form before it cools. A mold of

some sort is often used to aid him in making complex or uniform shapes. Since blowing causes an air-bubble to form within the mass, this process is used to make hollow items as tumblers, vases, bottles, etc. If stemware or other "footed" pieces are being made, a second mass is attached to the blown piece and is either pressed into shape between molds or formed with the aid of wooden paddles. The finished piece, still red-hot, is carefully detached from the blowpipe by the "crack-off" boy, trimmed to size with heated tools, and then sent through an annealing tunnel where it is gradually cooled to room temperature.

Highly ornate blown-glass center-pieces, such as glass ships, are usually made from heated glass tubes rather than from a blob at the end of a pipe.

Today the blower makes specialized pieces, for automatic machinery has been developed for the mass production of glass items. These machines duplicate most of the blower's functions; placing measured globs of molten glass on the ends of tubes, using compressed air to blow the glass within a mold, and breaking it off for annealing. The bulk of the cheaper blown glass items are now made with this machinery.

Pressed Glass. This process, which is applicable to some of the hollow shapes and all of the flat and solid shapes, consists merely of using a mold to shape the molten glass. Both hand processes and automatic machinery are used in making pressed glass, and tumblers and even stemware may be so made, provided that the opening in the finished piece is large enough to permit the escape of the mold piece used to shape the inside. Pressed pieces also go through an annealing tunnel to remove the internal stresses and safely reduce the glass temperature.

Once shaped and cooled, the glass piece made by either process may then be decorated, if this is desired.

Applied Color. Glass is, of course, made in different colors, but if a design rather than a solid color is desired, it must be applied later. Metals, such as gold or platinum, as well as pigments are used to decorate glass. The design is placed on the piece either by hand painting, silk screening, spraying, or some comparable process, and, in the case of the better glassware, is baked or fired so that it will not chip, peel, or wash off.

Cut Glass. In this process, designs are cut into the glass using various types of abrasive wheels. If not polished, it is called *gray cutting*, which, though suitable to some designs, lacks the sparkle and effect of a polished cut. Properly cut and properly polished, cut glass is clear and has a prismatic effect, adding color and sparkle to the piece as the cuts reflect and separate the light rays.

Because of the nature of the process, cut glass designs are pretty much elaborations of the straight line. During the Victorian era, cut glass was very popular and highly elaborate patterns were developed. Today's tastes are simpler and the craftsmen usually restrict themselves to plain mitre-cuts and flutes.

Etched Glass. Designs may also be cut in glass through the use of certain acids. The glass is first covered with a protective material, usually a wax, and the desired design cut through this layer. The glass is then immersed in the acid until the proper depth of design is reached. Etched designs are frosty or clouded in appearance and uniform in depth. The process permits delicate and elaborate work and floral patterns are commonly made in this manner.

Copper-Wheel Engraving. This difficult process comes more under the heading of art than industry, and by means of it are made the most beautiful pieces of worked glass. While abrasive wheels are used, they are capable of doing infinitely finer work than those used for ordinary cut glass. As in etching, the designs are usually frosted in appearance, but because different depths of cut may be more easily made than in etching, and because a variety of "grains" or types of frost are possible, the potentialities are endless. This process is confined to the more expensive glassware and it has produced many examples of magnificent art-work, the better products often going to museums.

Sand Blasting. This process is quite similar to etching, a stream of fine sand particles driven by compressed air being used to cut the glass. The design is first cut in a shield, somewhat like a stencil, which protects the rest of the glass during the blasting process.

Other Methods. There are many possible ways of effecting decorations in glass that have not been mentioned either because their use has been generally discarded or because they are not used for glassware of a type or price-range that is apt to be used in the kitchen or on the table. The so-called *spun glass*, for example, is made of colored glass rods bound in clear glass and twisted to form the desired effects. The possibilities of joining different colored glasses heated to a plastic state and then doing further things with them are endless. Different effects may also be obtained on the surface by dipping and by deliberately causing cracking and crazing. Designs may also be etched in relief or bas-relief; i.e., by cutting the surface below that of the design.

Many of these methods have been used for kitchenware in the past, but modern manufacturing methods have supplanted them and they are now found mainly in collections.

TYPES OF GLASSWARE

The range of glass-made objects is extensive, reaching into practically every phase of culinary work. Foods are preserved in glass jars and bottles (*see* CANNING), cooked in flame-resistant glass implements (*see* KITCHEN EQUIPMENT), and served on glass plates (*see* DISHES). Salt and pepper are dispensed from glass shakers, cigarettes served from glass boxes, and the table itself lighted from either glass candlesticks or glass fixtures.

Most of these items are made from other materials as well, and whether the object used be of glass, metal, plastics, ceramics, or some other material is largely a question of individual taste and circumstances. Most of those items are discussed under other headings, though, of course, the rules later given concerning glass should be applied to their purchase and care if that is the material selected.

There is, however, one field in which glass predominates; predominates so much, in fact, that the word "glass" has come to be a synonym for that type of object. The field is, of course, that of drinking vessels, and though they have been, are, and will be made from other materials, glass is still favored. There is little doubt that glass will continue to occupy that position, chiefly because of its scratch-resisting transparency.

A transparent drinking vessel offers two distinct advantages; the amount of fluid in the vessel is visible, and the beauty of the liquid may be observed. The first is more of a convenience than anything else, especially when pouring, but the second is a definite gastronomical aid.

By appealing to the eye, a food appeals to the stomach, and the rich, gay colors of fruit juices and the creamy coolness of milk appeal to the appetite. The sight and sound of ice cubes cl nking in a liquid are almost as much of a cooling aid as the actual temperature of the liquid.

Designs in drinking vessels will vary with the period and the manufacturer. A few specialized shapes have been developed to meet specific needs, and some other shapes have come, through tradition, to be associated with specific uses, but in the main, the only requirement of a drinking vessel is that it be of the proper capacity to hold the optimum serving of the liquid for which it is intended. The shape that capacity will take is subject to the whims of styling, and the capacity itself will vary as food tastes change.

A typical asso tment of glassware shapes is given in this book. It must be remembered that these are representative rather than arbitrary. The various glasses and their uses are described at length below and illustrated on pages 548 and 549.

In general, drinking vessels fall into three main groupings, depending on their physical appearance; stemware, tumblers, and handled vessels i.e., cups, mugs, or steins.

Stemware. This classification applies to those vessels which are constructed as a bowl set upon a stem, which, in turn, is mounted on a foot or base. As the capacity of the glass (and hence the size of the bowl) increases, there is a tendency for the stem to shorten as the bowl goes conical, to maintain the proper balance of the glass. Carried far enough, there is reached that neither region of the *footed tumbler*, where the stem is either non-existent or hardly worth mentioning. The difference between the two types being only a matter of length of stem, the two types are usually grouped together as a matter of convenience.

Whenever possible, stemware should be grasped by the stem and not by the bowl, thus keeping the heat of the hand from acting on the temperature of the contents. This, rather than appearance, is the basic purpose of stemware, though many pieces are now so designed as to make such a grip either impractical or impossible.

The more common types of stemware are shown in the drawing, *which see*. The

following discussion describes the most useful shapes.

Pony. This glass is intended for the serving of brandy which is served in small portions. The term is also applied generally to any glass which is smaller than the one normally used to hold the liquid being served, and for a unit of liquid measurement which is not now common (*see* WEIGHTS AND MEASURES).

Pousse Café, Cordial, and Brandy. These glasses have been specifically designed for ease in the construction of the Pousse Café (*which see*) type of drink, but is also used to serve cordials and liqueurs.

Note. These first three glasses may be used interchangeably, but difficulty will be encountered in making a Pousse Café in anything but the proper glass.

Sherry and Port. Though shown here plain, there is one school of thought which holds for cut glass for port service because of the prismatic effects produced. As a general rule, however, wine glasses should be plain.

Parfait. Though designed for the service of parfaits (*which see*), this glass may also be used for the service of sours (*which see*).

Claret. Should the family be restricted to only one set of wine glasses, a glass of this type is the best for all-round service.

Hollow Stem Champagne. This is a highly specialized glass type, being designed for serving sparkling wine. The hollow stem gives the bubbles a longer path to follow, greatly enhancing the physical beauty of the wine. They are, however, expensive and difficult to clean.

Rhine Wine. This is the traditional German glass for the service of the Rhine and Moselle wines, and is one of the few exceptions to the general rule of serving wine in clear glassware. The Germans hold that a tinted glass improves the flavor, while the French, rivals in wine growing as in other things, insist that the German notion stems from a desire to conceal the cloudiness of their wine.

High Sherbet. This glass may also be used to serve champagne.

Flip. This glass is particularly adapted to the service of flip (*which see*).

Ward Eight. Used in the serving of the Ward Eight (*which see*) drink, this glass shape has many other uses, especially for water and beer.

Brandy Inhaler. One of the most specialized of glasses, this is designed to give the connoisseur the utmost in enjoyment from

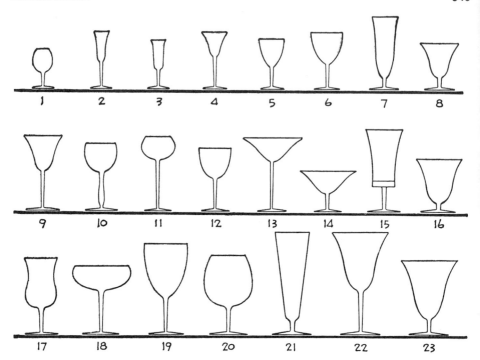

GLASSWARE 1. Pony ¾–1 oz. 2. Brandy, ¾–1 oz. 3. Pousse Cafe and Cordial, ¾–1 oz. 4. Sherry, 2 oz. 5. Port, 2–3 oz. 6. Cocktail, 3–4 oz. 7. Parfait, 3–6 oz. 8. Seafood or Fruit Cocktail, 4 oz. 9. Claret, 4 oz. 10. Hollow-stem Champagne, 4 oz. 11. Rhine Wine, 4 oz. 12. Rhine Wine and Sauterne, 4–5 oz. 13. High Sherbet, 4½–5½ oz. 14. Low Sherbet, 4½–5½ oz. 15. Flip, 5 oz. 16. Juice or Sour Tumbler, 5 oz. 17. Hot Toddy, 5–6 oz. 18. Saucer Champagne, 6 oz. 19. Ward Eight, 8 oz.

his brandy. A small portion of brandy (*which see*) is placed in the glass, and the inhaler cuddled in both hands. The heat thus generated vaporizes the brandy which is rolled about to wet the inner walls, and the relatively small size of the opening helps confine the vapors.

Tumblers. A tumbler is a drinking vessel that has neither stem nor foot nor handle. The name has an interesting derivation that harkens back to a much hardier day when there was a vogue for conical shaped drinking vessels. These vessels were built with either a rounded or a very small bottom making it impossible to set them down until they were empty, for a full vessel would "tumble." Today, however, tumblers are usually cylindrical or slightly tapered in shape, and, if designed with the correct proportion of base area to height, are difficult to tip.

There is little difference between tumblers, other than their size and capacity; factors that are governed largely by their intended use. Because they all have the same general appearance, it is often easier to use the same tumbler for different purposes than it is in the case of stemware, for certain stemware shapes have come to be identified with specific uses, making substitution more readily detected.

Whisky. The traditional "shot glass" or container for individual servings of straight whisky should not be confused with the measuring container, the jigger (*which see*), which is often quite similar in appearance. If the exact capacity of this glass is known, however, it may be used for measuring purposes. *See also* BARTENDING.

Old Fashioned. This glass has been developed for the preparation of the cocktail of the same name (*which see*), and is customarily restricted to that use.

Lemonade. This is one of the more useful of the tumblers, being also proper for serving individual eggnogs and punches. It may also be pressed into use to serve collinses and highballs, as well as any of

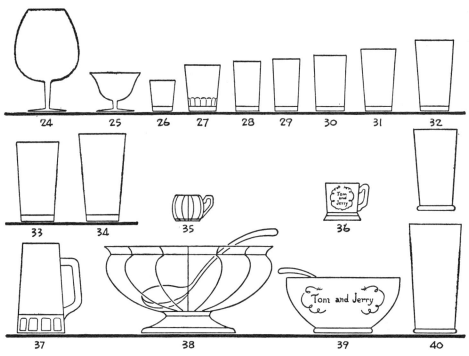

20. **Beer Goblet, 8–10 oz.**　21. **Pilsner Glass, 8–14 oz.**　22. **Water Goblet, 9 oz.**　23. **Water Tumbler, 9–12 oz.**　24. **Brandy Inhaler**　25. **Finger Bowl**　26. **Whisky, 1½–2½ oz.**　27. **Old Fashioned, 4–6 oz.**　28. **Delmonico, 5 oz.**　29. **Whisky Sour, 6 oz.**　30. **Fizz, 6–7 oz.**　31. **Highball, 8 oz.**　32. **Collins, 10 oz.**　33. **Lemonade, 12 oz.**　34. **Zombie, 14 oz.**　35. **Punch Cup, 4 oz.**　36. **Tom and Jerry Mug, 4–6 oz.**　37. **Beer Stein, 10 oz.** 38. **Punch Bowl**　39. **Tom and Jerry Bowl**　40. **Mixing Glass and Shaker**

the diluted fruit juice beverages and ice cream sodas.

Zombie. This, the tallest of the tumblers, has a rather limited use, being generally restricted to the preparation of the drink of the same name (*which see*).

Cups, Mugs and Steins. These are all handled drinking vessels, and though more often made of other materials, are found in glass. Mugs and steins with their thick, insulating walls are especially adapted to the serving of very hot or very cold beverages. The handle keeps the hand from contact with these temperature extremes, and the walls help maintain the liquid temperature. In the case of beverages, such as beer, which should be served chilled but do not permit dilution from melted ice, the mug or stein can first be packed in ice and the chilled walls will aid greatly in keeping the beverage cool.

Beer Stein. Though there are many sizes and shapes of beer steins, this has come to be the traditional American vessel. It is not to be confused with the "schooner," a stemware shape once highly popular for serving beer that has been largely replaced by the ten ounce tumbler.

Accessories. The range of glassware items is tremendous, and the examples given are merely those closest related to the other glassware shown.

Punch Bowl. Punch bowls are traditionally made of glass, the preference lying with cut crystal. It should match the punch cup. *See* PUNCH.

Tom and Jerry Bowl. Though this seasonal drink may be mixed and served in regular punch equipment, tradition decrees special utensils. *See* TOM AND JERRY.

Mixing Glass and Shaker. The heavy walled mixing glass is an invaluable aid in many phases of cooking and all phases of drink preparation. The size will vary, but they are usually made in pint and larger capacities. Graduated mixing glasses are to be preferred as an aid in measuring, though they are made plain as well. The shaker is not to be confused with the *combination shaker*, which is a complete instrument in itself (*see* COCKTAIL SHAKER), but is only an open container, usually made of metal, which fits over the mixing glass. *See also* BARTENDING.

PURCHASING GLASSWARE

Glassware is available in a wide range of design and price, running from antiques to modern mass-produced sets. In selecting glassware, the homemaker should look for the utmost in beauty and design within the price range that best fits the family budget. There are reasons other than the aesthetic for this; the careful design and good craftsmanship needed to produce beauty are not apt to be lavished on inferior products.

Every piece should be carefully checked for functional design. The piece should be able to do well the task for which it was made, and the proportions should be such that in addition to being pleasing to the eye, the piece is not easily tipped. Further, there should be no thin lips, handles, or other protuberances that will be easily chipped or broken off in use.

The decoration of the piece should be checked to see that it was properly done. Check cut crystal to see that the cuts were properly made, properly polished, and have a good prismatic effect. A good test of this is to inspect the glass carefully in strong sunlight against a white background, such as a damask tablecloth. Modern tastes lean towards simplicity, but if the ornate cuttings of the past are preferred, the quality of the glass itself should be carefully scrutinized, lest the ornamentation be used to conceal defects in the material. The same caution applies to etched glass, for etching is usually delicate and graceful, used with restraint; not heavy and deep, covering wide areas of glass.

Applied coloring of any sort should be baked into the glass so that it will not chip or wash off in use. It is well to avoid tinted glass in drinking vessels unless your taste prefers them, for through time, man has come to associate color with taste. Not only is the use of tinted glass apt to subconsciously confuse him, but with some people it actually impairs their enjoyment of the beverage within. If color is desired, it is better to choose opaque colors, for

then the eye and stomach are not confronted with the spectacle of green milk, for example. Tinted glass can be most fitting for uses other than drinking vessels, however.

Good glass should be crystal clear, and the best test of this is to place it against a pure white cloth in strong sunlight. The better the glass, the more pronounced the sparkle and luster, features that should be inspected in much the same manner. The artwork on the glass is another indication of the worth of the glass itself, as previously explained. Blown glass should give off a clear, bell-like tone when struck, though pressed glass may lack this feature.

Glass should be held to the light and checked for internal imperfections, such as air bubbles, impurities, etc. It should be looked through to see if there are any noticeable distortions of the light passing through. Such distortions are caused by stresses and strains within the material, and these are points of weakness that, in some cases, may even crack of themselves because of temperature changes.

The glass should be felt to see that there are no sharp edges, points, nicks, or roughness, especially about the rim. The piece should be inspected to see that there are no chips or scratches caused by poor handling, and finally it should be inspected for heavy ridges (parting lines) caused by improper mold closures, and other defects of faulty workmanship.

The patterns should be selected with an eye to their suitability with the rest of the tableware (*see* TABLE SETTING AND SERVICE), and finally some thought should be given to selecting an "open" pattern so that matching pieces may be added and broken pieces replaced in the future.

CARE AND CLEANING OF GLASSWARE

Though brittle by nature, if glass is treated with due respect it is as long-lived and durable as any of the materials; indeed, even more so than most since it is little effected by the actions of time and the elements. Manufacturers are continually working to bring out more durable grades of glass and there are many heavy duty types now available that will weather considerable abuse.

In general, the two main enemies of glass are impact and sudden or uneven extremes of temperature. With reasonable care both can be avoided and the life of the glass prolonged indefinitely. Other than that, little special care is required in the handling and storage of glassware.

Some thought should be given before pouring a hot fluid, such as coffee, into a glass. If the glass contains ice, or is chilled from other causes, a metal spoon should first be inserted to absorb some of the heat. Conversely, cold water should not be poured into a glass that has just held a hot fluid and has not had sufficient time to cool. Glass plates and other vessels should always be brought to room temperature before food that is either very hot or very cold is placed on or in them. A heated object should not be set on a piece of cold glassware and vice versa.

There are some special types of heat-resistant glass that have been developed especially for cooking and similar purposes. Instructions for proper care in use is normally supplied with such pieces and should be followed closely.

Drinking glasses, bowls, etc., should never be stacked one inside the other for there is danger of two or more pieces becoming stuck together. Should this happen, the pieces should not be separated by prying, for there is danger of breakage. Fill the inner glass with cold water and hold the outer one in warm water and, because of the expansion caused, the pieces should then separate easily.

A tiny nick or even a larger cutting edge caused by chipping may be smoothed down by careful rubbing with a piece of fine emery cloth.

Cleaning. Though glass does not corrode or tarnish, proper washing is most important for its proper appearance, since a dull or dirty surface impairs the sparkle, luster, and clarity that largely constitute the true beauty of glass. It is a characteristic of glass that minute spots or specks and films that would go unnoticed on other materials are readily visible.

Glassware should always be washed first, for the other tableware, and especially the cooking utensils, are prone to leave a deposit of grease in the dish water. The water should be warm, but not so hot that the bare hands cannot be comfortably immersed during the washing operations. A small amount of ammonia or a detergent may be used in the water. Light suds work well, but too much soap is apt to leave streaks on the glassware. A few drops of bluing in the water will aid greatly in restoring sparkle to the glass. A water softener may be added, not only to the washing water, but also to the rinse water. Drinking glasses may be made antiseptically clean and germ-free by adding three tablespoons of a bottled bleaching compound to an ordinary dishpan full of water.

A soft brush should be used to wash glassware that has either cut or pressed patterns to insure proper cleansing of the crevices. Gold-decorated glassware should never be washed or rinsed in scalding water, and a strong soap should never be used, for such soaps can actually eat away pure gold.

Never crowd glassware in a dishpan lest there be breakage caused by jostling. It is also a good plan never to place more than two stem glasses in the pan at one time. For double protection, especially if the pieces are valuable, a cloth or towel should be spread on the bottom of the pan and another on the drainboard to insulate against careless bumps.

Though good glass should withstand a rinse with boiling water, it is advisable to use rinse water of the same temperature as the wash water. The glasses should be drained on a rubber-covered rack, a rubber mat, or a thick towel.

Drying. If the glass has been washed with ammonia or a soapless detergent, it will airdry to a high luster. However, if soap or suds have been used, it must be wiped dry to prevent streaks and spots. Glasses should be wiped as soon as possible to minimize the danger of water spots. A dry towel made of linen or some other lintless material should be used, and it is well to follow up with a polishing, using a completely dry lintless towel. Glassware, incidently, should always be polished immediately prior to use to remove dust that will impair its appearance.

Stain Removal and other hints. In some regions, drinking water will leave a lime deposit in bottles and pitchers. As a preventative measure, water pitchers should be washed after every using and dried thoroughly both inside and out. Should such a deposit form, it may be removed by placing vinegar-soaked tea leaves in the pitcher or bottle and shaking them about until the deposit disappears.

The brown deposit that eventually appears in vinegar cruets may be removed with diluted ammonia.

Milk glasses should be rinsed with cool or lukewarm water as soon as possible after use. If they become sticky, or if stains appear, use lukewarm water softened with soda.

Wine glasses should be washed immediately after use.

It is obvious, of course, that chemicals, and never steel wool or other abrasives, should be used to remove stains and deposits from glass because of the possibilities of scratching.

GLAZE. To add luster by freezing or by heat. For example, we may glaze a fish under the flame of the broiling oven, to give a nicely browned shiny appearance. A baked ham, is glazed by spreading with brown sugar or a fruit purée. Tarts are glazed with melted jelly. See APRICOT for a typical glaze recipe.

GLOBE ARTICHOKE. Also known as French artichoke. See ARTICHOKE.

GLOBE ARTICHOKE

GLOBO DE ORO MELON. A round melon with light yellow rind and pink flesh. It is grown in the South and West. See MELON.

GLOIRE DES MONTAGNES CHEESE. Another name for the Hungarian cheese, Damen, which see.

GLORIA MUNDI. A sweetish wine from Madeira (which see).

GLOUCESTER CHEESE. An English cheese with a mild, rich flavor.

GLOW WINE PUNCH. A hot wine punch. See PUNCH.

GLUCOSE or DEXTROSE. A sugar found largely in the vegetable and fruit kingdom, in honey and in the animal organism, much less sweet than cane-sugar. It is prepared commercially by treating starch with sulfuric acid.

Glucose is present in almost all fruits, in the sweeter varieties of which it exists in large quantity. In peaches, pineapples, and strawberries it is found with cane sugar, and in grapes, cherries, and honey it occurs in connection with other varieties of sugars. In dried fruits, such as raisins or figs, glucose is present in a gummy form.

GLUMSE CHEESE. A German cottage cheese made from sour skim milk.

GLUTEN. Gluten is a valuable nitrogenous food product, separated in the process of making starch from wheat and other grains. The gluten retains the gas in dough —in excess it makes the flour soft and sticky. Gluten is capable of considerable expansion, and, as this power varies with different flours, it affects the quality of lightness of the bread. Some gluten expands four or five times as much as others. See FLOUR.

GLUTEN BREAD. See BREAD.

GLYCERINE. An oily, sweet, thick liquid compound of carbon, hydrogen, and oxygen, formed in the decomposition of fats, and used in making confectionery, soaps, etc.

GNOCCHI. An Italian dish of paste which may be filled with either ground meat, fish, cheese, poultry or vegetables, and served as a separate course.

GNOCCHI ROMANA (BAKED)·

2 cups milk
1 tsp salt
½ cup farina or flour
1 beaten egg
1 cup grated Parmesan cheese
3 tbsp butter

Scald the milk with the salt. Add the farina or flour, a tablespoon at a time, stirring constantly from the bottom of the pan to prevent lumping, and cook 10 minutes, stirring almost constantly. Add 1 tablespoon butter and half of the grated cheese. Remove from the fire and add the well-beaten egg, stirring vigorously. Roll the dough out on a floured board into a sheet one-half inch thick. Let it stand several hours; then cut into diamond-shaped pieces. Butter a baking dish and arrange in it a layer of *gnocchi*, sprinkle with grated cheese, dot with butter and repeat until the dish is full. Bake in a very hot oven (450° F.) for 20 to 25 minutes. Serve sizzling hot. (Serves 6)

GNOCCHI MILANAISE (BOILED)

4 tbsp olive oil
2 medium-sized onions, chopped fine
1 lb round steak, ground
1 tsp salt
⅛ tsp pepper
3 sprigs fresh parsley, minced fine
1 No. 2 can Italian tomatoes
3 cups mashed potatoes
2 cups sifted flour
1 tsp salt
2 qt boiling water or stock
½ cup grated Parmesan cheese

This dish should be prepared just when ready to serve, lest the *gnocchis* toughen. Brown the onions lightly in the olive oil in a heavy skillet; add the ground meat, and cook for five minutes, stirring almost constantly. Turn the mixture into a saucepan, and add the seasonings, parsley and tomatoes. Simmer for one hour, stirring frequently. Keep hot. Add the flour and salt to the potatoes and blend thoroughly. Knead the mixture into a soft dough; roll out on a floured board to ⅛ inch thick, then cut into 1½ to 2-inch squares. Drop into the boiling water (meat stock will add nourishment and flavor), and cook until each square comes to the top of the water. Skim out with perforated ladle or skimmer; drain thoroughly. Now place the *gnocchi*, thus boiled and hot, in a heated dish. Pour the hot tomato-meat sauce over them; sprinkle with grated cheese and serve immediately. (Serves 6)

GOAT. Seldom eaten by Americans, goat meat is very much relished by Italians and its preparation is about the same as that of lamb. For goat's milk, *see* MILK.

GOAT FISH. An edible American fish which belongs to the salmon family. It is also known under the name of "salmonette," under which name it is imported from Portugal. All the different methods of preparation of salmon may be applied to this fine fish.

GOAT'S MILK. *See* MILK.
GOAT'S MILK CHEESE. In goat's milk there is a softer curd and less fat than in cow's milk. This permits the making of delicious cheese. Some of the well-known names are: In France, *Chevret, Gavot, Fromage de Chevre*, and also the famous *Broccio* of Corsica; in Italy, the *Cacio Fiore*, and *Formaggio di Capri*; in the Caucasus, the *Eriwani*; in Macedonia, the *Ftinoporino*; in Scandinavia, the *Gjetost* and *Hvid Gjedeost*; in the German-speaking countries, the *Aiegenkase*; in the Carpathian Mountains district, the *Brinsen* or *Brinza* (locally known as "Landoch"); and others such as, *Zips, Siebenburgen, Neusohl, Altsohl*, and *Klencz*. *See also* CHEESE and MILK.

GOLD LABEL RUM. A general designation for a group of rums that are heavier and darker than the White Label Rums, but not as dark and heavy as the heavy-bodied tropical rums. *See* RUM.

GOLDBEERENAUSLESE. *See* AUSLESE.

GOLDEN CHASSELAS. A white table wine of the Chablis type made from Golden Chasselas (Gutedel) grapes. *See* CHABLIS.

GOLDEN FIZZ. An effervescent drink made using gin and egg yolk. *See* FIZZ.

GOLDEN MULLET. *See* MULLET.

GOLDWASSER. A strong liqueur made of a highly rectified spirit flavored with herbs and spices that is colorless but contains a very large number of minute fragments of gold leaf or a similar substance, from which it gets its name. The gold settles to the bottom, but when the liqueur is shaken, the specks permeate the liquid, dancing and flashing as the light strikes them.

In the olden days, gold was thought to be a nostrum, a cure for any and all ills, and was frequently prescribed as a medicine. This may well account for its appearance in a liqueur, for liqueurs were originally developed primarily for medicinal purposes (*see* LIQUEUR). The liqueur, which would taste as well without the gold particles, has survived in this form because of its colorful appearance.

GOMME SIRUP. Another name for Simple Sirup. *See* SIRUP.

GOOBER. A nickname for the peanut, *which see*.

GOOSE. An old proverb says, "The goose is a silly bird; too much for one, not enough for two." But geese on the American market today are usually big enough

GOOSE

554

to serve a family and guests. Allow about one and one-half pounds dressed weight for each serving.

Geese are classified as light when weighing from eight to eleven pounds; and heavy, when weighing 12 pounds or more. The half-grown goose is the most desirable.

American homemakers frequently, erroneously, consider the goose a greasy meat. European cooks have long appreciated it as a real delicacy and understand how to prepare it so as to have a savory meat, and utilize every bit of the soft, creamy fat. Goose fat, like chicken fat, makes excellent shortening for pastry and for many a special dainty.

Few dishes are more delicious than roast goose, home style, served with apricot, or apple and prune dressing. A stuffing containing some mild acid is desirable, as the acid serves to counteract the rich flavor of the meat. Goose is frequently stuffed with sauerkraut. Many of the old English cookbooks speak of the bird's being stuffed with apples and raisins. Apricot or prune dressing produces much the same flavor.

Much of the fat may be drained off if the goose, without stuffing, is first placed in a moderately hot oven (a good temperature is 425° F.), for a period of thirty minutes. The fat thus fried out, is then drained off, the goose stuffed as desired and the roasting completed. By following this method, you are assured of a deliciously tasty and tender, yet not greasy, bird. The legs of the goose are too short to permit trussing the same as with a turkey or chicken. Tie the trussing twine around one leg and then around the other, leaving about two inches of string between the legs. Bring the ends of the twine under the back, and then tie securely.

TRUSSED GOOSE

Wild Geese

White-Fronted Goose. Though occasionally met with on the Atlantic Coast and not uncommon in the Mississippi Valley, the white-fronted goose is essentially a bird of the West, and is particularly abundant in the Pacific Coast States. This is one of the geese which used to visit the wheat fields of California in such numbers as to threaten the crop, and which men were hired to kill and frighten away. The flocks of former days are now represented by comparatively small numbers, so the truly toothsome flesh of the bird is not enjoyed by as many gourmets today as in the past.

The nests of these geese are built on the grassy borders of ponds where the young can be quickly led into the seemingly protecting water. They feed on heath berries, hence their delicious flavor. Geese are strong of wing and of adventurous spirit, and to most of the tribe a migration of a thousand miles or so is a trifling matter.

Blue Goose. Also called Emperor Goose, this bird has a white head and neck, is much darker than the White-Front, and has pale bluish wings. Like its relatives, this species is a strict vegetarian and is particularly fond of the tender shoots of grass and of grain. It is a fine morsel and greatly esteemed by the gourmet.

When young and plump, a wild goose may be prepared in the fresh state. If old it should be allowed to hang for at least four days, when it may be roasted or still better, cooked *a l'estouffade* (that is, cooked like a smothered fowl).

Delicious entrées may be made when the bird is roasted and then cooled; the fillets are removed and may be prepared with different sauces, such as orange, anchovy, caper, bigarrade, currant jelly, etc. Wild goose seems to be predestined for salmi, as in fact are most of the game birds, except, of course, wild turkey. Most cooking methods applied to the domestic goose may also be used for the wild bird.

BRAISED GOOSE, FLEMISH METHOD

1 old goose
1 cup soft bread crumbs
Salt and black pepper
1 or 2 leaves each of sage, thyme and marjoram
2 tbsp butter
½ cup celery, parboiled and chopped fine
1 goose liver
White wine

1 cup chopped ham
Carrots, celery, onion
1 cup chicken stock
1 tsp gin

Combine all ingredients except the liver, wine, and the goose itself. Crush the liver with a fork, discarding all connective tissue, then add it to the stuffing and blend thoroughly, moistening with white wine to the consistency of any ordinary stuffing. Fill the body cavity of the bird which has been cleaned and singed with the mixture. Skewer or sew the vent, and truss.

Place in a braising kettle the raw ham, then the braising vegetables (carrots, celery, onion, etc.). Set the stuffed bird over these and pour over it a cup of good chicken or game stock to which the gin has been added. Cover closely and cook in a hot oven (400° F.) about 1½ hours without disturbing. Lift out the bird, place on a hot platter, brush over with melted fumet (*which see*) and keep hot.

Remove any excess fat from the braising kettle. Place over a hot fire and sprinkle in a scant tablespoon of flour. Bring to a rapid boil, stirring constantly. Add ½ cup of white wine, again bring to boiling point and strain through a fine sieve, pressing a little to extract all liquid from the vegetables. Add additional seasoning if necessary. Serve with the goose, accompanying this with plain boiled rice or wild rice and garnishing the serving platter with apple rings.

Comfit of Goose

For this really fine preserve, which keeps many months in a cool place, use a plump, fat goose—or several, if desired. For one goose proceed as follows:

Clean, singe, and cut the goose into four portions if small, or six if large—the legs and the breasts cut into two pieces, the carcass and the bones into two, likewise. Rub each piece with coarse salt, mixed with a little allspice, a pinch of thyme leaves, and a small piece of bay leaf, chopped very fine. Arrange in a deep dish, cover with salt, and cover with a small board with a heavy weight on it to keep the bird immersed in the brine. Let marinate at least 6 days. After this period, drain and wipe carefully with a damp cloth. Melt all the fat reserved from the bird in an enameled casserole. Arrange the pieces

of goose in the melted goose fat, and cook until nearly done—about 2½ hours—over a very low flame. (In some parts of Central Europe the entrails are added to the cooking meat.) Then turn the pieces of goose into a sterilized earthenware jar or crock and pour the fat from the cooking process over them. Cool. When thoroughly cold, add a layer of melted lard (1 inch thick), and allow it to solidify. Cover the jar or crock with a piece of paper, tie securely and place it in a cold dry place for future use. You may strain and clarify the goose fat before pouring it over the pieces of goose, if desired.

This method of preserving wild or domestic goose is advantageous in that by its use one may enjoy goose at any time of the year. Besides, this kind of conserve may be very useful for impromptu luncheons, as the goose pieces may be heated and served either on rice, noodles, purée of cabbage, red cabbage, spinach, etc., and even, when cubed small, served in patty shells, with cream sauce, to which mushrooms may be added.

Goose Neck Rocamadour

Rocamadour, known for its delicious and world-famed cheese, is also famous for its regional cookery. Those who have visited this picturesque little town in France, built on one of the many steep cliffs typical of the Massif Central, and sheltered from the north winds by three churches, one over-towering another, may have lunched or dined at the Hotel Sainte Marie and eaten stuffed goosenecks, a sensational regional dish that is nevertheless easily prepared at home.

The steps follow:

The Marinade

1 cup vinegar
1 liqueur glass brandy (applejack may be used)
1 glass white wine
2 cloves
2 small bay leaves
Small pinch of thyme leaves
1 small onion sliced fine
1 small carrot sliced fine
12 peppercorns, bruised
2 small cloves garlic, mashed
Salt to taste

Place all the ingredients together in a large bowl, and add the meat from 6 goose-necks from which the skin has been carefully removed (stripped to avoid tearing). Allow this to stand over night.

Clean the skins and put them in a separate dish for later use.

The Stuffing

1 lb sausage meat
2 duck livers
1 small truffle, finely chopped
Salt, white pepper and spices to taste
1 wineglass white wine
A little of the strained marinade
Meat of the marinated goose necks, finely chopped

Grind the meats thoroughly. Add seasoning and spices. Mix well. Moisten with the white wine, to which is added a little of the strained marinade liquor. Stuff the cleaned skins with the dressing. Tie securely, and cook very slowly in a little heated goose fat.

You may bake the stuffed gooseneck, instead of frying, in which case basting is imperative and should be profuse. Grilled and served with a foamy white wine sauce or any other kind of white wine sauce, this makes a very delicious dish. Cold and served with a green salad it makes an unusual luncheon.

JUGGED GOOSE IN SHERRY WINE

1 plump young goose
Water
Salt
Soup vegetables
1 egg, well beaten
2 tsp sherry
Bread crumbs

Draw and singe the goose and place it in a large soup kettle. Cover with cold salted water and add the vegetables. Simmer very slowly until tender, about 3 or 4 hours. Lift out the bird and let cool. Cut into serving portions. Beat the egg with the sherry and dip each piece of goose in the egg mixture and then in the crumbs. Broil on both sides until golden brown. Serve on a hot platter with the following sauce:

Sherry Sauce

1 tbsp sweet butter
1 tbsp flour
2 cups light cream or milk
Dash of nutmeg
1 whole clove
1 slice of garlic
1 bay leaf
1 tsp minced shallots
Salt and pepper
1 tbsp sherry
1 tbsp butter, additional

In a saucepan blend the butter and flour. Add the cream and the nutmeg, clove, garlic, bay leaf, and shallots. Bring to the boiling point, and cook for 15 minutes over a gentle flame, stirring occasionally. Strain through a fine sieve. Return to the stove and reduce the mixture to half its volume. Season with the salt and pepper and add the sherry and butter. Heat and serve immediately.

ROAST GOOSE

Clean, singe and draw a goose, preparing it in the same manner as for roast chicken. Season with salt, pepper and a little ground ginger and, if desired, rub over with a cut clove of garlic. Stuff, or not, as desired—apple stuffing is especially good. Place in a roasting pan on a rack and cook for half an hour in a hot oven (500° F.) after which reduce the heat to 300° F. Any excess fat in the pan should be strained off. With a young fat goose, no water is needed in the pan, but if old a little may be added while basting. Brown the bird first on one side, then on the other and occasionally prick the skin to let the fat fry out. The roasting time will vary considerably, depending on the age and tenderness of the goose. The giblets (liver, gizzard, heart and neck) may all be cooked in water with a little carrot and onion to form a gravy.

When the bird is done, drain off all but 2 tablespoons of fat from the pan. Add 2 tablespoons of flour to what remains together with the liquid in which the giblets were cooked. Bring the mixture to the boiling point and simmer 5 minutes. The giblets themselves may be finely chopped and added to the gravy.

Leftover Goose With Glazed Oranges. Cut leftover roast goose into portions, and heat in a little broth or gravy in a heavy skillet. Add a little grated orange rind, 2 or 3 spoonfuls of currant jelly, and some seedless raisins, say half a cup. Cover and simmer very gently for 15 to 20 minutes. Serve with a garnish of glazed oranges.

Glazed Oranges

2 large seedless oranges
½ cup sugar
3 tbsp water
1 tbsp corn sirup

Peel and section the oranges. Combine the sugar, water, and sirup, bring to a boil. Add the orange sections, and simmer for five minutes.

Stuffed Goose with Prunes

1 wild goose
1 small onion, minced
1 tbsp goose fat
1 cup soft bread crumbs
½ lb sausage meat
1 egg
3 doz small prunes
Chicken or veal stock
Salt
Black pepper
A pinch of sage
1 tbsp minced parsley
1 tbsp minced onion
Pinch of pulverized juniper berries
1 tsp brandy

Brown the onion in the goose fat. Add the crumbs and sausage meat, also the beaten egg and mix thoroughly over a low fire. Next put in the prunes which have been pitted, then soaked for 3 hours in hot stock to cover. Add also the seasonings and flavorings and when well blended use as a stuffing for the goose which has been cleaned and singed. Sew up the vent, truss, rub over with olive oil and roast in a moderate oven (350° F.), basting often with the goose fat in the pan. The time of roasting will depend on the age, size and tenderness of the bird.

For the gravy, drain all fat from the roasting pan, pour in 2½ cups of chicken stock, then reduce over a hot fire until only about 1 cupful is left. Stir constantly while reducing. Finally, add the juniper berries and brandy.

Wild Goose Daube

Put a dozen large chestnuts into a moderately hot oven for about 10 minutes, then remove both the shell and the inner brown skin and cook the nuts in milk to cover until almost tender. Drain them and glaze slightly in butter and sprinkle with granulated sugar. Fill the body cavity of an old goose which has been cleaned and completely skinned with the chestnuts. Sew or skewer up the vent and truss the bird as for roasting. Lard with narrow strips of bacon rolled in a mixture of parsley, chives, a tiny bit of garlic, a few sage, thyme and basil leaves, all finely chopped and seasoned with salt, pepper and grated nutmeg.

Place the bird thus prepared in a large pan, blanketing it all around with very thin slices of fat larding pork. Cover with a cup of strong chicken stock, ½ cup of good Moselle wine. Add a small veal knuckle cut into 3 or 4 pieces, 4 small carrots, 6 small white onions (2 of which should be stuck each with a whole clove), 1 small parsnip, halved, 1 bouquet garni, with a little salt, pepper and allspice. Cover closely, sealing the cover of an ordinary saucepan with a flour and water paste, and cook in a very moderate oven (325° F.) for three hours, without removing the lid. Now lift the bird carefully from the pan, remove the remains of the fat pork, skim off any excess fat and rub the sauce through a fine sieve. Return to the fire, add ½ cup of chicken stock and reduce to half its bulk over a hot fire. Cool, then clarify the jelly (reduced stock) with an unbeaten egg white and egg shell, then strain through a flannel cloth. Place the bird on a cold platter and when the jelly begins to set, pour it over. Chill and serve cold.

GOOSEBERRY. The gooseberry is a native of Europe and North Africa, which was introduced into England in the 16th century. The native American gooseberry bears small fruit, greenish purple, or black. It must be cooked, since it does not have the juiciness and sweetness of other berries. Stewed gooseberries sweetened and spiced with vinegar, cloves and cinnamon, then cooked to a jelly, are a surprisingly good

Food Value

| | Food Energy | Pro- tein | Fat | Carbo- hydrates | Cal- cium | Phos- phorus | Iron | Vit. A Value | Thia- mine | Ribo- flavin | Nia- cin | Ascor- bic Acid |
Water												
84.4	65	1.2	.8	13.2	36	34	.9	320	.03	.07	.3	23

variation of the sauces so often served with meats. Gooseberry marmalade or boiled puddings with sweet sauce, one versatile homemaker reports, can also be "things which in hungry mortal's eyes finds flavor."

GOOSEBERRY

Kinds of Gooseberries

Gooseberries belong either to the round variety or oblong. In either of these classes there are varieties with smooth, downy, or rough and hairy skin, and furthermore such differences occur in the four main classes of gooseberries. These are differentiated from each other by the color of the skin, as, when ripe, they are either red, yellow, green or white.

Hints on Buying

Gooseberries are sold by the ½ pint, pint or quart. One quart measures 3¾ cups and will serve four to six people. Buy bright, clean, fresh appearing berries, with each individual berry plump.

Hints on Preparation

To store gooseberries, spread them on a shallow tray without washing. Remove soft or moldy berries. Cover with waxed paper and put in refrigerator. Berries are very perishable. Wash just before using.

Compote of Green Gooseberries

For a quart of picked and washed green gooseberries, make a sirup as follows: put 16 tablespoons of granulated sugar into 2

cups of water and boil for 10 minutes. Then add a tablespoon of apricot jam and a sherry glassful of Kirsch. Add the gooseberries which you have first blanched for 2 minutes in boiling water, and let them simmer gently until they are tender. Then drain them, put them into a dish and strain the sirup over them, reducing it a little more if thought necessary. This compote should be served very cold.

Gooseberry Amber

4 tbsp butter
1 lb gooseberries
¼ lb powdered sugar
2 tbsp breadcrumbs
3 eggs, separated
3 level tbsp powdered sugar

Put the butter in a saucepan; add the gooseberries and sugar. Cook gently over the fire until the fruit is reduced to a soft thick mass, then stir in breadcrumbs previously rubbed through a wire sieve, and beat in well the yolks of the eggs. Turn the mixture into a greased pie plate. Bake the mixture in a moderate oven (350° F.) for about ½ hour. Beat up the whites of the eggs to a very stiff froth, adding the powdered sugar. Heap this mixture roughly all over the top, and sprinkle a little more powdered sugar over all. Put the dish in a cool oven (300° F.) and bake until the meringue is pale brown and crisp. Serve at once. (Serves 4 or 5)

Gooseberry Chutney

3 qt gooseberries
3 lb onions, chopped
1 lb currants
2 oz ginger root, chopped
¼ oz chili pepper, chopped
2⅔ cups sugar
1 tbsp salt
2 qt vinegar

Wash and drain gooseberries, and combine with rest of ingredients. Cover and simmer gently 6 or 7 hours, stirring occasionally. When thick pour into clean hot jars and seal at once. This chutney is better if stored 1 or 2 months before using. (Makes approximately 4 pint jars) *See also* CANNING and CHUTNEY.

GOOSEBERRY MARMALADE

Clean and wash the berries. Cut off the blossom ends and any stems. Place the fruit in a preserving kettle containing enough water to cover the bottom of the kettle. Cook slowly until the berries are soft. Measure, add an equal quantity of sugar and boil until the mixture is thick (about 20 minutes). Stir constantly to prevent burning. Turn into sterilized jars and seal.

For variety of flavor, rhubarb may be added, cooking it with the berries. *See* MARMALADE and JAM.

GOOSEBERRY PIE

3½ cups gooseberries (fresh or canned)
2 tbsp quick-cooking tapioca
1½ cups sugar
¼ tsp salt
1 tsp grated orange rind
2 tbsp melted butter
Pastry for a 2-crust pie

If using fresh gooseberries, remove the stem and blossom ends, then wash and drain the fruit. Add the tapioca, sugar, salt, orange rind, and butter and let stand 15 to 20 minutes. Line a 9-inch pie plate with pastry (*which see*). Fill with the gooseberry mixture, moisten the edge of the pastry with water, adjust the top crust and press edges firmly together. Make several slits to permit the escape of steam. Bake in a hot oven (450° F.) for 10 minutes, then decrease to moderate (350° F.) and continue baking 30 minutes longer. Serve cold, with or without whipped cream; or serve warm with hard sauce.

GOOSEBERRY PUDDING

3 cups green gooseberries
1 cup breadcrumbs
3 tbsp butter
4 tbsp sugar
3 eggs

Wash the gooseberries; cook them in a light sugar sirup till tender; rub them through a sieve. Add the breadcrumbs, butter, sugar, and eggs. Line a pie plate with short crust (*see* PASTRY) and pour in the mixture. Bake for about 40 minutes. Sprinkle with sugar and serve hot.

GOOSEBERRY TARTS

Pastry for 8-inch double crust
1 qt gooseberries
¾ to 1 cup sugar, depending on sourness of berries
4½ tsp flour
⅛ tsp salt
2 tbsp butter

Pick over the gooseberries, discarding any soft ones and removing stems and tails, then wash. Combine sugar, flour and salt. Sprinkle over berries, stirring to distribute. Roll out slightly more than half the pastry and line 5 individual tart pans. Turn berries into unbaked pastry shells, dot tops with butter. Roll pastry for upper crusts and cut a design for steam vents. Brush edge of pastry with water. Lay pastry over tarts. Press edge together and trim. Let rest 10 minutes and flute. Bake in a hot oven (450° F.) for 15 minutes or until crust is delicately browned. Then reduce heat to 325° F. (moderately slow) and continue cooking 20 to 30 minutes or until berries are tender. (Serves 5)

SPICED GOOSEBERRIES

5 lb gooseberries
8 cups sugar
2 cups vinegar
2 tbsp ground cinnamon
1 tbsp ground cloves
1 orange, grated rind and juice

Wash the gooseberries, add remaining ingredients and let stand several hours. Bring slowly to boiling point and cook about 2 hours, or until thick, stirring frequently. Pour into clean hot jars and seal at once. (Makes approximately 5 pint jars) *See also* CANNING.

GORGONZOLA CHEESE. A rennet cheese made from the whole milk of cows. The interior is mottled or veined like Roquefort, and the outer surface is covered with a thin coat resembling clay. It is wrapped in paper and packed with straw in wicker baskets. In shape the cheese is round—about 12 inches in diameter and 6 inches high. It is also known as *Stracchino di Gorgonzola.*

GOUDA CHEESE. A flat, pressed cheese which resembles Edam in flavor. Originally from Holland, it is now made in the United States.

GOULASH or **GULYAS.** The cooks of America have appropriated many foreign recipes and given them American twists so that a Hungarian gourmet might find the goulash of New York or San Francisco as different from the *gulyas* of the cafes on Budapest's Franz Joseph Quai as the visiting Chinese finds Manhattan chop suey different from the delectable viands of Peiping.

Goulash, as it is made in our restaurants and cafeterias, is as familiar to Americans as chop suey. It is generally free from any contact with sauerkraut, and often free from any trace of sour cream, though both are important ingredients of the national stew of Hungary. Although Americans are inclined favorably toward a succulent nest of sauerkraut with their pig's knuckles, they are suspicious of innovations and surprises and a canny chef knows that there would be wry faces and sniffs of disdain at the tang of sauerkraut blended in the sauce of a stew, though the genuine Magyar *gulyas* is a delicate and delicious composition.

Our American goulash seems generally to be made of beef—and nothing like an international situation should grow out of that—but the typical *gulyas* is founded on pork, and is more often of veal than of beef. The proud and temperamental Magyars have not melted readily in the continental cauldron. They are more Mongoloid than Teutonic, and their cooking has much of the mildness of the Balkans and the Levant—popular concepts of sauerkraut to the contrary notwithstanding.

HUNGARIAN GOULASH

Pork tenderloin, loin, or shoulder
3 or 4 medium-sized onions
3 tbsp lard
Paprika
Salt
Pinch marjoram
1 clove garlic

Boiling water
Sauerkraut
½ cup sour cream
1 liqueur glass kummel or tokay wine

Melt the lard in a skillet and slice the onions thinly. Cook the onions in the lard until they are golden brown. Cut the pork into 1-inch cubes. Skim out the onions and brown the meat in the lard. Turn the contents into a stew pan along with the onions. Season generously with the paprika, salt, marjoram, and garlic which should be crushed. Stir the meat to blend and add boiling water to cover. Let simmer for 30 minutes. Add the sauerkraut, using as much as there is meat. Continue simmering for 1 hour, or until the meat and sauerkraut are tender. If the sauce is too thin, thicken it with a roux (*which see*) of flour and butter. Add the kummel and the sour cream, and serve at once. Noodles are the traditional accompaniment to goulash but potatoes may be served.

Like the stews of all nations, goulash is subject to variations. Savory sausages may be combined with the meat. Veal may be used, using white wine as the seasoning. Beef alone, or combined with diced kidneys, may be used. And lamb and mutton also makes goulash.

GOURD. A melonlike inedible fruit with a hard rind; or the plant that bears it.

GOURMET. See EPICURE.

GOURNAY CHEESE. A soft, rennet cheese of France, usually three inches in diameter and three-quarters of an inch thick.

GOYA CHEESE. A rennet cheese made of whole or partly skimmed milk. It comes from Argentina.

GRAHAM BREAD. See BREAD.

GRAHAM FLOUR. See FLOUR.

GRAND MARNIER. A French cordial made in three colors: red, yellow, and green. This wonderfully delicious after dinner cordial may well be called "cordial of the gods." It is an orange brandy made with choice old cognac.

GRANITE. A frozen dessert similar to sherbet. The basic foundation is a very light fruit sirup (any kind) which gives its name to the granite. Neither fruit nor nut are added. Granite resembles the coarse texture of frappé (*which see*). It is prepared like frappé, and usually is served in chilled sherbet glasses.

GRANULATED SUGAR. See SUGAR.

GRAPE. Our first grapes came from scattered patches of wild vines, but today the grape is so widely cultivated that it ranks in commercial importance among our first four fruits. An American wine industry has been firmly established. The use of the grape as a table fruit, for making jelly and for paste confections is constantly expanding. And the grape still holds its own on the home-canning schedule.

The grape grew wild in America as far back as history records. Leif the Lucky, according to legend, was so impressed by the number of wild grapevines growing where he was supposed to have touched—Rhode Island or thereabouts—that he named the region "Vineland." Once colonized, the New World gave grape culture an important place. The early colonists brought with them the idea that grapes were only for wine, and this view continued until the middle of the last century and even later in some regions. Some colonists sent back to Europe for the varieties they knew, but these grapes did not take to the soil and climate of the Atlantic coast. The London Company, in 1621, tried to grow some continental varieties in Virginia, but they met failure there and elsewhere, because of insects and the lack of adaptability of the plants to this soil.

Meanwhile the Pacific coast was making grape history in what have since become the greatest vineyard areas in the world. The early Mission Fathers, going northward from Mexico, established the San Diego grape in 1769 and planted the Mission grape, a black variety said to have been known in Mexico as far back as 1520. The fruit was planted at the successive missions and proved to be the first successful culture of the European grape in the new land.

For the country as a whole the commercial era in grape culture began about 1800, but it was not until 1850 that the growing of native bunch grapes for table use began to receive serious attention. Many experiments, especially in Indiana, showed that one type of grape survived the new growing conditions and even improved as it developed. This was known as the *Cape* grape, and the culture of this variety foreshadowed the country's bunch-grape industry.

Grapes of many colors, from white through yellow, amber, pale green and dark green, to the red, and then the blues, purples, and blacks come from New York State, New Jersey, Pennsylvania, the south, and the Pacific coast. One of the greatest grape-growing areas in the world is the Chautauqua grape belt, the section which comprises the shore of Lake Erie in New York, Pennsylvania, and Ohio.

The Finger Lakes region of New York State comes next in size among grape areas in the United States. Champagne and still wines are produced there as well as table grapes. The Niagara region, along the end of Lake Erie and the south shore of Lake Ontario produces quantities for commercial uses. So does the Hudson Valley, which has been a grape section for more than 100 years.

Another source of grapes and wine, famous all over the world, is found on the islands of Lake Erie, near Sandusky, Ohio. For miles across the northern part of the state the lake breeze carries the fragrance of the blossoms and harvest. Motorists make holiday trips through that community to enjoy the spicy, sweet air.

VARIETIES OF GRAPES

1. *Vinifera* (A sweet type)
   a. Tokay—A large grape varying from green to deep red, according to stages of ripeness.
   b. Thompson's Seedless—A rather small greenish white grape without seeds.
   c. Malaga—Larger than Thompson's Seedless, of about the same color, and has seeds.
   d. Additional varieties—Emperor, Alexandria, Alicante Bouschet, Black Hamburg, Burger, Cabernet Sauvignon, Carignane, Chasselas de Fontainebleau, Cinsaut, Dodrelabi, Green Hungarian, Grenache, Listan, Mission, Mondeuse, Mourastel, Muscadelle du Bordelais, Olivette Blanche, Olivette Noire, Pedro Ximines,

FOOD VALUE

Water	Food Energy	Protein	Fat	Carbohydrates	Calcium	Phosphorus	Iron	Vit. A Value	Thiamine	Riboflavin	Niacin	Ascorbic Acid
81.6	74	.8	.4	16.7	17	21	.6	80	.05	.03	.4	4

Petit Syrah, Pineau de Chardonnay, Purple Damascus, St. Macaire, Sauvignon Very, Semillon, Sultana, Sultanina, Sylvaner, Traminer, Valdepenas, Veltliner, Vermentino, and Zinfandel.

2. *American Euvitis* (Not a sweet type) Of the 700 recognized varieties of this native type, seven varieties give the bulk of commercial production. They are described below. The last three named varieties produce inferior grapes.

a. Concord—The fruit of the Concord is a deep blue almost black, with a light bloom which readily rubs off. This grape is hardy and of high productivity under a wide range of climatic and soil conditions. It does not possess as good flavor as some other eastern varieties and is not so good a shipper. It rapidly loses its flavor after picking and the berries soon shell and crack.

b. Delaware—The Delaware, next in importance to Concord, is the standard of quality among the eastern grapes, as it has the best flavor and odor. The berries are of rather small size, and reddish color.

c. Niagara—The Niagara is the leading white variety of eastern grape, being grown chiefly in New York State. It is not of particularly high quality and its culture is difficult.

d. Catawba—This is a very attractive grape, the bunches being large, even and compact. The berries are medium in size, oval to round in shape, of a dull purplish red with lilac bloom and of excellent flavor.

e. Moore—This grape closely resembles the Concord, but the bunches are smaller, the individual berries larger, and the quality and texture not as good.

f. Worden—The Worden is an early grape similar to the Moore in appearance, but of somewhat better flavor.

g. Champion—This is an early blue variety. It is of distinctly poor quality, with a sour and rather disagreeable taste.

h. Additional varieties—The many other varieties of native grapes produce very little of the commercial supply. There is no reason against acceptance of any of these little known varieties, providing they are of good quality.

3. *Muscadine* (Peculiar musky odor)

a. Scuppernong—Produces the largest fruit of any cultivated grape, the fruit being twice the size of the largest Concord. It has sweet flesh, but is distinguished by a musky odor and flavor displeasing to

some. It is extensively cultivated in the south.

PREPARATION FOR MARKET

The proper stage of maturity for picking grapes may be judged by the color and taste. While a well colored grape is not necessarily a ripe one, the color is of great use to the picker in judging relative ripeness. Green or white varieties of grapes get more nearly white or yellow as they ripen. The color of red or black grapes usually becomes deeper and more brilliant as the ripening progresses.

Picking must be performed with great care. The bunches are easily crushed and bruised by rough handling, and damp berries are soon followed by mold and decay.

HINTS ON BUYING

Grapes found in the market are of two distinct types—the American, grown mainly in the eastern and central states, and the European or *Vinifera*, grown chiefly in California.

Western grapes usually have a higher sugar and solids content, and in many cases are larger than the eastern type. The skin and pulp of the western type do not separate, but the seeds separate readily from the pulp. Some varieties of western grapes were planted for table use and others for juice.

Eastern grapes are sold indiscriminately for both table and juice purposes. While the eastern type is shipped from many sources, the largest supplies come from New York, Michigan, and Pennsylvania. The *Concord* is used most extensively for juice purposes.

Eastern or native grapes injured by freezing, are shriveled and usually show a milky, opaque condition of the pulp. If the berry is pulled from the cap stem, the brush usually remains in the berry. Decay is indicated by mold, wet berries, and frequently by leaky and stained containers. Sometimes evidence of decay can be found on the berries at the stem. To be of good quality, table grapes should have a general appearance of freshness. They should be mature, and individual berries should be firmly attached to the stems. Mature grapes are usually plump. High color for variety is generally indicative of a well-developed sugar content and flavor.

Usually the white and green grapes of both American and European types are at their best for flavor and sweetness when they are turning to an amber color. A few good varieties of American grapes however, remain quite green in color when fully ripe.

For juice, the maturity of the grapes counts most. No consideration need be given to compactness of bunches or shattering of the berries from stems, provided the berries are not shriveled or dried.

For other uses, a few small, sunburned, wrinkled, raisined, or unripened berries do not affect the flavor or quality of the bunch as a whole, but they do detract from its appearance. Bunches of grapes that have dry and brittle stems usually shatter badly. A gentle shaking of a bunch will reveal the condition of the stem.

Grapes are graded according to the United States standards. U.S. Fancy Table Grapes are grapes of one variety which are well colored, mature, firmly attached to capstems, not shattered, split or otherwise damaged or diseased. U.S. No. 1 Table Grapes consist of grapes of one variety which are fairly well colored, and otherwise meet the standards for U.S. Fancy. U.S. No. 1 Juice Grapes are grapes of one variety, which are fairly well colored, mature, and free from serious damage. Any lot of grapes consisting of more than one variety which meets all other requirements of U.S. Fancy Table, U.S. No. 1 Table, or U.S. No. 1 Juice, may be designated as U.S. Fancy Table Mixed, U.S. No. 1 Table Mixed, and U.S. No. 1 Juice Mixed. Unclassified consists of grapes which have not been classified in accordance with any of the foregoing grades.

HINTS ON PREPARATION

In using the *Concord* grape, or one of the other juicy varieties for making jelly, the homemaker should keep in mind that "spikes" or crystals, will form if she does not let the juice stand overnight to permit precipitation, before she adds the required amount of sugar. If that precaution is taken, the high acid and pectin contents of this fruit will enable her to make smooth, translucent jelly. The blue-black *Concord*, native of Massachusetts and most widely known of the eastern "slipskins", has long been recognized as one of the finest jelly and grapejuice grapes.

The pomace or residue that is left after extracting the juice from cooked grapes, with its relatively high sugar content enables the economical homemaker to give free play to her talents, for she can use it as a basis for the preparation of grape paste, or dark, spicy butter or catsup, of sauce or vinegar, all of which will be only slightly less delicious than if they were made from the "first run" grapes.

GRAPE BAVARIAN

1 tbsp plain gelatin
2 cups concentrated grape juice
1/3 cup orange juice
1 tbsp lemon juice
1/4 cup sugar
2/3 cup whipping cream

Sprinkle gelatin over 1/4 cup of the cold grape juice and let soften 5 minutes. Heat over hot water, stirring until completely dissolved. Meanwhile combine rest of grape juice with orange juice, half the lemon juice and the sugar, stirring until sugar is dissolved; then stir in the liquid gelatin. Chill until thick and sirupy; then beat with rotary beater until light and fluffy. Have cream thoroughly chilled, beat until stiff, add rest of lemon juice and beat until very stiff. Fold thoroughly but lightly into grape gelatin and transfer to mold which has been rinsed with cold water. Chill until firm. Unmold onto cold serving plate. (Serves 5)

GRAPE CONSERVE

2 1/2 qt concord grapes
1 cup water
4 cups sugar
1 cup orange pulp
2 cups seedless raisins
2 cups drained, crushed canned pineapple
1 1/2 cups broken walnut meats

Wash and drain the grapes, then slip from the skins and cook the skins with the water for 15 minutes. Cook the grape pulp 10 minutes without water, then press through sieve to strain out seeds. Combine the two mixtures, add the sugar, orange pulp, raisins and pineapple, and cook over moderate heat for 45 minutes, stirring frequently. Skim, if necessary, add the nuts and turn into small sterilized jars and seal. (Makes about 6 pints) *See also* CANNING.

GRAPE COOLER

1 cup chilled grape juice
1 tbsp sugar
1 pinch salt
1 large scoop vanilla ice cream

Put grape juice, sugar, salt and ice cream into mixing bowl and beat until ice cream is half melted. Serve at once. (Serves 1)

GRAPE ICE

½ cup light corn sirup
½ cup sugar
1¼ cups cold water
1 tbsp plain gelatin
2 cups concentrated grape juice
½ cup orange juice
⅛ tsp salt
2 egg whites

Slowly boil sirup, sugar, and 1 cup of the water together for 10 minutes. Sprinkle gelatin over remaining cold water and let stand for 5 minutes. Add softened gelatin to the hot sirup and stir until completely dissolved. Cool and add the juices and salt. Pour into freezing tray of a mechanical refrigerator, set at coldest temperature and freeze. When the mixture becomes mushy, loosen from the sides of the pan, remove to a chilled bowl and beat hard with a rotary egg beater for a few seconds, then add stiffly beaten egg whites and again beat hard until well blended. Return immediately to the freezing compartment to finish freezing. *See also* ICE. (Serves 6)

GRAPE JAM

10 lb Concord grapes
¼ cup water
3 cups granulated sugar
2 tbsp lemon juice

Wash and stem the grapes. Place in a large preserving kettle, add water and heat very slowly until juice can be seen on bottom of kettle when grapes are lifted aside. Turn up heat to medium and continue

heating until juice flows freely (about 20 minutes). Remove from kettle and place in jelly bag; suspend over large bowl and let drip until no more juice flows. Do not squeeze. Put pulp and skins into a fine sieve, colander, or food mill and rub through as much as possible. Mix the pulp with the juice. To each quart of sieved pulp add 3 cups granulated sugar and lemon juice. Place in preserving kettle large enough to allow space for vigorous boiling. Cook rapidly with constant stirring for 20 minutes, or until mixture gives the jelly test (two drops sheeting from edge of metal spoon). Pour into sterilized glasses and seal while hot with melted paraffin. (Makes about 1 quart jam from each quart of pulp) *See also* JAM.

GRAPE JELLY

5 lb fully ripe Concord grapes
½ cup water
7½ cups sugar
½ bottle fruit pectin

To prepare the juice, stem the grapes and crush thoroughly. Add the water; cover and simmer 5 minutes. Turn into a jelly bag and drain out the juice. Measure the sugar and juice (there should be 4 cups) into a large saucepan. Mix well, bring to boiling point over the hottest fire, and at once add the pectin, stirring constantly. Bring to a full rolling boil and boil hard for ½ minute. Remove from the fire, skim and pour quickly into hot, sterilized glasses. Seal. *See also* JELLY.

GRAPE JUICE COCKTAIL

1½ tbsp sugar
1½ tbsp water
6 tbsp orange juice
½ cup grape juice
½ cup carbonated water
Crushed ice

Pour the ingredients into a cocktail shaker and shake vigorously. Put the ice in the glasses, and then pour the mixture over it. (Serves 4)

GRAPE MARMALADE

Wash the grapes and remove the stems. Press the pulp from the skins. Cook the pulp and press it through a sieve to remove the seeds. Add the skins to the pulp, measure, and add two-thirds the quantity of sugar. Cook until the skins are tender (about 20 minutes). Turn into sterilized jars and seal. *See also* CANNING.

GRAPE-ORANGE COCKTAIL

Mix equal portions of white grape juice and orange juice. Chill and serve in small cocktail glasses.

GRAPE PICKLE

10 lb large ripe grapes
6 lb sugar
1 qt vinegar
1 tbsp ground cloves
1 tsp ground cinnamon

Wash, stem, drain and pack the grapes in sterilized jars. Combine the sugar, vinegar and spices, bring to a boil, then pour immediately over the grapes and seal. (Makes 5 pints) *See also* CANNING.

GRAPE PIE

2 lb Concord grapes
¾ cup sugar
¼ cup flour
⅛ tsp salt
1 tbsp lemon juice
Pastry for 8-inch double crust

Wash grapes thoroughly, then stem (there should be 4 cups stemmed grapes). Press the clear pulp from the skins, saving the skins in a bowl and letting the pulp and juice drop into a saucepan. Cook the pulp over low heat for 5 minutes; then turn into a strainer or food mill and press the pulp through into the bowl containing the skins; discard the seeds. Mix sugar, flour and salt, and add the grapes. Stir in lemon juice. Pour cooled mixture into pastry-lined pie pan (*see* PASTRY). Roll out pastry for upper crust. Cut a design for steam vents. Moisten rim with cold water. Lay pastry over pie, press to seal edge, trim, turn under. Let rest 10 minutes and flute edge. Bake in a hot oven (450° F.) for 15 minutes; reduce heat to 325° F. (moderately slow) and bake 30 minutes longer until the crust is golden brown. Cool 3 or 4 hours on cake rack before cutting.

GRAPE SALADS

(1) Add whole seedless grapes to diced apples and combine with colored mayonnaise.

(2) Combine melon balls, grapefruit, and seeded or seedless grapes. Moisten with French dressing.

(3) Combine bananas with grapes, and moisten with boiled dressing to which have been added chopped red and green maraschino cherries.

(4) Combine diced crab apples, whole cooked or canned cranberries, and seeded or seedless grapes. Moisten with French dressing.

(5) Fill peeled large peach halves with cottage or cream cheese, and garnish with small seedless grapes. Pass French dressing separately.

(6) Fill peeled avocado halves with highly seasoned cream or cottage cheese, and cover the entire surface with seeded or seedless grapes. Sprinkle lightly with paprika, and pass spiced French dressing separately.

(7) Fill scooped-out orange halves with fruit salad or cubed fresh fruit. Top with mayonnaise or seasoned whipped cream, and "nail" the entire surface with small seedless grapes. Sprinkle lightly with paprika.

(8) Fill scooped-out baked or raw apples, with mixed chopped celery, green pepper and tomato cubes, moistened with French or any other favorite salad dressing. Garnish with seeded or seedless grapes.

(9) Garnish sections of pear (fresh or canned) and orange sections with seeded or seedless grapes. Serve with mayonnaise.

(10) Remove the cores of red-skinned apples (unpeeled). Slice apples thin, dip quickly in lemon juice, and top with seeded or seedless grapes mixed with equal parts of mayonnaise and red currant jelly. Sprinkle with finely chopped pistachio nuts.

(11) Slit large grapes, remove the seeds, and fill with cream cheese mixed with ground nut meats. Trim neatly, and place grapes thus filled on the top of split bananas, first dipped in French dressing.

(12) Slit large grapes, remove the seeds, and fill with guava jelly. Enrobe each grape in highly seasoned cream or cottage cheese. Place four balls on a slice of canned pineapple. Garnish with rosettes of green mayonnaise which has been forced through a pastry tube.

GRAPE JUICE

566

Grape Sauce

⅓ cup sugar
Pinch of salt
2 tbsp cornstarch
2 cups grape juice
1 tbsp lemon juice

Mix dry ingredients in saucepan; add grape juice and stir until blended. Cook over direct heat, stirring constantly until sauce boils and thickens. Remove from heat and add lemon juice and chill. Serve over ice cream. Also good over cottage pudding, leftover cake, baked custard, or sliced bananas. (Makes 1½ cups)

Grape Shrub

1 cup grape juice
4 tsp lemon juice
¼ cup cold water
4 tsp sugar
Dash of salt
½ pt sherbet, orange or lime

Combine all ingredients except sherbet and chill thoroughly. Serve in individual fruit juice glasses and float a scoop of sherbet in each. (Serves 4)

Hot Spiced Grape Juice

3 cups grape juice
2 cups water
2 tbsp sugar
1 tsp cinnamon
Pinch of ginger
2 tbsp lemon juice

Combine grape juice with remaining ingredients, except lemon juice. Heat slowly, stirring until sugar is dissolved. When hot, stir in lemon juice and serve immediately. (Makes 5 cups)

GRAPE JUICE. Unfermented grape juice is without doubt one of the most popular of the many fruit beverages. While it may be bought under any number of commercial labels, it is easily and inexpensively made at home.

The food value of grape juice depends upon the sugar present, since the finished juice contains only minute quantities of fats or nitrogenous elements. The many varieties of grapes vary widely in their sugar content, and the juice which may be made from them varies as widely.

Making Grape Juice in the Home

Two general methods are employed in preparing grape juice—the hot-press and the cold-press. The essential difference is indicated by the terms themselves. In the hot-press method, the crushed fruit is heated and the juice removed by pressing the fruit while it is hot; in the cold-press method no heat is employed while extracting the juice. By the cold-press method clear, brilliant juices are obtained, while the hot press method gives a somewhat larger yield of darker liquid.

The general process may be summarized as follows:

Select the fruit. In choosing fruit for making grape juice, it is necessary to consider the variety employed, since the choice of the variety determines the flavor, color, and general character of the juice. For characteristics of the varieties, *see* Grape. It is equally important to use only fruit which has fully ripened, in order that it may be at its height of sugar content, flavor, and color. The grapes should be clean and sound.

Crush the fruit. Unless the grapes really need it, do not wash them. They should be crushed as soon as possible after picking. While the best results are obtained if the berries are stripped from the stems, it is not necessary to do this. Working in the home, on a small scale, one may crush the grapes by hand or with a potato masher after they have been placed in a deep vessel or cloth bag. On a somewhat larger scale, it is better to use a small crusher, or even a cider press.

Press out the juice. Here the procedure varies, depending upon whether one chooses the cold-press or hot-press method.

For the cold-press method, proceed as follows: When the grapes are crushed, a considerable quantity of juice is released because of the separation of pulp and skins, and this liquid which is known as the free-run juice, may be drained off without exerting any pressure. This juice may be handled separately to make an ultra-fine product, or it may be combined with the juice obtained by pressing. When only a very small quantity of grapes is being handled, they may be placed in a bag of strong muslin or doubled cheese cloth, suspended over a vessel, and pressed by hand. Rubber gloves should be worn to prevent the juice staining the hands. This method is rather tedious if large quantities are to be made, and in this event, a small press should be used. The juice should be allowed to stand for 4 to 6 hours to allow it to settle.

For the hot-press method, proceed as follows: As quickly as possible after crushing, the pans of fruit should be placed on the stove and slowly heated to 175° F. The fruit should be stirred frequently and thoroughly to prevent its sticking to the bottom of the pan. Immediately after it reaches the required temperature, remove the pan from the stove, and pour the fruit into a bag, as in the cold-press method. Press while the fruit is still hot, using wooden paddles. The juice should then be allowed to stand until it is thoroughly cold and well settled.

Strain the juice. The juice should be filtered or strained through a clean double thickness of cheesecloth in such a manner as not to disturb the sediment which has formed. It may be siphoned off, or carefully dipped off. After passing through the cheesecloth, the juice should be still further clarified by straining through a flannel jelly bag.

Add sweetening if necessary. If a sweet variety of grape has been used, it will probably not be necessary to add additional sugar. If, however, the grape is acid, the addition of a level teaspoon of sugar per pint of juice is usually sufficient. However, the taste of the family should be considered, and if a particularly sweet product is desired, sugar should be added accordingly.

Place the juice in containers for storage. As soon as the juice is filtered, it should be placed in the containers in which it is to be stored. These may be half-gallon jars, bottles, or larger containers. In any event, they should be first washed and placed in cold water. They are then brought to the boil and allowed to boil rapidly for 30 minutes. If half-gallon jars are used, they should be filled with the juice no higher than the middle of the neck, in order to allow for the expansion of the juice in heating. The cover should be placed on the jars.

Pasteurize the juice. It is necessary to pasteurize the juice to prevent spoilage, due to the growth of yeasts or molds which are present in the air and on the fruit itself. A water bath is necessary to pasteurize the

juice successfully. For ordinary home use with moderate quantities of juice, a pasteurizer can be improvised by placing a false bottom made of wire netting or wooden slats in an ordinary washboiler or similar large vessel. A steam-pressure canning outfit, of course, makes the ideal apparatus. If the juice has been placed in jars, they should not be sealed until after the pasteurization; if, however, bottles are used, they should be sealed first.

Begin by putting the false bottom in the wash boiler. Place the boiler on the stove, and partially fill it with cold water. Put new rubber rings on the filled jars and cover with the lids, but do not clamp them down. Then set the jars of juice in the water bath and pour in enough additional water to bring the level of the water up to the neck of the jars. Then turn on the heat. The juice in the jars must reach a temperature of 180° F., and for this reason the temperature of the boiler will need to be somewhat higher. Test with a thermometer since the success or the failure in making grape juice that will keep depends on adequate pasteurization.

Seal the jars. As soon as the proper temperature has been reached, seal and remove the jars as rapidly as possible. In sealing, raise the clamp of each jar, or screw down the top, according to the type of jar used, first making sure that the rubber ring is in place. Then lift the jars out of the water, and place them where they will be protected from drafts until cool. Work rapidly.

Store the juice. Store the jars in a cool, dark, dry place, watching for several days for any that may have been improperly sealed which may begin to ferment. During the storage period the juice will undergo a further clarification, which will take anywhere from six weeks to a year. At the end of this period, the liquid in the jars will be clear, with a more or less compact sediment in the bottom of the jar. All that is necessary is to avoid disturbing the sediment in the bottle when pouring out the juice for use

In making the commercial product, the juice is allowed to stand in large containers until the end of this period, when it is drawn off into bottles, and again sterilized. It is then ready for sale.

GRAPE PRESS. A grape press is a device used to extract the juice from grapes by means of applied pressure. *See* WINE.

GRAPEFRUIT, with segmenting knife

GRAPEFRUIT. A large, round, or ob-long citrus fruit, an improved variety of the shaddock, the original *pamplemousse*, a name which is now made to serve for both shaddock and grapefruit.

A large part of our grapefruit supply comes from Florida, California, Texas, and Arizona; a fair supply comes to us from Puerto Rico and Cuba. Sometimes it is re-ferred to as "forbidden fruit" on account of a cordial by that name which has been made from the juice.

The steadily increasing use of canned grapefruit juice and grapefruit segments has been a boon to citrus growers. About ten years ago the culled fruit, unsuited for shipment because of shape or size, was hauled to the waste pile. Now the culls are turned into juice, and canning is an important part of the citrus industry. The marketing season has been lengthened from six months to the entire year.

The taste of canned grapefruit is slightly different from the fresh fruit, but this is due to the fully ripened grapefruit used for canning in contrast to the partially ripened fresh grapefruit. Canned grapefruit is a comparatively new product, but has be-come very popular for breakfast service and for salads. It is possible to purchase a combination of grapefruit and orange seg-ments, which is attractive for salad mak-ing.

Varieties of Grapefruit

There are a number of different varieties of grapefruit all of which belong to one or the other of two classes, the one having white pulp, the other pink or red. The col-ored varieties are known as *pomels* and are sweeter than the others.

Preparation for Market

Grapefruit is a year-round fruit The peak of the season is October to May. It is graded by the United States De-partment of Agriculture standards. U.S. Fancy consists of grapefruit of the same variety, which are mature, well-colored, firm, well formed, smooth textured, fairly thin skinned, free from decay, injury, dis-ease, dryness or mushiness. U.S. No. 1 is the same, except the skin of the fruit need not be as thin, nor the fruit so well colored. U.S. No. 2 consists of fruit which meets the requirements of U.S. Fancy, but to a lesser degree— i.e. the fruit can be fairly firm, fairly well formed, etc. U.S. Combination grade is any lot of grapefruit in which 40 percent meets the requirements of U.S. No. 1 and the remainder, U.S. No. 2. U.S. No. 3 consists of grapefruit which are mature, slightly colored, may be slightly spongy, misshapen, rough but not seriously lumpy, and free from decay, broken skins, disease, and serious damage. Unclassified is a name given to grapefruit which has not been classified in accordance with any of the foregoing grades.

Canned Grapefruit

The "groove run" or "culls" are used for canning. The fruit is superior to that sold fresh, as it is picked at a later stage of ripening. It may be misshapen, too large or too small, or may have marks on the skin which prevent its being sold as fresh fruit. It is hand picked with clippers and taken directly to the cannery, where it is washed and sorted according to size. It is then put in boiling water to loosen the skin, which is removed with the white membrane. Segmenters separate the sec-tions and remove seeds. The segments are then sorted according to their degree of wholeness and are then packed in cans and covered with cold sugar sirup, and sealed.

Canned grapefruit is graded according to the United States standards. Grade A (fancy) is composed of segments, 80 per-cent of which are whole, reasonably uni-form in size, bright in color, firm but not fibrous in texture. The sirup is reasonably clear. Grade B (choice) is composed of seg-

Food Value

	Wa-ter	Food Energy	Pro-tein	Fat	Car-bohy-drates	Cal-cium	Phos-phorus	Iron	Vit. A Value	Thia-mine	Ribo-flavin	Nia-cin	Ascor-bic Acid
Grape-fruit	88.8	44	.5	.2	10.1	17	18	.3	Trace	.04	.02	.2	40
Grape-fruit juice (canned)	89.4	41	.5	.2	9.4	8	12	.4	Trace	.03	.02	.2	35
Grape-fruit seg-ments (canned)	79.8	81	.6	.2	19.1	13	14	.3	Trace	.03	.02	.2	30

ments of which not less than 60 percent are whole, or practically whole. The other requirements are the same as Grade A, in general. United States Broken (broken) is composed of segments in which not over 15 percent shall be smaller than ½ inch in two dimensions. Off-grade grapefruit is grapefruit which fails to meet the requirements of the foregoing grades.

Hints on Buying

The color of grapefruit ranges from pale yellow to russet. The russeting is caused by the activity of the rust mite, a tiny insect that works on the skin of the fruit, but does not penetrate into the flesh. Russeting does not harm the quality of grapefruit. Decay, however, should be avoided since it affects the flavor. It may appear as a soft discolored area at the stem end, as well as by a puffy and spongy appearance. Round or slightly flattened fruits are superior to misshapen ones. Grapefruits are of good quality when they are firm, but springy to the touch.

Grapefruit is sold by the unit, dozen, pound or box. Each makes two servings. There are about twelve sections in every fruit.

Hints on Preparation

A full appreciation of the grapefruit assumes a knowledge of peeling it, and here the chief requirement is a sharp knife. Slice a thick layer off the top and bottom, and cut around the fruit deep enough to remove all the white membrane and to expose the flesh. The true grapefruit fancier never segments the fruit for salads and fruit cups before peeling it in the prescribed manner. Halved grapefruit should

be carefully prepared before serving in order to lessen the danger of "squirting." The most approved method is to leave the center pith, but remove the seeds with a sharp knife. Then cut around each segment, being careful not to separate the tough membrane from the outside rim. Powdered sugar may be added, although some people prefer salt.

Grapefruit may be practically stored by the crate or half crate, which is especially appreciated by big families. It should be sorted and stored at 40° F. to 60° F. and each should be individually wrapped in paper. Regularly it should be inspected, and any with soft spots removed.

Broiled Grapefruit

Cut grapefruit in halves. Remove core with a specially designed gadget for this, or clip around core with kitchen shears; lift out. With grapefruit knife or sharp paring knife, cut sections loose around sides. Sprinkle each half with 2 tablespoons granulated or light brown sugar and dot each with ½ teaspoon butter. Place under broiler for about 10 minutes until warm through and browned around edges. Overcooking tends to make grapefruit slightly bitter; it should be heated until fruit is just warm and sugar is well melted.

Candied Grapefruit Peel

Prepare grapefruit peel by pulling out all dividing membranes, and cutting into strips about ¼ inch wide. For a mild flavored peel, thick-skinned grapefruit should be chosen. For a bitter-flavored peel, preferred by some people, choose thin-skinned fruit, or cut away the inner white portion of the rind. Cover the peel with cold water, bring to a boil and drain. Repeat this, using fresh water each time, 4 times, or until peel is only slightly bitter. After last draining, measure peel and add an equal measure of granulated sugar. Place over low heat and gently toss around until the sugar is dissolved; then continue simmering until sirup reaches the soft ball stage (238° F.). Lift out peel, piece by piece, and roll in granulated sugar sifted on a plate or on waxed paper. Allow to cool and dry before storing.

CITRUS MARMALADE

1 grapefruit
1 orange
1 lemon
3½ qt cold water
5 lb sugar
1 tsp salt

Cut the fruit into thin slices, discarding the seeds. Cover with cold water and let stand overnight. Cook until tender. Let stand several hours, add the sugar and cook until the jellying point is reached. Turn into sterilized jars and seal.

A less bitter marmalade may be made by discarding the first water and replacing with fresh. See also MARMALADE.

GRAPEFRUIT CIDER PUNCH

2 cups grapefruit juice, chilled
1½ cups sweet cider, chilled
2 cups ice water
½ cup sugar
1 red apple

Combine all ingredients. Stir thoroughly. Serve with a garnish of thin slices of red apple rings. (Serves 8)

GRAPEFRUIT CONSERVE

2 large grapefruit
4 lemons
Boiling water
1½ cups halved seedless raisins
5 cups sugar
1 cup shredded coconut
½ tsp ground ginger

Peel both grapefruit and lemons thinly and shred the rinds, then slice the pulp of both fruit very thinly. Add boiling water to barely cover. Add also the raisins. Blend thoroughly and set aside overnight. In the morning, bring to boiling point, and cook until tender, stirring frequently, about 35 minutes. Strain, then boil down the juice rapidly to half its original bulk. Add the sugar, coconut and ginger, and the strained fruit. Simmer 5 minutes then turn into small sterilized jars and seal. (Makes about 6 pints) See also CANNING.

Coarsely chopped walnut may be added to the mixture with the sugar.

GRAPEFRUIT FLUFF

1 tbsp gelatin
¼ cup cold water
No. 2 can grapefruit sections
2 eggs, separated
¼ cup sugar
1 cup milk
2 tbsp sugar
1 tsp cornstarch
Pinch of salt
1 tbsp butter

Soften gelatin in the cold water for 5 minutes; then dissolve in a little boiling juice drained from the grapefruit. Add to rest of juice and the grapefruit which may be diced or left whole, as desired. Chill until liquid starts to congeal. Beat egg whites until stiff; then gradually beat in the ¼ cup sugar. Whip this meringue into the gelatin mixture. Chill until firm. Beat egg yolks, add milk and stir in the 2 tablespoons of sugar combined with the cornstarch. Cook over boiling water, stirring constantly until sauce thickens and coats a spoon. Stir in salt and butter and cool. Serve over the grapefruit fluff. (Serves 5 or 6)

GRAPEFRUIT FROSTING

1 egg yolk
1 tbsp grated orange rind
2 cups confectioner's sugar (about)
1½ tbsp grapefruit juice
Dash of salt

Mix together egg yolk, orange rind, grapefruit juice and salt; gradually stir in sugar until of proper consistency to spread. (Approximate yield: frosting for tops of 2 8-inch layers or 1½ dozen cup cakes)

GRAPEFRUIT JELLIES

2 grapefruit
Water to cover fruit
1 oz isinglass
1 tbsp sherry
1 lb sugar

Remove rinds of fruit and cut each into two parts. Carefully remove fleshy sections, removing white membrane and seeds. Place fruit in a small pan with the isinglass and cover with cold water. Reduce fruit to a pulp by gentle cooking. Add sherry and press through a small sieve or a jelly bag, according to whether you prefer cloudy or clear jellies. Return liquid to pan with scant pound of sugar and boil rapidly. Pour while still liquid, but cool, into serving glasses and chill.

GRAPEFRUIT JUICE

Serve fresh or canned grapefruit juice plain or mixed with other fruit juices in any desired combination. Add chopped mint for minted grapefruit juice, or add a few drops of peppermint oil.

GRAPEFRUIT MARMALADE

1 large grapefruit
3 large oranges
2 qt water
Sugar

Wash and slice fruit as thin as possible. Add the water and let stand overnight. Next day cook the mixture slowly until tender (about 2 hours). Measure, add an equal amount of sugar, and cook until the jellying point is reached. Turn into sterilized jars and seal. *See also* CANNING.

GRAPEFRUIT SALADS

(1) Add sections of grapefruit to plain lettuce and combine with French, or your favorite salad dressing.

(2) Add sections of grapefruit to endive, mixed with crisp watercress, and combine with your favorite dressing.

(3) Chicory or romaine, as well as crisp red or white cabbage finely shredded, go well with grapefruit sections; use either French or light mayonnaise dressing.

(4) Thinly sliced kumquats, watercress, and grapefruit sections go well with French dressing. Remove the seeds, but do not peel the kumquats.

(5) Orange sections, grapefruit sections, and quartered tomatoes, red or yellow, dressed neatly over shredded lettuce combine nicely with French or your favorite salad dressing.

(6) Tangerine sections, and pears—cubed or cut sticklike—mixed with grapefruit sections or cubes will prove unusual with either French or your favorite salad dressing.

(7) Grape halves (large ones) stuffed with cream or cottage cheese, mixed with shredded lettuce and finely chopped green pepper, combined with grapefruit sections go well with French dressing.

(8) Chopped celery, pimiento, shredded green pepper, and grapefruit sections or cubes combine with light mayonnaise or vinaigrette dressing.

(9) Canned or fresh sliced peaches, pineapple and grapefruit cubes, mixed with minced parsley or chives, all loosely packed in a scooped-out tomato, neatly arranged in a nest of crisp watercress may be served as a main course for a light luncheon. The appearance alone is appetizing. Serve with French dressing, or mayonnaise or with a sweetened whipped cream dressing.

(1) Sliced apple, kumquat, and grapefruit sections are excellent with French dressing.

(11) Apple cup, stuffed with grapefruit, celery, and crabmeat, mixed with mayonnaise combine well for a summer salad.

(12) Diced apple, seedless grapes, orange cubes, and grapefruit cubes, combined with a light mayonnaise make an unusual salad dressed on a slice of pineapple.

GRAPEFRUIT SAUCE

½ medium grapefruit
2 tsp sugar
Pinch of salt
1 tsp corn starch
1 tbsp water
1 tsp butter

Cut grapefruit and remove seeds. Pour juice and pulp (about ½ cup) into top of double boiler. Blend sugar, salt, cornstarch and water. Cook over hot water until sauce is slightly thickened and clear. Stir occasionally; add butter. Remove from heat and serve. This is especially good over parsnips.

GRAPEFRUIT SHORTCAKE

1¼ cups all-purpose flour
1½ tsp baking powder
½ tsp salt
3 tbsp shortening
⅜ cup milk (6 tbsp)
3 small grapefruit
¼ cup butter
1½ tbsp flour
¼ cup sugar
Pinch of salt
½ tsp vanilla
2 tbsp chopped maraschino cherries

Sift the flour, measure 1¼ cups, and resift 3 times with baking powder and salt. Cut in shortening, add milk and stir vigorously until dough just stiffens. Divide into 2 parts and roll each into a circle 7 inches in diameter and ⅜ inch thick on a lightly floured board. Place first portion on baking sheet; brush with melted butter and cover with second portion. Bake in hot oven (425° F.) for 20 minutes or until nicely browned. Peel and section grapefruit and cut in small pieces; drain off juice (should be ¾ cup, if not, add water). Melt the butter, stir in flour, and when smooth, add sugar, salt and grapefruit juice. Cook until sauce boils and thickens. Remove from heat and add vanilla. When ready to serve, break hot shortcake open, cover with half of grapefruit and sauce; replace top and cover with remaining fruit and sauce. Sprinkle with chopped cherries. Serve hot or cold as desired. (Serves 5)

GRAPEFRUIT JUICE. Besides unsweetened canned grapefruit juice, there is a grapefruit juice on the market that is sweetened with dextrose, a quick-energy sugar. Dextrose does not require any digesting, as it is one of the blood sugars and closely approaches the natural sugar of fruit. The addition of dextrose mellows the flavor of the grapefruit juice and smoothes that "too sharp taste," yet it does not nullify the pleasing tang of the natural fruit. Furthermore, dextrose sweetening retains a high percentage of the quality of the fresh fruit, because only a few hours elapse between harvesting the fruit and the sealing of the juice in the can. The juice is extracted by hand reaming, hence almost no rind oil, with its bitter tang, gets in by this method. Pasteurization is done by a process which sterilizes the juice by automatic control, thus eliminating that "cooked" flavor sometimes so noticeable in a canned product.

GRAPEFRUIT KNIFE. A grapefruit knife has a thin, curved blade, and is used to separate the individual fruit segments, once the fruit has been halved. *See* CUTLERY.

GRAPEFRUIT SPOON. *See* FLATWARE.

GRAPEFRUIT WINE. The grapefruit is called *grape*fruit because it frequently grows in large clusters, the same as grapes grow; and, like grapes, it is now being used as a source of wines, brandies, and cordials. Grapefruit champagne has already been served at public functions. Oranges are similarly utilized, and wines from these two fruits cannot be distinguished, although both possess a flavor distinct from that of grape wines. In either case, sugar must be added—a necessary process—for these citrus fruits do not contain enough natural sugars to ferment properly. In grapefruit, total sugars run from five to eight percent, while grapes contain from 12 to 25 percent sugar. High acid content in the citrus fruits is also a drawback, dry wines being excessively sour.

The juice from which wine is made is obtained from sound fruit which is of unmarketable size and color or has been frozen. Each grapefruit is cut in half and reamed on revolving burrs. Care must be taken to exclude the naringin, a bitter white crystalline glucoside, which in turn gives a bitter product. It has been found that baking the wine (cooking it) for two months at a temperature of about 125° F., imparts to it a sherrylike flavor. Citrus spirits and cordials are made from the wines by the usual methods.

Although the process has been commercialized for only a short time, the citrus wineries in Florida have a capacity of about 20,000 gallons a year.

GRATER. A grater is essentially a thin sheet, usually metal, that has variously shaped perforations punched through it. When a soft food, such as vegetables or cheese, is rubbed against the grater, it falls through from the other side in the form of particles, granules, or slices, depending on the shape of the perforations.

Graters are made in many different shapes and designs to meet almost any given need. One common grater design is that of a rectangular tube with a handle at one end and the other end open to let the grated food drop out. There is one, and in some cases more, different type of perforation on each of the four sides, thus making this a very versatile implement. Other graters are curved, some are round, some have handles, others are meant to be placed over a pot or pan, and they may all have one or more types of perforations, depending on their intended use.

Graters are commonly made of metal sheet thin enough to cut without being sharpened, yet stiff enough to stand up in use. Plastic graters are now being made that lessen the dangers of cut fingers. *See also* KITCHEN EQUIPMENT and GRINDER.

GRATIN (AU). *Au gratin* means, covered either with breadcrumbs, or cheese, or both, or with a cream sauce containing cheese, browned in the oven under the flame of the broiler.

GRATINATE. This means to prepare a dish *au gratin. See* GRATIN.

GRAVES. A grape growing district of the Gironde, which produces both red and white wines. The white wines, dry table wines, are usually called Graves Wines, while the red table wines are better known as Claret. *See also* BORDEAUX.

GRAVY. Good gravy is a most important addition to meat dishes, especially in winter, when there is need of both fat and flavor. Furthermore, unless we prepare good gravy from the juices left in the roasting pan or pot, we are wasting the valuable extractives emanating from the meat during the cooking process.

Pan gravy may be defined as a brown sauce made in the pan in which a roast of meat has been cooked. This may be an open pan, dry oven roast—a rib roast of beef, leg of lamb, shoulder of mutton or veal, or loin of pork. Or, pan gravy may result from cooking a pot roast in a closely-covered, deep kettle, by the moist process known as braising. Fowl, too, yields pan gravy with rich extractives which make chicken gravy so tempting.

Once the cooked meat is removed from the pan, the homemaker must consider the making of her gravy. If there is not enough liquid, more must be added, and this is one of the main reasons why a roast must be basted, and why the directions indicate that we should always add some sort of liquid to a roast to bathe the base of the roast. Should there be too much fat remaining in the pan some must be removed, leaving, for a family of six, about three tablespoons. The two chief faults to be found in gravy are excess of fat and lumpiness.

The making of good gravy is very simple. First, remove all excess fat by pouring it off into a small bowl, retaining only three tablespoons. Place the pan over a low flame and add to it three tablespoons of flour—that is, always the same amount of flour as there is fat. Stir the flour and fat together until smooth and brown, scraping the bottom and sides of the pan gently to loosen any particles which may adhere. While doing so, pour in slowly and gradually two and a half cups of hot water or stock, stirring and scraping constantly. Let all cook slowly about 10 minutes, stirring occasionally. Now add flavor or piquant sauce extract, which may be catsup, or any one indicated with salt and pepper to taste, then strain the whole through a fine sieve. (It is good policy to have one very fine sieve or strainer especially for sauces and gravies.) Serve piping hot.

If the gravy is rich and juicy in itself, no other flavor or color is necessary. But should it be weak and tasteless it becomes necessary to fortify it with added color and flavoring. In olden times, grandmother used to keep on hand what she called "browned flour" made ahead and stored in a jar or tin, hermetically closed until needed. To make this, a quantity of white flour was spread in a shallow pan and allowed to brown in a very moderate oven, frequently stirred until of a light cocoa or molasses tint. There is nothing wrong with this method today, if we have plenty of time and storage space for such items. But in keeping with the rapid short-cuts so characteristic of our times, even in cookery, it is often preferable to add color and flavor in a simpler way, either by the addition of a couple of beef bouillon cubes, or a few drops of some piquant sauce. There are many such flavor-seasonings in the grocery and delicatessen stores which will give excellent results such as mushroom sauce, Worcestershire, black walnut catsup, and the many tomato juices and pastes, and chili sauce.

Celery tops tied with fresh parsley and bay leaf, added to meat when setting it in the oven, yield a pleasant flavor when combined with onion and cut up vegetables; so does a clove of garlic and mushroom stems and peelings. Certain fruits may be used with care to arrive at quite novel gravies to accompany various meats.

Thus a handful of cranberries, added to an oven roast or pot roast will give an odd, sharp pleasant change. Canned or dried peaches, apricots, raisins and prunes, added to meat while it is cooking, give another tasty sauce. Raisin sauce (*see* RAISIN) is good with roast or baked ham, tongue, or any kind of smoked meat. In the same way apricots are good with roast lamb, etc., while lemons, oranges and grapefruit have long been accepted as accompaniments for over-rich meats.

To make brown gravy for poultry follow exactly the rules given above. The stock or liquid here is likely to be obtained by cooking the giblets (neck, heart, liver and gizzard) in water with or without added vegetables. The giblets themselves may be cooked and chopped and added to the gravy just before serving.

If a chestnut gravy is desired as for turkey, add to the brown gravy three-fourths cup of French or Italian chestnuts, cooked, skinned and mashed. In this case omit the chopped giblets.

It goes without saying that if a thicker gravy is desired a little more flour and fat should be used than the three tablespoons suggested. Or for a thinner gravy the quantites given should be slightly reduced. A roux (*which see*) may also be used to thicken gravy.

When you wish to make gravy or soup with the hot liquid in which meat has been cooked, wring a cloth out of cold water, and strain the liquor through it. The fat will remain in the cloth.

Add milk instead of water, to improve the flavor and nutrient value of meat and poultry gravies.

For never-fail, umpless gravy, put one cup of cold wa er or milk in a quart glass jar, and add two or three tablespoons of flour. Do not stir, but screw on the lid and shake vigorously until well blended. Then pour slowly into the browned fat and stir. Never put the flour in first. Always the water or milk first, then the flour.

CREAM GRAVY

3 tbsp fat
3 tbsp flour
½ cup chicken stock
1½ cups milk
Cooked chopped giblets
Salt and pepper

Leave the fat in the pan in which the chicken has been cooked. Stir in the flour and, when well blended but not browned, gradually add the stock and milk, stirring constantly over a low fire until smooth and thick Add the giblets and season to taste with salt and pepper. Especially good with chicken.

CREOLE GRAVY

1 tbsp butter
1 onion, chopped
1 green pepper, chopped
1 cup cooked fresh or canned tomatoes
Leftover gravy
Salt and pepper
A pinch each of cinnamon and sage

Melt the butter, add the onion and pepper, and cook gently until nearly tender. Add the tomatoes, gravy and seasonings and simmer gently for ten minutes or longer.

GIBLET GRAVY

Wash the giblets and the neck of the fowl, whether duck, chicken, turkey, etc.; cover with boiling water; season generously with salt, pepper, onion, celery, bay leaf, tied with a few sprigs of fresh parsley, and a clove or two. Simmer very gently. Remove the liver after 15 minutes, and continue the simmering for 2 hours (during the time the poultry roasts). When the bird is done remove it to a hot platter and keep hot. Pour off the fat from the roasting pan, and for each cup of gravy to be made, return 1 or 2 tablespoons of fat to the roasting pan, blend in an equal amount of flour, add gradually the strained giblet broth and cook until the gravy thickens, stirring constantly. Chop and add the giblets, with additional salt if necessary. Heat thoroughly, and serve with the roast.

CATSUP GRAVY

Pan-fry individual steaks or chops in a frying pan in butter. When done, add 2 tablespoons of water and 2 tablespoons of tomato catsup. Cover and simmer until thoroughly heated. Serve over the steaks or chops.

GRAVY BOAT. The name commonly given to a long, low, boat-shaped pitcher used to dispense gravies, sauces, etc., at the table. It is also called a sauce boat. *See* DISHES.

GRAVY LADLE. *See* FLATWARE.

GRAY CHEESE. A sour skim-milk product of the Tyrol. It has a gray appearance throughout, and comes in various shapes and sizes. Its taste is pleasant.

GRAY MULLET. *See* MULLET.

GRAY RIESLING. A white table wine of the Rhine Wine type made from Gray Riesling grapes. *See* RHINE WINE.

GRAY SNAPPER. An active carnivorous, basslike marine fish of the family Lutianidae. Most snappers are esteemed as food. *See* RED SNAPPER.

GRAYFISH. A modern name for the dogfish (*Squalus acanthias*), a small shark which was formerly considered an unmitigated curse by fishermen because of its frequent destruction of their nets and its voracious depredations on other fish and young crustaceans. In recent years it has acquired a good standing as a valuable food- fish, marketed fresh, smoked, canned, and dried. The average market weight is about seven pounds, the large specimens reaching 20 pounds and sometimes more. They are viviparous, the large sharks producing five to nine young at a birth The by-products of the grayfish are very important, its hide being utilized as *shagreen*, and its liver oil for dressing leather. It is best prepared like tuna, or any other kind of oily fish.

GRAYLING. A small troutlike fish, having a richly colored, long and high dorsal fin. It may be prepared in all the methods applied to trout.

GREASE. To rub a cooking utensil with grease, be it butter or any other kind of fat, preparatory to putting a food material in it to be cooked. A pan is most easily greased with a brush or a wad of soft paper dipped in the fat.

GREEN BUTTER. *See* BUTTER SAUCE.

GREEN CHEESE. A cheddar type of cheese that is either flavored with sage leaves, or colored green and flavored with sage extract. Cheese so treated is better known as Sage Cheese. It is also a term for *cream cheese*, which has to be eaten when fresh—similar to Neufchâtel, made from whole sweet milk enriched with cream, etc., containing up to 50 percent fat.

GREEN HUNGARIAN. A white table wine of the Rhine Wine type made from Green Hungarian grapes. *See* RHINE WINE.

GREEN LAVER. A water plant of the seaweed variety. *See* LAVER and SLOKE

GREEN PEPPER. *See* PEPPER.

GREEN SAUCE. *See* MAYONNAISE.

GREEN SLOKE. A seaweed sometimes used for food. *See* LAVER and SLOKE.

GREEN TEA. Unfermented teas, grown mostly in China and Japan. Those of Japan are considered superior and are sometimes called "the white wines of teas." *See* TEA.

GREEN TURTLE. *See* TURTLE.

GREENGAGE. *See* PLUM.

GREENS. The most common of the green leafy vegetables, which are collectively known as greens, are beet tops, broccoli, chard, chicory, collards, cress, dandelion, endive escaroli, kale, mustard, sorrel, spinach, and turnip tops. They are excellent sources of vitamins and minerals, and make an inexpensive vegetable. Various greens are in season at various times, and the supplies in the markets vary from time to time. All may be used raw in salads, or cooked in any manner suitable for spinach, *which see.*

GRENADINE SIRUP. A sweet sirup made from pomegranates, rather thick and sweetish, used for flavoring a number of beverages. It is manufactured in France under a secret formula.

GREY SOLE. A flat, small fish, with a flesh as white as snow, of fine texture and flavor. A luxury fillet, more expensive than any other filleted fish.

GRIDDLE. A griddle is a fairly thick, flat metal sheet, often equipped with a handle, on which certain types of cooking are done. The griddle heats evenly and holds the heat for a reasonable period. It is used much the same as the skillet or frying pan, but, being sideless, has the advantage of a more accessible working surface, and is usually much larger in area.

To prepare a new griddle for use, first wash it well in warm water and soap suds. The griddle is hot for baking when a small

GRIDDLE

piece of paper laid on it will brown. Adjust the heat, and start baking the cakes. With an electric griddle, preheat four minutes, then adjust the heat and start baking. Cakes often stick if the griddle is too hot. Wash the griddle after it has cooled in plenty of hot, soapy water, and wipe perectly dry before storing. With an electric griddle do not let the water come in contact with the element.

See also KITCHEN EQUIPMENT.

GRIDDLE CAKE. Most food historians believe that griddle cakes were among the first made dishes, and that they have their origin in the mixture of meal and water baked on a hot stone. During the early Christian era, they had already reached some importance by becoming an official meal of Shrove Tuesday—a custom still observed by many people.

It is thought that this came about through the fact that eggs, butter, lard, and milk were forbidden foods during the Lenten season; the homemaker therefore used up her supply of these things the day prior to the beginning of Lent. Shrove Tuesday was often referred to as Pancake Tuesday; and when the great stacks of the golden disks were ready, a bell, known as the pancake bell, summoned the family and servants to the feast.

Although griddle cakes, in one form or another, are included in the culinary delights of all nations, nowhere have they reached the heights of general popularity that they have attained in the United States.

Fifty years ago the proper place for a pancake was on the breakfast table. The pancake or griddle cake today, however, is just as likely to be served for luncheon or supper as for breafkast plate. Griddle cakes, pancakes, and waffles are practically first cousins, and the clever homemaker can manipulate her favorite griddle cake batter into a tantalizing, crispy waffle, while the average woman will turn to her waffle recipes when she wants to bake this aristocrat among hot breads.

HINTS AND SUGGESTIONS

For heavy, hearty pancakes make a thicker batter by using less liquid.

Use as little fat as possible on the griddle, only enough to prevent sticking.

Spoon the batter onto the griddle, using one generous spoonful to each cake.

Don't pat the cake, or otherwise disturb it, until ready to turn it.

Turn it once when the batter bubbles on the surface.

Take the pancakes from the griddle just as soon as they are browned on the under side.

In baking griddle cakes rub the hot griddle frequently with salt, tied firmly in a piece of cloth. The griddle will then be freed of bits of extra batter, and the cakes will be less likely to stick; moreover there will be less smoke.

Don't try to improve on a ready-prepared pancake mix by additions of your own. Follow mixing directions to the dot.

Don't stack pancakes. One minute of steaming gives the cheerful pancakes a glum appearance.

STANDARD GRIDDLE CAKES

2 cups sifted flour
2 tsp baking powder
1 tsp salt
1 tbsp sugar
2 eggs
1½ cups milk
4 tbsp melted butter or other shortening

Sift together the flour, baking powder and salt. Add the sugar. Beat the eggs, add them to the milk and beat again, then use this to moisten the dry mixture, adding the liquid gradually and beating thoroughly so as to el minate any lumps. Finally stir in the melted butter or other shortening and bake golden brown on a preheated griddle, greasing or not according to the type of griddle used.

Ham Pancakes. Add ½ cup of cooked, cold, minced ham to standard griddle cake batter, stirring in thoroughly. Or make standard griddle cakes rather thin, spread with minced cooked ham seasoned with a little mustard, roll up and serve hot.

Codfish Griddle Cakes. Add ½ cup of cold, cooked, shredded codfish to standard griddle cake batter, stirring in thoroughly.

Clam Griddle Cakes. Add ½ can of well drained, minced clams to standard griddle cake batter, stirring in thoroughly. Oysters may be substituted for clams if desired.

Fruit Griddle Cakes. Add ½ cup of blueberries, huckleberries, raspberries or other small tender fruit to standard griddle cake batter, stirring in gently and only enough to coat the fruit.

Rice Griddle Cakes. Add 1 cup cold cooked rice to standard griddle cake batter, stirring in thoroughly.

Nut Griddle Cakes. Add ½ cup of finely chopped or ground nut meats to standard griddle cake batter, stirring in thoroughly.

Any of the above variations are to be baked exactly as the standard griddle cakes.

Stuffed Griddle Cakes. Griddle cakes may be stuffed exactly as one would stuff a plain omelet. Bake the cakes as usual, then place a scant tablespoon of any desired cooked mixture, either sweet or savory, in the center, or spread over the cake, and fold together or roll up. With sweet fillings the cakes may be sprinkled with brown, granu-lated or maple sugar after being rolled up, then glazed quickly under the flame of the broiling oven. With savory mixtures pop into a hot oven for a minute or two before serving as all griddle cakes should be piping hot.

Good fillings would be: creamed chicken, fish or vegetables; minced meat reheated in its own sauce or heavy gravy. For sweet fillings use applesauce, heated crushed canned pineapple, marmalade or jam.

GRIGNOLINO. A red table wine made from Grignolino grapes. *See* WINE.

GRILL. *See* BROILING.

GRIND. To force food materials through a food chopper.

GRINDER. A grinder is a device that uses revolving wheels, teeth, or gears to reduce food to small particles. It may be turned by hand or motor.

Coffee Grinder. The coffee grinder or mill is used in many homes to grind coffee beans as they are needed, thus insuring the fresh-est possible coffee on the table. *See* COFFEE. Because of the toughness of the bean, those units turned by hand usually have a heavy flywheel, while the more modern devices have an electric motor.

Meat Grinder. The most commonly met home grinder, the meat grinder is chiefly used to prepare meats for use in hash, meat loaf, hamburger, etc. It can, however, handle most forms of food, making it, to that extent, more versatile than the grater, *which see.*

While an electric motor may be used, most home meat grinders are turned by hand. The food, cut into suitably sized chunks, is fed into a mouth or hopper at the top of the device, which opens over a

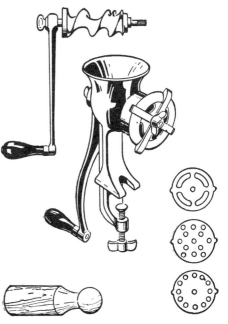

FOOD CHOPPER-GRINDER

revolving worm or screw. The worm has sharp blades which carry the food through a chamber and then through a set of re-volving teeth. By changing the teeth, the size of the finished particle may be varied. Different foods may be mixed in the grinder by dropping alternate pieces in the hopper. These grinders are made of some form of rustproof metal.

Pepper Grinder. The pepper grinder or mill is a standard table accessory for those who prefer the flavor of freshly ground pepper. These devices are not much larger than the standard salt or pepper shaker and are usually operated by either turning a small crank or twisting the base. They are filled with peppercorns which, as they are ground, drop down directly on the food. *See* PEPPER.

GRISSINI. A kind of Italian bread.

GRITS or GROATS. *See* HOMINY.

GROUND CHERRY. A plant of the genus *Physalis*; also known as *strawberry tomato.* The plant grows wild in many parts of the world, but in the United States it is most frequently seen in the lower Mis-sissippi Valley, and has recently been added to the list of cultivated crops. It has smooth, shining leaves. The spherical fruit, about the size of a cherry, is con-tained in a bladderlike husk, and varies in color from orange to red and purple. It matures inside the husk, and is often referred to as the winter cherry, because if left in the husk it may be kept through the winter. It is juicy, slightly acid, and is used for preserves and jams, and is also blended with chilipeppers in the making of chili sauce, and other flavorful combinations.

GROUND CHERRY

GROUNDNUT. The common European name for peanut, *which see.*

GROUPER. A general name for the fish belonging to the *Epinephelidae* family, which are a variety of sea bass, the most widely distributed and abundant of the finny tribe. Groupers range in size from two to twelve feet in length. About a dozen species are known along the southern coast of the United States, and in the West Indies under the various names of *Cabrillas, Chernas,* and *Guasas* by Spanish-speaking fishermen. In the British islands and at the Cape of Good Hope there is a certain spotted species called *Hinds.* Still another name for a part of the family is "jew fish" on the coasts of Florida and of California.

The black grouper of Key West is called *Aguaji* by the Spaniards, and is very popular among the native Cuban people. The red groupers are largely greenish-gray or orange-brown in color, varied with many blotches and stripes. They are found

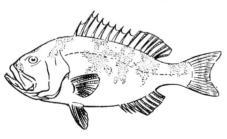

GROUPER

from Virginia to as far south as the coast of Brazil. This species averages about two feet in length and their colors deepen and spread with age. See RED GROUPERS.

The several methods employed in the preparation of bass, bluefish, pompano, whitefish, etc., may be adapted to this rich fish.

GROUSE. Scotch grouse is one of the favorite imported game birds, both for restaurant and home consumption. It is esteemed as an unmatched game delicacy when roasted like the pheasant or partridge, but when served, French style, in a casserole or in the Swedish method with sour-cream sauce and perhaps diced carrots and turnips, the bird of Scotland's fens and moors also wins the epicure's expressive dictum, *très recherché.*

The best method, the one universally accepted and recognized by gourmets and connoisseurs for this fine morsel, is roasting. However, all the different methods of preparation of the pheasant may be adapted to the larger grouse, while the small grouse may be prepared the same as partridge and quail. In most cases grouse should be eaten in the fresh state, unless otherwise indicated. The flesh of the female is more delicate, and the aroma more exquisite than that of the male.

Ruffed Grouse. This, the partridge of the northern woods, the pheasant of the South, may be called the "prince" of American game birds. Its high place, however, may soon be vacant, to be superseded by some lesser member of the game-bird galaxy, unless vigorous efforts are made to check its decrease. Possessed of a vigorous constitution the grouse is enabled to put up a brave fight for existence. Though usually enjoying an extensive domain of forested tracks, it is amazing how long the ruffed grouse will continue to live in leafy swamps of a few acres, or on little wooded islands, mere relics of its former forest home. Guns, dogs, natural diseases, sleety storms and unfavorable breeding seasons are decimating forces, however—to say nothing of the high market value placed on the bird— and all serve to reduce its numbers.

Spruce Grouse. At one time this bird was plentiful in the United States, especially in Michigan, the Adirondack region in New York and in northern New England, but now it is either rare or extinct. It is now chiefly to be found in the forests of northern Canada. The motherly, unsuspicious nature of this bird and its total disregard of danger from human beings, probably has had more to do with its thinning numbers than anything else. It is said that when a flock is surprised in trees, one bird after another can be shot down until the last one is gone.

Franklin's Grouse. This bird is named after Sir John Franklin, the English explorer, and is found in northwestern evergreen forests. It is very similar to the spruce grouse of the East, and possesses the same confiding disposition as that bird. This is attested by the fact that it will stand in amazed curiosity to watch the approaching foe intent upon its destruction. On this account it has earned the epithet, "fool hen." Like the ruffed grouse this bird is a drummer, but instead of sounding the roll from a rock or a log, the male drums by rapidly beating the air with his wings as he slowly sinks from some elevated station or mounts upward to it.

ROAST GROUSE

Wipe the bird clean with a damp cloth, inside and out. Sprinkle the inside lightly with salt. Fill two-thirds full with rice stuffing. Do not sew the opening. Cover the entire breast of the bird with thin slices of larding pork, fastening with string or toothpicks. Place on a rack in the roasting pan. Add a little water, or stock if available, and roast in a hot oven (450° F.) for 15 minutes. Reduce the heat to moderate (350° F.) and cook another 20 minutes, or until the bird is tender. Remove the fat. Rub with olive oil and dredge lightly with flour. Return to a hot oven (450° F.) and let brown for 10 minutes. Serve as hot as possible with currant jelly and bread sauce, *which see.*

GROUSE A LA MODE DE DUSSELDORF

Wipe the bird clean with a damp cloth. Rub inside and out with lemon juice mixed with an equal amount of white wine (Moselle wine). Fill the cavity with cooked rice, to which has been added the bird's liver and a tart apple, pared, then diced very small, and moistened with brandy. Season to taste with salt, black pepper and a little nutmeg. Sew up the vent and blanket the bird with a thin slice of fat larding pork, rubbed with minced parsley and chives, using a scant tablespoon of each.

Truss and roast in the usual way. Serve on a bed of red cabbage, cooked with an equal quantity of tart apples. Garnish with small triangles of bread fried in goose fat, alternating with small mushrooms, placed on slices of tomato also fried in goose fat. Serve with stewed cherries, bread sauce and guava jelly. *See* BREAD SAUCE.

GROWLER. (I) A colloquial American expression referring generally to any can, pitcher or bucket used to transport draft beer from the point of sale to the home. Specifically, it is applied to a type of metal can or bucket of pint or quart capacity that is fitted with a lid and a bail wire handle and was designed for this use.

Since draft beer is sold by measure, it was the practice of unscrupulous bartenders to draw the beer with as much "head" or foam as possible. To combat this, and in some cases as an equally unscrupulous measure on the part of the purchaser, the inside of the growler would sometimes be thinly coated with butter, making it impossible for the bartender to draw any head at all.

Because of the development of cardboard beer containers and the general acceptance of canned and bottled beers, the growler is fast passing from the American scene.

GROWLER. (II) A common name for the largemouthed black bass. *See* BASS.

GRUEL. A light, thin, cereal food for infants and invalids, easy to digest.

PLAIN OATMEAL GRUEL

3 tbsp oatmeal
1/8 tsp salt
1 scant tsp sugar
1 cup boiling water
1 cup rich milk

Mix the oatmeal, salt and sugar in a saucepan. Pour the boiling water over this and cook slowly for 30 minutes, stirring frequently. Strain the mixture through a fine sieve. Return the strained mixture to the stove and add the milk. Heat just to the boiling point. Serve hot.

GRUNT. Any of the numerous marine fishes of the genus *Haemulon*, and called grunts because when they are taken from the water they make a grunting noise. Many of these are valuable food fishes, such as the white and yellow, taken along the

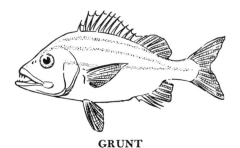

GRUNT

Florida coast and in the West Indies. The natives sometimes call them "red mouth." The flavor resembles that of the butterfish, and they are prepared for the table by all the methods adapted to that fish.

GRUYERE CHEESE. A variety of Emmental cheese of particularly fine flavor manufactured in France. There are three different qualities: whole milk, partly skimmed, and skimmed. Partly skimmed is the most popular.

GUAVA. Any of several tropical American small trees growing in the West Indies, Brazil, Mexico and other Spanish countries, as well as in the United States in Florida and California. It is a genus of the myrtle family and of the species *Psidium*, varying in height from 10 to 20 feet, and bearing fruit that is about the size of a small apple with a thin skin in shades from yellow to red, differing in shape slightly from oval to round. In substance the fruit is an aromatic pulp, sometimes sweet, sometimes slightly acid, which is mediocre in flavor until cooked when it becomes unusually delicious prepared as jelly, jam, paste, preserve, or sirup. There is a species in Brazil known as *P. Cattleyanum* bearing fruit of a fine, deep claret color that when prepared resembles the strawberry in flavor, and is therefore called strawberry guava which is highly prized; and in California there is a variety called pineapple guava, reminiscent of the flavor of pineapple. A vinegar is also made from guava

BAKED GUAVAS

3 guavas
½ cup sugar
Pinch of salt
2 tbsp lemon juice
1 tbsp butter
2 tbsp water

Wash guavas, peel and cut in half. Remove seedy pulp. Purée this pulp to remove seeds. Add sugar, salt, and lemon juice to the pulp. Mix and fill cavities of each half. Dot with butter. Arrange in baking dish, add water, cover and bake in a moderate oven (350° F.) for 20 to 25 minutes or until tender. Cool and serve. (Serves 6)

GUAVA JELLY

3 qt red guavas
Water
Sugar
Lemon juice

Slice the guavas. Cover with cold water, bring to boiling point, and simmer very gently for about 2 hours. Strain through a jelly bag. When cold, measure the juice and to each 2 cups add 1 ½ cups of sugar and 1 tablespoon of lemon juice. Cook gently to the jelly stage (about 1 ½ hours), then pour into hot, sterilized glasses and seal. *See* JELLY.

GUAVA MARMALADE

Use well-ripened or over-ripe guavas. Slice and place them with a little cold water in a kettle. Cook until soft, then press through a coarse sieve. Measure the pulp, add ¾ its bulk in sugar, with the juice of 1 lemon for each pint of pulp. Cook until thick, turn into sterilized jars and seal. *See* MARMALADE.

GUICHICHI DUCK. A wild duck, native of Panama. *See* DUCK.

GUINEA CORN. *See* SORGHUM.

GUAVA

GUINEA FOWL. Usually referred to as guinea hen, *Numida meleagris*, of North and West Africa, is related to the pheasants, and has been domesticated in most parts of the world. This bird was known to the ancients. The Greeks, Phoenicians and the Romans had it at their banquets, holding it in special favor.

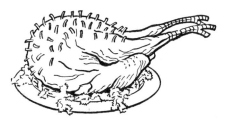

GUINEA HEN

There are two species of guinea fowl—both coming from Africa—one having wattles of turquoise blue, and the other with wattles of tender pink. The plumage of both is slaty gray variegated with white spots. One writer relates: "Whence the ancient Latin and modern specific name *meleagris*, the spots being fancifully taken for the tears shed by the sisters of Meleager at his fate." The guinea is agile, and with its symmetrical form and sparkling feathers it is an ornamental bird. Its screech, however, adds nothing of beauty to the domestic scene, but its cry is often lost in the chorus of the clucking turkey and the brass bands of roosters.

On our tables the guinea hen occupies a special place. The roast is indeed he favorite way to cook it, and it must be served with turnips. Select a young and tender bird, finely lard it or cover it with a thin sheet of pork fat and roast in a hot oven. Baste it with strictly fresh butter. Stuff with truffles for that extra savory flavor. For sheer goodness this tantalizing dish is the ultimate in pleasures of the eye and tongue. In Italy, especially in Messina, no Sunday dinner is complete without roast guinea hen accompanied by fresh soft figs and perfumed oranges.

The eggs of the guinea hen are greatly esteemed in Europe but they are not in special favor in the United States.

BREAST OF GUINEA HEN
IN PORT WINE

1 medium-sized guinea hen
1 small orange
2 slices onion
Port wine
Melted butter
⅓ cup bread crumbs

Clean the guinea hen and prepare as for roasting a chicken. Peel the orange and insert it with the onion slices in the cavity. Truss the bird. Roast in a moderately hot oven (375° F.) for about 30 or 35 minutes,

basting frequently with a mixture of equal parts of port wine and melted butter. At the end of the time, remove the bird from the oven. Cut off the breasts, leaving part of the wing on each piece. Brown the bread crumbs in a little butter, and place this mixture on the pieces of breast, patting into place. Heat in a little butter in a saucepan, over a very low flame, turning carefully to brown the crumbs.

Serve on toast with bread sauce (*which see*) and currant jelly. (Serves 2)

GUINEA HEN A LA CASTILLANE

1 good-sized guinea hen
Butter
Flour
Salt and pepper
1½ cupschicken broth
3 slices onion
3 sprigs parsley
1 bay leaf
4 tbsp olive oil
2 large onions, chopped
2 large green peppers, chopped
1 tbsp flour
1 cup fresh mushrooms, peeled and sliced
1 cup cooked strained tomatoes
Pinch powdered juniper berries
1 cup sweet cream

Clean the guinea hen and prepare for roasting. Season the flour with salt and pepper. Rub the bird with the butter and then with the seasoned flour. Place in a roasting pan and add ½ cup of the chicken broth, the onion slices, parsley, and bay leaf. Roast in a moderate oven (350° F.) for 20 minutes, basting frequently. Then add the rest of the chicken broth; turn the oven down to 300° (slow) and roast for 15 or 20 minutes longer, basting the bird frequently.

Remove the bird from the oven and disjoint. Pour off the broth into a pan and keep it hot. In a large saucepan, heat the olive oil and cook the onion and green pepper for 5 minutes, stirring constantly. Sprinkle in the flour, mix well, and add the mushrooms, tomatoes, and 1½ cups of the broth from the roasting pan. Cover and simmer for 20 minutes, until the vegetables are tender and the sauce thickened. Season to taste with salt, pepper, and the powdered juniper.

Scald the cream, and just before serving add the cream to the sauce. Heat to the boiling point, and put the pieces of guinea hen into the sauce. Heat thoroughly, but do not let boil. Serve immediately in a casserole.

GUINEA HEN. See GUINEA FOWL.

GUINEA PIG. This animal is not a pig, nor does it come from Guinea. It is a native of South America, and perhaps gets its name from Guiana, adjacent to Brazil; or it may have been given its name because it was carried by Guineamen in the slave trade. It is a compact, short-eared, almost tailless little animal, about seven inches long—black, white, and tawny color—which has been domesticated from the cavy (*Cavy porcellus*). In its wild state it produces litters only twice a year, but in captivity it breeds five or six times a year, and has three or four young at a time. It is used widely for bacteriological experiments.

The guinea pig does make good eating, however, its meat being tender, resembling the flavor of opossum. A five-months' old male, or a year old female will weigh between one and two pounds; they are best at these ages. It may be roasted or fricasseed the same as with chicken, after it has been cleaned, scalded and scraped.

GULPER EEL. See EEL.

GUM SIRUP. Another name for simple sirup. See SIRUP.

GUM TRAGACANTH. The name of a gum obtained from a mountain plant native to Asia Minor. The gum exudes through natural fissures and through incisions. It is reduced to a powder, and in that form is most generally used. When placed in water, the gum does not dissolve, but swells and becomes so distended as to occupy all of the water in which it is placed forming an adhesive, viscous mass. When used in ice cream it is usual first to soak the amount of gum to be used in warm water. Some prepare a stock by placing an ounce of gum in a quart of water, heating it until the entire mass is thick, and then adding about three pounds of sugar. The product will keep for several weeks. This gum, or one of similar composition, forms the base of most of the cold process ice cream powders or gelatinous mix desserts found on the market.

GUMBO. See OKRA.

GUMBO FILE. Dried sassafras leaves which are pulverized to make the rich green flour, much used in Creole cookery. The flavor is bland and delicate. If added to any mixture that is still on the fire it will turn to a sorry mess of ropey glue; but stir it in after the receptacle is taken off the stove and the result will be perfect and delightful. It is sold in small jars under the name of Gumbo File Powder.

GUNNEL. See BUTTERFISH

GUNPOWDER TEA. Pellets formed by rolling young, green tea leaves. See TEA.

GURNARD. See RED GURNARD

GURNET. See RED GURNARD.

GUSSING CHEESE. A skim milk cheese, weighing four to eight pounds. An Austrian cheese, it resembles very much the Brick cheese of the United States and is made in practically the same way.

GUTEDEL. A white table wine of the Rhine wine type made from Gutedel (Golden Chasselas) grapes. See RHINE WINE.

H

HACKBERRY. An American tree resembling the elm and having small, sweet, edible fruit, generally used for making preserves, jam, jelly, and the like.

HACKBERRY

HADDOCK. The haddock, which belongs to the cod family, weighs considerably less than the cod, averaging about four pounds, is differently mottled, and is distinguished by a black line running the entire length of the body on either side. Its back is dark brown and the belly is silver-white. The haddock is found in the same waters as cod and is always in their company, although the haddock is not so numerous. It has a smaller mouth than the cod, and feeds mainly on mollusks and crustaceans.

The haddock is in season throughout the year. It rates high in food value, whether fresh, salted, or smoked (in which case it is called Finnan Haddie). It has a firmer texture than the cod, but is somewhat inferior in flavor.

Both whole and filleted haddock are obtainable. Like cod, haddock may be broiled, pan fried, steamed, baked plain or with stuffing, or used in such dishes as haddock au gratin, pie, kedgeree (*which see*), à la vinaigrette, in puddings, loaves, and balls. The homemaker who owns a fish plank doubtless has tried planked haddock. Haddock is also available in frozen form. Kept at room temperature until thawed, the cooking time is comparatively short. The various methods of cooking cod, halibut, pike, whitefish, etc., may be adapted to haddock. *See also* FISH.

BOILED HADDOCK, EGG SAUCE

3 lb haddock
Boiling salted water
2 tsp vinegar
Sections of lemon
Parsley
Egg sauce

Cook the haddock in the boiling salted water to which the vinegar has been added, simmering gently to prevent breaking, and allowing 10 minutes per pound of fish. Drain and serve on a hot platter, garnishing with sections of lemon and parsley and passing egg sauce (*which see*) separately. If preferred, the sauce may be poured over the fish on the platter. (Serves 6)

CASSEROLE OF HADDOCK, ANCHOVY SAUCE

2 lb haddock fillets
3½ cups water
1½ tsp salt
½ tsp pepper
3 small onions, sliced
3 tbsp butter or substitute
3 tbsp flour
1½ cups milk, scalded
⅓ tsp salt, additional
⅛ tsp pepper
⅛ tsp each thyme and sage
½ tbsp anchovy paste
¾ tsp lemon juice
⅓ cup buttered crumbs
¼ cup grated American cheese

Poach the fillets in the water to which the salt, pepper and sliced onions have been added. Flake the cooked fish, watching carefully for bones. Melt the butter, add the flour and when smoothly blended, gradually add the milk and bring to boiling point, stirring constantly. Now put in all the seasonings and flavorings and again bring to boiling point. Arrange fish and sauce in layers in a casserole, top with the blended crumbs and cheese and bake in a moderate oven (350° F.) 25 to 30 minutes. Serve immediately. (Serves 4-6)

HADDOCK

HADDOCK ROE CROQUETTES

3 tbsp butter
⅓ cup flour
1¼ cups milk, scalded
1 tsp finely minced parsley
Slight grating of onion
½ tsp Worcestershire sauce
Salt and pepper
1½ lb haddock roes
1 egg
Dry bread crumbs

Make a thick white sauce of the butter, flour and milk, seasoning with the parsley, onion, Worcestershire sauce, salt, and pepper. Meanwhile cook the haddock roes in salted water. Drain, then break up finely with a silver fork and add to the sauce. Spread on a large platter and when cold form into small croquettes of any desired shape. Dip first in beaten egg, then roll in bread crumbs and at serving time cook golden brown in deep hot fat (375°–390° F.). Drain on soft crumpled paper. (Serves 6-8)

HAGGIS. The stomach of a sheep, stuffed with heart, etc., seasoned and boiled like a pudding. Unfortunately no one seems to know when the haggis became a Scottish symbol. Various tales are told— one is that in the old days the good wives of Scotland put together a paste of sheep "innards," sealed it up in a bit of bladder, and gave the package to their warrior husbands for battlefield rations. The mere fact that the Scots survived is sufficient testimony to the hardiness of the race.

In Scotland, however, the serving of the haggis became a ritual. To the skirl of bagpipes came the cook, flanked on either side by the pipers. Around the hall he marched, bearing aloft a platter upon which reposed the haggis, and halted before the honored guest, who had to recite:

"Fair fa' you honest, sonsie face,
Great chieftan o' the puddin' race!
Aboon them a' ye tak your place,
Painch, tripe, or thairm:
Weel are ye worthy o' a grace—
As lang's my arm."

With a perfectly straight face, the honored guest recited this bit o' verse from Bobby Burns and then handed two brimming mugs of Scottish dew to the pipers. Haggis is now more like a sausage, but the traditions are still associated with it.

HAKE. *See* WHITING.

HALIBUT. The habits of the halibut, sometimes called "ellbot" and "fletan," are remarkable. It has a skin which changes in color somewhat like that of the chameleon. The skin is soft and white on one side;

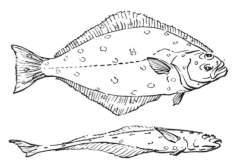

HALIBUT

on the other, light or dark gray. Its body is compressed, and its white flesh is firm and agreeable to the taste. The eyes, mounted on stalks, are located on the dark side of the pointed head. The halibut settles down on the bottom of the ocean, wiggles into the ooze, and lies there with its stalked eyes projecting above the ooze. When different lights strike those eyes, the skin changes color and becomes nearly invisible to the approaching fish. The cod hurries and scurries about all day hunting for food, while the lazy halibut lies at the bottom of the sea, camouflaged and invisible, until the cod comes within range. Then the halibut sweeps up fast, grabs the cod, and swallows it.

Like most other large sea fish, the halibut is usually crimped, which increases the firmness of its flesh and improves its flavor. As soon as caught, the large fish is incised transversely by numerous deep cuts on both sides of the body at intervals of about one and a half inches. On being plunged into ice-cold water for about an hour, the muscle fibers contract firmly and so remain. When the fish is cut immediately into sections after being caught, this incising is not necessary, but the sections are nevertheless plunged into ice-cold water for an hour.

The halibut, so much appreciated the world over, is one of the largest of the *Pleuronectidae* family. Specimens have been caught weighing 300 to 500 pounds. It is a delicious fish which is in season throughout the year. The halibut is exclusively a cold water fish and is found in the North Atlantic and North Pacific oceans, the specimens from either habitat being practically identical.

The various preparations of cod, haddock, whitefish, and in fact all the large white-fleshed fish may be adapted to this popular fish. *See also* FISH.

BAKED HALIBUT

3 lb halibut (one piece)
1 tsp salt
A few grains of cayenne
½ tsp paprika
Juice of a large lemon
2 medium-sized onions, minced
¼ cup olive oil
1 large green pepper, cut in strips
⅓ cup melted butter
1 tbsp sherry

Wipe the fish dry, then rub over with the blended seasonings and sprinkle with the lemon juice. Let stand in a cool place for an hour, turning 3 or 4 times. Brown the onions lightly in the oil. Place the marinated halibut in a buttered or oiled baking dish, spread the onions, with the oil in which they were cooked, over the surface, and top with the strips of green pepper. Pour in the sherry and bake in a hot oven (425° F.) about 30 minutes, or until the fish separates easily from the bone, basting three or four times with the melted butter and the liquid in the pan. Serve very hot, pouring the juices from the pan over the

fish. Garnish with sections of lemon and parsley and serve with a cucumber salad or other tart relish and plain boiled potatoes. (Serves 6 or 8)

BROILED HALIBUT, MAITRE D'HOTEL

Have the halibut cut into inch thick steaks or slices. Wipe with a damp cloth, then season with salt and pepper and brush over with softened butter. Place on the greased rack of the broiler and broil under moderate flame until golden brown, turning to brown the under side. Put a generous pat of maitre d'hotel butter or sauce (*see* BUTTER SAUCE) on each steak and garnish with parsley or water cress.

HAM. The legs of pork which are cured and smoked are called hams if they are the hind legs and picnic hams, or calas, if they are from the fore legs. Fresh hams are discussed under pork, *which see*. Ham is one of the most versatile of meats, being served equally well for breakfast, lunch, or dinner. And it is a most economical cut of meat since every bit can be used. Every last scrap of ham can be used in dishes of various sorts, and the bone may be boiled with split pea or lentil soup to give extra flavor.

TYPES OF HAM

Ham proper is of two kinds—short cut and long cut. Only plump, comparatively fat hams can be made into short-cut hams, but the majority of hogs which reach the Chicago market are of this type. In cutting these hams about half the pelvic bones remain on the ham, and the leg is cut off at the hock. Very fat hams are skinned and the fat trimmed down. The public has shown an increasing liking for hams prepared this way since it reduces the waste from the customer's point of view.

Long-cut hams come from hogs of the bacon type and are cut longer at both ends than are short-cut hams. The cuts are made at the joining of the pelvic bones to the backbone and at the fetlock joint. Italian-style hams are cut at the butt the same as short-cut hams, but long in the shank. Virginia-style or Smithfield hams are true long-cut hams.

Short-cut hams are graded into three grades, depending on their quality and conformation. *Fancy* hams have a plump rounded shape with thick firm lean meat of bright color, and solid fat not more than two inches thick. Second-grade hams are somewhat less perfect, but still satisfactory. Third-grade hams are too unsatisfactory to be used by the regular trade, being bruised, too thin, or coarse-fleshed.

These hams need to be soaked in water for 12 hours before cooking. They then should be covered with fresh water and simmered at least 3 hours, or until the bladebone is loose. The outer skin is then

WHOLE HAM

HALF HAM (BUTT END) HALF HAM (SHANK END)

SMOKED BOSTON STYLE BUTT ROLLED COTTAGE ROLL ROLLED BOSTON STYLE BUTT

HAM BUTT SLICE CENTER HAM SLICE

WHOLE PORK TENDERLOIN FRESH HAM ROAST ROLLED FRESH HAM ROAST FRESH OR SMOKED PICNIC SHOULDER CUSHION STYLE PICNIC SHOULDER ROLLED PICNIC SHOULDER

HAM CHART, showing principal cuts

Hams are also graded by weight, with a spread of two pounds in each grade, starting at 6 pounds. Very few hams weigh as little as 6 pounds, while few regular hams come over 16 pounds in weight. The larger hams, which are generally skinned, run as high as 24 pounds, and occasionally to 30 pounds.

Hams are cured, in either dry salt or sweet pickle, and smoked by any one of a number of different techniques. Smithfield or Virginia hams are dry cured, and then dried and aged. Italian-style hams are cured and dried, but not smoked. Because they are intended to be eaten without cooking, they are prepared under special regulations of the federal Bureau of Animal Industry. These are the *prosciutto* of Italian menus.

Kentucky Ham. These hams are from home-raised and butchered hogs. The freshly butchered hams are covered with salt and then hung in the smokehouse. A smudge fire of corncobs and hickory bark or sassafras wood is kept burning for three to five days in order to smoke the meat sufficiently. The hams are then hung in the smokehouse for about two years to age them and bring them to the state considered desirable. An icepick is inserted into the ham near the bone and by the odor of the pick the condition of the ham can be told.

removed and the ham trimmed of excess fat. It is then covered with brown sugar or sorghum molasses, cornmeal, and black pepper and baked as any other ham.

Virginia Ham. The special flavor and delicacy of these hams are due to a diet of acorns and peanuts. Like Kentucky hams, Virginia hams are aged after curing and smoking, and most Virginia hams carry a tag indicating their age. They should be soaked for 12 hours for each year of age and then scrubbed thoroughly with a stiff brush. They then need to be rinsed in several waters and dried and weighed. They are then covered with cold water and simmered very gently, allowing 25 minutes for each pound of ham. A Virginia ham is done when the bladebone at the large end is about two inches away from meat. The ham is then finished as any other ham.

Westphalian Ham, York Ham, Bayonne Ham, Italian Ham. These are all imported hams, ready to be served without additional cooking. They are usually served by slicing paper thin; in fact their goodness is lost if they are sliced too thick. They can be slightly warmed, if this seems desirable, but they should never be heated or cooked.

Tenderized Ham. Within recent years methods have been found of partially or entirely cooking a ham before it is marketed, thus saving the homemaker hours of boiling and preparation. Hams that are partially cooked need only roasting to finish them. Some, which are entirely cooked, need only to be warmed or glazed and baked for 30 minutes or so to heat. A label is always attached to these hams giving the directions for preparation, and it is well to follow these.

Smoked hams and shoulders may all be prepared in the same manner, depending on how they have been cured and whether they have been tenderized. See below for instructions for cooking a ham. Always

FOOD VALUE

Water	Food Energy	Pro- tein	Fat	Carbo- hydrate	Cal- cium	Phos- phorus	Iron	Vit. A Value	Thia- mine	Ribo- flavin	Nia- cin	Ascor- bic Acid
42	384	16.9	35	0	10	182	2.5	0	.78	.19	3.8	0

SMOKED SHOULDERS AND OTHER CUTS

The shoulders are cut in many different ways, each known by a different name. Regular shoulders have two ribs left on and the neck bone and short ribs removed; the leg is cut off at the knee joint. These shoulders are almost all cured, either with dry salt or pickle, and weigh on the average from 12 to 20 pounds. They are prepared and used like ham.

"New York" shoulders are cut two ribs wide, but the shank is removed between the knee and the brisket. They are made from hogs of the butcher and packing classes (see PORK) and average 8 to 14 pounds. They may be sold fresh or given a pickle cure. "New Orleans" shoulders are cut one and a half ribs wide from heavy hogs and weigh from 10 to 16 pounds. Skinned shoulders are cut like New York shoulders but have the skin removed to within four inches of the shank, and the excess fat trimmed off. They are given a pickle cure, and weigh from 6 to 16 pounds.

Picnic shoulders, or calas, are cut two and a half ribs wide, and the shank is cut off just above the knee. The butt is removed just above the neck of the shoulder blade, and the shoulder trimmed in the shape of a ham. They are made from good butcher and packing hogs and are usually pickle-cured. They weigh from 4 to 14 pounds.

The butts are made into Boston butts which include the middle portion of the shoulder blade, and boneless butts from which the blade is removed. Boston butts are usually sold fresh, but the boneless butts are rolled, cured, and smoked, and are then known as Cottage butts or rolls. These weigh from 1½ to 2 pounds.

The pork tenderloin may also be cured and smoked. It is usually boiled and then may be sliced and served hot or cold.

keep in mind that smoked or salted meat should be cooked slowly; always start it at a low temperature and increase the heat gradually. If ham is to be served cold, it should be allowed to cool in the cooking liquor.

While a whole ham may seem like a great deal of meat for the average family, it can be used in many ways and can be kept under refrigeration for a week or longer without detracting from its quality. When buying a whole ham it is a good idea, if the ham is too large for immediate use, to have the butcher cut it in two. The broad, or "butt" end can be baked and served as you would a whole ham.

Have the butcher slice several half-inch slices from the center. These are the choicest cuts of the ham and if bought separately command a fancy price. These slices can be broiled or sautéed for breakfast or luncheon dishes.

The "shank" end will yield ham for mincing or chopping to add to many dishes, and when only the bone is left it makes a fine basis for split pea or lentil soup, or it can be boiled with cabbage or other greens. The ham fat which is cut off should be carefully saved and rendered. Nothing is so good for drippings as ham fat, and many dishes rely for their flavor on the ham fat used in their preparation.

A slice one inch thick from the center of the ham is called a ham steak. This is ideal for braising in the oven, baking, or broiling. It will probably need extra fat if it is to be broiled, since the center slices have little fat except around the edges, and the meat will become dry during broiling. Try baking a ham steak using milk, fruit juice, cider, ginger ale, or wine in the baking dish. This makes a deliciously moist piece of meat with a different flavor. The steak may be garnished with mushrooms and served with a border of mashed sweet or white potatoes for a festive dish.

Ham sliced paper-thin is ham in its epicurean form. Italian-style hams and imported hams are intended to be eaten without further cooking. They are shaved into as thin slices as possible and make an attractive buffet supper dish. Ordinary ham may also be sliced thinly and served hot or cold in the same manner. For an appetizer de luxe serve paper-thin slices of ham with a wedge of sweet chilled cantaloupe.

Ham sliced somewhat thicker is the familiar fried or broiled ham which accompanies eggs, whether fried or in eggs benedict and similar dishes. A slice of broiled ham and a piece of broiled chicken served on toast and covered with a sauce such as hollandaise is another epicurean dish.

Baked ham may be glazed with brown sugar and studded with cloves. Or a purée of apricots or pineapple makes a fine glaze. Try baking slices of oranges on the ham. A raisin sauce goes well with ham. Or try basting the ham while it is baking with orange juice, or cider, or rum. The possibilities are limited only by one's imagination.

Leftover ham can be used in many ways. A quick luncheon dish can be made by spreading thin slices of ham with prepared mustard. Place a generous spoonful of baked beans on each slice and roll up, fastening with a toothpick. Heat for 10 minutes in a moderate oven (350° F.). Serve with sweet pickles.

Or ham, cut in chunks, may be used with baked beans instead of salt pork. Add the ham when you start baking the beans as you would use pork. Ham goes especially well with macaroni or noodles. Try a casserole of ham and noodles with a rich cheese sauce. Ham hash is an excellent way to use the last bits of ham. Take equal parts of chopped, not ground, cooked ham and potatoes. Add milk to moisten and cook slowly in a greased skillet. Season with pepper.

It is also possible to save the ends of a ham for future use in sandwiches and other dishes. Run the leftover bits of ham through the food chopper and pack into glass jars. Seal with a little melted ham fat. These jars will keep almost indefinitely in the refrigerator, and are ready for use at a moment's notice.

To Cook a Whole Ham

A whole ham which has not been tenderized should be soaked overnight in cold water, and then scrubbed thoroughly. It is then placed in cold water to cover and brought slowly to the boiling point. Cover the pan, reduce the heat, and simmer as gently as possible until done, allowing 25 to 30 minutes to the pound. A ham is done when the bladebone can be easily removed or is loose and protruding. The ham should be removed from the cooking water and the rind removed. This can usually be pulled off after starting with a sharp knife. Trim off any excess fat. The ham is then ready to serve hot. If it is to be served cold, return the skinned ham to the cooking water and let it cool in the water.

ROAST HAM GLAZED AND GARNISHED WITH PINEAPPLE

If the ham is to be baked, it should be boiled only 20 minutes to the pound. It is then skinned, the fat is removed in the same way, and it is ready to be scored and glazed with any desired topping. Place the ham on a rack in an open roasting pan and bake in a hot oven (400° F.) for 45 minutes or longer, basting several times with the drippings in the pan.

A tenderized ham needs only to have its rind removed and to be glazed and baked as above. However, it is easier to remove the rind if the ham is heated first by baking for 15 minutes or so in the oven. A ready-to-eat ham needs only to be glazed and heated through. However, the directions accompanying tenderized and ready-to-eat hams should be carefully read because different packers' processes differ somewhat in the result.

There are a number of toppings or glazes for baked ham:

(1) The simplest is to score the ham in diamonds, sprinkle with brown sugar, and stud with cloves.

(2) One cup of granulated sugar and 2 tablespoons of flour, thoroughly blended.

(3) One cup of strained honey or molasses.

(4) One-half cup of orange marmalade, peach preserves, currant jelly, or grape jelly, mixed with ¼ cup of ground nuts.

(5) One cup of brown sugar mixed with one tablespoon of dry mustard.

(6) One cup of sieved cooked, dried, or canned apricots, applesauce, sieved rhubarb, or half applesauce and half rhubarb.

(7) One cup of white or brown sugar and ½ cup maraschino cherry juice, cider, or fruit juice, sweet or pickled.

(8) One cup of white or brown sugar mixed with ¼ teaspoon each ground cloves, allspice, nutmeg, mace, and cinnamon.

(9) Dilute 1 tablespoon of dry or prepared mustard with a little water or fruit juice, cider, or tomato juice, and brush the surface of the ham with this mixture. Then sprinkle with either white or brown sugar.

(10) For a mysterious and delicate flavor score the fat in diamonds and insert narrow strips of sweet-sour gherkins or red pepper in the slits. Or wash narrow strips of anchovy fillets and use in the same way. Then glaze with white or brown sugar.

BAKED HAM WITH APPLE RINGS

3 thin slices ham
6 tbsp sugar
6 tbsp soft bread crumbs
½ cup pineapple juice
Sautéed apple rings
Parsley or water cress

Cut the slices of ham in halves and parboil for 10 minutes in water just to cover. Drain and arrange in a shallow buttered baking dish, sprinkling with the blended sugar and crumbs. Pour the pineapple juice over all and bake, uncovered, in a moderate oven (350° F.) about half an hour. Serve with sauteed apple rings; garnish with parsley or water cress. (Serves 6)

BAKED HAM CHASSEUR

10 to 12 lb ham
4 bay leaves
½ tsp thyme
1 cup brown sugar
1 tsp dry mustard
1 tbsp Worcestershire sauce
4 drops Tabasco sauce
1 slice canned pineapple
2 medium-sized oranges, peeled and sectioned
2 cups hard cider
1 cup rum

Boil the ham as directed (see above), adding the bay leaves and thyme to the cooking water. Place in a baking pan, carefully tear off the rind, and remove any excess fat. Combine the sugar, mustard, Worcestershire and tabasco sauces and spread over the entire surface of the ham, patting it down with the hand. Put the pineapple slice in the center of the ham, arrange the sections of orange around it, and sprinkle the entire surface with the blended cider and rum. Place in a very hot oven (400–450° F.), pouring any remaining cider and rum into the pan, and bake about three-fourths of an hour, basting occasionally with the liquid in the pan.

BAKED HAM AND SPAGHETTI RING

¾ cup spaghetti, broken into small pieces
Boiling salted water, or vegetable or meat stock
1 lb ground raw ham
1 tbsp grated onion
2 tbsp bacon drippings
¼ tsp salt
⅛ tsp pepper
⅛ tsp ground cinnamon
1 tsp minced parsley
1 tsp Worcestershire sauce
3 eggs, slightly beaten
½ cup evaporated milk

Cook the spaghetti in the boiling water or stock, draining as soon as tender. Combine it with the ham and onion which have been browned in the bacon drippings. Add also the seasonings and flavorings and moisten with the eggs and milk. Turn into a well greased ring mold, place this in a pan of hot water and bake in a moderate oven (350° F.) about 35 minutes, or until set. Unmold for service, filling the center of the ring with any desired cooked vegetable. (Serves 6)

BAKED HAM STEAK, COUNTRY STYLE

1 ham steak, cut 1-inch thick
Pepper
A pinch of thyme
1½ cups canned tomatoes
¼ lb grated American cheese
¼ cup minced onions
1 bay leaf
4 sprigs fresh parsley

Place the ham in a greased casserole or baking dish having a closely fitting cover. Sprinkle with pepper and thyme, then cover with the remaining ingredients all blended together. Cover closely and bake in a moderate oven (350° F.) about 45 minutes, turning once during the cooking process. Serve with plain boiled potatoes and cabbage or a green salad. (Serves 4)

BAKED STUFFED HAM EPICURE

10 to 12 lb tenderized ham
1 cup seedless raisins
4 cups toasted bread cubes
¼ tsp ground cloves
½ tsp salt
¼ tsp pepper
½ cup canned crushed pineapple, drained
½ cup canned red cherries, pitted and drained
1 cup chopped toasted nuts
1 cup strained honey

Have the butcher remove the bone from the ham. Soak the raisins in boiling water to cover for 10 to 15 minutes, then drain and combine with all the remaining ingredients to make a stuffing. Use this to fill the cavity in the ham, then sew up the opening and place the ham, fat side up, in a roasting pan with one cup of mixed vegetables (carrots, celery, onion, etc.), a bay leaf, two or three sprigs of parsley and a few of the green celery tops. Add one cup of water or stock, two whole cloves and eight peppercorns. Bake in a slow oven (300° F.) about three hours, basting frequently with the liquid in the bottom of the pan, and adding a little more water or stock, if needed.

An hour before serving time, remove the ham from the oven, score the top fat, then rub with brown sugar blended with a little ground cinnamon. Finally, stud with cloves and return to a hot oven (400° F.) to glaze. Garnish, if desired, with broiled quartered grapefruit, broiled peaches and crisp water cress.

BARBECUED HAM STEAK EN CASSEROLE

1 ham steak, cut 1-inch thick
2 tbsp dry mustard
2 tbsp brown sugar
4 drops Tabasco sauce
⅓ cup vinegar
A few grains cayenne
½ tsp paprika
2 tbsp hot water
3 tbsp currant jelly

Parboil the ham for five minutes in water barely to cover, drain, then sear on both sides under the flame of the broiling oven. Transfer to a greased casserole, which, if desired, may be rubbed over with a cut clove of garlic. Combine all remaining ingredients and spread over the ham. Pour in two or three tablespoons of water or stock, cover closely and cook in a moderate oven (350° F.) 35 to 40 minutes. Garnish with crisp water cress and serve with French fried potatoes and cabbage or sauerkraut. (Serves 4)

COTTAGE HAM KENTUCKY STYLE

1 cottage ham
2 quarts cold water
2 bay leaves
3 sprigs green celery tops
4 whole cloves
1 medium-sized onion, sliced
8 whole peppercorns, bruised
¼ tsp thyme

Scrub the ham well and place in a kettle with all remaining ingredients. Bring to boiling point, reduce the heat and simmer very gently, about two hours or until tender. Transfer to a roasting pan and bake in a moderate oven (375° F.) 25 to 30 minutes, basting frequently with a mixture of ½ cup of molasses, ½ teaspoon of dry mustard and ½ cup of orange juice. Serve with cooked greens. (Serves 6)

DEVILED HAM DUMPLINGS

1 can deviled ham
1 egg, slightly beaten
½ cup fine bread crumbs or cracker
    crumbs
Salt and pepper
A few grains paprika
Soup

Mix the deviled ham with the egg. Add
the bread or cracker crumbs, season with
salt, pepper, and paprika, and blend
thoroughly. Form into balls, the size of
a walnut, and drop into boiling soup.
Cook two or three minutes. If preferred,
seasoned minced corn beef may be substituted for the ham. They are appropriate
for service in bean or pea soup. They may
also be served as a garnish with cooked
spinach or other greens.

HAM BRAISED IN RED WINE

10 to 12 lb ham
¾ bottle red wine

Have the butcher saw off the shank bone
of the ham, then boil as directed until
tender. Transfer to a deep roasting pan,
remove the skin and crisscross the fat with
a sharp knife. Pour the wine over and bake
gently (300° F.) until the meat takes on a
dark reddish brown color, about one hour,
basting from time to time and turning the
ham over in the wine. Serve sizzling hot
with buttered spinach, candied sweet
potatoes, hot biscuits and the following
gravy:

Gravy

3 tbsp ham fat
3 tbsp flour
1 cup hot meat stock or canned bouillon
¼ bottle red wine, heated
Salt and pepper
1 tbsp paprika
½ cup of the wine from the pan

Melt the ham fat, blend in the flour and
when perfectly smooth add the stock,
alternately with the remainder of the red
wine. Season, stir until boiling, add the
half cup of liquor from the pan and continue simmering for five minutes, stirring
occasionally.

HAM AND EGG BALLS

3 hard-cooked eggs
½ tsp chopped chives
Salt
Paprika
Mayonnaise
¼ lb cooked lean ham
Cornflakes

Mash the egg yolks with a fork until
smooth. Add the chives and seasonings
and enough mayonnaise to moisten. Grind
the egg whites and ham, and add these to
the mixture. Shape the paste into 1-inch
balls, adding more mayonnaise if necessary. Roll the balls in crushed cornflakes,
and serve on toothpicks as hors d'oeuvres.

HAM MOUSSE

1 tbsp gelatin
¼ cup cold water
¾ cup hot water or strained ham stock
2 cups chopped cold boiled ham
Salt and white pepper
1 tsp mustard
¼ tsp paprika
½ cup heavy cream, whipped
Watercress
Quartered hard-cooked eggs
Sliced tomatoes
Stufed olives

Soften the gelatin in the cold water, then
dissolve in the hot water or stock. Cool
and when beginning to thicken, add the
chopped ham and seasonings and blend
thoroughly. Fold in the whipped cream
and turn into a previously wet mold. Chill.
Unmold and garnish with water cress,
quartered hard-cooked eggs, sliced tomatoes and stuffed olives. (Serves 4 to 6)

HAM AND POTATO CAKES

3 cups ground cooked ham or shoulder
3 cups mashed potatoes
3 tbsp chopped parsley
Salt and pepper
Drippings

Mix the meat, mashed potatoes and
parsley thoroughly and season to taste with
salt and pepper. Mold into flat cakes.

Heat the drippings in a skillet and fry the cakes until brown, turning once. (Serves 6)

HAM AND SPINACH SOUFFLE

4 slices white bread
Milk
3 tbsp butter
1 small onion, finely minced or grated
1 cup cooked spinach, drained and chopped
⅔ cup ground cooked ham
3 eggs, separated
Salt and pepper
Pinch of ground nutmeg

Soak the bread in milk to cover until soft. Drain, then combine with the butter and onion and cook until smooth, stirring constantly. Add the spinach, ham and well beaten egg yolks. Season with salt, pepper and nutmeg. Fold in the stiffly beaten egg whites and turn into a generously buttered soufflé dish. Set in a pan of hot water and bake in a moderate oven (350° F.) 45 to 50 minutes. Serve immediately with cream, egg, hollandaise or tomato sauce. (Serves 4)

PORK SHOULDER WITH RAISIN STUFFING

Select a cured picnic shoulder weighing 4 or 5 pounds. Skin it and remove the bones, or have the butcher do this. Make raisin stuffing as given below. Pile some of the stuffing into the shoulder and begin to sew the edges together to form a pocket. Gradually work in the rest of the stuffing, sewing as you go, but do not pack too tightly. Lay the stuffed shoulder, fat side up, on a rack in an open roasting pan. Do not add water and do not cover the pan. Bake in a very moderate oven (300°–325° F.) until the meat is tender, or about 4 hours. Turn the meat from time to time to permit even cooking and baste occasionally with the juice in the pan. Remove the strings before serving.

Raisin Stuffing

1 tbsp chopped onion
1 cup chopped celery and leaves
2 tbsp chopped parsley
2 tbsp drippings
½ lb seedless raisins

2½ cups soft bread crumbs
Salt and pepper

Melt the drippings in a skillet and cook the onion, celery, and parsley in the fat for a few minutes. Mix the raisins thoroughly with the bread crumbs and stir into the cooked vegetables. Season very lightly. The grated rind of a lemon is a good addition to this dressing.

A long-cut shoulder, weighing 8 or 9 pounds may be prepared in the same way. It will take 5 or 6 hours to bake and will use double the amount of stuffing. The smaller cut serves 6 to 8; the larger 12 to 15 people.

SUGGESTIONS FOR COLD HAM COMBINATIONS

(1) Ham, cole slaw, tomatoes, olives, pickles, rye bread.

(2) Ham, potato salad, sliced tomatoes, spiced pineapple, graham bread sandwiches with mayonnaise and cress.

(3) Ham, green bean and onion salad, celery stuffed with cream cheese, mustard pickles, orange bread.

(4) Ham sandwiches with mayonnaise, deviled eggs, potato chips, sweet and sour pickles.

(5) Ham, asparagus tips vinaigrette, radishes, scallions, crisp rolls.

(6) Ham rolls (cold thinly sliced ham spread with minced chicken, then rolled), sliced cucumbers with grated raw carrots (French dressing), hot biscuits.

(7) Ham with chutney, jellied vegetable salad, cottage cheese, melba toast.

(8) Jellied ham mousse with lettuce and tomatoes, prunes stuffed with cream cheese, bread and butter sandwiches.

(9) Ham, potato chips, molded lime gelatin salad, celery stuffed with roquefort cheese, clover leaf rolls.

(10) Sliced cold ham loaf, mixed vegetable salad, pickle relish, French bread.

(11) Ham, molded pear salad on shredded lettuce, radishes, cinnamon rolls.

(12) Ham, cabbage and pineapple salad with French dressing, radishes, hot tea biscuits.

(13) Thinly sliced ham piled with horseradish-seasoned cream cheese and sprinkled with paprika, string bean and onion salad, raisin bread sandwiches.

(14) Molded individual ham mousse, sliced tomatoes on shredded lettuce, as-

paragus tips, mayonnaise dressing, graham bread, celery and pecan sandwiches.

(15) Ham, potato and pimiento salad, peach halves stuffed with roquefort cheese blended with mayonnaise, bread sticks.

(16) Ham, cabbage and apple salad, radishes, popovers.

(17) Ham, with macaroni salad, either sliced or chopped in the salad.

HAMBURGER. Of the budget meat dishes, none are more adaptable than ground meats. The less expensive cuts of beef, lamb, mutton, veal, ham and pork may be tenderized by grinding and made into easily prepared meat dishes. In purchasing ground meats the homemaker may either select the already ground cuts or have the meat ground to order. The real hamburger as it was originally made in Hamburg, Germany, was something quite different. Today any kind of chopped meat is "hamburger," and the use of this name is so popular, although incorrect, that to change it would be impossible. True "Hamburger Steak" as served in Hamburg, is made as follows:

ORIGINAL HAMBURGER RECIPE

Procure thin slices of beef from the round. Pound gently until tender. Divide into serving portions the size of one's hand; sprinkle each portion with a little thyme, pepper, salt and grated onion, using about a teaspoon for each hamburger. Take a portion of veal kidney suet and form the hamburger into rolls with a bit of the suet in the center. Tie or skewer to keep in shape, roll in seasoned flour and place in a skillet in which butter or lard, the size of a small walnut, has been heated. Turn the meat rolls about to brown on all sides. Then carefully pour in a cup of beef stock, cover tightly and simmer gently for 10 minutes. Serve very hot, pouring the pan gravy over the rolls. The gravy may be thickened with a little browned flour.

Chopped steak, meat balls, meat loaves, meat patties, chili con carne, fresh beef hash, make-believe-steak, tamale, *koldomar*, *kottbollar*, chopped meat stew, picnic stew, *magnola*, steamed meat balls, etc. are all children of the hamburger family, and all are made with chopped or ground meat. Actually there are as many "hamburger" recipes and meat loaf recipes as there are people who make them. It is the bits of seasonings, the combination of meats and the way they are cooked that makes them varied and interesting.

Hamburgers, essentially, are patties made of ground meat either of one kind or a combination of several, be they made in croquette form, cake form, conic form, or cylindrical form. In the East it is customary to shape the meat into thin cakes and to spread the top with prepared mustard or some other condiment, before putting them under the broiler. In the West chopped onion and sage are added to the raw meat before shaping it into thick cakes for broiling or frying. The South has its own particular version of this extremely popular dish. It is a much fancier dish, with plenty of spices and condiments.

Hamburgers can be a fine food, and being also an inexpensive food, the wise budgeteer will feel justified in adding a few frills now and then. An extra pat of butter and a dash of paprika, slowly mingling with the pink juices of the well browned meat, or a mushroom or two for a sauce, for variety's sake, are all economies in the long run, since they will preserve the family's taste for the hamburger indefinitely.

See also MEAT LOAF.

ALBONDIGAS CON CHILE (MEXICAN)

1 lb hamburger
¼ cup white corn meal
1 egg
1 clove garlic, minced
1 small onion, minced
1¼ tsp coriander seed
1¼ tsp salt
½ tsp pepper

Mix the hamburger, corn meal, egg, and seasonings. Shape into tiny balls about ½ inch in diameter. Make the sauce as follows:

1 tbsp drippings
1 small onion chopped
1 clove garlic, minced
3 to 4 tbsp chili seasoning
3 cups tomato juice

Melt the fat in a large saucepan. Add the onion and garlic and cook slowly until lightly browned. Add the chili and tomato sauce and cook for 10 minutes. Drop the hamburger balls into the boiling sauce. Cover and simmer 5 minutes. (Serves 4)

BARBECUED BURGERS

1½ lb ground beef
1 cup soft bread crumbs
¾ cup cold milk
1 large onion, grated
1½ tbsp Worcestershire sauce
A pinch each of sage, thyme and allspice
2 tbsp minced parsley
1½ to 2 tbsp vinegar
⅓ cup tomato catsup
1 tsp salt
½ tsp black pepper

Combine all ingredients thoroughly. Form into patties and brown on both sides in hot fat, or broil under flame of the broiling oven, turning to brown both sides. Reduce the heat and allow the patties to cook through slowly. Serve very hot with French fried or cottage fried or mashed potatoes and a green vegetable or salad. (Serves 6)

BEEF BURGER CASSEROLE

1½ lb ground beef round
3 tbsp bacon drippings
4 raw potatoes, thinly sliced
2 medium-sized onions, thinly sliced
2 tsp salt
½ tsp black pepper
¼ cup minced green pepper
2 tbsp minced parsley
1 can tomato soup
½ can beef bouillon
1 tbsp Worcestershire sauce

Brown the meat in the bacon drippings, stirring frequently. Arrange in a casserole in layers half the meat, half the potatoes, half the onions and seasonings, following with a second layer of each. Pour in carefully the combined soup, bouillon and Worcestershire sauce. Cover and bake in a moderate oven (350° F.) about one hour. (Serves 6)

BEEF BURGER CHOP SUEY

½ package macaroni
Boiling salted water
2 cups chicken or beef broth or water
2 cups canned tomatoes or tomato juice
A small bay leaf

2 slices bacon
1 medium-sized onion, minced
1¼ to 1½ lb ground round beef
1½ tbsp minced green pepper
½ cup shredded celery
Salt and pepper
½ tsp Worcestershires sauce

Break the macaroni rather small and cook until tender in the boiling salted water. Drain.

Combine the broth or water, the tomatoes or tomato juice and the bay leaf and simmer 20 minutes. Meanwhile, dice the bacon and cook it with the onion until the bacon is crisp and the onion slightly browned, stirring occasionally. Add the beef and green pepper and cook, stirring constantly, about 10 minutes. Combine with the cooked, drained macaroni, the celery, tomato mixture, seasonings and flavorings, simmer 15 minutes longer and serve at once. (Serve 6)

BEEF BURGERS IN SOUR CREAM

1½ lb chopped chuck or beef
1 large onion, minced or grated
1 tsp salt
½ tsp black pepper
3 tbsp salad oil
1 large bay leaf
6 sprigs fresh parsley
¾ tsp prepared mustard
½ tsp soy sauce
¾ cup cream

Season the meat with the onion, salt and pepper; blend all thoroughly. Then form into six cakes and cook just until brown on both sides in the oil. Place in a very hot oven while preparing the sauce. For this add to the fat remaining in the pan, the bay leaf and parsley tied together for easy removal, the remaining seasonings and the cream. Bring to boiling point and simmer five minutes, scraping any brown particles of meat from the bottom of the pan. Strain over the burgers and serve immediately. (Serves 4)

BEEF BURGER TURNOVERS

1 lb ground beef round
½ tsp salt
¼ tsp black pepper

⅛ tsp ground nutmeg
1 tbsp finely chopped parsley
1 tbsp grated onion
1 tsp Worcestershire sauce
3 tbsp tomato puree
Pastry

Combine all ingredients except the pastry (*which see*). Roll this out thinly and cut into oblongs about two by four inches. Place a generous spoonful of the meat mixture on the lower half of each piece of pastry, moisten the edges with water, fold the pastry over the meat and pinch the edges firmly together. Prick once or twice on top with a fork, place on greased baking sheet and bake in a hot oven (400° F.) 20 to 25 minutes. Serve with shoestring or French fried potatoes and a creamed vegetable. (Serves 4 to 6)

Other meats, either raw or left over, may be similarly prepared.

BROILED BEEF BURGER CUTLETS

3 tbsp minced onion
1 tbsp butter
1 to 1½ lb chopped round or chuck of beef
¾ tsp salt
¼ tsp pepper
A pinch each of thyme, clove, sage, nutmeg and allspice
½ cup dry bread crumbs
1 egg, well beaten
¼ cup milk or evaporated milk

Cook the onion in the butter until yellow but not browned. Add the meat combined with all remaining ingredients and cook, stirring constantly, for five minutes. Remove from the fire. Cool and shape into six cutlets. Broil or pan-broil in a very lightly greased frying pan for 10 minutes, turning carefully to brown both sides. Garnish with toast points and water cress and serve with French fried potatoes. (Serves 6)

BURGERS WITH CREOLE SAUCE

1 lb chopped round of beef
1 cup fresh bread crumbs
2 tbsp grated onion
2 tbsp finely minced parsley
1 tsp salt
A few grains cayenne

A pinch each of thyme, clove and nutmeg
1 egg, well beaten
Butter or margarine

Combine all ingredients, blending very thoroughly, then form into small balls. Dust lightly with flour and cook in a little butter or shortening until browned. Transfer the frying pan to the oven and dot each ball with a pat of butter. Pour hot Creole sauce (*which see*) over and leave in a hot oven 10 to 15 minutes. Serve with steamed rice, mashed potatoes, or boiled noodles. (Serves 6)

HAMBURGERS WITH BROILED BANANAS

1½ lb round steak
2 tsp onion juice
1 tsp salt
⅛ tsp black pepper
A blade of sage
A blade of thyme
3 large bananas
Melted butter seasoned with salt, pepper and paprika

Have the meat passed through the chopper at least twice. Season with the onion juice, salt, pepper, sage and thyme. Blend very thoroughly, then form into six rather thin patties. Broil or pan-broil, turning to brown both sides. Arrange on a hot platter and place in the oven while preparing the bananas. Peel and halve these, dip them into the seasoned melted butter, then broil or pan-broil until golden brown and serve as a garnish to the meat. Pass tomato or curry sauce separately. (Serves 6)

INDIVIDUAL HAMBURGER PIES

1 tbsp beef fat
¾ lb ground beef round
2 medium-sized onions, thinly sliced
4 medium-sized raw potatoes, sliced very thin
1½ tsp salt
¼ tsp black pepper
A pinch each of thyme, sage and cloves
1 cup canned tomatoes with juice
Baking powder biscuit dough

Melt the fat in a heavy frying pan. Add the meat and onions and brown, stirring constantly. Next add the potatoes, seasonings and tomatoes. (If desired a teaspoon of minced parsley or chives and a little Worcestershire or other sauce may also be added.) Cover and simmer gently until the potatoes are almost cooked. Now divide into four individual baking dishes, top with rounds of biscuit dough (*which see*), brush the surface with melted shortening and bake in a hot oven (450° F.) 12–15 minutes. (Makes 4 pies)

MOUSAKA KREAS (Greek)

1 clove garlic
2 tbsp oil
1 lb hamburger
1 bay leaf, crumbled
1 tsp ground sage
Salt and pepper
6 cups thinly sliced raw potatoes
1 cup sliced onion
1 No. 2 can tomatoes
Paprika

Brown half a clove of sliced garlic in oil in large skillet. Remove the garlic and brown the meat slowly with bay leaf and sage. Add 1 teaspoon of salt and dash of pepper. Remove the meat. Brown the remaining half clove of garlic in the meat drippings. Add potatoes and brown, stirring often. Add the onions and 2 teaspoons of salt. Arrange layers of potato mixture, hamburger, and tomatoes in a 2½ quart casserole. The top layer should be potato and tomato. Cover and bake in a moderate oven (375° F.) for 1 hour, or until the potatoes are done. Sprinkle with paprika before serving. (Serves 6)

OW-YOK-SUNG (Chinese)

1 onion, minced
1 small clove garlic, minced
1 tbsp drippings
¾ lb hamburger
3 cups water
3 tbsp soy sauce
1 lb green beans
2½ tbsp corn starch

Brown the onion and garlic in the drippings in a heavy saucepan. Add the hamburger, and cook 3 minutes, stirring to break up the meat. Add the water and soy sauce. Heat to the boiling point. Dice the beans and add to the meat mixture. Cook

10 minutes. Make a paste of the cornstarch and a little cold water, and stir into the hot liquid. Cook, stirring constantly, until the liquid thickens and clears. Serve with rice. (Serves 4)

HAND CHEESE. A sour-milk cheese with a very sharp, pungent odor and taste. Local names are: Thuringin Caraway cheese; Olmützer Bierkäse; Dresdner Bierkäse; Berliner Kuhkäse; Alt Khukäse; Ihlefeld; Livlander; Satz; and Tyrol sour cheese.

HAPTULE. One of the finest, and highest priced teas grown on the Island of Ceylon.

HARD SAUCE. Hard sauce, an uncooked dessert sauce made from butter and sugar with flavoring as desired, has many variations. The longer the beating, the creamier the sauce. It should always be made well in advance in order to permit thorough chilling.

BASIC HARD SAUCE

1 cup butter
½ cup sugar
Flavoring extract

Cream the butter until light, gradually beating in the sugar which may be powdered, granulated, light or dark brown. One teaspoon or so of cream may be added with the sugar if desired to make mixing easier. Flavor as desired.

HARD SAUCE VARIATIONS

Date Hard Sauce. Use brown sugar for the basic sauce and add ½ cup of finely chopped dates.

Egg Hard Sauce. Use powdered sugar for the basic sauce, creaming in with the last sugar, one uncooked egg yolk.

Kirsch Hard Sauce. Use brown sugar for the basic sauce and add, after creaming, 2 tablespoons kirsch. Other liqueurs or wines may also be used, the sauce taking its name from them.

Lemon Hard Sauce. Use white sugar for the basic sauce and flavor with 1 tablespoon of grated lemon rind, working this in thoroughly.

Orange Hard Sauce. Follow directions for lemon hard sauce, substituting grated orange rind for the lemon.

Peach Hard Sauce. Cream ½ cup of butter gradually adding one cup of confectioners'

sugar. Beat in ⅓ cup of sieved peach pulp, fresh or canned, a dash of salt and 1 teaspoon of vanilla.

Pineapple Hard Sauce. Follow directions for peach hard sauce substituting well drained, crushed, canned pineapple for the peaches and flavoring with a tablespoon of brandy, rum, or lemon juice.

Rum Hard Sauce. Use white sugar for the basic sauce and flavor with 3 tablespoons of rum.

Spicy Molasses Hard Sauce. Cream ½ cup of butter, gradually adding ½ teaspoon of ground cinnamon, a dash of salt and 1 cup of powdered sugar. Finally work in 2 tablespoons of molasses, ½ teaspoon of grated orange rind and 1 teaspoon of vanilla.

Vanilla Pistachio Hard Sauce. Use white sugar for the basic sauce and add a teaspoon of vanilla and 3 tablespoons of blanched and finely chopped, pistachio nuts.

HARD TACK, or Ship Biscuits. As its name implies, hard biscuits or crackers, sometimes called "pilot crackers," used in New England for thickening chowders. Formerly used in army, navy, and on ships at sea.

HARE. In the South this game is called "old hare," no matter what its age may be. *See* Rabbit.

HARICOT. Original name of the kidney bean which constitutes a very serviceable article of diet, being one of the cheapest and best of all the dried beans. These beans must be thoroughly soaked until swollen and soft before boiling, and should only be eaten when wholly tender. Their flavor is heightened by the addition of onion, parsley, or other aromatic vegetables or herbs, and their nutritive value is increased by cooking them with pork. This is also the French word for bean. For fuller information, *see* Beans.

HARTFORD ELECTION CAKE. Well known in late nineteenth century New England as a traditional dessert around election time. *See* Yeast Raised Cakes *under* Cakes.

HARVEST FISH. *See* Whiting.

HARZE CHEESE. A hand cheese made in several sizes. It is a Belgian semicooked cheese similar to Port Salad and made at Harzé.

HARZKASE CHEESE. A sour milk cheese essentially the same as Bauden Cheese.

HASENPFEFFER. *See* Rabbit.

HASH. In cookery this is a mixture of chopped, warmed-up meat and vegetables. *See* Leftovers.

HASTY PUDDING. *See* Brose Pudding.

HAUT. A term sometimes used to indicate a sweet wine, especially in the case of Sauterne (*which see*).

HAUT-SAUTERNE. A sweet Sauterne (*which see*).

HAWS. The fruit of the hawthorn, a thorny shrub of the rose family, sometimes used for making desserts, but more frequently in jelly or jam.

HAY CHEESE. A skim-milk cheese. It is ten inches in diameter and two or three inches thick. Also known as Fromage de Foin. It is made in the Department of Seine-Inférieure, France. It derives its name from the fact that it is ripened on as freshly cut hay as possible. This gives a characteristic aroma to the cheese.

HAZEL HEN. A plump-breasted wild bird imported from Siberia. It is prepared like quail.

HAZELNUT. *See* Nuts, Cobnut, Filbert.

HEAD CHEESE. A jellied loaf made of the head, including the tongue and brains, of a calf or pig, highly seasoned, and molded in its natural aspic.

Head Cheese

1 calf's head (or a pig's head may be used)
Water
White wine
1 large onion, quartered
4 cloves
1 large bouquet garni
Salt
12 peppercorns
Cayenne pepper
Nutmeg
Sage

Have the butcher clean the head, taking out the brains and tongue. Scrub the head well and place in a deep kettle. Include the tongue but not the brains. Cover with equal parts of water and white wine. Add the onion, stuck with the cloves, the bouquet garni, salt, and peppercorns. Bring to a boil, skim carefully, and let simmer very slowly for about 4 hours or until the meat is very tender. The tongue may be done

with cayenne, nutmeg and sage. Toss thoroughly to mix well. Pack the mixture into a bread pan or other mold, pressing it in firmly. Pour over it 8 tbsp of the lukewarm broth. Cover the pan and weight it, and let cool. The mixture will jell as it cools. Chill at least 48 hours in the refrigerator before using.

Serve sliced, cold, with a salad or other appropriate garnish.

HEALTH FOOD COOKERY. Advocates of health foods believe that proper nutrition can not only maintain good health but prevent the development of disease in many cases. Some enthusiasts hold that many ailments can be substantially improved or cured by corrective diets and nutritional supplements.

In order to insure that individuals derive the greatest benefit from the foods consumed, health food advocates are concerned with (1) how foods are altered and nutrients destroyed through excessive refining or by the use of additives, (2) how foods may be prepared and cooked in order that as few nutrients as possible are lost and (3) what foods are particularly high in selected nutrients and what supplements can be taken to correct nutritional deficiencies.

ORGANICALLY GROWN FOODS

Health food specialists contend that so much food has been contaminated by the widespread use of insecticides, chemical fertilizers, preservatives, hormones and tranquilizers (in livestock) and so many nutrients have been lost during refining, grinding, processing and shipping that the food we eat is nutritionally inadequate and in some cases even harmful.

Many people believe that only organically grown vegetables and grains should be consumed. These are foods that have not been treated with artificial substances. Stone ground grains are preferred because the heat caused by industrial milling destroys nutrients and because the process itself removes the prime parts of the grains.

Cold pressed oils whose nutrients have likewise not been harmed by excessive heat, unbleached flours, fertilized eggs and foods which lack preservatives are preferred to the ordinarily marketed varieties.

Individuals who grow their own vegetables and herbs and raise their own chickens and livestock should take care to use only organic fertilizers and feed. Many organically grown products can be purchased at health food stores or through health food cooperatives.

Items should be purchased from a reliable store in which there is a frequent turnover of stock. Health foods, because they lack preservatives, turn rancid very quickly. Only fresh goods should be purchased. All items that go rancid should be discarded and nearly all health foods, including grains and oils, should be kept refrigerated.

The preparation and cooking of health foods follow the general principles for nutritional cookery. Nutrients are usually harmed by high heats and prolonged cooking. Raw foods are often emphasized in menus. See COOKING AND COOKERY and HEAT.

HEALTH FOODS

Certain foods have come to be known as health foods because they are thought to be rich in one or more nutrients that are essential to good health but largely unavailable in common foods. Some dispute exists, even among health food specialists, as to the merit of several foods, therefore only the most widely accepted health foods are listed here.

Beans. Dried and fresh beans, peas and lentils are rich in vitamin B1 (thiamin) and proteins. Newly sprouted beans are thought by some to be particularly rich.

Bone meal. Dried bones from healthy cows are ground into a meal that is used as a source of calcium. Bone meal is stirred into milk and other drinks and may be taken cooked or uncooked.

Brown rice. Rice that is unmilled (and, consequently, unpolished) retains its brown coating and a larger percentage of its nutrients, primarily the B vitamins.

Carob. Otherwise known as St. John's Bread, the fruit of the carob tree is used as a substitute for chocolate in milk and recipes. The plant flourishes in the Mediterranean region and may be purchased in powdered form.

Dried fruits. Apricots in particular are good sources of minerals and vitamin A. One-half cup of dried apricots contains 8,000 units of vitamin A, while a cup of apricots canned in heavy syrup supplies only 4,500 units of vitamin A and three medium size fresh apricots, only 2,900 units. Other preferred dried fruits are dates, figs, raisins and prunes. The sugar from these fruits is apt to cling to the teeth even more tenaciously than refined sugar, however.

Fish liver oils. Liver oils from fish such as cod and tuna are high in vitamins A and D. These may be taken in drinks or unmixed.

Honey. While honey is not extraordinarily rich in any of the nutrients, it is often preferred to sugar as a natural, unrefined sweetener.

Kelp. Dried seaweed, which is rich in iodine, is used powdered in salads and cooked dishes or mixed into a drink. It has, however, a very strong flavor and should, therefore, be used sparsely at first.

Liver. One of the most healthful of meats, liver contains vitamins A and B, iron and other minerals. Pork liver is particularly rich in iron. Dessicated liver may be purchased and is taken mixed into a fruit drink.

Molasses. Blackstrap molasses, rich in certain B vitamins, is used as a natural sweetener.

Nuts. Nuts are particularly good sources of proteins, vitamins B1 and E and certain minerals such as magnesium, potassium, manganese and zinc. Unsalted nuts are preferred to salted and nut butters made without hydrogenation or added preservatives are preferred to ordinary varieties.

Rice polish. A part of the grain removed by polishing, rice polish contains a variety of B vitamins. It may be used in drinks or cooked foods.

Rose hips. The bulb left on the rose bush after the petals have fallen is called a rose hip. These are found to be high in vitamin C and are often used as supplements. Wild rose hips are preferred.

Soybeans. Since soybeans and soy flour are rich in proteins, unsaturated fatty acids and vitamin A, an attempt is often made to introduce dishes made of these foods into the everyday diet. Soybean oil, particularly high in polyunsaturated fatty acids, is considered a good salad oil and soy sauce is a preferred flavoring.

Wheat germ. The kernel of the wheat which is discarded during milling carries a great many of the nutrients including certain B vitamins (since B vitamins are essential to the growth of the young plant, all seeds and grains carry them) and proteins. A cup of wheat germ supplies about 17 grams of protein alone.

Whole grain flours and cereals. These are preferred because they contain the nutrient rich part of the grains lost during ordinary milling. Whole wheat is highly nutritious as are rye, corn, oat and soy flours and meals.

Yeast. Though not commonly thought of as food, yeast is actually an exceptional source of complete proteins, many B vitamins and minerals. A number of varieties are available, including brewer's yeast and torula. These should be taken in small quantities at first since they may initially produce gas in individuals with poor digestion. Uncooked baker's yeast should not be used since it absorbs the body's supply of B vitamins. However, baked goods made with yeast are thought to be more nutritional than those made with soda. Yeast is usually taken mixed in a drink.

Yogurt. Clabbered or cultured milks such as yogurt contain all the nutrients of milk but are presumably easier to digest since they have, in a sense, been predigested by bacteria. Yogurt is also low in butterfat. It is a particularly good food for individuals who must take antibiotics over long periods of time since it keeps the natural bacteria in the intestines and mucous membranes from drying off. Buttermilk and sour cream are preferred milk products. Cottage cheese (*which see*) is particularly rich in proteins.

DIETARY SUPPLEMENTS

For those who decide to take vitamin, mineral or enzyme supplements on a regular basis, two factors should be kept in mind. Dietary supplements are not created to take the place of well-balanced meals and should only be taken in addition to an adequate daily diet. Moreover, since all the nutrients work in harmony in the body, it is unwise and even dangerous to create an unnatural imbalance by ingesting excessive amounts of only one nutrient.

A prolonged and excessive intake of one or two of the B vitamins, for example, will produce severe deficiencies in the other B vitamins. Similarly, certain minerals cannot be utilized without proper amounts of specified vitamins. Commercially sold vitamin supplements often do not indicate the additional nutrients required. In addition, an individual who decides to increase his intake of polyunsaturates and eliminate other fats should consult his doctor concerning the appropriate vitamin E supplement required.

SERVING SUGGESTIONS

Many health foods are already familiar to most cooks and appear in favorite recipes. Recipes for beans, honey, lentils, liver, molasses and soybeans may be found under the appropriate headings. Likewise, recipes for various nuts, dried fruits, grains and cereals will be found under specific headings.

Besides preparing health foods as main dishes, health food cookery advocates the use of various foods as healthful and tasty garnishes on familiar dishes. Wheat germ and rice polish may be eaten with milk as a cereal or sprinkled on hot cereals, cooked into breads and muffins, used in meat loaves and other foods instead of bread crumbs and used as topping on ice cream.

Soya granules can be cooked into foods or baked into baked goods much in the same way that nuts are added. Brown rice may be substituted for any recipe calling for rice (*which see*) if it is remembered that the cooking time of brown rice is nearly twice that of white rice.

Whole grain flours may be used to thicken gravies and sauces, to bread chops and cutlets and to make pancakes, breads and even cakes. Recipes utilizing whole grain flours include SWEDISH LIMPA BREAD, RYE BREAD and 100% WHOLE WHEAT BREAD (*See* BREAD), QUICK BUCKWHEAT CAKES and CAPE COD BUCKWHEAT CAKES (*see* BUCKWHEAT), OATMEAL BREAD and OATMEAL COOKIES (*see* OATMEAL), CORNMEAL FRUIT GEMS, CORNMEAL PANCAKES and CORNMEAL WAFFLES (*see* CORN), WHOLE WHEAT CAKE and DUTCH BREAD AND BUTTER CAKE (*see* CAKE) and NUT BREAD (*see* NUTS).

BAKED APPLES

Core 4 baking apples. Fill with a mixture of honey or maple syrup and allspice or cinnamon. (Honey and syrup may be thinned with water, apple or orange juice for a thinner syrup.) Bake uncovered until soft. Serve with condensed milk.

CARROT LOAF

1 cup walnuts, ground
1 cup carrots, ground
1½ cups whole wheat bread crumbs
1½ cups hot milk or thin white sauce
2 tbsp oil
1 onion, ground
2 eggs, well beaten
2 sprigs of parsley, chopped

Mix together all the ingredients. Pack into a greased loaf pan and bake in a moderate oven for 30 minutes or until done.

MIXED GRAINS BREAD

2 cups whole wheat flour
1½ cups unbleached white flour
¼ cup soy flour
¼ cup rye flour
1 to 1½ cakes compressed yeast
½ tsp salt
water
2 tbsp soybean oil
1 tbsp honey (optional)

Dissolve yeast in ¼ cup lukewarm water. Sift flours and mix together with salt. Make a well in flour and add yeast, oil and honey. Begin to knead, adding just enough water to form a dough. Set aside to rise. Form into 2 loaves and allow to rise until double. Bake in a moderate oven about an hour or until done. Different whole grain flours in different amounts may be used together with a large proportion of high gluten flour.

ORANGE-CINNAMON CHICKEN

1 quartered chicken
1 cup orange juice
1 tsp cinnamon
1 tbsp orange rind
⅓ cup honey or brown sugar
oil

Melt oil in a frying pan to cover. Fry chicken until half done and remove from pan. Melt sugar or honey in the pan with orange juice. Add cinnamon and orange rind and cook slowly for a minute until mixed. Arrange the chicken in pan. Pour orange sauce over the pieces   bake covered until done.

PIE TOPPING

½ cup brown sugar
⅓ cup whole wheat flour
¼ cup soy granules
2 tbsp butter or margarine

Mix together the brown sugar, flour and soy granules. Add the butter and work the mixture with fingers until it becomes crumbly. Spread liberally on top of any uncovered, unbaked fruit pie and bake as per instructions.

Soy Sauce Vegetables

Sautée onions until golden in vegetable oil. Add cut garlic or garlic powder and crushed peppercorns and mix. Add one cup of sliced sweet peppers and allow to cook a minute or so. Next add one cup of sliced zucchini and one cup of sliced eggplant without the skin. Cover and cook over low heat for about 3 minutes. Add 2 or more tablespoons of pure soy sauce to taste. Cover and finish cooking. Serve on rice.

Uncooked Fruit Bar

Finely chop equal amounts of dried fruits—apricots, pears, prunes, raisins, apples. Sprinkle with lemon or orange juice and grated lemon or orange rind. Mix in enough honey or molasses to enable the mixture to cohere. Cover the bottom of a cookie sheet with caraway or sesame seeds and pack the fruit mixture into the tray. Cover with more seeds and chill for 24 hours. Cut into bars.

Whole Wheat Liver

Allow ¼ pound of liver per person. Make a mixture of whole wheat bread crumbs, wheat germ and corn meal with fresh or dried parsley, freshly ground pepper, paprika and salt. Dip the slices of liver in milk or condensed milk and then dredge in the crumb mixture.

In a frying pan gently sautée onion slices in sesame or soybean oil. Place the liver in the pans and fry until done.

Yogurt Cucumber Dressing

Peel and grate one large cucumber. Sprinkle with salt and about a teaspoon of lemon juice. Stir the mixture into a pint of yogurt and sprinkle with curry powder. Use as a dressing on greens.

Yogurt Fruit Dressing

Mix 2 tablespoons of honey or molasses with 2 tablespoons of fruit juice or nectar— orange, lemon, grapefruit, grape, lime, apple, apricot, pineapple, etc. Mix a teaspoon of finely cut tart fruit rind into a cup of yogurt. Fold the yogurt into the honey mixture and serve on fresh fruits or with spicy meats.

Yogurt

To make yogurt mix about a quart of milk or reconstituted non-instant dry milk with a can of evaporated whole milk and 2 tablespoons of commercial yogurt or yogurt culture starter. The mixture must be heated to between 105 to 120 degrees Fahrenheit and kept at that temperature for about 4 hours or until solidified. A yogurt maker works best. But good results can also be obtained by keeping glasses filled with yogurt in a basin of warm water that is kept heated. Once the yogurt is solidified, it may be removed to the refrigerator to prevent further souring.

HEART. The heart of beef, veal, lamb and pork is a delicious, inexpensive dish when properly cooked. Beef heart is the largest and toughest, and small lamb hearts the most tender. But all must have long slow cooking with moist heat to be at their best.

Prepare hearts by washing in plenty of hot water. Then remove the veins, arteries, and fat, and any hard connective tissue. The heart may then be simmered slowly in seasoned stock and served sliced thin, hot or cold. Or they may be stuffed and braised, and served sliced hot.

Beef Heart With Rice Stuffing

1 beef heart
Salt and pepper
1¼ cups rice
½ cup chopped onions
¾ cup seedless raisins
1 tsp poultry seasoning
1 tbsp chopped parsley
1 egg
Bacon or ham drippings
1 No. 2½ can tomatoes
1 bay leaf
2 cloves
½ cup boiling water
¼ cup Pique seasoning

Prepare the heart and season inside and out with salt and pepper. Wash the rice in cold water and cook in boiling salted water for 15 minutes, or until half done. Parboil the raisins until plump and drain well. Mix the rice, raisins, onions, poultry seasoning, parsley, egg, and season to taste with salt and pepper. Stuff the heart lightly with part of the stuffing. Sew the edges of the heart together.

Heat the drippings in a Dutch oven and brown the heart well on all sides. Add the tomatoes, bay leaf, cloves, boiling water, and Pique seasoning. Cover and simmer gently for 3 hours. Add the remaining stuffing mixture to the sauce and continue cooking for 25 or 30 minutes longer. Slice the heart and serve with the sauce. (Serves 6)

HEAT. Cooking is defined as the preparation of foods by the application of heat. Proper control and use of heat in cooking helps produce the desired texture and flavor of cooked foods as well as maintaining a minimal loss of nutrients. In general, low heats contribute the least to the breakdown of nutrients and enzymes and the destruction of flavorsome juices in foods. In cooking vegetables, water should be brought to a boil as quickly as possible to prevent loss of vitamin C and other water soluable vitamins; then heat should be lowered to the simmering point to continue cooking. For discussions of cooking temperatures see individual entries.

Dry Heats. A cooking method is considered dry if no liquid is added to the foods during the cooking. The foods are actually cooked in their own internal juices. To the extent that the evaporated juices moisten the air surrounding the cooking foods, the cooking method is more or less dry. Foods are always roasted, baked or broiled in uncovered utensils to allow the foods to develop a crust which keeps in natural juices. If cooking utensils are covered, the foods will be steamed by their own juices rather than roasted. Likewise, in pan frying, sautéeing, and deep frying, the maintenance of a constant temperature allows foods to cook or brown without permitting juices to run into the pan or allowing grease to be absorbed by the cooking foods.

Moist Heat. Adding liquids to foods causes them to be cooked by moist heat which means that the heat is transferred to the food through the medium of a liquid. Boiling, simmering, scalding, poaching and pressure cooking are examples of moist heat cookery. Foods are cooked uncovered when maximum evaporation of liquids is desired (as in American-style casseroling or recipes that call for reduction of liquids). Since flavors and nutrients escape from the foods into the surrounding liquids, it is im-

portant to use as little additional liquid as possible (except in the case of soups where the liquid is also consumed) and to avoid overcooking, especially of vegetables.

HELMET CRAB. *See* CRAB.

HEN. *See* CHICKEN.

HERBS. Herbs are rather soft, juicy seed plants that do not develop the persistent woody tissue of trees. They were used medicinally in ancient times, and they are still used for this purpose to a lesser degree. They are used in cookery that they may impart aroma, flavor, or color to almost all foodstuffs. However, the use of the culinary herbs seems to be somewhat of a vanishing art.

The successful use of aromatic herbs is not difficult; nor is it shrouded in mystery—the French say that it depends primarily upon practice. Use just a soupçon (suspicion) remembering to heighten rather than disguise the flavor of the dish, and do not shy away from experimentation. A pinch of parsley or of chervil atop the mayonnaise—a pinch of tarragon in a sauce for fish or eggs—leaves and tips of basil in white sauces or in milk gravies—chopped leaves of dill added to a cream sauce—all of these are examples of inspired seasoning.

HERBS IN ANCIENT TIMES

Throughout history herbs have been held in high esteem. Innumerable legends have surrounded them, and all sorts of properties have been attributed to them. Tansy took its name from *athenasia*, signifying immortality; sesame, made famous by *Ali Baba and the Forty Thieves*, is a symbol of immortality to Brahmins. Thyme was once believed to be the source of courage, but the spiritual value attributed to it was diminished by Swinburne's line "There grows no herb of help to heal a coward heart."

Pliny referred to chervil's ability to stop hiccoughs. Believing basil to be efficacious in enlisting sympathy, Indian peasants wore sprigs of it behind their ears when visiting their beloveds. The ancient Greeks and Romans wore garlands of parsley to absorb fumes of wine and delay inebriation. More recently, colonists chewed dill seeds in church in order to stay awake.

CULTIVATING AND DRYING HERBS

Homemakers who have access to a few feet of earth will find a culinary herb garden a delightful and rewarding hobby. Herbs can be grown almost anywhere—in gardens, in window boxes, and even in pots on windowsills. Plan your herb garden in the spring. A single package of each variety of seed will be ample for an outdoor garden. When once well established, herbs require little care beyond an occasional weeding or turning over of the surface soil.

The following table provides a list of the most popular garden herbs and gives a general indication of their uses in cookery. See their individual listings for more particular information.

American homemakers used to hang bunches of aromatic herbs from kitchen rafters to be dried by the heat of their stoves. This was ornamental, but the dust that collected on them did not improve the flavors of the herbs. The preferred drying method nowadays is to spread the leaves on a tray made of screening, cover them with cheesecloth, and allow them to dry indoors. The tray is propped up so as to allow free circulation of air, and shaking it each morning will assure exposure of all leaf surfaces to the air. After the herbs have been dried (two or three days later), they

Common Name	Botanical Name	Annual, Biennial, or Perennial	Propagation	Uses
Angelica	Angelica archangelica	Biennial	Seed	Food
Anise	Pimpinella anisum	Annual	Seed	Food and beverage
Balm	Melissa officinalis	Perennial	Seed	Food and beverage
Basil	Ocimum	Annual	Seed	Food and beverage Seasoning
Borage	Borago officinalis	Annual	Seed	Food
Burnet	Sanguisorba minor	Perennial	Seed and division	Food
Camomile	Antemis nobilis	Perennial	Seed, rooting stems	Beverage
Caraway	Carum carvi	Biennial	Seed	Food
Chervil	Anthriscus	Annual	Seed	Food
Chives	Allium schoenoprasum	Perennial	Bulbs, seeds, and division of clumps	Food
Coriander	Coriandrum sativum	Annual	Seed	Food
Cress	Barbarea verna	Biennial	Seed	Food
Dill	Anethum graveolens	Annual	Seed	Food, pickling, vinegars
Fennel	Nigella sativa	Annual	Seed	Food, condiment
Horehound	Marrubium vulgare	Perennial	Seed	Beverage, candy
Horseradish	Armorica rusticana	Perennial	Root cuttings	Food, seasoning
Hyssop	Hyssopus officinalis	Perennial	Seed	Food, candy
Lemon verbena	Lippia citriodora	Perennial	Cuttings	Flavoring, salads
Parsley	Petroselinum hortense	Biennial	Cuttings, seed, divisions	Flavoring, garnishing
Peppermint	Mentha piperita	Perennial	Seed	Flavoring, candy
Rosemary	Rosmarinus officinalis	Perennial shrub	Seed	Flavoring
Saffron	Crocus sativus	Perennial	Seed, cuttings	Flavoring
Sage	Salvia officinalis	Perennial	Seed, corms	Flavoring
Sesame	Sesamum orientale	Annual	Seed, cuttings	Flavoring
Sorrel	Rumex acetosa	Perennial	Seed	Food flavoring
Spearmint	Mentha spicata	Perennial	Division	Flavoring, beverage
Tansy	Tanacetum vulgare	Perennial	Seed, division	Flavoring
Tarragon	Artemisia dracunculus	Perennial	Root cuttings	Flavoring, vinegar, salads, food
Thyme	Thymus (many varieties)	Perennial	Seed, cuttings	Flavoring food
Watercress	Nasturtium aquaticum	Perennial	Seed, cuttings	Salad, food, garnishing

are packed in glass jars or other tight-closing containers and stored in a cool, dry place.

The French recommend the following method for drying and keeping herbs: Gather them on a dry day just before they begin to flower. Dry them quickly before or near a fire, and then strip the leaves from the stalks. Put the leaves on baking pans, and place them in a moderately hot oven (325°–350° F.), door ajar, until they are thoroughly dry but not scorched. Then reduce them to powder between the palms of your hands. Place the powder in hot, dry bottles; cork these tightly, label them, and store them for winter use.

Use of Herbs in Cookery

Herbs are rich in vitamin content, they aid the digestive process, and from ancient times have been famed for their curative effects. Although particular curative effects are still recognized, the gourmet is primarily interested in the gastronomic uses of herbs. Although many of the powers formerly attributed to herbs are quite fantastic, modern scientists credit the old herbalists with knowing that savory odors tend to aid digestion and to refresh jaded nerves. Life manages to seem less complicated under the spell of the invigorating scent of lemon verbena or the spicy tang of rosemary.

The ancients believed that aromatic herbs were most potent and effective when picked under the signs of their respective planets. Modern homemakers know that a store of aromatic herbs, whenever picked, constitutes a little treasury to be drawn upon whenever garnishes or flavoring agents are called for. Herbs seem to be essential in stews and poultry stuffings. They give tang to cheese, salads, spaghetti, fish, lamb, and veal. They will add a new excitement to almost any of the so-called ordinary dishes. The art of using them is not difficult if you but know the fundamentals of Seasoning (*which see*).

There are numerous ways of flavoring with aromatic herbs. The herbs may be used fresh, dried, or as decoctions. They may be dropped in a minute before serving, as with soups. They can be mixed with the ingredients before cooking, as with meat balls. They may be added to the food while it is being cooked, as with stews. For cold drinks herbs should be wrapped in a cloth, bruised, and soaked in the liquid. If herbs are used, no condiments are necessary except sugar and salt and perhaps a little pepper. Herbs are sometimes used in combination with other herbs as in Curry Powder, Fines Herbs, and Bouquet Garnis (*which see*).

Either saffron or marigold will impart a rich yellow color to a pale-tinted food and render it more appetizing in appearance as well as in flavor.

HERMITS. A very popular type of cookie, made as follows:

⅔ cup butter, or substitute
1 cup brown sugar, firmly packed
2 eggs, well beaten
1¾ cups sifted pastry flour
1 tsp baking powder
1 tsp ground cinnamon
½ tsp salt
¼ cup chopped nut meats
¾ cup chopped seedless raisins

Cream the butter until light and fluffy, adding the sugar a little at a time. Work in the eggs, one at a time, beating well after each addition. Sift together the flour, baking powder, cinnamon and salt and add gradually to the first mixture, still beating. Fold in the nuts and raisins and drop by teaspoonfuls onto greased cookie sheets. Bake in a moderate oven (375° F.) 12 to 15 minutes. Cool on a wire rack. (Makes about 2 dozen)

Another popular version of Hermits is the following:

½ cup butter or substitute
1½ cups brown sugar, firmly packed
2 eggs, well beaten
3½ cups sifted pastry flour
3 tsp baking powder
¼ tsp baking soda
½ tsp salt
1 tsp ground cinnamon
½ tsp ground cloves
½ tsp ground nutmeg
About ½ cup evaporated milk
1 cup seedless raisins
½ cup ground walnuts

Cream the butter until light, gradually adding the sugar and continuing to cream each addition. Stir in the eggs, one at a time. Sift the dry ingredients and combine with the first mixture, alternately with the milk, beating after each addition. Finally fold in the raisins and nuts and drop from the tip of a spoon onto greased cookie sheets. Bake in a moderate oven (350°–375° F.) 12–14 minutes. Cool on a wire rack. (Makes about 6 dozen)

HERRGARDSOST CHEESE. The most popular cheese of Sweden. It is a hard cheese, weighing from 25 to 40 lbs., and is made in two qualities, full cream and half cream.

HERRING. In American history, as a result of different interpretations of the treaty signed between this country and England more than a hundred years ago, the right of United States fishermen to operate in Canadian waters was long a matter of dispute. Even a battle was named after this fish. During the Hundred Years' War, in the siege of Orleans then held by the French, the English attempted to transport a Lenten diet of herring to their soldiers. The French intercepted the supply train, but lost the fight, now known as the Battle of the Herrings. The overthrow of Charles I of England has been laid partly to the herring industry—following his interference with the free fishing rights of his own subjects, as well as the imposition of high taxes on English fishermen for the purpose of building a navy to destroy the great Dutch herring trade of the time. Holland's vast foreign trade of several centuries ago was built on the herring industry; her navy included many herring fishermen, and there was a saying that "the foundations of Amsterdam were laid on herring bones."

The spawning and feeding grounds of the herring have dictated the location of many cities and, through international disputes and other problems, have affected the destiny of nations. The expression "red herring" has come to have less gastronomic than political and literary meaning as a distraction or side issue.

Important in nearly every country with extensive fisheries, the herring genus, *Clupea*, numbers some 200 members. It is especially abundant in northern waters, from which Great Britain alone takes hundreds of thousands of tons annually. Great Yarmouth and Lowestoft, on the North Sea, have long been world-important centers of the herring trade. It was at Yarmouth that Nurse Peggoty told David Copperfield, in Dickens' book of that name, that she was "proud to call herself a Yar-

mouth bloater." In the North Sea and off the coast of Norway, herring fishing has long been a means of livelihood. At the beginning of the 11th century it was already an established industry, and the art of salting the herring dates back to the middle of the 14th century, while the smoking process was introduced the following century. Young herrings are canned as sardines.

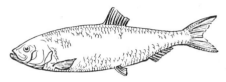

HERRING

In the North Atlantic herring fishing is possible from north of Cape Cod to Greenland, Iceland, and the White Sea. The herring is found all along our Eastern Atlantic seaboard as far south as the Carolinas, but never further south than 35 degrees latitude. Herring feed on minute organisms and crustaceans, which they strain from the water by means of their sieve-like gill-racker. They also feed on fry of their own and other species.

They are fast swimmers and are caught by millions during the quiet nights of spring, when they can be seen, especially in clear moonlight, advancing in close columns of several square miles. The surface of the sea then seems to be a gigantic carpet of enchanting brilliancy and beauty of colors, ranging from sapphire to emerald. The herring, full of sharp, slender bones like the shad, is a member of the same family. It is a migratory fish, which, when alive, is glaucous green on the back and silver-white on the sides and belly, with a kind of brilliantly-glazed metallic film covering its entire body. The green of the back turns blue immediately after death.

Herring are very prolific, the female laying an average of 50 million eggs annually, according to size. When spawning time approaches, the female swims toward shore and rubs herself against rocks, sand, and sea plants, on which the eggs remain for a while abandoned to Nature's care. Subsequently they are released by undercurrents and may be seen floating upon the sea, resembling a covering of sawdust. Scientists have estimated that if a single pair of herring were able to set up housekeeping and produce successive generations of offspring unmolested for about seven years, by that time they would choke up all the oceans, seas, and rivers of the world.

Useful as the herring is, and has been, in human diet, it is still more valuable in nature as a food source for such sea creatures as the cod, the haddock, the mackerel, the whale, the seal, as well as for birds like the gull and gannet. In fact, it has been estimated that the annual billions of herring which man takes from the seas is not more than five per cent of the total destruction wrought by that fish's natural enemies. Yet King Herring shows no signs of extinction, nor even of growing scarcer. Since it is by nature a pacifist, the answer lies neither in offensive nor defensive powers, but in sheer abundance. *See also* FISH.

Red Herring, a special grade of heavily salted fish, gets its rich brown color from long smoking; while Kippered Herring, first gutted and then lightly salted, are cured for twelve hours over a smoldering fire of oak chips. Canned in oil and shipped all over the world, kippered herring is a familiar breakfast dish from Stockholm to Cape Horn, and from New York to Hong Kong. A less tasty imitator of the true kipper is the Painted Lady, an ordinary split and salted herring, harmlessly dyed to resemble the golden brown of the genuine article.

DEVILED HERRINGS

6 fresh herrings
¾ tsp salt
1½ tbsp oil
2½ tbsp prepared mustard
A dash of cayenne
1 tsp grated onion
A pinch each of ground thyme and clove
3 or more tbsp fine bread crumbs
3 generous tbsp butter, melted
Anchovy paste, as large as a pea
Quartered lemon
Minced parsley

The fish dealer will scale and clean the fish, leaving the heads and tails on if you wish. Wipe the fish inside and out and pat dry. Score or make little slits on the flesh on each side, as this hastens the cooking and prevents the fish from curling up. Sprinkle with the combined salt, cayenne,

and spice. Brush with oil and spread the slits with the mustard blended with the anchovy paste. Preheat the broiler for five minutes; brush the rack with oil, and place the fish on it. Broil a few minutes, then sprinkle with the fine bread crumbs, and sprinkle them with the melted butter. Broil them until the flesh flakes and the crumbs brown delicately, basting often with the remaining melted butter. Serve upon a hot platter, garnished simply with lemon quarters and fresh parsley, after having sprinkled the minced parsley over the cooked fish. If desired, the fish may be pan fried. (Serves six)

KIPPERED HERRING IN CREAM

2 medium-sized onions, thinly sliced
3 tbsp butter
1 large can kippered herring
½ cup thin cream or evaporated milk
Paprika

Fry the onions in the butter until golden brown; then remove from the pan. Drain the herring and fry lightly on both sides, in the same pan. Add the cream or evaporated milk, and heat. Return the onions to the pan, placing them on top of the fish, dust with paprika, make piping hot and serve immediately. (Serves 4)

Note: Unless they are very small, kippers may be boned. If very salt, freshen by immersing in boiling water for 10 minutes, after which they may be broiled, baked, or pan-fried in butter.

HERVE CHEESE. A Belgian soft cheese, turned out in cubes.

HICKORY NUT. An American nut of the walnut family. Like the butternut, it contains a large amount of fat, and is frequently used in confections, cakes, and cookies. *See also* NUT.

HICKORY NUT

HIGHBALL. A drink made of diluted spirits served in a tall glass, usually with ice. The term is an American one; in fact, for a while America stood alone in insisting that ice be served in this type of drink.

The highball may be made of any spirituous liquor, though it is commonly made of one of the three whiskies—rye, scotch or bourbon. The customary proportions are one jigger of liquor placed in an eight ounce glass (see GLASSWARE) with one or two ice cubes, the glass then being filled with water, carbonated water, ginger ale or some other MIXER (which see). Sometimes a twist of lemon peel or a dash of bitters is added.

The highball is not unknown in other countries, though it will often be hidden under a local name. In England, for example, the preferred highball is known as "Scotch and Water," being just that; scotch diluted with room temperature water.

For a general discussion of drink preparation and a list of other drink types, see BARTENDING.

HIGH ALTITUDE COOKERY. Although Great-Aunt Hephzibah made the best baked beans to be had in Boston, when she moved to the Rocky Mountains she found that the same dish, made according to the same recipe, became not only unpalatable but the cause of acute indigestion as well. Other emigres from the lowlands had the same experiences with foods prepared by following tried formulas that previously had been more than satisfactory. Dried beans and other legumes were hard as nuts when cooked by the old time-tables—or were turned to mush by the time they became soft enough to eat; cakes seemed to be "hexed"—they fell unaccountably; even fresh vegetables and meats had to be boiled so long that they lost much of their flavor and many nourishing qualities.

There is no longer any great mystery concerning cooking at high altitudes. A great deal of information is to be had, based upon the experience of homemakers and the highly scientific experiments of the High Altitude Experiment Stations conducted by institutions such as Colorado A & M College, Fort Collins, Colorado, and the University of Wyoming, Laramie, Wyoming.

By acquainting herself with such information the homemaker, newly arrived from the lowlands, should soon be able to cook as well as in her old home. This article will forearm her with a basic understanding of the difficulties to be expected and methods of overcoming them.

Atmospheric Pressure in Relation to Altitude. Air has weight. The higher the homemaker goes the nearer she is to the top of the air mass, and the less air weight, or air pressure, there is surrounding her. The same amount of pressure surrounds the cake in the oven, the stew on the back of the range, and the coffee over the campfire.

At sea level the atmosphere exerts a weight of about fifteen pounds upon each square inch of matter that is exposed to it. As the altitude increases the pressure dwindles gradually until, at 13,000 feet (not uncommon in the Rocky Mountains), it amounts to only about seven and one-half pounds per square inch. However, the changes in pressure between sea level and altitudes of about 2,000 feet have very little effect on cookery; above that level they must be taken into account.

It is easy to see that most of our basic recipes, which were developed in the lowlands of Europe and America by trial and error methods, are suitable for use only at the altitudes in which they were worked out. When such recipes are not modified properly their use at high altitudes impairs the qualities of the foods that are cooked.

The foods that probably suffer most from changes in atmospheric pressure are those that require baking or boiling, and those containing a high percentage of sugar. They are treated briefly further on in this article. A few tested recipes are provided for cakes and icings.

Persons who are especially interested in this subject can obtain more detailed information by applying to the experimental stations that are maintained by state colleges in the mountainous areas of the West.

BAKING CAKE AT HIGH ALTITUDES

Effect of Air Pressure. Most breads, cakes, etc. depend upon leavening such as yeast or baking powder for the shapes and textures that are expected in properly baked foods. The leavening releases carbon dioxide gas. This gas forms bubbles within the mixture which inflate it and cause it to rise.

Because the weight of air grows less in proportion to the increase in elevation, less pressure is exerted upon doughs and batters at high altitudes than in the lowlands. Consequently, as the counteracting force of atmospheric pressure grows less the leavening is able to expand more. The gas bubbles become larger and more numerous, and the dough or batter walls between the bubbles become thinner and weaker. The result is that the walls of the bubbles collapse and the bread or cake falls. Leavening is not used in sponge cakes, but the air bubbles which cause it to rise are affected similarly.

Effect of Aridity. An overly dry, crumbly texture may be caused because moisture vaporizes at lower temperatures as air pressure is lessened. (*See* Boiling, in this article.) This effect becomes more acute in areas that are dry such as in the western plains and deserts.

Effect of Reduced Internal Temperature. Sogginess may result in cakes because, at high altitudes, the internal temperature of a baking cake is much lower than it is at sea level. At 10,000 feet the difference is at least 18° F. This causes a cake to be underbaked when it is made according to the directions of an uncorrected recipe. As will be seen in the recipes provided, oven temperatures are raised to overcome this trouble.

Correction of Adverse Factors. The remedy is to follow recipes that are especially designed for use in high altitudes. The proportions of the ingredients used in such recipes tend to strengthen the walls of the gas bubbles and to increase the specific gravity of the mixture. In this way the too sudden rise, and resultant fall, of the baked food is avoided.

Another remedy is for the homemaker to correct her old sea level recipes for use in the highlands. Since this alternative is, in itself, a complex subject, only basic information concerning it is given in this work.

PROPER USE OF SPECIAL RECIPES

Ingredients. Use fresh ingredients. Keep flour tightly covered to retain its natural moisture. If it is allowed to dry out it may cause baking failures. Baking powder loses strength with age. Keep it tightly covered.

Use cake flour unless instructed otherwise. Do not use prepared flour that already contains leavening unless it has been prepared especially for use at your altitude. If such flour is used, leave out the leavening required by the recipe. If ordinary cake flour is not available a substitute can be made by subtracting two tablespoonfuls of bread flour from the measured cup and replacing it with a like

quantity of cooking starch. Sift all flour before mixing.

Shortening may be butter or lard when the cake is relatively low in sugar and liquid. In richer cakes use hydrogenated shortenings, *which see.* This is done because natural shortenings, such as butter and lard, have a low water tolerance as compared with that of hydrogenated shortenings. Unless otherwise stated, hydrogenated shortenings have been used in working out the tested recipes that follow.

All ingredients should be at room temperature (65° to 72° F.) before mixing.

Measuring. Be especially careful when measuring the ingredients. Use standard measuring cups and spoons. When measuring dry ingredients heap the measure lightly and scrape it level with the edge of a knife or spatula. Dip sifted flour into the measure with a tablespoon. Do not shake or pack flour into the cup.

Each time a measurement is made there is the possibility of error. Therefore, when adjusting measurements to variations in altitude, follow directions carefully; they have been worked out to allow a minimum number of mistakes. For instance: the recipe for Lupine Sponge Cake calls for ¾ cup + 2 tbsp + 1 tsp of flour at 5,000 feet. This equals 14⅓ tablespoonfuls of flour. If the homemaker measures 14½ single tablespoonfuls she runs the risk of error fifteen times. If she follows directions she runs that risk only three times.

When subtracting ingredients (e.g. same recipe at 7,500 feet) be careful not to pack or heap the spoonfuls of dry ingredients that are dipped out. They should be dipped out carefully, without too much pressure, and scraped level with knife or spatula. The excess should be dropped back gently into the larger measure.

Mixing. Mixing may be done either by hand or by machine in preparing the recipes that follow. (Do not confuse beating with folding, *which see.*) Use a bowl that is large enough to hold the mixture easily. A bowl that is too large is better than one that is too small. Wooden spoons are best for mixing, and an egg beater is essential.

BAKING

The smaller internal bulk of sheet and layer cakes causes them to bake more evenly than loaf cakes. The tube pan used in baking sponge-type cakes helps to in crease the internal heat of the cakes and, therefore, to bake them more evenly than cakes of similar bulk which are baked in loaf tins.

Tube pans used for baking sponge-type cakes should not be greased.

Oiled waxed paper is convenient for lining the bottoms of pans used for baking cakes containing shortening.

Ovens should be at baking temperature when the cakes are put in.

Pans should be spaced in the oven so as to allow for adequate circulation of air.

Cake is done when its sides shrink from the sides of the pan, when it springs back after being pressed lightly with a finger, or when a cake tester or toothpick comes out clean.

BASIC CHANGES IN SEA-LEVEL RECIPES FOR CAKE

Following are the most important modifications that must be made when sea-level recipes for cake are adapted to use at high altitudes. Proportions vary with each increase in altitude.

(1) When the sugar and flour are to remain in the same proportions water must be added (add more milk or egg); leavening must be decreased (reduce baking powder or soda); and shortening either decreased or made more water tolerant (hydrogenated shortenings are more water tolerant than natural shortenings).

(2) When richer cakes are desired the proportions of shortening and flour remain unchanged. In this case, slightly less baking powder and soda must be used, sugar must be decreased, and water must be decreased (use less milk and egg).

Very rich cakes are made with butter and/or lard; but they are unable to tolerate much water. A mixture of hydrogenated shortening and natural shortening will make a rich cake and the batter will accept water. If the shortening cannot tolerate the amount of water used the batter will curdle.

ANGEL FOOD CAKE

1 cup less 1 tbsp cake flour
¼ tsp salt
Sugar (according to altitude)
1 tsp cream of tartar
1 cup egg whites
1 tsp vanilla

Beat egg whites until frothy. Add cream of tartar and salt. Continue beating until egg whites are glossy, fine grained, and will stand up in a stiff point as the beater is pulled off. With a wire whip, gradually fold in two-thirds of the sugar. Whip to a fluffy meringue. Sift flour and remaining sugar and gradually fold into meringue. Fold in vanilla. Pour batter into dry, ungreased 10-inch tube pan. With knife cut through batter to release large air bubbles and even up batter. Bake in a moderate oven about 35 minutes. Invert pan one hour and allow to cool.

Variations for Your Altitude

Altitude	Sugar	Oven Temperature
sea level	1¼ cups + 2¼ tbsp	350° F.
2,500 feet	1 cup + 3½ tbsp	350° F.
5,000 feet	1 cup + 1¾ tbsp	350° F.
7,500 feet	1 cup	350° F.
10,000 feet	¾ cup	360° F.

CHOCOLATE ANGEL FOOD CAKE

1 cup less 2 tbsp cake flour
⅓ tsp salt
1½ tsp cream of tartar
Sugar (according to altitude)
¼ cup cocoa
1½ cups egg whites
1¼ tsp vanilla

Beat egg whites until frothy. Add cream of tartar and salt. Continue beating until egg whites are glossy, fine grained, and will stand up in a stiff point as the beater is pulled off. With a wire whip, gradually fold in two-thirds of the sugar. Whip to a fluffy meringue. Sift flour, remaining sugar, and cocoa and fold into the meringue. Fold in vanilla. Pour into a dry, ungreased 10-inch tube pan. With knife, cut through batter to release large air bubbles and even up batter. Bake in a moderate oven about 35 minutes. Invert pan one hour and allow to cool.

Variations for Your Altitude

Altitude	Sugar	Oven Temperature
sea level	1¾ cups	350° F.
2,500 feet	1½ cups + 2 tbsp	350° F.
5,000 feet	1½ cups	350° F.
7,500 feet	1¼ cups + 2 tbsp	350° F.
10,000 feet	1¼ cups	360° F.

Burned-Sugar Cake

3/4 cup sugar
3/4 cup boiling water
3 cups cake flour
Soda (according to altitude)
1 tsp salt
Baking powder (according to altitude)
3/4 cup shortening
1 1/2 cups sugar
1 cup cold water
2 eggs, separated
1 tsp vanilla

Melt the 3/4 cup of sugar until it is very dark; add the boiling water. Dissolve well; remove from flame. Cream shortening and remaining 1 1/2 cups of sugar. Beat egg yolks and add to shortening mixture; beat well. Sift flour with soda, salt, and baking powder; add to shortening mixture alternately with cold water. Mix well. Save 3 tablespoons of burned-sugar sirup for icing; add rest of sirup to batter. Add vanilla to batter. Mix well. Fold into batter the stiffly beaten egg whites. Bake in moderate oven about 35 minutes. Makes three layers. Spread with Burned-sugar topping.

Variations for Your Altitude

Altitude	*Soda*	*Baking Powder*	*Oven Temperature*
sea level	1 1/8 tsp	3/4 tsp	350° F.
2,500 feet	1 tsp	3/4 tsp	350° F.
5,000 feet	3/4 tsp	1/2 tsp	350° F.
7,500 feet	1/2 tsp	1/4 tsp	350° F.
10,000 feet	1/4 tsp	1/8 tsp	360° F.

Colorado Birthday Cake

2 cups cake flour
Baking powder (according to altitude)
1 1/3 cups sugar
1 tsp salt
1/4 cup shortening
1/2 cup milk
6 egg whites
1 tsp vanilla

Cream shortening, gradually add one cup sugar. Cream well. Add sifted dry ingredients alternately with milk and vanilla; mix until smooth. Beat egg whites stiff, but not dry; gradually add 1/3 cup sugar. Fold into batter. Bake in moderate oven about 30 minutes.

Variations for Your Altitude

Altitude	*Baking Powder*	*Oven Temperature*
sea level	1 1/2 tsp.	350° F.
2,500 feet	1 1/4 tsp	350° F.
5,000 feet	1 tsp	350° F.
7,500 feet	1/4 tsp	350° F.
10,000 feet	1/8 tsp	360° F.

Gingerbread

Soda (according to altitude)
2 cups flour
1/3 cup sugar
3/4 tsp salt
1 1/4 tsp ginger
1/4 cup shortening
1 egg
2/3 cup molasses
1/2 cup milk

Cream shortening and sugar. Add egg and beat well. Combine molasses and milk Add alternately to shortening compound the sifted dry ingredients and molasse solution. Mix well. Bake in moderate oven about 45 minutes.

Variations for Your Altitude

Altitude	*Soda*	*Oven Temperature*
sea level	3/4 tsp	350° F
2,500 feet	3/4 tsp	350° F
5,000 feet	1/2 tsp	350° F
7,500 feet	1/4 tsp	350° F
10,000 feet	1/8 tsp	360° F

Mariposa Cake

2 cups cake flour
Baking powder (according to altitude)
3/4 cup plus 3 tbsp sugar
1 tsp salt
1/2 cup shortening
Milk (according to altitude)
1 tsp vanilla
2 eggs

Sift flour and baking powder together. Cream sugar, salt, and shortening until light. Beat in eggs alternately with flour and, finally, all except 1/4 cup of the milk. Beat until light. Then beat in remainder of the milk. Add vanilla. Mix well. Bake in moderate oven about 30 minutes.

Variations for Your Altitude

Altitude	Milk	Baking Powder	Oven Temperature
sea level	½ cup +1 tbsp	2 tsp	350° F.
2,500 feet	½ cup +1 tbsp	1¾ tsp	350° F.
5,000 feet	½ cup +1 tbsp	1⅓ tsp	350° F.
7,500 feet	½ cup +2 tbsp	¾ tsp	360° F.
10,000 feet	½ cup +3 tbsp	⅙ tsp	365° F.

MILK CHOCOLATE CAKE

Baking powder (according to altitude)
2 cups cake flour
1⅔ cups sugar
1 tsp salt
½ cup shortening
¾ cup milk
3 eggs
1 square melted chocolate
1 tsp vanilla

Cream shortening and sugar. Add eggs one at a time; beat until light and fluffy. Add sifted dry ingredients alternately with milk. Mix until smooth. Add melted chocolate and vanilla. Mix thoroughly. Bake in moderate oven about 30 minutes.

Variations for Your Altitude

Altitude	Baking Powder	Oven Temperature
sea level	1⅜ tsp	350° F.
2,500 feet	1⅛ tsp	350° F.
5,000 feet	⅞ tsp	350° F.
7,500 feet	½ tsp	350° F.
10,000 feet	¼ tsp	360° F.

RED DEVIL'S FOOD CAKE

Soda (according to altitude)
1¾ cups cake flour
1⅓ cups sugar
1 tsp salt
9 tbsp cocoa
⅓ cup plus 3½ tsp shortening
1 cup milk
¼ cup water
2 eggs
1 tsp vanilla

Sift flour, salt, sugar, soda and cocoa together. Add shortening, milk, and water. Cream until smooth (about 2 minutes). Add whole eggs and vanilla; continue beating until smooth (about 2 minutes). Bake in moderate oven about 30 minutes.

Variations for Your Altitude

Altitude	Soda	Oven Temperature
sea level	2⅝ tsp	350° F.
2,500 feet	2¼ tsp	350° F.
5,000 feet	1¾ tsp	350° F.
7,500 feet	½ tsp	350° F.
10,000 feet	¼ tsp	360° F.

MODIFIED SPONGE CAKE

1¼ cups plus 3 tbsp sugar
1 tsp salt
3 eggs
1 tbsp plus 2 tsp warm water
1¼ cups cake flour
Baking powder (according to altitude)
Milk (according to altitude)
1 tsp vanilla

Whip eggs, sugar, and salt until light. Add warm water. Add sifted cake flour and baking powder. Mix well. When batter begins to smooth out add milk and flavoring and mix well. Bake in moderate oven about 20 minutes.

Variations for Your Altitude

Altitude	Baking Powder	Milk	Oven Temperature
sea level	¾ tsp	2 tbsp	375° F.
2,500 feet	⅝ tsp	2 tbsp	375° F.
5,000 feet	½ tsp	2 tbsp	375° F.
7,500 feet	¼ tsp	2 tbsp	375° F.
10,000 feet	⅛ tsp	¼ cup	395° F.

SPICE CAKE

Baking powder (according to altitude)
2¼ cups cake flour
1 tsp salt
1 tsp cinnamon
¼ tsp cloves
½ tsp nutmeg
½ cup shortening
Milk (according to altitude)
Eggs (according to altitude)
¼ cup strained honey
½ cup light corn sirup
1 tsp vanilla

Beat eggs and honey together. Add corn sirup and beat a little. Add sifted flour, baking powder, and salt. Add shortening. Beat until smooth. Divide milk into three portions; soak spices in one portion. Stir batter while adding first two portions of milk. Add milk with soaked spices; beat until smooth. Add vanilla; stir thoroughly. Bake in moderate oven about 30 minutes.

Sift all dry ingredients except ¼ cup sugar. Blend ⅓ of mixture with lard. Add rest of sifted dry ingredients with ⅔ cup milk. Stir until smooth. Stir vanilla into remaining milk and add solution to batter

(SPICE CAKE) Variations for Your Altitude

Altitude	Baking Powder	Milk	Eggs	Oven Temperature
sea level	2 tsp	¾ cup	2	350° F.
2,500 feet	1¾ tsp	¾ cup	2	350° F.
5,000 feet	1⅓ tsp	¾ cup	2	350° F.
7,500 feet	¾ tsp	¾ cup + 1 tbsp	2	350° F.
10,000 feet	⅙ tsp	¾ cup	3	360° F.

SPONGE CAKE
(Whole Eggs)

⅔ cup sugar
¼ tsp salt
¼ tsp cream of tartar
4 eggs, separated
½ tsp vanilla
Water (according to altitude)
Cake flour (according to altitude)
Lemon juice and rind to taste

Add water, cream of tartar, salt, and vanilla to egg yolks and beat about twenty seconds. Add half of sugar and stir until mostly dissolved. Beat until mixture forms soft peaked meringue. Beat whites of eggs and other half of sugar to a meringue. Fold two meringues together. Fold in flour and lemon juice and rind (if latter are used). Bake in unlined, ungreased pan.

in two portions, stirring after each. Whip egg whites stiff and gradually add remaining ¼ cup of sugar. Fold egg whites into batter. Bake in moderate oven about 30 minutes.

Variations for Your Altitude

Altitude	Baking Powder	Oven Temperature
sea level	2¼ tsp	350° F.
2,500 feet	2 tsp	350° F.
5,000 feet	1½ tsp	350° F.
7,500 feet	½ tsp	350° F.
10,000 feet	¼ tsp	360° F.

YELLOW MESA CAKE

2 cups cake flour
Baking powder (according to altitude)
1¼ cups sugar
1 tsp salt

(SPONGE CAKE) Variations for Your Altitude

Altitude	Cake Flour	Water	Oven Temp.	Time (Minutes)
sea level to 4,500 feet	¾ cup + 1 tbsp + 2 tsp	1 tbsp + 1 tsp	330° F.	50 to 55
5,000 feet	¾ cup + 2 tbsp + 1 tsp	2 tbsp	340° F.	55 to 60
7,500 feet	1 cup − 1 tbsp − 2 tsp	2 tbsp	340° F.	55 to 60
10,000 feet	1 cup + 1 tbsp	2 tbsp + 1 tsp	350° F.	63 to 65

WHITE CAKE
(Lard)

2 cups cake flour
Baking powder (according to altitude)
1¼ cups sugar
1 tsp salt
⅓ cup lard
1 cup milk
3 egg whites
1 tsp vanilla

½ cup plus 2 tbsp shortening
¾ cup plus 1 tbsp milk
3 eggs
1 tsp vanilla

Cream shortening, gradually adding sugar. Add whole eggs. Cream well. Sift flour, baking powder, and salt. Add alternately to shortening mixture the sifted dry ingredients and milk. Add vanilla. Mix until smooth. Bake in moderate oven about 30 minutes.

Variations for Your Altitude

Altitude	Baking Powder	Oven Temperature
sea level	1½ tsp	350° F.
2,500 feet	1¼ tsp	350° F.
5,000 feet	1 tsp	350° F.
7,500 feet	⅛ tsp	350° F.
10,000 feet	⅙ tsp	360° F.

SPONGE CAKE
(Yolks Only)

8 egg yolks
Water (according to altitude)
⅔ cup sugar
¼ tsp salt
¼ tsp cream of tartar
½ tsp vanilla
Cake flour (according to altitude)

Mix egg yolks with water. Add sugar, salt, cream of tartar, and vanilla. Beat until mixture forms soft peaks when beater is removed. Fold flour into meringue. If desired, lemon juice and grated rind may be added using the juice to replace part of the water. Bake in unlined, ungreased pan; determine length of baking time according to your altitude.

SUGAR COOKERY AT HIGH ALTITUDES

When candies, frostings, and icings are cooked, the different stages of hardness are achieved at lower temperatures in the mountains than in the lowlands. These changes in temperature are fairly stable and can be calculated by allowing a decrease of 2° F. for each increase of 1,000 feet in altitude. For instance: A fudge icing is of the proper consistency when cooked to

(SPONGE CAKE) Variations for Your Altitude

Altitude	Cake Flour	Water	Oven Temp.	Time (Minutes)
sea level	1 cup + 2 tbsp	¼ cup + 2 tsp	330° F.	60 to 65
2,500 feet	1 cup + 2 tbsp	¼ cup + 1 tsp	330° F.	60 to 65
5,000 feet	1 cup + 2 tbsp	¼ cup + 1 tbsp + 2 tsp	340° F.	65 to 70
7,500 feet	1¼ cups + 2 tsp	¼ cup + 2 tbsp	340° F.	65 to 70
10,000 feet	1½ cups + 2 tsp	¼ cup + 2 tbsp + 2 tsp	350° F.	73 to 75

VARIATIONS IN TEMPERATURE FOR SUGAR COOKERY AT HIGH ALTITUDES

Finish Point for Candies (Water Test)	Type of Candy	FINISH TEMPERATURES (FAHRENHEIT)				
		Sea Level	2,500 Feet	5,000 Feet	7,500 Feet	10,000 Feet
		Degrees	Degrees	Degrees	Degrees	Degrees
Thread	Sirup	228–234	223–229	218–224	213–219	208–214
Very soft ball	Cocoa-fudge, sirup for boiled icing with egg white	234–235	229–230	224–225	219–220	214–215
Medium soft ball	Fudge, panocha	236–237	231–232	226–227	221–222	216–217
Soft ball	Sea foam, fondant	238–240	233–235	228–230	223–225	218–220
Medium firm ball	Divinity	240–242	235–237	230–232	225–227	220–222
Firm ball	Caramels	244–250	239–245	234–240	229–235	224–230
Hard ball	Toffee	250–255	245–250	240–245	235–240	230–235
Very hard ball	Taffy	256–265	251–260	246–255	241–250	236–245
Medium crack	Pulled mints	266–280	261–275	256–270	251–265	246–260
Hard crack	Butterscotch, lollipops	282–312	277–307	272–302	267–297	262–292
Caramel (very hard and brittle; loses sweetness at higher temperatures)	Coloring and flavoring	315–345	310–340	305–335	300–330	295–325

a temperature of 234 to 235° F. at sea level. The same formula, however, will need a "finish temperature" of only 220 to 222° for a similar consistency at 7,200 feet.

A candy thermometer is invaluable for preparing properly the various sugar foods that add so much to the dining table and to the snack dish. However, the old-fashioned cold water test is used exclusively by many successful cooks. Together, the cold water test and the candy thermometer form an unbeatable combination for the successful cooking of sugars in high altitudes.

The higher temperatures given in the table below should be used when it is raining or when it is very humid.

BURNED-SUGAR ICING
(Cooked)

3 tbsp sugar sirup
2 cups sugar
½ cup butter
½ cup sweet milk

See the recipe above for burned-sugar cake for the sirup. Boil all ingredients together until mixture reaches soft-ball stage. Cool and beat until mixture is of a consistency to spread. Put icing on cool cake.

BUTTER FROSTING
(Uncooked)

¼ cup butter
2 cups confectioners' sugar
2 egg yolks (may be omitted)
1 tsp vanilla
2 tbsp cream

Thoroughly cream butter and sugar. Stir in unbeaten egg yolks and vanilla. Add cream as frosting becomes thick.

Variations of Butter Frosting

Chocolate. Add 1½ squares unsweetened chocolate, melted, after first ¼ cup sugar has been added; stir until well blended.

Coffee-Cocoa or Mocha. Sift 3 tbsp cocoa with sugar; substitute strong coffee for the cream.

Orange. Substitute orange juice for cream, and grated rind of one orange for vanilla.

SEVEN-MINUTE ICING
(Cooked)

1 egg white
¾ cup sugar
⅛ tsp cream of tartar
3 tbsp water
½ tsp vanilla

Combine all ingredients, except vanilla, in top of double boiler; beat to completely blend. Place over boiling water and beat with rotary beater until mixture is fluffy and will hold its shape. This takes from 5 to 7 minutes, depending upon altitude. Remove from heat and blend in flavoring. (Enough for a two-layer cake)

COOKING VEGETABLES AT HIGH ALTITUDES

The studies that have been published concerning the cooking of vegetables at different elevations do not deal with a sufficient number of test points to provide timetables for various high altitudes. However, a perusal of this sub-article will give the homemaker basic information that will enable her to approach intelligently the problems she will encounter.

Baking. Variance in elevation seems to make little difference in the baking of vegetables. Oven temperatures and the length of time needed for successfully baked vegetables differ so little between low and high altitudes as to be negligible. The newcomer to mountain country should find satisfactory the recipes that are given elsewhere in this book, under the names of the vegetables concerned.

Boiling. As will be seen, boiling is probably the least satisfactory method of cooking vegetables at high altitudes. Baking, steaming, and pressure-cooking produce better results and should be used whenever possible.

Effect of Air Pressure on Boiling Point. When the temperature of water rises it expands proportionately and the surface of the water exerts a counter pressure against the air that rests upon it. When this pressure equals that of the atmosphere the water vaporizes or boils. Therefore, water will boil at a lower temperature in the mountains, where it is held down by a lesser weight of air, than it will in a valley where the atmosphere is heavier. Roughly, the drop in temperature amounts to 1° F. for each increase of 500 feet in elevation. The following table gives specific boiling points of water at key altitudes.

TEMPERATURE OF BOILING WATER AT
KEY ALTITUDES

Altitude	Degrees Fahrenheit
0 (Sea level)	212.0
2,500 feet	207.3
5,000 feet	202.8
7,500 feet	198.3
10,000 feet	194.0

Effect of Lowered Boiling Point. The immediate effect of the lowered boiling point upon foods is that they must be boiled longer in high altitudes than in the lowlands. When the homemaker is cooking soups and certain sauces, that require long simmering in covered kettles to bring out the full flavor, this need for longer cooking presents no great problem; but fresh vegetables that are to be served as such suffer the loss of vitamins and minerals.

The time element for boiling vegetables at high altitudes varies, not only with the elevation, but also with changes in the weather. Furthermore, the vegetables themselves react differently when boiled at varying altitudes. Tests conducted by the University of Wyoming, at 7,200 feet above sea level, show that while old carrots require as little as eleven percent of extra cooking time, cauliflower requires 58 percent, and new beets need up to 66 percent, as compared with the time required to cook these vegetables at an altitude of 600 feet. But the additional percentage of time required is not a constant factor at various altitudes.

Therefore, the homemaker must learn by the experience of her neighbors and by her own experiments, and devise time-tables to fit the conditions that exist in her own kitchen, Until she obtains this information, the homemaker may well rely upon the standard tests for determining when vegetables are cooked. These tests are given in this book under the names of the individual vegetables; they apply just as well in high altitudes as in the lowlands.

Tips on Boiling Vegetables at High Altitudes. Use garden-fresh vegetables whenever possible. Otherwise, use vegetables that have been stored in a cool place where the air is not too dry. This preserves natural moisture, flavor, and vitamins.

To preserve vitamins and minerals in your vegetables, avoid soaking them in water, and do not pare or cut away any more than is necessary. Water extracts these valuable elements, and others are removed by oxidation when large areas of cut surface are exposed to air.

Keep the boiling time to a minimum. The water must be at a rolling boil when the vegetables are put into it; it must be brought back to a boil as quickly as possible and kept boiling throughout the cooking period. In this way the vegetables retain as much food value as possible; vitamins will not be destroyed entirely by exposure to too much heat, and the vegetable will still retain a goodly portion of its normal mineral matter.

Serve the cooked vegetables as soon as possible. Natural color and vitamins are lost by overly long exposure to air.

PRESSURE COOKING

In cooking by steam pressure, the temperature within the cooker must be considered as well as the pressure. As previously explained, the pressure exerted on any boiling liquid controls the temperature of that liquid. However, in a cooker the identical pressure will produce a lower temperature at high altitudes than it will at sea level.

Since the cooking tables supplied with most commercial units are based upon the conditions existing at or near sea level, some adjustment must be made at high altitudes. It will be necessary to increase the pressure of the cooker beyond that normally used to achieve the correct result.

Though experience is the best teacher, the table below may be used as a guide in determining cooking pressures at approximate altitudes.

To use the table first see what temperature is produced at sea level using the pressure recommended for the food to be cooked. Next, consult the column under the altitude closest to that in which the cooker will be operated and locate the nearest equivalent temperature. By reading to the left, the proper pressure for the altitude will be found.

For example: a food that is to be cooked under a pressure of ten pounds will be subjected to a temperature of 240° F. at sea level. At an altitude of 6,000 feet this food must be cooked at a pressure of thirteen pounds to achieve approximately the same temperature.

The cooking period originally recommended may be used with the new temperature.

Should the bottom figure in the column under the correct altitude heading be lower than the required temperature, this indicates that a pressure greater than fifteen pounds is required to achieve the said temperature Inasmuch as few household cookers are designed to function at pressures greater than fifteen pounds, the user should experiment with extending the cooking time, unless the manufacturer has given specific instructions to cover the situation.

It is very important that the cooker not be operated at pressures beyond its stated capacity. Neglect of this warning may result in serious damage to the utensil or severe injury to the user. If a pressure cooker is handled right it is a useful tool, but it can be dangerous.

If it is established that pressures above fifteen pounds can be used safely, and there is need for higher temperatures than those shown in the table, they may be obtained by increasing the pressure by one-half pound for each additional degree Fahrenheit that is needed.

In order to maintain an even cooking pressure the air must be driven out of the cooker before the petcock is closed and cooking begins. The length of time needed to exhaust the cooker depends upon the size of the vessel as well as upon the altitude. At 7,200 feet this operation takes from ten to twelve minutes.

HIGH FREQUENCY COOKING.

While using a radio tube to cook food may seem to be carrying this modern age to extremes, that is essentially what happens when cooking is done by means of ultra high frequencies, one of the more recent offerings by science to a startled world. The basic idea is hardly new, for the principles of induction heating have been known and used for many years, but it was not until the Second World War that science had developed the equipment needed to apply those principles to food.

THEORY AND DEVELOPMENT

Waves of electrical force can be made to pass through almost any substance. Molecules are affected by these waves, and if the waves are strong enough and fluctuate fast enough, they can cause these molecules to vibrate. This molecular vibration, in turn, generates heat within the substance of which these molecules are a part.

That is the basis of induction heating which has had many industrial applications. At first, science had no satisfactory way of making waves that vibrated fast enough to cause food to heat, though they could even melt metal with the equipment on hand. This was due to a difference in the molecular make-up of food as opposed to more solid substances. An attempt was made to apply this principle to the field of cooking by heating the metal of the pans rather than the food, but this system did not offer enough advantages to outweigh the high cost of the equipment involved. As a result, this early induction cooking

APPROXIMATE TEMPERATURES WITHIN
PRESSURE COOKER AT DIFFERENT
ALTITUDES

Pressure Gauge Reading	Sea Level	3,000 Feet	4,000 Feet	5,000 Feet	6,000 Feet	7,200 Feet	8,008 Feet
	Degrees	Degrees	Degrees	Degrees	Degrees	Degrees	Degrees
5 lbs.	228	223	221	220	219	217	216
6 lbs.	230	226	224	223	221	220	219
7 lbs.	232	228	227	225	224	223	222
8 lbs.	235	231	229	228	227	225	225
9 lbs.	237	233	232	231	230	228	228
10 lbs.	240	236	235	234	232	231	230
11 lbs.	242	238	237	236	235	233	233
12 lbs.	244	240	239	238	237	236	235
13 lbs.	246	243	241	240	239	238	237
14 lbs.	248	245	244	243	242	240	240
15 lbs.	250	247	246	245	244	243	242

was confined to rather spectacular labora- tory demonstrations, such as frying eggs in a skillet resting on a cake of ice.

During World War II, the ultra high frequencies (UHF) came into their own with the development of the Magnetron, the tube that made advanced forms of radar possible. It was found that the Mag- netron-produced frequencies could heat food to cooking temperatures, as well as locate distant aircraft.

The problems then confronting science were three-fold: to apply this principle to cooking in a foolproof, practical mechan- ism; to produce the mechanism and the tube at a reasonable cost; and to develop cooking techniques suitable to this new principle.

Advantages and Disadvantages

As can readily be seen, electronic cook- ers differs radically from conventional methods. In all other methods of cooking, the heat is applied from the outside, and gradually works its way into the body of the food. As a result, the outside is always cooked more than the inside (unless the food be in such small pieces as to make this inconsequential), and it takes time for the food to be cooked thoroughly. Too great a heat cannot be applied, lest the surface be charred while the center is raw, and sufficient time must be allowed for the heat to reach and cook the interior portions.

When high frequencies are used, how- ever, the waves actually penetrate the food, generating heat almost 'simultaneously throughout the entire substance. The inter- ior is cooked almost as rapidly as the ex- terior.

Under this latter system, foods may be cooked at unbelievable speeds. For ex- ample, one early commercial unit grilled frankfurters in eight seconds, and cooked hamburgers in 35 seconds, while another unit cooked steaks in less than one minute, and half chickens in only two minutes. An experimental model could bring a pre- cooked, frozen dinner from its icy status to a temperature too hot to eat in ap- proximately 70 seconds.

Cooking at jet-propelled speeds with electrons involves some necessary changes in normal cooking procedure. The food must be physically prepared to best receive the waves. Seasoning procedures will be different, for the seasoning gets little chance to slowly permeate the body of the food. Perhaps the most noticeable difference is the lack of crisp crust or dark brown on the food surface, for the surface has little op- portunity to be browned under this system.

There are other problems peculiar to this method of cooking. Unbroken egg yolks have a tendency to explode because of the sudden formation of steam within the sac, and, in some cases, bones char before the surrounding meat is cooked.

Some of these difficulties can and are be- ing overcome by machine design as more is learned of the specific action of high fre- quencies on specific foods. An auxiliary unit of conventional design may be used to *toast* the food, putting a crust on pastries and searing steaks. It is obvious that mod- ifications of seasoning and preparation techniques must be developed.

Whether these differences will be ad- vantages or disadvantages is a question that can be settled only as specific units are brought on the market, and then only when these units are considered in light of their intended use. If a unit is to com- pete with the present kitchen Range (*which see*), it must be judged in view of versatility, convenience, and cost. Among the perti- nent factors will be the number and type of cooking operations it can do or duplicate, the range of foods that can be cooked there- in, and the maximum size of food which it will accept (though the speed of operation may well outbalance this). Time alone will tell whether high frequency cooking can be adapted to general use, or if it will be re- stricted to specialized tasks.

Whether the unit will be specialized or general, cost will be a factor. Magnetron tubes are expensive and do not last long. Just how economically these tubes can be made in mass production and how long their working life can be extended with de- velopment remains to be seen.

Because of the extremely brief cooking periods, the tube is not in constant opera- tion. It is said that a unit in a large restau- rant will only be on for a total of one hour in a normal working day.

The amount of energy used by the unit will be dependent on the unit size, but it is said that the units are 50% effective in converting the electrical energy into heat energy. This is a very high ratio, as cook- ing devices go, regardless of fuel.

The Magnetron offers more advantages in cookery than mere speed. It provides clean, smokeless cooking. The unit itself is water-cooled, and the only oven heat is in the food itself, and should have little effect on kitchen temperatures. It would seem that high frequency cooking has much to offer in the way of convenience and should eventually find a place in modern life.

APPLICATION

It will be some time before the average housewife will be cooking with radar, but commercial applications have already been made, while others are in the laboratories.

The present trend is to construct the units in the form of an oven, an electronic oven, as it were. This is necessary to guide and confine the waves, similar to those used in radar, which cause the food to heat. The tubes are water-cooled and require a brief warm-up before they are ready to operate. The food is inserted, the door closed, and the waves get to work. A timing device is essential because of the extremely brief cooking periods and the device either may be pre-set by the manufacturer or adjustable for varying foods.

The most common present use of these ovens is in restaurants, hotels, snack bars, and similar establishments serving great numbers of people. They offer a distinct advantage for this sort of operation, for not only are regular foods cooked in a matter of seconds, but frozen foods may be cooked in nearly the same periods without first going through a lengthy thawing process. This means that the establishment may keep all food supplies in a deep freeze, cooking them only on order, and in much less time than required by conventional methods.

Galley space is at a minimum in airliners, but hot, well cooked meals are an important passenger service. Some planes are equipped with these units, warming frozen, precooked meals while in flight.

This use of the high frequency oven with frozen foods (see also FREEZING FOODS), another development of science, holds much promise for the future. Not only can frozen raw foods be cooked in brief seconds without first being thawed, but precooked frozen foods can also be reconstituted to oven freshness by a brief exposure.

The visionary may, with some logic, predict a future where all food will go to processing centers instead of the market.

There some of it will be canned, frozen, and dehydrated for those who cling to the archaic methods, while the bulk of it will be prepared into tasty meals by master chefs. Once cooked, these meals will be frozen and stored for distribution. The housewife will then be able to purchase individual meals on disposable plates, popping them into an electronic oven as the family sits down at the table, and serving delicious, steaming dinners before they have hardly spread their napkins, with little more effort on her part than going to the store and deciding on the menu. But whether or not such a system of food handling is ever developed, whether or not the magnetron will ever replace the kitchen range, it is evident that science will give a new look to the present rituals of the kitchen.

HIGH TEA. A light meal, in the late afternoon, at which meats and relishes are served; tea is the beverage. It is also called Meat Tea. *See also* AFTERNOON TEA.

HILDESHEIMER SAUSAGE. *See* SAUSAGE.

HIND. The female of the red deer or stag. Also one of the various fish of the Grouper family.

HIND SHANK. The upper part of the hind leg of beef, lamb, or veal.

HIPPOCRAS. A scented and spiced wine preparation that took its name from the wool bag, or Hippocrates sleeve, through which it was filtered in its making. The Hippocras was extremely popular in medieval times when, it is believed, it was invented as a means of rendering palatable sour wine, of which there were great quantities in those days of inadequate storage and bottling methods. The sour wine was sweetened with honey, dosed with herbs and spices, and strained through a woolen bag.

RED HIPPOCRAS

2 oz cinnamon
2 drams coriander seeds
2 blades of mace
1 grated nutmeg
2 oz bruised ginger
6 musk mallow seeds
1 lemon, juice only
8 oz brandy
2 qt simple sirup or honey
2 bottles Claret
1 qt boiling water

The spices are ground together into a fine powder, the lemon juice and brandy added, and the mixture strained clear. Then the honey or sirup, claret, and boiling water are stirred in in the given order and the drink served while hot.

WHITE HIPPOCRAS

2 qt white wine
1 lb sugar
1 oz cinnamon
2 corns whole black pepper
1 blade of mace
1 lemon

The lemon is cut into quarters and the whole mixed and let stand for several hours. Following this, the mixture is strained 3 or 4 times through a cloth bag. If the mixture will not pass through the bag, a small quantity of milk may be added.

HOCK. A name generally given to all Rhine wine (*which see*). Though not proven, it is commonly accepted that the RHINE WINE (*which see*). Though not proven, it is commonly accepted that the name is a contraction of *Hochheim*, a village located on the right bank of the Main River, close to its junction with the Rhine, where many famous vineyards are situated.

HOE CAKE. An old-fashioned corn bread or cake, originally baked on the heated blade of a hoe.

HOHENHEIM CHEESE. A soft, round, German cheese, about four to six inches in diameter.

HOLLANDAISE SAUCE. This is a golden, rich sauce, largely composed of butter and egg yolks.

HOLLANDAISE SAUCE

½ cup butter
2 egg yolks
1 tbsp lemon juice
2 tbsp hot water
Salt and white pepper

Divide the butter into 2 portions, place of these in a bowl or the upper part of a double boiler. Add the egg yolks and lemon juice, place over hot water (not boiling) and stir constantly until the butter is melted. Add the remaining butter and continue stirring, preferably with a wire whisk, until this butter also is melted. Add

the hot water and cook, still stirring constantly, until thick. Remove from the heat and season with salt and white pepper.

One common reason for the failure of hollandaise is that it is made at too high temperature. Good hollandaise is not so much a matter of tricks as of good ingredients. Yolks of the very best grade of fresh eggs, and sweet butter, make the most difference. Some homemakers, and even some chefs, stretch hollandaise with cornstarch or flour, but that is not true hollandaise.

HOLLANDAISE SAUCE VARIATIONS

Figaro Sauce. To each 1½ cups of hollandaise, add 3 rounded tablespoons of tomato purée (canned or cooked), 1 tablespoon of finely chopped parsley, and a few grains of cayenne pepper. Salt to taste. Suitable for large pieces of fish.

Mousseline Sauce. To 1 cup of hollandaise, add 3 tablespoons of whipped cream. Suitable for small, tender fish such as trout, fillets of white fish, etc., and cooked asparagus.

Mustard Sauce. To 1 cup of hollandaise, add 1½ teaspoons of prepared mustard. This may also be made with a bechamel (white or cream) sauce base.

HOLLOW WARE. Also known as *dinnerware*; that class of table utensils that are hollow in form (plates, bowls, pitchers, candlesticks, etc.) as distinguished from the solid pieces of FLATWARE (*which see*). The term is most commonly applied to metallic objects; silver and silver plate, gold, brass, and pewter being among the metals used to make such utensils.

Hollow ware is also made from other materials, notably CERAMICS and PLASTICS (*which see*). The items of hollow ware embrace those discussed under DISHES (*which see*) plus tea or coffee sets, trays, steam dishes, food warmers, and other items whose design and function will vary with the manufacturer.

The field is too broad and entirely too dependent on individual circumstances for there to be any hard and fast rules as to what constitutes the essential hollow ware. Adequate service dishes must be provided for the foods prepared and the table should be attractive to the eye, but the homemaker has a wide option as to the size, style, and number of hollow ware items needed.

Not only is there a wide option in the type of items to be purchased, but there is an equally wide selection of available materials. Whether the items selected be of metal, glass, ceramics or plastics is a matter of individual taste. The purchase and care of these materials is discussed under the appropriate headings elsewhere. It should be remembered that regardless of the material selected, it must harmonize (though not necessarily match) with the other components of table furnishings (see TABLE SETTING AND SERVICE).

Hollow ware is by no means restricted to its stated use of food service, but is capable of filling many other ornamental and functional posts about the house. Pitchers, jugs, bowls and such can be used as flower vases, fruit holders, or alone as decorative pieces. Plates and small dishes can be used to hold sweets and nuts; water pitchers and coffee and tea sets can be used for beverage service of all types. These dual-function potentialities of hollow ware should not be overlooked, for not only is good hollow ware beautiful in itself, but it often represents a relatively large investment for the family and it is only sensible to get as much use as possible from the items.

See also SILVERWARE.

HOLLOW STEM CHAMPAGNE GLASS. See GLASSWARE, see also CHAMPAGNE.

HOLSTEIN HEALTH CHEESE. A German cooked cheese made from sour skim milk. Local name is *Holsteiner Gesundheitskäse.*

HOLSTEIN SKIM MILK CHEESE. A skim milk cheese, weighing 12 to 14 pounds.

HOLY-CROSS FISH. See CATFISH.

HOMINY. A cereal made of corn. There are various types of hominy on the market, differing mainly in fineness to which they have been ground. To prepare hominy by modern methods the dried corn is soaked enough to soften it somewhat. It is then passed through a machine called a degerminator which breaks the grain into coarse pieces and loosens the bran and germ. These are sifted out. The residue is dried and sold as hominy. When left in fairly large pieces, it is known as samp or pearl hominy. When ground to a coarse meal, it is called hominy grits. Hominy may be used like rice, as a cereal, or as a substitute for potatoes.

Old-fashioned lye hominy, or hulled corn, is a somewhat different preparation made by soaking the whole grain in water that contains lye, or in olden times, a bag of wood ashes, until the hulls are loosened. Then the hulled grains are washed in clear water and boiled. Lye hominy has a distinctive flavor, and may be used like other coarse hominy.

BOILED HOMINY GRITS

1 cup hominy grits
5 cups water
2 tsp salt

Add the grits slowly to the boiling salted water in the top of a double boiler. Boil 10 minutes directly over the flame and then place over the lower portion of the boiler. Continue cooking for 2 hours.

The boiled grits may be poured into a dish or molds and cooled and served with fruit or preserves for a simple dessert. It may also be sliced and fried like corn meal mush (*which see*).

BOILED SAMP

This coarse hominy requires long cooking. Soak 1 cup samp in 2 cups of water overnight. Add 6 cups boiling water and 3 teaspoons salt to the soaked hominy, and cook in the top of a double boiler for 5 or 6 hours. Samp may be advantageously cooked in a deep-well cooker. Use as a cereal or as a vegetable, served with salt and pepper and melted butter or gravy.

HOMINY AND CHEESE TIMBALES

2 cups drained canned hominy
⅔ cup grated cheese
2 eggs, beaten
¾ tsp salt
A dash of cayenne, pepper, or curry powder
2 tsp each of chopped green pepper and pimiento
2 tbsp chopped parsley
1 cup scalded milk

Combine all ingredients thoroughly Turn into individual greased baking dishes set these in a pan of hot water and bake i a moderate oven (350° F.) 30 minutes

Turn out and serve with tomato sauce, cheese sauce or Spanish sauce. (Serves 4 to 6)

Hominy Date Pudding

1 cup hominy grits
5 cups milk
1 tsp salt
⅛ cup sugar
1 cup chopped pitted dates
1 tsp vanilla

Add the salt and hominy grits to the milk and cook in a double boiler for one hour. Add the sugar, dates, and vanilla and mix well. Serve lukewarm with milk or cream. (Serves 6)

Hominy Fruit Scallop

1½ cups cooked hominy grits
1 cup stewed dried apricots
½ cup apricot juice
1 tbsp sugar
½ tbsp butter
1 tbsp sugar and cinnamon mixed

Grease a baking dish well. Mix the hominy grits with the apricot juice. Make layers of grits and stewed apricots until the dish is nearly full. Dot with the butter and sprinkle the sugar-cinnamon mixture over the top. Bake in a moderate oven (350° F.) until nicely browned. Serve hot or cold with cream, or a fruit sauce.

Peaches, pears, or almost any other fruit may be used and fresh or dried fruit, or preserves will work.

Hominy Muffins

1 cup cold boiled hominy grits
1 cup milk
1 egg
1¼ cups white flour
2 tsp baking powder
½ tsp salt
1 tbsp melted shortening

Beat the egg and milk into the hominy grits. Add the melted shortening, and the mixed and sifted dry ingredients. Mix well. Bake in greased muffin pans in a hot oven 400°–425° F.) for 30 minutes. (Makes 12 medium-sized muffins)

Scalloped Hominy

Arrange in a buttered casserole alternate layers of leftover cooked hominy and buttered crumbs. Pour over enough hot milk to barely cover. (If desired the milk may be seasoned by cooking with it while heating a bay leaf tied with a few sprigs of parsley and celery top, and one or two slices of onion.) Further flavor may be given by adding to the hominy itself a generous amount of grated cheese or a teaspoon of mustard or grated horseradish. Bake in a moderate oven (350° F.) about 30 minutes. Serve plain or with an accompanying sauce.

HOMOGENIZED MILK. A smooth easily digested Milk, *which see.*

HONEY. A long and interesting story could be told about honey, one of the oldest sweets known to mankind. Centuries ago it was held in high esteem by peoples of all races. The Old Testament describes the ideal land as one "flowing with milk and honey." Romans and Greeks referred to honey as food fit for the gods, and the Norsemen also wrote about its wonders. In early times, wild honey was commonly used. The bees stored this food in hollow trees and rock crevices. As the supply was limited, through necessity man soon learned to produce honey in greater quantities.

In the middle 19th century L. L. Langstroth, of Philadelphia, invented a movable frame hive, a device that stimulated the production of honey throughout the United States. Ten or more frames fit closely into the hive, and therein the busy army of bees deposit their honey. It is estimated that today there are five billion colonies of bees in this country.

Honey is defined by food chemists as the nectar and saccharine exudations of plants, gathered, modified, and stored in the comb by honey-bees. The flavor of honey depends upon the flowers from which the bees gather the nectar. Since there are so many different varieties of flowers, there are varied flavors of honey.

Some of the different varieties of flavor in honey are: Cotton blossom honey, from the fields of Alabama; clover honey, lima bean blossom honey, star thistle, orange blossom, and mountain lilac honeys, from California; mangrove and palm honeys from Florida; galberry honey from Georgia; clethra honey, from Massachusetts; buckwheat, locust, and raspberry honey from New York; horsemint and mesquite honey, from Texas; wild flower honey, from Cuba; linden and pie honey, from Czechoslovakia; clover and heather honey, from England; many flowers honey and lavender honey, from France; rose honey, from Greece; coffee plantation honey, from Guatemala; acacia honey from Hungary; black locust honey, from Italy; flower honey, from Palestine; and eucalyptus and white gum honey, from Australia; etc.

BENEFICIAL HINTS ABOUT HONEY

Pliny observed that honey mixed with fish oil constituted a splendid healing lotion for wounds. Such treatment had long been obsolete, but recently it was tested; and it was found that a mixture of honey and cod-liver oil was indeed an effective healing agency for minor wounds, burns, and skin eruptions.

According to pharmacopoeia, honey is a mixture of various alcohols, ethereal oils, formic, lactic, and vegetable acids, and very likely of hormones furnished by the bee itself. It has been reported that honey, even in weak solution, destroys a large number of bacilli. This healing substance has been successfully isolated and will doubtless prove a valuable ally to man in his battle with these foes.

Honey is assimilated completely and easily; even diabetics may partake of it without harm to themselves. The more we become acquainted with all the benefits this most interesting product confers upon man the more we are convinced that its praises cannot be sung too highly.

Honey may be substituted for any other form of sugar in the diet. Nutritionists regard honey as a wholesome food. Though it contains over 80 per cent carbohydrates, it is in a form that is readily digested and assimilated by the body. It is an excellent source of quick energy and fuel.

Honey is sold either as comb honey or extracted honey. Both are delicious and may be used interchangeably in the diet. Comb honey is difficult to ship and therefore not as easily obtained as the extracted variety. The latter may be shipped long distances and stored for long periods of time without deterioration.

The fact that honey takes up moisture rapidly may or may not be an advantage. Fruit cakes, steamed puddings, cookies,

and candies, stay moist longer if made with honey. But some confections and frostings, if made with honey, will remain soft and take up more moisture if the air is humid. This may make them too soft and sticky to be appetizing. Extracted honey contains water which will affect the amount of liquid used in a recipe when honey is substituted for sugar. The liquid must be reduced, however, more than the difference between the water content of the honey and dry sugar, according to the consistency of the honey and also according to the proportion of honey used. For example, if medium-thick honey is substituted for one-half the sugar in cake or quick-bread recipes, reduce the liquid by one-fourth. If honey is substituted for all the sugar, reduce the liquid one-half. If honey is very thin or very thick, this proportion may have to be adjusted. In making honey cakes and quick-breads, combine the honey with the liquid called for in the recipe, and bake at the lowest temperature possible. This prevents loss or change of flavor of the honey and also avoids too rapid browning.

Honey has much the same consistency as molasses and may be used in place of it, measure for measure, in gingerbread, brown bread, and steamed puddings. Because it contains less acid than molasses, baking soda is not needed. Add one teaspoon of baking powder for each one-quarter teaspoon of soda omitted.

Honey should be stored in a dry place. Low temperatures may cause the honey to become partly cloudy or partially crystallized. Most honey crystallizes on aging. Crystallized honey can easily be liquefied by warming the container in moderately hot water (not above 140° F.). Higher temperatures injure both the flavor and color of honey.

HONEY BALL MARLOW

18 marshmallows
1⅓ cups honey ball melon pulp
2 drops oil of cinnamon
2 tbsp lemon juice
4 tsp powdered sugar
3 stiffly beaten egg whites

Put the marshmallows and ⅓ cup of hot water in the top of a double boiler, and heat until they have melted. Rub the melon pulp through a fine sieve, and ad to the melted marshmallows. Add the oil of cinnamon and the lemon juice. Chill the mixture thoroughly. Beat the powdered sugar into the egg whites, and fold this mixture into the marshmallow mixture. Place in freezing tray of automatic refrigerator. Stir twice during the freezing. (Serves 4)

Honey Coconut Topping I

To ½ cup honey add 1 teaspoonful lemon juice and a light sprinkling of cinnamon, then ½ cup shredded coconut. Spread on warm cake and toast brown.

Honey Coconut Topping II

Mix thoroughly ½ cup honey and 1 cup coconut and spread on slightly warm cake. Broil under medium heat until golden brown.

Both of these toppings are excellent on a plain cake.

Honey Cream Pie with Apricot Meringue

2⅓ tbsp sifted pastry flour
2 cups milk
½ cup strained honey
¼ tsp salt
2 egg yolks
2 tsp grated lemon rind
2 tbsp butter
1 nine-inch pre-baked pie shell

Apricot Meringue

2 egg whites
¼ cup sugar
2 tbsp cooked, sieved, dried apricots

Moisten the flour with a very little of the milk. Scald the remaining milk, honey and salt. Pour over the moistened flour, stirring instantly. Then return to the double boiler with the beaten egg yolks and cook over hot water, stirring constantly, until thickened. Remove from the hot water, add the lemon rind, and butter, and when cool, turn into the pre-baked pie shell. Top with a meringue made from the stiffly beaten egg whites and sugar; fold in apricots, just before placing it on top of the pie. Place in a moderate oven (350° F.) to set, and delicately color the meringue.

Honey Jelly

3 cups honey
1 cup water
½ bottle fruit pectin

Measure the honey and water into a preserving kettle and mix. Bring to boiling point over the hottest fire, and at once add the pectin, stirring constantly. Bring to a full rolling boil and immediately remove from the fire. Skim, pour quickly into hot, sterilized glasses and seal.

Honey Muffins

1 cup milk
½ cup strained honey
½ cup sugar
3 cups sifted flour
3 tsp baking powder
¾ tsp salt
3 eggs, well beaten
¼ cup melted shortening

Blend the milk, honey and sugar, stirring very thoroughly. Combine with the sifted flour, baking powder and salt, add the eggs and shortening and mix very lightly and quickly. Bake in well greased muffin pans in a moderately hot oven (375°–400° F.) about 20 minutes.

Honey Sauce

¼ cup butter
2 tbsp cornstarch
1½ cups strained honey
¼ cup boiling water
8 marshmallows, quartered
1 tbsp lemon juice
¼ tsp salt

Melt the butter in a saucepan, add the cornstarch and when smoothly blended, the combined honey and water. Return to the fire and simmer for 5 minutes, stirring constantly. Fold in the marshmallows, lemon juice and salt and remove from the heat as soon as the marshmallows are melted.

HONEY BREAD. *See* Bread.

HONEY BALL MELON. Somewhat like the honeydew melon, but smaller. The honey ball melon is a round, slightly netted fruit, and may vary from a whitish-green, or gray, to yellow. Some of these melons are smooth; others are more or less netted. They keep well and can be bought and held for several days until ripe enough to eat.

HONEY BALL MELON

Prime quality honey balls have a thick, green-colored, sweet, fine-flavored flesh with a definite aroma. The rind has a light yellowish color and yields slightly to pressure. Frequently these melons have dark sunken spots on them, indicating the beginning of decay or breakdown. Such melons generally have flesh of excellent quality and flavor, provided spots have not penetrated beyond the rind into flesh.

Immaturity is generally indicated by hardness of the melon and the greenish-white color of rind. The flesh of such melons is hard, and the flavor is poor. Bruised melons and those with growth cracks should be avoided, as the flesh is likely to be soft and insipid. Decay is generally indicated by mold or dark, sunken, watery areas. *See also* HONEYDEW MELON.

HONEYDEW MELON. Bluntly oval in shape, honeydew melons vary somewhat in size. The rind is firm and usually very smooth, but may be somewhat netted. The color is a whitish green, changing to creamy yellow when fully ripe. They keep well and therefore may be bought before they are fully ripe.

A ripe honeydew has a creamy yellow color, and usually a small round scar or button at the blossom end, which yields to slight pressure when ripe. Ripeness also may be indicated by a slight pleasant odor. Since these melons are usually cut from the vine before they are fully ripe, the condition of the stem affords no indication of the stage of maturity.

The flesh of a full-ripe honeydew is greenish, very juicy, sweet, and of fine-

grained and melting texture. Immature fruit is firm, often hard, with a whitish-green color; the flesh is firm and not very juicy, and the sweet flavor is lacking. Decay appears in the form of sunken water-soaked spots, which may have dark-colored, pink, or black dots in them. These spots may be found anywhere on the surface. *See also* MELONS.

PREPARATION FOR MARKET

Honeydew and honey ball melons are graded according to the Department of Agriculture standards. U.S. No. 1 consists of melons which are mature, firm, well formed, free from decay, damage and disease. U.S. Commercial consists of honeydew or honey ball melons which meet the requirements of U.S. No. 1 to a lesser degree, while U.S. No. 2 consists of melons which are mature, fairly well formed, free from decay and serious damage. Unclassified consists of melons which have not been classified in accordance with the foregoing standards.

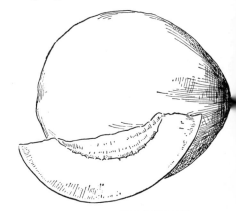

HONEYDEW MELON

HINTS ON BUYING

Honeydew melons and honey ball melons are sold by the unit or crate (6 lb.). One small melon serves two people. One large melon serves four to eight. Melons are available all year, but are most abundant in June and July.

HINTS ON PREPARATION

Honeydew and honey ball melons should be kept in a cool dry place, or wrapped several layers of waxed paper, or an oil-skin bag, and put in the refrigerator. For best flavor remove from refrigerator an hour or so before serving as the melon should be cool, but not ice cold. Never put ice into the cut melon.

HONEYDEW SUPREME

Take a ripe honeydew melon, and slice it into inch-thick rings. Remove any seeds and cut off the rind. Gather a few large, shiny leaves from the grape arbor or the maple tree. Wash and dry them, and place one on each plate. On the leaf, place the melon circle, and fill the center with large fresh black cherries that have been pitted, rolled in maraschino liqueur or sirup, then filled with a piece of blanched almond to resemble the pits. Serve thoroughly chilled with a section of lime.

HOODED MERGANSER DUCK. *See* DUCK.

HOPS. Hops are the flowers of the hop, a perennial climbing herb with opposite lobed leaves and scaly fruit, extensively cultivated in many parts of the United States, England, France, Belgium, Canada, Germany, Czechoslovakia, etc.

HOPS

A particularly rich and loamy soil is required for the successful growth of this plant, which also demands liberal supplies animal manure in highly concentrated rm. The hops are gathered in August. 'hen dried and closely packed in pockets bags, they become a solid mass of a ight or greenish-yellow color, with a fine oom or dust permeating it in which the incipal flavoring matter is found.

The best hops are of a bright color, between yellow and green. If they are very green, they were gathered too young; if very brown, they were allowed to ripen too long on the vine, or they have been over-dried and have consequently lost their individual flavor. They should have a powerful aromatic tang, particularly when rubbed between the fingers, should feel sticky to the hand, and should contain much of the yellow powder mentioned above. Porter brewers prefer hops of a brownish color, but ale and beer brewers use pale hops. New hops are reckoned as one-fourth or one-fifth stronger than old ones. When one year old, hops are vigorous; but after that every successive year takes away from their value, and after three or four years they are comparatively worthless.

The young shoot are good for the table, cut in the spring, when not more than five or six inches high; they are eaten as salad, or boiled and served as is asparagus, which they resemble. Prepared in this way they are delicious.

HOREHOUND. Horehound is an herb belonging to the mint family. It con ains a bitter aromatic juice that is used as a remedy for colds and also to flavor candies, confections, liquors, and cordials.

HOREHOUND

HORS D'OEUVRES. The French, now Americanized, hors d'oeuvres correspond to the Italian *antipasto* and the Scandinavian *smorgåsbord*. Hors d'oeuvres are tasty tidbits designed to tease the appetite. An endless variety of food combinations go into their making, but it is well to limit somewhat the different foods incorporated into one recipe. Assorted crisp vegetables, cold cuts, and stuffed tomatoes, eggs, and the like are popular servings. These may be charmingly decorated.

Trays of hors d'oeuvres may be passed at afternoon parties or at buffet suppers, or they may be served on individual plates in place of salads at informal dinner and supper parties. See also APPETIZERS, CANAPES, and COCKTAILS.

VEGETABLE BASE HORS D'OEUVRES

Among the more popular vegetable bases are tomatoes, cucumbers, onions, celery, lettuce, new cabbage, French endive, radishes, young carrots, small beets, cooked artichoke bottoms, and broiled mushroom caps. These may be cut into interesting shapes with a vegetable cutter, or they may be hollowed. Use fresh-looking vegetables of good color, and remove from them all inedible portions and blemishes. Chill uncooked vegetables; marinate cooked ones in French dressing, drain, and dry. Spread or fill these with a tasty mixture, garnish as desired, and serve on crisp lettuce or watercress.

Radishes can be made to resemble roses. Leave short pieces of stem on them. After washing them, cut the tops and cut thin slices from the root ends. Cut narrow, uniform strips of the skin without quite cutting through to the stems. Then place the radishes in ice water and allow the strips to curl back as petals.

TIDBITS ON TOOTHPICKS

Delicate pieces of any savory food may be served on toothpicks. Here are some suggestions.
   Hot ripe olives
   Tiny onions alternated with pieces of cocktail sausages
   Tiny broiled sausages seasoned with tartar sauce
   Squares of cheese (or cheese balls) alternated with halves of stuffed olives
   Rolled chipped beef
   Alternating blocks of sliced boiled ham and sliced Swiss or American cheese
   Shrimp slightly flavored with mustard and pieces of celery
   Alternating cubes of lemon-flavored avocado with cubes of tart apple

WRAPPED TIDBITS

Small pieces of a variety of foods can be served in bacon wrappers. Surround them with strips of bacon; fasten them with toothpicks; broil them until bacon is crisp, turning them often to assure uniform crisping; and serve them while they are still warm. Almost any savory morsel can be served in this manner—use your inventiveness and your leftovers. Here are some suggestions:
   Stuffed dates
   Stuffed olives
   Pickled pearl onions
   Watermelon pickle
   Sections of skinned grapefruit
   1-inch blocks of American cheese
   Sauteed chicken livers
   Oysters
   Shrimp
   Mashed sardines that have been seasoned with onion juice, mayonnaise, and mustard

HORSEFISH. See MOONFISH.

HORSE-MACKEREL. See TUNA FISH.

HORSEMEAT. Horsemeat is a nutritious meat for those who are not fastidious. It is consumed in large quantities by the poor in France, and to some extent in Austria, Denmark, Germany, and Sweden. It has found little favor in England or the United States, although during World War II there was some effort to popularize it. Most of the horseflesh sold in this country, by strictly licensed dealers is for feeding to dogs. It contains neurin and its excessive use may cause diarrhea in humans

HORSERADISH. Horseradish is coarse herb that bears white flowers. I was formerly known as German mustard because of the use in Germany of both i roots and leaves for food. Today it is culti vated for its peppery root which, some times extended with white turnip, is use as a condiment. It has a lively, punger flavor. It is favored as an ingredient sauces, particularly sauces for seafood cocktails because of its ability to stimula the appetite. Mixed with cream cheese, makes a delightful canapé spread.

Dehydrated or grated horseradish often thinned with vinegar to make mea sauces or relishes. Try substituting lemo juice for the vinegar, as this is more likel to enhance and preserve the flavor. Thi horseradish with cream if it is to be serve with boiled or roast beef; with applesauce, if it is to be served with ham. Horseradish and prepared mustard, mixed in equal portions, may be served instead of mustard. Horseradish is also used in the cooking of pickles and salads.

HORSE RADDISH

HORSERADISH SAUCE. *See* MAYONNAISE and WHITE SAUCE.

HORSESHOE CRAB. *See* CRAB.

HOSPITALITY. In prehistoric times, hospitality was unknown, but if we look backward through the period of history we find authentic documents, transmitted by contemporaries, traces left on monuments, stories from travellers, explorers, scientists, and writers, to which may be added the memoirs of missionaries to uncivilized countries, from all of which we may conclude that spontaneous and free hospitality preceded the institution of hostelries which made their appearance shortly after the dawn of civilization.

Among the Romans we find customs analogous to those of the Greeks as the Greek civilization met that of Rome. The banquets and feastings were on a munificent scale. The wealthy had their clubs as they have today, where friends were invited to sumptuous repasts.

During the persecution periods, the Western Christians fraternized with, and gave shelter to their brothers of the Orient, one helping the other when they were obliged to flee from the pagan.

In Western Europe, hospitality was also practised by the Celts, Gauls, and Anglo-Saxons. Among the Celtic people, the long-haired bards went from clan to clan, singing of the achievements of the heroes of present and past days. They were rewarded with horns filled with hydromel or ambrosia, and to them was given shelter and food with gracious generosity.

Religious orders were organized to entertain monks, pilgrims, crusaders, and paupers.

During the 13th century, the pilgrims and troubadours saw the drawbridges of somber manors and fierce-looking castles lowered to them; doors of homes large and small opened wide.

In every country, under all climates, all religions seem to have materially fostered the code of hospitality, to have established it as a duty. The stories of the various religions and the lives of their founders, prophets or ministers, Buddha, Moses, Jesus, Mohamet, Luther, Calvin, etc., are full of edifying and instructive anecdotes on hospitality.

HOTBREADS. Usually a quick bread, raised with baking powder. By following any good recipe for quick hot breads, and then baking at the right temperature, anyone can achieve perfect results. Butter always gives a characteristic flavor that most people find palatable. If the cost of butter is prohibitive, it is generally possible to use half butter and half other fat. The liquid to be used should be cold. It is important to have the mixture cool. If it is warm, the fat melts, and melted fat makes less tender products. Flakiness and tenderness depend upon the shortening being evenly distributed in the mix. This is best accomplished when cold fat is used. Folding and rolling the dough several times produces flakier biscuits than kneading it on the board, and the less flour used on the board the better. (*See* BREAD)

HOT BUTTERED RUM. *See under* TODDY.

"HOT DOG." This toothsome frankfurter is relished by children and adults from Maine to California and from Seattle to Miami; it has become as much a part of the American scene as chewing gum and baseball. Coney Island Red Hot, Frank, and Weenie are only a few of the many names by which it is known and it is enjoyed in even more forms than it has names. It becomes a main course when boiled and served with sauerkraut, a quick lunch when boiled or fried and tucked into a split roll and flavored with mustard, or a tasty snack when roasted whole over the campfire. *See* FRANKFURTER SAUSAGE, *under* SAUSAGE.

HOT FRUIT PUNCH. *See under* PUNCH, FRUIT.

HOT SLAW. A very popular winter dish made as follows:

To each 4 packed cups of cooked, shredded cabbage, add 1 cup of thin white sauce, to which has been added: 1 tablespoon of grated onion, 1 tablespoon of cider vinegar, 1 teaspoon of paprika, and

3 generous tablespoons of mayonnaise. Heat well but do not boil. Serve hot as a vegetable. (Serves 6) *See also* CABBAGE and COLE SLAW.

HOT PLATE. A small, portable cooking unit, heated by either gas or electricity. In its common form it has one or two burners or heating elements mounted on a low frame, and is sometimes equipped with a metal plate or grill. When used on a wood, or other combustible material, surface or table it is advisable to stand the hot plate on some type of protective pad, such as asbestos.

HUCKLEBERRY. *See* BLUEBERRY.

HULL. To remove or strip off the hull, or outer covering, as on corn or strawberries.

STRAWBERRY HULLER

HUMAN MILK. Discussed under milk, *which see.*

HULLER. A pair of small metal tweezers shaped to hull strawberries.

HUNTER SAUCE. *See* BROWN SAUCE.

HURTLEBERRY. *See* BLUEBERRY.

HUSHALLSOST CHEESE. A common cheese in Sweden, made in three varieties.

HVID GJEDEOST CHEESE. A Norwegian goat's milk cheese, which comes in forms nine or ten inches long, six inches broad, and four inches high.

HYDROGENATED FAT. Hydrogenated fat has the consistency of lard. It is made of one or more liquid fats (oils) such as coconut, cottonseed, peanut, sesame, and soybean oils. Lard is sometimes hydrogenated. The oils are hardened by exposure to hydrogen in the presence of heat and a catalyst.

Hydrogenated fats can be mixed with shortenings such as butter or lard to cut down expenses in cake making. They are preferred to the natural shortenings when cakes are baked at high altitudes because they have a much higher water tolerance than butter or lard. This facilitates the even distribution through the cake batter of water and water-bearing ingredients such as milk and eggs, and thus strengthens the structure of the cake. *See also* HIGH ALTITUDE COOKERY.

HYDROMEL. A mixture of honey and water with added herbs and spices. There is no standard recipe for Hydromel, it being compounded to suit the maker's taste. Hydromel also served as the basis for mead (*which see*).

HYSON. A name given to Chinese green tea, having a special twist. "Young hyson" is the early crop. The term has no reference to the quality of the tea.

HYSSOP

HYSSOP. Hyssop, a member of the mint family, bears aromatic, pungent leaves and violet-blue flowers. It is native to Europe, but it has been naturalized in America. Its leaves and flowers are used for flavoring salads, and the leaves are used in the making of absinthe as well. Hyssop is strong in both flavor and odor. It is also used to flavor soups, beverages and candy.

I

ICE. (I) Though mankind has long been aware of the beneficial nature of ice, it is only recently, as history goes, that he has been able fully to utilize frozen water in its many forms. The drawbacks have been those of successful manufacture, storage and distribution; and until methods were developed to meet those problems, ice was restricted to a luxury item for the wealthy. It was a highly seasonal, localized commodity.

HISTORY

The date and circumstances of man's first recognition of the usefulness of ice are not known, though it is generally assumed that primitive man somehow discovered that meat buried in a glacier or submerged in a glacial stream would keep longer than the same meat left lying in the open. Even today, stories, possibly true, come trickling out of the Arctic about mastodon meat being found that was still edible, despite its incredible age, because it had been frozen in the ice. Indeed, the remarkable preservation of these and other animals has often led to speculation on the possibilities of suspending life for long periods by a similar freezing.

In the Graeco-Roman days ice and snow from distant mountain tops was used to chill foods and drinks at banquets. In the year 50 B.C., the Romans dug snow from mountainsides and packed it in deep pits covered with straw and tree prunings to keep it for later use. The Roman emperors were fond of using mountain snow to chill their food, and Nero, in particular, had snow cellars built high in the Alps to store winter snow for summer use. The snow was carried to the city by slaves, and from what is known of Nero's tastes and habits, it is not too unlikely to suppose that a veritable bucket brigade of slaves was needed to keep the royal table properly iced.

Ice, or rather, the lack of ice, was almost directly responsible for the discovery of the New World, for the great surge of exploration in the 14th and 15th centuries was largely sparked by the need for quicker, cheaper routes to the spice-growing East.

Spices, at that time, were in great demand for use as food preservatives.

At first, man used both snow and ice, gathering them in the winter and storing them in caves lined with straw, chaff, or reeds, wrapping them in the same materials for safe delivery at the time of use. Gradually, as man learned to harvest and store ice from lakes and ponds, the used of snow was abandoned and natural ice was the only refrigerant used for many years.

Natural ice was, of course, restricted to those climes that were cold enough during the winter to freeze lakes and ponds. Warmer regions had to import their ice, an expensive and difficult procedure. Some chemicals were developed that, when mixed with water, could produce freezing temperatures, but they were not practical for large-scale use. It was only with the development of mechanical refrigeration (*see* REFRIGERATION) that man was able to manufacture ice at will in any season.

NATURAL ICE

When the air above a pond becomes cold, the upper layers of the water are chilled. This chilled surface water is heavier than the warmer water below, so it settles to the bottom; the process continuing until all of the water is cooled to four degrees Centigrade. As water attains its maximum density at that temperature, when the surface water goes below that temperature, it is actually lighter than the relatively warmer waters below and stays on the top. When the surface temperature reaches zero degrees Centigrade, ice begins to form. Ice, being even lighter than water, floats on the surface, and when any natural body of water freezes, the ice forms from the top down.

This freezing cycle is not without its great biological significance, for if water froze from the bottom up, virtually all of our present marine life would perish in the winter. As it is, the ice actually forms an insulating blanket and the lower depths of the pond are well protected against temperatures lower than four degrees Centigrade during the coldest of winters.

Ice frozen on still surfaces, such as ponds and small lakes, is opaque because of imprisoned air bubbles, minerals, and other impurities; while ice frozen on moving surfaces, as streams, etc., is usually clear. Salt water freezes with difficulty, requiring lower temperatures than fresh water, but once frozen, the ice will usually be found to contain relatively little salt.

During the 19th and the early part of the 20th centuries, ice harvesting was a seasonal event in northern America, being in much the same category as husking bees, sugaring-off parties, and other forms of communal agrarian activities. It was, in fact, a harvesting of one of nature's products, like all the others.

When the pond surface or ice field had reached a sufficient thickness (eight inches of ice will bear up to 150 pounds of weight), the snow was scraped off the top and squares marked off on the surface. Horse-drawn ice plows grooved the marks deep enough to permit the workers to pry the individual cakes free with hand tools.

The process changed little through the years. Mechanization has crept in to the point where portable power saws are used to cut the ice and an inclined conveyor (a power-driven device somewhat similar to an escalator) is used to lift the individual blocks from the water and into the ice house.

Once in the ice house, the blocks are packed closely together between layers of some insulating material, usually sawdust. The walls, roof, and floor of the structure are themselves well insulated and adequate provisions are made for drainage.

Though ice had long been harvested in America, it was not until 1802 that the first home delivery of natural ice was recorded. Prior to that time, the users had to harvest and store their own supply. The first long-distance ice shipment was made in 1799, with a shipment from New York to Charleston, S.C., but the business did not really get started until 1804 when Frederic Tudor of Boston shipped a cargo of 130 tons to Martinique in the West Indies. Shortly afterwards, his first competitor, also a Boston firm, introduced ice to the people of London.

When ice became commercially available, the demand began to grow. The requirements of towns and cities finally reached the point where local ponds were inadequate, making long-distance ship-

ments necessary. The South, of course, had to import all of its ice. By the last quarter of the 19th century, ice storage houses were built in virtually every industrial center and the natural ice business was prospering.

The demand kept growing until it evoked the natural laws of economics. A combination of a greater demand than could be supplied and high transportation costs sent natural ice prices spiraling, and ice seemed doomed to join the luxury class as in the days of old. Fortunately, manufactured ice appeared on the scene to meet the situation.

MANUFACTURED ICE

The first recorded research in the problem of making ice by mechanical means was done by Dr. William Cullen, of Scotland, in 1755. Many other workers developed methods and machines, and in 1851, Dr. John Gorrie, of Appalachicola, Fla., was granted the first American patent for a practical process of manufacturing ice. The good doctor, whose main concern had been the use of ice in the treatment of tropical fevers, suffered the traditional inventor's fate, dying a broken man in 1855, having reaped little profit from an industry which he made possible. Though the press and public had scorned his claims, Gorrie machines served as models and incentives to inventors around the world.

Other inventors developed other machines, among them being Ferdinand Carré, from France, who developed an ice making machine that used ammonia as a refrigerant and secured United States patents in 1860. His machines were used to produce ice for medical use under emergency conditions in the South during the Civil War when the Northern blockade had cut off ice supplies.

The census of 1870 reported a total of four operating commercial ice-making plants in the United States and the industry grew slowly until the year 1890 brought the greatest shortage of natural ice ever seen in the country. The industry was jolted into rapid growth that continued through the years, and, in 1944, some 6,800 ice manufacturing plants produced almost 50 million tons.

Ice is manufactured by using a system of mechanical refrigeration to produce freezing temperatures. The system, basically that described in the article on refrigeration (*which see*), uses ammonia as a refrigerant and has the evaporator coils suspended in a brine solution. Since brine freezes at temperatures lower than water, the coils are able to keep it at temperatures low enough to freeze the water without affecting the brine. The water is held in tapered cans of four or five hundred pound capacity that are lowered into the brine solution.

Opacity or cloudiness in ice is caused by imprisoned air bubbles, mineral particles, and items of a similar nature that are commonly found in water. Crystal clear ice may be made in two ways; either by freezing distilled water which is free from these impurities, or by agitating regular tap water during the freezing operation, even as Nature produces clear ice on the top of running streams. The water is agitated by introducing a stream of air through the bottom of the can. The water freezes from the sides of the can, forcing the cloud-causing substances into the unfrozen center. Near the end of the freezing period (if the brine is held at 16 degrees Fahrenheit, it takes about 45 hours to freeze the normal sized can) this remaining core of sediment-filled water is sucked out of the ice block and replaced with fresh water that is then allowed to freeze. The resulting block is almost optical in clarity, though in some cases a trailing "feather" may be noticed in the center along the path followed by the air bubbles during the agitation process.

When the freezing is completed, the cans are removed from the brine and the ice blocks dumped out onto conveyor belts (practically all of the handling is done by machinery today) which carry them into the storage room, an insulated area where a temperature of 22 degrees Fahrenheit is maintained by mechanical refrigeration. Because of the low temperature, there is no need to pack the ice in insulating material as there is in the ice house where natural ice is normally stored. When the ice is needed for distribution, the blocks are cut down to appropriate sizes for delivery.

Other Kinds of Ice

Ice, being solidified water, comes in a variety of forms. Snow, hail, and frost are actually all forms of ice, though seldom thought of as such. Snow was used for re- frigeration in the past, but the availability of cake ice has pretty much ruled it out of general use except for emergency purposes in snow regions. When the appearance of snow is desired (as a setting for some dishes, for example) it is far better to shave cake ice, since the resulting particles are much more solid and longer lasting than snowflakes would be. Frost, by its fragile nature, was never of applicable value as such, though the presence of frost on the exterior of glasses is sometimes desirable (*see* Bartending). Hail is not common enough to be considered a normal refrigerant, though it can be and has been used at times.

The most familiar form of ice, indeed, the one thought of when the word is mentioned, is block, cake, or solid ice. Ice may be either clear or cloudy and natural or manufactured, but there is no basic difference between the types. Several different types of ice have been produced in laboratories under different conditions of pressure, including one that is heavy enough to sink like iron when placed in water. These types are of little practical value, however, especially in the field of cookery.

Dry ice (*which see*) is actually not ice at all, being a solidified gas rather than solidified water.

Uses of Ice

As man becomes better acquainted with the workings of his environment, the problems and applications of temperature control assume even greater importance, and the growth of the ice industry offers mute testimony to the increasing use of ice.

At the moment, ice is chiefly being used in the fields of food and medicine. Ice is invaluable in certain types of therapy, being used in the form of packs, baths, and other applications. It has recently been shown that ice may be used in place of an anesthetic in certain types of surgery, particularly amputations. The area to be treated is packed with ice and, after a period of time, the cold numbs all possible pain sensations. Where applicable, this technique is of great value in the case of patients who are unable to take an anesthetic.

The major use of ice in the field of food is to preserve perishables, beginning at the moment of gathering and being used right on through the various phases of distribution and even in the home. Garden produce packed in ice in special box cars or trucks is shipped completely across the country, making possible the enjoyment of many foods out of their local season. Seafood, meats, and dairy products especially demand the use of ice. It finds much use in cooling beverages of all descriptions.

Florists, too, use ice to preserve the freshness of cut blossoms, and ice is also employed in many chemical and other industrial processes. Ice is used in some systems of air conditioning as well.

ICE IN THE KITCHEN

Ice is a valuable tool for the housewife. If she has an ice refrigerator (*which see*), she uses it to preserve her food. Regardless of her refrigerator type, she finds many uses for ice in her normal tasks.

If she has a mechanical refrigerator (*see* REFRIGERATOR), she can color and garnish the cubes that it makes, adding greater variety and more appeal to the beverages which the ice cubes are used to cool. She may even freeze ice in ornate cooky molds to supply unique table pieces and to give a distinctive touch to an ice bed used to serve some chilled dish.

If an ice refrigerator is used, ice for household requirements may either be purchased separately from the iceman or chipped from the block in the box. However, before using ice chipped from the ice refrigerator supply, it is well to first learn if it is safe to use that ice in beverages and in direct contact with food. It must be remembered that ice is not cold enough to kill all forms of bacteria, and if the water was polluted before freezing, many types of germs can adapt their physical structure to meet this new set of circumstances and lay dormant until chance again places them in an environment suitable for their activity.

In America, at least, it is a safe assumption that only pure water is used to make manufactured ice and the reputable natural ice merchant will select his source with care. There is, however, in some areas, a possibility that the water body from which the ice was taken was not definitely known to be pure.

This precaution is very pertinent in foreign countries, especially in the Orient where all water, regardless of source,

should be looked upon with high suspicion unless it is definitely known to have been boiled. Often, in the East, two types of ice will be made; one using regular water for refrigeration purposes only, and the other using the more expensive purified water suitable for use in beverages.

All ice chipped from the block within an ice refrigerator should be thoroughly rinsed in cold running water before being used in beverages or food. Due to absorbency, while in the unit the ice collects odors from the air circulating past, and unless these substances are washed off the wet surface of the ice, they are apt to impart undesirable flavors to the food with which they are used.

Ice is used on the table with some appetizers, leafy vegetables, etc., both to keep them properly chilled and to enhance their appearance. Because of the appearance factor, some care should be given to prepare the ice bed so that it looks neat and uniform. There are many tools available to assist the housewife in reducing ice to the desired size.

Ice Pick. A single-pointed, awl-like instrument used to cut relatively large pieces of ice. Since ice is a crystalline structure, it can be divided along the axis of the crystals and a few hard, well placed jabs of the pick will split the ice along definite lines. The task, however, grows more difficult as the size of the ice piece decreases.

Ice Chopper. A broad, flat-bladed, toothed instrument that can be used to split large blocks and also to break the ice into fairly small pieces.

Ice Plane. Designed somewhat like a carpenter's wood plane, this instrument shaves a thin layer off the top of the cake, to form a snow-like mass.

Ice Crusher. There are many different instruments on the market that will reduce cube-sized pieces to smaller particles. They all operate in different ways and some can be adjusted to produce different sized particles.

Perhaps the simplest way to crush ice, lacking a specialized instrument, is to wrap the ice in cloth and beat it with a hammer, ball bat or similar weapon.

Prepared ice is best kept under refrigeration until ready for use, but when in the room, it should be kept in a covered insulated container. It should be remembered that both the rate of melting and the rate of chilling are directly controlled by the size of the ice particle used, and the sizes selected should be appropriate.

Ice alone will never cause water to freeze, for it is obviously impossible for the ice to cause temperatures colder than that of the ice itself, and in actual practice it cannot be quite that efficient. However, a mixture of salt and ice will cause freezing temperatures, since the salt increases the melting rate and hence the rate of heat absorption of the ice. Crushed or chipped ice and rock salt are used in the proportion of three parts of ice to one part of salt. This principle is used today in ice cream freezers and similar devices. *See* ICE CREAM and FROZEN DESSERTS.

ICE. (II) The simplest of frozen desserts. It is usually made of fruit juice and water, sweetened, and then frozen. The mixture must be beaten or whipped to break up the ice crystals, and egg whites or other substances may be used to give a smooth texture. An ice is usually distinguished from a sherbet, which is made with milk or cream. *See* FROZEN DESSERT and individual fruits.

ICE CHEST. A type of ice refrigerator in which the ice and food lay side by side, separated by a perforated panel. It is small enough to permit an efficient convection current to be established in the air with the ice in that position instead of being above the food as in the icebox. *See also* ICE REFRIGERATOR.

ICE CHOPPER. A flat, toothed blade used to shave or chop ice into fine particles.

ICE CREAM. Ice cream is a frozen product made from cream, or a mixture of cream and milk, and sugar, and usually containing eggs. Since the advent of the automatic refrigerator ice creams, frozen custards, sherbets, frappés and mousses have become increasingly popular.

Mankind's predilection for chilling his palate is neither new nor localized. When Marco Polo returned from the Orient in the 14th century, he brought tales of slant-eyed men sitting on embroidered cushions, eating dishes of ice, brought from the mountains by camel pack, and flavored with exotic fruits. Adopted by the Italians, the custom of eating ices spread to France through the Medicis in the 16th century. French chefs improved water ices and developed ice creams. The formula went to England as a court secret, and came to America with the colonists early in the 18th century.

America's contribution was the practice of congealing the custard in mechanical freezers instead of placing it on ice, as we still do with certain parfaits, mousses, sherbets, etc. An entry in George Washington's account book for May 17, 1784, describes a "cream machine for making ice." And, showing the part that ice cream played in the early social and political history of our capital, is this comment on a party attended by the founding fathers at the second inauguration of President Madison: "Mrs. Madison always entertains brilliantly, but last night there was a sparkle in her eye that set astir an air of expectancy in her guests. . . . When finally the brilliant assemblage, America's best, entered the dining room, they beheld in the center, high on a silver platter, a large shining dome of pink ice cream."

The first newspaper advertisement for ice cream appeared in The New York *Gazette* on May 19, 1777. The first American patent on a freezer was issued in 1848. The confusion attendant on the birth of all great institutions was not missing. In 1849 the important step of blowing air into the ice-cream mix was discovered and forgotten in the fury of discussion of the cosmic problem of whether the dasher should revolve within the can or the can revolve around the dasher.

HOMEMADE ICE CREAM

There are ice creams, and ice creams, and the homemaker should know the most important pointers in making these delicious and refreshing dishes. Above all, she should understand what happens when cream or milk is frozen. The ingredients combined for ice cream making must be chosen with regard to freezing characteristics, texture, and flavor.

Functions of The Ingredients. The most important ingredients used are: (1) Milk, which gives body to the mixture, the solid substance in milk holding air bubbles and preventing crystallization. Evaporated milk may be substituted for sweet milk for richness, having the same properties and action as sweet milk. Condensed milk gives the same results as sweet or evaporated milk, plus a richness of texture and sweetness. Cream gives richness and smoothness, since its butter fat content prevents crystallization. (2) Eggs, acting as a binder, leavening, thickening and stabilizing ingredient, and giving texture as well as flavor. (3) Sugar, giving sweetness, and at the same time preventing crystallization. (4) Gelatin, acting as a stabilizer, and holding ice crystals apart. Marshmallow acts like· gelatin, being gelatin itself. (5) Flavorings, having no effect on the freezing. (6) Fruits, being solids, retard the freezing process, and thus should not be added until the mixture is half solid or half frozen. Nuts act in the same manner as fruits. (7) Starch, be it flour or cornstarch, is a stabilizer because it holds the ice crystals apart.

Preparation of Ingredients. Milk should always be scalded to reduce its water content and concentrate its protein. Evaporated milk and condensed milk used in making ice cream need not be scalded because their protein has already been concentrated during the manufacturing process, and the butter fat is evenly distributed or emulsified. The amount of sugar should be carefully measured as too sweet a mix will delay the freezing. Cream should be added when half beaten, as a too-well-beaten cream will not combine well. The cream should be beaten to a fluffy mixture, the consistency of boiled custard. Gelatin and marshmallows should always be dissolved.

To be smooth (free from crystals) ice cream must be frozen quickly, and so the refrigerator control should be set in the coldest position. As soon as the mixture is frozen, the control should be turned back to normal, so that the ice cream will not become too hard. An important point to be remembered is that all the ingredients used in ice cream making should be chilled thoroughly before combining them. If water is used in the recipe, the mixture should be beaten when it is frozen to a stiff mush, as this will break up any crystals that may have formed. Since the object of adding whipped egg whites or whipped cream is to incorporate air into the mixture, be sure to fold them in gently.

"Time" freezing just as you would roasting or broiling.

Using A Refrigerator. Most frozen desserts, such as mousses, parfaits, and in fact almost all desserts which merely require packing in salt and ice, can be easily made in a mechanical refrigerator without stirring. But it is wise always to consult the booklets issued by manufactures for exact information about using each make of mechanical refrigerator. However, whatever the make, always be certain that the temperature of the refrigerator can be made sufficiently low for freezing. (*See* REFRIGERATOR.) The motor may be set correctly for proper and correct refrigeration, and yet, not low enough for freezing desserts. A temperature control feature obviates any disappointment and allows temporary adjustment.

Ice cream made in a mechanical refrigerator must be beaten several times during the freezing process to break up the crystals and give a smooth finished product. When the mixture is partly frozen, scrape it out into a chilled bowl and beat with an egg beater until it is smooth. Return to the freezing tray and let freeze a second time. The beating process should be repeated two or three times for best results. It is important to work fast and have the utensils chilled so that the mixture does not thaw too much.

Using A Hand Freezer. There are many patterns of ice cream freezers that are well constructed and inexpensive. They are sold by the size, a two-quart freezer giving two quarts of the frozen cream, etc.

See that the crank is oiled and the whole apparatus clean. Have ready cracked ice and rock salt, usually in the proportion of one part salt to three parts of cracked ice. (Snow may be used.) Shavers or mallets or machines come for cutting the ice, but it is easy to pound or crack it in a strong bag or burlap. Set the freezer can, which should be well-chilled, in place, surround it with the cracked ice and coarse rock salt alternately, shaking down and packing them firmly. Have the cream mixture cool. Pour it in, having the can not more than three-quarters full, to allow for expansion. Put on the lid, cover with ice and salt, wait for five minutes, and then begin to turn the crank. Open and stir down once or twice, being careful to keep out the salt, lest the mixture be spoiled. Take out the dasher before the mixture becomes too stiff. Pack it firmly down in the can. See that the melted water is removed from the pail, put in more ice and rock salt, and leave for at least two hours, covered with an old blanket, bag, or burlap.

If ice cream is granular, too much salt was used in freezing, the can was too full or the crank was turned too rapidly. The turning of the crank should be slow and steady to insure a smooth, fine-grained mixture. After frozen to a mush (about ten minutes) the crank should be turned more rapidly until it turns with difficulty, showing that the mixture is frozen solid. The ice must be chopped fine. The new type of hand freezers have an easy action and may be obtained with an electrical connection which makes hand-turning unneccessary. The vacuum, sometimes known as still-freezers, may be used for desserts which have whipped cream as a base.

Three Types of Ice Cream. There are three general types of ice cream: (a) French ice cream, which is a rich egg yolk custard and heavy; (b) American ice cream, which is less rich than the French ice cream, and is also made of a custard base with or without flour or cornstarch; and (c) Philadelphia ice cream, which is made of thin cream, or cream and milk, and no eggs.

Ice cream may also be made using prepared powders and mixtures which require the addition of only milk or water and flavoring. These are usually designed to be frozen in the mechanical refrigerator, and the manufacturer's directions should be followed carefully.

See also FROZEN DESSERT and individual fruits and flavors.

BASIC ICE CREAM I
(American Type)

2 cups scalded milk
1 tbsp flour
1 cup granulated sugar
2 egg yolks, slightly beaten
¼ tsp salt
1½ tsp flavoring extract
4 cups thin cream or undiluted evaporated milk

Combine the flour, sugar and salt, and add to the slightly beaten egg yolks. Slowly pour the scalded milk over the egg mixture, stirring constantly. Turn into the top of a double boiler and cook over hot (not boiling) water for 10 minutes, stirring constantly, until the mixture coats the spoon. Strain the hot mixture through a double thickness of cheesecloth. Cool and add the cream or evaporated milk and flavoring. Freeze in a hand freezer, using 3 parts ice and 1 part rock salt, until solid. Pack in a mixture of 4 parts ice and 1 part rock salt.

Or, the mixture may be frozen in a mechanical refrigerator, beating the partially frozen mixture at least twice during the freezing process. (Makes approximately 2 quarts)

BASIC ICE CREAM II
(French Type)

2 cups scalded milk
4 egg yolks, slightly beaten
½ cup granulated sugar
1 cup heavy cream
1 tsp flavoring extract
⅛ tsp salt

Combine the sugar and salt and add the slightly beaten egg yolks. Beat until the sugar is dissolved. Slowly add the scalded milk, stirring constantly. Turn into the top of a double boiler and cook over hot (not boiling) water, stirring constantly, until the mixture coats the spoon. Strain through a double thickness of cheesecloth and cool. Add the unwhipped cream and flavoring extract. Freeze in a hand freezer, using 3 parts of ice and 1 part of rock salt, until stiff. Pack in 4 parts of ice and 1 part of rock salt.

Or, the mixture may be frozen in a mechanical refrigerator, beating the partially frozen mixture at least twice during the freezing process. (Makes approximately 1½ quarts)

BASIC ICE CREAM III
(Philadelphia Type)

1 qt light cream
1 cup granulated sugar
1 tsp salt
1½ tsp flavoring extract

Mix the ingredients thoroughly and freeze in a hand freezer, using 3 parts of ice to 1 part of rock salt, until stiff. Pack in 4 parts of ice and 1 part of rock salt.

Or freeze in a mechanical refrigerator, beating the partially frozen mixture at least twice during the freezing process. (Makes approximately 1½ quarts)

BASIC ICE CREAM IV
(Condensed Milk)

1 cup sweetened condensed milk
¾ cup cold water

⅛ tsp salt
1 cup heavy cream
1½ tsp flavoring extract

Combine the condensed milk, water, salt, and flavoring. Stir to blend thoroughly. Whip the cream until stiff and fold into the milk mixture. Freeze in a mechanical refrigerator until mushy. Remove the tray from the refrigerator, scrape the bottom and sides, and beat the mixture for 2 minutes, or until smooth. Return to the tray and freeze for 3½ hours (Makes approximately 1 quart)

BASIC ICE CREAM V
(Refrigerator Tray)

2 cups scalded milk
2½ tbsp quick-cooking tapioca
⅓ cup granulated sugar
2½ tbsp light corn sirup
¼ tsp salt
2 egg whites
2 tbsp powdered sugar
1 cup heavy cream
2 tsp flavoring extract

Scald the milk in the top of a double boiler. Add the tapioca to the hot milk and cook over boiling water for 10 minutes, stirring occasionally. Strain through a double thickness of cheesecloth. Mix the granulated sugar, salt, and corn sirup, and add to the milk. Chill. Beat the egg whites until stiff, beating in the powdered sugar. Whip the cream and add the flavoring. Add the beaten whites to the milk mixture, and then fold in the whipped cream. Freeze in a mechanical refrigerator, without stirring, for 4 hours. (Makes approximately 2 quarts)

VARIATIONS

An infinite variety of ice creams may be made by adding fruit pulp or various flavorings to these basic recipes. See the individual fruits and flavors for proportions.

ICE CREAM CROQUETTES

Shape any kind of your favorite ice cream into croquette shapes. Roll in toasted coconut. Serve with Chocolate Fudge Sauce (see FUDGE).

ICE CREAM PIE

1 qt vanilla ice cream
1 qt strawberries or raspberries
Sugar to taste
½ cup currant jelly
Whipped cream

Use homemade or commercial ice cream. Spread the ice cream about 2 inches thick on the bottom of a shallow mold with a tight-fitting cover. Press a deep plate into the ice cream to make an indentation similar to a pie shell. Place the cover on the mold, seal with cloth or paper, and pack in a mixture of 4 parts ice and 1 part rock salt for 2 hours.

When ready to serve, unmold the ice cream shell. Sweeten the berries to taste and arrange in the shell. Melt the currant jelly and brush over the berries. Decorate with whipped cream and serve immediately.

ICE CREAM SANDWICH

Bake sponge cake in a pan twice the size of the ice-cream tray if the ice cream is frozen in a mechanical refrigerator. After removing the cake from the pan, cut it into two pieces the size of the tray. Place one section of cake on a platter, lay the mold of ice cream on the cake, and place the second portion of cake on top. Serve the ice-cream sandwich plain, with chocolate, or other sweet sauce, or with fresh fruit.

ICE CREAM DISHER. The ice cream disher is an implement intended chiefly for use in serving ice cream, being a convenient means of getting neat, uniform, individual portions from a bulk container. It is sometimes known as a "scoop," as is the ball-like portion it serves.

There are two types of dishers or scoops in general use, one of which has moving parts. This type consists of a metal hemisphere set at the end of a handle. Inside the hemisphere is a thin blade, curved to conform to the bowl. The device is pressed or dragged through the bulk ice cream, gathering a ball in the bowl. When a lever set on the handle is pressed, the blade passes over the interior of the hemisphere, cutting or scraping the ice cream ball loose.

The second type of disher is much simpler in appearance and use. It is a deep-bowled spoon set on a sturdy handle. When it is·dragged over the ice cream, a ball is formed in the bowl, and, the sides of the bowl not being as high as in the other type of disher, the ice cream ball is easily removed from the device.

Dishers of the first type are also suited for serving mashed potatoes, boiled rice, and similar foods, while those of the second type will only function with soft, but firmly packed foods.

See also ICE CREAM and ICE CREAM SODA.

ICE CREAM SODA. An ice cream soda is a beverage made of carbonated water, a flavoring, and an undissolved lump of ice cream. It is generally named for the flavoring used, though fanciful names are sometimes coined to match complex constructions. Both a spoon and a straw are required to deal with a soda, since it is both eaten and drunk, and it is usually served in a ten-ounce glass, though paper cups are now coming into commercial favor because of their sanitary features.

HISTORY

Every nation or race has a set of symbols that identify it to the rest of the world. America is no exception, and chief among its symbols is the ice cream soda. This is most appropriate, for, like most things American, the ice cream soda is the offspring of emigrant parents that has risen to dizzy heights of fame and fortune in the New World.

The parents did not fare too badly, either. Both ice cream (*which see*) and soda water (*which see*), the principal ingredients of the beverage, were first developed in other lands. They came to America in the early days of the nation, and there they were fostered to their present gigantic growth.

As discussed in the article on soda water, artificially carbonated water made its first American appearance in the modernistic Philadelphia drug store of Elias Durand in 1825, and it is generally assumed that its mating with ice cream took place on the premises. At first, the beverage was considered a novelty.

Today there is a soda fountain in virtually every community in the nation. It is the accepted social center for youth, and the impact of the ice cream soda and its commercial surroundings upon our language, customs, and culture has been tremendous.

The first sodas were simple, flavored, effervescent beverages, mixed without the addition of ice cream. Gradually the custom of dropping in a scoop of ice cream spread, and this basic structure ʼwas further supplemented, until today, when many commercial establishments rival one another in making larger sodas that have more things in them than anywhere else. The basic sodas, however, are still highly popular, and their recipes have become standard.

HOMEMADE ICE CREAM SODA

A glittering fountain and professional skill are not essential to the making of good sodas. If the housewife will exercise the care she normally uses in following any recipe, and realize that eye appeal is almost as important as taste appeal, she can turn out excellent sodas that will solve many of her entertainment problems as well as offering novelty desserts to add zest to the menu.

Equipment. Ice cream sodas can be made in any drinking vessel, though tradition demands a tall glass. The ten-ounce tumbler is well suited for this task (*see* GLASSWARE). However, the possibilities of using mugs and other novelty vessels on appropriate occasions should not be overlooked. Also required are a number of straws and iced-tea spoons (*see* FLATWARE), for these are served with the individual drinks. Either an iced-tea spoon or a bar spoon (*which see*) may be used for mixing purposes. Long-handled spoons are required because of the depth of the glasses, though regular teaspoons may be used in emergencies or with shorter glasses.

A regulation ice cream scoop or disher is preferable if the ice cream is purchased in bulk form. While it is possible to use either a spoon or knife in that case, the disher gives a professional-looking ball. A rechargeable siphon bottle (*which see*) may be used in preference to commercially-bottled carbonated water, and a juice extractor and a beater for whipping cream are other often used items. A second rechargeable siphon may also be used to whip the cream.

Supplies. The essential supplies are: ice cream, carbonated water, and a flavoring sirup or extract. These, of course, may be varied by using ginger ale or some other flavored carbonated beverage in place of the last two essentials, and water ice or sherbet may also be used in conjunction with the ice cream. Milk is also required in some recipes.

Though not essential, the beverage is often garnished for various effects. Among the commonly used materials are whipped cream, marshmallow topping, chocolate chips or flakes, grated coconut, pineapple slices, and cherries.

Technique. Some care must be exercised to make a good soda. The flavoring should be mixed thoroughly and evenly with the carbonated water so that all portions of the beverage will have the same flavor, and the ice cream should be as intact and as little melted as possible.

All liquid ingredients should be chilled before using to keep the beverage at the proper temperature. Since the flavoring sirups are usually quite thick and heavy, they are inclined to resist mixing, especially because of the temperatures involved. For this reason, all of the necessary sirup is first placed in the glass, then just enough carbonated beverage to dilute it (usually about one-quarter to one-third of the glass) is added. These ingredients are thoroughly mixed before the ice cream is added.

The ice cream should be in as firm a ball or lump as is possible with the tools at hand. It is dropped gently into the mixture and the glass then filled to the brim with carbonated water or whatever mixer is being used. Because ice cream reacts rather violently to carbonated fluids, the mixer should be poured in gently, and the finished beverage stirred as gently and as little as possible to blend the flavors. If care is not exercised at this step, the glass may become filled with leathery, tasteless foam.

If desired, garnishings are then added to the top of the soda; if not, it is stirred just enough to give it an attractive topping of foam, if this has not already been accomplished in the mixing. The drink is served immediately with straws and an appropriately sized spoon. The mixer used should have been freshly opened to keep the drink from going "flat" or stale before it is consumed.

Recipes. As anyone familiar with a soda fountain knows, the field is wide open for imagination and experiment. The use of flavored ice cream in conjunction with flavored carbonated beverages, for example, offers many permutations and combinations. Restraint should be exercised, however, for a single predominating flavor is always to be preferred over a confused mélange of many that does little but bewilder the taster. Much can also be done in the way of garnishing, though the beverage should never become a sort of muddy fruit hash with ice cream floating on top or in the middle.

Following are some suggested basic recipes, the ones most commonly used.

CHOCOLATE SODA

2 tbsp chocolate sirup
1 tbsp milk or cream
1 large scoop chocolate or vanilla ice cream
Carbonated water (chilled)

Place the sirup, milk or cream, and ½ cup carbonated water in the bottom of a 10-ounce glass, and stir well. Add the ice cream, fill with carbonated water, and stir gently. Garnish with nutmeg, etc., if desired. Serve immediately with straw and long-handled spoon. (Serves 1)

If two scoops of ice cream are used, room is left at the top when the last of the carbonated water is poured in, and the second scoop added *after* the soda has been completely mixed.

When vanilla ice cream is used to make a chocolate soda, the beverage is frequently referred to as a Black and White Soda.

GRAPE SODA (PURPLE COW)

½ cup chilled grape juice
2 tbsp sugar (powdered preferred)
1 tbsp milk or cream
1 scoop vanilla ice cream
Chilled ginger ale

Mix and serve as above. (Serves 1)

PINEAPPLE SODA

2 tbsp crushed pineapple
1 tbsp sugar
1 tsp milk or cream
1 scoop vanilla ice cream
Chilled carbonated water

Mix and serve as above. (Serves 1)

ROOT BEER SODA (BLACK COW)

1 tbsp milk or cream
1 scoop vanilla ice cream
Chilled root beer

Mix the milk or cream with ½ cup root beer in the bottom of a 10-ounce glass, add the ice cream, fill with root beer, stir slightly, and serve immediately with straw and spoon. (Serves 1)

ICE CREAM FORK. See FLATWARE.

ICE CREAM FREEZER. An ice cream freezer is a device used to manufacture ice cream without the aid of mechanical refrigeration. It is based on the principle that if ice is made to melt at a forced rate through the use of chemicals (salt), it will draw enough heat from its surroundings to cause freezing temperatures.

The traditional ice cream freezer consisted of two main parts: an outer wooden bucket that held the ice, and an inner metal can that held the ice cream. The metal can was suspended from a metal frame so that it could be revolved in the ice mixture for even freezing, and there were dashers inside that churned the ice cream mixture during the early stages of freezing to keep it smooth and creamy. The metal can was revolved by means of a large crank.

Though ice cream is now being manufactured on a vast commercial scale, the home ice cream freezer is still in great demand, for the superiority of its product often outweighs the effort involved. The principles, and in some cases the form, of the traditional model are unchanged, but more compact and more easily turned units are now being made. Some units have small electric motors attached, while others have provisions for the can to be turned by means of a belt attached to an outside power source, such as the motor of a bench lathe. See also KITCHEN EQUIPMENT.

ICE CUBE. See REFRIGERATOR.

ICE CUBE TONGS. See FLATWARE; ee also BARTENDING.

ICE REFRIGERATOR. The ice refrigerator (icebox) is an insulated cabinet in which conditions proper for the safe storage of perishable foods are maintained through the use of ice. As discussed in the article on Food Preservation and Storage (which see), food structure is almost certain

to be attacked by molds, yeasts, and bacteria unless preventive steps are taken. A well made ice refrigerator, properly supplied with ice, will maintain temperatures of 50 degrees Fahrenheit or lower, sufficient to halt or retard the action of most of these microorganisms. Since perishable foods are high in water content, they are affected adversely by dehydration, and, it is claimed, the ice helps to prevent this water loss by maintaining proper conditions of humidity, as well as temperature, within the cabinet.

ICE CREAM FREEZER

ICEBERG LETTUCE. A large, firm-headed kind of lettuce with thick, broad, and wrinkled leaves, it is excellent for use in salads, sandwiches, and in cooking. See LETTUCE.

ICED DRINKS. See BEVERAGES and specific drinks such as BEER, CIDER, MILK, etc.

ICED TEA SPOON. See FLATWARE.

ICEFISH. A small, tasty smelt, also known as a Caplin. Prepare and serve like smelt, which see.

ICELAND MOSS. This is a lichen used as food, especially in arctic regions where it is dried, ground, and made into bread. It contains various bitter principles which must be eliminated by repeated washing and by steeping in hot water.

ICHANG. A fine China black tea, of the group known as "North China Congous." Ichangs, Keemuns, and Ningchows are often called the "Burgundies of China teas." Ichangs produce a full, rich brew with a slightly smoky flavor. All three of these teas have a superb bouquet.

ICING. See FROSTING, FILLING AND ICING.

IHLEFELD CHEESE. Another name for Hand Cheese, *which see.*

ILHA CHEESE. A moderately firm Portuguese cheese which is ten or twelve inches in diameter and four inches thick.

INCANESTRATO CHEESE. An Italian rennet cheese made of cow's, goat's, or sheep's milk, various spices, and olive oil. Also known as Majocchino cheese.

INDIAN-CRESS. The nasturtium (*which see*) is known in England by the name of Indian-Cress.

INDIAN CORN. Also known as maize. For various ways of preparing, *see* CORN.

INDIAN FIG. The edible fruit of the cactus. *See* CACTUS PEAR.

INDIAN MEAL. A meal made from corn or maize.

INDIAN PEAR. Edible fruit of the cactus. Known also as Indian fig and prickly pear. *See* CACTUS PEAR.

INVALID COOKERY. In preparing food for an invalid, one should bear in mind that it is of the utmost importance that the appetite of the patient be tempted. Large quantities of food should never be served to an invalid. The most attractive dishes procurable should be used, and the linen should be immaculate. A fresh flower adds color and daintiness to the tray. Hot dishes should be served very hot and cold dishes thoroughly chilled.

Never ask a patient what he would like for a meal but find out from the doctor what he may have; then surprise the invalid by serving something unexpected, nourishing, and dainty.

See also DIET.

IODINE. Iodine is essential for the formation of an organic iodine compound, thyrosin, which regulates the metabolic functions of the body. A lack of iodine prevents the formation of thyrosin and causes enlargement of the thyroid gland, or goiter. This disease results from an inadequate diet caused by a lack of iodine in the soil and a consequent lack of it in the foods grown in it. Sea water contains iodine and it is present in all sea plants, such as algae, agar-agar, Irish moss, and in fresh fish. Iodine is also present in minute quantities in many fruits and vegetables, such as cabbage, asparagus, garlic, leeks, sorrel, pineapple, and strawberries.

IRISH MOSS. A seaweed found along the coasts of New England and Ireland. It is used as a thickening agent in foods and medicines.

IRISH SODA BREAD. A leavened bread to which are added caraway seeds and raisins. Soda is used to neutralize the acidity of the dough. *See* BREAD.

IRISH STEW. There are many variations of this dish, but it is essentially composed of lamb, potatoes, other vegetables, and seasoning. *See also* LAMB.

IRISH STEW

2 lb breast of lamb
3 tbsp flour
1 tsp salt
⅛ tsp pepper
4 tbsp drippings
⅓ cup chopped onions
10 peppercorns
1 cup diced white turnip
1 stalk celery, diced
½ cup carrots, diced
3 medium-sized potatoes
2 small tomatoes
1 cup shredded cabbage
5 cups cold water

Cut the lamb into 2-inch pieces. Mix the flour, salt and pepper, and dredge the pieces of meat. Heat the drippings in a stew pan. Add the meat and sear lightly, turning to brown all sides. Add the onions and brown slightly. Then add the peppercorns, turnip, celery, carrots, the potatoes peeled and cut in quarters, the tomatoes peeled and quartered, the cabbage and the cold water. Cover the pan. Bring to a boil and simmer gently for an hour and a half. Taste and correct the seasoning. Serve very hot. (Serves 4 or 5)

IRISH MOSS

IRISH STEW
(Leftover Lamb)

2½ cups meat stock
1½ lb diced cooked lamb
1 tsp salt
¼ tsp pepper
2 medium-sized onions, sliced
1 white turnip, diced
2 medium-sized carrots, diced
Sprig of parsley
2 cups cubed raw potatoes

Place the diced lamb in a deep covered saucepan. Add the meat stock, or water in which bouillon cubes have been dissolved. Add the rest of the ingredients. Bring to a boil and simmer 35 or 40 minutes, until the vegetables are tender. Taste and correct seasoning. If desired, the gravy may be thickened with a little flour which has been rubbed to a paste with cold water. Serve the stew with dumplings, *which see.* (Serves 6)

IRISH WHISKY. *See* WHISKY.

IRON. Iron is the oxygen carrier of the blood. On account of its great affinity for oxygen, iron plays an important part in the human body as well as in the vegetable and animal worlds.

In the human body, iron serves to produce the hemoglobin of the red corpuscles and to assist the process of respiration. The hemoglobin carries the oxygen through the capillaries to all parts of the body, allowing the oxygen to oxidize the carbon of the ingested food stored in the tissue cells and change it into carbonic acid. This combines with the alkaline elements of the blood and is eliminated through the lungs.

The total amount of iron in the body is comparatively small and probably does not exceed 7 grams, or 75 grains, under normal conditions. Of this quantity, about 50 grains are contained in the blood, the remainder distributed in the marrow of the bones, the liver, and in the spleen. Iron is the most active element in the system and consequently needs to be renewed more frequently than the more stable elements of calcium and potassium in the bones and tissues.

The amount of blood in a normal adult man weighing 160 pounds is about 12 pounds—7½ percent of the body's weight —and contains about 50 grains of iron. With every pulse beat, nearly six ounces of blood are forced from the heart into the aorta, and in every half minute the entire amount of blood passes from the heart into the lungs and thence into the arteries and capillaries throughout the body. Accordingly, 50 grains of iron pass through the heart and lungs 120 times in an hour and 2,888 times a day. These 50 grains have to perform the function that 2,888 times 50, or more than 20 pounds of iron would perform. For this reason, an adequate daily supply of organic iron in the diet is most essential.

IRONWARE. Iron is one of the first materials to have been used to make cooking utensils, and though other materials have since largely supplanted it, there is still much to be said in its favor. It is inexpensive, not affected by heat, easy to clean, durable, practically ageless, and actually improves with use. It is heavy and cumbersome, but it also heats evenly and tends to hold the heat.

Iron is used to make skillets, Dutch ovens, kettles, and similar utensils, though, today, it is mainly used for the first two items.

The bulk of ironware is made from cast iron. Some sheet iron is used, but this material tends to buckle and warp. The casting should be sound, without defect, and the utensil itself properly designed for the purpose for which it is intended.

CARE AND CLEANING OF IRONWARE

New iron vessels are usually coated with lacquer to keep them from rusting. This must be removed before the vessel can be used, and it is advisable that the vessel be "seasoned" to keep it from rusting. The new vessel should be thoroughly scoured with hot water and a strong cleansing powder. As a further precaution, it should be filled with hot water that contains one teaspoon of baking soda per cup, covered, and let simmer for one hour. The vessel is then again scoured and is ready to be seasoned. It is coated with lard or some other form of unsalted fat or cooking oil and heated for several hours in a warm oven. The fat or oil is allowed to cool on the pan before it is cleaned off.

If an iron pan ever shows a tendency to rust, the spots should be removed with steel wool dipped in kerosene and the pan again seasoned. All ironware should be dry when stored away.

Some ironware is plated or has some other special finish. In these cases the manufacturer's directions should be carefully followed as to "breaking in" and seasoning.

Though cast iron is very durable, it can be broken by sharp impact, so reasonable care should be exercised in handling these heavy utensils.

See also KITCHEN EQUIPMENT.

ISIGNY CHEESE. Slightly larger than Camembert, but of the same shape. It also bears a close resemblance to Limburger. It is an American cheese, originating about 56 years ago in attempts to make Camembert. The proper ripening for Camembert was not obtained, hence a distinct name was given to the product.

ISINGLASS. Isinglass is derived from the membranes of the swimming bladder of the sturgeon and from other fishes. In its crude state, it is not very soluble in water but it is hygroscopic and swells in cold water. It may then be dissolved in boiling water. It will again harden when the water has evaporated. Isinglass has largely been superseded by the use of commercial gelatin.

ITALIAN PASTE. Inclusive term for alimentary pastes made in Italy and in America, such as macaroni, spaghetti, noodles, etc., *which see. See also* PASTE.

J

JACK CHEESE. A granular-curd Cheddar-type cheese made in America.
JACKFISH. Another name given to pike or pickerel.
JAM. A jam is a variation of a preserve. The product is cooked to a thick mass and the proportion of sugar used is less than that used for rich preserves. For jam, use one-half to three-quarters of a pound of sugar to each pound of fruit. Jams need constant stirring to prevent burning.

HINTS ON PREPARATION

Cook no more than 3 to 4 quarts of the fruit at a time. Wash fruit, cut or crush in tiny pieces, add small amount of water and cook 8 to 10 minutes. Measure fruit, add about ⅔ cup sugar for each cup of fruit and boil rapidly until jam is thick and clear, stirring until done, to prevent burning. When done, jam will fall cleanly away from spoon in thick stream. Pour into sterilized glasses and seal as for jelly, or pour into clean hot jars and seal at once. *See also* PRESERVES and individual fruits.
JAM AND BUTTER DISH. A round, saucer-like dish, divided in the middle, intended to hold both jam and butter for table service. *See* DISHES.
JAMAICA RUM. *See* RUM.
JAMBALAYA. A typical Creole dish of New Orleans which may be made of many types of fish, shellfish, or meat. The basic ingredient is rice.

CRAB JAMBALAYA

1 cup rice
½ lb lump crab meat
1 large onion
1 clove garlic
½ lb tomatoes
½ of a chili pepper
Salt, pepper, and cayenne pepper
Butter or oil

Boil the rice in boiling salted water until tender. Drain and rinse under cold water, and let stand to dry.
Heat the butter or oil in a skillet. Chop the onion and garlic and cook in the butter until golden brown. Quarter the tomatoes and add to the onions, pressing with a spoon to extract the juice. Put the rice in a deep heavy pan. Pour over the tomato sauce. Add the lumps of crab meat, and mix thoroughly with a wooden spoon. Season to taste with the salt, pepper, cayenne pepper and finely chopped chili pepper. Cover the pan and simmer very gently for 30 or 40 minutes, stirring frequently. Serve very hot. (Serves 4 or 6)
JAPANESE ARTICHOKE. A plant with small, edible roots, also known as Chinese artichoke. *See* ARTICHOKE.

JAPANESE ARTICHOKE

JAPANESE GELATIN. A gelatin prepared from seaweed, better known as agar agar, *which see.*
JARDINIERE. As applied to cookery, a dish garnished with several cooked vegetables. A French name meaning garden style.
JARDINIERE SAUCE. *See* BROWN SAUCE.
JAVA AND SUMATRA TEAS. When plucked in the dry season (July, August, and September), and from high altitudes, Java teas may be likened in richness and pungency to the better teas of North India and Ceylon. Teas from Sumatra are consistently good the year round. Like the Javas, they are very good blenders. *See* TEA.
JELLIED. Brought to a jelly; made gelatinous, but not necessarily sweet.
JELLIED SOUP. Primarily a summer soup, congealed through the use of gelatin and served chilled. *See* SOUP.
JELLY. Some fruits seem to have been designed by nature particularly for jelly making. They are juicy, pungent in flavor, and possess a quality which allows the strained, cooked juices to jell when cooked with sugar. Certain other fruits may have all the good qualities except the last. Mod-

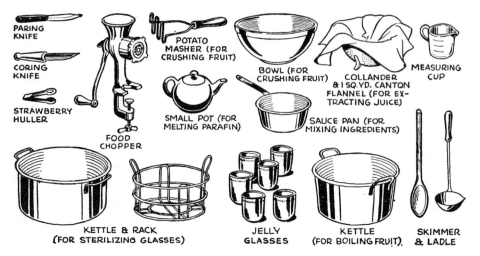

PARING KNIFE

CORING KNIFE

STRAWBERRY HULLER

FOOD CHOPPER

POTATO MASHER (FOR CRUSHING FRUIT)

SMALL POT (FOR MELTING PARAFIN)

BOWL (FOR CRUSHING FRUIT)

COLLANDER & 1 SQ.YD. CANTON FLANNEL (FOR EX-TRACTING JUICE)

SAUCE PAN (FOR MIXING INGREDIENTS)

MEASURING CUP

KETTLE & RACK (FOR STERILIZING GLASSES)

JELLY GLASSES

KETTLE (FOR BOILING FRUIT)

SKIMMER & LADLE

JELLY MAKING EQUIPMENT

ern science, however, has surmounted this difficulty, and we may now take advantage of their flavors and add to them fruit pectin (the jellying principle) in concentrated form.

Our great-grandmothers sometimes combined currant juice, which is very high in pectin, with raspberry or strawberry juice, either of which is very low. They also used green grapes and green apples for the same purpose. This is sometimes done today, but the results are less certain than when commercial pectin is used.

Test for Pectin

It is desirable to test fruit juice to determine whether it contains sufficient pectin which, in turn, will indicate the amount of sugar to be used.

1. To one tablespoon of cooked juice add one tablespoon of grain alcohol and stir slowly. Wood or denatured alcohol may •be used, but these are poison so DO NOT TASTE.

a. Juices rich in pectin form a large amount of heavy gelatinous matter.

b. Juices moderately rich in pectin form a small amount of separated gelatinous matter.

c. Juices poor in pectin form very small flaky particles of gelatinous matter.

2. Mix thoroughly one tablespoon of cooked fruit juice, one teaspoon of sugar and one and a half teaspoons of Epsom Salts. Stir thoroughly and let stand for 20 minutes. If the mixture forms a semi-solid mass, the juice contains enough pectin.

Test for Acid

Fruit juices may be rich in pectin yet lack sufficient acid to make a good jelly. The only method for testing this is tasting for tartness and adding lemon juice if necessary to give the acid content. Fruits with decided flavor may be combined with tart apples to give the necessary acidity.

Proportion of Sugar

For perfect jelly, the right proportion of sugar to juice must be used. For firm currants and green grapes, many still use the old-time rule of cup for cup, but usually three-fourths of a cup of sugar to a cup of juice will suffice. If too little sugar is used, the jelly will be ropy or sirupy.

The surest method, unless you are an expert jelly maker, is to combine commercial fruit pectin with fruit juices. Exact directions for the various fruits come with every container, whether liquid or dry pectin is used, and must be followed to the letter. It is essential that the jelly be turned into the sterilized glasses without delay, as it begins to set very rapidly. Due to the very short boiling required, a larger number of glasses can be made from a given quantity of fruit juice and sugar, the flavor will be richer, and the time consumption at a minimum.

Jelly without Added Pectin

The first consideration in making jelly is the selection of the fruit. A good fruit for jelly making is high both in pectin and acid. These two substances with the added sugar, plus cooking, bring about a jellying of the juice. Good fruit for jelly must also have good flavor. Of all the good jelly fruits, currants probably rate highest on all three counts—flavor, pectin, and acid. Others rating high are blackberries, gooseberries, raspberries, crab apples, grapes, and quinces.

Both pectin and acid are most abundant in fruit that is slightly underripe. Flavor is best in ripe fruits. To get a jelly that both tastes good and jells satisfactorily, combine ripe fruit with that which is slightly underripe.

One of the fundamental rules in jelly-making technique is to reduce cooking time to the minimum. Overlong cooking reduces the jelling power of the pectin, destroys fine flavor, and often spoils the color. For this reason, use a minimum of water. Excess water will have to be boiled off, and that will necessarily lengthen the cooking time.

In order to extract the juice, boil the fruits until they are soft. Naturally, the firmer the fruit the more water will be needed, and the longer will be the time of cooking. For example, quinces, a very firm fruit, take about two cups of water to a pound of fruit and need about 20 minutes to become tender. Red raspberries, on the other hand, need only to be crushed (with no water added) and they require only from five to ten minutes to cook to the right stage for extracting the juice.

After the fruit is fully softened, pour it at once into a jelly bag that has been wrung from hot water. Let the juice drip, and press the bag to squeeze out every bit of it. Clarify the juice by straining it again through a fresh bag, again wrung out of hot water.

Next comes the second period of cooking and it is here that modern jelly making differs from the old. Formerly it was the practice to cook the juice first, until it had become fairly concentrated, then to add sugar. Today jelly experts advise combining the sugar with the juice before heating. This cuts down the cooking time and the sugar also tends to prevent destruction of the pectin.

It's a good plan to use a large, flat-bottomed preserving kettle. Stir the sugar and juice until the sugar is dissolved. Then boil rapidly until the jelly stage is reached. How long this will take depends upon the fruit. With currants, for example, the juice and sugar usually need to be boiled only a short time. Other fruits, less rich in pectin and acid, take longer. We use the same satisfactory jelly test that grandmother learned from her mother.

Jelly Test. Dip a spoon in the boiling sirup, then hold it above the preserving kettle. At first a drop will form on the edge of the spoon and fall back. Later a drop will cling to the edge of the spoon, but the jelly is not ready to pour into the glasses until two drops will hang side by side and stay there. This is called sheeting.

When the homemaker gets to this point her job is nearly finished. She has only to remove quickly any scum that has formed on the sirup, then pour carefully into sterilized containers and seal. After the jelly is set, label and store in a cool, dry place. Pour the jelly directly from the kettle into the glasses, to within one-half inch of the top. Never overfill the glasses. This allows space for a paraffin seal. Dust is an enemy to the perfect preservation of jellies; consequently, just as soon as the jelly has been poured it should be covered with one-eighth inch layer of hot paraffin. Twirl the glass so the paraffin seals to the sides. When this is set, pour in a slightly thicker layer to finish the seal.

For melting paraffin use either a small teapot or a saucepan over hot water. As soon as the paraffin seal has set and the glasses are cool enough to handle, cover immediately with tin covers or with tightly pasted paper covers. Store jellies in a cool, dry place.

Fruits for Jelly Making

The juices from the following fruits may be used successfully alone to make jelly: green apples, crab apples, unripe grapes, blackberries, currants, gooseberries, raspberries (slightly underripe), cranberries, quinces, plums.

Juices from strawberries, peaches, pineapples, cherries, rhubarb, pears, and sweet apples lack either pectin or acid and must be combined with other juices to make good jelly. Consult the jelly table below for good juice combinations.

PROPORTIONS OF SUGAR AND FRUIT JUICE
FOR JELLY
(Showing approximate proportions of fruit
juices which will combine)

Fruit Juice	Proportions	Cups of Fruit Juice	Cups of Sugar	Color
(*) predominant flavor				
Apple*	—	1	¾	Light
Apple and	¾			
Blackberry*	¼	1	⅔	Dark
Apple and	½			
Blueberry*	½	1	¾	Dark
Apple and	½			
Black Raspberry*	½	1	⅔	Dark
Apple and	⅓			
Blueberry and	⅓			
Rhubarb*	⅓	1	⅔	Dark
Apple and	½			
Cherry*	½	1	⅔	Dark
Apple and	½			
Elderberry*	½	1	1	Dark
Apple and	½			
Peach*	½	1	⅔	Light
Apple and	½			
Pineapple*	½	1	⅔	Light
Apple and	½			
Quince*	½	1	⅔	Light
Apple and	⅓			
Quince and	⅓			
Cranberry*	⅓	1	¾	Dark
Apple and	½			
Rhubarb*	½	1	⅔	Light
Apple and	½			
Strawberry*	½	1	⅔	Light
Blueberry	—	1	⅔	Dark
Crabapple	—	1	¾	Light
Currant	—	1	¾–1	Dark
Gooseberry (green)	—	1	1	Light
Grape (underripe)	—	1	¾–1	Dark

EQUIPMENT FOR JELLY MAKING

A good fruit jar funnel
Long handled spoons—at least 3
An accurate kitchen scale
Food chopper
Potato masher
Small pot (for melting paraffin)
Jelly glasses
A standard measuring cup
A ladle
Several sharp knives
A grater—2 are more convenient
Orange and lemon squeezers
Preserving kettles of ample size
Bowls and crocks, various sizes
A cutting board
A wire strainer
Two colanders
Two jelly bags
See also PRESERVES and individual fruits.

JELLY FILLING AND FROSTING

¾ cup tart jelly
2 unbeaten egg whites
⅛ tsp salt

Place the jelly in the upper part of a double boiler and set over boiling water. As soon as melted, add the unbeaten egg whites and beat vigorously until the jelly is free from lumps. Now add the salt and continue beating until the mixture is stiff enough to stand in peaks. Use between layers or on top of a cake.

JELLY POWDER. There are many varieties of jelly (gelatin) powder on the market. Sweetened and flavored ones are used for desserts; savory ones for aspic, etc. See GELATIN.

JELLY ROLL. A very popular dessert cake with many variations. Because jelly

roll contains baking powder, and sometimes butter, it cannot be classified as true
sponge cake. After baking, the cake must
be rolled quickly to prevent crisping and
consequent cracking during rolling.

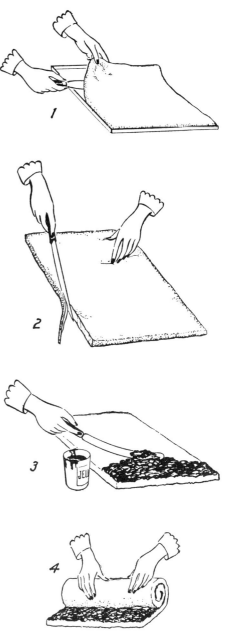

JELLY ROLL   1. Removing   2. Cutting
              3. Spreading   4. Rolling

FRENCH JELLY ROLL

  2 eggs, separated
  1 cup sugar
  Grated rind of 1 lemon
  1 tbsp lemon juice
  ½ cup boiling water
  1 cup sifted pastry flour
  2 tsp baking powder
  ¼ tsp salt
  Jelly

Line a shallow pan (10x15 inches) with
greased waxed paper, cut a trifle smaller
than the base of the pan. Do not grease the
sides of the pan.

Beat the egg yolks until thick and lemon
colored, gradually adding the sugar while
beating. Add also the lemon rind and juice
and beat again thoroughly. Now pour in
the boiling water and beat hard; then sift
in the dry ingredients which have been
sifted together twice. As soon as thoroughly
incorporated, fold in the stiffly beaten egg
whites. Pour the batter into the prepared
pan, tilting so that it runs to the corners.
Bake in a hot oven (400° F.) 12 to 15 minutes or until firm to the touch and slightly
shrunken from the pan.

Meanwhile spread a clean, dry cloth on
the table and sprinkle it lightly with sugar.
Invert the cake on it, quickly trim off crisp
edges with a sharp knife, and tear off the
paper. Spread the cake with jelly, which
may be whipped and very slightly warmed
to aid in spreading. Roll up the cake the
narrow way, using the cloth to aid in the
rolling. Cool on a wire rack. The cloth
may be left around the cake while cooling
to help keep it tender and preserve its
shape. Slice for service.

OLD-FASHIONED JELLY ROLL

  4 eggs
  ¾ tsp baking powder
  ¼ tsp salt
  ¾ cup sugar
  1 tsp vanilla
  ¾ cup sifted cake flour
  Jelly

Prepare the cake pan as directed for
French jelly roll. Combine the eggs, baking
powder, and salt in a bowl. Place this over
another bowl partly filled with hot water
and beat until thick, light and foamy,
gradually adding the sugar. Remove the

bowl from the hot water, add the vanilla and fold in the flour. Turn into the prepared pan and bake in a hot oven (400° F.) 12 to 15 minutes. Invert onto a sugar-sprinkled cloth, cut off the crisp edges of the cake, tear off the paper, spread with jelly and roll up quickly. Cool on a wire rack—the cloth may be left around the cake while cooling to help keep it tender and preserve the shape. Slice for service.

The jelly roll may be sprinkled with confectioners' sugar before serving, but no other topping is ordinarily used.

JELLY SERVER. See FLATWARE.

JELLYFISH. Another name given to the goosefish, *which see.*

JERKED BEEF. Beef or other meat which has been cut into strips and dried in the sun. See CHARQUI.

JEWFISH. A kind of grouper, *which see,* the jewfish is a large, voracious fish resembling the sea bass and is not as tasty as other fish in this family.

JIGGER. A unit of liquid measurement commonly used in mixing alcoholic drinks; *also,* a utensil used to measure intoxicating liquids.

The jigger is the accepted standard used in proportioning liquor in drinks. Since the amount of liquor served in a drink is often subject to local legislation and custom, the value of a jigger has fluctuated in time and place.

The jigger is now generally accepted to be one and one-half liquid ounces. That is the value assigned it in all recipes in this book, while a large jigger refers to two ounces and a small jigger only one.

The jigger, as a utensil, is made of metal, glass or plastic in several designs and sizes. Usually it is made of metal and greatly resembles a small whisky glass. See WEIGHTS AND MEASURES; *see also* BARTENDING.

JOHANNIS. An effervescent, pleasant tasting table water. See ALKALINE AND MINERAL WATERS.

JOHN COLLINS. An effervescent summer drink made of Hollands gin, lemon juice, sugar and carbonated water. Served in a tall glass with a straw and garnished with a cherry and other fruit, it differs from the popular Tom Collins only in the type of gin used. See COLLINS.

JOHN-DORY. A small food-fish, of compressed form and a prevailing yellow color, found off the Atlantic coast of Europe, the Mediterranean and Australian seas, but seldom seen in American waters.

JOHNNY CAKE. A bread made of Indian meal, eggs, milk, etc. Most of the busy homemakers of today, when thinking of corn bread or muffins, order corn meal from the grocer and let it go at that. The steel-cut and highly refined product comes in sealed packages, with printed recipes and instructions for the cook; but when the johnny cake is made and served, some critical person, of a reflective and nostalgic turn, recalls that the Rhode Island johnny cake of his earliest recollections was somehow different and indubitably better. Rhode Island johnny cake and Virginia hoe cake were made from water-ground meal, and that is why they were better. One can still get water-ground meal, usually made from sweet white corn, at the best grocery stores, but at an appreciable advance in price over the regular commercial product.

Monographs and essays without number have been written on Rhode Island johnny cake, which is so hedged about with legends and traditions that one must be bold to offer a casual recipe. Every family of Roger Williams' old colony has its own recipes, cherished and guarded like the corn-pone and spoon bread formulas of the Old Dominion and the Sunny South. In some homesteads of Washington and Newport counties you may eat johnny cake that has a superstructure of peculiar creamy consistency which mingles with melting butter on your breakfast plate and becomes a luscious custard upon a base of crisp but tender crust. Baking powder and other leavening agents rarely figure in the classic recipes for corn breads, either in New England or in the South, and in some of the most famous ones there is nothing but meal, water, and salt. See also CORN.

GRIDDLE-BAKED JOHNNY CAKE

2 cups water-ground white meal
1 tsp salt
Boiling water
Milk

Mix the cornmeal and salt and scald it with the boiling water. Drain and add sufficient cold milk to form a smooth soft batter. Drop from the tip of the spoon onto a hot greased griddle. Brown on both sides. Serve with sweet butter.

The johnny cake may be enriched by the addition of melted butter and beaten eggs.

PAN-BAKED JOHNNY CAKE

1¼ cups sifted flour
2 tsp baking powder
¾ tsp baking soda
1 tsp salt
2 tbsp sugar
1 cup corn meal
2 eggs
1¼ cups sour milk or buttermilk
3 tbsp melted butter

Sift together the flour, baking powder, soda, and salt, add the sugar and cornmeal, and mix thoroughly. Beat the eggs until light, combine with the milk and use to moisten the dry ingredients. Finally, stir in the melted butter. Turn into a greased pan (8x8x2 inches) and bake in a hot oven (425° F.) about 40 minutes.

JORDAN ALMONDS. A popular imported almond with long, plump kernel. *See* ALMONDS.

JOSEPHINE CHEESE. A soft-curd rennet cheese made from the whole milk of cows. It is marketed in small round packages and is a product of Silesia.

JOURNIAC CHEESE. A soft cheese resembling Roquefort. It is one of several types known as bleu cheese, *which see.*

JUG. (I) A narrow-necked, stout bulging vessel with a cork used for keeping or carrying liquids. Its capacity may vary.

JUG (II) A kind of stew, usually of game, made in an earthenware or stone cooking vessel, and often using the blood of the animal as an ingredient.

JUGGED HARE
(Southern Method)

1 good-sized hare or rabbit
3 large onions, sliced
Bacon drippings
Salt, pepper, and flour
¼ lb salt pork
2 tbsp parsley, chopped
2 tsp paprika
3 large tomatoes
1 cup beef stock
1 tbsp butter
1 tbsp flour
1½ tbsp currant jelly
Juice of 1 lemon
¼ cup sherry

Skin and clean the rabbit and cut into serving pieces. Heat the bacon drippings and brown one of the onions in the hot fat. Season the flour with salt and pepper and dredge the piece of rabbit. Brown the meat in the fat with the onion, and cook about 10 minutes. In a casserole, make a layer of the salt pork, cut in thin slices. Sprinkle in one more onion and half the parsley and paprika. Turn the meat and browned onions into the pan, but do not include the bacon fat. Sprinkle in the rest of the onion, parsley, and paprika. Peel and quarter the tomatoes and add to the meat mixture. Pour in the stock. Cover tightly and set the casserole in a pan of cold water. Bring slowly to a boil and let simmer for 3 hours.

Remove the pieces of rabbit and pork to a hot platter. Thicken the gravy with the flour and butter. Add the jelly, lemon juice and sherry. Let boil up once and pour over the meat. Serve immediately.

JUGGED HARE
(French Method)

1 good-sized rabbit
Liver and blood of the rabbit
Salt and pepper
Flour
¼ lb lean fresh pork
1 tbsp flour additional
1 small clove of garlic
1 bouquet garni
2 dozen small white onions
½ cup dry white wine
½ cup beef stock
2 doz small new potatoes
2 large tomatoes

Clean the rabbit and cut into serving pieces. Rub with a damp cloth. Season the flour with salt and pepper and dredge the pieces of meat. In an earthenware casserole fry the pork, cut into small cubes. When the fat is cooked out, remove the pork cubes and reserve. Brown the pieces of rabbit in the fat, turning until they are golden brown all over. Turn off the flame. Drain the fat out of the casserole. Sprinkle the tablespoon of flour over the meat. Add the garlic which has been chopped very fine, the bouquet garni, the white onions which have been peeled, salt and black pepper to taste, and pour in the wine and stock. Add the pork cubes. Light the flame again and let the mixture come slowly to a boil, stirring occasionally with a wooden spoon. Turn down the flame and let the mixture simmer very slowly. It is wise to put an asbestos mat under the casserole when cooking on top of the stove. Peel the potatoes and add them to the meat. Peel and quarter the tomatoes and add them. Let the rabbit simmer 50 minutes, or until the potatoes are tender. Just before serving, stir in the blood and the liver which has been rubbed through a sieve. Heat up and serve immediately.

JUGGED QUAIL
(English Method)

6 quail
Lemon juice
Salt and pepper
Pinch of allspice

Stuffing

1 cup bread crumbs
½ cup chopped fresh pork
2 hard-cooked egg yolks
1 tbsp minced celery
Onion juice
Salt and pepper

Clean the quail and singe them. Rub with a damp cloth and then with the lemon juice. Mix the salt and pepper and allspice and rub over the birds.

Make the stuffing by mixing together the crumbs, finely chopped pork, and egg yolks which have been rubbed through a sieve, and the celery. Season to taste with onion juice and salt and pepper. Stuff the birds loosely, sew the openings, and truss. Tie the wings and legs close to the bodies. Place the birds in a glass, earthenware, or agate vessel having a closely fitting cover. Place in a larger vessel of boiling water, deep enough to come almost to the top of the cooking vessel. Cook for 2½ hours, being careful that no water enters the vessel containing the birds.

Remove the birds and serve on toast, pouring over any juice which may have collected.

JUGGED WILD GOOSE IN RED WINE

1 good-sized wild goose
1½ doz small white onions
3 tbsp butter

¼ lb salt pork
Lemon juice
Salt and pepper
Pinch of allspice
1½ doz fresh mushrooms
6 sprigs of parsley, tied with
1 large bay leaf
1 clove garlic
2 cups claret
1 tsp fumet

The goose for this recipe need not be a young bird but it should be hung for 3 days. Clean the bird and singe it. Cut into pieces as for fricassee. Rub the pieces with lemon juice. Mix salt and pepper and allspice and rub into the pieces of goose.

In a deep heavy pot, melt the butter. Peel the onions and dice the salt pork. Cook the onions and salt pork in the butter until they are golden brown. Lift out the onions and pieces of pork and keep hot. Brown the pieces of goose in the butter, turning the pieces to brown all sides. Return the onions and pork to the goose. Peel and slice the mushrooms and add them. Add the parsley and bay leaf and the bruised clove of garlic. Stir gently, cover, and cook slowly for 20 minutes. Pour in the claret, cover, and bring to a boil. Simmer for 20 minutes, covered, or until the meat is tender.

Remove the pieces of goose to the serving platter and add the onions and mushrooms. Add the fumet (*which see*) to the remaining sauce, and reheat, but do not let boil. Pour the sauce over the goose. Serve with applesauce.

The traditional garnish for this dish is small triangles of bread which have been fried in butter and slices of orange.

JUICER. A juice extractor is a device designed to remove the juice from oranges, lemons, and limes as completely and as painlessly as possible. Because of the great popularity of the citrus juices, a wide variety of these devices has been developed.

The citrus fruits are alike in having a tough but flexible outer skin or rind, with the juice being contained in individual cells. These cells must be broken to release the juice, but the juice is quite apt to contain pulpy matter from the cells, as well as seeds and bits of cell wall. The extractor, then, must bring pressure to bear to burst the cells, and must contain some provision to strain the solid matter from the juice.

Reamer. Devices of the reamer type have a fluted dome that is forced into the cut half of the fruit with a twisting action. The fluted ridges break the cells, and the dome matches the fruit shape, insuring complete juice removal if the action is carried far enough. However, devices of this type also produce much pulp, fiber, and seeds that must be strained from the juice before use unless the reamer has an efficient strainer. The reamers are made in wall or table mounted units with the reamer being rotated by either an electric motor or a hand operated crank while the fruit half is pressed against it. Reamers of this type are the most expensive, but they will produce great volumes of juice with a minimum of effort.

There is a more inexpensive type of reamer, commonly made of glass, in which the reamer is stationary while the fruit half is pressed against it and rotated by hand. These devices either catch the juice in their bottom, or are made to be placed over a special cup or even a regular drinking glass that will catch the juice. They are more difficult to operate, and either have no strainer at all, or else are fitted with holes that are usually too large to be very efficient.

Squeezers. Another common type of juice extractor operates on a crushing or squeezing principle. Except for some units designed for commercial establishments, these devices are all manually operated. There are some that are mounted on the wall or table that crush the fruit half between two metal surfaces, one stationary, and the other moved by a long arm that exerts considerable leverage, thus requiring little effort.

The bulk of the squeezers operate on the pliers principle. Some crush the fruit half horizontally between two serrated jaws, while others force a perforated dome up vertically into the cut surface of the fruit.

The most inexpensive and simplest extractor of all consists merely of a perforated tube made of metal, plastic, or glass. The tube has a sharp, serrated end so that it may be forced up through the core of the fruit. It is important that these devices be inserted at the stem or navel so that they will cut through all of the segments on the inside. A glance at any cut citrus fruit will show the necessity for this, for unless all of the thick segment walls are cut, the juice will have difficulty reaching the walls of

the tube. When the tube is inserted, there will be a core inside which must be removed so the juicer can operate. The flexible fruit skin is manipulated by the hand, crushing the cells within, and causing the juice to flow to the tube where it passes through the perforations and out.

PURCHASING

Any juice extractor should be checked on five counts: how completely it removes the juice, how thoroughly it strains the juice, the ease of operation, the ease of cleaning, and soundness of construction.

The type of juicer selected will depend on family needs. While the electrical units are the most convenient to use, they are also the most expensive. The crank or lever operated type that are mounted to a wall or table are easier to use than the unmounted variety, while the ones that utilize no leverage are the most difficult to operate.

It is often convenient to have two or more squeezers of different types in the house to meet different needs. The kitchen unit should be mounted for convenience. Since the citrus juices are used in mixed drinks, and home bartending is often done in some room other than the kitchen, an auxiliary extractor is a great convenience. While a mounted extractor may be used here as well, many workers prefer some sort of portable device that can be carried to the scene and used to make the juice directly into individual glasses or cocktail shakers. Limes, being generally smaller than most other citrus fruits, are often difficult to manipulate on a regular extractor. For that reason, the smaller lime squeezer is helpful. This unit may also be used to squeeze small oranges or lemons, or pieces of larger fruit, thus eliminating the necessity of soiling an extra container to hold the juice for division among glasses.

Juicers are commonly made of either a coated metal, glass, or a plastic. Whatever the material, it must be stain-resisting and sturdy enough to stand up in use.

CARE AND USE

Citrus juice is highly acid. It is sticky and clings to anything that it touches, and can cause stains. If let dry it may ferment and will certainly attract flies and other insects.

JUNIPER

For that reason, great care should be exercised in cleaning the extractor after each use. It should be cleaned immediately, for, if the juice is given a chance to dry, the task will become more difficult.

The specific care given to an extractor will depend on the materials used in the unit. The various materials are discussed under their respective headings, *which see*.

Since, in most cases, the fruit must be cut for the extractor to work, a special cutting board (*which see*) and knife should be provided. The knife (*see* CUTLERY) may be of almost any shape, but the blade should either be stainless steel or a plastic. The board may also be used to hold glasses as they are filled because of the spillage danger. Both the knife and the board should be cleaned after using before the juice has had time to dry. If possible, they should be reserved for this single use.

The extractors are used mainly on oranges, lemons and limes. While grapefruit is also a citrus fruit, it is too large for the average extractor to handle. It may,

however, be cut into smaller pieces and thus handled by many extractors, especially those of the squeezer type. The extractors are not adapted to handle the other fruits; these are better handled in a blender (*which see*) or grape press.

See also ELECTRICAL EQUIPMENT and KITCHEN EQUIPMENT.

JUJUBE. One of several Old World shrubs of the buckthorn family, used in candy making.

JULEP. An intoxicating drink made with a liquor or wine and flavored by leaves from an aromatic plant, usually of the Mentha family. Juleps are fairly universal, but the American mint julep (*see* MINT) is, perhaps, the best known.

The word is derived from the Persian *gulab* and the Arabian *Julab*, or rose water, a highly aromatic liquid made by distilling rose petals and used in making perfume.

JULIENNE. A method of cutting meat, vegetables (especially potatoes), and fruits in small, match-like strips.

JUNIPER. The juniper is a hardy evergreen tree or shrub. Its fruit or berry is used by distillers to flavor gin. Juniper berries are especially good in sauces and stuffings for game. Use juniper as well in basting liquors for duck, lamb, or goose. A tiny dash will improve the flavor of any veal dish. The aromatic flavor of the juniper berry is very strong, so use it sparingly.

JUNKET. A dessert made of curds. Also, a drink made of cream, rennet, spice, and spirits. Junket pudding is usually made by the addition of commercial rennet powder to milk.

JUS. Plain pan gravy without thickening. *Au jus*, a French term, means served with natural gravy from a roast, a fowl, etc.

K

KAFFEE KLATSCH. (German; kah-fay-klahtch; literally, coffee gossip). Ladies' afternoon coffee party; or, any informal social gathering at which coffee is served—usually with cakes. Comparable to After-noon Tea, *which see.*

KAJMAR CHEESE. A Serbian cheese similar to cream cheese. The flavor varies greatly with age.

KALE. A variety of cabbage, also known as borecole, the leaves of which are finely toothed and curled, and which does not form a head. The leaves are used as greens, in the same manner as spinach. Kale is in the market during the winter months, and is usually cheaper than cabbage.

Using a medium-sized kettle, allow the ham bone to simmer in the boiling water

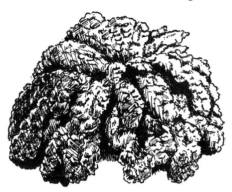

KALE

FOOD VALUE

Water	Food Energy	Pro-tein	Fat	Carbo-hydrates	Cal-cium	Phos-phorus	Iron	Vit. A Value	Thia-mine	Ribo-flavin	Nia-cin	Ascor-bic Acid
86.6	50	3.9	.6	7.2	225	62	2.2	7540	.12	.35	.8	115

Good quality kale is dark bluish green in color. A brownish color is caused by cold weather during the growing season, and while such kale is not attractive in appearance, the flavor is not changed, and it is perfectly wholesome. Avoid plants with wilted and yellowed leaves, unless there are so few of these that they can be trimmed off without being wasteful.

Kale is cooked by stripping the leaves from the tough mid-ribs. It should be cooked only until tender. Overcooking de-stroys the flavor. Kale may be prepared in a number of ways, plain boiled with salt and pepper, creamed, or cooked with salt pork or bacon as are turnip tops and mus-tard greens.

SOUTHERN KALE

3 cups boiling water
1 ham bone
1½ lb fresh kale, stripped
1 large bay leaf
6 sprigs fresh parsley
2 or 3 whole cloves
1 medium-sized onion, grated
Salt and pepper

for an hour. (If necessary, such a bone may be purchased for a few cents.) Cut the stems from the kale, discarding any imper-fect leaves. Wash thoroughly in lukewarm water to remove any sand, using several changes of water. Do not soak the kale for any length of time. Strip the leafy portions from the tough mid-ribs and discard the latter. Break the large leaves into pieces the same size as the small leaves, us.ng the small leaves and mid-ribs as they are. Re-move the ham bone; add the prepared kale, and the remaining ingredients. Cover and boil gently until tender, or about 25 minutes. Serve both kale and liquid in a rather deep vegetable dish. The liquid is considered good with cornbread, which is usually served with this dish. (Serves 6)

BUTTERED KALE

1½ lb kale
3 cups boiling salted water
3 tbsp butter or margarine
Salt and pepper
Nutmeg

Cut off the roots, and pick over the leaves of the kale. Wash thoroughly, then cook, covered, in the boiling salted water for 25 minutes, or until tender. Drain and chop as you would spinach. Add the butter or substitute and season to taste with salt, pepper, and a little nutmeg. (Serves 6)

KANTEN. A form in which agar agar (*which see*) is sold. The product is obtainable in either "bar kanten" or "slender kanten."

KARAB CHEESE. Another name for the Russian cheese, *Eriwani*, made from sheep's milk.

KARUT CHEESE. A very dry, hard, skim milk cheese of India.

KASACH CHEESE. Another name for Eriwani, which is made from sheep's milk. It is made in the Caucasus. Different local names are given to this product, such as, Karab, Tali, Kurini, and Elisavetpolem.

KASCAVAL CHEESE. A loaf-shaped rennet cheese made from sheep's milk, with goat's milk sometimes added. It weighs from 4 to 6 pounds. It is produced in Bulgaria, Rumania, and Transylvania. Considerable quantities of the cheese are exported.

KATI. (caa-tee) A Malayan weight used in weighing tea. It equals 1.43 pounds avoirdupois. *See also* CADDY, and CATTY.

KATSCHAWALJ CHEESE. A cream cheese made of sheep's milk in Serbia. It comes in various shapes and weighs about siz pounds.

KAVA. A native Polynesian intoxicating drink. *See* AVA.

KEBAB. A term used in Turkish cuisine, meaning "skewered." It is spelled in many different ways, *kabab, kaboub, kibbab saniah*, etc., according to the locality. *Kibbab saniah* is the Turkish and Syrian national dish. *Saniah* means "tray" in Arabic,

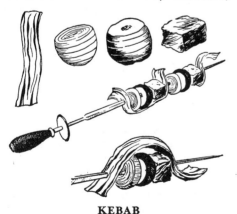

KEBAB

but we translate it as baking pan. In the United States it is also spelled *cabob*.

Grease the pan with olive oil and spread on it a thin layer of crushed wheat thoroughly washed in salt water. Add a layer of stuffing—chopped lamb and onions which have been sautéed in butter—another layer of wheat, another of stuffing, and so on to the top of the pan. The top layer is wheat. Over this scatter a handful of pignolia nuts. Bake the kebab to a flaky brown in a moderate oven, 350°–375° F., for 40 minutes. Eat with skewered lamb, or kebab.

Sheesh bakbab is another Near East dish, similar to our skewered kidney and mushrooms. Cut lean lamb in slices two inches thick and skewer with green and sweet peppers, whole mushrooms, quarters of tomato and quarters of onion, all salted, peppered, and broil.

KEDGEREE. Also spelled kidgeree or kedgery. A fish dish of East Indian origin, the selected fish giving its name to the dish. The original recipe consisted of fish sautéed in butter over a very low fire and served on a base of highly spiced boiled rice. The fish was covered with a rich velouté, or rich cream sauce seasoned with curry powder. Usually another dish of plain boiled rice was served with it.

The American version of this extremely popular fish dish is as follows:

KEDGEREE OF COD FISH

2 minced shallots or onions
4 tbsp butter
1 lb cooked cod
¼ cup fish broth
2 tsp finely minced parsley
1 tsp finely minced chives
3 cups cooked rice
3 hard-cooked eggs
Salt, cayenne, paprika

Sauté the shallots or onion in the butter until they begin to color. Pull the fish apart into flakes with a fork and combine it with the fish broth, parsley, and chives. Bring very slowly to boiling point. Simmer for 10 minutes, then add the rice and bring to a boil. Stir in the egg whites which have been coarsely chopped, season with salt and cayenne and make piping hot without actually boiling. Arrange in a pyramid on a hot platter and garnish with the sieved egg yolks. Dust lightly with paprika and serve very hot. Almost any leftover cooked fish, salmon, halibut, haddock, etc., may be substituted for the cod. (Serves 6)

VIRGINIA KEDGEREE

3 tbsp butter
1 thin slice of onion, finely minced
2 cups cooked rice
2 cups flaked, cooked fish
⅓ cup cream or evaporated milk
½ tsp curry powder
Salt and pepper
2 hard-cooked eggs, sliced

Heat the butter in a saucepan, add the onion and cook gently about three minutes, stirring almost constantly, but do not brown the onion. Add the rice and fish, then the cream or milk in which the curry powder has been stirred. Mix thoroughly and season with salt and pepper. Bring to the boiling point, add the eggs, and when these are hot serve at once. (Serves 4)

This is an old Colonial version of kedgeree, generally served as a breakfast dish.

KEFIR or KEPHIR MILK. A fermented milk. It is a pleasant beverage with medicinal qualities. *See* MILK.

KEG. A small, strong barrel, usually of five to ten gallon capacity.

KELLERABFULLUNG. Meaning literally "cellar bottling," this German word roughly corresponds to the French Château Bottled (*which see*), though it may not always carry the same connotations of quality.

KELLERABZUG. Found on German wine labels, this means "bottled at the cellar of," and is followed by the bottler's name. In this case the bottler is not necessarily the estate owner, as in the case of Kellerabfüllung (*which see*), but may also be the shipper or some other individual.

KENTUCKY HAM. The best hams cured in Kentucky are of fine quality and distinctive flavor. For ways of preparing and serving, *see* HAM.

KEROSENE RANGE. *See* RANGE.

KETCHUP. *See* CATSUP.

KETTLE. A large metal pot with a removable lid, used for many forms of cookery. It is provided with a bail wire handle for lifting, and may have additional small handles set on the sides. Some have small shaped lips for pouring. Though

at one time made of iron, that metal is now rarely used because of the weight factor. Aluminum, coated steel, and enamelware are commonly used. The individual metals are discussed under their own headings. *See also* KITCHEN EQUIPMENT.

KEWANE. One of the best of Japan's excellent green teas. The liquor is rich and flavorful and rather light in color.

KIDGEREE. Alternate spelling of kedgeree, *which see.*

KIDNEYS. Man seems to have known instinctively many facts about nutrition which have taken centuries to prove scientifically. For instance, it was the custom to reserve for the chief and the young warriors the liver, kidney, and heart of a freshly killed animal, which were believed to contribute to physical strength and a brave spirit.

Science has shown that these organs do play a most valuable part in nutrition. Liver has been found not only to contribute vital essentials to daily nutrition but also to be of value in the treatment of certain types of anemia. Recent reports indicate that kidneys apparently have a specific influence upon blood pressure and may also play a part in reducing weight caused by retention of water in the tissues.

Like liver, kidneys possess an ample supply of the essential vitamins, which places them in the list of those foods helping to prevent diseases caused by a dietary deficiency, prevalent among children and adults.

Kidneys, whether beef, lamb, pork, or veal, provide delicious and economical dishes. The thin, white covering tissue should be removed and is usually done by the butcher. The white centers and tubes, particularly in beef kidneys, must be cut out and the kidneys themselves soaked in cold salted water from one-half hour to three hours, depending upon the age of the animal from which they come. Lamb kidneys are ordinarily split almost through, or they may be cut in lengthwise slices. Veal kidneys are usually split. Beef kidneys may be cut into slices or into individual segments before cooking. Beef kidneys are most often stewed, and are more delicate if after the preliminary soaking they are covered with cold water, heated slowly to a point just below boiling, the water discarded, and the heating process repeated two or three times before the final cooking process.

Because of their close fiber and texture, kidneys should be cooked quickly and usually rather rare. Veal or lamb kidneys may be broiled, and often accompany a broiled chop.

BLANQUETTE OF LAMB KIDNEYS

1 doz lamb kidneys
½ tsp salt
¼ tsp white pepper
Cooking oil or butter
1 medium-sized onion, finely minced
3 tbsp butter or margarine
3 tbsp flour
1 tbsp each minced parsley and minced chives
⅛ tsp grated nutmeg
Juice ½ lemon
3 cups lamb, mutton or beef broth, canned or homemade
¼ cup heavy cream, heated
1 doz each, parboiled small onions and mushrooms

Remove skin and white centers from the kidneys and cut in thin, crosswise slices. Season with salt and pepper, then sauté with the onion in a little cooking oil or butter. As soon as the kidneys begin to lose their red, raw color, work in the butter, flour, parsley, chives, nutmeg, and lemon juice, all creamed together. Now add the heated broth, stirring constantly, and bring to simmering point. Cook gently for five minutes, then add the cream and cook two or three minutes longer. Finally put in the small onions and the mushrooms, these last sautéed in a little butter and thoroughly drained. Turn into a deep platter and surround with Roumanian corn meal dumplings. (Serves 6)

Roumanian Corn Meal Dumplings

Make 1 cup of heavy corn meal mush, using either water or milk as preferred (*see* CORN). Stir in 1 cup of grated cheese and season rather highly with salt and cayenne. Spread on a platter to cool and when cold but not yet firm, form into dumplings the size of a walnut. Chill. This may be prepared even a day in advance if desired; then, at the time of serving, fry the dumplings golden brown in butter or other preferred cooking fat.

BRANDIED SAUTEED VEAL KIDNEYS

3 veal kidneys
3 tbsp butter or margarine
1 wine glass brandy
1 wine glass sherry
6 fresh mushrooms
Cream
1 tbsp grated fresh horseradish

Wash, wipe, and cut the kidneys into slices, then brown in the butter. As soon as they have lost their red color, set them aflame with the brandy. When the flame has died out, pour over them the wine, add the mushrooms (peeled and sliced) with enough cream to barely cover. Add also the horseradish, bring to boiling point and serve at once either on toast or in heated patty shells. Garnish with parsley or water cress. (Serves 4)

BROILED KIDNEYS
(Veal or Lamb)

Remove the outer skin and split the kidneys; being young and tender they are less likely to require soaking. Allow 3 lamb kidneys or ½ to 1 veal kidney for each serving. Fasten the kidneys open with small wooden skewers, or the two halves will curl up during the cooking. Dip into a little cooking oil seasoned with salt, pepper, and paprika, then broil under a hot flame about 4 minutes on each side. Serve on hot buttered toast and place a pat of plain or maitre d'hôtel butter (*see* BUTTER SAUCE) on each of the kidneys. Garnish with broiled bacon and parsley or water cress.

KIDNEY STEW

1 beef kidney
1 tbsp minced onion
3 tbsp bacon drippings
1½ to 1¾ cups boiling water or consommé
1 large bay leaf tied with:
6 sprigs parsley
2 whole cloves
A pinch each of thyme and allspice
3 tbsp flour

Prepare, soak, and scald the kidney as directed above. After the second or third scalding, drain thoroughly and cook the kidney with the onion, in the heated bacon drippings until it begins to brown. Add the water or consommé with the herbs and spices and simmer very gently for 20 minutes. Then thicken the gravy with the flour made smooth with a little cold stock or water. Again bring to boiling point, simmer 10 minutes, and serve either on toast or in a border of mashed potatoes or boiled rice or noodles. (Serves 4–6)

PORK KIDNEYS PILAU

6 pork kidneys
Stock or canned bouillon
1 tbsp minced onion
2 tbsp butter
3 cups boiled rice
¾ cup curry sauce

Wipe and slice the kidneys, then cover with the stock or bouillon and simmer until tender. Meanwhile sauté the onion in the butter, then combine with the boiled rice. Arrange this on a hot platter. Lift the cooked kidneys from their stock, arrange on the rice and pour the curry sauce (*which see*) over all. (Serves 4–6)

KILKIE. Another name for sprat, *which see.*

KILL-DEVIL. The earliest form of rum, *which see.*

KING, A LA. A method of preparing poultry, using milk, eggs, mushrooms, seasoning, etc. For detailed recipe, see CHICKEN A LA KING.

KING CRAB. The various methods of preparing the common crab may be adapted to these giant crabs. *See* CRAB.

KING PIRATE. A name given to pike, *which see.*

KINGFISH. A member of the mackerel family, the kingfish is larger than the mackerel itself and is not oily. It is one of the most highly esteemed food fishes in northern markets on the Atlantic seaboard. The kingfish appears early in the spring, along with the weakfish which it frequently accompanies up the rivers to fresh water. A giant kingfish, called King Cero, is also delicious to eat and is found in the warmer parts of the Atlantic.

Kingfish run in schools and seem to prefer a hard, sandy bottom, the edge of channels, and the edges of sandbars. They gather about oyster beds and may be seen fighting among themselves for the small crustaceans dislodged in taking the oysters.

The various ways of preparing shad, herring, mackerel, and the like may be adapted to this excellent fish.

KINGFISH

KIN-PAN. Another name for kumquat, *which see.*

KIPPERED HERRING. Herring which has been preserved by salting and smoking. *See* HERRING.

KIRSCHWASSER. Among the best known of all liqueurs is the famous Kirschwasser of the Black Forest in Germany. A potent after-dinner cordial, it tastes of cherries and plums. *See also* LIQUEUR.

KISSES. Miniature meringues, classed among the cookies, and very popular and easily made at home. *See also* MERINGUE.

COCONUT KISSES

4 egg whites
½ tsp salt
1¼ cups powdered sugar
2 cups shredded coconut
Grated rind of half an orange or one lemon

Beat the egg whites until very stiff, gradually adding the salt and sugar while beating. Fold in the coconut and orange or lemon rind. Drop from the tip of a teaspoon onto cookie sheets lined with heavy ungreased paper. Bake in a slow oven (325° F.) 20 minutes or until delicately browned. Slip the paper onto a damp table or board, let stand a minute to steam, then loosen with a spatula and remove the kisses to a cooling rack. When cold, store in an airtight container. (Makes 3–4 dozen)

CREOLE KISSES

3 egg whites
½ cup granulated sugar
¾ cup brown sugar, firmly packed
1 tsp vanilla
1 tsp vinegar
½ cup chopped nuts

Beat whites until stiff but not dry. Add sugars gradually, beating constantly. Add vanilla and vinegar and beat thoroughly. Fold in nuts. Drop by teaspoonfuls onto baking sheets covered with smooth unglazed paper, about 1 inch apart. Bake in a very slow oven (250° F.) 20 minutes. Cool on cake racks. Put two kisses together with Maple Butter Cream, laying the two flat bottoms together. Makes about 2 dozen kisses.

Maple Butter Cream

1 tbsp butter
1 tbsp shortening
⅓ cup XXXX sugar, firmly packed
¼ tsp maple extract

Cream butter and shortening. Blend in sugar thoroughly, then flavoring.

MERINGUE KISSES

3 egg whites
1 cup granulated sugar, sifted
1 tsp vinegar
1 tsp vanilla

Start beating egg whites slowly, then increase speed and beat until stiff but not dry. Add sugar gradually, beating constantly. Add vinegar and vanilla, beat well. Drop from teaspoon onto baking sheets covered with smooth unglazed paper about 1 inch apart. Bake in a very slow oven (250° F.) for 20 minutes. (Makes 2 dozen) *Date Nut Kisses.* Make meringue kisses according to directions but fold in 1 cup finely cut dates and 1 cup chopped pecans before dropping on baking sheets. Then proceed as above.

Meringue Glacé. Shape mixture in large mounds. When baked, scoop out centers with spoon and place in oven to dry. Just before serving, fill shells with ice cream, crushed fruit or cream filling.

KISSINGEN WATER. A sparkling, salty, slightly astringent, natural mineral water from a spring in Bavaria. It has decided medicinal properties. *See also* ALKALINE AND MINERAL WATERS.

KITCHEN. Judged by any standards, the room in which the housewife spends a large portion of her working day preparing the family food is important enough to warrant special consideration.

In any early or pioneer culture, the typical house is usually a one-room affair. There are many reasons for this, and, naturally, all of the family activities are carried on in that one room. As soon as circumstances permit or the culture advances, the house expands, and separate rooms are built for specific activities. The kitchen, because of its heat and odors, is usually put in the rear or otherwise isolated from the main body of the house.

This arrangement is no longer necessary, nor is it very practical. Modern insulation and equipment design have done much to remove the objections of heat and odor that made an outcast of the kitchen. Comparatively few homes today can afford servants, and the modern housewife does not wish to be isolated from family activities.

The current trend in modern architecture is to unify the house; to break down the walls and divide it into areas rather than rooms, making the areas highly flexible and engineered to the household duties, but still a part of the whole. The kitchen area is divided from the living and playing area by only low walls, or even a trellis. The housewife is no longer shut off while cooking dinner; she can keep a watchful eye on her children, and even converse with her husband or guests.

As yet, few houses have been built on this principle. The majority of houses, even those of recent construction, cling to the traditional concept, though attempts are made to place the kitchen as close to the dining room as possible. It is quite possible that the modernistic concept of kitchen design may not be acceptable to many, even though it has much to offer in the way of convenience.

The kitchen, however, should never be permitted to become the step-child of architecture. No matter what style is followed in a house, the kitchen should be carefully planned to give the utmost in efficient working conditions and pleasant surroundings. Existing houses, especially the older ones, often have poorly thought-out kitchens. This may be due to the previous owner's tastes, the builder's desires to cut as many cost corners as possible, or simply because the kitchen was designed to handle equipment that has since become outmoded. Wherever possible, such kitchens should be redone. This can call for a complete remodeling with brand new equipment being installed, or can be as simple as a fresh coat of paint plus a few dime store decals stuck on cabinet doors; the individual circumstances will govern. It is, however, only good business that the housewife should be as proud and as happy in her kitchen as possible.

DECORATION

That the surroundings be pleasant is psychologically important. This fact, instinctively known by all women, has been validated by industrial psychology. Large concerns are now going to great trouble and expense to see that their factories have the proper color paint and the proper arrangement to be, in so far as possible, psychologically pleasing to the workers. There has been a trend in recent years for the kitchen to be as clean and white and grimly streamlined as the operating room of a hospital. All of this is fine from the sanitary aspect, but a colorful kitchen can be kept just as sanitary, and be much more pleasing to the housewife who must spend a good part of her day in the kitchen.

That is the whole secret of successful kitchen decoration—the user's tastes. The kitchen is, after all, the housewife's domain, and it should reflect her personality. Even if it is not possible to knock out walls and shift sinks, a few cans of paint, a few rolls of new wall paper, and possibly some painted tiles hung on the walls will work miracles. Books on interior decoration are filled with ideas for gay, colorful kitchens, and it should not be too difficult for the housewife to find some motif that both appeals to her and is practical under the circumstances, and then talk her husband into either doing it himself or calling in outside help.

PLANNING

Appearance is not the only important consideration of kitchen design; it should be efficient as well. An often cursed but highly practical development of our present culture has been the efficiency expert. Housewives may insist that they and they alone know how to manage a kitchen, but studies have shown conclusively that most old-fashioned kitchens are, in reality, woman-killers, a sort of slave-driving mechanism, instead of being built for the effortless, efficient production of food.

The chief consideration of kitchen layout is step-saving, and step-saving can be readily combined with space-saving to meet the challenge of today's cramped quarters. This does not mean that everything should be packed in as tightly as possible so that a person standing in one central point can have everything at finger's tip. That would be physically impossible, and highly impractical, could it be accomplished.

If the work of the kitchen is analyzed, it will be found to fall into three—and, in some cases, four—natural main divisions: food preparation, cooking, cleaning, and, sometimes, office work. Each of these operations will be found to center around one basic piece of kitchen equipment: the preparation starts when the food is taken from the refrigerator, cooking is done on the range, and cleaning, of course, is done in the sink. If the housewife keeps records (and they are virtually a necessity today), then she will need some sort of desk area and filing space.

If these divisions are studied, it will be seen that there is a natural flow from one to the other as the food is prepared. While there are always exceptions to any given rule, it follows that the assembly line technique, with all of its industry-proven advantages, is applicable to the kitchen. Kitchen equipment can, and should, be grouped for efficiency.

The exact layout of the equipment will, of course, depend on the circumstances. The physical structure of the kitchen is an established and often unalterable fact. Windows, doors, and walls must be accepted in their present positions, and the equipment arrangement modified to suit them. While major remodeling is a possibility, much can be done to an even hopeless looking layout, given a little thought.

Research has shown that there are six basic kitchen layouts, and almost any kitchen will fall under one of those groupings. These layouts are illustrated, together with suggested equipment arrangements. It is the relation of equipment to each other rather than the precise position of each item that is important. The positions will have to be varied to meet individual circumstances and even individual working habits, but if assembly line thinking is carried out, the amount of steps and effort saved in each working day will be astonishing.

The Preparation Center

The work of any meal begins when the housewife opens the refrigerator and starts taking out the components she will need. If she has to carry each item half way across the room to place it on a table or work-shelf, there are steps involved, many steps in the course of a day, steps that can be saved if she has a table or shelf of the proper height and width right beside the refrigerator, waiting to receive the components as they are removed and from which they need not be removed.

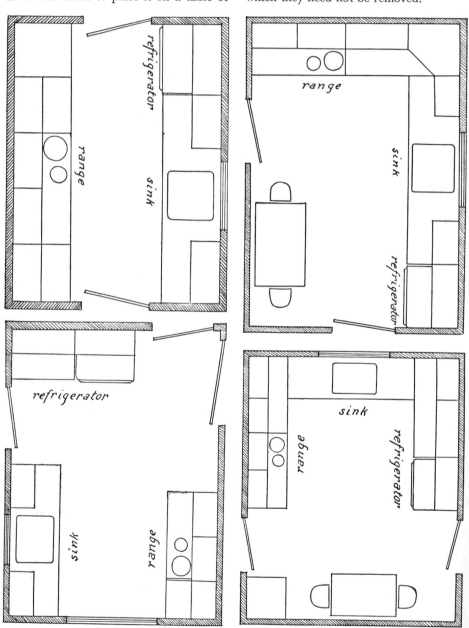

SIX BASIC KITCHEN LAYOUTS

It is only logical that she group within easy reach whatever else in the way of equipment, seasonings, and unrefrigerated foods will be needed in the work of preparation. Shelves and cupboards placed above and below the working area can hold these assorted items.

If the kitchen is large enough, the preparation center might well be broken down into further divisions suitable for specific types of food preparation. There might, for example, be a *mixing center* built around an electric mixer, which would have all of the batter ingredients, etc., within convenient reach, while further on, next to the sink, would be a *vegetable center*. Here, again, would be grouped the needed equipment, and there might well be a pull-out or drop-leaf shelf and a chair. Failing this there should be a stool so that the housewife may sit while she performs the sometimes tedious operations of peeling, husking, hulling, etc.

THE COOKING CENTER

When the food is ready, it naturally goes to the range to be cooked. Further equipment is needed, which should be convenient to the range. There should be some sort of working area here, as well, for the range top alone often does not suffice. Auxiliary cooking equipment, such as electric coffee makers, toasters, casseroles, etc., might well be grouped here, though they are sometimes used on the table.

The cooking center should be convenient to the dining room or wherever the food will be eaten. If there is room, it is con-

venient to have a *serving center* next to the cooking center. Here will be grouped the various serving dishes, utensils, etc., that are needed when the food is removed from the cooking vessels. The dishes may even be stored here. If there is no room, it is common practice to store the serving paraphernalia with the dishes.

THE CLEANING CENTER

Dirty dishes are the aftermath of any meal, and these are brought back to the sink. If there is an automatic dishwasher, that, too, is customarily located at the sink to be convenient to the plumbing. All equipment needed for washing and garbage disposal is grouped here. The cleaning center should be convenient to the preparation center, for many of the preparatory steps require water and washing as well as a means of refuse disposal. The preparation center produces its quota of dirty utensils, as does the cooking center. Household cleaning supplies other than those directly needed for dishes and utensils are conveniently grouped at the cleaning center.

THE BUSINESS CENTER

The housewife who regarded the budget as some nonsense or other invented by her

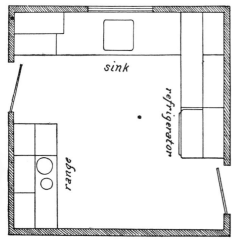

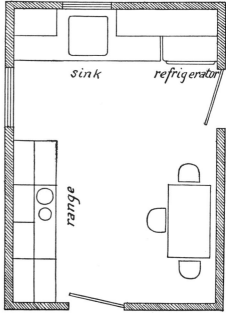

husband for no logical reason other than to annoy her is fast becoming a thing of the past, if, indeed, she ever did commonly exist outside of works of fiction. Food shortages and the general rise in prices have combined to make the average housewife a shrewd, hard businesswoman.

Even without wartime rationing, there is still plenty of paper work involved in running a well-organized kitchen. Records of bills due or paid, of food expenses, clippings of sale prices, recipes, menus, diets, instruction booklets that came with equipment, similar records and notes for all other phases of housework—the average housewife of today must take care of all of these. There is an amazing amount of paperwork involved in housework, and the housewife does well to keep it carefully organized at one central point. Because so much of it is directly concerned with food, because she will want to refer to recipes and cookbooks while she is preparing the meal, and because if it is convenient to the range she can get some of her bookkeeping done while waiting for the cake to brown, her "office" should be located in the kitchen, space permitting.

STORAGE SPACE

It can be readily seen that a major key to efficient kitchen operation is well-planned, adequate storage space. Closets, cupboards, and shelves—there can never be enough of them. Granted that every kitchen has spatial limitations, efficient design can do wonders in stretching what room there is available. Books and magazines dealing with interior decoration should be studied for ideas that will fit individual needs. The specific design of storage space is a problem that must be worked out by the individual.

There is, however, one valuable general rule as to the amount of overhead storage space that will be required. It is based on the number of people in the house, though it is safer to count the maximum possible number of beds, since that will tell you the greatest number of people that will ever live in the house. Add one to this total and multiply the figure by six square feet. To this answer add six square feet for entertainment accessories and six more square feet for accumulation. The total is the number of square feet of storage space *above counter level* needed for that house. As many

closets as possible should be built under the counters, but these are not figured in the above formula.

WORKING HEIGHT

The height of the various working surfaces is another important factor in kitchen planning. There is no point in forcing the housewife to stand at a task when she might just as well sit, and working at inconvenient heights is very tiring. The best height of the different working surfaces is an individual problem, for they must each be fitted to the user. There should also be a stool or chair available, as well as a small kitchen step-ladder which can be used to reach the top shelves.

LIGHTING

The science of proper lighting has come to be more fully understood in recent years, and fixtures have been designed that are in keeping with this increased knowledge. A single large fixture set in the middle of the ceiling does not constitute proper lighting, for the housewife will cast shadows on her work. There should be individual fixtures of proper design placed where needed to supplement, if not supplant, the overhead light. The lighting should be even, glareless, shadowless, and adequate. No one can do good work while suffering from eyestrain.

KITCHEN BOUQUET. A commercial flavoring for soups, stews, gravies, etc.

KITCHEN EQUIPMENT. While there are tools to every trade, it would be difficult to discover a profession that has a more abundant or varied array of implements at its disposal than cookery. A quick trip through the kitchen equipment section of any store will convince anyone not already acquainted with the subject that here, at the very least, there is variety and quantity.

However, not every new household has the funds to set up a kitchen complete with every implement on the market. New cooks, especially, must be selective in their purchases, buying only essentials at first and working up to a larger collection as need demands.

BASIC COOKING EQUIPMENT

To start with, only very few utensils, depending on the size of the family, are required. Two lidded saucepans, a 6-quart lidded pot, a medium size lidded frying pan, a shallow uncovered roasting pan with a rack, if possible, a sharp knife, a serrated-edge knife, a 2 cup liquid measure and several wooden mixing spoons will suffice to begin your cooking adventure. Add, as you wish, a colander, cutting board and grater.

If you have no cutting board, use an old plate or make one by sanding until smooth a block of wood. Season the wood by rubbing it with salad oil. Noodles can be strained with the aid of a pot cover or plate which is placed over the top of the pot as it is inverted. You don't need a board to roll out pastry either. Use a floured piece of canvas or muslin. Or sprinkle water on the counter top. A sheet of wax paper placed on the water will hold the paper securely in place while you roll the dough.

Aluminum foil can double as a pot cover if you have none. Or try covering a piece of cardboard with foil to use as a cover. Two knives can suffice for cutting in shortening when there is no pastry blender. If you misplace your measuring cup, almost any likely looking glass will suffice to give you proportions (except in baking). Or measure the amount the glass holds by using it to fill an empty milk container with water. If four glasses fill the container, the glass holds exactly a cup. A knife can be used to scrape or peel vegetables.

In a pinch, vegetables can be boiled in a frying pan, bacon can be cooked on top of the stove in a roasting pan. Spaghetti can be broken to fit into a smaller pot for cooking. A strainer can be used in place of a sifter. A potato peeler can often serve as a grater. A fork can be used to mash potatoes. A casserole can be cooked in a shallow roasting pan (more crust for everybody). Scout around the kitchen to find a utensil that will be up to the occasion. Or borrow expensive items that are infrequently used.

MATERIALS

Virtually every material known to man has been and is being used in the construction of kitchen equipment. It is interesting to note that while the newer materials have shouldered the older ones out of the prominent positions, few, if any, of the materials have been completely struck off the list.

The first pots were made of clay, and clay is still with us in many different forms. See CERAMICS. The first spoons were whittled from wood, and wood is still to be found in the kitchen. See WOODENWARE. About the only major casualty is stone. Flint knives are definitely passé, but even stone still survives in many homes as a knife sharpener (see CUTLERY).

So it goes with all of the materials. Iron pots, once so common, are now chiefly museum pieces, but the iron skillet can still be bought, and coated iron is widely used. See IRONWARE and ENAMELWARE.

Today, however, aluminum, glass, and plastics are the rising stars on the horizon. Cost, weight, and utility are the chief factors in their favor. These materials have made possible many new cooking techniques.

Each of the materials has advantages and disadvantages. There are some applications in which they excel, others in which they do merely a capable job, and some uses in which they just do not belong. They are all individuals and must be regarded as such. Like individuals they have their own talents and peculiarities, must be cared for in individual ways, and never should be pushed beyond their individual capacities.

Because these different materials may often be used interchangeably, the housewife may well be confused as to which is superior. It is important that she realize that there is no generally superior material. A given material will be superior in one given task, but inferior in another. The fact that a utensil made of one material may do an outstanding job does not mean that every utensil in the kitchen should be made of the same material. Conversely, if a material fails in one job, the housewife should not rule it out of her thinking and refuse to buy anything made of that substance thereafter.

Realization of this fact will save the housewife much time, money, and temper when it comes to purchasing and using kitchen equipment. She should have some idea of the capacities and characteristics of each specific material. Most of the materials commonly used in kitchen equipment are discussed under their own headings throughout the book. Experience is, perhaps, the best teacher in this respect, since the housewife's needs and working habits are such an individual proposition.

When purchasing any item of equipment then, the question to be asked is not, "Of what material is it made?", but rather, "How will the material of which this item is made stand up under the use which the item will be given?" The implement made of the materials that best fit the individual circumstances of intended use and budget limitations, then, is the one to be selected.

CONSTRUCTION AND DESIGN

Even as the materials should be considered in the light of their intended use, so should the construction and design of kitchen equipment be judged. For example, a pan thin enough for quick baking would be poorly suited for use as a griddle, while a glass thick enough to be used for mixing purposes would not make the best drinking vessel.

Since so much depends on the use which a given utensil will receive in a given home, it is difficult to establish overall rules for specific items. There are, however, some general principles that apply.

Shape. Unless specific use requires otherwise, all cooking vessels should have flat bottoms. This gives a sturdy support, and, for surface cooking, a more economical utilization of the heat.

The sides should be vertical and not tapered for the best surface cooking. However, it is preferable that the sides meet the bottom in a round curve rather than a right angle for more efficient stirring and better cleaning.

Size. The size of the vessels should be governed by two factors: family needs and the cooking unit. Broilers and pans must fit into the oven, and surface cooking utensils should be large enough to cover the burner, but not so large as to block off other burners or to project over onto the enameled surfaces of the range.

Finish. A smooth surface is always easier to clean than a rough one. Materials that need the protection should have a rust, stain, or corrosion-resisting coating. Some surface cooking vessels have copper-plated bottoms for more even heating. It must be remembered that a shiny surface will reflect radiant heat, while a dull or dark one will absorb heat. Dark or dull pans are better for many kinds of baking. Vessels used on an electric range should never have shiny, heat-reflecting bottoms.

The development of new non-stick plastic surfaces for nearly every kitchen utensil from baking tins to sauce pans is an advance of major consideration for homemakers. Utensils with non-stick surfaces cut clean up time and drudgery in half. In addition, individuals on restricted diets are provided with a range of utensils which they may employ for cooking greaseless meals. Clean them with soapy water and a sponge. Never use a scouring pad.

Weight. The material must be thick enough to be durable in its intended use. The weight factor, then, varies with the material and use. The vessel should never be too heavy to conveniently lift when full, and if it is, one made of a lighter material should be chosen.

Lids and Covers. There should be some convenient means of removing covers from hot pans. Wooden or plastic knobs are best for this use because of their insulating properties, but lids thus equipped are difficult to store flat. Hinged metal rings that lie flat when not in use are common, but these cannot be handled with the bare fingers when hot.

A dome-shaped lid will increase the capacity of the vessel as well as condensing the steam formed in cooking, but these are somewhat bulky to store.

Regardless of type, the lid should fit snugly if it is to be of value. If the lids are purchased separately, they should be of the proper size and shape to engage the rim of the vessel.

Rims. Most vessels have some sort of rolled rim both to protect the edge and to give it strength, enabling the vessel to hold its shape. Since the lid must engage the rim, there are many types of bevels and grooves used. These should match the lid. The rim, regardless of type, should be smooth to the fingers, not sharp, and be easy to clean.

Lips. Vessels used to hold liquids should have some sort of lip or spout for pouring purposes, while these are not required in utensils used for waterless cookery. A lip is more economical to manufacture than a spout, but rarely can a lipped vessel be fitted with a tight lid. The lip should be shaped for easy pouring; the more pronounced, the better. Double-lipped pans are quite convenient, for they may be poured by either hand.

Spouts. Spouts are more expensive to make than lips, being an added piece of material. They should be firmly attached, easily cleaned, and of a good pouring shape. Long, elaborate spouts should be avoided, especially on ceramic vessels.

Handles. Any handle should fit the hand with comfort. Metal handles often have sharp, cutting edges. While these may not be objectionable when the utensil is empty, they can be most uncomfortable when the vessel is full. The better handles have some type of insulation against the heat of cooking, so they may be touched by the bare hand. Plastics, hard rubber, and wood are often used for this reason. Under rough usage, however, these handles have a tendency to chip or break, and, in time, the paint will flake off a wooden handle. These materials are commonly placed over a metal core to give added strength. They should not be so low on the utensil as to be in danger of exposure to an open flame, and they should cover enough metal that there will be little possibility of the hand being accidently burned if the handle is not grasped in precisely the correct manner. While some composition handles are molded on their metal core, a screw arrangement is commonly used to attach the insulation. This device should be secure so there will be no danger of the handle coming loose and twisting in the hand when the utensil is lifted.

Composition and wooden handles must be removable if the utensil is to be used in the oven. Glass utensils for surface cooking also frequently have removable handles. Handles of this sort should be so designed that they may be easily replaced, even when the utensil is too hot to handle.

It is important that the handle, regardless of type, be properly balanced. This means that the vessel should stand by itself when empty, and not be tipped over by the weight of the handle. It is convenient for the handles to be fitted with holes, hooks, or screw eyes so the utensil may be hung up for storage.

SELECTION AND ARRANGEMENT

As has been said, there is a wide variety of kitchen equipment available today. Under conditions of normal production, these items are made in enough different materials so that, except for the more elaborate and expensive items, there is a wide range available to every budget. The equipment selected should be the best that the budget will allow, for it is false economy to purchase a poorly made, quickly damaged item. It is, however, possible to find inexpensive items, especially of enamelware, that will give reasonable service provided they are given proper care.

The type and number of items selected will be governed by individual circumstances. The size of the family, the type of permanent kitchen equipment available, the size of the kitchen, and the typical family menu must be considered as well as the budget.

It should be remembered that with a variety of equipment, it is possible to bring variety into the menu. Through equipment, it is also often possible to utilize leftovers or more inexpensive foods that would not be used unless they were prepared in an attractive manner.

The following lists are by no means intended to be complete and final; such would be impossible. They are, rather, mere guides. While there are some items that are basic and will be found in every kitchen, few cooks, either professional or household, will agree on what is essential and what is not.

There is a happy medium that each person must find. It is possible to get along with surprisingly little equipment, but there is little point to doing this unless there is need. On the other hand, it is very easy to acquire much that is either rarely used or is properly a gadget and not a utensil. These do no harm but do clutter up the kitchen.

Regardless of the personal preferences in equipment, the equipment should be grouped for efficiency. It has been established that an impressive amount of labor can be saved in the kitchen if only the equipment is properly arranged. *See* KITCHEN.

Following is a suggested arrangement of equipment. While the arrangement must be modified to fit individual cases and working habits, it will serve to indicate the type of efficient grouping that can help to leave the housewife fresh and vigorous at the end of a day's work.

PREPARATION CENTER

Beaters:
　Rotary
　Flat
Cutters:
　Biscuit

Cookie
Doughnut
Bread Board
Bread Box
Cake Box or Cover
Cake Coolers, Wire—4
Cake Decorator
Cake Pans:
  Tube—1
  Loaf—4
  8x8 inches square—2
  5x10 inches Oblong—1
  8 or 9 inch Layer—4
Cake Turner or Broad Spatula
Casseroles:
  Oven—2
  Individual—6
Chopper, Food
Chopping Board or Bowl
Cookie Jar
Cookie Sheets, 14x10 inches—2
Corn Stick Pan
Cups:
  Measuring—1 set
  Mary Ann—1 set
  Custard—6 or 8
Egg Slicer
Fruit Juice Extractor
Graters
Grinder, Meat
Knife Sharpener
Knives
Mixing Bowl—1 nest of 5
Mixing Glass
Muffin Pans
Nut Cracker and Pick
Pan with Trivet
Pastry Blender
Pastry Brush
Pie Plate:
  Large—2
  Individual—6
Poultry Needle
Refrigerator
Rolling Pin
Salad Molds
Shears, Kitchen
Sieve:
  Large—1
  Small—1
Sifter, Flour
Skewers—6 or 8
Spoons:
  Measuring—1 set
  Stirring—3 (1 wooden)
  Slotted—1
  Teaspoons
  Tablespoons

Storage Jars—1 set
Toothpicks
Twine on cutter
Supplemental: Blender
  Electrical Fruit Juice Extrac-
    tor
  Electric Mixer
  Frozen Food Chest
  Ice Cream Freezer

COOKING CENTER

Broiler
Chicken Fryer or Dutch Oven
Coffee Maker
Cutting Board
Deep Fat Fryer
Double Boiler, 1½ and 2 qts.
Egg Poacher
Forks, long and short
Griddle
Kettle, 6 to 10 qts.
Knives
Ladle, Slotted, or Wooden
Lids for Saucepans and Kettles
Lifter for Hot Pans and Vegetables
Potato Masher
Pot Holders
Range
Ricer
Roasting Pan
Saucepans:
  2 Lipped—pt. and qt.
  3 Covered—2, 3 and 4 qts.
Skillets:
  Double
  Small
Spatula, Large or Perforated Turner
Spoons:
  Measuring—1 set
  Large Bowl
  Slotted
  Tablespoons
  Teaspoons
Tea Kettle
Teapot
Thermometers:
  Candy
  Frying
  Oven
Toaster
Tray
Supplemental: Electric Casserole
  Pressure Cooker
  Serving Trays, 2
  Sizzling Steak Platter
  Timer
  Waffle Iron

CLEANING CENTER

Ammonia
Bottle Opener
Bowl Covers
Brushes:
  Bottle
  Household
  Vegetable
Can Opener
Cleansing Powder
Colander
Corkscrew
Corer, Apple
Cutting Board
Disinfectant
Dish Cloth
Dish Draining Rack
Dish Pan
Dish Towel
Drain Cleaner
Funnel
Garbage Pail
Ice Crusher
Jar Opener
Knives:
  Floating Blade Vegetable
  French Cook
  Paring—2
  Utility
Paper Bags
Paper Towels and Holder
Scraper
Soap
Steel Wool
Stool or Stepladder
Strainers:
  Large—1
  Sink—1
  Tea
Towel Rack
Trash Basket
Washing Soda
Waxed Paper
Supplemental: Dishwasher
  Garbage Disposal Unit
  Ventilator with Fan

BUSINESS CENTER

Blotters
Cook Books
File for Bills and Statements
Filing Box for menus
Hammer, Small
Pen and Ink
Pencils
Pencil Sharpener

Pliers
Ruler
Scissors
Scotch Tape
Screw Driver
Stationery and Memo Pads
String
Supplemental: Blackboard or Bulletin Board
  with Chalk or Thumbtacks.
  Clock
  Desk with Chair
  Stapler
  Telephone

KJARGAARD CHEESE. A hard, rennet cheese, made from the skim milk of cows It is a product of Denmark.

KLENCZ CHEESE. A rennet cheese made from sheep's milk, sometimes combined with goat's milk, and known also as Brinsen cheese.

KLOSTER CHEESE. A soft-ripened, rennet cheese made from the whole milk of cows. It has an unusual shape, being 1 inch by 1 inch by 4 inches, and weighs less than a quarter of a pound. It is made in France.

KNAOST CHEESE. A sour milk, rennet cheese made in Norway and called also pultost cheese.

KNEADING. Working a dough or paste, etc., with the hands or with an automatic mixer. The object is to blend the ingredients into a smooth elastic mass. *See* BREAD.

KNIFE. There are two general types encountered in cookery. Those with keen edges intended for carving, paring, and similar uses are usually spoken of as cutlery (*which see*), while the somewhat duller variety used by the individual diner are commonly called table knives (*see* FLATWARE).

KNIFE CASE. A knife case is commonly a box or other device that completely encloses a knife or matched set of cutlery (*which see*). While the knife rack (*which see*) merely holds the knives, the case offers protection against dust, atmosphere, etc., as well as being decorative in itself They are frequently lined with some sort of tarnish preventing cloth (*see* SILVERWARE) to keep the blades shiny and bright, especially if the handles are either plate or sterling. Because of their expense, cases are commonly used only for carving sets, though, in an earlier day, they were greatly used by travelers to carry their personal table gear.

A more modern type of case is being made for carving knives that have wooden handles. It is actually a wooden sheath, made of the same kind of wood as the knife handle, that holds only the blade. Cases of this sort may be set out on the table as part of the setting. Some of these cases contain built-in sharpeners that work as the blade is inserted or withdrawn from the case. There is, however, some possibility of wearing out the blade through excessive sharpening; depending, of course, on the construction of the sharpener.

KNIFE RACK. A knife rack is a device used to store knives of the cutlery (*which see*) class when they are not in use. It is a valuable kitchen accessory, for not only does it keep the knives from becoming lost in the depths of a jumbled drawer, but it protects both the edge of the knives and the fingers that might otherwise be cut while groping for the handle in a crowded drawer.

Though there are many variations in design, it is essentially a slotted board through which the knives are thrust, blade downwards, being supported by their handles which are too big to pass through the slots. The rack should be hung on the wall in a convenient place, but well out of the reach of children. It might be advisable to have several racks so that knives may be grouped at their proper working position. *See* KITCHEN. *See also* KNIFE CASE and KITCHEN EQUIPMENT.

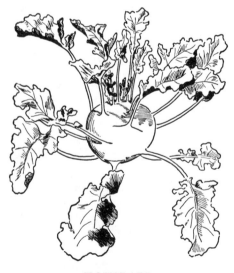

KOHLRABI

KNIFE SHARPENER. *See* CUTLERY.

KNUCKLE. The ankle-joint of pork, veal, etc. used in cookery. Knuckles, whether of pork or veal, make economical, nourishing, and delicious dishes. Pigs' knuckles are generally served with sauerkraut.

KOHLRABI, or Turnip Cabbage. A member of the cabbage family which is grown for the swollen stem which resembles white turnips in flavor, but is more delicate. While it has long been known and appreciated in Europe, it is only recently that American housewives have known and appreciated it.

The young, small globes, not over three inches in diameter, are the best and have the most delicate flavor. The young leaves of kohlrabi may be cooked like spinach. The globes are best steamed without peeling, but if the vegetable is not as young and fresh as it might be, it should be peeled before cooking. This is most easily done by inserting a knife under the tough fiber at the base of the globe and stripping off the skin. Cut into quarters or slices and boil in very little salted water.

Kohlrabi is delicious steamed until tender, peeled, and cut into julienne strips. Marinate the strips in French dressing while they are still warm and allow to cool in the marinade. Chill and serve as a salad with cold meat.

A simple and very good vegetable is made by cooking peeled, sliced kohlrabi in boiling salted water or bouillon until it is tender. Drain thoroughly and season with minced parsley, chives, a little lemon juice, and melted butter.

KOHLRABI IN SOUR CREAM

4 bunches young kohlrabi, peeled
1½ qt boiling salted water
2 tbsp butter
2 tsp grated onion
1½ tsp flour
¼ tsp salt
A dash of pepper
½ cup thick sour cream, scalded

Cook the kohlrabi in the boiling salted water until tender; drain thoroughly. Heat the butter, add the onion and cook for a moment over a low fire. Stir in the flour, salt and pepper, then the scalded cream. Cook until thickened, stirring constantly.

Pour over the drained kohlrabi and sprinkle with minced parsley or dust with paprika. (Serves 6)

Kohlrabi au Gratin. Follow recipe for kohlrabi in sour cream, then turn into a baking dish and top with buttered crumbs, plain or blended with an equal quantity of grated cheese. Bake in a moderately hot oven (375° F.) 10 to 15 minutes.

KOLA NUT. *See* COLA NUT.

KOLACHKY BREAD. The recipe for this delicious bread, more bun than bread, varies in the many homes in which it is made, for some like a sweet dough, while others prefer the bread unsweetened. Each Czechoslovakian or Bohemian family, whether at home or in the United States, has its own pet recipe, handed down through generations. After the dough is prepared, it is shaped into the *Kolachky,* a standard shape. For fluffy Kolachky, the dough should be a little soft.

KOLACHKY

1 yeast cake
¼ cup lukewarm water
2 cups lukewarm milk
6 cups, or more, sifted flour
½ cup butter
¾ cup sugar
1 tsp salt
2 large eggs, unbeaten

Soften the yeast in the lukewarm water, then add to the milk which has been scalded and cooled to lukewarm. Work in three cups of the flour and beat briskly until smooth. Cream the butter, gradually adding the sugar and salt, and when light and fluffy beat into the first mixture, blending very thoroughly until free from lumps. Now add the eggs, one at a time, beating after each addition, together with the remaining flour, or as much of it as is needed to make a light dough which can be kneaded. This added flour should be worked in spoonful by spoonful. Turn onto a floured board and knead until the dough is elastic and glossy but neither hard nor stiff, adding a little more flour if necessary. Place in a greased bowl, cover, and let rise in a warm place to double in bulk—about 2½ hours. Again turn out onto a slightly floured, warmed board, pat down lightly and roll one-fourth inch thick. Cut into 3-inch squares, place a tablespoon of any

desired filling on each, gather up the four corners and fold one over the other, square envelope fashion. (When correctly folded, the filling will peak through the four sides.) Place on greased cooking sheet about two inches apart, cover and again let rise until doubled in bulk. Bake in a moderate oven (375° F.) about 25 minutes. When cool sprinkle with powdered sugar.

KOLACHKY FILLINGS

Apple Filling. Four large apples, peeled, sliced, and cooked until tender but not mushy, with ⅓ cup of water and 3 tablespoons of red cinnamon candies.

Apricot Prune Filling. One-half pound each prunes and dried apricots, simmered until tender in water to cover, then drained and chopped together. Add sugar to taste with ½ cup of chopped nut-meats and 1 teaspoon grated orange or lemon rind.

Date and Nut Filling. Three-fourths pound of pitted dates, diced and simmered for 15 minutes in ½ cup of water with ½ teaspoon grated orange rind. When cool, beat slightly and add 1 tablespoon brown sugar and ½ cup (scant) chopped nut-meats.

Fig Nut Filling. Follow directions for date nut fillings, substituting figs for dates and flavoring with ½ teaspoon of almond extract.

Poppy Seed Filling. Cook 2 cups of ground poppy seeds with ½ cup of milk, ¼ cup of corn sirup, and 2 tablespoons of sugar, for about 5 minutes. Stir in 1 teaspoon of butter and ¼ teaspoon of powdered cinnamon.

Prune Cinnamon Filling. Simmer 1 pound of prunes until tender in water just to cover, adding two slices of lemon. Drain, remove pits and chop coarsely. Flavor with ¼ teaspoon ground cinnamon and 1 teaspoon of grated orange rind.

KOLOS-MONOSTOR CHEESE. A rectangular, rennet cheese made of sheep's milk. Its home is in Transylvania.

KOLOSVARER CHEESE. A cheese made from buffalo's milk It resembles Trappist cheese.

KOMIJNE KASS CHEESE. Another name for Leyden cheese, *which see.*

KOPPEN CHEESE. A goat's milk cheese with a sharp, pungent, slightly smoky flavor. *See also* BAUDEN CHEESE.

KOSHER. Kosher means "ceremonially clean." Beef, for example, is slaughtered according to prescribed Jewish rites. The animal is not stunned before the jugular vein is severed by a "Schochet," who does his killing painlessly. Orthodox Jews eat only the forequarters, and the meat is washed every third day until the twelfth when it is no longer used.

KOSHER CHEESE. A rennet, cow's milk cheese which is made in several countries for the Jewish trade. It resembles Limburger and is eaten fresh.

KUMBACH CHEESE. A soft-ripened, rennet cheese made from the whole or partly skimmed milk of cows. It is round in shape, six inches in diameter, three inches high, and weighs two pounds. It is a German product, made in upper Bavaria.

KUMISS. A fermented milk used as a beverage. See MILK.

KUMMEL. A popular white digestive liqueur made from a spirit flavored with caraway seeds and cumin and varying amounts of sweetening. A highly distilled spirit is used, obtained from grain or potatoes, but rarely from wine, as opposed to general liqueur practice. It is made in many countries, notably Holland, Germany and Russia, differing mainly in sweetness and never in appearance. See also LIQUEUR.

KUMMEL ECKAU. This liqueur is made in Russia. It is a white, potent cordial with an alcoholic content of 50 per cent, and sometimes used to flavor pastry, certain other beverages, and dessert dishes.

KUMQUAT. A small, citrus fruit, cultivated on a large scale in China and Japan.

KUMQUAT

It has been introduced into this country and is in season from December to the end of January. Kumquats are used in making preserves, pickles, and the like. They are also served whole as fresh fruit, sliced in salads, or candied whole. When buying this fruit, which is about the size of a large plum, choose those which are heavy for their size. The skin should be firm and unblemished. Wash carefully before using. See also ORANGE.

KUMQUAT JAM

Slice the kumquats and discard the seeds. Cook until tender in just enough water to keep from burning. Measure, then add an equal amount of sugar with a little lemon juice. Cook the mixture until thick, stirring constantly to prevent burning. Pour into hot, sterilized jars and seal. See JAM.

KUMQUAT PRESERVES

2 qt firm kumquats
1 qt boiling water
5 cups sugar

Remove stems and leaves from the kumquats. Wash and drain the fruit and prick each several times with a darning needle. Place prepared fruit in a saucepan with the boiling water, cover, and simmer over a low flame until the fruit can be pierced with a knife, shaking the saucepan frequently. Skim the fruit from the water. Stir the sugar into the water and when dissolved, boil five minutes. Add the drained fruit and cook gently for an hour, when the fruit should be clear. Transfer the fruit to a hot jar, cover with the hot sirup, using toothpicks to keep the fruit under the sirup. Let stand overnight to plump, after which drain the sirup from the fruit into a saucepan, boil until it thickens, then add the fruit and cook gently for five minutes. Turn into hot sterilized jars and seal. See also CANNING. (Makes 3 pints)

KURINI CHEESE. A Russian cheese made from sheep's milk, known also as Eriwani cheese.

KVASS. A refreshing home-brewed Russian beverage that has intoxicating properties. It is made from rye flour, malt, and mint.

L

LA BOUILLE. A French cheese made in Normandy.

LACRIMA CHRISTI. One of the most famous of Italian wines, this is made from grapes grown on the slopes of Mount Vesuvius. It is a sweet, delicate wine, highly prized by connoiseurs. It is made as both a red and a white wine, but the white or golden type is superior and produced in larger quantities.

Lagrima Cristi, Lacrymae Christi and *Lacrima Cristi* are but a few of the many different used spellings of this unusual name, but they all refer to the same wine. *See also* WINE.

LACTALBUMIN. The albumin present in milk, *which see*.

LACTIC ACID. The common agent in causing the coagulation of milk (*which see*). Lactic acid is always formed during the fermentation of milk sugar or lactose, as in the souring of milk, cheese-making, and the ripening of cream. Lactic acid is also found as a by-product in the fermentation of various sugars and other substances in the presence of protein. Lactic acid is neutralized by bicarbonate of sodium, the latter being also called baking soda (*which see*). The resulting salt is harmless.

LACTOSE. Lactose is a sugar present in some quantity in ordinary milk. It is also called sugar of milk. It forms a very important ingredient in the diet of the growing infant, who is unable to digest much starch during the first year of life, yet requires an easily assimilable form of carbohydrate. Cow's milk, as compared with human milk (*which see*) is deficient in lactose, and the latter should, therefore, be added in proper proportion to the milk of bottle-fed infants. It might be used for sweetening various articles of food, but it possesses no advantages over ordinary cane sugar, and in fact is more expensive and less sweet. It is mildly diuretic.

LADLE. A ladle is a deep-bowled spoon used to dispense liquids, and, in some cases, solids. It is distinguished from the other spoons by the shape of the bowl, and by the fact that the bowl is customarily set at a right angle to the handle, which may be straight or curved, depending on the intended function of the ladle.

Ladles are made of many materials and in many designs, depending on their use. Ladles made for table service are commonly constructed of silver or silver plate (*see also* FLATWARE) or of a ceramic material (*see also* DISHES), and are usually made to match a tureen, boat, or bowl. Ladles of appropriate design are used at the table to dispense soups, gravies, sauces, mayonnaise, punch, and even salt.

In the kitchen, where their use is strictly functional, ladles are made of plainer materials. They are usually larger and have longer handles than the tableware type, since they are used in bigger containers. In addition to their prime function of scooping up liquids, ladles are also used for stirring. Slotted ladles are used to remove solid objects from liquids. Ladles are sometimes used as cooking or warming vessels, for tasks like melting butter before it is added to a recipe. While wooden ladles cannot be used in this manner, they are best for use with enamelware, ceramic, or glass utensils because they are not apt to chip or break the material.

See also KITCHEN EQUIPMENT.

LADY FINGERS. A delicate pastry like a sponge cake, usually eaten with ice cream, or used as the foundation for more elaborate desserts. They are easily made at home.

LADY FINGERS

3 eggs, separated
¼ lb sifted, powdered sugar
½ tsp lemon juice
Pinch of salt
½ cup flour

Beat the egg yolks until light and creamy; add sugar and continue beating; add lemon juice. Add salt to egg whites and beat until very stiff. Stir flour lightly into yolks and fold in whites. Press the mixture through a pastry tube on a baking tin covered with paper, in portions ½ inch wide and 4 inches long. Sift a little powdered sugar on top of each cake. Bake from 10 to 15 minutes in moderate oven (350° F.). Do not let them brown. Remove from pan immediately; brush the flat surface of one cake with white of egg and press the underside of a second cake upon the first.

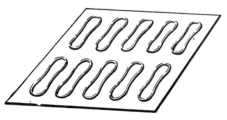

LADY FINGER PAN

LAGER BEER. *See* BEER.

LAGRIMA CRISTI. *See* LACRIMA CHRISTI.

LAGUIOLE CHEESE. A hard, rennet cheese, which · resembles Cantal and Roquefort. It derives its name from 'the village of Laguiole in the Department of Aveyron, France. The cheese is made extensively in the mountains of Aubrac, where it is said to have been made at the time of the Roman occupation.

LAKE HERRING. A fresh-water fish (*Argyrosomus artede*) also called Cisco, Greenback or Grayback depending on its color. It has a herring-shaped body and abounds in the Great Lakes where large quantities are caught and consumed. Its average weight is about one pound. Prepare it like whitefish (*which see*).

LAKE TROUT. *See* TROUT and FISH.

LAMB. In market terminology, lamb is a sheep less than twelve months old; after this age it is known as mutton. Spring lamb is very young lamb, generally born after December 31st and marketed in April of the same year. Spring lambs are entirely milk-fed and as a result their flesh is very white and delicate. Actually, although they are considered a great delicacy, spring lamb does not have a great deal of flavor and is not a particularly economic purchase. So-called genuine spring lamb is dressed with the head and pelt on, in distinction from older lamb which has the head and skin removed.

Lamb is inspected by government agents in the packing houses in the same manner as are other meats. Sheep are particularly susceptible to internal parasites and the carcasses are carefully inspected for freedom from such disease. Much lamb's liver is condemned for parasitic infection, making this liver rather scarce.

As is true with other meats, government grades have been established for lamb, although not all packers grade their meat in accordance with these grades. Often locally dressed lamb is available, particularly in the smaller cities and towns, and if the butcher is reputable and various local regulations have been complied with, such lamb is perfectly wholesome and an unusual treat.

UNITED STATES GRADES

One of the points by which the age and quality of lamb can be told is the break joint on the fore legs. In dressing sheep the shanks are left on the carcass, the feet being removed at the fetlock joint. In the development of the bones of the young animal, ossification begins at the three points in the long bone: one in the shaft and one at each extremity. As the animal grows older ossification proceeds until the hardening processes meet. In young lamb, before ossification is complete, the leg bone can be snapped off above the fetlock joint, where the lower hardening processes have not yet met. This is the break joint which shows as a broad, moist, dentated, pink surface on the bone. The attempt is sometimes made to imitate the break joint in older sheep, but this results in a white jagged break which does not resemble the true break joint.

Prime or Grade A-1. This is ideal lamb from the point of view of conformation, finish, and quality, and as a result there is very little of it to be found in the market. The general outline of the animal is remarkably symmetrical and the carcass is very compact and blocky. The legs are thick and plump, the backs are broad, and the loins and ribs are well fleshed. The fat is firm and white or slightly creamy in color, and may be tinged with pink. The exterior fat is evenly dispersed and there is adequate but not excessive internal fat. The flesh is firm, fine grained, and smooth and velvety to the touch; its color is a light pink. The bones are relatively small, soft, and tinged with blood. The break joints show four well defined, relatively soft and spongy red ridges.

Choice or Grade 1. This is excellent lamb from every point of view, and ordinarily the best grade available in the market. Generally speaking, it is slightly deficient in one or more standards as compared with prime lamb. The carcasses are relatively short and compact, and in general conformation resemble prime lamb. The fat is good quality, white or creamy, evenly dispersed and not excessive in any one place. The flesh is fine grained and firm and is light pink in color. The bones are relatively soft and small and tinged with blood. The break joint is as described for prime lamb.

Good or Grade 2. Carcasses of this grade are well proportioned and reasonably plump, but may be slightly deficient in breadth or depth at the hips, backs, or shoulders. The legs are inclined to be more tapering. The bones are soft and tinged with blood. The break joints show four well defined relatively soft red ridges. The outer covering of fat is smooth and even; the interior fat is usually unevenly distributed. The fat is good quality, white or creamy in color. The flesh is moderately firm, fine grained, and light pink in color.

Medium or Grade 3. Lamb of this grade is somewhat angular or rangy with moderately long thin necks and legs, and lacks plumpness of higher grades. The break joints show four well defined soft ridges,

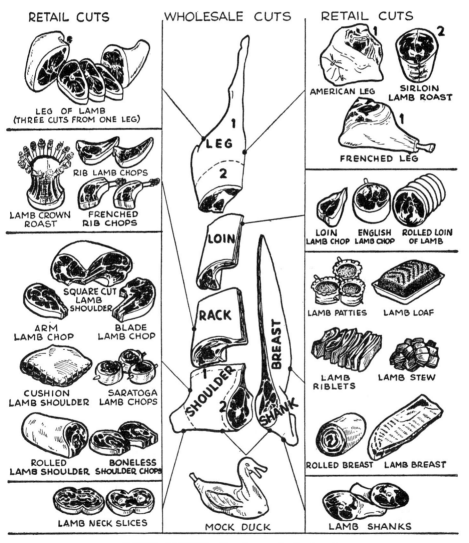

LAMB CHART, showing principal cuts

but these are almost white. The fat is not evenly distributed and is inclined to be scanty, except in heavier carcasses which are approaching yearling stage, where the fat is likely to be heavier. The flesh is usually soft, spongy, and moderately fine grained, but in older animals it may be firm. Its color varies from light to dark pink.

this temperature the meat can be held for some time in good condition.

For wholesale distribution, lamb is divided into two cuts, hind saddle and fore saddle, the division being made between the twelfth and thirteenth rib. The hind saddle is divided into the legs and loins; the fore saddle is divided into hotel racks, which include nine pairs of

FOOD VALUE

	Wa-ter	Food Energy	Pro-tein	Fat	Car-bohy-drates	Cal-cium	Phos-phorus	Iron	Vit. A Value	Thia-mine	Ribo-flavin	Nia-cin	Ascor-bic Acid
Choice	46.2	410	13.0	39.8	0	8	140	2.0	0	.15	.19	4.3	0
Medium	55.8	312	15.7	27.7	0	9	169	2.4	0	.18	.23	5.2	0
Common	66.3	202	17.1	14.8	0	10	184	2.6	0	.20	.25	5.6	0

Common or Grade 4. This is the lowest grade ordinarily found in market. The carcasses are angular and have poor conformation and finish. The bones are prominent and the animal is disproportionately long and narrow. There is little or no fat, either interior or exterior. Heavier and older carcasses may show fat in the region of the kidneys which will have a bluish tinge. The bones are usually soft, but lack the redness of better grades. The break joints show four well defined relatively soft ridges. The flesh is soft and spongy, and inclined to be watery. It appears coarse and fibrous, and its color may be dark pink or have a brownish tinge.

Cull or Grade 5. Lambs of this grade are not ordinarily found in market. They are most inferior and the proportion of bone to meat is very high. The flesh is dark, soft, coarse grained, and very fibrous.

PREPARATION FOR MARKET

In the slaughterhouse, lambs are killed and skinned. They are not ordinarily divided into sides or quarters as are beef and veal. The head is removed, although in the case of genuine spring lamb the carcass is dressed with both the head and pelt on.

The lamb carcasses are sent directly to the chilling room from the killing floor. Because of the comparative smallness of the carcass, it chills very rapidly. The sides of the animal are held open with sticks to facilitate the circulation of air and speed the cooling process. The temperature in the chilling is maintained at 38° and at

ribs, chucks, which includes the necks and breasts, including the shanks. As with all meats, there is a certain difference in terminology in different markets. The cut which include the chucks, breast, neck and shanks are also known as rattles stews, and slugs. A wing includes two shoulders, shanks, neck, and breasts. A bracelet includes the rack plus that portion of the breast which corresponds to the plate in beef.

The table below gives the wholesale cuts the most common retail cuts therefrom and the preferred cooking method.

RETAIL CUTS

Wholesale Cut	Retail Cut	Cooking Method
Leg	Leg	Roast or Braise
	Steak or Cutlet	Broil
	Sirloin	Roast
Loin	Loin Chop	Broil or Panbro
	English Chop	Broil or Panbro
	Rolled Loin	Roast
Rack	Crown Roast	Roast
	Rib Chops	Broil
Breast	Riblets	Braise or Stew
	Stew Meat	Stew
	Breast	Roast or Braise
	Rolled Breast	Roast or Braise
Shoulder	Arm Chop	Broil
	Square Cut Shoulder	Roast
	Blade Chop	Broil
	Cushion Shoulder	Roast
	Saratoga Chops	Broil
	Rolled Shoulder	Roast
	Boneless Chops	Broil
	Neck Slices	Braise
Shank	Shank	Braise or Stew

VARIETY MEATS

Brains. A delicacy which may be prepared in various ways. *See* BRAINS.

Heart. A lamb heart weighs approximately half a pound, and can be made into a very tasty dish either by stuffing and braising for an hour, or by cutting it in slices, in which case it will cook in less time. *See* HEART.

Kidneys. Lamb kidneys are often left attached to the loin, and they are included in English lamb chops, the meat being wrapped around the kidney. Such a chop is a great delicacy. Lamb kidneys are

tainers. They may be sliced and served cold or hot.

COOKING TIMES AND TEMPERATURE

Lamb should always be served medium well done. If a meat thermometer is used, it should register 175°-180° F. Lamb should be broiled at a temperature of 350° F. If the broiler has no regulator, light the flame full force and place the rack so that the surface of the meat will be about three inches from the flame. The temperature at this point will be approximately 350° F.

				Time (minutes)	
Cut	*Size*	*Method*	*Temperature*	*Medium*	*Well Done*
Chops or	¾–1 inch	Broil or	350° F.	12–25	15–35
Tender		Panbroil			
Steaks	1½ inch	Broil or Panb'l	350° F.	15–30	18–40
	2 inch	Broil or Panb'l	350° F.	18–32	20–40
	¾–1 inch	Fry	Moderate heat	12	18
Ground	1 inch	Broil or			
Patties		Panbroil	350° F.	18	20
Leg, Loin,					
Crown	6–7½ lbs.	Roast	300° F.	25–30	30–35 (per lb.)
Shoulder	4–6 inch	Roast	300° F.	25–30	30–35 (per lb.)
Rolled	3–4 inch	Roast	300° F.	35–40	40–45 (per lb.)
Cushion	3–4 inch	Roast	300° F.	25–30	30–35 (per lb.)
Stew	1 inch	Braise	Brown for	15 min.	
			Then simmer	1½–2 hours	
Breast			Brown for	15 min.	
Stuffed	2–3 lbs.	Braise	Then simmer	1½–2 hours	
Rolled	1½–2 inch	Braise	Brown for	15 min.	
			Then simmer	1½–2 hours	
Neck slices	¾ inch	Braise	Brown for	15 min.	
			Then simmer	45 min.	
Shanks	½ lb.	Braise	Brown for	15 min.	
			Then simmer	¾–1¼ hours	

tender enough to be broiled, either sliced, or cut in cubes and prepared en brochette. *See* KIDNEYS.

Liver. Lamb's liver is not so readily available as that from other animals. It compares in quality with calf's liver. Much lamb's liver is condemned at the packing house by government inspection because of infection with parasites. *See* LIVER.

Sweetbreads. Lamb sweetbreads compare with those from veal in quality. *See* SWEETBREADS.

Tongue. Lamb tongues are comparatively small and are ordinarily sold cooked and ready to serve in glass or tin con-

HINTS ON PREPARING LAMB

Practically any cut of spring lamb is tender enough to broil or roast. And the great advantage of lamb is that its size makes it right for the average amily. The butcher can cut a roast to suit almost any purpose or purse. Because lamb is the flesh of an immature animal it requires slow, even cooking and frequent basting to prevent its drying out in cooking.

The thin tissuelike skin on the surface of a leg of lamb or other cuts is called the fell. It may be removed if desired, but in a roast it should be left on since it helps to

LAMB

retain the juices. Except in very mature lamb, it will not affect the flavor. The fell should be removed from chops and steaks because it has a tendency to make the edges curl up. If it is not desired to remove it, gash the edge of the steak or chop several times.

Since one of the chief attractions of lamb is its delicate almost neutral flavor, this should never be lost or submerged by the addition of strong pungent vegetables or seasonings. Certain flavors go very well with lamb. The French cooks always insert a few slivers of garlic into a leg of lamb before roasting it. The very subtle flavor of garlic seems to enhance the lamb flavor. Lamb is most often served with mint sauce, which seems an ideal accompaniment, but for a change try a compote of apricots, raisins, or prunes, or a sweet spiced fruit conserve.

Lamb seems to go very well with either eggplant or curry, and there are many eastern dishes which use these ingredients. Ground raw lamb makes a pleasant change from hamburger, or for use in meat balls. Lamb patties, which are made of ground lamb, are available in many butcher shops. They should be cooked by broiling, as are hamburgers, but will take rather longer to cook than beef.

BARBECUED LAMB

4 lamb shanks (about 3 lb) trimmed
1 medium-sized onion, sliced
¾ cup cider or tarragon vinegar
¼ cup tomato catsup
1 tsp salt
Dash of cayenne

Have the butcher saw through the ends of the shanks. Tear off the skin and discard excess fat. Wipe the meat with a damp cloth, place in a heavy frying pan or casserole, cover with the sliced onion and bake uncovered in a slow oven (325° F.) until the fat begins to sizzle. Now turn the meat in the pan and cook, uncovered, for ½ hour longer, basting with the blended vinegar, catsup and seasonings and using about one-fourth of these. Cover, and bake until tender, about 2 hours, basting at intervals with the remaining sauce and any liquid in the pan and turning the meat 3 or 4 times. Serve very hot. (Serves 6)

BROWN LAMB STEW

2½ lb lamb
4 tbsp drippings
5 cups water or meat stock
6 white onions
6 carrots, halved
1 large turnip, cut into several pieces
Bouquet garni
2 whole cloves
Pinch of thyme
2 tsp salt
¼ tsp white pepper
6 potatoes

Use preferably shoulder or neck of lamb. Discard the fell and any excess fat and cut the meat into convenient pieces for serving. Heat the drippings and brown the meat in them. If desired, the meat may be rolled in seasoned flour before browning. Transfer to a stew pan, add the water or stock, the vegetables, except the potatoes, the bouquet garni and spices. Cover, bring to boiling point, then reduce the heat and simmer for 1½ hours. Now add the salt, pepper and potatoes, which if large may be halved. Increase the heat to a gentle boil and cook until the potatoes are tender, about 25 minutes. (Serves 6)

CROWN ROAST OF LAMB

A crown roast is made from the loin and rib chops, requiring enough ribs to make the crown. It is prepared by the butcher and usually weighs from 6 to 8 pounds. The ribs are separated at the backbone, but left together so that when carving, the knife slices down between the ribs, each then being lifted out and served as a portion.

To prepare a crown roast, wipe the meat with a damp cloth and rub with salt and pepper. A few slivers of garlic may be inserted in the fleshy parts if desired. Cover the ends of the ribs with large cubes of raw potato or salt pork, or wrap them with several thicknesses of waxed paper to prevent their scorching during roasting. Place on a rack in an open roaster and pour 1 cup hot water into the pan. Roast in a slow oven (300° F.) for 25 to 30 minutes to the pound, basting frequently.

If desired, the center of the crown may be stuffed with minced seasoned lamb before roasting. Otherwise, when ready to serve, fill the center cavity with small browned potato balls, fluffy mashed potatoes, or any other desired vegetable. Remove the potato or paper from the rib-ends and dress with paper frills. Serve very hot.

CURRIED LAMB

2 lb shoulder of lamb
3 tbsp flour
2 tbsp fat
1 small onion, sliced
1 tsp curry powder
½ tbsp lemon juice
½ cup boiling water
½ cup tomato juice
1 tsp salt

Cut the lamb into 1-inch cubes. Dredge the meat with the flour and brown in the fat in a deep skillet. Add all the remaining ingredients, cover, and simmer very slowly until the meat is tender. Serve with fluffy steamed rice. (Serves 6)

FRICASSEED LAMB WITH DILL

1½ lb lamb, cut from shoulder and shank
1 pt boiling water
12 small onions
2 new carrots, sliced
1 tsp salt
⅛ tsp pepper
3 or 4 tbsp flour
4 tbsp cold water
1 tbsp minced fresh dill

Wipe the meat, discard fat and bones and cut the meat into one inch cubes. Place both meat and bones in a saucepan, cover with the boiling water and bring all to boiling, after which reduce the heat and simmer about ¼ hour. Now add the vegetables and seasonings, cook until both they and the meat are tender and strain, discarding the bones. Return the broth to the pan and thicken with the flour and water rubbed smoothly together. Boil 5 minutes, add the dill, using somewhat more if a stronger flavor is desired, and reheat the meat and vegetables in this thickened broth. Serve very hot with rice or noodles. (Serves 4)

GRILLED LAMB STEAK

The steak or steaks are cut 1½ inches thick, from the leg and broiled on the rack for 15 minutes, as you would beef steak, always in a preheated broiling oven. They may be served with all the garnishing adapted to steaks; they may be planked and surrounded with a bouquet of cooked vegetables, or a border of smooth mashed potatoes may be arranged around the edge of the plank; or they may simply be garnished with broiled tomatoes, grilled bananas, stuffed small green peppers, broiled mushrooms, etc.

LAMB AND KIDNEY PIE

1½ lb shank or shoulder lamb
3 lamb kidneys
3 tbsp flour
1½ tsp salt
⅛ tsp pepper
3 tbsp fat
1 cup boiling water
Soup bouquet
9 small white onions
6 small carrots, quartered lengthwise
4 cups hot mashed potatoes
1 cup fresh-cooked peas
2 tbsp butter

Wipe the lamb and kidneys with a damp cloth. Remove any skin and cut the meat into 1-inch cubes, then add the flour, salt and pepper and toss lightly together. Heat the fat in a heavy frying pan, put in the meat and kidneys and brown on all sides. Place in saucepan, add the boiling water to the fat and browned flour in the pan and stir until smooth and slightly thick-ened, then pour over the meat. Add a soup bouquet (a piece of celery, one or two sprigs of parsley, 2 or 3 slices of onion and a small bay leaf, all tied together). Cover, simmer gently for about 20 minutes, remove the bouquet, add the onions and carrots and continue the cooking until the onions are tender but not broken.

Line a casserole with part of the mashed potatoes, arrange the meat and vegetables over them and make a rim of the remaining potato. Place under broiler flame for 5 minutes to brown and just before serving turn the fresh-cooked peas and the butter into the center. (Serves 6)

LAMB KEBAB

2 lb breast of lamb
12 small tomatoes
1 cup vinegar
⅓ cup olive oil
1 large onion, diced
1 large carrot, diced
2 tbsp chopped parsley
Salt
Black pepper

Cut the lamb into 1-inch cubes and place in a bowl. Mix together the vinegar, oil, and seasonings and pour over the lamb. Let marinate for several hours, turning the meat so that it is well seasoned. When ready to serve, string the meat on skewers, placing a small tomato at each end of the skewer. Broil in the broiler or over a grill, basting with the marinade. Serve hot with

Puree of Eggplant

2 good-sized eggplants
½ lb onions, chopped
¼ cup olive oil
1 lb tomatoes
Clove of garlic
Salt
Pepper

Parboil the eggplant in boiling water for 8 to 10 minutes. Heat the oil in a skillet, add the onions and cook until golden yellow, stirring constantly. Peel and quarter the tomatoes and add to the onions. Season with salt and pepper and let cook until it forms a pulp. Split the eggplant lengthwise, remove a little of the pulp, and stuff each half with the tomato-onion mixture. Place in a greased baking dish, and bake in a slow oven for 1 hour. Serves 4 to 6)

LAMB MOUSSE

2 cups cooked lamb, finely minced
1 cup lamb stock
3 egg yolks
1½ tbsp plain gelatin
¼ cup cold water
½ tsp salt
¼ tsp paprika

⅛ tsp cayenne
1 cup heavy cream, whipped
½ cup pecans, chopped

Discard all fat from the meat before mincing. Combine the lamb stock with the beaten egg yolks and cook over hot water in a double boiler until thickened. Soften the gelatin in the cold water, then dissolve in the lamb custard. Add seasonings, set aside to cool and when beginning to thicken, fold in the whipped cream, the meat and nuts. Turn into a previously wet mold and chill. Unmold and garnish with parsley and strips of pimiento. (Serves 6)

LAMB PAPRIKA

2 lb lean shoulder of lamb
1½ cups tomato, fresh or canned
1 cup sour cream
2 onions, minced
2 tbsp butter or margarine
1 tbsp chopped parsley
Paprika
Salt

Trim the fell and fat from the meat and cut into convenient morsels. Heat the butter in a heavy kettle and brown the onion slightly. Add the meat and brown it well. Add the tomato pulp, parsley, salt to taste, and paprika to taste. Cover and simmer gently for about 1½ hours, or until the meat is tender. If necessary add a little hot water or stock as required. Taste for seasonings, add the sour cream, and reheat just to the boiling point. Serve immediately with an accompaning dish of noodles. (Serves 4)

LAMB SHORTCAKE

Prepare standard baking powder biscuit dough. Roll out thinly, divided into 2 portions, brush the first one over with softened butter, lay the second on top and bake. Meanwhile, reheat diced, cold cooked lamb in gravy or cream sauce, seasoning with salt, pepper and Worcestershire sauce. If the amount of lamb is scant, 1 or 2 diced hard-cooked eggs may be added. Serve between and over the biscuit, which, if preferred may be cut into individual biscuits, rather than in one large shortcake.

LAMB SOUFFLE

2 tbsp butter
2 tbsp flour
¾ cup warm milk
¾ tsp dry mustard
½ tsp salt
1½ tsp sugar
Dash of cayenne
3 eggs, separated
1 cup minced cooked lamb

Blend the butter and flour in upper part of double boiler over hot water. When smooth, add the milk and seasoning and stir until thickened. Cool slightly, add the beaten egg yolks and when these are well blended, the minced lamb. Finally fold in the stiffly beaten egg whites. Turn into a buttered deep baking dish, set this in a pan of hot water and bake in a moderately hot oven (375°-400° F.) about ½ hour. (Serves 4)

LAMB STEAKS WITH WINE

Select the desired number of lamb steaks. Put a little butter or olive oil into a skillet, and, when heated, add a finely minced onion. When this is lightly browned, add the lamb and brown rapidly on both sides. Then add a cup of red wine, cover and simmer 20 minutes or until well done. Thicken the sauce with a tablespoon each of butter and flour rubbed smoothly together and season rather highly with salt and black pepper. If you wish to adventure a little, add a few chopped canned mushrooms or green ripe or stuffed olives, sliced. Serve with small browned potatoes and peas or string beans.

LAMB TERRAPIN

3 tbsp butter or substitute
3 tbsp flour
1 tbsp prepared mustard
1 tsp Worcestershire sauce
1½ cups lamb stock
2½ cups diced, cold cooked lamb
3 diced hard-cooked eggs
Toast
Parsley

Melt the butter or substitute and when hot add the flour, mustard, Worcester-

shire sauce and lamb stock which has been made from bones and trimmings of the meat. Simmer 5 minutes, stirring constantly, then add the lamb and hard-cooked eggs. Heat thoroughly without actually boiling, and serve on toast, garnishing with finely minced parsley, or with sieved egg yolk, reserving 1 yolk from the diced eggs for this purpose. (Serves 4 to 6)

SCOTCH BROTH

2 lb neck of lamb
2 qt cold water
1 small turnip
1 carrot
1 onion
2 stalks celery
2 tbsp barley
Salt and pepper
1 tsp minced parsley

Wipe the meat, cut into small pieces, place in a saucepan with the water, bring slowly to boiling point, then simmer for 1 hour, skimming occasionally. Add the diced vegetables, barley and seasonings and continue cooking until the vegetables are tender, about 1½ hours longer. Sprinkle with the parsley just before serving. (Serves 4 to 6)

SHEPHERD'S PIE WITH SWEET POTATO CRUST

2 cups mashed sweet potatoes
2 cups leftover roast lamb
Stock or gravy
Salt and pepper

Mince the meat, add the seasonings, and stock to moisten well. Place in a greased baking dish and cover with the mashed sweet potatoes. Roughen the surface of the potatoes with a fork. Bake in a moderately hot oven (375°-400° F.) until the dish is heated through and the potatoes are browned. (Serves 4)

STUFFED ROLLED SHOULDER OF LAMB

Shoulder of lamb
3 tbsp butter or shortening
1 small clove garlic, crushed
½ cup minced celery leaves and stalk

1 cup hot water or stock
½ cup ground lean pork
3 diced sour apples
¾ tsp salt
Few grains pepper and paprika
Dash of curry powder, optional
2 cups bread crumbs

Have the butcher bone the lamb. Prepare a stuffing by melting the butter or shortening and cooking the garlic and celery in it for 5 minutes. Add the water or stock, the pork, apples and seasonings, then stir in the crumbs and simmer 15 minutes.

Rub the meat over with a little salt and pepper, spread with the stuffing, roll up carefully and either tie or sew to hold in shape. Roast in a moderate oven (350° F.) allowing 30 minutes to the pound. Turn the meat once or twice during the cooking and baste frequently with a little stock or water.

If desired, breast of lamb may be substituted for the shoulder in which case 20 minutes to the pound will be sufficient time to allow for cooking. Otherwise it is handled the same. (Serves 6)

LAMB'S WOOL. An old English drink made with apples, spices and heated ale. It is mentioned in Pepys' Diary, and was a part of old Oxford tradition (*see also* BRASENOSE ALE).

LAMB'S WOOL

1 qt ale
6 or 8 apples (depending on size)
Ginger
Nutmeg
Sugar

The apples are roasted, skinned, cored and mashed. This pulp is mixed with the ale, which is first heated, the seasonings added to taste and the beverage served hot. If desired, the pulp can be well mixed with the ale, then strained out before the seasoning is added.

LAMOTHE-BOUGON. A French cheese made at *Poitou*. Also called LA MOTHE ST. HERAYE.

LAMPREY. An eel-like vertebrate. The epicures of ancient Rome had ever ready appetites for the lamprey. At that time the best lampreys in demand by the gourmets were found in the Strait of Reggio de Calabria, between Sicily and Sardinia, and a large supply of them were always kept in reserve in the exclusive fish ponds of the Roman nobility. History reports that the black Carrara marble fish pond constructed by Hirtius on the shores of his fabulous estate was the show place of hospitality to Julius Caesar, and that it

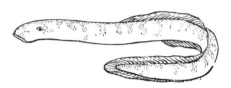

LAMPREY

contained thousands of plump lampreys, which were all eaten during that Emperor's reign, when the wealth of the world flowed into the treasury of Rome, and all natural resources were drained to the utmost to contribute to the feasting which rose to dimensions of almost incredible luxury.

The lamprey is a favorite dish in England and the story goes that Henry I was tremendously fond of it and died from over-indulgence in it. We cannot judge whether that statement was a slander of a delicious and exquisite fish, but at any rate that tragic happening did not deter succeeding kings of England and their subjects from enjoying a dish of lamprey. Probably there is no other country of the world where the lamprey has been and is so much appreciated.

At Gloucester an old custom dating back to the 16th century is still observed, of sending at Yuletide a huge lamprey pie to the King and Queen, which is always appreciatively accepted and eaten *en famille* with a certain ceremony by the royal family, despite what happened to their unlucky predecessor.

The lamprey belongs to the eel family, and like the eel is cylindrical in shape. It sometimes reaches great size; its head with its grotesque snout is unique; the body is trunk-like, without scales, greenish and slippery smooth on the back, with intermittent markings of dots and vaporous lines.

Lampreys are caught in large numbers from the month of March until the end of June, but are considered best in May and June. They are dark, rather dry, and somewhat insipid in taste if not highly seasoned.

While the lamprey is of much finer flesh than the eel, all the methods of preparing eel may be adapted to it. The skin should always be removed to facilitate cooking and render the fish more digestible. Whatever method of preparation is employed, the fish should first be placed in cold, strongly salted water to disgorge thoroughly, after which it is parboiled.

When small and fried in deep fat, the lamprey is a great delicacy. Combined with other fish in a classic fricassee, it is greatly preferable to the eel, especially if the white wine is not spared. When large, and braised on a bed of cut vegetables with a profusion of tomatoes, it is a delight to the appetite.

LANCASHIRE CHEESE. A hard, round, rennet cheese seven inches in diameter and nine inches high. The best of this cheese comes from the country north of the Ribble, bordering on the Irish sea coast.

LANDOCH CHEESE. Another name for BRINSEN (*which see.*)

LANGOUSTE. The langouste is very similar to the lobster (*which see*) in shape, flavor, and habits. The various methods employed in preparing lobster may be adapted to this crustacean.

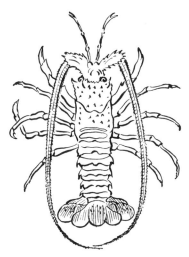

LANGOUSTE

LANGRES CHEESE. A soft, square, rennet cheese, five inches in diameter, eight inches high, and weighing one and a half to two pounds. Full-flavored, and strong scent. French.

LAPLAND CHEESE. A round, flat, hard cheese resembling a dumb-bell in shape.

LAQUEUILLE-BLUE CHEESE. A hard, rich cheese from France.

LARD. (I) The semisolid oil of hog's fat, after rendering. Economically, lard is one of the most important of our foodstuffs. Nearly one-sixth of the weight of the millions of hogs grown each year in America goes into the lard pail. That means about three billion pounds of lard is produced. Home use of lard has declined in the last ten years, but production has not. Lard ranks with butter in digestibility, and is excellent for pastry making, for hot breads, and for deep fat frying.

DIFFERENT FORMS OF LARD

Kettle-rendered leaf lard is made from the leaf fat, or the internal fat of the abdomen of the hog, excluding that adherent to the intestines. It is rendered in a steam-jacketed open kettle at a temperature of 230° to 250° F. This method of lard making is similar to the home method. It makes lard which is light in color, slightly grainy, with firm texture, mild and pleasing in flavor, and which keeps well.

Kettle-rendered lard is made from leaf and back fat, and rendered in a steam-jacketed open kettle at a temperature of 240° to 260° F. This lard is light in color, but somewhat darker than leaf lard, slightly grainy in texture, keeps well, and has a very pleasing flavor.

Prime steam lard is made from killing and cutting fats, rendered in direct contact with steam in a closed tank under a pressure of 30 to 50 lbs., or at a temperature of about 285° F. It is usually cooled rapidly over a chill roll or refrigerated drum, which produces a very smooth texture. It is whiter, and has a different flavor from kettle-rendered lard. This type of lard represents 80 per cent of the commercial product. Its keeping qualities are satisfactory, and it cost is usually less than that of the kettle-rendered lards. Of course, none of the above-mentioned lards keep quite as well as hydrogenated shortenings.

Hydrogenated lard has been marketed in recent years under brand names. It has been sold principally for home consumption and has not been used extensively in the hotel and restaurant trade. In hydrogenating lard the soft lard-like consistency is changed, and a firmer fat is produced. Furthermore, the lard-like flavor is changed because of the hydrogenation process.

LARD FOR DEEP-FAT FRYING

Lard used for deep-fat frying should not be heated to too high a temperature. Smoking lard means burning lard. On the other hand too low a temperature results in absorption of fat by the food being fried.

LARD (II). This is to introduce narrow strips of fat larding pork or bacon through the surface of the uncooked meat in order to nourish or tenderize and flavor it. Sweetbreads, tenderloin of beef, certain game birds, and liver are often prepared in this way.

LARDING NEEDLE. A long, steel needle with a large eye into which long, narrow strips of pork fat are threaded to lard meat, poultry, game etc. The length of the strips is from five inches to 15 inches.

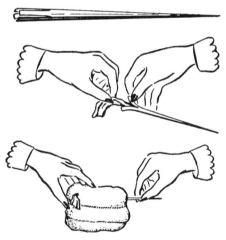

LARDING, showing use of needle

LARDING PORK. Pork fat especially used either to lard, to barde (enveiop), or to surround a food. Cooks sometimes envelop squab with a thin slice of larding pork.

LARK. It is related that a certain Doctor Lester, physician to Queen Anne of England and fond of good living, in speaking of the advantages of using scales in cookery, remarked: "If twelve larks do not weigh twelve ounces, they are scarcely

eatable; they are passable if they weigh twelve ounces; but if they weigh thirteen ounces, they may be considered plump and excellent."

The North American lark is widely distributed from ocean to ocean and from Mexico to Alaska, but is most abundant in the Mississippi Valley. It is a permanent resident wherever found, except in the northern part of its range, and its non-migratory habits and general adaptability have brought about a great deal of variation in the breeds living in different parts of the country. As many as 20 geographic varieties have been recognized in the United States.

The bird, for example, found along the Atlantic coast in summer, nesting in the Labrador and Hudson Bay region, is the common horned lark or shorelark. The bird of interior New England, New York, and the Mississippi Valley is the prairie horned lark. Farther west we find the pallid, the desert, the ruddy, the scorched, and dusky-horned lark.

During the breeding season, the male performs aerial evolutions which quite equal those of the skylark in daring if not in melody. Mounting upwards on a great spiral, the bird ascends until almost lost to view. Then poising for a few moments and breaking into song, it undertakes a thrilling dive toward the earth, closing its wings and dropping like a plummet, threatening to dash itself to pieces. But finally, when within four or five feet of the earth, it catches itself, swerves, and very gracefully lights.

The lark, a song bird, cannot legally be hunted or eaten in America. The pract ce, however, has been common in western and southern Europe. By means of a device composed of revolving mirrors the birds are decoyed and shot from ambush. Therefore they appear commonly in Continental markets.

Our meadow lark is not a true lark at all, and neither the meadow lark nor the horned lark is hunted in this country. In fact, such food is unknown here even to the connoisseur.

LASAGNA. Alternating layers of alimentary paste, such as that used for ravioli (*which see*) parboiled, then sauteed in either butter or meat glaze, to which is added a little tomato paste. The filling between layers may be meat sausage, cheese, pate de foie gras, ground poultry, etc. Baked, steamed or fried—they are typically Italian.

LASAGNA

½ lb lasagna macaroni or broad noodles
3 qt boiling water
2 tbsp salt
1 tbsp olive oil
1 lb cottage cheese
½ lb Muenster or mozzarella cheese, sliced
Tomato meat sauce (see below)
⅓ cup grated Parmesan cheese

Cook the lasagna in boiling salted water about 25 minutes, or until tender, stirring often. Drain well. Mix with the oil. Arrange in a shallow 2½-quart baking dish making three layers of each of the cooked lasagna, cottage cheese, sliced cheese, tomato-meat sauce, and grated cheese. Bake in a moderate oven (325° F.) for 45 minutes. (Serves 8)

TOMATO-MEAT SAUCE

¼ cup minced onion
2 cloves garlic, minced
¼ cup olive oil
1 lb hamburger
1 No. 2½ can tomatoes
1 6-oz can tomato paste
4 tsp salt
⅛ tsp cayenne pepper
2 cups water
1 tsp sugar
Pinch of basil
1 bay leaf

Brown the onion and garlic lightly in oil in a large saucepan. Add the hamburger and brown. Add the remaining ingredients. Cover uncovered, over a low flame for 1½ hours.

LAVENDER. See HERBS.
LAVER. A water plant; any of several purple seaweeds, the fronds of which are eaten in Europe, either pickled or stewed. Green laver, a sea lettuce of the genus *Ulva*, also used for food in Europe.
LAYER CAKE. See CAKE.
LAYER CAKE PAN. See CAKE PAN.
LEAF CHEESE. Another name for the Armenian cheese, *Tschil*, which is made from skimmed milk of cows or sheep. It is

also known as *Telpanier* or *Zwirn.*
LEANYKA. A light Hungarian table wine. There are two types; *Leanyka Szaraz*, which is dry, and *Leanyka Edes*, which is inclined to be sweet. See also WINE.
LEATHER CHEESE. A round cheese made from the skimmed milk of cows. It contains from five to ten percent buttermilk, and has small eyes throughout. It is made in Germany.
LEAVENING AGENTS. Leavens, either physical, chemical or biological, are used to make foods, especially of the bread or cake variety, light and porous. Physical leavens include steam or air which expands upon heating through baking, hence making the mixture light, popovers for example. Chemical leavens include commercial baking powders and baking soda, which combines with some acid as sour milk or buttermilk to form gas. Biological leavens include the yeast and bacteria family. Egg whites also have leavening qualities, due to their ability to hold air and release it during baking. See also EGGS.
LEBKUCHEN. A typical German cookie, which is most frequently served during the Christmas season. This cookie may be prepared several weeks in advance since it keeps well, and even improves with age. Keep in airtight containers.

LEBKUCHEN

1 lb or 1¼ cups strained honey
2 cups brown sugar, firmly packed
¼ cup water
7 cups all-purpose flour
½ tsp soda
¼ tsp cloves
¼ tsp nutmeg
1 tsp cinnamon
2 eggs, well beaten
½ lb almonds, blanched and slivered
⅓ cup chopped candied orange peel
¾ cup chopped moist citron
½ cup chopped glazed cherries

Boil honey, brown sugar and water 5 minutes. Cool. Sift flour, measure and resift 3 times with soda and spices. Reserve about 1 cup of the flour mixture to dredge fruits. Add eggs to cooled sugar mixture, then add sifted dry ingredients and mix thoroughly. Add nuts and fruits that are mixed with the 1 cup of flour; knead thoroughly. Wrap in waxed paper and store in a cool place, but not in refrigerator for 3 or 4 days. Divide into 4 portions. Roll out on a lightly floured board to ¼-inch thickness, cut into oblongs 3 inches by 2 inches. Bake in a moderate oven (350° F.) for 12 to 15 minutes. Cool. Ice with frosting made by mixing 1 cup sugar, 1 teaspoon white corn syrup, and enough water added by teaspoons to make a thick icing. Store in air tight containers to "ripen" for at least a month. (Makes 10 dozen)

LEEK. A member of the onion family, grown for its thick stalks, which have a very delicate onion flavor. The leek is the national emblem of Wales. Legend has it

LEEKS

that when Cadwalader, the Welsh leader, was about to meet Edwin, King of Northumbria, in battle, he ordered his men to wear a leek in their helmets to enable him to distinguish them from the enemy soldiers. The Welsh were victorious, and the leek was adopted as the emblem of the nation.

Leeks are served cooked, and may be prepared in any of the ways suitable for asparagus. In fact, they are often called the poor man's asparagus. Leeks make a number of delicious soups, either hot or cold for summer meals.

Leeks should be prepared by stripping off the outside leaves, cutting the green part down to five or six inches in length and cutting off the root. Leeks are very often full of sand or dirt, and should be thoroughly washed. Leeks cook quickly, in 15 to 20 minutes, in boiling salted water. They may then be served hot or cold. Young leeks and white onions, boiled together, may be served with milk or cream or with a mushroom sauce for a delicate and delicious vegetable.

Leeks, boiled in salted water, then drained and chilled are delicious with French dressing.

BRAISED LEEKS

1 large bunch of leeks
1 medium-sized carrot
4 sprigs fresh parsley
1 large bay leaf
½ cup minced celery
½ tsp salt
Pinch of thyme
⅛ tsp pepper
2 whole cloves
1½ cups stock or beef bouillon

Wash the leeks thoroughly and trim off the green tops to where they are tender. Peel the outside skin, and remove the root. Scrape the carrot and cut in thin slices. Place the leeks in the bottom of a baking dish and cover them with vegetables, spices, and seasoning. Add the stock or bouillon, cover tightly, and bake in a moderate oven (350°–375° F.) about 45 minutes. Drain and serve hot with the following sauce.

Sour Cream Sauce

2 eggs
¾ cup sour cream
½ tsp lemon juice
½ tsp salt
½ tsp paprika

Beat the eggs slightly, add the cream and seasonings, and cook in the top of a double boiler over hot water until the sauce thickens. (Serves 4)

This sauce is appropriate for such other vegetables as cauliflower, asparagus, or broccoli, or for plain boiled fish.

LEEKS WITH LEMON BUTTER

1 doz leeks
Well seasoned chicken or beef broth
3 tbsp butter or margarine
1 tsp lemon juice
Dash of tabasco

Cut off the green tops of the leeks to the tender portion, and trim the roots. Wash very thoroughly and cook, covered, in the broth until just tender (about 20 minutes). Drain thoroughly and place on a hot platter. Meanwhile, melt the butter, add the lemon juice, and tabasco, and pour over the leeks just before serving.
Instead of the lemon butter, the leeks may be sprinkled with buttered crumbs.

LEEK SOUP

6 leeks
3 tbsp butter
1 tbsp flour
1 qt boiling water
1 tsp salt
Dash of pepper
1 cup milk
1 egg yolk
Croutons

Trim, wash, and chop the leeks, then sauté in the butter about 3 minutes. Add the flour and brown slightly. Add the water, simmer 30 minutes, press through a sieve, season, and add the milk into which the egg yolk has been beaten. Heat without boiling, stirring constantly. Serve with croutons. (Serves 4)

LEEK SOUP—FLEMISH STYLE

Handful of sorrel
Same quantity of chervil
6 leeks
Small head of lettuce
6 medium-sized potatoes
Sprig of winter savory
Salt and pepper

Wash the vegetables thoroughly. Trim the leeks and cut into ½-inch slices. Shred the sorrel, chervil, and lettuce finely. Peel the potatoes and cut into quarters. Put all together into a pot, and add water just to cover. Season with salt and pepper, and

cover tightly. Cook very slowly until the potatoes have disintegrated (2 or 3 hours). The soup will be thick and creamy. (Serves 6)

LEEK SOUP—FRENCH STYLE

2 bunches leeks
4 tbsp butter or margarine
4 tbsp flour
4 cups rich milk

Trim the tops of the green portion and the root from the leeks, and wash thoroughly. Cut into ¼-inch slices. Scald the milk. Melt the butter or margarine in a saucepan and cook the sliced leeks in the hot butter for about 15 minutes, but do not let them brown. Stir in the flour and, stirring constantly, cook for another few minutes to blend the flour thoroughly. Carefully stir in 2 cups of the hot milk and simmer gently for 15 minutes, or until the leeks are very soft. Turn the contents of the saucepan into a sieve and force the leeks through. Return the purée to the saucepan and add the rest of the milk. Season with salt and pepper to taste, and bring to the boil again. Let simmer a few minutes, and serve very hot with croutons. (Serves 4)

LEEK SOUP—SCOTCH STYLE
(Cock-a-leekie)

2 qt chicken broth
1 tbsp oatmeal
6 leeks
Salt and pepper

Wash and trim the leeks and slice into fine pieces. Put the chicken broth into a pot and bring to a boil. Sprinkle in the oatmeal and the leeks. Season with salt and pepper. Let simmer until the oatmeal is thoroughly tender and the leeks likewise.

LEEK SOUP—WELSH STYLE

4 large leeks
4 medium-sized potatoes
6 cups water
1 medium-sized onion
2 tbsp butter or margarine
2 tbsp flour
A pinch of salt
2 egg yolks

Wash and trim the leeks. Cut them in half lengthwise, and then crosswise into fine pieces. Peel the potatoes and slice them. Put in a saucepan with the water and salt and simmer until tender. Peel and chop the onion finely. Melt the butter in a skillet and cook the leeks and onion in the butter until transparent, but do not brown. Stir in the flour and cook a few minutes longer to blend the flour. Moisten with a little of the potato water and stir to a smooth paste. Then put the leek and onion mixture into the saucepan with the potatoes and continue to simmer until the potatoes are very soft. Turn into a sieve and force the vegetables through. Return the purée to the saucepan and reheat. Beat the egg yolks and place in a soup tureen. Pour the hot soup on top of the eggs and stir in ½ cup cream, if desired. Serve immediately. (Serves 6)

LEES. The settling of any liquid. It is also the sediment or dregs resulting from wine or liquor manufacture.

LEFTOVERS. Leftovers often give the greatest problem, but at the same time they offer the greatest opportunity to infuse new flavors that make the second serving as palatable as the first. When you cook with one eye on the budget and the other on the pleasures of the table, you will find that you can get best results by concentrating your attention on preparing "made dishes" or leftovers. Escoffier, master of culinary art, once said that all the artistry, all the skill, and all the knowledge that any woman has, can be utilized in planning and preparing the perfect meal with leftovers. French cuisine is the acme of economy, and the French homemaker, having been trained along these lines, will unconsciously plan several meals ahead, especially in Summer, when preparing a family dinner. All that is needed is a little imagination and the knowledge which comes with experience.

The secret of making a delicious dish from the tasty end-of-the-roast pieces is to keep them moist. Too often a reheated piece of meat is overcooked and distinctly dry, or in the case of lamb, rubber-like. If it goes into a hot dish, protect the meat from over-cooking with a layer of mashed potatoes, cooked noodles, spinach, or whatever greens you may desire, a cream sauce, a curry sauce, a tomato sauce, a brown sauce, or a barbecue sauce perhaps. Cook it long enough to reheat the meat. Meat

pies, turnovers, croquettes, cutlets, meat balls, meat patties or loaves, and casserole dishes are all delectable concoctions from the end of the roast.

The first thing to remember in using canned or leftover meat is to reduce the second-cooking time to a minimum. That minimum is from eight to ten minutes. The meat already has been well cooked. After a certain point is reached, the longer meat is cooked the less savory and the less tender it becomes.

The bones go into the soup kettle. Cover them with cold water, add salt, a few cut up vegetables, seasonings, such as bay leaf, cloves, thyme, etc., and simmer gently for an hour or so. This delicious and nourishing broth, meat stock, or soup, may be used for the foundation of economical sauces. Place it in a glass jar in the refrigerator for tomorrow's use.

A proper proportion of made dishes to roasts is really essential to a satisfactory scheme of eating. The greatest steak-and-chop fancier alive will enjoy his steaks and chops better if they are spaced between savory scallops of leftover fish, a well-flavored ramekin of chicken, a timbale of fish, vegetable, cheese, or perhaps chicken livers, or an excellent hash now and then. And don't for a minute think that hash can't be excellent. A beefsteak is fine food —no doubt about that—but its remains, carefully made into a beautifully blended hash is every bit as fine.

True, the French have a hundred or so more sauces than we do, but you will never find a French hostess guilty of serving two sauces at the same meal. The French homemakers consider that enough is enough. Through several hundred years they have gauged to a nicety just how often the human palate craves a variation from legs of mutton and roasts of beef to a well-seasoned ragout (stew) or hash.

Looked at this way, these made dishes become something more than just a way of using up leftovers. No French home-maker need apologize for her ragout as many of us do (and with good reason) for our own hash. If all homemakers took the making of these dishes seriously, if they prepared their hash and their stews as carefully as they would a roast turkey, and if they spaced their dishes to be carved, with a judicious number of dishes to be spooned, then they could offer one or other to the highest and mightiest without misgivings. Look to the leftovers of yesterday's feast for today's easy economical dishes.

LEFTOVERS AS TESTS OF SKILL

Even if a bridge luncheon is something extra special, the homemaker may look deeply and find that the ham or chicken mousse, so beautifully presented, is apt to be made of leftovers. Skill in menu management makes leftovers not a problem, but rather an asset. Scalloped dishes by the score pop into the mind of the hostess as she opens the door of the refrigerator and studies its contents. For example: dice any leftover meat or poultry. If it happens to be chicken, use two cups for six servings. Then thicken a pint of chicken broth with two tablespoons each of blended flour and butter or a substitute. Season with salt and white pepper and stir in the chicken. Fill a generously buttered casserole with alternate layers of soft bread crumbs, creamy chicken, and cooked, sliced potatoes. (It will take about two cups of potatoes and two-thirds of a cup of bread crumbs). Top with buttered crumbs and bake in a moderate oven (350° F.) for 30 minutes. Or, if preferred, use six individual dishes and bake 15–20 minutes.

LEGUMES. Legumes rank next to cereals in importance as vegetable food. Legumes include one-celled, two-valved seed pods, containing one or more seeds. Legumes in their dry state have a very high percentage of protein, ranging from 18 to 25 percent, even more in the case of the soy bean. The composition of the mineral matter resembles that of cereals, showing a large amount of phosphate and magnesia, but is deficient in soda, lime, and iron. Only the lentil has an appreciable amount of iron. On account of their high content of proteins and carbohydrates and lack of alkaline elements, legumes are decidedly acid-forming. If used moderately and with discrimination, preferably with another food, legumes are a very valuable and economical source of protein. They should be cooked in soft, distilled, or rain water. If the water which is used for cooking is hard, due to the presence of carbonate of lime, one teaspoonful of baking soda per gallon may be added. If legumes are eaten too often, and to excess, and not in right combinations, they may produce flatulency and acidity of the blood. Out-

door workers can digest legumes better than sedentary workers.

Legumes require thorough mastication, for they are a bread. That is, they are very starchy, and improperly masticated starch is certain to cause digestive disturbances. Legumes are also a meat, for they are rich in building material—containing twice as much per pound as meat. *See also* BEANS, LENTILS, PEAS, PEANUTS.

LEGUMIN. Legumin is a vegetable ferment which is said to make milk highly digestible for invalids by converting casein into a soluble albuminoid. This substance is also given as a food to certain invalids, upon the prescription of a doctor.

LEICESTER CHEESE. A hard, rennet cheese made from the whole milk of cows. It resembles Cheshire and Cheddar, and like them, it also comes from England.

LEMON. According to reliable writers, it was in the foothills of the Himalaya Mountains, near the birthplace of Omar Khayyam, that the Arabs first discovered that lemons could be made into lemonade, and spread an industry that gives us that indispensable hot and cold weather fruit.

LEMON

Although there is doubt as to exactly when the lemon was brought to America, authorities agree that it was introduced by the Spanish explorers. Las Casas, Spanish historian, claims that Columbus brought lemon seeds with him on his second voyage, collecting these seeds at the island of Gomera, one of the Canary Islands, where he was waiting for favorable weather and taking on supplies. The first lemons grown in the New World were grown in Hispaniola, now known as Haiti. As this was the headquarters for Spanish exploration, it is only natural that lemons spread to all warm countries of the western hemisphere. From such beginnings lemons have grown into an industry of over a billion and a half dollars a year.

Lemon juice, as well as the rind, may be used to flavor bread, muffins and biscuit doughs, cake frostings and fillings, custards, chiffon pies or pudding, marshmallow combinations, ice creams, and a large number of gelatin desserts.

Lemon juice is a natural dressing for fruit—bananas, pears, and avocado—to mention but a few. Add a little lemon juice to water to which lettuce or other salad greens are freshened. It will revive and

FOOD VALUE

Water	Food Energy	Pro- tein	Fat	Carbo- hydrate	Cal- cium	Phos- phorus	Iron	Vit. A Value	Thia- mine	Ribo- flavin	Nia- cin	Ascor- bic Acid
89.3	44	.9	.6	8.7	14	10	.1	0	.04	Trace	.1	45

Originally Florida was our largest producer of lemons, but the freeze of 1895 killed her grooves and they were never replanted. Today California is our greatest lemon-growing state, producing about 85 percent of the lemons consumed in the United States and Canada.

Lemons rank with other citrus fruits as an excellent source of Vitamin C. The tang is citric acid, faintly muted with the natural sugar of the fruit. Aromatic oil wells in the rind offer their bounty for lemon flavoring extract. The rind goes into candy and other cookery. Few foods are as naturally refreshing as lemons. Indeed, these golden balls of juice seem almost designed by nature to serve as containers of aromatic, refreshing properties, which act miraculously to revive both jaded appetite and jaded nerves.

As a thirst quencher, the lemon is tops. The Army recognized this during World War I and when water ran short, lemon drops were handed out.

Practically every green salad is benefitted by the tang given by a generous amount of lemon juice, either sprinkled over the ingredients or included in the dressing. Vegetables seasoned with lemon juice tempt indifferent or laggard appetites. Some people like it on broccoli or spinach. Add lemon to the melted butter to pour over new cabbage. Use it also in the sauce for beets.

Lemon sherbet is delightfully cooling on scorching days, while lemon pudding, lemon gelatin, lemon pie, lemon fluff or whip, are other suggestions for the homemaker who wishes a light, refreshing finale to her menus.

crisp them. Whether served in the form of a refreshing drink, a tempting meringue pie, an artistic touch on the rim of a glass of iced tea, or an extra zest in a cup of hot tea, each of us has his own particular preference for the way we wish our lemon served.

Lemon juice may be substituted for vinegar in any recipe, except pickling, that calls for vinegar. A small amount of lemon juice and grated lemon rind gives zest to such dried fruits as prunes, figs and peaches. Added to apple sauce, especially when the apples lack flavor, it enhances it immediately.

HOUSEHOLD USES OF LEMON

When aluminum ware becomes dull or black, clean it with a cloth dipped in lemon juice. Then rinse it in warm water. To clean tarnished copper or brass use lemon rinds dipped in salt.

Immediately after dishwashing, drop a little lemon juice in the palm and rub well over the hands to keep them soft and white. This also removes odors, such as fish or onion.

To remove iron rust, fruit or ink stains from white linen, rub the spots lightly with lemon; then cover them with salt and place in the sun. Lemon rinds saved in water and dropped into the boiler on wash day will help to whiten white clothes, dishtowels, and handtowels particularly. Do not use them for colored pieces.

Lemon juice, applied with a toothbrush, cleans the teeth and hardens the gums. It also leaves the mouth with a fresh, wholesome feeling.

Have you ever tried lemon juice in your shampoo? It is really a necessity, in the rinse, to the proper care of the hair. It is the best of all brighteners, effective and harmless.

VARIETIES OF LEMON

a. The *Eureka* lemon is oblong in form, the apex being nippled, and the base tapering; the size is medium, the juice abundant, clear, strongly acid, with a good flavor. There are few seeds, often none.
b. The *Lisbon* lemon is oblong or obovate in shape, the apex being oblique and nippled with a characteristic crease to one side of the nipple. The base tapers sharply to the calyx, which is large. The rind is thin, smooth, and sweet; the juice abundant, clear and strongly flavored. There are few seeds, sometimes none.
c. Besides these two decidedly most important varieties, there are still grown a few of the *Villafranca*, the *Bonnie Brae*, the *Genoa*, the *Sicily*, the *Messina*, and the *Milan*.

PREPARATION FOR MARKET

Lemons are usually picked from ten to twelve times a year, the heaviest pickings coming in March and April and the lightest in August and September. They are picked with shears, according to size, rather than color. Lemons 2½ to 2¾ inches are picked. All fruit, green and yellow, that passes through the measuring ring is picked Those which have a waxy yellow color are considered the highest in grade. The best keeping fruit is picked green, trucked to the packing houses, scrubbed and cured in a special storage room where the temperature is 65° F., the humidity, 85 percent. Lemons are always handled very carefully, and the brush washer is about the only machinery through which they are allowed to pass. The yellow lemons are packed and shipped almost immediately, the others after varying periods of curing. When the lemons come from storage, they are sized and graded by hand and packed from trays into boxes.
California lemons are sorted into four grades: (1) Fancy, having good color, fine texture, no scars, thin skins, heavy, and juicy; (2) Choice, good but not perfect in all of the above respects; (3) Standard,

being discolored, irregular in shape, and scarred; (4) Culls, the poorest grade, used chiefly for production of citric acid, lemon juice, lemon oil, and marmalade.

HINTS ON BUYING LEMONS

The most practical way to judge lemons is by weight, heavy fruit containing the most juice. The skin should be oily and elastic. Lemons with large knobs at the ends will yield less juice than those having sharply pointed ends. Lemons that have a fine-textured skin, and are heavy for size are generally of better quality. Deep yellow-colored lemons are usually relatively mature and less acid than those of lighter or greenish-yellow hue; the deep yellow ones are also generally thinner skinned and may have a relatively larger proportion of juice, but are less desirable for acid flavor.
Four medium-sized lemons approximate one pound, and one medium-sized lemon yields about three tablespoons of juice. A standard commercial crate holds from 300 to 360 lemons. Decay appears either as mold or as a discolored soft area at the stem end. Fruits that have been mechanically injured are more or less subject to mold. Shriveled or hard-skinned fruits, or those which are soft or spongy to the touch, are not desirable. They may be aged, dried out, or affected by rot at the center of the fruit.

HINTS ON PREPARATION

Lemons should always be washed before being used for any purpose whatever. When used as a garnish, they may be cut in many attractive forms. It is often an economy to buy lemons in quantity to insure an adequate supply.
When lemons have become so dry that they are of little use, place them in the oven until they are heated through. It is surprising the amount of juice they will then give.
Lemon juice added to sweet, fresh milk, evaporated milk, or fresh cream, will sour it suitably for cooking. Add one-quarter cup of lemon juice to one cup of milk, fresh or evaporated, and one-third cup for cream.
Lemons are in season all during the year. They should always be kept in a refrigerator. When the homemaker needs only half

a lemon, she should wrap up the remaining half in transparent, moisture-proof paper. It keeps nicely. Whole lemons may be kept in a large fruit glass jar with the cover fastened tight, and the jar placed in the refrigerator.

LEMON WITH FISH

Add one tablespoon of lemon juice and one-half teaspoon of salt to each quart of water used for boiling fish.

Fish fritters, cakes, cutlets, or croquettes are extra delicious when a little lemon juice is added to the mixture before shaping. Of course, quartered lemons should be used also as a garnish.

Creamed or scalloped fish dishes are greatly enhanced in flavor when a little lemon juice is added to the sauce.

Cut lemons in halves and remove the pulp to make baskets or boats to be filled with mayonnaise or tartar sauce for fish, or with currant or grape jelly for chops or steaks.

LEMON WITH MEAT

Garnish any grilled meats with lemon dipped in finely chopped chives or parsley.

Marinate steaks in a blend of one-fourth cup of lemon juice, one-third cup salad oil, one tablespoon grated onion and one tablespoon Worcestershire sauce. Let stand in the mixture two or three hours, turning occasionally.

Immediately before serving steak, lamb or veal cutlet, pour over (the meat) melted butter blended with a little lemon juice and paprika.

LEMON SPREADS FOR CANAPES AND SANDWICHES

(1) Cream two tablespoons of lemon juice with one-half pound of butter. Blend thoroughly.

(2) Blend one package of cream cheese with two tablespoons of lemon juice, eight sprigs of minced, green, crisp water cress and one tablespoon finely minced green pepper, olives, celery, or ground nut meats.

(3) Blend thoroughly together the pulp of one ripe avocado with two tablespoons of lemon juice, salt to taste, a few grains of cayenne, and one generous tablespoon of minced chives.

LEMON BUTTER FROSTING

¼ cup butter
2 cups confectioners' sugar
¼ tsp salt
1 to 2 tsp lemon juice
½ tsp grated lemon rind

Cream butter until very soft and smooth, then add sugar gradually, creaming thoroughly. Add salt and lemon rind. Gradually work in the lemon juice, using just enough to produce a smooth spreading consistency. Spread on cake. This amount is enough to spread on two 8-inch layers.

LEMON CHEESE

This recipe was originally an old English one, brought over to America and guarded jealously by a few New England families. It was private property until recently.

Pour the juice of 6 lemons and the grated rind of 4 of them over 2 pounds of granulated sugar. Add ¼ pound of butter and 6 slightly beaten whole eggs. Stir this mixture over a very low fire until it thickens. When sugar is dissolved, and mixture begins to bubble, the lemon cheese is done.

This recipe is a generous one, but it can be kept in the icebox in a tightly covered jar for several weeks, ready for the moment when you need a delicacy in a hurry. You can use lemon cheese as a filling for open pastries, or as a spread for toast or tea sandwiches, or to take along for a picnic, camping and the like.

LEMON CHIFFON CUSTARD

3½ tbsp flour
⅔ cup sugar
2 tbsp butter
2 eggs, separated
3 tbsp lemon juice
⅔ cup milk

Mix flour and sugar together and add to creamed butter, blending thoroughly. Stir in beaten egg yolks, lemon juice and milk; and fold lightly but thoroughly into stiffly beaten egg whites. Fill individual custard cups ⅔ full, and set in a shallow pan, filled with enough hot water to come almost to the top of the cups. Bake in a moderately slow oven (325° F.) for 35 minutes, or until custard tests done. This custard separates into two distinct layers. (Serves 5)

LEMON CRACKER PUDDING

⅔ cup coarse cracker crumbs
1 cup sugar
½ tsp salt
3 tbsp lemon juice
½ tsp grated lemon rind
2 cups milk, scalded
2 tbsp melted butter
2 eggs, separated

Combine cracker crums, ¾ cup of the sugar, salt, 2 tablespoons of the lemon juice and the rind, and add slowly to scalded milk, stirring constantly. Stir in melted butter and beaten egg yolks. Pour into greased 4-cup baking dish and bake in a moderately slow oven (325° F.) for 45 minutes. Remove from oven; cover with meringue made by beating whites of eggs until stiff, gradually adding the remaining ¼ cup of sugar and the tablespoon of lemon juice. Return to oven. Bake at moderate (350° F.) heat until meringue is delicately brown (12 to 15 minutes). Serve warm or chilled. (Serves 5)

LEMON CREAM CHARLOTTE

3 eggs
1 cup sugar
1 lemon
Salt
1 doz lady fingers

Beat the egg yolks, add ½ the sugar, the juice and grated rind of the lemon and a dash of salt. Cook over hot water (double boiler) until thick, then fold in the egg whites stiffly beaten with the remaining sugar. Line a buttered mold with split lady fingers, pour in ½ the filling, arrange the remainder of the lady fingers over this, top with the balance of the filling, cover and chill 6 to 8 hours in the refrigerator. Unmold for service. (Serves 6)

LEMON CREAM FREEZE

14½ oz can evaporated milk
½ cup lemon juice
¾ cup sugar
1/16 tsp salt
2½ tsp lemon rind loosely packed

Freeze milk in refrigerator tray to an icy mush; remove to a cold bowl, add juice, beat until thick Add sugar and salt gradually, then rind, beating until mixture is stiff and fluffy. Turn immediately into chilled tray and freeze. (Serves 6)

LEMON CREAM PUDDING

1 cup sugar
1 cup cornstarch
⅛ tsp salt
1 cup cold water
¾ cup milk
3 eggs, separated
½ cup lemon juice
½ tsp grated lemon rind
Currant jelly

Thoroughly mix sugar, cornstarch, and salt in top of double boiler; add cold water, milk and blend until smooth. Stir constantly over direct heat until mixture boils and becomes transparent-looking. Place over boiling water, cover and cook 15 minutes. Separate eggs and beat the yolks; stir in lemon juice and rind. Stir a little of the hot mixture into the egg yolks then return to the double boiler and cook 2 minutes longer, stirring constantly. Remove from heat. While still warm, fold in the egg whites which have been beaten until just stiff. Chill and serve in sherbet glasses with a currant jelly garnish. (Serves 5 to 6)

LEMON EGGNOG

1 egg
2 tbsp sugar
2 tbsp lemon juice
Milk (fresh or evaporated)

Beat the egg white until stiff with half the sugar and fold ¾ths of it into the egg yolk, beaten with the lemon juice and remaining sugar. Pour into a tall glass, fill almost to the top with milk, stir well and top with the remainder of the beaten egg white. (Serves 1)

LEMON FILLING

¾ cup sugar
2 tbsp cornstarch
Dash of salt
1 egg yolk, slightly beaten

¾ cup water
3 tbsp lemon juice
1 tsp grated lemon rind
1 tbsp butter

Combine sugar, cornstarch and salt in top part of double boiler; stir in egg yolk, water and lemon juice, and cook over boiling water 5 minutes, stirring constantly; cook 10 minutes longer, or until mixture is thick, stirring occasionally. Remove from hot water and add grated lemon rind, and butter. Cool.

LEMON CREAM FILLING

When filling is cold, fold in ½ cup heavy cream, whipped. Put between layers, grating ½ square chocolate over top of filling, or omit chocolate, and fold in ½ cup plain or toasted coconut.

LEMON FLUFF

5 tsp plain gelatin
½ cup cold water
4 eggs, separated
1 cup sugar
1½ tsp grated lemon rind
⅓ cup lemon juice
¼ tsp salt
Pistachios

Soften gelatin in the cold water. Place over hot water until completely dissolved. Beat egg yolks thoroughly and gradually add sugar, beating until stiff. Add the lemon rind, juice and salt. Beat well, then add the gelatin and again whip until mixture is thoroughly blended. Beat the egg whites until stiff, then fold in the egg yolk mixture lightly but thoroughly. Turn into a 6-cup mold that has been rinsed in cold water. Cover and place in refrigerator to chill until firm. Unmold and serve with sweetened whipped cream and sprinkle with finely shaved pistachio nuts or almonds. (Serves 6)

LEMON ICE

½ cup lump sugar (tablets)
4 medium-sized thin-skinned lemons
1 cup hot water
2 cups cold water
¾ cups granulated sugar

Rub entire surface of lump sugar over rind of lemons which have been washed and sponged until dry. Over this lemon-flavored sugar lump, pour ½ cup of lemon juice, combined with the hot water, stir until sugar is thoroughly dissolved, then add the cold water into which has been stirred the granulated sugar. Strain and freeze in hand freezer, using 3 parts of ice and 1 part of rock salt. Serve in sherbet cups which have been well-chilled.

LEMON MARMALADE

Follow the directions for orange marmalade, reversing the quantities of lemons and oranges. (*See* ORANGE)

LEMON MERINGUE BREAD PUDDING

10 slices bread, cubed
3 eggs
½ cup granulated sugar
Grated rind of lemon
Juice of 1½ lemons
⅛ tsp nutmeg
2 cups milk
6 tbsp powdered sugar

Arrange the bread in a buttered casserole. Beat the egg yolks until light with the granulated sugar. Add the lemon rind, lemon juice, and nutmeg. Stir in the milk, then pour over the bread and bake in a moderate oven (350° F.) about 30 minutes. Make a meringue with the egg whites and powdered sugar and spread over the pudding. Return to the oven until delicately browned. (Serves 6)

LEMON MOUSSE

2 tbsp cornstarch
¼ cup granulated sugar
¼ tsp salt
1 cup cold milk
¾ cup granulated sugar
⅓ cup lemon juice
2 cups heavy cream, whipped stiff.
3 egg yolks, slightly beaten

Combine cornstarch, ¼ cup granulated sugar, salt and mix well. Stir in the cold milk and cook in double boiler for 15 minutes, or until mixture thickens, stirring constantly. Remove from hot water and beat in the egg yolks; return to hot water and cook, or rather allow to simmer gently for 1 short minute, stirring constantly. Strain through double cheesecloth, stir in the ¾ cup of granulated sugar and lemon juice, and strain again. Cool. Fold in the heavy cream, whipped stiffly, and place (molded or unmolded) in refrigerator tray. Chill 3 long hours without stirring. Or pack after molding in hand freezer tray, using equal parts ice and salt, and let stand for 2 to 2½ hours. You may pack in paper cases, or individual molds, and freeze as indicated for coffe mousse recipe (*which see*).

LEMON PIE

⅔ cup sifted pastry flour
1 cup sugar
¼ tsp salt
2 cups hot water
2 eggs
1 tbsp butter
⅓ cup lemon juice (unstrained)
1 tsp grated lemon rind
9-inch pre-baked pastry shell
2 tbsp sugar, additional

Sift the flour, sugar and salt, gradually add the water, stirring constantly, and cook in a double boiler, still stirring, until thick and smooth. Pour over the beaten egg yolks, still stirring. Add the butter, lemon juice and rind, blend thoroughly and when cool turn into the pre-baked pie shell. Top with a meringue made from the stiffly beaten egg whites and additional sugar. Place in a moderate oven (350° F.) to set and delicately color the meringue.

LEMON CHIFFON PIE

Of all chiffon pies, lemon is perhaps the most delectable. Actually it is a delicate spongy, fluffy gelatin mixture, firm enough to hold its shape, yet not in the slightest degree hard or tough. Its crust may be pastry or a crumb crust and naturally it is invariably served cold, usually topped with a thin layer of whipped cream, plain or slightly sweetened.

1 tbsp gelatin
¼ cup cold water
4 eggs
1 cup sugar

Dash of salt
1 tsp grated lemon r nd
½ cup lemon juice
1 9-inch pre-baked pie shell (*See* PASTRY)

Soften the gelatin in the cold water. Beat the egg yolks slightly and place with the sugar, salt, lemon rind and juice in the upper part of the double boiler. Cook over hot water, stirring constantly, until the mixture thickens. Remove from the fire, add the softened gelatin and stir until dissolved. Cool and as soon as the mixture begins to thicken fold in the egg whites beaten until stiff but not dry with the sugar. Turn into the pre-baked pie shell, chill and serve with whipped cream.

LEMON CRUMB PIE

1 cup sugar
½ cup all-purpose flour
⅛ tsp salt
1½ cups cold water
3 eggs, separated
¼ cup lemon juice
1 tsp grated lemon rind
1 tbsp butter
Chilled gingersnap pastry (*which see*)
⅓ cup sugar

Combine the 1 cup sugar, flour, and salt in saucepan; add water and stir until well blended; then cook over direct heat, stirring constantly until mixture boils and thickens. Remove from heat and stir a little of the mixture into the well beaten egg yolks; return to rest of hot mixture and cook 2 minutes over direct heat, stirring constantly. Remove from heat, add lemon juice gradually in small portions, mixing well after each addition. Stir in rind and the butter, then pour into chilled crust. Cool. Beat egg whites until stiff, then slowly beat in the ⅓ cup sugar until meringue is thick and smooth. Pile lightly and quickly over top of pie, touching edges all around and place pie pan on a baking sheet in a moderate oven (350° F.) for 12 to 15 minutes, or until meringue is nicely browned. Cool before cutting. (Serves 5 to 6)

LEMON PINEAPPLE FLUFF

1 package lemon-flavored gelatin
1¼ cups hot water
3 to 4 tbsp lemon juice (juice of 1 lemon)

No. 1 tin crushed pineapple (1⅓ cups undrained)
½ cup whipping cream
Pinch of salt

Dissolve gelatin in the hot water; add all but 1 teaspoon of the lemon juice, and the crushed pineapple. Chill until sirupy. Have the cream ice cold; turn into a bowl surrounded by cracked ice, and beat until thick. Then add the remaining 1 teaspoon of lemon juice and salt and continue beating until mixture just holds its shape. Whip the gelatin mixture; then fold in the whipped cream. Cover and continue chilling at least 1 hour; it does not become very stiff. Serve piled lightly in sherbet glasses. (Serves 5)

LEMON PUDDING

1 cup sugar
2½ tbsp cornstarch
¼ tsp salt
1½ cups boiling water
½ cup butter
Grated rind and strained juice 1 lemon
2 whole lemons
1½ cups sifted pastry flour
1½ tsp baking powder
½ tsp salt
½ cup sugar
1 beaten egg
½ cup milk
½ tsp lemon extract

Combine the first sugar, cornstarch and salt, pour the boiling water over, stirring constantly, then turn into a saucepan and cook, still stirring, for 5 minutes. Remove from the heat, add ½ the butter with the lemon rind and juice. Slice the remaining lemons thinly and arrange the slices around the sides and bottom of a greased mold or baking dish, as a lining. Pour in ½ the lemon mixture, spreading with a spatula to fill in the spaces between the slices of lemon.
Sift together the dry ingredients, add the egg, milk, remaining butter, melted, also the lemon extract. Beat to a smooth batter, then pour into the prepared baking dish. Bake in a moderate oven (350° F.) 35 to 40 minutes. Unmold and serve with the reserved lemon mixture which has been chilled as a sauce. (Serves 6)

LEMON RICE PUDDING

1½ cups cooked rice
Few grains of salt
½ cup sugar
2 slightly beaten eggs
3 cups milk
Grated rind and juice of 1 lemon

Combine all ingredients. Turn into a buttered baking dish and bake in a slow oven (300° F.) just until set. Serve warm with a fruit sauce. (Serves 4)

LEMON SAUCE

¾ cup water
¼ tsp salt
¼ cup sugar
Juice of 1 lemon
1 tbsp cornstarch
2 tbsp cold water, additional
1 tbsp butter

Combine the water, salt, sugar and lemon juice and bring to boiling point. Thicken with the cornstarch moistened with the 2 tablespoons of water. Again bring to boiling point, stirring constantly, simmer 5 minutes, then add the butter.

LEMON SHAKE

Shake together well the following: ¼ cup of lemon juice, ¼ cup of sugar, ½ cup of milk, and ½ cup of crushed ice. (4 ice cubes may be used).

LEMON SHERBET

2 cups water
¾ cup sugar
1 tsp grated lemon rind
2 tsp gelatin
4 tbsp cold water
1/6 tsp salt
⅓ cup lemon juice
2 egg whites

Combine the water, sugar and lemon rind, bring to boiling point and simmer 10 minutes. Remove from the fire, stir in the gelatin softened in the cold water, also the salt, then strain through doubled cheese cloth and chill. Finally, stir in the lemon juice, turn into refrigerator tray and hal freeze. Now stir down well and fold in the stiffly beaten egg whites. Pack smoothly in the tray and freeze until the mixture again begins to solidify, at which point stir thoroughly once more to break up the ice crystals, then complete the freezing. (Serves 6)

LEMON SNOWBALLS

1 cup sifted flour
1 tsp baking powder
¼ tsp salt
3 eggs, separated
1 cup granulated sugar
3 tbsp water
1 tsp grated lemon rind
2 tbsp lemon juice
Powdered sugar

Mix and sift flour, baking powder and salt. Beat egg yolks and granulated sugar gradually, beating until thick and light. Add water, lemon rind and juice; stir in flour and fold in stiffly beaten egg whites. Fill greased custard cups ⅔ full; tie greased paper over tops and steam 30 minutes. Turn from cups and roll in powdered sugar; serve with lemon sauce (*which see*) or any fruit sauce. (Serves 6 to 8)

LEMON SOUFFLE I

4 eggs, separated
¼ cup hot water
1 cup sugar
½ tsp salt
2 tbsp grated lemon rind
¼ cup lemon juice

Beat yolks until thick; add water gradually and continue beating; add sugar gradually, beating thoroughly after each addition. Add salt and lemon rind and juice, and fold in stiffly beaten egg whites. Turn into greased baking dish, set in pan of hot water and bake in moderate oven (350° F.) for 30 or to 45 minutes until firm. Serve at once with lemon sauce (*which see*). (Serves 6)

LEMON SOUFFLE II

3 eggs
⅔ cup sugar
Grated rind ½ lemon
1 tbsp gelatin

1 tbsp cold water
4 tbsp lemon juice

Beat the egg yolks until very thick, gradually adding the sugar and lemon rind. Soften the gelatin in the cold water, dissolve over boiling water, add the lemon juice, and combine with the first mixture. When thoroughly blended, fold in lightly the stiffly beaten egg whites. Turn into a serving dish and chill. Serve with whipped cream. (Serves 4)

LEMON SOUP

3 eggs well beaten
1 tsp salt
2 tbsp cold water
5 tbsp lemon juice
1½ qt quick Bouillon (bouillon cubes)

Combine eggs, salt, water and lemon juice; gradually stir in hot bouillon and heat to boiling point, stirring constantly. Serve at once. (Serves 6)

LEMON TAPIOCA WHIP

¾ cup quick-cooking tapioca
½ tsp salt
1½ cups sugar
3 cups boiling water
Juice of 2 lemons
3 egg whites

Cook the tapioca, salt and sugar in the water, until clear, using a double boiler and stirring frequently. Just before removing from the heat add the lemon juice. Cool slightly, then fold in the stiffly beaten egg whites. Turn into sherbet glasses and chill Serve with or without whipped cream or boiled custard. (Serves 6)

LEMON TARTS WITH RAISINS

1 recipe plain pastry
2½ lemons
2 cups raisins
1¼ cups sugar
1½ tbsp flour
¼ tsp salt
2 eggs, well beaten

Prepare pastry, using amounts for smaller recipe; line 8 tart shells with pastry. Squeeze juice from lemons and set aside (about ½ cup). Remove peel, cover with boiling water and cook 10 minutes; drain. Put peel and raisins through food chopper, using finest knife. Combine sugar, flour and salt, and stir in eggs and lemon juice; add to lemon peel-raisin mixture. Turn into pastry-lined tart pans. Bake in hot oven (450° F.) 10 minutes; then reduce heat to moderate (350° F.) and continue baking about 25 minutes. Makes approximately 8 (4-inch) tarts.

LEMON WAFFLES

Add two teaspoons grated lemon rind to egg yolk, milk mixture in waffle recipe (*see* WAFFLES). Serve with butter and marmalade, or top with ice cream and lemon sauce (*which see*).

LEMONADE

1 lemon
1 to 3 tbsp sugar or honey
1 glass cold water
Ice

Extract the lemon juice, add the sugar or honey to taste, stirring to blend. Add the water and serve over ice in a large glass. Garnish with a lemon slice on the rim. Add also a maraschino cherry, if desired. (Serves 1)

Hot Lemonade. Add to the juice of 2 lemons, 1 cup of boiling water. Sweeten to taste. This is often used to help relieve the discomfort of a common cold. Many who prescribe this for themselves add an ounce or two of whisky.

Lemon Fizz. Lemonade made with carbonated water. (*See* LEMONADE)

Lemon Float. Lemonade to which a dip of lemon sherbet is added. (*See* LEMONADE)

LEMON BALM. *See* BALM.

LEMON EXTRACT. *See* FLAVORING EXTRACTS.

LEMON FISH. *See* AMBER FISH. Related to Madregal.

LEMON FORK. *See* SERVING IMPLEMENTS *under* FLATWARE.

LEMON PICKLES. A commercial product found in some delicatessen and grocery stores, used as a condiment and garnish for cold fish, meat and poultry.

LEMON SOLE. *See* SOLE, *under* FISH.

LEMON VERBENA. This delicate aromatic herb is used in flavoring salads. Its leaves are lemon-scented.

LEMONADE GLASS. *See* GLASSWARE.

LENTIL. An Old World leguminous plant with pale-blue flowers and broad pods containing edible seeds. The lentil is one of the most ancient food plants. It has been used in the Mediterranean countries for thousands of years, but until recent times it was little known in the United States. The red lentil comes from Egypt, and the large purplish-green lentil from Central Europe. A small variety of the lentil is now grown in Arizona and New Mexico. Lentils are richer in iron than any

LENTIL

of the other legumes. Lately a legume similar to the lentil, the *Monantha vetch*, has been introduced into California. When cooked, it can hardly be distinguished from the real lentil in taste and color.

Lentils are beginning to find favor in the United States. They are very nutritious; lentil flour contains twice as much protein and nearly twice as much lime as that of wheat or oats. The Hindus rely on the lentil for its staying power when undertaking arduous journeys. Lentils belong to the body-building, regulating, and protective food group. They contain protein to build muscle and tissue, phosphorous to build up the nervous system, and Vitamin B to help appetite and growth, and prevent beri-beri.

Packaged lentils are usually perfect without stones, and much like split peas in appearance. When lentils are bought loose, they should be carefully picked over and

all foreign material and imperfect seeds
discarded. Lentils can be treated like dried,
split peas. They should be soaked overnight
in plenty of water, then cooked the next
day in fresh water to cover. The long soaking and change in water help to prevent
the digestive disturbances so often associated with dried legumes.

BAKED LENTILS

Soak 2 cups of lentils in water to cover.
In the morning drain, cover with cold
water, and simmer 30 minutes. Drain, season, turn into a baked bean pot, add an
onion stuck with cloves and a generous
piece of salt pork. Cover and bake in a slow
oven (325°. 350° F.) 3½ hours, removing
the cover for the last ½ hour of baking.
(Serves four)

CASSEROLE OF LENTILS

2 cups lentils
Salt and pepper
1 cup minced onion
4 strips bacon, diced
1 can condensed tomato soup
½ cup water

Soak the lentils overnight in water to
cover, then cook until almost tender. Drain,
season with salt and pepper, and place
half the lentils in a greased casserole. Add
half the onion, half the bacon and half the
soup blended with the water. Repeat the
layers topping with the remaining bacon.
Cover and bake in a moderate oven (350°
F.) one hour. 15 minutes before serving
remove the cover to brown the top bacon.
(Serves 4 to 6)

CURRIED LENTILS

1 lb lentils
4 large onions, sliced
½ cup bacon drippings
4 tsp curry powder
Boiled rice

Soak the lentils overnight in water to
cover, then cook until tender and drain.
Sauté the onions in the bacon drippings
until lightly browned. Add the curry powder, blend smoothly, combine with the
lentils and reheat. Serve over boiled rice.
(Serves 4 to 6)

HUNGARIAN LENTILS

½ lb lentils
1 onion, minced
2 tbsp bacon fat
2 tbsp flour
¼ cup cold water
1 tbsp sugar
½ tsp salt
2 tbsp vinegar
½ cup sour cream
Toast

Soak the lentils overnight in water to
cover, then cook until tender and drain.
Sauté the onion in the bacon fat, blend in
the flour, add all remaining ingredients,
bring to boiling point and cook 2 minutes.
Pour over the lentils and serve on hot
toast. (Serves 3 to 4)

LENTIL AND LIMA BEAN LOAF

1 cup dried lima beans
1 cup dried lentils
½ tsp salt
¼ tsp pepper
1 cup peanuts, finely chopped
¼ cup onion, finely chopped
2 tbsp green pepper, finely chopped
1 cup bread crumbs
2 tbsp melted butter
2 eggs and
½ cup milk, beaten together

Soak the lima beans and lentils overnight in water to cover. In the morning
bring to boiling point in the same water,
then simmer until tender. Drain and pass
through food chopper. Combine with all
remaining ingredients, turn into a well
greased bread pan or casserole and bake
in a moderate oven (350° F.) about 1
hour, basting occasionally with equal parts
of blended hot water and bacon fat or butter. (Serves 6)

LENTIL SOUP I

1½ cups lentils
2 qt cold water
½ cup diced bacon, salt pork, or ham
1 large onion, sliced
1 large carrot, sliced
½ cup diced celery

A small piece of bay leaf
Salt and pepper
Finely chopped parsley or chives
Lemon slices

Soak the lentils overnight in water to cover. Drain, place in a soup kettle with the water, bacon, salt pork or ham, the onion, carrot, celery and bay leaf. Cover and cook very slowly about 2 hours, or until the lentils are tender. Press through a sieve, season with salt and pepper, reheat and garnish with a dusting of finely chopped parsley or chives and lemon slices. (Serves 6)

LENTIL SOUP II

2 slices bacon
1 large onion, sliced
1 clove garlic
1 slice green pepper
2 qt water
½ lb lentils
1 carrot
1 leek
1 stalk celery
Salt and pepper
¼ tsp thyme
1 bay leaf
2 bouillon cubes
1 tsp sugar
1 tbsp minced parsley
½ cup cream
4 chicken livers
2 tsp butter

Fry together in a heavy saucepan the bacon, onion, garlic, and green pepper for about 3 minutes. Add the water with the lentils (which have been thoroughly washed, then soaked in cold water for 3 hours), the carrot, leek, celery, and seasonings, and simmer slowly about 2 hours. Press through a sieve, return to the fire with the bouillon cubes, sugar, parsley and cream, and simmer 2 minutes. Meanwhile, sauté the chicken livers in the butter, chop coarsely, add to the soup and cook 1 minute longer. (Serves 6)

SYRIAN RISHTAYA

1 lb neck of lamb
1 cup lentils, washed
7 cups boiling water

¼ lb broad egg noodles
½ lb spinach, washed and chopped
4 tbsp olive oil
1 large onion, chopped
3 tbsp chopped parsley
1 small bay leaf
Garlic
Salt and black pepper to taste

Rub the lamb very lightly with a clove of garlic; cut into 2 inch strips and sear in 1 tablespoon of olive oil over a very hot flame. Place lentils in the boiling water and add the lamb. Cover saucepan and allow lamb and lentils to simmer gently until lentils are almost done (about 45 minutes). Now add the spinach and noodles to the saucepan. Cover the pan and continue to simmer until the noodles are cooked to taste (about 15 to 18 minutes). Lightly brown the onion in the remaining olive oil, using the same pan in which the lamb was seared. Scrape the onions and oil into the saucepan; add the parsley, bay leaf, and salt and pepper. Cover the pan again and let cook for about 5 minutes. Rishtaya may be served immediately in hot dishes, although some homemakers prefer to chill it first. (Serves 6)

LES AYDES. A French cheese made in the *Orleanais*.

LESCIN CHEESE. A Russian rennet cheese which is made from sheep's milk.

LES LAUMES CHEESE. A French cheese made in Burgundy.

LETTUCE. A kind of salad, of which there are a number of varieties. Lettuce has had a long history. Herodotus, the Greek historian, tells us that it was served at royal tables 2500 years ago. The name, lettuce, comes from the Latin word for the salad *lactuca*, which in turn comes from the Latin word for milk. If you have ever cut lettuce in the garden, you probably know that the stem exudes a milky substance. For many centuries lettuce was considered too delicate a food for any but noblemen to eat, and woe unto serf or slave found surreptitiously trying its flavor. Thirty stripes was the punishment.

The Greeks served lettuce at the end of their meals; the Romans ate it as an appetizer, accompanied by eggs. So highly did the Romans cherish lettuce that in times of drought, when there was no water, they watered their lettuce beds with sweet wine. When the Dutch founded New Amsterdam, lettuce was included in the list of seeds ordered from Holland.

VARIETIES

Four types of lettuce are found in the markets: (a) the crisp head, which is represented by the New York variety, commonly (but erroneously) called Iceberg lettuce;

may penetrate to the interior of the head. Bruised or wilted leaves may be trimmed off without any waste, provided the balance of the head is good. Lettuce that has been kept in ice or wet too many times to freshen it, often takes on a red tinge in the stems. This is unattractive, and will lead to decay, thus cutting down the keeping quality of the head.

LETTUCE   1. Iceberg   2. Cos   3. Boston   4. Curly

(b) the butter head, which is usually the Big Boston, or White Big Boston varieties; (c) Cos or romaine; and (d) leaf lettuce. The crisp head type is the most popular, and the head is firmer, larger, and crisper than the butter-head type. Butter-head lettuce has a greener, smoother leaf. Cos or romaine is distinguished by its cylindrical or elongated head and its coarser leaf. Leaf lettuce, sometimes erroneously called butter lettuce, does not head, and may have a curled or smooth leaf.

Head lettuce of good quality is fresh looking, crisp, and tender, and the head is hard and firm when pressed. It should be free from decay, and the outer leaves will usually have been trimmed off.

Occasionally lettuce will be found that has gone to seed. Such lettuce is likely to be bitter in taste and wasteful. Even if the seed stem has not burst through the head, it can be detected by the wide spaces between the base of the outer leaves and a knoblike swelling which destroys the symmetry of the head.

Dark or discolored areas on the outer leaves may be an indication of decay which

Leaf lettuce should be fresh-looking, crisp and green. An odd wilted leaf can be trimmed away, but too many of them are wasteful.

HINTS ON PREPARATION

Lettuce needs little preparation. Often all that is necessary is to trim off the outer leaves and the base of the stem. A tightly formed head of lettuce does not ordinarily need washing. A head of iceberg lettuce may be separated into leaves easily by cut-cutting off the stem as far into the head as possible and holding the head upside down under cold running water. The force of the water will separate the leaves.

If lettuce is to be used for a salad it should be dried thoroughly after washing. This is most easily done by placing it in a wire salad basket which is whirled around, thus shaking out the water. Lacking a wire basket, a cheesecloth bag may be substituted. Or, as a last resort, the leaves may be patted dry in a towel. But this must be done very carefully, because pressure will bruise the leaves. Lettuce should be crisped

FOOD VALUE

	Wa-ter	Food Energy	Pro-tein	Fat	Car-bohy-drates	Cal-cium	Phos-phorus	Iron	Vit. A Value	Thia-mine	Ribo-flavin	Nia-cin	Ascor-bic Acid
Headed	94.8	18	1.2	.2	2.9	22	25	.5	540	.06	.07	.2	8
Other	94.8	18	1.2	.2	2.9	62	20	1.1	1620	.06	.07	.2	18

and chilled by storing in the compartment of the refrigerator designed for the purpose.

As will be seen from the table of food values, leaf lettuce contains more vitamin B than headed lettuce. And for the same reason, the green outer leaves contain more than the bleached inside leaves. The dark outer leaves should not be discarded, but should be thoroughly washed and trimmed and cooked. If there are only a few, they may be added to soups. A particularly delicious way of preparing fresh green peas is to cook them with a handful of lettuce leaves and a few tiny white onions.

For salad, lettuce may be served broken into conveniently sized pieces, in quarters, or smaller fractions of the head, or shredded. Lettuce needs no other dressing than a tart French dressing, but all sorts of combinations of greens and vegetables may be used with lettuce.

BELGIAN BRAISED LETTUCE

3 small heads Iceberg lettuce
2 tbsp butter or margarine
1 small carrot, thinly sliced
1 small onion, thinly sliced
3 sprigs of parsley, minced
⅛ tsp thyme
3 thin slices salt pork
1 cup well seasoned beef bouillon

Wash and drain the lettuce and tie the heads in shape with thread. Melt the butter in a casserole and add the carrot, onion, parsley, and thyme. Lay the heads of lettuce in the casserole and top each with a slice of salt pork. Pour in the bouillon, cover tightly, and cook in a moderate oven (350°–375° F.) about 45 minutes. If desired, the liquid in the casserole may be strained and slightly thickened before serving. (Serves 6)

BRAISED LETTUCE RAVIGOTE

1 large firm head Iceberg lettuce
½ cup stock, bouillon, or brown sauce
Salt

3 leaves green spinach
4 sprigs parsley
1 bay leaf
2 whole cloves
4 tbsp butter
½ tsp lemon juice
½ tsp onion juice
Cayenne pepper

Wash the lettuce, cut it in quarters and cook in boiling water to cover for 5 minutes. Drain thoroughly. Place in a baking dish, add the stock or brown sauce, and season with salt. Cover and bake in a hot oven (400° F.) for 30 to 35 minutes.

Meanwhile, prepare the ravigote butter by washing the spinach and parsley, and scalding in boiling water with the bay leaf and cloves. Drain and discard the bay leaf and cloves. Force the spinach and parsley through a fine sieve. Cream the butter, add the sieved vegetable, and season with the lemon juice, onion juice, and cayenne. Keep in a cold place until serving time, then spread over the hot lettuce. (Serves 4)

CREAMED LETTUCE

2 medium-sized heads Iceberg lettuce
1 cup well seasoned white sauce
1 cup heavy sour cream
1 tsp lemon juice

Wash the lettuce thoroughly and cut in thick slices. Heat the white sauce in a saucepan and add the sour cream and lemon juice. Place the lettuce in the sauce and simmer 7 or 8 minutes, until the lettuce is wilted. Serve very hot. (Serves 4)

LETTUCE SOUP

3 tbsp butter
1 leek
1 head of lettuce
1 qt chicken broth
2 cups cooked peas
¾ cup heavy cream

Salt and pepper
1 tbsp horseradish
Minced chives

Melt the butter in a saucepan and cook in it the leek and lettuce, both finely shredded, until tender. Add the broth and peas and simmer ½ hour. Press through a sieve, cool, and chill in the refrigerator. At serving time fold in the whipped cream, salt, pepper and horseradish. Serve in chilled cups, topping each portion with a sprinkling of minced chives. (Serves 4 to 6)

STUFFED LETTUCE, COUNTRY STYLE

1 large head of lettuce
2 tbsp Roquefort cheese
3 tbsp ground carrots
1 tbsp chopped pimiento
2 tbsp chopped green olives
1½ tbsp grated onion
1 tsp salt
⅛ tsp pepper
1 tsp lemon juice
¼ cup tomato catsup

Select a firm head of lettuce, and remove the center, leaving a good shell. Wash and drain the lettuce thoroughly. Chop the center very fine and mix with the remaining ingredients. Pack firmly but carefully into the lettuce shell. Wrap in waxed paper or cheesecloth and chill thoroughly. Slice and serve with French dressing. (Serves 6)

LEVEL. As applied to measurement of ingredients in cookery, level means that the ingredient must not rise over the rim of the container, be it teaspoon, tablespoon, cup, etc.

LEVEOUX CHEESE. A French cheese made in Berry.

LEVULOSE. Fruit sugar, or levulose, is now sold in crystalline form, for use in diabetes, on the ground that it is not known to reappear in the urine. It can be taken freely and in considerable quantity without disordering digestion, as saccharin often does after continued use.

LEYDEN CHEESE. A hard Dutch cheese, weighing about 25 pounds, which has cumin seed and cloves added. It is also known as *Komijne kaas, Liedsche Kaas,* or *Kummel.*

LICHEN. *See* ICELAND MOSS.

LID. A lid is a cover for a box or vessel and is usually made of the same material.

It may either be a separate unit or else hinged to the vessel which it covers. *See also* KITCHEN EQUIPMENT.

LIEDERKRANZ CHEESE. A cheese, ripened by red-slime growth, resembling Limburger in flavor. It is one and a half by two and a half by one inch. This cheese is native to America.

LIEDSCHE KAAS CHEESE. *See* LEYDEN CHEESE.

LIFTER. A lifter can be any device used to raise and carry things, especially objects tha are too hot to otherwise handle.

One common type of lifter is supplied with coal or wood-burning stoves or ranges, being used to manipulate the heated stove-lids. It consists of a simple metal handle that engages the lid in a special slot placed in the lid for that purpose.

There are many different designs of lifters used to remove bottles, vegetables, and other objects from boiling water. These consist essentially of some form of stiff wire spiral or grid that is inserted beneath the object and raised by means of a long handle.

Another type of lifter that can be used to handle hot pan lids, and even the vessels themselves, as well as to remove objects from boiling water, is built to resemble a pair of long-handled scissors. Instead of having blades, it is fitted with jaws or clamps for gripping purposes and gives a firm hold on unwieldy objects.

See also KITCHEN EQUIPMENT and RANGE.

LIGHTS. The lungs of the beef, lamb, hog, etc. They are nourishing and inexpensive but are not used much as food for humans in this country.

LIMA BEANS. These are of South American origin, and are flat and slightly kidney-shaped. The green seeded kind is generally preferred. The coastal regions of southern California grow more of these beans than any other part of the world. *See also* BEANS.

LIMBURGER CHEESE. A soft rennet cheese made from cow's milk. It has a very strong odor and taste. Local names are: *Algau, Lanark, Marianhof, Morin, Saint Michels, Schutzen, Tanzenberg, Carinthian, Grottenhof, Emmersdorf, Briol.*

LIME. A citrus fruit similar to the lemon. The lime is smaller, often less than half the size of an ordinary lemon, and nearly round in shape. The average lime contains about one-third more citric acid than the average lemon.

FOOD VALUE

Water	Food Energy	Pro- tein	Fat	Carbo- hydrates	Cal- cium	Phos- phorus	Iron	Vit. A Value	Thia- mine	Ribo- flavin	Nia- cin	Ascor- bic Acid
86.0	53	.8	.1	12.3	14	10	.1	0	.04	Trace	.1	27

VARIETIES OF LIME

Very few limes are grown in California; most of them come from Mexico and the West Indies. They are in season all the year, but are more plentiful in spring. There are two kinds of limes; the Persian or seedless lime, and the Dominican. Persian limes are larger, and most of them are shipped from Santo Domingo in barrels and packages.

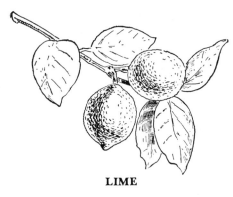

LIME

PREPARATION FOR MARKET

To make lime juice, fresh limes are pressed by machinery, and the seeds and pulp removed by straining and filtering. The juice is then boiled down to a high degree of concentration. Lime juice is carried by ships to prevent scurvy.

HINTS ON BUYING

The best limes are green in color and heavy for size. Deep yellow colored limes do not have the desired acidity. Limes are usually sold by the half dozen or dozen. One lime weighs approximately one and a half to two ounces. They are sometimes packed four to six to a basket for the retail market.

Limes often become spotted with purple-to-brown colored irregular shaped marks. Sometimes the whole fruit turns brown. This is the result of a defect called scald. Such fruit has a poor appearance and brings a lower price, but in many cases the flesh is not affected. Occasionally, however,

a tainted, moldy taste can be detected immediately below the spots.

HINTS ON PREPARATION

Limes are used in the same ways as lemons and a section of lime is often served with melon. They add flavor and zest to fruit beverages and salad dressings. Two limes may be used as the equivalent of one medium-sized lemon. However, the large green limes approximate the size of lemons. Limes, like lemons, should always be washed before using.

Limes are very perishable and should be kept in a cool, dry place, stored like lemons.

LIME CHIFFON PIE

1 tbsp gelatin
¼ cup water
4 eggs, separated
1 cup sugar
½ tsp salt
1 tsp grated lime rind
⅓ cup lime juice
1 baked 9-inch pastry
1 cup heavy cream, whipped

Soften gelatin in 2 tablespoons water. Combine slightly beaten egg yolks, ½ cup sugar, salt, lime rind and juice, and remaining 2 tablespoons water; cook over boiling water until mixture thickens, stirring constantly. Add softened gelatin, stirring until gelatin is dissolved; cool until mixture begins to thicken. Then gradually beat remaining ½ cup sugar into stiffly beaten egg whites and fold into lime-gelatin mixture. Turn into baked pastry shell and chill until firm. When ready to serve, top with whipped cream. (Makes 1 pie)

LIME FROSTING

1 egg yolk
¼ tsp grated lemon
1½ tbsp lime juice
Dash of salt
2 cups confectioners' sugar (about)
Green vegetable coloring

Mix together egg yolk, lemon rind, lime juice and salt, gradually add sugar, stirring, until of proper consistency to spread. Stir in coloring until frosting is light green. (Sufficient for two 8-inch layers)

LIME ICE

1½ tsp plain gelatin
1 tbsp cold water
3 cups water
1½ cups sugar
⅛ tsp salt
¾ cup strained lime juice (6 to 8 limes)
½ tsp grated lime rind
7 or 8 drops of green food coloring
Whites of 2 eggs, stiffly beaten

Soften gelatin in the 1 tablespoon of water for 5 minutes. Combine the 3 cups of water, sugar and salt in a saucepan and boil slowly for 5 minutes. Remove from heat, and softened gelatin and stir to dissolve and blend thoroughly. Cool. Add lime juice, rind and coloring and pour into freezer can. Freeze to a soft mush. Then open freezer can and add the egg whites and continue to freeze until firm. Makes about 2 quarts..

LIME SALAD DRESSING

¼ cup lemon juice
¼ cup lime juice
¾ tsp salt
⅛ tsp pepper
¼ tsp paprika
1 tbsp sugar
¾ cup salad oil

Combine ingredients in jar or large bottle, cover closely and shake vigorously, or make in bowl and beat with rotary egg beater. (Makes about 1 cup)

LIME HONEY FRUIT SALAD DRESSING

⅓ cup lime juice
⅓ cup strained honey
¼ tsp salt
1 cup salad oil
½ tsp paprika
¾ tsp prepared mustard
½ tsp seasoning salt
¼ tsp grated lime rind

Combine all ingredients in a bowl or fruit jar; beat with a rotary beater or shake thoroughly. Chill before serving with any fresh or canned fruit salad. This mixture will remain emulsified much longer than many other dressings, but should be shaken up or beaten just before serving. (Makes 1⅔ cups)

LIME SAUCE

¼ cup sugar
2 tsp cornstarch
¼ cup water
¼ cup fresh lime juice
⅛ tsp grated lime rind
2 drops green coloring
2 tbsp honey

Combine sugar and cornstarch. Then add water and lime juice and stir until smooth. Place over direct heat and heat until boiling, stirring constantly. Boil slowly bor 1 minute or until thick and transparent. Remove from heat, add rind coloring and honey. Stir well and cool. Serve over vanilla ice cream. (Makes about ⅔ cup)

LIME SHERBET

⅔ cup sugar
1½ cups water
1 tsp gelatin
1 tbsp cold water
4 drops green vegetable coloring
Juice of 5 fresh limes
2 egg whites
⅛ tsp salt

Combine the sugar and water and bring to boiling point, stirring until the sugar is thoroughly dissolved. Simmer 10 minutes, then add the gelatin softened in the cold water and stir until this also is dissolved. Chill. Add the green vegetable coloring, alternately with the lime juice (strained or unstrained), turn into refrigerator tray and half freeze. At the end of this time stir well and fold in the stiffly beaten egg whites and salt.

Pack smoothly in the tray and again freeze until mushy, at which point stir thoroughly once more to break up the ice crystals, then complete the freezing. (Serves 6)

LIME TAPIOCA FLUFF

Scant ⅓ cup quick-cooking tapioca
2½ cups water
¾ cup sugar
1 tbsp butter
½ tsp salt
¼ cup lime juice
½ tsp grated lime rind
2 egg whites

Mix tapioca, water, sugar, butter and salt in a saucepan and heat to boiling, stirring constantly. Remove from the heat and add lime juice and rind. Beat egg whites until stiff. Pour hot tapioca mixture slowly over them, beating well while pouring. Cool, then chill thoroughly before serving. (Serves 5)

LIMEADE

Juice of 1 lime
1 cup simple sirup
3½ cups water

Stir lime juice and simple sirup (*see* SIRUP) together, pour over cracked ice in 6 10-ounce glasses, fill with water. Garnish with mint leaves, orange slices, fresh berries or pineapple sticks; serve with straws. (Serves 6)

PINEAPPLE LIME PUNCH

2 cups currant jelly
2 cups boiling water
2 cups pineapple juice
1 cup orange juice
2 cups strained lime juice
1 qt ginger ale

Beat currant jelly with rotary beater until frothy; add hot water and continue beating until jelly is dissolved; add fruit juices and chill. Before serving add ginger ale and pour over a large piece of ice. (Makes approximately 3 quarts)

LIME SALTS. Lime salts and phosphates, when taken in food or drinking water in large quantities for several weeks or months, tend to cause the deposit of renal or vesical calculi. (Renal calculi are solid concretions formed in the kidney.)

LIME SQUEEZER. A plier-like instrument which extracts the juice from lime halves by crushing them between two serrated jaws. The juice is strained through a perforated shield attached to one of the jaws.

LIMEQUAT. A fruit obtained by crossing the round kumquat with the lime, the object being to overcome the extreme sensitiveness of the lime-tree to any suspicion of frost. The result is a fruit with juice and pulp possessing much of the true lime character, combined with that of the kumquat and its flavor.

LINEN DAMASK. The finest quality of table cloth, made from long flax fibers. It is commonly used for formal dinners. *See also* TABLE SETTING and SERVICE.

LING BERRY. The mountain cranberry. This name is also applied to several other berries, edible and otherwise.

LING-FISH. A member of the cod fish family.

LINGONBERRY. Another name for the mountain cranberry. It is also sometimes spelled Lingenberry.

LINK SAUSAGE. *See* SAUSAGE.

LIPSKI CHEESE. A Yugoslavian cheese.

LIPTAU. This cheese is made in the Provinces of Liptau, Saros, and Arva in Hungary, from sheep's milk. Condiments, especially red peppers, are usually added. It is rather greasy and has a sharp taste.

LIQUEUR. A potent spirit that is sweetened and flavored or scented or both. The term is also applied to some outstanding aged liquors fine enough to be enjoyed undiluted and unflavored, and also to some very sweet sirups used for flavoring purposes.

The first liqueurs, as the cordials, were developed more for their medicinal than their epicurean qualities. The monasteries in France, in particular, made great strides along these lines, and from them came the beginnings of an industry that has persisted even to the present day.

There are great numbers and varieties of liqueurs extant. The more important ones are listed alphabetically in this book. The French classify their liqueurs generally as *crèmes* (very sweet) and *eaux* or *elixirs* (not so sweet and more limpid). Liqueurs are named after the substance giving the predominant flavor (Creme de Menthe), its color (Liqueur Jaune), or the locale or maker (Chartreuse).

In addition to distinctive flavor, liqueurs frequently have striking colors, even spectacular colors, as in the case of Goldwasser.

While in common parlance the names cordial and liqueur have become almost interchangeable, there actually is a distinction between the two. All cordials are liqueurs, but, strictly speaking, all liqueurs are not cordials. A cordial is a stimulant that encourages blood circulation and otherwise acts on the heart. Liqueurs are stimulants, but not all are as effective as cordials, and many are more intended for use as a digestive.

There are three main processes by which liqueurs are made. All are based on a strong, pure, often neutral, spirit, and all are sweetened with either sugar or sirup. The difference lies in the manner in which the flavoring is added.

In the distillation or alcoholate method, the spirit is first infused with the aromatic flavoring substances and then distilled, often in the presence of solid pieces of the flavoring material, the alcoholate thus obtained sweetened and possibly colored to make the liqueur. The better liqueurs are made by this method.

In the essence method, the spirit is directly mixed with various flavoring essences and oils, sweetened, and then filtered. Products of this method are generally regarded as inferior.

Cordials are commonly made by the infusion process, whereby the spirit and sugar are added to fresh fruit juice or similar substances.

The exact formulation and manufacturing methods of many liqueurs are jealously guarded industrial secrets, but it is known that the making of fine liqueur can be a highly involved and delicate procedure.

Liqueurs have a wide range of alcoholic strengths, running from 27 percent for anisette to 80 percent for absinthe.

Though an improved pharmacopeia has largely supplanted their medicinal use, the cordials and liqueurs are still used as stimulants and digestives. Their greatest use lies in their appeal to eye and palate, however. Because of their sweetness and extreme strength, they are commonly used to flavor and color mixed drinks or, when served alone, are dispensed in relatively small portions, usually in special glasses (*see* GLASSWARE).

They are properly served as digestives, following the meal. Though delicious in their own right, there are some drinks, as the POUSSE CAFE (*which see*), whose appeal

is based largely on their eye-catching colors. *See also* CORDIAL.

Liqueur de Coing. A zestful liqueur, made in France, made with very old Cognac, the oil extracted from selected ripe and sound quinces and crushed bitter almond extract. Very sweet.

Liqueur d'Or. A form of GOLDWASSER (*which see*); a white liqueur containing bits of gold leaf that float about when agitated. Made in France, it is flavored with lemon peel, as opposed to Danziger Goldwasser, which derives its predominant flavor from orange rind.

Liqueur du Reverend Père de Montford. A golden, French liqueur with a subtle apricot-peach flavor. Highly aromatic, it has excellent reputation of more than six centuries' standing. It is commonly served as an after-dinner cordial. *See also* LIQUEUR.

Liqueur Jaune. A name commonly given to imitations of yellow CHARTREUSE (*which see*).

Liqueur Verte. A name commonly given to some of the imitations of green CHARTREUSE (*which see*).

LIQUOR. *See* BRANDY, GIN, RUM, WHISKY.

LIQUOR SAUCES. *See* BRANDY SAUCE, EGGNOG SAUCE.

LITCHI NUT. A Chinese nut resembling a strawberry, grown extensively in China. It is really a dried fruit surrounded

LITCHI NUT

by a nut-like shell. It is for sale in nearly all Chinese stores on the Pacific Coast, as well as in large cities where Chinese have settled.

LIVER. When we slice a piece of liver, we may see, if we look carefully, little round corpuscles, yellow in the center, with a red perimeter. These are the hepatic globules which contain the fat, bile pigments, etc., so necessary to life.

In human beings as well as in animals, the liver collects the venous blood and has many other functions of great importance, among which are: the secretion of bile, especially during digestion; the storing of sugars in the form of glycogen which is released into the blood stream as needed; and the elimination of inumerable poisons coming from the outside, in the shape of foods, as well as those generated in the system. Hence it has greater nutritive power than any other viscera of the animal kingdom.

However, since medical authorities have found out that liver was rich in Vitamins A, B, and C, this delicacy has jumped in price by leaps and bounds, and today calf's liver, which formerly used to be given away "to feed the cat," now fetches a high price. The reason given by the butcher is that the demand is greater than the production.

Beef, sheep, and pork livers are less in demand than calf's liver and therefore are lower in price—a point in their favor when cost must be considered. According to the findings of research scientists, these livers are fully as nutritious and potent in iron and vitamins as calf's liver.

HINTS ON PREPARATION

Liver is very tender except for the membrane or skin covering the outside and the tubes which run through it. These should be removed before cooking, particularly in beef liver, in order to give a tender dish. The membrane can be removed from the slices of liver by inserting the point of a knife beneath it and pulling it from the meat. The tubes may be cut out, or if the whole liver has been bought, they may be pulled out by loosening at one end and pulling the entire tube out of the liver. A sharp knife will aid in loosening the meat. This operation is easier if the hands are floured.

Liver should be cooked just until it loses its pink color. Overcooking makes it hard and tough. Slices should be of uniform thickness so that they cook evenly and are best cut fairly thin.

CHICKEN LIVER

Chicken livers are a special delicacy which may be obtained from the butcher or from dealers who sell poultry in parts. Look over the livers and carefully cut away any part that has been discolored by the gall. Chicken livers need only to be sautéed in a little butter or other fat. They go especially well with scrambled eggs, rice or noodles dishes, or in a spaghetti sauce.

BAKED LIVER BOHEMIAN STYLE

¾ lb boned veal shoulder
1 lb liver
Bouquet garni
1 cup thin sour cream
2 tbsp flour
1 tbsp paprika
Salt
2½ cups peas (a No. 2 can)

Dice the veal and simmer gently for half an hour with the bouquet garni (*which see*). Discard the bouquet garni and add the cream with which the flour, paprika and salt have been smoothly blended. Bring to the boiling point, stirring constantly, then add the peas, well drained, and the liver which has been wiped, scalded for a moment, then diced. Turn into a casserole and bake in a moderate oven (350° F.) 30 to 35 minutes. Serve with mashed potatoes. (Serves 6)

BAKED LIVER ROLLS

1½ cups soft bread crumbs
Salt and black pepper
1 tbsp finely minced parsley
½ cup ground ham
½ cup finely minced onions
4 tbsp bacon drippings
½ cup stock
12 thin slices liver

Combine the bread crumbs, salt, pepper, parsley and ham. Melt the drippings and when hot, cook the onions in it without browning. Add the bread crumb mixture and cook five minutes, stirring often from the bottom of the pan. Spread the dressing thinly on the slices of liver, roll up and skewer or tie with string. Arrange in a greased baking dish, pour over the stock and cover. Bake in a moderate oven (350° F.) 35 to 40 minutes. Baste occasionally with the stock in the dish and add more if necessary. Serve with spinach, topping this with buttered crumbs. (Serves 6)

BRAISED LIVER FARMER STYLE

2½ lb liver (in one piece)
Seasoned flour
Bacon drippings
3 small onions, quartered
½ cup diced celery
1 cup diced carrots
½ cup diced yellow turnip
1 large green pepper, diced
2½ cups tomatoes (a No. 2 can)
6 slices bacon, diced
1 cup tomato juice
Bouquet garni
1 cup diced, raw string beans
Salt and pepper
4 large potatoes, quartered

Wipe, scald and remove the thin outer skin and any veins from the liver. Roll in seasoned flour, then sear on all sides in the bacon drippings. Place in a large casserole with all remaining ingredients except the potatoes. Cover and bake in a moderate oven (350° F.) for 2 hours. Arrange the potatoes on top of the other vegetables about 40 minutes before serving time. (Serves 8)

BROILED LIVER BEARNAISE

6 thick slices liver
Seasoned flour
4 tbsp bacon drippings
3 tbsp very finely minced onions
2 tbsp tarragon vinegar
3 egg yolks
Salt and black pepper
Dash of cayenne
2 tbsp chopped parsley
1 tbsp chopped pickles

Wipe and scald the liver; roll in seasoned flour and sauté on both sides in the bacon drippings. Meanwhile prepare the sauce by cooking the onions (shallots are preferable) in the vinegar for five minutes. Do this in a double boiler and after cooking the onions, set over hot water and add the egg yolks, one at a time, beating after each addition. Cook until of the consistency of a custard, stirring constantly and keeping the water in the lower vessel under the boiling point. Add the seasonings and flavorings and when serving place a tablespoon of the sauce on each slice of liver. Garnish with small triangles of fried bread or toast. (Serves 6)

BROILED LIVER SPANISH STYLE

6 thick slices liver
Seasoned flour
4 tbsp olive oil

Wipe and scald the liver, then dredge with seasoned flour. Pour the olive oil over and let stand 10 minutes, turning once. Lift from the oil and broil under moderate heat until the liver begins to exude little droplets of pink blood. Serve very hot, topping each portion with a slice of broiled tomato. Garnish with French fried onion rings and fried parsley. (Serves 6)

BROILED LIVER STEAK

6 thick slices liver
4 tbsp olive oil
1 tbsp lemon juice
Salt and pepper
A small piece bay leaf
1 small thinly sliced onion
1 small thinly sliced carrot
4 tbsp butter
2 tbsp minced parsley
Few drops onion juice
1 tsp Worcestershire sauce

Wipe and scald the liver, then pound with a rolling pin to break the fibers. Combine the olive oil, lemon juice, salt, pepper, bay leaf, onion and carrot and marinate the liver in this mixture for 1 hour, turning 3 or 4 times. Broil very slowly, about five minutes, turning occasionally. Top with the butter creamed with the parsley, onion juice and Worcestershire sauce. (Serves 6)

DANISH LIVER LOAF

1½ lb liver
Slices of fat salt pork
6 anchovy fillets

3 eggs
2 medium-sized onions, finely chopped
1 tbsp minced green pepper
Salt and pepper
A dash of nutmeg
2 tsp Worcestershire sauce

Wipe and scald the liver. Cook 3 or 4 minutes in boiling salted water, then drain and discard any veins. Cut into small pieces and pass through the food chopper with two slices of fat salt pork and the anchovy fillets, washed and patted dry. Now combine with the beaten eggs, the onions, green pepper, seasonings and flavorings. Mix all thoroughly, then pass a second time through the food chopper to insure smoothness and thorough blending. Arrange three or four slices of fat salt pork in the bottom of a loaf pan and place the liver mixture on these. Cover with buttered paper and bake in a slow oven (300° F.) for two hours, removing the paper half an hour before the loaf is done.

Cool in the dish and slice for service with Andalouse sauce. For this combine 1 cup of mayonnaise, ⅓ cup of thick tomato purée, 1 tablespoon of finely minced green pepper and salt and cayenne to taste. (Serves 6)

Fried Breaded Liver

6 slices liver
Beaten egg
Bread or cracker crumbs
5 tbsp butter or bacon fat
Tomato sauce

Wipe and scald the liver. Dip first into beaten egg, then into crumbs, and sauté gently in the butter or bacon fat. Serve with tomato sauce, corn fritters, and fried onions. (Serves 6)

Fried Breaded Liver Creole

Substitute a Creole sauce (which see) for the tomato sauce in the recipe above and sprinkle chopped parsley over all at the moment of serving.

Fried Liver Steak a la Minute

6 slices liver
Salt and black pepper
4 tbsp butter or margarine

2 tbsp beef stock
A few drops lemon juice
1 scant tsp meat extract
Finely minced parsley

Wipe, scald and remove any veins from the liver, then pound with a rolling pin until quite thin. Season with salt and pepper and sauté in the butter. Remove the liver to a hot platter, then add to the butter in the pan the stock, lemon juice, and meat extract. Bring to boiling point, pour over the liver and dust with parsley. (Serves 6)

Liver Balls

¼ lb liver, ground
2 tbsp chopped onion
2 tbsp chopped parsley
1 cup soft bread crumbs
¼ tsp pepper
1 tsp salt
2 cups boiling salted water (or stock)

Combine all the above ingredients, except the water, in the order given. Form into small balls and cook in boiling, salted water or stock (meat, poultry, broth from corned beef, broth of cooked ham, etc.) for 3 minutes. Add to the soup, or serve with spaghetti, noodles, mashed potatoes, or other vegetables.

Liver Dumplings (Dutch Method)

1 large soup bone (about 2 lb)
2 qt cold water
Salt and pepper
12 sprigs celery tops
6 sprigs fresh parsley
3 whole cloves
1 lb beef liver
2 medium-sized onions, finely minced
2 tbsp butter
2 eggs, slightly beaten
1 cup milk
2 cups flour

Have the butcher saw the bone moderately small. Cook with the water, seasonings, and flavorings for 2 hours, simmering slowly and keeping the pan covered during the cooking; then strain and reserve the broth. Scrape the liver so as to eliminate all tissue and fiber. Cook the onions in butter until tender and yellow but not brown, stirring frequently; then add the liver, and cook two minutes, stirring constantly. Beat the eggs and milk, then stir into them enough flour to make a light soft dough. Combine this with the onion and liver mixture, and shape into balls the size of an egg. Bring the soup stock again to the boiling point, drop in the dumplings, and cook, uncovered, for 18 to 20 minutes.

These are appropriate to serve with noodles, macaroni or spaghetti or with various cooked vegetables, or plain with stock. (Serves 6)

LIVER LOAF COUNTRY STYLE

6 slices diced bacon
1¾ lb liver
1¼ cups bread crumbs
¾ cup beef stock
1 egg yolk
1 tbsp finely minced parsley
1 finely minced onion
1 small clove garlic
Salt and pepper
A dash of nutmeg and thyme
1 scant tsp poultry seasoning
1 tsp Worcestershire sauce

Cook the bacon until crisp, lift out and set aside. Wipe, scald and remove any veins from the liver and slice thinly. Cook in the bacon drippings about 3 minutes. Soak the crumbs in the stock, then pass liver, bacon and crumbs through the food chopper, using the coarse knife. Add the egg yolk, parsley, onion, garlic and seasonings, and again pass through the food chopper. Turn into a greased loaf pan, cover with buttered paper and bake in a moderately hot oven (350°–375° F.) 45 to 50 minutes. Cool in the pan. Serve cold with a spiced mayonnaise and garnish with sliced tomatoes, hard-cooked eggs, and parsley. (Serves 6 or 8)

LIVER STEW FAMILY STYLE

1¾ lb liver
6 slices bacon, diced
Salt and pepper
A dash of nutmeg
½ can mushrooms, drained
1 diced green pepper
Bouquet garni
2½ cups tomatoes (a No. 2 can)

Wipe, scald, remove veins from the liver and cut into large cubes. Arrange in a casserole which can be sent to table, first the bacon, then the liver seasoned with salt, pepper, and nutmeg. Pour the mushrooms over this, sprinkle with the diced green pepper, add the bouquet garni and finally the tomatoes, seasoning these with salt and pepper. Bring quickly to boiling point, then cook, covered, in a moderate oven (350° F.) 1¼ hours. Should there be any excess of fat on the surface, skim this off before serving.

LIVER SAUSAGE. *See* SAUSAGE.

LIVERWURST. *See* SAUSAGE.

LIVLANDER CHEESE. A German sour milk cheese with a very sharp, pungent odor and taste. It has a variety of other names, the commonest being hand cheese.

LOACH. A small fresh water fish, like a minnow.

LOAF (MEAT). A baked loaf of chopped or ground meat. *See* MEAT LOAF.

LOAF PAN. A deep, rectangular pan used to bake bread, cake, fish, meat, or vegetable loaves.

LOAF PAN

LOAF CHEESE. Also called process cheese. A clean, sound, heated product made by pulverizing and blending, with the aid of heat and water, with or without salt, one or more lots of cheese into a homogeneous, plastic mass. It is reported that one-half of all cheese made in this country is marketed as loaf or process cheese— American Cheddar, Swiss, Brick, L mburg, Camembert. Twenty percent white American cheese is often blended with Swiss to give proper texture. Cheese processed in this fashion gives a uniform product which does not continue to age.

LOAF PAN. *See* CAKE PAN.

LOBSTER. The lobster heads the list of shellfish belonging to the *Decapodae*

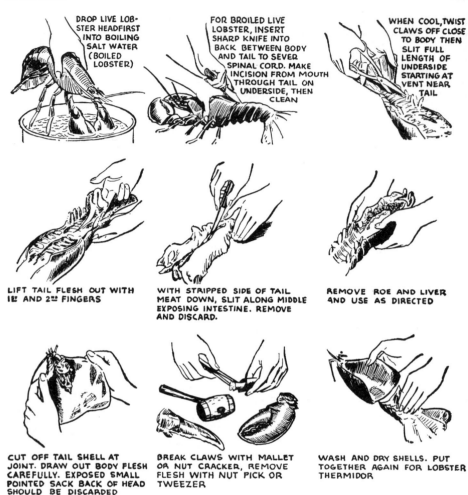

KILLING AND CLEANING A LOBSTER

family and, like the crab, is a scavenger of the ocean. Lobsters are found in most parts of the world—along our shores from Labrador southward to Delaware Bay, usually near the rocky shores at depths of from 60 to 120 feet. They feed at this level, seldom rising more than a few feet above the bottom.

Specimens have been found weighing 16 to 25 pounds, but such huge lobsters apparently are now extinct along our coasts. The average weight of a lobster is two pounds and the length from 10 to 15 inches. Lobsters are largest and most abundant from June to September, but are obtainable all the year round. When taken from the water, the shells are of mottled, dark green color, except when the lobster is found on sandy bottoms, when the shell is quite red.

SELECTING AND PREPARING LOBSTER

In choosing a live lobster, remember that there is a greater shrinkage than in any other fish. If the lobster is already cooked, pick it up, and if it is heavy in proportion to its size, the lobster is fresh. Straighten the tail, and if it springs back to its former place, the lobster was alive (as it should have been) when it was put into the pot for boiling.

In boiling a lobster, have salted water, or whatever other liquid the recipe calls for, boiling rapidly in a large fish kettle. Plunge the lobsters into the boiling liquid, head first, one at a time, bringing the liquid back to the boiling point between each addition. Lobsters should be entirely immersed in the liquid. The time usually required for cooking lobster is about 15 to 20 minutes, depending on the size. Do not stop the rapid boiling as this will make the meat tough.

In opening a cooked lobster first remove the large claws, then the small claws and tail. The tail meat may sometimes, after a little practice, be drawn out whole with a fork or a skewer, but more often it is necessary to cut the thin shell in the under part of the tail with a pair of kitchen scissors, before the tail meat can be removed.

Divide the tail meat through the center and remove the small intestinal vein which runs along the entire length. Hold the body of the shell firmly in the left hand, and with first two fingers and thumb of the right hand, draw out the body, leaving in the shell the stomach, which is not edible. The green liver is a particular delicacy. Discard the lungs. Break the body through the middle, and separate the body bones, picking out the meat that lies between them, which is the sweetest and tenderest part of the lobster. Separate the claws at the joints.

LIVE LOBSTER

Live lobsters may be dressed for broiling at the fish store or may be prepared at home. Cross the large claws and hold them firmly with the left hand. Insert a sharp knife into the back between the body and the tail shells. This kills the lobster by severing the spinal cord. Place the lobster on its back and make a deep incision immediately below its mouth and draw the knife through the body and the entire length of the tail. (For Bouillabaisse, *which see*, the body should be cut again crosswise.) Remove the small stomach from just back of the head and the intestinal tract which runs from the stomach to the end of the tail. Remove also the spongy lungs; the latter lie between the meat and the shell. Crack the claw shells with a nutcracker, mallet, or cleaver.

COLD LOBSTER

Cold lobster makes a good addition to a summer luncheon and may be served with

any one of the cold fish sauces (*See* MAYONNAISE), using either canned or fresh lobster. When serving cold lobster, take care to have it well chilled. Its usual and most popular sauce, however, is mayonnaise.

Cold lobster is usually served in its shell from which it has been first loosened, and the claws cracked with a mallet or cleaver. The dish may be garnished with cups of crisp lettuce, containing mayonnaise which may be forced through a pastry bag with fancy tube. Quartered hard-cooked eggs are also used for garnishing. A few capers too may be sprinkled over the mayonnaise. Crisp, fresh parsley or young watercress is a good garnish for a dish of cold lobster; well chilled slices of red beets, strips of gherkins, or strips of green pepper may also serve as decoration.

BAKED LIVE LOBSTER

Split a 2-pound live lobster and place in a baking pan. Season highly with salt, cayenne and Worcestershire sauce, pour 4 tablespoons of melted butter over the lobster and bake in a hot oven (450° F.) about 15 minutes. Any juices remaining in the pan may be added to the cooked lobster with a tiny bit of onion juice.

BROILED LIVE LOBSTER GOURMET

Split the live lobster lengthwise and crack the claws. Brush with olive oil or melted butter, even to the claws to keep the meat inside from drying out. Sprinkle with paprika and broil 8 minutes on the flesh side; then turn and broil 6 minutes on the shell side, basting frequently while cooking with melted butter to which a little minced parsley and a tiny bit of garlic have been added. Serve very hot with melted butter and French fried or shoestring potatoes. (Serves 2)

LOBSTER COCKTAIL

Cook the lobster meat, cut it in pieces, chill thoroughly, and serve in cocktail glasses with cocktail sauce (*see* COCKTAIL) or with highly seasoned mayonnaise.

LOBSTER CURRY SOUFFLE

2 tbsp butter
3 tbsp flour

1 cup milk
¾ tsp salt
½ tsp curry powder
Few drops tabasco sauce
1 tsp minced parsley
1 tsp Angostura bitters
1 tsp lemon juice
1 can (6 oz) lobster meat
3 eggs

Make a white sauce of the butter, flour and milk. Add the seasonings and flavorings, the lobster meat, cut in small pieces but not chopped, and the well beaten egg yolks. Finally fold in the stiffly beaten egg whites and turn into an oiled or buttered casserole. Place this in a pan of hot water and bake in a very moderate oven (325° F.) 50 minutes. (Serves 4)

LOBSTER MOUSSE

2 cups lobster meat
½ cup white sauce
2 eggs
Salt, pepper and paprika
3 tbsp cooking sherry

Pass the lobster meat (quick-frozen, canned, or fresh cooked) through the food chopper as often as necessary to produce a smooth mass. Blend with the white sauce (*which see*), beaten eggs, seasonings, and sherry. Turn into individual buttered molds or into one large buttered mold or casserole. Place in a pan of hot water, cover with buttered paper and bake in a moderate oven (350° F.) about 20 minutes for small molds, 35 to 40 minutes for one large mold. Unmold and serve with mushroom sauce or lobster sauce. *See* WHITE SAUCE. (Serves 4)

Shrimp or crabmeat mousse may be made by the same recipe using these fish.

LOBSTER NEWBURG

2 lb lobster (cooked)
¼ cup butter
1 tbsp flour
Salt and paprika
Dash of nutmeg
1 cup thin cream
3 egg yolks
2 tbsp sherry

Remove the lobster meat from the shell and dice it. Melt the butter, add the flour and seasonings, and when smoothly blended, gradually add the cream. Bring to boiling point, stir in the lobster meat and when thoroughly heated, add the beaten egg yolks and the sherry and cook over hot water (double boiler) just until thickened, but not boiling. Serve on toast. (Serves 2 or 3)

LOBSTER THERMIDOR

2 (1½ lb) lobsters (cooked)
2 tbsp butter
2 tbsp flour
1 tsp dry mustard
¼ tsp salt
Dash of cayenne
1 tbsp minced parsley
1 cup thin cream
⅓ cup white wine
Grated Parmesan cheese

Cut the lobsters in halves lengthwise. Remove and cube the meat. Sauté it in the butter about 5 minutes, then add the flour, seasonings and cream. Heat and blend thoroughly. Add the wine, then return the mixture to the lobster shells, sprinkle with the cheese and bake in a hot oven about 10 minutes, or brown under the broiler. If desired, ¼ cup of sliced mushrooms may be sautéed in the butter before adding the lobster. (Serves 2 or 4)

LOGANBERRY. Loganberries were named after Judge J. H. Logan who dis-

LOGANBERRY

covered what was apparently a cross between blackberries and red raspberries,
in 1881. They resemble blackberries in
shape, but have the color and flavor of red
raspberries, except that they are more tart.
They are seldom found in great quantity
in the market, the entire, or almost the entire production of the Pacific coast being
canned. They are very perishable and
should be stored in a cool, dry place. They
are used as breakfast fruit, for dessert, in
pies, ices, and beverages, exactly like
blackberries and other berries. They
should be thoroughly washed before being
used. The dark purplish-red are the ripest.

LOGANBERRY ICE CREAM

½ cup loganberries
⅔ cup sweetened condensed milk
½ cup water
1 tbsp lemon juice
1 cup heavy cream, whipped

Wash and pick over the berries and force
through a sieve. Mix the pulp, milk water
and lemon juice and chill. Fold in whipped
cream. Turn into freezing tray of automatic refrigerator and freeze 2 to 4 hours,
or until firm. Stir well twice during freezing. (Makes approximately 1 quart)

LOGANBERRY TAPIOCA

⅓ cup quick-cooking tapioca
½ cup sugar
¼ tsp salt
12 oz can loganberry juice
¾ cup water
4½ tsp lemon juice
Coffee cream

Mix the tapioca, sugar, salt, loganberry
juice and water. Stir well and cook over
direct heat, stirring constantly, until it
reaches a full rolling boil. Remove from
heat and stir in lemon juice. Chill, stirring
occasionally as it cools. It becomes much
thicker when cold. Serve with cream.
(Serves 5)

LOIN. *See* BEEF, LAMB, MEAT, PORK.

LOIN CHOP. A chop taken from the
loin of the animal.

LOLLIPOP. A large clear taffy or candy, usually impaled on a stick.

LONGFIN FISH. Name given to several long-finned fishes (*Serranidae* family) of
Australia. It is not found in this hemisphere.

LORRAINE CHEESE. A small, hard
cheese, made with sour milk and seasoned
with pepper, salt, and pistachio nuts. In
size it is usually about two ounces. It is
made in Lorraine, France, and sells at a
very high price.

LOQUAT. A low-growing pomaceous
fruit, cultivated in the Gulf states for preserving.

LOQUAT

LOUISIANA CALAS. A delicious confection, a favorite among the Creoles of
New Orleans during the Mardi Gras celebration. They are sold hot in the streets and
cannot travel very far from the frying
kettle.

CALAS

½ cup rice
3 cups water
Salt
1 yeast cake
2 tbsp lukewarm water
3 eggs
½ cup sugar
3 tbsp flour
Frying fat
Powdered sugar

Boil the rice in the water, slightly salted,
until very soft and mushy. When cold, add
the yeast liquefied in the lukewarm water.
Let rise overnight. In the morning, add
the well beaten eggs with the sugar and
flour and beat thoroughly; the mixture
should be of the consistency of a thick batter. Set aside to rise for about 15 minutes,
then drop by tablespoonsfuls into deep hot
fat (360°–357° F.). Cook to a light golden
color, turning several times. Drain on soft,
crumpled paper, sprinkle with powdered
sugar, and serve very hot.

In Louisiana the Negroes hawk the calas through the streets in the early morning in covered baskets crying "calas, belle calas, tout chaud:"

LOVAGE. See HERBS.

LOVING CUP. A large, ceremonial, two-handled drinking cup, formerly passed around the table at banquets and similar functions. In the olden days elaborate local rituals were often built up around the passing of the loving cup. For example, each guest, on receiving the cup, would rise, bow to the assembly in a prescribed routine, make a toast, quaff, and then wipe the rim before passing it on to his neighbor. The cup is double handled for ease in passing.

The loving cup has pretty much passed out of the present social system as a drinking vessel and is now chiefly used as an athletic award. There are, however, some drinks, mostly wine mixtures, which are still called "loving cups" because they had originally been developed for use in this communal bowl. See WINE CUP.

LUKEWARM. As applied to cookery this means a that liquid or a food is moderately warm, tepid.

LUNCH or **LUNCHEON.** A light meal between other meals, usually second consideration in planning the meals for the day. Here flexibility of menu is essential. The family luncheon is served in homes to every member of the family or more often to the children and mother when father does not come home. The bridge or party luncheon and the formal luncheon have both gained favor in recent years. See TABLE SETTING AND SERVICE.

No brain worker can digest a hearty meal and concentrate at the same time. The manual laborer must avoid overeating at lunch, for physical work also retards digestion. In both cases the nerve energy necessary to digest the food is diverted. The hearty meal of the day should be taken when the cares and hard work of the day are done.

LUNCH CHEESE. A German cheese of the Limburger type, round in shape, and about three inches in diameter. It is also known as Fruhstuck cheese.

LUNCHBOX. Of all food forms, the sandwich is best adapted to lunchbox use. Its simplicity and economy of preparation, its ease in carrying and convenience in eating are all geared to the demands of modern life.

The rules of common sense apply to the preparation of the lunch-box meal. The homemaker must balance the materials on hand with the tastes of her family. She must be economical, but not frugal. The lunch-box sandwich is essentially a practical thing, and while imagination should be used in its preparation, the object is to provide "eating food," not appetizers or bridge party novelties.

To ease the morning duties, the sandwiches may be prepared the night before, if the filling used will lend itself to this treatment. They should be well wrapped in waxed paper, immediately after making, to keep them fresh. Individual sandwich bags designed for this purpose are on the market. They should then be stored in a cool, dry place—sometimes the refrigerator—until morning.

The cold, covered type of sandwich should be used. The sandwich should be so constructed as to stand up under a normal amount of rough treatment while being carried. Three-decker, or club, sandwiches are not recommended for that reason.

For a description of sandwiches, their preparation, recipes, garnishes, etc., see SANDWICHES and PICNICS.

LUNCHEON FORK. See FLATWARE.

LUNCHEON KNIFE. See FLATWARE.

LUNCHEON PLATE. A flat plate, usually seven inches in diameter. See DISHES; see also TABLE SETTING AND SERVICE.

LUNEBERG CHEESE. A German cheese which is a cross between Emmenthaler and Limburger.

LUNEL. A tawny, delicate, unfortified, sweet dessert wine made in the vineyards of Lunel on the French side of the Pyrenees Mountains. See WINE.

M

MACADAMIA NUTS. Exotic is the word that describes the Hawaiian macadamia nuts that are now marketed in America, roasted, salted, and vacuum packed. This really delicious nut was first discovered to be edible by Dr. John Macadam, secretary of the Philosophical Institute of Melbourne, Australia, where, strangely enough, the nut is almost unknown, even today. In 1892, the seeds were taken to Hawaii by a man named Jordan to plant in his back-yard. It was fourteen years later that several thousand trees were planted with the purpose of creating a new industry. Now there are many groves.

The macadamia is a hard nut to crack. The kernel is buried in a fibrous husk, ¼ inch thick, under which there is a second line of fortification hard enough to break a nut cracker. Before cracking, the macadamia nuts go into a dehydrating unit for a period of days to reduce their moisture content—then to the cracking machine, which grades, cracks, and sorts with a quick precision. After shelling, the kernels are again dehydrated until the moisture is less than 2 percent.

This new nut provides the newest cocktail bite. It is golden brown and tastes like an almond, but resembles a clean-shaven, overgrown hazel nut. To add to the confusion of the description, it has the faint aroma of freshly roasted coffee beans.

MACARONI. There are practically all shapes and sizes of macaroni, some formed into long straight sticks, some in small elbows, sea shells of various sizes, baskets and alphabets, all, however, having the same food value.

To be truly flavorsome and delicious, macaroni should not be overcooked. It is tender if, when a piece of it is cut, the end does not look chalky white. Overcooking develops a soft and shapeless mass which is very unappetizing. Always have the water boiling hard before adding macaroni, or spaghetti, and then regulate the heat to keep the water boiling steadily and constantly.

Drain immediately after cooking by turning the whole into a colander. Some cooks like to run cold water over the macaroni or spaghetti to make the sections stand apart. The Italians, who are expert in cooking macaroni and spaghetti, say: It should be cooked "al dente"—sufficiently firm to be felt "under the tooth." Italians are as particular about the time of cooking macaroni and spaghetti as we are about eggs.

For an eight ounce package of macaroni, which easily serves six or eight, use six cups of water with one scant teaspoon of salt and cook about nine minutes. To prevent boiling over, put a tablespoon of butter or margarine into the cooking water, or wipe the inside edge of the saucepan with greased paper. See also PASTES and SPAGHETTI.

SERVING SUGGESTIONS

(1) Combine in any desired proportions creamed macaroni, baby lima beans, and ham or tongue. Bake in a casserole in a hot oven (400° F.) 35 to 40 minutes.

(2) Use creamed macaroni, macaroni and cheese or spaghetti and tomatoes as a stuffing for green peppers, tomatoes or onions, topping with buttered crumbs or crumbs and grated cheese. Bake.

(3) Add cooked mushrooms and diced chicken or calf's liver to macaroni or spaghetti with tomato sauce. Season to taste and heat thoroughly.

(4) Blend chopped pimientoes and seedless raisins with cooked macaroni, add a cheese sauce and bake in a moderate oven (350° F.) 30 minutes.

MACADAMIA NUT

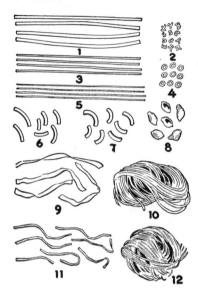

TYPES OF MACARONI 1. Macaroni
2. Alphabet 3. Spaghetti 4. Macaroni
Rings 5. Vermicelli 6. Elbow Spaghetti
7. Elbow Macaroni 8. Macaroni Shells
9. Wide Egg Noodles 10. Large Twisted
Vermicelli 11. Fine Egg Noodles 12.
Fine Twisted Vermicelli

(5) Use cooked macaroni, spaghetti, or
noodles, with butter, poppy seeds, and
chopped blanched almonds as a stuffing for
chicken or turkey.

(6) Combine cooked shell macaroni
with cream sauce, mushrooms, chopped
veal, chicken or pork, and grated cheese.
Bake in a casserole in a moderately hot
oven (375° F.) about half an hour.

(7) Form cooked macaroni, spaghetti
or noodles into nests for individual service
and fill with creamed chipped beef and
sliced mushrooms.

MACARONI COMBINATION SALAD

2 cups cooked, seasoned, chilled macaroni
½ cup shredded raw carrots
½ cup shredded green pepper or pimiento
½ cup diced celery
½ cup cooked peas or lima beans

Cut the macaroni into convenient sized
pieces after cooking. Chill thoroughly, then
combine with the various vegetables, also
chilled, and season rather highly. Moisten

with Russian dressing. Pile high in lettuce
cups and garnish with cheese balls and
radish roses. (Serves 6)

MACARONI LUNCHEON LOAF

½ lb macaroni
Boiling salted water
1 cup cottage cheese
1 cup cooked spinach
½ cup soft bread crumbs
½ tsp salt
¼ tsp pepper
2 tsp grated onion
2 eggs

Cook the macaroni in boiling salted
water until tender. Drain and cut into inch
lengths. Add the cheese, spinach (well
drained and chopped), the crumbs, seasonings and onion. Moisten with the slightly beaten eggs, turn into a well greased loaf
pan and bake in a moderate oven (350°
F.) about 45 minutes. Unmold and mask
with cheese sauce (*which see*) into which a
little diced pimiento has been stirred.
(Serves 6)

MACARONI WITH OLIVE MUSHROOM SAUCE

2 tbsp oil
1 minced onion
1 No. 2 can tomatoes
1 tsp sugar
¼ tsp salt
1 can condensed cream of mushroom
soup
⅛ tsp pepper
½ cup sliced stuffed olives
1 package macaroni
Boiling salted water
¼ cup grated cheese
¼ cup buttered crumbs

Heat the oil and cook the onion in it for
three minutes. Add the tomatoes and seasonings and simmer gently for 20 minutes.
Add the soup and olives and stir until well
blended.

Cook the macaroni until just tender in
boiling salted water. Drain. Arrange alternate layers of macaroni and sauce in a
greased baking dish. Combine the cheese
and crumbs and sprinkle over the top.
Bake in a moderate oven (350° F.) about
half an hour. (Serves 6)

Old-fashioned Macaroni and Cheese

½ package macaroni
Boiling salted water
3 tbsp butter or margarine
3 tbsp flour
3 cups milk
Salt and pepper
1½ cups grated or diced cheese

Cook the macaroni until tender in boiling salted water. Drain. Blend the butter with the flour and add the milk gradually. Stir until boiling and cook until thickened, still stirring constantly. Season. Add ⅔ of the cheese and when this is melted pour the sauce over the macaroni which has been turned into a well greased baking dish or casserole. Sprinkle the remaining cheese over the surface and bake in a moderate oven (375° F.) until piping hot and delicately browned. (Serves 4 to 6)

Many prefer macaroni cooked with tomato sauce, in which case substitute good tomato sauce for the white sauce in the above recipe.

MACAROON. There are several varieties of these rich crunchy cookies. Originally they were a highly complicated French delicacy, but many recipes have been devised simplifying them for home baking. The oven door should never be opened during the baking period.

Cajun Macaroons

½ lb almond paste
3 egg whites
½ cup sifted pastry flour
½ cup fine granulated sugar
½ cup powdered sugar

These should be baked a few days in advance. They will keep several months when kept in a closed tin in a cool, dry place.

Work the almond paste with a wooden spoon until it is smooth. Add the egg whites, slightly beaten, and blend thoroughly. Add pastry flour, resifted with the granulated sugar and the powdered sugar. Cover a cooky sheet or sheets with plain white paper. The cooky mixture may be dropped from the tip of a teaspoon and shaped on the paper, or may be pressed through a cooky press, or shaped with a pastry bag and tube. Bake in a slow oven (300° F.) about 30 minutes. The cakes

may be removed from the paper by means of a spatula while still warm.

Variations. Finely chopped or ground candied fruits may be added to the mixture before baking. Or the tops of the macaroons may be decorated before baking by placing in the center of each a nut half, a raisin (seedless, black or white), or a bit of candied fruit—such as a bit of angelica—cut fancifully or by sprinkling with finely chopped nut meats. The cakes may be decorated after baking by dainty frosting designs formed with the help of a cake decorator or a pastry tube

Cocoa Macaroons

2 egg whites
3 tbsp cocoa
¼ tsp salt
¾ cup sugar
1½ cups cornflakes
½ cup moist shredded coconut

Beat egg whites until just stiff enough to hold moist peaks. Sift cocoa, salt and sugar together and add gradually to egg whites, continuing to beat until mixture will stand in soft peaks. Then lightly fold in cornflakes and coconut with a fork or wire whip. Drop from a teaspoon onto a baking sheet covered with smooth unglazed paper. Bake in a slow oven (300° F.) for 20 to 30 minutes or until well dried. Remove to cake racks and cool. (Makes about 2 dozen)

Coconut Macaroons

3 egg whites
1½ cups sugar
½ tsp salt
⅓ tsp almond extract
½ tsp vanilla
3 cups flaked cereal
½ cup shredded coconut
1 tsp grated lemon rind

Beat the egg whites until stiff, gradually adding the sugar and salt and beating well after each addition. The mixture should be stiff enough to hold its shape when all the sugar is added. Put in the flavorings, the combined flaked cereal, coconut and lemon rind, blend thoroughly and drop from the tip of a spoon onto well greased baking sheets. Bake in a very moderate oven (350°

F.) 20 to 25 minutes. Remove from the pan as soon as taken from the oven. (Makes 50)

FRENCH MACAROONS

½ lb almonds
2 egg whites, unbeaten
⅔ cup sugar
1 tsp vanilla
1 stiffly beaten egg white

Blanch and thoroughly dry the almonds, then pound them or pass through the food chopper, using the finest knife. Add gradually the unbeaten egg whites, alternately with the sugar and vanilla. Work in the stiffly beaten egg white, a little at a time, mixing thoroughly between additions. Turn the paste into a pastry bag fitted with a plain tube, and press small balls the size of a walnut onto waxed paper, on a cooky sheet. Lacking a pastry bag, the mixture may be dropped from the tip of a spoon. Bake in a slow oven (275°–300° F.) 15 to 20 minutes. Cool, then tear off the paper and join the macaroons by placing the flat bases together in pairs.

Other flavoring extracts may be substituted for vanilla, and other nuts, such as walnuts, hazelnuts, or cashews, for the almonds.

For soft macaroons add 2 teaspoons of cornstarch or potato starch to the above mixture. (Makes 18)

RICE MACAROONS

2 cups crisp rice flakes
4 egg whites
1½ cups sugar
¼ tsp salt
½ tsp vanilla
¼ tsp almond extract
1 cup shredded coconut
½ cup finely chopped nut meats

Toast and cool the rice flakes. Beat the egg whites until stiff, gradually adding the sugar and salt. Combine with the rice flakes, the flavorings, coconut and nut meats. Drop by teaspoonfuls onto well greased baking sheets and bake in a moderate oven (350° F.) for 25 minutes. Remove from the pans as soon as taken from the oven.

If the macaroons become hardened on the pan they may be softened by replacing

them in the oven for a few minutes. (Makes 36)

MACE. Mace forms an aril around nutmeg seeds (*see* NUTMEG). In this natural form it has a red color, but this fades to a light orange as the product is dried for commercial use. Mace has a mild, fragrant flavor. The aroma of ground mace is, naturally enough, similar to that of nutmeg; but the two spices differ in flavor and in use.

MACE

Mace is recommended for use in a variety of foods. It imparts a delicious flavor to oyster stew, cherry pie, and all chocolate dishes. It is used widely in baking, especially to flavor cakes and cookies. It serves as well to enhance the color of all yellow cakes and to flavor loaf cakes. Try adding a teaspoon of ground mace to a pint of whipped cream.

Blades of mace add their fragrance to fish sauces and stuffings, meat stuffings and gravies, soups, pickles, and preserves. A single blade, chopped, will lend interest to fruit jellies, Welsh rarebit, gingerbread dough, and stewed cherries.

MACEDOINE. As applied to cookery, this French term means a mixture of fruits or vegetables, served as a cocktail, a salad, a dessert, or as a sauce or garnish.

MACERATE. To soften or separate the parts of a food by steeping it in a fluid.

MACKEREL. Mackerel fishing played an important part in the early history of this country, both from a commercial standpoint and as the basis for treaties with Great Britain. In 1671 the laws of the Colony of Plymouth were revised to provide for the improvement of fishing for mackerel. Penalties were imposed for taking them at other than specified times. Mackerel were important to the early settlers both as food and as an article of commerce.

COMMON MACKEREL

This sea fish, belonging to the *Scombereidae* family, lives north of he equator. Like the pike and bluefish, the mackerel is one of the most predatory and voracious of the migratory fish which travel in groups, and after a shoal of mackerel passes, no small fish are to be found, all having been consumed by the larger gluttons. The common mackerel ordinarily has five false fins, but no bladder fins. When taken out of salt water, it is a beautiful metal-blue color, changing almost immediately on contact with the air to iris-green, and reflecting gold and purple. These colors are beautifully accentuated by intervening undulated black stripes, and all the rest of the body is a silver-white shade. Although mackerel measuring from 16 to 18 inches are caught, the usual length is less. The common weight is from three-quarters of a pound to one and three-quarters pounds.

Mackerel may be prepared in an endless variety of delicious ways and accompanied by most any kind of sauce. However, it is never better than when grilled and served with plenty of clarified or drawn butter.

VARIETIES OF MACKEREL

Bonito Mackerel. This distant relative of the mackerel ranges the Atlantic Coast of North and Central America. It is a large fish, weighing from five to twelve pounds, and is taken throughout summer and autumn. Owing to its stronger flavor, the bonito mackerel is not very popular as a food fish in this country. Its larger cousin, the California, or Pacific, Bonito, is found in the Pacific Ocean from California to Japan where it is important commercially.

Frozen Mackerel. Mackerel for freezing is caught in the autumn, at the peak of the season when its quality is of the best. It is rushed immediately to the refrigerating plants, which usually are located just off the docks. First the mackerel are washed, placed in huge pans, then conveyed into the freezers, which are kept at a temperature of 15 degrees below zero. They remain there for 24 hours. When removed from the freezers they are taken out of the pans in cakes—about 20 fish to the cake—and carefully glazed. Glazing takes place at a low temperature, in water at the freezing point.

The simplest way to defrost a mackerel is by immersing it in cold water. It should be gutted as soon as possible after defrosting, and then prepared in the same way that one would the fresh mackerel. Frozen fish tends to spoil more rapidly than the fresh product.

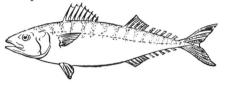

MACKEREL

Salt Mackerel. This fish must be freshened before cooking, allowing at least 24 hours for the process. Put the fish in a large amount of fresh water, meat side down. It is a good practice to place it on a rack, a few inches from the bottom of the vessel, so that the salt may drop away from the fish. Change the water a few times.

When the fish is to be broiled or fried it is necessary to freshen it longer than when it is to be boiled or cooked with milk, as the latter methods themselves lessen the salty flavor. To hurry the freshening process, it is helpful to cut out the bones of the mackerel or to make several gashes in the flesh.

Spanish Mackerel. A southern fish in season from November to May. The U.S. Government Bureau of Fisheries lists this fish of distinctive flavor among the leading varieties of fish marketed in the United States. In weight the fish vary from one and one half to six pounds, with an average weight of three pounds or less. The rich, firm flesh of the oily-meated Spanish mackerel is cooked by all the methods applied to other fish. It is more expensive than the common mackerel. *See also* FISH.

BAKED SAVORY FRESH MACKEREL

2 small fresh mackerel
4 tbsp butter
1 tsp salt
2 tbsp lemon juice
½ cup chopped pickle
½ cup chopped onions
1 tbsp minced parsley
⅔ cup water

Place the mackerel in a greased baking dish. Melt the butter and combine with all remaining ingredients except the water. Spread over the fish, pour the water around and bake in a moderately hot oven (375° F.) about 30 minutes, basting two or three times with the liquid in the pan. (Serves 4)

BAKED STUFFED SPANISH MACKEREL

1 finely chopped onion
¼ cup butter
3 cups soft bread crumbs
1 tbsp poultry seasoning
1 tsp salt
⅛ tsp pepper
2½ to 3 lb Spanish mackerel
Bacon or salt pork

Cook the onion in the butter for 5 minutes without browning. Add the crumbs and seasonings and use to stuff the fish which has been wiped and rubbed with salt, inside and out. Sew up or skewer to keep in the stuffing. Place in a greased baking dish. Arrange the bacon or salt pork over the top and bake in a moderate oven (350° F.) about 50 minutes. (Serves 6)

BROILED FILLETS OF FRESH MACKEREL, CUCUMBER SAUCE

3 small mackerel
Melted fat
1½ cups drained, grated cucumber pulp
½ tsp salt
Dash of paprika
⅛ tsp prepared mustard
1½ tbsp olive oil
Juice 1 large lemon

Have the fish dealer split the mackerel, and remove the back bones. Wipe, brush over with melted fat and season lightly with salt and pepper. Broil on a well greased rack about 20 minutes.

For the sauce peel and grate the cucumber and drain off any excess liquid. Add all remaining ingredients and chill thoroughly. Serve with the mackerel. (Serves 6)

BROILED FRESH MACKEREL WITH BLACK BUTTER

1 large fresh mackerel, split
Salt and pepper
3 tbsp butter
1 tbsp vinegar
2 tbsp finely minced chives or onion

Wipe the mackerel and season with salt and pepper. Place flesh side up on a well greased broiler rack and brush over with 1 tablespoon of the butter, melted. Broil about 20 minutes under low flame. Remove fish to serving platter. Add remaining butter to pan in which fish was cooked and place over the fire, cooking until it turns almost black. Add the vinegar and chives and pour over the fish. (Serves 4)

PLANKED SPANISH MACKEREL

3 lb Spanish mackerel
Salt, celery salt, and paprika
Juice of 1 lemon
¼ cup melted butter
3 cups seasoned mashed potatoes
½ cup grated cheese

Have the mackerel split down the back and the back bone removed. Arrange flesh side up on a greased heated plank. Dust with salt, celery salt, and paprika and pour the lemon juice over all. Bake in a hot oven (400° F.) 20 minutes, basting twice with melted butter. Meanwhile prepare the potatoes, adding half the cheese to them. Arrange as a border around the edge of the plank. Sprinkle with the remaining cheese and set under the broiler flame long enough to melt the cheese and brown the potatoes. Garnish with lemon slices. (Serves 6)

MACCONNAIS CHEESE. A goat's milk cheese, made in France.

MACQUELINE CHEESE. A soft rennet cheese of the Camembert type, made from whole or partly skimmed milk. It weighs about one-quarter of a pound and is four inches in diameter and one and one-quarter inches thick. It is produced in the region of Senlis, in the Department of Oise, France.

MADE DISH. See LEFTOVERS.

MADEIRA SAUCE. See BROWN SAUCE.

MADEIRA WINE. The island of Madeira, from which Madeira wine takes its name, belongs to Portugal, and lies off the northwest coast of Africa. Extending nearly 30 miles in length, it is often called the "Pearl of the European Atlantic," for it is a place of almost unequaled scenic beauty.

Madeira wine is an American favorite. The choice old wines possess a peculiar charm and have a haunting fragrance. The driest types are excellent served with soups. Used as an appetizer, Madeira is the wine par excellence as a stand-by, one to be on every sideboard, ready to welcome the friend who happens to call.

The method of wine culture in Madeira differs little, if any, from that of most wine-growing countries, the chief difference lying in the primitive methods and customs which prevail in Portugal. Large vineyards are practically non-existent in Madeira, most of the grapes being cultivated by small vineyard owners on small, well-kept, terraced vineyards on the slopes of the volcanic mountains which cover this picturesque isle. Wines from different districts, and of different vintages, vary so greatly, and the quantities of each type are so small that vintage Madeiras are seldom exported, but generally used for blending purposes. The peculiar characteristics of each one thus serve to add greater flavor, bouquet, fragrance, and perfume to the others.

For many years it was believed that to obtain perfect Madeira wine it was necessary to send it on a long sea voyage. The heat of the ship's hold, coupled with the motion of the vessel, was supposed to give the fine flavor and softness to the wine, at the same time checking the process of fermentation. Today, this is not done—in fact, for the past 25 years it has been demonstrated that heat and motion may be applied at the source with the best results.

Madeira wine varies in color from flame-red to amber and from the driest type to the sweetest. It has remarkable lasting qualities which improve with age. Some of the most widely known brands are:

Boal. A delicious wine, luscious, rich in bouquet and fragrance, of a flame-red color.

Caravela. A wine of the dry variety, usually served as an aperitif. It is of a beautiful, light amber color, one of the best of the Madeira family.

Duke of Clarence Malmsey. A very dry wine, of a light amber-reddish color, produced by the use of several kinds of grapes. It has a tang which pleases, and it possesses a wonderful bouquet. It is often served as an aperitif, and goes well with any cheese except cream cheese.

El Rei Sarcial. A very fine, dry, highly bouqueted wine, appropriate for an aperitif.

Gloria Mundi. A clear, flame-reddish, fragrant, fruity, and deliciously bouqueted wine. More sweet than dry, it is sometimes used in certain cocktails.

Malmsey. A deliciously perfumed and sweetened wine, having a fine bouquet, an unequaled softness, and an excellent flavor. It is almost a liqueur, and is usually served with the soup or dessert.

South Side. A highly aromatic and full bouqueted wine, produced in the southern part of the island of Madeira, hence the name. It is one of the best of the Madeiras, possessing remarkable lasting qualities, some of it being as much as 100 years old. In its light amber color it resembles French brandy.

MADELEINE. A French tea-cake shaped scallop-style in special molds.

MADELEINE

2½ cups pastry flour
½ tsp salt
½ cup butter
2¼ cups powdered sugar
1 tsp grated lemon rind
2 egg yolks, slightly beaten with
2 whole eggs
Beaten egg white
Powdered sugar

Sift the flour and salt twice. Cream the butter, sugar and lemon rind until very light and fluffy, gradually adding the beaten egg yolks and whole eggs, creaming and beating after each addition. Next add the flour and continue beating until very creamy and thoroughly blended. Bake, in buttered madeleine molds, in a moderate oven (350° F.) 20 to 25 minutes. When done arrange on a cookie sheet, brush over with a little stiffly beaten egg white, then sprinkle with powdered sugar and return to the oven or place under flame of the broiler until delicately glazed.

MADRAS TEA. Black teas from the province of Madras, South India. These teas are used in many popular blends. They are somewhat stronger than the Travancores and vary in quality according to the

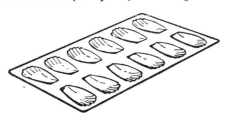

MADELEINE MOLDS

district in which they are produced. Brews of teas from the Nilgiris district are somewhat "thin" (lacking in color and strength) but are still pungent and of fine flavor. *See* TEA.

MADREGALS. *See* AMBER FISH.

MADRILENE. A jellied consommé. *See* CONSOMME.

MAGNESIUM. Magnesium, a salt, is found in the body, principally in the bones, as phosphate of magnesia which contains about 50 percent of phosphate of lime and one percent of phosphate of magnesia. Yet this comparatively small quantity gives the skeleton its firmness and prevents softening of the bony tissues. Our teeth are harder than our bones because they contain 1½ percent, or ½ percent more phosphate of magnesia than the bones. Magnesium, as well as calcium, iron, and sulphur, also take part in the formation of the albumen of the blood. Healthy lungs show twice as much magnesium as lime. Magnesium is a cell-builder, particularly of the nervous system and lung tissues. Magnesium salts assist in reducing foreign matter and waste, and in carrying them out of the system, thus invigorating the excretory organs and producing pressure, without which metabolism would be impossible.

Magnesium salts can exert their nourishing functions only with the presence of calcium salts, while in the absence of the latter, they have an injurious effect. This absence of magnesium salts leads to a gradual stoppage of all further development and to final exhaustion.

MAID. *See* TABLE SETTING AND SERVICE.

MAIGRE. The French term for lean, meaning not fat.

MAIGRE CHEESE. Another name for farm cheese, (*which see*).

MAILE CHEESE. A rennet cheese made of sheep's milk, produced in the Crimea. The ripened cheese will keep a year, and has a crumbly texture and agreeable taste.

MAINAUER CHEESE. A German semi-hard, full-cream cheese, round in shape, and weighing about three pounds. It is red outside and yellow inside.

MAINZ HAND CHEESE. A typical hand cheese, which is sometimes called pimp. It is marketed in a jar or keg.

MAITRE D'HOTEL. (may'tr doetel) Literally, a steward or head servant. A sauce of lemon or vinegar, melted butter, salt, pepper, and chopped parsley which is used with meats, fish, etc. *See* BUTTER SAUCES.

MAIZE. *See* CORN.

MAJOCCHINO CHEESE. An Italian rennet cheese made from the milk of cows, goats, sheep, plus various spices and olive oil. It is also called Incanestrato cheese.

MALAGA. A fine dessert wine made in two types, white and dusky garnet color. It contains about 15 percent alcohol. It is made in Spain, France, and the United States. *See* WINE.

MALAGA GRAPES. *See* GRAPES.

MALAKOFF CHEESE. A form of Neufchatel cheese, made in Normandy, France. It is two inches in diameter and a half inch thick.

MALLARD DUCK. *See* DUCK.

MALLOBET. A frozen dessert, on the order of a sherbet containing marshmallows.

MALMSEY WINE. A sweetened wine from Madeira (*see* MADEIRA).

MALT. The name given to any germinating cereal, particularly in brewing. To prepare it for beer brewing, malt is made from barley grains as follows: The grain is steeped in water at a temperature which causes germination and the development of diastase (*which see*). It is next couched and "floored," during which process germination continues, and it is finally kiln-dried. Malt is then ready, after sifting, blowing, and mashing, for the manufacture of beer (*which see*).

MALT EXTRACTS AND MALTED FOODS. A variety of malt extracts and malted foods are prepared for invalids, many of which possess intrinsic value for nutrition and tonic action. They are especially useful in chronic and subacute ailments and in convalescence from protracted fevers. All malted foods are deficient in fats and protein. Farinaceous meal of any kind, mixed with one-eighth of its weight of ground malt, forms a highly digestible combination.

MALT SIRUP. A sirup made by the action of malt on starch, the result being a mild sweet sirup without any malt flavor.

MALTED MILK. A powdered, sterilized preparation of pure cow's milk and extracts of malted barley and wheat, the starch of which has been converted into dextrin, the mixture then being dried in a vacuum. Malted milk keeps well, is always ready for use, and in it dextrin takes the place of additional fat; hence, its great popularity.

When preparing malted beverages, have all liquid ingredients thoroughly chilled but do not put ice itself into the drinks.

CHOCOLATE MALTED MILK

Combine in a shaker 1 to 1½ ounces of chocolate sirup, 3 rounded teaspoons of malted milk, a small scoop of ice cream and 1 cup of milk. Shake thoroughly. Top with whipped cream. (Serves 1)

COFFEE MALTED MILK

Proceed as directed for chocolate malted milk, substituting 1½ ounces of coffee sirup for chocolate sirup. (Serves 1)

HOT MALTED MILK

Combine in a mug 1 ounce of any preferred sirup (chocolate, coffee or vanilla), 3 tablespoons of malted milk, a dash of salt and 2 tablespoons of hot water. When smoothly blended fill the mug with scalding water or milk. Dust the surface with cinnamon or nutmeg, or top with whipped cream. (Serves 1)

IMPERIAL MALTED MILK

Put 1½ ounces of pineapple sirup into an electric mixer or a shaker, add 1 tablespoon of malted milk, 1 scoop of vanilla ice cream, and ¾ cup of cold milk. Set the beater at full speed, if using the mixer, or shake vigorously if using a shaker. When thoroughly blended, pour into a tall glass. Top with whipped cream and dust with grated nutmeg. (Serves 1)

MALTED MILK EGG SHAKE

Combine in a shaker 1 ounce of chocolate, coffee, vanilla, or sugar sirup, according to taste. Add 1 tablespoon of malted milk. Break a fresh egg into this, fill the shaker with cold milk, adding a little ice, and shake. Strain into a tall glass and dust with a little cinnamon or nutmeg. (Serves 1)

MALTED MILK GINGER ALE SHAKE

Combine in a shaker 1 tablespoon of sugar sirup, 1 tablespoon of malted milk, a small scoop of vanilla ice cream and ¼ glass of ginger ale. Shake vigorously, pour into a tall glass and fill up with ginger ale. Serve with straws. (Serves 1)

MALTOSE. Sugar obtained from starch by the action of diastase (*which see*) and/or malt (*which see*). The action of the diastase of malt resembles that of the ptyalin of the saliva and the amylopsin of the pancreatic juice, which alter starches into dextrin and maltose.

MAMMEE APPLE or **MAMEY APPLE.** This is a rather inferior but edible fruit with a brownish rind and yellow pulp. It grows on a large and rather beautiful tree in the West Indies, in South and Central America, and on the west coast of Africa. The fruit is round, about four to six inches in diameter, and tastes something like an apricot. In the West Indies it is eaten raw, or with wine and sugar. It is also known as the Santo Domingo apricot or the South American apricot. A spirituous liquor called "Eau de Créole" is distilled from its flowers, and the gum exuding from the bark is used by natives of the West Indies for destroying chigoes in the feet.

MAMMEE SAPOTA. An oval shaped fruit about five or six inches long, belonging to the sapodilla family. The flesh is somewhat similar to that of the cantaloupe, either yellow or salmon color. There are from one to three long, jet black seeds. The skin is rough and light

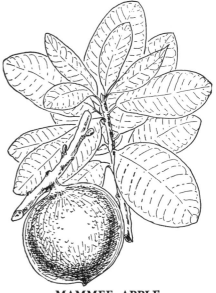

MAMMEE APPLE

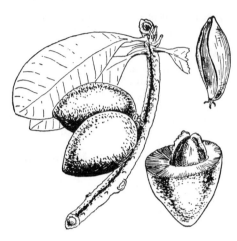

MAMMEE SAPOTA

brown in color. The average weight is about ten ounces. It is grown in Central America, South America, and in the West Indies.

MANATEE. An aquatic mammal, found in the rivers of Florida, Mexico, Central America, and the West Indies. It is whale-like, except the tail, which is broad and rounded. It may be nine to thirteen feet long. The flesh is white and delicate, and said to resemble pork.

MANDARIN. A variety of orange, (*which see*).

MANDARINE. A sweet, tangerine-flavored liqueur. *See also* LIQUEUR.

MANDRAKE. An herb of southern Europe and northern Africa, with large leaves and thick roots and whitish or bluish flowers. It is used medicinally, and

the superstitious attribute aphrodisiac qualities to it. In America the May Apple (*which see*) is called a "mandrake."

MANDUVIRA. Fruit of a tree in South America. The Indians there toast it before eating it.

MANGANESE. This metal resembles iron in its physical and chemical properties. It is contained in the red blood corpuscles, though in much smaller quantities than iron, and seems to have a decided influence on the vegetative functions and the glands in general, enabling them to improve the quality of their secretions.

MANGLER. A meat-chopping machine.

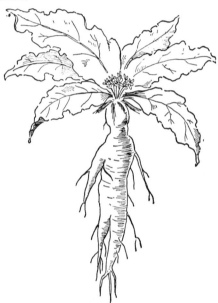

MANDRAKE

MANGO. The mango is the fruit of a tree (*mangifera indica*) believed to be a native of India, which is now grown in most tropical countries. The tree usually grows to a height of 30 to 40 feet.

The fruit grows in various shapes, some round, some long and narrow, others shaped like a kidney. Sizes vary from large ones weighing five pounds or more down to small ones the size of a peach. Colors range from green to yellow or red, orange color being perhaps the most common. The quality varies greatly, the flavor of choice magnos rivaling any fruit in the world, the pulp, juicy, aromatic and usually orange colored, while poor mangos have a large

MANGO

seed stone and pulp full of fiber which tastes like nothing so much as rope soaked in turpentine.

Mangos should not be cut until just before serving. The easiest method is to halve the fruit lengthwise, remove the stone, and serve the two halves as is usually done with cantaloupe. However, some of the aroma escapes, and to prevent this you may serve it whole with the skin cut, letting the person served turn back the skin and eat the pulp with a spoon.

In addition to its use as a fresh fruit, the mango forms the basis of most East-Indian chutneys, and is also canned and otherwise preserved.

MANGO FISH. A handsome, yellow-colored, edible fish of the Ganges River in India, some of which are canned and imported in the United States.

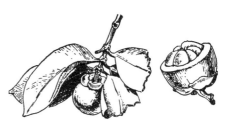

MANGOSTEEN

ported to the United States. Its bark is used in tannin.

MANHATTAN COCKTAIL. A cocktail that ranks with the martini (*which see*) in popularity, but is made with rye instead of gin. Like the martini, the Manhattan recipe can be varied to different degrees of dryness or sweetness.

MANHATTAN COCKTAIL

2 parts rye
1 part sweet vermouth
1 dash Angostura bitters

The ingredients are placed in a mixing glass with cracked ice, stirred gently but thoroughly, and strained into a cocktail glass. Serve with a cherry in the glass.

MANGO MELON

MANGO MELON. A melon (*cucumis melo*) which is sliced and cooked like eggplant. It is not edible raw. It is grown largely for preserving and making mango pickles. The skin is yellow and the flesh white or pale yellow. Other names are orange melon and vegetable peach.

MANGO SQUASH. Another name for chayote (*which see*).

MANGOSTEEN. A delicious fruit, the size of an orange, which grows in Australia, West Indies, Java and the Moluccas, and is imported into the United States. Its taste is best when picked when dead ripe and eaten immediately.

MANGROVE. (I) A fish. *See* RED SNAPPER.

MANGROVE. (II) A fruit from the East Indies and West Indies which is im-

MANGROVE FRUIT

DRY MANHATTAN

Make as above, substituting dry for sweet vermouth and garnishing with a twist of lemon peel rather than a cherry.

SWEET MANHATTAN

1 part rye
1 part sweet vermouth
1 dash orange bitters

Mix and serve as in basic recipe.
See BARTENDING; *see also* COCKTAIL.

MANICAMP CHEESE. A French cheese made in Flanders.

MANIOC. A tropical plant from the roots of which cassava and tapioca (*which see*) are prepared.

MANNA. A name given by the Israelites to the food miraculously supplied in the wilderness (Ex.xvi.15). Also sweet, laxative juice exuded from certain species of ash tree of southern Europe.

MANNITE. Mannite is obtained from the sweet juice of the stems of the ash tree. It is also contained in beet roots and some other vegetables. Like sucrose, it crystalizes, and is white and free from odor. It does not ferment with yeast. It is laxative, and doctors may prescribe it in diabetes.

MANURI CHEESE. A Yugoslavian cheese made from sheep's or cow's milk.

MAPLE. Maple sirup is a strictly American institution. There are maple trees in other parts of the world, but it is chiefly in America that the stately sugar maple spreads its broad leaves to the sun and stores up a sugar crop worth harvesting commercially.

MANIOC

Although all species of maple trees yield sweet sap, only a few produce it in paying quantities. The sugar maple and black maple are the principal species used for commercial purposes. The quantity of sap from the red, silver, and Oregon maples and the box elder, which is related to the maple, is too small to be of importance.

The black maple is generally regarded as the best sap producer. It is similar to the sugar maple in general appearance, except that it seems to prefer lower land, such as river bottoms, and the banks of streams. It grows in Vermont, on the shores of Lake Champlain, and ranges southward, west of the Alleghenies, from Minnesota to Arkansas and eastern Kansas.

The maple tree is confined to the eastern and northern United States and the neighboring parts of Canada as a tree for the commercial production of maple sirup and sugar. Twenty-two states produce maple products on a commercial basis but three states—New York, Vermont, and Ohio—produce a large share of the total. Of course, the production of maple sirup and sugar is small compared with the production of sugar from cane and beets.

Vermont occupies first place in the maple hall of fame. From Vermont comes a legendary story about the discovery of maple sugar. The story is that an Indian squaw was preparing moose meat for her brave, boiling it in the sweet water that came from a tree near her wigwam. She was an industrious squaw. While the meat boiled, she busied herself with a pair of moccasins. She became so engrossed in her work that she forgot about the meat. When it suddenly occurred to her that her husband's dinner was about to burn up, she was terror stricken. But it was not burned. Later she wept for joy, for not only was the moose meat done to a turn, but the sweet water had turned into a brown sirup. She tasted it, and nothing sweeter had ever passed her lips. When her warrior returned, she told him about it. He ate as he had never eaten before. Like a dutiful husband, proud of his wife's culinary efforts, he went out and told the neighbors. They tapped the tree again for some of the sweet water, and every day was feast day while the sap ran. The Indians decided that the recipe was heaven sent, and that was the beginning of maple sugar.

The spring task of tapping the maple trees for their sap is begun while last year's leaves are still heavy under foot. A half inch hole is driven into the trunk of the tree, and the sap is collected in large, galvanized buckets through a drain called a "spiel." The sap-laden buckets are emptied, as soon as they are full, into other buckets which are carried to the hauling tank for transportation to the sugar house. The original bucket goes back into place on the tree for another filling. The sugar house is a wooden contrivance into which the sap is poured, and its water content removed by evaporation. By the time the sap has flowed to the farthest end of the evaporator it has been reduced to sirup and is drained off.

Sugar parties are a popular pastime in the north woods of Vermont. After the sirup has been boiled to the proper temperature, it is poured on snow or cracked ice and permitted to harden. The resultant candy is delicious, but hard on the teeth.

The greatest use of the sirup is in its own form with hot biscuits, griddle cakes, waffles, or French toast. It is also delicious for flavoring frozen and custard desserts, and for frostings and candies. The maple sugar itself, when made according to modern methods, makes a soft and creamy confection. It may be scraped and used with hot bread, boiled rice, hot and cold breakfast cereals, and of course makes delicious candy.

Maple Frosting

2 cups sugar
½ cup water
1 tbsp light corn sirup
2 egg whites
Dash of salt
⅔ cup maple sirup

Put the sugar, water, corn sirup, and maple sirup in a saucepan and stir over low heat until the sugar is dissolved. Boil, covered, about 3 minutes; then boil, uncovered and without stirring until a small amount of sirup forms a soft ball when dropped into cold water (240° F.). Remove sirup from the heat. Quickly beat the egg whites until stiff, then pour the sirup in a fine stream over the egg whites, beating constantly. Add salt and continue beating until frosting is cool and of proper consistency to spread. If frosting hardens before spreading, beat in a few drops of hot water. One-eighth teaspoon of cream of tartar.

may be used instead of corn sirup. (Makes enough frosting for tops and sides of two 9-inch layers.) On a rainy or humid day, boil the sirup to a higher temperature.

Maple Gingerbread

1 egg
1 cup maple sirup
1 cup sour cream
2⅓ cups sifted flour
1 tsp baking soda
1½ tsp ground ginger
½ tsp salt
4 tbsp melted butter

Beat the egg well, blend with the sirup and sour cream. Measure the sifted flour and resift with baking soda, ginger, and salt. Stir the liquid mixture into sifted ingredients, beating well until smooth. Add the melted butter and beat thoroughly. Pour batter into oblong pan lined with wax paper and bake in moderate oven (350° F.) for 30 minutes. When cool cover with maple frosting.

Maple Mousse

1 cup maple sirup
4 egg yolks
⅛ tsp salt
2 cups undiluted evaporated milk

Boil the maple sirup 5 minutes. Remove from the fire, and immediately pour very slowly, over egg yolks which have been beaten until thick with the salt, beating briskly and constantly. Cool. Whip the evaporated milk. When cold, fold in the whipped milk. Freeze in the refrigerator tray, or mold and freeze either in refrigerator tray for 3½ hours, or in hand freezer pail, using equal parts ice and salt, for 2½ hours. (Makes 1 quart)

Maple Parfait

¾ cup maple sirup
4 eggs
1 pt heavy cream
¼ tsp salt

Heat the maple sirup, but do not boil. Beat the whole eggs in the top of a double boiler until they are light yellow. Pour the hot sirup over the eggs, beating briskly and constantly. Place the boiler over hot water and cook, stirring constantly, until the mixture coats the spoon. Whip the cream until stiff, adding the salt. Cool the maple mixture and fold in the whipped cream. Freeze in the tray of a mechanical refrigerator until firm, or about 2½ hours. Or pack in molds and place in a mixture of equal parts of ice and salt for 2 hours if small molds are used, or 3 to 3½ hours for a single large mold. (Makes approximately 1 quart)

MAPLE SAUCE

1½ cups maple sugar
½ cup milk
2 tbsp butter

Bring the maple sugar and milk slowly to the boiling point, stirring frequently. Simmer about seven minutes, then add the butter. Serve hot on ice cream or hot desserts.

MAPLE WALNUT ICE CREAM

1 cup maple sirup
3 eggs
¼ tsp salt
1 tsp vanilla extract
1 cup heavy cream
½ cup chopped, skinned walnuts

Place the maple sirup in the upper part of double boiler, and heat, but do not boil, over hot water. Separate the eggs, beating the whites until stiff and the yolks until light. Then, stir in the egg yolks until well-blended. Cook, stirring constantly, over hot water, until mixture thickens. Remove from water, and add vanilla extract. Chill. When cold, fold in the stiffly beaten egg whites, alternately with the heavy cream which has been beaten to a custard-like consistency. Freeze in the refrigerator tray, to a mushy consistency, or until a layer is frozen 1 inch from sides of tray. Remove from refrigerator and scrape and stir from bottom and sides of tray. Then beat until smooth, incorporating at the same time the chopped, skinned walnut meats. Return to refrigerator and freeze for 3 hours.

MAQUEE CHEESE. A soft, rennet, brick-shaped cheese made from cow's milk. It comes from Belgium where it is known as fromage mou.

MARASCA CHERRY. A world-famous cherry grown in Dalmatia, Yugoslavia. It is used to make maraschino, which see.

MARASCHINO. A delicate, crystal clear, after-dinner cordial made from a distinctive type of cherry known as the Marasca cherry, which grows in Dalmatia, Yugoslavia. It is very sweet and widely used as a flavoring for many cocktails, in cooking (desserts), in cups, punches, and the like. It is a cordial with centuries of good reputation. It is also made in Italy. See also LIQUEUR.

MARASCHINO CHERRY. In America maraschino cherries are prepared from Royal Anne cherries which are picked before fully ripe, pitted, cooked in sugar sirup, and artificially colored and flavored. They are used mainly as a garnish in fruit cups, and in puddings, cakes, frosting, and the like.

MARASCHINO APPLE JAM

4 cups green apples, chopped
1 cup maraschino cherries, chopped
2 tbsp lemon juice
6 cups sugar
Pectin

Barely cover fruits with water, stir in sugar, and boil 2 minutes. Add lemon juice. Test for jellying quality (see JELLY) and add pectin if indicated. Seal in hot jars. (Makes about 4 pint jars)

MARC. The residue of skins, pulp, seeds, etc., left in the press after wine or cider is made; also, a highly potent spirit distilled from this residue that usually requires many years of mellowing before the spirit even approaches a palatal state. See also CIDER and WINE.

MARGARINE. Margarine or oleomargarine is a product made to resemble butter in which one or more optional fat ingredients are used along with or in place of the butterfat. Margarine was first made in France in 1870 when Napoleon III offered a prize for a butter substitute. Margarine, like butter, is a water-in-oil emulsion and must contain 80 percent fat. In making margarine, the melted fat is agitated with skim milk that has been pasteurized and which may have been cultured with a bacterial starter.

The flavor of margarine at one time depended to a large extent upon the treatment of the milk. Today, flavor is obtained principally by adding flavoring substances permitted under Federal standards of identity. Salt, preservatives, emulsifiers, vitamins A and D may be used as additives. The addition of 15,000 units of vitamin A per pound (which is the average amount found in butter), although not mandatory, is almost universal.

On the market are margarines significantly reduced in calories. These are plainly marked as imitation margarine, and they only contain about half the amount of fat that real margarine must contain. Consequently the calories present in imitation margarine are about half of the amount found in margarine. Because of aeration, whipped margarine contains only about two-thirds of the calories in an equal volume of plain margarine.

Butter and margarine contain water and rancidity may be due to enzyme action or to micro–organisms that break down the fat and water into glycerol and fatty acid. If short-chain fatty acids are present, this breakdown will result in a rancid odor that can be detected at room temperature.

Since butter and margarine absorb odors so noticeably, they should be stored in covered containers in the refrigerator.

Margarine may be substituted for butter in most cooking operations, and where it is to be used for cooking, it is not necessary to color it. It is marketed under various trade names.

MARGHERITA CHEESE. A soft, small cream cheese made in Italy.

MARINADE. A preparation containing spices, condiments, vegetables and aromatic herbs with a liquid in which food is allowed to lie for a certain length of time to enhance its flavor.

The word "marinade" comes from an old Spanish word meaning "to pickle," and it is the acid of the marinade that does the work, adding new flavor, softening tough fibers, increasing their natural sapidity through the action of penetration, lifting ordinary foods out of the commonplace in flavor.

There are several types of marinade:

Light Marinade. This is used for small game, fish, meats, vegetables, and fruits. (It is also called "instantaneous marinade.") It may be plain and consist of only a little lemon juice, vinegar mixed with a little oil, and a few spices and seasonings. An example of a light marinade is salad dressing.

Tomato juice, French dressing, vinegar, fruit juices (especially the citrus kinds), spicy sauces (cooked or uncooked), and sour cream make the light marinade most used in cookery.

LIGHT MARINADE

1 small thinly sliced lemon
1 thinly sliced small raw carrot
1 tbsp vinegar
1 tbsp oil
1 sprig of thyme
2 small bay leaves
3 whole cloves, slightly bruised
1 or 2 sprigs parsley
12 peppercorns, crushed
Salt

All the above ingredients are placed in a flat-bottomed dish, usually of earthenware, then the meat, fish, vegetable, or game is placed in it. This recipe may be doubled or trebled if necessary.

Ordinary Marinade. This type of marinade may be used hot or cold, according to directions. The ingredients are practically the same as for a light marinade, and are prepared in the same way, except that they are heated, cooled, then poured cold over the fish, meat, or game to be marinated. The purpose of cooking is to precipitate more rapidly the essences, aromas, and extracts from the ingredients used, thus producing a stronger effect.

Marinade for Large Pieces. This is used for meat, game, etc. (but seldom fish). The marinade may be hot or cold according to indications in the recipe. It is employed mostly for large pieces of meat or game, such as whole ribs of beef, or wild boar, deer, bear, reindeer, etc. In it are included additional aromatic herbs, such as rosemary, sarriette, sweet basil, salt, mace, sage, etc. The directions are the same as for light marinade and ordinary marinade, except that the proportions are much larger, according to need. If the meat or game is to remain several days in the marinade, the quantity of vinegar is smaller in proportion to the other liquids; if of short duration, the vinegar is equal or thereabouts. Keep in a cool place covered with a cheesecloth for the required length of time.

MARINATE. To let lie, as meat or fish, in a brine or marinade. Also to season with

MARJORAM

French dressing some hours before adding mayonnaise for a salad.

MARJORAM. Marjoram is an aromatic herb belonging to the mint family. It is native to Europe, but wild marjoram, also known as oregano (*which see*), has been naturalized in North America. Sweet and pot marjoram are used fresh, dried, or as extracts for flavoring. The dried herb is favored because this form seems to facilitate its permeation of the food.

Majoram is extremely adaptable; it blends well with cheese dishes, meats, poultry, fish, vegetables, egg dishes, and with other herbs for stews, soups, sauces, stuffings, and green and vegetable salads. In fact, it blends well with almost everything. It should be pounded into veal cutlets, and it should always be used with lamb and mutton. Add it to the basting liquor when roasting beef and poultry. A dash of marjoram will enliven the flavor of green lima beans, string beans, peas, hash, casseroles, meat pies, scalloped potatoes, and squash. Sprinkle it over the vegetables during the cooking. Its flavor is strong, so use it sparingly.

MARKETING. *See* PURCHASING FOOD.

MARKISCH HAND CHEESE. A German cheese similar to hand cheese, *which see.*

MARMALADES. There is no clear-cut division between the definitions of marmalade and jam. The generally accepted distinction is that jams are made from crushed fruits, while marmalades are made from sliced or stripped fruits or whole small berries. The latter are sometimes called conserves or preserves. In other words, a marmalade is a variation of a preserve. Marmalades are usually made from citrus fruits, oranges being the most common. *See* ORANGE, GRAPEFRUIT, and other fruits for recipes.

MAROILLES CHEESE. A French semi-hard, fermented, whole milk cheese, about five inches square and two inches thick. The rind is brownish red and the center yellow. It has a sharp smell.

MARQUISE. A frozen dessert made by combining a fruit sherbet which has been flavored with kirsch, rum, or brandy with whipped cream. The fruit juice used is usually strawberry, pineapple, or raspberry. The sherbet is made in the usual manner (*see* SHERBET) and when ready to serve, stiffly whipped cream is folded into the sherbet. The marquise is then served in punch or sherbet glasses.

MARRON GLACE. (Glazed Chestnuts). A good recipe for these deliciously rich confections is as follows:

MARRON GLACE

Peel off the outer skin, taking care not to cut the chestnuts. Put them into an enameled strainer, then put the strainer into a copper or aluminum pan filled with cold water. Do not use an iron vessel, since this will blacken the chestnuts. Heat gently until the water is close to the boiling point, the temperature to be maintained during the cooking. Do not let the water actually boil for this will cause the chestnuts to break or open out.

When the water begins to grow red from the tannin which the chestnut contains, lift out the strainer, and put it in another pan containing boiling water in which has been stirred a little flour mixed with a little cold water. (The flour is not absolutely necessary, but it facilitates the washing.) It takes nearly two hours to wash the chestnuts. They are cooked enough when they can be crushed easily with the fingers. Change the water then once more, and keep them in this water, which should be very hot, while removing the skins with a small pointed knife. This must be done with great care, without squeezing the nuts, and commencing at the big vein near the point.

Put the peeled chestnuts in flat-bottomed pans, not too many at a time. Flavor stock sirup (*see* SIRUP) with vanilla and cover the nuts with the sirup. Place the pans over very low heat, and add additional sirup as it evaporates. The chestnut is preserved when the sirup forms a thin film on the outside. If a candy thermometer is used, it should register 230° F., or the thread stage. Turn off the heat, cool the nuts, and store in covered glass jars.

MARRON GLACE ICE CREAM

1 lb chestnuts
5 egg yolks
1½ cups granulated sugar
½ tsp salt
3 cups milk
¼ cup pineapple sirup
2 cups undiluted evaporated milk

Prepare the chestnuts by cutting a ½-inch slit on the flat side. Put the nuts in a heavy pan and add ½ teaspoon of oil or butter for each cup of nuts. Shake over the fire for 5 minutes, then set in a moderate oven (350° F.) for 5 minutes longer. Remove from the oven, and shell while still hot, using a sharp knife. Remove the brown skins. Place the skinned chestnuts in a pan and cover with boiling salted water. Cook gently for 15 or 20 minutes. Drain the nuts and put through the ricer. There should be 1½ cups of pulp.

Scald the milk. Beat the egg yolks in the top of a double boiler until light and beat in the sugar and salt. Pour the hot milk over the egg mixture, stirring rapidly and constantly. Cook over hot water until the mixture thickens, stirring constantly. Strain through a double thickness of cheesecloth. Cool the mixture. Add the evaporated milk alternately with the pineapple sirup and the riced chestnuts.

Freeze in a hand freezer, using 3 parts of ice and 1 part of salt until firm and solid. Pack in 4 parts of ice and 1 part of rock salt for 2 hours. (Makes approximately 1½ quarts)

MARROW BEAN. *See* BEAN.
MARROW. (I) The soft material filling animal bones. Bone marrow is an easily digestible and wholesome fat which has long been used as a food. The long bones of beef are cut crosswise in pieces about two inches long, and cooked with the marrow within them. The marrow slides out easily and can then be served on freshly made toast. It makes a very delicious appetizer with the addition of a little salt.

MARROW BALL DUMPLINGS

½ cup beef marrow
1 cup bread or cracker crumbs
Salt and pepper
2 unbeaten eggs
A dash of cayenne
½ tsp finely minced parsley

Place the marrow in a small bowl and set over hot water to melt, after which, with a spoon, press it through a fine strainer. Set aside to cool, and when of about the consistency of cream, stir in ⅓ of the crumbs. Blend thoroughly. Add the eggs, one at a time, and mix well with a fork. Add seasonings, then more of the crumbs, adding a little at a time and mixing well after each addition. Take ⅓ teaspoon of the mixture, roll into a small ball and drop into boiling salted water. If the dumpling falls apart, add a few more crumbs and test again. Cook in very small balls in boiling soup, about 10 minutes or just until firm and set.

These dumplings also may be used as a garnish for soups or stews or as a main dish with noodles, macaroni or spaghetti, or other vegetables.

MARROW. (II) A variety of summer squash, which may be prepared and served in the same way as summer squash. *See* SQUASH.

MARROW

MARSALA. The best known dessert wine produced in Sicily and Italy. It is a fortified wine containing from 16 to 20 percent alcohol. It somewhat resembles sherry and Madeira wines. A wine of a brilliant golden-yellow hue, it is excellent to serve with cake. *See also* WINE.

MARSHMALLOW. Originally, the confection which bears this name was a product of the gelatinous roots of the familiar plant, the marshmallow. Gardeners know this decorative shrub, with its large, spectacular, hibiscus flowers in all shades of rose, red, and crimson. The alert wayfarer also recognizes it among the marshes near the seacoast. A decoction from its roots gives a colorless, tasteless gum, formerly used in medicine, and by the confectioner.

Today, however, the slow and expensive method of extracting the root sirup has been replaced by a process which utilizes other natural starches, such as corn sirup, or glucose, cane sugar, and some animal gelatin. This natural sugar-starch mixture is then flavored with vanilla and pressed into the cube-like candies so familiar to picknicker and homemaker alike. Being starch, the cells of this confection, under heat, or toasting, expand and burst—hence the puffy quality of the toasted marshmallow.

Marshmallow "cream" which is used as a topping or icing is nothing more than marshmallows of a spreadable consistency, so packaged for convenience. It is this special, velvety, cream-like consistency which is perhaps the marshmallow's chief asset, and the one quality which has made it popular indoors as well as out. Being glucose, the marshmallow has all the body and smoothness which glucose gives to a mixture, thereby preventing the formation of crystals or separation in sirups. Hence marshmallows are not only a confection to be eaten out-of-hand, but a standard ingredient for the one to whom perfect cake fillings and frostings, or frozen desserts, are a matter of special interest and pride. The addition of marshmallows, when cut in pieces, or beaten into a hot sirup, insures that the resulting frosting or sauce will be velvet-smooth, and neither flaky nor hard.

HINTS ON USING

Since marshmallows form a perfect starch, we cannot cook or heat them over a direct flame without too great a danger of scorching them. Hence, when using this ingredient, in whatever form, always melt it over hot water, as in a double boiler. Marshmallows may be cut into quarters for greater convenience and more rapid melting. Use sharp shears, first dipped into cold water or flour. The melting or beating must not continue too long or the marshmallows will return to their original colorless liquid. Watch carefully, and remove from the heat when the marshmallows are only partially dissolved. Finish by beating them smooth with a spoon or egg beater.

As mentioned, the consistency of marshmallows is a spready or sirupy one, and thus is ideal for frostings, and also for making all types of frozen desserts. A refrigerator mixture to which marshmallows have been added will never split or form ice crystals. If left to stand, the mixture will tend to become stiff and solid, as in ice cream. In many recipes the mixture is allowed to chill, then is beaten, and the whipped cream folded in last. This gives a perfect texture to all frozen desserts of this type.

Because of its quality of puffing under the action of direct heat or flame, the marshmallow makes an interesting topping or garnish for many foods. In its uncooked form the marshmallow can be combined into favors for the table, using the white surface as the "face" and nuts, fruits, and other candies to form unique figurines or place-card holders.

Although it combines with almost any other food material, the marshmallow seems a perfect accompaniment to sweet, starchy foods, like sweet potatoes, bananas, rice, etc. Also, it blends well with the sub-acid fruits like pineapple or cherries.

MARSHMALLOW FILLING

10 marshmallows
¼ cup raisins
2 tsp cream
2 tbsp chopped nuts
½ tsp grated orange rind

Cut the marshmallows into quarters with scissors dipped in hot water. Place in the top of a double boiler, add the raisins, and steam over hot water until the marshmallows have melted. Remove from the heat and stir in the cream thoroughly. Add nut meats and orange rind and stir to distribute evenly. Spread between cake layers. (Enough for two 8- or 9-inch layers)

MARSHMALLOW RASPBERRY PARFAIT

15 marshmallows, quartered
1 cup rich milk
1 tsp vanilla extract
⅛ tsp salt
1¼ cups heavy cream

Scald the milk and add quartered marshmallows. Beat with rotary egg beater until thoroughly blended, then chill until slightly thickened. Stir in the salt, vanilla extract, and stiffly whipped heavy cream. Place in refrigerator tray and freeze for 3½ hours. When ready to serve, have ready one of the raspberry sauces. *See* RASPBERRY.

Place a generous tablespoon of the raspberry sauce in the bottom of a chilled parfait glass. Over this place 2 or 3 tablespoons of the frozen parfait, and top with more raspberry sauce. Or you may alternate layers of sauce, parfait mixture, and so on until chilled glasses are full. Top each glass, if desired, with either a fresh or preserved raspberry.

MARSHMALLOW SAUCE

¼ cup water
½ cup sugar
8 marshmallows, quartered
1 egg white

Cook the water and sugar together to a thin sirup (220° F.). Add the marshmallows and when light and fluffy pour all carefully over the stiffly beaten egg white. Flavor, if desired, with a few drops of vanilla.

MARTINI. This is one of the favorite cocktails, and perhaps the most commonly used appetizer. Its recipe closely resembles that of the Bronx (*which see*) without the orange juice. There are many martini recipes which vary the sweetness or dryness of the drink, and of them, the Dry Martini seems to be the most popular.

DRY MARTINI

2 parts dry gin
1 part dry vermouth
2 dashes orange bitters

Place in a mixing glass with cracked ice and mix by stirring gently. Strain into a cocktail glass and garnish with an olive or small pickled onion.

To make a very dry martini, use three parts of gin to one part of vermouth.

Should the formula given be too dry, a medium martini may be made instead.

MEDIUM MARTINI

2 parts dry gin
1 part dry vermouth
1 part sweet vermouth

Mix as above. Strain and serve with olive and dash of lemon juice.

To make a sweeter martini, use four, instead of two, parts of gin with the Medium Martini recipe.

All of the above drinks are properly called martinis. It is a matter of local custom or individual taste to decide which of the above is *the* martini, and which the sweet and the dry. Martinis are sometimes served with small peeled onions instead of olives. *See* BARTENDING; *see also* COCKTAIL.

MARY ANN PAN. *See* CAKE PAN.

MARZIPAN. An almond paste which may be made at home or bought already prepared. It is widely used in candy making. Almond paste is the chief essential in making this rich and delicious sweetmeat so characteristic of holiday candy assortments.

MARZIPAN

1 cup (½ lb) almond paste
3 cups confectioners' sugar
2 tbsp lemon juice
1 egg white
1 tsp powdered sugar
1 tsp cocoa
1 square sweet chocolate, grated
Vegetable coloring

Knead into the almond paste the sifted confectioners' sugar, lemon juice, and unbeaten egg white, working until very smooth. Divide mixture into several portions, keeping each cold until ready to mold. Then, shape some of the plain mixture into small oval potatoes about the size of marbles, and roll them in a mixture of cocoa and powdered sugar. Form eyes by pressing with a toothpick. Color another portion with orange coloring, and then shape into small carrots or pumpkins. Shape another portion into acorns and dip the ends into grated sweet chocolate for the acorn cups. Fruits such as small apples, oranges, pears, bananas, strawberries, or raspberries can be made by using corresponding vegetable colorings.

MASCONE CHEESE. A white, soft Italian cheese made from fresh cream.

MASH. To make a soft or pulpy mass of a food.

MASHER. A kitchen utensil used to mash food. A potato masher is the commonest example.

POTATO MASHER

MASK. To cover one food completely with another, as with a cream sauce, etc.

MASTICATION. The chewing of food in preparation for swallowing it. Food not thoroughly masticated cannot be properly digested or assimilated. Mastication is the first process of digestion. Unless food is chemically and mechanically prepared in the mouth for the next stage of digestion, it will never be properly digested and assimilated. Improper mastication and hurried eating are the greatest causes of overeating. All solid foods require thorough mastication. No food should enter the stomach except as a liquid. This is especially true of starches—bread, potatoes, cereals, and animal foods.

MATE. Called also Paraguay tea, this shrub grows in Argentina, Brazil, and Paraguay. It is the dried leaves of a plant resembling holly. Steeped and made into a tea, it is a mildly stimulating beverage which contains theine, but it has no special dietetic advantages over tea or coffee.

MATZOTH. An unleavened bread made from flour and water only. The eating of the matzoth is the most symbolic feature of the Passover, the Jewish festival

MATE

commemorating the Hebrew's liberation from Egyptian bondage. Fleeing Egypt hurriedly, the Jews had no time to leaven their bread. Thus they have eaten matzoths for thousands of years, remembering them as the bread of affliction.

Matzoth, the meal that is used in so many varieties of rich or simple food, has a tradition that goes back to early Biblical times. History says that it was Pharoah's wife who finally persuaded her cruel husband to permit Moses to lead the Jews out of Egypt away from his persecution. When the march to the Red Sea was hurriedly begun, all possessions were left behind. Flour was the food most easily carried. When the marchers carried flour mixed with water in vessels on their heads to ward off sunstroke, the heat of the blazing Egyptian sun baked the flour and water to a crust, and the Jews were surprised to discover that it was palatable. From this evolved the idea of mixing flour and water and spreading a thin paste in the sun to dry.

Later, when it was possible to have soup, the women made the paste into little dumplings, called matzoth balls, and served them with soup—a practice that has come down to our time. Matzoth balls are made of matzoth meal, eggs, a little chicken fat, fried onions, and seasonings mixed into a dough and rolled into balls. They are boiled to serve in soups, stews, and the like.

Two well known variations of matzoth are chrimsels and blintzes. Chrimsels are made of matzoth, first soaked in water, then mixed with nuts, raisins, and eggs, shaped into pancakes and fried. Blintzes are flat squares of matzoth dough folded, omelet fashion, over jelly and sweetened cottage cheese, then fried in either chicken fat or butter.

The manufacture of matzoth is very simple: Flour and water are measured into a mixing tub. Kneaders work the dough, and rollers press it into a thick sheet, three feet wide. Automatically it moves through a series of kneading rollers, which roll it to one-eighth inch thick. This moving sheet passes along to the dotters for its hemstitching effect. The bread speeds into a 90-foot oven, heated between 700° and 800° F. In two minutes the matzoths emerge thoroughly baked, well browned, traveling on special trays and into packages. Just eleven minutes have elapsed from the mixing of the flour and water until the baked matzoths are sealed into packages and cased. It is the quickest baked bread in the world, and untouched by human hands.

MAVRODAPHNE. A sweet, fortified, red Greek dessert wine. *See also* WINE.

MAY APPLE. An egg-shaped, yellowish, fleshy fruit about the size of a large cherry, containing numerous seeds, produced by a woodland herb known as the American mandrake. The term "mandrake," thus used, is a misnomer, as the mandrake proper, a plant growing in southern Europe, is poisonous. The American may apple is used especially to make marmalade. In some regions it is called hog-apple, wild lemon, may-pop, etc. It is very common east of the Mississippi.

MAY WINE. A German beverage popular all over the world. It is sometimes called May Bowl. It is made as follows:

Carefully select fresh young woodruff (an aromatic herb) before it is in bloom. Wash and pick it over carefully. Tie a handful in a muslin bag and place it, together with one pound of sugar and a bottle of Rhine wine, in a container having a close-fitting cover. Cover tightly, and allow it to remain five to six hours in a cool dry place, to mellow. Remove the bag and discard it. Add another bottle of Rhine wine, one of claret, and one of good champagne, together with some strawberries (preferably the wild ones), a juicy orange, sliced, and one small, fresh pineapple, also sliced. Stir and serve at once.

MAYONNAISE. Mayonnaise is an emulsion consisting of oil, egg, vinegar, condiments, and spices. Nothing else.

Unlike French dressing, it is a stable emulsion, which is formed when the tiny drops of oil are held in solution. Since oil and water will not mix, it is necessary to keep these drops of oil separated by adding a substance which is dissolved in one solution but not in the other, and which will form a covering for these tiny droplets of oil. One such substance is yolk of egg but gelatin, condensed milk, or a cooked starch paste will have the same effect.

Egg yolks are as a rule used in mayonnaise because they form a heavier emulsion and produce a deeper yellow color. Whole eggs give a thinner dressing, while egg whites give a dressing which is entirely unlike mayonnaise. Frozen eggs may be used, but eggs which are the least bit stale will not form a stable mayonnaise. A certain amount of salt is necessary for flavor,

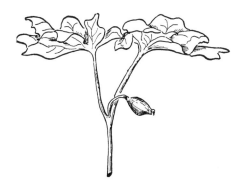

MAY APPLE

but an excessive amount may break the solution. Sugar helps to hold the emulsion. Some cooks add a small amount of hot stock to the mayonnaise at the very end of the beating, which is said to keep the dressing from separating.

The care of mayonnaise is very important. It should be stored at a temperature of 60° to 75° F. and kept covered. Glass or earthenware crocks are suitable containers. If the containers are not tightly covered, the contents should be protected by a damp cloth to prevent the surface from turning dark.

If mayonnaise is frozen, it will separate on thawing, or if it is exposed to too much heat, the same thing will happen. Sudden changes of temperature will cause separation—that is, mayonnaise, which has been kept in a refrigerator when brought into a warm room or placed on a hot plate, often separates. The most practical solution is to keep it in a cool place of even temperature, or in a refrigerator with properly regulated temperature.

If the egg yolks separate into tiny lumps instead of forming a smooth paste with the oil, the emulsion may be restored in either of two ways: (1) Beat additional egg yolks, then beat in the curdled mixture gradually, and proceed as in the first place until it becomes a smooth paste. (2) Use one tablespoon of water or vinegar in place of the egg and beat the curdled mixture into water or vinegar. If a film of oil forms on top of mayonnaise, do not stir it in, because so doing will cause the entire mass to separate, but rather remove the layer of oil and use the remaining dressing.

The flavor of any salad dressing is improved when it has stood for at least a few hours after making. Experiments have proved that a temperature of 70° F. is best for mixing mayonnaise. One safeguard against failure is to have the oil at that temperature before starting the dressing, and the egg strictly fresh. Ingredients should be measured accurately, and the process should not be hurried, for best results.

BASIC MAYONNAISE DRESSING

½ tsp prepared mustard
½ tsp sugar, optional
Few grains cayenne or white pepper
Few grains salt
1 egg yolk
1 tbsp vinegar
1 tbsp strained lemon juice
1 cup olive oil

Place the mustard, sugar if used, pepper and salt in a bowl. Add the egg yolk, mix thoroughly, then pour in the vinegar slowly, while stirring constantly. Add the oil, 1 teaspoon at a time, beating thoroughly and constantly. When the mayonnaise thickens, add the lemon juice and remaining oil rapidly. The whole process should only take about 10 minutes.

CONDENSED MILK MAYONNAISE

⅔ cup sweetened condensed milk
¼ cup vinegar or lemon juice
¼ cup oil
1 egg yolk
½ tsp salt
Few grains cayenne
1 tsp dry mustard

Combine all ingredients in a bowl and beat with a rotary beater until the mixture thickens. Or, place in a jar, cover tightly, and shake vigorously for 2 minutes.

MAYONNAISE WITH COOKED BASE

2½ tbsp flour
1 tsp dry mustard
½ tsp salt
½ tsp white pepper
1 tbsp olive oil
1 tbsp strained lemon juice
1 cup boiling water
2 egg yolks
1 cup olive oil

Combine the dry ingredients with the tablespoon of oil to form a paste. Add the lemon juice and boiling water, stir well while adding, then cook, in double boiler, until thick. Cool, add the well beaten egg yolks and remaining oil, gradually, beating constantly while adding. Chill before using.

MAYONNAISE WITH GELATIN

1 tbsp gelatin
3 tbsp cold water
1 tsp dry mustard
1 tsp salt
½ tsp white pepper
2 egg yolks
1 tbsp strained lemon juice
2 cups olive oil

Soften the gelatin in the cold water, then dissolve over boiling water. Combine the seasonings and egg yolks, then add 1 teaspoon of the lemon juice with the dissolved gelatin. Cool, then add the oil gradually, beating constantly. As the mixture thickens, add the remaining lemon juice.

MAYONNAISE VARIATIONS

Astoria Dressing. Gradually beat ¼ cup of French dressing into ¼ cup of mayonnaise, beating constantly while adding. Stir in 2 tablespoons of tomato catsup, 1 teaspoon of finely minced green pepper and 2 drops of tabasco.

Caper Dressing. To 1 cup of mayonnaise add a scant ½ cup of finely chopped, well-washed capers. Blend thoroughly.

Cavalier Dressing. To 1 cup of mayonnaise add 1 tablespoon of catsup, 2 tablespoons of crumbled Roquefort cheese, 1 teaspoon of tarragon vinegar, and 1 teaspoon of finely chopped olives. Blend.

Caviar Anchovy Dressing. To 1 cup of mayonnaise add 2 tablespoons of caviar and 4 anchovy fillets, washed, dried, and finely minced.

Caviar Dressing. To 1 cup of mayonnaise add 1 tablespoon of caviar. Blend thoroughly.

Caviar Dressing à la Russe. To 1 cup of mayonnaise add 2 tablespoons caviar, 1 hard-cooked egg white, finely chopped, and 1 tablespoon of finely minced chives.

Caviar Horseradish Dressing. To 1 cup of mayonnaise add 1 tablespoon each of caviar and well-drained prepared horse-radish.

Chutney Dressing. To 1 cup of mayonnaise add 2 tablespoons of chutney. Blend thoroughly.

Cream Mayonnaise Dressing. To 1 cup of mayonnaise add, immediately before serving, 3 tablespoons of whipped cream.

Cranberry Dressing. To 1 cup of mayonnaise add 2 tablespoons of well-beaten cranberry jelly and 1 teaspoon of grated orange rind. Blend thoroughly.

Cumberland Dressing. To 1 cup of mayonnaise add 1 tablespoon of well-beaten currant jelly and 1 teaspoon of grated lemon rind. Blend thoroughly.

Egg Dressing. To 1 cup of mayonnaise add 1 chopped hard-cooked egg and 1 teaspoon of grated onion. Blend thoroughly.

Gherkin Dressing. To 1 cup of mayonnaise add ½ cup of sweet-sour gherkins, finely chopped, and 1 teaspoon of chopped olives.

Green Dressing. Color 1 cup of mayonnaise with juices expressed from water cress and parsley, using twice as much parsley as water cress. To obtain the coloring, break the greens in pieces, pound them in a mortar until thoroughly macerated, then squeeze them through a cheese cloth. This method of coloring is preferable to the use of artificial coloring, as it contains all the mineral salts of the greens. If desired, add also 2 tablespoons of well-washed capers.

Horseradish Dressing. To 1 cup of mayonnaise add 3 tablespoons of prepared horseradish, or 2 tablespoons of freshly scraped, fresh horseradish root with ½ teaspoon of sugar if desired. Blend thoroughly. Excellent with cold meat, especially beef.

Ideal Dressing. To 1 cup of mayonnaise add 1 teaspoon of strained, prepared horseradish, 1 teaspoon of prepared mustard and ½ teaspoon of finely chopped shallot. Blend thoroughly. Ideal for cold fish and shellfish.

Minted Dressing. To 1 cup of mayonnaise add 1 tablespoon of mint jelly, chopped fine, or 1 teaspoon of fresh mint leaves, finely minced.

Olga's Dressing. To 1 cup of mayonnaise add 2 well-washed, dried and finely chopped fillets of anchovy and 1 teaspoon of finely chopped chives. Blend thoroughly.

Olive Dressing. To 1 cup of mayonnaise add 1 tablespoon of finely chopped black olives, 1 teaspoon each of finely chopped green olives, boiled cranberries, and parsley. Blend thoroughly.

Perfect Dressing. To 1 cup of mayonnaise add a small clove of finely chopped garlic, 1 teaspoon of finely chopped shallot, 1 teaspoon of finely chopped washed capers, and 1 teaspoon of very finely chopped onion. Blend thoroughly, and let stand an hour before using.

Piquante Dressing. To 1 cup of mayonnaise add 1 teaspoon each of finely chopped green olives, sour pickles, well washed capers, chervil, onion, and chives, with a scant teaspoon of prepared mustard. Blend.

Red Dressing (I). To 1 cup of mayonnaise add 1 tablespoon of strained beet juice and 2 tablespoons of finely chopped cooked beets. Blend thoroughly and chill.

Red Dressing (II). To 1 cup of mayonnaise add 1 tablespoon or more of pounded lobster coral rubbed through a fine sieve. Blend thoroughly. Good with fish salads.

Rum Cream Dressing. To 1 cup of mayonnaise add 1 teaspoon of rum. Combine with ½ cup of whipped cream, then stir in ¼ cup of chopped, blanched, roasted almonds. A fine fruit salad dressing.

Russian Dressing (I). To 1 cup of mayonnaise add 1 tablespoon of chili sauce, 1 tablespoon of finely chopped India relish, and a pinch of sugar. Blend thoroughly.

Russian Dressing (II). To 1 cup of mayonnaise add 1 tablespoon of chili sauce and 1 tablespoon each of finely chopped celery (white part only), pimiento, green pepper and parsley. Blend thoroughly.

Russian Dressing (III). To 1 cup of mayonnaise add 1 tablespoon of chili sauce, 1 teaspoon of grated onion, 1 tablespoon of finely minced sour pickles, a pinch of sugar, and 1 tablespoon each of finely chopped pimiento and green olives. Blend thoroughly.

Russian Dressing (IV). To 1 cup of mayonnaise add 1 hard-cooked egg, finely chopped, 1 tablespoon of chili sauce, 1 tablespoon each of finely chopped green pepper, pimiento, and shallot, and 1 tablespoon of caviar. Blend thoroughly.

Roquefort Cheese Dressing. To 1 cup of mayonnaise add 2 tablespoons of crumbled Roquefort cheese, a few drops of Worcestershire sauce, 1 tablespoon of French dressing, and 1 tablespoon of finely chopped chives. Blend thoroughly.

Sour Cream Dressing (I). To ½ cup of mayonnaise add ½ cup thick sour cream, 1 teaspoon prepared mustard, 1 teaspoon of finely chopped olives and ½ teaspoon of sugar. Blend thoroughly.

Sour Cream Dressing (II). To ½ cup of mayonnaise add ½ cup of thick sour cream and ½ cup of chopped walnut meats. Blend thoroughly.

Sour Cream Dressing (III). To ½ cup of mayonnaise add ½ cup of heavy sour cream, 1 tablespoon of tarragon vinegar, a few drops of onion juice, ½ teaspoon of prepared mustard, 1 teaspoon of finely chopped chives, and 1 teaspoon of finely chopped chervil or parsley. Blend thoroughly, then add a few drops each of lemon juice and Worcestershire sauce.

Sour Cream Dressing (IV). To ½ cup of mayonnaise add ½ cup of heavy sour cream, 1 coarsely chopped hard-cooked egg, and 1 tablespoon of finely chopped shallot. Blend thoroughly.

Thousand Island Dressing (I). To ½ cup of mayonnaise add 1 tablespoon of Chili sauce, and 1 tablespoon each finely chopped celery, pimiento and green pepper, with 1 tablespoon of coarsely chopped hard-cooked egg. Finally fold in ½ cup of whipped cream.

Thousand Island Dressing (II). To ½ cup of mayonnaise add the same ingredients as indicated for Thousand Island dressing I, also 1 tablespoon of finely chopped green olives, and 1 teaspoon of finely chopped sweet-sour pickle. Finally fold in ½ cup of whipped cream.

Thousand Island Dressing (III). To ½ cup of mayonnaise add 1 tablespoon each of finely chopped green maraschino cherries, red maraschino cherries, candied ginger, candied pineapple and pistachio nuts. Finally fold in a scant cup of whipped cream. Especially good for fruit salads.

Thousand Island Dressing (IV). To 1 cup of mayonnaise add 1 tablespoon of finely chopped seedless raisins, 1 tablespoon each of chopped red and green maraschino cherries, pineapple and candied apricot, with 1 teaspoon of finely chopped angelica. Finally fold in 1 cup of whipped cream colored with a little grenadine. Especially good for fruit salads.

Victory Dressing. To 1 cup of mayonnaise add the same ingredients as indicated for Thousand Island dressing IV, with ⅓ cup of shredded coconut or 3 tablespoons of finely chopped blanched almonds, and flavor the added cup of whipped cream with creme de menthe or maraschino.

COLD SAUCES FOR FISH

Andalouse Sauce. To 1 cup of mayonnaise add 3 tablespoons of tomato purée and 2 tablespoons each of julienne strips of green pepper and pimiento. Also used with Danish Liver Loaf, *which see* under LIVER.

Caper Cocktail Sauce. To ⅓ cup of mayonnaise add 1 teaspoon of anchovy pea, tablespoon of well drained, chopped drained capers with 2 tablespoons of the liquid from the bottle, 1 tablespoon of lemon juice, 1 teaspoon of prepared horseradish and a dash each of tabasco, salt, and paprika. When well blended and just before serving fold in ¼ cup of whipped cream.

Cucumber Mayonnaise. Add to 1 cup of mayonnaise, anchovy paste the size of a pea, tablespoon of well drained, chopped capers, 1 teaspoon each of minced chives and onion, cup of chopped raw cucumber and ¼ cup of chopped dill pickle, with salt, pepper and a dash of cayenne.

Green Sauce (Sauce Verte). To ¾ cup of mayonnaise add 1 teaspoon each of tarragon vinegar, minced chives, parsley and onion, with 2 handfuls of fresh, raw, young spinach which has been chopped very fine, or, better still, passed through the food chopper, using both the spinach itself and the exuding juice. Serve very cold.

Horseradish Sauce. Combine ½ cup of mayonnaise and ½ cup of whipped cream. Season highly with tabasco and a few drops of Worcestershire sauce, then stir in ⅛ teaspoon of dry mustard and ⅓ cup of drained, prepared horseradish.

Mayonnaise Cocktail Sauce. Combine ½ cup mayonnaise and ½ cup of whipped cream. Add 1½ teaspoons of caviar, 1 tablespoon of minced hard-cooked egg, 1 teaspoon each of chopped onion, parsley, chives and chervil, with ⅛ teaspoon of grated lemon rind. Serve very cold.

Orientale Sauce. To ½ cup of mayonnaise add 2 tablespoons of French dressing, 1 tablespoon each of chili sauce, chopped olives, and dill pickles, with 1 teaspoon of curry powder moistened with a little oil. Blend thoroughly and serve very cold.

Sauce Tartare. To ¾ cup of mayonnaise add 1 tablespoon each of chopped pickle, capers, and olives, and 1 teaspoon of grated onion. Also good for cold meats.

Seafood Cocktail Sauce. To ½ cup of mayonnaise add ½ cup of chili sauce, 2 tablespoons of India relish, 1 chopped hard-cooked egg and 1 teaspoon each of minced parsley, green pepper, celery, onion, and prepared mustard.

MAYONNAISE LADLE. *See* FLATWARE.

MEAD. A very ancient beverage once popular in northern Europe and England, especially in the days of the Saxons. Mead is a mild, alcoholic beverage made of fermented honey, seasoned with various spices. Often referred to by the ancients as mead wine, there were many types, depending on the seasonings used. Of these, sack mead, flavored with hops, and cowslip mead, seasoned with cowslip blossoms were the most common.

MEAL. (I) As applied to cereals, meal is a ground cereal, as corn meal.

MEAL. (II) A number of dishes assembled for a repast constitute a meal, and their assembly requires a skill quite different from that needed to make one simple dish, which may also constitute a meal by itself. Three meals a day—breakfast, luncheon, and dinner—are the conventional rule because most people eat that way. Sometimes a fourth meal is included, afternoon tea, or supper late in the evening.

A menu being decided upon, it needs an accurate sense of time, forethought, and promptness to have a variety of dishes ready at the same time, or in proper sequence if several courses are served. Such questions as the following must be answered: (a) What steps in preparation can be taken ahead of time, such as washing, paring, cutting, etc.? (b) What dishes take the longest to cook? (c) Which dishes must be served the moment they are done? (d) Which foods can be kept hot for some time without injury? (e) Which dishes can be finished and cooled, perhaps several hours ahead? (f) Do the dishes selected require the same utensils at the same time, and if so, how had the menu best be changed? (g) What is to be the order of serving?

To understand fully the bearing of these questions, the homemaker will need to select a menu and make a plan for preparing it. It is obvious that in preparing a meal she cannot finish preparation of dishes one at a time, and that steps individual to each dish must be interwoven with one another, so that she is often doing parts of half a dozen things at once.

The homemaker will devise many ways of easing and shortening the labor just before the meal is served, avoiding haste and anxiety in this way. For example, a dessert can be prepared and be cooking while the breakfast dishes are washed. Even while leftovers are being put away they can be arranged ready to re-serve, as in the case of meat or poultry to be served cold. While the preparation of the midday meal is in progress, often something can be done for dinner too.

Each dish should be perfectly prepared, neither overcooked nor undercooked. All hot dishes should be hot, and cold dishes cold. Lukewarm food is not agreeable. Bread, cake, some kinds of pastry, and red wine are the only foods that should be served at room temperature. Sliced meats and salads should be cold.

A warming oven above a coal, gas, or electric range is made to keep food hot. A double boiler is a help, and one utensil may be set in a larger, filled with boiling water. Some dishes can be set back on the stove, or over a simmering gas burner with an asbestos mat underneath. The oven may be used sometimes, with the door set ajar. The food may be kept covered until it will steam, in which case cover it with a towel. Serve hot food in hot dishes.

To keep food cool, leave in the refrigerator until the last possible moment. Sometimes serve it with ice—this is a good practice to keep butter firm in warm weather. Moreover cold foods should be served in chilled dishes.

MEALY. As applied to food, the term means having the dry, crumbly qualities of meal. For example, a potato or an egg yolk becomes mealy with long boiling.

MEASURE. See WEIGHTS AND MEASURES. For measuring liqueurs and cordials, see LIQUEURS AND CORDIALS. For measuring beverages, see BEVERAGES.

MEASURING CUP. A measuring cup is a cup of known capacity, used to measure out like quantities of any suitable material. The measuring cup may have a graduated scale on its side, or it may be part of a set, each cup having a different capacity. While measuring cups can be made or marked to any volume scale, the unit commonly used is that of the cup, rather than ounces (see WEIGHTS AND MEASURES). See also CUP and KITCHEN EQUIPMENT.

MEASURING GLASS. A glass with markings on the side to indicate levels of known capacity, usually in terms of liquid measure (see WEIGHTS AND MEASURES). It may be used solely as a measuring device, but is commonly built sturdily enough to function as a mixing glass (which see) as well. See also KITCHEN EQUIPMENT.

MEASURING SPOON. Measuring spoons are spoons that are made to hold specified amounts for measuring purposes. The spoon may have a large bowl that is marked off with a graduated scale, and there are a few patented units that can be adjusted to hold different amounts by means of sliding parts. The most common form of measuring spoon, however, is a set of differently sized spoons, usually held together by means of a ring through all of the handles. The spoons are usually graduated in terms of tablespoons, teaspoons, and fractions thereof, but may also include liquid ounces (*see* WEIGHTS AND MEASURES). They are made of metal or plastic, and the capacity should be clearly indicated in some permanent, easily read fashion. The sets mounted on rings are the most convenient for kitchen use, especially because the set may be hung up, and there is little possibility of individual spoons being lost. *See also* KITCHEN EQUIPMENT and SPOON.

MEAT. Nature's way of indicating what she requires man to eat is through the appetite. And one of the strongest human appetites is the liking for meat. Sit a big, husky, he-man down to a meatless dinner, and watch him glance around expectantly, wondering when the "food" will begin to appear! Leave a two-year child alone for a few minutes with his feeding bowl, and when you return he will have eaten all the meat with his fingers while the rest of the plate remains untouched! That is indisputable testimony to the fact that no one food has such great instinct-appeal and contributes so much palate-appeal to the diet as meat.

Practically everyone loves the rich flavor of meat, and after a meal of a juicy, well-cooked piece of meat, we feel well fed. The tantalizing flavor of meat is due to a class of substances known as "extractives," so called because they may be extracted from the meat by water. Extractives have relatively little food value in themselves, but they act as powerful stimulants to the digestive juices, especially the gastric juice, and thus they are an aid to digestion. Meat also gives the body a sense of physical well-being, obtained from no other food.

KINDS AND QUALITY OF MEAT

Beef, lamb, mutton, pork, and veal are the principal meats which the butcher handles. In cookery certain meats are classified as dark, including beef and mutton; and light, pork, lamb, and veal.

When grilled, braised, sautéed, or cooked by any of the different methods of cooking, the succulent qualities of dark meat must be retained, and this is accomplished only when the meat has not been too recently slaughtered, and the cooking process not overdone. The light meats, be they boiled, braised, sautéed, grilled, roasted, or stewed, should be sufficiently cooked, so that when carved the juice is not reddish or pinkish in color.

Meat in good condition is firm, bulky, and odorless. The color should be clear and fairly bright, not purplish or dull. For the different qualities of good meat, see each one in its alphabetical order.

MEAT AS A FOOD

As a food, meat is invaluable. From the standpoint of nutrition it supplies protein for building and rebuilding body tissues, fat for producing heat and energy, mineral salts, without which life cannot be sustained, and vitamins essential to the maintenance of good health and the building up of resistance to disease.

Of all these valuable constitutents, protein is the most important. The body tissues are composed largely of substances containing nitrogen, which are known as proteins. These tissues are not fixed and indestructible, but are constantly undergoing a process of change—regeneration and reconstruction. To rebuild these worn-out tissues, protein is necessary. Meat is one of the few complete proteins, which means that it is sufficient to support the growth and repair of the protein tissues of the body. Since so few proteins are complete, it is safe to say that no other food can take the place of meat. Meat is Nature's own principal source of food protein for human beings. In the assimilation of meat protein, there is little waste, because the meat protein is well balanced, and is so nearly like the protein which makes up the human body.

In addition to its splendid protein, meat also contains energy value in its fat and sugar content. The fat in meat is an excellent fuel food that is necessary for heat, vitality, and energy. The fats of meat are twice as valuable as starch and sugar for the production of heat, energy, and fat in the body.

Meat is extremely valuable, also, as a source of iron, phosphorus, sulphur, sodium, and iodine—minerals necessary to keep the body well regulated and in good physical condition.

Besides protein, fats, and minerals, meat also contains vitamins A, B, C, D, and G. Because there are so many ways in which it serves the nutritive requirements of the body, not only in health but in sickness and convalescence as well, meat may very properly be considered a protective food.

PURCHASING MEAT

One of the problems facing every home-maker anxious to satisfy the tastes of the whole family, is the intelligent selection of meats, which figure so importantly in the well-balanced meal. As every cook knows, there are two main classes of meats: the prime cuts, which come chiefly from inner, protected portions of the food animal, and the less expensive cuts, taken from exposed and hence more muscular and fibrous tissues.

If the family is a large one, from six to eight persons, then a large choice prime cut does not cost so much per person. But the real problem arises when the family is small, two or three persons when a large roast is so big that it will last all week and make the family tired of it despite dis-guises—hot, cold sliced, hash, soup, etc. Is it possible to have a real roast on Sunday without having to face it every day the following week?

A choice beef roast can be bought in one-, two-, or three-rib sections, as de-sired, with a roast of two ribs conveniently serving four persons. Ask the dealer to cut what is called a Newport Roast—that is, a rib roast from which a few inches of the end bones are cut. That can be braised separately to produce a delicious, tasty "Beef Ribs a la this or that."

A roast shoulder of lamb or veal is an-other prime cut which goes far, especially if it is boned and the resulting pocket stuffed. Use the big bone, cracked well, as a base for soups or broths, with a thicken-ing of cereals like whole barley, rice, or grits, and you have an entire additional meal in the soup kettle.

Even the prime leg of lamb, weighing about six or seven pounds, may be used as a three-way meat. Purchase the leg on Thursday, have the butcher cut off the first four chops or small cutlets, and use them grilled for one meal. Have the shank end sawed off with a good portion of meat, and use it in a casserole dish with carrots, onions, and white turnips—possibly adding a top crust of mashed potatoes or pastry on another day. That leaves a thick center roast, of choice texture, the best suitable for slicing.

And now for the cheaper cuts or muscles of meat, and the so-called "organs," which bring in any and all muscular cuts, plus the liver, heart, kidneys, tripe, and others —each described at its alphabetical place. Here, we may say, "enter the casserole," or baking dish. For it is only by means of a heat-resistant closed vessel or pot, whether of clay, glass, or other material, that we can tenderize tough cuts and make them truly palatable.

Casserole cooking is oven cooking, and at its best when done slowly and for a con-tinued period at uniform, low heat. There must be a tight lid to keep the steam in, to retain food fragrances. It is, perhaps, the ideal meat-cooking method, because all kinds of vegetables, spices, and herbs, can be combined with the meat while it is cook-ing, and thus result in a blended "bouquet."

Stews are slow cookers that cannot be hurried. Take time. Do not be worried. A good stew is a good brew if done right, and it helps to keep within the budget. The neck, chuck, shoulder clod, and the round, or bottom round are the muscular parts used for stews. Stews are a reminder of dumplings. They must swim and never sink—float like a boat on the kettle's brink.

Take a flank steak for baked stuffed flank steak, and for beef a la mode take the round, rump, chuck, or brisket. For boiled beef use the brisket, short ribs, neck, or chuck. The spiced beef requires the chuck, rump, or flank. The "burger" steak de-mands the neck, lower round, flank meat (ground), and the salisbury steak uses the very same muscular parts. For beef soup, the neck, shank, and bottom round are used, while the popular Pot Roast employs chuck, brisket, round, and rump.

All in all, the choice cuts comprise only 27 percent of a side of beef. That leaves 73 percent of the side for less popular cuts, almost all of which belong to the muscular or organ parts. Nevertheless when proper-ly cooked, with trappings of garlic, spices, vegetables and herbs, these become excel-lent dishes.

Fresh meat, be it prime or muscular cuts, should never be tightly covered in storage.

Put it into a shallow dish and set it in the refrigerator, with no more than a piece of oiled paper on top, not wrapped around it. The cut surface of fresh meat is already so moist that it is susceptible to contamination. Do not blame your butcher for giving you tough meats. If you want it tender, whatever the cut, take it out of your refrigerator about half or three-quarters of an hour before you start to cook it. You will be surprised at the results. To put meat directly from a cold box or refrigerator into a hot pan will certainly toughen it.

DIGESTIBILITY OF MEAT

Meat is readily digested because it comes in almost complete contact with the digestive juices. It is 97 percent digestible. The connective tissues which determine the degree of tenderness in meat, are quickly dissolved by the gastric juice. Experiments show that the protein of meats is digested as easily as that of milk and eggs. Lean meat is more quickly digested than meat with an excess of fat. Less tender, inexpensive cuts of meat, if properly cooked, are every bit as easily digested as the more tender and more costly cuts. Research has shown that if two meats of varying tenderness contain the same amount of nutritive materials, the body will ultimately derive as much benefit from the less tender as from the tender cut.

There was a time when some Americans held the opinion that veal was less digestible than beef or lamb. Research has shown, however, that veal acts very much the same in the stomach as beef and lamb do. Occasionally some individual cannot assimilate veal properly, but this may also be true of other foods, and the fact in no way affects the digestibility of veal for persons in general. In many European countries veal holds a high place among meats, and is considered preferable in many respects to beef. Veal is even included in the invalid's diet.

This also applies to pork. Fat pork, however, will digest more slowly, but this does not mean it is in any way less digestible. Pork is a highly nutritious food that should be included in the diet for variety.

Experiments show that chicken, stewed, roasted, or fried, remains in the stomach fully as long as beef or mutton. So there is little foundation for the belief that chicken is more digestible than beef or mutton.

THE GOVERNMENT STAMP

When we consider that more money is spent for meat than for any other food, and that meat is perishable, it is not surprising that the United States Government maintains a rigid control over the meat industry. Governmental control, however, is exercised only when the product of the packing houses is handled in interstate or foreign shipment. About 65 percent of the meat sold in this country is U.S. Government inspected. Look for the U.S. Government Inspection Stamp when buying meat. See the individual meats for the various standards.

MEAT BALLS. *See* HAMBURGER.

MEAT LOAF. There are so many meat loaves which may be made with one meat, or with a combination of two or more, that the following suggestions may help the homemaker to concoct her own version of this popular, economcal, and nourishing dish.

In French kitchens food choppers are rarely used, so to vie with French cooks, you must use a sharp knife to cut the meat in very small cubes. It's going to take longer, to be sure, and the result will be different from a loaf made with ground meat. Meat loaf can be an interesting dish if the home maker will but exert her originality. Actually, there are as many meat loaf recipes as there are people who make them. It is the variation of the seasonings used, the combination of meats, the way they're baked that makes them varied and interesting.

For example: If you have a familiar meat combination that gives you good results (say three-quarters beef and one-quarter pork) you can still vary it by adding one-half cup of chopped olives one time, six chopped sweet pickles another, whole hard-cooked eggs another, or chopped celery and pimiento still another. Each of these additions merely enhances the original flavor. Another good idea is to pour a can of soup over the loaf as it bakes, not all at once, but a little at a time as you'd baste a roast. Vegetable soup, mushroom soup, tomato soup, or onion soup are all good for this purpose.

Another suggestion for introducing variety is in the baking. If you like lots of crust, shape the loaf in a roll or loaf shape, and bake it in a flat pan with a few strips of bacon or salt pork over the top. Or, if you like less crust, bake it in a deep bread pan lined with wax or parchment paper to facilitate removing the loaf whole.

One of the most important points in making a meat loaf juicy and tender is to bake it slowly, for at least an hour or more, depending on the size of the loaf, basting it with the oup or its own drippings, or, if you have leftover gravy, so much he better. This slow baking is one sure secret of success.

If you relish meat served with appropriate vegetable concomitants—and have the courage to fly in the face of convention—try a meat and vegetable loaf, and forget the bread crumbs.

BEEF AND HAM LOAF

1½ lb round steak
½ lb raw lean ham
Beef suet the size of a small egg
1 minced green pepper
1 can corn (vacuum packed)
¼ tsp each thyme and cloves
1 medium-sized onion, minced
1 cup minced celery leaves
1½ tsp salt
½ tsp pepper
1 tbsp minced parsley
¼ cup tomato soup or juice (about)

Pass the two meats and the suet through the food chopper. Add all remaining ingredients except the soup and grind a second time. Moisten with the soup or tomato juice. Pack into a well greased loaf pan, cover with buttered paper and bake in a moderate oven (350° F.) for 2 hours, removing the paper for the last 15 minutes of baking. Serve plain or with mushroom sauce. (Serves 6 or 8)

BEEF AND PORK LOAF

8 slices bacon
1½ lb bottom round of beef, ground
1 lb lean pork, ground
1 tsp salt
1 tbsp parsley, minced
½ cup minced celery
1 small clove garlic
½ cup finely minced onions
⅛ tsp each cloves, thyme, sage, allspice
    and marjoram
½ cup soft bread crumbs

Arrange part of the bacon lattice-fashion in the bottom of a greased loaf pan. Thoroughly combine all remaining ingredients except the eggs and soup and turn into the prepared loaf pan. Top with more slices of bacon. Cover with a buttered paper and bake in a moderate oven (350° F.) for 2 hours, removing the paper during the last 15 minutes of baking. Serve plain or with tomato or mushroom sauce. (Serves 6 or 8)

BEEF AND SAUSAGE MEAT LOAF

2 eggs, slightly beaten
1 cup condensed tomato soup (canned)
1½ lb bottom round of beef
1 lb pork sausage meat
3 good-sized potatoes
2 medium-sized onions, ground
1 small can pimientoes
1 tbsp minced chives
1 tart apple, pared, cored and grated
1½ tsp salt
½ tsp pepper
1 tbsp parsley, minced
1 cup thin cream or undiluted evapo-
    rated milk

Grind the two meats once, then combine with all remaining ingredients except the cream or milk and grind a second time. Moisten with the cream or milk. Pack into a well greased loaf pan, cover with buttered paper and bake in a moderate oven (350° F.) 2 hours, removing the paper for the last 15 minutes of baking. Serve with onion sauce. (Serves 6 or 8)

COLD MEAT LOAF

1 tbsp gelatin
½ cup cold water
1 cup well-seasoned stock
½ onion, thinly sliced
1 stalk celery, finely chopped
½ tsp salt
⅛ tsp white pepper
½ tsp Worcestershire sauce
1 tbsp lemon juice
1 cup chopped (not ground) cold cooked
    chicken, veal, lamb, beef or ham
¼ cup pimientoes, cut in thin strips
1 tsp finely chopped chives
1 tsp finely minced parsley

Soften the gelatin in the cold water. Combine the stock, onion, celery, salt and pepper and Worcestershire sauce; bring to boiling point and cook three minutes. Then strain through a fine sieve. Add the softened gelatin and stir until completely dissolved, reheating if necessary. Now add the lemon juice and cool until beginning to thicken. Fold in the meat, pimientos, chives and parsley and when blended turn into a previously wet mold. Chill. Unmold and cut into slices for serving. Garnish with shredded lettuce, small stuffed tomatoes or sliced tomatoes.

If beef alone is used for the loaf, double the Worcestershire sauce and omit the lemon juice; with lamb, a little minced mint may be added to the loaf itself; with ham, a little grated horseradish would give good flavor. (Serves 4 to 6)

MEAT OR FISH LOAF IN BREAD SHELL

Use a large or small loaf of bread, depending on the number to be served. A 10-ounce loaf serves 6 generously, possibly 8, depending on appetites. For the small family, only half a loaf may suffice. All the crust is cut off, and a slice about ½-inch thick is cut from the top of the loaf to make a cover; then the crumbs are scooped from the inside, leaving a shell of a scant inch, or better still, half an inch on the sides and bottom. Soft butter is spread on the outside to aid in browning. The loaf is now ready to be stuffed with the meat, fish, poultry, or vegetable—even fruit—mixture, which is always put in warm. After filling, the top edge is brushed over with an egg, beaten with a tablespoon of milk, the cover adjusted and this, too, moistened with egg and milk. The loaf is placed on a generously greased baking sheet and baked in a hot oven (400° F.) for 30 minutes or until attractively golden brown. This loaf may be served hot or cold. If hot, serve with a hot tomato sauce or gravy; if cold, with a green salad and Russian dressing.

When it comes to stuffings for the loaf, there is almost no end to the varieties that may be made. A few suggestions follow:

BEEF STUFFING

2 onions, chopped
2 tbsp bacon drippings
1 cup gravy or thick white sauce
3 cups cooked beef, ground
1½ cups soft bread crumbs
2 tbsp chili sauce
½ cup seedless raisins
2 eggs, beaten slightly
3 thin slices cheese

Brown the onions in the bacon drippings. Add the gravy, ground beef, bread crumbs, chili sauce, and raisins. Heat. Add the eggs and place mixture in a hollowed-out loaf of bread. Spread slices of cheese on top, adjust cover and bake as directed above.

DRIED BEEF STUFFING

2 cups medium white sauce
½ lb chipped dried beef
1 cup cheese, cut fine, grated, or put through sieve

Add the chipped dried beef and cheese to the white sauce, place in hollowed-out loaf of bread, adjust cover, and bake as directed above.

HAM STUFFING

1 small onion, chopped
1 tbsp green pepper, chopped
2 tbsp bacon drippings
1 cup canned cream of tomato soup
3 cups cooked ham, chopped
1½ cups soft bread crumbs
3 sprigs parsley, minced
1 tbsp prepared mustard
¼ tsp pepper
2 eggs, beaten slightly

Brown the onion and green pepper in the bacon drippings. Add the soup and ham. Stir in the bread crumbs, and heat. Then add the parsley, mustard, pepper, and eggs. Stuff and bake as above.

LAMB STUFFING

1 cup canned pea soup
1 tbsp onion, grated
3 cups cooked lamb, ground
1½ cups soft bread crumbs
½ tsp salt

Combine the soup, add onion, meat, bread crumbs, and salt. Heat and add eggs. Stuff and bake as above.

PORK STUFFING

2 eggs, beaten slightly
1/4 onion, chopped fine
3 tbsp green pepper, chopped
2 tbsp bacon drippings
1 cup canned tomato soup
2 cups cooked pork, ground
1 cup cooked ham, ground
1 1/2 cups soft bread crumbs
1 tsp salt
2 eggs, beaten slightly

Brown the onion and green pepper in the bacon drippings, add the soup, stir in the meat, bread crumbs, and salt. Heat. Add the eggs. Stuff and bake as above.

TUNA FISH OR SALMON STUFFING

1 cup thick white sauce
2 cups canned tuna fish or salmon
1 tbsp lemon juice
Few gratings lemon rind
1/2 tsp salt
2 tbsp minced parsley
1 1/2 cups soft bread crumbs
2 hard-cooked eggs, minced

Combine all ingredients in the order given. Stuff and bake as above.

MEAT AND VEGETABLE LOAF

1 lb fresh, lean round of beef
1 tbsp ground beef suet
1 medium-sized onion, chopped
1 cup tomatoes, canned or fresh stewed
1/2 lb fresh string beans, coarsely ground or chopped
4 stalks celery, coarsely ground or chopped
1/4 lb mushrooms
2 medium-sized carrots, coarsely grated
2 tbsp chopped parsley
2 tbsp butter
2 tsp salt
1/2 tsp fresh ground pepper
1/4 tsp thyme
1/2 tsp dry mustard
3 tbsp Chinese soy sauce or
2 tbsp Worcestershire sauce
1 egg
1/2 cup milk

Combine the meat, vegetables and seasonings, blending very thoroughly. Moisten with the egg yolk beaten with the milk (undiluted evaporated milk may be used) and finally fold in the stiffly beaten egg white. Turn into a well greased baking dish generously sprinkled with bread crumbs. Cover and set the dish in a pan of hot water. Bake 2 hours, having the oven hot (400° F.) for the first half hour, then reducing to moderate (350° F.) for the remainder of the baking. Unmold, garnish with parsley or water cress and serve with brown gravy or tomato sauce. (Serves 6)

THREE-MEAT LOAF

2 cups soft bread crumbs
1 lb round of beef, ground
1/2 lb lean ground pork
1/2 lb lean ground veal
2 tbsp flour
2 tsp salt
2/3 tsp pepper
1 tsp paprika
1 medium-sized onion, minced
2 tbsp parsley, minced
2 eggs, slightly beaten
1/2 cup milk

Combine and blend thoroughly the crumbs, meats, flour, seasonings and flavorings and pass through the food chopper. Moisten with the beaten eggs and milk and grind a second time to insure smoothness and lightness. Pack in a well greased loaf pan, cover with buttered paper and bake in a moderate oven (350° F.) for 2 hours, removing the paper for the last 15 minutes of baking. Serve with a brown or mushroom sauce. (Serves 6 or 8)

MEAT MOUSSE. The word "mousse" means "moss" or "froth." Meat mousse, whether its foundation be of ham, beef, tongue, poultry, or game, is always made in the same way. Ham mousse is given here as an example of a hot mousse, while turkey mousse is a good example of a cold one.

HAM MOUSSE

2 cups ground cooked ham
2 eggs
A dash each of nutmeg, white pepper and cayenne
1 cup heavy cream
1 small glass sherry

Remove all gristle and fat from the meat and grind, using the finest possible knife of the food chopper. Then press through a fine sieve. Beat in the egg yolks and seasonings. Next add the cream, slightly beaten and blended with the wine. Finally fold in the stiffly beaten egg whites and turn carefully into a buttered mold or soufflé dish. Set this in a pan containing hot water and bake in a very moderate oven (300°–350° F.) until set like a custard. Unmold onto a hot platter, garnish with parsley or water cress and serve with hollandaise, béchamel or any other preferred sauce. See additional recipes under HAM and LAMB. (Serves 6)

TURKEY MOUSSE

1½ tbsp gelatin
2 tbsp cold water
1 cup hot chicken broth or stock
Salt, celery salt and paprika
1 tbsp minced olives
1 cup ground cooked turkey
1 cup heavy cream, whipped
2 egg whites, stiffly beaten

Soften the gelatin in the cold water, add the hot broth or stock and stir until dissolved. Add the seasonings and cool. When almost at the setting point, beat with a rotary beater until very light, then fold in the olives, turkey, cream and, finally, the stiffly beaten egg whites. Turn into a previously wet mold and chill. Unmold and garnish with water cress, sliced tomatoes, stuffed olives, etc. (Serves 6)

MEAT GRINDER. See GRINDER.

MEAT PASTES. Commercial products, usually in paste form, made from meat, poultry, game, etc. They are often referred to as potted meats.

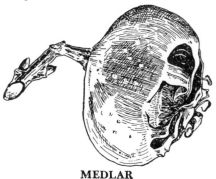

MEDLAR

MEAT PIE. An almost infinite variety of fillings and crusts can be used. Leftovers are at their best under a crust, and no freshly purchased food is too good for the purpose. Perhaps most meat pies conceal what was left of Sunday's roast, but that should not be held against them, for tender meat, combined with well-seasoned gravy, vegetables, and a crust, are a savory and appetizing food.

For crusts, you may choose between plain and rich pastry, biscuit or short-cake dough, mashed white or sweet potatoes, alone or in combination with mashed turnips or carrots, minced onion, or parsley, or both. Less usual, but very good, are toasted bread rings, diamonds or triangles.

A pastry crust is easier to handle if added to a cold mixture. Biscuit and other crusts cook and brown better on a hot dish.

The easiest meat pie is made from a stew, a fricassee, or pot roast leftover. The wise homemaker makes enough of these dishes to serve twice, once plain and once under a crust. Variety may be obtained by adding a new vegetable, or mushrooms, to the original stew.

MECKLENBURG SKIM CHEESE. A Mecklenburg rennet cheese made from skim milk. Saffron is added for coloring.

MEDLAR. A small fruit of the rose family. It is grown in England, is picked in November, and is not edible until about two weeks after it is picked.

MELANGE. This delicious French fruit preserve should be put up in the month of June. Proceed as follows:

To every pound of fruit take one pound of sugar. No cooking at all is required and the directions are very simple. Begin with strawberries. Buy some of the largest and soundest berries in the market. Wash and pick out two pounds of them and lay them in a two-gallon stone jar. Cover with two pounds of granulated sugar. Remove pits from as many pounds of red, black, or white cherries as you wish to use, adding an equal amount by weight of sugar. You may also use bananas, pineapples, or oranges. Seed the oranges carefully. Be sure to weigh each additional amount of fruit and add a corresponding weight of sugar. Pour over the fruit a pint of brandy. Stir well. Later add peaches, apricots, raspberries, blackberries, red currants, greengages, purple or red plums, in season. Be sure to add the same amount of sugar as you do fruit, but no more alcohol. Keep in a dry, cool place. As the fruit is used, more fruit and sugar may be added, keeping the jar going indefinitely. There is always a surplus of sirup, which makes excellent pudding sauces, by adding a little water and thickening. This sirup is also good for waffles and pancakes.

MELBA. A sauce named for the famous singer, which is made of fresh raspberries. It is the sauce used in Peach Melba.

MELBA SAUCE

1 cup of pulp and juice of fresh raspberries, rubbed through a sieve to remove seeds
1 small glass jar currant jelly
½ cup granulated sugar
⅛ tsp salt
½ tbsp arrowroot or cornstarch
1 tbsp cold water
¼ tsp lemon juice

Combine currant jelly, sugar, and pulp and juice of berries. Place over direct flame and bring to boiling point (212° F.). Add salt, arrowroot or cornstarch, and cook, stirring constantly, until mixture thickens and becomes clear. Strain through double cheesecloth. Cool.

MELBA TOAST. Cut two- or three-day-old bread with a very sharp knife into slices not more than ⅙-inch thick. Remove crusts. Place slices on rack in a very slow oven (200° F.) and allow to dry thoroughly. The toast will be crisp and a light brown throughout when done.

MELON. A plant of the cucumber family (gourd). The story of the melon is interesting. A fruit that originally grew wild in India and Africa, during the 8th century it was brought to China. Later the plant was introduced into Europe, finally reaching the United States.

Today large areas of land in many parts of the United States are devoted to the cultivation of various types of melons. The leading producing states are California, Colorado, Georgia, New Jersey, Texas, Delaware, Maryland, Michigan, Indiana, North Carolina, and South Carolina. The watermelon, the muskmelon or cantaloupe, and the honeydew melon are perhaps the best known varieties. Other melons include: Burrell Gem, Cannon Ball, Casaba, Globo de Orb, Hales Best, Heart of Gold, Honey Ball, Montreal, Netty Gem, Osage, Persian, Pollock, Rocky Ford, Santa Claus, Tip Top, and Winter Pineapple.

GENERAL HINTS ON BUYING MELONS

Selection of melons for quality and flavor is not easy; it often tests the skill of the experienced homemaker. Sweetness and flavor in melons are not fully developed until the fully ripe stage of maturity is reached. Ripeness in almost all kinds of melons is indicated by the softening of that part of the fruit which surrounds the "eye" or "button" at the blossom end, and which yields to pressure of the finger. Usually the odor that most melons diffuse becomes stronger and is most perceptible when the full stage of ripeness is reached. In some melons a change of color to a more or less yellowish tinge is also a sign of ripeness. No one indication is infallible. Sometimes one, and sometimes a combination of indications must be considered as a guide.

Unripe melons should never be chilled, because they do not then fully ripen. Melons should be kept at a temperature of 70° F. until ripe, and then chilled just before serving. A cut melon should always be wrapped in cellophane or wax paper before it is put into refrigerator to prevent its odor permeating other foods.

TO SERVE MELONS

Melons may be served fresh in the shell or may be cut into various shapes and served in fruit cups, salads, etc. The pulp and inner rind may be made into preserves and pickles in the same way as indicated for watermelon. Canteloupe should always be chilled before serving, but should not be cooled to such a degree that it loses its flavor. In serving "iced cantaloupe" the fruit should be chilled, and if desired, served on ice, but the cavity should never be filled with ice because that injures the fruit and dilutes the flavor. Salt, lemon, or lime may be served with melon, or a scoop of ice cream may be placed in the center, à la mode style. The outside of canteloupes should be scrubbed with a brush to remove all sand, before the melon is cut.

Artful chefs sometimes cut honeydew melons lengthwise and serve them garnished with maraschino cherries, peeled white grapes, and fresh currants covered with confectioners' sugar, the whole sprinkled with chopped pistachio nuts.

MELLOW 748

Melon a la Gonneau

Small melon
Hot ginger sirup
Whipped cream
Preserved pineapple, cubed

Cut the melon in half and soak in hot ginger sirup. Then chill. Fill with whipped cream and cubes of preserved pineapple.

Melon Cup Cocktails

The fleshy part of the melon may be shaped into balls with a vegetable ball cutter, or it may be cut in cubes.

Melon mint cocktails. Prepare sugar sirup by boiling ½ cup of sugar and ½ cup of water for 5 minutes. Pour the sirup over 3 chopped mint leaves, cool, and strain it. Add the juice of 1 lemon and of 1 orange, and chill. Place cantaloupe and watermelon balls in cocktail glasses, and pour the sirup over them. Garnish with sprigs of mint.

Or, mix the cubes of 2 small melons with about 2 dozen broken afterdinner mints.

Cantaloupe baskets. Cut 2 pieces from each cantaloupe, leaving the remainder in the shape of a basket with a handle. Remove the seeds and dice the pulp. Combine it with an equal amount of strawberries, seeded cherries, or diced pineapple, or of a combination of the fruits. Sweeten slightly, and add French dressing if desired. Serve the fruit in the baskets. Garnish with preserved green grapes.

Raspberry-melon cup. Divide 3 cups of chilled diced watermelon among 6 cocktail glasses, and pour raspberry purée over the melon. Prepare the purée by covering 1½ cups of raspberries with ½ cup of sugar, chilling for about an hour, and then forcing through a sieve.

Watermelon cup. Divide 3 cups of watermelon cubes or balls among 6 sherbet glasses. Over these sprinkle the juice of 2 limes and 3 tablespoons of chopped mint leaves. Chill thoroughly.

Melon Ice

1 large honeydew melon
3 tbsp lemon juice
1 cup sugar
2 cups water
⅛ tsp salt

¾ cup dry sherry
½ cup heavy cream, whipped

Cut the melon, remove the seeds, and scoop out the pulp; place the shell in refrigerator. Force the pulp through sieve and add the lemon juice. Heat the sugar and water to boiling point; add melon and salt and cool. Freeze in a mechanical refrigerator until of mushlike consistency. Add the sherry and fold in the cream. Freeze until firm. Serve in melon shells and garnish with mint. (Makes approximately 2 quarts)

MELLOW. A fruit so described is fully ripe—not hard, harsh, or rigid. It is unctuous, soft, loamy, and of rich quality.

MENHADEN. A shad-like fish caught off the northeastern coast of the United States. It is oily and bony, and not ordinarily used for food.

MENTHA. The technical name for that genus or family of highly aromatic herbs, having opposing leaves and small flowers, that includes the mints. Peppermint, spearmint, mint, etc., are of this genus. Mint is widely used in cooking, both as a garnish and as an ingredient. *See* Mint.

MENU PLANNING. A menu is a meal plan. It should be a plan for combining foods to make a wholesome, digestible, and appealing meal. Since we eat primarily to maintain bodily health, our first concern in menu planning is the provision of a nourishing diet. We are then concerned with digestibility. This, like nutritive value and appeal, is achieved through proper selection and preparation. All of these phases are discussed under diet (*which see*). No more than one food somewhat difficult to digest should be served at a single meal. Highly seasoned foods are included in this group and should be used sparingly.

Many of our eating habits are worthy of being cultivated or preserved. Fresh fruit for breakfast stimulates the appetite and helps to prevent or overcome constipation. Cereal is better enjoyed before highly flavored foods have been eaten. Soup at the beginning of a meal tends to condition the stomach for the digestion of the food that follows. Bread and butter afford a good combination of fat and carbohydrate. Cheese is highly concentrated and is more digestible when served with crackers or sauce than when unaccompanied. Ice cream is less likely to chill the stomach at the end of a meal than at the beginning.

APPEALING MEALS

Our third concern is with palatability, and significant in this connection are color, flavor, and variety. Just as there are pleasant combinations of sound, so there are harmonies of flavor, color, and odor; and their achievement is an art. Try to introduce attractive color contrasts into your meals; avoid serving several foods of the same color at a single meal. Pale dishes can be made to look more colorful through the addition of garnishes such as parsley sprigs.

Certain flavors seem naturally to complement one another, so utilize these. Habit has much to do with food combinations. A Frenchman would not cook beans with molasses as does the Bostonian; nor would a Chinaman eat sugar on rice. It is interesting to experiment with food combinations in order to introduce new ones as well as to discover why old ones are pleasing. Why, for example, do we like crackers with chowder? Butter on bread? Toast with eggs? Peas with lamb chops? Mint with roast lamb? The introduction of new combinations will help you to avoid the monotony of stereotyped meals.

Food combinations may be designed to add the appetizing characteristics of some foods to other wholesome but unappetizing foods. The less attractive but nourishing foods may also be served to better advantage when the appetite is strong; but try generally to serve food that is appealing in itself.

Variety is the keynote of appealing meals. Avoid a repetition of one food in a single meal, and don't use just one type of foodstuff such as starchy foods. Try to vary the texture, flavor, garnishes, and methods of preparation involved in the single meal—combine soft and solid, tart and sweet, hot and cold foods. This does not, however, mean that you should serve a great variety of foods at each meal. The most favorable variety is obtained by serving a few carefully selected foods.

It is not sufficient to provide variety in a single meal or even among the meals of a single day. It is better to limit the variety of foods served in a day in order to allow for a greater range of foods in the course of a week. Try to prevent the monotony of frequent or regular repetitions of foods or combinations of foods. By all means use your leftovers, but try to make these reappear in a new form.

Among the factors entering into the degree of satisfaction to be derived from a meal are the surroundings and the method of service. Of course you don't want to "starve" your guests, but it is equally important that you don't serve too much food; small portions tend to be more appetizing than large ones. An attractive arrangement lends eye appeal. And be sure to serve each dish at the proper temperature.

ORIGINATING YOUR OWN MENUS

You can, of course, obtain no end of menu plans that have been preformulated by food experts. However, if you plan carefully, you yourself are by far your best menu-maker. The preformulated menu plans must at least be adapted for personal use, but it is most advisable to originate your own.

In planning menus you must consider a number of personal, geographical, and climatic conditions of which your food expert can have no knowledge. The food expert has no knowledge, for example, of the individual tastes, allergies, or dietary requirements of those whose food you prepare. Nor can she plan to spare you the embarrassment that can result from serving guests foods that their religions may forbid them to eat.

You must also determine whether the difficulty and time involved in preparing and serving certain dishes is too great. If you have no help, it is advisable to plan meals to facilitate preparation and service, and it is not advisable to undertake too elaborate a menu.

The cost of food must also be considered. Fruits and vegetables are more reasonably priced when they are in season, so try to use them at that time. And local produce is usually less expensive, as well as fresher, than that which must be imported from other sections.

Appetites are usually heavier during the winter than during the summer, and winter foods should be chosen to increase the fuel value. Main dishes and some desserts need to be substantial, strengthening, and warmth-giving, but these high-fuel foods must not supplant the required fruits, vegetables, and milk. If children crave sweets, don't discourage them unduly. Sweet fruits, jams, honey, and jellies are good winter foods for active children.

The following forms can serve as a basis for menu planning.

Breakfast
Fruit
Cereal
Meat, if desired
Eggs, if desired
Toast with butter, if desired
Beverage

Dinner
Soup, if desired
Meat
Potatoes or a substitute
Another vegetable
Salad, if desired
Bread with butter
Dessert
Beverage

Supper or Luncheon
Meat or a substitute
Potato or a substitute
Another vegetable or a salad
Bread with butter
Dessert
Beverage

The question of appetizers is largely left to the discrimination of the individual. For a wealth of suggestions in this connection *see* APPETIZERS, CANAPES, COCKTAILS, and HORS D'OEUVRES.

The above outlines are intended as an aid in menu planning, but it is by no means necessary to follow them exactly. Simple substitutions such as that of rolls or biscuits for bread can be made at any time. It is of utmost importance, however, that when you have planned your menus you check them against the normal diet outline (*see* DIET) in order to insure an adequate daily intake of nutrients. If one meal is particularly light, it should be compensated for in another.

It is recommended that breakfast be a fairly substantial meal providing one-fourth to one-third of the food consumed throughout the day. It should always include fruit, milk, and something hot. A bird-sized breakfast is not satisfactory even for one who is trying to lose weight.

It is impossible to plan each meal independently of the others if the daily diet is to provide the proper nutritive value, and it is impossible to plan menus for but a single day if the food for the week is to have the proper variety. The most satis-

factory procedure is to work out a series of menus at one time. This practice will serve as a marketing aid as well as to insure an adequate diet and variety of foods.

A SAMPLE OF MENU PLANNING

The following market list and menus for a week were prepared by the Bureau of Human Nutrition and Home Economics of the Department of Agriculture (Bulletin AIS–54) and are recommended for purposes of economy. They are adapted to a family of four, two adults and two children of pre-school age.

Marketing list.
2 heads of lettuce
1½ lb. snap beans
2 bunches carrots
2½ lb. spinach
1 lb. squash
1 head of cabbage, small
1 No 2 can green peas
1 pkg. green lima beans (frozen)

4½ to 5 lb. oranges
2 grapefruit
1 46½-oz. can tomato juice
2 or 3 lemons or 1 small can lemon juice

2 lb. sweet potatoes
6 lb. potatoes

2 lb. apples
1 No. 2 can applesauce
1 No. 2½ can peaches
1 lb. prunes
½ lb. raisins
3 lb. other fruit in season or canned
1 bunch celery
1 lb. beets
1 lb. onions

1½ to 2 lb. sugar
½ to 1 pt. molasses, honey, jelly, or preserves

17 qt. fresh whole milk
1 14½-oz. can evaporated milk
¼ lb. cheddar cheese
½ to 1 lb. cottage cheese
1 pt. ice cream

3 to 3½ lb. chuck roast of beef
2 to 3 lb. shoulder of lamb
¾ lb. liver
1 lb. fish (haddock, cod, halibut)

2 doz. eggs

8 oz. split peas
4 oz. peanut butter

3 loaves enriched bread
3 loaves whole-wheat bread
1 loaf rye bread
¼ lb. rolled oats or whole-wheat cereal
1 small pkg. ready-to-eat cereal
1 lb. enriched flour
2 lb. macaroni or corn meal
1 box graham or other crackers

½ lb. bacon
½ lb. table fat (butter or margarine)
½ lb. shortening
½ pt. salad dressing or salad oil

1 lb coffee
¼ lb. tea

MENUS
Sunday
Breakfast.
Orange juice
Scrambled eggs
Toast
Butter or margarine
Preserves
Milk for children
Coffee for adults

Dinner.
Pot roast cooked with carrots, potatoes,
    and onions
Chopped spinach
Bread
Butter or margarine
2-egg sponge cake with ice cream
Milk for children
Coffee or tea for adults

Supper.
Open-faced grilled cheese and bacon sand-
    wiches for adults
Hot wheat cereal with milk for children
Shredded cabbage and raisin salad
Fruit in season
Milk

Monday
Breakfast.
Prunes with orange slices
Hot oatmeal with milk
Toast
Table fat
Milk for children
Coffee or tea for adults

Lunch.
Cream of tomato soup with toast squares
Shirred eggs
Spinach
Bread
Table fat
Baked Indian pudding
Milk

Dinner.
Beef casserole with mounds of mashed po-
    tatoes (beef left from Sunday roast)
Green peas
Fruit salad
Bread and table fat
Sponge cake with honey sauce
Milk

Tuesday.
Breakfast.
Grapefruit sections
Soft-cooked eggs
Toast and table fat
Milk for children
Coffee or tea for adults

Lunch.
Baked macaroni
Green beans and shredded raw carrots
Bread and table fat
Oatmeal and prune pudding
    (oatmeal left from Sunday breakfast)
Milk

Dinner.
Broiled liver or liver pattie
Baked potato and baked squash
Tossed green salad flavored with chopped
    crisp bacon
Bread and table fat
Fruit in season
Milk

Wednesday
Breakfast.
Orange
Ready-to-eat cereal with milk
Toast, table fat, and preserves
Milk for children
Coffee or tea for adults

Lunch.
Split pea soup
Apple, cabbage, and raisin salad
Bread and table fat
Baked Indian pudding
Milk for children
Coffee or tea for adults

Dinner.
Beef hash with potatoes (beef left from Sunday)
Creamed carrots and peas
Celery
Bread and table fat
Fruit cup
Milk

Thursday

Breakfast.
Tomato juice
Hot oatmeal with milk
Toast and table fat
Milk for children
Coffee or tea for adults

Lunch.
Creamed eggs on toast, or soft-cooked eggs with toast
Jellied fruit salad
Molasses cookies
Milk

Dinner.
Baked shoulder of lamb
Baked sweet potato
Green lima beans
Cole slaw
Bread and table fat
Canned peaches and graham crackers
Milk

Friday

Breakfast.
Orange
Hot wheat cereal with raisins and milk
Toast and table fat
Milk for children
Coffee or tea for adults

Lunch.
Split pea soup
Cottage cheese and peach salad
Bread and table fat
Cookies
Milk for children
Coffee or tea for adults

Dinner.
Baked fish (haddock, cod, or halibut)
Sliced beets
Baked potato
Celery
Bread and table fat
Lemon snow with custard sauce
Milk for children
Coffee or tea for adults

Saturday

Breakfast.
Tomato juice
Ready-to-eat cereal with milk
Toast, table fat, and preserves
Milk for children
Coffee or tea for adults

Lunch.
Peanut butter and celery sandwiches
Vegetable salad
Floating island or junket
Milk for children
Coffee or tea for adults

Dinner.
Minced lamb on riced potatoes (lamb left from Thursday dinner)
Hearts of lettuce with dressing
Green beans
Applesauce and graham crackers
Milk

SAMPLE MENUS FOR SPECIAL OCCASIONS

Sunday breakfast
Fruit juice
Little pork sausages
French toast
Raspberry jam
Coffee

Club luncheon
Grapefruit segments in wine
A casserole dish
Green salad
Carrot sticks
Hot cheese biscuits
Fruit
Salted nuts
Mints
Coffee

Informal dinner
Cocktail
Toasted crackers
Molded fruit salad
Chicken casserole
Steamed rice
Buttered peas
Hot rolls
Individual lemon pies
Coffee

Semi-formal dinner
Mock turtle soup
Toasted crackers
Celery, olives, pickles
Orange and avocado salad

Broiled chicken
Buttered asparagus
Steamed rice with chopped parsley
Hot dinner rolls
Spiced apricots
Chilled white table wine
Lemon sherbet
Tiny frosted cup-cakes

Special occasion dinner
Consommé
Toasted crackers
Celery and olives
Baked ham
Oven-browned sweet potatoes
String beans and mushrooms
Diced apple and dill pickle salad
Hot bran rolls with apricot jam
Chilled sparkling burgundy wine
Angel cake à la mode
Coffee
Salted nuts

Meatless meal
Salad-stuffed tomatoes
Fillets of sole
French fried potatoes
Buttered green lima beans
Toasted cheese rolls
Sauterne wine
Peaches with whipped cream
Coffee

Grill or barbecue supper
Barbecues or grilled steaks
Hot buttered rolls
Raw onion rings
Scalloped potatoes (prepared in kitchen)
Lettuce bowl
Fresh fruits
Gingersnaps
Coffee

Easy buffet supper
Spaghetti-meat casserole
Hot French bread
Claret or burgundy wine
Relish platter—pickles, raw carrot strips,
   celery curls, olives, green onions, rad-
   ishes
Cheese atop warm apple pie
Coffee

Holiday dinner
Oysters and clear soup
Wafers
Roast turkey and stuffing
Giblet gravy

Sweet potatoes
Cranberry jelly
Lima beans
Spinach
Salad of pears in minted gelatin with may-
   onnaise thinned with lemon juice
Hot plum pudding with sauce
Raisins and salted nuts
Coffee

Basket picnic
Tuna fish salad in lettuce cups
Corned beef sandwiches made with whole-
   wheat bread
Potato chips
Sweet pickles
Ice tea in thermos jug
Fruit
Salted nuts

Informal teas
Tea, coffee or cocoa
Open-faced sandwiches or canapés
Small pieces of cake

MERGANSER DUCK. A wild duck.
See DUCK.

MERINGUE. A delicate, fluffy mixture
of stiffly beaten egg whites plus sugar, commonly used as a topping for desserts; sometimes individually baked as for meringue
glacé.

The recipe for meringue depends upon
the type to be used. If you want it to
tower to the skies and to be dry, one tablespoon of sugar should be used to each well-
beaten egg white. If you prefer a sweeter
and more flavorful topping, you may use
from two to three tablespoons of sugar to
each egg white.

There is another point besides the
amount of sugar, however, which must be
considered in making perfect meringue of
any type. The oven temperature must be
low; otherwise you will have a tough product. Besides this, if you use a hot oven and
short cooking, your beautiful meringue
may shrink almost to nothingness. Like
other rules, this one has one exception.
When making a Baked Alaska (*which see*)
you must have a hot oven, as the ice cream
will not hold up during the longer time
necessary for the browning with a low
temperature.

MERINGUE TOPPING

When making a meringue for topping,
use 2 tablespoons of sugar to each egg

white. Add the sugar gradually. Beat until the mixture is very smooth. Have egg whites cold but not chilled. Beat until they are stiff enough to stand up in points when the beater is removed. Another test is to invert the bowl and if the whites do not run out they are stiff enough. Beat constantly, while adding sugar, until the whites are stiff but still glassy. Do not let them reach the "dry" stage. A very little salt or cream of tartar may be added during the beating; flavoring may be added if desired.

If you need a greater amount of meringue, use an electric mixer, and beat in second speed with the wire beater. Do not add any sugar to the whites. Beat to a medium dry stiffness, to the point where the egg whites start to pull away from the bowl sides, then if making an uncooked meringue add the required amount of sugar gradually and slowly, while still beating in second speed.

Hot Sirup Meringue

For hot sirup meringue, proceed as indicated for a large amount of meringue, and substitute a sirup for sugar. This sirup should be hot and should be poured in very slowly, in a heavy, thread-like stream, while the machine is still beating in second speed. This hot meringue increases the amount to almost double that made by the cold method. Beat the mixture one minute or so after all the sirup has been added. This type of meringue is very appropriate for butterscotch, custard, sabayon, and brandied fruit pies, as well as all the chocolate pie tribe. Add any desired flavoring just before the beaten egg whites are removed. If used on citrus pies, such as lemon, lime, grapefruit, or orange, the flavoring may be the juice of the fruit used in the pie.

This hot sirup meringue will appear somewhat softer than the plain sugar meringue, but it will set firm and dry after it is placed on the pies. Another advantage of this boiled meringue is that it is foolproof as regards leaking, cracking, or shrinking. Again, like other rules, this method has an exception. It should be baked in a hot oven or at 425°–450° F. as it will not keep fluffy long, and it should be put on at once. Spread the meringue immediately on the pies, making sure that it touches the rim on all sides. Do not have, unless desired, the meringue with a smooth,

even surface, but rather what has been described as "mountain and valley" effect. Or you may force the meringue through a pastry bag; or you may work a fork or spoon through the meringue to make an attractive but not fussy appearance. A swirled effect is most attractive.

When making cold meringue, be sure not to add sugar before the eggs are beaten sufficiently, lest the meringue be watery. Tough meringue may be caused by too little sugar or by baking in too hot an oven.

Meringue Hints

A teaspoon of cold water added to the white of each egg will make it whip more easily, and also increase the quantity.

Grated orange peel gives a delightful flavor to meringue.

Meringue will always stand up high and perfect if a generous pinch of baking soda is added to beaten egg whites.

Egg whites separate from the yolk easily when the egg is cold, but they whip better at room temperature.

Pie meringues become flat when too much sugar is used in them, when they are baked in too hot an oven, or when they are not baked enough. A quarter of a teaspoon of cream of tartar, mixed with each two egg whites, will help to keep the meringue firm.

Grated apples are often used in meringues. Peel the apples whole, then press them onto a regular grater, turning the apple around in your hand until everything but the core has been grated.

Do you ever make berry pies with a meringue on top instead of a top crust? Blueberry pies, for example, done this way, are excellent.

Try sprinkling shredded coconut (which may be tinted) over meringue before browning in the oven.

For one-crust pies which take a meringue or whipped cream topping, instead of covering the entire filling, pipe a "collar" of the meringue or whipped cream around the outer edge. This leaves a bit of the filling exposed to view, and presents a most attractive appearance. *See also* Kisses.

MERISETTE. A liqueur made in France. It is a highly bouqueted after-dinner cordial in which a wild cherry flavor predominates with that of cherry kernels.

MERMEN. A cowfish belonging to the skate family, dressed and sold as skate wings or saddles.

MERO. *See* GROUPER.

MESCAL. A highly potent Mexican and South American spirit that is distilled from the sap of the maguey or American aloe.

MESITRA CHEESE. A soft, unsalted cheese made of sheep's milk, which is produced in the Crimea. The cheese is often eaten fresh and unsalted.

MESOST CHEESE. A sweet whey cheese made in Sweden.

METHEGLIN. A Welsh mead *which see.*

METTON CHEESE. A variety of French cheese made in the winter.

METTWURST. *See* SAUSAGE.

MEUNIERE BUTTER. *See* BUTTER SAUCE.

MIGNOT CHEESE. A soft, rennet cheese, which may be either round or square in shape. There are two types: White, a fresh cheese; passé, a ripened cheese. It has been made in the Department of Calvados, France, for more than 100 years and resembles Pont l' Évêque and Livarot.

MILDEW. A decayed condition of food, produced by small fungi.

MILK. On a wall long buried in Babylon and recently excavated, there is a frieze of cows and their calves and a man milking a cow into tall jars. The frieze is five thousand years old. On the side of a cave in the Pyrenees is a crude drawing of a cow. Archeologists say it is twenty thousand years old. Among the oldest writings still preserved are the Vedic hymns of India, inscribed four or five thousand years ago. They are records of Hindu folklore. They sing the praises of the cow as the greatest benefactor of the human race.

Whenever you draw the curtain from the past, in whatever time or place, you will find some reference to the animals which produce milk. When civiliaztion opened the New World, the cow went with it. There were no cattle on the western continent five hundred years ago. De Soto left some in the Mississippi valley shortly before he died of fever and wounds in 1542. Coronado, seeking the Seven Golden Cities, left a few somewhere along the Rio Grande before he disappeared from history about 1549. Later, the English colonists

brought cattle on their boats in the 17th century. There were some at Jamestown in 1611 and at Plymouth Rock in 1624. By 1650, the New England colonies had ceased to import butter and cheese and were exporting these products instead. As the early pioneers moved westward, the cow was a familiar sight behind each wagon, an invaluable member of the pioneer family.

The housewife made butter at home pounding a dasher in a wood churn. But American inventiveness was always making improvements. In the early days of the United States, the U.S. Patent Office reported, on an average, a new dairy machine every two weeks.

Today, the United States is the greatest dairy country in the world. Over 26,-000,000 cows supply it with milk. The milk industry, including all its products, represents one of the largest in the nation, with an output valued at several billion dollars a year.

In France in 1860, Louis Pasteur found a way to destroy harmful bacteria by heat, and within the next half century pasteurization became an almost universal requirement among municipal departments of health. Pasteur's was probably the most important contribution to the milk industry and to public health since milk was first used as a food.

MILK AS A FOOD

The milk of several animals, such as cows, goats, asses, mares, and camels, may be used for food, but in America cow's milk is by far the most popular. Varieties of milk differ slightly in chemical composition, odor, and taste, but they all contain the elements necessary to sustain life in fairly economical proportion. For infants, milk is a "complete" food, meeting the requirements of the growing body, and even for adults milk can be the principal food in the diet.

Milk ranks among the most important of all foods. A pint of milk may be said to equal approximately the nutrition contained in six ounces of beef, mutton, or pork. Although such a valuable food, milk is by no means essential to a diet designed to increased bodily strength and is usually omitted from the menus of athletes in active training. Infants and children tire of milk less easily than adults. The adult needs 23 ounces of water-free food per day

day to maintain a healthful equilibrium, and he must consume nine pints of milk to obtain it. The excess of albumin, fat, and water which he would thus obtain is wasteful for him. Milk, however, leaves no coarse residue in the intestine, such as the indigestible fiber of meat or the cellulose of vegetable and fruits.

Milk contains Vitamins A, B, C, G, in varying amounts, and Vitamin D is often added artifically to increase its nutritive value.

COMPOSITION

Milk is composed principally of water, protein, fat, carbohydrates, and ash. The fat, suspended in a casein solution with other proteins, lactose, and inorganic salts, is mainly formed of glycerides of palmitic and oleic acids, the latter constituting about 50 per cent of the fat content, and five or six other fatty acids, such as myristic and stearic, represented in minute quantity.

The percentage of fat in milk is about four percent, but in cream it is considerably higher. Cream is not pure fat, however. It is simply an aggregate of the oil globules in the top portion of the milk with a little protein and carbohydrate. Average milk contains from eight to ten percent cream. Good milk should form a layer of cream about two and one-half inches thick as it stands in a quart bottle. The fuel value (calories) of a pint of cream is not far from 1,425 calories, or about the same as 11.8 lbs. of bread, 1½ dozen bananas, or 4½ lbs. of potatoes.

Casein. The principal protein of milk is casein, but there are a half dozen others. Casein itself is noncoagulable by heat, even by boiling, but it is coagulated into firm, tough clots by acids, such as gastric juice and the many organic acids which occur as products of malfermentation in the stomach. Lactic acid is the common agent in forming the coagulae. Casein is also coagulated, but less firmly, by the milk-curdling ferment, rennin present in the infant's stomach. The casein clot formed by rennin is not redissolved by neutralization with alkalis. Casein is present in milk chiefly in an alkaline form, as potassium caseinate, and in conjunction with calcium phosphate.

Lactalbumin. There is an albumin present called lactalbumin which is coagulable by heat and forms the tenacious skin which floats on top of boiled milk. This albumin plays an important role by surrounding the minute oil globules of the milk and preventing them from agglutination, keeping them in fine emulsion. It is contained in solution in whey.

Lactose. Lactose is an important ingredient of milk. Called also milk sugar, it is hard, transparent, white, and crystalline, when chemically pure. It has a diuretic effect when given therapeutically, has a faintly sweetish taste, and is allied to both sucrose and starch in its properties. In human milk, its chief function is to supply energy for heat production in an infant whose muscles are not yet active in developing this force, and it constitutes about one-half of the total solids of milk, exclusive of fat The quantity present in cow's milk varies greatly, but it can generally be said that it bears an inverse ratio to the amount of fat and casein present. It is less liable than cane sugar to ferment in the stomach and alone is not susceptible to alcoholic fermentation. In the presence of nitrogenous material, however, it is converted into lactic acid and sours the milk. It is promptly absorbed from the alimentary canal, not remaining over an hour in the stomach.

Strippings. Strippings is the name given to residual milk, which may be drawn off shortly after ordinary milking has been completed. Contrary to popular belief, it possesses no advantage as food over the rest of the milk, and what little difference in composition exists can be artificially produced. It is richer in fat but poorer in casein than milk first drawn. For infant use, it should be diluted with two parts of water.

PRESERVING AND PURIFYING MILK

Good cow's milk should be almost neutral, reddening blue litmus paper very slightly, if at all. The normal color is white and is due to the fat globules, but it may be slightly yellow, particularly when the cow has been feeding in wheat fields. The taste of good milk is sweet and the odor faint and fresh.

Bad milk has a bad odor, either sour or derived from absorption of some other matter. Milk easily acquires other odors and even other flavors. Left in a refrigerator with cheese, onions, decomposing meat or fish, it will spoil. Milk absorbs odors of tobacco, camphor, turpentine, or any volatile substance. It is sour to the taste, reddens blue litmus paper distinctly, and if held to the light in a test tube or small thin glass, it may have a bluish or reddish tinge and appear watery. It curdles in tough, stringy, or glutinous yellowish lumps of large size. The color of milk is affected by various substances eaten by the cow: madder turns it saffron, rhubarb makes it red or yellow, and some medicinal plants turn milk blue.

Boiled Milk. Good, clean, uncontaminated milk should keep fresh, at a temperature 68° F., for 48 hours without souring or coagulating. If the air is much warmer, or if the milk is tainted in any way, it will sour in a few hours. Boiled milk stays fresh more than half as long again as raw milk and boiling keeps the number of harmful bacteria present at a safe number. The introduction of air into boiled milk—pouring the milk back and forth a few times between two cups held a short distance apart is a good way—will remove "flat" taste. Boiling milk expels some of the gases in milk, altering the taste and making it "flat."

Sterilized Milk. The sterilization of milk is accomplished by heating it to the boiling point, 212° F. In a vacuum, this can be accomplished with a slightly lower temperature. The taste of sterilized milk resembles that of boiled milk. If put in bottles which have been sterilized in boiling water or steam and stopped with pledgets of absorbent cotton which have been baked, the milk will stay fresh for a number of days. It has been found that when churning sterilized milk, butter forms more slowly than from raw milk. This is attributed to the toughening of the albumin envelopes (lactalbumin) of the fat globules by the heat.

Pasteurized Milk. Pasteurized milk is prepared in a fashion similar to sterilized milk and is, in fact, sterile, but the temperature is only raised for twenty minutes to about 145° F , instead of to the boiling point. It is somewhat more digestible than sterilized milk, but does not keep as long and spoils in one or two days. It has the advantage of tasting more like fresh milk. The heat of pasteurization is sufficient to destroy most harmful bacteria without altering the properties of the milk. Pasteurized milk is finally cooled rapidly to below 50° F. to arrest development of bacteria.

FORMS OF MILK

Acidophilus Milk. A milk fermented by the introduction of bacteria *lactobacillus acidophilus* and prescribed for its beneficial effect in certain gastro-intestinal disorders. It is similar in taste to buttermilk.

Buttermilk. Technically, the liquid left after butter has been churned from milk. Buttermilk, as used in most homes, is a pleasant and nutritious beverage made from skim or whole milk. It is fermented by the addition of bacteria cultures, and the lactic acid produced by the action of the bacteria sours the milk. Buttermilk is then churned to break up the curd. It is at least equal to sweet milk in nutriment value and is more easily digested, the casein having broken up by souring and churning. Buttermilk is a good source of readily digestible protein.

Buttermilk should be kept in glass, paper, or chinaware containers, for the lactic acid may possibly react upon other materials.

Condensed Milk. This is prepared by slowly evaporating the water content of milk by moderate heat in a vacuum. After evaporation, cane sugar is added as a preservative. Condensed milk is of the consistency of molasses or honey. Good quality condensed milk is composed of about 30 percent milk fat and solids, 42 percent sugar, and 28 percent water. In sealed cans, it will keep safely for long periods of time.

Dried Milk. Either whole milk or skim milk is obtainable in dried form. In this process the water has been evaporated from the milk. One pound of dried whole milk furnishes the same quantity of milk solids as three and a half quarts of fresh whole milk. Four and one-half ounces of dried whole milk mixed with three and a half cups of water makes one quart of whole milk. If high quality dried milk is used, the reconstituted milk tastes and looks sufficiently like fresh pasteurized milk to be a pleasing drink. One pound of dried skim milk furnishes the same quantity of milk solids as four and three-quarters quarts of skim milk. Because of the fat content of the dried whole milk, it does not keep so well as the skim milk powder, and should be stored in a cool place.

Evaporated Milk. The water content of milk is reduced for evaporated milk in a manner similar to condensed milk. While hot and sterilized, it is sealed in cans and will keep well for a long time. Evaporated milk is less thick than condensed milk, having a content of about 26 percent fat and solids and 74 percent water; no sugar is added to evaporated milk.

Goat's Milk. The breeding of milk goats in the United States has reached large proportions only during the past forty years. Goat's milk has been steadily growing in popularity but it is still in much less demand than cow's milk. Most of the goat's milk sold in American cities comes from Toggenburg and Saanen goats, the herds usually being mixed, for these two breeds give milk similar in composition.

Various studies have shown that the content of goat's milk is closely akin to that of cow's milk. There is no marked difference in the casein contained in each, and the amount of calcium, phosphorus, and iron is about the same. Neither is there any significant difference in vitamin content. The curd of goat's milk is softer than that of cow's milk, however, and the fat globules are smaller, making it easier to digest. Many infants can digest goat's milk who cannot tolerate cow's milk. The butterfat content of goat's milk varies with the breed, and crossbreeding has produced goats which yield milk with a high butterfat content.

Goat's milk is white and has an agreeable taste, but those used to cow's milk will find it a new and different beverage. Many cheeses are made from goat's milk (*see* CHEESE), and excellent butter can be made from the butterfat extracted by a separator.

Goat farms in the United States produce milk under the same regulations laid down for certified cow's milk.

Homogenized Milk. In this process, milk is passed through a homogenizer, a machine which forces the liquid through fine openings against a hard surface to break up the fat globules and casein, making a smoother milk and increasing digestibility. The cream does not separate out of homogenized milk.

Human Milk. Human milk differs from cow's milk in several important particulars. It is sweeter by one-third and contains slightly less than one-half as much casein— hence the importance of diluting cow's milk when using it for infant feeding. The casein in human milk, moreover, forms smaller curds in the stomach and is more easily digested. The normal reaction of human milk is alkaline, while cow's milk varies from mildly alkaline to neutral and may become acid, particularly when the animal is not pasture-fed. There is more fat in human milk, and the globules exist in a finer emulsion; it requires more acid to precipitate the protein from human than from cow's milk.

Kefir. Milk fermented by the action of certain bacteria and fungi. It is similar to kumiss (*which see*), better known in America than kefir.

Kumiss. (Also called koumiss.) Originally, a fermented, intoxicating beverage made from mare's or camel's milk. The drink is of ancient origin; Herodotus refers to the use of "kumys" by the Scythians (about 650 B.C.). In America, kumiss is made from cow's milk, fermented by lactic acid and yeast cultures. It is a mild, palatable, nourishing beverage with the consistency of buttermilk. Kumiss can usually be purchased in drugstores.

Yoghurt. Yoghurt is another type of fermented milk similar to kumiss and kefir. It is milk in a more concentrated form, however, and is often eaten as a food. Yoghurt contains a higher percentage of lactic acid than other fermented milks, and fermentation is brought about by the addition of *lactobacillus bulgaricus* bacteria after the milk has been partially evaporated. Yoghurt can be of a semisolid consistency and eaten by itself or used as a spread, but many prefer it in the fluid state, where it resembles thick cream.

GRADING MILK

Fresh whole milk is graded by municipal ordinance in the important markets of the United States according to grades recommended by the U.S. Department of Agriculture.

Certified Milk. In 1930 the American Association of Medical Milk Commissions set up methods and standards for the production and distribution of certified milk. A milk commission, organized under these standards, certifies the milk so produced. In general, the milk is guaranteed to be from clean, healthy, well groomed cows, produced in clean, well ventilated, well conducted stables, and promptly cooled, bottled, and delivered in the most sanitary manner and with the greatest possible expedition.

Grade A Milk. This is milk produced from healthy cows, as determined by a tuberculin test and physical examination within not exceeding one year by a qualified veterinarian, from dairies meeting the standards set up by the Department of Agriculture, and containing not more than a certain specified bacteria count.

Grade B Milk. This is milk produced from healthy cows as determined by physical examination within not exceeding one year by a properly qualified veterinarian, from dairies that score slightly lower than for Grade A, and containing a somewhat higher bacteria count. All Grade B milk must be pasteurized.

CREAM

When milk stands undisturbed, the globules of butterfat rise to the surface in the form of cream. This takes place because the specific gravity of fat is lower than that of the rest of the milk.

Dairies do not wait for this process to take place, and draw off the cream by means of a separator, but cream is best obtained at home by placing the milk in broad, shallow pans. Churning the milk causes the fat globules to coagulate in small lumps and form butter. Contrary to a popular belief, warm water added to the milk will not increase cream production. It lessens the specific gravity of the milk and hastens the rising of the globules, but the ultimate amount of cream produced is not increased.

Cream, according to federal standards, should not contain less than 18 percent butterfat, but many good farms and dairies sell cream with a fat content exceeding 20 percent. Likewise, cream should not form less than five percent of the total volume of milk. If the cream content is less, the milk has been watered. Milk usually contains eight to ten percent cream, but rich milk may contain much more.

Housewives can usually buy two grades of cream, light cream and heavy cream. Heavy cream is more expensive but it can be stretched by the addition of milk and still be used as light cream.

Sour Cream. Soured cream used to be a calamity in many households, a useless waste to be thrown out as soon as possible.

Fortunately, sour cream (and sour milk) have now returned to favor, and their use in cooking is well known. When used in the preparation of many foods, with meats, fish, vegetables, breads, pastries, and desserts, hot, cold, or frozen, they turn an ordinary dish into something new and light and delectable. Used either as a basic component of a recipe or as part of a sauce, sour cream adds a zest and flavor to biscuits, waffles, a sauce for vegetables, and makes a pedestrian dish a creation.

If sour milk is called for in a recipe, and the milk has not naturally soured, this may be done by adding a teaspoon of vinegar or lemon juice to a cup of milk and standing it in a warm place for thirty minutes or so. Do not heat the milk.

WHIPPED CREAM

Cream for whipping should be at least 12 hours old. Both bowl and beater, as well as the cream itself, should be thoroughly chilled, especially when only a small amount of cream is being whipped. If beaten in a warm bowl, in a warm place, cream is apt to turn to butter. It is best to whip not more cream at one time than will be used up quickly. Cream which is hard to whip will thicken more quickly if a few drops of lemon juice are added to it.

For variety of flavor add any of the following: a slight grating of orange rind; a teaspoon of strained honey to each cup of whipped cream; a dash of powdered cinnamon; a few drops of black walnut extract, especially where the cream is to be used as a topping for chocolate pie; a few chopped nut meats, especially walnuts or Brazil nuts.

For added fluffiness use equal parts of whipped cream and stiffly beaten egg whites—it's economical, too;

WHIPPED EVAPORATED MILK

To whip evaporated milk for use in place of cream, have the milk itself, the bowl and the beater all thoroughly chilled. If cold enough it will whip readily. In a warm room the chilled milk may be placed in a bowl, this in turn being set in another bowl of cracked ice. Scalding evaporated milk makes it easier to whip but is not really essential. If it is to be scalded, heat the milk in a double boiler for from five to ten minutes, then chill quickly. Where the flavor of lemon is not objectionable add two tablespoons of lemon juice to each cup of evaporated milk and whip as directed. The lemon juice will give a stiffer and more permanent texture.

MILK BREAD. Any bread in which milk, rather than water, is used in preparation of the dough. *See* BREAD.

MILK SHAKE. A milk shake is a cool beverage made of milk and flavoring that is mixed, beaten, or shaken until frothy. It is usually named after the predominant flavor used. Ice cream is frequently used in making milk shakes, both for flavor and richness. In most cases, the ice cream is so well mixed with the rest of the ingredients that a spoon is not required to consume the beverage.

In soda fountain parlance, a milk shake that contains dissolved ice cream is known as a "frosted," while one that has undissolved ice cream in the manner of an ice cream soda (*which see*) is called a "float."

Malted milk powder is sometimes used in making milk shakes, giving a beverage that is definitely richer. Such drinks are known as "malted milk," or "malteds," "malts," rather than milk shakes, with, again, the name of the chief flavoring prefixed to the title.

HINTS ON PREPARATION

There are a number of ways to make any member of the milk shake family. Perhaps the most efficient method is to use the blender (*which see*). The use of this device permits the addition of solids like cut fruits, ice cubes, etc., with the assurance that they will be liquefied and blended into the beverage. The timing must be carefully watched, however, lest the device be in operation too long, making the drink too frothy for most tastes.

Special electric mixers have been designed to make milk shakes, but these are so specialized in application as to be practical only for soda fountains. Any regular electric mixer (*which see*) will make good milk shakes. Beaters (*which see*) may also be used, but their action is so slow as to make them a bit impractical.

Cocktail shakers (*which see*) and similar devices may also be used. However, considerable effort is required, especially if ice cream is being dissolved in the beverage. Some shakers have been recently designed

that impart a swirling motion to the fluid by virtue of their internal shape, and it is claimed that these do a superior job.

Whatever utensil or implement is used, it must be remembered that the ideal milk shake is a compromise between froth and liquid, and that it must be cool, if not actually cold. The ingredients should be chilled before use, and the worker should be fast, to keep them from getting too warm. Milk shakes are served immediately after being made, before the froth has had a chance to subside. They may be served with or without straws, depending on individual tastes, but a spoon should be required only in the case of floats.

As a general rule, milk shakes are not garnished, though spices may be sprinkled on the surface if desired.

BANANA MILK SHAKE

1 cup chilled milk
1 medium banana, mashed (if blender is not used)
⅓ cup orange juice
1 tsp sugar (powdered preferred)
1 large serving vanilla ice cream
Pinch of salt

Mix well and serve in tall glass with chocolate wafers. (Serves 1)

BUTTERMILK SHAKE

3 cups chilled buttermilk
½ cup cold lemon juice
Pinch of salt
½ cup sugar
⅛ tsp lemon rind
2 small servings ice cream

Shake well and serve with a dash of ginger. (Serves 3)

CHOCOLATE MALTED MILK

¼ cup cold chocolate sirup
1½ to 2 tbsp malted milk powder
1 to 1½ cups chilled milk
1 large serving vanilla or chocolate ice cream

Mix until frothy and sprinkle with nutmeg or grated chocolate, if desired. (Serves 1)

CHOCO-MINT SHAKE

2 tbsp chocolate sirup
1 cup milk
1 large serving peppermint ice cream

Shake thoroughly until ice cream dissolves. (Serves 1)

MAPLE MILK SHAKE

2 to 3 tbsp maple sirup
¼ tsp vanilla
1 cup milk
1 large serving vanilla ice cream

Mix all but the ice cream together first, then add ice cream and shake as before (Serves 1)

PRUNE SHAKE

⅓ cup prune purée
⅓ cup orange juice
1 cup chilled milk
Pinch of salt
1 tsp lemon juice
1 tbsp sugar
1 large serving vanilla ice cream

Mix the prune purée, orange juice, and milk together before adding other ingredients, then proceed as before. (Serves 1)

MOLASSES MILK SHAKE

2 tbsp light molasses
2 tbsp lemon juice
1 tsp sugar
¼ tsp grated lemon peel
1 cup chilled milk
1 large serving vanilla ice cream

Place all but the ice cream in a shaker, mix well, and add ice cream. Shake well, serve with butter wafers or sugar cookies. (Serves 1)

Any of the given milk shakes may be made into a float simply by adding another lump of ice cream after the beverage is mixed. They may also be made into malteds by adding malted milk powder to taste.

MILK SUGAR. A popular name for lactose, an important constituent of milk, *which see.*

MILK TOAST. Toast soaked in milk, to which butter, salt, sugar, or spices are sometimes added. It is used in the diet of invalids and convalescents. *See* TOAST.

MILLE FEUILLES. The term, meaning literally "a thousand leaves", is used for a French pastry made of puff paste, usually spread with thin layers of pastry cream. It is similar to, but not so fine as, a Napoleon. To make:

MILLE FEUILLES

Roll puff paste to paper thinness. Cut in 6-inch rounds or circles, prick with a fork, and bake on a cookie sheet lined with ungreased white paper in a hot oven (450° F.) 10 to 12 minutes. Cool. Make as many circles as desired, 8, 10, and even 12 being sometimes used in *mille feuilles.*

Spread one circle with coconut-flavored cream, place another pastry circle over this and repeat, varying the fillings according to individual taste. For example, the second circle might be spread with raspberry jam or peach preserves, the third with coconut cream again, etc. Almond or any other flavored cream may be substituted for the coconut. The top circle should be spread with white frosting and decorated with candied fruits, chocolate sprills, etc.

MILLET. A grain-bearing grass cultivated for forage and as a cereal. The grains are hulled like barley and ground into flour, used plain or blended with bread flour. There are many sub-varieties. Millet contains, on an average, over seven percent fat, nearly ten percent each of protein and dextrin, sixty percent starch, and two percent sugar.

MILLET

MILT. The male spermatic glands of a fish, or the secretion therefrom. It may be prepared like roe, *which see.*

MINCEMEAT. Long before New England was settled and the first Thanksgiving celebrated, mincemeat pies were a favorite dish in Old England. Every member of the family helped chop beef and apples, seed raisins, and blend spices for the mincemeat, which was then stored in crocks for the winter's use. The spices which gave mincemeat its delicious flavor were luxuries indeed. When a ship from the East docked in London, bringing a sweet-smelling cargo from the spice isles, the king was privileged to choose any spices he desired before the owners could sell to the eager merchants.

The first mincemeat recipe which we have dates from 1486, and contained "a hare, a pheasant, two partridges, two pigeons, and two conies," suitably spiced and cooked, then "made craftily into the likeness of a bird's body," the meat stuffed into a pastry shell and feathers placed over all.

Two centuries later, the famous Christmas pie now contained eggs, raisins, orange and lemon peel, as well as meat and spices. It was closer to what we know today, "a mixture strange of suet, currants, meats, and spices, where various tastes combine, the greasy and the sweet. . . ."

There is still much controversy as to what belongs rightfully in a mince pie, but the following recipes may be of help to those who wish to prepare their own mincemeat. Remember, too, that mincemeat can be used in tarts, muffins, and as a filling for cookies, cakes, etc.

Mincemeat may be purchased in cans or jars, or dried. To use dry mincemeat, break the package into pieces in a saucepan and add one-half cup cold water. Place over the heat and stir until all lumps are broken up. Boil briskly for three minutes, or until the mixture is practically dry, stirring constantly. Cool and use like ordinary mincemeat.

CRANBERRY MINCEMEAT

1 (9 oz) package dry mincemeat
1½ cups water
1½ cups whole fruit cranberry sauce

Break the mincemeat up into small pieces, add the water and cook over a low flame, stirring constantly until smooth. Bring to a rapid boil and continue boiling for three minutes. Cool and combine with the cranberry sauce. Bake as a lattice-top pie.

GREEN TOMATO MINCEMEAT

4 qt finely chopped green tomatoes
2 qt pared, finely chopped tart apples
1 lb raisins
4 tbsp minced orange or lemon peel
1 tbsp ground cinnamon
2 tsp salt
¼ tsp ground allspice
¼ tsp ground cloves
2 cups firmly packed brown sugar
3 cups granulated sugar
¾ cup vinegar
½ cup lemon juice
2 cups water

Combine all the ingredients and cook the mixture slowly until tender, stirring frequently. When it is slightly thickened, pour into hot sterile jars, filling to the top and seal. (Makes approximately 4 quarts)

MINCEMEAT

½ lb lean boiled beef, chopped
½ lb beef kidney suet, chopped
3¾ lb raw apples, pared and chopped
½ lb currants
1 lb seeded raisins, chopped
1 tbsp salt
3 oz each candied orange rind, lemon rind and citron, chopped
Grated rind of 2 lemons
5 cups brown sugar
3 tbsp cinnamon
2 tsp nutmeg
1 tsp ginger
½ tsp ground cloves
5 cups cider

Combine all ingredients in the order given, in a large heavy pan, and simmer very gently for 2 hours, stirring occasionally. The placing of an asbestos pad under the kettle prevents scorching. When cold turn into jars, cover tightly, and keep in a dry, cool place. This will keep six months. (Sufficient for five 9-inch pies)

Brandy may be added before baking the pie but its flavor will evaporate;

therefore, if you are partial to a brandied mincemeat, here is the way to proceed: After the pie is baked, carefully pour a a little brandy, or brandy and sherry, into the slits of the top crust. Mince pies with a lattice (criss-cross) top crust are obviously easier to flavor.

MINCEMEAT (FRENCH)

½ lb raw lean beef
Water
2½ tsp salt
½ lb veal kidney suet, chopped
5 cups raw apples, pared and chopped
1 lb seedless white raisins, chopped
2½ cups dried apricots, chopped
2½ cups canned, crushed pineapple
2½ oz candied citron, chopped
2½ oz candied orange rind, chopped
2½ oz candied lemon rind, chopped
1¼ cups granulated sugar
⅝ cup strained honey
⅝ cup lemon juice
2½ cups white wine
1 tbsp mace
2 tsp nutmeg
1⅓ tbsp cinnamon
2 tsp allspice
1 tsp cloves (ground)
1¼ cups toasted almonds, chopped

Cover meat with water; add the salt and simmer until tender, or about 30 minutes. Cool in the water in which it has been cooked. Chop the meat fine and combine with the chopped veal kidney suet and apples. Add all remaining ingredients and simmer very gently for 2 hours, placing an asbestos pad under the pan to prevent scorching. Stir occasionally. The mixture will be almost dry. Cool. Pack in fruit jars or a stone crock, and do not use for three weeks. (Sufficient for five 9-inch pies)

MINCEMEAT BROWN BETTY

Use recipe for Apple Betty (see APPLE) substituting 1 cup of mincemeat and 4 apples.

MINCEMEAT CAKE

1 cup sifted flour
1 cup white cornmeal

2 tsp baking powder
⅛ tsp salt
⅓ cup shortening
⅔ cup sugar
2 eggs, separated
½ cup milk
1⅓ cups mincemeat

Mix and sift the flour, cornmeal, baking powder, and salt. Cream the shortening until soft and smooth; gradually add sugar, creaming until fluffy, then beat in egg yolks. Add flour-cornmeal mixture alternately with milk, beating until smooth after each addition; beat in mincemeat. Fold in thoroughly the stiffly beaten egg whites. Turn into greased, 8-inch square pan and bake in moderate oven (350° F.) about 1 hour. Cover top and sides with any desired icing (see FROSTING).

MINCEMEAT PIE

Line a 9-inch pie plate with any preferred pastry. (Cheese pastry is especially good.) Fill with mincemeat, either homemade or commercial. Wet the edges of the crust, adjust the top crust, press edges firmly together and make several slits in the top. Bake in a hot oven (450° F.) for 10 minutes, then decrease to moderate (350° F.) and continue baking about 30 minutes longer. While the pie is still hot insert a small funnel into one of the incisions and pour in 3 tablespoons brandy or equal parts brandy and sherry. The liquid will spread over the filling. Return the pie to the oven for 3 or 4 minutes. Serve warm with cheese.

MINERALS. The mineral constituents of the human body are potassium, sodium, calcium, magnesium, iron and manganese. They are known as the acid-binding (alkaline) elements, while phosphorus, sulphur, silicon, chlorine, and fluorine make up the acid-forming elements. Beside these, there are minute quantities of iodine, aluminum, arsenic, and bromine.

It has long been known that certain substances called mineral salts are required in the diet. The commonest of these is sodium chloride, ordinary table salt. These salts furnish the material needed to build new red corpuscles, bone, teeth, thyroxin, and acid for the stomach.

The red corpuscles of the blood stream are a host of tiny disc-like affairs of complex structure and can be seen only by means of a microscope. As these corpuscles pass through the lungs, each takes up a small load of oxygen and carries it to various parts of the body. On the return trip, these tiny carriers bring back carbon dioxide, the principal gas exhaled from the lungs.

One of the main components of the corpuscles is iron. The diet must contain enough of this element to keep the corpuscle count high. Greens and leafy vegetables help supply iron, for most of them contain some form of it, but the doctors may prescribe additional iron if a run-down, tired feeling persists.

Phosphorus is another element that is essential in the diet, for building both teeth and bones. During dentition periods, children should have a diet rich in phosphorus, as well as calcium. Prunes have a high content of iron and phosphorus, and also sodium and potassium. Peanuts and carrots are among the best foods containing calcium.

The importance of iodine in the diet must also be recognized. There is a gland in the neck called the thyroid, which produces a substance called thyroxin. This is a complex iodine compound which influences metabolism (the chemical changes in the cells of the body) and plays an important part in the physical and mental development of the young. An upset in the balance of the thyroid's activity can cause one or another form of goiter, a swelling in the neck which can have serious consequences.

An adequate supply of iodine in the diet helps maintain the normal activity of the thyroid. Some drinking water contains traces of iodine, as do certain foods, particularly fish. Table salt known as "iodized table salt" contains a small amount of potassium iodide, a compound which the body can assimilate. The human system requires only a small amount of iodine, and regular consumption of foods having this important element is the best way of providing it.

The normal and healthy development of the body depends, in large part, on an adequate supply of all the aforementioned elements. The alkaline elements, particularly sodium, potassium, calcium, magnesium, iron, and manganese, insure an adequate supply of life-giving oxygen and the prompt removal of poisonous wastes

from the system. The control of the voluntary and involuntary muscles is also influenced by the salts of calcium, magnesium, potassium, and sodium, contained in the blood.

No system of diet will give permanently beneficial results which does not give consideration to the quantity and proportion of mineral salts.

MINERAL WATERS. Waters containing a marked amount of certain mineral salts or carbon dioxide. *See* ALKALINE AND MINERAL WATERS for a list of these.

MINESTRONE. A thick, flavorful soup made with barley, verimicelli, or other paste, and vegetables.

MINESTRONE SOUP

3 medium-sized potatoes, sliced
3 small onions, chopped
$\frac{1}{4}$ head cabbage, shredded
$\frac{1}{2}$ lb string beans
3 qt boiling water
1 tbsp salt
$\frac{1}{4}$ lb spaghetti
1 medium can kidney beans
1 cup chopped green celery
$\frac{1}{4}$ cup brown sugar
3 tbsp butter
3 tbsp olive oil
3 tbsp Parmesan cheese
1 small clove garlic, minced
$\frac{1}{2}$ tsp minced parsley
Salt and pepper
$\frac{1}{4}$ cup cream

Cook together for 10 minutes the potatoes, onions, cabbage, string beans, boiling water, and salt. Add the spaghetti, broken into inch pieces, and cook 15 minutes longer, after which put in the kidney beans, celery, and sugar, and cook until the celery is tender.

For the pesto, cream the butter and oil together in a bowl, stir in the cheese, garlic, and seasonings, then slowly add the cream. Stir this mixture into the soup, cook a few minutes longer and serve in bowls with Italian bread, olives and grated Parmesan cheese. (Serves 6 or 8)

MINT. This name is applied to a number of aromatic herbs belonging to the genus *Mentha*. Among these are dittany, horehound, hyssop, marjoram, oregano, peppermint, rosemary, spearmint, and thyme, all of *which see*. Members of the mint family usually have a fragrant aroma and a pleasant taste. Either orange mint or apple mint may be used in any recipe calling for mint; they are more delicate and more fragrant than spearmint. Hyssop leaves are mildly bitter.

Mint sauce or jelly is often served with lamb or mutton. Mint sauce is said to have been invented early in the 16th Century by English women who were forced by law to serve bitter vinegar and mint leaves with every portion of lamb. The intent of the law was to render lamb less palatable and thus conserve British flocks.

Mint is also used to make herb teas, candies, and fruit cups. Sprigs of fresh mint are used to garnish foods and beverages. Peas or carrots served with a sprinkling of finely chopped mint leaves are a taste experience.

MINT

CANDIED MINT LEAVES

Perfect mint leaves
White of 1 egg
½ tsp lemon or orange juice
Fine granulated sugar

Wash and dry the mint leaves, being careful not to bruise them. Beat the egg white slightly with the fruit juice. Brush each leaf with the egg white and roll in sugar. Spread out on waxed paper to dry.

MINT BUTTER

Mint creamed with butter to form a delicious sauce. *See* BUTTER SAUCE.

MINT ICE

2 cups sugar
1 qt water
2 or 3 tbsp dried mint leaves
Juice of 2 lemons
A few drops green vegetable coloring

Boil the sugar and water together to a sirup, cooking for 5 minutes after boiling point is reached. Add the mint, using more, or less, depending on its strength. Cover and leave until cold. Strain, Add the lemon juice and coloring and turn into refrigerator tray. Freeze about 3 hours, stirring once when mushy. Especially good with lamb or mutton. (Serves 6 or 8)

MINT JELLY

1 cup water
½ cup vinegar
3½ cups sugar
½ cup mint leaves
½ cup fruit pectin
Green coloring

Place the water, mint leaves, and vinegar in a saucepan and color the mixture to a rich green with the coloring. Add the sugar and bring to a racing boil, stirring constantly. Add the pectin as soon as the mixture boils hard and continue boiling for ½ minute. Strain, and pour the liquid into hot, sterilized glasses. Seal.

MINT MOUSSE I

1 cup granulated sugar
3 tbsp cornstarch
¼ tsp salt
2 tbsp butter
2 tbsp lemon juice
2 cups boiling water
1 tsp mint extract, or 4 drops oil of peppermint
Green vegetable coloring
¾ cup heavy cream, stiffly whipped
2 egg whites, stiffly beaten

Combine sugar, cornstarch, salt, butter, and lemon juice, and blend thoroughly. Gradually pour over the boiling water, stirring briskly and constantly, and cook, over hot water (double boiler) until mixture is thick and clear, stirring constantly to prevent lumping. Strain while hot, through a fine sieve. Cool a little and add mint extract or oil of peppermint and a few drops of green vegetable coloring so as to obtain the desired hue. Chill. Fold in combined stiffly whipped heavy cream and stiffly beaten egg whites. Freeze, either in hand freezer pail, after molding, using equal parts ice and rock salt, for 2¾ to 3 hours; or freeze in refrigerator tray, or mold in large or small molds or paper cases, and freeze in refrigerator tray for 2½ hours, if small molds, and 3½ to 4 hours for large mold or directly in refrigerator tray (unmolded).

MINT MOUSSE II

1 cup fresh milk
20 marshmallows, cut small
1 cup heavy cream
⅛ tsp salt
4 drops oil of peppermint
Green vegetable coloring

Place milk and marshmallows, which have been cut small, using a pair of scissors dipped in flour, in top of double boiler. Scald, stirring constantly, so as to melt the marshmallows. Remove from hot water, cool, then chill. Lastly fold in the stiffly whipped cream to which has been added the salt, oil of peppermint and a few drops of green vegetable coloring. Freeze as indicated in recipe for mint mousse I.

MINT SAUCE

½ cup vinegar
1 to 2 tbsp sugar
¼ cup minced mint leaves

Scald the vinegar, add the sugar and stir until this is dissolved. Add the minced mint and allow the sauce to stand for an hour or more before using.

Currant Mint Sauce
1 cup currant jelly
1 tsp grated orange rind
2 tbsp finely chopped mint

Combine all ingredients and let stand several hours before serving to extract the flavor of the mint. Especially good with lamb.

Orange Mint Sauce

⅔ cup orange marmalade
2 tbsp finely minced mint

Combine the marmalade and mint and let stand at least one hour before serving. Especially good with lamb.

MINT SIRUP

4 cups sugar
2 cups water
½ cup light corn sirup
40 stalks fresh mint

Combine the sugar, water, and corn sirup in a saucepan. Crush the mint stalks and add to the sugar mixture. Place over direct heat and stir until the sugar is dissolved. Simmer 20 minutes. Strain through flannel and turn into a hot sterilized jar. Keep covered in the refrigerator. (Makes 1 quart).

This sirup can be used in the making of mint sauce or mint jelly.

MINT WAFERS

1 cup remelted fondant
3 drops oil of mint

Remelt the fondant (*which see*) and add the flavoring. Blend thoroughly. Drop from the tip of a teaspoon onto waxed paper or a marble slab. When firm, lift off carefully.

Wintergreen wafers are made in the same manner, substituting oil of wintergreen and tinting the fondant pink or green with vegetable coloring.

PEPPERMINT CREAM BROWNIES

⅔ cup all-purpose flour
¼ tsp baking powder
⅛ tsp salt
⅓ cup butter
¾ cup sugar
½ tsp vanilla
2 eggs, well beaten
2 squares unsweetened chocolate, melted

1 tbsp milk
½ cup chopped walnuts
½ cup chopped raisins

Sift the flour, measure, and resift 3 times with baking powder and salt. Cream the butter, add the sugar gradually and blend thoroughly. Add the vanilla and eggs and mix thoroughly. Stir in chocolate. Mix in the sifted dry ingredients and milk. Add nuts and raisins. Spread into two 8-inch square pans lined with wax paper. Bake in moderate oven (350° F.) for 20 minutes. Cool. Put layers together, bottom sides facing, with peppermint butter cream:

1 tbsp butter
1 cup unsifted XXXX sugar, firmly packed
2 tbsp hot milk
⅛ tsp peppermint extract or 2 drops oil of peppermint

Cream the butter and mix thoroughly with sugar. Add milk and flavoring. Blend until smooth and thick. Spread over bottom of one layer, top with second layer. Dust with powdered sugar and cut into bars. Store in a tightly covered container. (Makes 18 bars)

PEPPERMINT ICE CREAM

1 cup undiluted evaporated milk
1 lb peppermint candy
1 pt heavy cream
¼ tsp salt

Pour the undiluted evaporated milk over the peppermint candy. Let stand overnight in refrigerator. Next day pour the mixture through double cheesecloth to remove any undissolved particles of candy. Fold in the heavy cream which has been whipped stiff with the salt, and freeze in hand freezer, using 3 parts ice and 1 part rock salt, until firm. Mold in melon mold. Pack 2 hours in 4 parts ice and 1 part rock salt. (Makes approximately 1 quart)

MINT JULIP. By far the most famous and the most controversial of American drinks. There has been, is, and will be almost as much debate on the proper manner of making this whisky, sugar and mint mixture as on any disputed subject in any field.

Most ardent julep fans think of julep making as they would a sacred rite, hallowed and prescribed by tradition and time. Their feelings on the ritual and the sacramentals used are correspondingly intense. There are different schools of julep making; there are schisms within those schools; and there are heretics outside that do such things in the name of julep as to make all these dissenting factions collectively shudder.

There is, for example, the matter of the vessel; should it be of thin glass or of silver? And the whisky; rye or bourbon? And the mint itself; to crush or not to crush, to leave in the drink, or to remove the bruised leaves before serving, once the essence has been pressed out? And finally, the garnishes. Should miscellaneous fruits and vegetables be arranged in the glass with tender care to the delight of eye and tongue, or should they be carefully avoided? The debate rages on these and similar matters; problems that have never been settled by majority vote, problems that probably never will be settled as long as there are at least two people, from different families, who mix mint juleps.

Under the circumstances, it would be sheer folly to offer a standard recipe for the mint julep. It is also quite impossible to trace the one, the only, the original recipe. And it is equally impossible, due to space limitations, to give all known variations. Julep recipes appear to be a matter of taste, heritage, and training. However, they are all alike in many basic respects, and the majority produce a drink that is truly delicious and potent. Their potency is often overlooked because of their exceptional flavor, a fatal mistake.

A mint julep, regardless of recipe, requires considerable care in the making; but the finished product, drinkers agree, more than justifies the effort. As a cooling summer drink, as a unique taste experience, the mint julep has evoked such paeans of published praise as to make the reader wonder if its origin were not, perhaps, celestial.

MINT JULEP

A 14- or 16-ounce thin-walled glass or silver julep cup is used, and is first frosted. *See* BARTENDING.

Place 4 to 6 fresh mint sprigs on the bottom; add just enough sugar to cover and just enough water to melt the sugar. Muddle until mint is crushed and sugar melted. The sides of the glass should be well smeared with this mixture. The crushed mint may or may not then be removed, depending on your beliefs. Fill the glass a little over half way with finely crushed ice and pour in 2 jiggers of rye or bourbon (again a matter of contested opinion), and top with 2 or more bushy mint sprigs. These topping sprigs may or may not be slightly bruised to release the odor, again a question of local option. (Serves 1)

Mint Julep II

Place from 10 to 12 mint sprigs in a mixing bowl, cover with sugar, moisten with water, and muddle until sugar is melted and mint well crushed. Remove the mint. Fill a frosted julep glass or silver cup about half way with finely cracked ice. Pour in the melted sugar, then 2 jiggers of the desired whisky. Decorate as above. (Serves 1)

Mint Julep III

Make as last given, but pack the crushed mint leaves among the cracked ice. The order of adding the sugar and whisky may be varied in either case.

Mint Julep IV

Melt sugar (½ teaspoon or more, depending on taste) separately in enough water to give it a sirupy consistency. Prepare a frosted julep glass or cup by crushing mint leaves against sides and bottom, taking care that the entire surface is thus treated. These crushed leaves may then be thrown away or packed among the finely crushed ice that is then added. Two jiggers of the desired whisky are then poured into the ice and let cool. The sugar is then added and topping mint sprigs placed as above. (Serves 1)

Garnishing the Julep

The true Southerner rarely adds anything further in the way of trimmings, but certain developments have taken place in other regions. Cherries, pineapple, and even spices, are sometimes added. There are those who even go so far as to add a small quantity, a teaspoon or so, of brandy. The mint julep is sometimes served with straws, but the true addict prefers to bury his nose deeply among the mint to get the full aroma while drinking.

Hints

Regardless of how a julep is made, there are certain things that must be done if the drink is to be worthy of its noble lineage.

It must be served cold. The glass or silver cup should be frosted and the ice used should be finely crushed. Once made, the julep should be allowed to stand for a while before serving, some people even placing them in a refrigerator an hour or so before serving.

A julep should never be stirred, the natural action of standing and melting ice will mix the ingredients. Regardless of the whisky used, it should be of the best quality practical, since the julep, like a highball, quickly exposes inferior grades of liquor.

If fruit garnishing is desired, by all means garnish, but with restraint. Garnishes should never be used to the extent that they overshadow the original characteristics of the drink, julep or otherwise.

Never rush your work; a good julep is more an act of creation than a mere assembly job. If there is a julep addict among your guests, let him make them, or at least his own, lest there be bloodshed.

See also Julep.

MINUTE STEAK. A steak without any bone, cut one-fourth inch thick, broiled or pan fried for no lonter than two minutes.

Its preparation is as follows: Broil or pan fry the steaks. Have ready for four steaks, one teaspoon each of minced shallots, parsley, and chives. When the steaks are cooked, place immediately on a sizzling hot platter, spread with one tablespoon of butter and sprinkle the minced seasonings over the surface.

MIRABELLE DE LORRAINE. A delicious liqueur made from pure, old spirits redistilled with the extract of fresh greengages, small, tasty plums of France. It is served as an after-dinner liqueur.

See also Liqueur.

MIREPOIX. A seasoning used mainly in braising meat. It is usually composed of carrots, onion, and ham, sautéed in butter, with bay leaves and thyme added.

MIRONTON. A French beef stew, made as follows:

MIRONTON

2 lb tender, lean stewing meat
Water, or beef stock, to cover
Lard
2 tbsp butter
2 tbsp flour
1 cup good red wine
Salt and pepper
1 large bay leaf
2 whole cloves
1 cup peeled, thinly sliced onions
1 cup small mushroom buttons

Cut the beef into 1-inch squares. Sear it in a little lard until it is thoroughly browned on all sides. Turn it into the stew pot, barely covering it with the water or stock. Stew as gently as possible for 1 hour. Drain and reserve the stock. Melt the butter, blend in the flour, and brown well. Gradually stir in 2½ cups of the broth from the meat, stirring constantly until the mixture becomes slightly thick. Let it boil rapidly for 3 or 4 minutes to thoroughly cook the flour. Add all the remaining ingredients, and simmer, covered, for a half hour. Serve in a deep dish, using rice as a border. (Serves 6)

MIXED GRILL. Restaurant cooks who prepare meat over hot coals or charcoal, speak of "grilled" steaks or chops. Homemakers usually use the term "broil" rather than "grill" because of the fact that they cook meats in the broiler of the gas or electric stove and not over an open flame. In either case, however, a mixed grill, or broil, is a combination of several meats which broil well, together with several vegetables.

As a one-dish meal, the mixed grill has few peers, but its components should be chosen carefully with regard to appearance, shape, and texture, as well as taste and food value. With a first course of soup or appetizer and a dessert a complete meal is easily arranged. Bread of some kind and a beverage should be served, however.

SAMPLE MIXED GRILL

Lamb chops
Calf's liver
Little pork sausages

Thinly sliced bacon
Mushrooms
Tomatoes
French fried potatoes
Watercress
Toast

Have the lamb chops cut thick and tell the butcher to French them. Broil under the flame or over a bed of hot coals for ten to fifteen minutes. Season with salt and pepper and place on triangles of hot toast. Brush the calf's liver with seasoned melted butter and broil it.

Cut tomatoes in halves, brush with melted butter, season with salt and pepper, and broil.

Pan-broil or broil the sausages, allowing two for each plate.

Pan-broil or broil the mushrooms (large caps), one for each plate.

French-fry the potatoes in the usual way, and drain them. Plain, boiled new potatoes may be substituted if desired. Dip the boiled potatoes in melted butter and roll in minced parsley.

Arrange all on hot plates, garnish with watercress, add two strips of crisp, broiled bacon, and serve at once.

Other foods may well be substituted for those mentioned. For example, kidneys may replace liver, small minute steaks instead of lamb chops, and peas, string beans, or peas and carrots, may be added. Seafood can also provide the basis for excellent mixed grills.

SAMPLE SEAFOOD MIXED GRILL

Broiled bluefish
Broiled bacon
Baked stuffed potato
Pickled beets
Cole slaw
Buttered carrots
Watercress

Prepare, arrange, and serve in the manner described for a regular mixed grill.

MIXER. (I) A mechanical device to beat, blend, mix, etc. When used properly, these electric mixers are efficient and thorough. See ELECTRIC EQUIPMENT and ELECTRIC MIXER.

MIXER. (II) A colloquial expression referring to any effervescent liquid used to dilute or flavor an intoxicating drink. See *also* AERATED WATER and ALKALINE AND MINERAL WATERS.

MIXING BOWL. A mixing bowl is a plain, round bowl, with no corners or crevices to catch the food, made of any material sturdy enough to stand up under mixing operations. They are usually sold in nesting sets of differing capacities so that the appropriate size may be selected for each mixing, and they are sometimes made with lips for easier pouring of liquids. As a general rule, they are not suited for cooking purposes. *See also* KITCHEN EQUIPMENT.

MIXING GLASS. A heavy-walled glass vessel in which substances, primarily liquids, are combined by stirring or beating. It may also be graduated to serve as a measuring glass (*which see*), but this is not always done. Mixing glasses are used in bartending (*which see*); alone to mix wine drinks, and in combination with a metal vessel to form a cocktail shaker (*which see*). They are also greatly used in the kitchen. *See* GLASSWARE; *see also* KITCHEN EQUIPMENT.

MIXTURE. A compound or mass formed by blending foods, solid or liquid, especially where the particles of each ingredient retain their separate identity.

MIZITRA CHEESE. A Yugoslavian soft cheese, made of sheep's milk.

MOCHA. A flavoring made by combining chocolate and coffee, or sometimes coffee is used alone.

MOCHA BISCUIT

3 cups milk
1 cup strong coffee
2 tbsp flour
½ cup sugar
5 eggs, slightly beaten
1 tsp vanilla

Combine the milk and coffee. Mix the flour and sugar and add milk-coffee mixture slowly, mixing well. Cook over hot water 15 minutes, or until smooth and slightly thickened. Stir a small amount into the eggs, mixing well; return to remaining hot mixture and cook 5 minutes longer, stirring constantly. Add the vanilla and chill. Turn mixture into paper cases and freeze in trays of automatic refrigerator 2 to 3 hours, or until firm. Garnish with whipped cream. Sprinkle with chopped nuts, if desired. (Serves 8)

MOCHA CHIFFON PIE

1 tbsp gelatin
¼ cup cold water
⅓ cup dry cocoa
1 cup sugar
Dash of salt
4 eggs
1 tsp vanilla
1 cup strong coffee
1 pre-baked 9-inch pie shell

Soften the gelatin in the cold water. Combine the cocoa, half the sugar and the salt, then add the egg yolks, slightly beaten with the coffee. Cook over hot water until thickened. Add the softened gelatin and stir until dissolved. Cool, and when beginning to thicken, fold in the egg whites beaten with the remaining sugar until stiff but not dry, and the vanilla. Turn into the pre-baked pie shell. Chill, and spread with a topping of whipped cream.

MOCHA FROSTING

⅓ cup medium-grind coffee
1 cup water
¼ cup butter
2 cups sifted confectioners' sugar firmly packed
¼ tsp salt

Add the coffee to the water and heat just to boiling. Remove from heat immediately and let stand 2 minutes. Then strain through very fine strainer or through cheesecloth to remove all grounds. Cool. (Never use leftover regular coffee. This strong infusion is necessary for a good rich coffee flavor.) Cream butter until soft and smooth, and gradually blend in sugar and salt. Slowly work in the fresh coffee infusion (about 3 tablespoons) until mixture is the proper consistency for spreading. Spread between layers and on top and sides of cake. (Sufficient for two 8-inch layers)

MOCHA SPONGE

¼ cup cold water
1 tbsp sparkling gelatin
¾ cup granulated sugar
Pinch of salt
1½ cups very strong black coffee

2 tbsp strained lemon juice
2 egg whites
Whipped cream

Pour the water over the gelatin. Let stand 5 minutes to soften. Add sugar, salt and stir, then pour in coffee as hot as possible without being actually boiling. Stir until gelatin and sugar are entirely dissolved, adding, meanwhile, the lemon juice. Cool until nearly set, then beat with a rotary egg beater. When quite stiff, fold in the stiffly beaten egg whites, a little at a time, continuing to beat until the mixture holds its shape. Turn into a fancy mold previously rinsed in cold water, and chill in refrigerator for several hours. To serve, unmold on a cold glass platter and decorate with tufts of whipped cream. For additional flavor and crunchiness, stir into the stiff gelatin mixture, ¼ cup each, chopped, toasted, cooled, blanched almonds and toasted, cooled long threads of coconut.

MOCK CRUSTA. A non-intoxicating version of a traditional drink type. It is made with fruit juices and is heavily iced and garnished. See FRUIT DRINKS.

MOCK TURTLE. A combination of meat, usually calf's head, and condiments made to imitate real turtle. Mock turtle soup is the most common dish employing this combination.

MOCK TURTLE SOUP

1 calf's head
1 lb lean beef
1 or 2 veal bones
12 onions
Butter or margarine
Flour
White pepper
6 whole cloves
Dash of cayenne pepper
Dash of mace
1 shallot
Pinch of basil
Pinch of sage
Rind of 1 lemon
½ glass sherry or Madeira
Juice of 2 lemons

Split the calf's head and take out the tongue and brains. Blanch thoroughly in several waters. Place the halves of the head in a large pan, cover with cold water, and bring to a boil. Skim several times, until no more scum rises. When the meat is tender, take the head out of the liquor and cool it. Remove the meat from the bones. Put the meat, the tongue and brains, the beef, and veal bones back into the stock, and continue the cooking several hours until all are tender. Strain the stock and let stand until cold. Lift off the fat which will have risen to the top. The stock should be practically jellied.

Place the stock in a saucepan. Slice the onions and brown them in a little butter or margarine. Add the onions, a tablespoon or so of flour, the white and cayenne pepper, cloves, mace, the shallot minced, the basil, sage, and lemon rind. Simmer for 1 hour. Strain into another pan. Add the meat and tongue which have been cut into ½-inch cubes. Add the wine and the lemon juice. Heat just to boiling and serve immediately.

MODE, A LA. From the French, "in the fashion of". As applied to beef, à la mode designates a roast which has been larded before braising, and simmered in a pan with vegetables, the vegetables later being included in the sauce or gravy. See BEEF.

Pie or fruit served with a scoop of ice cream is also called à la mode.

MOLASSES. Molasses, though popularly thought of as typically American, is actually much older than the Pilgrim Fathers. It was probably first extracted in India or China, where sugar cane was first grown.

Molasses was an important commodity in 18th and early 19th century America, and the principal sweetener in American homes. Every cabin and covered wagon had its molasses jug, and the molasses pitcher went to the table along with the vinegar cruet and sugar bowl. It was added to doughnuts, to cornbread, puddings, pie; men and women ate it on their griddle cakes and on their bread.

Improvements in the refining of sugar, an abundant and cheap supply of sugar cane, spelled the decline in popularity of this old time sweetener. Today, molasses is homemade scarcely anywhere, even in the South where once the pressing of the sugar cane stalks was a common household activity. The old open-kettle method has been supplanted by modern, large-scale processing methods.

Now, giant crushers squeeze the juice from the stalks. This juice—the essence of the cane—is then purified and concentrated, usually by boiling. Some mills use different methods of evaporation. When the natural sugar crystallizes, the molasses is drawn off, or "spun out" in some mills.

Molasses from the first boiling is the finest grade, from which only a small part of the sugar has been removed. First-boil molasses is mostly for table use. When the molasses is boiled again it takes on a darker color, is less sweet, and has a more pronounced flavor. This second-boil molasses is used for the most part in cake and candy making. Third-boil molasses, often called "blackstrap," has only a commercial value in the manufacture of cattle feed, the production of alcohol, and other industrial uses.

MOLASSES IN COOKING

Today, molasses is used more for flavoring than for sweetening. Its rich, mellow flavor cannot be duplicated; it hints of golden cane fields under a hot sun. Remember, however, that molasses has sweetening power. A cupful of molasses is comparable to about three-quarters of a cup of granulated sugar. When substituting molasses for sugar, take into account that a cupful of molasses adds about 2½ fluid ounces to the recipe, and compensation should be made, particularly in baking recipes, by decreasing the water, milk, or other liquid ingredient accordingly. In baking, bicarbonate of soda neutralizes the acid in the molasses thereby providing the leavening gas. This action is similar to that of sour cream or buttermilk and baking soda.

Treacle, though specifically the residual molasses which is drained from the molds used in the refining process, is often meant in certain parts of the South to designate either table or cooking molasses. Both treacle and molasses contain a larger amount of acids, extractives, mineral salts, nitrogen compounds, and other matter, than does refined sugar. They also have a slightly aperient effect.

MOLASSES FROSTING

¾ cup sugar
⅛ tsp salt

3 tbsp water
2 tbsp molasses
1 egg white

Combine all the ingredients in the top of a double boiler. Mix thoroughly. Beat over boiling water with a rotary beater or electric mixer until mixture will stand in firm peaks. (Upper pan should not touch surface of water.) Spread on cooled cake. (Sufficient for 8-inch square cake)

MOLASSES MOUSSE

4 whole eggs, slightly beaten
1 cup molasses
2 tbsp orange juice
⅛ tsp salt
2 cups heavy cream
½ tsp ground cinnamon

Stir the slightly beaten eggs into the molasses, and cook in double boiler until mixture thickens, stirring constantly. Place the top of double boiler in a pan of ice and stir briskly, until mixture is creamy and cool. Then, add orange juice, cinnamon, and salt. Blend well. Chill. Whip the cream until stiff. When thoroughly chilled fold in the whipped cream. Mold and freeze in hand freezer pail, using 4 parts ice and 1 part rock salt. Do not churn, just pack for 4 hours. *See also* MOUSSE.

MOLASSES PIE

Pastry
1 cup sieved bread crumbs
1 cup seedless raisins
1 cup molasses
6 tbsp brown sugar
1 tbsp grated lemon rind
3 tbsp sifted pastry flour
2 tsp ground cinnamon

For the Topping:

2 tbsp shortening
¼ cup brown sugar
6 tbsp pastry flour
⅛ tsp salt

Line a 9-inch pie plate wish pastry *which see*. Arrange in it in the order given; first the crumbs, next the raisins, then the molasses, combined with the sugar, lemon rind, flour, and cinnamon. Have ready the topping, working all ingredients together with the fingers. Spread this over the filling and arrange strips of pastry, lattice-fashion, over all. Brush with water or milk and bake in a moderate oven (350° F.) 40 to 45 minutes. Serve cold. If desired, a few chopped nut-meats may be added to the molasses mixture.

OLD-FASHIONED SOFT MOLASSES COOKIES

6 cups all-purpose flour
1 tsp baking powder
1½ tsp ground ginger
½ tsp ground cinnamon
1 tsp salt
1 cup lard
2 cups brown sugar, firmly packed
3 eggs
1 cup dark molasses
1 tsp baking soda
1½ cups hot water
Granulated sugar

Sift the flour, measure and resift with next 4 ingredients 3 times. Cream lard and brown sugar thoroughly. Add eggs, one at a time and beat mixture thoroughly after each addition. Stir in molasses. Stir in the flour mixture, then add the combined soda and water. Mix thoroughly. Drop by heaping teaspoonfuls onto greased baking sheets and sprinkle with granulated sugar. Bake at 375° F. (moderate) 8 to 10 minutes. Remove to cake racks to cool before serving or storing. (Makes 8 to 9 dozen cookies)

SOFT MOLASSES COOKIES

3 cups all-purpose flour
4 tsp ginger
2 tsp cinnamon
1 tsp salt
½ cup rendered goose grease or chicken fat
1 cup molasses
1 tsp soda
1 tbsp hot water

Sift the flour, measure and resift 3 times with spices and salt. Combine goose grease with molasses and beat well. Add soda to the hot water and combine with molasses mixture. Add the sifted dry ingredients and stir until dry ingredients are thoroughly blended. Chill. Divide into 2 portions and roll to about ⅜ inch thickness. Cut with a 3-inch cutter. Bake on an ungreased cookie sheet in a moderate oven (350° F.) for 8 to 10 minutes or until done. Cool on cake racks. (Makes 2½ dozen)

MOLD. (I) The fuzzy growth which appears on fruits, vegetables, , bread, and meat, that is too long unprotected, is mold, caused by the activity of minute fungi. These thrive best in a dark, damp, warm atmosphere, where they are left undisturbed.

The accumulation cannot be prevented, indefinitely, but it can be retarded by keeping food in a dry place with good circulation of air about it, and by keeping food under refrigeration. Mold destroys food by decomposing it, with the aid of yeasts and bacteria, but a light covering of mold is not harmful if it is removed promptly and the food subsequently cooked. Mold does not putrefy food, and in the case of cheese different molds are used to give individual cheeses their distinctive flavors. Roquefort, Camembert, and other highly flavored cheeses owe their piquancy to the action of certain molds.

Mold in early stages is generally soft and white, but the deeper the fungi penetrate the food the denser the mold becomes and the deeper its color. The bluish-green mold on bread, cheese, and other soft foods and the black mold on fresh fruit and preserves are common sights.

Yeasts. Yeasts are another type of fungi (genus *Saccharomyces*) which have the ability to reproduce themselves quickly in liquids containing sugar or in sugar solutions. Though of varying shape, these fungi are one-celled organisms and cannot be seen by the naked eye except when massed together—in which case they appear as froth on the surface or, in larger accumulation, as a thick sediment.

With the help of enzymes, complex substances present in the cells, the yeasts cause the sugar to break down into carbon dioxide and alcohol, the process known as *fermentation.*

Yeast cells grow most rapidly in warm temperatures (above 70 degrees Fahrenheit), so that refrigeration will greatly retard their propagation. In spite of their reaction on sugar, however, yeasts will not ferment pure, dry sugar or thick jam, though they will cause jelly to ferment. Keeping the sugar can tightly shut and the jam well covered will prevent excessive moisture from entering. Moist sugars are vulnerable to yeast action.

Controlled fermentation by yeast is important to the homemaker. It is the action of carbon dioxide liberated by the yeast which causes bread dough to rise, and it is fermentation which converts grape juice into wine for the table and for cooking. For various uses of yeast and forms in which it is obtainable, see YEAST.

MOLD. (II) To mold is to shape a food by packing into a form. After it is congealed, the food is turned out and retains the shape of the mold. Molded dishes may be hot or cold.

Cold molds are usually solidified by the addition of gelatin or by freezing, as in the case of frozen desserts. In the case of gelatin molds, the process of unmolding is simplified if the mold has been rinsed in cold water before the food is placed in it. For hot molded dishes, such as rice rings, or timbales, the molds should be well greased.

To unmold a cold dish, immerse the mold for a second in very hot water, taking care that the water does not come over the of the mold. This will melt a thin surface layer of the congealed food and allow it to slip out easily. Or, turn the mold upside down on the serving platter, and place a cloth wrung out of very hor water on the mold for an instant until the food drops out.

Instructions for making moulded gelatin dishes are given under gelatin, *which see*. Frozen moulded desserts, such as mousses and parfaits are treated under their own headings.

MONKEY NUT. An English colloquialism for peanut, *which see*.

MONKFISH. Another name for the spadefish, angelfish, or porgy (*which see*).

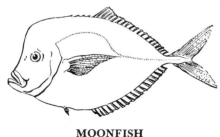

MOONFISH

MONK'S HEAD CHEESE. A soft, rennet cheese made in Switzerland. It is also called Bellelay Cheese, *which see*.

MONTASIO CHEESE. This Italian cheese has a sharp taste and characteristic odor. When fresh it is almost white, but when it gets old, it turns yellow. It is soft and creamy.

MONTAVONER CHEESE. A cheese made of sour milk and dried herbs, in Austria.

MONT CENIS. A hard, rennet cheese made in France of cow's, sheep's, and goat's milk. It resembles the imitation Roqueforts, such as Gex and Septmoncel.

MONTEPULCIANO. A red Italian *dessert wine* made from Muscat grapes. *See* WINE.

MONTILLA. A very dry, light, nutty wine of the sherry type made from grapes grown in the Montilla Mountains about one hundred miles from Jerez, Spain, heart of the Sherry country. *See* SHERRY.

MONTLHERY CHEESE. A soft, rennet cheese of France made of cow's milk. It is two inches thick, fourteen inches in diameter, and weighs approximately five and a half pounds. Smaller-sized cheeses weigh about three pounds.

MOONFISH. The moonfish, commonly called "horsefish," and in certain localities "horsehead," belongs to the pompano family. It is of silvery color, has a compressed body, and seldom grows more than a foot in length. It is found abundantly off both the Atlantic and Pacific Coasts.

This fish passes through a remarkable series of transformations in growth, being so thin when young as to be useless for food, though it is well liked as a pan fish when mature. A species closely related, known around New York as "blunt-nosed shiner," is highly esteemed by fish connoisseurs and gourmets.

The various methods employed in the preparation of bass, flounder (when filleted), mackerel and, of course, pompano may be adapted to this really delicious and fine fish.

MOOR COCK. The male of the red grouse. Also moor fowl.

MOOR HEN. A small European game bird, dark brown above and grey colored in the lower portions, with white tail coverts, the moor hen makes excellent eating, particularly in a salmi (*which see*), but it also can be roasted and prepared like other fowl. Its flesh is slightly gamy, well flavored, and lends itself well to game cookery.

The moor hen haunts pools, streams, and lakes, and is a voracious eater. The moor hens are sometimes imported into the United States.

MOONSHINE. Spirits made in the United States illegally. Prior to Prohibition the illicit product was chiefly made in the mountains of Tennessee and Kentucky, where the stills were often raided by revenue officers. The name was derived from the secrecy involved in the manufacture, principally at night.

MOOSE. The moose which is related to the European Elk, but not the American, is one of the largest of the ruminants of the deer family or *covides*, and sometimes reaches the size of a horse. Only the male wears antlers, more or less subdivided, the weight of which sometimes reaches 50 pounds.

This animal, which lives in small bands, distinguishes itself among all other deer by its short, but robust neck, which allows it to carry the enormous weight of its antlers; by the shape of its head; by its swelled snout; by the thick, prolongated upper lip, which possesses a great mobility; and finally by the shape of its forequarter, which is higher than the hind one. The male has under the throat a protuberance from which grows a long, black shock of hair which resembles a beard. Its general color is of a deep gray, while the hair of its mane and tail, which is very short, is of a still deeper gray. These animals sometimes reach fabulous size.

The moose loves the damp and marshy woodland of North America. During the hot summer months it sometimes remains all day long in boggy water, its head out, to protect itself against the sting of the ox-fly and other insects. From September to April it is found on higher land, where it browses, preferably on the young shoots and leaves of trees. The length of its front legs and the shortness of its neck compel it, when it wants to browse on grass, to swerve its forelegs or even to kneel. Its steps are a kind of rapid trot, which is usually accompanied by a cracking noise, which is attributed to the clashing of his hoofs.

The flesh of the moose is very light, digestible, and nourishing, and the Canadians hold it in great esteem. It is appreciated by those who appreciate game and who like a roast buttock, or round of moose, simmered gently in red wine with onions plentifully stuck with cloves, parsnips, turnips, and leeks, until the wine is almost reduced to nothing. Then it may be served with a sweet-sour shallot sauce. A moose steak, from the round, should be pounded, marinated in white wine overnight, and slowly broiled, then served with a Hungarian sauce. It may be prepared in any way suitable for beef. For further information *see* ELK and GAME.

MORI. A good green tea of Japan, best when plucked in May or June. *See* TEA.

MORINO CREAM CHEESE. A very rich, soft cheese from France. It should be eaten as soon after purchasing as possible.

MORNAY. A cream sauce made with cheese. This is especially good with fish.

MORNAY SAUCE

1 cup cream sauce I
¾ cup white wine court bouillon
1 generous tbsp grated Parmesan cheese
1 scant tbsp grated Swiss Cheese
1 tbsp sweet butter

To the cream sauce (*which see*) add white wine court bouillon (*which see*). Reduce over a hot fire to ⅓ the volume, stirring constantly. Stir in cheese. Finally add, off the fire, the tablespoon of butter.

MORRO CRAB. *See* CRAB.

MORTAR. A small, strong vessel of metal or porcelain in which spices and other dry substances are ground into fine powder with a pestle.

MOSCATEL. A general name for sweet wines made from muscat grapes in Spain and South America. *See also* WINE.

MOSCATELLO. A general name for sweet Italian dessert wines made from muscat grapes. These wines are also called Moscato. *See also* WINE.

MOSCATO. *See* MOSCATELLO.

MOSELLE. Germany, like France, is divided traditionally into different wine-growing regions. In France the divisions are usually along political boundaries, while in Germany, the wines are usually grouped by river valleys. Thus, Moselle wines are those grown along the banks of the Moselle River, while the Rhine wines come from vineyards in the Rhine valley.

In appearance and taste, Moselle wines greatly resemble Rhine wine (*which see*) As a general rule, they are not, however, as long lasting as their Rhenish brothers, and for that reason, not too many are exported.

They are usually clear white table wines with a greenish color and are served in the same way as Rhine wine. Many of the Moselle wines are effervescent or appear to be. *See also* WINE.

MOU CHEESE. Another name for farm cheese, *which see*.

MOUNTAIN HERRING. *See* WHITE-FISH.

MOUNTAIN MINT. *See* BASIL.

MOUSSE. A rich concoction, usually served cold and molded, based on whipped cream. Gelatin is sometimes added as a stabilizer. Mousses are of two types. Dessert mousses are sweet mixtures usually frozen in fancy shapes. A mousse may also be made of meat, fish, or vegetables. In this case gelatin is usually added and the mold is chilled but not frozen. For typical mousses, *see* HAM and TURKEY. For dessert mousses, see the various fruits and flavors.

Frozen mousses may be made in the refrigerator tray, stirring and beating the mixture twice during the first hour of freezing. Or the molds may be packed in a mixture of three parts of ice and one part rock salt.

CHANTILLY MOUSSE

1 cup heavy cream
¼ cup powdered sugar
⅛ tsp salt
1 egg white
½ tsp vanilla
1 cup crumbled macaroons

Whip the cream until quite thick, add the sugar and salt and continue beating until stiff. Fold in the stiffly beaten egg whites to which the vanilla has been added, alternately with the crumbled macaroons. Turn into refrigerator tray or small paper cups and freeze about 3 hours. (Serves 4 to 6)

MOUSSELINE SAUCE. *See* HOLLANDAISE SAUCE.

MOZARINELLI CHEESE. A soft, rennet cheese, made in Italy, from cow's milk.

MUDDLE. In drink mixing, the act of grinding or mashing sugar, fruit slices, etc., in liquid at the bottom of a glass using a thick wooden rod or pestle designed for the purpose and known as a muddler.

MUDDLER. A thick, heavy rod or pestle, used to crush and mix fruit slices, mint, sugar, etc. *See* STIRRER.

MUENCHNER WIESSWURT SAUSAGE. *See* SAUSAGE.

MUFFIN. Of all the quick breads, muffins take the least time to make. The chief secret of their success lies in the mixing. Stirring the batter to a point where the gluten of the flour becomes toughened is a common mistake. Good cooks say that pitfall can be avoided if the mixture is stirred only enough to moisten the ingredients, leaving the batter with a rough appearance. For good food value, flavor, and texture, milk is the best liquid to use. Any mild-flavored fat makes a suitable shortening, and whole-grain wheat flour may be substituted for white flour.

Muffin pans should always be generously buttered or oiled, and the baking should be done in a hot oven (400° to 450° F.) for 20 to 25 minutes, the muffins being immediately turned out of the pans and served piping hot.

STANDARD MUFFINS

2 cups sifted flour
2 tsp baking powder
½ tsp salt
2 tbsp sugar
1 egg, beaten
1 cup milk
2 tbsp shortening, melted

Sift the dry ingredients, then moisten with the combined egg, milk, and shortening. Stir only enough to thoroughly blend and bake in well greased muffin pans in a hot oven (400° to 350° F.) 20 to 25 minutes. (Makes 1 dozen)

VARIATIONS

Bran Muffins. Follow recipe for standard muffins, substituting 1 cup of bran for 1 cup of the flour, molasses for the sugar and using ¾ cup instead of 1 cup of milk.

Cornmeal Muffins. Follow recipe for standard muffins, substituting 1 cup of cornmeal for 1 cup of the flour. If desired, bake in special "corn cob" pans.

Dried Fruit Muffins. Follow recipe for standard muffins, adding ½ cup of seedless raisins, sliced dates or pitted prunes, coarsely cut figs, etc. to the sifted dry ingredients.

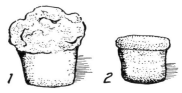

MUFFINS   1. Good   2. Bad

Fresh Berry Muffins. Follow recipe for standard muffins, adding to the sifted dry ingredients ½ cup of washed, drained, stemmed berries, as blueberries, huckleberries or cranberries.

Nut or Coconut Muffins. Follow recipe for standard muffins, adding ½ cup of chopped nut meats, or ⅓ cup of shredded coconut, to the sifted dry ingredients.

Sour Milk or Buttermilk Muffins. Follow recipe for standard muffins, reducing the baking powder to 1 teaspoon, adding ½ teaspoon of baking soda and substituting sour milk or buttermilk for sweet milk.

Spiced Muffins. Follow recipe for standard muffins adding ¼ of a teaspoon each of ground ginger, cinnamon and cloves to the flour before sifting.

Whole Kernel Corn Muffins. Follow recipe for standard muffins, stirring in ½ cup of canned whole kernel corn (drained) for each 2 cups of flour.

Whole Wheat or Graham Muffins. Follow recipe for standard muffins, substituting whole wheat or Graham flour for white flour and slightly increasing the quantity of milk used.

MUFFIN DISH. A large, flat, usually round dish that is fitted with a cover. It is used to serve heated muffins, toast, etc., at the table, the cover keeping the contents warm until served. *See* DISHES.

MUFFIN PAN. A baking pan made of thin metal, with a number of cavities shaped to hold individual muffins or cupcakes. It is sometimes called a muffin tin. *See* MUFFIN; *see also* KITCHEN EQUIPMENT

MUG. A drinking vessel equipped with a large handle, and usually lipless and

cylindrical in shape. Mugs are distinguished from cups by their shape, and by the size of the handle, which is usually designed to be grasped by the entire hand rather than a few fingers. They are traditionally made of earthenware or metal, though any other suitable material may be used. *See* GLASSWARE; *see also* STEIN.

MULBERRY. The native American mulberry is the fruit of the red mulberry tree. There are several different varieties which bear bluish-purple, red, or reddish-black fruit. The flavor is sub-acid.

Although it is excellent for cooking and is wholesome and agreeable when eaten raw, it has never become popular in the United States.

MULBERRY

MULLED BEVERAGES. A "mulled" drink is always served hot. It is a beverage very appropriate to the winter months, as it is claimed to stimulate body-heat. It is also said to be a good digestive. All beers, wines, liqueurs, and cordials may be "mulled" and the kind selected usually gives its name to the drink. The other ingredients are sugar, spices, and condiments. Sometimes eggs are added, thereby enhancing the nutritive value of the drink.

MULLED PORT

Put ½ pint of water into a saucepan, with 3 ounces of sugar, a little nutmeg and a few cloves. Boil all together for a few minutes, then add from 10 to 12 wineglassfuls of rich port wine and let it come up to the boiling point, but not actively boil. Stir and serve as hot as possible (Serves 4)

MULLED CIDER

Infuse in ½ pint of boiling water, just removed from the fire, ⅛ teaspoon of nut-

MUFFIN TIN

meg (more if desired), 4 or 5 bruised whole cloves, ⅛ teaspoon of ground cinnamon and sugar to taste. Strain and add 1 pint of hot cider. (Serves 2 to 3)

MULLED CLARET

Bring to the boiling point ½ cup of water, 4 ounces of sugar, the rind of 2 small lemons, a 4-inch stick of cinnamon and 4 or 5 whole cloves. Strain and combine with 2 bottles of good claret which have also been brought to the boiling point. Finally stir in 1 glass of good brandy or rum. (Serves 8)

MULLED GRAPE JUICE

Tie mixed whole spices (a 4-inch stick of cinnamon, 4 whole cloves and 3 or 4 allspice) in a cheesecloth bag and drop this into a saucepan containing 2 quarts of grape juice. Bring to a boil, allow to stand 10 minutes, or longer if a strong spicy mulled drink is desired, then strain. Serve in heated glass cups. (Serves about 10)

MULLET. There are several varieties of the mullet, among which the striped mullet is most plentiful. It is in season from September to May, and is usually very fat; but it has a rather unpleasant flavor, and is not so much esteemed for the table. The golden mullet, or mullet sucker, is a beautiful fresh water fish, in season during the winter and spring months. The flesh is sweet, but rather dry, and quite full of small bones. The plain red mullet is abundant in summer, and may be had throughout the year. The white or gray mullet is also very fine.

All the recipes applied to bass, catfish, mackerel, and perch may be adapted to this fish.

MULLIGATAWNY. The word mulligatawny means "pepper water," consequently the soup should be highly seasoned. The original recipe, an East Indian one, consisted of a rich thin cream

soup flavored with curry powder and plenty of spices, garnished with small pieces of chicken and served with a side dish of rice, cooked Indian style, that is rather highly seasoned. This, however, has degenerated into the following:

MULLIGATAWNY

1 to 2½ lb chicken
¼ lb diced salt pork
1 tbsp flour
1¾ tsp curry powder
2¼ qt veal stock
1 cup diced carrots
¼ cup diced onions
1 large bay leaf
6 sprigs parsley
3 whole cloves
6 whole peppercorns, slightly bruised
Salt, pepper and cayenne

Wipe and cut up the chicken as for fricassee, but in smaller pieces. Try out the pork, then fry the chicken lightly in the pork fat, turning to brown on all sides. Sprinkle over it the blended flour and curry powder, and continue cooking, stirring and turning the pieces of chicken frequently, until the meat is firm, but not quite done. Turn into a soup kettle and add the stock, a little at a time, still stirring frequently, also the vegetables and seasonings. Bring to a boil and simmer very gently for one hour. Strain.

Meanwhile prepare the garnish for which will be needed:

½ eggplant
Butter or margarine
1 cup sliced leeks
1 cup diced cooked white meat of chicken
3 tbsp cooked rice

Parboil the eggplant, then peel, dice and sauté it in a little butter until half cooked. Sauté the leeks, but do not brown them, in the same butter. Then add these, with the chicken and rice to the strained soup and reheat. Serve very hot with a side dish of plain boiled rice. (Serves 6)

MULLIGATAWNY, TAMIL STYLE

1 to 3 lb young fowl
¼ cup butter or margarine

MULLET

¼ cup sliced onions
¼ cup diced celery
¼ cup diced carrots
½ cup finely chopped green pepper
2 tart apples, peeled, cored and sliced
1 tbsp flour
2 tsp curry powder
1 tsp salt
¼ tsp white pepper
1 tsp chopped parsley
1 tsp granulated sugar
⅛ tsp mace
2 qt chicken stock
1 cup tomato pulp

Cut the chicken into individual portions as for fricassee. Brown in the heated butter. Add the vegetables and apples and cook until the mixture begins to brown, stirring frequently. Stir in the flour blended with the curry powder and seasonings. When thoroughly mixed add the stock and tomato pulp and bring to boiling point, stirring constantly. Cover and cook very slowly until the chicken is tender. Lift out the chicken and dice the meat. Strain the soup, forcing the vegetables through the sieve. Add the diced chicken, and serve very hot, with a side dish of plain boiled rice. (Serves 6)

MULLIGATAWNY SOUP

1 cup uncooked chicken, diced
1 small onion, sliced
⅓ cup diced carrot
⅓ cup diced celery
⅓ cup minced green pepper
1 apple, thinly sliced
¼ cup fat
¼ cup flour
2 tbsp minced parsley
1 tsp curry powder
1 blade mace
4 cloves
1 cup tomato pulp
1½ qt chicken stock
1 tsp salt
½ tsp pepper
1 cup cooked rice

Brown the chicken, vegetables (except parsley and tomato), and apple in the fat. Add all remaining ingredients (except the rice) in the order given. Simmer gently for

1 hour. Strain, take out the pieces of chicken, press the vegetables through a sieve and combine the soup itself, the chicken, and the puréed vegetables. Just before serving add the rice and serve very hot. (Serves 4 to 6)

MULSE. An old-fashioned beverage made of claret and honey, brought to the boiling point.

MUM. A kind of very strong ale brewed from a mixture of malted wheat, oatmeal, ground beans, and various herbs.

MUNG BEAN. *See* BEAN SPROUTS.

MUNSTER CHEESE. A rennet cheese, made of the whole milk of cows. It is also called "Gerome," "Colmar," and "Strassburg." It is semi-hard, and cylindrical in shape with a brick red rind. It is produced in France and also in western Germany. It is generally flavored with caraway or anise seed.

MUSCADEL. A sweet dessert wine made from muscat grapes, that is quite similar to California muscatel, *which see.*

MUSCATEL. A white dessert wine having the flavor, aroma and sweetness of the muscat grape from which it is made. A medium-bodied, fortified, California wine with a color ranging from gold to amber, it is properly served either with desserts or between meals with fruit. It can be served either chilled or at room temperature. *See* WINE.

The name is also given to a sweet, white, English sparkling wine usually flavored with elderberry flower essence.

MUSH. Cornmeal or Indian meal, white or yellow, boiled as a cereal in slightly salted water.

FRIED MUSH

1 qt boiling water
1 tsp salt
1 cup white or yellow cornmeal

Shake the cornmeal very gently into the boiling salted water, stirring constantly. Cook over direct heat until the mixture thickens, still stirring. Turn into a previously wet or greased shallow pan and when cold cut into slices. Roll in flour and sauté in a little hot fat, turning to brown both sides. Serve with maple sirup, cheese sauce, or as an accompaniment to sausages, bacon or other meat.

MUSHROOM. The name given to all forms of edible fungus. The origin of the

MUSHROOMS

mushroom is lost in antiquity, but it was known as far back as there is any written record. Hippocrates, in 400 B.C., wrote that mushrooms were eaten in large quantities and were exported as an article of commerce. For centuries they have been used in the cookery of Russia, France, Germany, Italy, China, and Japan. The early colonists in America found them growing wild and quickly learned to use the harmless varieties.

The mushroom, as we know it, is the fruit of the fungus which grows below ground. This underground plant is a white or bluish mold called "spawn" which resembles a mass of thin roots. The fruit grows up through the ground, forming the familiar caps. Mushrooms reproduce by spores which are minute powdery seeds which are borne on the underside of the caps in the gills.

The commercial production of mushrooms in the United States started in the late 1890's when a group of florists in Chester County, Pennsylvania started growing the common mushroom under the benches of their greenhouses. The idea spread until today mushrooms are grown commercially in most parts of the country. The greatest event in the history of mushroom culture in the United States occurred in 1926, when a farmer found a clump of pure white mushrooms in a bed of uniformly cream-colored fungi. From this spore has descended most of the mushrooms grown today, and market men prefer the snow white appearance.

Mushrooms are easily grown in cool moist surroundings, away from direct light. Many people grow sufficient to supply their own needs in a cellar. On a commercial scale, mushrooms are raised in caves or closed tunnels, or in specially constructed houses which are built partly above and partly below ground.

The mushroom makes no claim to nutrition. Analysis indicates that the fungus contains few elements of nutritive value, chiefly iron and copper, and these few are so diluted by the water which forms most of its structure that they hardly count. A mushroom exists to give grace and fragrance to plainer food.

The mushrooms which are found in the market are cultivated mushrooms and are always wholesome food unless they are spoiled by over-keeping. They are marketed in two forms, buttons, and caps. Button mushrooms are the young mushrooms, picked before the cap has flattened out, and with the gills still covered over. They are considered more delicate and so command a higher price. The caps are the more mature mushroom which has opened out into the typical umbrella-shape. Since the cap is more tender than the stem, mushrooms with longer stems are generally cheaper. The stems may be used for soup or sauces, or cut small, will be as tender as the caps. Mushrooms, to be in good condition, and worth purchasing, should be white and without spots. Since they deteriorate very rapidly they are not worth buying if they have started to darken.

TYPES OF MUSHROOMS

Wild Mushrooms. Many types of wild mushrooms and other fungi are edible, but others are deadly poison. Unless one is very familiar with the harmless kinds it is risky to eat mushrooms that have not been purchased in the market. Even when one knows the harmless kinds well, buttons should not be picked since positive identification depends upon the gills which are not visible before the cap has opened out.

Cèpes. A large fleshy mushroom which is found in France and canned for the export trade. The cap of this edible *Boletus* is six inches or more in diameter and yellowish or reddish brown in color. It is usually canned preserved in olive oil or other sauce, and has a somewhat stronger flavor than the common mushroom.

Truffles. Usually considered in a category by themselves, truffles are fungus which grows entirely underground. *See* TRUFFLE.

Canned Mushrooms. Mushrooms are canned in various forms. Small buttons pickled for use as hors d'oeuvres. Caps are canned in brine, or broiled in butter, for use in many dishes. Canned mushroom soup, aside from its use as a delicious soup, makes an excellent quick sauce for chicken, veal, or tuna fish.

Dried Mushrooms. These are most often found in foreign grocery stores, and are dark shriveled-looking things. However, their flavor is very concentrated, and three or four dried mushrooms added to a stew or sauce will give a flavor which is equal to that of a considerable quantity of fresh mushrooms. They are particularly useful during the seasons when fresh mushrooms are expensive.

HINTS ON PREPARATION

Fresh mushrooms need little preparation, and should be cooked quickly. All that is necessary is to peel the skin from the caps—this pulls off easily in strips. The caps should be cut from the stems and the tougher bottom portion of the stem cut off. If the mushrooms are large they may be cut in slices. If they are button size they are best left whole. The tender stems may be sliced and cooked with the caps. The skins and tough portion of the stem may be boiled in a little water to give a stock for flavoring soups or sauces.

Peeled mushrooms darken quickly when exposed to air. If they are to be used in stew, it is permissible to prepare them ahead of time and drop them in cold water containing a little lemon juice or vinegar until ready to use them. If they are to be sautéed or broiled, they should not be prepared until just time to cook them.

Overcooking toughens mushrooms. Fresh mushrooms will cook sufficiently in eight minutes; three or four minutes will heat canned mushrooms sufficiently. Mushrooms sautéed in butter are a luxurious addition to many dishes such as scrambled eggs, rice, or spaghetti. Mushrooms are a fine addition to fricassee of chicken or veal, or a beef stew. And a few dried mushrooms make all the difference in a fine sauce for spaghetti.

CREAM OF MUSHROOM SOUP

1 lb mushrooms
¼ cup butter
1 medium-sized onion, chopped
1½ tbsp flour
6 cups milk

1 bay leaf
4 sprigs parsley
1 whole clove
Salt and pepper
Dash of cayenne
Dash of mace
½ cup heavy cream
2 egg yolks, well beaten

Peel the mushrooms, cut off the tough ends of the stems, and put the balance through a food chopper. Melt the butter in the top of a double boiler and add the chopped onion and the mushrooms. Cook for 5 minutes over direct heat, stirring constantly. Sprinkle in the flour and blend well. Scald the milk with the bayleaf, parsley, and clove, and strain. Gradually stir the scalded milk into the mushroom mixture and cook, stirring constantly, until the mixture boils and thickens. Season to taste with salt, pepper, cayenne, and mace. Place the top of the boiler over boiling water and let simmer for 20 minutes, stirring frequently. Turn into a fine-meshed wire sieve and rub through into a fresh saucepan. Return to the stove, taste for seasoning. Scald the cream and stir in the egg yolks. Add to the soup mixture and stir thoroughly. Reheat, but do not boil again. Serve with croutons. (Serves 6)

CREAMED MUSHROOMS ON TOAST

1 lb mushrooms
4 tbsp butter or margarine
3 tbsp flour
1 tsp salt
⅛ tsp pepper
1 cup milk
½ cup mushroom stock
¼ cup light cream
1 tsp onion juice

Wash the mushrooms and peel the caps. Slice the caps and tender portion of the stems. Cook the peel and the tougher portion of the stem in ¾ cup of water for 10 minutes. Melt the butter in a saucepan, add the sliced mushrooms, and cook over a low flame for three minutes, stirring to prevent burning. Add the flour, salt, and pepper, and blend well with the butter. Then carefully stir in the milk and the strained mushroom stock. Stir constantly over low heat until the mixture thickens and boils. Then add the cream and onion juice. Reheat, but do not boil again. Serve on toast. (Serves 4)

FLAMED MUSHROOMS

1 lb mushroom caps
Salt
6 tbsp butter or margarine
1 cup dry sherry
2 tbsp brandy
¼ cup heavy cream

Wash the mushrooms, peel them, and trim off the tough portion of the stems. In a chafing dish melt the butter and sauté the mushrooms until brown. Pour in the sherry and let simmer until nearly dry. Pour the brandy over the mushrooms and light it. When the flame has gone out, stir in the cream. Season with a little salt. Serve on toast. A green salad is a good accompaniment for this supper dish. (Serves 4)

GRILLED MUSHROOMS

¼ cup butter or margarine
2 tbsp grated horseradish
1½ doz large mushrooms
Salt and pepper

Cream the butter with the horseradish. Wash, dry, and stem the mushrooms, and peel the caps. Melt a little butter in a dish and dip each mushroom cap into it. Place the caps, one by one, cup side up, in a flat heat-proof dish. Salt and pepper them lightly. Place about three inches away from the broiler flame and broil them four minutes; then turn and broil four minutes on the other side. Dot with the horseradish butter, and place in the oven just long enough to melt the butter. Serve at once on hot buttered toast. (Serves 4)

HOT MUSHROOM PUFFS

2 tbsp butter or margarine
2 tbsp flour
¾ tsp curry powder
½ cup milk
1½ tsp Worcestershire sauce
1 raw egg, slightly beaten
2 tbsp cracker crumbs
1 cup chopped mushrooms
½ tsp salt
⅛ tsp pepper

Melt the butter. Blend in the flour and curry powder and cook for one minute, stirring constantly. Add the milk and continue cooking, stirring constantly, until smooth and very thick. Remove from the fire and add all the remaining ingredients. Allow to cool thoroughly. Form into small balls and roll in additional fine cracker crumbs. Fry in deep hot fat (390° F.) until golden brown. Impale on colored toothpicks and use as hors d'oeuvres. (Makes 2 dozen)

JELLIED MUSHROOM BOUILLON

1 tbsp gelatin
4 cups water
½ lb fresh mushrooms
2 thin slices mild onion
Salt and pepper
2 tbsp sherry, optional
1 hard-cooked egg, thinly sliced
2 tbsp minced parsley

Soften the gelatin in ¼ cup of the water. Pass mushrooms and onion twice through the food chopper, saving all juice. Add remaining water to the mushrooms and simmer 15 minutes. Strain, pressing all possible juices through the strainer—there should be 2½ cups of liquid. Add the softened gelatin, stir until dissolved, season and flavor with the salt, pepper, and sherry if used, and chill. Serve in bouillon cups, garnishing with the egg and parsley. (Serves 4)

MARINATED MUSHROOMS

1 lb small firm mushrooms
Salted water
Juice of 1 lemon

Wash the mushrooms and dry quickly. Cut off the tough parts of the stems. Peel the mushrooms and drop them into a saucepan containing salted water and the juice of a lemon. Bring quickly to a boil. Cover and simmer for eight minutes. Drain. Let cold water run over the mushrooms for a second, drain again, and place in a bowl. Strain over them the boiling hot marinade, made as follows:

¾ cup vinegar
⅓ cup olive oil
1 clove of garlic, crushed
A pinch of thyme

A small piece of bay leaf
½ tsp coarsely ground black pepper
½ tsp salt
A sprig of parsley
A few coriander seeds
Chopped chervil or fennel

Simmer together for five minutes the vinegar, oil, garlic, thyme, bay leaf, pepper, salt, parsley, and coriander seeds. When cold, place in the refrigerator and chill for several hours before serving. Dust lightly with chopped chervil or fennel just before serving. Use as hors d'oeuvres. (Serves 6)

MUSHROOMS BAKED IN CREAM

16 or so large mushrooms
Butter or margarine
Salt and paprika
1 cup light cream
Small rounds of hot dry toast

Remove the mushroom stems and peel the caps, reserving the peel and stems for flavoring stock or sauces. Place the mushrooms, cup side up, in a shallow buttered casserole. Dot with butter, sprinkle with salt and paprika, and pour in the cream. Bake 10 minutes in a hot oven (375°–400° F.). Place on small rounds of toast and pour the cream over them. Serve immediately. (Serves 4)

MUSHROOM BISQUE

4 tbsp butter
3 tbsp flour
¼ tsp dry mustard
1 tsp salt
¼ tsp pepper
5 cups boiling water
¾ lb mushrooms
¼ cup sherry
Paprika
Whipped cream

Blend half the butter with the flour and seasonings until smooth, gradually add the water and bring to boiling point, stirring constantly. Add the mushroom stems, washed and finely chopped. Cover, and simmer ½ hour, then strain. Meanwhile, sauté the peeled and sliced mushroom caps in the remaining butter. Turn them into the upper part of a double boiler, add the strained thickened liquor in which the

stems were cooked and cook 10 minutes over hot water. Add the sherry slowly and serve in individual bowls, topping each portion with paprika-flavored whipped cream. If desired, the cream may be sprinkled with thinly sliced unsalted pistachio nuts or blanched shredded almonds, or may be flavored with a dash of bitters. (Serves 4)

MUSHROOM CUTLETS

½ lb mixed green pepper, celery, and carrots, in equal amounts
1 lb mushrooms
2 large onions
2 tbsp olive oil
1 cup fresh bread crumbs
2 eggs
1 additional egg yolk
Salt and pepper
A small clove of garlic

Peel and chop the mushrooms, onions, and garlic. Chop the mixed vegetables very fine and add in the mushrooms, onions, and garlic, continuing to chop to blend thoroughly. Add the remaining ingredients and mix thoroughly. Shape into 6 cutlets. Place in a well greased baking dish and bake in a moderately hot oven (375° F.) for 25 minutes, until well heated and nicely browned. (Serves 6)

MUSHROOM AND POTATO PIE

3 tbsp butter or margarine
3 cups coarsely chopped, peeled mushrooms
1½ cups brown sauce
4 cups cold mashed potatoes
1 egg, beaten
Salt and pepper to taste
½ cup grated American cheese

Melt the butter. Put in the chopped mushrooms and sauté them until browned. Add the brown sauce (*which see*), and heat over a low flame. Combine the mashed potatoes and egg. Cover the bottom and sides of a greased baking dish with the prepared potatoes and fill the center with the mushroom mixture. Cover the top with the remaining potatoes and sprinkle with the grated cheese. Bake in a hot oven (375° F.) for 30 minutes, or until brown on top. Serve as the main dish for luncheon or supper. (Serves 6)

MUSHROOM SOUFFLE

3 tbsp butter or margarine
½ lb mushrooms, finely chopped
2 tbsp minced onion
2 tbsp flour
½ tsp salt
¼ tsp pepper
½ cup milk
2 tbsp minced parsley
1 tbsp lemon juice
2 egg yolks, well beaten
3 egg whites, stiffly beaten

Melt one tablespoon of the butter, add the mushrooms and onion, and cook over a low flame about 5 minutes, until tender but not brown. Melt the remaining butter in a small saucepan, stir in the flour, salt, and pepper. When well blended, slowly stir in the milk and stir constantly over a low flame until the mixture boils and thickens. Remove from the heat and add the mushrooms, parsley, and lemon juice, and the beaten egg yolks. Fold in the stiffly beaten egg whites and pour into a greased baking dish. Bake in a moderately hot oven (375° F.) 30 to 35 minutes. (Serves 4)

MUSHROOM SOUP

2 qt chicken stock
3 cups coarsely chopped fresh mushrooms
¼ tsp onion juice
½ tsp lemon juice
2 dashes celery salt
Salt and pepper
½ cup broiled mushroom caps
3 tbsp sherry

Combine the stock and chopped mushrooms and simmer gently about 1 hour. Strain through doubled cheesecloth, pressing out all possible juice. There should be 1½ quarts of stock. Add to this the onion and lemon juices with the seasonings, finely diced broiled mushroom caps and the sherry. (Serves 6)

NEAPOLITAN MUSHROOMS

Peel and boil as many mushrooms as desired in salted water for a few minutes.

When tender, drain thoroughly and sauté in olive oil with a little garlic and sliced tomatoes, all well seasoned with salt and pepper.

MUSK DEER. A small, hornless deer. The male yields musk, which is used in perfumes.

MUSKELLUNGE. The muskellunge is a fresh water fish belonging to the pike and pickerel family, found in the Great Lakes and the upper St. Lawrence river. It is seldom seen in the East, being marketed mostly in the Middle West.

The muskellunge is of a dark gray color with black dots. It may reach a length of eight feet and a weight of seventy-five pounds, but its average weight is from five to six pounds and its length two and one-half feet. Considered one of the best food fishes of the region, it is a delicacy and may be prepared like the pike, salmon (which it resembles slightly in flavor but not in color), and whitefish.

MUSKMELON. See CANTALOUPE.

MUSKRAT. "A North American aquatic rodent, yielding a valuable fur." So the dictionary defines this animal. But down on the Eastern Shore of Maryland, where muskrat raising has grown into a profitable industry, breeders would add "edible game."

Not so long ago, muskrat, or marsh-rabbit, meat was considered fit for only the poor to eat. The Negroes living on the Eastern Shore, after the Civil War, would catch these plump, furry animals, skin them, sell their pelts for 10 cents apiece, and then eat the carcass. When it was discovered by the well-to-do inhabitants that muskrat flesh was delicious if properly cooked, a new source of revenue in muskrat-raising was introduced. A wealthy financier, upon buying acreage in this locality, is said to have stocked his estate with muskrats.

Several hotels make a specialty of serving muskrat in season. The meat is either roasted, baked, or stewed and served in a pie. But menus do not list the dishes as muskrat, but as "marsh rabbit," the more appetizing name used by Marylanders.

MUSSELS. A small bivalve mollusk. In the year 1237, as the story goes, a ship carrying a cargo of English mutton foundered off the coast of France. The skipper, named Patrick Walton, managed to swim ashore and soon set about finding a means of living. To his favorite pastime of fishing

MUSKELLUNGE

he added that of hunting wild birds which, he noticed, flew very low over the water during the night and which he captured by attaching a large net onto high sticks which he placed in the sand at low tide. These sticks were soon covered with hundreds of young mussels which, in this new location, grew much faster than when left in their usual ocean beds. The fishermen in this neighborhood today get their mussels in exactly the same manner.

The edible sea mussels are gregarious and are found in great masses, closely crowded together, adhering to rocks, and attached to one another by the very tough byssus—the entire beds being practically bound together. When young, the mussels move about, but they soon anchor themselves by the byssus and remain thus throughout life. These delicious and nourishing shellfish are generally found in shallow water, and are often exposed at low tide. The shell—black on the outside and blue inside—is oblong and generallly about three inches long by one and one half inches wide, although some are found nearly double these dimensions.

Sea mussels are found in enormous quantities from New Brunswick as far as North Carolina and are at their best from October until the end of April, after which they spawn and are rather indigestible.

HINTS ON PREPARATION

Place the mussels in cold water and scrape with a knife, removing all seaweed which may adhere. Rinse in several waters, rejecting any open mussels. Discard the hairy beards. Place the mussels in a large kettle with a finely chopped onion, a small bunch of fresh parsley, or a large parsley root tied with a large bay leaf and a dozen crushed peppercorns. Add one-half cup of white wine for every 50 mussels. Cover closely and set on a hot fire. One or two minutes are quite sufficient to open the shells. Remove from the fire and when cooled a little, shell the mussels and place in a bowl, covering with the strained liquor from the kettle.

MUSSEL CHOWDER

4 doz mussels
2 small onions, minced
4 tbsp butter
1 qt light cream, milk, or part evaporated milk
Salt and pepper
¼ cup fine cracker crumbs

Scrub the mussels removing the "beards", then steam until the shells open freely. Take out the meats and save the liquor. Fry the onions lightly in half the butter, stir in the cream, or cream and milk, and add the mussell liquor. Simmer 10 minutes or until the onions are tender. Season, add the mussel meats and heat through, but do not actually boil. Just before serving add the crumbs and the remaining butter. (Serves 6)

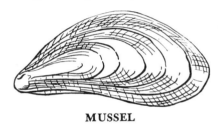

MUSSEL

MUSSELS MARINIERE

3 qt mussels in shells
1 cup dry white wine
1 tsp each minced shallots and parsley
A few grains cayenne
1 tbsp butter
Chopped parsley, additional

The mussels must be absolutely fresh, heavy, and with the shells tightly closed. Wash them thoroughly, scraping the shells with a knife and changing the water several times. Place in a saucepan with the wine, shallots, parsley, cayenne and butter. Cover tightly and steam over a hot fire until the shells open, taking care that they are not overdone. Drain (reserve the liquor), remove the empty shell of each mussel, leaving those with flesh in them. Arrange in a serving dish and keep warm. Pour the reserved liquor into a saucepan, taking care not to mix in any sediment. Boil down to ¾ of a cup. Add butter and seasoning, if necessary, and pour over the mussels.

Sprinkle more chopped parsley on top and serve very hot.

MUSSEL PATTIES

Cook 3 dozen mussels as directed. Discard shells; strain the liquor through fine cloth and use it in preparing a cream sauce which should be made with sweet butter, half milk and half mussel liquor, with a generous squeeze of lemon juice. Sauté ½ cup sliced fresh mushrooms in a little butter, drain and add them to the sauce. Reheat the mussels in this sauce and use to fill puff paste patty shells. Dust with paprika, garnish with parsley and quartered lemon and serve with shoe string potatoes. (Serves 6)

MUSSELS POULETTE

3½ to 4 doz small mussels
½ lb butter
1 tbsp each finely chopped parsley and chives
1 tbsp flour
1 cup each of white wine and fish stock
Sauce Poulette

Scrape, wash and thoroughly clean the mussels, rejecting any opened ones. Place in a large stock pot (without water) over a hot fire, allowing the heat to force open the shells. Then shell the mussels. Place in a saucepan with the butter, chopped parsley and chives. Set on a low fire, stirring constantly, and when the butter begins to melt, sprinkle the flour over the mussels. Pour in the white wine and fish stock and simmer gently for 20 minutes. Meanwhile prepare Sauce Poulette (*see* WHITE SAUCE), place the prepared mussels in it, heat thoroughly and serve on a hot platter, garnishing with small triangles of fried bread and lemon slices. Serve with plain boiled potato balls.

MUST. Unfermented, expressed grape juice. *See also* WINE.

MUSTARD. From the earliest times mustard has been known as a condiment and as a medicine. Today the United States Pharmacopoeia describes mustard as a digestive stimulant and as a warming application in a bath or as a poultice. But although mustard has been appreciated since Biblical times, it is used to a greater extent today and in more variety than ever before. On the grocery shelves one can find German mustards, French mustards, English mustards, Swedish mustards, as well as the American favorites, the difference being in the seasonings and spices that are added to the mustard seeds.

The custom of grinding the seeds and sifting them to a fine powder, the form in which we use mustard so frequently today, dates back to 1720, when an English woman known to history simply as "Mrs. Clements of Durham," experimented and found it tasty.

There are two varieties of mustard plants, one yielding black or brown seeds and the other white or yellow seeds. The best seeds are the brown seeds of Holland, England, France, and California, which are used for what is known as prepared mustard. The yellow seeds are milder and are used whole in pickling and for mustard salad dressings. The young leaves of the mustard plant are used for salad or as cooked greens, and are more popular in the south than elsewhere.

Mustard, the condiment, is marketed in two forms—as a flour and as a paste. Mustard flour is variously described as powdered mustard, or pulverized mustard, and reaches the consumer in the form of a yellow, rather oily powder. To bring out its real value as a condiment, it is necessary to add water or milk. Mustard in paste form is generally known as prepared mustard and consists of the seeds thoroughly mixed with vinegar and spices; it is then ground between heavy stones, from which it trickles in a semi-liquid state. Good prepared mustard is a delicate mixture of the choicest seeds. These are dried in the sun—not in kilns—so that they are rich and full-flavored.

HINTS ON USING MUSTARD

Mustard gives flavor to many dishes. As an accompaniment to cold meat, or hot, powdered mustard is easily fixed. To prepare it, the liquid must be added slowly and the mixture thoroughly mashed and blended with the back of a spoon until it is the consistency of thick batter and perfectly smooth. The simplest preparation is to mix it with water, adding ½ teaspoon of salt for each 2 ounces of powdered mustard. Some people like powdered sugar added in the same proportion as salt. Milk, used instead of water, makes a smooth pungent condiment. Cream will make a less pun-

gent mixture. The milk or cream mixtures will not keep, so only enough should
be prepared to use at the time. Vinegar
and oil, mixed with the powdered mustard,
give a sharp flavor which is enjoyed by
many people. It is desirable to moisten
the mustard first with a very little cold
water before adding the other ingredients
to bring out the best flavor.

Prepared mustard needs no further preparation before its use. There are many
brands, differing in the combination of
spices which have been used. Some are
mild, and some very sharp. It is a matter
of sampling to find the brand which is preferred.

In cooking, mustard adds unsuspected
flavor to many otherwise bland dishes. In
making cream sauces for hard-boiled eggs,
chicken à la king, or leftover meats, try
the addition of a half teaspoon of powdered
mustard to the flour used for thickening.
Cheese dishes are usually the better for a
bit of mustard. A bit of powdered mustard
added to a cheese souffle is an improvement; two teaspoons of prepared mustard
give zest to a Welsh rarebit. When making
cheese biscuits try adding two teaspoons of
prepared mustard to the milk before working it into the dry ingredients.

In broiling steaks or chops, rub a little
prepared mustard on the meat before placing it under the broiler. Ham is delicious
rubbed with mustard before baking or
broiling. In fact, there are few dishes, except desserts, which cannot be improved
by the judicious addition of a bit of mustard.

MUSTARD GREENS. Bunches of fresh
mustard greens, bearing some yellow flowers, find their way into the markets in the
spring. The tenderest of the leaves are an
addition to the salad bowl, giving a sharp
pungent taste which combines well with
the blander salad greens. The rest of the
leaves, tender stems, and flower heads may
be cooked as a vegetable, either alone or in
combination with less strongly flavored
greens. Mustard greens are used to a greater extent in the south than elsewhere,
but they are an inexpensive and very
healthful vegetable.

FOOD VALUE

MUSTARD

Mustard greens, to be worth buying,
should be fresh looking, tender, and crisp,
and should have a good green color. Mustard which is old and wasteful will have
wilted and discolored leaves. If seed heads
are visible, the mustard is old and will be
very strongly flavored.

Some cooks favor cooking mustard
greens in salted water and seasoning them
at serving time. Others maintain that the
greens should be cooked in water in which
salt pork, corned beef, or ham has been
simmered.

MUSTARD GREENS AND POTATOES
(Southern method)
⅛ lb mild salt pork
1½ qt cold water
2 qt mustard greens
1 doz new potatoes
Salt and pepper
Slice the pork into very thin slices and
simmer, covered, in the water for an hour.

	Food Energy	Pro-tein	Fat	Carbo-hydrate	Cal-cium	Phos-phorus	Iron	Vit. A Value	Thia-mine	Ribo-flavin	Nia-cin	Ascor-bic Acid
Water												
92.2	28	2.3	.3	4.0	220	38	2.9	6460	.09	.20	.8	102

Wash and clean the mustard greens, removing the tender heads, and cutting the stalks into convenient pieces. Wash and scrape the potatoes. When the pork has simmered the hour, add the stalks of the mustard and cook about 15 minutes. Then add the potatoes and the heads of the mustard. Cook 15 or 20 minutes longer, until the potatoes are tender. Season with salt and pepper. Serve all together with some of the pot liquor. (Serves 6)

MUSTARD POT. A small serving pot designed to hold mustard. See DISHES.

MUTTON. The flesh of sheep too mature to be classified as lamb (*which see*) is known as mutton. The best mutton is that known as yearling mutton, which comes from animals between twelve and twenty-four months of age, and in all respects is close in quality to lamb. More mature mutton is divided into classes by sex, being wether, buck, or ewe mutton, and in general shows similar characteristics of maturity.

The break joint of the forelegs which is the sign of young lamb is also present in yearling mutton, although the bone end in mutton shows whiter, more porous, and drier than in lamb. In more mature mutton the bone has ossified so that the foot must be removed at the fetlock joint, an l as a result the rounded bone end is visible and no break is possible.

GOVERNMENT GRADES

Yearling mutton is graded by Federal inspectors into six classes, on much the same basis as is lamb.

Prime or Grade A-1. In many respects this grade is similar to prime lamb, differing only in having somewhat longer carcasses in proportion to the width. Because of the greater maturity, the bones are harder and whiter, the flesh is somewhat coarser, and there is a greater amount of fat, both internally and externally. The fat is firm and white, slightly creamy in color, and the flesh is a medium pink in color.

Choice or Grade 1. Mutton of this grade has excellent conformation and quality. The ratio of length to breadth is good, but the animal is relatively heavier in the forequarters than lamb of the same grade. The bones are whiter than lamb, and the break joint shows as a rough, dry, and comparatively hard surface. The fat covering is well distributed over the carcass; interior fat is apt to be more localized. The fat is white or creamy in color; the flesh is a medium to dark pink.

Good or Grade 2. This grade of mutton corresponds to the same grade of lamb, with the difference that the animal has proportionately longer body and legs, a larger abdominal cavity, and more distended ribs. The bones are white, and the break joint is rough and dry. The outer covering of fat is generally well distributed, but it may be somewhat irregular. The flesh is firm and deep pink or light red in color.

Medium or Grade 3. These are fair grade animals which generally lack the plumpness found in better grade mutton. The shoulders are generally thin, and the neck and legs are inclined to be rangy. The exterior fat is localized over the shoulders, loins, ribs, and breast, and interior fat is scanty. The flesh is moderately fine grained, but usually rather moist. The color varies from deep pink to light red.

Common or Grade 4. This is the lowest grade mutton ordinarily offered for sale. The percentage of bone to flesh is very high and there is little fat generally. The flesh is moist, soft, and flabby, and usually dark red in color.

Cull or Grade 5. Mutton of this grade is all that the word "cull" implies. The bones are very prominent and the flesh is dark, coarse, soft, and watery. It is not ordinarily found in market.

More mature mutton is graded into the same six classes, allowances being made for maturity. In general, the differences are in the bones which are much harder and whiter, and in the flesh which is darker in color, ranging from light red to very dark in the poorer grades. The feet are removed at the ankle joint, and there is no break joint. The fat is generally more plentiful than in younger animals, and in the best grades is firm and somewhat brittle; its color ranges from creamy to yellowish.

HINTS ON USING MUTTON

The food value of mutton is generally like that of lamb, *which see.* However, mutton is not used in the United States to the extent that lamb is used, the belief being prevalent that it is strong in flavor and inclined to be tough. Yearling mutton is by no means tough, and when an Englishman or Australian praises mutton, it is

yearling mutton he is talking about. The
more mature the animal the progressively
stronger and tougher the flesh; but this is
true of other animals than sheep.

Mutton, like beef, is the better for being
aged before use; hanging for several weeks
will improve the flavor and tenderness. If
the mutton flavor is considered too strong,
it can be lessened by removing the outer
fat before cooking the meat. It also may be
removed by rubbing the meat with lemon
before broiling or roasting, or by putting
several slices of lemon in the water in which
mutton is to be boiled.

The cuts of mutton are generally the
same as those for lamb, *which see*. Because
of its greater maturity, mutton should be
cooked by boiling or braising, although
chops from yearling mutton can safely be
broiled. The so-called English mutton
chop, with the kidney in the center, is especially to be broiled.

Mutton is used in many dishes of near-
eastern origin, and the original shish kebab
used mutton. The English also use mutton
to a considerable extent and have many
characteristic recipes.

BOILED LEG OF MUTTON WITH CAPER SAUCE
(English Style)

Leg of mutton
1 bay leaf
1 medium-sized onion, sliced
2 slices lemon
1 tsp salt

Have the butcher trim and prepare the
meat for boiling. Place it in a large kettle
and add the bay leaf, onion, and lemon
slices. Cover with boiling water and boil
hard for 8 or 10 minutes. Skim the liquid.
Cover the kettle and let the meat simmer
until tender, allowing 30 minutes to the
pound. Add the salt when the meat is half
cooked. When tender, remove from the
liquid and keep warm. Skim the fat from
the liquid and strain the stock. Serve the
meat with

Caper Sauce
3 tbsp butter or margarine
3 tbsp flour
½ tsp salt
⅛ tsp pepper
1½ cups mutton stock
2 tbsp butter, additional

3 tbsp capers
1 tsp lemon juice

Melt the butter in a saucepan and gradually blend in the flour, salt, and pepper.
Add the hot mutton stock, stirring constantly, and bring to the boiling point.
Let boil for 5 minutes, or until thickened,
stirring all the time. Remove from the
stove, stir in the remaining butter, the
capers which have been drained, and the
lemon juice. Mix thoroughly and serve immediately.

BRAISED SHOULDER OF MUTTON

Shoulder of mutton
2 onions, sliced
2 carrots, sliced
2 cups chopped celery, stalks and leaves
1 tsp thyme, finely chopped
1 tsp parsley, finely chopped
12 peppercorns
2 bay leaves
3 whole cloves
1 blade of mace
Claret
Stock

Trim the shoulder of mutton of excess
fat and the fell, if any. Place it in a casserole
with a tightly fitting cover and add the
vegetables and seasonings. Cover with
equal parts of claret and stock. Bring the
mixture to a boil, then close the casserole
tightly and place in a moderate oven (350°
F.). Bake for 2½ or 3 hours, or until the
meat is tender. When done, transfer the
meat to a heated platter and keep warm.
Strain the sauce and taste for seasonings.
Reheat and pass with the meat.

CHINESE MUTTON STEW

2 lb leg of mutton, sliced
4 cups water
1 tbsp sherry
1 tbsp soy sauce
1 tbsp candied orange peel, chopped
1 small piece ginger root
1 tsp salt

Cut the meat into convenient pieces and
place in a saucepan with the water. Bring
to a boil and add the sherry, orange peel,
and ginger. Simmer, covered, very slowly
until the meat is tender. Add the soy sauce

and salt, and taste for seasonings. Remove the meat, and strain the sauce. Boil up again, and if desired, thicken the sauce with a very little corn starch. Serve very hot with rice or potatoes. (Serves 4)

ENGLISH MUTTON GRILL

1 mutton chop
1 lamb kidney
1 pork sausage
1 slice bacon
1 thick slice tomato

This is for one portion; multiply the quantities by as many as are to be served. Light the broiler and place the rack so that the surface of the food will be about 3 inches below the flame. Start the chops to broil first as they will take from 20 to 25 minutes to cook. When they are half done, start the kidneys which have been split. Dip the tomato slices in fine bread crumbs and grate a little onion juice over each slice. Add the sausages and the tomato slices to the grill. Baste the tomato occasionally with drippings from the pan. Add the bacon just at the end, since it takes only a minute or two. Turn all the ingredients once during the broiling. Season with salt and pepper and transfer immediately to a heated serving plate. Serve immediately.

MUTTON BROTH

1 lb lean raw mutton
3 cups cold water
1 cup diced vegetables (celery, carrot, onion, etc.)
Salt and pepper

Free the meat of all fat and cut into small pieces. Add the water and let stand in the refrigerator for several hours. Then transfer to a saucepan, add the vegetables, and simmer very slowly, using the same water, for at least 2 hours. A teaspoon of barley may also be added at the start of the cooking period. Strain, or not, as desired, cool the broth and skim off all the fat. Reheat and season to taste. Mutton broth may be reheated with a little barley.

MUTTON COLLOPS

6 slices roast or boiled mutton
1 tsp lemon juice
Salt and pepper
1 tsp each finely chopped parsley, chervil and tarragon
Few grains mace
2 finely chopped shallots
4 tbsp butter or margarine
2 tbsp flour
1½ cups broth

Trim the meat into rounds, rub with the lemon juice, season with salt and pepper, and dust with the herbs and shallots. Let stand one hour in a cool place. Heat the butter in a frying pan and fry the meat quickly in it, then arrange them on a hot platter. Add the flour to the remaining butter in the pan, and when well blended, pour in the broth. Bring to boiling point, stirring constantly, simmer three minutes, season and pour over the meat. (Serves 6)

SHOULDER OF MUTTON WITH TURNIPS

Rolled shoulder of mutton
1 clove
Stock or hot water
2 lb white turnips
Pinch of ground ginger
Salt and pepper
2 tbsp drippings

Season the meat with salt, pepper, and the ground ginger. Melt the drippings in a heavy kettle with a tightly fitting cover. Brown the meat and add stock or hot water barely to cover. Bring to a boil, cover the kettle, and simmer very gently until tender, allowing 15 minutes per pound. About 30 minutes before the meat is done, peel the turnips, and if they are large cut in several pieces. Add to the meat. Add the clove and salt and pepper. Cover and cook until meat and turnips are tender. Serve very hot. (Serves 6)

MYSOST CHEESE. A Scandinavian cheese made from whey. It is light brown in color and has a buttery consistency and a mild, sweetish taste. It is usually round in shape and is wrapped in tinfoil.

N

NAARTJE. South Africa's Tangerine (*which see*), and probably the country's best citrus fruit. It is eaten as a dessert fruit, in fruit salads, as a preserve, and crystallized (i.e. coated with sugar).

NAGELKAZEN (Friesche Cheese). This cheese is made from skimmed milk mixed with cloves and cumin seed. It is the trade name of a Holland species. *See also* CHEESE.

NAMAYCUSH. Indian name for the Great American Trout. *See also* FISH.

NANTAIS. An all-the-year round French cheese manufactured in Brittany, also known as FROMAGE DU CURE. *See also* CHEESE.

NANTZ. A name commonly used in England during the 18th century for French brandy, because during that period large quantities of brandy were shipped from the port of Nantes on the River Loire.

NAPAREULI. A Caucasian (USSR) white wine. *See also* WINE.

NAPOLEON BRANDY. A greatly abused name. The genuine stock was placed in the wood in the time of Napoleon the First, and consequently is more than 100 years old. Any other brandy sold under this name is a misnomer. Very few bottles, if any, are to be found in this country. *See also* BRANDY.

NAPOLEON. As applied to pastry, a French pastry made with puff paste and filled with pastry cream.

NAPOLEON

Double the amount of the recipe for Puff Paste (*which see*). Divide in thirds and roll each third as thin as possible and of equal size. Prick each sheet with a fork and bake in a hot oven (450° F.) until delicately browned. When cool, put together as three layers, using the following cream filling.

⅞ cup sugar
⅓ cup cake flour
⅓ tsp salt
2 eggs, or 4 egg yolks
2 cups scalded milk
1 tsp vanilla

Combine the dry ingredients, add the eggs slightly beaten, also the scalded milk. Cook 15 minutes in a double boiler, stirring constantly until thickened, stirring occasionally afterwards. Cool and flavor.

For the frosting, moisten confectioners' sugar with a very little boiling water to make it of spreading consistency. Flavor with vanilla and spread over the top layer of the Napoleon. Mark the frosting to cut the Napoleons into slices 2½ by 4¼ inches. Cut with a very sharp knife.

Sometimes Napoleons are sprinkled with powdered sugar instead of being frosted. Again the puff paste layers may be put together with sweetened and flavored whipped cream. The important thing about Napoleons is the pastry which must be light and tender.

NASCOL. One of Sardinia's best wines. *See also* WINE.

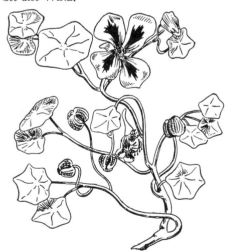

NASTURTIUM

NASTURTIUM. The red, orange, and yellow flowers of the Dwarf Nasturtium form an attractive, brightly colored garden border; its climbing cousin decorates many a trellis or fence in the Western Hemisphere and in England. However, from the gourmet's point of view, the most important quality of the Nasturtium lies in the unusual flavor of the leaves when used as a garnish or as a salad. The flowers have a distinctly spicy flavor. They are tasty when served between thin slices of buttered bread as part of a light lunch in summer or as snacks between meals.

In England the plant is called Indiancress. Its immature fruits are pickled and sold under that name as a substitute for CAPERS, *which see*.

NASTURTIUM SALAD. Combine a quantity of nasturtium leaves with finely shredded lettuce, add 2 quartered, hard-cooked eggs and dress with oil, vinegar, salt, and pepper. Garnish with nasturtium flowers.

NATURE, NATUR. French and German words, respectively, descriptive of unsweetened wine. *See also* WINE.

NAVEL ORANGE. A type of seedless orange characterized by a navel-like pit at its apex and grown extensively in California. *See also* ORANGE.

NAVY BEAN. The standard baked bean (*which see*). Any small or medium sized bean is included in this type. *See also* BEAN.

NEBBIOLO. A black grape grown in northern Italy from which some of the country's best red wine is made. *See also* WINE.

NECTAR. In classic mythology, the wine of the gods. The name is also given to the honey of plants and any delicious beverage.

NECTARINE

NECTARINE. A variety of peach (*which see*) having a smooth, waxy skin, and a firm aromatic pulp. Peaches sometimes grow from nectarine seeds and nectarines from peach seeds. In America, they are grown mainly in California and Oregon, and are chiefly canned or dried, due to their perishability.

They are sold by the pound, dozen or six-pound basket, and are in season from May to October. Nectarines of good quality are firm, free from cuts, and decayed spots. Underripe fruit can be ripened in a warm room, although green fruit will shrivel rather than ripen Mature fruit should be covered and stored in the refrigerator.

NEEDLEFISH. A fish with long, narrow jaws and an elongate, pikel ke body; related to the gar, *which see*. *See also* FISH.

NELSON'S BLOOD. A slang expression referring to the rum served as a daily ration on vessels of the British Navy.

Also, a drink made by mixing one jigger of a dark, heavy bodied 190 proof rum (similar to British Naval Rum) in a highball glass (*see* GLASSWARE) with ice and ginger ale.

NEMES KADARKA. One of Hungary's best red wines. *See also* WINE.

NESSEL CHEESE. A round, very thin, soft-cured, rennet cheese made from the whole milk of cows. It is an English product.

NESSELRODE PUDDING. A frozen dessert, created by Count Nesselrode, Chamberlain at the court of Belgium during the reign of King Leopold the First. This dessert is very rich and is most appropriate for an adult party. Since it is based on a custard, it should be considered an integral part of the meal and not merely a light, terminating touch. The following is a modernized version of the original recipe:

3 cups milk
1½ cups sugar
5 egg yolks
½ tsp salt
2 cups light cream or 1 cup heavy cream and 1 cup evaporated milk
¼ cup pineapple juice, fresh or canned
1½ cups boiled chestnuts
½ cup assorted candied fruit
½ cup seedless raisins
8 or 10 chestnuts, additional
Whipped cream for garnishing

Make a boiled custard (*which see*) with the milk, sugar, egg yolks and salt. While still hot, strain through a fine sieve. Add the light cream or the heavy cream and evaporated milk (undiluted); the pineapple juice and the chestnuts which have been forced through a sieve. Freeze. If using a hand freezer use the proportions of 3 parts of ice to 1 part of rock salt and freeze solid. With automatic refrigeration proceed as usual, that is, freeze the mixture to a mush, turn out into a bowl, beat vigorously, then return to the tray and complete the freezing which will take at least 2½ hours.

Now line a 2-quart melon mold with part of the frozen mixture. To the remainder add the candied fruit, cut small; the raisins previously soaked in boiling water until plump then thoroughly drained, also the 8 or 10 chestnuts prepared as directed below.

Fill the mold to the very top with this mixture, cover with a buttered paper, adjust the cover and seal with a strip of adhesive tape or by smearing butter around the rim. Bury the mold in equal parts of ice and salt for 3½ to 4 hours. Drain off the salt water from time to time before it reaches the top of the mold. If using automatic refrigeration, place the sealed mold in the freezing chamber for at least 7 hours or even overnight.

To serve, unmold onto a chilled platter, first dipping the mold quickly in and out of hot water. Garnish with unsweetened, unflavored whipped cream forced through a pastry bag.

To prepare the chestnuts, cut a ½-inch gash in the flat side of each. Place them in a heavy pan, adding ½ teaspoon of butter, oil or other fat for each cup of nuts. Shake over the fire for 5 minues, then set in a slow oven (275° F.) for 5 minutes. Remove from the oven and strip off the shells and inner skins with a sharp knife. Now cover the shelled chestnuts with slightly salted water, and cook over a gentle flame for about 20 minutes, more or less, according to the size of the nuts. Drain, then soak for 3 hours in Maraschino liqueur, and break into pieces.

Nesselrode pudding as made in the United States is a totally different version from that given above.

AMERICAN NESSELRODE PUDDING

2 tbsp gelatin
1 cup cold water
2 cups milk

5 eggs
¾ cup sugar
¼ lb toasted, blanched almonds, coarsely chopped
1 doz macaroons, crumbled
¼ tsp salt
2 tbsp brandy
½ tsp vanilla

Soften the gelatin in the cold water. Scald the milk, then pour it over the egg yolks and sugar beaten together until very light. Return to the fire (double boiler) and cook to a custard, stirring constantly. Add the softened gelatin, cool, then stir in the almonds, macaroons and salt. When almost at the setting point, fold in the egg whites, stiffly beaten and flavored with the brandy and vanilla. Freeze.

NETTY GEM MELON. A round melon grown all over the United States. It has a grayish rind and pink or green flesh. *See also* MELON.

NEUFCHATEL CHEESE. A soft, rennet cheese originally from Normandy, France, made from whole or skimmed milk. It is made in the same manner as Cream cheese. The standard package is round, wrapped in tinfoil, and weighs 2½ or 3 ounces. The dimensions of the standard package are 1½ by 2½ inches. *Bondon, Malakoff, Petit Carre*, and *Petit Suisse* are essentially the same but have different shapes.

NEUSOHL CHEESE. A rennet cheese made from sheep's milk, or a mixture of sheep's and goat's milk. It is made in the Carpathian Mountains, and is also called Brinsen or Brinza. *See also* CHEESE.

NEW ENGLAND CODFISH CAKES. Codfish and potato balls flattened and fried or sautéed. Almost any other fish may be substituted. *See* FISH CAKES.

NEW ENGLAND FISH BALLS. Small balls made up of fish stock, potatoes, egg and flavoring, and cooked in hot fat. *See* FISH BALLS.

NEW YORK SOUR. A variation of the Whisky Sour. *See under* SOUR.

NEW ENGLAND SPINACH. A tender annual vegetable of the southern hemisphere, now cultivated in the United States. It resembles ordinary spinach in appearance and flavor, but has several advantages for the gardener. It thrives in hot weather which spinach cannot stand, and it bears repeated cutting through the summer. Because its growth is more open than spinach, it is not so likely to be sandy. Its preparation is identical with that of spinach, *which see*.

NEW ZEALAND SPINACH

NEWBERG. Certain dishes made in Newburg fashion, with Newburg sauce (*which see*).

NEWBURG SAUCE. A sauce made of cream, egg yolks, wine, brandy, and butter. It is used with almost any kind of reheated food, but was especially conceived by Pascal, the chef of the old Delmonico's Restaurant, as a tasty adjunct to lobster.

NEWBURG SAUCE

1 boiled lobster, weighing 2 lb
6 tbsp sweet butter
3 tbsp oil
Salt and cayenne pepper
2 tbsp brandy
¾ cup Madeira or sherry wine
¾ cup heavy cream
½ cup fish stock
2 egg yolks

Split the lobster and remove the coral and liver. Remove the meat and cut into suitable pieces. Pound the coral and liver with 3 tablespoons of the butter and set aside. Heat the rest of the butter with the oil in a skillet. Season the pieces of lobster with salt and cayenne pepper and saute in the oil. When the lobster is cooked, drain out the oil. Pour in the brandy and wine, and turn the flame slightly higher. Cook, stirring occasionally, until the liquid is re-

duced to ⅔ its volume. Scald the cream and add it to the lobster, and add the fish stock. Cover and simmer very gently for 25 minutes, stirring occasionally. Just before ready to serve, stir in the egg yolks, one at a time, stirring well after each addition. Add the butter mixed with the coral and heat thorough y, adding additional seasoning if necessary. Never allow the sauce to boil after the egg yolks are added.

SHORT-CUT NEWBURG SAUCE

1 cup medium white sauce
½ cup heavy cream
4 egg yolks
Salt and pepper
2 tbsp wine

Have the white sauce hot in the upper part of a double boiler. Scald and add the cream, then the egg yolks one at a time, beating well after each addition. Season with salt and white pepper and add the wine immediately before serving. Do not allow the sauce to boil after adding the egg yolks.

NICKEL SILVER. *See* SILVERWARE.

NIEHEIM CHEESE. A sour milk cheese, made in Germany. *See also* CHEESE.

NIERDERUNGSKASE. A hard, rennet cheese made from cow's milk. Also known as ELBING and WERDERKASE (*which see*).

NIGHTSHADE. The name is given to a number of plants belonging to the same family, among them the deadly nightshade, or belladonna, which is a deadly poison. Some of the nightshades are harmless, although cases have been recorded of children being made ill by eating the berries. In some parts of the world the green leaves are used like spinach.

NIOLO. A French cheese manufactured in Corsica from October through May. *See also* CHEESE.

NIP. A quarter bottle. *See also* WEIGHTS AND MEASURES.

NIPPLEWORT. A weed of the dandelion order which can be used n salads, or cooked as a vegetable preferably combined with a less bitter and leafier one such as spinach or endive.

NOEL RED CLARET PUNCH. A hot wine punch in which the final mixing is done by igniting the ingredients with the bowl placed on the table and the lights extinguished. Not only a delicious beverage, it also provides a pleasant, warming spectacle well suited to the Noel season. *See also* PUNCH.

NOEKKELOST. A hard, flat pressed, all-the-year round Norwegian cheese similar in quality to rich DUTCH GOUDA, *which see. See also* CHEESE.

NOGG. Short name for Eggnog, *which see.*

NOGGIN. An English measure equivalent to a pint. *See also* WEIGHTS AND MEASURES.

NOISETTES. Tiny, choice pieces of lean meat, usually the eyes of chops.

NONNATS. French name for Whitebait (*which see*).

NOODLES. A kind of dried paste (*which see*) cut in long, narrow strips, and sold packaged like macaroni or spaghetti.

BAKED NOODLES WITH CHEESE

1½ cups thin white sauce
2 eggs
½ tsp onion juice
Dash of salt
1¼ cups grated cheese
¼ lb medium noodles, cooked
¼ cup buttered crumbs

Pour the hot white sauce slowly over the beaten egg yolks, stirring while pouring. Add the onion juice, salt, and 1 cup of the cheese and fold in gently the beaten egg whites. Combine the noodles and sauce, turn into a buttered baking dish and top with the crumbs blended with the remaining cheese. Bake in a moderate oven (350° F.) about ½ hour, or until the sauce bubbles and the crumbs and cheese topping brown delicately. (Serves 6)

The cheese may be a sharp cheddar, store cheese, or one of the packaged cheeses of mild flavor.

DEVILED CREAMED NOODLES

1 or 2 slices onion, minced
3 tbsp fat
3 tbsp flour
2½ cups milk
2¾ oz (small can) deviled ham or potted meat
½ lb noodles, cooked
3 tbsp grated cheese

Cook the onion in the fat just until it begins to turn color. Stir in the flour, then add the milk and cook, stirring constantly until thickened. Now add the deviled ham or potted meat, with salt and pepper if needed. Arrange the noodles in a baking dish, pour the sauce over, sprinkle with the cheese and bake in a moderate oven (350° F.) 20 to 25 minutes. (Serves 6)

EGG NOODLES

1 egg
½ egg shell cold water
½ tsp salt
Flour (about 1 cup)

Break the egg into a cup, add the half egg shell of water and the salt and mix lightly. Sift ⅔ of the flour into a bowl, make a hollow in the center and pour in the egg mixture. Stir, with a knife, in one direction, adding flour until the dough is so stiff that stirring is difficult. Turn onto a floured board and knead until smooth and elastic. Then roll out as thin as possible, turning the dough about to prevent its sticking to the board. Flour the board lightly and let the dough stand ½ hour to dry. If a cutter is available, run it evenly across the dough, and shake the noodle lengths apart. If no cutter is at hand, cut the dough into halves, roll each like a jelly roll, then slice thin or wide as desired. Shake the slices apart. Let the noodles dry.

To cook drop the noodles into boiling soup or stew, and boil for 20 minutes. Or drop them, a few at a time, into hot fat and quickly fry them until brown and crisp, then drain on soft crumpled paper. Noodles are very good in a soup made from turkey or chicken carcass.

FRIED NOODLES

Fry uncooked noodles in deep hot fat (375° F.) until golden brown. Drain on soft crumpled paper and sprinkle with salt.

MOLDED NOODLES WITH CREAMED EGGS

1 package broad noodles
Boiling salted water
2 cups white sauce
1 tsp onion juice
1 tbsp minced parsley
4 to 6 hard-cooked eggs

Cook the noodles until just tender in boiling salted water. Drain, turn into the well greased top of the double boiler, and let stand over hot water for ½ hour. Then unmold onto a hot platter, pour the white sauce (o which the onion juice and parsley have been added) around the noodles, and arrange the eggs, halved or quartered, in the sauce. (Serves 6)

NOODLES WITH MEAT SAUCE

½ lb lean round steak
3 tbsp olive oil
1 small onion, minced
1 clove garlic, minced
¼ lb mushrooms, sliced
2 tbsp flour
1½ cups strong broth
2 tbsp dry white wine
1 tsp tomato paste
½ bay leaf
¼ tsp thyme
1 tsp chopped parsley
Salt and pepper
½ lb thin noodles
Parmesan cheese

Pass the meat through the food chopper or have this done by the butcher. Heat the oil in a frying pan, and brown in it the meat, onion, garlic, and mushrooms. Add the flour, mix thoroughly, then pour in the broth, wine and tomato paste, with the herbs and seasonings. Simmer ½ hour, combine with the noodles which have been cooked until tender in boiling salted water and drained. Turn onto a hot platter and serve with grated Parmesan cheese.

NOSTRALE CHEESE. A hard, rennet, Italian cheese made from cow's milk. It is also known as Raschera. *See also* CHEESE.

NOTRUSCHKI CHEESE. Another name for TWOROG, a sour milk cheese, made in Russia. *See also* CHEESE.

NOUGAT. A confection wh:ch originated in the towns of Nougat and Monte-limar, France, composed of almonds, pistachio nuts, sugar and honey.

FRENCH CHOCOLATE NOUGATINETTES

1 tbsp honey
1 cup powdered sugar
1 cup coarsely chopped blanched almonds
⅛ tsp salt
½ tsp vanilla
½ tsp almond extract
Melted dipping chocolate

Warm the honey in a heavy, shallow pan, add the sugar and stir constantly until it is melted. Now add the almonds over wh:ch the salt has been sprinkled and continue stirring over a very gentle heat until the mixture turns to a delicate light brownish color. Stir in the flavorings and drop small portions from the tip of a teaspoon onto a buttered slab or platter and when cold dip in melted chocolate.

NUBBIN. A small or imperfect ear of maize (corn).

NUN'S TOAST. Pan fried bread. *See* FRENCH TOAST.

NUTS. Too little thought is given to nuts as a food, except as they terminate a "soup to nuts" meal. It is as absurd to end a hearty meal with nuts, which are rich in fat and building elements, as it would be to end the meal with a dessert of fat beefsteak. Eating nuts in this manner, as well as eating them late at night or when not needed for their nutriment, has given nuts an undeserved reputation for causing indigestion.

Nuts contain protein, with some starch, more or less fat, and very little water. From 55 to 65 percent of the common nuts is shell. With the exception of the coconut, chestnut, almond, and so-called English walnut, the varieties eaten in this country furnish but little nutriment. Their chief value is to stimulate the appetite and afford variety in the diet. Excepting chestnuts and coconuts, they are usually eaten raw, as dessert, but they are much used in confectionery as well as in certain hot dishes.

Nuts, especially English walnuts, coconuts, hickory, pecan, and Brazil nuts, all contain a good deal of vegetable oil. The oil of nuts which have been kept too long sometimes becomes rancid and unwholesome. Coconut oil is principally used in Oriental countries. Peanut oil is used to some extent in this country, like cottonseed oil, mainly to replace olive oil, which is much more expensive.

Nutritive Value. Nuts are very concentrated in nutritive value, one pound equaling about two and one half pounds of beefsteak, and should be eaten in mall quantities. Two ounces of nut meats are sufficient for one meal. They should be eaten

only as a part of a meal, and can be substituted for meat. Nuts are used in about
the same combinations as meat with other
foods, that is, they may be eaten with fresh
or dried fruit and raw or cooked vegetables.
If the teeth are defective, nuts should be
ground in a handmill or food chopper.
Most of the nut foods on the market are
largely, sometimes entirely, made of peanut , because peanuts cost considerably less
than true nuts. (Peanuts are the seeds of an
herb of the family *Leguminosae*, and they
mature underground.)

Nuts and nut produc's are steadily becoming more abundant in the markets of
the United States. Four kinds of nuts, including the peanut, are produced on a
commercially impo tant scale in this country. Arranged in the order of the quantity
produced, they are the peanut, Persian
(English) walnut, pecan, and almond.
However, the production of the filbert is
increasing, and many other nuts that grow
wild or in small orchards are used as food.
Other nuts, imported into this country in
considerable quantities, are the Brazil nut
from South America, the cashew from India, and the chestnut, mainly from southern Europe.

Purchasing and Storage. Nuts are somewhat
cheaper and less liable to contamination
when purchased in the shell, but the buying of shelled nuts saves considerable time,
labor, and storage space. When the weight
of the shell and the labor involved in c ack-
ing are considered, nuts purchased as kernels are probably cheaper per unit than
are the same nuts purchased in the shell.
Some nuts with heavy shells are generally
sold shelled.

Hints on Using Nuts

To Salt Almonds or Other Nuts. There are
three effective methods of salting nuts.

1. Place nuts in a baking pan, allowing
one teaspoon of butter or salad oil for each
cup of nuts. Bake in a moderate oven (350°
F.), stirring occasionally, until brown—
about five to ten minutes. Brazil nuts do
not need butter or oil. Sprinkle with salt.

2. Allow one pint of oil per pound of
nuts. Heat the oil to 360 degrees in a deep
frying pan and cook the nuts in this until
delicate brown Drain on absorbent paper
and sprinkle with salt.

3. Allow one egg white for each half
pound of shelled nuts. Beat the egg whites

slightly, shake the nuts in it, and place on
a baking sheet. Bake in a moderate oven
(350° F.) 15 minutes, or until brown, stirring occasionally. Sprinkle with salt.

To chop nuts: Place nuts in wooden bowl
and chop with vegetable-chopping knife.

To grind nuts: Use regular vegetable
grater, meat chopper, or special nut meat
chopper.

To slice nuts: A sharp knife is all that is
needed.

To shred nuts: A vegetable shredding
knife is best, but any sharp knife will do the
work.

To toast chopped nuts: Chopped nuts to be
toasted should be chopped medium fine
rather than ground. Spread the chopped
nuts over the bottom of a baking sheet and
set in a moderate oven (350° F.), stirring
frequently, until the nuts are golden brown.
Remove at once and transfer them to a
cold, dry baking sheet. Any kind of nut
may be prepared in this way.

To blanch nuts: Essentially, blanching is
the process of removing the skins of nuts by
placing them in boiling water. The length
of time required to blanch different kinds
of nuts varies, and certain thin-skinned
varieties, as the English walnut, the peanut, and the pecan, can be used without
blanching.

Nuts in Salad, Sandwich Fillings and Ice Cream

Nuts add to the appearance, flavor, and
food value of salads. Roasted peanuts give
an especially good flavor to chopped
vegetable and pickle salads. Pecans and
blanched almonds are good in meat salads.
Chopped pistachios, because of their green
color, are especially attractive; and
blanched nuts, such as almonds, are also
decorative. Cheese balls, or pieces of bananas, covered with mayonnaise, may be
rolled in finely chopped nuts. Most nuts
are good with fruit salads or in whipped-
cream dressing served with fruit salad.
Some nuts, such as hickory, black walnuts,
and Persian (English) walnuts, if used in a
salad, should be added just before serving,
otherwise they may discolor and darken
the whole mixture.

Nuts can be used with cheese, dried
fruit, and other foods for sandwich fillings
in innumerable varieties. The following are
suggestive merely of the many possible
combinations:

a Chopped nuts, dates (or other dried fruits) with lemon juice to season and moisten.

b Chopped nuts, honey and butter, with chopped whole orange if desired.

c Nuts and jelly or jam.

d Almond and chicken, tuna, or crab meat.

e Cream cheese and peanuts or pecans.

f Chopped carrots, cabbage, apples, or combinations of these with chopped peanuts or pecans.

g Chopped olives and nuts.

h Chopped ham and Persian (English) walnuts.

Nuts with pronounced flavor, such as black walnuts and pistachios, or nuts especially prepared, such as butter pecan, peanut brittle, and burnt almond, give a delicious flavor to ice cream. Add about one-half cup of nuts to one quart of ice-cream.

NUT BREAD

3 tsp baking powder
1 tsp soda
1 tsp cinnamon
1½ tsp salt
3 cups whole wheat flour
⅓ cup brown sugar
½ cup dark molasses
1 cup milk
½ cup water
1 cup broken walnut meats
2 tbsp melted butter or shortening

Mix the dry ingredients—baking powder, soda, salt, cinnamon, brown sugar, and flour—and combine with the molasses, milk and water. Blend thoroughly. Add the nuts and melted butter to the ingredients and beat well. Pour the mixture into one large (or two small) bread pans which have been thoroughly greased. Let stand at room temperature for 20 minutes; then bake in a slow oven (300°–325° F.) until the bread is brown and shrinks slightly from the sides of the pan. If baked in one pan the baking will take 1 hour; if baked in two pans, 40 to 50 minutes. Turn onto a rack and as soon as it is cool enough to handle, remove the paper.

Buttered nut bread fingers spread with cream cheese are a perfect teatime refreshment.

Or nut bread may be spread with butter creamed with honey for a tea sandwich.

NUT BRITTLE

2 cups nuts
2 cups sugar
¼ tsp salt
¼ tsp baking soda
1 tsp vanilla

Heat the sugar gradually in a heavy frying pan, stirring constantly with the bowl of the spoon until a golden sirup is formed. Remove from the fire and stir in quickly the salt, soda and vanilla. Pour the sirup over a layer of nuts in a greased pan and when cold, break into small pieces.

NUT DATE LOAF

3 cups sifted all-purpose flour
3 tsp baking powder
1 tsp salt
½ cup brown sugar
1 cup finely cut dates
½ cup broken walnut meats
1 egg, well beaten
1 cup milk
4 tbsp melted butter or shortening

Sift flour, baking powder and salt together and add the sugar, dates and nuts. Mix all together and add the combined egg, milk, melted butter or shortening. Stir the mixture enough to blend all ingredients. Turn into a greased loaf pan and bake in a moderately hot oven (350°–375° F.) about 1 hour. Remove from the oven and let stand for 5 minutes then turn out of pan onto a rack and when cold, store in a covered container.

This makes a delicious sandwich when spread with cream cheese.

NUT MOLASSES SQUARES

2 tbsp butter
1 cup molasses
⅓ cup sugar
½ cup chopped nuts, any kind
Salt

Melt the butter in a saucepan, add the molasses and sugar and cook to the medium crack stage (270° F.), stirring frequently. Add the nuts, lightly sprinkled with salt, turn into a buttered pan and when cool, mark into squares or break into pieces.

NUT ORANGE BREAD

1 cup pecans, or hickory nuts, chopped
½ cup orange marmalade
2½ cups sifted all-purpose flour
1 tbsp baking powder
1¼ tsp salt
1 cup milk
2 eggs, beaten
2 tbsp melted butter or shortening

Sift the dry ingredients and add the nuts. Add the milk and eggs, stir them until just moistened. Stir in the orange marmalade and the selected shortening, and pou this into a well-greased bread pan. Bake in a moderate oven (350° F.) for about 1 hour.

NUT PATTIES

1 cup chopped nuts, any kind
1 egg, well beaten
½ cup evaporated milk
1 tsp salt
¼ tsp pepper
3 cups dry bread crumbs

Combine the nuts, egg, milk, seasonings and 2 cups of the crumbs. Let stand ½ hour that the crumbs may absorb the milk, then shape into patties, roll in the remaining crumbs and sauté or fry golden brown in deep hot fat (390° F.). Drain on soft crumpled paper. Serve with tomato sauce or cheese sauce. (Makes 8 patties about 2 inches in diameter.)

NUT PRALINES

1 cup brown sugar, packed
2 cups granulated sugar
3 tbsp corn sirup
¾ cup evaporated milk
½ cup water
2 tsp mapleine
1 cup pecans, chopped
½ cup pecans, halved

Combine and cook all of the above ingredients, except the nuts, to the softball stage (236° F.) and allow to cool. Add the chopped nuts and beat until the mixture is soft and creamy. With a spoon, drop onto a buttered cooking sheet so as to form 4-inch diameter patties. Arrange the pecan halves on top of each pattie and press in place. The pralines should harden at once,

and be wrapped in waxed paper immediately. Makes about 12.

NUT AND RICE LOAF

1 egg
½ cup milk
1 cup soft bread crumbs
½ cup chili sauce
1½ cups cooked rice
1 cup chopped nuts
½ tsp sage
1 tsp salt
⅛ tsp pepper
2 cups tomato sauce

Beat the egg and combine with all ingredients except the tomato sauce. Blend thoroughly, pack in a well greased loaf pan and bake in a moderately hot oven (375° F.) 45 minutes. Unmold and serve with tomato sauce. (Serves 6)

NUT SAUSAGE

1 cup soft bread crumbs
1 tbsp butter
1 cup cooked rice
2 tsp sage
½ tsp paprika
1½ cups chopped nuts, any kind
2 eggs, beaten
½ tsp salt
¼ tsp celery seed
1 tsp minced onion

Combine all ingredients thoroughly. Shape as sausages and sauté golden brown in a little hot fat. Garnish with crisp bacon and, if desired, serve with a white sauce, tomato sauce or cheese sauce (Serves 6 to 8)

NUT STUFFING
(For Turkey)

2 minced onions
½ cup fat
Salt and pepper
Sage or other herbs
8 cups soft bread crumbs
2 cups sliced Brazil nuts

Cook the onions for 2 minutes in the fat. Combine with the seasonings, crumbs, and nuts. Use dry, or if a moist stuffing is desired, add water or stock. See STUFFING.

**BLACK WALNUT OR BUTTERNUT
MOLASSES TAFFY**

1½ cups sugar
½ cup molasses
1½ cups water
2 tbsp vinegar
½ tsp cream of tartar
4 tbsp butter
⅛ tsp salt
¼ tsp baking soda

Cook the sugar, molasses, water, vinegar and cream of tartar together to the medium crack stage (270° F.). Add the butter, salt and soda, stir gently to thoroughly blend, then pour onto a greased platter or slab. When cool enough to handle pull until light in color (first greasing the fingers). Add the nuts and work them into the mass by kneading. Pull into strips of desired thickness and cut into inch lengths with buttered scissors.

DIPPED NUTS

Melt fondant (*which see* under CANDY) over hot water, turning it from time to time, but avoiding stirring. When the whole mass has become mobile but still thick, remove from the hot water and start dipping. Hold each nut separately with tweezers or a wire dipping fork, and dip into the fondant. Drain, and place on waxed paper. If the fondan becomes too thick, it may be reheated and a few drops of water or glycerin added.

The fondant-covered nuts, as well as plain nuts, may be coated with chocolate in the following manner:

Break dipping chocolate in small pieces, and place in a shallow dish over hot water. As soon as the chocolate begins to soften, remove it from the hot water, and stir until it is all melted. Dip the candies or nuts into the chocolate, and place them on waxed paper to dry.

FILLED PECANS OR WALNUTS

Use perfect, unbroken halves of large nuts. Spread them with one of the following pastes, or use a concoction of your own. Then press the halves together sandwich-fashion. Chill before serving.

Roquefort spread. Work Roquefort cheese into a smooth paste, and moisten it with a

few drops of lemon juice or cream.

Blended-cheese spread. Work ¼ cup of blended Cheddar cheese and 1 tab'espoon of pimiento cheese spread into a smooth paste. Stir in 1 tablespoon of chopped green olives.

GLACE NUTS

2 cups sugar
¼ tsp cream of tartar
1 cup hot water
⅛ tsp salt
1½ cups perfect nut meats

Combine the sugar, cream of tartar, hot water, and salt in a small saucepan and place over a hot fire. Stir until the sugar is dissolved, then cook to the hard crack stage (290° F.). Remove from the fire at once, and place in a pan of hot water while dipping the nuts. Hold these separately with tweezers or on a wire dipping fork, and dip into the sirup. Place on waxed paper or a greased slab to dry. Reheat the sirup carefully if it becomes too thick.

SUGARED NUTS

1½ cups sugar
¼ cup honey
½ cup water
3 cups halved walnuts or Brazil nuts
½ tsp vanilla

Combine the sugar, honey, and water in a saucepan, and cook to the firm ball stage (242° F.). Remove from the fire, add the nuts and vanilla, and stir until the sirup has become creamy and thick. Turn onto waxed paper to harden, then break into individual pieces. A little grated orange rind or cinnamon may be added to the sirup for variety of flavor.

VEGETABLE NUT LOAF I

3 tbsp melted butter or substitute
1¾ cups soft bread crumbs
1 cup chopped celery, cooked 10 minutes
1 cup diced cooked carrots
1¼ tsp salt
½ cup chopped nuts, any kind
1 cup cooked or canned peas or string beans
4 tbsp liquid from vegetables

2 eggs, well beaten
⅛ tsp pepper
1½ tsp Worcestershire or similar sauce
¼ cup buttered crumbs

Combine all ingredients except the buttered crumbs. After blending, thoroughly pack into a greased loaf pan (8x4x2 inches). Top with the buttered crumbs and press a few perfect walnut halves into the top of the loaf. Bake in a moderately hot oven (375°–400° F.) about 45 minutes. Unmold and garnish with parsley and orange slices. (Serves 6)

VEGETABLE NUT LOAF II

1 cup cooked tomatoes
1 cup cooked peas
1 cup cooked carrots, diced
½ cup nut meats, chopped
1 tsp salt
3 tbsp minced onion
1 cup soft bread crumbs
½ cup milk
2 eggs, beaten
1 tbsp melted butter
⅛ tsp pepper

Combine and thoroughly mix all of the above ingredients. Turn into a buttered loaf pan (8x4x2 inches). If desired, top with additional nut meats, halved. Bake in a moderate oven (350° F.) for 60 minutes. (Serves 8)

NUT BRITTLE TAPIOCA CREAM. See TAPIOCA.

NUT BUTTER. The making of nut butters is not a difficult process. At present peanuts and almonds are chiefly used for this purpose, but Brazil nuts, pignolias, filberts and walnuts also make fine butters, although some of these nuts cannot easily be blanched. The blanching of peanuts and almonds is now done on a large scale by special machinery, and the blanched nuts can be procured in nearly all the larger cities. The nuts should be broken into small pieces by running them through a food chopper, after which they are put into a moderately hot oven (325°–350° F.) for a few minutes to dry and crisp them before they are run through the tightly adjusted nut mill or food chopper. Care should be taken not to have the nuts too brown; they should merely be crisped. In this condition they make smooth, palatable nut butters.

If the nuts are too moist, they will form a stiff paste and clog the mill or food chopper.

NUT BUTTER SAUCE. See BUTTER SAUCES.

NUTCRACKER. A nutcracker is an instrument designed to open nuts by bursting their shells through applied pressure. While there are many elaborate variations, in its basic form, the nutcracker consists of a pair of levers, hinged together at one end to form a fulcrum. The nut is placed between the levers, as close to the fulcrum as possible, the inside of the levers being serrated to hold the nut which is cracked by squeezing the levers together. Nutcrackers are usually made of metal, though some are made of hardwood.

A *pick* (a small metal point) is used to separate the nut meat from the broken shell. Nutcrackers and picks are also used to remove the meat from lobster claws. *See also* KITCHEN EQUIPMENT and NUTS.

NUT PASTRY. In any recipe for plain piecrust, substitute finely ground pecans for ½ the shortening. Mix and bake in the usual way. This makes a very good crust for a cream filling. If desired, chopped nuts may be sprinkled over a meringue just before serving.

NUTMEG. The nutmeg is the fruit of a species of evergreen tree that is usually cultivated in the Molucca Islands. It is the only single fruit yielding two spices. On ripening, the fruit husk splits to expose a lacy red aril that is commercially known as mace. This surrounds the hard inner shell that encloses the nutmeg proper. The ripe fleshy fruit is removed before these spices are prepared for market. The MACE (*which see*) is dried in the sun. The nutmeg pits are dried over slow fires for several weeks until the kernels rattle within their shells, the shells are cracked, and the kernels are removed and assorted according to size. The larger ones are sold whole and the smaller ones are ground.

Today most nutmeg is sold in ground form. Nutmeg's greatest use is in confections, baked products, and applesauce. It is excellent with rice puddings. Other puddings can be made with maple sugar instead of sugar and then flavored with nutmeg. It is very popular with desserts—custards, fruits, fruit pies, pumpkin pie, baked apples, bananas with cream, etc. It enhances the flavor of sauces for seafood cocktails, and it is also used to flavor fish, meats, poultry, game, cauliflower, cab-

NUTMEG

bage, spinach, sweet potato dishes, consomme, and cream soups. A sprinkling of nutmeg adds the finishing touch to such

beverages as milk punches, and egg nogs, and flips.

NUTMEG SAUCE. A dessert sauce.

NUTMEG SAUCE

½ cup sugar
1 tbsp cornstarch
Pinch of salt
1 cup boiling water
1 tbsp butter
¼ tsp grated nutmeg

Combine sugar, cornstarch and salt. Gradually pour the boiling water over them and cook over direct heat, stirring constantly, until boiling, then continue the cooking about 5 minutes longer. Remove from the heat and add the butter and nutmeg.

NUWARA EILYAS. One of the outstanding Black teas of Ceylon, *which see.*

O

OATMEAL. Oatmeal is a cereal made from hulled oats and should contain not more than 12 percent of moisture. The grains are softened by steaming, after which they are flattened between steel rollers to make rolled oats. Steaming and drying processes render the starch in the grains more soluble. Quick-cooking rolled oats are partially cooked by a greater application of heat and steam in the process of manufacture. *See also* CEREAL.

OATMEAL BREAD

½ lb all-purpose flour
½ lb oatmeal
1 tsp salt
1 tsp baking soda
1 tsp cream of tartar
1 cup buttermilk

Soak the oatmeal in the buttermilk for 2 hours, then add the flour mixed with the other dry ingredients. Knead lightly, form into a loaf, and bake in a hot oven (400° F.) for 30 to 40 minutes.

OATMEAL COOKIES

2 cups all-purpose flour
¼ tsp salt
1 tsp soda
1 tsp cinnamon
½ tsp nutmeg
1 egg
1 cup sugar
⅓ cup butter, melted with
⅓ cup lard
2 tbsp molasses
2 tbsp water
2 cups rolled oats
½ cup chopped raisins
½ cup chopped pecans

Sift flour, measure and resift 3 times with salt, soda and spices. Beat egg, add sugar and mix well. Then add melted shortenings, molasses and water, and beat vigorously. Add flour mixture, mix well. Stir in rolled oats, raisins, and pecans thoroughly. Drop mixture from tablespoon onto lightly greased baking sheet far enough apart to allow for spreading or shape with fingers into rounds (about 2 inches in diameter) and flatten to about ¼ inch thickness with the tines of a fork. Bake in moderate oven (350° F.) 12 to 15 minutes. Remove from baking sheet onto a cake rack while slightly warm. (Makes about 4 dozen medium-sized cookies)

OATMEAL SAUCER. A wide, deep saucer used for individual servings of oatmeal and other heated cereals. *See* DISHES.

OCA or **OKA.** A South American tuberous plant which produces a number of small tubers about the size of a walnut. It is edible and quite delicious, although it has not achieved any popularity in the United States. The freshly dug tubers are not edible, since they contain an acid which disappears with drying. In Peru, where they are native, the tubers are dried in the sun for a few days. They are then cooked and served like new potatoes and have the flavor of a fine sweet potato. They are also dried more thoroughly, when they resemble a fig in appearance and taste, and are used like figs.

OIL. There are several kinds of cooking and salad oils, among which are:

Coconut Oil. This oil is used principally in Oriental countries.

Corn Oil. An excellent and widely used oil is made from corn (maize) and has become very popular in America. It is obtained from the germ of the kernel of Indian corn and, when refined, is made into salad oil, cooking oil, and shortening for pastry.

Cottonseed Oil. Cottonseed oil, and to some extent the oils of other fatty grains, vegetables, or seeds are now largely substituted for olive oil in the preparation of salad oil or cooking oil. Cottonseed oil is not to be considered rancid because its flavor and odor differ from those of olive oil. Cottonseed oil has been greatly improved since it was first manufactured. When the product is absolutely pure, both flavor and odor are delicious.

Miscellaneous Oils. Oils such as poppyseed, rapeseed, sesame, and soy bean (edible oils) also are used in salad making and for cooking purposes. They are sold as "salad or cooking oils" or under their own names.

Olive Oil. Olive oil is labeled "pure olive oil," even though it may be high grade, medium grade, or low grade. Two or more olive oils with characteristic flavors are often mixed in order to produce a certain blend—just as in coffee—but no other oils than those pressed from ripe olives are ever included and labeled "olive oil."

The product of highest quality is known in the market as "virgin olive oil." It is drained from the slightly crushed pulp of the olives. Oil of ordinary quality is made by grinding and pressing pulp and seeds together after the virgin oil is extracted. A third oil is also obtained by adding boiling water to the pulp residue and again subjecting it to pressure. The oil thus produced is more likely to become rancid than the top two grades.

The cheaper grades are sometimes adulterated with corn oil or cottonseed oil, which have the same food value but should be sold under their correct names and at a lower price than for pure olive oil.

The fat content of olive oil is 100 percent, its fuel value being equal to that of lard used in cookery. Olive oil is made on a large scale in Italy, France, Spain, and California, the oils from different countries differing somewhat in flavor. Imported olive oil is usually more expensive than that produced in California.

Nut Oils. English walnuts, hickory, pecan, and Brazil nuts, more than other varieties, contain excellent vegetable oil. However, when kept too long, these oils turn rancid.

Peanut Oil. This oil has a fine flavor when pure. As its name implies it is made from peanuts. It is extensively used in America an in many European countries.

Tin cans are used for packing many oils to protect them against the act on of light, which may cause deterioration. Oil will not become rancid if the can is tightly closed and kept in a cool place.

A half-gallon can is the most convenient for use, but a five-gallon can is more economical when buying salad or cooking oil. And there is no difference between salad, table, or vegetable oil. Any one of them may be used for cooking.

See also FAT.

OIL RANGE. *See* RANGE.

OKA CHEESE. Another name for Trappist cheese, (*which see*).

OKOLEHAO. This is a very potent, native Hawaiian whisky. It is a distillate, obtained from fermented mash of the proper proportions of sugar-cane molasses, Koji rice lees, and the juice of baked *ti-root* (the root of taro plant) with water added. It is of a dark color with a smoky aroma and flavor. The whisky can be drunk neat, but it has been more widely used in continental America in cocktails and punches.

A popular punch is made under the name of Okolehao Punch, consisting of gin, pineapple juice, lemon juice, coconut milk, and a dash of curacao. This is served in scooped-out, dried coconut shells.

OKRA. There are a number of species of okra, but that generally used in the United States and West Indies as a vegetable is the *Hibiscus esculentus* which bears an attractive mallow-like flower and is often grown as an ornament in the garden. The seed pods are the "okra" which is marketed. In the West Indies, it is called "gobbo" and is an important ingredient of Pepper Pot. In Louisiana okra is used in Creole cookery and is the "gumbo" of so many dishes.

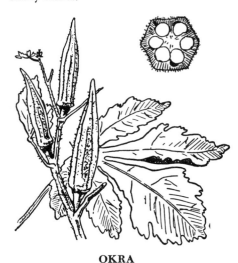

OKRA

Good quality okra has pods two to four inches long which are fresh and clean looking. The pods will snap easily when broken. Pods which are too old will look dull and dry and will be hard and woody. If they have been in the market too long, the pods will be shriveled and withered. Be careful, in purchasing okra, that it is not stuffed into a bag so hard as to crush the pods.

Formerly okra was dried for use out of season. Now it is available canned, either

FOOD VALUE

Water	Food Energy	Pro- tein	Fat	Carbo- hydrate	Cal- cium	Phos- phorus	Iron	Vit. A Value	Thia- mine	Ribo- flavin	Nia- cin	Ascor- bic Acid
89.8	39	1.8	.2	7.4	82	62	.7	740	.12	.10	.7	30

sliced or in the whole pods, and is more satisfactory than the dried pods.

Okra may be cooked and served with lemon and butter, creamed, or scalloped; it may be combined with onion and tomatoes, or corn and tomatoes in a stew. It may be pan-fried or French fried. For a salad, the tender pods are boiled in salted water, drained and chilled, and served with French dressing. The stems, which may be left on the pods, serve as handles to dip the okra in the dressing. Cut into slices, crosswise, okra has an attractive starlike shape, and makes an attractive and delicious addition to vegetable soups.

Okra should preferably be cooked in agate, aluminum, porcelain, or earthenware or glass utensils. Copper, brass, iron, or tin will cause the okra to discolor, turning black and unappetizing-looking. No harm is done, only to the appearance.

BAKED OKRA, RICE, AND TOMATOES

1 qt young okra
¼ cup rice
1 qt cooked tomatoes
1½ tsp salt
Pepper
Curry powder
Butter

Wash the okra, cut off the tips and stems, and cut into thin slices. Grease a baking dish. Sprinkle about 1 tablespoon of the washed rice in the bottom of the dish, cover with a layer of okra, and then with a layer of tomatoes. Season with salt, pepper, curry powder and dot with butter. Repeat the layers until the dish is filled. Cover and bake in a very moderate oven (325° F.) until the rice is tender (about 45 minutes). Remove the cover at the end to allow the top to brown slightly. (Serves 6)

CHICKEN GUMBO

1 qt young okra
1 frying chicken, 3 to 4 lb in weight
1 slice ham, about 1 lb in weight
4 tbsp butter or other fat

4 cups fresh tomatoes, peeled and chopped, or canned tomatoes
1 large onion, chopped
1 sprig parsley
3 qts boiling water
Salt
Cayenne pepper

Wash and stem the okra and cut in ½-inch slices. Cut the chicken up as for fricasee. Cut ham into dice. In a large kettle melt 2 tablespoons of the fat and cook the okra slices in it until lightly browned. Remove the okra. Melt the remaining fat in the kettle. Add the chicken and ham, cover closely, and cook for about 10 minutes, turning as necessary to brown it slightly. Add the tomatoes, onion, parsley, water and browned okra. Simmer for an hour, or until the chicken and ham are very tender. Salt to taste, and add a few grains of cayenne pepper. Serve in soup plates with fluffy rice. (Serves 6 or 8)

FRIED OKRA

Cut off the stem end and the tip of okra pods and wash them thoroughly. Parboil in salted water for 8 minutes. Drain carefully, wiping each pod on a dry cloth. Roll in cornmeal, seasoned to taste with salt and pepper and a few grains of cayenne. Fry in deep fat or sauté in butter. Drain on soft crumpled paper, and serve at once.

OKRA AND BEEF STEW

2 cups okra
2 lb lean beef
Salt and pepper
¼ lb fat
1 large onion, chopped
2 qt cold water

Wash the okra, trim off the ends, and chop rather small. Cut the beef in small pieces and season with salt and pepper. Melt the fat in a large kettle, add the meat and onion, and stir until lightly browned. Add the cold water and simmer, covered, until the meat is tender. Add the okra, and continue simmering until the okra is tender. Taste and add more seasoning if necessary. A No. 3 can of tomatoes may be used in place of 1 quart of water. (Serves 6)

OKRA AND EGGPLANT

1 doz large okra pods
1 medium-sized eggplant
1 medium-sized onion
2 large tomatoes
1 tbsp butter or margarine
Salt and pepper
2 tbsp finely chopped parsley

Wash the okra, cut off the ends, and slice thinly. Peel the eggplant and cut it in small dice. Peel and slice the onion, and peel and quarter the tomatoes. Put all together in a saucepan and simmer over very low heat, stirring occasionally to prevent sticking. Add the butter, seasonings, and parsley, cover, and simmer until thoroughly blended and tender (about 30 or 40 minutes). This dish may be prepared in a casserole and baked in a moderate oven for about an hour. In either case, serve piping hot, directly from the cooking dish. (Serves 4)

OKRA AU GRATIN

1 lb fresh okra
2 cups boiling salted water
1½ cups medium white sauce, well seasoned
¼ cup bread crumbs
1½ tbsp melted butter
¼ cup grated cheese

Wash the okra carefully and cut off the stem end and tip of each pod. Have the water boiling briskly and salt to taste, using about 1 teaspoon of salt. Drop the okra into the rapidly boiling water, stirring with a wooden spoon until every pod is immersed. Cover and boil steadily until the pods can be pierced with a fork, but are not broken (about 15 minutes). Okra cooks very quickly; be careful not to overcook it. Drain the liquid, reserving it for soup. Cool the pods slightly. Arrange the pods in a shallow buttered baking dish, leaving the small pods whole and cutting the larger ones in half crosswise. Pour the hot white sauce over the okra, sprinkle the bread crumbs, melted butter, and cheese over the

top, and bake in a moderately hot oven (375° F.) until the sauce bubbles and the crumbs are brown (about 20 minutes). Serve sizzling hot. (Serves 6)

SAVORY OKRA

1 qt okra
3 tbsp butter
1 small onion, minced
1 cup tomatoes, canned or fresh
1 tsp salt
6 sprigs of parsley
1 large bay leaf
4 tbsp vinegar

Wash the okra and cut off the ends. Cut the pods in slices about ⅓ inch thick. Parboil in boiling salted water for three minutes. Drain and rinse with cold water. Melt the butter in a saucepan and cook the minced onion in it until soft and yellow. Then add the drained okra, the tomatoes, salt, a few grains each of pepper, nutmeg, and thyme, and the parsley tied up with the bay leaf. Mix lightly and turn into a buttered baking dish. Sprinkle the vinegar over the dish. Cover, and bake in a moderate oven (350° F.) for about an hour. Serve hot from the baking dish. (Serves 6)

SCALLOPED OKRA AND CORN

3 cups sliced okra
4 tbsp butter or margarine
2 cups cooked or canned corn
1 tsp salt
Pepper
2 tbsp flour
1 cup milk
¼ lb sharp cheese, grated
1 cup fine dry bread crumbs

Melt 2 tablespoons of the butter in a skillet and fry the sliced okra for about 10 minutes, stirring frequently to prevent burning. Make a cream sauce of the remaining 2 tablespoons of butter and flour and milk. Season with salt and pepper. Stir in the grated cheese and stir until the cheese has melted. In a greased baking dish make alternate layers of the okra and corn. Pour the sauce over the vegetables and cover with the bread crumbs. Bake in a moderate oven (350° F.) until the mixture is hot and the crumbs are brown. (Serves 6)

SCALLOPED OKRA AND TOMATOES

1 qt young okra
4 tbsp butter or margarine
1 small onion, chopped
1 qt peeled and chopped tomatoes
2 tsp salt
Pepper
1 cup fine dry bread crumbs

Wash the okra, remove the tips, and cut in ½-inch slices. Melt 2 tablespoons of the butter in a skillet, add the onion and okra, and cook until they are slightly brown, stirring frequently. Add the tomatoes, salt, and pepper, and simmer for about 10 minutes. Pour the mixture into a greased shallow baking dish. Cover with the bread crumbs mixed with the remaining 2 tablespoons of melted butter. Bake in a moderate oven (350° F.) for 15 minutes, or until the okra is tender and the crumbs are brown. Serve hot from the baking dish. (Serves 6)

OLD ENGLISH CHEESE. The trade name of a distinctive processed cheese.

OLD-FASHIONED. As applied to cookery, this means a dish prepared by the old method. It is often applied to such items as bread pudding, doughnuts, shortcake, and candy.

OLD FASHIONED COCKTAIL. A cocktail made of whisky, bitters and fruit, served in a special glass, that ranks with the martini and manhattan in popularity.

OLD FASHIONED COCKTAIL

1 jigger whisky
2 dashes angostura bitters
1 lump sugar
1 slice orange
1 slice lemon
1 stick pineapple
1 maraschino cherry

Place the sugar, bitters, orange and lemon in the bottom of an old fashioned glass (*see* GLASSWARE). Muddle thoroughly until sugar is dissolved. Add one or two ice cubes, whisky, pineapple and cherry. (Serves 1)

As in the case of all mixed drinks, there is considerable controversy over the correct manner of mixing an Old Fashioned. Some object to the quantity of fruit in the drink; others will add even more varieties. In some cases, two dashes of curaçao are added with the bitters.

The drink is not stirred when the whisky is added, but is served with a stirrer in the glass, permitting the guest to stir to his personal satisfaction and to further crush the fruit, should he so desire. Toothpicks or anchovy spears are customarily provided to aid in handling the fruit, which is meant to be eaten. *See also* BARTENDING.

OLD TOM GIN. A sweet white Gin, popular in England, also known as tom gin and Plymouth gin. *See* GIN.

OLEASTER. A small tree or low shrub of southern Europe, bearing olive-shaped, bitter fruit. The term is used erroneously to describe the wild olive.

OLEOMARGARINE. *See* MARGARINE.

OLIVE. The olive has played an important and romantic role in food history ever since Biblical times. In Eastern countries notably lacking in many of our common foods of today, it was always regarded as a chief source of nutriment and as the most valuable of fruit trees.

For many centuries the olive tree has been cultivated in groves in Italy, Spain, France, Greece and the Orient, because of the remarkably sweet and nut-like oil which can be pressed from its ripe fruits. Used as the chief cooking and frying oil, as a salad dressing, and for other household uses, olive oil has been the most important culinary fat in the semitropical countries, in whose milder frost-free climates the tree best thrives.

Not only was the oil extracted from the ripe, dark or green, small fruits, but they were also treated to various processes of salting, curing, pickling, etc., a wrinkled and briny olive, pickled Spanish fashion, for example, being little different from a pickled peach such as our homemakers know and use as a meat savory.

It was only in 1901 that American experts discovered that the ripe olive could be canned. This was quite a revolutionary idea, although it now appears simple. In its modern canned form the ripe olive comes to the pantry shelf in many sizes and also in various forms. There is just as much flavor to olives in the small sizes as in the large.

Most of our green olives are imported from Spain, but a few come from France and Italy. They are brought to this country in large casks or in sacks. Here they are graded, pickled and packed. Queen olives are those of the best quality. Most of the ripe olives in our markets are grown in California and packed there.

Not only may whole ripe olives be purchased in different sizes, but the pulp has

Sevillano. This is the variety from which the largest Queen olives of Spain are made. The largest specimens excel the Ascolano in size. It is of typical olive shape. It has a large pit and is deeply colored like the

FOOD VALUE

Water	Food Energy	Pro-tein	Fat	Carbo-hydrate	Cal-cium	Phos-phorus	Iron	Vit. A Value	Thia-mine	Ribo-flavin	Nia-cin	Ascor-bic Acid
75.2	144	1.5	13.5	4.0	101	15	2.0	420	Trace	. . . .		

now been packed, freed from its stone, in such modes as sliced olives, chopped olive pulp, etc.—all forms convenient for the popular sandwich or salad uses.

The olive must be considered as a true fruit tree, and its small oval fruit ranks with plums, peaches, apricots and other hard-pit fruits. But different from these other allied fruits whose flesh or pulp is chiefly watery, as in plums and peaches, the firm pulp of the olive is packed chock full of edible oils of great delicacy as well as high energy content.

VARIETIES OF OLIVES

Mission. The fruit of the common or broad-leaved Mission is typically olive-shaped, slightly oblique and pointed. Its deep color when ripe makes it suitable for ripe pickles. The ripe fruit is very bitter but it is firm and easy to pickle. It is one of the best oil olives, both in quantity and quality. More than half of the olives of California are of this variety.

Ascolano. This variety, the largest of all the California olives, comes from Italy. It has a very small pit. It is sometimes called the "white olive of Ascoli" because it has very little color even when perfectly ripe. Since its flesh is somewhat tender, its large size makes special care and skill necessary in preparing the ripe pickles.

Manzanillo (No. 1). This olive is of Spanish origin, and as its name indicates, it is apple-shaped. It is deeply colored and bitter when ripe and requires treatment with strong lye, but as it softens easily in pickling, great care is needed. It is on the average a little larger than the Mission, and its oil is somewhat inferior both in quantity and quality.

Manzanillo (No. 2). This is the variety usually pickled in Spain. It is of excellent quality but too small for the American market.

Mission. It is particularly suited for making both green and ripe pickles, but its large size makes special care necessary in the process.

Macrocarpa and Polymorpha. These are very large and suitable for ripe pickles, but are very liable to a disease causing spotting or softening of the flesh, which much decreases their value.

Other large-fruited varieties which have been tried and which have given good results in some sections are *Obliza, Salonica, Regalias, Empeltre,* and *Columbella.* These are not being largely planted now, as they are excelled in most respects by the four preferred varieties.

Among smaller varieties which under favorable conditions produce fruit large enough for pickling are the *Nevadillo Blanco, Oblonga, Pendulina,* and *Uvaria.* The *Neva-*

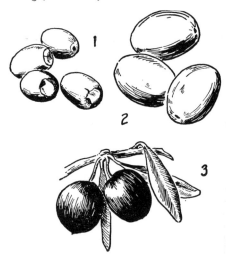

OLIVES 1. Stuffed Spanish 2. Green
3. Ripe

dillo especially was planted largely at one time and under suitable conditions is one of the best oil olives. It is, however, sensitive to cold, subject to dry-rot of the fruit and in many sections an unreliable bearer.

The Picholine. A variety used in France for "olive farcies" gives excellent fruit in California but has been little planted. The so-called Redding Picholine, which was largely planted some years ago is a seedling whose fruit is very small and useless.

PREPARATION FOR MARKET

As a rule, the ripening season extends from two or three to several weeks, depending on the size of the crop, the locality, and the variety. Three or four pickings are usually necessary where the crop is heavy, especially if the orchard lies within the range of cool sea breezes, where ripening of the fruit progresses slowly. To obtain a uniformly good quality of ripe pickles, well-matured fruit is necessary. The most practical guide for the picker is the color of the fruit. For making ripe pickles, care ful handling of the fruit during harvest has been recognized for many years as of first importance. Badly bruised or punctured fruit cannot be used for pickles and must be utilized for oil. The fruit is therefore gathered by hand and placed carefully in picking baskets or buckets and transferred to lug boxes for hauling to the pickling plant. Further to insure against bruises, some packers place some water in the picking bucket to serve as a cushion for the falling fruit. While somewhat less care is taken in harvesting fruit for oil making, it is recognized that only sound, well-matured fruit will render first-class oil. For making green pickles, which is a sizable industry in this country, large fruits only are used, and these are gathered as soon as they are full sized or when a light-yellow color indicating approaching maturity appears.

Grading. When the fruit reaches the pickling plant it is first run through a sizing machine and separated into different sizes. Great care must be used and the machine adjusted to prevent bruising the fruit. Fruit of different varieties is kept separate throughout the pickling process. This is necessary, not only for marketing but also because the fruit of different varieties is different in texture and quality.

HINTS ON PREPARATION

The homemaker who slices her own olives may wish to learn the simple technique of getting the most pulp away from the stone, as practiced originally by Spanish homemakers. Quarter each olive by cutting against the seed with a sharp knife, then insert the point of the knife blade at the end opposite the stem and bring away the easily separated flesh with four quick turns of the knife. In other cases, where it is more convenient to slice the olives, slice against the stone in segments of eighths, and remove as in quarter sections.

Black olives are picked green, therefore there is a little loss of flavor. Mold, softening, and darkening, are forms of spoilage. To get rid of this, wash thoroughly, renew the brine, and expose the fruit to direct sunlight. Repeat this for several days. It is advisable to remove mold as soon as it appears on top of the brine.

Olives should always be taken in the fingers. It is told that Cardinal Richelieu once drove from his table a guest who was posing as a nobleman, because the man helped himself to olives with a fork.

Heating improves the flavor of ripe olives. Adding a small amount of oil, vinegar, and garlic just before heating makes them even better.

HINTS ON USING RIPE OLIVES

The oval or ball-like fruits are good friends to the hostess who likes decorative dishes, and whose salads and similar hot weather dishes are enhanced by the clever use of ripe olives as topping for the potato salad, as a row down the back of a meat loaf, and as points of color contrast on many other plates.

The size and form of the ripe olive lend it equally well to use as a relish, pickle, and appetizer, whether wrapped and broiled in a bacon sliver, or otherwise treated for the cocktail hour.

But as a flavor—and a texture—the hostess and gourmet should learn to know it in sauces and as a topping or dressing of the most delectable kind. Ripe olives sliced in any gravy—beef, or other meat, sauces, or juices—make it the equal of the esteemed mushroom gravy so dear to the epicure. Or, simmering in a spicy tomato sauce, its smooth but firm pulp greatly enhances the deliciousness of the Spanish and barbecue sauces so valued by the hot-climate homemakers.

In making stuffings, also, the ripe olive comes to the fore, giving the dressing color, flavor, and texture. Many of the recipes for all uses of olives naturally come from Spain, Italy, France, Greece, or Arabia—countries long familiar with olive lore and cooking skill. The use of olives and eggs in combination is one to appeal especially to the gourmets. Olives in soufflés or casserole form, with fish, game, ham, poultry, meat, corn, or vegetables, are delicious.

In many recipes calling for similar dressings, and piquant and contrasting sauces for fish, game, poultry, etc., sliced or chopped olives may be substituted occasionally for chopped gherkins, or a combination of the two may be made, giving a new taste to old familiar recipes.

The ripe olive gives a new note to vegetables and salads when added to hot or cold dressings and mayonnaise. Tomatoes, broccoli, asparagus, squash, etc., are made into a vegetarian dream when a spicy ripe-olive mayonnaise (hot or cold) is poured over them.

Chili powder, Spanish and Mexican, is another excellent condiment with which to tone up the milder dishes of hot weather especially if chopped or sliced olives are added to them.

Chopped olives enhance the flavor of almost any sandwich filling.

OLIVE APPETIZER

Roll bacon around a large green olive that has been stuffed with cheese. Broil carefully until bacon is done. Serve hot.

OLIVE-CHEESE CUSTARD

5 slices bread, crusts removed
2 tbsp butter
1 cup grated American cheese
½ cup sliced stuffed olives
3 eggs, slightly beaten
⅛ tsp dry mustard
⅓ cup olive liquor
2 cups milk, scalded

Spread bread with 1 tablespoon butter; cut in cubes and scatter ⅓ over bottom of greased casserole. Arrange layers of ⅓ cup cheese and ¼ cup olives over crumbs; repeat. Then cover with remaining bread cubes and top with remaining ⅓ cup cheese; dot with remaining tablespoon of butter. Combine eggs, mustard, and olive liquor; gradually stir in hot milk. Pour

over mixture in casserole and bake in slow oven (300° F.) about 1 hour, or until knife inserted comes out clean. Serve as main luncheon dish. (Serves 6)

OLIVE STUFFING FOR TOMATOES

Mix together raw carrot, minced stuffed olive, and tomato pulp, and cream cheese. Moisten with cream and season with salt and pepper. Wash medium-sized firm, ripe tomatoes; peel, if desired, and scoop out centers. Sprinkle insides with salt, invert and chill in refrigerator. Fill with stuffing, serve on crisp salad greens with salad dressing, and garnish as desired.

OLIVE FORK. See FLATWARE.

OLIVET CHEESE. A soft, rennet cheese made from cow's milk. It resembles Camembert, and is made in France.

OLLA PODRIDA. The national dish of Spain. A stew made of meat sausages, chick peas, cabbage, etc., with many variations.

OLMUTZER QUARGEL CHEESE. A German hand cheese containing caraway seeds. Its manufacture is identical with hand cheese, which see.

OLOROSO. One of the more famous types of sherry wine. It is sweet, full-bodied, and golden. See also SHERRY.

OMELET. See EGG.

OMELET DESSERTS. Once the rum omelet and the jelly omelet were among the specialties of great hotels and popular chop houses, and they will come again as time rolls on, for the experienced chef can prepare them to a king's taste, while the amateur cook of light touch and some native skill may also achieve masterpieces out of commonplace materials.

Desserts are a problem, at home or abroad. The homemaker's repertory is soon exhausted and made drearily familiar. You may be having one of the light home dinners that end with salad, and the unexpected guest arrives—a good trencherman. The pastry shop is closed and you hesitate about the corner drugstore ice cream, but there are eggs in the pantry and there must be a flask of Jamaica rum in the cupboard—for rum is more important than vanilla among the flavorings. Well, then, after the chops and salad have gone their way, mysteriously declare a recess for cigarettes and small talk and retire to the kitchen. Make one of the following sweet omelets.

CHOCOLATE OMELET

1 oz chocolate, melted
4 tbsp rich cream
3 tbsp powdered sugar
6 eggs
1 wine glass rum
1 wine glass creme de cacao

Blend the chocolate, cream, and sugar with the beaten eggs. Pour mixture into a large, well buttered, hot frying pan, and keep it hot as you move it about over a moderate flame to guard against scorching. Lift the edges of the omelet, and break the bubbles until the custard is uniformly firm but still soft. Then fold it from the two sides toward the middle with a wide spatula, shape it nicely, and turn it out by inverting the pan over a fireproof glass or earthenware platter. Sugar the top well and then carry it to the table on a tray with a wine glass of rum and another wine glass of crème de cacao, topped with half an inch of heavy unwhipped cream. Burn the rum until the fire flashes out, then let the cordial and the cream flow smoothly over the smoldering omelet. Serve immediately. (Serves 6)

JELLY OR JAM OMELET

6 eggs
1/8 tsp salt
4 tbsp powdered sugar
6 tbsp ice water
Butter
2 tbsp jam

Jelly or jam omelets may be simple or elaborate, but they are always effective if the homemaker has any skill at all. If an emergency catches you with nothing more than eggs and strawberry or raspberry jam, proceed as for a rum omelet (*see below*), but put 2 heaping tablespoons of the jam on the omelet in the pan before you fold it, with plenty of butter, and it will melt into a delicious sauce before you turn it out. Glaze the top with butter and sugar, and sear it in stripes with the hot iron, then serve at once. (Serves 6)

If you keep an assortment of cordials and a collection of jams and jellies, the variety of your sweet omelet may be limited only by your imagination.

Apricot Rum Omelet. Proceed as for Jelly Omelet but put in 2 tablespoons of rich apricot jam, scatter powdered sugar on top, and set it blazing with a wine glass of rum or brandy. Then as the flames die out, pour on a libation of apricot brandy, and serve. (Serves 6)

Other Variations. Use fine orange marmalade for filling, and top off with curaçao or grand marnier. For a spring luncheon or dinner, fill the omelet with crushed fresh strawberries or raspberries, or cherries. Burn with rum, and finish with a glass of kirsch.

RUM OMELET

6 eggs
1/8 tsp salt
4 tbsp powdered sugar
6 tbsp ice water
Butter
Rum

Break the eggs into a bowl and beat them just enough to blend. Add salt, 2 rounded tablespoons of powdered sugar and the ice water. Then beat again until the mixture is smooth and creamy, but not foaming. Pour it into a large, well buttered, hot frying pan, and keep it hot as you move it about over a moderate flame to guard against scorching. Lift the edges of the omelet, and break the bubbles until the custard is uniformly firm, but still soft. Then fold it from the two sides toward the middle with a wide spatula, shape it nicely, and turn it out by inverting the pan over a fireproof glass or earthenware platter. Quickly spread soft butter and 2 more rounded tablespoons of powdered sugar over the top, and sear the surface at 1-inch intervals from end to end with a red hot poker, as a professional decorative touch. Now, pour a large wine glass of good rum over the omelet and set it on fire with a match. Serve immediately. The spirit burns out quickly, as you ladle the burning rum over the sugary surface until you have a rich and luscious sirup. As the last tongue of blue flame flickers out, serve the omelet with its sauce.

ONE YARD OF FLANNEL. The name sometimes given to an English ale drink of the flip type. *See* FLIP.

ONION. Not more delicious to the palate than hateful for the odor which it imparts to the breath, the onion has been

FOOD VALUE

Water	Food Energy	Pro- tein	Fat	Carbo- hydrate	Cal- cium	Phos- phorus	Iron	Vit. A Value	Thia- mine	Ribo- flavin	Nia- cin	Ascor- bic Acid
87.5	49	1.4	.2	10.3	32	44	.5	50	.03	.02	.1	9

at once a source of joy and despair to the epicure. The test of a good cook, someone has said, lies in his seasonings. And this might almost be taken to mean whether or not she is skillful in her use of onions, knowing how to add them sparingly for some dishes, or lavishly for others. A glance through any good cookbook reveals few recipes, apart from desserts, which do not include a suspicion of onion.

From the earliest recorded time, the onion has been highly esteemed. The original home of the onion was probably southern Asia or the shores of the Mediterranean, and in the desert regions it was used as a preventative of thirst by travelers and soldiers on the march.

KINDS AND VARIETIES

Although leeks, chives, garlic, and shallots belong to the onion family, they are covered under their own headings, *which see*. We are concerned here only with the green onion, or scallion, and the mature dried onions.

The young green onions, or scallions, are marketed in bunches. They may be eaten raw, with salt, or cut into salads, or they may be boiled and served like asparagus.

Onions are divided by size and flavor into various types suitable for different purposes. The smallest size, which may be white- or yellow-skinned, is the pickling onion. These are also known as pearl, or button, onions. The next larger size is the boiling onion which is usually an inch to an inch and a quarter in diameter. The larger onions with increasingly strong flavor are used to chop or grate for flavor. The very large Spanish or Bermuda onions, which are characteristically flatter in shape than the stronger varieties, are very mild and sweet in flavor. Their color varies from white to yellow, and occasionally red. In size they average 2½ to 2¾ inches in diameter.

HINTS ON BUYING

The bulbous onions have been dried after pulling and before marketing. For this reason, they keep well if kept in a dry cool place. Dampness and too much heat will cause them to rot or sprout. Good quality mature onions are bright and clean looking, well shaped, hard, and with dry skins. The color may be white, yellow, reddish, or brownish. Decay appears as a rot attacking the outer scales or the center of the bulb. When it is outside it is fairly evident. Moisture at the neck of the onion indicates decay in the interior. Misshapen onions are not necessarily bad, but they are liable to be wasteful.

Green onions should have fresh green tops, and should be well blanched for two or three inches from the root. Wilted tops are unimportant, since they can be trimmed off, if the balance of the onion is fresh- and good-looking.

HINTS ON PREPARATION

It is well to have a small chopping board reserved for onions and garlic. In this way, the flavor will not inadvertently get into food for which it is not intended. After peeling and chopping onions, wash the knife and your hands in cold water. If the onions were strong, make a paste of baking soda and water or salt and water, and rub it thoroughly into your hands. Rinse off with cold water, and the odor will have disappeared. Dry mustard rubbed on the hands and then rinsed off will also remove the odor.

Holding onions under cold water while peeling them prevents the volatile oils from rising and causing tears. If you have a number of onions to peel, cover them with hot water, let stand a minute or two, and then drain. The thin skin which is sometimes so difficult to get off can be peeled off easily.

Onions should also be sliced crosswise into rings. An easy way to mince onion is to peel the onion, slice down through the onion at right angles, making a checkerboard of eighth-inch squares, and then cut across. The little dice will fall out easily.

To extract onion juice, peel the onion and cut off one slice. Press the raw surface against a fine grater and move slightly back and forth. The juice will run off and can be caught in a spoon.

While onion may be added raw to many dishes which involve long cooking, the flavor is improved if the onion is chopped fine and browned in butter or margarine before being added to the other ingredients.

In the wintertime, when chives and green onions are not available, an excellent garnish for salads, etc. may be achieved by allowing onions to sprout. Choose several large onions which show indications of sprouting, and leave in the light near a window. Within a few days the sprouts will have grown to several inches in length. They may be cut off and chopped and used like chives or scallions. The onion will continue sprouting and growing until the substance in the bulb has been entirely used.

Onion rings, to be used raw in salads, or with hamburgers, may be crisped by dropping in iced water and chilling. Drain them well before serving.

APPLE AND ONION SCALLOP

9 medium-sized onions
6 medium-sized cooking apples
12 slices bacon, cut in small pieces
¾ tsp salt
1 cup water
½ cup buttered crumbs

Peel the onions and apples; slice them about ⅛ inch thick. Fry the cut-up bacon in a frying pan until the fat is extracted and the bacon is crisp. In a greased baking dish make alternate layers of onions, apples, and bacon, having two layers of each. Sprinkle with the salt, add the water and top with the crumbs. Cover and bake in a moderately hot oven (375° F.) about 45 minutes, then uncover and brown. If desired the crumbs may be moistened with bacon fat instead of butter. (Serves 6)

CREAM OF ONION SOUP

3 or 4 large onions
1 tbsp butter or margarine
1 tbsp flour
1 quart milk
Minced parsley

Peel the onions and slice thinly. In the top of a double boiler, melt the butter and stir in the onions. Cook, stirring constantly, until the onions are pale yellow. Stir in the flour and cook until it is blended. Scald the milk. Gradually stir into the onion mixture, and season to taste with salt and pepper. Place the top of the boiler over boiling water and continue cooking for 20 minutes until the onions are tender. Serve immediately with croutons. This makes an excellent luncheon dish, served with a green salad. (Serves 4)

CREAMED ONIONS

1 lb small white onions
6 cups boiling water
1½ tsp salt
1 cup thin cream or white sauce
Salt and pepper

Select onions of uniform size so that they will cook in the same length of time. Peel the onions, and cook them rapidly, uncovered, in the boiling salted water, until just tender, 15 or 20 minutes. Drain the onions. Place in a heat-proof serving dish and pour over the cream sauce (which see), adding additional seasoning if necessary. Reheat. Sprinkle with minced parsley before serving and serve from the dish in which they were heated. (Serves 6)

FRENCH FRIED ONIONS

Peel medium-sized Bermuda onions and slice crosswise in ¼-inch slices. Separate the rings carefully. Soak the rings in milk for 15 minutes. Mix together ⅔ cup corn meal and ⅓ cup white flour. Season with salt and pepper. Drain the onion rings and roll in the corn meal mixture. Fry in deep hot fat (375° F.) for 2 minutes, until delicately browned. Drain on soft crumpled paper. This makes thin crisp rings.

For thicker-coated rings, make a batter of ½ cup corn meal and ½ cup flour. Add salt and pepper, 1 egg well beaten, and ½ cup milk. Stir and blend thoroughly. Fold in 2 tbsp melted shortening. Dip the drained onion rings in this batter and fry as above.

GLAZED ONIONS

12 to 16 white onions
1 qt boiling water
1 tsp salt

½ cup brown sugar
1 cup boiling water or stock
¼ tsp salt
1 tbsp butter or margarine
Finely minced parsley

Select onions of uniform size, those about the size of a walnut being most desirable for this dish. Peel the onions and drop in the boiling salted water. Cook until barely tender. Drain thoroughly. In a shallow saucepan combine the · sugar, water or stock, salt and butter. Add the drained onions and continue cooking until the onions are tender. Remove the onions to a serving dish, then boil the remaining liquid down quickly and pour over the onions. Garnish with the minced parsley, and serve immediately. (Serves 6)

ONION CUSTARD PIE

8 medium-sized white onions
Boiling salted water
1 pint milk
2 eggs, beaten slightly
½ tsp salt
¼ tsp pepper
Baking powder biscuit dough

Peel the onions and simmer in the boiling salted water until just tender, about 15 minutes. Drain and place in a deep baking dish. Combine the milk, eggs, and seasonings, and pour over the onions. Make a recipe of baking powder biscuit dough (*which see*) and roll it out about ½ inch thick. Cover the baking dish with the biscuit crust, making a slit in the center for steam to escape. Bake in a moderate oven (350° F.) about 45 minutes, or until the custard is set and the crust is brown. A delicious luncheon or supper dish. (Serves 6)

ONION PIZZA

Plain pastry
Ripe olives
1 clove
Filleted anchovies
4 to 5 large onions
Olive oil
1 clove of garlic, minced
Salt and pepper
1 bay leaf

Peel the onions and slice thinly. Heat 2 or 3 tablespoons of olive oil in a frying pan. Add the onions, clove, garlic, salt and bay leaf. Sauté very slowly until the onions are a light golden brown. Line a pie plate with pastry (*which see*). Spread thickly with the onions from which the bay leaf and clove have been removed. Cut up the ripe olives and sprinkle over the top of the onions. Dot with the anchovy fillets. Bake in a medium hot oven (375° F.) for 15 or 20 minutes. Serve very hot, cut in thin strips.

ONION AND POTATO SOUP

4 medium-sized potatoes, diced
4 onions, chopped
2 tbsp butter
2 tbsp flour
3 cups scalded milk
Salt, pepper, celery salt
1 tbsp minced parsley

Cook the potatoes and onions together until tender. Strain, pressing all possible pulp through a sieve, and reserve 1 cup of the liquid in which the cooking was done. Melt the butter, add the flour, and when smoothly blended, the reserved cooking liquid. Combine with the milk, vegetable purée and seasonings and strain once more. Top with minced parsley and, if desired, crisp fried bacon dice. (Serves 4)

ONION SHORTCAKE

2 cups finely sliced onions
2 tbsp butter
2 tbsp water
2 cups sifted flour
2 tsp baking powder
½ tsp salt
6 tbsp shortening
¾ cup milk (approximately)
1 egg, well beaten
½ cup thick sour cream
Salt and pepper

Saute the onions in the butter until pale brown. Add the water and cook, stirring often so that the onions color evenly. Prepare a shortcake dough by sifting the dry ingredients, working in the shortening and mixing with milk to make a light soft dough. Roll or pat about ½ inch thick and fit into a greased pan 8 x 8 inches. Spread the onions over the dough. Mix the beaten egg with the sour cream and season with salt and pepper. Spread over the onions. Bake in a hot oven (400° F.) until golden brown. Serve piping hot. (Serves 6)

ONION SOUFFLE

2 tbsp butter
2 tbsp flour
1 cup milk
¾ tsp salt
¼ tsp pepper
3 eggs, separated
6 medium-sized onions

Peel the onions and quarter them. Cook in boiling salted water until very tender. Drain, and chop finely, and drain again. Prepare a white sauce with the butter, flour, milk and seasonings. Cool slightly, and add the beaten yolks of the eggs and the onions. Beat the whites until stiff and fold into the onion mixture. Turn into a buttered baking dish and bake in a moderate oven (350° F.) 25 to 30 minutes. This is excellent with broiled steak. (Serves 6)

ONION SOUP

3 large onions
4 tbsp butter or margarine
2 qts beef stock
Salt and pepper

Peel the onions and slice them thin. Melt the butter in a saucepan and sauté the onions until they are golden brown. Gradually stir in the stock, and season to taste with salt and pepper. Cover and cook gently for 20 minutes. Serve in individual tureens, garnished with a toasted round of French bread topped with grated Swiss or Parmesan cheese. Additional grated cheese may be passed. (Serves 6 or 8)

FRENCH ONION SOUP

1½ lb onions
⅝ cup butter
1 tbsp flour
2½ qt consommé or beef stock
Salt and freshly ground pepper
Slices of toasted French bread
½ cup heavy cream
1½ lb grated Parmesan or Swiss cheese

Slice the onions and sauté slowly in the butter until delicately browned. Add the flour, simmer 2 or 3 minutes, then cook with the consommé and seasonings for 25 minutes.

Moisten the toasted slices of French bread with heavy cream. Pour the soup over them, sprinkle the toast with grated cheese and place in the oven or under the broiler to brown, being sure that the soup does not actually come to a boil.

According to the real Lyonnaise recipe, eggs are poached in the soup itself just before serving. (Serves 8 to 10)

ONIONS WITH CRUMB SAUCE

12 medium-sized onions
2 tsp butter
2 tsp lemon juice
½ tsp salt
Dash of pepper
⅓ cup buttered crumbs

Peel the onions and cook in boiling salted water until tender. Drain and transfer to a buttered baking dish. Add the butter, lemon juice, salt and pepper and top with the crumbs. Bake in a moderately hot oven (375° F.) about 10 minutes, or until the crumbs are delicately browned. (Serves 6)

SMOTHERED ONIONS

1½ lb onions
¼ cup butter or drippings
½ tsp salt
⅛ tsp pepper

Peel and slice the onions thinly. Sauté in the butter or drippings until golden brown, stirring often to prevent burning. Season rather highly with salt and pepper, and cover the pan to cook the onions through. Serve as an accompaniment to steak. (Serves 6)

SPRING ONIONS ON TOAST

2 bunches young green onions
3 cups boiling water
½ tsp salt
4 thin slices hot buttered toast
1 cup medium white sauce
3 tbsp grated cheese

Trim the roots and tops from the onions, leaving two or three inches of the green top. Wash, and drain, and cut into inch-and-a-half lengths. Cook in boiling salted water until just tender. Drain thoroughly and arrange on the toast in an oven proof dish. Pour the white sauce over and sprinkle with the cheese. Place under the broiler flame until the cheese melts and browns slightly. Serve immediately. (Serves 4)

Texas Stuffed Onions

Peel 6 large mild onions and parboil in boiling salted water until barely tender. Drain and scoop out the centers, leaving a substantial wall. Brush the onions with melted butter or margarine, and sprinkle with salt and pepper. Fill with a stuffing made as follows:

Chop equal parts of chicken livers and cooked ham and sauté in a little butter or margarine. Season with a dash of thyme and nutmeg. Fill the onion cavities, mounding up the stuffing. Brush melted butter over the surface and place in a shallow baking dish. Cover tightly and bake in a very slow oven (300° F.) until tender, about 45 minutes. A little sherry may be poured over the onions immediately before serving. (Serves 6)

OOLONG TEA. Semifermented teas; a cross between the fully-fermented black teas and the unfermented green teas. They are produced in China and Formosa, teas from the latter being of higher quality. *See* Tea.

OPAH. Another name for kingfish, *which see.*

OPOSSUM. Also commonly called possum. An American and Australian marsupial, carnivorous animal greatly liked by the Negroes, especially in Mississippi, Arkansas, etc. Usually roasted. It is a nocturnal animal. When caught, it acts as if dead; hence the phrase "to play possum," meaning to avoid detection by keeping quiet.

Roasted Possum Ozark Method

An extremely delicious dish for the most discriminating gourmets. First catch your possum alive. Fatten it with mashed persimmons and warm water for a week. Then kill as you would a little piglet. Stuff with a mixture of equal parts of persimmons,

sweet potatoes, bread crumbs, and the usual spices used for a savory stuffing (thyme, sage, parsley, chopped celery leaves, allspice, bay leaves, and a little rosemary), moistened with beef stock or canned bouillon. Sew up the opening. Make two or three gashes three inches long on each side of the backbone, then place on a rack in a roasting pan. Sprinkle with salt and pepper and brush over with melted butter. Pour 2 cups of boiling water around the possum, and cover with buttered paper. Now sear the possum for 15 to 20 minutes in a very hot oven (475°–500° F.), after which reduce the heat to slow (300° F.) and cook until the meat is tender (about 25 minutes to the pound) basting frequently with the liquid in the pan. Remove the paper after cooking 2 to 2½ hours, and brush the possum over with heavy cream. Then continue roasting until delicately browned. Serve on a large, sizzling hot platter, garnished with sweet potatoes and stewed persimmons.

ORANGE. Introduced into Europe from China, the Malta, Portugal or common Orange (*citrus sinensis*) is now cultivated extensively. A grove of glossy-leaved, healthy citrus fruit trees, with its wealth of golden fruit, is a joy to behold. The blossoms appear in February and again in June, filling the air with exquisite perfume. In February it is not an uncommon sight to see the golden oranges and the waxy white blossoms on the trees at the same time.

Varieties of Oranges

California.

1. The Washington Navel ripens in the fall and winter and is packed and shipped from November to May. It is round and has a deep golden color, is seedless and is characterized by a navel formation at the end opposite the stem. It takes from nine to ten months to ripen. This is the only orange that can be divided into large attractive sections.

2. The Valencia ripens from April to November, is lighter in color, more oblong and not entirely seedless. The fruit of this tree does not ripen until a year or more after it blossoms. In the spring, both ripe fruit and blossoms can be seen on the tree at the same time.

3. Some miscellaneous varieties whose crops are limited and relatively unimpor

tant are: the Blood Orange, St. Michael, Seedlings, Mediterranean Sweet, Thompson Improved Navel, and the Smith Early.
Florida.
1. The Parson Brown ripens in October and will remain on the trees until June. It is the earliest commercial variety.

Sometimes the fires are built in metal containers. The fuel may be bamboo, roots, dead branches, pine knots or palmetto stalks.
The fruit is picked by professionals, from November to April. It is cut from the tree with pruning shears, loaded into trucks,

ORANGES   1. Navel   2. Hamlin   3. Temple

2. The Pineapple is the principal mid-season variety, maturing from late December to early March.
3. The Valencia is the late-growing variety, ripening from March to May.
4. Satsuma, marketed from October to November, has a loose skin.
5. Other varieties are the Homosassa, the Lue Gim Gong, Dancy tangerine and the King.

Preparation for Market

When the trees are planted, they are generally pruned back to about 18 or 20 inches to assure low branching. Low-branched trees are the easiest to handle when the fruits are gathered. After the trees have become established, they are thinned out so as to leave only four or five branches for framework. The sun must always be allowed to penetrate to the center of the tree.
The bane of the grove is the frost that creeps in on a clear night. If the night is cloudy, the trees are not so apt to be injured if the temperature goes down; but on a clear night, if the mercury drops, then the smudge pots must be lighted. Generally these are just low fires built on the ground throughout the grove, which must be kept smouldering all through the night. It is the smoke that protects the trees.

and taken to the packing house. There it is placed upon racks. The fruit rolls from the rack into a hot water bath in which there may be a solution of borax, and is thoroughly scrubbed with a rotary brush, then rolled into the drying machine, where a vapor wax envelops each piece of fruit. It is polished with an 18-foot horsehair polisher, and passed over a wide belt where graders examine it and separate it into classes according to grade requirements. The oranges that pass muster go into the sizer, from which the smallest ones drop first, and the largest, last. The fruit is usually wrapped individually before being packed in boxes for shipment.
The grade divisions of oranges, are first, the top grade, U.S. Fancy, which consists of fruit of similar variety, which is mature, well-colored, firm, well formed, smooth, thin-skinned, and free of disease, injury and decay. Next, U.S. No. 1 to which the same standards are applied, only to a lesser degree, i.e., the oranges may be fairly well-colored, fairly well-formed, etc. Unclassified oranges are those which do not conform to the foregoing grades.

Hints on Buying

Oranges of the best quality are firm and heavy, have a fine-textured skin for

FOOD VALUE

	Wa-ter	Food Energy	Pro-tein	Fat	Car-bohy-drate	Cal-cium	Phos-phorus	Iron	Vit. A Value	Thia-mine	Ribo-flavin	Nia-cin	Ascor-bic Acid
Orange	87.2	50	.9	.2	11.2	33	23	.4	190	.08	.03	.2	49
Canned Orange Juice	86	55	.6	.1	12.9	33	23	.4	100	.07	.02	.2	42

their variety, and are well-colored. Such fruits (even with a few surface blemishes, such as scars, scratches and slight discolorations) are much to be preferred to oranges that have badly creased skin or are puffy or spongy and light in weight.

Puffy oranges are likely to be light in weight, lacking in juice and of generally poor quality. Exceptions occur in the tangerines (of which Dancy is the principal variety), satsumas, King, and mandarin types and varieties. These oranges are usually thin-skinned and flattened at the ends. Because of the looseness of the skin these oranges are likely to feel puffy; therefore judgment as to quality should be based mainly on weight for size and deep yellow or orange color of the skin.

When present, decay is usually in the form of soft areas on the surface of the fruit that appear to be water-soaked. These areas may be covered by a mold. In the early stages of development the skin in the affected area may be so soft and tender that it breaks easily under pressure. Oranges that have been mechanically injured should be carefully examined. Decay may be present at the point of injury.

Wilted, or shriveled, or flabby fruit is sometimes found. Age or injury may cause these conditions. Oranges so affected are not desirable.

For years pomologists have puzzled over green oranges whose ripeness belies their appearance. The green tinge is a peculiarity of the California Valencia. In winter, fruit of this variety grows in size, and is a true orange color while still unripe. The green tinge occurs frequently in fruit which hangs on the tree waiting for late-summer shipment. All California oranges are tree-ripened and these Valencias have to be ripe before taking on the misleading green complexion. Usually it is even juicier and sweeter than that purchased earlier in the season, for it has developed more natural sugar.

Florida and Texas oranges are often designated as "bright" or "russet" de-

pending upon the extent of the russeting or discoloration of the surface. The russeting does not affect the flavor. California oranges are not subject to russeting. Oranges are received in bulk in many markets, many bulk oranges being shipped by motor truck. Such fruit is usually not graded or sized, and is known as "grove or orchard run." Frequently considerable saving can be made by buying such fruit, if the quality is suited to the use for which the oranges are intended.

The juice of one orange equals approximately three ounces; of six oranges, one pound; of one crate, eighteen quarts.

HINTS ON PREPARATION

To segment an orange. Cut a thick layer of skin off the top and one off the bottom of the orange, and then cut off sections of peel from sides, inserting the knife deep enough to remove all white membrane and to leave the fruit exposed. Loosen each segment, cutting along the membrane. Lift out each segment and remove the seeds.

To make an orange basket. Cut the orange in hal and remove the contents of the two half shells. With a sharp knife, cut around one of the halves half an inch from the top leaving one inch uncut on each side of the shell. Raise the two cut strips in loops above the hollowed half, and tie them together with a narrow ribbon. Repeat the process with the other half shell. Thus one orange makes two baskets.

To make an orange cup. With a sharp knife or spoon, scoop the meat from halves of a clean-skinned orange of good size. Flute o scallop the edge using scissors. One orange makes two cups.

To make an orange cup, chrysanthemum shape. With scissors cut orange skins three quarters of the way down in strips, one third of an inch wide, being careful not to break the strips apart. Remove orang meat. Curl each strip of orange peel a trifle inward. One orange makes one cup

Hot breads and rolls fresh from the oven. Cupcakes and muffins and pies. Luscious, two-layer frosted confections. Now streamlined recipes and modern kitchen equipment make the baking of longtime favorites such as orange bread, garland cake, raisin muffins and coconut sponge cake easier than ever — and fun, too!

Soup becomes a main dish when it's chicken gumbo, mushroom bisque or New England clam chowder. Creamy and rich in vegetables, these dishes are more like stew than soup. Serve them with rolls, crackers, fresh salad vegetables and white wine.

For dessert try Baba au Rhum, as beautiful to look at as it is delicious to eat. Or surprise your family with a chocolate layer cake. Homebaked desserts, made with fresh, whole products, taste better than commercial goods and are better for you, too.

Breakstone Sugar Creek Foods

For perfect broiled fish, brush fillets with orange sauce or butter. Then cook about 4 inches from the source of heat for 10 minutes or until the meat flakes easily. Remove the fillets or whole fish carefully to a heated platter, garnish with greens and serve with sauce or relish.

o make quick cream of tomato soup
ombine 2 cups of cooked or canned
omatoes and 3 cups of milk in the
op of a double boiler. Heat slowly
ut do not boil. Season with 1 teaspoon
ach of salt and sugar, a dash of
epper and 1 tablespoon of butter or
margarine. Serve at once. To enhance
he flavor of canned tomato soup,
orinkle with grated Cheddar or smoked
heese and chopped chives. Add thin
ices of onion, small balls of chopped
eat or small chunks of par-boiled
otatoes to cooking tomato soup.

Part of the pleasure of cooking is setting an attractive
table. The cheerful design of modern china adds warmth
and distinctiveness to dinnertime. Arabia's "Paratiisi"
dinnerware, designed by Birger Kaipiainen, is typi
cal of the exciting new motifs in modern design
available today. Even fine bone china is easily
cared for and may be washed in an automatic
dishwasher, cutting down immensely on
tiresome, after dinner chores.

A good meal always tastes better when it's attractively arranged. Plan meals with a view toward variety in color, texture and taste. Decorative salads, garnishes and sauces stimulate the appetite and enhance the flavors of foods. Including foods from all four food groups—meat, dairy, fruits and vegetables and grains—guarantees a meal of variety and balanced nutrients. Pieces of leftovers can be used to decorate dishes — boiled egg slices, celery tops, grated carrot. Lemon adds zest to lamb and veal. Paprika can be used liberally on chicken.

Pizza is usually made with bread dough but in a pinch try pastry. Place the dough
a shallow pie pan; spread with tomato sauce, oregano, grated Parmesan chees
and olive oil. Bake until the crust is done. For variety add anchovies, pepperor
salami, mushrooms, peppers or sausage with the sauce.

It's fun to experiment making fane
pastry desserts that look as thoug
they're "bakery bought" goods. Frien
and family will be delighted when y
bring out this tasty Swedish tea ri
(recipe on page 1036).

Breakstone Sugar Creek Foods

Never squeeze an orange and let the juice stand. It loses Vitamin C that way.

To make one orange go as far as possible for a baby, cut a small piece off one end, and squeeze the juice from that end-piece for one feeding; turn the cut surface of the orange into a plate or saucer, and set it in a cool place until the baby's next feeding time. Then cut off another small piece of the orange, squeeze out of it another spoonful or two of juice, and again turn the cut surface into the plate.

AMBROSIA

3 oranges
3 bananas
½ cup shredded coconut

Section the oranges carefully, removing every particle of skin and white connecting fiber. Peel and slice the bananas and combine with the orange. Chill and just before serving sprinkle the coconut over all. (Serves 6)

BAKED WHOLE ORANGES

Slightly grate the rinds of oranges, then simmer the fruit for 30 minutes. Cool. This is done to make the skins tender.

Cut a slice from the blossom end of each orange and remove the core, then place in each one a teaspoon of butter and a tablespoon of sugar creamed together. Place in a baking dish with water to come half way up the sides of the orange, and bake, covered, in a moderately hot oven (375° F.) about one and a half hours.

For an accompanying sauce measure the liquid remaining in the dish, and for each three-quarters cup add one tablespoon of cornstarch moistened with one quarter cup of orange juice. Bring to boiling point, stirring constantly, and simmer three minutes.

NUT-STUFFED BAKED ORANGES

6 oranges
18 dates, sliced
2 tbsp coconut
1 cup chopped walnuts
6 marshmallows

Cut a slice from the top of each orange, scoop out the pulp and combine this with the dates, coconut and nuts. Refill the oranges with the mixture, place in a deep pan, pour a little water around and bake in a moderate oven (350° F.) 30 to 45 minutes, topping each with a marshmallow 10 minutes before the baking is completed. (Serves 6)

CANDIED ORANGE PEEL

Rind of 4 heavy-skinned oranges
2 cups sugar
Water

Wash, then cut the rinds into ¼-inch strips. Cover with cold water and bring slowly to boiling point. Then continue as for grapefruit peel, *which see.*

GLAZED ORANGES

2 large seedless oranges
½ cup sugar
3 tbsp water
1 tbsp cor sirup

Slice the oranges across into slices about ½ inch thick. Do not peel. Combine the sugar, water, and sirup, and bring to a boil. Add the slices of orange and simmer for five minutes, or until the skins become transparent. Drain, and serve as a garnish with roast duck, goose, or pork.

ORANGE BAVARIAN

1 tbsp plain gelatin (1 envelope)
¼ cup cold water
¼ tsp grated orange rind
1 cup orange juice
1½ tbsp lemon juice
Pinch of salt
½ cup sugar

Soften gelatin in the cold water; then place over hot water and heat until gelatin is dissolved. Allow orange rind to stand in orange juice for 2 minutes. Strain. Discard rind. Combine orange juice with lemon juice (saving out 1 teaspoon lemon juice), salt and sugar. Add gelatin, stir thoroughly, and chill until thick and sirupy. Then whip with egg beater until light and fluffy. Whip chilled cream until thick, then add the 1 teaspoon lemon juice and continue beating until stiff. Fold whipped cream thoroughly but lightly into gelatin and turn into a mold which has been rinsed with cold water. Chill until firm. Unmold onto a chilled serving plate. Garnish with sections of peeled orange and whipped cream, if desired. (Serves 5)

ORANGE BRAN COOKIES

1½ cups butter
2 cups light brown sugar
2 eggs, well beaten
1 cup bran
Grated rind 1 large orange
3 cups flour
2 tsp baking powder

Cream butter with sugar. Add well-beaten eggs and bran. Add orange rind and flour sifted with baking powder. Form into a long roll, wrap in heavy waxed paper and place in refrigerator overnight. Slice thin and bake on lightly buttered tins about 10 minutes in a hot oven (400°-450° F.).

ORANGE BREAD

1½ cups sifted all-purpose flour
2½ tsp baking powder
½ tsp salt
½ cup minced, candied orange peel
2 tbsp shortening
¼ cup sugar
1 egg
½ cup milk
¼ cup orange juice

Mix and sift flour, baking powder, and salt; stir in candied orange peel. Cream shortening; gradually add sugar, creaming until well mixed, and beat in egg. Add flour mixture alternately with milk, beating well after each addition; stir in orange juice. Turn into greased loaf pan and bake in moderate oven (350° F.) about 1 hour. (Makes 1 loaf)

ORANGE BUTTER FROSTING

¼ cup butter
2 cups confectioners' XXXX sugar
¼ tsp salt
2 tbsp orange juice
1 tsp grated orange rind

Cream butter until very soft and smooth; then add sugar gradually, creaming thoroughly. Add salt and orange rind. Gradually work in the orange juice using just enough to produce a smooth spreading consistency. Spread on cake (Sufficient for two 8-inch layers)

ORANGE BUTTERMILK PUDDING

½ cup strained orange juice
1 tbsp lemon juice
1½ cups fresh buttermilk
Pinch of salt
About ⅓ cup sugar (or to suit taste)
1 tbsp plain gelatin (1 envelope)
3 tbsp cold water

Combine orange and lemon juice with buttermilk and salt and sweeten to suit the taste (depending on sweetness of orange juice). Soften gelatin in cold water; then heat over hot water until dissolved. Stir into buttermilk mixture. Pour into a mold or bowl and chill until firm. Unmold and garnish with orange sections and serve with whipped cream if desired. (Serves 5)

ORANGE CHARLOTTE RUSSE

2 cups milk
2 eggs, separated
¾ tsp salt
⅔ cup sugar
2 tbsp cornstarch
1 package orange-flavored gelatin
1 pt coffee cream
1 tbsp lemon juice
½ cup orange juice
2 tsp grated orange rind
15-oz angel food cake (bought)

Pour milk into the top of a double boiler, add the egg yolks and beat well to mix. Blend the salt, sugar and cornstarch, and stir into the milk. Cook mixture over hot water, stirring until mixture is smooth and thickened. Add the gelatin and stir until it is dissolved; add cream, fruit juices, rind. Cool until slightly congealed. Then beat egg whites until stiff and fold into the orange mixture. Slice the cake into wedges, and line the bottom and sides of a 9-inch spring-form pan. Fill the pan with thr orange mixture and set in the refrigerator for several hours to congeal and chill. Serve with whipped cream if desired. (Serves 10 or 12)

ORANGE CHIFFON PIE

Follow directions for lemon chiffon pie (*see* LEMON) substituting orange juice and rind for the lemon juice and lemon rind, but adding also 1 tablespoon of lemon juice.

ORANGE CUSTARD I

3/4 cup sugar
3 tbsp cornstarch
Few grains of salt
2 cups milk
2 eggs
1/3 tsp almond extract
3 oranges

Combine 1/2 cup of the sugar with the cornstarch and salt. Blend thoroughly, add the milk, then cook in the upper part of the double boiler for 20 minutes, stirring constantly, until the mixture thickens. Add the beaten egg yolks and cook one minute longer, then remove from the fire and add the almond extract. Halve the oranges crosswise and carefully remove the pulp with a small sharp knife. Place the pulp in a shallow baking dish, carefully discarding all white connecting fiber. Pour the custard over all and top with a meringue made by beating the egg whites until stiff with the remaining sugar. Bake in a moderate oven (350° F.) until the meringue is set and delicately colored. (Serves 4)

ORANGE CUSTARD II

1 tbsp gelatin
1/4 cup cold water
1 cup hot water
1/2 cup sugar
4 egg yolks, beaten very light
1 cup strained orange juice
2 tbsp lemon juice
1/4 tsp salt
1/8 tsp ground nutmeg
1/2 tsp grated orange rind

Soften the gelatin in the cold water, then add the hot water and stir until dissolved. Add the sugar and the well-beaten egg yolks, then cook over hot water (double

boiler), stirring constantly until the mixture thickens. Remove immediately from the hot water and add the orange juice, lemon juice, salt, nutmeg and orange rind. Stir occasionally until the mixture is almost at the setting point, then turn into small, previously wet individual molds, and chill. Unmold and serve with sponge drops, lady fingers or plain cookies. (Serves 6)

ORANGE FILLING

1 1/2 cups sugar
1/3 cup flour
Dash of salt
2 tbsp softened butter
2 eggs, beaten
2/3 cup strained orange juice (2 to 4 oranges)
4 tsp lemon juice
3 tsp grated orange rind
1/4 tsp grated lemon rind

Blend sugar, flour and salt into the butter thoroughly. Add eggs and orange juice and beat until well-blended. Cook over medium heat until thick and smooth. Stir constantly. Remove from heat, add lemon juice and orange rind. Cool slightly before spreading on cake. (Sufficient for two 8- or 9-inch layers)

ORANGE FRUITCAKE

1 1/2 medium oranges
2 1/4 cups sugar
1 cup nuts
1 1/2 cups seeded raisins
3 cups sifted flour
1 1/2 tsp baking soda
1 tsp salt
2/3 cup shortening
1 tsp vanilla
3 eggs, well beaten
1 cup sour milk, or buttermilk

Squeeze juice from oranges and add 3/4 cup sugar. Cut the orange skins in quarters and remove all of white pulp and membrane; put the yellow rind, nuts and raisins through food chopper, using the finest knife. Mix and sift flour, soda and salt. Cream the shortening until soft and smooth, gradually add remaining 1 1/2 cups sugar, creaming until fluffy; beat in vanilla and eggs, then fruit-nut mixture. Add the flour alternately with the sour milk, beating well after each addition. Turn into 2 greased loaf pans and bake in slow oven (300° F.) about 1½ hours. Remove from the oven and immediately pour the orange juice-sugar mixture over cakes. Cool in pans and allow to stand several hours or overnight before cutting.

ORANGE ICE

2 cups granulated sugar
4 cups cold water
2 cups orange juice
¼ cup lemon juice
Grated rind of 2 oranges

Make a sirup with cold water and sugar, and allow it to boil for 5 minutes. Cool slightly, then add orange and lemon juice and grated orange rind. Cool, strain, and freeze in hand freezer, using 3 parts of ice and 1 part of rock salt. Serve in chilled orange baskets, or in chilled sherbet glasses.

ORANGE MARMALADE

12 thin-skinned oranges
3 lemons
3 qts water
Sugar

Wash and slice the oranges and lemons as thin as possible. Add the water and let stand overnight. Next day cook the mixture slowly until tender (2 to 2½ hours). Measure, add an equal measure of sugar, and cook until the jellying point is reached. Turn into sterilized jars and seal. *See also* CANNING.

QUICK ORANGE MARMALADE

3 large oranges (about 1¾ lb)
2 lemons
3 tbsp lemon juice
5 cups water
6 cups granulated sugar

Choose sound, juicy oranges, preferably seedless. They may be any size but a large size is easier to prepare. If only a mildly bitter product is desired, scrape the surface of the oranges with a sharp knife to open the cells. Boil for 3 minutes in 2 quarts of water. Cool in cold water. Cut oranges

and the 2 lemons into 8 sections each; scoop out the pulp removing any seeds, cut up and put into kettle. Then slice the rind paper-thin and add to kettle. Add the additional lemon juice and water; bring to boil, simmer 1 hour uncovered. Add sugar, stir until dissolved, and return to heat; again bring to boil and simmer for about 50 minutes longer. Remove pan from heat. Test for doneness by dropping a teaspoonful of the hot liquid onto a thoroughly chilled plate and place in refrigerator for 5 minutes; if jellied by the end of this time, the marmalade is done; if not, continue cooking for a few minutes longer, and again test for doneness. When done, pour into hot sterilized jelly glasses and cover immediately with paraffin. When cool, add another thin layer of paraffin. (Makes about 4 pints of marmalade)

ORANGE MARMALADE SOUFFLE

4 eggs, separated
½ to ¾ cup orange marmalade
¼ tsp salt
2 tbsp sugar
1½ cups milk
⅛ tsp salt
3 tbsp sugar
1 tbsp vanilla
½ tsp flour
Almonds

Beat egg whites until very stiff. Fold in the marmalade, the teaspoon salt, and the 2 tablespoons sugar very lightly but thoroughly. Turn into the well-greased top of a double boiler (preferably one with a round bottom). Cover and cook over simmering water about 1 hour and 20 minutes, or until done. When a knife inserted in center comes out clean, the soufflé is done.

Meanwhile prepare custard sauce by scalding the milk with the ⅛ teaspoon salt and 3 tablespoons sugar. Beat egg yolks well, add flour and stir until smooth. Pour a small amount of hot milk into yolks, stir well and return to large amount of hot liquid. Cook over simmering water until custard coats a spoon. Remove custard from heat, cool and stir in vanilla. When soufflé is done, turn out onto a serving plate, pour on the custard sauce and serve. Garnish with slivered, salted, toasted almonds, if desired. (Serves 5 or 6)

ORANGE MILK SHERBET

2 cups undiluted, well-chilled evaporated milk
1 cup boiling water
1¾ cups granulated sugar
2 cups orange juice
4 tbsp lemon juice
⅛ tsp salt

Boil sugar and water for 5 long minutes. Cool, then chill. Add orange and lemon juice, mix thoroughly, then combine, while beating gently, with chilled undiluted evaporated milk and salt. Freeze in hand freezer, using 4 parts ice and 1 part salt, until solid, but not too hard. Serve in chilled sherbet glasses or orange cups.

ORANGE OATMEAL COOKIES

2 cups all-purpose flour
1 tsp baking soda
¾ tsp salt
½ tsp ground cinnamon
⅛ tsp allspice
1 cup shortening
½ cup granulated sugar
½ cup light brown sugar, firmly packed
2 eggs
2 cups quick-cooking rolled oats
⅓ cup orange juice
1 cup seedless raisins, washed and dried
½ cup coarsely cut nuts
2 tsp grated orange rind

Sift flour, measure and resift 3 times with soda, salt and spices. Cream shortening until smooth and soft. Add both sugars gradually and beat until thoroughly blended. Add eggs one at a time, and beat until very light. Stir in the oats; add flour mixture and orange juice alternately in 2 or 3 portions and beat well after each addition. Stir in the raisins, nuts and rind. Drop by teaspoonfuls onto greased baking sheets and bake in a 350° F. oven for 10 to 12 minutes. (Makes 8 dozen small cookies)

ORANGE PUDDING I

5 tbsp butter
¾ cup sugar
2 eggs

1 tbsp grated orange rind
1 cup orange juice (about)
1½ cups sifted flour
1½ tsp baking powder
⅛ tsp salt

Cream the butter, gradually adding the sugar and continuing the beating until fluffy. Add the well-beaten eggs, then the grated orange rind and juice, alternately with the flour previously sifted with the baking powder and salt. The batter should be moist enough to drop easily from the spoon. Turn into one large buttered mold (or individual custard cups) having this about two-thirds full. Cover with waxed paper, then set in a pan containing one inch of hot water. Bake in a moderate oven (350° F.) about one hour, or until set. Unmold and serve with any preferred sauce. (Serves 6)

ORANGE PUDDING II

3 eggs
6 tbsp sugar
½ tsp grated orange rind
¼ tsp grated lemon rind
¾ cup orange juice
3 tbsp lemon juice
2 tbsp water
1 tsp gelatin
1 tbsp water
16 small lady fingers

Beat the egg yolks in the upper part of the double boiler, gradually beating in 4 tablespoons of the sugar. Add orange and lemon rinds and slowly stir in the orange juice, lemon juice and water. Place over boiling water and cook, stirring constantly, until the mixture thickens slightly, about 10 minutes. Now add the gelatin which has been softened in the cold water, then when thoroughly blended, cool the whole slightly and fold in the egg whites which have been beaten very stiff with the remaining sugar. Arrange the split lady fingers in a refrigerator tray, pour the orange mixture over. Chill very thoroughly and unmold for service. (Serves 4 to 6)

ORANGE REFRIGERATOR CAKE

32 to 34 strips of day-old angel food cake
1 tbsp gelatin

ORANGE

1½ cups orange juice
½ cup sugar
¼ cup butter, melted
Pinch of salt
12 marshmallows, cut fine
½ cup orange segments
1 tsp lemon juice
½ cup heavy cream

1 cake compressed yeast
7½ cups sifted flour (about)
2 well beaten eggs
1 tsp salt
½ cup sugar
2 tbsp grated orange rind
⅓ cup orange juice
¼ cup shortening, melted

Line sides and bottom of an 8-inch spring mold pan with strips of cake. Soften gelatin in ¼ cup of the orange juice. Bring ½ cup orange juice and sugar to boil, remove from heat. Add gelatin and stir until dissolved. Add butter, remaining orange juice, and salt. Set in a pan of cracked ice and beat thoroughly with a rotary beater. Chill until slightly congealed, beating at intervals to keep butter from forming into lumps. Add marshmallows, orange segments and lemon juice to the slightly congealed mixture. Whip cream until it holds its shape. Fold into the gelatin mixture thoroughly. Turn into cake-lined pan. Chill several hours before serving. (Serves 8)

ORANGE REFRIGERATOR COOKIES

1¾ cups all-purpose flour
½ tsp soda
½ tsp salt
½ cup butter
½ cup granulated sugar
½ cup brown sugar, firmly packed
1 egg
1 tsp grated orange rind
½ tsp orange extract

Sift flour, measure and resift 3 times with soda and salt. Cream butter. Add both sugars gradually and beat until fluffy. Add egg and beat well. Stir in dry ingredients, rind, and flavoring. Shape in rolls, wrap in waxed paper and chill overnight or for at least 4 hours. Slice ⅛ inch thick with a thin-bladed, very sharp knife. Place on ungreased baking sheet, and bake in a moderate oven (375° F.) 7 to 8 minutes. Remove to racks to cool. (Makes·12 dozen tiny cookies)

ORANGE ROLLS

1 cup mashed potatoes
1¾ cups milk, scalded

Force mashed potatoes through fine sieve into large mixing bowl and stir in hot milk; when lukewarm, add crumbled yeastcake and 4 cups flour, and beat thoroughly; cover and let rise in warm place until doubled in bulk (about 4 hours). Combine eggs, salt, sugar, orange rind, juice, and shortening; add to light sponge and beat well; gradually stir in remaining flour and knead until smooth. Put in greased bowl and cover. Let rise in warm place until doubled in bulk (for 2 to 4 hours). Knead, shape as desired and place in greased pan; brush with melted shortening. Cover and let rise in warm place until very light (for 1 to 2 hours). Bake in hot oven (400°–425° F.) for 15 to 20 minutes. (Makes approximately 3 to 4 dozen rolls)

ORANGE SALADS

Orange and Asparagus Salad

Arrange on lettuce for individual service 6 orange segments alternating these with an equal number of cooked asparagus tips. Garnish with sliced stuffed olives or pimiento strips, passing any preferred dressing separately.

Orange Flower Salad

Peel and separate oranges into sections. Arrange for individual service on crisp lettuce, a mound of mayonnaise in the center, then radiating orange sections with a thin strip of pimiento or maraschino cherry between each two.

Orange and Onion Salad

Peel and thinly slice small sweet onions and small seedless oranges. Arrange in alternate slices on romaine or lettuce and serve with French dressing.
The large sweet Bermuda onions may also be used.

ORANGE SAUCE

3 tbsp cornstarch
1 cup sugar
¼ tsp salt
1 cup orange juice
½ cup water
1 egg yolk
1 tsp grated orange rind

Combine the cornstarch, sugar and salt, add the orange juice and water gradually, then cook over hot water (double boiler) stirring constantly until thick and clear, about 10 minutes. Pour over the well-beaten egg yolk, beating while pouring, and add the grated orange rind.

ORANGE SHORTBREAD

6 oz butter
8 oz flour
2 oz sugar
Grated rind of 1 orange

Rub butter into flour and add sugar and orange rind, grated. Work together into stiff dough. Turn out on floured board and knead thoroughly till smooth. Roll out thinly, cut in rounds of 2½-inch diameter. Prick well with fork. Bake in moderate oven till pale brown. Can be brushed with egg if liked and an almond, split, placed on each, or piece of candied orange peel.

ORANGE SOUFFLE I

½ cup sifted flour
1 cup orange juice
4 eggs
½ cup sugar
1 tbsp lemon juice
1 tbsp grated orange rind

Moisten the flour with the orange juice, adding it slowly and mixing until perfectly smooth. Cook over moderate heat until the mixture thickens, then remove from the fire, add the egg yolks, unbeaten, one at a time, and beat well after each addition. Add also half the sugar, the lemon juice and the orange rind. Beat the egg whites until stiff with the remaining sugar, then turn into a casserole, well-buttered and sprinkled with a heavy coating of granulated sugar. Bake in a moderately hot oven (400° F.) about 30 minutes. Serve immediately with a thin orange sauce. (Serves 6)

ORANGE SOUFFLE II

¼ cup butter, melted
½ cup dry bread crumbs
1 cup milk
Grated rind 1 orange
3 eggs
2 tbsp sugar

Combine in the upper part of a double boiler the butter, crumbs, milk, and orange rind. Cook 20 minutes over boiling water, then add to the egg yolks and sugar which have been beaten together lightly. Fold in the stiffly beaten egg whites. Turn into a buttered casserole, place this in a pan of hot water and bake about 40 minutes in a moderate oven (375° F.). Serve with orange-flavored hard sauce. (Serves 4 to 6)

ORANGE SOUP

2 tbsp gelatin
4 tbsp cold water
3 cups orange juice
¾ cup sugar
2 tbsp lime juice
Pulp of 3 oranges
2 tbsp sweet cordial, optional
Mint

Soften the gelatin in the cold water. Heat 1 cup of the orange juice and dissolve both sugar and gelatin in it. Strain into the remaining orange juice combined with the lime juice, and chill. When almost at setting point beat with a rotary beater and combine with the orange pulp, and cordial, if used. The mixture must be blended before the gelatin fully sets. Immediately before serving beat again thoroughly with rotary beater. Serve in bouillon cups or in the orange shells, garnishing with sections of orange and sprigs of mint. (Serves 4 to 6)

ORANGE SPONGE

1 tbsp plain gelatin (1 envelope)
¼ cup cold water
1 cup boiling water

⅓ cup sugar
⅛ tsp salt
1 cup orange juice
2 tsp lemon juice
¼ tsp lemon rind
½ tsp orange rind
2 egg whites

Soften gelatin in the cold water for 5 minutes. Add boiling water, sugar, and salt and stir until dissolved. Cool slightly and add juices and rinds. Allow to partly congeal, then beat with rotary beater until fluffy. Fold in stiffly beaten egg whites. Chill 5 to 6 hours until firm. Serve cold. (Serves 4 or 6)

ORANGE TAPIOCA

1 egg, separated
2 cups milk
½ cup cream
¼ cup quick-cooking tapioca
½ cup sugar
¼ tsp salt
½ tsp grated orange rind
½ cup orange juice
2 tbsp lemon juice
1 seedless orange

Add egg yolk to milk in top of double boiler. Beat well. Add cream, tapioca, sugar and salt and cook over boiling water for 12 to 15 minutes, stirring frequently. Remove from heat, add orange rind and juices. Beat egg white until stiff and fold lightly but thoroughly into hot tapioca mixture. Chill and serve garnished with orange slices or with cream. (Serves 5)

The orange may be cut into small bits and stirred into the cooked tapioca.

ORANGE WALDORF SALAD

1 large seedless orange
Lettuce or romaine
1 cup peeled and diced apples
1 cup diced celery
¼ cup chopped pecans
Salt to taste
2 tbsp mayonnaise
2 tbsp boiled salad dressing

Peel orange, cut into 5 slices, and place in lettuce cups on individual plates. Combine other ingredients, tossing lightly together, and pile in light heaps on orange slices. Serve at once. See SALAD DRESSING for boiled dressing. (Serves 5)

ORANGE WINE

Squeeze as many oranges as necessary to make 8 quarts of juice. Strain. Remove the pulp from half of the orange peels and cut rinds in very fine strips. Beat 2 egg whites, add the lightly crushed shells, 6 pounds granulated sugar, and 2 quarts of water; bring to the boiling point, and cook, stirring constantly, until sugar is thoroughly dissolved and the liquid is clear. Pour over orange rind strips and let stand 1 day. Then, add orange juice mixed with 1 quart of lemon juice and strain through a flannel bag. Crumble ½ yeast cake (compressed) into ½ cup of the liquid (cold) and stir until dissolved, then add to the remaining liquid, stir well and pour into a crock. Tie a cloth over crock until fermentation ceases. Skim carefully, pour into small cask and bung tightly. Allow to stand 9 months. Then bottle, cap or cork tightly, and let stand 3 to 4 months before using.

POACHED ORANGE SLICES

Combine 1 cup water, 2 cups sugar and the juice of 1 lemon (3 tablespoons) in a 10-inch aluminum skillet or a shallow sauce pan and simmer five minutes. Wash and cut into slices about ⅜ inch thick, seedless oranges, and drop them into the hot sirup; simmer until tender. Lift out and serve hot with bacon or sausage. These also make an attractive garnish for baked ham. The sirup may be used several times if a little more water and sugar are added each time. (Serves 5)

ORANGE BITTERS. A widely used flavoring for mixed drinks, such as cocktails, cups, punches, etc. A product of England, it is very tonic and stomachic, having a bittersweet, quinine-orange peel taste. It is claimed that a few drops on a lump of sugar facilitate digestion. Diluted with fresh water, it is a very refreshing beverage, especially in summer.

ORANGE EXTRACT. See FLAVORING EXTRACTS.

ORANGE FLOWER OIL. An oil produced from orange blossoms, used in confections and pastry.

ORANGE FLOWER WATER. A product distilled from orange blossoms, found in almost every drugstore. Used in pastry and confections.

ORANGE MELON. Another name for mango melon, *which see.*

ORANGE POMANDER. An orange, studded with cloves, used to perfume clothes.

ORANGE RATAFIA. Ratafia is a term which was used long years ago in France to designate liqueurs of the after-dinner type, but the term has long been discarded. The Louisiana Ratafias are home-made cordials, generally prepared with a good brandy as a base.

ORANGE RATAFIA

3 oranges
1 pt brandy
1 lb sugar

Grate the rind of the oranges very lightly. Place this oil, or zest, which is thus secured, on lumps of sugar in a jar. Add one pint of good brandy and the juice of the three oranges, seeds removed. Let the mixture stand for three days; then filter and bottle.

ORANGE PEKOE TEA. Unbroken, black tea, with a fairly well-twisted leaf. The term has no bearing on the quality of tea. *See also* TEA.

ORCHARD. An enclosure of fruit trees, or trees which yield nuts or maple sugar.

ORCIN. A coloring substance obtained from lichens.

OREANDA. A very good dessert wine of a beautiful amber color. It is very popular in Russia where it is made.

OREGANO. *Orégano* is the Spanish name for wild marjoram. It is a necessary ingredient of chili con carne, and it is used in spaghetti sauce and many other Italian dishes. It can be used to a greater extent than it is in cookery, nicely replacing thyme in any recipe. It blends particularly well with veal, lamb, pork, scrambled eggs, omelets, salads, and cream cheese. *See* MARJORAM.

ORGANIC SALTS. Although organic salts constitute only a comparatively small part of the body—about five percent—they are nevertheless essential constituents, and every element has some distinct physiological function to perform. The organic salts enter the system as fully oxidized compounds and therefore furnish practically

no heat and energy. Still they hold the key to nearly all of the material manifestations of life. They are the builders of healthy cells and tissues, giving them firmness and form. They are the carriers of the life-giving oxygen to all parts of the body. They are essential factors in digestion and assimilation, and important ingredients of the digestive juices, regulating the osmotic exchange between lymph and blood and cells—in short, they are indispensable for the proper physiological functioning of all the glands of the body. The body of a normal man, weighing 150 pounds, is composed of about:

90 lb		of oxygen
36 lb		of carbon
14 lb		of hydrogen
3 lb	8	oz of nitrogen
3 lb	12	oz of calcium
1 lb	14	oz of phosphorus
4		oz of chlorine
$3\frac{1}{2}$		oz of sulphur
3		oz of potassium
$2\frac{1}{2}$		oz of sodium
2		oz of fluorine
$1\frac{1}{2}$		oz of magnesium
$\frac{1}{4}$		oz of silicon
$\frac{1}{6}$		oz of iron

Plus traces of manganese, iodine, aluminum, and arsenic.

The phosphate of lime and the carbonate of lime of the skeleton, the iron contained in the red corpuscles of the blood, the phosphate of sodium, chloride of potassium, and the sodium found in the blood serum have a certain duration of life, during which they have vital functions to perform. Sooner or later they must be supplanted by fresh material. The proteins in the body are always combined with mineral elements, whereby the former acquired specific properties.

ORGEAT. A sirup made of an emulsion of almonds for sweetening drinks.

ORIENTAL SAUCE. *See* MAYONNAISE.

ORPINE. A succulent plant with fleshy leaves. Some species have yellow flowers.

ORTOLAN. A very small bird, allied to the bunting. In Europe it is highly esteemed for its flesh, but such birds cannot be killed for food in America.

OSAGE MELON. A round melon with grayish rind and pink or green flesh. It is grown in all parts of the United States. *See also* MELON.

OSMAZONE. A great service which chemistry has rendered to the science of food is in exactly defining osmazone. It is that eminently sapid part of meat which is soluble in cold water, and which is distinguished from the extractive part, because the latter is soluble only in boiling water.

Osmazone is the thing that gives good soups their special merit. And when osmazone passes into a state resembling caramel, it causes the browning of meat, and also the crisp brown of roast meat. From it arises the odor of game.

Osmazone is derived mainly from full-grown animals with dark reddish flesh, such as beef. It is absent (or found only in very small quantities) in lamb, young pigs, and fowls. It is for this reason that real connoisseurs have always preferred the thick part of the thigh; their instinctive taste anticipated science.

OSMOSIS. The process of diffusion whereby gases and fluids pass through a membrane dividing two solutions of the body, tending to equalize their concentrations.

OSOYE. A wine that was popular in England during the days of Chaucer. Its origin, taste, and appearance are unknown.

OSSEIN. See GELATIN.

OSSETIN CHEESE. A Russian cheese made from sheep's or cow's milk. It is also known as Tuschinsk and Kasack. It is made in the Caucasus.

OSTIEPEK CHEESE. A cheese made from sheep's milk in the Carpathian Mountains. The process of manufacture is said to be the same as that used by the Italians in making the better-known caccio cavallo.

OUNCE or **OZ.** A unit of measure—one-sixteenth of a pound.

OUTDOOR COOKERY. See BARBECUE, CAMP COOKERY, and PICNIC.

OUZO. An anisette-flavored apéritif popular in Greece. In appearance and manner of serving, it greatly resembles absinthe.

OVAL DISH. A name used for relatively flat, oval-shaped dishes of varying sizes, used more for serving than eating. Such a dish is more commonly called a platter. See DISHES.

OVAL SOUP SPOON. See FLATWARE.

OVAR CHEESE. A Hungarian cheese made of cow's milk. It is reddish yellow with a reddish brown crust, mild in taste, and weighs about ten pounds.

OVCJI SIR CHEESE. A rennet cheese, made of sheep's milk, weighing from six to ten pounds. It is made in the Slovenian Alps.

OVEN. An oven is a heated chamber in which food is cooked, primarily by means of dry heat, though it may be adapted to other forms of cookery. An oven may take a surprising number of sizes, shapes, and forms, be built from any one of a variety of materials, and utilize just about any efficient heat source.

TYPES

Ovens may be heated internally or externally, and they may be separate units or incorporated into some other device. They are universally known and one of the oldest of cooking devices, so it is only natural that they should have assumed different forms at different times in different cultures.

The most commonly used oven in the modern American home is the type that is incorporated into the kitchen range (see RANGE). The design and functioning of this oven depends upon the type of range of which it is a feature.

Another fairly common type is the so-called Dutch oven (which see), a separate, usually portable unit. These ovens may have their own heat source (coal or wood) but many are built of stamped metal with an open bottom, and are designed to be placed over some outside heat source. These ovens are commonly used over the burners of an oven-less range, though they are also handy as an auxiliary unit to augment the regular range oven. They are also invaluable to campers for they may be used, not only in conjunction with portable oil or gasoline stoves, but also with open fires.

The *reflector oven* is an unusual and somewhat rare type, being confined almost exclusively to camping and other out-of-door use. It differs from the normal oven in being open rather than closed. The interior is lined with sheets of highly polished metal arranged to catch and reflect radiant heat, concentrating it on the food which is placed inside.

In its most common form, the reflector oven is a highly portable item, collapsing to a compact, light-weight bundle that fits easily into a pack. It is intended to be assembled and set up close to a fire which supplies the necessary heat. *See* CAMP COOKERY. It may also be built as a permanent unit using an electric heating element. Experimental reflector ovens have frequently been designed to utilize the heat of the sun, but while these may function, they are so far of little practical value.

The large, outdoor oven, built of brick or clay, complete with fire pit and chimney has largely passed out of existence in modern America. These ovens, used primarily to bake bread, and to roast large quantities of meat, are rarely required these days, even where there is sufficient ground area to build them.

In the days before the cellar furnace, ovens were sometimes built into chimneys or the fireplace wall, but modern units and modern living have supplanted these.

The *high frequency oven* is the latest arrival on the scene, but is still largely in the development stage. While it is not yet practical for home use, some limited commercial applications have been made. *See* HIGH-FREQUENCY COOKING.

HINTS ON USING THE OVEN

The oven is primarily used for baking, roasting, and, where design permits, broiling, though this latter is not an essential oven function. These uses are all discussed specifically under their own headings, *which see*. Other forms of cooking, such as steaming, may be done in the oven if the occasion should so require, but unless the foods involved are components of an oven meal, it is more economical to cook them over the surface burners, since the heat is applied more efficiently, with consequent fuel savings.

In general, all oven cookery is done on a basis of time and temperature. It is a bad practice to constantly open the oven door to "peek," for not only does this lower the oven temperature by permitting the heat to escape, but the vibration and sudden flow of air can well cause cakes and similar mixtures to collapse. As a concession to human nature which somehow cannot bear the thought of operations going on behind closed doors, and also to facilitate matters in those operations such as browning that do require observation, some manufacturers equip their ovens with windows.

Temperature control is one of the two keys to successful oven cookery, and it must be constant, even, and exact. Many ovens are equipped with a thermometer, and if there is none provided, an oven thermometer (*see* KITCHEN EQUIPMENT) should be purchased in the interests of good cooking. Most modern gas and electric ranges are equipped with a thermostat that automatically keeps the oven at a predetermined temperature. While a thermometer is not essential in that case, it is well to have one on hand to occasionally check the accuracy of the thermostat settings.

The test of a good oven is the ease and accuracy with which the temperature may be regulated and maintained. This depends on both oven construction and the heat source, and is a fact that should be carefully considered when a kitchen range or separate oven is purchased.

Temperature may also be controlled to some extent by the position of the food in the oven. This is especially true of gas and electric ovens that are heated by elements or burners placed on the inside. Most ovens are equipped with removable, adjustable racks so that large objects may be accommodated and distance from food to heating unit regulated. The position of the heating element in some electric ovens may also be changed.

The recommended oven temperatures for the various types of oven cookery are given in the articles dealing with such cooking. Recipes are sometimes encountered that give the oven temperatures in descriptive terms rather than degrees. This practice stems back to the early ovens where temperature control was not so exact a science as it is in modern models. These terms are, however, fairly standard and in general correspond to specific degrees as follows:

OVEN TEMPERATURES

Very slow	250° F.
Slow	300° F.
Moderately slow	325° F.
Moderate	350° F.
Moderately hot	375° F.
Hot	400°–425° F.
Very hot	450°–500° F.

Timing is the other key to successful oven cookery and it also marks the point where science and art meet. Temperature and timing both have a great deal to do with the flavor, texture and appearance of the finished product; temperature controlling the rate of cooking, while timing controls the duration. Were all food uniform, it would be possible to set up exact time and temperature tables to produce the best possible results. Food, unfortunately, will vary. The texture and the amount of fat and gristle in a steak, for example, will vary, while the ratio of bone to meat in chickens is hardly standardized. Doughs and batters have their discrepancies, as well. Since the food is not consistent, either the time or the temperature must be altered to compensate, and of the two, time is the preferred element.

This does not mean that time and temperature tables are useless; far from it. They are excellent guides and will produce consistently good results. They should be followed until the user has gained the experience that will tell her when the time element should be varied and then by how much. Indeed, most time tables are given in terms of a tentative range spread rather than an exact interval for just that reason, that the proper time will lie somewhere between the two mentioned intervals, but its exact location will vary with the food in the oven and the family taste.

Though good timing does require a touch of the artist, it should be done in a scientific way. Approximate methods can produce only approximate results no matter what task is being performed.

Oven cooking should be timed by some manner other than guesswork. Many modern ovens are equipped with automatic timers that will actually shut them off at the end of the cooking period and, in some cases, even turn them on at the beginning. Other ranges are equipped with timers that function somewhat like an alarm clock, making some sort of warning sound when the desired interval is over. Such units may also be purchased separately, if the range is not already so equipped. Failing a special timer, a regular alarm clock may be used, or the kitchen wall clock consulted. This last is a potentially dangerous practice, however, for there is a tendency to become so engrossed in some phase of housework as to forget about the oven, unless bells are rung or some other warning noise given.

It must be remembered that most types of ovens require pre-heating. Once lit or placed over a burner (depending on type) it takes a short period for these ovens to reach the proper internal temperature. For proper timing, then, the oven must first be allowed to reach the correct temperature before the food is inserted, or, if the food is placed inside before the pre-heating is done, due allowances must be made.

After an oven has been used, the door should be left open slightly (many ovens have an arrangement to hold the door slightly ajar during broiling operations) so that it may cool without causing the moisture resulting from cooking to condense on the oven walls. As explained in the article on ranges, the oven should be kept clean at all times.

EQUIPMENT

As previously mentioned in this article, an oven thermometer and a timer are important pieces of auxiliary equipment for use with an oven. Many modern ovens are equipped with interior lights. If the bulb is exposed, care should be taken not to touch it with a cold damp cloth while it is hot. Though the commonly used bulb is heat resistant, sudden temperature differences could cause it to crack. Only the proper type of bulb should be used as a replacement, when the original one is burned out.

The pans used for baking should be made of light and medium weight materials that are smooth and even. If metallic, the pans should be bright and shiny, for dark colored, black pans absorb too much heat and cause uneven browning of cakes and similar foods. Warped, uneven, or dented pans should be avoided. The pan walls should not be so high as to shield the top of the baking food, for this, too, will cause uneven browning.

A baking sheet without sides gives the best results for cookies, small rolls and biscuits, though a pan with low sides (about a quarter of an inch) may be used with biscuits and small rolls. High sides interfere with heat circulation and browning.

Both shallow, uncovered pans, and larger, covered ones made of glass or metal are used for roasting. Covered pans of almost any heat-transmitting material are used for steaming and moist-heat cooking. *Under no conditions are plastic dishes ever to be used in the oven.*

Oven pans should be kept spotlessly clean to prevent undesirable blackening.

Discretion should be exercised in using them for any other than their primary function. Layer cake pans, for example, should never be used as a grill to pan-broil bacon, etc. When used in the oven, the food-filled pans should be carefully arranged to permit free heat circulation on all sides. Pans should never be allowed to touch each other or the sides or back of the oven during cooking.

OVEREATING AND OVERDRINK-ING. Both these excesses may be temporary—that is, the result of an occasional debauch, or chronic.

Temporary overeating may apply to the excessive consumption of a mixed diet, or of particular articles of food. The former causes dyspepsia, or, in extreme cases, acute gastro-enteritis. The latter may also cause dyspepsia and diarrhea, or such affections may be produced as glycosuria, from excessive indulgence in candy and sweets; acne and other skin diseases, from the too liberal consumption of fats.

Temporary overeating at one or two meals may not produce any serious ill effect, but if the excess in feeding be long continued a variety of ills result, attributable directly to overloading of the alimentary canal. There is a limit to the quantity of every food which can be digested in a given time. Beyond this the food, whether starches, fats, sugars, or protein, may decompose, or pass away unaltered. Or, if the excess be absorbed the blood is overwhelmed, and the excretory organs are overworked.

The inability to sing with precision after a too hearty meal is often attributed to temporary congestion of the vocal cords. While this is observed in the thickened speech of alcoholism, the difficulty in singing caused by overeating is mainly due to inability to regulate the actions of the diaphragm and other respiratory muscles when the stomach is too greatly distended.

Overeating, especially among the well-to-do, is the commonest dietetic error, and looking at the question in its broadest aspects, it is quite certain that the foundation for more disease is laid by this habit than by overdrinking.

Overdrinking, except of alcohol, is not common, and is mainly confined to the excessive consumption of tea and coffee, which results in insomnia, cardiac palpitations, and various neuroses. Dilation of the stomach has been attributed in some cases to overindulgence in mineral waters, but such instances are very unusual. Polyuria and diabetes insipidus have also been ascribed to the abnormal consumption of fluids, but without strong proof. Excessive use of milk as a beverage usually results in "biliousness" and constipation, but for the reason that it is really a solid food—that is, it becomes such immediately on entering the stomach.

OVERHEAT. To heat more than the indicated directions, or more than is necessary.

OX TONGUE. Another name for beef tongue. *See* Tongue.

OXTAIL. The tail of the beef. Although it contains very little meat, it is used in soups to give flavor, and it may also be braised.

BRAISED OXTAIL

2 oxtails
1 tbsp chopped onion
Salt and pepper
2 cups stewed tomatoes
2 slices lemon
2 tbsp butter or margarine
1 tbsp chopped green pepper
Flour
½ tsp ginger
Water or stock

Heat the butter and sauté the onion and green pepper until soft, but not brown. Cut the oxtail in serving pieces and cover with boiling water. Let stand for a few minutes and then drain. Dry the pieces. Season the flour with salt and pepper, and roll the pieces of oxtail in the seasoned flour. Brown in the butter with the onions and pepper. Pour in a scant 2 cups of water or stock, add the tomatoes and ginger. Cover the pan and simmer gently until the meat falls away from the bones. (Serves 6)

OXTAIL SOUP

2 or 3 oxtails
3 tbsp bacon fat or drippings
Water
1 bay leaf
Salt and pepper
1 qt diced mixed vegetables
1 tbsp Worcestershire sauce

Wash, dry, and disjoint the oxtails, then brown in the bacon fat or drippings. Cover with water, add the bay leaf and a little salt, and simmer until the meat is quite tender. Strain, add the diced vegetables—carrots, onion, turnip, potatoes, celery—and simmer until these are tender, but not broken. Meanwhile, chop the meat, return it to the soup, reheat, and if necessary add additional salt and pepper, with the Worcestershire sauce. (Serves 6)

OXYGENEE. The name given to an aniseed liqueur designed as a substitute for absinthe, when the sale of the latter was prohibited in France. The name, which has no relevant meaning, has since been discarded.

OYSTER. The ancient Greeks considered the oyster the perfect prelude to a meal, and the Romans called it the "dainty manna of the sea." After Caesar's conquest of Britain, British oysters were transported in bags packed in snow and ice for service at Roman banquets. The ancient peoples of the New World appreciated the oyster, witness the ancient shellmounds found in many places in the United States.

Oyster fishing and farming have grown to be a considerable industry in the United States, and three commercial species are grown in American waters. These are the native eastern oyster, the Olympia which is native to the Pacific coast, and the Japanese oyster which is grown on the Pacific coast from seed imported from Japan.

COMMERCIAL OYSTER FISHING

The adult oyster is usually attached to some hard object, such as old oyster shells, rocks, pilings, etc. Spawning takes place at water temperatures of 68° to 70° F. during the summer months, and over a longer period of time in the Gulf of Mexico. The female oyster lays an incredible number of eggs during the season, and the newly hatched oyster is so small as to be barely visible with the naked eye. For about two weeks it is free-swimming. Then if conditions of temperature and water are satisfactory, it sinks to the bottom, and attaches itself to some hard object. It remains fixed and growing until it is of marketable length, generally two to four years.

About 60 percent of the American oyster harvest is from cultivated bottoms owned outright or leased from the government.

Some bottoms are reserved for getting a set of seed oysters, the very tiny young oysters which have just settled. The oyster farmer transplants the seed oysters to

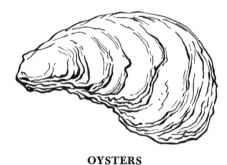

OYSTERS

growing grounds. As they increase in size, he thins them out, replanting the surface, and finally moving them to maturing grounds for fattening for market. During this time he runs constant risk of damage from starfish and other natural enemies of the oyster, and from hurricanes and other storms.

Oysters grow in brackish and salt water in coves, bays, the mouths of rivers, and such comparatively shallow water. The saltier the water in which they grow, the saltier the taste of the oyster. The oysters are harvested with tongs and dredges and taken immediately to the shucking houses for preparation for shipment.

Oysters which are to be marketed in the shell are carefully selected for size and shape of shell and good meats. They are graded for size and packed tightly in barrels to keep the shells closed and thus prevent loss of the oyster liquor.

Oysters which are to be shucked are opened, the meat removed, and particles of shell removed by washing and agitation in air. The meats are then packed in new metal cans, usually of one gallon capacity, packed in ice, and shipped to market. Oyster meats are also quick-frozen and canned.

Oysters keep remarkably well under proper refrigeration. Oysters in the shell remain good for several months if they are kept below a temperature of 41° F. Oyster meats which have been properly chilled and kept at 32° F. will remain good for three weeks or longer. However, at room temperature they will spoil in two days. A spoiled oyster can cause serious illness, so do not take a chance.

SIZES AND GRADES

The most conspicuous difference between oysters from the consumer's point of view is their size. The Pacific oyster, which is very small, will measure between 1600 and 2400 meats to a gallon. The eastern oyster varies between 150 and 600 meats, and the Japanese oyster from 40 to 160 to the gallon.

The eastern oyster is further graded into recognized size classifications as follows:

Trade name	Size	Count per Gallon
Counts or plants	Extra large	Not more than 160
Extra selects	Large	161–210
Selects	Medium	211–300
Standards	Small	301–500
"Standards"	Very small	Over 500

HINTS ON USING OYSTERS

One of the superstitions that is fast losing ground is that oysters should not be eaten in the summer months—those months not containing the letter R. This legend is probably due to the fact that the early colonists were familiar with the English oyster which has different spawning habits. The English oyster retains the developing young within the body of the female for a

from a reliable dealer contain a minimum of free liquor. The oysters are usually left in the cans in which they are packed, the cans being surrounded with ice, and the oysters sold from the can.

Oysters should never be really cooked, just heated through sufficiently to plump them up. Cooking until the "edges curl" is a good test. Overcooking an oyster has the same effect as overcooking an egg—making it tough and leathery.

Quick-frozen oysters should not be thawed until they are ready to be used. Once thawed, they should never be refrozen. In purchasing oysters, remember that for six persons you will need at least three dozen shell oysters, one quart of shucked oysters, or two No. 1 cans.

HOW TO SHUCK AN OYSTER

Wash and rinse the oysters thoroughly in cold water. Place the oyster on the table, flat shell up and holding it with the left hand. With the right hand force an oyster knife between the shells at or near the thin end. The knife is easier to insert if the thin end or "bill" is broken off with a hammer. Cut the large muscle close to the flat upper shell in which it is attached, and remove the shell. Cut the lower end of the same muscle which is attached to the deep half of the shell and leave the oyster

FOOD VALUE

Water	Food Energy	Pro- tein	Fat	Carbo- hydrate	Cal- cium	Phos- phorus	Iron	Vit. A Value	Thia- mine	Ribo- flavin	Nia- cin	Ascor- bic Acid
87.1	50	6.0	1.2	3.7	68	172	7.1	—	.18	.23	1.2	—

week or more, during which the young develop the rudiments of the shell. In the eastern oyster the sex elements of the male and female oysters are discharged into the sea and the young oyster hatches and forms independently of the adult.

Of course, in the early days before modern refrigeration, it was difficult to ship oysters during the warm months without fear of spoilage but this objection has largely been done away with. The oyster farmers foster the superstition as an aid in conservation, but with modern quick-freezing and canning methods, it is possible to enjoy oysters during the summer which have been harvested earlier in the year.

In purchasing oysters, freshness is the most important factor. Oysters purchased

loose in the deep half if it is to be served on the half shell. Examine the oyster for bits of shell which sometimes adhere to the muscle.

CHAFING DISH OYSTERS

½ cup butter
1 tsp dry mustard
Salt, pepper, and celery salt
1½ cups finely chopped celery
3 cups light cream
2 doz oysters
2 tbsp sherry or Madeira

Combine the butter and seasonings in the upper part of a double boiler or chafing dish. When the butter is melted, add the celery and cook until this is almost tender. Add the cream slowly and bring to boiling point. Pick over and add the oysters and cook just until the edges begin to curl. Finally add the sherry or Madeira and serve plain or on toast, garnishing with parsley. (Serves 4 to 6)

CREAMED OYSTERS IN CASES

1½ doz oysters
3 tbsp butter
3 tbsp flour
½ cup milk
¼ cup cream
Salt and pepper
Dash of Worcestershire sauce
6 patty shells or bread cases

Chop one dozen of the oysters and reserve the others whole. Prepare a white sauce (*which see*) with the butter, flour, milk and cream, and seasonings. Add the chopped oysters and set over hot water to heat and slightly cook the oysters. Meanwhile broil the remaining whole oysters just until the edges begin to curl. Divide the creamed mixture among the pastry or bread cases, top each with a broiled oyster and garnish with parsley and cut lemon. (Serves 6)

For the bread cases cut day-old bread into two-inch thick slices. Trim the edges and with a sharp knife remove the centers to form shells or cases. Brush over with softened butter, inside and out, and crisp in the oven.

CURRIED OYSTERS

3 doz shucked oysters
2 tbsp butter
2 tbsp flour
Liquor from oysters and enough cream
  to make 1 cup
1 cup milk
1 bay leaf
Salt and cayenne
½ tsp curry powder mixed to a paste
  with milk or water
4 cups hot cooked rice

Pick over the oysters and pat dry. Prepare a white sauce (*which see*) with the butter, flour, cream and oyster liquor, milk, seasonings and flavorings. When

thoroughly cooked, add the oysters, place over hot water and heat. Serve with the rice, seasoned with salt, pepper, melted butter, and a few drops of onion juice. Pass chutney separately. (Serves 6)

CURRIED OYSTERS
(As Made in Ceylon)

4 shallots
1 small clove of garlic
½ medium-sized green pepper
3 tbsp butter
1 tbsp curry powder
1 inch stick cinnamon
1 small bay leaf
2 whole cloves, heads removed
1 cup coconut milk or cream
Salt
1 doz large oysters
Juice 1 medium-sized lemon
Boiled rice

Mince the shallots, garlic, and green pepper and brown them in the butter in an iron skillet. Add the curry powder, cinnamon, bay leaf and cloves and when these are blended, the coconut milk or cream (*see* COCONUT) and salt to taste. Cook for three minutes. Add the cleaned oysters and cook gently three minutes longer. Remove from the fire, stir in the lemon juice and serve with an abundance of boiled rice. (Serves 2)

OYSTER BISQUE

3 cups milk
1 slice onion
2 stalks celery, diced
1 sprig parsley
1 bay leaf
1 cup oysters
¼ cup soda cracker crumbs
3 tbsp butter
2 tsp salt
Paprika

Scald the milk with the onion, celery, parsley, and bay leaf for 15 minutes. Strain. Pick over and heat the oysters in their own liquor just until the edges begin to curl. Chop finely and add to the milk with the cracker crumbs, butter, and salt. Serve immediately in bowls, dusting each portion with paprika. (Serves 3 or 4)

Oysters Casino

Select large oysters and have them opened on the deep shell. Allow about eight to each portion. Arrange the oysters in their shells in a shallow baking pan, which has been filled with a layer of rock salt. Imbed the oysters firmly in the salt, as this will hold them steady while cooking. Season with salt, cayenne, and paprika. To each oyster add ½ teaspoon each of finely chopped green pepper and pimiento, and top with a slice of bacon cut the same size as the oyster. Broil under a moderate flame. The bacon will cook first, so when both sides are broiled, remove it to a warm dish while the oysters and peppers cook a few minutes longer. Keep the oysters moist by adding a bit of butter or oyster liquor while cooking. Serve in the shells, garnishing with the broiled bacon and parsley.

Oysters on the Half-Shell

3 doz oysters on the half-shell
Cocktail sauce
Lemon
Ice

Serve the oysters with their shells imbedded in the ice and thoroughly chilled, allowing 2 tablespoons of cocktail sauce for each serving. Garnish with lemon sections. (Serves 6)

Cocktail Sauce

2 tbsp horseradish
6 tbsp tomato catsup
4 tbsp lemon juice
Celery salt
Tabasco sauce

Combine all ingredients and chill thoroughly.

Oyster Gumbo

1 pt shucked or canned oysters
1 qt fish stock
2 tbsp butter
2 tbsp finely chopped onion
1 cup cooked or canned okra
2 cups cooked or canned tomatoes
Salt, pepper, and thyme
2 tbsp sweet butter

Clean and pick over the oysters; parboil in their own liquor until the edges curl. Drain the oysters and reserve. Add to the oyster liquor the fish stock and heat in a saucepan. In a skillet melt the butter and cook the minced onion until it is pale yellow, stirring frequently. Add the butter and onion to the stock, together with the okra and tomatoes. Season to taste with salt, pepper, and thyme. Bring to a boil and let simmer a few minutes until the vegetables are well mixed. Remove from the stove and stir in the oysters and the sweet butter. Serve immediately with toasted crackers. (Serves 6)

Oyster Pie

1 cup sliced mushrooms
3 tbsp butter
3 tbsp flour
1 cup milk
½ tsp salt
¼ tsp celery salt
Dash of pepper
1 tsp lemon juice
2 doz oysters
Baking powder biscuit dough

Cook the mushrooms in the butter for five minutes. Stir in the flour and when smoothly blended, gradually add the milk and cook until thickened, stirring constantly. Add the seasonings, lemon juice and oysters and heat all thoroughly. Line the bottom and sides of a small casserole with baking powder biscuit dough (*which see*) rolled out thinly. Fill with the oyster mixture, top with more biscuit dough, press edges firmly together and make two or three slits in the top to permit the escape of steam. Bake in a hot oven (450° F.) for 15 minutes, after which reduce the meat to moderate (350° F.) and bake 10 to 15 minutes longer. (Serves 4)

Oysters Rockefeller

2 doz medium-sized oysters
3 tbsp butter
1 tbsp finely chopped shallot or onion
1 tbsp finely chopped parsley
Salt and cayenne
2 tbsp minced bacon
½ cup spinach purée
Fine bread crumbs

Have the oysters opened on the deep shell. Imbed them in a shallow baking pan which has been prepared with a layer of rock salt as this will hold them steady while baking. Cream half the butter, and add the shallot or onion and parsley to it. Dot each oyster with a bit of this butter, season with salt and cayenne and put a pinch of minced bacon on each oyster. Spread the finely chopped (puréed) spinach over each oyster. Cover with fine bread crumbs and dot with the remaining butter. Bake in a moderate oven (350° F.) about 15 minutes. Serve with quartered lemon. (Serves 4)

OYSTER STEW

4 tsp butter
6 oysters (with liquor)
¾ cup milk, scalded
Salt or celery salt and pepper
Paprika
Oyster crackers

Drain the oysters, reserving the liquor. Heat half the butter in a heavy saucepan, add the drained oysters (carefully picked over) and cook until the edges just begin to curl. Now add the reserved oyster liquor and bring to boiling point. Combine with the scalded milk, season, and serve in a bowl topping with the remaining butter and a generous dusting of paprika. Serve with oyster crackers. (Serves 1)

SAVORY OYSTER STEW

1 peeled clove of garlic
1 halved onion
4 tbsp butter
1 tsp Worcestershire sauce
1 qt raw oysters
1 qt milk, scalded
1½ tsp salt
⅛ tsp pepper
Few grains mace

Rub the inside of the saucepan well with the garlic and onion, and remove them. Melt the butter in this saucepan, add the Worcestershire sauce and the oysters (carefully picked over) and heat just until the edges begin to curl. Finally add the scalded milk and seasonings and serve immediately. (Serves 6)

OYSTER STUFFING
(For Chicken)

4 cups soft bread crumbs
½ cup melted butter
2 tsp salt
½ tsp pepper
1 tbsp lemon juice
2 tbsp minced green pepper
1 pt oysters

Combine all ingredients and blend thoroughly. See STUFFING.

SCALLOPED OYSTERS

Butter a baking dish generously and cover the bottom of it with bread crumbs or crushed oyster crackers. Arrange a layer of picked-over and drained oysters over this and top with butter. Sprinkle with salt and pour in half the reserved oyster liquor. Repeat the layers, finishing with a final topping of butter and crumbs. Pour 1 cup of milk into the dish and bake in a hot oven (400° F.) 25 to 30 minutes.

Do not have more than two layers of oysters lest those on the bottom and top layers become over cooked, while the middle one remains more or less raw.

OYSTER CRAB. A very small crab which lives in the oyster shell with the oyster, obtaining its food as the oyster draws in its food. See CRAB.

OYSTER FORK. See FLATWARE; see also TABLE SETTING AND SERVICE.

OYSTER KNIFE. An oyster knife has a short, narrow, heavy blade set in a husky wooden handle. It is used to pry open clams and oysters. See also CUTLERY.

OYSTER PLANT. Another name for salsify, which see.

OYSTERETTES. A small unleavened cracker usually served as a side dish with oysters.

OYSTER-FISH. See BLACKFISH.

P

PADDLE-FISH. An edible fish of the sturgeon family, with a scaleless body, found in the Mississippi Valley.

PADDY. Rice in the husk, whether growing or gathered.

PAGLIA CHEESE. A very soft cheese with an aromatic flavor; an imitation of Gorgonzola. It is eight inches in diameter and two inches thick. It is made in the Canton of Ticino, Switzerland.

PAGO CHEESE. An Austrian rennet cheese, made from sheep's milk. It weighs from half a pound to eight pounds.

PAK CHOI. Chinese cabbage.

PAKLING. A fine green tea of South China. *See* PANYON TEA.

PAKLUM. One of the best green teas of South China. *See* PANYON TEA.

PALADRU CHEESE. A French cheese made in Savoie.

PALAMONTE. A compound made in Turkey from ground up acorns, sugar, spices, and aromatics. A food called racahout is made from it.

PALATABLE. Means agreeable to the taste, savory.

PALE ALE. *See* BEER.

PALMETTO. *See* CABBAGE PALM.

PALM TREE CABBAGE. *See* CABBAGE PALM.

PALM WINE. The name given to any alcoholic beverage made by fermenting the sap of a palm tree. Sap from the date palm or the coconut palm is most commonly used.

PALPUSZTA CHEESE. A strong-smelling Hungarian cheese similar to Limburger.

PAN. A shallow metallic or earthernware vessel. *See* KITCHEN EQUIPMENT.

PAN-BROIL. The cooking of meat in a hot frying pan without any fat. This method is for tender cuts only.

PANCAKE. A quick bread batter cooked on a griddle. It may be used as a main dish or dessert. *See* GRIDDLE CAKES *and* BUCKWHEAT.

CHOCOLATE NUT PANCAKES

1½ cups prepared pancake mix
½ cup sugar
½ cup chopped nuts
1½ cups milk
1 egg
1 square cooking chocolate

Combine the pancake mix, sugar, and nuts. Beat the egg well and combine with the milk. Melt the chocolate over hot water. Add half the milk mixture to the dry ingredients and blend well. Add the melted chocolate and the remaining milk mixture. Stir to blend thoroughly. Bake on a hot, lightly greased griddle, turning only once. Serve warm with hard sauce or cold with foamy sauce. (Makes two dozen 3-inch pancakes)

FRENCH PANCAKES

3 eggs separated
1 tsp sugar
½ tsp salt
1 cup milk
½ cup all-purpose flour
1 tbsp melted butter

Separate the eggs and beat the yolks until lemon colored. Add the sugar, salt and ½ cup of the milk; beat to mix. Sift the flour, measure and add to the egg yolk mixture. Add the remaining milk and beat with rotary beater until smooth. Stir in the melted butter. Fold in the stiffly beaten egg whites. Pour ½ cup batter into a heated, lightly greased skillet, spread with back of spoon to fill pan. When brown on underside, turn and brown on other side. Spread with jelly and roll. Sprinkle with powdered sugar if desired. Serve at once—for breakfast, for luncheon, or as a dessert. This batter may also be used to make regular breakfast size pancakes. (Makes about 5 eight-inch pancakes)

OLD-TIME EGG PANCAKE

3 eggs
⅓ cup milk
⅓ cup flour
¼ tsp salt
2 tbsp shortening
¼ cup thinly sliced apple

Beat eggs slightly. Add milk, then combined flour and salt, beating with a rotary beater until smooth. Have shortening heated in a heavy ten-inch skillet; tilt skillet from side to side so all surfaces will be coated with the fat. Quickly turn egg mixture into hot skillet and sprinkle apple slices over top. Bake in a moderately hot oven (400° F.) uncovered, for 20 minutes. Remove from oven onto a dinner plate and serve immediately with a sprinkling of sugar or sugar combined with cinnamon. (Serves 2)

SWEDISH STUFFED PANCAKES

2 tbsp goose fat or butter
1½ tbsp flour
1 thin slice garlic, thinly chopped
1 tsp grated onion
½ tsp sugar
Salt and Paprika to taste
1 scant cup beef stock
1 cup chopped fresh mushrooms
2 tbsp thick cream
2 slightly beaten eggs

Heat goose fat or butter in a saucepan. Blend in flour, garlic, onion, sugar, and salt and paprika. When the mixture is well browned, stir in one scant cup beef stock, stirring constantly; when it is boiling, stir in mushrooms. Cook gently, stirring constantly until the mixture boils and thickens, then stir in cream. Spread the mixture over a chilled platter until it is lukewarm, then beat in two slightly beaten eggs, blending thoroughly.

Make thin pancakes and brown them on one side only. Remove to a platter, cover the browned side with the above stuffing, and roll the pancake. Cut the stuffed pancakes in two-inch pieces, roll them in beaten egg and then in fine cracker meal, and fry them in hot, clear fat until are nicely browned. Serve hot with a side dish of mushroom sauce.

PANCREAS. A large, fleshy gland, situated under and behind the stomach, secreting a fluid that assists in the process of digestion. In veal it is known as Sweetbread (*which see*).

PANCREATIN. The name given to a complex fermentative preparation derived from the pancreatic gland of animals. It is available as a dry powder and as a solution or liquor.

PAN-FRY. Cooking in a frying pan with a small amount of fat. With meats this method is for tender cuts only. *See also* FRYING.

PANTRY. A provision closet or a closet for glassware, china, etc.

PANYON TEA. A black tea of South China, good for blends, and possessing fine aroma and flavor. The Pakling and Paklum varieties are sometimes called the "Clarets of China teas."

PAP. Soft food for infants or invalids, such as bread softened in milk or water.

PAPAIN. A proteolytic enzyme in the juice of the papaya which is used as a digestant. Extended study of the reactions of the vegetable ferment papain shows that it is composed essentially of a mixture of vegetable globulin, albumoses, and peptone, with which is associated the ferments characteristic of the preparation. *See also* PAPAYA.

Caroid is a vegetable digestive ferment made, like papain, from the papaya or pawpaw, in the form of a dry, yellowish powder. According to analysis, it retains a strong proteolytic action in acid, neutral, or alkaline mediums. It softens and disintegrates proteins, coagulates milk like rennet, and is also amylolytic.

PAPAYA or Papaw or Pawpaw. A subtropical tree, the fruit of which usually is six to twelve inches long. The form is globular to oblong or melon-shaped. Very large specimens may weight as much as 20 pounds. This delicious product of the tropics is rapidly coming to the fore as the source of many useful products. Papayas are eaten like melons, with salt and pepper or with sugar. The seeds are eaten as a delicacy and the natives of the tropics often chew them to quench their thirst. The fruit may be cooked and eaten as a vegetable in the green state. The bark of the papaya is used in the manufacture of rope, while the roots yield a juice that is said to be an excellent nerve tonic. At the end of approximately three years, when the tree has become unproductive, it is cut down and the soft, pithy heart carefully removed, grated and served in about the same manner as a coconut (*which see*). The milky fruit juice which is obtained from the green fruit is used by the natives of the tropics in the treatment of eczema, warts, intestinal worms, ulcers, sores, etc.

Except for food and the production of papain from the fruit for the drug trade,

no single use of this plant is so common as
that of rendering tough meats tender. The
reasons for this unusual quality of the
papaya is that the juices of the tree
are rich in papain, which possesses the
power of digesting protein materials, such
as meat, egg white, the curd of milk, and so
on. The action is similar to the two well-
known body ferments in the human
stomach—pepsin and trypsin. On account
of the efficiency of papain, it is largely replacing pepsin in the drug field.

The method followed in obtaining this
valuable papain is to dry the milk that
exudes from the rind of the green papaya.
The milk, containing the papain, is best
obtained from the still green, full-grown,
well-developed papaya by scratching or
making shallow cuts in the rind with an
ivory, wooden, or bone knife. From young
fruit comes a milk that is rather weak in
digestive power, while the ripe fruit gives
little, if any, milky juice. The juice that
flows from the cut fruit is collected in a
glass or china vessel, which must be
scrupulously clean. After a short while, the
juice will cease to flow, because of the
coagulation of the milk in the cut. In a few
days the cut heals over, and apparently
the process has little effect upon the quality
of the fruit produced. Additional cuts may
be made in the fruit after four or five days,
or until the fruit shows signs of ripening.
Under no condition are steel knives used
for making the incisions, as the resulting
papain would be of dark color.

The tapping is done in the early hours
of the morning and is always finished
before ten o'clock, which gives plenty of
time for drying the same day. Shortly
after collection, the whole mass of juice
coagulates, forming a pure, white curd.
This must be rapidly dried, lest decomposition should set in, completely spoiling
the material. A good average yield of
papain from an acre of papayas is 175
pounds of powder yearly.

RAISING PAPAYAS

The papaya belongs to a genus of about
20 species which is native to tropical and
subtropical America, with the commonest
species (*Carica Papaya*) occurring, naturalized, through the keys of south Florida.
The plant has been carried around the
world, however, until it is known in almost all tropical regions.

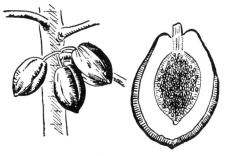

PAPAYA

The fruiting is comparatively continuous
over a period of three or four years. The
fruit ranges in size from that of a quart
measure to that of a large water bucket,
weighing from three to as much as fifteen
pounds. Many species are round in shape,
while others are elongated. The latter are
the best type for shipping.

The cultivator has several problems. The
most important one, when raising the fruit
for food purposes, is that of establishing a
strain of papayas which is uniform in
quality. The papaya produces three types
of plants bearing, respectively, staminate,
pistillate, and perfect flowers. The first are
useless for fruiting, and the second must be
polinated by male, or perfect, flowers.

It is unfortunate that a plant having
such great possibilities for culture in the
southern portions of the United States,
especially in southern Florida, should be
beset by so many perils. Being strictly
tropical, the papaya must be grown out of
reach of frost. It cannot stand flooding or
a high water level, yet it requires a constant supply of moisture. However, the
greatest danger lies in the activities of the
papaya fruit fly, an insect that deposits its
eggs beneath the skin of the papaya, where
they later hatch and prey upon the pulp
within. One tends to use superlatives to
describe a fruit which has so many qualities
to recommend it. But, after all, the papaya
is nothing but a melon, and the man who
said that it struck him as being "a glorified
melon which has climbed into a tree to display its superior qualities," spoke with
considerable justification.

PAPER COOKERY. This method of
cooking to retain flavor and odor is very
popular. It is appropriate for small fish—
brook trout, perch, lake bass, sea bass, or
mackerel. The fish should be cleaned but
the heads and tails retained. Season the in-

side of the fish with salt and pepper. Next cut heavy, brown, unglazed paper large enough to envelop the fish. Rub the paper on both sides with cooking oil or soft butter. Fold the paper in the center and lay one fish thereon, bring the edges together and fold and crimp them until there is no opening in the paper. Repeat this procedure for each fish.

Place the fish on a rack in a moderate oven (400° F.) and bake for 20 to 30 minutes, depending on the size of the fish. The paper will be scorched, but have no fear that it will catch fire or impart any flavor to the fish— the cooking oil on the paper prevents that.

This method of cookery has been known in France for centuries and is called "papiette." It need not be confined exclusively to small fish. Halibut, cod, salmon, and swordfish steaks may be cooked this way with the same fine results —and with no pans to scour afterward.

PAPER TOWELS. Paper towels are of thick, absorbent paper, perforated so that individual sheets may be torn off at need. Originally intended as a disposable hand towel, the paper towel has found many other uses in the kitchen, thanks to its ability to absorb grease. Paper towels are excellent for draining fried foods, cleaning dirty pans, etc., not only because they are highly absorbent, but because they can be thrown away, making a minimum of grease and mess in the kitchen. *See also* Kitchen Equipment.

PAPRIKA. Paprika is a red, powdery spice obtained by grinding the ripe dried fruits of the bonnet pepper (*Capsicum tettragonum*). The extreme mildness of the paprika sold in this country permits its almost unrestricted use. It enhances the flavor of seafood, meats, salads, and eggs, and it is excellent as a garnish for hors d'oeuvres and canapés. Its color renders it decorative as well as flavorsome and you might do well to sprinkle it over pale-colored dishes to make them more attractive. Try a mixture of paprika and cinnamon in a sweet-potato dish. The brighter the color, the better the quality of this spice. The highest grade is that imported from Hungary.

PAPRIKA BUTTER. *See* Butter Sauces.

PARAGUAY TEA. *See* Mate.

PARBOIL. To partially cook food in water or stock.

PARCHED CORN. This highly nutritious food is light in weight and is ideally suited for use in the out-of-doors. *See* Pinole.

PARENCIA CHEESE. A sheep's milk cheese made in Hungary.

PARE. To cut off the outer coating, such as the skins of fruits.

PARFAIT. (par-fey) Parfait, the French word for "perfect," differs from ice cream in that it is less cold and more creamy, consequently more delicate. The name parfait, which used to apply exclusively to Café Parfait, is now used for many other combinations. Parfaits may be molded or served in special chilled glasses. They may be made with almost any kind of fruit, canned, fresh, or dried, as well as with almost any kind of sweet cordial or liqueur or dessert wine. Whisky, however, is not recommended.

To freeze a parfait in an automatic refrigerator, pack in tray or mold and freeze until firm, about two and a half hours. Or fill a mold to overflowing, cover, and seal with buttered muslin or cheesecloth or with a strip of adhesive tape to prevent salt water from entering. Bury in equal parts of ice and salt for three to three and a half hours for large molds and about two hours for individual molds, pouring off the salt water as it accumulates, before it reaches the top of the mold.

In almost every parfait recipe, the basic foundation is a sugar sirup cooked to the indicated stage and enriched with eggs, cream, or undiluted evaporated milk. In some recipes gelatin is used as a stabilizer.

Angel Food Parfait

1 tsp gelatin
2 tbsp cold water
½ cup sugar
½ cup water
2 egg whites
1½ cups heavy cream
¼ tsp salt
½ tsp almond extract
3 tbsp orange juice
¼ cup each candied cherries, candied pineapple, candied citron, and candied apricots, cut small

Soften the gelatin in the two tablespoons of cold water for five minutes. Make a sugar sirup with the sugar and water, boiling them until the sirup spins a thread when dropped from the tip of a spoon (230° F.). Add the softened gelatin, and as soon as this is dissolved, pour in a fine stream onto the stiffly beaten egg whites, beating steadily while pouring. Continue the beating until the mixture is cool and begins to set; then fold in the stiffly whipped cream, to which the salt and almond extract have been added, with the orange juice and candied fruit. Freeze in automatic refrigerator or bury in ice and salt as directed. (Serves 6 to 8)

GOLDEN PARFAIT

¾ cup granulated sugar
⅓ cup boiling water
3 egg yolks
⅛ tsp salt
2 cups heavy cream, whipped stiff
1¾ tsp vanilla extract

Make a sugar sirup with water and sugar, cooking it until it spins a thread from the tip of a spoon (230° F.). Immediately pour in a fine stream onto egg yolks, which have been beaten with salt until light, beating briskly and constantly until mixture is cool. Chill, then fold in stiffly whipped heavy cream and vanilla extract, and freese as directed. (Serves 6)

ITALIAN MERINGUE PARFAIT

¼ cup water
½ cup granulated sugar
3 egg whites
¼ tsp salt
¼ tsp granulated gelatine
¾ cup heavy cream
1½ tsp vanilla extract

Beat egg whites with salt until stiff. Make sugar sirup with water and sugar, boiling five minutes or until sirup spins a thread when dropped from the tip of a spoon (230° F.). Immediately pour in a fine stream onto egg whites in a pan in ice water. Beat briskly and constantly and until cold. Dissolve granulated gelatin in a small amount of boiling water and strain into the mixture. Add stiffly whipped cream and vanilla extract, and freeze as directed. (Serves 2)

PARFAIT AMOUR. A sweet, violet-colored liqueur that tastes of both violets and vanilla. It is not very common in this country. *See also* LIQUEUR.

PARFAIT GLASS. A glass for serving parfaits. *See* GLASSWARE.

PARING KNIFE. See CUTLERY.

PARISIENNE, A LA. The French expression for "as it is made in Paris."

PARMESAN CHEESE. There are two distinct kinds of Parmesan cheese— *Lodigiano* and *Reggiano*. In grated form, this cheese is used to garnish soups and macaroni. Parmesan is considered the hardest cheese in the world.

PARSLEY. Parsley is an aromatic garden herb. Its leaves are used both as a seasoning and as a garnish. Its roots are used for flavoring alone. The curly-leaf variety is preferred for garnishing, while the plain-leaf is preferred for flavoring. Do not use wild parsley, which, although it resembles the plain-leaf variety, is poisonous. Domestic parsley has curlier leaves than Italian parsley; the Italian variety is darker green and more pungent than the domestic.

Parsley sprigs are probably the most popular of garnishes, and they are used largely with fish, meat, and poultry. Their ability to stimulate the appetite recommends their use with hors d'oeuvres and canapés. The leaves should be fresh and green. Yellowed or wilted leaves are almost worthless. However, slightly wilted parsley may be revived if it is put in cold water.

Parsley is very versatile; it seems to go well with everything but sweetmeats. Ever-increasing is its use in flavoring soups, stews, stuffings, sauces, and salad seasonings.

PARSLEY JELLY

To make parsley jelly, a delicious change from other jellies, choose fresh,

PARSLEY

young parsley. Wash it thoroughly in cold water after removing the stalks. Place in a deep enamel saucepan with enough cold water to barely cover the parsley. Bring to a boil, reduce the heat, and allow to simmer very gently for 30 minutes. Strain through a fine sieve or a flannel cloth. Return the liquid to the fire, and allow it simmer for another 15 minutes. Now take cup for cup of the juice and granulated sugar, and boil until the mixture jellies. Flavor with vanilla, lemon, orange, or any other desired flavoring extract, using one-half teaspoon of extract for each cup of jelly. Turn into small sterilized jars and seal. Store in a cool, dark place.

Parsley Sauce

3 tbsp butter
1½ tbsp flour
1 cup hot water
Dash of nutmeg
Salt and pepper
4 tbsp finely chopped parsley
2 tsp lemon juice

Melt the butter, add the flour, and when smoothly blended, gradually stir in the water. Bring to boiling point, cook two minutes, season with the nutmeg, salt, and pepper, and just before serving, stir in the parsley and lemon juice.

PARSNIP. A winter vegetable which does not receive the attention to which it is entitled. Parsnips do not develop their full flavor until they have been touched with frost. For this reason, they do not appear in the market until late fall. When properly cooked—and this means steamed, not boiled—parsnips have a sweet, nutty flavor.

Parsnips are generally sold by the bunch. They resemble carrots in shape. Their skin is yellowish brown. Smooth, firm, well shaped roots of small to medium size are the most desirable. Soft or shriveled roots are of poor quality. Very large roots are likely to be overgrown and have woody cores which must be removed in cooking.

To obtain the full flavor of parsnips, they should be steamed in their skins until tender. Then they may be peeled and slit lengthwise. If the core is large, scoop it out with the point of a knife; it will be tender, but is rather tasteless and detracts from the flavor of the rest of the root. The parsnips are then ready to be put through the ricer and served like mashed potatoes. Or they may be sliced and glazed like sweet potatoes, pan-fried, creamed, or French fried.

Farmer Pie

8 medium-size parsnips, cooked
3 medium-size potatoes, cooked
½ cup cooked or canned peas
½ cup cooked or canned string beans
⅓ cup diced salt pork
1½ cups medium white sauce
1 tbsp chopped green pepper
1 tbsp chopped parsley
1 tbsp minced onion
Baking powder biscuits

This is an excellent way to use leftover vegetables. Cut the parsnips and potatoes in dice. In a frying pan, cook the diced salt pork until the fat is extracted and the pork is crisp and brown. In a greased baking dish, make layers of parsnips, potatoes, and salt pork, repeating the layers. Mix the peas and beans and spread in the dish. Season the medium white sauce (*which see*) with salt, pepper, a little nutmeg, and a dash of thyme, and stir in the green pepper, parsley, and onion. Pour carefully into the baking dish. Cover the top with small baking powder biscuits, (*which see*). Brush the tops of the biscuits with cold milk and bake in a hot oven (400° F.) about 20 minutes or until the biscuits are nicely browned. Serve piping hot from the baking dish. (Serves 4 to 6)

Parsnip Chips

Select medium-size parsnips and scrape; do not peel them. Cut off the stem and root ends. Slice in very thin lengthwise slices, discarding the core. Drop the slices in ice water as you prepare them. Put in the refrigerator in the ice water to chill for

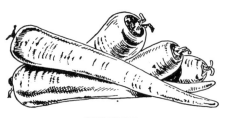

PARSNIP

FOOD VALUE

Water	Food Energy	Pro- tein	Fat	Carbo- hydrate	Cal- cium	Phos- phorus	Iron	Vit. A Value	Thia- mine	Ribo- flavin	Nia- cin	Ascor- bic Acid
78.6	83	1.5	.5	18.2	57	80	.7	0	.11	.09	.2	18

at least 30 minutes. Drain and dry thoroughly. Fry, a few at a time, in deep, hot fat (390° F.) until golden brown. Skim out with a perforated ladle and drain on soft, crumpled paper. These chips may be served hot or cold.

PARSNIP CROQUETTES

Wash parsnips and steam unpeeled until just tender. Drain and peel and cut in two, lengthwise. Remove the core. Chop coarsely. Have ready enough thick white sauce (which see) to bind the chopped parsnips. Spread three-quarters of an inch thick on a platter and allow to cool. When cold, shape into croquettes. Beat an egg slightly with a pinch of salt. Dip the croquettes into crumbs, then into the beaten egg, and again into the crumbs. Fry in deep hot fat (375° F.) until golden brown. Drain on soft crumpled paper. Serve very hot.

PARSNIP PIE

Wash the parsnips and steam unpeeled until very tender. Drain and peel. Cut in half lengthwise and remove the core. Force the parsnips through a ricer. Season with salt and pepper and add one tablespoon of butter or margarine for each medium-size parsnip. Whip the mixture until light and fluffy. Grease a pie plate and pile the parsnips into it. Sprinkle the top with bread crumbs and dot with butter or margarine. Heat in a hot oven (400° F.) until the crumbs brown and the mixture is heated through.

This pie may be varied in a number of ways. Try whipping grated cheese into the parsnip. Finely minced left-over ham makes a more satisfying addition. Sautéed mushrooms, cut in small bits, make an epicurean dish.

PARSNIP WINE

Wash, scrape, and clean one peck of parsnips. Cut them into very small pieces and put into two gallons of water. Boil two

hours. Then strain through a flannel bag of four thicknesses. Add six pounds of granulated sugar or brown sugar. (Brown sugar makes it stronger but darker.) Let mixture cool and add one cake of compressed yeast. Stir well and set aside for one week to ferment. Then cork and put away in a dark place for six months.

SAUTEED PARSNIPS

Wash the parsnips well, but do not peel. Steam until tender, or about 40 minutes. Drain and peel. Slice in half lengthwise and remove the core. Cut into lengthwise slices and roll in flour which has been seasoned with salt and pepper. Sauté until golden brown in butter, bacon drippings, ham, or chicken fat.

SCALLOPED PARSNIPS AND CHEESE

2 lb parsnips
½ cup bread crumbs
1 small green pepper, chopped
1 small onion, grated
1 tbsp minced parsley
1 tsp salt
⅛ tsp white pepper
2 cups medium white sauce
½ cup grated American cheese
3 tbsp buttered crumbs

Wash the parsnips and steam unpeeled until tender. Drain and peel. Remove the core and cut into dice. Put the parsnips in a buttered baking dish in layers, first parsnips, then bread crumbs, then the mixed green pepper, onion, parsley, and seasonings. Repeat, making two layers of each. Pour the medium white sauce (which see) over all. Mix the grated cheese with the buttered crumbs and cover the top of the dish. Bake in a moderate oven (350° F.) about 30 minutes. (Serves 6)

PARTRIDGE. From the Himalaya Mountains, via China, came the ancestors of the Chukars or Asiatic partridges, which we find today in our markets. Representatives of the breed have been in the United

States only a short time, and it was only a few years ago that three pairs were taken as the nucleus of a flock to be raised in America for market. A little smaller than a pheasant, one partridge is large enough to serve two persons. The meat is white, and the flavor pleasantly gamy.

The wild Redleg and Grayleg partridges, along with wild duck and quail, vie with the pheasant for the place of honor among game specialists. Partridge pie and grilled partridge have their partisans, but the most popular way of preparing this bird, like the pheasant, is by roasting. Roasted and basted with butter, or split and broiled, it is often served on buttered toast and garnished with a slice of lemon or orange and plenty of crisp, green, young water cress.

The name partridge is also used in the southern part of the United States for the Bob-white or Quail, *which see.*

GRILLED PARTRIDGE
(English Method)

Clean as many partridges as are required. Singe, cut off the legs, split open down the back (but without separating), and flatten with a cleaver. Marinate for at least 20 minutes in olive oil to which has been added salt, pepper, a large bay leaf, a small clove of garlic, four sprigs of parsley, and a few drops of Tabasco sauce. Grill the birds under a very hot flame, turning them twice during the cooking process. Turn onto a hot platter, spread maitre d'hôtel butter over them, and serve with Remoulade Sauce, *which see.*

NEW METHOD PERDREAUX AUX CHOUX
(Partridge with Cabbage)

6 young partridges
½ cup fumet
½ cup butter
1 tbsp flour
Meat stock
¼ lb diced salt pork
6 sprigs parsley
1 large bay leaf
3 small new cabbages
1 lb lean fresh pork, sliced
Salt and pepper
Pork sausages

Clean, singe, and truss the partridges. Brown delicately in the combined fumet

and butter, turning the birds so as to brown on all sides and sprinkling with the flour while cooking. Now add three cups of stock with the diced pork and with the parsley and bay leaf tied together. Simmer 15 minutes. Meanwhile, parboil the cabbage, first removing the heavy ribs. After cooking five minutes, lift out with a perforated skimmer and add to the partridges with the fresh pork slices and more meat stock, using enough to cover the birds. Season with salt and pepper, cover tightly, and bake in a moderate oven (350° F.) about half an hour (longer if the birds are old).

To serve, arrange the cabbage in nests on a hot platter, place a partridge in each nest and surround each with small pork sausages sautéed in butter.

OLD METHOD PERDREAUX AUX CHOUX

Prepare six partridges as indicated above to the point of adding the cabbage. By this old method, the cabbage, with the large ribs removed, is cooked with three-fourths of a pound of bacon and two tablespoons of lard for 15 minutes. While the cabbage is cooking, slice thinly four carrots and one French cervelat or Bologna sausage. Butter a large braising kettle and arrange in it first the carrots, then the cervelat or Bologna. Line the sides of the kettle with the bacon, which was cooked with the cabbage. Drain the cabbage and arrange a layer of it over the carrots and sausage. Now add the partridges, placing between each two a slice of lean fresh pork, using one pound in all. Cover with the remaining cabbage and moisten with the stock in which the partridges were first cooked. Cover and set in a hot oven (400° F.) for 30 minutes.

To serve, invert a platter over the braising kettle and turn upside down gently so that the whole retains its shape on the platter.

PAN-FRIED PARTRIDGE MOTHER PULLIG

Select young partridges; if large use three, if small six. Clean and wipe the birds with a damp cloth, then rub with orange juice, black pepper and salt. Cut up as for chicken fricassee and sauté in plenty of butter in a heavy frying pan over a medium heat, stirring occasionally to brown on all sides. This will take about half an hour. Drain and garnish on the platter with six

artichoke bottoms previously sautéed in
brown butter, two dozen small potato
balls previously parboiled and browned in
butter, two dozen small white onions
glazed rather brown, six small mounds of
steamed wild rice, fried parsley, and thin
slices of lemon dipped in paprika.

For the accompanying sauce, add to the
buttery glaze remaining in the frying pan
one cup of veal stock, bring to boiling
point, then add a small wineglass of sweet
white wine and one scant teaspoon of
fumet.

PARTRIDGE CASSEROLE MADAME
METZELTHIN

Partridges
Small white onions, peeled
Juniper berries
Thin strips of cooked tongue
Larding pork
2 cups braising vegetables
1 cup brown sauce
1 pony good brandy
Salt and pepper
1 bay leaf
Pinch of thyme
1 doz fresh mushrooms
Boiled wild rice

Clean and wipe the birds with a damp
cloth. Stuff each with one small onion, one
juniper berry, and six strips of tongue.
Truss, then cover the breasts with thinly
sliced larding pork, and arrange in a braising kettle (of a type which can be sent to
table) on the usual braising vegetables (see
BRAISE). Add the brown sauce and brandy,
which may be set alight to add flavor. Add
salt and pepper to taste, the bay leaf,
thyme, one dozen small white onions, and
the mushrooms. Cover closely, and braise
in a hot oven (400° F.) for 40 minutes
without disturbing. Serve wild rice separately.

ROAST PARTRIDGE YANKEE STYLE

Clean four partridges very carefully and
tie over the breast of each a slice of bacon
about two inches long. Rub the partridges,
inside and out, with salt and pepper, and
place inside each a slice of lemon cut thin
and without seeds. Arrange in a buttered
baking dish with three-fourths cup of
chicken bouillon, fresh or canned but clear.

PASSION FRUIT

Roast in a moderate oven (350°–375° F.)
for 25 to 30 minutes, basting frequently.
When the birds and gravy are a rich brown,
pour over them three-fourths cup of slightly sour heavy cream. Let the cream bubble
up in the pan for one minute, basting twice.
Serve with the gravy from the baking dish,
bread sauce, and a side dish of parsley jelly,
which see.

PASKI CHEESE. A Yugoslavian
cheese.

PASSION FRUIT. Early Italian and
Spanish explorers discovered the Passion
Flower in South America and declared it
to be symbolic of the Passion of Christ by
reason of the shape and arrangement of
its parts.

Possibly half a dozen species of edible
Passion fruit have been in cultivation in
Hawaii for the last half century. It is
coming into importance in California orchards. The fruit is plum-size and purple
in color when ripe. It has a tough hull, the
inside of which contains small black seeds
surrounded by aromatic, yellow pulp. Its
taste somewhat resembles the peach with
a tinge of apricot flavor and the exotic
tang of guava. The six principal varieties
of edible Passion fruits are the Purple Passion fruit, the Yellow Passion fruit, the
Sweet Granadilla or Waterlemon, the
Giant Granadilla, The Bell-apple, and the
Sweet Calabash. These are distinguishable
mainly by the size of the fruit, which varies
from the two and a half inch diameter of

the Sweet Calabash to the nine to ten inch diameter of the Giant Granadilla.

A very little of the juice goes a long way because of its penetrating flavor. It may be used in almost any cocktail, in punch, or a drop or two—no more—in a fresh fruit cup. In a salad dressing, in pie, and in flavoring fruit desserts, from cream to custards, it is unsurpassed. The taste lingers like a happy memory. The juice is pressed from the pure pulp of Passion Fruit. Sugar is added, but no water or preservative is used.

PASSITI. The name given to several sweet Italian dessert wines. *See also* WINE.

PASSOVER BREAD. *See* MATZOTH.

PASSOVER WINE. A very dark and very sweet red wine made, in America, from the Concord grape. Though fully fermented, the wine is not fortified but is sweetened with added sugar. *See also* WINE.

PASTE. Macaroni, spaghetti, noodles, and the other so-called pastes have had such an important place in the food history of the world that nations vie with one another for the honor of their invention.

While we usually associate macaroni and spaghetti with Italy and noodles with Germany, the evidence seems to show that the honors belong to the Orient—probably to China, although the Japanese claim that their rice paste is the oldest product of the kind. For the European and American types of paste, a hard wheat, known as durum or semolina, is used, entirely or in part. The flour is moistened and thoroughly mixed by machinery, after which it is kneaded and flattened under pressure. The shape into which it is molded decides its name. There are more than 50 shapes, including fish, animals, crescents, flowers, shells, crowns, and letters, besides the commoner spaghetti of various thicknesses and the tubular macaroni. Some of these are colored with eggs, spinach, or beet juice. American products are less varied. In Italy the pastes are usually dried out of doors, but in America our factories have heated drying rooms through which washed and filtered air is continually blown.

Macaroni is seldom served alone. Being a bland food without much taste, it combines well with many other foods. It may be served blended with cheese in timbales, with crab meat or any other kind of seafood, as ramekins, with nuts, in a cheese and tomato casserole, with mushrooms and chopped meat, with chopped liver, etc.

Spaghetti is similarly served. All pastes should be cooked until tender, yet firm. If overcooked, they lose much of their character and attractiveness. Both macaroni and spaghetti are of the highest quality if they break evenly without splintering. An eight-ounce box of macaroni will make eight servings. *See also* MACARONI, NOODLES, PASTRY, PIES, SPAGHETTI, *and* VERMICELLI.

PASTEURIZATION. A technique of using heat to partially sterilize a liquid. While the temperatures employed 131° to 158° F.) are high enough to kill many harmful bacteria, they do not cause radical chemical or physical changes within the fluid.

Pasteurization is perhaps best known for its use in purifying milk (*which see*), but the process is also applied to other foods. It is named in honor of Dr. Louis Pasteur, who developed the technique while seeking a cure for certain wine diseases.

PASTEURIZED MILK. A sterile, yet easily digested milk which is prepared by the method developed by Louis Pasteur. *See* MILK.

PASTIES. A kind of pastry, usually shaped like a turnover, which may contain almost anything in the way of meat, fish, poultry, fruits, or vegetables.

PASTING. As applied to wine or cider-making, pasting is a professional word meaning clarifying or fining. *See* WINE.

PASTRAMI. Pastrami is derived from the navel section of beef. It must be boned, trimmed of fat, cured with spices for ten days, and smoked for eight hours before it is ready for use. It is then a delicious meat having an extremely spicy taste. The meat may be served either hot or cold. Its chief use is in pastrami sandwiches, but it is sometimes served with beans or with eggs.

PASTRY. Pastry-making began in ages so remote that no records remain of the earliest recipes and formulas. Where did pastry originate? Legend says from Greece, where an ancient pastry-cook, with primitive, hand-made tools and utensils, produced delicious honey cakes.

From Greece the art of pastry-making was introduced into Italy. Good living was unknown to the Romans as long as they were fighting to secure their independence. But when their conquests were extended to Africa and Greece, they brought back to Rome the art of preparing delicious pastry.

From Italy the art of pastry-making went to Gaul. The first Capetian kings had at their court an officer called *Patissier-Bouche* and four assistant pastry-cooks. The first corporation or trade union of pastry-makers was created in Paris in 1270 and extended all over the French kingdom. The final status granted by the king in 1566 gave to all its members the title of "Master Pastry-Cook" with franchise and privileges, as well as severe and rigorous by-laws. Before the Revolution, the trade union of Master Pastry-Cooks was divided into several branches or specialties, such as wafer-makers (*oublieurs*) and cream-makers (*darioleurs*), and no branch had any right to encroach upon the specialties of another.

Real pastry, as it is known today, was created about 1790 and was not developed to its present-day standard of proficiency until the beginning of the 19th century. Pastry-making was introduced in America by the Pilgrims and its story is closely related to our traditions, customs, and progress.

PLAIN PASTRY

Plain pastry is generally used for dessert pies, but also may be used for meat or fish pies, tarts, dumplings, turnovers, cobblers, and deep-dish pies.

Shortening. Butter, lard, or any of the commercial shortenings may be used in making pastry. However, each has its own characteristics, which influence the results.

Butter, although it adds flavor, is the most expensive shortening. Even in expensive hotels and restaurants, pastry made with butter is extremely rare. When substituting butter for lard or other shortenings in pastry, remember that butter is not 100 percent fat, and so more butter than lard should be used. In general *two* additional tablespoons of butter should be added for each cup of pure fat called for. When butter is used, the moisture present develops the gluten of the flour and makes tough pastry. However, when butter is washed to remove all the buttermilk, it gives a tender pastry with a flavor not obtained with any other shortening. Some cooks prefer to melt the butter, remove the curds (which settle), cool the remaining butterfat, and use it in a semi-solid condition. This is practiced by French and Italian pastry makers.

Lard is extremely soft and not always uniform in quality. Quite often lard tends to separate from the dough and work out

on the board during the rolling, thereby requiring the use of considerable additional flour, which, of course, produces an inferior crust. Yet it is the favorite shortening for pie pastry.

Hydrogenated shortenings, which include lard and vegetable shortenings, have a bland, neutral flavor and a firm consistency which makes them ideal for pastry, since they blend easily and well with the flour.

Various other shortenings, such as *margarine, chicken fat, sour cream*, and *suet* may be employed, but their use is limited and often impractical. See also SHORTENING.

Flour. Any good all-purpose flour is suitable for use in pastry. See also FLOUR.

Water. The ticklish business of adding water to the fat-flour mixture in making pastry would be much simpler if an exact measure of water would give just the right degree of moisture for a given amount of fat and flour. However, this cannot be done, for the measure varies with the temperature and firmness of the ingredients and the rate of adding the water. The amount is less for warm ingredients than for cold, less for finely divided particles than for coarse, and more when the water is added slowly than when it is added quickly.

A small quantity of water tends to produce a crust which is crumbly rather than flaky, while too much makes for toughness. The important point is that the water be added in such a way as to distribute it evenly among all the fat-flour particles. They tend to absorb more water than is really necessary. If this happens, the mixture will have to be stirred more vigorously, or more flour will have to be added in order to make a dough which can be rolled out. In either case, the crust will be tough and rubbery.

CUTTING IN SHORTENING

PASTRY JAGGER OR WHEEL

To distribute the water evenly, sprinkle it over the fat-flour mixture. The water should be ice cold. To determine when enough water has been added, press the dampened particles gently to see whether they tend to stick together; set aside the small lumps of dough which form; sprinkle the water over the next layer; and so on. If the process has been successfully carried out, you should have a ball of dough which is easy to handle, being neither sticky nor crumbly, and which will yield tender, flaky pastry. Otherwise, there is nothing to do but start over again. Repairing dough at this stage simply does not work.

In blending the ingredients, remember that a stirring motion will develop the gluten of the flour, making a tough pastry, while a cutting-in or chopping motion with a wooden fork or spoon tends to produce a light and tender pastry. The less the shortening and flour are mixed, the more water the dough will take and the tougher the resulting pastry.

If the room is cool and you work quickly, all you need do is keep the fat in the refrigerator until you are ready to use it and to have the water ice-cold. However, if the room is hot and damp, set the fat-flour mixture in the refrigerator to chill before adding the ice water, and, if necessary, chill the dough before rolling it. In other words, keep the mixture so cool that the fat shows no tendency to melt.

There is a difference of opinion as to the best rolling surface. Some bakers prefer smooth hardwood, some canvas, and others a marble slab. The latter is very satisfactory because it remains cold and is easily cleaned. A wooden or glass rolling pin is generally used. Some homemakers use a cloth cover on the rolling pin to prevent sticking.

Flour the board or slab lightly. Press the dough lightly into a disk rather than a ball. Allow no cracks in the edges. Do not knead or pat the dough. With the lightest possible springy motion, roll it from the center to the edge, then in the opposite direction, and then criss-cross, so that every part is rolled evenly. If the dough begins to stick—that is, if it does not spread out from the center when rolled—loosen it with a pastry scraper or spatula. Never turn the pastry over during the rolling process, since there is danger of rolling in too much flour. Roll out to a thickness of one-eight of an inch for both under and upper crusts.

After the dough has been rolled to the desired thickness, fold one half over the other, forming a semi-circle. Do not grease the plate. Remember that "good pastry greases its own pan." Lift it carefully to pan or pie plate, laying the crease in the center, and unfold it so that it covers the entire surface of the plate, having the bottom crust about two inches larger than the pie plate. With the right hand, press the pastry to the pie plate so that it fits like the proverbial paper on the wall. The left hand should lift the pastry from the pan or plate to permit the escape of any air which will cause bulging of the crust in baking. Never stretch the pastry, but take enough in the beginning to insure covering the entire surface. From now on, the treatment of the crust will depend on the type of pie for which it is to be used.

PROCEDURE FOR PARTICULAR CRUSTS

Two-Crust Pie. The dough for the bottom crust should be about two inches larger than the diameter of the top of the pie plate. Trim it by running a knife around the outer rim of the plate. Do not trim too closely or the pastry may not cover the outer edge of the plate when the filling is put in, particularly if the pastry has been stretched or has not been fitted properly into the plate. Put in the filling. Add butter, if the recipe calls for it. Roll out the top crust as you did the bottom crust, allowing an inch more than the diameter of the top of the plate. Fold one half over the other, and place the upper crust gently and carefully on the plate, so that it will completely cover the pie when unfolded. Put it on loosely, and do not stretch. Press the

FLUTING PIE CRUST

edges of the two crusts together firmly, and trim off the surplus pastry. A good pastry cook will have few trimmings left. To finish the edges, they may be pressed together with the tines of a fork or a pastry roller or trimmer. The most common method of crimping is by pressing the edge between the thumb and forefinger of the left hand. With a sharp knife, cut several slits in the top crust to act as steam vents. Brush the top with ice water, milk, cream, or beaten egg if a glazed crust is desired.

One-Crust Pie. Roll the dough to one-eighth of an inch thickness and allow five inches more than the diameter of the top of the pie plate. Fit the pastry snugly to the plate, leaving no air underneath. The edge may be folded, fluted, and trimmed in one operation. With the left hand fold the rim of the pastry at the outer edge of the pan, using the forefinger of the right hand to make the fluted edge. As the forefinger of the left hand presses down on the edge of the pan, the surplus pastry breaks off. Prick the pie shell to remove air, which will cause it to bulge when baking. If the surface puffs up during baking, it may be pricked again.

If you prefer, a second pie plate of the same size may be placed inside the shell during the first part of the baking and then removed to brown the surface. The crust may also be baked on an inverted pie plate, but must be pricked carefully before baking. A one-crust pie shell should be baked in a very hot oven (420° F.) for 15 to 20 minutes.

Unbaked One-Crust Pie. In a one-crust pie for which the shell is not baked before the filling is added, the problem arises of how to avoid a soggy undercrust. Make your crust as indicated for the one-crust pie. Any of the following suggestions may help to keep the filling from soaking the crust. (1) Let the shell stand for at least an hour or even overnight in the refrigerator before adding the filling. (2) Brush the surface with slightly beaten egg white, and place it in the oven until the egg sets. (3) Brush a little flour over the crust before adding the filling.

Criss-Cross Top Crust. Prepare the bottom of a two-crust pie. Roll the balance of the pastry into a long strip one-eighth of an inch thick, and cut it into one-half-inch strips. Put the filling into the crust, and add butter if indicated in recipe. Brush the rim with milk or water. Lay the strips across the pie, parallel and one inch apart. Press the ends of the strips tightly to the rim, brush the strips with milk or water, and lay the same number of strips at right angles to the first. Place a long strip of pastry around the rim to cover the ends and make a rim which may be pressed with a fork or fluted. Brush with milk or water again, and bake in a hot oven (400°–450° F.) for ten minutes; then finish baking according to the requirements of the filling.

Baking the Pie. The correct oven temperature is important for many reasons. Tough texture, coarse grain, heaviness, cracks, burned edges—all these are ills which befall the pie baked at too high or too low a temperature.

If you do not have an oven thermometer, tests may be made to indicate the heat of the oven. Set a pan sprinkled with flour in the oven. In a slow oven (250°–300° F.) it becomes a delicate brown in five minutes; in a moderate oven (325°–375° F.) it turns golden brown in five minutes; in a hot oven (400°–425° F.) the flour turns a deep dark brown in five minutes; in a very hot oven (425°–500° F.) the flour turns a deep dark brown in three minutes. These same tests may be made with white tissue paper.

HINTS ON PLAIN PASTRY AND FILLINGS

In general, the secret of good pastry lies in the use of the right amount and kind of flour and shortening, in not overmixing or overhandling the ingredients, in enclosing as much air as possible while mixing, and in using as little water as possible.

Tenderness of pastry depends upon the kind of flour, the amount of shortening, and the handling.

Flakiness is determined by the method of combining the ingredients.

Do not turn pastry. If it sticks, lift it from the board or table with a spatula. Turning the pastry works in too much flour and often makes for a rough surface.

To allow for shrinkage in the upper crust, leave the upper crust one inch larger than the pan.

To glaze pie crust, brush it over before baking with milk, cream, or warm, melted butter. This will add to the appearance and flavor. For a browner glaze, brush it with combined melted butter and egg. Always allow the glazing to dry before baking the pie.

To prevent air bubbles in a baked pastry shell, prick the bottom and side of the crust with a fork before placing it in the oven.

Tough pie crust may be due to too much water being added to the dough while mixing it, to too little water, to too little fat in proportion to the flour, or to too much flour used for dusting when rolling out.

Before you roll out pie dough, chill the dough thoroughly. This makes it easier to handle. Then roll out just enough dough for one pie at a time. Work quickly and roll from the center to the outside. Try to keep the shape as round as possible.

Sift together salt, sugar (if any), flour, and spices (if any) before adding shortening.

The proportion of flour to shortening varies, but is usually three or four to one by volume, or two to one by weight. Three quarts (three pounds) of sifted flour with three cups (one and one-half pounds) of shortening will give twelve shells or six two-crust pies nine inches in diameter.

Always use the *same kind of flour* for dusting the table or board as is used in the pastry.

When using half shortening and half butter in pastry, cut the chilled shortening into the flour with two knives or a pastry blender until the mixture looks like meal. Then add the chilled butter, and continue cutting and blending until the pieces are about the size of a small pea.

For a flaky texture, shortening should be evenly distributed and the mixture kept light and airy.

When a recipe calls for melted shortening, measure after melting.

Always use as little ice water as possible.

When making cream filling for pies, do not allow the mixture to cool in the pan in which it has been cooked. Transfer it as soon as possible to a shallow, cold container, This will prevent souring or separating, especially in summer.

To prevent souring or separating of cream or custard filling, beat air into the filling when lukewarm by adding a meringue made of one egg white beaten stiffly and then sweetened with two tablespoons of powdered sugar. This increases the lightness of the cream filling, helps to prevent souring and separating, and does not in the least affect the consistency or flavor of the filling because the air cells disappear when the mixture cools.

To prevent liquid from berry pies or other juicy pies from running out into the oven, place small heatproof funnels (three-inch lengths of macaroni will do) upright in slits cut in the top crust; thus the juice can bubble up but will not run out. Or, sprinkle one to two tablespoons of quick cooking tapioca into the filling with the sugar.

To prevent fruit filling from soaking into the bottom crust, dust the bottom crust with a little flour mixed with an equal part of sugar before adding the fruit. You may also brush the bottom and sides of the with unbeaten egg white.

BOILING WATER PASTRY

¼ cup boiling water
½ cup shortening
1½ cups sifted pastry flour
¼ tsp salt

Pour the boiling water over the shortening, stir well, and when melted, gradually add the sifted flour and salt, stirring vigorously after each addition. Mix thoroughly, yet with as little handling as possible. Chill before rolling out. (Makes a nine-inch pie with lattice top)

BRAZIL NUT PASTRY

1½ cups finely ground Brazil nuts
3 tbsp sugar

Mix nuts and sugar well. Press evenly over bottom and sides of pie plate. Use without baking, for cream pie. (Makes pastry for one eight-inch pie)

BREAD CRUMB PIE CRUST

⅓ cup soft butter or margarine
¼ cup light brown sugar
1 cup fresh, fine, dry bread crumbs
1 tsp cinnamon
¼ cup chopped nuts, if desired

Mix all ingredients until well blended. Press firmly in layer of uniform thickness over bottom and sides of a buttered eight-inch pie pan. Make sure the rim of the crust is uniform in thickness and symmetrical in shape. Bake in a moderate oven (350° F.) for ten minutes. Cool and fill with any pre-cooked or chiffon pie filling. (Makes one eight-inch crust)

CHEESE PASTRY

2 cups sifted pastry flour
½ tsp salt
½ cup shortening
1 cup grated American cheese
5 to 6 tbsp water

Sift together the flour and salt, cut in the shortening as for short pastry, work in the cheese lightly with a fork, then add the water, using only just enough to bind the mixture. Roll out on a lightly floured board. Brush the bottom crust either with melted shortening or a little egg white to prevent soaking. Bake as directed for plain pastry. (Makes a two-crust, nine-inch pie)

FLAKY PASTRY—STANDARD PIE CRUST

2 cups sifted pastry flour
⅔ tsp salt
½ cup shortening
6 tbsp water

Sift together the flour and salt; chill shortening thoroughly, then cut it in quickly and lightly until the mix resembles peas in size.

There is a knack to this method of mixing, especially if done by hand, in which case it should be done very quickly because the heat of the hands may melt the shortening. A pastry blender or chopping knife may be used, but hand manipulation seems best. The fat particles are rubbed with the fingers so that they are flattened between layers of flour, rather than being squeezed together. More air is incorporated in this way. The essential thing is to work quickly but not to overmix; also, see that all ingredients are thoroughly chilled. Add the water quickly and chill before rolling out. (Makes a two-crust nine-inch pie)

GINGERSNAP PIE CRUST

1¼ cups fine gingersnap crumbs
¼ cup soft butter or margarine
Dash of salt

Lay gingersnaps between two sheets of waxed paper and crush with a rolling pin to make fine crumbs. Combine with the butter and salt and mix well. Press firmly in a layer of uniform thickness over bottom and sides of a buttered eight-inch pie pan. Chill thoroughly in refrigerator for at least 45 minutes before filling with pre-cooked or chiffon pie fillings. If pie is to be topped with meringue, spread on meringue and bake at 325° F. for six to eight minutes. (Makes one eight-inch crust)

GRAHAM CRACKER PIE CRUST

16 graham crackers
2 tbsp sugar
1 tsp flour
¼ cup melted butter or margarine

Lay crackers between two sheets of waxed paper and crush with a rolling pin to make fine crumbs. Add remaining ingredients and mix well. Press firmly into a nine-inch buttered pie pan to make an even layer of uniform thickness and a rim with a symmetrical shape. If pie is to be topped with meringue, spread on meringue and bake as usual. Chill for at least 45 minutes in refrigerator before filling with a cooled, pre-cooked or chiffon filling. (Makes one nine-inch crust)

PASTRY MIX

8 cups (2 qt) sifted flour
1 tbsp salt
2½ cups shortening

For unforeseen occasions, and to have on hand a foundation for pastry which needs only the proper amount of water added when ready to mix a pie, tarts, etc., make up and store, preferably in the refrigerator, the following mix:

Sift together the flour and salt, cut in the shortening with a pastry blender, a little at a time, until the mixture approximates cornmeal in texture.

For pastry shells, use one and one-quarter cups of this mix; for each two-crust pie, use two and one-half cups. Add the necessary amount of water and proceed as for any other pastry. These quantities will make a reserve of pie crust for ten shells. Covered and stored in the refrigerator, the mix will keep several weeks.

POTATO PIE CRUST

1 cup all-purpose flour
½ tsp salt
½ tsp sugar
½ cup cold mashed potatoes
6 tbsp shortening

Sift flour, measure, and resift with salt and sugar. Add potatoes, unseasoned and without milk or butter, and mix in with a fork till achieving the consistency of cornmeal. Cut in shortening with two knives or pastry blender until pieces are the size of rice grains, then gather up the mixture and press into a ball. Wrap in waxed paper and chill for one-half hour. Roll out dough to one-eighth inch thickness to fit an eight-inch pie pan. Trim edge, turn under, and flute. Prick pastry closely all over and bake in a moderately hot oven (400° F.) for 10 to 12 minutes. Cool before filling. (Serves 4 to 6)

SHORT PASTRY—STANDARD PIE CRUST

2 cups sifted pastry flour
⅔ tsp salt
½ cup shortening
6 tbsp water

Sift together the flour and salt and work in half the shortening, blending thoroughly; the resulting mixture will be light and cream colored. Now add the remainder of the shortening and work to the pebbly stage. The mixing at this point will not toughen the dough, provided the first mixture has been thoroughly blended. Add the water, a little at a time, and chill thoroughly before rolling out. (Makes a two-crust nine-inch pie)

VANILLA WAFER PASTRY

¾ cup finely crushed vanilla wafers
7 whole vanilla wafers

Cover bottom of pie plate with crumbs and stand up whole wafers, cut in halves, around edges. Use, without baking, for pie.

USING PASTRY TUBE IN DECORATING A BIRTHDAY CAKE

PASTRY BAG. A cornucopia made of thin, tough paper and used for making elaborate decorations on cakes, etc., with frosting. For this purpose, typing paper, sized 8½ x 11 inches, may be cut diagonally in two. By holding a long point in either hand and wrapping the cornucopia so that the three corners are brought together at the open end, you can make a very sharp point in the middle of the long side. The shape may be held firm by folding in the open tips. The point may be cut round for a plain tube, pointed for a leaf tube, and serrated for a star tube.

PASTRY BLENDER. A pastry blender is an instrument used to mix pastry dough. It usually consists of a slotted strip of metal or a number of stiff wires bent into the form of a U, with a handle across the open end. *See also* KITCHEN EQUIPMENT.

PASTRY BRUSH. *See* BRUSHES.

PASTRY SERVER. *See* FLATWARE.

PASTRY TUBE. This is a small tube made of metal and used for elaborate decoration of cakes. The openings come in different shapes. The sizes indicate their use. *See* CAKE DECORATOR.

PATE DE FOIE GRAS. A pleasant result of the French Revolution is that during those fateful years of turmoil and change, *foie gras* (fat goose-liver paste) ceased to be a delicacy known only to the aristocrats. Before 1789 *paté de foie gras* had been a luxury of the select few. It was enjoyed by the aristocrats of Alsace who were fortunate enough to be invited to the

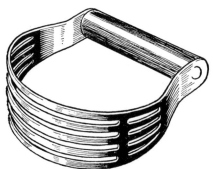

PASTRY BLENDER

Governor's table. Invented in Strasbourg about 1762, *paté de foie gras* had been served there regularly for more than two decades before the Revolution, invariably provoking surprise and admiration. The formula for preparing it was as jealuosly guarded as a state secret.

After the Revolution, Jean Pierre Clause, the inventor of the delicious paté, left the service of his noble master, the Marshal de Contades, Royal Chamberlain and Governor of Alsace, to embark upon a business career in which he could use his great capabilities as a chef. He opened a restaurant in Strasbourg with *paté de foie gras* as its specialty. Popularity and success came at once. When a man dined *Chez Clause*, no embarrassing questions were asked about his rank or pedigree. Everyone able to pay was served, and that is how *paté de foie gras* became the food of commoners, peasants, and tradesfolk—a minor triumph of the French Revolution that no gourmet will belittle.

The motto of Clause's restaurant was *Moult Foie, Moult Espoir*, which means, "Much liver, much hope." However, it includes a play on words, since *foie* (liver) and *foi* (faith) are pronounced exactly the same way. Had an American invented *paté de foie gras*, he might have chosen as his slogan that triple play on words so appreciated by William James: "Is life worth living? It all depends on the liver!"

A short time after Clause opened his restaurant, another and vitally important event influenced the destiny of *paté de foie gras*. This was its marriage with truffles, the latter heightening the flavor of *paté de foie gras* and making it even more palatable. This felicitous union was made by Nicholas François Doyen, a Paris-born chef who had settled in Bordeaux.

The Revolution uprooted him and Doyen moved to Strasbourg, where, in 1792, he joined the truffles of Perigord with the *paté de foie gras* of Alsace. Since then *paté de foie gras* with truffles has circumnavigated the globe, invaded every country, and made conquests in every clime.

MAKING THE PATE

Formerly, the raising and fattening of geese for the preparation of *paté de foie gras* was essentially a home industry. It still is in thousands of peasant homes, not only

in Perigord and Alsace, but in Gascony, Lorraine, and other provinces as well. But furnishing *paté de foie gras* to the world has developed into a large-scale business. World-famous houses, some of them a century old, exist in Strasbourg, Perigueux, Cahors, and Mirande.

Paté de foie gras is an intricate concoction. Every paté house has its own secret recipe, handing it down from father to son. Soaking, mincing, simmering, seasoning—all this is a complicated and almost sacred process. Timing, dosing, and adding have developed into solemn rituals.

In addition to truffles, most patés contain salt, pepper, butter, *fines herbes* (garden herbs), parsley, mushrooms, and goose fat, of course. But the proportions vary, and a comparison of recipes is impossible. No specialist in *paté de foie gras*, be he peasant or industrialist, wishes to give his secret away.

To stimulate the production of *foie gras*, electric feeding machines have been introduced in Alsace. The electric feeder is equipped with a nozzle which forces a steady stream of corn into the bill of the goose until the bird is almost out of breath. Since exercise interferes with the fattening process, the geese are kept in small pens that permit no movement. In front of each pen is a constant and generous flow of fresh, clean water. Twice a day, sometimes three times, the bird is gorged. This is kept up for a month. After the twenty-second day, a little oil is usually sprinkled on the corn. The goose is compelled to grow fat. Resistance is useless, escape impossible. Within thirty or forty days, the goose doubles in weight and its liver weighs a full pound, sometimes more.

Much sympathy has been bestowed upon the geese exposed to this fattening process. But the average French peasant, who knows how to feed his geese, dismisses such scruples as misdirected and maudlin. His observation convinces him that the goose experiences no pain whatsoever. In the process of forcible feeding, there is nothing resembling martyrdom. On the contrary, the goose clucks with pleasure at feeding time.

For many decades experts have disagreed as to the proper place of *paté de foie gras* in a well-balanced meal. Curnonsky, who has the title Prince of Gastronomes, asserts that *paté de foie gras* should be served at the beginning of a meal, when the diner is still hungry and can fully appreciate its delicacy. Many French hostesses frequently serve the *paté de foie gras* with the hors d'oeuvre. At any rate, no salad or spicy food should be served with this smooth, unctuous concoction. It is best served in canapé form or from the pot in which it is packed. It should never be eaten icy cold, but at room temperature.

Prosper Montagne, master caterer and prolific writer on gastronomic subjects, states his opposing viewpoint as follows: "... *Paté de foie gras* is the summit of gastronomy. Eating a meal is like mountain climbing—you should always begin at the bottom and move upward. For this reason, *paté de foie gras* should always come after the fowl, and at big banquets it should be the fifth dish. Oysters (if in season) should be first; then the consommé, the fish, the turkey, and only then the *foie gras*."

PATENT PEELER. *See* Floating Blade Vegetable Knife.

PEELING GADGET

PATO REAL. A wild duck. *See* Duck.
PAVE DE MOYAUX CHEESE. A French cheese made in Normandy.
PAWPAW. *See* Papaya.
PEA. Like many other familiar foods, peas have had a long and sometimes romantic history extending back into prehistoric times. Some authorities claim they were eaten in the Stone Age. Dried peas were discovered in a tomb at Thebes, and they were uncovered among the ruins of ancient Troy, where they had been buried in pottery jars for some thirty-four centuries. Certainly they were well known in Greece and Rome, and in the Middle Ages peas were grown as an insurance crop against the frequent famines and were included in the rations of the armies of the time.

So common was the use of peas in England that the terms "pottage" and "porridge" came to mean pease porridge, as in the old nursery rhyme. The oldest use of peas was in the form of the dried seed. It was not until the Middle Ages that people began to use the green peas, cooking the pods whole and eating the peas from the pod.

Green peas shelled from the pod before cooking marked the last step in the evolution of pea-eating, and this new method of cooking peas was taken up as a fad by the French court in the time of the Louis'. Writings of the time are full of amusing commentaries on the heights of folly which the taste for green peas reached. In a letter of 1696, Madame de Maintenon wrote, "The subject of peas continues to absorb all others. The anxiety to eat them, the pleasure of having eaten them, and the desire to eat them again are the three great matters which have been discussed for four days past by our Princes. Some ladies, even after having supped at the Royal table, and supped well, too, returning to their homes ...will again eat peas before going to bed. It is both a fashion and a madness."

It is probably because of this Royal madness for the delicate taste of the small green peas, famous as the French *petits pois*, that green peas were formerly considered a typical French vegetable de luxe.

The French liked small round peas. The English, however, liked their peas bigger, smoother, and unwrinkled. Indeed, the first, and later the most extensive, development of the pea plant occurred in England, and two of today's best known varieties were originated by English horticulturists. As colonial settlers in America, the English brought with them a large variety of peas. In 1629, the Reverend Francis Higginson wrote, "There is in Massachusetts a store of green peas, as good as ever I ate in England, now growing in the Governor's garden."

Today peas are grown all over the United States and form one of the most important commercial canning industries.

Hints on Buying

Fresh Peas. Peas grown for market are of two basic types, the early smooth-skinned varieties and the later, larger, wrinkled-skin peas. In either case, peas of the best quality are young, tender, and sweet. Peas lose their sweetness as they mature and very rapidly after they are picked, so the choicest peas are those freshly picked while young. The pod should be bright green and fresh looking, and the peas should be well developed within the pod. Some varieties have large pods which stand away from the peas so that it is necessary to break one open to judge the con-

FOOD VALUE

	Wa-ter	Food Energy	Pro-tein	Fat	Car-bohy-drates	Cal-cium	Phos-phorus	Iron	Vit. A Value	Thia-mine	Ribo-flavin	Nia-cin	Ascor-bic Acid
Fresh	74.3	101	6.7	.4	17.7	22	122	1.9	680	.36	.18	2.1	26
Canned	82.3	69	3.4	.4	12.9	25	67	1.8	540	.11	.06	.9	8
Dried	10.0	354	24.5	1.0	61.7	73	397	6.0	370	.87	.29	3.0	2

tents. Immature peas, which will lack flavor, have flat pods and are likely to be darker green in color. Yellowed pods indicate age or damage in shipping and storing. The peas within will be tasteless and probably tough.

Sugar Peas are a particular type of peas, otherwise known as edible-pod peas. They are better known in England than in America. The pods are more tender than the shelling pea, and when the peas are very young, they are picked, the tips nipped off, and then cooked like string beans and eaten pods and all.

Canned Peas. Peas grown for canning fall within the two classifications of the small unwrinkled and the larger wrinkled varieties. Because the unwrinkled peas stand up better under the canning process, their appearance is more attractive and they sell at a higher price than the larger, wrinkled peas, which actually have a better flavor.

Canned peas are graded according to size and quality. The standards of quality are (1) Fancy, young tender peas uniform in color and size; (2) Standard, peas slightly more mature and somewhat less even in size; and (3) Ungraded, peas packed as they come without sorting for size or uniform maturity. There are six grades for size, ranging from a diameter of 9/32 of an inch to 13/32 of an inch and larger, with No. 1 being the smallest and No. 6 the largest.

Good quality canned peas should have a clear liquid, although a slight sediment at at the bottom of the can is not important. Cloudy liquid indicates that the peas were overcooked in the canning process.

Canned peas should be bought with their use in mind. It is obviously foolish to buy No. 1 fancy peas to make a cream of pea soup. On the other hand, large ungraded peas are perfectly wholesome food, but do not make an attractive vegetable for the special dinner when everything must be just perfect.

Quick-frozen Peas. Within recent years, the quick-freezing industry has perfected the freezing of peas to the point where they are practically comparable to choice peas fresh picked from the vine. Generally the larger types are frozen, although it is possible to find the very small peas in the market. Frozen peas should be cooked in as little water as possible in order to capture all their flavor. Otherwise, they are treated as fresh peas.

Dried Peas. Ordinarily known as split peas, dried peas are used for soups and other dishes which form effective meat substitutes. Dried peas come in both green and yellow varieties and are available unsplit. Formerly, dried peas required overnight soaking and long preparation, but quick-cooking types are now available.

HINTS ON PREPARATION

Fresh Peas. A pound of fresh peas will give about 1⅛ cups of shelled peas. Fresh peas should be cooked as soon as possible after picking or purchasing. They need no washing. Shell the peas and cook in as little water as possible until tender, about 15 minutes, depending on the size and age of the peas. If you suspect that the peas may not be as sweet as possible, a teaspoon of sugar should be added to the cooking water. Green peas need no more than salt and pepper and butter to be delicious, but there are a number of other ways of preparing them. Try sprinkling the cooked peas with finely chopped mint leaves just before serving them. Peas in cream are easily made by cooking two cups of peas until tender and draining off the liquid. Add to the peas two teaspoonfuls of butter or margarine and one-half cup scalded cream. Allow to boil up once and serve immediately. Do not discard the water in which peas have been cooked. There should be so little that it is served with the peas, but if there is an unusual quantity, use it in soup or sauce.

An old fashioned use for pea pods as coloring for soups is well worth trying. Use firm, fresh pods and wash them before shelling the peas. Lay the empty pods on a cooky sheet and place in a very cool oven (300° F.) until the pods are thoroughly dried and well browned. Turn the pods once or twice to brown them evenly. Allow to get quite dark brown without burning. After drying, the pods may be kept in an airtight jar or tin cannister in a dry place almost indefinitely. Three or four pods cooked in a pot of bouillon or consomme will give a pleasing color to otherwise pale stock. Use instead of commercial colorings.

Canned Peas. Canned peas really need nothing more than heating and seasoning, in any of the styles appropriate for fresh peas. (Be careful not to cook them again as they will become mushy.) Again, do not discard any of the liquid which comes in the can, since much of the valuable food elements of the peas have cooked into the liquid during the canning process. If it cannot be used in a sauce for the peas, save it for soups or sauces.

Quick-frozen Peas. Frozen peas should be dropped, still frozen, into a small amount of boiling, salted water, and cooked until just tender. They may then be treated like fresh peas.

Dried Peas. If dried peas are bought in packages, they probably need little cleaning. However, if they are bought loose, they should be picked over. They may or may not need soaking, according to the instructions on the package. Modern methods of preparation give a quick-cooking product which does not need overnight soaking. In any event, they should be well washed in lukewarm water before cooking.

CREAM OF PEA PODS SOUP

2 qt young tender pea pods, shelled
1 qt boiling water
1 cup shredded lettuce
1 large onion, minced
1 qt milk
1 bay leaf
4 sprigs parsley
Salt and pepper
Dash of nutmeg
2 egg yolks
1 tbsp butter or margarine
1 tsp flour

Pick over and wash the pea pods. Boil covered with the lettuce and onion in the quart of water until the pods are very tender. Rub through a wire sieve into a fresh saucepan. Scald the milk with the bay leaf and parsley, and strain, discarding the herbs. Add the milk to the pea purée, and bring to a boil. Season to taste with salt, pepper, and a dash of nutmeg, and remove from the fire. Beat the egg yolks well. Knead the butter with the flour. Add the egg yolks alternately with the butter and flour mixture, beating thoroughly. Reheat, but do not let boil. Serve with croutons. (Serves 6)

CREAMED PEAS AND CUCUMBERS

4 cups shelled green peas
1 medium-sized onion, sliced
1 tsp salt
2 cups boiling water
2 small cucumbers, peeled and diced
3 tbsp butter or margarine
1 cup cream or rich milk, scalded

Combine the peas, onion, and salt in a saucepan, add the boiling water, and cook, covered, until the peas are almost tender, about 15 minutes. Add the cucumbers and continue cooking until these also are tender. Drain, reserving the liquid for soup. Add the butter and scalded cream, and let boil up once. Serve very hot. Sour cream may be used for a particularly delicious and unusual dish. (Serves 6 generously)

GREEN PEA SOUP

2 cups shelled peas, somewhat old and hard
4 cups boiling water
1 small onion, minced
2 small potatoes, peeled and sliced thinly
Salt and pepper
1 tbsp butter or margarine
1 yolk of egg

Boil the peas in the boiling water until they are tender. Drain and save the water. Press the peas through a fine sieve, discarding the skins. Brown the onion in the butter. In a saucepan put the cooking water, the puréed peas, the onion and butter, and the sliced potatoes. Season with salt and pepper. Bring to a boil and simmer, covered, for 30 minutes, or until the potatoes have disintegrated. Just be-fore serving, stir in the well beaten yolk of an egg. Serve hot. (Serves 6)

NEW·PEAS, FRENCH STYLE

2 cups shelled peas
1 small head of lettuce
8 small white onions
1 tsp sugar
2 tbsp water
Salt and pepper
Butter or margarine

Place the peas, the lettuce separated into leaves, the onions peeled but left whole, and the sugar and water in a heavy saucepan or earthenware casserole. Cover tightly. Bring to the boiling point and sim-mer gently until the peas are tender and the liquid almost all absorbed. Season to taste with salt, pepper, and a good lump of butter or margarine. Serve hot. (Serves 4)

PEAS ALSATIENNE

2½ cups shelled peas (1 No. 2 can)
1 small onion, finely minced
½ cup finely shredded lettuce leaves
1 tbsp butter or margarine
½ tsp sugar
½ tsp salt
Dash of black pepper
3 tbsp minced parsley
½ cup thin cream or evaporated milk, scalded

Combine all the ingredients except the cream or evaporated milk in the top of a double boiler. If canned peas are used, heat thoroughly. If fresh peas are used, cook until the peas are tender. Add the cream or milk and reheat. Serve immedi-ately. (Serves 6)

PEAS CREOLE

3 strips bacon, diced
1 medium-size onion, minced
1 green pepper, finely chopped
1 tbsp minced parsley
½ tsp salt
¼ tsp pepper
Dash of cayenne
1 can concentrated tomato soup
½ cup liquid from peas
2 cups cooked or canned peas
2 tbsp grated Parmesan cheese

Fry the bacon until crisp and remove from the pan. Cook the onion, green pepper, parsley, and seasonings in the bacon fat for ten minutes. Add the soup and liquid from the peas and simmer five minutes. Then add the peas themselves and the cheese and let heat up thoroughly. Serve piping hot, sprinkling the crisp bacon over the dish. (Serves 6)

PEA LOAF

Either dried peas or green peas which are somewhat past their prime may be used. If dried peas are used, they should be soaked overnight in cold water ·to cover, unless a quick-cooking brand is used. In either case, cook the dried or fresh peas until tender in salted water with a small sprig of mint. Drain and press through a sieve, discarding the skins of the fresh peas.

For each two cups of pulp add one cup fine bread crumbs, one beaten egg, one teaspoon of minced parsley, salt and pep-per to taste, and one and one-half cups milk or evaporated milk. Turn into a well greased casserole and bake in a moderate oven (350° F.) 45 to 50 minutes. Serve hot with a cream sauce (which see). (Serves 6 when made with two cups of pea pulp)

PEA SOUFFLE

1 No. 2 can large peas, or 2½ cups cooked peas
1 tbsp granulated sugar
½ tsp salt
Dash of pepper
2 or 3 thin slices of onion
Speck of dried thyme
2 tbsp butter or margarine
3 eggs separated
1 additional egg white
1 cup dried bread crumbs, soaked in milk

Heat the peas, sugar, salt, pepper, onion, and thyme in a saucepan until the peas are very tender. Drain thoroughly, and rub through a fine sieve, discarding the skins. Add the butter to the pulp and beat in the egg yolks one at a time, beating well after each addition. Soak the bread crumbs in a little milk and squeeze them dry. Add to the pea mixture and mix thoroughly. Beat the four egg whites until very stiff, adding a few grains of salt while beating. Fold into the pea mixture. Turn the mixture into a well-greased casserole, and bake in a hot oven (400° F.) for 35 minutes. (Serves 6)

EAST INDIAN SPLIT PEAS

1 lb yellow split peas
1 tsp salt
1 or 2 tsp curry powder
2 cups sour cream

Wash the peas thoroughly and soak in cold water if desired. Drain and cover with fresh water and cook gently until the water is all absorbed and the peas are tender. Season to taste with salt, add the curry powder and sour cream, and heat thoroughly. Serve hot or cold. (Serves 6)

SPLIT PEA SOUP I

2 cups split peas
2 qt meat stock
1 carrot
1 onion
1 stalk of celery

Soak the peas overnight in cold water to cover, if necessary. In a pot, place the peas and the stock (plain water may be used and a ham bone cooked in the pot) and the vegetables which have been cut in small pieces. Bring to a boil and simmer until the peas are very tender. Rub through a sieve into a fresh saucepan, rectify the seasonings, and reheat. Just before serving,

PEACH

stir in two tablespoons of heavy cream. Serve hot with croutons or with slices of frankfurters in the plate. (Serves 6)

SPLIT PEA SOUP II

1 cup split peas
1 smoked ham butt or bone
¼ cup diced carrot
1 stalk celery
1 medium-size onion, sliced
4 peppercorns
1 bay leaf
8 cups boiling water
Pepper, and salt if needed
½ cup cream or evaporated milk, scalded

Wash and soak the peas overnight in water to cover. Drain and place with the ham bone or butt, vegetables, seasonings, and boiling water in a large saucepan. Cover and simmer gently until the peas are tender, stirring frequently to prevent burning. Strain through a sieve and if necessary add more water to give the desired consistency. Season with pepper and a little salt if needed. Just before serving, add the scalded cream or milk. (Serves 6)

PEA BEAN. Another name for Cowpeas. See BEANS.

PEACH. Botanically, according to certain specialists, the peach belongs to the prune family. Another group of scientists classify it with the almond, the nectarine, and the apricot. Seeds of the peach will produce nectarines and vice versa, and nectarines and peaches may mature on the same branch of a tree. To add to the confusion, peaches and nectarines can be budded on plum or almond sticks.

The controversy among horticulturists as to present classification is equalled by their despair at not being able to supply any accurate information as to the origin of the peach. One group holds that the peach was probably Chinese, grown from a long-cultivated species. Another theory is that the wild almond may be the source of the peach as well as of the present cultivated almonds, nectarines, and apricots. At any rate, its Latin name is *Prunus persica*, meaning Plum from Persia. The peach is mentioned in documents of the tenth century before the Christian era. The Greeks of Alexander's time wrote of it, both as a garden embellishment and as a fruit for feasting. In all probability the peach, in a well-developed stage, was introduced to the West from Asia Minor or Persia. It was brought to America by the earliest Spanish explorers. By 1600 it was common in Mexico and spread northward. There are no less than 2,181 varieties of peaches, differing in size, shape, flavor, and color.

Brillat-Savarin, the gourmet philosopher, in attempting to analyze the sensation of taste, uses the peach as an example: "He who eats the peach is at first agreeably struck by the odor which emanates from it; he puts it in his mouth and feels the sensation of freshness and of sourness which induces him to continue. But it is only at the moment when he swallows it that the perfume is revealed to him. This completes the sensation which a peach ought to produce. Finally it is only when it has been swallowed that the taster says to himself, 'How delicious!' "

Wherever it originated, the peach is now thoroughly Americanized. Nowhere else in the world does it thrive as it does in the United States. It likes our soil so well that there was a widespread escape from cultivation into the wild; in fact, early botanists found so many peach trees outside orchards that they considered it a native. With the orange and the grape, it ranks next to the apple among fruits of commercial importance, the annual crop having a value of more than $45,000,000.

eral use, although hand sizing is still practiced extensively, particularly in the smaller orchards. In the United States standards for peaches, the size is based on the minimum diameter taken through the center and at right angles to a line running from stem to blossom end.

United States standards for grading peaches include the following grade classifications: U.S. Fancy, U.S. Extra No. 1, U.S. No. 1, U.S. No. 2, and Unclassified. These standards define in detail the requirements of the various grades. The size of the peach is stated separately from the grade. Thus peaches of any size may be U.S. Fancy, U.S. Extra No. 1, etc.

HINTS ON BUYING

In the white-fleshed and yellow-fleshed classes of peaches, there are also many varieties of clingstones and freestones. The freestone varieties of both classes are most popular for dessert, home canning and general culinary use. The clingstones are not so popular for dessert but are used to some extent for slicing and home pickling. They are used mainly for commercial canning.

A peach of fine quality should be firm, free from blemishes, and have a fresh appearance, a color that is either whitish or yellowish and sometimes possesses a blush or red color, depending on the

FOOD VALUE

	Wa-ter	Food Energy	Pro-tein	Fat	Car-bohy-drates	Cal-cium	Phos-phorus	Iron	Vit. A Value	Thia-mine	Ribo-flavin	Nia-cin	Ascor-bic Acid
Fresh	86.9	51	.5	.1	12.0	8	22	.6	880	.02	.05	.9	8
Canned	80.9	75	.4	.1	18.2	5	14	.4	450	.01	.02	.7	4
Dried	24	295	3.0	.6	69.4	44	126	6.9	3,250	.01	.20	5.4	19

PREPARATION FOR MARKET

Great care must be used in picking such a tender fruit as the peach to prevent bruising and consequent deterioration and loss. Damage to fruit frequently results from careless handling by pickers in tossing the peaches into baskets on the ground or pouring them from the picking utensils into the orchard boxes or baskets used for hauling the fruit to the packing house.

In most of the important peach-producing areas, sizing machines are in gen-

variety. This blush, however is not a true indication of maturity. Round, plump peaches are superior to flat ones, as flatness in shape means flatness in flavor. Peaches are very perishable and for long-distance shipment are picked when slightly immature. Immature peaches may develop a pale, weak color and will shrivel. Generally the flesh becomes tough, rubbery, and lacking in flavor. For immediate consumption, over-mature or soft peaches may be bought. However, they bruise easily, soon spoil, and are wasteful. Worm injury may often be detected by the unevenness of the form of the peach and the small punctures from which gum exudes, generally giving the appearance of premature ripeness.

Evaporated or dried peaches are sometimes sold peeled. The peeling makes them more expensive but adds to their desirability. They are usually treated with sulfur fumes in the drying to promote their self-preserving qualities. Since the fruit for drying is tree ripened, they have a good flavor. They are less expensive than canned fruit and may be used frequently in low cost menus. *See also* DRIED FRUITS.

HINTS ON PREPARATION

Fresh peaches are usually peeled, sliced, and served with cream and sugar. With some varieties the skin may be removed easily, but with others it is necessary to plunge them into boiling water for a few seconds and then into cold water in order to loosen the skins. They should be peeled and served at once. When it is necessary to prepare them in large quantities, they may be peeled and kept in milk, or heavy fruit juice, and sliced as needed. Powdered sugar should be sprinkled on peaches as soon as they are sliced.

One pound of peaches (four to six) yields two, to two and a half cups of slices, or three to four portions. A bushel of peaches averages 15 quarts when canned.

Fresh peaches are very perishable and should be handled carefully. Store at 40° F. and you may be able to keep them for a week, but for the best flavor, peaches should be tree-ripened and used as soon as possible after they are picked.

PEACHES AS GARNISHES

Hot peach halves, plain or dressed-up, make superb garnishes and accompaniments for all sorts of meat dishes, chicken, turkey, fish, eggs, salads, and sandwiches. Both fresh and canned peaches may be used. A few suggestions follow:

Simply heat the peaches in their own sirup, either by dropping the can in boiling water for 20 minutes or by emptying the peach halves into a saucepan and heating gently.

Drain the sirup from a can of peach halves, add sugar (about three-quarters of a cup to the sirup from a No. 2½ can), and boil until rather thick. Add the peach halves and a few drops of lemon juice, and cook until slightly glazed.

Fry drained, canned peach halves in a little butter or meat drippings for about ten minutes, turning as necessary. Sprinkle with brown sugar and a dash of ground cinnamon while cooking.

Pour a little of the canned peach sirup into a baking dish, put in the peach halves cut-side up, dot with butter, and bake about 20 minutes in a hot oven (400° F.). The cavities of the peach may be filled before baking with jelly or relish. Those filled with sharp relishes (chutney, chili sauce, catsup, or French dressing) are especially good with steaks, roasts, salmon, or tuna loaf, or croquettes.

Remove halves of canned peaches from sirup. Arrange them cut-side up in a shallow pan. Brush them with melted butter, and broil them under moderate flame until peach halves are delicately browned. The peach halves may be stuck with whole cloves, and filled with sugar mixed with a little grated lemon or orange rind. Or, a dash of ground cinnamon and sugar on each one will make delicious, spiced peaches, particularly nice with ham, roast pork, smoked pork tenderloin, or fresh pork chops.

To serve with fish, fill the cavities of hot peach halves with tartar sauce after removing from the oven.

Roll drained peach halves in melted butter, then in finely chopped nuts or coconut or crushed corn flakes, and bake gently. Serve with any kind of meat, preferably veal or chicken.

Peach and fresh berries combine well in fruit cups.

Combine diced canned peaches with banana or avocado, or both, cut similarly. Serve in sherbet glasses, topped with a thin dressing made of mayonnaise, whipped cream, and tomato catsup to suit taste.

Save the sirup from canned peaches to use for gelatins, punches, frozen desserts, for liquid in cooking tapioca, rice, for jelly, and for basting smoked meats.

Ginger ale or cider poured over chilled and drained peaches makes an excellent beginning to a dinner. Add a bit of sugar and a dash of powdered ginger of desired. Excellent when frozen semi-solid.

Peach Shortcake. Cover layers of plain cake (home or bakery made) with sweetened whipped cream and sliced peaches. Serve cold.

Peach Cardinal. On a square of sponge cake, put a peach half, rounded side up. Pour raspberry sauce (canned raspberries strained and cooked down to a sirup) over all, and serve.

Peach Delight. Crumble graham crackers over canned peaches, halves or sliced, in serving dishes (individual dishes if desired). Add whipped cream and another sprinkling of graham crumbs (or vanilla or chocolate wafers, crumbled) and serve. Coconut or macaroon crumbs or ground or coarsely chopped nuts may be substituted for graham crackers.

Mix chilled, canned, sliced peaches with sliced bananas, and serve in small cantaloupe halves. Sprinkle with powdered sugar, and serve with lemon or lime quarters.

Add diced, canned peaches to chopped cabbage. Mix this with your favorite salad dressing.

A stuffing for salads may be made from peach halves with diced marshmallows, chopped dates, and nuts.

BRANDIED PEACHES

4 lb fine peaches
6 cups sugar
1½ cups water
Brandy

Plunge a few peaches at a time into boiling water, then into cold water, and remove the skins. Combine sugar and water in a preserving kettle, stir until the sugar is dissolved, then boil hard for five minutes. Drop the peaches as they are peeled into this hot sirup and simmer gently until the fruit is easily pierced but not really soft; then lift out into another container. When all the peaches are cooked, drain off from them any juice back into the sirup and boil this rapidly until it begins to thicken, about ten minutes. Pour over the peaches and let all stand together until cold. Now lift the fruit with a perforated skimmer and place in hot sterilized jars. Measure the sirup, add an equal amount of brandy, and pour over the fruit in the jars. Seal. (Makes two quarts)

DELMONICO PEACHES

6 medium-size peaches
4 green apples

Grated rind 1 lemon
½ to ¾ cup sugar
⅛ tsp nutmeg
½ cup macaroon crumbs
1 tbsp butter

Peel and slice the peaches and apples, add the lemon rind, and mix with the sugar and nutmeg. Arrange alternate layers of fruit and macaroon crumbs in a baking dish, dot the top with butter, and bake in a moderate oven (350° F.) for about 30 minutes. Serve warm, with cream if desired. (Serves 6)

FROZEN PEACH CUSTARD

2 cups milk
4 egg yolks
4 tbsp sugar
¼ tsp salt
2 cups ripe peach pulp
½ tsp almond extract
1 cup sugar, additional
2 cups heavy cream

Scald the milk, then pour it over the egg yolks beaten with the first sugar and the salt. Strain into a double boiler and cook until as thick as custard. Cool. Crush the peaches thoroughly with the additional sugar, press through a coarse sieve, and add the almond extract. Combine the two mixtures. Add the cream, and freeze. (Serves 8)

GLAZED PEACHES

4 peaches
Juice of 1 lemon
1 tbsp butter
2 tbsp sugar

Peel and halve the peaches, arrange cut-sides up in a buttered baking dish, then sprinkle with the lemon juice and top with the butter and sugar creamed together. Bake in a moderate oven (350° F.) for about 30 minutes.

ORIENTAL PEACHES

Peel and halve peaches, then cook until tender in a heavy sugar and water sirup. Flavor with kirsch and a dash of maraschino. Drain and chill. Serve on slices of vanilla ice cream, filling the hollows of the peaches with raspberry ice.

Peach Bread Pudding

1 large can evaporated milk, scalded
1⅔ cups water
2 eggs
½ cup sugar
½ tsp nutmeg
½ tsp vanilla extract
½ tsp almond extract
½ tsp salt
4 slices buttered bread
1¼ cups sliced, sugared, ripe peaches

Combine the scalded milk and water and pour over the eggs beaten with the sugar, flavorings, and salt; beat while pouring. Place one slice of bread in a casserole, cover with peaches, moisten with the milk mixture, and continue until all ingredients are used. Set the casserole in a pan of hot water and bake in a moderate oven (375° F.) about 40 minutes, or until set. (Serves 4 to 6)

Peach Frappe

See recipe for APRICOT FRAPPE, substituting peaches for apricots.

Peach Ice Cream

2 cups ripe peach pulp
¼ cup granulated sugar
1⅓ cups (1 can) sweetened condensed milk
¼ tsp salt
1 cup undiluted evaporated milk
1 cup cold water
1 tbsp lemon juice
2 tbsp ground fresh peach kernels

Sprinkle granulated sugar over fresh peach pulp and let stand for ten minutes until sugar is dissolved. Combine sweetened condensed milk, salt, undiluted evaporated milk, and water; stir in peach pulp mixture, lemon juice, and ground peach kernels. Freeze in hand freezer, using three parts ice and one part rock salt, until firm and solid. Pack or mold in four parts ice and one part rock salt for two hours.

Peach Jam

3 pt peach pulp
4 cups sugar

3 peach kernels
1½ in. ginger root
3 in. stick cinnamon
¾ tsp whole allspice
1½ tsp whole cloves

Dip the peaches into boiling water, using a strainer for easy removal, then cold-dip and remove the skins and pits. Crush the pulp; add the sugar, peach kernels, and the spices (tied in a bag). Cook until thick and clear. Remove the spice bag and pour into hot, sterilized jars, and seal.

Peach Jelly

About 3½ lb very ripe peaches
½ cup water
6½ cups sugar
1 bottle fruit pectin

Remove the pits from the peaches but do not peel. Crush; add the water, bring to boiling point, and simmer five minutes. Turn into a jelly bag and press out the juice. Measure the sugar and juice (there should be three cups) into a large preserving kettle, mix well, bring to boiling point over the hottest fire, and at once add the pectin, stirring constantly. Bring to a full rolling boil and boil hard for half a minute. Quickly remove from the fire, skim, pour into hot, sterilized glasses, and seal.

Peach Melba

For each serving, take a round of sponge cake. Place on it a scoop of vanilla ice cream and top with a preserved or canned peach. Pour over it a tablespoon or two of Melba Sauce, garnish with small rosettes of whipped cream, forced through a pastry bag with a fancy tube.

Melba Sauce

1 cup pulp and juice of fresh raspberries
1 small jar currant jelly
½ cup granulated sugar
⅛ tsp salt
½ tbsp arrowroot or cornstarch
1 tbsp cold water
¼ tsp lemon juice

Rub fresh raspberries through a sieve to remove the seeds. Retain the pulp and juice. Combine currant jelly, sugar, and pulp and juice of berries. Place over direct flame and bring to boiling point (212° F.). Add salt, arrowroot or cornstarch, lemon and water, and cook, stirring constantly, until mixture thickens and becomes clear. Strain through double cheesecloth. Cool.

PEACH MELBA—FRENCH STYLE

Master Escoffier, the celebrated chef, invented the world-famous "Peach Melba" in honor of the Australian diva, Madame Melba, while in London, where he directed the famous kitchen of the Ritz-Carlton Hotel. He subsequently made it according to two recipes, which follow:
(1) Having peeled fresh, luscious, free-stone peaches, poach them in a vanilla-flavored sugar sirup for three minutes. Lift out with a perforated skimmer. Put a layer of vanilla ice cream in a large, stemmed glass, or in a flat, individual, glass dish. Lay the peaches on the ice cream, and cover with raspberry purée, which may be blended with a little whipped cream or may consist simply of raspberries and powdered sugar crushed together. (A Melba sauce, ready prepared, is on sale in first-class grocery stores.)
(2) His second method uses fresh, peeled peaches, sprinkled with powdered sugar and allowed to stand for at least 30 minutes. Then, after draining off the liquid, proceed as above. During the green almond season you may, if desired, stick the peaches with finely shredded almonds, but never use dried ones.
Peach Melba is a very simple dessert that never fails to find favor.

PEACH MERINGUE

6 canned peach halves
6 rounds of cake
2 egg whites
1/4 cup powdered sugar
1/4 tsp vanilla

Drain the peaches and arrange round side up on the rounds of cake in a buttered baking pan. Make a meringue by beating the egg whites until stiff, gradually adding the powdered sugar and flavoring with the vanilla. Cover the peaches with meringue and place in a moderate oven (350° F.) until delicately browned (10 to 15 minutes). Serve immediately. (Serves 6)

PEACH MOUSSE

2/3 cup granulated sugar
2 cups peeled, sliced peaches
1/2 tsp granulated gelatin
1 tbsp cold water
1/3 cup evaporated milk
2/3 cup warm water
1/2 tsp salt
1 tbsp cornstarch
1 tsp vanilla extract
2 egg yolks, beaten thick
2/3 cup undiluted evaporated milk, whipped

Sprinkle sugar over sliced peaches and let stand for 30 minutes, then force through a coarse sieve. Soak granulated gelatin in cold water for five minutes. Combine one-third cup undiluted evaporated milk and warm water, scald in the usual way, and pour over the softened gelatin. Then add salt, vanilla, and cornstarch, which have been mixed with enough cold water to form a smooth, thin paste. Cook over hot water, stirring constantly, until mixture coats the spoon; then pour creamy mixture over thickly beaten egg yolks; return to double boiler and cook a few minutes longer, or until mixture is thick. Chill. When cold, fold in the sieved peach pulp and juice alternately with the whipped, undiluted evaporated milk. Freeze either in hand freezer, using equal parts ice and rock salt, for two and one-half to three hours, or in the refrigerator tray, either molded or right in the tray. If small molds are used, freeze for two to two and one-half hours; if large mold or mixture is frozen right in the tray, freeze for three and a half to four hours.

PEACH AND ORANGE CONSERVE

6 medium-size oranges
2 doz fresh peaches
4 cups sugar
1/2 cup blanched, chopped, toasted almonds

Quarter the oranges and discard seeds, if any; then pass through food chopper, using medium knife, and saving all juice. Scald, peel, pit, and slice the peaches. Combine the two fruits, add sugar, and cook over a gentle heat, stirring frequently, until thick, about one hour. Skim if necessary, then add the almonds. Turn into sterilized jars and seal. (About four pints)

PEACH AND ORANGE MARMALADE

2 doz large peaches
6 oranges
Water
Juice 1 lemon
Sugar

Peel the peaches and oranges. Cut the rinds of three of the oranges into small pieces, cover with water, and boil gently until tender. Drain and run the rinds through the food chopper. Cut the peaches and oranges into small pieces, add the lemon juice and three-fourths of a pound of sugar for each pound of fruit. Cook until transparent (one to one and a half hours). Turn into sterilized jars and seal.

PEACH PARFAIT

1½ tsp granulated gelatin
2 tbsp cold water
¼ cup water
½ cup granulated sugar
2 egg whites, stiffly beaten
1 cup sieved peaches, canned or fresh
¼ cup orange juice
1 cup heavy cream, whipped stiff
½ tsp vanilla extract
¼ tsp salt

Boil the one-quarter cup water and sugar until sirup spins a thread when dropped from the tip of a spoon. Immediately pour in a fine stream onto the stiffly beaten egg whites, while beating briskly and constantly until almost cold. Then add gelatin, which has been soaked in cold water and softened over boiling water, and stir until thoroughly blended and gelatin is dissolved. Continue beating until mixture is cold and begins to set, then fold in the sieved peaches combined with orange juice alternately with the heavy cream, stiffly whipped with vanilla and salt. Freeze as directed in the article on Parfait (which see).

PEACH, RASPBERRY AND PLUM COMPOTE

1 cup water
¾ cup sugar

1 lemon sliced
2 ripe peaches
4 plums
½ cup seedless grapes
1 pt box red raspberries
¼ cup sherry

Combine the water, sugar, and sliced lemon and cook to a sirup. Meanwhile, peel and slice the peaches, and prick the plums. Then cook with the grapes in the sirup over a moderate heat until almost tender. Add the raspberries for the last few minutes of cooking. Finally remove the lemon slices, stir in the sherry, and chill. If fresh raspberries are not available, quick-frozen ones are satisfactory.

PEACH SHERBET

⅔ cup sweetened condensed milk
2 tbsp lemon juice
2 tbsp slightly melted butter
½ cup cold water
1 cup sieved peach pulp
⅛ tsp salt
2 egg whites, stiffly beaten

Have all the above ingredients except the butter well chilled. Combine peach pulp, milk, lemon juice, salt, melted butter, and cold water. Fold in the stiffly beaten egg whites and freeze until mushy, as indicated under Sherbet, which see. Then scrape and beat for one minute, or until smooth. Return to refrigerator (if using hand freezer, you do not need to remove from the pan; simply scrape and beat until smooth) and freeze until solid. Serve in chilled sherbet glasses.

OLD-FASHIONED PEACH SHORTCAKE

1½ cups sifted flour
1½ tsp baking powder
½ tsp salt
1 tbsp sugar
¼ cup shortening
1 egg well beaten
6 tbsp milk
Softened butter
Sugared sliced peaches
Cream

Mix and sift the dry ingredients. Work in the shortening and mix to a soft dough with the egg and milk. Turn onto a slightly floured board, roll one-third inch thick, and cut into two rounds. Brush one round with softened butter and place the remaining one on top. Bake in a very hot oven (450° F.) 15 to 18 minutes. Split the layers, spread the split sides with butter, put the peaches between and on top of the layers, and serve immediately with plain or whipped cream. (Serves 6)

PEACH SOUFFLE

1 cup peach pulp
Grated rind 1 lemon
1 tbsp lemon juice
½ cup sugar
⅛ tsp salt
3 egg whites

To make the pulp, peel peaches and press through a coarse sieve. Add the lemon rind and juice, half the sugar and the salt. Beat the egg whites until stiff but not dry, beating in the remaining sugar. Fold in the peach pulp, turn into a buttered baking dish, set this in a pan of hot water, and bake in a moderate oven (375° F.) for 30 minutes, or until set. Serve immediately with fresh, sliced peaches.

PEACH TAPIOCA PUDDING

1 No. 2 can peaches
Water
4 tbsp quick-cooking tapioca
⅓ cup sugar
¼ tsp salt
2 tbsp lemon juice

Drain the peaches of their juice, measure the juice, and add water to make two and a half cups. Add this to the tapioca, sugar, and salt in a saucepan, stir thoroughly, and bring to a full boil over a direct heat, stirring constantly. The mixture will be thin, but it thickens on cooling. Remove from the fire, add one and a half cups of the peaches, diced, and the lemon juice. Cool, stirring occasionally; then chill and serve in sherbet glasses with plain or whipped cream. (Serves 6)

PICKLED PEACHES

3 lb sugar
2 cups vinegar
2 tsp whole mace
1 tsp whole allspice
2 3-in. sticks cinnamon
1 tsp whole cloves
6 lb peaches

Combine the sugar, vinegar, and spices (tied in a cheesecloth bag), and bring to boiling point. Scald the peaches, peel, then drop a few at a time into the boiling sirup. Cook gently just until tender but not in the least broken. Take out with a perforated skimmer and pack in sterilized jars. When all the peaches are cooked, boil down the sirup until thick, pour it over the fruit and seal. (Makes 1½ pints)

PEACH BRANDY

Peel a peck of very ripe, juicy peaches. Remove the pits, crack, take out the kernels, blanch like almonds, and put them to soak in a quart of brandy, allowing them to stand in the sunshine a full day in order to extract the flavor. Weigh, then pack down the fruit in an earthen crock with an equal weight of sugar. Let stand for 24 hours, then place over a moderate heat in a preserving kettle and simmer very slowly until the fruit is absolutely broken down, adding a little water occasionally to make up for the evaporation. (If a spicy brandy is desired, simmer with the fruit a little mace and a few whole cloves and peppercorns. This is not essential; it depends on the taste of the maker.) Strain without pressing to avoid cloudiness. There should be a gallon of fruit juice. While still hot, combine with the brandy and blanched kernels. Add also a quart of whiskey. Stir thoroughly, let cool, and bottle, taking care to apportion the kernels equally in the containers. They will sink to the bottom, but the liquor will acquire a delicate almond fragrance and flavor.

PEACH CORDIAL

Use ripe peaches. Remove the pits and crush the fruit in a crock. Add 30 pounds of sugar and two yeast cakes to each bushel of peaches. Mash, stir, and add water to make up to ten gallons. Let stand until all fermentation has ceased (this varies from three weeks to a month or more), then strain off the liquor into bottles or a barrel. Let stand a month before using.

PEACH DUMPLING. A pastry that may be made by substituting peaches for apples in recipe given under APPLE DUMPLINGS, *which see.*

PEACH PALM. *See* PEJIBAVE.

PEACOCK or Peafowl. A gallinaceous bird with handsome plumage. The Peacock is strictly an ornamental bird. It has such wild habits and eats so much that it is seldom raised to be eaten. When old, or even when mature, the flesh is tough and rank; but the flesh of the peachick is both tender and agreeable in flavor. Some gourmets and connoisseurs pronounce it superior to that of turkey. It may be prepared, cooked, and served as directed for turkey. The female of the peacock is the peahen.

PEA CRAB. *See* CRAB.

PEANUT. More than a billion pounds of peanuts are grown in this country annually. That's a lot of peanuts. The peanut's fancy name is *Arachis hypogaea* (family *Leguminosae*). However, this fruit which is called a nut is commonly known, aside from peanut, as ground nut, earth nut, monkey nut, and goober. The original home of peanuts is uncertain, but it was probably Brazil. Peanuts were also grown

PEANUT

in Peru at about the same time they were discovered in Brazil.

Peanuts spread to other countries from South America by slave ships, reaching this country from Brazil by way of Africa in the early slave ships. They were first grown in Virginia and North Carolina. When the boll weevil became a menace to cotton, farmers in other states turned to peanuts, which, curiously enough, are immune to any known disease.

The Virginia varieties—Runner, Jumbo, and Bunch—are the largest and are grown chiefly in southeastern Virginia, northeastern North Carolina, and central Tennessee. The Spanish peanut, a much smaller and rounder variety, is grown in the rest of the South. The plant thrives in a light, sandy soil. After the flower of the plant has withered,the flower stalk has the peculiarity of elongating and bending down, forcing the young pods underground, where the seed matures.

We are quite familiar with peanuts in the roasted state and in peanut butter, but they also have uses other than as food for man or beast. The oil is used in soap making, for lubrication, and sometimes for illumination. The ground shell is used for polishing tin plate, and the ash of the shells is used for fertilizer.

Peanut flour is made from the ground and bolted nuts, and it is claimed that a pound of it contains as much nutritive material as three pounds of beef or two pounds of peas. Pancakes may be made from it. Peanut grits may be boiled like oatmeal or made into biscuits. A form of peanut meal prepared for diabetics is said to contain little or no carbohydrate.

Peanut oil is an important product of the peanut. It can be used like other vegetable oils for cooking, salad dressings, and in hundreds of other ways. It is sometimes used in the preparation of oleomargarine. The meal left over after the extraction of the oil is a valuable food for animals. Pigs are partial to peanuts and waste peanuts are often fed to them. Sometimes portions of peanut patches are fenced off and pigs turned into the enclosures, where they root up the seeds for themselves. Also, peanut tops are used for hay.

Today, of course, there is machinery for harvesting and shelling peanuts. It was not until this machinery was developed on a large scale that peanuts became an important commercial crop. Since 1900 the uses and production of peanuts have increased tremendously.

Peanuts, like peas and beans, are rich in protein, and, like nuts, they are rich in fat and contain a surprisingly small percentage of starch and water. They are a good source of phosphorus and Vitamin B and a fair source of iron. They combine pleasingly with a large variety of bland and spicy foods, and properly prepared they are delicious. Peanut dishes are not only digestible, nutritious, varied, and different, but they are almost spectacular aids to the budget.

PEANUT BRITTLE MOUSSE

2 whole eggs, slightly beaten
½ cup maple sirup, heated
1 cup heavy cream, whipped stiff
⅛ tsp salt
¼ generous cup ground or pin-rolled peanut brittle

Over the slightly beaten, whole eggs, pour slowly the hot maple sirup; cook over hot water until mixture thickens, beating constantly with rotary egg beater. Cool, then chill. Lastly, add stiffly whipped heavy cream into which the salt and ground peanut brittle have been folded. Fill paper cases or place directly into freezing tray, and freeze until solid. If paper cases are used, freeze from two to two and one-half hours; if poured directly into the refrigerator tray, freeze three and one-half to four hours.

Any other kind of nut brittle may be used, if desired.

PEANUT BUTTER BREAD

2 cups all-purpose flour
2 tsp baking powder
½ cup sugar
¾ tsp salt
½ cup peanut butter
1 tbsp shortening
1 egg, beaten
1¼ cups milk
1 tsp grated orange rind
½ cup raisins

Sift flour, measure and resift three times with baking powder, sugar, and salt. Add peanut butter and shortening and cut into

dry ingredients with a fork until mixture is crumbly. Beat egg, add milk and orange rind, and add all at once to the flour mixture. Beat until well mixed. Stir in raisins. Pour into well greased loaf pan, 8x4x2½ inches. Bake in a moderate oven (350° F.) for 60 to 70 minutes or until loaf tests done. Cool on wire rack. (Makes 1 loaf)

PEANUT BUTTER COOKIES

1¼ cups all-purpose flour
¾ tsp baking powder
½ cup butter
½ cup granulated sugar
½ cup brown sugar
1 egg beaten slightly
½ cup peanut butter

Sift flour, measure and resift three times with baking powder. Cream butter and both sugars until soft and well blended but not fluffy. Add egg and peanut butter, mix thoroughly, then add flour. Knead in the bowl only long enough to form a smooth dough. Divide into two parts and roll each part into a roll about one inch in diameter. Cut into one-inch pieces. Place the pieces cut-side down and one inch apart on ungreased baking sheets; press with the tip of a fork to form crisscrosses on top. Or to make a cookie with a less porous surface, roll the one-inch pieces between the palms of hands to form smooth balls; lay on cookie sheets one inch apart and press with tip of fork to make criss-crosses. Bake in a moderate oven (350° F.) for 12 to 15 minutes. (Makes 4 dozen cookies one and one-half to two inches in diameter)

PEANUT BUTTER ROLLS

Combine six tablespoons of peanut butter with one-half teaspoon of Worcestershire sauce and enough chili sauce to make a stiff paste. Broil 12 slices of bacon until crisp, and spread them with the paste immediately. Roll the slices and fasten them with toothpicks. Serve hot. (Makes 12)

PEANUT CARAMEL SHERBET

1 cup granulated sugar, caramelized
1 cup hot water
1 cup milk, scalded

¼ tsp salt
1 tsp vanilla extract
1 cup chilled milk
½ cup ground roasted peanuts
3 whole eggs, well beaten

Caramelize granulated sugar in the usual way, stirring constantly, over a low flame. (See CARAMEL.) Add boiling water slowly, while stirring constantly, until caramelized sugar is thoroughly dissolved. Set aside in a warm place. Combine scalded milk, well beaten eggs, and salt in top of a double boiler. Pour caramelized mixture in a fine stream onto the egg mixture over hot water stirring constantly, until mixture coats the spoon. Remove from hot water and add vanilla extract combined with chilled milk and roasted ground peanuts. Freeze in refrigerator tray until mushy; then scrape bottom and sides and beat one short minute. Return to tray and freeze until solid but not too hard, or about two and one-half hours. Serve in chilled sherbet glasses. Use almonds if desired.

PEANUT ICE CREAM
(Hand freezer)

4 whole eggs
1 cup granulated sugar
2 cups fresh milk, scalded
¼ tsp salt
1 pt heavy cream
¾ tsp vanilla extract
¼ scant tsp almond extract
1 cup peanut butter

Break whole eggs in top of double boiler, and beat slightly with sugar and salt. Gradually add hot scalded milk, stirring rapidly and constantly. Cook over hot water until mixture begins to thicken. Remove from hot water, stir in unwhipped heavy cream, strain through a double cheesecloth. Cool. Combine and add flavoring extracts, and add peanut butter. Freeze in hand freezer, using three parts ice and one part rock salt, until firm. Pack or mold, using four parts ice and one part rock salt, for two hours. You may use roasted, ground, or sifted peanuts instead of peanut butter.

PEANUT BUTTER. See NUT BUTTERS.
PEANUT FLOUR. See PEANUTS.
PEANUT MEAL. See PEANUTS. One kind of meal is made for diabetic.
PEANUT OIL. See OIL.

PEAR. Practically all varieties of pears are descended from the *Pyrrus communis*, or common pear. The Chinese Sand Pear, another species, furnishes several sorts of attractive fruits, but most are almost inedible until cooked and even then are of little value.

VARIETIES

Bartlett is the leading pear in America for all purposes—shipping, home use, and canning. It has excellent quality, with melting, juicy, aromatic flesh. Its surface is uneven, and the fruit is rather large and yellow.

Kieffer is an oval, yellow, granular fruit which cans well, but is poor for dessert.

Seckel, though small, is perhaps the most desirable of all pears, and with its trim obovate shape and bronze color, it is a favorite wherever it is grown.

Clapp Favorite is a large, yellow fruit with a red blush. The flesh is melting, juicy, and of very good quality.

Beurre d'Anjou is large and is an attractive winter pear of high quality.

Beurre Clairgeau is an attractive pale yellow with pinkish red cheek. The flesh is firm, granular, and of only fair quality. Clairgeau is a standard fall and winter pear.

Winter Nelis. The appearance of this pear detracts from its value; it is russet, with a long, curved stem. However, it is the most esteemed winter variety.

Flemish Beauty is dull yellow blushed with red on the exposed cheek, very good in quality.

Doyenne du comice is one of the finest varieties of pears. The fruit is in season in late October and November. It is large, clear yellow, blushed with red.

Howell is medium in size, lemon-yellow with a faint blush, very good in quality, and in season in late September and October.

PREPARATION FOR MARKET

When the fruit loses its grass-green color, it is ready to be gathered. When it is mature it will separate from the stem without difficulty. The pickers stand on ladders and drop the fruit into the picking bags which they carry. Two and sometimes three pickings are made from a tree. In commercial sections of the West, great

Food Value

	Water	Food Energy	Protein	Fat	Carbohydrates	Calcium	Phosphorus	Iron	Vit. A Value	Thiamine	Riboflavin	Niacin	Ascorbic Acid
Fresh	82.7	70	.7	.4	15.8	13	16	.3	20	.02	.04	.1	4
Canned	81.1	75	.2	.1	18.4	—	—	—	Trace	.01	.02	.1	2

importance has been placed upon the exact time of picking, and the mechanical-pressure tester is used to determine the degree of maturity. The vast majority of the fruit is sized by hand, because of its shape. Sorting is done by hand into different trays as the fruit passes on slowly moving canvas trays. Packing is done from the trays as they pass the packers.

Pears are graded according to the U.S. Department of Agriculture Standards. U.S. No. 1 consists of pears of one variety which are mature but not overripe, clean, fairly well formed, and free from decay, injury, or disease and mechanical damage. U.S. No. 2 is made up of pears of one variety which are mature but not overripe, clean, not seriously deformed, and free from decay, injury, and serious damage. U.S. Combination Grade is a combination of U.S. No. 1 and U.S. No. 2. Pears which are not in conformity with any of these grades are unclassified.

Hints on Buying

Pears are normally picked when somewhat immature and ripened in a cool, dark place. The flesh of storage-ripened pears is usually of fine texture, while that of tree-ripened fruit is often coarse and, in some varieties, gritty.

Good quality pears are generally firm or fairly firm, but not hard, free from blemish and clean, and not misshapen or wilted.

Some varieties are in prime condition while still green or greenish-yellow in color; others may be yellow and yet too immature for eating. Pears that are soft or that yield readily to pressure at the base of the stem are usually mature and ready for immediate consumption but are too ripe to hold for future use.

Some varieties are affected by scald, which in mild cases discolors the skin and superficially affects the flesh.

Pears that have a water-soaked appearance should be avoided as they are usually mushy and wasteful.

The fruit is often affected by a form of injury known as "limb rubs," caused by the pressure or rubbing of a tree limb while the fruit was in the course of development. This injury appears as a roughening of the surface of the fruit which causes hard, woody spots in the flesh just below the injury and sometimes causes the fruit to be misshapen.

Hints on Preparation

Pears, having a distinct but rather bland and mild flavor, will blend with foods that are distinctly flavored. They also make splendid carriers for flavors that are sharp and perhaps a bit acrid.

Pears have insufficient pectin for jellies but make delicious preserves. Those grown in the Southeast are usually less expensive than the Bartlett and hold their shape well when canned. For preserving, wash, core, and cut the pears into small, uniform pieces. To each pound of prepared fruit add three-quarters of a pound of sugar, after which immediately add one-quarter cup of

PEAR

water, and cook. Another way is merely to combine the pears and sugar in alternate layers, leave them overnight, and cook them in their own juice the next day. In either case, they must be stirred carefully until they reach the boiling point. Then they are boiled rapidly with constant stirring until the sirup is somewhat thick, and finally are packed in sterilized jars, and sealed.

BAKED PEARS PARISIENNE

16 marshmallows, quartered
1½ cups boiling water
Pinch of salt
½ tbsp lemon juice
6 tender pears, peeled
⅓ cup fresh grated or shredded coconut
Grated rind 1 small orange
6 whole walnut meats

Heat the marshmallows, water and salt, then beat with a rotary beater until smooth. Add the lemon juice. Wipe, core, and peel the pears. Place in a baking dish, pour the hot sauce over them, cover and bake in a moderate oven (350° F.) until tender, about 25 minutes. Blend the coconut and orange rind thoroughly, rubbing the two together to color the former. Sprinkle over the hot pears and garnish with the walnuts. Serve warm. (Serves 6)

BAKED PEARS WITH GINGER SAUCE

4 large, firm Bartlett pears
1½ tbsp butter
3 tbsp brown sugar
3 tbsp water

Wipe the pears with a damp cloth but do not remove stems or skins. Arrange in a baking dish large enough to hold them without their touching one another. Put a dot of butter and a sprinkling of brown sugar on each pear. Add the water, cover, and bake in a moderately hot oven (375° F.) until tender, basting several times with the liquid in the dish and uncovering for a few minutes before taking from the oven.

Sauce

½ cup sugar
¼ tsp ground ginger

⅛ tsp salt
2 tsp cornstarch
1 cup boiling water
1 tbsp butter

Blend the sugar, ginger, salt, and cornstarch in a small saucepan. Slowly add the water, stirring constantly, bring to boiling point, and cook five minutes. Add the butter and the liquor from around the pears.

If desired, honey, molasses, or sirup from ginger preserves may be substituted for part of the sugar.

BAKED PEARS WITH SABAYON SAUCE

6 large ripe pears
6 small macaroons, crushed
1 oz angelica, chopped
1 oz candied citron, chopped
1 pony kirsch

Wipe, core, and peel the pears, then fill the cavities with the blended macaroons, angelica, and citron moistened with the kirsch. Arrange in a baking pan, cover, and bake in a moderate oven (350° F.) about half an hour, or until tender. Serve with sabayon sauce. (Serves 6)

Sabayon Sauce

4 egg yolks
3 tbsp sugar
1 cup wine
1 pony brandy
6 drops lemon juice
Pinch of salt

Beat the egg yolk with the sugar until very light. Add the wine, brandy, lemon juice, and salt, and cook to custard consistency in a double boiler, beating constantly.

CURRIED PEARS

4 ripe cooking pears
¼ cup butter
¼ cup brown sugar
2 tbsp curry powder
¼ tsp salt

Wipe, core, peel, and halve the pears, and arrange in a greased, shallow pan. Cream the butter, add the sugar, curry powder, and salt, and use to fill the pear cavities. Bake in a moderate oven (350° F.) or broil until tender. Serve as a meat garnish.

FLAMING PEARS

Peel pears and cook gently in a heavy sugar sirup until tender. Arrange in a deep dish with the sirup, and just before serving, pour a glass of brandy over all and ignite.

FRENCH FRIED PEARS

1 cup sifted flour
1 tsp baking powder
½ tsp salt
1 tsp sugar
3 eggs, well beaten
1 cup milk
6 large ripe pears
Lemon sauce

Mix and sift flour, baking powder, salt, and sugar. Combine eggs and milk and add to flour mixture, stirring until smooth. Pare, halve, and core pears. Dip pears into batter, covering pears completely, and fry in hot, deep fat (360° F.) for two minutes, or until browned. Drain on unglazed paper. Serve with lemon juice, or Lemon Sauce (*which see*). (Serves 6)

MINCEMEAT-STUFFED PEARS

Wipe, core, and peel pears. Stuff the cavities with mincemeat. Place in a baking dish, sprinkle with sugar, add a little water, and bake in a moderate oven (350° F.) about 45 minutes, basting two or three times with the sirup in the pan. Serve hot with cream or cream cheese.

MINTED PEARS

1 cup sugar
1 cup hot water
2 tsp gelatin
2 tbsp cold water
¼ cup mint leaves
Green vegetable coloring
4 firm, ripe Bartlett pears

Bring the sugar and hot water to boiling point, stirring until the sugar is dissolved, then boil five minutes. Soften the gelatin

in the cold water. Combine the two mixtures and stir until the gelatin is dissolved. Add the mint and let stand five minutes. Strain and add just enough coloring to tint a delicate green. Wipe, peel, core, and halve the pears. Arrange in a serving dish, pour the gelatin mixture over, and chill. Serve very cold. (Serves 4)

PEAR CONDÉ

1 cup rice
2 cups boiling water
1 cup milk
⅔ tsp salt
Canned pear halves
Crushed sweetened berries
Whipped cream

Wash the rice thoroughly, then cook in a double boiler with the combined water, milk, and salt until all the liquid is absorbed. Turn the rice into a wet mold, cool, then chill. Unmold and serve surrounded by the pear halves. Fill the cavities of the pears with such fresh berries as strawberries, raspberries, or blueberries. Additional crushed, sweetened berries should be poured over the rice and the whole garnished with whipped cream. (Serves 6)

PEARS IN PORT

8 ripe pears, peeled and cored
4 cups water
2 cups sugar
1 cup port wine
Rind of 1 orange, thinly sliced

As the pears are peeled and cored, drop them into cold water containing a little lemon juice. Boil the water and sugar together until they become sirup. Add the wine, orange rind, and drained pears, and simmer until the fruit is tender but not broken. Serve hot or cold. (Serves 8)

PICKLED PEARS

2 lb brown sugar
1 pt vinegar
4 in. stick cinnamon
1 tsp whole cloves
2 qt firm pears

Combine the sugar, vinegar, and spices (tied in cheesecloth). Bring to boiling point and boil ten minutes. Peel the pears thinly and cook a few at a time in the sirup just until tender. Lift out with a perforated skimmer and pack in sterilized jars. Boil down the sirup a little, then pour it into the jars, filling them to overflowing. Seal. (Makes 4 pints)

POACHED DATE-STUFFED PEARS

6 pears
Juice and grated rind of 1 lemon
2 cups sugar
2 cups water
Dash of ground ginger
½ pkg dates, chopped
¼ cup nuts, chopped

Wipe, peel, halve the pears, then sprinkle with the lemon juice. Combine the sugar, water, lemon rind, and ginger in a skillet and bring to boiling point. Arrange the pear halves cut-sides down in the sirup, cover, and simmer ten minutes. Then, turn the fruit and fill the cavities with the combined dates and nuts. Cover again and continue simmering ten to fifteen minutes, or until the pears are tender. Serve hot or cold.

If preferred, the pears may be arranged in a casserole with the sugar sirup and baked in a moderate oven (350° F.). (Serves 6)

STUFFED MOLDED PEARS

2 pkg lime-flavored gelatin
1 qt water
12 canned pear halves
1 pkg (3 oz) cream cheese
¼ cup finely chopped nut meats

Prepare the gelatin according to directions on the package. Cool. Drain the pear halves well. Fill the cavities with the blended cream cheese and nuts. Place the pears in a shallow, wet dish. When the cooling gelatin is almost at the setting point, pour it carefully around the pears. Chill, cut into squares, allowing a pear half to each portion, arrange on lettuce, and garnish with mayonnaise. (Serves 12)

IMPERIAL PEAR SALAD

1 pkg lemon or lime gelatin
1 cup hot water

1 cup pear juice
1 tbsp vinegar
¼ tsp salt
⅛ tsp ginger
3 pear halves, diced

Dissolve the gelatin in the hot water. Add the pear juice, vinegar, salt, and ginger, and chill. When slightly thickened, fold in the pears, turn into wet individual molds, and chill. Unmold onto crisp lettuce and garnish with cream cheese dressing or with mayonnaise and cream cheese balls. (Serves 6)

PEARL BARLEY. See BARLEY.

PEARL TAPIOCA. A spurious article made from potato starch. See also TAPIOCA.

PECAN. Two-thirds of the world's supply of pecans is estimated to come from the states of Texas and Oklahoma. The pecan is the oldest crop known in Texas. Cabeza de Vaca, the Spanish explorer, reported after his visit to Texas in 1528 that the Indians along the gulf coast retired each autumn to the river bottoms and ate pecans to ward off starvation. Several years ago the pecan was adopted as the Texas State Tree.

Until about 30 years ago, pecans were just nuts. Few people outside of the areas where they grew realized that they had commerical possibilities. Even in the localities where they grew wild little effort was made to harvest them. There are many legends of their origin as a commercial product. In Oklahoma they say that a group of New Yorkers were inspecting some potential oil properties one day, and while roaming over a hillside they picked up some of these nuts. One of them asked the native Oklahoman who was with them what the nuts were, and he said: "Just pecans—good to eat." The banker is reported to have eaten some, liked them, put a few in his pocket, and brought them home. His family liked them so well that he wrote and asked his friend in Oklahoma to gather a bushel or two and send them East by express. The banker's friends tried and liked them, and soon there was a canned for shipment, or salted and sold in sprouted, and owners of vacant land began gathering seeds and planting groves.

Today there are regular nut factories in Oklahoma, Texas, and other southern states. The nuts are gathered, shelled, and canned for shipment, of salted and sold in attractive packages. Processors and brokers in Texas have over a half-million dollars invested, and at the height of the autumn season employ more than 35,000 persons. *See also* NUTS.

PECAN

PECAN PIE

⅓ cup butter
½ cup sugar
½ cup light corn sirup
½ cup maple sirup
3 eggs, well beaten
1¼ cups broken pecans
¼ tsp salt
¾ tsp vanilla
9-inch pie shell, partially baked

Cream the butter, add the sugar, and continue creaming while adding the combined sirups. Blend all thoroughly, then beat in the eggs with the nuts, salt, and vanilla. Turn into the partially baked pastry shell and return to a moderate oven (350° F.) for 20 minutes, or until no filling adheres to the tip of a knife. Serve cold, with or without a whipped cream topping.

PECAN MAPLE SAUCE

1 lb maple sugar
Pinch of salt
½ cup water
½ cup pecans

Boil the sugar, salt, and water together to the thread stage (230° F.). Remove from the fire and add the nuts broken into small pieces.

PECAN ORANGE MUFFINS

1¾ cups sifted cake flour
3 tsp baking powder
¼ tsp salt
⅓ cup shortening
¾ cup sugar
2 eggs, separated
¼ cup milk
¾ tsp grated orange rind
¼ cup orange juice
¾ cup chopped pecan meats

Mix and sift flour, baking powder, and salt. Cream shortening until soft and smooth, and gradually add sugar, cream-

ing until fluffy. Beat in well beaten egg yolks. Add flour alternately with mixture of milk, orange rind, and juice, beating until smooth after each addition. Stir in nuts and fold in stiffly beaten egg whites. Turn into greased muffin pans, filling them two-thirds full. Bake in moderately hot oven (375° F.) about 20 minutes. (Makes 1 dozen medium-sized muffins)

PECORINO CHEESE. An Italian sheep's milk cheese which comes in several varieties. Cacio Pecorino Romano, or merely Romano, is the most common. The interior is slightly greenish, somewhat granular, and devoid of eyes or holes. It weighs from two to 25 pounds. Pecorino Dolce is artificially colored with annatto. Pecorino Tuscano is smaller than Romano, weighing from two to five pounds. Local names are: Ancona, Cotrone, Iglesias, Leonessa, Puglia, and Viterbo. It is the chief article exported from Sardinia.

PECTIN. According to an old Irish superstition, pooka is the fairy that makes the juices of fruits jell. We modern Americans call it pectin but it still works magic.

Pectin is a carbohydrate substance found in pulpy fruits. It causes fruit to gelatinize when boiled. It has a wide distribution in nature, as it occurs in many fruits, berries, and even vegetables. The chief commercial sources of pectin today are from the peel of citrus fruits and from apple pomace. When one eats any of the citrus fruits, very little pectin is obtained, since the peel is discarded, but when an apple is eaten, a large amount of pectin is ingested. In fact, green-apple colic, so prevalent during the early part of the apple season, is due to an overdose of pectin.

USES OF PECTIN

Every homemaker wishes to make perfect jelly. But just what stands for perfection in a jelly or jam? Flavor, texture, color, and clearness. Flavor and texture are the most important. Flavor is defined as the flavor of fresh, fully ripe fruit, while perfect texture is one which holds its shape when turned out on a plate but quivers when the plate is moved.

Specifically, jelly is a product obtained from cooking fruit juices and sugar together. But not all jellies come to a successful jell. Some are runny, others are gummy, still others show crystallization, and cloudiness may spoil what should be a clear translucency. This is because each kind of fruit contains varying amounts of pectin.

In general, pectin is obtained more plentifully from under-ripe acid fruits. Green grapes will jell, whereas ripe raspberries or mature peaches often will not. Again, fruits made into juice or jelly the day they are picked will behave otherwise than after a lapse of some days between picking and preserving. All of these variations make jelly-making a hazard. But a fruit juice with the proper balance between pectin and acid will jell when it is cooked with the proper proportion of sugar. The most reliable way to secure this proper balance is to use true, natural fruit pectin in bottled or powdered form, thus bringing the chief variable in jelly-making under control.

Another important advantage of using commercial pectin is that it enables you to use mature, fully ripened, and hence more flavorful, fruits that will jell to perfection without adding a proportion of under-ripe fruit, as was done formerly. Still another convenience is that you may extract juice or cook down fruits in summer when the supply is plentiful, pack the juice or fruits in jars, and later, at your

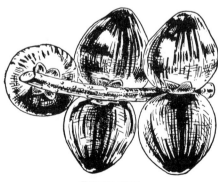

PEJIBAVE

leisure, turn them into jellies and jams. Likewise, any commerically bottled or canned fruit juice, such as grape juice or pineapple juice, or canned fruits, such as apricots or peaches, may be quickly cooked up with pectin to form tasty jellies.

But remember, to insure success always follow exactly the recipes given with the pectin for each individual fruit used. *See also* JELLY.

PEEL. To remove the outer coating— skin, rind, or bark—from food, such as potatoes, fruits, etc.

PEJIBAVE. This is the fruit of a tall palm tree of South America. It is oval, the size of a small plum, and has a thin skin varying from light to dark brown and, generally, a single black seed and dry, somewhat mealy flesh. The best varieties are seedless. In South America, where it is a food staple, it is boiled in salted water. Its dry flesh, which suggests the chestnut, is very popular. Its food value lies chiefly in its large percentage of starchy matter with a fair proportion of fat. It is used for stuffing game and poultry. It is also dried, ground into meal, and made into cakes, bread, and pastry.

PEKOE TEA. A leaf grade of black teas. *See* ORANGE PEKOE TEA; *see also* TEA.

PELARDON DE RIOMS CHEESE. A French cheese made in Languedoc.

PEMMICAN. This is said to be a Cree Indian word which, roughly translated, means "the least food with the most nourishment." The Crees certainly had a word for it! For Pemmican is best known as the food of highest possible caloric content for its weight and the space it occupies. It was prepared by the Indians of North America long before the white man came and was used extensively by them as an emergency ration in times of war and on long journeys. The explorers of the American frontier were quick to learn its value and to make use of it. Formerly the components were venison or the meat of bison, fat, and berries. Due to its availability, beef has gradually displaced the other meats as the basic ingredient.

Pemmican is simple to prepare. In arid regions lean meat is cut into thin slices and thoroughly dried in the sun. In more humid climates the meat will not dry properly unless it is smoked. This is done by building a horizontal latticework of branches three or four feet above a low fire of hickory, ash, or other non-resinous woods. (Pine, balsam, etc. are not used because the oily smoke contributes an unpleasant flavor to the Pemmican.) The fire is kept low; a hot fire will cook the meat rather than dry it. The meat is spread on the lattice-work over the smoke and heat of the fire until it becomes brittle. The drying may take from a few hours to more than a day, depending upon the amount of moisture in the air.

The meat, whether dried by sun or smoke, now is laid upon a flat rock and pounded with a stone until broken down to a coarse powder. Hot fat is added and kneaded thoroughly into the powder until a uniformly thick, doughy consistency is obtained. If dried fruits—berries, currants, raisins, or even apricots or prunes—are available, they are pounded in with the meat powder before the fat is added. The fruits must be thoroughly dry, however, or they will be likely to cause fermentation of the Pemmican.

When the Pemmican filling is completed, it is shaped into a round loaf or a large sausage and is wrapped tightly in skin or canvas. The American Indians frequently used the large intestines of deer or bison as casings for Pemmican. The intestines were washed thoroughly inside and out and then dried carefully with grasses. The filling was stuffed inside the still pliable casings, the ends of which were then tied tightly with rawhide thongs. Finally, the casing was rubbed well with grease to make it water-proof and hung up until needed.

When made in sausage shape, the casing such as the Indians used is best. A less satisfactory wrapping for the sausage-shaped Pemmican is made of long strips of rawhide or even of heavy canvas at least two inches wide. These are wrapped in overlapping spirals around the filling; the wrapping is then sewn tightly at the ends and the whole thing dipped into warm tallow or else rubbed thoroughly with animal fat to make it water-tight.

Loaf pemmican is laid upon a large piece of rawhide or canvas. The covering is pulled up over the sides and bunched at the top and tied tightly with rawhide thongs or stout cord so that it resembles an old-fashioned plum pudding. It is given a water-tight coating and then is ready for storage or use. The loaf was often made by the Indians and is as good as the sausage shape made with casing. However, the

second method of making the sausage-shaped pemmican will do when neither an intestinal casing nor a large piece of canvas or rawhide is available.

When properly made, Pemmican will keep indefinitely, regardless of climate, as long as it is kept dry. Slices or chunks may be cut off as neeeded and either cooked or eaten raw. It is easily masticated, and the acidity of the fruit promotes the flow of digestive juices. The remainder of this dried food should then be rewrapped and sealed against moisture until it is to be used again.

Pemmican is still used on long voyages, especially to the polar regions where a fatty diet is essential to furnish heat and to enable the body to withstand the rigor of the climate. *See also* CAMP COOKERY.

PENNSYLVANIA POT CHEESE. *See* COOKED CHEESE.

PENSACOLA SNAPPER. *See* RED SNAPPER.

PENTELE CHEESE. A sheep's milk cheese made in Rumania.

PEPO (peé poe). The cucumber, pumpkin, squash, or any other fruit of the gourd family.

PEPPER. (I) The hot pungent spice called pepper comes from quite a different plant than the green or red garden peppers. Botanically, the spice is *Piper nigrum*, a tropical vine bearing spike-shaped clusters of fruit, which contain the round peppercorns.

According to history, pepper was discovered growing in the Malabar province of India, and that section, together with certain islands in the Dutch East Indies and parts of Malaya, are still the chief sources of pepper. Legends indicate that it may have been an article of trade between Asia and Africa as early as 2000 B.C. Records show that it was known to the Greeks in the 4th century B.C. Like other products which trickled into Europe over the caravan trails from the mysterious East, pepper was imbued with a certain glamour. Medical properties were ascribed to it. One physician of the early days recommended eating five peppercorns every morning to cure a stomach-ache, and another advised the use of a mixture of pepper, fennel, and cloves to alleviate failing eyesight.

In the tropical Orient, pepper's primary use was as a food preservative, especially in preserving meats, which spoiled rapidly before the days of refrigeration. Southern Europe, the western end of the caravan routes, also had its problems of food spoilage and probably first welcomed pepper as a preservative. Out of this use came a new food delicacy which is still a favorite— sausage. In the ancient sausages, as in modern varieties, a mixture of spices was used, but pepper was always the most important.

As trading with the Orient increased during the early centuries of the Christian era, Venice and Genoa became the chief centers of trade. As caravan terminals, these cities controlled the spice industry and therefore the pepper market. Fortunes were made from the pepper trade— fortunes that other nations envied and which spurred them to the search for quicker, surer routes to the lands of the East where the pepper grew. The Genoese and Venetian monopoly was not broken, however, until 1497, when Portugal opened up a water route to India through the successful voyage of Vasco da Gama around the Cape of Good Hope. Thereafter Lisbon became the pepper center of the world and grew to riches on the proceeds of the trade.

England, Holland, France, and Denmark each chartered East India companies in an effort to win the lucrative trade from Portugal. Then followed an era of warfare between these nations on land and piracy between their ships on the sea. Ultimately, in the 18th century, the Dutch and English triumphed, the Netherlands gaining control of the East Indies and England of India, the two chief sources of pepper.

Throughout the Middle Ages, pepper was a form of wealth. Taxes, tributes, doweries, and rents often included levies of pepper. In the siege of Rome by Alaric, King of the Goths, the ransom of the city was 5000 pounds of gold, 3000 pounds of pepper, and 30,000 pounds of silver. Pepper was literally worth its weight in gold and, as in the case of gold, severe penalties were attached to stealing of it. So closely guarded were the porters who unloaded pepper cargoes in England during Queen Elizabeth's day that even their uniforms were made without pockets. Tenants paid part of their rent in stated quantities of pepper. A pepper guild existed in the time of Henry II, the traders in the condiment being known as pepperers.

THE MODERN INDUSTRY

The price of pepper came down, of course, as transportation became more regular and quicker. But it was not until the day of the clipper ships was past that pepper and the other spices lost most of the glamour connected with their commerce.

Although the halo of great riches no longer surrounds the industry, pepper still retains first place among the spices. Imports to the United States equal the amount of all other spices combined. Something like 35,000,000 pounds are consumed annually in the United States by commercial and household users. The annual world consumption is estimated at 120,000,000 pounds. The bulk of this pepper goes into commercially prepared food products. The meat packing, canning, pickling, and condiment industries use the major share. Pepper appears, with salt, on every dining table. Its primary kitchen uses are for seasoning meats, soups, sauces, gravies, and salads, and for home pickling. It is always an ingredient in the mixture usually called pickling spice.

PREPARATION FOR MARKET

In its wild state, the pepper vine grows to a height of 20 feet, supporting itself on tree trunks. When cultivated, as most of the commercially grown product is today, the vine is kept to a height of eight to 12 feet, and is usually supported on posts. The peppercorns are the fruit of the vine, growing in long clusters. The peppercorns are first green, then red, and finally yellow. For the spice trade, the peppercorns are picked just before they turn red. The entire spike is plucked from the vine and dried. Various methods of drying are used; airdrying in the sun is the usual method, and drying near a low fire is another. As they dry, the peppercorns become black-brown in color and the skin becomes wrinkled and very hard. When dry they are stripped from the spikes.

Whole peppercorns. These are the whole dried berry, cleaned and packaged for use in the home. Peppercorns are used in making soups and stews and give a rather more pungent flavor than ground pepper. Freshly ground pepper is obtained by the use of a small handmill, which grinds the peppercorns rather more coarsely than the

  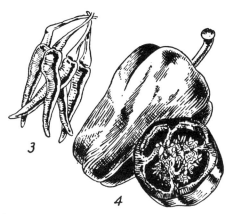

PEPPERS   1. Pimiento   2. Cayenne   3. Tabasco   4. Sweet

commercially ground pepper. Because pepper has a tendency to lose its pungency after it is ground and allowed to remain in an opened package, freshly ground pepper adds extra flavor to salads, sliced tomatoes, or almost any dish where the stronger flavor is desired.

Black Pepper. This is the whole dried peppercorn ground and packaged either at the plantations or by merchants who buy the whole peppercorns and grind and package them themselves. This is the common black pepper of the trade.

White pepper. This is made by removing the outer skin of the peppercorn, leaving the white kernel. Most white pepper comes from the island of Banka, where the pepper berries grow unusually large and thus give a larger kernel. The outer layers are removed by soaking or by machinery, and only the white interior is ground. For this reason, white pepper is somewhat more expensive than black pepper. It is a little less pungent because the dark outer layers are stronger in flavor than the interior. White pepper should be used in white sauces and other dishes where the dark specks of black pepper are unsightly.

Cayenne, paprika, and tabasco are products of the capsicum, related to the edible red and green peppers. They are discussed under their own names.

PEPPER. (II) The green and red peppers of the vegetable markets and temperate gardens are not related to the pepper of the spice trade. Botanically they are *Capsicum frutescens* and apparently are native to tropical America, although they were widely cultivated in Europe before they became popular in the United States.

For many years peppers have been grown on a small scale in the homegarden for use in pickles, salads, as a fresh vegetable and in other ways. It was not until the last quarter of a century that raising peppers commercially became a sizable industry. Besides the peppers grown for marketing fresh, considerable acreage in the Southeast is devoted to the pimiento type of pepper, which is grown for canning.

TYPES AND VARIETIES FOR MARKET

The pepper plant grows between one and two and a half feet in height. The fruit varies in size and shape among the different varieties, most of which are green when immature and red when ripe. Some varieties are yellow when immature, turning red at maturity. Peppers are divided into two general types, sweet or mild flavored and hot or pungent.

A number of varieties of sweet pepper are grown for the market; for instance, California Wonder, Worldbeater, King of the North, Ruby King, and Perfection. Perfection is the heart-shaped pepper which is canned as pimiento. All of these peppers are green when immature, which is the state in which they are marketed for fresh peppers. Occasionally some of them have begun to streak with red when sent to market; such a pepper is still sweet and makes an attractive color addition to a salad or creamed dish. Oshkosh is a type that is yellow in color when mature.

The hot peppers all have red flesh when they are mature. They include the tabasco pepper which is very small and very hot. Red Chili peppers are small finger-shaped

FOOD VALUE

Water	Food Energy	Pro- tein	Fat	Carbo- hydrate	Cal- cium	Phos- phorus	Iron	Vit. A Value	Thia- mine	Ribo- flavin	Nia- cin	Ascor- bic Acid
92.4	29	1.2	.2	5.7	11	25	.4	630	.07	.04	.4	120

peppers, also very hot. Cayenne is also very hot, with somewhat larger fruits. Hungarian wax pappers are semi-hot; as they are banana-shaped and are yellow when immature, they are often called banana peppers. The Hungarian paprika pepper is a milder form of red pepper, deep red in color when mature. Its pungency is mainly in the seeds and membranes.

USING PEPPERS

Sweet peppers are offered in the markets when they are mature but still green. The varieties vary in shape; some are long and slender and others are more chunky. The latter are more desirable for stuffed peppers. As the peppers continue to mature they turn to a bronzy or bright red color without becoming hot. Good quality peppers are firm, thick-fleshed, and with a good fresh color. Immature peppers are soft, thin-fleshed, and pale in color. Shriveling and softness indicate aging. Crooked and deformed peppers are liable to be wasteful, as are those with surface blemishes.

Hot peppers are marketed in either the red or green stage but are most generally used when red. They are not so thick-fleshed as the sweet varieties. Chili and cayenne peppers are sometimes strung on cords and dried before marketing. In foreign markets one will sometimes find the whole pepper plant with the peppers still attached, dried and ready for use.

In using the sweet peppers, it is well to remember that the seeds and the membranes to which they are attached are often much sharper than the green flesh. If these are completely removed the pepper will be sweet when cooked or chopped raw in salad or sauce. One of these seeds can be as hot as chili or cayenne pepper.

Stuffed peppers. In this form, peppers are stuffed with leftovers and made into an economical and appetizing dish. They should be cut in two lengthwise and all the seeds and membranes removed. Parboil the peppers three or four minutes and drain thoroughly. Stuff with any desired com-

bination or meat, poultry, fish, vegetables, or rice, top with crumbs or grated cheese, and bake in a hot oven (350° F.) for fifteen minutes or so.

French Fried. Peppers may be French fried in strips or rings. Remove the seeds and whitish membranes completely. Dip the slices in egg and crumbs and fry in deep hot fat until delicately brown. Drain on soft crumpled paper and serve hot.

Salad. Green peppers may be sliced into salad. A particularly attractive garnish for salad may be made by cutting the end off a pepper and carefully removing the seeds and membranes. Pack the pepper with cream cheese, flavored as desired. Chill in the refrigerator for several hours, and then cut crosswise into thin slices.

BAKED RICE AND PEPPERS

3 cups cooked rice
2 large green peppers, chopped
1 small onion, minced
3 tbsp margarine or drippings
3 tbsp catsup
1 cup tomato juice
½ tsp salt
⅛ tsp pepper

Grease a casserole well. Saute the pepper and onion in the margarine or drippings until brown. Add the rice, catsup, tomato juice, and seasonings, and mix well. Turn into the casserole. Bake in a moderate oven (350° F.) for 25 or 30 minutes. Serve from the casserole as a luncheon or supper dish. (Serves 6)

STUFFED GREEN PEPPERS NEAPOLITAN

6 small green peppers, evenly sized
3 cooking apples, peeled and diced
¼ cup seedless raisins
2 tbsp chopped peanuts or pignolia nuts
¼ cup olive oil
Thyme leaves, a few
4 tbsp grated Parmesan cheese
1 tsp sugar
Salt and black pepper

1 small clove of garlic
6 anchovy fillets

Sauce

4 tbsp olive oil
4 tbsp stock
1 tsp beef extract
1 tbsp minced onion
Salt, pepper, and allspice

Slice the top from the peppers and carefully remove the membrane and seeds. Wash the peppers in cold water and drain. Rub a mixing bowl with the garlic and combine all the rest of the ingredients down to the anchovies. Mix thoroughly and fill the peppers with the mixture. Place an anchovy fillet on top of each cup and replace the cap. Stand the peppers upright in a baking dish and pour around them a sauce made by combining the balance of the ingredients. Set the baking dish in a moderate over (350° F.) for about an hour, basting the peppers frequently with the liquid. Serve hot. (Serves 6)

CHICKEN AND RICE STUFFING

2 cups cooked chicken
¼ cup seedless raisins
1 cup cooked rice
1 tbsp melted butter or margarine
2 eggs, well beaten
½ tsp salt
⅛ tsp pepper
1 tsp chili powder
¼ cup grated cheese

Combine all the ingredients. Prepare green peppers by cutting a slice off the tem end and scooping out the seeds and membranes. Parboil for ten or fifteen minutes and drain well. Stuff with the chicken mixture and bake in a moderate oven 350° F.) for 25 or 30 minutes. (Sufficient or 6 small peppers)

COTTAGE CHEESE STUFFING

½ cups dry cottage cheese
 eggs, well beaten
¼ tsp onion juice
⅛ tsp paprika
nough crushed cornflakes to make a firm mixture

Combine all the ingredients and stuff into previously prepared green peppers. Bake as above. (Sufficient for 6 peppers)

HAMBURGER STUFFING

2 tbsp margarine or drippings
1 medium-size onion, chopped
½ lb hamburger
2 fresh tomatoes
1 tsp salt
Dash of pepper
1 cup coarse bread crumbs
⅓ cup fine buttered crumbs

Saute the onion, hamburger, and the tomatoes, peeled and cut into pieces, in the drippings until the onion is soft and the meat grayish in color. Season with salt and pepper and add the coarse bread crumbs. Stuff into previously prepared green peppers, and top with the buttered crumbs. Bake as above. (Sufficient for 5 peppers)

RICE AND HAM STUFFING

1 tbsp chopped onion
2 tbsp chopped celery
2 tbsp ham drippings
2 tsp flour
½ cup milk
1½ cups cooked rice
½ lb slice of boiled ham
Salt and pepper
¼ cup grated cheese

Saute the onion and celery in the ham drippings until golden brown. Stir in the flour and blend well. Add the milk gradually, stirring constantly over a low flame until thick. Put the ham through the food chopper. Add the ham and cooked rice to the sauce mixture. Season with salt and pepper. Prepare green peppers and stuff with the mixture. Sprinkle the tops with grated cheese. Bake as above. (Sufficient for 4 peppers)

SHRIMP STUFFING

1 egg yolk, slightly beaten
¼ cup French dressing
1 cup cooked macaroni in small pieces
½ lb shrimp, boiled, peeled, cut small pieces
¼ cup grated cheese

Mix the first four ingredients and stir thoroughly. Stuff into prepared green peppers and top with grated cheese. Bake in a moderately hot oven (400° F.) for 30 minutes. (Sufficient for 4 peppers)

SWEET PEPPER CONSOMME

3 medium-size sweet peppers
2 tomatoes
1 large onion
2 qt boiling water
¾ tsp salt
1 whole clove

Either green or red peppers may be used. Cut the peppers in quarters and remove the seeds and membrane. Quarter the tomatoes and the onion. Put all the ingredients in a kettle and bring to a boil. Simmer, covered, for one and one-half hours. Strain and taste for seasoning. A delicate and delicious broth for summer meals, which may be served hot or cold. (Serves 6)

PEPPER CREAM CHEESE. A Neufchatel cheese, in which one pound of red peppers is used for every ten pounds of cheese.

PEPPERCORNS. See PEPPER (I).

PEPPERCRESS. This is a popular name for WATER CRESS, which see.

PEPPERGRASS. The name peppergrass refers to certain weeds of the mustard family. About 100 species of peppergrass exist, and some of these are native to North America. Some are pests, others are fed to birds, and one species, garden cress (which see), is cultivated in gardens.

PEPPER MILL. See GRINDER; see also PEPPER.

PEPPERMINT. (I) Peppermint is an aromatic herb belonging to the mint family. The oil derived from its leaves and stem is pleasantly pungent in odor and taste. It is used to flavor candy and chewing gum and to disguise the unpleasant tastes of certain medicines. White peppermint is generally considered to be superior to the more common black peppermint. See also MINT.

PEPPERMINT. (II) A candy. See CANDY and MINT.

PEPPERMINT GLACIAL. An after-dinner cordial, made in two colors, white and green. It is made of pure spirits of wine and the essential oil of Mentha Veridis, supposed to be the Mint of the Holy

Scriptures, with which the Paschal Lamb was eaten. A very strong digestive and refreshing beverage. A product of France.

PEPPER POT. A stew prepared in two different ways. In the West Indies it is made with vegetables, fish or meat, and cassareep. The stew that is often called Philadelphia Pepper Pot is made with tripe, meat, vegetables, and dumplings— all highly seasoned.

PHILADELPHIA PEPPER POT

3 to 4 lb tripe
2 qt water
1 knuckle of veal
2 potatoes
1½ tsp sweet marjoram
Small pinch of basil and thyme
Salt and pepper
Dumplings

Wash and scrape the tripe, place in a large saucepan with the water, bring to a boil, and simmer four hours. Meanwhile, in another pan, simmer the knuckle of veal with water to cover until the meat separates from the bone, about four hours. Strain. When the tripe is cooked, take it out of the water and set aside. Combine the water in which the tripe was cooked with the veal liquor and set aside until next day. One hour before serving time lift any fat from the broth, cut the tripe into half-inch dice, and add to the broth with the potatoes, peeled, washed, and diced in the same manner as the tripe. Add also the herbs and seasonings. Cook 15 to 20 minutes, add dumplings (which see) and cook, closely covered, an additional 15 minutes. (Serves 6 to 8)

PEPPERSTEAK. Beef chuck baked in a spicy sauce.

PEPSIN. A hydrolytic ferment which is found in the cells of the tubules of the gastric mucous membrane, chiefly near the cardiac portion. It exists in these cells in an antecedent form as a granular pro enzyme, which is called pepsinogen or pro pepsin. The agent which is believed to convert the pro-pepsin into true pepsin, the active ferment is hydrochloric acid. Pepsin digests coagulated egg albumin (the white) even better than fibrin, gluten casein, myosin and gelatin. The standard of the United States Pharmacopoeia requires that pepsin shall dissolve three thousand times its own weight of coagula ed disintegrated egg albumin. Pepsin reaches its maximum activity at a temperature considerably higher than that of the body—namely, 130° F. Its action is suspended below 40° F., and destroyed between 160° and 170° F.

PEPTIC. Pertaining to or promoting digestion.

PEPTONE. The product of the action of pepsin. *See* BEEF PEPTONE.

PERCH. The perch belongs to the bass family and is a common, spiny-finned, fresh water fish found throughout the Northern Hemisphere where the bass belongs.

The perch may be recognized by the compressed body, the two dorsal fins, the small hard and rough scales, and the simple, conical teeth. Its weight does not usually exceed four or four and a half pounds. Its color is greenish, covered with broad vertical black bands, and the ventral and anal fins are a beautiful red. Perch love clean water and feed on smaller fish, eggs, and insects. The perch is a singularly voracious lake fish.

The name perch is applied to various other fresh and salt water fish, which have only a more or less distant relationship to the true perch. Among these are the pike-perch, so called from a superficial resemblance to the pike and the perch, and several others. The yellow-perch, found in the North, is delicious and may be served in a variety of ways.

As a general rule, the small perch are fried, and the medium size are baked, broiled, filleted, or prepared with a court-bouillon, while the various methods employed in the preparation of bass, catfish, mullet, pike or pickerel, whitefish, whiting, and similar fish may be adapted to the large perch. *See also* FISH.

PERCOLATOR. There are any number of makes of this coffee maker, and whether you use a drip pot, glass coffee maker, vacuum filter, or an old-fashioned tin or enamel coffee pot, you will undoubtedly want to add a percolator to your kitchen equipment. *See also* COFFEE MAKER and COFFEE.

PERIGUEUX SAUCE. *See* BROWN SAUCE.

PERIWINKLE. A small, univalve mollusk.

PERRY. A fermented drink made from the juice of pears, as cider is made from apples.

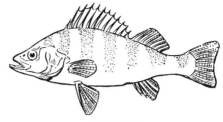

PERCH

PERSIAN MELON. An oval melon grown in the Southwest. It has a greenish rind and pale pink flesh. *See also* MELONS.

PERSILLE DE SAVOIE CHEESE. A French cheese made in Savoie.

PERSIMMON. The persimmon was the first native American fruit to be described and praised by early explorers. De Soto published an account of it in 1557. The following year, Jan de Laet described the persimmon in his work on Virginia. John Smith's report of the resources of the New World written during the first years of the seventeenth century included a long discussion of the persimmon. His comment, "If it be not ripe, it will draw a man's mouth awrie with much torment," covers completely the effect of eating an immature persimmon.

The American persimmon is a yellowish-red fruit not exceeding three inches in diameter which may or may not have seeds. It is a wild fruit, very astringent when green on account of the large amount of tannin present. This may be counteracted to some extent if soda is added to the pulp before it is heated. The quantity of soda to use varies with the degree of ripeness and the variety of the fruit, but one-fourth teaspoon of soda to one cup of persimmon pulp is the average. Persimmons will discolor if cooked in tin utensils.

Very few persimmon trees are found west of eastern Kansas. The more favored localities are southern Iowa and southeastern Nebraska.

The Japanese persimmon is now being cultivated in America. The fruit is of two types—non-astringent, with crisp, sweet flesh, or hard and astringent until fully ripe, when the flesh becomes sweet and juicy. The color of both types varies from yellow to dark red, and the shape from round to oblong. The average size is about that of an apple or tomato. The non-astringent persimmons are best for use in preserving.

SERVING PERSIMMONS

Served raw, the persimmon should be accompanied by a sharp pointed spoon, so that it may be easily dug out of its skin and wine may be added to give flavor. The Japanese add saki when serving the fruit. Other people prefer quarters of lemon or lime with it. The skin may be marked in quarters and peeled back, forming an attractive service. The fruit should always be washed and chilled before serving.

Persimmons may also be added to salads. Some varieties should not be cooked, as heat develops their astringency. To avoid this, mash the pulp and add it to cooked desserts, such as rice or cornstarch puddings, after the mixture has been allowed to cool slightly. The pulp of persimmons is excellent in ice creams, milk drinks, jellies, pudding sauces, and pies.

BAKED PERSIMMON PUDDING

2 cups persimmon pulp
3 eggs
1¾ cups milk
2 cups sifted flour
½ tsp soda
1 tsp salt
½ tsp cinnamon
½ tsp nutmeg
1½ cups sugar
3 tbsp melted butter

Mix the persimmon pulp, beaten eggs, and milk. Sift the dry ingredients together

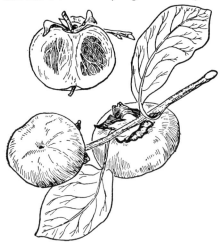

PERSIMMON

and pour the liquid mixture into them. Stir in the melted butter, and pour into a shallow greased pan to the depth of about two inches. Bake for about one hour in a very moderate oven (300° to 325°). When cold, cut into squares and serve with plain or whipped cream.

ENDIVE, WATER CRESS, AND PERSIMMON SALAD

Arrange endive and water cress attractively in a shallow salad bowl. Cut the stem ends from very ripe persimmons and scoop out the jellylike pulp onto the bed of greens. Serve with chilled French dressing slightly sweetened with a little honey or a honey cream dressing.

JELLIED PERSIMMONS

1½ cups ripe persimmon pulp
½ cup crushed pineapple and juice (canned)
¼ cup sugar
Dash of salt
1 tsp lemon juice, optional
1 tbsp gelatin
¼ cup cold water
½ cup heavy cream, whipped
½ tbsp sugar
¼ cup chopped pecans

Carefully remove the peel from ripe persimmons (four or five, according to size) Press the fruit through a sieve, measur the pulp into a bowl, add the crushed pine apple and juice, the sugar, salt, and lemo juice. Soften the gelatin in the cold wate then dissolve over hot water. Add to th fruit mixture, and when almost at settir point, turn into previously wet individu molds. Chill, unmold, and serve with th slightly sweetened whipped cream, which the pecans have been adde (Serves 6)

PERSIMMON CAKE

½ cup shortening
1 cup sugar
1 cup persimmon pulp
2 eggs
¼ tsp soda
2 cups sifted flour
3 tsp baking powder
½ tsp salt

Cream the shortening and sugar together, add the persimmon pulp and beaten eggs. Sift the dry ingredients and add to the liquid mixture. Beat well, pour into a greased pan, and bake in a moderate oven (325°–375° F.) for about one hour.

PERSIMMON CORNSTARCH PUDDING

½ cup sugar
⅓ cup cornstarch
⅛ tsp salt
½ cup cold water
1½ cups boiling water
¼ tsp soda
1 cup pulp
¼ tsp cinnamon
1 tbsp lemon juice

Mix the sugar, cornstarch, salt, and cold water thoroughly in a double boiler. Add the boiling water, and stir until the mixture thickens. Add the soda to the persimmon pulp and combine with the cornstarch mixture. Cover and cook for 15 minutes. Add the cinnamon and lemon juice, pour into a mold, and chill. Serve plain or with cream.

PERSIMMON CUSTARD

2 cups pulp
½ cup sugar
½ tsp soda
2 egg yolks, beaten slightly
¼ tsp cinnamon
⅛ tsp nutmeg
1/16 tsp salt

Combine the ingredients, pour into a baking dish surrounded by hot water, and bake in a slow oven (250°–300° F.) for about 15 minutes.

Make a meringue, using two egg whites, one-fourth cup of sugar, and one-sixteenth teaspoon of salt. Place on top of the custard and bake in a slow oven (250°–300° F.) until slightly browned.

PERSIMMON JELLY DESSERT

1 tbsp gelatin
¼ cup cold water
¼ cup sugar
Pinch of salt
1¼ cups persimmon pulp

½ cup drained, crushed canned pineapple
Sweetened whipped cream
¼ cup chopped pecans

Soften the gelatin in the water, then dissolve over hot water, adding the sugar and salt and stirring until these also are dissolved. Combine with the persimmon pulp, pressed through a ricer or strainer, and the pineapple. Blend all thoroughly, turn into a previously wet mold, and chill. Serve with the cream into which the nuts have been stirred. (Serves 4)

PERSIMMON WHIP

1 cup pulp
½ cup sugar
5 egg whites
¼ tsp salt
3 tbsp lemon juice

Heat the persimmon pulp with the sugar. Fold the hot mixture into the stiffly beaten egg whites, to which the salt has been added. Mix in the lemon juice, place in a baking dish surrounded by hot water, and bake in a very slow oven (225°–250° F.) for about one hour.

STEAMED PERSIMMON PUDDING

¼ cup butter
½ cup sugar
2 eggs
1½ cups pulp
⅜ tsp soda
½ cup sifted flour
2 tsp baking powder
¼ tsp salt

Cream the butter, add the sugar, beaten eggs, and persimmon pulp. Sift the remaining dry ingredients and combine with the first mixture. Pour into a greased mold, cover, and steam for one and one-half hours.

PESTLE. An instrument used with a Mortar (*which see*) for grinding spices into powder.

PET DE NONNE. A typically French dessert. It consists of a rich batter with many egg yolks, fried golden brown in deep hot fat, then dusted with sugar, tucked into a folded napkin, and served piping hot. Of all the rich pastries which on holidays perfume the kitchens and adorn the dinner tables of France, there is none more delicate and more charming than the *Pet de Nonne*.

The following legend is told to account for its origin. The ancient Abbey of Marmoutier stood on the River Loire in the sunshine of Touraine, in France. The Reverend Abbess, a godly woman, knew so well not only the secrets of heaven but also those of the kitchen, that there came to the door a constant procession of bishops, gourmets, monks plump as capons, vicars with triple chins, and canons fat and rubicund. There was in the Abbey a young probationer named Agnes. Because she had remarkable aptitude for preparing delicious foods, the Reverend Abbess raised Agnes to practise the culinary art.

On St. Martin's Day, the Archbishop of Tours himself was expected to come in pomp. There was great excitement and preparation, with swarms of nuns in their grey robes, veils, and headdresses bustling to and fro. The Abbess herself lent a helping hand, and Sister Agnes listened to her learned instructions, while playing with a small ball of paste in a spoon. Suddenly the ball of paste tumbled into a kettle of hot fat. The nuns looked on aghast. But the ball, crackling and swelling, turned golden, beautiful, and round. One by one they all tried the new and savory morsel. It was immediately named *Pet de Nonne*.

PETIT CARRE CHEESE. See NEUFCHATEL.

PETITE MARMITE. A French soup similar to the national *Pot au Feu* (Pot on the fire), served in individual casseroles or marmites, to which is added, just before serving, a slice of beef marrow. It is garnished with small pieces of toast, topped with grated Swiss cheese.

PETITE MARMITE

2 lb beef plate (lean)
1 5-lb young fowl
4 qt water
Salt
6 medium-size carrots
3 white turnips
4 stalks celery
½ small cabbage, optional
1 white onion
2 leeks
4 cloves

2 tbsp fat
4 slices marrow
Pinch of chervil
Toasted bread
Grated cheese

Cook the beef and fowl in a large pot, preferably earthenware, with the water and a little salt. Simmer two hours, carefully removing any scum which forms. Add the carrots, turnips, celery, and cabbage, if used, all cut into inch-long strips. Stick both onion and leeks with the cloves and brown in the fat. Add to the soup, and simmer all gently about two and one-half hours. Take out beef and chicken, and when cool enough to handle, cut the meat (except chicken legs, which may be reserved for other use) into cubes or strips. Return to the cooking soup, and just before serving, add the marrow and chervil. Remove from the fire, take out the onion and leeks and serve accompanied by toasted bread and grated cheese. (Serves 8)

PETIT FOURS. Petit fours are tiny cakes made by cutting thin layers of French almond cake or plain butter cake (*which see*) into fancy shapes. It takes care and skill to give them a professional look. Cake is cut, bottom-side up, into one-inch strips crosswise, then into one-inch squares, small triangles, and oblongs, or diamonds, circles, half-circles, stars, or other fancy shapes. Use a sharp knife and wipe it with a damp cloth before cutting each piece. Coat cakes one at a time with apricot glaze (*which see*). Insert a fork into the side of the small cakes and dip them into the glaze, covering all but the top, and arrange four in a row on a wire cake rack with uncovered surface down, placing them one-half inch apart. Place the rack on a marble slab or over a plain surface covered with waxed paper. This coating keeps the cake moist, gives a gloss to the frosting, and helps keep it from peeling off.

Pour Fondant Frosting (*which see*) from a pan onto the center of the cakes, moving from cake to cake and back again to cover generously but gradually. It will require about one cup of frosting for four cakes. What overflows can be scraped up and used again. Shake the rack gently to remove the frosting that clings to it and put in a warm place to set. When dry, remove cakes with a spatula and trim the frosting from their bottoms. Cakes are dry by the time the next series of four is ready.

To decorate cakes, make a cone of cooking paper or vegetable parchment and cut a tiny opening at the tip, or use a pastry bag and tube with a small opening. Fill about one-third full with decorative Boiled Frosting (*which see*), and press it out in fine lines to make scrolls or any desired design. The frosting may be colored with vegetable color paste or with melted chocolate. Decorations such as nuts, candied orange peel, cherries, angelica, ginger, candied rose petals, or violets may be used.

PETITE SIRAH. A red table wine of the Burgundy type made from Petite Sirah grapes. A Californian wine.

PETIT GRUYERE CHEESE. A soft, rich, yellowish cheese with a nutty flavor, made in Denmark.

PETIT SUISSE CHEESE. A soft, rich, unsalted cream cheese, cylindrical in shape, made in France.

PE TSAI. See CHINESE CABBAGE.

PEWTER WARE. Pewter is an alloy of tin and other metals, usually lead or copper. The origin of pewter is uncertain. Specimens of Roman pewter have been found in England, and it is said that the alloy was known to the Egyptians, Greeks, and even the Chinese. Pewter was very popular in England and surrounding countries because of the availability of the required metals.

Pewter was used to make all manner of table service, drinking vessels, and even church vessels, but it is not suited for cooking utensils. Though the composition of the alloy varies, it is inclined to be soft, malleable, and easily scratched. If there is too great a proportion of lead in the alloy, it is apt to cause toxic reaction in highly acid foods. In 1348 the Pewter Makers Guild in England passed laws to prevent this dangerous debasing of the alloy.

The nature of pewter is such that it is best suited for simple shapes and ornamentation. In time, it has been largely supplanted by other materials. Silver is more durable and capable of more complicated decoration, while Chinaware can be made more cheaply and in greater quantity. Pewter ware today is commonly purchased for its antique value rather than for actual use.

PFEFFERNEUSSE. A German word, meaning peppernuts, given to a traditional Christmas cookie. The nuts are highly spiced and shaped in round balls. They are crisp and hard, rather than chewy.

PFEFFERNEUSSE

2 cups all-purpose flour
½ tsp salt
½ tsp baking powder
⅛ tsp white or black pepper
2 eggs, separated
1 cup granulated sugar
½ tsp grated lemon rind
½ cup finely cut citron
Juice of 1 orange
Sugar

Sift flour, measure and resift three times with salt, baking powder, and pepper. Beat egg whites until stiff with a rotary beater. Add egg yolks and sugar and beat at low speed on electric mixer or by hand for ten minutes. Add lemon rind, and then fold in flour mixture gradually. Add citron and mix thoroughly. Chill. Pinch off small pieces about one-half the size of walnuts and roll into balls. Dip top into orange juice, then into sugar, either granulated or powdered. Place sugar-side up about two inches apart on greased baking sheet. Bake in a slow oven (325° F.) until a delicate brown, about 20 minutes. Cool on racks. Store in air-tight containers. (Makes 5 dozen)

PFISTER CHEESE. A cheese of the Emmenthaler group, made from fresh skim milk of cows. It is drum-shaped and weighs 50 pounds. It is made in Switzerland.

PHEASANT. Dispensers of good cheer often wonder if the casual epicure gets as much enjoyment out of eating game as the hunter did in bagging it. To rise at dawn and crouch on the reedy brink or some lake or pond, awaiting the honk of wary geese or watching the circling mallards and hoping they will tarry a bit on their flight south, is to live a phase of life that can be gained in no vicarious way.

The game tradition of America is as old as the country itself. In the civilized world, America is still nearest to the time when killing game was necessary for the maintenance of life. From the time the first wild turkey was brought down by a Pilgrim's blunderbuss, game has been our heritage.

A bird eaten within three days after killing is less delicate than a pullet, less savory than a quail, but when allowed to hang and ripen, its flesh is tender, sublimely gamey, and reminiscent of both chicken and venison. Its aroma arises from an oil which, to become developed, requires a slight degree of fermentation, just as the essential oil of coffee is obtained only by roasting the bean.

The right moment reveals itself to the uninitiated by a slight odor and a change in the color of the belly of the bird, but the gourmet divines it by instinct. When a pheasant has arrived at the right stage— but not before—it ought to be plucked and larded carefully with the freshest and firmest pork fat. It is important not to pluck a pheasant too early; careful experiments have revealed that those kept in their feathers are more highly perfumed than those plucked earlier. This is either because the contact of the air neutralizes some part of the aroma or because a part of the juice used for nourishing the feathers is absorbed again and serves to give more flavor to the meat.

HISTORY OF THE PHEASANT

The pheasant is a native of Asia. Ascending the Phase to reach the Colchis, the Argonauts saw this magnificent bird for the first time. They brought it to Greece, thus endowing Europe with a conquest more precious than that of the Golden Fleece.

First introduced from China into the United States in 1881, the pheasant is now found in nearly every state of the Union. This splendid game bird has not escaped censure on the score of its damage to crops, for it has a keen appetite for corn, peas, grain, and even potatoes. Pheasants are naturally hardy and prolific, and once established in a region they need only reasonable protection to ensure their preservation for all time—and for our tables.

The pheasant is always in itself a regal dish, whether served roasted, braised, as a game pie or loaf, or in any number of ways with sauces enriched with truffles. Below is an ancient recipe which survived the sacking of the library of the Convent of Alcantara, Spain, by Napoleon's soldiers. It was originally intended for partridge.

PHEASANT A LA MODE D'ALCANTARA

Clean a plump, freshly plucked pheasant, removing the breastbone as you would that of a small broiler. After the bird has been well cleansed and rubbed with lemon inside and out, stuff it with a whole duck liver mixed with one-third its bulk of chopped black truffles, previously cooked in port wine for five minutes. Sew up carefully. Truss, and marinate for three or four days in a bath of port wine, keeping the bird constantly submerged. Drain and cook in a casserole as you would an ordinary chicken, with plenty of butter (about one-fourth pound). Take one and a half cups of the marinade, place over a hot fire, and reduce to half its volume. Add six small, black truffles to the reduced wine with a teaspoon of fumet (*which see*), and allow all to simmer gently for 15 minutes. Serve at once with the port wine sauce and the truffles.

No mention is made of a garnishing. However, it is presumed that the monks, who had a reputation as gourmets and connoisseurs, must have served the bird of birds with the usual garnish, which is bread crumb sauce and jelly. A pheasant prepared in this manner ought to be washed down with some of the best Burgundy, such as Clos de Citeaux.

PAN FRIED PHEASANT WITH SAUERKRAUT

Select a young pheasant and let it hang for four or five days. Pick, clean, and wipe with a damp cloth. Place two juniper berries and a small white onion in the cavity. Sew and truss, then cook in a casserole for 35 minutes (the pheasant should be a little rare) in plenty of butter, turning the bird often to brown on all sides. Serve on a hot platter on a bed of well drained sauerkraut, generously seasoned with goose fat or butter. Garnish with small squares of fresh pork cooked with the sauerkraut, and serve with a sauce made as follows:

To the butter left in the casserole, add one scant cup of game stock made from trimmings, and bring to a boil, stirring from the bottom of the casserole. Add one teaspoon of fumet (*which see*). Stir, bring to a boil, and serve.

PHEASANT A LA LECZINSKI

During the reign of its last Duke Stanislas, King of Poland, the Duchy of Lorraine not only held a distinguished rank in Letters and Arts but also in Culinary Art. It was at a famous feast given by the King in his castle of Luneville that the delicious Pheasant à la Leczinski was served for the first time. The modernized recipe for this dish follows.

Bone two snipe. Take the meat, liver, and entrails, and pound all in a mortar with three duck livers and five ounces of cooked ham fat, moistening with a wine glass of Moselle and seasoning to taste with salt and pepper. Take half of this stuffing and fill the cavity of a young pheasant which has been hung five days, plucked, cleaned, singed, and rubbed inside and out first with brandy and then with salt and pepper. Sew and truss. Spread a piece of freshly made toast with the remainder of the stuffing, place this in a baking pan, and set the bird on it. Bake in a hot oven (400° F.) about 35 minutes, basting often with melted fumet (*which see*). Serve toast and bird on a hot platter immediately, without any accompaniment.

PHILADELPHIA PEPPER POT. *See* Pepper Pot.

PHOSPHATE BAKING POWDER. *See* Baking Powder.

PHOSPHORUS. Phosphorus is the third of the three minerals to which we should give most thought when planning meals. Phosphorus works with calcium to supply the salts which make the bones and teeth strong and sturdy. These two minerals are so intertwined that it is not only necessary to have a full quota of each, but to have each in such a proportion that it balances the other. In the absence of this, the skeleton of the body may grow to be normal in size but not in strength.

The foods which supply phosphorus most liberally are milk, cheese, eggs, vegetables, nuts, some of the fruits, and whole cereals. All but the latter are sources of calcium to a greater or lesser extent. Among fruits we find peaches, bananas, grapefruit, oranges, pineapple, prunes, and berries high in phosphorus, while among vegetables navy beans, carrots, lentils, and sweet potatoes are at the head of the list.

The quality of minerals in foods is not affected to any large extent by cooking, if proper methods are used. One of the reasons for cooking vegetables in very little water is to preserve the mineral content, which may be partly drawn out into the liquid.

A shortage of either calcium or phosphorus, a poor balance between them, or the lack of Vitamin D, which has the property of stimulating the deposit of these minerals in the bones, may result in rickets.

A mild form of rickets is not uncommon among children, while acute rickets attack undernourished children, especially those who do not get enough sun.

PICCALILLI. *See* Pickles.

PICK. *See* Nutcracker.

PICKEREL. A very delicious fresh water fish found everywhere, the pickerel belongs to the pike family and is known under different names according to localities. The banded pickerel found in Mississippi reaches 12 inches in length, and is very variable in color. In Tennessee and Arkansas, the pickerel reaches a length of 24 inches and is of a golden-green color marked with numerous dark lines and streaks, for the greater part horizontal.

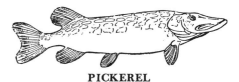

PICKEREL

The pickerel of the coast streams from Massachusetts to Florida is about 12 inches long and is of a dark greenish color, with about 20 dark, curved bars on the sides. The various methods employed in the preparation of small bass, pike, smelts and whiting may be adapted to this delicious and delicate fish.

The pickerel is not the most respected fish in the world. He is not honored by good eaters in the spring and summer when the wild rainbow and native trout are to be had. It is not so in winter. As the memory of trout fades from the palate, the thought of pickerel returns, and you may hear these epicures murmuring that the pickerel is not so bad after all and that he is better eating, in any event, than fish from the salt sea.

PICKLED PIGS' FEET. *See* Pork.

PICKLES and PICKLING. Pickles, as a rule, are combinations of several ingredients, such as vegetables, fruits, and spices, chopped and blended, and marinated in the spiced and seasoned vinegar which gives them their flavor. Few pickles can be successfully made in a hurry. Their preparation requires care, patience, and good judgment. The tang of crisp, spiced pickles adds interest and palatability to any meal; and used in moderation, they play an important part in the diet because they stimulate the flow of saliva and gastric juices, thus aiding digestion.

Though the last twenty years have ushered in many new ways of serving the tomato, it has been a stand-by in the pickle jar since it first became accepted as an accredited food. And, while there are many manufactured brands available, homemakers often prefer their own recipes, even though their preparation requires hours of work.

Each country has its favorite pickled foods. In England cold catsup, a tomato-and-vegetable combination, is highly esteemed as a complement to cold roast beef and other cold cuts, and many Americans like the condiment. Pickled melon rinds, peaches, and pears are truly American. Old recipe books tell us that the peeled rinds or fruits must lie for three days and nights in the boiled, spiced sirup of vinegar and sugar, and that this sirup is poured off each morning and boiled down. Then the fruit is again covered with the hot, concentrated liquid. If this method is strictly adhered to, and a final boiling up is given to both fruit and sirup, the pickled rinds, peaches, or pears appear dark and firm, and they keep indefinitely unsealed, lying in the rich, golden-brown sirup afloat with whole cloves and stick cinnamon.

The American farmer of a generation ago always had a supply of mustard pickle to serve with hot or cold roast ham or with smoked tongue. Mustard pickle is still a prime favorite. It is readily made at home and is composed of such vegetables as onions, cucumbers, cauliflowers, peppers, and green tomatoes. These are cut in rather large pieces, steeped in brine, drained, and added to a thick, boiled sauce of mustard, vinegar, sugar, flour and tumeric. It requires skill to produce a smooth, creamy sauce of exactly the right thickness.

There are no hard and fast classifications among pickled vegetables. The small whole cucumbers have no other name than pickles. The mixed sliced vegetables, however, are sometimes known as pickles and sometimes as relishes. Often relishes carry the name of the vegetable used in the largest amount, as tomato relish. The name bread and butter pickles was given that very popular kind of pickles perhaps because they make good filling for canapes and sandwiches.

The better quality of commercial pickles are usually put up in cider, wine, or malt vinegar. Cider vinegar is commonly used because of its cheapness and flavor. As a rule, genuine dill pickles do not keep for more than six months.

HOMEMADE PICKLES

Spices should be bought fresh for each year's pickling. A mixture of spices commonly known as pickling spices may be obtained loose or in package, or they may be blended at home. They should include whole cloves, peppercorns, stick cinnamon, mace, tiny red peppers, mustard seeds, allspice, bay leaves, and root ginger. Spices are usually tied in a square of cheesecloth and cooked with the pickles. Glass top jars are the best containers for pickles and other products that have a strong acid, vinegar, or salt solution. If metal top jars are used, they should never be inverted to test for seal.

More satisfactory results can be obtained if the homemaker understands what causes some of the troubles encountered in pickling, such as the following:

1. Tough, shriveled pickles are the result of too much salt or sugar, or too strong a vinegar.
2. Soft pickles are the result of too strong a vinegar or too weak a brine.
3. Hollow pickles are due to imperfect cucumbers or too long a lapse of time between picking and pickling.
4. Slippery pickles are the result of letting the cucumbers stand above the brine. This will also cause them to be soft.
5. Off color is the result of using the wrong kind of vinegar or cooking in a copper kettle.
6. Use high grade cider vinegar or pure grain vinegar 40 to 60 percent strength.
7. Avoid water having an excess of minerals.
8. Cloudy appearance is caused by using fine table salt, since this salt contains some starch. Common or coarse salt which is not caked is the best to use.
9. If it is necessary to use hard water, add a little vinegar before making up the brine.
10. Some homemakers, during the busy season, prefer to brine their cucumbers and make pickles at a less busy time. Brined cucumbers will make pickles of higher quality. Perfect brining or curing requires from six to eight weeks. Brine for pickles is made by adding one pint of clean, coarse salt to nine pints of water (soft preferred—rain water can be used if boiled and

cooled). This is a ten percent solution and should barely float a new laid egg. Accurate measurement is essential to avoid either softening or toughening.

Do not wash cucumbers unless necessary. If washed, dry them well. Put the cucumbers in brine, using a round board or plate with a weight to keep cucumbers below the surface. On the following day put a scant pint of salt on top. At the end of each succeeding week for five weeks, put a half cup of salt on the top. Skim off any scum as it forms. Before making pickles, cucumbers must be freshened by soaking in from three to five changes of fresh water, as most of the salt must be removed. The cucumbers are now ready for pickling as specified in individual recipes, but omit the brining and salting specified in the recipes when using cucumbers prepared as above.

11. *Pickling Vinegar.* Frequently pickles are spoiled by the use of inferior vinegar. Select a good, clear vinegar of 40 to 60 grain strength (four to six percent of acetic acid). If fruit vinegar is used, it should be filtered to remove sediment. If filter paper is not available, filter through double flannel.

12. *Honey Vinegar.* To make honey vinegar, mix one quart of strained honey and eight quarts of warm water. Allow the mixture to stand in a warm place until fermentation ceases. Seal in clean jars. The resulting vinegar is white and of excellent quality.

13. *Spiced Vinegar.* Mix together the following:

1 qt vinegar
2 cups sugar
1 tbsp cinnamon
1 tbsp allspice
1 tbsp white mustard seeds
1 tsp cloves
1 tsp salt

Combine, bring to a boil, and pour mixture over the pickles.

BREAD AND BUTTER PICKLES

20 medium-sized cucumbers
12 medium-sized onions
1 cup salt
4 cups vinegar
4 cups water
3 cups sugar

4 tsp celery seed
2 tsp mustard seed
2 tsp ground ginger
1 tsp turmeric

Wash the cucumbers and cut them into thin slices without peeling. Peel and slice the onions. Combine with the salt, and let stand for 2 hours. Combine all remaining ingredients, and heat to boiling point. Rinse off the vegetables, drain, and add them to the boiling sirup. Simmer about 30 minutes or until tender, then pack in sterilized jars and seal. (Makes 6 pints)

DILL PICKLES

Carefully select and wash good cucumbers about 5 or 6 inches long. Pack them in earthenware jars. Between the layers of cucumbers, place thin layers of dill, using stalks, leaves, and seed balls. Cover with brine (using about 1 pound of salt to 3 pints of water). Place a layer of grape or horseradish leaves on top and weight down with a large earthen plate. Let stand several weeks before using.

DUTCH PICKLES

3 sweet red peppers
2 stalks celery
1½ qt finely chopped ripe tomatoes
1½ qt finely chopped green tomatoes
1½ qt thinly sliced cabbage
1½ qt chopped onions
½ cup salt
3 cups sugar
3 pt vinegar
½ tsp cloves
1 tsp cinnamon
½ cup mustard seed
½ cup prepared horseradish

Discard seeds and white connecting fiber of the peppers; scrub the celery, then pass both through the food chopper using the coarse knife. Combine with the remaining vegetables and salt, blend thoroughly, then turn into doubled cheesecloth and hang up to drain overnight. In the morning make a sirup of the sugar, vinegar and spices by boiling these together for 10 minutes. Add the drained vegetables and horseradish and simmer ½ hour. Turn immediately into sterilized jars and seal. (Makes 8 pints)

INDIA RELISH

2½ lb diced watermelon rind
Cold water
Salt
4 sweet red peppers
5 small hard white cabbages
5 Spanish or Bermuda onions
¼ cup salt
2 cups light brown sugar
1 qt vinegar
1 tbsp curry powder
1 tbsp celery seeds
2 tbsp white mustard seeds
1 tbsp paprika
2 tbsp mace
2 tbsp cinnamon
1 tbsp salt

Discard green outer portion of water-melon rind, also soft pink inner portion, cut the firm white part into large dice, cover with brine (¼ cup salt to 1 quart cold water) and let stand overnight.

Discard the seeds and white connecting fiber of the peppers and chop these together with the cabbages and onions. Sprinkle with ¼ cup of salt and let stand overnight also.

Next day rinse the watermelon rind with fresh cold water, drain, pat dry in a cloth and chop fine. Drain the vegetable mixture, pressing with the hands to extract all the liquid. Now combine the watermelon rind and vegetables with the sugar, vinegar, spices and seasonings. Cook gently until thick, about 1 hour. Turn into sterilized jars and seal. (Makes 6 pints)

PICCALILLI

½ peck green peppers
½ bushel green tomatoes
½ peck onions
2 firm white cabbages
1½ cups salt
3 lb light brown sugar
4 3-inch sticks cinnamon
2 oz whole cloves
2 oz whole allspice
2 oz white mustard seed
Vinegar

Wash, quarter and discard seeds and white connecting fiber of peppers. Wash

and remove stems from tomatoes. Peel onions and cut cabbages small. Pass all vegetables separately through the food chopper, using coarse knife. Arrange in layers, sprinkling each with salt. Cover and let stand overnight. In the morning, drain very thoroughly and add the sugar, the spices tied together in a cheesecloth bag, and vinegar barely to cover. Bring to boiling point and simmer very gently for 6 hours. Remove the spice bag, turn into sterilized jars and seal. (Makes 4 to 5 quarts)

PUERTO RICO PICKLES

3 lb small green tomatoes
2 large cans sliced pineapple
1 cup pineapple juice
2 lb sugar
1 cup honey
4 cups cider vinegar
6 in. stick cinamon
1 tbsp whole allspice
1 tbsp whole cloves
2 tbsp yellow mustard seed
A few blades mace

Wash, dry and cut the tomatoes into moderately thick slices. Cut the pineapple through into thinner slices. Place together in a large bowl. Combine the pineapple juice, sugar, honey and vinegar, add the spices, tied in cheesecloth, and bring slowly to boiling point, stirring occasionally. Pour over the prepared tomatoes and pineapple, cover, and let stand 24 hours. Drain off the liquid, bring it again to boiling point, add the tomatoes and pineapple, but discard the spices. Simmer until the tomatoes are clear, about 1 hour. Transfer tomatoes and pineapple to sterilized jars with a perforated skimmer. Boil down the sirup until thick, then pour over the fruit, and seal. (Makes 3 pints)

STUFFED DILL PICKLES

Cut the ends from dill pickles, and remove the pickle centers with a small apple corer. Fill the hollows with pencil-shaped pieces of spiced sausage that have been spread with cream cheese, or ground cooked meat seasoned and then thinned with a little cream, or liverwurst spread (*which see*). Chill the pickles, and cut them in crosswise slices about ⅛-inch thick.

SWEET MUSTARD PICKLES

1 qt green tomatoes, chopped
1 qt cabbage, chopped coarsely
1 qt tiny onions, peeled
1 qt green peppers, chopped
1 qt cucumbers, chopped
¼ cup salt
3 cups sugar
1 cup flour
¼ lb dry mustard
2 tsp turmeric
5 pt vinegar, heated

Combine the prepared vegetables, sprinkle with the salt and let stand overnight. In the morning drain very thoroughly. Combine in a saucepan the sugar, flour, mustard and tumeric, add a little of the vinegar, mixing smoothly, then add the remaining vinegar and bring to boiling point, stirring constantly. Cook until the sauce thickens, add the prepared vegetables and heat thoroughly. Turn into sterilized jars and seal. (Makes 8 pints)

PICKLE FORK. *See* FLATWARE.

PICNIC. *See also* BARBECUE, CAMP COOKERY, SANDWICHES and LUNCH BOX SANDWICHES. Open-air dining, or lunching, or the *al fresco* meal partaken of against a background of natural scenery is nothing new, for the Roman poet Horace often sang its praises and its delights. The frequent enjoyment of this informal, outdoor and camp type of meal seems particularly and peculiarly native to America. Relic, perhaps, of our not so distant pioneer days, of our trappers, guides and scouts, of the picturesque periods when great sections of population were always on the move.

The automobile, of course, has played a stellar role in helping us to span distances and in encouraging families to pack up their troubles in the old picnic basket. No wonder then, that the frequent request for "let's have a picnic" brings the homemaker actively into the recreational spotlight, not only to provision the miniature expedition, but also to share in its fun.

But here is the rub. Getting a picnic together is often so hurried and so laborious that much of the carefree anticipation is lost, even before the party goes out of the front door. Further, after the day is over, there is a tired scramble to get holiday belongings back into place. At the end

of a long gypsy day, putting the picnic to bed is likely to be more than a chore.

Yet the cause of haste and useless effort here is, as it is on so many other occasions, lack of organization. For, after all, a picnic is a true meal, and does require napery and plates and drinking vessels, although of a different type. And it does demand foods and serving dishes and beverages.

In a sense the first meal that man ever ate was a picnic. For the essence of picnics is that they use the open air as sauce. But people who live in houses, and particularly people who live in paved or macadamized cities, are the people who have kept the custom of the picnic alive. As soon as hot weather and its attendant annoyances descend on us, many feel an urge to get into the country or by the sea for a meal. It may be only hot dogs and iced coffee, tea, beer, wine, or soda bought along the road, or it may be a repast eaten from hampers carefully packed in advance. Any basket will do—a humble sturdy market basket which has been given two coats of shellac or an outside coat of a gay lacquer is excellent for heavy duty. The basket lunch is still the favorite form of the picnic meal. But instead of a large hamper stuffed with sandwiches, there is available a basket lined with tin and insulated. This is divided into compartments, one of which to contain dry ice for keeping ice cubes and bottles of beverages. The rest of the basket may contain a casserole of some sea food or chicken mixture, a salad, cold meat (a leg of lamb or a cut of roast beef), fruit, squares of cake or cookies. The foods are separately wrapped in waxed paper.

What makes a picnic depends entirely on your own appraisal of what a picnic should be. People quickly fall into definite types as they interpret their ideas in answer to the question. Let the true nature-lover tuck two slices of buttered bread with ham or cheese between them in one pocket, and an orange or apple in another pocket, and he is off to a good start toward what to him means picnic perfection. Then there is the other extreme, the person who never even considers having a picnic until his equipment is pretentious. Between, are two distinct types. First are those to whom a picnic is always a condescension. The other type is represented by those who really love the novelty of eating out under the trees or stars but who also like good food and pride themselves on serving it.

PICNIC

In the elaborate picnic baskets popular today, all foods become foods that travel. Vacuum jugs take care of salads, beverages, soup. Cold bricks take care of butter and salad dressing. Tightly closed compartments take care of sandwiches and meats. A picnic today can have great variety.

For a *between-meals picnic* sandwiches are best. Made carefully, with any too-heavy crust removed and with the filling spread evenly over each slice, they make a satisfying food. The jokes about them are due to the scanty use of spread, too thin slices of too dry bread, or a dry filling.

For an *evening meal picnic* in cool weather, a fire is almost a necessity if it is not unlawful in the state or locality. Make use of it for food. In some states regular picnic parks now provide elaborately for picnickers. Open fireplaces with built-in grills, wood piles, and rubbish cans are located at comfortably distant intervals to insure privacy. Rude wooden tables and benches are at hand, and their use is free to all who respect the property on which they stand. Carry along a stew, a kettle to heat it in, and a long wooden spoon to stir it. If made early in the day, cooled, and then chilled until the gravy sets before it is packed, stew will not spill or leak, and the flavor will be the better for reheating. Biscuits or rolls may be split, perhaps toasted over the fire, and served with the stew, are perfect and travel with ease. Plenty of crisp, well-cleaned celery, packed in wet parchment paper, radishes in twists of paper with a little salt, or a cole slaw in one of the vacuum bottles will give a picnic air. A cake, or some cookies, is sufficient for dessert. Make coffee over the fire if the local water supply is safe. If not, carry enough in a vacuum jug. The new jugs with spigots at the bottom are particularly handy. There may also be fresh fruit or cheese for those still hungry.

For a *noontime picnic* corned beef hash, or broiled liver sliced at home and browned in a skillet over a charcoal fire in a little butter or bacon fat is good, or it may be a cold meat loaf, packed in cardboard. Ripe tomatoes, hard-boiled eggs and one or two cans of sardines appeal to almost everyone. Lemonade, iced tea, coffee or beer, well chilled before being packed, will do for beverage. A potato salad garnished with bits of smoked herring and tomatoes is popular. Doughnuts and fruit, canned or fresh, complete the menu.

PICNIC HINTS

1. First make a list (and don't forget the salt) when you pack the basket. If there are sandwiches, have each variety in a separate box, plainly labeled. Or follow the individual package school, and give each person his private assortment of sandwiches, wrapped separately in waxed paper.

2. When taking hot dishes, such as baked beans, scalloped potatoes, chicken à la king, etc., to a not-too-far-away picnic ground, wrap the dishes in six or eight thicknesses of newspaper. You'll find the food and container hot when you reach your destination.

3. For the late afternoon picnic in the country, hot tea in a thermos bottle, milk in another for the youngsters, sliced tomatoes and stuffed eggs, with sandwiches, make a fine meal.

4. For cooking in the open, two fires are often more convenient than one. Use one for the coffee, the other for roasting corn or frying ham and eggs. (*See* BARBECUE and CAMP COOKERY.)

5. Split picnic buns, spread them with deviled ham, then toast them. Put a slice of crisp bacon in each bun.

6. Don't peel the potatoes for use in salads until after you have cooked them. Then peel and dice or cut them into thin slices. Don't prepare salads with too much dressing. Carry an extra supply in a jar to pass around at the picnic.

7. Mix a half cup of butter, one teaspoon each of dry mustard, salt, paprika, horseradish, and chili sauce. When your steak, cooked over a campfire, is ready, heat the above sauce and pour it over the steak. We can do without a good many of the implements of civilization at an outdoor meal, but seasonings are vital. Fingers were used before forks, and so were spices. Picnic foods need to be savory, and it is important to include the makings of fine flavor in the lunch basket.

8. Charcoal used for outdoor cooking should be red hot. To broil meats over it, place the grill about four inches above the charcoal. Put the meat on it, quickly searing it on both sides to prevent losing the juice. Then turn and cook the meat until it is done.

9. For your outdoor culinary efforts, use a long-handled, open-and-shut broiler, easy to carry; a small, outdoor grill stove; or simply cut a hickory or apple twig for

cooking equipment, especially if you are having only bacon or frankfurters for the meat course.

Last Minute Picnic. When you do not want to bother with fussy preparations, and you do not have time to make up many sandwiches, this is a good plan to select. Take a can of spaghetti along for each person, and lots of fruit. All that is needed is a small fire to heat the spaghetti and to make a pot of coffee. The picnic requisites are:

Spaghetti with tomato sauce and cheese
Romaine or leaf lettuce
Buttered rolls
Basket of fruit
Coffee

The Men-Cook-Picnic. Cooking at the picnic will be much less tedious if you do some of the work at home and let the men finish. In this case equal parts of pasteurized buttermilk and tomato juice may be poured into a fruit jar. Cooked potatoes and raw onions may be chopped and packed in jars. Freshly made coffee should be poured into a thermos bottle. A wire toaster rack is a great convenience for broiling the steaks. Doughnuts and cheese are a fitting conclusion to this picnic. Here is what to take:

Tomato juice and buttermilk cocktail
Cube steaks
Fried potatoes and onions
Garden relish
Radishes
Sandwiches
Doughnuts
Cheese
Coffee

Youngsters' Favorite Picnic. The youngsters usually prefer hot dogs or wieners to anything else when going on a picnic. Green twigs whittled down to points make good toasting forks for the frankfurters and the marshmallows.

Frankfurters
Long buttered rolls
Mustard
Dill pickles
Spice cake
Grapefruit juice
Pineapple juice
Marshmallows (to toast)

Picnic for the Crowd. This picnic requires a minimum of work at home. You do not even have to take a basket along, just pack all you need in paper bags: cans of beans, whole ripe tomatoes, onions, salt and pepper, loaf of bread (possibly some of several different kinds, as white, raisin, rye, whole

wheat, etc.) butter, some cheese, coffee, sugar, cream, paper plates, napkins, cups, a knife, spoon, can opener, coffee pot, and a box of turnovers.

Apple sauce turnovers are very easy to make. See TURNOVER. If there is no time to make the turnovers, take with you a few cans of apple sauce, cookies, and doughnuts.

Make-Your-Own-Sandwich Picnic. Be sure to bring a variety of items, for everybody does not relish the same food: assorted cheese, sliced for convenience, a jar each of peanut butter and jelly, bananas, and cookies. If you take cookies along, be sure to wrap three or four together in wax paper. The picnic may include the following:

Assorted cold cuts
Assorted cookies
Assorted sliced cheese
Bread and butter
Cole slaw
Bananas
Coffee in thermos bottle
Beer

Nothing-To-Cook Picnic. No cooking is required for this outing. The sandwiches can be made on the picnic grounds, but the bread can be buttered at home and wrapped in wax paper. Put ginger ale in a bucket of ice and the cans of corned beef on top, because corned beef is easy to slice when it is cold. To have cold watermelon, chill it thoroughly in the refrigerator, wrap it in several layers of damp newspaper, and wrap again with a gunny sack or an old piece of carpet. The picnic essentials include:

Cold sliced corned beef
Rye bread and butter
Sandwiches
Whole cold tomatoes
Pickle relish
Potato chips
Cold watermelon
Ginger ale

Picnic De Luxe. This is a good supper to serve on the porch or at a card party some warm evening. Cut a thick slice from the top of a loaf of bread. Remove the inside of the loaf, leaving walls about half an inch thick. Butter the inside walls generously with soft butter; fill with chicken salad. Butter the under side of the top crust; place it on top of the salad, and put it in the refrigerator to chill thoroughly until ready to slice.

Angel food cake carries well in the tin in which it was baked. Wrap the freezer of ice cream with several thicknesses of newspaper, and cover it with burlap. The complete supper includes:

Chicken salad bread box
Celery hearts
Ripe and stuffed olives
Freezer of peach ice cream
Angel food cake
Coffee

Sunday Dinner Picnic. After the chicken is cooked, allow it to cool to room temperature before packing it in wax paper. Do not put it in the refrigerator to chill. When the corn bread is baked, turn it out of the pan, remove the wax paper, and cool. When cold, return corn bread to the pan and wrap it in a towel or wax paper. The salad is more crisp if prepared at the picnic. A can of pineapple sticks may be purchased or you may use a fresh pineapple prepared at home, sprinkled with sugar, and packed in a preserving jar.

Diced celery, avocado, and tomato salad
Fried chicken
Boiled Canadian bacon
Pan of corn bread
Butter
Fresh or canned pineapple sticks
Apricots
Plums
Iced coffee or tea

Back-Yard Picnic. It is just as much fun to eat this combination in the back yard as on the picnic grounds. The back yard has some advantages, as things can be kept in the refrigerator until the last minute, and the coffee can be made when needed.

Minute steaks
Baked potatoes
Fried onions
Rolled lettuce leaves, stuffed
with pickle relish
Buttered rolls
Caramel layer cake
Pot of coffee
Iced beer

Sunday School or Club Picnic. When a big group of people comprising a number of families go on a picnic, each family usually brings one item, such as meat, salad, cake, etc. There is bound to be an abundance, but the food usually disappears before the picnic is over. The following list is a suggestion for such an outing. To make sure that not too much of one thing is brought and not enough of another, there should

be a meeting of the families going to decide what each group will bring.

Whole baked ham or hams
Cold meat loaf
Chicken salad
Deviled eggs
Sliced tomatoes
Cole slaw
Potato salad
Baked beans
Sliced bologna and liverwurst
Mustard, olives, pickles
Preserves
Assorted cheese
Bread and butter
Buttered rolls
Freezers of ice cream
Chocolate sauce
Fresh fruit sauce
Devils food cake
Lady Baltimore cake
Assorted frosted cup cakes
Watermelons
Lemonade, iced tea, milk
Hot coffee

SANDWICHES TO BE MADE AT THE PICNIC

Choose three or four kinds of bread. If you are going to use lettuce, wash the whole head and wrap it in a damp towel. Here is a variety of sandwiches: Peanut butter and sliced bananas; bean and cole slaw; cheese and grilled bacon; tomato, bacon, and lettuce; cream cheese and mint jelly; hamburger and onion; cucumber, tomato, and lettuce with salad dressing; grilled steak; fried egg and ham; lettuce and sliced tomato with sandwich spread; toasted cheese; grilled ham.

SANDWICHES THAT ARE EASY TO PACK

The following sandwiches are easy to pack in wax paper in a basket: Chopped cheese and chili sauce; cream cheese and chopped, stuffed olives; cottage cheese, green pepper, and onion; crabmeat with sandwich spread; cream cheese, cucumber, and green onion; egg salad; sliced ham and swiss cheese; liverwurst and horseradish mustard; peanut butter and marmalade; chopped corned beef and pickle relish; salmon and cucumber salad; sliced egg and dried beef with salad dressing; cold cuts of meat with relish; chicken salad; sardine or tuna fish with salad dressing; preserves and cream cheese.

PICNIC HAM. *See* CALI BUTT under HAM.

PICODON DE DIEULEFIT CHEESE. A French cheese made in the Dauphine district.

PIE. Pastry crust (*see* PASTRY) with various kinds of fillings. Pies are divided into five main types: chiffon; custard; cream (or soft); fruit; and deep dish. Boston Cream pie is actually made from two layers of rich sponge cake put together with cream filling or chocolate filling, the top layer being sprinkled with powdered sugar. Occasionally one sees a Boston cream pie topped with sweetened whipped cream and for a deluxe Boston cream pie, fresh whole raspberries or strawberries are used to garnish the whipped cream topping. Another version is Washington Pie. Here raspberry jam is a must between the layers.

poured into a pre-baked pastry shell and allowed to settle, the pie should be thoroughly chilled in the refrigerator before serving.

CUSTARD PIE

A perfect custard pie is a delight both to the eye and the palate, a thin watery pie or one which is curdled is little short of a catastrophe.

The correct proportions of eggs and milk used in custard pies are three whole eggs to each pint of milk or equal part of milk and coffee cream. Four eggs, however, will give a somewhat richer flavor and smoother body.

The eggs should only be slightly beaten to avoid too many air bubbles in the custard, then combined with the milk, sweet-

OVEN TEMPERATURE FOR PIE SHELLS AND FRUITS

	Degrees (Fahr.)	Time (Minutes)
For pie shells	450	15
For tart shells	450	10–15
For berry and fruit (canned or fresh)	450	10–15
and then	350	20–30
For custard, pumpkin, etc. (uncooked mixture) baked in		
uncooked pastry	450	10–15
and then	350	20–25
For dried fruit	425–450	10–15
and then	350	25–30

In general, all pastry should be baked in a hot oven (450° F,) for 10 to 15 minutes, the heat then reduced to medium (350° F.) and baking finished according to the time indicated in the recipe.

For toppings, such as meringue and whipped cream, see the separate entries.

CHIFFON PIE

Chiffon pie is one of the handsomest, most delicate and richest of all pies. Great variations are possible in the garnishing, crust and shape. Most fillings are mixtures of egg yolk and either milk or cream, sweetened, together with the desired flavoring of chocolate, coffee, rum or fruit juice. Enough gelatin is added to support the filling. The name denotes the texture which is extremely light and is secured by folding in stiffly beaten egg whites or whipped cream. After the mixture is

ening and flavoring, and the whole turned into an unbaked pastry shell which has been brushed over with egg white to prevent soaking. The top is dusted with nutmeg and the pie immediately set in a hot oven (450° F.) for ten minutes, to set the crust, after which the temperature should be lowered to 325° F. and the baking continued for 30 minutes longer.

A good custard pie filling resembles a good fruit jelly in that it is tender, and quivery, yet keeps its angles when cut and does not weep on standing. Furthermore, it has a delicate golden-brown surface entirely free from the heavy, dark-brown layer sometimes observed on this type of pie.

If the temperature of the oven is not reduced after the crust has set, the filling will be tough and have a tendency to weep; whereas if it is too low, the filling will soak into the crust unless the latter has been pre-baked before the filling is added. Cool custard pies on a cake cooler to prevent the crust from steaming after the pie is baked.

CREAM OR SOFT PIES

Cream or soft pies depend on smoothness of the filling for quality. It should be firm enough to hold its shape when cut, yet soft enough to maintain its creamy consistency.

FRUIT PIE

The best fruit pie is made of the highest quality fruits, with a crisp pastry. It should be eaten within three or four hours after it has been cooked, as it begins to lose flavor after that. If it must be kept, refrigerate it and heat for 5 to 10 minutes, about a half hour before serving.

DEEP DISH PIES

The deep dish pie is, generally speaking, a one-crust pie with the crust arranged over instead of under the fruit. Fresh fruit, sweetened, and with water added if the fruit is at all dry, is placed in a deep baking dish of the casserole type. Often a small inverted cup or custard cup is placed in the dish to draw some of the juices up into itself during the baking and prevent boiling over. Any desired pastry may be used, this being placed over the top of the fruit, one or two gashes made in it to allow for escape of steam and the pie then baked as any pie, having the oven hot (450° F.) for the first 10 minutes, then reducing to moderate (350° F.) to complete the baking of both crust and fruit.

PIE BIRD. A pie bird is a small, hollow figurine which, when inserted into the upper crust of a two-crust pie, acts as a steam vent during the baking and as an ornament during the serving. The use of these devices eliminates the need of cutting steam vents in the top crust, giving a more pleasing appearance to the finished pie. They are, of course, not required in the case of criss-crossed or perforated crusts.

The figurines are commonly made of a ceramic material, and are painted in keeping with their design, with a paint that is baked into the ceramic to eliminate the dangers of flaking while on the pie. They may be quite simple, resembling a small

funnel in appearance, but usually they are shaped and painted in the form of birds, animals or small cooks. Traditionally, however, they are made in the form of open-mouthed birds because of the nursery rhyme concerning the "four and twenty blackbirds baked in a pie."

PIE CRUST. See PASTRY.

PIE PLANT. Another name for Rhubarb, *which see.*

PIE PLATE. A pie plate is a dish in which pies are baked. It is usually made of metal, with tin being so commonly used that the plates are frequently referred to as pie "tins," regardless of the material used. Pie plates are also made of aluminum, ceramics and glass, though these are heavier than the metal ones. See PIE; *see also* KITCHEN EQUIPMENT.

PIED PIPER. See RED GURNARD.

PIERCED BLADE PASTRY SERVER. See FLATWARE.

PIG. The swine—especially the young. *See recipes under* PORK.

PIGEONS. (SQUABS) Young pigeons or squabs have light, red flesh upon the breast, and full, fresh-colored and moist legs. When the legs are thin and the breast very dark, the bird is old. The only difference between pigeons and squabs is that squabs are never more than four weeks old. At that age the flesh is milky and delicate, but once they have learned to leave the nest and have begun to walk or fly about a little, they lose the special squab characteristics, become lean, and are then pigeons.

When purchasing squabs, look for plumpness and light flesh. See that there are no bruises. Squabs are on the market all year. The average weight per squab is one pound, while pigeons sometimes reach one and a half, even one and three-quarters pounds, and are less tender than squabs.

Both pigeons and squabs may be broiled, roasted, served en casserole or potted.

POTTED PIGEONS

For 6 servings clean and wash a half dozen pigeons, each weighing about 1½ pounds, but always figure on one pigeon per person. Pack (necks down) in an earthenware pot with a slice of onion on each bird. Pour 1 cup of cider vinegar over and let stand in the refrigerator overnight. Next morning lift out the pigeons and drain thoroughly, discarding the vinegar and onion. Dredge the birds with seasoned flour; then fry 3 or 4 slices of fat salt pork in a Dutch oven or other heavy kettle. When the fat is extracted, remove the pork and add to the fat in the pan 3 medium-sized onions, thinly sliced. Arrange the pigeons over the onions, cover and cook very slowly, turning once, for about 15 minutes. Now pour over them 1 quart of boiling stock or water, cover and simmer for 2 hours over the lowest possible flame. Add additional seasoning, if needed, and thicken the gravy with a tablespoon of flour moistened with a little cold water. Simmer ½ hour longer. When ready to serve add 2 tablespoons of sherry and serve on a hot platter, dusting the birds with minced parsley and a little chives. Additional gravy may be passed separately and currant jelly is a good accompaniment to the dish.

If squabs are used instead of pigeons reduce slightly the amount of liquid used for gravy and simmer only 1 to 1½ hours. In any case garnish the platter with crisp water cress.

Roast Stuffed Squabs

Select birds of the same size. Wash, dry, then rub the insides with salt, followed by rubbing with a piece of cut lemon. Stuff loosely, sew up the opening and truss. Spread softened butter on breasts and legs to prevent scorching or burning, place the birds on the rack in a roasting pan and roast in a slow oven (300° F.) about 1 hour, depending on the size of the birds. Baste frequently with hot water in which a little butter has been melted. Serve very hot, garnishing with water cress.

Stuffing (I)

3 cups freshly cooked rice
⅓ cup melted butter
1 small onion, grated
1 tsp salt
⅓ tsp pepper
½ tsp poultry seasoning
1 tbsp minced parsley
Grated rind 1 orange
3 tbsp seedless raisins

Combine all ingredients, first parboiling and draining the raisins if they seem at all dry.

Stuffing (II)

1 cup soft bread crumbs
¼ cup stock or bouillon
½ lb sausage meat
2 tbsp minced parsley
2 tbsp minced chives
Salt and pepper
Dash of grated nutmeg
Pinch of poultry seasoning

Combine all ingredients and use as any stuffing.

PIGMENTS. Artificial coloring matters are added to foods, both to deceive intentionally and also merely to make different substances, such as preserved green vegetables, candies, or confections, appear more attractive to the eye. Formerly highly injurious copper or zinc salts were used to color canned peas and beans, and not infrequently they were found in poisonous quantities, but the green plant pigment, chlorophyll, is so much cheaper, and is so abundant and harmless, that it has almost entirely superseded them since its introduction for this purpose in 1877.

Ultramarine is much used to color sirups; safranin, eosin, fuchsin, anilin violet, and many other anilins are employed in the manufacture of candies; so also is cochineal.

The pigments most in vogue to color butter and cream are turmeric, saffron, sulphonated anilin yellow, and annatto. Annatto, as used by certain dairymen to color milk and cream is not harmful.

PIGNOLIA NUTS. A small nut imported from Spain, used in pastry and confections. They are already shelled and blanched and can be used for making nut butter without further preparation except washing and drying in a moderately hot oven (350° F.) for a few minutes, to make them crisp.

PIG-NUT. The sweetish-bitter nut of a species of hickory. It is also another name for the ground chestnut.

PIG'S FEET. *See* Pork.

PIKE. An insatiable fish, ever ready to fight, it is justly called the "King Pirate" of the fresh waters. It spares no fish, large or small, its voracious mouth ever open to gulp down its prey indiscriminately, not sparing its own kind. The pike darts, lightning-fast, after its prey, seizes it, thrashes it, then swallows it in a jiffy. Its

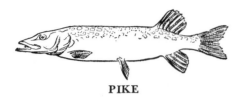

PIKE

digestion is as speedy as its assault, its appetite is never ending. It thins out its own empire but it reproduces prolifically. Were this not so, the gourmets would be deprived to a great extent of its delicious meat.

But, if the pike is a ferocious and cannibalistic fish, its flesh is of a supreme delicacy with which a real chef may work magic and which many of the thousands of sauces known in culinary art adorn and ennoble.

There exists in the Amazon River, South America, a giant species of pike. This colossus, always hungry, possesses a formidable saw-like mouth with hundreds of sharp teeth. Its flesh is one of the most delicate there is, especially delectable when boiled or court-bouilloned in white wine and served with a side dish of soft, smooth, creamy Hollandaise sauce.

It is claimed that pike, like carp, live to be very old, and it has been stated, although never proved, that pike have been caught in the River Volga, in Russia, weighing 60 pounds and measuring 7 and 8 feet.

According to a most extraordinary fish story, it has been established that the oldest pike ever caught alive, was taken during the year 1497, at Kaiserslautern, near Mannheim, in Germany. The skeleton was for many years kept in a museum of that town. This famous pike reached 20 feet in length and weighed nearly 975 lbs. Moreover, it was found that a gilded ring which was found in the monster bore the following inscription, engraved in German: "I am the first fish which has been thrown into this water by the hands of Emperor Frederick II, October the 5th, 1262." Consequently, when caught, this Methuselah was 235 years of age!

All the methods of preparation of Bass, Lamprey, Carp, Perch, and Whitefish may be adapted to the Pike. See also FISH.

PILAFF or **PILAU.** These stews and soups represent concentrated nourishment in Oriental form for almost any season. The thousand and one savory stews of the world's kitchens are bound together in one of the major orders of foods, and Irish stew is a first cousin to the ragouts of France and the pilaffs of the Levant. All are filling, soothing, gratifying to the tired, empty stomach, but in those of the mysterious East lurks the subtle charm of Persian gardens and the perfumes of the bazaars.

The term *pilaff* indicates the general Levantine pronunciation, and *pilau* is found more or less from Baghdad to Madras. The pleasant tang of curry grows more evident as one nears the equator and enters into most of the Indian pilaus, but the Turkish taste inclines to a milder delicacy, and a pilaff may be as bland as milk and honey.

Pilaff may come to the table in a soup tureen or on a covered platter with mounds of rice, and there is a spectacular form which is easily confused with the elaborate risotto (*which see* under RICE) that masks a prize of meat and assorted dainties. For a summer soup course, a pilaff or pilau is an unusual satisfaction when properly prepared.

PILAU (I)

1 cup rice
2 qt stock, chicken or veal
1 cup chicken, raw
Oil or butter
2 lamb kidneys, or chicken liver and heart
1 small onion
½ cup watercress, chopped
Salt
White pepper
Coriander, crushed
¼ tsp saffron, rubbed to powder

Wash the rice in several waters and then cook in enough stock to cover until tender. Saute the cup of diced raw chicken in butter or oil, add the lamb kidneys skinned and diced with minced onion (or the diced chicken liver and heart), and the chopped water cress, then cook 5 minutes. Now add

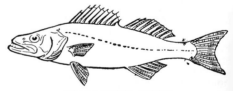

WALLEYED PIKE

the 2 quarts of stock and bring to a boil, then add the cooked rice. Season with the salt, pepper, coriander and saffron. Serve as hot as possible. (Serves 6)

PILAU (II)

1 cup rice
Oil or butter
2 qt stock, chicken or veal
1 fowl, boiled or roasted and diced
1 green apple, diced
½ cup sultana raisins
¼ cup almonds, blanched and sliced
6 small shallots or 2 small onions
1 cup tomato puree
Salt
White pepper
Coriander, crushed
Saffron, powdered

Wash the rice thoroughly in several waters and then cook in oil or butter (as for risotto, *which see*), until every grain is golden brown. Add the stock and simmer until the rice is tender, moistening with more stock if necessary. Brown the diced meat of the fowl (both light and dark meat) in oil with the diced apple, raisins, almonds, and shallots or onions. Moisten with more stock and add the tomato puree. Form a pyramid of this in a low, shallow casserole and mask completely with the cooked rice. Season with the salt, pepper, coriander and saffron.

BOMBAY PILAU

This is an adaptation of the recipe for Pilau II, *which see*, to which is added the following:

2 to 3 tbsp curry powder
3 to 4 pieces preserved ginger
2 doz almonds, blanched
⅓ cup sultana raisins
1 doz onion rings
1 doz ripe olives
2 to 3 hard boiled eggs, sliced
6 sprigs water cress
6 sprigs parsley

As indicated above, follow the recipe for Pilau II, up to the point of forming the pyramid. Then add the curry powder and the ginger, sliced wafer thin. Form the

pyramid in the casserole and mask with the rice. Keep hot in the oven until ready to serve. Then garnish with the almonds and raisins after they have been sauted together in oil or butter. Also garnish with the onion rings French-fried, and the olives made bright with oil. Ornament the base of the pyramid with the slices of hard boiled egg, water cress and parsley. Keep the pilau moist with the seasoned stock and serve sizzling hot.

If the curry powder is left out, this dish would be Stamboul Pilau.

LEVANTINE PILAFF

2 lb lamb, lean
Oil or butter
3 small onions, sliced
6 shallots, minced
1 cup rice
1 small eggplant
2 cups lamb broth
1 cup tomato paste
Salt
Pepper
Saffron, powdered
Coriander, bruised

Dice the lamb and brown in oil or butter with the onions and shallots. Thoroughly wash and drain the rice and cook with the meat until colored. Peel, dice and saute the eggplant in oil or butter and then add to the meat and rice mixture with the lamb broth and tomato paste. Simmer all this gently and then season with the salt, pepper, saffron and coriander. Thicken with a brown roux (*which see*) and turn into a well buttered or oiled casserole. Cook in a very hot oven (450° F.) for 12 to 15 minutes. Serve in a covered dish. (Serves 6)

PILCHARD. A salt water, edible fish, resembling the herring, used fresh or canned.

PILON. French name for a pestle, of wood or metal, used in the kitchen to pound, grind, or mix, either in a mixing bowl or a mortar.

PILOT BISCUIT. *See* CRACKER.

PILOT FISH. Another name for whitefish, *which see*.

PILOT WAFERS. *See* HARDTACK.

PIMENTA. *See* ALLSPICE.

PIMENTO. Pimentos are the dried, unripe, aromatic berries of a West Indian tree. *See* ALLSPICE. This name also refers, but erroneously, to the Spanish paprika or pimiento.

PIMENTO CHEESE. Any kind of cheese to which pimientos or Spanish peppers have been added.

PIMIENTO. The sweet pepper, the fruit of which is used as a relish, for stuffing olives, garnishing salads, etc. It is usually sold in canned form. *See also* PEPPER.

PIMIENTO SAUCE. *See* WHITE SAUCE.

PIMP CHEESE. Another name for Mainz hand cheese (*which see*).

PINA. A sweet Cuban drink, prepared from pineapples.

PINCH. As applied to food, the amount of salt, pepper, condiment or spice that can be held between the thumb and the forefinger.

PINDAR. A nickname for peanuts (*which see*).

PINE NUT. The small seed contained in the cone of certain trees of the genus *Pinus*, usually roasted and salted and served as a tidbit. It contains a large percentage of fat.

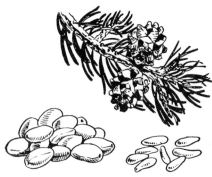

PINE NUT

PINEAPPLE. The pineapple belongs to the order *Bromeliaceae*, the members of which are either tropical or subtropical. They grow on a plant which consists of a short stem covered with leaves arranged in whorls and supported by roots which are directly attached. The root system is shallow, and in certain soils is restricted to a somewhat narrow region around the plant. The pineapple is a multiple fruit, that is, it is really a group of individual fruits which become fused together.

The history of a now familiar and popular food is often another version of the history of man in his role as an intrepid pioneer. Thus pineapples were discovered for the first time, when, late in the fall of 1493, Columbus and his men on their sec-

ond voyage westward, reached the island of Guadaloupe, as it was to be known henceforth. Here among the wonders of this island, they noted the strange tropical beauty of the pineapple. It was an experience for Columbus to remember and to mention in Spain many months later. And Peter Martyr, confidant of Spanish royalty and nobles and an indefatigable letter writer, recorded what Columbus had seen and thus gave us the first known account of this royal fruit of the tropical west.

It is another diarist, Don Francisco Paula y Marin, who several centuries later records the presence of pineapples in a different place—this time in Hawaii. How they got there, or when, remains a mystery. But they were not native there. We know that, from the Hawaiian name for them, *holakahiki*. The first part of the word comes from "hala," meaning "screw pine." But the second part, "kahiki," means a foreign land. So sometime, somehow, "foreign" pineapples were brought to Hawaii. But no trace of their "foreignness" is left today, for the soil and climate have made Hawaii a pineapple paradise and the center of pineapple industry.

The fruit was known to the aboriginal Indians of tropical America as *na-na*, meaning fragrance. The Spanish explorers called the fruit *pina* because of its resemblance to the cone of the pine. Before the 16th century the Portuguese and Spanish missionaries and navigators had introduced the pineapple into India, Africa, China, and the East Indies. The Hollanders were the first to grow it on European soil. According to the diary of John Evelyn, the first pineapples ever seen in England were sent to Oliver Cromwell in 1657. The first English-grown pineapple was hot-house raised in 1720 and served to King George I.

CULTIVATION IN HAWAII

The exact date of the first planting of a pineapple in the Hawaiian Islands is unknown. But, whatever the date, that first pineapple felt right at home. Soon it was flourishing wild over the Kona district. The wild fruit was small, acidulous, woody as to fiber, but evidently sweet to taste, for the first settlers recognized its possibilities and shipped supplies to America during the gold rush days. But from Kona to Honolulu, then to California, was a long journey, and most of the fruit spoiled on

FOOD VALUE

	Wa-ter	Food Energy	Pro-tein	Fat	Car-bohy-drates	Cal-cium	Phos-phorus	Iron	Vit. A Value	Thia-mine	Ribo-flavin	Nia-cin	Ascor-bic Acid
Fresh Pineapple	85.3	58	.4	.2	13.7	16	11	.3	130	.08	.02	.2	24
Pineapple Juice	86.2	54	.3	.1	13.0	15	8	.5	80	.05	.02	.2	9
Canned Pineapple	78.0	87	.4	.1	21.1	29	7	.6	80	.07	.02	.2	9

the way. To shorten the transportation distance to market, an English horticulturist, Captain John Kidwell, planted four acres of pineapples on the Island of Oahu, now the fashionable residential district of Honolulu. The captain noticed that under cultivation the pineapple grew larger, and yet remained woody fibered. Knowing that other varieties grew in other parts of the world, he ordered from Jamaica a thousand slips of the smooth Cayenne pineapple. He tried other varieties, too, but of some thirty kinds, the smooth Cayenne proved superior to all. There was one drawback—spoilage before the crop could reach the California coast. The obvious answer was canning the fruit. The first cannery was opened on the islands in 1892.

The real foundation of the pineapple industry was laid a few years later in 1901, when a young Bostonian, homesteading a 60-acre tract of land near Honolulu, organized a pineapple company and planted 12 acres. Today this company has 25,000 acres under cultivation.

It is only at the final degree of ripeness that fresh pineapples are picked for the cannery. Otherwise, since they spoil within 24 hours from the field, fresh pineapples for the market are of necessity picked green and let ripen en route. They change color, they have the appearance of ripe fruit, but the flavor is never up to that of the plant-ripened pine. Fruit canned in Hawaii within a day of picking shows an average of 12.6 percent sugar, against 3.6 percent in fruit picked and shipped into market green. Canned pineapple of top quality is usually superior in flavor to choice fruit bought fresh.

VARIETIES

Red Spanish. Reddish yellow fruit of fair quality. In Cuba, Florida and Puerto Rico, it is regarded as the most profitable variety to grow.

Smooth Cayenne. Large orange yellow fruit of very good quality. This variety is grown extensively in Hawaii and the Azores.

Puerto Rico, Cabezona, or Bull Head. Large orange yellow fruit of good quality, which is excellent for canning.

Sugar Leaf. Bears a small yellow fruit of very good quality, but is mostly restricted to Cuban consumption, as it does not ship well.

Antigua Black. Bears a small oblong bronze colored fruit of the best quality.

PINEAPPLE

Antigua White. A medium-sized yellow fruit of good quality.

PREPARATION FOR MARKET

The fruit is full sized before it is picked and the more nearly mature it is, the better flavor it has. It is snapped off the stem or cut with an inch or two of stem attached. The pickers wear long sleeved heavy canvas gloves to protect their hands. The fruit is collected in baskets, great care being exercised to prevent the fruit from being bruised or injured in any way which would detract from the quality.

Pineapples are graded for market according to the United States Department of Agriculture standards. U.S. Fancy consists of pineapples of one variety, which are mature, dry, free from disease, decay, and damage. The fruit is firm, well formed, with well developed eyes. U.S. No. 1 consists of pineapples of one variety which are mature, fairly dry and free from damage, disease and decay. U.S. No. 2 consists of pineapples of one variety which are mature and free from decay, damage and disease. The fruit is firm, fairly well formed and the eyes are fairly well developed.

Pineapples which are not graded in conformity with any of the foregoing grades are unclassified.

HINTS ON PURCHASING

Size has little to do with flavor. Square shouldered fruits are more economical than long tapering ones. Color and odor determine quality. Ripe pineapple in good condition is indicated by fresh appearance, distinctive dark orange yellow color; fragrant odor; eyes flat, and almost hollow; heavy weight in proportion to size, and leaves which pull out easily. If picked when too immature, the fruit presents a dull, lifeless appearance, the eyes are poorly developed and often somewhat pointed, and the flavor is very acid. Bruises show as discolored areas and may develop into decay. Decay appears as soft watery areas, and may often be moldy, usually around the eyes. Sour odor usually accompanies decay. Sunburn causes pineapple to be hard, pithy, and dry, marked by color lighter than normal. It is often found where tops have grown at a decided angle. Overmaturity is frequently shown by decay at the base of the pineapple.

HINTS ON PREPARATION

Pineapples should be kept at moderate temperature until ripe, 65°–70° F. being considered best. Chill just before serving. Fresh pineapple contains an enzyme which destroys gelatin. Consequently such a combination will not solidify unless the fresh pineapple has been heated to destroy this enzyme.

If the fruit weighs about 2 pounds, the homemaker can count on having 4 cups of grated fresh pineapple or about 2½ cups of small cubes. With this formula she can estimate pretty closely for parties or occasions requiring large amounts of the fruit.

To pare a fresh pineapple, proceed as follows: with scissors trim off the top of the spikes. Then, holding the pineapple in the left hand by the remaining leaves, begin paring with a sharp knife at the other end, removing all the skin and digging out eyes with the point of the knife. Skin and eyes should never be eaten because they are very sour. The hard core is discarded in slicing and grating. However, the West Indians cover the parings with water and allow it to stand several hours. Then they pour off this water, chill it, and add charged water just before serving over cracked ice. The result is a very pleasing, delicately flavored pineapple drink. The slightly astringent quality which is characteristic of pineapple makes it a particularly good accompaniment for meat, especially smoked meat.

In its canned form, pineapple has become an all-the-year-round staple. You may choose rings, fingers, diced or crushed fruit, with or without extra sweetening. Pineapple juice, in its natural form or with extra sugar, has made a place for itself since it came on the market as a breakfast beverage and as an ingredient for punches and other mixed drinks, soft or potent. Quick-frozen pineapple is also available.

Meats and fish acquire an elusive and different flavor when pineapple juice has been added to their preparation. Baked ham, smoked tenderloin, and smoked tongue in pineapple juice are delicious. Chicken and pineapple go together excellently.

Ices and ice creams of a distinct pineapple flavor, sometimes with the addition of a subtle dash of mint, are a perfect finale to a somewhat rich and heavy meal. A delicious fruit salad dressing can be prepared simply by adding pineapple juice to whipped cream salad dressing, or to mayonnaise.

In addition to paring the whole fruit and then slicing across in thin sections, there are other variations. Cut the entire pineapple in half lengthwise, through the brush as well. Carefully scoop out the entire pulp, leaving two shells. Dice the pulp small, and return to shell. Dust lightly with powdered sugar. Or, combine the cut pineapple with other fruits in a fruit salad mixture, and put the mixture in the shells. A still more glamorous idea is to fill the shells with diced pineapple and ice cream, and garnish with cherries.

In tropical countries, a favorite way of serving is to dig into the whole fruit, around each eye, cutting a cone-shaped wedge, which is left in the pineapple. This leaves the fruit solid, with easily removed sections, which may be pulled out and dipped in powdered sugar, either plain or flavored with vanilla.

BAKED PINEAPPLE AND PEACHES

6 slices canned pineapple
6 canned peach halves
2 tbsp butter
3 tbsp maraschino cherry sirup
Juice ½ lemon

Place the pineapple slices on a shallow buttered pie plate. Arrange the peach halves on them, hollow sides up. Dot with butter, pour the maraschino sirup and lemon juice over and bake in a moderately hot oven (375° F.) about 15 minutes. At serving time place one whole cherry in each peach cavity. (Serves 6)

FRENCH PINEAPPLE SALAD

1 large pineapple
2 oranges
2 peaches
1 banana
1 apple
1 pt strawberries

Cut pineapple in halves lengthwise, and scoop out the pulp. Dice pulp and other fruits and slice the strawberries, Dust lightly with sugar and chill. Replace in pineapple shells. Serve whipped cream mayonnaise separately. (Serves 6 to 8)

FROZEN PINEAPPLE NUT PUDDING

4 tbsp blanched chopped almonds
4 tbsp chopped pecans
½ cup halved candied cherries
½ cup drained shredded pineapple
½ cup sherry
2 cups boiled custard
2 cups heavy cream

Mix the nuts, cherries, and pineapple in a bowl and pour over the sherry. Let stand over night. Make the custard (which see) and chill it. Whip the cream. Combine the nut mixture with the custard and whipped cream. Freeze in the refrigerator tray without stirring. Serve with the following sauce:

2 egg yolks
2 tbsp powdered sugar
1 tbsp brandy
½ cup heavy cream

Beat the yolks with the sugar and cook over hot water until the egg thickens slightly. Remove from the heat and beat until it is cold. Add the brandy. Just before serving add the cream which has been whipped to a stiff froth. (Serves 6 or 8)

GINGER PINEAPPLE SALAD

6 slices canned pineapple, halved
1 package cream cheese (3½ oz)
4 tbsp shredded crystallized ginger
2 tbsp light cream
Lettuce

Spread half of the pineapple sections with the cream cheese blended with the ginger and cream. Top, sandwich fashion, with the remaining pineapple sections. Serve on shredded lettuce, passing fruit French dressing (see FRENCH DRESSING) separately. (Serves 6)

HAWAIIAN SHERBET

½ cup shredded pineapple
½ cup granulated sugar
1 cup pineapple juice
2 tbsp lemon juice
2 cups cold milk
1½ tsp granulated gelatin
2 tbsp cold water

Make a sugar sirup of sugar and pineapple juice. Boil 10 minutes. While hot add the gelatin which has been soaked in cold water and stir until gelatin is thoroughly dissolved. Then add the lemon juice, the shredded pineapple to which have been added a few grains of salt, alternately with the milk. Chill. Freeze, if using hand freezer, with 3 parts ice, and 1 part rock salt, for 1½ to 2 hours. Pack, using 5 parts ice and 1 part rock salt, for 1 short hour to mellow and ripen. If using refrigerator tray, freeze, without stirring, for 3 hours. Serve in chilled sherbet glasses or in orange cups. (Serves 6)

PINEAPPLE BAVARIAN

1 tbsp plain gelatin (1 envelope)
¼ cup cold water
No. 1 flat can crushed pineapple
  (1⅓ cups)
1 cup whipping cream
Juice of 1 lemon (3 tbsp)
¼ cup sugar

Soften the gelatin in the cold water for 5 minutes. Drain the juice from the pineapple and heat to boiling; stir in gelatin until dissolved and set aside to cool. Have the cream throughly chilled, either by pouring into freezing tray of refrigerator for an hour or two, or by placing in a bowl of cracked ice and salt. Beat in chilled bowl with rotary beater until fluffy, then add lemon juice and sugar and beat until very stiff. Fold in gelatin mixture and crushed pineapple lightly but thoroughly. Cover and chill in refrigerator until firm. Serve in chilled sherbet or parfait glasses. (Serves 5)

PINEAPPLE BETTY

1 cup cake crumbs
1½ cups crushed pineapple
½ cup pineapple juice

Arrange alternate layers of cake crumbs and crushed pineapple in a buttered casserole. Sprinkle each layer lightly with cinnamon and 1 tablespoon of brown sugar. Top with a layer of buttered cake crumbs, and pour ½ cup of pineapple juice over all. Bake in a moderate oven (350° F.) for 20 to 25 minutes. Serve with light cream. (Serves 4)

PINEAPPLE CHERRY COMPOTE

1 medium-sized pineapple
1½ cups water (about)
1 lb cherries
½ cup sugar

Peel and slice the pineapple, removing the eyes and cutting the fruit into cubes. Place in a saucepan with water barely to cover, bring to boiling point and simmer ten minutes. Pit the cherries, add to the pineapple and continue simmering for a further ten minutes, adding the sugar during the last 5 minutes of cooking. Chill before serving.

PINEAPPLE CHERRY CUP

1 ripe fresh pineapple
½ lb pitted red cherries (fresh)
¾ cup sugar

Peel the pineapple, remove all eyes. Score closely, up and down and around with a knife, then pull the flesh away from the core with a fork. Combine the fruits and sugar and chill before serving.

PINEAPPLE CHIFFON PIE

Follow directions for lemon chiffon pie (*see* LEMON) but use 1 cup of crushed canned pineapple with its juice in place of the lemon or orange juice. Add also 1 tablespoon of lemon juice, and if desired, substitute ½ cup of whipped cream for the white of 1 egg.

PINEAPPLE CREAM FLUFF

4 slices canned pineapple
12 marshmallows
1 cup heavy cream
½ cup fresh grated, or shredded coconut

Dice the pineapple, quarter the marshmallows, combine and chill thoroughly. Drain and just before serving fold into the whipped cream and sprinkle with the coconut. (Serves 4)

PINEAPPLE FRITTERS

1½ cups sifted flour
1½ tsp baking powder
2 tsp sugar

½ tsp salt
1 egg
6 tbsp milk
½ tbsp salad oil
½ cup drained, crushed pineapple

Combine the dry ingredients, then mix to a batter with the beaten egg, milk, and oil. Fold in the pineapple, then drop from the tip of a tablespoon into deep hot fat (375° F.). When brown on all sides, drain on soft crumpled paper and serve with a sauce made by boiling together 1 cup of the pineapple juice and two tablespoons of lemon juice with ⅔ cup of sugar until slightly thickened. (Serves 4)

PINEAPPLE GINGER ALE JELLY

2 tbsp gelatin
1½ cups canned pineapple juice
½ cup sugar
1¾ cups ginger ale
1 cup orange sections
½ cup sliced strawberries

Soften the gelatin in ¼ cup of the pineapple juice. Heat the remaining juice and dissolve the softened gelatin and the sugar in it. When cold but not set, add the ginger ale. Chill, and as soon as the mixture begins to congeal, fold in the fruit. Turn into a previously wet mold and chill. Unmold and garnish with additional orange sections and whole berries.

Be careful not to add the fruits until the gelatin is almost at the setting point that they may remain in suspension instead of sinking to the bottom of the mold.

Again, if desired, instead of adding the fruits to the gelatin mixture pour a thin layer of the gelatin into the bottom of the mold; when firm arrange part of the fruit over it, cover with more gelatin, and so on, until all are used. Be careful, however, not to let the gelatin become too firm and set, otherwise the layers may separate when unmolding. (Serves 4 or 6)

PINEAPPLE GOURMET

Whole fresh pineapple
Strawberries, soaked in port wine
Vanilla ice cream
Whipped cream, flavored with wild strawberry preserves
Jamaica rum

Split the pineapple lengthwise, scoop out the fruit and dice it. Then blend with the strawberries, previously soaked in the wine. Put this mixture into the pineapple shells, top with the ice cream to which the strawberry-flavored whipped cream has been added and pour the rum over all. Serve immediately.

PINEAPPLE LIME VELVET

1 package lime-flavored gelatin
1 cup boiling water
3 oz package cream cheese
⅔ cup crushed pineapple with its juice
½ cup finely cut celery
½ cup heavy cream, whipped
Maraschino or bing cherries

Add the gelatin to the water and stir until dissolved. Add cheese and beat with a rotary beater until cheese is well blended. Chill until slightly congealed, then add pineapple and celery. Fold in whipped cream lightly but thoroughly. Turn into 3 to 4 cup mold that has been rinsed in cold water. Chill until firm. Unmold and serve on watercress. Garnish with cherries. (Serves 6 or 8)

PINEAPPLE JUICE

Peel a pineapple and cut it into cubes. Put these through a grinder to extract the juice. Strain, and serve with crushed ice. Garnish with sprigs of mint.

Or combine pineapple juice with an equal portion of chilled loganberry juice.

PINEAPPLE MACAROON CHARLOTTE

1 cup crushed canned pineapple
¼ cup sugar
1 tsp lemon juice
1 tbsp gelatin
¼ cup cold water
½ cup heavy cream
¼ cup macaroon crumbs

Scald the pineapple juice with the sugar. Add the lemon juice and dissolve in it the gelatin previously softened in the cold water. Chill, and when almost at the setting point, fold in the stiffly beaten cream and the macaroon crumbs. Pile high either in sherbet glasses or a deep serving dish. (Serves 4)

Pineapple Madeira

1 medium-sized fresh pineapple
1 cup sugar
1 cup Madeira

Pare and dice the pineapple. Add the sugar and toss lightly with two forks. Turn into a serving dish. Pour the Madeira over and chill 2 hours before serving. (Serves 4)

Pineapple Marlow

1 cup canned pineapple juice
⅓ cup water
20 marshmallows
2 tbsp lemon juice
2 tbsp sugar
¼ cup egg whites
Few grains of salt

Combine the pineapple juice, water, and marshmallows in the upper part of the double boiler. Set over hot water until the marshmallows dissolve. Beat slightly to blend. Add the lemon juice and half the sugar and set aside to cool. Beat the egg whites with the remaining sugar and the salt. Fold into the first mixture, turn into the tray of an automatic refrigerator and freeze without stirring. (Serves 4)

Pineapple Marshmallow Filling

½ lb marshmallows
1 cup shredded canned pineapple
A few grains of salt
½ cup chopped dates
½ cup chopped nut meats

Melt marshmallows in top of double boiler and add well drained pineapple, dates, salt, and nut meats. Blend thoroughly but do not let boil. Cool slightly before spreading between layers of cake. (Sufficient for two 8-inch layers)

Pineapple Melange

1 cup fresh or canned peaches, sliced
6 apricot halves, canned
6 slices fresh or canned pineapple
3 bananas, sliced
1 glass raspberry jelly

Combine all the fruits. Melt the jelly and pour it over. Chill thoroughly, then arrange in sherbet glasses and top each with one perfect blackberry, raspberry, or ripe strawberry.

Pineapple Milk Sherbet

1½ cups pineapple juice (canned)
½ cup granulated sugar
⅛ generous tsp salt
2 egg whites, stiffly beaten
½ cup thin cream or evaporated milk
3 tbsp lemon juice

Combine the pineapple juice, sugar and salt and bring to the boiling point; then boil for 5 minutes. Pour this hot sirup over the stiffly beaten egg whites, stirring briskly and constantly. Chill. Combine chilled thin cream or undiluted evaporated milk with lemon juice and stir into the chilled pineapple mixture. Freeze either in hand freezer or refrigerator tray as indicated for Hawaiian sherbet (*see above*) without stirring, for 3 hours, if using refrigerator tray, and until solid, but not too stiff, if using hand freezer. Serve in chilled sherbet glasses.

Pineapple Mint Salad

1 package lime gelatin
1 cup hot water
1 cup canned pineapple juice
⅛ tsp spearmint extract
1 cup crushed canned pineapple
1 cup finely shaved white cabbage

Dissolve the gelatin in the hot water. Cool, and add the pineapple juice and spearmint extract. When almost at the setting point fold in the crushed pineapple and cabbage. Turn into a previously wet ring mold and chill. Unmold and garnish with shredded lettuce, passing mayonnaise or a semi-sweet salad dressing separately. (Serves 6)

Pineapple Mousse

1 cup whipping cream
2 tsp plain gelatin
3 tbsp cold water
1 cup pineapple juice
⅛ tsp salt
3 tbsp lemon juice
1¼ cups crushed pineapple

Chill the cream thoroughly. Meanwhile soften the gelatin in the cold water for 5 minutes. Heat the pineapple juice to simmering, add gelatin and stir until dissolved. Add the salt and cool. Then add the lemon juice and pineapple. Chill until thick. Place cream in a cold bowl and beat until stiff. Fold lightly but thoroughly into pineapple mixture. Turn into chilled refrigerator tray; set refrigerator at coldest temperature and freeze for several hours in freezing compartment until firm. Return controls to normal refrigerator temperature and ripen until ready to serve. Serve in chilled dishes. (Serves 8 to 12)

PINEAPPLE-NUT REFRIGERATOR CAKE

1 cup butter
1½ cups powdered sugar
½ cup finely chopped nut meats
1 cup drained, shredded pineapple
2 egg whites, stiffly beaten
3 doz vanilla wafers
Heavy cream, whipped

Cream together butter and sugar, add nuts and pineapple and blend thoroughly; fold in egg whites. Line a cake pan with wafers and cover with part of the fruit-nut mixture. Add a layer of wafers and repeat until all ingredients are used, having a layer of wafers on top. Chill in refrigerator at least 12 hours. Serve with whipped cream. (Serves 6 or 8)

PINEAPPLE RICE BAVARIAN

½ cup rice
1½ cups milk
¼ tsp salt
1 tbsp gelatin
3 tbsp canned pineapple juice
1 cup canned pineapple, diced or crushed
1 cup heavy cream

Cook the rice in the salted milk about 45 minutes or until tender. Soften the gelatin in the pineapple juice, then dissolve over hot water. Combine with the hot rice, blending thoroughly; then add the pineapple with additional sugar if desired. Cool, fold in the whipped cream and turn into a previously wet mold. Chill, unmold and garnish with additional pineapple. (Serves 6)

PINEAPPLE SABAYON

3 egg yolks
3 tbsp sugar
¾ cup pineapple juice
⅛ tsp salt
1½ tsp lemon juice
¾ tsp vanilla
Few drops of sherry

Beat the egg yolks until very light. Add the sugar and cook over hot water (double boiler), beating continuously with a rotary beater until thick and foamy. Add the pineapple juice, salt and flavorings. Remove the beater and stir with a wooden spoon 2 minutes longer. Be careful to keep the water in the lower vessel below boiling point lest the mixture curdle. Serve hot in parfait glasses. (Serves 4)

PINEAPPLE SAUCE

1 cup sugar
½ cup hot water
1 cup crushed pineapple (canned)
Pinch of salt

Bring the sugar and water together to boiling point and cook for three minutes. Remove from the heat, add the drained pineapple and salt, and when cold, store in the refrigerator.

PINEAPPLE AND STRAWBERRY CUP

1 medium-sized ripe fresh pineapple
1 qt strawberries
1 to 1½ cups powdered sugar
Fresh mint

Peel and remove eyes from the pineapple and shred the fruit with a fork. Add the sugar. Blend and chill very thoroughly. Wash, drain, hull and slice the strawberries; sweeten them to taste and chill. At serving time combine the two fruits and arrange in sherbet glasses, garnishing with fresh mint. (Serves 6 or 8)

PINEAPPLE STUFFING
(For Crown Roast of Lamb or Pork)

1 carrot
1 onion
½ cup celery

2 tbsp lard
1 cup cooked rice
1 cup drained crushed pineapple
½ cup raisins
2 cups bread crumbs
Salt, pepper, and paprika

Chop the carrot, onion, and celery finely, and brown in the hot lard. Add all remaining ingredients and toss lightly together in the pan. *See* STUFFING.

PINEAPPLE AND SWEET POTATO SOUFFLE

3 cups hot mashed potatoes
3 tbsp butter
½ tsp each salt and grated lemon rind
2 eggs, separated
¾ cup well drained, crushed, canned pineapple

Using hot potatoes beat in the butter, salt, emon rind, and beaten egg yolks. Beat all until light and fluffy. Fold in the pineapple and, when cool, the stiffly beaten egg whites. Bake in a well-greased baking dish in a moderate oven (350° F.) about 40 minutes. (Serves 6)

PINEAPPLE UPSIDE-DOWN CAKE

1 cup sugar
3 tbsp cornstarch
1¾ cups crushed pineapple (No. 1 tall tin)
2 tbsp melted butter
½ cup maraschino cherries
1⅔ cups all-purpose flour
½ tsp salt
2¼ tsp baking powder
⅓ cup shortening
2 eggs, beaten
½ tsp vanilla
½ cup milk

Mix ⅓ cup of the sugar with the cornstarch. Add the juice drained from the pineapple, and cook over direct heat in heavy 10-inch skillet which has an ovenproof handle. Stir constantly until sauce boils and becomes clear. Add the drained pineapple and butter. Drain the cherries thoroughly and arrange in a pattern in the pineapple mixture. Sift the flour, measure, and resift 3 times with salt and baking powder. Cream the shortening until soft,

add the remaining ⅔ cup sugar and the eggs, and beat vigorously until smooth and fluffy. Stir in the vanilla. Add flour mixture and milk alternately, beginning and ending with flour, and beating well after each addition. Pour batter into skillet over pineapple and bake in a moderate oven (350° F.) for 35 to 40 minutes, or until center of cake is springy when lightly pressed with finger tips. Cool in pan on cake rack about 10 minutes; then turn out onto a serving plate. Serve warm with whipped cream if desired. (Serves 6 or 8)

PINEAPPLE CHEESE. A highly colored, hard, rennet cheese, made from the whole milk of cows. It is a domestic cheese.

PINEAPPLE CREAM CHEESE. Cream cheese, flavored with pineapple.

PINK LADY. A gin cocktail so named because of its pinkish color, made as follows:

PINK LADY

1 large jigger dry gin
1 tbsp grenadine
1 egg white

Shake the ingredients well with cracked ice until egg white is thoroughly mixed, strain into cocktail glass. (Serves 1)
A more elaborate version of the same drink may be made as follows:

PINK LADY VARIATION

1 jigger dry gin
1 tsp grenadine
1 egg white
1 tsp lemon juice
1 tsp brandy

Mix and serve as above. (Serves 1)
For a general discussion of drink mixing and recipes, *see* BARTENDING, and COCKTAIL, ALCOHOLIC.

PINOLE (pee-noé-lay). The Indians of Mexico and of the Southwestern United States prepared this concentrated food by parching the grains of various native edible grass seeds and grinding them to a fine meal. The meal, thus prepared, was light in weight and would keep indefinitely. With pemmican (*which see*) it made an ideal food for carrying on long journeys and as an emergency ration in times of war.
Pinole meal can be eaten dry, but it is more tasty when mixed with two or three

times its own bulk of cold water. The flavor and nutritional quality vary with the kind of seed from which the ground meal is made. When made of parched corn, pinole is more nourishing than when prepared from most other seeds. Parched corn was a standard food carried by Daniel Boone and other American pioneers who would sometimes keep going on as little as a small handful a day. *See also* Camp Cookery.

PINOT BLANC. A white table wine of the Chablis type made from Pinot Blanc grapes. *See* Chablis.

PINOT NOIR. A red table wine of the Burgundy type, made from Pinot Noir grapes. *See* Burgundy.

PINT. A unit of measure which equals two cups or one-half a quart in liquid measurement.

PINTO BEAN. *See* Bean.

PINWHEEL. As applied to food, such as cookies, sandwiches, etc., the term means a cookie or a sandwich rolled pinwheel-like.

PIP. The seed of an apple, an orange, etc.

PIPERINE. The active principle of black pepper. An alkaloid of pepper, which stimulates perspiration, thus having a cooling effect on the body if a sufficient amount is eaten. For this reason, pepper is widely used in seasoning food in hot countries.

PIPPIN. A variety of apple, *which see*.

PIQUANCY. The state or quality of a food being piquant or pleasantly sharp so that it tends to stimulate the appetite.

PIQUANT BUTTER. *See* Butter Sauce.

PIQUANTE SAUCE. *See* Brown Sauce.

PIQUE (peek). A proprietary seasoning for gravies, soups, meats, etc. *See also* Seasoning.

PIQUETTE. The French term for an imitation wine made from the grape husks left after the juice is pressed for the real wine. The husks are steeped in water, sugar added and fermentation caused by brewer's yeast. *See also* Wine.

PISCO. A highly potent spirit distilled from wine in Peru. A milder form is made for export sale.

PISTACHIO. Pistachio nuts are imported, Syria, Persia (Iran), the British West Indies, and Italy providing the largest quantities. Smaller amounts come from Egypt, Arabia, and Turkey, and a few are grown in California. The nut has a greenish, almond-like kernel and is chiefly used

in fancy cookery for its color and its delicate flavor. Pistachios are very rich in iron —a fact which may account for their inclusion in certain diets. *See also* Nuts.

PISTACHIO PARFAIT

¼ cup water
1 cup granulated sugar
3 egg whites, stiffly beaten with
¼ tsp salt
2 tsp vanilla extract
¾ tsp almond extract
2 cups heavy cream, whipped stiff and colored with
2 or 3 drops green vegetable coloring
½ cup coarsely ground pistachio nut meats

Make a sugar sirup with water and sugar, and boil until sirup spins a thread when dropped from the tip of a spoon. Immediately pour the hot sirup in a fine stream over the stiffly beaten egg whites, while beating briskly and constantly, until mixture is cold. Then add combined vanilla and almond extracts. Add stiffly whipped heavy cream which has been colored with green vegetable coloring to the desired tender hue, alternately with the coarsely ground pistachio nut meats. Freeze as directed for parfaits (*which see*).

PIZZA. (peets za) An Italian open-faced pie whose basic ingredients consist of paste, cheese, tomatoes, and olive oil. It may be further embellished with fish (anchovy), meat (sausage), etc.

PLACE MAT. A small, oblong mat that is used in place of a table cloth. One is placed before each seat and they are large enough to comfortably hold all the components of an individual place setting. *See* Table Setting and Service.

PLACE PLATE. The basic plate of an individual table setting. It is used as a marker or guide for the silverware and other components of the place setting and functions as a service plate (*which see*) when

PISTACHIO NUTS

the food is served. *See* TABLE SETTING AND SERVICE.

PLAICE. The plaice, more often called "fluke," belongs to the flounder family, and is found abundantly on the Atlantic seaboard. The plaice is sold in the markets during the same months as the flounder and is a very economical fish. The skin on both sides of the eyes is of a grayish-brown color, with oval and round reddish-orange dots. Its composition is similar to that of the flounder, but not quite so delicate, and the various methods employed in the prep-

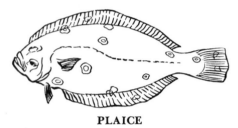

PLAICE

aration of all the flat fish may be adapted to this popular fish. *See* FLOUNDER. The large ones may be cooked in court-bouillon (*which see*) and served with any of the sauces appropriate to flat fish.

PLANKING. Cooking by means of a plank was invented by the Indians, and the early settlers, finding it convenient and delicious, adopted it. But along with the disappearance of the big open fireplace and the evolution of the kitchen range the plank vanished. Just recently it has been slightly revived.

Planking is really practical, inexpensive, and adaptable to any home. The plank itself should be made of well seasoned, hard wood—maple, oak, or hickory—and be either oblong or oval in shape. It should be grooved so that the juices can be retained and not lost in the oven. Any fish suitable for boiling or broiling may be prepared on the plank—trout, shad, mackerel, pickerel, pike, and all the white fish. Salmon or halibut steaks, and even cod or haddock can be cooked successfully this way.

In using the plank, first heat it in the oven, and then oil it thoroughly with olive oil, melted butter, or other fat—but olive oil is preferable. Split the fish. Wash, dry, and season it, and arrange it on the plank with bits of butter, bacon, or pork. Then it is ready to bake in a hot oven, or to be broiled at some distance from the gas

flame, charcoal, or electric broiler. A plank, used over charcoal or wood, will absorb the delightful odors of both, and assume an elusive delicacy of flavor that is unequaled. When the fish is done, it is conventionally decorated with duchesse potato (creamy mashed potato made smooth by adding one egg yolk to each cup of potato), put on with a pastry tube or bag, then browned under heat; and some vegetables, as broiled tomato or tomato slices, stuffed peppers, baked stuffed onions, or buttered string beans or peas, which last may be placed in hollowed-out carrots, beets, or small cooked turnips. The whole is then garnished with parsley and lemon.

Although this sounds rather elaborate, it can be modified to everyday living. A large plank may be purchased for a dollar or so, or an oblong meat board will serve admirably. It is not necessary to put on the potato with a pastry tube or bag—it can be piled lightly about the edge or made into rough nests or balls. The regular dinner vegetable may serve as garnish, and radishes can be used for decorating.

MEAT DISHES

A vegetable plate may also be served on a plank as can any kind of steak from Hamburg to Filet Mignon. Of course a plank which is used for fish should not be used for meat or vegetables.

The plank should never be washed, but scraped, wiped with a bit of bread to absorb superfluous grease, and then rubbed with crumpled soft paper until clean. It is most valuable after years of service, and the homemaker who possesses among her treasures an old, charred plank, is indeed fortunate.

There is nothing quite so good in the entire culinary repertory as a fine two- or three-inch steak, either of the Delmonico, the porterhouse, or the Chateaubriand type, and nothing is less in need of a sauce. The steak is cooked in advance on the griddle, pan, or broiler. The meat is then placed on the greased, heated plank, and vegetables, also cooked separately, are arranged around it, after which the entire ensemble is placed in the oven for a final browning of everything and served immediately.

PLANTAIN. A tropical, edible fruit similar to the banana (*which see*), which may be prepared by the same methods adapted to bananas. The banana is really a variety of the plantain, but the fruit is not so large or so hard as that commonly called "plantain," while the flavor is more delicate than that of the true plantain.

PLANTER'S PUNCH. A rum and lime juice drink that originated among the Jamaica sugar planters. The original punch recipe has been modified with time to make cocktails and coolers.

PLANTER'S PUNCH (ORIGINAL RECIPE)

1 part sour (fresh lime juice)
2 parts sweet (sugar or sugar sirup)
3 parts strong (Jamaica rum)
4 parts weak (water and ice)

PLANTER'S PUNCH COCKTAIL

4 parts Jamaica rum
2 parts lime juice
1 part sugar

The ingredients are mixed in a cocktail shaker with ice and either are poured unstrained into cocktail glass or strained into cocktail glass filled with cracked ice. The drink is garnished with fruit.

PLANTER'S PUNCH COOLER

2 jiggers Jamaica rum
½ lemon (juice)
1 dash grenadine

The ingredients are stirred in a ten-ounce glass filled with cracked ice. Carbonated water is added. Serve garnished with fruit to taste, including a cherry, and straws. An equivalent amount of lime juice may be used instead of the lemon if preferred. (Serves 1) *See also* BARTENDING.

PLASTICS. The name given to a group of synthetic materials that can be formed into usable shapes under conditions of heat and pressure. Developments of organic chemistry, they have come to be widely used in the modern kitchen, even though they are comparatively young as materials go. Present indications are that plastics will find even greater use in this field in the future.

There are two main groupings of plastics, the classification being based on the nature of the materials. These groupings are the *thermosetting* and the *thermoplastic* materials.

Thermosetting Materials. These are plastics which, when subjected to certain conditions of heat and pressure, undergo chemical reactions that change them to their finished form. Once these reactions have taken place, the material can be cut, drilled, or otherwise mechanically altered, but never re-used or reworked; even as cement, once set, cannot be re-poured. Under extremes of heat they may char or burn, but they will not soften or melt.

Thermosetting materials are easily recognized by their rigidity and by the fact that the known materials are never transparent. Their most common uses are described on the accompanying chart and are usually based on the ability of thermosetting materials to withstand heat.

Thermoplastic Materials. These are compounds which are also formed into usable shape by conditions of heat and pressure, but without involving a chemical change. The thermoplastics act somewhat like a wax which can be softened and reshaped under heat.

Thermoplastic materials may be recognized by their flexibility. This characteristic ranges from extreme pliableness in some cases to near rigidity in others, but any thermoplastic will bend if in a thin enough section, whereas a thermosetting material would break before bending. The thermoplastics are lighter than the thermosetting materials, and, in general are more easily scratched and have more brilliant colors. They are the only plastics yet known that are transparent, and have a complete color range including opaque and translucent colors as well.

At the present, due to more economical manufacturing methods and greater availability of material, the bulk of the plastic kitchenware found in the stores is made of the thermoplastic materials, excluding those items that come in direct contact with heat sources.

PURCHASING PLASTICS

When purchasing any item, the prospective buyer should look for good workmanship. In plastics this means that all edges should be smooth and clean with no thin fins of excess material (flash) projecting from the article, that there should be no unduly large ridge (parting line) where the mold halves joined, and that the surface should be free from scratches. Defects of this sort do not necessarily mean that the object itself is defective, but they are indications of poor workmanship and inadequate factory inspection, and they imply that the article should be carefully checked before buying.

If the article has been made of parts that have been glued together, the joints should be checked for proper gluing since this is a potential weakness. For the same reason, all seams in an article made of flexible sheet or film should also be checked.

The surface of the plastic should be free from all blisters and signs of peeling, and pliable film should be free from dirt specks and holes in the material as well as rough spots on the surface.

CARE OF PLASTIC ARTICLES

The most important thing to remember in caring for a plastic object is to use it only for the purpose for which it was made, for the plastic materials are selected for their ability to do a specific job well, rather than their adaptability to all-round usage. Thus, a plastic cake knife will cut cake beautifully for years of use, but will break the first time it is used to pry open a jar lid, and a plastic refrigerator dish will serve well until someone tries to boil water in it.

Food and only food should be put in plastic food containers; not dry cleaning compounds, paints, etc. Some plastics have amazing powers of chemical resistance, but it takes a technician to tell which plastic may be safely used in conjunction with which chemical. Should it be desired to use a plastic bowl to hold chemicals, it would be well to first test a small section of the outside to see if anything happens, if the color of the plastic runs or discolors, or if the plastic is softened, it is not safe to use them together.

In the case of gasoline, benzine, turpentine, dry-cleaning compounds and other aromatic hydrocarbons, use either a thermosetting plastic or a container made of *polyethylene*, for these are the only plastics commonly used to make kitchenware bowls that will resist those chemicals. Polyethylene may be recognized by its flexibility (see chart), its usually dull colors, and its "waxy" feel, a characteristic peculiar to this plastic. Polyethylene is practically chemically inert and almost anything can

be safely stored in a vessel made of this material.

While plastic colors (unless they have been sprayed on to form a design) are one with the material and will never chip or flake, most plastic surfaces are susceptible to scratching, especially the thermoplastics. Scratching mars the surface and causes clear or transparent surfaces to cloud. Scratches can be removed only by resurfacing the object, so reasonable care should be exercised in handling and storage to avoid this hazard.

Thermoplastic articles should never be subjected to temperatures greater than 160 degrees Fahrenheit unless permission has been clearly given on the label or the object has been designed for some specific use that does involve higher temperatures. Thus, boiling hot foods should never be placed in thermoplastic bowls or other containers, thermoplastic articles should never be placed on radiators to dry, etc. If a plastic tablecloth is used, hot objects, such as tea pots, should never be placed directly on the material.

While no object made of ordinary plastic should ever be used for cooking, new heat resistant plastics are being developed to provide pots with easy to clean, non–stick surfaces. *See* KITCHEN EQUIPMENT.

Plastic objects should be washed in warm soapy water with a soft cloth. The water can be hot, but never so hot that the bare hands cannot be comfortably held in the water while washing (this automatically protects all thermoplastic objects), and scalding rinses, etc., should not be used. Steel wool, scouring powder, and other abrasives should never be used because they scratch. Likewise if a food scraper is used, it should be made of either soft rubber or a soft plastic.

Many plastics can be warped or deformed if pushed out of shape by a great enough pressure over a long enough period of time. For this reason, plastic articles should always be stored in their natural or "flat" positions and never under any weights.

An attempt is being made throughout the plastics industry to have all plastic articles labeled as to the material used and its proper care and treatment. The purchaser should insist on this, whenever possible, for his or her own protection, and the instructions on any such label should always be carefully followed.

PLASTICS IN THE KITCHEN

Type	Technical & Trade Name		Characteristics	Uses	Special Care
THERMO-SETTING					
Molding Powders	Phenol	Durez Durite Resinox	Rigid Colors: dull to brilliant, often mottled; opaque, translucent, NEVER transparent Withstands high temperatures Chars or burns, but never melts	Handles, especially for heat insulation Electrical parts Dishes Trays Ash trays Lamp shades Radio cabinets	Avoid dropping or sharp blows
	Urea Melamine	Beetle Plaskin			
Cast Resins	Phenol	Catalin Marbelette	As above, but heavier, usually brilliant colors	As above Mainly used for handles	As above
Laminates	Phenol	Micarta Synthane	Extremely hard and rigid	Table tops Machine gears	
	Melamine		Opaque colors only, sometimes has pattern (usually a fabric) on surface Cross-section often shows layers of material Withstands high temperatures Chars or burns, but never melts	Electrical and heavy duty parts	
THERMO-PLASTIC					
Molding & Extrusion Powders	Acetate	Tenite I Lumarith	Semi-Rigid Colors: complete range, opaque, translucent, transparent; usually bright Surface: varies, but usually fairly easy to scratch as compared to thermosetting materials Lower temperature range than thermosetting Melts, burns, or distorts under heat and fire	Refrigerator dishes Egg cups and trays Bowls, dishes, etc. Place mats Pastry knives Spoons Drink stirrers Graters Juicers Clothespins Most "dime store" kitchen equipment	Avoid temperatures over 160° F. Avoid scratching Avoid chemicals unless known to be safe
	Acrylic	Lucite Plexiglass			
	Butyrate Cellulose	Tenite II			
	Nitrate Ethyl Cellulose	Celluloid Ethocel			
	Polystyrene	Styron Lustron			
	Polyethylene	Polyethylene Polythene			
	Rigid Vinyl Vinylidene Chloride	Vinylite Saran			
Elastomeric	Vinyl	Geon Koroseal Vinylite	Flexible Rest as above	Sheets and films Aprons Curtains Dish covers Tablecloths Flexible molded objects	Avoid temperatures over 160° F. Avoid contact with sharp edges If stiff from cold, warm before bending
	Polyethylene*	Polyethylene Polythene			

PLATE   914

It must be remembered that new plastics and improvements on old plastics are continually appearing, and the future may well see developments that will be the complete contradiction of the facts set forth here. The industry, for example, is working on a thermoplastic that will stand up under boiling water. Thus, the label should always be consulted and the instructions followed, even though they be the reverse of previous procedure.

PLATE. (I) In beef—the thin underportion just behind the brisket. *See* BEEF.

PLATE. (II) A shallow, usually round dish of various sizes used for the service of food. *See* DISHES; *see also* TABLE SETTING AND SERVICE.

The term plate is also applied to tableware made of gold or silver. *See* HOLLOWWARE; *see also* SILVERWARE.

PLATTER. The common name for any large, relatively flat dish on which food is served, especially the meats. The shape, size and design vary according to purpose. Platters are also called oval dishes, fish dishes, and chop dishes. *See* DISHES.

PLOVER. In Holland the plover is venerated, not only as a gastronomic dish, but also for the great services it renders to the country which is criss-crossed by canals and dikes. The teredo, or ship-worm, allied to the oyster and mussel, with its scissorlike tool, hidden under its microscopic shell, penetrates into the wood of the dikes and wooden bottom boats. Greedy for sawdust, this parasite rapidly turns the hull of a boat into a sieve. Against this dangerous insect, Nature has provided a fearless adversary: the plover. Very fond of this mollusc, this bird seeks it unceasingly with its sharp bill. In the United States no plover can be killed legally, as the breed is easily wiped out if hunted as game.

It is in October, when rested and plump, that the European plover is most succulent. It is a pleasure to see the elegant bird promenading along the meadows, stamping the moist soil to make the worms crawl out of the ground. It is also a pleasure to see it along the rivulets, bouncing with sudden movements of its nervous wings, then flying up with a strange noise like a winnowing basket—whence comes its name *vanneau* in French, meaning winnowing. But it is a far greater pleasure, to the epicure, to see this bird on the table covered with a golden crust of succulent crackling, or under a gilded crust, fried in butter.

As its flesh is succulent, so are its eggs. The late Tsarina of Russia was exceptionally fond of them delicately scrambled, then served on a silver dish garnished with strips of breast of hazel-hen, intermingled with thin slivers of perfumed black truffles, and finally sprinkled with a few drops of essence of truffle added to a glazed game sauce. It is said that this dish was regularly served to the Empress twice a week. *See also* GAME.

PLUCK. (I) To remove the feathers of a bird.

PLUCK. (II) A popular term for the heart, liver, and lungs of calves and sheep.

PLUM. A drupe, or true stone fruit of the genus *Prunus*. (*See* PRUNES.) Those cultivated in America can be roughly divided into the groups of European, Japanese and native American.

The European fruits are various colors and sizes, ranging from the tiny Damsons, to the big Yellow-Egg. They are raised in quantity in California and New York. Japanese plums are grown mainly in the south. They are generally yellow or reddish, large, firm and inclined to be pointed. Throughout the east and central west are found the American plums. This yellow or reddish-yellow fruit is usually small, and often hard and bitter.

HINTS ON BUYING

The leading dessert varieties of plums are Burbank, Bradshaw, Golden Drop, Jefferson, Reine Claude (Green Gage), Diamond, Wickson, Tragedy, Santa Rosa and Kelsey.

For cooking use, the leading varieties are: Lombard, Golden Drop, Grand Duke, Italian Prune and Reine Claude. Because of their tart flavor, Damson plums are excellent for jam and jelly making.

In purchasing plums note whether the flesh is shriveled or not. Shriveled flesh usually indicates a leathery texture and poor flavor. Sunburn is generally indicated by brownish or reddish brown color on the cheek. Softening at the tip is a good sign of maturity. Overmature fruit is generally soft, easily bruised, often leaky and insipid in flavor. Moisture or stains on the container may be evidence of crushing, overripeness, or decay. With very few exceptions, all plums are canned with the pits. Removing pits from plums is difficult, and pitted plums are not attractive in appear-

Food Value

Type	Wa-ter	Food Energy	Pro-tein	Fat	Car-bohy-drates	Cal-cium	Phos-phorus	Iron	Vit. A Value	Thia-mine	Ribo-flavin	Nia-cin	Ascor-bic Acid
Fresh plum	85.7	56	.7	.2	12.9	17	20	.5	350	.15	.03	.6	5
Canned plum; Italian prune	78.6	84	.4	.1	20.4	8	12	1.1	230	.03	.03	.4	1

ance. Canned unpitted plums are better not held over from one year to the next, therefore make a careful estimate of your needs before purchasing in large quantities. For use raw, plums should be fully ripe (tree ripened if possible) with unbroken skin and free from bruises. For canning, preserving or for use in pies or cooked desserts, it is better to select those not quite ripe. Plums average 10 to 16 to a pound. Stewed, they average five portions to the pound. If the skins are unbroken, plums may be kept in storage for two or even three weeks. However, it is better to use them as soon as they are ripe, because the flavor deteriorates rapidly.

Hints on Preparation

The sweet varieties of plum such as Lombard and Yellow Egg, may be served raw as breakfast or dessert fruit. Sweet plums may be used in fruit cups and salads. If you plan to serve the whole fruit in stewed form, use just enough water to barely cover the fruit, and do not add the sugar until the fruit is tender. This method will help preserve the shape.

The pulp of either very fresh plums, or of those which have been cooked, makes good sauces, for rice pudding, ice cream, cottage pudding, and the like.

Plum and Apple Betty

2 cups day-old bread crumbs
2 cups peeled, sliced apples
1 cup sugar
1/4 tsp ground cinnamon
1 cup halved, pitted, ripe plums
3 tbsp butter
3 tbsp flour

Butter a large baking dish and sprinkle 1/3 of the crumbs on its bottom and sides.

Then arrange in the dish half of the apples, sweetened and flavored with part of the blended sugar and cinnamon. Over this arrange the prepared plums, then another third of the crumbs with a little sugar, and finally the remainder of the sweetened, flavored apples. Blend the remaining crumbs and sugar with the butter and flour to a crumbly consistency, and spread this over the apples. Cover and bake in a moderate oven (350° F.) for about 45 minutes, removing the cover for the last 15 minutes of baking. (Serves 4)

Plum Bavarian Cream

2 tbsp gelatin
1/3 cup cold water
2 cups plum pulp
3/4 cup sugar
Juice 1 lemon
1 cup heavy cream

Soften the gelatin in the cold water. Combine the plum pulp and sugar and bring to boiling point. Dissolve the gelatin in this, cool slightly, add the lemon juice and when almost at the setting point, fold

PLUMS

in the whipped cream. Turn into a previously wet mold and chill. Unmold and serve with light cream or custard. (Serves 4 to 6)

PLUM BETTY

2½ cups coarse bread crumbs
8 red plums
¼ cup chopped nuts
½ cup sugar
2 tbsp butter

Lightly toast crumbs in oven. Wash and cut plums up coarsely, discarding the pits. Sprinkle bottom of a greased glass baking pan (3½x7½x2½ inches) with a layer of crumbs. Then arrange alternate layers of plums, nuts, and crumbs, sprinkling each layer with sugar until all is used. Finish with a layer of crumbs. Dot with butter, bake uncovered in a moderate oven (350° F.) for 20 minutes or until the betty is nicely browned. Serve warm with slightly sweetened cream sprinkled with cinnamon. (Serves 4)

PLUM CONSERVE

2 lb fresh plums
1½ cups seedless raisins
½ medium sized lemon
1½ oranges
4 cups sugar
1 cup chopped nut meats

Wash, quarter and pit the plums; pass raisins and lemon rind through food chopper; slice the oranges very thin and quarter the slices. Combine all in a preserving kettle with the lemon juice and sugar. Cook very gently, stirring frequently, about 1 hour, add the nut meats and cook 5 minutes longer. Skim if necessary and turn into sterilized jars and seal. (About 8 eight-ounce glasses)

PLUM JAM

3 pt plums
4 cups sugar

Wash the plums (Damson plums are best) and remove the pits, if desired. Add the sugar and cook until thick and clear. Pour immediately into hot, sterilized jars and seal.

PLUM KUCHEN

1 cup all-purpose flour
2 tsp baking powder
½ tsp salt
1 tbsp sugar
3 tbsp shortening
⅓ cup milk
1 lb Italian blue plums, halved and pitted
Dash of salt
2 tbsp chopped nuts
¼ cup sugar
1 tbsp butter

Sift the flour, measure and resift 3 times with baking powder, salt and sugar. Work in the shortening with a pastry blender or 2 knives until particles are the size of rice grains. Add the milk all at once, stir quickly enough to dampen the dry ingredients. Spread dough in the bottom of an 8-inch greased pie pan. Arrange the halved plums, skin side down, over the dough. Sprinkle salt, nuts, and sugar over the top and dot with butter. Bake in a moderately hot oven (400° F.) for 20 to 25 minutes. Serve warm. (Serves 6)

PLUM PORRIDGE

1 qt fresh plums
½ cup sugar
1½ cups water
3½ tbsp cornstarch

Scald the plums and remove skins and pits. Cook with the sugar and water until soft but not mushy. Moisten the cornstarch with a little cold water (additional) then add to the hot fruit mixture and cook, stirring constantly until thickened and clear. Cool, turn into a dessert dish and chill before serving. A little sugar sprinkled on top prevents the formation of a firm skin. (Serves 4 to 6)

PLUM SOUP

1 qt plums
5 cups water
½ lemon, thinly sliced
1 tsp ground cinnamon
¼ cup sugar
2 tbsp quick-cooking tapioca
2 beaten eggs

Pit the plums, then cook with 1 quart of the water, the lemon, cinnamon and sugar, for about 15 minutes. Meanwhile sprinkle the tapioca into the remaining water and cook, stirring frequently, until the tapioca is transparent and tender, adding more water if necessary. Combine the two mixtures, bring to boiling point, then gradually pour over the eggs, stirring while pouring. Chill and serve cold. (Serves 6)

PLUM SPONGE

1½ tbsp gelatin
½ cup cold water
1 cup hot canned plum juice
½ cup sieved plum pulp
½ cup sugar
½ cup orange juice
1 stiffly beaten egg white

Soften the gelatin in the cold water, then dissolve in the hot plum juice. Add the plum pulp and sugar and stir until the sugar is dissolved. Cool and add the orange juice. Chill until almost at the setting point, then beat until foamy and finally fold in the egg white. Pile high in a serving dish and chill thoroughly. Serve with light cream or custard. (Serves 4)

PLUM TART

Line a pie plate with any preferred pastry. Fill with stoned, cooked, sweetened plums and decorate lattice-fashion with narrow strips of pastry. Bake in a hot oven (450° F.) about 15 minutes. Serve plain or with whipped cream.

BAKED CANNED PLUMS ANGOSTURA

1 No. 1 can plums
½ cup sugar
½ cup hot water
1 tbsp Angostura bitters
3 cups sifted flour
3 tsp baking powder
½ tsp salt
2 tbsp sugar, additional
½ cup shortening
1 egg
1 cup milk

Use preferably dark red plums. Drain, pit, then chop coarsely. Combine the plum juice, ½ cup of sugar, water and bitters in a heavy iron frying pan and cook 5 minutes over a slow fire. Meanwhile sift together the flour, baking powder, and salt, work in the shortening, add the 2 tablespoons of sugar and moisten with the beaten egg and milk. Roll out into a rectangular shape about ⅔-inch thick. Spread with the chopped plums and roll like a jelly roll. Cut into 1-inch slices and place these cut sides up and down in the hot sirup. Dot with butter, and sprinkle with cinnamon and sugar. Bake in a hot oven (400° F.) until golden brown, basting occasionally during the last few minutes of baking with a little of the sirup in the pan. Serve with Angostura-flavored whipped cream. (Serves 4 to 6)

FRESH PLUM DUMPLINGS

1½ lb plums
½ cup water
¾ cup sugar
Dumpling dough

Wash the plums, add the water and cook covered, until the pits separate from the fruit, and come to the top of the pan. Skim these out, add the sugar, and drop dumpling dough from the tip of a tablespoon into the hot fruit mixture. (*See* DUMPLINGS.) Cover and cook gently for 15 minutes. Serve hot. (Serves 4)

FRESH PLUM PUFF

8 large, fresh plums, halved and pitted
1⅓ cups sugar
2 tbsp quick-cooking tapioca
½ cup water
2 eggs
Dash of salt
¼ tsp cream of tartar
6 tbsp sifted cake flour

Combine the plums with 1 cup of the sugar, the tapioca, and the water in a saucepan and cook about 5 minutes or until the tapioca is clear. Turn into a buttered casserole. Beat the egg yolks until thick and lemon colored, add the remaining sugar and beat again. Combine with the egg whites which have been beaten until foamy, the salt and cream of tartar added and the beating continued until the egg whites are stiff. Gradually fold in the flour and pour the batter over the plums.

Bake in a moderate oven (350° F.) about 45 minutes. Serve cold, plain or with whipped cream. (Serves 6)

GREEN GAGE MIXED COMPOTE

1 No. 2½ can whole apricots
1 No. 2½ can Royal Anne cherries
1 No. 2 can green gage plums
½ cup sugar
½ lemon, rind and juice
2 tbsp diced candied ginger

Drain the juice from the fruits, and add the sugar. Peel the lemon in thin strips, discarding the white pith. Add the peel, lemon juice, and ginger to the fruit juice, and bring it to the boiling point. Simmer about 10 minutes. Add it to the fruit, and chill for several hours before serving.

GREEN GAGE PLUM JAM

Wash the plums, discard the pits, but not the skins; place fruit in a preserving kettle containing enough water to cover the bottom of the kettle. Cook until tender. Measure and add half as much sugar as fruit. Boil until thick, stirring, constantly to prevent burning. Pour into hot, sterilized jars and seal.

STEWED OR POACHED PLUMS

Wash 1½ pounds of plums. Halve and remove the pits, then place in a saucepan with sugar to taste, a dash of salt and about ⅓ cup of water. Simmer gently until the fruit is tender, about 10 minutes. (Serves 4)

PLUM PUDDING. A traditional holiday pudding rich with dried fruits, but not actually containing plums.

FROZEN PLUM PUDDING

¼ cup currants
¼ cup seeded raisins
¼ cup finely shredded citron
12 maraschino cherries, chopped
3 tbsp shredded dates
3 tbsp shredded figs
½ cup maraschino cordial
3 tbsp blanched chopped almonds
1 qt chocolate ice cream

Wash currants, add raisins, and steam or simmer in small amount of water 5 minutes, or until plump; drain and cool. Marinate all other fruits in maraschino cordial 6 hours; combine fruits and nuts, and mix into ice cream. Turn into freezing trays of automatic refrigerator and freeze 2 to 4 hours, or until firm. Makes 3 pints.

STEAMED PLUM PUDDING

1½ lb seedless raisins
2 oz citron, cut fine
½ cup fruit juice
½ cup brandy
1 cup sifted flour
1 tsp salt
1 tsp ground cinnamon
½ tsp each ground cloves and allspice
½ cup sugar
1 cup molasses
1½ cups dry bread crumbs
1 cup suet, chopped fine
Grated rind 1 lemon
1 cup chopped Brazil nuts or almonds
2 tart apples, cut fine

Soak the raisins and citron overnight in the combined fruit juice and brandy. In the morning, sift together the flour, salt and spices, then blend all ingredients thoroughly. Turn into well greased molds, cover closely, and steam about 5 hours. Serve with hard or liquid sauce. (Makes 2 puddings)

PLUMP. As applied to food means round and sleek with fullness of flesh, like a soaked prune.

PLUMY. A term applied to an edible bird, meaning feathery.

PLUNGE. To suddenly put an article of food into water or other liquid.

PLYMOUTH GIN. *See* GIN.

POACH. The method of cooking food in a hot liquid which is kept just below the boiling point. Poaching is done on top of the stove. Eggs may be poached in water or milk; fish may be poached in a court bouillon (*which see*); fruits may be poached in a light sirup or wine. The temperature of the liquid is kept so that bubbles form on the bottom of the pan, but do not break the surface.

Beginners have difficulty in poaching eggs so that they come out attractively shaped. One of the simplest kitchen gadgets is an egg poacher, which is set into a pan of simmering water. The eggs are broken, one at a time, in a saucer, and then slid into the depressions in the poacher. When the eggs are done, the poacher is lifted out of the pan, the water drained out, and the eggs removed with a broad spatula.

Eggs may also be poached in a shallow pan, such as a skillet, by placing shallow metal rings, such as English muffin rings, in the water and dropping the eggs in the rings. It is also possible to use a pan of deeper water. When the water is at the proper temperature set it into a swirling motion with a spoon. Drop the egg into the center of the swirl. The action of the water will shape the white into a circular mass and by the time the water stops moving the egg will be set. Only strictly fresh eggs can be poached successfully, since the white of less fresh eggs has a tendency to run out in strings.

POCHARD. The sea duck.

POD. The pericarp, or the covering of the seed of certain plants, such as the legumes, etc. Podding means the action of removing the shells of peas, etc.

POELE. A French word meaning sautéed.

POHENICHNAYA. A very fiery Russian vodka made of wheat. It is used as an after-dinner cordial. *See* VODKA.

POI. A food of the Hawaiian islands which is made by pounding taro (*which see*) and allowing it to ferment.

POKEWEED. A strong-smelling perennial that grows from four to eight feet tall. The root and berries are poisonous, but the first thick succulent shoots that appear in the spring are a great delicacy. In color they are green to reddish purple and are fixed like asparagus (*which see*). The vegetable is popular in certain local markets such as Cincinnati and Philadelphia.

POLAND WATER. A plain, carbonic-acid water. *See also* ALKALINE AND MINERAL WATERS.

POLENTA. A mush, pudding, or porridge which may be made of various granulated cereals such as farina or cornmeal. In Italy, especially in the fall, chestnut meal is used.

CORNMEAL POLENTA

1 qt water
1 tsp salt
1 cup cornmeal

POKEWEED

2 tbsp butter or olive oil
1 cup grated cheese
2 cups tomato sauce

Place salt in water in top of double boiler and bring to boiling point. Add the cornmeal gently and cook to a mush, stirring constantly until smooth and thickened, after which it may be placed over boiling water and cooked with occasional stirring for 25 minutes. Beat in the butter or olive oil and serve with grated cheese and previously heated tomato sauce. For a more pronounced cheese flavor, an additional cup of grated cheese may be stirred into the mixture just before taking from the fire. (Serves 6 or 8)

POLLACK or **POLLOCK.** A member of the cod family approximately three feet in length and weighing up to 25 pounds. It is consumed both fresh and salted, and may be cooked by all the different methods applied to cod (*which see*). The fish is also known as green codfish. *See also* FISH.

POLLOCK MELON. A round melon grown all over the United States. It has a grayish rind and pink or green flesh. *See* MELON.

POME. A fleshy fruit such as the apple or the pear.

POMEGRANATE. While the pomegranate is by no means one of our most important fruits, it is one of the most ancient. There are frequent references to the pomegranate in the Old Testament. Homer mentioned it in the *Odyssey*, and the name appears in Sanskrit writings.

According to many authorities, the fruit is probably a native of Persia. It has been grown in Africa and throughout the East for many centuries. Today it is receiving attention as a market crop in California, Arizona, Georgia, Alabama, Nevada, Utah, and Florida.

The pomegranate is usually about the size of an orange, but somewhat flattened. It has a thin, tough, leathery rind and varies in color from pale yellow to purple. The rind is always thin, but it is lined with a layer of rag or pulp which may be relatively thick or thin. Inside this are found the large seeds coated with pulpy flesh. It is in season from October to the end of January.

Most of the fruit is harvested before it is fully ripe, because of its tendency to split. In some varieties the fruit bursts wide open on approaching maturity, while in others it cracks, both of which spoil the fruit. The fruit keeps well in cold storage, where it ripens and the quality improves, the flavor becoming richer, the rind thinner and tougher, and the amount of rag diminishes. The fruit may also be hung in a dry room, where it will keep for several months.

In buying pomegranates remember that the ideal fruit should be of medium or large size, pink or bright red. The rind should be thin and tough. There should be an abundance of bright red or crimson flesh, and a small amount of rag or pulp, for this is apt to be bitter in flavor. The seeds must be tender, easy to eat, and small in proportion to the covering of juicy matter which surrounds them. The juice should be abundant and the flesh rich, vinous, and sub-acid.

When the fruit is eaten raw, it is broken open, the kernels are dislodged, usually

POMEGRANATE

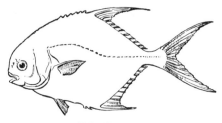

POMPANO

with a nut pick, and the flesh is sucked from the pits. These same ruby-red kernels are used as a garnish for desserts and salads. The juice may be used in beverages and ices.

From the rind is made an ink that one writer described as "unfading till the world's end." From the rind, also, is brewed a bitter draught that many an adventurer and explorer has found invaluable in combating tapeworm or dysentery.

The juice is highly prized in the making of beverages. Grenadine, indispensable in the flavoring of drinks, is made from pomegranate juice. The juice is also used in the making of gelatin desserts, icing for cakes, fruit drinks, and pudding sauces.

POMEGRANATE COCKTAIL

Boil the seeds of 1 large pomegranate with 2 slices of lemon in 3 cups of water until the water has absorbed the color and flavor from the seeds (about 15 minutes). Add ½ cup of sugar, and boil for 5 minutes more. Strain through a double thickness of cheesecloth, add 1 tablespoon of lemon juice, and chill. (Serves 6)

POMELO. A small variety of grapefruit.

POMMEL CHEESE. A soft, rich cheese, made in France. It should be served as soon as possible after purchasing.

POMPANO. The name given in the United States to several members of the *Carangidae* family, fishes which are found in the warmer coastal sea waters. The commonest and best known of the American species is the Florida pompano which enters the bays and estuaries of the South Atlantic and Gulf states to spawn in the spring. The Florida pompano is considered to be one of the most delicately flavored fish and suggests a cross between the salmon, shad, and turbot in flavor. Although it is a year-round fish, the heaviest catches are marketed in December, January, and February.

Specimens reach an average of about eighteen inches and are ovate in form and vertically flattened. The color is a strikingly beautiful silvery blue.

The various methods of preparing flat fish such as carp, sturgeon, turbot, plaice, and sole may be adapted to the pompano, as well as those for small salmon. There are also a number of special methods of fixing this delicious fish.

POMPANO COOKED IN WHITE WINE

1 pompano, weighing about 1 lb
1 medium-sized onion
Salt
Whole peppercorns
Several sprigs of fresh dill
White wine

Place a rack in the kettle. Place the sprigs of dill in the cavity of the fish and lay it on the rack. Add white wine just to the level of the rack. Add the onion, left whole, salt, and peppercorns. Steam the fish for 40 minutes. Remove from the pan, discard the dill, and skin the fish. Serve with the following sauce:

2 tbsp freshly ground horseradish
3 tbsp unsweetened whipped cream

Mix together and serve with the pompano. (Serves 4)

POMPANO PAPILLOTTE

1 large pompano
Salt, pepper and lemon juice
1 cup dry white wine
1 medium-sized onion
½ tbsp butter
6 mushrooms
1 cup heavy cream

Wipe, split and bone the fish. Place in a heavy, well buttered frying pan, season with salt, pepper and lemon juice and pour the wine over and around. Bake in a moderately hot oven (350°–375° F.) 10 minutes. Remove from the oven and keep hot while preparing the stuffing.

For this, mince the onion and cook for a minute or two in the butter until soft but not browned. Add the mushrooms, finely chopped, and cook five minutes longer. Pour over this the liquid from the pan in which the pompano was baked, stirring constantly while pouring. Simmer five minutes, add the cream and simmer 10 minutes longer. Now take a sheet of heavy brown paper, cut into the shape of a large heart, butter it well and place the fish on half of the paper, flesh side up. Cover with with the stuffing and fold the paper over, bringing the two edges together and sealing by folding the ends very tightly, but allowing a space around the fish. Place in a generously buttered shallow pan and bake in a very hot oven (450° F.) for five minutes. (Serves 6)

PONT L'EVEQUE CHEESE. A semi-hard fermented cheese made in the Pont l'Eveque district of Normandy. It is made in small molds about four inches square and one and a half inches thick. Yellow coloring and a good deal of salt is added during the making. It is a cheddar-type cheese, depending upon the natural rennin for its maturation; no mold is added to it. It varies in quality depending on the quality of the milks used.

PONY. A very small drinking glass of stem shape used to serve brandy and other liqueuers (see GLASSWARE). The term is generally applied to any glass that is smaller than the one normally used to serve a given beverage, as, for example, today's "short" beer. It is also given to a unit of measurement in drink mixing derived from these smaller glasses (see WEIGHTS AND MEASURES).

POP. A colloquial name for any non-intoxicating, effervescent beverage, given because of the characteristic sound made by a cork as it is withdrawn or expelled from a bottle that has gas pressure inside. The term has persisted, though corks have been largely supplanted by crimped bottle caps. See also SODA POP and SOFT DRINK.

POPCORN. Special corn for popping may be bought in packages or cans, or in the country it may be freshly shucked from the ear. Packaged popcorn is often rather dry and does not pop out in full white fluffy bits, but this condition is quickly remedied by sprinkling the corn with a little water before popping.

When ready to pop the corn, cover the bottom of the utensil you choose (which may be a wire shaker, a frying pan or heavy saucepan or an electric popper) and shake it constantly over a slow steady heat until the corn pops. If using a frying pan or saucepan be sure to have a close fitting cover. As the corn is popped, empty it into a large bowl (warmed) and pour melted butter over it. Toss with a spoon or fork to coat all the corn and sprinkle generously with salt.

Popcorn may be served as a cold cereal with sugar and cream; a few grains may also be used as a topping for cream soups in place of croutons.

MOLASSES POPCORN BALLS

2 qt freshly popped corn
1 cup broken nut-meats (optional)
2 cups brown sugar
1 cup water
2 tbsp cider vinegar
Dash of salt

Have the corn popped before preparing the sirup, and if the nut-meats are used, stir them into the popcorn. Boil sugar, water, vinegar and salt together to the hard crack stage (300° F.), stirring only until the sugar is dissolved. Pour in a slow stream over the corn, mixing and stirring it in with a heavy spoon. As soon as cool enough to handle, oil the hands lightly and form the mixture into small balls or flat patties. Wrap in waxed paper when cool.

SUGARED POPCORN

2 qt freshly popped corn
1½ cups sugar
1 cup water
Dash of salt

Have the corn popped before preparing the sirup. Boil the sugar, water and salt together to the firm ball stage (242° F.). Remove at once from the fire and stir

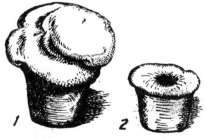

POPOVER   1. Good   2. Bad

until the mixture just begins to grain around the edges. Pour over the corn and stir quickly and thoroughly until each grain is coated with the sugar. If desired the sirup may be colored red or green with a few drops of vegetable coloring.

POPOVER. It is rather difficult to describe this delectable American creation. It is a very light muffin which rises high above the top of the pan. The thickness of the batter should be that of rich cream. Too thick a batter will keep the popovers from fully rising. The best pans to use for them are heavy, old-fashioned iron or earthenware ones. Modern oven-proof glass or heavy aluminum pans are also good but they must be heavy and of the right shape—higher than their width. The pans must be generously greased and should also be sizzling hot when the batter is poured into them. Fill them about half full—they should then rise well above the tops of the pans. Have the oven hot at the beginning of the baking (425°–450° F.), and after 15 minutes lower the heat to 375° F. for an additional 15 to 20 minutes.

POPOVERS

1 cup sifted flour
½ tsp salt
1 large egg
1 cup milk

Sift together the flour and salt. Beat the eggs slightly, and add the milk. Then combine the dry and liquid ingredients, beating only enough to make a smooth batter. Turn into the prepared pans and bake as directed. (Makes 8)

POPPER. Any device made to cook popcorn, *which see.* There are two types of corn poppers in general use. One consists simply of an enclosed wire basket at the end of a fairly long handle. A small quantity of popcorn is placed inside the basket and shaken gently over a fire, gas burner, or any other heat source, the basket being covered to keep the kernels from flying out as they explode.

Another common device consists of a covered metal drum or pan set over an electric heating element. Poppers of this sort have a crank-turned wire or some similar device that stirs the popcorn, keeping the individual kernels from sticking to the bottom and burning.

POPPY SEEDS. Tiny black poppy seeds come from a variety of the poppy plant that differs from that which yields opium. The seeds are so tiny that there are, according to spice tradesmen, more than 900,000 to a pound. They have a distinctive, appealing flavor with virtually no fragrance.

Because the seeds tend to stimulate the appetite they are excellent in canapés. You may sprinkle them over the tops of the canapés or mix them with canapé spreads.

Baked poppy seeds have a delightful nutty flavor and are, consequently, very often used in baking rolls, cookies, breads, and cakes. Add a bit of cold water to a beaten egg yolk, brush this over the baked products, and then sprinkle with poppy seeds.

In this country poppy seeds are most often used as a topping for baked products, but in some European cookery they are used as the base of rich pastry fillings. Try mixing ½ cup each of sugar and milk with ½ pound of poppy seeds. Boil the mixture for about ten minutes while stirring constantly. Allow it to cool, spread it over the dough, dot with butter, and bake. You may experiment with poppy seed fillings to suit your taste. Other recommended ingredients are honey, sirup, and ground nut meats. Determine your own preferred combinations and proportions.

In addition to their use in baking and in appetizers, poppy seeds are sometimes used to give a pleasant flavor to noodles, pickles, preserves, and beverages.

POPPY SEED COOKIES

3 cups all-purpose flour
¾ tsp soda
½ tsp salt
¼ cup butter
¼ cup shortening
1 cup sugar
1 egg, beaten
½ cup buttermilk
2 tbsp lemon juice
2 tsp grated lemon rind
¼ cup whole poppy seeds

Sift the flour; measure and resift 3 times with soda and salt. Cream the butter with shortening until smooth and soft; blend in sugar gradually. Add egg, beat until fluffy. Add flour mixture in 3 portions alternately with buttermilk, beginning and ending with flour and beating well after each addition. Add lemon juice, rind, and poppy seeds, mixing thoroughly. Chill dough at least 1 hour, then roll out thin on a floured board. Cut out, and transfer to lightly greased baking sheets. Bake in a moderately hot oven (425° F.) for 6 to 8 minutes, or until delicately browned. Remove to cake racks to cool. (Makes 4 to 6 dozen, depending on size)

POPPY SEED OIL. An oil obtained from the poppy seeds. See OIL.

PORCELAIN. The finest type of ceramic material, it is subject to exquisite coloring and extensive ornamentation. Because of its great cost, it is usually confined to decorative rather than functional uses, but may be encountered in dinner services, etc. See CERAMICS; see also DISHES.

PORCUPINE. The porcupine, sometimes called quill-pig or hedge hog, is a large, sluggish rodent and is found in the forests of North America north of the 40° line, excepting in the Rocky Mountains where he ranges as far south as the Mexican border.

Although he attains a total length of up to 40 inches and a weight of from 15 to 40 pounds, his actual bulk is not as much as it would seem at first glance. This is due to his pelage of long, soft, brownish or slaty black hairs from which protrude the lighter colored quills or spines that are porky's defensive and offensive weapons.

While the old story that the porcupine can "shoot" his quills at his enemies has been exploded as pure bunk, he is still a formidable opponent when at close quarters and placed on the defensive. His quills are attached very loosely to his skin and, with a flick of his tail, he can bury barbed quills in anything soft that they touch. To attempt to grab him is to turn one's hand into a pincushion. The porcupine's habit is to turn his back on his enemy and wait for the latter to attack. When dogs or inexperienced wild carnivores attack, they usually retreat with a mouthful of quills that may cause them to starve to death.

To satisfy his appetite for salt the porcupine will chew up a shirt or other garment that has dried, salty perspiration on it. He has even been known to chew off the butt of a gun for the same reason. The camper's ham, bacon, and salt pork are considered delicacies by the animal, and a cake of soap is an acceptable tidbit. Ordinarily, he manages to soothe the pangs of hunger by nibbling on soft shoots and buds of trees and shrubs. Sometimes he will eat so much bark from a tree that it is girdled; this kills the tree—but not the porcupine.

Although his eating habits cause porky to be considered a minor nuisance, in some states he is protected by law. For the porcupine is probably the only fair sized mammal that can be killed easily by a blow from a club. This fact makes him a good source of emergency rations for any unarmed person who is lost in the woods. But, however grateful a starving man might be to see a porcupine waddle into view, his flesh is not generally accepted as a delicacy.

If ever the need—and opportunity— arises to make a meal of a porcupine, the hunter should procure a club and approach the animal cautiously so as not to frighten it. Getting within range is not too difficult to achieve; this rodent seems to be some- what near sighted and he doesn't pay too much attention to cautiously moving objects. But, if he is startled by a sudden motion or sound, porky will usually head for a tree. He is an excellent climber and will quickly find his way to branches that are too flimsy to support the weight of a man.

When proximity is achieved, the animal can be stunned by a sharp blow to the nose, and a couple more to the skull will finish him. Skinning and dressing the animal requires caution if the hunter is to come off unpunctured. The directions should be followed carefully.

PREPARING THE PORCUPINE

With the club turn the body on its back. Press the point of your knife deeply through

the lower jaw so that the brain is pene- trated. Cut the throat; then hang up the body by one hind leg until bleeding ceases.

The next step is to skin the porcupine. With your knife make a long incision in the outer layer of skin on the un-quilled belly. Do not cut through the inner skin, or abdominal wall. Insert your fingers into the opening and pull and cut the skin loose from the carcass. (This is a slippery job. Rub a little corn meal, or even sandy soil on your hands; it will help you to get a grip on skin and carcass). Be sure to work from the inside of the skin so that the quills do not touch your hands. Sever the bones of the tail, feet, and neck. Cut away the glands of reproduction and the anal region. (This is important; if it is not done thoroughly the meat will have an objectionable flavor.) Now draw the carcass away from the skin; the append- ages are left attached.

Now the carcass may be disembowled— or this operation may be accomplished at the time of making the first incision. However, the job is less messy if this method is followed. Be sure that all internal glands and organs are removed.

Wash the carcass, disjoint the legs, and cut up the body as you would a rabbit, *which see.* Although not absolutely neces- sary, the meat will be more tender if it is parboiled. The pieces may be stuck on a pointed stick and broiled over an open fire. (*See* CAMP COOKERY.)

In skinning a porcupine you may be stuck by some of the quills. These should be removed from the wound immediately as they tend to work farther into the flesh. If the penetration is slight a good tug will pull them out. If they are in deeply, work some oil or fat of any sort into the quills as closely as possible to the skin. (Melted fat from the carcass will do.) The oil softens the barbs and allows them to be removed more easily, and less painfully.

PORGY. The original name of this fish was "scup" which was given to it by the American Indians. The porgy is common all along the Atlantic coast and resembles the sheepshead. It is a good food fish, and may be prepared in the same manner as catfish or sheepshead. *See also* FISH.

PORK. The pig has been used for food since time immemorial. Chinese legend, according to Charles Lamb, tells of the origin of roast pork in the accidental death

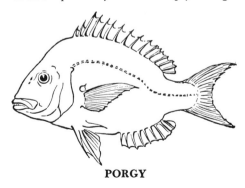

PORGY

of a pig in a burning house. An old rustic custom of Lorraine concerned the butchering of a pig. The daughter of the house sent to her betrothed the foot of the pig tied up with blue ribbons and bay leaves as a symbol of her love. On the other hand, if she wished to indicate her lack of interest, she sent the tail of the pig tied up with a pickle, the symbol of indifference and mockery.

The popular belief that pigs impart an unpleasant flavor to their flesh by rolling in mire is entirely without foundation. The pig is actually a very clean animal, and under modern methods of raising hogs for market, there is very little chance of the flesh being contaminated.

Pork is, however, a source of infection with trichinosis, a disease resulting from infection with trichina worms. The only sure prevention against infection is the thorough cooking of pork, and for this reason pork should never be eaten raw or partially cooked. It must be well done to be absolutely safe. Infection with trichinosis is very widespread, and undoubtedly thousands of people are infected without realizing it. In its acute stage the illness resembles typhoid fever, "intestinal flu," rheumatism, or any one of a number of other diseases. The parasites eventually work into the muscles, particularly of the chest and abdomen, and the acute stage subsides, to be followed by subsequent period of reduced health which will probably continue for the rest of the victim's life. Depending on the extent of the infection, the symptoms may be mild or aggravated, but there is no known cure for the disease.

Government Grades

Pork is not definitely graded by federal standards as are beef, veal, lamb, and mutton. The grades are largely a matter of utility and weight, with considerable difference in quality resulting from a difference in feeding the animals. A hog that has been fed on corn and alfalfa yields a firm carcass. Its flesh is pink and fine grained, and the fat is firm and white. The cuts trim out cleanly, and the hams have a proper depth of fat and flesh. This is the kind of hog that is most often found in the Chicago packing houses. On the other hand, a hog that has been fed on slops, nuts, and acorns yields a soft carcass that no amount of chilling will firm. The fat is flabby and brownish, and the flesh lacks firmness and fine grain. Such hogs are most often found in the southern markets, while northern markets prefer the corn-fed hogs. This is not intended to imply that such hogs are inferior.

Hogs are divided into classes, depending on the cuts which will be the chief product. Loin hogs and packing hogs have a considerable width of back in proportion to their length, and have smooth meaty hams and shoulders. Bacon hogs are just the opposite, having long deep sides and narrow backs, indicating less development of fat. Heavy loin hogs are heavy hogs of the highest quality. They produce heavy loins for which there has been a decreasing demand over the years as American families now desire smaller cuts of meat than formerly. The hams from such hogs are usually skinned to reduce the weight; and the shoulders are cut into calas, butts, and plates. Butcher, or light loin hogs furnish the greatest percentage of retail fresh pork cuts. Their quality is as good as the heavier animals, but the size of the cuts is more in keeping with the demand. Packing hogs are deficient in quality, and not ordinarily marketed as fresh pork. Hogs of the bacon type are becoming the most popular, because of the public demand for lean pork, in small-sized cuts. Shipper pigs and roasting pigs are marketed whole, the former mainly for export, and the latter for sale as "suckling pigs" for the holiday trade and other specialized markets.

Food Value

	Wa-ter	Food Energy	Pro-tein	Fat	Car-bohy-drates	Cal-cium	Phos-phorus	Iron	Vit. A Value	Thia-mine	Ribo-flavin	Nia-cin	Ascor-bic Acid
Fat	35	534	9.8	55	0	6	106	1.5	0	.62	.12	2.6	0
Medium	42	453	11.9	45	0	7	128	1.8	0	.75	.15	3.2	0
Thin	50	371	14.1	35	0	8	152	2.1	0	.89	.18	3.8	0

The quality of fresh pork can be told by four characteristics. The skin of good quality pork is smooth, white, thin, and flexib.e. The fat is firm and white and evenly distributed over the body. The flesh should be fine grained, bright light red in color, and firm in texture. The bones should be small in size, red and soft.

PREPARATION FOR MARKET

In the packing house, hogs are slaughtered and bled, and then scalded to remove the hair from the skin. Further operations of polishing and singeing are necessary to completely remove all of the hair. The head is then partially severed and the animal slit open along the underside. Government inspectors examine the internal organs for any sign of disease. The hog is then eviscerated, and the edible organs separated out. The carcass is then braced open and the leaf fat removed. The leaf, which is a thin layer of tissue heavily deposited with fat of very fine quality, lies against the abdominal cavity on either side. This fat is pulled out by hand, readily coming away from the carcass, and goes for the manufacture of lard, *which see*. The hog is then split in two down the backbone. Ordinarily half of the spinal bones remain in each half. However, for certain cuts, primarily for the export trade, the spine is removed, and this is done at this time.

The hams are then "faced," an operation which consists of removing a strip of fat and skin about an inch wide from the flank side of the ham and about three inches wide from the cushion side. Hams chill much better when treated this way, and present a more attractive appearance. The fat trimmed off, and any loose fat scraped from inside the carcass is sent to the rendering tanks. The head is then removed from the hog and the carcass goes into the chill room.

Fresh pork must be handled rapidly and under very sanitary conditions to remain wholesome. Bruises and other injury rapidly spoil and meat showing such injury is discarded. If the fresh pork is not to be marketed immediately, it cannot be kept without being frozen. Ordinarily it is not kept in the chill room more than forty-eight hours, after which time it begins to deteriorate. At the packing houses, the cuts which are intended for curing are sent to the curing cellars and placed in cure the same day. Fresh pork is handled equally fast. Loins, butts, and shoulders are usually wrapped individually in oiled paper and packed in crates or barrels. Spareribs are packed in barrels or boxes, and tenderloins are usually packed in tin pails. All such fresh pork must be kept under constant refrigeration to prevent spoiling.

The thawing of frozen pork is just as careful an operation as the preliminary freezing. It may be done by returning the meat to the chill room where it is kept at a temperature of 34° to 38° F., which gives the best results. Sometimes in order to thaw it more quickly, it is done in a steam-heated room at a temperature of about 80° F., but this process requires constant watching lest the meat become overheated.

Pork is cut into an infinite variety of cuts, and new cuts are constantly being worked out to suit new trends in buying. Some of the more common cuts are:

Rough side. The entire side of a hog carcass as it comes to the cutting floor. It is not marketed as such.

Ham. The most posterior part of the side, including part of the pelvic bones and the leg above the hock.

Shoulder. The most anterior portion of the side, including the greater part of the shoulder blade and the foreleg above the knee.

Short rib. The rough short rib is the rough side from which the ham and shoulder have been removed. The regular short rib has had the backbone removed and the pelvic bone and breastbone cut even with the side. The extra short rib has had the loin removed.

The clear. The long clear is a side from which the ham, jowl, and all bones have been removed, the flank cut straight, and the foreshank cut off close to the breast. The extra long clear has had the long loin removed. The short clear is the same as the long clear, with the shoulder removed. The extra short clear has also had the loin removed.

Loin. The muscular part of the back extending from the ham to the shoulder and containing the ribs and the backbone.

Fat back. The fat portion of the back lying outside the loin and above the belly and extending from ham to shoulder.

The *rib back* is the fat back and loin together.

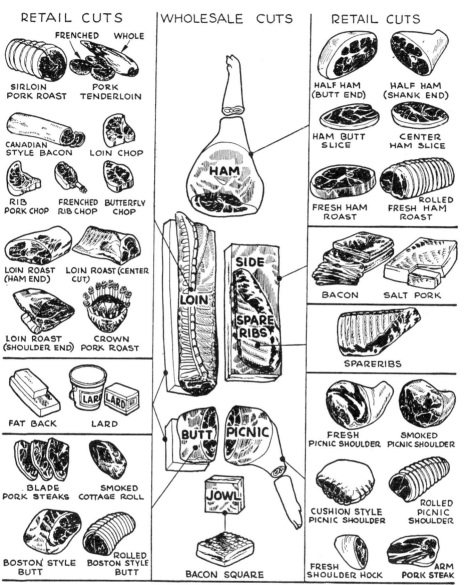

PORK CHART, showing principal cuts

The *belly* may be either a rib belly, which includes the lower ends of the ribs, or a clear belly, which has had the ribs removed.

Spareribs. That part of the ribs lying below the loin and attached to the rib belly.

Pigs' feet. The extremities of the legs below the knee and hock.

Cala or Picnic "hams." The lower part of the shoulder cut off just above the shoulder joint and including the lower extremity of the shoulder blade, and all the arm bones to the knee. They are trimmed and rounded to resemble a small ham. They are also smoked like ham.

The *plate* is the fat portion of the shoulder above the cala and outside the butt.

The *butt* is the lean portion of the shoulder above the cala.

The *jowl* is the fat portion lying in front of the shoulder and outside the jaw.

Retail Cuts

Wholesale Cut	Retail Cut	Cooking Method
Ham	Half Ham, Butt or Shank end	Bake or Simmer
	Half Slice	Broil or Panbroil
	Fresh Roast	Roast
	Rolled Fresh Roast	Roast
Loin	Sirloin Roast	Roast
	Tenderloin	Broil or Braise
	Canadian Style Bacon	Broil
	Loin Chop	Broil or Braise
	Rib Chop	Broil or Braise
	Butterfly Chop	Broil or Braise
	Loin Roast—Ham End	Roast
	Center Cut	Roast
	Shoulder End	Roast
	Crown Roast	Roast
Fat Back	Salt Pork	Broil or for Seasoning
Side	Bacon	Broil or Panbroil
	Salt Pork	Broil or Panbroil or for Seasoning
Spareribs	Spareribs	Simmer, Braise, or Roast
Butt	Blade Steak	Braise
	Smoked Cottage Roll	Bake or Panbroil
	Boston Style Butt	Roast
	Rolled Boston Butt	Roast
Picnic Shoulder	Fresh Picnic Shoulder	Roast
	Smoked Picnic Shoulder	Bake or Simmer
	Cushion Style Shoulder	Roast
	Rolled Shoulder	Roast
	Fresh Hock	Roast
	Arm Steak	Braise
Jowl	Bacon Square	Panbroil or for Seasoning

Variety Meats

Brains. A great delicacy which may be prepared in various ways. *See* Brains.

Ears. A great delicacy in the south, which is seldom seen in the north.

Feet. Often pickled, and cooked and served with sauerkraut.

Head. Generally used to make Head-cheese, *which see.*

Heart. A pork heart weighs from ¾ to one pound and can be cooked in any of the ways suitable for the heart of other animals. *See* Heart.

Kidneys. Pork kidneys are not ordinarily tender and mildly enough flavored to be broiled. They should be braised, or cooked in water. *See* Kidney.

Knuckles. Pig's knuckles are the ankle-joints, which make delicious, nourishing, and economical meals. See the recipes below for suggestions.

Liver. Pork liver contains the higest per-centage of iron of any liver, and for this reason, and for its generally lower price, it is the most economical buy in liver. *See* Liver.

Tongue. Pork tongue is usually sold pickled, salted, or smoked, and comes ready to serve. *See* Tongue.

Hints on Preparation

Pork must always be thoroughly cooked. This means that the pork will have lost its pink color and be white. Don't eat pink pork. Thick cuts of pork will need to be cooked a minimum of 30 minutes to the pound, smaller cuts proportionately long. If a meat thermometer is used, it should register 185° F. in order for the pork to be safe.

Pork should be cooked more slowly than beef. Because of the great amount of fat, it is practically self-basting, and no additional fat needs to be added during the cooking process. Pork is sometimes considered indigestible, but this is because of the high fat content. If it is properly cooked, most of the excess fat will have cooked out, and the moist tender meat is just as digestible as any other kind. If pork chops are to be broiled, they should be done rather more slowly than lamb or veal chops because they are inclined to become dry if the fat is cooked out of them too quickly.

Directions for preparing the special cuts of pork such as bacon, ham, and spareribs are given under their own headings. Many cuts of pork, such as hams, shoulders, tenderloins, etc. are available either smoked or fresh. Recipes using fresh pork are given under this heading; those for smoked hams and shoulders are given under ham, *which see.* If the instructions for cooking pork are carefully followed, it will be found perfectly digestible.

Pork should be cooked to an internal temperature of 185° F. if a meat thermometer is used. Otherwise, the times given in the chart below should be scrupulously followed. Pork should be broiled at a temperature of 350° F. If the broiler has no regulator, this temperature is arrived at by turning the flame on high and placing the broiler rack so that the meat will be 3 inches from the flame.

CRANBERRY PORK CHOPS

6 pork chops
½ tsp salt
4 cups cranberries, ground
¾ cup honey
½ tsp cloves

Brown chops quickly on both sides in hot frying pan and sprinkle with salt; place three chops in greased baking dish. Combine cranberries, honey and cloves, spread ½ over chops in baker. Arrange remaining 3 chops on top and cover with remaining cranberry mixture. Cover and bake in moderate oven (350° F.) about 1 hour. (Serves 6)

CROWN ROAST OF PORK WITH PRUNE DRESSING

Crown roast of pork (12 ribs)
Salt and pepper
1 cup prunes

COOKING TIMES AND TEMPERATURE

Cut	Size	Method	Temperature	Time (minutes)
Chops	1 inch	Broil or Panbroil	350° F.	20–25
		Braise	Sauté for Then simmer for	10 40–55
	2 inch	Braise	Sauté for Then simmer for	10 45–60
		Bake	300°–350° F.	30–45
Loin				
Center Cut	3–4 lb.	Roast	350° F.	35–40 per lb.
End Cuts	3–4 lb.	Roast	350° F.	45–50 per lb.
Crown Roast or entire Loin	12–15 lb.	Roast	350° F.	15–20 per lb.
Shoulder (fresh)				
Whole	12–14 lb.	Roast	350° F.	30–35 per lb.
Rolled	4–6 lb.	Roast	350° F.	40–45 per lb.
Cushion	4–6 lb.	Roast	350° F.	34–40 per lb.
Steaks	¾ inch	Braise	Sauté for Then simmer for	10 30–40
Fresh Ham	10–12 lb.	Roast	350° F.	30–35 per lb.
Fresh Butt	4–6 lb.	Roast	350° F.	40–45 per lb.
Tenderloin	¾–1 lb.	Braise	Sauté for Then simmer for	15 30–45
Sliced (fillets)	½ inch	Braise	Sauté for Then simmer for	10 20
Spareribs	2–3 lb.	Roast	350° F.	60
		Braise	Sauté for Then simmer for	15 75
Double (stuffed)	4–6 lb.	Roast	350° F.	90

5 cups cubed bread
2 onions, diced
1½ cups diced celery
1 green pepper, minced
Water or stock

Have the butcher trim and prepare the roast. Season with salt and pepper and roast in a moderate oven (350° F.) for 1½ hours. Remove from the oven, fill the cavity with dressing, and return to the oven. Roast 1 hour longer, basting frequently with a little stock, water, or the drippings from the poasting pan.

Prune Dressing

Simmer the prunes in water to cover for about 10 minutes. Remove the pits and cut the prunes into small pieces. Combine with the bread, onion, celery, green pepper, and salt and pepper. Moisten with stock or water and blend thoroughly. Any dressing which does not fit into the roast may be baked in a separate pan or in muffin tins and served with the roast.

FRENCHED PORK TENDERLOINS

Have the butcher cut 2 pork tenderloins into thick crosswise slices; then pound them to flatten until they are half their original thickness. Sauté in a little butter or drippings, turning to brown both sides. Then cover and cook slowly for about 15 minutes longer. Season with salt and pepper when about half done. Remove to a hot platter and keep warm. Add 1½ tablespoons of flour to the fat remaining in the pan, and stir constantly while it cooks and browns. Stir in gradually 1½ cups of water. Bring to the boiling point, stirring constantly, and let simmer 3 or 4 minutes, until the sauce is thickened. Pour over the meat and serve immediately. Fried apple rings are a good accompaniment for this dish. (Serves 4)

PHILADELPHIA SCRAPPLE

1¼ lb lean pork
½ lb pork liver
Water
½ lb corn meal
1 tbsp salt
½ tsp pepper
2 tbsp onion juice

Simmer the pork and liver in water to cover until tender. Drain and reserve the the liquor in which the meat was cooked. Grind the meat and liver very fine. Measure the liquor and add enough water to make 2 quarts. Bring the liquor to a boil and gradually stir in the cornmeal. Cook until thick, stirring constantly. Add the meat and seasonings and cook together about 15 minutes longer, stirring constantly. Then cook 30 minutes longer, stirring occasionally. If a double boiler is used, the pan may be placed over hot water for this last 30 minutes, in which case no stirring is necessary. Rinse a bread pan in cold water and shake dry. Pour in the cornmeal mixture and allow to cool. To serve scrapple, slice the loaf and fry like mush.

PIG'S KNUCKLES DINNER

5 medium-sized pig's knuckles (about 3 lb)
2 medium-sized onions, sliced
2 large bay leaves
6 sprigs parsley
4 sprigs green celery tops
1 small clove garlic, crushed
⅛ tsp thyme
⅛ tsp each allspice and sage
3 whole cloves
8 whole peppercorns, bruised
2 tsp salt

Scald the knuckles in boiling water, then scrub with a brush in lukewarm water. Remove any hairs by singeing. Place the knuckles in a large stew pan with all remaining ingredients, first tieing together the bay leaves, parsley, and celery tops. Cover with water to an inch above the contents of the pan. Bring slowly to boiling point and boil five minutes, then reduce the heat and simmer (covered) for 2 hours, skimming occasionally. When the meat is ready to fall from the bones, lift out the knuckles and drain well. Serve with mustard sauce and red cabbage, or sauerkraut, and steamed potatoes. (Serves 6)

FRIED PIG'S KNUCKLES

4 pig's knuckles
1 qt boiling water, or vegetable stock
2 large bay leaves
6 sprigs parsley

4 sprigs green celery tops
1 tsp salt
6 whole peppercorns, bruised
3 whole cloves
1 clove garlic
1 large onion, chopped or thinly sliced
¼ cup flour
2 eggs, well beaten
1 cup bread crumbs
¼ cup oil

Have the butcher split each knuckle into four pieces. Wash, scald and singe, removing any hair which may adhere. Place in a stew pan, cover with the water or stock. Add all the ingredients, including the onion, tying together the bay leaves, parsley, and celery tops. Simmer two to two and a half hours or until tender. Remove the knuckles from the broth and cool. Reserve the broth for soup or sauce. Separate the meat from the bones and dip the meat first into the flour then into the well beaten eggs and, finally, into the bread crumbs. Sauté in the oil about ten minutes or until golden brown. Serve with hot sauerkraut, hot cole slaw, hot mashed potatoes, or hot shredded red cabbage cooked with apple, pouring ¼ cup of melted butter, blended with the juice of 1 lemon and 1 tablespoon of minced parsley, over the knuckles. (Serves 6)

PIG'S KNUCKLES AND SAUERKRAUT

3 lb (about 5) pig's knuckles
2 lb raw sauerkraut
1½ qt cold water
2 large bay leaves
6 sprigs fresh parsley
6 sprigs green celery tops
1 tbsp caraway seeds, optional

Wash, scald, and singe the knuckles. Then simmer the knuckles, sauerkraut, and water for 3½ hours, with the bay leaves tied with the parsley and celery tops (these last may be omitted if desired). If caraway seeds are used, add them to the boiling kettle 15 minutes before serving. Drain, reserving the broth for soup. Serve with mashed potatoes. (Serves 6)

PORK AND APPLE PIE

1½ lb pork shoulder
1 tbsp flour

1 tsp sage
½ tsp salt
2 tbsp finely chopped salt pork or bacon
3 medium-sized cooking apples
1 cup water
Baking powder biscuit dough

Cut the pork into small dice. Blend the flour with the sage and salt, and roll the pork in this mixture. Try out the salt pork or bacon and sauté the diced pork in the fat, turning to sear all sides. Place the meat in a casserole. Pare and core the apples and slice them thickly. Place on top of the meat. Pour in the water. Cover with biscuit dough (which see) which has been rolled out to fit. Make three or four slits to allow steam to escape. Bake in a hot oven (450° F.) for 15 minutes. Then turn the oven to 350° F. and continue to cook for 1 hour. (Serves 4 to 6)

PORK AND APPLE CASSEROLE

Place a layer of apple sauce or very thinly sliced, pared, cored apples in the bottom of a buttered baking dish. Cover with diced or sliced cold cooked pork and stuffing. Add leftover brown gravy, thinned with a little water or stock. Taste for seasoning, and add salt and pepper if needed. Top with a layer of leftover mashed sweet potatoes and turnips. Dot with butter and bake in a moderate oven (350° F.) for 25 to 30 minutes, or until the contents of the casserole are thoroughly heated and the crust is delicately browned.

PORK CHOPS BOLOGNESE

4 thin pork chops
Juice of 1 lemon
Salt and pepper
1 egg, slightly beaten
Fine breadcrumbs
3 tbsp drippings
¼ cup shaved Gruyére cheese
1 cup stock

Trim the pork chops, removing any excess fat. Put the juice of the lemon, well seasoned with salt and pepper, into a dish and marinate the chops for several hours, turning once or twice. Drain the cutlets well, dip in the beaten egg and then in breadcrumbs. Heat the drippings in a heavy skillet and add the chops. Brown well on one side and then turn over. On the browned side heap the cheese which should be slivered, not grated. Add the stock carefully, and place the skillet in a moderate oven (350° F.) to continue cooking. The chops are done when they are thoroughly cooked and the cheese is melted, about 15 or 20 minutes. Serve from the baking dish, with the pan gravy. (Serves 4)

PORK CHOP CASSEROLE

4 loin chops
4 tbsp chopped onion
4 tbsp chopped celery
2 tbsp chopped green pepper
2/3 tsp salt
1/3 tsp pepper
1 cup water
3 tbsp catsup

Sear the chops on both sides in a hot skillet which has a cover. Add all the remaining ingredients, cover tightly, and cook very gently until the chops are tender (about 30 minutes). Serve with mashed potatoes or buttered noodles. (Serves 4)

PORK CHOPS CASSEROLE, COTTAGE STYLE

6 pork chops
2 tbsp flour
1 tsp salt
1/3 tsp pepper
1 tbsp minced parsley
2 cups sliced raw potatoes
2 cups hot milk

Brown the chops on both sides in a hot frying pan. Grease a deep casserole and place 3 of the chops in the casserole. Combine the flour, salt, pepper, and parsley, and sprinkle half of this over the 3 chops. Cover with half of the potatoes. Repeat the layers and pour in the milk. Cover and bake in a moderate oven (350° F.) for 1½ hours, uncovering for the last 20 minutes to brown the top. (Serves 6)

PORK CHOPS CHARCUTIERE

6 pork chops
Salt and pepper
2 tbsp drippings

Melt the drippings in a heavy skillet and add the chops. Brown well on each side,

and season with salt and pepper. Then cover the pan and cook very slowly for 20 to 25 minutes, until the chops are well done. Then serve with the following sauce:

1 large onion, chopped
2 tbsp lard
1 tsp flour
½ cup dry white wine
1 cup stock
1 tsp dry mustard
2 tbsp sliced gherkins
Salt
4 or 5 peppercorns

Melt the lard in a small saucepan and cook the chopped onion, stirring constantly, until golden brown. Sprinkle in the flour and continue to stir until the flour browns. Gradually add the stock and wine, stirring constantly. Add a dash of salt and the peppercorns. Bring to a boil, stirring well, and skim off the froth. Cover the pan and simmer gently for 30 minutes. Strain the sauce, and return to the saucepan. Add the mustard and gherkins and reheat just to the boiling point. Pour over the chops and serve immediately. (Serves 6)

PORK CHOPS FLORENTINE

6 shoulder pork chops
Flour
Salt and pepper
2 cups hot cooked spinach
2 cups medium white sauce
2 egg yolks
Grated cheese

Season the flour with salt and pepper and dredge the chops. Sear the chops in a hot frying pan on both sides until well browned. Reduce the heat, cover the pan, and cook gently until the meat is tender, about 20 minutes. Grease a shallow baking dish. Season the spinach with salt and pepper and a dash of nutmeg and place in the bottom of the baking dish. Place the chops on top of the spinach. Beat the egg yolks and stir into the white sauce. Pour over the chops. Sprinkle the top with grated cheese. Place in a hot oven (450° F.) or under the broiler flame until the cheese melts and browns slightly. Serve very hot. (Serves 6)

PORK IN SOUR CREAM

2 pork tenderloins
4 tbsp drippings
½ cup sour cream
Salt and pepper
1 tbsp flour
1 tbsp chopped capers
2 tbsp tomato paste
2 tbsp stock

Cut the tenderloins into thin slices slightly on the diagonal. Heat the drippings in a saucepan and brown the slices of pork, turning to brown on both sides. Cover the pan and simmer very gently for 10 minutes. Add the sour cream and continue to simmer for 15 minutes longer, seasoning with salt and pepper. Remove the pork slices to a hot dish and keep warm. Stir the flour into the sauce and add the other ingredients. Mix thoroughly and bring just to a boil. Pour the sauce over the meat and serve immediately. (Serves 4)

PORK STEW WITH SWEET POTATO BISCUITS

3 cups cubed leftover pork
3 tbsp drippings or margarine
2 cups stock (or water and bouillon cubes)
¼ tsp salt
⅛ tsp sage
Dash of pepper
1 cup small boiled onions
1½ tbsp quick-cooking tapioca

Cut the pork into 1-inch cubes and brown in the drippings. Add the stock and seasonings and simmer, covered, for 10 minutes. Add the onions and tapioca and bring to a quick boil, stirring constantly. Cook until tapioca is clear and the sauce thickened. Serve very hot, arranging sweet potato biscuits (see SWEET POTATO) around the dish. (Serves 4)

PORK TAMALE PIE

2 lb diced pork shoulder
1 diced onion
½ cup diced celery
1 green pepper, diced
1 clove garlic, minced
1 cup tomato juice
4 cups hot water
2 tsp chili powder
1 tsp salt
2 tbsp flour
3 tbsp cold water
2 canned pimientos, sliced
1 cup sliced olives
4 cups cornmeal mush
2 tbsp butter
2 eggs

Brown the meat in its own fat in a heavy saucepan. Add the vegetables, tomato juice, and hot water. Cover and simmer gently until tender. Mix together the chili powder, salt, and flour with the cold water, and stir into the pork mixture. Cook, stirring constantly, until the sauce thickens slightly. Add the pimientos and olives. Have ready the cornmeal mush (which see). Beat the eggs and add to the mush with the butter. Line a baking dish with part of the mush. Fill with the meat mixture and top with the remaining cornmeal. Bake in a moderate oven (350°–375° F.) about 30 minutes, or until the sauce draws up through the cornmeal topping. Serve very hot. (Serves 6–8)

PORK TENDERLOIN WITH SWEET POTATOES

Wipe two pork tenderloins and place in a roasting pan. Place in a moderate oven (350° F.) and roast for about 20 minutes. Meanwhile parboil 4 sweet potatoes; peel and cut into thick slices. Arrange around the meat, and dot each slice with butter or drippings. Bake about 45 minutes longer, basting both meat and potatoes every 15 minutes with hot water mixed with a little drippings. Season with salt and pepper when half done. (Serves 4)

ROAST SUCKLING PIG

The butcher will prepare the suckling pig by scraping and thoroughly cleaning it. He will force the mouth open and insert a piece of wood to keep it open while roasting.

Wash the pig in cold water and dry thoroughly. Then stuff with either of the suggested dressings (see below) and sew up the opening. Place on a rack in an open roasting pan, having the forefeet extending out straight. Fold the hind legs under, tying or skewering them in place. Rub the pig with softened butter or sausage drippings, sprinkle with salt and pepper, and dust with a little flour. Roast in a moderate oven (350° F.) for 3 to 3½ hours, basting every 15 minutes with hot water and drippings.

When done, remove to a hot platter. Take the piece of wood from the mouth and substitute a bright red apple. Place two bright red cranberries in the eye sockets, and garnish the platter with parsley or watercress. Serve with tart applesauce.

Prune-Apple Stuffing

4 to 6 cups dry bread crumbs
2 cups chopped cooked prunes
2 cups pared, chopped tart apples
1 tsp salt
¼ tsp pepper
¼ tsp cinnamon
Water

Mix all the ingredients together, adding enough water to make a moist but not wet dressing.

Sausage Stuffing

1 lb sausage meat
4 cups boiled rice or stale bread crumbs
2 tbsp chopped celery leaves
2 tbsp sausage drippings
1 tbsp chopped parsley
1 onion, grated
1 tbsp poultry seasoning
1 tsp salt
¼ tsp pepper
Water

Cook the sausage meat in a skillet over a moderate flame until the fat is extracted, and drain off the fat. Add the rest of the ingredients, using only enough water to moisten. Mix thoroughly.

Any extra dressing may be baked in a separate pan and served with the pig.

ROAST LOIN OF PORK

Be sure that the butcher cracks the bones thoroughly for ease in carving. Wipe the meat with a damp cloth, and rub well with salt and pepper. Place, fat side up, on a rack in an open roasting pan. If desired, one or two sliced onions may be arranged over the surface of the meat. Roast in a moderate oven (350° F.), allowing 30

minutes to the pound, and basting frequently with the drippings in the pan. Increase the heat to 375° during the last 15 minutes of cooking to brown and crisp the fat surface. Serve with brown gravy and apple sauce.

ROAST STUFFED FRESH HAM

A fresh ham, 10-12 lb
Salt and pepper
4 cups any desired dressing
2 tbsp flour
2 medium-sized onions, sliced

Have the butcher bone the ham. Fill the cavity from which the bone was removed with stuffing (*which see*), leaving room for the dressing to swell. Sew or tie the opening to keep the meat in shape. Rub the ham lightly with salt and pepper and the flour. Place fat side up on a rack in an open roasting pan and arrange the slices of onion over the ham. Cook in a moderate oven (350° F.) allowing 30 minutes to the pound. Baste frequently with the pan drippings. Serve with brown gravy and apple sauce.

SWEET AND SOUR PORK (CHINESE)

2 lb pork cutlets
1 cup mixed sweet pickles
2 cups flour
2 eggs
2 tbsp water
2 cloves garlic
1½ cups vinegar
½ cup sugar
Soy sauce
1 tbsp cornstarch
Salt and pepper
Cooking oil

Heat a little cooking oil in a skillet and sprinkle in a little salt. Crush the cloves of garlic with a knife and cook in the oil for 1 minute. Remove the garlic and discard. Pour the vinegar into the skillet carefully, because it will boil up. Add the sugar, the soy sauce, and a dash of pepper. Cook, stirring constantly until the sugar is dissolved Sprinkle in the cornstarch, and continue to cook, stirring constantly, until the cornstarch clears and the mixture thickens. Take off the heat until ready to use.

Cut the pork cutlets into pieces ¾ inch wide and 1½ inches long. Season with salt and pepper and dredge with the flour. Beat up the eggs with the water and pour over the pieces of pork. Mix thoroughly so that all pieces are we l coated. Heat cooking oil in a deep kettle to 375° F. Fry the pork pieces for 15 minutes in the deep fat, stirring occasionally to brown them evenly. Drain thoroughly.

Reheat the sauce, and when boiling, add the pork and the pickles which have been cut in small bits. Stir for a minute or so and serve immediately. (Serves 4 to 6)

PORRIDGE. Oatmeal (*which see*) boiled slowly in salted water until it thickens.

PORRINGER. A small bowl-shaped dish for eating porridge. Children frequently have silver porringers.

PORT. A fortified sweet, dessert wine (*see* WINE) originally from the valley of Douro, Portugal. Though Portuguese by birth and name (derived from either the country or the town of Oporto from which the wine is shipped), its upbringing, education and sponsorship have been exclusively British.

Port was first introduced into England in 1689, and in 1703 was given a preferential duty under a mutual trade pact between the countries. But the original port was not too agreeable to the British taste, and it was found that by fortification the wine could be made both sweeter and stronger. This modified version received tremendous popularity and, under British sponsorship, the wine was spread around the world.

The British consumption of port became phenomenal. It was on the one hand hailed as a medicine of unparalleled virtues and on the other as an evil. Dr. Johnson summed up his views with the oft quoted "claret is for boys, pure port for men and women, and brandy for heroes."

The fortification was, in many cases, carried to extremes. This, in turn, lead to another famous quotation, that of a tavern keeper who took offense when the quality of his port was questioned. "I say it is black and it makes you drunk; is it not then good port?"

Under a treaty made in 1916, England refused to admit any wine as port unless it is produced in a certain area in Portugal (a 30 by 60 mile area of the Douro Valley) and shipped from either Oporto or Vila Nova de Gaia. Port is, however, made in

PORRINGER

many other countries, though this fact is usually specified on the label. It is even made in England from imported wines, though this wine is felt by some to be inferior to the true port.

Port is a blended wine, made sweet by arresting the fermentation while the wine still contains sugar, by adding a small amount of grape brandy. The Portuguese port contains very little brandy and the wine's total alcoholic content is about the same as that of the common French table wines. Port made for export, however, may contain more, depending on the market for which it is intended.

There are three common varieties of Port; *crusted*, *tawny* and *ruby*. Crusted port does most of its aging in the bottle, for that reason depositing a very heavy sediment in the form of a crust. The other two are primarily aged in wood, and are named according to their color.

Port is a sediment-forming wine, and the older it is, the greater the sediment in the bottle. For that reason, care should be taken in the pouring.

Though primarily a dessert wine, it may be served in a variety of ways (*see* WINE) and also used for cooking.

The signs of a good port differ somewhat from the qualifications set down by the anonymous tavern keeper. It should be lively on the palate; dry-flavored, but bordering on sweetness; perfectly transparent, with a color ranging from pale rose to bright purple; mellow in age, with the rose color turning tawny and the purple going ruby. Perhaps the simplest test of a good Port is to draw the cork and let it dry. If the Port is really good, crystals of tartar should form where the cork had been wet.

HOMEMADE PORT WINE

Wash 20 pounds of Concord grapes, remove them from stems and crush. Allow to stand 2 hours or longer and then drain off juice. Strain it through flannel cloth several times until clear, or put it in a cloth bag and allow it to drip overnight. Measure 4 quarts of juice, and add 2 pounds each of washed prunes and washed seedless raisins, chopped together, 8 pounds of granulated sugar, and 6 quarts of boiling water. Stir until sugar is thoroughly dissolved; add to juice and let stand, lightly covered at room temperature for 3 days, skimming and stirring 3 times a day. Then strain through a flannel cloth, and bottle, corking loosely until fermentation stops. Then cork tightly and let stand 4 months before using.

PORTABLE COOK STOVES. *See* CAMP COOKERY.

PORT DU SALUT. A French, rennet cheese made from cow's milk. It has a soft, homogenous interior, a hard rind, and is similar in taste to Swiss cheese. Oval shaped, it measures seven to ten inches in diameter. *See also* CHEESE.

PORTERHOUSE STEAK. The name given to a thick steak cut from the loin of beef (*which see*) from which part of the tenderloin has been removed and the ends trimmed. This name was given to such a steak served in English public houses where porter, ale, beer, etc. were retailed.

PORT GLASS. *See* GLASSWARE.

POSSET. Milk curdled with ale, molasses, wine, etc.

ALE POSSET

Boil 1 pint of fresh milk with a slice of toasted bread. Following this, pour a bottle of mild ale into a bowl, sweeten to add a pinch of spice such as nutmeg, etc., and then pour in the boiling milk. A fine bead or froth should rise. Serve very hot. (Serves 4)

MOLASSES (TREACLE) POSSET

Set 1 cup of fresh milk and 1 cup of water on the fire in a saucepan. Stir in 2 tablespoons of molasses and bring to a boil. Serve very hot. This posset may be made entirely of milk if a richer brew is desired. (Serves 2)

SACK POSSET

Add grated biscuits to 1 pint of cream and boil. Season with pinches of cinnamon, nutmeg and sugar to taste. Now, warm but do not boil 2 wineglassfuls of good sherry and stir into the hot cream. Pour the whole mixture rapidly from one vessel to another until perfectly smooth. Eggs may be substituted for the cream if desired. (Serves 4)

POSSUM. *See* OPOSSUM.

POT. A rounded metallic or earthen vessel. *See* KITCHEN EQUIPMENT.

POT AU FEU. Literally "pot on the fire," the French pot au feu is a rich soup made of meat and vegetables.

POT AU FEU

1 soup bone
2 lb lean meat
2½ qt water
Salt
2 carrots
1 turnip
1 onion, stuck with a clove
1 small parsnip
1 stalk celery
2 leeks
Bouquet garni
Toasted French bread

Wipe the bone and meat and place in a large kettle with the water and a little salt. Bring slowly to boiling point, remove any scum which may form, add the vegetables and the bouquet garni, this last tied together with the leeks. Simmer gently, partly covered, about 3 hours. Skim carefully, remove the leeks and bouquet garni, season to taste, and serve with toasted French bread. (Serves 6)

POT CHEESE. Another name given to cottage cheese, *which see.*

POT LIQUOR. A thin broth obtained from boiling meat—a favorite of Southerners, usually served with greens.

POT PIE. A deep-dish pie of meat or poultry, usually topped with crust or dumplings.

POT ROAST. Meat cooked in a pot with very little liquid. Pot roasting is a method similar to braising (*which see*) except that the vessel is kept on top of the stove and direct heat is used instead of radiant heat. The meat, or game, or fowl is usually seared, then placed in a covered kettle, or a Dutch oven, and the braise and liquid added. The process of cooking is a slow one and is usually applied to less tender cuts.

Round of beef (top or bottom), rump, eye of round, shank, chuck (top, bottom, or rib), crossrib, neck (boneless), and shortribs may be used for an economical pot roast. Vegetables may be added and puffed seedless raisins, etc. The pot roast may be a spicy one, or again it may be cooked in tomato juice, instead of plain water or meat stock, or sour cream may be added when the meat has been removed from the kettle. In other words a pot roast is a kind of stew, the meat being left whole instead of cut into serving pieces.

See also BRAISE and SAUERBRAUTEN

POT ROAST OF BEEF

5 lb rump, round, or chuck of beef
1 large onion sliced
Seasoned flour
2 cups boiling water or tomato juice
1 tbsp butter
1 tbsp flour

Have the meat in one piece, rolled and compactly tied by the butcher. Wipe with a damp cloth, dredge with seasoned flour, and brown in a heavy kettle on all sides in its own fat, with the sliced onion. If fat is lacking on the meat, use either bacon drippings, or ham fat, or beef suet which has been tried out. Add the boiling liquid, slowly, while stirring gently from the bottom of the kettle, scraping the sediments which may be attached to the kettle. Cover and simmer over a very low flame about 3½ to 4 hours, or until tender. Remove the meat to a hot platter. Cream the butter and flour together, and stir into the hot gravy. Cook, stirring constantly, until the gravy thickens slightly. Slice the roast thinly for service. (Serves 8)

COUNTRY POT ROAST

4 lb pot roast, top round or rump
1½ cups hot water
1 stalk celery, with leaves
1 large carrot, scraped and sliced
1 large bay leaf, tied with
6 sprigs fresh parsley
6 whole peppercorns, bruised
⅛ tsp each ground thyme, mace and allspice
2 tsp salt
½ cup tomato juice

1 small clove garlic
1 doz small whole white onions, peeled

Have the meat in one piece, rolled and compactly tied. Wipe with a damp cloth, then brown on all sides in its own fat in a heavy skillet. Do not hurry the browning. Transfer to a casserole having a tight-fitting cover, and add all remaining ingredients. Pour off the fat from the skillet, add a little water, and scrape bottom and sides so as to detach any particles of meat. Boil up once and pour over the meat. Cover and simmer for three hours. Lift out the meat and place it on a very hot platter. Into the remaining gravy, stir 1 tablespoon of flour creamed or kneaded with 1 tablespoon of butter. Boil a few minutes, then serve with the meat and vegetables, with plain boiled potatoes and a separately cooked green vegetable. (Serves 6)

POTASSIUM. Potassium, in the form of phosphate of potassium, is the mineral basis of all muscular tissues, giving them their characteristic pliancy. In the synthetic processes of organic combinations potassium salts are indispensable. They play an important part in the formation of glycogen from glucose, of fats from glycogen, and of proteins from peptones. The liver, which is the principal factor in glycogen-formation, contains twice as much potassium as sodium. Potassium is also a predominant element in red blood corpuscles and in the brain.

POTATO. A native of the Americas, the white potato was found growing in Peru by the early Spanish explorers. It was introduced into Spain in 1538 by the explorer Sieza de Leon who referred to it as ". . . this ground nut which when boiled becomes as soft as a cooked chestnut, but which has no thicker skin than a truffle." From Spain it was introduced into central Europe, thence to Germany, and from there it was brought to France by Antoine Auguste Parmentier, whose name is still given to mashed potatoes in France. It was constantly developed so that by the time the English colonists brought the potato back to America it was quite a different vegetable from the "ground nut" of the conquistadores.

Potatoes, like most new and unknown foods, were called poisonous by the early physicians. Marie Antoinette wore potato flowers in her hair and was imitated by the ladies-in-waiting of her court. But Louis

POTATOES   1. Idaho   2. New   3. Irish Cobbler

XIV had difficulty persuading his subjects that potatoes were wholesome food. But gradually, particularly in Germany and Ireland, the potato became a staple crop. In 1847, when the blight hit the potato crop in Ireland, so dependent had the people become on this article of food that starvation faced the country, and over a million and a half Irish emigrated to America.

Today more than five and a half billion bushels of potatoes are harvested yearly throughout the world. The United States leads with an average harvest of some 475 million bushels a year. The potato has become a staff of life—like bread and rice—and today runs rice a close second as the world's chief food crop.

Although many people spurn the potato as starchy and fattening, nutrition experts have disproved this theory. Potatoes do contain starch, and starch when taken in too large quantities can be fattening, but potatoes contain less starch then rice, peas, or lentils. Potato starch is more digestible than many other starches, and when the potato is properly cooked the starch granules become tender and mealy. When potatoes are improperly cooked they are hard and soggy and generally indigestible.

New potatoes, or early potatoes, are dug before they reach full maturity and are marketed immediately. Because of their immaturity and the warm weather during which they are packed and shipped, they will not keep and should be used as soon as possible. Their skins are delicate, often ruddy in color, and are inclined to rough up in little flakes. Often it i possible to find in the markets little new potatoes, all about one inch in diameter, which have been sorted for size. These make an attractive dish, cooked whole in their jackets.

Old potatoes are the later crop of more mature potatoes. These are the potatoes which are stored and shipped during the winter and are available all year around. Their skins are browner and tougher than the new potatoes.

Lately canned potatoes have come into the markets. Both full-sized potatoes and small round potato balls the size of a large marble are available in cans. They have been partially cooked in the canning process and need only finishing up to be served. They make a useful adjunct to the emergency shelf.

With the development of the frozen foods industry, packers have discovered ways of freezing potatoes, already cooked

FOOD VALUE

Water	Food Energy	Pro-tein	Fat	Carbo-hydrate	Cal-cium	Phos-phorus	Iron	Vit. A Value	Thia-mine	Ribo-flavin	Nia-cin	Ascor-bic Acid
77.8	85	2.0	.1	19.1	11	56	.7	20	.11	.04	1.2	17

MARKET TYPES

Potatoes are classified in two types, the long type, a mealy potato, and the round or intermediate type, which is a harder waxier potato. The mealy potatoes are best for baking and mashing, the harder potatoes for boiling and other uses. The so-called Idaho potato is a particularly large fine potato excellent for baking.

various ways, so that the housewife need only heat according to the directions on the package. French fried potatoes and mashed potato puffs are two products currently on the market.

HINTS ON BUYING

Good quality potatoes are sound, smooth skinned, with shallow eyes and reasonably clean. Formerly potatoes were marketed with a good deal of earth clinging to them; more recently the potatoes are cleaned so that one does not pay for a measure of earth in a pound of potatoes. Potato varieties vary considerably in size, shape, and color, and it is almost impossible to tell from the outside what the characteristics of the potato are. Most of the medium-sized potatoes found in American markets are good for boiling and other purposes. The best baking potatoes are the large oval "Idaho" potatoes, which need not come from Idaho, but are usually marketed scrubbed and wrapped individually in paper.

Wilted or discolored potatoes should be avoided. They were either dug too early and improperly stored, or otherwise injured. Potatoes with deep eyes are wasteful, since so much must be cut away. Potatoes which have green coloring on some portion of the skin should be avoided. This condition is known as "sunburn" and is caused by long exposure to light either while growing or in storage. The green parts are very bitter due to the presence of a substance called solanin. While there is some doubt as to whether they are actually poisonous, such potatoes are certainly unpalatable. The same substance is also found in potatoes which have begun to sprout.

Occasionally potatoes are found with hollow centers, or with black, slimy centers. These diseases of the potato cannot be detected from the outside, and can only be found by cutting the potato in two. Potatoes which have been damaged by freezing will show a black ring just inside the skin. Frozen potatoes are tasteless when cooked and often turn dark in boiling. If the freezing is very bad it can be detected from the outside by the potato being wet and leaky.

Potatoes must be stored in a dark cool, not cold, place to keep successfully. If exposed to the light they will sprout. Before storing any quantity of potatoes, look them over and pick out any decayed or soft specimens, since these will infect other potatoes.

Hints on Preparation

Since much of the minerals and other nutritive worth of the potato is just beneath the skin, potatoes should be cooked in their jackets whenever possible. In any case, they should be peeled very thinly. New potatoes need only washing and scrubbing. Old potatoes, particularly if there is any doubt of their quality, might better be peeled and cut in pieces before boiling in order to find any with bad centers.

Choose potatoes of uniform size, or cut them into uniform pieces so that they will cook in the same amount of time. Potatoes should be cooked in boiling salted water. Drop the potatoes into a pan of rapidly boiling water to cover, and continue to cook at a low boil until the potatoes are tender when pierced by a fork—about 20 minutes for medium-sized potatoes. Drain thoroughly and then hold the pan containing the potatoes over the stove, shaking the potatoes about for a few minutes to dry them out. Do not place directly on the heat, because they will stick to the pan. This drying is the secret of flaky boiled potatoes, and works equally well for potatoes cooked peeled or in the jackets. If they have been cooked in their jackets, this is the time to peel them. The jackets will strip off easily while still hot.

Very small new potatoes may be well washed and cooked in their jackets and served without peeling, with butter and parsley or chopped chives.

To make fluffy mashed potatoes, cook in boiling salted water until very tender, drain and dry thoroughly and peel. Put through a ricer, being careful not to fill the ricer too full so that the mashed potatoes remain fluffy. Then the potatoes should be seasoned with additional salt, if necessary, pepper, butter or margarine and a little hot milk or cream, and beaten lightly with a wooden spoon until creamy and fluffy.

To bake potatoes, scrub uniform-sized potatoes and bake in a hot oven (425° F.) for 40 to 60 minutes, until the potatoes can be pinched and appear tender. Prick the potatoes with a fork in several places after they have cooked about half the time. This allows the steam to escape and makes a fluffier potato. If you like the skins soft, rub with a little fat or oil before baking.

Potatoes should not be peeled too far ahead of cooking, since they will discolor. If they must be prepared ahead of time for stews or other dishes in which peeled potatoes are necessary, drop the potatoes into cold salted water to cover until ready to use.

In deep-frying potatoes, whether in strips or cut into fancy shapes, drop the peeled prepared slices into ice water and chill for 30 minutes or so before frying. Dry thoroughly between towels and drop into deep hot fat. The potatoes will puff and become crisp and delectable.

BAKED STUFFED POTATOES

6 large baking potatoes
1 cup grated cheese
⅓ cup milk
⅛ tsp paprika
1 tsp salt

Scrub the potatoes and bake in a hot oven (425° F.) until tender. Halve the potatoes lengthwise, scoop out the centers, and put through the ricer. Heat the milk and cheese together, and combine with the potato pulp. Season with salt and paprika, and beat with a wooden spoon until light and fluffy. Pile back into the potato shells and return to a hot oven (400° F.) until delicately browned. (Serves 6)

BROILED POTATOES

Boil medium-sized potatoes until just tender. Drain, dry, and peel if the potatoes have been cooked in their skins. Let cool. Leftover boiled potatoes may be used equally well. Cut the potatoes in lengthwise slices and dip in melted butter or margarine. Place on the broiler and broil, turning once, until the potatoes are nicely browned. Sprinkle lightly with salt and pepper and serve very hot.

COTTAGE FRIED POTATOES

Dice cold boiled potatoes. Brown in a little fat in a heavy frying pan. Season to taste with salt and pepper, and cook until heated through. A little minced onion may be browned in the fat before adding the potatoes.

CREAM OF POTATO SOUP

6 cups sliced raw potatoes
1 good-sized onion
3 tsp salt
4 tbsp butter or margarine
3 cups milk
1 tbsp parsley

Slice the onion and put the potatoes and onion into a saucepan. Barely cover with cold water. Add the salt, cover, and bring to a boil. Let simmer for 10 minutes, or until the potatoes are very tender. Mash the potatoes and onions in the liquid. Add the butter and the milk. Taste for seasoning. Reheat, but do not let boil. Just before serving, add the chopped parsley. Serve hot. (Serves 6)

CURRIED POTATO DUMPLINGS

4 tbsp butter or margarine
1 egg yolk
Pinch of salt
Pinch of nutmeg
½ tsp curry powder
¾ cup cold mashed potatoes
4 tbsp flour

Cream the butter and add the egg yolk, beating until the mixture is light and fluffy. Add the seasonings. Stir in the potatoes alternately with the flour. Beat until smooth. Shape into balls the size of a marble. Have the consomme at a rolling boil, and about 8 minutes before serving, drop in the dumplings. Cover the pot and let simmer until the balls rise to the surface. Serve the soup immediately, serving several dumplings in each plate. (Serves 6)

DUCHESSE POTATOES

2 cups hot riced potatoes
2 tbsp butter or margarine
½ tsp salt
2 egg yolks, well beaten
Hot cream or milk

Add the butter, salt, and egg yolks to the riced potatoes and stir in enough hot milk or cream to moisten. Form into mounds on a greased baking sheet, or make fancy shapes with a pastry bag. Brush the tops with a little beaten egg diluted with milk, and brown in a hot oven (425° F.)

FRANCONIA OR RISSOLE POTATOES

Select medium-sized potatoes of even size. Peel the potatoes, wash them, and dry thoroughly. Arrange in the roasting pan with the meat, preferably a roast of beef or lamb, and cook at the same time as the meat, basting and turning during the cooking so they are evenly browned on all sides. Sprinkle lightly with salt before serving.

FRENCH FRIED POTATOES

Select firm sound potatoes. Peel and cut into uniform sticks, keeping rather thin. Drop into ice water and chill for 30 minutes. Drain and pat dry between towels. Have ready a kettle of cooking oil or fat, heated to 375° F., and drop in the potato strips a few at a time. Fry until crisp and golden brown. Skim out and drain on soft crumpled paper. Sprinkle with salt and serve very hot. The secret of good French fried potatoes is to cut the strips thin enough so that they cook through, and to fry only a few at a time so they do not stick together, but brown evenly. True French fried potatoes are crisp through, and not soft and mealy inside as is often the case.

HUNGARIAN STUFFED POTATOES
6 large potatoes
1 cup cooked minced pork
3 tbsp cooked rice
1 cup smoked sausage, sliced
3 good-sized onions
3 tbsp lard
Salt and paprika
1 cup sour cream

Peel the potatoes and cut in halves lengthwise. With a sharp knife, remove the centers, leaving a shell ⅛-inch thick. Put the scooped-out center through the meat grinder, using the coarsest blade. Melt 2 tablespoons of the lard in a skillet and brown the minced pork and rice. Season well with salt and paprika, and fill the potato shells with the mixture. Melt the remaining lard in the skillet. Dice the onions and mix with the ground potato. Brown the sliced sausage in the fat, remove, and brown the onions and potatoes in the same pan. In a large casserole, make a layer of onions and potatoes, then a layer of the sausage, and place the stuffed potatoes on top. Pour in a little water. Sprinkle the potatoes with paprika, and cover the casserole. Bake in a moderate oven (350° F.) for 45 minutes to an hour, or until the potatoes are tender. Just before they are done, open the casserole, pour in the sour cream, and continue cooking until ready to serve. Do not overcook lest the potato cases fall apart. (Serves 6)

JULIENNE POTATOES

Cut raw potatoes into very thin matchlike strips. Soak in ice water for one hour. Pat dry between towels and fry, a few at a time, in deep hot fat (375°–390° F.) until golden brown. Drain on soft crumpled paper and serve very hot. Julienne potatoes are more crisp than French fried potatoes.

LEEK AND POTATO SOUP

4 medium-sized potatoes
4 small leeks
2 cups water
4 cups milk
1 tbsp flour
2 tsp salt
1 tbsp butter or margarine

Peel the potatoes and cut into small dice. Trim the leeks and cut into thin slices. Put the potatoes, leeks, and water into a saucepan. Cover and bring to a boil. Simmer 10 minutes, or until very tender. With ½ cup of the milk make a smooth paste with the flour and salt. Mash the potatoes and leeks. Add the 3½ cups of milk, and then stir in the flour paste. Stir well and add the butter. Reheat, stirring constantly, until the mixture bubbles, and let simmer for a few minutes to cook the flour. Serve hot or cold. (Serves 5)

NEW POTATOES WITH LEMON-CHIVE BUTTER

3 lb small new potatoes
4 tbsp butter or margarine
Grated rind of 1 lemon
2 tbsp lemon juice
1 tbsp chopped chives
Salt and pepper and nutmeg

Scrub the potatoes, cook in boiling salted water until tender. Drain, dry, and peel. Melt the butter and add the remaining ingredients. Pour over the hot potatoes and toss and mix until the potatoes are completely coated. Serve immediately. (Serves 6)

O'BRIEN POTATOES

3 tbsp bacon fat
2 tbsp minced green pepper
2 tbsp minced onion

2 tbsp minced celery
3 cups diced cooked potatoes
1 tbsp minced parsley
3 tbsp milk
Salt and paprika

Melt the fat in a skillet and cook the green pepper, onion, and celery in the hot fat for about 5 minutes, or until beginning to brown. Add the remaining ingredients and toss together until heated thoroughly. Pat together into an oval, covering half the frying pan, and allow to brown on the underside. Invert onto a hot platter for service. (Serves 6)

OVEN FRIED POTATOES

Peel and slice potatoes into lengthwise strips as for French fried potatoes. Soak in ice water for thirty minutes or an hour. Drain and pat dry between towels. Place the potato strips in a well greased, shallow baking pan, and sprinkle lightly with cooking oil. Bake in a hot oven (450°–500° F.) about 45 minutes, turning and tossing about several times so that the strips brown evenly. Drain on soft crumpled paper, sprinkle with salt, and serve very hot.

PAN-SCALLOPED POTATOES

3 tbsp butter or margarine
3 cups diced raw potatoes
2 cups milk
Salt and pepper to taste

Melt the butter in a frying pan, add the potatoes, and stir over a low flame until the fat is absorbed. Add the milk and seasonings, and cook very slowly about 30 minutes, adding more milk if needed. (Serves 4)

PARSLEY POTATOES

Dice raw peeled potatoes or cut into balls with a vegetable cutter; or use very small new potatoes. Boil in slightly salted water until tender, drain, and dry. Season with salt and pepper, add plenty of melted butter or margarine and chopped parsley, and shake about until the potatoes are evenly coated.

For *Browned Parsley Potatoes*, dice or cut the potatoes into balls as directed above. Fry in deep hot fat (375°–390° F.) until golden brown. In a saucepan melt some

butter or margarine, add minced parsley, and then the fried potatoes. Toss about until the potatoes are coated.

For *Minted Potatoes*, substitute chopped fresh mint leaves for parsley in either of the above recipes.

POMMES SOUFFLES
(Potatoes Soufflés)

Choose firm potatoes of medium size. Peel and slice crosswise as thin as possible and of uniform thickness. Do not wash the potatoes, but wipe clean and dry with a towel. Have two pans of deep fat ready, one heated to 350° F. and the other smoking hot, about 400° F. Plunge the potatoes into the first pan, and let them cook 4 or 5 minutes, stirring them about. When they rise to the surface and begin to puff, skim them out and let them cool slightly. Then plunge into the hotter fat. They will puff up immediately, and should be cooked until nicely browned. Skim them out, drain on soft crumpled paper, and sprinkle with salt. Serve very hot.

The potatoes may also be prepared using only one kettle of fat. Have the fat at 350° F. and drop the potatoes in, a few at a time so that the temperature is not lowered too much. Cook 4 or 5 minutes, skim out, and place in a colander. When all the potatoes have been prepared this far, heat the fat to 400° F. Again drop in the partly cooked potatoes, a few at a time, and cook as above.

For a professional appearance the slices of potatoes should be trimmed to a pointed oval shape so that when they puff in cooking they resemble a football in shape. Pommes soufflés are not difficult to make, despite their exotic appearance, if the temperature of the two pans of fat is carefully controlled.

PORTUGUESE POTATO SOUP

2 qt meat stock
4 good-sized potatoes
1 bunch of water cress
4 egg yolks
1 cup milk, scalded
Salt and pepper
4 tbsp grated cheese

Grate the raw potatoes. Bring the stock to a boil and add the potatoes. Let simmer for 30 minutes. Then rub through a sieve and put back into the saucepan. Keep hot. A few minutes before serving, chop the water cress finely and add to the soup. Season to taste with salt and pepper. Put the yolks of the eggs into a soup tureen and stir in the milk. Stir in a few spoonfuls of the hot soup and then pour in the rest of the soup. Sprinkle with the grated cheese. Serve hot. (Serves 6)

POTATO AND CARROT CHOWDER

2 tbsp diced salt pork
1 medium-sized onion, diced
2 cups raw potatoes, diced
2 cups boiling water
Salt and pepper
1/4 tsp paprika
2 carrots diced
2 cups milk, scalded
1 tbsp flour
2 tbsp butter or margarine

Try out the salt pork, and brown the onion in the fat. Add the potatoes, carrots, boiling water. Cover and bring to a boil. Let simmer about 15 minutes, until the potatoes are tender. Mix the flour with the butter and stir into the soup mixture. Add the milk. Season to taste with salt and pepper and the paprika. Cook about 5 minutes longer, stirring constantly, until smooth and thickened. (Serves 6)

POTATO AND CHEESE SOUFFLE

6 medium-sized potatoes
2 medium-sized onions
1 tbsp butter or margarine
1 cup milk, heated
1 cup grated cheese
1 tsp salt
Pepper
2 eggs, separated

Cook the potatoes and onions together in slightly salted boiling water until tender. Pass through a ricer. Add the butter, milk, 3/4 of the cheese, salt, pepper, and the beaten egg yolks. Beat together thoroughly. Beat the egg whites until stiff and fold into the potato mixture. Turn into a greased baking dish and sprinkle with the remaining cheese. Bake in a moderately hot oven (375° F.) about 30 minutes, or until golden brown. Serve immediately. (Serves 6)

POTATO AND WALNUT CROQUETTES

1 cup soft bread crumbs
1 cup blanched ground walnuts
1 cup milk, scalded
2 egg yolks
2 cups hot mashed potatoes
Salt, pepper, and nutmeg

Combine the bread crumbs, walnuts, and scalded milk in the top of a double boiler. Cook over hot water, stirring constantly, until the mixture thickens. Remove from the heat. Beat in the egg yolks, one at a time, alternately with the potatoes. Season to taste with salt, pepper, and a dash of nutmeg. Beat briskly to blend thoroughly. Spread the mixture on a platter to cool. When cold, form into ovals the size of an egg. Roll in fine crumbs, then in egg beaten with a little milk, and again in crumbs. Plunge into deep hot fat (375°–390° F.) a few at a time, and fry until golden brown. Drain on soft crumpled paper, and serve very hot.

POTATO AND YELLOW TURNIP SOUP

1 lb yellow turnips
1½ cups water
2½ tsp salt
1 lb potatoes
1 tsp sugar
2 cups milk
2 tbsp butter or margarine
Dash of pepper

Peel the turnip and cut into thin slices. Put into a saucepan with the water and 1 teaspoon of the salt. Cover the pan and bring to a boil. Let simmer 20 or 25 minutes. Meanwhile peel the potatoes and slice them thinly. Add to the turnips and continue simmering until potatoes and turnips are very tender. Mash in their liquid. Add the rest of the salt, sugar, butter, and pepper. Stir in the milk. Reheat, but do not allow to boil. Serve immediately. (Serves 4)

POTATO CAKES

Use leftover mashed potatoes. If desired, add some chopped cooked meat or fish or some grated cheese to them. Stir in a well-beaten egg. Form into small cakes. Roll in beaten egg and fine crumbs. Fry in a little fat until golden brown.

POTATO CASSOLETTES

2 lb hot boiled potatoes
3 tbsp thin cream or milk
4 tbsp butter
2 eggs
Salt, pepper, and nutmeg
Crushed cereal crumbs

Rice the potatoes while still hot. Season with the cream, butter, salt, pepper, and nutmeg. Add the eggs, one at a time, beating after each addition. Stir vigorously over moderate heat for about 10 minutes. Turn the mixture onto a platter to cool, spreading flat as for croquettes. When cold and set, form into balls the size of a billiard ball and flatten two sides so they will stand evenly. Cut around the upper surface with a pastry cutter or sharp knife, to form a cover, leaving a standing rim. Roll carefully in flour, then in beaten egg, and finally in crumbs. Let stand for 30 minutes, and then fry in deep hot fat (375°–390° F.) until golden brown, using a frying basket if you have it to prevent their breaking. Drain on soft crumpled paper. Remove the lids and scoop out the soft inside. Fill with creamed mushrooms, oysters, chicken, or other food, and replace the lids. Serve very hot. (Serves 6)

While this sounds somewhat complicated, it is actually easy to prepare, and the cases are more interesting than the usual pastry shell.

POTATO CHAHKEE (INDIAN)

1 lb potatoes
⅓ cup mustard oil
4 tsp minced onion
1 tsp ground chili peppers
½ tsp ground turmeric
¼ tsp garlic salt
1¼ tsp salt
1 cup water

Heat the mustard oil in a saucepan. Brown the onion and peppers in the oil, adding the other seasonings. Peel the potatoes and quarter them. Add to the hot mixture, and cook for 10 or 15 minutes, stirring frequently. Pour in the water, cover the pan, and simmer until the potatoes are tender. This is a true Indian vegetable curry. (Serves 4)

POTATO CHOWDER

2 slices salt pork, diced
1 slice onion
2 cups diced potatoes
2 cups water
1 cup corn
1 qt scalded milk
Salt and pepper
3 tbsp butter
Crackers

Fry the pork until crisp. Cook the onion in the fat about 5 minutes, but do not brown. Parboil the potatoes in the water for five minutes, add both potatoes and water to the onions and continue cooking until the potatoes are tender. Put in the corn, milk, seasonings, and butter, and bring just to boiling point. Pour over crackers in the serving dishes and sprinkle with the bits of crisp salt pork. (Serves 4 or 6)

POTATO CROQUETTES

2 tbsp milk
1½ tsp salt
Dash of pepper
1 tsp minced onion
2 tbsp melted butter or margarine
4 cups cooked riced potatoes
2 egg yolks
1 whole egg
1 tbsp water
Fine bread crumbs

Heat together the milk, seasonings and butter, and add to the riced potatoes with the beaten egg yolks. Beat thoroughly with a wooden spoon. When well blended, chill until firm. Form into balls or cylinders. Roll first in crumbs, then in the egg and water which have been beaten together, and again in crumbs. Fry, a few at a time, in deep hot fat (375°–390° F.) using a basket, until golden brown. Drain on soft crumpled paper. Serve very hot. (Serves 6)

POTATO CRUST

Grease a baking dish and line it with cold mashed potatoes. Fill the center with stew, or leftover meat or vegetables. Cover with mashed potatoes. Bake in a hot oven (400° F.) until hot through and delicately brown on top. If there is not enough potato for two crusts, make deep-dish style with only a top crust of the potato.

POTATO DUMPLINGS

6 large potatoes
Salt and pepper
Pinch of nutmeg
Pinch of marjoram
2 tbsp flour
2 tbsp melted butter or margarine
2 tbsp bread crumbs
4 eggs

Cook the potatoes in their jackets in boiling salted water until just tender. Drain, dry, and peel, and put through the ricer. Season with salt, pepper, nutmeg, and marjoram. Add the flour, butter, and crumbs, and the eggs, one at a time, beating thoroughly after each egg is added. Form into balls with a tablespoon, drop gently into boiling salted water and cook, covered, about 12 minutes. Lift out carefully with a skimmer and serve at once. Especially good with pot roast or sauerbraten. (Serves 6)

POTATO FRITTO MISTO

Leftover meat, fish, poultry, or vegetables
Thick white sauce
4 medium-sized potatoes
2 egg yolks
⅓ cup milk
1 bay leaf
2 sprigs parsley
2 slices onion
Salt, pepper, and nutmeg
1 tsp curry powder
½ cup grated cheese

Mince up whatever leftovers are desired, keeping each kind separate. Mix each with enough thick white sauce (which see) to bind the morsels together, and let cool. Boil the potatoes in their skins and drain, dry, and peel. Put through the ricer. Scald the milk with the bay leaf, parsley, and onion, and then discard the seasonings. To the riced potatoes, add the egg yolks, one

at a time, beating well after each addition. Stir in the scalded milk and mix thoroughly. Season to taste with salt, pepper, and nutmeg and add the curry powder and the grated cheese. Mix well. Spread on a platter to cool.

When the mixture is cold, take pieces the size of a walnut. Insert bits of the creamed filling, and shape into a ball, covering the filling completely. Roll the balls in fine crumbs, then in egg beaten with a little milk, and again in crumbs. Fry in deep hot fat (375°–390° F.), a few at a time, until golden brown. Drain on soft crumpled paper and serve very hot. (Serves 6)

POTATO GNOCCHIS

2 lb potatoes
2 eggs
1 slice cooked ham
2 tbsp butter or margarine
2 tbsp grated Parmesan cheese
Flour

Boil the potatoes, drain, dry and peel. Put through the ricer. Put the ham through a food chopper and mix the chopped ham, cheese, and butter with the riced potatoes. Beat the eggs and add to the potato mixture, beating thoroughly. Beat in enough flour to make a thick paste. Flour the hands and form the potato mixture into small balls the size of a hazelnut. Drop the balls into rapidly boiling salted water and cook until they rise to the surface. Skim out and drain thoroughly. Place in a serving dish, cover with a well-seasoned tomato sauce, and sprinkle with additional grated cheese. (Serves 6)

POTATO PANCAKES

1 egg
½ tsp salt
⅛ tsp pepper
¼ tsp onion juice
2 cups grated raw potato
Flour

Beat the egg until light and pale yellow, add the seasonings and the grated potato. Stir in flour, a tablespoon at a time, using only enough to make a thick batter. Drop by spoonfuls into a frying pan containing a little hot fat and brown slowly on both sides. Potato pancakes are especially good with pot roast or sauerbrauten. (Serves 6)

POTATO SALAD

2 lb small new potatoes
2 medium-sized onions, diced
1 cup diced celery
Salt and pepper
1 cup French dressing
½ cup mayonnaise

Scrub the potatoes and cook in boiling salted water until tender. Drain, dry, and peel. Slice into even slices into a salad bowl. Add the onions and celery. Pour the French dressing over the hot potatoes and toss thoroughly. Set aside to cool, turning the potatoes several times so that they absorb the dressing. When the potatoes are thoroughly cooled, taste for seasoning, adding salt and pepper as needed. Mix in the mayonnaise. Set the salad in the refrigerator to chill. By marinating the hot potatoes in the French dressing, the flavor is absorbed into the slices of potato. Serve on crisp lettuce, garnishing as desired. (Serves 6)

HOT POTATO SALAD I

3 cups diced hot potatoes
1 clove garlic
⅓ cup sweet pickles with juice
⅓ cup mayonnaise
1 tsp salt
Dash pepper
2 hard-cooked eggs, chopped
½ cup celery, diced
¼ cup radishes, diced
2 tbsp minced onion

Cook the potatoes in their jackets in boiling salted water until done. Drain, dry, peel, and cut into dice. Cut the clove of garlic in two and rub the inside of the salad bowl thoroughly. Chop the pickles. Use about ¼ cup of pickle juice. Put the potatoes into the salad bowl, mix all the other ingredients, and add to the potatoes. Toss together until thoroughly mixed. Serve hot. (Serves 6)

HOT POTATO SALAD II

8 good-sized potatoes
6 slices bacon

1 tbsp flour
½ cup water
¾ cup vinegar
3 tsp salt
1 tsp sugar
1 onion, minced

Scrub the potatoes and cook until tender in boiling salted water. Make the dressing by sautéing the bacon until crisp and draining it on soft crumpled paper. To the drippings in the pan, add the flour, stirring well, and stir in the water and vinegar. Cook over direct heat, stirring constantly, until the mixture boils and thickens. Add the salt, sugar, and onion. When the potatoes are done, drain, then dry and peel, and cut into small dice. Crumble the bacon and mix with the potatoes in a bowl. Pour the hot dressing over the potato and mix thoroughly. Serve hot. (Serves 6)

HOT POTATO SALAD III

Cook firm potatoes in their skins just until tender. Drain and, when cool enough to handle, peel, then cut into thin slices. Have ready a baking dish and arrange in it first a layer of the sliced potatoes, then a generous sprinkling of blended finely chopped celery leaves, parsley, onion and tarragon. Repeat the layers. Pour ½ cup of French dressing over all. Place over gentle heat and bring slowly to boiling point. Serve with additional French dressing.

POTATO SALAD CALIFORNIA METHOD

3 cups diced hot potatoes
2 chopped hard-cooked eggs
2 tbsp grated onion
1 tbsp minced green pepper
1 tbsp minced pimiento
¾ cup diced celery
2 tbsp minced chives
Salt and pepper
¾ cup French dressing

Use freshly cooked potatoes and freshly cooked eggs and, while both are still warm, combine with all remaining salad ingredients. Pour the dressing over all and chill. Just before serving sprinkle with blended paprika, minced parsley and chives. (Serves 6 or 8)

Potato Salad with Caraway and Sour Cream

3 cups hot cubed potatoes
¼ cup minced green onion
2 tbsp minced radishes
2 hard-cooked eggs, diced
¼ cup mayonnaise
¼ cup sour cream
2 tbsp vinegar
¼ tsp sugar
1 tsp salt
½ tsp caraway seeds

Mix the potatoes, green onion, radishes, and eggs in a salad bowl. Blend together the remaining ingredients and mix thoroughly with the potato mixture. Cover and let stand at least 30 minutes in the refrigerator to blend and chill. Serve in crisp lettuce cups. (Serves 6)

Mashed Potato Salad

3 cups hot mashed potatoes
¼ cup mayonnaise
2 tsp vinegar
¾ tsp salt
1 tbsp chopped green pepper
1 tbsp chopped radishes
½ cup minced celery
¼ cup minced green onions

Combine all the ingredients and mix thoroughly. This salad may be served warm or cold. It may also be molded by packing in small molds while warm, then chilling.

Hot Mashed Potato Salad

4 slices bacon
2 tsp chopped onion
1 tsp celery salt
½ tsp salt
¼ tsp pepper
1 tsp sugar
3 tbsp vinegar
¼ cup mayonnaise
2½ cups hot mashed potatoes

Sauté the bacon until crisp and remove from the pan. Drain on soft crumpled paper. Combine 2 tbsp of the hot bacon drippings with the seasonings, sugar, vinegar and mayonnaise. Pour over the potatoes and mix thoroughly. Serve hot, crumbling the bacon over the top. (Serves 4)

Potato Scones

2 cups sifted flour
1 tsp salt
3 tsp baking powder
3 tbsp shortening
1 cup cold mashed potatoes
1 egg
⅓ cup milk

Sift together the flour, salt, and baking powder. Cut in the shortening with 2 knives or a pastry blender. Mix in the cold potatoes. Beat the egg and stir in the milk; add to the potato mixture. Mix only enough to blend well. Roll ⅜ inch thick on a floured board and cut into squares. Bake slowly on a hot griddle or a greased frying pan. Turn several times so that the cakes brown on both sides and cook through. (Makes 10 or 12 scones)

For a luncheon or supper dish, creamed meat, fish, or vegetables may be served over the scones.

Potato Soup with Oatmeal

4 cups meat stock (water and bouillon cubes may be used)
2 cups raw diced potatoes
½ cup sliced onions
1 cup sliced carrots
½ cup chopped celery
½ cup rolled oats
1 cup cooked tomatoes
Salt and pepper

Wash and peel the vegetables and cut into small pieces. Add them to the stock and bring to the boiling point. Gradually stir in the rolled oats. Simmer 20 minutes, or until the vegetables and oatmeal are tender. Add the tomatoes. Season to taste with salt and pepper, and continue to simmer until ready to serve. (Serves 6)

Potatoes Anna

Peel medium-sized potatoes and slice them very thinly crosswise. Soak in iced water for ten or fifteen minutes. Drain and dry between towels. Grease a straight-sided baking dish with a tightly fitting cover. Place the sliced potatoes in the dish in layers, seasoning each layer with salt and pepper, and dotting with butter or margarine. When the dish is full, spread the top with plenty of butter or margarine and put on the lid. Bake in a slow oven (325° F.) for 45 minutes. Take out the dish; turn the cake carefully upside down, being careful not to lose the melted butter. Re-cover and place in the oven for 45 minutes more. To serve, turn out the potatoes, which will have amalgamated into a golden cake, and pour the butter over the top. Serve very hot.

POTATOES AU GRATIN

6 medium-sized cooked potatoes
3 tbsp butter or margarine
3 tbsp flour
1½ tsp salt
Pepper
2 cups milk, heated
1 cup grated cheese

Dice the cooked potatoes. Make a white sauce by melting the butter in a saucepan and stirring in the flour and seasonings. Cook, stirring constantly, until the mixture bubbles. Gradually add the milk, and cook over a low flame, stirring constantly until the sauce boils and thickens. Stir in ¾ cup of grated cheese and the diced potatoes. Turn into a baking dish, top with the rest of the cheese, and bake in a moderately hot oven (375° F.) about 15 minutes, until the cheese melts and browns. Serve very hot. (Serves 6)

POTATOES COOKED WITH PORK

2 lb small potatoes
¾ lb lean breast of pork
2 large onions
1 tbsp flour
4 cups water
1 bouquet garni
1 stalk celery

Choose very small potatoes, all of even size. Peel the potatoes and place in an earthenware baking dish with a tightly fitting cover. Cut the pork into large cubes. Peel and quarter the onions. Melt a little pork fat in a skillet and brown the pork cubes and onions. Sprinkle the flour into

the skillet, stir, and allow to blend thoroughly. Pour in the water slowly, add the bouquet garni (which see) and the stalk of celery. Allow the mixture to simmer for a few minutes and then pour over the potatoes. Cover the baking dish and put over direct heat. Bring to a rapid boil. Season to taste with salt and pepper. Re-cover the dish and place in a moderately hot oven (350° F.) for 35 minutes. Do not remove the cover while baking. Serve from the baking dish, very hot. The potatoes will be delicately flavored, and the whole dish exceptionally delicious and unusual. (Serves 6)

POTATOES DAUPHINOISE

6 good-sized potatoes
½ cup grated Gruyere cheese
Milk
Salt and pepper
1 clove garlic
3 tbsp melted butter or margarine

Rub the entire surface of an earthenware baking dish with the garlic, and grease the dish with butter or margarine. Peel the potatoes and cut into rather thick slices. Lay half of them in the dish, sprinkle with salt and pepper, and half the cheese, and make a second layer the same way. Pour in enough milk to barely come to the surface of the potatoes. Pour the melted butter over the top. Bake in a moderate oven (350° F.) uncovered until the potatoes are tender and nicely browned. It may be necessary to add more milk while baking, but only enough so that it is all absorbed in the cooking. Serve very hot from the cooking dish. (Serves 6)

POTATOES HASHED IN CREAM

4 large cooked potatoes
1 cup cream or milk
Salt, pepper, and cayenne
2 tbsp butter or margarine

Dice the cooked potatoes and season rather highly with salt, pepper, and cayenne. Arrange in a buttered baking dish, and pour in the milk or cream. Dot with the butter or margarine. Bake in a moderate oven (350° F.) for an hour. If desired, a little onion juice may be added to the mixture. (Serves 4)

POTATOES IN SOUR CREAM

2 lb potatoes
1 medium-sized onion
2 tbsp butter or margarine
4 tbsp grated cheese
4 tbsp bread crumbs
1 cup sour cream
2 eggs
Salt and pepper

Scrub the potatoes and cook in boiling salted water until tender. Drain, dry and peel, and slice in thin slices. Melt the butter in a skillet and brown the onion which has been minced. Put the potatoes into a baking dish and add the onion, bread crumbs and grated cheese. Beat the eggs and stir into the sour cream. Pour over the potatoes. Bake in a moderate oven (350° F.) for 15 or 20 minutes, until well heated and slightly brown.

POTATOES IN SOUR SAUCE

2 tbsp butter or margarine
1 tbsp minced onion
1 tbsp flour
2 tbsp vinegar
½ cup stock
Peel of a large lemon, cut in strips
1 bay leaf
Salt and pepper
4 medium-sized potatoes

Scrub the potatoes and cook in boiling salted water until tender. Meanwhile make the sauce by melting the butter in a pan and cooking the onion in it until brown. Sprinkle in the flour, and continue cooking, stirring constantly, until the flour browns. Add the hot stock gradually, and then the vinegar, lemon peel, bay leaf, and salt and pepper. Let the sauce simmer for 30 minutes. When the potatoes are done, drain, dry and peel them, and cut into small dice. Add the potatoes to the sauce and let simmer for 5 minutes. Remove the lemon peel and bay leaf, and serve immediately. (Serves 4)

POTATOES LYONNAISE

3 tbsp butter or bacon fat
3 tbsp minced onion
3 cups diced cooked potatoes
½ tsp salt
⅛ tsp pepper
1 tsp minced parsley

Heat the butter or bacon fat in a heavy frying pan. Add the onion and cook, covered, until just beginning to color, about 5 minutes. Add the diced potatoes and salt and pepper, and toss lightly until coated with the fat. Cover and cook 5 minutes; then remove the cover and continue cooking until the potatoes are brown. Sprinkle in the minced parsley and serve immediately. (Serves 6)

SARATOGA POTATOES

Peel evenly sized potatoes and slice as thinly as possible, crosswise, using a slicer. Drop into ice water and let stand one hour, changing the water twice during this period, or adding more ice cubes. Pat dry between towels and fry, a few at a time, in deep hot fat (375°–390° F.) until golden brown and floating on the surface. Drain on soft crumpled paper and sprinkle with salt. Saratoga chips may be served hot or cold.

SCALLOPED POTATOES

Peel and wash medium-sized potatoes and slice crosswise into slices of even thickness. Drain thoroughly. Arrange in a shallow baking dish, first a layer of potatoes, next a sprinkling of flour, salt and pepper with a few dots of butter or margarine, and repeat the layers until all the potatoes are used. Pour in hot milk to come level with the top of the potatoes. Cover and bake in a slow oven (300° F.) about one hour, or until the potatoes are tender and slightly browned on top. It may be necessary to add a little more milk during the cooking. Sprinkle with minced parsley and serve very hot.

SCALLOPED POTATOES AND FRANKFURTERS

4 large potatoes
½ lb frankfurters
1 cup diced celery
2 tbsp butter
2½ tbsp flour
2 tsp prepared mustard
½ tsp salt
2 cups milk

Peel and slice the potatoes. Slice the frankfurters into ½-inch slices. Grease a baking dish and arrange alternate layers of sliced potatoes, frankfurters, and celery. Make a cream sauce of the butter, flour, mustard, salt, and milk. When it boils and thickens, pour over the contents of the baking dish. Cover the dish and bake in a moderate oven (350° F.) about an hour, until the potatoes are tender. Uncover for the last few minutes to brown the top. Serve from the casserole. (Serves 6)

Leftover ham may be used in place of the frankfurters.

SHOE STRING POTATOES

These are simply French fried potatoes, cut very thin and matchlike. Because of their thinness they cook more quickly than the larger pieces.

STRAW POTATOES

Slice raw potatoes paper-thin, preferably on a cutting board, and then slice the other way into threadlike strips. Plunge into deep hot fat (375°–390°) and fry until golden brown. They will cook almost instantaneously. Drain on soft crumpled paper and serve, sprinkled with salt, with broiled chops or steaks.

POTATO APPLE. The yellowish or purplish fruit or seed pod of the potato plant. It is about the size of a small gooseberry, and one fruit contains as many as three hundred small seeds. It is known in certain parts of Europe as "gadelles" and is pickled, made into marmalade, and sometimes eaten raw with pot cheese and sugar. It has almost disappeared in the United States because of commercial practices in raising potatoes which do not allow the plants to go to seed.

POTATO CHEESE. A rennet cheese, made from the sour milk of cows with caraway seeds added. Sometimes sheep's or goat's milk is used. It is native to Germany.

POTATO MASHER. A potato masher is an implement used to break boiled potatoes into a creamy, even mass. They are made of either wood or metal, and in a great variety of designs. Some are used with a straight thrusting motion, while others are also adapted for a beating or whipping action. *See* POTATO; *see also* KITCHEN EQUIPMENT.

POTHEEN. Irish "moonshine"; a whisky made by an illegal still, often using a potato mash. *See also* WHISKY.

POTTED CHEESE. This cheese is prepared from well-ripened Cheddar, butter, condiments, spirits, etc. It is wrapped in waxed paper and tin or lead foil and is often known as club cheese.

POTTED MEATS. Commercial products, usually in paste form, made from meat, poultry, game, etc.

POTTERY. The designation for the coarsest type of ceramic material found in kitchen utensils, dishes, etc. *See* CERAMICS.

POUCHONG TEA. Oolong tea that has been scented with the blossoms of gardenia, jasmine, or Chinese magnolia shrubs. Layers of the petals are placed in chests alternately with layers of tea leaves. The best Pouchong teas come from Formosa. *See also* TEA.

POULETTE SAUCE. *See* WHITE SAUCE.

POULTRY. By poultry we understand all the edible domestic birds that are cooked except squabs, which are classed as game. There follow a few important points for the cooking of poultry:

Poultry, as a rule, should never be cooked until six to eight hours after it has been killed, but it should be plucked and drawn as soon as possible. If plunged in a kettle of scalding-hot water, the feathers are easily plucked off, after which the hair is singed.

Remember that poultry is classified among the white meats, and as such, like pork, veal, and young lamb, should always be well done.

Basting is as important as seasoning. *See* SEASONING *and* BASTING.

Poultry, of whatever kind, when roasted needs no searing. To brown, raise the temperature during the last half hour or so of roasting, basting often.

A braised bird is prepared as for roasting. time, allowing a few minutes additional when the bird is stuffed.

Generously half fill the bird with the chosen stuffing. This permits expansion during roasting and prevents bursting of the skin.

Never attempt to roast an old, tough bird. One too old to roast is very good boiled or braised.

A braised bird is prepared as for roasting It may be stuffed, should be covered closely, and should be allowed to braise (*which see*) very slowly in a moderate oven (300°–325° F.), allowing 40 minutes per pound, using the undrawn weight to figure time. The flavor of an old bird is enhanced when the breast is covered with a thin slice of fat larding pork. This prevents dryness. Do not baste a braising food. The basting is done automatically.

Birds, except the goose and duck, may be stuffed front and rear and are always trussed. A roasted, boiled, or braised bird is not presentable if it has not been securely fastened into good shape before being cooked.

When a bird is not stuffed, but simply roasted, it is advisable to place in the cavity a small piece of celery or onion or carrot, or all three. For a duck, pieces of apple may be added. This will greatly enhance the flavor and prevent dryness in cooking.

When boiling a bird, it is advisable to tie it in a piece of muslin or cheesecloth, wrung out of cold water, to keep it in good shape and simplify lifting it out of the broth. A boiled bird may be stuffed or not as preferred. Barely cover with water, or the indicated liquid, when boiling a bird, if you desire a rich, good stock.

The fat from a roasting bird, especially duck or goose, should not be allowed to accumulate in the roasting pan, lest the duck or goose become greasy and therefore difficult to digest. As the fat melts in any quantity, it should be drained from the pan, leaving just enough for basting.

When adding bread or a quantity of bread crumbs to a stuffing, it is of the utmost importance to squeeze it after soaking and then toss it to loosen it. By this method a stuffing will always be light, moist, and easy to digest.

Try basting a goose or duck with orange juice after removing all the fat drippings in the pan.

The legs of the goose are too short to truss like chicken or turkey. Tie the trussing twine around one leg and then around the other, leaving about two inches of string between the legs, bring the ends of the twine under the back, and then tie securely.

When roasting a bird, always place it breast-side-up on the rack of the open roasting pan. Turn the bird once on each side during the cooking process to obtain an even browning. Do not forget to baste it occasionally.

If you are planning to serve chicken or turkey to a number of persons, figure three-quarters to one pound per person when you are buying it. Figure a broiler for two persons, and a squab or pigeon for one or two persons, according to size.

Poultry, as a rule, should be served sizzling hot, or, if served cold, should be very cold. There is no intermediate stage if you want to enjoy the full flavor.

Bland and tart sauces, smooth or sharp, hot or cold, may be served with hot or cold poultry.

Small poultry may be advantageously cooked whole in an earthenware casserole (*which see*), either on the range or in the oven, and may or may not be stuffed in either case. This affords variation to roast, broiled or baked poultry. Small poultry may or may not be boned, as preferred.

An old bird may be used for a stew, but never sauteed or fried. These two methods would only render it tougher.

Poultry livers afford many a delicious preparation. They may be sautéed, served en brochette (on skewers), on toast, au gratin, in shells or ramekins, or in small individual casseroles, in pie forms, in an omelet, etc. The same may be done with poultry trimmings. They are economical, besides being delicious and nourishing.

Broilers, if loosely disjointed but not taken apart, will heat through faster and be handled more easily by the eater.

Giblets, neck, and feet make an inexpensive and delicious chicken broth.

Thin slices of salt pork, cooked to a crisp, are savory with chicken cooked in cream.

Popovers may be slit and filled with creamed chicken.

A light dusting of nutmeg gives chicken soup a distinctive flavor.

Try cheese biscuit crust to top chicken, turkey, or squab pies, and press tiny stuffed green olives in rows in top crust for an attractive garnish. Or make a lattice crust and after baking fill each hole in the lattice with a stuffed ripe olive.

Did you ever try rubbing broiling chickens with butter mixed with onion juice and powdered ginger? Or baking chickens with anchovy paste (adding no salt or pepper of course) mixed with dry mustard? If you try this idea on your next chicken, add half a cupful of sliced olives, either ripe or pimento-stuffed, to the gravy.

Chicken hash is well known to all. But have you served it in biscuit shells, topped with cream sauce, sprinkled with grated cheese, and brought to perfection under the flame of the broiling oven?

POULTRY NEEDLE. A poultry needle has a long, heavy shaft, and an eye large enough to take string rather than thread. It is used to sew up poultry, meats, or fish, especially when they have been stuffed.

POULTRY SEASONING. A mixture of different spices and herbs, sold in small packages at almost all grocery stores.

POUND. A unit of measure consisting of 16 ounces.

POUSSE CAFE. (I) A deep-brown after-dinner cordial, sweet and sirupy, packaged in a beautiful bottle, usually served at room temperature.

poured first, thus making the effect possible. In making a pousse café, the exact order of pouring given in the recipe must be followed, if the pouring is to be a success.

The making of pousse cafés is not recommended for the average amateur bartender. Not only is considerable skill required in the pouring, but the ingredients are costly and, for the most part, rarely used for other purposes, and special glassware is needed.

There are a great many recipes known as "pousse café," while others are given names, often fanciful, suggested by the appearance of the finished product. Some typical recipes are listed here.

POUSSE CAFE

POUSSE CAFE. (II) The original French meaning referred to a brandy or liqueur served with black coffee at the close of a dinner, and in America the term has been applied to a specific class of drinks served as after-dinner liqueurs.

The pousse café, American style, is made by carefully pouring various liqueurs, cordials and other fluids into a pousse café glass (*See* GLASSWARE) in such a manner that they form separate, colorful layers. *See* BARTENDING.

The ingredients are arranged in order of their specific gravities, the heaviest being

POUSSE CAFE I

1 part grenadine
1 part yellow chartreuse
1 part Creme de Yvette
1 part white creme de menthe
1 part green chartreuse
1 part brandy

POUSSE CAFE II

1 part grenadine
1 part maraschino
1 part vanilla

1 part curacao
1 part yellow chartreuse
1 part cognac

STARS AND STRIPES POUSSE CAFE

1 part grenadine
1 part white creme de menthe
1 part Creme de Yvette

POUSSE CAFE GLASS. *See* GLASS-
WARE; *see also* POUSSE CAFE.
POUT. A variety of codfish.
PRAIRIE HEN. This bird is a lover of
the open prairie and as a substitute readily
accepted the wheat and corn fields of the
early settlers in America, in which it was,
and still is, a valuable ally of agriculture.
However, great as its value is to the
farmer, if we are to judge from present
appearance, the prairie hen must soon be
written of in the past tense. Formerly
it was abundant in the Mississippi region,
from Manitoba south to Louisiana and
Texas, and extending as far west as Colorado. Today a scant remnant of its former
number is left, and this remnant is rapidly
dwindling. Ranging only a short distance
of our boundaries, the prairie hen is in
the strict sense of the word an American
game bird, and one must go far to find
a finer. Being nonmigratory, it is State
property, and its fate rests solely with the
individual States within which it resides.
Considering its past abundance, the fine
sport its pursuit affords to the legitimate
sportsman, its delicacy for the table, and
the valuable service it renders the farmers
in destroying his insect enemies, the record
of its treatment is a shameful one. In many
states no protection or little was given this
precious bird, till its extinction was practically assured, while in the states in which
adequate legislation has been enacted,
open seasons, too large bag limits, and
inadequate enforcement of the laws have
produced their inevitable effect.

COWBOY'S FRICASSEE OF PRAIRIE HEN

2 prairie hens
2 tbsp fat
1 tbsp flour
3 small carrots, sliced
1 medium-sized onion, sliced
1 small clove garlic, crushed

3 large tomatoes, peeled and quartered
1 bouquet garni
Pinch each of marjoram and thyme
Dash of grated nutmeg
Salt
Freshly ground peppercorns
1 wineglass each dry white wine and
stock

Pick, clean, singe, and cut each bird into
six pieces. Cook in the fat, first the neck,
wings, gizzard and liver, then the remaining portions, browning all slightly.
Drain off any remaining fat and sprinkle
the flour over the meat. Add the vegetables,
tomatoes and seasonings. Moisten them
with the wine and stock. Cover closely and
cook just until vegetables and birds are
tender. (Serves 4)
PRAIRIE OYSTER. A nonalcoholic
concoction often used by drinkers as a
medicine on the morning following over-
indulgence. As the name would imply, it
is regarded as an old American tradition.

PRAIRIE OYSTER

1 whole egg
½ tsp vinegar
Salt and pepper to taste

The egg is dropped into a wineglass,
care being taken not to break the yolk.
The vinegar is then dropped gently down
inside the glass and the salt and pepper
added. It is drunk in such a way that the
egg is swallowed first, before the vinegar.
(Serves 1)
One variation calls for a teaspoon of
Worcestershire sauce to be placed on the
egg before the vinegar is added.
There are other, more complicated variations of this basic recipe.

PRAIRIE OYSTER VARIATION

1 whole egg
1 tsp Worcestershire sauce
1 tsp tomato catsup
½ tsp vinegar
1 drop tabasco sauce

This is made and drunk as above. (Serves
1)
While at first reading the idea of the
Prairie Oyster may sound repulsive,
especially in view of the notoriously queasy

state of the hangover stomach and mind, it is based on sound reasoning and usually affords some measure of relief. The substances used, the egg especially, tend to counteract the action of alcohol on the human system.

PRALINE. A confection of nuts and caramelized sugar.

BURNT SUGAR PRALINES

3½ cups sugar
⅛ tsp salt
2 cups hot water
Dash of grated nutmeg
2 tbsp butter
2 cups blanched toasted almonds or other nuts

Place 1 cup of the sugar, with the salt, in a heavy iron frying pan and stir constantly over a moderate heat until the sugar melts and is of a pale yellow color. Remove from the fire and let this carameled sugar stand for 5 minutes, stirring once or twice; then add the remaining sugar, water and nutmeg. Stir from the bottom of the pan and bring all to the boiling point. Add the butter and cook, stirring constantly, always from the bottom of the pan, to the soft ball stage (238° F.). Remove from the fire, let stand 5 minutes, then stir until the mixture becomes cloudy. Now add the nuts and continue stirring until the praline becomes creamy. Be careful not to continue this too long lest the mixture become thick and heavy. Drop from the tip of a teaspoon in small mounds, a little distance apart, on waxed paper.

CREOLE PRALINES

3 cups granulated sugar
½ cup top milk
½ cup undiluted evaporated milk
¼ tsp salt
2 tsp grated orange rind
1 cup brown sugar
1 tsp vanilla
1 cup broken pecans

Combine the granulated sugar, milks, salt, and orange rind and bring slowly to boiling point, stirring until the sugar is entirely dissolved; then cook to the soft ball stage (238° F.). Melt the brown sugar in a heavy iron frying pan, stirring constantly, and as soon as it is all melted and caramelized, combine the two mixtures in the saucepan slowly, stirring constantly. The mixture will probably foam and sputter. Return to the fire and again bring to the soft ball stage (238° F.). Cool to lukewarm, add the vanilla and pecans and beat briskly until creamy. Then drop by tablespoonfuls onto waxed paper.

PRALINE COOKIES

½ cup butter
1½ cups brown sugar, firmly packed
1 egg
1 tsp vanilla
1½ cups sifted all-purpose flour
1 cup chopped pecans

Cream butter until smooth, add sugar and egg and beat until smooth and fluffy. Add vanilla. Sift in flour and blend thoroughly. Stir in nuts until well distributed. Shape dough in small balls and flatten out with a flat-bottomed glass covered with a clean, slightly dampened cloth, to about ⅛-inch thickness on a greased baking sheet. They should be at least 1 inch apart when flattened. Bake in a moderate oven (375° F.) for 12 minutes, or until nicely browned. Cool on the pan for 2 to 3 minutes; then transfer to cake racks. (Makes about 3 dozen cookies)

PRAWN. A large shrimp, *which see.*

PRESERVATIVES. The preservative substances long familiar are salt, sugar, molasses, sirup, wood smoke, spices, vinegar and alcohol. While a small amount of sugar is necessary in the fermentation process, a large amount acts as a preservative, as in candied fruit. It is an interesting fact that alcohol and vinegar, products of fermentation processes, tend (when sufficiently concentrated) to stop the growth of the fermentation organisms. Molasses, like sirup, is a good preservative. It has been used to preserve potatoes in layers. Brine and saltpeter are also preservatives.

The application of preservative substances is another common and important method of preserving meats. The substances which have been most used for this purpose are salt, saltpeter, and other nitrates and nitrites, boric acid or borates, sulfites, vinegar, wood smoke, and sugar. Frequently two or more preservatives are used in the curing of a single product.

Thus hams are cured in a sweet pickle (brine), containing sugar, salt, and saltpeter; and bacon is packed in watertight vats with sugar, salt, and sodium nitrate or nitrite before preservation is completed by exposure to wood smoke. Salt, sugar, vinegar, and wood smoke are condimental as well as preservative in their properties, and there is no restriction upon their use. Saltpeter in addition to its preservative action has the property of maintaining, or even intensifying, the red color of meat. Under the present federal food laws it has been ruled that saltpeter may be used pending further investigation regarding its wholesomeness. According to recent reports, sodium nitrite not only fixes the color of hams but has been found particularly effective in preventing the growth of the organisms which cause souring. Boric acid and borax, which, when used, are employed purely for their preservative effect, and sulfites, which act both to preserve and to give the meat a bright appearance, are not permitted under the present United States meat inspection law. In England and Canada, on the other hand, no objection is made to the use of limited amounts of boric acid or of borax.

PRESERVE JARS. Small pots or jars designed to hold honey, jam, etc., for serving at the table. *See* DISHES.

PRESERVES. A good preserve is one in which the fruit or pieces of fruit remain whole, tender, clear, and plump, in a thick transparent sirup. The approximate proportion of sugar to fruit in preserves is three-quarters of a pound of sugar to one pound of fruit. As with jams and other canned foods, preserves should always be stored in a cool, dark, dry place.
See also CANNING, JAM, JELLY, MARMALADE, and individual fruits.

PRESERVING. *See* CANNING. *See also* FREEZING FOODS.

PRESSURE COOKER. A new technique of cooking has come into being with the development of the pressure cooker, a vessel that utilizes steam pressure to cook foods faster. It is said that the pressure cooker is more than just a time saver; that, due to the quickness of cooking and the small amount of water involved, the natural appearance and flavor of the food is preserved. It is also said that the foods retain more of their natural vitamin and mineral content than in most other cooking methods, that less fuel is required to do the cooking, and that the tougher (and more economical) cuts of meat can be utilized, being rendered suitably tender and flavorsome.

There is much to be said for these claims. Much, of course, depends on the skill of the user, for, unless the manufacturer's directions are followed, the results can be just

PRESSURE COOKER

as unsatisfactory as are the results of any cooking method that is poorly done. The techniques are not difficult to learn, however, and the pressure cooker is definitely suited to the pace of modern living.

The device is by no means new, for the principles involved have long been known and used. Its wide popularity, however, has been a recent development, for until not so many years ago, pressure cookers were rather rare and quite expensive. Much research has been put into the technique, and today many manufacturers are competing in the race to bring better and cheaper cookers to the market. As a result, the techniques of pressure cooking have been fairly well explored and standardized, and the devices themselves are now within the reach of most family budgets.

THEORY OF PRESSURE COOKING

In pressure cooking, the cooking is done by live steam acting under pressure. Because of the pressure, the steam penetrates the food quickly and effectively, and also because of the pressure, the temperatures involved range from 16 to 38 degrees higher than those used in most other forms of cooking with water. As a result, the foods are cooked much quicker, and though moist heat is used, there is less opportunity for the food elements to be dissolved out of the food itself as there is when the food is immersed in boiling water.

These higher temperatures are possible because, while water cannot be heated hotter than its boiling point, the boiling point is controlled by the pressure exerted on the surface of the liquid. The boiling point of water is normally given as 212 degrees Fahrenheit, or 100 degrees Centigrade, but this applies only to water boiled under an atmospheric pressure of 14.7 pounds per square inch, the normal air pressure at sea level. If that pressure is lessened, by, for example, going to a higher altitude, the water will be found to boil at a lower temperature (*see* HIGH ALTITUDE COOKING). If the pressure is increased, however, the temperature at which the water will boil will also increase.

In pressure cooking, the water is boiled in a sealed container. Anyone familiar with the steam engine will realize that, as the steam is given off, it builds up pressure within the container. This pressure has two effects: it causes the temperature to increase by raising the boiling point, and it forces the steam into the food.

CONSTRUCTION

There are three essential parts to any pressure cooker: a vessel, a lid, and a valve.

Depending on need, the vessel may range in size from a small saucepan to a large kettle or pot, for the shape and size are not vital to the principle of pressure cooking. The vessel may be made of any metal strong enough to withstand the pressure involved, and yet not too heavy to handle.

The lid may be of any shape, but it, too, must be strong enough to stand the pressures, and it must be fitted to an airtight seal with the vessel. Unless the seal is perfect, the cooker will not operate in the proper manner. Gaskets of some sort are commonly used to insure the seal, and the lid may be held in place by clamps, threads, or else fit under a restraining rim on the inside of the vessel.

The valve must be such to maintain a constant, known pressure within the vessel. Usually, these valves may, in some manner or other, be adjusted to maintain different pressures for different foods. The valve may be a simple weight resting on an open vent tube, or it may be more complicated.

Some of the larger pressure cookers are also equipped with a pressure guage. These are needed for only certain types of operations, however, and usually an accurate, adjustable valve is sufficient.

Because of the dangers of excessive pressures, most pressure cookers are equipped with some sort of safety device that will release the pressure if it reaches the danger point. This may be a subsidiary unit, or may be incorporated into the design of the valve. It usually takes the form of a special plug that will be blown out if the pressure reaches a certain point.

The valve, gauge, and safety device are commonly installed in the lid.

USE

The food is prepared in the manner recommended by the manufacturer and placed in the cooker with the prescribed amount of water. The amount of water used will be the same regardless of how little or how much food is cooked. While as little food as desired may be cooked, there is a limit to the maximum amount that may be placed in the cooker at any one time. There must be a certain amount of air space left in the vessel if it is to function properly. While it will vary with the cooker, the vessels are usually not to be filled beyond the two-thirds level.

When the cooker is loaded, the lid is placed in position, care being taken to see that it is seated properly to make a tight seal. The valve is either opened or left off, depending on the design. The cooker is then placed on the range and heated with a high or intense heat, except when otherwise indicated in the instructions. When a steady stream of steam comes out of the open valve, indicating that all of the air has been forced out of the cooker, the valve is closed and carefully watched until it jiggles or otherwise indicates that proper pressure has been reached within the vessel.

The cooking time is counted from the moment the proper pressure is reached and not from any time before that point. While a high flame is used to bring the cooker to the proper pressure as quickly as possible, once that pressure has been reached, it takes surprisingly little heat to maintain it. The burner, then, should be turned down as soon as the pressure has been built up to the proper level, thus saving fuel and keeping the water from being boiled away needlessly. The burner is turned down as low as possible, with the valve still indicating that the correct pressure is being maintained.

If steam escapes from around the edges of the rim, or if the correct pressure is not built up in a reasonable time, it means that the lid is not correctly seated to form an airtight seal. This must be adjusted for the cooker to function.

The time should be watched very carefully, for, due to the speed with which a pressure cooker operates, it is easy for a careless worker to overcook the food. The times given in the instruction booklet should be followed exactly, even where fractions of a minute are indicated. Many foods require less than five minutes to cook, and some even less than a minute. An accurate timer (*which see*) will be found to be a valuable aid in many cases.

When the proper time has elapsed, the burner is turned off. The cover or lid should not be removed until the pressure has been reduced. There are two methods of reducing pressure: instantaneous and gradual. The pressure is reduced instantaneously by holding the cooker under a stream of cold water, and it is reduced gradually simply by letting the cooker stand for a reasonable period, usually from five to ten minutes. Since the cooking continues as long as there is pressure in the unit, it is important that the method used is the one indicated for that particular type of food.

It can be seen that there are several factors to be controlled in pressure cooking. There is the manner in which the food is prepared and the amount of water placed in the unit. There is the pressure at which the food is cooked, the length of cooking time, and the manner in which the pressure is reduced. Since these factors will vary according to the design of the unit used, it is difficult to give a general chart that will hold for all cases. The user should consult and religiously follow the instruction booklet supplied with the unit. If this booklet is lost, another should be obtained by writing the manufacturer. Under no circumstances should a book for a different make cooker be used.

Practically every food may be cooked in a pressure cooker. Foods may be cooked separately, or several at the same time. Dividers may, in many cases, be purchased which partition the interior off into two or more sections to hold different foods. Many dishes, sauces, etc. may also be prepared in the unit. In some cases, virtually all of the components of a meal may be prepared in the same cooking. Where appropriate, such recipes will be found in the instruction booklet.

The pressure cooker is not restricted to use with food, but, by adding racks and stands, may be used to sterilize various objects, and for canning operations.

CARE

When a pressure cooker is purchased, the buyer should make certain that an instruction booklet is supplied. This booklet should be carefully read before any attempt is made to use the implement, and it should be saved for future reference.

A new cooker should be cleaned before use. All labels should be removed by soaking and not by scratching with sharp or pointed instruments. The cooker should be scoured both inside and outside with a cleaner suited to the material.

The cooker should be cleaned after each use. It is important that it be kept clean for proper operation. Among the points to be checked are the valve mechanism, the gasket, and the rim of the lid or cover. Bits of dried food or dirt at any of these points can have serious consequences.

The cooker should be carefully dried before being put away. It should never be assembled as for cooking unless it is actually being used for that purpose. Storing it with the lid in place will cause the gasket to wear out sooner than it would in normal use.

Care should be taken not to pour hot liquids into a cold cooker and vice versa, lest the thick metal be cracked. If the user is ever called out of the kitchen while the cooker is in operation, the burner should be turned off, for the user may well be detained longer than the stated cooking period.

The unit, or parts of the unit, should never be dropped or banged around if it can be helped. The specific care of the individual components will vary with the unit, and this is discussed in the instruction booklet. Those instructions should be followed.

When parts become worn or damaged, they should be replaced only with parts made by the original manufacturer. If the safety plug is ever removed or blown out, it should be replaced either by the manufacturer or according to his directions.

In general, it must be remembered that a pressure cooker is a precision instrument, and not just another pot or pan. It must be treated as a precision instrument. Further, it must be remembered that steam pressure can become dangerous if it ever gets out of hand. While all pressure cookers are engineered for safety and have adequate protective devices, accidents may happen if the user is careless and permits the device to become damaged or fouled with dirt of some sort. *See also* KITCHEN EQUIPMENT.

PRESSURE OF ATMOSPHERE IN RELATION TO COOKERY. The pressure of the atmosphere (air pressure) is 14.7 pounds per square inch at sea level. It is inversely related to increases in altitude.

Air pressure has a distinct effect upon food cooked by moisture. When subjected to a normal atmospheric pressure of 14.7 pounds per square inch at sea level, water reaches its maximum temperature at 212 degrees Fahrenheit; that is, at its boiling point. However, when, by artificial means, water is subjected to an additional five pounds of pressure at the same elevation, the temperature rises to 227.5° F.

Contrariwise, when the atmospheric pressure is reduced, the temperature of boiling water follows down the scale. Thus, at 10,000 feet above sea level, where the air pressure is only 10.16 pounds per square inch, the boiling point of water is only 194.0° F.

Because of the heightened temperature, foods cook much faster under artificial pressure and, therefore, retain vitamins, minerals, and flavors that are lost when they are subjected to longer periods of heat and moisture.

Conversely, when pressure and, therefore, temperature is lowered, foods require longer to cook and lose many valuable qualities.

Changes in atmospheric pressure have little effect on foods that are cooked by dry-heat methods such as broiling, roasting, etc. *See also* HIGH-ALTITUDE COOKERY, and PRESSURE COOKER.

PRESTOST CHEESE. A rennet cheese made from the fresh milk of cows. It is cylindrical in shape and weighs from five to thirty pounds. It is also called Saaland Pfarr.

PRETZEL. The pretzel was known in the days of the ancient Romans, and in its long journey down to these days has acquired a very impressive collection of traditions. It obtained the name by which we know it in Germany, but the name "pretzel," according to some who have delved into its history, comes from a Latin word meaning "*a little reward.*" Others declare that the word has the same derivation as the word "*prayer.*" The two stories, interestingly, come together in the third story that priests, many, many years ago, gave pretzels to children who learned their prayers properly.

Pretzels seem to have had some kind of religious significance, probably long before priests put them to especially praiseworthy use. Pretzels once appeared in the shape of large rings to be worn about the neck before they were eaten. They were supposed to keep evil spirits away. Pretzels sometimes were hung on fruit trees with the expectation that, somehow, they would help the trees to bear well. Even today an old superstition about pretzels survives. If one breaks a pretzel ceremoniously while he makes a wish, the wish will come true. The ceremony probably derives from the same superstition that still leads people to cooperate in the breaking of the wishbones of fowls. Pretzels are manufactured with water and flour, similar to matzoths (*which see*) except they are baked in a hot oven until very hard, then glazed, which operation the matzoths do not require.

PRICKLY PEAR. *See* CACTUS PEAR.

PRIME RIBS. *See* BEEF.

PRIMOST CHEESE. Another name for Mysost cheese, *which see.*

PRIMULA CHEESE. A delicate Norwegian cheese.

PROFITEROLLE. In the ancient cuisine, profiterolles were nothing more than small balls of ordinary bread crumbs, used for garnishing potages (or thick soups), until 1373 when William (Guillaume) Tirel, nicknamed "Taillevent," the name under which he is better known, created profiterolles, made of a paste forced through a pastry tube. Later on, these little puffs were made of all sorts of food—fish, meat, poultry, and even vegetables.

Kitchen helper in the kitchen of Queen Jeanne d'Evreux, William Tirel became a great chef. Successively he was Esquire of Cuisine to Philipe le Valois; of Monsignor, the Dauphine de Vienne, then Esquire of

Cuisine to the Duc de Normandie. In 1373, he was made Esquire of all the Royal Cuisines of the Kingdom of France by Charles VI, King of France; and it was while in that high situation that he wrote his famous Cookbook, "The Viandier," then the "Cookbook of Taillevent, Esquire of All the Cuisines of the King of France." Taillevent died in 1395 and was buried near Saint Germain-en-Laye, a suburb near Paris. His tomb, richly carved and kept in the Saint Germain Museum, represents him as a warrior between his two wives, Jeanne Bonnard and Isabeau Le Chandelier. On the shield which he holds, three large kettles are surrounded each with six carved roses.

It was Taillevent who created Dodine Rouge which is a mixture used for stuffing ducks or water fowls. It is made as follows: Toast enough bread slices on both sides. Soak the toast in Chambertin wine. Fry finely sliced onions in a little salted lard, until golden brown; season highly with salt, pepper, cloves, cinnamon, and add a little duck fat. Let simmer until the mixture begins to thicken. Cool. Fill the cavity of the duck.

Having some of this paste left over, Taillevent decided to make use of it. He forced it through a pastry bag onto a greased baking sheet, placed this in a medium hot oven—at that time they did not have modern ovens as we have today. Their oven consisted of placing their utensil containing the ingredient to be baked between two fires—fire under and fire over—as they used to say. The result was astonishing. Light, fluffy little golden marbles resulted. Profiterolles were created.

From the small one to the large one, there was only one step. And today we use the *pâté a chouxe* as the French call the paste, for almost anything, from fish, meat, fruit custard, and ice cream.

PARISIAN PROFITEROLLES AU CHOCOLATE

½ cup water
¼ cup butter
1 tsp salt
1 tsp sugar
½ cup sifted flour
2 eggs
1 tsp vanilla

Combine the water, butter, salt, and sugar in a saucepan and heat. When boiling, add the flour, all at once, stirring vigorously, and cook until the mixture forms a smooth ball which leaves the sides of the pan clean. Turn into a mixing bowl and beat the eggs in thoroughly, one at a time. Add the vanilla and continue beating until the mixture is thick and shiny and breaks off when the spoon is raised. Drop by half teaspoonfuls onto greased paper on a baking sheet and bake in a very hot oven (450° F.) 10 minutes, then reduce the heat to moderate (350° F.) and bake 20 minutes longer. Cool. Cut a slit in each, and fill with whipped cream or ice cream. Serve with thin chocolate sauce.

CHOCOLATE SAUCE

4 squares cooking chocolate, grated
½ cup warm water
1½ cups light cream or evaporated milk
½ tsp salt
¾ tsp vanilla

Melt the chocolate in the warm water. Add the cream or milk and stir until thickened and well blended. Remove from the fire, add the salt and vanilla and serve either warm or cold. (Makes about 2 cups)

PROOF SPIRIT. A term which is applied to an alcoholic beverage which contains at least 50 percent alcohol by volume. A spirit weaker than "proof" is said to be so many degrees percent "underproof." A spirit stronger than proof is said to be so many degrees percent "overproof."

Here the term percent is not employed in its proper arithmetical sense, but merely to mean "strength to one hundred," which is the assumed numerical value of proof strength. For instance, a liquor which is 25 percent overproof (O.P.) is a quarter stronger than "proof"; or, in other words, it contains 75 parts of alcohol out of the possible 100, the remainder being water and flavoring material.

PROTEIN. About fifty different proteins have been isolated and studied. They are all made up of compounds of similar structure, called amino acids. Seventeen different kinds of amino acids have been determined so far; they can be crystallized and do not show the colloidal character of the protein molecule and are, therefore, easily dissolved. Nitrogenous compounds, chiefly found in the various forms of protein, have a highly complicated organic structure. Among their constituents are:

Carbon	50 to 55 %
Oxygen	19 to 24 %
Hydrogen	6.6 to 7.3%
Sulphur	3 to 2.4%

The more complex forms of protein also contain small quantities of phosphorus and iron.

Proteins are needed for growth and for the replacement of destroyed body tissues. If taken in larger quantities than required, the surplus is made into liver sugar or liver starch (glycogen) and often into fat. The extra amount of protein means overwork for the liver and kidneys and increased blood pressure.

Proteins, as well as carbohydrates (starches and sugar) and fats, are a fuel food. Every gram of pure protein provides four calories—an equal amount to what a gram of carbohydrates provides and about half as much as a gram of fat gives us. Some persons believe that protein does not provide calories. The reason for the first supposition is that protein is always included in liberal amounts in a reducing diet. This is for the sake of its other attributes as well as for the sake of its calories. The body needs protein every day in some degree to rebuild the tissues which are each day worn by the burden of every-day life.

Children need an extra amount to build new tissue while growing. Any protein that is not used for building may be burned as fuel which is used for heating the body to a normal temperature and to supply the energy needed for the body processes and for exercise.

Experience has shown, however, that protein should be used moderately in a well-balanced diet. About 10 percent of the calories in a day's diet—which averages about 2,400 calories—is the usual standard for the protein requirement. Some authorities allow an increase over that amount, and others feel that it is larger than necessary. When calories are cut down to 1,200–1,300, as they sometimes are in a reducing diet, the proportion of protein increases although the total amount eaten remains about the same as in an average diet. In fact, the so-called high-protein diets are generally favored as safer reducing diets.

The following table gives the protein calories in the 100-calory portions of some common food materials:

DISTRIBUTION OF CALORIES IN 100-CALORY PORTIONS OF COMMON FOOD MATERIALS

Food Materials	Weight	Protein	Fat	Carbohydrate
	(Ounces)	(Percent)	(Percent)	(Percent)
Almond, shelled	0.5	13	77	10
Apples, fresh	7.5	2	6	92
Bacon	0.5	6	94	—
Bananas	5.5	5	6	89
Beans, dried	1.0	26	5	69
Beef, lean round	2.5	54	46	—
Bread	1.4	14	4	82
Butter	0.5	1	99	—
Cabbage	13.3	21	7	72
Carrots	10.1	10	5	85
Cheese, American	0.8	27	73	—
Cod, salt, boneless	3.1	98	2	—
Cornmeal	1.0	10	5	85
Eggs, whole	2.7	36	64	—
Flour, white	1.0	12	3	85
Lamb chops	1.3	23	77	—
Lentils	1.0	29	4	67
Macaroni	1.0	15	2	83
Milk, whole	5.1	19	52	29
Milk, skimmed	9.6	37	7	56
Oats, rolled	0.9	17	16	67
Peanuts, shelled	0.6	19	63	18
Peas, canned	6.4	26	3	71
Peas, dried	1.0	27	3	70
Salmon, canned	2.4	54	46	—
Veal	3.2	70	30	—
Walnuts, shelled	0.5	10	82	8

The supply of protein is largely obtained from animal foods, milk, eggs, fish, meat, and cheese. Nuts and the legumes—peas, beans, and lentils—are a chief source of vegetable proteins. Animal proteins are more complete in themselves and are more completely utilized than those from vegetable sources. Proteins are much more complicated in construction than are fats and carbohydrates. Protein is made up of large numbers of substances which are known chemically as amino acids. The efficiency of a protein depends upon the number of these acids and the proportion of each. Certain protein foods supplement each other, as for instance, the protein in milk and that in cereals which are often eaten together. If milk is allowed in an otherwise vegetarian diet, the result will be satisfactory. There is, however, no good reason for persons in normal health to avoid any of the animal proteins, since the body is equipped to take care of certain waste products which are found in the digestion of meat and fish. When the organs lose some of this efficiency in later life, it is sometimes necessary to cut down on the amount of protein we have been accustomed to taking.

Nitrogen in the form of protein is necessary to the life of every cell in the body. From protein, too, muscle is built, though we cannot build good muscle merely by eating protein. A diet moderate in its amount of protein, but with plenty of fuel for healthy exercise, is best for muscle building. Under all ordinary conditions, if 10 to 15 calories in every hundred (10 to 15 percent of the total calories) are from protein, the need for this kind of building material will be met. Thus, a family requiring 10,000 calories per day, should have from 1,000 to 1,500 of these as protein calories.

Note that some foods, like bread, have about the right proportion of protein calories; others, like beef, beans, and peas, are very high in protein calories.

By combining some foods, high in protein, with others containing little or none, we can get the right proportion. Thus, 100 calories of beef, combined with 400 each of bread and butter, will give 900 calories, of which 114, or 12.7 percent, are from protein.

Beef   54 protein calories total 100 calories
Bread   56 protein calories total 400 calories

Butter   4 protein calories total 400 calories
Total 114 ÷ 900 equal 0.127 or 12.7 percent

It is interesting to work out other combinations which give these excellent proportions.

Proteins are a vital constituent of every cell. They make life possible and furnish the constructive materials for repair in the event of illness, injury, or disease. But we cannot store them in the human system as we can fats and starches. Any excess over daily bodily needs is immediately thrown off via the excretory organs. If there is a deficiency of protein, the muscles are called on to give up their supply and fatigue results. Any combination of food which excludes meat, fish, eggs, and cheese will fail to hold an individual in perfect nutritional balance. We can exist comfortably on a minimum intake of protein if adequate starches and fats are provided, but we must have that minimum of protein.

PROVIDENCE CHEESE. A French cheese resembling Port du Salut. It is eight inches in diameter and one and one-half inches thick.

PROVOLONI. An Italian cheese made from cow's milk. A special rennet is used and the cheese is smoked and cured in salt brine for 24 hours before being hung to cure. As a result it has a sharp smoky flavor. It is a hard cheese and will keep almost indefinitely without refrigeration. Giant provoloni is made in cylinders which weigh approximately 350 pounds. Pear-shaped provoloni is somewhat smaller and tapered. Provolette is the same cheese made into small apple-like shapes weighing from two to five pounds.

PRUNE. The dried plum of certain cultivated varieties. Prunes were introduced into America in California in 1856, when Louis Pellier grafted the French prune scion to the rootstocks of our native plum. Commercial planting began in 1870. The original *prune d'agen* is still the chief California prune and Santa Clara valley, where it originated, is still the greatest center of its production.

For varieties of prunes, *see* PLUMS.

PREPARATION FOR MARKET

Most prunes grown in California are sun dried, although in modern times a growing number are dried in evaporators.

Food Value

Water	Food Energy	Pro-tein	Fat	Carbo-hydrate	Cal-cium	Phos-phorus	Iron	Vit. A Value	Thia-mine	Ribo-flavin	Nia-cin	Ascor-bic Acid
24	299	2.3	.6	71.0	54	85	3.9	1,890	.10	.16	1.7	3

In any case, prunes are generally allowed to fall to the ground when ripe and are then picked up and put into lug boxes. They are taken to the dipper where they are immersed in a hot solution of lye. The dip should remove all the bloom or wax from the surface of the fruit and slightly check or crack the skin. After this, the prunes are rinsed in clean water. They are then separated into two sizes, and placed on drying trays. If sun-dried, the drying process takes from ten days to two weeks. When the prune has become firm in texture and the

PRUNES

pit cannot be separated from the flesh by rolling between the thumb and first two fingers, it is usually considered cured.

Hints on Buying

The leading dessert varieties of prunes are the Italian prune, and Agen, or French, prune.

Prunes of good quality are plump, clean, of fresh appearance, full-colored for the variety, and yield to slight pressure.

One pound of dried prunes yields two to three cups.

Prunes are less expensive than most other dried fruits. The California varieties in general are more sweet and tender than the large tart Italian prunes from Oregon. Tenderized prunes have had moisture added. Small prunes are less expensive than large prunes and usually give more meat for the same amount of money.

Hints on Preparation

Prunes should be cooked very slowly without ever reaching the boiling point and just until tender.

No sugar is needed for good California prunes. Those of the Oregon type are generally improved by about 1 tablespoonful for each pound.

Chocolate Prune Drops

2 cups uncooked prunes
2 cups granulated sugar
¼ cup white corn sirup
1 cup water
4 egg whites
1 cup finely cut citron
¾ lb dipping chocolate

Wash prunes in hot water, dry with cloth, and cut from pits in small pieces. Combine sugar, corn sirup and water in a deep saucepan or kettle and cook to 238° F., or until sirup forms a soft ball when a small amount is dropped into cold water. Beat egg whites until very stiff and add hot sirup slowly, beating continuously with a rotary beater. When firm, add prunes and citron. Beat with heavy spoon until very thick; cool. Cut chocolate fine and dissolve over lukewarm water, stirring to dissolve lumps. When chocolate is creamy, add egg mixture, a small amount at a time, and blend thoroughly. Drop by teaspoonfuls onto a waxed paper to harden. (Makes about 6 dozen drops)

Fried Prune Turnovers

1 recipe baking powder biscuits
2½ cups chopped cooked prunes

½ cup chopped nuts
1 tbsp lemon juice

Roll biscuit dough (*which see*) ½ inch thick; cut in rectangular pieces 4x2 inches. Mix together remaining ingredients; place 1 tablespoon filling on half of each piece, fold over and press edges together with floured fork. Fry in hot, deep fat (375° F.) about 3 minutes or until lightly browned.

Frozen Prune Pudding

1 package vanilla pudding powder
2 cups milk
½ cup confectioners' sugar
1 cup chopped, cooked prunes
¼ cup chopped pistachio nuts
1 cup heavy cream, whipped

Mix vanilla pudding powder with milk and cook in a double boiler for 15 minutes, or until smooth, stirring constantly; add sugar and cool. Fold in prunes, nuts and whipped cream; turn into trays of automatic refrigerator and freeze 2 to 4 hours, or until firm. (Makes 1 quart)

Prune Apricot Betty

1½ cups chopped, cooked prunes
1 cup cooked apricot pulp
Grated rind of 1 orange
Juice of 1 lemon
1½ cups fine bread crumbs
½ cup brown sugar
2 tbsp melted butter

Combine the prunes, apricot pulp, orange rind, and lemon juice. Place in a greased baking dish. Mix the crumbs and sugar, and add the butter. Sprinkle the crumb mixture over the fruit, and bake in a moderate oven (350°–375° F.) for 20 minutes or until browned. Serve with light cream. (Serves 6)

Prune Bavarian

1¼ tsp gelatin
½ cup water
½ lemon, grated rind and juice
¼ cup sugar
⅛ tsp salt
2¼ cups sieved prunes
1 cup heavy cream

Soften the gelatin in half the water. Simmer the lemon rind in the remaining water for 2 minutes, take out the lemon and dissolve the gelatin in this boiling water. Add the lemon juice, sugar, salt and fruit, and let stand until almost at the setting point. Fold in the cream, whipped, and turn into previously wet individual molds. Chill. Unmold, and serve with additional light cream or boiled custard. (Serves 6)

Prune Bread

⅓ cup sugar
¼ cup lukewarm water
1 package dry granular yeast or 1 cake compressed yeast
2 tsp salt
1¾ cups milk, scalded
6½ cups sifted all-purpose flour
3 tbsp melted shortening
1 egg
1 cup chopped cooked prunes

Stir 1 teaspoon of the sugar into the lukewarm water. Add yeast and let stand 10 minutes. Stir to blend well. Add remaining sugar and salt to the hot milk. Cool to lukewarm. Combine yeast and milk mixtures and stir well. Add 2½ cups of the flour and beat well. Add the cooled shortening and the egg and beat vigorously. Add the prunes and the remaining flour, turn dough onto floured board. Cover dough with bowl and let rest 10 minutes, then knead quickly and lightly for 10 minutes. Divide dough in two equal portions. Round up each portion, cover with a bowl and let rest for 10 minutes. Shape into loaves. Place in greased bread pans 8¼x 4½x2¾ inches. Cover and let rise in a warm place (86° F.) until double in bulk (about 1¼ hours). Bake in a moderate oven (375° F.) for 50 minutes. Remove from pan to rack; cool uncovered and away from drafts. A delicious tea or sandwich bread. (Makes 2 loaves)

Prune Coffee Cake

Sponge

1 cup milk
4 compressed yeast cakes
1 tbsp salt
2 cups all-purpose flour (sifted)

Heat milk to lukewarm, add crumbled yeast and stir until dissolved. Add salt and flour, and beat. Cover, and let rise in warm place 1 hour.

Batter

1½ cups uncooked prunes
1 cup water
¾ cup granulated sugar
½ cup butter
½ tsp cinnamon
2 eggs
3½ cups sifted all-purpose flour

Wash the prunes, drain and cut in small pieces. Add the water and let stand 1 hour. Cream sugar, butter, cinnamon and combine with sponge. Add prunes (do not drain), beaten eggs, flour and beat well. Cover and let rise in warm place 1 hour. Beat down, pour into well-greased pan (about 10x10x2¼ inches), and let rise 40 minutes. Bake for 30 minutes at 400 degrees F.

Top. If desired, remove from oven after 20 minutes and cover with ⅓ cup granulated sugar moistened with 3 tablespoons cream and ½ teaspoon vanilla. Return to oven and bake 15 minutes longer. Serve hot.

PRUNE ICE CREAM

2 cups uncooked prunes
1 cup milk
½ cup granulated sugar
1 tsp granulated gelatin
1 tbsp cold water
4 eggs
1 tbsp vanilla
¼ tsp salt
1 cup whipping cream

Wash prunes in hot water, cut from pits and put through food chopper using a fine knife. Combine milk and sugar and heat to boiling. Moisten gelatin in cold water, add to milk and stir until dissolved. Pour the hot mixture over well-beaten eggs, stirring to prevent curdling; add vanilla, salt, cream, prunes and beat until well blended. Freeze in freezing tray of automatic refrigerator with temperature control at coldest setting until firm enough to serve, or pack in rock salt and finely crushed ice. Requires 5 to 6 hours or may stand over-

night (will not become icy). *See also* ICE CREAM. (Serves 6)

PRUNE JUICE GELATIN

2 cups prune juice
½ cup granulated sugar
3 tbsp lemon juice
4 tsp granulated gelatin
3 tbsp cold water

Combine prune juice, sugar, lemon juice, and heat to boiling point. Moisten gelatin in cold water, add to hot juice and stir until dissolved. Pour into mold and chill. Serve with plain or whipped cream. (Serves 6)

PRUNE AND MARMALADE WHIP

1½ cups pitted, cooked prunes, diced
¼ cup orange marmalade
2 tbsp lemon juice
2 egg whites
¼ tsp salt
2 tbsp sugar

Combine the prunes, marmalade, and lemon juice. Beat the egg whites until stiff, gradually beating in the blended sugar and salt. Combine the two mixtures and again beat until thoroughly mixed. Pile in a serving dish and sprinkle with chopped nuts if desired. Serve immediately. (Serves 4)

PRUNE AND OLIVE APPETIZERS

Steam or cook large prunes until they are soft but not mushy, remove their pits, and insert a small stuffed olive in each. Wrap each prune in a small piece of bacon and secure with a toothpick. Broil until bacon is crisp, turning to assure uniform crisping. Serve at once.

PRUNE RICE CUSTARD

⅓ cup rice
3 cups milk
¼ tsp salt
Grated rind of 1 orange
½ cup sugar
2 eggs
2 cups stewed prunes, pitted
4 tbsp sugar, additional

Cook the rice, milk, salt, and orange rind in the upper part of the double boiler, until the rice is tender. Add the sugar and beaten egg yolks. Arrange the prunes in a baking dish, pour the rice custard over, and bake in a moderate oven (350° F.) for 10 minutes. Top with a meringue made from the egg whites with the additional sugar and a dash of salt, and return to the oven to set and delicately color the meringue. Serve warm. (Serves 6)

PRUNE SOUFFLE

5 egg whites
1 cup sweetened prune pulp
¼ tsp salt
1 tsp lemon juice
½ tsp grated lemon rind

Beat the egg whites until stiff, fold in the prune pulp (stewed prunes pressed through a sieve) with the salt, lemon juice, and rind. Turn into a deep, well-greased double boiler. Cover, and cook over hot water about 1 hour. Unmold and serve with slightly sweetened whipped cream. (Serves 6)

Slightly sweetened cooked apricot, cranberry, or peach pulp may replace the prunes.

PRUNE WHIP

3 egg whites
½ cup powdered sugar
1 cup cooked prunes

Whip the egg whites until stiff, gradually adding the sugar while beating continuously. Fold in the prunes, pitted and chopped, and continue beating until light. Turn into a buttered baking dish and bake in a moderate oven (350° F.) for about 15 minutes. Serve warm with soft custard (made from the egg yolks), or with cream. (Serves 3 or 4)

SAUSAGE–STUFFED PRUNES

Steam or cook large prunes until they are almost tender, remove their pits, and fill each with a tiny cocktail sausage. Place them in a well-buttered dish and bake them in a very hot oven (450° F.) until the sausages begin to brown. Serve on toothpicks when slightly cooled.

STEWED PRUNES

Wash prunes and, if dry, soak overnight in water to cover; otherwise add water, bring immediately to boiling point and simmer just until tender. One or two slices of lemon may be cooked with the fruit. Sweeten as desired; usually 1 to 2 tablespoons of sugar to the cup will be found sufficient.

STUFFED PRUNES IN CUSTARD SAUCE

8 stewed prunes
1 small apple
1 cup boiled custard

Remove the pits from the prunes and stuff them with bits of peeled apple. Arrange the prunes in a dish, and pour the custard (*which see*) around them. Serve very cold. (Serves 2)

PRUNELLE. A yellow-brown, sweet, fragrant liqueur, flavored with sloe berries, usually served as an after-dinner cordial. It is made in the same manner as gin, that is, distilled several times over sloe berries, to which is added the essential oil of different aromatic herbs. It is claimed to be a very digestive liqueur.

PTARMIGAN. A grouse of the northern hemisphere, with the winter plumage chiefly pure white. It is prepared like any other kind of grouse (*which see*).

PTOMAINE. Ptomaines are substances, resembling alkaloids, which are formed in the alimentary canal by the decomposition or putrefaction of nitrogenous foods. They may also form in such food outside of the body. This decomposition is the result of the action of certain microorganisms. The artificial cultivation of these microorganisms has proved that they are capable of forming poisonous substances which have distinct physiological actions.

Many of these microorganisms flourish in beef juice, milk, and various solutions of nitrogenous material. In the alimentary canal, when such food is taken, all the most favorable conditions are present for the development of toxins. When the poisonous germs are ingested, their toxins are readily absorbed by the intestinal mucous membrane, and it is probable that ptomaine poisoning would occur very much oftener were it not that the liver, acting as it does as a gateway for the admission of nutritive matter for the body, is capable of destroying many poisons which enter it from the intestines. Corroboration of this statement is found in the fact that snake bites of the surface of the body may prove highly poisonous by immediate absorption of toxic material into the circulation, whereas snake poison may be swallowed with impunity, for if it is absorbed from the alimentary canal it is destroyed in the liver before reaching the nervous system. The same is true of the action of putrefying meat, which in very small quantities may not produce severe gastro-intestinal symptoms or constitutional disturbances, and yet if inoculated through a cut in the finger may cause symptoms of a violent septic character. Ptomaines may be developed from a variety of foods, but the principal ones from which poisoning from time to time occurs are spoiled meat, milk, shellfish, and fish.

PUDDING. Puddings—those subtle blends of flavor, defying analysis; those spicy, fragrant mixtures or mild delicate ones—topped with just the right sauce—become epicurean desserts. And they allow for almost unlimited ingenuity and originality on the part of the maker. Though for generations puddings have been closely related to cold weather, they are right at any season, providing they suit the season—heavier ones for winter, of course, and lighter, daintier, less filling types in warm weather.

Puddings should be considered an integral part of the meal. If the pudding is rich in flour, eggs, milk, and fat, serve smaller amounts of these foods in the main course. More green vegetables should be included when a starchy dessert is served. If the pudding has suet in it, serve one of the leaner meats in the main course. A dessert high in eggs means that less protein need be served in the main course.

There are so many kinds of puddings that it is almost impossible to consider them all. Some are made in the double boiler, thickened by some starchy substance, such as cornstarch, flour or arrowroot—or eggs, as in the case of custards. Or the steamed fruit pudding may have a batter which is more like a cake. There are Indian puddings, made with cornmeal, baked rice or bread puddings, gelatin puddings, which are not baked at all, and the delicate pudding of the Spanish cream or Bavarian type. For a lighter pudding, one of the most delicious and delicate is the

custard soufflé with its many variations. *See* STEAMED PUDDINGS.

CORNSTARCH PUDDINGS

When cornstarch pudding is properly prepared, it cannot be rivaled in appearance or flavor, and certainly the cost is low. There are points to guide one in making it, however, just as in making and baking custards. To be quivery and jelly-like in consistency, just the right proportion of cornstarch to milk must be used. If a slightly thicker pudding is preferred, slightly increase the quantity of cornstarch. For a stiffly molded pudding, use four tablespoons (one-fourth cup) more of cornstarch to the same amount of milk. Always scald the milk in the top of the double boiler while you mix smoothly the sugar, salt, and cornstarch with some of the cold milk reserved for that purpose. Otherwise the contrast of the cold milk would delay or retard the cooking, and possibly cause lumping or scorching, this applying to almost every kind of pudding made over a direct flame or in a double boiler. This is then added to the scalded milk and cooked 20 minutes or so, being stirred constantly. If eggs are to be used, they are very gradually added to the mixture at this time, not before or after, first warming the eggs with a little of the hot mixture so that they will not be heated too quickly and become stringy. Cook only a minute or two after adding the eggs, still stirring constantly to prevent curdling. Then pour into cold, wet mold or molds to chill.

PUDDING SUGGESTIONS

The best results are obtained when a moderately hot oven is used for pudding baking.

A plain pudding to serve both the very youthful members of the family, who are not permitted to have spices, and also the elders, who may have what they please, may be made by providing brandy sauce or something heady for the elders, and a simple sauce, such as a fruit sauce, for the children.

Try baking a custard, then topping it with meringue.

Cover the bottom of a glass pudding dish with fresh ripe fruit, sprinkle with sugar, and cover with boiled custard, then with meringue.

The family won't know it is eating bread pudding if, after making and cooling regular bread custard pudding, you spread it with currant jelly or plum jam, then with a meringue.

PUDDING, molded and garnished

A bowl of cold boiled rice becomes a delicious cold pudding when you add to 2 cups of the rice, 1 cup of whipped cream and half a can of drained, canned red raspberries. Mix well and chill. Serve with a rich sauce made with the remainder of the fruit juice, sweetened if necessary, and boiled down until slightly thickened.

A baked vanilla custard, cooled and topped with fresh berries or canned fruits, is a hot-weather pudding you will like.

Sweeten 2 cups of applesauce and stir in 2 beaten egg yolks. Turn into individual dishes and bake in a moderate oven (350° F.) 15 minutes; then top with meringue made from the egg whites.

For a delicious summer pudding, pour creamy tapioca pudding over sweetened strawberries, cleaned and hulled, but left whole. Chill.

To unmold cornstarch pudding easily, add one tablespoon of butter to the mixture just before it is removed from the stove. Be sure, too, to rinse the molds with cold water just before you fill them.

Rhubarb makes delicious tapioca or brown betty pudding and shortcake. It is also good with sliced bananas.

Spread softened jelly over any simple pudding, such as rice, bread, tapioca, and apple brown betty, after baking. Top with meringue.

Hot applesauce with marshmallows folded in gives children special pleasure.

When you make an old-fashioned fruit pudding or betty, put layers of shredded

coconut between and on top of the layers of fruit and crumbs.

When making bread pudding, add one or two sliced, cored apples to the mixture, and thus change the flavor.

Crumble a few macaroons in the bottom of a baking dish before pouring in a custard to be baked, and note the difference in flavor.

Add a little grated orange rind to almost any baked pudding. This enhances the flavor, especially of bread, rice, and brown betty puddings.

See also individual fruits and flavors for pudding recipes.

BROWN PUDDING

2 tbsp softened butter
1 cup dark brown sugar
1 cup sifted flour
1 tsp baking powder
1 tsp ground cinnamon
¼ tsp salt
¾ cup milk
1 cup halved, seeded raisins
1 cup coarsely broken nut-meats
Sugar sirup

Combine the butter and sugar, then sift and add the dry ingredients alternately with the milk. Fold in the raisins and nuts, turn into a greased baking dish and drizzle the sugar sirup (*see below*) over. Bake in a moderate oven (350° F.) about 45 minutes. If desired, serve with light cream. (Serves 6)

For the sugar sirup boil together 1 cup of light brown sugar, 2 cups of boiling water, 1 tablespoon of butter and a dash of salt, stirring until the sugar is dissolved.

COTTAGE PUDDING

¼ cup butter
⅔ cup sugar
1 egg
2¼ cups sifted flour
2½ tsp baking powder
½ tsp salt
1 cup milk

Cream the butter and gradually add the sugar, then the egg, and finally the sifted dry ingredients alternately with the milk. Beat and whip until the mixture is smooth and fluffy. Turn into a greased dish and bake in a moderate oven (350° F.) about 40 minutes. Serve with any preferred sauce. (Serves 4 to 6)

Fruit Cottage Pudding. Cover the bottom of a buttered baking dish with any desired tender fresh, canned, or stewed fruit, as for example, pared, cored, sliced or diced apples; sliced bananas; canned pineapple; drained, pitted canned cherries; peeled, sliced fresh peaches; canned peach or apricot halves, etc. Top with cottage pudding batter (*see above*) and bake as directed. Serve with any appropriate sauce.

INDIAN PUDDING

3 cups milk
5 tbsp yellow cornmeal
½ tsp salt
1 tbsp butter
1 beaten egg
⅛ tsp ground ginger
3 tbsp sugar
2 tbsp molasses

Scald the milk in the upper part of the double boiler. Sprinkle in the cornmeal, stirring constantly. Add the salt and stir until thickened, then cook for 30 minutes with occasional stirring. Remove from the fire, cool slightly, and add the butter, then the egg, ginger, and sugar beaten together with the molasses. Turn into a buttered baking dish. Set in a pan containing hot water to come about half way up the sides of the dish, and bake in a slow oven (325° F.) until set like custard, about 2 hours. Serve warm with cream, hard sauce, or a small scoop of vanilla ice cream. (Serves 6)

MOLASSES PUDDING

1¾ cups sifted flour
½ tsp salt
1 tsp each ground ginger and cinnamon
1 cup molasses
1 tsp baking soda
1 egg
⅔ cup boiling water

Sift together the flour, salt and spices. Beat the molasses and soda together until light and frothy, then stir in the well-beaten egg and water. Combine with the dry ingredients and beat with rotary beater until smooth—the mixture will be very thin. Pour into a well-greased large mold,

cover closely, and steam 1½ hours. Serve with hard or liquid sauce, or with whipped cream. (Serves 6)

OLD-FASHIONED BAG PUDDING

1 cup lard
½ cup flour
4 eggs, well beaten
½ cup sugar
1 qt milk

Use a pudding bag of extra heavy unbleached muslin, 14 inches long and 8 inches wide. Rub all the lard into the bag, covering it completely; then rub the flour into the lard. Turn the bag inside out. Have a deep kettle, well filled with boiling water. Beat the eggs. Add the sugar and milk. Holding the bag so that the bottom touches the boiling water, pour the custard into it; tie it securely because the pudding will swell. Submerge the bag completely in the water. Cover it, and boil slowly until the custard is set, which will take about 20 minutes. Serve with Blackberry Sauce, made as follows:

1 cup seedless raisins
1 cup water
1 cup blackberry jelly or jam
Juice of 1 lemon

Simmer the raisins for 10 minutes in the water in a saucepan. Slowly pour them over the jelly or jam, beaten in a bowl. Add the lemon juice. Untie the bag and turn the pudding into a dish. Slice it, and pour the sauce over it. Serve hot or cold. (Serves 6)

PUFF. *See* CREAM PUFF.

PUFF PASTE. A rich, very flaky type of pastry used for roses, vol au vent, pâté shells, napoleons, cream horns, or turnovers. It is not difficult to make but is more expensive than plain pastry and requires greater care in handling.

PUFF PASTE

1 lb butter
1 lb sifted pastry flour
½ tsp salt
About ¾ cup ice water

All ingredients used in puff paste should be thoroughly chilled. The work must be done rapidly and the dough handled lightly and as little as possible.

First wash the butter by placing it in a mixing bowl, holding it under cold running water, and squeezing and pressing, preferably with the hands, until it is pliable and waxy, after which it should be chilled thoroughly before using.

ROLL TO SCANT ¼" THICKNESS KEEP CORNERS SQ. PLACE BUTTER IN CENTER OF LOWER HALF. FOLD UPPER HALF OVER LOWER HALF.

FOLD LEFT ⅓ UNDER. FOLD RIGHT ⅓ OVER. TURN FOLDED DOUGH ¼ TURN. REPEAT WHOLE PROCESS THREE MORE TIMES, THEN FINISH WITH STEP NO. 1.

PUFF PASTE

Sift the flour twice, adding the salt at the second sifting, then mix to a light dough with the water, adding only enough to moisten thoroughly. Form into a compact ball without over-working and set aside for 20 to 25 minutes. Roll out on a lightly floured board into a rectangular shape and about ¼ inch thick. Now place the washed butter in the center of the lower half of the paste, fold the upper half over the butter, press the edges firmly together and again roll out to approximately one-fourth inch thick. Fold together in three, as you would fold a sheet of paper to fit a business envelope. Again press the edges firmly together, place on a platter, cover with a napkin wrung out of cold water and chill in the refrigerator (but not directly on ice) for about 20 minutes. Now place on the board again and repeat the folding, rolling and chilling four times altogether, the last chilling lasting about one hour.

The rolling out should always be done in the opposite direction from the last, so as to spread and combine the butter evenly. Use for any recipe requiring puff paste, such as for pâtés, pies, turnovers, dumplings, or wherever a rich, light pastry is desired.

PUFFED RICE. *See* CEREALS.
PUFFED WHEAT. *See* CEREALS.
PUFFY. As applied to food, the term puffy means distended by the introduction of air bubbles, as by the addition of beaten egg whites or whipped cream. Certain other foods puff and become light when heat is applied.

PULLET. A young hen, usually under a year old. *See* CHICKEN.

PULQUE. An intoxicating beverage popular in Mexico, made by fermenting the sap of the Maguey and other aloes. *See also* MESCAL.

PULSE. *See* LEGUME.

PULTOST CHEESE. A Norwegian cheese made from sour milk with the addition of rennet. It is also called Knaost.

PUMPERNICKEL. *See* BREAD.

PUMPKIN. Although related to the cucumber, the pumpkin has been greatly modified by cultivation. Pumpkins vary in size from that of a large grapefruit to 50 or 100 pounds in weight. They belong to the gourd family. Pumpkin is extensively used in the United States, especially for pies, soups, etc. It contains much water and a good deal of coarse fiber.

The month of October brings awareness of the pause before autumn succumbs to winter. To the student of folklore, it may mean reflections on the ancient Druidic custom of lighting bonfires on hills and sacrificing to the moon god for protection against witches and spirits of the dead, both of which haunted the earth on the night

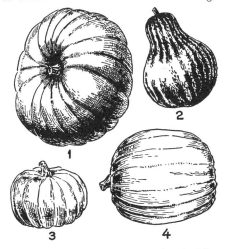

PUMPKINS   1. Mammouth   2. Pie
3. Sugar   4. Field

that later Christian eras knew as All Hallows' Eve. To the country dweller it may mean thoughts of harvest and Hallowe'en, as they are symbolized in the pumpkins that glow warmly from the lintels of white houses. To the boys of America it may mean jack-o'-lanterns and an excuse to lift gates from their hinges. But to a public that likes pumpkin pies, these are all subsidiary interests; the primary fact is that Hallowe'en is here to mark the traditional opening of the pumpkin season.

Though the largest pumpkins may make the most terrifying jack-o'-lanterns at this time, experts say that the medium-sized ones, 10 to 12 inches in diameter, sound, heavy for their size and bright in color, make the most satisfactory eating. The brilliant Sweet Sugar, or New England, pie pumpkin and the lighter yellow Winter Luxury are among the tastiest varieties on the market at that time, and the Connecticut Field, and the tan Big Cheese types run them a close second. Contrary to James Whitcomb Riley's poetical fancy, none of these is actually improved when the frost is on the pumpkin. The Bureau of Home Economics declares frost does not bring out the flavor of the big gourd as was popularly supposed, and it does injure its keeping qualities. But sound, ripe pumpkins will keep for a year or more, and retain their flavor, if they are stored in a cool dry place, separated from one another and wiped off occasionally with a dry cloth.

until tender when pierced with a sharp fork right through the skin. Then remove seeds and fibers and scoop out the flesh and press through a potato ricer. If the juice is pressed out first and kept separate from the pulp, it may conveniently be evaporated by boiling to almost nothing, and then mixed with the pulp.

PUMPKIN PIE

To the initiate, pumpkin pie is the first and most important of the pumpkin dishes. And indeed, the honorable history of New England's "favorite pie vegetable" is ample testimony of its perennial popularity. From earliest colonial days it has been as traditionally a part of the national diet as corn and cranberry sauce for Thanksgiving and Christmas as well as New Year's.

The one-crust pumpkin pie that begins its reign as queen of the dessert world is really an open tart, what the French term a "flan." But the culinary disputes that center around this dessert arise less from etymological disagreement than from individual differences of opinion about proper ingredients and methods of baking. Some cooks champion the cause of pumpkin chiffon pie made with egg whites or gela-

FOOD VALUE

Type	Water	Food Energy	Protein	Fat	Carbohydrates	Calcium	Phosphorus	Iron	Vit. A Value	Thiamine	Riboflavin	Niacin	Ascorbic Acid
Fresh	90.5	112	3.8	.6	22.8	66	138	2.5	10,640	.15	.24	1.8	26
Canned	90.2	174	4.5	1.4	35.9	91	163	3.2	15,440	.07	.28	2.5	0

HINTS ON BUYING

Pumpkins are sold by the pound or unit. One pound makes ¾ cup cooked pulp, and serves two people. Pumpkins are in season from September to March. In purchasing, look for deep yellow, fine-grained flesh. Large varieties may be covered with russet netting. Smaller pumpkins are preferable. Store pumpkins in a cool, dark, dry place with good air circulation.

HINTS ON PREPARATION

To prepare a mature pie pumpkin for purée, wash it and cut in halves. Do not scoop out seeds and fibers, but rub the cut surfaces with shortening and place the halves cut-side down on a baking sheet. Bake in a moderately hot oven (400° F.)

tin. Some vary the ordinary taste by adding a little cider, good brandy, or sherry to the custard. Often cream is substituted for part of the milk in a recipe, to make a rich pumpkin pie, or ginger, for at least part of the cinnamon and allspice that are most commonly used. The variety and amount of spices mixed into the custard depend largely on the homemaker's preferences and ingenuity.

One group of homemakers and cooks will bake crust and filling together, with a little nutmeg and sugar sifted over the top; another will pre-bake the pastry shell because they prefer a crisp to a soggy undercrust. But all wise homemakers and cooks will agree that the watery pumpkin should be cooked in as little water as possible and perhaps even steamed in a double boiler to remove the excess moisture and to bring out the true pumpkin flavor. They know that a strip of cloth dipped in cold water and bound around the edge of the pie-plate will keep the filling from overflow-ing, and they warn the apprentice home-maker-baker to have her custard filling moist enough to prevent cracks from ap-pearing in the finished golden brown prod-uct.

No less in the choice and combination of primary ingredients, the variety of acces-sories that may be served as embellishments for plain pumpkin pie is wide, and admits of personal preference. Quince preserves or quince jelly or guava preserves and guava jelly or paste, or cheese and whipped cream, singly or together, chopped nut meats or preserved ginger, ginger sirup, or currant jelly that shines darkly beneath a curlicue of whipped cream, all add their attractive harmony to the variations of the pumpkin pie theme.

OTHER USES

But though pumpkin pie may be the first pumpkin dish in the hearts of Americans, it is by no means the last. Here, as in other countries, pumpkin has always been used in many of the same ways as the summer squash or the winter squash from which is made a pie almost exactly like the pump-kin in taste. In South Wales pumpkin is added to hashed meat, made into pies with apples, pears, rhubarb, or other fruits. In France and many European countries pumpkin is made into a delicious soup, sometimes mixed with puréed carrots, or carrot pieces, sliced onions and leeks, chopped celery, parsley, etc.

Seasoned and baked, or boiled in salted water and served with drawn butter or sweet herbs, young pumpkin brings to the palate the joys of summer squash. Like squash, the pumpkin can also be sieved, stewed, mashed, fried in egg and crumbs, or baked au gratin with results that will surprise and please those whose acquaint-anceship with the pumpkin has hitherto been confined to the circumscribed area of a pie-crust.

For an unusual pumpkin dish try baked stuffed pumpkin. The seeds are removed and the pulp is scraped from the shell of a young pumpkin that has been simmered whole for 10 minutes and then quartered. A chopped onion and 2 cups of chopped shrimp, or any other kind of fish, even

meat, are fried lightly in 2 teaspoons of bacon drippings. A minced, large, ripe to-mato, a clove of garlic, some ground thyme, a pinch of ground nutmeg, parsley and a few bay leaves are added. Then the pressed pumpkin pulp, which has been mixed with a cup of dry bread crumbs, salt, pepper, and a whole, well-beaten egg, is added. The mixture is stirred constantly for 10 minutes, then put into the shells, sprinkled with crumbs (to which grated cheese may be added, or buttered crumbs used), and baked until delicately brown. Whatever ingenuities of ingredients the homemaker may devise, the dish must be served oven-hot if its distinctive flavor is to be best appreciated.

Pumpkin combined with rice, in layers of cooked rice and layers of thinly sliced or chopped, cooked pumpkin, and a rich, thick sauce, made of cheese and white sauce in the usual way, is another novelty. With minced green pepper in it, it is delicious.

PUMPKIN BREAD

2 packages dry granular yeast or 2 cakes compressed yeast
¼ cup lukewarm water
¼ cup sugar
1¾ cups milk, scalded
1 tbsp salt
8 to 8½ cups sifted all-purpose flour
2 cups puréed cooked pumpkin (or canned)
¼ cup melted shortening

Soften yeast in the water with 1 tea-spoon of the sugar. Let stand 10 minutes. Combine hot milk, salt, and the remaining sugar. Stir and cool until lukewarm. Com-bine yeast and cooled-milk mixtures and stir to blend. Add 2½ cups of the flour and beat until batter is very smooth. Add the pumpkin and the cooled shortening and mix well. Add enough of the remaining flour to make a stiff dough; use any re-maining flour on the board for kneading and shaping the dough. Turn dough out on a lightly floured board. Cover dough with bowl, let rest 10 minutes, then knead until smooth and elastic, about 10 minutes. Round up and place in a greased bowl, turn once to bring greased side up. Cover and let stand in a warm place (86° F.) and let rise until double in bulk (about 1 hour). Punch down dough, turn over in bowl and let rise again until double in bulk (about 45 minutes). Turn out on board and divide into 3 equal portions. Quickly round up each portion, cover with bowls and let rest for 10 minutes on board. Shape into loaves. Place in greased loaf pans. Cover and let rise in a warm place (86° F.) until double in bulk, sides of dough reach the top of pan, and center is well rounded (1 hour). Bake in a moderately hot oven (400° F.) for 15 minutes, reduce heat to moderate (375° F.) and continue baking 20 to 30 minutes longer until well browned. Turn out on racks to cool, uncovered and away from drafts. (Makes 3 loaves)

PUMPKIN CAKE

2½ cups cake flour
½ cup shortening
1½ cups sugar
4 tsp baking powder
1 tsp salt
1 tsp cinnamon
¼ tsp ground cardamo seedsm
¼ tsp ground clove
3 eggs, slightly beaten
1 cup fresh cooked or canned pumpkin
    purée
⅓ cup milk

Sift the flour, measure, and resift into a large mixing bowl. Cut in the shortening with pastry blender or two knives until the particles are the size of coarse cornmeal. Sift together the sugar, baking powder, salt, cinnamon, cardamom, and cloves, and add to flour mixture. Stir to mix. Add the eggs and beat until smooth. Add the pumpkin and again beat until smooth. Gradually add the milk and blend well. Turn into 8-inch layer-cake pans—bottoms lined with thin, plain paper. Bake at 375° F. (moderate) for 25 minutes or until cake tests done. Cool 5 minutes in pan, turn out on cake rack and cool thoroughly. Put together with rum-nut frosting (see RUM) between layers and on top and sides.

PUMPKIN CAKES WITH BACON

2 cups mashed pumpkin
½ tsp salt
Dash of paprika
1 tsp sugar
1 tsp catsup
¼ cup milk
2 tbsp melted butter
Bacon

Mix all ingredients together and shape into patties. Fry 6 to 12 strips of bacon; drain on unglazed paper and keep hot; pour off all but 2 tablespoons of the bacon drippings in pan. Sauté patties in bacon fat and serve with crisp bacon. Makes approximately 6 portions, or 12 small patties.

PUMPKIN CHIFFON PIE

1 recipe Brazil Nut Pastry
1 tbsp gelatin
¼ cup cold water
1½ cups cooked pumpkin
½ cup sugar
¾ tsp salt
1 tsp cinnamon
½ tsp ginger
2 eggs, separated
1 cup milk
¼ cup shredded Brazil nuts, toasted

Line 8-inch pie plate with nut pastry (see PASTRY). Soften gelatin in cold water. Combine pumpkin, ¼ cup sugar, salt, spices, slightly beaten egg yolks and milk. Cook over boiling water 5 minutes, stirring constantly. Add softened gelatin and stir until gelatin is dissolved. Chill until slightly thickened. Then gradually beat remaining ¼ cup sugar into stiffly beaten egg whites; fold into thickened pumpkin-gelatin mixture. Put into prepared plate and top with shredded nuts. Chill until firm.

PUMPKIN CUSTARD

1 cup canned or fresh cooked pumpkin
2 eggs, slightly beaten
½ cup light brown sugar, firmly packed
½ tsp salt
Dash of ginger
½ tsp cinnamon
1 cup cream or milk
⅛ tsp grated orange rind

Mix pumpkin with eggs, sugar, salt and spices. Stir in cream and orange rind, and pour mixture into custard cups. Set cups in a shallow pan of hot water high enough to come almost to the top of the cups. Bake in a moderately slow oven (325° F.) about

40 minutes, or until custard tests done. (Serves 4)

FROZEN PUMPKIN CUSTARD

2 eggs, separated
½ tsp salt
½ cup brown sugar
1½ cups cooked or canned pumpkin
1¼ tsp cinnamon
1 tsp ginger
⅛ tsp cloves
Dash of nutmeg
¼ cup boiling water
½ cup granulated sugar
1 tall can evaporated milk (1⅔ cups), chilled

Beat the egg yolks. Add the salt, brown sugar, and pumpkin and mix well. Soak spices in the boiling water for a few minutes, then add to pumpkin mixture. Chill. Beat egg whites until foamy. Add the granulated sugar a little at a time and continue beating until the meringue is very stiff. Whip milk very stiff. Fold meringue and whipped milk into pumpkin mixture. Pour at once into cold freezing trays and freeze in the refrigerator without stirring until stiff. (Makes 3 pints)

PUMPKIN PIE

2 cups freshly cooked pumpkin
1 cup brown sugar
¼ cup granulated sugar
1 tsp each ground cloves and cinnamon
½ tsp ground nutmeg
¼ cup pastry flour
1 tsp salt
1 cup milk
3 eggs
A 9-inch pre-baked pie shell

Blend the pumpkin, sugars, spices, flour and salt. Gradually add the milk. Combine with the slightly beaten egg yolks, and stir constantly until the mixture is smooth; then cook in the double boiler until thick, stirring almost constantly. Cool to lukewarm, turn into the pre-baked pie shell and top with a meringue made with the beaten egg whites and 5 tablespoons of confectioners' sugar. Place in a moderate oven (350° F.) to set and delicately color the meringue.

PUMPKIN SOUP

2 tbsp chopped onion
2 tsp chopped green pepper
2 tbsp margarine or butter
2 cups milk
1 cup cooked pumpkin
¾ tsp salt
Pepper
⅛ tsp Worcestershire Sauce
Chopped parsley

Sauté onion and green pepper slowly in the margarine for 5 minutes. Add next five ingredients and cook over hot water until very hot. Add parsley just before serving. (Serves 4)

PUNCH. Punch, usually a quantity drink mixed in a large bowl, has long been known as an extremely popular social beverage. The name is attributed variously to the Persian *Punj* and the Hindustani *Paunch*, both words meaning five and referring to the five properties of punch: hot, cold, sweet, bitter, and strong. One of the earliest of punch recipes called for tea, water, sugar, lemon and arrack, thus supplying the traditional five properties.

Punch making was once considered almost a fine art, and often days of preparation went into the making of a punch. Ingredients were laboriously boiled down, or set aside to steep and mellow before being combined in the bowl.

Punch is primarily a social drink, made in large quantities to serve many people. Perhaps the largest single punch on record was one prepared for a formal gathering held by a British naval official in 1694. Some 6,000 people attended the function and the quantities involved were so great that the punch was actually mixed in an outdoor fountain and ladled out by a boy who floated on the surface in a small boat.

While such extremes are rare, punch is ideal for serving large groups of twenty or more. It only requires one mixing and iced punches will stand for considerable periods. The bowl and glasses (*see* GLASSWARE) can be set out for the guests to serve themselves, thus relieving the host from bartending duties, and, while servants may be stationed at the punch bowl if the affair is very formal, they are not necessary.

Some of the older recipes produced truly delicious punches, but, unfortunately, the ingredients demanded and the time required are not in keeping with contemporary life. *See also* BARTENDING, BOWL, PLANTER'S PUNCH, TOM AND JERRY, TODDY, WASSAIL, and WINE CUP EGGNOG.

PUNCH (OLD RECIPE)

1 qt brandy
1 qt whisky
1 pt Jamaica Rum
8 oz dry sherry
8 oz chartreuse
6 lb sugar
2 doz oranges
1 doz lemons
1 pineapple
2 qt strawberries
Wine, additional

The oranges and lemons are first scrubbed thoroughly, then peeled so the rind comes off in thin slices. The peels are placed in a container and covered by the brandy, whisky, rum, sherry, and chartreuse. The fruits themselves are squeezed and the juice strained into four pounds of sugar in a separate container. In two other containers the pineapple finely shredded, and the strawberries washed and hulled, are each covered with a pound of sugar. All of the containers are placed in a cool dry spot and let stand for 3 days.

After standing, the fruit juices are all strained into one container, the strawberries being mashed to release all of the juice. One gallon of weak green tea is then prepared and strained, boiling hot, into the container with the peel and liquor, which, well mixed, is added to the fruit juices and the whole allowed to cool.

This, however, is only the basic mixture. Equal parts of the basic mixture and a wine, preferably claret, are placed in a large punch bowl with a large piece of ice, and allowed to stand one half hour. Before serving, carbonated water—the same amount as the wine, or as desired—is added, and the whole garnished with fruit, particularly with cucumber rind slices.

Punch may be simple or compounded. Simple punches are those made of only one liqueur or wine or infusion. They may be made with all kinds of liqueurs: wines, red or white, still or sparkling; tea; cider; etc. Punches are usually served hot during the cold months, and cold during the summer months. Punches should never be permitted to boil. The heat should be applied gently and gradually, as too intense a flame will cause the spirit or wine used to lose its flavor. Heat until the spirit or wine or liqueur is covered with a fine white foam; then remove and cover it to retain the heat and flavor. The traditional lemon or orange slice so frequently included in punch recipes is more a flavoring than a garnish; it adds its essential oil to those of the beverage. Butter is sometimes added to soften a punch, the proportions being, 1 pat of butter to 1 quart of liquid.

ARCHBISHOP'S PUNCH

1 large orange
12 cloves
1 qt white wine or claret
Sugar to taste

The orange should be stuck with the cloves, then roasted under the flame of the broiler or in a hot oven (400° F.) until it has acquired a rich dark-brown color and is delicately flavored with cloves. Cut it in halves and remove the seeds. Place the halves in a saucepan, and pour the selected wine over them. Sweeten to taste and simmer until a white foam appears on the surface, but do not allow it to boil. Remove from the fire and serve in glass punch cups.

ARTILLERY PUNCH

1 qt claret
1 qt sherry
1 qt whisky (bourbon, rye or scotch)
1 qt brandy
6 lemons (juice)
1 cup sugar
2 tbsp bitters

The ingredients are mixed well and let stand in punch bowl with a large piece of ice until thoroughly chilled. One quart of carbonated water is added immediately before serving. (Serves 30)

BEADLE'S PUNCH

A dash each of ground cinnamon, cloves, ginger and salt
1 cup sugar
2 cups boiling water
2 egg yolks
1 cup red wine
1 full bottle white wine

Combine the spices, salt, sugar and boiling water and bring to a boil over a hot flame, then strain through fine cheesecloth. While still hot pour gradually over the beaten egg yolks, beating continuously. Add the wines, return all to the fire and bring slowly to simmering point, stirring until a white foam appears on the surface. Serve in glass punch cups. (Serves 10)

BEER PUNCH (TRANSYLVANIAN)

3 bottles good beer
2 cups milk
6 egg yolks
¾ cup sugar

Heat the beer and milk in separate saucepans. Beat the egg yolks with the sugar until very light, then gradually add the hot milk, stirring vigorously and constantly, lest the egg curdle. Finally add the hot beer, still stirring constantly. Serve very hot in glass cups. (Serves 6)

BRANDY PUNCH

1 qt brandy
1 large jigger curacao
½ jigger grenadine
1¼ cups sugar
7 lemons
2 oranges

A block of ice is placed in a punch bowl, the above added, stirred until mixed and chilled, and one quart of carbonated water is stirred in immediately before serving. (Serves 20)

CARDINAL'S PUNCH I

3 large oranges, sliced thin
3 whole cloves, heads removed
1 blade mace
3 drops essence of nutmeg
3 bruised cardamom seeds
4 oz dissolved barley sugar
2 cups boiling water
1 bottle good Rhine wine

Place in a saucepan all ingredients except the wine. Cover, bring to boiling point, then leave over the lowest possible flame for 10 minutes, after which strain into another saucepan, pressing the fruit so as to extract all possible juice. Add the wine, cover and simmer gently, without actually boiling, until a white foam appears on the surface. Serve as hot as possible in glass punch cups. (Serves 8)

CARDINAL'S PUNCH II

2 oranges
2 doz cloves
1 qt champagne
Sugar to taste

Press the cloves into the oranges, carefully removing the heads of the cloves. Roast under the broiler or in the oven until the oranges have acquired a rich dark-brown color, after which cut in halves and remove the seeds. Place in a saucepan with the champagne and sugar to taste. Bring to the scalding point over a gentle heat without actually boiling. When a white foam appears on the surface serve in glass punch cups with an orange quarter in each cup. (Serves 6)

CHORISTER'S PUNCH

½ cup white wine
About ½ cup sugar
1 cup cold water
3 egg yolks

Combine the wine, sugar and ¾ cup of the water in a saucepan. Stir well and bring slowly to the simmering point. As soon as a white foam appears on the surface, remove from the fire and pour over the egg yolks which have been beaten with the remaining water, beating while pouring. Strain and serve in glass punch cups. (Serves 2)

CHURCHWARDEN'S PUNCH

1 large lemon
6 whole cloves
1 pt unsweetened weak tea
¾ lb sugar
1 bottle Bordeaux wine

Stick the lemon with the cloves, then roast in a hot oven to a rich, dark-brown color. Place it whole in a saucepan with the tea and sugar, stir well, add the wine, cover and bring slowly to simmering point. When a white foam appears on the surface, remove from the fire and press the lemon gently to extract the juice. Serve in glass punch cups. (Serves 10)

FISH HOUSE PUNCH

This punch has been brewed by the "State in Schuylkill," Pennsylvania, since 1732. One old recipe says: "Slack three-fourths pound of loaf sugar in a large punch bowl. When entirely dissolved, add one quart of lemon juice, then two quarts of Jamaica rum, one bottle of brandy, two quarts of water, and one wineglass of peach brandy. Put a large piece of solid ice in the punch bowl and allow the mixture to brew for about two hours, stirring occasionally."

In winter when the ice melts slowly, more water may be used; in summer, less, as the melting dilutes the mixture sufficiently.

A later version of the same punch is:

1 jigger bitters
1 pt lemon juice
3 lb sugar (dissolved in as little water as possible)
1 qt brandy
1 pt peach liqueur
1 qt Jamaica Rum
1 gal carbonated water

The ingredients are mixed in an ice-filled punch bowl in the order given. (Serves 24)

FIVE O'CLOCK PUNCH
(FRENCH METHOD)

1 pineapple
½ lb strawberries
1½ bottles Champagne
Powdered sugar

Select a medium-sized, ripe, fresh pineapple; peel, slice as thinly as possible, and core, using an apple corer. Arrange the slices in a deep, flat-bottomed, crystal punch bowl, sprinkling each layer with powdered sugar. Let stand overnight to mellow, keeping the bowl covered and in a cool place. Next day, pour a bottle of champagne or other sweet wine over it.

Early in the morning, take the wild strawberries (garden berries may be used if the wild ones are not available), carefully hull and wash them, then roll in powdered sugar and add to the pineapple mixture. Allow them to bathe in this ambrosia for at least six hours, still keeping the bowl and its contents in a cool place. Fifteen minutes before serving, turn into a glass pitcher a half bottle of champagne and a large piece of ice and put a further piece of ice into the punch bowl with the prepared fruits.

The hostess herself serves the punch as follows: using a silver fork and a silver ladle, she places in the bottom of each glass a little of the strawberry mixture over a slice of the pineapple, then with her ladle fills up the glass with the iced champagne from the pitcher. (Serves 15)

FLAMING TEA PUNCH

1 qt freshly made green tea
½ pt rum
½ pt brandy
Juice 1 large lemon
½ lb sugar

Use about one ounce of tea to the quart of boiling water. Heat the punch bowl, then pour in the rum, brandy, lemon juice, and sugar. Set the liquid aflame and pour in the tea slowly, mixing thoroughly with a ladle. The mixture will continue to burn briefly. It should be poured, still flaming, into warmed glass punch cups. (Serves 12)

GIN PUNCH

3 bottles dry gin
2 large jiggers sloe gin
3 lemons (juice)
6 oranges (juice)
Sugar to taste

A large block of clear ice is placed in a punch bowl. The above ingredients are poured in and mixed until chilled. Carbonated water in the same amount as the dry gin is added immediately before serving. (Serves 20)

GLOW WINE PUNCH

2 bottles red Bordeaux wine
1 cup sugar
6 whole cloves
Thinly peeled rind 1 large lemon
2 or 3 oranges, sliced and seeded

Pour the wine into a saucepan and bring slowly to boiling point; when a white foam forms on the surface, remove from the fire, and add the sugar, cloves, and lemon rind. Stir well, cover and let stand a few minutes to infuse. Serve in glass cups, adding a slice of orange to each glass. (Serves 18)

HOT WINE AND ORANGE PUNCH

1 cup boiling water
¾ lb sugar
Grated rind of 2 small oranges
1 bottle red Burgundy wine
¼ cup brandy, optional
Thinly sliced orange

Pour the water over the sugar and stir until dissolved. Add the orange rind and Burgundy which has been heated in the upper part of the double boiler. If brandy is used, add it with the wine. Serve in glass cups, placing a slice of orange in each. (Serves 8)

HOT WINE PUNCH A LA FRANCAISE

3 bottles good red wine
1 lb sugar
3-inch stick cinnamon
2 or 3 blades mace
6 small bay leaves
Thinly peeled rind 2 lemons

Scald the wine with the sugar, then add all remaining ingredients and boil up once, stirring occasionally to be sure that the sugar is entirely melted. Remove from the fire, ignite and allow the punch to burn for three minutes. Strain into glasses. (Serves 20)

NOEL RED CLARET PUNCH

1 qt tea
1 bottle red Bordeaux wine
Juice of 1 small lemon and 1 orange
1 lb loaf or lump sugar
1 pt best rum

Plain tea, either black or green, linden, or camomile tea may be used, according to taste. After brewing, strain it carefully, twice to insure clearness. Add the wine and the fruit juices, and heat thoroughly without actually boiling. Then pour into a punch bowl of porcelain or heatproof glass. Place over the bowl a pair of fire tongs (or two heavy metal bars). Arrange the sugar on these, pour over it a wineglass of the rum. Set afire and feed the flame constantly with the gradually added remaining rum, pouring it very slowly and gradually over the melting, flaming sugar. This is usually done in the dining room where all lights have previously been extinguished. The alcohol fades away in the blue flame. Serve in glass cups. (Serves 10)

PUNCH BOWL. A large, usually ornate bowl intended for the mixing and serving of punch, *which see*. See GLASSWARE.

PUNCH BOWL AND GLASSES

PUNCH, FRUIT. Though punch (*which see*) contains intoxicants, this by no means rules out the possibility of making similar beverages from combinations of fruit juices or fruit juices and tea. Many truly delicious beverages can be made in this manner and they all are of definite value to the busy hostess.

Punch is distinguished from the "ades" and other juice-based beverages on three counts. It is usually prepared in larger quantities, it is usually more heavily garnished than the other fruit drinks, and it has a combination of tastes rather than one predominating flavor.

Though possibly involving more work than the other beverages because of the quantity involved and the number of ingredients, punch offers distinct advantages to the hostess. For one thing, the cold punches can usually be mixed, either wholly or in part, well in advance of the social function, thus relieving last-minute pressure of preparations. For another, while punch may be served in heavily garnished and carefully arranged glasses, it is commonly served by the simple expedient of either ladling or pouring into punch cups or small glasses.

Fruit punches are especially ideal for children's and teen-agers' parties. They are delicious "party drinks" that need no apologies and are relatively inexpensive compared to other beverages frequently served. If the children are old enough, they may do the serving themselves, increasing their enjoyment of the function and giving the adult more time for general supervision rather than specific tasks. In the case of teen-agers, they satisfy the desire for a "grown-up" drink, and, by their simplicity of service, enable the adolescent to gradually learn gracious entertaining.

FRUIT PUNCH

2 cups orange juice
1 lemon, grated peel and juice
1 cup pineapple juice
2 cups water
½ cup simple sirup
1 tbsp honey
½ tsp powdered cloves
½ tsp nutmeg
½ tsp cinnamon
½ tsp allspice
3 small bottles ginger ale

All of the ingredients except the ginger ale are mixed together, warmed over a low flame and let steep for three hours. The mixture is then strained over a large block of ice in a punch bowl and, when chilled, the ginger ale is added. Whole cloves may be substituted for the powdered cloves, the simple sirup replaced by honey, and the fruit juices varied to taste. Garnish with fruit slices to taste. (Serves 20)

HOT FRUIT PUNCH

3 cups pineapple juice
3 cups grapefruit juice
3 cups orange juice
3 cups crushed pineapple
2 cups sugar
4 cups water

The sugar, water, pineapple juice and crushed pineapple are mixed over a low fire and brought to a boil. The grapefruit

and orange juices are added, and the mixture reheated, if necessary, to make it hot. Canned juices and pineapple may be used; if fresh fruits are used, the juices should be strained. If garnishings are used they should be simple. Spices may be dusted on the surface as the punch is served. (Serves 20)

Other fruit punch recipes will be found under the headings of the individual fruits used. *See also* FRUIT DRINKS.

PUNGENT. As applied to tea; puckery —of an astringent nature; the characteristically pungent flavor of tea is caused by tannin. (*See* TEA) As applied to other beverages or food, pungent refers to the stinging or prickling sensations caused by strong spices such as mustard, pepper, red chili, etc. A beverage which is too strong in alcoholic content is said to be pungent.

PUREE. The pulp of a boiled food which has been rubbed through a sieve. Almost any kind of food may be puréed, including farinaceous and fibrous foods, meat, fowl, fish, etc. Soup is called purée when it has been thickened with its sieved pulpy ingredients.

PURSLANE. Purslane is a weed, both wild and cultivated varieties of which are used as food. The leaves may be used in

PURSLANE

soups and salads like sorrel (*which see*). They may be oiled as a potherb. Or they may be served alone as greens; these are surprisingly appealing when served with butter sauce or French dressing. It is sometimes called "pussley."

Q

QUACHEQ CHEESE. A sheep's milk cheese, made in Macedonia.

QUAHAUG or **Quahog.** A thick-shelled American clam (*Venus mercenaria*). See CLAM.

QUAIL. The bob-white or common quail of America (*Ortyx Virginiana*), fattened on the late summer's grain gleaned from the furrows, the blood-red partridge berries taken on upland slopes, and the succulent wild grapes from rambling stone walls, presents itself as one of the most tempting game birds for the palate of the epicure.

There are many species of quail. Nearly all are natives of the Eastern Hemisphere. They were known to the ancients, and it is said that the people of Egypt could not eat all the birds that appeared in that country, so they shipped many to nearby nations. Several species have been brought to the Western Hemisphere in the past, but none has thrived so well as the bob-white. This migratory, gallinaceous game bird has variegated chestnut-brown plumage with buff or whitish stripes over its upper parts. It differs slightly in markings from its European cousin and also from the California quail, but the general contour of all these birds is similar. The Eastern Hemisphere species, however, measures only about seven inches in length, while the Western Hemisphere species measures up to ten inches.

There is some confusion in the nomenclature of the birds in the eastern United States; wherever the ruffed grouse (*Bonasa umbellus*) is called pheasant, the bob-white is called partridge; and where the grouse is called partridge, the bob-white goes under the name of quail. As a rule, too, Northerners call it quail, and Southerners call it partridge.

PREPARATION OF QUAIL

Quail are always prepared in their fresh state; they may, however, hang for a couple of days, but seldom more than three, since they should not be allowed to mortify. Like almost all game birds, they should be cooked rather rare, so as to retain their full gamy flavor.

Quail should be plump, with white, firm, fat flesh. Roasted they are delicious, especially when the spit method is used, which unfortunately is almost impossible unless one lives in the country or prepares the birds where they are shot. However, quail may be prepared in all the different delicious methods that are used in connection with partridge, prairie chicken, snipe, woodcock, and other game birds. Quail has an affinity for veal, especially veal stock, so it is advisable to have this on hand when preparing the bird; the stock also goes well with snipe and woodcock. As with almost all kinds of game birds, bread sauce and jelly should be served, even if there is another sauce indicated.

BRANDIED QUAIL

Clean as many quail as desired. Singe and rub them inside and out with olive oil, and then with salt and black pepper. Place in the cavity of each bird a small truffle cooked in champagne for five minutes. Truss, then place the birds in a casserole, allowing for each one-half teaspoon of sweet butter and one-half teaspoon of olive oil. Cover tightly and cook in a hot oven (425° F.) for 20 minutes. Lift out the birds and keep hot. Remove any excess fat, and place the casserole over a low flame. Add one-fourth cup of brandy, ignite, and allow the flame to burn out. Then stir from the bottom of the casserole all the gelatinous particles which may adhere to the dish. Pour in one-half cup of good Madeira wine, bring to a rapid boil, and replace the birds in this sauce. Cover and set aside to mellow for a few minutes. Serve on toast, spread with the quail liver, which has been cooked for two minutes.

CASSEROLE OF QUAIL WITH CHERRIES

6 quail
Butter
1 tsp brandy
3 tbsp port
1 tbsp grated orange rind
5 tbsp veal stock
2 tbsp currant jelly
5 doz sour cherries

Prepare the quail as for roasting but without any blanket of larding pork, merely cleaning and trussing. Pan-roast in an earthen casserole in plenty of butter for about 25 minutes. Lift out the birds and keep hot. To the butter remaining in the casserole, add the brandy and port and stir until the mixture boils up, then add the orange rind, stock, jelly, and sour cherries (pitted and cooked in a light sirup, then cooled and drained). Return the quail to this sauce, cover and heat all to the boiling point. If too sweet, add a few drops of lemon juice. Serve with bread sauce but without jelly. (Serves 3)

ENGLISH JUGGED QUAIL

Clean six plump quail. Singe and wipe with a damp cloth inside and out, then rub with lemon juice, and again with a mixture of salt, pepper, and allspice. Finally stuff with a forcemeat of bread crumbs, chopped fat pork, the sieved yolks of two hard-cooked eggs, and a tablespoon of minced boiled celery, with onion juice, salt, and pepper to taste. Sew and truss, tying the wings and legs close to the bodies. Pack into the upper part of a double boiler with a well-fitting cover and cook over boiling water for two and a half hours. Serve with orange-mint sauce, fried bread crumbs, and red currant jelly, passed separately. (Serves 6)

QUAIL A LA CRAPAUDINE

Split birds open, empty, and singe. After flattening place them in a dish, season with salt and pepper, a pinch of mixed spice, broken bay leaf, parsley, thyme, and a few slices of onion. Now add juice of lemon and two tablespoons of olive oil. Marinate quail in this mixture for several hours, after which drain off liquid and roll birds in either fresh or browned bread crumbs, mixed with pepper and salt. Grill gently. Turn often and moisten with drops of butter. (*A la crapaudine* is French for "cut open and broiled.")

QUAIL RAGOUT

Select the number of birds desired, clean them, cut in two, and put them in a pan for a couple of minutes with a little pork fat and a sprinkle of flour. Add a cup of consommé or veal stock, salt, pepper, bou-

quet, and a few fresh mushrooms and pieces of globe artichokes. Cook slowly. When about ready to serve, add the juice of an orange.

QUAIL WITH GRAPES

Wrap each quail in a vine leaf (soaked beforehand in cognac) and a snow-white covering of bacon fat. Make a paste of the following ingredients: Quail's liver, a little chopped bacon, some bread crumbs soaked in cognac. Fill the birds with this. Cook in butter in a hot oven for about ten minutes; then add a dozen grapes for each bird to the baking dish or tin. The grapes should be fresh and should have their skins and pips removed. Add a small glass of brandy and cover the pan, leaving it in a moderately hot oven for another five or six minutes. Take the birds out and remove their wrappings. Put hem in a serving dish with the grapes and brandy gravy in which they were cooked, and serve hot.

ROAST QUAIL

Cover the breasts of the birds with vine leaves, then wrap in thin rashers of bacon. Roast for about 15 minutes in a good oven, basting constantly with butter, and seasoning with salt and pepper. When done, do not remove either leaves or bacon. Serve each bird on a fried croûton or on hot rounds of buttered toast.

QUARENDEN or **Quarrender.** A deep-red early cider apple, similar to the "Bloody Turk."

QUART. Two pints, or four cups, or one-quarter gallon. A liquid measure of capacity. *See* WEIGHTS AND MEASURES.

QUARTER. To divide a fruit or a vegetable or any food material into four equal parts or quarters.

QUEENSLAND NUT. An Australian nut, and another name for the Macadamia nut. *See* NUTS.

QUENELLES. A French name for small, tiny dumplings, made of forcemeat or a mixture of flour and water. *See also* DUMPLINGS.

QUESO DE CINCHO CHEESE. A sour-milk cheese from Venezuela. It comes in the form of balls and is wrapped in palm leaves.

QUESO DE HOJA CHEESE. A Puerto Rican cheese made from fresh cow's milk. When cut into, it appears to be in layers.

QUESO DE MANO CHEESE. A sour-milk cheese which resembles hand cheese. It is made in Venezuela.

QUESO DE PRENSA CHEESE. A hard, rennet cheese made from the whole milk of cows. It is made in Puerto Rico and comes in forms about 11 inches long, five and one-half inches wide, and three inches thick. It weighs about five pounds.

QUESO DE PUNA CHEESE. A Puerto Rican cheese which resembles Cottage or Dutch cheese. It should always be eaten when fresh. It is five inches in diameter and one and one-quarter inches deep.

QUESO ENCHILADO CHEESE. A hard, Mexican cheese in loaf form.

QUETSCH D'ALSACE. An excellent after-dinner cordial, served straight in a pony glass, or poured over finely shaved ice in a cordial glass. It is made of sloe berries distilled with pure spirits of wine, to which are added the crushed pits of the berries and certain aromatic herbs. It is rather fiery and contains about 50 percent alcohol. It is a strong digestive product of France.

QUICK-COOKING TAPIOCA. *See* Tapioca.

QUILL PIG. Another name for Porcupine, *which see.*

QUINCE

QUINCE. The ripe quince resembles nothing so much as a large, pale-golden apple with a slightly malformed blossom end. In fact, the Greek name is *Chrysomelon*, meaning the golden apple. Many learned writers assert that quinces were the Golden Apples of the Hesperides and were the fruit that the swift-footed Atalanta paused ɔ retrieve. Still others assert that it was the beauty and delightful fragrance of the quince that tempted Mother Eve. The fruit, which has been under cultivation for centuries, was probably native to ancient Persia and was one of the earliest of the garden fruits. In ancient times quinces were used as tokens of love, and their presence at wedding feasts was said to insure happiness to those being married. Our word marmalade is derived from the Portuguese word for this fruit, *marmelo*. The first quince seeds were probably brought to America by Governor Endicott when he landed on the shores of Massachusetts in 1628, for we find quince kernels listed in the manifest.

There are many varieties of this excellent fruit, the most esteemed being the apple-quince, the pear-quince, and the Portugal-quince. The apple- or orange-quince, as it is sometimes called, is the tenderest and has an excellent flavor; the Portugal-quince is rather scarce; and the pear-quince is somewhat hard and tough, but it is the most perfect in appearance and has a flavor equal to any other variety.

When selecting quinces, choose the large smooth ones; the small, knotty ones are tough, worm-eaten, and wasteful. The quince season is from October to the end of December, and our best quince-producing localities are California and western New York. Quinces are graded according to size and quality into fancy, choice, and standard and are sold either by the piece or in baskets that measure from one peck to one bushel. The fruit should be stored in a cool, dry place and will keep for a considerable length of time if wiped with a dry cloth occasionally, provided the skins are not bruised and each quince rests separately.

Quinces are an age-old standby of the home apothecary. Numerous wines and sirups for the relief of colds, coughs, and ailing throats have been made from this fruit. Perfumes have been distilled from the blossoms, and today many hand and hair lotions have a quince or quince-seed base.

Perhaps the best-known of the quince products is the reddish-golden jelly. There are also preserves, jams, honey, and marmalade. The fact that quinces blend easily with other fruits, especially apples, has added many delightful combinations to the fruit cabinet. Among these are apple and quince chips, quince and tangerine jam, and orange and quince conserve.

The quince also makes mouth-watering desserts. It may be baked and scalloped, made into roly-polies, dumplings, pies, pastries, steamed batter pudding, quince sauce, quince apple sauce, quince ice cream, cream cheese with stewed or preserved quinces, etc. From Latin America we get the delightful *mambrilla pasta*, or quince paste, made in the same way as guava paste. And then there is a very sweet quince candy.

Unlike most other fruits, quinces should be cooked until they are clear and transparent in a small amount of water before the sugar is added, unless you wish to use a large amount of thin sirup and then cook until the sirup is thick. Marmalade and preserves are made in the same way, although for marmalade the fruit is cut into small pieces, while for preserves large sections are used. In preparing quinces for any use they should be pared and every seed and every bit of the core should be carefully removed, as these parts contain a gummy substance that will destroy the texture of the marmalade. Quinces are indigestible unless they are very thoroughly cooked.

HINTS ON BUYING

Quinces are old by the unit, pound, peck, 12 pound, or bushel. One pound is equivalent to three medium fruits.

In purchasing quince look for greenish-yellow to yellow fruit of firm but not hard consistency. The presence of worms is shown by punctures in the skin. Bruises or spots should be avoided.

Store quinces in a cool, dark, dry place.

BAKED QUINCES

6 small quinces
½ cup sugar
A few grains salt
1⅓ cups hot water

Peel, core, and slice the quinces. Arrange all ingredients in a baking dish, cover closely, and cook in a slow oven (325° F.) about two hours, or until tender and of a deep red color. Remove the cover, sprinkle with an additional one-quarter cup of sugar and continue baking, uncovered, until the sirup is somewhat thickened. Serve either hot or cold. (Serves 6)

QUINCE COMPOTE

4 medium-size quinces
3 cups cold water
Juice and rind of ½ lemon
Pinch of salt
3 cups sugar

Wash, peel, core, and quarter the quinces, then slice them very thinly into the combined water, lemon juice, salt, and thinly sliced lemon rind. Cook gently until tender but not broken. Skim out the fruit, add the sugar to the hot liquid, and bring to a boil. Return the fruit to this sirup and simmer gently about 30 minutes, when the fruit should have turned a beautiful red color. Chill, and serve plain or with light cream. (Serves 6)

QUINCE JAM

Pare, quarter, and core fruit. To each pound of prepared quinces allow three-quarters pound of sugar and two tablespoons of lemon juice. Crush the fruit and combine with the sugar in alternate layers, and let stand until some of the juice is extracted, that is about three to four hours. Then heat slowly until the sugar is dissolved, stirring meanwhile. Bring to boiling and cook, stirring constantly, until the fruit is clear and the jam somewhat thick. Pour into hot sterilized jars, and seal.

QUINCE JELLY

Do not pare the quinces but cut them into small pieces, first removing cores and seeds. Add sufficient water to cover and cook until tender. Quinces require long cooking to become tender and to bring out their flavor and deep rich color. Drain off and measure the juice. Use two-thirds as much sugar as fruit juice, and follow general directions for making apple jelly. The pulp may be utilized for making conserve or fruit butter.

If preferred, equal parts of quince and apple juice may be used, or one-third quince and two-thirds apple juice, or equal parts of quince, cranberry, and apple juice.

QUINNAT. Another name for the Chinook salmon of the coasts of the North Pacific. It averages about 22 pounds in weight—larger ones are often taken. It is the most important species of salmon.

R

RAAB. A kind of broccoli, also called turnip tops, widely cultivated in Virginia and the Carolinas. It resembles broccoli in flavor, and on that account is sometimes referred to as broccoli-raab, but the stems are smaller than broccoli, and there is no head. It is found in the markets at the beginning of spring. It is cooked like any other greens, such as spinach. It is sometimes spelled rab.

RABACAL CHEESE. A round, firm cheese, made from the milk of sheep or goats. It is four or five inches in diameter and one inch thick. Rabacal cheese is made in Portugal.

RABBIT or HARE. In the south they refer to rabbit as Old Hare, without regard to the age of the animal. In the North and West it is rabbit, whether it is tame or wild.

The flesh of rabbit or hare when more than a year old is dry and somewhat tough; the young ones, when nearly full-grown and fat, are tender and make rather delicate eating. A young rabbit has soft paws which are not fully opened, while the paws of an old rabbit are open and worn. The ears of a young one are very soft, while those of an old one are stiff and comparatively rough. A rabbit, in common with almost every other game tastes better when it is a little seasoned, aged, or when the flesh is what is called high; but it must not be too much so. When the body is rather stiff, the flesh is good, but when the body is limber and the flesh has a black-bluish appearance, it is best to examine it carefully, as the meat is probably tainted.

A young rabbit that is cut into small serving pieces and cooked in a strong broth, spiced with a bouquet garni (*which see*), a little mace, cloves, pepper, thyme, and onion, before it is fried in a butter and claret mixture, makes a stew that turns a cold autumn night into a heartwarming occasion. And a good rabbit pie, a helping of the universally acclaimed hasenpfeffer, a serving of fried rabbit and tarter sauce, or a roast rabbit, is guaranteed to be a propitious introduction for those whose knowledge of this long-eared little animal is bounded by the covers of "Uncle Remus."

SKINNING AND CLEANING A RABBIT

1. Opening cut, from about breast bone to base of tail. Cut outer skin only, not the flesh of the abdomen.

2. Loosen the skin from the flesh along the sides of the cut, using the fingers. A pinch of dry cornmeal in the opening will make movement of the skin easier.

3. Work skin loose from the knee and upper leg so that the knee-joint may be thrust upward. Disjoint leg at knee and work skin back as far as it will go.

4. Clean flesh from lower part of leg. Skin out other leg in same manner. With a knife or scissors, cut away any tissue at base of tail and work the skin of the tail loose.

5. Hold flesh at base of tail with firm grasp and pull steadily on skin until freed from entire after-section. Roll skin back until forelegs are reached. Work forelegs free, disjoint and clean as in steps 3 and 4.

6. Roll skin back to base of ears. Cut off ears as close to head as possible. Work skin over head and cut eyelids free. Avoid cutting the lid, especially if the fur is to be sold. Cut skin free at the nose by cutting the cartilage, not the bones, of the nose. Free skin from flesh at lips, remove all fat, and turn inside out.

7. Slice open abdomen, from chest to tail and remove entrails.

8. Cut off head and other parts of body to form portions as desired.

BARECUED RABBIT OR HARE

2 cups water
2 cups vinegar
12 whole peppercorns, bruised
1⅓ tbsp salt
Thinly peeled rind 1 large lemon
12 sprigs parsley tied with
2 large bay leaves
1 large onion, thinly sliced
1 medium-size raw carrot, thinly sliced
Scant ½ tsp thyme
3 whole cloves, heads removed
¼ tsp allspice
1 blade sage
¼ tsp celery seeds

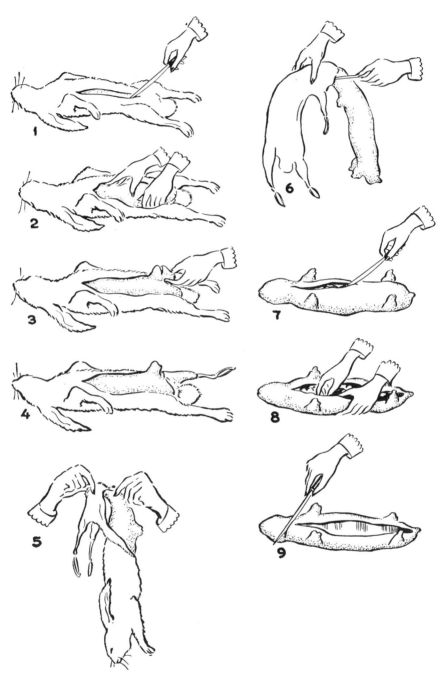

SKINNING AND CLEANING A RABBIT 1. Opening cut 2. Loosening skin
3. Skinning and disjointing leg 4. Leg disjointed and Lesh cleaned from lower end
5. Skinning tail 6. Cutting of ears and skinning head 7. Cutting abdomen
8. Removing entrails 9. Cutting into portions

Skin, clean, and wipe the rabbit or hare. Trim, clean, and thoroughly scrape the bluish skin with a knife. Prepare a marinade with the ingredients above. Combine all ingredients and bring to a rapid boil. Cool to lukewarm, then pour over the rabbit in a large earthen crock or bowl. Cover and let stand for 48 hours— less if a milder flavor is desired. Lift the animal out, pat dry, and rub lightly with salt and pepper. Envelope it with thin stripes of bacon and place in a roasting pan which has been very thoroughly greased, preferably with bacon drippings. Add one cup of the strained marinade and roast in a moderate oven (375° F.) about 40 minutes, basting often with the liquid in the pan. Keep hot while preparing the barbecue sauce.

Barbecue Sauce

Liquid in roasting pan
2 small cloves garlic
2 tbsp catsup
1½ tsp Worcestershire sauce
Dash of Tabasco
2 tsp brandy
2 tbsp butter
1 tbsp flour

Discard any excess fat from the liquid in the roasting pan. Measure and add enough more of the marinade to make one cup. Boil this up once with the garlic (peeled but left whole), the catsup, Worcestershire sauce, and tabasco. Strain and return to the fire with the brandy, also the butter into which the flour has been rubbed. Bring to boiling point, add more seasoning if desired, pour over the rabbit or hare, and garnish with watercress and quartered lemon.

CIVET OF RABBIT OR HARE

1 rabbit or hare
4 tbsp brandy
1¾ cups oil
Salt and pepper
3 medium-size onions
½ lb lean pork (fresh)
3 tbsp butter
3 tbsp flour
Red wine
1 bouquet garni

1 small clove garlic
2 doz small onions
2 doz mushrooms
Fried bread croutons

Skin, clean, wipe, and cut up the rabbit or hare. Save all blood, with the liver, having first carefully removed the gall. Place the meat in a large bowl with the brandy, oil, seasonings, and one onion cut into thin rings. Allow these to marinate for two hours, stirring frequently, then lift out the meat and pat dry. Dice the pork and brown it in the butter until delicately colored; lift out and set aside. Brown the two remaining onions, peeled and quartered, in the same fat. Sprinkle in the flour and cook until both butter and flour are thoroughly browned and blended. Add the rabbit or hare and sear on all sides. Half cover with red wine, add the bouquet garni and garlic, cover, and simmer gently for 45 minutes. Five minutes before serving, add the blood, which has been slightly heated with a little of the sauce, and the liver, cut in small cubes. Arrange for service on a hot platter, garnishing with the cubes of pork, the small, white, glazed onions the mushrooms (peeled and cooked in butter), and the heart-shaped croutons of bread fried in butter.

CURRIED RABBIT OR HARE

1 rabbit or hare
2 tbsp flour
2 tsp salt
⅔ tsp black pepper
Pinch of allspice
4 tbsp lard
Stock
4 whole cloves
1 tbsp butter
1 finely minced onion
½ cup rice
1 tbsp curry powder

Skin, clean, and wipe the rabbit or hare. Cut into serving portions, setting aside the head, heart, and liver for the making of stock. Roll each piece of meat in the blended flour and seasonings, then sear in the lard until thoroughly browned. Transfer the meat to a large kettle and pour over it enough stock (made from the head and trimmings) barely to half cover. Add the cloves, then reduce the heat, cover closely, bring to a rapid boil, and simmer 20 minutes. Meanwhile, heat the butter in a separate pan and lightly brown the onion in it. Add the rice, washed and drained, and stir all together for three minutes, then cook, stirring occasionally for 20 minutes. Sprinkle in the curry powder, moisten the rice with a little stock, then pour it over the rabbit or hare. The rice and meat should be just covered with the liquid in the kettle. Again cover closely and cook in a hot oven (400° F.) for 30 minutes. Lift the meat carefully to a serving dish, shaking off any rice which adheres. Arrange the rice itself around the meat and serve with any preferred chutney.

HASENPFEFFER

1 rabbit or hare
Vinegar
Water
3 slices onion
1 doz whole cloves
3 bay leaves
Salt and black pepper
3 tbsp lard
1 cup heavy sour cream
Fried bread triangles
Stewed prunes or other fruit

Skin, clean, wipe, and cut up the rabbit or hare. Place in a bowl and cover with vinegar and water in equal parts. Add the onion, cloves, bay leaves, and seasonings. Marinate for two days, turning the meat frequently but keeping it entirely covered with the liquid. Lift out the meat, pat dry, sear on all sides in the hot lard, drain off the fat, and add enough of the marinade to cover the pieces of meat. Cover and simmer until tender, about half an hour. Just before serving, add the sour cream, bring to a rapid boil, discard the bay leaves, pour the sauce over, and serve on a hot platter, garnished with the bread triangles. Serve the fruit separately.

JUGGED RABBIT OR HARE

1 rabbit or hare
3 onions
Bacon drippings
Flour, salt and pepper

½ lb salt pork, sliced thin
2 tbsp minced parsley
2 tsp paprika
3 tomatoes
1 cup beef stock
1 tbsp butter
1 tbsp flour
1½ tbsp currant jelly
Juice of 1 lemon
¼ cup sherry
Triangles of fried hominy

Skin, clean, wipe, and disjoint the rabbit or hare. Cut the back into two portions and sever every joint. Slice one onion and fry light brown in the bacon drippings, then roll the meat in the seasoned flour and sear it in the same fat. Place the meat in a large saucepan, in the bottom of which have been arranged half the pork, parsley and paprika, and one of the remaining onions, sliced. Top with the remaining pork, parsley, paprika, and onion, put in the tomatoes, peeled and quartered, and pour over all the beef stock, generously seasoned with celery and celery seeds. Cover closely, set in a vessel of cold water, bring slowly to boiling point, and cook three hours. To serve, arrange the rabbit or hare and pork in a deep hot platter. Thicken the gravy with the butter and flour rubbed smoothly together, and finally add the currant jelly, lemon juice, and sherry. Pour over the meat and garnish with triangles of fried hominy.

RABBIT PIE

1 rabbit
Cold water
1 bouquet garni
1 small clove garlic
A pinch each of thyme, mace, and allspice
Salt
¼ cup lemon juice
2 cups diced raw potato
2 or 3 diced carrots
2 tbsp flour
Baking powder biscuit dough or pastry

Skin, clean, wipe, and cut up the rabbit. Cover with cold water, add the bouquet garni, garlic, spices, salt, and lemon juice, and let stand overnight. In the morning, cook the rabbit until tender in the mixture in which it was marinated. As soon as tender, remove the meat and add the potato and carrots to the liquor remaining in the kettle. Cook these just until tender, then thicken the gravy slightly with the flour moistened with a little cold water. Meanwhile, take the bones from the meat, arrange the meat in a baking dish, add the vegetables and stock almost to cover. Top with biscuit dough or pastry and bake about 25 minutes, having the oven hot (450° F.) for the first ten minutes and reduced to moderate (350° F.) for the remainder of the baking period.

RACHAHOUT. A Turkish dish made from *palamoute*, a compound of dried acorns, sugar, spices, and aromatics.

RACCOON. The raccoon, a nocturnal carnivore, is identified easily by the black "robber's mask" that extends across his eyes. His fur is grayish, brown, or black; his tail is circled with dark rings. The raccoon, like opposum, may be prepared in all the different ways applied to hare or rabbit. This animal is more frequently seen on the table in the South than in other parts of the country, but it occasionally makes its appearance in the East. It is in season during the fall and winter months. The full grown raccoon

RADISH

weighs from 7 to 12 pounds, and its flesh is both rank and tough. The young are better, but even these are not good if very fat.

RADEN CHEESE. A hard, rennet cheese, made from skim milk and resembling Emmenthaler. It is 16 inches in diameter, four inches thick, and weighs 32 pounds. Raden cheese is made in Germany.

RADISH. This vegetable has been highly prized since the days of ancient Egypt. Its crisp, fleshy root, which has very little nutriment, is pleasantly pungent, and the outer rim is antiscorbutic. Radishes are mostly eaten raw as an agreeable relish, and they add a stimulating tang when sliced in a mixed salad. When cooked with a cream sauce they have a flavor somewhat like that of young, white turnips. The young seedling leaves may be used in a salad; they were formerly boiled and eaten as greens. The seed-pods when pickled alone resemble capers in flavor; they are often pickled with string beans.

There are several varieties of radishes, but they are generally divided into the turnip or round and the spindle-rooted. Many are forced for the early market, and they are one of the first vegetables to make their appearance in the spring. Their season commences in April and continues with a succession of crops until cold weather. The black Spanish and other varieties can be buried in dry sand for winter use and, in fact, can be kept until the new radishes appear. The color of radishes varies greatly, passing from white through red and dark purple to almost black. They will grow in almost any soil.

Of the early turnip-shaped varieties, the Scarlet, Olive-shaped, and White turnip-rooted are the best. The long scarlet Short top and the long white Naples are the most desirable of the long-rooted kinds. The rose-colored Chinese is good for winter forcing.

RAGOUT. The French word for stew (*which see*).

RAIL. The king rail, the largest and handsomest bird of its family, is trim of form, moves with an air of conscious grace, and is tastefully garbed in soft brown and black, which harmonize wonderfully well with the vegetation of swamp and meadow where it passes its life. It lives exclusively in fresh-water meadows.

The clapper rail prefers the salt-water marshes of Long Island. A closely allied species is the California clapper rail. As the name implies, clapper rails are noisy birds, and their harsh notes are often heard coming from the thick reeds when the birds themselves are invisible. As food, the clapper rail, or meadow hen, is inferior to the sora rail but very tender and well flavored when in good condition. It is best in September and October.

The Virginia rail is a denizen of both fresh and brackish water marshes, though with a decided preference for the former, especially in the nesting season. Its thin, wedge-shaped body eminently adapts it for a life among sedge and tule, through the stems of which it glides so swiftly that the sharpest observer rarely catches a glimpse of it. Its grunting note, which may be compared to the sound of a hungry pig, is its downfall. The Virginia rail, or little mud hen, is occasionally found in the markets in April and May and again in September and October. It is considered best in the latter months.

The sora rail, or Carolina rail, is not very plentiful but is much sought after. Its flesh has an exceedingly delicate flavor. It is best in September.

These birds may be prepared in the ways described for Quail and Grouse.

RAISINS. Raisins are grapes dried in the sun or by artificial heat. They have a long history. Subjects of King David are said to have brought "asses laden with cheese and raisins" to pay their taxes. The Kingdom of Armenia had a flourishing raisin business in 400 B.C. but 500 years later Asia Minor was the center of production. Raisins held a place on the elaborate menus served at the Bacchanalian feasts of Nero's time. By A.D. 1300 Spain and Hungary were competing for leadership in the world's raisin markets. Then for centuries Spain, Asia Minor, and Greece furnished the world's supply of this fruit.

In 1878 California had a crop of 500 tons, by 1892 the tonnage was 30,000 tons, sufficient to displace Spain as the leader in production. For the past several years the raisin production in California has averaged about 200,000 tons annually. Raisins are also produced in Arizona, Utah, and New Mexico, but in limited quantities.

VARIETIES OF RAISINS

The Alexandria is the most important raisin variety. Sultanina is, next to Alexandria, the most important. Sultana is important in production of seedless raisins. Other large berried varieties that have been dried in limited quantities are not commercially important.

PREPARATION FOR MARKET

Drying is the most ancient and primitive of fruit-preserving methods. Dried fruit contains much more nutritive value in proportion to its bulk than fresh fruit. In the raisin district of this country, grapes are ripe by the middle of August and the season often lasts into November. The average time necessary for drying and curing a tray of raisins is about three weeks. The method is very simple. Immediately after being cut from the vines, the grapes are dipped in clear water to rinse them and are then immersed in a boiling alkaline mixture called *legia* (lye) until they show an almost imperceptible cracking of the skin. Dipping and scalding accomplish several purposes —cleansing the fruit, hastening its drying, and giving the dried fruit a lighter color. The bunches are then placed in shallow trays and allowed to sun-dry, being turned over from time to time.

SEEDED RAISINS

The invention of a raisin-seeding machine in the early '70's had a wonderful effect on the industry, and seeded raisins are now its most important branch. The machine flattens the raisins between rubber rollers while an impaling device catches and removes the seeds. Seeded raisins have a more pronounced flavor than the seedless ones. At the packing house, loose raisins and those that are to be shipped as dried

FOOD VALUE

Water	Food Energy	Pro-tein	Fat	Carbo-hydrate	Cal-cium	Phos-phorus	Iron	Vit. A Value	Thia-mine	Ribo-flavin	Nia-cin	Ascor-bic Acid
24	298	2.3	.5	71.2	78	129	3.3	50	.15	.08	.5	Trace

grapes are run through a stemmer and grader, which stems, cleans, and sorts raisins into three or four different grades. Then they are packed and shipped. Cluster or layer raisins are packed in sweat boxes and stored in equalizing rooms, where they are usually left from 10 to 30 days, long enough for over-dried berries to absorb moisture from under-dried ones. The sweating also properly softens and toughens the stems, which prevents their breaking and enables them to hold the berries better. After this, the raisins are sorted into the different grades, pressed, and stacked in piles ready for packing.

HINTS ON PREPARATION

A pound of raisins yields two to two and a half cups.

To plump raisins, wash and turn into colander. Cover, place over boiling water, and let steam for five minutes.

There are so many ways of using raisins that you will have no difficulty thinking up raisin dishes for the table. Three types of packaged raisins are available: Seeded, seedless, and cluster.

Seedless raisins may be added whole, by the handful, or by the cupful to almost any recipe for bread, cake, candy, cookies, muffins, or puddings. They are good in stuffing for meat or poultry and in meat and dessert sauces. They should be sliced with scissors, however, before being added to a thin, light cake batter or to icing. Chopped seeded raisins were an important ingredient in the boiled icing spread between and over the layers of an old-fashioned cake. Seeded raisins are sticky and are usually left whole and added to puddings. Cluster raisins are usually eaten as a confection.

APPLE AND RAISIN SALAD

5 tart, red, juicy apples
½ cup raisins plumped
⅓ cup mayonnaise
Lettuce

Wash but do not peel apples; core, julienne, or dice. Immediately toss with raisins and mayonnaise. Pile lightly into lettuce cups on individual salad plates.

Note: One quarter teaspoon cinnamon and one tablespoon lemon juice are flavorful additions to the mayonnaise.

RAISIN BREAD

10 oz whole wheat flour
¾ lb all-purpose flour
3 tsp baking powder
1½ tsp salt
4 to 6 oz sugar
1½ cups milk
6 oz seedless raisins
1 egg

Mix the wholewheat flour, flour, baking powder, sugar, and salt. Add the raisins, which have been mixed with a little flour, and make a well in the center of these dry ingredients. Pour in the milk and the egg slightly beaten, and form into a dough. Put into two greased breadpans and bake in a moderate oven (375° F.) about three quarters hour or until done.

RAISIN AND CRANBERRY JAM

1 cup seeded raisins
4 cups water
4 cups cranberries
2½ cups sugar

Cook raisins with four cups of water until liquid is reduced one half. Add cranberries and sugar. Pour into hot sterilized jars and seal. (Makes approximately 4 half-pint jars)

RAISIN DELICIOUS

½ cup brown sugar, firmly packed
½ cup granulated sugar
1½ cups boiling water
1 tbsp butter
¼ tsp cinnamon
¼ tsp salt
¾ cup moist raisins
1 tsp vanilla
1 tbsp butter
⅓ cup granulated sugar
¾ cup all-purpose flour
1 tsp baking powder
¼ tsp salt
⅓ cup milk
⅓ cup coarsely chopped nutmeats
Cream

Mix first seven ingredients in saucepan and boil to a medium sirup, about 15 minutes. Remove from heat and add vanilla. Meanwhile prepare drop batter as follows: Cream butter, add the one-third cup of sugar, and mix until blended. Sift flour, measure and resift three times with baking powder and salt. Add to sugar-butter mixture and combine well. Add milk all at once and stir until dry ingredients are thoroughly blended. Drop batter from tablespoon into a well-greased baking pan (7x11x1½ inches), and pour the raisin sirup over it. Sprinkle with nuts and bake in a moderate oven (350° F.) for about 30 minutes, or until golden brown. Serve warm or cold with cream. (Serves 5)

RAISIN PIE

2 to 2½ cups plumped raisins
½ to ¾ cup prune juice
¼ to ¾ cup sugar
1 tbsp butter
1 to 2 tbsp flour, cornstarch, or quick-cooking tapioca
¼ tsp salt
1 recipe pastry

Mix raisins, juice, and combined dry ingredients. Line pie plate with pastry (which see) and fill with fruit mixture. Dot with butter and adjust top crust, or arrange lattice of pastry strips on top. Bake in hot oven (450° F.) ten minutes, then reduce heat to moderate (350° F.) and bake about 25 minutes longer. (Makes 1 two-crust nine-inch pie)

RAISIN TARTLETS

1 recipe plain pastry
1 lb raisins
10 walnut halves
3 tbsp lemon juice
¼ cup firmly packed brown sugar

Prepare pastry (which see). Line tiny muffin pans with pastry. Put raisins and nuts through food chopper, using medium knife. Moisten with lemon juice and add one-half of brown sugar. Turn into pastry-lined muffin pans; sprinkle with remaining brown sugar. Bake in hot oven (400° F.) for 15 to 20 minutes. (Makes 20)

RAISIN WINE

Put eight pounds of Smyrna raisins in a large tub and cover with one gallon of cold water. Stir thoroughly every day for a month. Then press the raisins through a very fine jelly bag of several thicknesses of cloth. Put the liquor into a small cask and let it stand until it has finished hissing; then pour in a bottle of the best brandy, seal the cask, and let stand for 12 months. Rack off the wine, filter it through a bag of flannel of four folds, and pour into it a quart of brandy. Seal or stopper up the cask again and let stand for three years. Then the wine will be right for drinking.

SCOTCH RAISIN SQUARES

2 cups seedless raisins
2 cups water
⅓ cup sugar
½ tsp cinnamon
⅛ tsp salt
3 tbsp cornstarch
¼ cup cold water
2 tbsp lemon juice
½ tsp grated lemon rind
Pastry for 8-inch double-crust pie

Wash raisins and simmer in water until soft and plump, about ten minutes. Meanwhile blend sugar, cinnamon, salt, and cornstarch together and combine with the one-quarter cup of cold water. Bring raisins to a boil; slowly add the sugar mixture, stirring continuously. Boil for two minutes. Remove from heat, add lemon juice and rind, and cool. Divide the pastry in two portions. Roll out to one-eighth inch thickness; cut a rectangular piece to fit the bottom of an 8x12 inch pan. Then pour raisin filling into pan. Top with rectangular crust made from remaining pastry. Let rest ten minutes. Prick top or cut any desired design in pastry for steam vents. Bake for 25 to 30 minutes in a hot oven (425° F.). Cut into eight squares and serve warm or cold. (Serves 8)

RAMEKIN. A small, individual casserole without a lid.

RAMPION. A perennial cultivated in gardens for its root, which is eaten as a salad.

RANCID. Said of a food having the peculiar tainted smell of oily substances that have begun to spoil—rank, sour.

RANGE. The modern kitchen range is a device on and in which virtually all forms of cookery may be done. Range designs and types are legion, for practically every

RAMPION

known heat source has at one time or another been more or less successfully adapted to the needs of cookery. It is possible to find a range that will meet almost any given requirements of fuel supply and cooking needs.

HISTORY

It is not known just when, where, or how man first learned the wonderful effects that heat can have when applied to raw foods, though, as Charles Lamb has suggested in his famous dissertation on roast pig, the discovery was inevitable once man had overcome his primeval fear of fire and had begun to use it for heat, protection, and light.

The modern range, with its precisely controlled heats, its oven, and its broiler, is indeed a far cry from the first open cooking fires. Though a cooking tool, its development was largely caused by forces of economics, climate, and home construction, and it is only recently that all its elements were assembled in one compact, specialized unit.

In the early days, meats were roasted over open fires and glowing beds of coals by being turned slowly on spits or held on grates. Fish and vegetables were wrapped in mud and thrown into the fire to bake or else buried in the ground beneath the fire. Stews and soups were cooked in pots that

were hung over or near the fire. The oven was gradually developed in different climes in different ways. The Egyptians, for example, used clay pots that were buried in the ground and heated by building fires inside them.

Most old cooking methods seem crude today, but the ancients were actually making the best possible use of the tools of their cultures. Their methods did work and are still working in many regions today.

In the warmer climes, heat was not needed in the house—indeed, it was to be avoided as much as possible. Cooking was done over small fires in the open or, in rainy weather, on a porch or under some form of shelter. When the fire was brought indoors, it was kept as small as possible, for the oriental structure does not have smoke removing facilities and grass and bamboo structures are all too inflammable.

In the colder climates, heat of some sort was essential in the house. At first this took the form of an open fireplace, and it was only natural to utilize this fire for cooking rather than to build additional fires. Pothooks were built into the fireplace and there was often a large kettle of stew or soup bubbling away continuously. The word *range* is believed to have been first applied to a hinged iron grate that was lowered down over the fire to hold pots and pans and was swung back out of the way when not needed.

It was a logical step to incorporate the oven in the chimney or otherwise to locate it so as to use the heat of the main fire. In some places, instead of a fireplace there was a long bench or shelf-like arrangement that cooked and baked while it heated the room. In the very cold climates, this shelf was sometimes large enough to hold beds as well, central heating and the electric blanket being unknown.

In regions of variable climate where it was not necessary to heat the house during the summer, the oven was moved outside. Baking usually requires higher heat of longer duration than the other forms of cooking, and the outdoor brick or clay oven meant that some degree of comfort could be maintained in the house during the hot season.

Stoves were first developed as heating sources in order to get all possible benefit from the fuel. The stove was much more practical than the fireplace; it radiated heat better, made better use of the fuel, made for better smoke elimination, was to some extent portable, and offered other conveniences. The first stages of stove development were centered around the problem of getting the most out of the fire—and, in some countries, of ornamenting them profusely. Some early stoves are still renowned for their great beauty.

As the stove began to displace the open fire, it was only natural to use it for cooking as well as heating. Thus, in time, the kitchen stove came to replace the hearthside as the center of family life.

Central heating has had much to do with the present form of the range. When central heating was developed, the stove or range was free to become a specialized cooking instrument. Where it was once designed to radiate heat freely, it was now insulated to hold the heat in and concentrate it on the task at hand. With the hot water tank banished to the basement, where it was heated by the furnace in the winter and an auxiliary stove in the summer, the range had to be lit only when actually cooking, permitting more economical use of modern fuels.

Though range is the most general term, the words range and stove are often used interchangeably. It is difficult to draw an exact line between the two words, for authorities are inclined to disagree in definitions and usage has affected the meaning of the words. According to some, a stove is a heating device that may also be used for cooking, while a range is a cooking device that may also be used for heating; others hold that a stove has an oven opening from two ends while a range has an oven that opens only from one. Still another version is that a stove is mounted upon feet, while a range rests upon a pedestal.

See also CAMP COOKERY, KITCHEN EQUIPMENT, and OVEN.

TYPES

The essential requirements of a range are a source of heat and a means of applying the heat to pots, pans, and the like and to an oven. In addition, most ranges have some provision for broiling (which see). A range may also heat a room, supply hot water, and, in modern units, have timing devices, temperature controls, built-in pressure cookers, and so-called fireless cookers.

Since the chief function of all ranges is the same—to cook food—ranges are usually classified by the type of fuel which they burn.

Wood Range. In its most common form, the wood-burning range is a box-like structure made of cast iron and set on legs. It generally has a shelf over it and is designed to be placed against a wall, through which the stovepipe is passed. The fire pit is placed in one side of the box with the ash pit immediately below, and the oven or ovens are set beside the ash and fire pits, usually occupying most of the remaining box space. A large portion of the top surface is fitted with removable sections, and the fire is fed either through one of those sections or by means of a door set in the front side, while the ashes are removed by means of a lower door. There is an air passage between the top surface and the oven top that leads from the fire pit and almost completely encircles the oven before reaching the stovepipe at the rear of the range.

In operation, the air enters through the ash pit, is heated by the fire, and then goes through the passageway, where it heats both the oven and the top cooking surface before it passes out through the pipe, carrying the smoke and fumes of the fire along with it. A range of this type will also heat the room, since it radiates heat from all its cast-iron surfaces. For this reason, the wall and floor areas near it are usually covered with metal sheets to protect the wood. Various types of hot water tanks may also be incorporated into a range of this design.

Broiling can be done on this range by removing the section of top surface immediately above the fire pit and replacing it with a metal grill. Oven temperatures are regulated by controlling the fire, by means of air vents in the oven door, and even by opening and closing the oven door itself. Temperatures on the top cooking surface can be controlled to some extent by regulating the fire, but mostly by varying the position of the pan in relation to the fire pit. The top area is also provided with round lids of different sizes which may be removed to let the heat act directly on the bottom of the pot, pan, or kettle.

Coal Range. Coal-burning ranges are identical to wood-burning ranges in all respects save for the grate in the fire pit. A coal fire requires a different type of grate to give it proper support and ventilation.

and different types of coal will even require different types of grates. The grates in a range can be changed to meet specific fuel requirements, and it is difficult to get satisfactory results unless the proper grate is used with a given fuel. The coal range is superior to the wood range only in so far as coal gives a better, more even fire than wood.

Gas Range. Coal and wood-burning ranges have largely been supplanted by the gas-burning range, which is now, perhaps, the most commonly used type. Though the gas range is by far a more efficient cooking device than its smoke-snorting elders, its general use was made possible largely by causes unrelated to cooking. Illuminating gas, as the name implies, first came into general use as a source of light. The gas jet and mantle proved themselves so far superior to the oil lamp and candle that the public overcame its initial fear of gas and took it into their homes. Expensive pipes and mains were laid, and manufacturing and distributing systems were established in most large communities. Once gas was available, it was easily applied to other uses.

As the central heating system came into general popularity, it was possible to develop specialized ranges that would only cook. These ranges freed the housewife from the drudgery of fire-tending and saved the gas industry from economic extinction when the electric light replaced the Wellsbach mantle.

The gas range differs from the two preceding types not only in the fuel used but in its more specialized function. While the first two were built to radiate heat from their cast-iron sides, the gas range was equipped with an insulated oven, thus not only keeping the kitchen cooler but also getting more cooking use out of the heat produced.

In physical appearance, the gas range takes many forms, but all have two basic sections. There are the top burners, which produce small concentrated flames, individually regulated and intended for the heating of individual cooking vessels, and the insulated oven, heated by a self-contained burner of much larger dimensions than the top burners, that can be used for broiling as well as baking.

Because it is heated independently, the oven may be located above or below the level of the top burners or in any other de-

sired position. The remaining cubic area in the body of the range may be used as storage space for utensils and accessories even while the unit is in operation, thanks to the oven insulation and the design of the individual burners. However, there is often a drawer located immediately under the top burners that may be used as a warming area for plates, buns, etc. while the meal is being cooked. The oven top or other top surface area that is not used to hold burners is cool enough to be used as a working area or even for some types of storage.

The operation of the gas stove is based on the individual burner, a device which blends the gas with the proper amount of air and releases the mixture for combustion. Many burners are designed to produce a concentrated flame of a given size, shape, and motion, while others merely restrict the flame to a given area. All burners are subject to individual control, and they are designed to perform specific heating functions.

The nature of the fuel and the operation of the burners are such that the burner need be lit only when in actual use, thus conserving fuel. Most modern ranges are equipped with pilot lights, however. These are small gas jets that are always burning and will light the main burners whenever desired. Pilot lights consume little fuel, and though not designed for cooking, they may in some cases be used as warmers.

The burners themselves do not support the cooking vessels but are set below grates or racks. There is always some arrangement, usually a large pan, set below the burners to catch any spillage.

One development incorporated in many models of gas ranges is the so-called fireless cooker. This is a covered, heavily insulated well or pot set into the body of the range in place of one of the regular top burners. A variety of vessels and other accessories may be fitted into the well for specialized cooking functions. The well is heated by a special burner placed underneath. Once the cooking process has started, relatively little additional outside heat is needed, thanks to the insulation and cover. This permits the burner to be turned down to a much smaller flame with consequent fuel savings.

The gas will vary with its source and the pressure at which it is supplied, but the burners and fittings can be adjusted to meet conditions. By special fittings, the burners can also be adapted to the bottled gas which is supplied in portable tanks. However, regardless of chemical composition and method of supply, the fuel used must be gaseous.

Oil Range. Though often outwardly resembling the gas range in appearance, the oil range is designed to operate on liquid fuels, the most common being kerosene. The flame produced by the burners is quite similar to that of gas burners, but their construction is different. The typical burner is a good deal larger than that of the gas range and often uses a circular wick and an outer chimney to vaporize the fuel. The fuel itself is fed by gravity from tanks that are mounted in or on the stove or, in some cases, outside the house.

There are two general types of oil ranges, one consisting only of burners and the other incorporating an oven. A Dutch oven (*which see*) can be used with the former, however.

The nature of the burners is such that no broiling can be done on an oil range.

Gasoline Range. The gasoline range differs from the oil range in the burners and fuel tank. Gasoline can produce clean, effi ient fires of intense heat, but the fuel requires special handling to be properly and safely used. It is fed to the burners under air pressure and is there vaporized and mixed with air before combustion. Neither a wick nor a pilot light can be used with this fuel.

The availability of the fuel and the efficiency of the flame has made this range a favorite of campers and travellers, for whom special portable models have been developed.

Electric Range. It was inevitable that electricity should follow in the steps of gas, its predecessor, first entering the home as a source of light and then being put to other uses.

Electricity generates heat by passing through a resistance, which is, non-technically, any substance that tends to retard the current. The amount of heat generated can be controlled by varying either the resistance or the current.

The electric range applies its heat in much the same manner as the gas range, though it utilizes heating elements rather than gas burners. There are two types of heating elements generally used for what corresponds to the top burners of the gas range. In one type, the resistance lies in spiral grooves cut in the surface of a circular porcelain block. The pots and pans are held over this heating element by grates in an arrangement similar to that of the gas range. In the other type the resistance is imbedded in heating coils—broad spirals of ribbon-like metal that directly support the cooking vessels. There is usually a polished metal reflector placed below units of this type to further concentrate the heat.

The oven has one or more heating units, depending on the design; these consist of resistances arranged to radiate heat evenly over a large area. In some cases these units may also be used for broiling.

The electric range frequently has a deep-well cooker as part of its standard equipment. This device is quite similar to the one used in gas ranges, but the heating element at the bottom is located inside the well. These elements are commonly designed so that they may be raised and used as a surface unit when needed. Some newer models incorporate a pressure cooker in the deep well.

Many electric ranges are fitted with devices which turn heating elements on and off at predetermined times. Thus it is possible to prepare a meal in advance, leave it on the cold range, and have it cooked at a certain time even though no one is in the house.

An interesting development of the electric range is the field of induction or electronic cooking, which has yet to be fully exploited. The principle involved is again that of passing electricity through a resistance, but the application is a bit different. In the induction range, an early experiment, the metal cooking vessel itself became the resistance, while in the more recent electronic range, the heat is actually generated within the food. *See* HIGH FREQUENCY COOKING.

Combination Ranges. There are many circumstances in which specialization is not desirable. At a camp cottage, for example, water must be heated and the cottage itself must be heated during the winter. A coal or wood range that would perform these functions as well as cook the food has decided disadvantages, and other fuels convenient for cooking are not versatile enough to assume the additional functions.

For these reasons, combination ranges have been developed that use two different fuels. These ranges are made with every workable combination of fuels to meet almost every conceivable need.

Solar Range. Regardless of form, almost all the energy found on this planet can be traced directly or indirectly to the sun. In addition it lavishes untold volumes of energy on us that go unused. Since much of this energy comes to us directly in the form of heat, efforts have been concentrated largely on using it as heat. Cooking is one obvious use and man has devised many gadgets, some ingenious, some rather fantastic, that more or less successfully boil water, fry eggs, and broil steaks. Most of these devices are alike in principle, they use lenses or reflectors to collect and concentrate a usable amount of natural heat at a given point. The methods of applying the heat differ. Many of these devices have performed satisfactorily under testing conditions, but their commercial practicability has yet to be established. The first hurdle to clear is the necessity for cloudless skies and a shining sun. But science may yet bring sunlight into the kitchen to heat the morning coffee.

USE AND CARE

Except for rare developments, the basic principles of cookery remain unchanged regardless of the instrument used. Cooking is principally a matter of time and temperature control, and the housewife's main concern with any range is to make it produce a desired temperature for a desired length of time. The techniques differ with each type of fuel and often for various models using the same fuel. The instruction booklet usually provided by the manufacturer is the best guide.

One of the most common sources of range trouble is the oven door. When swung open, it forms a convenient and tempting resting place for such things as heavy roasts while on the way in or out of the oven. In some models this is an intended convenience, but if the door has not been designed to carry weights, the frame is sprung out of position, which creates a faulty seal and a resulting loss of heat.

Wood and Coal Ranges. Ranges of this type require fairly constant attention, since the fuel is not supplied automatically. The fire should be lit and tended exactly as any other fire of the same materials. The fire pit functions just as the fire pit in a furnace —all vents below the grate act as accelerators and all vents above the grate retard or check the action of the fire. The fire pit should not be overloaded with fuel, for this accomplishes nothing but waste, and the ash pit should be emptied daily, for if it is clogged it will hamper the proper circulation of the air. The passageway used by the air in heating the range should be cleaned occasionally, for in time soot will collect and block it. If the range is clean and properly adjusted but the fire does not function correctly, the trouble will very likely be found in the chimney.

While the metal used in these ranges can stand quite intensive heats, the range should be warmed gradually, for sudden heating causes uneven expansion and hence cracking in the metal. Cold liquids should not be spilled on the heated surface for the same reason, nor should the range parts be washed while still hot. The manufacturer will suggest various ways of treating the metal to give it a polish and an easily cleaned surface. The range should be set level on the floor, especially if there is a hot water reservoir in the unit, and the nearby woodwork should be shielded from the heat.

Oil Ranges. It is most important that only the proper fuel be used in an oil range lest fire or explosion result. The proper fuel properly used, however, presents no hazards. Since these ranges are gravity fed, they must be set absolutely level on the floor.

Gasoline Range. Here again, only the proper fuel should be used. Many types of gasoline contain lead and other chemicals which, while fine for a motor, will clog up the delicate valves of a range. Intelligent care should be exercised in handling the fuel because of its potential dangers.

The two most common causes of failure in a gasoline range are insufficient pressure in the fuel tank and clogged fuel lines and valves. When lighting, the procedure outlined by the manufacturer should always be followed, especially in regard to priming. The fuel pipe must be heated at a certain point to vaporize the gas before it enters the burners; no gasoline range will function correctly until this is done. Methods of heating or priming will vary, and carelessness at this point may well be dangerous.

A gasoline burner should give a clean, bright, steady, blue flame. If it does not and if the flame does not correct itself after burning for a few moments, the trouble should be found and cured before use:

CLEANING RANGES 1. Wiping burner top, burner grate removed 2. Wiping aeration pan 3. Wiping burner box, burners removed 4. Wiping porcelain around raised element

Gas Range. Gas is by no means a standard product. Both the chemical composition and the pressure at which it is supplied will vary in different localities. It is important, then, that when a range is first installed it be properly adjusted by a competent serviceman to meet the individual circumstances. Should a range be moved to a different gas supply system, as in a different city, it will probably require readjusting. Ranges using butane or propane air or bottled gas require special fixtures, and while the basic range may in many cases be used with any of these fuels, the burners must be adapted to the specific fuel involved.

The common kitchen range is designed to be set against a wall. For efficient operation, the location selected should be well lighted and free from all drafts. The range should be set absolutely level so the food will be uniformly thick in all vessels, permitting even cooking. The actual installation should be done by someone from the gas company or some other experienced person because of the importance of correct adjustments and the potential dangers of an amateur's handling gas under pressure.

When properly adjusted, the burner flame will show a distinct inner cone, with the outer flame reaching high enough to touch the bottom of a cooking vessel placed on the burner grate when the burner is turned on full. When a vessel is actually placed over the flame, the flame should spread out to a circle about six inches in diameter.

A solid blue flame that is too high is getting too much gas, while one that is too low is not getting enough gas. If the flame has yellow tips, it is not getting enough air while a flame that lifts and sputters and a flame that pops when turned off are getting too much air.

Pilot lights, too, must be adjusted according to the manufacturer's specifications. If the range is so equipped, when the individual burners are turned on some of the gas mixture is diverted to the open flame of the pilot light, causing the burner to light automatically. Some ranges have pilot lights for the top burners but none for the oven. If there is no pilot light for either the top burners or the oven, the burners must be lit manually. The important thing in lighting a burner manually is to ignite the gas before much of it has had a chance

to escape and collect. A large volume of gas in open air will flare up, while a volume of gas in a confined space, such as an oven, can stage an explosion, the intensity of which will vary with the volume and pressure of the gas.

If matches are used, they should be lit and held near the burner *before* the gas is turned on. A long, twisted paper "spill" may be used to light the oven burners if no special lighting provisions have been made. There are also several designs of oven and range lighters that use flint and steel to produce sparks.

The top burners should never be turned up so high as to spill flame over the edges of the pan. This merely wastes fuel, for the heat must be applied under the pan to be effective. Nor is it necessary to keep the flame high during all the cooking operation, for once a substance starts boiling, that is as hot as it will ever get and a small flame will suffice to keep it boiling. For further fuel economy, when possible, the flame should not be lit until the vessel is in place and should be turned off before the pan is removed.

The range should be kept clean, not only for neatness, but for efficient operation. Vessels should not be overloaded, their outside should be wiped clean before placing them on the range, and temperatures should be watched to prevent boiling over. Any spillage should be wiped up as soon as possible. Food particles in the burner area can clog the gas holes and the heat will char them, making them difficult to remove later. Food acids can permanently stain porcelain surfaces if permitted to lie on them long enough.

The range should be cleaned each time it is used, and at least once a month should be given a thorough going-over. Porcelain surfaces should be washed with mild soap and water, wiped with a cloth rinsed in clear water, and polished with a clean, dry, soft cloth. Porcelain should never be cleaned while warm, for sudden changes in temperature can cause the surface to crack or check due to uneven expansion.

The burner grates should be removed and washed, using a mild abrasive, if necessary, to remove charred food particles. The burners themselves may be removed and washed, but they should be thoroughly dry before they are replaced. Drying can be done in the oven. All burner holes should be kept clear and can be cleaned with a fine wire, needle, or pin. It is not advisable to use steel wool on a burner, since small pieces of metal can easily break off and lodge in the gas ports.

The oven door should be left open for a short time after each use of the oven to let cooking moisture evaporate. All spillage should be cleaned up as soon as possible, and, after broiling or roasting, the broiling rack, pan, and oven lining should be cleaned thoroughly to remove all grease. Grease or food particles left in the oven will burn, and the resulting fumes will affect the cooking food when the oven is next used. The inside of the oven should be cleaned in the same manner as the outer porcelain, using mild abrasives only when necessary to remove charred foods. All portholes of the oven burner should be checked with a piece of wire or a long pin at least twice a year to make certain that they are still open.

If an oven has become excessively dirty, it can be cleaned by placing about a half cup of household ammonia in a shallow dish in the bottom of the oven. The door is closed and the dish allowed to stand in the cold oven overnight, or from six to eight hours. The ammonia fumes will soften the greasy deposit on the oven lining and racks, thus simplifying removal.

Should there be noticeable gas odors in the kitchen, the range should be checked to see that all burner controls are at the off position and that pilot lights, if any, are all lit. If the odors persist, either the gas company or a repairman should be notified at once. If the odors are very strong, the kitchen windows and doors should be opened to dissipate the gas and the pilot light extinguished to prevent possible explosions.

Electric Range. Before an electric range is installed, the lighting company should be consulted to make certain that the house has the proper wiring. The range should be given a convenient, well lighted position in the kitchen, and, like all ranges, should be level to give the best cooking results. The manufacturer's instruction book should be carefully studied to learn the best working procedure for the particular range.

The cooking vessels should have flat bottoms and straight sides and be large enough to cover fully the heating area of the units. To get the most from the heat, especially if the heating unit is of the type that directly supports the vessel, there should be no dents or unevenness in the vessel bottom. There are specially designed wire grids that, when placed between the heating unit and a vessel made of heat-resisting glass, increase cooking efficiency.

The cleaning procedure for an electric range is much the same as that for the gas range, except for the heating units. Here, because of design differences, the manufacturer's booklet should be consulted.

RANGIPORT CHEESE is similar to Port du Salut cheese. It is six inches in diameter, two and one-half inches thick, and weighs two and one-half pounds. It is made in France.

RANGPUR. A citrus fruit similar to the lemon and lime in acidity. It is about the size of a small lemon, globular, sometimes flattened at the poles, and has reddish skin and orange-colored flesh.

RAPE

RAPE. A plant of the cabbage species, the fleshy stem and leaves of which are sometimes used in the same manner as spinach, in salads, etc. It is hardly fit to use until touched by frost and is not cultivated in the United States to any considerable extent, hence it is seldom obtainable in the markets. Its flavor is warm and aromatic, but its chief value lies in its oil-yielding seeds. Rape oil is thick and brownish-yellow. It is used in India for illuminating and lubricating purposes.

RAREBIT. A rarebit is a dish consisting of melted cheese poured over toasted bread or crackers. It is often mixed with ale or beer. Many different ingredients may be added to vary the basic recipe. *See* CHEESE.

RASCHERA CHEESE. Another name for the Italian cheese, Nostrale, *which see.*

RASHER. A thin slice of bacon.

RASPBERRY. The raspberry is considered one of the most delicately flavored fruits and is a general favorite. It makes excellent jam, jellies, and preserves and is used in confectionery in making ice cream, tarts, pies, puddings, sauces, etc. It is also valuable in the compounding of liqueurs.

not graded in conformity with either of the aforementioned grades remain unclassified.

Raspberries are in season from May to the end of July. Quality is indicated by a

FOOD VALUE

Water	Food Energy	Pro- tein	Fat	Carbo- hydrate	Cal- cium	Phos- phorus	Iron	Vit. A Value	Thia- mine	Ribo- flavin	Nia- cin	Ascor- bic Acid
84.4	65	1.2	.8	13.2	36	34	.9	320	.03	—	—	23

RASPBERRIES

VARIETIES OF RASPBERRIES

The red berry is the type most familiar as a fresh fruit, but the native black raspberry or black cap is used widely for both canning and evaporating. It is a very pleasing fruit, although not as delicate or select as the red. Some regions produce yellow and purple raspberries to a limited extent; the latter is a hybrid of the red and black fruits. Red raspberries grow on erect canes, black and purple fruit on arched canes. New York and Michigan are the chief producing states.

PREPARATION FOR MARKET

Raspberries are graded for market according to U.S. Department of Agriculture standards. U.S. No. 1 consists of raspberries of one color which are well colored, well developed, and not soft, overripe, or broken and which are free from decay, disease, and damage. U.S. No. 2 consists of raspberries of one variety which are not graded according to U.S. No. 1 standards but do not contain more than 10% by volume of berries that have been seriously damaged by any cause (not more than one-fifth of this amount may be affected by mold or decay). Any raspberries

bright, clean, fresh appearance combined with a solid, full color and plumpness of the individual berry. Beware of stained boxes and soft berries, which are indications of decay. Overripe berries are usually very dull in color, soft, and sometimes leaky. Such fruit is a wasteful buy. Natural breakdown, decay, bruising, and crushing may cause berries to be soft and leaky. Decay can easily be detected by the presence of molds on the surface of berries. A berry that has a number of cells green or off-color will not have as good flavor as the naturally ripened berry.

When buying raspberries, see that they have no caps, because that indicates that they were picked before they were fully ripe. They should be naturally fragrant. Berries are usually sold by the quart or pint. Buy only for immediate consumption, as raspberries are extremely perishable and lose their flavor rapidly. They should be spread out in thin layers when it is necessary to store them and should be rinsed in cold water just before serving.

Of the red and black raspberries, the red raspberry is preferred for canning purposes. Heavy sirup shrinks the fruit, therefore Fancy or drained weight will not be as heavy as Choice or Standard.

All the different methods of serving strawberries may be applied to this delicate fruit.

BLACK RASPBERRY COBBLER

1 qt black raspberries
½ cup sugar
2 tbsp flour
1 tbsp lemon juice
1 cup all-purpose flour
½ tsp salt
1¼ tsp baking powder
¼ cup shortening
½ cup milk minus 1 tbsp

Wash and drain fruit. Combine sugar and two tablespoons flour, and mix with berries. Add lemon juice and turn into buttered deep-pie dish. Sift flour, measure and resift with salt and baking powder. Cut in shortening with a pastry blender or two knives and add milk all at once, stirring with a fork until dough clings together. Pat or roll out dough to one-quarter-inch thickness and place it on top of fruit mixture. Trim edges and cut a design in center for steam to escape. Bake in a hot oven (450° F.) for 15 minutes, reduce heat to moderately slow (325)° F.), and continue baking until berries are cooked through, about 20 minutes. Plain pastry (*which see*) may be used instead of biscuit dough for crust. Serve warm. (Serves 5)

RASPBERRY BAVARIAN CREAM

1 tbsp gelatin
2 tbsp cold water
1 cup crushed raspberries
1 cup heavy cream, whipped
¾ cup powdered sugar
Ladyfingers
6 whole raspberries

Soften gelatin in cold water five minutes; heat over hot water, stirring until dissolved. Add to raspberries, mixing well, and chill until slightly thickened. Fold in cream, sweetened with sugar, and chill mixture until thick enough to hold its shape. Line parfait glasses with ladyfingers, fill with gelatin mixture, and top with a large berry. Chill. (Serves 6)

RASPBERRY BOMBE

2 qt red raspberries
1 cup sugar
1 cup water
1 lemon
1 pt stiffly whipped cream
Vanilla

Crush and strain raspberries through a cheese cloth. Make a sirup of one cup of sugar and one of water, cook together for five minutes after starting to boil. Add the sirup to the fruit juice, and when cool, add the lemon juice and freeze hard. Line a two-quart mold about two inches deep, bottom and sides, with the raspberry ice and fill with one pint of stiffly whipped

cream which has been sweetened to taste and flavored with vanilla. Cover with three sheets of wax paper and see that the lid is pressed down tight. Pack in salt and ice, using salt freely, for at least three hours. Unmold on platter and surround with red raspberries well powdered with sugar. Serve with a light cake.

RASPBERRY CHIFFON PIE

1½ cups boiling water
1 pkg raspberry-flavored gelatin
½ pt fresh raspberries
¼ cup sugar
Pinch of salt
2 egg whites, stiffly beaten
Chilled graham cracker or bread crumb pastry

Slowly pour one cup of boiling water over the gelatin and stir until dissolved. Set aside to cool until slightly congealed, thick, and sirupy. Pick over and wash the raspberries. Press one-quarter cup of the berries through a sieve into a small pan and then pour the remaining one-half cup of the water through the sieve to insure no loss of raspberry flavor; add the sugar and salt to the juice and boil for five minutes. Gradually pour this over the beaten egg whites, beating continuously until mixture is very thick, fluffy, and slightly cool. Whip the gelatin until light and foamy, then fold in the beaten egg white mixture. Fold in the remaining raspberries and pour into the chilled, crumb-lined pan. Set pie in refrigerator to chill until firm, two or three hours. Serve with whipped cream if desired, and garnish with a few whole perfect berries. (Serves 6)

RASPBERRIES AND CHOCOLATE

Whip two and one-half cups of cream stiff with one cup grated chocolate and sifted sugar to taste; pick over one quart red raspberries; wash them, and fold them in the chocolate cream. Serve cold.

RASPBERRY ICE

1 qt raspberries
1 cup granulated sugar
1 cup cold water
2 tbsp lemon juice
⅛ tsp salt

Pick over raspberries, run them under cold water, and sponge dry. Sprinkle sugar over raspberries; cover and allow to stand for at least two hours. Then mash and squeeze through double cheesecloth or fine muslin cloth. To this juice add water which has been mixed with lemon juice and salt, and freeze in hand freezer, using three parts of ice and one part of rock salt. Serve in well chilled sherbet glasses.

RASPBERRY ICE CREAM

1 pt fresh raspberries
½ cup cold water
½ cup sugar
⅛ tsp salt
½ tsp grated lemon rind
2 cups heavy sour cream

Wash, pick over, and coarsely mash the berries. Combine with the water and sugar, and cook five minutes. Strain immediately through doubled cheesecloth and chill. Add the salt and lemon rind, then fold into the stiffly beaten sour cream. Freeze in refrigerator tray until mushy. Scrape and beat until smooth, then complete freezing in automatic refrigerator, about three hours. This cream may also be frozen in a hand freezer. (Serves 6)

RASPBERRY JAM

Wash, crush, and measure the raspberries. If berries are tart, add an equal measure of sugar; if sweet, use three-quarters as much sugar as fruit. Cook until thick, stirring constantly to prevent burning. Boil rapidly as long cooking tends to darken the jam. Pour into hot, sterilized jars and seal.

RASPBERRY JELLY

3 qt fully ripe raspberries
3½ cups sugar
1 bottle fruit pectin

To prepare the juice, crush thoroughly or grind the berries. Place in a jelly bag and press out the juice. Measure juice (there should be four cups) and sugar into a large preserving kettle. Mix well, bring to boiling point over the hottest fire, and at once add the pectin, stirring constantly. Bring to a full rolling boil and boil hard for half

a minute. Quickly remove from the fire, skim, pour into hot, sterilized glasses and seal.

RASPBERRY AND STRAWBERRY JELLY

1½ qt each fully ripe raspberries and strawberries
3½ cups sugar
1 bottle fruit pectin

To prepare the juice, crush thoroughly or grind the fruit. Turn into a jelly bag and press out the juice. Measure juice (there should be four cups) and sugar into a large preserving kettle, mix well, bring to a full rolling boil over the hottest fire, and boil hard for at least one minute, stirring constantly. Add the pectin, bring again to a full rolling boil, and boil hard for half a minute. Remove from the fire, skim, and pour into hot, sterilized glasses. Seal.

RASPBERRY MOUSSE

1½ cups raspberry juice
Juice of ½ lemon
20 marshmallows
1½ cups of cream

Strain and heat the juice. Cut up the marshmallows and dissolve in the juice. Cool. Add the lemon juice and the cream, which has been whipped stiff. Fill sherbet glasses with the mousse, and cool.

RASPBERRY PRESERVES

Pick over, wash, and thoroughly drain as many red raspberries are desired. Half fill quart glass jars with them, then fill the jars right to the top with sugar. Cover closely but do not seal. Place in the refrigerator, and in two or three days, if the sugar should settle, fill up again with additional sugar. Again close tightly and leave for several months. The sugar will preserve the berries, they will be whole, and there will be an abundance of sirup.

RASPBERRY PUDDING

Pastry
1 qt raspberries
1 qt currants
Sugar

Lemon juice
1 glassful water

Line a buttered pie-dish with pastry (*which see*) and put in half the raspberries and the same quantity of currants, red if the raspberries are red, white if the raspberries are yellow. Then put a good coating of sugar and the juice of half a lemon over the fruit. Fill up the dish with the rest of the raspberries and currants mixed, with sugar and more lemon juice on top. Add the glassful of water. Roll out the pastry for the lid, moisten the edges and place on top. Ioin the lining pastry and the lid, press round the edges, trim with a knife, cover with a well-floured cloth, and boil for two and one-half to three hours.

RASPBERRY PUNCH

2 cups fresh red raspberries
Mint sprigs
4 cups lime juice
4 cups simple sirup
6 cups water

The berries and mint are muddled in the lime juice, and the water and simple sirup, previously mixed, are added. This mixture is strained into a punch bowl holding a large block of ice and is garnished with whole mint sprigs. (Serves 20)

RASPBERRY RATAFIA

2 lb raspberries
½ gallon brandy
2 lb sugar
1 qt water

Crush the berries well. Steep them for at least two weeks in the brandy, and then add a boiled sirup of the sugar and water. Bottle.

RASPBERRY SHERBET

2 tbsp gelatin
3 cups cold water
1 cup boiling water
1 cup sugar
1 cup strained raspberry juice
3 tbsp lemon juice

Soften gelatin in one-half cup cold water; dissolve in boiling water, and add

sugar, fruit juices, and remaining cold water. Strain and freeze. (Makes approximately two quarts sherbet)

RASPBERRY SPONGE

½ pt red raspberries
⅔ cup sugar
3 tbsp lemon juice
1 tbsp plain gelatin
3 tbsp cold water
½ cup boiling water
2 egg whites

Wash and crush berries, add sugar and lemon juice and stir until sugar is dissolved. Soften gelatin in the cold water for five minutes; add boiling water and stir until dissolved. Add to raspberries and stir well. Chill until mixture begins to congeal. Beat egg whites until stiff; add raspberry mixture and continue beating until thoroughly blended. Cover. Chill until firm. Serve in sherbet glasses with cream, if desired. Frozen berries may be used if they are first thawed in the refrigerator. If they have been frozen with sugar, omit further sugar from the ingredients. (Serves 5)

RASPBERRY VINEGAR. A sweet concentrate that has innumerable uses. Not only is it an admirable flavoring ingredient, but, when diluted to taste with water and ice, it makes a delicious beverage.

3 lb ripe raspberries
1 qt white wine or cider vinegar
Sugar

Place one pound of berries in a bowl and bruise well. Pour in the vinegar (cider vinegar can be used, but wine vinegar yields a better taste) and led stand overnight. The following day place another pound of berries in another bowl and bruise well. Strain the liquid in the first bowl through a cloth into the second bowl, taking care not to crush the berries too much lest fermentation result. Let the second bowl stand overnight and, the following day, repeat the process with the remaining pound of berries. When the last pound of berries has been steeped overnight, strain through a cloth into an earthenware vessel and add one pound of sugar for every pint of liquid. When the sugar has dissolved, place the earthenware vessel in a container of water and put on the stove. Let the water simmer and keep skimming the raspberry vinegar until it is clear, then remove and let cool. Bottle and keep in a cool place until needed. *See also* FRUIT DRINKS.

RATAFIA. A general name, no longer common in America, for a liqueur or cordial made by the infusion method (*see* LIQUEUR). During the Victorian era, especially in England, Ratafias were very popular and were usually homemade.

RAVIGOTE. One of the most popular French sauces for cold boiled fish.

3 hard-cooked egg yolks
2 raw egg yolks
Small pinch each of paprika, dry English mustard, and granulated sugar
1 tsp each of finely chopped onion, shallot, parsley, chives, and burnet
⅔ cup mayonnaise

Force hard-cooked egg yolks through a sieve and mix them with raw egg yolks, paprika, English mustard, sugar, onion, shallot, parsley, and chives. Beat the mixture thoroughly and fold into it the two-thirds cup mayonnaise.

RAVIGOTE BUTTER. A relish also called *Beurre Vert*, or Green Butter. To make this, combine equal parts of parsley, chervil, tarragon herbs, chives, and burnet, and chop very fine. Blanch these ingredients in a little water, drain, and pat dry in a cloth and combine with a teaspoon of finely minced shallot and as much butter as there are mixed herbs. Chill, then serve on any broiled meat or game.

RAVIOLI. An Italian dish which may be used as an appetizer or may be served as a main course.

RAVIOLI I

3 cups sifted bread flour
2 eggs
Warm water
½ cup bread or cracker crumbs
½ cup ground cooked meat
Salt and pepper
Tomato sauce
Grated Parmesan or other cheese

Return the flour to the sifter and sift it onto a board in a small mound. Make a depression in the center and break one egg

into this. Mix well, moisten with enough warm water to make a stiff dough, knead until smooth, and then roll out very thin and cut into three-inch squares. Combine the crumbs, meat, and remaining egg. Season, and place a small mound on half of the squares. Moisten the edges, top with the remaining dough, and press the edges firmly together. Cook 10 minutes in boiling water or in meat, fish, or chicken stock. Drain, and serve with tomato sauce and grated cheese. (Serves 6)

RAVIOLI II

2 cups sifted bread flour
½ tsp salt
2 whole eggs plus 1 egg yolk
1 tbsp oil
⅓ cup cold water

Sift the flour and salt together onto a board as directed above. Drop the eggs into the center, add the oil and mix thoroughly, adding water gradually to make a firm paste. Knead for ten minutes, cover with a dry cloth, and let stand for half an hour. Roll out very thin with a lightly floured rolling pin, and cut into three-inch rounds. Put a teaspoon of the desired filling on one half of each round, brush the edges with a little beaten egg white, and fold the other half of the paste over the filling, pressing the edges tightly together. Drop rapidly into boiling salted water or stock and cook 15 to 20 minutes. Skim out, drain on a cloth and serve with hot butter and grated Parmesan, Gruyère, or American cheese. Such sauces as tomato, mushroom, and cheese, or the gravy left over from a roast are all appropriate for serving with ravioli.

RAVIOLI FILLING I

2 slices onion, minced
2 tsp minced parsley
2 tsp oil
½ lb cooked cold meat, ground
1 egg
Salt and pepper

Brown the onion and parsley in the oil. Add the meat blended with the egg and seasonings. Cook, stirring constantly, about five minutes.

Ravioli Filling II

½ cup cooked spinach
½ cup cooked chicken
2 tbsp grated cheese
Salt, pepper, and cayenne

Thoroughly drain the spinach, then pass through the food chopper with the chicken. Add the cheese and seasonings.

RAY FISH. *See* Skates.

RAYON CHEESE. An exceedingly dry, hard cheese used for grating. It is of the Emmenthaler type and is made in Switzerland.

REAMER. A type of fruit juice extractor, *which see.*

REBLOCHON CHEESE. A soft, rennet cheese, made from fresh whole milk. It weighs one to two pounds. An imitation of Reblochon is known as Brizecon.

RECHAUFFE. A French word for made-over dishes or reheated food.

RECIPE. Conditions favor the modern housekeeper, whether she cooks by electricity or carries her fuel from the woodpile. She has a hundred conveniences that her great-grandmother never dreamed of, to say nothing of the excellent markets where raw materials and prepared foods may be had in abundance. She needs plan her meals only from day to day, and if some essential ingredient should be missing from the pantry shelf, the telephone will generally bring it to her in time for dinner. However, markets, conveniences, and books on cookery will never set a good meal on the table without the skill and devotion of a genuine cook. The management of the oven, the exact consistency of custards, the nice browning of baked or roasted meats and pastry—these are details which nothing but experience and practice can teach and without which a good meal, a balanced and healthful meal, can hardly be prepared. Written instructions can only point out the way which each one must follow for herself.

The Cookbook

The observance of a few general principles in planning a single dish or a full menu will greatly lighten the labor of cooking. First of all, if you do not know your recipe by heart, place your cookbook on the table and keep it open. Then choose from your supplies everything that you will use—even the kitchen utensils—and set them within easy reach. Proceed to think out the various steps of measuring, mixing, heating, beating, basting, and so forth, in their proper order. See that your fire or oven is just as you wish it and that nothing has been overlooked that will save you time and prevent mistakes.

Remember that the apparent nonchalance with which an expert cook will sometimes throw together an attractive meal is proof that he or she knows just what to do and how to do it so well that preparations go forward with astonishing speed to their orderly and triumphant conclusion. It would be difficult, as it is unnecessary, to memorize all the recipes which you may use in the course of a year or even a month. Experienced cooks know by heart scores of recipes, but they are likely to forget almost as many as they remember. When in doubt or seeking fresh suggestions, they refer to the recipe book. Beginners, therefore, should not feel ashamed in accepting help from their friends who are good cooks or in gleaning valuable information from reliable books.

What Is a Recipe?

A recipe is the fruit of practical experience. The cook who experimented at one time in the distant past perhaps failed the first time but finally succeeded and passed on the information to others. Some recipes have been handed down from as far off as Roman times. Modern recipes are much more accurate than the old ones, as may be seen by consulting old cookbooks.

When first using a recipe, follow the directions exactly. Notice the proportions and read carefully the directions for combining the ingredients—there are always important points to note. Have the whole process well in mind before you begin work. It is poor technique to refer to the printed page at every move. If the use of a recipe is preceded by a simple experiment that makes the basic principle clear, it is much easier to use the recipe with intelligence. When one is no longer a novice, one may take liberties with a recipe, even a new one, scanning it with critical eye and perhaps giving it a cool welcome. It may not be a new one at all, for there are few absolutely original formulas, despite their variety of garbs. Learn these and then, with experience, you will become inventive.

The word recipe is from the Latin meaning *take* Take or bring together on the worktable whatever materials are needed. As you gather the materials together, measure and weigh the exact amounts.

The preparation of a number of dishes assembled for a meal requires a skill quite different from that necessary for the making of a single dish. A menu needs forethought, an accurate sense of time, and promptness in order to have a number of dishes ready simultaneously or in proper sequence. It is obvious that in preparing a meal the dishes cannot be finished one at a time, but that steps peculiar to each dish must be interwoven with others. All the courses of the meal are on the mind of the housekeeper, who must attend to half a dozen things at once.

RED GROUPER. The red groupers belong to the bass family but are much larger than bass. They are found in the warm waters of the Atlantic seaboard from Virginia to Brazil. An excellent fish, the red grouper is similar in flavor to the bass. The methods employed in the preparation of bass, catfish, pickerel, perch, and whiting may be adapted to this delicate fish. *See* GROUPER.

RED GURNARD. The reputation of the red gurnard dates back to the Roman Empire, when the poets extolled the gurnard's magnificent colors and the sophisticated gourmets regaled themselves with its exquisite and incomparable flesh served on gold and silver platters. The demands of the Roman gastronomes caused this luxury to soar to such ridiculous prices that even Cicero in one of his pamphlets reproached their insane ostentation and berated the Roman nobles vigorously.

It is recorded that Suetonius under the reign of Tiberius paid for three small red gurnards the incredible sum of 30,000 sestercii, which represents about $360 of our currency. Since the days of Suetonius and Cicero, the gurnard has become more common and hence less expensive, while its deliciousness has not altered one whit. The price has fallen to 20 cents a pound, and one does not have to be a Caesar to enjoy and relish a delicious dish of red gurnard properly grilled and served with maître d'hotel butter.

The red gurnard, or gurnet, as it is sometimes called, is a spiny-rayed fish of the *Triglidae* family and is found abundantly in the waters of the Eastern Atlantic sea-

board from Maine to South Carolina. The name is suggestive of the sound made by the fish when it is taken from the water.

There are many other species, such as the cuckoo gurnard, the flying gurnard, the pied piper, the bat fish, and the sea swallow, which, like the red gurnard, never exceed 16 inches in length; the average length of the red gurnard is about eight inches and the average weight one pound. The red gurnard should never be scaled, for unscaled it keeps better its incomparable delicacy and aroma.

Broiled Red Gurnard

Slash the backs of six one-pound red gurnards. (This prevents the fish from curling.) Roll in melted, seasoned butter, and broil under a medium flame for ten minutes on each side. Serve very hot, sprinkling each fish with a few drops of tarragon vinegar, then with a teaspoon of chopped sweet-sour gherkins, and finally pouring over each fish a tablespoon of sizzling hot brown butter. Serve with French fried potatoes and fried green cabbage.

Red Gurnard en Papillote a l'Italienne

6 1-lb red gurnards

Marinade

1 cup oil
1 tbsp lemon juice
1 tbsp fennel, finely minced
1 small clove garlic, crushed
1 large bay leaf
3 sprigs parsley
3 sprigs celery top
Salt and pepper

Stuffing

½ lb fresh pork fat
3 or 4 sprigs parsley
1 tbsp coarsely cut chives
2 sprigs fennel
1 slice onion
2 small shallots
1 cup tomato sauce

Clean the gurnards, then marinate for one hour in the combined marinade ingredients. Meanwhile, pass through the food chopper, using the fine knife, the pork fat, parsley, chives, fennel, onion, and shallots. Season with salt and pepper, and moisten to spreading consistency with a little of the liquid of the marinade. Divide this paste into six equal portions and spread each on a square of oiled paper large enough to completely envelop a fish. Lay the fish on the stuffing, fold the paper completely over and around it, then arrange in a shallow pan with half the marinade, leaving the various flavoring ingredients in it. Bake in a moderate oven (350° to 375° F.) about 20 minutes, basting frequently with the liquid in the pan and turning the fish after 15 minutes of baking. Carefully remove the paper from the fish, scrape the spreading paste from the paper into a saucepan, add the tomato sauce, and bring to a rapid boil. Pour this into a shallow hot platter and arrange the fish on it, each overlapping the next. Garnish with parsley and lemon quarters. (Serves 6)

In New Orleans the snapper is called "the king of the fish market." Spices are generally used in its preparation. These are put into the water when the fish is poached or cut; the shape of a letter S is made on the back to prevent shrinking. Then the snapper is stuffed with a highly seasoned stuffing, including thyme, cloves, bayleaf, and soaked bread and is rubbed with olive oil or butter and baked in a hot oven (400° F.). Or it may be baked in a Creole sauce. The sauce may also be made separately and served with the fish.

RED SWIZZLE. A red colored, intoxicating, tropical drink mixed with a swizzle stick. *See* SWIZZLE.

RED TABLE WINES. A classification referring to those still wines that are red in color and best suited for use with food. *See* WINE.

REDFISH. (1) The blue-backed salmon which ascends the rivers of Alaska and as far south as the Columbia River.

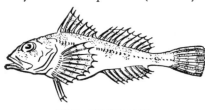

RED GURNARD

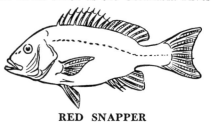

RED SNAPPER

RED LAVER. A species of seaweed, sometimes used for food.

RED MULLET. *See* MULLET.

RED PEPPER. *See* CAPSICUM *and* PEPPERS. (II).

RED PERCH. *See* PERCH.

RED SNAPPER. The red snapper is an important food fish related to the sea bass and found on rocky banks in the warm seas. It reaches the length of about two feet. The species found from the Gulf Coast up to New Jersey are deep water fish and include the mangrove or gray snapper, also called Pensacola snapper, which, like the red snapper, is a very delicate morsel. This variety attains an average weight of about two pounds, although some specimens weigh more. It is very abundant and is not carnivorous, as are certain snappers found in the West Indies, but it is voracious and bites quickly at food—hence its name. The various methods employed in the preparation of bass, herring, pickerel, pompano, and whitefish may be adapted to these fish. (*See also* FISH).

(2) The red drum or southern red horse, an important food fish, common to the Atlantic coast southward from Chesapeake Bay. It is several feet long. Its flesh is lacking in flavor. (3) The red perch or rosefish. *See* PERCH.

REEDBIRD. Another name for the bobolink. These excellent little birds were once brought to market picked and strung together in bunches. It is now unlawful to hunt them. Thirty years ago they were most abundant in the Pennsylvania markets, especially in Philadelphia, which is near their feeding grounds. They are commonly known there as reedbirds, but in the Charleston and Savannah markets, where they were also abundant, they were called ricebirds. They were in best condition for the table during September and October and were cooked in the same way as rail or quail.

REFLECTOR OVEN. An open oven whose function is based on the principle of reflected heat. *See* OVEN and CAMP COOKERY.

REFRIGERATION. Any process whereby a substance is cooled, chilled, or frozen is a form of refrigeration. These processes have been put to many an advantageous use, not the least of them being to keep perishable foods from spoiling (*see* FOOD PRESERVATION AND STORAGE). Man has, through the years, developed many methods of temperature control, both natural and artificial.

Some degree of refrigeration may be achieved by insulating against heat and through the use of caves, springs, wells, and other naturally cool locations. Satisfactory results may be achieved through the use of ice (*which see*), though the available temperature ranges are limited. There are also certain chemicals which, when mixed with water in the proper proportions, can cause freezing temperatures, but here the application is rather limited.

Man has overlooked few possibilities in his quest for controlled coolness. The powers of evaporation have been utilized in many ways—porous water bottles and bags, for example—and even fire has been put to use. Sweltering GI's stationed in the ice-less tropics would bury their beer in the ground and build fires over the spot. The fire would actually draw the heat from the surrounding ground, and when the beer was unearthed, though not chilled, it was at least cooled.

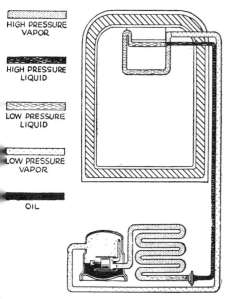

HIGH PRESSURE VAPOR

HIGH PRESSURE LIQUID

LOW PRESSURE LIQUID

LOW PRESSURE VAPOR

OIL

ELECTRIC REFRIGERATOR SYSTEM

Of all the available methods, mechanical refrigeration is by far the most flexible, both in application and ease of control. Through it, mechanical power of any sort, or even heat itself, can be used to produce almost any desired degree of cold.

PRINCIPLES OF MECHANICAL
REFRIGERATION

The same basic principles of physics are utilized in all present refrigeration machines. Cold is a negative rather than a positive state, being only the absence of heat. Even as water will always flow to a lower level, heat will always pass to those regions where it is not, unless there is some barrier (insulation) in the way.

All matter is made up of molecules which are constantly in motion. If a liquid is to turn into a gas (boil or vaporize), these molecules must absorb additional energy in the form of heat. Conversely, if a gas is to become a liquid (condense), energy must be given off in the form of heat.

Liquids have different boiling points, some very low, others exceedingly high. The pressure exerted on a liquid controls the boiling point, since, if the pressure is low the molecules need less energy to fight their way clear of the liquid than they would if the pressure were high. Thus, a high pressure means that the boiling point is raised, and a low pressure means that the boiling point is dropped.

These principles are applied by using a liquid that has a low boiling point in a sealed network of pipes divided into two sections, the evaporator and the compressor.

Evaporator. This normally consists of a series of coils and is the cooling or freezing unit in any refrigeration system. The liquid in the coils has an extremely low boiling point, lower than the freezing point of water. The coils are so arranged that the pressure on the liquid is low enough to let the temperature of whatever surrounds the coils cause the liquid to boil or evaporate. But to boil, the refrigerant must absorb heat, and this heat is drawn from whatever surrounds the coils—usually the air in the refrigerator.

Compressor. The refrigerant, now a gas, goes to the compressor, which is located outside of the insulated, refrigerated zone. Here the gas is compressed back into a liquid, and the heat, which the gas had been carrying, is literally wrung from it in the process.

The liquid refrigerant, still considerably hotter than it was before it entered the evaporator coils, goes to another set of coils—a radiator or some similar device—where its excess heat is carried away. Once the refrigerant has lost this cargo of heat, it is ready for another trip to the evaporator.

The most common means of compressing the refrigerant is to use a pump. There is one system, however, in which this is accomplished by heat from an outside source. This system is a bit more complex, but it uses the same basic principles of the evaporator and compressor and uses the outside heat to supply the energy needed to push the refrigerant through the different steps of the cycle.

APPLICATIONS

When first developed, these machines were on the bulky side. They were used principally to make ice, which, in turn, was used for various types of refrigeration. As more compact and more efficient machines were developed they began to replace ice in many forms of refrigeration, especially in those cases where temperatures lower than that of ice were needed. They were used widely in the cold storage industry and in home food storage (see REFRIGERATOR). As even better machines were developed and as more was learned about the effect of cold on foods, another method of food preservation was developed; that of freezing food, which see.

Naturally, the design of the machine will be varied to fit specific uses, but all mechanical refrigerators now in use are based on the principles explained. Though mechanization is now in the fore, ice itself is still heavily and properly used in many forms of refrigeration. See REFRIGERATOR and ICE REFRIGERATOR.

REFRIGERATOR. A refrigerator may be correctly defined as any box, room, or device used to keep things cool. Though the word is quite inclusive in meaning, through usage it has come to be generally accepted as applying specifically to the mechanical home storage unit. In this sense, a refrigerator is an insulated cabinet fitted with an automatically regulated mechanism that both keeps the cabinet

temperature at the proper level for the safe storage of perishable foods and also provides a supply of ice.

DEVELOPMENT OF THE REFRIGERATOR

The present home storage units were made possible as the principles of mechanical refrigeration were perfected (see REFRIGERATION). In the beginning, mechanical refrigeration was used to make ice for use, among other things, in the ice refrigerator (which see), but ice-making units compact enough to go into the home were finally developed in the early days of this century.

At first these home units were made in two sections—the evaporator or freezing apparatus that went into the kitchen, often fitting into the ice compartment of the regular icebox, and the condensing unit, complete with bulky motor, that was installed in the basement. These two sections were connected with pipes so that the refrigerant could circulate between them.

In time, components compact enough to fit into one unit were developed. These units functioned more or less like the ice refrigerator; the evaporator coils were placed near the top of the cabinet interior. These coils were wrapped around a small compartment and served the dual functions of chilling the air within the cabinet and making ice within the smaller compartment.

More recent trends in refrigerator design, however, are making greater use of the flexibility inherent in mechanical refrigeration. In addition to trying to give greater storage space in relation to the cubic size of the unit, manufacturers are developing specialized areas within the unit for the more efficient storage of specific types of food. Among the more recent developments are, for example, special compartments for the preparation and storage of frozen foods.

REFRIGERATOR OPERATION

The present home refrigerator consists of four basic parts: An insulated cabinet, a freezing unit or evaporator, a condensing unit, and a thermostat.

Insulated Cabinet. Since heat will always pass to areas of lower temperatures if at all possible, a well insulated cabinet is essential, for efficiency and economy.

Freezing and Condensing Units. The operation of these essential units is described in the article on refrigeration. A refrigerator may have more than one set of evaporator coils, but their basic operation will be the same.

Thermostat. If the cabinet is properly insulated, there is no need for the refrigerant to circulate constantly to maintain the proper temperature. For this reason, all household refrigerators are fitted with an automatic, temperature-sensitive control. When the proper temperature has been established, this control automatically shuts off the motor or otherwise halts the action until the temperature rises above the prescribed limit. Then the control starts the apparatus going again. Each set of coils has its own thermostat.

There are only two kinds of refrigerators generally made for household use—the electrical and the flame-operated types. The electrical types all use a pump of some sort to compress the gas in the condensor; also electricity is the only practical power for intermittent, economical operation. The flame-operated types have no moving parts, they use the heat of the flame to make the refrigerant circulate. The intensity of the flame can be varied by the thermostat.

Refrigerators will differ in design and internal arrangement, but all use wire-rack shelves to permit air circulation, and all will have at least one set of evaporator coils and an ice cube compartment. However, refrigerators using only one set of coils tend to dry out the foods that are stored in them. This dehydration is largely due to the temperature of the coils, which must be below freezing if ice cubes are to be made. The air circulating through the cabinet picks up moisture from the food, and when it comes to the freezing coils, the moisture is deposited on them in the form of ice and frost and the air is ready to pick up more moisture when it again passes over the food.

The obvious answer is to keep the air from circulating, but this is not practicable, since the food is cooled by circulating air. If, however, the food is placed in a container and the circulating air cools the food through the container rather than directly, the problem is partially solved.

Another solution is to use two sets of evaporator coils. One set is kept at freezing temperature and makes the ice. By expanding the ice compartment and bringing the coil temperature near the zero level, it is also possible to handle frozen foods. This freezing area is separated from the rest of the cabinet, and a second set of coils is used to chill the main storage compartment. By keeping this set just above freezing, it is possible to maintain ideal storage temperatures (38° to 40° F.) without freezing the moisture out of the air.

In practice, manufacturers are using a combination of these principles in their better models in order to provide a frozen food section and areas with different degrees of humidity. Some refrigerators have specialized storage space for butter, dry storage bins for vegetables, etc.

There is much competition among manufacturers to offer the most usable storage space in relation to the size of the box. Shelves are removable and can be re-arranged to take bulky objects, and there are ingenious devices for utilizing nooks, crannies, and even the back of the door.

FOOD STORAGE IN THE REFRIGERATOR

With few exceptions, all perishable foods not only can but should be given refrigerated storage. The food should be placed in the refrigerator as soon as possible after purchase or preparation; cooked foods, however, should be cooled first.

All bags and other bulky store wrappings should be removed, especially from meats, fish, and poultry, because untreated paper soaks up moisture and insulates against refrigeration. In some cases, such as cheese, eggs, etc., food may be stored for some time in cardboard cartons.

The food should not be tossed indiscriminately into the cabinet, but should be arranged with some care and planning. Since effective refrigeration depends upon air circulation and contact with freezing surfaces, a too tight packing of the cabinet will defeat its purpose. Foods should also be arranged with some eye to accessibility, and, most important of all, each food should go in its proper place.

In the icebox, which has humid air but higher temperatures (*see* ICE REFRIGERATOR), the problem is to get the more perishable foods in the coldest zones of the cabinet. The refrigerator, however, is different. The temperatures are lower, but the humidity of the air will vary, so the main problem is to see that each food is placed in its proper "climate."

Since manufacturers differ in their approach to this problem, the storage methods will vary with the make and model of refrigerator used. This fact should be borne in mind, for foods should not be stored in a refrigerator in the same manner in which they are stored in an icebox, and should a person already accustomed to one model get a different one, he should learn the proper storage procedure for the new machine.

The manufacturer generally supplies an instruction booklet with each machine. It should be studied and followed closely. It should be stored somewhere in the family archives where it will not get lost. If there is no booklet, the dealer or manufacturer will be glad to send one.

In general, all foods that have strong aromas should be well wrapped in waxed paper, foil, or some similar airtight covering, and placed on one of the upper shelves to prevent possible transfer of odors and flavors to the rest of the foods. The ex-

ARRANGEMENT OF FOOD IN REFRIGERATOR

tremely perishable foods, such as meats and dairy products, require colder temperatures than the others. Moist foods or foods with high water content must either be placed in a humid area or stored in a covered container to keep from drying out.

The instructions that follow apply generally, they should be varied to meet the conditions of individual refrigerator models.

Batters (muffin, waffle, pancake). Store in a covered refrigerator dish.

Berries (blackberries, blueberries, boysenberries, loganberries, raspberries, strawberries). Sort, place on plate, and cover lightly with waxed paper. Store near freezer coils. Do not wash or hull until ready for use. Do not keep more than a day or so; freeze for longer periods.

Biscuit and Pie Mixes (made with animal shortening). Store in a covered dish.

Bottled Beverages (other than dairy products). Wipe bottles before storing. There is usually a place for tall bottles. Bottles may be placed in the frozen-food compartment for quick chilling but should not be permitted to freeze.

Butter. Leave in carton or place in covered dish. Butter must be kept covered, for it absorbs flavors and odors. If special butter container is used, wash it frequently.

Casserole Dishes, Scalloped Foods (ready for cooking). These may be prepared a few hours in advance of cooking and stored in an uncovered dish.

Cheese. Store in a covered dish (a thin coating of butter will keep cut surfaces fresh), the original container, or some sort of airtight wrapping.

Chocolates. Leave in carton and place on any convenient shelf.

Dough (yeast rolls and bread). Store in covered container large enough to permit expansion.

Dry Sausage. Store without cover.

Eggs. Whole eggs should be stored in their original carton, or in any similar protective box. Egg yolks may be stored in an uncovered dish if there is a humid area or covered with water in a covered dish if there is none. Egg whites will keep for several days in a tightly covered glass jar.

Evaporated and Condensed Milk. The can should be cleaned before storing, especially the top where the pouring holes are punched. Once opened, store with the milk.

Fish and Shellfish. Wash with water or wipe clean with damp cloth, and wrap in waxed paper or similar covering. Place in refrigerator as soon as possible, storing in meat compartment or ice-cube tray. Fish that is to be kept over 24 hours should be frozen or, if there is no freezer, go into the ice-cube compartment.

Frozen Foods. Some refrigerators have special compartments to care for these foods. Treatment will vary with the model and the manufacturer's instructions should be followed, especially in regard to maximum storage periods. If there is no such compartment, frozen foods may be stored for reasonable periods in the ice-cube compartment. To thaw, place frozen food in regular compartment some hours before desired use. Once thawed, frozen food should be treated like fresh food. (*See also* HOME FREEZING.)

Fruits. Those with thick protective covers (oranges, lemons, etc.) should be washed, dried, and placed on the most convenient shelf. If cut, they should either be given humid storage, be wrapped in waxed paper, or be placed on a dish with the cut side down.

Thin-skinned fruits (peaches, grapes, etc) should be stored in a humid area.

Opened packages of dried fruits may be stored on any convenient shelf.

Bananas should never be put in the refrigerator.

Ice Cream. Since sugar and fat do not freeze easily, it is sometimes difficult to keep ice cream solid in a home refrigerator. It should be stored in the frozen food section or the ice-cube compartment. In either case, the container should be in direct contact with the metal floor of the compartment to get the maximum chilling effect. Since round containers allow little surface contact, the ice cream should be transferred from them to a freezer tray or an ice cube tray without grids.

Jams and Jellies. Store covered in original jars.

Juices (fruit and vegetable). Store in covered containers.

Leftovers. Let cool before storing, place in covered container or in moist storage if they are to be kept for more than a few hours. Unused, opened, bottled foods may be stored covered in their original containers.

Mayonnaise. Store in covered jar as far away from freezer coils as possible.

Meat. Remove from original wrappings as soon as possible. (Butcher's paper absorbs the juices but a waterproof wrapping may be left on.) Wipe clean with damp cloth and place in meat compartment. If this is not possible, place on a plate or in a dish, cover lightly with waxed paper, and store in coldest section of the refrigerator. Ground and glandular meats should be stored in the freezer or ice-cube compartment to prevent spoilage.

Following are the maximum storage periods for fresh meat as recommended by the National Live Stock and Meat Board. These figures are based on an assumed average home-refrigerator temperature of 38° to 40° F.

Fresh beef (steaks, chops, roasts)	4 to 5 days
Fresh pork	2 to 3 days
Fresh veal	3 to 4 days
Fresh lamb	3 to 4 days
Smoked hams and bacon	10 days to 2 wks
Cooked hams	1 wk. to 10 days
Variety meats	not over 48 hrs.
All ground fresh meats	not over 48 hrs.

Bacon and other smoked meats should be wrapped in waxed paper and stored in the meat tray; if to be kept for the maximum period, they should be covered tightly and kept away from the fresh meats.

Cooked meats are treated as leftovers.

Milk and Cream. Wash caps and bottles, store immediately. Remove as infrequently as possible, replace as soon as possible. There is usually a special place provided for milk bottles; if none, store close to the freezer coils. Milk will keep for three or four days, depending on its freshness at the time of purchase and the amount of time it has been kept out of the refrigerator. Cream can be kept for the same period but is more easily spoiled. Keep both covered.

Nut Meats. Store in a tightly covered glass container.

Olives and Pickles. Store in their own liquor in covered containers.

Pastries and Breads (baked). Some refrigerators have humid storage areas that will keep these items fresh.

Pie Dough. Store in covered dish or wrap in waxed paper. Leave ready-prepared dough in carton.

Poultry. Do not wash. Wipe with damp cloth and store in the same manner as meat. Do not keep for more than two or three days without freezing.

Salad Dressing (other than mayonnaise). Store in covered container in bottle storage space.

Sandwiches. Wrap in waxed paper.

Sirups. Store in covered container.

Vegetables. All fresh vegetables, except potatoes, dry onions, squash, and rutabagas, should be stored in the refrigerator. Since vegetables have notably high water contents, they require humid storage. If the refrigerator does not have a space designed for vegetable storage, covered enamelware pans made for this purpose can be purchased and placed in the refrigerator on one of the lower shelves. Vegetables (except corn on the cob) should be prepared for storage by trimming off unusable parts such as stems and tops and by washing. (Before trimmings are discarded, they should be considered for use for garnishing or soups.)

Green, leafy, and root vegetables should be stored with the water that clings to them, while head vegetables (cabbage, head lettuce, cauliflower, etc.) should be drained.

To keep things under control, green onions and leeks should be cleaned, washed, and wrapped in airtight paper before being stored. Cut dry onions should also get the waxed-paper treatment before being put in with the rest of the foods.

ICE CUBES

One of the advantages of the refrigerator is that, in addition to preserving the food, it also manufactures a quantity of ice. Sometimes it also offers great trials of temper, patience, and strength, as anyone who has ever wrestled with a stuck ice-cube tray well knows.

Manufacturers have tried many approaches to this last problem, ranging from trays built of rubber and flexible plastics to metal trays equipped with various levers, prying devices, and everything short of small charges of blasting powder. In general, all these devices have merit, provided they are used and cared for in the manner described by the manufacturer.

To make ice cubes, first wash the trays in warm (never hot) soapy water and rinse well. Fill with cold water, taking care to leave at least a quarter of an inch at the top to allow for expansion. The trays go either on the bottom of the frozen food compartment or in special racks of their own. If fast freezing is desired, wet the tray bottom to insure the best possible contact with the freezing surfaces of the ice-making compartment.

This last step can be carried to extremes, however, for if too great an accumulation of ice forms on the floor of the freezing compartment, it will act as an insulator and retard the action. Too much water can also weld the trays into position when it freezes.

In many models it is possible to adjust the temperature of this compartment, using a lower range for faster action. The controls should be set back to the normal position once the ice is made.

Methods of cube removal will vary with the tray used. If the cubes shatter because of their intense coldness, let the tray warm up for a few minutes by exposure to room temperatures or pass it quickly under water tap.

If large quantities are desired, the cubes may be made in installments and the finished cubes stored in a refrigerator dish in or close to the freezing compartment. If the cubes are removed from the trays quickly and placed back in the refrigerator before they have had a chance to melt, they are not apt to stick together.

Crystal clear cubes may be made by using distilled water (*see* ICE). The ice-cube department of the refrigerator offers many intriguing possibilities. Things may be frozen inside individual cubes to make attractive garnishes. With the dividers removed, larger blocks of ice may be frozen in the trays for use in cooling punches, etc., and these too are subject to decoration. Cubes may also be tinted by adding coloring matter to the water. Iced tea and iced coffee may be made by freezing double-strength solutions of the beverages and pouring milk or water over the cubes in the glass.

Frozen desserts may also be prepared in this section. There are many prepared mixes designed for this purpose. Instructions should always be followed, for if the desserts are not frozen correctly, they will turn out flaky and filled with ice chips.

CARE AND MAINTENANCE

When a refrigerator is purchased, it should be installed and set in operation by a competent mechanic. The instructions booklet that comes with the machine should be carefully studied and saved for future reference.

In time, ice and frost will form on any freezer coils. If this icy layer is permitted to get sufficiently thick, it will act as an insulator and impair the efficiency of the machine. Not only will the motor have to run for longer periods to cool the box, but the average interior temperature will rise.

For these reasons, the refrigerator should be defrosted at regular intervals. The correct intervals for this operation and the proper procedure will vary with individual models, so the manufacturer's advice should always be followed. Hot water should never be used to melt the ice, nor should it be chipped away with sharp or pointed instruments, for this might seriously damage the mechanism.

The refrigerator should also be emptied and cleaned periodically to prevent odors and to catch any food particles that might present health hazards. Since the materials used in refrigeration construction will vary, it is well to follow the manufacturer's advice on cleaning procedure lest harm be done to the surfaces. In general, use warm, soapy water for all metal, plastic, and glass parts, and clean porcelain with a mixture of baking soda and lukewarm water. Acid foods should never be permitted to rest too long on a porcelain surface, and soaps and scouring powders should never be used on that material.

In some cases, waxes and polishes may be used on the exterior of the cabinet, but the instruction booklet should first be consulted.

When a refrigerator is first installed or when it has been disconnected for a considerable period, the motor will have to run steadily until the temperature within the box has reached the proper level. Once this temperature is established, however, the motor should have to function only at intervals.

If the motor continues to run steadily or for unusually long periods, the refrigerator may need defrosting, the air circulation may be checked by overcrowding or by paper spread on the shelves, hot foods may have been placed inside, the thermostat may not be set properly, or the door may be improperly closed or opened too often. If none of these is causing the motor to run too much, the dealer or an authorized repairman should be consulted.

Conversely, the dealer or repairman should also be called if the motor does not run and a check shows that the refrigerator is connected, that there is current in the lines, that there are no blown fuses, and that all controls are set at their proper positions.

Other symptoms of trouble are overheating or faulty action of the motor and rise of the cabinet temperature. It is wise to check the cabinet temperature periodically with a thermometer to see that it corresponds to the setting on the thermostat controls, especially if foods begin to spoil before their normal storage period has expired. Another danger sign is chemical odors in the vicinity of the refrigerator, or, in the case of an odorless refrigerant, a hissing sound, as of escaping gas.

Either the dealer or a competent repairman should always be consulted if a refrigerator breaks down or exhibits unhappy symptoms. The amateur repairman should confine his activities to mere onlooking. The refrigerator mechanism consists essentially of a gas or liquid held under varying degrees of pressure in a system of pipes and coils. Some refrigerants are toxic; and in any case, if the gas escapes, the mechanism will not function. Such a mechanism calls for the proper knowledge and the proper tools if it is to be successfully repaired.

The same general precautions apply to flame-operated refrigerators, though since there is no sound, it is difficult to tell if the mechanism is running too often. The best check is to watch cabinet temperatures; a sudden increase in the gas bill may be an indication of trouble. If kerosene or bottled gas is used for fuel, there is a direct check on consumption rate.

In the flame-operated refrigerator, care should be taken that the air vents near the burner are always clear of dust and other possible obstructions. If the refrigerator is fed by a regular gas line, the housewife should familiarize herself with the steps to be taken in case the gas supply should fail.

Since in normal use there is rarely any food spoilage in a refrigerator, the housewife might forget that foods do have maximum storage periods. Hence, it is often wise to make certain that no food items have been tucked away on a back shelf and forgotten. This check-up can be combined with the weekly cleaning of the cabinet. It follows, of course, that no perishable items should be left in storage, unless they are frozen, while the family is away on vacation.

REFRIGERATOR BAG. A refrigerator bag is a container made of some flexible, airtight material, usually a plastic, in which foods are placed before being put in the refrigerator. These bags keep the food from drying out and prevent the transfer of odors.

REFRIGERATOR CAKE. The exact origin of this popular dessert is not clear. The English have long had a somewhat similar medley of fruits, whipped cream, and cake, familiar under the names of syllabub and trifle. But the chilled refrigerator cake is probably the product of automatic refrigeration.

The ingredients are crushed fruits, cake or cake crumbs, and cream or an equivalent food stabilizer, such as gelatin, beaten egg white, etc. The difficulty lies in so blending and chilling these items that the resulting texture is a smooth, creamy velvet with no dividing line between the cake and the cream.

One of the best molds for making this special type of chilled cake is known as a springform cake-pan. It consists of a tin collar or sides and the usual tin bottom of any deep cake-pan. The sides fall apart when a pin is taken out, and the cake is easily removed. However, any plain, tin loaf-pan, or brick-pan, will give a convenient oblong shape which slices neatly and efficiently. A fancy mold with a stamped design is not good because it sticks.

To achieve the single, velvety consistency the cake used should be light and porous. Sponge cake is ideal, and next comes the wide assortment of wafers and light, spongy cookies. Of these, the vanilla wafer is perhaps the best because of its neutral flavor and thin delicate quality. Any cake or wafers used must be very fresh, delicate, and moist, or they will absorb too much of the liquid or fruit mixture and the dessert will be all cake.

The contrast to the cake is some kind of sweetened, crushed fruit. You may use fresh berries or the crushed or shredded forms of many canned fruits. Tart fruits, such as strawberries, pineapples, green gage plums, and blueberries, give the greatest and most pleasing contrast.

The fruit must be slightly sweetened and there must not be an excess of juice. Any extra juice may be used for dipping the cake, so that its outer surface will begin to combine with the cream. While some cream is usually called for, it is quite possible to make delicious refrigerator cake by using only condensed milk, whipped egg whites, or gelatin dissolved in other ingredients such as fruit juice. Each and all of these items give body and are spoken of as stabilizers when used in ice cream and similar desserts. (*See* FROZEN DESSERTS.) All ingredients except the cream or the egg whites should be well blended and cooled; then the whipped cream or whites are folded in very gently. While this seems a very simple dish, it requires attention and care.

Sometimes a custard (*which see*) is the base or stabilizer—often a three-egg custard, cooked in a double boiler, cooled, and then added to the crushed fruit. The thinner the fruit the more need for a custard or thick base. Of course, the cake itself is also a thickening agent, but it must be bound with the cream. Many recipes call for cake to be used in crumb form, so that these smaller particles will combine evenly. However, for best results, cake or other crumbs should not be rolled too fine, they should be crumbs and not flour-like in their texture.

The bottom of the mold will become the top when the cake is unmolded and set on the serving platter. Cake or lady fingers or wafers are generally used as a lining for the mold. After lining, pour in one thin layer of the liquid mixture, then insert a cake layer, and continue alternating—but always end with a cake layer. The cream and cake must have time to combine completely, which means from six or eight hours to overnight in the refrigerator.

CELLOPHANE REFRIGERATOR CAKE

½ cup sweetened condensed milk
¼ cup raspberry or strawberry jam
1 tbsp lemon juice
½ cup heavy cream, whipped
1 pkg cellophane wrapped cookies

Blend milk, jam, and lemon juice; fold in whipped cream. Open top of cellophane roll and remove all but bottom cooky. Drop a spoonful of filling on this cooky, add another cooky, pressing it down gently; repeat until all cookies are used. Close top of package tightly and chill in refrigerator

12 hours or longer. To serve, unwrap, cut in diagonal slices and top with additional cream. (Makes 6 portions)

REFRIGERATOR DISH. A bowl or similar container, usually covered, designed for storing food in a refrigerator (*which see*). These containers are usually rectangular in shape and may be made of almost any material.

The term is also applied generally to any dish that requires refrigeration as a necessary step in its preparation.

REGGIANO CHEESE. An Italian cheese of the Parmesan type, but considered of superior quaity to Parmesan. It is used for grating.

REGIMEN. A special diet. A systematized plan of feeding.

REINDEER. Reindeer is distinguished among the numerous members of the deer family by its antlers, which are divided into several branches. The antlers are slender and sharply pointed in the young, but become enlarged, palmate, and toothed with age. Antlers are found on both male and female but are smaller on the female. The reindeer is approximately the same size as an ordinary deer but more thickly set. Its legs are shorter and bigger, its feet larger, and its hoofs resemble those of a camel. Its hair is brown in the summer and whitish in winter, thus affording protection from hunters.

During the summer the reindeer browses on the buds and leaves of young trees, but during the long winter months it feeds solely on a kind of moss, which its sharp sense of smell discovers under the snow.

Besides occurring in great numbers in northern America, the reindeer is found in Scandinavia, Siberia, and Greenland. Outside its native climate, the reindeer does not reproduce and soon dies.

The reindeer is very gentle and domesticates easily. The Laplanders, Siberians, Alaskans, Esquimos, and, in fact, all the northern inhabitants of the world make use of every part of this animal. Its pelt provides an impenetrable fur against the biting cold. The hair can be woven to make warm clothing. Its flesh is nourishing and delicate. Its milk is strengthening and is the source of a delicious cheese.

From the culinary viewpoint, reindeer is almost equal to beef, and the various methods of preparing beef may be adapted to it. Reindeer is best, however, when larded, marinated for several hours, and braised with part of its marinade. While braising, add a little red wine and turn the meat occasionally. Serve with vegetables and blackberry jam, and small ham dumplings or homemade noodles.

REINDEER IN AMERICA

The reindeer herds of Alaska, introduced by government agencies to supply food for the natives, have now developed until they are looked upon as the most practical agricultural industry of Alaska. In 1920 the Bureau of Biological Survey was authorized to conduct investigations, and since then studies have been made of various phases of range and herd management, time and method of slaughtering, cold-storage practices in Alaska, and the shipment of carcasses.

These herds now furnish not only a large proportion of Alaska's meat supply but also increasing quantities for export. Marketed first in the Northwest and then on transcontinental trains and in metropolitan hotels, reindeer meat is now being more generally distributed. Studies on the best methods of preparation have been made by the Bureau of Home Economics, and the results are given here in the form of recipes.

In proximate composition, reindeer meat differs little from beef or veal of the same grade. In general it contains less fat and slightly more protein. Feeding conditions, however, produce differences in vitamin and mineral content. The flavor of reindeer is characteristic, different from beef or veal, gamy but not strong. The texture is fine, and most of the meat is tender.

The reindeer is different in size and shape from either beef cattle or sheep, and the cuts vary accordingly. The most desirable cut is the round. It may be used as steaks and is the most satisfactory piece for roasting. The lower end of the round is less tender and is best used as a pot roast, or for making soup. The loin and rib cuts, thinner than in beef, make satisfactory small steaks or—from the smaller animal—chops. The tenderloin may be stripped out and used as such, and the other portion of the loin and the rib section after boning can be rolled and stuffed or made into cutlets. Rib chops similar to those from lamb and mutton can be cut from this portion if desired. The double loin may be prepared either boned or unboned as a saddle. The shoulder is larger than the corresponding part in either a small beef or a mutton carcass and makes a satisfactory roast if boned and stuffed. The foreshank and the knuckle portion of the neck and the foreleg may be used for stews or pot roasts. For quick cooking, the steaks, chops, and cutlets are most satisfactory.

Reindeer meat is shipped frozen and must be handled with the same care as any other frozen meat. It should be allowed to thaw slowly at a low temperature.

Rolled Reindeer Chops. In the smaller animals, the loin and rib cuts are too small for steaks, and need added fat for successful cooking. These portions can best be used by cutting them in pieces of the thickness desired and rolling them in bacon. Skewer tightly in shape, and broil in the same way as other chops.

Breaded Reindeer Cutlets. Small steaks or chops from loin, rib end, rib, or shoulder may be prepared as cutlets. Wipe the meat, cut into serving portions, dip into beaten egg, roll in seasoned bread crumbs, and allow the surface to dry. Cook in hot fat until golden brown, then lower the heat and continue cooking until done. For cutlets one inch thick, 20 to 25 minutes total cooking time will be required. Drain on soft crumpled paper and serve garnished with parsley.

Fried Reindeer Liver. Slice the liver about one-half inch thick. Place in boiling water over a low flame for one minute, remove, sprinkle lightly with salt and pepper, dip in flour, and fry golden brown in any well-flavored fat.

Broiled Reindeer Liver. Parboil slices of reindeer liver as for frying. Sprinkle with salt and pepper, dip in melted butter, and boil under a low flame for five minutes or more, depending on the thickness of the slices. Serve with melted butter.

Roast Round of Reindeer. The leg of a very young reindeer may be roasted in the same way as a leg of lamb, but in the older animals it is too large for such a method to be successful. The most satisfactory roast is cut from the upper end of the round, the thickness (five inches or more) depending upon the size of roast desired. Such roasts will vary from seven to twelve pounds. Roasts from fat animals may be cooked without larding. Wipe

them carefully, rub them with salt, pepper, and flour, then place on a rack in an open pan. If a roasting thermometer is available, the cooking can be regulated more satisfactorily. The thermometer should be inserted so that the bulb is approximately in the center of the roast where the cooking will be slowest. Place the roast in a hot oven (480° F.) for 25 minutes to sear the outside and develop flavor. Lower the heat to about 350° F., and continue the cooking until the thermometer in the meat registers the desired temperature. A rare roast should be removed when the thermometer reaches 140° F., continue to 160° F. for medium, and to 180° F. for well-done meat. The time will vary depending upon the size and the shape of the roast and the temperature at which the cooking is finished, but it will generally require about 25 minutes to the pound to cook to the rare stage.

Broiled Reindeer Steaks and Chops. Remove the thin, paperlike tissue (sometimes referred to as fell) from the steaks or chops, and wipe them thoroughly. Place on a greased broiler about two inches from the flame. Sear on one side, then turn, When well browned on both sides, lower the flame and cook more slowly until the meat reaches the desired degree of cooking. A steak or chop one inch thick will required about ten minutes to cook well done; if two inches thick, the time required will vary from 20 to 40 minutes, depending upon the degree of rareness desired. Place the broiled meat on a hot platter, sprinkle with salt and pepper, pour melted butter over, and garnish with water cress.

Swiss Steak of Reindeer. Less tender steaks or chops need longer, slower cooking, and may be prepared as Swiss steak. The meat may be left in the form of steak or cut into portions for serving. Into each side, pound as much flour as possible, mixed with salt to season. Brown on both sides in a small quantity of fat, then add water or tomato juice and pulp to cover it, and simmer until the meat is tender. This will require from one and a half to two hours, depending upon the thickness of the steak.

Tenderloin of Reindeer. Tenderloin strips make a tasty dish. Wipe the meat with a damp cloth, season with salt and pepper, dust with flour, arrange in a lightly greased pan, and place strips of salt pork or bacon over the top. Bake in a hot oven (475° F.) for 15 minutes, then reduce to moderate

(350° F.) and continue cooking from 30 to 40 minutes longer. Serve with tart cranberry sauce.

Boned Rib Roast of Reindeer with Apple Stuffing

½ cup diced salt pork
1 cup chopped celery
1 cup chopped onion
½ cup chopped parsley
9 tart apples, diced
1 cup sugar
2 cups dry bread crumbs
1½ tsp salt
¼ tsp pepper
7 or 8 lb rib of reindeer, boned

Fry the pork until crisp. Set aside the pieces and cook the celery, onion, and parsley in the same fat. Take these out also and replace with the apples, sprinkling them with the sugar. Cover and cook until tender, then remove the cover and continue cooking until the juice evaporates and the pieces of apple are somewhat candied. Combine with all remaining ingredients, except the meat.

Wipe the meat with a damp cloth, pack the hot stuffing into the boned cavity and sew up the opening. Place the meat on a rack in a roasting pan and sear in a hot oven (475° F.) for 25 minutes, then reduce the temperature to moderate (350° F.), sprinkle the meat with salt and pepper, and continue to cook for three hours.

Cranberry Stuffing

½ cup finely chopped suet
1 qt cranberries, chopped
1½ cups sugar
2 cups dry bread crumbs
1½ tsp salt
¼ tsp pepper

Cook the suet in a frying pan until crisp. Add the cranberries, sprinkle with the sugar, and cook until clear. Combine with remaining ingredients and use in place of apple stuffing for boned rib roast of reindeer.

Reindeer Stew

1 cup diced salt pork
2 lb reindeer meat, cut in inch cubes

Flour
2 tsp salt
¾ tsp pepper
½ tsp poultry seasoning
1 cup chopped celery
½ cup chopped onion
2 tbsp chopped green pepper
1 tbsp chopped parsley
3 cups water or stock
1 bay leaf
2 potatoes, diced

Fry the pork until crisp, remove from the fat, and brown the meat in the remaining fat, first rolling it in the combined flour, salt, pepper, and poultry seasoning. Next cook the celery, onion, green pepper, and parsley for two or three minutes in the fat remaining in the pan. Add the water or stock with the bay leaf. Cover and simmer until the meat is almost tender, then stir in the crisp salt pork and the potatoes and continue cooking until the potatoes are tender.

REINDEER MILK. This contains 18 percent solids. Generally speaking, animals living farthest north have the most solids in their milk.

REINDEER MILK CHEESE. A rennet cheese from Norway and Sweden.

RELEVER. A French term meaning to impart to a sauce or any food a piquant flavor, through seasoning.

RELISH. A side dish which is usually served with meat and is usually sweet-sour. It is generally composed of different vegetables. Its purpose is to give zest to the food with which it is served. *See* Pickle.

REMOULADE. A cold sauce, highly spiced, and usually served with cold fish or meat.

1½ cups mayonnaise
1 tsp prepared mustard
1 scant tbsp finely chopped sweet gherkins
1 tsp finely chopped capers
1 scant tsp each of finely chopped parsley, chervil, and tarragon
Anchovy paste the size of a small hazelnut

Add mustard, gherkins, capers (pressed through a cloth to extract the liquid), and seasonings to the mayonnaise, and mix. Finally add anchovy paste. Serve cold.

RENNET. The gastric juice of calves extracted from the inner membrane of the fourth stomach. It is used for coagulating milk, and in powder form for making certain desserts. Where it is used in curdling milk for the purpose of making cheese, the result is referred to as rennet cheese. Rennet rapidly loses its properties when heated above 60° C.

REVENIR. A French word meaning to give color to food by heating in a fat.

RHENISH. This was the name given to rhine wines (*which see*) by the English up to the 18th century. After that time they were called Hock.

RHINE WINE. Strictly speaking, this name applies only to wines made from grapes grown in the Rhine valley. However, since many German wines are of the same type, the term is often applied to wines grown along the Moselle and in other places. At one time these wines were called Rhenish, but the name Hock has now come into common use.

Made from many grape varieties, but most often from the Riesling, Rhine wines have great lasting qualities. They are usually light in alcoholic strength. Their virtues do not depend so much on aging as is the case with so many other wines. In the past, Rhine wines were traditionally aged in huge, fantastically ornamented Heidelberg casks.

They are white table wines, dry and tart, pale gold or green in color, fruity in taste. A few, such as *Assmannshausen*, are red. They go well with white meats and seafood, and are served either chilled or at room temperature.

The Rhine wines are among the few that are traditionally served in colored glasses. The proper glass is a small, round goblet set on a stem that is rather long in proportion to the goblet (*see* GLASSWARE). The Germans claim that the use of a tinted glass improves the flavor, while others, notably the French, insist that the glass is colored to hide a cloudiness in the wine. *See also* WINE.

RHINE WINE GLASS. *See* GLASSWARE and RHINE WINE.

RHUBARB. Although often regarded as a fruit, rhubarb is really a vegetable. The first mention of it in this country, according to one authority, was made in 1778. It is an immigrant from the colder parts of Asia, probably Siberia, by way of Italy.

Rhubarb is one of the most wholesome of all the products of the garden. The rhubarb plant, often referred to as pie plant, is a strong perennial. The stalks average from 12 to 18 inches in length. The large leaves at the end of each stalk are discarded, as they contain injurious amounts of oxalic acid, but the leafstalks, with or without skinning, depending on the age of the rhubarb, can be converted into marvelous dishes appropriate for breakfast, luncheon, or dinner. At first, rhubarb was highly pized for its medicinal properties. It is still prescribed in certain ailments today, as it has mild laxative properties. It is used in diet of those suffering from constipation.

VARIETIES OF RHUBARB

There are two kinds of rhubarb, forced and field or garden grown Forced rhubarb comes in quantities from Pacific

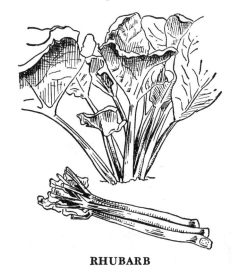

RHUBARB

FOOD VALUE

Water	Food Energy	Pro-tein	Fat	Carbo-hydrate	Cal-cium	Phos-phorus	Iron	Vit. A Value	Thia-mine	Ribo-flavin	Nia-cin	Ascor-bic Acid
94.9	18	.5	.1	3.8	—	25	.5	30	.01	—	.1	9

coast states and Michigan. Field grown is dark red, and rich in color, with a coarse, deep-green foliage; forced is of a light, pale pinkish, or reddish color, and has yellowish-green, under-developed foliage.

PREPARATION FOR MARKET

The commercial rhubarb season is short, rarely extending over more than two months. Only the largest and best stalks are harvested. The leafstalks separate readily from the crown and are easily harvested by grasping them near the base and pulling slightly to one side in the direction in which the stalks stand. The smaller stalks are often thinned somewhat to permit better development of those remaining. A heavy crop of rhubarb in any year depends to a large extent on the strong leafgrowth of the year before.

From two to five stalks, depending on their size, are tied in a bunch for market. United States standards for field grown rhubarb have been established. U.S. Fancy consists of stalks of rhubarb of the same variety which are well colored, fresh, tender, straight, clean, well trimmed, not pithy and are free of decay and damage. U.S. No. 1 consists of stalks of rhubarb of the same variety which are similar in quality to those of U.S. Fancy but not so highly colored. U.S. No. 2 consists of stalks which are fairly well colored, fresh, fairly straight, clean, well trimmed, not pithy, and are free of decay and serious damage.

Stalks of rhubarb that are well colored are usually well flavored. Stale rhubarb usually has a wilted, flabby appearance and is stringy and poor in flavor when cooked. Old rhubarb or that which has grown too long may be pithy, tough, and stringy, with much waste. Tenderness and crispness may be tested by puncturing the stalks. The younger stems are less acid than the older ones.

Rhubarb is a favorite in the early spring before other fruits come on the market. The hot house or strawberry has a decided pink color as compared with the green stalks of the home-grown varieties. Rhubarb is in season from February to the end of June.

BAKED RHUBARB

4 cups diced rhubarb
1¼ cups sugar

¼ tsp ground cinnamon
½ tsp ground mace
1 orange

Wipe and dice the rhubarb but do not peel. Place with the sugar and spices and the juice, pulp, and grated rind of the orange in a casserole. Cover and bake in a moderate oven (350° F.) about 45 minutes, or until tender. If desired, the cover may be removed during the last 15 minutes of cooking. (Serves 6)

JELLIED RHUBARB MOLD

1½ lb tender young rhubarb
¾ to 1 cup sugar
½ cup boiling water
3 tsp gelatin
1½ tbsp cold water
½ cup heavy cream, whipped
Grated rind of ½ orange

Wash but do not peel the rhubarb, dice, then place in a heavy saucepan with the sugar and water. Cover closely and cook over a low flame about 15 minutes, stirring occasionally. Drain off the hot juice and add to gelatin, previously softened in the cold water. Stir until thoroughly dissolved, then pour over the rhubarb itself which has been divided among individual serving glasses. When cold, chill in the refrigerator and serve topped with a puff of slightly sweetened whipped cream flavored with the grated orange rind. (Serves 4 to 6)

RHUBARB BROWN BETTY

Use recipe for Apple Betty (*see* APPLE), substituting two and one half cups of stewed rhubarb for the apples.

RHUBARB CREAM PUDDING

2 tbsp cornstarch
½ cup sugar
⅛ tsp salt
2 cups milk
3 eggs, beaten

Mix cornstarch, sugar, and salt in top of a double boiler. Add cold milk and stir until smooth. Cook over direct heat, stirring constantly until mixture boils and thickens. Slowly stir part of the hot mixture into the beaten eggs. Return to hot mixture in top of double boiler and continue cooking over boiling water for two minutes, stirring constantly to keep smooth. Remove from heat and cool Prepare rhubarb sauce as described below to serve with this cooled cream pudding.

1 lb rhubarb
1 tbsp water
½ cup sugar
1 tbsp cornstarch

Wash rhubarb, discard stem ends and leaves. Slice stalks in one-inch lengths. Add water, cover, and cook slowly until rhubarb is soft. Mix sugar and cornstarch thoroughly, and stir into the rhubarb; stir constantly over low heat until mixture boils and thickens. Chill, and when ready to serve, stir rhubarb sauce into chilled cream pudding. (Serves 5)

RHUBARB DATE PUDDING

2 cups diced rhubarb
1 cup chopped, pitted dates
¼ cup water
½ cup sugar
1 cup soft bread crumbs
1 tsp butter
6 quartered marshmallows

Cook together the rhubarb, dates, and water for about ten minutes. Add the sugar, crumbs, and butter, and turn into a buttered baking dish. Top with the marshmallows and bake in a moderate oven (350° F.) about 20 minutes. (Serves 4)

RHUBARB HIGHBALL

1 cup water
2 cups sugar
3 cups diced rhubarb

Place the sugar and water in a double boiler and heat. Add the rhubarb before the mixture boils and let simmer until the rhubarb is tender. Then force the mixture through a sieve. The resulting purée may be kept in a closed jar in the refrigerator until needed, but should not be kept more than a few days. Combine one large jigger purée and one large jigger orange juice in a glass. Stir well, add cracked ice, and fill with carbonated water. (Serves 1)

RHUBARB MARMALADE

2 lb rhubarb
2 lemons
5 cups sugar

Cut the rhubarb finely. Remove outer (yellow) half of the lemon rinds and slice finely. Mix rhubarb, lemon rind, and sugar, and let stand overnight. Next day squeeze lemons, strain juice, add juice to mixture, and cook until quite thick, stirring almost constantly to prevent burning. Turn into sterilized jars and seal.

RHUBARB SCALLOP WITH MERINGUE

½ lb rhubarb
1 cup granulated sugar
Grated rind of 1 orange
¼ tsp salt
1 small sponge cake
2 egg whites
2 tbsp powdered sugar

Wash and peel rhubarb and cut in one-inch pieces; add sugar, orange rind, and salt, mixing well. Cut sponge cake in thin slices; line bottom of greased baking dish with three or four slices; cover with one-fourth of rhubarb. Continue to make alternate layers of cake and fruit until material is used. Cover and bake in moderate oven (350° F.) for 30 minutes. Beat egg whites until stiff, add sugar slowly, beating until blended. Pile on baked pudding and bake 15 minutes longer, or until meringue is slightly browned. (Serves 6)

RHUBARB SHERBET

½ cup stewed rhubarb
⅓ cup (generous) lemon juice
⅛ tsp salt
½ cup granulated sugar
¼ cup light corn sirup
1 cup chilled milk
1 tsp granulated gelatin
1 tbsp cold water
½ cup heavy cream, whipped stiff

To the unmashed, cold, stewed rhubarb, add lemon juice, salt, sugar, and corn sirup. Blend carefully but thoroughly with the milk. Then add gelatin soaked in cold water for five minutes and dissolved over hot water. Mix well and chill. Lastly, fold in the stiffly whipped heavy cream, and freeze as indicated for Hawaiian Sherbet (*see* PINEAPPLE) until mushy. Stir from bottom and sides, beat one-half minute, then continue freezing until solid but not too hard. Serve either in chilled sherbet glasses, orange cups, or cantaloupe halves which have been chilled.

RHUBARB SPONGE CUSTARD

1 cup diced fresh rhubarb
¼ cup water
½ cup sugar
¼ cup all-purpose flour
¼ tsp salt
¼ cup sugar
2 tbsp butter
2 eggs, separated
1 tbsp lemon juice

Put rhubarb in saucepan, add water and sugar. Cover and cook until tender. (Makes about one cup thick sauce.) Sift flour, measure and resift with remaining dry ingredients. Add to the creamed butter and mix well. Add the beaten egg yolks and lemon juice and beat until light and fluffy. Add cooked rhubarb and mix well. Beat the egg whites until stiff. Fold lightly but thoroughly into the rhubarb mixture. Pour into custard cups and set in a pan of hot water that comes almost to the top of the cups. Bake in a moderately slow oven (325° F.) for 30 minutes. Sauce will separate and remain at bottom with a fluffy cake-like topping. Serve warm or chilled.

RHUBARB TAPIOCA PUDDING

2 tbsp quick-cooking tapioca
¾ cup boiling water
¾ cup sugar
½ tsp salt
2 cups diced rhubarb

Combine in the upper part of a double boiler the tapioca, water, sugar, and salt, and cook over hot water until the tapioca is clear. Add the rhubarb and continue cooking until tender. Serve hot or cold with light cream. (Serves 4 to 6)

RHUBARB WHIP

4 cups diced rhubarb
¼ cup water

Sugar
2 cups heavy cream, stiffly beaten
Lady fingers or sponge cake

Simmer the rhubarb gently with the water until soft, add the sugar, and when this is dissolved, press through a fine sieve and chill. Just before serving, fold in the whipped cream and serve in sherbet glasses with split lady fingers or strips of sponge cake around the edge. (Serves 6)

STEWED RHUBARB

3 cups diced rhubarb
1 cup boiling water
1 cup sugar
1 two-inch stick cinnamon

Cover the rhubarb with boiling water, let stand five minutes, then drain. Meanwhile make a sirup with the cup of boiling water, the sugar, and the cinnamon. Add the drained fruit and cook gently until the fruit is tender but not broken.

For stewed Rhubarb and Strawberries, prepare the rhubarb as directed above, and when almost tender, add one-half pint of strawberries (washed, hulled, and halved) and cook three minutes longer. (Serves 4 to 6)

RIABINOVKA. An excellent Russian after-dinner cordial, made from the essential oil of ashberries distilled with Vodka. The oil, which is extracted from the pit of the olive-like ashberries, is very aromatic, tonic, and astringent.

RIBS. For pork, see SPARERIBS. See also ROAST, BEEF, and LAMB.

RICE. A true cereal, rice constitutes the staple food of a majority of the world's inhabitants. It was first introduced into America in 1694 and is now grown chiefly in Louisiana, Texas, Arkansas, and California.

PREPARATION FOR MARKET

There are three types of rice grown in the United States. Long-grain rice, which is raised mainly in Mississippi and Louisiana, gives the lowest yield per acre of any of the types. For this reason, and because the long grains are considered the most attractive for table use, it commands the highest price. Round-grain rice, also known as Japanese, is grown most extensively in California. Its chief advantage is that its tougher grains do not break in the milling operation as often as is the case with the other types. The short-grain rice, which is intermediate in size between the other two, combines many of the advantages of both and gives a greater yield per acre.

All three types may be prepared for sale as brown, unpolished, polished, or coated rice.

Brown Rice. The rough rice grain, which is called paddy, consists of the edible kernel inclosed in a very hard shell-like hull. The hull is easily removed once it is broken. The kernel consists of a hard endosperm surrounded by seven relatively soft bran layers. The preparation of rice for market consists of removing the hull and also the outer layers of bran in varying amounts, depending on the products desired.

The rough rice is fed into a scalper, which removes sticks, stones, and other foreign matter and blows out the dust. The next machine, the clipper, cuts off the beards and stems from the rough grains The monitor machine draws off blighted grains, which are light in weight. The grain is then fed into the hulling stones. The upper stone revolves and splits the hulls, and the kernels drop out. The mixture then passes to the stone reel, a fine wire mesh that sifts out broken hulls, germ, and bran. The hulls, kernels, and any unbroken rough rice go on to the paddy machine, which shakes out the heavier, unhulled grains and leaves the kernels, which still contain practically all the bran. At this point the rice is marketed as brown rice which has more flavor and contains more nutritive elements than white rice.

Unpolished White Rice. The unbroken, rough rice from the paddy machine is fed through another set of milling stones which remove any remaining hulls. Then the brown rice is fed into the hullers. A huller consists of two cylinders, one inside the other; the inner cylinder rotates. The brown rice passes through the space between the cylinders, and a portion of the

RICE

bran coat is rubbed off. The rice then passes through a reel, which sifts out the bran. The operation is repeated to remove more and more of the bran. The last of the bran is removed by a pearling cone—a conical millstone revolving within a fine wire cone. At this point, the rice is known as unpolished rice. Almost white, it has a rough surface. A small amount is marketed in this form, since some people feel that it contains enough of the bran to be dietetically valuable.

Polished White Rice. At this point the rice has become heated from the friction of the milling operation and is stored in large bins to cool off. It is then fed into the brush machine—a drum covered with soft leather which revolves inside a fine wire cylinder. The rice passes between the cylinder walls and is polished. An air stream blows off the fine dust and cools the grains. The rice is now called polished rice, and this is the form in which much of it is marketed.

Coated Rice. Some rice is coated with a mixture of glucose and talc. The coating

FOOD VALUE

	Wa-ter	Food Energy	Pro-tein	Fat	Car-bohy-drates	Cal-cium	Phos-phorus	Iron	Vit. A Value	Thia-mine	Ribo-flavin	Nia-cin	Ascor-bic Acid
Brown	12.0	356	7.5	1.7	77.7	39	303	5.5	0	.29	.05	4.6	—
Convert-ed	12.3	351	7.6	.3	79.4	9	92	.7	0	.23	.04	3.8	—
White	12.3	351	7.6	.3	86.4	12	12	1.0	0	.05	.03	1.4	—

improves the appearance and the self-preserving qualities of the rice. It is perfectly harmless, and most of it goes when the rice is washed for cooking.

Converted Rice. Within recent years a new method of preparing white rice so that it is much easier to cook has been developed. In preparing it for market, the paddy is cleaned of foreign material and then soaked for several hours in hot, circulating water. It is then dried and steamed and dried again. The rice then goes through the usual hulling and milling operation, but only the pearling cone is used. Much less of the bran is removed and the finished grains have a slightly yellowish look. However, the rice cooks up almost as white as the rice prepared by the older process.

Wild Rice. This is not a true rice at all, but the grains of a perennial grass native to North America. *See* WILD RICE.

HINTS ON PREPARATION

The ideal in rice cookery is to obtain a thoroughly cooked, plump, fluffy grain which is separate from its neighbors and unbroken. Remember that a pound of rice, which is two and one-half cups, will swell to eight cups when it is cooked.

There are several "only" ways to cook rice. Brown rice is cooked in the same way as white but requires almost twice as much time. It is a good idea to soak brown rice for an hour or so before cooking in order to soften the bran; this shortens the cooking time. In either case, the rice should be washed in several changes of cold water until the water runs clear. For the American method of cooking—the simplest—proceed as follows:

For one cup of uncooked rice, put two quarts of water in a large pan and add three teaspoons of salt. Bring to the boil. Drop the rice in slowly so that the water does not stop boiling, and stir with a wooden fork or spoon to prevent the grains sticking to the pan. Continue boiling. Do not cover the pot, since the rice has a tendency to foam up and boil over if it is covered. After about twelve minutes, test a few grains. Continue testing every few minutes until the grains crush between the fingers, at which time the rice is done. Drain the rice into a colander. Place the colander over a pan containing a little boiling water, cover with a thin cloth, and let the rice steam until fluffy and ready to serve. You can keep it hot almost indefinitely this way, and the kernels will not stick together.

The oriental method of cooking rice consists of using so little water that it is all absorbed in the cooking process. For one cup of rice use one and one-half cups of water and one teaspoon of salt. Wash the rice and drain it. Place the rice, salt, and water in a heavy kettle over direct heat. Cover and bring to a boil, stirring once or twice to make sure the grains are not sticking. When the water boils, turn the heat very low and continue cooking about 40 minutes, or until all the liquid is absorbed and the rice is fluffy.

To cook converted rice, no washing is necessary. In a heavy kettle, or the top of a double boiler, place one cup rice, one and one-half cups water, and one teaspoon of salt. Cover and place over boiling water. Cook for about 40 minutes without stirring. The rice should be tender and each grain separate.

Rice must always be cooked in liquid, but the liquid need not always be water. Rice may be cooked in milk for use as a cereal, or to give additional nutrition. Cooking it in tomato juice, chicken stock, or other meat or vegetable stock, gives a flavorful dish which is a change from plain rice. Canned tomatoes, grated cheese, and crisp bacon turn rice into a one-dish meal.

RISOTTO

A risotto in its simplest form represents merely an admirable way of cooking rice. In the hands of talented chefs it may mean something quite complicated and wonderful. One memorable Italian restaurant made a daily special of risotto en surprise. It was served in a casserole, blanketed with golden cheese. When you broke the crust on a fast day, you found fresh shrimp, lobster, crabmeat, and sweet peppers nested in a bed of richly seasoned rice. On another day the surprise might be a savory mixture of diced chicken, sweetbreads, chicken livers, and mushrooms.

To prepare a risotto, wash a pound of ordinary rice in a number of waters, rubbing the grains between the hands, to remove the excess starch, until the water runs clear. Heat olive oil in an iron skillet, and when it is hot put in the rice. Do not fry it, but let it heat slowly, and stir it gently but constantly with a wooden fork or spoon. Presently the rice will begin to show a yellow tinge. As it absorbs the oil, add more to keep it moist. Little by little the grains take on a peculiar gloss and glisten like jewels. Don't let them scorch; keep stirring until each separate grain is the color of ripe yellow corn. Meantime prepare a quart of soup stock in which has been steeped a crust of bread rubbed with garlic. Brown some minced onions or shallots in a little oil and add to the strained stock. Pour the hot stock over the rice— you will be amazed to see how swiftly the liquid is absorbed. Continue until the dish is well moistened and the grains are covered with stock. Stir well to blend. Season to your taste. A tin of Italian tomato paste may be added to the stock and a half cup of grated Parmesan cheese stirred in. A pinch of sweet basil helps. Some Italian and Spanish cooks add Spanish saffron, pinch by pinch.

Transfer the risotto to a casserole, or leave in the skillet, and bake it in a moderate oven (350° F.) for about 30 minutes. It is done when the rice is soft, but still firm, with the grains separate and distinct. Serve from the casserole with a rich tomato sauce and plenty of grated cheese. The variations are limitless, but the Italains are usually content with a simple garnish of sliced cervelat or salami.

PILAW

A pilaw (also spelled pilaf, pillau, and other variations) is the East Indian method of cooking rice, somewhat akin to the risotto. For a basic pilaw use:

1 cup rice
2 small onions
2 tbsp seedless raisins
1 tbsp almonds
1 cup butter
Few small pieces of stick cinnamon
2 cardamon seeds
1 or 2 bay leaves
Saffron, salt, and peppercorns

Put 4 tablespoons of the butter in a saucepan and when it is hot fry the sliced onions until golden brown. Then add the rice with the rest of the butter, and cook, stirring frequently, until the rice has absorbed most of the butter and turns golden. Be careful not to let it burn. Add all the ingredients except the saffron, and just

cover with boiling water. Put the lid on the saucepan and let simmer until the rice is tender. Transfer the rice to a casserole and bake in a moderate oven (350° F.) until the moisture has evaporated. Ten minutes before serving, sprinkle with the saffron. Pilaws can be made with any sort of meat or poultry, using the appropriate stock in place of water, and serving the pieces of meat with the prepared rice.

BAKED RICE AU GRATIN

2 cups cooked rice
2 cups medium white sauce
½ tsp Worcestershire sauce
Dash of thyme
1 cup grated cheese
¼ cup buttered crumbs

Season the white sauce with the thyme and Worcestershire sauce. Grease a casserole and make a layer of rice in the bottom. Cover with part of the sauce. Sprinkle generously with cheese. Repeat the layers until all is used, finishing with a layer of cheese. Top with the crumbs and bake in a moderate oven (350° F.) for 20 minutes, or until the cheese is melted and the crumbs delicately browned. (Serves 6)

CASSEROLE OF RICE

2 large green peppers
1 small onion, minced
3 tbsp fat
3 cups cooked rice
1 cup canned tomato juice
3 tbsp tomato catsup
½ tsp salt
⅛ tsp pepper

Remove the seeds and membrane from the peppers, chop them, and cook with the onion in the fat until golden brown. Combine with the rice, add all the remaining ingredients, blend thoroughly, and turn into a casserole. Bake in a moderate oven (350° F.) for 20 or 25 minutes. (Serves 6)

CREOLE RICE FRITTERS

½ cup rice
3 cups boiling water
3 eggs
3 tbsp flour

½ cup sugar
1 yeastcake

Cook the rice in the boiling water until very soft and almost mushy. Drain and dry the rice and let cool. Dissolve the yeast cake in a little warm water, and mix it with the cold rice. Let rise in a warm place over night. In the morning, beat the eggs thoroughly, and add to the rice with the sugar and flour. Beat well to make a thick batter. Set aside to rise for another 15 minutes. Have ready a pan of deep hot fat (375°–390° F.) and drop the mixture in by tablespoons, cooking only a few cakes at a time. Fry until golden brown in color. Remove from the fat, drain well, sprinkle with sugar, and serve very hot.

FRIED RICE RING

1 cup rice
¼ cup butter or margarine
2 cups boiling water
1 tsp salt

Wash and dry the rice, then cook slowly in the butter until golden brown, stirring frequently. Add the water, cover the pan, and bring to a rapid boil. Simmer until the rice is tender, about 15 minutes. Remove the cover, add the salt, and continue cooking until all the water is absorbed. Press into a ring mold. Unmold and serve with any desired creamed or curried mixture.

JAMBALAYA

1 cup raw rice
½ lb sausages, boiled shrimp, or left-over chicken
1 large onion, chopped
1 clove of garlic, minced
2 tbsp butter or margarine
½ lb tomatoes
½ of a chili pepper, minced
Salt, pepper, and cayenne pepper

Cook the rice until tender. Drain and steam until dry and fluffy. Melt the butter in a skillet and cook the onion and garlic until they are golden brown. Peel and quarter the tomatoes, and add to the onion mixture, mashing with a spoon. Brown the sausages, shrimp, cut-up chicken, or other meat in additional butter or margarine.

Place the rice and tomato in a deep skillet, together with the onion and the garlic and the butter in which they were cooked. Add the meat, and season with the salt, pepper, cayenne pepper, and chili pepper. Mix thoroughly. Cover the pan tightly and let simmer very gently for 35 or 40 minutes, stirring frequently. (Serves 4)

JAPANESE FIELD RICE

2 cups cooked rice
2 cups left over chicken, cut in ½ inch dice
Chopped bamboo shoots
Chopped mushrooms
½ tsp sugar
1 cup stock or water
2 tsp soy sauce

Mix all the ingredients except the soy sauce into a deep skillet. Simmer gently for 30 minutes, stirring occasionally. When the stock is all absorbed, add the soy sauce, and mix. Serve very hot. (Serves 6)

QUICK PILAW

3 cups cooked rice
2 small tomatoes, peeled and quartered
1 small onion, minced
1½ cups stock or water
2 cups leftover lamb or mutton, cut in small dice
3 tbsp buttered crumbs

Mix together the rice, tomatoes, onion, and stock. Grease a casserole. Make alternate layers of the rice mixture and the meat until the casserole is filled. Top with the crumbs. Bake in a moderate oven (350° F.) about 30 minutes, until heated through and nicely browned on top. (Serves 6)

RICE CHEESE RING

2 eggs
2 tbsp melted butter
½ tsp salt
⅛ tsp pepper
¼ tsp onion juice
1½ cups milk
1½ cups cooked rice
1½ cups grated cheese
2 cups medium white sauce
1 pimiento, minced

Beat the eggs until light, add the butter, seasonings, milk, rice and cheese. Blend thoroughly, and turn into a buttered ring mold, filling it only ¾ full. Set in a pan of hot water and bake in a moderate oven (350° F.) until firm, about 30 minutes. Unmold and fill the center with the hot cream sauce into which the pimiento has been stirred. Tomato sauce may be used instead of the white sauce. (Serves 6)

2 cups dry cooked rice
1 cup well seasoned thick white sauce
1 tsp onion juice
½ tsp salt
1 tsp Worcestershire sauce
2 tbsp minced parsley
1 cup fine dry bread crumbs
1 egg
2 tbsp cold water

Combine the rice, white sauce, and seasonings. Spread 1½ inches thick on a platter and chill. Divide into 12 portions and form into croquettes. Dip first into crumbs, then into the egg slightly beaten with the water, and again into the crumbs. Fry golden brown in deep hot fat (390° F.). Drain on soft crumpled paper. Serve with tomato or mushroom sauce. (Serves 6)

RICE FRITTERS

1½ cups sifted flour
2 tsp baking powder
¾ tsp salt
Dash of pepper
1 egg
¾ cup milk
1 cup boiled rice
Paprika

Sift together the dry ingredients. Add the beaten egg and milk and mix to a smooth batter. Stir in the rice. Drop by tablespoonfuls into deep hot fat (390° F.). Cook until golden brown. Drain on soft crumpled paper. Serve with a cheese sauce and a green salad. (Serves 4 to 6)

RICE MUFFINS

1 cup flour
1 tbsp sugar

2 tsp baking powder
½ tsp salt
1 egg
⅔ cup milk
1 cup cooked rice
3 tbsp melted shortening

Sift the flour before measuring. Then sift together the flour, sugar, baking powder, and salt. Beat the egg well, and stir in the milk and rice. Add the shortening and the flour mixture. Stir until just mixed. Spoon into greased muffin tins, filling them ⅔ full. Bake in a moderately hot oven (325° F.) for 15 or 20 minutes, depending on the size, until nicely browned. (Makes 10 medium sized muffins)

RICE PUDDING

1 cup rice
2 cups milk
1 tsp salt
Shaved maple sugar
Cream

Wash and drain the rice. Put with the salt and milk in the top of a double boiler and cook over hot water until the rice has absorbed all the milk and is tender and fluffy, about 30 minutes. Serve with shaved maple sugar and cream.

DUNDEE RICE PUDDING

1½ cups raw rice cooked in milk until ender
Marmalade
3 tbsp butter
3 tbsp sugar
Yolks of 5 eggs

Put the cooked rice into a baking dish and sread a thin layer of marmalade over the top. Leave a shallow well in the center, center, and prepare the sauce.
Melt the butter. Beat the egg yolks until light, then beat in the sugar and add to the melted butter. Pour the mixture over the top of the pudding. Bake the pudding in a medium oven (350° F.) for 30 minutes, or until the topping is a delicate brown.

OLD FASHIONED RICE PUDDING

½ cup raw rice
4 cups milk

½ cup sugar
½ tsp salt
Dash of nutmeg
½ cup seeded raisins

Wash the rice thoroughly. Grease a baking dish and put in it the rice, milk, sugar and salt. Bake, uncovered, in a slow oven (250°–275° F.) for an hour, stirring well with a fork several times. Add the nutmeg and raisins and continue baking for an hour or two longer, stirring whenever a brown film forms on top of the pudding. The pudding is done when the rice is tender. Let the last brown skin remain and become delicately colored. (Serves 6)

RICE PUDDING WITH MERINGUE

¾ cup uncooked rice
3 cups boiling water
4 eggs, separated
¾ cup sugar
½ tsp salt
½ tsp vanilla extract
4 cups milk, scalded

Boil the rice in the water until tender. Drain and steam dry. Beat the yolks of the eggs until thick and light in the top of a double boiler and add the sugar, salt and vanilla extract. Stir in the scalded milk and cook over hot water, stirring constantly, until the mixture coats the spoon. Add the rice, mix thoroughly, and turn into a greased baking dish.

Make a meringue by beating the 4 egg whites until stiff, and beating in a few grains of salt, 4 tablespoons of sugar and ¼ teaspoon of vanilla extract. Spread over the pudding, and brown in a slow oven (325° F.) for 12 to 15 minutes.

Chill this dessert before serving. (Serves 6)

For a mocha rice pudding, use equal parts of milk and strong coffee in place of all milk.

QUICK RICE PUDDING

1 cup cooked rice
2 cups milk
2 eggs
½ cup sugar
Pinch of salt
Dash of nutmeg
½ cup raisins

Heat the rice and milk in the top of a double boiler, over hot water. Separate the eggs. Beat the whites until stiff and the yolks until thick and lemon colored. To the beaten yolks add the sugar, salt and nutmeg. Spoon about ½ cup of the hot rice-milk mixture into the egg yolk mixture; then stir it all into the remaining mixture in the double boiler. Add the raisins. Cook over hot water, stirring occasionally, for 3 to 5 minutes, or until the mixture thickens. Take off the stove and cool slightly. Fold into the stiffly beaten egg whites and chill before serving.

The pudding may be served plain or with cream. (Serves 6)

RICE RING

1 cup rice
2 tbsp butter
1 tsp salt
Pinch of pepper

Wash and cook the rice. When tender and dry, add the butter and seasonings. Pack firmly into a buttered ring mold. If not to be used immediately, keep hot by placing in a pan of hot water. Unmold when ready to serve and fill the center with any desired creamed mixture (meat, poultry, fish, etc.).

RICE AND SAUSAGE CASSEROLE

¾ lb pork sausage
2 tbsp hot water
1½ cups cracker crumbs
1½ cups cooked rice
1½ cups cooked or canned tomatoes
¼ cup green pepper, chopped
3 tbsp celery leaves, minced
1½ tbsp minced onion
1½ tsp salt
¼ tsp pepper
2 tbsp butter

Cut the sausage into small pieces and fry until browned, stirring to prevent burning. Add the water. Combine the other ingredients except the butter and stir into the sausage. Grease a casserole and turn the mixture into it.

Dot with the butter and bake in a moderately hot oven (375° F.) for a period of 30 minutes, or until heated completely through. (Serves 6)

RICE STUFFING
(For Goose and Duck)

2 cups uncooked rice
½ cup cooking oil
1 cup chopped celery
1 cup chopped onion
2 cups tomato juice or meat stock
2 tsp salt
½ tsp pepper
1 tbsp catsup
1 tbsp Worcestershire sauce
1 tbsp chopped parsley

Wash and dry the rice, then cook in the oil with the celery and onion, stirring frequently, until the rice is golden brown. Add the tomato juice or stock, cover closely, and cook very gently for ½ hour. Add the seasonings. *See* STUFFING.

RICE VALENCIENNE

4 tbsp butter or margarine
1 tbsp minced onion
1 tbsp chopped lean ham
1 cup rice
3 cups chicken broth
2 whole tomatoes, peeled and diced
½ tsp salt
Pinch of pepper
1 sprig of parsley
1 bay leaf
1 sprig thyme

Heat the butter, but do not let it brown. Add the onion and ham and cook for 10 minutes. Add the rice, washed and drained, the broth, tomatoes, and seasonings. Tie the parsley, bayleaf, and thyme together, and add them. Simmer for 10 minutes. Remove the bouquet, cover, and bake in a moderate oven (350° F.) 20 or 25 minutes, until the rice is tender. Rice prepared in this manner is delicious with chicken, veal, turkey, or guinea hen. (Serves 6)

RICE WINE

2¼ lb rice
4 lb granulated sugar
1 package (lb) seeded raisins
1 package (lb) seedless raisins
2 oranges, each cut into 8 pieces
6 qt lukewarm water
1½ yeast cakes

Combine all ingredients in a large container. Let stand for 3 weeks, stirring every 5 days. Strain through filter paper, bottle and seal.

SAVORY RICE AND MUSHROOMS

1 cup brown rice
2 cups water
1 tsp salt
3 tbsp oil or butter
½ cup diced onion
1 large green pepper, diced
1 pimiento, diced
1 cup diced mushrooms
2 eggs
⅔ cup grated Parmesan cheese
½ cup buttered crumbs

Wash the rice thoroughly. Cook with the salt and water in the top of a double boiler until tender (about 1½ hours if the rice was not soaked first.) Heat the oil or butter and cook the onion, green pepper, pimiento, and mushrooms in it for 5 minutes. Add to the rice with the beaten egg. Stir until thoroughly mixed, and finally blend in the grated cheese. Turn into a well greased casserole and sprinkle the buttered crumbs over the surface. Bake in a moderate oven (350° F.) about 30 minutes.

SCALLOPED RICE WITH CHEESE

6 medium-sized onions, chopped
2 tbsp butter or margarine
1½ cups uncooked rice
1½ tsp salt
2½ cups boiling water
2 cups tomato soup
1 chopped green pepper
1 cup diced soft American cheese

Fry the onions in the butter until golden brown. Then add the rice, salt and boiling water. Cook until the rice is nearly tender, then add the tomato soup. When the rice has absorbed all the liquid, stir in gently the green pepper and cheese. Transfer to a well greased casserole and bake in a moderate oven (350° F.) about 15 minutes. (Serves 6)

SCRAMBLED RICE

12 slices bacon
3 cups cooked rice

3 eggs
3 tbsp milk
1 tsp salt
⅛ tsp pepper

Saute the bacon until it is crisp. Remove from the fat, drain on soft crumpled paper, and keep hot. Turn the rice into the hot bacon fat and mix well. Beat the eggs well, add the milk and seasonings and turn into the rice. Mix well. Cook over a low flame until the eggs thicken, stirring frequently. Garnish with the bacon. (Serves 6)

SPANISH RICE

1 cup uncooked rice
4 tbsp oil
1 mild onion, sliced
1 green pepper, sliced
1 slice garlic
4 cups canned tomatoes
2 tsp salt
1 tsp chili powder
⅛ tsp sweet marjoram

Wash, drain, and dry the rice thoroughly. Heat the oil in a heavy frying pan and cook the rice, stirring constantly, until it is light brown. Add the onion, pepper, and garlic and continue cooking about 5 minutes. Transfer to a casserole. Heat the tomatoes with the seasonings and pour over the rice, mixing well. Cover and bake in a moderate oven (350° F.) about 45 minutes, until the rice is tender and the liquid absorbed. Do not stir while cooking. If the liquid should cook away before the rice is tender, add a few spoonfuls of hot water. The kernels should be separate but there should be no excessive liquid. (Serves 6)

RICE BIRD. See REED BIRD.

RICE FLOUR. A flour made from rice.

RICER. A ricer is an instrument that forces cooked potatoes and like soft vegetables through perforations, giving them a shape that is somewhat granular and resembles cooked rice. It is commonly built in the form of a perforated metal basket with a snug fitting wooden or metal plunger to exert pressure on the vegetables within. See also KITCHEN EQUIPMENT.

RICING. Pressing vegetables or tubers, such as potatoes, through a special utensil called a ricer, thus producing rice-like pellets.

RICKEY. A refreshing summer beverage made of a liquor (usually gin), lime juice and carbonated water. The Rickies are noted for their fresh, tart flavor, which makes them excellent thirst quenchers.

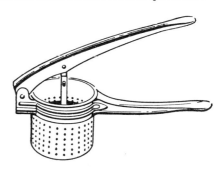

RICER

RICKEY

½ lime (juice)
1 jigger desired liquor (gin, rum, whisky)

The lime half is squeezed and then dropped into a 6-or 8-ounce glass containing cracked ice or 1 or 2 ice cubes, the liquor and carbonated water to fill are added and the whole stirred gently. Sugar may be added to taste, if too tart. (Serves 1)

For a discussion of drink mixing and serving, see BARTENDING.

RIESENGEBIRGE CHEESE. A soft, rennet cheese, made from goat's milk in the mountains on the northern border of Bohemia.

RIJSTAFEL. A Javanese dish, or rather a whole meal, with a Dutch name, which is a favorite with Dutch planters. It is too elaborate for home preparation, consisting of many dishes served by a succession of waiters. Basically, it includes a chicken sauteed in many condiments and herbs served with a curry sauce. Accompanying it are twenty or thirty side dishes of such things as plain boiled rice, shrimps, fried bananas, chutney, fried eggplant, tamarind preserves, coconut, tomatoes, mangoes, dried fish, and many others.

A simplified rijstafel may be served as a buffet supper, by setting out a large bowl of fluffy boiled rice, a dish of chicken curry, and small dishes of as many accompaniments as may be come by in the markets. A suggested list includes mango chutney,

Bombay duck, hard-boiled egg chopped in small bits, freshly grated coconut, orange peel and grapefruit peel chopped finely, mild onion chopped finely, shredded ripe pineapple, chopped nuts (peanuts, cashews or almonds), plumped raisins, fried sliced bananas. The guests help themselves to a portion of rice, put the curried chicken on top of the rice, and make a selection of the condiments.

RIND. The skin or outer coat that may be peeled, grated or taken off certain citrus fruits, such as the rind of lemon or orange. It is used to flavor dishes and beverages.

RING MOLD. A kitchen utensil often made of tin, aluminum or glass, used for molding food in ring shape.

RING-NECKED DUCK. This is a tender wild duck similar to the Canvasback. It is a fresh-water species, an excellent diver and is fond of wild celery.

RINNEN CHEESE. A cheese made from sour milk and caraway seed. It was known in the eighteenth century. It is made in Pomerania and derives its name from the wooden trough in which it is laid to drain.

RIOLA CHEESE. This cheese is made from sheep's or goat's milk. It has a soft texture and strong flavor, and resembles *Mont d'Or*.

RIPE. As applied to food, ripe means brought to maturity, fit for use.

RIPEN. To make ripe; to bring to perfection.

RISHTAYA. A Syrian dish of lamb, noodles, and lentils. See LENTILS.

RISOTTO. See RICE.

RISSOLE. A French term meaning to obtain a crackling food by means of heat. Example: to rissole potatoes is to cook them to a golden-brown crispness in fat.

ROAST. Cooking of meat (or other foods) in the oven by the application of indirect dry heat, using an uncovered pan. This method is for tender cuts only.

The processes of roasting and grilling or broiling, when performed over a hot fire, result in cooking the meat in a manner which is in some respects analogous to stewing. In fact, the interior portions of the meat are stewed in their own juices instead of in water. A coating (searing) of coagulated albumin forms upon the outer surface of the meat, while the material of the interior is gradually warmed and more slowly coagulated. The outer coating prevents the evaporation of the juices of the meat

which, together with the other materials, are retained and add flavor to it. Roasted meats, therefore, have a decided advantage in flavor as well as in nutritive value over meat which has been boiled for a long time, although the latter may be more tender and easily digested.

The process of roasting is conducted mainly by radiant heat, although there is slight convection through the air. The main object of an oven is to prevent burning by uneven cooking. In other words, the meat is cooked by the action of radiant heat projected towards it from all sides while it is immersed in an atmosphere nearly saturated with its own vapor. The air which surrounds the roasting meat is constantly removing the water which tends to evaporate upon its surface, and therefore dries the outer surface of the meat. From 20 to 24 per cent of the water content is lost in this manner, and the meat therefore weighs less. This should be remembered by the homemaker when buying meat. The evaporation of this water, which continually passes from the interior of the meat toward the outer surface, produces a loss of heat in the meat itself which keeps the interior from becoming overheated. If the roasting is long continued, the water gradually passes out more and more from the interior of the mass, which finally becomes dry and hardened or burned. If too much air surrounds the meat, it is poorly roasted, dry, and leathery; whereas if the heat is applied more directly by radiation from glowing embers, from bright flame or glowing electric heat, the sudden hardening of the outer coating of the meat, even though it be slightly burned, forms a barrier against the evaporation of water from the interior.

The roasting of any meat, however, cannot be accomplished without the effusion some of the meat juice and the melting of a portion of the more superficial fat and of gelatin. These substances, together, constitute the meat gravy, the most natural sauce known, which is itself quite nutritious and is advantageously used for basting the meat to prevent excess drying.

In over-roasted or burned meat, the external layers become scorched or charred. This is due chiefly to the carbonizing of the fat through the omission of basting. Before the fat has become fully burned, certain volatile fatty acids are liberated which have a very disagreeable odor, and various products are developed which are not only of no value for nutrition, but also may be irritating to the digestive system.

Game or meat which is high, or slightly turned, is extremely repulsive if cooked by boiling or stewing, for then it more or less disintegrates, and the elements of decomposition pass into and flavor the whole mass. Such meat, however, is often palatable and wholesome if cooked by roasting, when the external layers which have first commenced to decompose are thoroughly browned and thereby disinfected. A real gourmet prefers that a leg of mutton should be hung until it becomes slightly odorous before it is roasted, but it must be fresh for boiling or stewing.

METHODS OF ROASTING

There is no subject in cookery upon which there is more difference of opinion than that of meat, and especially when it comes to roasting.

The length of time the meat has been hung, the amount of fat, and the shape of the roast itself—all affect the time of cooking. Meat that is well ripened will cook in a comparatively short time. The more fat on the meat, the longer the time it will take for the heat to begin to penetrate. A boned and rolled roast takes longer than a short or standing rib roast. The higher the temperature, the more shrinkage, and for this reason some authorities advise the use of a moderate temperature throughout the entire period of roasting.

The use of a meat thermometer, which is inserted into the meat, will insure consistent results for roasting any kind of meat. It should read 140° F. for rare beef, 160° for medium, and 180° for well done meat. The readings should be 165° F. for veal, 180° for lamb, 185° for pork, 160° for ham.

Also, remember that meat continues cooking after it is removed from the oven; and if for any reason, it is not to be served immediately, allowance should be made for this important point.

Beef Rib Roast. Wipe the meat with a damp cloth and then rub it with mixed salt and pepper. Do not use flour. Place the meat fat side up in an uncovered roasting pan. If a meat thermometer is to be used, make a hole with skewer or ice pick through the fat side, and then insert the thermometer so that the bulb will be in the center of the fleshy part of the roast but not touching the bone.

Cook the meat at the same temperature throughout. Place the meat, fat side up, in a moderately slow oven (325°–350° F.) and keep the oven at this temperature. Baste every 15 minutes. The cooking time will be: 22 minutes per pound for a roast weighing over 5 pounds for rare, 28 minutes for medium, and 35 minutes for well done. For a smaller roast, increase the time by 3 to 5 minutes per pound.

Leg of Lamb Roast. Wipe the meat with a damp cloth. Do not remove the fell (thin skin covering the meat). Rub the leg of lamb with mixed salt and pepper to taste, but do not use flour. Place it fat side up in an uncovered roaster. If the meat thermometer is used, insert it in the thick part of the roast, not touching the bone.

Proceed as described for beef. If you do not have a meat thermometer, the cooking time is as follows: For a roast weighing over 6 pounds allow 30 minutes per pound for rare, 33 minutes for medium, and 45 minutes for well done. For a smaller roast increase the time by 4 or 5 minutes per pound. Baste frequently. The addition of a braise (*which see*) will add to the flavor of the roast.

Roast Veal. Wipe the meat with a damp cloth. Rub it with salt and pepper. Do not use flour. Place the meat skin side up in an uncovered roaster. The addition of a braise (*which see*) will improve the flavor. Insert the meat thermometer. Veal should always be very well done, the thermometer registering 172° F. Place the meat in a moderately slow oven (325° F.) allowing 35 minutes per pound. Baste the roast frequently.

Roast Fresh Pork. Wipe the meat with a damp cloth. Rub it with mixed salt and pepper. Do not use any flour. Place it fat side up in an uncovered roaster. Insert a meat thermometer if you use one. Pork should always be very well done, the thermometer registering 190° F.

Roast in a moderately slow oven (325° F.), allowing 35 minutes per pound for a large roast and 45 minutes for a small roast. The roast should be basted frequently.

Boned and Rolled Roasts. A greater length of time should be allowed for cooking roasts which have been boned and rolled because it takes longer for the heat to penetrate through the layers of solid meat.

ROASTER. (I) *See* KITCHEN EQUIPMENT.

ROASTER. (II) As applied to chicken, *see* CHICKEN.

ROASTING PAN. A roasting pan is a large, metal container, in which meats are roasted. Because of the size and weight of the meats commonly handled, these pans are made of substantial stock, and often are fitted with handles. Various sizes are available, usually rectangular in shape. Recently, heat-resistant glass models have been made.

ROASTING PANS

ROBERT. One of the oldest of French brown sauces, used with goose, pork, and sometimes venison. To bechamel sauce (*which see*) add 3 large onions very finely chopped, per tablespoon of flour used to make bechamel. Moisten with bouillon, season well, simmer for ½ hour, and add when ready to serve, a suspicion of good wine vinegar and French mustard as desired.

ROCAMADOUR CHEESE. A rennet cheese made of sheep's milk.

ROCAMBOLE. Spanish shallot used in salad seasoning.

ROCK AND RYE. An American, sweetish mixture found ready prepared in market, and easily made at home. For individual servings, stir a spoonful of rock candy sirup, home made or commercial, into a wine glass of good rye whisky (any other spirit may be used). Add a thin slice slice of seeded lemon.

ROCK-COD. *See* CODFISH.

ROCK EEL. *See* BUTTERFISH.

ROCKET. A member of the mustard family with pink, purple, and white flowers. The leaves are used in salads.

ROCKFISH. Another name for striped bass, (*which see*).

ROCKFORD or Rockyford Melon. A round melon grown in Colorado. It has a gray rind and pink flesh. *See also* MELON.

ROCKY MOUNTAIN WHITEFISH. *See* WHITEFISH.

ROE. (I) European deer not known in the United States.

ROE. (II) The eggs of fish or crustaceans, which are removed intact from the body of the fish. The roe is a great delicacy.

It is prepared by first parboiling in salted water, then either broiling or sautéing in butter.

DEVILED ROE

Mix 1 tablespoon of melted butter, ⅓ teaspoon of mustard, 1¼ teaspoons of Worcestershire sauce, and salt to taste. Drain 4 pieces of canned fish roe, and roll these in the mixture. Mash the roe, spread it on toast, and place it in a hot oven (425° F.) for 5 minutes. Garnish with thin lemon slices. (Serves 6)

ROGNONS. French name for cock's kidneys often used in classical cookery as a garnish. *See also* KIDNEY.

ROLL (I). To spread flat with a rolling pin, as in rolling out pastry, dough, etc. Also, to roll up, as a jelly roll.

ROLL (II). A kind of small fancy bread.

FRENCH ROLLS

For French Rolls, use the same ingredients as for French Bread (*see* BREAD). For each roll, take two and a half to three ounces of dough and shape according to fancy. Bake in a moderately hot oven (375°–400° F.) 15 to 20 minutes.

PARKER HOUSE ROLLS

1½ cups milk
½ yeast cake
4 cups sifted flour
1 tbsp sugar
1 tsp salt
1 egg
3 tbsp melted shortening

Scald, then cool the milk to lukewarm. Dissolve the yeast in one-half cup of this. Sift the dry ingredients together, make a hollow in the center and pour in the dissolved yeast, with the beaten egg, remaining milk, and shortening. Mix to a light dough and knead until smooth and elastic. Place in a greased bowl, brush over with melted shortening, cover lightly with a cloth, and set aside in a warm place to rise until doubled in bulk, about four hours. Turn onto a floured board and, if necessary, work in a little additional flour. Roll out into a sheet about three-fourths inch thick, cut into rounds with a large biscuit cutter, brush with melted butter, fold over in half, and place a little distance apart on greased baking pans. Brush the tops with melted butter, cover lightly, and again allow to rise until very light. Bake in a moderately hot oven (375°–400° F.) 15 to 20 minutes.

PLAIN ROLL DOUGH

2 pkg dry granular yeast or 2 cakes compressed yeast
1 cup lukewarm water
1 tsp sugar
2 cups milk, scalded
1 tbsp salt
⅓ cup sugar
2 eggs beaten
9¼ cups sifted all-purpose flour
¼ cup shortening, melted and cooled

Soften yeast in the water with the one teaspoon sugar. Let stand ten minutes. Combine hot milk, salt, and the one-third cup sugar. Cool to lukewarm. Combine yeast mixture, cooled milk, and eggs, and beat vigorously until thoroughly blended. Add half the flour and beat until smooth. Beat in shortening, add all but about two tablespoons of the remaining flour, and mix thoroughly. Use the remaining flour for kneading and shaping rolls. Turn out on very lightly floured board. Cover dough and let it rest ten minutes before kneading. Do not add more flour. Knead until dough is smooth and elastic with tiny bubbles on surface (about ten minutes) adding not more than two tablespoons flour for knead-ing. Shape into smooth ball, place in a clean, greased bowl, turn once in bowl to coat top with melted fat. Cover and let rise in a warm place (about 86° F.) until doubled in bulk, about one and one-half hours. Divide dough in three equal por-tions, each weighing about one pound, eight ounces, and shape into rolls as de-sired. (Makes 4 to 5 dozen dinner rolls)

BRAIDED ROLLS

After the first rising, turn plain roll dough onto lightly floured board. Cut off pieces of dough the size of a golf ball for each strip to be used in the braid, and with the outstretched fingers of both hands roll out into ten-inch lengths, about one-fourth inch in diameter. Place three strips side by side on the board, pressing the far ends

firmly together, and braid in the usual way, making the braid moderately loose. Cut into four-inch lengths, pressing cut ends firmly together. Place braids on greased baking sheet, brush with melted butter, cover and let rise in a warm place until doubled in bulk. Bake in a moderate oven 375° F.) for 15 to 20 minutes. Serve hot.

BUTTERFLY ROLLS

After the first rising, do not punch down plain roll dough but turn out on lightly floured board and roll dough into rectangle that is twice as long as it is wide and about one-fourth inch thick. Spread with soft-ened butter. Roll up tightly like a jelly roll and cut into slices one to one and one-fourth inches wide. Lay handle of knife or wooden spoon across center of each slice parallel with the cut surfaces and press down firmly. When pressure is lifted, roll will take butterfly shape. Place on greased baking sheet. Cover and let rise until double in bulk. Bake in a moderate oven (375° F.) for 15 to 20 minutes. Serve hot.

BUTTERHORN ROLLS

After first rising, turn plain roll dough out on to lightly floured board. Do not punch down. Divide into portions which will roll out into round sheets about ten inches in diameter and three-eighths inch thick. Brush with melted butter and cut each circle into twelve pie-shaped pieces. Roll up each piece, beginning at the wide end, stretching dough slightly as you roll. Lay straight or in cresent shape on greased baking sheet with tip underneath to keep from unrolling. Cover, set in warm place to double in bulk, brush with milk, bake in a moderate oven (375° F.) for 15 to 20 min-utes. Serve hot.

VARIOUS SHAPES FROM PLAIN ROLL DOUGH

Clothespin Rolls. After the first rising, re-move the desired amount of dough; cover and let rest ten minutes. Roll into a rec-tangular shape to one-fourth inch thickness and about eight inches long. Cut into strips eight inches long and one-fourth inch wide. Dip clean, round, all-wood clothes-pins into melted shortening. Immediately wind a strip of dough around each clothes-pin, starting just below knob. Tuck both ends in to prevent unwinding. Place rolls on greased baking sheet; brush with melted shortening, cover, let rise until double in bulk. Bake in a moderate oven (357° F.) for 15 to 20 minutes. While warm, slip clothespins carefully out of rolls.

Cloverleaf Rolls. After the first rising, cut off small pieces of dough and shape into smooth balls about the size of small walnuts or large marbles (size should be determined by size of muffin pans and size of roll desired). Place three in each greased muffin pan. Cover, let rise until doubled in bulk. Bake in a moderate oven (375° F.) for 15 to 20 minutes. Serve hot. Two larger balls or four small ones may be used for each roll if preferred. Mixing balls of white and whole wheat dough in the same roll makes an attractive variation.

Crooked Miles. After the first rising, cut off pieces of dough large enough to roll into cylinders six inches long and about three-fourths inch in diameter. Tie a loose knot close to one end of the strip; then pull rest of strip through center of knot; repeat pulling dough through center until strip is used up. Place on greased baking sheet, brush with melted butter, cover, and let rise until doubled in bulk. Bake in a moderate oven (375° F.) for 15 to 20 minutes. Serve hot.

Fan Tan Rolls. After first rising, turn dough onto lightly floured board, cover and let rest ten minutes. Roll into a rectangle 22 by 9 by ¼ inches thick. Brush with melted butter and cut into strips 1½ inches wide, making six strips 22 inches long. Pile one on top of other, turning the top strip butter side down. Press lightly into place, let stand a minute, then cut into pieces 1¼ inches wide. Lay cut side down into greased muffin tins (2¾ inches in diameter). Cover and let stand in warm place (86° F.) until double in bulk (about 45 minutes). Bake in a moderate oven (375° F.) for 15 to 20 minutes. Serve hot.

Knots. After the first rising, roll pieces of dough with the palm of the hands to form strips about one-half inch thick and ten inches long. Cut strips into five-inch lengths. Holding strip by both ends, stretch lightly and tie into a loose knot. Place on a greased baking sheet, brush with melted butter, cover and let rise until doubled in bulk. Bake in a moderate oven (375° F.) for 15 to 20 minutes. Serve hot.

Pan Rolls. Pan rolls are the easiest kind of rolls to make. Once you have learned to make balls of dough of an even size, you have mastered all there is to know of the shaping technique. Make them from plain roll dough. Place them in a greased pan—metal or glass, square or round. Allow them enough room to double in bulk in a warm place (86° F.) for about an hour, then bake at 400° F. for 20 to 25 minutes.

RICH ROLL DOUGH

1 pkg dry granular yeast or 1 cake compressed yeast
¼ cup lukewarm water
⅓ cup sugar
1 tsp salt
¾ cup milk, scalded
2 eggs, beaten
1 tsp grated lemon rind
4 cups sifted all-purpose flour
½ tsp mace or ground cardamon (optional)
¼ cup butter or shortening melted

Soften yeast in the lukewarm water with one-half teaspoon of the sugar. Let stand ten minutes. Add remaining sugar and salt to hot milk, stir and cool to lukewarm. Combine softened yeast with cooked milk mixture and stir well. Add eggs, lemon rind, and half the flour sifted with spice, and beat until smooth. Beat in the cooled butter, then add remaining flour and stir thoroughly. Turn out on lightly floured board. Cover the dough, and let it rest ten minutes before kneading. Knead until smooth and elastic (about ten minutes) using not more than one-fourth cup additional flour for kneading. Do not add excess flour on board. Sweet roll dough must be soft and too much flour kneaded in will make the finished rolls bready instead of delicate, light, and flaky. Round up into a smooth ball, place in a clean, greased bowl, turn once to bring greased side to top. Cover with waxed paper and a clean towel and let rise in a warm place (about 86° F.) until doubled in bulk, about one and one-half to two hours. Dough is then ready to be shaped into plain rolls, or various kinds of sweet rolls and coffee cakes. (Makes about 2½ dozen plain rolls)

BUTTERSCOTCH PECAN ROLLS

½ yeast cake
⅛ cup lukewarm water

¼ cup granulated sugar
¼ cup shortening
1 egg
1 cup milk, scalded and cooled
About 4 cups sifted flour
¾ tsp salt
¼ cup melted shortening
¼ cup butter
1 cup brown sugar
1 cup pecans, chopped

Soften the yeast in the water, adding about one-half teaspoon of the granulated sugar. Cream the shortening, add the remaining granulated sugar, beaten egg, and the milk, then the yeast. Add the flour, sifted with the salt, using enough to make a dough stiff enough to knead. Turn onto a floured board and knead 10 to 15 minutes, or until the dough is smooth and elastic. Place in a greased bowl, brush over with melted shortening, cover, and let rise in a warm place until doubled in bulk, about four hours. Turn onto a lightly floured board, knead slightly, and roll out thinly into a rectangular shape. Spread with softened butter, sprinkle generously with brown sugar, then with the chopped pecans. Roll up like a jelly roll, cut into one inch to one inch and a half slices, and place slices flat in well greased muffin pans on top of one-half teaspoon of butter, two teaspoons of brown sugar, and a few pieces of nut. Press down the slices of dough to make the nuts stick. Cover and let stand in a warm place until doubled in bulk, about four hours, then bake in a moderate oven (350° F.) about 20 minutes. As soon as baked, turn immediately bottom side up. Spread over any remaining sirup.

FINGER ROLLS

Use Parker House roll dough. When ready for molding, pinch off pieces about the size of a small egg. Roll each piece in the hands to form a round ball; then place on a floured board and roll with the palm of the hand till each is about four and a half inches long and tapering towards the ends. Place in greased finger-roll pans or arrange about one inch apart on lightly greased baking sheets. Let rise until very light, brush the tops over with beaten egg to which a little milk has been added, and bake in a moderately hot oven (375°–400° F.) 15 to 20 minutes.

SWEET POTATO ROLLS

2 tbsp sugar
1 tbsp salt
2 tbsp shortening
2 cups mashed, cooked sweet potatoes
About 6 cups sifted flour
1 yeast cake
1½ cups lukewarm milk

Add the sugar, salt, and shortening to the potatoes while these are still warm. Blend thoroughly, then add one cup of the flour and the yeast, dissolved in the milk. Beat until smooth, cover, and set in a warm place to rise for about one hour. Now add gradually the remainer of the flour, work to a dough, knead, place in a greased bowl in a warm place, cover and let rise until doubled in bulk, about four hours. The dough must be rather stiff, as the potatoes help to moisten it while rising. Roll out into a sheet about three-fourths inch thick, cut with biscuit cutter, brush with melted butter, fold over in half and place on greased pans, a little distance apart, to rise until very light. Bake in moderately hot oven (375°–400° F.) 15 to 20 minutes.

WHITE POTATO ROLLS

1 tbsp sugar
1 tbsp salt
2 tbsp shortening
1 cup hot milk
1 yeast cake
4 cups sifted flour
4 cups cooked, riced potatoes

Add the sugar, salt, and shortening to the hot milk. Let stand until lukewarm, then add the yeast and stir until this is dissolved. Gradually add the flour and potatoes, mix and knead to a smooth, elastic dough; this should be somewhat stiffer than bread dough, as the potatoes soften it while rising. Place in a greased bowl, cover, set in a warm place, and let rise until doubled in bulk, about four hours. Knead lightly on a floured board, adding more flour if the dough is too soft. Roll out three-fourths inch thick, cut with large biscuit cutter, spread with melted butter, fold over in half, arrange on greased pans a little distance apart, cover, and let rise until very light. Bake in a moderately hot oven (375°–400° F.) 15 to 20 minutes. When almost done, brush over with melted butter or water in which a little sugar has been dissolved and return to the oven to finish baking.

SWEDISH TEA RING

Use one-half recipe Rich Roll Dough to make one ring. Roll out into a 15 inch by 8 inch rectangle about ⅜ inch thick. Spread with two tablespoons softened butter. Sprinkle with a mixture of one-half teaspoon cinnamon and one-fourth cup sugar, one-half cup almonds, blanched, slivered and toasted lightly in oven, and one-fourth cup raisins, plumped. Roll up like a jelly roll, seal edge, turn underneath. Place roll on greased baking sheet, stretch slightly and shape into a ring. Pinch ends together to form a perfect circle. Using a kitchen shears, start at outside of ring and at one inch intervals, cut about three-fourths way through roll toward center. Twist each section in the same direction, so it will lie flat, cut-side up, the sections overlapping slightly. Brush with melted butter, cover lightly, and let rise until doubled in bulk, about one hour at 86° F. Bake in moderate oven (375° F.) 25 to 30 minutes or until golden brown. Remove to rack to cool. Ice with Confectioners' Icing (*which see*).

ROLL CHEESE. A hard, rennet cheese, made from the whole milk of cows. It is round in shape and is nine inches in diameter, eight inches high, and weighs twenty pounds. It is made in England.

ROLLING PIN. A rolling pin is an implement used to flatten dough into smooth, even sheets. As the name would imply, it is essentially a roller. There are four general types.

The simplest of all is the French type, which is nothing but a plain wooden rod,

tapered so that the middle is thicker than the ends. While it can be put to general use, it is especially adapted for the preparation of fancy pastries.

Perhaps the most familiar of all rolling pins, especially to readers of the comic strips, is the handle variety. This is made of wood in the form of a heavy cylinder or rod that has a small handle set on either end. The cylinder may revolve on the handles, or the entire implement may be turned down from one piece of wood.

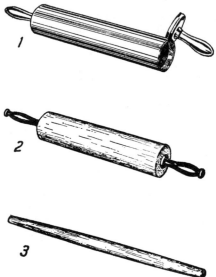

ROLLING PINS 1. Hollow (Ice Filled Keeps Dough Chilled) 2. Free-Wheeling 3. French (Tapered Ends)

One well-known variation is the hollow rolling pin. While it outwardly resembles the handle-pin, it is made of either glass or metal, and the rolling cylinder is hollow. One end is removable so that the cylinder may be filled with cracked ice to keep certain types of dough chilled.

A less common variation is a handle-pin made of wood with a series of designs cut into the surface of the cylinder. Pins of this sort are used to make a fancy cookie known as Springerle, which is popular in parts of Pennsylvania. When the dough is rolled into a sheet with one of these pins, a series of raised designs is eft on the surface. These designs are separated with a knife to form the individual cookies.

See also PASTRY *and* KITCHEN EQUIPMENT.

ROLL MOPS. A delicatessen product, sold in glass jars. It is made of small

ROLLING PIN FOR SHAPING FANCY COOKIES

herrings marinated in highly spiced brine. Roll mops are served as appetizers.

ROLLO. An old-fashioned pudding similar to Roly-Poly (*which see*).

ROLLOT CHEESE. A soft, rennet cheese from France. It is two and a half inches in diameter and two inches thick.

ROLY-POLY. A jam pudding made with a baking-powder-biscuit dough, spread with jam or sweetened fresh berries, rolled up tightly, and brushed over with melted butter and baked. Serve sliced, with cream or any preferred sweet sauce.

ROMADOUR CHEESE or Remoudou or Romatur Cheese. This is similar to, but a little finer than, Limburger. It is four and a half by two by two inches, and weighs one pound. It comes from Germany.

ROMAINE. *See* Lettuce.

ROMANO CHEESE. A hard cheese, similar to Parmesan. It is used mainly for cooking and comes from Italy.

ROOK. See "Ruddy Duck" under Duck.

ROOT BEER. A refreshing, hot weather drink which may be purchased commercially or made at home through the use of a commercially prepared root-beer extract. A quick method is to make a simple sirup with two pounds of sugar and one quart of cold water. Add to this the contents of a bottle of root-beer extract and keep tightly corked in a cold place. To serve, pour the desired amount of flavored sirup into a glass, then fill the glass with carbonated water.

ROQUEFORT CHEESE. A soft rennet cheese, made from the milk of sheep. The interior has a mottled or marbled appearance. It weighs four and a half or five pounds. There are many imitations of this cheese; two of them are Gex and Septmoncel. The original Roquefort is made in France. American Roquefort is made from cow's milk. It comes wrapped in lined tinfoil.

See also French Dressing.

ROSE AUX FRUITS. A delicious, pinkish dessert wine, made of the finest Medoc white wine and the extract of several fruits, the infusion of which is made rapidly so as to capture the flavor and perfume of the fruit extract. It is a product of France.

ROSEFISH. A species of perch also known as ocean perch, under which name it is very popular. Its average weight is

from one and a half to two pounds. It is prepared similarly to perch (*which see*).

ROSEMARY. Rosemary is a fragrant evergreen shrub belonging to the mint family. Native to the Mediterranean region, rosemary is widely cultivated and used as a flavoring agent. Fresh rosemary is usually used in chopped form, dry

ROSEMARY

rosemary in ground form. Dried rosemary should be dipped in hot and then in cold water before it is used; this will enliven it. Sprigs of rosemary, sometimes combined with thyme and chives, are used to garnish green salads. Rosemary is strong and piny in fragrance and flavor, and used sparingly it is a wonderful addition to many dishes.

Rosemary will give a delicious flavor to vegetables, soups, stews, and meats, and as a seasoning for poultry stuffing it has no equal. Try adding it to the basting liquor when you are roasting lamb, beef, veal, or pork. It adds the epicurean touch to fricassees and broilers. It serves as a base for tisanes (herb teas) and herb soups.

Rosemary agreeably adds its fragrance to both biscuit dough for meat pie and dumplings to be served with chicken fricassee. For the latter, add one teaspoonful of rosemary to a standard biscuit recipe.

Rosemary wine is also used in cookery. Small quantities added to or used as a basting liquor lend an interesting flavor to broiler fish. Try adding two teaspoons of this wine to a soup or stew for six. Prepare the wine by loosely packing two-thirds of a cup of rosemary sprigs in a pint jar, filling it with dry white wine or very dry red wine, and storing, tightly sealed, in a cool, dark place (not a refrigerator). Store for a week and then strain through filter paper.

ROULADE. The French name for a delicious, economical beef dish.

2 lb round steak
6 slices raw bacon
6 strips raw carrot, cut the length of the meat
6 strips dill pickle, cut the length of the meat
1 tbsp minced parsley
1 tbsp minced onion
1 tsp salt
¼ tsp black pepper
⅛ tsp each ground thyme, cloves and mace
4 tbsp fat
2 cups brown sauce
A thick crust of sour rye bread

Have the steak cut in one large piece and as thin as possible. Pound it even thinner, then cut into six equal pieces. Place these on a wet board and spread each as follows: A slice of bacon, a strip of carrot, and one of pickle, then a generous sprinkling of the combined parsley, onion, seasonings, and spices. Roll up and tie the meat firmly with this filling inside. Brown in the hot fat, transfer to a Dutch oven or stewpot, pour the brown sauce over (*see* SAUCE), add the rye bread, cover closely and simmer for two hours. Or, if desired, cook in a moderate oven (350 F.). To serve, arrange the meat on a hot platter, cut off the strings, discard any of the rye bread which is left (some of it will have disintegrated in the gravy) and pour the sauce over all. (Serves 6)

ROUND OF BEEF. *See* BEEF.

ROUND SERVER. *See* FLATWARE.

ROUND SOUP SPOONS. *See* FLATWARE.

ROUND STEAK. A steak cut from the round of beef.

ROUNDFISH. *See* WHITEFISH.

ROUX. The French name for a mixture of flour and butter used for thickening sauces, gravies, and soups. It is made by melting slowly two tablespoonfuls of butter over a very low flame. When the butter is thoroughly melted, add two tablespoonfuls of all-purpose flour a little at a time, while stirring almost constantly. Continue stirring as the mixture browns slowly. When the right color has been achieved, or when the roux is almost dry, it may be stored in a small, covered dish for future use.

The dark *roux* is used to thicken the more highly seasoned sauces, gravies, and soups, while the light-toned roux (*roux blond*) is mixed with the more delicately flavored sauces, etc. Whatever the liquid used, it should be poured gently into the *roux* (do not pour the *roux* into the basic liquid) while over a gentle flame and while stirring constantly. If the *roux* has been made previously, it should be warmed in a double boiler (to prevent further darkening) before the sauce, gravy, or soup is added.

The amount of butter used determines the thickness of the *roux*. Therefore, if a thinner *roux* is desired, use two parts of butter to one of flour rather than one of each. The drippings of the meat with which the sauce is to be served may be substituted for the butter, and, in the opinion of some people, a *roux* so made adds more flavor than the one made with butter. *See* SAUCE, SOUP, *and* GRAVY.

ROYAL FIZZ. An effervescent drink made with gin and eggs. *See* FIZZ.

RUBY PORT. A type of Port wine distinguished chiefly by its color. *See* PORT.

RUDDY DUCK. A wild duck. *See* DUCK.

RUE. A small, bushy herb with bitter leaves, used for decoction. *See also* HERBS.

RUFF. An Old World sand-piper. In the breeding season the male has a frill of elongated feathers about the neck. The female is called a reeve. A delicious bird.

RUFFED GROUSE. *See* GROUSE.

RUM. A spirit distilled from fermented molasses and other sugar-cane products. Though a favored drink in cold climes, rum is of tropical origin, having developed and grown up with the sugar industry, of which it is a by-product.

The British are largely responsible for the development of rum from a crude, raw, native drink called Kill-Devil into its present potable form, even as they were responsible for the development of port. When the West Indies were first colonized, the British planters did not think too highly of the local spirit, preferring to import Nantz brandy for their own consumption. However, the warming qualities of the liquor, so well suited for northern countries, became known and the fame of the "comfortable waters of Barbados" spread, largely through the sailors and travelers who touched there. Commercial pressure and the natural desire of the planters to utilize their by-products led to the refinement and development of more palatable grades of rum.

Though the English were not alone in their whole-hearted adoption of these "comfortable waters," they have, in many ways, made the spirit their own. When punch was at the height of its popularity, few self-respecting Englishmen would consider mixing a punch that did not contain rum. Indeed, some definitions of punch still specify that the mixture must contain rum.

Rum is still served today as a daily ration to the common seamen on the ships of the Royal Navy. Each sailor gets his choice of either his daily grog or a small sum of money. He is not, incidentally, permitted to let his grog ration accumulate, and if he waives it on any given day, he automatically receives the stipend instead.

A stream of rum flows through American history. Though an official definition of Rum has been given as "a spirit distilled direct from sugar-cane products in sugar-cane growing countries," the domestic manufacture of rum began in the eighteenth century, chiefly in New England, using imported molasses for the ferment. This industry has flourished and has continued even to the present day. Much mention has been made of New England rum in early Americana, and a daily grog ration, similar to the British, was long served on American naval vessels.

The origins of the name rum are somewhat obscure. It is often supposed to be American, and, indeed, the word is deeply ingrained in the American vocabulary, where it is frequently used to describe any and all kinds of spirits. During prohibition, the terms rumrunner and Rum Row came into common use. The British, however, claim it to be a British contraction of a British word. The spirit was first known in England as Barbados Waters and in the West Indies as Kill-Devil. This latter name, however, was a poor word from a commercial viewpoint, and the spirit came to be known as *Rumbullion*, said to be a Devonshire word meaning "a great tumult." In time, this word was shortened to the present rum.

TYPES OF RUM

There are several different kinds of rum. They are variously classified according to place of manufacture, as Jamaica, New England, etc.; or manufacturing method, as Jamaica or Demerara; or by some brand names used by distillers who have developed distinctive rums. They are also classified according to their alcoholic content, color, body, and flavor. Under the last system, the White Label Rums are generally light in color and taste, the Gold Label Rums darker and heavier, and the heavy-bodied tropical rums the strongest, the heaviest, and the darkest.

While some rum is distilled directly from the juice of the sugar cane, most of it is made as a by-product of sugar manufacturing. There are two distinct systems used, the products being called Jamaica Rum and Demerara Rum.

There are three elements to the ferment used in making Jamaica Rum—the skimmings from boiled cane-juice, the molasses left after the sugar crystals are extracted from the juice, and the dunder or residue from previous distillations. This mixture is allowed to ferment slowly from six to twelve days, to permit both the primary fermentation of sugar into alcohol and various secondary fermentations that give flavor and aroma.

In the making of Demerara Rum, a slightly acid, watered solution of molasses is fermented. Usually, this fermentation is much quicker than for Jamaica Rum.

These two ferments are distilled in the usual manner, though the pot still is preferred to the more economical modern methods. The product is colorless and must be aged. It acquires some coloring from the wood of the casks and may be further colored by the addition of caramel or burnt sugar before bottling.

Rums are also made artificially, a practice which led to the precise wording of the official British definition, specifying that rum must be made in a cane-growing country.

Rum has a great many uses, both as a liquor and as a flavoring ingredient in cookery. As a liquor, it is served straight, diluted, or in a great variety of mixtures. *See* DAIQUIRI, PUNCH, and TODDY.

RUM FONDANT FILLING
AND FROSTING

3 tbsp good rum (more if desired)
3 tbsp heavy cream
3 cups confectioner's sugar

Add the rum and cream to the sugar. Beat vigorously to spreading consistency, adding more rum or cream, if necessary. Spread between the layers and on top and sides of the cake.

RUM NUT FROSTING

¼ cup butter
2 cups sifted confectioner's sugar, firmly packed
1 tsp rum
2 tbsp hot water
¼ cup chopped walnuts

Heat butter in skillet until delicately browned. Blend into sugar and mix thoroughly. Add rum. Stir in hot water, a teaspoon at a time, until icing is of proper consistency to spread easily. Stir in chopped nuts. Spread between layers and on sides and top of cake. Enough for two eight-inch layers. A quarter of a teaspoon of rum flavoring may be substituted for rum if desired.

RUM AND COKE. An intoxicating tropical beverage made by mixing one jigger of rum in a ten-ounce glass filled with ice and cola. It is a Cuba Libre (*which see*) without lime.

RUM CAKE. See BABA AU RHUM.

RUM COLLINS. A cooling summer drink made of rum, served in a tall glass. A Tom Collins made with rum instead of gin. See COLLINS.

RUM CRUSTAS. An iced rum drink, very similar to a cocktail, that is served in a glass completely lined with lemon peel. See CRUSTAS.

RUM RICKEY. A thirst-quenching drink made of rum, lime juice, and carbonated water. See RICKEY.

RUM SOUR. A slightly sour rum drink. See SOUR.

RUM SWIZZLE. A tropical rum drink that is mixed with a swizzle stick. See SWIZZLE.

RUM TODDY. A type of hot or cold rum drink. See TODDY.

RUMP. The rump steak of beef is taken from the round. In Chicago the whole round is also called the rump. The rump or round is located between the sirloin or loin and the horseshoe or heel of the hind back of beef. Good steaks are cut from the back of the rump. They are solid meat, the most economical of the steaks for broiling. They must be cooked very rare, because, if well done, they are tough and stringy. See BEEF.

RUNNER. A long strip of cloth, lace, or other material that is placed on the center of a table to hold centerpieces, ornaments, and serving dishes. It is used in conjunction with place mats when a table cloth is not spread. See TABLE SETTING AND SERVICE.

RUSK. See CRACKERS.

RUSSET. An apple of a greenishs color, mottled with brown. *See also* APPLES.

RUSSIAN DRESSING. *See* SALAD DRESSINGS.

RUTABAGA

RUTABAGA. A winter vegetable, more commonly known as yellow turnip. See TURNIP.

RYE BREAD. See BREAD.

RYE FLOUR. See FLOUR.

RYE WHISKY. See WHISKY.

S

SAALAND PFARR CHEESE. Another name for Prestost cheese, *which see*.

SAANEN CHEESE. A type of Emmenthaler cheese made from cow's milk. The eyes are few and small. It is also known as *Hartkase*, *Reibkase*, and *Walliskase*.

SABAYON. A sweet sauce used mainly for pudding and often with vanilla ice cream. This sauce must not boil.

SABAYON SAUCE

4 egg yolks
3 tbsp sifted sugar
2 wineglassfuls of Marsala wine

Put into a saucepan the 4 yolks and the sugar; place the saucepan on a hot stove and beat the yolks and sugar briskly with a wire whisk for 2 minutes. Pour in the wine slowly (Madeira may be substituted), stirring all the time; then take the pan from the fire and strain the sauce through a fine sieve over the pudding with which it is to be served.

SACCHARIN. A crystalline, organic-acid substance, containing in addition to the elements carbon, hydrogen, and oxygen, a little sulphur, and nitrogen. It was introduced about 50 years ago as a substitute for sugar, and it is especially useful in cases of obesity, rheumatism, gout, and diabetes, when the withdrawal of sugar is followed by intense craving for it, or a refusal to eat those foods which are customarily flavored with it. It is antiseptic, and has the property of acidifying the urine, being eliminated unaltered by the kidneys. It may be used for months at a time without danger, if the quantity as prescribed by doctors does not exceed more than 1 or 2 grains, three times a day. More than this may cause gastric derangement. It may be added to food in cooking.

SACK. A wine that was highly popular in England, especially in the 16th century. It is generally supposed to have been a dry, amber wine. The name was originally spelled seck, believed to be an anglicized version of the French sec (*which see*), meaning dry. In addition to plain sack, there was also mention of sherris-sack, canary

sack and malligo sack as being in use in the olden days.

There is some doubt as to just what sack really was. It is claimed that it was sherry (*which see*) and, in England, sherry is sometimes called that even today. There are those, however, who claim that this is a fallacy, for sherry of the dry type was little known at that time. Another group of authorities say that sack was a general term, first applied to any and all wine of certain characteristics, that later came to be narrowed down to sherry alone, as the outstanding member of the group.

SACK POSSET. An intoxicating drink made by curdling cream with sherry wine and other ingredients. *See also* POSSET.

SADDLE. The upper back portion of an animal carcass, including the loins. *See* LAMB.

SAFFRON. Saffron is a species of purple crocus, the mildly pungent aromatic stigmas of which are used to color and flavor foods. It is used primarily to impart a yellow color to certain confections, vegetables, and alcoholic beverages. It is also used to season breads, pickles, sauces, fish, meat, and poultry. This extremely sweet-smelling herb is cultivated largely for ornament in America. *See also* HERBS.

SAFFRON BREAD

2 lb 14 oz white flour
2 cups lukewarm milk
1½ oz yeast
1 tsp saffron
5 oz butter
6 oz sugar
1 egg
2 tbsp ground almonds
6 pounded bitter almonds
3½ oz raisins or
1½ oz chopped candied peel

Covering: 1 egg, 2 tbsp chopped almonds, 2 tbsp granulated sugar.

Work part of the flour, tepid milk and yeast into a dough. Let rise to twice its size. Dry saffron in a very cool oven, pound finely with a little sugar, stir with a little milk and add to the dough. Cream sugar and butter and beat the egg. Work into the dough together with almonds and raisins, previously soaked in warm water and stoned. Add more flour if necessary and when well worked in, leave again to rise. Remove to floured board, knead well and divide into eight portions. Roll out, shape into strands and twist into a plait, which might be shaped into a wreath. Place on greased pan and let rise until doubled in bulk. Brush with lightly-beaten egg, sprinkle with finely chopped almonds and sugar

SAGE. Sage is an aromatic herb of the mint family, the dried leaves of which are used for seasoning. These must be stored in airtight containers if they are to retain their aroma. They are used to season stuffings and dressings for meat and poultry. They are also used with onions, dried beans, fish, stews, and sauces, and with tomato, veal, or cheese dishes. The fresh leaves are sometimes used with cottage cheese. Sage is stronger in flavor than any other herb except parsley.

It is almost always used with pork and sausage because the salviol that it contains aids the digestive process and prevents the harmful effects that these rich meats might otherwise have. Generally speaking sage is overworked, and in many dishes it might well be replaced by savory (*which see*).

SAGE AND ONION STUFFING
(For Duck, Goose, Pork)

6 onions
1 tbsp powdered sage
½ tsp poultry seasoning
1 tsp salt
¼ tsp pepper
2 cups crumbled bread

Cook the onions until tender, chop fine, then combine with all remaining ingredients. See STUFFING.

SAGE CHEESE. A cheese made in America by the Cheddar process. The interior has a green, mottled appearance, and the flavor is obtained by the addition of sage extract. It comes in various shapes and sizes.

SAGE HEN. The sage hen, largest of the grouse family in the United States, lives on the barren plains where the *Artemisia*, or sage brush, grows in abundance. This aromatic plant furnishes both safe cover and food. In fact, because the sage

hen's diet includes such a large porportion of sage leaves, the flesh becomes strongly tainted to the point that it is not palatable. However, the flesh of young birds is much more delicate and not so overpowering in the flavor of sage. Accordingly, young sage hens are considered excellent eating and are in demand when and where available. Because they are rather tame and large in size, they are easily shot and will soon become rare unless preservation measures are effected. *See also* GROUSE.

SAGE

SAGO. An easily digested form of starch, sago is derived from the pith in the trunks of the sago and other tropical palms. After the tree is felled the pith is powdered, and the dried sago flour is later treated with water and worked into a paste. This is granulated by being forced through sieves. The granules acquire a spherical form as they fall into a shallow iron pan held over a fire. They are known commercially as pearl sago.

Sago is an important native food, and the wild sago derived from a Floridian palmlike plant is used as a food by the Seminoles. Sago has an agreeable flavor more delicate than that of tapioca, and it is an invaluable adjunct to the invalid dietary. Sago is combined with milk, cream, and eggs and made into tasty and nutritious puddings. It is used like tapioca (*which see*).

SAGUARO. The giant cactus of Mexico, producing a fruit from which Mexican Indians make an alcoholic liquor.

SAIGON. *See* CINNAMON.

SAINT AGATHON CHEESE. A French cheese made in Brittany.

SAINT BENOIT CHEESE. A soft rennet cheese, which resembles Olivet.

SAINT CLAUDE CHEESE. A small, square goat's milk cheese, made in France.

SAINT FLORENTIN CHEESE. A French cheese made in Burgundy.

SAINT HONORE. A delicious French pastry, too complicated to be made at home.

SAINT MARCELLIN CHEESE. A goat's milk cheese, made in France.

SAINT MAURE CHEESE. A French cheese, made in Touraine.

SAINT NECTAIRE CHEESE. A soft, rich, rennet cheese made of whole milk.

SAINT PATRICK SOUP. A combination soup made by combining a can of cream of spinach soup and a can of cream of mushroom soup. Mix thoroughly and top it with minced chives or parsley.

SAINT REMY CHEESE. A soft, rennet cheese made in France. It is very similar to *Pont L'Eveque*.

SAKE. The national liquor of Japan, strong and fiery, produced from rice. It is used by the natives of Japan, China, and India, especially at their festivities. One of the most impressive of these is the Feast of the Bear at which the blood of a young cub, imprisoned in a gilded cage and fattened for the occasion, is drunk in a solemn ritual from a special totemic spoon made by the native Ainos of the island of Yeso. This liquor is also called *"saki."*

SALAD. The word "salad" derives from a term meaning "salt" and probably first referred to a plate of uncooked greens garnished with salt. Today's salads are among the most versatile of dishes. Of endless variety, quick and easy to prepare, salads may be adapted to suit any meal in any season or they may constitute meals in themselves.

Since raw, dark green leafy vegetables are the primary—often sole—source in the diet of such valuable nutrients as vitamin A, it is nutritionally wise to develop the habit of serving salad with at least one meal a day. Proper handling and preparation of salad greens and vegetables is crucial in order to insure that these foods retain their nutrients. Since warmth, water and oxygen contribute to the destruction of nutrients, care should be taken that vegetables are kept dry and chilled.

PREPARATION

Select fresh vegetables and greens which have been trimmed the least. Break rather than cut off the number of leaves needed for the salad. Wash these quickly and with a minimum of handling in cold water. Immediately dry the greens by whirling them about in a towel or napkin. Never soak greens or vegetables as many nutrients, being water soluble, pass out of the vegetables into the soaking water. Return the thoroughly dried greens to the refrigerator in a covered pan or plastic bag and chill.

To prepare carrots, turnips and beets scrub the skin with a special brush and rinse in cold water. Refrain from peeling vegetables since many nutrients reside in the skins. Mushrooms, since they absorb water so quickly, should only be wiped with a damp cloth.

TOSSED GREEN SALAD

Rub a wooden salad bowl with a broken clove of garlic and a selection of crushed, fresh herbs (*which see*) if available or prepare a chapon (*which see*). Break the thoroughly chilled greens into the bowl. Use a variety of greens including romaine, chicory, field salad, dandelion, pursalane, watercress, lettuce, spinach, cabbages, and chard. Try the top of radishes, young beets and turnips, celery, green onions, scallions and chives for variety.

For a family size salad sprinkle about three tablespoons of salad oil on the greens and toss them lightly for fully 10 minutes or until all the leaves glisten with oil. Tossing with oil insures that the greens remain crisp and retain their nutrients when the sour seasoning is added.

Season the salad with salt, freshly ground peppercorn, oregano and dry mustard. Add about a tablespoon of vinegar or lemon juice and toss again lightly. Garnish the tossed salad with cubes of Cheddar and toasted croutons. Serve at once.

The classic proportions of oil to vinegar in a tossed salad dressing are 3 to 1 as indicated here. However, these elements may be manipulated to taste, as always.

SALAD SUGGESTIONS

Salad may be limited to only greens or may include other vegetables as well. Greeks, for example, make a salad without greens, using only plump tomatoes, onions, olives, peppers, native feta cheese, oil and seasonings.

Cucumbers, sweet peppers, zucchini, celery, radishes, chives, scallions, onions, slivers or curls of carrot, turnip, beet or kohlrabi, may be added for interest and nutritional value. Use cherry tomatoes, Bermuda onion slices, shredded red cabbage and parsley for color and texture.

Cooked vegetables, cubed or crumbled cheese, anchovies or sprats, cubes and strips of cooked meat and poultry, cauliflower or broccoli flowerets, nut meats, olives and grapes may be added according to taste.

Fragile ingredients such as avocado and hard boiled egg slices may be used as garnishes after the salad has been tossed. If cut tomatoes are used, add them to the salad after the other ingredients and just before tossing or use them as garnishes.

When all the salad ingredients are assembled in the bowl, proceed as for tossed green salad or choose an appropriate dressing (*which see*).

Apple. Combine quantities of cubed red apple, shredded carrot, celery slices, and walnut meats. Toss with a mayonnaise dressing and serve in a bowl lined with bib lettuce.

Avocado. Arrange slices of ripe tomato and avocado on a bed of spinach leaves. Garnish with lemon slices and black olives. Use an oil and lemon juice dressing.

Spinach. Cut raw mushrooms into a bowl of well washed, dried and chilled spinach leaves. Crumble bits of cooked bacon into the salad and garnish with hard boiled egg slices. Use an oil and vinegar dressing.

Tuna. Combine iceberg lettuce, romaine and chicory in a bowl. Add cucumber slices, radish slices, pot cheese, chopped ripe tomatoes and a can of tuna with oil. Toss well and season with cider vinegar, salt, pepper and basil. Garnish with sliced stuffed olives and Bermuda onion rings.

FINGER SALAD

These are perfect for informal dinners or for use as appetizers. Children seem to prefer finger salads to tossed salads, also. For the best effect use a variety of colors, textures, shapes and flavors. A combination of carrot and celery sticks, quartered or sliced cucumbers, wedges or slices of tomato, hard boiled egg, sweet pepper rings and scallions may be attractively arranged on a bed of crisp, dark greens.

Choose a small enough plate so that the salad does not look scanty and garnish the vegetables and greens liberally with a selection of olives, radish slices, fruit slices, parsley, chives, onion rings, cheeses and pickles. For variety include stuffed celery stalks (*which see*), cucumber-cheese slices (*which see*) or stuffed tomatoes (*which see*).

Finger salads may be left undressed or seasoned only with salt. A bowl of French dressing is sometimes supplied for dipping. Or the elements of the salad may be marinated for an hour or so in a chosen dressing and served with toothpicks.

SALAD BASKET. Usually made of woven wire, about the size of a colander, a salad basket is used for washing and draining salad greens.

SALAD BOWL. A special bowl which may be made of porcelain, glass, or wood, used for serving salads. New wooden bowls are seasoned by being rubbed with salad oil which is allowed to remain on the wood for half an hour. The bowl is then washed with lukewarm water and a mild soap, if desired, and thoroughly dried.

Wooden salad bowls are often rubbed with cut cloves of garlic or crushed fresh herbs before use. To clean simply wipe the bowl with a damp cloth. Store in a cool place.

SALAD DRESSING. The success of a salad depends largely upon the dressing, which in turn derives its flavor from the quality of the ingredients used. These are: Oils, acids, such as vinegar, lemon juice, or other fruit juices, salt, pepper, and other condiments.

One should never lose sight of the fact that salad dressings serve two purposes: to give or develop flavor, and to bind the ingredients and raise their food value.

SALAD BOWL WITH SPOON AND FORK

Too little dressing makes an insipid salad, while too much produces equally undesirable results. The Spaniards are convinced that, ". . . to make a perfect salad, one should be a spendthrift for oil, a miser for vinegar, a wise man for salt, and a madcap to mix the ingredients together."

CHOICE OF DRESSING

The dressing to be used in salad-making depends upon the texture of the ingredients and the place of the salad on the menu. For example, the salad used as a first course should merely whet the appetite. A heavy dressing should never be used here, but rather a spicy French dressing, or merely fruit juices. Salad used as a main course may have a heavier dressing, such as mayonnaise, boiled, or a whipped cream mixture. A dinner salad should be light, and served with a tart dressing. Especially after a fish main course a tart dressing is preferable to one of the bland type. The dessert salad is somewhat of an innovation, but is becoming increasingly popular with the ladies. Usually it is a fruit, or fruit and cheese salad, with whipped cream or mayonnaise or a boiled dressing, or it may be a frozen salad.

In general, the uses of salad dressings are as follows:

Plain French Dressing: With fresh salad greens, vegetables, fish, fruit, and cheese.

French Dressing with variations: With fresh salad greens, vegetables, fruit and cheese, fish or shell fish.

Plain Mayonnaise: With meat, fish, shellfish, egg, and vegetables.

Mayonnaise with variations: With fish, shellfish, egg, cheese, fruit, and vegetables.

Sour Cream Dressing: With cucumbers and all the aqueous vegetables and fruit.

FRENCH DRESSING

French dressing is a temporary emulsion, which can be explained thus: If you pour oil and water together they will not mix, but if you shake them violently little drops of oil can be seen suspended throughout the liquid. That is exactly what happens in making French dressing, and the finer these droplets, the less likely will be a separation. For this reason French dressing should be shaken in a jar or bottle when a quantity is needed, and mixed in an electric mixer when a large quantity is re-

quired. French dressing will be less likely to separate if the ingredients are cold when combined. It is also well to have the mixing bowl surrounded by ice during the mixing or beating. French dressing is called a temporary emulsion because it contains no substance which maintains the drops of oil suspended in the liquid, as in mayonnaise.

BOILED WALTHAM DRESSING

1 cup heavy sour cream
1 egg
¼ cup tarragon vinegar
1½ tsp salt
1½ tsp powdered sugar
1 tsp prepared mustard
Dash of cayenne
2 tbsp finely chopped hickory nuts

Combine in the double boiler all the ingredients except the nuts and cook, stirring constantly, until the mixture thickens. Cool, then fold in the nuts.

HORSERADISH CREAM DRESSING

½ cup heavy cream
3 tbsp wine vinegar
Dash each of salt and pepper
2 tbsp grated horseradish
1 tsp finely minced shallot

Beat the cream until very stiff, then gradually add the wine vinegar, still beating. Season and fold in the horseradish and shallot.

INDIAN DRESSING

2 hard-cooked egg yolks
Dash each of paprika, cayenne, white pepper, and salt
1 tsp powdered sugar
1 tbsp lemon juice
2 tbsp tarragon vinegar
½ cup oil
1 tbsp each finely chopped pimiento, green pepper and pickled beets
1 tsp finely minced parsley
1 tbsp finely chopped walnut meats

Press the egg yolks through a fine sieve. Add the seasonings, sugar, lemon juice, vinegar, and oil and shake thoroughly. Add all remaining ingredients and chill.

Marshmallow Nut Cream Dressing

3 egg yolks
½ cup strained honey
3 tbsp lemon juice
½ cup heavy cream
Dash of salt
6 soft marshmallows, quartered
1 tbsp chopped blanched almonds or pistachio nuts

Beat the eggs in the double boiler until light, gradually adding the honey alternately with the lemon juice. Cook, stirring constantly, until the mixture thickens. Remove from the fire and, when cold, fold in the cream, whipped until stiff with the salt, marshmallows and nuts.

Mustard Dressing

1 cup tomato catsup
¼ cup sweetened condensed milk
¾ cup prepared mustard
1 tbsp each chopped parsley and chives
Salt and pepper

Combine all ingredients, beating until well blended with a rotary beater. Chill.

Pot Cheese Dressing

½ cup pot cheese
¼ cup evaporated milk
1 tsp salt
Dash of pepper
1 egg yolk
1 tbsp sugar
3 tbsp vinegar

Press the cheese through a sieve and moisten it with a little of the milk. Add the seasonings, egg yolk beaten with the sugar, and, last of all, the remaining milk. Beat until smooth.

Suzette's Dressing

1 to 3½ oz packaged cream cheese
½ cup currant jelly
Juice 1 lemon
Salt and pepper
1 cup whipped cream
2 tbsp chopped pistachio nuts

Combine the cheese and jelly, gradually adding the lemon juice. Beat well with a rotary beater, season, then fold in the cream and nuts.

Sweet Sour Dressing

½ cup sugar
½ cup tarragon vinegar
2 tbsp salad oil
1 tbsp each minced onion, chives, celery, green pepper, pimiento and parsley
1 tsp salt
¼ tsp pepper
1 tsp prepared mustard
1 tsp paprika
½ tsp Worcestershire sauce

Combine all ingredients in the order given. Add a piece of ice and beat until thickened. Especially good with fish salads.

Whipped Cream Dressings

Whipped cream (or whipped evaporated milk) may be used either as a sweet or savory salad dressing by the addition of flavorings and seasonings. If desired it may also be delicately tinted with a very small amount of liquid or paste coloring. In any case whipped cream for dressings should be chilled and the dressing added to the salad immediately before serving so that it does not separate.

1. To 1 cup of whipped cream, add, just before serving, ½ cup of tart red jelly such as currant, cranberry, raspberry, etc.

2. To 1 cup of whipped cream, add, just before serving, 3 tablespoons of chopped nut meats.

3. To 1 cup of whipped cream, add, just before serving, 1 tablespoon of minced assorted candied fruit and 1 teaspoon of grated lemon rind.

4. To 1 cup of whipped cream, add, just before serving, 1 tablespoon each of finely minced figs, dates, and raisins.

5. To 1 cup of whipped cream, add, just before serving 1 teaspoon of chopped, candied ginger, and 1 teaspoon of grated lemon rind.

6. To 1 cup of whipped cream, add, just before serving, ⅓ cup of minced green pepper and 2 tablespoons of minced pimiento.

7. To 1 cup of whipped cream, add, just

before serving, a bit of anchovy paste the size of a large pea. Here the addition of a little minced parsley* or chives, or both, is most desirable.

8. To 1 cup of whipped cream, add, just before serving, 3 anchovy fillets, washed, dried, then minced fine, and 1 teaspoon of grated lemon rind.

9. To 1 cup of whipped cream, add, just before serving, 1 tablespoon of capers, well washed then finely minced, 1 tablespoon of finely minced sweet-sour gherkins, and 1 teaspoon of grated orange rind.

10. To 1 cup of whipped cream, add, just before serving, 1 tablespoon of either black, red, or white caviar, and a few drops of onion juice.

11. To 1 cup of whipped cream, add, just before serving, 4 tablespoons of minced cooked tongue, 1 tablespoon of minced capers, and 1 tablespoon of grated lemon rind.

See also MAYONNAISE.

SALAD SETS. *See* FLATWARE.

SALAMANA CHEESE. A soft, sheep's milk cheese from Italy. It has a very pronounced flavor and is eaten spread on bread, or is mixed with corn meal and cooked.

SALAMI. *See* SAUSAGES.

SALEP. A starchy food, which is obtained from the tubercles of certain Oriental orchids. It is a mixture of starch and mucilage from which is made a favorite beverage of the Orientals.

SALERATUS. *See* BAKING SODA.

SALINE WATERS. Natural purges from springs in Europe and America. *See* ALKALINE AND MINERAL WATERS.

SALISBURY STEAK. Name given to a broiled Hamburger steak.

SALLY LUNN. A Southern bread which may be made with either yeast or baking powder, and baked either in greased muffin pans or in a large shallow pan, then cut into squares like corn bread.

RAISED SALLY LUNN

1 cup milk
3 tbsp butter
3 tbsp shortening
2 tbsp sugar
1 tsp salt
1 yeast cake
½ cup lukewarm water

3 eggs
4 cups sifted flour

Scald the milk, add the butter, shortening, sugar and salt. Stir until these are dissolved, then cool to lukewarm. Soften the yeast in the lukewarm water, then add to the first mixture. Beat and add the eggs, alternately with the sifted flour, beating until well blended. Cover, and set in a warm place to rise until doubled in bulk, about 3 hours. Work down, divide into portions if to be baked in greased muffin pans, or turn into one larger-sized greased pan. Allow the mixture to rise again until doubled in bulk, then bake in a hot oven (425° F.) 15 minutes if in muffin pans, 25 minutes if in one large pan. Serve hot. (Serves 6 to 8)

QUICK SALLY LUNN

½ cup shortening
½ cup sugar
3 eggs
1 cup milk
2 cups sifted flour
2 tsp baking powder
¾ tsp salt

Cream the shortening and sugar. Beat and add the eggs alternately with the milk. Sift the dry ingredients and add to the first mixture beating gently but thoroughly until smooth. Bake either in greased muffin pans or one large shallow pan in a hot oven (425° F.) 15 minutes if in muffin pans, 25 minutes if in one pan. (Serves 6)

SALMAGUNDI. Although obscure, the origin of this word is believed to be a corruption of the French *salmigondis*, which in turn stems from a very special *salmis* which was first concocted by an 18th century chef named Gondis or Gonde. Because salmis in France is usually a *chaudfroid* of leftover meat, game or poultry, it would seem that the chef attained his fame by the device of making a fancy hash. It must have been better than good because authorities claim that salmis de Gondis (or salmis de Gonde) was one of the most popular viands among continental gourmets for a century or more. Supposedly, its content was a combination of game and chicken with fillets of anchovies, in a sauce of eggs, shallots, garlic, fines herbes and white wine.

Somewhat better known, Salmagundi is the name of a venerable and distinguished club with branches all over the United States. Allegedly, the members are qualified critics of food.

Current dictionaries authorize use of the word to denote almost any mixture: hot, cold, sweet, sour, bland or savory. At the club of the same name, one of several delectable dishes so honored consists of a cup of chilled melon and cantaloupe balls in assorted colors of green, pink and white, all laced with a fruit sirup including marachino, curacao or other cordial.

For a hearty salad course, a salmagundi may be made by taking ½-inch cubes of chicken, lamb or veal combined with smaller quantities of diced carrot, boiled potato, eggplant, peas and beans and marinating the mixture in oil with vinegar or lemon juice, grated onion, salt, pepper and a touch of tarragon vinegar. Drain well, toss with fresh mayonnaise and serve with hearts of lettuce or crisp watercress. Anchovy fillets may be added effectively, in keeping with the original formula.

SALMI. A spiced dish of birds or game, roasted, minced, and stewed in wine. A kind of stew.

SALMON. Of all the edible fish, the salmon is best equipped with regard to teeth. Its snout is pointed, its jaws nearly equal, the head small and the body elongated, with a thick and gracefully curved back. The ordinary length of this fish is from two and one-half to three feet, and the average weight from 15 to 25 pounds, although many have been caught weighing considerable more. Below the lateral line, the color is of a bluish-slate, melting delicately away into a silver-white, blended with shading of an iris hue over the rest of the body.

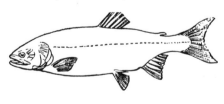

SALMON

The salmon is extremely abundant in the oceans as far north as the Arctic Ocean. Each spring it migrates in countless numbers, the troops forming two long lines, the female always preceding the male, the fish swimming generally with terrific noise, going slowly, unless menaced by danger.

During its migratory maneuvers, the salmon ascends waterfalls of a great height. If it fails at the first attempt, it is not discouraged, striving again and again until successful, when the fish disappears over the cataract into the river. It sometimes scales a height of 25 feet. The fish continue up river until the female has found a suitable spot to spawn. Then she prepares a sort of nest where she leaves her eggs, which the male impregnates. These are hatched by the heat of the sun. When the spawning is over, the salmon seem exhausted, their bodies are covered with red spots, they swim so feebly that the tide of the river drags them and they return to the ocean where they will spend the winter.

At first the young ones feed on the yolk which is in the egg, and later on small plants and animals. The salmon grow up very rapidly. They wear, like the trout, a kind of tunic ,or livery, marked with brown vertical stripes, which disappear as they grow older. When the young are grown to about a foot in length, they abandon the fresh water of the rivers and go to the sea.

Salmon fishing constitutes one of the most important and profitable industries in America. It is established at the mouth of the rivers, when these delicious fish leave the sea. Salmon are in season from May until September, but frozen salmon may be obtained during most months of the year.

The flesh, of a pinkish orange color, is excellent and very nutritious and may be eaten fresh, salted, smoked, dried, or canned in oil. *See also* FISH.

PREPARING SALMON

Large cuts and slices of salmon are generally boiled in a vinegar court bouillon (*which see*) though the slices may also be broiled, baked, or sautéed. A sauce usually accompanies boiled salmon, those suitable for this popular and delicious fish being: anchovy, brown butter, caper, egg, hollandaise, lobster, oyster, mousseline, ravigote, venetian, etc. Cucumber salad with French dressing is also a traditional accompaniment.

When salmon is prepared to be served cold, at luncheon or supper, for instance, it is preferable to have the fish boiled whole and allowed to cool in its broth. In this way, both flavor and quality are preserved. When boiled in slices, hot or cold, the skin is removed when lukewarm and before dressing on the service platter, to facilitate garnishing. Any of the cold fish sauces may be served with cold salmon, as well as any kind of green or vegetable salad, including the above mentioned cucumber.

Garnishes best suited to cold salmon are: small tomatoes, peeled, scooped out and filled with a vegetable salad; hard-boiled eggs, quartered or sliced, or stuffed by having the yolk removed and replaced by any preferred filling, such as chopped olives and gherkins moistened with mayonnaise, or a sour cream dressing; leftover fish, such as crab, lobster, or shrimp, moistened with mayonnaise, sour cream dressing, catsup, French dressing, etc., formed into balls, sprinkled with paprika, and topped with a small slice of red beet, black olive or radish, a caper, or a truffle. Or, a small cucumber cut in fancy shape and garnished with lobster coral or fish roe; a small cooked red beet, scooped out and filled with any savory mixture; a ring of anchovy with an olive in the center; or a few slices of lemon dipped half in paprika and half in finely chopped parsley, or half in paprika and half in ground nutmeg, or three tints may be used, red, brown, and green, etc. All of this being left to the ingenuity and taste of the homemaker.

The various methods employed in the preparation of pompano, pike, muskalonge, turbot, and the like, may be adapted to this universally popular and nourishing fish.

BAKED SALMON

1 onion, minced
½ clove garlic, minced
2 tbsp butter
½ green pepper, finely chopped
1 tsp Worcestershire sauce
½ tsp salt
¼ tsp pepper
1 cup canned tomatoes
1 bay leaf
1 slice salmon, 1 to 2½ lb
4 slices bacon

Cook the onion and garlic for 5 minutes in the butter. Add the green pepper, Worcestershire sauce, seasonings, tomatoes, and bay leaf, and simmer all gently about 10 minutes. Pour into a casserole, place the salmon (wiped and patted dry) in the sauce, top with the bacon and bake, covered, in a slow oven (300° F.) about 1 hour, removing the cover during the last 15 minutes of baking. (Serves 6)

BAKED SALMON IN SOUR CREAM

3 to 4 lb salmon, in one piece
2 tsp onion juice
Juice 1 lemon
Salt and pepper
1 cup sour cream

Wipe the salmon with a damp cloth, place in a baking dish, skin side down, and pour over it the combined onion and lemon juices to which salt and pepper have been added. Pour the cream over all and bake in a hot oven (400° F.) about ¾ hour. Serve with parsley potatoes, steamed broccoli, and pickled beets. (Serves 6)

BROILED SALMON STEAK

Have the fish cut about ¾-inch thick. Season lightly with salt and pepper and brush over with oil. Broil under a moderate flame, allowing about 12 minutes for each side. Baste 2 or 3 times during the broiling with a little butter. When done, add the juice of 1 lemon to the broiling pan, blend it with any remaining butter and oil, and when thoroughly heated, pour over the fish, sprinkle with finely chopped parsley, and garnish with sections of lemon.

PLANKED SALMON LOAF

2 cups canned salmon
½ cup soft bread crumbs
2 eggs
¼ cup light cream
4 tbsp butter, melted
1 tbsp lemon juice
1 tbsp minced parsley
1 tsp scraped onion
½ tsp salt
Dash of pepper
Buttered crumbs

Pick over and flake the salmon, discarding any bone or skin. Add all remaining ingredients, except the buttered crumbs, and blend thoroughly. Shape into a loaf in the center of a plank which has been oiled and heated for 10 minutes in the oven. Bake in a hot oven (400°–425° F.) about 25 minutes, then sprinkle the buttered crumbs over the loaf and brown either in the oven or under the broiler about 5 minutes. (Serves 6)

SALMON CAKES

1 No. 1 can salmon
1½ cups bread crumbs
¼ cup flour
1 tsp baking powder
1 tsp salt
⅓ tsp pepper
2 eggs
1 cup milk

Pick over and flake the salmon. Combine with the crumbs, flour, baking powder and seasonings. Beat the eggs, blend with the milk, then add to the first mixture and let stand a few minutes for the crumbs and flour to absorb the moisture. Shape into cakes and sauté in a little fat, turning to brown both sides. (Serves 6)

SALMON AND CORN PIE

3 tbsp butter
3 tbsp flour
½ tsp salt
Dash of pepper
2 cups milk
1 No. 1 can salmon
2 tbsp minced onion
1 cup grated cheese
1 can vacuum-packed corn
½ cup buttered crumbs

Make a white sauce with the butter, flour, seasonings and milk. Pick over and flake the salmon. Place ⅓ in a buttered casserole, add ⅓ of the sauce to which the onion has been added, and sprinkle with ⅓ of the cheese. Repeat the layers twice. Spread the corn over all and top with the buttered crumbs. Bake in a moderately hot oven (375° F.) about 20 minutes. (Serves 6)

SALMON AU COURT BOUILLON

2 qt water
2 tbsp salt
2 tbsp vinegar
3 or 4 carrots, cubed
3 or 4 onions, minced
3 stalks celery
3 or 4 sprigs parsley
Few sprigs thyme
½ bay leaf
6 or 8 whole peppercorns
2 lb slice salmon

Combine all ingredients except the salmon. Simmer for 1 hour, strain, return the liquid to the pan, and bring to a boil. Wipe the fish with a damp cloth, put it in the pan, and simmer 20 minutes. Then lift the fish carefully from the bouillon and remove skin and bone. Set aside to cool, then chill in the refrigerator. Serve garnished with lettuce, mixed vegetable salad, and mayonnaise. (Serves 6)

SALMON CUSTARD

2 cups milk
2 tbsp minced onion
1 cup soft bread crumbs
3 tbsp butter
1 No. 1 can salmon
½ tsp salt
¼ tsp pepper
Dash of nutmeg
3 eggs, beaten

Scald the milk with the onion, add the crumbs and butter, cover and let stand for 10 minutes. Pick over and flake the salmon, and add to the first mixture with all remaining ingredients. Blend lightly but thoroughly, turn into greased custard cups, set these in a pan of hot water and bake in a moderate oven (375° F.) 30 to 40 minutes. (Serves 6)

SALMON LOAF

1 No. 1 can salmon
¼ cup milk
¾ cup soft bread crumbs
2 tbsp melted butter
1 egg
Juice of ½ lemon
1 tbsp scraped onion
½ cup finely minced green pepper
½ tsp salt
⅛ tsp pepper

Pick over and flake the salmon. Scald the milk, add the bread crumbs and butter and let stand 5 minutes. Beat until smooth, then combine with the salmon, the egg yolk, seasonings and flavorings. Finally, stir in the beaten egg white, transfer to a greased loaf pan and bake in a moderate oven (350° F.) about 35 minutes. Unmold and serve hot with tomato sauce, or cool, then chill, and garnish with lettuce, passing mayonnaise separately. (Serves 6)

SALMON PIE

2 No. 1 cans salmon
1 cup crushed crackers
2 eggs
1 cup medium white sauce
1 tsp salt
Dash of pepper
½ tsp scraped onion
1 tbsp minced parsley
2 tbsp minced green pepper
3 cups mashed potatoes

Pick over and flake the salmon. Combine with the crackers, beaten eggs, white sauce, seasonings and flavorings. Turn into a baking dish, top with the potatoes, carefully mashed and seasoned, and roughen the top with a fork. Bake in a moderate oven (375° F.) about 25 minutes. (Serves 6 to 8)

SALMON-NUT SALAD

2 tbsp gelatin
½ cup cold water
2 cups boiling water
1 tsp salt
½ cup sugar
½ cup vinegar
2 tbsp lemon juice
¾ cup cooked or canned salmon
¾ cup chopped cabbage
½ cup broken nut meats
Lettuce
Mayonnaise or French dressing

Soften the gelatin in the cold water, then dissolve in the boiling water. Add the seasonings and flavorings and stir until dissolved. Set aside to cool and when almost at the setting point fold in the salmon, carefully picked over, drained and flaked. Add the cabbage and the nuts. Turn into

previously wet individual molds, chill, unmold and serve on lettuce, passing the dressing separately. (Serves 6)

SALMON SOUFFLE

2 tbsp butter
2 tbsp flour
½ cup milk
½ tsp each salt, celery salt, and paprika
3 eggs
1 cup fresh cooked or canned salmon

Prepare a thick white sauce with the butter, flour, milk and seasonings. Cool slightly, add the beaten egg yolks, and the salmon (picked over and flaked). Cool, fold in the stiffly beaten egg whites, turn into a greased baking dish and bake in a moderately hot oven (375°–400° F.) about ½ hour. Serve immediately with or without an accompanying sauce. (Serves 4)

SWEET-SOUR FRESH SALMON

2 lb fresh salmon (in one piece)
3 cups boiling water
3 large onions, sliced
¾ cup raisins
1 tsp salt
Juice of 1½ lemons
¼ cup vinegar
1½ tbsp sugar
1 egg yolk

Wipe the salmon, place in a shallow pan, pour the water over, add the onion and raisins, and sprinkle with the salt. Simmer 20 minutes, turn the fish, add the lemon juice, vinegar and sugar and cook 20 minutes longer, basting the fish several times with the liquid in the pan. Remove the salmon carefully to a glass dish. Strain the sauce, reheat, and when boiling, pour slowly over the beaten egg yolk, then pour all over the fish and chill in the refrigerator.

SALMON BUTTER. *See* BUTTER SAUCES.
SALMON TROUT. *See* TROUT.
SALOIO CHEESE. Portuguese cheese, hand made from cow's skim milk.
SALOOP. An infusion of sassafras-chips or similar aromatic herbs, formerly used as a cure for rheumatism, and still so used in the South.
SALSIFY. A root with a mild, sweet flavor somewhat similar to the parsnip. Its

peculiar flavor, somewhat like that of the oyster, is the reason it is sometimes called oyster plant. Its chemical composition is almost identical to that of the carrot. It can be French-fried, or it may be prepared in cream, or by any of the recipes given for carrots or parsnips.

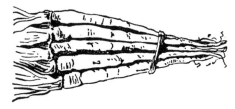

SALSIFY

Salsify should always be put in cold, slightly acidulated water (1 scant tablespoon of lemon juice to each quart of water) immediately after scraping, to prevent discoloring. Then cook it in rapidly boiling water.

The leaves may be used as a salad or cooked as greens.

SALT. Since ancient times salt has been one of the most important seasonings in the world. One of the oldest roads in Italy was called "Via Salaria" because this important commodity was transported over it. Cakes of salt have served as currency in Abyssinia and Tibet. A daily payment of salt known as *salarium* was given to Roman soldiers, and from this word is derived our modern salary. Marco Polo mentioned the importance of salt in his report on the financial system of the Mongolian emperors. Primitive tribesmen have traded members of their families into slavery in order to acquire salt.

Common salt is sodium chloride. It occurs abundantly in the sea, in natural brines, and in a crystalline form as rock salt. It is obtained by freezing or evaporating the water of the ocean, or that of saline lakes, springs, and wells, or it is obtained by mining beds of rock salt. Table salt is finer than common salt and it is usually iodized, i.e., treated with iodine or an iodide. Many cases of goiter used to occur in inland sections because of the deficiency of iodine in the food products, and health officers attacked this problem by adding minute quantities of iodine to table salt.

Common table salt is extremely useful. It is the chief source of baking soda and caustic soda, and it is used to preserve foods, in the making of ice cream, and in the curing of meat. We are primarily concerned with its use as a seasoning for any food that might be included in the diet. It serves to stimulate the appetite and to aid digestion. It fulfills the latter function not only by increasing the amount of hydrochloric acid, but also by acting locally in the stomach to promote its secretion and to induce the conversion of pepsinogen into active pepsin. The frequency of salt tablet dispensers about gymnasiums and swimming pools, and in places where people work under very high temperatures, indicates a recognition of the worth of this commodity in combating fatigue.

The inclusion of some table salt in the diet is considered to be essential. Continued deprivation of any one of the common salts will have no seriously harmful effects so long as others are furnished in reasonable abundance in the food. If, however, all of the salts are reduced in quantity or entirely excluded from the diet, malnutrition will soon be manifested.

SALTED ALMONDS. *See* NUTS.

SALTED AND SMOKED FISH. *See* FISH.

SALTPETER. Mineral salt consisting of nitric acid and potassium used in curing meat.

SALT PORK. *See* PORK. *See also* BEANS.

SALT TONGUE. *See* TONGUE.

SAMOVAR (saam-oh-vahr; Russian, meaning self-boiler). The Samovar is a metal urn which is used for boiling water for tea after the Russian method. It stands upon a charcoal grate which holds constantly glowing coals, and a pipe, which passes vertically through the urn, exposes the water to the heat of the fire over a concentrated area inside the urn. A faucet at the bottom of the urn is used to draw off the water.

Usually a tea pot, containing concentrated tea, is set on the top of the urn to be kept hot. Some tea is poured from the teapot into glasses which are then filled with boiling water from the urn. However, sometimes fresh tea leaves are placed directly in the drinking glass and boiling water from the urn poured over them. This latter method insures freshly made tea.

The tea is drunk plain, or with the addition of a slice of lemon, or with a spoonful of jam or rum. If sugar is used, a small quantity is placed upon the drinker's tongue before each sip of tea is taken.

Samovars are usually made of copper or brass, but many are of silver. The metal frequently is embossed beautifully, and the teapot, urn, and grate are designed so as to appear to be a single, graceful unit.

SAMOVAR

The objections to the Samovar method of making tea are that the water is over boiled and also, when the teapot is used, the tea is usually allowed to steep too long. *See also* TEA.

SAMP. A food typical of eastern Long Island cookery about 1875. It was actually coarsely broken maize, which was either boiled alone and eaten with milk, or boiled in combination with beans or the seeds of other legumes and salt pork. The current equivalent might be called large hominy. It often serves as an alternate for potatoes and is generally more popular in the South where it is better known. *See also* HOMINY.

SAMSHU. A Chinese rice beer, somewhat similar to the Japanese *Saké, which see.*

SAND EEL. *See* WHITEBAIT.

SAND GROUSE. *See* GROUSE.

SAND SKATE. *See* SKATE.

SANDERLING. The sanderling is well named beach bird for sandy beaches are its favorite place of resort. No prettier sight can be imagined than a flock of these little white birds, when busily engaged in hunting for food. As the foam-topped breakers of the sea rush up the beach, and retreat to gather force for another dash, they plough up the sand, and expose for a few brief seconds multitudes of sand fleas and minute shell fish. These are the chosen food of the delicious sanderlings, and to gather their harvest, they keep pace with the progress of the waves, now advancing, now

retreating, ever ready to snatch any helpless creature less nimble than they. The law forbids their hunting.

SANDFISH. *See* WHITING.

SANDPIPER. Any of the small shore birds, distinguished from the plover by the longer bill which is flexible at the tip. Under conservation laws they may not be killed for market.

SANDROCK. *See* SKATE.

SANDWICH. The Greeks and the Romans enjoyed a wedge of meat between two slabs of bread, and so without a doubt, did the Babylonians, but it was the fourth Earl of Sandwich who made the English people sandwich-minded and gave the world a habit-forming luncheon. However, it was actually the invention of the great Jewish teacher, Rabbi Hillel.

The Jewish people during the Passover feast ritual still follow Hillel's custom of eating a sandwich made of two pieces of *matzoh* (unleavened bread) containing *mohror* (bitter herbs) and *haroseth* (chopped nuts and apple, to resemble the mortar of the Egyptians), as a reminder of Hebrew suffering before the Deliverance from Egypt. This merely by way of proof that sandwiches are as old as bread and cheese, and Romans, Danes, Saxons, and Normans must have eaten them from one end of England to the other.

Sandwiches today are (or ought to be) real food, served in a convenient form, when knives and forks are out of place. Even a tea sandwich should be good no less than dainty. Remember that sandwiches, which are in existence to assuage the pangs of hunger, should not be made paper-thin and practically tasteless. Sandwiches are not canapés, and canapés are not sandwiches.

HINTS ON PREPARATION

Traditionally, day-old bread is supposed to be used, because it is easier to cut, but if you have a sharp knife and keep it horizontal as you cut with a sawing motion, even fresh bread may easily be cut into either thick or thin slices. The slicing of bread should be done ahead of time. Then comes the spread or spreads which may be plain butter, creamed butter, one of the spreads used for canapés, or one of your own creation. These spreads should be soft enough to be spread thinly and evenly with a knife blade or spatula.

In spreading fillings, be sure all four corners of the bread are covered. This means a proper distribution of the fillings in the sandwich, so that when one is biting near the edge he will find something besides bread. The filling may be topped with crisp lettuce, cabbage (red or green), water cress, cole slaw, or other greens. These greens as well as filling should not protrude over the sides of the bread, but should be neatly trimmed.

Sandwiches prepared in advance should be kept in a cool place, wrapped in a damp towel. However, never prepare salad or fruit or any really moist-filled sandwiches far in advance lest they become soggy.

There are many types of sandwiches for service hot or cold, on plain bread, fancy bread, on toast, or on a sliced roll; open-faced, double or triple decked, pinwheel, and the loaf or layer sandwich. The pinwheel and loaf or layer sandwich may be prepared in advance and sliced to order.

Under no circumstances use stale bread unless specially requested. Where toast is used for a sandwich, butter the toast promptly after making. This preserves the moisture and keeps it from drying too quickly. Cold, dry toast should never be used. Reserve it for croutons for soup, or for pudding. Save also the bread and toast trimmings for the same purpose and for crumbing. Burned toast or scraped burned toast should never be used.

SANDWICH GARNISHINGS

The difference which garnishings make to a dish, be it plain or elaborate, is simply unbelievable until you see it. Garnishing, decorating, and trimming are to the decorative ensemble of a dish what accessories are to a dress ensemble. They should be chosen with taste, with a sure sense of their appropriateness. The shape, color, and edible texture of these accessories should always be suited to the dish on which they are used, and should harmonize with the decorative color scheme of the dish. There are so many attractive yet inexpensive garnishes for sandwiches that it would be impossible to .ist them all. A few suggestions are:

Apples. Cubed, in balls, in rings, rolled in paprika, minced parsley or chives.

Cheese. Cubed, rolled into small balls, then rolled in paprika, minced parsley or chives, or finely minced nuts.

Dill Pickles. Slivered, cut fan-like, or in diagonal thin slices.

Green Pepper. Minced or sliced in rings.

Hard-boiled Eggs. Quartered, chopped, sliced, or sieved. Sometimes blended with minced parsley, chives, chopped dill, or capers.

Horseradish. Added to cream or cottage cheese, plain or blended with prepared mustard or dressing, then formed into small balls and rolled in minced parsley or chives.

Lemon. Sliced thin then dipped in paprika, minced parsley or chives.

Lettuce. Shredded, or the whole tender heart leaves.

Mint. Fresh mint leaves or minted jelly.

Olives. Black, green, or stuffed.

Parsley. In sprig or minced.

Pimiento. Sliced or minced.

Radishes. Plain scraped or as radish roses.

Water Cress. Sprays.

HOT AND COLD SANDWICHES

Note: Unless otherwise indicated, all recipes are individual.

American Cheese and Broiled Ham Sandwich. Toast two slices of bread and cover each with thin, sliced American cheese. Place under the broiler until the cheese begins to melt—about one and a half minutes. Place a slice of broiled ham on top of one half, put the two halves together and serve immediately.

American Cheese and Fried Bacon Sandwich. Use rye bread. Cover with sliced cheese, then with thin, crisp, fried, or broiled bacon. Top the bacon with crisp lettuce and garnish with a dill pickle, cut fan-like.

Bacon and Tomato Sandwich. Broil three slices of bacon and arrange between slices of toast with crisp lettuce and sliced tomato, the latter raw or broiled with the bacon.

Baked Bean Cheesewich. Spread heated baked beans (canned or home-prepared) on a slice of toast. Top with a thin slice of American cheese and place under the broiler until the cheese melts. Cover with two strips of broiled bacon, then with crisp lettuce, and top with a second piece of toast.

Boiled Beef Sandwich. Place a slice of bread in the center of a hot plate, cover with a slice of hot boiled beef, spread with prepared horseradish, and top with a second slice of bread. Garnish with section of dill pickle.

Boiled Ham Sandwich. Place a thin slice of broiled ham between two thin slices of bread with crisp lettuce and a little mustard. Garnish with a pickle and a slice of ripe tomato

Broiled Tomato Sandwich. Wash a ripe tomato, slice thick, season with salt and pepper, and dip in oil or bacon fat. Broil on both sides and place between slices of buttered toast, previously covered with crisp lettuce.

Cape Cod Sandwich. Cover a slice of buttered hot toast with a generous layer of creamed flaked crabmeat, not too moist. Lay a slice of American cheese over this and set in the broiling oven until the cheese is melted. Top with a second piece of toast and serve immediately, cut into quarters and garnish with a slice of dill pickle.

Chicken Sandwich. Using hot sliced chicken, follow directions for roast beef sandwich (*which see*) pouring over all a gravy made from chicken stock.

Corned Beef Sandwich. Follow directions for boiled beef sandwich (*which see*). Serve with hot horseradish sauce and garnish with a slice of dill pickle.

Cottage Cheese and Marmalade Sandwich. Use brown bread. Spread one slice generously with well-drained cottage cheese seasoned with salt, pepper, and onion juice. Top with lettuce. Spread another slice of bread with orange marmalade and adjust over the first slice. Cut into four triangular sections and garnish with a small slice of tomato, topped with a slice of hard-cooked egg, again topped with a slice of stuffed olive.

Club or Three Decker Sandwich. These are made of three slices of bread which may be plain, toasted, buttered, or spread with a creamed (compounded) butter (*which see*). Serve cold or hot. They may be cut into halves, diagonally; in thirds; or quarters. Cover the first slice of bread or toast with a spread or filling, top with a second slice of bread or toast, then another spread or filling, and finally top with a third slice of bread or toast. Gently press together with the tips of the fingers and the sandwich knife, then cut as indicated above. When cut in thirds or quarters, they may be held together with toothpicks. Hot club or three-decker sandwiches should be served on hot plates. Both hot or cold club sandwiches, and in fact any kind of sandwich, should be attractively garnished before serving.

Whether or not to remove the crust from the bread depends upon the occasion. This may be done if the sandwiches are to be served for tea, but these club and three-decker sandwiches being almost a meal, many persons prefer to have the crust left on.

Denver Sandwich. Blend 1 pound of chopped (not ground) raw ham with 2 well-beaten eggs, 1 teaspoon of onion juice and a dash of pepper. Heat a tablespoon of bacon fat in a frying pan, turning the mixture into the pan and cook over a low flame for 5 minutes, stirring occasionally. Spread on slices of buttered toast, cover with further slices of toast, and serve immediately, garnishing with cole slaw. (Serves 6)

Fish Cake Sandwich. Place one or two thin freshly cooked fish cakes between two slices of bread. Cover with tomato sauce and garnish with a black olive.

Roast Beef Sandwich. Place a slice of bread, unbuttered, in the center of a hot plate. Cover with a slice of hot roast beef (three to three and a half ounces), and pour over this a rich brown gravy made from the stock of the roast. Garnish with a strip of dill pickle.

QUANTITY SANDWICH FILLINGS

Note: In the following suggestions remember that 1 cup of filling will be sufficient for about 6 sandwiches. The bread or toast used for spreading these fillings may be spread first with either plain butter or one of the compounded butters. *See* BUTTER SAUCE.

Apple and Peanut Butter Filling. To 1 cup of pared, cored, finely chopped, crisp apple add quickly 1 teaspoon of lemon juice and moisten with equal quantities of blended peanut butter and mayonnaise, about 4 tablespoons. Whole wheat bread.

Avocado Filling. To 1 cup of sieved avocado pulp add 2 teaspoons of lemon juice, ½ teaspoon of onion juice and a dash of salt and paprika. Rye bread.

Chicken Filling. Pass through the food chopper enough cold cooked chicken to make ½ cup, with 3 olives, a strip of green pepper and 2 hard-boiled eggs. Add 2 teaspoons of chili sauce, 3 tablespoons of mayonnaise and a few drops of Worcestershire sauce. Blend thoroughly. Toast.

Crabmeat Filling. To 1 cup of flaked cooked or canned crabmeat add ⅓ cup of finely minced celery, a few drops of onion juice, ⅓ cup of mayonnaise, with salt and pepper to taste. Chill before using. Any preferred bread or toast. Lobster, shrimp, tuna fish and salmon filling may be similarly prepared.

Egg Mayonnaise Filling. To the finely chopped whites of 6 hard-boiled eggs add the yolks pressed through a sieve. Season and moisten with mayonnaise (or boiled dressing). Graham bread.

Fig and Date Filling. Combine ½ cup of dates and ½ cup of figs both passed through the food chopper using the coarse knife. Add water to barely cover and cook, stirring constantly, until smooth. Add 1 tablespoon of lemon juice. Cool. Graham, brown, or nut bread.

Ham and Raw Vegetable Filling. To ½ cup of grated mixed raw vegetables (carrots, onion or chives, green pepper, celery, etc.) add ½ cup of ground ham and moisten with mayonnaise, then season with salt, pepper, and horseradish. Rye bread.

Liver and Bacon Filling. Broil 8 slices of bacon and ¼ pound of beef liver. Pass both through the food chopper with a slice of onion. Add salt, pepper and a teaspoon of Worcestershire sauce, and blend thoroughly. Rye or Boston brown bread.

Prune and Nut Filling. To ½ cup of sieved prune pulp add 1 teaspoon of lemon juice and ½ cup of ground nut-meats with a few drops of almond extract, optional. Cracked wheat or white bread.

Roquefort Cheese Filling. Combine ½ cup of Roquefort cheese, ½ cup of American cheese and 1 teaspoon of Worcestershire sauce. Season highly with pepper, lightly with salt. Any preferred bread.

Roquefort Cheese and Nut Filling. Follow directions for Roquefort cheese filling, adding ¼ cup of chopped nut-meats. Rye or Boston brown bread.

Spicy Salmon Filling. Combine ¾ cup of finely flaked canned or fresh cooked salmon with a dash of nutmeg, a few drops of lemon juice and ⅓ cup of sour cream, mayonnaise, or boiled dressing. Any preferred bread or toast.

While for every filling the type of bread is indicated, this is not a rigid ruling, and remember that all hot sandwich fillings may be served on hot waffles or freshly made toast, while all creamy sandwich fillings may be used as canapé spreads. *See also* Lunch-Box Sandwiches and Picnic.

SANDWICH NUT CHEESE. Cream or uncured Neufchatel cheese, mixed with chopped nuts.

SANDWICH TOASTER. A sandwich toaster is a device used to toast or grill completed sandwiches. *See* Electric Toaster and Toasting Fork.

SANGAREE. A type of alcoholic cocktail made of spirits and wine. The brandy, gin and whisky sangarees are all made following a basic recipe.

Sangaree (Basic Recipe)

1 jigger desired liquor (brandy, gin or whisky)
1 tsp powdered sugar
1 tbsp port wine

The liquor and sugar are placed in a cocktail shaker, cracked ice added, and the whole shaken vigorously, then strained into a cocktail glass where the wine is floated on top of the drink before serving. (Serves 1)

Sherry Sangaree

1 jigger sherry wine
1 tbsp brandy
1 tsp powdered sugar
1 tbsp port wine

The sherry, brandy and sugar are placed in a cocktail shaker and mixed as above, the port wine being floated on the finished drink in the same manner. This cocktail is an exception to the general rule that wine drinks should be mixed by stirring, not shaking. *See* Bartending; *see also* Cocktail, Alcoholic. (Serves 1)

SANGUE DI GIUDA. A red table wine made in Italy that has a blood-like appearance. *See* Wine.

SAN SEVERO. A very dry white table wine made in Italy. *See* Wine.

SANTA CLAUS or **CHRISTMAS MELON.** The newest variety and best keeper of winter melons. It is oblong in shape; the rind is green, with broad bands of slight netting. Because of its good keeping qualities, it can be bought and held until it ripens thoroughly.

Santa Claus melons of good quality have a thick, sweet, firm, juicy, light yellowish-green flesh, and a fine aroma. The melon does not attain its fine quality until fully ripe. Ripeness is indicated by a slight yellowing of the rind and softening at the blossom end. Immaturity is indicated by the green color of the rind and a general

SANTA CLAUS MELON

firmness with no indication of softness at the blossom end. Decay may be present in the form of sunken, water-soaked areas which may penetrate rind and affect the flesh. See also MELON.

SANTE CHEESE. A brand of cream cheese and farmer cheese (cottage cheese) made according to Kosher standards, manufactured in America by a special "culture process" that merely hastens the natural fermentation that takes place in milk and cream, and keeps it under control. By means of that process, all the natural flavor of the sweet, fresh milk and cream is retained.

SAP SAGO CHEESE. A small, hard, green cheese, made from sour skimmed cow's milk and flavored with a species of clover. It is shaped like a truncated cone, four inches high and three inches in diameter. A product of Switzerland.

SAPODILLA

SAPODILLA. A large evergreen tree of the West Indies and Central America, producing a luscious, apple-shaped fruit. The tree also yields chickle from which chewing gum is made.

SARATOGA CHIPS. See POTATO.
SARATOGA WATER. A mineral water from the springs at Saratoga, New York. See ALKALINE AND MINERAL WATER.
SARAWAK. This is another name for white pepper. See PEPPER.
SARDINE. Small fish of the herring family which are caught in enormous quantities off the coast of Sardinia and in other parts of the Mediterranean Sea. They are also found in the Atlantic and Pacific Oceans.

Sardines are sometimes imported in brine, but generally they are preserved in oil in small tins containing from one to two dozen fish and weighing from one-half to one pound. When fresh, sardines constitute a delicious dish and may be

SARDINE

prepared in many ways, including those applied to whitefish (which see).

The *French sardine* is a handsome, silvery little fish, distinguished by the good oil used in packing it, and by the presence of spices, truffles, pickles, and herbs, used to season it. Epicures say that no French sardine should be sold until it is at least a year old, when the spices have ripened and seasoned, and when the fish, oil, and flavoring have blended properly.

The *Portuguese sardine* is also of high quality, the fish principally used being the young pilchard, a relative of the herring family.

The *American or domestic sardine* is canned on both the East and West coasts. On the Atlantic, small herring are used, while on the Pacific various young fish, including the California sardine, are used and packed in mustard, tomato sauce, and other spices.

Norway, land of the midnight sun and midnight-blue fjords, sends us large shipments of two kinds of sardines: the *brisling* (sometimes called the sprat), and the *sild*. Norwegian sardines taste of smoke, since they are dried or smoked over special wood fires, and it is this delicious wood-smoke flavor which makes the Norwegian sardine so savory.

The *brisling* sardines have very tender flesh, which often makes it a little difficult to remove them whole from the can. But this is because the brisling is so oily and rich, with no bones to crunch, and no scales. The brisling is smoked, soft, juicy, and of a delicate texture, and a peculiar fine mellowness which makes it a savory tidbit. The *sild*, on the other hand, is firmer in its flesh or texture, and since it is the most abundant catch, the sild sardine generally costs less than the brisling, although both are packed by the same process.

Canned sardines, then, can be regarded as compact, savory mouthfuls of nourishment. There is practically no waste to a sardine, and by including it in or on the vegetable or starchy dish, we easily secure a simple, economical, pre-cooked protein food. The sardine appetizer is a smart way to start off a luncheon or dinner. Combined with cucumbers or other juicy vegetables, and slightly grilled, the sardine appetizer becomes a sophisticated morsel.

Another food with which canned sardines combine in a most pleasing manner is cheese. There are many delicious recipes for cheese-sardine tidbits, after the manner of a cheese rarebit.

BROILED SARDINES ON TOAST

1 large can sardines
¼ cup butter or margarine
¼ cup soft bread crumbs
1 cup milk
Salt and pepper
Paprika
2 hard-cooked eggs

Melt the butter in the top of a double boiler over hot water. Add the crumbs and milk and mix thoroughly. Season to taste with salt, pepper, and paprika, and keep hot, but do not let boil.

Drain the excess oil from the sardines and broil the fish until delicately brown (about 5 minutes). Place the sardines on hot buttered toast and pour the sauce over. Garnish with the sliced hard-cooked eggs. (Serves 6)

SARDINE RAREBIT

Make a Welsh rarebit (*see* CHEESE). Drain the excess oil from a can of sardines and arrange on pieces of hot buttered toast. Place under the broiler for two or three minutes. Pour the rarebit over the hot sardines and serve immediately.

SARSAPARILLA. The dried roots of a tropical American, climbing plant, from which a refreshing popular beverage is made. It is also used in medicinal preparations.

SASSAFRAS. The sassafras is an American tree belonging to the laurel family. Its bark, twigs, and roots are used for flavoring and in medicine. It is closely related to the spicebush. Highly fragrant, it was referred to as "smelling stick" by the Onondago Indians. From the leaves of the tree is derived filé powder (*which see*). The bark yields an oil that is used in making soaps and perfumes. The dried bark of its root acts as a sudorific, goes into the making of aromatic bitters, and serves as a flavoring agent.

Sassafras is an integral part of Creole cookery, and its spicy flavor adds to confections, soups, vegetables, fish, meat, game, and beverages. It is also used in making sassafras tea and root beer.

SASSENAGE CHEESE. A hard, rennet cheese made from cow's milk. It is 12 inches in diameter and 3 inches thick. It is identical with Gex and Septmoncel and is native to France.

SATSUMA. A variety of Mandarin orange. *See* ORANGE.

SATA CHEESE. Another name for Hand cheese, *which see*.

SAUCE. A liquid, or semi-liquid food which enhances the flavor and appearance of other foods. Most sauces are composed of a basic substance; such as cream, butter, or stock, and a binder, usually eggs; and flavoring.

A perfect sauce is always a triumph. A bit of this, a sprinkle of that, a dash of imagination and the most prosaic food is "saucily served." Good sauce is a most important addition to any kind of dish with which it is served.

The corporation of sauciers (saucecooks) in Paris in the reign of Louis XI ran the risks of cooking and seasoning too much or too little, or of committing gustatory crimes against discriminating palates that commended or censured certain combinations of flavors. According to our standards today, a sauce should be smooth, light without being liquid, glossy to the eye, and decided as to taste. No effort is too great when it comes to the preparation of a fine sauce. A good sauce requires precision, patience, time and watching. It also demands smelling and tasting. Obviously, unless a sauce tastes good, why bother to eat it?

The "ambrosia," which the Greeks claimed to be the food of their god , was probably only a clever way with garic. Anyone who knows about seasoning must agree that a discreet use of garlic might very well turn out something that tastes as fine as ambrosia sounds. When it comes to seasoning, however, most cooks are either too cautious or too venturesome. The cautious school sticks closely to salt and pepper (and not very much of either) only occasionally risking some dull cook book's directions for ⅛ teaspoonful of onion juice, while the amateur cooks, who fancy themselves as sauce-makers and tossers-up of exotic stews, sauces, etc., having discovered what garlic and onion can do for a sauce, completely lose their heads and use those virile seasonings in almost everything. A skilled cook strikes a happy medium.

Hints on Preparation

For delicacy, potato flour is often used in making flour sauces. It tends to reduce the saltiness caused by over-simmering, which sometimes results when ordinary flour is used. Also, it makes a smoother sauce, which is able to stand up well.

Where called for in the recipe, egg yolks should first be beaten with a teaspoonful of cold water, then a small quantity of the sauce stirred into them. Remove the saucepan from the fire and stir this egg yolk mixture into the rest of the sauce slowly, and until well blended. Return to the double boiler and stir constantly to prevent curdling, never allowing the mixture to boil.

To remove fat from a sauce, turn the heat down low, and the fat will rise to the surface when a few drops of cold water are thrown in the pan. This can easily be skimmed off with a spoon.

Only the best quality of foods should be used in sauce-making, in order to produce the best quality sauce.

Fish Sauces

Sauces for fish predicate an artist's knowledge of and respect for white sauce, parent to almost all good fish sauces. Experts agree that really good sauce making requires a maximum amount of care and cooking instinct. Sauce making should be approached with what Escoffier called "the proper reverence."

Butter sauce, flavored with mustard and a teaspoon of tarragon vinegar, for instance, masks the flavor of fat in broiled fish, such as fresh herring or mackerel, and enhances the flavor of most of the coarser-fleshed fish. One or two chopped hard-cooked eggs often give the finishing touch to the characteristic white sauce. Tiny specks of green or butter-browned parsley add color and flavor to white sauces for mackerel or halibut, and the more aromatic chervil harmonizes with sauces to be used on delicately flavored fish.

Horseradish, grated cheese, curry paste or powder, when judiciously added, lend pleasing flavor to white sauces for boiled or broiled fish.

Basic Sauces

The basic sauces are brown sauce, butter sauce, and white, or cream, sauce, all of which have infinite variations. They should be seen under their own headings.

Foamy Egg Sauce

3 eggs, separated
½ cup powdered sugar
Pinch of salt
⅛ tsp grated orange rind

Beat the egg yolks until thick and light colored. Gradually beat in the sugar and add the salt. Add the orange rind and fold in the stiffly beaten egg whites. Pile lightly in bowl and serve at once. Flavor with 2 tablespoons finely chopped preserved ginger, and 1 teaspoon ginger sirup; 2 tablespoons sherry; or 1 tablespoon brandy, if desired. (Makes approximately 1½ cups)

Foamy Yellow Sauce

½ cup butter or margarine
1 cup confectioners' sugar
1 egg, separated
¼ cup orange juice

Cream the butter until soft. Gradually beat in the sugar, then the egg yolk and orange juice. Just before serving, fold in the stiffly beaten egg white. For variety, flavor with 1 tablespoon brandy, or substitute sherry for orange juice. Serve with a steamed fruit pudding. (Makes approximately ¾ cup)

SOUR CREAM SAUCE

2 egg yolks
¾ cup sour cream
1 tsp tarragon vinegar

Beat the egg yolks lightly. Combine with the cream and vinegar and cook until thickened over hot, not boiling, water. Sweet cream with additional vinegar may be substituted for the sour cream. Suitable for such vegetables as cabbage, broccoli, etc. (Makes approximately 1 cup)

SWEET-SOUR SAUCE

½ cup water
¾ tsp cornstarch
2 tbsp sugar
¼ tsp salt
1½ tbsp lemon juice
1 tbsp butter

Bring the water to boiling point. Combine the cornstarch, sugar and salt and pour the boiling water over, stirring constantly. Return to the fire and cook until thickened. Add the lemon juice and butter. Suitable for beets and carrots. (Makes approximately ½ cup)

SAUCE BOAT. The name given to a type of pitcher used to dispense sauces, gravies, etc., at the table. It is also called a *gravy boat* because in shape it somewhat resembles the hull of a ship. See DISH.

SAUCE CHASSEUR. See BROWN SAUCE.

SAUCE TUREEN. A covered vessel, similar in design to the soup tureen, but smaller, that is used to dispense sauces, gravies, etc., at the table. It is fitted with a lid to keep the contents warm and a ladle or spoon is used to do the serving. See DISH.

SAUCEPAN. A saucepan is a simple cooking vessel with a single, long, straight handle. It is intended primarily for surface cooking of liquids, and is not well adapted for other uses. Depending on use, saucepans may be lipped or covered. They are made of glass and most forms of metal, and

in a wide range of sizes. See also KITCHEN EQUIPMENT.

SAUERBRATEN. (Sour Pot Roast) In purchasing beef from which to prepare sauerbraten, select a cut with a generous amount of fat, preferably from the rump or round.

SAUERBRATEN

4 lb rump or round of beef, in one piece
Salt and pepper
2 cups water
2 cups vinegar
2 large onions, sliced
3 bay leaves
6 sprigs celery tops
12 peppercorns
1 large carrot, sliced
¼ tsp thyme
4 whole cloves
3 tbsp sugar
⅓ cup seedless raisins
4 or 5 ginger snaps
1 cup thick sour cream

Rub the meat with salt and pepper; place in a large bowl with the water, vinegar, onions, the bay leaves tied with the celery tops, the peppercorns, carrot, thyme and cloves. Cover with doubled cheesecloth and let marinate for 3 days, 4 if a specially spicy flavor is desired, turning the meat twice a day in the marinade.

To cook, first sear the meat on all sides in a little drippings, then turn into a saucepan with the vegetables and liquor in which it was marinated. Cover and simmer very gently for at least three hours, adding more water if necessary.

Melt the sugar in a heavy frying pan, gradually add the strained liquid from the cooking pot, stirring while adding. Put in also the raisins, first plumped in a little boiling water, and the ginger snaps, crumbled. Cook about 10 minutes or until smooth and thickened. Add more seasoning if necessary and finally stir in the scalded sour cream. Pour part of the sauce over the sliced meat, and serve the remainder separately.

Usually plain boiled potatoes and a green vegetable or a dish of sauerkraut accompany sauerbraten.

SAUERKRAUT. Sauerkraut is made by placing salt between layers of finely shredded cabbage and then subjecting the whole to pressure, which bruises the cabbage and squeezes out its juices. The mass then ferments.

Fresh sauerkraut needs only to be washed in several cold waters to partially remove the brine, but old kraut should remain in cold water several hours before cooking, and should be well squeezed after being washed in several changes of cold water, then shaken and loosened. The addition of a few grains of juniper enhances the flavor. When cooking kraut, use very little water, and, if you add a ham bone, you will enjoy a delicious dish.

Sauerkraut is also delicious cooked with one or two tart apples which have been peeled and cored and sliced small. Cook the kraut only until it is thoroughly heated; it should remain crisp.

SAUERKRAUT IN SOUR CREAM

2 lb sauerkraut
½ cup boiling water
¼ cup pique seasoning
2 tart apples
¼ cup chopped onions
Bacon drippings
1 cup thick sour cream
1 bay leaf
3 sprigs parsley

Cook the sauerkraut in a saucepan with the boiling water, Pique seasoning, and the apples which have been peeled, cored, and cut in small slices. Heat the drippings and cook the onions until slightly brown. When the sauerkraut is cooked almost dry (about 30 minutes over gentle heat) stir in the onions. Scald the sour cream with the bay leaf and parsley and then discard the seasonings. Stir the cream into the sauerkraut and heat thoroughly. Serve hot. (Serves 6)

SAUERKRAUT JUICE

Season 1½ cups of sauerkraut juice with lemon juice, and chill thoroughly.

Or, mix ¾ cup of sauerkraut juice with an equal amount of tomato juice, and season with horseradish, if desired.

SAUERKRAUT WITH RAISINS

½ cup bacon drippings
2½ lb sauerkraut
1 tsp celery seed
½ cup chopped onions
½ clove garlic
½ cup boiling water
½ cup pique seasoning
3 tbsp grated raw potato
8 peppercorns
¾ cup seedless raisins

Heat the drippings in a pan and cook the onion until slightly yellow. Add the well drained sauerkraut, the celery seed, the clove of garlic mashed to a pulp, and the boiling water and pique seasoning. Mix well and cook gently for 30 minutes, stirring frequently to separate the sauerkraut. Plump the raisins in a little boiling water and squeeze them dry. Add to the sauerkraut with the grated potato and the crushed peppercorns. Cover and cook 10 minutes longer. Serve hot. (Serves 6 or 8)

SAVORY SAUERKRAUT

¼ cup ham or bacon drippings
1 qt sauerkraut
¼ tsp celery or caraway seed

Heat the fat in a skillet until golden brown. Add the sauerkraut and the seasoning. Mix well with a fork, separating the kraut. Cover and cook for 5 minutes. Serve hot. (Serves 6)

SAUSAGE. Homemakers searching for new and different items with which to add variety to their menus, are discovering more and more the convenience and adaptability of sausage. With a meat dish as the basis of every important meal, and with only four major meats available, this increase in the use of sausage indicates that women rapidly are appreciating the fact that the 20 or 30 different kinds of sausage on the market add an almost unlimited variety.

One of the most popular sausage items is pork sausage. Undoubtedly every homemaker is familiar with several uses for pork sausage links. A second and virtually new type of pork sausage is the cocktail link which is small enough to be served on a toothpick. A third type of pork sausage is "country style." The primary difference between country style pork sausage and regular sausage links is that this sausage is larger in diameter, and is in one continuous length. The fourth—and one of the most interesting types of pork sausage—is smoked pork sausage. The hardwood smoke flavor adds a tang to the taste of the sausage which is something to experience. Other sausages found in the markets are sausage bologna style; sausage cervelat style; sausage liver style; sausage Vienna style; Thuringer sausage style; dry salami, etc. and, last, but by no means least, the ever popular frankfurter.

PORK SAUSAGE

Among the hearty dishes which so admirably satisfy wind-sharpened appetites at moderate cost, pork sausage holds a high and valued place. Indeed, when we turn over the calendar leaf to November, we can safely say it is the open season for all types of sausage dishes.

Sausage may be bought in either bulk form or in individual links protected by sanitary transparent casings. These links may be large, medium, or small, but whatever the size, be sure the sausage is pure pork. For not all sausage is choice pork and nothing else, but may be composed of blended pork and cereal. So select a well-known brand for sausage quality and flavor.

What makes one sausage taste better than another is the quality of the meat, the right moderate proportion of fat to lean meat, and the character and blending of the spices. Sausages containing too much fat are likely to be greasy, and in sausage containing too many spices, the meat will be peppery and coarse in flavor. Carefully seasoned and freshly prepared, good sausage is rushed to the dealer in modern refrigerator cars and is a safe, saving, and satisfying winter meal.

Probably the best way in which to cook and serve sausage is always to broil or pan-fry the links after the manner of broiled steaks or chops. Prick each sausage with a fork, place it on the broiling rack which is adjusted to 4 inches beneath a moderate flame, and broil about 12 minutes, turning once. Serve on a very hot platter, if desired on a bed of mashed potatoes, or spinach, or purée of peas, etc.

For pan-fried sausage, have the pan very hot. Lay in the sausages and turn to brown on all sides.

Since sausage meat is solid protein and fat, it requires the accompaniment of starch and a mineral or watery food to make a complete meal. Potatoes, rice, macaroni, spaghetti, noodles, and bread may be used for the starch; and any green vegetables, particularly any members of the cabbage family, or apples, cranberries, or other tart fruits, seem "naturals" with sausage meals. Sausages and pancakes make a royal breakfast.

FRANKFURTER SAUSAGE

It is about 100 years since the wienerwurst, frankfurter, "hot dog," whatever you choose to call it, first came to this country. The deliciousness of the frankfurter is due largely to the fact that its casing is a natural meat product. While the casing's function is primarily that of giving the sausage meat the proper size and shape, it also is the only method of achieving proper smoking and complete smoke vapor permeation of the entire sausage during the smoking process. When natural casings are used there is no hard coating of albumen on the outside of the meat, and the sausages do not have to be skinned before eating.

The great-grandfather of all hot dogs was beloved by man 3,000 years ago. It was a plain sausage, without spice. It lacked the fire and hot temper of the present breed. It was called *salsus* from the Latin word for salted.

Greek writers after Homer frequently referred to *oryae* which was their name for the ancient forbear of the hot dog. Constantine the Great, as Emperor of Rome, considered it too good for common people.

In the Middle Ages sausage artists came into their own. They experimented with spices and produced a wide variety of tricky meats, all blood brothers of the modern hot dog. In many cases these progenitors of the American favorite took on the names of the cities where they were first introduced. The *wienerwurst*, which is the foreign name of the hot dog, took its name from the city of Vienna, or Wien as it is called by natives. One school of genealogists insists that Frankfort-am-Main was its birthplace, but any honest resident of Frankfort, to this day, still calls it *wienerwurst*.

BOLOGNA

One of the most popular and varied types of domestic sausage. Originally, the sausage came from Bologna, Italy, but domestic packers have rung a number of changes on the original model. Beef bologna is made of beef, veal, and pork trimmings which are chopped very finely, spiced, and stuffed into casings which may be small or large. Ham bologna is made of pork shoulder or shoulder butt. Sometimes ham bologna has cubes of meat in it.

It may be eaten cold, or substituted for frankfurters in any recipe. Chunks of bologna baked with beans make an interesting variation to salt pork.

BRATWURST

This is made of finely chopped, lean fresh pork trimmings, highly seasoned with spices, such as nutmeg, ginger, cloves, and mace, and herbs like sage. It is stuffed into small hog casings, and sold in small links. This sausage goes well served with boiled cabbage, spinach, mashed potatoes, buttered kale, mashed turnips, or onions. It must be cooked and served hot.

BRAUNSCHWEIGER

Made by the same method as the liverwurst, this sausage has a little more liver in it and spreads easily on sandwiches, crackers, or toast. It has a trifle more spice, a bit less meat, and is a fine choice for frying.

It is made in two kinds: fresh or smoked. Either kind is good with griddle cakes, waffles, or pancakes. It is a favorite on the cold cuts platter, and is used as a spread, in some hot dishes, and as a stuffing for roast fowl, fresh pork, crown of lamb, veal, and baked stuffed potatoes, green pepper, squash or kale.

CAMBRIDGE SAUSAGE

A sausage formerly made in England. This is a beef sausage with a small amount of pork in it, a very little seasoning, and almost no spice. It is a dry, chewy meat of pinkish tones, with very little fat. The skins are tender and must be carefully pricked with a fork before frying or broiling, or they will stick and tear.

CERVELAT

The generic name of a number of sausages which resemble salami in their preparation. The meat is generally more finely chopped, and hog or beef casings are used. Cervelat is a smoked sausage. *Thuringer* sausage is usually a fresh cervelat. *Holstein* is coarsely chopped and shaped into a horseshoe. *Farmer* sausage is like Holstein, but in straight lengths. *Goteborg* is a Swedish cervelat which is coarsely chopped, salty, and heavily smoked.

HILDESHEIMER SAUSAGE

A pure pork sausage, made of 65 percent belly fat to make it soft and spreadable, and 35 percent pork liver, lightly spiced. This sausage is used for sandwiches, canapés, and snacks. It is also used to garnish mashed potatoes, sauerkraut, mashed turnips, cabbage cooked in any style—especially red cabbage with apple, mashed squash, etc.

LIVERWURST

As its name implies, liverwurst sausage should be made with liver—only pork liver and pork meat. Some makers use beef in place of pork pieces, and some use a liver other than hog's, but it is pork liver and pork meat that make the true liverwurst. This sausage is highly seasoned with salt, pepper, cardamom, and a secret mixed seasoning specially made for liverwurst. After thorough mixing and blending the casings are filled and then exposed to hickory-wood smoke for three hours or more.

It is best served with cabbage, mashed potatoes, mashed turnips, or as an appetizer, when sliced thin, or spread on bread, toast, or crackers. It is sold both fresh and smoked.

An excellent substitute for paté de foie gras may be made by mashing good quality liverwurst with mayonnaise to make a smooth, spreadable mixture. Serve heaped in a bowl with crackers for a cocktail snack.

METTWURST

Made with chopped fine pork and liver, cooked with spices, this sausage is put into beef casings and then smoked. It is a popular spread for sandwiches, canapés, and the like. It is also used to accompany sauerkraut, cabbage, mashed potatoes, mashed turnips, etc.

Muenchner Weisswurst

A white sausage made of pork and veal, but mostly veal, slightly spiced, and very popular broiled, baked, or steamed.

Salami

The type of dry sausage called salami is made in many countries. There are Italian salamis, Hungarian, and German, with variations of each. Italian salami is made of two-thirds pork and one-third beef which is chopped finely and moistened with red wine or grape juice. It is highly seasoned with garlic and other spices and then stuffed into beef casings. This sausage is air-dried, and with proper attention will keep for years without refrigeration.

German and Hungarian salamis are smoked instead of air-dried and are less highly spiced than Italian salami.

Bologna Tiers

1 package (3 oz) cream cheese
2 tbsp cream
1 tbsp fresh grated horesradish
½ lb thinly sliced bologna

Mix the cheese, cream, and horseradish thoroughly, and spread slices of bologna with this mixture. Stack 6 slices, wrap them in waxed paper, and set them in the refrigerator to chill. Cut into 6 pie-shaped pieces. Serve as an hors d'oeuvre.

Barbecued Frankfurters with Bacon

1 doz. frankfurters
Slices of broiled bacon
1 tbsp butter
½ onion, chopped
½ tsp pepper
4 tsp sugar
1 tsp mustard
1 tsp paprika
½ cup catsup
¼ cup vinegar
⅓ cup water
4 tsp Worcestershire sauce
1 tsp tabasco

Melt the butter, add the onion and cook until clear but not browned. Add all remaining ingredients except the frankfurters and bacon and bring to boiling point. With a sharp knife cut a 3-inch slit in each frankfurter and place in a shallow baking pan, slit side up. Pour the sauce over and bake in a moderate oven (350° F.) about 25 minutes, basting once or twice with the sauce. Garnish with broiled bacon. (Serves 6)

Frankfurter Casserole

1 lb frankfurters
Mild sliced onions
1 can tomato soup
½ cup hot water

Arrange the frankfurters in a casserole or baking dish. Fill up the dish with onions. Pour the blended soup and water over all. Cover and cook in a moderate oven (350° F.) until the onions are thoroughly tender, about 1 hour, after which remove the cover and slightly brown the surface. Usually the seasoning of the frankfurters themselves are enough to season the entire dish. (Serves 4 or 6)

Frankfurter Platter

6 tenderized frankfurters
6 slices canned pineapple
2 tbsp butter
1½ cups cooked string beans, sliced
1½ cups canned or fresh cooked corn
Salt and pepper
6 thin squares toast

Grill the frankfurters and sauté the pineapple in the butter. Combine the beans and corn; season and heat, then pile in the center of a large platter. Surround with the toast, each square topped with a slice of pineapple and a frankfurter. (Serves 6)

Frankfurters and Caraway Cabbage

4 cups shredded cabbage
¼ cup melted butter or margarine
¾ cup buttered crumbs
1 tsp caraway seeds
1 doz frankfurters

Cook the cabbage 7 or 8 minutes in a very little water, adding a dash each of salt and sugar. Drain and add the melted butter. Pile in the center of a serving dish. Sprinkle with the crumbs and caraway seeds. Serve with the frankfurters grilled in a slightly greased frying pan. (Serves 6)

FRANKFURTERS WITH SAUERKRAUT

Partially fill a casserole with sauerkraut, and add a layer of frankfurters, and then another layer of sauerkraut. Cover, and bake in a moderate oven (350° F.) about 25 minutes.

FRANKFURTER SAVORY

Broil cocktail frankfurters, and slit each halfway down on one side. Spread them with a mixture of horseradish and mustard, using ½ teaspoon of horseradish to each tablespoon of mustard. Serve on toothpicks.

LIVER SAUSAGE COUNTRY STYLE

6 tbsp vacuum packed corn
6 tbsp chopped liver sausage
6 eggs
1 tsp salt
⅛ tsp pepper
1 tsp minced parsley
1 cup cream
2 tsp grated Parmesan cheese

Arrange in each of 6 individual buttered baking dishes first a tablespoon of the corn, then a tablespoon of the sausage. Break an egg on top. Sprinkle with the salt, pepper and parsley, and pour in the cream. Sprinkle the surface with the cheese and bake in a moderate oven (350° F.) about 20 minutes. (Serves 6)

SAUSAGE BAKED WITH SWEET POTATOES

3 cups sliced cooked sweet potatoes
1 tsp salt
⅛ tsp pepper
1 cup sliced tender apples or crushed pineapple
½ cup hot water or pineapple juice
1 lb pork sausage meat

Arrange the potatoes in a shallow greased baking dish, sprinkling them with half the salt and pepper. Cover with the apples or pineapple and pour in the hot water or pineapple juice. Season the saus-age meat with the remaining salt and pepper. Form into thin cakes of even size and lay these on top of the fruit, leaving a little space between the cakes. Cover and bake in a moderate oven (350° F.) about 30 minutes, then remove the cover and press the meat down into the fruit and potatoes. Return to the oven and complete the baking, uncovered, browning quickly. (Serves 4 or 6)

SAUSAGE CAKES WITH APPLE

1½ lb pork sausage meat
4 apples
⅓ cup brown sugar

Shape the sausage meat into small flat cakes. Core the apples and cut into slices. Arrange the sausage in the center of a baking pan, placing the slices of apple around. Sprinkle with the brown sugar and bake in a moderately hot oven (375°–400° F.) 25 to 30 minutes, basting 2 or 3 times during the cooking with the liquid in the pan or with a little melted sausage fat and hot water. (Serves 6)

SAUSAGE, OYSTER AND MACARONI CASSEROLE

3 cups uncooked elbow macaroni
1 lb pork sausages
½ cup chopped onion
2 cans cream of mushroom soup
1½ tsp salt
¼ tsp pepper
⅛ tsp cayenne pepper
1 cup milk
½ cup chopped parsley
1 pt small oysters and liquid

Cook macaroni in boiling salted water until tender. Drain and keep hot. Cut the sausages into 1-inch pieces. Fry slowly until lightly browned. Remove the pieces of sausage and pour off half the fat. Add the onion and cook slowly in the fat until golden brown. Add the soup, seasonings, milk, and parsley. Cook, stirring occasionally, until thoroughly heated. Add the oysters and half the sausages. In a 3-quart casserole, make alternate layers of the cooked macaroni, and oyster-sausage sauce. Top with the remaining sausages. Bake in a moderate oven (350° F.) for 30 minutes. Serve very hot. (Serves 8)

SAUSAGE AND POTATO BALLS

Shape sausage meat into 1-inch balls, and coat these with mashed potatoes. Roll them in 1 egg diluted with 1 tablespoon of water, and then in sifted and seasoned breadcrumbs. Repeat the coating, rolling the balls in each again. Allow them to dry, and then cook them in deep fat (390° F.) until they become brown. Serve on toothpicks.

SAUSAGE PRUNE LOAF

1½ cups uncooked prunes
1½ lb pork sausage
1 large sweet pepper
1 cup sliced celery
2½ cups cooked rice
2 tbsp Worcestershire sauce
1 tbsp Angostura bitters
Salt and pepper
2 eggs

Scald the prunes; drain, remove the pits, and pass the fruit through the food chopper using the medium knife. Fry together the sausage meat, the pepper (seeds and fiber removed and pepper passed through food chopper), also the sliced celery, until the sausage is cooked through but not crisp. Drain off any excess fat. Add the prunes, rice, seasonings, flavorings and slightly beaten eggs. Blend all thoroughly. Pack in a greased loaf pan and bake in a moderately hot oven (375° F.) about 40 minutes, after which reduce the heat and continue baking 25 minutes longer at about 300° F. (Serves 6)

SAUSAGE SCRAPPLE

½ lb pork sausage meat
2½ cups meat broth or water
1 cup corn meal
1 tsp salt
¼ tsp pepper
1 tsp poultry seasoning

Cook the sausage meat in a large frying pan about 5 minutes, stirring and tossing it about in the pan with a fork. Drain off any excess fat. Add the liquid, bring to boiling point, then sift in the corn meal slowly, stirring constantly, and cook until the mixture thickens. Season, cover, and cook very slowly for 15 minutes. Turn into

a small, previously wet, loaf pan. Cool, chill, then slice and brown in a little hot fat. Serve with tomato sauce or brown gravy. (Serves 6)

SAUTE. A French culinary term meaning to fry quickly in a small amount of fat. This method should be applied only to tender pieces of meat, fish, vegetables, and sometimes fruits.

SAUTERNE. One of the more popular white table wine types. In France, sauternes are made in the Sauterne district and are one of the white Bordeaux (which see) wines. Sauternes are made in other countries as well, and a great variety of grapes are used. In taste, they range from the dry to the very sweet, dessert wine class. They are full-bodied, and golden in color. They are all served chilled. The drier types are especially suited for table use with white meats and seafood.

Haut Sauterne. The commercial designation for a sweet sauterne. These wines are served chilled and may be used as either a dessert wine or a white table wine (*see* WINE).

Château Sauterne. A designation frequently given to the very sweet sauternes that are primarily used as dessert wines, though some palates will accept them as table wines.

Château Yquem (d'Yquem). A sweet sauterne that is acknowledged to be the best in the field. Many epicures even rate it as superior to champagne. It is made only at the Château Yquem vineyards in France.

SAVORY. This herb of the mint family is dried and used in cookery. It was once known as the "bean herb" because it is the perfect seasoning for all members of the bean-pea-lentil family. It is used alone or in combination with other herbs to season meats or meat dishes. It will also add a subtle flavor to salads, vegetable cocktails, soups, and scrambled eggs, and it tends to refresh left-over dishes. Try substituting it for the overworked sage in stuffings for meat and poultry and in meat balls, stews, and gravies. One tablespoonful of savory will add a pleasant flavor to poultry stuffing.

SAVOY CABBAGE. A kind of cabbage, *which see.*

SCALD. To heat a liquid over hot water or direct heat to a temperature just below the boiling point. Milk is scalded when a thin skin forms on the surface. No bubbles form, and the temperature is thus below that of simmering, *which see.*

SCALE. (I) A scale is a device used to measure weight. Though a great many different types of scales have been developed since the instrument was originated in 5000 B.C., there are only two kinds that are commonly used in kitchens today.

Beam Balance. Scales of this type have a removable pan, used to hold the material to be weighed, resting on one end of a system of linked levers. A sliding weight is used to balance the material, being shifted until the beam is level. This weight may be supplemented by others that are placed in a pan that is linked with the levers. On more expensive models, the weight may be indicated by a pointer moving across a card, but usually the weight is determined by shifting the weights until the beam is level and then noting the position of the weights. These scales have provisions for adjustment, and are highly accurate.

Spring Scale. A typical kitchen spring scale has a movable platform set on top of a box that contains the weighing mechanism. The object to be weighed is placed on the platform, and the amount by which it compresses a spring within the box is translated into pounds by a pointer moving across a dial on the front side of the mechanism. Scales of this type are more inexpensive than the beam balance type, and, as a general rule, not nearly as accurate. They are more apt to wear out and get out of adjustment, in time, than the former type. They are, however, entirely satisfactory for kitchen work.

The better spring scales have an adjusting screw or knob that can alter the position of the pointer. This adjusting screw is very useful in kitchen work, for it enables the user to compensate for the weight of the containers used to hold food. The container is first set on the scale, empty, and the pointer is turned back to the zero mark. When the full container is later weighed, the scale then gives only the weight of the contents. If the scale does not have this feature, the weight of the empty container must be learned and subtracted from future weighings.

Scales of both types should be checked periodically with known weights to make certain that they are accurate. There are many factors such as a change in temperature, that can put a scale out of adjustment, even though it is not used, especially the more delicate ones. For this reason, a scale should not be assumed to be accurate unless it has been checked in a reasonable period.

See also WEIGHTS AND MEASURES.

SCALE. (II) A thin, flat, horny, membranous or bony outgrowth of the skin of various fish.

SCALE. (III) To remove the scales, as from a fish. *See* FISH.

SCALLION. A bulbless onion with a long thick neck, like a leek. *See* ONION and SHALLOT.

SCALLOP. (I) To bake in a dish. The term is applied to the combining of cooked meat, vegetables, or both, or to raw fruit, fish, meat, or vegetables alone or in combination, in a casserole, baking dish, ramekin, etc., with sauce, or juice, slightly thickened. Scallop shells were first used for this method of cooking.

SCALLOPS. (II) Without doubt the most fascinating life history among our marine mollusks is that of the common or shallow water scallop. Of the four species of scallop found on the Atlantic Coast, only two are of commercial importance in New England, the shallow water scallop and the deep sea or giant sea scallop.

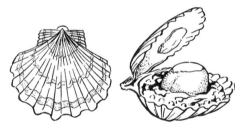

SCALLOPS

The scallop shell consists of two valves of equal curvature joined together on the dorsal edge by means of a thin V-shaped ligament in the central part of the hinge which tends to keep the valves apart like a piece of rubber in the hinge of a door. The shell is well adapted to the mobile life of the scallop; being light in weight, it is suitable for movement through the water, while its outline offers the least resistance in swimming.

The scallop has a well-developed system consisting of gills, digestive, nervous, circulatory, excretory systems, and reproductive organs. It has many well-developed eyes, brilliantly colored with blue and brown pigments. They appear to be keenly sensitive to any change in light and shade, possibly observing the approach of an enemy by its shadow or movement in the water.

The digestive system of the scallop is comparatively simple. From the mouth, its food opens into a short gullet which leads into a gourd-shaped stomach, thence into the intestines and liver, and finally ends in the posterior portion of the shell.

The scallop has a blood system extending over the whole body and through the gills, where the blood is aerated. The heart is a three-chambered organ which pumps blood through the different arteries to all parts of the body, whence it is returned through the nervous system to the gills, and finally back to the heart. The nervous system of the scallop is quite complicated.

The normal life of the scallop is from 20 to 26 months, relatively few passing the two year limit. About the first of March, the adult scallops begin to die. In the natural scallop beds, the majority of the scallops are caught by this time, while most of the remainder die a natural death before May.

The large muscle which opens and closes the shell is the only part which is used for food and constitutes but a small part of the entire animal within the shell. The rest of the animal is thrown away.

One bushel of average scallops will yield 2½ to 3 quarts of meats, and an average opener can open 8 to 10 gallons a day. The greater part of the scallop catch is taken by dredging, which is the most profitable method. The dredge consists of an iron framework about 3 x 1½ feet with a netting bag attached which will hold from one to two bushels of scallops. Sailboats or power boats towing from 6 to 10 dredges cruise the scallop grounds.

HINTS ON PREPARATION

The best scallops are cream-colored and not white. Bay or Cape scallops are small, while sea scallops are considerably larger. Usually, scallops are purchased already shelled from the fish dealer's ice chest. Their price may seem a bit high by the pound, but it must be recalled that every bit of the opened scallops is edible meat. You may dip them in egg and crumbs, then sauté them in butter, or fry them in deep

fat. A tartare sauce is usually served with scallops. Chives or minced onions, and either minced olives or pickles make this sauce savory. Scallops are in season during the "R" months.

Scallops combine well with other seafoods and are excellent by themselves, as a scallop casserole or a la poulette (a delicately tangy cream sauce).

Cold cooked scallops may be made into a delicious fish salad. Cut the scallops in small bits and dress with French dressing or mayonnaise.

DEVILED SCALLOPS

1½ lb scallops
3 tbsp butter
1½ tbsp prepared mustard
½ tsp salt
Dash of cayenne
½ cup liquid drained from scallops
Few drops tabasco
1 tsp minced parsley
½ tsp onion juice
Buttered crumbs

Pick over the scallops, add ½ cup of water and heat to boiling point. Drain, reserving the liquid, and chop the scallops coarsely. Cream together the butter and mustard, add the seasonings, and the ½ cup of reserved liquid, with the tabasco, parsley, and onion juice. Combine with the scallops and let stand for 1 hour to marinate, then turn the whole into a shallow baking dish or into scallop shells. Dot with buttered crumbs and bake in a moderately hot oven (375° F.) about 20 minutes. Serve immediately. (Serves 6)

FRIED SCALLOPS

Pick over and drain scallops. Dip first into crumbs, then into beaten egg, then into crumbs again. Sauté in a small amount of butter or other fat, or fry in deep hot fat. Drain on soft crumpled paper, and serve with tartare sauce and broiled bacon, if desired.

MINCED SCALLOPS AU GRATIN

1½ lb scallops
1 tsp grated onion
½ cup white wine
½ tsp salt

Dash of cayenne
3 tbsp butter or margarine
3 tbsp flour
1 cup hot scallop stock
½ cup heavy cream, scalded
½ cup grated American cheese
2 hard-cooked eggs, chopped
½ cup buttered crumbs

Drain the scallops, reserving any liquid. Rinse quickly in cold water and chop fine but do not grind. Place in a saucepan with the liquid, grated onion, wine, salt, and cayenne and simmer for 10 minutes, then drain, reserving all liquid for sauce. If scallops are dry a very little water may be added.

Melt the butter in a saucepan or double boiler. Add the flour, and, when smoothly blended, the combined stock and cream. Stir constantly until smooth and thick, then stir in the cheese a little at a time, blending very thoroughly to prevent any lumping. Add the eggs and chopped scallops and turn the mixture into a buttered shallow baking dish or into buttered shells. Top with the crumbs and brown in a hot oven (400° F.) about 15 minutes. Serve immediately. (Serves 6)

SCALLOPS EN BROCHETTE

These are not only delicious, but if one is the fortunate possessor of metal skewers with ornamental hilts, like swords or daggers, they make a spectacular luncheon or supper dish.

Cut large scallops into half inch slices of uniform shape and size; if small, they may be used whole. Sauté mushroom caps in butter until slightly browned. Slice cooked Virginia ham, not too thinly, and cut into pieces to match the scallops and mushrooms in size. Arrange on the skewers, first a scallop, then ham, then mushroom, continuing the operation until the skewers are filled almost to the point. Dip the filled skewers into melted butter seasoned with finely minced parsley and Worcestershire sauce, turning about until well covered. Roll in fine crumbs, and broil, turning and basting with the remaining butter, until well browned. Serve on long strips of plain or French toast, garnishing with watercress or parsley, and sections of lemon. The pieces may be slipped from the skewers before serving or served on the skewer.

SCALLOPED SCALLOPS

1½ lb scallops
¼ cup butter
4 cups soft bread crumbs
1¼ tsp salt
1 tsp grated onion
1 tsp finely minced parsley
1 tsp finely minced chives
1 tbsp lemon juice

If large scallops are used, quarter or slice them. Melt the butter, add all remaining ingredients, and toss together thoroughly. Arrange in a generously buttered baking dish alternate layers of scallops and the crumb mixture, having crumbs for the top layer. Bake in a hot oven (400° F.) about 20 minutes, or until delicately browned. (Serves 6)

SCENTED TEA. See POUCHONG; see also TEA.

SCHABZIEGER CHEESE. A hard, skimmed-milk cheese made in Switzerland. At first it is green in color, due to melilot green leaves which are cooked into it in making, but it turns brown with age. It is used chiefly as grated cheese in cooking.

SCHAMSER CHEESE. A rennet cheese, made from the skimmed milk of cows. It is eighteen inches in diameter, five inches thick, and weighs 40 to 45 pounds. It is also known as Rheinwald and is made in Switzerland.

SCHAPZIEGER CHEESE. A hard skimmed-milk cheese of Switzerland, generally used for flavoring soups or grated in cooking.

SCHAUM TORTE. A pastry made of meringue in the form of layers with crushed fruit between.

SCHAUM TORTE

4 egg whites
1 cup granulated sugar
1 tsp vinegar
1 tsp flavoring extract

Sift the sugar, before measuring it. Fine powdered sugar such as is used for fruits will make a smoother meringue. Beat the egg whites slowly until stiff. Beat in the sugar, adding in four parts, and beating well after each addition. Beat in the vinegar and the flavoring.

Place a sheet of heavy white paper on a cookie sheet. Draw two 8-inch circles on the paper. Drop the meringue by spoonfuls into the circles, shaping the edges and smoothing the top into attractive swirls. Bake in a very slow oven (300° F.) for 30 minutes, leaving the oven door slightly ajar. Turn off the oven at the end of the time and allow the meringue to cool in the oven for another 30 minutes.

Carefully remove from the paper and place one layer on a serving plate. Spread it with crushed sweetened fruit, strawberries, raspberries, peaches, or whatever is desired. Place the second layer on top and garnish the top with additional fruit. Slice for serving like a cake. (Serves 8 or 10)

SCHLOSS, SCHLOSSKASE, or **CASTLE CHEESE.** This is a cheese of the Limburg type. It is a soft-cured rennet cheese, about four by two by two inches, and is wrapped in tinfoil for marketing. It is produced in the northern part of Austria.

SCHOONER. To a generation now passing, the expression "schooners passing over the bar" was not a line of nautical verse, but had reference to a type of beer vessel now virtually extinct. The schooner is, or was, a beer goblet of generou· capacity. It belonged to a not-too-distant era when a nickel was a lot of money and the free lunch assumed the proportions of a seven course dinner. It, like the growler (*which see*) fell under the impact of changing economics and different customs. The physical form of the schooner has survived in smaller editions, but the expression has virtually passed from the living language. *See* GLASSWARE; *see also* BEER and STEIN.

SCHWARZENBERG CHEESE. A rennet cheese, made from the partly skimmed milk of cows, in southern Bohemia and western Hungary.

SCOLYMUS. This member of the salsify family is also called Spanish oyster plant, Spanish salsify, or golden thistle. It is prepared like salsify, *which see.*

SCONE. A typically Scotch hot bread or cake, baked on a griddle or in the oven. The original Scotch scone is made as follows:

SCONES

2 cups wheat meal or flour
1 tsp cream of tartar
1 tsp baking soda
½ tsp salt

2 tsp sugar, optional
½ cup butter
¾ cup light cream or rich milk

The true Scot would use wheaten meal. Whole wheat flour will prove a good substitute, or bread flour may be used. Sift or thoroughly mix (depending on whether whole wheat or bread flour is used) the flour with the cream of tartar, soda, salt and sugar, if used. Work in the butter with the tips of the fingers or cut it in with the blades of two knives. When the mixture looks like coarse meal, moisten to a light, tender dough with the cream or milk (slightly more will be required with whole wheat flour than with white flour). Divide into two portions. Pat out on a floured board into a round about ¾ inch thick and cut across in both directions making 4 pie-shaped sections. Place on a lightly greased baking sheet and bake in a hot oven (400° F.) 12 to 15 minutes, or bake on a preheated greased griddle. In the latter instance the dough may be rolled a little thinner than for oven baking. Split, butter generously, and serve with or without jam.

Oven-baked scones may have the surface brushed with beaten egg or milk to give a rich color. Scones may be baked together as four and split after baking, or they may be separated before baking. Griddle scones must be turned as soon as well raised in order to cook through thoroughly. Oven-baked scones may be turned if desired, or may be baked as originally laid on the pan.

SCOOP. To ladle out, to remove or excavate with a scoop; to hollow a fruit, a potato, etc., in order to fill it up with other food material.

SCORE. A culinary term meaning to mark a food—a fish, meat, fowl, etc.—with small cut , notches, lines or stripes, sometimes to prevent the food from curling, folding, or crumpling, and other times to make designs which tend to make the food more tempting and appetizing in appearance.

SCOTCH AND WATER. The traditional British highball made of scotch whisky and plain water served at room temperature. *See also* HIGHBALL.

SCOTCH GROUSE. *See* GROUSE.

SCOTCH WHISKY. *See* WHISKY.

SCRAPER. A scraper is a piece of stiff but soft material, usually rubber or a plastic, so shaped that it may be used to scrape food from plates and cooking vessels prior to washing. The material has to be stiff enough to be effective, but still cannot be so hard that it would scratch. *See also* KITCHEN EQUIPMENT.

SCRAPPLE. *See* PORK.

SCROD. A young codfish, (*which see*).

SCUP. *See* PORGY.

SCUPPERNONG. An American grape. A variety of sweet grape cultivated in the southern United States. It is also a white wine made from the scuppernong grape.

SEA BASS. *See* BASS.

SEA COCONUT. *See* COCO DE MER.

SEA COW. Another name for the manatee, (*which see*).

SEA CUCUMBER. *See* TREPANG.

SEA FOOD. A general term applied to any kind of fish from the sea, including the shellfish and crustaceans.

SEA FOOD COCKTAIL SAUCE. *See* MAYONNAISE.

SEA KALE. *See* CABBAGE.

SEA LETTUCE. A green seaweed, sometimes used for food.

SEA PHEASANT. Another name for the pintail duck. *See* DUCK.

SEA PERCH. *See* BASS.

SEA ROBIN. *See* RED GURNARD.

SEA SWALLOW. *See* RED GURNARD.

SEA TROUT. *See* WEAKFISH.

SEA WOLF. *See* BASS.

SCORING FISH

SEAR. As applied to cookery, especially to the cooking of meat, to sear is to expose the food to a high temperature in the oven, thus producing a firm coagulation, a kind of caramelization of the outer layers. The natural juices of the meat are almost completely retained within the crust thus formed.

Formerly it was believed that roasts should first be seared and then the cooking finished at a lower temperature in order to prevent the escape of the juices. It is now known that this method of cooking is wasteful since it causes a greater shrinkage in weight than when the meat is cooked at a constant lower temperature, and that far from making the meat juicier, it actually dries out the piece. *See also* ROAST.

SEASONING. Seasoning refers to the addition of condiments, spices, sauces, dressings (all of *which see*), and other stimulants to foodstuffs. Certain seasonings increase the palatibility of certain foods, but the cook must be careful to avoid underseasoning or overseasoning. The seasoning is added not that it may impart its own flavor to the dish, but rather to enhance the flavor of the principal ingredient and to add an indistinguishable aroma.

The number of flavors that may be achieved through seasoning is limitless. Each seasoning agent has its particular flavor, and these are modified when used in combination with others. Even a distinctly disagreeable flavor can become appealing when combined with stronger ones. Then again, a pleasant flavor can become unpleasant if used in too great a quantity.

Seasoning directions must often of necessity be flexible, the amount to be used to be determined by the tastes of the cook. This is particularly understandable in the case of salt. The salt used in different localities varies considerably in taste and 'saltiness." Hence the frequent occurence in recipes of the expression "salt and pepper to taste."

The aromatic oils of spices and herbs are strong, and these should, generally speaking, be used sparingly. The dried herbs are about four times as strong as fresh ones; one-quarter of a teaspoonful of the dried products is usually sufficient to season four servings of a dish. Don't use more than two highly flavored seasonings in any one meal.

To achieve the best flavor, powder dried herbs and chop fresh ones finely before using them. Spices and herbs should be blended with food during its preparation and not simply served with it. Herbs tend to lose their flavor during long cooking periods, so it is best to add them during the final hour of cooking. To season cold salads or beverages, let herbs or spices stand in them for several hours or even overnite.

All spices and herbs should be kept dry in tightly-covered glass containers, and they should not be exposed to more heat than is necessary. Keep them on a low shelf rather than a high one.

For more particular information about spice and herb seasonings see them under their individual listings.

SEC. A French word meaning dry, i.e., the absence of sugar in a beverage. However, it means exactly the opposite in the case of champagne (*which see*).

SELTZER WATER. A highly effervescent mineral water from Nieder Selters, in the Wiesbaden district of Germany. The term is also applied to artificially aerbonated waters of a similar lively effervescence, especially sold in siphon bottles. The long and lively duration of the effervescence makes these waters well suited for beverage use. See ALKALINE AND MINERAL WATER and AERATED WATER; *see also* SIPHON BOTTLE.

SELTZER WATER BOTTLE. A type of siphon bottle (*which see*) in which seltzer and similar carbonated waters are commonly distributed.

SELTZOGENE MACHINE. A name applied generally to early devices used to manufacture carbonated or soda water (*which see*). They generated a gas by means of a chemical reaction and mixed it with water. The name stems from the resemblance of carbonated water to seltzer water (*which see*), a naturally effervescent liquid. The term is now in disuse and the machines to which it was applied have been supplanted by more modern mechanisms. See SIPHON BOTTLE and SODA FOUNTAIN.

SEMI-FERMENTED TEA. Better known as Oolong tea. See TEA.

SEMOLINA. A name having two applications. In France it denotes the hard, central substance of the wheat grains which is retained in the bolting machine after the finer portions have passed through; but in Italy the word is used to denote the finer portion itself, consisting of fine, hard granules rounded by grinding. The larger sizes contain much gluten, and may be used to thicken soups, gravies, and sauces since the granules swell in water. When the grinding and sifting process is carried still further, the starch granules are obtained in the fine powder which constitutes flour.

Semolina is used extensively in the manufacture of what are called alimentary pastes. *See* PASTES.

SEMILLON. A white table wine of the sauterne (*which see*) type, made from Semillon grapes. It may be either dry or semi-sweet.

SEPTMONCEL CHEESE. A hard rennet cheese of France made from cow's milk. Its manufacture is identical with Roquefort, and it resembles both Gex and Sassenage. It is also known as "Jura blue."

SERRA DA ESTRELLA CHEESE. A Portuguese cheese made from the milk of sheep. It is soft, and has a pleasant, acid taste. It is 10 inches in diameter, 2 inches thick, and weighs about 5 pounds.

SERVANTS. See TABLE SETTING AND SERVICE.

SERVICE. A term applied to both the manner of serving food (*see* TABLE SETTING AND SERVICE) and the impliments used in serving (*see* SILVERWARE).

SERVICE BERRY. See JUNEBERRY.

SERVICE PLATE. A plate that is used to hold another plate instead of having food placed directly on it. Any plate can function as a service plate, but it should be in keeping with the plate, cup, bowl, saucer or dish that is placed on it. See TABLE SETTING AND SERVICE.

SERVING FORK. See FLATWARE.

SERVING SPOON. See FLATWARE.

SESAME. The sesame is an East Indian aromatic herb that has been naturalized in some parts of the United States. In the Orient it is cultivated for the oil derived from its seeds, but the seeds themselves are valuable as a condiment. Their slightly pungent, nutlike flavor especially recommends their addition to pastries. They are baked on rolls, breads, cookies, and cakes, and they are also used with certain desserts. Their use in baking is similar to that of poppy seeds (*which see*). *See also* OIL.

SETUBAL. A Portuguese dessert wine. It is made from Muscatel grapes and is white or amber in color. See WINE.

SHAD. In the early days, the shad was looked upon as an inferior fish. Only the poor utilized it as food and the epithet "shad eater" became indicative of poverty. In 1736 shad was advertized in Boston for a penny apiece. Public opinion has changed so that today shad is a great delicacy.

Shad is a salt water fish. The males spend two to five years at sea and the females four to six years before they move into the rivers to spawn. They start to move upriver when the river water is a few degrees warmer than the sea; if they spawn in the rivers below the fresh water line, it is because they find the necessary warmth there. In the Hudson, James, Potomac, and Delaware they are usually above the fresh water line. The shad that get through to the fresh water spawn and then swim back to the open sea. They are then flabby and useless for food.

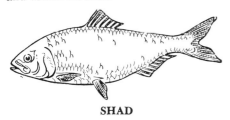

SHAD

The shad season starts in Florida about the first of December. By January the Florida run is on, and by the middle of the month Georgia is sending shad to market from the Savannah and Altamaha rivers. The season moves up the coast. Delaware shad is at the peak of its season in April. San Francisco Bay shad arrives in April. Hudson river shad is usually in season in late April and May.

SHAD ROE

Shad roe is a great delicacy. Because of the size of the fish, the roe is a good size, and the individual eggs are about the size of a good-sized pin head. As a result the texture is a cross between moistness and crispness which is very delicious. Shad roe may be broiled, baked, sautéed, planked, made into croquettes, or mixed with an omelet.

It is best prepared by parboiling for a few minutes in slightly salted water to which a little vinegar or lemon juice has been added. The proper proportions are one teaspoon of salt and one tablespoon of vinegar to a quart of water. The roe is sufficiently done when it blanches (whitens) slightly. The roe is then drained and dried and prepared in any manner desired.

HINTS ON PREPARATION

Shad has a great many bones, and is most satisfactory when it has been filleted. Most fish markets will do this when the shad is bought if it is ordered that way.

Shad is marketed as the buck male) or roe (female) shad. The roe shad may be either cut or whole. If cut, the roe has been removed. Roe shad is usually more expensive than cut roe or buck shad, but the roe itself may always be used for a second meal. The roe is sold separately, usually by the pair—a pair coming from one fish.

BAKED STUFFED SHAD

1 shad (3 lb)
3 cups soft bread crumbs
3 tbsp minced parsley
½ cup minced celery
½ green pepper, minced
Salt, pepper, paprika
⅓ cup melted butter
2 cups white grape juice

Wipe the fish and remove the center bone if it has not been filleted. Combine the crumbs, parsley, celery, green pepper, and seasonings, and moisten with the butter; then use to stuff the fish, sewing or fastening the edges with wooden toothpicks. Dust with flour, and place in a greased baking pan. Pour the grape juice over the fish and bake in a moderate oven (350° F.) about 40 minutes, basting frequently with the liquid in the pan. If desired, the liquid may be slightly thickened with flour rubbed smooth with a little cold water and used as an accompanying gravy or sauce. (Serves 4 or 6)

BROILED SHAD

Wipe and split the fish. Place on a well greased broiler rack flesh side up, and brush generously with melted butter or oil seasoned with salt and paprika. Broil until well browned, then turn and broil the under side, or complete the cooking in a very hot oven. Pour a little melted butter over the fish on the serving platter and garnish with parsley and cut lemon.

BROILED SHAD ROE

Wipe the roe and sprinkle with salt, pepper and a few drops of lemon juice. Place on a well greased broiler and broil 5 minutes, basting with melted butter and lemon juice. Turn and broil an additional 5 minutes on the under side, again basting with the butter and lemon juice. Serve with maitre d' hôtel butter. (*See* BUTTER SAUCE). If desired, the roe may be par-boiled before broiling.

SHAD BAKED IN WINE

1 shad (4 lb)
1 cup bread or cracker crumbs
2 tbsp butter or margarine
Salt and pepper
1 tbsp finely minced parsley
Pinch of crushed, dried tarragon
1½ cups water
¼ cup butter
1 tbsp catsup
1 tbsp browned flour
Juice of 1 lemon
⅓ cup sherry or Madeira

Wipe and dry the fish, leaving the head and tail on. Prepare a stuffing by combining the crumbs, melted butter, salt and pepper, parsley and tarragon and use to fill the cavity. Skewer or sew the edges together. Place upright on a rack in a baking pan and pour around the fish one cup of hot water. Bake about 40 minutes, having the oven hot (400° F.) for the first 10 minutes, then reducing to 325° F., and baste frequently while cooking. Transfer the fish to a serving dish and keep hot.

Add the remaining ½ cup of water and the catsup to the gravy in the pan and thicken with the browned flour moistened with 2 tablespoons of cold water. Stir until boiling. Cook 5 minutes, and add the lemon juice and wine. Do not allow the gravy to boil after the wine is added. The sauce may be poured over the fish or served separately. Garnish with lemon and water cress. (Serves 6)

SHADDOCK. A member of the grapefruit family. The round shaddock is the grapefruit or pomelo of the United States, and derives its name from Captain Shaddock who brought it to America. *See* GRAPEFRUIT.

SHAD-WAITER. A local name for the whitefish, (*which see*).

SHALLOT. The shallot is a member of the onion family, but it is milder and more aromatic than the onion. It is believed to have been developed during the early part of the Christian era, and it was introduced into Europe from Syria by knights of France during the Crusades.

It is pear-shaped and smaller than the average onion; its thick outer skin is reddish or grey; and the inside is green at the top and purplish at the bottom. Small red onions are sometimes marketed as

shallots. The Jersey shallot, also known as the "false shallot," is larger than the true shallot, and it has a thin reddish skin and a purple or white interior. Shallots are used fresh as a flavoring agent in any case where fresh onions might be used, and the two are sometimes used together.

SHALLOT

SHANDYGAFF. An English drink made by mixing ale or beer with equal portions of ginger ale or ginger beer. It was introduced into India to be drunk with curry dishes. The ingredients must be stirred very gently while being mixed.

SHANK. The upper part of the foreleg or the hindleg of beef, veal, or lamb.

SHEDDER. Another name given the crab, *which see*.

SHEEP. *See* MUTTON.

SHEEPBERRY. A wild, edible fruit native to the United States. *See* BLACK HAW.

SHEEPSHEAD. The sheepshead of the porgy family is found along the Atlantic Coast from Cape Cod to Texas. The name is derived from the shape of the head and the prominent incisor teeth.

It grows to a length of about 30 inches and weighs on an average from six to seven pounds, although specimens have been found weighing twenty pounds. The body is deep and marked by seven or eight dark transverse bands, most evident in the young.

Except during the spawning season from March to June, the sheepshead is gregarious in habit. It feeds on small crustaceans and shellfish which it detaches from the sea bottom by means of its incisors, and also on seaweeds.

Perhaps the ham is such a favorite with cooks because, apart from considerations of economy and even taste, ham always makes such an attractive dish. These admirable legs of pork naturally lend themselves to decorative glazing and garnishing. Spicy apple rings, brandied apricots, sirupy pineapple slices look equally tempting pinned to the ham itself or ranged about the rim of the serving platter. Creating glazes for smoked ham can be a delightful imaginative exercise. Honey, brown sugar, orange marmalade and fruit preserves, spiced with the traditional cloves, cinnamon, nutmeg, mace and allspice, are special favorites. Accompaniments for ham include sweet potato pie, New England baked beans, strings beans and glazed carrots. Serve cider to complete the festive meal. Leftover ham has uses, too. It becomes a casserole with asparagus or rice. Cold ham goes into sandwiches, salads and spreads. Ground cooked ham enhances a spinach souffle or potato pancakes. Even ham bones are useful — for making lentil soup, of course.

Casserole American-style is the magician of the kitchen. With the aid of this cooking technique, the most humble leftovers become transformed into princes of the dining-room table. The casserole recipe usually employs a starch food, such as rice, noodles, beans or potatoes, as a base to which are added vegetables or meats and a sauce. Richer sauces such as cream sauce, cheese sauce and tomato sauce are best suited to casserole cookery. For a simple casserole, mix precooked rice with frozen vegetables and cheese sauce. Sprinkle buttered bread crumbs on top and bake uncovered.

Good tasting and high in protein, nuts make interesting garnishes for foods. Make a sundae sirup by browning ½ cup chopped pecans or walnuts in butter. Add ¼ cup of brown sugar and 2 tablespoons each of water and light corn sirup. Simmer 2 minutes. Serve hot over ice cream.

Borscht, the beloved beet stew of Russian peasantry, is equally delicious served cold with sour cream as an appetizer or hot with boiled potatoes as a luncheon dish.

Whip up a delightful artichoke casserole in less than 30 minutes. Cut in half the artichoke hearts from one 15 ounce can and place in a shallow, well-greased 1 ½ quart casserole. Cover with 4 ounces of drained, sliced mushrooms (unless these are used in the sauce) and one pound of crab meat or chopped cooked chicken. Pour over all, your favorite sauce—onion, poulette, Swedish, mushroom white. Or make a wine sauce by melting 2 tablespoons of butter or margarine in a saucepan. Blend in 2 ½ tablespoons flour, salt and a dash of cayenne pepper. Add 1 ½ cups of cream gradually and cook until thick, stirring constantly. Stir in 2 tablespoons of sherry and pour the sauce over the casserole. Garnish with grated cheese, cracker crumbs and paprika. Then bake until bubbly.

Nothing adds such distinction to a dinner or party as a flambé dessert or cook-it-yourself dish. Fondue in a chafing dish, shish kebab on a hibachi and the incomparable crêpes Suzette are fun to prepare and generate an excitement all their own. For shish kebab set out bowls filled with chunks of lamb, tomato, green pepper, onion, orange, lemon, olives chicken livers wrapped in bacon and scallops. Pre-cook longer cooking food to insure that cooking time of all foods i approximately the same. Serve shish kebabs with a tossed green salad topped with pickled garnishes and for dessert try baked whole oranges or nut stuffed baked oranges. For delightful, fun to make, citrus desserts, cakes, pies and puddings see recipes under Lemon Lime, Grapefruit and Orange.

Late winter just coming on spring is full of gastronomical delights. Sweet fresh berries and melons are just beginning to appear. Lettuces and asparagus are at their peak. Still the winter favorites linger on—citrus fruits and peppers, onions, squashes and tubers. It's a fine time to experiment with food ideas when the appetite as well as the spirit rises to the expectation of a new year.

The same name is given in the west to the drum, a fresh water fish of silvery grey hue with obscure oblique streaks on the sides, which in Texas and Louisiana is very popular, but in the north is not eaten. This fish sometimes reaches a weight of fifty to sixty pounds.

In certain parts of the United States, the sheepshead is known under the name gaspergou croaker, and in others white perch.

The various methods employed in the preparation of catfish, porgy, and smelts may be adapted to this fish. *See also* FISH.

SHEFFIELD PLATE. A form of silver plate. *See* SILVERWARE.

SHELLFISH. A general name for all the fish having shells, such as clams, oysters, mussels, etc., all of *which see*.

SHERBET. The sherbet originated in Turkey, where it is very popular. In a sherbet there is a very large proportion of liquid or fruit juice, hence special treatment is required to keep the texture smooth. Beaten egg whites, marshmallows, or gelatin are used as a stabilizer.

Sherbets frozen in the automatic refrigerator should be stirred once or twice while freezing after they are about half frozen or mushy. They should be scraped up from the sides and bottom of the tray, then returned to the refrigerator to complete the freezing. If stirred too soon the mixture will return to its original liquid state. All mixtures to be frozen should first be thoroughly chilled as this saves time in freezing. Never fill either refrigerator tray of freezer can more than three-fourths full, as the stirring or agitation during the freezing process beats in air, causing the mixture to increase in bulk.

When freezing sherbets in a hand freezer use three parts of ice to one part of salt, turning the crank slowly and steadily to insure a smooth fine-grained texture. After freezing, wipe off and remove the cover, of the freezer can, take out the dasher and pack the mixture down in the can. Replace the cover, closing the opening in the lid with a cork; then repack in ice and salt in the proportions of three or four parts of ice to one of salt, covering the can completely with the mixture. Protect with a piece of burlap or carpet and leave one and a half to two hours to ripen and mellow.

Sherbets are usually served in special sherbet glasses, either as an appetizer, a digestive, or a dessert. If to aid digestion, serve immediately after the roast, and eat very slowly. See the individual fruits and flavors for sherbet recipes.

CITRUS SHERBET

3 cups sugar
3 cups water
Grated rind of 1 orange
3 bananas
¼ tsp salt
Juice of 3 oranges
Juice of 3 lemons
3 egg whites

Combine the sugar, water and orange rind. Bring to boiling point and boil 5 minutes. Chill. Press the bananas through a fine sieve and combine with the salt and orange and lemon juice. Then combine with the first mixture. Finally fold in the stiffly beaten egg whites and freeze in automatic refrigerator or hand freezer as directed. (Serves 6 or 8)

SHERRY. True sherry wine comes from Spain, from a district of which Jerez de la Frontera is the center, a district which lies within an imaginary line drawn from Puerto de Santa Maria to Rota, San Lucar de Barrameda, Tribujena, Lebrija, Arcos, then back to Puerto de Santa Maria.

The grapes are gathered and crushed in September; then after pressing, they are allowed to ferment. A handful or two of *yeso* is sprinkled over the thick mass in the press. This *yeso* is a native earth burned to a dust. The earth is found in large quantities in the neighborhood of Jerez de la Frontera, and consists almost entirely of sulphate of lime. It is added in the proportion of about two pounds to a ton of freshly crushed grapes, a quantity of grapes which will give a *botto* of 126 gallons of must. The addition of sulphate of lime is peculiar to Jerez de la Frontera, and has a marked beneficial influence on the quality and strength of the sherry.

The fermentation of the newly pressed grapes goes on violently for about three weeks, then proceeds at a slower pace during the ensuing eight weeks or so. The wine is then racked into new casks, and although it is still called *mosto*, it is no longer must, but young wine, although not yet sherry. The casks are then stored in above-ground cellars called *bodegas* and left to mature.

No one can guess how the young wine inside the casks is going to turn out. It may become sour or vapid; it may develop into a delicate *Fino* or a generous *Oloroso*. Time alone will tell.

In January the new wine becomes brighter; then another racking takes place and a little brandy, distilled from the grapes which yield the wine, may be added to it. For eighteen months longer the wine will ferment at varying rates, with the result that there will not be two casks of wine identical, although made from the very same grapes on the very same day. In some casks the wine will be clean, clear, dry, and most delicate; this is the *Fino* sherry. In some others, the wine will be coarse but rich; this is the *Raya* sherry. Yet the wine maker cannot label all his wine either coarse or delicate. Some of the casks will contain a wine nearly as clean as the *Fino* and yet as full-bodied as the *Raya*. In this case a blend is made, and it is here that the fine art of the wine maker manifests itself. From the blending of his choices comes the *Palo Cortado*.

Sherry wine is seldom shipped under the names of *Fino*, *Raya*, or *Palo Cortado*, but under the names of Amontillado, Vino de Pasto, Amoroso, Golden Sherry, etc., which are blends of the three types. In each case the blending of different wines of different years is carried on slowly and judiciously year by year.

The luscious taste, which all but the very dry, pale sherries possess to a more or less marked degree, is due to the fact that most exported sherries are blended further with a sweet wine, Pedro Ximenez, which is prevented from fermenting by the addition of grape spirits.

Pale dry sherries make excellent appetizers, and may be served cold as an aperitif before meals or with the soup course. The medium-dry may be chilled slightly, if desired, and may also be served like the pale dry sherries. The richer, brown wines should not be chilled, but served at room temperature as afternoon drinks or after dinner. *See also* WINE.

SHERRY BAVARIAN CREAM

1 tbsp gelatin
2 tbsp cold water
½ cup sugar

¾ cup boiling water
1 tbsp lemon juice
Pinch of salt
½ cup good sherry
1 cup heavy cream, whipped

Soften the gelatin in the cold water for ten minutes, then dissolve with the sugar in the boiling water. Add the lemon juice. Cool slightly, then add the salt and sherry. When almost at the setting point, fold in the whipped cream. Turn into one large mold or several individual molds previously moistened with cold water, and chill thoroughly. Unmold for serving and garnish with sliced bananas, green or red maraschino cherries, sections of canned pineapple, slices of orange, or any other desired fruit. (Serves 4 or 6)

SHERRY SHERBET

2 cups boiling water
1 cup granulated sugar
¼ scant tsp salt
2 tsp granulated gelatin
2 tbsp cold water
Juice of 4 lemons
Grated rind of 1 lemon
¼ cup orange juice
1 cup (scant) sherry wine
2 egg whites, stiffly beaten
Green vegetable coloring (optional)

Boil sugar and boiling water until sirup spins a thread. Remove from the fire and add gelatin which has been soaked in cold water for 5 minutes, and stir until gelatin is thoroughly dssolved. Then add lemon juice and rind, salt and orange juice, and blend well. Strain through a double cheesecloth, and chill. Add sherry wine and 3 or 4 drops of vegetable coloring, remembering that freezing or cooking lessens all colors. The mixture should be a pretty pale green when served. Freeze in hand freezer, using 4 parts ice and 1 part rock salt until mushy, then stir in the stiffly beaten egg whites, and continue freezing until solid, but not too hard. Serve in chilled sherbet glasses or orange cups.

SHIN OF BEEF. *See* BEEF.

SHIP BISCUIT. *See* HARD TACK.

SHIRR. To bake, or cook, in a ramekin or small, shallow casserole. Shirred eggs are one of the commonest examples of this method of cooking.

SHIVOWITZA. A Hungarian liqueur made from the shiva plum. *See also* LIQUEUR.

SHORT RIBS. *See* BEEF.

SHORTBREAD. A rich cookie, typical of Scotland, made with butter.

SCOTCH SHORTBREAD

1 cup butter
½ cup XXXX sugar, packed in cup, then sifted
2 cups sifted all-purpose flour

Cream the butter thoroughly. Blend in sugar gradually. Add flour gradually, then knead to blend well. Roll out to ¼-inch-thick rectangle on lightly floured board. Prick or press any desired design on top. Cut into squares 2 inches by 2 inches. Place on ungreased baking sheets ¼ inch apart. Bake in moderate oven (350° F.) for 18 to 20 minutes, to a delicate golden color. Cool on cake racks. (Makes about 3 dozen)

SHORTBREAD ROYAL FANS

1 cup butter
⅔ cup brown sugar, firmly packed, then sifted
2⅛ cups sifted all-purpose flour
1 egg yolk
2 tbsp milk

Cream the butter till soft and fluffy. Blend in sugar gradually. Add flour and knead to a smooth dough. Roll out on lightly floured board to ¼ inch thickness. Cut with a fluted cutter 4 or 5 inches in diameter. Cut each round into quarters.

SHIRRED EGGS IN RAMEKIN

Mark each quarter with lines to represent fans. Brush with egg yolk mixed with milk. Place on ungreased baking sheets ¼ inch apart. Bake in moderate oven (350° F.) 20 to 23 minutes or to a delicate brown color. (Makes 2½ dozen)

SHORTCAKE. A dessert that is 100 percent American. It consists of merely a simple biscuit dough, a box of berries, and cream. Shortcake is the ideal summer dessert because it is easy to make, easily digested, and has such a dignified and

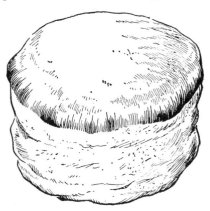

BISCUIT. A good shape for shortcake

colorful appearance. With its red or plum-colored berry jewels, it graces the table like a coronation crown and makes the plainest menu seem a guest occasion.

There is some controversy as to which is the preferable shortcake basis—a genuine biscuit dough, or a spongecake. Both alternatives have stout adherents. However, biscuit dough shortcake is a native form of bread cookery, and its hot, moist, buttery biscuit provides more contrast than any cold, dry-textured spongecake could possibly give when used with chilled and watery acid fruits.

How did this luscious combination of hot biscuit and cold fruit happen to originate? Quite possibly a homemaker had some baking powder biscuit dough and some berries left over and served them together to use them up. Happy chance! Now the two are indissolubly linked as the great American dessert—fruit shortcake—which is liked by our English cousins and admired by our French friends.

The housewife who can make good biscuits has any shortcake at the tip of her spoon—or in this case, at the tip of her kitchen case-knife. For success in making shortcake dough depends on the skill and rapidity with which it is cut with a knife rolled, and baked.

HINTS ON PREPARATION

The dry ingredients of flour, salt, baking powder, and perhaps a suspicion of sugar, must be sifted several times to insure even blending, so that the dough will be porous, light, and of even texture throughout. The shortening must be very cold, and added to the flour in tiny bits, which are then cut in with a flexible knife.

Some cooks, those who are born cooks only, may use their fingers in manipulating shortcake dough, but the rest of us should be wise and use a stout case-knife or pastry blender for cutting in the fat, until we too become artists. A too heavy pressure from the fingers makes a too heavy dough.

The liquid, too, which is added to bind the dough, should also be chilled. Only the least possible amount should be added, almost drop by drop, until the desired soft dough stage is reached. It must be moist, and yet permit rapid handling. In making a single, large shortcake, toss the mass of soft dough on a floured board, and divide it into two parts. Pat it into shape, or roll it lightly until one inch thick. For individual portions, use a cutter slightly larger than a biscuit cutter, and having a scalloped edge to give a pretty effect.

The dough may be baked in a well greased pie tin; but often there is more success if the dough is baked on top of an inverted tin or on a cookie sheet. This allows a free and even circulation of hot air to strike all around the biscuit while it is baking. The oven for shortcakes should always be pre-heated—what is called "a quick oven." This means, for those who wisely use temperature in their baking, 450° F. for 15 minutes when the shortcakes are small, or 425° F. for 20 to 25 minutes when the shortcake is a large, single cake. The two layers may be placed on top of each other and baked together, after making sure that the dough was generously spread with melted butter before baking, so that the layers will split apart easily.

All fruits for shortcakes should be ripe and slightly crushed. Sprinkle them with sugar—½ cup of sugar to each cup of crushed fruit and juice—and allow to stand for about two hours before serving. A teaspoon or two of butter may be added to give richness. A few drops of lemon juice will help bring out the fruit flavor. Put the shortcake together while still hot so that the juices may soak in.

OLD-FASHIONED BISCUIT SHORTCAKE

2 cups sifted flour
2 tsp baking powder
1 tsp salt
5 tbsp shortening
About ¾ cup milk
Butter
Sweetened berries
Whipped cream

Sift the dry ingredients together twice. Work or cut in the shortening until the mixture resembles coarse meal, then add milk to make a soft dough. Turn onto a floured board and divide into 2 parts. Knead slightly, then pat into ¾ inch thick rounds. Brush 1 over with softened butter, lay the second round on top, and bake on a greased pan in a hot oven (425° F.) 15 to 20 minutes. Separate the layers, spread the lower 1 generously with butter, then with sweetened berries. Set the top layer in place over the berries and garnish with whipped cream, preferably using a pastry bag, and whole berries.

For individual shortcakes, roll the dough 1 inch thick and cut into rounds slightly larger than baking powder biscuits.

SHORTENING. Fat or oil which is used to make pastry crisp, such as lard, butter, or vegetable oil preparations. *See* FAT and PASTRY.

SHOT GLASS. A colloquial name often given to the small whisky glass used to dispense individual servings of liquor. *See* GLASSWARE.

SHOULDER. See the specific kinds of meat. For a smoked pork shoulder, *see* HAM.

SHRIMP. Closely allied to the crayfish and prawn, the shrimp belongs to the *Carididae* family. Of elongated form, tapering and arched as if hunchback, the whole structure is delicate, almost translucent. The colors are such that the shrimp may escape observation, whether resting on a sandy bottom or swimming. Their natural color tint is greenish-gray, speckled with brown. The quick darting movements of these little shellfish betray them to one who looks attentively into a pool of water left by the tide. When alarmed, they bury themselves in the sand by a peculiar movement of the fanlike fin.

Shrimp are found abundantly in America, off the Atlantic and Pacific seaboards, wherever the bottom is sandy. Swarming in untold millions, they form a considerable part of the food of the flatfish and other shallow sea-water species. The largest and best specimens, called by epicures "bouquet," come from the region of Lake Pontchartrain, in Louisiana, and are about two inches long.

Shrimp are in season from May first to October first. Of the 125,000,000 (average) pounds of shrimp caught annually in the United States, 95 percent of the total catch, sold to canning factories and wholesale fish dealers, comes from the warm waters of the South Atlantic and Gulf States. Louisiana's fishing grounds and picturesque fishermen account for about half of that catch.

Almost half of the total annual catch goes directly to government-inspected canning factories, where the shrimp are headed, washed, and then blanched in boiling brine. They are shelled when cold, graded in sifting machines, as small, medium, and large, and packed for shipment. A good proportion of the rest of the catch is sent to the fish markets as fresh headless shrimp.

Shrimp dishes have a special value, for shrimp, like other fish products, are rich in calcium, phosphorus, copper, and sulphur, all of which are necessary body-building elements. They have as high a percentage of all necessary digestible proteins as any fish food. And in addition they contain Vitamins A, B, and D, natural protectives against winter health trials, plus a considerable amount of iodine.

HINTS ON PREPARATION

Although the popularity of the shrimp grows constantly, few homemakers explore the possibilities of shrimp cookery. Their culinary interests often take them no further than a cocktail, a salad, or an occasional excursion into the realms of the exotic by way of a shrimp chop suey. Yet the canned or fresh varieties can be prepared in a great number of other ways.

There is a certain art even in the boiling of fresh shrimp. To bring out the best flavor, the cook should add to a quart of boiling water, 2 cups of minced celery, 1 tablespoon of whole black pepper, 1 generous tablespoon of salt, and ¼ cup of chopped onion. This mixture is simmered for half an hour, with 3 slices of lemon

added during the last 5 minutes, and then strained. Then 2 or more quarts of fresh water are added to the liquid and when it boils again, the washed, cleaned shrimp are put in and cooked until tender, generally about 5 minutes, depending on size. Drain the shrimp and cool until they can be handled. Remove the shells and the black intestinal vein which runs down the center of the back.

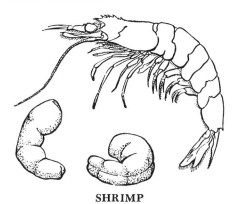

SHRIMP

Shrimp are now ready to be creamed, stewed, fricasseed, jellied, or baked, with results that will appeal to anyone who likes the flavor of these small crustaceans. If ordinary aspics have lost their charm, shrimp will bring new life to them. Cooked à la Creole as they so often are in Louisiana, or with tomatoes, green peppers, and mushrooms, they make a main dish that goes far toward relieving the monotony of both winter or summer menus.

Good shrimp wiggle, made by adding a pound of diced, cooked shrimp to thickened tomato soup, enriched with the flavor of onions that have been browned in butter, then served with toasted hard crackers, warms the cockles of a frost-bitten heart.

Shrimp that have been soaked in lemon juice and seasoning, dipped in egg and cracker or fine bread crumbs, and French fried, gladden the epicure. Curried shrimp is one of those never-failing, hurry-up dishes. Served with boiled or Spanish rice, or risotto, it usually pleases those who like both seafood and spicy cookery, which is, remember, very cooling on a hot summer day.

An unusual shrimp dish is pumpkin that has been quartered and baked with a stuffing made of a spicy mixture which includes chopped shrimp.

Shrimp is also available canned and quick-frozen either shelled or in the shell— cooked or raw.

CURRIED SHRIMP WITH RICE

2 tbsp finely chopped onion
2 tbsp butter
2 tbsp flour
1 tbsp curry powder
1 tsp salt
1 cup boiling water
1 cup evaporated milk
2 cups canned shrimp
¾ cup raw rice
½ cup freshly cooked peas
1 diced pimiento

Cook the onion slowly in the butter for 5 minutes without browning. Add the combined flour, curry powder, and salt, and blend smoothly. Gradually add the boiling water and again bring to boiling point, stirring until smooth, after which put in the milk and the shrimp (carefully picked over). Cook over boiling water until thickened. Meanwhile, cook the rice in boiling salted water until tender. Drain, and rinse with hot water. Toss lightly with the peas and pimiento; press into a ring mold and invert onto a serving dish. Pour the curried shrimp into the center. (Serves 6)

MINCED SHRIMP LOUISIANA

1 lb shrimp
1 tbsp minced onion
2 tbsp butter
2 cups canned cream of tomato soup
½ tsp salt
Dash of cayenne
1 tsp Worcestershire sauce
Patty shells or toast

Cook the shrimp in boiling salted water for 15 minutes. Drain, remove the shells and black intestinal veins, and cut into small pieces. Cook the onion in the butter for 5 minutes without browning. Add the soup and seasonings, and bring to boiling point. Add the shrimp and heat all thoroughly. Serve in patty shells or on freshly made toast. Canned shrimp may be substituted for fresh, needing only to be picked over and minced. (Serves 6)

SHRIMP ASPIC

1 qt water
1 onion
1 clove garlic
3 peppercorns
1 tsp sugar
1 tsp salt
1½ lb uncooked shrimp
2½ cups bouillon
1 tsp chopped celery
1 tsp minced parsley
A drop of tabasco
Salt and pepper
¾ tbsp gelatin
1 bunch water cress
1 tsp chopped chives
1 cup mayonnaise

Bring to the boiling point the water, onion (reserve one slice), garlic, peppercorns, sugar, and salt, and let boil 3 minutes. Add the washed shrimp and cook for 10 minutes. Remove the shrimp, shell them, and remove the black veins. Strain the cooking liquid. Soften the gelatin in a tablespoon of cold water. Combine the shrimp liquid, celery, parsley, minced slice of onion, tabasco, and salt and pepper to taste. Bring slowly to the boiling point, but do not let boil. Pour over the gelatin and stir until dissolved. Let cool.

Wet a mold with cold water and arrange the shrimp in the mold. Pour the cooled broth over them and chill in the refrigerator for 3 or 4 hours. Unmold onto a chilled platter and garnish with water cress. Shred the remaining water cress and add with the chives to the mayonnaise. Pass this sauce separately or use part to garnish the dish. (Serves 6)

SHRIMP CHOW MEIN

1 lb raw shrimp
2 tbsp oil
2 tbsp soy sauce
2 cups sliced celery
2 cups sliced onions
1 tbsp Chinese brown sauce
1 medium can water chestnuts or bean sprouts
2 or 3 tsp cornstarch
3 tbsp cold water
Fried noodles

If using canned chow mein noodles reheat them briefly in a shallow pan in a moderately hot oven. If desired, package noodles may be used, first boiling them, draining them, and spreading loosely in a cloth to dry. Then fry golden brown in deep hot fat and drain on soft crumpled paper.

Pick over and rinse the shrimp, then parboil 2 minutes in boiling salted water. Drain, remove the shells and black intestinal veins. Rinse quickly and dry, then fry in the oil in a heavy saucepan for 5 minutes, turning to cook both sides. Add 1 tablespoon of the soy sauce, remove from the pan, and keep warm. Add to the oil remaining in the saucepan, the onions, celery, brown and remaining soy sauces, with the liquid from the chestnuts or bean sprouts. Cover and cook just until the vegetables are readily pierced with a knife, about 20 minutes. Add the chestnuts or bean sprouts and the shrimp. Moisten the cornstarch with the water, add to the mixture in the pan, and stir until slightly thickened. Serve very hot over the hot fried noodles and garnish with strips of green pepper. Pass soy sauce separately. (Serves 6)

Shrimp Cocktail

Cook fresh shrimps for 15 minutes in boiling water to which salt has been added. Drain and clean them. Remove shells and intestinal veins. Break them into small pieces and mix these with cocktail sauce (*which see*), or serve whole and garnish with sauce, or put sauce in center of dish and surround with shrimps. Serve in cocktail glasses, green pepper cases, or in grapefruit shells. Shrimps may be surrounded with crushed ice and garnished with lemon slices. Allow ¼ cup for each serving.

Shrimp Creole

1 lb cooked shrimp
2 tbsp butter
Salt and pepper
Boiled rice or toast
2 cups canned tomatoes
1 minced green pepper
2 minced onions
½ cup sliced mushrooms
½ cup stock

2 tbsp minced ham
2 tbsp flour
2 tbsp butter

Melt the butter, add the shrimp, and cook together for 2 minutes. Add to the Creole sauce, simmer 5 minutes, and serve with boiled rice, or on toast.

For the sauce, cook the tomatoes, pepper, onion, and mushrooms for 10 minutes. Add the stock and ham and cook 2 minutes longer. Thicken with the flour lightly creamed with the butter and stir until thick and smooth. (Serves 6)

Shrimp Fried in Batter

1½ cups sifted flour
¼ tsp salt
1½ tsp baking powder
1 egg
½ cup evaporated milk
Drained canned, or fresh cooked shrimp

Sift together the flour, salt, and baking powder, and mix to a batter with the beaten egg and milk—it should be thick enough to readily coat the shrimp. Pat the shrimp dry, dip each into the batter, completely coating it. Fry golden brown in deep hot fat (360°–375° F.), and drain on soft crumpled paper. Garnish with parsley. (Serves 6)

Shrimp a la King

1 lb fresh mushrooms
5 tbsp butter
⅓ cup flour
1 cup chicken broth
1½ cups top milk or cream
3 tbsp minced canned pimientoes
Salt and pepper
2 cups fresh cooked or canned shrimp
2 egg yolks

Slice or quarter the mushrooms and cook in the butter in the upper part of a double boiler, placed over direct heat, about 5 minutes. Stir in the flour and, when smoothly blended, add the chicken broth and milk or cream, still stirring constantly. Place over hot water and cook until thickened, stirring occasionally. Add the pimientoes, seasonings and shrimp from which the black intestinal veins have been removed. Heat thoroughly. Finally, just before serving, pour a little of the hot sauce over the beaten egg yolks, stirring while pouring. Return all to the double boiler and heat, but do not actually boil. Serve on toast. (Serves 6)

SHRIMP LOAF

2 cups chopped celery
1 tbsp finely chopped onion
2 tbsp butter
1 cup chopped, cooked shrimp
3 cups mashed potatoes
Salt and pepper
2 beaten eggs
¼ cup minced parsley

Cook the celery and onion in the butter for 10 minutes, without browning. Combine with the shrimp, potatoes, seasoning, beaten eggs and parsley. Blend all thoroughly, pack into a well-greased loaf pan and bake in a moderately hot oven (350°–375° F.) for 1 hour. (Serves 6)

SHRIMP A LA NEWBURG

2 lb cooked shrimp
½ lb mushroom caps
¼ cup sherry
¼ cup butter
2 tbsp flour
1¼ cups light cream
2 egg yolks
Dash each of salt, paprika, and nutmeg
2 tbsp brandy

Cut the shrimp into large dice. Wash and drain the mushrooms and cut into quarters. Add to the shrimp, pour the sherry over, and let stand for 1 hour. At serving time melt the butter in a saucepan, add the shrimp-mushroom mixture and cook 5 minutes. Sprinkle in the flour, add 1 cup of the cream, and stir until thickened. Beat the egg yolks with the remaining cream and add to the shrimp mixture. Stir and cook for a moment. Add the seasonings and brandy. Serve on toast. (Serves 6)

SHRIMP PIE

4 cups cooked shrimp
3 ears of corn, grated

1 cup cracker crumbs
3 tbsp butter
1 tsp salt
Dash of pepper
1 cup light cream

In a greased baking dish arrange in alternate layers the shrimp, corn, and cracker crumbs mixed with the butter and seasonings, having 2 or 3 layers of each. Pour the cream over all and bake in a moderate oven (350° F.) about 40 minutes or until brown.

SHRIMP AND RICE CASSEROLE

1 lb cooked shrimp
4 cups cooked rice
2 beaten eggs
1 minced onion
2 tbsp melted butter
Salt and pepper

Cut the shrimp into large dice. Combine with the rice, eggs, onion, butter, and seasonings, and turn into a greased casserole. Bake in a moderate oven (350° F.) about half an hour. If desired, a dash of either curry powder or nutmeg may be added, and canned shrimp may be substituted for the fresh. (Serves 6)

SHRIMP BUTTER. *See* BUTTER SAUCE.

SHRIMP SAUCE. *See* WHITE SAUCE.

SHRUB. A beverage made of sweetened fruit juice, usually with added alcohol to preserve it; also, a home-made cordial. It is sweet, strong, and heavy; and is sometimes drunk straight as a liqueur, but more often served diluted or used as a flavoring ingredient in other drinks.

SHRUB

1 gal rum or brandy
1 qt lemon juice
3 oranges, peels only
3 lemons, peels only
Sugar

The orange and lemon peels are cut as thin as possible, so that no white inner skin still adheres, and are then cut into fairly small pieces. The peels, lemon juice and liquor are mixed together and put aside to stand for about 60 days in a covered container in a cool place. It is then sugared to taste, and, if desired, "cut" with water to a thinner consistency. The mixture is then strained clear and bottled.

BRANDY SHRUB

3 lemons
1 qt brandy
1 pt sherry
1 lb sugar

The lemons are squeezed, the juice strained and mixed with the brandy. The peel of one lemon is prepared as described above and also added. The mixture is placed in a covered container and let stand in a cool place for 3 days. The sherry and sugar are then added, the whole mixed well, strained, and bottled.

RASPBERRY SHRUB

1 qt fresh raspberries
½ pt vinegar
Sugar

The berries and vinegar are mixed and let stand for 2 days, then thoroughly mashed and strained clear. The sugar is added in the proportion of 1 pound to 1 pint of liquid, the mixture boiled for 20 minutes, skimmed, and bottled. This shrub is served diluted with either plain or carbonated water and ice, 2 tablespoons of shrub to a glass.

SIDECAR. A popular, pleasantly flavored cocktail made of Cointreau and brandy.

SIDECAR

1 part cointreau
1 part brandy
1 part lemon juice

Shake well with cracked ice, strain.

A variation on the sidecar recipe is to substitute a few drops of lime juice for the lemon juice. *See* BARTENDING; *see also* COCKTAIL, ALCOHOLIC.

SIEBENBURGEN CHEESE. A local name for Brinsen cheese, (*which see*).

SIEVE. A sieve is a mesh made of any suitable material, fitted into a frame or holder, that is used to screen substances so that those particles fine enough to pass through the mesh are separated from the rest. The sieve is an ancient device, the mesh being made of hair, textiles, and natural fibers in the past. Today, however, the majority of sieves are made from wire, though the older materials are still used in some specialized cases.

The classic form of the sieve is that of a round basket that is open at the top and has a screen for a bottom. Another common type has the mesh or screen built in the form of a hemisphere set in some sort of handle. Sieves are also incorporated in more elaborate devices (*see* FLOUR SIFTER).

Perhaps the most common kitchen use of the sieve is to sift flour and other powdered solids. They are also used to purée foods, and as strainers to drain off liquids from solids.

HINTS ON PURCHASING

While the meshes are all quite fine, there is some variance, and the openings should be of a size suitable for the need. The openings should be uniform throughout the entire surface of the screen, but if they are not, the largest should not be too large, lest it defeat the entire purpose of the sieve. The sieve should be strongly made so that the holes will not be forced to a larger size in use. The sieve should be made of rust-resisting materials.

The manner in which the screen is joined to the body of the sieve should be critically inspected to see that it is strong enough to last and that there are no projecting ends of wire to endanger the fingers. *See also* COLANDER, KITCHEN EQUIPMENT, and STRAINER.

SIFTER. A flour sifter is a sieve (*which see*) that is especially adapted for use with flour. It is commonly built in the form of a metal cup with a screen bottom, and contains some sort of mechanism to force the flour through the mesh. This mechanism usually consists of wires that either revolve or rub against the screen, being operated by a crank or a lever. Some flour sifters have a graduated scale on their sides as an aid in sifting measured amounts of flour into a mixing bowl. The flour sifter is pretty much a specialized tool, the construction of the instrument and the size of the mesh not being suited for use with many materials other than flour. *See also* KITCHEN EQUIPMENT.

SILD. *See* SARDINE.

SILENCE CLOTH. A large, soft cloth that is spread on a table underneath a linen damask tablecloth as a sort of buffer. to keep the dishes and silverware from clattering against the table. *See* TABLE SETTING AND SERVICE.

SILESIAN CHEESE. A German cheese, made from the skim milk of cows. Onions or caraway seed are added also. It closely resembles Hand cheese.

SILVER FIZZ. A highly effervescent summer drink made of gin, egg white and carbonated water. *See* FIZZ.

SILVER PLATE. *See* SILVERWARE.

SILVERWARE. Though descriptive of any article made of silver, this term has come to be especially applied to knives, forks, spoons, and other items made for use in the kitchen and on the table. Through usage, it has come to be applied to knives, forks, and spoons in general, even though they be made of materials other than silver.

All silverware used in connection with food is divided into two general classes: *flatware*, which includes the knives, forks, spoons, and serving implements; and *hollow ware* (*holloware*) or *dinner ware* which, as the names imply, cover the field of bowls, pitchers, trays, platters, candlesticks, etc.

HISTORY

Silver, the "Queen of Metals," has long been loved by man because of its beauty. In addition to its beauty, silver is long-lasting, is easily worked into ornate shapes, and (though classified as a precious metal and priced accordingly) is found in reasonably large quantities. For these reasons, the metal has always been a favorite of the craftsman.

Written descriptions of the art of silversmithing that date back to 2500 B.C. have been found in Egypt, while actual pieces made in approximately 1900 B.C. have been found in other places. The history of silversmithing is, in many ways, the history of art and the history of civilization.

The silversmith is by no means a stranger to American history. Among the early silversmiths in this country, there are records of a Thomas Howard in Jamestown, Va., in 1620 and a John Mansfield in Charlestown, Mass., in 1634. John Hull of Boston set up the first mint in this country in 1652, striking the famed pine tree shilling under a rather profitable arrangement whereby he kept one out of every 20 coins

made. Paul Revere would be known today for his craft in that metal even had he not made his famous ride. It is interesting to note that his often overlooked companion in that venture, one William Dawes, who alerted a different portion of the countryside but was never immortalized in verse, was also a silversmith.

The Colonial craftsmen, working with limited tools and resources, gave birth to distinctive stylings that are ranked with the best ever produced and still greatly influence modern design. The modern silver industry is largely centered in the east, as was the old. Upper New York State, Connecticut, Massachusetts, and Rhode Island produce the bulk of modern American silverware.

TYPES

Most modern silverware falls under two main headings; *sterling* and *silver plate*. There are other types, of course, and there are also many imitations that contain no actual silver.

Sterling. Completely pure metallic silver is too soft (ductable) for practical use. To overcome this, the silver is alloyed with a base metal, usually copper, making it harder. Sterling is such an alloy, being fixed by law at 925 parts of pure silver to 75 parts of a base metal. The name is generally believed to be a contraction of *Easterling*, the name given to a group of merchants from eastern Germany who traded in England during the Twelfth Century, in the reign of Richard I. These merchants offered, in return for goods, silver tokens that were noted for the uniformity and purity of the metal. The British silver trade adopted the standards set by these tokens, and, in 1907, the United States adopted legislation setting the same standards here for sterling silver: 925/1000 pure.

To be stamped "sterling," an object must be solid sterling throughout.

Silver Plate. Sterling objects, being solid silver, are expensive, so a natural alternative was to apply a coating of silver to a cheaper metal. This was first done by fusing and rolling sheets of silver on the surface of copper sheets, the product being known as *Sheffield Plate*. When the electroplating process became commercially practical around the year 1840, this earlier method was, for the most part, abandoned.

In this later process, finished metal objects are suspended in a chemical solution together with bars of pure silver. An electrical current flows from the silver to the object, depositing a layer of .999 pure silver on the surface of the object. This layer can be built to any desired thickness by varying the intensity of the current or the length of the operation.

Coin Silver. This is a silver alloy on the order of sterling, but usually of a lower silver content to give the alloy greater hardness. In the United States, the standard is now set at 900/1000 pure silver. The colonial smith, faced with a supply problem, often made objects (especially spoons) from melted coins, which were almost pure silver and consequently softer than modern alloys.

Dutch Silver. A common name for silverware imported from Holland. It is usually cast, and the silver used is an alloy, but not always of sterling standard.

Fine Silver. Technically used, this term refers to absolutely pure silver.

Nickel Silver. Also called *German Silver.* An alloy that greatly resembles silver, but actually contains none. It is made of copper, zinc and nickel, and is commonly used as a base for silver plate as well as a substitute for the metal itself.

PURCHASING SILVERWARE

The first question that usually arises when contemplating the purchase of silverware is whether to get sterling or silver plate. Sterling is quite expensive in terms of its purchase price, but it will last for generations. Silver plate is not as costly and matches the appearance of sterling, but it does wear out in time. Its life expectancy hinges largely on the thickness of the silver with which it is covered, and good silver plate can stand up under a great many years of normal usage.

The common tactics of newly-weds who want but cannot afford good silverware of either the sterling or silver plate variety is to first purchase a cheaper set, and then, as circumstances permit, build their good set piece by piece. The basic thought is that this type of purchasing is relatively painless, and, by the time the initial set is worn out, the family will have their good set complete.

Design is an important element to be considered when purchasing silverware.

The silverware does not have to match the chinaware, table linens, and other dining room furnishings, but it should harmonize. More important, the pattern selected should be such that the family will not tire of seeing it daily for many years.

The pattern selected should be an "open" one; i.e., one that will be manufactured for years to come. Pieces may get lost, family requirements may grow, or the set may be built up through the years a piece at a time. Only by selecting an open pattern can the purchaser be certain of always being able to obtain matching pieces.

"Bargains" in silverware should be approached cautiously. Silver as a metal has a fairly standard value, and the worth of a piece is determined largely by the amount of metal in it and the workmanship needed to shape it. Too low a price may indicate a skimping on either of these elements. It may also mean that the pattern is "closed" or will be closed shortly.

Only those pieces that are solid silver throughout can legally be stamped "sterling." Silver plate may be said to be solid silver, but this refers only to the plating and not the entire piece. Sterling should be fairly substantial if it is to last. A thick sheet may be genuine sterling, but it may also be subject to dents, bending, and even tearing.

As in all buying, it is best to consult a reputable dealer when purchasing silverware. Such purchases usually represent considerable outlays for the family involved, and it really takes an expert to tell whether or not real value is being given for the money.

ENGRAVING

It is a common and long cherished practice, when buying a set of good silverware of any type, to have it engraved with the family initials. The exact initials and design used will vary with the individual's taste and local tradition. In general practice, either single initials or two or three-letter monograms are used.

Single Initials. The initial of either bride or the groom's family name is used.

Two-Letter Monogram. The initials of the two family names are used, with a small star or cross between them.

Three-Letter Monogram. When done in a line or linked, either the initials of the bride's full maiden name or her first and last initials and the initials of the groom's family name are used. In some cases, the initials of the pair's first names are engraved in small letters separated by either a star or a cross, set above a single large initial which is the first letter of the groom's family name.

CARE OF SILVERWARE

Unlike the base metals, silver does not rust. However, it does tarnish through contact with sulfur and other elements. Eggs, smoke, rubber, and salt are the things commonly met that will cause tarnish. When not in use, silverware should be stored in some sort of reasonably airtight container and out of all possible contact with the mentioned substances. There are a great many cloth bags, rolls, and wrappings; papers; and even lined chests that have been specially treated so that silverware may be stored in them without danger of tarnish.

The best method of preventing tarnish is to wash silverware often, and especially to wash it as soon as possible after contact with food. Silverware should be washed in hot, soapy water; rinsed in hot, clear water; and wiped with a clean, dry towel. It is not a good policy to let silverware dry by standing, nor is it well to let it remain in water for long periods of time, for any steel components (e.g., knife blades) are apt to be rusted.

Silverware should also be cleaned occasionally with a silver polish. This should be done as a preventative measure whether there is tarnish present or not, and it will be found that by using frequent washings and occasional polishings, the total effort needed to keep the silver gleaming is much less than if the silver were allowed to get tarnished before being cleaned.

A good grade of polish should be used; one that is not too abrasive. The pieces should be rubbed in a lengthwise motion; never crosswise or circular. The polish should be removed by washing in the regular manner, using a brush to remove the polish from crevices such as are found in the ornamentation.

Some patterns of silverware have areas that are deliberately oxidized or blackened to bring out the design details. These dark areas should not be removed lest the appearance of the design suffer.

Silverware may also be cleaned by placing it in a salt, soda, and water mixture in an aluminum pan and boiling. If an aluminum pan is not used, a piece of aluminum should be dropped in the water and all pieces of silver must either touch the aluminum or another piece of silver that is in contact with the aluminum. The action is somewhat on the order of electroplating in reverse and does remove the tarnish. However, it also removes the so-called "aging tone," a greyish cast silver acquires through the years that is thought by some to be desirable, and it also removes the intentional oxidation previously mentioned, thereby spoiling the design. Whether this method may be safely used or not depends on the individual pieces.

Under no circumstances should steel wool or scouring powder be used on silverware, for these and similar materials would cause marring scratches. It is also not a good policy to put too much silverware in the sink at once or to let it jostle together, since this, too, can cause scratches.

If silverware is scratched, the marks can be removed by carefully rubbing with a silver polish. Most abrasives would only cause further scratching, or, possibly, wear away more of the surface than required.

Not only is a certain amount of scratching unavoidable in silverware, but it is actually desirable. New pieces rapidly acquire minute scratches in normal use. While they may not look well at first, the surface will gradually come to be completely covered by these fine marks, giving it a softness and patina that will actually enhance the beauty of the piece.

The most important rule to remember in caring for silverware is simply to use it. Constant use simplifies the tarnishing problem because it automatically provides constant washing and polishing. Use also "mellows" the silverware as previously explained. Then too, it is rather pointless to make a major investment for a rarely used commodity. It takes several generations to wear out sterling, and silver plate, depending on the quality, can also have considerable longevity.

Of course, not all items of silverware are naturally subject to daily use, but those that are should be utilized. If, as is usually the case, a family has more flatware than is needed for a complete table setting, the pieces should be carefully rotated so that all will receive equal use. Not only does this help to prevent tarnish, but, when there is company and the extra pieces are used, they will all look equally aged. *See* FLATWARE and HOLLOW WARE; *see also* TABLE SETTING AND SERVICE.

SIMMER. To cook at a temperature slightly under the boiling point.

SIMPLE SIRUP. A sugar and water sirup used in cases where granulated sugar is difficult to dissolve, as in cold drinks. *See* SIRUP.

SINGAPORE SLING. A cooling, intoxicating tropical drink. *See* SLING.

SINGE. To burn lightly or scorch the outside so that the fine hair or feathers are removed. *See also* CHICKEN.

SINK. The sink is as basic and as important a piece of kitchen equipment as is the range or the refrigerator. It has as vital a role to play in the daily work as they do, and improper design and lack of facilities in the sink can greatly hamper the housewife. In recent years, much thought has been given to sink design, causing it to be changed from a functional ugly duckling to a thing of useful beauty.

In the first place, the sink should be conveniently located to carry on its duties as the heart of the cleaning center (*see* KITCHEN). When remodeling, because of the plumbing involved, it is sometimes easier to modify the kitchen plan than to shift the sink location.

The sink should be surrounded with adequate working space above and beyond the drain boards. The ideal unit is set in a continuous row of work shelves and cabinets, but if the sink is of the older style, it may be possible to place tables and cabinets in handy, adjacent positions. If possible, there should be cabinet space below the sink to hold garbage pails, trash buckets, dish pans, cleaning equipment, etc., and some of these items may be placed there even if the sink is not enclosed.

While one sink basin may be made to serve, it is better to have two, placed side by side, each having a separate drain board. This arrangement greatly facilitates dishwashing (*which see*) and other sink operations. There should be ledges and racks above for soap, dish rags, towels, and other often used equipment.

The most practical plumbing system is the type where the two faucets flow out through the same spout, thus enabling the user to regulate the water temperature with greater accuracy than if the two separate streams are mixed in the basin. This spout should swivel so that the stream of water may be directed to a specific point, and attachments may be purchased that vary the flow from a solid stream to a shower spray for different uses.

Chief among the accessories that can be installed in the sink to extend its usefulness are the garbage disposal unit (*which see*) and the dishwasher (*which see*). A special water heater (*which see*) may also be attached to the faucet if there is no other source of hot water. There are also many miscellaneous cleaning aids, garbage handling devices, etc. that are used in conjunction with the sink.

CONSTRUCTION

Kitchen sinks are commonly made of heavy enamel, though laundry or basement sinks may also be made of sheet metal and even concrete. Special metal alloys are being used to make some kitchen sinks.

The drain board of a modern unit will often be surrounded by a working surface made of linoleum, with metal or plastic binding strips on the edges. If the sink is so designed, it should be put together in such a way that there is no possibility of moisture collecting in cracks.

HINTS ON USE

The most important element in sink care is that it must be kept clean. It should be cleaned after each use and thoroughly scrubbed down once a week, whether it seems to need it or not. Another important rule is that no solid substances should be forced down the drain. Each drain is protected by some sort of strainer (*see* SINK STRAINER), and that should be left in place except when being cleaned. If it is lost or broken, another should be purchased, and never should the user try to force anything down the drain that would not normally pass the screen.

Some discretion should be used in pouring materials down the drain, even though they might go past the strainer. If there is any possibility of the material balling up in the pipe and blocking it, the substance should be poured in slowly, and flushed through with plenty of water. If possible, the material should be thrown in the garbage can, instead. *See also* KITCHEN EQUIPMENT.

SINK STRAINER. There are two types of sink strainers in general use; one which is usually incorporated into the sink proper, and the other, which is actually an accessory.

The former is a perforated metal plate or basket that is set in or over the main opening of the sink drainpipe. It is placed there to keep large objects from falling into the drain and either becoming lost, if their fall was accidental, or blocking the pipe. These units can be removed for cleaning purposes, and are sometimes backed up by a fine wire screen placed across the pipe underneath the strainer.

The second type consists of a high-walled, triangular container, usually made of hard rubber or a plastic, that has a perforated bottom. This unit is used to drain the liquids from plate scrapings and garbage so the solid refuse may be thrown in the garbage pail with a minimum of mess. *See also* DISHWASHING, KITCHEN EQUIPMENT, and SINK.

SIPHON BOTTLE. A bottle especially designed for carbonated or effervescent liquids wherein the fluid is drawn off by using gas pressure to force it through a siphon arrangement. There is a long, slender, open glass or metal tube inside the bottle that nearly touches the bottom, and is connected to a pouring spout in the cap. The cap is so constructed that the liquid can escape only through the tube and spout, which are sealed by means of a lever operated valve closed under spring tension.

When the bottle is filled at the factory, a small air space is left at the top. Gas escapes from the liquid until enough pressure is built up in the air space to stop the effervescing. When the lever is pressed, opening the valve, this gas pressure, which is always pushing down on the liquid, forces the fluid up the tube and out through the spout.

There are two general types of siphon bottles; one (often called a seltzer water bottle) that must be filled at the factory where there is adequate equipment to keep the liquids under constant pressure during the process, and another kind in which plain water and other fluids may be carbonated at home or place of use.

This latter kind has a removable cap and tube, so that the bottle may be filled. In filling, an air space is left at the top, as above, so that gas pressure may be built up. The gas, highly compressed in small cylinders, is introduced through a special valve that feeds into the siphon tube. The bottle should be shaken vigorously while the gas, carbon dioxide, is admitted slowly so that it emerges from the bottom of the tube in small bubbles. This is done to dissolve as much of the gas as possible in the liquid, giving better carbonation.

There are two common types of these "self-charging" siphon bottles. Those best suited for home use a very small gas capsule which is tapped by means of a puncturing device on the valve. One capsule contains the proper amount of gas for one charging. Another kind, better adapted to commercial establishments, takes its gas from a larger cylinder using hand valves, and using a pressure gauge to indicate when the proper amount of gas has been admitted to the bottle.

Since they depend on gas pressure for successful operation, siphon bottles are only used for effervescent or carbonated fluids. There, however, they are ideal, since the liquid is always kept under pressure (necessary to preserve carbonation) and they offer a convenient method of service. Their disadvantages are bulk in storage, expense, and the ever-present danger of accidental discharge through pressure on the valve lever.

Siphon bottles of the factory-filled type are used mainly for carbonated or seltzer water. The rechargeable type are also used to make whipped cream and do other labor saving tricks. They may also be used to carbonate otherwise plain beverages. *See* AERATED WATER and SELTZER WATER; *see also* BARTENDING.

SIR IZ MJESINE CHEESE. A Dalmatian cheese made from the skim milk of cheese. It usually comes eight inches square and two inches thick, although larger sizes are made. It is sometimes eaten while fresh.

SIR MASTNY CHEESE. A rennet cheese made of sheep's milk.

SIR POSNY CHEESE. A hard white rennet cheese made from the skimmed milk of sheep. It has many small holes. It is made in Montenegro where it is also called lord, or mrsav cheese.

SIRAZ CHEESE. A smooth eyeless cheese made in Servia from whole milk. It is made four to six inches in diameter and one inch thick. It is semi-hard.

SIRLOIN. Probably derived from the old French *sur longe*, meaning superloin, or over-loin. According to legend, the loin of beef was knighted "Sir Loin" by James I, of England, who was especially fond of that cut of meat. More likely, the present version of the French words is an Anglicized spelling which may, in turn, have given rise to the story. At any rate, the loin of beef is one of the choice cuts of the meat and lies immediately behind the porterhouse. *See* BEEF.

SIRLOIN STEAK. A steak which may be cut thick or thin and is taken from the loin of BEEF, *which see.*

SIRUP. Liquid sweetening is called sirup. It may be a sirup of cane sugar, corn sirup or maple sirup. Fruit and other sweet sirups may also be made to provide thirst quenchers by the addition of water or carbonated beverages.

One of the most important points in beverage-making is the proper use of sugar with fruit juices and other cold ingredients. Granulated sugar will not readily dissolve in cold liquids and so only a portion of the full sugar sweetness is obtained. It is far better to make up ahead of time a supply of simple sirup or stock sirup which can be used for such purposes. Such sirup is easy to make.

SIMPLE SIRUP

This is also known as bar sirup, gomme sirup, and gum sirup. Dissolve granulated sugar in cold water, using the proportion of four cups of sugar to one of water. Bring to a boil, stirring only until the sugar dissolves, and simmer until the sugar is dissolved and the liquid clears. If desired, the sirup may be clarified by adding the well beaten white of one egg to the above quantity, and skimming the mixture until clear. Cool and bottle. If the sirup is kept airtight, it need not be kept under refrigeration.

STOCK SIRUP

This is a somewhat less sweet sirup which may be used when the sweetness of simple sirup is not required. Combine two cups of sugar and two cups of water in a saucepan and bring to a boil, stirring only until the sugar is dissolved. Remove any scum from the surface as it rises. Cover the saucepan and boil for four minutes to allow the steam to wash the sugar crystals from the sides of the pan. Uncover and let simmer gently for 25 minutes. Cool slightly, and strain into a sterilized jar. Keep tightly covered in a cool, dark place.

LEMON SIRUP

4 cups sugar
2 cups hot water
4 tbsp corn sirup
6 tbsp grated lemon rind

Combine the ingredients in a saucepan. Place over direct heat, stir only until the sugar is dissolved, and simmer gently for 25 minutes. Strain through flannel. Turn into hot sterilized jars and keep tightly covered in the refrigerator. (Makes 1 quart)

Lime Sirup. Proceed as directed for lemon sirup, substituting lime rind for lemon rind.

Orange Sirup. Proceed as directed for lemon sirup, substituting orange rind.

MINT SIRUP

4 cups sugar
2 cups water
¼ cup corn sirup
40 stalks of crushed fresh mint

Combine the ingredients in a saucepan over direct heat. Stir until the sugar is dissolved, and then simmer for 20 minutes. Strain through flannel and turn into hot sterilized jars. Keep tightly covered in the refrigerator. (Makes 1 quart)

This sirup may be used in the making of mint sauce or mint jelly to accompany lamb. It may also be used to sweeten iced tea. A very small amount of green vegetable coloring may be added to the sirup after cooking is completed.

PINEAPPLE SIRUP

2 cans crushed pineapple
2 tbsp grated orange rind
1 tsp grated lemon rind
12 whole cloves
¼ cup corn sirup
1 cup sugar
2 cups cold water

Combine the ingredients in a saucepan and place over direct heat. Stir until the sugar is dissolved. Simmer for 25 minutes. Remove the cloves and turn the sirup into hot sterilized jars. Keep tightly covered in the refrigerator. (Makes 1 quart)

This sirup is good not only for beverages but as a topping for ice cream and puddings.

RASPBERRY SIRUP

2 qt fresh raspberries
4 cups sugar
3 cups cold water

Pick over and wash the raspberries. Drain well and mash. Add the sugar. Cover and let stand over night. Next morning, add the water and bring slowly to the boiling point over direct heat. Stir occasionally. Simmer for 20 minutes. Press through a fine sieve and then strain through flannel. Return to the fire and bring to the boiling point. Skim, and turn into hot sterilized jars, filling them to overflowing. Keep closely covered in the refrigerator. (Makes 1 quart)

This sirup is good not only for beverages but as a base for dessert sauces and ices. Quick-frozen raspberries may be used in place of the fresh. Thaw them and drain thoroughly before measuring.

Strawberry Sirup. Proceed as directed for raspberry sirup, substituting fresh or frozen strawberries.

SIZZLING PLATTER. A sizzling platter is a special metal platter, usually made of cast aluminum (*see* ALUMINUM) on which meats may be broiled and served. There are indentations on the bottom to drain off the juices released in cooking. Usually these indentations are in the form of a pattern for appearance's sake, the "well and tree" design being the most popular.

SKATE. The skate is a ray of the genus *Raja*. It has a disk-like body, horizontally flattened. The eyes are sometimes above, and sometimes on the side of the head; its mouth, situated on the ventral side, is armed with long, thin, closely-set teeth, which may attain great size. The skin is very thin and generally soft.

There are two common species of skate known on the markets: the small dotted skate, sometimes called sand skate or sand-rock, and the buckled skate, the skin of which is usually covered with excrescences.

Another variety called torpedo, or ray-fish, also edible, possesses an apparatus somewhat similar to an electric battery. This apparatus is composed of several membranous tubes, close together, similar to a honey-comb, and disposed in two layers. These tubes are divided by horizontal diaphragms into small cells which are full of mucus. The apparatus is ani-

mated by many nerves, which centralize in the same vulnerable, electric spot and a discharge takes place at the will of the skate and with a sure precision against the fish which the skate preys upon for nourishment, or to defend itself against any enemy. The electrical commotion caused

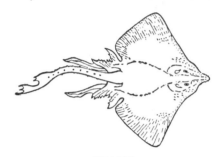

SKATE

by the discharge of this unusual torpedo is rather strong, and even in the human being it results in a well-defined numbness in the point of contact, which, while not dangerous, is very painful. Owing to this phenomenon, the most wide-spread, fantastic stories have been recounted about the torpedo skate.

When buying skate, demand either sand-rock skate or buckled skate, which are the best known of the species. Also, insist on getting the liver of the fish, as it is a great delicacy and may be prepared in many delicious ways. It contains the valuable Vitamins A and B. Skate should be strictly fresh; if you entertain any doubt on this point, abstain from buying.

Only the wings, or fins, of the larger skates are used for food.

See also RAY.

HINTS ON PREPARATION

One of the choicest ways of serving skate is with sizzling hot black butter, especially when the fish has been cooked in a court-bouillon.

Always add a few drops of vinegar or lemon juice to the salted water in which the fish is cooked, and remember that after cooking the fish should be well drained, skinned and served immediately to prevent discoloration. If, for any reason, it must be kept standing let it remain in the cooking liquor until it can be served. Should the fish have a reddish appearance before cooking, place it in cold water for 1 or 2 hours to disgorge and to lessen the strong flavor.

If only the fins of skate are to be served, they may be cooked without special preliminary preparation but if the dorsal is used always parboil in slightly acidulated, salted water.

BAKED SKATE WITH SWISS CHEESE

2 skate fins
Lemon juice
Salt and pepper
1 cup milk
1 clove
Bouquet garni
1 tsp finely minced shallot or onion
Thin slice garlic
Grated Swiss cheese
Cream sauce
2 tbsp butter

Wipe the skate fins and rub over with lemon juice and sprinkle with salt and coarse black pepper. Place in a deep skillet. Pour in the milk and add the clove, bouquet garni, shallot or onion, and garlic. Bring quickly to the boiling point and simmer gently for 15 minutes. Lift out the fish and place in a buttered baking dish or casserole sprinkled with the cheese. Use the milk in which the fish was simmered in preparing the cream sauce (*which see*); pour this over the fish, dot with the butter and place in a hot oven (400° F.) about 10 minutes to brown. Serve from the baking dish. (Serves 4 or 6)

BOILED SKATE WITH BLACK BUTTER

2 skate fins
Vinegar court-bouillon
2 tsp finely minced parsley
3 or 4 tbsp butter
1 tbsp tarragon vinegar

Wipe the skate fins and place in a saucepan with the court-bouillon (*which see*) almost to cover. Bring to boiling point, reduce the heat and simmer gently for 10 minutes. Lift out the fish and drain thoroughly. Place on serving platter and sprinkle with the parsley. Set in an open oven to dry a little while preparing the black butter.

For this let the butter brown very thoroughly in a frying pan, then holding the pan as far as possible from you to avoid

being burned by spluttering, pour in the tarragon vinegar gently. As soon as boiling, pour over the fish. Garnish with fresh parsley and quartered lemon. (Serves 4 or 6)

FRIED SKATE

Wipe, then cook a 3½ to 4 pound skate, as directed, in court-bouillon (*which see*). Immediately it boils reduce the heat and simmer very gently for 20 minutes. Drain, place on a hot platter, skin and immediately (to avoid discoloration) cut into 3-inch pieces. Roll in flour, and sauté in butter, turning frequently until golden brown. Serve at once, garnishing with small potato balls, small glazed onions, parsley and quartered lemon. Serve separately pats of lemon butter (butter into which a little lemon juice and a very little grated lemon rind has been beaten, the whole then chilled). (Serves 6)

SKATE MEUNIERE

Select a 3½ to 4 pound skate, preferably a buckled skate, thick in proportion to length. Cut the fins, open the coffer by cutting the skin in the middle to clean, and remove the liver without breaking; cut the fish into 3 portions, wash thorough-

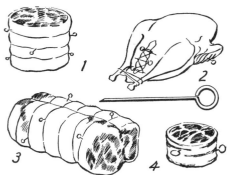

**SKEWER USES   1. Pot Roast   2. Fowl
3. Rolled and Boned Shoulder
4. Filet Mignon**

ly in several waters, and fillet. Place in a fish kettle with boiling court-boui1on (*which see*) to almost cover. As soon a; this again reaches boiling point, reduce the heat and simmer very gently for 10 minutes. Lift out the fish, drain, pat dry, and roll in seasoned flour, then brown rapidly by sautéing in ⅓ cup of hot butter. Lift from this butter as soon as browned, place on a hot serving platter and season highly with freshly ground pepper, minced parsley and 2 tablespoons of chopped capers. Squeeze the juice of 1 lemon over all and finally pour the boiling hot, strained browned butter over all. Garnish with fresh parsley and quartered lemon. (Serves 6)

SKEWER. A skewer is a short, sharp metal pin used to hold meat together while it is being roasted.

SKILLET. Though the term skillet once applied to any metal cooking vessel that had a handle, the term has come, in America especially, to be applied exclusively to the metal frying pan, *which see*. See *also* SPIDER.

SKILLET

SKIM. To remove floating matter from the surface of a liquid with a spoon or ladle which is usually perforated.

SKIP MACKEREL. *See* BLUEFISH.

SKIPJACK. *See* BLUEFISH.

SKUNK CABBAGE. The first plant to bloom in the spring. It is good eating when the thick, almost white leaf stalks are boiled, and the water is changed two or three times. Cooked tender, seasoned with butter, pepper and salt, all the offensiveness disappears with the boiling. In cream or other sauce, or cold in salad form, the skunk cabbage is delicious.

SLAW. The Dutch word for cabbage. *See* COLE SLAW.

SLICING KNIFE. *See* CUTLERY; *see also* CARVING.

SLING. A class of rather strong, simply prepared alcoholic drinks, popular in some sections of the tropics. These drinks, especially the gin sling, have acquired considerable repute through their mention in literature and drama with a tropical locale.

As is customary in the case of a family of drinks based on the same recipe, simple slings are named after the liquor used; viz., brandy sling, gin sling, etc.

SLING (Basic Recipe)

1 tsp powdered sugar
1 jigger desired liquor (brandy, gin, etc.)

The sugar is first dissolved in a teaspoon of water in the bottom of an old fashioned or similar glass *see* GLASSWARE), two ice cubes or equivalent are added, and the liquor poured in. The drink is garnished with a twist of lemon peel. (Serves 1)

Slings are sometimes served in highball glasses with carbonated water added. In some cases where the drink is served in this manner, the sugar is eliminated, but it is then actually a highball (*which see*) rather than a sling, though it may be referred to as such.

Of the many sling variations, the most famous by far is the *Singapore sling*, both from its virtues as a drink and its romantic connotations.

SINGAPORE SLING

1 tsp powdered sugar
½ lemon (juice)
1 jigger dry gin
1 jigger cherry brandy

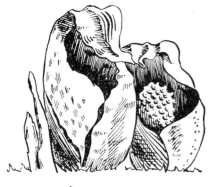

SKUNK CABBAGE, open and closed

These ingredients are placed in a collins glass (*see* GLASSWARE) with cracked ice or ice cubes and stirred until the sugar is dissolved. Carbonated water is added, the whole stirred gently and decorated to taste with fresh fruit. (Serves 1)

For further discussion of drinks and drink mixing, *see* BARTENDING.

SLIPCOTE CHEESE. A soft, unripened, rennet cheese, made from cow's milk, in Rutlandshire, England. It is an old variety, well known in the middle of the 18th century.

SLIT. To make an incision in a food material, as in pie crust, to allow the steam generated in cooking to escape.

SLIVER. To cut or split a fruit, a piece of meat, or vegetable into long thin pieces.

SLIVOVITZ. An excellent brandy-type liquor, made in Hungary of plums.

SLOE BERRY. A small, plum-like, astringent fruit from a shrub, much used in the manufacture of gin.

SLOE GIN. Sloe gin is really a liqueur made with sloe berries, which grow on bushes in the southern and midwestern sections of the United States. The bush is known in some regions under various names, such as haw bush, blackthorn, or bullace tree, etc. It grows wild in rich dry woodlands, and in the spring makes a pretty sight with its splashes of white and pinkish-white blossoms. Today the sloetree is cultivated for the berries, not only in the United States but also in England. In France the sloe berries (*prunellier*) are utilized in making a delicious liqueur called "Eau de Vie de Prunelle des Vosges," (*which see*).

SLOKE. Edible marine algae, such as sea lettuce, red laver and Irish moss. *See* LAVER.

SMALTOST CHEESE. A soft Swedish cheese.

SMASH. A brandy, gin, or whisky drink made with crushed mint sprigs. It is usually named after the liquor used.

SMASH (Basic Recipe)

1 large jigger desired liquor (brandy, gin or whisky)
1 tsp powdered sugar
4 sprigs fresh mint
1 jigger water, carbonated or plain

The mint, sugar and water are placed in the bottom of an old fashioned or similar glass (*see* GLASSWARE) and muddled thoroughly until mint is well crushed and sugar dissolved. An ice cube or equivalent amount of cracked ice is added and the liquor poured in. It is garnished with a cherry, orange slice and a twist of lemon peel. (Serves 1)

For further discussion of drinks and drink recipes, *see* BARTENDING.

SMEARCASE CHEESE or **SMIERKASE CHEESE.** Another name for cottage cheese, *which see*.

SMELT. The smelt is a small fish of the salmon family, characterized by the elongated body, the wide mouth cleft, the moderately-sized scales, and well-developed teeth.

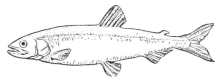

SMELT

These exceedingly prolific fish spawn in brackish water, and are frequently found at the mouth of the rivers. The smelt does not exceed 10 to 12 inches in length. Its bony back is colored a beautiful olive-green, the sides and belly are silvery with a more pronounced silvery band running along each side. These fish are found on both the Atlantic and Pacific Seaboards in temperate waters. New Brunswick and Maine send large quantities of smelts to the Eastern markets. Their sale is prohibited from March 15th to June 1st, which is spawning time for these very popular little fish.

Owing to their small size, smelts, which are really delicious, do not lend themselves to many variations in cookery. When very small, they may be fried "en brochette"— that is, threaded on a skewer, three or four at a time, and plunged into deep boiling fat, then dressed bush-like, similar to the whitebait or anchovy, on a platter covered with a napkin, with the usual fried green parsley and quartered lemon as the only garnishing. A tartare sauce, or any of the other tangy sauces served with fried fish, may be passed with the fish. The various methods of preparation of red gurnard, anchovy, sardines, and whitebait may be adapted to this fish. *See also* FISH.

SMITANE SAUCE. A Russian sauce, used with game and other foods.

SMITANE SAUCE

1 tbsp butter
1½ tbsp grated onion
½ cup dry white wine
1¼ cups sour cream
Salt and pepper

Melt the butter and sauté the onion until it is soft but not browned, stirring constantly. Add the wine and let simmer until the wine is evaporated. Stir in the sour cream, and bring to a boil, stirring constantly. Strain through a fine sieve and season to taste with salt and pepper. Serve very hot. (Makes 1 generous cup)

SMOKED BEEF. See CHIPPED BEEF.

SMOKED FISH. See FISH.

SMOKED HAM. See HAM.

SMORGASBORD. A Swedish platter or buffet of appetizers. The smorgasbord has been expanded into an elaborate collation of various hot and cold foods, pickled, jellied, in salad, and prepared in innumerable other ways. A whole meal may be made of small portions of the various dishes and will need only dessert and coffee to finish it off.

SMOTHER. As applied in cookery, smother means to cook in a covered dish or in a close mass, as smothered onions.

SNACK. A quick repast, usually between meals. See also HORS D'OEUVRE.

SNAILS. Snails which feed solely on soft leaves in the spring, summer, and fall are among the cleanest of the edible shelled creatures. During the winter months, they hibernate and fast under ground, first sealing themselves securely in their shells.

Whether taken from the vines of Ohio, the fields of hops in the Middle West, the bushes of Virginia, or imported from Europe, the inexpensive snail is always delicious and deserves to appear on the tables of rich and poor alike.

PREPARATION

When the snails are collected from bush or vine, they are kept in a cool cellar for a week and fed on tender green lettuce, growing plump and firm on such fare. They are then thrown into a pail containing salt and vinegar, and stirred vigorously with a stick. Through this procedure, the inedible secretions are cast off, and the snails are washed under running water until the liquid is perfectly clear.

The snails are now plunged into a kettle of violently boiling salted water, and allowed to boil for a good half hour, then turned into a large colander to drain. The next operation consists of pulling them out of their shells (which are set aside for later use) and removing the green gall or intestine.

Now comes the most delicate and artistic part of the preparation. Place the snails in a clean kettle, and add the traditional *bouquet garni* of fresh parsley, bay leaves, and thyme, then a large onion, sliced, a clove of garlic, and half a wine glass of cognac for every 6 dozen snails. Cover the mixture with cold water, season to taste with salt and white pepper (the latter generously) and set on a gentle fire for 6 to 7 hours, tightly covered.

Meanwhile, wash and thoroughly dry the shells, and into each pour skillfully good meat juice, without fat and slightly heated. Then return a snail to each shell, closing the opening with a thick coat of beaten butter profusely mixed with chives, shallots, and parsley very finely chopped, then seasoned with salt and white pepper. (You may flavor the butter with a morsel of very finely chopped garlic.)

Arrange in a ring all the little domes which shelter these perfumed preparations on a flat baking tin, and set them in an open oven, until the butter melts and runs, and the aromas penetrate through the limp flesh. Serve the snails ring-shape on a platter without garnishing. This authentic French preparation of the widely defamed snail is a culinary treat.

Snails may also be fried in deep hot oil; they may be chopped and prepared as for corn fritters; they may be served as cutlets or croquettes and they are delicious in patty shells especially when sliced mushrooms have been added. They are also very tasty à la Poulette, or à la Newburg.

SNAP BEAN. Another term for the string bean. See BEAN.

SNAPPER. See BLUEFISH.

SNAPPING TURTLE. See TURTLE.

SNIPE. Of all game birds snipe are the most difficult to hunt because the cunning little fellows seem to know that the hunter is hungry for a good morsel. Apparently in order to delay his capture he rises straight from the ground, makes several swift zigzags before flying away horizontally, and, if the hunter is not quick, escapes, at least for the time being.

The snipe has a very long, straight, flexible, smooth and soft bill which is extremely sensitive. The eyes are large and placed far back, the legs rather long for such a fragile mite. The male and female are alike in plumage, but the female is rather larger and plumper than the male. The general color of the upper parts of the body is blackish brown, blended with pale brown and a rich buff.

The snipe hides in the marshes and bogs amongst the high rushes. It is there that the grey and brownish black or sometimes greenish eggs are laid in a grassy depression in the ground.

While snipe is usually roasted, gourmets prefer it en salmis. The following recipe, which may be adapted to the woodcock, is, when the directions are followed, not a simple dish, but a revelation. *See also* GAME.

SALMIS OF SNIPE A LA RABELAIS

Roast, without drawing, a snipe until it is very underdone. Remove the legs and wings carefully and set aside. Discard the head, gall and gizzard. Pound the remainder of the bird to an unctuous and firm paste, adding enough stock or consommé to make this of the consistency of a rather thick cream. Press through a fine sieve, preferably a hair sieve. For each snipe thus reduced to a paste and strained, add the size of a small walnut of kneaded butter (equal parts of butter and flour kneaded together) and ½ wineglass of red claret, 2 whole small shallots, skin removed, 1 small bouquet garni (4 or 5 sprigs of parsley tied up with a small bay leaf), 1 crushed clove, 4 bruised peppercorns, and 1 thin slice of garlic, pounded. Bring this sauce to a slow boil over a moderate fire. When boiling, reduce the temperature and simmer gently for 25 minutes. Strain and add 1 tablespoon of olive oil, the juice of ½ lemon, and salt to taste. Into this soft sauce, place the 4 limbs of the snipe and heat, but do not boil. Serve on fried squares of bread, pouring the nectar of a sauce over all.

SODA. *See* BICARBONATE OF SODA and BAKING SODA.

SODA FOUNTAIN. The soda fountain is essentially and originally a machine that makes soda water (*which see*) by dissolving a neutral gas into water under pressure, and dispenses the product through a tap.

The first soda fountains were crude affairs, but highly complex in their action.

The gas was generated through a chemical reaction, and then mixed with the water in tanks that were rocked back and forth during the process. They were known variously as cylinders (because of the mixing tanks), seltzogene machines (an early name for mechanisms that carbonated fluids), and fountains (because of their appearance as the soda water was dispensed).

When the fountains came into general use, they soon became ornate, and accessories were added. One of the first developments was to install a large marble top or counter, and this tradition has persisted. Containers were needed to hold sirups and fruit, and shelves and racks were needed for glassware and other equipment. A sink was soon added, as well as compartments for ice and ice cream. Sirup-dispensing devices were developed, and when mechanical refrigeration (*which see*) came along, it, too, was incorporated into the growing fountain. Among the more recent additions have been devices that automatically mix the sirup and the soda water as it emerges from the tap, and others that make and dispense whipped cream. Steam tables, coffee makers, and other food preparing devices are sometimes installed in the fountain, but they are not an essential part, and are usually made as separate units.

The soda fountain has grown greatly in size and scope since its inception at the beginning of the 19th century, but it has grown little in grandeur. From the days of the first marble top until now, the soda fountain has always been designed to impress—the style may have changed from Victorian to modern, but the intent is the same.

Despite its many added attractions, the soda fountain is still a device that manufactures soda water. This process has been greatly simplified by modern methods. The gas is no longer manufactured in the machine, but is delivered in steel cylinders, and it is no longer necessary to agitate the mixing tanks as the gas is dissolved into the water.

HISTORY

There was a time when druggists were called apothecaries, and you could buy only drugs at their shops. Today, the typical drugstore is a cross between an old-time general store and a restaurant, while the prescription counter is usually tucked away in the rear between the lending library and the toy department. The soda fountain and a man named Elias Magloire Durand are largely responsible for this change.

It was only natural that the druggists should be among the first to make and use soda water, for it was first made and thought of as a type of medicine, and the equipment used was such as to require the skilled hand of a chemist, principally to generate the gas. That is why the fountains were in the drugstores when people began thinking of soda water as a beverage. The ice cream soda was a natural development of the fountain, and it followed that the druggist should then become the chief retail vendor of ice cream, both in sodas and other forms. By this time the pattern was established, and it was only a question of development before the soda fountain was elaborated into a small short order restaurant, and the "drug store lunch" became an accepted part of city life.

When the soda fountains were first installed, it did not take the druggist long to realize that there were other things that could be sold at a profit—some of them, like photographic services, being allied to his chemical background.

Durand might well be called the father of the "modern" drugstore. A former pharmacist in Napoleon's army, he had come to America in exile, and eventually gravitated to Philadelphia, which had a growing French colony in addition to being, then, America's largest city and chief drug center. After working at various chemist's jobs, he decided to go into business for himself, reasoning that a store that sold cigars and beverages as well as drugs might be profitable. He sent to France for equipment and supplies, and, in 1825, opened his establishment near Independence Hall. His store created quite a sensation in its time, having a glass front, mirrors, and other "modern" touches. In addition to a marble counter, he had the first soda fountain to be set up in an American drugstore. He is generally credited with having a hand in the first ice cream soda (which see).

As the popularity of soda water and soda water products grew, and as the fountains became simpler to operate, establishments out of the drug field, especially those already selling cooked food, began installing soda fountains. Theaters, bowling alleys, skating rinks, and other places of amusement where the patrons were likely to

thirst for nonalcoholic refreshment also installed fountains. The ice cream parlor of yesteryear made such great use of the fountain that it is now generally known as a "soda fountain" instead of the older title. These last institutions have become an important social factor in their role as the social center for youth, especially teen-aged youth.

SODA POP. A name given colloquially to any and all nonalcoholic carbonated beverages, especially when bottled. The name stems from both the fact that soda water (*which see*) is commonly used in the manufacture of these beverages, and from the popping sound made by a cork as it is withdrawn from a bottle that has pressure within. *See also* SOFT DRINK and POP.

SODA WATER. Soda water is a name applied generally, in America, to artificially carbonated water used to make various effervescent beverages. The water owes its bubbling characteristic to the presence of carbon dioxide gas, dissolved in the liquid under pressure. When this pressure is released, the gas escapes in the form of tiny bubbles that appear, as if by magic, within the water (*see* AERATED WATER).

HISTORY

Soda water was first produced in the latter half of the 18th century by the famous scientific pioneer, Dr. Joseph Priestley, who was then experimenting with the gas given off by fermenting beer. Further experimenting was done, and effervescent water was produced on a commercial basis in 1790 by Paul in Geneva, and, shortly afterwards, by Schweppe, in London. Similar experiments were being conducted in other countries, and the water was known as soda water because carbonated soda was used in its manufacture.

The beverage was first produced as a table water having certain medicinal properties, and flavoring was sometimes added to make it a more palatable drink.

It is generally conceded that soda water first came to the United States in Philadelphia, where it was sold in drug and perfume stores. Soda water is largely responsible for the amazing metamorphosis of the American drugstore to its present form from its beginnings as an apothecary shop (*see* SODA FOUNTAIN).

A Philadelphia physician, Dr. Philip Syng Physick, heard of Priestley's experiments and got a local chemist to make carbonated water for his patients. The chemist, Townsend Speakman, flavored the water with fruit juice, and the carbonated beverage industry in America may be said to date from that time, 1807.

In 1825, an exiled French pharmacist opened a drugstore in Philadelphia that had, among other innovations, the first soda fountain seen in America. The chemist, Elias Magloire Durand, had experimented with soda water, and had even devised a machine for its production, while an apprentice in France.

Durand's store soon became a social center, partially because of his personality and social position (Lafayette was an old friend of his), and partially because of his wonderful soda fountain.

From its beginnings as a medicine and a novelty, soda water gradually became an accepted beverage. The apparatus for making the water was greatly simplified and improved with time, and complicated but efficient bottling devices were later developed to meet the needs of the growing soft drink industry. Today, soda water is the basis of a major American industrial field.

USES

Soda water is no longer thought of as a medicine; indeed, it now usually consists of plain tap water that has been carbonated. Mixed with sirups for sweetness and flavor, soda water becomes the highly popular soft drink or soda pop, as carbonated beverages are commonly called. It is an important ingredient of the ice cream soda (*which see*), and, either plain or as a carbonated beverage, is greatly used as a mixer in many alcoholic beverages (*see* BARTENDING). It may be purchased in bottled form, and there are even devices that enable the user to carbonate water in the home (*see* SIPHON BOTTLE).

SODIUM. A soft, whitish element, an alkali, occurring abundantly, always combined, as in common salt. In the human organism, sodium has many important functions to perform. It serves to make the lime and magnesia salts in our food, and consequently, in the blood, more soluble. Lime and magnesia, if not kept liquid by sodium, are soon deposited in various parts of the body, thereby causing obstruction of the capillaries. Sodium protects the blood from becoming too easily coagulated,

as it does in case of milk, where it keeps the casein, which is combined with lime and magnesia, in a liquid state.

Sodium helps in the formation of saliva, the pancreatic juice, and the bile. It carries the excretion of carbonic acid. Sodium is a purifier, but is only of value to the system when supplied in organic form.

SODIUM BICARBONATE. Bicarbonate of soda. *See also* BAKING SODA.

SOFT DRINK. In America, the term soft drink is commonly applied to the nonalcoholic carbonated beverages, to distinguish them from the alcoholic or hard drinks. As the names would imply, at one time root beer, birch beer, ginger beer, and similar effervescent beverages were alcoholic in nature, being made by a process of fermentation (*which see*). When soda water (*which see*) became commercially available, it was possible to duplicate these beverages, using nonalcoholic ingredients.

SOFT SHELL CRAB. *See* CRAB.

SOLE. This supremely delicate fish belongs to the *Malacopterygae Subbrachiae* family. Unfortunately it is not found in American waters, and due to the fact that it has to be imported, thus commands a rather

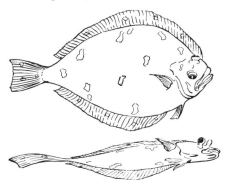

SOLE

high price. So most of the fillets of sole found in our markets are not fillets of genuine sole, but from flounder, fluke, and other flat, white-fleshed fish found in our waters. While these provide an excellent substitute, they cannot compare with the real sole.

As a general rule, sole remains at the bottom of the water along the shores in close propinquity to the sand or mud in which these fish find their nourishment.

The head of the sole is not symmetrical. Both eyes are situated on the same side of the head, which side is always uppermost when the fish swims. This characteristic is found also in the flounder, fluke, and some other flat fish. The eyeless side of the fish is whitish, and on this side is the mouth, twisted, and rather bulldoggish. The teeth are fine, velvety, and very close together. The general contour is oblong, with a rounded, protruding snout.

The chemical composition of an edible portion of sole is similar to that of the cod, including calories and vitamins. Sole may be prepared in any form of cooking applied to fish fillets. *See* FLOUNDER and FISH.

SOLAR RANGE. *See* RANGE.

SOMATOSE. *See* BEEF SOMATOSE.

SORBAIS CHEESE. A high-smelling, semi-hard, whole-milk French cheese. It is square in shape, the center yellow, and the rind reddish brown. It is a little smaller than Maroilles cheese which it resembles in shape and flavor.

SORGHUM. A cane-like grass, resembling broom corn, yielding sugar. Molasses (*which see*) may be prepared from the juice of sorghum.

SORREL. A relative of the dock, this herb has a pungent or acid flavor which is much enjoyed by many people and as much disliked by others. Properly prepared, as an accompaniment for mild-flavored dishes, it is a delicious vegetable. The young tender leaves may be added to salads, and the older plants cooked as a vegetable or in soup. Several delicious soups, among them the French *potage santé*, or health soup, are made of sorrel. Sorrel proper is not to be confused with the troublesome sheep sorrel or with wood sorrel.

COLD SORREL SOUP

4 cups chicken bouillon, or water and bouillon cubes
½ lb fresh sorrel
6 egg yolks
1 pt cream, or rich milk
Celery salt
1 tsp fresh tarragon, chopped, or ½ tsp dried tarragon

Wash the sorrel and discard the stems. Bring the bouillon to a boil and add the sorrel. Simmer for several minutes or until the sorrel is tender. Beat the egg yolks and stir in the cream. Slowly add ½ cup of the bouillon to the egg mixture. Then pour this back into the bouillon, very slowly,

stirring constantly. Season to taste with celery salt, and add the tarragon. Cook, not letting the mixture boil, and stirring constantly, until the mixture coats the spoon. Remove from the stove, cool, and then chill in the refrigerator until ready to serve. Serve very cold in cups. (Serves 6)

PUREE OF SORREL

Trim 4 pounds of fresh sorrel, discarding the stems. Wash it well in several waters and place it in a saucepan. Do not add any more water than clings to the leaves. Cover the pan and cook very slowly for 30 minutes, when the sorrel will have wilted considerably. Stir in 4 tablespoons of flour and 2 tablespoons of butter, and add 4 cups of meat stock. Season to taste with salt and pepper, and add 1 teaspoon of sugar. Cover the pan and let simmer for another 30 minutes. Put the whole mixture through a sieve. Reheat the purée. If desired, several egg yolks may be stirred into the sorrel just before serving, or a little cream may be added. Prepared this way, sorrel is a fine basis for poached eggs, or sliced veal, or a white fish. (Serves 4 to 6)

SORREL SOUP I
(Potage Santé)

6 handfuls of fresh sorrel
2 tbsp butter
4 cups milk
Salt and pepper
2 egg yolks
2 tbsp cream
Croutons

Remove the stems from the sorrel and wash thoroughly in several waters. Place the butter and the sorrel in a saucepan over a low flame. Cook, stirring constantly, until the butter melts and the sorrel wilts. Add the milk, a little at a time, season with salt and pepper, and bring to a boil, but do not allow to boil. Beat in the egg yolks and add the cream. Warm a soup tureen and place the egg yolks in the bottom. Pour in the hot soup, stir well, and serve immediately with croutons. (Serves 6)

SORREL SOUP II

1 lb sorrel, chopped
1 head lettuce, chopped
1 bunch water cress or chervil, chopped

Juice of 2 lemons
3 tbsp butter
1 qt seasoned chicken broth
1 cup diced white meat of chicken
2 egg yolks
1¼ cups heavy cream
Buttered bread or toast strips

Simmer the sorrel, lettuce, water cress or chervil, lemon juice and butter for 10 minutes, stirring frequently. Add the broth and diced chicken and cook 10 minutes. Beat the eggs and cream thoroughly together, combine slowly with the hot soup and cook 2 minutes more without actually boiling. Pour over the bread or toast strips and serve at once. (Serves 4)

SORTE MAGGENGA CHEESE. Another name for Parmesan cheese (*which see*).

SORTE VERMENGA CHEESE. Another name for Parmesan cheese, (*which see*).

SOUBISE SAUCE. *See* WHITE SAUCE.

SOUDAN COFFEE. *See* COLA NUT.

SOUFFLE. Usually a dessert, although there are also fish, meat, poultry, and vegetable soufflés.

There is a popular misconception that soufflés are difficult to make and that the chances of producing a perfect dish are less than even. The main trouble is that a soufflé is apt to fall in the center before it reaches the table; because a soufflé is composed largely of stiffly beaten egg whites on which it depends for its lightness, it must be baked with special care. Keep your oven temperature steadily between 350° and 375° F. in order to insure a light soufflé in which the egg whites will not separate nor fall. Furthermore, allow enough baking time so that the soufflé may be fully cooked right through to the center. A soufflé should be put into the oven to bake just as soon as the ingredients are combined, planning the time so that it will be cooked as nearly as possible at the moment of serving.

The basic foundation of a soufflé is a very heavy white sauce made with 3 tablespoons of butter and 4 tablespoons of flour to 1 cup of milk. Prepare exactly as a white sauce (*which see*). Then if the soufflé is to be a plain sweet one, add ¼ cup of sugar and cool. Beat in, one at a time, the yolks of 4 eggs, mixing each in thoroughly. Now add the desired flavoring, a teaspoon of

vanilla for example, and finally, fold in very gently the stiffly beaten whites of 4 eggs. Bake in a generously buttered soufflé dish and serve immediately, plain, or with a sauce of fruit, chocolate, or cream.

Never over-fill the baking dish because a properly made soufflé will rise almost treble its original bulk. And, never plan on a soufflé for dessert unless you know that the family or guests will be at table promptly; for while the guest may be kept waiting, the soufflé cannot.

With the suggested sauce base leftovers may well be used in a soufflé. To the quantities given, for instance, one cup of flaked cooked fish, canned or fresh cooked, or the same quantity of meat (chicken, lamb or veal) may be added after the egg yolks with appropriate flavoring and seasoning.

Desserts of the puff or whip type are also often designated as soufflés, as are certain cold desserts with a gelatin base.

See also individual meats, fish, vegetables, fruits and flavors.

SOUFFLE DES SEIGNEURS

8 lady fingers
Kirsch
½ cup shredded candied fruit
Brandy
3 tbsp butter
3 tbsp flour
Salt
1¼ cups milk
½ cup sugar
1 tsp vanilla
4 egg yolks
5 egg whites

Soak the lady fingers in kirsch and the candied fruits in brandy. Prepare a white sauce (*which see*) with the butter, flour, salt, and milk. When thickened, add the sugar and stir until dissolved. Cool slightly. Add the vanilla and the beaten egg yolks. Then fold in the egg whites, beaten to a light froth. Butter a large casserole, dust it with flour, and line with the lady fingers and fruit. Pour the custard into the center and bake in a moderate oven (375° F.) about 25 minutes. Serve immediately upon taking from the oven as the soufflé falls quickly. (Serves 6)

SOUP. Not so many years ago every kitchen had a coal range with a stock pot simmering on it. Soup making then was easy. The advent of gas and electric ranges, however, has made soup making a forgotten art, and in these high pressure times with leisurely dining a Victorian memory, the can opener has superseded the stockpot. Light soups serve as appetizers; heavier ones may be a main course.

The line between stews and soups is sometimes hard to define. England's boiled beef started in the soup pot, and stews and soups go back hand in hand in the world's cuisine until antiquity swallows them up. When the subject is explored the relation between soups and puddings emerges, too. One of the earliest references in English describes "soops" as "a kind of sweet, pleasant broth, made rich with fruit, or vegetables, and spices." These popular, sweetened soups gradually thickened until bread and rice puddings evolved.

Custard soups of continental cuisines indicate steps along the way. Travelers tell of the sweetened fruit juice soups of Europe and of the soaked prunes floating in one of Holland's soups. An iced claret soup is traced to Denmark by one compiler of cooking lore. Yet traditional ingredients linger. Bread and rice or tapioca, or vermicelli are still used as thickening agents and as accessories; so are slices of bread in the French onion soup, fragments of toast or cubes, "croutons" as the French call them. Little custard squares in the consommé are reminders of the egg-thickened soups which antedated the use of cornstarch or flour.

The only edible soup, or form of soup, the gourmet concedes, is freshly made from fresh materials—lean meat, a shin bone of beef, and vegetables or soup greens—and unquestionably the principles he defends do underly certain peerless soups, fortifying to the system and delicious to the palate.

Soup, you know, is not to be entrusted to just anyone. It is a job for an expert cook. In big hotel kitchens noted for good food, to be the master of the soup pot is a top office, next to that of the sauce cook himself. In commercial soup companies the soupmaker is the head man, chosen from master chefs the world over. His job is to develop the master recipes by which the different soups are made and to maintain the high standard of those long on the market.

Perhaps one of the sure tests of a good homemaker is her choice of soup in relation to the rest of the meal. The purpose of soup in the meal is two-fold: first, to stimulate appetite, second, to provide nourishment. A heavy meal should begin with a thin soup, one that will enliven even the most jaded appetite for the other good things to come. A light meal may well begin with a heavy soup, and sometimes the soup, as we have noted, may serve as the entire main course.

All soup recipes may, generally speaking, be classified into three main groups, as follows:

(I) Thin, clear soups which stimulate appetite; consommé, bouillon, broth, julienne, chicken, etc., to which may be added the fruit soups.

(II) Thin, light, delicate cream soups; cream of tomato, pea, asparagus, celery, watercress, lettuce, etc. For thickening soups, roux (which see) may be used.

(III) Heavy, thick soups or chowders, bisques, fish soups; pepper pot, Scotch broth, mulligatawny, vegetable soups, etc. To make soup thicker, use roux.

A fourth, supplementary class may be added, consisting of the jellied soups, usually served on hot summer days.

Meat Stock

Fresh, uncooked beef with the addition of cracked bones makes the best stock, the glutinous matter contained in them adding to the strength, richness, and thickness of the soup. Two ounces of bones contain as much gelatin as one pound of meat, but it can only be released by long, slow, moist cooking. Breaking or chopping the bones causes the gelatin to be released more easily and quickly. An abundance of gelatin causes the stock to jelly when cold. The flesh of mature animals is more flavorful than that of young ones.

To make the stock cut the meat small and place it with the bones in cold water with a little salt. Bring slowly to boiling point and skim, after which vegetables may be added to improve the flavor but only after the meat has boiled at least once and the scum has been removed. Generally speaking, the proportions to be used are as follows:

For each quart of water 1¼ to 1½ pounds of lean beef.

For each pound of meat, ½ pound of beef bone.

For each quart of liquid 1 level tablespoon of salt.

For each quart of liquid 2 cups of mixed vegetables.

Chicken stock is made exactly as meat stock, chicken being substituted for the beef, weight for weight. For white stock to be used in the preparation of white soups, substitute veal, poultry trimmings, and a little lean ham in place of the beef. The latter, when seared, gives brown stock.

Bouillon or Consommé. To clarify stock for bouillon or consommé, after the stock is made, strained and chilled, remove the fat which will have hardened on top. Measure the quantity of stock to be clarified and place in a saucepan with the slightly beaten white and shell of 1 egg to each quart. Bring slowly to the boiling point, stirring constantly. Boil 2 minutes, reduce the heat, and allow the stock to simmer 15 minutes. A heavy scum will appear on the surface. Skim this off carefully, then strain the bouillon through doubled cheesecloth or a flannel bag.

Vegetable Stock. This is a combination of the liquids in which a variety of vegetables have been cooked.

CANNED SOUPS

These are of two varieties: condensed or concentrated, requiring the addition of an equal volume of water or milk; and soups ready to serve after either heating or chilling. Canned bouillon, consommé or chicken soup will be found very useful in preparing recipes which demand "a cup of stock." Many meat dishes requiring added liquid will gain variety of flavor if canned soup is used in place of water. Again when making sauces canned soups may often substitute for water.

CREAM SOUP

These must be of distinctive flavor and are usually prepared with a foundation of white sauce, cream sauce, or béchamel sauce plus the puréed cooked vegetable or blend of vegetables. Cream soups must be well seasoned. They may also be made from the pulp of canned vegetables, such as peas, tomatoes, carrots, beets, asparagus, etc. See the various vegetables for recipes.

FRUIT SOUPS

One frequently finds fruit soups served on the Continent, a custom which might well be adopted by us, especially in summer. *See* recipes under fruits such as lemon, and below.

JELLIED SOUPS

Jellied soups are excellent appetizers in summertime. They are usually of the consommé or bouillon type; either a strong home made stock (veal or chicken) may be jellied, or one may add gelatin to canned bouillon or consommé. Serve such soups in bouillon cups, breaking up the jelly lightly with a fork and garnishing with a teaspoon of salted whipped cream, or with a light sprinkling of minced parsley or chives and a small section of fresh lemon.

VEGETABLE SOUPS

Every country has its own variation of the vegetable soup. Like meat soups, vegetable soups should simmer gently for several hours so as to extract all the mineral salts from the numerous vegetables used. The vegetables should be cut very small, and the addition of a meat bone will enhance the flavor of any vegetable soup. *See* MINESTRONE, PEPPER POT, etc.

CANNED SOUP COMBINATIONS

There are so many varieties of canned soups that one can serve a different soup almost every day of the month. Brand new soups can be created by merely combining a couple of cans of different, yet harmonizing, flavors. Extend concentrated soups according to directions on the containers; use others as they come from the can. A few good combinations follow:

Clam Chowder Creole Style. Equal parts clam chowder and chicken gumbo Creole.

Chicken Gumbo Paysanne. Equal parts chicken gumbo Creole and vegetable soup.

Cottage Vegetable Soup. Equal parts vegetable soup and tomato soup.

Corn Chowder Berkshire. Equal parts corn chowder and tomato soup.

Cream of Celery Country Style. Equal parts cream of celery soup and chicken noodle soup.

Cream of Oyster Louisiana. Equal parts cream of oyster soup and cream of mushroom soup.

Cream of Tomato Soup Traymore. Equal parts cream of tomato soup and cream of celery soup.

Indian Corn Chowder. Equal parts corn chowder and onion soup.

Old-Fashioned Mushroom Soup. Equal parts mushroom soup and chicken noodle soup. Top with minced parsley.

Onion Soup Creole. Equal parts onion soup and chicken gumbo Creole.

Oyster Bisque Home Style. Equal parts sieved cream of oyster soup and cream of mushroom soup, also sieved. Garnish with croutons.

Pittsburgh Pepper-Pot. Equal parts pepper-pot and canned vegetable soup.

Saint Patrick Soup. Equal parts cream of spinach soup and cream of mushroom soup. Top with minced chives or parsley.

Tomato Mongole. Equal parts cream of tomato soup and green pea soup.

And so on ad infinitum, according to imagination, taste, and emergency.

JELLIED FRUIT SOUP

¾ cup cherry juice
¾ cup pineapple juice
½ cup orange juice
2½ tbsp lemon juice
2 tbsp gelatin
1½ cups cold water
Dash of salt
Sugar to taste
Chopped fresh mint

Combine the fruit juices. Soften the gelatin in ½ cup of the cold water, then dissolve with salt and sugar in the remaining (boiling) water. Combine with the fruit juices, and chill. At serving time break up with a fork, stir in the chopped mint, and serve in bouillon cups or cocktail glasses. (Serves 4 to 6)

JEWISH FRUIT SOUP

½ cup finely diced oranges
½ cup finely diced pineapple
½ cup finely diced peaches
½ cup finely diced strawberries
½ cup finely diced rhubarb
1 cup sugar
½ tsp salt
1 qt water
½ cup sour cream

Simmer the fruits, sugar, and salt with the water for 10 minutes. Add the sour cream, blend thoroughly, and serve hot. If preferred, chill the fruit mixture and add the sour cream immediately before serving. (Serves 6)

SCANDINAVIAN FRUIT SOUP

1½ qt water
¼ cup cornstarch
1 tsp salt
3 tbsp lemon juice
1 stick cinnamon
¼ lb prunes
½ cup seedless raisins
½ cup tart apples, diced
¼ cup sugar
1 cup cherry or grape juice
¼ cup sweet red wine

Mix the water, cornstarch, and salt in a saucepan and bring to a boil, stirring constantly. Add the remaining ingredients, except the wine. Simmer 30 minutes until the prunes are tender, stirring occasionally. Cool the mixture and chill several hours or over night. Just before serving add the wine and additional salt and lemon juice, if needed. (Serves 6)

VEGETABLE SOUP

1½ lb shin of beef
2 qt cold water
Bouquet garni
½ cup carrot
½ cup string beans
½ cup lima beans
⅓ cup onion
⅓ cup cabbage
⅓ cup celery
⅓ cup shelled peas
1½ tsp salt
⅛ tsp pepper

The amounts and varieties of vegetables may vary according to taste and season.

Wash the meat, place in a saucepan with the water and add the bouquet garni. Bring slowly to boiling point, skim, and simmer until the meat falls from the bones, about 3 hours. Strain, add the vegetables, all diced to about the size of the peas—even the lima beans may be halved or quartered if large. Simmer until the vegetables are tender but not broken. If desired, some of the meat may be diced and added to the soup. Season and serve with grated Parmesan cheese and crusty bread. (Serves 6 or 8)

SOUP CUP. A large, double-handled cup that is sometimes used instead of a soup dish or bowl for individual soup servings. It frequently has a removable lid to keep the contents warm. *See* DISHES; *see also* TABLE SETTING AND SERVICE.

SOUP DISH. A large shallow bowl or deep plate that is used for individual soup servings. *See* DISHES; *see also* TABLE SETTING AND SERVICE.

SOUP LADLE. *See* FLATWARE.

SOUP SPOON. There are three different types of soup spoons in general use: round, oval, and cream. *See* FLATWARE.

SOUP TUREEN. A large, covered bowl, often highly ornate, used to serve soups at the table. The tureen is filled and placed on the table, the soup being ladled out in individual portions at the proper time. *See* DISHES.

SOUR. The family name for a group of intoxicating drinks, distinguished by their sour taste. Sours are especially good for freshening an unpleasant flavor in the mouth, as caused by overindulgence, for example, or as thirst quenchers.

In the case of the basic recipe, the sour usually takes its name from the used liquor; viz, brandy sour, gin sour, rum sour, whisky sour, etc. Of these, the whisky sour is, perhaps, the most common.

SOUR (Basic Recipe)

1 large jigger desired liquor (applejack, brandy, gin, rum, whisky, etc.)
½ lemon (juice)
½ tsp powdered sugar

These ingredients are well shaken with cracked ice and strained into a sour glass (*see* GLASSWARE) which is then filled with carbonated water and garnished with a lemon slice and cherry. (Serves 1)

There are many elaborations and variations of this basic recipe, many of a strictly local nature.

BOSTON SOUR

1 large jigger rye or bourbon
½ lemon (juice)
1 egg white
1 tsp sugar

Mix the ingredients and pour into an 8-ounce glass. Add an ice cube and stir. (Serves 1)

DOUBLE STANDARD SOUR

½ lemon (juice) or 1 lime (juice)
½ tsp powdered sugar
½ tsp grenadine
½ jigger rye or bourbon
½ jigger dry gin

This is served in the regular sour glass, garnished as in the basic recipe. (Serves 1)

EGG SOUR

1 whole egg
1 tsp sugar
½ lemon (juice)
1 jigger brandy
¼ tsp curacao

This sour is served in an eight ounce highball glass without the usual sour garnishings. (Serves 1)

New York Sour. This is made in much the same manner as the whisky sour (*see* basic recipe), except that the carbonated water is left out, and a half jigger of claret is floated on top of the finished drink.

For further discussion of drinks and drink mixing, *see* BARTENDING.

SOUR MASH. Sour mash is one of the two methods of fermentation used in the production of American type whisky. The other is known as sweet mash. The "sweet" and "sour" mash designations are the result of differences in the process of fermentation. For the sweet variety, the mash is mixed with fresh water and yeast in the fermenting vats and the operation is completed in 48 hours. In the sour mash process, the yeast used is taken from the "spent" beer of a former fermentation. By "spent" beer is meant a beer from which the alcohol has been removed in its passage through the still. The fermentation in this case requires 72 hours. While the sour mash process yields a distinctive flavor which is highly prized by connoisseurs, the sweet method yields a greater quantity of whisky.

SOUTH SIDE WINE. A light amber colored wine from Madeira (*which see*).

SOY BEAN. Current scientific research confirms ancient Oriental records of the medicinal value of beans, especially of soy beans. A twenty-five thousand year old food of eastern Asia and one of the five sacred grains of ancient China, soy beans are now grown on more than five million acres in the United States, and seem destined for innumerable uses "from hay to hairpins." According to prediction one of the surprises science may soon spring on the American public is that city back-yard farmers may even in future grow their own clothes, the "wool" coming from the heart of the soy bean! The casein of milk is already being used in the manufacture of artificial wool so protein-rich soy beans may provide a plentiful and less expensive substitute for the milk casein.

The soy bean may replace cows and sheep just as the automobile has ousted the horse. Chemical studies show that their protein has a high nutritive value, practically equivalent to that of milk, and that they contain vitamins B and G. Especially significant is the use of soy beans in infant foods as the sole source of protein for those children who are allergic or hypersensitive to animal protein. Normal infants are also fed with milk and solids of the bean and it is steadily finding wider use in diets for diabetics.

Soy beans must be thoroughly soaked until swollen soft before boiling and should only be eaten when wholly tender. When cooking the beans, or in fact any kind of dry vegetables, salt should be added after cooking, as salting at the beginning of the cooking shrinks the pores of the pellicles and delays the cooking process. This, incidentally, applies to all beans.

Soybean Souffle

3 eggs
3 cups cooked sieved soy beans
1 tbsp minced onion
1 tsp salt
1 tsp minced chives
2 tbsp minced parsley
⅛ tsp white pepper

Separate the yolks from the whites of the eggs. Beat the yolks thoroughly, and combine them with the bean pulp, seasonings, and flavorings. Blend all very thoroughly and finally fold in gently the stiffly beaten egg whites. Turn into a well-buttered casserole or soufflé dish and bake in a moderate oven (325°–350° F.) from 30 to 35 minutes, or until set and puffy. Serve immediately.

SOY SAUCE. A commercial product, the foundation of which is made with soy beans, and sold in almost any grocery. It is used in Oriental cookery.

SPADE-FISH. See PORGY.

SPAGHETTI. One of the most delectable of wheat foods, the nutritious *pasta* of Italy, that comes to us most often as macaroni, spaghetti and vermicelli, may be served in any or every course of a dinner from soup to savory, as garnishment, vegetable, entrée, dessert, or even a piquant and truly American savory in ramekins.

The best spaghetti—the word means little cords, whereas vermicelli means little worms—is made from the glutinous semolina meal, ground from the hard durum wheat of southern Europe and northern Africa. Some of our Italian immigrants never ate it before coming to this country, but regarded it as a luxury of the rich, and had to content themselves with the sustaining ration of polenta, which is corn meal. However, it is one of the familiar commodities in most civilized lands, and research in the cook books of the world probably would show a thousand fashions for serving it. It lends itself readily to the simplest methods, and is particularly good when treated only with melted butter and grated cheese, and particularly delicious in a béchamel sauce, white sauce, or cream sauce, with grated cheese sprinkled over it.

Between the simplest and the most elaborate sauces there is a vast host of comparatively insipid, uninspiring forms; and it is a sorry reflection on our easy acceptance of things put before us that certain of the ready-made concoctions of spaghetti sauce are merely palatable messes of tomato paste and cheese calculated neither to offend nor to excite unduly the unsophisticated tastes of the multitude.

Italian Spaghetti

Tomato paste is precious stuff, invaluable—but so is milk, and so is water. Buy some good Italian tomato paste if you would electrify a party of chosen guests with a proper dish of spaghetti, but buy also three pounds of good lean beef, a veal knuckle, a slice of ham, some fat bacon, and leeks, celery, carrots, parsley, chervil, and garlic. Thrifty Italians grow sweet basil in their gardens; and you should get some of the fresh herb if you can; otherwise use a pinch of dried basil. Then, proceed as follows:

Fry the ham and bacon, which you have coarsely chopped, using about 3 slices of bacon and one slice of ham and turn the

WINDING SPAGHETTI ON FORK

mixture, which should be drained of all its fat, into a stew pan. Dredge the beef rather lightly with powdered sugar, and sear it fiercely in the hot fat remaining from the bacon and ham, turning it over and over till it is nearly black and all crusty and glistening. Put it in the pot with the chopped ham and bacon, and the knuckle veal, and add all the vegetables, cut up small. Use the whole bunch of leeks, three stalks of celery, two carrots, and a tablespoon each of parsley and chervil. Two cloves of garlic will do, sliced thinly; but if you have scruples you may substitute six shallots. Season with a tablespoon of salt, one of black peppercorns, four cloves, three bay leaves, a large pinch of thyme and either the fresh or dry basil. Then pour on enough boiling water to cover it, and simmer three of four hours, or until the fiber of the meat is broken down and all its essence is in the sauce. Expensive! yes, but remember it is for a party of at least eight guests, and it should be good; your spaghetti should put on airs. Strain the sauce through a coarse sieve, pressing through all the soft pulp and discarding only the lumps and shreds, and add a cup of the tomato paste and a half cup of Marsala, sherry, or Madeira wine.

Take one medium truffle (optional) from a tin, wash and brush it, slice it thinly,

and cut it in julienne strips. Peel half a pound of mushrooms, chop the stems, and slice the caps thinly in transverse sections. Add all these to the sauce, and simmer all slowly while the spaghette is boiling.

Now for the spaghetti. Use a large kettle of salted, boiling water, and put 2 packages of spaghetti in without breaking it. Ten to 20 minutes will cook it, depending on the hardness of the paste. Italians prefer it not too tender, not too soft; but some Americans like is as soft as boiled rice. While it boils, grate your cheese, about 1 pound of it, rubbing the granite-like block of Parmesan furiously on a fine grater till you have a mountain of light and feathery flakes. The dry and tasteless Parmesan that comes in bottles is an insult to spaghetti and to cheese. Incidentally, if Parmesan is a bit too much for you, in bouquet and tang, you may grate a little Swiss, gruyère, or old cheddar along with it, say half and half.

When the spaghetti is done, drain it, pile on a huge platter, and pour the golden bronze sauce over it with luxurious abandon. Then make a small mountain of the cheese in the middle, and have an extra dish of cheese on the table. How to eat it? Well, an Italian can do the trick with elegance by catching up the strands on a fork and twirling them into a neat bolus in the bowl of a soup spoon. This is a royal spaghetti party. You may call it a spaghetti festival.

Spaghetti with Bacon Sauce

1 8-oz package spaghetti
Boiling salted water
1½ cups diced bacon
½ cup minced green pepper
½ cup minced onion
2 cups thin tomato sauce
1 tsp chili powder
Salt
½ cup grated cheese

Cook the spaghetti in boiling salted water according to directions on the package. Drain thoroughly. For the sauce, fry the bacon slightly, add the green pepper and onion and sauté until the onion is light brown. Add the tomato sauce, chili powder and a little salt and cook 10 minutes. Turn the spaghetti into a casserole or individual baking dishes. Pour the sauce over, sprinkle with the cheese and set in a moderate oven (350° F.) just until the cheese is melted. (Serves 6)

SPAGHETTI MALNATTI

1 onion, minced
2 tbsp cooking oil or butter
1 No. 2 can tomatoes
1 tsp sugar
¼ tsp salt
⅛ tsp pepper
1 can condensed cream of mushroom soup
½ cup sliced stuffed olives
1 8-oz package spaghetti
¼ cup grated cheese
¼ cup buttered crumbs

Cook the onion in the fat until it begins to turn color. Add the tomatoes and seasonings and simmer 15 minutes. Combine with the mushroom soup and olives. Cook the spaghetti in boiling salted water according to the directions on the package; drain thoroughly. Arrange alternate layers of spaghetti and sauce in a greased baking dish, top with the combined cheese and crumbs, and bake in a moderate oven (350° F.) 20 to 30 minutes. (Serves 6)

SPAGHETTI MILANAISE

1 8-oz package spaghetti
1 No. 2 can tomatoes
1 can tomato sauce or purée
1 cup stock
½ tsp salt
½ tsp minced garlic
⅛ tsp pepper
1 tsp paprika
1 bay leaf
1 tsp Worcestershire sauce
2 thin slices boiled ham
6 thin slices boiled tongue
1 cup canned mushrooms, thinly sliced
1 tbsp butter
Grated Parmesan cheese

Cook the spaghetti in boiling salted water according to directions on the package. Drain thoroughly. Meanwhile prepare a sauce by simmering together for 20 minutes the canned tomatoes, tomato sauce or purée, stock, seasonings and flavorings.

Add the ham and tongue, both cut in julienne strips, with the mushrooms. Simmer 10 minutes longer. Add the drained spaghetti to the sauce and mix thoroughly, and just before serving add the butter. Pass cheese separately. (Serves 6)

If fresh mushrooms are used they must be thinly sliced and sautéed in a little butter before being added to the sauce.

SPAGHETTI TUNA DINNER

1 7-oz can tuna fish
1 clove garlic, crushed
4 large tomatoes, peeled and quartered
½ cup stock
¼ tsp sugar
1 tbsp minced parsley
A pinch each of saffron and dried basil
8 ripe olives, sliced
1 8-oz package spaghetti, cooked
Grated cheese

Flake the fish and sauté in its own oil for 5 minutes. Add the garlic, tomatoes, stock, seasonings and flavorings. Cover and simmer gently until thick. Just before serving stir in the olives with the spaghetti (cooked according to directions on the package, then well drained). Pass cheese separately. (Serves 6)

SAUCE FOR SPAGHETTI

2 or 3 onions, sliced
1 clove garlic, minced
2 tbsp oil or butter
1¼ lb chopped round steak
1 large can imported Italian tomatoes
½ can tomato paste
Salt, pepper, cayenne
¼ cup sugar
1 tsp minced basil
Pinch of thyme
Slight grating lemon rind
½ cup sliced mushrooms or minced green pepper, optional

Brown the onions and garlic in the oil or butter. Add the meat and brown this also. Combine with the tomatoes and tomato paste and cook down until thick, simmering gently and adding a little water if necessary. Cook about 1½ hours. Add seasonings and flavorings, pour over cooked spaghetti and serve with grated

Parmesan cheese. If the mushrooms or green pepper are used add with the tomatoes and tomato paste.

SPALEN CHEESE. A type of Emmenthaler cheese sometimes known as stringer. It weighs 35 to 40 pounds.

SPANISH BAYONET or SPANISH DAGGER. A wild, edible plant of the yucca family. *See* YUCCA.

SPANISH CREAM. A gelatin custard. Its basis is a soft custard stiffened with gelatin. As in the whips, stiffly beaten egg whites are folded into the partially set gelatin custard, making Spanish cream really a gelatin custard whip.

SPANISH CREAM

1 tbsp gelatin
3 cups milk
½ cup sugar
3 eggs
⅓ tsp salt
1 tsp vanilla

Soften the gelatin in one cup of the milk (cold). Scald the remaining milk, add the softened gelatin and the sugar, and stir until both are dissolved. Pour slowly over the egg yolks beaten with the salt, beating while pouring. Return to the double boiler and cook, stirring constantly, until thickened. Remove from the fire, cool a little and add the vanilla. When partly cold but not set, fold in gently the stiffly beaten egg whites. Turn into one large or several individual previously wet molds and chill.

Made in this manner the mixture will separate and form a jelly on the bottom with custard on the top. If this separation is not desired, allow the custard to cool thoroughly before folding in the egg whites. Unmold and serve with whipped cream or any preferred fruit. (Serves 6)

VARIATIONS

Chocolate Spanish Cream. Follow directions for Spanish cream adding 2 squares (ounces) of melted chocolate or 6 tablespoons of cocoa to the milk before scalding.

Coffee Spanish Cream. Follow directions for Spanish cream using 2 cups of strong coffee for a similar amount of milk and slightly increasing the sugar.

Orange Spanish Cream. Follow directions for Spanish cream substituting 1 cup of

orange juice for 1 cup of the milk, adding this after the custard is removed from the fire. Serve with sliced or cubed oranges and cream.

Macaroon or Nut Spanish Cream. Follow directions for Spanish cream adding ¾ cup of macaroons, dried and rolled, or chopped nuts just before turning into individual molds. Garnish with candied cherries or fresh or canned fruit.

SPANISH MACKEREL. *See* MACKEREL.

SPANISH OMELET. *See* EGG.

SPANISH SAUCE. *See* TOMATO.

SPANISH TOAST. Another name for French toast, *which see.*

SPARERIBS. Spareribs are all the ribs from the side of pork, somewhat closely

SPARERIBS

trimmed. Besides being very economical they are delicious and nutritious. They are sold fresh, pickled, or smoked.

BARBECUED SPARERIBS

4 to 5 lb fresh spareribs
1 cup tomato catsup
¼ cup vinegar
¼ cup Worcestershire sauce
1 tsp salt
1 tsp freshly ground black pepper
2 tsp chili powder
¼ tsp cayenne
1 or 2 finely chopped onions
1½ cups water

Wipe the spareribs, and lay in a roasting pan. Blend all remaining ingredients and pour over the meat. Cover, and bake in a moderate oven (350° F.) about 1½ hours, uncovering during the last 30 minutes of baking. The meat should be turned and basted at frequent intervals. Serve with parsley potatoes and a green salad. (Serves 6)

SPARERIBS BAKED WITH NAVY BEANS

1½ lb navy beans
2 qt water
1½ lb spareribs
½ small onion, minced
5 tbsp molasses
1 tsp salt
2 tbsp prepared mustard

Wash and soak the beans overnight in the water. In the morning simmer for 2 hours in the same water. Add the spareribs and onions and simmer 30 minutes longer. Blend the molasses, salt and mustard and stir into the mixture. Turn into a bean pot or baking pan. Slip the bones from the spareribs and cut the meat into convenient-sized pieces; bury in the beans. Cover and bake in a slow oven (300° F.) about 2 hours. Uncover and brown. Serve hot with brown bread. (Serves 6)

SPARERIBS WITH APPLES AND SAUERKRAUT

Arrange sauerkraut over the bottom of a covered roasting pan. Put cored apples, the cavities filled with brown sugar, down in the bed of sauerkraut. Arrange spareribs over all, season with salt and pepper, and roast in a moderate oven (350° F.) 1 to 1½ hours.

STUFFED SPARERIBS

3 lb fresh spareribs
2 cups soft bread crumbs
½ cup butter
2 tsp salt
½ tsp pepper
2 minced onions

Have the spareribs cut in two portions. Wipe, lay one in a greased roasting pan. Prepare a stuffing with all remaining ingredients and spread over the meat. Top with the second portion of meat and pour 1 cup of stock or water around. Cover and bake in a moderate oven (350° F.) about 2 hours, removing the cover during the last half hour of baking. If desired, omit the water and baste frequently with barbecue sauce (which see). (Serves 4)

SPARKLING BURGUNDY. A red sparkling wine (see WINE). Light-bodied and slightly sweet, it is made from one or more varieties of grapes. It may be served at any time, with or without food, and is always served chilled. See also BURGUNDY.

SPARKLING WINE. See WINE.

SPATULA. A spatula is an implement consisting of a flat, thin blade set in a handle. Though it may resemble a knife in appearance, the spatula has no sharpened cutting edge, and the blade is often flexible. It is made in many sizes and shapes for different specific uses.

Spatulas are used in many different ways, and are among the handiest of kitchen tools. The thinness and flexibility of the blade makes them ideal for slipping between or under things, as to free a cake from its pan or to turn over foods in a frying pan or on a griddle. Broad blades are preferred for turning or serving purposes, while narrow ones are handy for tight corners or delicate operations. Spatulas are also used for spreading substances and for scraping. They should not be used to scrape an easily scratched surface, however, unless the blade is made of a plastic or similar soft material. See also KITCHEN EQUIPMENT.

SPEARFISH. A salt-water fish with a long, sword-shaped snout, related to the swordfish (which see) and prepared in the same ways.

SPEARMINT. This aromatic herb of the mint family is native to Europe, but it has been naturalized in the United States. It is sometimes referred to as garden mint or lamb mint. Its leaves are used to make a mint sauce for lamb (see MINT), and from them is derived an oil that is made into a flavoring extract. The extract is used in chewing gum, medicines, and beverages. Spearmint leaves are a principal ingredient of the mint julep.

SPECK. A German term for bacon.

SPELT. A cereal intermediate between wheat and barley.

SPERRKASE CHEESE. Another name for dry cheese, which see.

SPICE. This is a general name for all varieties of spicy, pungent, aromatic vegetable substances. They are used in medicines and wines as well as in cookery. Spices are derived from no particular part of a plant or tree, but from whichever parts happen to be richest in flavor. They are used either as powders or as decoctions.

Spices have been regarded as a luxury, or at least have been held in high esteem, throughout history. Arabia was known as "Araby the blest" because of the fact that it served as a distributing point for spices. The spice trade promoted the expansion of the Roman empire, and it was responsible for the period of exploration that resulted in the discovery of the "new world." Most spices are of tropical origin, but some have been naturalized elsewhere.

The use of spices in cookery is parallel to the use of make-up in grooming. Both

SPEARMINT

should be used subtly in order to achieve a particular effect without becoming too noticeable. They can then achieve an intriguing elusiveness.

Tightly covered spices will retain their full body and strength for months. However, spices that have been exposed to the air over a period of time, or that have been allowed to stand for over a year in a kitchen closet will have lost most of their value as

seasoners. The delicate aromatic oils that give spices their appetizing qualities must be protected from the air if they are to be preserved. *See also* SEASONING.

SPICED LEYDEN CHEESE. An Edam cheese (*which see*), spiced with caraway seeds.

SPICY. Containing spices, or flavored or fragrant with spices.

SPIDER. A spider is a cast-iron skillet or frying pan, *which see*. At one time, this cooking vessel had three long metal legs, enabling it to be set directly over the coals of a hearth fire. It was from these legs, since discarded, that the utensil received its name. Though the legs were discarded with the coming of the range, the name has clung in many localities, referring to the cast-iron vessel only.

SPINACH. Not many years ago the world learned that spinach contained iron, and as a result countless children were urged to eat spinach because it would make them strong. Comic-strip heroes attributed their superhuman feats to the consumption of spinach. True, spinach is very healthful, but as the sorry mess in which it is sometimes served, it can be most unappetizing.

In buying spinach, look for well-developed, stocky plants with dark green, crisp leaves. Wilted spinach is not worth buying. Spinach with yellowed leaves or showing seed stems is liable to be overgrown and tough.

HINTS ON PREPARATION

Spinach must be thoroughly washed in several lukewarm waters to remove the sand which clings to the leaves. Remove the large tough stems, if any, and cook the spinach in a covered pan until just tender in only the water which clings to the leaves. Do not overcook the spinach; it should retain a certain character and not be a nondescript mass of green. Spinach may be served *en branches* or as a purée, the former being more desirable when the spinach is to be used as a vegetable.

To prepare it in this fashion, cook the spinach until just tender as above. Drain any excess water (but there should not be any) and use in soup or sauce. Chop the spinach coarsely with a knife or put it through a food chopper. Season to taste with salt and pepper, and reheat with a good lump of butter or margarine. The

FOOD VALUE

Water	Food Energy	Pro- tein	Fat	Carbo- hydrate	Cal- cium	Phos- phorus	Iron	Vit. A Value	Thia- mine	Ribo- flavin	Nia- cin	Ascor- bic Acid
92.7	25	2.3	.3	3.2	81	55	3.0	9420	.12	.24	.7	59

spinach may be creamed by adding a tablespoon or two of flour and a little milk to the chopped spinach and heating until the flour cooks and thickens. A dash of nutmeg or of mace gives a particularly good flavor to spinach. Some people like spinach seasoned with a little vinegar.

If the spinach is to be used in a soufflé or soup, or as a bed for poached eggs, it is best puréed. To do this, cook the spinach a little longer than ordinary. Chop finely, season with salt and pepper, reheat with a little butter or margarine, and then press the whole mixture through a sieve.

SPINACH

The very young tender leaves of spinach may be used raw in salads, mixing them with other greens and serving with French dressing. In cooking spinach, remember that one pound of raw spinach gives two cups of the cooked vegetable.

A simple luncheon or supper dish is made with spinach and eggs. Grease a number of individual baking dishes. Fill them with hot cooked spinach, leaving a slight hollow in the center. Carefully break an egg into the hollow. Sprinkle with salt and pepper, and cover with a good dash of grated cheese. Set in a moderately hot oven (400° F.) until the egg is set and the cheese melted. Serve immediately.

BAKED SPINACH WITH BACON

3 cups cooked drained spinach
2 cups drained canned tomatoes
1 medium-sized onion, chopped

¼ cup chili sauce
1 cup cracker crumbs
1 tsp salt
¼ tsp paprika
½ lb American cheese, sliced thin
6 slices bacon

Grease a baking dish. Place a layer of spinach in the dish, next a layer of tomatoes, a sprinkling of onion, chili sauce, crumbs, and the seasonings. Then make a layer of cheese. Repeat until all the ingredients are used, and sprinkle more crumbs on the top. Arrange the slices of bacon over the top of the dish and bake in a moderate oven (350° F.) for 25 minutes, or until the cheese melts and the bacon is crisp. Serve hot. (Serves 6)

CHEESE SPINACH CASSEROLE

2 cups of cooked, chopped spinach
1 cup sieved cottage cheese
2 whole eggs, slightly beaten
2 tbsp butter
2 tsp grated onion
Salt and pepper to taste
½ cup buttered bread or cracker crumbs

Combine all the above ingredients, except the crumbs, and blend well. Arrange in a shallow buttered casserole. Sprinkle the buttered crumbs over all, and bake in a moderate oven (350° F.) for about 30 minutes. (Serves 6)

CREAM OF SPINACH SOUP

2 qt spinach
1 qt chicken stock, or water and bouillon cubes
1 tbsp butter or margarine
1 tbsp flour
1 cup cream or rich milk
1 small bay leaf
4 slices onion
3 sprigs parsley
1 whole clove
Salt and pepper
2 egg yolks

Wash the spinach, pick off the tough stems, and chop the raw spinach as finely as possible. Put in a good-sized saucepan and cook covered without adding any water until the spinach is very tender. Press through a sieve into a saucepan. Stir in the chicken stock and bring the mixture to a boil. Let simmer for 15 minutes. Meanwhile scald the milk or cream with the bay leaf, onion, parsley, and clove, and then strain out the seasonings. In a small saucepan, melt the butter and blend in the flour, stirring constantly. Gradually pour in the scalded mlik and cook, stirring constantly until the mixture boils and thickens. Add a half cup or so of the spinach mixture to the cream mixture, stirring until smooth, and then add all the milk to the soup, stirring constantly. Season to taste with salt and pepper, and let the soup boil up once. Remove from the stove. Beat in the 2 egg yolks, one at a time, beating thoroughly after each addition. Serve immediately. (Serves 6)

CREAMED SPINACH

2 lb spinach
1 small onion, chopped
1½ tbsp butter or margarine
¼ cup evaporated milk
½ tsp salt

Wash the spinach thoroughly, remove any tough stems, and cook until tender. Drain any excess water. Cook the onion in the butter until soft but not browned. Chop the spinach very fine. Add the onion, milk, and salt to the spinach and mix thoroughly. A dash of nutmeg may be added if desired. Reheat and serve. (Serves 6)

FRIED SPINACH BALLS

3 cups chopped cooked spinach
2 tbsp butter or margarine
2 tbsp grated cheese
2 tbsp grated onion
1 cup fine bread crumbs
1 egg
⅛ tsp cayenne pepper
Dash of paprika

Mix all the ingredients together, blending thoroughly. Allow to stand until thoroughly cold. Shape into balls. Roll in crumbs, then in egg beaten with a little

water, and again in crumbs. Fry in deep hot fat (375°–390° F.) until golden brown. Serve very hot. (Serves 6)

SPINACH CHEESE DUMPLINGS

3 cups chopped cooked spinach
3 tbsp melted butter or margarine
½ tsp salt
Dash of pepper and nutmeg
1¼ cups cottage cheese
2 tbsp flour
3 egg yolks
2 qts boiling water
¼ cup melted butter (additional)
1 cup grated Parmesan cheese

Drain the spinach very thoroughly. Combine with the 3 tablespoons of butter, seasonings, cottage cheese, flour, and beaten egg yolks. Chill the mixture thoroughly. Form into small balls the size of a walnut, roll in flour, and drop into the rapidly boiling water. As soon as the dumplings rise to the top, skim them out and drain. Serve very hot with the melted butter and grated cheese. (Makes 1½ dozen dumplings)

SPINACH DUBROVNIK

2 tbsp butter
1 tbsp flour
1 cup milk, scalded
4 eggs, separated
2 cups cooked puréed spinach
Salt, pepper, and nutmeg
Fine bread crumbs
Butter, or margarine
½ cup chopped cooked ham
1 cup sour cream
Grated Parmesan cheese

Melt the butter in a saucepan, add the flour, and stir until smooth. Gradually pour in the scalded milk, and cook for several minutes, stirring constantly. Remove from the stove, and let cool slightly. Beat the egg whites until stiff and the yolks until thick and lemon-colored. Beat the egg yolks into the milk and then stir in the spinach. Season to taste with salt, pepper, and nutmeg. Fold in the stiffly beaten egg whites.
Cover the bottom of a long, shallow baking dish with a sheet of greased paper,

allowing the ends to protrude over the ends of the dish. Cover the paper with a thin layer of bread crumbs and spread a few dots of butter or margarine over the crumbs. Pour in the spinach mixture, spreading it evenly in the dish. Bake in a hot oven (400°–425° F.) for 15 minutes. Remove the dish from the oven. Spread the chopped ham over the spinach, and pour the sour cream over all. Roll into two folds with the aid of the paper and roll onto a hot platter. Sprinkle with grated Parmesan cheese and serve at once. Although this sounds complicated, it is very simple to do if the paper has sufficient overhang to give a working grasp. (Serves 4 or 5)

SPINACH NICOISE

2 cups purée of spinach
1 small tin of skinless, boneless sardines
½ cup bread crumbs
1 egg
Salt and pepper

Break the sardines into small bits and mix all the ingredients together, including the oil from the sardines. Put into a shallow baking dish. Sprinkle additional crumbs on top, and bake in a moderate oven (350° F.) about 20 minutes, or until heated through. (Serves 4)

SPINACH SOUFFLE

2 tbsp butter
2 tbsp flour
½ tsp salt
¼ tsp pepper
½ cup milk
1 cup grated cheese
½ tsp Worcestershire sauce
1 cup puréed spinach
3 eggs, separated

Make a thick white sauce with the butter, flour, milk and seasonings. Add the cheese and Worcestershire sauce, and stir over a low heat until the cheese melts. Stir in the spinach and mix thoroughly. Beat the whites of the eggs until stiff and the yolks until thick and yellow. Add the yolks to the spinach mixture, and lastly, fold in the whites. Turn into a well-greased casserole and bake in a moderately hot oven (400° F.) for 30 minutes. (Serves 4)

SPINACH TIMBALES

2 cups chopped cooked spinach
2 tbsp melted butter
2 eggs, slightly beaten
1 cup milk
⅔ tsp salt
Dash of cayenne pepper
½ tsp onion juice
2 tsp vinegar or lemon juice

Combine all the ingredients and mix thoroughly. Turn into well-greased timbale molds or custard cups. Set these in a pan of hot water and bake in a moderate oven (350° F.) about 20 minutes, or until a knife inserted in the center comes out clean. Unmold onto rounds of toast and serve with tomato, cream, or hollandaise sauce. (Serves 6)

SPINACH WITH SOUR CREAM

2 lb spinach
1 tsp salt
Dash of pepper
Dash of nutmeg
¾ cup sour cream

Wash the spinach, take off any tough stems, and cook without adding water until the spinach is just tender. Drain thoroughly. Whip the sour cream and season to taste with salt, pepper, and nutmeg. Mix the cream into the spinach and serve immediately. (Serves 4 or 5)

WILTED SPINACH

5 slices bacon
4 tbsp chopped onion
2 tbsp flour
¾ cup water
⅓ cup vinegar
1 tsp salt
2 tsp sugar
Dash of pepper
4 cups shredded raw spinach, tightly packed
¾ cup chopped celery

Cut the bacon into small bits and sauté with the onion for 10 minutes. Lift out the bacon and drain on soft crumpled paper. Stir the flour into the fat remaining in the pan. Add the liquids gradually, and cook over a low flame, stirring constantly, until the mixture boils and thickens. Add the seasonings, and then stir in the spinach and celery. Toss lightly until the spinach is coated with the sauce, and then cook over a very low flame until the spinach is warmed through. Sprinkle the crisped bacon over the top and serve immediately. (Serves 6)

SPINACH-DOCK. See SORREL.

SPIRITS. See BRANDY, GIN, RUM, WHISKY.

SPITZ CHEESE. A small, round, rennet cheese from Switzerland.

SPLIT. To divide a piece of food, such as an apple, a roll, etc., into two or more parts.

SPONGE. As applied to dessert, a jelly dessert made of gelatin, combined with stiffly beaten egg whites or whipped cream. As applied to dough, the light "sponge" mixture which is the basis of the raised dough used in bread and other yeast pastry.

SPONGE CAKE. See CAKE.

SPOOM. The spooms are sherbets prepared with a light sirup, and may be made with fruit juices or with almost any kind of dessert wine. A meringue, double the amount of the sherbet, is folded into the mixture to render it light and foamy, and the spooms are served in chilled sherbet glasses. See SHERBET.

SPOON. A spoon is an instrument consisting of a relatively shallow bowl set at the end of a handle, usually in line with the shaft. It is one of the oldest culinary instruments known to man, being possibly preceded by only the knife, and being in general use much before the fork. It was, of necessity, an early development, for it represents the only practical method of handling liquid foods. Nearly every culture has developed some form of spoon.

Spoons are used, not only with liquids, but with every other food form that cannot be conveniently handled by a fork. The most obvious use of the spoon is at the table, both as a serving implement and as an individual tool, and many different types and shapes have been developed to handle specific foods. See FLATWARE.

Spoons are also used in the kitchen for stirring and other operations. The kitchen spoons are usually larger than those for the table, and many have slotted bowls or other functional shapes.

Through the years, spoons have become so standardized that the teaspoon and

tablespoon are now accepted units of measurement. See MEASURING SPOONS and WEIGHTS AND MEASURES.

SLOTTED SPOON

At one time or another, spoons have been made from practically every known material. Today, they are commonly made from rust-resisting forms of metal, with silver preferred for table use. See SILVERWARE. Kitchen spoons are generally made of baser metals, and wooden spoons are widely used for mixing purposes, especially in containers made of fragile substances. Plastic spoons are the latest development, and these are finding many uses. See PLASTICS. See also KITCHEN EQUIPMENT.

SPOON BREAD. See CORN.

SPOSI CHEESE. A soft Italian cream cheese, small in size.

SPRAT. A small fish of the herring family, usually smoked, or prepared in brine. See also FISH and SARDINE.

SPRIG. As applied to food the term means one small branch, as a sprig of parsley, of thyme, of celery top, etc.

SPRING FORM PAN. See CAKE PAN.

SPRING LAMB. See LAMB.

SPRINGERLE. A traditional German cookie imprinted with raised designs. A special rolling pin is used which has the designs carved on it. The cookie dough is first rolled out with a plain roller. Then designs are imprinted with the springerle roller.

SPRINGERLE

2 cups sifted sugar
4 eggs, separated
1 cube ammonium carbonate
20 drops oil of anise
1 tsp grated lemon rind
4 cups sifted all-purpose flour
Anise seeds

Stir sugar into beaten egg yolks. Beat whites until stiff, add to egg yolks and sugar, and stir vigorously for 10 minutes either by hand or on an electric mixer using slow speed. Crush ammonium carbonate thoroughly and add to mixture, along with anise oil and lemon rind. Add flour in several portions, combining well. Chill the dough.

Divide into 3 or 4 portions; turn one onto floured board and replace the others in the refrigerator. Roll out ¼ inch thick. Dust springerle roll by tying a spoonful of cornstarch into a twist of cheesecloth and striking it lightly against the roll. Imprint the cookie dough. Cut cookies apart between designs and transfer them to a lightly floured board or cookie sheet. Cover with a dry towel, and let stand overnight.

When ready to bake, brush flour from dried surface with a camel hair brush, and rub underside carefully with cold water. Place cookies on a buttered baking sheet sprinkled lightly with anise seeds. Bake in a slow oven (275° F.) until cookies are a delicate straw color, about 40 minutes. Cool on baking sheet; then store in covered jar or box. Springerle may be eaten immediately, but they improve with age. They are a hard cookie. (Makes about 6 to 8 dozen cookies, depending on size and thickness)

SPRINKLE. As applied to food, to sprinkle means to scatter in drops or small particles, such as chopped parsley sprinkled over a finished dish or lemon juice sprinkled over fish.

SPRUCE BEER. A slightly alcoholic beverage flavored with essence of spruce or the green tips of the spruce tree. It is similar to root beer.

SPRUCE GROUSE. See GROUSE.

SPUMONI. An Italian ice cream usually containing chopped nuts and fruit.

SPUN SUGAR. Spun sugar which lends such an air to desserts is not very difficult to make. First three pounds of sugar—less if desired—is put to boil with a pint (2 cups) of water in an enamel or copper kettle. In fifteen minutes, the furiously bubbling sirup should reach 320° F. by the candy thermometer. But just before that moment, the juice of half a lemon is squeezed in to keep the sirup from crystallizing.

To make a nest for ice cream or a frozen dessert, the spun sugar may be colored by adding a few drops of the desired coloring —pale green, soft rose, or any other delicate shade. While the sirup bubbles to its climax, the worker lays out three steel bars on a stainless-steel-topped table, two bars arranged to overlay the third like an unfinished square. These two catch the sugar strands. Everything is ready now. There is a special whip for spinning out the sugar. This is like a miniature hearth broom in shape; the brush part is of steel instead of straw.

Gently dip the whip into the sirup pot, then raise it a second to let the sirup drip. The spinner's movements should be slow and rhythmic. Raise the arm high, flinging the sirup high over the head. It will shoot out in little silver arrows then come to rest across the bars.

SQUAB-CHICKEN

The threads may scatter to the floor where a large sheet of white paper should have been placed so that none are lost or soiled. When the spinning is sufficient for a nest, the worker cuts the filmy mass into lengths with a carving knife. Now a ball is formed, as large as desired, the center is hollowed, and a cardboard base laid in. Over this is placed a doily or frame for the frozen ice cream.

SQUAB. See PIGEON.

SQUAB-PIGEON

SQUASH. The *Cucurbita* includes the squashes, pumpkins, and gourds, all of which are native to the western hemisphere. Several varieties of squash were known to the Indians of America centuries before the white men came. Today the term squash is used for several quite different members of the family, which are divided roughly into summer and winter squashes.

are very susceptible to decay. Sometimes the injured part can be cut away without undue waste. Summer squash should not be stored, except in the refrigerator; winter squash, if it is perfectly sound and

Food Value

Type	Wa-ter	Food Energy	Pro-tein	Fat	Car-bohy-drate	Cal-cium	Phos-phorus	Iron	Vit. A Value	Tha-mine	Ribo-flavin	Nia-cin	Ascor-bic Acid
Summer	95.0	19	.6	.1	3.9	15	15	.4	260	.04	.05	1.1	17
Winter	88.6	44	1.5	.3	8.8	19	28	.6	4950	.05	.08	.6	8

Varieties

Summer squash. There are three varieties of summer squash ordinarily found in the markets. The flat white disk-shaped squash is known as pattypan or cymling. The yellow squashes are generally long and crook-necked, although within recent years horticulturists have developed varieties which grow straight. The green or green-striped varieties are known as vegetable marrow, Italian squash, or zucchini.

Winter squash. Again there are three main varieties. The acorn squash is small and fluted, dark green in color, and generally shaped like an acorn. The sweet potato squash, marrow, and other similar squashes are paler green in color, streaked with white, and medium-sized. The Hubbard squash is the largest of the winter varieties and has a dark green, roughened skin, often touched with orange color.

Hints on Purchasing

Summer squash is usually picked and marketed before it is fully mature. At this time the seeds and skin are tender, and the whole squash may be cooked without peeling or wastage. For this reason the summer squashes should be clean and free from blemish, and the skin should be easily pierceable with the nail. The squash should be heavy for its size. Overripe summer squash, with its hard rind, will have hard seeds and fibrous flesh.

Winter squash, on the contrary, is allowed to develop on the vine until fully ripe. The rind is therefore very hard and cannot be pierced with a fingernail. The seeds are also hard, but they are discarded in preparing the squash.

All varieties of squash should be free from bruising or other injury, since they

dry, may be stored in a cool dark place for a considerable time.

In purchasing squash, remember that a medium-sized summer squash will yield one and a half cups of cooked squash; one pound of winter squash will give one cup of cooked squash.

Hints on Preparation

Like most other vegetables, squash should be steamed, never boiled. This is particularly true of the summer squashes, which have a sweet delicate flavor which is entirely lost when the vegetable is cooked in large quantities of water. To steam summer squash, wash well and wipe dry. Cut in convenient pieces, removing the stem attachment. Do not peel, unless the squash is old and tough. Place in a saucepan with just enough boiling water to prevent scorching. Cover the pan tightly and let the squash cook in its own steam for about 15 minutes. It should then be tender enough to mash. It need only be seasoned with salt and pepper and a little butter or margarine. It may also be creamed by stirring in a little hot milk or cream just before serving. Summer squash may also be fried or baked in many variations.

Winter squash must be handled differently because of its hard skin. The little acorn squashes are usually cut in half, the seeds scooped out, and the squash baked, usually with a little water in the bottom of the pan to prevent drying of the flesh during baking. It will take 45 minutes to an hour to cook the squash this way. A quicker way to prepare it is to place the halves of squash, cut sides down, in the baking pan with a little water in the bottom of the pan and bake for fifteen or twenty minutes. This will steam the squash and cook it almost tender. Then the halves may be turned right side up, the desired filling put in, and the baking continued until the squash is tender. Acorn squash needs no more than a sprinkling of salt and pepper and a good piece of butter or

squash may also be served as a vegetable, seasoning them with salt and pepper and spreading with butter or margarine. Serve a piece as a portion, and let the guest scoop the soft pulp from the shell as he would an acorn squash.

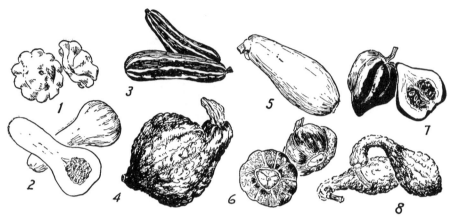

**SQUASH   1. White Scallop   2. Butternut   3. Cocozelle   4. Hubbard   5. Straightneck
6. Buttercup   7. Acorn   8. Crookneck**

margarine in the cavity to be delicious. But for a more substantial dish, pork sausage meat or sliced apples may be put in the cavity during the latter part of the cooking.

The larger winter squashes must be cut in pieces and either steamed or baked in order to soften the flesh. Cut the squash in two and remove all the seeds and stringy portion. Do not peel the squash (a rather difficult job at best) but cut into convenient pieces. Put in a good-sized kettle with a very little boiling water. Cover the kettle and steam over a low flame until the pulp is tender. Drain the squash, and scoop the pulp out of the shell. Mash, or put through a ricer or strainer. Season to taste with salt and pepper and butter or margarine and serve as a vegetable.

An even easier way to prepare winter squash is to bake the pieces in the oven. Cut the squash in two, remove the seeds and stringy portion, and then cut into convenient pieces. Arrange in a shallow baking pan, with a little water in the bottom. Bake in a moderately hot oven (375° F.) for 40 to 60 minutes, or until the squash is tender. Scoop out the pulp and proceed as with steamed squash.

The strained pulp of the winter squash makes an excellent substitute for pumpkin in pies or puddings. The pieces of baked

Squash blossoms make an unusual and delicious vegetable. They may be dipped in thin batter and fried in deep hot fat, or the unopened yellow buds may be sautéed. They will open in the pan, and make an attractive and unusual garnish for omelets and other egg dishes.

Squash soup is an epicure's delight, and many combinations of squash and other vegetables can be made.

Baked Summer Squash

**6 very small white pattypan squashes
1 cup cream cheese
1 green onion, minced
½ tsp minced parsley
1 tbsp heavy cream
½ tsp salt
⅛ tsp pepper
Dash of paprika**

Cook the whole squashes until tender in boiling salted water. Drain. Scoop out the centers, leaving a substantial wall. Mix the scooped-out pulp with the remaining ingredients and refill the shells. Arrange in a well-greased shallow baking pan, pour in a little milk, and bake in a moderate oven (350° F.) about 20 minutes. (Serves 6)

BAKED ZUCCHINI AND TOMATOES

2 medium-sized zucchini
2 medium-sized tomatoes
2 medium-sized mild onions
Salt and pepper
Butter or margarine
1 cup buttered crumbs

Wash the zucchini; do not peel it unless the skin is hard. Peel the tomatoes and the onions. Slice the vegetables into very thin crosswise slices. In a greased baking dish make alternate layers of zucchini, tomatoes, and onions, sprinkling each layer with a little salt and pepper and dotting with butter or margarine. Spread the top with buttered crumbs. Bake in a moderate oven (350° F.) until the vegetables are tender. (Serves 4)

FRIED SQUASH

2 lb summer squash
1 egg
¼ cup milk
Cracker crumbs
Salt and pepper

Cut young tender summer squash into ½-inch slices. Beat the egg with the milk and seasonings. Dip the slices in the egg mixture, and then in crumbs. Fry in a skillet in butter or bacon drippings until golden brown and tender. (Serves 5)

SQUASH AU GRATIN

2 lb tender summer squash
1 cup boiling salted water
1 cup sliced onions
3 tbsp butter or margarine
1 cup crumbled cheese crackers
1 additional tbsp butter or margarine
Pepper

Wash the squash and cut into ½-inch cubes, discarding stem and blossom ends. Do not peel. Cook in boiling salted water until just tender and then drain. Season with pepper and additional salt, if needed. Meanwhile sauté the onions in the 3 tablespoons of butter in a covered saucepan until transparent but not browned. Arrange half the squash in a buttered baking dish, cover with half the onions, and repeat the layers, using all the butter in

which the onions were cooked. Sprinkle with the crumbs and dot with the remaining butter. Bake in a moderately hot oven (400° F.) about 15 minutes. (Serves 4)

SQUASH CUSTARD

1½ lb yellow summer squash
1 medium-sized onion, chopped
1 cup medium white sauce
½ cup grated American cheese
2 eggs, slightly beaten
1 cup buttered crumbs
2 tbsp grated Parmesan cheese

Wash and cube the squash. Cook with the onion until tender in a very little boiling salted water. Drain thoroughly and combine with the white sauce, American cheese, and eggs. Turn into a greased baking dish, sprinkle with the buttered crumbs and the Parmesan cheese. Bake in a moderate oven (350° F.) about 30 minutes, or until browned. (Serves 4)

SQUASH FRITTERS

Cut pattypan squash into ½-inch slices. Dip in a thin fritter batter (*see* FRITTER) and sauté in a little butter or margarine until golden brown and tender.

SQUASH SOUP

2 medium-sized yellow or white squashes
1 cup boiling water
4 cups milk
Salt and pepper
2 tbsp butter or margarine

Wash the squash, but do not peel it if it is young and tender. Cut in small pieces and cook in the boiling water until very tender. Scald the milk. When the squash is tender, mash it thoroughly so that only pulp remains. Stir in the scalded milk, season to taste with salt and pepper, and add the butter. Heat thoroughly, but do not boil. Serve immediately. (Serves 4)

SQUASH SUPREME

6 small pattypan squashes
2 cups cooked green beans
¼ lb American cheese, grated
Salt and pepper
Buttered crumbs

Parboil squashes in salted water until tender. Scoop out the centers, and dice the pulp. Combine the pulp with the beans, cheese, and seasonings, and stuff the squash shells with the mixture. Top with buttered crumbs and bake in a hot oven (400° F.) about 20 minutes. The squash may be placed under a low broiler flame during the last few minutes of baking to brown the tops. (Serves 6)

SQUASH TORTE

4 lb zucchini
2 tbsp butter
6 tbsp oil
6 eggs
2 tbsp grated Parmesan cheese
½ tsp salt
Dash of pepper
¼ tsp nutmeg

Wash the squash, and if it is young and tender do not peel it. If the skin is tough, peel it. Slice thinly crosswise. Melt half the butter and oil in a heavy skillet and cook the squash slowly until it is tender. Beat the eggs and add to the cooked squash. Stir in the cheese and the seasonings. Heat the remaining butter and oil in a heavy frying pan. When it is hot pour in the mixture from the other pan. Cook slowly until firm and omelet-like. Turn onto a hot platter and garnish with parsley. (Serves 6)

STUFFED ACORN SQUASH

3 acorn squashes
1 cup diced celery
1 cup diced carrots
4 tbsp minced onion
½ cup diced green pepper
3 tbsp butter, margarine, or bacon fat
2 tbsp hot water or stock

Halve the squashes, remove the seeds and stringy pulp, and bake in the oven (400° F.) until almost tender. Heat the fat in a skillet and sauté the mixed vegetables for 10 minutes. Pour over the water or stock and mix thoroughly. Fill the centers of the squash and return to the oven. Continue baking until the squash is very tender. Serve garnished with crisp bacon. (Serves 6)

WHIPPED SQUASH

4 cups peeled, diced Hubbard squash
Salt and pepper
1 tsp sugar
1 tbsp heavy cream
2 tbsp butter
Chopped parsley

Place the squash in a colander over a pan of boiling water. Cover tightly and steam for 20 minutes, until the squash is very tender. Drain thoroughly. Mash the squash, or put it through a ricer, and transfer it to a saucepan. Season to taste with salt, pepper, and the sugar. Beat in the cream and butter, and continue beating over a very low flame until the squash is light and heated through. Serve at once, sprinkled with the parsley. (Serves 6)

SQUAW GRASS. An edible wild plant found in the United States and southwestern Canada. It is also called bear grass, *which see.*

SQUETEAGUE. See WEAKFISH.

SQUID. The squid or cuttlefish is found throughout the oceans of the world. This cousin of the octopus is a *cephalopod*, the highest class of mollusks. It is an elongated creature, having ten muscular arms which extend from around the front of the dark, hooded head. Other than the head, which contains an ink sac, the animal's coloring varies from a milky translucence to tints of reddish and brownish hue. There are numerous families of squid which vary in length from less than an inch to a reputed seventy-five feet. Old maps were often decorated with pictures of sailing ships being crushed by the animals. However, the common squid found off the coast of the United States grows to be only about eighteen inches long. It makes admirable bait.

Although most Americans shudder at the thought of eating the squid, the flesh is considered delicious by many who have tried it. Squids are easy to prepare and, according to the skipper of a fishing schooner out of Boston Harbor, "they are twice as sweet as lobster and only half the trouble to fix." This is how he cooks them.

BOILED SQUID A LA CAP'N IVAR

A handful of table salt is added to a five- or ten-gallon caldron of sea water. (A solution approximating the salinity of weak sea water can be made by adding a generous ¼ cup of common salt to each gallon of fresh water.) The water is brought to a violent boil and a pailful of very fresh squids is dropped into it. Use young, tender squids about eight inches long. The squids are boiled for from 15 to 20 minutes. They are removed from the caldron and their heads, with tentacles attached, are removed. The intestinal tracts are then scooped from the body and the squid is eaten hot, usually without sauce or seasoning.

SQUIRREL. This slender rodent is well relished in the South. The meat is white with somewhat the flavor of chicken crossed with rabbit. Squirrel may be prepared by all the methods applied to chicken and rabbit. The following recipe is a sample of the way it is done in the South:

CASSEROLE OF SQUIRREL

2 squirrels
Seasoned flour
¼ cup wild rice
2 minced green peppers
1½ cups diced celery
1 cup diced tart apple
Boiling water

Disjoint the squirrels and roll in seasoned flour. Arrange in a generously greased casserole and sprinkle over them the rice, peppers, celery and apple. Cover with boiling water and bake, closely covered, in a slow oven (300° F.) about 1 hour, or until tender. (Serves 4)

STAG BUSH. A wild shrub of the Unites States which bears a sweet, edible berry. See BLACK HAW.

STAINLESS STEEL WARE. An alloy of steel, chromium and nickel that resists acid or alkaline stains, stainless steel is more durable than aluminum of the same weight. However, the material heats slowly and conducts the heat unevenly. Food cooked in stainless steel utensils must be watched to keep it from sticking and scorching.

PURCHASING STAINLESS STEEL WARE

Because of the uneven heating properties of stainless steel, some utensils are made with thicker bottoms than sides. A better expedient is to provide them with copper-clad bottoms, for copper is an excellent heat conductor. In addition to material choice, the utensils should also be considered for their suitability for various jobs. See KITCHEN EQUIPMENT.

CARE OF STAINLESS STEEL

Stainless steel vessels are washed in the normal manner, taking care to use only mild abrasives. If the bottom is copper-clad and does not have a further coating, the copper may be brightened by rubbing with salt and a piece of lemon.

STALE. As applied to food, stale means having lost its original freshness, as with stale bread. The food is not necessarily spoiled.

STALK. The stem of an herbaceous plant, such as celery.

STARCH. The term applied to the fecula or granular material found in fruits, roots, and tubers, and in the cellular tissue of plants. The structure and form of the starch granules vary, and those from different plants may be distinguished by microscopic examination.

Farinaceous foods are composed of flour of different kinds, and constitute a subdivision of starchy foods. The different starchy and farinaceous foods are derived from a variety of plant structures, including roots, tubers, bulbs, stems, pith, flowers, seeds, fleshy fruits, etc. Some, like the banana and certain vegetables, are eaten raw, but the majority require cooking, and the starches derived from grain-bearing plants of the grass tribe, or cerealia, usually must be prepared by grinding and milling before cooking.

Foods upon which we depend particularly for fuel are starches, sugars, and fats. Starch is a white, odorless, tasteless substance, insoluble in cold water, alcohol, or other liquids.

STEAK. See BEEF.

STEAK KNIFE. The name of steak knife is given to both a small carving knife (see CUTLERY and CARVING) and to a special table knife which has a keen cutting edge (see FLATWARE). Both varieties of the steak knife are intended, as the name would imply, for use on steaks.

STEAM. To cook in a closed vessel using only enough water to generate steam. This is the preferred method for cooking vegetables.

STEAM-BAKE. To steam-bake means to place the pan of food to be baked in another shallow pan of hot water in the oven. This method is used for cooking soufflés, timbales and similar dishes which require slow baking. Fruit cakes are steam-baked by placing a pan of water in the oven with them to keep the cake moist during the long baking period.

STEAMED PUDDING. There are so many kinds of steamed puddings that it is almost impossible to describe them.

While practically all puddings have the same basis of flour and suet, variations of fruits and spices, the use of sugar or molasses, or the inclusion of nuts will produce differences in richness and flavor. Both Scotch and German recipes call for grated carrots as well as fruit. English recipes sometimes call for brandy, rum, or sherry as part of the liquid.

In these modern days we seldom wrap our puddings in cloths and boil them according to the old-fashioned method. Instead, we fill greased bowls or cans three-fourths full and cover them tightly before the steaming. Oiled paper, by the way, held closely to the bowl with a rubber band, will do just as well as a closely fitted cover.

It is very important that the water be kept boiling rapidly in the steamer during the whole cooking period. Large puddings should be steamed from five to six hours; smaller ones demand about an hour less time. When they are done, if not to be served at once, any covers should be removed at once, but may be replaced after the puddings are cold. They may then be reheated from half an hour to an hour before serving time.

Today we may pour rum or brandy over the pudding when ready to take it to the table, and carry it, flaming, according to tradition, to the festive board. And, fully as important as the pudding itself is the sauce. Hard sauce, liberally flavored with brandy or rum, or a rich creamy sauce may be used.

See the individual fruits and flavors for recipes. *See also* PUDDING.

STEEL. A steel is a steel rod fitted into a handle and equipped with finger guards, that is used to sharpen carving knives and other forms of cutlery. *See* CARVING and CUTLERY.

STEEL WARE. Steel is an exceedingly durable form of metal that can be made into medium-weight utensils that are not affected by the temperatures of cooking. Steel vessels are moderately priced and duplicate the functions of ironware (*which see*) though they are made from sheet stock and not cast. Steel is fairly easy to clean, but it is subject to corrosion and staining. Because of this, stainless steel ware (*which see*) is more commonly used, despite its higher cost.

STEEL WOOL. Steel wool is a mass of fine steel threads, so named because of its wool-like appearance. Because it makes an excellent abrasive and is convenient to handle, it is widely used for cleaning, scouring, and some polishing purposes.

Steel wool may be purchased in bulk rolls, in individual pads or similar hand-sized bundles. It can be purchased plain, or impregnated with a special soap. There are also various holders designed for use with the material.

USE AND CARE

Because the material is very susceptible to rusting, it should be stored in a dry place, and no more than the amount actually needed used at any one time. The used pad should have a special resting place at the sink, preferably in a disposable soap dish, for a wet pad will leave rust marks wherever it is stored.

Steel wool may be used dry for many types of scouring operations. However, if there is much material to be removed, it is often better to use it with water. If there is any grease present, soap should also be used. While the material may be used with any sort of soap, it is better to use the special soap that is provided with the steel wool either as a separate cake or else actually mixed in with the material.

Steel wool may be used to remove almost any type of food soil or stain, especially charred foods, and will even remove tarnish. It must be remembered, however, that the material is an abrasive and does its work by wearing away the substance against which it is rubbed. Thus, not only the spot, but also a portion of the surface is removed. For this reason, steel wool should never be used on any coated metal, ceramic, glass, or plastic, except as the last resort, and then very cautiously. It should never be used on any material where a scratch will either mar the appearance, or expose substances beneath that are easily corroded. It can, however, be used freely on solid metals such as aluminum, cast iron, or stainless steel, unless they have a smooth, highly polished surface.

It is used, whether wet or dry, with a scrubbing, scouring motion, with only enough pressure to do the task at hand, and not so much pressure as to needlessly wear away the surface. It should be handled with some respect, for the threads are apt to act like splinters on the bare fingers. The vessel should always be carefully washed after steel wool is used, going over it with a cloth and plenty of water, to make certain that none of the metal bits that break off from the wad are still clinging to the surface.

As a last word of caution, steel wool is unmatched in its proper place, but the user should never become so enthusiastic as to use it on the family silver or glassware. *See also* DISHWASHING.

STEEP. To allow a dry substance to stand in liquid to extract flavor, as in steeping tea.

STEIN. Derived from the German word for stone, a stein is, properly speaking, an earthenware mug (*which see*) of approximately pint capacity, designed for the serving of beer. Through usage, the term has come to be loosely applied to any beer mug of any material and capacity, some holding as much as a quart or a liter.

The true stein is well suited for its role as a beer vessel. The earthenware walls are thick, affording ample insulation to keep the beer chilled though it be sipped slowly or ignored for a time in the heat of discussion. Some connoisseurs prefer to have their steins chilled and the beer drawn at room temperature, claiming this presents the beer at the peak of its flavor and heightens its thirst-quenching properties. Whether this be so or not, a well-chilled stein keeps the beer cooler longer.

Some advanced models of the stein are equipped with lids which are permanently attached by means of hinges and are lifted clear of nose and lip by levers so placed as to fall naturally under the thumb when the handle is grasped.

Stein handles themselves show the same careful thought and planning that has gone into stein development. They are large and easily grasped by the most unsteady of hands, there is no need for the fingers to contact the chilled walls of the

mug, and they afford a firm, well balanced grip, though the stein grow heavier and the trip from table to mouth longer as the evening progresses.

Steins are sturdily built so they may be thumped with impunity. Indeed, steins are often thumped in the normal course of events; thumped when empty to summon the waiter, thumped when full to emphasize a well-made point in argument, and banged lustily to mark the rhythm of a boisterous song. It is also said by many that steins are sometimes thumped on heads that refuse to admit the logic of an advanced argument.

Steins are traditionally associated with beer drinking in many parts of the world, especially in Germany where the art of stein decoration has, perhaps, reached its peak. In America, home of the cocktail (*which see*), the stein is not too prevalent, the schooner (*which see*) and the simple 10-ounce tumbler taking precedence. *See* GLASSWARE; *see also* BEER.

STEINBERGER. A Rhine wine (*which see*).

STEINBUSCHER-KASE CHEESE. A semi-hard, full-cream cheese which is mildly sour and pungent, made in Germany.

STEINWEIN. One of the Moselle white table wines, Steinwein is dry, full-bodied and potent. It improves with age, developing a fine bouquet reminiscent of primroses. It is usually sold in the distinctive *bocksbeutel*, a flat, squat, broad-bottomed bottle made of green glass. *See* MOSELLE and WINE.

STEMWARE. The name given to that class of drinking vessels made with a bowl set on a stem and foot. *See* GLASSWARE.

STEPLADDER. The common kitchen stepladder is designed to double as a stool when the steps are not in use. Since kitchens usually have a great deal of overhead storage space (*see* KITCHEN), some sort of ladder of step arrangement is needed to enable the housewife to reach the upper shelves with ease. If these shelves are not accessible, they are of little practical value.

The normal stepladder being much too bulky and heavy to be convenient for this use, the kitchen stepladder was developed to serve two purposes. It is light enough to be moved without too much effort, and when the steps are swung out of the body, the seat becomes the top step. While they are not as high as the regular ladder, they are high enough to enable the user to reach most kitchen shelves.

STEPPES CHEESE. A Russian cheese made from whole milk. It is usually 10 by 5½ by 7 inches.

STERILIZE. To kill bacteria by the action of heat. Jars for canning and jams and preserves are sterilized by boiling in water for a specified time. Milk may be sterilized by heating to a temperature somewhat higher than that used for pasteurizing. *See* CANNING and MILK.

STERLING. *See* SILVERWARE.

STEW. Stewing differs from boiling in the fact that the juices of the meat or vegetables are dissolved in the heated liquid, whereas in boiling the juices are prevented from passing out into the water by the coagulation of the external surface of the food mass produced by immersing it suddenly into boiling water. The proper temperature for stewing is between 150° and 170° F. In thick stews the juices dissolved in the water are eaten together with the cooked food, but in some instances, as in the making of beef tea and some kinds of soups, the aqueous solution only is used. Obviously, the more the food is subdivided the greater the surface exposed to the solvent action of the water, hence the process of thoroughly mincing the meat which is to be used in preparing beef tea.

The manner in which stewing differs from other processes of cooking may be described as follows: Instead of the meat itself surrounding and enveloping the meat juices, as it should when boiled, roasted, grilled, or fried, in a stew we demand that the juices shall surround or envelop the meat. And more or less water enters the substance of the meat to replace the juices which have passed out by osmosis and diffusion into the surrounding fluid.

After meat has stewed a while, a scum, containing coagulated albumin and fat, is usually seen floating upon the surface. Unfortunately the cook sometimes removes this, thus robbing the stew of nutritious material, although it may be done in preparing beef tea for invalids in order to make it more palatable and agreeable to the eye.

Stews are an economical way of preparing food. Nothing is lost by evaporation and nothing is thrown away but the bones, and they only after they have furnished their nourishing substances.

Stew, of course, is of many natures; it is a slow cooker and can't be hurried. Beef stew is but one of a galaxy. In culinary parlance a stew is half way between a soup and a meat dish. The vegetables, which may vary according to taste, are usually added at the last, so that they never cook to death, but the good garden flavor is saved. Those same vegetables may be cut fancifully, using a French vegetable cutter.

There are countless recipes for stews; among them, the following: the goulashes; the pot roasts; the Brunswick stew, made of squirrel way down South, and of chicken up North; the Bohemian style, thickened with pumpernickel crumbs; the Calabrese beef stew, made with tomato juice instead of water, etc. For lamb, there is the delicious Irish stew with its white gravy. Then there are pork stew, ham stew, etc. All of them are made in much the same way, browned and cooked slowly in plenty of liquid—with vegetables, or rice, or noodles, or sometimes with no vegetables at all, as in the famous Carbonade which has a thick brown gravy, made with part beef and part meat stock or water.

See BEEF, LAMB, and other meats.

STILL WINE. A wine that is not effervescent (sparkling). *See* WINE.

STILTON CHEESE. This English cheese is related to roquefort and gorgonzola, the same penicillium mold being used. Stilton is made from May to September of rich milk with added cream. It is not milled or pressed like cheddar, and consequently is a semi-hard cheese. Good stilton is white in color with veins of blue mold evenly distributed over the whole surface. The rind is brown and well crinkled. Stilton is at its best when fully ripe, certainly not less than six months old.

STINGER. A drink made of brandy and créme de menthe that is sometimes used as a cocktail, but more properly served as an after-dinner liqueur.

STINGER

1 part white crème de menthe
2 parts brandy

Place in a cocktail shaker with cracked ice, shake well, strain into cocktail glasses.

See Bartending; *see also* Cocktail, Alcoholic.

STIR. Stirring is blending several ingredients by moving their positions by means of a spoon or other implement. To stir, move the tool round and round, using a circular motion. In stirring a cooking mixture to prevent it from sticking or

STIRRING

scorching, use a crosswise motion, going first to the far side of the pan, then bringing the spoon or wire whisk toward you, back and forth, keeping the movement even, steady and rather slow, covering the entire area of the pan. A thickening ingredient such as egg yolk should be stirred briskly and constantly to prevent curdling.

STIRRER. Also known as a bar stirrer or drink stirrer. A small, slender rod used to stir drinks, usually alcoholic, in the individual glass. It usually has a small knob at one end to be used in crushing sugar granules, but is not to be confused with either the muddler (*which see*) or the swizzle stick (*which see*), two other stirring implements which have distinct uses. The stirrer is commonly used with the highball and similar drinks.

STOCK. *See* Soup.

STOCK POT. A large pot in which to cook chicken, soup, or any kind of stock. *See also* Kitchen Equipment.

STOCKFISH. *See* Codfish.

STONE. As long as knives have been made, stone has been one of the most popular abrasives used to sharpen them. The name stone is generally given to all sharpeners made of that material, though

it may also be qualified to fit some specific sharpener. Stones may be used exactly as supplied by nature, may be ground down to a special surface, or may be shaped to meet some specific need. Stones may also be made artificially, by compressing and binding stone particles and other elements to produce a surface of desired characteristics.

Types

Grinding Stone. The old rotary grinding stone, once a common household sight, is now rarely seen unless there is a well-equipped workshop in the cellar. It is, however, still brought from door to door, either on the back or in a truck, by itinerant "grinders" who live by sharpening knives and scissors. It is simply a wheel-shaped stone, made with a number of different surfaces, and powered in many different ways.

Whetstone. A whetstone has a comparatively coarse surface and must have a film of water on its surface for its most efficient operation.

Oilstone. Oilstones are made with finer surfaces than whetstones, and use a film of oil on their surface for effective sharpening. Oilstones are used primarily for honing and can produce the keenest edge of all stone sharpeners. They are commonly used to hone razors, etc.

Both oilstones and whetstones are made in many different shapes and surface grades to suit different needs. For household use, however, they are commonly met as a plain oblong block, sometimes with different types of surface on either side.

Hints on Use

Stones are always used with a cutting motion; i.e., the blade travels across the stone in the direction of the knife edge. An equal number of strokes are made with both sides of the blade. There is a certain amount of manual skill required to sharpen a knife, the edge being determined by the angle at which the knife is held against the stone. Since the exact shape of the cutting edge is a matter of individual taste, it is difficult to establish any hard and fast rules, only to say that the user must determine for himself the correct angle to achieve the best results for any given knife. A thin, razor edge will be wanted for carving; but a broader, huskier one will be required for other types of work.

Few stones are used without a lubricant of some sort, either oil or water, except for those of the carborundum type, *which see.* *See also* CARVING and CUTLERY.

STORE CHEESE. A kind of domestic cheddar cheese, *which see.*

STOUT. *See* BEER.

STOVE. Cook stoves used in the kitchen are discussed under range, *which see.* *See also* BARBECUE and CAMP COOKERY.

STRACCHINO CHEESE. Several forms of Italian soft cheeses. Stracchino crescenza is very soft and highly colored, and is usually eaten when fresh. Other names are: stracchino di gorgonzola, stracchino de Milano, fresco, quardo, and quartirola.

STRAFFORD SAUCE. This is good with broiled meats and chicken.

STRAFFORD SAUCE

½ cup whipped cream, sweet or sour
2 tbsp grated horseradish
2 tbsp grated apple
Salt and cayenne

Combine all ingredients and chill thoroughly.

STRAINER. Strainers are devices used primarily to separate liquids from solids. They function on the principle of providing openings through which the liquid may pass, but which are small enough to hold back the solid matter. There are a great many designs and types of strainers built to meet differing needs. Because they are used in conjunction with liquids, they must be made of some appropriate rust-proof material.

In some cases, the strainer consists of a mesh or screen, similar to the sieve (*which see*). Strainers of this type may either be an independent unit (*see* TEA STRAINER), or they may be incorporated into a larger device, usually being set in the pouring spout.

Perforations and slots are also greatly used. *See* COLANDER and SINK STRAINER. In other cases, as in making jelly, for example, cloth pads or bags are more appropriate. Spun glass and other materials are sometimes utilized in specialized cases. All of these types may be made as separate units or incorporated into a vessel or similar utensil.

The effectiveness of a strainer will, of course, depend on its design, but as a general rule, they are made to be used with fairly large sizes of food. If minute particles are to be removed from a liquid, a filter (*which see*) is usually needed.

See also KITCHEN EQUIPMENT.

STRAWBERRY. These berries are so named because they were originally brought to market strung on straws. Records indicate that their cultivation began in the 15th century, and they have long been a popular item of food for all classes of people all over the world.

The wild strawberry, which still grows over large areas of the United States, Asia, and Europe, has been vastly improved by cultivation. This is evidenced by the fact that in this country the average annual

STRAWBERRY

production is about 300 million quarts. They are grown in every state, with Arkansas, California, and Tennessee leading in production. Their season is from April to the end of June, but in some modern markets they are obtainable throughout the year, due to improved methods of transportation.

The strawberry is considered one of the finest berries, because of its flavor, large size, and colorful pulp. It contains rich stores of food lime, and food iron, both responsible for the sharp but pleasing tang of the strawberry flavor. The strawberry contains both citric acid, found in lemons, and malic acid, found in apples. That is why strawberries are so wholesome, so cleansing and should be used often while the real season lasts. They are suitable in salads, in desserts, as sauces, and as rich flavoring for other foods and beverages.

Owing to this same tart quality, the strawberry blends with blander fruits, such as the banana, or in dishes with corn-starch, rice, tapioca, and all the shortcakes (*see* SHORTCAKE).

Many million dollars' worth of straw-berry products are manufactured each year. Among the more important of these are preserves, jams, essences for flavoring for candies and for use as flavoring ex-tracts, sirup for soda fountains, and crushed fruit for flavoring ice cream and sauces. Large quantities of strawberries are canned.

they are to reach the market in the best condition. The field should be picked over at least every other day, and at the height of the season it will often be necessary to pick daily. One soft berry in a basket may spoil the entire contents and one spoiled basket of berries may spoil the looks of the crate by the time it reaches the market. Each berry, therefore, should be placed carefully in the basket.

Strawberries are graded according to the United States Department of Agri-

FOOD VALUE

Water	Food Energy	Pro-tein	Fat	Carbo-hydrate	Cal-cium	Phos-phorus	Iron	Vit. A Value	Thia-mine	Ribo-flavin	Nia-cin	Ascor-bic Acid
90.0	41	.8	.6	8.1	28	27	.8	60	.03	.07	.3	60

PREPARATION FOR MARKET

Plants may be set at any time in the spring or summer if moisture conditions are favorable; these are usually best in early spring, and most of the planting is done then. There are two main systems of training strawberries, the hill system and the matted-row system. The hill system is the method of training under which all runners are removed from the plants as they appear, so that at the fruiting season there are no more plants than were originally set. Such plants become much larger than those grown under the matted-row system and bear more than do the individual plants in matted rows, where the runners are allowed to remain and take root. Under the matted-row system the plants are set in rows and all or part of the runners which form during the summer are allowed to take root in the spaces be-tween the original plants. By the end of the season a mat of plants will have formed.

The different varieties of strawberries differ somewhat in the degree of maturity at which they should be picked. Varieties with soft flesh must be picked before they are very ripe, in order to get them to market in good condition. Firm varieties, however, may be left on the plants until thoroughly ripe, and will have a better ap-pearance on the market than those picked when not fully ripe. Varieties also differ greatly in the length of the picking season, and in the frequency with which they need to be picked.

After berries of the best grade are grown they must be handled with great care if

culture standards. U.S. No. 1 consists of strawberries of one variety, with the cap attached, which are firm, free from decay, disease, and damage. Each strawberry must have three-quarters of its surface pink or red, and the minimum size shall be not less than ¾ inch in diameter. U.S. No. 2 consists of strawberries which are free from decay and serious damage. Each strawberry must have at least half of its surface showing a pink or red color. Un-less otherwise specified, the minimum size shall be not less than ⅝ inch in diameter. U.S. Combination is made up of any lot of strawberries when not less than 80 per-cent by volume meet the requirements of U.S. No. 1 and the remainder meet the requirements of U.S. No. 2 except for size. Unless otherwise specified the minimum size shall be not less than ¾ inch in di-ameter.

HINTS ON PURCHASING

When purchasing strawberries, care-fully examine all those without caps. They may have been roughly handled, or they may be overmature. Such berries are likely to break down rapidly and are a wasteful buy. Conspicuous green or white tips are indicative of lack of flavor, unless typical of the variety. Avoid sandy fruit, as the sand is extremely hard to remove. Juice stains on the box may indicate overripe-ness or decay. Decay is easily detected by the presence of mold on the surface of the berries. It may be found anywhere in the container, and is not always evident in the top layer. Medium to large berries are best for eating raw. Medium-sized, tart-flavored are best for canning. Strawberries are packed in pint and quart baskets, and a full quart averages 20 ounces.

HINTS ON PREPARATION

Like other small fruits, strawberries are highly perishable and deteriorate rapidly. Berries must be kept cool and dry and should not be washed until ready for use. In washing strawberries, raspberries, and the like, do not let water from the faucet play on them. They are too tender to stand such treatment. Instead, put them in a large bowl of water and lift them out of the water with the fingers spread apart a little to act as a strainer. The sand and soil on the berries will settle to the bottom of the container. For that reason, do not pour the water off the berries. Unless they are quite dirty, two such rinses are usually sufficient. Above all things, do not let the berries stand long in water, or they will lose color and flavor.

If you are opposed to washing berries, here is a dry method: Tie one end of a large piece of cheesecloth to a heavy piece of kitchen furniture, such as a table leg or faucet, in hammock fashion, holding the other end in your hand. Drop berries into the center of the cheesecloth. Then raise and lower the end in your hand so that the berries roll back and forth, giving the cloth a little shake as the berries roll. The porous cheesecloth will catch all the particles of sand and soil and remove them from berries. Do this a few times, and the berries will be thoroughly free of foreign matter.

After hulling, sprinkle the berries lightly with sugar and set them in a warm place, not in the refrigerator, in order to draw out the juice. If you wish to sweeten the berries before serving them, cut them in halves, or chop rather than crush them, so as to keep them as attractive as possible. For richest flavor, never touch strawberries with a steel knife—use a silver knife, as the steel taints the true berry flavor. Use fine powdered sugar to sweeten them.

Save green or inferior berries for stewing, or for making some of the unusual conserves or jams and jellies. Chopped mint blends well with fresh strawberries and diced fresh pineapple. Add two tablespoons of mint to each quart of fruit, and serve as an appetizer, salad, or dessert.

FRAIDE A LA NEIGE
(Strawberries in Snow)

Large ripe strawberries
1 cup heavy cream, whipped
4 tsp confectioners' sugar
3 tsp chopped mint leaves
2 tsp aromatic bitters, or less
1 cup shredded coconut

Rinse the berries thoroughly to remove all sand. Hull all but the six largest. Chill. Combine the cream, sugar, mint and bitters and chill. Arrange in alternate layers in sherbet glasses first a spoonful of the cream, then berries, until the glasses are filled, having cream for the top layer. Sprinkle with the coconut, and place one of the reserved berries in the center of each glass. (Serves 6)

FROZEN STRAWBERRY CUSTARD

1 qt strawberries
1¼ cups sugar
2 egg yolks, slightly beaten
1 tsp gelatin
2 tbsp cold water
2 cups heavy cream, whipped
½ tsp vanilla

Wash and hull the berries. Crush them and add the sugar. Let stand 3 hours. Press half the berries through thin cloth. Add the juice to the egg yolks and cook over hot water 5 minutes or until slightly thickened, stirring constantly. Soften the gelatin in cold water, add to hot mixture and stir until dissolved; cool. Add the remaining berries and fold in cream and vanilla. Turn into mold or into freezing trays of automatic refrigerator; freeze 2 to 4 hours. (Makes 3 pints)

FROZEN STRAWBERRY FLUFF

1 cup fresh ripe strawberries
¾ cup sugar
¼ cup water
Dash of salt
2 egg whites, stiffly beaten
1 cup heavy cream, whipped
⅛ tsp vanilla

Wash, hull, and drain the berries, then crush. Cook the sugar, water and salt

until the mixture spins a fine thread (232°
F.). Pour this sirup slowly, in a steady
stream, over the stiffly beaten egg white,
beating constantly until the mixture stands
in peaks. Fold in the vanilla-flavored
whipped cream and the crushed berries.
Turn into refrigerator tray and freeze. Cut
into small squares for serving.

If preferred, the fluff may be frozen in
small paper cups, these in turn being set in
the refrigerator tray to freeze. Garnish, if
desired, with large, whole, fresh berries
and a green leaf. (Serves 6)

FRENCH STRAWBERRY AND CHERRY COMPOTE

1 lb cherries
1 pt strawberries
1½ cups sugar
¾ cup red wine
Heavy cream

Wash the fruit, pit the cherries and hull
the strawberries. Place together in a bowl
and cover with the sugar. After 35 minutes, drain off the sirup and boil 5 minutes
over a hot fire. Pour over the fruit and
add the wine. Chill until icy cold and serve
with u sweetened plain cream passed separately. (Serves 6)

HOT STRAWBERRY DUMPLINGS

Roll out biscuit dough (*which see*) about
¼ inch thick. Cut into 4-inch squares, and
place on each 1 tablespoon of sliced,
sweetened strawberries. Wet the edges,
press together and place smooth side uppermost in a buttered baking pan. Bake in a
moderate oven (375° F.) about 25 minutes. Serve with cream or hard sauce or
with crushed sweetened strawberries.

HOT STRAWBERRY SAUCE

1 cup strawberry juice
½ tbsp lemon juice
½ tbsp cornstarch
½ cup sugar

Combine the strawberry and lemon
juices and bring to boiling point. Thicken
with the cornstarch moistened in a little
cold water. Add the sugar and bring all to
boiling point, stirring constantly. Simmer
three minutes.

STRAWBERRY BAVARIAN CREAM

1 tbsp gelatin
2 tbsp cold water
1 cup crushed strawberries
1 cup heavy cream, whipped
¾ cup powdered sugar
Ladyfingers
6 whole strawberries

Soften the gelatin in cold water 5 minutes; heat over hot water, stirring until
dissolved. Add to strawberries, mixing
well, and chill until slightly thickened.
Fold in cream, sweetened with sugar, and
chill mixture until thick enough to hold its
shape. Line parfait glasses with ladyfingers,
fill with gelatin mixture and top with a
large berry. Chill. (Serves 6)

STRAWBERRY CHEESE SALAD

½ lb cottage or cream cheese
Thick cream
3 tbsp honey
3 tbsp oil
5 tbsp lemon juice
½ tsp salt
Lettuce
1 pt ripe strawberries

Beat the cheese until smooth and
creamy, adding thick cream to slightly
moisten. Pack into a heart-shaped mold
and chill.

For the dressing combine the honey, oil,
lemon juice, and salt and blend thoroughly. Use a little of this dressing to
marinate the strawberries.

To serve, unmold the cream cheese onto
a platter, garnish with heart leaves of
lettuce, arrange the strawberries around
the heart and pass the remaining dressing
separately. (Serves 6)

STRAWBERRY COTTAGE PUDDING

½ cup butter or shortening
1 cup sugar
1 egg
1¾ cups sifted flour
1¾ tsp baking powder
½ tsp salt
½ cup milk
Crushed sweetened strawberries
Light or whipped cream

Cream the butter, gradually adding the sugar. Add the egg and, when well blended, the sifted dry ingredients alternately with the milk. Turn into a buttered and floured shallow pan and bake in a moderate oven (350° F.) about 30 minutes. Cut into squares and top with crushed sweetened strawberries and cream or with a hot strawberry sauce. (Serves 6)

STRAWBERRY CREAM PIE

3 tbsp butter
1 tbsp cornstarch
2 tbsp flour
¼ cup sugar
1½ cups milk
2 egg yolks
½ tsp vanilla extract
1 pt strawberries
Baked 8-inch pie shell
½ cup whipping cream

Melt the butter in the top of a double boiler; blend in the cornstarch, flour and sugar until smooth. Add the milk and cook over boiling water with constant stirring for 10 minutes. Add a small amount of the hot mixture to the well-beaten egg yolks, return to double boiler and cook 2 minutes longer, stirring constantly. Remove from heat and stir in vanilla. Pour immediately into cooled baked pie shell (*see* PASTRY) and chill. Wash strawberries, hull and slice, sprinkle with ¼ cup sugar and let stand for 15 to 30 minutes. Then arrange berries over the cream filling, top with whipped cream and garnish with a few whole strawberries. Serve at once. (Serves 5 or 6)

STRAWBERRY DAINTY

1 pt strawberries
1 cup diced pineapple, fresh or canned
½ cup sweetened condensed milk
½ cup pineapple juice
¼ cup orange juice
1 tbsp lemon juice

Wash and hull the berries; cut in quarters and place in 6 sherbet glasses; add pineapple. Add fruit juices to condensed milk and beat until well mixed. Pour over berries and chill thoroughly. Garnish with a whole berry. (Serves 6)

STRAWBERRIES EPICURE

6 eggs
1 cup confectioners' sugar
1 jigger benedictine (or 3 tbsp)
½ jigger creme de menthe
2 qt ripe strawberries (with stems attached)

Beat the egg whites until very stiff, gradually adding the sugar. In another bowl beat the egg yolks until creamy then fold into the egg whites. Add the benedictine and creme de menthe, and chill thoroughly. Rinse and dry the strawberries without removing the stems and chill. Serve the berries and sauce separately in deep dessert dishes, dipping the berries into the sauce, holding them by the stems. (Serves 6 to 8)

STRAWBERRY FROSTING

¼ cup butter
2 cups powdered sugar
1 tbsp lemon juice
Dash of salt
⅓ cup fresh strawberry pulp (with canned fruit, decrease sugar)

Cream the butter until soft; gradually stir in 1 cup of the sugar, then the lemon juice and salt. Add remaining sugar alternately with the strawberry pulp, beating until smooth after each addition, and adding enough strawberry pulp for proper consistency to spread.

STRAWBERRY JAM

Pick over and hull the berries. Measure, and for each 4 cups of fruit allow 3 cups of sugar. Place the fruit in a preserving kettle and crush while heating. Bring to boiling point, stirring frequently, and crushing any berries which still remain whole. Add the sugar, then cook until thick, not over 20 minutes, stirring constantly to prevent burning. Pour into hot, sterilized jars and seal. *See also* JAM.

STRAWBERRY JELLY

2 lb strawberries
2 tbsp water
2 cups sugar
⅔ cup pectin extract

Wash the berries thoroughly and remove the caps. Add the water to the berries, boil rapidly for a few minutes until the berries are soft, and strain through a jelly bag. (This yields about 2 cups of juice.) Mix the 2 cups of strawberry juice with the sugar and pectin extract. If the berries are especially lacking in acid, add 1 teaspoon of lemon juice to each cup of the juice. Boil rapidly until the jelly stage is reached and pour into hot sterilized glasses. *See also* JELLY.

STRAWBERRY MERINGUE

2 egg whites
⅛ tsp salt
½ cup sugar
1 tsp lemon juice
1½ cups sliced strawberries

Beat egg whites until stiff, but not dry. Blend in salt, sugar and lemon juice. Continue beating until meringue stands in peaks and is well blended. Fold in strawberries. Pile on sponge cake or angel food cake. (Sufficient for one 8-inch cake)

STRAWBERRY MERINGUE PUDDING

¾ cup cake flour
1 tsp baking powder
⅛ tsp salt
2 eggs
½ cup sugar
½ tsp vanilla
1 pt strawberries, sliced and sweetened to taste
2 egg whites
Dash of salt
Custard sauce

Sift the flour; measure and resift three times with baking powder and salt. Beat whole eggs until light and lemon colored; add ¼ cup of the sugar gradually, beating constantly. Add the vanilla. Sift the dry ingredients into the egg mixture gradually, and fold in carefully. Turn batter into a greased 8-inch layer cake pan and bake in a moderate oven (350° F.) for 20 to 25 minutes. Cool 5 minutes in pan, then turn out on cake rack to cool.

Place cake on large flat baking sheet and spread berries over top. Cover completely with a meringue made by adding a dash of salt to the egg whites and beating until

stiff but not dry, and gradually beating in the remaining ¼ cup sugar until thick and smooth. Return to oven and bake for 15 additional minutes at 350° F. or until meringue is golden brown. This may be served warm or cold with a custard sauce (*which see*). (The 2 remaining egg yolks may be used for the custard sauce.) (Serves 5 or 6)

STRAWBERRY MOUSSE

4 cups whole fresh strawberries
1 cup granulated sugar
2 tbsp cornstarch
2 tbsp cold water
¼ tsp salt
1 cup undiluted evaporated milk, whipped stiff
6 drops vanilla extract
2 egg whites, whipped stiff

Wash, stem, and press fresh, ripe strawberries through a sieve; add the sugar, and heat to the boiling point. Combine the cornstarch, salt, and cold water to form a smooth thin paste, and add to hot mixture, stirring constantly while pouring to prevent lumping. Cook, continuing stirring constantly, until mixture thickens, that is, coats a spoon. Strain, while hot, through a fine sieve. Chill; then fold in milk that has been whipped, alternately with the stiffly beaten egg whites, and add vanilla. Freeze in refrigerator tray, or mold, for 3½ to 4 hours; if individual molds, or paper cases are used, freeze 2 to 2½ hours. If hand freezer tray pail is used, pack, using equal parts of ice and salt, and let stand for 2 hours for individual, and 3 hours for large molds.

STRAWBERRY PIE

Pastry for 9-inch double crust pie
1 qt strawberries
1 cup sugar
¼ tsp salt
½ cup water
3 tbsp cornstarch
2 tsp lemon juice

Line a pie pan with pastry (*which see*) leaving edge plain. Prick very thoroughly over bottom, in the angles and up sides of pastry, and bake in a moderately hot oven (425° F.) for 15 to 18 minutes or until golden brown. Cool.

Meanwhile, wash and hull the berries. Thoroughly chill all but 1 cupful. Mash these, add the sugar, salt and ¼ cupful of the water. Heat to boiling. Blend the cornstarch with the remaining water. Combine with the boiling mixture and cook, stirring until clear. Remove from heat, strain and chill. Add lemon to cooked mixture and combine with chilled berries. Turn into baked shell.

Roll out remaining pastry for upper crust. Moisten rim of lower crust with water. Cut a design for steam vents and lay over the top of the pie. Press gently to the baked crust, trim, but don't flute edge. Place pie on a baking sheet. This prevents further baking of lower crust. Bake on the top shelf of a very hot oven (475° F.) for 15 to 18 minutes, just long enough to bake upper crust. Watch carefully at this high temperature. This method will produce a flaky, crisp bottom crust and whole berries that are cooked enough so they will have the highest possible appeal. Cool on cake rack before cutting. (Serves 6 to 8)

STRAWBERRY-PINEAPPLE PRESERVES

2 qt strawberries
2 large oranges
1 fresh pineapple, or 1 large can pineapple slices
Sugar

Wash, drain, and hull the berries. Grind the orange peel and cut the orange pulp and pineapple into small pieces. Measure the fruit and peel into a large saucepan and add the sugar, allowing ⅔ cup for each cup of fruit mixture. Let stand 2 hours, stirring two or three times; then bring slowly to boiling point, keeping an asbestos mat under the pan. Continue to cook slowly until the mixture thickens like marmalade, then turn into hot steri- lized jars and seal. (Makes 1 quart) *See also* CANNING.

STRAWBERRY PRESERVES

1 qt stemmed strawberries
Sugar
1 tbsp lemon juice

Select fine, ripe berries of uniform size; rinse quickly in a colander, then drain, and measure. Place fruit and sugar in alternate layers in a preserving kettle. For a heavy sirup allow equal parts of sugar and fruit; for a lighter sirup ¾ cup of sugar to each cup of fruit will suffice. Cover, let stand overnight, and, in the morning, set over a low flame. When boiling point is reached, place an asbestos mat under the pot and cook 15 minutes, making sure that the preserve does not boil over. Remove from the fire, add the lemon juice, cover with cheesecloth and let the preserve stand until the next morning. Bring again to boiling point, skim if necessary, and turn into hot steri- lized jars. Seal immediately. (Makes 1 quart) *See also* CANNING.

STRAWBERRY REFRIGERATOR CAKE

1 qt strawberries
½ cup butter
3 cups sifted confectioners' sugar
1 whole egg, beaten
3 eggs, separated
3 to 4 tbsp lemon juice
Pinch salt
Day old sponge cake

Wash and hull the berries; select 12 to 18 perfect whole berries for garnishing, and mash the rest to use in filling. Cream the butter, add 1 cup of the sugar and blend well. Add the one whole beaten egg and about ½ cup sugar and beat; then add 1 egg yolk, some of the crushed berries, lemon juice and more sugar; repeat until all are used, beating thoroughly after each addition until mixture is smooth and fluffy. Add salt to the 3 egg whites and beat until stiff; fold into first mixture. Line bottom and sides of spring-form pan with slices of cake and pour in half of the filling; add another layer of cake slices and rest of filling. Top with more cake slices. Place in refrigerator overnight, or for at least 3 hours. To serve, remove sides of pan. Garnish with whole strawberries or straw- berry halves and whipped cream if de- sired. (Serves 10)

STRAWBERRIES ROMANOFF

Marinate fine ripe strawberries, washed, drained, and hulled, in a blend of equal parts of orange juice and curaçao. At serving time arrange the fruit in a silver dish packed in ice, and cover with whipped cream.

Strawberry Sherbet

2½ cups strawberry pulp and juice
¾ cup granulated sugar
⅛ tsp salt
2 egg whites, stiffly beaten

Combine strawberry pulp and juice with sugar and salt, and chill for 1 hour; then freeze in the refrigerator tray until mushy. Stir in the stiffly beaten egg whites, and continue freezing until solid, but not too hard. Serve in chilled sherbet glasses or orange cups.

Strawberry Shortcake

3 cups strawberries
Sugar
Baking powder biscuit dough

Crush the berries very lightly with a fork. Sweeten to taste and let stand in a warm room for 2 or 3 hours to draw out the juice. Prepare biscuit shortcakes (*see* Shortcake). When baked, split, and spread the crushed berries between. Pour additional berries over the top and serve with plain or whipped cream. (Serves 6)

Strawberry Whip

1 cup strawberries
1 cup sugar
1 egg white
½ cup heavy cream, whipped

Wash, drain, and hull the berries. Place them with the sugar and unbeaten egg white in a bowl, and beat with a whisk for about 10 minutes or until the mixture is thick. Fold in the whipped cream and chill. Serve in sherbet glasses with cake or cookies. (Serves 4)

STREGA. A sweet, perfumed, golden-yellow after-dinner cordial, made in Italy. For full appreciation of its wonderful aroma and bouquet, it should be served at room temperature. *See also* Cordial and Liqueur.

STRING BEANS. *See* Beans.

STRINGER CHEESE. Another name for Spalen cheese, *which see.*

STRIPED BASS. *See* Bass.

STRIPED MULLET. *See* Mullet.

STRIPPINGS. *See* Milk.

STRUDEL. A pastry, made by rolling and baking a paper-thin sheet of dough spread with a filling, usually of fruits, but sometimes of cheese.

Apple Strudel

1 lb butter or other shortening
2 tsp salt
Ice water
1 lb pastry flour, sifted

If salt butter is used, wash it to remove the salt. To do this, wash the hands in water as hot as possible, rinse them in cold water, and knead the butter in ice water in a scalded bowl until all the salt is drawn out. At first the butter will crumble, but when free from salt, it will cling and mass together. Pat and fold it until dry and formed into a compact mass. Reserve 2 tablespoons, and put the rest into the refrigerator until needed.

Work the 2 tablespoons of shortening into the sifted flour and salt with the tips of the fingers. Mix to a dough with ice water. Turn onto a slightly floured board, pat smooth, and divide into two portions. Roll these out to the same size and thickness. Over one sprinkle a little flour. Take the remaining shortening from the refrigerator, and form into a sausage-like roll. Dredge with flour, and roll out very

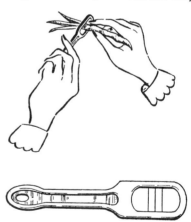

**GADGET FOR FRENCHING
STRING BEANS**

thin, as nearly like the sheets of dough in shape as possible. Flour both board and rolling pin, so that the shortening will not adhere to them. Place the shortening between the two sheets of dough, then roll as thin as possible without allowing the fat to break through. When the sheet becomes thin, fold in the sides until they meet, turn half around and roll out. Fold and roll in this way twice, then chill in the refrigerator for 15 minutes. Repeat the rolling and cooling three times more. Then roll out and spread with the following mixture, pressing it in lightly with a rolling pin:

1 cup fine, dry bread crumbs
¼ cup butter or other shortening
2 cups finely chopped peeled apples
½ cup chopped raisins
½ cup chopped almonds
½ cup sugar
1 tsp cinnamon

Brown the crumbs in the butter, combine with all remaining ingredients and cook until the apples are soft.

Roll up like a jelly roll, transfer to a well-greased, shallow pan and bake in a hot oven (400°–450° F.) until the crust is golden brown. Serve sliced, hot or cold, plain, or with a lemon sauce or whipped cream.

BOHEMIAN STRUDEL

2¼ cups sifted flour
Dash of salt
1 tsp olive oil
1 egg, slightly beaten
1 tbsp vinegar
½ cup lukewarm water

Sift the flour and salt. Add all remaining ingredients, and stir together quickly. Turn out onto a floured board and knead until smooth, 2 or 3 minutes, working in a little more flour if necessary. Place in a buttered bowl, brush with melted butter, cover with a towel, and leave in a warm place for about 1 hour. Cut the dough into two equal portions; leave one in the bowl and roll the other into an 8-inch square on a well-floured cloth spread on a large table. Brush the top generously with butter, and lift the dough on the backs of your well-floured hands. Stretch the dough gently from the center, letting it fall over the hands and stretch from its own weight. As it increases in size, lay it on the table, and run the palms under the dough. Work from the center out, not so much pulling the dough as letting it run

from one hand to the other. (This is very important. Do not leave either hand too long in one place or it will tear the dough.) Work as quickly as possible, stretching heavier areas to make the sheet evenly thin throughout. If particularly thin spots appear and seem to be drying, brush them lightly with melted butter. When pulled to transparency, the dough should cover a table 36″ x 26″. Cut away any thick edges with a sharp knife, stretch them as thin as possible, and cut them into squares. Working quickly, brush the entire surface with melted butter, sprinkle with fine, dry bread crumbs and cinnamon, and lay the pulled squares of dough over the surface. Butter them quickly. Spread the filling in bar shape along one end of the dough. Lift the cloth to bring the dough over the filling, and by raising the cloth higher and higher, roll the filling over and over, wrapping it in the fragile strudel dough. Cut the roll into lengths convenient for baking. Place on an ungreased baking sheet, brush with melted butter, and bake in a very hot oven (450° F.) for 10 minutes. Repeat the process with remaining dough.

CHEESE STRUDEL

1½ cups sifted flour
¼ tsp salt
1 egg
⅓ cup lukewarm water
Melted butter

Sift the flour and salt and moisten with the slightly beaten egg and warm water. The dough should be tender but firm. Knead on a board for 15 to 20 minutes or until the dough is full of bubbles and leaves both board and hands clean. Spread a little warm lard or butter over the surface and set aside in a warm place for half an hour. Cover a large table with a cloth, dust this with flour and put the dough in the center. Brush it over with melted butter, then pull and stretch gradually and evenly all around the table until the dough is as thin as tissue paper. Trim off any dough that extends over the edges and brush the entire surface with melted butter. Spread the cheese filling over and roll up like a jelly roll. Trim the edges. Place the roll on a greased baking sheet, twisting to fit into the pan. Brush once more with melted butter and bake in a hot oven

(400° F.) about 30 minutes. Sprinkle with powdered sugar and serve warm, cut in slices.

For the filling:

2 lb cottage cheese
4 egg yolks
2 egg whites
¼ tsp salt
3 tbsp sour cream
½ cup sugar

Press the cheese through a sieve, then add all remaining ingredients.

STUFFING. Erroneously called "dressing," stuffing is needed to upholster the inner cavities of poultry so that the bird will be kept extended in its natural shape. It also makes the bird go further at table. Moreover, the inner padding also serves as a slow distillator of its own spicy flavors back into the meat while at the same time absorbing juices and fats as they exude and trickle downwards during the roasting process.

Not only is this seasoned mixture desirable with roast, but sometimes also with braised, poultry. It can also be used frequently with meat such as steaks and chops; or as a filling for a crown roast of pork or lamb, a shoulder of veal, or as the herb-fragrant accompaniment to many fish recipes.

The type of stuffing to be used depends on the exact nature of the meat, poultry, or fish; but in general, stuffings are either pronouncedly "wet" or "dry." Bread is the most commonly used base for dry stuffings, but mashed potatoes, boiled rice, mashed cooked chestnuts, corn, or cornmeal, etc., are additional starchy fillings to which aromatic herbs and spices and other seasonings, such as fruits, are added.

As a rule the more rich and oily the meat, the more simple or more fruity the stuffing. Thus, stuffings including chopped apples, prunes, cranberries, pineapple, etc. are most suitable for goose, pork, duck, and similar meat; while dry, white-meated turkey, chicken, etc. may have oysters, sausage, or other rich mixtures. Those for fish should always have a sharp ingredient such as cucumber or pickle added to the bread base.

In any case most stuffing meriting the name contains a generous portion of onion, garlic, or shallots. It is a common practice to pan-fry the onions in butter, likewise the garlic or shallots, together with some herbs, as parsley, celery tops, etc.; but no chef or professional cook will ever fry these seasonings. For best results, they should be chopped, and mixed raw with the other ingredients. This keeps the "bite" and "sparkle" in their true flavor and strength.

HINTS ON PREPARATION

It is well to remember that stuffings, no matter of what kind, expand greatly during the cooking process, and if they do not have room to expand, they will become soggy masses or burst the meat. It is therefore recommended to stuff lightly and to bake any excess stuffing in a separate, greased baking pan or dish, as a second-helping supply.

Spices make the stuffing, and no homemaker should be guilty of using old or long-opened spices and herbs, which fail to yield full strength and fragrance. And, when the stuffing takes flavor from the bird or meat, it does not follow that the stuffing spoils the flavor of the meat. When stuffings are high in egg or fat value, or both, these ingredients form a seal against the wall of the bird or meat and prevent the juices from dripping into the stuffing.

Almost any one of the following stuffings may be used for stuffing vegetables, like eggplant, tomatoes, large onions, etc. For variation, a teaspoon of curry powder may be added to a plain bread stuffing; it gives an interesting and different flavor, and while it can be used with any kind of meat or bird, or vegetable, it is best with veal, lamb, or pork.

TO STUFF A BIRD

In stuffing, day-old bread is preferred for crumbs. Chop the onion, celery, parsley and other herbs, and combine them with the crumbs. Whatever other ingredients are indicated should then be added, and the crop cavity filled with a portion of the stuffing. The skin of the neck should be pulled back over the opening and fastened down. (The neck itself and the giblets are cooked in highly seasoned water to make broth for the gravy.) The body cavity is then filled with the remaining stuffing and the bird is trussed, the surface brushed with softened butter or oil and rubbed with salt. The bird is then ready for the oven. *See also* OYSTER, CHESTNUT, and various meats for additional recipes.

APPLE STUFFING
(For Duck or Goose)

1 slice onion
2 tbsp butter or margarine
½ cup chopped celery
½ cup bread crumbs
½ cup peeled, chopped tart apples
Salt and pepper

Melt the butter in a skillet and brown the onion. Add the rest of the ingredients, seasoning to taste, and mix thoroughly. Heat through. Stuff the bird as directed. (Sufficient for a duck)

BREAD STUFFING
(For Turkey)

6 to 8 cups crumbled day-old bread
1 tbsp salt
¼ tsp pepper
2 tsp poultry seasoning
¼ cup minced onions
½ to ¾ cup butter, melted
¾ cup giblet stock, or hot water
1 egg

Combine the bread, seasonings, the onions (first cooked, but not browned, for 5 minutes in 2 tablespoons of the butter) and the stock. Blend thoroughly, add the remaining butter with the beaten egg. The chopped cooked giblets may be added also, if desired. For chicken, reduce the amounts one-half.

GIBLET STUFFING
(For Turkey)

2 qt crumbled, day-old bread
2 tsp salt
½ tsp pepper
1 tsp sage
¾ cup butter
1 onion, finely minced
3 tbsp finely minced celery
Minced cooked giblets (heart, liver, gizzard)
Milk or giblet broth, optional

Combine the crumbs and seasonings with the onion and celery first, simmer until tender, but not brown, in 2 tablespoons of the butter. Add the remaining butter with the minced cooked giblets. If a moist stuffing is desired, add milk or giblet broth, otherwise omit this.

SAGE STUFFING

1 cup cracker crumbs
⅓ cup butter or margarine
⅓ cup stock
Salt and pepper
½ tsp powdered sage
1 blade marjoram

Heat the stock and melt the butter in the liquid. Add the crumbs and seasonings, using salt and pepper to taste. Mix thoroughly and stuff the bird as directed. (Sufficient for a chicken)

WILD RICE STUFFING
(For Turkey, Duck or Wild Birds)

2 cups raw wild rice
½ cup oil
1 cup chopped celery
1 cup chopped onion
½ cup button mushrooms
½ cup minced green pepper
2 cups stock
2 tsp salt
½ tsp Worcestershire sauce
½ tsp catsup
1 tbsp minced parsley

Wash the rice and drain thoroughly. Heat the oil in a heavy skillet and add the rice, celery, and onion. Cook, stirring constantly, until the rice is golden brown. Add the stock and all the rest of the ingredients. Cover and simmer for 30 minutes. Stuff the bird as directed. (Sufficient for a turkey)

STURGEON. The sturgeon belongs to the *Canoidae* family. It is found abundantly in America at the mouths of large rivers, as well as along the shore of both the Pacific and Atlantic Oceans, and is in great demand as food. The flesh of the young fish is much finer than that of the older fish. Both resemble veal and are similar to the tuna, although not quite so fine and delicate as the latter.

The American species are large and sluggish. The body is long and narrow with five rows of bony shields on the back. Their average length seldom exceeds five feet. They feed on crustaceans, mollusks, and the like, which they rout out from soft bottoms with their snout.

The large sturgeon which is found in the seas of Europe, Asia, and India, and which

STURGEON

ascends the large rivers, feeds on herring, mackerel, cod, salmon, and other fish. At the commencement of the spring season, they ascend rivers in large schools, similar to the salmon, to deposit their eggs. During that time they feed exclusively on the salmon, which migrate up the rivers at the same time.

Their strength is tremendous and they may knock a man down with a stroke of the tail. Their fecundity is remarkable, and it has been found that many females produce more than a million eggs annually. The eggs of the large sturgeon are so abundant that they form one-third of the weight of the fish. This sturgeon sometimes reaches a length of 20 feet and weighs a thousand pounds.

After birth the young fish immediately migrate to the sea and do not return to fresh water until maturity.

Sturgeon may be eaten fresh, dried, smoked, or canned. It is from the eggs of sturgeon that true caviar is prepared, and a sort of fish gelatin called *vesiga*, frequently used in Russian cookery, is obtained from the spinal marrow. The chemical composition of the edible portion of sturgeon is similar to that of salmon.

The various methods of preparation of tuna may be adapted to sturgeon. On account of its large size, it is usually cut either in slices or in pieces weighing three or four pounds each. However, small sturgeons of about four pounds may be found in the markets, and these are generally cooked whole. *See also* FISH.

SUCCOTASH. A combination of cooked sweet corn and lima beans.

SUCCOTASH

1 cup lima beans
1 cup cooked cut corn
3 tbsp butter
Salt and pepper

Wash the lima beans and drop them into boiling water. Cover and let them simmer about 25 minutes, until tender. Drain off liquid and save it. Add the corn which has been cut off the cob, and mix. Add enough of the bean liquid so that it is even with top of corn and beans. Simmer until most of the liquid is evaporated. Add the butter and salt and pepper to taste. (Serves 4 to 6)

Succotash may be varied by the addition of chopped pimientos or green peppers to give color and flavor.

SUCKER. One of the various fish with thick and fleshy lips, adapted for sucking in food such as plants and small animals. Among them is the blackhorse, a fish of the Mississippi Valley, also known as the Missouri or gourd-seed sucker. It is about two feet long, with a small head suggesting, in profile, that of a horse. It becomes almost jet-black in Spring. All the recipes applied to catfish may be applied to this really delicate fish.

SUCKLING PIG. *See* PORK.

SUET. The fatty tissues about the loins and kidneys of animals used for food. Specifically, it applies to beef fat. *See also* SHORTENING and FAT.

STEAMED SUET PUDDING

1 cup suet, chopped
½ lb figs, finely chopped
1 cup brown sugar
½ cup flour
2 tsp baking powder
1 tsp salt
¾ tsp ground cinnamon
½ tsp ground nutmeg
½ cup seeded raisins, halved
½ cup chopped nuts, optional
2½ cups stale bread crumbs
¾ cup milk
4 eggs

Be sure that the suet is very finely chopped. Add to it the figs, sugar, sifted flour, baking powder, salt and spices, the raisins and nuts, if used. Soak the crumbs in the milk and add to the first mixture with the well beaten eggs. Turn into two well greased molds, cover, and steam about 3 hours. Serve with hard sauce. (Makes 2 puddings)

SUGAR. Sugar ranks high in food value, producing energy and heat. It has been demonstrated that during muscular activity the consumption of sugar in the body is increased fourfold. If one pound of pure sugar were burned in the laboratory so as to utilize all the heat, it would raise the temperature of five gallons of water from freezing to the boiling point.

Sugar eaten to excess is fattening because the body stores the extra amount. However, a certain amount of sugar must be included in the diet to provide energy and to keep the body warm.

Sugar is usually thought of as coming from sugar cane, but sugars are also obtained from the sugar beet, the sugar maple, and from grapes, as well as corn and other vegetables.

HISTORY

The origin of sugar goes back into unrecorded history, but some historians believe that India was the first country to produce sugar from cane. It was introduced into Europe by the eastern traders and brought to the New World in Columbus' expedition. Its culture in the West Indies began in 1550.

In the middle ages, in France, fine cooks used sugar in dishes which a modern cook would not dream of sweetening. A recipe dated 1540 describes a dish made of eggs, chicken livers, red wine, aromatic herbs, and sweetened with sugar. Another early recipe for cooking perch suggests that the fish be cooked in water, then pounded with bitter almonds. It is then moistened with some of the cooking liquor, and set on the stove to simmer. The dish is then sweetened to taste with sugar.

DISCOVERY OF BEET SUGAR

For centuries it was believed that only sugar cane, which grows in a tropical climate, could provide sugar. But about 1740 a German chemist, Margraff, discovered sugar in some of the plants of the temperate zone, among others, the beet. At the beginning of the 19th century circumstances in Europe made cane sugar scarce, and the French government encouraged investigation into its manufacture from other plants. As a result beet sugar became the substitute for cane sugar.

Because of the cheapness of modern cane sugar, beet sugar is not used to as great an extent as cane sugar. The process of manufacturing it is similar to cane sugar, and the two sugars may be used interchangeably in recipes calling for sugar. It was formerly believed that beet sugar could not be used in jelly making because the sirup would not jell; this has been demonstrated to be false.

OTHER TYPES OF SUGAR

Tablet and cube sugar. These are made by moistening the granulated sugar with a high grade cane liquor and pressing it into a mold by means of a roller, the contents of the mold being pushed out into trays and placed in ovens to dry. Tablet sugar dissolves quickly and is preferred by restaurants as a matter of economy.

Powdered sugar. This comes in various grades. They are made by grinding granulated sugar in mills and passing it through fine meshed screens. They are grain sugars, but of minute grain, and have fast solubility.

Four X confectioners' sugar. This is the finest grade of powdered sugar. It is used for icings and candies, such as fondants, etc. Some kinds contain starch; others do not. The addition of three percent starch keeps it from lumping. This sugar is finer than flour, and it absorbs moisture like a sponge.

Brown sugar. This comes in two types— *light* and *dark*. They are made in the same manner as the granulated sugars, but the sirup is boiled at lower temperatures. The result is sugar containing a considerable amount of sirup which gives the pleasant flavor, the soft texture. Light brown sugar is for baking, for icings, for candy—when a not too dark molasses flavor is desired. Dark brown sugar is for sweets like soft molasses cookies, and other batters coarse of texture, heavy of spice. Both light and dark brown sugars are made from sugar cane or beet juice. Brown sugar should be stored in an airtight container. Place a slice of fresh bread, section of apple, or fresh lettuce leaf with the sugar to keep it properly moistened. This will prevent caking or will restore the normal texture if the sugar is caked already. *See also* MAPLE, SIRUP, and CORN.

SUGAR BOWL. *See* DISH.

SUGAR SPOON. *See* FLATWARE.

SUGAR TONGS. *See* FLATWARE.

SULPHUR WATERS. Mineral waters found in natural springs flowing in Europe and America. *See* Alkaline and Mineral Waters.

SULTANA RAISINS. *See* Raisins.

SUMATRA TEA. *See* Java and Sumatra Tea.

SUN VALLEY CHEESE. A soft, rich, Norwegian cheese with a creamy texture.

SUNDAE. An ice cream served with a dressing or topping of fruit or sirups, or both, or with a sauce poured over it. This famous and truly American creation is said to have been originated at a time when the state of Massachusetts passed and enforced stringent laws prohibiting the sale of soft beverages of all kinds on Sunday. An enterprising confectioner is said to have merely omitted the carbonated water from the ice cream soda, thus literally complying with the law. The name "sundae" was applied to this new product, and it made a pleasing and palatable dish on weekdays as well as Sundays. The possible combinations are endless.

SUNFISH. A North American freshwater fish of the perch family. Also known as blue gill.

SUNNYFISH. *See* Bream.

SUPPER. A relatively light meal eaten in the evening when dinner has been served at noon, or eaten very late in the evening, usually following some sort of social activity. *See* Table Setting and Service.

SUPREME. A rich white sauce, made of velouté (*which see*) to which fresh cream is added just before serving.

SURINAM CHERRY. The red, soft, aromatic, subacid and juicy fruit of a large, decorative Brazilian shrub, cultivated in southern Florida and southern California with great success. It is subglobose, ribbed, and from half an inch to an inch in diameter. It is eaten fresh or preserved. Surinam cherry jelly is an unusual delicacy. Also called Brazilian cherry.

SVECIAOST CHEESE. The most popular cheese of Sweden. It is made in three grades, full-cream, three-quarters-cream, and half-cream. It weighs from 25 to 30 pounds. It is ready for consumption after about six weeks, but is not safe to keep after it is six months old.

SWEDISH SAUCE. *See* White Sauce.

SWEET ALMOND. *See* Almond.

SWEET BASIL. *See* Basil.

SWEET CICELY. An aromatic herb sometimes used in cookery.

SWEET FENNEL. *See* Fennel.

SWEET MARJORAM. *See* Marjoram.

SWEET POTATO. The sweet potato is a native of tropical America and was known to the Indians before the time of Columbus. The Spanish explorers took the plant back to Europe, where it met with immediate success. There are two types of sweet potato, one with pale yellow flesh which cooks dry and mealy and the other, often incorrectly called yam, with deeper orange flesh which is much sweeter and moister. The true yam is an entirely different plant, a native of Africa. The sweet potato makes a fine substitute for white potatoes, although it is not related botanically.

HINTS ON BUYING

The two types of sweet potatoes are distinguishable in the market. The dry yellow potatoes have a yellowish fawn-colored skin, while the darker moister potatoes have a whitish or reddish skin. The varieties vary considerably in shape and in size, and in their cooking characteristics so that it is not desirable to buy mixed

SURINAM CHERRY

varieties. Sweet potatoes are shipped either as the new crop, or dried and stored for winter use. Either crop is equally good. The new crop potatoes are likely to have more delicate skins and thus bruise more easily; sweet potatoes are very susceptible to damage from bruising and spoil very quickly after an injury is received.

Good quality sweet potatoes are smooth, well shaped and firm; misshapen potatoes and those with cracks are likely to be wasteful. Potatoes with decayed spots should be avoided because the decay gives an unpleasant flavor even to the unaffected parts of the tuber.

Some potatoes are difficult to keep under ordinary home conditions. For this reason, buy only what will be used in a day or two. To keep satisfactorily, sweet potatoes need a dry storage place with a temperature between 55 and 60 degrees. Dampness will cause them to spoil readily.

material; for this reason it is best to put the cooked sweet potatoes through the ricer, thus removing the fiber, rather than mashing with a potato masher.

Cold mashed sweet potatoes may be used as a substitute for pumpkin or squash in pies and puddings.

To boil sweet potatoes, scrub them thoroughly and place in a kettle of boiling salted water. Cover the pot and boil until the potatoes are tender. Drain off the water, dry the potatoes by shaking the

Food Value

Water	Food Energy	Pro-tein	Fat	Carbo-hydrate	Cal-cium	Phos-phorus	Iron	Vit. A Value	Thia-mine	Ribo-flavin	Nia-cin	Ascor-bic Acid
68.5	125	1.8	.7	27.9	30	49	.7	7700	.10	.06	.7	22

Canned sweet potatoes. Canned sweet potatoes are available in markets now, and are a convenience and a source of supply when the fresh potatoes are not in season. The canned potatoes are peeled and processed so that they need only finishing by mashing or other preparation, and heating, to be ready to serve.

Dehydrated sweet potatoes. These may be used in any of the ways in which fresh or canned sweet potatoes are used. It is important to remember to keep the sweet potatoes completely covered during the soaking process and then bring them slowly to a boil. They should be cooked, covered, very slowly until tender and plump. The instructions on the package should be carefully followed.

Hints on Preparation

Sweet potatoes should be cooked in their jackets whenever possible. Not only does this preserve the nutriments just under the skin, but the potato is much easier to peel than when raw. Also, if sweet potatoes are peeled before cooking some of the sweetness escapes into the cooking water.

If it is necessary to peel sweet potatoes before cooking, drop the pared potatoes into cold salted water to keep from darkening. Cook as quickly as possible. Sweet potatoes are delicious baked in their jackets and served with salt and pepper and a lump of butter or margarine. Boiled sweet potatoes may be mashed just like white potatoes. Sometimes the large tubers contain a certain amount of fibrous stringy

pan for a moment over the stove, and then pull off the skins. The potatoes are now ready for preparation in many ways.

Mash boiled sweet potatoes, season with salt and pepper and beat in a little hot milk until the potatoes are smooth and fluffy. For variety, shape the mashed potatoes into small nests and brown in the oven. For still further variety, use orange juice in place of milk, and grate a little orange rind into the potatoes. For a special occasion, try sherry instead of other liquid.

To bake sweet potatoes, scrub them thoroughly and dry the skins. Bake in a hot oven (435° F.) until tender, 35 to 60 minutes, depending on the size. When

SWEET POTATO

they are about half done, prick the potatoes several times with a fork to allow the steam to escape. If you like the skins soft, rub the potatoes with a little fat before baking them.

Baked sweet potatoes may be stuffed by cutting large potatoes in half lengthwise and carefully scooping out the soft insides. Leave a little potato for a shell because the skin of the sweet potato is much thinner than that of the white potato. Mix the pulp with chopped leftover ham or chopped peanuts, or with a tablespoon of peanut butter. Stuff back into the shell, brush the top with a little melted fat and reheat in a hot oven (425° F.). Baked sweet potatoes may also be seasoned with a dash of tabasco sauce for a different flavor.

CANDIED SWEET POTATOES

Boil sweet potatoes; drain, and dry, and peel. Cut in lengthwise slices and arrange in layers in a greased baking dish. Sprinkle generously with maple sirup or brown sugar and dot each layer with butter. Bake in a moderate oven (350° F.) about 30 minutes, basting occasionally with the sirup. If desired, one or two cloves may be baked with the potatoes.

GLAZED MASHED SWEET POTATOES

Peel and mash boiled sweet potatoes. Season generously with salt and pepper and butter or margarine. Whip until light and fluffy. Pile in a glass baking dish, spread generously with brown sugar and dots of butter or margarine. Sprinkle chopped pecans over the top and place in a hot oven (400° F.) to melt the sugar mixture. Serve very hot.

GRILLED SWEET POTATOES

Boil sweet potatoes in their jackets until just tender. Drain, dry, and peel the potatoes. Cut into thick lengthwise slices. Brush with melted butter and place on a baking pan under the broiler flame. Broil, turning several times, until golden brown. Sprinkle with salt and pepper.

MARSHMALLOW SWEET POTATOES

Boil sweet potatoes in their jackets. Drain, dry, and peel. Put through the ricer. For each 4 cups of potato add 1 teaspoon of salt and 3 tablespoons of butter. Beat until light. Turn into a well greased baking dish and cover the surface with marshmallows. Bake in a moderate oven (350° F.) until the marshmallows melt, then brown quickly under a low broiler flame. Serve immediately.

SCALLOPED SWEET POTATOES

6 small sweet potatoes
1½ seedless oranges
½ lemon
12 chestnuts
½ cup light brown sugar
½ cup granulated sugar
½ cup butter or margarine
1 jigger of brandy

Parboil the potatoes in their jackets in boiling salted water for 10 minutes. Drain, dry, peel, and slice. Boil the chestnuts until tender and peel them. Slice the oranges and lemon thinly. In a greased baking dish arrange a layer of half the potatoes, then half the fruit slices, and half the chestnuts. Sprinkle with the white and brown sugar mixed, and dot with butter or margarine. Repeat the layers. Pour in the brandy. Bake in a moderate oven (350° F.) about 60 minutes, basting frequently with the sirup. Should this cook away too rapidly, add a little more sugar and water or brandy. If it is not desired to use brandy, a jigger of cider or plain water may be substituted. Delicious with game or baked ham. (Serves 6)

SWEET POTATO AND APPLE CASSEROLE

Place a thick layer of sliced cooked sweet potatoes in a buttered baking dish. Cover with a layer of sliced raw apple, peeled and core. Add two or three slices of lemon. Sprinkle with brown sugar and red cinnamon candies. Repeat the layers twice. Top with dots of butter or margarine and marshmallows. Bake in a moderate oven (350° F.) until the apples are tender and the marshmallows brown.

SWEET POTATO BISCUITS

1½ cups sifted flour
1½ tsp baking powder
½ tsp salt
3 tbsp butter or other shortening
½ cup cold mashed sweet potatoes
6 tbsp milk (about)

Sift together the dry ingredients, work in the shortening, and cut in the sweet potatoes. Moisten with the milk, using only enough to form a soft tender dough.

Turn onto a slightly floured board, knead until just smooth, and roll out ½-inch thick. Cut into very small biscuits. Bake in a hot oven (450° F.) until browned.

SWEET POTATO CROQUETTES

3 large sweet potatoes, boiled and peeled
⅓ tsp salt
2 eggs, separated
½ cup shredded almonds
Sifted flour

Mash the potatoes thoroughly, add the salt and egg yolks, and beat until smooth. Cool the mixture. Form into croquettes. Beat the egg whites until foamy. Dip the croquettes in the flour, then in the egg whites, and finally roll them in the shredded almonds. Fry in deep hot fat (375° F.) until golden brown. Drain on soft crumpled paper. (Serves 6)

SWEET POTATO PIE

1½ cups mashed sweet potatoes
⅔ cup brown sugar
1 tbsp melted butter or margarine
1 egg, slightly beaten
1 cup milk
1 tsp cinnamon
½ tsp ginger
⅓ tsp allspice
⅛ tsp salt
Pastry for single crust pie

Line a pie plate with pastry, forming a high collar. Combine all the other ingredients in the order given and turn into the pastry. Bake for 45 minutes, having the oven hot (450° F.) for the first 15 minutes, and then reducing the temperature to moderate (350° F.) for the remainder of the time. Bake until a knife inserted in the middle comes out clean, and the crust is nicely browned. (Serves 6)

SWEET POTATO PUDDING

1½ cups grated raw sweet potato
1½ cups cold water
¼ cup sugar
¼ tsp cinnamon
⅛ tsp allspice
3 tbsp melted butter or margarine
Grated rind of ½ orange

Combine the potato with the water, sugar, salt, and spices. Stir in the melted butter and orange rind. Turn into a greased casserole and bake in a moderate oven (350° F.) for 30 minutes, keeping the dish covered. Then uncover the dish and bake for another 30 minutes, or until a knife inserted in the center comes out clean. (Serves 6)

SWEET POTATO ROLLS

2 cups hot mashed sweet potatoes
3 tbsp butter or margarine
1 tsp salt
1 egg
3 tbsp sugar
1 yeast cake
1 cup lukewarm water
2 cups flour

Beat the butter in the hot sweet potatoes and let cool to lukewarm. Soften the yeast cake in the warm water. Add the salt, well beaten egg, sugar, and yeast mixture to the sweet potatoes. Add the flour and knead until smooth. Cover and let the dough rise in a warm place until it has doubled in bulk. Knead down again. Break off small balls and place in well greased muffin tins. Put aside to rise again until doubled in bulk. Bake in a moderate oven (350° F.) until delicately browned (12 to 20 minutes, depending on the size of the rolls).

SWEET POTATO SHEAVES

6 parboiled sweet potatoes
6 orange slices, centers removed
1 cup sugar
½ cup water

Make a sirup of the sugar and water and cook the orange slices in the sirup until tender. Drain and reserve. Cut the sweet potatoes in narrow lengthwise strips and fry in deep hot fat (375° F.) until golden brown. Drain on soft crumpled paper. Arrange the sweet potatoes in sheaves or bundles, and insert them in the orange rings. Use as a garnish for ham or turkey. (Serves 6)

SWEET WOODRUFF. *See* WOODRUFF.

SWEETBREAD. Only calf's and lamb's sweetbreads are generally used in cookery, although beef sweetbreads may be used advantageously when mixed with other meats, especially in meat pies, meat patties, garnishings, etc.

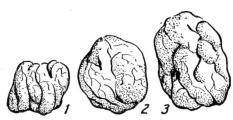

**SWEETBREADS   1. Lamb   2. Veal
3. Beef**

Sweetbreads, always believed a bit costly in cities, are too rarely found on the home table, and seem to be tacitly accepted as a delicacy peculiar to the rich, and to the better hotel restaurants, where adroit chefs know precisely what to do with them.

Each animal possesses two kinds of sweetbreads: one found in the throat and the other in the body proper. The first called throat sweetbreads are of elongated shape, while the other called heart or belly sweetbreads are of rounded contour.

Some dealers try to substitute sweetbreads from young steer for those of veal, which are quite different in quality and color, as are the lamb sweetbreads. Veal and lamb sweetbread are white and tender, while those of the steer are reddish and tough under pressure of the fingers.

Sweetbreads must be strictly fresh otherwise they are unfit to eat. Soft gland tissue always deteriorates and decomposes rapidly.

PREPARATION

Just as soon as sweetbreads come from the butcher, plunge them immediately into lukewarm water to draw out the blood, allowing them to remain in the water for at least 1 hour and changing it several times. Now place them in a pan, cover with cold water, add a dash of salt and the juice of ½ lemon for each pair of sweetbreads. Bring slowly to boiling point and simmer gently for 15 minutes—this is termed blanching. Return them to cold water to complete the blanching. Then carefully take out the tubes and membranes, avoiding tearing the tissues. When cold, place in the refrigerator but use as quickly as possible as they easily absorb the flavors of other foods with which they come in contact. Before their final cooking (broiling, creaming, etc.) pat dry.

BRAISED SWEETBREADS

3 pair sweetbreads
¼ lb salt pork
2 chopped carrots
1 celery stalk, chopped
1 tbsp chopped parsley
1 cup stock
½ cup cream
1 small can mushrooms

Parboil the prepared sweetbreads. Lard with the salt pork. Arrange on the carrots, celery and parsley in a casserole, and pour the stock over. Cover and bake in a moderate oven (350° F.) about 45 minutes. Place the sweetbreads on a hot platter. Press the vegetables through a coarse sieve, add the cream and mushrooms, reheat and pour over the sweetbreads. (Serves 4 to 6)

SWEETBREADS IN EGG SAUCE

1 pair sweetbreads
1½ cups stock
Salt and pepper
1 tsp onion juice
2 eggs
1 tbsp flour
2 tbsp cold water
1 tsp lemon juice
1 tsp minced parsley

Parboil the prepared sweetbreads, and cut into large cubes. Heat the stock in a double boiler. Season with salt, pepper and lemon juice. Then thicken with the slightly beaten eggs and the flour moistened with the cold water. When as thick as custard, add the lemon juice and parsley. Heat the sweetbreads in this sauce and serve on toast. (Serves 2)

SWEETBREADS SOUS CLOCHE

Ambitious? Willing to work? Then try something like this. Lard the blanched sweetbreads with larding pork, using a larding needle. (*See* LARDING) Have as many individual glazed earthen baking dishes as you will need, and the same number of small bell glasses to fit the dishes.

Having larded the sweetbreads lightly with a small-sized needle, put them in a stew pan with two or three times as many large mushroom caps as you have dishes; season with salt, pepper, and a sprinkle of Worcestershire sauce. Pour over them (for each 3 pair of sweetbreads) a pint of heavy cream and a pint of milk. Bring to a boil and simmer gently for 20 minutes. Take out the sweetbreads and mushrooms, and thicken the cream slightly with a prepared roux (*which see*) of butter and flour.

Slice cooked lean Virginia ham ½ inch thick to fit the dishes under the bells. Arrange the sweetbreads on the ham, with the mushrooms, and garnish with small disks of thinly sliced truffles. Be sure that the cream sauce is well seasoned, and pour it into the dishes, then fit the bells into place. Put the dishes in the oven (moderately hot) and bake 10 minutes after the sauce is seen to bubble through the glass. The dishes are placed before the guests "with the bells on," but beware of burned fingers!

Hot buttered rolls, brioche, or croissants are appropriate accompaniments, and a bottle of cool Chablis or Montrachet would never be amiss with sweetbreads sous cloches.

SWEETS. A common term for candies and the like.

SWISS CHARD. *See* CHARD.

SWISS CHEESE. If you ask a grocer or delicatessen dealer for Swiss cheese, he will likely ask, "imported or domestic?" And if your answer is "imported," you will probably get a full-flavored cheese with the characteristic holes or "eyes" running throughout the piece. But it may or may not have been made abroad. There are two kinds of Swiss cheese; that with the eyes, which is called imported type, and that without, which is called domestic type.

The "eyes" in Swiss cheese are what determine its grade and consequently its price, for, to a large extent, they indicate the quality of the flavor. These eyes should be neither too large nor too small, uniform in size and appearance, each produced by a different kind of bacteria working at a different stage of the ripening process—like runners in a relay race. All were needed to produce its distinctive sweetish flavor.

The domestic processed Swiss cheese does not have those eyes. It is made of various grades of Swiss and Cheddar cheeses ground up, melted, and then run into molds of various sizes, sometimes into glasses or into small bricks to be wrapped in tinfoil for merchandising in a form convenient to spread.

Imported Swiss cheese should be sliced in thick portions, not thin slices, before it is brought to the table. But it is the only cheese that should be so served.

The Swiss in Wisconsin make cheese so much like the originals that few people can tell the difference. As a result the imported product is now known as Switzerland cheese. The Wisconsin cheese makers still call their product Swiss cheese. It has the same rich, nutty flavor, and few cheese buyers can tell them apart without looking at the name stamped on the label.

Swiss cheese, unlike other cheeses, is not made in vats but in shining copper kettles, each holding 2,000 pounds of milk, enough to yield 300 pounds of curds, which shrink eventually into 200 pounds of cheese. The curds are very slowly stirred with a strange contraption called a "cheese harp." Suddenly, one of the kettles of curds gets ripe. The cheese man folds a cloth over a spring-steel blade and with a lightning-like movement scoops up the curds, ties a deft knot, hooks on an overhead crane, gives a heave, and there is the cheese hanging in a huge, dripping blob in the air. Another heave, and it is dropped into a round wooden form, slipped under a press, and the whey squeezed out. Next day it comes off the table and goes into a brine tank for three days. After that it goes onto a shelf in the curing cellar for six to eight weeks. The eyes are the result of the natural fermentation in the cheese.

SWISS STEAK. A method of braising less tender cuts of beef, veal, or lamb.

SWISS STEAK

Either beef, veal or lamb may be used—about 3 pounds, cut into 1½ inch thick steaks. Dip the meat into water, drain but do not dry. Have ready ½ cup of flour in a bowl or on a platter, lay the meat in this and press and knead as much flour as possible into the meat itself. Now brown thoroughly in drippings, turning to brown both sides. Transfer to a stew pan large enough to hold the meat easily. Add 1 cup of water or stock to the frying pan in which the meat was browned, allow this to come to boiling point, then pour over the meat in the stewpan. Add 1 medium-sized onion finely minced, a can of tomatoes, salt and pepper. Cover closely and simmer very gently at least 2 hours. The cooking may be done either over a low top-of-the-range burner, or in a slow oven (300° F.).

The flour used in browning the meat will help thicken the gravy. If desired a bay leaf, a clove or a pinch of thyme may be added to the cooking meat. Serve with plain boiled potatoes, rice or noodles. (Serves 6 or 8)

SWITZERLAND CHEESE. A trade name for genuine imported Swiss cheese, (*which see*).

SWIZZLE. A tropical drink made of liquor, bitters, lime juice and sugar, mixed with finely crushed or shaven ice so as to make it intensely cold.

The swizzle originated in the West Indies where a large percentage of the Caribbean Islands claim to be the birth place, and where a great variety of swizzles have been invented and perfected. In those regions the swizzles are all mixed in the traditional manner of placing the ingredients and ice in a glass pitcher and stirring by means of a swizzle stick (*which see*) twirled rapidly between the palms until the pitcher is well frosted. Traditionally, too, the finished drink is tossed down rapidly, while still extremely cold.

Since the swizzle stick is native to the Caribbeans, other regions have evolved different techniques for mixing these drinks. Perhaps the most effective alternative is the use of the cocktail shaker.

Swizzles are usually named after the basic liquor ingredient (brandy swizzle, gin swizzle, rum swizzle, whisky swizzle, etc.) or the color (green swizzle red swizzle) and, regardless of the mixing method used, are all based on the same formula.

SWIZZLE (Basic Recipe)

1 jigger desired liquor (brandy, gin, rum, whisky, etc.)

1 lime (juice)

1 tsp powdered sugar

2 to 6 dashes Angostura bitters (depending on taste preference)

There are several possible ways of pre-

paring this drink. The ingredients may be mixed in a pitcher with a swizzle stick, as described above. They may be mixed in a cocktail shaker and then strained into a cocktail glass. They may also be prepared in a Tom Collins glass by first mixing the sugar and lime juice with a small quantity of carbonated water in the glass and filling the glass with finely shaven ice. Then the liquor and bitters are poured in and as much carbonated water as the glass will hold, leaving a little margin for stirring. The drink is then served with a swizzle stick and the guest does the final "swizzling" himself. (Serves 1)

Green Swizzle. Made as above, with one tablespoon of green creme de menthe added.

Red Swizzle. Basic recipe with one tablespoon of grenadine added.

For a further discussion of drink recipes and drink preparation, *see* BARTENDING.

SWIZZLE STICK. A stirring device, originally made from a dried Caribbean plant, used to mix those intoxicating drinks known as swizzles (*which see*). The

SWIZZLE STICK

plant, found in the West Indies, has many forked, radiating branches, which are well suited for agitating heavily iced mixtures. In regions where swizzles are popular and the plant unavailable, swizzle sticks are sometimes made of fine metal wire. The term is wrongly applied to stirrers and muddlers, *which see*.

SWORDFISH. This fish has flourished for centuries and was well known to both the Greeks and Romans. The swordfish season in north Atlantic waters begins in May, reaches its peak in July and August, and tapers off in the fall. Southern Atlantic fishing lasts throughout the year. The waters of the Pacific, too, provide swordfish abundantly. The fish is sold around the calendar, but in the winter the fish is frozen and those who speak with authority insist that frozen swordfish is less delicate in flavor and tougher of flesh.

A relative of the mackerel, the swordfish is one of several fish having an elongated snout forming a flattened, sharp-edged sword-like beak. This weapon is about

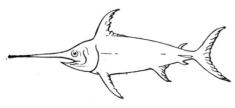

SWORDFISH

half as long as the body and becomes so strong that it may be driven far through the planking of a row boat or even a sailing vessel.

Not so long ago this fish with the polished, metal-like hide was a drug on the fish market in the United States, selling for about a cent and a half a pound. Then came the summer of 1927 when a buyer for a restaurant took a fancy to the fish, and served it broiled. It became fashionable, and, before the summer ended, his restaurant was serving hundreds of pounds of swordfish steaks.

The average length of the swordfish in the Atlantic Ocean is about seven feet, and the weight reaches several hundred pounds. The fish uses its sword to forage for a meal. Rising up suddenly among a school of mackerel, bluefish, or herring, he strikes right and left and then returns to gorge.

SWORDFISH STEAK

To enjoy a swordfish steak, the equivalent of a fine juicy sirloin or porterhouse, have a fresh steak cut 2 inches thick. Broil or pan-fry slowly to a rich golden brown, basting frequently with butter. A quarter or half section, cut thick, is worth a whole round cut thin. Serve as you would a good steak, that is, with French fried potatoes.

BAKED SWORDFISH SKIPPER'S METHOD

½ cup chopped onions
3 tbsp oil
1½ cups canned tomato
½ cup tomato juice
3 whole cloves
½ tbsp sugar
¾ tsp salt
1 large bay leaf
6 sprigs celery tops
6 sprigs parsley
12 sprigs chives
6 whole peppercorns, crushed
3 tbsp flour
3 tbsp cold water
½ cup sliced stuffed olives
1 tbsp minced green pepper
2 tbsp capers
2½ lb swordfish (in one piece)

Cook the onions in the oil in a large, heavy skillet. Add the tomato pulp, juice, cloves, sugar, salt, the bay leaf, celery, parsley and chives tied together, and the peppercorns. Simmer 5 minutes, then turn into a baking dish. Moisten the flour with the water and stir slowly into the mixture, cooking 5 minutes longer, stirring occasionally to prevent scorching. Discard the bouquet of herbs and add the olives, green pepper, and capers. Wipe the fish and bury it in the sauce. Bake in a moderately hot oven (375° F.) 40 minutes, covering the dish with a greased paper during the first half of the cooking period. Serve right from the baking dish accompanied by plain boiled potatoes and a green salad. (Serves 6 or 8)

SYCAMINE. The black mulberry, *which see.*

SYCAMORE FIG. The fruit of a bushy tree of Syria and Egypt.

SYLLABUB. Also spelled sillabub or sillilub. A very old drink of milk and wine or cider. Sweeten the milk with sugar and add wine to taste, but not enough to curdle it. Serve in tall glasses and top with whipped cream.

SYRUP. *See* SIRUP.

SZANORODNER. A delicious, pale-golden, dry, fiery Tokay-type wine of Hungary, usually served as a dessert wine also as an after-dinner cordial, or for afternoon tea with cakes and cookies. *See* WINE.

SZEKELY CHEESE. A soft Hungarian cheese made from ewe's milk. It is sold in sausage skins.

T

TABASCO SAUCE. A very hot, sharp seasoning made of capsicum.

TABLE CLOTH. A decorative and protective covering that is spread over a table before the individual pieces are set. There are many different kinds of table cloths, all suited for different occasions. Though originally only cloth was used for this purpose, the term has come to be applied to coverings made of oilcloth, plastics, and other such substances. *See* TABLE SETTING AND SERVICE.

TABLE KNIFE. That type of knife which is designed to be used by the individual diner to cut the food on his plate, spread butter, etc. *See* FLATWARE.

TABLE LINEN. A term used generally to describe all table cloths and napkins, though the cloth may be a material other than linen. *See* TABLE SETTING AND SERVICE.

TABLE SETTING AND SERVICE. Table setting and service has a very important role to play in dietetics; a role almost as vital as that of menu planning and food preparation. It is the background for the meal. The chief function of background is to establish the proper mood or atmosphere in which the meal will be eaten. If the mood or atmosphere is harmonious, it will never be noticed in itself, but the actual meal will be enhanced a thousand fold. If the mood is not proper, again it will not be self-evident, but there will be a distinct air of wrongness about the dinner.

With the proper atmosphere established at the table, eating becomes an enjoyable experience and not a mere task that must be done three times daily because of the demands of nature. The very color of the dining room walls can have a decided effect on the diner's appetite, and food that is haphazardly thrown on unmatched plates on a cluttered table certainly does not appeal to the eye.

Meals eaten under an atmosphere of tension and haste are not good meals. Unless the diner has a very strong constitution, they are not properly digested, and a succession of improperly digested meals is a sure route to stomach disorders.

Under the pressures of modern living, however, too often the family meals lapse into a dull routine. They become an annoying task that must daily be faced because people seem to get hungry, and for no other reason. They become mere ordeals to be rushed through quickly, dirtying as few dishes as possible, so that there will be as little work as possible for all involved, even the diners.

The wise homemaker fights this tendency. She knows how important it is for the health of her family that the atmosphere at table be relaxed, leisurely, and cheerful. She knows how important it is for the health of her children that the meals be enjoyable and not trials-by-fire. She knows that if her children come to look upon food as something that must be eaten so they can then leave the table, and not as part of an enjoyable experience, they will not get the proper nourishment and may even build up intense dislikes for certain foods that will affect them all of their lives.

A smart homemaker knows well how major a role the table plays in a happy family life, and she also knows that by approaching it in this manner she can make meal-time an exciting challenge rather than a daily drudgery as far as she, herself, is concerned.

She knows these things and approaches the challenge in many ways. The menu is an important element. She makes it varied and interesting, full of little tricks and surprises, and knows the power that little touches have in taking the curse of monotony away from the inexpensive staple dishes that economics often force on the table.

But she knows, too, how well table setting and service can help her in her task. An orderly, well-set table is in itself an inducement to sit down and eat. It is neither cramped, crowded, nor chaotic. But orderly settings can, in themselves, be monotonous as any ex-serviceman knows.

By varying the decoration of the table it is possible to relieve that monotony, to make every setting appear unique and distinctive. The decorations need not be elaborate, indeed, it is better if they are not. A simple centerpiece, a dish of fruit, a few flowers, a figurine or two; any small **touch** that will establish a mood. And it is mood that is desired on the table, not mere visual decoration; a mood that is established in the decorations, reflected in the dishes and setting, enhanced by the food, and established in the diners themselves. A few fresh flowers, for example, when placed on a breakfast table, can establish a mood of cheerful freshness that will not only make the food taste better, but actually make the entire morning seem brighter.

The wise homemaker knows that these tricks are not saved for company use only, but are tools to be used in her everyday care and feeding of the family. She practices settings and decorations, she studies the pages of women's magazines for table settings applicable to her circumstances and, even as she does with unique recipes, keeps a scrap book or other file of those she likes for future inspiration. Then, when guests are expected for dinner, she is able to entertain them in a royal manner without casting a marring pall of worry that all will not go well.

Table Accessories

Table Linen. This term is used generally to apply to all cloth—table cloths, napkins, etc.—used at the table.

Table Cloth. There are many materials used to cover tables, chief of which is linen damask. This cloth is made of long flaxen fibers and is usually white and unembroidered, though it may have both color and needlework. It is the finest and most expensive cloth, though in the long run it is economical because it is long wearing and does very little shrinking. Shrinkage is an important factor, for in a cloth of that size it take relatively little shrinkage per foot to hopelessly distort the piece. Linen also ages well, and with proper laundering and ironing will always look crisp, fresh, and new. When buying linen, the thread count (number of threads per square inch) largely determines the value. In addition to damask, there is the so-called peasant linen, which is made of a shorter fiber.

Lace is another material commonly used for table cloths, and some cloths may have lace insets. Actually, any cloth may be used for a table covering, and table cloths may be economically made at home from regular yard goods.

Cloths may be embroidered or plain, colored or white; the possibilities are end-less. Only plain white cloths, usually linen or lace, are used at formal functions, but color is often used for informal settings. The table cloth, more than any other single item of setting, sets the fundamental mood of the meal. It can be bright and gay or dignified and restrained; vivid and bold or delicate and refined—but always it must fulfil two requirements. It must be harmonious with the rest of the setting and it must never predominate.

The table cloth should be of such a size and shape that it will overhang the table from 12 to 15 inches. Lace cloths are permitted more overhang, if desired, but they should never interfere with the diner's knees. When lace cloths or cloths with lace insets are used at other than formal functions, a colored undercloth that is a bit smaller in size than the table cloth itself may also be used. Whenever a damask cloth is spread, it is customary to first lay down a soft silence cloth unless felt pads or similar devices are placed under the damask.

Table cloths made of plastic, oilcloth, and other treated materials are colorful and practical, but are not used for formal events.

Place Mats and Runners. These are used as substitutes for a table cloth, especially in the summer when the cooling appearance of a bare table is desired. They are made of a variety of materials in a variety of patterns and should be selected in much the same way as table cloths. The mats are used for the individual settings, while the runner goes in the center of the table.

Dinnerware or *Chinaware.* These should echo the mood of the meal and the setting. *See* DISHES.

Silverware. This, too, should harmonize. *See* SILVERWARE.

Decorations. While almost anything can be used to decorate the table, the most common decorations are built around matched bowls, comports, compotiers, vases, etc. Unusual effects may be achieved by using mirrors, figurines, and even toys. Whatever the decorations are, they should be kept simple, should not be allowed to predominate, and should be kept under 14 inches in height so as not to screen off the diners at opposite sides of the table.

Lighting. The lighting should be carefully planned; neither too brilliant nor too dim, but adequate for visual enjoyment of the food. It should not shine into the guest's eyes, and it must be remembered that a broad expanse of white linen can reflect considerable glare unless the lighting is properly arranged.

Candles add an attractive touch to the table and are almost required equipment for a formal meal. They should be provided in sufficient numbers, however, lest the guests be forced to grope their way about in the dark. Two candles are used only on a small table set for two. Four candles should be used for up to six guests, and the number increased in the proportion of one candle for every two or three additional guests. The arrangement of the places will also affect the number of candles required. Candles violate the general rule of low decorations and should stand at least 16 inches high to keep them from shining directly into the eyes of the guests. Either candles or electricity should be used; never both.

SETTING THE TABLE

When a table is set, the table cloth or place mats are first put on. If a damask cloth is used, a silence cloth is placed beneath it, and in the case of lace or other perforated cloths, a colored undercloth may be used on all but formal occasions. Both the silence cloth and the undercloth are smaller than the outer cloth, to keep them from projecting below the cloth.

If the occasion is informal, a transparent plastic cloth may also be laid over the table cloth, to keep the cloth clean should there be any spillage at the table. If this plastic cloth is used, hot pads must be placed under all hot serving vessels that are later set on the table (*see* PLASTICS).

If place mats are used, they should be evenly spaced and set close to the edge of the table. Runners are often used in conjunction with mats, but if the shape of the table does not lend itself to this treatment, or if the runner would be too crowded, it should be left off, and dish pads substituted.

A service plate is then set at each place, with at least two feet between the centers of adjacent plates, thus giving each diner sufficient elbow room. The plates should be set in straight lines, one inch from the edge of the table.

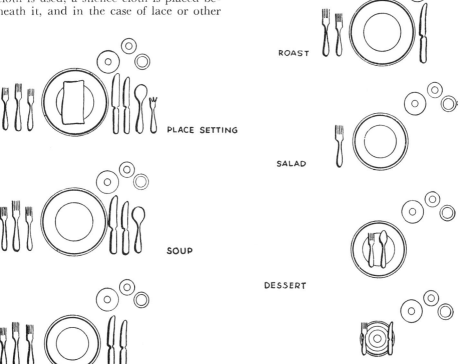

PLACE SETTING

ROAST

SOUP

SALAD

DESSERT

FISH

TABLE SETTINGS

INFORMAL TABLE SETTING

The silverware is next laid down, set at right angles to the line of the table, also one inch from the edge. Even though the table may be round, the silver and plates of each setting are in a straight line.

Forks are placed to the left of the plate, tines up, and knives and spoons go to the right. The knives are set next to the plate, cutting edges of the blades facing the plate, and the spoons are laid with the open sides of the bowls facing up.

The only two exceptions to this general placement order are the oyster fork and the butter spreader. The oyster fork, when used, does not go with the other forks, but is placed to the extreme right of the spoons; while the butter spreader is placed on the bread and butter plate, if there is one, or, lacking that, is set on the table above the service plate, centered, handle to the right, blade parallel to the table's edge.

The pieces are always laid out in the order of use so that, as the meal progresses from course to course, the diner will always find the knife, fork, or spoon required at the outer extremities of the setting. Not all of the silver required for the meal is set on table at the initial setting, however. The dessert silver, for example, is always brought in with that course. If there are more than three other courses on the menu, only the silver for the first three is set out, the rest being brought in as needed.

Another important rule is that no piece of silver that is not required by the menu is ever set on the table. The table is supposed to be the showcase for food, not the accessories, no matter how beautiful they may be. Setting excess silver on the table is unfair to the guests for it leads them to expect courses that are never served, and they may well have not eaten their fill of the courses that were served in order to leave room for these phantom foods.

After the silver is in position, the water glass or goblet is placed at the top of and in a line with the innermost knife. This position may be varied slightly if, for any reason, it would be a precarious perch for the glass. If wine, ice tea, or other beverages requiring special glasses are to be served, these additional glasses are arranged in a triangle to the right of the water glass. Here, too, the rule of three is followed. If more than that number of additional glasses will be required, they are brought out at the proper time instead of being placed at the initial setting.

If coffee or tea is to be served during the meal, the cup and saucer are placed to the right of the spoons. The tea spoon may be either laid on the saucer or placed in proper order among the other spoons, depending on the amount of silver on the table.

The bread and butter plate, if used, is placed to the left, and slightly above, the forks. The butter spreader is always placed on this plate. The position of the spreader should be harmonious, though not always conforming to the lines established by the other silver, and should be uniformly placed on each plate.

If salad is served as a side dish, and not as a separate course, the salad plate is located to the left of the forks.

The napkin is placed either on the service plate or on the table to the left of the forks. It is always neatly folded, but the exact manner of folding is more a matter of local tradition than general rule.

Individual items, such as salt and pepper shakers, ash trays, match boxes, cigarette boxes, name cards, etc., are placed directly above the service plate.

Not all of the items previously discussed will be required by any one menu, of course, and like the silverware, unnecessary items should not be placed on the table. The table should have as free and uncluttered an atmosphere as possible. It should also be orderly. All silver (except,

possibly, the butter spreader) should be set in straight lines either at right angles or parallel to the table edge (which is imagined to be straight if it is actually curved), cup handles are aligned the same way, and the individual place settings are all lined up. While it is not necessary to go to the extremes of using a piece of string or a chalk line to set the table, reasonable care should be taken to see that everything is correctly aligned.

When the places have been set, the table is decorated, as previously discussed. It must be remembered that the important effect is one of mood or atmosphere. The basic trend should have been established by the selection of table cloth, napkins, china and silver; it remains only for the decorations to point it up. If the only effect desired is one of fresh, pleasant beauty, perhaps the simplest centerpiece is a carefully heaped dish of fruit. The container should be either distinctive or unobtrusively plain, and the fruit can later serve as a dessert course. Cut flowers are always good decorations, and for an unusual effect, may be put out in the form of blossoms floating in bowls of water.

Whatever the ornamentation, it should be kept simple, low, and should never clutter the table. It is a good general rule to see that the decorations never take up

NEAR-FORMAL TABLE SETTING

more than one third of the table space left clear after the settings are placed.

The settings just given were the basic placements, applicable to all meals. The specific meals will vary, of course, in accordance with their needs.

Often slighted, breakfast is really a very important meal. The gap between dinner or supper and breakfast is usually the longest period of the day in which a person abstains from food, and breakfast must supply him with energy enough to last till noon. Since the modern luncheon is too often a fast sandwich and a malted milk, breakfast assumes considerable importance in the dietetic scheme.

Too often breakfast is looked upon as just another of the many hurdles in the race to reach school or work at the appointed hour. Under modern conditions breakfast can never be a truly leisurely meal, except on weekends, and for that very reason, the meal and the table settings should be as attractive as possible. Not only does this induce the mental attitudes for proper digestion and sometimes urges the family to eat more than they would normally, but, if breakfast is sufficiently attractive, the family might even rise a bit earlier so they might properly enjoy the meal.

The breakfast table should be bright and gay; simple, not cluttered. Brightly colored cloths or place mats and gaily ornamented dishes should be used. Fresh flowers are preferred as a decoration to carry out the clean, fresh, pleasant motif.

Breakfast settings are fairly simple. Usually a luncheon plate is large enough for use. A luncheon knife and fork, a teaspoon, a butter spreader and, if needed, a cereal spoon, a fruit spoon and an egg spoon are the normal silver needs. A bread and butter plate and a cup and saucer, as well as water or milk glass complete the setting. The teaspoon may either be placed on its appropriate saucer or laid in proper order among the spoons, and the butter spreader goes in its normal place. The serving dishes, of course, depend on the nature of the menu.

If circumstances permit making a leisurely affair of the meal, or if guests are present, it is traditional that the host serve the main course, while the hostess, as always, pours the tea or coffee. At break-

fast, she may also serve the toast, making it at the table as needed. Toast may also be made in advance and served on a plate or special toast rack. Heated muffins are usually served in a covered muffin dish.

Breakfast dishes are usually of a nature that permits serving with a fork and spoon. The tray or platter bearing the course is set before the host, with the serving implements arranged in a line at an angle to the right of his water glass. The coffee or tea equipment is placed before the hostess, usually on a tray. In this case, the cups and saucers are not set out at the individual places, but come in on the tray, and are passed, filled, to the guest.

If fruit juice is served, it is sometimes served in a glass nesting in an ice-filled bowl. These ice-filled bowls are also used for fruits and similar foods, maintaining the crisp, cool, attractive note of breakfast.

If there is a maid in attendance, the host does not serve the entree. The maid brings in filled plates and also takes over the duties of toast-making. The hostess, however, is still expected to do the pouring.

Buffet Breakfast. When large groups are entertained, it is often more convenient to serve a buffet breakfast, handled much the same as a buffet supper. The food is placed on a buffet in covered dishes and special hot plates which keep it warm and appetizing. If the gathering is small, places are set at the table in the regular manner and, when the guest comes down, he takes his plate and either serves himself or, if there is a servant, is served at the buffet, returning to his place to eat. If the gathering is extremely large, the plates and silverware are arranged in a convenient manner on the sideboard.

If the affair is informal, the food is merely set out and the guests are free to come down when they wish to arise, instead of meeting at a stated time. This permits everyone to follow their own inclinations for the morning, and the hostess is not required to be in attendance.

If the affair is conducted in a semiformal manner, the usual hours are from 11 A.M. to 2 P.M., and the hostess is required to be in attendance. Tradition demands that she do the pouring, while either servants or the guests themselves serve the food from the sideboard. In these cases, the tea and coffee things are set up at a separate table to permit the hostess to be seated at her duties, but not giving all of her attention to one particular group that would otherwise be sitting with her. A friend or servant can, of course, relieve the hostess if she wishes to mingle with the guests. At affairs of this nature it is also proper to invite neighbors and friends instead of restricting it solely to house guests.

LUNCHEON

Since the bulk of the household is usually off to school and work during the noon hour, the institution of luncheon parties has come to be largely a feminine affair. These are always light, informal affairs and, for that reason, the table is never spread with a formal damask cloth. Place mats, lace or embroidered table cloths are preferred. The object is to make the event as colorful as possible, still keeping the meal light. There are rarely more than three or four courses served at a luncheon; a juice, melon or soup, a simple main dish, a salad and some sort of light dessert and coffee.

It is proper to serve cocktails at a luncheon, but a better touch is to serve a sherry. A luncheon menu should be unique, but not so fanciful as to render the food unrecognizable as such. Unusual fruit and vegetable dishes and juices, tricks like tossing a salad at the table, casserole dishes; all of these are appropriate.

The basic setting again applies, here with accent on the frills and unique decoration. Individual smoker's accessories, use of a soup cup rather than a soup dish, bowls of ice for cold things, are all elements to be considered. A luncheon plate is used as a service plate, being removed with the soup dishes to make way for the salad plate. Bread and butter plates are used, but coffee is generally not served with the food, and the cups are not put out. A luncheon knife and fork, a salad fork, a soup spoon and a butter spreader are the typical silver requirements for the place setting.

Except for the glasses, the table is cleared and crumbed after the salad course. The dessert course is then brought on, complete with knife and fork or whatever combination of silver is required to eat it. The silverware is brought in on the plate, to be removed and placed by the guests themselves. The usual routine is to bring the silver in on a service plate, and come around again with the actual dessert.

If a finger bowl is used, it, rather than the dessert, is brought in with the silver on the dessert service plate. The whole assembly is placed before the guest, who removes and places the silver, then removes the finger bowl and the doily on which it is always set, using both hands, and places them in the position normally occupied by the bread and butter plate, thus clearing the service plate for the dessert.

Coffee or tea is usually served in the living room, rather than at the table, but may be brought on following the dessert, if desired. If there is a maid in attendance, she does all of the serving while the hostess pours but if there is no maid, it is customary for a friend to do the pouring while the hostess does the serving.

Luncheon may also be served buffet style—a convenient arrangement for large groups—and also helpful for small gatherings because it takes some of the duties of serving away from the hostess, letting her spend more time with her guests.

TEA

Among the British, afternoon tea is rated as a necessity, being considered one of the regular meals of the day. Among Americans, however, that custom has not attained as strong a foothold and tea is regarded more as a social event than a regular meal.

But as a social event, tea has an important part in the American pattern of hospitality. It is highly convenient, for not only is the hour suitable for most women, but also it is an agreeable method of maintaining social contact without imposing too great a burden of preparation on the hostess.

The most important element of a tea is, of course, the tea itself which should be brewed correctly (*see* TEA). Coffee or chocolate may also be served, provided that the tastes of the guests are known.

The food served with the tea may be fanciful, but it should be kept simple to the extent that it may be readily handled with the fingers or a small fork. In countries where tea is considered a meal, they have especially prepared cakes and even tiny individual meat pies for the occasion, but in America the tendency has been to serve sandwiches (*which see*) of an elaborate nature, cakes, nuts and candy.

Tea is commonly served in the buffet manner, with the food elements and necessary dishes arranged on a sideboard or table for the guests' convenience, and the tea things set on a small table for the hostess to pour. Sometimes, too, the foodstuffs are passed around on trays, particularly if there are servants in the house. As a general rule, tables are not required for informal teas, though such provision should be made if the food element is considerable.

In the summer time, it is customary to provide facilities for iced tea and coffee as well as for hot beverages.

At-Home Tea. Ideal for week ends and holidays when the men of the house are at home, this is a combination tea and cocktail party. The tea things and the necessary cocktail equipment are set up on two separate tables, with the hostess pouring the tea while the host presides at the impromptu bar. The food served should include canapés, olives, salted nuts, and sandwiches that are somewhat more substantial than those normally served with tea. *See also* BARTENDING.

Bridge Tea. Tea is customarily served at the close of an afternoon of bridge playing, and there are many possible ways of handling the service. While it is possible to set up in another room, the simplest expedient is to bring in the tea things on a tray and use the bridge tables that are already set up. The tea may also be served buffet style throughout the game; a good system if there is a large gathering. This enables individual tables to break off play and have tea at their own discretion and also permits the ardent players to continue their game, while the one who is dummy is taking tea.

DINNER

The main meal of the day, most often served in the evening, dinner is by far the most important of the meals. It is the chief occasion of formal hospitality and frequently about the only time of day when all the members of the family are grouped in one place and not in a hurry to go elsewhere. It should be a time of pleasant conversation and interchange of experience, as well as one of enjoyable food. If at all possible, dinner should not be rushed nor should even the impression of haste be given. It should be a time of unhurried enjoyment, if only for the stomach's sake.

Family Dinner. The basic table settings are used, with practicality rather than etiquette the chief concern. It should be made as enjoyable as possible.

Informal Dinner. Perhaps the most common means of entertaining in our age is to have guests in for dinner. Since maid service is the exception rather than the general rule, the serving must, necessarily, be done by the hostess or possibly a daughter. It should be a time of enjoyment and relaxation, but far too many an otherwise perfect dinner has been ruined by the hostess trying too hard to see that everything goes off all right.

The first thing to remember in planning an informal dinner is to keep it as simple as possible. It is best to invite only a small number of guests until the knack is learned. The menu itself should be simple; some sort of appetizer or soup, a main dish with vegetables, a salad course and a dessert.

If liquor is served in the house, the host provides cocktails or an appetizer wine when the guests gather. This sound practice gives everyone a chance to relax and move out from under the strain of being formal, while it whets the appetite for the meal to come. It also gives the hostess a chance to slip quietly out and put the final touches to the cooking food and the table setting.

The table is set according to the basic plan, as suits the courses scheduled for the evening. The formal damask cloth may be used as well as candlelight, but if this mood is established, the china and other accoutrements should be in keeping. The hostess makes sure that the table is properly set, the glasses filled, and the relishes, jellies, etc., in place. If candles are used, she makes sure they are properly lit and really burning.

If a cold appetizer is planned, she then sets it out. If the first course is to be a hot soup or something similar, it is best to wait until everyone is seated before serving it. There may be some delay in getting the guests from the living room into the dining room, and hot things cool quicker than cold things warm.

The guests are then summoned and seated, with the host at the head of the table and the hostess at the foot. Formal seating arrangements of the guests may be followed, but are rarely needed because of the small number and the circumstances. In some cases, the hostess may have to sit in other than her traditional place to gain more ready access to the kitchen,

When the appetizer is finished, the hostess removes the dishes and brings in the main dish, setting it before the host. If the host is not confident of his carving ability, it is better to plan a casserole dish or something else that can be served with fork or spoon. The carving can, of course, be done in the kitchen and full plates brought out for the guests, but this gives them little option as to quantity. The vegetables and other side dishes may be either passed around or served by either the host or hostess.

The dinner plate may have been used as a service plate for the appetizer course, but if hot plates are required by the nature of the main course, they should be brought on only immediately prior to use.

When the salad course is finished, the table is cleared and crumbed before the dessert dishes are brought in, in the manner described for luncheon. The simplest type of dessert for such a function is a bowl of fruit, which may have been used as a centerpiece, or a good cheese with a variety of crackers. If a pie or other heavy dessert is served, it is preferable to serve the coffee in the living room, taking the guests away from the disarranged table and leaving the dishes to be done later. The coffee may, of course, be served at the table.

Informal Dinner with One Maid. With a properly trained maid to do the serving, the duties of the hostess are greatly simplified. The duties of the maid are not so complicated that a high school girl or other part-time worker cannot be quickly trained for use on state occasions.

The maid sets the table and announces the dinner when all is in readiness. The first course is not set out, but is brought in only after the guests have been seated.

In serving, plates and foods are served and removed from the guest's left side, while water, wine, and other beverages are served from the right to avoid upsetting the glasses. The maid removes the appetizer service dish from the left, using her left hand, and immediately replaces it with a fresh hot dish for the main course, using her right hand.

With a maid, the roast may be pre-carved in the kitchen and then offered on a platter to the guests in turn, to serve themselves as they later do with the vegetables. The maid should present trays and dishes held flat on the palm of her hand, using a folded napkin to insulate the hot ones. Special serving utensils, a fork or spoon or both, are placed in each dish before it is passed around so that the guests will not have to use their own silver to serve themselves.

If the host desires to carve the roast, the maid stands by with an additional plate in her hand after having placed dinner plates before each guest. When the host has carved a serving and placed it on the plate in front of him, the maid takes the full plate (replacing it with the empty plate) and serves it to a guest, taking his empty plate. This process is continued until everyone has been served, at which time the remaining empty plate is retired to the kitchen.

The main course is always offered to the guest a second time at informal dinners. The order of serving is first to the lady at the host's right, and then around the table, serving first the ladies and then the men, and serving the host last.

Sometime during the meal the maid cleans up the living room where the cocktails were served and prepares it for the service of after-dinner coffee. By serving the coffee there, the maid then has a chance to clean up the table and finish her duties at an early hour.

A competent maid can serve up to six guests with no difficulty or undue delay, but for larger gatherings more servants are advisable if the service is to be at all prompt.

Formal Dinner. Tradition has imposed a stricter rule of etiquette on the formal dinner than it has on any other social function. The formal dinner is, indeed, more of a social function than a meal, but the food element should not be overlooked. If guests are invited for an evening of their best manners and most brilliant conversation the least they can expect in return is to be properly fed. The courses should be edible and filling as well as attractive to the eye and proper for the occasion. Sometimes that detail is overlooked in the press of other worries.

But the formal dinner is still primarily a social function and, for that reason, the concern is largely with the traditions involved. Some of those traditions, largely those of specific dress and toasts, are gradually becoming casualties to altered time and circumstances, because they are deeply rooted in the past, but the majority persist and should be respected.

Because of its involved nature, a formal dinner should never be attempted unless there are at least two competent servants on hand; more if the assembly is larger than 12. In households where formal dinners are given as a matter of course, everything runs as well-oiled clockwork, but it is definitely not an activity for amateurs. Far better an elaborate informal dinner than a disastrous formal function.

The table is spread with the formal linen damask cloth, though lace may also be used. During the summer, formal place mats on a bare table are sometimes used. The formal dinner is the one occasion when bread and butter plates are never used, but butter spreaders are sometimes provided unless buttered rolls are served.

The guests dress for dinner, the exact nature of the formal attire being prescribed by local custom. At large affairs each man is given a small card on entering the house, the card bearing the name of the lady whom he is to escort to dinner and who will sit at his right. He is sometimes also shown a device holding small slips of paper bearing the guests' names and indicating their exact positions at the table. If the diagram is not used, the letters "R" and "L" are written on the card he is given to indicate the side of the table on which he is seated.

As may be gathered, the seating arrangement of a formal dinner is very important, for on that hinges the success or failure of the function. Since the meal is rather long, the diner must depend on the conversation of the person on either side for entertainment, and it is the duty of the hostess to see that compatible types are seated next to each other. Though this is no reflection, husbands and wives are traditionally parted at these affairs.

The host sits at the head of the table with the lady guest of honor (the oldest lady present, if there is no actual guest of honor) to his right, and the hostess sits at the foot of the table with the male guest of honor to her right. It depends on the skill of the hostess to make a harmonious matching of the couples between, always alternating the sexes in the seating arrangement.

When dinner is announced, the men seek out the ladies whom they are to escort and form a procession going into the dining room, the host leading and escorting the lady guest of honor, the others more or less in order of whatever rank (if any) prevails

in the gathering, and the hostess last. It is customary for gentlemen to offer the ladies their arms as they escort them in.

The places are set, but the goblets are empty and there is no food on the table as the guests are seated. In some cases, a roll is folded in the napkin, so it is always well to check this feature before pulling the napkin off the plate.

A very strict procedure is followed in formal dinner service. For one thing, there is extended use of the service plate. The table in front of the guest is never permitted to be plateless except when the table is crumbed before the dessert is served. But a used plate is never immediately replaced by a full plate. When it is removed, a service plate (any plate on which other dishes are placed) is laid down and the full plate is either put on top of that or used to replace it.

The hostess is frequently served first at formal functions. This may seem a bit unhospitable, but it is a long-standing tradition that once served a very practical purpose. It, like many of our present social niceties, was once a rule of conduct followed in a more violent age so that people who did not trust one another could meet with some degree of safety when circumstances warranted. Since a very popular method of eliminating enemies was to invite them up for dinner under circumstances in which they could not refuse and then see that they got the poisoned soup, the hostess used to taste everything before it was served so the guests could proceed with reasonable assurances of a ptomaine-less evening.

Because of the numbers involved and because etiquette says that ladies should be served first and also the more honored of the guests before the others, there have been several systems of service devised. Sometimes the waiters make two circuits of the table, serving first the ladies, then the men; sometimes there are two simultaneous servings, one starting with the lady guest of honor and the other with the hostess, then serving the men when each rounds his respective end of the table; and in large gatherings the assembly is served in groups. In the last case, it is not required that everyone wait until everyone else has been served, but groups of six may begin eating as soon as they are served.

Table conversation is supposed to begin with the lady on the right, and there is a rite known as "turning the table" which is done at the discretion of the hostess. When she feels it timely, she turns to the man on her right, and everyone at the table is supposed to switch over so that no one will be left to stare silently at his plate.

Courses are not, as in the informal dinner, offered a second time. In the vast majority of the cases, there is no carving done at the table, but filled plates are presented to the guests. The number and nature of the courses served will vary with the desires of the hostess, but usually number no more than eight, including coffee, and are now frequently less.

In some cases, instead of serving individual plates, the course is brought around on a tray for the guests to serve themselves. Often the chef gives full freedom to his creative instincts for these courses, and the food comes out in the form of statuary, landscapes, architecture; anything but food. The guest is then confronted with the problem as to just what is edible and what is not, since he is expected to despoil these masterpieces to get his serving. The object should be carefully studied before selection is made. As a general rule, stands and holding apparatus are not edible, while rings and garnishes are. If the artwork is clearly divided into sections smaller than the diner's plate, then each one is usually a portion. Cardboard and other obvious indigestibles should be left on the tray, but if any does show up on the plate, it is merely pushed to one side in silence.

Candles are nearly always used on a formal dinner table, as well as place cards. The practice of smoking during the meal varies with regional tradition, and individual ash trays are provided at the proper time. Individual salt and pepper shakers are not set out, but sets are placed at every other seat. Vegetables are never served in separate saucers, and the salad is usually treated as a separate course. All condiments, relishes, etc., are served in special dishes.

Following the dessert course, the ladies retire to the drawing room for coffee and conversation, while the men will either go to the smoking room (if there is one) or remain at the table for port and cigars or their equivalent. If the men remain at the table, they naturally consolidate to make conversation easier.

The duties of a hostess at such an affair are quite rigorous, since the success or failure of the entire venture is largely a question of her generalship. Perhaps the most stringent rule of all is that she should never become concerned if anything goes wrong, but merely try to correct the situation (if possible) or simply ignore it, while the guests do likewise. It is said that if the house were to catch on fire, the good hostess would merely suggest, in a pleasant tone of voice, that the company might find it cooler if the coffee were served on the lawn.

The duties of the guest have been prescribed through time as well. He is expected to be punctual, on his best behavior, and apparently oblivious of mishaps that might occur. The guest should never arrive too early, lest he impede last-minute preparations, but really should appear on the stroke of the appointed hour. If he is late, the dinner need not be delayed more than a reasonable time, for the other guests must be considered and the food itself deteriorates rapidly if not served at the proper time.

If the tardy guest arrives while the dinner is in progress, he makes his way to the hostess, bows, and makes his apologies. The hostess is not expected to rise to greet him. The guest is then seated and begins the meal at the course which is then being served. He is not served the missed courses because this would cause further delay.

If a guest accepts an invitation to dinner, it is expected that he will come, and only the most extreme of emergencies will properly excuse his absence. The reasons for this are obvious if one considers the care and planning that go into the seating arrangements for a formal dinner. It is not like other social functions where one more or less in the group does not really matter. For the same reasons, a guest should never show up with a guest of his own in tow, unless the hostess has been notified well in advance and has given her consent.

If there is an actual guest of honor at a formal dinner, he should be prompt because etiquette forces the hostess to delay the dinner until his coming, unless, of course, he is extremely late. Whether or not entertainment has been planned following the dinner, etiquette also rules that no one leaves until the guest of honor has departed.

SUPPER

When the main meal of the day is served at the noon hour, a light meal called supper is served in the evening. Supper is also served as a fourth meal of the day, late at night or even early in the morning, following evening social activity.

Supper is always an informal affair and is usually handled the same as the family dinner or the informal dinner, depending on the circumstances.

Buffet Supper. This popular method of serving supper is commonly employed for after-theater meals and similar events. It is especially popular in cities, for buffet service is admirably suited to the confined space and fast tempo of city life.

Because the circumstances vary so much with the individual household, it is difficult to establish any set rules for buffet suppers. Usually the food and necessary implements are arranged on a table or sideboard in a convenient manner and the hostess does the pouring. Normally, tables are provided for the guests, though numbers or circumstances may rule this out.

The menu should be such that it is visually attractive, but still convenient to handle on a single plate. The meal should be kept simple and the effort centered on producing one good main dish rather than a great variety of ordinary dishes.

Servants may be used at buffet suppers; indeed, they are almost required if the gathering is at all large.

The buffet principle of serving, incidentally, is applicable to many different social gatherings, especially parties and lawn affairs. Among its many advantages, it offers the least work for the hostess and the most freedom of movement for the guests. The very atmosphere of a buffet function does much to dispel the icy air of formality that is apt to descend on social gatherings.

TABLESPOON. *See* FLATWARE; *see also* WEIGHTS AND MEASURES.

TABLE WATERS. A predominantly British term used to designate those bottled mineral waters which are suited for mealtime use. *See* ALKALINE AND MINERAL WATER.

TABLE WINES. Both red and white wines which are especially adapted for serving with food. *See* WINE.

TAFFY. A chewy candy made with brown sugar or molasses boiled down with butter (or equivalent). Some types are pulled after cooking to secure the desired consistency. Butter the hands and stretch the taffy until it is light and porous. *See* CANDY.

CHOCOLATE NUT TAFFY

2 cups sugar
1½ cups light corn sirup
1½ cups undiluted evaporated milk or light cream
⅛ tsp salt
3 tbsp butter
1 tsp vanilla
1½ cups coarsely chopped, toasted, blanched almonds
6 squares (oz) melted chocolate

Combine the sugar, sirup, milk or cream and salt in a large saucepan. Bring slowly to boiling point, stirring constantly until the sugar is dissolved, then cook to the firm ball stage (246° F.). Add the butter and continue cooking to the hard ball stage (265°–270° F.). Remove from the fire, stir in the vanilla and half the almonds, mix well, then beat for 2 minutes and turn into a buttered shallow pan. When cool, pour the chocolate over the surface and sprinkle with the remaining almonds. When cold, break into small pieces, and store in an airtight container.

OLD-FASHIONED HONEY TAFFY

1 lb honey
1 cup sugar
½ cup top milk or undiluted evaporated milk

Combine the honey, sugar and milk in a large saucepan and bring slowly to boiling point, stirring until the sugar is thoroughly dissolved. Then cook very slowly, stirring occasionally, to the hard crack stage (300° F.), skimming while cooking if necessary. Turn onto a generously buttered platter or pan and, as soon as cool enough to handle, pull and cut into pieces with buttered shears and wrap each in waxed paper.

OLD-FASHIONED MOLASSES TAFFY

⅔ cup molasses
⅓ cup light corn sirup
1½ cups brown sugar
1½ tbsp cider vinegar
½ cup water
¼ tsp salt
½ tsp soda
¼ cup butter

Combine the molasses, sirup, sugar, vinegar, water and salt and bring slowly to boiling point, stirring until the sugar is dissolved; then cook to the hard ball stage (258°–260° F.). Remove from the fire, add the soda and butter and stir just enough to blend. Turn into a large shallow buttered pan and, when cool enough to handle, pull quickly until it changes from brown to light yellow. Twist into braids or cut into individual pieces, using scissors dipped in butter. When cold wrap each piece in waxed paper.

TAFIA. A fiery, heady, yet sweet liquor made in India, where it is very popular. It is drunk both as an after-dinner cordial and between meals.

TALI CHEESE. Another name for the Russian cheese, *Eriwani*, made from sheep's milk.

TAMALES. A rather hot Mexican dish, made with a special corn meal called *nixtamal*. In Mexico the real *tamales de cazuela* (tamales casserole) is made with freshly boiled chicken, but in Central America leftover beef or pork is often used.

TAMALE PIE

2 small roasting chickens, disjointed
Butter or oil
Clove of garlic, minced
4 large ripe tomatoes, peeled
2 onions, sliced thin
1 lime or ½ orange, juiced
1 green pepper, minced
1 sweet red pepper, minced
1 tbsp parsley, minced
1 tbsp chili powder
Salt and pepper
1 cup corn pulp

Fry the chickens in the butter or oil with the garlic, until golden brown and tender. Then bone and dice the chicken meat, and place in a stew pan with the tomatoes, onions, lime or orange juice, minced peppers, parsley and chili powder. Add salt and pepper to taste and simmer gently until vegetables are tender. Then add the corn pulp and continue cooking over a low flame, stirring occasionally, until consistency is good. Make a paste crust by mixing 1 cup of corn meal and 2 large eggs, well beaten, with salt and pepper to taste. Roll out this crust and line a brown earthenware casserole or similar baking

dish. Pour in the meat mixture, set the casserole in a pan of hot water, in a very hot oven (425° F.) and bake until crust is nicely browned. This can be eaten hot or cold, but is usually served hot. (Serves 6)

TAMARIND

TAMARIND. The tamarind is a tropical tree the fruit of which is really a seed pod. This contains an acrid-sweet pulp that is used medicinally, and from one to twelve hard, glossy seeds. The usual method of preparation for market involves shelling the pods and packing the pulp and seeds in large kegs filled with boiling sirup. The tamarinds are imported in these kegs and then repacked for retail sale by the distributors. Tamarinds of a higher quality are packed in sugar.

Tamarinds are used in making chutneys, curries, and other East Indian dishes. The juice is used for pickling fish, the pulp is used in making preserves, and highly diluted tamarind sirup makes a cooling summer beverage.

TANGELO. *See* ORANGE.

TANGERINE. A small orange (*which see*), containing very sweet juice and a loose, easily detachable rind; grown chiefly in North Africa. A variety of the tangerine is the Clementine which is not quite as sweet, contains no seeds and has a closer rind.

TANGERINE

TANGERINE PRESERVES

2 lb sugar
1 cup water
6 lemons
6 tangerines
½ lb shelled almonds

Bring the sugar and water together to boiling point, stirring until the sugar is dissolved. Add the lemons and tangerines, first peeling and discarding most of the white portion of the skin, then shredding. Discard also the seeds and white connecting fiber of the pulp. Bring slowly to boiling point, reduce the heat, and simmer until thickened, about 45 minutes, stirring frequently. Add the almonds, blanched and split lengthwise, cook 5 minutes longer, then turn into hot sterilized jars and seal. (Makes 2½ quarts)

TANGO COCKTAIL. A gin, vermouth and orange juice cocktail that is almost identical to the Bronx cocktail, *which see.*

TANGO COCKTAIL

1 small jigger dry gin
½ small jigger sweet vermouth
½ small jigger dry vermouth
½ small jigger orange juice
½ tsp curacao

Place in a cocktail shaker with cracked ice, mix by shaking well, strain into cocktail glass. (Serves 1)
See BARTENDING; *see also* COCKTAIL, ALCOHOLIC.

TANNIN. Tannin, or Tannic Acid, is found in most fruits and nuts, in tea, coffee,

red wines, and in nonedible vegetation. When quite pure, it is a white or faintly yellowish, crystalline substance that is soluble in water and in alcohol. On exposure to air it becomes brown. Either in solution or in crystalline form it is highly astringent.

Tannin possesses no nutritive value whatever, and is mainly of interest to the dietitian because of the harm it may cause if taken too freely. In strong solution, it precipitates the ferment of the gastric juices and renders them inert. It also gives rise to constipation by its astringency which affects the mucous membrane of the intestine. For these reasons, very strong tea, or tea drunk to excess, materially hinders digestion.

Tannin in Coffee. It is said that the tannin in coffee interferes with the digestion of fresh meat, and to a lesser degree with that of dried or smoked meat, such as tongue or ham, the fibers of which are already shrunken by curing. Paradoxically, the tannin in coffee sometimes acts as a laxative. *See* COFFEE.

Tannin in Tea. Because it carries a much higher proportion of tannin than does coffee, the effect of very strong tea upon the human digestive system may be even more pronounced than that of coffee. However, its effect on the alimentary canal is that of a binder rather than that of a laxative.

Tannin is the chemical component of tea that is responsible for both color and the pungent taste of the brew. A cup of black tea, infused five minutes, contains about two grains of tannin and, of this quantity, about one and one-half are astringent. However, the astringent effect of tannin in tea is practically removed by the addition of milk. *See* TEA.

TANSY. Tansy is an aromatic herb that is native to Europe, but it has been naturalized in America. It is extremely ornamental and has a bitter taste. It was used in such old-fashioned dishes as tansy puddings, and tansy tea formerly served as a household medicine. Today it is used as a potherb and as a salad herb. It is greatly used by the British and French as a flavoring for stuffings for poultry and veal.

TAPIOCA. Tapioca is made from the rhizoma (fleshy root) of the Manioc or Manihot or Cassava, a common plant found in temperate and tropical regions. It is extensively grown in South and Central America, Africa, and the West Indies.

TANSY

Manioc flour forms the basic food of the natives, and, when made into bread and cakes, it replaces the wheat bread of Europe and North America. Cassava contains a poisonous juice that must be drained off.

Tapioca, which is purified cassava, like sago, is an almost pure starch. The granules are very easily digested and form one of the most satisfactory starchy foods for persons of weak digestion. Tapioca may be eaten in the form of puddings with cream or fruit, and it may also be used to thicken broths or soups.

TARRAGON

TAPIOCA CREAM

¼ cup sugar
Dash of salt
3 tbsp quick-cooking tapioca
2 cups milk, scalded
1 egg plus 1 egg yolk
½ tsp vanilla

Blend the sugar, salt, and tapioca in the upper part of a double boiler. Gradually add the scalded milk, stirring briskly while adding. Place over hot water and cook, stirring constantly, until the mixture thickens and the tapioca is clear. Add the beaten egg and egg yolk and cook a moment longer. Cool, stirring occasionally, and add the vanilla. Chill thoroughly and serve plain or with light cream or a fruit sauce. (Serves 4)

VARIATIONS

Berry Fluff. Fold whipped cream and slightly crushed fresh raspberries or strawberries into tapioca cream before chilling. Serve in sherbet glasses, topping with berries or whipped cream.

Chocolate Tapioca Cream. Melt one square (ounce) of unsweetened chocolate with the milk when scalding, then follow directions for tapioca cream.

Golden Tapioca Cream. Fold blanched, chopped, toasted almonds into tapioca cream before chilling. At serving time top with sweetened cooked apricots and garnish with additional almonds and whipped cream.

Nut Brittle Tapioca Cream. Fold coarsely crushed nut brittle into tapioca cream before chilling. Serve in sherbet glasses, topping with additional crushed brittle and garnishing with whipped cream.

TARO. A starch-bearing root of the Arum family, used for food in the South Sea Islands. Like dasheen and yautia, taros form large underground rootstocks, or corms, of spherical shape but slightly pointed toward the top, sometimes weighing over five pounds. They contain, on an average, about 70 percent of water, from 2 to 3 percent protein, 3 to 28 percent starch and 1 to 1.3 percent mineral matter. The starch granules are very much smaller than those of potatoes and other starchy roots. *Poi,* the cooked and slightly fermented paste of the grated taro, is a favorite dish of the Hawaiians.

TARPON. Local name given to the Kingfish.

TARRAGON. Tarragon is a European herb closely related to wormwood. Its somewhat bitter, aromatic foliage is used to season vinegar, pickles, fish, salads, stuffings, meat stews, gravies, sauces, soups, broilers, beets and spinach. It should be used sparingly. Try adding a few chopped fresh leaves to mushroom or egg dishes. Tarragon adds the master's touch to lobster thermidor and chicken à la king.

TART. (I) "Having a sharp, sour taste."

TART. (II) As applied to pastry, usually a diminutive or full-size open pie with a filling of fruit, jelly or jam.

Any good pastry or fragments of leftover pastry may be made into tart or tartlet shells. Bake these over muffin pans or fluted patty pans, or over inverted muffin pans, pricking the pastry well before baking that it may retain its shape. Such tart shells may be made fresh for immediate use or reheated at the time of serving. Fill with chilled, sweetened, fresh or cooked fruit, lemon pie filling, one of the prepared pudding mixes or a rich preserve. Any of the above may, if desired, be topped with meringue or with slightly sweetened, flavored whipped cream. *See* PASTRY.

TARTAR. An acid substance deposited from grape juice during fermentation from which tartaric acid is derived. It is used in the manufacture of cream of tartar, *which see.*

TARTARE SAUCE. A rich sauce that is especially delicious with fish and cold cuts of meat, chicken, and with shellfish. It should be highly seasoned and absolutely smooth. Serve hot with hot foods and chilled with cold foods.

ORIGINAL TARTARE SAUCE

2 hard cooked egg yolks
Salt and pepper
1 cup olive oil
3 tbsp wine vinegar
1 tbsp pounded green onion tops or chives
2 tbsp mayonnaise

Pound the egg yolks until quite smooth. Season, then beat in gradually and alternately the oil and vinegar. When perfectly smooth, add the onion blended with the mayonnaise.

QUICK TARTARE SAUCE

½ cup mayonnaise
2 tsp chopped capers
2 tsp chopped olives
2 tsp chopped parsley
2 tsp chopped sweet pickle
2 tsp minced onion
2 tsp minced cucumber

Mix all the ingredients together and serve immediately.

TARTRATE BAKING POWDER. *See* BAKING POWDER.

TASTE. Taste itself may be considered under three aspects. In physical man it is the mechanism by means of which he appreciates savors. Considered in moral man, it is the sensation which any organ impressed by a savory body excites in the common center. Finally, considered under its material aspect, taste is the property which a body possesses to impress an organ and to originate sensation.

Taste appears to have two principal uses: It invites us, by pleasure, to repair the continual losses which we suffer by the action of life; and it aids us in selecting among the various substances which Nature presents to us, those which are nutritious. In this choice we can see that taste is powerfully aided by the sense of smell. It may be laid down as a general principle that nutritive substances are repulsive neither to smell nor to taste.

TAUTOG. *See* BLACKFISH.

TAWNY. A rich brown color characteristic of some wines, especially Port. It is often a sign of age and an indication of a mellowness in taste as well as color. Only the red wines can become tawny, and not all of them are capable of the change. The word is used as a qualifying adjective in the wine name, even as a Dry Sherry or a Ruby Port. *See* WINE.

TAWNY PORT. *See* PORT; *see also* TAWNY.

T-BONE STEAK. A juicy steak cut from the short loin of beef and from which the tenderloin has been removed. It contains a T-shaped bone from which it gets its name. *See* BEEF.

TEA. (I) Although tea has been long a world-wide popular beverage, most of us take it for granted without knowing much about the origin and history of this delicious and always refreshing beverage. The lore of tea is a fascinating subject.

TEA IN THE ORIENT

China. A Chinese legend has it that the first cup of tea was produced by accident about 2700 B.C. According to the tale, an old philosopher, while boiling water over a fire made of tea branches, dropped some of the dry leaves into the pot and found that they made a delightful, stimulating beverage. It was hundreds of years later that the rest of the world was permitted to enjoy the taste of tea.

While there are numerous ancient Chinese records of beverages made from the leaves of wild and cultivated plants, it is open to question as to whether they all refer to tea. This is due to the fact that there was no generally accepted name for tea until about the 7th century A.D. when the word *ch'a* came into prominence. Plants and beverages, that may or may not have been tea, were mentioned in early documents under the names of *chuan* or *ming*, *kia*, *k'u t'u*, and *t'u*. The last name was the one most used. In 350 A.D. *kia*, or *k'u t'u*, was described by the Chinese scholar *Kuo P'o* in such a way as to leave no doubt that he was writing about tea.

The *Ch'a Ching*, or Tea Memoir, was published in 780 A.D. This book was the work of *Lu Yu*, a Chinese scholar, and was a compilation of all available information on the cultivation, harvest, preparation, and service of *ch'a*, or tea.

Japan. Despite legends and records of the previous discovery and use of tea, Japanese legends credited a Buddhist saint called Daruma with causing the miraculous growth of the first tea plant.

It seems that during Daruma's efforts to keep awake throughout meditations, that had already lasted for five sleepless years, his heavy eyelids closed. In vexation, he tore them from his eyes and flung them to the ground. A green leafed, white flowered plant sprang up from the very spot where the offending lids had landed. The good man quickly discovered the stimulating qualities of the plant (which was, of course, tea), and it is presumed that he completed his meditations in pleasant wakefulness induced by the brew he prepared from it.

In the first half of the 6th century A.D. Daruma is supposed to have introduced tea to Japan.

Early history records tea as a rarity that was reserved for princes and members of the priesthood who drank it mainly for the almost magical medicinal qualities ascribed to it. It was not used generally as a beverage in China until the 6th century A.D.; and not until after Japan began growing her own tea plants (about 800 A D) was tea available in that country as a purely social drink.

The news of the delicious brew became known generally in Europe in the middle of the 16th century. It was described lavishly by travelers as a panacea for practically all of mankind's ills, and gradually aroused the interest of merchants. By the early 1600's the dried herb itself was being imported into Europe; but the secret of its preparation was guarded jealously by the Chinese.

For the next two hundred years the British and Dutch East India Companies had almost a monopoly on the tea trade to Western Europe and to America.

India. Although native tea had been known long to the inhabitants of India, and although a few attempts were made by Englishmen to plant there the seeds of China tea, the East India Company successfully guarded her prized trade with China until 1833. In that year China refused to renew her trade treaty with England. By this act she unwittingly forced British India to the fore as a competitor in the sale of tea.

Despite China's reluctance to part with the secrets of tea growing and manufacture, skilled workmen and quantities of seeds were brought from there to India.

At about the same time it was ascertained that the tea plants native to India were suitable for the European market, but they were neglected in favor of seeds and plants of China stock. However, these did not flourish as well as had been hoped, and gradually their cultivation dwindled as the propagation of the tea indigenous to India increased.

From about 1860 on, the tea business of India grew slowly and steadily, like a great tree, stretching its branches into the foreign markets, and finally overshadowing China's older industry. Today, India exports almost four times the quantity of tea exported by China, although she actually grows only about half as much as China.

TEA IN EUROPE AND EARLY AMERICA

In the 16th century A.D., Venice was one of the chief commercial ports of the world. It was here that a Persian merchant told of drinking tea in China and of the therapeutic values ascribed to it. A Venetian scholar, Giambattista Ramusio, published the story in 1559, and soon samples of tea leaves started to trickle into Europe.

Fifty years later, in 1610, Dutch merchants brought sizable shipments of the herb back to Holland. It was still another 50 years before the English started to show an interest in tea. But, though slow to start, English merchants were the first to advertise the brew in a newspaper (1658) and coffee houses, which served "That Excellent, and by all Phyfitians approved, China Drink, called by the Chineans, Tcha, by other Nations Tay alias Tee . . ." were besieged by eager Londoners who wanted to enjoy the flavor of tea, or who hoped to cure physical ailments by drinking it. Although tea by the pound was too expensive for the common man, most people were able to become familiar with the drink by buying it ready-made in a cup.

In 1662, Queen Catherine of England, introduced tea to society as a temperance drink, and its use soon became quite fashionable. Ever since, it has played an important part in advancing the social graces of the Western world.

During the 18th century the popularity of tea continued to grow in England and also spread to America. But the tax assessed by the Crown on all tea imported into the colonies resulted in the famous Boston Tea Party of 1773, when irate citizens made a potent brew by adding 342 chests of tea to the salty waters of Boston Harbor. More or less the same action was taken in half a dozen other port cities of America, and many historians consider that these were the sparks that set off the American War for Independence.

The all-powerful East India Company had a tight monopoly on trading in those days—and it was not until the 19th century that freedom of trade with both India and China was opened to all adventurers. That was the era of the clipper ships with their dangerous and romantic exploits.

Cultivation of Tea

The tea plant (*Thea sinensis*) belongs to the camelia family. The large, white, fragrant flowers could easily double for that popular favorite of Milady's corsage, the gardenia.

There are innumerable varieties and sub-varieties of tea plants, and various scientific names have been assigned to them by botanists. More familiar, and of more importance to the homemaker, are the names given to teas that are different because of the variations in the processes to which they are subjected after they are plucked. *See* Types of Tea in this article.

The primitive method of harvesting tea leaves was to cut down the tree, which rises, in its natural state, to a height of from 15 to 70 feet. The leaves were plucked and another tree sought for further cutting and picking.

Centuries ago, when the cultivation of the plant began, the wasteful practice of destroying the tree gave way to the sensible one of pruning the plants down to a height

of about four feet. This system still prevails and the tender leaves on shrubs in present-day tea gardens are within easy reach of the pickers. The plants are set out in symmetrical lines and generally bear their first crop when they are four years old. With scientific care a tea shrub may live and produce for 100 years. A year before the first crop is expected the bush is cut down to a foot in height, and again cut down about three months before ripening in order to increase the number of young shoots which furnish the most tender and succulent leaves.

Tea shrubs grow well in almost any climate, but are best suited to the high altitudes of tropical or semitropical areas where there is an abundance of rain. Given a humid atmosphere, the plants will survive extremes of temperature ranging from below 0° F. to above 130° F. For proper drainage it is necessary to set the plants in stony or sandy soil.

The climate and soil in which the bush grows, and the care given to it, influence the quality of the leaves it produces. Thus, new properties may be developed in the leaves of a shrub simply by planting it in an environment that is foreign to the one to which it is normally accustomed. It is for this reason that the names of tea growing countries, and even districts, are often combined with the names of the teas produced. Typical examples of this practice are the teas called Assam Black, China Black, Foochow Oolong, Formosa Oolong, etc.

Types of Tea

The three main types of tea are Black, or fermented tea; Oolong, or semifermented tea; and Green, or unfermented tea. All three types of tea leaves may start life on the same bush; it is the difference in their later treatment that gives the most noticeable characteristics to the different types.

Black Tea. The United States consumes almost 100 million pounds of tea a year, and about 90 percent of this is Black tea. Most of it comes from India and Ceylon.

After being plucked from the shrub, leaves for Black tea are withered for up to 24 hours. During this time the leaves darken, become sticky, and lose a small percentage of their moisture. The leaves are then rolled, either by machine or by hand. The bruised leaves lose more moisture and assume a twisted or ball-like form. The rolling process may last several hours before the leaves are removed, run through the roll-breaker (which breaks up lumps), and finally graded according to size by means of wire mesh screens. During the rolling operation the leaves start to ferment.

To hasten the process of fermentation, the tea leaves are spread on smooth, wide tables or floors, in rooms where the air is very humid and where the temperature ranges from 70° F. to 80° F. In from 30 minutes to almost five hours the leaves turn to a bright, coppery red color. The exact point of fermentation that the leaves are allowed to reach is a most important factor in determing the quality of the tea. Insufficient fermentation results in raw and bitter tea, and too much destroys flavor. The process is halted by firing—that is, by exposing the leaves to dry heat.

Black teas generally make stronger brews than Oolong or Green teas. They are richly red or golden in color, not dark. The flavor is rich and the liquor is almost sirupy. Broken leaves, preferred by the British, give a darker color to the tea than when leaf grades are used. The latter are preferred in Europe and the United States.

A few of the favorite kinds of black tea are known as *Assam*, *Cachar*, *Darjeeling*, *Dikoya*, *Dooar*, *Haptule*, *Ichang*, *Java*, *Madras*, *Nuwara*, *Panyon*, *Sumatra*, and *Travancore*. These varieties are described elsewhere in this book under their own titles.

Green Tea. Although China produces about 900 million pounds per year (almost one half of the world's supply of tea) she consumes most of her own tea and leaves only about 100 million pounds for export. Japan exports approximately 20 million pounds per year. Most of the Green tea consumed throughout the world comes from these two countries.

The processes used in the manufacture of Green tea are much the same as those followed in making Black tea, excepting that fermentation is not allowed to take place. The leaves are steamed immediately after they are plucked. This treatment eliminates the possibility of fermentation. The leaves are then rolled and fired. Green teas are not subjected to as high a degree of heat as is used in making Black tea. The finer leaves of Green tea usually emerge from processing with their normal color of clear green. However, the coarser leaves frequently turn a dark gray.

When properly made into a beverage, good grades of Green tea become a greenish-golden colored liquor that has a delicate aroma and flavor.

The *Panyon* of China, and the *Kewane* and *Mori* of Japan are among the favored varieties of Green teas. These teas are described under their own titles.

Oolong Tea. Although Oolong tea was originated in the Foochow District of China, most of this delectable leaf now comes from Formosa where unique conditions of soil and climate contribute to the production of a superior tea.

Oolong teas are slightly withered and fermented before the leaves darken slightly and a fragrance like that of a cut apple is emitted. At this point (not more than five hours after plucking) fermentation is stopped by drying the tea in hot pans for a few minutes. Panning also adds to the strength of Oolong and makes the leaves less moist and, therefore, easier to roll.

Rolling Oolong tea is still a hand process in Formosa. The principle followed is the same as that used in the manufacture of black tea, but the operation takes a few minutes rather than a few hours. Several firings are required to make the tea ready for sorting and packing.

The delicately flavored Formosa Oolongs are considered among the finest teas of the world. They are aptly termed the champagnes of teas. Oolongs are still made in the Foochow District of China, but they are not as popular as the Formosa varieties.

Oolong makes a delicately amber colored beverage. *See also* FORMOSA, and FOOCHOW.

Pouchong or Scented Tea. Oolong teas mixed with the petals of gardenia and jasmine are known as Pouchong or Scented Teas. The larger, less tightly rolled leaves of Oolong are used and the teas are manufactured in both China and Formosa.

Pouchong teas are flavorous and aromatic in relation to the proportions of the flower petals used in manufacture.

Blended Tea. Most tea is blended before it reaches the retail market. Some teas that are not suitable for consumption in unadulterated forms are sought by tea brokers for the fine qualities they impart to blends. There are blends on the market that are composed of as many as thirty varieties of tea; each kind contributes its part whether it be color, bouquet, flavor, or strength. Most popular, packaged teas are blends.

Standards. The standards for tea imported into the United States are set by the U.S. Board of Tea Experts, which body operates under the Food and Drug Administration of the United States Government. These are the highest standards for tea decreed by any country in the world.

Seasonal Qualities. The quality of even the choicest tea varies according to the season in which it is harvested or plucked. Therefore, the homemaker who is a connoisseur of tea is as much interested in the season of plucking as the gourmet is in the vintage of wine.

Among the Black teas of India, *Assam, Darjeeling, Dooar,* and *Cochar* are best when plucked in the months of June, July, September, and October; *Travancore* and *Madras* in December and January. Ceylon Blacks are best in February, March, April, July, August, and September; Java and Sumatra Blacks in July, August, and September. China Blacks, some of which are known as *Ichang, Keemun, Lapsang Souchong, Paklam,* and *Panyon,* are best in April through October.

Of the Green teas, Japan's *Mori* and *Kewane* are best when plucked in May and June; China's *Panyon* in June and July; Formosa teas are best also in June and July.

Orange Pekoe. This term is quite familiar to most homemakers in America; it appears on the packages of various brands of tea and is misunderstood by many persons who accept it as meaning that the package necessarily contains choice tea. Actually, Orange Pekoe is indicative of the size of the leaf rather than of the quality of the tea, which may be either exceptionally good or as low as is allowed by the standards of the country in which it is sold.

Quality and Individual Preference. In the long run, the tea best suited to each family will be determined by individual taste and economic status. Price usually increases in proportion to flavor; however, as one pound of tea makes from 150 to 200 cupfuls, the slight extra cost per cup of really good tea is usually more than compensated by the additional enjoyment it gives.

HINTS ON PREPARATION OF TEA

Brewing Tea. Tea is easy to prepare, but a few simple rules must be observed if the full goodness of the leaves is to be enjoyed with each cup of the beverage.

In the following basic recipes it will be noted that there is a reason for each step described. If the method is followed with care a delicious, invigorating brew will result.

POT METHOD
(Basic Recipe)

1. Bring fresh, cold water to a fierce boil; pour upon the tea leaves the moment it reaches a full boil, which should occur simultaneously with the completion of step 3, below.

Fresh, cold tap water has more air in it than water that has been standing or previously heated; it imparts a pleasantly brisk flavor to the tea.

The water is boiling as soon as the entire surface is violently agitated. Heating longer will not increase the temperature, but, due to loss of vapor, will cause the brew to have a flat flavor. If the water does not reach a full boil, some of the flavor will be left in the leaves.

Water boils at 212° F. at sea level, and at proportionately lower temperatures as the altitude grows higher. If tea is prepared in high altitudes, water boiled under pressure will give best results. *See* HIGH ALTITUDE COOKERY.

2. While the tea water is heating, fill a china, pottery, or glass tea pot with scalding water, cover with the lid, and allow to stand until the pot is heated thoroughly.

Although the infusion of tea should not be boiled, the heat of the boiling water should be retained as long as possible. Preheating the pot helps to do this. The practice may be carried further by following the British custom of using a tea cozy, or by wrapping a napkin or towel around the pot.

Pots of china, pottery, or glass hold heat longer and, therefore, are preferred to pots of metal. Also, pots made of some metals give the tea an unpleasant metallic flavor.

3. Using one slightly rounded, standard teaspoonful of fresh tea leaves for each standard cupful of water, or 1 tea bag for each 1½ cups of water, put the tea into the preheated pot, re-cover the pot, and allow the tea to wilt until the tea water is ready.

The rounded teaspoonful is more practical as a measure than the old "level teaspoonful per cup, plus one for the pot"; with the latter method the strength of the brew varies according to the number of cupfuls prepared.

Unless the pot is to be filled, measure the cold water before pouring it into the kettle. In this way heat will be retained that would ordinarily be lost while measuring the boiled water. This method saves fuel also; for only the amount of water needed will be heated.

Ordinarily, govern the strength of the brew by varying the quantity of tea leaves used—not by the time allowed for steeping. The exceptions are explained under step 4.

Fresh leaves are necessary for good tea; leaves that have been used previously yield little but tannin in a second infusion.

Wilting the leaves causes them to yield a richer bouquet and flavor when the boiling water is added.

4. Pour the boiling tea water upon the wilted leaves. Allow the well covered pot to stand while the brew steeps; 5 minutes for Black tea; 3 minutes for Green tea or Oolong. If the boiling water is exceptionally soft, the steeping period may be shortened slightly.

The quality of the liquor is impaired when the steeping period is either too short or too long. In the first case, the aromatic oil and the stimulating caffeine are not drained fully from the leaves. In the second, the delicacy of flavor is destroyed by an infusion of excess tannin. Black tea is steeped longer than Green and Oolong teas because the extra tannin added lends flavor—and is not harmful to the mucous membrane when milk is used, as is usual with fermented teas. If milk is not used with Black tea, the period of infusion should be shortened to 3 or, at the most, 4 minutes. On the other hand, if milk is used with Green or Oolong teas, the infusion should be continued for up to 5 minutes.

Very soft water extracts the flavor of tea faster than hard water, and, in this case, the steeping period may be shortened. Contrariwise, the period of steeping may be prolonged slightly to compensate for the slower action of unusually hard water. Ordinarily, the difference in the finished brew is imperceptible.

5. Separate the liquor from the tea leaves and serve at once in preheated cups.

CUP METHOD
(Basic Recipe)

The metal tea ball, and the more modern and popular tea bag are the answers to a haste-conscious public's clamor for a means of preparing a single cup of tea in a minimum of time.

Usually, the hastening clock demands that the tea bag be dangled into a cup of more or less hot water for a minute, and that the resulting excuse for tea be downed without regard for bouquet, flavor or stimulating qualities—all of which are lessened, if not entirely lost.

For the person who can afford an extra few minutes, a very good, stimulating cup of tea can be made.

The steps (and reasons for them) are basically the same as those described in this article for the Pot Method.

(1) Bring fresh, cold water to a fierce boil.

(2) Scald the tea cup. (Do this while the tea water is heating.)

(3) Put the tea bag into the preheated cup and cover with a saucer.

(4) At the moment it reaches a full boil pour the tea water upon the tea bag and re-cover the cup. Allow Black tea to steep for 5 minutes; allow Green tea and Oolong 3 minutes.

(5) Remove the tea bag and serve.

(6) Relax a moment and enjoy the bouquet and flavor of the drink.

RECIPES FOR TEA

There are untold thousands of recipes for preparing tea. In England, it is prepared much like the basic recipe which we call Pot Method, excepting that a stronger brew is generally preferred. The Russians traditionally make tea in the Samovar, and the Chinese usually infuse their tea directly in small, handleless cups.

In some parts of China and Tibet the leaves are used to make a beverage, and then are mixed with butter or grease, molded into cakes, and fried or baked for use as a solid food. In other parts of Asia the dry leaves are chewed and the juices swallowed. Some Australians simmer the tea all day over the fire and consider it just right for drinking when it is time for the evening meal.

Belgium, Germany, Finland, France, and the countries of Southern Europe consume comparatively little tea; but there are few other places in the world where it is not popular—and each locality has its own manner of making the brew. A few recipes are given below:

Char. It is interesting to note that though most other armies lean to the use of alcoholic stimulants when their troops are subjected to extreme conditions of hardship and fatigue, the British military prefer the use of tea, not only for their home armies, but for their colonial troops as well.

This is a well founded preference; for not only was hot tea a warming stimulant in the bone-chilling, water-filled trenches of the First World War, but its sweat-inducing properties afforded safe, cooling relief from the heat and humidity in the steaming jungles of World War II.

The average American is not especially noted for his tea-drinking habits; but, during the two World Wars, many came to respect the body and morale building qualities of the milky, heart-warming Char, as "Tommy" called his army brewed tea.

Char is to tea what Army Coffee is to home brewed coffee; it has a distinctive flavor and properties unto itself. It is brewed more by expediency than by rule; the materials at hand and the prevailing conditions governing the method of making. Some common recipes are:

CHAR

1 tsp fresh tea leaves
½ pt fresh milk, or substitute

Boil the milk. Place tea leaves in a scalded pot and add the boiled milk. Steep for 7 minutes. Serve immediately, adding sugar to taste. Condensed, evaporated or dried milk may be mixed with water to the desired consistency, and used as substitutes for fresh milk.

BOILED CHAR

(Although this recipe violates the usual caution that tea leaves are not to be boiled, it is preferred by some hardy souls who like the biting flavor of tannin. It is also practical when used in countries where the water, milk, and even the tea leaves might be polluted.)

10 rounded tsp fresh tea leaves
10 cups (5 pt) fresh milk, or substitute
Sugar to taste

Place all ingredients (including sugar) in covered vessel and bring to a gentle boil. Continue to boil for 10 minutes or longer. Stir and strain into heated cups. (Serves 10)

CHAR WITH WATER

2 rounded tsp fresh tea leaves
½ pt fresh milk, or substitute
½ pt fresh cold water

Bring milk and water to a boil in separate vessels. Place tea leaves in scalded pot and add boiled milk. Steep 4 minutes. Add the boiled water. Stir and strain into heated cups. (Serves 2)

Dessert Flavoring of Tea. All kinds of tea can be used to flavor and color desserts. The flavoring is made by powdering 1 teaspoonful of the best obtainable tea leaves in a MORTAR (*which see*) and adding just enough warm water to make a thin paste. (Do not use boiling water as flavor and aroma will thus be lost.) The paste is blended thoroughly with the liquid part of the dessert or cake mixture, and substituted for other flavoring called for in the chosen recipe. Two teaspoonfuls of the flavoring are sufficient to give a characteristic taste of tea to two quarts of ice cream or 1 quart of sherbet; the same quantity will also flavor a single average sized butter cake, white cake, etc. Extra sugar may be required to satisfy individual taste.

The dried skins of lemon, lime, orange, or tangerine may be powdered also and added to the powdered tea for variety. However, the proportion of powdered fruit skin should be small—not more than one part to five parts of powdered tea.

Extract of Tea. When large quantities of tea are required, as for a dinner party, it is usually a convenience to use an extract of tea. It can be made easily by varying the Pot Method as follows:

EXTRACT OF TEA

12 tsp (slightly rounded) fresh tea leaves
3 cups freshly boiled water (measured before boiling)
9 additional cups freshly boiled water (in second kettle)

Bring fresh, cold water to fierce boil. Heat the tea pot.

Wilt the tea leaves in covered pot. (Use 8 tea bags if preferred.)

Pour the boiling water from the first kettle upon wilted leaves. Allow tea to steep: 5 minutes for Black tea; 3 minutes for Green or Oolong tea.

Strain ¼ cup of the extract into each of 12 preheated cups.

Fill the cups with freshly boiled water from second kettle; serve immediately. (By boiling 2 kettles of water the second kettleful should be ready just as the tea has finished steeping. This insures a freshness of flavor for each cup. (Serves 12)

Any quantity of extract may be made by using more or less water and tea, as long as the proportions are maintained (4 tea-spoons of tea leaves to 1 cup of water, for a total of 4 cups of tea; or 2 tea bags to ¾ cups of water, for a total of 3 cups of tea).

Extract of tea may be made also for Iced Tea.

Iced Tea. This is a typically American drink, although said to have been first prepared by an English tea promotor, Richard Blechynden, on a hot summer's day at the St. Louis, Mo., Exposition of 1904. It quickly became popular and, today, about 2½ billion glasses of the cooling beverage are consumed in the United States each summer.

ICED TEA

4 cups extract of tea
8 slices lemon
Powdered sugar to taste
Cracked ice

Make Extract of Tea. Fill 8 tall glasses with cracked ice and pour into each glass ½ cup of the hot extract. Add more cracked ice to replace that which has melted. Slit each slice of lemon crosswise from one side to the center and slip onto the rim of each glass. Serve with long handled spoons and straws. Powdered sugar may be added by each individual to suit his own taste. (Serves 8)

HINTS ON MAKING ICED TEA

Chill Glasses. To keep the drinks cold, chill the glasses with cold water, or by standing them in the refrigerator for half an hour before serving.

Cloudy Iced Tea. Excess tannin, which is extracted from tea when it is steeped too

long, may cause cloudiness in iced tea. Steep only three minutes for Green and Oolong teas; five minutes for Black tea.

Cold Extract. If preferred, the extract may be chilled and then diluted before serving. Ice cubes should be added for further chilling as well as for the psycholog-ically cooling effect of the sound of ice tinkling against glass.

Flavors Added to Iced Tea. A dozen fresh mint leaves, a twisted quarter of orange peel, or one or two whole cloves may be added to the hot extract for a few minutes while steeping They should be removed before serving. A tantalizingly delicate goodness will be added to the flavor as a result.

Hot Extract. To avoid cracking the glass the hot extract should be poured directly onto the cracked ice, or on a long spoon. Never pour any hot liquid directly on cooled glass. By following this tip the tea will also be chilled more readily.

Sugar. Powdered, rather than granu-lated sugar is served with iced tea because it melts more rapidly in the cold drink. However, if granulated sugar is to be used, it is more economical to mix the proper amount of sugar with the hot ex-tract before pouring over the ice. One-third cup of sugar should be about right for four cups of extract.

Lemon Tea. Although the English gen-erally prefer milk with their tea, the fol-lowing recipe is known well to England:

LEMON TEA

2 rounded tsp fresh, Black tea leaves
½ small lemon, sliced thin
1 cup freshly boiled water
2 cups freshly boiled water, in second kettle

Heat tea pot and wilt leaves as directed by Pot Method. Place all but 3 slices of lemon in pot with tea leaves. Add 1 cup boiling water and allow to steep 4 min-utes. Be sure pot is covered. Add contents of second kettle (which should boil just in time) and allow to steep 3 minutes more. Stir well, strain into preheated cups, and add one of the extra slices of lemon to con-tents of each cup. Serve plain or with sugar to taste. (Serves 3)

(Limes, oranges, tangerines, or any combination, may be substituted for lemons.)

Lime Tea. Follow recipe for Lemon Tea, substituting 1 lime for the lemon.

Orange Tea. Follow recipe for Lemon Tea, substituting ½ small orange for the lemon.

Russian Style Tea. The Russians prefer tea made in a Samovar, *which see.* The same method is used in Turkey, and in other countries of the Near East.

Tangerine Tea. Follow recipe for Lemon Tea, substituting ½ tangerine for the lemon.

TEA PUNCH (I)

3 cups strong Black tea
4 cups orange juice
1 cup lemon juice
2 cups raspberry sirup
1 cup crushed pineapple
Sugar to taste
2 qt carbonated water

If fresh fruit juices are used, they should be strained. The ingredients are mixed in a punch bowl with a large block of ice, the carbonated water being added last, after other elements are well chilled. If desired, lime juice may be substituted for the lemon, and grenadine used instead of raspberry sirup. (Serves 20)

TEA PUNCH (II)

3 cups strong tea
3 cups sweetened strawberry juice
1½ cups orange juice
½ cup lemon juice
3 small bottles ginger ale

The ingredients are mixed in the usual punch manner and are garnished with fruit slices, berries in season, and mint sprigs. *See also* PUNCH, FRUIT (Serves 15)

SERVING TEA

Tea is becoming an increasingly popular beverage in the United States. It is most commonly served hot with meals, and either hot or iced in the afternoon and evening for its mild, pleasantly stimulating qualities. About 100 million pounds (enough to make almost 20 billion cups) are used in this country each year.

Although the true connoisseur of tea prefers to savor the unadulterated flavor of the beverage (this is true especially of the drinker of Green and Oolong teas) the majority of Americans like to add one or more ingredients for flavor. The homemaker will do well to understand the proper use of the few favorites which are listed below.

Sugar. About 70 percent of American tea drinkers like varying quantities of sugar in their tea. In order to dissolve it thoroughly, sugar should be placed in the bottom of the tea cup or other vessel before the hot tea is added. If milk, cream, lemon juice, or other flavorings are used, they should be added later.

Milk. Of America's tea drinkers, slightly more than one-third use milk or cream in the beverage. As a matter of fact, milk should be served with all black teas. The casein in milk renders insoluble the small quantity of tannin that comes from the leaf and thus protects the human mucous membrane from the astringent effects of the tannin.

As Green and Oolong teas are not steeped long enough to extract much tannin the protective effect of milk is unnecessary, and the flavor of these teas is generally considered to be better when taken alone.

Cold milk should not be served with hot tea. The addition of slightly warmed milk to hot Black tea not only helps to retain the heat, but adds to the flavor; also, the milk is less likely to curdle. Milk should not be added until the sugar, if any, has been dissolved in the tea.

Lemon. A few drops of lemon juice add a tang to hot tea that is enjoyed by about one-fifth of American tea drinkers. The additional flavor of lemon is especially suited to Green and Oolong teas, although the Chinese, who are the greatest consumers, generally prefer to drink these teas plain.

More of an aroma, and a distinctly different flavor, is added when a twist of lemon peel is used without juice.

Thin slices of lemon are especially good with iced tea. They are usually split halfway across and slipped onto the edge of the glass.

Mint. The leaves of fresh garden mint add a pleasing aroma and flavor to hot or cold tea. The mint leaves should be bruised and floated upon the surface of hot tea.

When used with iced tea a few mint leaves are bruised (to release flavor) and the entire sprig of mint is stood in the glass. A few more mint leaves may be rubbed on the edge of the glass for added aroma.

Vanilla. Our grandmothers used to keep whole vanilla beans with their tea in tightly closed caddies. The dry tea leaves absorbed the flavor of the beans and released a delightful bouquet when steeped in hot water.

Flower Petals. The petals of gardenias, roses, and other aromatic flowers may be added to the contents of the tea pot, or used in the caddy like vanilla. The fragrance and flavor are fairly similar to those of Pouchong tea but somewhat less subtle.

TEA. (II) The name given to a light afternoon repast, usually served about 4 p.m., and usually centered around hot, freshly brewed Tea, *which see*. Though predominately British, the custom is fairly universal.

In America, afternoon tea is not commonly served and when it is, it is usually more of a social function and not as one of the regular meals of the day, as it is regarded in other parts of the world. *See* TABLE SETTING AND SERVICE.

TEA BAG. A tea bag is a small cloth or paper sack that contains tea leaves, usually enough to make a single cup of tea of average strength, though they are also made in larger sizes. The sack has a length of thread or fine cord attached to it so the unit may be recovered from the cup when the tea has reached the proper strength, and the bag is discarded after use. Because of the great convenience which it offers, the tea bag, a comparatively recent innovation, has become extremely popular. *See* TEA; *see also* TEA BALL and TEA STRAINER.

TEA BALL. A tea ball is a perforated, hollow metal container, usually made in the shape of a ball or egg, used to confine the tea leaves during the brewing process (*see* TEA). The container comes apart, usually having a screwtop, so the leaves may be inserted and removed, and is equipped with a length of fine chain so that it may be recovered from the boiling water. While they may be made of many metals, silver is preferred, and tea balls are often quite ornate in appearance, to match the rest of the service. *See also* TEA BAG and TEA STRAINER.

TEA COZY. A cloth cover for a teapot. The very practical purpose of the tea cozy is to hold heat in tea while it is steeping. The cozy frequently is quilted, and is widely used throughout the British Commonwealth. It is especially handy during winter in homes that lack central heating, where the teapot is likely to be subjected to drafts of cool air during the process of steeping. *See also* TEA.

TEA STRAINER. A tea strainer is a small, fine-meshed, wire sieve used to hold tea leaves. It has a relatively long handle, and the frame is fitted with hooks so the strainer may be rested securely on a cup while hot water is poured over the leaves. *See* SIEVE and TEA; *see also* TEA BALL.

TEACUP. *See* CHINAWARE.

TEAKETTLE. A teakettle is a simple metal vessel, equipped with lid, spout and handle, used to boil water and to make tea. It may be quite plain or highly ornate, although they are usually plain for they are not generally used to serve the tea. Some have a special cap that contains a whistle and fits over the spout. When the water boils, the steam comes out of the spout with considerable pressure, causing the whistle to blow shrilly, informing the housewife that the water is now ready. *See also* TEA.

TEAPOT. A teapot is a vessel used to make and serve tea, but not, as a general rule, to boil the water. They are made of metal or ceramic materials, and usually strive for beauty as well as utility in their design They sometimes take on unusual shapes, but have a lid, handle and pouring spout. *See also* TEA and TEA KETTLE.

TEASPOON. *See* FLATWARE, *see* WEIGHTS AND MEASURES; *see also* TABLE SETTING AND SERVICE.

TELEME CHEESE. A Rumanian cheese, made from sheep's milk. It is also known as *Branza de Braila*.

TELLICHERRY. Black pepper is known by this name. *See* PEPPER, CONDIMENT.

TELPANIER CHEESE. Another name for Tschil cheese. It is made from the skim milk of cows or sheep. It is also known as Leaf or Zwirn cheese.

TEMPETE CHEESE. Another name for Canquillote cheese, *which see*.

TEMPLE ORANGE. *See* ORANGE.

TENCH. The tench is a fresh-water fish of the carp family which, owing to its somewhat muddy flavor, enjoys but slight popularity in America. However, it is a

good, wholesome fish when, after parboiling, it is prepared au gratin, a la
Meuniere, stewed, plain boiled, etc. The
various methods employed in the preparation of carp, sole or any of the flat fish
may be adapted to the tench.

TENDERLOIN. The tender part of the
loin as of beef, pork, etc., *which see. See also*
CHATEAUBRIAND.

TENTHIDID. Another name for the
Barber Fish, or Barber Sturgeon. *See*
STURGEON.

TEPID. Moderately warm, lukewarm.

TEQUILA. A harsh, potent Mexican
spirit distilled from PULQUE (*which see*).

TERRAPIN. *See* TURTLE.

TERRINE. When applied to a utensil
terrine means an earthen mixing dish.
When applied to food it means potted
meats, game, fowl, or fish. Sometimes the
French word *Paté* meaning loaf is used instead of the word terrine. These terrines or
patés may be served cold or hot.

TERRINE DE FOIE DE VEAU
(Veal Liver Paté)

2 lb calf's liver
½ lb pork fat
¾ lb lean raw veal
1 tbsp brandy
Juice of 1 medium-sized lemon
A generous grating nutmeg
A generous pinch each powdered thyme
  and nutmeg
Salt and pepper
Thin slices fat pork back

Discard any skin and fiber from the
liver. Pass it through the food chopper
with the pork fat and veal. Work in the
brandy, lemon juice, flavorings and seasonings. Line an earthen baking dish or
terrine with thin large slices fat pork back.
Pack the mixture in solidly and cover the
top with more of the pork back. Put on the
cover, set the whole in a pan containing
hot water almost to reach the top of the
mold and bake in a moderate oven (375°
F.) 2 hours.

After taking from the oven drain off
any liquid fat, place a heavy weight on
top and cool overnight. Next day warm
just enough to unmold, wipe the pan, return the loaf to the mold and chill thoroughly, or, if desired, reheat for hot service.

Such a terrine may be kept for several
weeks if one pours over and on the sides of
the mold melted lard blended in equal
parts with the drained-off fat. Cover with
a sheet of white paper, then replace the
cover of the terrine and store in the
refrigerator.

Serve hot or cold. If cold, slice thinly
and arrange with other cold cuts and
serve with a green salad. If hot, unmold
after heating, slice and serve with mashed
potatoes, spinach or other green, and a hot
sauce, preferably a tomato sauce.

Game, poultry or other meats may be
similarly prepared.

TETE DE MAURE CHEESE. Another
name for EDAM CHEESE, *which see.*

TETE DE MOINE CHEESE. A Swiss
cheese, also called BELLELAY CHEESE,
which see.

TEXEL CHEESE. A sheep's milk,
green cheese. It is produced in Holland
and was known in the 17th century.

THENAY CHEESE. A soft, rennet
cheese, which resembles Camembert and
Vendôme, and is made in the region of
Thenay, France. It is of comparatively
recent origin, and its consumption is
limited practically to the region in which it
is produced.

THERMOMETER. A thermometer is
an instrument used to measure temperatures. This is done in a number of different
ways, but only two methods are suitable
for kitchen use.

TYPES

The Mercury Type. Thermometers of this
type consist essentially of a sealed, hollow
glass tube containing a measured quantity
of mercury, colored alcohol, or some other
visible fluid. One end of the tube termi-
nates in a ball or reservoir which is also
filled with fluid and is connected with the
interior of the main tube. When the fluid
is heated, it espands, and as a result, rises
in the tube, for there is no other direction
in which it can travel. As the fluid is
cooled, it contracts, and the liquid level
falls. By checking the height of the liquid
against a calibrated scale, the temperature
may be read.

The scale may be marked directly on
the glass tube itself, but, for ease in reading,
it is usually printed on a card or metal
tag that is firmly affixed to the tube. The
tube may be covered with metal or other

materials to give it protection, for as long as the heat of the material to be measured contacts the bulb or reservoir, and the level of the liquid is visible, the thermometer will function.

The Metallic Type. Like the mercury thermometer, the metallic type functions by measuring the expansion of materials, but here the expanding materials are solid, rather than liquid. Two strips of different kinds of metals are firmly fastened together to form the vital part of the mechanism. Since the two metals expand and contract at different rates, it follows that the combined strip will bend in the direction of the side that has expanded the least or contracted the most. By attaching one end of this combined strip to the body of the unit and using the free end to activate a pointer, the temperature can be indicated on a printed scale.

Both of the basic types can be made in various shapes to meet specialized needs. What is more important, the scales may also be differently calibrated to meet special needs. Each type has its peculiar advantages and drawbacks, but they can be used interchangeably, provided that each has an appropriate scale.

There are four specialized kitchen thermometers, not counting the traditional wall thermometer which, while not directly used in cooking, is not without its functions.

Candy. The candy thermometer is designed so that it may be securely fastened to the side of the cooking vessel, with one end inserted in the cooking candy. Thus, constant temperature readings are given, and there is little possibility of the thermometer slipping down to the bottom of the vessel. They are used because cooking temperatures are vital to successful candy making (*see* CANDY).

Fat. The fat, or frying thermometer is used to check the temperature of the boiling fat used in deep fat frying (*see* FRYING). It greatly resembles the candy thermometer and is used in an identical manner, though, of course, the scale is different, for the temperatures involved are higher.

Meat. The meat thermometer is used to measure the internal temperatures of roasting meats. This, of course, calls for a different design than as before. The sensitive element of the thermometer is encased in a slender metal point that is thrust deep into the meat to get the read-

ing. The scale, which is appropriate for temperatures met, is on the upper end of the shaft and does not penetrate the roast.

MEAT THERMOMETER
Showing position in standing rib roast

Oven. Most modern ranges have an oven thermometer incorporated into the body of the unit. In many cases, there is also a thermostatic temperature control, but this is generally a separate unit. If the oven lacks a thermometer, a separate unit may be purchased to be placed inside when a temperature reading is desired. *See* OVEN.

PURCHASING

While it is not true in every case, the thermometer buyer is sometimes confronted with a choice between the two basic types of instrument. There are many disadvantages inherent in the mercury type thermometer. Being made of glass, it is subject to breakage. If the scale card ever slips out of place, the thermometer is useless unless it can be put back in its original position.

As a general rule, the metallic thermometer is a sturdier, more easily read instrument, but it is usually more expensive. Both are equally accurate, if properly made.

In selecting a thermometer, the buyer should make certain that it is soundly made, and especially that the scale card is firmly attached and not apt to come loose. The scale should be easily read, and it should be appropriate to the intended function of the instrument. Some scales are even given in terms of cooking times instead of degrees Fahrenheit or Centigrade. The instrument should be built to withstand reasonable use, and it should be easily cleaned. Remember that they will be used around grease, liquids and high temperatures, and that they must be especially built for the purpose.

CARE

A thermometer should never be dropped, especially those of the glass variety. It should never be used for other than its intended purpose. If a thermometer is subjected to temperatures higher than those for which it was made, not only will it fail to give a proper reading, but it can be damaged beyond repair. *See also* KITCHEN EQUIPMENT.

THICK. Said of the liquor produced by certain Black teas to describe the quality of strength and color. A thick tea is full flavored, and is possessed of a clear, deep red tone. *See also* TEA.

THIN. An infusion of tea that lacks body and color; in other words—weak, watery looking tea. *See also* TEA.

THOMAR CHEESE. A Portuguese cheese which closely resembles Saloio cheese, *which see.*

THURINGIA CARAWAY CHEESE. Another name for Hand cheese, *which see.*

THYME. Thyme is an aromatic herb belonging to the mint family. It bears piney, pungent, aromatic leaves and pinkish flowers. Certain varieties are cultivated for their decorativeness, for an oil that is used in perfumery and for seasoning. Leaves of thyme are extremely popular as a seasoning for soups, stews, meat, poultry, fish, game, picklings and stuffings, and they increase the taste appeal of most vegetables. The extremely versatile thyme is an integral part of the New Orleans cuisine, especially the *bouquet garni.*

TIBET CHEESE. A hard sheep's milk cheese, used for grating.

TIGNARD CHEESE. A hard, rennet cheese made from sheep's or goat's milk. This French cheese resembles Bex and Sassenage.

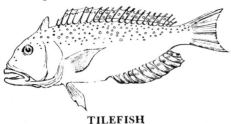

TILEFISH

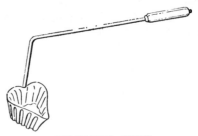

TIMBALE IRON

TILEFISH. One of the low-priced fresh fish, in season throughout the year, but in greatest abundance during winter and spring. In weight it averages from 15 to 30 pounds and is usually cut into steaks to fry, bake or boil. The tilefish is a recent arrival on the food fish list, and is abundant along the coast of Maine. Tilefish may be prepared in all the methods applied to swordfish, *which see.*

TILSIT CHEESE. A hard, rennet cheese resembling Brick cheese and sometimes called Ragnit. It is made in Germany, Yugoslavia, Hungary, Denmark, and Switzerland.

TIMBALE. Term applied to almost any kind of food cooked on a small timbale iron.

TIMBALE IRON. A long handled utensil which is equipped with a small cup-shaped head. The head is dipped into batter which adheres to it and which is cooked in the form of small pastry shell by lowering the batter coated head of the timbale iron into hot oil. *See also* FRYING.

TIMER. A timer is any device that can be used to indicate the passage of a definite period of time. While a regular clock or watch may be used for this function, there are also separate units made just for this purpose.

The timer is hardly a luxury item, even though it is possible to get by without one. Certain types of cooking (boiling eggs, for example) require one if the results are to be consistent. In other cases, such as baking or roasting, they are valuable aids. The most careful of cooks will burn an occasional cake if the matter is left to her memory. The phone rings, a salesman calls, or the children come home from school, and sometime after that, smoke from the burned food begins to fill the kitchen.

Egg. The typical egg timer is patterned after the traditional hourglass. It consists of two glass globes joined by a very small opening, and holding a measured amount of fine sand. It is usually mounted so it can be reversed, and the eggs are cooked for the length of time that it takes the sand to run from the top globe to the bottom one. Egg timers are made in several sizes, so that they may be used to time both soft-cooked and hard-cooked eggs, and they frequently have two different sized glasses mounted on one board. *See also* EGG.

Clock. Since there is usually a clock of some sort in the kitchen, that may be used to time cooking operations. This, however, is not the best possible practice, for the housewife may either forget the time that the operation started, or else let the finishing time slip by, unnoticed. An alarm clock is better, for it can be set to ring when the interval is over.

Most modern ranges are equipped with clocks, and the bulk of these clocks have some sort of timing arrangement as part of their works. These function somewhat as an alarm clock, emitting a warning note or ring when the selected interval is over. Some clock timers on electric ranges can also be adjusted to turn the heating elements on or off at desired times.

The latest development is a separate electric clock that, in addition to making warning noises, can also be set to turn off or on any electrical unit that is plugged into the clock in a special receptacle provided for that purpose.

Laboratory. These devices do not tell time as such, but are made solely to indicate the passage of a selected interval or period of time. This has advantages, for the user does not have to add or subtract the desired interval from the actual time of day, but can set the device for the desired number of minutes, starting from zero. They are usually operated by clockworks and are highly accurate, though, in most cases, their warning tones are neither loud nor as insistent as those of the previously described units. They can be obtained in most houseware supply stores. *See also* KITCHEN EQUIPMENT.

TINTILLA DE ROTA. The darkest of the Spanish red wines. While sold in its natural state, it is more commonly used as a blending agent with the lighter wines. *See also* WINE.

TINWARE. Tin itself is much too soft a metal for utensil use, but because of its corrosion-resisting powers, it is used to cover iron and steel. When used as a plating, tin scratches and wears with use. It darkens in time and tends to discolor any highly acid foods that are cooked in it. This darkening is not a disadvantage, however, for dark pans will brown baked goods more quickly and evenly than light ones. Because of its color and because it heats quickly and but does not hold the heat long, tinware is often used for baking pans. It is also used to make measuring cups and small saucepans as well as other utensils.

PURCHASING TINWARE

Tin plate is fashioned into pans by two different methods. In the cheaper method, the pieces are cut in two or more separate sections and are usually assembled by soldering. This method leaves sharp, raw edges, and such pans readily rust and leak. The more expensive method is to fold the pans from one single sheet, leaving smooth, watertight corners and edges.

Block tin is by far better, though it is also more expensive. The utensils are fashioned from uncoated steel, and are then dipped into molten tin to give them their covering.

Regardless of the method used, the steel or iron stock must be sturdy enough to resist warping or denting. Good tinware is expensive.

CARE AND CLEANING OF TINWARE

New baking pans should be darkened by placing in a very slow oven for several hours when first purchased. Tinware is washed in the normal manner, but only mild abrasives should be used, and then only gently. Harsh rubbing or harsh abrasives can easily remove the tin plate, exposing the metal beneath.

TIP TOP MELON. An oval melon grown all over the country. It has a grayish rind and pink flesh. *See also* MELON.

TISANE. When ladies were ladies and never women, and a leg was discreetly called a limb, and it was fashionable for members of the feminine gender to be pale and delicate, and to faint prettily when afflicted with "vapours," the mildly stimulating tea called tisane was used to revive them. The tea was brewed with the leaves of CAMOMILE, *which see.* Tisane is also used as a name for herb teas in general.

TOAST. For dry crisp toast, bread should be at least one day old and must be browned slowly. For the crisp, shiny finish desirable for grilled sandwiches, butter one side of the bread before toasting and put the sandwiches together, buttered side out. To make crisp, dry Melba toast, cut the bread as thin as possible and brown slowly in a very slow oven.

BALTIMORE TOAST

2 well-beaten eggs
½ cup sugar
2 cups milk
Dash of salt
2 tsp ground cinnamon
12 slices bread

Combine the eggs, sugar, milk, salt and cinnamon. Dip the slices of bread into this mixture, then into flour. Fry in deep hot fat and serve hot with jelly or jam.

BUTTERSCOTCH TOAST

Toast triangles of decrusted bread on one side. Spread the untoasted side with a mixture of creamed butter and brown sugar. Set under the broiler until the topping becomes hot and bubbly. Sprinkle with cinnamon and serve very hot.

CHEESE TOAST

½ lb rich cheese, diced
1 tsp salt
½ tsp prepared mustard
1 tsp paprika
1 egg
¾ to 1 cup milk
Toast

Place the cheese in a buttered pan with the seasonings. Combine the beaten egg and milk and pour over the cheese. Bake in a moderate oven (350° F.) 10 to 15 minutes or until the cheese has melted and is slightly brown. Serve on freshly made toast.

CINNAMON TOAST STRIPS

Slices of bread 1¼ in. thick
Melted butter
½ cup confectioners' sugar
2 tbsp ground cinnamon

Remove crusts from the bread and cut each slice into three strips making oblong blocks. Toast on all sides in the oven. Dip first into melted butter, then into the blended sugar and cinnamon. Serve very hot.

HONEY TOAST

Combine 2 teaspoons of cinnamon with ⅓ cup of strained honey and spread generously on hot buttered toast.

FRENCH TOAST

2 beaten eggs
1½ cups milk
Bread
Butter or drippings

Beat the eggs, add the milk and moisten 2-day-old bread thoroughly in the mixture. Sauté in butter or drippings and serve with sugar, maple sugar or jelly.

FRIED TOAST

Instead of toasting the bread, sauté or pan-fry in bacon fat. Serve with fried eggs and bacon.

MAPLE SUGAR TOAST

Spread freshly made toast lightly with softened butter and crushed maple sugar. Place in the oven until the sugar melts. Top each slice with a spoon of whipped cream.

MELBA TOAST

Slice 2- or 3-day-old bread not more than ⅛ inch thick. Remove crusts, place bread on a rack in a very slow oven (200° F.) and allow it to dry until crisp and golden brown throughout.

MILK TOAST

Pour over freshly made toast scalded milk, lightly seasoned with salt, white pepper and paprika, using about ¾ cup for each slice of toast.

TOAST RACK. Used mainly by the British, a toast rack is a device which holds several slices of toast in an upright position for serving purposes. In design and appearance it is quite similar to certain types of letter racks and phonograph record racks. *See* TOAST; *see also* TOASTER, TOASTING FORK, and TOASTING RACK.

TOASTER. Electrical toasters have come a long way from the grandfather of such implements, which features a heating device encased in a wire cage.

Today's toasters can accommodate two, four or more slices of bread, toasting the pieces on both sides with controllable heat and raising the toast automatically when it's done.

When purchasing a toaster it is wise to look for wide toast slots, multiple toast settings and an easy to clean crumb tray. Most modern appliances have heat resistant controls, handles and feet and an insulated base to protect table tops.

The crumb tray should be kept in place during use to protect the table top. A slightly darker toast setting may be needed for whole wheat and other rich breads and frozen waffles than will be needed for white bread. Knives and forks should never be inserted into a toaster to remove bread. Not only can the heating element be damaged by such a procedure but the person involved may receïve a shock. Aluminum foil packages should not be placed in a toaster.

The toaster should be unplugged and cooled before being cleaned or stored. Frequent removal of crumbs from the crumb tray by means of brushing is desirable. The tray may be wiped with a damp sponge and then thoroughly dried.

TOASTER

TOASTING FORK. A toasting fork is a long handled implement used to hold foods, especially bread or sandwiches, over a fire or other heat source for toasting or grilling purposes. They are commonly made of wire, with a wooden or otherwise insulated handle. They may have tines for impaling the food, but usually have some sort of grid on which the food is rested, or a wire cage which may be opened to receive the food. The latter type is the best, since there is little danger of the food falling out or off of the device, and it may be turned to do both sides without handling the food. *See also* TOASTING RACK, TOASTER and TOAST.

TOASTING RACK. A toasting rack is a metal frame that can be placed over a gas burner or similar heat source and used to toast bread. It has upright metal sheets which become heated and, in turn, toast the bread, which is supported parallel to the heated surface. *See* TOAST; *see also* TOASTER, TOASTING FORK, and TOAST RACK.

TODDY. (I) There are two types of toddies, hot and cold. Both are intoxicating, being made of brandy, gin, rum or whisky, and they are identified by the liquor used.

The cold toddy is made exactly as the basic SLING (*which see*) with one jigger of plain water added.

The hot toddy has a formula of its own, and in addition to being a pleasant cold weather drink, is often used for medicinal purposes to induce perspiration. The hot toddy is mixed in a toddy mug or other thick walled stein. *See* GLASSWARE.

HOT TODDY

1 lump sugar (or equivalent)
1 large jigger desired liquor (brandy, gin, rum or whisky)

These ingredients are placed in the toddy mug which is then filled $\frac{2}{3}$ with boiling water and stirred. The drink is garnished with a slice of lemon, a piece of cinnamon and some cloves, with nutmeg sprinkled on top. (Serves 1)

Hot Buttered Rum. A winter rum drink that belongs in the toddy family.

HOT BUTTERED RUM

1 large jigger Gold Label rum
1 lump sugar (or equivalent)
1 pat butter (or equivalent)

The ingredients are mixed in a toddy mug which may first be prepared by coating the inside with a thin layer of butter. The sugar is placed in first, boiling water added to fill $\frac{3}{8}$ full, the rum and butter added, and the mixture stirred gently. (Serves 1)

For further discussion of drinks and drink recipes, see BARTENDING; see also TOM AND JERRY.

TODDY. (II) A name which, in the tropics, is applied to both the sap of palms and the beverages which are fermented therefrom. These beverages are generally made and consumed only by the natives.

TOFFEE. A type of chewy candy. See CANDY.

TOKAY. There are two distinctly different wines known by this name, one made only from the Furmint grape, the other being a blend of several sweet wines.

Often called Royal or Imperial because it has been the favored drink of crowned princes, true Tokay is a Hungarian wine that has received enthusiastic praise since the 15th century. It comes from a district comprised of 31 villages, of which Tokay is the center, located among the foothills of the Carpathian Mountains, and is made from a species of blue grape called Furmint.

The secret of this wine's exceptional flavor lies in the use of *trockenbeeren* (over-ripe grapes) gathered in wooden trays of approximately 25 quart capacity called *puttonyos*, judiciously added to the regular grapes at the time of pressing. The number of puttonyos added per cask is indicated on the label; the larger the number, the richer the wine. Rarely are more than 5 puttonyos of trockenbeeren (approximately 50 per cent of the total amount of grapes) used, except in some years of exceptional vintage when 6 will be added.

Tokay is a delicate, rich wine, with a pale tint, extremely sweet but not cloying, and with an aroma somewhat like that of green tea. Imperial Tokay has often been called a liqueur rather than a wine. It will keep longer than any other wine, and, contrary to general practice, seems to improve indefinitely with age (see WINE). Those fortunate enough to taste Tokay that had passed the century mark are almost incoherent in their search for praise great enough to do it due honor.

There are, of course, other grades of Tokay made in Hungary; some more properly table wines than dessert wines. Since good Tokay is produced in relatively small quantities, and improves with extreme age, it is difficult to obtain, and the price is often prohibitive to all but the wealthy.

There is also an amber-colored dessert wine (see WINE) called Tokay, made, notably in California, by blending various sweet wines, usually a combination of Angelica, Port, and Sherry. It is medium-bodied, has a nutty flavor, and lies between Port and Sherry in sweetness. It is served with or following desserts and between meals, chilled or at room temperature.

TOM AND JERRY. A traditional American winter drink that is mixed in a special bowl and served in matching cups. See GLASSWARE. The Tom and Jerry is made by diluting small portions of a basic egg batter in hot milk or water and liquors in a heated individual mug.

TOM AND JERRY BATTER

6 eggs
2 jiggers Jamaica rum
Powdered sugar
1 large pinch baking soda
½ tsp allspice

The egg parts are separated, beaten, then combined by heating with enough powdered sugar to make a stiff batter. The other ingredients are added and the whole beaten again with enough more sugar added to restiffen the batter. The baking soda is used only as a preservative so if the batter will be used up soon, it may be left out.

TOM AND JERRY SERVING

1 tbsp Tom and Jerry batter
1 jigger Jamaica rum
½ jigger brandy

The batter is dissolved in the bottom of a heated Tom and Jerry mug with a little hot water or milk. The rum is added and the mug filled with hot water or milk, the brandy floated on top and the whole sprinkled with cinnamon.

If the brandy is not desired in the individual drink, one jigger of brandy is mixed into the basic batter at the time of making. (Serves 1)

For other drink recipes, see BARTENDING; see also TODDY.

TOM AND JERRY BOWL. See TOM AND JERRY and GLASSWARE.

TOMATO. The exact origin of the tomato is still in doubt. Various legends say that it comes from Africa, from India, or from China. However, some historians claim that the tomato was first found in Peru where the Spaniards, searching for Inca treasures, saw it growing in the gardens. The tomato was first believed to be poisonous, and was called love apple or paradise apple. It was not until about 1830 that it began to be used as food. In many European countries it is still a luxury and is sold as a fruit.

HINTS ON PURCHASING

Tomatoes, in order to ship satisfactorily and arrive in good condition, must be picked before they are fully ripe. They are allowed to stay on the vine until they are mature, but still green. At this stage they will continue to ripen after they have reached the market. However, the flavor of tomatoes ripened in this way does not compare with that of vine-ripened tomatoes, and whenever the local crop is available, it is much to be preferred.

Tomatoes which are shipped from distant growers usually arrive wholly green or tinged with yellow. Such tomatoes should be firm, with a clear, dark green color, and feel and look polished. Immature tomatoes usually appear shriveled and have a whitish color. Such tomatoes will not ripen satisfactorily. Tomatoes are best ripened by leaving in the light on a window sill or similar place, turning frequently, until the fruit is evenly reddened and ripe.

Good quality tomatoes are firm, not overripe, well formed and without serious blemish. Scars around the blossom end are not serious except as they affect the appearance of the tomato for salads, etc. Puffy fruit is watery and wasteful. Tomatoes that have started to spoil are not worth purchasing.

So-called home grown tomatoes are likely to be less perfect, with more irregular shape and cracks, than the tomatoes shipped in from large commercial growers.

There are a number of novel forms of tomatoes which are occasionally found in the markets: the cherry tomato, which is about the size of a good-sized cherry; the egg tomato, which is the size and shape of a pullet's egg; and the yellow tomatoes which may be conventional pear or egg-shaped. All of these make interesting variations in salads or raw vegetable platters.

TOMATO

Since their novelty lies in the size, shape, or color, it is foolish to use them for cooking, except for the yellow tomatoes which make a distinctive tomato juice.

Canned tomatoes. Tomatoes are canned either as the whole peeled fruit or as the cut-up fruit which gives a fairly liquid sauce with chunks of the pulp suspended in it. The best quality of canned tomatoes consists of very large chunks, all of uniform ripeness. Italian-style tomatoes are canned tomatoes which have been seasoned with basil; use these in making spaghetti sauce or other dishes in which the flavor of basil is desired.

Tomato purée, or tomato paste, is a concentrated form of canned tomatoes in which most of the water has been removed. It adds the highly concentrated flavor of tomatoes to sauces, etc. without adding unnecessary liquid.

Tomato juice is actually a misnomer. It is the pulp and liquid of the tomatoes, only the skin and seeds having been removed, cooked to the point where the whole is a liquid. Tomato cocktail is the juice with various seasonings and flavorings added.

FOOD VALUE

	Water	Food Energy	Protein	Fat	Carbohydrates	Calcium	Phosphorus	Iron	Vit. A Value	Thiamine	Riboflavin	Niacin	Ascorbic Acid
Fresh	94.1	23	1.0	.3	4.0	11	27	.6	1100	.06	.04	.6	23
Canned	94.2	21	1.0	.2	3.9	11	27	.6	1050	.05	.03	.7	16

TOMATO

Hints on Preparation

Fine ripe tomatoes are at their best in a salad served with a simple, tart French dressing. While the skin of tomatoes is edible, it is sometimes a little tough and raw tomatoes are more appetizing if they are peeled. This is easily done in one of three ways.

Impale the tomato on a fork (at the stem end) and rotate over a flame until the skin blisters and cracks. It may then be peeled off easily with a knife. Do not heat the tomato too long, and chill again in the refrigerator after peeling. Or the tomato may be dipped for a moment in boiling water and then plunged into cold water. The skin will slip off easily. Again the tomato should be chilled again before serving. If the tomatoes are quite ripe it may only be necessary to rub over them firmly but gently with the back of a knife. Then the skin may be slit and removed quite easily.

In preparing sliced tomatoes, cut around the stem and remove the somewhat hard core. Then slice crosswise. The older varieties of tomatoes had a considerable amount of thin watery pulp surrounding the seeds which was difficult to handle when slicing tomatoes. Newer varieties have more solid meat and slice more attractively.

In adding fresh tomatoes to a stew or other dish, peel the fruit and cut it into chunks. It will cook away quite quickly. In using canned tomatoes in such dishes, it may be desirable to drain away part of the liquid, lest it make the dish too thin.

Green tomatoes may be used in a number of ways: for preserves and relishes, fried, in a form of mincemeat for pies, or in various combinations of meat and other dishes.

Once tomatoes are ripened, keep them in the refrigerator until ready to use. Do not peel them too far ahead of time, and keep them covered once they have been peeled.

When stewing tomatoes or making tomato soup, a teaspoon or two of sugar added to the tomatoes during the cooking will bring out the flavor and take away the slightly acid flavor whch some tomatoes have.

When making stewed tomatoes, try thickening them with a little flour or cornstarch or with soft bread crumbs. Do not overthicken; the point is only to prevent their being too liquid.

Baked Curried Tomatoes

6 tomatoes
1 cup tomato sauce
2 tsp curry powder
1 tbsp currant jelly
1 tsp salt
Dash of pepper
¼ cup grated American cheese
¼ cup buttered crumbs
6 slices bacon

Scald and peel the tomatoes, and remove the stem end. Arrange in a deep greased baking dish. Combine the tomato sauce, curry powder, and jelly, and cook for 5 minutes. Season with salt and pepper and pour over the tomatoes. Mix the cheese and crumbs and sprinkle over the top. Bake in a moderate oven (375° F.) about 20 minutes. Top with the slices of bacon and return to the oven until the bacon is crisp and browned. (Serves 6)

Baked Tomato Surprise

6 tomatoes
Salt and pepper
6 eggs
2 tsp minced onion
2 tsp minced parsley
2 tbsp oil or butter
6 thin squares of bacon

Wash the tomatoes and cut a thin slice from the blossom end of each. Scoop out the pulp from the centers and set aside for other use. Sprinkle the tomatoes with salt and pepper. Drop a raw egg into each tomato. Heat the oil or butter and cook the onion and parsley for 5 minutes. Cover the eggs with a little of the cooked mixture and top with a piece of bacon. Arrange in a baking dish and bake in a moderate oven (375° F.) about 20 minutes. (Serves 6)

Broiled Tomatoes

Cut firm tomatoes into thick slices, season with salt and pepper, top with buttered crumbs and broil under moderate heat.

Deviled Tomatoes. Top the broiled slices with the following sauce:

2 tbsp oil
½ tsp mustard
Dash of cayenne
½ tsp sugar
3 tbsp mild vinegar

Heat the ingredients together and pour over the hot tomatoes. Serve very hot.

Variations of Broiled Tomatoes. Spread thick slices of tomato, before broiling, with any of the following:
1. Buttered crumbs, grated onion, sage, thyme, salt and pepper.
2. Minced onion sprinkled liberally with curry powder, salt and pepper.
3. Grated onion, salt, pepper and sugar.
4. Grated cheese, soft crumbs, salt and pepper.
5. Buttered crumbs seasoned with powdered ginger, salt, pepper, a little sugar and grated lemon rind.
6. Potted meat, deviled ham, peanut butter or chopped crisp bacon.
7. Highly seasoned French dressing.
8. Grated onion and cheese mixed with salad dressing.

CLEAR TOMATO SOUP

1½ qt fresh or canned tomatoes
½ bay leaf
¼ cup chopped onion
4 cloves
1 tbsp melted butter or margarine
1 tbsp flour
1 tsp sugar
1 tsp salt
Dash of pepper

Cook together the tomatoes, bay leaf, onion, and cloves—about 20 minutes for fresh tomatoes and 10 for canned. Press through a sieve. Blend the butter, flour and sugar in a saucepan. Gradually add the cooled, sieved tomatoes. Cook over low heat, stirring constantly, for about 5 minutes. Season with salt and pepper and serve hot. (Serves 6)

CREAM OF TOMATO SOUP

3½ cups fresh or canned tomatoes
¼ cup chopped onion
2 tbsp butter or margarine
3 tbsp flour
½ tsp sugar
3 cups milk, scalded
1 tsp salt

Cook the tomatoes and onion together for 20 minutes if fresh tomatoes are used, about 10 for canned tomatoes. Press through a sieve. Melt the butter and blend in the flour and sugar. Gradually add the cooled, sieved tomatoes. Cook over low heat, stirring constantly, until thickened. Gradually add the scalded milk, stirring constantly. Reheat but do not boil. Season to taste with salt. Serve at once. (Serves 6)

FRIED TOMATOES

6 medium-sized ripe or green tomatoes
1 egg
½ cup fine dry bread crumbs
½ tsp salt
Dash of pepper

Slice the tomatoes about ½ inch thick. Beat the egg slightly, and season with salt and pepper. Dip the tomato slices in the crumbs, then in the seasoned egg, and again in the crumbs. Fry in a small amount of fat in a skillet until delicately brown on both sides. (Serves 6)

FROZEN TOMATOES

Thoroughly crush 1 quart of canned tomatoes, discarding all hard portions. Season highly with salt, pepper, and minced onion, and add a generous tablespoon of finely chopped parsley. Turn into refrigerator tray and freeze to a mush, then scrape into a bowl, beat vigorously and return to the freezing chamber until serving time. If convenient, the scraping and beating may be repeated once or even twice more. The mixture should be frozen only to the mushy stage. Serve in sherbet cups, topping each with a spoon of mayonnaise.

GREEN TOMATO CURRY

1 onion, sliced
3 tbsp drippings, or other fat
4 cups sliced green tomatoes
3 cups chopped cooked meat
2 tsp curry powder
Salt

Cook the onion in the fat. Add the green tomatoes, cover and cook until tender. Add the meat and heat thoroughly. If the mixture is too thick, thin it slightly with meat broth, gravy or water. Season to taste with curry powder and salt. Serve with boiled rice or noodles. (Serves 6)

GREEN TOMATO MARMALADE

3 qt sliced green tomatoes
6 cups sugar
1 tsp salt
6 lemons
1 cup water

Combine tomatoes, sugar and salt. Peel the lemons and slice the peel very thin. Boil in the cup of water for 5 minutes and drain. Slice the lemon pulp and remove the seeds. Add with the rind to tomato mixture. Heat slowly to boiling, then cook rapidly, stirring constantly, for 45 to 60 minutes or until thickened. Pour into hot sterile jars (see JAMS AND JELLIES). Seal and store in a cool, dark place. (Makes about 4 pints)

GREEN TOMATO MINCEMEAT

4 qt finely chopped green tomatoes
2 qt pared finely chopped tart apples
1 lb seedless raisins
4 tbsp minced citron, lemon, or orange peel
1 tbsp ground cinnamon
2 tsp salt
1/4 tsp ground allspice
1/4 tsp ground cloves
2 cups firmly packed brown sugar
3 cups granulated sugar
3/4 cup vinegar
1/4 to 1/2 cup lemon juice
2 cups water

Combine all the ingredients and cook mixture slowly until tender and slightly thickened. Stir frequently to prevent sticking. Pour into hot sterile jars (see JAMS AND JELLIES), filling jars to the top, and seal. Store in a cool, dark place. (Makes 4 qts.)

GREEN TOMATO PIE

Pastry for 9-inch double-crust pie
6 or 8 medium-sized green tomatoes

2 tbsp lemon juice
1 tsp grated lemon or orange rind
1/2 tsp salt
1/4 tsp cinnamon
3/4 cup sugar
2 tbsp cornstarch
1 tbsp butter or margarine

Wash the tomatoes, remove the stem ends, and slice. Combine with the lemon juice, rind, salt and cinnamon in a saucepan and cook for 15 minutes, stirring frequently. Mix the sugar and cornstarch. Add it to the tomato mixture and cook until clear, stirring constantly. Add the butter. Cool slightly. Line a pie pan with pastry. Pour in the mixture. Cover with pastry, seal the edges, and cut several gashes to allow the steam to escape. Bake in a hot oven (435° F.) for 40 to 50 minutes.

JELLIED TOMATO BOUILLON

1 1/4 tbsp gelatin
1/4 cup cold water
2 1/2 cups well-seasoned tomato juice
2 bouillon cubes
2 tbsp minced parsley
2 tbsp sherry
Green pepper or pimiento

Soften the gelatin in the cold water. Heat the tomato juice (highly seasoned with onion juice and celery salt), add the bouillon cubes and softened gelatin and stir until both are dissolved. Cool, add the parsley and wine, and chill. Beat lightly with a fork before serving to break up the jelly. (Serves 4)

JELLIED TOMATO LOAF

1 No. 2 can tomatoes
1 stalk celery
1 medium-sized onion
Small piece bay leaf
2 cloves
2 tsp salt
2 tbsp vinegar
2 tbsp sugar
2 tbsp gelatin
1/2 cup cold water

Simmer the tomato, celery, onion, and seasonings together until tender. Press through a sieve and reheat. Soften the gelatin in the cold water and add to the hot mixture, stirring until the gelatin is all dissolved. Cool, and when the mixture begins to set, turn into a loaf pan which has been wet with cold water. Chill in the refrigerator until set. Unmold and garnish with any preferred salad green. Serve with mayonnaise. (Serves 6)

JELLIED TOMATO SALAD

2 cups canned tomatoes
1 small bay leaf
2 whole cloves
½ tsp salt
Dash of black pepper
1 tbsp gelatin
¼ cup cold water
1 tbsp mild vinegar or lemon juice
1 tbsp onion juice
Few drops tabasco
Lettuce
Mayonnaise

Combine the tomatoes, bay leaf, cloves, salt and pepper and cook 10 minutes. Meanwhile, soften the gelatin in the cold water and when the tomatoes are cooked combine the 2 mixtures and stir until the gelatin is dissolved. Now add the vinegar or lemon juice, tabasco and onion juice, bring just to boiling point and strain through a fine sieve rubbing through as much of the vegetable pulp as possible. Cool, and when almost at setting point, turn into one large or several small previously wet molds and chill. At serving time unmold onto lettuce, plain or shredded, and garnish with a dot of mayonnaise; or, chill the mixture in a large shallow pan and when firm cut into any desired shapes with a sharp cutter; or break up lightly with a fork if to be used as a garnish for salads or cold platters of meat, fish or poultry. (Serves 6)

When fresh tomatoes are plentiful substitute these for the canned tomato. Concentrated tomato soup extended with an equal amount of water, or tomato juice, or tomato juice cocktail may also be used.

Favorite Salad. When the tomato jelly begins to stiffen add ½ cup of diced (not chopped) celery and ½ cup of chopped blanched almonds or other nut meats.

Christmas Salad. Chill the jellied tomato salad in a shallow pan, having it about ½-inch deep. When firm, cut into stars with cutter or very sharp knife and serve as individual salads on lettuce, with a small ball of cream cheese and a stuffed olive in the center of each star. Pass any preferred dressing separately. The trimmings may be remelted, reset and used to cut additional stars.

Perfection Salad. When the tomato jelly begins to stiffen stir into it one cup of finely shredded cabbage, ½ cup of diced celery and ½ cup of finely chopped green pepper.

Tomato and Fish Salad. When the tomato jelly begins to stiffen stir into it gently 1 cup of shredded, boned, drained fish (fresh or canned) with ½ cup of green pepper and ½ cup of canned pimientoes, both finely chopped. Serve with mayonnaise or whipped cream flavored with lemon juice.

JELLIED TOMATO SOUP

2 cups fresh or canned tomatoes
1 onion, sliced
2 stalks celery
¼ cup chopped green pepper
1 tbsp minced parsley
¼ cup water
1 tbsp gelatin
½ tsp salt
1 tsp sugar
4 whole cloves
1 bay leaf

Combine together the tomatoes, vegetables and seasonings and bring to a boil. Simmer, covered, for 20 minutes and strain through a fine sieve. Soften the gelatin in the water and add to the hot liquid. Stir until thoroughly dissolved. Pour into a shallow dish and chill until firm. Arrange by spoonfuls in bouillon cups. Serve very cold with a slice of lemon. (Serves 4 or 5)

QUICK CREAM OF TOMATO SOUP

2 cups cooked or canned tomatoes
3 cups milk
1 tsp salt
1 tsp sugar
Dash of pepper
1 tbsp butter or margarine

Combine the tomatoes and milk in the top of a double boiler and heat slowly but do not boil. Season with salt, sugar, pepper, and butter. Serve immediately. (Serves 5)

RIPE TOMATO CONSERVE

Peel and cut up 12 medium sized tomatoes. Weigh them and add ¾ pound of sugar for each pound of tomato, together with the juice of 2 lemons and 2 oranges, 1 teaspoon of ground cinnamon and ½ teaspoon ground cloves. Cook gently, stirring frequently, until quite thick, about 1 hour, then add 1 cup seeded raisins and ½ cup each candied orange rind and candied ginger, finely diced. Cook 5 minutes longer, then turn into sterilized jars and seal.

SCALLOPED TOMATOES WITH MUSHROOMS

⅛ tsp minced garlic or onion
2 tbsp butter or margarine
1 cup minced mushrooms
1 cup soft bread crumbs
2 tbsp butter, additional
2 tbsp minced parsley
Salt and pepper
6 tomatoes, peeled and quartered

Cook the garlic or onion slowly in the butter until it yellows. Add the mushrooms and stir until thoroughly heated. Remove from the fire, add the crumbs, the remaining butter, and the parsley, salt, and pepper. Arrange the quartered tomatoes in a shallow greased baking dish, top with the mushroom-crumb mixture and bake in a hot oven (400° F.) about 20 minutes. Delicious with broiled steak. (Serves 6)

SCALLOPED TOMATOES WITH SPINACH

1 No. 2 can tomatoes
1 tsp salt
⅛ tsp pepper
2 tsp minced onion
1 tbsp sugar
2 cups soft bread cubes
¼ cup melted butter or margarine
2 cups cooked, seasoned spinach

Combine the tomatoes, salt, pepper, onion, and sugar. Place an inverted cup in the center of a greased casserole. Arrange around it in alternate layers the tomato mixture and the bread cubes, having bread for the top layer. Pour the melted butter over all and bake in a moderate oven (375° F.) about 25 minutes. Remove from the oven, lift out the cup, and fill the center with the hot cooked spinach which has been well seasoned with butter and a little lemon juice. (Serves 6)

SPANISH SAUCE

2 tbsp chopped onion
2 tbsp fat
1 tbsp flour
2½ cups fresh or canned tomatoes
½ cup chopped celery
½ cup chopped green pepper
1 tbsp chopped parsley
1 tsp salt
Dash of pepper

Cook the onion in the fat until lightly browned. Blend in the flour. Add the tomatoes, celery, green pepper, parsley, and seasonings. Cook 15 or 20 minutes, stirring frequently. Serve over meat loaf, cooked spaghetti, fish, or omelet.

STUFFED TOMATO APPETIZERS

Use small, firm tomatoes for cups. Peel them, cut off the stem ends, scoop out the centers, salt them, and invert them to drain. Use one of the following fillings or one of your own selection. Among popular fillings are chicken salad and crabmeat salad. Cheese is a popular garnish for many stuffed-tomato recipes.

Cottage cheese filling. Combine the cottage cheese with blanched shredded almonds or pecan meats. Garnish with stuffed olives and a sprig of parsley. Serve with mayonnaise.

Egg-tomato appetizer. Stuff tomatoes with caviar-egg spread, *which see*. Spread Worcestershire butter on·toast rounds, and place the stuffed tomatoes on top of these. Garnish with a mixture of mayonnaise and caviar.

Tomato-liver paste cups. Stuff tomatoes with chicken liver spread, *which see*. Serve them on lettuce, and garnish with strips of tomato.

STUFFED TOMATO SALAD

6 medium-sized tomatoes, well chilled
½ cup chopped celery

½ cup chopped cucumber
1 tbsp minced onion
1 tbsp chopped green pepper
2 hard-cooked eggs, chopped
2 tbsp mayonnaise or salad dressing
1 tsp salt
Pepper

Wash tomatoes and remove the stem ends. Scoop out the center, leaving a shell about ¼ inch thick. Turn upside down on plate to drain and place in refrigerator to keep cold. Dice the tomato pulp and combine with the other ingredients. Stuff the tomatoes. Serve on lettuce or other salad greens. Serve very cold. (Serves 6)
For a meat stuffing:

1 cup diced cooked meat or poultry
1 cup diced cooked potatoes
1 tbsp chopped parsley
1 tbsp minced onion
2 tbsp chopped green pepper
1 tsp salt
Dash of pepper
2 tbsp mayonnaise or salad dressing

Combine all the ingredients and stuff into tomatoes. Serve very cold.

TOMATO ASPIC WITH VEGETABLES

1 tbsp gelatin
2 tbsp cold water
2 tsp sugar
Salt and pepper
1½ cups hot strained tomato
1 cup mixed cooked vegetables
Shredded lettuce
French dressing
Mayonnaise

Soften the gelatin in the cold water and dissolve with the sugar and seasonings in the tomato. When almost at setting point, put a little of the jelly mixture into a previously wet ring mold. Allow this to almost set, then arrange on it a layer of the vegetables—peas, cauliflower flowerets, lima or string beans, carrot slices, etc. Fill up the mold with alternate layers of jelly and vegetables and chill. Unmold, and garnish with crisp shredded lettuce, filling the center with additional vegetables moistened with French dressing. Pass mayonnaise separately. (Serves 6)

TOMATO GELATIN

1½ tbsp gelatin
½ cup cold water
2 cups tomato juice
1 tsp sugar
Salt and pepper
1 cup diced celery
2 tbsp minced green pepper (optional)
Lettuce
Mayonnaise or boiled dressing

Soften the gelatin in the cold water. Bring the tomato juice to boiling point, add the gelatin, sugar and seasonings, and stir until dissolved. Cool, and when almost at setting point add the celery and green pepper, if used. Turn into a previously wet mold and chill. Unmold onto shredded lettuce and garnish with stiff mayonnaise, or pass boiled dressing separately. (Serves 4)

TOMATO CHRISTMAS SALAD

Take Jellied Tomato Salad (which see) and chill the salad in a shallow pan, having it about ½ inch deep. When firm, cut into stars with cutter or very sharp knife and serve as individual salads on lettuce, with a small ball of cream cheese and a stuffed olive in the center of each star. Pass any preferred dressing separately. The trimmings may be remelted, reset, and used to cut additional stars.

TOMATO, HAM AND CHEESE LOAF

3 cups tomato juice
1 small onion, minced
1 tsp sugar
1 tsp salt
⅛ tsp pepper
2 tbsp gelatin
½ cup cold water
1 cup chopped cooked ham
1 tsp prepared mustard
Mayonnaise
3 packages cream cheese
2 tbsp heavy sour cream
Water cress
Hard-cooked eggs

Simmer the tomato juice and onion with the sugar, salt, and pepper for 5 minutes. Soften the gelatin in the cold water and add to the hot mixture. Strain and cool. Combine the ham and mustard and moisten with a little mayonnaise. When the tomato mixture approaches the setting point, wet a loaf pan with cold water and pour in ⅓ of the tomato mixture. Chill again until firm. Arrange the ham mixture on this layer and pour over it another ⅓ of the tomato mixture. Chill again until firm. Mix the cream cheese with the sour cream and add a dash of salt. Spread this on the tomato layer, and cover with the last ⅓ of the tomato mixture. Chill thoroughly until ready to serve. Unmold and garnish with water cress and quartered hard-cooked eggs. (Serves 6 to 8)

TOMATO JELLY CANAPES

1 tbsp gelatin
¼ cup cold water
2 cups canned tomatoes
1 tbsp grated horseradish
1 tbsp onion juice
1 tsp salt
½ cup cucumber, peeled, chopped and drained
½ cup celery hearts, cut small
Dash of tabasco sauce (optional)

Soften the gelatin in the cold water, then dissolve by setting the bowl containing it over hot water and stirring until dissolved. Pass the tomatoes through a strainer, rubbing through as much as possible of the pulp, add all remaining ingredients and combine with the dissolved gelatin. Blend very thoroughly. Stir frequently and, when beginning to thicken, turn into a shallow, previously wet pan. When quite firm cut with fancy cutters into rounds, squares, diamonds, ovals, etc., using a cutter first dipped in cold water. Serve on wafers crisped in the oven, then cooled, or on rounds or squares of the gelatin mixture cut a little larger than the small fancy designs themselves. Garnish with water cress.

TOMATO JUICE COCKTAIL

3½ cups fresh or canned tomatoes
1 cup chopped celery
¼ cup chopped green pepper
½ bay leaf
1 tbsp chopped onion
½ tsp salt
1 tsp Worcestershire sauce
½ tsp horseradish

Cook together the tomatoes, celery, green pepper, bay leaf, and onions—about 20 minutes for fresh tomatoes and 10 minutes for canned. Press through a sieve. Add the salt, Worcestershire sauce, and horseradish to the sieved tomatoes. Mix well and chill. Shake thoroughly before serving. (Makes 3 cups)

TOMATO CREAM COCKTAIL

2 cups chilled tomato juice
1 cup chilled cream
1 grated onion
¼ cup crushed ice
4 grated celery ribs
Salt
Tabasco sauce
Cayenne

Put all of the ingredients into a cocktail shaker, using very small amounts of the seasonings, and shake vigorously. Put the ice into the glasses, and pour the mixture over it. (Makes 6)

TOMATO BUTTERMILK

5 cups chilled tomato juice
3 cups chilled buttermilk
1 tsp salt
6 drops Worcestershire sauce

Mix the ingredients together and serve at once. (Serves 8)

TOMATO MILK

3 cups chilled evaporated milk
1½ cups ice water
5 cups chilled tomato juice
2 tsp celery salt

Mix the milk and water, then slowly stir in the tomato juice. Stir in the celery salt and serve immediately. (Serves 8)

TOMATO MARMALADE

3 qt sliced, peeled tomatoes
6 cups sugar
1 tsp salt
2 oranges
2 lemons

2 cups water
4 sticks cinnamon
2 tsp whole cloves

Combine the tomatoes, sugar, and salt. Peel the oranges and lemons. Slice the peel very thin and boil in the 2 cups of water for 5 minutes. Drain. Slice the orange and lemon pulp and remove the seeds. Add with the rind to the tomato mixture. Put the spices in a thin white cloth and tie the top tightly. Add to the tomato mixture. Heat slowly to boiling, then cook rapidly, stirring constantly, for 45 to 60 minutes, or until thickened. Remove spice bag. Pour the marmalade into hot sterile jars (see JAMS AND JELLIES). Seal and store in a cool dark place. (Makes about 5 pints)

TOMATO AND ORANGE SALAD

1½ cups diced peeled tomatoes
1 cup diced orange
1 tbsp finely minced onion
¾ cup diced celery
1 tbsp minced green pepper
1 tbsp minced parsley
½ cup French dressing (made with lemon juice)
Lettuce or water cress

Peel and dice the tomatoes, discarding any excess juice. Combine with all remaining salad ingredients, add the French dressing and chill thoroughly. Arrange for individual service on lettuce, plain or shredded, or garnish with water cress. If desired, pass mayonnaise or boiled dressing separately. (Serves 6)

TOMATO PICKLE
(Sweet)

1 peck green tomatoes
6 large onions
1 cup salt
2 qt water
3 qt vinegar
2 lb brown sugar
2 tbsp cloves
2 tbsp allspice
2 tbsp ginger
2 tbsp cinnamon
2 tbsp mustard seed
½ tsp cayenne, or less

Wipe the tomatoes, then slice about ⅓-inch thick. Peel the onions and slice as thinly as possible. Place together in a bowl, sprinkle with the salt, cover and let stand 12 hours. Drain well, turn into a saucepan, add the water and 1 quart of the vinegar and cook about 15 minutes or until almost tender. Drain again. Combine the remaining vinegar, sugar and ground spices, tied in cheesecloth. Bring to boiling point and cook about 15 minutes. Pack the drained tomatoes and onions in sterilized jars and fill to overflowing with the sirup, from which the spice bag has been removed. (Makes 8 pints)

TOMATO RABBIT

½ cup finely chopped celery
¼ cup chopped green pepper
¼ cup chopped onion
2 tbsp fat
2 tbsp flour
2½ cups fresh or canned tomatoes
1 cup grated cheese
1 tsp salt
2 eggs
Dash of tabasco

Cook the celery, green pepper, and onion in the fat for 8 or 10 minutes, stirring frequently. Blend in the flour. Add the tomatoes, cheese, and salt. Cook over low heat, stirring constantly, until the mixture thickens and the cheese melts. Beat the eggs and gradually add a little of the tomato mixture. Mix well and return to the tomato mixture. Continue to cook over low heat, stirring constantly until thickened and creamy. Serve on toast or crackers. (Serves 6)

TOMATO SAUCE

2½ cups fresh or canned tomatoes
¼ cup chopped onion
½ tsp sugar
¼ bay leaf
2 whole cloves
Flour
Fat
½ tsp salt
Dash of pepper

Cook together the tomatoes, onion, sugar, bay leaf, and cloves about 20 minutes. Press through a sieve and measure. For each cup of sieved tomatoes, blend 1 tablespoon flour and 1 tablespoon melted fat. Gradually add the cooled sieved tomatoes. Cook over low heat, stirring constantly, about 5 minutes, or until thickened. Season with salt and pepper. Serve over meat loaf, croquettes, fish, spaghetti, or omelet.

TOMATO SOUFFLE

2 tbsp flour
2 tbsp butter or margarine
⅓ tsp salt
Dash of pepper
½ cup milk
½ cup thick tomato pulp
2 eggs, separated

Prepare a white sauce with the butter, flour, seasonings, and milk. When smooth and creamy add the tomato pulp and beaten egg yolks. Blend thoroughly. Beat the egg whites until stiff and fold into the tomato mixture. Turn into buttered ramekins and set in a pan of hot water. Bake in a moderate oven (350° F.) 20 to 25 minutes. Turn out of ramekins and serve immediately. (Serves 4)

TOMATO SOUP

2 cups canned tomatoes
2 cups brown stock
3 tbsp butter
2 tbsp flour
1 carrot
2 stalks celery
1 small turnip
¼ cup of cooked lean ham
2 leeks
1 tbsp finely chopped chives
Bouquet garni
Salt and pepper

Stir the flour into 2 tablespoons of heated butter, then add brown stock and stir more. Chop carrot, celery, turnip, and leeks up fine and add to mixture. Put in ham and bouquet garni and simmer for about ½ hour. Add tomatoes, season with salt and pepper, bring slowly to boiling point, and then simmer for 20 minutes. Strain through seive, add rest of butter and chives, stir, and serve.

YELLOW TOMATO PRESERVES

Wash small firm yellow tomatoes. For each pound of tomatoes take:

¾ cup water
¾ lb sugar
¼ lemon, thinly sliced
1 piece of ginger root

Boil the lemon for 5 minutes in a little of the water. Boil the remainder of the water with the sugar for 5 minutes to make a sirup. Add the tomatoes, ginger root, lemon, and the water in which the lemon was cooked. Boil until the tomatoes are clear and the sirup somewhat thick. Remove scum, and pour the preserves into hot sterile glasses (*see* JAMS AND JELLIES). Seal and store in a cool dark place.

TOMCOD. *See* COD.

TOM COLLINS. A tall, cool, sparkling summer drink, made of gin, lemon juice, sugar and carbonated water, served with straws and fruit garnishing. *See* COLLINS.

TOMME CHEESE. A French cow's milk cheese, made in Savoy. Other names are *Tomme Boudane*, *Tomme des Beauges*, and *Tomme au Fenouil*.

TONGUE. Beef, lamb or mutton, pork, or veal tongues, fresh and smoked, are found in our markets, and may be prepared in countless delicious ways. Tongue, like heart, has received considerable exercise and thus developed connective tissue. For this reason, it is necessary to cook tongue gently by moist heat. This is often preliminary to further preparation.

First, the tongue should be thoroughly washed in warm water. (Smoked or pickled tongue should be soaked for several hours before cooking.) The heavy skin and roots are not removed until the tongue is cooked. Fresh tongue should be covered with salted water, one teaspoon of salt for each quart of water, and cooked at a simmering temperature until tender. It will require three to four hours for a large beef tongue.

Tongues, like hams, are lightly cured or smoked nowadays, and the soaking reshapes the tongue which during the curing or smoking will have shrunk. A tongue weighing about four pounds will provide four people of average appetite with hot meat for two meals and leftovers for a salad or sandwiches for the third meal. There is little waste to be considered in buying tongue, and its preparation for the table is quite simple.

Never discard the butt of a tongue nor the water in which the tongue was cooked. This last may be used as a stock for pea, bean, and lentil soups, adding a delicious flavor. Or the broth may be used as the foundation for a sauce to be served with the tongue.

BAKED FRESH TONGUE

1 small fresh beef tongue, about 4 lb
3 qt boiling water
1 onion
3 whole cloves
1 carrot, sliced
1 stalk celery
1 bay leaf
6 peppercorns
2 or 3 tsp salt
1 cup tomato or brown sauce

Wash the tongue thoroughly. Place in a saucepan, cover with the boiling water, add the onion stock with the cloves, the carrot, celery, bay leaf and peppercorns. Bring slowly to boiling point, allow it to boil 5 minutes, skim, reduce the heat and simmer for 1 hour. Add the salt and continue simmering until tender. Lift out and carefully strip off the tough skin. Trim, removing the fat and tough portions near the heavy throat end. Place in a greased baking dish, pour the sauce over and bake in a moderate oven (375° F.) about 25 minutes, basting frequently. Serve with mashed potatoes and spinach. (Serves 6)

BRAISED FRESH BEEF TONGUE

1 beef tongue, about 4 lb
¼ cup chopped onion
¼ cup chopped celery
½ cup chopped carrot
3 tbsp butter
3 tbsp flour
3 cups tongue water
1 tsp Worcestershire sauce
Salt and pepper
¼ cup chopped sour pickles

Wash, then cover the tongue with boiling water and simmer for 2 hours. Remove the skin and trim. Place the tongue in a deep casserole with the onion, celery and carrot. Prepare a sauce by blending the butter and flour, gradually adding the tongue water and stirring until boiling. Season with the Worcestershire sauce, salt, pepper, and pickles. Pour over the tongue in the casserole and bake, covered, in a moderate oven (350° F.) for 2 hours. Serve on a hot platter with the strained sauce from the casserole. (Serves 6)

JELLIED FRESH TONGUE

2 tbsp gelatin
2 tbsp cold water
2 cups boiling water
1 tsp salt
⅛ tsp pepper
1 tbsp prepared mustard
1 tbsp lemon juice
1 tsp Worcestershire sauce
2 cups cooked tongue, chopped
2 hard-cooked eggs
4 tbsp chopped pickles
¼ cup mayonnaise

Soften the gelatin in the cold water, then dissolve in the boiling water. Add the seasonings. Chill and, when almost at setting point, fold in the combined tongue, eggs, pickles, and mayonnaise. Turn into a previously wet mold, chill until firm, unmold, and garnish with any preferred salad green and serve with salad dressing. (Serves 6)

POTTED LAMB TONGUES

6 lamb tongues
2 cloves garlic
¼ tsp pepper
1 tsp salt
2 tbsp vinegar
2 tbsp olive oil
1 bay leaf
2 cups water
1 No. 2 can tomatoes
1 tbsp flour
2 tbsp cold water
6 pitted olives, sliced

Wipe the tongue with a damp cloth, rub with the garlic, pepper, and salt. Place in a heavy saucepan with the vinegar, oil, bay leaf, and water, and simmer until the tongue is tender and beginning to peel. Remove from the saucepan and skin. Return to the pan, add the tomatoes and simmer for 1 hour. Serve on a hot platter, pouring over the sauce thickened with the flour rubbed smoothly with the cold water and with the olives added at the last moment. (Serves 6)

SMOKED BEEF TONGUE CASSEROLE

1 smoked beef tongue, about 3 lb
1 tsp salt
¼ tsp pepper
2 cloves
1 bay leaf
2 tbsp butter
2 tbsp flour
2 cups tongue broth
1 cup diced carrots
1 cup diced turnips
1 cup diced celery
1 cup cooked peas

Wash the tongue, soak for several hours in cold water, then simmer for 3 hours with the seasonings in boiling water to cover. Drain, reserving 2 cups of the liquor. Remove the skin and trim. Place the tongue in a casserole, making a sauce of the butter, flour and tongue broth. Arrange the vegetables around the meat in the casserole, pour the sauce over all, cover and bake in a moderate oven (350° F.) about ¾ hour or until the vegetables are tender. Serve with a green salad. (Serves 6)

SMOKED BEEF TONGUE IN PRUNE JUICE

1 smoked tongue, 3½ to 4 lb
Boiling water
1½ cups prune juice

Wash the tongue, soak in cold water for several hours, then place in a saucepan, cover with boiling water and simmer about 3½ hours or until tender. Remove from the fire and let the tongue stand in the liquor until cool. Skin, trim, and place tongue in a covered baking dish. Add the prune juice. Cover and cook in a moderate oven (350° F.) about 45 minutes, turning once during the baking. Fresh tongue may be similarly prepared, if desired. (Serves 6)

SMOKED BEEF TONGUE WITH RAISIN SAUCE

1 smoked tongue, 3 or 4 lb
1 bay leaf

1 onion
3 or 4 cloves
3 or 4 slices lemon
Raisin sauce

Wash the tongue, soak in cold water for several hours, place in a deep kettle with the bay leaf, onion, cloves, and lemon. Add water to cover and simmer about 3 hours or until tender. Skin and trim. Have ready raisin sauce (*which see*), reheat in this and serve very hot. (Serves 6)

SPICED VEAL TONGUE

2 veal tongues, about 2 lb each
3 whole peppercorns
6 whole cloves
2 tsp salt
2 bay leaves
1 tbsp vinegar

Wash the tongues thoroughly, then simmer in water to cover about 1 hour. Add the peppercorns, cloves, salt, bay leaves, and vinegar. Cover and continue cooking until tender, about 2 hours. Remove skin and trim the tongues. Cool in the broth. Serve sliced, garnishing with stuffed tomatoes, quartered hard-cooked eggs and any preferred salad green. (Serves 6)

SWEET-SOUR FRESH BEEF TONGUE

1 medium-sized fresh beef tongue
Water
4 or 5 slices bacon, chopped
3 medium-sized onions, chopped
1 small bay leaf
Rind of 1 lemon
3 peppercorns
1 qt tongue stock, strained
1 tbsp vinegar
1 tbsp sugar
2½ cups rolled gingersnaps
6 prunes, cooked and sieved
½ cup raisins
½ cup sliced blanched almonds

Wash the tongue and simmer in water to cover until tender, about 3 hours. Skin and trim. Prepare a sauce by frying the bacon and onion together in a heavy pan, then adding the bay leaf, lemon, peppercorns, tongue stock, vinegar, sugar, gingersnaps and sieved cooked prunes. Simmer for 15 minutes, strain, add the raisins and almonds. Slice the tongue and reheat it in the sauce. (Serves 6)

To Salt Fresh Beef Tongue

1 fresh tongue
Salt and saltpeter
1 large bay leaf
6 sprigs parsley
Pinch of thyme
2 whole cloves, bruised
1 tsp brown sugar

Make an incision about ½ inch deep and 2½ inches long under the heavy part of a fresh tongue. Make several similar incisions superficially on both sides. Rub the tongue well with salt mixed with 1/10 its volume of saltpeter; then place it in a flat-bottomed container with all remaining ingredients. Cover with a further thin layer of salt, then with a small board to weight it down. Turn the tongue over every day for approximately a week. If left beyond this time the meat will deteriorate. (If the tongue remains in the brine more than 4 days it should be soaked several hours in cold water before using.)

Veal, lamb, and sheep's tongues may also be salted at home in the same manner. Veal tongue should not remain in the brine for longer than 5 days; 3 days is the maximum time for lamb and sheep's tongue. Fresh tongue is always much improved by preliminary salting, afterwards being boiled, braised, or steamed.

TONKA BEANS or **Tonqua Beans.** These are also called *Coumara nuts.* They are dark, aromatic seeds produced by a tall tropical South American tree, having an essential oil known as *Coumarin* or *Coumarine*, called *Coumarouna* in Brazil. This essential oil is a white substance found in small crystals coating the lobes. On account of the similarity in aroma, tonka beans and the oil are often employed in the manufacture of imitation vanilla extract, although they are heavier and coarser in flavor than vanilla beans.

TOPPEN CHEESE. A sour milk cheese, produced in Germany, made from skim milk. It comes in small packages weighing about an ounce.

TOPPING. The term is applied to the ingredients sprinkled or poured over a food, as a topping for a baked cake or bun.

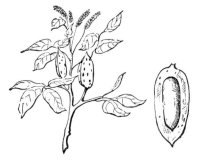

TONKA BEAN

TORPEDO SKATE. *See* Skate.

TORRE GIULIA. One of the better Italian white table wines (*see* Wines). It is dry, full-bodied, and fragrant.

TORTE. A dessert of the meringue or cake type, usually rich in eggs and nuts.

Blitz Torte

½ cup butter
1¼ cups sugar
4 eggs
1 tsp vanilla
1 cup sifted pastry flour
1 tsp baking powder
3 tbsp milk
½ cup chopped or sliced, blanched almonds

Cream the shortening with ½ the sugar. Add the beaten egg yolks and vanilla, then the flour sifted with the baking powder alternately with the milk. Spread the mixture in 2 round, shallow, greased baking pans. Top with a meringue made by beating the egg whites until very stiff, gradually adding the remaining sugar. Sprinkle this with the almonds and bake in a moderate oven (350° F.) about 30 minutes. When cool put together with custard filling flavored with orange or lemon.

Schaum Torte

6 egg whites
2 cups sugar
1 tbsp vinegar
1 tbsp vanilla

Beat the egg whites until stiff, add the sugar gradually, then the vinegar and vanilla, still beating constantly. Bake in 2 greased spring forms in a very slow oven (275°–300° F.) 45 to 60 minutes. Put together with sweetened whipped cream into which berries have been stirred, or omit the berries and reinforce the cream with a few tablespoons of rich jam.

VIENNA TORTE

Here's the answer to your dessert problem when you want something really delicious. The foundation is a simple butter sponge cake (*which see*) baked in 3 layers. For the filling you will need:

2¼ cups milk
½ cup sugar
½ cup flour
½ lb sweet butter
1¼ cups confectioners' sugar
Almond or vanilla extract
5 tsp cocoa

Scald 2 cups of the milk in a double boiler. Add the sugar and flour blended and moistened with the remaining milk. Cook until quite thick, stirring constantly both during cooking and cooling to prevent lumpiness. Add the butter and confectioners' sugar creamed together, with the flavoring. Reserve 2 cups of this mixture and to the remainder add the sifted cocoa, blending it in smoothly. Use this as a filling, spreading it between the layers of sponge cake. Frost top and sides with the plain mixture.

TORTILLAS. Tortillas are the form of bread used by the Mexican people. In Texas, they are in great favor. They are made from corn or maize and nothing else, but their palatability depends upon the way they are handled in the making. The corn should be white, and is soaked with enough lime to soften the hull. This takes from five to six weeks. It is then thoroughly washed in clear water and drained. Next it is ground, forming a clear paste like putty. This is called *masa* and can be purchased at any Spanish or Italian food store.

To make tortillas, place a lump of *masa* on a flat grinding stone, and rub it back and forth with a rolling pin until it becomes pliable and somewhat fluffy. A small piece the size of an egg is taken between the hands and patted back and forth until it is as thin as pie crust. It is then laid on a hot iron, usually heated by charcoal, and baked.

TOSS. In cookery, tossing refers to the mixing of ingredients, especially those of a salad. It is done by lifting the ingredients repeatedly and allowing them to fall lightly. This is usually done with a fork, although a spoon and a fork are sometimes used together.

TOUAREG CHEESE. A rennet cheese, made from skimmed milk by the Berber tribes, from the Barbary States to Lake Tohad, in Africa.

TRAGACANTH. *See* GUM TRAGACANTH.

TRAPPIST CHEESE. A pale, soft, yellow cheese with a milk taste. It is made by Trappist monks in the monasteries.

TRAVANCORE. A variety of Black teas grown in South India. Although the teas of this variety are of good strength and flavor, they are not as distinguished as the finer teas of North India. Their chief value is as blenders.

TRAVNICKI CHEESE. A soft, eyeless, rennet cheese, made from the whole milk of sheep. Made in Yugoslavia.

TREACLE. *See* MOLASSES.

TREPANG. A Chinese delicacy. Also an East Indian fish delicacy.

TREPANG

TRICHINA SPIRALIS. A parasitic worm found in meat insufficiently cooked and causing the frequently fatal disease commonly known as trichinosis. It is common in pork and pork products and is easily transmitted from those sources to the muscle tissues of human beings.

Although there is no known means of ridding the system of the worms when once they have lodged in the body for a few days, they can be prevented from gaining entry by simply cooking thoroughly all pork and pork products before even tasting them. Large pieces of pork must be cooked long enough to be sure that the center is thoroughly done. Smoking does not destroy the worm in bacon and ham, and, with sausage, these meats are always a possible source of infection unless subjected to heat. It must be remembered that hamburger, too, may be prepared with pork;

unless the homemaker knows positively that her ground beef contains no pork she will be doing herself and family a favor by serving the meat well done. *See also* PORK.

TRIFLE. An English dessert simply made, but rather expensive. It may be a ceremonial dessert or may be made simply with almost any kind of fresh or canned fruit, arranged over cookies or pieces of cake. The real and original trifle, as still made in England, is made as follows:

Line a silver or crystal bowl with uniform slices of sponge cake, and make an ornamental border of split lady fingers. Within that border arrange another of macaroons, spaced carefully with some attention to design. Spread with 1 cup of rich preserves—apricot, quince, peach, strawberry or raspberry. Pour slowly over all 1 cup of good sherry or Madeira and let stand until the cake has absorbed this. Make a standard boiled custard of 6 egg yolks with ⅓ cup sugar, 3 cups of scalded milk, and the grated rind of ½ medium-sized lemon. When cool, add 1 teaspoon of vanilla and 1 small glass of brandy. Turn carefully over the preserves, and chill.

The pyramid within the bowl is completed with a carefully arranged pinnacle of sweetened whipped cream, and the trifle is done, except for the garnishing. Crisp bright angelica may be cut in fancy forms to give flashes of emerald in contrast with the ruby of candied cherries. All around the border, among the lady fingers and macaroons, should be slender Jordan almonds, blanched, and some jewels of cubed apricot jelly, glacé Malaga grapes, and a few more candied cherries.

This, however plain or elaborate you may care to make it, will be a typical English trifle but there are, as already said, hundreds of recipes and you can always make up your own. Fine cordials may enter into the flavoring, and color schemes may be lively or subdued. Fresh strawberries, drenched with kirsch, may take the place of jam, and in the season of ripe peaches, the very thinly sliced fresh fruit should be piled on the custard, and flavored with a jigger of Noyau Cordial and a dash of fine peach brandy.

TRIPE. Tripe, like certain alluring vices, is enjoyed by society's two extremes, the topmost and the lowermost strata, while the multitudinous middle classes of the world look upon it with genteel disdain and noses tilted. Patricians relished tripe in Babylon's gardens, plebeians have always welcomed it as something good and cheap, and always the peasant cook has taught the prince how to eat it.

No one can tell logically why so many persons despise the clean, white tissue of a steer's stomach that is called tripe, but some almost shudder at the word. Yet the same squeamish ones devour "hot dogs" in their cases, and other mysterious compounds of gland tissue and organic bodies, with gusto. There is, however, a dish which ranks with the distinguished viands of the world, and it is celebrated as Tripe à la Mode de Caen. Its preparation is a matter of arduous labor and infinite pains, and one burns the midnight gas in the long process, but joy and the triumph of art come in the morning!

TRIPE A LA MODE DE CAEN
(Original Recipe)

Start with 3 pounds of fresh, honeycomb tripe, and wash it well in 2 or 3 changes of cold water. Drain, and cut it neatly into strips about as long and as wide as a man's thumb. Use a large casserole or a huge bean pot—a metal Dutch oven with a tight cover will do, if you have no earthen pot— and line the bottom of it with thin slices of fat salt pork. Next, put in 2 diced carrots, 2 sliced onions, 2 leeks, and 2 celery stalks, minced rather finely, with a large green pepper. On this vegetable layer arrange the strips of tripe, and add 2 calf's feet, cut into small pieces, using both meat and bones. Season with a tablespoon of minced parsley, generous pinches of thyme and marjoram, 1 piece of mace, 2 bay leaves, 6 whole peppercorns, gently bruised, 2 whole cloves, and 1 teaspoon of salt.

All this should nearly fill the pot. Cover the mixture with equal parts of rich soup stock and white wine or cider. The next step is the magical secret of the dish, developed through the ages in Norman kitchens. Mix a very stiff, plain dough of flour and water, and roll it quickly into a thick rope as long as the circumference of your pot cover. Arrange it carefully around the rim of the pot, moisten it with water, and fit the cover upon it, pressing it down firmly. If there are ventilating holes in the cover, seal them with bits of dough. Thus the pot is hermetically sealed, and neither juices nor aromas can escape.

Let the oven be as slow as you can make it. Bake the dish overnight, without disturbing it under any circumstances. 12 hours will do a pretty good job, but distinguished authorities advocate from 12 to 18 hours. When you break the seal and lift the lid, Olympian vapors will assail your nostrils, and you will behold ambrosia richer than ragouts of green turtle or of terrapin. A final step remains. Add 6 finely minced shallots, cooked lightly in butter, 1 cup of strained tomato paste, and 1 glass of sherry. Serve in the casserole, or on a deep platter which should be sizzling hot. Garnish with puff paste croutons and parsley. Some French chefs prefer cognac or calvados, to sherry, but that is for you to decide.

FRIED PICKLED TRIPE

Cut pickled tripe in pieces for serving. Wash carefully and cover with boiling water. Simmer gently for 20 minutes. Drain, cover with equal parts of milk and water and bring to boiling point. Drain, dry on a cloth, sprinkle with salt and pepper and brush with melted butter. Dip in fritter batter, and fry in deep hot fat until delicately browned. Drain on soft crumpled paper.

For the fritter batter: sift ½ cup of flour, ¼ teaspoon of salt and a few grains of pepper. Gradually add ⅓ cup of milk, beaten with 1 egg yolk, ½ tablespoon of melted butter or shortening, and 1 stiffly beaten egg white.

TRIPE CREOLE

2 lb fresh honeycomb tripe
Slices of salt pork (about ½ lb)
1 whole carrot
1 whole stalk celery
1 whole clove garlic
1 tbsp minced parsley
1 onion
3 whole cloves
1 bay leaf
1 sprig thyme
2 pig's feet
Salt, pepper, and cayenne
1 wine glass cognac
Flour

Cover the tripe with salted water, bring to the boiling point, drain, cover with fresh, boiling, salted water, cook for 15 minutes and drain again. Line an earthenware pot with slices of salt pork, fill with the tripe (cubed) in layers alternating with the vegetables and herbs, and seasoning with salt and cayenne. Lay the pig's feet, which have been cut in two lengthwise, on top of all, season with salt and pepper, and place a slice of salt pork on top. Pour the cognac over all and put on a close-fitting lid, sealing it with flour paste. Cook in a moderate oven (350° F.) for 5 hours. Unseal, remove the celery, carrot, and garlic, and serve very hot from the cooking pot. (Serves 8)

TRIPE AND ONION STEW

2 lb honeycomb tripe
Boiling water
1 sprig parsley
1 sliced carrot
1 small bay leaf
Few celery leaves
6 peppercorns
1 clove
20 small white onions
3 cups cream sauce
⅓ cup tripe stock

Wash the tripe thoroughly; then cut into 1½-inch squares. Cover with boiling water, add the parsley, carrot, bay leaf, celery, peppercorns and clove. Cover and simmer very gently until tender, about 3 hours. Meanwhile peel the onions, cover with boiling salted water and cook until tender, about 20 minutes. Prepare a cream sauce and flavor it with the tripe stock. Transfer the tripe and onions to the cream sauce, bring all to boiling point and serve immediately. (Serves 6)

TRIPLE AURORE CHEESE. A French cheese made in Normandy.

TRIPLE-SEC. A type of curacao (*which see*) liqueur, sold uncolored, usually in squarish flagons.

TRIVET. A trivet is a dish or support, usually made of metal and quite ornate, with short legs, used to hold hot pans or dishes on the table. It is often supplied with a matching pan that can be used as a cooking utensil.

TROCKENKASE CHEESE. Another name for dry cheese, *which see*.

TROO CHEESE. A French cheese made in Touraine.

TROTTERS. The feet of calves, pigs, sheep, etc., used for food.

TROUT. This most completely toothed of all fish belongs to the *Salmonidae* family. The jaws of the lake trout are nearly equal, the mouth is wide and large with a pointed snout, the head rather small, the body elongated and the back thick and rounded.

The sea trout has sides sprinkled with small crescent-shaped spots on a silvered base. Its flesh is of a yellowish-orange color, resembling that of the salmon to which it may be compared as regards delicacy, hence its name salmon trout.

The brook trout, always caught in clear, running brooks, is considered superior to the two varieties mentioned above. Its flesh is snow white, it has brown spots on its back, and red spots outlined with shadowy circles, on the sides. This fish seldom reaches seven inches in length, although some have been caught measuring nearly a foot.

The most important specimens of lake trout, the largest of the three varieties mentioned, are to be found in Lakes Huron, Michigan, and Superior, but splendid specimens are also found in many other lakes throughout the United States.

About forty-five years ago, a new trout was brought into this country by a European. This, the brown trout, is one of the hardiest and most adaptable of our freshwater fish. The brown trout grows to an immense size and is a fairly satisfactory game fish, making itself at home in ponds as well as in rivers and small streams.

Sea trout, commonly known as weakfish, is a delectable seafood, plentiful at low cost during most of the year. They are taken in southern waters and are very similar to our weakfish, except that they have purplish spots along their sides. They are good fighters.

New to our markets also are smoked rainbow trout which have spent two or more years in spring-fed pools and tumbling mountain streams in Colorado. Fed upon ground shrimp from Louisiana, and salmon eggs from Seattle, they have all of the flavor of wild trout. These rainbows are smoked by a secret process and emerge from the smoke house with a definite smokiness, but less pronounced than that of finnan haddie or of smoked butterfish. They are prepared like finnan haddie, *which see.*

Trout are in season and on the markets from April to August, although many are found there much later. (*See also* FISH.) The chemical composition of an edible portion of sea trout is similar to that of the salmon, and that of the brook trout is as follows:

Water	77.6	percent
Protein	19.2	
Fat	2.1	
Total carbohydrates	none	
Ash	1.1	
	———	
Total	100.00	percent
Fuel value per pound (calories)		445
Vitamins		A & B

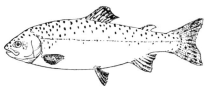

TROUT

From the culinary point of view, trout may be divided into two distinct classes: the large and the small. The large ones are the salmon trout and the sea trout; the small, the brook trout and the lake trout.

Trout, the queen of lakes, rivers and sea, may be dressed in an endless variety of ways and with a variety of sauces. Truite Chambord, which is marinated in old Sauterne, is smartly dressed with sweetbreads and adorned with crayfish; Trout à la Hussarde is first bathed in a highly seasoned sauce, then lightly grilled.

The various methods, garnishings, and sauces employed in the preparation of salmon, hot or cold, may be adapted to the Salmon Trout; however, being an exiguous fish, the Salmon Trout may be sliced but rarely is. As a general rule it is served whole or filleted.

BOILED LAKE TROUT AU BLEU

2 lake trout, 2 lb each
Vinegar court-bouillon
Parsley
Lemon
Boiled potato balls
Hollandaise sauce

Wipe the trout, then plunge quickly into boiling court-bouillon (*which see*). Simmer very gently 15 to 20 minutes. Arrange on a hot platter, surrounding the fish with a wreath of parsley, quartered lemon and plain boiled potato balls. Serve with hollandaise sauce and a green salad. (Serves 4 to 6)

BRAISED SALMON TROUT PARISIENNE

1 salmon trout, about 3 lb
Salt, peppercorns, and nutmeg
Larding pork
White wine
1 tsp raw mushrooms, chopped
2 tbsp thick tomato purée
3 tbsp fresh cream, scalded
2 tbsp sweet butter
Lemon and parsley

Clean, wipe and trim the fish, rub with the salt, crushed peppercorns and nutmeg. Wrap in thin slices of larding pork, place in a well-buttered baking dish with white wine almost to cover. Add the mushrooms and cover with buttered paper. Bake in a moderate oven (350° F.) 25 to 30 minutes, basting occasionally. Remove the paper and cook the fish 5 minutes longer, basting again during this period. Serve on a hot platter with a sauce made by adding to the liquid in the baking dish, the tomato purée and cream. Simmer 5 minutes, add the butter and additional seasonings, if necessary. Pour a little of the sauce over the fish, garnish with quartered lemon and parsley, and serve the remaining sauce separately, with plain boiled potatoes. (Serves 4)

BROILED FILLET OF SEA TROUT

3 sea trout, 1½ lb each
Lemon juice
Salt and pepper
Butter
Lemon and parsley

Have the fish carefully filleted. Wash, pat dry, then rub with the lemon juice, salt and pepper, and brush generously with melted butter. Broil, turning and basting frequently with additional butter. Cover with brown butter sauce, garnish with quartered lemon and parsley, and serve with plain boiled potatoes. (Serves 4)

TROUVILLE CHEESE. A soft, rennet cheese, made from fresh, whole milk, in France. It is of the same nature as Pont l' Evêque, of the same region, but of superior quality.

TROYES CHEESE. A French cheese made in Touraine. Two kinds of cheese are referred to by this name, one a washed cheese with a yellow rind known as Ervy, and the other, resembling Camembert, known as Barbery.

TRUCKLES CHEESE. Two English cheeses have this name. One is a full-cream Cheddar made in the western part of England. The other is a blue veiny cheese similar to Blue Vinny, made in Wiltshire.

TRUFFLE. Superstitious Romans thought that truffles were sown by thunderbolts in autumn storms. And there is a pretty French legend about truffles which follows:

In the 15th century, a French peasant offered to share his frugal meal of potatoes with a starving woman, who turned them into delicious truffles. The guest's rather cavalier treatment of the fare provided by her host was forgiven when the peasant discovered his land was covered with truffles. The peasant and his family quickly grew rich—so rich that when their guest returned, they haughtily turned her from the door. In the twinkling of an eye, they were turned into pigs and had to burrow for their truffles thereafter.

TRUFFLE

The truffle is a fleshy, underground fungus, much esteemed as a table delicacy. The most famous species is the Perigord. It varies in size from that of a walnut to a lemon, is generally round in shape and black or brown in color. It has a rough, warty exterior. A truffle hunt is a picturesque expedition and has remained so for centuries. Pigs are cleverer than men at locating ripe truffles, so farmers follow their trained truffle-hunting pigs from tree to tree and relieve the luckless porkers of their booty at the crucial moment. In some regions of France dogs have been trained to replace the pigs. Rather inferior types of truffles are found in England, Germany, Spain, and California.

The delicate flavor of the black truffle is often conserved by cooking for an hour over a slow fire with lard, thyme, bay leaves, salt, and pepper. The truffle so prepared is then sliced into flat disks for garnishings and sauces, diced for inserting into pieces of meat, pate de foie gras or terrine, or left whole or minced for dressing for fowl or game.

The canned product is by no means to be despised. It is often used in the preparation of grand dinners, and is decidedly reminiscent of the Thackeray quotation: ". . . Presently, we were aware of an odour gradually coming towards us, something musky, fiery, savoury, mysterious—a hot, drousy smell, that lulls the senses, and yet enflames them—the truffles were coming . . ."

TRUSS. To fasten a fowl with skewers or twine before cooking. *See also* CHICKEN.

TRY. To brown small cubes of pork, bacon, or the like in a skillet, over a very low flame, stirring frequently. The purpose of this process is to extract as much as possible of the fat to be used for cooking purposes. The remaining cubes, if it is pork, bacon, suet, or kidney fat, are called cracklings and may be used to season peas, lentils, legumes in general, or soups.

TSCHIL CHEESE. A cheese made in Armenia from the skim milk of cows or sheep. It is also known as Leaf, Telpanier, and Zwirn.

TUBE PAN. *See* CAKE PAN.

TUMBLER. *See* GLASSWARE.

TUNA CHEESE. A confection rather than a cheese, it is made from the fruit of the *Tuna cardona* or *Tuna pachona*. It has a chocolate color and a pleasant taste.

TUNA FISH. The Tuna fish belongs to the *scomberoidae* family. It is distinguished from the mackerel by a corselet made of scales softer and much smaller than those of the mackerel. The common tuna fish is of a bluish-black color on the back, and grayish with silver dots on the stomach. Specimens are sometimes three feet in length, and some tuna have been caught that weighed a thousand pounds.

Tuna fish travel in schools and spend the winter at the bottom of the ocean. When spring comes, they rise to the surface near the shore where there is warmer water, to spawn.

It is rather interesting the way fishermen catch tuna by the thousands in the spring. Two common methods are employed.

When a school of tuna is discovered near shore, several fishing boats, commanded by one individual, are maneuvered into a long curved line in the shape of a half moon with the ends toward shore. Nets are dropped into the sea so as to form an enclosure several miles long, and into this the fish are drawn by a tremendous noise made by the boat's crew at either end of the enclosure. The frightened tuna fish gather in the center of the enclosure, where there is no noise, but also no exit. At a signal from the commander of the fleet, the ends of the enclosure are moved toward shore and then along the shore until they meet. When surrounded the tuna are pulled onto the boats by nets.

Another method of catching a shoal of tuna fish is to string nets to form several alleys toward shore. Then boats dragging vertical nets move up the alleys toward shore sweeping the fish before them and trapping them.

The four varieties of tuna used for canning are the Albacore tuna, the yellow fin, the blue fin, and the striped tuna. They vary in color, and the flesh may be white, pink, or darkish tan. Fresh tuna and canned tuna contain the same food elements. Tuna fish contains about 11 percent fat in easily digested form. This substance provides the body with heat and energy. Maine fishermen call the type of tuna which they catch horse mackerel and insist that the flavor is more like that of pork or veal than the usual fish. Epicures consider tuna of lighter color more delicate in flavor, and for this reason this finest is called chicken of the sea.

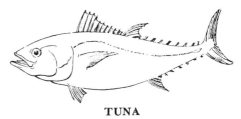

TUNA

The flesh of this popular fish resembles veal in flavor and texture, and the flesh over the stomach is still more delicate. Its chemical composition is similar to that of the salmon.

The tuna fish may be salted, preserved in oil, or cooked in its fresh state. Tuna should always be well washed, if necessary using a hard brush to remove the blood which sometimes accumulates on the surface of the fish. *See also* FISH.

BAKED TUNA CASSEROLE

4 tbsp butter
4 tbsp flour
¾ tsp salt
Pepper
½ tsp Worcestershire sauce
2 cups milk
2 pimientoes
1 (13 oz) can tuna fish
¼ cup buttered crumbs

Prepare a white sauce with the butter, flour, seasonings, Worcestershire sauce, and milk. Cut 6 strips of the pimiento and set aside as a garnish. Dice the remaining pimiento and add to the sauce with the fish, carefully picked over. Turn into a greased baking dish, top with the buttered crumbs, and bake in a moderate oven (350° F.) about 20 minutes. Garnish with the reserved pimiento strips. (Serves 6)

BROILED TUNA WITH LIME BUTTER

3 lb fresh tuna
2 tsp salt
½ tsp paprika
⅓ cup lime juice
½ cup melted butter
⅓ cup hot water

Have the tuna in slices about 1 inch thick. Wipe carefully, sprinkle with the salt and paprika and broil, turning once, until tender and evenly browned, basting while cooking with the lime juice, melted butter and hot water. (Serves 6)

TUNA CROQUETTES

4 cups flaked canned tuna
Boiling water
2 cups thick white sauce
2 tbsp minced parsley
½ tsp salt
¼ tsp cayenne
1 tbsp lemon juice
Potato-chip crumbs
1 egg
1 tbsp water

Pour boiling water over the fish in a colander to eliminate fishy taste. Drain thoroughly, combine with the white sauce and seasonings and chill. Form into croquettes, roll in finely crushed potato chips, dip in the egg, beaten with the water, and again roll in the chip crumbs. If possible chill for 1 hour. Fry, a few at a time, in deep hot fat (375° F.) until golden brown. Drain on soft crumpled paper. (Serves 6)

TUNA AU GRATIN

1 large can tuna fish
1½ cups cream sauce
1 cup grated cheese
1 tsp paprika
¼ cup buttered crumbs

Arrange the fish in a casserole and pour over it the sauce to which the grated cheese and paprika have been added. Top with the crumbs and bake in a hot oven (400° F.) about 30 minutes. (Serves 6)

TUNA A LA KING

2 cups white sauce
1 cup or 1 small can flaked tuna
¼ cup chopped, cooked or canned mushrooms
1 chopped hard-cooked egg
1 tbsp chopped pimiento
Salt, pepper, and paprika
1 tbsp lemon juice

Combine all ingredients, heat thoroughly and serve. If using fresh mushrooms, these should be sautéed for 10 minutes in a little butter before adding to the sauce. (Serves 6)

TURBOT. In bygone days a large turbot was the traditional dish at a festivity or family reunion, especially during the Lenten period. After careful preparation it was served with due ceremony on a long porcelain dish garnished with a lace-like necklace of green curled parsley; first slightly moistened, then dipped in paprika. This simple adornment, through the contrast of colors to the whiteness of the flesh of the fish, accentuated and enhanced its beauty.

The turbot, frequently called halibut in America, has a body of almost square proportions, which is roughcast on the left side. The turbot found near rocky shores is much superior in flavor to those which inhabit muddy shores.

Large turbots are usually boiled in a milk or cream court-bouillon (*which see*) and are dressed on a platter covered with a napkin, the garnishings being a crisp bunch of green parsley and slices of lemon. Just before serving, after the skin is removed, it is advisable to brush the fish with melted butter to give it more brilliancy and appetizing appearance.

Before you start to cook it, to prevent disfigurement of the fish, both sides should be slashed slightly to permit the breaking of the collar bone. This also hastens cooking.

The liquid containing the fish should be brought slowly and gradually to a boil, and then the heat immediately reduced so that it will only simmer gently and thus ensure uniform and thorough cooking. That is very important to the success of the dish, and also to prevent indigestion caused by insufficiently cooked fish. Those same directions also apply to slices of fish cooked in the same way.

Invariably, the usual accompaniment of boiled hot turbot, whole or in slices, is plain boiled potatoes, and the most appropriate sauces are those indicated for boiled salmon, *which see.*

The turbot, being a gelatinous fish, should not be boiled too long in advance when served cold, especially if in slices, as it may become tough, shrink, and the flavor may be greatly impaired. The usual sauces for cold turbot are the same as for cold salmon. For large turbot, the various methods of preparation of boiled, braised, or grilled salmon may be used.

Small and medium-sized turbot may be braised, but the ingredients should be prepared in advance, cooled, and then added to the fish, which should be basted frequently to ensure tenderness and uniform flavor.

Turbot is in season January to March.

BOILED TURBOT

3 to 4 lb piece turbot
White wine court-bouillon
Melted butter
Lemon and parsley

Wipe the fish thoroughly, place in a fish kettle, cover with court-bouillon (*which see*), bring to boiling point, and simmer

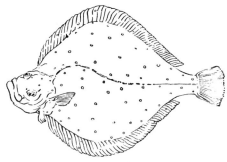

TURBOT

gently for 25 minutes. Drain, and remove the skin. Brush the fish over with melted butter, garnish with quartered lemon and parsley, and serve with plain boiled potato balls, hollandaise sauce, and cucumber salad with French dressing. (Serves 6)

GRILLED TURBOT, LOBSTER SAUCE

6 slices turbot (7 to 8 oz each)
Salt and pepper
Oil or melted butter
Lemon and parsley
Lobster sauce

Wipe and pat the fish dry. Season, brush with oil or melted butter, place on a double broiler, set this on a rack in the broiling oven and cook very slowly, turning and basting frequently with oil or melted butter. Serve very hot, garnishing with quartered lemon and parsley, and serving also French fried potatoes, cucumber salad with French dressing, and lobster sauce (*which see*) separately. (Serves 6)

TURBOT SOUFFLE

4 cups freshly poached turbot
Few mussels
Few oysters
Cooked mushrooms and truffles
2 tbsp hot, thick béchamel sauce
Salt and pepper
3 egg yolks
4 egg whites

Finely pound the turbot, mussels, oysters, cooked mushrooms, and truffles. Add, little by little, the béchamel sauce *which see.* When very smooth, season, place in a saucepan and add the beaten egg yolks. Finally fold in the stiffly beaten egg whites. Turn into a buttered soufflé dish, and bake in a moderate oven (350° F.) for 30 minutes. (Serves 6)

TUREEN. A large vessel, usually covered and made of a ceramic material, that is used to hold soup at the table. Similar vessels, in smaller sizes, are sometimes used to hold gravies, sauces, etc. The liquid must be ladled from the tureen, for the vessel is not designed for pouring use. *See* DISHES.

TURKEY. Turkey is obtainable all year round, but is best from late fall until the beginning of spring. The skin should be dry, firm, but tender. Dark, dull color of skin and flesh usually indicates improper bleeding or a bird none too fresh, Choose a well-fleshed, plump turkey with a well-distributed coating of fat, rather than one having hard fat deposits such as result from hurriedly fattening range turkeys just prior to killing.

Always seek a straight, long breast bone, because the longer the keel or breast bone, the more white meat it carries. Turkey furnishes a larger proportion of choice white meat than any other kind of poultry. The tips of the pelvic bones should also be well covered with fat, with the breast bone and back both straight and level. Avoid birds with bluish coloring around the tail and the rear portion of the back.

As to size, allow from three-fourths to one pound of turkey, as purchased, for each person to be served. As purchased means with head and feet on and not drawn. Both hens and toms are good, the former having a deeper, wider breast, but there is no difference in meat quality. For an average family it is not advisable to buy the so-called most popular bronze turkey which is the largest breed unless one wishes to indulge in turkey for several meals. The standard weight of a young bronze turkey (tom) is around 25 pounds; that of a hen is about 15 pounds. A good "family" turkey weight is from 10 to 12 pounds.

TERMS USED FOR TURKEYS

1 *Young hens*—usually less than a year old, soft-meated and with flexible breast bone.

2 *Old hens*—mature, more than a year old, with toughened flesh, and hardened breast bone.

3 *Young toms*—same age, etc., as young hens.

4 *Old toms*—same age, etc., as old hens.

REMARKS

There is a vast difference in the flavor and weight of turkeys due to feeding. Minnesota and California grain-fed turkeys are popular.

In purchasing notice the fullness of the breast and under wings. A well developed bird yields more portions.

Old toms may be tough and dry. These are best gently simmered to tender them, before roasting

Turkey season: young birds from August to November; roasters from November to January; old birds, all year.

PREPARING AND ROASTING A TURKEY

Have the turkey drawn at the store. The butcher should slit the skin down the back of the neck from shoulder to the head; disjoint the neck at the shoulders, and remove it. The neck is usually cooked with the giblets to give a rich stock for the gravy. Singe the turkey, remove the pin feathers, wash thoroughly, inside and out, wipe dry, and sprinkle the inside with salt and pepper.

To stuff, fill the breast cavity with the selected stuffing, then fill the inside from the rear. Stuffing packed too tightly will burst the skin in cooking. Truss the bird with string to hold it in shape, folding the wings back on the skin of the neck, tieing legs and tail together. Brush with melted butter and place the trussed, stuffed turkey, breast side up, on a rack in an open roasting pan. If roasting French method, add the same ingredients as indicated for roasting a fowl, *which see*. If using the American method, do not add any liquid or vegetables. Roast in a moderate oven (325°–350° F.) until the turkey is tender, keeping the same temperature steadily through the roasting process. Baste frequently, if not using the French method, with melted butter and pan drippings; if using the French method, use the liquid in the pan.

Allow 20 minutes per pound for 8 to 12 pound birds, and 15 minutes per pound for 12 to 16 pound birds. Use undrawn weight to figure the time. Salt and pepper the bird before roasting, or during the last

30 minutes of cooking (American method). For gravy *see* GRAVY.

ROASTING A HALF TURKEY

1. Follow the same steps in preparing a half turkey as you would for a whole bird. Lace up the gash made by drawing so as to form a cavity to hold the stuffing. Tie the end of the leg to the tail. Dip double-thick cheesecloth in melted fat and wrap around the tail end. Tie the wing to the breast. Put one or two tablespoons of the stuffing selected into the neck (do not fill too full) and then pull the neck skin over the stuffing. Next stuff the cavity and securely tie a sheet of parchment paper over the cavity with about four cords passing completely around the bird. Put, parchment down, on a rack in an open roaster and brush with melted fat. Dip cloth in melted fat and cover bird completely. Roast in a slow oven (300° F.), allowing 20 to 25 minutes per pound. Baste every half hour. Remove the cloth cover for last 20 minutes, for browning.

2. Truss as directed above. Do not stuff. Place, skin side up, on rack in open roaster and cook in slow oven (300° F.) until well browned. Remove from the oven and fill the cavity with selected stuffing. Cover and securely tie parchment paper over the cavity as directed above. Replace the bird in the roaster, skin side down, and complete the cooking, allowing a total of 20 to 25 minutes per pound.

The following recipe for stuffing has been devised especially for use with half a turkey.

YORKSHIRE GOLDEN RAISIN BREAD STUFFING

1 qt golden seedless raisins
1½ qt hot water
4 eggs, beaten
1½ gal soft ½-inch bread cubes
¾ cup melted butter or margarine
2 tsp salt
2 tsp celery salt
¼ tsp pepper
1½ tbsp sage
1⅓ cups turkey or chicken bouillon

Soak the raisins in hot water for ten minutes; drain. Combine washed raisins, beaten eggs, soft bread cubes, butter, salt, celery salt, pepper and sage. Add turkey bouillon and mix well. Mound stuffing on greased double thickness of heavy waxed paper cut approximately the shape of the half turkey's cavity. When the turkey is half roasted, remove from oven and place paper with stuffing on rack. Replace partially roasted half turkey over the stuffing and continue roasting until done. Bake extra stuffing in a greased casserole for forty minutes. Cut in squares and place around edge of serving platter. Serve with each portion of turkey.

(Note: Extra stuffing will be needed because it is impossible to stuff the breast of the half turkey.)

Yield: 3 quarts stuffing.

BAKED TURKEY ROLL

2¼ cups minced roast turkey
2 tsp finely minced onion
2 cups turkey gravy
2 cups sifted flour
2 tsp baking powder
½ tsp salt
⅓ cup shortening
¾ cup milk

Put 1½ cups of the turkey into a bowl, add the onion and moisten slightly with a little of the gravy. Add seasoning if necessary. Prepare a baking powder biscuit dough with the flour, baking powder, salt, shortening and milk. Roll out about ½-inch thick, spread with the turkey mixture, almost to the edges. Roll up as for jelly roll. Place on a lightly greased baking pan and bake golden brown in a hot oven (400° F.) about 20 minutes. Heat the remaining turkey and gravy together and pass separately with cranberry sauce. Other left-over poultry may be similarly prepared. (Serves 6)

INDIVIDUAL TURKEY PIES

1 thick slice onion, finely minced
4 tbsp butter or other fat
4 tbsp flour
1 tsp salt
¼ tsp pepper
2 cups scalded milk
2 cups diced turkey
2 cups cooked or canned vegetables
Pastry

Cook the onion in the butter or fat for 2 minutes. Blend in the flour and seasonings, add the scalded milk gradually, and cook until thickened, stirring constantly. Add the turkey and the drained cooked or canned vegetables. (A combination of celery, carrots, peas, etc. is good with a few cooked, diced small potatoes, or canned mushroom buttons.) Turn into 6 individual casseroles, cover with pastry and bake in a very hot oven (450° F.) for 10 minutes, then reduce the heat to moderate (350° F.) and continue baking 15 to 20 minutes longer. (Serves 6)

TURKEY SOUFFLE

1 medium-sized onion, finely minced
3 tbsp butter
3 tbsp flour
¾ cup scalded milk
3 egg yolks, well beaten
Dash of cayenne or curry
½ tsp salt
⅛ tsp pepper
1 cup minced cooked turkey
3 egg whites, stiffly beaten

Cook the onion in the butter for 3 minutes without browning. Add the flour, then the milk and stir constantly until the sauce reaches boiling point. Add the egg yolks beaten with the seasonings and the minced turkey and cool. Finally fold in the stiffly beaten egg whites. Turn into a buttered souffle dish, set in a pan of hot water and bake in a moderate oven (350° F.) 40 minutes. Serve immediately. (Serves 4)

TURKISH PASTE. Turkish paste, also known as Turkish delight, is a gelatinous

TURK'S HEAD PAN

confection. It is prepared by adding gelatin to sweetened fruit juice and allowing the mixture to stand until it reaches a consistency suitable for cutting. Before serving, it is cut into squares and dusted with sugar.

TURK'S-HEAD PAN. A round cake pan with spiral-shaped indentations in the walls. There is a central tube that permits even heating. The pan is so named because it resembles, somewhat, a certain type of Oriental turban. *See* CAKE; *see also* KITCHEN EQUIPMENT.

TURMERIC. Turmeric is the rootstalk of an Oriental aromatic herb belonging to the ginger family. From the roots of the plant is derived a yellow powder having an appetizing gingerlike odor. This is used to color delicately tinted foods such as pastries, butter, cheese, and egg dishes, and it is used as well in pickles and condiments. In the East it is the most common base for curry powder. In the United States it is used to flavor mustard pickles and to extend mustard.

TURNER. A turner is an instrument designed for use in flipping over cooking foods and removing them from their pans, especially pancakes, fried eggs, hamburgers, and other easily broken foods. Turners usually have broad, thin, flat blades, and long, insulated handles. However, they are also made in specialized shapes for specific needs, perforations being common. *See also* KITCHEN EQUIPMENT and SPATULA.

TURNIP. A plant grown mainly for its roots, the turnip is related to the mustards and cabbages. There are many varieties of turnips, some used for human food, and some fit only for cattle. The white turnips are comparatively small globular roots with white flesh. The yellow turnip, or rutabaga, forms larger roots somewhat more elongated in shape and with yellow flesh. The green tops of young turnips are an interesting change from other greens.

HINTS ON BUYING

Turnips are marketed as the early and late crops. The early turnips, usually from local sources, are sold in bunches with the tops attached. These early turnips are much smaller than the later crop which is usually sold with the tops removed. Although most of the turnips available in the winter are the late crop, because of the variety of climate in the United States, new

FOOD VALUE

	Water	Food Energy	Protein	Fat	Carbohydrates	Calcium	Phosphorus	Iron	Vit. A Value	Thiamine	Riboflavin	Niacin	Ascorbic Acid
Roots	90.9	35	1.1	.2	7.1	40	34	.5	Trace	.06	.06	.5	28
Greens	89.5	37	2.9	.4	5.4	259	50	2.4	9540	.10	.56	.8	136

turnips will be found almost all year around.

Good quality turnips are smooth and firm with comparatively few fibrous roots at the base. If the turnips are bunched, the tops should be young and fresh and green. If they are yellowed or wilted, it may indicate that the turnips have been kept too long. These bunched turnips are not so mature and have not been dried as are the turnips stored for later marketing. Large overgrown turnips are likely to be woody, hollow, or strong in flavor. Good turnips are heavy for their size.

Turnip greens should be purchased as are other greens: the leaves should be crisp and tender and clean. Large coarse leaves are likely to be tough and stringy. Wilted leaves are not worth purchasing.

HINTS ON PREPARATION

White and yellow turnips are cooked in the same way. Turnips are one of the few vegetables which must be peeled before cooking. Scrub the turnips, peel them as thinly as possible, and cut in large pieces if they are to be mashed or into dice if they are to be creamed or prepared in similar fashion. Cook in a large quantity of boiling salted water, uncovered, until the turnips are tender. Young turnips will cook tender in 20 to 30 minutes; older roots will take longer. Drain the liquid off, mash the turnips, and season with salt, pepper, and butter or margarine.

The turnip is rather neglected as a vegetable in this country. It makes an admirable addition to stews and soups, having a characteristic of enhancing the flavor of the dish in which it is cooked while improving its own flavor. It may be served in fritters, in puddings, and pancakes, French fried, glazed, and in many casserole dishes. Try baking white turnips as you would potatoes. Or prepare them O'Brien, as for potatoes. Mashed turnip, sprinkled with grated cheese, and browned under the broiler, is a simple and delicious dish. Duck

TURNIP

cooked with white turnips is an epicure's delight.

FLUFFY MASHED TURNIPS

3 cups cooked mashed yellow or white turnips
Salt and pepper
3 eggs, separated

Season the turnips to taste with salt and pepper. Beat the egg whites until stiff, and the yolks until thick and lemon coloreb. Add the yolks to the turnips, mixing well, and then fold in the whites. Turn into a greased casserole and bake in a hot oven (400° F) until lightly browned. If a crusty surface is desired, sprinkle the top with a little brown sugar before baking. Serve very hot. (Serves 6)

GLAZED TURNIPS

Peel and cube yellow or white turnips and cook in boiling salted water until just tender. Drain well. Melt a little butter or margarine in a skillet and add the turnips. Cook a few minutes, stirring frequently. Sprinkle with a little sugar and continue cooking over a very low flame. Sprinkle with a little more sugar, cook a bit longer, and continue adding sugar and cooking until the turnips are nicely glazed. Serve at once.

TURNIP CASSEROLE

4 cups cooked diced yellow turnips
¾ cup cooking water

¾ cup evaporated milk
2 tbsp butter
1 cup coarse bread crumbs
½ cup grated American cheese
½ cup buttered bread crumbs

Cook the turnips in boiling salted water until just tender. Drain and reserve ¾ cup of the liquid. Mix this with the evaporated milk. Melt the butter and stir in the cup of coarse crumbs. Then stir in the grated cheese Gradually add the milk mixture, stirring constantly, until the sauce boils and thickens Add the diced turnip, mix well, and turn into a well greased casserole. Sprinkle with the buttered crumbs and bake in a moderate oven (375° F.) for 15 or 20 minutes, or until the top is nicely browned. Serve immediately. (Serves 6)

TURNIP CUSTARD

3 eggs
1½ cups grated raw turnip, white or yellow
3 cups milk, scalded
Salt, pepper, and nutmeg
1 tsp grated onion
1 tsp chopped parsley
1 tsp minced green pepper
3 tbsp melted butter or margarine

Beat the eggs slightly and stir in the grated turnip alternately with the scalded milk. Season to taste with salt, pepper, and nutmeg. Beat briskly until the mixture is foamy. Stir in the rest of the ingredients. Turn into a well greased baking dish, sprinkle the top with a little granulated sugar, and bake in a moderate oven (350° F.) for about 45 minutes, or until a knife inserted in the center comes out clean. Serve at once. (Serves 6)

TURNOVER. A small pastry, usually triangular, which may be filled with almost anything edible. They may be made large or small, used as a snack, a main dish, or a dessert, according to filling. The dough may be either short, or puff paste.

APPLE TURNOVER
(With Spice Pastry)

2 cups sifted flour
¼ tsp salt
1 tsp nutmeg
⅔ cup shortening

Ice water
Sliced apples
Sugar
Butter

Sift together the flour, salt, and nutmeg. Work in half the shortening thoroughly, then add the remaining shortening and chop in just enough to break up. Moisten with ice water using only enough to hold the mixture together. Chill, roll out thinly and cut into squares. On each portion pile sweetened sliced apples (or other fruit), dot with butter, and fold the remaining pastry over the apples. Moisten the edges and press together well to hold in the juice. Prick several times with a fork and bake about 25 minutes, having the oven hot (450° F.) for the first 10 minutes, then reducing to moderate (350° F.) for the remainder of the baking period.

APPLE SAUCE TURNOVERS

As many squares of pastry as desired, a spoonful of canned apple sauce for each square of pastry, and a dash of nutmeg Fold the pastry into triangles, crimp the edges, and bake in a very hot oven (450° F.) until brown.

TURTLE. The Green turtle and its numerous relatives among the edible turtles are the most highly esteemed as food; then come Terrapins, Snapping turtles, and other fresh water turtles.

Green turtles are not green. The name is derived from the color of its fat, used in making turtle soup The green turtle may attain a weight of 350 pounds. It is a vegetable-eating sea turtle which occasionally makes its way as far north as Long Island Sound. Its principal food is eelgrass. The eggs are buried in the sand along the shores of the islands of the South Atlantic. Female green turtles, some of which weigh 500 pounds or more, go ashore during moonlight nights from April to July and dig two-foot holes in the sand above the highwater mark. Into the hole they drop up to 250 eggs. They replace the sand and crawl back to the sea, leaving nature, through the heat of the sand, to hatch the eggs. The turtles are captured while ashore at night laying the eggs, or more often are taken in nets, and are transported alive to northern markets.

The terrapin is a fresh-water turtle, and feeds partly on vegetable food, but also devours fish and other aquatic animals. The family of the terrapin is represented in the United States by about 20 popular species. The word terrapin has no confined significance, but in America it is more commonly applied to the Diamond Back terrapin of gray color, with black markings, found in salt marshes from New York to Texas, its flesh being high in favor as a table delicacy.

The snapping turtle is a large freshwater turtle noted for its fierceness, with jaws so large and strong that it is often lifted from the ground by the object bitten. This turtle sometimes exceeds three feet in length, although at average age it is about half that size.

Several species of soft-shell turtles are widely regarded as delicious food. They seldom reach the large city markets, but are sold in the areas they frequent. Many other species of fresh-water turtles are used as food, as the Mississippi and common map turtles, the Pacific pond turtle, the Mobile turtle, the Suwannee turtle, the red-bellied and yellow-bellied turtles, the chicken turtle and Troost's turtle. Wood turtles and painted turtles also are eaten locally at times.

Turtles found in the markets range in weight from about four to twenty-five pounds, although they have been known to attain three times the latter weight, and even more. The smaller turtles are more tender and are preferred for food.

PREPARATION

In order to soften and dissolve the foreign matter attached to the flesh and shell, place the live turtle in a pan containing sufficient water to allow it to swim easily. Renew the water several times and allow the turtle to remain thus for about an hour.

Remove the animal from the water and place it on its back on a stout board or chopping block. Stand by quietly with a sharp axe or cleaver poised above the block in the area immediately in front of the shell. In a few moments the turtle will extend its head in an effort to right itself. Do not move until the head is fully out of the shell. Then, with one quick blow, cut through the neck. Immediately plunge the turtle's head and body into a pan of very cold water. (Do not be alarmed if the turtle moves after the head is severed, for this is only a muscular reaction that is not

an unusual occurrence in the lower animals when they meet sudden death.)

When bleeding has stopped change the water and thoroughly scrub the shell and flesh with a brush; then place the head and body in unsalted water that is boiling rapidly. Continue to boil until the skin of the head and feet becomes white.

Cook the turtle in fresh, unsalted water or in a pressure cooker. The time will vary according to size, although more than three-quarters of an hour should not be necessary for an ordinary sized turtle of good quality. The turtle is cooked when the feet are soft under pressure of the fingers.

Once cooked to the required point, the turtle is set aside to cool; then the nails are pulled from the feet. The under shell is cut loose from the upper shell and the flesh is carefully removed. The feet are separated from the body, cut in small pieces, and set aside. The upper shell is emptied and the gall bladder discarded. (Any small particle of the gall-bladder remaining in the meat will impart a bitter flavor to the dish.) The sandbag, heart, tail, and intestines, as well as the white muscles of the inside, are also discarded.

The eggs are carefully removed and set aside with the feet and liver, and these are immediately sprinkled with salt and coarse black pepper, placed in a kettle with the turtle meat and covered with cold salted water, a few slices of carrot and onion, a bay leaf and two whole slightly bruised cloves are added and the covered kettle is set on the fire for 20 minutes, to boil rapidly, then transferred into a moderate oven (350° F.), still covered and the cooking process continued for another 20 or 25 minutes.

If the turtle thus cooked is not to be used immediately, it should be packed into a bowl, or porcelain container, tightly covered and kept in the refrigerator until wanted

TERRAPIN BALTIMORE

3/4 cup white stock
1½ tbsp sherry wine
1 terrapin
1½ tbsp butter
Salt and black pepper
2 egg yolks
Toast

Combine the stock and wine and cook in it the terrapin, with the bones, cut in small pieces. Simmer very gently until the liquor is reduced to half its original volume. Add the liver, cut small, the butter, seasonings and, finally, the well-beaten egg yolks, stirring while adding. Turn immediately into a deep hot platter and serve with crisp dry toast. (Serves 4)

TERRAPIN MARYLAND

Proceed as directed for Terrapin Baltimore but thicken the liquor with 1 tablespoon each of butter and flour kneaded together. Add ½ cup of thick cream, scalded, and use 2 additional egg yolks (4 in all) with 1½ teaspoons of lemon juice. Just before serving, add 1½ tablespoons of sherry and serve garnished with small triangles of bread fried in butter.

TERRAPIN WASHINGTON

1½ tbsp butter
1½ tbsp flour
1 cup thick cream, scalded
1 terrapin
2 terrapin eggs
1 hard-cooked egg, coarsely chopped
½ cup finely chopped mushrooms
Salt and pepper
2 egg yolks
2 tbsp sherry
Toast

Blend the butter and flour smoothly, add the cream and bring to boiling point, stirring constantly. Put in the terrapin meat with bones and liver, all cut into small pieces. Add also the terrapin eggs, the hard-cooked egg, mushrooms and seasonings. Simmer gently, without boiling, for 5 minutes Just before serving, add the beaten egg yolks, stirring while adding, and, finally, the wine. Serve in a deep platter garnishing with crescents or triangles of golden brown toast, which has been spread liberally with butter. (Serves 4)

TURTLE A LA KING

6 hard-cooked eggs
2 tbsp butter
2 cups light cream
Dash of pepper, allspice, and nutmeg

½ tsp salt
2 cups chopped, cooked turtle meat

Press the egg yolks through a sieve, then cream with the butter. Scald the cream in a double boiler, add the seasonings, then beat in the egg yolk-butter mixture. Add the turtle meat, cover, and heat thoroughly. Serve very hot, garnishing with the egg whites. (Serves 4)

TURTLE SOUP

The preparation of turtle soup is so complex that it would be almost impossible for the homemaker to prepare it, nor is it a dish which would often be in demand in the home. Here, however, is a simplified method, using previously prepared turtle meat.

1 qt brown stock
2 egg whites, slightly beaten
Shredded rind ½ lemon
1 lb diced turtle meat
Salt and pepper
¼ cup sherry

Combine the stock, liquid from the turtle, egg whites, and lemon rind, and bring to boiling point, beating continuously with a wire whisk, Simmer 5 minutes, then leave 15 minutes to settle. Strain through a jelly bag or doubled cheesecloth and, just before serving, add the diced turtle meat and reheat without boiling. Season and stir in the wine at the moment of serving. (Serves 4)

TUSCHINSK CHEESE. A Russian cheese made from milk of sheep or cows. It is also known as Ossetin cheese.

TUTTI FRUTTI. A term applied to a dessert in which several fruits are combined, either whole, crushed, or frozen. Also a confection, and chewing gum made with different fruit flavorings.

TWANKEY TEA. A size of green tea—not a guide to quality. *See* TEA.

TWIST. A loaf of bread or any pastry formed of thin strips, twisted before baking.

TWOROG CHEESE. A sour milk cheese made in Russia. It is often called Notruschki.

TYROL SOUR CHEESE. A sour milk cheese with a sharp, pungent odor and taste. Another name for hand cheese.

UV

ULLAGE. The amount that a cask, bottle or other liquid container lacks of being full; also used to refer directly to a bottle which, through a faulty cork, has lost part of the original contents.

UNFERMENTED TEA. Green tea, most of which comes from China and Japan. *See* TEA.

URI CHEESE. A hard, rennet cheese made of cow's milk. It is produced in the canton of Uri, Switzerland.

URTICARIA. Acute erythema or urticaria, or hives, may be caused in some persons by eating fish, particularly shellfish and crustaceans such as oysters, clams, lobsters, shrimps, and crabs. It is also produced in some people by strawberries, bananas, and other kinds of fruit. Crustaceans and strawberries are perhaps the most common excitants. According to medical authorities the whole matter seems to be influenced solely by idiosyncrasy.

USQUEBAUGH. The Celtic word (literally: *water of life*) from which came the modern term whisky (*which see*).

UTENSILS FOR THE KITCHEN. *See* KITCHEN EQUIPMENT and ELECTRIC EQUIPMENT.

VACHERIN CHEESE. Two cheeses bear this name. Vacherin à la main, from Switzerland and France, is a rennet cheese, which is 12 inches in diameter, 5 or 6 inches high, and weighs 5 to 10 pounds. The rind is firm and hard and the interior is liquid in consistency. It is either spread on bread or eaten with a spoon. It is known locally as *tome de montagne*. Vacherin fondu is much the same as emmenthaler

VACUUM COFFEE MAKER. An electrical apparatus for making coffee and keeping it hot. A special control makes it automatic. *See* COFFEE.

VALENCIA. *See* ORANGE.

VALENCIA ALMOND. *See* ALMOND.

VAN DER HUM. A south African liqueur, considered by many to be the best produced in that country. It is made with cape brandy, flavored with fruits and herbs, the *naartje* (South African tangerine) predominating. *See also* LIQUEUR

VANILLA BEAN. The dried bean of an orchid, used for flavoring, grown in Mexico, Java, and other tropical regions. It makes an agreeable flavoring extract for foods, especially desserts, such as puddings, custards, blancmange, or ice cream, because unlike the spices, it is very bland. *See also* FLAVORING EXTRACTS.

VANILLA BAVARIAN CREAM

2 tbsp gelatin
½ cup cold water
2 cups milk, scalded
4 egg yolks, well beaten
½ cup sugar
¼ tsp salt
1 tsp vanilla extract
1 pt heavy cream, whipped

Soften the gelatin in the cold water for ten minutes. Make a soft custard (*which see*) in upper part of double boiler, using the milk, egg yolks, sugar, salt, and vanilla extract. When the custard coats the spoon, add the softened gelatin and stir until dissolved. Strain and cool. When the mixture begins to thicken, fold in the whipped cream. Turn into a mold, or individual molds which have been moistened with cold water. Chill, and unmold. (Serves 6)

VANILLA BEANS

FROZEN VANILLA CUSTARD

1 egg, separated
1/4 cup sugar
1/2 tsp vanilla extract
1 small can evaporated milk, (2/3 cup, chilled)

Beat the egg yolk. Add the sugar and vanilla. Beat until the sugar is dissolved. Beat egg white stiff and fold into yolk mixture. Whip milk very stiff. Fold in egg mixture lightly. Pour at once into cold freezing tray. (Makes 1 pint)

VARIATIONS

Chocolate Chip. Fold in 2 squares semi-sweet chocolate, shaved or grated, after combining egg and sugar mixture with whipped milk.

Cocoa. Omit sugar. Use in its place a sirup made by blending 1/4 cup sugar, 1/4 cup cocoa and 1/2 cup water and boiling until thick. Chill sirup, then add to the beaten egg yolk.

Peanut Brittle. Fold 2/3 cup crushed peanut brittle into egg and sugar mixture, then add to whipped milk.

VANILLA CRISPS

1 1/3 cups all-purpose flour
1 1/4 tsp baking powder
1/2 tsp salt
1/2 cup shortening (half butter)
1 cup sugar
2 eggs, beaten
1 1/2 tsp vanilla

Sift the flour; measure and resift 3 times with baking powder and salt. Cream the shortenings and blend in the sugar well. Add the eggs and beat until fluffy. Stir in the vanilla. Stir dry ingredients into creamed mixture and mix well. Drop by teaspoonfuls onto a well greased baking sheet. Bake in a moderately hot oven (400° F.) for about 8 minutes or until delicately browned. (Makes about 5 dozen cookies about 2 inches in diameter).

VANILLA ICE CREAM)
(American Method)

1 tbsp flour
1 cup sugar

1/4 tsp salt
2 egg yolks
2 cups scalded milk
1 qt thin cream, or undiluted evaporated milk
1 1/2 tsp vanilla extract

Combine the flour, sugar, and salt, and add the slightly beaten egg yolks; then slowly, while stirring briskly and constantly, pour the scalded milk over the egg mixture. Turn into the top of a double boiler and cook over hot water 10 minutes, stirring constantly, until the custard mixture coats the spoon. Strain through doubled cheesecloth while still hot. Chill and add the cream or evaporated milk and the vanilla. Freeze in a hand freezer, using 3 parts of ice to 1 part of salt. Pack or mold in 4 parts ice and 1 part salt. Or freeze in tray of automatic refrigerator, scraping down when the mixture reaches a half frozen consistency. (Serves 8) *See also* ICE CREAM.

VANILLA ICE CREAM
(French Method)

1/2 cup sugar
1/8 tsp salt
4 egg yolks
2 cups rich milk, scalded
1 cup heavy cream
1 tsp vanilla

Combine the sugar and salt with the slightly beaten egg yolks, beating gently until the sugar is dissolved and the mixture thoroughly blended. Pour the milk over slowly, while stirring briskly and constantly. Turn this creamy custard into the top of a double boiler and cook over simmering water, stirring constantly, until the mixture coats the spoon. Strain through doubled cheesecloth, cool, then chill. Add the heavy cream, unwhipped, and the vanilla, and freeze in a hand freezer, using 3 parts of ice and 1 part salt. Pack or mold using 4 parts ice and 1 part salt. Or freeze in tray of automatic refrigerator, scraping down when the mixture reaches a half frozen consistency. (Serves 6)

VANILLA ICE CREAM PIE

Have ready or purchase 1 quart of vanilla ice cream. Spread it quickly, about

2 inches thick in the bottom of a shallow mold, having a tight-fitting lid or cover, about the size of an ordinary 8- or 9-inch pie plate. Now, operating rapidly, press a meat plate into the cream in such a way as to form an indentation in the center similar to a baked pie shell. Seal on the lid, or cover with a piece of cloth or muslin, dipped in melted butter, and as an additional precaution, spread some butter over the cloth. Pack in 4 parts of ice and 1 part rock salt for 2 hours. When ready to serve, unmold or rather turn over the ice cream shell to serving platter, lifting out the plate. Fill the shell with sweetened raspberries or strawberries. Rapidly brush the berries with a small jar of melted currant jelly. Serve immediately, decorated with whipped cream, sweetened and flavored to taste.

VANILLA MOUSSE

1 cup heavy cream whipped stiff
1/4 scant cup powdered sugar
1/8 tsp salt
1/2 tsp vanilla extract
1 egg white, stiffly beaten

Fold into the stiffly whipped heavy cream, the powdered sugar, salt and vanilla extract; then fold in the stiffly beaten egg white. Freeze in the refrigerator tray or individual molds. See also MOUSSE.

VANILLA SAUCE

1 cup milk
1 cup cream
2 egg yolks
Scant 1/2 cup sugar
1 tsp vanilla

Scald the milk and cream together. Beat the egg yolks and sugar, then pour the scalded mixture over them, beating while pouring. Return to the fire and bring just to boiling point without actually boiling. Cool and add the vanilla. (Makes 2 cups)

VANILLA FOAMY SAUCE

1 egg yolk
1/4 cup brown sugar, firmly packed
Pinch of salt
1/4 cup cream, whipped
1/2 tsp vanilla

Beat the egg yolk until light with half the sugar. Add the salt to the egg white and beat until foamy. Add the remaining sugar to this, a tablespoon at a time, beating after each addition. When the sugar is all added, continue beating until stiff. Combine the two mixtures, fold in the whipped cream and vanilla. (Makes 1 cup)

VANILLA SUGAR. Sugar flavored with vanilla. It may be made easily at home by placing one or two vanilla beans in a jar containing granulated sugar and having a tightly fitting cover. It may be used in pastry, desserts, and for sweetening fresh berries.

VAPID. As applied to food, the term implies having lost flavor and quality, hence being flat and insipid.

VASTERBOTTENSOST CHEESE. A Swedish cheese also called West Bothian cheese. It has a pungent, rather bitter taste, and is not ready to eat until twelve to eighteen months old. It is made in northern Sweden.

VASTGOTAOST CHEESE. A Swedish semi-hard, pressed cheese also called West Gothland cheese. It weighs about 25 pounds, and takes about 6 months to ripen.

VAPORIZING POINT OF WATER. This is another term for the boiling point of water. It is reached when the pressure of heating water equals that of the surrounding atmosphere. See HIGH-ALTITUDE COOKERY.

VEAL. Veal is young beef. The most desirable veal comes from milk-fed calves between six and eight weeks old. After this age, the calves begin to eat grass and this darkens the flesh. Like the flesh of any immature animal, veal has very little fat, and is therefore likely to be dry unless moisture is applied during the cooking process. For this reason, veal, even the most tender cuts, should never be broiled. The bland flavor and smooth texture of veal suggests the use of tart, stimulating seasonings in its preparation. Like pork, veal should always be well done. The old idea of its being indigestible has been completely disproved; veal well cooked is delicious and easily digested.

Like other meats, veal that is slaughtered by the major packing houses is government inspected and may be government graded. Occasionally, in the smaller towns local veal is available in the market. This, of course, has not been federally inspected, but there usually are state or local regulations governing the sale of such meat. If the butcher is reputable, such veal can be a particularly delicious treat.

UNITED STATES GRADES

Prime or Grade A-1. Prime veal represents the very best in quality and finish and results only from the highest type of breeding and care. As a result, very little of this grade appears in the markets. Prime veal is short, thick, blocky, and very compact. The bones are soft and red and there is an abundance of creamy white fat. The flesh is firm, fine grained, and velvety and a rich pinkish brown in color.

Choice or Grade 1. The highest grade ordinarily found in market, choice veal has excellent conformation and finish. It is relatively short and chunky, with broad shoulders, back, and hips. The legs and shoulders are heavily fleshed. The bones are soft and red and there is a good amount of creamy white fat both in the interior and over the back. The flesh is fine grained, firm, and without the moisture which appears in the lower grades. Its color is pinkish brown.

Good or Grade 2. This grade of veal is in all respects above average. The major difference between Choice and Good veal is in the conformation, good veal being less full in the rounds, loins, and ribs, and having slight deficiencies in the quantity and distribution of fat. The bones are soft and red and the flesh is moderately fine grained and firm, but may be slightly moist. Its color is a pinkish brown.

Medium or Grade 3. This grade of veal is fair or average, and is generally less chunky and well fleshed than the higher grades. The bones are soft, but not usually red. There is much less fat, and this is white, lacking the creamy tinge of the higher grades. The flesh is slightly soft and moist and in color varies from pinkish brown to light tan.

Common or Grade 4. This is the lowest grade of veal sold for fresh meat. The carcass is bony and angular, and has comparatively little flesh. The bones are soft, but pale in color. There is almost no exterior fat, and the interior fat is coarse. The flesh is coarse grained, soft, and flabby, and inclined to be watery. The color varies from pinkish tan to dark tan, and cut surfaces darken very quickly.

Cull or Grade 5. This grade of veal is not ordinarily sold as fresh meat. It is thin and bony, lacking fat, and with coarse, dark, watery flesh. The meat is used principally for sausage, veal loaf, and other prepared meat products.

After the animal reaches 12 or 14 weeks of age, it is known in the meat trade as calf, rather than veal. The same grading applies, except that the animal is more mature.

PREPARATION FOR MARKET

Calves are slaughtered in the same way as other animals, by being stunned and bled. Calves are dressed with the hide on to prevent the drying out and discoloration of the flesh. If a calf carcass is skinned before chilling the flesh will dry out and become very dark in color. If the meat is chilled with the hide on, it maintains the bright moist appearance which the customer considers attractive. Calves are subjected to the usual inspection for diseased or otherwise undesirable animals. In general, veal is handled in the same way as beef, *which see.*

Again, like beef, there is considerable difference in the methods of cutting the carcass into wholesale and retail cuts. In general, the carcass is not divided into cuts at the slaughterhouse, but is shipped to the consuming centers as the whole carcass or as sides, that is, the carcass which has been split in two along the backbone. The principal wholesale cuts of veal are the hind saddle and fore saddle. In the so-

FOOD VALUE

Grade	Water	Food Energy	Protein	Fat	Carbohydrates	Calcium	Phosphorus	Iron	Vit. A Value	Thiamine	Riboflavin	Niacin	Ascorbic Acid
Choice	65	218	18.5	16	0	11	199	2.8	0	.17	.26	6.1	0
Medium	68	184	19.1	12	0	11	206	2.9	0	.17	.27	6.3	0
Common	71	151	19.7	8	0	11	212	3.0	0	.18	.28	6.5	0

called Chicago method, which is the one most widely used, the division is made along the ribs, leaving one rib on the hind saddle. The hind saddles are divided into legs and loins; and the fore saddles are divided into racks and chucks. The chuck may be further divided.

VARIETY MEATS

Brains. A great delicacy which may be prepared in various ways. *See* BRAINS.

Heart. The calf's heart is smaller and more tender than a beef heart. While it is prepared in much the same way, it takes less cooking, and does not provide so many servings. *See* HEART.

Kidneys. Veal kidneys are sometimes cut with the chops, as a kidney chop. They are also available separately and are the most delicately flavored of the kidneys. *See* KIDNEY.

Knuckles. These may be prepared in any of the ways suggested for pig's knuckles, *which see.*

Liver. Calf's liver is the most tender and delicious kind of liver available; for this reason it is also the most expensive. Its food

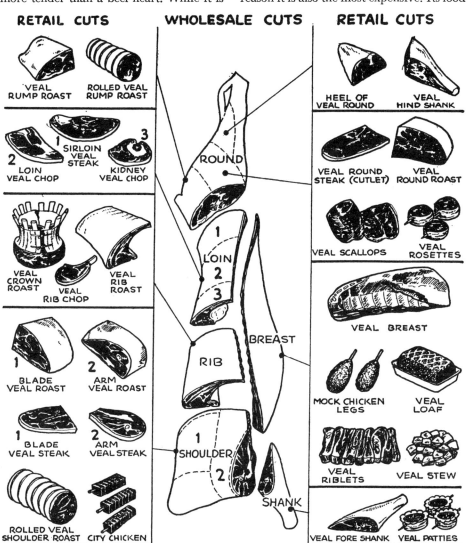

RETAIL CUTS **WHOLESALE CUTS** **RETAIL CUTS**

VEAL RUMP ROAST ROLLED VEAL RUMP ROAST

HEEL OF VEAL ROUND VEAL HIND SHANK

SIRLOIN VEAL STEAK LOIN VEAL CHOP KIDNEY VEAL CHOP

ROUND

VEAL ROUND STEAK (CUTLET) VEAL ROUND ROAST

VEAL CROWN ROAST VEAL RIB CHOP VEAL RIB ROAST

LOIN

VEAL SCALLOPS VEAL ROSETTES

BLADE VEAL ROAST ARM VEAL ROAST

BREAST

RIB

VEAL BREAST

BLADE VEAL STEAK ARM VEAL STEAK

SHOULDER

MOCK CHICKEN LEGS VEAL LOAF

SHANK

ROLLED VEAL SHOULDER ROAST CITY CHICKEN

VEAL RIBLETS VEAL STEW

VEAL FORE SHANK VEAL PATTIES

VEAL CHART, showing principal cuts

RETAIL CUTS

Wholesale Cut	Retail Cut	Cooking Method
Leg or Round	Rump Roast	Roast or Braise
	Rolled Rump Roast	Roast or Braise
	Heel of Round	Braise or Stew
	Hind Shank	Braise or Stew
	Round Steak (Cutlet)	Braise
	Round Roast	Roast or Braise
	Scallops	Braise
	Rosettes	Braise
Loin	Loin Chop	Braise
	Sirloin Steak	Braise
	Kidney Chop	Braise
Rib	Crown Roast	Roast
	Rib Chop	Braise
	Rib Roast	Roast
Breast	Breast	Braise or Stew
	Riblets	Braise or Stew
Shoulder	Blade Roast	Roast or Braise
	Arm Roast	Roast or Braise
	Blade Steak	Braise
	Arm Steak	Braise
	Rolled Shoulder Roast	Roast or Braise
Shank	Fore Shank	Stew

value does not differ from that of other animals, and unless the budget can well afford it, calf's liver is an extravagance. *See* LIVER.

Lights. These are the lungs of the animal, which are not ordinarily used for food in this country. They are inexpensive, very nourishing, and can be mixed with other meats in appetizing dishes.

Sweetbreads. Calf's sweetbreads (the thymus gland) are a great delicacy, and correspondingly expensive. They can, with advantage, be extended by using part beef sweetbreads. *See* SWEETBREAD.

Tongue. Calf's tongues are sold in the same forms as beef tongue—fresh, pickled, salted, or smoked. They are somewhat smaller than beef tongues, and therefore desirable for the smaller family. *See* TONGUE.

Calf's Head. The head of the calf is used in making a number of dishes, among them mock turtle soup, head cheese, and calf's head vinaigrette. To prepare a calf's head have the butcher clean it, split it, and take out the brain and tongue. At home, set the brain and tongue aside. Tie the head in cheesecloth and blanch it for a few minutes in boiling water. Then untie and rinse thoroughly in cold running water. Drain and pat dry. Cut into convenient portions and rub each piece all over with a halved lemon to prevent discoloration. If the brain and tongue are to be used with the calf's head, parboil the brain for 10 or 12 minutes, and cook the tongue separately until tender. Serve hot or cold with a vinaigrette sauce. *See also* HEAD CHEESE.

Calf's Feet. A natural aspic is obtained from the long boiling of calf's feet. After clarifying and straining, flavoring may be added in the form of any of the sweet wines such as sherry, Madeira, port, etc. This is the calf's foot jelly of invalid cookery.

HINTS ON PREPARING VEAL

Remember that veal comes from an immature animal and the flesh is likely to be dry. Therefore, it should never be broiled, although certain pieces may be roasted. Preferably it should be braised. Cuts such as chops and cutlets may be breaded and sautéed. Veal for stew may first be browned in fat, or, particularly in the preparation of blanquette de veau, cooked without browning, giving a delicate creamy dish.

Since veal is very delicate meat it bruises easily, and such bruises spoil rapidly. Hence it should be handled carefully and always kept under refrigeration.

In roasting veal, if it is very lean, additional fat may be added, or the piece of meat may be larded (*which see*). Veal should always be roasted with moderate heat and never seared because searing dries out the meat too much.

Veal may be pounded with a mallet to break down the fibers and make a thin tender morsel. This is usually done to the cutlets in the preparation of wiener schnitzel and scalopini.

Cooking Times and Temperature

If a meat thermometer is used in roasting veal, it should register 170°, or well done, in order for the veal to be thoroughly cooked. The table below gives approximate cooking times for various cuts.

2 sprigs parsley
4 peppercorns
2 tsp salt
1 cup mushrooms, sliced
1 doz small onions
5 tbsp butter
4 tbsp flour
2 tbsp lemon juice
2 egg yolks, slightly beaten
1 tbsp chopped parsley
2 whole cloves

Stick the cloves into the onion. Wipe the meat, then cut into 2 inch pieces. Simmer until tender, about 1 hour, with the water, onion, carrot, herbs, peppercorns, and salt. Drain off the liquid, Cook the mushrooms in a little of this liquid in a double boiler, about 15 minutes. Meanwhile cook the small onions in 2 tablespoons of butter in a covered heavy saucepan 20 to 30 minutes or until tender. Melt the remain-

Cut	Size	Method	Temperature	Time Well Done
Rib and Loin Chops	1 inch	Pan broil (rub with fat)	350°	15–20 min.
Cutlet or Steak	½ inch	Fry (breaded)	Sauté slowly	30 min.
	1 inch	Braise	Brown for Then simmer	15 min. 60 min.
Leg	7–8 lb.	Roast	300°	25 min. per lb.
Loin	4–5 lb.	Roast	300°	30–35 min. per lb.
Rack	3 lb.	Roast	300°	30–35 min. per lb.
Shoulder	7 lb.	Roast	300°	25 min. per lb.
Rolled	5 lb.	Roast	300°	40–45 min. per lb.
Pot Roast	2–3 lb.	Braise	Brown for Then simmer	15 min. 60–90 min.
Stew	Cubes	Simmer		60–90 min.
Chops	½–¾ inch	Braise	Sauté slowly	45–60 min.
Breast	3–4 lb.	Braise	Brown for Then simmer	15 min. 1¼–2 hrs.
Rolled	2–3 lb.	Braise	Brown for Then simmer	15 min. 1¼–2 hrs.
Birds	½ inch	Braise	Brown for Then simmer	15 min. 30–45 min.

Blanquette of Veal
(French Creamed Veal Stew)

2 lb stewing veal
1 qt boiling water
1 large onion,
¼ cup chopped carrot
1 bay leaf
1 sprig thyme

ing butter, add the flour, and when well blended, 3 cups of the veal stock. Bring slowly to boiling point, stirring constantly and cook gently for 5 minutes. Add the lemon juice, and egg yolks with the veal and parsley and reheat without actually boiling. Garnish with the onions and mushrooms. Dumplings or noodles are a good accompaniment. (Serves 4)

BRAISED SHOULDER OF VEAL

1 shoulder of veal
Bread stuffing
1 tsp salt
⅓ tsp pepper
2 tbsp flour
Salt pork fat
½ cup diced carrot
½ cup diced celery
1 onion, sliced
12 peppercorns
A pinch each of thyme and marjoram
2 cups hot water
Flour

Have the butcher bone the shoulder of veal. Wipe, then fill the cavity with the stuffing (*which see*) and sew up the opening. Rub over with the blended salt, pepper and flour and brown the entire surface in the rendered salt pork fat (or other fat). Transfer to a heavy kettle with the carrot, celery, onion, peppercorns, thyme and marjoram. Pour the water over, cover closely, and cook in a slow oven (300° F.) about 3 hours, turning once during the cooking. Strain the liquor from the casserole and thicken with a little flour rubbed smooth with cold water, using 1 tablespoon of flour to each cup of liquid. Bring again to boiling point, season with salt and pepper and serve with the veal. (Serves 8)

CURRIED VEAL

2 lb veal shoulder
1½ qt water
2 cups chopped onions
1½ cups chopped celery
½ cup oil
1 tbsp curry powder
¾ tsp salt
⅛ tsp pepper
½ tsp ginger
½ tsp tabasco sauce
1 tsp Worcestershire sauce
1 qt veal broth
4 tbsp flour
Hot boiled rice

Wipe the meat and simmer gently until tender in the water. Cut into cubes, discarding any fat—there should be about 3 cups of meat and 1 quart of broth. Cook the onion and celery gently in the oil until slightly browned. Add the seasonings and simmer 5 minutes longer, then add the broth. Moisten the flour with a little cold water. Stir into the broth and cook, stirring constantly, until thickened. Add the veal, reheat and serve with plenty of hot boiled rice. (Serves 6)

JELLIED VEAL

2 lb shank of veal, bone in
1 small carrot
1 small onion
Salt and pepper
1 stalk celery
2 qt water

Season the meat with the salt and pepper and place it in a kettle with all the other ingredients. Bring to a boil and simmer, covered, very slowly until the meat falls from the bones. Strain the liquid, remove all the bone, and cut the meat and vegetables into small evenly sized pieces. Put the liquid in a pan and boil it until it is reduced to half its volume. Rinse a mold with water and place the meat and vegetables in it. Turn in the liquid, and chill. Stir the mixture several times before it sets to keep the solid parts from settling at the bottom. Cut into slices when it is cold and firm and serve with salad or other appropriate garnish.

JELLIED VEAL KNUCKLE

3 lb lean veal and a veal knuckle bone
1 large onion, thinly sliced
1 large bay leaf tied with
1 parsley root and
4 sprigs green celery tops
6 whole peppercorns, bruised
2 or 3 whole cloves
1 small clove garlic
Water

Wash the meat thoroughly. Combine with all remaining ingredients, add water to cover, and simmer about 2 hours, or until the meat is tender. Strain the liquor; allow it to cool, then skim off all fat and measure. Cut the meat into large dice with a sharp knife or scissors. Season the broth with salt and pepper, add the cubed meat, and bring to boiling point. For each quart of broth add 1 tablespoon of gelatin, softened first in a little of the cold broth. Add for each quart 2 tablespoons of minced parsley and chives and 1 tablespoon of finely chopped capers (optional). Stir until the gelatin is dissolved. Cool, and when almost at setting point, turn into a bread pan rinsed in cold water. Chill. Unmold and slice for service, garnishing with quartered hard-cooked eggs and water cress. (Serves 6 or 8)

VEAL MOUSSE

1½ lb veal and a veal knuckle bone
1 large onion, sliced
1 small carrot, quartered
6 sprigs parsley
1 large bay leaf
8 whole peppercorns
1 tsp salt
5 cups cold water
1 tbsp gelatin
2 egg yolks
¼ tsp salt
Dash of cayenne
½ cup whipped evaporated milk

Cook the veal, the knuckle bone, onion, carrot, parsley, bay leaf, peppercorns, salt and water until the meat is tender. Strain and cool the broth and skim off any fat. Pass the cooked meat through the food chopper—there should be about 1½ cups of meat and the same quantity of broth. Soften the gelatin in ¼ cup of this cold broth. Heat the remainder in a double boiler, then pour over the beaten egg yolks and return to the double boiler and cook to custard consistency, or until a little will coat the back of the stirring spoon. Add the softened gelatin, stir until dissolved, then combine with the meat and additional seasonings. Cool, and when almost at setting point fold in the whipped evaporated milk. Turn into a wet mold, chill and serve as a main dish, garnishing with lettuce, sliced tomatoes, and mayonnaise; or serve with hot vegetables, such as creamed potatoes and peas or string beans

For a lighter, fluffier mixture, the whites of the eggs may be beaten until stiff and folded into the mousse after the evaporated milk has been added.

Be sure to chill the evaporated milk before whipping. (Serves 4 or 6)

STUFFED BREAST OF VEAL

3 lb breast of veal
2 tbsp minced onion
1 tbsp minced celery
2 tbsp fat
2¼ cups soft bread crumbs
¼ cup ground smoked ham
Dash each of thyme and marjoram
2 tsp salt
¼ tsp pepper
1 cup hot water
4 tbsp fat, additional

Have the butcher bone and cut a pocket in the meat. Wipe with a damp cloth, sprinkle the inside of the pocket with a little salt and pepper, and fill loosely with stuffing. For this cook the onion and celery for 10 minutes in the fat, then combine with the crumbs, ham, seasonings, and flavorings. Sew up the meat and place on a rack in a roasting pan. Roast in a slow oven (300° F.), basting frequently with the combined hot water and fat and allowing about 30 minutes to the pound of meat. Serve with brown gravy or brown mushroom sauce. (Serves 6)

A cushion of veal (a piece cut from the upper part of the leg) may be similarly stuffed and roasted, then served with the same accompaniments.

STUFFED SHOULDER OF VEAL

5 lb veal shoulder
2 tsp salt
¼ tsp pepper
½ cup fat
1 cup chopped celery
1 tbsp chopped onion
2 tbsp chopped parsley
4 cups soft bread crumbs
½ cup dried apricots

Have the veal boned by the butcher, cutting it so as to make a large pocket. Wipe, then rub inside and out with salt and pepper. Heat ⅔ of the fat and cook the celery, onion, and parsley in it for 5 minutes. Add the crumbs and apricots, which have been soaked in hot water to cover and then coarsely chopped. Season lightly and fill the pocket in the veal. Sew up the opening securely, rub the meat over with the remaining fat and sprinkle with flour. Place on a rack in a roasting pan and bake in a moderate oven (350° F.), allowing 2½ hours and turning several times during the baking. Serve hot with brown gravy, or cold with a green salad. (Serves 8 or 10)

VEAL FRICANDEAU

4 lb piece veal cutlet
2 carrots, sliced
3 onions, sliced
2 stalks celery, sliced
1 sprig thyme
4 sprigs parsley
1 pt white wine
Salt and pepper
2 cloves garlic, sliced

Have the meat cut about 2 inches thick and have the butcher lard it on the cut sides. Prepare a marinade of the carrots, onions, celery, thyme, and parsley, with the wine, seasonings, and garlic. Lay the meat in a receptacle just large enough to contain it easily, pour the marinade over, cover, and leave in a cool place for 3 hours, turning it 2 or 3 times during that period. Lift out and brown on all sides in a little hot fat. Pour the marinade, vegetables and liquid, over the meat. Cover, and cook gently until tender. Strain out the vegetables and use the liquid as a sauce. Serve with sorrel or spinach. (Serves 6 or 8)

VEAL PAPRIKA

2½ lb veal cut in inch cubes
1 large onion, minced
2 tbsp butter or margarine
2 tsp salt
½ tsp pepper
1 tbsp paprika
2 cups boiling water
2 tbsp flour
2 tbsp cold water
½ cup sour cream

Sauté the onion in the butter in a heavy skillet until golden color. Add the veal and brown it slightly, stirring constantly. Sprinkle in the seasonings, add the boiling water, cover the skillet and simmer for 1½ hours or until the meat is tender. Mix the

flour and cold water to form a smooth paste. Stir in a little of the hot liquid, and then return all to the stew, stirring constantly until the sauce is smooth and thickened. Stir in the sour cream, and bring just to the boiling point. Serve immediately. (Serves 6)

VEAL POT PIE

2 lb veal neck
Salted water
2 tbsp melted butter or margarine
2 tbsp flour
1½ cups combined milk and stock
Salt and pepper
Baking powder biscuit dough

Wipe the meat and cook gently in salted water until tender. Take out the bones. Prepare a sauce by blending the butter and flour, adding the combined milk and stock (liquid in which the meat was cooked). Bring to the boiling point, stirring constantly. Add the seasoning. Add the meat and turn into a baking dish. Cover with biscuit dough (*which see*). Cut several slits in the crust for the escape of steam, and bake in a moderately hot oven (375°–400° F.) 20 to 25 minutes. Serve with mashed potatoes and peas. If preferred add pre-cooked potato balls and peas to the pot pie with the meat. (Serves 4 or 6)

VEAL ROLLS

2 thin slices veal cutlet, about 1½ lb
¾ tsp salt
⅛ tsp pepper
1 cup minced chicken and giblets
2 slices bread, moistened and crumbled
2 tbsp minced onion
2 tbsp minced parsley
3 tbsp fat
⅓ cup hot water

Wipe, then pound the veal until very thin and cut it into pieces about 4 inches square. Season lightly with salt and pepper, then spread on each portion of meat a forcemeat made from the chicken and giblets, the bread, onion, parsley, remaining seasonings, and 1 tablespoon of the fat. Roll up each piece of meat tightly and tie or skewer with small wooden toothpicks. Heat the remaining fat in a frying pan, lay the rolls in this and brown on all sides. Add the water, cover, and simmer gently until very tender, after which remove the cover and allow any moisture to evaporate. Serve with a garnish of tomato wedges and, if possible, with sliced Italian squash steamed in butter. (Serves 4 or 6)

VEAL SCALOPINI

6 thin escalopes (veal cutlets pounded and cut in ovals)
½ cup melted butter or margarine
¼ cup grated Parmesan cheese
1 cup thinly sliced mushroom caps
Salt and pepper
1 bouillon cube
2 tbsp boiling water
1 tbsp butter
4 tbsp sherry

Dip the veal slices into the melted butter and then into the grated cheese. Heat the remaining butter and sauté the veal until browned on both sides. In a separate pan, melt a little butter or margarine and cook the mushrooms, stirring and turning them frequently. When the mushrooms are tender, add the bouillon cube, boiling water, butter, and sherry, and bring just to the boiling point. Do not allow to boil. season the veal with salt and pepper and serve with the mushroom sauce. (Serves 6)

WIENER SCHNITZEL
(Veal Cutlet Viennese Style)

Have medium-sized veal cutlets cut about ¾ inch thick. Place the cutlets on a board and rub them lightly with English mustard moistened with a dash of Worcestershire sauce. Then pound the cutlets with a rolling pin or potato masher. Turn the cutlets over, rub the other side with the mustard mixture and continue the pounding until the cutlets are half their original thickness. Season the cutlets highly with salt and black pepper. Dip each cutlet first into flour, then into slightly beaten egg, and then into fine crumbs. Sauté in butter or other fat, turning until the meat is well browned and cooked through. Serve with the following sauce:

1 small can tomato paste
1 bay leaf
Pinch of thyme
1 tbsp minced celery
1 small onion, minced
Salt
Black pepper
⅔ cup cream sauce
¼ cup cream

Heat the tomato paste with the seasonings, and allow to simmer for 15 minutes. Strain through a sieve. Scald the cream, and have the cream sauce hot. Combine the tomato mixture with the cream sauce and cream and stir well. Pass with the cutlets.

VEGETABLE. Each vegetable is treated under its individual heading. The recipes which follow use a combination of vegetables.

VEGETABLE PIES

A vegetable medley in a cheese sauce, baked under a pastry or biscuit cover, makes a hearty luncheon main dish any day. The vegetables may be fresh cooked or leftovers, or a combination of fresh-cooked and leftover vegetables. Should the refrigerator hold two or more kinds of vegetables left from previous meals, the preparation of the pie will take little time and effort.

Some good combinations are: (1) carrots, lima beans, onions; (2) peas, carrots, turnips, and string beans; (3) beans, mushrooms, celery, and tomatoes; (4) asparagus, onions, snap beans, and potatoes; (5) tomatoes, a little chopped green pepper, and parsley, rice, or cooked buttered noodles, etc. Vermicelli or rice may replace the pastry, biscuit or potato topping; or bread crumbs, combined with equal parts of grated cheese, may replace the other toppings.

Combine the vegetables with seasonings and flavorings and moisten with cheese sauce (see WHITE SAUCE) using one cup of sauce to each three cups of vegetables, then turn into a casserole. (If preferred the vegetables may be placed in the casserole in layers and the sauce poured over all.) Top with biscuit rings or pastry triangles and bake in a hot oven 12 to 15 minutes.

If preferred the cheese may be added to the biscuit dough in which case plain white sauce would be used with the vegetables.

Vegetable Shortcake

Use any of the vegetable combinations indicated for vegetable pie. Moisten with white or cheese sauce and serve between and on top of layers of biscuit shortcake (*which see*).

Vegetable Souffle

1½ cups vegetable purée
1 cup very thick white sauce or cheese sauce
Salt and pepper
1 tsp grated onion
A few grains thyme, cloves and mace
4 eggs

For the purée press any leftover vegetables through a sieve, being careful to drain them thoroughly. Combine with the sauce. Add seasonings and flavorings, then the slightly beaten egg yolks and when these are thoroughly blended, fold in the stiffly beaten egg whites. Turn into a well buttered soufflé or baking dish. Set in a pan of hot water and bake in a moderate oven (350°–375° F.) 40 to 45 minutes. Serve immediately.

If for adults, a little curry powder may be added to the sauce. (Serves 4)

VEGETABLE COLORING. This is used to color whipped cream, beaten egg white, and other dishes. It may be made by squeezing the juice from spinach or the like to secure green coloring, and by using beet juice for red or pink coloring. Commercial vegetable colorings are available in both liquid and paste form.

VEGETABLE DISH A large dish used to hold vegetables for serving at the table.

VEGETABLE PLATE

They come in many shapes and designs and are often fitted with removable covers to keep the contents warm. Vegetable dishes that do not have covers are sometimes called *bakers*. See Dishes.

VEGETABLE JUICE. The juice squeezed from uncooked spinach, carrots, parsley, celery, and other greens contains the concentrated goodness of the lot. A glass of juice represents the minerals and vitamins of a pound or more of vegetables, which if eaten as such would be too bulky for the digestive system to take care of easily.

The whole line of humble garden products from cabbage up is used, blended in fruit juices or served separately. Usually those who drink the raw juices are also devoted to the raw vegetable plate. As many as six colorful garden products may be assembled on such plates as they are now served at home tables and in restaurants.

The juices call for mixing to please the taste. Any vegetables can be used, but those preferred are spinach, parsley, celery, with the golden carrot and the ruby beet for color. Lettuce and parsley juices with a dash of lemon juice make one of the most popular cocktails. The rule is to squeeze as much as is to be consumed at the time, and no more.

Though people as a rule do not tire of tomato juice, you may wish to vary your manner of serving it once in a while. Combine it with some of the other vegetable juices that also come in small cans— celery, parsley, beet, carrot, spinach, etc., as well as sauerkraut. Season tomato juice with lemon juice, celery salt, a little sugar and a dash of Worcestershire sauce. Spinach juice and tomato juice blend well, as do sauerkraut juice and tomato juice.

VEGETABLE MARROW. A form of squash, *which see.*

VEGETABLE PEACH. Another name for mango melon, *which see.*

VEGETABLE PLATE. Generally this dish contains from three to five vegetables such as potatoes, spinach, cut corn, squash, carrots, peas, lima beans, etc. These are usually boiled or baked, but may be broiled.

The vegetables may be either fresh or canned and can be extremely tasty when served with plenty of butter or cream sauce.

In high favor with the vegetarians, the

vegetable plate is also esteemed by home-makers at times when the price of meat forces the latter dish from the table. However, most men are suspicious of plain vegetables and usually want them to be accompanied by more substantial food such as meat, fish, or cheese. *See* VEGE-TARIANISM.

VEGETARIANISM. The custom of living on a diet of vegetables and abstaining from all animal foods is as old as the history of man. It is still practiced by religious and lay groups.

True vegetarians abstain from eating not only flesh, but also all animal products such as butter, cheese, eggs, and milk. There are others who feel that the use of dairy products and eggs does not conflict with their determination not to eat meat, and still others who admit fish to their diets. Rather more strict are the views of vegetarians who exclude underground roots and tubers from their tables, and others who avoid eating cooked foods of any kind.

VELOUTE. Also called *sauce blanche grasse* or fat white sauce, or rich white sauce. There are three different kinds: *velouté for meat*, *velouté for poultry*, and *velouté for fish*. A Velouté, be it for meat, fish, or poultry is a rich, velvety sauce usually used for compounded sauces.

VELOUTE ORDINAIRE (ORDINARY VELOUTE)

For white sauces used to accompany a white meat such as veal, pork, and the like, a *vol-au-vent* (patty shell filled with white meat, poultry, sweetbreads, etc.) or a veal stew, such as a blanquette of veal, you may, in a strict sense, use a plain white sauce or a cream sauce, but the sauce will not have the richness or smoothness of one made with veal stock, chicken stock, or fish stock. The making of this sauce requires three distinct operations: (a) the stock; (b) the white roux; and (c) the combining of the two.

STOCK

4 or 5 slice raw carrot
4 or 5 slices onion
1 lb shin of veal with bone
2 chicken necks
2 chicken gizzards
Bouquet garni
2 tbsp fresh mushroom peelings
5 cups water

Combine in a heavy saucepan the carrot, onion, meat and bone, chicken necks and gizzards, bouquet garni, and mushroom peelings. Cover and cook very gently about 10 minutes. Add 2 cups of the water with a little salt, cover and bring to boiling point. Cook until the liquid is almost all evaporated, stirring occasionally. Add the remaining water (hot) with additional salt and bring again to a boil, stirring all well from the bottom and sides of the kettle so as to loosen any particles that might have adhered to it. Reduce the heat, cover, and simmer gently 2 hours. Strain through flannel, and, when cold, turn into a glass jar, cover closely and store in the refrigerator. This will keep a week to ten days.

WHITE ROUX

Stir constantly together in a heavy saucepan until well blended but not at all browned, 1 tablespoon each of flour and butter. *See also* ROUX.

MAKING THE SAUCE

Add 1 cup of the heated stock gradually to the roux, stirring constantly until the mixture thickens. Place over hot water (double boiler) and simmer very gently 20 to 25 minutes. Strain through flannel without pressing. Cool, then keep covered in the refrigerator until needed. This also will keep a week to 10 days.

If to be used at once combine the velouté with the indicated sauce or liquid.

Velouté de volaille (Chicken velouté). Proceed as indicated for velouté ordinaire, except that chicken is used instead of veal.

Velouté de poisson (fish velouté). Proceed as indicated for veloute ordinaire, except that fish stock is used instead of veal.

VENDOME CHEESE. A soft, rennet cheese which resembles Camembert, and is made in the region of Vendôme, in France. Its principal market is Paris.

VENISON. The flesh of any edible animal game especially of deer. *See also* GAME.

VERJUICE. The sour juice of green fruit.

VERMICELLI. A preparation of wheat flour very similar to macaroni (*which see*) made in the same way, except that cheese, egg yolks, and saffron are added to the paste. It is of Italian origin, and the name means "little worms." Good vermicelli should be of a slightly yellowish color, so white denotes an inferior quality. It should be fresh, as it becomes musty when kept too long. *See also* ALIMENTARY PASTES.

VERMOUTH. Vermouth is an excellent wine by itself, containing about 20 percent alcohol. It is slightly bitter, fairly rich in sugar, and has a pleasing stimulating flavor. The vermouth made in France is dry, that is, less sweet, while that made in Italy is sweeter.

French vermouth is made from at least 80 percent white wines, called *Picpouls* and *Clairettes*, and more than sixteen herbs, among them the following:

Alder, which is very bitter and aromatic.

Aniseed, which has an agreeable, warm, sweetish taste.

Centaury, which by itself is used to produce a spirit called "Gentian."

Chinchona, or quinine.

Cinnamon.

Clove.

Colombine, a bitter herb which is sometimes used in making sarsaparilla.

Coriander, which has a sweet aromatic flavor.

Elder, of which the volatile oils of the leaves and stems are used.

Galanga, which possesses aromatic qualities similar to ginger.

Nutmeg.

Orange Peel.

Quassia, which has an extremely bitter taste.

Tansy, which is very bitter and aromatic.

Wormwood, very bitter and strong in odor.

In Europe, vermouth is served by itself, straight, or as a long drink, diluted with water or seltzer. It is sometimes mixed with sirup (grenadine, cassis, lemon, etc.). Vermouth is not to be gulped down; it must be sipped slowly to be thoroughly enjoyed.

When served as an appetizer wine (*see* WINE), it is chilled. Vermouth is also used in a great many cocktails and other mixed drinks. *See* BRONX and MARTINI.

VIAND. An article of food.

VIC-EN-BIGORRE CHEESE. A French cheese made in Béarn.

VICHY. A mineral water imported from France. *See* ALAKLINE AND MINERAL WATERS.

VICHYSSOISE. A cream soup made of leeks and potatoes, usually served cold.

It is one of the most delicious summer soups.

VICHYSSOISE

3 leeks
1 onion
¼ cup butter or margarine
1 qt chicken stock
2 medium-sized potatoes, cut small
Salt and pepper
1 cup rich milk or cream

Discard any tough green part of the leeks, split down the center, wash very thoroughly, then chop both leeks and onion fine. Melt half the butter in a saucepan and cook leeks and onion in it until yellow but not browned. Add the chicken stock, potatoes, and seasonings, and cook until the potatoes are thoroughly tender. Press through a fine sieve, add the milk or cream and reheat in a double boiler. Serve hot or thoroughly chilled, garnished with minced chives. (Serves 4)

VICTUAL. (Pronounced *vit'l*.) A dialectal word meaning food prepared for human consumption.

VIDONIA. A golden Madeira wine which is very dry and fruity. It is a product of the Canary Islands. It is usually served as an appetizer before a meal and sometimes with the soup and fish.

VINAIGRETTE SAUCE. This is especially suitable for vegetables, and for cold fish and other bland dishes.

VINAIGRETTE SAUCE

1 tsp salt
½ tsp paprika
⅛ tsp pepper
½ tbsp dry mustard
½ tsp sugar
1 tbsp tarragon vinegar
2 tbsp cider vinegar
¼ cup olive oil
1 tbsp minced pickles
1 tbsp chopped stuffed olives

Combine all the ingredients and beat thoroughly. Serve cold with cold meats, or heat to boiling point and serve with broccoli, artichokes, and asparagus.

VINEGAR. Vinegar is made from wine, beer, cider, various fruits, and even from the dry distillation of wood. It contains, besides acetic acid, traces of dextrin, sugar, organic acids, pigment, extractives, and acetic ether. The acetic acid in good French vinegar exists in the proportion of 5 per cent. Ordinary table vinegar contains between 2 and 7 per cent.

The acidity enables this condiment to soften muscle fiber so that the digestion of tough meat is facilitated as in the case of boiled beef and other foods with firm fiber, like salmon and lobster.

The action of mild acids, such as vinegar, favors the digestion of tough cellulose, and aids the formation of sugar. For this reason vinegar is a wholesome addition to coarse, fibrous, or stringy vegetables, such as beets, cabbage, spinach, lettuce, celery, etc. and to raw vegetables, such as cucumbers, cole, lettuce and like food materials used in salads. If vinegar taken in a salad dressing disagrees, white wine or lemon juice may be substituted.

Vinegar has a well-known antiseptic and preservative action, hence its use for pickling fish, oysters, fruits and vegetables.

Flavored Vinegars

Cayenne Vinegar. Put from a ¼ to ½ ounce of the best cayenne pepper into a bottle. Pour on it a pint of strong vinegar. Cork it closely, and shake it well every 2 or 3 days. It may remain any length of time before straining off but will be ready for use in 2 weeks.

Celery Vinegar. Add to a pint of boiling vinegar a few grains of cayenne pepper, or ½ ounce of peppercorns, a teaspoon of salt, and 2 cups of the white portion of the roots and stems of fresh celery, sliced thin. Let all boil for 2 or 3 minutes, turn into a stone jar and close tightly as soon as cold. It may be strained off and bottled in 3 or 4 weeks, but may remain as many months in the jar without injury.

Chili or Capsicum Vinegar. Put an ounce of chilies or capsicums into a pint of vinegar, cover closely, and let stand 2 weeks. After straining, the vinegar will then be ready for use. If a stronger flavor is preferred, let the mixture infuse for 2 weeks longer.

Cucumber Vinegar. First wipe, then without paring, slice young cucumbers into a stone jar. Pour on sufficient boiling vinegar to cover. Add a teaspoon of salt and ⅔ the quantity of peppercorns to 1½ pints of vinegar. The mixture may remain thus for a month, or even two months if well protected from the air. It should then be strained, allowed to settle, and poured quite clear into small dry bottles, which should be tightly corked. A mild onion may be mixed with the cucumbers, if its flavor is desired.

Horseradish Vinegar. On 4 ounces of young and freshly scraped horseradish pour a quart of boiling vinegar, and cover closely. The vinegar will be ready for use in 3 or 4 days, but the mixtures may remain for weeks or months before straining. An ounce of minced shallot may be substituted for one ounce of the horseradish, if the flavor is preferred.

Mint Vinegar. Slightly chop or bruise the young leaves of freshly gathered mint; pack in bottles, filling nearly to the neck, pour in vinegar to cover the mint. In 50 days strain off and bottle for use.

Nasturtium Vinegar. Loosely fill a quart jar with clean nasturtium flowers. Add a finely chopped shallot, a very small piece of garlic, and a piece of red pepper. Fill the jar with cold cider vinegar. Cover closely and let stand for 2 months. Add 1 teaspoon of salt, strain through several thicknesses of cheesecloth, and store in sterilized containers closely sealed.

Onion Vinegar. Proceed as directed for shallot vinegar, substituting onion for shallot.

Raspberry Vinegar. Crush 4 quarts of raspberries and cover with 4 quarts of mild vinegar. After 2 days strain through doubled cheesecloth and pour the same vinegar over a further 4 quarts of berries. Let stand again for 2 days. Strain, measure, add 2 pounds of sugar for each quart of liquid, bring slowly to boiling point, boil 10 minutes, skim, turn into sterilized bottles, and seal. Use from 2 to 3 tablespoons in a large glass of iced water to make a pleasant summer beverage.

Raspberry and Strawberry Vinegar. Raspberries and strawberries, mixed, will make a vinegar of very pleasant flavor. Follow directions indicated for raspberry vinegar, using half the quantity of each fruit.

Shallot Vinegar. Over 4 to 6 ounces of shallots, peeled and bruised, pour a quart of good vinegar. Cover closely and in 2 or 3 weeks the vinegar may be strained off for use. A few drops will give sufficient flavor to salad dressing, sauce, etc.

Garlic Vinegar. Make in the same way as shallot vinegar, above, using only ½ the quantity of garlic.

Tarragon Vinegar. Strip the tarragon from the larger stalks. Put it into small stone jars or wide-necked bottles, and in doing this twist some of the branches so as to bruise the leaves and tear them apart. Pour in enough very pale vinegar to cover the tarragon. Allow to infuse for 2 months or more, the longer the better. Strain into small dry bottles and cork. An excellent vinegar for green and vegetable salads.

VINTAGE. See WINE.

VIRGINIA HAM. See HAM.

VISHNEVAIA. A liqueur made in Russia. A cherry brandy, made with vodka distilled over crushed wild cherries, the pits of which have been pounded; it is then filtered several times and aged.

VITAMIN. Vitamins are chemical compounds that are necessary to normal nutrition. They occur in the normal diet only in minute amounts, but they are nonetheless necessary for the maintenance of health. They are in themselves essential to health, and they also serve to facilitate the utilization of other healthful food factors.

Our knowledge of the properties and characteristics of the various vitamins is relatively new. The name vitamins first appeared in 1912, and since then research has progressed rapidly. These substances have in the past been designated by letters of the alphabet, but as we become more familiar with their chemical composition the tendency is to call them by their chemical names.

Although our knowledge of these important substances is new, the need for them is as old as life itself. It is now known that fish-liver oils contain vitamins A and D, but cod-liver oil has served as a tonic for centuries without anyone's knowing the reason. It is now known that vitamin C is responsible for the antiscorbutic power of citrus fruit juices; but in 1747, long before vitamins were known, James Lind, a surgeon in the british Navy, discovered that lemon or lime juice would prevent or cure scurvy. When this fact was recognized, it became customary for all English vessels to carry a supply of limes to be rationed to the seamen. Hence, the name "limey" for a British sailor.

An adequate vitamin supply is extremely important to people of all ages, but it is of special importance in the state of pregnancy and during the periods of growth and development. Each vitamin has a particular function in the body, and the

prolonged absence of any one will cause a deficiency disease. Many people experience periods of vitamin shortages without showing any marked deficiency symptoms; but even a moderate vitamin deficiency can effect an impairment of health, efficiency, and resistance to infection.

A lack of vitamins in the diet can weaken the system generally and make one susceptible to diseases that could be easily overcome were the vitamin intake normal. This is especially true in the case of tuberculosis. Tuberculosis germs attack ordinary person many times throughout his life, but if his physical condition is as it should be these germs will be destroyed automatically.

Because the presence or absence of vitamins in the diet has exhibited startling contrasts, interest has soared and vitamins have been widely publicized. It is generally good that people have become vitamin-conscious, but some commercial claims must be taken with a grain of salt. Cod-liver oil distributing agents, for example, have commercialized the discovery that this product is vitamin-rich, and some have made exaggerated claims as to the benefits to be derived from it. Supplementary vitamin medication is often recommended in special diets, but an adequate balanced diet (*which see*), properly prepared, will provide the normal vitamin requirements.

Vitamins are present in almost all natural foods, and when possible they should be derived from these rather than from synthetic vitamin concentrates, pills, and tablets. It is probable that natural foods provide unknown nutrients that are not contained in the synthetic preparations. Furthermore, the regular use of synthetic preparations is most uneconomical. They should be used only on the recommendation of a competent physician in cases of known deficiency, pregnancy, lactation, and disease.

VITAMIN A

Functions. Vitamin A is essential for normal growth, for normal functioning of the body's internal and external surface membranes, and for normal vision in dim light or darkness. It also aids the body in resisting infection.

Results of deficiency. Night blindness and abnormal growth are among the many undesirable conditions that can result from a shortage of this vitamin. A rather severe deficiency will increase the susceptibility to infection of the skin and of the mucous membranes of the respiratory tract, digestive system, and excretory system. It can also produce an abnormal condition of the eye membranes which is known as xerophthalmia or conjunctivitis. If the deficiency is severe and prolonged, total blindness may even result. Although this occurrence is infrequent, many people get a supply that is insufficient for the best possible eyesight performance.

Sources. Carotene, a yellow pigment substance formed in green plants, can be converted into vitamin A within the body. The green coloring matter of the plants usually supersedes it to make it invisible, but it sometimes manifests itself in yellow vegetables. Because of this carotene content, green leafy and yellow vegetables are known as sources of vitamin A. Kale, chard, collards, broccoli, spinach, green lettuce, turnip tops, green peas, green beans, yellow squash, carrots, sweet potatoes, and other green leafy and yellow vegetables are excellent sources.

The best sources of pre-formed vitamin A are liver, egg yolks, butter, cheese, fish roe, canned sardine and salmon, apricots, prunes, yellow peaches, red tomatoes, milk and cream. Fish-liver oils contain tremendous amounts of this vitamin and are used to treat severe deficiencies.

THIAMIN (VITAMIN B₁)

Functions. Thiamin is essential to the proper utilization of the fuel foodstuffs in the body and to the normal functioning of the digestive tract and of the nervous system. It promotes normal growth and tends to stimulate the appetite.

Results of deficiency. If the thiamin intake is insufficient for the amount of sugar and starchy foods in the diet, disturbances of metabolism will result. These can manifest themselves in various nervous symptoms— loss of appetite, indigestion, irritability, disinterest in important matters, pains in the limbs, ready fatigue, and even in mental and physical incompetence. Lack of thiamin can also effect a slowing of the heart rate. A severe deficiency produces the disease known as polyneuritis, or beri-beri, with its accompanying functional paralysis.

Cases of severe deficiency were less frequent before modern methods of refining foods were introduced. Raw, unhusked rice grains contain thiamin, but the substance is removed in the process of polishing. Whole wheat flour and wheat bran are thiamin-rich, but ordinary white bread flour is not since thiamin is removed from wheat during the milling process. The polishings from rice and the germ portions of grain are among the best sources of this vitamin. For this reason beri-beri is common where polished rice is eaten.

Cases of severe thiamin deficiency are infrequent in the United States, but prolonged mild shortages are common. This is one of the reasons for the all-too-common occurrence of heart and nerve disturbances in this country. This situation has recently been somewhat alleviated by the movement to enrich white flour and bread. People who consume little bread or cereal must give particular attention to the inclusion of thiamin-rich foods in their diets.

Sources. Lean meat (especially pork), liver, chicken, whole grain cereals, enriched flour and bread, milk, egg yolks, peanuts, pears, prunes, pineapples, oranges, apples, dates, and many of the green vegetables are good food sources. Yeast is also rich in thiamin.

RIBOFLAVIN (VITAMIN B₂ OR G)

Functions. This vitamin, like thiamin, is necessary to the derivation of energy from fuel foodstuffs. It is also important to normal growth and normal digestion.

Results of deficiency. Riboflavin deficiency can cause mouth irritation, redness of the tongue, and soreness and cracking of the lips. It is also likely to cause visual disturbances manifesting such symptoms as bloodshot eyes, undue sensitivity to light, and dim vision. A severe deficiency can cause pellagra with its accompanying skin lesions, nervous symptoms, and gastrointestinal disorders. This disease has been largely conquered in the United States, but many diets, especially in the southern states, are low in riboflavin content.

Sources. Liver and other animal organs, lean muscle meats, eggs, milk, cheese, peanuts, whole grain cereals, and green leafy vegetables are excellent sources of riboflavin, but it is contained in small amounts in many foods.

NIACIN (NICOTINIC ACID)

Functions. Like the other vitamins of the B group, niacin plays an important role in the conversion of fuel foodstuffs into energy. It also helps to maintain good digestion, steady nerves, and healthy skin.

Results of deficiency. The earliest effects of a shortage of niacin are the appearance of various nervous symptoms such as loss of appetite, forgetfulness, and mental depression, and the appearance of either diarrhea or constipation. Later there may be a condition of the mouth that is reminiscent of trench mouth. A severe and prolonged deficiency is one of the causes of pellagra.

Sources. Lean meats, liver, haddock, salmon, chicken, eggs, milk, tomato juice, and green leafy vegetables are good sources of this vitamin.

(VITAMIN C) ASCORBIC ACID

Functions. Ascorbic, or antiscorbutic, acid is so called because it serves to prevent and to cure scurvy, but it would be an extremely important nutritional element even if this disease had never existed. This vitamin is responsible for maintaining the integrity of the cementing substance of the body; among the duties involved therein are the regulation of the heart muscle, the prevention of hemorrhages, and the prevention of certain forms of anemia. It is also important in the processes of oxidation and reduction and in the formation of healthy teeth, gums, and bones. Liberal amounts of vitamin C strengthen the body's resistance to bacterial diseases.

Results of deficiency. The first evidence of a lack of this vitamin is usually a marked weakening of the capillary blood vessels; in the presence of this condition minor injuries can produce large bruises. Decay and loosening of the teeth also occur early in the absence of vitamin C. Loss of weight and ready fatigue are additional symptoms. A prolonged deficiency causes scurvy. In this disease the aforementioned symptoms occur in an intensified form. It has been prevalent among seamen, but it does not seem to appear when people live on a fresh food diet. Many people get less ascorbic acid than is recommended for optimum health and efficiency although they escape severe deficiency.

Sources. The richest sources of vitamin C are fresh citrus fruits, strawberries, raspberries, currants, gooseberries, tomatoes, peppers, cabbage, and other leafy green vegetables. Since high losses result from cooking, the diet should contain an abundance of fresh fruits and vegetables in order to insure an adequate intake of this vitamin. It cannot be stored in the body to any extent, so it is necessary to provide a regular intake of the foods containing it.

Milk is not an important source of vitamin C since pasteurization destroys most of that present. Therefore it is important to provide children with a good source such as orange juice or tomato juice early in life. This is particularly important in the case of artificially-fed infants. Milk is a fairly good source, however, when it is used in large quantities. It is interesting to note that cow's milk usually contains about three times more of this vitamin during the summer, when there is an abundance of fresh green material, than it does during the winter months.

VITAMIN D

Functions. Vitamin D is necessary for proper calcium and phosphorus metabolism, and thus it contributes to the formation and maintenance of healthy teeth and bones. Adequate amounts assist in the prevention or arrest of tooth decay.

Results of deficiency. Dental decay and bone deformities result from an insufficient intake of this vitamin. It causes the disease known as rickets. The name is derived from the old English word "wrikken," meaning "to twist or bend," and the disease is so called because of the twisted condition of the bones that seems to characterize it. It is primarily a children's disease, but it sometimes attacks adults in a milder manner. In adults a deficiency of vitamin D is more likely to effect muscular fatigue and a condition of extreme nervousness.

Sources. Ample amounts of this vitamin can be produced in the body by a sufficient exposure of the skin to direct sunlight or to artificial light containing ultraviolet rays, but the supply must usually be provided, or at least supplemented, by the diet. The best dietetic sources are egg yolks and fish-liver oils. Other good sources are salmon, herring, sardines, oysters, eggs, butter, cream, irradiated evaporated or whole milk, and liver.

Vitamin Contents of Particular Foods

Food	Vitamin A	Thiamin	Riboflavin	Niacin	Vitamin C	Vitamin D
Dairy products, eggs						
Butter	x					x
Cheese	x		x			
Cream	x					x
Eggs, whole	x	x	x	x		x
Egg yolk	x	x		x		x
Milk, whole	x	x	x	x		x
Meat, poultry, fish						
Beef, lean		x	x	x		
Chicken		x		x		
Codfish		x	x			
Fish-liver oils	x					x
Haddock				x		
Kidney	x	x	x		x	
Liver	x	x	x	x	x	x
Mutton, lean		x	x	x		
Pork, lean		x		x		
Roe, fish	x	x	x			
Salmon	x	x		x		x
Sardines	x	x				x
Fruit						
Apples		x	x		x	
Apricots	x	x	x		x	
Avocados	x	x	x		x	
Bananas	x	x	x		x	
Blackberries	x	x				
Blueberries	x					
Cantaloupe	x	x	x		x	
Cherries					x	
Cranberries					x	
Currants, black	x				x	
Dates	x	x				
Figs		x	x			
Gooseberries					x	
Grapefruit		x	x		x	
Lemons					x	
Oranges	x	x	x		x	
Olives, green and ripe	x					
Peaches	x		x		x	
Pears			x	x		
Pineapples	x	x			x	
Plums	x	x				
Prunes	x	x	x			
Raspberries		x			x	
Strawberries	x		x		x	
Tangerines	x	x	x	x	x	
Tomatoes		x	x		x	
Watermelon	x	x			x	
Vegetables						
Asparagus, green	x				x	
Beans, lima			x	x		
Beans, navy			x	x		
Beans, snap	x	x	x		x	
Beet greens	x		x			
Broccoli	x	x	x			x
Brussels sprouts	x	x				x
Cabbage	x	x	x	x	x	x
Carrots	x	x	x			
Cauliflower		x	x			x
Chard	x					
Collards	x	x	x	x	x	x
Corn, sweet	x					
Cowpeas		x	x	x		
Dandelion greens	x					x
Dock	x	x				x
Eggplant		x				
Endive	x		x			x
Kale	x	x	x	x	x	x
Kohlrabi		x				x
Leeks		x				x
Lettuce, green	x	x	x			
Mushrooms		x				
Mustard greens	x	x	x	x	x	x
Okra	x					
Onions		x				x
Parsnips		x				x
Peanuts		x	x	x		
Peas, dried		x	x	x		
Peas, green	x	x	x	x		x
Peppers, sweet	x	x				x
Potatoes		x				x
Radishes						x
Rhubarb						x
Rutabagas		x				x
Soybeans		x	x	x		
Spinach	x	x	x	x	x	x
Squash, yellow	x	x				
Sweet potatoes	x	x	x	x	x	x
Turnip greens	x	x	x	x	x	x
Water cress	x	x	x			x
Cereals						
Corn meal, yellow	x	x	x			
Whole grains		x	x			

A check under the vitamin in the vertical column indicates that it is contained in the food listed in the corresponding horizontal column. The chart will enable you to evaluate particular foods in regard to their vitamin content.

OTHER VITAMINS

Among the other known vitamins are additional members of the B family and vitamins E and K, but we need not be concerned with all of the vitamins that are required in the diet for normal nutrition. We are interested only in those that are of practical importance in diet planning. It is reasonable to assume that if the dietary provides adequate amounts of vitamins A, B, C, and D, there will be no ill effects resulting from a deficiency of any of the others.

THE PRESERVATION OF VITAMIN VALUES

Storage. The necessary temporary storage of food always involves certain vitamin losses. Riboflavin, niacin, and vitamin D are little affected during storage; vitamin A and thiamin are slowly destroyed; and vitamin C losses may be serious. For this reason, try to avoid long storage periods for foods that are rich in destructible vitamins. Vitamin C losses are not very great, however, in the case of acid foods. Tomatoes, citrus fruits, and rhubarb, for example, can be stored in a refrigerator for several days without undergoing any serious vitamin losses. Keep foods cold until you are ready to serve or cook them; heat tends to decompose vitamins.

Methods of food preservation. Freezing seems to have no destructive action on vitamins, and the losses attributed to it are due to improper handling before and after freezing. In connection with this process, fast freezing, storage at a temperature below 0° F., and fast thawing are recommended as aids to the preservation of vitamins. Cooking should generally begin while the food is still frozen. Foods should not be allowed to stand but should be consumed as soon as possible after thawing.

Drying results in losses of vitamin A, thiamin, and especially of vitamin C. Sun drying effects losses of vitamins A and C more than does artificial dehydration. The indications are that drying causes no appreciable destruction of riboflavin or of vitamin D.

Proper canning methods do not destroy vitamins. There are no appreciable losses so long as air is excluded from the hot food as much as possible. Losses result from oxidation, and they are prevented by removing air from the containers before processing begins. Acid foods tend to retain vitamins more than do the non-acid foods.

Preparation and cooking. The following vitamin-conserving suggestions are of the most practical value to the homemaker:

Prepare chopped fruit and vegetable salads just before serving. Bruising, peeling, cutting, chopping, or shredding of these foods accelerates their loss of vitamin C.

When cooking green vegetables, don't add soda to preserve their color. Soda destroys thiamin and vitamin C

Don't cook foods containing vitamin C in a copper vessel.

Don't use long cooking methods such as stewing when shorter methods are possible. To boil, put vegetables into boiling water and bring the water back to the boiling point as rapidly as possible. Cook vegetables until they are tender but no longer.

Since cooking liquid absorbs vitamins and minerals, it should not be discarded. Serve it with the vegetables, or use it to make gravies, soups, or sauces.

Use food as soon as possible after it has been prepared.

VITELLIN. The albumenoid substance in the egg yolks.

VITICULTURE. Vine culture. *See* GRAPE and WINE.

VODKA. The national drink of Russia, which is made in several varieties and is the base of various delicious liqueurs and beverages. Prior to World War I, it was usually made from potatoes and was strongly alcoholic (90–100 proof). Today, under government monopoly, vodka is made of selected wheat and carefully distilled by modern methods.

Vodka is usually served as an after-dinner cordial, and should be drunk cold. In Russia it is most often used as an apéritif or with the hors d'oeuvres or the fish. It is crystal-clear and rather fiery. Diluted in cold water, in the summer, it makes a very delicious as well as a very refreshing and thirst-quenching beverage. With hot water in winter it makes delicious grogs and punches.

VOL AU VENT. The French name for a patty shell made of puff paste, *which see.*

VOLATILE OIL. A substance evaporating rapidly on exposure, as oil of onion, garlic or shallot; also of fruits, as lemon, etc.

W

WAFER. A thin sweet cookie, which is sometimes baked on a special iron called a rosette iron. This is heated by dipping in hot oil, and the wafer batter dipped into the mold. Because it is very thin, it cooks almost instantaneously.

OUBLIES
(French Wafers)

6 oz sweet butter
½ lb powdered sugar
2 eggs, separated
½ cup white wine
1 lb pastry flour
1 tsp ground cinnamon
½ tsp salt

Cream butter with powdered sugar until very light. Then, using a wooden spoon, cream in egg yolks, adding one at a time, and beat well after each addition. Add the white wine; beat briskly until thoroughly blended and fluffy. Then fold in gently but thoroughly the stiffly beaten egg whites, alternately with the pastry flour, previously sifted with 1 teaspoon of cinnamon and ½ teaspoon of salt. Beat steadily for 2 minutes, or until batter is light and of the consistency of heavy cream, adding more white wine as needed. Pour by tablespoons into a heated, buttered rosette iron, and cook from 1 to 1½ minutes. Remove immediately, and while still hot roll around the handle of a knife or a wooden spoon.

WAFERS
(English)

6 oz flour
1 tsp ground ginger
½ tsp baking powder
2 oz molasses
2 oz butter
2 oz powdered sugar, or soft brown sugar

Melt the butter, sugar, and molasses together in pan very slowly until blended but do not overheat. Sift the flour with the baking powder, add the ginger; then mix all ingredients together to stiff paste. Divide into three portions. Roll out each portion as thinly as possible on floured board; cut in rounds with small cutter, and place on a cookie sheet. Bake in very moderate oven till firm and lightly colored. Store in covered containers. This dough is easier to handle if used while still warm.

WAFFLE. Waffles are made from a batter somewhat heavier than pancake batter, cooked in a specially constructed iron. Waffles may be plain or rich and made with bread flour or cake or pastry flour, or again with one of the commercial mixes. In making the batter, yolks and whites of eggs should always be separated, the stiffly beaten (but not dry) whites being folded in at the last moment, this giving a more foamy batter and subsequently a lighter waffle. It is well also to have the shortening sizzling hot and to pour it into the batter just before the final hard beating.

The preliminary preparation of the waffle iron depends on the type used and the manufacturer's directions should be closely followed. Generally speaking, however, a waffle iron should be greased, preferably with an unsalted fat, before it is used for the first time. Subsequently, provided enough shortening is added to the batter, greasing is unnecessary. Waffle irons should be thoroughly preheated before pouring in the batter. Many types have an indicator showing when the iron is ready for baking and when the waffle is done to perfection. If the batter is baked quickly in a very hot iron a soft waffle results, while a crisp one follows slow baking for a longer time.

Upon completion of the baking, heat the waffle iron for a few minutes to burn off any fat which may cause rancidity. If there are crumbs, brush them off with a steel brush especially designed for the purpose and leave the iron open until cold.

And remember that waffles may be served not only with butter and sirup but with such creamed mixtures as creamed dried beef, creamed shrimps, oysters, chicken, vegetables, etc.; also with a rich chocolate or butterscotch sauce, with whipped cream, melted honey, or ice cream. Again one may waffleize a cake batter, a gingerbread, or such a simple mixture as a cottage pudding.

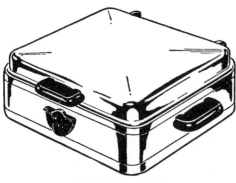

WAFFLE IRON

PLAIN WAFFLES

2 cups sifted flour
2 tsp baking powder
⅔ tsp salt
2 eggs
1¼ cups milk
6 tbsp melted shortening

Sift the dry ingredients and mix to a light batter with the beaten egg yolks, milk, and melted shortening. Beat the egg whites until stiff, fold into the batter, and bake in a preheated waffle iron, about 3 minutes. Serve hot with butter and sirup; as a base for various creamed dishes (vegetables, fish or meat); or topped with ice cream or a dessert sauce. (Makes 6 to 8 waffles)

VARIATIONS

Apple Waffles. Stir into plain waffle batter, before folding in the beaten egg whites, 2 cups of peeled, diced apples.
Banana Waffles. Stir into plain waffle batter, before folding in the beaten egg whites, 1½ cups of sliced bananas.
Cheese Waffles. Stir into plain waffle batter before folding in the stiffly beaten egg whites, 1 cup of grated cheese.
Chocolate Waffles. Substitute 3 tablespoons of cocoa for 3 tablespoons of the flour when preparing plain waffle batter.
Cinnamon Waffles. Sift 1½ teaspoons of cinnamon with the dry ingredients when preparing plain waffle batter.
Nut Waffles. Stir into plain waffle batter before folding in the beaten egg whites, ¾ cup of any preferred finely chopped nut meats.
Bake any of these waffles as directed for plain waffles.

WAFFLE IRON. A waffle iron is a utensil designed specifically for the cooking of waffles. It has two metal parts, hinged together, that, when closed, form the cavity in which the waffle is cooked. These parts have rows of projecting studs that produce the characteristic indentations on the finished waffle (*which see*). Though they can be designed to be heated by other fuels, virtually all waffle irons now in common use are electrically heated. *See also* ELECTRICAL EQUIPMENT and KITCHEN EQUIPMENT.

WALDMEISTER. An aromatic herb used for flavoring beverages, such as May wine. It is imported in dry form, but is also found fresh in the Pennsylvania woods, making its spring appearance in late May or the beginning of June.

WALDO CHEESE. A soft Italian cheese which should be eaten while fresh.

WALNUT. Indigenous to Persia, walnuts are mentioned in civilization's earliest history. The Phoenicians traded in them, and the Romans deified them, calling them the "nut of the gods." These large, creamy, wrinkled nuts with the sweet interior were eventually carried to all parts of the world in English trading ships and thus gained the misnomer of "English" walnuts.

The same Spanish padres who brought the first orange and lemon trees to southern California and thus inaugurated the gigantic citrus industry in the United States, also brought the first walnut trees to California, where 90 percent of our supply is now produced.

Water in abundance is needed to produce plump, tender walnut kernels. Normal rainfall does not supply enough, and growers must irrigate often. And just *any* water is not good enough—it must be free from alkali. Everyone likes walnuts—even orchard pests. So sprayers and dusters must be employed frequently to destroy these threats to quality. Spray towers 30 feet high are used, to reach the tops of the highest trees. For some pests a chemical "dust" is used, and powerful fans blow it throughout the entire grove.

Walnuts reach maturity early in the fall. As the husks split open, pickers shake the branches with long, hooked poles, and the nuts fall to the ground. Then they are dried, either on large trays spread in the sun, or in mechanical dehydrators, where circulating currents of warm air blown by fans dry them much more rapidly.

From the grove the walnuts are taken to packing plants where the nuts are first passed under a vacuum machine which automatically lifts out all nuts with empty or part-filled shells. Human eyes cannot tell by looking at a walnut whether there is a sound kernel inside, but these machines practically "look through the shells" with uncanny accuracy. From the vacuum machines, the nuts pass to trained inspectors, who remove nuts with external defects. Then the shells are washed, and then inspected again, and nuts with defects revealed in washing are removed. In all, there are three of these hand-sortings, to make sure that only the finest walnuts reach market.

The nuts are next graded mechanically for size. Spiral graders, 18 feet long and 40 inches in diameter, having over 18,000 openings, separate the nuts into three size grades. Only medium and large sizes are sold in the shell, and these must pass another test in which 300 nuts from each lot are cracked and the kernels inspected. Shelled walnuts are packed in vacuum-sealed tins. An automatic weighing machine fills each can with the exact weight of nuts. The cans then pass through a complicated machine which extracts all air and tightly seals the cans. The absence of air insures the kernels' retaining their freshness indefinitely in any climate. Paper-shell walnuts have particularly thin skins.

HINTS ON USE

Walnuts can be used in many dishes where the richer, oilier nuts are undesirable. Unless a recipe specifically calls for grinding the nuts, walnuts should be broken in rather coarse pieces.

Try adding broken walnut meats to a bread dressing for chicken or turkey. Add broken meats to an apple betty pudding.

Walnuts may be bought in the shell, shelled whole meats, or broken meats. They are cheapest in the shell, and most expensive as shelled whole meats. If you plan to use the meats for cooking, it is uneconomical to buy the whole meats. *See also* NUTS.

WALNUT STICKS

1¼ cups all-purpose flour
½ cup butter
½ cup brown sugar, firmly packed

Sift the flour; measure and resift once. Cream the butter and add the brown sugar gradually. Add the flour and mix to a smooth stiff dough. Pat into a shallow pan (12x8½x½ inches). Bake in a moderate oven (350° F.) for 15 minutes. Cool thoroughly before adding part two:

1 egg
¾ cup brown sugar, firmly packed
¼ cup short shredded moist coconut
2 tbsp flour
½ cup chopped walnuts
½ tsp baking powder
½ tsp vanilla
¼ tsp almond extract

Beat the egg, add the brown sugar and mix thoroughly; then add remaining ingredients. Stir to blend well. Spread over cooled baked layer. Return to oven (350° F.) for 20 minutes; the top will look slightly unbaked. Cool thoroughly and dust with powdered sugar. Cut into bars or sticks. Store in a tightly covered container. (Makes 25 bars about 2½ inches by 1½ inches)

WARD EIGHT. A cocktail which originated, at least in name, in the eighth ward in Boston, Mass.

WALNUTS 1. English 2. Japan 3. Black

WARD EIGHT

1 jigger whisky (rye or bourbon)
1 small lemon (juice)
1 tsp powdered sugar
2 tsp grenadine

The ingredients are mixed by shaking with cracked ice, strained into a ward eight glass (see GLASSWARE) and two ice cubes added. The drink is garnished with orange and lemon slices, a maraschino cherry, and served with straws. See also BARTENDING. (Serves 1)

WASSAIL BOWL. A festive bowl, or beverage, that was served during the Christmas season under old English traditions. It was a very old custom, dating back to the days of the Saxons, in whose language was-hael! meant "Health to you!" This became a drinking toast, the proper reply being, drinc-hael! The term wassail came to be applied to festive occasions in general, where drinking was done, and to the yuletide season in particular. There were wassail songs and wassail singers and wassail cups and wassail bowls, these latter beverages usually being served in the form of a loving cup (which see). Though there were many recipes for these beverages, they were generally based on heated, spiced ale or beer.

WASSAIL BOWL

1 qt ale or beer
1 tbsp grated nutmeg
1 tbsp grated ginger
1 tbsp grated cinnamon
1 pt sherry
1 lemon, juice and skin
2 roasted apples
2 slices toast
Sugar

The ale is heated, placed in a punch bowl or large loving cup and the spices, sherry, and lemon juice added. The lemon peel is first prepared by slicing in long spirals, as thin as possible, so that no white skin is left on the rind, and then added. The apples are cored before roasting and may be either skinned and pulped or tossed in whole, to float in the mixture. It is sugared to taste, and the slices of toast are dropped on the surface. It is served hot, either as a punch, or as a loving cup pass-ing round the table, giving each guest an opportunity to toast the gathering. See also PUNCH. (Serves 8)

WATER. Man can live without food for considerable length of time, if he has to do so. But deprivation from water affects him very seriously after a short time. While this colorless liquid has no value which can be measured in calories, all of the body's tissues contain it, and it is an essential part of the blood and digestive juices. It is estimated that water composes about 70 percent of the entire body weight, and it is an almost universal solvent. Its importance to the system, therefore, cannot be overrated. The elasticity or pliability of muscles, cartilages, and tendons, and even of bones, is in a large part due to the water these tissues contain.

The amount of water required by a healthy person in 24 hours averages between 65 and 70 ounces, besides about 20 ounces taken in as an ingredient of solid food, thus making a total of 85 to 90 ounces. The elimination of this water is divided as follows: 28 percent through the skin; 20 percent through the lungs; 50 percent through the urine; and 2 percent through other secretions and the feces. This of course is a very general computation, for there is constant variation in the activity of different organs.

A large proportion of the water is taken in the form of beverages composed chiefly of it, and many persons substitute such beverages for plain water altogether. In some countries light wines, beer, and other fermented drinks almost wholly replace drinking water. This may be due to habit or custom, or to necessity from lack of pure natural water, but in all cases the quantity of water required to maintain the functions of the body in healthful activity remains the same, whether it be drunk pure or in beverages, or taken in succulent fruits and vegetables, or in milk, etc.

One of the most universal dietetic failings is a neglect to take enough water into the system. The uses of water in the body may be summarized as follows:

It enters into the chemical composition of the tissues.

It forms the chief ingredient of all the fluids of the body and maintains their proper degree of dilution.

By moistening various surfaces of the body, such as the mucous and serous membranes, it prevents friction and the uncomfortable symptoms which might result from their drying.

It furnishes in the blood and lymph a fluid medium by which nourishment may be taken to remote parts of the body and the waste matter removed, thus promoting rapid tissue changes.

It serves as a distributor of body heat.

It regulates the body temperature by the physical processes of absorption and evacuation.

You may drink just as much water as you like and not be obliged to worry about its being a factor in producing extra weight. It is a common fallacy to believe that water is fattening. Actually, it plays a part in weight only when salt is eaten in excessively large quantities. Both salt and water are necessary for body efficiency.

There is no reliable evidence that ice water (35° to 50° F.) causes chronic injury to the alimentary tract. Taken in large quantities with a meal, it may, through its coolness, slow down gastric digestion for a few minutes. But this is probably of little significance.

DRINKING WATER

For drinking purposes water containing a moderate quantity of mineral salts, 4 or 5 grains to the gallon, is not to be regarded as impure, though the composition as well as the quantity of these salts affect its power as a solvent in the tissues, and may exert a very decided influence upon the digestive system when present in the proportion of 60 or 70 grains to the gallon. The mineral waters may contain much more. Water is usually unwholesome for drinking when derived from volcanic and basaltic mountain regions, and because of organic impurities water is bad in marshy regions.

Hard and Soft Water. An excess of lime salts and of other mineral matter in water produces constipation, flatulence, indigestion, and favors the formation of calcareous deposits in various parts of the body. *Hard water* unites with soap and makes it less soluble, so that it is difficult to cleanse the hands with it. It also roughens the skin and dries the mucous membranes. The hardness of water, which is due to the presence of earthy carbonates, is diminished by boiling, for the carbonic acid, which aids in holding them in suspension, is driven off. Water is also improved for drinking by

being filtered, either through a filter paper, or clean absorbent cotton placed in a funnel.

Soft water is simply water which is free from objectionable salts. It is more wholesome than hard water. Hard and soft waters have well-known characteristics in regard to their effects upon the cooking of food.

Rain Water. Next to clear mountain-spring water which has run through gravel and been well aerated, rain water at the close of a shower is the purest form of natural water, excepting where it has fallen through a very dusty or smoky atmosphere or has run over a dirty roof. The first drops of a shower carry down with them the impurities of the air, including traces of ammonia and nitric acid. No natural water possesses absolute chemical purity, but water collected at the end of a hard or long shower is very pure, having been distilled by previous evaporation. It is very good for cooking vegetables, including tubers and roots.

River Water. The water which has run over a rocky or gravel bed, and has been well aerated, is quite pure if properly protected from sources of pollution. Free oxidation makes much organic matter harmless. Flowing water by oxidation and dilution becomes purified to a great extent of injurious organic matter, but is not necessarily deprived of living germs of contagion, such as those of typhoid fever or cholera, and the question whether their number and virulence are at all diminished in such water is still a matter of controversy. When boiled and cooled, this water may be safely drunk or used for cooking.

Distilled Water. Distilled water is absolutely pure, but it has a flat or metallic taste, due to absence of air or salts. It is now supplied widely for drinking, and is generally used on vessels at sea. Modern naval vessels carry apparatus for its preparation.

Filtered Water. Filtration, as employed to render drinking water more pure, is a very delusive process, unless great care is taken in the construction of the filter and the rate of filtration.

Boiled Water. Boiled water is antifermentative and antiseptic. The object of boiling water which is to be used for drinking purposes, or in the preparation of food, is to free it from all organic impurities, and in some cases to precipitate salts of lime.

There are no forms of germs, and there are no ferments which are not killed by longer or shorter boiling, or exposure to the temperature of boiling water. The process consists in the application of heat to water in sufficient degree to expand the air which it naturally absorbs and cause it to rise to the surface in bubbles of various sizes. If the water contains gases of decomposition, they are expelled, and the odor is most foul just before the boiling point is reached; later the odor passes off, thereby showing when the water is fit to drink or to be used for cooking food. When boiled water, cooled, is drunk, it tastes flat or insipid, but it may be freshened by pouring it through the air from one vessel to another. Drinking water should always be boiled if there is the slightest suspicion as to its purity.

WATER HEATER. The importance of an adequate supply of sufficiently hot water is perhaps best grasped when one is either deprived of it, or forced to heat it at need over a gas burner or other heating element. It is especially needed in cleaning operations, for without it, it is difficult to remove grease.

Several different types of water heaters have been developed to meet different needs. With few exceptions, they require a regular water pressure system to operate successfully.

TYPES

Reservoir. A reservoir or tank was commonly built into wood and coal ranges so that they could heat a supply of water while performing other functions. *See* RANGE.

Hot Water Tank. The hot water tank is an improvement over the reservoir, for it insures a larger supply of heated water. The metal tank itself is built large enough to care for the estimated family needs, and is connected at top and bottom to a length of coiled pipe, usually copper. The tank is held in a position higher than the coil, and the coil is built into some sort of heating device. This device may be a separate coal, wood, oil, or gas stove, or the coil may be included in the regular furnace. When the water in the coil is heated, it rises to the top, being lighter than the cold water surrounding it. The hot water goes to the top of the tank and is replaced by cold water from the bottom. Theoretically, this process continues until all of the water in the tank is at the same temperature, and that as hot as the heat source can make it. When hot water is drawn from the tank, it is automatically replaced with cold water from the mains.

Flash Heater. The flash heater eliminates the hot water tank, the water flowing directly from the main to the coil and thence to the faucet. The coil and the heater, usually gas, are so designed that the water will be heated to a pre-set temperature as it passes through. Usually ignited by means of a pilot light, the heater functions only when the water faucet is turned on.

Immersion heater. The immersion heater is powered by electricity and is lowered into any vessel filled with the water to be heated. There are two types of immersion heaters. One consists of a sealed cartridge which contains the heating element, but does not admit the water. Units of this type are turned off and on by means of a switch.

A second type of immersion heater has an exposed heating element. When the unit is dipped in the water, which is a conductor of electricity, the circuit is actually completed by the water, causing the unit to heat up and to stay in operation as long as it is under the surface.

This same principle is also utilized in bottle warmers and some other similar devices. These units consist of a receptacle that holds the object to be heated, having a porcelain inside and an exposed heating element on the bottom. When a measured amount of water is poured in, the unit automatically starts to function, working only until the water has boiled away and no longer completes the circuit. Thus, the heat can be controlled by varying the amount of water poured into the device.

Instantaneous Heater. This is a variation of the flash heater, but is operated by electricity and is made as a separate unit to be connected to the end of the faucet. Inside the unit there are two sets of metal plates, between which or through which the water must flow when the faucet is turned on. These plates do not touch each other, and are so connected to an attachment wire as to form the halves of a broken circuit. When the water flows, it completes the circuit and becomes heated to a temperature which is controlled by adjusting the distance between the two sets of plates. *See also* DISHWASHING and ELECTRICAL EQUIPMENT.

WATER ICE. *See* ICE.

WATER SOFTENER. Water is said to be "hard" when it contains an excess of mineral salts, notably calcium and magnesium (*see* WATER.) Not only is it difficult to get a good soap lather (*see* DISHWASHING) with hard water, but it also leaves a hard, scaly deposit in the bottom of all the vessels in which it is used. If the water supplied in a community is hard, relief from the situation may be obtained by installing a special unit in the house water line that will remove the objectionable minerals by chemical means. Known by a variety of trade names, as well as filters (*see* FILTER) and water softeners, some of these units must have their chemicals replaced periodically, while others may be "recharged" by flushing with a saline mixture.

WATERCRESS. Watercress is a hardy, aquatic herb belonging to the mustard family. It is cultivated in Europe, and varieties of wild watercress are found in brooks in some sections of the United States. The peppery leaves of the plant are eaten raw as salads or garnishes, or they are chopped or ground and used as a seasoning agent. Cream of watercress soup, which may be made like cream of sorrel soup, is both delicious and nutritious. Watercress butter (*see* BUTTER SAUCE) makes an interesting sauce for hot diced beets.

WATERMELON. Watermelon originated in Africa, where it is greatly appreciated by both natives and the wild beasts. In America, the southern states and California are the chief commercial growers. Properly chilled watermelon is a delicious and refreshing fruit, one of the most popular desserts on the summer menu. Pickled watermelon and pickled watermelon rind also make appetizing

WATERCRESS

relishes and are easily made at home. A tea from watermelon seeds has been used in the treatment of kidney trouble, because of its refreshing and cooling qualities. The juice of the watermelon is used in several diseases by Russian peasants, and it has been practically the only remedy used by the ancient and modern Egyptians in case of fever.

VARIETIES OF WATERMELON

There are numerous varieties of watermelon which differ considerably in coloring, shape and quality, but in size and flavor they are all very similar. There are several kinds distinguished by their bright yellow flesh, but the flavor and other characteristics are practically the same. News in the melon field is the recent development of watermelons in reduced sizes to answer the ever-persistent demand for a melon to fit the modern refrigerator and families of two. One of these new varieties is Northern Sweet, developed by the Minnesota Agricultural Experiment station from seeds imported from the Volga region of Russia. The melon weighs but 9 to 10 pounds, is rich in color, sweet, and free from fiber.

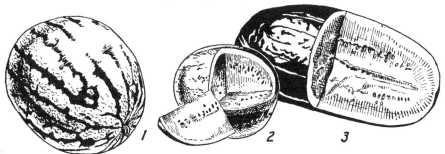

WATERMELONS   1. Dixie Queen   2. Ice Box   3. Kleckley

Food Value

Water	Food Energy	Pro- tein	Fat	Carbo- hydrate	Cal- cium	Phos- phorus	Iron	Vit. A Value	Thia- mine	Ribo- flavin	Nia- cin	Ascor- bic Acid
92.1	31	.5	.2	6.9	7	12	.2	590	.05	.05	.2	6

Preparation for Market

Rich sandy loam soils are considered best for watermelons, but good crops are often grown on almost any type of well-drained, warm and fertile soil. Watermelons are not an exacting crop as regards their cultivation, but it is essential that the land be well plowed before planting. A pound of good watermelon seed is sufficient for planting an acre, with a small amount left for replanting. Planting dates vary with the locality. Because the young plants are easily injured by frost, the seed should not be planted until the soil is warm and the danger of frost is past. Growers of high-grade watermelons prune the watermelons so that the entire vigor of the vine goes into the development of the melons that are left; this usually results in the production of a high percentage of marketable melons. Exterior indications are the only practical ones by which to judge the maturity of the individual melons. The best one is that of the change in color, especially that of the lower part of the melon where it rests upon the ground. This consists of a slight yellowing of the white background. The usual method of loading the melons from small piles to the wagon or truck is to have two men on the ground and two on the wagon or truck and simply pass the melons, one at a time, from the ground to the wagon or truck. All melons cut from the vines during the day, should be placed in the car, and not allowed to remain in the field. Watermelons are shipped in stock cars, ordinary box cars, ventilated fruit cars, and in special cases of long haul, refrigerator cars are employed.

Watermelons are graded for the market according to the standards of the United States Department of Agriculture. U.S. No. 1 consists of watermelons of the same variety which are mature but not overripe, fairly well-formed, and free from decay, disease, and damage. U.S. Commercial consists of watermelons which meet all the requirements of U.S. No. 1 and are free from anthracnose. U.S. No.

2 consists of watermelons of the same variety which are mature but not overripe, not badly misshapen, and free from serious damage. U.S. No. 3 consists of watermelons which are mature but not overripe, and free from any defect that seriously affects the internal quality of the watermelon.

Any lot of watermelon which does not meet the requirements of the above grades remains unclassified.

Hints on Buying

When buying watermelon look for regular shape; good-looking melons are generally the best. A fully ripe melon usually has a dull rather than a bright, shiny appearance, and a thin outer skin that peels easily. Ripe melons have a bloom over a velvety surface and are deep solid green to gray in color, according to the variety. The underside is pale yellow. Thumping produces a dull, muffled sound. Immature watermelons usually present a hard, greenish, unripe appearance. The underside is pale green. Thumping produces a hollow ring. Overmature watermelons are dull and lifeless, and soft and springy to the touch.

Hints on Preparation

Serve watermelon ice cold. Or dip out the red heart balls, and add their flavor to a fruit cup. For a garden party or buffet supper there is cool beauty in a fruit-basket centerpiece, made of a watermelon shell. The upper half of the rind is removed in two sections, leaving a crosswise strip 2 inches wide, to form the basket handle. The pulp is cut into small balls and replaced along with balls of honeydew and cantaloupe, with seedless grapes, each arranged in a section of the holder. White wine is poured over all this just before serving.

A slice of melon cut lengthwise, or melon halved crosswise and filled with berries, makes either an attractive dessert or introduction to a meal. Chilled and served sliced, diced, or cubed, as in cocktails or sherbets, it is the ideal dessert for sultry summer days.

Watermelon honey, made by straining the crushed flesh and mixing it into ordinary honey, has an appeal. Watermelon pickle is quite popular and has considerable commercial value. The white part of the rind is pickled in sugar, vinegar, and spices, and makes a very acceptable accompaniment to meats. Watermelon juice also has been made into a successful and delicious vinegar, but this process found no commercial possibilities.

PINEAPPLE AND WATERMELON ROYAL

On a shiny green leaf place a slice of fresh pineapple, which has been sprinkled first with a little brown sugar and then with one teaspoon of brandy. On the pineapple place a round of chilled watermelon, cut from a thick slice of melon with a fancy cookie cutter. Top with one tablespoon of fresh, cleaned, hulled raspberries, and garnish with sprigs of fresh mint leaves. Pass powdered sugar separately.

WATERMELON MILK SHERBET

2 tbsp lemon juice
½ tsp grated lemon rind
½ cup granulated sugar
4 cups diced watermelon
⅛ tsp salt
1¼ cups undiluted evaporated milk
2 tbsp sherry wine (optional)
2 egg whites, stiffly beaten

Combine lemon juice, grated rind, sugar and watermelon pulp. Mix well and let stand in refrigerator for 30 minutes. Rub this through a sieve; then add well-chilled undiluted evaporated milk slowly to watermelon mixture. Freeze to a mush in the refrigerator tray; remove from tray and scrape bottom and sides. Then fold in the stiffly beaten egg whites with the sherry wine. Continue freezing for at least 4 hours. Serve in chilled sherbet glasses. (Serves 4 to 6)

WATERMELON PICKLE I

7 lb prepared watermelon rind (about 30 lb melon if rind is thin; slightly less if thick)

2¼ qt water
⅓ cup salt
6½ cups sugar
2 cups vinegar
1 cup water
1 tbsp whole cloves
1 stick cinnamon
2 tsp cassia buds
1 lemon, sliced paper thin.

Prepare watermelon rind by cutting into inch strips. Slice away pink flesh, peel off the green rind, then cut strips neatly into diamonds, squares, or triangles. Stir water and salt until salt dissolves and pour over the rind in an enamelware bowl. Brine should cover the melon. Cover bowl and let stand over night. Next morning rinse in several cold waters. Drain and turn into an aluminum or enamelware preserving kettle. Barely cover melon with cold water. Cover and heat to boiling. Reduce heat and simmer until rind is tender when pricked with a fork (from 40 to 60 minutes), the time depending on thickness of rind. Turn into colander to drain. Have ready a sirup made by heating 5½ cups of sugar, vinegar and 1 cup water to boiling in the same preserving kettle. Add the drained hot rind and heat to boiling. Reduce heat, and simmer uncovered for about 1 hour or until melon begins to take on transparent appearance. Add the spices last 10 minutes of cooking. Remove from heat, cover and let stand overnight. Drain off sirup, add lemon slices, and remaining 1 cup sugar. Reheat to boiling, and again pour over melon. Cover, let stand again over night. Drain off sirup, and heat to boiling. Pour over rind packed in hot sterilized jars. Seal and process 10 minutes in boiling water bath. (Makes 6 pints) *See also* CANNING.

WATERMELON PICKLE II

Pare off the thin green rind, and cut out the red meat, leaving just a tiny line of pink. Cut this into small cubes. Weigh, and cook, until nearly transparent (about 1 hour), in clear water to which a teaspoon of salt has been added. Drain very thoroughly—there should be a quart of liquid for each 2 pounds of raw peel. If not, add additional hot water to make up the quantity. Add the sugar to this, allowing 1 pound for each 2 pounds of fruit, weighed when raw. Bring to boiling point, add the prepared rind, with 2 lemons, thinly sliced, and simmer about 2 hours or until the sirup is thickened and the rind clear. Turn into hot sterilized jars and seal. *See also* CANNING.

WATERMELON SALAD

With a French vegetable cutter, cut balls from the melon, which should be very ripe and of good red color. Remove all seeds carefully. Place the balls in the refrigerator to chill. At serving time, arrange them in cups of small crisp lettuce and garnish with sprigs of mint. Serve with French dressing. This salad is very attractive in a bed of fresh, green watercress.

WATER-PEPPER. The common smartweed. An allied species without acrid leaves, hence called "mild water-pepper," is used in some parts of the South as a salad.

WAX BEAN. *See* BEAN.

WAX MYRTLE. Another name for bayberry, *which see.*

WAXED PAPER. Waxed paper is paper that has been impregnated with wax to make it airtight. It is available in both sheets and rolls, and has a great many kitchen uses, chief of them being to wrap foods for storage.

WEAKFISH. So-called because of its very tender mouth, this fish is also known as deep water trout or sea trout. The Indians called it *squeteague*. The weakfish is found all along the eastern seaboard, coming near the shores to spawn in May. The fish is a pale brownish color on the back with a greenish tinge, grading into silvery along the sides and belly. It is splotched with brown, some of which form undulating lines running forward and downward. Its average weight is four or five pounds.

Although it is called sea trout, it is not a trout and does not have the delicacy of trout. However, it is a very delicious fish and may be prepared in any of the ways appropriate for trout or other white fishes. *See also* FISH.

WEDDING CAKE. Fashions in wedding refreshments change. However, the basic recipes for the cake itself seem to be just about the same from one generation to the next. A cake that deserves to be called a wedding cake should be superlatively good—a rich fruit cake, which is usually the centerpiece of the bridal table. The bride always cuts the first slice and shares it with the bridegroom.

The wedding cake is a direct survival of a particular kind of cake used in Roman times among patrician families. At the aristocratic Roman *confarreation* the bride and groom not only ate together, but feasted the guests, and a fragment of the cake of *confarreation* was broken over the bride's head as a symbol of plentifulness. Each of the guests took a piece to insure plentifulness to himself.

With the Anglo-Saxons, the wedding guests brought to the wedding small spiced buns which were piled in a huge mound on the table. It was a popular custom for the bride and groom to attempt to kiss each other over this mound, and if they succeeded they were assured life-long prosperity. The wedding cake, as we know it today, was the idea of a French chef who was traveling through England. Stopping for a while in London, he noted the inconvenience of piling hundreds of small spice cakes into one mound and thereupon he conceived the idea of icing this mound in one solid mass. So the wedding cake was created.

A unique Bermuda wedding tradition involves the imbedding of a tiny cedar tree in the third tier of the cake. Prior to cutting, the bride must plant the tree, in order that it may thrive and therefore bless the newlyweds with everlasting happiness. *See* CAKE for recipes.

WEDGE. To cut fruit, meat, vegetables, etc., in the shape of a wedge. Also a triangular portion of a round pie or cake.

WEIGHTS AND MEASURES. Weights and measures are arbitrary systems or standards used to determine the quantity of substances. Any unit desired may be used as the standard, provided that it does not change, and that it is understood and accepted by others. In this respect, weights and measures are very much like languages; indeed, they originated and developed much as did languages.

HISTORY

As each race or tribal unit developed its language, it also developed some system of weights and measures. These systems were usually based on parts of the body, length of stride or reach, etc. When food was gathered in bundles or baskets, these were gradually standardized for trading purposes. Not all of these systems were too accurate or efficient, and they all suffered in being local, rather than general in their acceptance.

As the races mingled and trade was established on a world basis, the need for uniform measuring systems became apparent, and gradually a few of the better systems became generally accepted as "standard." However, many of the old or local systems have clung on, even to today, creating occasional confusion.

The *metric system* was developed and an attempt was made to have it adopted universally. While it is a most convenient system to use, it has never made much headway in the United States, except in scientific circles.

Culinary. Since food figures prominently in trade, weighing and measuring standards were quickly developed for use in the market place. Except for a few foods that are sold by the bunch, such as radishes or celery, standard measures and weights are used. While some foods, such as oranges, are sold in terms of crates or boxes at the wholesale level, they are sold by the pound or by count at the retail level.

Confusion has reigned in the field of recipes, however, until quite recently. When one is following a recipe, it is obvious that one should know how much of a particular food should be used, but when recipes were first recorded, the instructions called vaguely for "some" of this and "a goodly portion" of that. As time went on, recipes began to be a bit more specific, speaking of a "pinch" of salt and a "lump of butter the size of a walnut." This was better, but still not too efficient, since a "pinch" will vary, even when measured by the same person, and walnuts grow to many sizes.

This condition prevailed largely because cooking was an art handed down from mother to daughter, or done by specialists who measured by taste, instinct, and inspiration. It was not until a very short time ago that domestic *science* became an accepted field, and serious attempts were made to find the best cooking techniques and standardize them for all to use. Recipes were then expressed in terms of definite units.

But the kitchen had developed a language all its own, so it followed that this language should be used in its measurements. As a result, recipes are given in terms of teaspoons, tablespoons, dashes, and cups. These, however, have been standardized and are as exact units as are liters, yards, or drams.

IMPORTANCE

The importance of weights and measures cannot be minimized. Their importance when purchasing food is, of course, obvious, and needs no discussion. But their importance in cooking, unfortunately, is sometimes overlooked.

Weights and measures are invaluable kitchen tools. Through their intelligent use, the housewife is able to get the best results, consistently. She can judge the cooking time of a piece of meat through its weight. She can estimate the correct quantities to purchase and prepare to serve a given number of people by means of weights and measures. And by following a recipe carefully, she can be certain of getting pretty much the same results every time she prepares a given dish.

EQUIPMENT

The equipment needed for accurate kitchen measurement is simple, small in number, and usually quite inexpensive. The equipment is basic, and most items are essential for good cooking practice. *See also* KITCHEN EQUIPMENT.

Jigger. A small glass of 1, 1½, or 2 ounce capacity, used primarily in the preparation of alcoholic beverages, and sometimes for measuring salad oil and other cooking liquids that are used in small quantities. Since jiggers are made in various capacities, but are rarely marked, its exact capacity should be determined before use. *See* BARTENDING; *see also* JIGGER.

Knife. A knife is a handy tool for leveling off the contents of measuring devices. Either edge of the blade may be used, but the edge must be straight, and sufficiently long to reach across the vessel. Since it is not used for cutting, a table knife may be used.

Measuring Cups. There are two types of measuring cups made: one has a graduated scale on the side to indicate different amounts, while the other is made to hold an exact amount when filled to the brim, and comes as part of a nested set, each cup having a different capacity. The first type is used to measure liquids, the level of a measured amount falling below the edge of the rim, thus eliminating the danger of spillage, while the second type is used to measure solids, which have to be smoothed on the surface to give an accurate measure. Both types are needed. *See* MEASURING CUP.

Since, in this sense, a cup is a unit of measure and not a drinking vessel, regular tea or coffee cups (*see* DISHES) should not be used for measuring purposes, unless their exact capacity is known. Drinking cups are designed for appearance and not to hold an exact amount.

Measuring Spoons. All that has been said for measuring cups applies to measuring spoons. These are also made in two types for the same reasons, and both types are needed. The teaspoons and tablespoons made for table use are often not accurate as measuring devices, and their bowls are frequently too shallow to be practical in use. *See* MEASURING SPOON: *see also* FLATWARE.

Mixing Glass. Mixing glasses (*which see*) often have graduated scales on their sides so they may be used for measuring purposes. When so marked, they are also called measuring glasses and graduates. They are usually marked in terms of fluid ounces rather than cups, though both scales may be used, and they should have a good pouring lip.

Recipe File. Recipes come from many sources other than cook books. They are clipped from newspapers and magazines, written down by neighbors, and even discovered by experimentation or accident. It is well to have some storage place for these miscellaneous scraps of paper, either a box or a paper folder. All variations on basic recipes should be noted down, as well.

Scale. A scale is not essential, but it is a handy thing to have. One can keep a record of the weight of meat at the time of purchase and estimate the differences made by boning or fat removal, but the scale will give an accurate measure of the final weight of the prepared roast for use with a time-temperature table. It may also be used to check the accuracy and honesty of the butcher and other food vendors who sell their produce by the pound. Few

recipes are given in units of weight, however, and one should never confuse fluid ounces with ounces avoirdupois, the former being a unit of volume, and the latter a unit of weight. *See* SCALE.

Scoop. These are needed to remove flour, sugar, cereal, etc., from their storage containers.

Sifter. A sifter is needed to prepare flour for accurate measuring. *See* SIFTER.

Spatula. This may be used, in place of the knife, to level dry foods in measuring devices, and also to handle butter, lard, shortening, etc.

There are many other measuring devices available in the stores; some of these are quite ingenious, others are mere gadgets. The devices mentioned are basic, but that does not preclude the use of other items, if they are desired. Dry measures—bushels, pecks, and quarts—may, in some cases, be required. There are devices which, when placed on bottles, will only permit a measured amount to be poured.

In addition, there are many basic kitchen utensils that can be used as measures, though that is not their prime function. A ladle, bowl, cup, pan, etc., can be used, provided that its capacity is first determined by checking it with an accurate measure. In some cases graduations or levels may be marked on the side of the vessel, and, in the case of an often used metal pan, discoloration may prove to be a sufficiently accurate mark. These markings need not be in terms of cups or other specific units, but in terms of use—for example, filling a coffee maker to a certain level to produce enough coffee of the desired strength to serve the family at breakfast.

Purchasing. As most basic items are inexpensive, there is little excuse for not getting good ones. Good, in this case, means sturdy, accurate, easily read devices. There are many items that are convenient and "showy," but these are usually more expensive. Since the basic implements can serve the same purpose (though, in some cases, less conveniently), their selection is a matter of individual circumstances.

It is most important that the markings be accurate and easily read. Most of the foods handled have a tendency to cling to the sides of the vessels and obscure markings, especially if they are small or faint. It is not a good policy to have too many markings on any one vessel, lest the user become confused and select the wrong one. Nesting cups and spoons should be clearly marked so that the wrong one will not be selected.

The devices should have rings or holes so they may be hung in convenient positions. Utensils used with liquids should have good pouring lips, and all of the devices should have large, sturdy handles, so that none of a measured amount will be spilled in carrying or pouring.

Virtually every material is used to make these devices, and both the materials and the devices are discussed under their individual headings, *which see*. As a general rule, either glass or clear plastic vessels are to be preferred for use with liquids, for they are easier to read than are opaque devices.

Care. Each device should receive the care proper to the material of which it is made. All devices should be cleaned after each use, to prevent contamination when next used. Devices should be dried carefully before use, lest any powdery, dry substance cling to the instrument, and not go into the food where it is needed.

If a measuring device becomes dented or warped, it is no longer accurate, and should either be returned to its original shape or discarded. If the markings become obliterated and cannot be restored, the device should also be discarded.

Above all, measuring devices should never be used as cooking vessels, or for any purpose other than measuring.

Measuring Methods

Instructions given in the recipe should be followed closely. A *heaping* measure indicates that there is more than the stated capacity of the measure, the surplus material lying in a mound above the edge of the instrument. Heaping measures are best obtained in the nesting rather than graduated instruments, the "heap" being as much material as will conveniently lie on the top without falling as the vessel is moved. Unless otherwise specified, however, all measures are *level*, and this is best found by resting the container on an even surface, in the case of liquids, and scraping the top, in the case of solids.

Fractional parts of a teaspoon or tablespoon may be found by first taking a level spoonful of the substance and using a knife

to halve or quarter the contents of the spoon, discarding the unwanted portions. Greater accuracy may be obtained, however, by using special measuring devices.

Flour. Flour should be sifted once before measuring, so that it will be packed properly and evenly. Once sifted, the flour is lightly scooped into a measuring cup of the nesting type until it has reached the "heaping" stage. The cup is then leveled off, using a knife or spatula to scrape the surplus flour back into the container. Care must be taken not to shake, tap, or set the container down too hard during the process, thus causing the flour to pack or settle.

Liquids (Milk, Water, Juice, etc.). These are best measured in a graduated clear vessel, with the level of the liquid lying below the rim. The vessel should be set on a level surface and the markings read at eye-level to insure accuracy.

Oils and Sirups. These are measured in the same manner as liquids. Because these substances tend to cling to the sides of their container, care must be taken to see that all of the fluid is poured out of the measuring device. A pastry brush (*which see*) is useful in urging the fluid to leave.

Powders and Granules. Baking powders, salt, cereals, etc., are handled in somewhat the same manner as flour, without the preliminary sifting. The container is first shaken to see that the contents are uniformly packed, the material scooped up in heaping measures, and then leveled off with a straightedge.

Shortening. All solid greases, including butter, are packed firmly in the measuring vessel with the aid of a spoon or spatula, to make certain that all air pockets are eliminated. The measure is filled to the "heaping" point, and then leveled off in the usual manner. The material will handle better if it is on the soft side.

Sugar. Most sugars are measured in the same manner as the powders and granules. Brown sugar, however, must be handled like shortening.

Caution: while weight and measurement scales are standard, it must be remembered that there is often more than one scale for the same measurement. The English quart, for example, is larger than the American quart. Also, the same terms are sometimes used for different types of measurements; viz., a quart can be both liquid and dry measure, both different. Before following any recipe, then, the housewife should be certain that she understands the type of measures called for. This caution applies particularly to old recipes and recipes culled from foreign books.

AVOIRDUPOIS WEIGHT

While there are many different systems used to measure weight (troy, metric, etc.), the avoirdupois scale is the one commonly used with food.

16 drams=1 ounce (oz.)
16 oz.=1 pound (lb)
2,000 lbs.=1 ton
2,240 lbs.=1 long ton

DRY MEASURE

2 cups=1 pint (pt)
2 pts. =1 quart (qt)
4 qts. =1 peck (pk)
4 pks. =1 bushel (bu)

N.B. The American bushel contains 2150.42 cubic inches while the English bushel holds 2218.92 cubic inches.

LIQUID MEASURE

16 fluid ounces=1 pint (pt)
4 gills=1 pt
2 pts.=1 quart (qt)
4 qts.=1 gallon (gal)
31 gals.=1 barrel (bbl)*
63 gals.=1 hogshead (hhd)*

* These are the legal capacities of those vessels, in America, when used for measuring purposes. The actual containers themselves are frequently made in different capacities.

N.B. The British quart (Imperial Quart) contains 40 ounces.

KITCHEN MEASURES

A few drops=less than ⅛ teaspoon (tsp)
A dash=¼ tsp.
60 liquid drops=1 tsp
3 tsp=1 tablespoon (tbsp)
2 tbsp=1 fluid ounce
16 tbsp=1 cup
2 cups=1 pint
2 cups (liquid)=1 pound

KITCHEN EQUIVALENTS

While not all of the following equivalents are absolutely accurate under all circumstances, they are close enough for all

practical purposes, and their intelligent use can save the housewife much time in her cooking preparations.

1 tsp   =⅙ oz
1 tbsp   =½ oz
1 oz   =2 tbsp
2 oz   =¼ cup
4 oz   =½ cup
6 oz   =¾ cup
8 oz   =1 cup
6 egg yolks =½ cup
5–6 egg whites=½ cup
10 eggs in shell=1 pound

COMMERCIAL CAN SIZES

Can Size	Weight	Cups
8 oz	8 oz	1
#1	11 oz	1½
#1½	16 oz	2
2	20 oz	2½
2½	28 oz	3½
3	33 oz	4
10	106 oz	13

BARTENDING

Like the kitchen, bartending (*which see*) has developed a system uniquely its own as far as measurements are concerned. The system is based on the glasses used to serve the drinks (*see* GLASSWARE), which are, of course, the most convenient measuring devices when the drinks are being prepared. However, the styles of glasses change through the years, as does their capacity, and the system is by no means standardized. Today, virtually all measuring is done by the jigger (*which see*), and even that varies. However, old recipes will call for the ingredients in the old terms, and the figures given below are an approximation of the quantities involved.

1 small jigger   =1 oz
1 jigger   =1½ oz
1 large jigger   =2 oz
1 pony   =1 oz
1 liqueur glass   =1 oz
1 sherry or port glass=2 oz
1 cocktail glass =2 oz
1 wine glass   =4 oz
1 champagne glass =5 oz
1 tumbler   =8 oz

BOTTLES

A bottle may be made in virtually any shape, and to hold any desired amount.

KITCHEN EQUIVALENTS (*Continued*)

	tsp	tbsp	1/4 cup	1/2 cup	3/4 cup	1 cup	1 pound
Butter	1/6 oz	1/2 oz	2 oz	4 oz	6 oz	8 oz	2 cups
Cheese:							
Amer'n, grated	1/15 oz	1/5 oz	4/5 oz	1-3/5 oz	2-2/5 oz	3-1/15 oz	5 cups
Cream	1/6 oz	1/2 oz	2 oz	4 oz	6 oz	8 oz	2 cups
Cottage	1/7 oz	1/2 oz	1¾ oz	3½ oz	5¼ oz	7 oz	2-2/7 cups
Coffee, Med. Gr'd	1/14 oz	1/7 oz	6/7 oz	1½ oz	2½ oz	3-1/5 oz	5 cups
Flour:							
Bread	1/12 oz	¼ oz	1 oz	2⅛ oz	3¼ oz	4¼ oz	3¾ cups
Cake	1/12 oz	¼ oz	1 oz	2 oz	3 oz	4 oz	4 cups
Graham	1/10 oz	⅓ oz	1-1/17 oz	2⅓ oz	3½ oz	4½ oz	3½ cups
Pastry	1/12 oz	¼ oz	1 oz	2 oz	3 oz	4 oz	4 cups
Lard	1/6 oz	1/2 oz	2 oz	4 oz	6 oz	8 oz	2 cups
Milk:							
Fresh	1/6 oz	1/2 oz	2 oz	4 oz	6 oz	8 oz	2 cups
Malted	1/6 oz	⅓ oz	1¼ oz	2½ oz	3¾ oz	5 oz	3⅓ cups
Powdered	1/5 oz	1/2 oz	1⅛ oz	2⅜ oz	3½ oz	4¾ oz	3⅓ cups
Shortening	1/6 oz	1/2 oz	2 oz	4 oz	6 oz	8 oz	2 cups
Sugar:							
Brown	1/9 oz	⅓ oz	1⅓ oz	2⅔ oz	4 oz	5⅓ oz	3 cups
Confectioners'	1/10 oz	⅓ oz	1-1/7 oz	2⅓ oz	3½ oz	4½ oz	3½ cups
Granulated	1/6 oz	1/2 oz	2 oz	4 oz	6 oz	8 oz	2 cups
Powdered	1/10 oz	⅓ oz	1-1/7 oz	2⅓ oz	4½ oz	4½ oz	3½ cups
Sirup	¼ oz	¾ oz	3 oz	6 oz	9 oz	12 oz	1⅓ cups

Certain sizes and shapes of bottles have become traditionally associated with certain beverages, and are now the accepted unit of sale, but these are usually local or national traditions. The contents of a bottle are not always too accurate, because bottles are never filled to the brim, and certain beverages, especially the wines, contain unusable dregs or lees in the bottom.

In America, it is required by law that the amount of liquid in the bottle be indicated on the label.

Liquor. Liquor is usually packed in terms of quarts and fractions thereof, though, in some countries, ounces may be used. The common liquor bottles are:

Pint =16 oz
Fifth =26 oz
Quart=32 oz (American)
        =40 oz (British and Canadian)

Wine. There is, perhaps, more discrepancy here than in any other field. This is because wine (*which see*) is grown in so many different countries, causing many different traditions and bottling techniques to develop. One is best advised to consult the label to learn the amount in the bottle, though there is some standardization in the field.

In Europe, the standard wine bottle, if there can be said to be such a thing, usually contains about 26⅔ fluid ounces. The amount is based on the reputed wine quart, which is one sixth of an imperial gallon (160 ounces). There are also quarter bottles and half bottles, based on this bottle.

Many elaborate and out-sized bottles have been developed, the larger ones being used more for display purposes than anything else. These bottles have acquired nicknames, and their capacity is commonly a multiple of the basic 26⅔ ounce bottle.

Name	Capacity
Magnum	2 bottles
Double Magnum	4 bottles
Tappit-Hen	3 imperial quarts
Jeroboam	4 bottles
Rehoboam	6 bottles
Methuselah	8 bottles
Salmanazar	12 bottles
Balthazar	16 bottles
Nebuchadnezzar	20 bottles

Certain wines have become associated with certain bottle shapes, and, in some cases, these shapes have been standardized as to capacity. These figures especially apply in America.

Vermouth bottle	30 oz
Chianti bottle	30 oz
Champagne bottle	24 to 26 oz
Champagne half-bottle	12 to 13 oz

PURCHASING GUIDE

Item	Market Unit	Approx. Measure as Purchased	Approx. No. of Servings per Unit
BEVERAGES			
Chocolate	1 lb	16 squares	60
Cocoa	1 lb	4 cups	100
Coffee	1 lb	5 cups	50
Lemonade	1 doz lemons	2 cups (juice)	16
Tea	1 lb	6–8 cups	300
CEREALS			
Bread	1 lb	12–16 slices	
Corn Flakes	1 lb	18–24 cups	20 (4/5 cup)
Corn Meal and other farina	1 lb	3 cups	25 (2/3 cup)
Grapenuts	12 oz	3 cups	12 (1/4 cup)
Hominy grits	1 lb	2½ cups	15 (2/3 cup)
Macaroni	1 lb	4–5 cups	18 (2/3 cup)
Noodles	1 lb	6–8 cups	18 (2/3 cup)
Rice	1 lb	2¼ cups	12 (2/3 cup)
Rolled Oats	1 lb	5 cups	12 (2/3 cup)
Spaghetti	1 lb	4–5 cups	15 (2/3 cup)
DAIRY PRODUCTS			
Butter	1 lb	2 cups	48 squares (1/3 oz)
Cheese, American	1 lb	4 cups grated	25 (depends on use)
Cheese, Cottage	1 lb	2 cups	6
Cream, coffee	1 quart	4 cups (64 Tbsp)	50 (for coffee)
Cream, whipping	1 quart	4 cups (8 cups whipped)	50
Milk	1 quart	4 cups	
Milk, condensed	1 can (15 oz)	1⅓ cups	Equals 2½ cups milk 8 tbsp sugar
Dry whole milk	1 lb	3½ cups	Equals 3½ qts milk
Milk, evaporated	1 can (14½ oz)	1⅓ cups	Equals 3½ cups milk
Nonfat dry milk solids	1 lb	4 cups	Equals 5 qts milk
Ice Cream	1 quart		6–8
FRUIT, DRIED			
Apples	1 lb		20 (½ cup)
Currants	1 lb	3 cups	
Dates	1 lb	2½ cups (60)	
Figs	1 lb	3 cups (44)	10
Peaches	1 lb	3 cups	12 (½ cup)
Prunes	1 lb	2½ cups	8
Raisins	1 lb	3 cups seedless 2½ cups seeded	
FRUIT, FRESH			
Apples	1 lb	3 medium	3
Apricots	1 lb	8–12	5
Avocado	1 lb	1	2
Banana	1 lb	3	3
Berries—Strawberries	1 quart		4
Blueberries	1 quart		6
Cranberries	1 lb	1 quart	16 (⅛ cup)
Cherries, red	1 quart	2 cups pitted	6
Grapefruit	1 lb	1 medium	2
Grapes—Concord	1 lb	1 quart	4
Tokay	1 lb	2¾ cups seeded	
Lemons	1 doz medium	3 lb	Yields 1 pt juice
Oranges	1 doz medium	6 lb	Yields 1 qt juice 3 quarts diced

Item	Market Unit	Approx. Measure as Purchased	Approx. No. of Serving per Unit
	FRUIT, FRESH (Cont'd)		
Peaches	1 lb	4 medium	4
Pears	1 lb	4 medium	4
Pineapple	2 lb	1 medium	6 (½ cup)
Plums	1 lb	8–20	4
Rhubarb	1 lb	4–8 stalks	5
	MEATS		
Boned or ground meat—	1 lb	—	3 to 4
Flank, clod, beef roll, tenderloin, boneless loin, sirloin butt, sirloin strip, heel of round, liver, heart, kidneys, brains, sweetbread, tongue, sausages, wieners			
Meat with medium amount of bone—	1 lb	—	2 to 3
Steaks, ham slices, rib roasts, chuck, chops, rump roasts, loin roast			
Meat with large amount of bone—	1 lb	—	1 to 2
Shoulder cuts, short ribs, neck, breasts, plate, brisket, shank			
	VEGETABLES, DRIED		
Kidney beans	1 lb	2⅓ cups	12
Lima beans	1 lb	2⅓–3 cups	10
Navy beans	1 lb	2–2½ cups	10
Split peas	1 lb	2 cups	10
	VEGETABLES, FRESH		
Asparagus	1 lb	16–20 stalks	4
Beans, lima in pod	1 lb	⅔ cups shelled	2
Beans, lima shelled	1 lb	2 cups	6
Beans, snap	1 lb	3 cups	5
Beets	1 lb	2 cups diced	4
Broccoli	1 lb	—	3
Brussels sprouts	1 lb	1 quart or less	5
Cabbage—Served raw	1 lb	½ small head	7
Served cooked	1 lb	—	4
Carrots	1 lb	4 cups diced or shredded	5
Cauliflower	1 lb	1½ cups	2
Celery	1 lb	2 med. bunches 4 cups diced	4 (cooked)
Corn, cut	1 lb	—	5
Corn, ears	12 medium	3 cups cut	6
Eggplant	1 lb	4½ cups diced 11½ inch slices	5
Greens	1 lb	—	4
Mushrooms	1 lb	35–45	6
Onions	1 lb	3 large	4
Parsnips	1 lb	4 medium	4
Peas, in pod	1 lb	1 cup shelled	2
Potato, sweet	1 lb	3 medium	3
Potato, white	1 lb	3 medium 2½ cups diced	3
Rutabaga	1 lb	2⅔ cups sliced	4
Squash, Hubbard	1 lb	—	2
Squash, Summer	1 lb	—	3
Tomato	1 lb	4 small 16 slices	3 (cooked) 4 (raw)
Turnip	1 lb	3 medium	4

Table wine split	6 and 6.4 oz
Champagne split	6.2 and 8 oz
Chianti split	8 oz
Miniatures	2, 3, and 4 oz

WINE CONTAINERS

Wine, being made by a bulk process, is frequently packed and shipped in large containers. These containers, being available, are often used for other liquids, and the names of the containers are frequently encountered.

Puncheon	84 to 160 gal
Pipe	117 to 140 gal
Butt	100 to 140 gal
Barrel (average)	50 gal
Keg	15, 10, 5, 3, 2, and 1 gal
Demijohn	4.9, 3, and 2 gal

WELSH RAREBIT. Also called Welsh rabbit. *See* CHEESE.

WENSLEYDALE CHEESE. A round, rennet cheese, made from the whole milk of cows. It weighs anywhere from five to 15 pounds. It derives its name from the valley in Yorkshire, England, in which it originated. If allowed to ripen it develops blue veins like Stilton, but it may also be eaten fresh.

WHEAT. Botanically wheat is related to grass, and there are at least a thousand varieties of wheat and wheat-like grasses known all over the world. The commonly cultivated wheats are roughly divided into bread wheats and durum wheats. Wheat is further divided into winter and spring wheats. Winter wheat, which is grown in warmer climates, is planted in the fall and harvested early in the next summer. Spring wheat, the wheat of colder climates, is planted in the spring and harvested at the end of the summer. In the United States seventy percent of the wheat grown is winter wheat, and ninety-three percent of the wheat crop is bread wheat.

HARD AND SOFT WHEAT

Bread wheat is soft or semi-soft wheat. The hardness of the kernel of wheat is governed by the character of the endosperm, the hard kernels being more difficult to break in the milling process. Soft wheat has a white starchy kernel which yields a good color flour. Durum wheat has a very high gluten content and makes a strong flour of yellow or grayish color. Its use for bread is undesirable because it makes a dingy looking loaf. However, it is used in the manufacture of macaroni and other pastes which require a very elastic dough. It is also blended in with other wheat flours.

STRUCTURE OF THE WHEAT BERRY

The wheat berry is folded in shape so that it has a crease running along one side. At one end of the berry is a brush of tiny hairs, and at the other end is the wheat germ. The starchy cells which form flour are contained in six layers of coating, which constitute the bran. Within these coats, the germ itself and the endosperm, which is the starchy part, are contained. The endosperm is divided into a number of comparatively large cells which are packed with starch and gluten granules. The tightness of the packing determines whether the wheat is hard or soft. Flour which contains the germ is yellow in color and has poor keeping qualities because of the fat content.

The object in making flour is to separate as much as possible of the endosperm from the germ and bran coatings. To obtain a white flour, it is necessary to remove some of the outer portions of the endosperm, so that in effect only seventy percent of the wheat kernel becomes flour. The bran usually amounts to fourteen percent. The germ and the remainder of the bran and endosperm forms an inseparable mixture called shorts.

The amount of protein in the wheat kernel decreases toward the center, so that the whitest flours which contain the least amount of the outer portion of the endosperm, will contain the lowest amount of gluten. However, this gluten is of better quality, and the best flours for baking purposes are made of the inner portions of the kernel only.

PRODUCING FLOUR

Originally wheat was ground between two large flat stones which revolved upon each other. However, this process makes it almost impossible to separate the wheat from the bran, and modern milling is accomplished by a highly complex system of roller mills and successive gradual reductions.

The wheat grains, which have been cleaned on their arrival at the elevators, are cleaned once more before starting the milling process. This may be done by a sieve and air machine, or the wheat may be washed. Some mills separate the wheat grains by size, grinding the larger ones separately. Some millers mix the varieties of wheat before milling; more prefer to mix the flours after milling to obtain standard flour.

The first operation of milling proper is called scouring. In this process part of the outer coat is removed by friction in a cylinder. Large beaters force the kernels against the casing and air currents carry off the dust. However, in the case of soft wheat, this process may break up much of the grain. This is prevented by tempering the wheat after one or two scourings.

Tempering, or conditioning, consists of dampening the wheat with water or steam to toughen the bran and mellow the floury part. As a result the rolls will separate the endosperm from the coatings without shattering them.

The first step in the milling process itself is passing the wheat through the first break rolls. These rolls do little more than crack open the wheat kernel. The material is then sifted and the coarse material which contains most of the bran goes on to a second break roll. Again the material is sifted and the coarser part goes on to a third break. This process is repeated, usually through five breaks, the successive rollers being set closer together and flattening and cutting the bran more. The sifters are flat sieves made of silk or wire cloth over which the meal travels from one end called the head to the other end, called the tail. The material that passes through the meshes of the cloth is called throughs; that which is too coarse and passes out over the tail is called tailings or overtails. The process of sifting is also known as bolting.

The broken material then goes through a series of reductions—grinding on increasingly fine rollers, followed by the sifting out of the coarser portions which go on to additional rollers. The reduction rolls are named according to the type of material they grind, and in a modern flour mill may run from five to fourteen or more. The term middlings, or semolinas, is used to designate the middle-sized particles which result from the first sifting process. This is usually subdivided into sizings, which are the largest particles; tailings which are the portion which pass over the

end of the sifter and contain a great deal of bran; middlings proper are clean white particles; low-grade, or red dog, is the mixture of flour and shorts which is the product of the last role.

As the stock from each break or reduction is sifted, there is separated more or less flour. A thoroughly white flour, as free as possible from dirt and bran specks, is the desired product. Therefore the break flour is treated in a flour dresser which frees it of any coarse material and from lumps. The flour then must be bleached.

Flour which is allowed to stand for a certain amount of time bleaches naturally. The object of bleaching is to hasten this process artificially. This is done by a number of different processes using various chemicals. The finished flour is then blended with flours from other types of wheat to give a uniform market product.

TYPES OF WHEAT FLOUR

Flour is the fine, clean, sound product made by bolting wheat meal, which is the product of grinding the whole grain. Graham flour is unbolted wheat meal. Entire, or whole, wheat flour is actually a misnomer; these terms refer to the product after removal of the outer coat of bran. Gluten flour is wheat flour from which a large proportion of the starch has been removed.

White flour is ordinarily graded into patent, straight, clear, and low-grade flours. Patent flour originally referred to the method of producing flour by high rollers and the middlings purifier. However, it has now come to mean the flour produced from the cleanest and best particles, excluding the first and last breaks and tailings. Straight flour is the total flour produced in the mill run, excluding the low-grade. Clear flour is straight flour, excluding the flour included in the patent grade. Low-grade flour is the last two or three percent of flour obtained at the end of the milling process. See FLOUR.

WHEY. The residium of milk, from which casein and fat have been removed as cheese by the action of rennin or otherwise. It contains, in addition to water, salts (mineral) especially of potassium, a little lactalbumin, and lactose. It is apt to turn sour, but is fairly digestible even then, and its taste may be disguised by the addition of nutmeg and sugar. It makes a palatable, mildly diuretic drink, which is enjoyed by invalids. In Europe, several "whey cures" have been established for the treatment of renal disease and dropsical affections; but according to recent discoveries whey is not in any case a specific, and its dietetic value is greatly overrated.

WHIP. A dessert made light by the addition of beaten white of egg or whipped cream. Whips may also be made of gelatin puddings, whipped with an egg beater before the gelatin is entirely set. See PRUNE for a typical recipe.

WHIPPED CREAM. Directions for whipping cream and evaporated milk are given under the heading MILK, *which see.*

WIRE WHISK

WHISK. A device, usually made of wire, used to beat or stir liquid foods. *See* BEATER, *see also* KITCHEN EQUIPMENT.

WHISKY. American whisky traces its ancestry back to the *Usquebaugh* of Scotland and Ireland, but with some difficulty. No Scotsman or Irishman in the distilling industry admits that the American products, rye or bourbon, made with bases of rye, grain, or corn, show any but the slightest relationship to the good family of malt whisky.

Scotch whisky is made from pure barley malt, while Irish whisky is made from malted and unmalted grains. The essential difference lies in the smoky taste of Scotch whisky. Four regions—the Highlands, the Lowlands, Campbeltown, and Islay—produce whisky, each with a distinctive character.

Malt is made by moistening the grains and laying them out in a warm place until they just start to sprout. The sprouting of the grains is a very particular procedure which must be carried just so far and no farther. When the sprouts are of the proper length, the growth is stopped by rapid drying, which is done in a kiln, on metal plates over a fire, or by electricity.

The fire is anthracite coal in Ireland and most American distilleries, which communicates little taste or odor to the malt. Some of the most modern distilleries use electricity. In Scotland the fire is made with blocks of peat which burn with a glow and emit a fragrant smoke. This smoke passes up through holes provided in the plates and communicates a characteristic taste to the malt. In the later distillation the smoky taste remains to identify Scotch whisky.

All whiskies, no matter what the base of the mash—malt, green barley, rye, or corn—are colorless when raw. From time immemorial, however, men have believed that whisky should be deep amber-flame in color, and so all commercial whiskies follow this tradition. In Scotland and Ireland the coloring is achieved in one of two ways, or even by a combination of both. The raw whisky or "highwine" is poured off into casks whose staves and bottoms are saturated with wine, usually sherry. Sometimes fluid caramel or burnt sugar is added in small quantities to brighten the color. Sherry wine casks, besides coloring the whisky, absorb the fusel oil and other insoluble bodies which mar the taste and flavor of whisky.

American whisky is made in exactly the same way as Scotch or Irish, with the difference that, instead of malted cereals, grain is used as the basic ingredient. American distillers, instead of pouring the raw whisky into sherry wine casks, use charred white oak casks. This gives American whisky its beautiful flame-red color and its delicate flavor.

When these operations are completed, the cask is sealed and stored away. From four to eight or more years later, depending on the quality desired, the contents are tapped and drawn off into bottles. Age, after that, makes no difference, for whisky, unlike wine, does not mellow or mature in glass. Artificial maturing methods have been "discovered" from time to time, only to take their places, one by one, in the realm of dreams which could not come true.

STRAIGHT AND BLENDED WHISKY

Whisky, whether called "straight" or "blended," is composed of approximately half water and half ethyl alcohol, plus a color and a flavor, and the only substantial difference between the two consists in the percentage of fusel oil and tannic acid, which exist in straight whiskies in a larger amount than in blended whiskies.

It should be understood that the practice of blending whiskies is done for the purpose of producing a smooth, rich, mellow finished product by bringing together the characteristics of several whiskies—frequently as many as fifteen different kinds—resulting in a single blend that will meet the favor of the public. In other words, "blends" are combinations that may contain different whiskies, neutral spirits, distilled water, wine juices, burned sugar, and caramel. A whisky used in a blend becomes a "cut whisky."

Whisky mixtures are known as "rectified spirits." Any whisky which is pure—that is, as it left the still, whether aged or raw—with the possible addition of distilled water, is straight whisky. The first run of the grain alcohol during the distilling process is called the "heads," the last run is called "tails," and between them are the "neutral spirits."

According to the ruling of the United States Pharmacopoeia, whisky to be used for medical purposes must be matured at least four years and contain from 44 to 55 percent alcohol—equivalent to 88 to 110 proof (see Proof). It may be a blend, but in that case it must be made up of whiskies of similar age and purity, altered only by the addition of distilled water to bring the proof down to the proper level. The addition of neutral spirits takes it out of the field of whiskies which may be labelled "bottled in bond."

WHISKY GLASS. See GLASSWARE.

WHITE CHEESE. A round, rennet, skimmed milk cheese, made in France during the summer months. The cheese is consumed while fresh, and may or may not be salted.

WHITEBAIT. The Atlantic and Pacific whitebait, although analogous to the Mediterranean whitebait and the English specimens from the mouth of the Thames River, is a zoologic enigma. Certain naturalists maintain that the whitebait is only a fry, and it has never been clearly ascertained from what fish it is produced. Certain authorities claim it is from the herring, but their claims are not entirely convincing.

Whitebait is known under several different local or national names, such as "blanchaille," "nonnats," "fry," "sandeel," "small fish," etc.

Whitebait does not accommodate itself to many ways of preparation and is at its best when fried. It must be handled very carefully as it breaks easily. Whitebait is not cleaned. It should be strictly fresh, and so should be the frying fat. After washing the fish in clear running water, pat dry, and then roll in plenty of seasoned flour, the excess of which is eliminated by shaking the fish in a fine wire frying basket. Then plunge the fish into clear, clean, smoking deep fat, a few at a time, lest they stick together. After a short time, lift them out quickly, drain, and serve on a folded white napkin placed on a hot platter, with a garnish of fried, green, curled parsley and quartered lemon. They should be eaten piping hot.

The various methods for the preparation of anchovies, small smelts, and sardines may be adapted to this delicate fish.

WHITEFISH. A fresh-water fish of which approximately fifteen species are known the world over under different names.

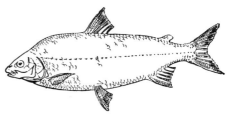

WHITEFISH

Whitefish has an elongated and compressed body, a conical head with projecting snout and small toothless mouth, the teeth having been shed before maturity. The scales are larger than in the salmon, the caudal fin is deeply forked, and the dorsal fin is followed by an adipose dorsal. The fish is of a bluish-olive color on the back, silvery on the sides and belly.

This most important and popular fresh-water fish is found in enormous numbers throughout the Great Lakes and adjacent waters. While the average weight is from three to three and a half pounds, whitefish have been caught weighing 15 and even 20 pounds.

Whitefish remain for the most part in deep water but in the fall, which is the spawning season, and at certain other times for purposes which are not yet clear, they migrate to shallower water in very great shoals. A single fish will yield as many as 75,000 eggs, never less than 35,000. They feed mainly on crustaceans, mollusks, insects and larvae.

The Rocky Mountain whitefish, known also as mountain herring, is a real delicacy and is found as far as the Pacific coast. The whitefish taken from Lake Winnipeg and as far as Labrador, called sometimes Sault whitefish, is a very fine delicacy, loving clear water.

The New England lakes contain a valuable species of darker color, known under various names such as roundfish, shad-waiter, Menominee whitefish, pilot-fish, etc.

Whitefish is smoked, and used as a tidbit for canapés and appetizers, and also as a sandwich filling. It is particularly delicious in this form.

The various methods employed in the preparation of bass, flounder, pike, weak-fish, and large whiting may be adapted to this popular fish.

BAKED STUFFED LAKE WHITEFISH

1 whitefish, 2½ to 3 lb
2 cups bread crumbs
1 medium-sized onion, minced
1 tsp salt
1 egg
1 stalk celery, chopped
⅛ tsp each ground thyme and sage
⅛ tsp pepper
½ cup butter
Bacon

Have the fish scaled and cleaned but do not remove the head and tail. Wash thoroughly and wipe dry. Combine all remaining ingredients except bacon and stuff the fish with them. Sew up the fish. Place the stuffed fish on a well-greased rack in an open roasting pan. Lay strips of bacon over it, pour in ½ cup of water and bake in a slow oven (300° F.) about 1 hour, basting occasionally with the liquid in the pan. (Serves 4 to 6)

PLANKED LAKE WHITEFISH

1 whitefish, 3½ to 4 lb
½ cup melted butter
2 tbsp lemon juice
Salt and tabasco

Hot mashed potatoes
1 egg, slightly beaten

Wash and scale the fish, removing head and tail. Clean and then split lengthwise down the back, without actually separating the two halves. Heat a large plank thoroughly, and brush with melted butter. Lay the fish on it, skin side down. Brush over the fleshy surface with melted butter and bake in a hot oven (425° F.) about 35 minutes, basting every few minutes with the blended lemon juice, salt, and tabasco. Remove from the oven and garnish the plank with a border of hot mashed potatoes passed through a pastry bag. Brush this over with slightly beaten egg and return to the oven to brown the potato. Garnish with cut lemon and parsley. Serve on the plank, placing this on a large platter. (Serves 6)

SMOKED WHITEFISH BAKED IN TOMATO SOUP

1 large smoked whitefish, about 3 lb
2 medium-sized onions, thinly sliced
1 green pepper, finely chopped
Salt and pepper
½ tsp lemon juice
1 can condensed tomato soup
¼ cup water
1 or 2 small dill leaves, fresh or dry, optional

Wipe the fish and place in a greased baking dish. Combine all remaining ingredients and pour over and around it. Bake in a slow oven (300° F.) about 30 minutes. (Serves 6)

SMOKED WHITEFISH FILLETS IN CREAM

3½ lb smoked whitefish
1 onion, thinly sliced
Salt and pepper
A few grains thyme
1 large bay leaf
6 sprigs parsley
1 tall can eavporated milk

Wipe the fish, then cut into six fillets. Place these in a buttered shallow pan and arrange over them the onion and seasonings. Add the bay leaf and parsley tied together. Pour the milk over all and bake in a slow oven (300° F.) for ½ hour. Discard the bay leaf and parsley, and serve from the baking dish. If desired, ½ cup of blended grated cheese and buttered crumbs may be sprinkled over the fish after the first half of the baking is completed. (Serves 6)

WHITE LABEL RUM. A general designation for the lighter rums. *See* RUM.

WHITE SAUCE. There are three white sauces in common use, thin, medium, and thick, all made on a basis of one cup of liquid, the difference lying in the proportion of butter and flour used in the one cup of milk or cream. Sometimes they are referred to as White Sauce Number One, White Sauce Number Two, and White Sauce Number Three—a simple definition, because in White Sauce One, we use 1 tablespoon of butter and flour; in White Sauce Two, 2 tablespoons each, and in White Sauce Three, 3 tablespoons each, always to 1 cup of milk.

BASIC WHITE SAUCES

	No. 1 *Thin*	*No. 2* *Medium*	*No. 3* *Thick*
Butter	1 tbsp	2 tbsp	3 tbsp
Flour	1 tbsp	2 tbsp	3 tbsp
Cream or scalded milk	1 cup	1 cup	1 cup
Salt	½ tsp	½ tsp	½ tsp
White pepper	⅛ tsp	⅛ tsp	⅛ tsp

Melt the butter, add the flour and blend thoroughly. When perfectly smooth and free from lumps but not in the least browned, add the seasonings then gradually the scalded milk. Stir constantly over a low flame until the sauce boils. Cook 5 minutes. This sauce may be made in larger quantity and will keep several days under refrigeration.

Cream sauce is an enriched type of white sauce, made like white sauce with a little cream, or sometimes even beaten egg yolk added after the cooking is completed.

Bechamel sauce (*which see*) is a similar type of sauce made with a base of stock instead of milk or cream.

WHITE SAUCE VARIATIONS

Aurore Sauce. To 1 cup of white, cream, or bechamel sauce, add ¼ cup of tomato purée and, immediately before serving, 1

tablespoon of butter, bit by bit. Suitable for eggs, white meat, and poultry.

Caper Sauce. To 1 cup of white, cream, or bechamel sauce, add ¼ cup of coarsely chopped capers (scalded before chopping) and, immediately before serving, 1 tablespoon of butter, bit by bit. Suitable for boiled meat, especially lamb, and fish.

Cardinal Sauce. To 1 cup of white, cream, or bechamel sauce, add ¼ cup of strong fish stock, (1 cup cooked down to ¼ its volume) if for fish, or chicken stock in the same proportions if for poultry; with 1 scant teaspoon essence of truffle, and ¼ cup of scalded heavy cream. Immediately before serving add 1 tablespoon of butter, bit by bit. A very rich sauce suitable for boiled chicken and fish.

Cheese Sauce. To 1 cup of white, cream, or bechamel sauce, add ¼ cup of grated American or Swiss cheese, stirring constantly while adding. Suitable for fish, eggs, and vegetables.

Cucumber Sauce. To 1 cup of white, cream, or bechamel sauce, add 1 teaspoon of lemon juice, ¼ teaspoon of paprika, ¼ teaspoon of cider vinegar and ½ cup thinly sliced or cubed, peeled, raw cucumber. Suitable for boiled chicken or boiled fish.

Egg Sauce. To 1 cup of white, cream or bechamel sauce add 1 hard-cooked egg, chopped or crushed, and 1 teaspoon of minced parsley or chives. Suitable for boiled fish, hot asparagus, and peas and carrots.

French Sauce. To 1 cup of bechamel or rich cream sauce, add ½ cup of strong chicken stock (1 cup cooked down to half its volume) and 1 wineglass of sherry. Remove from the fire, then add 2 tablespoons of whipped cream alternately with 1 tablespoon of grated Parmesan or other cheese. Suitable for cooked chicken, game and lobster.

This sauce may be poured over the chicken, game or lobster, grated cheese sprinkled over all and the whole placed under the broiler to brown.

Horseradish Sauce. To 1 cup of white, cream, or bechamel sauce, add 3 tablespoons of well-drained prepared horseradish and, immediately before serving, 1 tablespoon of butter, bit by bit. Suitable for boiled fish, boiled meat, or poultry, or smoked meats.

Lobster Sauce. To 1 cup of white, cream, or bechamel sauce, add ¼ cup of cooked, chopped lobster meat and, immediately before serving, 1 tablespoon of butter, bit by bit. Suitable for any kind of boiled fish.

Mornay Sauce. To 1 cup of bechamel sauce add ¼ cup of strained stock: for fish, fish stock; for vegetables, vegetable stock; with 3 tablespoons of grated Parmesan or Swiss cheese and, immediately before serving, 1 tablespoon of butter, bit by bit. Suitable for fish, fowl, and vegetables, especially au gratin.

Mushroom White Sauce. To 1 cup of white or cream sauce add ½ cup of mushroom stock (mushroom trimmings cooked with water), ¼ cup of cooked, sliced mushrooms, and 1 teaspoon of minced onion cooked in butter until tender but not browned. Suitable for fowl, fish, and eggs.

Olive Sauce. To 1 cup of white or cream sauce add ¼ cup of chopped stuffed olives, 1 tablespoon of chopped green pepper, and immediately before serving, 1 tablespoon of butter, bit by bit. Suitable for eggs, fish, vegetables and boiled fowl.

Onion Sauce. To 1 cup of white or cream sauce add ¼ cup of rich chicken or veal stock, ⅓ cup of thinly sliced onions (cooked in chicken stock until tender, then drained), a dash of sugar and ½ cup scalded light cream. Suitable for chicken, boiled meat, eggs, fish and vegetables.

Oyster Sauce. To 1 cup of white or cream sauce add 1 dozen small oysters poached in their own liquor (use both oysters and liquor), ¼ cup scalded light cream, and a few drops of lemon juice. Suitable for any kind of boiled fish.

Pimiento Sauce. To 1 cup of white or cream sauce add 2 tablespoons of minced onion cooked in butter until clear, 1 teaspoon minced parsley, ¼ cup of minced pimiento, and immediately before serving, 1 tablespoon of butter, bit by bit. Suitable for vegetables, hard-cooked eggs, fish and boiled fowl.

Poulette Sauce. To 1 cup of white, cream or bechamel sauce, add ¼ cup of appropriate stock: fish, if for fish; oyster, if for oyster; chicken if for chicken, etc.; with ¼ cup of scalded light cream, a dash each

of nutmeg and cayenne, 1 teaspoon of lemon juice, and ½ cup cooked, sliced mushrooms. Suitable for fish and shellfish, mushrooms and fowl.

Shrimp sauce. To 1 cup of white or cream sauce add 1 dozen cooked, coarsely chopped shrimps and a dash of nutmeg. Suitable for fish.

Soubise Sauce. To 1 cup of white, cream, or bechamel sauce, add ¼ cup of scalded light cream to which has been added ¼ teaspoon of sugar, ½ cup of sieved cooked onions, ¼ cup of sieved cooked rice, 1 or 2 tablespoons of tomato purée (optional), and, immediately before serving, 1 tablespoon of butter, bit by bit. Suitable for boiled chicken, meat, fish, eggs, and vegetables.

Swedish Sauce. To 1 cup of white or cream sauce, add 1 tablespoon of minced onion (cooked in butter until tender, but not browned), ¼ cup of scalded heavy cream, 1 teaspoon of lemon juice, a few grains of cayenne, ¼ cup of cooked, sliced mushrooms, also cooked in butter then well drained, and immediately before serving, 1 tablespoon of butter, bit by bit, and 1 tablespoon of sherry. Suitable for large pieces of boiled white fish.

WHITE TABLE WINES. Those still wines that are white, green or gold in color and are best suited for use with food. *See* WINE.

WHITING. The whiting, or silver hake as it is also called, is a native of the north Atlantic waters. Strangely enough, it is not popular in the eastern states as a food fish, its greatest market being in the middle west where it is the chief fish used for "fish fries."

The whiting is a relative of the cod. It is a slender dark gray fish with silver under-parts. The average market weight is one and a half or two pounds. Its flavor is very delicate, and the flesh is fine and white. The whiting may be prepared by frying, broiling, or baking.

WHOLE WHEAT. *See* BREAD and WHEAT.

WHORTLEBERRY. *See* BLUEBERRY.

WEINER SAUSAGE. *See* SAUSAGE.

WEINER SCHNITZEL. *See* VEAL.

WILD BOAR. A wild pig, the native hog of the Old World. To roast the wild boar, it is necessary that he should be very young, from eight to ten months old. If the meat is tender, it is excellent; if tough, it is detestable. Choose a little saddle,

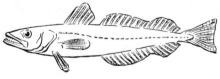

WHITING

which should be covered with a layer of fat. When roasted it should be served with gooseberry sauce and its natural gravy.

As to the grown-up boar's head, it is best cooked simply (*au naturel*), admitting, however, that the stuffed head is more luxurious, but also more costly, complicated, and difficult to prepare.

Though boar's head does not appeal to all tastes, it has always been a favorite with gourmets. The gods in Valhalla used to eat a wild boar every evening, a wild boar which had the property of being restored to life every morning, to be eaten again the following night; and even the ascetic Buddha fell a victim to its succulence, for he is said to have died from a meal of dried boar's flesh.

But it is not alone to one's palate that the sight of the boar's heads in restaurant windows appeals. On the contrary, for some of us its appeal is mainly to the imagination. It recalls all sorts of historic and literary memories. Indeed, the wild boar may be said to be only secondarily an article of diet, and primarily an heraldic and romantic animal. It belongs rather to Shakespeare and Scott, to royal huntsmen and tavern signs, than to the world of reality.

Probably our first thought at the mention of it is the Boar's Head Tavern in Eastcheap, England, kept by a certain Dame Quickly, and the favorite haunt of that fat rogue, Sir John Falstaff, boon companion of the wild young Prince of Wales, and those other rogues who cut purses with him on the highway. The sign that swung over their revels was the crest of the Gordons, whose ancestor had slain a ferocious wild boar in the forest of Huntley in 1093.

Or we think of the young Scottish archer, Quentin Durward, saving the life of Louis XI, of France, from a particularly formidable boar, when the King was out hunting one day in the Normandy woods, and so making his fortune. The wild boar in literature would make a long story.

They still sing, "*Caput apri defero, Reddens laudes Domino,*" and march in with the pipes and fiddles and the smoking boar's head in English universities and at some yuletide feasts this side of the ocean; but turkey is our meat for the holidays.

Actually, the wild boar does not exist in America, although there are herds of wild pigs or wild hogs in many parts of the United States. However, hunting the wild boar—let us give the wild pigs or hogs found in America that name—is distinctly a man's sport and a dangerous one at that. Down along the Tennessee-North Carolina border where the razor-tusked wild pigs grow up to weigh a quarter of a ton, hunting them in the treacherous mountain underbrush is even more hazardous than it is in India, where British Army officers go in for "pig-sticking." The mere sight of one of the ferocious-looking beasts crashing its way clumsily but swiftly through the woods has made many a sportsman take to the nearest tree.

At any rate, when they have succeeded in bringing down one of these wild beasts, and when later they smell the luscious flavor of a broiled boar steak, guests need no cocktail to stimulate the appetite.

BROILED BOAR STEAK

Have the steak cut thick, sear it on both sides under a high flame, after which reduce the heat and broil to the desired degree of doneness. Dust with salt and pepper and serve with a sauce made as follows:

> 1 large red onion
> ½ lb fresh large mushrooms
> 1 large green pepper
> Boar fat
> 1 cup claret
> 1 large bay leaf
> 6 sprigs parsley
> 3 sprigs celery tops
> 2 or 3 whole cloves
> 1 blade garlic
> ½ cup beef bouillon
> Salt
> Dash of tabasco
> 1 glass red currant jelly
> A pony glass brandy

Slice the onion, mushrooms, and pepper very thin and sauté in a little of the heated boar fat, stirring constantly until the mixture is soft, but not browned. Add the claret, with the bay leaf, parsley and celery tied together, also the cloves, garlic, and bouillon. Blend thoroughly and simmer gently, closely covered, for 20 minutes. Season to taste with salt and tabasco, then stir in the jelly blended with the brandy. Remove the bouquet and pour the hot sauce over the steak.

WILD CHERRY. One of two wild fruits native to North America. The choke-cherry is the fruit of a shrub belonging to the rose family, bright red in color. It is quite astringent in flavor, and in some parts of the country is used in making preserves.

The so-called wild cherry is the fruit of a tree, blue-black in color and very sour. It is used in making jelly and a homemade wine. Because the fruit has little juice it is necessary to add a considerable amount of water in making jelly.

WILD ONION. The wild onion, and kindred members of the genus *Allium*, are found throughout North America. The bulbs and leaves of these herbs are edible and were used as food by the Indian before the advent of the white man.

Small, bellshaped flowers adorn the head of the bright green stem and may be yellow, white, pink, red, or even blue in color. The leaves are long and slender; they may be either rounded or flat; they issue from the base of the stem.

Although the plants are smaller than the domestic herbs bearing the same names, they may be eaten raw or cooked in the same manner as their cultivated cousins. The cook should remember that the wild varieties are much stronger in flavor than the cultivated varieties.

WILD PLANTS. *See* EDIBLE WILD PLANTS.

WILD RICE

WILD RICE. The botanical name of wild rice is *Zizania aquatica*, and it is a native of the United States. It is found in fresh water and in brackish swamps from New England to Texas and North Dakota, but its center of abundance is in Minnesota and Wisconsin. It grows in nearly every state east of the Rocky Mountains. It has some sixty local names, and the fact that many of them are Indian shows its close association with the red men. In Connecticut, wild rice is known as "blackbird oats," in Louisiana and Wisconsin as "fool oats," in Delaware and Pennsylvania as "Indian oats" and "Indian rice," in Texas as "duck rice," and in North Carolina as "wild oats." In addition wild rice bears eleven Chinese and Japanese names. It has been taken to both China and Japan and now grows in both countries.

The first white settlers in the present states of Minnesota and Wisconsin found the Indians using wild rice and followed their example. Its fame spread to Europe and about 1823 some of it was sent to Europe to be planted.

The Indians harvested wild rice in a rather primitive but nonetheless effective way. Two squaws went out in a canoe, and while one paddled, the other bent rice stalks over the canoe and struck them with a stick, knocking the grain into the canoe. The rice was taken ashore and dried in the sun or over a fire. It was threshed by beating with sticks or trampling with the feet. Then it was winnowed in birchbark trays and stored for winter use in bags of skin or cloth.

The plant is the *folleavoine* of the French explorers and the *menomin* of the Northwest Indians. Indeed, it gave that name to one tribe—the Menominee, which means, literally, wild rice men. That tribe formerly lived in northern Wisconsin and Michigan, chiefly along the Menominee River, and is now on a reservation near Green Bay, Wisconsin. There is a city of Menominee in Michigan and a city of Menominie in Wisconsin.

Wild rice, long a staple food of the Indians of that region, and a favorite of the wild duck, has been gaining in popularity as a delicacy for our dinner tables. It is now marketed, processed, and shipped to all sections of the country. Several years ago it appeared that a too thorough harvesting threatened to wipe out the wild rice supply. So the Wild Rice Producers

Association was organized, and legislation was enacted setting dates of the harvest and other regulations. The rice grows in the shallow waters of lakes and rivers, and good crops are insured when water levels remain stable.

Wild rice reaches its greatest size in the southeastern states, where it may grow twelve feet high, with a stalk two inches in diameter. It may grow no higher than three or four feet in its northern range. On the whole, it prefers deep, rich soil.

In general, wild rice is cooked like white or brown rice, but it takes much longer to become tender. *See also* RICE.

STEAMED WILD RICE WITH CHICKEN LIVERS

4 large onions, minced
1 cup butter
10 to 12 chicken livers and hearts
2 tsp salt
¼ tsp black pepper
2 cups washed wild rice
6 cups boiling water

Sauté the onions in the butter until well browned. Wash, pat dry, and mince the livers, then add with the hearts and seasonings and toss all together over a moderate heat, about 5 minutes, or until browned. Add the rice and water, cover, and cook gently over a low heat, stirring occasionally, about 40 minutes or until all liquid is absorbed and the rice is tender. Serve very hot. (Serves 6)

WILD RICE CROQUETTES

1 cup washed wild rice
3 cups soup stock
4 egg yolks, well beaten
1 tbsp minced parsley
1 tsp salt

Cook the rice and stock together over hot water (double boiler), stirring occasionally, until all liquid is absorbed and the rice is tender (about 45 minutes). Combine the egg yolks, parsley and salt, and blend with the cooked rice. Cool, then chill thoroughly. Form into croquettes and fry in deep hot fat (390° F.) about 2 minutes or until browned. Drain on soft crumpled paper and serve immediately. (Serves 6)

WILD RICE WITH MUSHROOMS

1 cup washed wild rice
2 cups water
½ tsp salt
1 tbsp minced onion
¼ lb sliced mushrooms
3 tbsp butter

Cook the rice in the salted water in a covered pan until tender. Meanwhile cook the onion and mushrooms for 5 minutes in the butter. Combine the two mixtures and serve very hot. (Serves 4)

WILD RICE AND SHAD ROE EN CASSEROLE

3 cups cooked wild rice
1 can (8 oz) shad roe
½ cup chopped parsley
2 tbsp butter
2 tbsp flour
1 cup heavy cream
1 tsp salt
Pinch of black pepper

Arrange the rice and shad roe in alternate layers in a casserole, sprinkling each layer of the roe with parsley. Prepare a white sauce (*which see*) with the butter, flour, cream, and seasonings. Pour this over the contents of the casserole and bake in a moderate oven (350° F.) 20 minutes. (Serves 6)

WILSTERMARSCH CHEESE. A German full-cream, semi-hard cheese.

WINE. Properly speaking, the term applies only to the fermented juice of the grape. There are, however, many "wines" that are made from other fruits (and even, in certain cases, vegetables) whose manufacture and appearance are quite similar to those of the grape. These are generally homemade, and are commercially identified by prefixing the name of the fruit used before the word "wine" on the label. (*See* WINE, HOMEMADE.)

The fermented juice of the grape is one of the oldest intoxicants known to man. It is made by natural processes that can take place in the simplest of equipment, and is made wherever grapes are grown, though some regions produce superior products. Wine is the most universal of made beverages, and, in one form or another, certainly one of the oldest.

History of Wine

Little is known of the first actual discovery of wine, an event shrouded in the mists of antiquity. It was an inevitable accident, and most likely occurred independently in several civilizations.

Wine has ever played an important role in the history of the world. It has influenced religion, economics, and literature, to name but a few of its manifold effects.

To the unschooled mind, the production of wine is indeed an awe-inspiring and mystical thing. A container of grape juice, for no apparent cause, goes through a series of violent changes and then is no longer grape juice. The effects of this new liquid, taken in quantity, are startling, to say the least, and totally inexplicable to one who knows nothing of the science of alcohol.

It is no wonder, then, that the mystery of the grape should join the mystery of growth in the early, naturalistic religions of the pagans. Special deities were established to account for wine. The beverage was considered, along with the first fruits of the harvest, as a most suitable offering in religious rites. This ancient convention assumed new importance with the coming of the New Testament.

Commercially, wine is one of the few products that can be made without machinery, is susceptible to shipment in skins and earthen jars, and will find a market in almost any type of culture. For these reasons it became an important item of trade in the very early days of agrarian economy, and, as such, had considerable influence on world events. It is the businessman, rather than the adventurer, who has been responsible for the bulk of exploration, colonization, and the eventual integration of colonies through trade.

The first traces of Egyptian-wine-making date from about 2400 B.C., and China is known to have made wine sometime before 2000 B.C. The Greeks, of course, had a word for it, and even wrote handbooks on the subject. The Phoenician crafts that had nosed inquisitively around the Adriatic, Mediterranean, and other waters carried wine merchants among their passengers, and they are supposed to have brought grape culture to France in 600 B.C.

The wine trade was among the first to be established among the nations of the world. When the English conquered parts of France, following the battle of Hastings, the vineyards of Bordeaux were among the British prizes.

For the most part, the English imported their wines, and, in the 14th century, when a law was passed forbidding the exportation of actual currency out of the country, the foreign merchants stopped coming to the island. As a result, the British merchant fleet was considerably expanded, making two yearly convoys to Europe to bring in wine. Many authorities say this expansion had a great influence on England's eventual rise to sea superiority.

During many periods in history, wine has functioned as a currency. It has been legal tender for debts and taxes. The wine industry itself has a long-standing history of government regulations and controls, especially concerning taxation.

Other larger industries have since grown up in world trade, but the vineyard produce still accounts for an amazingly large percentage of the yearly trade dollars.

Wine in America

When, back in the year 1000 A.D., Leif Erickson discovered a new land some distance off Iceland, he and his crew were mainly impressed by the abundance of grapes they found there. This land they called *Vinland,* or, *Wineland.*

The later explorers and colonists were equally impressed, and, in many cases, vineyards were started as the first attempt to establish two-way trade with the mother countries. Wine was made of native grapes in Florida in 1564. The first recorded attempt to establish a standard vineyard was made in Virginia in 1620. In 1648 an English publication told of three different wines being made from native grapes in what is now Delaware. William Penn instituted vineyards in Philadelphia in 1683.

The Spaniards, settling in Mexico and Lower California, brought their wine-making traditions with them. In 1769, Father Serra, the Franciscan priest who pioneered the Californian missions, planted the first grapevines in San Diego. These, as opposed to the native vines of the East, were Spanish vines brought up from Mexico, where they had been transplanted.

While there is an abundance of native American grapes, they are found primarily in the eastern and middle states. The vineyards in the west are mainly stocked with European varieties.

Wine-making in the United States did not really become a sizable commercial venture until the last half of the 19th century. In 1829, an Episcopalian minister, Rev. William Bostwich, had planted cuttings of Isabella and Catawba grapes at Hammondsport, and, as a result, vineyards were started in northern New York State. In 1856, some two tons of grapes from the Lake Keuka region were shipped to New York City, marking the beginning of large-scale operations in the east.

In the west, a Hungarian nobleman, Colonel Agoston Haraszthy, was sent to Europe in 1861 by the California State legislature. When the colonel returned with 100,000 cuttings representing 1,400 European grape varieties, the governing body, split internally by the Civil War, refused to pay his expenses, amounting to $12,000, so he sold the cuttings at general sale, scattering them throughout the state.

When, in 1850 and 1860, the plant louse *Phylloxera* attacked and nearly destroyed the grapevines of Europe, it was found that native American grapevines were hardier than their overseas kin, and able to resist the insect pest. Cuttings were transplanted from America, saving the Old World vineyards from extinction. It was further found that these American cuttings resulted in bigger and better European grapes.

While grapes are now grown in at least 44 American states, wines are commercially made in only 27. Of these, California leads with 95 percent of the production, and New York State comes second. Ohio, Delaware, and Michigan are among the others.

Wine Names

Wine production is a world-wide enterprise, and so, too, is wine-naming. There are far too many wine names to list in this book; the important ones are treated under their alphabetical headings.

Some wines, notably the French, are named after the districts where the grapes are grown; e.g., champagne and sauterne (*which see*). Others are more specifically named after the vineyard in which they are grown, as is chateau d' yquem (*which see*), the best of the sauternes. Still other wines take their names from the grapes

used to make them, as does catawba (*which see*), and then there are those wines that are named because of their appearance or because of some interesting legend, true or untrue, connected with their past, like Est Est Est (*which see*).

The practice of naming a wine after the place of growth has lead to some confusion, for, when similar wines are made elsewhere, they are frequently given the old name. This situation is especially true with the French wines. The Gallic vintners have gone on record claiming that these names, sauterne, for example, are applicable only to wines grown in that region. But foreign growers have argued that, if they can produce a wine that duplicates the French sauterne, it has a legal right to that title.

In America today, the country of origin is specified on the bottle label. Thus we have New York State port, California sherry, and Chilean riesling, to name but a few.

Types of Wine

Wines are said to be *sweet* or *dry*, depending on the amount of sugar they contain. However, there is also a legal practice of using these same two terms to indicate the relative alcoholic content of wines for taxation purposes. These two different interpretations should not be confused, for while it is often true that the sweet-tasting wines contain more alcohol than those lacking in sweetness, this is not always the case. A *dry* sherry, for example, may contain more than 20 percent alcohol, while a very *sweet* sauterne may have as little as 10 percent.

In appearance, wines are usually said to be either *red* or *white*. A *red* wine can be rather pale or very dark, while there is no truly *white* wine, that term being applied to colors that range from gold and yellow on through various shades of green. There are also *amber* wines, *pink* or *rose* wines, and *tawny* wines, but their numbers are few in comparison with the many and variedr red and white.

Wines are also *sparkling* (effervescent) or *still*. Then there are the wines called *crackling*, or, by the French, *petillant*, which are only slightly effervescent, and there are a few hocks (*which see*) referred to as *spritzig*, which are actually still, but taste as though they might be effervescent.

In recent years, the wine industry has come to further classify wines by their table use. This system, though not perfect, is highly practical, since the bulk of wine consumption is with food, and the system further serves as a convenient guide to the inexperienced buyer.

When classified according to use, the industry divides wine into five general groups: appetizer wines, red table wines, white table wines, dessert wines, and sparkling wines.

Appetizer Wines. These are light, highly flavored wines that are usually served alone before dinner, or with appetizers and soups. Though varying, their alcoholic content is rather high, generally ranging from 15 to 20 percent, most often in the higher bracket. Dubonnet, Madeira (dry), sherry (dry) and vermouth are typical of this class. They are usually served chilled.

Red Table Wines. Dry, slightly tart, astringent wines served at room temperature, these red wines are usually served with the heavier entrées: meats, game, pasty or starchy foods, etc. Their alcoholic content, on the average, ranges from 10 to 14 percent. In this class are claret (Bordeaux), burgundy, chianti, and that great variety of common table wines just called "red."

White Table Wines. Having delicate flavors, these wines, usually served chilled, are better suited for the lighter entrées, fish, fowl (especially the white meat), eggs, etc. Their alcoholic content is the same as the red table wines. The sauternes and Rhine wines are common examples of this class, which also includes the white varieties of the wines listed as red table wines.

Dessert Wines. Sweeter and heavier than the table wines, these are served with desserts, fruits, nuts, etc., or alone, after the meal. Their alcoholic content is higher than that of the table wines, usually being about 20 percent. Incidentally, for taxation purposes, wines above 14 percent in alcoholic content are sometimes listed as dessert wines, though this means of classification also includes many of the appetizer wines. Among the true dessert wines are Bordeaux (sweet), Madeira (sweet or medium), muscatel, angelica, port, sherry (sweet or medium), sauterne (sweet), and tokay.

Sparkling Wines. Effervescent or bubbling wines that can be served at any time, alone or with food. Because of their expense, these wines find their greatest use at festive occasions, but they are actually highly versatile. Their alcoholic content generally ranges from 10 to 14 percent. They are served chilled. Champagne and sparkling Burgundy are the most common sparkling wines, but any still wine can be made effervescent by means of a second fermentation in the bottle.

MAKING OF WINE

Wine is made by a natural process of fermentation; i.e., by the conversion of sugar into alcohol and carbon dioxide gas through the action of living organisms called yeasts. Actually, the process is more complicated than that, for the grape juice contains a great number of organic and mineral elements in addition to sugar. During fermentation and aging, these substances react in a myriad of subtle secondary processes that produce esters, acids, salts and other compounds, giving the wine its unique flavor, aroma, body, and all those other qualities that are readily appreciated by the palate but so difficult to describe.

Wine has often been described as Nature's method of preserving grape juice, for the alcohol does have just that effect. It would almost seem that Nature wants wine to be made, for she has so set the scene that grape juice will automatically become wine unless vigorous countermeasures are taken.

The fully ripened grape is rich in natural sugar. When the grape is ripe, the surface of each one is covered with an eye-catching "bloom," a whitish film that is made up of minute yeast organisms. The only step necessary is to unite the two by crushing and then sit back and let Nature run her course.

The grapes are gathered when they have reached that stage of ripeness or even overripeness that best suits the type of wine being made. They are crushed or pressed to form a *must*, a mixture of juice and skin, which is collected in huge vats. After a period of time which varies with the individual must and the prevailing conditions, a crust or *cap* forms on the surface of the must, the temperature of the liquid rises as the rate of fermentation increases, and the must begins to bubble as the gas is given off. Often the must will bubble vigorously as though it were boiling, and if the vat is open, it is dangerous to approach at this time because of the quantity of gas, which, though not in itself toxic, has driven off the air that would normally be present. When this boiling stops, again after a varying period of time, the crust or cap settles to the bottom and the must has become young wine.

This young wine is carefully drained off into other containers to go through a period of aging. The *lees* or *pomace*, i.e., the grape skins left in the bottom of the vat, are taken to a wine press where the residual wine is extracted under pressure. This pressed wine is either aged and sold as a cheaper grade, or is distilled to make brandy (*which see*).

From the remaining lees and the incrustations on the fermenting vats, from the wood of the aging casks, and from the sediments left in aging, the industry reclaims valuable by-products, notably the *tartars*, used for cooking and other purposes.

The young wine, once removed from the fermenting vats, goes through a period of aging in casks. During this aging period the subtle processes mentioned before continue to go on, forming sediment, and giving the wine character. Because of this, the wine is *fined*, i.e., clarified by using albumin, isinglass and similar substances to force the sediment to the bottom (*see* FINING), and *racked*, i.e., drained or siphoned off into fresh casks, leaving the sediment behind.

When the wine has matured sufficiently, again a varying period, it is bottled and the process of aging continues. Wine, incidentally, is the only known beverage that will age in glass. After it has aged in the bottle for a sufficient period, it is distributed for sale.

It is due to this quality of aging in glass that some wines form sediments in the bottle. This sediment is by no means harmful, it is merely an indication of advanced age. However, it does necessitate certain care in the handling, storage, and shipment of the wine, since the sediment should be settled and not mixed with the liquid.

Some wines, then, are subject, as are some people, to travel-sickness. They become cloudy and must be given a chance to rest before they are fit for use. The care in storage and serving will be discussed further on in this article.

The "pushed-up" or "false" bottom often found in wine bottles, incidentally, is not an attempt at deception as to quantity, but rather an expedient used to form crevices in which the sediment may settle.

VARIATIONS IN THE PROCESS

This, then, is the basic method of making wine. However, certain other steps are often taken, either to refine the process, or to produce a specific type of wine.

Blending. Wines are like individuals; each has characteristics of its own. Wines made of the same type of grape but grown at two separate vineyards will differ, so will different vintages of the same vineyard. Wines are blended for two reasons; to insure a uniform product, and to make a superior wine by combining several wines with different characteristics. For example, sherry (*which see*), made by the *solero* method, is a blend of different vintages, and champagne was first developed because none of the wines of the district were, by themselves, wholly satisfactory.

Controlled Fermentation. While Nature unaided will produce wine, her product is rarely consistent. Man, then, endeavors to improve by standardizing the process in its most perfect form. This he does by scientifically testing the sugar content of the growing grape to determine the best picking time, by controlling the temperature of the must (thus regulating the rate of fermentation), and by killing off the natural yeast in the must (which is variable to the extreme) and substituting measured amounts of a known yeast culture carefully raised for just that purpose.

Fortified Wines. Wines to which alcohol has been added in the form of brandy. Usually, only brandy that has been distilled from the same kind of wine that is being fortified is used. The amount added is determined by the purpose of fortification, and is sometimes controlled by law. Wines are usually fortified so they will keep better, since the alcoholic content directly controls a wine's lasting qualities and its ability to stand rough treatment. Wines are also fortified for reasons of flavor or potency.

Sparkling Wines. These are wines that are effervescent because of imprisoned carbon dioxide gas. Though this gas is produced during fermentation, it is permitted to escape, and all wines are first made as still wines. The traditional manner of making a sparkling wine is to induce a second fermentation once the wine is sealed in the bottle. This is done by adding sugar and possibly yeast to the wine when it is being bottled. (*See* CHAMPAGNE.) Since this requires much hand labor, the price of a sparkling wine is correspondingly higher than that of a still wine. In an attempt to cut down production costs, a "bulk process" has been developed, whereby the wine is given the secondary fermentation in large, sealed glass-lined tanks, and is bottled under pressure. It is mainly used for champagne, and its use is usually indicated on the label of the bottle. Still wines may also be artificially carbonated, even as are club soda or similar beverages.

Sweet Wines. In most cases, if the fermentation of a must be permitted to run its natural course, most, if not all, of the grape sugar will be converted into alcohol, leaving the wine dry. There are a number of ways of producing a sweet wine, the most obvious being to add pure cane sugar to the finished wine. The preferred method, however, is to halt the fermentation while there is still the desired amount of sugar in the wine. The fermentation can be halted by several methods, since all that is required is to kill the yeast. The wine may be pasturized or else have small quantities of a sulfur compound added. Since these methods leave the wines low in alcoholic content, hence subject to spoilage, etc., the most commonly used method is to introduce a small quantity of brandy which effectively checks the yeast action.

White Wines. Since a wine derives its color from the skin of the grape, white wines may be made from either dark or light grapes. If dark grapes are used, only the juice is used in the must, or, if the skins are used, they are removed after a very short period. If light grapes are used, the skins are either excluded or removed, depending on the exact shade of wine desired.

BUYING WINE

If one has had no previous experience in wine buying, it is well to find a reputable dealer and follow his advice. Be guided by the advice of those competent in the field until you have acquired sufficient experience to make sound decisions, then follow the dictates of personal taste.

If one is merely seeking one or two good all round table and cooking wines, the problem is simple and easily solved. If, however, one wishes to serve a variety of wines and possibly to become a connoisseur, some experimentation will be necessary before major purchases are made.

As an aid to the novice, the dealer often has a variety of assortments of various wines packed in small bottles which can serve for testing purposes. If he has none available, the majority of dealers are willing to arrange such assortments so the beginner may learn where his taste lies.

There are certain things that should be remembered, pertinent to wine, when purchasing.

Age. Possibly because literature has made a fetish of praising old wine, a belief has grown up that the older a wine is, the better it is. There is only some truth in that statement. Wines are astonishingly like people in many respects. They are individuals, and as individuals they age differently. There is a prime, a high point, in every man's life, which once passed, is never again attained. Wines are the same. Some find their prime in rich, full-blooded youth, and then pass on to a weak, bitter old age. Others find their maturity later in life, and a few, a very few indeed, are at their best only in the mellowness and wisdom of age. But every wine has a point beyond which it loses quality and eventually spoils. That is why the prime vintages of the past are now but memories.

The age of the wine, then, should only be considered in relation to that particular wine. While wine is rarely sold at too young an age, the buyer who is interested can easily learn the best ages for the various types.

Vintage. Because it has a number of meanings and uses, the term vintage is sometimes misunderstood by the novice. The word can refer to the grape on the vine, the gathering of the grapes, or the pressing and making of the wine, and in all cases carries connotations of year or season. Hence, every wine is of the vintage of the year in which it was made, and every wine may be referred to as being a vintage, without it following that it is a superior wine.

However, in Europe especially, primarily due to the influence of the weather on the quality of the grape crop, the quality of the wine will fluctuate from year to year. When the conditions have been favorable and a wine of exceptional quality is produced, that year is referred to as a "vintage year," and the wine called a "vintage wine" or "of good vintage."

When buying, the purchaser should be careful how the word is used, lest he be deceived, either through design or his own misconception. It would be well to learn the outstanding vintage years of each area as a guide to fine wines he might encounter. If the vintage years are learned, the question of wine age should also be considered, lest he purchase a bottle of excellent vintage, but a little too late in its life span to be properly enjoyed.

Label. Any food or beverage product sold in the United States must, of course, comply with Federal labeling regulations. The points of interest on the label for the wine buyer are the kind of wine, the country or place of origin, the date of vintage, the name of the vineyard, vintner, or bottler, and, in the case of foreign wines, the name of the importer. The date of vintage, rarely seen on American wine labels, is a common sight on European ones. Because of the varying grape quality from year to year, this date is very important.

Quantity. While it is always cheaper to buy in quantity, there are times when this may prove to be false economy. The larger bottle sizes may prove cheaper, but no wine will keep long once the bottle has been opened. Thus, if wine is consumed only infrequently and in small quantities, the smaller bottles should be purchased. If suitable storage space is available in the home, economies can be effected through the purchase of case lots and even in laying down wines to age. This will be discussed further in Home Wine Cellar below.

STORAGE

Wines, as has been inferred throughout this article, are inclined to be somewhat sensitive to outside conditions, and there are minimums of care that must be given them if they are to keep well. Sunlight, vibrations, temperature fluctuations, and temperature extremes can damage them. Corks have a tendency to dry out and shrink from the sides of the bottle, thus admitting air and causing eventual weakness, spoiling, and, in the case of sparkling wines, loss of carbonation.

For these reasons, wines are stored where it is reasonably cool (55° F. is the ideal temperature), dark, and free from vibration. A reasonable amount of dampness will not affect stored wines, but fruit and vegetable odors may, and these should be avoided, if possible. Corked wines are laid on their sides, though bottles with screw caps and dessert wines may be stored upright. Since the shelves nearest the floor are the coolest, the more delicate wines are stored there. The best arrangement is to place the sparkling wines on the lowest shelves, and, in ascending order, the white table wines, the red table wines, and finally, the dessert wines on top.

Home Wine Cellar. A cellar is the best possible place to store wines. However, in this age of modern living, cellars are not always available, but it does not follow that wine cannot be stored in the home.

A home wine cellar can be anywhere, as long as it fulfills the previously given conditions. It can be a closet, a cabinet, or even a chest; whichever is best suited to the circumstances.

A closet is most often the best solution. There should be no steam or hot water pipes running in or near the closet chosen, and it should be in that part of the house that is freest from street vibrations.

Not too much modification is required, merely the installation of shelves. Since many wines are stored on their sides, shelves of the "pigeonhole" type are the best since this allows the removal of individual bottles without disturbing the others. It might be well to have the shelves tipped slightly back to prevent mishap. Such shelves can be purchased in many stores, or can be made without too much difficulty.

Why bother with a wine cellar in this age of modern distribution when the wines of the world are no farther away than the corner store? Part of the answer has already been given—economy. Case lots may be purchased and safely stored. Advantage may be taken of special sales. Wines may be put down to age.

This last is one of the more interesting features of owning a wine cellar. As previously explained, some wines improve considerably with age. If the buyer has sufficient space to lay away young wines, he can get them at fairly reasonable prices and is spared the premium the dealer would justly ask had he, and not the buyer, stored them away. If a wine should age exceptionally well, the future market

WINE

1258

price may even rise higher because of competitive demand.

Laying wine away need not be thought of purely as an economy measure. It can be done on a very small scale purely as a hobby or a matter of curiosity. In many countries, this practice forms part of the overall traditions that knit families together and make home life the important element to living. A number of bottles of choice wine are laid down when each child is born, to be used later to celebrate important moments in the person's life. A wedding toast drunk with a simple wine that had been stored away at birth for just this occasion can have much, much more meaning than a toast drunk with the finest of champagne brought in by the caterers.

The Cellar Book. If a wine cellar is to be instituted, either as a measure of economy, like the pantry shelf, or as a hobby, a "cellar book" should be kept that the cellar may be used to the best advantage. It is essentially a ledger in which is kept a record of all wine purchases. Each bottle is entered with such details as the type, the name of grower or vintner, name of dealer, date of purchase, and price. When the bottle is consumed, a further entry is made, giving the date of consumption and pertinent remarks anent quality, aroma, etc., as well as any other memoranda that might seem fitting.

The book, then, serves a number of functions. It is at once a stock record showing what bottles the owner has in storage, and a guide to further purchasing. It is also a scrap book of taste experiences, and even of memorable events, and will be of increasing interest to the keeper as time goes by. Even if a wine cellar is not possible and wines are bought as needed, the cellar book may still be kept in a modified form.

Further Storage Tips. If vibrations are excessive and unavoidable in the house, the more sensitive wines, especially the sparkling variety, should be bedded in sand.

Exposure to the air hurts any wine, though the action is relatively slower if the wine has a high alcoholic content. If a bottle is opened but not entirely consumed, the remaining wine should be poured into a smaller bottle to minimize the air content, and tightly corked. Storage in a refrigerator does not help too much, because the trouble comes from exposure and not bacteria.

The dessert wines can be kept in decanters for reasonable periods, but they should be carefully watched. If wines are kept in a cask or barrel, the container should always be filled to a high level to cut down on the air space.

SERVING WINE

Wine is essentially one of the simplest of beverages to prepare and serve. The bottle is merely brought to the proper temperature (often that of the room), opened, and poured. Any elaborations on this are done to keep the contents pure and the sediment undisturbed.

Wines should always be allowed to rest a day or so after being brought home from the store, to give any sediment that might be present a chance to settle. In handling, they should never be agitated or sloshed about, and the cork should be withdrawn with care.

If there is foil or cellulose around the cork, that is first removed, usually by cutting, since that leaves a neat looking band around the neck of the bottle. The neck of the bottle and the exposed cork are carefully wiped before the corkscrew (*which see*) is inserted, and the cork is withdrawn with as steady and smooth a motion as possible. If possible, the cork should be removed in one piece. After the cork has been extracted, the bottle mouth is again wiped to minimize the dangers of dust or sediment.

When wine is poured, a little bit is always first poured into the host's glass. This is done every time a bottle is opened, and only on the first pouring from a bottle. It is not a violation of the general rule of hospitality that says the host should be served last, but serves several rather practical purposes. If there are any bits of cork, dust, or· sediment floating on the surface of the bottle's content, the host, and not the guests, will get them. It also gives the host an opportunity to first inspect, smell, and taste the wine to make certain it is of a quality worthy to be set before his guests. In every restaurant where wine is served correctly, the waiter will always make the first pouring in the host's glass and wait for his approval before serving the other members of the party.

Wine glasses are filled to the half, two-thirds or three-quarters level, but never to the brim. This is done to leave an area of glass exposed, enabling the drinker to roll the wine around, wetting this area and thus releasing the aroma, an important part of true wine enjoyment. On succeeding rounds, it is customary to fill every glass to this level, whether it has been emptied or not.

The bottle is poured carefully so as not to disturb the sediment. Usually it is gripped in the vicinity of the label to insure a steady hold and even pouring. Dripping may be prevented by gently twisting the bottle as the last drops are poured into a glass and the neck raised.

If a bottle is properly poured, only a little wine will remain among the lees, dreg, or "heel" in the bottom. This need not be thrown away, but should be saved for use in cooking.

There is no need to wrap a towel or napkin around a bottle while pouring; indeed, there are those who might think the host is ashamed of the quality of the wine and trying to conceal the label. The only purpose of the towel is to absorb the moisture found on the surface of chilled bottles, especially those that have been packed in ice. This moisture can just as well be wiped off before pouring.

Heavy Sediment. As previously explained, some wines form sediment in the bottle while aging. Special care must be taken in pouring these wines, to keep them clear. They, in particular, should be well rested before they are served. They should be gently withdrawn from the shelf, and, when carried, held at the same angle as the one in which they had lain. Bottle baskets or cradles made of wicker are sometimes used for this purpose. They are so constructed that the bottle rests in them on its side, and they have a handle so the bottle may be carried in them, placed on the table, and then poured without removal or disturbance. Cradles are made in different sizes for different bottles, so if one is used, it should be the proper size for the bottle, else the bottle may slip. If the wine has been agitated, or merely as a precautionary measure, it may be *decanted* instead of directly poured.

Decanting. This is a measure usually taken when a wine has a heavy sediment, or when bits of cork or other foreign bodies have fallen into the bottle. It may also be done simply for appearance sake. Decanters are usually made of cut crystal and are shaped along the lines of a full-bodied bottle. They are equipped with a stopper, usually also of glass (*see* GLASSWARE). Decanting consists in pouring the wine into a decanter or similar stoppered container, straining it through a piece of fine linen or cambric cloth as it is poured. Wines, especially of high alcoholic strength, may be left in a decanter for reasonable periods of time without suffering, but never for an undue period. The wine dealer should be consulted if a wine is intended to be left in a decanter more than a day or so, to learn how long would it be safe for that particular wine.

Champagne. The technique of handling a bottle of champagne or other sparkling wine, differs somewhat because of the effervescent nature of the wine. There is considerable pressure within the bottle and the cork is usually held in place by means of a wire hood beneath the foil wrapping. There is a special wire loop attached to the hood enabling both the hood and the foil to be removed in one motion. When the hood is, removed, a thumb is held on the cork to keep it from inadvertantly popping out. The bottle is held at a 45-degree angle and the cork removed by twisting gently until the internal gas pressure forces it out. A firm grip should be kept on the cork at all times to keep it from flying off and striking someone as it is forced out. There are two opposing schools of thought on the matter of champagne corks. Some prefer to have them emerge with a loud, spectacular bang, while the older, traditional school holds that a properly removed champagne cork will emerge soundlessly. Once uncorked, the wine is poured in two motions; the glass filling with foam on the first pouring, being brought to the proper level (two-thirds to three-quarters full) with the second, once the foam has subsided. Between servings, the champagne is kept in an ice-filled bucket to keep it at the proper temperature.

Temperature. Wines are served at three general temperature levels; *cellar, room,* and *chilled. Cellar* temperature is slightly lower than that of the room, being wine that is brought directly from the cellar and promptly served. Wines are brought to *room* temperature by letting them stand in the room for a few hours before serving. *Under no circumstances should a wine be warmed over a fire or otherwise heated to bring it to the proper temperature.* Some wines improve in flavor if they are opened during this standing period, others should remain corked until the time of serving. A wine dealer can advise on this.

There is no exact temperature for a *chilled* wine, for it varies too greatly with taste for general rules. The temperature should be somewhere around 45 degrees, however. Wines are easiest chilled by placing them in a refrigerator some time before serving. They may also be packed in an ice and salt mixture, usually held in a metal bucket. The ice bucket is commonly used in restaurants, being placed on a stand beside the table. It is very convenient, for the wine can remain in it and be kept at the proper temperature between servings. If a wine is not pre-chilled, usually twenty minutes in the ice bucket will bring it to the proper temperature.

Ice is never placed *in* wine, unless the wine is served in the form of a mixed drink containing other ingredients. This rule can be broken at the dictates of personal taste, but the host should never put ice in a guest's wine without first consulting him, for the vast majority of wine drinkers look on this practice as the ruination of wine.

Glasses. Wine may be, and usually is, served in any type of glass desired. Tradition has, however, prescribed certain glass shapes for certain types of wine, usually with due cause, and on formal occasions, wine is usually served in those. They are discussed in the article on glassware, *which see.* Inspection will prove that it is not even necessary to buy all of the various types of glasses for formal service; two or three types can usually suffice, depending on the need.

Wine glasses are, for the most part, traditionally made of thin, clear crystal. This is because the connoisseur derives much enjoyment from the visual inspection of the wine, and the glass is intended to act more as a setting for a jewel than as an ornate package which is, in itself, beautiful. If colored glasses are used, as in the case of the Rhine wines (*which see*), they should be tinted rather than opaque.

WINE WITH FOOD

By far the greatest percentage of all wine consumed is taken as a meal-time beverage. Its use is by no means restricted to the

wealthy, there being table wines suited to every purse in every clime.

The selection of table wines can be either a matter of taste alone, or taste guided by tradition. In everyday practice, only one wine is served with the meal. Here, the novice's choice is simple. He finds a wine that he likes and one that, to him, best harmonizes with the foods normally served at his table, and he uses it.

There are a few time-hallowed traditions that can guide him in making his selection: red wines with dark meats; white wines with light meats; dry wines with salts, sweet wines with sweets.

However, it has been established with time that certain wines compliment best certain foods. At formal functions, where two or more wines are served, the purpose is to match the wine with the food it best suits to the general taste. A general chart is given below which shows this breakdown.

It can be seen from the chart that a different wine may be served with each course of the meal; usually, however, only two or three different wines are served on formal occasions, though the function may be as elaborate as the host desires.

It is not a good policy, when wine is served with food, to preface the meal with cocktails made with any form of liquor even though wine may be one of the ingredients. Connoisseurs object because liquor has the effect of marring the full enjoyment of the wine which may follow. For this same reason, true wine lovers will refrain from smoking, before, or while drinking, wine, until the final stage of after-dinner port is reached.

As a general rule, a liqueur (*which see*), and not a wine, is served with coffee. Coffee is too strong and authoritative to be complimented by the subtle flavor and delicate aroma characteristic of most wines.

When more than one wine is served at a formal function, they are normally served in ascending order of alcoholic content and sweetness, so that the memory of the last wine will not overshadow the enjoyment of the one at hand.

For a description of the arrangement of formal wine glasses at special occasions, *see* TABLE SETTING AND SERVICE.

WINE IN DRINKS

Though purists may insist that wine should be drunk as wine, it forms either the basis or an ingredient of many delicious drinks. Wine is used in punches, coolers, cocktails, sangarees, flips, and a whole host of other cooling or warming beverages.

Because of the relatively low alcoholic content of many such wine drinks, they are much favored by those who prefer colorful, flavorful, but mild beverages.

Recipes will be found under their pertinent headings throughout this book.

Wine in Cooking

Many famous chefs look upon wine as they do salt and pepper; an essential seasoning to most dishes. Whether or not this is an extreme view is a matter of personal taste, but it is established that wine used in cooking does improve a great many dishes.

Oddly enough, when wine is used in cooking, the finished product does not taste of wine at all, but has taken on new, subtle flavors, describable only in terms of themselves. Nor can a cooked wine dish be termed intoxicating or even alcoholic, for the heat of cooking drives off the alcohol in the form of vapors, leaving only the wine-borne flavors behind.

There are many recipes in which wine is an ingredient given in this book. Should the home-maker wish to experiment with wine in cooking in a dish for which she has no recipe calling for wine, as a general rule, the same kind of wine that is served with the food on the table, is the proper one to use in cooking that food. While wine may be purchased specifically for cooking use, the "heels" of table wines may also be economically used. A wine that is sour, spoiled or has absorbed odors, is never used in cooking, however.

The appetizer wines, such as vermouth, which have been altered with herbs, spices, etc., are rarely used in cooking.

Wine Service Table

Food	Wine	Temperature
When wine is served alone as an appetizer	Champagne	Chilled
	Dubonnet	Chilled
	Sherry (dry)	Chilled
	Vermouth	Chilled
Appetizers	Champagne	Chilled
Soups	Sherry	Chilled
	Vermouth	Chilled
Eggs	Chablis (White Burgundy)	Cellar or Chilled
Light main course dishes	Graves (White Bordeaux)	Cellar or Chilled
Fowl (light meat and domesticated)	Moselle	Chilled
Seafood	Rhine Wines	Chilled
	Sauterne (dry)	Chilled
	Any other white table wine	
Cheese dishes	Burgundy	Cellar
Game (including dark fowl meat)	Chianti	Cellar or Room
Heavy main course dishes	Claret (Red Bordeaux)	Room
Meat	Any other red table wine	
Pastes (Spaghetti, etc.)		
Desserts	Champagne (if dessert is not overly sweet)	Chilled
	Haut (Sweet) Sauterne	Chilled
	Muscatel	Cellar
	Port	Room
	Sparkling Burgundy	Chilled
	Tokay	Almost Room
	Any other sweet dessert wine	
Cheese (alone)	Burgundy	Cellar
	Port	Room
Nuts	Port	Room
Alone at end of meal	Port	Room
	Sherry	Cellar or Chilled
	Any Sparkling Wine	
	Any sweet dessert wine	

WINE CUP. A cooling summer drink, pleasing to both eye and palate, that is made somewhat along the same lines as a punch (*which see*) though in smaller quantities. A wine cup is usually mixed in a pitcher and takes its name from the particular wine used. A good basic recipe for all wine cups is:

WINE CUP

1 large jigger brandy
½ small jigger triple sec
½ small jigger curacao
4 tsp sugar
1 small bottle (5 or 6 oz) carbonated water
1 pt desired wine

The ingredients are placed in a large glass pitcher, together with a quantity of ice cubes or lumps, and stirred gently but thoroughly. It is garnished with as many different kinds of fruit as are desired or available, including one or two small slices of cucumber rind, slit lengthwise and thrust over the side of the pitcher, and mint sprigs floating on the surface. It is served in claret glasses (*see* GLASSWARE).

Champagne Cup. The above recipe made with champagne.

Claret Cup. The above recipe made with claret.

Loving Cup. Another name for the champagne cup.

Sauterne and Rhine wine are two other wines often used in making wine cups. *See also* BARTENDING.

WINE JELLY. A molded dessert flavored with wine.

WINE JELLY

1 tbsp gelatin
¼ cup cold water
½ cup sugar
⅛ tsp salt
½ cup hot water
¼ cup orange juice
1 tbsp lemon juice
¾ cup wine (red, white, sherry, port, or Madeira)

Soften the gelatin in the cold water. Add the sugar, salt and hot water, and stir until all are dissolved, placing over hot water for a moment if necessary. Add the combined fruit juices and wine. Turn into previously wet mold (or individual molds) and chill. (Serves 4)

Sometimes a wine jelly is passed through a ricer and used as an edible garnish over ice cream. Again one may cut the center from a sponge cake, leaving the bottom and sides thick enough to hold the jelly which is turned into this shell as it begins to thicken, the whole being then chilled and served topped with whipped cream.

WINE, HOMEMADE. In the cities with their apartments and restricted back yard, home wine making is fast becoming another lost art. In the country, however, where small vineyards or orchards are possible, the practice still persists, not only providing pleasant but economical beverages for the table, but also utilizing the fruits that might otherwise be left over from the normal canning and preserve needs. Wines may be made in city homes from market produce, but the home must have adequate space for the operation.

If wines are made in the home, they should really be made in the cellar; a cool, roomy cellar, though any other working and storage area will suffice, provided that it has a cool, even temperature. Also required are several clean wooden casks or kegs, a wine press of some sort, a special siphon designed for this use, and, if possible, some sort of mill for mashing the grapes.

The grapes should be well ripened, and all of one kind, either light or dark. The clusters are carefully picked over, removing all unripe, dried, or damaged grapes, and then are mashed or milled. If a mill is used, it should be so adjusted that the seeds will not be mashed (thus giving a bitter taste to the wine), and if they are mashed by hand, the action should be thorough so that all the grapes are ruptured.

The longer this skin and juice mixture is permitted to stand in the tub before being pressed, the darker will be the color of the finished wine. Immediate pressing will yield a white wine, a few hours standing will give a rose wine, etc. Because this varies with the type grape used, it is impossible to give any rules for standing time, other than the precaution that the mixture cannot stand too long, else fermentation may begin.

The mixture is placed in the press and the juice expressed into clean tubs for transfer into clean casks. The cask or casks should be filled to within ten inches of the bung. The special siphon fits into the bunghole, making an airtight seal. The free end of the siphon is then placed in a pail, lower than the cask, and covered with at least four inches of water.

If properly made, the must will undergo fermentation, similar to that described in the article on wine (*which see*). The purpose of the siphon and water pail arrangement is to let the gases of fermentation escape with no danger of air getting into the must and possibly contaminating it, or otherwise impairing its quality. When the fermentation is completed (usually in a little over two weeks), *rack* the wine into a clean cask of such a size that it is well filled, bung it loosely for about a week, and then make the bung airtight.

The wine is now let stand to age and clarify itself, usually a five month period, and then is racked into clean casks and bunged up tightly. It is now ready for consumption, and may be left in the cask or, if desired, bottled. If left in the cask, it should be racked every nine months, or so.

Different qualities of wines may be made from the same batch of grapes by separating the different runs of the press. The first pressing yields the finest wine for immediate consumption, but it begins to deteriorate after two or three years. If the different runs are all mixed together, the wine will be inclined to be rough during its first year, but will have better body and flavor during the second and third years and keep on improving with age for several more years.

There are, of course, variations on the above method. Practically every home where wine is made has its own special technique, perfected through the years and handed down from generation to generation. There are different things that can be added to the must, and little tricks like dropping raisins into the bottle when the wine is put up, that can produce wines of unique flavor. The method given, however, is basic, and will produce a thoroughly satisfactory wine.

Another feature about homemade wines is that they frequently ignore the grape. Many delicious beverages are fermented from different fruits and even blossoms that are commonly called wine. Technically speaking, wine is only that beverage fermented from the juice of the grape, but these other brewings have many wine-like

WINTERGREEN

qualities, and it would, indeed, be difficult to call them anything else.

It is unfortunate that many of these home brewings are not commonly available through commercial channels, for they are truly delicious in their own right and fully entitled to a just and honest hearing. Modern civilization has given us many aids to enjoyable living, but, unfortunately, it too often shoulders aside some of the better things of the past. *See* recipes under individual fruits.

WINTERGREEN. An aromatic, creeping wild plant, bearing bright red berries, which grows in dry woods. The fresh leaves have a pungent, tart taste, and are often used in flavoring candies and chewing gums. As they are only good when fresh, they are not usually procurable in market. The plant has medicinal qualities as a tonic and diuretic.

WITHANIA CHEESE. A rennet cheese, flavored with withania berries, native to India.

WITLOOF. A type of chicory, *which see*.

WOOD APPLE. *See* BAEL QUINCE.

WOODCHUCK. Also called groundhog. A sn.all, stout, brown animal which weighs from eight to twelve pounds. In the Fall it is very fat, when the flesh of the young is said to be quite palatable, tasting like pig. The old ones are tolerably good, but are much better after having been frozen for some time. Cook the young as directed for pork, and the old ones like opossum, *which see*.

WOODCOCK. The woodcock, another member of the royal family among game, is found almost exclusively in the United States, although some woodcock cross our northern border to breed.

As a prerequisite to its presence, the woodcock requires soft, moist earth in which to probe for earthworms, and its range may be said to be largely determined by the presence or absence of this favorite food. Study this bird at what season you will, meet him where you may, the woodcock is always an interesting bird in every way. His spring-flight song, given as the hours of darkness approach, is unique among the long-billed, long-legged fraternity, and many details connected with his housekeeping are well worth attention.

And what a thrill to the sportsman's heart it is to bag this many-hued denizen of swamp and hillside in fair, sportsmanlike fashion. The first rain in March brings a flight of woodcocks to the Jersey mountains. The males arrive first, the females a few days later, but pause only long enough to feed and then continue migrating toward the north. A shot at a woodcock is the hunter's first treat of the season, which commences early in July and finishes at the end of October.

Woodcock and snipe are prepared in the same ways. They should be slightly "high," and never be cleaned; only the giblets are removed. The best method for trussing a woodcock or snipe is to pass the string through and through, to keep the legs crossed. Both snipe and woodcock should be blanketed with a thin slice of fat larding pork. The woodcock, when roasted, requires 15 to 18 minutes cooking, in a hot oven (400° F.). Woodcock may be prepared by all the different methods given for partridge, quail, and grouse, *which see.*

Woodcock and snipe require rather high seasoning, and the preferred wines to serve with them are burgundy and champagne. Unless otherwise indicated, both birds are placed on a piece of toast just before being served, so that the liquid which runs from them will be absorbed by the bread, giving it an exquisite flavor. Large woodcock will serve two persons, while small ones, or snipe, will be enough for only one person. *See also* GAME.

BRAISED WOODCOCK

1 plump woodcock
Peel of 1 orange
Salt and black pepper
2 rings of onion
1 small piece bay leaf
Pinch of thyme
1 tbsp minced celery leaves
Pinch of allspice
1 juniper berry
1 pat butter
1 cup braising vegetables
½ cup veal stock
¼ cup port wine
Cayenne pepper
½ cup cream
1 tbsp fumet

Clean and singe the woodcock and rub inside and out with the orange peel. Then rub with salt and black pepper. In the cavity of the bird place its liver, the onion, bay leaf, thyme, celery leaves, allspice, butter, and juniper berry. Sew and truss the bird. In a casserole make a layer of braising vegetables (*see* BRAISE) and lay in the bird. Pour in the stock and wine and season with cayenne pepper. Cover and place in a hot oven (400° F.) for 30 minutes. Lift out the bird and place on a hot platter. Keep hot while straining the sauce into a saucepan. Bring to a boil and stir in the cream. Then add the fumet (*which see*). Pass the sauce separately. (Serves 2)

BROILED WOODCOCK

Clean, split down the back, and broil over a clear flame or over wood fire if cooking in the open. Butter, salt, and pepper highly when done. If the full flavor is desired, place the broiled bird between two hot platters before serving.

CASSEROLE OF WOODCOCK

1 plump woodcock
4 small truffles
1 glass Madeira wine
1 tsp fumet
3 tbsp diced raw chicken liver
Thin slice larding pork
2 tbsp butter
Salt and black pepper
½ glass game stock

In an earthenware casserole, cook the truffles, fumet (*which see*), and half the glass of Madeira for 5 minutes. Add the liver and cook for 2 minutes. Clean the woodcock, singe it, and rub inside and out with a damp cloth or lemon juice. Fill the cavity with the truffles and liver. Cover the bird with the larding pork and truss. Heat the butter in the casserole and brown the bird all over. Then pour in the rest of the Madeira, the game stock, and season to taste with salt and black pepper. Cover the casserole tightly and set in a hot oven (400° F.) for 15 minutes. Serve in the casserole. (Serves 2)

ROAST WOODCOCK

This is the orthodox English way of roasting woodcock. Do not draw them, merely wipe with a soft cloth. Truss them with the head under wing and the bill laid down close to the breast. Pass a small skewer through the thighs, catch the ends with a bit of skin, and tie it across to keep the legs straight. Suspend the bird feet downwards on a bird-spit; flour well, and baste with butter, which should be already melted in the pan or ladle before the trail begins to drop, which it will do as soon as the bird is well heated. Lay a piece of toast in the pan under the bird to catch the trail, as this is considered finer eating than even the flesh of the bird. Continue the basting, letting the butter fall from bird to pan where it will soak into the toast. With a brisk fire the birds will be done in from 15 to 18 minutes. Then place toast in a hot dish and the bird on it. Pour a little gravy around the head, and send more gravy to the table in a gravy dish.

ROAST WOODCOCK MONACO

1 plump woodcock
1 tbsp minced fresh pork
3 chicken livers
½ cup fine bread crumbs
Pinch allspice
Pinch nutmeg
1 blade thyme
2 tbsp spicy tomato sauce
1 tsp fumet
2 slices of toast
Spanish sauce

The woodcock should be hung for 5 days. Clean and roast the bird as directed above. Meanwhile, fry out the pork in a heavy skillet. Add the giblets of the woodcock and the chicken livers. Stir and cook slowly over a low flame. Add the bread crumbs, herbs, tomato sauce, and fumet (*which see*). Cook for several minutes, stirring constantly. Rub through a fine sieve, and spread the mixture on the slices of toast. Split the roasted bird in half and dress half on each slice of toast. Pour 1 tablespoon of Spanish sauce (*see* TOMATO) over each serving and pass additional sauce separately. (Serves 2)

WOODCOCK ALEXANDER DUMAS

1 plump woodcock
1 pat butter
Salt and black pepper
2 tbsp butter
1 cup heavy cream

Clean and singe the bird thoroughly, reserving the liver. Sew the skin of the neck so that the opening is tightly closed. Place the liver and pat of butter into the cavity of the bird, season well inside with salt and black pepper. Sew the cavity and truss the bird. Place on a rack in an open roaster and place in a moderate oven (375° F.) for 25 minutes. After the first 10 minutes pour the cream and the rest of the butter into the roasting pan and baste the bird constantly with the mixture. Serve the bird on a hot platter and garnish with triangles of bread fried in butter. Strain the sauce and pass separately. (Serves 2)

WOODEN WARE. Much kitchen equipment was made of wood before metal and ceramic manufacturing techniques were developed. While wood is cheap, abundant, and often beautiful, there are many limitations in its use.

It is obvious that wood cannot be subjected to any form of direct flame or even intense heat, thus making its use in cooking vessels impossible. Because wood is porous, it will, in time, become permeated by grease, liquids, and similar materials. This, in addition to its softness, rules it out for dinner plate use.

Wood is chiefly used to make handles; cutting boards; salad and mixing bowls; forks, spoons, and other utensils used for stirring, mixing, and serving; serving trays; and many items whose purpose is more decorative than functional.

CARE AND CLEANING

There are many different kinds of wood, each with different properties. There are also many different ways of processing wood; of staining, painting, oiling, etc. For these reasons, the purchaser would do well to learn the proper care of each wooden item purchased at the time of buying.

In general, except for stirring spoons, excess moisture should be avoided, for this is usually harmful to wood. Bowls, boards, and other wooden objects and surfaces should be cleaned by wiping with damp cloths rather than by washing in a dishpan as is done with other materials. All wood objects should be handled with

WOODRUFF

some care to prevent denting, chipping, and splitting.

WOODRUFF. Woodruff is a sweet-scented European herb that is used to flavor candies, confections, wines, and punches.

WORCESTERSHIRE SAUCE (woos-tehr-shihr). Worcestershire sauce was used freely by the ancient Phoenicians, and after that by the early Romans, primarily as a self-starter for the morning. It is then traced to ancient India, where it was used for centuries. Later the English made the product in Worcester, England, whence it gets its present name. So it is not actually of English origin, and is in the same category as Irish potatoes, English walnuts, and such other food items that have traveled for years under mercantile names.

Worchestershire sauce is a product which represents the skillful cooking, steeping, blending, and aging of over one hundred ingredients, many of them from farflung corners of the earth. It is especially used to enhance a sauce, a soup, or a dressing.

WORMWOOD. A woody herb with a very bitter astringent flavor. Its chief use was in making absinthe, *which see*.

WORT. A plant of the cabbage family; also the saccharine infusion of malt which ferments and makes beer. Also an aromatic herb.

WRASSE. A bony, brightly colored food fish of tropical waters, seldom seen in American markets except canned.

XYZ

XANTHIA COCKTAIL. A cocktail made of brandy, gin and wine.

XANTHIA COCKTAIL

½ jigger dry gin
½ jigger cherry brandy
½ jigger yellow chartreuse

The ingredients are placed in a mixing glass with cracked ice, stirred well and strained into a cocktail glass. *See* BARTENDING; *see also* COCKTAIL, ALCOHOLIC. (Serves 1)

XERES COCKTAIL. A wine and bitters cocktail suitable for serving as an appetizer.

XERES COCKTAIL

1 large jigger sherry
1 dash orange bitters

The ingredients are placed in a mixing glass with cracked ice, stirred until chilled and strained into a cocktail glass. *See* BARTENDING; *see also* COCKTAIL, ALCOHOLIC. (Serves 1)

YAM. A tuber of African origin, allied to the sweet potato, but with moist texture and high sugar content, and a whitish to reddish color skin and greenish-yellow to reddish or orange tint flesh. There is a wide variation in shape. The yam closely resembles the sweet potato, but grows much larger; it is the tuberous root of a different plant.

YAPON. A kind of holly, the leaves of which are used as tea. Also called South Sea Islands Tea.

YAVA. Another name for ava (*which see*), an intoxicating drink made by the Polynesian natives.

YEAST. A fungus growth consisting of minute vegetable cells that increase by division in contact with saccharine liquids, producing alcoholic fermentation when used in beverages as well as in dough. There are two forms of yeast from which the homemaker may choose: compressed yeast and dry yeast. In reality yeast is a one-celled plant or organism (fungus) requiring definite conditions of temperature, food, and moisture for its growth. It feeds upon sugar and starch. The temperature best suited to the multiplication of yeast cells and consequent leavening and lightening of the dough in which it is used is between 70° and 90° F. (room temperature). Yeast is destroyed by heat at a temperature (oven temperature) of 132° F., and by cold at approximately 40° F. At the temperature indicated yeast grows rapidly and this growth process causes fermentation and the development of carbonic-acid gas which causes the dough to rise. *See also* BREAD and FERMENTATION.

YELLOW PERCH. The typical yellow perch has a greenish-brown back with yellow and dark bars on the sides, while the under part is white. Good sized specimens reach a length of 14 inches but such large fish are not so desirable as to flavor. The fish is generally bony, with flesh of poor quality. It is in season all the year round.

YELLOW TURNIP. *See* TURNIP.

YERBA MATE. Also called Paraguay tea. *See* MATE.

YOGHOORT, YOGHURT, or **YOGURT.** A fermented, concentrated milk, *which see.*

YORKSHIRE PUDDING. An English pudding usually served with roast beef.

A Yorkshire pudding batter and a popover batter are practically identical. Popovers are always baked in small heavy pre-heated pans—Yorkshire pudding *may* be baked in this manner but more frequently is cooked in a shallow baking pan into which three or four tablespoons of the drippings from the roasting beef have been

YAM

poured. In the old days when meat was roasted in front of the fire the baking pudding was placed under the roast for the last few minutes of cooking that it might absorb the last rich drippings or essence from the beef itself. It is served cut into squares and either placed around the roast or on a separate dish.

Certain variations call for the addition either of a little coarsely grated onion and a sprinkling of sage, in which case the pudding is referred to as "savory pudding"; or again a handful of plump seedless raisins may be stirred into the batter just before baking.

YORKSHIRE PUDDING

1 cup sifted flour
½ tsp salt
2 eggs
1 cup milk

Sift the flour and salt and mix to a batter with the unbeaten eggs and milk, beating until the mixture is smooth and creamy. If made an hour or more before baking, the pudding will be lighter than if prepared at the last moment. Turn into a shallow pan into which beef drippings have been poured and the pan placed in the oven until sizzling hot. Bake about 45 minutes, having the oven hot (450° F.) for the first 15 minutes, after which reduce the heat to 375° F.

YQUEM, CHATEAU D'. The finest of all French sweet white wines. Yquem is in the Sauternes district. The grapes are picked one at a time, when fully ripe, instead of by bunches.

YUCCA. A wild plant family of southwestern and southern parts of the United States. Edible members of the family are called Spanish bayonet or Spanish dagger (*Yucca baccata*), Broad-Leaved yucca (*Yucca macrocarpa*), Adam's needle or bear grass (*Yucca glauca*), and Eve's darning needle (*Yucca filamentosa*).

The short stalk of Spanish bayonet is surrounded by a barrier of wide, fibrous, dark green leaves that are stiff and sharply pointed. The stalk is crowned by a mass of small, yellowish flowers that appear luminescent when seen at night. (Other edible yuccas have the same general appearance, but have tall stalks which sometimes rise to a height of eight feet.)

The fruit of Spanish bayonet ripens in the autumn and varies from yellow to a dark purple and is shaped somewhat like the papaya, *which see*. It has a sweet flavor when peeled and eaten raw although the Indians of the Southwest generally roasted it before eating, and sometimes dried the raw, sliced fruit in the sun for future use.

When young, the stalks of yucca may be prepared like asparagus.

ZABAGLIONE. *See* SABAYON.

ZANZIBAR COCKTAIL. A gin, vermouth, and lemon juice mixture suitable for serving as an appetizer.

ZANZIBAR COCKTAIL

1 jigger dry gin
1 jigger dry vermouth
1 jigger lemon juice
½ tsp powdered sugar
2 dashes orange bitters

The ingredients are placed in a cocktail shaker together with cracked ice, shaken vigorously, strained into cocktail glasses and garnished with lemon slices. *See also* BARTENDING and COCKTAIL, ALCOHOLIC. (Serves 1)

ZAPOTE. Another name for the sapodilla, *which see*.

ZAZA COCKTAIL. A cocktail made of gin and dubonnet.

ZAZA COCKTAIL

2 jiggers dry gin
1 jigger Dubonnet

The ingredients are placed in a mixing glass with cracked ice, stirred until chilled, strained into cocktail glasses and garnished with twists of lemon peel. *See also* BARTENDING and COCKTAIL, ALCOHOLIC. (Serves 2)

ZEST. To give zest or relish to a food or a dish is to make a dish or preparation piquant. The zest of a lemon is the oil grated from the skin.

ZIEGEL CHEESE. A German cheese made from the whole milk of cows.

ZIEGENKASE CHEESE. A German goat's cheese, also called Gaiskasli cheese. It is a soft cheese never exported.

ZIPS CHEESE. Another name for Brinsen cheese, *which see*.

ZOMBIE. Named for the walking dead of West African and West Indian voodoo lore, to refer to this rum drink as intoxicating is, almost, an understatement. Being a mixture of several types of rum, it is extremely potent. Introduced to America chiefly as a novelty drink, different commercial establishments have evolved separate recipes, all producing pretty much the same effect.

ZOMBIE I

1 small jigger tropical heavy bodied rum
1 large jigger Gold Label rum
1 small jigger White Label rum
2 tsp apricot brandy
½ jigger unsweetened pineapple juice
½ jigger papaya juice
1 tsp sugar
1 lime, juice and skin

The ingredients are mixed extra well in a cocktail shaker and poured, unstrained, into a 14-ounce zombie glass (*see* GLASSWARE). A half jigger of 151 proof rum is floated on top, and the drink is garnished with a green cherry, a small square of pineapple, a red cherry and a sprig of mint that has been dipped in powdered sugar. It is served with straws. (Serves 1)

ZOMBIE II

1 small jigger passion fruit juice
1 small jigger plum or apricot juice
1 lime, juice and skin

1 tsp powdered sugar
1 dash bitters
1 medium orange (juice)
½ small jigger anisette
1 jigger and 1 small jigger West Indian rum
½ small jigger apricot brandy
½ jigger 151 proof rum
1 small jigger Jamaica rum
1 small jigger Porto Rico rum

The ingredients are well shaken with cracked ice, as above, and strained into frosted 14-ounce zombie glass. Garnished and served as above with the exception of the rum floated on top. (Serves 1)

ZOOLAK. *See* MILK.

ZUBROWKA. A Russian drink made from vodka, by steeping some Zubrowka grass in it, to give it a little color, aromatic bouquet, and bitterish taste which vodka does not have.

ZUCCHINI. Italian name for a certain species of squash *which see*.

ZUCCO. A dessert wine from Sicily.

ZWIEBACK. A toast made from especially baked bread, the dough of which is usually prepared with milk, butter, eggs, sometimes sweetened with sugar, and flavored with lemon and cinnamon. The loaves are sliced when cool, and the slices toasted in the oven at low temperatures.

ZWIRN CHEESE. Another name for Tschil cheese, *which see*.

ZYTHUM. An ancient beverage made from malt and wheat; a kind of beer.

Glossary

This section contains an explanation and clarification
of uncommon and foreign words found
on restaurant menus

AAL. Eel. (German)

AAM CHATNI. Mango chutney. (Hindi)

ABAISSE. A thin pastry undercrust. (French)

ABATIS. Giblets. (French)

ABRICOTS. Apricots. (French)

ACCIUGHE. Anchovies. (Italian)

ACEITUNAS. Olives. (Spanish)

ACEMITA. Brown bread. (Spanish)

ACHAR. Pickled relish. (Hindi)

ADEREZO. Garnishing. (Spanish)

AGLIO. Garlic. (Italian)

AGNEAU. Lamb. (French)

AGNEAU DE LAIT. Spring lamb. (French)

AGNELLO. Lamb. (Italian)

AGNELLO DI LATTE. Spring lamb. (Italian)

AGUACATE. Avocado. (Spanish)

AHORNSIRUP. Maple sirup. (German)

AHORNZUCKER. Maple sugar. (German)

AIGRE-DOUX. Indicates a sour-sweet taste. (French)

AIGUILLETTE. A small slice or strip of cooked fish, meat, bacon, etc. (French)

AIL. Garlic. (French)

AILE. Wing. (French)

AILLOLIS. This indicates a Provencale sauce of olive oil with garlic pounded into it. (French)

AIRELLES ROUGES. Cranberries. (French)

AJI. Chilies. (Spanish)

AJO. Garlic. (Spanish)

A LA or **A L'.** Means "in the manner, fashion, or style of," "with" or "in." (French)

A LA BELLEVUE. Indicates a food prepared in an aspic in such a manner that the food can be clearly seen. (French)

A LA BIGARADE. Indicates the use of orange juice or orange peel for flavoring. (French)

A LA BORDELAISE. Made with Bordeaux wine. (French)

A LA BOULANGIRE. Means served with potatoes and fried onions. (French)

A LA BRIOCHE. Cooked on a skewer. (French)

A LA CALEDONIAN. Usually applied to finnan haddie, this expression means that the food in question is boiled slowly in plain water, and then is baked with a dressing of butter, chopped parsley, and lemon juice. (French)

A LA CARTE. This expression on the menu indicates that the diner is free to select individual items, paying for each, rather than taking a prescribed dinner. (French)

A LA CLERMONT. This refers to a garnish of fried artichokes, farced onions, etc. (French)

A LA CONDE. Refers to dishes of stewed fruit served with rice. (French)

A LA COQUE. Boiled, refers chiefly to eggs. (French)

A LA COQUELICOT. Made to resemble a poppy in shape. (French)

A LA DUCHESSE. Implies: in sauce, Béchame with mushrooms and ham; in soup, thick poultry stock with asparagus tips and truffles; with meats, servings of Duchesse potatoes and braised lettuce; and with fish, oyster sauce. (French)

A LA DUGLERE. Signifies the use of onions, shallots, and tomatoes. (French)

A LA FINANCIERE. Means, in sauce, brown sauce with truffles and mushrooms; in garnishing, mushrooms, olives, and cucumbers; and in soup, goose liver cream with croûtons. (French)

A LA FLAMANDE. Eggs with brussels sprouts; butter sauce with mustard, parsley, and lemon juice; fish poached in wine and butter, and served with fines herbes and browned, rasped bread, with slices of lemon, or meats with carrots, turnips, and brussels sprouts. (French)

A LA HOLSTEIN. Indicates that the food is fried, and served with a fried egg, pickled beets, capers, and pickles. (French)

A LA KING. Usually applied to meat or fowl to indicate that they are served in a cream sauce to which mushrooms and pimientos or green peppers have been added. (French)

A L'ALSACIENNE. Applied to meats to signify garnishings of potatoes, pickled herring, and thin slices of apple. (French)

A LA MARYLAND. This expression means that the food is either made or served with a butter and cream sauce that sometimes contains wine. (French)

A LA MEUNIERE. Either, in soups, a velouté of fish with croûtons, or fish dipped in flour, sautéed in butter, and served with butter sauce and lemon, and sprinkled in parsley. (French)

A LA MEYERBEER. Applied to eggs, this expression means shirred and served with broiled kidney and truffle sauce. (French)

A LA MILANAISE. Depending on use, implies either Allemand sauce made pink with tomato purée, or, in the case of spaghetti or macaroni, garnishings of tomato sauce, slices of ham, tongue, and truffles. (French)

A LA MODE. This expression indicates that the dish is prepared in the current or common fashion. In the case of beef, however, it usually signifies marianating, and in the case of pie, it means that it is served with a scoop of ice cream. (French)

A LA MOUTARDE. In a mustard sauce. (French)

A LA NAPOLITAINE. Signifies meat served with eggplant and tomatoes au gratin, a wine and tomato sauce, or spaghetti served with tomato sauce and cheese. (French)

A L'ANCIENNE. "In the old-fashioned way." Applied to sauce to signify Hollandaise with cucumbers, mushrooms, and truffles; to garnishings, to signify poached fish with capers, truffles, and sliced gherkins; and to consommé to signify a poultry base, croûtons, and Parmesan. (French)

A L'ANDALOUSE. Referring to a section of southern Spain, this expression implies in consommé and soups, the use of tomatoes and rice; in garnishing, the use of tomatoes, eggplant, rice, and red peppers; in sauce, the use of mayonnaise with tomatoes and red peppers; and in *salads*, the use of Spanish onions, to-

matoes, cucumbers, oil, eggs, and vinegar. (French)

A LA NEIGE. This expression means that the food is either prepared or served in such a way as to suggest snow. It frequently indicates the use of beaten egg whites or balls of white boiled rice. (French)

A LA NESSELRODE. Indicates the use of chestnuts. (French)

A L'ANGLAISE. Meaning "in the English manner," this expression is applied to garnishings of turnips, cabbage, carrots, and boiled potatoes; to boiled potatoes; to breaded cutlets; and to poached or shirred eggs. (French)

A LA NORMANDE. In the case of fish, it signifies shellfish with slices of fried fish; in soup, vegetables; and in sauce, velouté of fish with mushrooms. (French)

A LA ORLY. Fried in batter; usually applied to strips of fish or meat. (French)

A LA PARISIENNE. Usually signifies the following: in consommé, a poultry base with vegetables and seasoning; in fish, poached, using three separate sauces; in meat, served with Parisienne potatoes, asparagus tips or stuffed artichoke bottoms, truffles, and mushrooms; in potatoes, small, round, and brown; in sauce, Espagnole sauce with shallots and lemon juice; in salad, chopped beef, potatoes, and hard-cooked eggs. (French)

A LA PARMENTIER. Signifies the use of potatoes. (French)

A LA PERIGUEUX. Made or served with truffles or truffle sauce. (French)

A LA POLONAISE. Signifies the following: in sauce, velouté, horse raddish, sour cream, and lemon juice; in garnishing, rasped bread, beurre noir, and hashed hard-cooked eggs. (French)

A LA PROVENCALE. Signifies, in sauce, white or brown sauce with mushrooms, tomatoes, garlic, and onions; and in garnishing, the use of mushrooms and tomatoes. (French)

A LA REINE. Meaning "to the Queen's taste," this expression is usually applied to soup to indicate the presence of puréed white meat of chicken. (French)

A L'ARGENTEUIL. This expression signifies the use of asparagus in or with the food to which it is applied. (French)

A LA RICHELIEU. Signifies, in sauce, Allemande with added tomato; and in garnishing, braised lettuce, mushrooms, olive potatoes, and artichokes. (French)

A LA SAINT GERMAIN. Indicates the use of peas. (French)

A LA SOUBISE. Signifies the use of onion purée or sauce. (French)

A LA TARTARE. Signifies a hot, spiced dish. (French)

A LA VICHY. Implies the use of carrots. (French)

ALBICOCCHE. Apricots. (Italian)

ALCACHOFAS. Artichokes. (Spanish)

AL DENTE. Firm or hard. This expression is applied to spaghetti to indicate that it is not cooked long enough to make it completely soft, but retains some firmness in the center. (Italian)

A L'HUILE. Indicates the use of olive oil or olive oil dressing. (French)

A L'INDIENNE. Means a dish prepared in the East Indian fashion, a curried Allemand sauce, or a curried rice garnishing. (French)

A L'ITALIENNE. Means a dish prepared in the Italian manner, or, specifically, a rich, brown sauce with mushrooms, truffles, tomatoes, herbs, and ham; or a garnishing of artichoke bottoms and macaroni croquettes fried in oil. (French)

ALLUMETTES. Meaning "matches," this term is applied to foods cut into fine strips. (French)

ALMEJAS. Clams. (Spanish)

ALMENDRADOS. Macaroons. (Spanish)

ALMENDRAS. Almonds. (Spanish)

ALOSA. Shad. (Spanish)

ALOSE. Shad. (French)

ALSE. Shad. (German)

AMANDES. Almonds. (French)

AMARETTI. Macaroons. (Italian)

AMERICAINE. Signifies that the dish is prepared in the American style. (French)

ANANAS. Pineapple. (German)

ANAS. Pineapple. (French)

ANCHOAS. Anchovies. (Spanish)

ANCHOIS. Anchovies. (French)

ANDA. Hard-cooked eggs. (East Indian)

ANGLAISE. English. (French)

ANGUILA. Eel. (Spanish)

ANGUILLA. Eel. (Italian)

ANGUILLE. Eel. (French)

ANIMELLA. Sweetbread. (Italian)

ANITRA. Duck. (Italian)

ANITRA SELVATICA. Wild duck. (Italian)

ANSARON. Gosling. (Spanish)

ANTIPASTI. The name of an Italian appetizer course. (Italian)

ANTIPASTO. Depending on use, means either a mixture of mushrooms, tuna fish, and pimiento, or the first or appetizer course of an Italian dinner. (Italian)

AP. Duck. (Chinese)

APFEL. Apples. (German)

APFELSINEN. Oranges. (German)

APFELWEIN. Cider. (German)

APIO. Celery. (Spanish)

ARACHIDES. Peanuts. (French)

ARANCI. Oranges. (Italian)

ARENQUE. Herring. (Spanish)

ARENQUE AHUMADO. Smoked or kippered herring. (Spanish)

ARENQUE EN ESCABECHE. Pickled herring. (Spanish)

ARINGA. Herring. (Italian)

ARINGA AFFUMICATA. Kippered or smoked herring. (Italian)

AROMATES. Aromatic herbs. (French)

ARROSTO. Roast. (Italian)

ARROZ. Rice. (Spanish)

ARTICHAUTS. Artichokes. (French)

ASADO. Baked or roasted; applied only to fish or meats. (South American, Spanish)

ASPERGES. Asparagus. (French)

ASSAISSONNEMENT. Seasoning. (French)

ASSIETTE. Plate. (French)

ASSIETTE PARISIENNE. Small relishes or appetizers served on small plates. (French)

ASTACO. Lobster. (Italian)

ATTEREAUX. Pieces of meat cooked together on a skewer. (French)

AU. Depending on use, means "with," "in," or "of," or, in some cases, "in the manner of." (French)

AUBERGINE. Eggplant. (French)

AU BLEU. To cook by boiling; applies correctly only to fresh-water fish that has been treated with vinegar to make the skin turn blue. (French)

AU FOUR. This expression means "baked in the oven." (French)

AU GRAS. Means cooked in a rich broth or gravy. (French)

AU GRATIN. Meaning "with a crust," it implies either a cheese or bread crumb crust, or both. (French)

AU KARI. Curried. (French)

AU NATUREL. Prepared in a simple manner; sometimes raw. (French)

AU PARMESAN. Made or served with grated Parmesan cheese. (French)

AUSTERN. Oysters. (German)

AU VIN BLANC. Made or served in or with white wine. (French)

AUX. Plural of au. (French)

AUX CROUTONS. Served with croutons. (French)

A V E L I N E S. Filberts or Hazelnuts. (French)

BACALAO. Codfish. (Spanish)

BACCALA. Codfish. (Italian)

BACCHE. Berries. (Italian)

BACKPFLAUMEN. Prunes. (German)

BACKWERT. Pastry. (German)

BAIES. Berries. (French)

BALLOTINE. Refers to round-shaped, boned, individual servings of meat or poultry, and also to small game birds stuffed with forcemeat. (French)

BANANES. Bananas. (French)

BARBEAU. Bass. (French)

BARDE. Means either larded or covered with bacon or salt pork. (French)

BARQUETTE. Bread cut in the shape of a boat and toasted; used to hold other foods. (French)

BARQUILLOS. Waffles. (Spanish)

BARSZCZ. Beet soup. (Polish)

BARWARKA. Cambric tea. (Polish)

BATATAS. Sweet potatoes. (Spanish)

BATATE. Sweet potatoes. (Italian)

BATATEN. Sweet potatoes. (German)

BAVAROIS. Whipped cream stiffened with gelatin; also, Bavarian. (French)

BAVETTE. A macaroni shape larger than perciatelli. (Italian)

BAYAS. Berries. (Spanish)

BEEREN. Berries. (German)

BEIGNET. A fritter. (French)

BELLEVUE, "A pleasing sight." Usually refers to aspics. (French)

BERENJENA. Eggplant. (Spanish)

BERRO. Water cress. (Spanish)

BEURRE. Butter. (French)

BEURRE DE CUISINE. Cooking butter. (French)

B E U R R E F O N D U. Melted butter. (French)

BEURRE SALE. Salt Butter. (French)

BHUJIYA. A very hot, spicy, vegetable dish. (East Indian)

BIEN CUIT. Well done. (French)

BIER. Beer. (German)

BIFF. Meat (Norse)

BIFF STROGONAFF. Beef tenderloin cut into strips and served with rich sour cream and mushroom sauce. (Russian)

BIFTEC. Steak. (Spanish)

BIFTECK. Beefsteak. (French)

BIRNEN. Pears. (German)

BISTECCA. Steak. (Italian)

BIZCOCHOS. Biscuits. (Spanish)

BLANCS D'OEUF. Egg whites. (French)

BLANCHI. Means blanched or parboiled. (French)

BLE. Wheat. (French)

BLINI. Pancakes. (Russian)

B L U M E N K O H L. Cauliflower. (German)

BOEUF. Beef. (French)

BOEUF EPICE. Spiced Beef. (French)

BOEUF FUME. Dried or smoked beef. (French)

BOEUF ROTI. Roast beef. (French)

BOEUF SALE. Corned beef. (French)

BOHNEN. Beans. (German)

BOMBE. A ball-shaped, filled, frozen dessert. (French)

BON GOUT. Meaning "good taste," this term is often applied to highly seasoned dishes. (French)

BONNE FEMME. Meaning "good wife," this term is often applied to simple or "home cooking" type dishes. (French)

BONOR. Beans. (Swedish)

BOR. Wine. (Hungarian)

BOUCHEE. A "mouthful," i.e., a small patty or cake. (French)

BOUILLI. Depending on use, means either boiled, or boiled beef, especially beef that has been used to make soup. (French)

BOURGEOISE. A term used to denote family or "home" style cooking. (French)

BRACIUOLA. Steak. (Italian)

BRATEN. Roast. (German)

BRATHUHN. Roasting chicken. (German)

BRINJAL. Eggplant. (East Indian)

BROCHETTES. Pieces of meat that have been cooked on a skewer. (French)

BRODO. Broth. (Italian)

BROSCHEN. Sweetbread. (German)

BROT. Bread. (German)

BROTCHEN. Rolls. (German)

BROUILLE. Mixed, mingled, or scrambled. (French)

BRUGNON. Nectarine. (French)

BRUNEDE KARTOFLER. Browned potatoes. (Danish)

BRUNNENKRESSE. Water cress. (German)

BUCHWEIZEN. Buckwheat. (German)

BUDDING. Pudding. (Danish)

BUISSON. A pyramid or mound-shaped arrangement of food. (French)

BURAKI. Beet purée. (Polish)

CABEZA. Head. (Spanish)

CABILLAUD. Codfish. (French)

CACAHUETES. Peanuts. (Spanish)

CACAO. Cocoa. (French)

CACCIATORE. Indicates that the specified meat (usually veal or chicken) is cut into pieces and cooked in a tomato sauce. (Italian)

CAFE. Coffee. (French)

CAFE AU KIRSCH. After-dinner coffee with cherry cordial. (French)

CAFE AU LAIT. Coffee with hot milk. (French)

CAFE BRULE. After-dinner coffee made with brandy and sugar. (French)

CAFE NOIR. Black coffee. (French)

CAFE ROYALE. After-dinner coffee with brandy. (French)

CAFE TURQUE. Turkish coffee. (French)

CAILLE. Quail. (French)

CALABAZA. Pumpkin or squash. (Spanish)

CALDO. Broth. (Spanish)

CAMARONES. Prawns or shrimps. (Spanish)

CANARD. Duck. (French)

CANARD SAUVAGE. Wild duck. (French)

CANETON. Duckling. (French)

CANGREJO. Crab. (Spanish)

CANGREJO BLANDO. Soft-shelled crab. (Spanish)

CANNELLE. Cinnamon. (French)

CANNELONS. Small, stuffed rolls, made of pastry or starchy vegetables. (French)

CAPPONE. Capon. (Italian)

CARACOLES. Snails. (Spanish)

CARCIOFI. Artichokes. (Italian)

CARNE. Meat. (Italian and Spanish)

CARNE DE CARNERO. Mutton. (Spanish)

CARNE DE CORDERO. Lamb. (Spanish)

CARNE DE PUERCO. Pork. (Spanish)

CARNE DE TERNERA. Veal. (Spanish)

CARNE DE VACA. Beef. (Spanish)

CARNE DE VENADO. Venison. (Spanish)

CAROTE. Carrots. (Italian)

CARP POLONAIS. Carp prepared or served with raisin sauce. (French)

CARRE. Rack. (French)

CARTE DU JOUR. Bill of fare for a given day. (French)

CASTRATO. Mutton. (Italian)

CASUELA. Implies the use of a casserole, especially one with a lid. (South American)

CAVOLI SALATI. Sauerkraut. (Italian)

CAVOLO. Cabbage. (Italian)

CAVOLO FIORE. Cauliflower. (Italian)

CAVOLO RICCIO. Kale. (Italian)

CEBOLLAS. Onions. (Spanish)

CECINA. Corned beef. (Spanish)

CEDRAT CONFIT. Candied citron. (French)

CEREZAS. Cherries. (Spanish)

CERISES. Cherries. (French)

CERVELLE. Brains. (French)

CERVELLE DE VEAU. Calf's brains. (French)

CERVEZA. Beer. (Spanish and South American)

CETRIUOLI. Cucumber. (Italian)

CHA. Tea. (Chinese)

CHAI. Tea. (East Indian)

CHAMPIGNONS. Mushrooms. (French)

CHAPON. Capon. (French)

CHAPPATI. Thin, flat, unleavened bread. (East Indian)

CHA SHIU. Roast pork. (Chinese)

CHASSEUR. Means either served with or made of game or mushrooms. (French)

CHATEAUBRIAND. Depending on use, either a thick, tenderloin steak, or a brown sauce with fat, lemon juice, parsley, and Spanish sauce. (French)

CHATEAU POTATOES. Cut olive-shaped, boiled, and then browned in butter. (French)

CHAUD. Hot. (French)

CHAUDFROID. Meaning "hot-cold," this term is applied chiefly to pressed fowl that is covered with sauce and eaten cold. (French)

CHAWL. Rice. (East Indian)

CHEPPIA. Shad. (Italian)

CHICCHE. Candy. (Italian)

CHIFFONADE. Means either made of or served with shredded vegetables. (French)

CHILES. Chilies. (Spanish)

CHIRIVIA. Parsnips. (Spanish)

CHOU. Cabbage. (French)

CHOUCROUTE. Sauerkraut. (French)

CHOU DE SAVOIE. Savoy cabbage. (French)

CHOUFLEUR. Cauliflower. (French)

CHOU VERT FRISE. Kale. (French)

CHOUX DE BRUXELLES. Brussels sprouts. (French)

CHU CHAI. Suckling pig. (Chinese)

CHUEN KUEN. Egg rolls. (Chinese)

CHULETAS. Cutlets or chops. (Spanish)

CIALDE. Waffles. (Italian)

CIDRE. Cider. (French)

CILIEGIE. Cherries. (Italian)

CIMIER DE VENAISON. Haunch of venison. (French)

CIPOLLE. Onions. (Italian)

CITRON. Lemon. (French)
CITRONNAT. Candied lemon peel. (French)
CITROUILLE. Pumpkin. (French)
COCHON DE LAIT. Suckling pig. (French)
CODA DI BUE. Oxtail. (Italian)
COEUR. Heart. (French)
COHOMBRO. Cucumber. (Spanish)
COING. Quince. (French)
COL. Cabbage. (Spanish)
COL ACIDA. Sauerkraut. (Spanish)
COLIFLOR. Cauliflower. (Spanish)
CON. With. (Spanish)
CONCOMBRE. Cucumber. (French)
CONCOMBRES CONFITS. Pickled cucumbers. (French)
CONIGLIO. Rabbit. (Italian)
CONFITES. Candy. (Spanish)
CONFITURE. Jam. (French)
CONSERVES. Preserves. (French)
CONTREFILET. Boned sirloin. (French)
CONTRE-FILET. Slices of boned sirloin. (French)
CORAZON. Heart. (Spanish)
CORAZONES DE ALCACHOFA. Artichoke bottoms. (Spanish)
CORDERILLO. Spring lamb. (Spanish)
CORDON BLEU. An exceptional cook. (French)
CORNICHONS. Gherkins. (French)
COSCIA. Leg. (Italian)
COSTILLAS DE CERDO. Spareribs. (Spanish)
COSTOLA. Rib. (Italian)
COSTOLETTE. Cutlets or chops. (Italian)
COTE. Rib. (French)
COTELETTE. Cutlet or chop. (French)
COU. Neck. (French)
COURGE. Squash. (French)
COUVERT. Depending on use, either a cover of some sort, the table equipment for one diner, or a cover charge. (French)
CRABE MOU. Soft-shelled crab. (French)
CRAPAUDINE. Usually applied to broiled, small fowl, this expression means to flatten and truss to give the food a frog-like appearance. (French)
CRAUTI. Sauerkraut. (Italian)
CRECY. This expression usually signifies the use of carrots. (French)
CREMA. Cream. (Italian)
CREMA GHIACCIATA. Ice cream. (Italian)
CREME. Cream. (French)
CRESSON DE FONTAINE. Water cress. (French)

CREVETTES. Shrimps or prawns. (French)
CROQUETTES. Any kind of meat that is minced and shaped. (French)
CROSTATA. Pie or tart. (Italian)
CROUSTADE. A container cut from bread and toasted that is used to serve creamed foods. (French)
CRUSTACES. Shellfish. (French)
CUISSE. Leg. (French)
CUISSES DE GRENOUILLES. Frogs' legs. (French)
CUISSOT. Leg. (French)
CUL. Bottom, especially of vegetables. (French)
CULATTA. Rump. (Italian)
CULOTTE. Rump. (French)
CULS D'ARTICHAUTS. Artichoke bottoms. (French)
CUMIN DES PRES. Caraway seed. (French)
CUORE. Heart. (Italian)
CUT MEZZANI. A heavy macaroni shape cut into short lengths. (Italian)
CUT ZITA. A macaroni shape that is cut into short lengths. (Italian)
DAL. Lentils. (East Indian)
DAMPFNUDELN. Steamed noodles. (German)
DANSK KAGE. Danish pastry. (Danish)
DARNE. Slice. (French)
DATTERI. Dates. (Italian)
DATTERI DI MARE. Mussels. (Italian)
DATTES. Dates. (French)
DEJEUNER. Breakfast. (French)
DEJEUNER A LA FOURCHETTE. Luncheon. (French)
DE JOUR. Meaning "of the day," this expression is used to indicate some dish that, for some reason or another, is being stressed on a particular menu. (French)
DE LA MAISON. An expression used to indicate a dish that is a specialty of the restaurant, usually one made from the chef's private recipe. (French)
DELICES DE RUSSIE. An assortment of barquettes filled with some form of fish. (French)
DEMI-DEUIL. Means that a dish has been made to have a black and white effect; usually truffles contrasted with white meat or a white sauce. (French)
DEMI-GLACE. Rich, thick gravy. (French)
DIABLE. A term applied to highly spiced, or "deviled," dishes. (French)
DILLGURKEN. Dill pickles. (German)
DINDE. Turkey. (French)

DINDONNEAU. Young turkey. (French)
DINER. Dinner. (French)
DITALI. A macaroni shape. (Italian)
DOLCI. Candy. (Italian)
DUCHESSE POTATOES. Mashed potatoes mixed with egg and forced through a pastry tube. (French)
DUDH. Milk. (East Indian)
DUGLERE. Usually refers to the use of tomatoes. (French)
DURAZNOS. Peaches. (Spanish)
EAU. Water. (French)
EAUX GAZEUSES. Carbonated waters. (French)
EAUX MINERALES. Mineral waters (French)
ECHALOTE. Shallot. (French)
ECORCE DE CITRON. Lemon peel. (French)
ECREVISSES. Crayfish. (French)
EGGS A LA SUISSE. Eggs baked with cheese. (French)
EGGS COCOTTE. Eggs cooked in sweet cream. (French)
EGREFIN. Haddock. (French)
EGREFIN FUME. Finnan Haddie or smoked haddock. (French)
EIER. Eggs. (German)
EIERPFLANZE. Eggplant. (German)
EISCREME. Ice Cream. (German)
EMINCE. Means sliced small, or, in some cases, hashed. (French)
EN BORDURE. Applied to any dish served with a border or ring of vegetables. (French)
EN CAISSE. Means served in some sort of non-edible case, such as paper, etc. (French)
EN CARAFE. Usually refers to wine served in open wine pitchers, the wine having been drawn from casks or other large vessels. (French)
EN CASSEROLE. Means served in a casserole or similar covered vessel. (French)
EN CHEMISE. Usually applied to potatoes, this expression means served with the skins on. (French)
ENCHILADES. Tortillas that are filled with beans, fried in oil, and served with chili sauce. (Mexican)
EN COCOTTE. Served in an individual casserole. (French)
EN COQUILLES. Made to resemble a shell or served in a shell. (French)
ENCURTIDOS CON ENELDO. Dill pickles. (Spanish)
EN DAUBE. Braised or stewed. (French)

ENDIBIA. Endive. (Spanish)
EN PAPILLOTES. Made or served in paper casings or trimmings. (French)
EN PENSION. Indicates the so-called "American Plan," i.e., the price of the room includes the price of the meals. (French)
ENSALADA. Salad. (Spanish)
ENSALADA DE COL. Cole slaw. (Spanish)
EN TASSE. In a cup. (French)
ENTE. Duck. (German)
ENTRECOTE. A rib or sirloin steak. (French)
ENTREE. One of the subordinate courses of a formal dinner, and the main course at luncheon. (French)
ENTREMESES VARIADOS. Hors d' oeuvres. (Spanish and South American)
ENTREMET. As used in America, this refers to the sweet course. (French)
ENTREMETS DE DOUCEUR. Sweet dishes. (French)
ENTREMETS DE LEGUMES. A vegetable course. (French)
EPAULE. Shoulder. (French)
EPICE. Spice. (French)
EPIGRAMME. Two pieces of meat, prepared differently but usually cooked together, that are served together as an entrée. (French)
EPINARDS. Spinach. (French)
ERBAGGIO. Herbs. (Italian)
ERBSEN. Peas. (German)
ERDBEEREN. Strawberries. (German)
ESCALOPE. A thin slice. (French)
ESCALLOP. To bake, usually with a mixture of white sauce and an au gratin crust, in a baking dish or a scallop shell. (French)
ESCARGOT. Snail. (French)
ESPALDILLA. Shoulder. (Spanish)
ESPARRAGOS. Asparagus. (Spanish)
ESPICIA. Spice. (Spanish)
ESPINACA. Spinach. (Spanish)
ESTOFADO. A stew of meat or fish. (South American)
ETOFFE. Stewed or braised; also means pot roast. (French)
ETUVEE. Stewed or braised; also means pot roast. (French)
EXTRAIT. Extract. (French)
FADENNUDELN. Vermicelli. (German)
FAGIANO. Pheasant. (Italian)
FAGIUOLI. Beans, especially kidney beans. (Italian)
FAGIUOLI GIOVANI. Green beans. (Italian)

FAGIUOLINI. String beans. (Italian)
FAGIUOLINI GIALLI. Wax beans. (Italian)
FAGIUOLI SECCHI. Navy beans. (Italian)
FAISAN. Pheasant. (French)
FAN. Rice. (Chinese)
FAN SI. Rice noodles. (Chinese)
FARCE. Stuffing. (French)
FARCI. Stuffed. (French)
FARINE D'AVOINE. Oatmeal. (French)
FAUSSE-TORTUE. Mock turtle. (French)
FAVE. Beans. (Italian)
FEGATO. Liver. (Italian)
FEKETE KAVE. Coffee. (Hungarian)
FERMIERE. Meaning "farmer's wife," this expression denotes plain or country-style cooking. (French)
FETTA. Slice. (Italian)
FEVES. Beans. (French)
FICHI. Figs. (Italian)
FIDEOS. Vermicelli. (Spanish)
FIGUES. Figs. (French)
FILBUNKE. Clabber. (Swedish)
FILET. A boneless piece of beef tenderlion, mutton, veal, pork, or fish. (French)
FILET MIGNON. A piece of beef tenderloin without the bone. (French)
FILETTO. Tenderloin. (Italian)
FINES HERBES. Sweet herbs; also, a mixture of finely chopped herbs used in many kinds of cooking. (French)
FISCH. Fish. (German)
FISKE. Fish. (Norse)
FISKEBOLLER. Fish balls. (Norse)
FISKESUPPE. Fish soup. (Norse)
FLAGEOLETS. Young green beans. (French)
FLAMBE. The name given to a dessert covered with burning spirits that is served before the flames have died out. (French)
FLEISCHSAFT. Gravy. (German)
FOCACCIA. Cake. (Italian)
FOET BURGONYA. Boiled potatoes. (Hungarian)
FOIE. Liver. (French)
FOIE DE VEAU. Calf's liver. (French)
FOND. Bottom. (French)
FONDS D'ARTICHAUTS. Artichoke bottoms. (French)
FONDU. Melted. (French)
FOO YONG. Indicates the use of eggs, especially in omelet or scrambled form. (Chinese)
FORELLE. Trout. (German)
FORLORNE EGG. Poached egg. (Norse)

FORMAGGIO. Cheese. (Italian)
FORMAGGIO GRATTATO. Grated cheese. (Italian)
FRAGOLE. Strawberries. (Italian)
FRAI. Hard roe. (French)
FRAISES. Strawberries. (French)
FRAMBOISES. Raspberries. (French)
FRAMBUESAS. Raspberries. (Spanish)
FRAPPE. Partly frozen. (French)
FRESAS. Strawberries. (Spanish)
FRIANDISE. A small, dainty dish. (French)
FRICANDEAU. A piece of larded and braised meat, often veal. (French)
FRICASSEE. To cook meat by braising, the meat usually being cut into small pieces. (French)
FRIJOLES. Beans, especially Kidney beans. (Spanish)
FRIKADELLER. Meat balls. (Danish)
FRIT. Fried. (French)
FROID. Cold. (French)
FROMAGE. Cheese. (French)
FROMAGE A LA CREME. Cream cheese. (French)
FROMAGE DE PORC. Headcheese. (French)
FROMAGE RAPE. Grated Cheese. (French)
FROSCHSCHENKEL. Frogs' legs. (German)
FRUCHT. Fruit. (German)
FRUITS GLACES. Candied fruit. (French)
FRUITS SECS. Dried fruit. (French)
FRUKOST. Breakfast. (Swedish)
FRUTAS CONFITADAS. Candied fruit. (Spanish)
FUME. Smoked. (French)
FUMET. Extract. (French)
FUNGHI. Mushrooms. (Italian)
GABELFRUEHSTUECK. A second breakfast traditionally taken between 10 and 11. (Austrian)
GALLETAS. Biscuits. (Spanish)
GALLETTO. Spring chicken. (Italian)
GALLINA. Hen. (Italian and Spanish)
GAMBA. Leg. (Italian)
GAMBERETTI DI MARE. Prawns. (Italian)
GAMBERETTINI. Shrimps. (Italian)
GAMBERO D'ACQUA DOLCE. Crayfish. (Italian)
GAMBERO MARINO. Lobster. (Italian)
GANS. Goose. (German)
GANSO. Goose. (Spanish)
GARNEELEN. Shrimps or prawns. (German)

GARNIERT. Garnished. (Austrian)
GARNIERUNG. Garnishing. (German)
GARNITURE. Garnishing. (French)
GASTRIC. A mixture of white wine or vinegar with crushed peppers, shallots, and spices. (French)
GATEAU. Cake. (French)
GATEAU AUX FRAISES. Strawberry shortcake. (French)
GATEAUX ASSORTIS. Assorted cakes. (French)
GAUFRES. Waffles. (French)
GEBACH. Pastries. (Austrian)
GEFLUGEL. Poultry. (German)
GELATO. Ice cream or sherbert. (Italian)
GELEE. Jelly. (French)
GESELCHTES. Smoked or cured pork. (German)
GESIER. Gizzard. (French)
GETROCKNETE BOHNEN. Navy beans. (German)
GHEE. Rendered butter. (East Indian)
GHIACCIO. Ice. (Italian)
GIAMBONE. Ham. (Italian)
GIBIER. Game. (French)
GIGOT. Leg. (French)
GINGEMBRE. Ginger. (French)
GIROFLES. Cloves. (French)
GLACAGE. Cooked icing. (French)
GLACE. Depending on use, means frozen, glazed with meat extract, covered with a sugar frosting, or candied. (French)
GLACE A LA CREME. Ice cream. (French)
GLACE ROYAL. Frosting. (French)
GOLDAPFEL. Tomato. (German)
GOMBAUT. Okra. (French)
GOSHT. Meat. (East Indian)
GOYAVE. Guava. (French)
GRAINS DE POIVRE. Peppercorns. (French)
GRAISSE. Fat. (French)
GRAISSE DE MOUTON. Mutton suet. (French)
GRAISSE DE ROGNON DE BOEUF. Beef suet. (French)
GRANATAPFEL. Pomegranate. (German)
GRANCHIO. Crab. (Italian)
GRANCHIO A GUSCIO MOLLE. Soft-shelled crab. (Italian)
GRANCHIOLINI. Prawns or shrimps. (Italian)
GRENADE. Pomegranate. (French)
GRENADIN. Means either a small frican-deau, or pomegranate sirup, depending on use. (French)
GRILLE. Grilled. (French)

GROSEILLES. Fresh currants. (French)
GROSEILLES A MAQUEREAU. Goose-berries. (French)
GRUNE BOHNEN. String beans. (German)
GUACO. Grouse. (Spanish)
GUARNIZIONE. Garnishing. (Italian)
GUAYABA. Guava. (Spanish)
GUISADO. A boiled stew. (South American)
GUISANTES. Peas. (Spanish)
GUISANTES PARTIDOS. Split peas. (Spanish)
GUISANTES VERDES. Green peas. (Spanish)
GUISO. A boiled stew. (South American)
GULYAS. Goulash, especially when made of beef or fowl. (Hungarian)
HABAS. Lima beans. (Spanish)
HABICHEULAS. Beans. (Spanish)
HACHE. Minced or chopped. (French)
HACHIS. Hash. (French)
HA K'AU. Small, fluted dumplings formed from a dough containing shrimp, water chestnuts, bamboo shoots, and seasoning. (Chinese)
HAMMELFLEISCH. Mutton. (German)
HAM PAU. A bun stuffed with spiced, wine-cured pork. (Chinese)
HAM TAN. Preserved eggs, aged for about three months in a packing of salt and charcoal. Unlike pei tan, ham tan are cooked before being eaten. (Chinese)
HANG YAN PEANG. Almond cookie. (Chinese)
HERBATA. Tea. (Polish)
HARENG. Herring. (French)
HARENG MARINE. Pickled herring. (French)
HARENG SAUR. Smoked or kippered herring. (French)
HARICOTS. Kidney beans. (French)
HARICOTS A COSSE JAUNE. Wax beans. (French)
HARICOTS BLANCS SECS. Navy beans. (French)
HARICOTS DE LIMA. Lima beans. (French)
HARICOTS DE MOUTON. Mutton stew with vegetables. (French)
HARICOTS VERTS. String beans. (French)
HECHT. Pike. (German)
HELADO. Ice cream. (Spanish)
HERBES AROMATIQUES. Sweet herbs. (French)
HERING. Herring. (German)
HERZ. Heart. (German)

HIELO. Ice. (Spanish)
HIERBAS. Herbs. (Spanish)
HIGADO. Liver. (Spanish)
HIGOS. Figs. (Spanish)
HIMBEEREN. Raspberries. (German)
HOMARD. Lobster. (French)
HONGOS. Mushrooms. (Spanish)
HONSE. Chicken. (Danish)
HOY SIN CHEUNG. A sea food sauce. (Chinese)
HUEVA. Hard roe. (Spanish)
HUEVOS. Eggs. (Spanish)
HUHN. Hen or chicken. (German)
HUILE. Oil. (French)
HUILE DE TABLE. Sweet oil. (French)
HUITRES. Oysters. (French)
HUITRES A LA NORVEGIENNE. Oysters served on crushed ice with quarters of lemon and parsley. (French)
HUMMER. Lobster. (German)
ILI. Or. (Russian)
INDIENNE. Implies the use of curry or other East Indian seasonings. (French)
INDIVIA. Endive. (Italian)
INSALATA. Salad. (Italian)
INSALATA. DI CAVOLO. Cole slaw (Italian)
JAATELOA. Ice cream. (Finnish)
JALEA. Jelly. (Spanish)
JALEBEES. Sweets. (East Indian)
JAMBON. Ham. (French)
JAMON. Ham. (Spanish)
JARABE. Sirup. (Spanish)
JARABE DE ARCE. Maple sirup. (Spanish)
JARDINIERE. Prepared or served with a variety of vegetables. (French)
JAUNES D'OEUF. Egg yolks. (French)
JUDIAS. Kidney beans. (Spanish)
JUDIAS BLANCAS SECAS. Navy beans. (Spanish)
JUDIAS DE VAINA AMARILLA. Wax beans. (Spanish)
JUDIAS TIERNAS. Young green beans. (Spanish)
JUGO. Juice. (Spanish)
JULIENNE. Means either shredded vegetables, especially potatoes, or the use of shredded vegetables. (French)
JUNGES HUHN. Spring chicken. (German)
JUS. Juice. (French)
JUS DE CITRON. Lemon juice. (French)
JUS DE LA VIANDE. Gravy. (French)
KABELJAU. Codfish. (German)
KAFFE. Coffee. (Norse)
KAHVIA. Coffee. (Finnish)
KAI. Chicken. (Chinese)

K'AI LAT. Mustard. (Chinese)
KAISERSCHMARREN. Pancakes. (Austrian)
KALBFLEISCH. Veal. (German)
KALDAUNEN. Tripe. (German)
KAMMUSCHEL. Scallops. (German)
KANAPKI. Canapes. (Polish)
KANINCHEN. Rabbit. (German)
KARP PO POLSKU. Carp Polonais. (Polish)
KARTOFFELN. Potatoes. (German)
KARTOFFELPUREE. Mashed potatoes. (Austrian)
KARTOFLE PRZYPIEKANE. Browned potatoes. (Polish)
KARTOFLER. Potatoes. (Danish)
KASHA. A type of mush. (Russian)
KAWA. Coffee. (Polish)
KEITETTYJA PERUNOITA. Boiled potatoes. (Finnish)
KELVIRAG. Cauliflower. (Hungarian)
KESAKEITTO. Cream soup made by cooking vegetables in butter and then adding milk. (Finnish)
KIELBAZA. Sausage. (Polish)
KIRSCHEN. Cherries. (German)
KNACKEBROD. Hard Bread. (Swedish)
KNEDLIKY. Dumplings. (Czech)
KNOBLAUCH. Garlic. (German)
KOAL. Cabbage. (Danish)
KOGTE. Boiled. (Danish)
KOHL. Cabbage. (German)
KOHLSALAT. Cole slaw. (German)
KOKTE POTETER. Boiled potatoes. (Norse)
KOKT POTATIS. Boiled potatoes. (Swedish)
KOLACLAY. Tarts. (Czech)
KOLT BORD. Smorgasbord. (Norse)
KOPFSALAT. Lettuce. (German)
KOTELETT. Cutlet. (German)
KOTTBULLAR. Meat balls. (Swedish)
KRAFTOR. Crayfish. (Swedish)
KRAUSKOHL. Kale. (German)
KRAUT. Cabbage. (German)
KRINGLE. Cookies. (Norse)
KRUPI. Barley. (Polish)
KUCHEN. Cake. (German)
KUTTELFLECKE. Tripe. (Austrian)
KWAS. A sour beverage or liquor made from fermented cereal that is often used in Polish cookery. (Polish)
KWASNE MLEKOR. Sour, clabbered milk. (Polish)
KYLLING. Roast chicken. (Norse)
LABERDAN. Salt cod. (German)
LACHS. Salmon. (German)
LAIB. Loaf. (German)

LAIT. Milk. (French)
LAITANCE. Soft roe. (French)
LAIT DE BEURRE. Buttermilk. (French)
LAITUE. Lettuce. (French)
LAMM. Lamb. (German)
LAMPONI. Raspberries. (Italian)
LANGOSTA. Lobster. (Spanish)
LANGOSTINES. Crayfish. (Spanish)
LANGUE. Tongue. (French)
LAP CHEUNG. Wine-cured sausages. (Chinese)
LAPIN. Rabbit. (French)
LARD. Bacon. (French)
LARDO. Bacon. (Italian)
LARDONE. Salt pork. (Italian)
LASAGNA. A heavy, broad, flat strip of dried flour paste on the order of spaghetti; also, a special dish made using lasagna. (Italian)
LATTE. Milk. (Italian)
LATTE DI PESCE. Soft roe. (Italian)
LATTUGA. Lettuce. (Italian)
LEBER. Liver. (German)
LEBKUCHEN. Gingerbread or honey cake. (German)
LECHE. Milk. (Spanish)
LECHECILLA DE PEZ. Soft roe. (Spanish)
LECHECILLAS. Sweetbread. (Spanish)
LECHONCILLO. Pig's tongue. (Spanish)
LECHUGA. Lettuce. (Spanish)
LEFSE. Waffles. (Norse)
LEGUMBRES. Vegetables. (Spanish)
LEGUMES. Vegetables. (French)
LEGUMES VERTS. Green vegetables. (French)
LEGUMI. Vegetables. (Italian)
LENGUA. Tongue. (Spanish)
LENGUADO. Sole. (Spanish)
LENTEJAS. Lentils. (Spanish)
LEVRE. Yeast. (French)
LIEVRE. Hare. (French)
LIHALIENTA. Bouillon. (Finnish)
LIMA-BOHNEN. Lima Beans. (German)
LIMPA. A heavy rye bread. (Swedish)
LINGUA. Tongue. (Italian)
LINGUINI. A thick spaghetti shape. (Italian)
LOG. Onion sauce. (Danish)
LOK. Onion. (Norse)
LOMBO. Loin. (Italian)
LOMO. Loin. (Spanish)
LO MEIN. Noodles. (Chinese)
LONGE. Loin. (French)
LUCINES. Clams. (French)
LUCINES ORANGEES. Hard clams. (French)

LUCINES PAPILLONS. Soft clams. (French)
LUCULLUS. A term applied to rich sauces. (French)
LUMACHE. Snails. (Italian)
LUNG HA. Lobster. (Chinese)
LYONNAISE. Means that the dish contains onions. (French)
MACARELA. Mackerel. (Spanish)
MACARRONES. Macaroni. (Spanish)
MACCHERONI. Macaroni. (Italian)
MACEDOINE. A mixture of cut fruits or vegetables. (French)
MAELK. Milk. (Danish)
MAIFISCH. Shad. (German)
MAIGRE. Depending on use, means a dish that contains neither meat nor animal fats, lean meat, little meat, or thin, poor, or scanty. (French)
MAIS. Corn or maize. (German)
MAIS. Maize or corn. (French)
MAITOA Milk. (Finnish)
MAITRE D'HOTEL. Usually implies the use of chopped parsley as a flavoring or garnishing. (French)
MAIZ. Corn. (Spanish)
MAKSALAATIKKO. Liver pudding. (Finnish)
MANTECA DE VACA. Butter. (Spanish)
MANTECADO. Ice cream. (Spanish)
MANTEQUILLA. Butter. (Spanish)
MANZANAS. Apples. (Spanish)
MANZO. Beef. (Italian)
MANZO AROMATICO. Spiced beef. (Italian)
MANZO ARROSTO. Roast beef. (Italian)
MANZO SALATO. Corned beef. (Italian)
MANZO SECCATO. Dried beef. (Italian)
MAQUEREAU. Mackerel. (French)
MARINE. Pickled. (French)
MARISCOS. Shellfish. (Spanish)
MARRONS. Chestnuts. (French)
MASQUE. Means covered, i.e., with a sauce, jelly, etc. (French)
MATELOTE. Made of or served with a variety of fish. (French)
MECHADA. Larded. (South American)
MED. With. (Danish, Norse, Swedish)
MEERFISCH. Salt water fish. (German)
MEERRETTICH. Horse-radish. (German)
MEJILLONES. Mussels. (Spanish)
MELANZANA. Eggplant. (Italian)
MELASSE. Molasses. (French)

MELE. Apples. (Italian)
MELLONE. Melon. (Italian)
MELON D'EAU. Watermelon. (French)
MENTHE POIVREE. Peppermint. (French)
MENUDILLOS DE AVES. Giblets. (Spanish)
MERLUZZO. Haddock. (Italian)
MOSTACCIOLI. A heavy macaroni shape. (Italian)
MOSTRICH. Mustard. (German)
MOULES. Mussels. (French)
MOUSSE. Meaning "froth" or "foamy," this expression is applied to very light, airy dishes, usually those made with whipped cream or egg whites. (French)
MOUT. Grape juice. (French)
MOUTARDE. Mustard. (French)
MOUTON. Mutton. (French)
MURES. Mulberries. (French)
MURES DE HAIE. Blackberries. (French)
MUSCADE. Nutmeg. (French)
MUSCHELN. Mussels or clams. (German)
MUSS. Sauce. (German)
MYRTILS. Blueberries or huckleberries. (French)
NABOS. Turnips. (Spanish)
NACHTISCH. Dessert. (German)
NAKKILEIPAA. Hard bread. (Finnish)
NARANJAS. Oranges. (Spanish)
NATA. Cream. (Spanish)
NAVETS. Turnips. (French)
NEAPOLITAN. When applied to ice cream, this indicates solid bricks consisting of three differently colored and flavored layers. (French)
NESSELRODE. Containing chestnuts. (French)
NIERE. Kidney. (German)
NIVERNAISE. Carrot garnishing. (French)
NOCI. Walnuts. (Italian)
NOCKERL. Dumplings. (Austrian)
NOISETTE. A small piece of lean meat; often a boneless chop. (French)
NOIX. Nuts, especially walnuts. (French)
NOIX DE COCO. Coconut. (French)
NOUILLES. Noodles. (French)
NUDELN. Noodles. (German)
NUECES. Nuts, especially walnuts. (Spanish)
O. Or. (Spanish)
OCA. Goose. (Italian)
OBED. Evening meal. (Russian)
OCH. With or and. (Swedish)
OCHSENSCHWANZ. Oxtail. (German)
OEUF, Egg. (French)

OEUFS A LA COQUE. Boiled eggs. (French)
OEUFS BROUILLES. Scrambled eggs. (French)
OEUFS FARCIS. Stuffed eggs. (French)
OEUFS FRITS. Fried eggs. (French)
OEUFS POCHES. Poached eggs. (French)
OEUFS SUR LE PLAT. Shirred eggs. (French)
OIE. Goose. (French)
OIGNONS. Onions. (French)
OISON. Gosling. (French)
OKUNG. Perch. (Russian)
OLUTTA. Beer. (Finnish)
ORGE. Barley. (French)
OS. Bone. (French)
OS A MOELLE. Marrowbone. (French)
OSEILLE. Sorrel. (French)
OST. Cheese. (Norse, Swedish)
OSTIONES. Large oysters. (Spanish)
OSTRAS. Oysters. (Spanish)
OSTRICHE. Oysters. (Italian)
PAILLES. Thin strips or "straws," especially of cheese. (French)
PAIN. Bread. (French)
PAIN BIS. Brown bread. (French)
PAIN BLANC. White bread. (French)
PAIN D' EPICE. Gingerbread. (French)
PAIN DE SEIGLE. Rye bread. (French)
PAIN ROTI. Toast. (French)
PAK CHOY. Cabbage. (Chinese)
PALOMA. Pigeon. (Spanish)
PAMPELIMOSSA. Grapefruit. (Italian)
PAMPLEMOUSSE. Grapefruit. (French)
PAN. Bread. (Spanish)
PANACHE. An expression meaning "of mixed colors." (French)
PANAIS. Parsnips. (French)
PANE. Bread. (Italian)
PANECILLOS. Rolls. (Spanish)
PANI. Water. (East Indian)
PANINO. Roll. (Italian)
PAPAS. Potatoes. (Spanish)
PAPERO. Gosling. (Italian)
PAPILLOTE. A paper frill used to decorate food. (French)
PARADIESAPFEL. Tomato. (German)
PARISIENNE POTATOES. Potatoes that are cut into small rounds with a scoop and browned. (French)
PARMIGIANNE. Indicates that the food is covered with melted parmesan cheese. (Italian)
PASTEL. Cake or pie. (Spanish)
PASTEL DE FRESAS. Strawberry short-cake. (Spanish)
PASTELERIA. Pastry. (Spanish)

PASTELILLO. Patty. (Spanish)
PASTICCERIA. Pastry. (Italian)
PASTICCETTO. Patty. (Italian)
PASTICCIO. Pie. (Italian)
PASTINACA. Parsnips. (Spanish)
PASTINACHE. Parsnips. (Italian)
PASTINAKE. Parsnips. (German
PATA. Leg. (Spanish)
PATAS DE RANA. Frogs' legs. (Spanish)
PATATAS. Potatoes. (Spanish)
PATATE. Potatoes. (Italian)
PATATE DOLCI. Sweet potatoes. (Italian)
PATATES. Sweet potatoes. (French)
PEPERONI COMMUNI. Sweet peppers. (Italian)
PEPINILLOS. Gherkins. (Spanish)
PEPINO. Cucumber. (Spanish)
PERAS. Pears. (Spanish)
PERCIATELLI. A thin macaroni shape. (Italian)
PERDIZ. Partridge. (Spanish)
PERDRIX. Partridge. (French)
PERE. Pears. (Italian)
PEREJIL. Parsley. (Spanish)
PERIGORD. Made or served with truffles or truffle sauce. (French)
PERNIL. Shoulder of pork. (Spanish)
PERSIL. Parsley. (French)
PERSILLADE. Signifies the use of parsley. (French)
PESCA. Peach. (Italian)
PESCADO. Fish. (Spanish)
PESCE. Fish. (Italian)
PETERSILIE. Parsley. (German)
PETIT. Small or "new." (French)
PETITE MARMITE. A strong consommé made with beef, chicken, and vegetables. (French)
PETITS-FOURS. Small cakes. (French)
PETITS PAINS. Rolls. (French)
PETITS POIS. Green peas. (French)
PETONCLES. Scallops. (French)
PETTINI. Clams. (Italian)
PETTONCHI. Scallops. (Italian)
PICALILLO. Cut up into little pieces. (South American)
PICCIONE. Pigeon. (Italian)
PICHON. Squab. (Spanish)
PIECE DE RESISTANCE. The main dish of a meal. (French)
PIEROGS. Pastry stuffed with chopped cabbage, eggs, meat, etc. (Russian)
PIEROZHKI. Turnovers made of noodle dough, stuffed with meats or sweets. (Polish)
PLATTAR. Pancakes. (Swedish)

POCHE. Poached. (French)
POINTES D'ASPERGES. Asparagus tips. (French)
POIREAUX. Leeks. (French)
POIRE D'AVOCAT. Avocado. (French)
POIRES. Pears. (French)
POIS. Peas. (French)
POIS CASSES. Split peas. (French)
POISSON. Fish. (French)
POISSON D'EAU DOUCE. Fresh-water fish. (French)
POISSON DE MER. Salt-water fish. (French)
POITRINE. Breast. (French)
POIVRADE. Pepper sauce. (French)
POIVRE. Pepper. (French)
POIVRE BLANC. White pepper. (French)
POIVRE DE GUINEE. Cayenne pepper. (French)
POIVRE NOIR. Black pepper. (French)
POIVRE ROUGE. Red pepper. (French)
POIVRONS DE GUINEE. Chilies. (French)
POLLASTRINO. Spring chicken. (Italian)
POLLO. Chicken. (Italian and Spanish)
POLLO TIERNO. Spring chicken. (Spanish)
POLNISH. Usually applied to fish, especially carp, this expression indicates that the food is cooked in beer with a sweet-sour gingerbread sauce, and served in an aspic. (German)
POMMES. Apples. (French)
POMMES A COUTEAU. Eating apples. (French)
POMMES DE TERRE. Potatoes. (French)
POMMES SAUVAGES. Crab apples. (French)
PONCIRE. Citron. (French)
PORCELLINO LATTANTE. Suckling pig. (Italian)
PORC FRAIS. Fresh pork. (French)
PORC SALE. Corned or salt pork. (French)
PORKOLT. A goulash made using browned or scorched meat, and that contains more onions (finely chopped) and has a thicker gravy than gulyas. (Hungarian)
POSPASTO. Dessert. (Italian)
POSTRES. Dessert. (Spanish)
POTAGE. Soup. (French)
POT POURRIE. A mixture of highly seasoned meat. (French)
POULE. Hen. (French)
POULET A ROTIR. Roasting chicken. (French)

POULET A SAUTER. Frying chicken. (French)
POULET DE GRAIN. Spring chicken. (French)
PRALINE. Signifies the use of burnt almonds. (French)
PRESSGURKA. Cucumber salad. (Swedish)
PREZZEMOLO. Parsley. (Italian)
PRINTANIER. Made with spring vegetables. (French)
PROSCIUTTO. Ham. (Italian)
PROVENCALE. Signifies the use of garlic or onions and olive oil, as well as mushrooms, herbs, etc. (French)
PRUNEAUX. Prunes. (French)
PRUNES. Plums. (French)
PUNTAS DE ESPARRAGO. Asparagus tips. (Spanish)
PUTER. Turkey. (German)
QUARTIER DE DERRIERE. Hindquarter. (French)
QUARTIER DE DEVANT. Forequarter. (French)
QUESADILLA. Cheese cake. (Spanish)
QUESO. Cheese. (Spanish)
QUESO DE CERDO. Headcheese. (Spanish)
QUESO FRESCO. Cream cheese. (Spanish)
QUESO RALLADO. Grated cheese. (Spanish)
QUEUE DE BOEUF. Oxtail. (French)
RABANOS. Radishes. (Spanish)
RABANO SILVESTRE. Horse-radish. (Spanish)
RABO DE BUEY. Oxtail. (Spanish)
RADIS. Radishes. (French)
RAGOUT. Stew. (French)
RAHM. Cream. (German)
RAIFORT. Horse-radish. (French)
RAISINS. Grapes. (French)
RAISINS DE CORINTHE. Dried currants. (French)
RAISINS SECS. Raisins. (French)
RAKI. Crabs. (Russian)
RAPE. Turnips. (Italian)
RAVANELLI. Radishes. (Italian)
RAVES. Turnips. (French)
REBANADA. Slice. (Spanish)
REBHUHN. Partridge. (German)
REIS. Rice. (German)
RELEVE. A name sometimes given to a course of a large roast or a large fowl. (French)
RELLENO. Stuffing. (Spanish)
RETTICHEN. Radishes. (German)
RINDERBRATEN. Roast beef. (German)

RINDFLEISCH. Beef. (German)
RINONES. Kidney. (Spanish)
RIPIENO. Stuffing. (Italian)
RIPPCHEN. Chops or cutlets. (German)
RIPPE. Rib. (German)
RIS. Rice. (Danish) Sweetbread. (French)
RIS DE VEAU. Calf's sweetbread. (French)
RISO. Rice. (Italian)
RISSOLE POTATOES. Potatoes that are cut into the shape of large nuts with a scoop, and browned. (French)
RIZ. Rice. (French)
ROBALO. Haddock. (Spanish)
ROGEN. Hard roe. (German)
ROGGEN. Rye. (German)
ROGGENBROT. Rye bread. (German)
ROGNON. Kidney. (French)
ROGNONE. Kidney. (Italian)
ROSBIF. Roast beef. (French)
ROSENKOHL. Brussels sprouts. (German)
ROSINEN. Raisins. (German)
ROTI. Unleavened bread. (East Indian)
ROTI. Roast. (French)
ROUELLE. Round (French)
ROULADE. Rolled meat. (French)
ROUX. A mixture of flour and fat used to thicken sauces and gravies. (French)
RYPER. Grouse. (Norse)
SANCOCHO. A meat or fish stew. (South American)
SANDIA. Watermelon. (Spanish)
SARAZIN. Buckwheat. (French)
SAUCISSE. Sausage. (French)
SAUGE. Sage. (French)
SAUMON. Salmon. (French)
SAUS. Gravy. (Norse)
SCALLOPINE. Indicates that the food is prepared with a covering of melted cheese. (Italian)
SCHALTIERE. Shellfish. (German)
SCHELLFISCH. Haddock. (German)
SCHINKEN. Ham. (German)
SCHLAGOBERS. Whipped cream. (Austrian)
SCHLOGSAHNE. Whipped cream. (German)
SCHNITZEL. Usually applied to veal, this means a thin slice of meat. (German)
SCHOLLE. Sole. (German)
SCHWARZBROT. Dark bread. (German)
SCHWEINEFLEISCH. Pork. (German)
SCIROPPO DI ACERO. Maple sirup. (Italian)
SEB CHATNI. Apple chutney. (East Indian)
SEDANO. Celery. (Italian)

SEEZUNGE. Sole. (German)
SEIGLE. Rye. (French)
SEL. Salt. (French)
SELLE. Saddle. (French)
SELOTKA. Herring. (Russian)
SIROP D'ERABLE. Maple sirup. (French)
SMETANA. Sour cream. (Russian)
SMORREBROD. Smorgasbord. (Danish)
SNAPS. Appetizer spirits. (Swedish)
SOGLIUOLA. Sole. (Italian)
SOLOMO. Rump. (Spanish)
SOPA. Soup. (Spanish)
SOR. Beer. (Hungarian)
SORBET. Sherbet. (French)
SOUDE. Soda. (French)
SOUFFLE. A very light or "puffed" dish. (French)
SOUPER. Supper. (French)
SOUS CLOCHE. Means served or cooked "under cover." (French)
SPAGHETTINI. Thin rods of dried flour paste, thicker than vermicelli, but thinner than spaghetti. (Italian)
SPANFERKEL. Suckling pig. (German)
SPARGEL. Asparagus. (German)
SPARGELKOHL. Broccoli. (German)
SPECK. Bacon. (German)
SPEKEKJOTT. Dried mutton. (Norse)
SPINAT. Spinach. (German)
SPUMONI. The Italian form of ice cream. (Italian)
STOCKFISCH. Dried codfish. (German)
STORIONE. Sturgeon. (Italian)
SUBGUM. Indicates a mixture of assorted meats and vegetables. (Chinese)
SUCCO. Juice. (Italian)
SUCRE. Sugar. (French)
SUCRE BRUT. Brown sugar. (French)
SUCRE D'ERABLE. Maple sugar. (French)
SUCRE EN MORCEAUX. Lump sugar. (French)
SUCRE EN POUDRE. Powdered sugar. (French)
SUCRE GRANULE. Granulated sugar. (French)
SUCRERIES. Candy. (French)
SUERO DE LECHE. Buttermilk. (Spanish)
SUGO. Juice. (Italian)
SUIF. Mutton suet. (French)
SUPPE. Soup. (Danish, German)
SUSSWASSERFISCH. Fresh-water fish. (German)
SUZETTE POTATO. One baked on the half shell with a whole egg and bread crumbs. (French)

SVAMP. Mushrooms. (Swedish)
SZEKELY GULYAS. A goulash made by using pork or a mixture of meats. (Hungarian)
TABLE D'HOTE. This expression on a menu indicates a meal of a fixed number of courses, selected by the management. There is usually a choice of dishes within each course, but a set price is charged for the meal. (French)
TACCHINO. Turkey. (Italian)
TARTELETTE. Tart. (French)
TARTUFI. Truffles. (Italian)
TAUBE. Pigeon. (German)
TCHAI. Tea. (Russian)
TE. Tea. (Italian and Spanish)
TEETA. Tea. (Finnish)
TEEWURST. Sausage made of finely ground pork tenderloin. (German)
TEIG. Paste. (German)
TELLER. Plate. (German)
TETE. Head. (French)
TETRAS. Grouse. (French)
THE. Tea. (Norse)
THE. Tea. (French)
THEE. Tea. (German)
T'IM PAU. A bun stuffed with ground soybeans and brown sugar. (Chinese)
TOCINO. Bacon. (Spanish)
TOCINO FRESCO. Fresh pork. (Spanish)
TOKANY. A goulash that has smaller pieces of meat than those used in gulyas, and less onions than are found in porkolt. (Hungarian)
TOMATE. Tomato. (German)
TORONJA. Grapefruit. (Spanish)
TORTE. Tart. (German)
TORTILLAS. Thin, crisp pancakes made of corn meal, often used as bread in Mexican cookery. (Mexican)
TORTUE DE MER. Turtle. (French)
TORTUE DE TERRE OU D'EAU DOUCE. Tortoise. (French)
TORTUGA. Turtle. (Spanish)
TOSTADA. Toast. (Spanish)
TOSTADOS. Stuffed tortillas. (Mexican)
TOURTE. Pie. (French)
TOW-FU. Soybean curd. (Chinese)
TRAUBEN. Grapes. (German)
TRAUBENSAFT. Grape juice. (German)
TRIFLE. A second-course sweet dish, usually composed of sponge cake soaked in wine or liqueur, macaroons, whipped cream, and fruit jams. (French)
TRIPPA. Tripe. (Italian)
TROTA. Trout. (Italian)
TRUCHA. Trout. (Spanish)
TRUFAS. Truffles. (Spanish)

TRUITE. Trout. (French)
TRUMEAU. Leg. (French)
TRUTHAHN. Turkey. (German)
TUNKE. Sauce or gravy. (German)
TUTTI-FRUITTI. "Various kinds of fruits;" usually mixed, as in certain types of ice cream. (Italian)
TVOROZHNIKI. Cakes made of cream cheese, eggs, and sugar, that are fried in butter. (Russian)
UCHA. A fish soup. (Russian)
UOVA. Eggs. (Italian)
UOVA DI PESCE. Hard roe. (Italian)
USZKA. Small pierozhki used in soup. (Polish)
UTRENNIY ZAVTRAK. Breakfast. (Russian)
UVA. Grapes. (Italian)
UVAS. Grapes. (Spanish)
VARIANTES. An assortment of French beans, spring onions, artichoke bottoms, pimientos, gherkins, etc., strongly marinated in oil, vinegar, English mustard, and coriander. (French)
VARMA KORVAR. Hot dogs. (Swedish)
VEAU. Veal. (French)
VECERE. Dinner. (Czech)
VECHERNIY TCHAI. A late evening meal or tea taken at about 10 p.m. (Russian)
VENAISON. Venison. (French)
VENERAS. Scallops. (Spanish)
VENUSMUSCHELN. Hard clams. (German)
VERDI. Green. This is applied to spaghetti and other pastes when ground spinach has been mixed with the basic flour to give the resulting shape a green color. (Italian)
VERDURA. Green vegetables. (Italian and Spanish)
VERMICELLI. Long, fine rods of dried flour paste, similar to spaghetti, but thinner. (Italian)
VIANDE. Meat. (French)
VIINIA. Wine. (Finnish)
VILII. Clabbered milk. (Finnish)
VINAIGRE. Vinegar. (French)
VINAIGRETTE. Means that the dish is made or served with a vinegar sauce. (French)
VITELLO. Veal. (Italian)
VOILEIPAPOYTA. Smorgasbord. (Finnish)
VOLAILLE. Poultry. (French)
WACHS-BOHNEN. Wax beans. (German)
WACHTEL. Quail. (German)

WAFFELN. Waffles. (German)
WEICHMUSCHELN. Soft clams. (German)
WEIN. Wine. (German)
WEISSBROT. White bread. (German)
WELSCHE BOHNEN. Kidney beans. (German)
WICKEL. Roll or cake. (German)
WIENER. Vienna. (German)
WIENERBROD. Danish pastry. (Danish)
WIENER SCHNITZEL. Viennese veal steak; i.e., a slice of veal that is breaded and fried. (German)
WILDENTE. Wild duck. (German)
WINDBEUTEL. Cream puffs. (German)
WONTON. A meat preparation on the order of ravioli. (Chinese)
WURST. Sausage. (German)
Y. And. (Spanish)
YERBABUENA. Peppermint. (Spanish)
YIN WO. Birds' nests. (Chinese)
YIT PEANG. "Moon cakes," a type of stuffed or filled pastry. (Chinese)
YOW CHIEN QUEI. A cruller shaped like two cigars lying side by side. (Chinese)
YU CHEE. Shark fins. (Chinese)
Z'AFRANI CHAWL. Rice cooked brown with raisins. (East Indian)
ZAKONSKI. Russian hors d'oeuvres that are traditionally taken before dinner being served from a buffet with all kinds of liquors. (Russian)
ZAKUSKA. A service of hors d'oeuvres. (Russian)
ZAMPONI. Stuffed, salted pigs' feet. (Italian)
ZANAHORIAS. Carrots. (Spanish)
ZARZAMORA. Blackberries. (Spanish)
ZAVTRAK. Principal meal of the day. (Russian)
ZESTE. Orange or lemon peel; specifically, the colored outer portion of the rind. (French)
ZOLLEN. Crusts. (German)
ZRAZY. Beef or veal slices fried with butter, shallots, spices and potatoes. (Polish)
ZUCCA. Squash. (Italian)
ZUCKERWERK. Candy. (German)
ZU KOCHEN. To boil. (German)
ZUMO DE UVAS. Grape juice. (Spanish)
ZUNGE. Tongue. (German)
ZUNGENSHEIBER. Sliced tongue. (German)
ZUPPA. Soup. (Italian)
ZWIEBEL. Onion. (German)

Index

Clam *(Continued)*
  Juice, 305
  Kitchen Clambake, 305
  Spread, 305
Claret
  Cobbler, 308
  Cup, 1262
  Mulled, 778
  Punch, Noel Red, **977**
Cobbler (Beverage)
  Applejack, 308
  Catawba, 308
  Champagne, 308
  Claret, 308
  Port Wine, 308
  Sherry, 309
  Whisky, 309
Cobbler (Pudding)
  Apple, 17
  Blackberry, 98
  Black Raspberry, **999**
  Cherry, 261
Cock-a-Leekie, 685
Cocktail
  Avocado, 38
  Cantaloupe, 217
  Cape Cod, 310
  Citrus Fruit, 310
  Clam Juice, 305
  Crabmeat, 358
  Cranberry Juice, 363
  Grape Juice, 564
  Grape-Orange, 565
  Grapefruit and Strawberry, 310
  Lobster, 711
  Melon, 745
  Orange Fruit, 310
  Peach, 310
  Pineapple Mint, 310
  Pomegranate, 920
  Sauces, 311, 835
  Shrimp, 1081
  Tomato Cream, 1184
  Tomato Juice, 1184
Cocktail, Alcoholic
  Bronx, 130
  Champagne, 245
  Clover Club, 307
  Crustas, 374
  Cuba Libre, 374
  Daiquiri, 387
  Daisy, 387
  Fizz, 466
  Flip, 472
  Frozen Daiquiri, 387
  Gimlet, 539
  Manhattan, 725
  Martini, 733
  Old-Fashioned, 807
  Pink Lady, 908
  Sangaree, 1056
  Sidecar, 1083
  Sour, 1103
  Stinger, 1122

Cocktail, Alcoholic *(Continued)*
  Swizzle, 1143
  Tango, 1158
  Tom Collins, 331
  Ward Eight, 1228
  Xanthia, 1267
  Xeres, 1267
  Zanzibar, 1268
  Zaza, 1268
  Zombie, 1268
Coconut
  Ambrosia, 819
  Apricot, Custard Pie, 30
  Blanc Mange, 101
  Cake, Fresh, 316
  Cantaloupe Mold, 217
  Cherry Divinity, 408
  Chocolate Dreams, 314
  Chocolate Pudding, 289
  Cones, 314
  Cream Filling, 519
  Cream Pie, 314
  Custard, 382
  Custard Pie, 383
  Fingers, 315
  Honey Topping, 623
  Icing, 315
  Jumbles, 332
  Kisses, 657
  Lemon Cookies, 315
  Macaroons, 717
  Milk, 315
  Muffins, 777
  Orange Creams, 315
  Orange Salad, 316
  Pie, Chocolate, 293
  Refrigerator Cookies, Lemon, 337
  Sponge Cake, 157
Cod
  Baked Stuffed, 317
  Baked with Crabmeat Dressing, 317
  Boiled, 318
  Brandade, 318
  Broiled, 318
  Fried, 318
  Griddle Cakes, 576
  Kedgeree, 319, 654
  New England Codfish Cakes, 466
Coffee
  Bavarian, 323
  Cafe Brule, 322
  Chocolate Punch, Mexican, 322
  Cream Filling, 519
  Cream Pie, 368
  Custard, 382
  Custard Cake, 158
  Custard Pie, 383
  Flip, 322
  Frappe, 323
  Frosted, 322
  Fruit Frosting, 323
  Ice Cream, 323
  Iced, 322
  Iced Russian, 322

Mush, Fried, 779
Mushroom
  and Chicken with Biscuit Rings, 275
  and Potato Pie, 783
  and Savory Rice, 1028
  Baked in Cream, 783
  Bisque, 783
  Bouillon, Jellied, 782
  Brown Sauce, 132
  Catsup, 233
  Creamed, on Toast, 781
  Cutlets, 783
  Eggs with Peas and, 435
  Flamed, 782
  Grilled, 782
  Marinated, 782
  Neapolitan, 784
  Puffs, 782
  Scalloped with Tomatoes, 1182
  Souffle, 784
  Soup, 784
  Soup, Cream of, 781
  Soup, Old-Fashioned, 1102
  White Sauce, 1248
  with Wild Rice, 1251
Mussel
  Chowder, 785
  Mariniere, 785
  Patties, 786
  Poulette, 786
Mustard
  Butter, 187
  Greens and Potatoes, 787
  Pickles, Sweet, 890
  Salad Dressing, 1046
Mutton
  Boiled Leg with Caper Sauce, 789
  Braised Shoulder, 789
  Broth, 790
  Collops, 790
  English Grill, 790
  Shoulder with Turnips, 790
  Stew, Chinese, 789

N

Napoleon, 791
Nasturium Vinegar, 1219
Nesselrode Pudding, 792
Newburg
  Banana, 49
  Lobster, 712
  Sauce, 794
  Shrimp a la, 1082
Noodles
  Baked with Cheese, 795
  Deviled Creamed, 795
  Egg, 795
  Fried, 795
  Molded, with Creamed Eggs, 795
  with Meat Sauce, 796
Nut
  and Prune Sandwich Filling, 1056
  and Rice Loaf, 799

Nut (*Continued*)
  and Roquefort Sandwich Filling, 1056
  Apricot Nut Bread, 29
  Banana Nut Cake, 49
  Bread, 798
  Brittle Tapioca Cream, 1159
  Butter, 187
  Butter Balls, 334
  Butter Sauce, 143
  Cake, Austrian, 157
  Cake, Old-fashioned, 162
  Caramels, 221
  Chocolate-Nut Taffy, 1156
  Cottage Cheese Loaf, 257
  Date Loaf, 798
  Dipped, 800
  Filled, 800
  Frosting, Chocolate, 290
  Glace, 800
  Griddle Cakes, 577
  Hot Cheese Balls, 258
  Molasses Squares, 798
  Molasses Taffy, 800
  Muffins, 777
  Nibbles, 333
  Orange Bread, 799
  Pancakes, Chocolate, 837
  Pastry, Brazil, 850
  Patties, 479, 799
  Pecan Pie, 873
  Pineapple Refrigerator Cake, 907
  Potato and Walnut Croquettes, 943
  Pralines, 799
  Pudding, Frozen Pineapple, 903
  Rum Frosting, 1040
  Salmon Salad, 1051
  Salted, 797
  Sausage, 799
  Souffle, Chocolate, 294
  Spanish Cream, 1107
  Stuffed Baked Oranges, 819
  Stuffing, 799
  Sugared, 800
  Vegetable Loaf, 800
  Waffles, 1226
  Walnut Sticks, 1227

O

Oatmeal
  and Potato Soup, 947
  Bread, 803
  Cookies, 803
  Cookies, Orange, 823
  Gruel, 579
Okra
  and Beef Stew, 805
  and Corn, Scalloped, 806
  and Eggplant, 806
  and Tomatoes, Scalloped, 806
  au Gratin, 806
  Baked, Rice and Tomatoes, 805
  Chicken Gumbo, 805